THE

PRACTICAL WORKS

OF

RICHARD BAXTER:

WITH A PREFACE, GIVING SOME ACCOUNT OF THE AUTHOR,
AND OF THIS EDITION OF HIS PRACTICAL WORKS:

AN

ESSAY ON HIS GENIUS, WORKS, AND TIMES;

AND A PORTRAIT

IN FOUR VOLUMES.

VOL. IV.

Soli Deo Gloria Publications
"...for instruction in righteousness..."

Soli Deo Gloria Publications
213 W. Vincent St., Ligonier, PA. 15658
(412) 238-7741

*

The Practical Works of Richard Baxter
in 4 Volumes
19th Century Reprint by George Virtue, London
This Soli Deo Gloria Reprint 1990-91

*

Volume 4
ISBN 1-877611-36-0

4 Volume Set
ISBN 1-877611-37-9

Introduction to Volume 4 of Richard Baxter's Practical Works

by Dr. J. I. Packer

1991 is the three-hundredth anniversary of Richard Baxter's death. For me, the great joy of this year is that it sees the completion of Soli Deo Gloria's reprint of his incomparable Practical Works.

The contents of these four volumes follow the arrangement of the original edition of 1707, of which William Wilberforce, evangelical politician extraordinary and hero of the battle against the slave trade, wrote in his Practical View (full title: A Practical View of the Prevailing Religious System of Professed Christians, in the Higher and Middle Classes of this Country, Contrasted with Real Christianity, 1797): "His (Baxter's) writings, in four massy folios, are a treasury of Christian wisdom...the writings of few, if any, uninspired men, have been the instruments of such great and extensive benefit to mankind, as those of Mr. Baxter."

That the evangelical religion of the eighteenth century was firmly rooted in the Puritan religion of the seventeenth century is a fact that should be better known than it is. That Wilberforce, in particular, knew his Puritans well appears from his further statement: "The writings of the Puritans are prolix, and, according to the fashion of their age, rendered rather perplexed than clear, by multiplied divisions and subdivisions; yet they are a mine of wealth, in which anyone who will submit to some degree of labour, will find himself well rewarded for his pains. In particular, the writings of Dr. (John) Owen, Mr. (John) Howe, and Mr. (John) Flavel, well deserve this character..." But, for Wilberforce, "this great man" (Baxter) stood at the head of the line of Puritan devotional divines, and his Practical Works had pride of place in the Puritan literary legacy.

It is clear that the original compilers thought carefully about the arrangement of the four volumes, and we see a logical order in their layout. The first volume contains the classic Christian Directory, a compendium of practical Christianity in all its aspects. Volume two collects material on evangelism, conversion, and assurance. Volume three gives us a series of analyses of the life of faith, repentance (self-denial), and communion with God, including The Saints' Everlasting Rest, Baxter's sprawling masterpiece on the power of "heavenly meditation." Finally, volume four offers resource material for nurture and pastoral care in the church, and in families from the cradle to the grave, backed by white-hot exhortations to the clergy throughout The Reformed Pastor. (We should remember that "Reformed" here means, for Baxter, what "Revived" and "Renewed" mean for us.) Baxter's coverage of what Wilberforce called "Real Christianity" is as full as anyone could wish.

No Puritan is so skillful and strong when it comes to searching and stirring sluggish consciences as Richard Baxter. Some are more majestic than he in exposition, but none has more electrifying energy in application. As the massiveness of John Owen's theological constructions gives some of his work an impact comparable to that of the Grand Canyon, so the torrential flow of Baxter's four volumes, first to last, renders them a hortatory Niagara Falls. The holy passion that fires Baxter's pleading for a morally realistic commitment to the grace of the triune God is simply overwhelming.

Puritan piety was, from one standpoint, a sustained protest against all modes of formalism and formality. Down-to-earth realism was its temper, honesty before God was its spirit, holiness was its central concern, "heart-work and heaven-work" (Baxter's phrase to describe the meditation he taught) was its very essence. Faith, hope, love, humility, repentance, self-denial, patient endurance, obedience to the truth one had learned accompanied by desire to learn more, the sanctifying of all relationships, starting at home, and prayerful, enterprising zeal for the glory of God and the good of others in church and community, were the principal Puritan requirements; and Puritan pastoral strategy was designed to produce a pattern of godliness that met these specifications.

In that strategy, education of mind and conscience through pulpit instruction, the catechizing of young and old, the disciplines of reviewing ("repeating") sermons in company and reading Christian books, and the experience of being under discipline in one's local church, were basic. The Puritans knew that, once people see that they are lost as they are, and that God calls them to repentance and conversion, and that Christ saves those who close with him in sincerity, there is hope that they will come to a genuine commitment and discipleship, but not otherwise. Baxter says in one place that, while you can find the road to heaven without Hebrew and Greek, "in the darkness of ignorance you can never hit it." The dispelling of ignorance, and the errors and follies that ignorance brings, is what the material in this volume, starting with the three catechism-books for home use, and ending with six burial sermons designed to enrich and sustain the living, is really all about.

What Puritan Christianity, then and now, boils down to becomes plain in the closing directives of the sermon Baxter wrote (but was not permitted to preach) as his enforced farewell to his Kidderminster congregation in 1662.

> Spend most of your studies in confirming your belief of the truth of the gospel, the immortality of the soul, and the life to come, and in exercising that belief, and laying up your treasure in heaven . . .
>
> Make it the sum of all your religion, care, and business, to be ready for a safe and comfortable death. . .
>
> Live as in a constant war against all fleshly lusts, and love not the world, as it cherisheth those lusts . . . Take heed of the love of money . . . think of riches with more fear than desire. . . .
>
> Make not too great a matter of sufferings, especially poverty, or wrongs from men . . .
>
> Take heed of a self-conceited, unhumbled understanding, and of hasty and rash conclusions. Humble doubting is much safer than confident erring . . .
>
> Maintain union and communion with all true Christians on earth . . .
>
> Be sure that you maintain due honour and subjection to your governors . . .

> Be sure that you keep up family religion; especially in the careful education of youth. Read the Scriptures and good books, and call upon God, and sing his praise; and recreate youth with reading the history of the church, and the lives of holy men and martyrs: instruct them in catechisms and fundamentals. . . .
>
> Above all, live in love to God and man . . . (IV, pp.1026 ff.).

I commend this volume, and the entire reprint, as a truly invaluable resource to all for whom Puritan Christianity, and Puritan pastoral strategy, make sense. May there be many such; for today's church and world stand in desperate need of people of this kind.

J.I. Packer

CONTENTS

OF THE FOURTH VOLUME.

COMPASSIONATE COUNSEL TO ALL YOUNG MEN.

THE CATECHISING OF FAMILIES.

THE POOR MAN'S FAMILY BOOK.

SACRED HYMNS.

CONFIRMATION AND RESTAURATION,

THE NECESSARY MEANS OF

REFORMATION AND RECONCILIATION.

A GENERAL RULE TO GUIDE REFORMERS.

THE REFORMED PASTOR.

CHAPTER I.

CHAPTER II.

CHAPTER III.

CHAPTER IV.

CHAPTER V.

CHAPTER VI.

CHAPTER VII.

CHAPTER VIII.

THE VAIN RELIGION OF THE FORMAL HYPOCRITE.

CAIN AND ABEL MALIGNITY.

KNOWLEDGE AND LOVE COMPARED.

PART I.

FALSELY PRETENDED KNOWLEDGE.

PART II.

TRUE SAVING KNOWLEDGE.

THE ONE THING NECESSARY.

DIRECTIONS TO JUSTICES OF PEACE,

COMPASSIONATE COUNSEL

TO ALL

YOUNG MEN:

ESPECIALLY,

I. LONDON APPRENTICES;
II. STUDENTS OF DIVINITY, PHYSIC, AND LAW;
III. THE SONS OF MAGISTRATES AND RICH MEN.

CHAPTER I.

There is no man that ever understood the interest of mankind, of families, cities, kingdoms, churches, and of Jesus Christ the King and Saviour, but he must needs know that the right instruction, education, and sanctification of youth, is of unspeakable consequence to them all. In the place where God most blessed my labours, (at Kidderminster, in Worcestershire,) my first and greatest success was upon the youth. And (which was a marvellous way of divine mercy) when God had touched the hearts of young men and girls with a love of goodness, and delightful obedience to the truth, the parents and grandfathers, who had grown old in an ignorant, worldly state, did many of them fall into liking and love of piety, induced by the love of their children, whom they perceived to be made by it much wiser and better, and more dutiful to them. And God, by his unexpected disposing providence, having now twenty years placed me in and near London, where, in variety of places and conditions, (sometimes under restraint by men, and sometimes at more liberty,) I have preached but as to strangers, in other men's pulpits as I could, and not to any special flock of mine, I have been less capable of judging of my success: but by much experience I have been made more sensible of the necessity of warning and instructing youth than I was before. The sad reports of fame have taught it me: the sad complaints of mournful parents have taught it me: the sad observation of the wilful impenitence of some of my acquaintance tells it me: the many score (if not hundred) bills that have been publicly put up to me to pray for wicked and obstinate children, have told it me: and, by the grace of God, the penitent confessions, lamentations, and restitutions of many converts have more particularly acquainted me with their case. Which moved me on my Thursday's lecture awhile to design, the first of every month, to speak to youth and those that educate them.

And though I have already loaded the world with books, finding that God seems to be about ending my life and labours, I am urged in my mind by the greatness of the case to add yet this epistle to the younger sort. Which shall contain, I. The great importance of the case of youth. II. How it stands with them in matter of fact. III. What are the causes of their sin and dangerous degeneracy. IV. How great a blessing wise and godly youth are to themselves and others. V. How great a plague and calamity the ungodly are. VI. What great reason ungodly, sensual youth have, presently to repent and turn to God. VII. Directions to them how to do it. VIII. And some directions to parents about their education. And all must be with the brevity of an epistle.

CHAPTER II

TO BEGIN BETIMES TO LIVE TO GOD, IS OF UNSPEAKABLE IMPORTANCE TO YOURSELVES.

For, 1. You were betimes solemnly dedicated to God, as your God, your Father, your Saviour, and your Sanctifier, by your baptismal vow. And as that was a great mercy, it obliged you to great duty: you were capable in infancy of that holy dedication and relation; and your parents were presently obliged, as to dedicate you to God, so to educate you for God: and as soon as you are capable of performance, the vow is upon yourselves to do it. If your childhood is not presently obliged to holiness, according to your natural capacity, no doubt your vow and baptism should have been also delayed. Little think many that talk against anabaptists, how they condemn themselves by the sacred name of christians, while they by perfidious sacrilege deny God that which they vowed to him.

2. All your time and life is given you by God, for one end and use; and all is little enough; and will you alienate the very beginning, and be rebels so soon?

3. The youngest have not assurance of life for a day, or an hour. Thousands go out of the world in youth. Alas, the flesh of young men is corruptible, liable to hundreds of diseases, as well as the old. How quickly may a vein break, and cold seize on your head and lungs, and turn to an uncurable consumption! How quickly may a fever, a pleurisy, an imposthume, or one of a thousand accidents, turn your bodies to corruption! And oh that I knew how to make you sensible how dreadful a thing it is to die in an unholy state, and in the guilt of any unpardoned sin! An unsanctified soul, that hath lived here but to the flesh and the world, will be but fuel for the fire of hell, and the wrathful justice of the most holy God. And though in the course of undisturbed nature, young men may live longer than the old, yet nature hath so many disturbances and crosses, that our lives are still like a candle in a broken lantern, which a blast of wind may soon blow out. To tell you that you are not certain in an unsanctified state to be one day or hour more out of hell, I expect, will not move you so much as the weight of the case deserveth, because mere *possibility* of the greatest hurt doth not affect men when they think there is no *probability* of it. You have long been well, and long you hope to be so: but did you think how many hundred veins, arteries, nerves, must be kept constantly in order, and all the blood and humours in due temper; and how the stopping of one vein, or distemper of the blood, may quickly end you; it would rather teach you to admire the merciful providence of God, that such a body should be kept alive one year.

4. But were you sure to live to maturity of age, alas, how quickly will it come! What haste makes time! How fast do days and years roll on! Methinks it is but as a few days, since I was playing with my school-fellows, who now am in the sixty-sixth year of my age: had I no service done for God that I could now look back upon, I should seem as if I had not lived. A thousand years, and one hour, are all one (that is, nothing) when they are past. And every year, day, and hour of your lives, hath its proper work; and how will you answer for it? Every day offereth you more and more mercies; and will you despise and lose them? If you were heirs to land, or had an annuity, which amounted but to a hundred pounds a year, and you were every day to receive a proportionable part of it, or lose it; would you lose it through neglect, and say, I will begin to receive it when I am old? Poor labourers will work hard all the day, that at night they may have their wages: and will you contemptuously lose your every day's mercies, your safety, your communion with God, your daily blessings and his grace, which you should daily beg and may daily receive?

5. Either you will repent and live to God, or not; if not, you are undone for ever. Oh how much less miserable is a dog, or a toad, than such a sinner! But if God will show you so great mercy, oh how will it grieve you to think of the precious time of youth which you madly cast away in sin! Then you will think, Oh what knowledge, what holiness might I then have gotten! What a comfortable life might I have lived! Oh what days and years of mercy did I cast away for nothing! Yea, when God hath given you the pardon of your sin, the taste of his love, and the hopes of heaven, it will wound your hearts to think that you should so long, so unthankfully, so heinously offend so good a God, and neglect so merciful a Saviour, and trample upon infinite divine love, for the love of so base a fleshly pleasure,—that ever you should be so bad, as to find more pleasure in sinning than in living unto God.

6. And be it known to you, if God in mercy convert and save you, yet the bitter fruit of your youthful folly may follow you in this world to the grave. God may forgive the pains of hell to a penitent sinner, and not forgive the temporal chastisement to his flesh. If you waste your estate in youth, you may be poor at age. If you marry a wicked wife, you may feel it till death, notwithstanding your repentance. If by drinking, gluttony, idleness, or filthy lust, you contract any uncurable diseases in youth, repentance may not cure them till death. All this might easily have been prevented, if you had but had foreseeing wisdom. Beggary, prisons, shame, consumptions, dropsies, stone, gout, pox, which make the lives of many miserable, are usually caused by youthful sins.

7. If ever you think to be men of any great wisdom, and usefulness in the world to yourselves or others, your preparations must be made in youth. Great wisdom is not got in a little time. Who ever was an able lawyer, physician, or philosopher, without long and hard study? If you will not learn in the grammar-schools in your childhood, you will be unfit for the university at riper age; and if, when you should be doctors, you are to learn to spell and read, your shame will tell you that you should have sooner begun. Oh that you well knew how much of the safety, fruitfulness, and comfort of all your after-life, dependeth on the preparations of your youth, on the wisdom and the grace which you should then obtain! as men's after-trading doth on their apprenticeship.

8. And oh what a dreadful danger is it, lest your youthful sin become remediless, and custom harden you, and deceivers blind you, and God forsake you for your wilful resistance of his grace! God may convert old hardened sinners: but how ordinarily do we find, that age doth but answer the preparations of youth, and the vessel ever after savoureth of the liquor which first thoroughly tainted it! And men are but such as they learned to be and do at first. If you will be perfidious breakers of your baptismal vows, it is just with God to leave you to yourselves, to a deluded understanding, to think evil good, and good evil, to a seared conscience, and a hardened heart, and, as "past feeling, to work uncleanness with greediness," Eph. iv. 19; and to fight against grace and your own salvation, till death and hell convince you of your madness. O sport not with the justice of a sin-hating God! Play not with sin, and with the unquenchable fire! Forsaking God, is the way to be forsaken of him. And what is a forsaken soul, but a miserable slave of Satan?

9. Yea, did you but know of what moment it is to prevent all the heinous sins that else you will commit, you would make haste to repent, though you were sure to be forgiven. Forgiveness maketh not sin to be no sin, or to be no evil, no shame or grief to the soul that hath committed it. You will cry out, Oh that I had never known it! To look back on such an ill-spent life, will be no pleasant thought. Repentance, though a healing work, is bitter; yea, oftentimes exceedingly bitter: make not work for it, if you love your peace.

10. And is it a small thing to you, that you are all this

while doing hurt to others, and drawing them to sin, and plunging them into that dangerous guilt which can no way be pardoned but by the blood of Christ, upon true conversion? And when they have joined with you in lust and fleshly pleasure, it is not in your power to turn them, that they may join with you in sound repentance; and if not, they must lie in hell for ever. And can you make a sport of your own and other men's damnation?

But this leadeth me to the second point. I have showed you of what vast concernment it is to yourselves to begin betimes a holy life. I will next show you of what concernment it is to others.

CHAPTER III.

OF WHAT PUBLIC CONCERNMENT THE QUALITY OF YOUTH IS.

SECT. 1. The welfare of the world is of far greater worth than of any one single person; and he hath put off humanity who doth not more earnestly desire it. If this world consisted but of one generation, then to make that generation wise and good would be enough to make it a happy world. But it is not so. In heaven, and in the future glorious kingdom, "there is neither marrying, nor giving in marriage, but they are as the angels," in a fixed everlasting state, and one continued generation maketh up the new Jerusalem: being once holy and happy, they are so for ever. But here it is not so: one generation cometh, and another goeth: if the father be as wise as Solomon, the son may be as foolish as Rehoboam. Oh what a great work is it to make a man truly wise and good! How many years' study doth it usually require! What wisdom and diligence in teachers! What teachableness and diligence in learners; and especially the grace of God! And when all is done, the man quickly dieth, and obtaineth his ends in another world. But his children are born as ignorant, and perhaps as bad, as he was born: he can neither leave them his knowledge, nor his grace. They must have all the same teaching, and labour, and blessing as he had, to bring them to the same attainments. The mercy and covenant of God taketh them into his church, where they have great advantages and helps; and promiseth them more mercy for their relation to a faithful parent, if he or they do make no forfeiture of it. But as their nature is the same with others, so their actual wisdom must come by God's blessing on the use of the same means, which are necessary to the children of the worst men. A christian's child is born with no more knowledge than a heathen's, and must have as much labour and study to make him wise.

Sect. 2. It is certain then, that the welfare of this world lieth on a good succession of the several generations; and that all the endeavours of one generation, with God's greatest blessing on them, will not serve for the ages following. All must begin anew, and be done over again, or all will be as undone to the next age. And it is not the least blessing on the faithful, that their faith and godliness dispose them to have a care of posterity, and to devote their children wholly to God, as well as themselves, and to educate them in his fear. If nature had not taught birds and beasts to feed their young, as well as to generate them, their kind would be soon extinct. Oh what a blessed world were it, if the blessings of men famous for wisdom and godliness were entailed on all that should spring from them! and if this were the common case!

Sect. 3. But the doleful miseries of the world have come from the degenerating of good men's posterity. Adam hath his Cain, and Noah his Ham, and David his Absalom; Solomon, Hezekiah, and Josiah, left not their like behind them. The present state of the Eastern churches is a dreadful instance. What places on earth were more honourable for faith and piety than Alexandria, Antioch, Jerusalem, Constantinople, Ephesus, Philadelphia, and the rest of those great and noble countries? and these also strengthened with the powerfullest christian empire that ever was on earth. And now they are places of barbarism, tyranny, and foolish Mahometanism, where the name of Christ is made a scorn, and the few christians that keep up that sacred profession, by tyranny kept in so great ignorance, that, alas! the vices of most of them dishonour their profession, as much as their enemies' persecutions do. Oh what a doleful difference is there between that great part of the world now, and what it was fourteen hundred or a thousand years ago!

And alas! were it not for the name of a pompous christian church, how plain an instance would Rome be of the same degeneracy! And some countries that received the blessing of reformation, have revolted into the darkness of popery. What a change was in England by Queen Mary's reign! And how many particular cities and towns are grown ignorant and malignant, which in former times were famous for religion! The Lord grant it may never be the case of London! Yea, how many persons of honourable and great families have so far degenerated from the famous wisdom and piety of their grandfathers, yea, and fathers, as to hate that which their parents loved, and persecute those whom their ancestors honoured! The names of many great men stand honoured in history for their holiness to God, and their service to their several countries, whose posterity are the men that we are most in danger of. Alas! in how few such houses hath piety kept any long succession! Yea, some take their fathers' virtues to be so much their dishonour, that they turn malignant persecutors, to free themselves from the supposed reproach of their relations. Yea, some preachers of the gospel, devoted to God by pious parents, become revilers of their own parents, and despisers of their piety, as the effect of factious ignorance.

Sect. 4. And on the other side, when piety hath successively, as a river, kept its course, what a blessing hath it proved! (But how rare is that!) And when children have proved better than their parents, it hath been the beginning of welfare to the places where they lived. How marvellously did the Reformation prevail in Germany in Luther's time, when God brought out of popish monasteries many excellent instruments of his service; and princes became wise and pious, whose parents had been blind or impious! Godliness or wickedness, welfare or calamity, follow the changes and quality of posterity.

And men live so short a time, that the work of educating youth aright is one half of the great business of man's life. He that hath a plantation of oaks, may work for twenty generations: but he that planteth gardens and orchards with plants that live but a little time, must be still planting, watering, and defending them.

Sect. 5. Among the ancient sages of the world, the Greeks and Romans, and much more among the Israelites, the care of posterity and public welfare was the great thing which differenced the virtuous and laudable, from those of a base, selfish, sensual disposition. He was the bravest citizen of Rome that did most love and best serve his country. And he was the saint among the Jews who most loved Sion, and the security and succession of its holy and peaceable posterity. And the christian faith, hope, and interest, do lead us herein to a much higher pitch, and to a greater zeal for public good, in following Him that whipped out profaners from the temple,—even a zeal of God's house which eateth us up. It teacheth us, by the cross, most effectually to deny ourselves, and to think nothing too dear to part with to edify the church of God; nor any labour or suffering too great for common good. It teacheth us to pray for the hallowing of God's name, the coming of his kingdom, and the doing of his will on earth, as it is done in heaven, before our daily bread, and any other personal interest of our own. Therefore the families of christians should be as so many schools or churches, to train up a succession of persons meet for the great communicative works to which God calleth all believers, in their several measures: it is eminently teachers, but it is also all others in their several ranks, who must be "the salt of the earth, and the lights of the world." And indeed the spirit of holiness is so eminently the spirit of love to God and man, that it inclineth every sanctified person to a communicative zeal, to make others wise, and good, and happy.

Sect. 6. And God in great mercy hath planted, yet more deeply and fixedly, the natural love of parents to their children, that it might be in them a spring of all this duty; so that though fleshly vice may make men mistake their children's good, as most ungodly men do their own, and think that it consisteth in that in which it doth not; yet still the general desire of their children's welfare, as well as of their own, is deeply rooted, and will work for their welfare, as soon as they well know wherein it doth consist. And God hath not given them this love, only for the good of the individual children, but much more for the commonwealth and church; that as many sticks make one fire, and many exercised soldiers one army, so many well-educated children may make up one peaceable and holy society.

Sect. 7. And accordingly it is much to be observed, that God hath not given children a natural love and submissiveness to parents, only for the personal benefit of their provision, and other helps; but especially that hereby they may be teachable and obedient to those instructions of their parents by which they may become blessings in their generations, and may conjunctly make up wise and holy societies, families, churches, and commonwealths. For these ends it is, that God hath bound you, as to reverence your masters, tutors, and pastors, so especially both to reverence and love your parents, that you may be the more capable of their necessary instruction and advice.

Sect. 8. Yea, the great strictness of God, in condemning polygamy, adultery, and fornication, seemeth to be especially for the securing of the good education of children, for their souls and for the public good. For it is notorious, that confusion in marriages and generation would many ways tend to the depraving of human education, while mothers had not the necessary encouragement to perform their part. The younger women would be awhile esteemed, and afterwards be cast off and made most miserable; and families be like wandering beggars, or like exposed orphans; disorder and confusion would deprive children of much of their necessary helps, and barbarousness and brutishness corrupt mankind.

By all this it is most evident, that the great means of the welfare of the world must be the faithful and holy endeavours of parents, and the willing teachableness and obedience of children, that they may escape the snares of folly and fleshly lusts, and may betimes get that wisdom and love of goodness which may make them fit to be blessings to the places where they live.

CHAPTER IV.

HOW THE CASE STANDETH WITH OUR YOUTH IN MATTER OF FACT.

Sect. 1. Through the great mercy of God, many families are sacred nurseries for church and kingdom; and many parents have great comfort in the grace of God appearing in their children. From their early childhood many are of humble, obedient dispositions, and have a love to knowledge, and a love to the word of God, and to those that are good and virtuous persons. They have inward convictions of the evil of sin, and a fear of sinning, and a great dislike of wicked persons, and a great love and reverend obedience to their parents; and when they grow up, they diligently learn in private and in public: they increase in their love to the Scriptures and good books, and to godly teachers and godly company; and God saveth them from temptations, and worldly deceits, and fleshly lusts; and they live to God, and are blessings to the land, the joy of their friends, and exemplary and useful to those whom they converse with.

Sect. 2. But all, even religious parents, have not the like blessing in their children. 1. Some of them, though religious otherwise, are lamentably careless of the duty which they promised to perform (at baptism) in the education of their children, and do but superficially and formally instruct them; and are too faulty as to the example which they should give them, and seem to think that God must bless them because they are theirs, and because they are baptized, while they neglect their promised endeavours. 2. And some children when they grow up, and are bound to resist temptations, and to use God's appointed means for their own good, do wilfully resist God's grace, and run into temptations, and neglect and wretchedly betray themselves, and forfeit the mercies which they needed.

Sect. 3. In all my observation, God hath most blessed the children of those parents who have educated them as followeth: 1. Those that have been particularly sensible what they promised for them in the baptismal vow, and made conscience of performing it. 2. Those that have had more care for their souls than of their outward wealth. 3. Those that have been most careful to teach them the pravity of corrupted nature by original sin, and to humble them, and teach them the need of a Saviour, and his renewing as well as pardoning grace, and to tell them the work of the Spirit of sanctification, and teach them above all to look to the inward state of their souls. 4. Those that have most seriously minded them of death, judgment, and the life to come. 5. Those that have always spoken of God with the greatest reverence, affection, and delight. 6. Those that have most wisely laboured to make all the knowledge and practice of religion pleasant unto them, by the suitableness of doctrines and duties to their capacity. 7. Those that have most disgraced sin to them, especially base and fleshly pleasures. 8. Those that have kept them from the baits of sensuality, not gratifying their appetites in meats and drink, to bring them to an unruly habit; but used them to a habit of temperance, and neglect of appetite. 9. Those that have most disgraced worldliness and pride to them, and used them to low things in apparel and possession, and told them how the proud are hateful to God, and set before them the example of a crucified Christ, and opened to them the doctrine of mortification, and self-denial, and the great necessity of true humility. 10. Those that have been most watchful to know their children's particular inclinations and temptations, and apply answerable remedies, and not carelessly leave them to themselves. 11. Those that have been most careful to keep them from ill company, especially, (1.) Of wicked youths, of their own growth and neighbourhood; (2) And of tempting women. 12. Those that have most wisely used them to the meetest public teachers, and helped them to remember and understand what they hear, especially the fundamental truths in the catechism. 13. Those that have most wisely engaged them into the familiarity and frequent converse of some suitable, godly, exemplary companions. 14. Those that have most conscionably spent the Lord's days in public and in their families. 15. Those that have done all this, as with reverend gravity, so especially with tender endearing love to their children; convincing them that it is all done for their own good; and that do not by imprudent weaknesses, ignorance, passions, or scandal, frustrate their own endeavours. 16. Those that use not their children as mere patients, only to hear what their parents say; but engage them to constant endeavours of their own, for their own good; especially in the reading of Scripture, and the most suitable books, and meditating on them, and daily personal prayer to God. 17. Lastly, those that pray most heartily and believingly for God's grace and his blessing on their endeavours.—Such men's children are usually blessed.

Sect. 4. But it is no wonder, where such means are neglected, (much more when parents are ungodly, fleshly, worldly persons, and perhaps enemies to a holy life,) if the children of such are ignorant, deluded, ungodly, and drowned in fleshly lusts. And alas! it is the multitude of such, and their sad conditions, which is the occasion of my writing this epistle.

Sect. 5. 1. We see to our grief, that many children are of a stupid and unteachable disposition, and almost uncapable of instruction, who yet can as quickly learn to talk of common matters as other persons, and can as easily learn a trade, or how to do any ordinary business. And though some inconsiderate persons overlook the causality of the more immediate parents' sins, in such judgments on their children, as if it were only Adam's sin that hurt them, I have elsewhere proved, that this is their great and dangerous mistake. As David's child died for the father's sin, the children of gluttons, drunkards, fornicators, oft contract such bodily distempers as greatly tend to stupify or further vitiate the mind. And their souls may have sad additions to the common human pravity.

2. Accordingly many children have more violent passions, and carnal desires, than others, which run them into wicked ways impetuously, as if they were almost brutes, that had no reason or power to resist. And all words and corrections are to them of little force; but they are as blocks, that, when you have said and done what you can, go away as if they had not heard you.

3. And some have cross and crooked natures, addicted to that which is naught, and the more, by how much the more you do contradict them: froward and obstinate, as if it were a desirable victory to them to overcome their parents, and escape all that would make them wise and good: dogged, sour, proud, self-willed, and utterly disobedient.

4. And too many have so great an enmity and averseness to all that is holy, spiritual, and heavenly, that they are weary to hear you talk of it; and you persuade them to learn, to read, to pray, to meditate or consider, as you persuade a sick man to meat which he doth loathe, or a man to dwell with those that he hateth. They have no appetite to such things, no pleasure in them; when you have said all of God, and Christ, and glory, they believe it not, or they savour it not: they are things above their reach and love, yea, things against their carnal minds. You tire them worse than if you talked in a strange language to them,—such enmity is in the heart of corrupted man to God and heaven, till the grace of the Great Reconciler overcome it by a new life, and light, and love.

5. And when custom is added to all these vicious dispositions, alas, what slaves and drudges of Satan doth it make them! For instance,

(1.) Some are so corrupted with the love of sport, that gaming or stage-plays, or one such foolery or another, becometh so pleasant to them, that they can understand or believe nothing that is said against it by God or man; their diseased fantasy hath so conquered reason, that they cannot restrain themselves; but in their callings and in religious exercises they are weary, and long to be at their sports, and must be gone: neither God, nor holiness, nor the joys of heaven are half so sweet to their thoughts as these are. For they have that mark of misery, (2 Tim. iii. 4,) "They are lovers of pleasures more than lovers of God."

The same I say of sinful mirth, and the company which doth cherish it. Little do they believe Solomon: Eccl. vii. 2—4, "It is better to go to the house of mourning, than to go to the house of feasting: for that is the end of all men, and the living will lay it to his heart. Sorrow is better than laughter: for by the sadness of the countenance the heart is made better. The heart of the wise is in the house of mourning, but the heart of fools is in the house of mirth. It is better to hear the rebuke of the wise, than for a man to hear the song of fools: for as the crackling of thorns under a pot, so is the laughter of fools."

It is true, that mirth is very desirable to nature; and God is not against it, but much more for it than sinners will believe. But it is a rational mirth which beseemeth a rational creature, and such as he can justify, and as will make him better, and tends to felicity and everlasting mirth; and not the causeless mirth of mad-men, who set their house on fire, and then laugh and sing over it; nor like the mirth of a drunken man, whose shame exposeth him to pity or derision; nor any such mirth as leadeth a man from God to sin, and keepeth him from the way of manlike and everlasting joy, and prepareth for the greatest sorrows.

(2.) There are some so enslaved to their appetites, that their reason hath no power to rule them; but, like brutes, they must needs have what the belly and throat desire. And if they be the children of the rich, (who have always full and pleasant food,) constant flesh-pleasing and true gluttony is taken for no sin: and, like swine, they do but live to eat, whereas they should but eat to live, and cheerfully serve God.

But it is never so dangerous as when it turneth to

the love of drink. Then the pleasing of the throat, and the pleasing of the brain by mirth, going together, do so much corrupt the appetite and fancy, that their thoughts run after it, and reason hath no power to shut their mouths, nor keep them from the house of sin. Some sin against an accusing conscience, and under their convictions and terrors do drink on; which yet they could forbear, if they knew there were poison in the cup. Some are more miserable, and have sinned themselves into searedness of conscience and past feeling, and perhaps into infidelity and a blinded mind, persuading them that there is no great harm or danger in the sin, and that it is but some precise people that make so great a matter of it. And some, that have purposes to forsake the sin when appetite stirs, forget it all; and when company enticeth, and when they see the cup, they have no power to forbear. Oh what a pitiful sight it is to see men in the flower of youth and strength, when they should most rejoice in God and holiness, to be still thirsty after a forbidden pleasure, and hasting to the tavern or ale-house, as a bird to the snare of the fowler, and sweetly and greedily swallowing the poisonous cup which God forbiddeth! And that false repentance which conscience and experience force them to sometimes, is forgotten the next day when the temptation is renewed: yea, the throat madness, and the merry and belly devils are within them a continual temptation, which the miserable slaves cannot resist.

(3.) And these beastly, fleshly sins do usually make them weary of their callings, and of any honest labour: the devil hath by this time got possession of their thoughts, by the bias of delight and sinful lust; and they are thinking of meat or drink, or play, or merry company, when they should be diligently at work: and so idleness becomes the nursery of temptation, and of all their other vice, as well as a constant sin of omission and loss of hasty, precious time. And custom increaseth the habits, and maketh them good for nothing, and like dead men to all that life is given them for, and only alive to prepare by sin for endless misery.

(4.) And usually pride also takes its part, to make the sin of Sodom in them complete: Ezek. xvi. 49, "Pride, fulness, and idleness." They that must be in their jovial company, must not seem despicable among them, but must be in the mode and fashion, whatever it cost. When they make themselves odious in the sight of God, and the pity of all wise men, and a terror to themselves, yet they must be somebody to their sottish companions, especially of the female sex; lest the image of the devil, and his victory over them, should not be perfect, if pride were left out, how unreasonable soever.

(5.) And by this time they have (usually here amongst the rich and idle) a further step towards hell to go, and yet a deep gulf to fall into; fleshly lust next entangleth them in immodest converse with women, and thence into filthy fornication. The devil will seldom lose a soul for want of a temptation: either he will provide them one abroad, among their lewd companions, or at home some daughter or servant of the house, where they can oft get opportunity, first for uncivil sights and touches, and then for actual fornication. And if they have done it once, they are usually like the bird that is fast in the lime-twigs: conscience may struggle, but lust holds them fast, and the devil saith, If once may be pardoned, why not twice, and if twice, why not thrice? "And so they go on as an ox to the slaughter, and as a fool to the correction of the stocks, and know not that it is for their lives," Prov. vii. 21—23. "Till they mourn at last (perhaps) when flesh and body are consumed, and say, How have I hated instruction, and my heart despised reproof, and have not obeyed the voice of my teachers, nor inclined my ears to them that instructed me! I was almost in all evil," &c. Prov. v. 12—14. And it is well for the wretches if this repentance be true and in time, that though the flesh be destroyed, the spirit may be saved: for Solomon saith, Prov. ii. 18, 19, "Her house inclineth to death, and her paths to the dead: none that go unto her return again, neither take they hold of the path of life."

God, I doubt not, recovereth some, but the case is dangerous. For though age and sickness cure lust, usually before that the conscience is seared and debauched, and "they being past feeling, work uncleanness with greediness;" and, forsaking God, are so forsaken by him that all other sin, sensuality, and enmity against a holy life, prevail against them, and the unclean devil lets in many more. Most debauched drunkards, gluttons, and fornicators, are so enslaved to Satan, that they think, say, and do what he would have them, and become the enemies and persecutors of those that are against their sin; and the blinded Sodomites go on to grope for the door of Lot, as one that reproveth them, till the flames of justice stop the rage.

(6.) And when all these sins have enslaved sensual youths, they must have money to maintain them; and if they have it not of their own, and be not the sons of great men, who will maintain them in the service of the flesh, they must steal to get it, which usually is either by thievish borrowing when they cannot pay, or by robbing their parents or masters. If all the masters in London knew what thieves their apprentices' vices are, for their own sakes they would take greater care to watch over them, and keep them from ill company, drunkenness, and plays, and would teach them to seek pleasure in good books, good company, and serving God. I had not known it myself if the confessions and restitution of many penitent converts had not made me know it. I thank God that he recovereth any, yea, so many; but I must tell foolish youth, that repentance itself, especially when it must have restitution, is so bitter, that they would prevent that need of it, if they had but the use of reason and foresight. Oh what heart-tearing confessions and sad letters have I had from many young apprentices in this city! Much ado to escape utter despair they had, when conscience was awakened to remember all their sin and danger! And when they knew that they must restore (if possible) all that ever they deceived or robbed their masters or any others of, oh what difficulties hath it put them to, both as to the shame of confession and the actual restitution! Some have not money; and to go and confess the sin and debt, and to promise to pay it if ever they were able, seemeth hard, but must be done. Some have rough masters, that will disgrace them when they confess it. Some have parents that paid dear to set them apprentices, and would go near to cast them off if they knew their case. Some marry after, and it will grieve their wives to know what they have been, and how much they must restore. Wisdom might have prevented this; but if the thorn be got into the conscience it must come out, and if the poison be swallowed it must come up, what gripes soever the vomit cost. There is no playing with hell-fire, nor jesting with the justice of the most holy God. One penitent review of fleshly lust and sinful pleasure, of falsehood and deceit, (though wholesome, if true and timely,) will turn it all into gall and wormwood: for the end of sinful mirth is sorrow.

(7.) And too many there be who escape the gross and disgraceful part of the aforesaid sensuality and unrighteousness, that yet do but choose another idol, and set themselves wholly to rise in the world; and riches, preferment, and honour have almost all their hearts and care: that have no delight in God and holiness; nor doth the state of their souls, or the thought of their everlasting state, affect them in any measure according to its unspeakable weight, nor so much as these shadows which they pursue. And when great travellers that have seen much of the world, and old men and dying men that have had all that it can do, are forced by experience to call all vanity and vexation, unexperienced youth that are taken up with the hopes of long prosperity, and provision for all that the flesh desireth, have other thoughts of it, and will not know that it is deceitful vanity till it hath deceived them of their chiefest hope and treasure. And when they have overtaken the shadow which they pursue so greedily, they find it (what others have done before them) the sweeter the more dangerous, and the parting will be the more bitter. Whereas had they sought first God's kingdom and its righteousness, and six days laboured in obedience to God, and referred all corporal blessings to spiritual uses and everlasting ends, taking them as from God to serve him by them, they might have had enough as an overplus to their satisfying treasure.

CHAPTER V.

HOW SAD A CASE IT IS THAT I HAVE DESCRIBED.

I HAVE told you the very lamentable case of too many young men, especially rich men's sons, and apprentices in this city: I told you before of what concern the state of youth is to themselves and others. From thence (and, alas! from sad experience) it is easy to gather the dolefulness of the case of those that are drowned in fleshly lust, and have sinned themselves into the guilt and danger which I have described. But I will name some parts of the misery more particularly again.

Review the second chapter, and think what a doleful case this is to yourselves.

Sect. 1. Do you not know that you are not beasts, but men who have reason given them to know, and love, and serve their Maker? And how sad is it to see a man forget all this, and wilfully brutify himself! Were the poets' fictions true of men turned into trees, and birds, and beasts, how small were the misery in comparison of yours! It is no sin in brutes to lust, or to eat and drink too much. They have not reason to restrain and rule them; but lest they should kill themselves by excess, God hath made reasonable man their governor, and moderateth their appetite in the temper of their natures. But for a reasonable creature to subject himself to fleshly appetite, and wilfully degrade his soul to the rank of brutes, is worse than if he had been made with the body and the unreasonableness of brutes. Are you capable of no better things than these?

Sect. 2. And what an odious thing is it,—when God hath chosen you out of the world to be members of his visible church, and given you the great privilege of early entrance into his holy covenant, and washed you in the laver of visible regeneration, and you are vowed to Christ, renouncing the lusts of the flesh, of the world, and the devil, that you might follow a crucified Christ in the way of holiness to everlasting life,—that you should so soon prove false, perfidious traitors and rebels against him that is your only hope, and, by wickedness and covenant-breaking, make your sin greater than that of infidels, Turks, and heathens, who never were taken into the church and covenant of Christ, nor ever broke the vows which you have broken, nor so cast away the mercies which you had received!

Sect. 3. And what a doleful case is it, that so much of your minds, and love, and delight, which were all made for God, should be so misemployed, even in your strength, when they should be most vigorous; and all worse than cast away on filth and folly! If your souls be more worth than your money, it is more folly and loss to misemploy and abuse your souls, your reason, love, and your delight, than to abuse or cast away your money. And what a traitor or murderer deserveth, that would give his money to hire one to kill the king, or his neighbour, I suppose you know; and what deserveth he that will use, not only his money, but himself, his soul, his thoughts, his love, his desire and pleasure, against the most glorious God that made him? That you cannot hurt him is no thanks to you while you break his laws, and deny him your love and duty, and love more that one thing which only he hateth, and will never be reconciled to.

Sect. 4. And how doleful a case is it that all the care, and love, and labour of your parents, masters, and teachers should be lost upon you! God hath made all this their great duty for your good; and will you despise God and them, and wilfully for nothing reject it all? Shall all the pain of a child-bearing mother, and all her trouble and labour to breed you up, and all the care of your parents to provide for you, be but to breed up a slave for the flesh, the world, and the devil, and a firebrand for hell? Shall godly parents' prayers for you, and teaching and counsel of you, and all their desire and care for your salvation, be despised by you, and all forgotten and cast away for a swinish lust?

Sect. 5. And how doleful a case is it, that so much of so short a life should be lost, and a thousand times worse than lost,—even turned into sin, to prepare for misery, when, alas! the longest life is little enough for our important work, and quickly gone, and the reckoning and Judge are hard at hand! All the wealth, wit, or power in the world, cannot bring or buy you back one hour of all that precious time which you now so basely cast away. Oh how glad would you be of a little of it, ere long, on the terms that now you have it, when you lie dying, and perceive that your souls are unready to appear before a righteous God! Then oh for one year more of precious time! oh that you knew how to call again that time which you cast away on sin! You will then perceive with a terrified conscience, that time was not so little worth as you once thought it, nor given you for so base a work. Yea, if God in mercy bring you hereafter to true conversion, oh how it will wound your hearts to think how much of your youth was so madly cast away, while your God, your souls, and everlasting hopes, were all neglected and despised!

Sect. 6. And, alas, if you should be cut off in that unholy, miserable state, no heart on earth can sufficiently bewail your case! How many thousands die young, that promised themselves longer pleasure in sin, and repentance after it! O foolish sinners! cannot you so long borrow the use of your reason, as to think seriously whither you must go next? Do you never think when the small-pox or a fever hath taken away one of your companions, whither it is that his soul is gone? Have you your wit for nothing but to taste the sweetness of drink or lust, which is as pleasant to a dog or swine as to you? O, little do you know what it is to die! what it is for a soul to leave the body, and enter into an endless world, to come to judgment for all his sins, and all his ill-spent days and hours, and for choosing the pleasures of a swine before heaven and the pleasures of a saint! Little know you what it is for devils presently to take away to hell a wretched soul which they have long deceived! I tell you, the thought of appearing before God, and Christ, and angels in another world, and entering on an endless state, is so dreadful, even to many that have spent their lives in holy preparation, and are indeed in a safe condition, that they have much ado to overcome the terror of death. Even some of God's own faithful servants are almost overwhelmed, when they think of so great a change: and though the belief of God's love and the heavenly glory do support them, and should make them long to be with Christ, yet, alas! faith is weak, and the change is great beyond our comprehension, and therefore feared. Oh then in what case is a wicked, unpardoned, unprepared wretch, when his guilty soul must be torn from his body, and dragged in terror to hear its doom, and so to the dreadful execution! Sinners! is this a light matter to you? Doth it not concern you? Are you not here mortal? Do you not know what flesh is, and what a grave is? And are not your abused souls immortal? Are you so mad as to forget this, or so bad as not to believe it? Will your not believing it, make void the justice and the law of God, and save you from that hell which only believing could have saved you from? Will not the fire burn you, or the sea drown you, if you can but run into it drunk or winking? Is feeling, remediless feeling, easier than believing God in time? Alas! what should your believing friends do to save you? They see by faith whither you are posting. They foresee your terror and undone case; and fain, if possible, they would prevent it: but they cannot do it without you. If you will not consent and help yourselves, it is not the holiest nor wisest friends in the world that can help you. They would pull you out of the fire in fear, and out of the mouth of the roaring lion, but you will not be delivered! They call and cry to you, O fear God, and turn to him while there is hope; and you will not let conscience and reason be awakened. But those that go asleep to hell, will be past sleeping there for ever. O run not madly into the everlasting fire!

Sect. 7. And indeed your sleepy security and presumption do make your case more dangerous in itself, and more pitiful to all that know it. Oh what a sight is it to see a man go merry and laughing towards damnation, and make a jest of his own undoing! to see him at the brink of hell, and will not believe it! like a mad-man boasting of his wit, or a drunken man of his sobriety; or as the swine is delighted, when the butcher is shaving his throat to cut it; or as the fatted lambs are skipping in the pasture, that to-morrow must be killed and eaten; or as the bird sits singing when the gun is levelled to kill him; or as the greedy fish run striving which shall catch the bait, that must presently be snatched out of her element, and lie dying on the bank.

But because I touched much of this in the second chapter, I will pass by the rest of your own concerns, and a little further consider how sad the case of such wretched youths is also unto others.

Sect. 8. And if parents be wise and godly, and understand such children's case, what a grief must it needs be to their hearts to think that they have begotten and bred up a child for sin and hell, and cannot make him willing to prevent it! to see their counsel set at nought, their teaching lost, their tears despised, and an obstinate lad seem wiser to himself than all his teachers, even when he is swallowing the devil's bait, and cruelly murdering his own soul! Ah! thinks a believing father and mother, have I brought thee into the world for this? Hath all my tender, natural love so sad an issue? Is this the fruit of all my sorrows, my care and kindness, to see the child of my bowels, whom I dedicated in baptism to Christ,—to make himself the child of the devil, the slave of the flesh and world, the enemy of God and holiness, and his own destroyer? and all this wilfully, obstinately, and against all the counsel and means that I can use! Alas! must I breed up a child to become an enemy to the church of God into which he was baptized, and a soldier for Satan against Christ? Must I breed up a child for hell, and see him miserable for ever, and cannot persuade him to be willing to be saved? Oh what a heart-breaking must this be to those whom nature and grace have taught to love them with tenderness, even as themselves!

Sect. 9. But if they be wicked parents, and as bad as themselves, the misery is far greater, though they yet feel it not: for,

1. As the thief on the cross said to his companion, "Thou art in the same condemnation, and we suffer justly; for we receive the due reward of our deeds," Luke xxiii. 40, 41; wicked parents and wicked children are in the same gall of bitterness and bond of iniquity. They sinned together, and they must suffer for ever together, if true faith and conversion do not prevent it.

2. And it is their wickedness which was much of the cause of their children's sin and misery; and their own deep guilt will be more to them than their children's suffering. God and conscience will say to them ere long, O cruel parents, that had no mercy on your children or yourselves! What did nature teach you to love more than yourselves and your children? and would you wilfully and obstinately be the ruin of both? You would not have done as the mad idolaters, that offered their children in fire to Moloch: and will you offer them by sin to Satan and to hell? Had a serpent stung them, or a bear devoured them, they had done but according to their nature: but was it natural in you to further their damnation? This was work too bloody for a cannibal, too cruel for an enemy, fitter for a devil than a father or mother. As your child had from you his vicious nature, it was your part to have endeavoured his sanctification and recovery. You should have taught him betimes to know the corruption of his nature, and to seek and beg the grace of Christ; to know his God, his duty, the evil of sin, the danger of temptations, and his everlasting hopes and fears. You should have taught him to know what man hath done against himself, by disobeying and departing from his God, and what Jesus Christ hath done for his redemption, and what he himself must do to be saved. You should have taught him early how to live and how to die, what to seek and what to shun. You should have given him the example of a holy and heavenly mind and life. You should have watched over him for his safety, and unweariedly instructed him for his salvation. But you led him the way to despise God's word, and set light by Christ, and holiness, and heaven, to hate instruction and reproof, to spend the Lord's day in idleness or worldly vanity, and to seek first the world and the prosperity of the body, and glut the flesh with sinful pleasure. What wonder if a serpent breed a serpent, and quickly teach him to hiss and sting, and if swine teach their young to feed on dung and wallow in the

mire? This is part of the fruit of your worldliness, fleshliness, ungodliness, and neglect of your own salvation and your child's. Now he is as you are, a slave of sin and an heir of hell. Was this it that you vowed him for to God in baptism? was it to serve the flesh, the world, and the devil, against our God, our Saviour, and our Sanctifier? or did the mistake of the liturgy deceive you, to think that it was not you, but the godfathers, that were bound by charge and vow to bring him up in the faith and fear of God, and teach him all that a christian should know for his soul's health? Was it not you whom God bound to all this? The sin and misery of your child now is so far your curse, as you are guilty of it, and will add to your misery for ever.—Such are the sorrows that wicked parents and wicked children do prepare and heap on one another. Such miseries will come; but woe to those by whom they come! it had been good for that man that he had never been born.

Sect. 10. And it is no small grief to faithful ministers, to see their labour so much lost; and to see so much evil among their flocks, and such sad prognostics of worse to come. He is no true minister of Christ, (as to his own acceptance and salvation,) whose heart is not set on the winning, and sanctifying, and saving of souls. What else do we study for, preach for, live for, long for, or suffer for in our work? All faithful teachers can say with Paul, that they "are willing to spend and be spent for them," and "now we live if ye stand fast in the Lord," 2 Cor. xii. 15; 1 Thess. iii. 8. He told them, "weeping, of those that were enemies to the cross of Christ, whose God was their belly, who glory in their shame, and mind earthly things," instead of a conversation in heaven, Phil. iii. 18, 19. When God hath blessed us with the comfortable enjoyment of many ancient, holy christians, who are the beauty and honour of the assemblies, and death calls home one of them after another to Christ, and the rest are ready to depart, alas! must a seed of serpents come after them? Must those take their places to our grief and shame, who are bred up to the world and flesh, in drunkenness, fornication, and enmity to God and a holy life? Oh what a woeful change is this!

And if any be like to be the stain and plague of the church, it is such as these. If we preach holy truth to them, lust cannot love it. If we tell them of God's word, the fleshly mind doth not savour it, nor can be subject to it, Rom. viii. 5—7. If we reprove them sharply, they smart and hate us. If we call them to confession and repentance, their pride and carnality cannot bear it. If we excommunicate them for impenitency, as Christ requireth, or but deny them the sacrament as unmeet, they rage against us as our fiercest enemies. If we neglect discipline, and admit swine to the communion of saints, we harden and deceive them, and flatter them in their sin, pollute the church, and endanger our souls by displeasing the Chief Pastor. What then shall we do with these self-murdering, ungodly men?

Many of them have so much reverence of a sacrament, or so little regard of it, that they never seek it, but keep away themselves. Perhaps they are afraid lest they eat and drink damnation to themselves, by the profanation of holy things. But do they think that it is safe to be out of the church and communion of saints, because it is dangerous to abuse it? Are infidels safe because false-hearted christians perish? What! if breaking your vows and covenant be damnable, is it not so to be out of the holy covenant? What! if God be a consuming fire to those that draw near him in unrepented heinous sin, is it therefore wise or safe to avoid him? Neither those that come not to him, nor those that come in their hypocrisy and reigning sin, shall be saved.

And yet, what to do with these self-suspenders, we know not. Are they still members of the churches, or are they not? If they are, we are bound to call them to repentance for forsaking the communion of saints in Christ's commanded ordinance. If they are not, we should make it known, that christians and no christians may not be confounded, and they themselves may understand their case. And neither of these can they endure; but for dwelling in the parish, and hearing the liturgy and sermons, must still pass for church members, lest discipline should exasperate and further lose them. This is that discipline which is thought worthy the honour of episcopal dignity and revenues, and is supposed to make the church of England the best in the world, by the same men that would rage, were discipline exercised on them; and must either be admitted to the sacrament in a life of fornication, drunkenness, sensuality, and profaneness, without any open confession, repentance, and reformation, or else must pass for church members without any exercise of discipline, while they shun the sacramental communion of the church. Such work doth wickedness make among us!

Sect. 11. Indeed these are the men that are the trouble of families, the trouble of neighbours, the trouble of good magistrates, the shame of bad ones, and the great danger of the land. All the foreign enemies whom we talk so much against, and fear, are not so hurtful and dangerous to us as these,—these that spring out of your own bowels; these that are bred up with care, and tenderness, and cost in your houses; these that should succeed godly ancestors in wisdom and well-doing, and be their glory. Who plot against us but homebred sinners? Who more hate the good, and persecute them? Who are more malignant enemies of godliness, and scorners of a holy life, and hinderers of the word of God, and patrons of profaneness, and of ministers and people that are of the same mind? If England be undone, (as the Eastern churches, and much of the Western, are undone,) it will be by your own carnal, ungodly posterity.

He that is once a slave to Satan and his fleshly lust, is ready, for preferment or a reward, to be a slave to the lust of any other. He that is false to his God and Saviour, after his baptismal vows, is unlike to be true to his country or his king, if he have but the bait of a strong temptation: and he that will sell his soul, his God, and heaven, for a whore, or for to please his appetite, it is like will not stick to betray church or state, or his dearest friend, for provision to satisfy these lusts. Can you expect that he should love any man better than himself? A wicked, fleshly, worldly man is a soil for Satan to sow the seeds in of any sort of actual sin, and is fuel dried, or tinder for the sparks of hell to kindle in. Will he suffer much for God or his country, who will sell heaven for nothing? An evil tree bringeth forth evil fruit. If he have the heart of an Achan, a Gehazi, an Ahithophel, no wonder if he hath their actions and their reward. If he be a thief and bear the bag, no wonder if Judas sell his master.

Sect. 12. And these wretches, if they live, are likely to be a plague to their own posterity. Woe to the woman that hath such a husband! And how are the children like to be bred, that have such a father? Doth not God threaten punishment to the third and fourth generation of them that hate him, and to visit the iniquities of the fathers on the children? Were not the children of the old world drowned, and those of Sodom and Gomorrah burned, and Achan's stoned, and Dathan's and Abiram's swallowed up, and Gehazi's struck with leprosy, &c. for their fathers' sins? And the Amalekites' children all destroyed, and the posterity of the infidel Jews forsaken, the curse coming on them and on their children? And as their children are like to speed the worse for such parents' sins, so are such parents like to be requited by their children. As you shamed and grieved the hearts of your parents, so may your children do by you. And by that time, it is like, if grace convert you not, though you have no hatred to your own sins, worldly interest may make you dislike your children's. Their lust and appetite do not tempt and deceive you, as your own did. Perhaps when they shame your family, debauch themselves with drink and whores, and consume the estates which you sold your souls for, you may perceive that sin is an evil and destructive thing; especially when they proceed to despise and abuse your persons also, and to desire your death, and be weary of you. Sooner or later you shall know better what sin is.

CHAPTER VI.

THE JOYFUL STATE AND BLESSING OF GOOD CHILDREN, TO THEMSELVES AND OTHERS.

Sect. 1. From what is said in the second and fifth chapters, it is easy to gather how joyful a case to themselves, and what a blessing to parents and others, it is when children betimes are sober, wise, godly, and obedient. The difference doth most appear at age, and when they come to bring forth to themselves and others the fruits of their dispositions. And the end, and life to come, will show the greatest difference; but yet, even here, and that betimes, the difference is very great.

Sect. 2. I. As to themselves: how blessed a state is it to be quickly delivered from the danger of damnation, and God's displeasure, that they need not lie down and rise in fear lest they be in hell whenever death removeth them from the body! Can one too soon be out of so dreadful a state? Can one who is in a house on fire, or fallen into the sea, make too much haste to be delivered? If a man deep in debt be restless till it be paid, and glad when it is discharged; if a man in danger of sickness, or a condemning sentence of the judge, be glad when the fear of death is over; how glad should you be to be safe from the great danger of damnation! And till you are sanctified by grace, you are far from safety.

Sect. 3. And if a man's sickness, pain, or distraction be a calamity, the cure of which brings ease and joy; how much more ease and joy may it bring, to be cured from all the grievous maladies of reigning sin! Sanctification will cure your minds of spiritual blindness and madness, that is, of damnable ignorance, unbelief, and error. It will cure your affections of idolatrous, distracting, carnal love; of the itch of fleshly desires or lusts, of the fever of revengeful passions, and malignant hatred to goodness and good men; and of self-vexing envy and malice against others, of the greedy worm of covetousness, and the drunken desire of ambitious and imperious minds. It will cure your wills of their fleshly servitude and bias, and of that mortal backwardness to God and holy things, and that sluggish dulness and lothness to choose and do what you are convinced must be done. It will make good things easy and pleasant to you; so that you will no more think you have need to beg mirth from the devil or steal it from sin,—as if God, grace, and glory had none for you. But it will be so easy to you to love and find pleasure in the Bible and good books, in good company and good discourse, in spiritual meditations and thoughts, in holy sermons, prayers, and church communion and sacraments, even in Christ, in God, and the forethoughts of heaven, that you will be sorry and ashamed to think that ever you forsook such joys for fleshly pleasure, and defiled your souls with filthy and forbidden things. And is not the itch of lust better cured than scratched? is not the feverish and dropsical thirst after drink, wealth, and honour, better cured than pleased to the sinner's death? And is not a lazy backwardness to duty better cured by spiritual health than pleased with idleness and sleep?

Sect. 4. And certainly you cannot too soon attain the delights of faith, hope, and love, of holy knowledge and communion with God and saints. You cannot too soon have the great blessing of righteousness, peace, and joy in the Holy Ghost; and live night and day in peace of conscience,—in assurance that all your sins are pardoned, and that you are the adopted sons of God and heirs of heaven, sealed by his Spirit, accepted in your prayers, welcome to God through Christ, and when you die shall be with him. Can you make too great haste from the folly and filth of sin, and the danger of hell, into so safe and good a state as this?

Sect. 5. And it will be a great comfort to you thus to find, at age and use of reason, that your baptismal blessings ceased not with your infancy by your own rejection, but that you are now by your own consent in the bond of God's covenant, and have a right to all the blessings of it, which the sacrament of Christ's body and blood will confirm; as you had your entrance by your parent's consent and accepted dedication: for the covenant of grace is our certain charter for grace and glory.

Sect. 6. And is it not a joy to you to be your parents' joy, to find them love you not only as their children, but as God's? Love maketh it sweet to us to please and be beloved by those whom we love. If it be not your grief to grieve your parents, and your pleasure to please them, you love them not, but are void of natural affection.

Sect. 7. And oh what a mercy will you find it, when you come to age and business in the world! 1. That you come with a clear conscience, not clogged, terrified, and shamed with the sins of your youth. 2. And that you come not utterly unfurnished with the knowledge, righteousness, and virtue, which you must make use of in every condition, all your lives; when others are like lads who will go to the universities before they can so much as read or write. To live in a family of your own, and to trade and converse in the world, and especially to go to church, to hear, to pray, to communicate, to pray in private, to meditate, in a word, to live or die like a christian, like a man, without the furniture of wisdom, faith, and serious godliness,—is more impossible and unwise than to go to sea without provision, or to war without arms, or to become a priest without book or understanding.

Sect. 8. II. And you that are young men, can scarce conceive what a joy a wise and godly child is to his wise and godly parents. Read but Prov. x. 1; xiii. 1; xvii. 2, 25; xix. 13, 26; xxvii. 11; xxiii. 15, 19, 24, &c. The prayers and instructions of your parents are comfortable to them, when they see the happy fruit and answer. They fear not God's judgments upon their houses, as they would do if you were Cains, or Hams, or Absaloms: they labour comfortably, and comfortably leave you their estates at death, when they see that they do not get and leave it for those that will serve the devil with it, and consume it on their lusts; but will use it for God, for the gospel, and their salvation. If you fall sick and die before them, they can rejoice that you are gone to Christ; and need not mourn as David for Absalom, that you go to hell. If you overlive them, they leave the world the easier, when they leave as it were part of themselves here behind them, who will carry on the work of God which they lived for, and be blessings to the world when they are gone.

Sect. 9. III. And oh what a mercy is it to church and state, to have our posterity prove better than we have been, and do God more service than we have done, and take warning by our faults to avoid the like! Solomon tells us of one poor wise man that saved a city; and God would have spared Sodom, had there been but ten righteous persons in it. Wherever yet I lived, a few persons have proved the great blessings of the place,—to be teachers, guides, and exemplary to others, as the little leaven that leaveneth the lump, and as the stomach, liver, and other nutritive parts are to the body. Blessed is that church, that city, that country, that kingdom, which hath a wise, just, and holy people! The nearest good and evil are the greatest: our estates are not so near us as wives and children, nor they so near us as our bodies, nor they so much to us as our souls. It is more to a person, house, or country, what they are, than what they have, or what others do for them or against them.

It is these that are God's children as well as ours, who are the blessing so often mentioned in the Scripture, who will, as the Rechabites, obey their fathers' wholesome counsels, rather than their lusts and carnal companions, and God before all:—"Who walk not in the counsel of the ungodly, nor stand in the way of sinners, nor sit in the seat of the scornful. But their delight is in the law of the Lord, and in that law they meditate day and night," Psal. i. "Lo, such children are an heritage of the Lord; such fruit of the womb is his reward. They are as arrows in the hand of a mighty man. Happy is the man that hath his quiver full of them. They shall not be ashamed; but they shall speak with the enemies in the gate," Psal. cxxvii. 3—5. Were it not for wise and godly children to succeed us, religion, peace, and all public good, would be but as we frail mortals are,—like the grass or flowers of a few days' or years' continuance; and the difference between a church and no church, between a kingdom of christians and of infidels, would be but like the difference between our waking and our sleeping time, so short as would make it the less considerable.

CHAPTER VII.

UNDENIABLE REASONS FOR THE REPENTANCE AND SPEEDY AMENDMENT OF THOSE THAT HAVE LIVED A FLESHLY AND UNGODLY LIFE: BY WAY OF EXHORTATION.

SECT. 1. And now the commands of God, the love of my country and the church, the love of piety, true prosperity, and peace, and the love of mankind, even of your own souls and bodies, do all command me to become once more an earnest suitor to the youth of this land, especially of London, who have hitherto miscarried, and lived a fleshly, sinful life. Thousands such as you are dead in sin, and past our warning, and past all hope and help for ever. Thousands that laughed at judgment and damnation, are now feeling that which they would not believe. By the great mercy of God it is not yet the case of you who read these words; but how soon it may be, if you are yet unsanctified, you little know. Oh that you knew what a mercy it is to be yet alive, and, after so many sins and dangers, to have one to warn you, and offer you salvation, and to be yet in possibility, and in a state of hope! In the name of Christ I most earnestly entreat you, a little while try to use your reason, and use it seriously in retired, sober consideration, till you have first well perused the whole course of your lives, and remembered what you have done and how, till you have thought what you have got or lost by sinning, and why you did it, and whether it was justifiable reason which led you to it, and such as you will stand to in your sober thoughts, yea, such as you will stand to before God at last. Consider seriously what comes next, and whither you are going, and whether your life have fitted you for your journey's end, and how your ways will be reviewed ere long, and how they will appear to you, and taste at death, judgment, and in the world to come. Hold on and think soberly a little while, what is in your hearts, and what is their condition, what you most love, and what you hate, and whether God or sinful pleasure be dearer and more delightful to you, and how you stand affected and related to the world that you are very near. Sure reason would be reason if you would but use it; sure light would come in, if you would not shut the windows, and draw the curtains on you, and rather choose to sleep in darkness. Is there nothing within you that grudgeth at your folly, and threateneth you for being wilfully beside yourselves? If you would but spend one half hour in a day, or a week, in sober thinking whither you are going, and what you have done, and what you are, and what you must shortly see and be; how could you choose but be deeply offended with yourselves, for living like men quite void of understanding, against your God, against yourselves, against all the ends and obligations of life, and this for nothing?

But, it may be, the distinctness of your consideration may make it the more effectual: and if I put my motives by way of questions, will you consider them till you have well answered them all?

Sect. 2. *Quest.* 1. Are you not fully convinced, that there is a God of infinite power, knowledge, and goodness, who is the perfect Governor of all the world? God forbid that any of you should be so bad and so mad, as seriously to doubt of this, which the devils believe, while they would draw you to unbelief. To doubt of a perfect governing God, is to wink and doubt whether there be a sun, to stop your ears against the notorious testimony of heaven and earth, and every creature. You may next doubt whether there be any thing, if you doubt of God. For atoms and shadows are hardlier perceived with certainty, than the earth, the heavens, and sun.

Quest. 2. If you believe that there is a governing God, do you not believe that he hath governing laws or notifications of his will, and that we owe this God more full, more absolute, exact obedience, than can be due to any prince on earth, and greater love than to our dearest friend, He being infinitely good and love itself? Can you owe more to your flesh, or to any, than to your God that made you men, by whom you have life, and health, and time, and all the good that ever you received? And can you give him too much love and obedience? or can you think that you need to fear being losers by him, and that your faithful duty should be in vain?

Quest. 3. Is it God that needeth you, or you that need him? Can you give him any thing that he wants, or do you want what he hath to give? Can you live an hour without him? or be kept without him from pain, misery, or death? Is it not for your own need, and your own good, that he requireth your service? Do you know what his service is? It is thankfully to receive his greatest gifts, to take his medicines to save your souls, and to feast on his prepared comforts. He calls you to far better and needfuller obedience for yourselves, than when you command your child to take his meat, or wear his clothes, or, when he is sick, to take a necessary remedy. And is such obedience to be refused?

Quest. 4. Hath not nature taught you to love yourselves? Surely you cannot be willing to be damned, nor be indifferent whether you go to heaven or hell! And can you believe, that God would set you on that which would do you hurt, and that the devil is your friend and would save you from him? Can you believe that to please your throat and lust, till death snatch away your souls to judgment, is more for your own good than to live here in holiness and the love of God, and hereafter to live for ever in glory? Do you think you have lived as if you truly loved yourselves, or as self-destroyers? All the devils in hell, or enemies on earth, could never have done so much against you, as, by your sensuality, ungodliness, and sloth, you have done against yourselves. O poor sinner, as ever thou wouldst have mercy from God in thy extremity, be entreated to show some mercy on thyself!

Quest. 5. Hath not nature deeply taught all the world, to make a great difference between virtue and vice, between moral good and evil? If the good and bad do not greatly differ, what makes all mankind, even the sons of pride, to be so impatient of being called or accounted bad, and love to be accounted wise and good? How tenderly do most men bear a reproof, or to hear that they do amiss! To be called a wicked man, a liar, a perjured man, a knave, how ill is it taken by all mankind! This certainly proveth that the conscience of the great difference between the GOOD and the BAD, is a common natural notice. And will not God make a greater difference, who better knoweth it than man?

Quest. 6. If God had only commanded you duty, even a holy, righteous, and sober life, and forbidden you the contrary, and had only bidden you to seek everlasting happiness, and made you no promise of it, should you not in reason seek it cheerfully in hope? Our folly leadeth us to do much in vain; but God setteth no man on any vain employment. If he do but bid you resist temptation, mortify lust, learn his word, pray to him, and praise him, you may be sure it is not to your loss. A reward you may be sure of, though you know not what it will be. Yea, if he set you upon the hardest work, or to pass the greatest danger, or serve him at the dearest rate, or lose your estate for him, and life itself, what reason can there be for fear of being losers by obeying God? Yea, the dearest service hath the greatest reward. But when he hath moreover ascertained your reward by a promise, a covenant sworn and sealed by his miracles, by Christ's blood, by his sacraments, by his Spirit, if yet you will be ungodly because you cannot trust him, you have no excuse.

Quest. 7. Do you know the difference between a man and a brute? Brutes have no capacity to think of a God, and a Saviour, and a life to come, and to know God's law, and study obedience, and fear hell and sin; nor reason to rule their appetites and lusts, nor any hope or joy in foreseen glory. But man is made capable of all this: and can you think God maketh such noble faculties in vain? Or should we live like brutes that have none such?

Quest. 8. Do you not certainly know, that you must die? All the world cannot hinder it: YOU MUST DIE. And is it not near, as well as sure? How swift is time! Oh how quickly shall we all be at our race and warfare's end! And where then is the pleasure of pride, and appetite, and lust? Neither the dismal carcass, nor the dust or bones, retain or taste it: and alas! the unconverted soul must pay for it for ever. And can you think that so short a brutish pleasure, that hath so sure and sad an end, is worthy the grieving of your friends, the offending God, the hazard of your souls, the loss of heaven, and the suffering of God's justice in hell for ever? O foolish sinners! I beseech you think in time how mad a bargain you are making. Oh what an exchange! for a filthy lust or fleshly pleasure, to sell a God, a Saviour, a Comforter, a soul, a heaven, and all your hopes!

Quest. 9. If the devil or deceivers should make you doubt whether there be any judgment and life to come, should not the mere possibility and probability of such a day and life be far more regarded by you than all fleshly pleasure, which is certainly short and base? Did you ever hear a man so mad as to say, I am sure there is no heaven or hell for souls? But you are sure that your flesh must rot in a dark grave; you are sure that death will quickly put an end to all that this world can afford you. House and land, and all that now deceive poor worldlings, will be nothing to you, (no more than if you had never seen them,) save the terrible reckoning that the soul must make. Sport and mirth, and meat and drink, and filthy lusts, are ready all to leave you to the final sentence of your Judge. And is not even an uncertain hope of heaven more worth than certain transitory vanity? Is not an uncertain hell to be more feared and avoided, than the forsaking of these certain trifles and deceits? Much more when God hath so certainly revealed to us the life to come!

Quest. 10. Is it a wise and reasonable expectation, that the righteous God should give that man everlasting glory, who will not leave his whores, his drunkenness, or the basest vanity, for all his love and for all his mercies, for the sake of Christ or for the hopes of all this glory? Heaven is the greatest reward of holiness, and of the diligent and patient seekers of it: heaven is the greatest gift of the great love of God: and can you believe that he will give it to the slaves of the devil, and to contemning, wilful rebels? May not you next think, that the devils may be saved? If you say that "God is merciful," it is most true; and this will be the unconverted man's damnation,—that he would for a base lust offend so MERCIFUL a GOD, and sell everlasting mercy for nothing, and abuse so much MERCY all his life. Abused and refused mercy will be the fuel to feed the flames of hell, and torment the conscience of the impenitent for ever. Doth not God know his own mercy better than you do? Can he not be merciful, and yet be holy and just? Is the king unmerciful, if he make use of jails and gallows for malefactors? It is mercy to the land to destroy such as would destroy others. The bosom of Eternal Love is not a place for any but the holy. The heavenly paradise is not like Mahomet's,—a place of lust and sensual delights. You blaspheme the most just and holy God, if you make him seem indifferent to the holy and the unholy, to his faithful servants and to the despisers of his grace.

Quest. 11. If there were any possibility, that unsanctified souls should be sanctified and saved in another world, is it not a madness to cast everlasting life upon so great uncertainty or improbability, when we have life, and time, and helps to make our salvation sure? God hath called you to "give all diligence to make it sure," 2 Peter i. 10. He hath made infallible promises of it to sanctified believers: he calleth you to examine and judge yourselves, 2 Cor. xiii. 5. And do you know the difference between CERTAINTY and UNCERTAINTY in so great a case? O none can now sufficiently conceive what a difference there is, between a soul that is going out of the body with a joyful assurance that Christ will presently receive him, and a soul that, in the guilt of sin, must say, I am going to an endless life, and know not but it may be an endless misery! I am here now, and know not but I may be presently with devils that here deceived me! Just fear of passing presently to hell-fire, is a dreadful case, to be avoided above all earthly sufferings, Luke xii. 4; xiv. 33; much more when God's threatenings to the impenitent are most sure.

Quest. 12. Do you think in your hearts that you have more pleasure, and sound content, and peace, with your whores, and in your sports, and drink, or riches, than true believers have in God and Christ, in a holy life and the hopes of everlasting glory? Judge but by the cause; is not the love of that God who is the Lord of life, and death, and all, and the pleasure of pleasing him, and the sense of pardon and mercy through Christ, and the firm expectation of endless joy by a promise of God sealed by his Son, his sacraments, and Spirit; I say, is not all this matter more worthy to rejoice a soul, than money, and meat, and drink, and lust? Have not you those secret gripes of conscience, when you think how short the sport will be, and that for all these things you must come to judgment, which much abateth the pleasure of your sin? Had you spent that time in seeking first the kingdom of God and its righteousness, and in honest, obedient labouring in your callings, you need not have looked back on it with the gripes of an accusing conscience. If you see a true believer sorrowful, it is not for serving and obeying God, or being holy and hating sin; but for serving God no better, and hating sin no more.

Quest. 13. Have you not often secret wishes in your hearts, that you were in the case of those persons whom you judge to be of the most holy and heavenly hearts and conversations? Do you not think they are in a far safer and better case than you? Unless you are forsaken to blindness of mind, it is certainly so. And doth not this show that you choose and follow that which is worse, when your consciences tell you it is worse, and refuse that which your consciences tell you is best? But it is not such sluggish wishes that will serve: to lie still and live idle, and to wish yourselves as rich as the industrious, is not the way to make you so.

Quest. 14. At least, if you have no such wishes now, do you not think that you shall wish it at death or judgment? Do not your consciences now tell you that you shall shortly wish, Oh that I had hated sinful pleasure! Oh that I had spent my short life in obeying and trusting God! Will you not say with Balaam, "Let me die the death of the righteous, and let my last end be like his?" Oh that I were in the case of those that mortified the flesh, and lived to God, and laid not up their treasure on earth, but in heaven? And why choose you not now that which you know you shall deeply wish that you had chosen?

Quest. 15. I take it for granted, that your merry, and sensual, and worldly tempters and companions deride all this, and persuade you to despise it, as if it were but needless, melancholy, troublesome talk. But tell me, do you think in conscience that it is sound reason that they give you, and such as should satisfy a sober man, who careth what becomes of his soul for ever? If it be, I make a motion to you. Bring any of them to me, or any such man, and in your hearing let the case be soberly debated. I will hear all that they can say against a holy, sober life, for the world, and for their fleshly pleasure, and you shall hear what I can say on the contrary: and then do but use the reason of a man, and judge as you see cause. As Elias said to the Israelites, "Why halt you between two opinions? If the Lord be God, follow him; if Baal be God, follow him." If money, preferment, drink, and lust be best, take it: but if God, heaven, Christ, faith, hope, and holiness be best, at your peril refuse them not, and halt no longer. I suppose you sometimes think of the case, or else you are dead in sin: I pray you, tell me, or tell yourselves, which cause seemeth best upon the deepest thoughts and consideration? But if you will take the laughter or scorns of ignorant sots, instead of reason, and instead of sober consideration, you are well worthy of the damnation which you so wilfully choose.

Quest. 16. But if you think highly of their wit or learning, who sin as you, and who encourage and deceive you, I pray you answer these two questions.

1. Which side is Christ, and his prophets and apostles on? Which side doth the Scripture speak for? Which way went all the saints whose names are now honoured? Were they for the fleshly or the spiritual life? Were they for the love of pleasures more than God? Doth Christ from heaven teach you an earthly or a heavenly choice and life? Did he come to cherish sin, or to destroy it and save us from it? You can make no doubt of this, if ever you read or heard the Bible. And,

2. Which do you think were the wiser and better men, and worthy to be believed and followed,—whether Christ, and all his apostles and saints, that ever were in the world, to this day; or the drunkards, and whoremongers, and worldlings, who deride the doctrine sent from heaven? If there be a heaven, is drunkenness or sobriety liker to be the way to it? But if indeed you will take the mocks of a swinish sot to be wiser than God, than Christ, than prophets and apostles, and all that ever went to heaven, and their jeers to be more credible than all God's word, what can a man say to convince such wretches with any hope?

Quest. 17. I further ask you, Have you not some secret purposes hereafter to repent? If not, alas! how far are you from it, and how forlorn is your case! But if you have, conscience is a witness against you, that you choose and live in that case and course which you know is worst. Were it not worst, you need not purpose to repent of it. And will you wilfully choose known evil, when the very nature of man's will is to love good?

Quest 18. If you believe that the faithful are in a happier case than you, tell me, what hindereth yet but you may be like them, and yet be happy as well as they? Hath God put any exception against you in his word? Are not mercy and salvation proclaimed and offered to you, as freely as to them? Did any thing make you so bad as you are, but your own choice and doing? And can any thing yet hinder you from pardon and salvation, if you yourselves were but truly willing? What if your parents were bad, and bred you up amiss? God hath told you, in Ezek. xviii. and xxxiii. that if you will but do your own part yet, and take warning and avoid your parents' sin, and give up yourselves unfeignedly to him, he will save you, whatever your parents were. What if princes, or lords, or learned men should be your tempters, by words or example? None of them can force you to one sin. God is greater and wiser than they, and more to be believed and obeyed; and your salvation is not in any of their power. What if your old companions tempt you! They can but TEMPT you; they cannot CONSTRAIN you to any evil. All the devils in hell, or men on earth, cannot damn you; no, nor make you sinners, if you do it not yourselves. Refuse not Christ, and he will not refuse you. And when he is willing, if you be but willing,—truly willing to be saved from sin and misery, and to have Christ, grace, and glory in the use of the means which God hath appointed you,—neither earth nor hell can hinder your salvation. Who, but yourselves, keep you from forsaking the company, house, or baits which have deceived you? Who, but yourselves, keep you from lamenting your sin and flying to Christ, from begging mercy and giving yourselves to God? If you think that serious christians are the happiest, refuse not to be such yourselves. It will be your own doing, your own wilful obstinacy, if you perish. But of this I have already said more in my "Call to the Unconverted."

Quest. 19. Dare you deliberate, resolve, or bargain to take your fleshly pleasures for your part, instead of all your hopes of heaven? I hope none of you are yet so mad. I think it is but few (if any) of the witches that make so express a bargain with the devil. If they did, oh how they would tremble when they see their glass almost run out, and death at hand! If you dare not make such a bargain in plain words, oh do not do the same in the choice of your hearts, and in the practice of your lives, and deceive yourselves by thinking that you do it not, when you do. It is God (and not you) that maketh the conditions of salvation and damnation. If you choose that life which, God hath told us, is the condition of damnation, and finally refuse that life which God hath made the condition of salvation, it will in effect be all one as to choose damnation and refuse salvation. He that chooseth deadly poison, or refuseth his necessary food, chooseth death, and refuseth life, in effect. God hath said, "If ye live after the flesh, ye shall die; but if, by the Spirit, ye mortify the deeds of the body, you shall live," Rom. viii. Christ tells you, that, unless you are born again and converted, you cannot enter into his kingdom, John iii. 3, 5; Matt. xviii. 3; and that "without holiness none shall see God." Refuse these, and choose the world and sinful pleasures, and you refuse salvation, and shall have no better than you choose. What you judge best, choose resolvedly; and do not cheat yourselves.

Quest. 20. Have you no natural love to your parents, or your country? Oh what inhuman cruelty is it, to break the hearts of those from whom you had your being, and who were tender of you when you could not help yourselves! Doubtless, one reason why God hath put so strong a love in parents to their children, and made your birth and breeding so costly to your mother, and made the milk which is formed in her own body to be the first nourishment of your lives, is, to oblige you to answerable love and obedience. And if, after all this, you prove worse than brutes, and become the grief of their souls who thus bred, and loved, and nourished you, do you think God will not at last make this far sadder to YOU, than ever it was to THEM? If cruelty to an enemy (much more to a stranger, to a neighbour, to a friend!) be so hateful to the God of love that it goeth not unrevenged, oh what will unnatural cruelty to parents bring upon you! Yea, even in this life, as honouring father and mother hath a special promise of prosperity and long life, so dishonouring and grieving parents is usually punished with some notable calamity, as a forerunner of the GREAT REVENGE hereafter.

And you cannot but perceive that such as live in sensuality, and lust, and wickedness, are the great troublers of the church and state. God himself hath said it, "There is no peace to the wicked," Isa. xlviii. 22. "For the wicked are like the troubled sea when it cannot rest, whose waters cast up mire and dirt. There is no peace, saith my God, to the wicked.—The way of peace they know not; there is no judgment in their goings: they have made them crooked paths: whosoever goeth therein shall not know peace," Isa. lvii. 20, 21; lix. 8. They give no peace to others, and God will deny peace to themselves. Yea, the nature of their own sin denieth it them, as broken bones and griping sickness deny ease to the body. And can you think you shall become the shame of the church and the troublers of the land, and that God will not trouble you for it? If you will be enemies of God and your country, you will prove the sorest enemies to yourselves.

And who is the gainer by all this? No one in the world; unless you will call it the devil's gain, to have his malicious, cruel will fulfilled. And sure the pleasing the devil and a fleshly lust, fancy, or appetite, can never compensate all your losses, nor comfort you under the sufferings which you wilfully bring upon yourselves.

Young men, the reason I thus deal with you by way of question is, that I may, if possible, engage your own thoughts in answering them. For I find most are aptest to learn of themselves: and indeed, without yourselves and your own serious thoughts, we cannot help you to true understanding. He that readeth the wisest lecture to boys or men who take no heed to what is said, yea, or who will not make it their own study to understand and remember, doth but cast away his labour. It is hard saving any man from himself; but there is no saving any man without himself, and his own consent and labour. If you will but now take these twenty questions in secret into your serious thoughts, and consider of them till you can give them such an answer as reason should allow, and as you will stand to before God when the mouth of all iniquity shall be stopped, I should not doubt but you will reap the benefit.

Oh what should a man do, who pitieth blind and wilful sinners, to make them willing of their own recovery! Here all stops. And must it stop at this? Are you not willing? And will you not so much as consider of the reasons that should make you willing, when heaven or hell must be the consequence? Oh what a thing is a blind mind, and a dead and hardened heart! What a befooling thing is fleshly lust! Oh what need had mankind of a Saviour! And what need have all of a sanctifier, and of his holy word, and of all the holy means of grace!

Poor sinners! O let not your teachers' and your parents' counsel and tears be brought in as witnesses against you to your condemnation! O add not this to all their griefs, that their counsel and their sorrows must sink you deeper into hell! Alas, it were sadness enough to them to see that it is all in vain! Let not this counsel of mine to you be rejected to the increase of your guilt and misery: if it do you no good, it will leave you worse. Were I present with you, I should not think it too much, would that prevail, to kneel to you, to beg that you would but well consider your own case and ways, and think before of what will follow, and that you will study a wise and satisfactory answer to the questions put to you, till you are resolved. Your case is not desperate; mercy is yet offered you; the day of grace is not yet past; God is not unwilling to receive you; Christ is not unwilling to be your Saviour, if you consent. No difficulty in the world maketh us afraid of your damnation, but your own foolish choice and wicked wills. Our care is not to make God merciful, nor to make Christ's merits and sacrifice sufficient, nor to get God to promise you pardon if you repent and come to him by Christ: all this is done already. But that which is undone, is, to make you considerate and truly willing, and to live as those that indeed are willing to let go the poisonous pleasures of sin, to take God and heaven for your hope and portion, and to be saved and ruled by Christ and sanctified by his Spirit, and to receive his daily help and mercies to this end, in the use of his appointed means; and, without this, you are undone for ever. And is there any hurt in all this? If there were, is it worse than the filth of sin, and the plagues that follow here and for ever? Worthy is he to hear at last, "Depart from me, thou worker of iniquity," and to be thrust away from the hopes of heaven, who, after all that can be said and done, chooseth sin as more desirable than this God, this Saviour, this Sanctifier, and this glory.

CHAPTER VIII.

GENERAL DIRECTIONS TO THE WILLING.

Though the blindness and obstinacy of fleshly sinners too oft frustrate great endeavours, yet we may well hope that the prayers and tears of parents, and the calls of God, may prevail with many; and I may hope, that some that have read what is before written, will say, We are willing to hear and learn that we may be saved: tell us what it is that we must do. And on that hope, I shall give such miscarrying youth some general advice, and some counsel about their particular cases, and all as briefly as I may. Oh that the Lord would make you who read this truly willing to practise these ten directions following! How happy yet you may be!

I. Set your understandings seriously and diligently to the work which they are made for, and consider well what is your interest and your duty, till you come to a fixed resolution what is for your good, and what is for your hurt, and what that good or hurt will be.

Should it be a hard thing to persuade a man in his wits to love himself, and to think what is good or hurtful to himself, especially for everlasting? Why are you men, if you live like dogs? What do you with understandings, if you will not use them? What will you use them for, if not for your own good and to avoid misery? What good will you desire, if not everlasting joy and glory? And what hurt will you avoid, if not hell-fire? Have you reason, and can you live as if these were not worth the thinking on? Will you bestow your thoughts all the day and year upon you know not what nor why, and not one hour soberly think of such important things as these? O sirs! will you go out of the world before you well think whither you must go? Will you appear before the Judge of souls, to give up your great account, before you think of it, and how it must be done? Is he worthy of the help of GRACE, that will not use his natural REASON? I beg it of you, as ever you care what becomes of you for ever, that you will some time alone set yourselves for one hour seriously to think, who made you, and why; what you owe him; how much you depend on him; what you have done against him; how you have spent your time; what case your souls are in; what Christ hath done for you; and what he is or would be to you; whether you are sanctified and forgiven; what God's Spirit must do for you; and what you must be and do, if you will be saved; and if it be otherwise, whither it is that you must go.

II. Therefore I next advise you and entreat you, that you live not as at a great distance from eternity, nor foolishly flatter yourselves with the deceitful promises of long life: and were it sure to be a hundred years, remember how quickly and certainly they will end. Oh! time is nothing! therefore think of nothing in this world as separated from the world to come. Whatever you are doing, or saying, or thinking, the boat is hastening to the gulf. You are posting to death and judgment: which way ever you go, by wealth or poverty, health or sickness, busy or idle, single or married, you are going still to the grave and to eternity. Judge then of every thing as it tendeth to that end; and think of nothing as not relating, as a means, to the near and everlasting end. O choose and do that which reason and conscience tell you, that you will at last earnestly wish that you had chosen and done! When you are tempted to be prayerless and averse to good, or to run to lust or sinful pleasure, ask yourselves seriously, How will this look in the final review? What shall I think of this at last? Will it be my comfort, or my torment? O judge as you will judge at last.

III. My third counsel is, If your consciences tell you that you have foolishly sinned against God and your salvation, make not light of it; but, presently and openly, go to your parents or masters, and penitently confess your sinful life in general, and your known or open sins particularly. But such secret sins which wronged not them and will blast your reputation, you are not bound to confess openly, unless the ease or future direction of your doubtful and troubled consciences require it. But when your vicious fleshly life is known, excuse it not, hide not the evil by lies or extenuation. When you have wronged your parents or masters by disobedience, and by robbing them of part of your time and service, if not also of their money or goods, go to them with sorrow and shame, and confess how foolishly you have served the flesh, to the injury of them, to the offending of God, and to the unspeakable hurt of your own souls. Lament your sin, and ask them forgiveness, and entreat their prayers, and their careful government of you for the time to come, and sincerely promise them reformation and obedience.

Yea, if you have had familiar companions in your sin, go to them, and tell them, God and reason have convinced me of my sinful folly, that for brutish, fleshly pleasure, have wilfully broken the laws of my Creator and Redeemer, and, for nothing, undone and lost my soul, if Christ do not recover me by sound repentance. Oh how madly have we despised our salvation! How easily might we have known, had we but searched and considered the word of God, that we were displeasing God, undoing ourselves, and making work for future sorrows! Should I, when I know this, and when I know that I am going to death and judgment, yet obstinately go on and be a hardened rebel against Christ and grace, what can I expect but to be forsaken of God and lost for ever? O therefore, as we have sinned together, let us repent together! You have been a snare to me, and I to you. We have been agents of the devil to draw each other to sin and misery: certainly all this must sooner or later be repented of. O let us join together in sorrow, and reformation, and a holy, obedient life. If you will not consent, I here declare to you before God, (for I know that he seeth and heareth me,) that I will be your companion in sin no more. I beg pardon for tempting you. I resolve by God's grace to prefer my salvation and my obedience to God, before a base and beastly pleasure. Whatever you say against it, I will never more forsake my salvation to follow you, nor ever take you to be wiser than God, nor better friends to me than my Saviour, nor your words more regardable than God's word, nor a whore, or a merry cup, or vanity, to be better than heaven, nor temperance and holiness to be worse than hell. If you will not be undeceived with me, I will pray for you; but I renounce your sinful company, and my warning will be a witness against you to your confusion.

Stick not at the scorn of fools, nor at the shame of such repentance and confession; it may profit others. But, however, it is no more than, in duty, you owe them whom you have wronged and endangered by sin. And it will lay some new obligation on yourselves to amend, by doing what you have so professed: and sure conscience and shame will somewhat the more hinder you from ever more joining with them in the sin which you have so bewailed and renounced. And think not this too much, for there is no jesting with God, and with everlasting joy or misery.

IV. My next counsel is, Presently, understandingly, and considerately, renew the covenant which you made in baptism with God your Creator, Redeemer, and Sanctifier.

Consider whether to be a christian is not necessary to your salvation; and then consider what it is to be a christian, and whether it be not a far higher thing, than merely to take that name upon you, and be of that party, and to join with the right church, and to have the bare words and picture of believers: and then consider whether God will be mocked with shows, and ceremonies, and dead formalities, and false professions; and whether the lifeless carcass or image of christianity will be taken by God instead of the life and power of it, and will ever save a soul: yea, whether a false, counterfeit christian, bred up under christian instructions and examples, does not make your guilt far greater, and your case more miserable, than Americans or Indians, who never heard what you have heard: and when perhaps you have spoken against hypocrites yourselves, whether there be any more notorious hypocrites than such as you, who say you are christians, and yet live to the flesh in the odious sins which Christ abhorreth. Think what a dreadful thing it is, to profess a religion which condemneth you, and to say over that creed which you believe not, and those petitions in the Lord's prayer which you desire not, and those commandments which you break and will condemn you;—to rebel against God, while you say you believe in him; to despise Christ's government, while you say you trust him for salvation; to ask for his grace, when you would not have it to sanctify you and save you from your sin; to beg mercy of God, and to reject this mercy, and to have no mercy on yourselves! O think what a doleful case it is to see distracted sinners such hypocrites, playing with such contradictions so near God's bar and in his sight; and to make no better use of prayers, and the name of christians, and the profession of the truth, than to give the devil more matter to accuse you, and conscience to torment you, and a righteous God to say to you at last, Out of thy own mouth will I judge thee, thou wicked rebel! Didst thou not confess, that Jesus was the Christ, and that thou didst believe the gospel and the life to come? and yet didst live in the wilful disobeying of Christ and the gospel, and base contempt of God and thy salvation.

And when you have considered the sad case of hypocrites, that call themselves CHRISTIANS to their own condemnation when they are none such, then think seriously what the covenant was which was made for you in your baptism, and you have taken on you to own. Think what it is devotedly to trust to God as your reconciled Father, and devotedly to trust to Christ as your Saviour, your great Teacher, Governor, and Mediator with the Father; what it is devotedly to trust the Holy Spirit to illuminate, to sanctify, and quicken you in a holy life, and to strengthen and comfort you against and under all your trials. Consider what it is to take the flesh, the world, and the devil, (as they are against this holy life and heavenly hope,) for your enemies, and to enlist yourselves under Christ, in avowed war to the death against them. Think how you have perfidiously broken this covenant, on which all the hope of your salvation lieth. And then, if you dare not utterly renounce all that hope, presently and resolvedly renew this covenant. Lament your violation of it to God: do it, not only in a passion, but upon serious considerations make that choice and resolution which you dare stand to at a dying hour, and on which you may believe that God, for Christ's sake, will accept you, and forgive you. O think what a mercy it is to have a Saviour, who, after all your heinous sins, will bring you reconciled as sons to God, for the merits of his sacrifice and righteousness, and by his powerful intercession; and will send from heaven the Spirit of God into your hearts, to renew those blind, dead, carnal minds to God's holy image; and will dwell in you and carry on your sanctification to the end. Thankfully, joyfully accept this covenant and grace, and again give up yourselves to God, your Father, Saviour, and Sanctifier; but be sure that you do it absolutely, without deceitful exceptions and reserves; and that you do it resolvedly, and not only in a frightened mood; and yet that you do it as in the strength of the grace of Christ, not trusting the stedfastness of your own deceitful, mutable hearts. And when you can truly say, that you unfeignedly consent, and renew this covenant in your hearts, then go the next opportunity to the sacrament of the Lord's supper, and there penitently and faithfully renew it openly in the solemn way that Christ hath appointed you; thankfully profess your trust in Christ, and receive a sealed pardon of your sins, and title to everlasting life; and settle your conversation in the communion of saints, as you hope to live with such for ever.

V. Henceforward set yourselves, as the true scholars of Christ, to learn his doctrine; and as his true subjects, to know his laws; and as those that trust their souls into his hand, to understand and firmly believe his promises for this life and that which is to come; and as the blessed man, "to delight in the law of the Lord, and meditate in it day and night," Psal. i.

2, 3. As you were wont to steal some hours from God and your masters, to go to the house of sin and death, so now get such hours as lawfully you can from your other employments and diversions, but especially on the Lord's days; and get alone, and beg mercy and grace from God, and set yourselves to read the Bible, and with it read some catechisms, and some sound and serious treatises of divinity, which are most suitable to your state.

It is young men who have miscarried, and being convinced, are willing to turn to God, whom I am now directing. And therefore supposing that you will ask me what books I would commend to you, I will answer you accordingly, supposing still that you prefer the Bible.

1. For the full resolving of your hearts to a sound repentance and a holy life, read Joseph Allen's book of Conversion, Richard Allen's Vindication of Godliness, and their book of Covenanting with God, and his Victory over the World; Mr. Whateley's New Birth; and some of the old sermons of Repentance, such as Mr. Stock's, Mr. Perkins's, Mr. Dikes's, and Mr. Marbury's; Bunny's Correction of Parson's Book for Resolution; John Rogers's Doctrine of Faith; William Fenner's books; Samuel Smith on the first and the fifty-first Psalms, and his Great Assize, and on the Eunuch's Conversion; Bifield's Marrow, Mr. Howe's Blessedness of the Righteous, and of Delighting in God.

And if you would have any of mine, read the Call to the Unconverted, or the Treatise of Conversion, and the Directions for a Sound Conversion, and Now or Never, and A Saint or a Brute, or which of all these God's providence shall afford you.

2. If you would have help to try your hearts lest they be deceived, read Allen's foresaid Book of the Covenant, and Pinke's Trial of Sincere Love to Christ. Many books of marks are extant, Bifield's, Rogers's, Harsnet's, Berries's, &c. and Mr. Chishull and Mr. Mead of being Almost Christians. If you would have any of mine, read the Right Method for Peace of Conscience, and Directions for Weak Christians, where are the characters of the false, the weak, and the strong.

3. For the daily government of heart and life, read the Practice of Piety, Scuder's Daily Walk, Mr. Reyner's Directions, (three excellent books,) and Mr. Corbet's small Private Thoughts. And if you would have any of mine, read my Family Book, and The Divine Life, the Life of Faith, or the Saints' Rest, and, for those that can read great ones, my Christian Directory.

4. And it will not be unuseful to read some profitable history, especially the lives of exemplary persons, and the funeral sermons which characterize them. I have prefaced to two, which are eminently worth your reading, and most true,—both young men,—that is, John Janeway's Life, and Joseph Allen's; and given you the true exemplary characters (in their funeral sermons) of Mr. Ashurst, (an excellent pattern for apprentices and tradesmen,) Mr. Stubs, Mr. Corbet, Mr. Wadsworth, and Mrs. Baker. Read Mr. Samuel Clark's Lives, and his Martyrology, and his Mirror, Dr. Beard's Examples, or Fox's Book of Martyrs. Some church history, and history of the Reformation, and the history of our own country, will be useful.

5. As you grow up to more judgment, you may read methodical sums of divinity, especially Ames's Marrow, and his Cases of Conscience, (which are in English translated,) and Commentaries.

Great store of all sorts of good books (through the great mercy of God) are common among us: he that cannot buy, may borrow.

But take heed that you lose not your time in reading romances, play-books, vain jests, or seducing or reviling disputes, or needless controversies.

This course of reading Scripture and good books will be many ways to your great advantage.

1. It will, above all other ways, increase your knowledge.

2. It will help your resolutions and holy affections, and direct your lives.

3. It will make your lives pleasant. The knowledge, the usefulness, the variety, will be a continual recreation to you, unless you are utterly besotted or debauched.

4. The pleasure of this will turn you from your filthy, fleshly pleasure. You will have no need to go for delight to a play-house, a drinking-house, or to beastly lusts.

5. It will keep you from the sinful loss of time, by idleness or unprofitable employment or pastimes. You will cast away cards and dice, when you find the sweetness of useful learning.

But be sure that you choose the most useful and necessary subjects, and that you seek knowledge for the love of holiness and obedience.

VI. The sixth part of my advice is, forsake ill company; and converse with such as will be helps to your knowledge, holiness, and obedience, and not such as will draw you to sin and misery.

You have found by sad experience what power ill company hath on fools; with such a merry tale, a laugh, a jest, a scorn, a merry cup, and a bad example and persuasion, do more than reason, or God's authority, or the love of their souls. A physician may go among the sick and mad to cure them; and a wise man that seeth these will pity them, and hate sin the more. But what do you do there, where you have already caught the infection of their disease? The mind of a man is known much by the company which he chooseth; and if you choose ill, no wonder if you speed ill. "He that walketh with wise men shall be wise; but a companion of fools shall be destroyed," Prov. xiii. 20. "Whoso keepeth the law is a wise son, but he that is a companion of riotous men shameth his father," Prov. xxviii. 7. David saith, "I am a companion of all them that fear thee, and of them that keep thy precepts," Psalm cxix. 63. "I have not sat with vain persons, neither will I go in with dissemblers, I have hated the congregation of evil-doers, and will not sit with the wicked," Psalm xxvi. 4, 5. "Depart from me, ye evil-doers, for I will keep the commandments of my God," Psalm cxix. 115.

VII. Especially be sure that you run not wilfully upon temptation, but keep as far from every tempting bait and object as you can. Fire and gunpowder, or straw, must be kept at a sufficient distance. No man is long safe at the very brink of danger, especially if it be a sin that his nature is much inclined to. No wise man will trust corrupted nature very far, especially where he hath often fallen already. The best man that is, should live in fear when an enticing bait of sin is near him. If David, who prayed, "Turn away mine eyes from beholding vanity," had better practised it, oh what heinous sin had he escaped! Had he "made a covenant with his eyes," as Job did, what wounds had he prevented! The feast that you see not, the cup that is a mile off, the person that is far distant, the words which you hear not, are not they that you are most in danger of. But when tempting meat and drink are before you, and the tempting person hath secret familiarity with you, and tempting or provoking words are at your ears, then, alas! many have need of more grace, resolution, and mortification than they have.

If you knew well what sin is, and what is the consequence, you would be more watchful and resolved against temptations than against thieves, and fire, or the places infected by the plague.

VIII. Make it the chief study of your lives to understand what man's everlasting hope is, and to get a lively, well-settled belief of it, and to bring your souls to take it joyfully for your true felicity and end, and thence daily to fetch the powerful motives of your duty and your patience, and your contenting comfort in life and at your death.

1. The end is the life of all the means. If heavenly blessedness be not the chief end that you live, hope, and labour for in the world, your whole lives will be but carnal, vain, and the way to misery: for the means can be no better than the end. God, that is the BEGINNING, is our END; we are made and governed by him and for him. Heavenly glory is the sight of his glory, and the everlasting perfection and pleasure of joyful, mutual love.

But we are not the noblest creatures, next to God in excellency and desert, yea, we are sinners who have deserved to be cast out from his love. And therefore, as in the way we must come to him by a Saviour, so at the blessed end we must enjoy him by a Mediator. And to see God's glory in Christ, and the heavenly Jerusalem, the blessed society of saints and angels, continually flaming in love, joy, and praises to the most holy God,—this, this is the felicity for which we labour, suffer, and hope.

2. And oh how great and how needful a work it is, to search, study, and pray for so firm a belief of this unseen glory, as may so resolve, engage, and comfort us in some good measure, as if we had seen it with these eyes! Oh what men would one hour's being in heaven make us, or one clear sight of it! Faith hath a greater work to do than a dreaming or dead opinion can perform. If it be not well grounded first, and well exercised upon God's love, promise, and glory from day to day, you will find cause sadly to lament the weakness of it. For this use you have great need of the help of such books, as open clearly the evident proofs of the christian verity, which I have briefly done in the beginning of the second part of my "Life of Faith," and more largely in two other books, viz. "The Unreasonableness of Infidelity," and "The Reasons of the Christian Religion." A firm belief of the world to come, is it that must make us serious christians, and overcome the snares of worldly vanity.

And your faith being well settled, set yourselves daily to use it, and live by it: dwell in the joyful hopes of the heavenly glory. What is a man that liveth not in the use of reason? And you must know that you have as daily use for your FAITH, as for your REASON. Without reason, you can neither safely eat or drink; nor converse with men as a man, but as a Bedlamite; nor do any business that concerneth you; and therefore you must live by your reason. And without faith you cannot please God, nor obtain salvation; no, nor use your reason for any thing higher than to serve your appetites and purvey for the flesh: and therefore you must "live by faith," or live like beasts, and worse than beasts; and cannot otherwise live to God, nor live in the hopes of blessedness hereafter. O consider that the difference between living chiefly upon and for an earthly, fleshly felicity, or a heavenly, is the great difference between the holy and the unholy, and the foregoer of the difference between those in heaven and those in hell.

IX. Still remember that the GREAT MEANS of all the good that here or hereafter you can expect, is the GREAT MEDIATOR, the GREAT TEACHER, RULER, and INTERCESSOR for his people; and therefore, out of him you can do nothing. All duty that you offer to God, must be by his mediation; and so must all mercy which you receive from God. "To come to God by him, who is the way, the truth, and the life," must be your daily work of faith. His blood must wash you from all sin past, and from the guilt of daily failings and infirmities. None but he can effectually teach you to know God and yourselves, your duty and your everlasting hopes. None but he can render your persons, praises, and actions acceptable to God; because you are sinners, and unmeet for God's acceptance without a Mediator. "All power in heaven and earth is given him," and your lives and souls are at his will. And it is he that must judge you, and with whom you hope to live in glory. Therefore you must so "live by the faith of the Son of God, who hath loved you and given himself for you," that you may say it is he that liveth in you, Gal. ii. 20, 21. This is the fountain from whence you must daily fetch your strength and comfort.

X. And still remember that it is by the operation of the HOLY SPIRIT that the Father and the Son do sanctify souls, and regenerate and breed them up for glory. It is by the Holy Ghost that God dwelleth in us by love, and Christ by faith. Therefore see that you rest not in corrupted nature, and trust not to yourselves or to the flesh. Your souls are dead to God and holiness, and your duties dead, till the Spirit of Christ do quicken them. You are blind to God and mad in sin, till the Spirit illuminate you, and give you understanding. You are like enemies, out of love with God, heaven, and holiness, till this Spirit reconcile you, and sanctify your wills. You will have no man-like, spiritual, holy pleasure, till the Holy Spirit renew your hearts, and make them fit to delight in God. Oh that men knew the great necessity of the illuminating, quickening, sanctifying, comforting influence of the Spirit of God, how far would they be from deriding it, as some profane ones do! By this Holy Spirit the sacred records were written; and by miracles of Christ and his apostles, and evangelists and prophets, sealed and delivered to the churches. And by this Spirit, the orders and government of the church were settled; and by Him we are enlightened to understand the Scriptures, and inclined to love them, and delightfully to believe them and obey them. Study therefore obediently these writings of the Holy Ghost, and confidently trust them. O be not found among the resisters or neglecters of the Spirit's help and motions, when proud self-confidence or fleshly lust do rise against them.

Christ's bodily presence is taken from the earth; he promised instead of it, (which was but in one place at once,) to send his Spirit, which is to the soul more than the sun's light to the eye, and can shine in all the world at once. This is his agent on earth, by whom (in teachers and learners) he carrieth on his saving work. This is his advocate, who pleadeth his cause effectually against unbelief, and fleshly lusts, and worldly wisdom. This is the "well of living water, springing up in us to everlasting life;" the name, the mark of God on souls; the divine regenerator, the author of God's holy image; and the divine nature, even divine life, and light, and love; the conqueror of the world and flesh, the strengthener of the weak, the confirmer of the wavering, the comforter of the sad, and the pledge, earnest, and first-fruits of everlasting life. O therefore pray earnestly for the Spirit of grace, and carefully obey him, and joyfully praise God, in the sense of his holy encouragement and help!

CHAPTER IX.

ADDITIONAL COUNSEL TO YOUNG MEN, WHO ARE BRED UP TO LEARNING, AND PUBLIC WORK, ESPECIALLY TO THE SACRED MINISTRY, IN THE UNIVERSITIES AND SCHOOLS.

SECT. 1. It was the case of the London apprentices, who are nearest me, and I have oft to do with, which first provoked me to this work; and therefore which was the chief in my intention. But had I as near opportunity to be a counsellor to others, there are three sorts whom I should have preferred, for the sake of the church and kingdom, to which they are of greater signification:—

1. Those in the schools and universities, who are bred up for the sacred ministry.

2. Those there, and in the inns of court, who are bred up to the knowledge of the law.

3. The sons of noblemen, knights and others, who are bred up for some places of government in the kingdom, according to their several ranks. And of these it is the first that I shall most freely speak to.

Sect. 2. And *first* I shall mention the importance of their case; and *secondly* the danger that they are in of miscarrying, and what they should do to escape it.

Sect. 3. I. And indeed their condition, as they prove good or bad, is of unspeakable importance.

1. To the church and the souls of men.

2. To the peace of the kingdom.

3. To themselves. And,

4. To their parents, above the common case of others.

Sect. 4. 1. Of how great importance the quality of the clergy is to the church and men's salvation, many thousands have found to their joy and happiness; and, I fear, many more thousands to their sorrow and destruction. And then of what importance the quality of scholars and young candidates is to the soundness of the clergy, I need not many words to make men of reason and experience know.

Sect. 5. 2. God, who hath instituted the sacred office, and by his Spirit qualifieth men for the work, doth usually work according to the fitness of their work and qualifications. As he doth the works of nature according to the fitness of natural second causes, (giving more light by the sun, than by a star or candle, &c.) so he doth the works of morality according to the fitness of moral causes. Holiness is the true morality, and usually wrought by holy means. And though it be so supernatural in several respects, (as it is wrought by the supernatural revelation or doctrine, or a supernatural teacher, Christ, by the operation of the Holy Ghost, a supernatural agent, commonly called infusion, and raising the soul to God, a supernatural object, and to a better state than that of corrupted nature,) yet we are natural recipients and agents, and it is our natural faculties which grace reneweth; and, being renewed, exercise the acts of holiness. And God worketh on us according to our nature, and by causes suited to our capacities and to the work. As he useth not to give men the knowledge of languages, philosophy, or any art, by the teaching of the ignorant and unskilful, so much as by learned and skilful teachers, we must say the same of our teachers of sacred truth; and though grace be the gift of the Holy Ghost, experience constraineth all sorts of christians almost to acknowledge what I here assert. Why else do they so earnestly contend, that they may live under the teachers which they count the best? Will heretics teach men the truth as well as the orthodox? Why then is there such a stir made against heretics in the world? And why are the clergy so eager to silence such as preach down that which they approve? Will papists choose protestant teachers, or protestants choose papists?

And as men are unfit to teach others that which they know not themselves, so unbelieving men and unholy men are far less fit to persuade the hearers to faith and holiness, than believing, holy teachers are. Though some of them may be furnished with the same notions and words which serious, godly teachers use, yet usually, even in that, they are greatly wanting; because they have not so thoroughly studied saving truth, nor perceived its evidence, nor set their hearts upon it, nor deeply received and retained it. For serious affection quickeneth the mind to serious consideration, and causeth men speedily and deeply to receive that truth which others receive but slowly, superficially, or not at all. How eagerly and prosperously do men study that which they strongly love! And how hardly do they learn that in which they have no delight, much more which they hate, and their very natures are against.

But if a hypocrite should have good notions and words, yet he will usually be greatly wanting in that serious delivery which is ordinarily needful to make the hearers serious christians. It seldom reacheth the heart of the hearer, which cometh not from the heart of the speaker. As light causeth light, so heat causeth heat; and the dead are unfit to generate life. The arrow will not go far or deep, if both the bow and arm be not strong that shoot it. Constant experience telleth us undeniably of the different success of the reading or saying of a pulpit lesson, or a dull or a mere affected speech, and of the judicious, serious explication and application of well-chosen matter, which the experienced speaker well understandeth, and which he uttereth from the feeling of his soul. And the love of a benefice, no, nor of applause neither, will not make a man preach in that manner, as the love of God, and the lively belief of heaven and hell, and as the desire of saving souls will do. The means will be chosen and used, and the work done, agreeably to the principle and the end.

But if a stage hypocrite should learn the knack or art of preaching, with affected fervency and seeming zeal, yet art and paint will not reach the power and beauty of nature. Usually affectation bewrayeth itself; and, when it is discerned, the hypocrisy is loathed. And it faileth ordinarily, in point of constancy: "Will the hypocrite pray always?" Job xxvii. 10. Art will not hold out like nature: when the motives of gain (which is their godliness) ceaseth, the pleasure of applause, the means, will cease. Yea, it usually turneth to a malignant reviling of the serious piety which they counterfeited before, or of the persons whose applause they did affect. For where the hypocrisy of the preacher is discovered by his contrary self-condemning words or life, and the people accordingly judge of him as he is, his proud heart cannot bear it, but he turneth a malicious reproacher of these whose applause he sought, thinking by disgracing them, to defend his own esteem, by making their censure of him incredible or contemptible.

And if the hypocrite should hold on his stage affectation with plausible art, yet it will not reach to an answerable discharge of the rest of his ministerial work. It is from MEN that he expecteth his reward; and in the sight of men, on the public stage, that he appeareth in his borrowed glory. But in his family, or his conversation, or his ministerial duty to men in private, he answereth not his public show. He will not set himself to instruct and win the ignorant and impenitent, and zealously to save men from their sins, and to raise men's earthly minds to heaven, by praying with them, and by a heavenly discourse, and by a heavenly conversation; nor will he be at much cost or labour to do good.

Sect. 6. But, alas! the far greatest part of bad, unexperienced clergymen do prove so hurtful to the church, that they have not so much as the hypocrite's seeming zeal and holiness to cloak their sin or profit their people with. The sad case of the christian world proclaimeth this; not only in the Southern and Eastern churches, Abassia, Egypt, Syria, Armenia, the Greeks, Muscovites, &c.; nor only the papist priests in the West; but too great a number in the reformed churches. And it is more lamentable than wonderful; for there goeth so much to the general planting of a worthy, faithful ministry, that it is the great mercy of God that such are not more rare.

1. If they have not natural capacity, there is not matter for art and ordinary grace to elevate.

2. And if this capacity be not improved by diligent and long study, (which most will not undergo,) it is no wonder if it be useless, or much worse.

3. And if it be not directed by a sound and skilful teacher, but fall into the hands of an erroneous or bad guide, you may conjecture what the fruits will be.

4. And if that good parts and studies be not kept from the mischievous enmity of a worldly mind and fleshly lusts, how easily are they corrupted, and turned against their use and end, to the great hurt of the church, and of themselves!

5. And if those that choose prelates or church governors, should be either of currupted judgments, wicked hearts, or vicious lives, how probable is it that they will choose such as themselves, or, at least, such as will not much cross their lusts!

6. And if such worldly and wicked prelates be the ordainers, examiners, judges, and institutors of the inferior clergy, or be their rulers, it is easy to know what sort of men they will introduce and countenance, and what sort they will silence and discourage.

7. And if lay patrons have the choice of parish pastors, and most or many of them should be such as Christ tells us the rich most usually are,—a worldly and sensual sort of men, or such as have no lively sense of heavenly things,—we may easily conjecture what men such are likely to present.

8. And if the people have any where (as anciently) the choice, when most of them are bad, what men will they choose? Or if they have not the choice, yet they are so considerable, that their consent or dissent, love or hatred, will sway much with those that much live among them. But I must afterward say more of these impediments.

Sect. 7. And as all these impediments are like to make worthy pastors to be rare, so it is certain that the naughtiness of such is like to make them exceeding hurtful, which is easily gathered from,

1. What they will be.

2. What they will do.

3. In what manner they will do it. In all which, the effects may be probably foreseen. And,

First, It is supposed, 1. That they will be worldly-minded men, that will take gain for godliness, and will judge that to be the best cause, and those the best persons, who most befriend their worldly interest. They will love the fleece more than the safety of the flock; and their benefices more than the benefit of the people's souls; they will serve their bellies more than Christ, Phil. iii. 18; Rom. xvi. 17; and being lovers of the world, they will be real enemies to God. "The love of money in them will be the root of all evil." As Achan and Gehazi, they will think they have reason for what they do; and, if tempted, will with Judas betray their Master.

2. And their fleshly desires will have little restraints, but what one sin doth put upon another, or God's controlling providence give them. Their reputation may make them avoid that which would be their disgrace. But, secretly, they will serve their appetites and fleshly lusts. For they will not have God's effectual grace, nor much tenderness of conscience, to restrain them.

3. And pride will be their very nature. Esteem and applause will be taken for their due, and seem as necessary to them, almost, as the air, and as water to a fish. Ambition will be their complexion, and will actuate their thoughts. And all these vices will so corrupt their judgments, that there will want little more than worldly interest and temptations, to turn them to any heresy, or ill design.

And it is much to be feared that their profanation of holy things will make them worse and more impenitent than other men: partly, by the righteous judgment of God forsaking them; and partly, by the hardening of their own hearts, by long abuse of that truth which should have sanctified them. For when they have imprisoned it in unrighteousness, and long played, as hypocrites, with that which they preached and professed to believe, custom will so harden them, that their knowledge will have little power on their hearts.

Sect. 8. Secondly, And no wonder if the fruit be like the tree. These vices will not be idle; nor bring forth holy or just effects.

1. It is likely they will make it the chief care of their minds, to get that which they most love; and that they will study preferment (which is the clergyman's nearest way to wealth).

2. And then they must be flatterers of those that can prefer them; or, at least, must not seriously call them to repentance, or tell them of their sin.

3. In all differences, of what consequence soever, they will usually pass their judgment on the side of such as can prefer or hurt them.

4. In religious controversies, they will usually be on the side that is for their worldly interest, be it right or wrong.

5. They will harden great men in their sins, by flattering them.

6. They will harden the profane, by pleasing them in their ignorance and ungodliness, to get them on their side.

7. They will be enemies to the serious, religious people, because they discern the vice and hypocrisy which they would conceal; and because they honour such as fear the Lord, while vile persons are contemned in their eyes, Psal. xv. 4.

8. They will turn their preaching against such, partly to vent their malignant spleen, and partly to overcome them as their enemies. Hereupon they will describe their serious piety as faction, self-opinion, and hypocrisy, and will raise jealousies against them in the minds of rulers, and increase the rabble's malignity and rage, and will extenuate the sin and danger of the most ungodly sort who take their own part.

9. They will shame their office and profession by base mutability, turning with the time and tide as temptations from their worldly interest lead them.

10. They will, by their making light of godliness, and by the scandal or unholiness of their own conversations, make the vulgar believe that godliness is either a cheat, or a matter of mere words and outward observances, and to be of the religion of their rulers, and a thing to keep men in some awe and order in a worldly life.

11. Their ignorance oft makes them unfit for hard controversies; and yet their pride and malignity will make them forward to talk of what they understand not, and to take thence an occasion to revile those whom they dislike; and, speaking evil of what they never knew, they will make up their want of knowledge with outward titles, pretended authority, confident affirmation, censorious reproach, and violently oppressing by power the gainsayers.

12. And if any man's conscience be awakened, to call him to true repentance, they will either tell him it is needless, melancholy trouble, and give him an opiate of some flattering, false comfort, or preach him asleep again with unsuitable things, or a cold, dull, formal kind of managing holy things.

Sect. 9. Thirdly, And such are too often the plagues of the church and state, as well as injurious to individual souls.

1. Their ignorance or scandalous ambition, covetousness, and other sins, do render them so contemptible in the eyes of many, that it tends to make the church and all religion so. And when nobles, gentlemen, and people think basely of the ministry, church, and religion for their sakes, how sad is the case of such a people! The gospel is half taken away from a nation when it is taken out of their esteem and brought under their reproach and scorn. And a scorned clergy will prepare for the scorning of religion; and an ignorant, or worldly, ambitious, fleshly, scandalous clergy, will be a scorned clergy with too many. Erasmus much disgraced the German protestants, when he described some of them as having a bottle of wine at their girdle, and his translation of the New Testament in their hands, ready to dispute for it with blows. And so do many, that tell the world how many of the Lutheran ministers are given to excess of drink, and unpeaceable reviling of dissenters. And the same Erasmus much depreciated either bishops or Scotists, when, speaking of the Scotist bishop of London, who was Dr. Collett's adversary, he saith, I have known some such whom I would not call *knaves*, but never one whom I could call a *christian*. Not only drunkenness and brutish sins, but factiousness, envy, unpeaceableness, contentiousness, and especially a proud and worldly mind, will be, in most men's eyes, more ugly in a minister than others. For where there is a double dedication to God, that which is common will seem unclean; and when there should be a double holiness, sin will appear to be double sin.

2. And indeed a carnal, worldly clergy are oft the most powerful and obstinate hinderers of the peace and quietness of church and state.

(1.) By fitting themselves to the humours of those in whose power their preferments are, be it never so much to the injury of men's souls, bodies, or estates, or against the public good and safety! Or else, leading the people into error, for popular applause.

(2.) By a domineering humour in matters of religion; taking themselves lawgivers to others; and taking their wits and wills for uncontrollable; laying heaven and hell upon their own inventions or conceits, and the controversies which they endlessly make, but understand not; and hereticating or anathematizing such as take them not for oracles, or rabbies that must not be gainsaid.

(3.) And by corrupting the christian religion and church, by departing from the christian simplicity and purity; and forming doctrine, worship, and government, according to their own carnal, worldly minds and interest.

(4.) And then militating against the best that contradict them or stoop not to them, though it be to the distraction and division of the churches. And usually they are the hardest to be brought to peace and reconciliation, and do most against it whenever it is attempted by peace-makers, who pity the woeful case of such a self-disturbing people.

Sect. 10. All this hath been so long manifested to the sad experience of mankind, in most nations and ages of the christian world, that it is not to be denied or concealed. And should we pretend the honour of the church and clergy for the denying or the hiding of such grievous sins, it would but make us partakers of the guilt, and displease the most holy God, who will have sin in whomsoever shamed, to warn others who are ready to imitate them. The holy Scriptures open and shame the sins even of Adam, of Noah, of Lot, of David, of Solomon, of Peter, and of God's chosen people the Jews: and this was not a faulty uncovering of their nakedness, but a necessary disgrace of sin, and manifestation of the holiness and justice of God, and a warning to others that we should not sin with such examples before our eyes, 1 Cor. x. 6—8.

I have written the history of the bishops and councils of former ages, in which, with their virtues, I have opened their miscarriages. Some blame it, as if it were uncovering their nakedness. But I have said nothing but what is openly proclaimed of them long ago, by their own greatest flatterers; and it was Christ himself that said, "Remember Lot's wife." The pit which so many have fallen into must be uncovered; and God and holiness must be honoured, rather than those that dishonour them by sin. Sin, confessed and forsaken, is not so dangerous, as sin denied and extenuated. He that hideth it, shall not prosper. "Sin is a reproach to any people," Prov. xiv. 34; vi. 33. Even God that forgiveth it to the penitent, will shame it,—to keep others from committing it. He that minceth or hideth it, tempteth others to imitate it.

Alas! what work have a worldly, proud, and ignorant clergy made in most christian nations, these thirteen hundred years! Athanasius, Chrysostom, Isidore-Pelusiota, &c. but especially, excellent Gregory Nazianzen have told it us, even of their flourishing times, more plainly than I now intend to do:—They have loved this present world; some set themselves, by venting new and odd opinions, to draw disciples after them for applause; some furiously hereticating those that differed from them by ambiguous words, and making themselves lords of the faith of others, and making their ignorant dictates the oracles of the church; striving who should be thought wisest and best, but especially who should be greatest, as if Christ had never judged in that controversy; flattering emperors and princes, till they got wealth and power by them, and then overtopping them, and troubling the world by rebellions and wars; tearing the churches in pieces on pretence of union, killing and burning men on pretence of faith and charity, and cursing from Christ his faithful servants on pretence of using the keys of Christ's kingdom; setting up themselves and a worldly kingdom, on pretence of the spiritual government of Christ; making merchandise of souls, on pretence of feeding and ruling them; cherishing the people in ignorance, and sloth, and carnality, that they might be more obedient to their tyranny, and less capable of opposing it; hating and destroying the most conscionable christians, as heretics, or schismatics, because they are the greatest enemies to their sin, and desirous of reformation; provoking princes to become the bloody persecutors of such, for the upholding of their worldly state and dignity; yea, making them their lictors or executioners, to destroy such as they condemn.

Such work as this hath destroyed the Greeks, or Eastern churches, set up Turkish tyranny by dividing christians, weakening and ruining the emperors, making religion a mere image of lifeless formality and ceremony, and a powerless, dying thing. Such a clergy have darkened and lamentably brought low the christian churches in Muscovy, Armenia, Georgia, Mongrelia, Syria, Abassia, and extirpated them in Nubia, and brought them in Italy, Poland, Hungary, Spain, France, and most of Germany, to what they are: such a clergy have brought Ireland from the laudable state in which it was in the days of Malachias, as Bernard described it, into the barbarous, brutish ignorance and bloody inhumanity at which it is now arrived; and had the chief hand in the murder of two hundred thousand persons in the late rebellious insurrection. Such a clergy had a chief hand in the civil wars in England in the reign of William Rufus, King Stephen, Henry the Third, King John, &c.—the subject of Pryn's History of the Treasons of Prelates. And, alas! such a corrupt sort of ministers keep up the division of the German protestants, under the name of Lutherans and Calvinists, about consubstantiation, church images, and doctrines of predestination not understood. And had the Low Countries ever had the stirs between remonstrants and contra-remonstrants, or England and Scotland ever had the miserable contentions, wars, and cruelties between the former episcopal parties and the Laudians, or between them and the presbyterians and independents, and all the silencings, and woeful contentions and schisms that have thence followed, if the vices of the clergy had not been the cause? And had we continued in this case these twenty years last, silencing, reviling, and prosecuting about two thousand conscientious preachers, and writing and preaching still for executing the laws against them, and the prosecuted people flying from such a clergy as ravening wolves, and some censuring the innocent with the guilty,—could all this have been done by a wise, holy, and peaceable clergy, that served God in self-denial, and knew what it is to seek the good of church and souls? When we yet continue under the same distractions and convulsions, and all cry out that a flood of misery is breaking in on the land and like to overwhelm us all, still it is the clergy who cannot or will not be reconciled, but animate rulers and people against each other, and cannot or will not find the way of peace. Yea, all would soon be healed, in probability, could the nation but procure the clergy to consent. Certainly there is some grievous disease in ourselves, which is like to prove mortal to such a kingdom, and that while so many pray and strive for peace. Those men that have no more skill or will to heal the wounds and stop the blood of a fainting church and state, nor will by any reason or humble importunity be entreated to consent to the cheap and necessary cure, no, nor to hold their hands from continued tearing of us, do tell all the world that they are sadly wanting in fitness for their sacred office, and that this unfitness is like to cost an endangered nation dear.

Woe, woe, woe, to that church that hath hypocrites, ungodly, unexperienced, proud, worldly, fleshly, unskilful, unfaithful, and malignant pastors, and that hath wolves instead of shepherds! Woe to the land that hath such! Woe to the prince and states that have and follow such counsellors, and to the souls that are subverted by them! Alas! from a bad clergy have sprung the greatest calamities of the churches, in all places, to this very day.

Sect. 11. But will such men's sins prove less woeful to themselves than others?

No. 1. It is the sin and guilt itself which is the greatest evil.

2. They aggravate their sin and guilt by a perfidious violating a double vow,—their baptismal vow of christianity, and their ordination vow to be faithful ministers of Christ.

3. They aggravate their guilt by their nearness to God in their office and works, as Aaron's two sons that were struck dead, Lev. x. 2, 3. "For God will be sanctified in them that come nigh him, and before all the people he will be glorified." The examples of the Bethshemites, Uzza, Uzziah, the bad priests and false prophets of old, are terrible.

4. And it greatly addeth to the guilt, to do all this or much of it as in the name of God, or by his commission. This is a dreadful taking of God's name in vain, for which he will not hold them guiltless. To pretend, that it is by God's command that they set up that which he abhorreth; that they corrupt his doctrine, or worship, or church order; that they set up their own wills and sinful laws instead of and against his laws; that they tear his church by proud impositions and wicked anathemas, and interdicts of whole kingdoms, excommunicating and deposing kings, absolving men from their oaths of allegiance, tormenting and murdering godly men as heretics, silencing faithful ministers, smiting the shepherds and scattering the flocks, and then reviling them as schismatics,—and all this to uphold a worldly kingdom of their own, and keep up their pride, domination, and self-will, and to have riches for provision for fleshly lusts;—I say, to do all this as in the name of Christ, with a *Sic dicit Dominus*, and as for the church, truth, and souls, is a most heinous aggravation.

5. Indeed, while a poor blind clergyman as his trade, for applause and gain, doth study and preach that word of God, which is against him, how dreadful is it to think how all that he doth and saith is self-condemnation, and that out of his own mouth he must be judged, and that all the woes which he pronounceth against hypocrites and impenitent, carnal, worldly men, his own tongue pronounceth them against himself.

Sect. 12. And when Satan hath once got such instruments, how great an advantage hath he for the success against themselves, against the flock, and against the church and cause of Christ, above what he might expect by other servants!

1. They are far hardlier brought to repentance than others.

(1.) Because they have, by wit and study, bended that doctrine to defend their sin which should be used to bring them to repentance.

(2.) Because their aggravated sin against light doth most forfeit that help of grace which should work repentance in them.

(3.) And because, being taken for wise, learned men, and preachers of truth, and teachers of others, and reprovers of errors, their reputation is much concerned in it, and their unhumbled souls, which look all others should assent and consent to their prescripts, will hardly be brought to confess sin and error; but will sooner (as papists) plead infallibility, or conclude, as some councils have done, that a layman must not accuse a clergyman, be he never so bad. Repentance is hard to all men of carnal interest, but to few more than to an unhumbled clergyman.

And, 2. Whoever accuseth or reproveth them of sin, will be represented as an enemy to the church, and a dishonourer of his ghostly fathers, and one that openeth their nakedness which he should cover. And so their ulcers are as a *noli me tangere;* and fret as a gangreen unremedied.

3. And their place, office, titles, and learning with many will give sin reputation and advantage. If a drunkard in the ale-house deride godly men, as heretics, schismatics, hypocrites, or puritans, sober men will not much regard it; but they think they owe more belief and reverence to a learned, reverend preacher in the pulpit, even when he preacheth against preaching, and against those that practise what he teacheth them at other times. Oh how much of his work hath Satan done in the world by corrupting sacred offices, and by getting HIS SERVANTS INTO RULE AND MINISTRY, TO DO HIS WORK AS FOR CHRIST and his church, and by his authority and in his name! Our natural enmity with the serpent dissuadeth him from speaking or sending to us in his own name. Should one say in the pulpit, Thus saith the devil, Hate Christ's servants, silence his ministers, call serious godliness hypocrisy, (which is the contrary to hypocrisy,) I should not much fear his success with any. But if he be a lying spirit in the mouth of Ahab's prophets, and get a prophet to smite Micaiah for pretending to more of the Spirit than he had; or if he can get men in the sacred office to say, "Thus saith the Lord," when they speak for sin or against the Lord, this is the devil's prosperous way.

Sect. 13. II. I have told you what plagues bad clergymen will be, and still have been, to themselves, to the souls of men, and to the public state of churches and kingdoms; and, were it not lest my writing should be too large, I should tell you what blessings on the contrary able and faithful ministers are.

Briefly, 1. Christ maketh them the chief instruments for the propagating of his truth and kingdom in the world, for the gathering of churches, and preserving and defending contradicted truth. "They are the lights of the world, and the salt of the earth." All christians are bound to teach or help each other in charity; but Christ's ministers are set in his church, (as parents in families,) to do it by office: and therefore must be qualified above others for it, and be wholly dedicated to it, and attend continually on it. As a physician differeth from every neighbour, who may help you in your sores or sickness as they can, so do the pastors of the church differ from private helpers of your souls. The Scripture is preserved and delivered down by the private means of all the faithful, but, eminently, by the public office of the pastors. It may be expounded and applied privately by any able christians, but the pastors do it, eminently, by office; and to them especially (though to all christians commonly) are committed the oracles of God. "The priest's lips must preserve knowledge, and men should inquire of the law at his mouth; for he is the messenger of the Lord of hosts," Mal. ii. 7. Never yet was the gospel well propagated nor continued in any country in the world, but by the means of the ministers of Christ. And oh what difference hath there been in their successes as they differed in ability, piety, and diligence! And how great an honour is it to be such blessed instruments of building up the house of God, and propagating the gospel and the kingdom of Christ, and the christian faith and godliness in the world!

2. And thus God useth them as his special instruments for the convincing, converting, edifying, comforting, and saving of souls. Others may be blest herein; but the special blessing goeth along with those that are specially obliged to the work,—which is parents in families, and pastors in the churches. Oh how many thousand souls in heaven will for ever rejoice in the effects of the labours of faithful ministers, and bless God for them! And what an honour, what a comfort is it to have a hand in such a work! "He that converteth a sinner from the error of his way, doth save a soul from death, and cover a multitude of sins," James v. 20.

3. And in this they are co-workers with Jesus Christ, the great Saviour of souls, and with the Holy Spirit, the Regenerator and Sanctifier. Yea, Christ doth very much of the work of his salvation by them: when he ascended on high he gave gifts to men, for the edifying of his body, till they come to a perfect man, Eph. iv. 6—16; and "when the Chief Shepherd shall appear, they shall receive a crown of glory that fadeth not away," 1 Pet. v. 4; and shall hear, "Well done, good and faithful servant." Hence are the streams of consolation, that make glad the city of God, and daily refresh many thousand precious souls. For "how shall men believe without a preacher? And how shall they preach unless they be sent" (qualified, obliged, and authorized by Christ)? Rom. x.

4. In a word, churches, states, and christian kingdoms, are chiefly blessed and preserved by the labour of the faithful part of the ministry: for, (1.) If we have the rare blessing of a wise, holy, and loving magistracy, it is usually by the success of the labours of the ministry. (2.) And there is no better means to bring the subjects to the conscientious performance of their duty to superiors. (3.) And, by the blessing of their labour, the sins of a nation are prevented or healed, which would else bring down God's heavy judgments. (4.) They teach people to live in love and peace with one another; and to abhor contention, cruelty, oppression, injury, and revenge; and all to do their several duties to promote the common good. (5.) When the ignorant, and slothful, and scandalous sort of bad ministers betray souls and would bring the ministry and religion into contempt, it is a wise and holy ministry that counter-worketh them, by labouring while others are idle, and doing that wisely which others do foolishly, and showing in their lives the power of that truth which others disgrace, and the reality of that holiness, love, justice, peace, and concord, which others would banish out of the world by making it seem but a name or image. (6.) When proud men tear the church by the engines of their domineering wits and wills, these humble pastors, as the servants of all, will labour to heal it, by christian meekness and condescension. When malignant priests seek to strengthen themselves by the multitude of the ungodly, and to bring serious piety (which doth molest them) into contempt, these faithful pastors open the just disgrace of sin, and the great necessity and honour of holiness, endeavouring that vile persons may be contemned, and those may be honoured that fear the Lord, Psal. xv. 4; and distinguishing the precious from the vile, the righteous from the wicked, and him that sweareth from him that feareth an oath, and him that serveth God from him that serv-

eth him not, God saith, They are as his mouth, Jer. xv. 19; Mal. iii. 17, 18; Eccles. ix. 2.

To be short, as an ignorant, worldly, carnal, proud, unholy sort of prelates and priests, are and have been the great plague of the churches these thirteen hundred years at least, so the skilful, holy, humble, faithful, laborious, patient ministers of Christ, have been and still are, the great blessings of the world; for saving souls, promoting knowledge, faith, holiness, love, and peace; opposing error, pride, oppression, worldliness, sensuality, and contention; diverting God's judgments by faith and prayer; forsaking all for Christ, and patiently suffering for well-doing; and by doctrine and example teaching men to difference the Creator from the creature, holiness from sin, heaven from earth, the soul from the body, the spirit from the flesh, and helping men to prepare, by a mortified, heavenly heart and life, for a comfortable death and endless happiness. Of such vast importance is it to the world whether the clergy be good or bad, skilful or unskilful, holy or worldly; and he is not a true christian that is insensible of the difference, or thinks it small.

And now, do I need to say any more, to show young men designed for the ministry of what importance it is that they be well prepared and qualified for it? God can and sometimes doth turn wolves into faithful shepherds, and convert those that, being unconverted, undertake the work that should convert others, and give wisdom and grace to ignorant and graceless preachers of wisdom and grace. But this is not ordinarily to be expected. But as youth are trained up and disposed, they commonly prove when they come to age. Their first notions lie deepest, and make way for their like, and resist all that is contrary, be it never so true, and good, and necessary. Experience tells this to all the world,—those who in youth are trained in heathenism, Mahometanism, popery, or any distinct sect of christians, they commonly continue such; especially if they live among those who are for it, and so make it their interest in reputation or wealth. And if the rulers and times should be but erroneous, heretical, or malignant, at enmity to truth and serious holiness, alas! how hard is it for ill-taught youth to resist the stream! How hard is it to unteach them the errors which they first learned! A vomit may easily bring up that which was but lately eaten; but the yellow and the green humours that lie deep, must cost heart-gripes before they will be cast up. False opinions, as well as truths, are usually linked together; and the chain is neither easily cast off nor broken. And they that have received errors, have received their defensatives: these are like the shell-fish, that carry their house about them. They have studied what to say for it, but not what can be said against it; or, which is worse, by a slight and false consideration of the arguments for truth, they have disabled them from doing them any good.

And if they had never so true notions in their memories, if they come not in power on their hearts, and make them not new, spiritual, holy men, these will not master fleshly lusts, nor overcome ambitious and worldly inclinations, nor make men fit to propagate that faith and holiness which they never had.

And it is now that you must get those eminent qualifications of knowledge and holiness which you must after use. And how will you use that which you have not?

And yet proud hearts, how empty soever, will be desirous of esteem and reputation, and will hardly bear vilifying, contempt, or disregard. Whenas, though some few prudent hearers will encourage such young as they think are hopeful, yet most will judge of things and persons as they find them; the ignorant, dry, and lifeless orations of unexperienced, carnal preachers, will not be magnified by such as know what judgment and holy seriousness that place and sacred work require. Few will much praise or feed on unsavoury or insipid food, merely to flatter and please the cook.

And then when you find that you are slighted for your slight and unskilful work, your stomachs will rise against those that slight you, and so by selfishness you will turn malignant, and become enemies to those that you take for enemies to you, because they are not contented with your unholy trifling. And all your enmity will turn against yourself, and be like Satan's against the members of Christ,—which is but his own self-tormenting.

Sect. 15. II. The case being so important, I shall briefly conjoin your danger and your remedy, beseeching you (as you have any care for your souls, your country, or the church of God, or any thing which faith or reason should regard) that you will soberly weigh the counsel that I give you.

The first of your dangers which I shall mention, lieth in a too hasty resolving for the sacred ministry. Pious and prudent desires and purposes I would not discourage. But two sorts of parents in this prove greatly injurious to the church: First, Worldly men, that send their sons to the universities in order to their worldly maintenance and preferment, looking at the ministry merely as a profession or trade by which they may be able to live: Secondly, And many honest, godly parents ignorantly think it a good work to design their children to the ministry, and call it a devoting them to God, without due considering whether they are like to be fit for it or not. And when they have been some years at the university, they thing a parsonage or vicarage is their due; ordained they must be; what have they else studied for? It is too late now to change their purposes, when they have been at seven years' cost and labour to prepare for the ministry. They are too old and too proud to go apprentices or servants. Husbandmen they cannot be; they are used to an idler kind of life. To be lawyers will cost them more time and study than they can now afford, having lost so much; and there are more already than can have practice. Physicians are already so many that the younger sort know not how to live, though they would, for money, venture on their neighbours' lives, to their greater danger than I am willing to express. So that there is no way left but for a benefice, to become church mountebanks and quacks, and undertake the pastoral care of souls, before they well know what souls are, or what they are made for, or whither they are going, or how they must be conducted and prepared for their endless state. And it seems to some the glory of a nation, to have many thousand such lads at the universities, (more than there be cures or churches in the land,) all expecting that their friends should procure them benefices. And they must be very ignorant and bad indeed, that cannot find some ministers so bad as to certify that they are sober and of good lives, and some patrons so bad as to like such as they, and, for favour, or somewhat worse, to present them; and some bishops' chaplain bad enough to be favourable in examining them, and then some bishop bad enough to ordain and institute them. And by that time nine thousand such youths have got benefices, alas! what a case will the churches and the poor people's souls be in!

Sect. 16. I. And what remedy is there for this? That which I have now to propose is, first to tell you, Who they be that should be devoted to the ministry; and next what both parents and you should do.

The work is so high, and requireth such qualifications, and miscarrying in it is of such dreadful consequence, that no youth should be resolvedly devoted to the ministry, that hath not all these following endowments:

1. He must have a good natural wit and capacity. It should be somewhat above the ordinary degree; but it must needs be of the better rank of ordinary wits: for grace supposeth nature, and, by sanctifying it, turns it the right way; but doth not use to make wise teachers of natural drones or weak-headed lads, that have not wit enough to learn. How many and how great things have they to learn and teach!

2. They must have some competent readiness of speech, to utter the knowledge they have got. One that cannot readily speak his mind in common things, is not like to come to that ready utterance which will be necessary to a preacher.

3. He must be one that is so far hopeful for godliness,

(1.) As to be captivated by no gross sin.

(2.) To have a love not only to learning, but to religion, to the word of God, and good company, and prayer, and good books; and a settled dislike of the things, words, and persons, that are against these.

(3.) And he must show some sense of the concerns of his soul, and regard of the life to come, and that his conscience is under some effectual convictions of the evil of sin, and the goodness and necessity of a godly life. The youth that hath not these three qualifications, should not be intended or devoted to the ministry. To devote an uncapable person, an ungodly person, to such a holy state and work, is worse than of old to have offered God the unclean, which he abhorred, for a sacrifice. And to design a graceless lad for the ministry, on pretence of hoping that he may have grace hereafter, is a presumptuous profanation, and worse than to design a coward to be a soldier, a wicked, unsuitable person to be a husband or wife, in hope they may be fit hereafter.

Sect. 17. II. Therefore if your parents have been so unwise as to devote that to God which was unfit for his acceptance, it concerneth you quickly to look better to yourselves, and not to run into the consuming fire. You should be conscious of your own condition. If you may know that you want,

1. A competency of natural capacity and ingenuity.

2. Or of ready speech.

3. Or of serious piety, love to godliness, and heart-devotedness to God;—do not meddle with that calling which requireth all these.

Sect. 18. *Obj.* But, you may say, what shall we do? We have gone so far that we are fit for nothing else.

Answ. You are less fit for the ministry than for any thing. That which requireth the highest qualifications, will most shame you and condemn you if you them want. If you are not fit for physic or law, be some great man's servant; if not that, it is better that you turn to the basest trade or laborious employment, than to run into the sad case of Hophni and Phinehas, or Nadab and Abihu, to the utter undoing of yourselves and the loss and danger of many others! But if your unfitness be not in your DISABILITY, but your UNGODLINESS, whether you be ministers or not, you will be for ever miserable unless you consider well the great things that should change your hearts and lives, and turn unfeignedly to God; and when that is done, I am no discourager of you. But I believe it is far better to be a cobbler or a chimney-sweeper, or to beg your bread, than to be an ungodly clergyman, with the greatest preferments, riches, and applause.

Sect. 19. *Obj.* But, parents may say, if we devote none to the ministry till godliness appear in them, how few will be so devoted! Children seldom show much savour of religion, and some that seem young saints prove old devils.

Answ. 1. At the present we have so many supernumeraries, that we need not fear a want of number.

2. Children cannot be expected to show that understanding in religion which men must have. But if they show not a love to it, and a conscience regardful of God's authority and the life to come, and a dislike of ungodliness and sin, you have no reason to presume that they will be fit for the ministry. If they had never been baptized, you ought not to baptize them in such a state. They must credibly profess faith and repentance before they can be adult christians, and so dedicated to God in baptism, much more before they are dedicated to him as the guides of the christian churches.

3. And you can judge but according to probabilities; if they prove bad after a probable profession, it will not be charged upon you. But we all know that a hopeful youth is a great preparation to an honest age.

Sect. 20. II. My next advice to you is, Abhor sloth and idleness. When you are at country schools, your masters drive you on by fear. But when you are in the universities and at riper age, you are more trusted with yourselves; and then all the diligence which fear constrained will be left off; and if you be not carried on with constant pleasure and love of knowledge, the flesh will prefer its ease, and unwillingness and weariness will go so slow a pace, as will bring you to no high degree of wisdom. And when you have spent your appointed time, and are void of that which you should have attained, your emptiness and ignorance will presently appear, when you are called out to the use of that knowledge which you have not. And it is not your canonical habit, nor seven or seventeen years spent in the university, nor the title of master of arts, bachelor of divinity, or doctor, no, nor bishop, that will pass with men in their right wits, instead of knowledge, diligence, humility, patience, and charity; nor that without these will do the work to which you are devoted. And then when you find that other men discern that weakness and badness which you are loth to know yourselves, it will be like to exasperate you into diabolical malignity. Believe it, the high and needful accomplishments of a true divine, are not easily or speedily attained.

Sect. 21. III. My next warning is, Fear and fly from sensuality, and fleshly lusts, and all the baits and temptations that may endanger you therein.

Sense and appetite is born with us, and it is inordinate in our corrupted nature; and the reason and will that should resist and rule it, are weakened and depraved. Labouring, poor countrymen are not in such danger in this as you are. Your bodies are not tired and tamed with labours, nor your thoughts taken up with wants and cares. While your bodies are at ease, and your studies are arbitrary, fleshly lust and appetite hath time and room to solicit your fancies, and incline you to interrupt your studies, and think of the matters of sensual delight, either with what to please your appetite in eating, or of strong drinks or wine that also exhilirates, or of some needless or hurtful pastime called recreation, cards, dice, gaming, &c. or to think of women and filthy lusts, or to read romances, play-books, or other corrupting vanities. More idle scholars far, are strongly haunted with temptations to self-pollution and other filthy lusts, than the poor and afflicted sort of men.

And if these should prevail, alas! you are undone; they will offend God, expel his grace, either wound or scare your consciences, destroy all spiritual affections and delights, turn down your hearts from heaven and holiness to filth and folly; and beasts will be unfit for the pleasures or the work of saints.

Sect. 22. Away therefore from idleness! pamper not the flesh with fulness or delights; abhor all time-wasting, needless recreations. Away from the baits of fleshly lust! Be no more indifferent herein and unresolved, than you would be about drinking poison, or leaping into a coal-pit, or wilfully going among murderers or thieves. Presume not on your own strength: he is safest that is furthest from the danger. Gunpowder must not stand near the fire.

Sect. 23. IV. Be sure to make a prudent choice of your companions, especially of your bosom friends.

It is supposed that a man loveth the company which he chooseth, though not which he constrainedly is cast upon. And love and familiarity will give them great advantage over you: if they be wise, they will teach you wisdom; if they be holy and spiritual, they will be drawing you towards God, and settling you in the resolved hatred of sin and love of holiness. But if they be worldly and ambitious, they will be filling your heads with ambitious, worldly projects; and if they be ungodly hypocrites that have but the dead image and name of christians, they will be opposing or deriding serious godliness, and pleading for the carcass and formalities of piety as better than serious spiritual devotion; and if they be hardened malignants, they will be trying to make you such as they, by lies, revilings, or plausible cavils against the things and persons that are spiritually contrary to their fleshly minds and interests. And while you hear not what can be said on the other side, it will possess your minds (if God preserve you not) with false thoughts of God's servants, and with scorn or contempt of such as you hear described falsely. As papists think of protestants as heretics, you will take serious godliness for fanatical self-conceit, and think of the best christians as you do of quakers or others, that are mad with fear or pride.

Wise and religious companions, and bosom friends, are an unspeakable blessing; but the merciful providence of God doth usually choose them for us, yet so as that usually we must also be faithful choosers for ourselves. Ill company is a dangerous snare, and God often trieth us by casting us where such are; but if we choose it not, and love it not, God will provide us of an antidote; and we may converse with him even in the presence of the ungodly; and he will teach us by the experience of their folly and sin, to dislike it more than if we had never seen it.

Sect. 24. V. Especially be most careful in the choice of your tutors and instructors.

Though it be first your parents' part to choose them for you, it is yours to do your best herein, to save yourselves, if your parents by ignorance or malignity do mischoose. And the rulers that allow not men to choose their own pastors, yet hitherto allow the parents or the sons to choose their own tutors and domestic instructors.

But this is the grand danger and misery of mankind, that the ignorant know not what teachers to choose; yea, the more they need the help of the best, the less they know who they are: but I will tell you as far as you are capable of discerning.

1. Usually the common report of men that are sober and impartial, commendeth worthy men above others; for knowledge and goodness is like light, a self-discovering thing.

2. Choose not a teacher that preferreth human wisdom before divine, but one that maketh it his business to expound the Scripture, and teach you what is the will of God, and how to please him and to be saved.

3. Choose not one that is of a worldly and ambitious mind, and will teach you that which most conduceth to get preferment and worldly wealth, and not that which best helpeth you to heaven.

4. Choose not one that is factious and uncharitable, violent for a party, either because it is uppermost, or because it standeth for some odd opinion or causeless singularity; but one that is of a christian, catholic charity, and loveth a godly man as such, even as himself, and is for wronging none, but doing good to all, and maintaining unity and peace.

Sect. 25. VI. Watch with great fear against pride, ambition, and worldly ends, in your own hearts and lives.

The roots of these mortal sins are born in us, and lie very deep; and they not only live, but damnably reign where they are little discerned, bewailed, or suspected: but woe to him that is conquered by them! "Ye cannot serve God and mammon. The love of the world is enmity to God. If any man love the world, the love of the Father is not in him." Paul spake, weeping, of such, "whose God was their belly, who gloried in their shame, who minded earthly things, being enemies to the cross of Christ, when their conversation should have been in heaven," Phil. iii. 18—20. A surprise in passion, even of an ugly sin, is less dangerous than such a habit of worldliness and pride. And, alas! how many that have escaped the temptations of sloth and sensuality, have been flattered and overcome by this! Those that have had better wits than others, and got more learning, have thought now that preferment is their due. And if they fall into times (which have not been rare) when the malignity of church or state governors hath made it the way to preferment, to declaim against some truth, or the most religious men, that are against a carnal, sinful interest, and to revile God's best servants, and cry up some notion or error of their own, and magnify the worst that promote their worldly ends and hopes, alas! how doth this stream carry down the pregnantest wits into the gulf of perdition!

Yea, some that seemed very humble and mortified, when they had no great temptation, when wealth and honour have been set before them, have lost virtue and wit before they were well aware. And worldly interest hath secretly bribed and biassed their understandings, to take the greatest truth for error, duty for sin, and error for truth, and sin for duty. And they have talked, and preached, and wrote for it, and seem to believe that indeed they are in the right; and cannot discern that they are perverted by interest, when an impartial stander-by may easily see the bias by the current of their course. And if you be servants of the flesh and the world, woe to you when your masters turn you off, and you must receive your wages!

Sect. 26. VII. Above all, therefore, choose like real christians, and take God and heaven for your hope, your all.

If you do not so, you are not christians indeed, nor stand to your baptismal covenant; and if you be here fixed, by the grace of God, and your sober consideration and belief, you will then know what to choose and do. It will teach you to refer all worldly things to spiritual and heavenly ends and uses, and to count all things loss and dung for Christ, and "to choose the one thing needful, which shall never be taken from you," even that which will guide you in just and safe ways, and save you from the greatest evil, and give your minds continual peace, even that which passeth understanding, and will be best at last, when sinners are forsaken.

Sect. 27. VIII. My next counsel, therefore, is for the order of your studies. Begin then with your catechism and practical divinity, to settle your own souls in a safe condition for life or death. And deal not so foolishly as to waste many years in inferior arts and sciences, before you have studied how to please God and to be saved. I unfeignedly thank God, that, by sickness and his grace, he called me early to learn how to die, and therefore to learn what I must be and how to live, and thereby drew me to study the sacred Scriptures, and abundance of practical, spiritual English books, till I had somewhat settled the resolution and the peace of my own soul, before I had gone far in human learning. And then I found more leisure and more capacity to take in subservient knowledge in its proper time and place. And, indeed, I had lost most of my studies of philosophy, and difficult controversies in theology, if I had fallen on them too young, before I came to due capacity; and so had been prepossessed with crude or unsound notions, for they had kept out that which required a riper judgment to receive it. Such books as I before commended to the apprentices, contain the essentials of religion, plainly, affectionately, and practically delivered, in a manner tending to deep impression, renovation of the soul, and spiritual experience, without which you will be but "like sounding brass or a tinkling cymbal." The art of theology, without the POWER, (consisting in holy life, and light, and love,) is the make of the hypocrite.

Yet before you come to lay exact systems of theology in due method in your minds, much help of subservient arts and sciences is necessary; however a council of ancient bishops once forbad the reading of the gentiles' books.

Sect. 28. IX. And here next I advise you, thoroughly to study the evidences and nature of the christian faith; but not to hasten too soon over-confidently on hard controversies, as if your judgment of them at maturity must have no change; but still suppose, that greater light, by longer study, may cause in you much different thoughts of such difficulties.

Sect. 29. Lastly, I advise you, that you begin not the exercise of your ministry too boldly, in public, great, or judicious auditories. Over-much confidence signifieth pride and ignorance of your imperfection, and of the greatness of the work, and the dreadfulness of the Most Holy Majesty. But (if you can) at first settle a competent time in the house with some ancient experienced pastor, that hath some small country chapel, that needs your help. And,

1. There you may learn as well as teach, and learn by his practice that which you must practise; which, in a great house, as a chaplain, you will hardly do, but must cast yourself into a far different mould.

2. By preaching some years to a small, ignorant people, where you fear not critical judgments, you will get boldness of speech, and freedom of utterance, without that servile study of words, and learning your written notes without book, which will be tiresome, time-wasting, and lifeless. And when freedom and use hath brought you to a habit of ready speaking of the great and necessary things, and acquaintance with ignorant country people hath taught you to understand their case, you will have a better preparation for more public places, (when you are clearly called to them,) than you were ever like to get either in universities, among scholars, or in great men's houses.

Compassion to the church that is plagued with bad ministers, and by the weak undergo exceeding great loss; and the sense of the grand importance of the pastors' qualifications to the happiness or misery of souls and kingdoms, have drawn me to say more to young students that intend the ministry, than I at first intended. And therefore with the other two sorts I shall be very brief.

One earnest warning to you, and all young men, I add: Know that one of the most common and pernicious maladies of mankind, is an unhumbled understanding, rashly confident of its own apprehensions, through false, hasty judging and prefidence, the brat of ignorance and pride. Of a multitude of persons differing, how few are not obstinately confident that they are in the right, even lads that are past twenty years of age! O dread this vice, and suspect your understanding. Be humble; take time, and try, and hear, before you judge. Labour for knowledge; but take not on you to be sure where you are not, but doubt and try till you are sure.

CHAPTER X.

COUNSEL TO YOUNG STUDENTS IN PHYSIC.

SUPPOSING what is said to others, which equally concerneth you, I briefly add,

I. Make not the getting of money, and your own worldly prosperity, so much of your end as the doing good in the world, by the preservation of men's health and lives, and the pleasing of God thereby. Selfish, low ends show a selfish mind, that liveth not to God or public good.

II. Undertake not the practice of physic without all these qualifications:

1. A special sagacity, or natural searching, conjecturing judgment. For almost all your work lieth in the dark, and is managed by conjecture.

2. Much reading, especially of observators, that you may know what hath been the experience of all ages, and eminent men before you.

3. The experience of other men's practice: and therefore, if possible, stay some time first in the house with some eminent practitioner, whose experiences you may see, and hear his counsel.

III. Begin with plain and easy cases, and meddle only with safe and harmless remedies; and think not yourselves physicians indeed, till you have got considerable experience yourselves: there is no satisfactory trusting to other men's experiences alone.

IV. In cases too hard for you, send your patients to abler physicians, and prefer not your reputation or gain before their lives.

V. Study simples thoroughly, especially the most powerful; and affect not such compositions, as by the mixture of the less powerful, do frustrate the ingredients, which would else be more effectual.

VI. Forget not the poverty of most patients, who have not money to pay large chargeable bills of the apothecary, nor give large fees to a physician. Multitudes neglect physic and venture without it, because physicians require so much, and are so much for their apothecaries' gain, that they have it not to pay.

VII. Take heed of self-conceitedness, and rash confidence, and too hasty judging. Most of your work is hard; many things, which you think not on, may occasion your mistake. Causes and diseases have marvellous diversities. Most that are quick judges, and suddenly confident that all their first apprehensions are true, do prove but proud, self-ignorant fools, and kill more by ignorance and temerity, than high-way robbers or designing murderers do. And though the grave hide your mistakes, they are known to God.

VIII. Give not too much physic; nor too often, or without need; nor venture on things dangerous. Man's life is precious; and nature is the chief physician, which art must but help. The body is tender and easily distempered: rather do too little than too much. Oft tampering useth to kill at last: as he that daily washeth a glass, at last breaketh it; and as seamen are bold, because they have oft escaped, but many, if not most, are drowned at last; and as soldiers that have oft escaped are bold to venture, but killed at last. It is usually so with them that oft take physic, except from very cautelous, skilful men. Therefore, were I a woman, I would not marry a physician, lest his nearness and kindness should cause him to be tampering with me so oft, till a mistake did kill me. All your neighbours may mistake your disease without your hurt, but your physician's mistake may be your present death.

IX. Direct men first, as faithful friends, to the things which may prevent the need of physic: viz.

1. A temperate and wholesome diet, avoiding fulness and hurtful things.

2. Sufficient labour to suscitate natural heat, keep pure the humours, and expel excrements; avoiding idleness.

3. Keeping warm, and avoiding occasions of cold, especially cold drink, cold places, and cold clothing, either when they are hot, or in winter, when nature needeth help.

4. Contentedness and quietness of mind, and cheerful converse.

5. Direct them to such familiar remedies at home, in their drinks and diet, as is suitable to their distempers for preservation, and are safe and harmless, and put them not to a needless dependence on your frequent help; make not use of weak women's fears, to make them miserable by needless medicining, and so to make them as tenants to you, to pay you a constant rent to quiet them.

X. Give them good counsel for their souls that need it; flatter them not with false hopes of life, when it tendeth to hinder their preparations for death. They and you are hasting to so great a change, as requireth great and careful fore-thoughts. It is sad to go out of the world, and not at all to know whither, and what will be their next habitation; much more to be in a certain state of misery. Those will hear a physician that will not send for a divine, and it is not a work unbeseeming your profession, but such as christian faith and charity bespeaks.

CHAPTER XI.

COUNSEL TO YOUNG STUDENTS OF THE LAW IN LONDON.

God hath made much use of honest lawyers, as the instruments of our safety, and of the just and orderly government of the land.

1. They are not bred up in mere idleness and luxury, as too many are of higher birth, but in such diligent study as improveth their understandings, and keepeth them from that debauchery which idleness and fulness cherish.

2. And their studies and callings make it their interest, as to know, so also to maintain the laws; and that is to maintain propriety, just liberty and order, and so to preserve justice and the common peace, except in countries that have pernicious laws. Injustice in judges and lawyers is like heresy, ungodliness, and persecution in pastors of the church; clean contrary to their very calling and profession; but more easily and commonly seen and hated, because it is against the well-known interest of mankind. Shame therefore and common hatred of the unjust, is here a great restraint of evil.

But bad men, for all this, will do badly, and turn even the rules of justice into oppression, to serve the wills and lusts of those that can promote them, that by them they may serve their own. Therefore that young men, that study the law, may prove wise and honest, is of great importance to the common good, as well as to their own.

I. And here, first, I warn all such to take heed of the sins of sensuality. Alas! London doth so abound with temptations, that, without grace and wise resolution, you are unsafe. There are so many sensual, proud, and ungodly young men ready to entice you; so many play-houses, taverns, and filthy houses to entertain you; that if you go without grace and wit, the flesh and the devil will soon precipitate you into the slavery of brutish flesh. And then you forfeit God's favour and protection; and he may leave you to more sin and misery, or to grow up to be the servants of oppression, the enemies of piety, and the plagues of the commonwealth.

II. Study hard; for idleness never made good lawyers, nor very useful men.

III. Abhor and avoid ill company, especially of two sorts:

1. Those that would entice you to the places and practices aforesaid of voluptuousness.

2. Those that being themselves deceived would deceive you, against religion and your salvation. It is too well known that such persons in London are not rare, though the danger by them is not known enough. Even those that are so unchristian and inhuman as to prate against the christian faith, the truth, the authority or sufficiency of the sacred Scripture, the life to come, the soul's immortality, if not also against the government and providence of God, will yet talk as confidently as if they were in their wits, yea, and were the greatest wits among us. For my part, I could never yet get one man of them soberly to join with me in a fair disquisition of the truth, and follow it on till we came to see the just conclusion. Commonly they will fly from me, and refuse disputes, or turn all to some rambling rant or jest; or when they are sated, be gone, and go no further, and come no more.

Young unfurnished heads are unfit to dispute with the devil, or any such messengers of his. A pest-house is not more dangerous to you. But if they have perplexed you, desire some well-studied minister of Christ either to meet them, or to resolve your doubts. And if you will read what I have written on that subject, you may find enough to resolve if it be justly received, viz.

1. In my "Reasons for the Christian Religion."
2. In my "Unreasonabless of Infidelity."
3. In my "Life of Faith."
4. In "More Reasons for the Christian Religion."

And avoid also the snares of those that would draw you into uncharitable factions, on pretence of right religion, to hate, or censure, or fly from all that are not just of their sect and way; especially the proud faction of church tyrants, that on pretence of order and piety, would set up a lifeless image of formality, and burn, banish, silence, or persecute all that are not for domination, and usurpation, and worldly interest.

4. Let not rising and riches be the chief end of your studies, but to serve God in the just service of your king and country, to promote justice, and do good in the world.

5. Live in the familiarity of the most useful men of your profession, that is, the wisest and the most conscionable; and choose those pastors, for your best helpers in religion, who keep closest to God's word, and warp not after any dangerous singularities, or worldly preferments, or unpeaceable, tearing impositions on their brethren; and that live as they preach,—in love, peace, and holiness,—as men that set their hearts and hopes on future blessedness, and labour for the church's edification and concord, and the saving men's souls.

CHAPTER XII.

COUNSEL TO THE SONS OF THE NOBILITY AND MAGISTRATES.

THOUGH men of your rank are furthest out of the hearing of such as I, and usually the greatest contemners of our counsel, yet will not that excuse us from due compassion to the land of our nativity, nor from love and pity to yourselves, nor from any probable ministerial attempt to do you good.

Your dangers are much greater than other men's; or else Christ had never so often told us, how hard it is for rich men to be saved; and how few such escape the idolatrous damning love of the world, and become sincere believers and followers of a crucified Saviour, Luke xii; xvi. &c.

I. One part of your great danger is, that you are commonly bred up among the baits of sensuality. It is not for nothing that "fulness of bread" is made one of the sins of Sodom, Ezek. xvi. 49; and that he that after lay in the flames of hell, is described as "richly clothed and faring sumptuously every day." Not that all rich clothes, or sumptuous, seasonable feasting, is a sin; but that these use both to signify sensuality and to cherish it. It is the sure brand of the ungodly, to be "lovers of pleasure more than of God." They that but seldom come where tempting plenty is of delicious meats and drinks, are too often overcome. But they that are bred up where plenty of both these is daily before them, are in greater danger lest their table and their drink become a snare.

Feast not therefore without fear; remember that flesh-pleasing sensuality is as damnable in the rich as in the poor; and that the greatest wealth will not allow you to take any more for quantity or quality, than standeth with temperance, and truly tendeth to fit you for your duty. Your riches are given you in trust as God's stewards, to serve your country, and relieve the poor, and to promote good uses; but not to serve your fleshly lusts, nor to be abused to excess, or cherish sin. To be sober and temperate, is the interest of your own souls and bodies, and, under your great temptations, the more laudable.

II. Another of your dangers is, the ill examples of too many persons of your rank. You are apt to think that their wealth, and pomp, and power, makes them more imitable than others, as being more honourable. And if they wallow in drunkenness or filthy lust, or talk profanely, you may think that such sins are the less disgraceful.

But can you dream that they are the less dangerous and damnable? Will God fear them or spare them? Must they not die and be judged as well as the lowest? Is it not an aggravation of their sin, that it is done by men that had the greatest mercies, and were put in trust and honour purposely to suppress sin in the world? As their places signify more than others, so do their sins; and accordingly shall they be punished. Doth the quondam wealth, honour, or pleasures of a Dives, a Pharaoh, an Ahab, a Herod, a Pilate, a Nero, ease a lost, tormented soul.

III. Another of your temptations will be pride, and overvaluing of yourselves, because of wealth and worldly honour. But this is so foolish a sin, and against such notorious humbling evidence, that, as it is the devil's image, it is nature's shame. Is not your flesh as corruptible as a beggar's? Do you not think what is within that skin; and how a leprosy or the small-pox would make you look; and how you must shortly leave all your glory, and your bodies become unpleasant spectacles? Do you not think what is it to lie rotting in a grave and turn to earth? And do you not know how much more loathsome a thing all the vice and unholiness of your souls is; and what it is to have to do with a holy God, and to be near to judgment and an endless state? He is mad in sin, that such considerations will not humble.

IV. Another of your dangers is from flatterers, that will be pleasing and praising you, but never tell you of that which should humble you, and awake you to the sense of your everlasting concerns. But none here are so dangerous as a flattering clergy, who, being themselves carnal worldlings, would serve that flesh which is their master, by your favour and beneficence. Ahab had such prophets, that said, "Go and prosper;" in whose mouths the devil was a lying spirit. How many sincere men have been undone by such!

Remember then what it is to be a sinful man, and what need you have of vigilant friends and pastors, that will deal faithfully with you, as if it were on your death-bed: and encourage such, and abhor worldly flatterers. Your souls have need of as strong physic, and as plain dealing, as the poorest men's, and therefore bear it, and thankfully accept it.

V. And one of your greatest dangers here will be, that your own fleshly minds, and this worldly sort of men, (especially if of the clergy,) will be drawing you to false, contemptuous thoughts of serious godliness, and of serious, godly men. Whenas if you be not such yourselves, you are undone for ever, and all your flatterers, your big names, wealth, and honour, will neither save you, nor ease your pains in hell. As ever you believe there is a God, believe that you owe him the utmost reverence, obedience, and love, that your faculties can perform. And as ever you care what becomes of you for ever, pay him this great due, and hate all that would divert you; and much more all those diabolical suggestions, which would draw you to think that a needless thing which must be your life and all.

VI. But above all, I beseech you fear and watch, lest you be drawn to espouse any thing as your interest, which is against the interest and command of Christ, and against his kingdom, or the good of his church, or the commonwealth. As the devil first undid the world, by making deceived Eve believe, that God's command was against her interest, so doth he to this day; but with none so much as with nobles and rich men. God hath commanded you nothing but what is for your own good, nor forbidden you any thing but what is for your own and others' hurt. He needs not you, or any; but you must allow him to be God, and therefore to be wiser and better than you, and to know better what is best and fittest for you and others: but Satan will slander to you God's laws, ways, and servants; for he is for your enmity and separation from God, and therefore would draw you to believe, that he and his ways are enemies to you, and against your pleasure, honour, domination, commodity, or ease. Oh how many princes and great men have been utterly undone by believing the flesh, the devil, and his ministers, that christianity is against their power, honour, or other interests, and that the Scripture is too precise, and that conscience, obeying God before them, is against their power and prerogative, and so have set them as enemies to keep under conscience and serious godliness, lest obedience to their wills be thereby hindered.

Yea, how many also so dote, as to think that the interest of head, heart, stomach, and members of rulers and subjects, stand not in union, but in contrariety and victory against each other! Woe to the land that hath such rulers, and to the poor tenants that have such landlords! But much more woe to such selfish oppressors, that had rather be feared than loved, and take it for their honour to be free and able to do mischief, and destroy those, whose common welfare should be more pleasant to them than their own! And to them especially, that take serious godliness and godly men to be against them, and therefore bend their wit and power to suppress them; as if they said, as Luke xix. 27, "We will not have this man reign over us;" whom Christ will destroy as his unthankful enemies, and "will break them with his iron rod, and dash in pieces as a potter's vessel," Psal. ii.

VII. As you love yourselves and the common good, get good men about you. Read Psal. ci.; xv.; xvi. Especially faithful teachers, and next godly friends, and servants, and companions. And read much the histories of the lives of wise and godly men, such as King Edward the Sixth, and the Lord Harrington, young men: imitate such excellent persons as Scripture and other history justly commend to your imitation. It will be profitable to read lives of worthy men, such as are gathered by Mr. Clark, Dr. Fuller, Thuanus, Beza, yea of the martyrs, and of such christian princes as Constantine, M. Theodosius, &c.; Maximilian II. Emperor, John Frederick of Saxony, Philip of Hessia, Ludov. Pius of France; yea, such heathens as Titus, Trajan, Adrian, but especially M. Aurel., Antonine, and Alex. Severus; yea, and such lawyers, philosophers, physicians, but especially divines, as Melchior Adamus in four volumes hath recorded; and of such bishops as Cyprian, Nazianzen, Ambrose, Austin, Basil, Chrysostom, and our Usher, and such others.

VIII. Live not in idleness, as the sons of rich men too oft do; for that will rust and corrupt your minds, and cherish besotting, damning lusts, and render you worthless and useless in the world, and consequently the greatest plagues of your country, to which you should be the greatest helps and blessings. Make as much conscience of improving your hours, as if you were the poorest men: you have most wages, and should do God most work. Let holy and useful studies one part of the day, and doing good to others another part, and necessary refreshment and exercise another, take up your time; you have none allowed you for any thing unprofitable, much less hurtful.

Oh what a blessing to the world are wise, godly magistrates! and what a curse are the foolish and ungodly!

IX. Remember that the grand design of the devil, and all deceivers, is to delude and corrupt the rulers of the people, knowing how much they signify by their laws, power, and examples; and how sad it will be to be judged as a persecutor, or a captain of iniquity. And therefore you must have a greater self-suspicion, and fear of seduction and sin, than others; and must watch more carefully against wicked counsel and example, but especially the temptations of your own flesh and corrupted nature, and of your wealth and place.

CHAPTER XIII.

COUNSEL TO PARENTS AND TUTORS OF YOUTH.

Should I now say to parents and teachers what on their parts is necessary to their great duty, and the good of youth, it would be more than all that I have said already; but that is not the present work, and you may see much of it done in my "Christian Directory." But because so much lieth on their hands, I beseech all such that read these lines, to remember,

I. How near their relation to their children is; and that for a parent to betray their souls to sin and hell, by neglect or by ill means, seems more unexcusable cruelty than for the devil, a known enemy, to do it.

II. How very much their welfare is intrusted to your care. You have the teaching of them before the ministers, and have them always nearer with you, and have greater power over them. Oh that you knew what holy instructions, and heavenly excitations, and good example God requireth of you for their good, and how much of the hopes of the church and world lie on the holy skill and fidelity of parents, in the right education of youth!

III. O feed not their sinful desires and lusts; use them not to pride, to idleness, to too much fulness or pleasing of the appetite; but teach them the reasons of temperance and mortification, and the sin and mischief of all sensuality.

IV. Yet use them with tender, fatherly love, and make them perceive that it is for their own good, and cherish their profitable delights; study how to make all good delightful to them, encourage and reward them. Tell them of the wisdom and goodness of God's word, and let them read the lives of holy men.

V. Choose them both callings, habitations, and relations which make most for the common good, and for the advantage of their souls; and not those that most serve covetousness, pride, or slothfulness.

VI. Know their particular inclinations, corruptions, and temptations, and accordingly watch and keep them, as you would do against death.

VII. Settle them under wise and godly pastors, and in the familiar company of godly persons, especially of their age and usual converse.

VIII. Keep them as much as possible from temptations at home and abroad, especially those that tend to sensuality, and to impiety, or corrupting their judgments against religion. Thrust them not beyond sea or elsewhere unfortified among deceivers, for a mere ornament, as some cruelly do.

IX. Remember how you dedicated them to Christ in baptism, and what was promised, and what renounced, and what you bound yourselves to do.

X. Remember still how much the happiness or misery of church, and kingdoms, and of the world, doth lie on the right or wrong educating of youth, by PARENTS, much more than our UNIVERSITIES or SCHOOLS.

XI. Remember that your own comfort or sorrow in them lieth most on your own duty or neglect. If they prove wicked and plagues of the world, and you are the cause, it may tear your hearts. But what a joy is it to be the means of their salvation, and of their public service in the world!

XII. Disgrace sin to them, and commend holiness by word and practice; and be yourselves what you would have them be; and pray daily for them and yourselves. The Lord bless this counsel to them and you!

CHAPTER XIV.

WHAT ARE MEN'S DUTIES TO EACH OTHER AS ELDER AND YOUNGER.

SECT. 1. It is most clear in Scripture and reason that there are many special duties, which the elder and younger, as such, owe to each other. The elder are bound,

1. To be wiser than the younger, as having longer time, and so to be their instructors in their several places.

2. And especially, to deliver down to them the sacred Scripture which they received, and the memorials of God's works done for his church in their days, and which they received from their fathers.

3. And to go before them in the example of a holy and heavenly life; Job xxxii. 4; viii. 8; Heb. v. 14; Tit. ii. 2, 3; 1 John ii. 13, 14; Judges vi. 13; Psalm xliv. 1; lxxviii. 3, 5; Deut. i. 21; Exod. xii. 26; Deut. xi. 19; Josh. iv. 6, 21, 22; Joel i. 3.

Sect. 2. And nature and Scripture tells us, that the younger owe much duty to the elder, summed up, "Ye younger, submit yourselves to the elder," 1 Peter v. 5. This submission includeth especially, a reverence to their judgments, preferring them before their own, and supposing that ordinarily they are wiser than the younger, and therefore living towards their elders in a humble, learning disposition, and not proudly setting their unfurnished wits against their greater experience without very evident reason. For the understanding of which, note,

Sect. 3. 1. That it is certain that mere age doth not make men wise or good: none are more sottishly and uncurably ignorant, than the aged ignorants; and few so bad, as the old, obstinate sinners. For they grow worse, deceiving and being deceived, and more and more abuse God's mercy, and are still going further from him, as the faithful are growing better and nearer to him.

2. And it is certain that God greatly blesseth some young men's understandings, and maketh them wiser than the aged and their teachers.

3. And such a one is not bound to think, that he knoweth not what he knoweth; nor to believe, that every old man is wiser than he; all this we grant.

Sect. 4. But though "Better is a poor and wise child than an old and foolish king who will no more be admonished," (Eccles. iv. 13,) yet,

1. It is certain that knowledge cometh much by experience; and long experience and use is far more powerful than the short; and time and converse are necessary to it. Naturally or ordinarily, long learning and use increase knowledge. Do not all take it for granted, that, usually, the boys who have been many years at school, are better scholars than beginners? And so in all other acquisitions. Therefore it was the elders that were commonly the rulers of the people in church and commonwealth; and the pastors and rulers are thence called elders: and if they were not ordinarily the wisest, why did not God make the children the ordinary teachers and rulers of their parents, but the parents of the children? Old men may be ignorant and erroneous, as well as wicked; but young men cannot be ripe in wisdom without a miracle. We are not, therefore, now to suppose unusual things to be usual. Ordinarily, youth is ignorant and raw; their conceptions undigested, not well fixed or improved: it is but few things that they know; and their ignorance of the rest maketh them liable to many errors. "For the time, ye ought to have been teachers," Heb. v. 12; fitness to teach supposeth time; the young cannot digest strong meats. A novice must not be a bishop; the reason may seem strange,—"Lest he be lift up with pride, and fall into the condemnation of the devil," 1 Tim. iii. 6. One would think youth should be most humble, as conscious of defectiveness. But because the ignorant know not that more is to be known than ever they attained, therefore they know not their own ignorance.

2. And this proud ignorance is so odious a sin, and the nurse of so many more, and so great an enemy to wisdom and all good, that it is no wonder that it is the way to "the condemnation of the devil."

Sect. 5. Therefore though young men should not receive any falsehood, heresy, or ill example from the aged, yet they should still remember, that, *cæteris paribus*, age hath the great advantage for knowledge, and youth must needs live in a humble, teachable sense of ignorance; other men's abuse of time, and aged folly, will not prove them miraculously wise. The aged are always the wisest, if they equally improve time and helps.

Sect. 6. It is so odious a sin for lads and young students to be self-conceited and unteachable, and set up their apprehensions with ungrounded confidence against their elders, that all should be very fearful of that guilt, and have such humble thoughts of their own understandings, as to be jealous of their conceptions. For all these vices make up their self-conceited prefidence:

1. It is both great IGNORANCE of the darkness of men's understanding, and great ignorance of themselves,—to be ignorant that they are ignorant, and to think they are sure of that which they know not.

2. It is an odious sort of PRIDE, to overvalue an ignorant understanding, and to be proudly confident of that which they have not.

3. It is FOLLY, to think that truth can be known, without sufficient time and trial, and contrary to the world's continual experience.

4. It is as absurd and inhuman a SUBVERTING OF THE ORDER OF THE WORLD, for lads to set up their wits by groundless self-conceitedness against their elders, as for subjects to set their wills against rulers.

5. It is a continual unrighteousness; there is a justice required in our common private judging, as well as in judges' public judgment. And all should be heard and tried before we peremptorily judge.

6. It is a nest of continual ERROR in the mind, which is the soul's deformity, and contrary to nature's love of truth.

Sect. 7. And it hath abundance of mischievous effects.

1. It keepeth out that truth or knowledge which should be received. It obstinately resisteth necessary teaching, whereas the willingest entertainment is little enough to get true knowledge, even by slow degrees. As God giveth birds an instinct to feed their young, so the young ones by instinct hunger, and open their mouths. But if they abhorred their meat, and must be crammed, they would commonly perish; that knowledge that such get, must be from themselves,—in their own thinking and observation only; where their minds are yet unfurnished with those truths that must let in more, and daily objects will occasion error or confusion in the minds that are unprepared to improve them; and their own lusts will pervert them, and one error draw in more; whereas the help of those that by long and successful study have rightly ordered and digested their conceptions, might be an exceeding help to willing learners.

2. And such by pride do forfeit the grace of God which he giveth to the humble, "and resisteth the proud;" and are oft given up to the self-conceitedness which they so defend, till their own counsels and ways be their confusion.

3. And the devil hath advantage to set in and even possess such proud, prepared, ignorant minds, and become their teacher, and lead them almost to what he will, against truth, and the church, and themselves, and God.

4. And self-conceit and hasty confidence maketh them continual liars; even while they rage for what they say as true: for being usually mistaken for want of patient trial, they say what they think, and are not to be much believed in their prefidence.

Sect. 8. But seeing many old men are ignorant and erroneous, and some young men have sounder understandings, how shall I know when I am guilty of pride, self-conceit, and prefidence, and refusing others' judgment? *Answ.* 1. When you rashly neglect their judgment and counsel, who have had as good helps and parts as you, and far longer time and experience, without so much as hearing what they have to say, and taking time to try the cause according to its weight, especially if they be such as nature or relation obliged you to learn of. 2. When you easilier suspect such than your own understandings. 3. When your confidence of your understandings is so unproportionable to your time and studies, that you must suppose you know by a miracle or some rare capacity and wit; as if you had got more in a few years than the rest of mankind doth in many. 4. When you judge suddenly before you take time to think, and may know that you never heard what may be said against you.

5. When you talk most in a bold asserting or a teaching way, as if you were oracles to be heard and reverenced; and not in a humble, inquiring way, with that necessary doubting which beseemeth learners. "Except ye become as little children" in teachable humility, you are not fit for the school of Christ, Matt. xviii. 3. Even he that is a teacher, must be a learner still, as conscious of his remaining ignorance, and not think himself above it, nor set himself to dispute against all that he understands not, but continue humbly to search and try. 6. When those reasons of your own seem good and cogent, which are sufficiently confuted, and you cannot see it, or which men of the most approved learning and fitness to judge, do judge to be but folly; and when other men's soundest reasons seem light to you, because you judge by a proud and selfish understanding, confident and tenacious of all that is your own, and contemning that which is against you.

7. When you can too easily without certain cogent reason dissent from the judgment, not only of those whose light and integrity hath by self-manifestation convinced the world, but also from the generality of such as are commonly known to be the wise, godly, and impartial; yea, perhaps from all the church of Christ.

8. When the most and wisest men that know you, think you not so wise as you think yourselves, nor your reason so good, but pity your self-conceitedness, and yet this brings you not to suspect and try.

9. When you are hardly and rarely brought to a humble confession of your errors, but in all debates you seem still, whatever the cause be, to be in the right, and when you have once said it, you will stand to it, and justify untruths, or extenuate and excuse them.

10. When you too much affect the esteem of wisdom, and love to have your judgments a rule to others, and are unfit for true subjection.

In a word, when instead of being "swift to hear, slow to speak, and slow to wrath," you are swift to speak and dictate, slow to hear and learn, and swift to wrathful censure of dissenters.

Sect. 9. So common and hurtful is this sin in mankind, that you should still be duly fearful of it. Error, I fear, taketh up the greater half of the thoughts of men, and most are rather deceived than in the right; and man's mind in flesh is in great darkness, and therefore PROUD IGNORANCE is a monstrous and pernicious vice; and most of the confusion and miseries of the world, of kingdoms, churches, and all societies, come from it. Yea, though it seems quite contrary to scepticism, it tendeth at last to infidelity or atheism. For when experience hath convinced such, that their most confident rage was but a mistake, they turn to think that there is nothing certain, and deny the greatest truths. It is by this one sin of proud self-conceitedness in false thoughts that kingdoms, churches, and the world, by obstinacy, seem remediless, and the wisest men that would cure them can do no good, but on themselves and few.

Sect. 10. But it is no where more unnatural than in children against their parents' counsel, and scholars against their tutors, and ignorant persons against the common consent of the most able, godly pastors. What an odious thing is it to see an ignorant lad run against all his father's words, and think that he is wiser and always in the right; and to hear ignorant persons magisterially judge and despise their wise and faithful teachers, before they are capable to understand them, or the matter of which they talk of! Oh! how happily might parents, and pastors, and wise men, promote knowledge and goodness in the world, were it not for this selfish prefidence, which shuts the door against their necessary helps.

CHAPTER XV.

THE CONCLUSION, TO MINISTERS.

There is another sort of helpers, on whom the welfare of youth much depends;—even the ministers of Christ. But I presume not here to teach them. In my "Reformed Pastor" I have spoken somewhat freely when I had leave. I cannot expect that those that silence me should hear me; nor will I think that able faithful ministers need my counsel. But all that I will now say, is, humbly to entreat those who take no great pains with the young persons in their parishes, and will not be admonished by such as I, but to read Martin Bucer, (who had so great a hand in counselling our reformers that made the Liturgy,) his book de Regno Dei, this Censure of the Liturgy, especially of baptism, confirmation, ordination, and discipline; and his vehement pressing the necessity of congregational discipline, and denying the sacrament to the unmeet, and the necessity of keeping baptized youths among the catechumens, till at age they come to true understanding of the covenant, which they made and must renew, and till they give credible signs of real godliness by a godly life; and of what mischievous effects it is to confirm them, and admit them to the Lord's supper, on their bare saying the words of the catechism, the creeds, Lord's prayer, and decalogue, without tried understanding and serious piety; and what a wrong it is to the christian church and religion, to confound and corrupt our communion for want of parish discipline and distinctions; and how little good all canons or laws for reformation or religious duty will do, if the ministry be ignorant, worldly, and ungodly, and the churches be not taught and guided by able, godly, humble, self-denying, and loving pastors.

I beseech you read him diligently; he was no violent man, and his books here mentioned were purposely written for King Edward, and the bishops and church of England, and accepted kindly by them. His burnt bones were honourably vindicated by the public praise, and his memory by many in Cambridge solemnly commended to posterity. I beseech you let his counsel in these books be revived, and true reformation be tried by their light. I hope they will hear that great and moderate reformer that will not hear me, or such as I. And if you will add the reading of old Salvian, and of Nic. Clemangis, it may do you good, and excite you to do good to others, and promote the ends of this ADVICE TO YOUTH.

March 25, 1681.

THE

MOTHER'S CATECHISM;

OR, A FAMILIAR WAY OF

CATECHISING OF CHILDREN

IN THE

KNOWLEDGE OF GOD, THEMSELVES, AND THE HOLY SCRIPTURES.

THE PREFACE TO THE READER.

Candid Reader,

This is the errand of this preface, to assure thee that this treatise was left under Mr. Baxter's own hand, which now is exposed to thy view from the press. It was Timothy's great commendation and advantage, "That from a child he had known the holy Scriptures, which were able to make him wise to salvation, through faith which is in Christ Jesus," 2 Tim. iii. 15. Early draughts from this spring will give us such a relish of the waters issuing from thence, as will render our most diligent reading of them both profitable and delightful to us. This book at once may profit both the mother and the child: and the contents thereof may, with greater ease and pleasure, impress themselves upon their minds and memories, by frequent reading of them, and discourse about them, than if children were confined to get large portions of catechisms without book. At least the former would greatly prepare them for the latter. Had Mr. Baxter completed what he did design herein, the reader might have been more advantaged thereby.

All that the author left thou hast. And, if it be desired, the continuation may possibly be exposed to view hereafter, by another hand. Pray heartily for the publisher; for none more need and crave it, than

Thine, in the best of bonds and services,

MATT. SYLVESTER.

THE FAMILIAR WAY

OF

CATECHISING CHILDREN.

Mother. Come, child, are you willing to be taught your catechism?

Child. What is the catechism, mother?

M. It is those things which you must know above all other.

C. Why must I needs know them?

M. Because God made you to know them, and without such knowledge you cannot be good, nor blessed of God.

C. Cannot I do as well without learning as other children do?

M. Those that do not learn that which God would have them learn, are all naught, and miserable, worse than beasts.

C. But I find that I had rather play, and talk of somewhat else than learn my catechism: I do not love it.

M. That is because you are foolish and naught; and it is by learning that you must become wise and better, or else you will be undone for ever, and wish that you had never been born.

C. What is it that I must learn?

M. You must learn to be wise, and good, and happy for ever, and to escape hell, misery, and sin.

C. I would fain be wise, and good, and happy: how shall I learn that?

M. Not by knowing how to eat and drink, laugh and play; and those little common things which beasts and fools know: but it must be by knowing great, and excellent, and needful things.

C. What are those things?

M. The first thing you must know is, what you are yourself, and what you are made for. Do you know how man doth differ from all sorts of beasts and birds?

C. Yes, I know a man from a beast as soon as I see them.

M. You see how the shape of their bodies differ; but that is a small difference. It is their souls that differ, which you cannot see; their flesh and ours little differ, but in shape: the soul is the man, or his chiefest part; the body is but like clothing to the soul.

C. What is a soul, mother?

M. The soul is a spirit, and cannot be seen; but it is that which hath all the power: the body is but earth, and water, and air, and when the soul is gone, it rots and turns to earth.

C. How do you know that we have souls?

M. We know it by that which the soul doth in us: do not you know that you are alive, and that you hear me now, and that you feel when you are hot or cold, well or ill, hungry or thirsty? It is the soul by which you live, and see, and feel.

C. Dogs and beasts do see and feel, have they souls?

M. Yes; they have souls, or else they would be but dead carcasses: but their souls and ours greatly differ. And this is the difference which you must know.

C. What is the difference between our souls and theirs?

M. You may see some of the difference outwardly between our works and theirs. Beasts do not talk as we do, nor write books, nor study laws and other learning, nor make ships, nor build cities, nor govern kingdoms, as men do. But yet because they do somewhat like these, it is a greater difference than all these that you must know.

C. What is that greater difference?

M. Beasts, and birds, and fishes, are all made but for the use of man, and therefore their souls can do nothing but feed and preserve their bodies, and serve us: they never think of God or another world; they live not by a law, but by the inclination of their nature; they have no hopes of heaven or fear of hell, nor any conscience within to tell them of duty to God or sin against him: nor do they knowingly worship, serve, and seek him. But the soul of man is made for all this; even to know God and his law, and our duty, and to think of and prepare for another life after death, and to fear punishment then, and hope and prepare for everlasting happiness, and to serve and obey God that we may obtain it. This is the difference.

C. Are you sure that a man is made for all this?

M. Yes: do you not see that good men do all this? Do they not teach and learn God's law, and obey him, and worship him, and hope for heaven hereafter? Good men could not do this if God had not made them fit to do it.

But I must teach you how to know all this better hereafter, when I come to tell you what God saith of it in his word: I cannot teach you all at once.

The Second Part of the Catechism.—To know God.

M. I have told you first what you must know of yourself, and what a man is: I must next tell you what God is; for if you know not God, it were as good you knew nothing at all.

C. What is God?

M. God is not a body, nor like any thing that we can see: you must have no such thought of him.

C. How then shall I know what he is?

M. You must know him by his works, and especially by knowing yourself, and the soul of man, which is called God's image.

C. How can I know him when I do not see him?

M. Nothing but the lowest or basest things are seen besides the light. You never saw the wind; and yet you see and feel what it doth; how it can overthrow trees and houses; and by that you know that it is strong. You see roses, and other flowers, and apple trees, and pear trees; and you see and taste how one differs from another in flower and fruit; but you do not see that within them which causeth all the beauty, and sweetness, and difference, that appeareth without. You do not see that inward soul of birds and beasts, by which they live and move; nor (as I told you) you do not see my soul, nor your own. But you may know much of things unseen by what they do.

C. What be the works of God, by which I may know him?

M. All that you see in the world: God made them all, and God doth preserve them all. Do you not see all the country about you? This earth is many thousand and thousand times bigger than you see; and it stands upon nothing, but it is round like a ball, and hangs in the air, and the heavens are round about it, as far as you see them over it. All England is as much less than the whole earth, as a pin is less than all this house. And you see how the ground doth bring forth all sorts of trees, and herbs, and corn, and flowers: how many thousand thousands of birds, beasts, sheep, and other living things, do live in all countries, and how many thousand thousand men. All these God made, and feeds and keeps them: and yet all this earth is next to nothing, in comparison of the heavens, and the rest of the world. Yonder sun that you see doth give light and heat to all this earth, and yet it is many thousand miles from hence: it goeth round about the earth every day and night, and goeth many thousand miles every hour; and yet it is many thousand times bigger than all the earth: many of the stars seem little to you, because they are many thousand miles from us, and yet are many hundred times bigger than all this earth: and no man can tell how many thousand thousand miles there may be beyond all the stars which we can see. Do you not look up and wonder at all this?

C. O yes, I wonder at it: but how shall I know God by all this?

M. Are not you sure that he that doth all this must needs be great and almighty, and have more power than all the world? How could he make such a world, and give all this power to sun, and moon, and stars, and sea, and land, if he had not more than they all himself? No one can give more than he hath to give.

C. I know God must needs be great and powerful.

M. And do you not perceive that God is most wise, and knoweth more than all the world? How else could he make heaven and earth in such admirable order, and keep them in the same course through all generations? How could he make nights and days, winter and summer? Yea, the very body of every man and beast is so wonderfully ordered, that the wisest men in the world are posed in searching into the work of God therein. We know not how a man is made, nor how he digesteth his meat into blood and flesh, nor any such like. All the men in the world cannot make one flower or grass, nor one bird or fly: and it is God that giveth all men and angels all the knowledge and wisdom which they have; and therefore he must needs have more himself: he must needs know all the secret thoughts of all men in the world, because they cannot think a thought without him. Do you not perceive, then, that God is infinitely wise, and knoweth all things?

C. Yes; he that made all, must needs know all.

M. And you must know by his works that God is as good as he is great and wise, and that he is better than all the world besides, both heaven and earth. For all things are good that he hath made: the sun is good; without its light, and heat, and motion, what were the earth but a dungeon and a grave? The moon and stars are good, heaven and earth are good, sea and land are good, and the fruits of the earth and all living things are good, save that man's sin hath brought a curse on them for his punishment: and among men, learning and virtue are good; our food and clothing, our parents and friends, and all good people are good. And could God make the world good, if he were not good?

C. I know God must needs be powerful, and wise, and good, above all; but yet I do not know him.

M. I told you that God is not of a bodily substance and shape, like things seen. He is a Spirit, and the Maker of all bodies and spirits. And therefore I next told you, that you must know him partly by knowing yourself, that is, your soul.

C. Is God like me, or like a man?

M. God hath made the soul of man in his own image, in some little likeness to himself: and so you may know somewhat of God by yourself, as you may see one's face in a glass.

C. Wherein is man's soul like God?

M. In many things: 1. Our souls are spirits, and cannot be seen, and so is God. 2. Yet it is by the soul that the body liveth, and moveth, and feeleth. It can do nothing without the soul; nor can any thing in the world without God: it is God that doth all that sun and moon, sea and land, wind and rain, men and beasts, and all things do. 3. Our souls have life to move us, and understandings to know good and evil, and wills to love the good and hate the evil: and in this they are God's image; for God is life itself, and knoweth all things, and loveth good, and hateth evil, more than we. So that as our souls are unseen spirits, of life, and understanding, and will, in our bodies; so God is more than a soul to the whole world, to heaven, and earth, and sun, and moon, and stars, and to every soul and body that is.

C. I understand you that God is a spirit, that hath more power, and knowledge, and goodness, than all the world besides, but yet methinks I do not know him.

M. No one in the world knoweth God perfectly, but we may know so much of him as may make us wise, and good, and happy; and you must increase in knowing God more and more as long as you live. If you are willing to learn, God will help you to know him a great deal better hereafter than you can do now while you are but a child. You do not know how to build houses, nor write books, nor do any other thing which you see men do, and how then should a child know as much of God as a man may know? When you come to understand the Bible, which is God's word, you will know God better. Therefore I must next teach you to know what God's word is, that it may teach you more.

The Third Lesson.—To know God's Word.

C. What is it that you call the word of God?

M. Because we are dull, and cannot sufficiently know God and his will by his works alone; therefore God hath more fully and plainly told it us from heaven.

C. Did God speak it himself?

M. God is not like a man, nor doth he talk as men do: but God can many ways make known his mind to us. As your soul doth talk by your tongue, and not of itself without it, so God hath sometimes spoken by angels, and sometimes by prophets, to whom he inwardly maketh known his will, as you inwardly know now what you think or see. And some part of God's word he did write himself; that is, the ten commandments: and all this is written for us in the Bible, which is God's book.

C. Who did God speak this to, and when was it?

M. Not all at once, nor all to one man; but by degrees, as I teach you some one day, and some another. He first spake to Adam and Eve, and after to others, especially to Noah, and after that to Moses; and he taught Moses to write down all that God had said to him, and all that he said from the beginning of the world, which was meet for us to know: and he wrote the ten commandments in two tables of stone, and gave them to Moses to keep, and many other laws he spake to him by angels: and after that in many ages, when he had any new thing to make known, or sinful people to reprove, he often sent some prophet to them: and, last of all, he sent his Son from heaven, to tell us more than all before had told us.

C. What is a prophet?

M. One that God tells his mind to, either inwardly himself, or outwardly by an angel, and then sendeth him to tell others as from God.

C. How were men sure that God sent these prophets?

M. God did bring to pass all that he sent them to foretell; and the laws which he commanded by Moses, and by Jesus Christ, he owned by many great miracles before all the people, such as none can do but by the power of God, which I shall tell you more fully when I tell you the history of the Bible. Besides that, the Bible is such a book for matter and manner, as none could write, if God had not taught it them.

C. How come we to have this book?

M. Those that God gave it to did give it to their children; and so it hath been delivered from one generation to another, as the laws of this land are, by which men hold their estates; and God made it the office of ministers to keep and preach his word.

C. Are no other books God's word but the Bible?

M. That which our teachers do take out of the Bible and teach the meaning of it, is so far God's word as it is in the Bible whence they take it: and good books to expound this word of God to us, and help us to practise it.

C. Is all true that is written in the Bible?

M. Some part of the Bible tells us what lies the devil and wicked men have used to deceive men with: it is true that such lies were told. And all that God said must needs be true, for it is impossible for God to lie.

C. Why is it impossible?

M. Because God is perfect: all lying is either for want of knowledge of the truth, or because men are naught, and love not the truth; or for want of power to attain their wills without a lie. But God wanteth neither knowledge, nor goodness, nor power, and he hateth liars, and condemneth them, and therefore cannot lie himself.

The Fourth Lesson.—Of the Creation.

C. What is it that the Bible tells us?

M. The first thing is, how God made the world.

C. I would fain know that. How was it?

M. In the beginning, God made the heaven and the earth. And the earth was first like a great puddle of dirty water, without light or shape; and God did take six days' time to shape it out of this confused heap, and to adorn it with all the creatures which it possesseth.

C. Why did God take just six days to do it?

M. We must not ask why God doth it; his will must satisfy us: but this helpeth us the more distinctly to take notice of God's work.

C. What did God make the first day?

M. The light.

C. How did God make it?

M. As he did all the rest, by the power of his bare will and word. He said, Let there be light, and there was light.

C. What did God make the second day?

M. He made the firmament, which is called heaven.

C. What did he make the third day?

M. He gathered the waters by themselves, which is the sea, and made the land dry, which is the earth. And he made the earth to bear grass, herbs, and trees, with seed.

C. What did God make the fourth day?

M. He made the sun, and moon, and stars, to be lights, and otherwise useful to the earth.

C. Had he not made light before?

M. As he made earth, in one mass, before he shaped it; but now he formed it into all these parts which we call sun, moon, and stars.

C. What did he make the fifth day?

M. Fishes and fowls, with power to beget more and multiply.

C. What did he make the sixth day?

M. All sorts of beasts on the earth; and, lastly, man.

C. How did God make man?

M. He made his body of the earth, and then breathed his soul into it.

C. Did not God make woman?

M. When he made the man, he took a rib out of his side, and made it a woman, to be his wife, to show that a man and his wife should be, as it were, one.

C. Who were the first man and woman?

M. Adam and Eve.

C. Did God make them good or bad?

M. He made all things good, and he made man in his own image, with life for action, understanding for knowledge, and free-will to choose good and refuse evil; and he put them in a most pleasant garden, called Paradise.

C. What did he bid them do there?

M. God being man's governor, gave him, in nature, a law to keep: and also commanded him to dress and keep the garden, and gave him all lower creatures for his use; only, to try his obedience, he charged him not to eat the fruit of one tree, which was called the tree of knowledge, on pain of death.

C. And what did Adam and Eve do then?

M. God suffered the devil to tempt Eve in the shape of a serpent, to eat of that one forbidden fruit, and she did eat, and persuaded Adam to eat also, and so they broke the law of God.

C. How did the devil tempt her to it?

M. He told her that eating of the tree of knowledge would make her wise, and to be like God himself in knowledge; and that God forbade it them because he would not have them know so much; and that God would not put them to death as he had threatened, but they might safely eat it. And so because the fruit was pleasant, and she thought it would increase her knowledge, she did eat, and gave it Adam to eat.

C. What did God do with them then?

M. God reproved and judged them, and cast them out of Paradise, and cursed the earth to them, and judged them to labour and sorrow, pain and death. But yet, in mercy, so far forgave them as that he promised them a Saviour to deliver them from hell and everlasting misery, if they would believe him and repent, and sincerely obey him for time to come.

C. Did eating of one tree deserve so great a punishment?

M. Yes: for it was God Almighty that they sinned against. And they believed the devil before God, and took God to be a liar, and to be their envious enemy, and the devil to be more their friend: and this they did when they were new-made good, and able to do better, and had all things given them by God to serve them.

C. But why did God curse the earth?

M. For a punishment to man; that it should bear briers, and be barren without his toil, and be a place of sorrow to him.

C. But must all men suffer and die because Adam sinned?

M. All that were since born came out of Adam and Eve: and when they were guilty, and naught, we must needs be born so too, for they could beget no better than they were themselves: and hence it is that the nature of all mankind is become naught, and turned from God; and this is called our original sin.

C. But what did God do to the devil for deceiving them?

M. The devils were once angels, and fell by sin themselves, and therefore did bear malice both to God and man; and he would make all others as bad and miserable as himself: and ever since then he hath sought man's destruction; but God promised a Saviour that should overcome him, and deliver us.

C. What did God do on the seventh day?

M. Having made the world in six days, God appointed the seventh to be the sabbath day, in which man should rest from his labours, and worship God in remembrance of the creation.

C. And what doth God ever since?

M. He preserveth and governeth the world which he made, both heaven and earth. And he enjoyeth himself, and needeth nothing; but all need him.

The Fifth Lesson.—More of the Scripture History.

M. Do you remember what I taught you last?

C. You told me how God made the world, and how Adam and Eve sinned by the devil's temptation, and how we are all born in sin, and how God judged man to suffering and death, but pronounced a Saviour to deliver believers. But what did men do after Adam's fall?

M. Adam had two sons, Cain, the elder, and Abel, the younger. Adam had taught them both to worship God; but Cain was a bad man, and did not serve God with all his heart, but as bad men do now; but Abel was a good man, and served God heartily with the best he had. And God accepted Abel's service, and refused Cain's; and therefore, Cain envied and hated Abel, and killed him: and God forsook Cain, and punished his posterity.

C. Did the first man that was born kill his own brother? What made him kill him?

M. God suffered this to tell us all ever after, that the world will still have two sorts of men; bad men, that are the servants of the devil, and good men, that serve God; and that the bad will hate and persecute the good, because they are like the devil, and the good are the children of God; and their hearts and lives are contrary to one another.

C. But if God loved Abel better, why would he not save him from being killed?

M. It was no loss to him to be killed, for God took his soul to heaven: he was the first man that went to heaven, and the first martyr; and God giveth the best place in heaven to the martyrs, that suffer and die by wicked men for serving God. God loveth all good men, and yet he will not keep them all from being hated, and persecuted, and killed by the wicked. This doth but try them, as gold is tried in the fire, and prepare them for greater glory in heaven than other good men have.

C. What did the rest of the world do after?

M. God gave Adam another good son in Abel's stead, called Seth; and many of his posterity served God, and especially Enoch was so holy a man, that God took him up to heaven without dying; but Cain's posterity, and most others, proved so bad, that at last all the good men were worn out, saving one called Noah and his household: and then God would bear with them no longer, but drowned them all with a flood of rain from heaven.

C. I pray tell me how they were drowned, and how Noah escaped?

M. God told Noah beforehand what he would do, and bid him prepare an ark, and taught him how to make it, like a ship with many rooms, and covered; and bid him take into that ark two of all sorts of beasts and birds, and meat for them, and for himself, and his wife, and his three sons, and their three wives. And Noah believed God, and made the ark as God bade him; and he preached to those about him, to persuade them to believe and repent, a long time while he was making the ark; but they would not believe him, till the flood came and drowned all, both man and beast; but Noah, and his household in the ark, were carried about, as in a ship on the water, till all the rest were drowned, and the waters dried up, and then he came out.

C. And what came of him after?

M. He was a husbandman, and planted a vineyard, and made wine; and once, by temptation, he was drunk with the wine, and laid himself naked in his drink; and one of his sons, called Ham, in mockage, told the other two, called Shem and Japheth; and they, in reverence to their father, would not see his nakedness, but covered him with their faces backward; wherefore Noah blessed Shem and Japheth, and their posterity, and cursed Ham and his posterity, and they proved wicked men.

C. It is strange that so good a man would be drunk?

M. It was but once, and thereby we are warned to take heed of fleshly temptations, and to beg God's grace to keep us, and not to trust ourselves.

C. Did all the world come from Noah?

M. Yes; and when they increased to great numbers, one great man, called Nimrod, would needs build a tower so high, that if another flood came, it should not reach the top of it to drown them. And when abundance of men had worked at it long, God derided them, and stopped them.

C. How did he stop them?

M. He made them forget the language which they all spake before, and made them speak every man a language of his own, so that they understood not one another: and hence came many languages into the world.

C. And what did they next?

M. Most men grew worse and worse, and forsook God, and worshipped creatures and devils; but some of Shem's and Japheth's posterity served God; but especially one called Abraham: but I must tell you his story the next time.

The Sixth Lesson.—The History of Abraham and his seed.

C. You told me, that you would next tell me the history of Abraham. I pray you how was that?

M. When the world grew worse and worse, Abraham being one of the posterity of Shem, was so good a man, that God singled him out for a special blessing.

C. Why, what did Abraham do?

M. He forsook idols, and served and obeyed God: and yet he lived till he was a hundred years old, and his wife Sarah fourscore and ten, before he had any child by her. And then God told him that he would give him a son, from whom should spring a great nation, which should be God's special people, chosen before all the world; and that Christ the Saviour should be of his seed, in whom all the nations of the earth should be blessed. Abraham and Sarah thought this strange at first, that a man of a hundred years old, and a woman of fourscore and ten, should have a son, and a nation spring from him; but seeing God said it, he believed God, knowing that nothing is impossible to him: and God took this so well, that Abraham did so fully trust him, that he imputed it to him for righteousness, and renewed his promise to him, and gave him a son called Isaac: and Abraham having an elder son called Ishmael, by another woman, that son abused Isaac, and God bid Abraham cast him out of his house; but yet a great nation sprung from Ishmael. When Isaac grew up he had two sons by his wife Rebecca at a birth, Esau and Jacob; and God chose Jacob, and not Esau, to be the heir of those great blessings which he had promised Abraham: and Esau hated and persecuted Jacob, because God preferred him. And when Jacob grew up, he had twelve sons and a daughter; and ten of these sons fed sheep and cattle in the commons far off, and the two youngest, Joseph and Benjamin, being loved best by their father, stayed at home. And God revealed things to come to Joseph in his dreams; and when Jacob sent Joseph to see how his brethren did, he told them his dreams. One dream was, that they were binding sheaves in the field, and Joseph's sheaf stood upright and all their sheaves bowed to it; signifying that all they should bow to him. Another dream was, that the sun, and moon, and seven stars, (signifying his father, and mother, and brethren,) did bow to him. And his brethren hated him because of his dreams, and because his father loved him more than them. And once when his father sent him to see how they did, when they saw him they plotted how to kill him; and Reuben, the eldest, desiring to save him, got them to cast him into a dry pit: and presently some merchant carriers passed by that way, who carried spices into Egypt to sell; and Judah, the fourth brother, got the rest to sell him to these carriers; and so they took his coat, and dipped it in blood, and sent it to his father, making him believe that some wild beast had torn and devoured Joseph; but while Jacob mourned, Joseph was carried into Egypt, and sold there to Potiphar, who was chief marshal to Pharaoh. And Joseph being Potiphar's servant, God blessed all that he was trusted with; so that his master prospered extraordinarily in house and field, so that he made Joseph his steward, and trusted him with all that he had. Now Joseph was a very comely, well-favoured man, and his mistress fell in love with him, and tempted him to lie with her; but he feared God, and still denied her. At last, when he was alone, she took hold of his coat, and said, Lie with me; but he ran away, and left his coat with her. When she saw this, to hide her own lust and sin, she called out to the servants, and told them that Joseph would have forced her to lie with him: and making Potiphar, her husband, believe it, he was angry, and put Joseph in a prison. When Joseph was in prison, God made the gaoler kind to him, so that he trusted him to keep all the rest of the prisoners, and he had the rule of all, and God prospered all that he did. At that time the king was displeased with his chief butler and chief baker, and put them into the same prison where Joseph was: and at last both of them had a special dream, but they could not tell the meaning of them. And God gave Joseph the gift to expound dreams. And Joseph expounded their dreams to them, and told them that the baker's dream signified that he should be hanged, but the butler's dream signified that he should be restored to his place; and he prayed him then to remember him: and so it came to pass; but the butler did not remember Joseph. After this king Pharaoh himself had a great dream, which troubled him, and none could expound it. He dreamed that he saw in a meadow seven fat kine, and there came seven lean kine, and did eat them up: then he saw seven full ears of corn, and seven thin, blasted ears came and eat them up. Then his butler remembered Joseph, and told the king how he had expounded their dreams in prison. And the king sent for him, and brought him out of the dungeon, and told him his dreams. And Joseph answered him, that God had made known to him what he would do; that there should be seven years of great plenty, and next seven years of great famine in many countries; and therefore he advised the king to choose a wise man, to set officers over all the land of Egypt, to take up the fifth part of all the food of the land, the first seven years, that there might be food enough for the seven years of famine. And the king believed him, and liked the motion, and thought no man so fit as Joseph, that had the Spirit of God. So he made Joseph ruler over all his house, and the next person to himself, and put his ring on his hand, and a gold chain about his neck, and made all men bow to him, and obey him, and made him ruler over all the land, and appointed him to gather up the fruit and corn into storehouses all over the land, till the famine should come, that they might not perish: and thus God began to fulfil Joseph's dream; but his father and brethren dwelt in Canaan, another land, and knew none of all this: but I must tell you the rest the next time, and not too much at once.

The Seventh Lesson.—The rest of the History of Joseph and Jacob.

C. I long to hear the rest of the history of Joseph.

M. When Joseph had been seven years ruler, next the king, over all the land of Egypt, his old father, Jacob, thinking all the time he had been dead, the seven years' famine came next, as Joseph had foretold; and when all the corn was eaten up, the people all lived on the stores that Joseph had laid up; and they were fain to sell their cattle and lands to the king to buy them bread, that they might not famish, and after that to sell themselves to be the king's servants; and so Joseph gave them corn to sow the ground: and ever after it became a law that the fifth part of all the fruit of the land should be the king's, except the priests' lands.

C. Were not they, and their cattle and land, the king's before?

M. No; not till they sold it him, with themselves. The king was their ruler; but they, and their lands, and goods, and cattle, were their own, not his.

C. And what became of Joseph's father and brethren?

M. The famine was also in their land; and when it was so great that they were ready to famish, and they heard that there was corn in Egypt, Jacob sent his ten sons to buy corn there, keeping the youngest, Benjamin, whom he best loved, at home with him; and when they came into Egypt they were brought to Joseph to buy corn. Now Joseph was grown up, and the king had changed his name, and they knew him not, nor what was become of him; but Joseph knew all them when he saw them. And Joseph carried it sourly to them, and took on him that he did not know them, and asked them whence they came; and they bowed to him, and told him they came from the land of Canaan to buy corn: and he took on him to take them for enemies and spies; and they told him they were twelve brethren, the sons of one man, and one was dead, and the youngest was at home with his father. And he bid them send one and fetch their young brother, and then he would believe them. And he put them three days in prison: and at the end of three days he granted that they should all go home, and bring corn to their father, save one that he would keep in prison, as a pledge, till they returned; for he remembered how cruelly they had thought to murder him, and had sold him, and what his dream was, that they should bow to him. And when they were all in prison, and thus in danger, then they remembered their sin against Joseph and repented, and said one to another, "We are verily guilty concerning our brother, in that we saw the anguish of his soul, when he entreated us, and we would not hear: therefore is this distress come upon us. And Reuben said, Did not I speak to you, and say, Do not sin against the child, and you would not hear: therefore his blood is now required." Thus God makes men's consciences condemn them for their sin, when punishment comes, that before would take no warning. All this while Joseph heard them, and they thought that he understood not what they said, because he spake in the language of Egypt: and he turned away from them, and wept to hear them bewail their sin, and then came to them again.

C. And what did those that he sent home?

M. He kept Simeon prisoner; and when the other nine were to go, he made his servants fill their bags with corn, and give them provision for the way, but secretly to put every man's money into his bag, to the corn. And when they came to their inn, and opened their bags for provender for their asses, they found their money; and then their hearts sunk yet more, for they feared God did it to punish them; but they went home to their father Jacob, and told him all that had befallen them, and how the ruler of the land took them for spies, and spake roughly to them, and kept Simeon prisoner till they should bring Benjamin to him. And Jacob lamented, and asked them why they would tell him that they had another brother. And they said, Could we know that he would say, Bring your brother?

C. And did they bring him?

M. Jacob resolved that he should not go, till the famine was so great that they must send to Egypt for more corn, or die, and there was no remedy; and they durst not go without their brother, for Joseph said, "Ye shall not see my face, unless you bring your brother with you." And when there was no remedy, Jacob let him go, and sent them for more corn, with double money, to restore that which was put into their bags again.

C. And how did Joseph receive them next?

M. They took a present of balsam and spices with them, beside their money. And when they came to him, Joseph told his steward that those men should dine with him, and bid him make full provision for them. And when he came home at noon they gave him their present, and bowed to the ground. He asked them how their father did. And when they saw they must dine with him, they were afraid lest he would charge the money on them that they had, and keep them prisoners; and they told the steward what had befallen them, and how they had found their money in their bags; but the steward bid them fear not, for he had their money. And when Joseph saw his young brother Benjamin, he spake kindly to him, but was fain to get away into his chamber to weep; and when he had wept awhile he washed his face, and came out to them again. And at dinner he set them by themselves, every one according to his age, and they marvelled at it; and he sent every one of them of the best from his own table, but twice as much to Benjamin as to the rest: and because he would keep them longer, and affect them more, he made his steward fill all their sacks with corn, and again put their money into their sacks; and into Benjamin's sack he put his own silver drinking cup. And when they were gone out of town, in the morning, he sent his servant after them, to charge them with stealing his cup, and to bring them back. At this they were amazed, and said, "God forbid that we should do so: let him die that hath the cup, and let us be my lord's servants: but when they were searched, the cup was found in Benjamin's bag. Then they were all confounded, and came back to Joseph; and when he accused them for stealing his cup, they fell to the ground and said, "God hath found out our iniquity; we are all thy servants." But he said, No; none shall be my servant but he with whom the cup was found: but Judah told him how hardly he had got his father to consent that Benjamin should go with them, and that he was fain to undertake to bring him back, and that his father would die with grief if he returned not; and therefore besought him that the lad might go home, and that he might be a bond-servant in his stead. Then Joseph could no longer refrain, but made all his servants go forth, and he wept so loud that the king's house heard him: and he opened himself to his brethren, and said, I am Joseph; doth my father yet live? But they could not answer him, for they were troubled at his presence, remembering their sin against him. But he comforted them, and said, "I am Joseph, your brother, whom you sold into Egypt; but be not grieved nor angry with yourselves, for God sent me hither before you to preserve life:" and he told them all that God had done for him, and that there were two years of famine yet to come: so he wept over them, and kissed them, and bid them make haste home, and tell his father all this; and bid him come away with all his children's children, and his flocks, and he would give them the best place in Egypt, because of the famine that was yet to come. And when the king heard that Joseph and his brethren were there, he commanded also that their father and they should come and dwell in Egypt, in the best place that Joseph would choose for them. So Joseph gave them waggons and provision, and a present to his father, and sent for them all away.

C. Sure Jacob would be very glad of this.

M. You may easily think how it would transport him with joy; but at first he could not believe it, that Joseph was lord of Egypt, who, he thought, had been many years dead; but when he saw the waggons, and that all was true, the old man's heart revived in him with joy and thankfulness to God: and so he and all his children's children went into Egypt, and there Pharaoh welcomed them; and Joseph placed them in Goshen, the best part of the land.

The Eighth Lesson.—The History of Sodom and Lot.

C. I would fain know what God did with all the other countries all this while.

M. We can know no more of that than God hath told us in his word. But this we know, that God had every where some righteous men whom he loved; and in every nation, they that feared God, and did righteously, were accepted of him. But the most proved wicked men, and idolaters, and hated them that were good. And to show this, I will next tell you the history of Sodom and of Lot, which should have gone before, but that I would put Abraham, Isaac, and Jacob's history together.

C. What was the case of Sodom?

M. In Abraham's days there were four kings joined together, and made war on many countries, and destroyed many people near the place where Abraham dwelt: and there were five kings went out to fight against them, the king of Sodom, and of Gomorrah, and of Admah, and of Zeboim, and of Zoar: and the four kings conquered these five, and carried away the people and their goods. In Sodom, Abraham had a brother's son dwelt, called Lot, and he was carried away prisoner with the rest. When Abraham heard of it, he armed all his servants, (who were three hundred and eighteen,) and got some neighbours to join with him, and by night followed the four conquering kings, and overtook them, and fought with them, and destroyed them, and rescued Lot, and all the persons and goods that they had taken; and when he had done, he gave them all back to the kings that had lost them, and would keep nothing of it to himself. Then there was one Melchizedek, that was king of Salem, and priest of the most high God, that came out and blessed Abraham, and Abraham gave him tithes of all. Yet after this great deliverance, Sodom and Gomorrah, and the other cities and kings that were delivered, continued very wicked men, till God destroyed them.

C. How did God destroy them?

M. As Abraham was sitting in his tent door, three angels, in likeness of travellers, passed by; and Abraham being used to entertain strangers, bowed to them, and entreated them to stay and eat with him. They consented; and he killed a calf, and made them a feast: upon this the Lord renewed his promise to him, to give all that country to his seed; and told him what he would do to Sodom, and said he would not hide it from Abraham, because he would command his children and his household after him, to keep the way of the Lord: so he told him that in Sodom and Gomorrah were so very wicked men, that he would destroy them all. Abraham remembered his cousin Lot in Sodom, and he humbly made his prayer to the Lord, that he would not destroy the righteous with the wicked, but would spare the city for the righteous' sake, if there were but fifty righteous in it: and the Lord promised to spare it, if there were but fifty. Then Abraham prayed that he would spare the city, if there were but forty-five; and the Lord granted it. Then Abraham prayed that he would spare it, if there were but forty; and again, if there were but thirty; and again, if there were but twenty; and the Lord still granted it. Then Abraham begged of God not to be offended, if he once more asked, that he would spare it, if there were but ten righteous; and the Lord promised that also. Then Abraham knew that there was no remedy.

C. And what became of Lot in Sodom?

M. Two angels, like men, came to Sodom, to Lot's house; and the men of Sodom were so unnaturally wicked, that they commanded Lot to bring out the two strange men, that they might abuse them like women; but Lot humbly entreated them not to do so wickedly with strangers: but they reviled Lot, (just as the wicked do godly men now,) and said, "This one fellow came in to sojourn, and he will needs be a judge: now will we deal worse with thee, than with them." And as they crowded towards the door to break in, the angels pulled in Lot, and struck them all with blindness; and yet this miracle did not stop them, but they groped to find the door. Then the angels told Lot who they were, and that they came to destroy the city; but God had mercy on him; and therefore bid him take his wife, and his children, and his two sons-in-law, and presently fly out of the city, for his life; but his sons-in-law would not believe the danger, but took it for a fanatic mockage. And while Lot lingered, the angels took hold of him, and his wife, and two daughters, and brought them out of the city, and bid them fly for their lives to the mountains, and look not back behind them; but Lot prayed the Lord to let him escape to Zoar, the least of the five cities; and God heard him, and saved that city for his sake. But God rained fire and brimstone upon Sodom and Gomorrah, and consumed all the cities and the people there, and round about it. But Lot's wife that was forbidden did look behind her, and God turned her into a pillar of salt, to warn us not to disobey God. But Abraham stood afar off, to see what would become of Sodom and Gomorrah, and saw the smoke of it like a great furnace, rise up toward heaven. And the place where these cities stood, and all the plain about them, remaineth ever since to this day a dead sea, or stinking, pitchy lake, which nothing can live in; and travellers familiarly see it that go that way.

Thus you see, by the example of Sodom, how God hateth sin, and how he will use the wicked at the last; and yet that in this very wicked city of Sodom, Abraham thought there might have been fifty righteous persons; and that one man's family that was righteous, and mourned for their wickedness, God would not forget, but saved him.

The Ninth Lesson.—The Israelites' Deliverance out of Egypt.

C. Will you tell me what became of the children of Jacob and Joseph in Egypt?

M. When they were planted in Goshen, God did so greatly prosper them, that they increased more than the Egyptians, and were so many, that after some ages, when the old ones were all dead, another king arose, that knew not Joseph; and he was afraid lest in time they should grow too strong for him, and he endeavoured to destroy them.

C. What did he to them?

M. First he gave the midwives command to kill all the sons that were born to them at their birth; but God put his fear in the midwives, and they made excuses, and said that the women (then called Hebrews and Israelites) were delivered before they came, and so did not obey the bloody king. Then the king made them to be his slaves and drudges, and he made them daily labour in making brick, with which he built great, stately monuments; and he set taskmasters over them, that should beat them, if they made not as many bricks as he required of them; and thus they were used cruelly, like beasts, and cried, in their bondage, to God for deliverance; and God did hear, and did deliver them.

C. How did he do it?

M. One of the Hebrew women, to keep her new-born son from being murdered, made a basket of bulrushes, and daubed it with slime and pitch, and put the child into it, and put it into the flags by the river's brink; (when she had hid it three months, and could hide it no longer;) and his sister stood afar off to see what would become of him. And God so ordered it that the king's daughter came that way with her maids to wash herself in the river, and they saw the basket, and opened it, and found a comely child, and he wept. The king's daughter said, "This is one of the Hebrews' children:" the child's sister said, "Shall I go and call a nurse of the Hebrew women to nurse it for thee? And she said, Go." So his sister ran and called his own mother; and so she nursed her own child for king Pharaoh's daughter, and she called his name Moses, and he was bred up as her son: and when he was a man, God made him the captain and deliverer of the Hebrews, called Israelites.

C. How did he deliver them?

M. God stirred him up; and one day, when he saw an Egyptian abuse an Israelite, he killed the Egyptian, and saved the Israelite. The next day two of the Israelites were striving, and Moses said to him that did the wrong, "Why strikest thou thy fellow?" And it being a bad man, he said to Moses, "Who made thee a prince and a judge over us? Wilt thou kill me as thou didst the Egyptian?" Thus bad men cannot endure to be reproved. And when Moses heard that it was known, he was fain to fly out of the land, for fear of Pharaoh and the Egyptians, till that king died. And Moses married a daughter of Jethro, priest of Midian. And when he kept his father-in-law's flock in the wilderness, an angel of God appeared to him in a flame of fire, in a bush, which burned and was not consumed; and God by the angel spake to him out of the fire, and said, "I am the God of Abraham, Isaac, and Jacob; I have seen the affliction of my people in Egypt, and have heard their cry by reason of their task-masters, and am come to deliver them, and to bring them out of Egypt into a good land which I promised Abraham. And I will send thee to Pharaoh that thou mayst bring them out." And Moses said, "Who am I, that I should go to king Pharaoh, and bring them out?" But God charged him to go and tell the Hebrews, and tell the king, that the Lord God had sent him to bid them come and sacrifice to him in that wilderness. And God told him, "I am sure that Pharaoh will not let them go; but I will smite Egypt with all my wonders, and then he will let them go." And Moses said, "They will not believe me, that God appeared to me." And God said, "Cast down the rod that is in thy hand;" and he did, and it became a serpent; and Moses was afraid of it. And God said, "Take it by the tail;" and he did, and it became a rod again. And God said, "Put thy hand in thy bosom," and he did; and when he took it out it was all leprous. And God said, "Put thy hand in thy bosom again;" and he did, and it was whole as before. This was to encourage Moses to trust God's power and word, and that he might do the same, and other miracles, before the people, to make them believe. But Moses made excuses, and said he was slow of speech, and prayed God to send some one else. And God reproved him, and said, "Aaron thy brother can speak well, and he shall be thy mouth, and thou shalt speak from God to him, and take this rod in thy hand, and with it thou shalt do signs (or wonders)." So Moses took his wife and children, and the rod of God, and went back into Egypt; for they were all dead that sought his life. And Moses told his brother Aaron all that God had said; and Moses and Aaron called all the elders of Israel together, and told them; and they believed, and were glad that God would deliver them.

C. But what said the king to them?

M. Moses and Aaron went to king Pharaoh, and said, "Thus saith the Lord, the God of Israel, Let my people go, that they may hold a feast to me in the wilderness." And the king said, "Who is the Lord, that I should obey his voice to let Israel go? I know not the Lord, neither will I let them go."

C. Why would he not let them go?

M. Because they were his servants, and did his work, as our horses and oxen do for us. And the king reviled Moses and Aaron for hindering the people from their work, and bid the taskmasters lay more burdens and work upon them; and whereas before they had straw given them to burn their brick with, he bid them gather stubble themselves, and they should make all their task of brick, and have no straw; for they talked of going into the wilderness to serve God, because they were idle. And now their case was far worse than before; for they were beaten when they could not make as much brick as they did before. And when the people complained to the king that they were beaten for not making brick without straw, the king said, "Ye are idle, ye are idle, and therefore talk of going to serve God; you shall have no straw, and yet have none of your task abated." And when the people found themselves in so bad a case, they were impatient with Moses and Aaron, and laid the fault on them, as making the king abhor them. And Moses complained to God for sending him to make the people more miserable than before. But thus doth God often use to make his servants' sufferings greater, when he is about to deliver them.

C. Why doth he so?

M. To humble them, and try their faith and patience, and to try their enemies; and to show his power the more in their deliverance.

C. And what did they do next?

M. Then God said to Moses, "Now you shall see what I will do;" and bid him go tell the Israelites, that the Lord doth promise to deliver them. But the anguish of their hearts was so great, that they would not hear Moses and Aaron.

C. What did they then?

M. Then God bid Moses go again to Pharaoh the king, and say, "Let my people go;" and if he ask for a sign, cast down thy rod, and it shall become a serpent. And they did so; and the king had some enchanters, or witches, about him, and they did so too, and their rods turned into serpents; and therefore the king refused to obey God and let the people go.

C. By what power did the witches do this?

M. By the devil's power, which God suffered, to show his own the more; for when they were all turned to serpents, Moses' and Aaron's rod devoured all theirs.

C. And what did they after this?

M. The first plague was this: God bid Moses put forth his rod, that was turned to a serpent, over the river, in the sight of the king; and the waters were turned to blood, and the fish died and stunk; and their ponds were turned to blood, and the people had no water. Yet the king's heart was hardened, because his conjurers did the same; God suffering it to make his power yet more known.

The second plague was this: God bid Moses stretch forth his rod over the waters, and it should fill the land with frogs; and he did so, and the frogs swarmed over the land, and in the king's house and bedchamber; and the conjurers did the like. Then the king called Moses and Aaron, and said, "Entreat the Lord to take away the frogs, and I will let the people go." So Moses prayed, and God heard them, and the frogs died; but the dead heaps made the land to stink. And when the king saw that he was delivered of them, his heart was hardened again.

Then God sent the third plague: Aaron stretched forth his rod in the dust of the land, and the dust turned all to lice, which swarmed over all the land: and the conjurers tried to do the same, but could not; and therefore told the king, "This is the finger of God." And yet his heart was hardened, and he would not let them go.

Then God sent a fourth plague, even such swarms of flies as destroyed all the fruit of the land. But in Goshen, where the Hebrews dwelt, there were none. Then the king called Moses, and bid them go and sacrifice to God in Egypt. But Moses said, "Nay; but they would go out three days' journey." The king bid them go, so they would not go far off. So they prayed to God, and God took away all the flies. But the king's heart was hardened still; and God sent the fifth plague, which was a great murrain upon the cattle, that all the horses, oxen, and sheep, &c. of the Egyptians died; but not one of the Israelites' cattle died. And yet the king would not let them go.

Then God sent the sixth plague: Moses and Aaron took a handful of ashes before the king, and sprinkled it in the air, and it turned to boils upon men and beasts, even on the conjurers themselves. And yet the king would not let them go.

Then God sent the seventh plague: Moses told the king, "To-morrow I will send hail that will kill all the cattle that are not fetched home out of the field." And those Egyptians that believed God fetched home their cattle: and the rest were killed with hail, fire, lightning, and thunder. But there was none in Goshen, among the Israelites. Then the king repented and said, "I and my people have sinned, and the Lord is righteous, I will let you go: pray God to cease the hail and thunder." But when the thunder ceased, his heart was hardened again, and he would not let them go.

Then God sent the eighth plague: they told Pharaoh, that locusts, or caterpillars, should so swarm as to darken the land, and eat up every green thing that was left. Then the Egyptians petitioned the king to let the Hebrews go, before all the land was destroyed. And the king consented that the men should go, but not their wives and children; but they would go all or none. And then he reviled them, as if they made religion a cloak for rebellion to be gone. But God sent the locusts, and they ate up all that was green in the land. Then the king called Moses and Aaron, and said, "I have sinned; pray God to deliver me this once," and they did; and God sent a wind that carried away all the locusts. Yet the king's heart was hardened, and God sent the ninth plague, and darkness came upon all the land, that for three days they could not see or stir. Then the king bid them go, with children and all, so they would leave their cattle behind (for death or darkness was not in Goshen); but they would not leave a hoof behind. Then Pharaoh bid Moses come near him no more, for if he came again he should die. And Moses said, "Content, I will see thy face no more." Then God said to Moses, I will send but one plague more, and then they will thrust you out. Therefore let all the people borrow silver, and gold, and jewels, of their neighbours, and take them with them.

C. But was not that stealing?

M. Yes, if God had not bid them; but all things are God's, and he may give them to whom he will.

C. And what was this last plague?

M. About midnight, God killed the eldest sons in all the houses of Egypt, even the king's and all. And there was a great cry over all the land, and they came and entreated the Israelites to be gone. And this was the night of their deliverance, which

God commanded them to keep in remembrance to all generations.

C. How were they to keep it in remembrance?

M. By a feast and sacrament, which God appointed. For God, by Moses, bid all the Israelites make ready that night, and every house was to kill a lamb, and with hyssop strike the blood on the door-posts without, and to eat the flesh roasted with unleavened bread and bitter herbs; they must eat it girded and shod, with their staves in their hands, in haste, as ready to be gone. And every door that had this blood on, God's angel passed by, that night, when he killed all the first-born of Egypt. And that all generations should keep this great deliverance in remembrance, God commanded them to do this again in the same manner once a year, on that same day, for ever.

C. And how and whither did they go?

M. When every house had one dead, the king and people thrust them out, and they lent them their jewels. And they carried their dough unleavened, and all their cattle: six hundred thousand men went, besides children, and a mixed multitude. God had before told Abraham that his seed should sojourn four hundred and thirty years, and then he would give them deliverance, and the land of Canaan; and the very day when the four hundred and thirty years were accomplished, God brought them out. And they had a great wilderness to go through, and the Red sea between them and it, before they could come to the promised land.

C. How, then, did they get over?

M. God was resolved to make this deliverance so great, that they and their children should never forget it: and though there was a nearer way than over the sea, God would not let them go that way. But his angel caused a pillar of fire by night, and of cloud by day, to go before them all the way, to show them which way they should go. And when they were gone, Pharaoh's heart was hardened, and he repented that he let them go from serving him: and he made ready his chariots and armies, and followed after them, and came near them; so that the sea was before them, and the king and his army at their backs, to kill them.

C. What did they do then?

M. This new danger made the Israelites again, in fear and unbelief, to cry out against Moses and Aaron for bringing them out to die in the wilderness, but God did it to show his power. For Moses cried to the Lord, and the angel of God that went before Israel, removed, and went behind them, and was a dark cloud between them and Pharaoh, so that he could not see them. And God bid Moses hold his rod over the sea, and the sea divided to the right hand and to the left, and was as a wall of water on either side, and dry ground between; and God made the Israelites go through it on foot: and Pharaoh's heart was hardened, and he followed them into the sea; and the angel took off their chariot wheels and stopped them, and then they would have fled back, but could not: for as soon as the Israelites were over, Moses stretched out his hand over the sea, and it came to its place, and drowned the king and all his army, so that one man of them did not escape.

C. Sure the people would never forget this, nor displease or distrust such a God any more.

M. They presently made a psalm of praise to God; but how they behaved themselves in the wilderness I shall tell you next.

The Tenth Lesson.—Israel's Travels in the Wilderness.

C. What did Moses with them when they were got through the sea?

M. For all the power of God that they had seen, Moses could not quiet the people, nor get them to trust God in any danger, want, or difficulty. And God purposely tried them whether they could trust him.

C. How did he try them?

M. First when they came into the wilderness, they went three days and found no water; and when they found water at Marah, it was bitter, and then they murmured again against Moses, and God showed him a tree, which he cast into the water, and it made the water sweet to drink.

C. How were they next tried?

M. When they had no meat in the wilderness, and they murmured again against Moses, and wished they had died in Egypt, where they had meat enough. And God said to Moses, I will rain bread from heaven for them, and they shall go out and gather it every day; but on the sixth day they shall gather for two days, and none shall go out to gather on the sabbath day. And God's glory appeared to reprove them for their murmuring; and God said at evening, you shall eat flesh, and in the morning you shall be filled with bread, that you may know that I am the Lord. So at evening abundance of quails fell among them, and they had flesh enough: and in the morning a dew fell and left a little round thing behind it like coriander seed, called manna. And this God gave them for bread: but he forbade them to keep it till morning, that they might receive it every day from God. But some would needs try, and that which they kept till morning had worms, and stunk. And when God bid them gather enough for two days before the sabbath, it did not stink on the sabbath day. And some of them did not obey God, but went out to gather manna on the sabbath day, but they found none, and God reproved them. This bread God fed them with in the wilderness forty years: the taste of it was like wafers made with honey.

C. What was their next trial?

M. They came to another place where was no water, and they murmured against Moses for bringing them thither to kill them with thirst: and Moses was too much troubled himself at their murmurings, and said to God, What shall I do with this people, they are ready to stone me? And God was displeased with them, and with Moses himself, for trusting him no better, and showing it by his impatience and complaint: and God bid him go, and with his rod strike the rock of mount Horeb before the people: and he did, and water flowed out enough for them all.

C. And what was their next trial?

M. Next a people, called Amalek, came and fought against them; and Moses sent Joshua and his men to fight with them. And Moses stood on the hill with the rod of God in his hand, and (he being above fourscore years old) when his hands fell down Amalek prevailed, and while his hands held up Israel prevailed: and Aaron and Hur set him a stone to sit on, and they two held up his hands till sunset, and so Amalek was overthrown by Joshua.

C. What did they next?

M. Next Moses' father-in-law, Jethro, priest of Midian, came to see him, and Moses told him all that God had done; and he saw how Moses was overwhelmed with judging all the people alone, and he advised him to choose able men, such as fear God, men of truth, hating covetousness, and set them over thousands, and hundreds, and fifties, and tens, to judge the smaller matters, while Moses inquired of God, and told them his laws, and judged of greater matters, (if God commanded this,) and so Moses did.

C. And what did they next?

M. Next God, by Moses, called all the people, to

know whether they would make a covenant with God to obey him for ever, and he would be their God, and take them for his peculiar people above all others on earth. And the people consented, and God and they made a solemn covenant. And when they had promised to obey him, God called Moses up to mount Sinai, and came, by his angel, in fire and thunder, and the mountain trembled and smoked, and God forbade the people to come near it, but they trembled at the sight and noise: and there God spake to Moses the ten commandments, and then spake to him many other particular laws by which he would rule the people of Israel, which were presently written down. And the people saw as it were the glory of God, and promised to be obedient to all his laws; and so became a settled commonwealth, of which God himself was the lawgiver, and chose him that should be chief commander under him, and entailed the priesthood on Aaron and his line, and the tribe of Levi. And the Lord kept Moses forty days in the mount, and wrote in two tables of stone the ten commandments.

C. What were these ten commandments?

M. I will tell you the rest of the history first, and then I will tell you what they are afterward.

C. Sure the people durst not break God's law after such a terrible sight as all this?

M. No: they did not forbear sinning so long as Moses was in the mount with God: because he stayed forty days, they said, We know not what is become of him. And they brought gold to Aaron, and compelled him to make an idol of it in the shape of a calf, and called that their God that brought them out of Egypt, and worshipped it: so bad is man, if God leave him to himself.

C. What became of them for this?

M. God was offended, and would have destroyed them all presently, but that Moses prayed for them. And when Moses came down and saw their sin, his anger kindled, and he cast down the tables of stone that God had written, and brake them; and he chid Aaron, and he caused three thousand of the people to be presently killed: and God plagued the people for this golden calf; and Moses burned it, and cast the dust on the water, and made them drink it. And God made the two tables to be written out anew.

C. And what did they next?

M. Moses desired to see God, and God hid him in a rock while he showed him a glimpse of his glory at his back parts; and as he past by, proclaimed his name by which he would be known to all?

C. What was that?

M. "The Lord, the Lord God, merciful and gracious, long-suffering, and abundant in goodness and truth, keeping mercy for thousands, forgiving iniquity, and transgression, and sin, and that will by no means clear the guilty; visiting the iniquity of the fathers on the children, and upon the children's children, unto the third and to the fourth generation."

C. What did they next?

M. Next God taught them to make a tabernacle, like a tent, which they could carry about, to be as a temple, a place where God would still be sought: and it was made with great art and cost; and a cloud stood before it; and there God was sought to by Moses and the priest, and there he told them his mind, and answered them. And in an ark in that tabernacle God made them keep the two tables of stone that were the ten commandments, and a pot of the manna with which God fed them, and Moses' rod with which he did his miracles, that their children after them might see that all those things were true.

C. What did they next?

M. When God, by Moses, had delivered them all his laws, a wilderness life was hard; and the people complained, and God was offended, and sent a fire that burnt up some of them, till Moses prayed.

But after this they grew weary of eating manna, having no other meat, and their appetite longed for flesh, or other meat; and they again murmured against Moses: and Moses grew impatient of their murmurings, and prayed God to set some other over them, and not leave all this burden upon him; and God bid Moses call threescore and ten of the elders, that had been officers over the people, and bring them to the door of the tabernacle, and there God spake to Moses, and took of the spirit (of power) which was on Moses, and put on them, and so made them partners with Moses in the government. And then God gave the people flesh, but with his wrath, because they lusted, and were not content with his provision.

C. What was it he gave them?

M. He told them they should have flesh a whole month together, till they loathed it; and Moses said, They are six hundred thousand men, and whence shall they have flesh? And God said, Is my hand shortened? And God made a wind from the sea bring quails, that fell all about them, and a day's journey round them, and they lay a yard thick upon the ground, and the people gathered them for meat. But while the flesh was in their mouths, God sent a plague among them, which killed many of the murmurers.

C. What did they next?

M. Moses married an Ethiopian woman, (a black,) perhaps to typify that the God of the Israelites would also be the God of other nations, and call them. And Miriam, Moses' sister, and Aaron his brother, murmured, and spake against him for it: and God was offended, and struck Miriam with a leprosy, but Moses prayed, and God restored her in seven days.

C. What did they after this?

M. When they drew towards the land of Canaan, which God had promised to give them, Moses chose twelve men out of the twelve tribes, to go as spies unknown, and see what a land it was, and to bring the people word. So they were forty days searching the land, and when they returned, ten of them discouraged all the people, and told them it was a good land, but the cities were walled, and the people many and strong, and giants among them, and they should never be able to overcome them. But two of them, Caleb and Joshua, brought of the grapes, and told them it was an excellent land, and the people of it would be but as bread to them, and bid them fear not, God would deliver them into their hands. But the people believed the other ten, before these two, and were frightened, and mutinied more than ever, even against God himself, for bringing them, and their wives and children, to be destroyed by the sword; and wished they had died in Egypt; and they consulted of making them a captain to go back to Egypt; and when Caleb and Joshua would have encouraged them, they cried out, "Stone them." And in this rebellion the glory of God appeared at the tabernacle; and God said, "How long will this people provoke me, and not believe me for all the signs that I have done among them?" and God was about to destroy them all with the plague, had not Moses stopped it by earnest prayer. But God decreed that never one of them should enter into that land, save Caleb and Joshua, and their children that were but twenty years old, but that they should all die in the wilderness for their unbelief, and murmuring; yea, even Moses and Aaron: but their children should possess it.

And the ten men that had searched the land, and disheartened the people, all died presently of the plague.

C. What did the people then?

M. When they heard God's sentence, that all above twenty years old should wander forty years in the wilderness, and there die, then they mourned, and repented of their mutiny, when it was too late, and then they would needs go suddenly, and fight to get the land. But Moses forbade them, and told them, now God was against their going, and if they went they should be overthrown: but they obeyed not God; (for they would go when God forbade them,) and they were beaten by their enemies.

C. What did they then?

M. Worse and worse: then Korah a Levite, with Dathan and Abiram, two great men, got two hundred and fifty chief men to join with them; and they drew the people into rebellion against Moses and Aaron, and accused them of deceiving and destroying the people; and said they took too much upon them for Moses to make himself their prince, and Aaron priest, when all the congregation were God's people, as well as they: and said they promised them a good land, and performed nothing, but brought them to perish in the wilderness; and would put out the people's eyes. When Moses heard this, and saw the rebellion, he bid Korah, and his Levites, come and offer incense to God, and Aaron should do so too, and God would show which of them he had chosen.

Then God offered to destroy them all, but Moses prayed to him to spare the people: then God sent him to tell Dathan and Abiram what God would do to them, and to charge all the people to get far enough from them, unless they would die with them: and as soon as Moses had spoken, the ground opened, and swallowed up these leaders, and their wives and children, and all that belonged to them; and then the earth closed again. And the people ran away at their cry, lest the earth should also swallow up them. And the two hundred and fifty that were to offer incense were all burnt up as they offered, by a fire from the Lord.

C. Sure they would take warning after all this?

M. No, the next day all the congregation got together against Moses, and said, You have killed the people of the Lord. Then God again offered to kill them all, and sent a plague, but Moses prayed to God and stopped it: but the plague first killed fourteen thousand and seven hundred rebels.

C. What a wicked people was this! had God no better people in the world than these?

M. No; all the rest of the nations were worse: by them we may see what a blind mind, and naughty heart, is in us and all men, till God's grace sanctify us: they judged by their own blind reason, and their selfish interest, as most men do.

C. Did this quiet them, and make them obedient?

M. When they saw that there was no remedy, they cried out, We all die, we perish; God kills us all that come near the tabernacle; instead of bewailing their own sin.

And to convince the murmurers, whom God had chosen to rule them, God bade Moses call twelve chief men of the twelve tribes, and bade every man bring a rod (or wand) and lay them all in the tabernacle, and Aaron's rod had his name written on it: and in the morning they found that Aaron's rod (and no other) did spring forth with buds, and blossoms, and almonds; to show them whom God did choose.

C. Were they quiet after this?

M. Then God made them turn back into the wilderness, and they came again to a place that had no water; and they again murmured against Moses and Aaron, as promise-breakers, and said they had brought them to a place that had neither seed, fruit, nor water; and wished they had been killed with the rebels, or died in Egypt: so hard is it to be patient in suffering, and to trust God when no outward help is seen.

Then God bade Moses strike the rock as formerly, and plenty of water gushed out. But Moses and Aaron did not there honour God, by so strong a faith as they should have done; for God told them that they should die in the wilderness; and Aaron died shortly after.

C. What did they then?

M. The Edomites would not let them pass through their country, so that they were fain to go a great way about. And then some Canaanites fought with them; but God gave Israel the victory, and they destroyed king Arad, and his cities.

But again they were impatient with the long way, and having so many years no bread but manna, and they murmured against Moses for bringing them out of Egypt, to die by famine, in a wilderness. Then God sent fiery serpents among them, that stung many of them to death; and then they repented and begged for mercy: and God bade Moses make the likeness of a serpent in brass, and set it up on a pole; and every one that was stung was cured, when he looked up on the brazen serpent, which was a type of Christ.

C. What did they next?

M. When they had long travelled, Sihon, king of the Amorites in Heshbon, and Og, king of Bashan, would not let them go through their country, but fought with them; and God delivered them and their cities to the Israelites, and they killed them, and possessed their land: and now they had some place besides a wilderness to dwell in: but this was but in the way to the promised land, the river Jordan being between it and them.

C. What did they next?

M. The land of Moab was near them, and the king, called Balak, was afraid of the Israelites; and there was a man called Balaam, not far off, that could prophesy, and king Balak sent some lords to him to entreat him to come and curse the Israelites, that he might hope to overcome them; and he would give him great rewards. Balaam bid them stay all night, and in the morning he would answer them. And in the night God charged Balaam not to go with them, nor curse Israel, for God would bless them. So Balaam gave them their answer, and sent them away. But king Balak sent other greater men, and offered him greater things if he would come. He told them, that if they would give him a house full of silver and gold, he could not go beyond the word of the Lord; but bid them stay till morning for their answer. And in the night God bid him go with them, but be sure to say nothing but what God put into his mouth; so he went with them. But because his heart was to have got the money and honour by cursing Israel, if God would suffer him, therefore God sent an angel that stood with a sword in his way: his ass saw the angel, and Balaam did not; and the ass went out of the way to pass by the angel, and Balaam beat his ass: then the angel stood in a narrower way between two walls, and the ass hurt his foot up to the wall, to go by the angel; and Balaam beat the ass again. Then the angel stood in so narrow a way that there was no passage by; and then the ass lay down, and Balaam beat him again, and God made the ass to speak, and reprove Balaam for striking him. And God opened Balaam's eyes to see the angel; and when the angel reproved him, he offered to turn back again; but God bid him go on, but be sure to say but what he bid him. And when he was come, king Balak met him, and told him his desire, and took him to a high hill, that he might see Israel and curse them. And Balaam caused seven altars to be there built, and offered sacrifice on every one, to hear what God would bid him say. And God made him pronounce a blessing on Israel, instead of a curse. And king Balak was angry with him for blessing them that he called him to curse. And he brought him to another hill, and built seven altars also there, and sacrificed; and God made him bless them from thence yet more. And king Balak took him to another hill, and there they built seven altars, and sacrificed; but there God made Balaam prophesy of all the prosperity of Israel, and bless them more. And the king was in a rage and bid him be gone; God had kept him from honour.

C. What did the people after this?

M. They sinned again: when they saw the women of Moab, they began to commit whoredom with them; and these women tempted them to come to the service of their idols, or false gods; and so the Israelites were tempted to do as they saw the idolaters do: and God was offended, and commanded to kill them: and Phinehas, the priest's son, killed one man and woman; and the plague ceased when it had killed four-and-twenty thousand. Yea, God made Moses make war against the Midianites, whose women had tempted the people to whoredom and idolatry; and they killed five of their kings, and burnt their cities, and took all that they had, and brought away the women and children. And Moses made them kill all the male children, and every woman that had lain with a man, and so revenge that sin.

C. What else was done by them?

M. God made Moses to set Joshua to be chief ruler in his place when he was dead; and gave commandment that all the Canaanites, whose land God would give Israel, should be killed; because they had been idolaters, and committed all manner of wickedness, which God would revenge, and not forgive.

C. And what came next?

M. Last of all, Moses repeated God's laws, and left them written for the people, and gave to two tribes and a half their inheritance in the land that he had taken on that side Jordan; and God called him up to mount Nebo, to die, at six-score years old, and God buried him; and Joshua was to bring them over Jordan, into the rest of the promised land.

The Eleventh Lesson.—Joshua's Conquest of Canaan.

C. What did God do with them when Moses was dead?

M. God made Joshua their captain, and charged him to be courageous, and obey his law, and promised to be with him. Jericho being the first city that Joshua was to take, he sent spies to search it: and a woman called Rahab, believing that God would give it them, hid them; and she and all her friends with her were therefore spared. But they must first pass over the river Jordan, where God confirmed their faith by a miracle, like that at the Red sea: as soon as the priests that bare the ark touched the waters, they divided, and stood on a heap, till the Israelites were all past over on dry ground. And Joshua set up twelve great stones, that their posterity might believe it.

C. And how did they take Jericho?

M. First, Joshua and all the people renewed their covenant with God, and circumcised all the males; (for they had not been circumcised in the wilderness, of forty years, that were born there;) and celebrated the passover, and then they had manna no more, but eat of the corn of the land. And God sent an angel to Joshua, to bid him but go round about the city six days with the ark, by seven priests, and blow trumpets made of rams' horns, and the seventh day go seven times, and the walls should fall down: and so they did. And God made them kill all the people, save Rahab and her company, and burn all their goods, save the gold, silver, and brass, for God's treasure; and they did so.

But one man, called Achan, was covetous; and when he saw a wedge of gold, and a rich garment, he stole and hid them, which cost them dear.

C. Why, what came of it?

M. They went next to take a city called Ai, but God left them, and the men of Ai beat them; and then their hearts were down, and Joshua lamented, and prayed to God; and God told him there was sin among them, and he would be with them no more till the sinner were destroyed. So Joshua called them together, and cast lots, and the lot found out Achan; and he confessed it, and he and his sons and daughters, his cattle, the stolen gold and silver, and all that he had, they burnt, when they had stoned him; and so God's wrath was turned away.

C. This seemed but a little fault?

M. It is no little fault to break the law of God wilfully. Afterward they conquered Ai. But the Gibeonites saved themselves by craft: they sent ambassadors to Joshua with old shoes and clothes, who told him they dwelt in so far a country, that their clothes were worn out in coming to him, and that they came to make a league with him, because they heard that God was with him; so Joshua believed them, and swore a league with them. And when he knew that they were Canaanites that had deceived him, he durst not break his oath, but made them servants. And after this many kings, for fear, joined together, and fought against Joshua and Gibeon, and Joshua overcame them; and God rained great hailstones on them, and killed many. And Joshua prayed that the sun might not go down till they had been avenged on their enemies; and so the sun and moon (or the light at least) staid a whole day extraordinary: and Joshua killed the five kings, and took many cities. Then many other kings joined to fight against Israel, (for most great cities had their kings in those times,) and God gave them all, and their cities and lands, into Joshua's hands; and then Joshua divided the land among them, to every tribe their part by lot. And at Shiloh they set up God's tabernacle, where they were to inquire of his will: but much of the promised land was much unconquered. And Joshua rehearsed to the people all God's mercies, and exhorted them to obey his laws, and so died at a hundred and ten years old. And Israel obeyed God, and prospered, all the days of Joshua, and while the elders lived, that with Joshua had seen the wonders of God.

The Twelfth Lesson.—The History of the Judges after Joshua.

C. What did they when Joshua was dead?

M. God sent them to conquer and possess the rest of the land, but commanded them to drive out all the Canaanites, and other old inhabitants, and make no league with them, lest they should draw Israel to worship their false gods, and learn their wicked customs. But the Israelites did not obey God, but were contented to make most of the Canaanites tributaries to them, and suffered them to dwell among them, because they met with difficulties in conquering them. For this, God was offended, and sent an angel to tell them that these Canaanites that dwelt among them, should henceforth be thorns in their sides, and a tempting snare to them. And so it proved.

C. Why, what came of it?

M. When the old men were dead, another generation sprung up, that knew not the Lord, nor the wonders that he had done for Israel. And they were tempted by the Canaanites to worship their idols, and forsake the Lord; and God forsook them, and gave the Canaanites power against them, to overcome them, and make them servants. But when affliction made them repent, then God sent a judge to deliver them. And when the judge was dead, they turned to idolatry and sin again.

C. Who were these judges?

M. First God gave the king of Mesopotamia a victory over the Israelites, and they were eight years his servants. Then they cried to God, and he sent Othniel, Caleb's brother's son, to be their captain; and he delivered them, and they had quietness forty years. Then they fell to sin again, and God gave them up to Eglon, king of Moab, eighteen years. Then they cried to God for help, and he raised up one Ehud, who took on him to bring the king a present, and stabbed him, and escaped, and raised the Israelites in arms, and killed ten thousand Moabites; and after this they were quiet fourscore years. And after him rose up Shamgar, and slew many of the Philistines that had afflicted them. When Ehud was dead they fell to sin again; and God gave them to Jabin, king of Hazor, who oppressed them twenty years. Then Deborah, a woman prophetess, judged them, and she called Barak to be their captain: and she and Barak conquered Sisera's general; and he fled and hid himself in the tent of Jael a woman, who spake him fair, and laid him to sleep, and then struck a nail in his head, and killed him. Then they were quiet forty years.

But they turned to sin again, and God gave them up to the Midianites and Amalekites, that destroyed their fields, and took their cattle: then they cried to God again, and God sent first a prophet to reprove them, and next an angel to deliver them; and the angel appeared to Gideon, and made him captain: but Gideon was afraid, till God wrought a miracle to encourage him; and God gave him a victory with a very few men. The Midianites fled, and killed one another; and Oreb and Zeeb, two of their princes, were slain, and a hundred and twenty thousand, and Zeba and Zalmunna, their kings. Then they had rest forty years. But when Gideon was dead, they worshipped the idol Baal again.

C. Who ruled them next?

M. Gideon had threescore and ten sons, by several wives, and one (Abimelek) by a concubine. This one son enticed the men of the city of Shechem to make him their king; and he went and killed all his brethren, except Jotham, who escaped. But God revenged the murder, and the men of Shechem turned against him, and one Gaal led them, and he destroyed them that made him king, and their city: and when he attempted to burn them that fled to a tower at Thebez, a woman cast down a piece of a millstone on his head; and when he saw he must die, he made his armour-bearer kill him.

After him Tola judged Israel twenty-and-three years. After him Jair twenty-two years. But the Israelites forsook God, and served the idol gods of all the countries about them. And God gave the Philistines and Ammonites power to oppress part of them eighteen years. Then they cried to God for help, and God reproved them for their sin, and threatened to deliver them no more, and bid them go cry to their idols to help them. But they confessed their sins, and put away their idols, and begged God this once to save them: and God raised up Jephthah, and he was their captain, to fight against the king of Ammon, and had the victory. But a rash vow troubled him.

C. What was that?

M. He vowed to God, if he would give him the victory, that he would offer as a sacrifice the first thing that met him out of his house; and his daughter came with joy to meet him, which grieved him; but by her consent he kept his vow. And a greater mischief followed than this: when the men of Ephraim saw that Jephthah had conquered the Ammonites, they mutinied against him in pride, because he had not called them with him, insomuch that it came to a war, and forty-two thousand Ephraimites were killed.

C. What came next?

M. When Jephthah had ruled six years, he died. Then Ibzan ruled seven years, and died. Then Elon ruled ten years, and died. Then Abdon ruled eight years, and died. Then Israel fell to sin again, and God gave the Philistines power over them.

C. How were they delivered then?

M. Then there was a man named Manoah, and his wife was barren; and God sent an angel to promise her a son that should deliver Israel. The angel appeared twice to them; and when they sacrificed, he went up from them in the flame: so God gave them a son called Samson, who had the strength of many men; and he judged Israel twenty years, and slew many of the Philistines, but at last was betrayed into their hands by a harlot that he fell in love with: and they took him and put out his eyes; and at one of their great meetings they sent for him to make sport with him. But he prayed to God for strength, and pulled down two great pillars of the house, near which they set him, and the house fell and killed their lords, and more people with him than he had killed in his life.

C. Who judged them next?

M. They were long after this without any judge, but not without sin and punishment; for a Levite and his wife lodging in Gibeah, a city of Benjamin, some wicked men abused his wife to death: and he cut her body into twelve pieces, and sent them to all the tribes of Israel, to summon them to come and revenge her death; and the foolish Benjamites revenged the malefactors, and the rest of the tribes went to war against them, in which were slain forty thousand Israelites, and twenty-five thousand Benjamites, and the city burnt: such is the fruit of sin.

C. Who judged them after this?

M. They had long no king or judge, but were in much subjection to the Philistines; but they had priests, that in Shiloh waited at the tabernacle and sacrificed, and inquired for them of God. And Eli being then chief priest, he had two sons, called Hophni and Phinehas, priests under him, that were very wicked men, and oppressed and robbed the sacrifices, and lay with the women that assembled at the tabernacle door, so that God's worship grew contemptible, and the priests and offerings were loathed by the people: and Eli their father reproved his sons, but did not punish them as God required; and God was greatly displeased with him and them. And there was a woman named Hannah, the wife of Elkanah, that had no child, and earnestly begged for a child of God, and vowed to dedicate him to God. So God gave her a son called Samuel; and she dedicated him to serve God at the tabernacle: and God sent a prophet to old Eli to denounce God's judgment against his sons, and against him for suffering them. And while Samuel was yet but a youth, God in a vision called to him by his name, and he thought it had been Eli, and went to him; and when he told him that he called him not, he lay down again: and God called him again; and he went to Eli, and said, "Thou didst call me:" then Eli perceived that it was a vision, and bid him next say, "Speak, Lord, for thy servant heareth." Then God told Samuel of all the punishment he would bring on Eli and his sons, and how he would cast out his house. And Samuel was loth to tell it to Eli till he urged him. Then Eli said, "It is the Lord, let him do what seemeth him good." And shortly after God destroyed them as he had threatened.

C. How did he destroy them?

M. The Philistines fought against Israel, and killed at first four thousand of them. Then the Israelites fetched God's ark from Shiloh, and took it with them when they went to fight, thinking that God would deliver them for his ark's sake; like foolish people now, that think God will save wicked men for the outside of religion: but the Philistines killed thirty thousand of them, and also took the ark of God; and the two wicked priests, Hophni and Phinehas, were killed. And when old Eli heard all this, especially that the ark was taken, he fell off his seat with grief, and broke his neck, and died at ninety-eight years old, when he had judged Israel forty years.

C. And what became of the ark after this?

M. The Philistines carried it away in triumph, and set it up by their idol called Dagon (which was an image). But in the morning Dagon was fallen on his face before the ark: then they set up their image in its place again; but the next morning they found him fallen again, and the head and hands broken off. And God smote the men of that city with a sore disease; and they would keep the ark no longer, but sent it away to another city. Then God struck the men of that city also with the same disease, called the emerods; then that city sent it away to another city; but that city was afraid, and durst not keep it: and when it had been seven months, they advised with their wizards what to do with it; and they bid them send it home again to Israel, but send it not empty, but gold cast into the shape of the emerods and mice that afflicted them. And they bid them take two kine that had calves, and had never been yoked, and put them to draw the ark in a new cart, and keep the calves at home, and leave them to go which way they would; for if they went from their calves towards Israel, then they might be sure it was God that afflicted them: and so they did; and the kine went straight to the Israelites with the ark, but lowing as they went, for their calves. And the men of Bethshemesh (a town of Israel) rejoiced when they saw the ark, and they offered the two kine in sacrifice to God. But the men of Bethshemesh did unreverently presume to look into the ark, which they ought not to do, and God killed many thousands of them; and they were afraid, and sent away the ark to another city, where it staid twenty years.

C. Who judged Israel all this while?

M. Samuel: for God made him a holy prophet, and all the people saw that God had chosen him. And Samuel called them all to fast and pray, and put away all their idol images, and God was reconciled to them; and the Philistines came again to fight against them, and Samuel prayed, and God destroyed the Philistines with thunder and with the sword; and they came no more against Israel all the days of Samuel.

C. And who ruled them after Samuel?

M. When Samuel was very old, he made his sons judges, and they proved not like their father, but were covetous, and took bribes; and the people were weary of them, and they desired to have a king, like other countries, which displeased God.

C. Why was God displeased at this?

M. It was their happiness, above all other nations, to be ruled so by God himself, that as he made their laws, so he chose their rulers and judges by prophets, or visions, or heavenly revelation, or inspiration, as it pleased him: but the people would needs have a king that should have greater power than the judges, and should rule them by force, and leave the crown to his successors, like other nations: so that it was a departing from God's prophetical and extraordinary government, and this on their own heads, without God's call or warrant. They should have made no such change without God's consent and conduct. It was he, and not they, that should appoint their government. But of their kings I will tell you more the next time.

The Thirteenth Lesson.—The History of King Saul.

C. Who was the first king of Israel?

M. Saul.

C. How came he to be king?

M. The people rebelliously, without God, came and told Samuel they would have a king like other nations: and Samuel was displeased at it; and he prayed to God, and God said, "They have not rejected thee, but they have rejected me, that I should not reign over them:" yet God bid him hearken to them, and let their own will be their punishment, and tell them what should be the manner of their king, that he would make their sons and daughters his servants, and make them do his work, and take tithes of them for his servants; and that then they should cry out, because of the king which they had chosen, and the Lord will not hear them. But the people were set upon it, and would have a king.

C. Why? Should there not be such kings as these?

M. While they might have been free, they should have chosen it rather, and continued under God's prophetical government, without such servitude. But where God appoints such, they must be obeyed.

C. And how was Saul chosen?

M. Saul was the goodliest proper man in Israel, higher from the shoulders upward than any of the people. And his father's asses being lost, he came to Samuel the prophet, to know of him what was become of them: and God told Samuel, "This is the man that shall be king, and fight against the Philistines." And Samuel anointed Saul, and told him who should meet him in the way, and what signs he should see, and how he should prophesy among the prophets; which all came to pass. And he bid Saul go to Gilgal, and tarry seven days, till he came to him to offer sacrifice. And God gave Saul another spirit. Then Samuel called the people together, and told them, that they had rejected God in choosing to have a king, but bid them all come and see whom God would choose by a lot: and the lot chose Saul, but he hid himself, and they found him out, and made him king; and God moved the hearts of many to follow and obey him. After this the king of Ammon came in war against them, and would not make peace with them, unless they would have their right eyes put out for a reproach and mark of servitude. But God stirred up Saul, and he called all Israel together, and fought with the Ammonites, and destroyed them. Then they settled Saul in the kingdom. But Samuel called them, and appealed to God and them, whether ever he had taken ox or ass from them, or defrauded or oppressed any, or taken any bribe; and he preached to them, and told them, that if they would not keep God's commandments, his hand would be against them: and that they might know God spake by him, they should suddenly see it witnessed by thunder and rain (at an unusual time): so it did so thunder and rain, that the people were humbled, and believed him, "That their wickedness was great in the sight of the Lord," in asking a king. And they feared, and desired Samuel to pray to God not to destroy them, confessing that they had added this to all their sins, to ask a king. And Samuel promised to pray for them, though they had done this wickedness, and told them God would not yet forsake them, if they would fear God, and serve him with all their heart; but if they would still do wickedly, both they and their king should be consumed.

C. And how did Saul rule then?

M. When he had been king two years, he kept three thousand soldiers with him, and his son Jonathan; and Jonathan smote a garrison of the Philistines, who thereupon gathered so huge an army against Israel as put the people into great fear; so that they hid themselves in caves, and thickets, and rocks; and they that were with Saul trembled: and Samuel not coming, as he appointed, in seven days, to offer sacrifice and prayer to God, Saul ventured to do it without him, when he saw the people scattered from him. And then Samuel came and reproved him, and told him God would choose another king, because he had thus disobeyed God; for it did not belong to him to sacrifice.

C. Sure Saul thought he did well: was not this a little fault?

M. God must be carefully obeyed; and thinking we do well will not save us, if we will venture to do ill. So there did but six hundred men stay with Saul; and the Philistines had so mastered Israel, that they let them have no smith in all the land, and no one but Saul and Jonathan had so much as a sword or spear.

And one day only Jonathan and his armour-bearer went up to a garrison of the Philistines, and killed twenty men; and God sent a terror among all the rest, and they trembled, and fought against each other; and the Israelites that were hid came out and fell upon them. But Saul, in a blind zeal, said, "Cursed be the man that eateth any food till evening, that I may be avenged of mine enemies." And the people were all faint; and Jonathan heard not when his father charged the people with the oath; and he saw some honey, and, eating some, was refreshed. But the people were so hungry that, after the victory, they ran upon the spoil, and did kill and eat things raw, with the blood; and Saul reproved them for the sin. And he inquired of God whether they should again pursue the Philistines, and God answered him not: then he thought that some one had broke the oath of fasting, and he cast lots to know who it was, and the lot took his son Jonathan: and Saul vowed he should die, to keep his oath; but the people swore he should not die, and so delivered him. After this, God sent Samuel to command Saul to go fight against the country called Amalek, and to kill man and woman, oxen and sheep, camels and asses, because they were wicked men, and had fought against Israel coming out of Egypt; and Saul obeyed not: he went and conquered the Amalekites, and took their king, Agag, prisoner, and brought away the best of the sheep and cattle, and killed none but the worst. And for this disobedience God sent Samuel to reprove him, for saving the king, and the sheep, and the oxen, which he should have killed: but Saul said he had done as God bid him, save that the people saved the best of the sheep and oxen to offer to God in sacrifice. But Samuel told him that obedience was better than sacrifice, and rebellion against God's command was as the sin of witchcraft and idolatry; and he told him for this God had taken the kingdom from him, and would give it to one that was better than he. So Samuel killed Agag; and he came no more to Saul, but mourned for him to the last.

C. Was it not better to save the sheep and oxen than kill them: why should they be lost? Sure this was a very little sin: would not God forgive thus much?

M. It is not a small sin for a man to set his reason and will against God's. God is the owner of all things, and may do what he will with his own; and he knows what is good or evil better than we do. We must not do what we think best, but what God thinks best. And kings must be examples of obedience to God, to all their subjects, or else their sin is worse than others'.

C. And what became of Saul after this?

M. God sent Samuel to anoint one of the sons of Jesse, of Bethlehem; and he was to cover it with going thither to sacrifice, lest Saul should know it, and kill him. Jesse had eight sons; and when Samuel called seven of them, one by one, God told him that none of these were the man that he had chosen. There was no more but the youngest, keeping sheep, which was David; and when they sent for him, God said to Samuel, "This is he:" so Samuel anointed him to be king afterward. Upon this, the Spirit of the Lord came upon David; but it departed from Saul, and an evil spirit had power from God to terrify and trouble him, as a melancholy man. And Saul's servants persuaded him to seek out a good musician, that could play well upon the harp, to drive away the trouble of his spirit; and they chose David, (not knowing that Samuel had anointed him,) and when the evil spirit troubled Saul, it departed when David played on the harp; and Saul loved him, and made him his armour-bearer awhile.

C. And what did he with him after?

M. David went home again to keep sheep, till Saul had forgot him. And after this the Philistines came to fight against Israel; and when the two armies were near, Goliath, a Philistine giant, that was stronger than many men, dared the Israelites to send a man to fight with him, and he that got the better should carry the day with the whole armies. And the Israelites feared him, and none of them durst fight with him. And Saul offered to give his daughter to wife, and great riches, to him that could conquer Goliath: and David's brethren being in the army, he brought them provision; and hearing what was said, he offered to fight with Goliath; but Saul told him he was not able, being but a youth, to fight with a giant bred up to war. But David answered him, "That while he kept his father's sheep, there came a lion and a bear, and took a lamb, and he went after him, and killed the lion and the bear, and rescued the lamb; and he believed that God would make this Philistine like one of them, seeing he had defied the army of the living God." So Saul bid him go, and put on him his armour, a helmet of brass, and a coat of mail, and his sword; but David put them off, and said, "I cannot go with these, for I have not proved them." And he took his staff and sling, and took five smooth stones out of the brook, and drew near Goliath, who despised him, and said, "Am I a dog, that thou comest to me with staves?" And he cursed him by his gods, and told him he would give his flesh to birds and beasts. But David said, "I come to thee in the name of the Lord of hosts, and the Lord will deliver thee into my hand." And David did sling a stone, which sunk into his forehead, and he fell down dead; and

David, with Goliath's own sword, cut off his head; and the Philistines fled; and David brought the head to Jerusalem, and kept the armour.

C. And what reward had David for this?

M. Saul took him to his house, and would let him go home no more; and Jonathan, Saul's son, loved David as his own soul, and gave him his very garments, his sword and bow; and they two made a covenant of dearest friendship. And Saul set him over the men of war; but the women in their songs said, "Saul hath killed his thousands, and David his ten thousands." And this turned the proud heart of Saul into envy and jealousy against him, (for he did not know that Samuel had anointed David,) and from that day Saul sought to kill him. And when he next fell into his mad fit, by an evil spirit, and David played on his harp, Saul sought to kill him with his javelin; but David avoided him. Then Saul made him captain of a thousand, that he might fall by the enemies; and he gave him Michal his daughter to wife, to be a snare to him, on condition he would bring him a hundred foreskins of the Philistines. And David and his men killed two hundred, and he married Saul's daughter.

Then Saul was more afraid of David, and spake to Jonathan, and to all his servants, to kill David; but Jonathan awhile appeased his father's wrath, till more war arose, and David got more honour by slaying the Philistines; and then Saul, in his disturbed fit of melancholy, attempted again to kill David, as he was playing before him; and when he escaped, he sent after him to kill him in his own house; but Michal, his wife, let him down through a window, and put an image in his bed; and when Saul bid them bring him to him, that he might kill him, he saw how his daughter had deceived him. Then David fled and dwelt with old Samuel in Ramah; and Saul sent men to fetch him thence; and when they came, they found Samuel, and many prophets, prophesying, and the Spirit of God came on the messengers, and they prophesied with them. Then Saul sent other messengers to fetch him; and when they came, they prophesied as the first. Then he sent others the third time, and those prophesied too. Then he went himself, and before he came thither, the Spirit of prophecy fell upon him, and he stripped himself naked, and prophesied among them.

C. I thought none had been prophets, and had God's Spirit, but good men?

M. None but good men are made good and godly by God's Spirit; but others may prophesy, and do miracles.

C. And what did Saul and David then?

M. David fled to Jonathan, who pleaded for him to his father, till his father reviled him for defending David against his own hope of the kingdom, as his heir. And Saul sought to kill David again; but Jonathan told David of all his father's purposes, and saved him. Then David fled to Ahimelech, the priest, and made him believe he was sent of business by the king: and Ahimelech, having no other, gave him of the consecrated bread, and Goliath's sword, and he fled to a Philistine king, to Gath. But Doeg, a servant of Saul, saw all this, and told Saul; and Saul sent for the priests, and charged them of confederating with a rebel, or not telling him when David fled, and commanded his guard to kill the priests; but they would not do it. But Doeg, when the king bade him, killed fourscore and five of them for this.

C. And what did David among the Philistines?

M. He heard them tell their king how many of them he had killed, and he was afraid, and took on him to be a mad-man, and the king turned him away. And he got again into Israel; and his kindred, and all that were in debt, and discontented, came to him, and he became their captain, and had about four hundred men. And he got the king of Moab to receive his father and mother, and being warned by a prophet, he went into the country of Judah. And Saul destroyed the whole city of Nob, men, women, and children, where the priests dwelt, because Ahimelech gave David bread; but Abiathar, one of Ahimelech's sons, escaped to David, and was his priest. After this the Philistines fought against a town called Keilah, and God bid David go and deliver them; and he went and conquered the Philistines, and delivered Keilah. Then Saul thought to besiege, and take David in, Keilah; but David inquired of God, by the priest, whether the men of Keilah would give him into the hands of Saul; and God said "They will." So David, with six hundred men, fled from thence to a wood in the wilderness, and Saul hunted after him; but Jonathan came secretly to David, and encouraged him, and made a covenant with him, knowing he would be king. Then the men of Ziph told Saul where David was, and offered to deliver him to him, and Saul was glad, and pursued him hard; but then the Philistines invaded the land, and Saul was fain first to go fight with them. And after that he pursued David again; and as he hunted him on the craggy mountains, Saul found a great cave, into which he went for his ease, and David and his men were in the inside of the cave; and David's men persuaded him now to kill Saul, but he said, "God forbid that I should lay my hand on the Lord's anointed!" only he secretly cut off some of his robe. And when Saul was gone out, he called to him from the hill, and showed him how his life was in his hand, and pleaded with him why he sought his life, that intended him no hurt. Then Saul relented, and confessed his fault, and said, now he knew David would be king after him; and made him enter into an oath, that he would not cut off his seed after him; and so they parted.

C. What did David then?

M. He durst not trust Saul, but kept with his men in the wilderness, where they wanted food; and there was near a rich man, called Nabal, that had a great feast for his sheep-shearers, and David sent his men to ask him for some part of his provision; but Nabal answered them with reproach, and asked why he should give his provision to fugitives, whom he knew not. And David at this was over angry, and rashly swore that he would destroy him and all his; but his wife Abigail was a discreet woman, and perceived their danger, and went out with some servants, and met David with provision, and appeased him; and David thanked God and her that had kept him from rash shedding blood. And when she came back to Nabal, he was drunk at his great feast, and she told him nothing till the morning, and then she told him all; and it struck him to the heart, and ten days after he died; and David took Abigail to be his wife. After this, Saul again pursued David in the wilderness, near Ziph; and David from a mountain saw Saul's camp, and where he lay, and in the night he and Abishai came secretly into the camp, and they were all in a dead sleep; and David came to Saul, and took away his spear and cruse, and went his way. Abishai would have had leave to kill him, but David said, "God forbid; let us stay till he die; let God's hand do it, and not mine."

Then David again pleaded with Saul from the hill; and Saul again relented, and confessed his fault.

But David being weary to be thus hunted, went again with his six hundred men to Achish, a Philistine king of Gath. And he received him, and gave him a town called Ziklag, where he dwelt a year and four months. And David went out with his soldiers, and smote many places of the Amalekites, and other people, and killed them all, and brought away their cattle, and made king Achish believe he had smitten the Israelites, and so was hateful to his own country, that he might trust him.

C. Was it well done of David to tell so many lies?

M. No; he did ill, and we must not imitate him in this. God forbade it by his law, and did not justify David in it, though he had mercy on him. After this, the Philistines gathered an army against Saul, and David was to go with them, and Saul was afraid of them, and Samuel was dead; and Saul inquired of God what he should do, but God gave him no answer. And Saul heard of a witch, or conjuring woman, at Endor, and he masked himself, and went to her unknown, to know his fortune. And he desired her to raise up Samuel; and she caused the shape of Samuel to appear to him, which told him that he and his sons should to-morrow be with him, and Israel be overthrown; and so it came to pass Saul and Jonathan were killed.

C. What did David do the while?

M. He would have gone out with the Philistines, but the lords durst not trust him, but sent him back; and so God kept him out of that battle. But when David was absent, the Amalekites took Ziklag, and burnt it, and took David's wives, and his soldiers' wives and children, which so grieved their hearts that, in their rage, his men talked of stoning David; but he pursued the Amalekites, and overtook them, and recovered all the captives again, and took all the spoil, and destroyed all the Amalekites. But David's kingdom must be told you next.

The Fourteenth Lesson.—The Kingdom of David.

M. When the battle was over, an Amalekite came to David, and thought to please him by telling him that Saul and Jonathan were dead; and that Saul, leaning on his spear, wounded, prayed this man to kill him; and that he did it, and brought his crown and bracelet to David. But David, instead of rewarding him, caused him to be put to death, for killing the Lord's anointed. And he greatly lamented that overthrow, and made a song of lamentation, especially for Jonathan. And God bid David go to Hebron, in Judah, and there they made him king of Judah; but Saul's captain, Abner, and the most of Israel, made Ishbosheth, a son of Saul's, their king. And thus some years the kingdom was divided, till, after long war, Ishbosheth angered Abner, the general, and he vowed to deliver up the kingdom to David: and he came to him to do it; but Joab, David's captain, killed Abner, because he had killed a brother of his: but David detested and lamented the fact. Then two other of Ishbosheth's captains murdered him, and brought his head to David, thinking to be rewarded by him; and he charged them for the murder. Then all Israel made David king. He reigned over Judah only seven years and a half, and over all Israel thirty-three years.

C. And what did he after he was king of all?

M. First, he took mount Zion from the Jebusites of Jerusalem. Then he twice overthrew the Philistines that came against him in battle: and then he fetched the ark of God from the house of Abinadab, in Gibeah, where it had long staid; and oxen drew it on a cart; and when the oxen stumbled, Uzzah, one of Abinadab's sons, put forth his hand to hold the ark, and God struck him dead in the place for his rashness.

C. Why, what great harm was that?

M. The ark was holy, and God would have none presume to meddle with it, but by his appointment. And by this God teacheth us that he will be trusted himself with his worship; and men must not pretend to save it from supposed dangers by their own wit, and will, and way, but only by his appointed means and way.

C. And what did they then with the ark?

M. David was displeased that God killed Uzzah, and was afraid, and durst not receive it, but brought it to the house of Obed-Edom. But when he heard that God blessed Obed-Edom's house because of the ark, then he sent again, and with great music, and dancing, and joy, brought it to mount Zion. And when David lived in peace, he purposed to build a house, or temple, for the tabernacle and ark, and the solemn worship of God. But God forbade him by the prophet Nathan, but promised to build him a house, and that his seed should succeed him on his throne, and not be cut off as the seed of Saul was, and that his son should build a temple for God. After this, David conquered the Philistines, the Moabites, the Ammonites, the Edomites, the Syrians of Damascus, the king of Zobah, and made them tributary, and set garrisons among them, and took their gold and silver, and dedicated it to God. And when they again renewed the war, he conquered the Ammonites and Syrians again: and he found out a lame son of Jonathan's, called Mephibosheth, and gave him all Saul's land, and made him sit at his own table. And yet, after all this, temptation drew him into a heinous sin, which blotted all his glory.

C. What was that?

M. While Joab, his general, was conquering the Ammonites, and besieging their city Rabbah, David, being at the top of prosperity, staid idle at home; and one day, walking on the top of his house, he saw a beautiful woman washing herself, and he suffered lust to possess his heart; and he sent to know who she was, and lay with her, and she was with child by him, while her husband, Uriah, was at the siege in the war. And because adultery was a heinous sin, which God would have punished with shame and death, to hide his own crime, David sent for Uriah, as it were to know the news, and bid him go to his house, thinking that, by laying with his wife, the thing should be concealed; but Uriah lay among the king's servants, and said, while the king's captains lie on the ground and in tents, he would not go eat and drink, and lie with his wife. Then David made him drunk, hoping that then he would have gone home; but still he refused. Then David sent him with a letter to Joab in the army, bidding Joab set him in a place of danger, that he might be killed; which Joab did, and Uriah was killed, and divers with him; and David took his wife to be his wife. So that here he was guilty of lust, adultery, hypocrisy, drunkenness, and murder.

C. Sure he was a very bad man that would do all this.

M. His sad example tells us what a good man may come to by temptation, if he be not watchful, and God do not save him from himself; and it tells how dangerous it is to let in temptation at the first, and to have an ungoverned eye, and to look upon any tempting thing or person in an immodest manner: for when one spark of lust taketh fire on the heart, the flame soon grows great, and is hardly quenched; and one sin draweth men on to another, and another to hide it, and escape the shame and punishment, when all do but increase the mischief which they would avoid.

C. But what did God do with David for this?

M. He sent Nathan the prophet to him, to open the greatness of his sin, and to tell him that for this the sword should never depart from his house, and that God would raise up evil against him out of his own house, even one that should take his wives, and lie with them in the sight of all the people. And then David was struck with deep repentance, and confessed his sin, and begged God's mercy; and God so far forgave him as not to damn, or kill, or depose him; but he killed his child that was begotten in adultery; and he followed him with affliction for it, which brought him low.

C. How did God afflict him?

M. By his own children. First, his son Absalom had a beautiful sister, and Amnon, her brother, by another wife, fell into lust, called love, with her: and when he could not tempt her to lie with him, he forced her; and when he had forced her he hated her: and in revenge for this, her brother Absalom killed his brother Amnon, and fled into another land three years. And when his father pardoned him at last, he flattered the people, and stole their hearts from David, and rebelled against him, and was proclaimed by them king in Hebron. So that David was fain to fly from Jerusalem into the wilderness, from his son Absalom. And Absalom got David's chief counsellor, Ahithophel, on his side, who advised him to follow David suddenly, and destroy him before he gathered strength. But David had a friend called Hushai, that took on him to be for Absalom, and gave him contrary counsel, to stay till all Israel could be gathered together, to make sure work of the battle. And God overruled the rebels' hearts to follow this counsel of Hushai. And when Ahithophel saw that his counsel was not followed, he hanged himself. And when the day of battle came, David's men conquered Absalom's; and Absalom's mule carried him under a thick oak, where he was hanged by the head, and Joab killed him. But David loved him, and mourned for his death. This rebellion of Absalom showed God's justice in punishing David for his sin against Uriah; and it showed the unconstancy and untrustiness of the multitude, that so suddenly, for nothing, would forsake that king that had ruled them with extraordinary success, and sought his life whom they had valued above all men. Yea, after this battle was over, one Sheba rebelled, and the people followed him till he was killed.

C. And what befell them after this?

M. After this God sent a famine on the land three years together. And David inquired of God what was the cause; and God told him that it was because Saul would have destroyed the Gibeonites, to whom Joshua had made a covenant of peace, and so would break the oath of Joshua. And David asked the Gibeonites what satisfaction they would have; and they demanded the lives of seven of Saul's posterity, whom David gave them, and they hanged them up. And after this David had many battles with the Philistines, in which he overcame them.

Lastly. God being offended with Israel for sin, left David to the temptation of Satan, to take the number of all the people, in a carnal confidence in human strength: for which sin, and the people's, God's angel, by a plague, destroyed threescore and ten thousand.

C. Was not the book of Psalms written by David?

M. Most of them were: by which it appeared that he was a prophet and a holy man, devoted to God and his service.

C. For what use was the book of Psalms written?

M. First, to exercise the writer's zeal towards God, by confession of sin, prayers for mercy, thanksgivings and praises unto God; and, next, to be a help for others in the same cases; but especially to be the public liturgy of the Jewish church, in their worship of God in the synagogues and temple.

The Fifteenth Lesson.—Of the Reign and Writings of Solomon.

C. Who was king next after David?

M. Adonijah, a son of David, sought it, which cost him his life; and Joab and Abiathar helped him; whereupon Joab was killed for his former murders of Abner and Amasa, and Abiathar was put from the priesthood. For David, before he died, made Solomon, his younger son, king, by the advice of Nathan the prophet.

C. Did not the kingdom belong, by right, to the eldest?

M. No: for God kept the choice in his own hand, and it was in the people's under him; and he turned the hearts of the people to follow whom he chose. God preferred Solomon before his elder brethren, as he had done David before his elder brethren, and before the sons of Saul; and Moses, the younger, before Aaron, the elder brother; and Judah and Joseph before Reuben, and Jacob before Esau, and Isaac before Ishmael, and Shem before Ham, and Seth and Abel before Cain; and so of many others.

C. What did Solomon do?

M. When he prayed to God, God bade him ask what he should give him, and he asked wisdom. And it pleased God that he preferred that before riches, and honour, and long life; and God gave him greater wisdom than any king of Israel had before or after him; and he gave him with it all the rest. And he abounded in riches and honour, and he built a most rich and beautiful temple at Jerusalem, to be the chief place of God's public worship for all the land, where prayer was made, and sacrifices offered, and priests and Levites employed about them as their officers.

C. How could all the people out of all the countries come so far, and meet in one place?

M. It was a small country, so that they had not very far to travel, and they were to come but very seldom, at some great feasts, and they were not to be all at once in the temple. And their ordinary worship was performed in lesser assemblies at home.

C. What else did Solomon?

M. He governed wisely, and prospered greatly, being the only king that reigned over the twelve tribes in full prosperity and peace. But his prosperity proved a dangerous temptation to him, and he lived in all sorts of fleshly pleasure, and especially had multitudes of wives and concubines; and when he grew old, his wives drew him into the guilt of idolatry; for they were women of several other nations, and worshipped their several idols. And Solomon built, or allowed them, high places for the worship of these idols, and so provoked God against him.

C. Did not you say, that he was the wisest of all the kings of Israel? And could a wise man do so bad?

M. He had more knowledge than any of them, as many great scholars now know more than better men; but it appeareth by their lives, that David, Hezekiah, and Josiah, had more than he of that practical wisdom which consisteth in holiness. And, 2. Wise men may, by temptation, be drawn to folly; and as the wisest man is a fool when he is drunk, so he is when temptations prevail against his wisdom.

C. What books did Solomon write, to show his wisdom?

M. He wrote many: of which God hath preserved us three in the Bible. First, the Book of Proverbs, which containeth the praise of wisdom, and many excellent lessons, especially for young men. Secondly, the Song of Solomon. Thirdly, the book called Ecclesiastes, which seemeth to speak his repentance after his fall; in which he showeth, from his own experience, that all the profits, honours, and pleasures of this world are mere vanity and vexation, and all can give men no more than to eat, and drink, and be merry; that so the flattering world may not deceive us when we should prepare for God's judgments and the life to come.

C. Did not God punish Solomon for so great sin?

M. Yes, he cut off ten of the twelve tribes from the kingdom of his son; who foolishly followed the counsel of rash and bad young men, and had not learned his father's wisdom.

The Sixteenth Lesson.—Of the other Kings of Judah and Israel.

C. How did God cut off the ten tribes from Solomon's son?

M. His son Rehoboam was proud and foolish; and because Solomon, by his great buildings and pomp, had laid great burdens of service and taxes on the people, and they now desired to be eased of them; the old counsellors advised Rehoboam to speak kindly to them, and to ease them, and win their hearts. But the young counsellors advised him to speak roughly to them, and rule them by fear, and keep up his power. And he hearkened to these; whereupon the ten tribes all forsook him, and chose one Jeroboam king.

C. And how did Jeroboam reign?

M. He thought, that if the people went yearly up to Jerusalem to worship, they would be in the power of Rehoboam, and would turn to him again. Therefore he made new places for worship, and made two golden images, like calves, and set them to represent their God; and made priests for them of the basest of the people, who were not of the tribe of Levi. And thus he drew the ten tribes into a course of sin which was their ruin, and for which God at last forsook them.

But God sent a prophet, to prophesy to them, that the altar made for their idol should have their priests burnt on it, and men's bones, by Josiah by name. And when king Jeroboam heard him, he stretched out his hand, and said, "Lay hold on him;" and his hand was dried up, so that he could not pull it to him; and he entreated the prophet to pray for him, which he did, and his hand was restored; and the altar rent, to verify his word: and the king invited him home, and would have rewarded him; but he refused, because God had bid him not to eat or drink in that place. But an old lying prophet went after him, and told him that God bid him call him back, to eat and drink with him; and he believed him, and did so. But because he disobeyed God, a lion killed him as he returned home. By which we see that all men must not be believed that take on them to be sent of God; and that they that preach to others may be destroyed, if they disobey God's word themselves.

C. Did the kingdom continue thus divided?

M. Yes, to the last. Israel had one king, and Judah another. And there was war between Rehoboam and Jeroboam all their days; and both of their people lived in wickedness and idol worship. And the king of Egypt came against Jerusalem, and took away all the rich vessels of gold, that Solomon made.

C. Who were the next kings after them?

M. Rehoboam's son, Abijam, a bad man, succeeded him. And Asa, his son, a better man, succeeded him. And Jehoshaphat, a good king, succeeded him. And Jehoram, a bad man, succeeded him. And Ahaziah, a bad man, was next him; and he being killed, his mother, Athaliah, killed all the royal line, save Joash, that was secretly saved, and she usurped the kingdom; and she was killed. And Joash, a good king, reigned next; and he was murdered. And Amaziah reigned next, and did well; yet he was murdered. And his son, Azariah, reigned next (called also Uzziah); and God made him a leper, for invading the priest's office, by offering; and his son Jotham ruled, and, when he was dead, reigned next; and Ahaz, a bad man, succeeded him; and Hezekiah, a good king, came next him. Manasseh, a most wicked man, was next. Amon, a bad man, was next him; and he being murdered, his son Josiah, a good king, was next. Jehoahaz was next him; he was wicked, and the king of Egypt took him, and set his brother Eliakim, called Jehoiakim, in his stead: he was bad, and made subject to Nebuchadnezzar: and his son Jehoiachin was next. He was wicked; and Nebuchadnezzar carried him, and all the chief of the people, captives to Babylon; and over the rest he made his uncle, Mattaniah, king, called Zedekiah. He was wicked, and rebelled against Nebuchadnezzar, who took him, and put out his eyes, and killed his sons, and destroyed Jerusalem; and carried him, and all the chief of the people left, to Babylon; and set one Gedaliah over the poor in the country, who was presently murdered. And thus ended the kingdom of Judah, by captivity.

C. And who succeeded Jeroboam, and what became of the kingdom of the ten tribes of Israel?

M. All that came after Jeroboam followed him, in his sin of idolatry, to keep the people from going to Jerusalem. Nadab came next Jeroboam. Baasha murdered him, and came next. Elah was next. Zimri murdered him, when he found him drunken, and reigned next; he killed also the king's kindred, and reigned but a week, before Omri was chosen king by the people; who besieged Zimri, and made him set fire to his house, and burn himself. Omri, a wicked man, was next. And Ahab, more wicked, next him. Ahaziah was next. His brother, Jehoram, was next. Jehu killed him, and was next. Jehoahaz was next. Joash was next. Another Jeroboam was next. Next him, was Zechariah. Shallum murdered him, and was next. Menahem killed him, and was next. Then Pekahiah. Pekah killed him, and was next. Hoshea killed him, and was next; and in his days Shalmaneser, king of Assyria, carried him, and all the chief people, away, and sent men of other countries into the land; who together feared God, and worshipped their own idols. And so ended the kingdom of Israel, before that of Judah.

C. But what great things fell out in all this time?

M. The greatest thing for our notice was, the many prophets that God sent to warn them, and what they did, and how they were used by these kings.

C. Who were these prophets?

M. 1. Ahijah was sent to prophesy Jeroboam's reign against Solomon, when he sinned. 2. Shemaiah was sent to forbid Judah to fight against Jeroboam, for Rehoboam. 3. A man of God was sent from Judah to foretell Jeroboam that Josiah should destroy his altar, and burn his priests on it. 4. When Jeroboam's son, Abijah, was sick, Ahijah, the prophet, foretold his death, and the destruction of Jeroboam's wicked house. 5. Azariah is sent to Asa, to rid Judah of idols. 6. Hanani was sent to reprove Asa, for trusting to Syria for help; and, though otherwise he had done well, he was in a rage against the prophet, and imprisoned him, and oppressed some of the people; and in his sickness sought not to God, but to the physicians. 7. Jehoshaphat sent his princes and Levites, to teach the law of the Lord in the cities of Judah; and when he joined with Ahab in war, the prophet Jehu was sent to reprove him. 8. The same Jehu is sent to prophesy against king Baasha. 9. Elijah, in Ahab's days, prophesieth, that Israel should have no rain, but famine, three years. And when he fled to a brook-side, God sent ravens, to carry to him bread and flesh twice a-day. Then the brook was dried up; and God sent him to Zarephath, near Sidon, to a widow woman, to be fed. And the woman had nothing left but a little meal and oil, to make one cake for herself and son, before they died. And Elijah bid her make one for him first, and told her from God, that the meal and the oil should not waste and fail till rain came. And the woman believed him, and they all lived on that meal and oil a full year, and it wasted not, for God secretly renewed it. Then the woman's son died: and Elijah prayed to God, and laid himself upon the child, and God restored the soul and life of the child.

And the third year, God bid Elijah go show himself to Ahab: and wicked Ahab had a more wicked wife, Jezebel, who killed the prophets of the Lord. But yet he had a governor of his house, called Obadiah, who greatly feared God, and hid two hundred prophets, by fifties, in a cave, and fed them. To this Obadiah Elijah appeared, and bid him go tell Ahab of him; and promised to appear to him. And the king met Elijah, and said, "Art thou he that troubleth Israel?" And Elijah said, "I have not troubled Israel, but thou and thy father's house, in that you have forsaken the Lord, and followed Baalim." And to convince him, he bid him gather Israel and Baal's prophets to mount Carmel. So he gathered eight hundred and fifty false prophets, that Jezebel maintained. And Elijah said to all the people, "How long halt ye between two opinions? If the Lord be God, follow him; but if Baal be God, follow him." And he said, "I only remain a prophet of the Lord, and Baal's prophets are four hundred and fifty;" the other four hundred belonged to the groves. So he bid them take a bullock, and cut him in pieces for a sacrifice, and lay it on wood without fire, and he would do the same by another bullock; and let each call on his God, and let him that answereth by fire be their God. And they did so; and Baal's prophets cried, "O Baal, hear us!" and Elijah mocked them, and said, their god was talking, or pursuing, or in a journey, or asleep, and must be awaked. And they cried, and cut themselves till they bled, as their manner was, but no fire came. Then Elijah repaired God's altar, and laid on the wood and sacrifice, and made a trench about the altar, and he made them pour water on the sacrifice and wood three times, till the trench was full; and he prayed to God, and a fire came and consumed the flesh, and the wood, and the stones, and the water. And when the people saw it, they fell on their faces and cried, "The Lord he is God! the Lord he is God!" And Elijah bade the people kill all the prophets of Baal; and they obeyed him, and killed them. Then Elijah bade king Ahab haste up, for rain was coming, and it rained plentifully.

C. But how did the king take the death of his prophets?

M. He told his wife Jezebel, and she swore that she would take away the life of Elijah the next day: and Elijah fled into Judah, and went into the wilderness, and prayed God to end his life; and he fell asleep, and an angel waked him, and bid him arise and eat. And he saw by him a cake baked on coals, and a cruse of water, and he did eat and drink, and slept again: and the angel came again, and bid him eat and drink, for he had far to go. And he went to Horeb, the mount of God, forty days, in the strength of that meat. As he was there in a cave, God spake to him and said, "What dost thou here, Elijah?" and he said, "I have been very jealous for the Lord, because the children of Israel have forsaken thy covenant, thrown down thine altars, and slain the prophets, and I only am left, and they seek my life also." And after a wind, that tore the rocks, and an earthquake, and a fire, had passed by him, God spake in a still, small voice, and bid him go and anoint Hazael king over Syria, and Jehu king over Israel, and Elisha to be a prophet in his stead; and God told him, he had yet seven thousand in Israel that had not bowed to Baal. So Elijah went, and did but cast his mantle on Elisha, and he left, and followed, and served him.

C. But what became of king Ahab, and Jezebel?

M. Shortly after, Benhadad, king of Syria, raised an army against him, and commanded him to surrender to him all that he had: Ahab was ready to yield, but the elders of Israel were against it; and though Ahab was wicked, God, in mercy, sent a prophet to him, to bid him not to fear that great multitude, for God would deliver them into his hand; and he told him how to order the battle: and so the Syrians were overthrown. And the prophet told Ahab, that at the return of the year they would come again, and bid him prepare. And so it came to pass, for the Syrians told their king, that the gods of Israel were gods of the hills, but, if he would fight in the plains, he should be too hard for them. But God would not put up that reproach, but sent a prophet to bid Ahab fight with them again, and he should conquer; which he did, and then the Syrians fled into a city, and a wall fell upon twenty and seven thousand of them that were left. And Benhadad and his servants came in sackcloth, with ropes on their heads, to beg for life of Ahab; and he let him go: whereupon God sent another prophet to tell Ahab, that because he had dismissed one whom God had appointed to destruction, his life should go for his life.

After this Naboth, a subject of Ahab, had a vineyard, which lay near to Ahab's house, and Ahab desired it, to make him a garden, and offered him money, or a better, for it. But Naboth refused, because it had been the inheritance of his fathers. This so offended Ahab that he took to his bed, (and would not eat,) in discontent. But his wife Jezebel told him that this was unmeet for a king, and bid him be merry, and she would give him Naboth's vineyard. So she wrote letters to the nobles and elders of the city where Naboth dwelt, in Ahab's name, and sealed them with his seal, requiring them to proclaim a fast, and set up Naboth, and get two wicked men to swear that he blasphemed God and the king, and so to stone him to death as guilty. And they did all that was required of them.

C. Could not the king have taken it without this?

M. No; God had given the people their inheritances, and they knew that the king might not take them from any that did not forfeit them: and they that were so wicked as to obey the king in perjury and murder, yet would not give him an arbitrary power over their inheritances and lives. But God sent Elijah to Ahab, when he went to take possession of the vineyard: and he said, "Hast thou killed, and taken possession?" and Ahab said, "Hast thou found me, O my enemy?" And Elijah said, "I have found thee, because thou hast sold thyself to work evil:" and he told him, that in the place where dogs licked the blood of Naboth, they should lick his blood, and all his house should be destroyed; and that the dogs should eat Jezebel by the wall of Jezreel, and dogs and birds should eat his household. And when Ahab heard this, he humbled himself in sackcloth, with fasting: and God so far suspended his judgments as to tell Elijah that, because he humbled himself, this destruction of his house should not come till he was dead.

C. And how did God execute this judgment?

M. After three years, Ahab had a mind to recover Ramoth, a bordering city, from the Syrians; and Jehoshaphat, king of Judah, coming to visit him, he persuaded him to join with him in the war, which he did: and Jehoshaphat desired him first to inquire of the Lord, what they should do; and king Ahab gathered four hundred of his own prophets, and inquired of them, and they bid him go, for God would deliver the city into his hand. But Jehoshaphat asked whether there was never a prophet of the Lord to inquire of, and Ahab said, "There is one Micaiah, but I hate him, for he doth not prophesy good of me, but evil." Jehoshaphat said, "Let not the king say so:" so the two kings sat in their robes, and all the prophets prophesied good to them; and said, "Go and prosper:" and one of them, Zedekiah, made iron horns, and said, "With these shalt thou push the Syrians till thou hast consumed them." And they that went to call Micaiah, told him what all the prophets said, and persuaded him to be conformable, and say as the rest did: but he protested that he would speak the word of God, whatever it should be. And when the king demanded it of him, he said, "I saw all Israel scattered on the hills, as sheep without a shepherd;" and the Lord said, "These have no master, let them return in peace." And Ahab said to Jehoshaphat, "Did not I tell thee that he would prophesy no good of me, but evil?" And Micaiah told him, that he saw the Lord on his throne, and the host of heaven about him, and that he gave leave to an evil spirit to be a lying spirit in the mouth of all Ahab's prophets, to persuade him to go and fall at Ramoth. And Zedekiah struck Micaiah, and said, "Which way went the Spirit of the Lord from me to speak to thee?" And Micaiah told him, that he should see in that day when he should go into an inner chamber to hide himself. And king Ahab said, "Put this fellow in prison, and feed him with the bread and water of affliction, till I return in peace:" and Micaiah said, "If thou return in peace, the Lord hath not spoken by me;" and bid the people all to hear this. So Ahab and Jehoshaphat went out to war, and Ahab was mortally wounded with an arrow, and was carried to Samaria, and died there, and the dogs licked his blood, but Jehoshaphat escaped. But Jehu the prophet was sent thus to reprove him, "Shouldest thou help the ungodly, and love them that hate the Lord? therefore is wrath upon thee from before the Lord."

10. After this, divers nations joined in war against Jehoshaphat, and he prayed earnestly to God, and God raised a prophet, Jehaziel, to bid them not fear, for God would deliver them without fighting; and they believed the prophet, and went towards their enemies with songs of praise to God; and God made their enemies fight with one another, so that the Jews found them dead on the ground, and were three days gathering all the spoil: and they returned home with psalms of praise, and Jehoshaphat set just judges and teachers through all the land.

11. Yet did this good king, after all this, join himself with Ahaziah, king of Israel, who succeeded Ahab, in sending out a fleet of ships to sea: and God sent Eliezer, a prophet, to tell him that for this God would break his ships; and so it came to pass.

12. Ahaziah, king of Israel, fell from an upper chamber; and was sick; and he sent to inquire of idols whether he should recover; and Elijah met his messengers, and bid them tell him that for this he should die, and not come down from his bed. And the king sent a captain, with fifty soldiers, to fetch Elijah, and at the word of Elijah, God sent down fire from heaven, which consumed the captain and all his soldiers. Then the king sent another captain with fifty more, and fire from heaven consumed them also. And the king sent yet another captain with fifty more; and this captain fell on his knees, and entreated Elijah to spare his life. And an angel of God spake to Elijah, and bid him go to the king and fear not. And he went and told him, that for inquiring of Baal, and not of God, he should die: and so he did; and Jehoram reigned in his stead.

13. After this came the time that Elijah must depart from earth; and he prayed Elisha to tarry where he was, for God had sent him to Bethel. But he would not, but went with him: and the sons of the prophets told Elisha that God would take away his master that day; and he said, "I know it; hold your peace." And Elijah said to Elisha, "Tarry here, I pray thee, for the Lord hath sent me to Jericho;" but he would not leave him. And the prophets of Jericho told him, that the Lord would take away his master that day; and he said, "I know it; hold ye your peace." And Elijah said, "Tarry here, I pray thee, for the Lord hath sent me to Jordan;" but he would not leave him. And fifty prophets followed them at a distance, to see the issue: and Elijah, with his mantle, smote the waters of Jordan, and they divided, and they two went over dry. And Elijah said to Elisha, "Ask what I shall do for thee before I be taken away from thee:" and he asked that a double portion of his spirit might be upon him. Elijah said, "Thou hast asked a hard thing; but if thou see me when I am taken from thee, it shall be so to thee, else not." And there appeared a chariot of fire, and horses of fire, and parted them; and Elijah went up by a whirlwind into heaven, and Elisha saw, and cried out, "My father, my father, the chariot of Israel, and the horsemen thereof." And he saw them no more; and he rent his own clothes, and took up the mantle of Elijah that fell from him, and with it he struck the waters of Jordan, and said, "Where is the Lord God of Elijah?" and the waters parted, and he returned over dry. And when the sons of the prophets saw it, they said, "The spirit of Elijah resteth on Elisha;" and they bowed to him. And they entreated that fifty men might go to see whether God had not cast Elijah on some mountain: and Elisha forbade them, but after yielded to their importunity. And they went and searched, but found him not. And so Elisha became like him.

14. The first miracle that Elisha did after the dividing of the waters of Jordan was this: the city Jericho was pleasantly situate, but the waters were naught, and the land barren. And he cast salt into the water, and said, "Thus saith the Lord, I have healed these waters;" and they were forthwith healed.

15. And as he went from thence little children mocked him, and said, "Go up, thou bald-head." And God moved him to curse them, and there came two bears out of the wood, and tore forty-and-two children.

C. Was not that too cruel a revenge?

M. It was God that did it, who can do no wrong, and knoweth what he doth. And it is like he did it rather to be a warning to children afterward, to take heed of mocking any, but especially holy men.

16. After king Ahaziah, Jehoram reigned, and in his days Moab rebelled against Israel, and the king of Israel got Jehoshaphat, king of Judah, and the king of Edom, to help him in war: but when they passed seven days through the wilderness, the three

kings, and their armies, and horses, were like to perish, because they found no water. But Jehoshaphat asked for a prophet of the Lord to inquire of, and king Jehoram called Elisha: and Elisha said to him, "What have I to do with thee? get thee to the prophets of thy father and mother. Surely were it not that I regard the presence of Jehoshaphat king of Judah, I would not look toward thee, nor see thee. Then Elisha said, Make this valley full of ditches: for thus saith the Lord, You shall not see wind or rain, yet the valley shall be filled with water: and also God will deliver the Moabites into your hand."

And so it came to pass: water came from towards Edom, and filled the country; and they overthrew the Moabites, and destroyed much of their country. And the king of Moab sacrificed his son and heir to his idol god on the wall before them, and so they left him.

17. After this a prophet's widow was in debt, and the creditors came to take her two sons as bondmen for the debt; and she sought to Elisha: and he asked her what she had in the house; and she said, "Nothing, save a pot of oil:" and he bid her go borrow empty vessels enough, and pour out the oil into them; and she did so, and the oil ran as long as she had ever a vessel to receive it: and he bid her go sell the oil and pay the creditors, and live on the rest.

18. Then Elisha went to Shunem, where was a great woman, who constrained him to come in, and eat with her, which he did as oft as he passed by: and she said to her husband, "I perceive that this is a holy man of God that oft passeth by us: let us make for him a little chamber on the wall, and set a bed, and a table, and a stool, and a candlestick, that he may turn in hither:" and they did so. And he called the woman, and asked her what he should do for her: but she said that she lived among her own people, and wanted nothing: but Gehazi, his servant, told him she had no child, and her husband was old: and the prophet told her that "at that season she should bear a son;" and she did so. And when the child was grown up, as he went to his father to the reapers, he was taken with the head-ache, and shortly died; and she laid him on Elisha's bed, and rode speedily to Elisha, and constrained him to go home with her; but he sent his man Gehazi before with a staff, and bid him lay it on the face of the child, but he revived not: and when Elisha came he went up and lay on the child, and put his mouth on his mouth, and his eyes on his eyes, and his hands on his hands, and the flesh of the child waxed warm; and he walked awhile, and then did so again, and the child revived, and he gave him to the mother.

19. After this, in a dearth, many sons of the prophets came to him, and he bid his servant make pottage for them: and he ignorantly gathered wild gourds (a horrid, bitter, violent plant); and they cried out, "There is death in the pot:" and he bid them cast in meal, and the pottage after had no harm in it.

20. After this, he multiplied a little food, to satisfy many people.

21. The king of Syria had a great man, captain of his army, called Naaman, but he had the leprosy: and a little maid of Israel, whom they had taken among the captives, waited on his wife: and she said, "Would my lord were with the prophet that is in Samaria; for he would recover him of his leprosy:" and Naaman was told what she said, and the king of Syria bid him go to Samaria, and he would write a letter from him to the king of Israel: which was that he would cure Naaman of his leprosy. But the king of Israel thought he did it to pick a quarrel with him: when Elisha heard of it, he sent to the king, saying, "Let him come to me, and he shall know that there is a prophet in Israel." Now Naaman brought with him ten talents of silver, and six thousand pieces of gold, and ten changes of raiment; and he came to the door of Elisha, and Elisha sent a messenger to him, and said, "Go wash seven times in Jordan, and thy flesh shall come again, and thou shalt be clean." But Naaman went away in rage, and said, "I thought he would have come out to me, and called on his God, and moved his hand over the place, and recover it: are not the waters of Damascus better than all the waters of Israel?" but his servants humbly appeased him, saying, "If the prophet had bid thee do some great thing, wouldst thou not have done it? How much rather when he saith to thee, Wash and be clean." So he went and dipped himself seven times in Jordan, and was healed. Then he returned to the prophet and said, "Now I know that there is no God in all the earth but the God of Israel." And he urged him to take a gift of his money; but the prophet utterly refused it. And Naaman desired to have two mules' load of the earth of Israel, that on it he might sacrifice to God when he came home. But when he was gone, the prophet's servant, Gehazi, coveted his money, and thought it was his master's weakness to refuse it from so great a man; and he ran after him with a lie, and told him that even now two young men, sons of the prophets, were come to his master, and he desired him to give them a talent of silver, and two changes of raiment: and Naaman made him take two talents. And when he came in to his master, he asked him where he had been; and he lied again, and said he went no whither. But Elisha said, "Went not my heart with thee when the man turned again from his chariot to meet thee? Is this a time to receive money, &c. The leprosy of Naaman shall cleave to thee, and to thy seed for ever: and he went out from his presence a leper."

22. After this the young prophets desired him that they might go to Jordan, and make there a larger house for them and him to dwell together in; and he went with them: and as they cut down wood by the river side, one man's axe-head fell into the water; and he said, "Alas, master! it was borrowed;" and Elisha made the iron to rise and swim, and they took it up.

23. After this, the king of Syria oft attempted a war against the king of Israel: and Elisha still told him which way the king of Syria would come, so that he still avoided him. Then the king of Syria thought that some of his servants betrayed him; but they said, "It is the prophet that tells the king of Israel what thou sayst in thy bedchamber." And the king of Syria sent spies to know where to find and take Elisha: and finding him in Dothan, they beset the city in the night with an army, and in the morning his servant rose and saw them, and cried out, "Alas, master! what shall we do?" And Elisha said, "Fear not, fear not: for they that be with us are more than they that be against us:" and he prayed God to open his man's eyes, and he saw mountains full of horses and chariots of fire about Elisha: and Elisha prayed God to strike the Syrian army with blindness, and it was done. And Elisha went to them, and told them they were out of the way, and bid them follow him, and he would bring them to the place where the prophet was. And he led them into the midst of Samaria, the king's chief city; and then prayed God to open their eyes, and they found themselves in Samaria: and the king of Israel would have killed them; but the prophet made him set them meat, and send them home.

24. After this, the king of Syria besieged Samaria so long, till the famine was so extreme, that a woman cried to the king for justice, because another woman and she agreed to kill, and boil, and eat, their sons by turn; and when they had eaten hers, the other woman hid her son. This put the king of Israel past patience, and he vowed to kill Elisha, because God did not deliver them. And Elisha was sitting in his house with the elders, and he said to them, "This son of a murderer hath sent to take away my head; but shut the door when the messenger cometh." And the king said, "This evil is of the Lord; why should I wait any longer?" And Elisha said, "Thus saith the Lord, To-morrow about this time shall a measure of fine flour be sold for a shekel, and two measures of barley for a shekel." And one of the king's lords said, "If the Lord would make windows in heaven how could this be?" And Elisha said, "Thou shalt see it with thine eyes, but shalt not eat of it." And there were four lepers at the gate of Samaria, and they agreed to cast themselves on the mercy of the Syrians, having no other hope of life. And when they came where the camp was, there was no one there, for God had made them hear as the noise of many armies, and they thought the Israelites had hired the Egyptians against them, and they all fled in fear, and left their provisions behind them. And when the four lepers had eaten and drunk their fill, they brought the news into the city (having taken and hid as much silver and gold as they would): and when the king heard it, he thought the Syrians had retired in craft to entice them out and take them; and he sent a few horsemen to see; who found all the way to Jordan where they fled, spread with garments cast away: so the city went out, and had all their treasure and provisions; and all was as cheap as the prophet had foretold. And the king set that lord that spake against the prophet's words, in the gate of the city, and there the crowding people trod him to death.

25. After this, the woman of Shunem, whose son Elisha restored to life, was told by him the famine would continue seven years, and he bid her go sojourn elsewhere; and she went among the Philistines till the seven years were expired; and her house and land, in the mean time, were possessed by others, and she went to petition the king that they might be restored: and just when she came, Gehazi was telling the king how Elisha restored her son to life, and he said, "This is the woman, and this is her son:" and the king caused all to be restored to her.

26. After this, Elisha went to Damascus, in Syria; and king Benhadad heard of it, and he lay sick, and he sent Hazael to the prophet to know whether he should recover. And the prophet said, he may recover, (as to his disease,) but he shall surely die: and he looked on Hazael, and wept: and he asked him why he wept? "And he said, I know the evil thou wilt do to Israel: thou wilt kill men and children, and rip up the women: and Hazael said, Am I a dog, that I should do this? And Elisha said, God hath showed me that thou shalt be king of Syria." And when he heard this, he went home, and killed the king (stifling him by spreading a wet cloth on his face). And he reigned in his stead.

27. After this, Jehoram, king of Israel, was wounded in a war at Ramoth, against Hazael, and he went to Jezreel to be healed; and Elisha called a young prophet, and said, "Go to Ramoth, to Jehu, (one of the king's captains,) and call him into an inner chamber, and pour this box of oil on his head, and say, Thus saith the Lord, I have anointed thee king over Israel; and when thou hast done, flee away:" and he did so, and told him he must cut off all the house of Ahab for their sin. And the rest of the captains made Jehu tell them what he said, and when they heard it, all their hearts were turned to fulfil the prophecy; and they set up Jehu, and marched with him against his master Jehoram, and he met him at Naboth's vineyard and killed him, and cast his carcass there, as God had foretold: and he killed Ahaziah, king of Judah, that had come to visit Jehoram: and he went to Jezreel, and made them throw down Jezebel through a window, where she died, and the dogs ate her flesh, all save her palms of her hands, and her feet, and skull; and caused all Ahab's sons to be killed, even seventy persons, and all his kindred and priests, and great men; and he killed forty-two of the brethren of Ahaziah, king of Judah, that were going to visit king Jehoram's sons; and he took on that yet he would worship Baal, and made all Baal's prophets come to sacrifice; and he killed them all, and made Baal's house a draught house, and burnt all their images with the fire. But he yet continued in Jeroboam's sin of false worship.

28. Before this, Jehoram, king of Judah, was wicked, and worshipped Baal, and killed his brethren; and Elisha sent a letter to him to tell him that God would cut off his dominions by Hazael, and would strike him with a sickness, so that his bowels should fall out; and so all this came to pass.

29. And in Judah, when king Ahaziah was killed, and his wicked mother, Athaliah, killed his brethren, that she might reign, his sister, that was wife to Jehoiada, the priest, had a young son, Joash, six years old; and in the seventh year Jehoiada, the priest, got many on his side, and killed Athaliah, and made Joash king at seven years old: but the high priest ruled in his name, and put down the idols, and set up the worship of God: and Joash did well all the days of Jehoiada; but when he was dead, the princes about him drew him from God to idolatry. And God sent Zechariah, the son of Jehoiada, to say to them, "Why transgress ye the command of the Lord, that ye cannot prosper? because you have forsaken the Lord, he also hath forsaken you." But they stoned this prophet to death by this unthankful king's commandment, even in the court of the house of the Lord; and when he died, he said, "The Lord look upon it, and require it." And so he did: for at the end of the year the Syrians came with a small army, and destroyed all the princes from among the people, and sent away the spoil: and the king was diseased, and his servants killed him, who had turned from God, and murdered the son of him that saved his life, and made him king; God avenging his cruel ingratitude.

30. And when his son, king Amaziah, preparing for a war with Edom, trusting to numbers, hired a hundred thousand Israelites for a hundred talents, to help him, and God sent a prophet to bid him send home the Israelites, for God was not with them: but the king was loth to lose his hundred talents; but the prophet prevailed, and he sent them home: and he went with his own men, and conquered and destroyed the Edomites: yet was he so sottish as to carry home the idol gods of Edom, and worship them as his gods. And God sent a prophet to ask him why he would seek to the gods that could not save their own people? But the king proudly answered him, "Art thou made of the king's counsel? forbear, why shouldst thou be smitten?" and the prophet forbore, but told him that he knew God had determined to destroy him, because of this his sin and disobedience. And so it fell out; for he provoked the king of Israel to fight with him (for

the soldiers which he hired and dismissed had, in anger, plundered his country). And he was conquered, and Jerusalem pillaged, and the walls broken down; and after this his own servants murdered him.

31. In Israel, the Syrians grievously oppressed them; and when Elisha lay dying, Josiah the king came to visit him, and lament over him. And he bid the king open the window and shoot an arrow, and strike the ground, and he struck thrice. And the prophet was angry, and told him now he should conquer the Syrians but thrice; but if he had struck six or seven times he should have consumed them. And when Elisha was dead and buried, the Moabites invaded the land, and being burying a dead man in haste, they put him into Elisha's sepulchre, and when the dead body touched his bones he revived, and stood up.

32. When Uzziah (called Azariah) was king in Judah, and did well and prospered, at last his heart was puffed up, and he would needs burn incense to the Lord: and when the priests told him it belonged not to him, but was their office, he was wroth with them; and suddenly God struck him with a leprosy, and they thrust him out, and he hasted out himself, and was shut up as a leper to the day of his death.

33. Before Israel was carried away captive by the Assyrians, in the reign of Hoshea, all the prophets called them from their sin, and foretold God's judgments, but they would not hear them.

34. In the reign of good king Hezekiah, the king of Assyria sent an army against Jerusalem, where Rabshakeh blasphemed God, and bid the people not to trust in him, for no God could save his people from the Assyrian power. And God sent Isaiah the prophet to tell Hezekiah, that as he prayed to God, and trusted in him, God would deliver him, and put his hook in the nostrils of the Assyrian king. And that night the angel of the Lord killed a hundred and fourscore and five thousand of the Assyrian army, and in the morning they were all found dead. And shortly after, when their king, Sennacherib, at Nineveh, was worshipping in the house of his idol god, his own sons killed him.

35. After this, Hezekiah was dangerously sick, and he earnestly prayed to God to spare him, and God sent Isaiah, the prophet, to tell him of a medicine to cure him, and to promise him fifteen years' longer time to live. And when Hezekiah desired a sign to confirm his belief, God made the dial's shadow go backward ten degrees to satisfy him. But after this God was not pleased that Hezekiah showed the king of Babylon's ambassadors all his treasure; and he sent Isaiah to tell him that all that, with his posterity, should be carried to Babylon.

36. When his son, Manasseh, proved a wicked, bloody idolater, worse than the heathens, God sent his prophets to tell them that he would cast them off as he had done the Israelites. Yet this wicked king, when he lay a prisoner in the fetters of the Assyrians, humbled himself to God, and repented, and God heard his prayers, and delivered him.

37. When his son Ammon, a bad man, was killed, his son Josiah reigned, and restored the true religion. And Hilkiah, the priest, sent him the book of Moses' law, where, reading God's threatenings, he humbled himself. and made all the land reform and pray. And God sent him word by Huldah, a prophetess, that for the great sins that had been done, God would give up the Jews into captivity, but because he had humbled himself, it should not be done in his days. Yet after this, even this good Josiah would needs rashly go out to war against the king of Egypt, against God's warning of him, and was killed, on which occasion, Jeremiah wrote his lamentation.

38. In the reign of Uzziah, Jotham, Ahaz, Hezekiah, the prophet Isaiah reproved the sins of the Jews, and prophesied of their punishments, and of Christ and his kingdom.

39. In the reign of Josiah, Jehoiakim, and Zedekiah, did Jeremiah prophesy against their sin, and of their punishment, and captivity, and was cruelly used for it, till the Babylonians delivered him.

40. In the captivity, Ezekiel prophesied: and Hosea, Joel, Amos, Obadiah, Jonah, Micah, Nahum, Habakkuk, Zephaniah, Haggai, Zechariah, and Malachi, some before, and some in the captivity.

The Seventeenth Lesson.—The History of the Captivated Jews.

C. What became of the Jews after that they were carried captives to Babylon?

M. The most that we are concerned to know of them is contained in the books of Daniel, Esther, Ezra, Nehemiah, and in the Apocryphal book of the Maccabees, and other common history.

C. What saith the book of Daniel of them?

M. 1. When Nebuchadnezzar carried them to Babylon, he gave order to Ashpenaz to choose some of the most comely and ingenious children of the Jews, and teach them the Chaldean tongue, and nourish and breed them, to be fit to stand before the king. So he chose Daniel, and Hananiah, and Mishael, and Azariah; but the Jews being forbidden by God to eat some such meat as the king sent them, they refused them, and the king's wine, and craved leave to feed on pulse and water; and by this they became fairer and fatter than all the rest. And God gave to Daniel an extraordinary spirit to prophesy, and interpret dreams: and the king having an extraordinary dream, required all his soothsayers and wise men to tell him both what the dream was and what its interpretation was, or else he would destroy them. And when none of them could do it, Daniel undertaketh it, and telleth the king both; and for this the king advanced him to be chief in government over his sages, and the other three were made rulers also at his request.

But the king, being an idolater, made a golden image, and commanded all to worship it. But these three religious Jews refused, though he threatened to burn them in a furnace. They told him that the God whom they served was able to deliver them out of his hand; but if he would not, yet be it known to him, they would not worship his image. Upon this, he caused a furnace to be made extraordinary hot, and them to be cast into it. And the flame catched and burnt up those that cast them in. But God kept the flame from hurting them; and the king saw them walk unburnt in the flaming furnace, and one with them that was glorious, like an angel, called the Son of God. And he being astonished, called them out, and made a decree, that all his subjects should honour the true God, that had saved them; and whoever would speak against him should be cut in pieces, and their houses made dunghills. After this Nebuchadnezzar had an extraordinary dream, which did portend his own fall, and that he should be cast out of his kingdom, among brutes. And Daniel expounded it to him, when no other could. And accordingly it came to pass; for a year after, as he was proudly boasting of Babylon, and the glory of his kingdom, a voice from heaven told him, that the kingdom was departed from him; and his understanding was taken from him, and they drove him among the beasts. But his reason returned to him, and he was restored, and praised God.

After this, Belshazzar, another king, made a great feast for his lords; and as they were drinking riotously, in the holy vessels that were taken from God's temple at Jerusalem, a hand appeared, writing upon the wall, signifying that his kingdom should be taken from him, and given to the Medes and Persians. And none but Daniel could expound the words. And that very night Belshazzar was killed, and Darius took the kingdom.

After this, Darius set a hundred and twenty princes over his kingdom, and, over these, three presidents, of whom Daniel was chief. And these princes envied Daniel, and sought to find some accusation against him, to destroy him; but he was so blameless, that they could find none. Therefore they resolved to fetch somewhat against him for his religion, concerning the law of God. And they saw that he was much in prayer; and they got the king, by importunity, to pass a decree, that no man should put up any petition to God, or man, save only to the king, for thirty days, on pain of being cast to the lions, in their den. When Daniel knew that the decree was signed, he opened his window, and thrice a day prayed in his house, as he was wont. Then these lords accused him to the king, for breaking the law; and the king was sorry, and would have saved him, but upon their importunity he yielded, and Daniel was cast into the lions' den; but they hurt him not. The king passed the night in trouble, and early in the morning went to the den, and cried, "O Daniel, is thy God, whom thou servest, able to deliver thee from the lions?" And Daniel said, "My God hath sent his angel, and shut the mouths of the lions, that they have not hurt me, because before him I was innocent, and before thee have done no hurt." Then the king was glad, and caused Daniel to be taken up, and those to be cast in that accused him, with their wives and children; and the lions broke their bones in pieces, ere they came to the ground. And the king made a decree, that all should fear and honour the God of Daniel.

This Daniel was a holy man, and spent much of his time in fasting and prayer; and God sent an angel to him, that told him of the great changes of the kingdoms of the world that were to come, and told him the very time when Christ was to come, and to be put to death.

C. What saith the book of Ezra of the Jews?

M. It tells us how king Cyrus, before named by Jeremiah, was stirred up by God to rebuild the temple at Jerusalem; and how he restored the captive Jews to their own land; and how Zerubbabel and Joshua set upon the work; and how malicious enemies hindered them; and how Darius prosecuted the work, though the enemies accused the builders, as contriving a rebellion: and how the building was finished; and how king Artaxerxes after sent Ezra, with the rest of the captives, who, by fasting, and prayer, and confession of sin, and teaching the people the law of God, restored religion, which was almost lost in the captivity.

C. What doth the book of Nehemiah tell us?

M. It tells us how king Artaxerxes sent Nehemiah to build up the wall of the city Jerusalem; and how he and the people unweariedly carried on the work; and how malignant enemies accused and hindered them; and how he, with Ezra and the chief of the people, by fasting, and prayer, and repentance, engaged all in a covenant with God to keep his law; and how they informed the people, and instructed them, and restored religion.

C. What doth the book of Esther tell us?

M. It tells us how king Ahasuerus, putting away his queen, chose Esther, a Jew, in her stead; and how Mordecai, her kinsman, that bred her up, was preferred hereupon; and how proud Haman, who was greatest with the king, hated him, because he bowed not to him; and how Haman, that he might destroy Mordecai, made the king believe, that the Jews were a rebellious people, against the king's profit, and got a commission to destroy them all: but Esther petitioned the king, and obtained their deliverance. And Mordecai, having discovered a conspiracy against the king, the king resolved to advance him more, and asked Haman how that man should be used, whom the king did delight to honour? And Haman, thinking it could be none but himself, said, "Let the royal apparel be brought which the king useth to wear, and the horse that the king rideth upon, and the crown royal that is set upon his head, and let them be delivered to the hand of one of the king's most noble princes, that they may array the man with them, and bring him on horseback through the streets of the city, and proclaim before him, Thus shall it be done to the man whom the king delighteth to honour:" and the king commanded Haman himself to do all this to Mordecai whom he hated, which broke his heart, but he dared not disobey. After this, queen Esther told the king, how Haman had got his commission to destroy all the Jews, and the king's wrath was kindled against him, and he caused him to be hanged on a very high gallows, which Haman had made to hang Mordecai on. And also the queen procured a commission from the king, giving power to the Jews to kill all their malicious enemies that would have destroyed them; which they executed.

C. What is it that the history of the Maccabees tells us?

M. It tells us the state of the Jews that returned and dwelt in Judea, and how they were governed by the high priest, and what wars they had with many great princes: but because this book is no part of the Bible, I will say no more of it; though you may profitably read it, to know the state of the Jews, till the birth of Jesus Christ.

C. But why must I know all these stories? What are they to me any more than any other history?

M. I shall tell you that the next time: all this is to prepare you to know one that is God and man, Jesus Christ; and what he hath done and will do for the salvation of man.

The Eighteenth Lesson.—The History of Christ's Incarnation, Life, and Death.

M. You must know that all the Jewish and Old Testament history is but preparatory to the history of the gospel of Jesus Christ; as all the types and ceremonies were but preparatory to his revelation, mediation, and kingdom. The Jews were themselves a small and sinful people; but their state of peculiarity, as under a more special government of God, made them a fit type, and preparatory to the catholic church of Christ. The law of Moses was just, but rigorous, and burdensome in multitudes of ceremonies; but its purity and divinity made it fit, as a schoolmaster, to lead them to Christ, who is the end of their policy and law.

C. Who is Jesus Christ?

M. He is the Eternal Word, Wisdom, and Son of God, who took the nature of man, and so is God and man in one person, that he might be a Mediator between God and man, to reconcile and recover fallen, miserable man to God, and save his church from sin, and death, and hell, and bring them to glory in the heavenly kingdom.

C. Is there more Gods than one?

M. No: but in God there are three persons, called the Father, the Son, and the Holy Ghost.

C. How can three persons be one God?

M. As well as one sun can have light, and heat, and motion. For a person in the Godhead is not like the persons of men, which are so many substances divided from one another; but this is the greatest mystery, which you must learn better hereafter, when you are riper, and more capable.

C. And how can God be made a man?

M. As well as our souls can dwell and act in our bodies; (though there be difference;) not by any change of God, but by uniting himself to the human nature of Jesus.

How doth the fire become a candle? The fire or flame is not the wick or tallow; but yet it is so united to them, that it is with them one and the same candle.

C. Hath God a Son?

M. Yes: but not begotten, as we men are, by our parents.

C. How then?

M. No similitude can show us clearly these great, unsearchable mysteries; but some may a little help us to understand somewhat of them. Do you know how the sun begetteth, or causeth, the beams of light? or do you know how a man begetteth, or causeth, his own thoughts? This showeth us a little how God the Father begets his Son, which is called his Word and Wisdom, from all eternity: and then when this Son, or Word, became a man, that was another begetting.

C. Was Christ begotten of his Father?

M. Yes: the first was before all time and worlds, from eternity. This is Christ's Godhead, by which he and his Father are as truly one God as the sun and its light are one sun, or as a man's soul and his understanding are one soul.

C. And what was the other begetting of Christ?

M. God by his Spirit did beget Jesus Christ, without any other father, in the womb of the Virgin Mary, in which the Eternal Word, or Son of God, did take to himself the substance and nature of man, and so was made and born a man.

C. Did he take only the flesh and body of a man, or the soul of a man also?

M. He took both body and soul of man; and his Godhead was as nearly united to his soul (and more than a soul to that soul) as our souls are to our bodies. And so as we have a soul and body, Christ had a Godhead, and a soul, and a body.

C. Was he born as other men are?

M. Yes: but not begotten nor conceived as others.

C. Where was he born, and how?

M. He was born at Bethlehem, a little city in Judea, in a common inn, and that in a stable.

C. How came that to pass?

M. His mother, after she was with child of him by the Holy Ghost, was married to a man called Joseph, who was taken for his father, and was but a carpenter; but both he and Mary his mother were of the blood royal, descended from king David: and at that time the Romans that had conquered a great part of the world, had also conquered Judea, and were rulers there; and their emperor Augustus made a decree, that the names of all his subjects must be taken, and enrolled in the places where they were born; and so Joseph, who was gone to live in Galilee, far off, was put to travel with his wife to Bethlehem, to be enrolled; and there was no room in the inn, and so Mary was delivered of her Son Jesus in the stable.

C. But if Jesus was God, why should he be born of so poor a woman, and in so poor a manner?

M. Oh! this was part of the reason of his coming into the world: he came to suffer for our sins, and not to live as earthly kings, in pomp and pleasure; and therefore he began his life in a low and suffering state, and so he passed it on to the end. And also he came to teach us all how to suffer, and to live above the love and vanity of this world, that we may obtain a better world after we are dead, and not to make us great men on earth, or to pamper and pleasure our flesh.

C. But how was it known that God begat Jesus?

M. God did many ways reveal it. He sent an angel to Zachary, a priest, to tell him that his wife should bear a son, which was John the Baptist, who should be a prophet, to prepare men to believe in Christ; and Zachary hardly believing it, the angel told him that he should be dumb till the child was born, and so he was; and when John was born Zachary's tongue was loosed, and he prophesied of Christ. Also God sent his angel to Mary, to tell her, that she should be with child by the Holy Ghost; and she believed and prophesied, praising God. Also, at the time of Christ's birth, angels appeared to some shepherds, that were watching their flocks in the field by night, and told them that Christ was then born at Bethlehem, and they might find him laid in a stable. And the angels sung this praise to God, saying, "Glory to God in the highest; on earth peace, and to men good will." And the shepherds came and found him there.

Also there were three wise astronomers of another country, in the East, that by a new star were taught, by God, to know it; and the star went before them, and led them to the very place where they found him, and offered gifts, as to a new-born king. It is like an angel was the conductor of that star.

C. How was Christ received when he was born?

M. King Herod, being told by these wise men that he was born king, intended to murder him, and bid the wise men find him out, and then come and tell him, that he might worship him; but God bid them go home another way. And when Herod saw that he was deceived, he sent and murdered all the children about Bethlehem, that were but two years old. But God first told Joseph, and bid him fly, with Mary and the child, to Egypt, till Herod's death.

C. What did Christ do when he was a little child?

M. He obeyed his supposed father and his mother, to be an example to all children, to teach them to obey their parents. If he that was God in flesh would obey, how much are all children bound to obedience!

C. But why would Christ become so weak at first, as an infant, and not be made a man first, as Adam was?

M. He that came to redeem all ages, young and old, would sanctify all, by taking both childhood and riper age upon himself, and show us that children are saved by him.

C. How could Christ be our Teacher, King, and Saviour, when he was an infant?

M. The work of our redemption was not to be done all at once, but by degrees and parts. His infant humiliation, next his incarnation, was a part, but the great part was to be done at age, in its proper season. A child may be a king, or a lord, though he cannot do that which a king, or lord, at age, can do. An infant may be the owner of an inheritance, or lands, in right, though he be not capable of knowing or using it. And as Christ was the Head of the church in his infancy, so infants may be infant members of it, though they know it not.

C. What did Christ do after, when he came to fuller age?

M. He grew up in wisdom as he grew in age, as to his bodily manner of knowing; and he disputed with the doctors; but he did not openly declare himself to be Christ, and exercise his office, till he was thirty years old.

C. How did he do it then?

M. He was first baptized by John Baptist, who was his harbinger, to show that the kingdom of Christ was now coming, and to prepare the Jews, by preaching repentance, and baptizing the penitent, to be fit receivers of this heavenly King. And God, by a voice from heaven, proclaimed him to be his beloved Son, in whom he was pleased, commanding us to hear him; and the Holy Ghost descended on him visibly, as in the likeness of a dove.

C. What did he when he was baptized?

M. He went into the wilderness, and fasted forty days and nights, as Moses did when he received the law; and then Satan was permitted to tempt him, that if he could have drawn him to any sin he might have hindered our redemption.

C. What did the devil tempt him to?

M. To break God's order, and tempt God, by commanding stones to be made bread, to satisfy his hunger; and to cast himself headlong from a pinnacle of the temple, to show that God could preserve him; and to worship the devil, upon promise that he would give him all the kingdoms of the world.

C. How did the devil find any means for such foul temptations?

M. By citing some texts of Scripture falsely perverted.

C. Did Christ yield to any of his temptations?

M. No; he never sinned in thought, word, or deed.

C. How did Christ answer the tempter?

M. By Scripture, rightly alleged; and, at last, by detesting his motions, and commanding him to be gone.

C. Why would Christ be tempted to such odious sins?

M. The world was overthrown, and Paradise lost, by the devil's overcoming Eve and Adam by his temptations: and Christ, that came to recover sinful man, was to conquer the tempter, who, by temptation, had conquered man.

C. What did Christ after that?

M. He went abroad preaching to sinners, to prepare them, by repentance, to believe that the promised Redeemer was come, and joyfully to receive the heavenly King that came to save them. And before he told them that he was the Christ, he proved it by his works, going about to do that which none could do, but by the power of God. He healed the blind, the lame, the palsy, the lepers, and all diseases, by his bare word or touch. He did, by command, heal those that were mad and possessed by devils. He raised the dead to life again; and then he declared that he was the Christ. And he sent forth twelve chosen chief messengers, and seventy other disciples, to preach the same doctrine, and to work such miracles as he had done; which they did.

C. And how was he received? did they believe him?

M. The multitude admired him, and cried him up, and followed him to see his miracles, and to be healed of their diseases: but none but those that were ordained to eternal life did so believe in him, as to forsake their sin, and to be saved; for he came to preach repentance and holiness.

C. Who were they that believed him not?

M. Especially the rulers, and great men, and priests, and Sadducees; and next the wicked sort of the rabble.

C. Why were the rulers and priests against him?

M. The Roman empire had conquered the Jews, and ruled over them, and were the powerfullest in the world; and Christ was called the King of the Jews, because he came to be their Saviour; and they thought that if the Romans did but hear of a king risen up among them, they would send their armies and destroy them: and the common people, seeing Christ's miracles, would have made him a king, but that he refused it, and therefore the rulers plotted to kill him.

C. And how did they use him at last?

M. The priests and the rabble joined together to desire Pilate, the Roman governor, to put him to death: and they called him a blasphemer, because he told them that he was the Son of God. And when Pilate told them he found no fault in him, they cried out with rage, instead of reason, "Crucify him, crucify him!" And when they could no otherwise prevail with Pilate, they told him that if he did not crucify Christ, he was an enemy to Cæsar, the Roman emperor, whom the Jews were subject to, because Christ called himself the King of the Jews. And then Pilate durst forbear no longer, but judged him to be crucified.

And then when he was in their power, king Herod, and the soldiers, and the rabble, abused and scorned him, and put a crown of thorns on his head, and a purple robe on him, and a reed in his hand, as a sceptre, and bowed to him in scorn, and blindfolded him and struck him, and bid him read who struck him; and after much scorn and scourging they crucified him.

C. What is crucifying?

M. It was the manner of the Romans' putting malefactors to death, like our hanging men. They set in the ground a long piece of timber, and nailed a cross piece near the top; and they nailed men's hands, spread out on the cross-bar, and the feet to the lower part of the upright piece, that they might so hang in pain till they died: and so they did by Jesus, writing over his head his accusation, "Jesus of Nazareth, King of the Jews."

C. What did his disciples do, when they saw him hanged on a cross?

M. Peter himself denied him, and forswore him, and the rest forsook him and fled, save that John and his mother, and some women, or few others, stood mourning by him.

C. I doubt if I had seen him crucified and dead, I should not have believed that he was the Son of God?

M. But what if you had seen the proof that followed? He was crucified between two thieves. One of them reviled him, and so did the people, for not saving himself that had saved others; but the other was converted, and believed in Christ, and prayed him to remember him when he came into his kingdom; and Christ promised him, "This day shalt thou be with me in paradise." And as he hung on the cross, the sun was darkened, the earth trembled, the veil of the temple was rent from the top to the bottom, and many dead bodies rose, and appeared to many.

C. It is wonder, then, that they did not all believe?

M. The captain of the guard of soldiers was convinced; but a wicked, hardened heart resisteth reason and sense.

C. What did they, then, with the body of Jesus?

M. Two of the rulers, that had secretly believed him, now owned him, Joseph of Arimathea, and Nicodemus. And Joseph begged his body of Pilate, and buried it in a grave hewn in stone, in a garden, which he had prepared for himself; and they wrapped the body with spices, to keep it.

C. What day of the week died Christ?

M. On a Friday, so called now, that is, the fifth day; on the yearly day commonly called Good Friday.

C. What became of him after this?

M. His soul went to paradise, and to ——, that is, among departed souls, and his body lay in the grave till the third day, which was the first day of the week, now commonly called Sunday. And then he rose from the dead, of which I shall speak to you the next time.

C. But could not Christ have saved himself from death?

M. Yes, very easily, as he saved others. But he came into the world on purpose to die; and not only to die, but to suffer in his soul the greater pain of the displeasure and justice of God, for the sins of man, which he voluntarily undertook to bear: of which I must also further teach you, but will not load you with too much at once.

The Nineteenth Lesson.—The History of Christ's Resurrection, and his Commission to the Apostles, and his Ascension.

C. When did Christ rise again from the dead?

M. Early in the morning, on the first day of the week, now called, by christians, the Lord's day; which is kept in remembrance of it ever since.

C. How did Christ rise?

M. His Godhead was Almighty, and his soul, which was in paradise, by and with his Godhead, again entered into his body.

C. How was his rising known?

M. Because Christ had often told them that he would rise again the third day, the rulers set a seal on the stone that was at the entrance of the sepulchre, and set a guard of soldiers to watch it. And an angel came and frighted away the soldiers, and rolled away the stone; and the rulers hired the soldiers to say that Christ's disciples came by night and stole him away, while they were asleep, and the people believed this.

C. Who saw him when he was risen?

M. First Mary Magdalene, and some other women; and after, five hundred at once, on a mountain in Galilee. And he oft appeared to his disciples, on the first days of each week, when they were met with doors shut on them. And Thomas once being absent, he told the rest that he would not believe it, unless he saw the wound in his side, (which the soldiers had made with a spear,) and those in his hands and feet, and might put his finger into them. And the next time he bid Thomas come and put his finger into his side and wounds, and not be faithless, but believing. And Thomas cried out, "My Lord and my God!" At another time he appeared to two of them on the way, and opened to them the old scripture, which foretold his sufferings and his glory.

And another time he came to them at the sea-side where they were fishing, and brought a huge draught of great fishes into their net, and then did eat with them on the shore.

C. How long staid he on earth when he was risen?

M. Forty days; from Easter day to Ascension day.

C. What did he all that while on earth?

M. He appeared to men, not constantly, but at certain times: and before he went, he gave his apostles their commission what to do when he was gone.

C. What were they appointed to do?

M. To go as far as they could into all the world, and preach the gospel to all nations, and to make them Christ's disciples, and to baptize them in the name of the Father, the Son, and the Holy Ghost. And, having baptized them, to teach them to observe all that he had commanded them, and live after his laws.

C. What is baptizing?

M. It is a solemn covenant made between God the Father, the Son, and Holy Ghost, and him that is baptized; which is signified by washing the person with water.

C. How were they washed?

M. The minister brought them to some water, and dipped them over head, and then they rose up: which was to signify that they trusted in Christ, that had been dead and buried, and risen again; and that they did now, by covenant, become as dead men to the world, and to their fleshly, sinful life, and did enter upon a new life of faith and holiness, in hope of heaven.

C. Must they be so baptized now?

M. They must be so washed to the same signification and covenant: but the same quantity of water, and dipping over head, is not necessary in our cold country, where it may destroy life, as was used in that hot country, where it was a pleasure: for it is the washing, and signification, and covenant, that is necessary; and God will have mercy rather than sacrifice and outward ceremony.

C. What is the covenant that is made by baptism?

M. God the Father, Son, and Holy Ghost, doth consent and promise to the baptized, to be his God and Father, his Saviour, and his Sanctifier and Comforter, if he will consent, unfeignedly and practically, so to take him; and forsaking the devil, the world, and the flesh, so far as they are against him, will consent to live in faith, love, and holy obedience, to him; in which he will strengthen him, and will forgive his sin, and give him an everlasting life of blessedness in heaven.

C. Were little children to be baptized?

M. Yes, if the parents were baptized christians, and, desiring it, did dedicate them to God in Christ: for nations were to be made disciples, and baptized; and children are parts of nations.

C. What did Christ after the forty days on earth?

M. He ascended up into heaven.

C. How did he go up?

M. By the power of his Godhead, in the sight of his disciples. He called them together, and gave them his commands and his blessing, and promised to send down the Holy Ghost on them and on other believers, and to enable them to speak those languages (to propagate the gospel) which they had never learned; and to work miracles, to confirm their doctrine and testimony of Christ. And he commanded them to stay at Jerusalem till the Holy Ghost was sent down upon them. And then he went bodily to heaven, while they looked up and gazed after him: and an angel stood by them, and said, "Why stand ye gazing up into heaven? This same Jesus shall come again as you have seen him go."

C. But did Christ ever come again?

M. That is to be done at the end of this world, when Christ shall come to judgment.

C. Did Christ take up his body that he had on earth?

M. Yes: but it is changed from corruptible flesh into a spiritual, incorruptible, glorious body.

C. And what doth Christ do now in heaven?

M. He is above all angels and men, the Lord of all, and all power is given to him to gather and save his elect, and to subdue his enemies, and punish the ungodly.

C. Why did Christ stay forty days before he ascended up.

M. To leave men a full proof that he was risen.

C. But why did he not show himself to all the Jews, as well as to his disciples.

M. We must take heed of asking God a reason of his doings: he doth all things in perfect wisdom, but maketh not us his counsellors, or judges of his doings. But we may conceive that the malignant, self-cursed Jews were unworthy and unfit to be the witnesses of his resurrection: and seeing the witnesses of it were to be sent abroad through the world, to testify what they had seen themselves, none were so fit for this office as those that had been with him, and heard his doctrine, and seen his miracles, and by sanctification were fitted to be his messengers, and by self-denial and patience to propagate his saving gospel to the world.

Chapter Twenty.—Of the coming down of the Holy Spirit, and the Works of the Apostles thereby.

C. What is that Holy Ghost that Christ promised to send down?

M. He is the Spirit of God the Father and the Son, sent to do those strange works on men which no man or angel was able to do, to fit men to further their own and other men's salvation, and propagate the grace and kingdom of Christ in the world.

C. What were those strange gifts and works?

M. The Holy Spirit filled them with a lively belief of that they were to preach; and brought all to their remembrance that Christ had taught them, and taught the apostles infallibly that which they were to deliver as Christ's truth, by word or writing to the world. And he enabled them to speak the languages which they had never learned, that they might be able to preach to men of divers languages and nations. And to convince all men that they were sent by God, they had the gift of doing miracles, to heal the sick, and lame, and blind, and raise the dead to life again. And with these gifts they were sent to preach the gospel to the world.

C. Could they heal all the sick, and raise all the dead?

M. No: but the same Holy Spirit that gave them the power, told them when to use it: it was not to be common, nor at their own will; but when God, by miracles, would have unbelievers convinced, that would not be convinced by other means, and so Christ and his gospel proved to be true.

C. Had not good men the Spirit of God before?

M. Yes, in a lower measure, agreeable to that measure of means that God then afforded them: but they had this eminent, extraordinary gift of the Spirit, which Christ gave after his ascension, for the proof and success of his gospel.

C. When and how did they receive this gift of the Spirit?

M. On the Lord's day, which we call Whitsunday, when all the believers were assembled to worship God, suddenly a noise, like a rushing, mighty wind from heaven, filled all the house; and there appeared like cloven tongues of fire, and sat upon each of them, and they were filled with the Holy Ghost, and spake with other tongues, as the Spirit gave them utterance, the works and praise of God: so that the people of many nations, that were then at Jerusalem, wondered to hear them speak in all their several languages.

C. Did this convince the Jews?

M. The most of the priests and rulers were hardened, and believed not: but Peter made a speech to them to prove that this miraculous gift of the Spirit was sent from Christ as the witness to his word: and three thousand were converted and were baptized that day.

C. What more did the apostles do to prove the gospel to be true?

M. There was a poor man born lame, and had so lived above forty years, that was carried to beg at the gate of the temple, and he asked an alms of Peter and John, that were going in to prayer. And the Spirit of God moved Peter to say, "In the name of Jesus, stand up and walk;" and he was presently healed, and walked, and leaped, praising God: and the people wondering, Peter preached another sermon to them, and the converts were then five thousand.

C. Did not this convert the rulers and priests?

M. No: but being in a rage to see so many converted, they laid hold on the apostles, and the next day examined them, by what power they did this miracle: and when Peter told them that it was by the name of Jesus, they knew not what to say, but commanded them to preach Christ no more.

C. And did they obey him, and give over preaching?

M. No: but they came to the rest of the believers, and gave God thanks for his wonders of mercy. And the Holy Ghost again fell on the hearers, and they magnified and praised God. And they went on preaching, and the rulers put them in prison, and the angel of God opened the prison doors, and let them out, and bid them go and preach in the temple; which they did.

C. Did not this convince them?

M. No: they did but rage the more, and threatened the apostles for preaching, when they forbade them; and were plotting to kill them; but one of them, Gamaliel, stopped them, by telling them what it is to fight against God.

C. But did none believe them after these miracles?

M. Yes, those whose hearts God changed; many thousands joined with the apostles as a church, in their doctrine and communion and prayer: and were, by the Spirit, so filled with love, that they sold their inheritances, and brought the money to the apostles, and all lived and fed together on the common stock; and no one called any thing his own.

C. But what did they when the stock was spent?

M. This was not to continue; but to show the power of the Spirit of love at first. God, that moved them to it, knew that they would quickly be persecuted out of the land, and could not carry their inheritance away with them.

C. Were all willing thus to part with their estates?

M. God made them willing by love: but one called Ananias, and his wife, Sapphira, brought but part that they sold their land for, and lied, and said that it was all: and, by the Spirit of God, Peter pronounced the sentence of death on them for lying, and thinking that the Holy Ghost in the apostles knew it not; and for keeping that which they took on them to devote to God.

C. Did not this frighten men from being christians?

M. It frightened men from being hypocrites, and from coming with a false, divided heart. But the good that the apostles did drew abundance the more to them.

C. What was that good they did?

M. They rejoiced sinners with the glad tidings of pardon and salvation by Christ; and they healed them of all diseases: insomuch that men carried the sick on beds and couches into the streets, that at least the shadow of Peter passing by might overshadow them; and multitudes of the sick, and possessed with devils, were brought out of other cities about; and they were healed every one. And men love their bodies so well, that this turned to the good of their souls, and winning them to believe.

C. What did the apostles next?

M. They made seven good men deacons, to distribute the church's stock, and take care of the poor. And one of these, called Stephen, was full of the Holy Ghost, and confounded the unbelievers, by proving the truth of Christ; which filled them so full of rage, that they brought false witness against him, as for blasphemy, and stoned him to death: and this was the first martyr that was killed for the faith of Christ.

C. How did he die?

M. Praying for his murderers that God "would not lay that sin to their charge," (that is, not so as to deny them repentance, and the further tenders of his grace,) and he prayed the Lord Jesus to receive his spirit. For before they killed him, he saw heaven opened, and Christ sitting on the right hand of God: no wonder, then, that he died with joy.

C. Who were they that did this cruel murder?

M. One of the leaders of this malignant rabble was Saul; who did not stop here, but went on to persecute the rest; and made havoc of the church, and entering into every house, haled out men and women, and committed them to prison: and so scattered the christians from Jerusalem into other parts.

C. What did they when they were driven away from Jerusalem?

M. They went abroad several ways preaching the gospel. Philip went to Samaria, the chief city of the ten tribes, where were a mongrel sort of erroneous Jews; where he so preached, that the generality of the city gave heed to him, and after were baptized as believers, both men and women; for his miracles convinced them: he cast out devils from many that were possessed by them; and he healed palsies, lameness, and other diseases, and convinced Simon that had bewitched them.

C. Who was that Simon?

M. He was a famous wizard, that, by the power of the devil, had done such strange things among them, that they called him the great power of God, and were commonly deluded by him.

And when he saw the miracles of Philip, he himself believed, and was baptized as a christian; but yet his heart was false, and not truly converted and sanctified.

C. How was that known?

M. Though Philip, that was but a deacon, and many others, worked miracles, yet God made it a special gift to the apostles, that, by laying on of their hands, the Holy Ghost should be given to others, to enable them to work miracles. And when the Samaritans believed, Peter and John came to them, and laid their hands on them with prayer, and they had presently this miraculous gift of the Holy Ghost. And when Simon the conjuror saw this, he wondered, and offered them money, if they would give him the power to give the Holy Ghost to others, which showed a proud, ungodly heart.

C. And what answer did they give him?

M. Peter said to him, "Thy money perish with thee, because thou hast thought that the gift of God might be bought with money;" and he told him that his heart was not right, and that he had no part in that matter; but for all his believing and baptism, he was yet in the gall of bitterness and bond of iniquity, and bid him repent and pray, if, perhaps, he might be forgiven. And Simon being afraid of this threatening, entreated them to pray for him, lest it should fall upon him. And thus the great city Samaria joyfully received the christian faith.

C. What other miracles followed this?

M. When Philip had converted the Samaritans, an angel of God bid him go toward the south, for further work, which God had thus to do. There was a great man that was a treasurer to a queen of Ethiopia, who, being a proselyte, had been worshipping at Jerusalem, and going home, was reading in his chariot part of Isaiah liii. which is a prophecy of Christ's sufferings, but understood it not: and God bid Philip go to him and teach him. And the great man took Philip into his chariot, and Philip expounded it to him, and preached Christ to him, and he was converted, and baptized.

C. But what became of bloody Saul, that persecuted the church?

M. Oh! God made him the greatest example of his mercy that ever was heard of. While he raged against the church in his blind zeal, he was not content to drive them from Jerusalem, but he got letters from the high priest to pursue them to Damascus, the chief city of Syria, and to bring them bound to Jerusalem; but as he journeyed and came near to Damascus, (a famous city in Syria,) suddenly, at midday, a light from heaven, above the brightness of the sun, shone round about him; whereupon he fell to the earth, and he heard a voice, (but they who were with him only heard the noise,) saying to him, "Saul, Saul, why persecutest thou me? It is hard for thee to kick against the pricks." Saul, trembling and astonished, said, "Who art thou, Lord?" And, being informed that it was Jesus of Nazareth whom he was persecuting, by this same Jesus he was ordered to arise, and to go into the city, (Damascus,) where he should know more. He, lodging there, in the street called Straight, in the house of Judas, remained blind three days, fasting and praying. Thither the Lord, in a vision, sent Ananias, a disciple at Damascus, who, having heard of Saul's fury, and errand to Damascus from the high priest, was loth to go, till better satisfied by the Lord concerning him. But when he understood that Christ had fixed on him to be a chosen vessel to himself for extraordinary service, he goes to Saul; and telling Saul what Christ told him, Saul is baptized by him, and recovers his sight: and, after some days' abode with the disciples at Damascus, he preached Christ in the synagogues, that he was the Son of God. And thenceforward he became the most eminent of Christ's servants and apostles, converting souls, edifying churches, and ordering things and persons to their greatest advantage: and his Lord all along owned and prospered him, till he at last sealed his doctrine with martyrdom.

But the course of his ministry, the substance of his doctrine, the dates and occasions of his epistles, with their main scope, sense, and force, his sufferings, with his wisdom and behaviour upon all accounts, as the New Testament informs us, require good time, and close thought.

THE CATECHISING OF FAMILIES.

A TEACHER OF HOUSEHOLDERS

HOW TO

TEACH THEIR HOUSEHOLDS:

USEFUL ALSO TO

SCHOOLMASTERS, AND TUTORS OF YOUTH.

FOR THOSE THAT ARE PAST THE COMMON SMALL CATECHISMS, AND WOULD GROW TO A MORE ROOTED FAITH, AND TO THE FULLER UNDERSTANDING OF ALL THAT IS COMMONLY NEEDFUL TO A SAFE, HOLY, COMFORTABLE, AND PROFITABLE LIFE.

THE REASONS AND USE OF THIS BOOK.

MAN is born without knowledge, but not without a capacity and faculty of knowing; this is his excellency and essence: nature, experience, and God's word, tell us the great necessity of knowledge. As the soul's essential form is the virtue of vital action, understanding, and will, conjunct; so holiness is holy life, light, and love, conjunct. The wisest men are the best, and the best the wisest; but a counterfeit of knowledge is the great deceiver of the world. Millions take the knowledge of bare words, with the grammatical and logical sense, instead of the knowledge of the things themselves, which by these are signified; as if the glass would nourish without the wine, or the dish without the meat, or the clothing or skin were all the man. God, and holiness, and heaven, are better known by many serious unlearned christians, that cannot accurately dispute about them, than by many learned men, who can excellently speak of that which their souls are unacquainted with. The hypocrite's religion is but an art; the true christian's is a habit, which is a divine nature.

But yet the words are signs, by which we are helped to know the things, and must diligently be learned to that end; and though men cannot reach the heart, God hath appointed parents, and masters, and teachers, to instruct their inferiors by words, and hath written the Scripture to that use, that by them his Spirit may teach or illuminate the mind, and renew the heart: God worketh on man as man; and we must know by signs, till we know by intuition.

It is a thing well known, that the church aboundeth with catechisms, and systems of divinity; and doth there yet need more? Their scope and substance is the same; they differ most, 1. In choice of matter, that there be nothing left out that is needful, nor needless uncertainties and disputes put in. 2. That the method or order of them be true, agreeable to the matter and sacred Scripture. 3. And that they be not blotted with any drops of disgraceful error. These are the requisites to desirable catechisms.

No doubt but they should be sorted into three degrees, suited to the childhood, youth, and maturer age of christians. I. The essentials of christianity are all contained generally in baptism; this must be understood, and therefore expounded. The creed, Lord's prayer, and decalogue, the summaries of things to be believed, desired, (in hope,) and practised, were from the beginning taken for a good exposition to those that were to be baptized: these three, as expounding baptism, are themselves a good catechism, the understanding of the Lord's supper being added for communicants. II. But here also children will be childish, and learn the words while they are mindless of the sense; therefore an explication of these in other words hath ever been thought a great part of the work of a teaching ministry; whence the ancients have left us their expositions of the creed, &c.

But here the difficulty is made insuperable by the learner's indisposition: if such a catechism be short, and much put in few words, the vulgar cannot understand it; if it be long, and in many words, they cannot learn and remember it. III. For remedy of this, a larger catechism yet is needful; not to be learnt without book, but to be a full exposition of the shorter which they learn; that they may have recourse to this for a more full and particular understanding of a shorter, whose general words they can remember.

Accordingly, having in my "Poor Man's Family Book" written two catechisms of the former rank, I here add the third, for those that have learned the two first. Far am I from thinking that I have done any one of these to perfection; I never yet saw a catechism without some notable imperfection; and no doubt mine are not free from such. But while I avoid what I see amiss in others, I hope God will illuminate some to do yet better, and to avoid what is amiss in mine. The degree which yet pretendeth to greater accurateness in method, I have given in a Latin "Methodus Theologiæ."

The uses for which I have written this are these. I. For masters of families, who should endeavour to raise their children and servants to a good degree of knowledge. I have divided it into short chapters, that on the Lord's days, or at nights, when they have leisure, the master may read to them one chapter at a time, that is, the exposition of one article of the creed, one petition of the Lord's prayer, and one commandment expounded.

II. For schoolmasters to cause their riper rank of scholars to learn. I am past doubt, that it is a heinous crime in the schoolmasters of England, that they devote but one hour or two in a week to the learning of the catechism, while all the rest of the week is devoted to the learning of Lilly, Ovid, Virgil, Horace, Cicero, Livy, Terence, and such like: besides the loss and sinful omission, it seduceth youth to think that common knowledge (which is only subsidiary and ornamental) is more excellent or necessary than to know God, Christ, the gospel, duty, and salvation; besides which, all knowledge (further than it helpeth or serveth this) is but fooling and doting, and as dangerous diversion and perversion of the mind, as grosser sensual delights. He is not worthy the name of a christian schoolmaster, who maketh it not his chief work to teach his scholars the knowledge of Christ, and life everlasting.

III. But if they go from the country schools before they are capable of the larger catechisms, (as to their great loss most make too much haste away,) why may not their next tutors make it their chief work to train up their pupils as the disciples of Jesus; and yet not neglect either Aristotle, or any natural light? To our present universities, I am not so vain as to offer such instructions; (though to some small part of them I directed my "Methodus Theologiæ;") I learned not of them, and I presume not to make myself their teacher: their late guides, their worldly interest, and their genius, have made my writings odious to many, even that which they like they will not read. But I have oft, with lamentation, wondered why godly ministers do no more of the work now appropriated to universities for their own sons? Those men whose church zeal would ruin nonconformists, if they teach many, either boys or men, have no law against parents teaching their own children.

1. Are you fit for the ministry yourselves? If so, cannot you teach others what you know? If you are defective in some useful knowledge, let them elsewhere learn that afterwards.

2. Is there any so greatly obliged to take care of them as yourselves? Will you be like those parents who set godfathers at the font, to vow and promise to do the parents' part? And how do such undertakers use to perform it? Or will you be like the women of this unnatural age, who get children, and (not through disability, but wealth, pride, and coyness) disdain to nurse them, but cast that on hired women, as obliged more by money, than themselves by nature, to all that care.

3. Cannot you do more at least to ground them well in religion, before you send them from you for other learning? Or are you of the mind, that to cant over the catechism is divinity enough, before they have read Aristotle, or studied the sciences? And that they must be proficients in logic and philosophy, before they make sure of their salvation; and must read Smiglecius, Ariago, Zabarel, Suarez, or be fooled by Cartesius, Gassendus, or Hobbs, before they will study the gospel and cross of Jesus Christ?

I am no undervaluer of any academical advantages: when the stream of academies runs pure and holy, they are blessed helps to men's salvation: when their stream is sensual, worldly, corrupt, and malignant, they are seminaries for hell, and the devil's schools, to train up his most powerful soldiers to fight against serious godliness in Christ's own livery and name; and to send youth thither, is worse than to send them to a brothel-house, or a pest-house.

4. Are there not fewer temptations in your own houses, than they are like to find abroad in the world? You can keep them from the company of sensual, voluptuous lads; and of learned, reverend enemies of serious christianity; and of worldly men, whose godliness is gain, and would draw them ambitiously to study preferment, and espouse them to the world, which, in baptism, they renounced: if you cannot keep them from such snares, how shall they be kept where such abound?

5. And one of the greatest motives of all, for your keeping them long enough at home, is, that you will thereby have time to judge whether they are like to become fit for the ministry, or not. Oh, how many good men send plagues into the church, by devoting unproved lads to the ministry, hoping that God will hereafter give them grace, and make them fit, who never promised it! When you send them at fifteen or sixteen years of age to the university, from under your own eye, you are unlikely to know what they will prove, unless it be some few that are very early sanctified by grace; and when they have been a few years at the university, be they never so unmeet, they will thrust themselves into the ministry, and, (miserable men,) for a benefice, take the charge of souls; whereas, if you will keep them with you till twenty years of age, you may see what they are like to prove, and dispose of them accordingly.

If you say, they will lose the advantage of their degrees, it is an objection unfit for a christian's mouth: will you prefer names, and airy titles, before wisdom, piety, and men's salvation, and the church's good? Must they go out of their way for a peacock's feather, when they are in a race as for life or death?

If you say, they will lose their time at home, the shame then is yours, or they are like to lose it more abroad: teach them to read the Scriptures (at least the gospel) in the original tongues, and to understand and practise things necessary to salvation, which all arts and sciences must subserve, and they do not lose their time; and at ripeness of age they will get more other learning in a year, than before they will do in many; and what they learn will be their own, when boys learn words without the sense.

If you say, they will want the advantage of academical disputes; I answer, if reading fill them with matter, nature and common use will teach them how to utter it: the world hath too many disputers; books may soon teach them the true order of disputing, and a few days' experience may show the rest.

If you say, you have not time to teach them; I answer, you have no greater work to do, and a little time will serve with willing, teachable youth, and no other are to be intended for the ministry. What boys get by hearing their tutors they oft bestow small labour to digest, but take up with bare words, and second notions: but when they are set to get it from their books themselves, harder study better digesteth it; it is they that must bestow much time, the teacher need not bestow very much: country schools may teach them Latin, Greek, and Hebrew, let them stay there till they attain it; you may then teach them the common rudiments of logic, and see them well settled in divinity and serious religion; and then, if academies prove safe and needful, they will go out better fortified against all the temptations which they must expect.

It is certain, that inconveniences are not so bad as mischiefs: and it is certain that all our natures, as corrupt, are dark, carnal, and malignant, and need the sanctifying grace of Christ: and it is certain, that as grace useth all things to its increase, so this serpentine nature will turn studies, learning, and all such things, to serve itself; and that carnal, sensual, malignant nature, cultivated by human learning, is too usually ripened and sublimated into diabolism, and maketh the most potent servants of the devil against Christ; and if this be but gilded with sacred ornaments and titles, and pretences of the church's peace and order, it is garrisoned and fortified, and a stronger hold for sin and Satan than open vice: and it is certain, that as the rage of drunkards is raised in their riotous meetings, and as conjunction, example, and noise put more valour into armies than separated persons have; so combined societies of learned, reverenced malignity do confirm the individuals, and raise them to the height of wickedness: so that universities are either, if holy, a copy of paradise, or, if malignant, the chief militia of the malicious enemy of man, except a malignant hierarchy or clergy, who are malignant academies grown up to maturity.

If any say that there is no great and solid learning to be got elsewhere, let them think where great Augustin, and most of the great lights of the church for four hundred years, attained their knowledge; and whether the Scaligers, Salmasius, Grotius, Selden, and such others, got not more by laborious, secret reading, than by academical tutors and disputes: and whether such famous men as John Reignolds, Blondel, &c. even in the universities, got not their great learning by searching the same books which may be read in another place. If any say, that I speak against that which I want myself, I only desire that it may not be those who cast by my "Catholic Theology," "Methodus Theologiæ," &c. with no other accusation, but because they are too scholastical, accurate, and hard for them.

I here bewail it as my great sin against God, that in the youth of my ministry, pride made me often blush with shame for want of academical degrees; but usually God will not have us bring our own human honour to his service, but fetch honour from him, in faithful serving him: fringes and laces must be last set on, when the garment is made, and not be the ground, or *stamen*, of it. There have been men that have desired their sons to learn all the oriental tongues, and the rare antiquities, and critical, applauded sort of learning, not for its own worth, but that they might preach the gospel with the advantage of a greater name and honour: and this course hath so taken up and formed such students into the quality of their studies, when their souls should have been taken up with faith and love, and heavenly desires and hopes, that it hath overthrown the end to which it was intended, and rendered such students unfit for the sacred ministry, and caused them to turn to other things: when others, who (as Usher, Bochart, Blondel, &c.) have first taken in a digested body of saving truth, have after added these critical studies at full maturity, and have become rare blessings to the church.

Let those that think all this digressive, or unmeet for the preface to a catechism, pardon that which the world's miscarriages and necessities bespeak.

If at least masters of families, by such helps, diligently used, will keep up knowledge and religion in their houses, it is not public failings in ministers, nor the want of what is desirable in the assemblies, that will root out religion from the land: but if the faithful prove few, they must be content with their personal comforts and rewards; there is nothing amiss in the heavenly society, and the world which we are entering into. Come, Lord Jesus, come quickly. Amen.

London, Oct. 3, 1682.

THE

CATECHISING OF FAMILIES.

[The Questions are the Learner's, and the Answers the Teachers.]

CHAPTER I.

THE INTRODUCTION.

Q. 1. What is it which must be taught and learned?

A. All must be taught, and must learn, 1. What to know and believe. 2. What to love, and choose, and hope for. 3. What they must do, or practise.[a]

Q. 2. What is it that we must learn to know and believe?

A. We must learn to know ourselves, and our concerns.[b]

Q. 3. What must we know of ourselves?

A. We must know what we are, and what condition we are in.[c]

Q. 4. What mean you by our concerns, which we must know?

A. We must know, 1. Whence we are, or who made us. 2. And whither we are going, or for what end he hath made us. 3. And which is the

[a] Psal. xxv. 4, 5; xxvii. 11; cxix. 12, 33, 66.

[b] Job xxxiv. 32.

[c] Heb. vi. 1—3.

way, or what means must be used, to attain that end.[d]

Q. 5. What must we learn to love, and choose, and hope for?

A. We must learn to love best that which is best in itself, and best to us and others, and to choose the means by which it must be attained; which implieth hating and refusing the contraries.[e]

Q. 6. What must we learn to practise?

A. We must practise the means to obtain the end of our lives, and that is our obedience to him that made us.[f]

Q. 7. Cannot we learn this of ourselves, without teachers?

A. There is some part of this which nature itself will teach you, as soon as you come to the free use of reason, and look about you in the world. And there is some part of it that nature alone will not teach you, without a higher teaching from above. And even that which nature teacheth you, you have also need of a teacher's help to learn it speedily and truly. For nature doth not teach all things alike easily, speedily, and surely: it quickly teacheth a child to suck; it quickly teacheth us to eat and drink, and to go and talk; and yet here there is need of help; children learn not to speak without teaching. It teacheth men how to do their worldly business; and yet they have need of masters to teach it them, and will serve an apprenticeship to learn some. Some things nature will teach to none but good wits, upon diligent search and study, and honest willingness to know; which dullards, and slothful, and bad men, reach not.[g]

Q. 8. Who be they that must teach, and who must learn?

A. None is able to teach more than they know themselves; and all that are ignorant have need to learn. But nature hath put all children under a necessity of learning; for, though they are born with a capacity to know, yet not with actual knowledge. And nature hath made it the duty of parents to be the teachers of their children first, and then to get the help of others.[h]

Q. 9. May we give over learning when we are past childhood?[i]

A. No; we must go on to learn as long as we live; for we know but in part, and therefore still have need of more. But those that have neglected to learn in their childhood, have most need of all; it being sinful and unnatural to be ignorant at full age, and signifieth great neglect.[k]

Q. 10. Who must teach us at age?

A. Parents and masters must teach their households, and public teachers are officers to teach all publicly; and all that have wisdom should take all fit opportunities, in charity, to teach and edify one another; knowledge and goodness have a communicative nature.[l]

Q. 11. How must parents teach their households?

A. Very familiarly and plainly, according to their capacities, beginning with the plain and necessary things; and this is it which we call catechising, which is nothing but the choosing out of the few plain, necessary matters from all the rest, and in due method, or order, teaching them to the ignorant.[m]

[d] Tit. ii. 3. [e] Psal. xxxiv. 11; xxxii. 8.
[f] 1 Kings viii. 36; Micah iv. 2.
[g] Isa. xxviii. 26; 1 Cor. xi. 14; Job xii. 7, 8; Heb. v. 12.
[h] 2 Tim. ii. 2; Job xxxii. 17; Tit. ii. 21; Deut. vi. 7, 8; xi. 19, 20.
[i] Prov. i. 5; ix. 9; vi. 21, 22.
[k] Psalm cxix. 99; Heb. v. 11, 12; Prov. v. 13.
[l] Gal. vi. 6; Deut. vi. 7; 1 Tim. ii. 7; 2 Tim. i. 11; Eph. iv. 11; Tit. ii. 3.

Q. 12. What need we catechisms, while we have the Bible?

A. Because the Bible containeth all the whole body of religious truths, which the ripest christians should know, but are not all of equal necessity to salvation with the greatest points. And it cannot be expected that ignorant persons can cull out these most necessary points from the rest without help. A man is not a man without a head and heart; but he may be a man if he lose a finger, or a hand, but not an entire man; nor a comely man without hair, nails, and nature's ornaments. So a man cannot be a christian, or a good or happy man, without the great and most necessary points in the Bible; nor an entire christian without the rest. Life and death lieth not on all alike. And the skilful must gather the most necessary for the ignorant, which is a catechism.[n]

Q. 13. But is not knowledge the gift of God?

A. Yes; but he giveth it by means. Three things must concur. 1. A right presenting to the learner, which is the teacher's work. 2. A fitness in the learner, by capacity, willingness, and diligence. 3. The blessing of God, without which no man can be wise.[o]

And therefore three sorts will be ignorant and erroneous. 1. Those that have not the happiness of true teachers, nor truth presented to them. 2. Those that by sottishness, pride, sensuality, malignity, or sloth, are uncapable, or unwilling, to learn. 3. Those that, by wilful sinning against God, are deprived of the necessary blessing of his help and illumination.[p]

CHAPTER II.

HOW TO KNOW OURSELVES BY NATURE.

Q. 1. WHAT is the first thing that a man must know?

A. The first in being and excellency is God. But the first in time known by man, or the lowest step where our knowledge beginneth, are the sensible things near us, which we see, hear, feel, &c. and especially ourselves.[a]

Q. 2. What know we of the things which we see, and feel, &c.?

A. A man of sound senses and understanding knoweth them to be such as sense apprehendeth, while they are rightly set before him; the eye seeth light and colours, the ear heareth sounds and words, and so of the rest; and the sound understanding judgeth them to be such as the sense perceiveth, unless distance, or false mediums, deceive us.[b]

Q. 3. But how know you that sense is not deceived? You say that is bread and wine in the sacrament, which the papists say is not.

A. God hath given us no other faculties but sense, by which to judge of sensible things, as light and darkness, heat and cold, sweet and bitter, soft and hard, &c. Therefore if we be here deceived, God is

[m] Heb. iii. 13; Ezra vii. 25; Col. iii. 16; Heb. v. 11, 12; vi. 1, 2; 2 Tim. i. 13.
[n] Matt. xii. 30, 31, 33; xix. 19; xxii. 37, 39; Rom. xiii. 9; Matt. xxviii. 19; xxiii. 23; James i. 27.
[o] Isa. xxx. 29; Matt. xxviii. 19, 20; 1 Tim. i. 3; iii. 2; vi. 2, 3.
[p] 2 Tim. ii. 2, 24; Acts xx. 20; 2 Tim. iii. 17; Heb. v. 12, 13; 1 John ii. 27; 1 Thess. iv. 9.
[a] 1 John i. 2, 3; Acts i. 3; iv. 20; xxvi. 16.
[b] John xx. 20, 25, 27.

our deceiver, and we are remediless; even faith and reason suppose our senses, and their true perception; and if that first perception be false, faith and reason could be no truer. God expecteth not that we should judge by other faculties than such as he hath given us for the perception of those objects.

Q. 4. What doth a man first perceive of himself?

A. We first feel that we are real beings; and we perceive that we use and have our senses, that we see, hear, feel, smell, taste; and then we perceive that we understand and think of the things so seen, felt, &c. And that we gather one thing from another, and that we love good, and hate evil, and choose, refuse, and do accordingly.

Q. 5. What do you next know of yourselves?

A. When we perceive that we see, feel, &c. and think, love, hate, &c. we know that we have a power of soul to do all this, for no one doth that which he is not made able to do.

Q. 6. And what do you next know of yourself?

A. When I know what I do, and that I can do it, I know next that I am a substance, endued with this power; for nothing hath no power, nor act, it can do nothing.

Q. 7. What know you next of yourself?

A. I know that this substance, which thinketh, understandeth, and willeth, is an unseen substance; for neither I, nor any mortal man, seeth it; and that is it which is called a spirit.

Q. 8. What next perceive you of yourself?

A. I perceive that in this one substance there is a threefold power, marvellously but one, and yet three, as named from the objects and effects; that is, 1. A power of mere growing motion, common to plants. 2. A power of sense common to beasts. 3. And a power of understanding and reason, about things above sense, proper to a man; three powers in one spiritual substance.

Q. 9. What else do you find in yourself?

A. I find that my spiritual substance, as intellectual, hath also a threefold power in one; that is, 1. Intellectual life, by which I move and act my faculties, and execute my purposes. 2. Understanding. 3. And will, and that these are marvellously diverse, and yet one.

Q. 10. What else find you by yourself?

A. I find that this unseen spirit is here united to a human body, and is in love with it, and careth for it, and is much limited by it, in its perceivings, willings, and workings; and so that a man is an incorporate, understanding spirit, or a human soul and body.

Q. 11. What else perceive you by yourself?

A. I perceive that my higher powers are given me to rule the lower, my reason to rule my senses and appetite, my soul to rule and use my body, as man is made to rule the beasts.

Q. 12. What know you of yourself as related to others?

A. I see that I am a member of the world of mankind, and that others are better than I, and multitudes better than one; and that the welfare of mankind depends much on their duty to one another; and therefore that I should love all according to their worth, and faithfully endeavour the good of all.

Q. 13. What else know you of yourself?

A. I know that I made not myself, and maintain not myself in life and safety, and therefore that another made me and maintaineth me; and I know that I must die by the separation of my soul and body.

Q. 14. And can we tell what then becomes of the soul?

A. I am now to tell you but how much of it our nature tells us, the rest I shall tell you afterward; we may know, 1. That the soul, being a substance in the body, will be a substance out of it, unless God should destroy it, which we have no cause to think he will. 2. That life, understanding, and will, being its very nature, it will be the same after death, and not a thing of some other kind. 3. That the soul, being naturally active, and the world full of objects, it will not be a sleepy or unactive thing. 4. That its nature here being to mind its interest in another life, by hopes or fears of what will follow, God made not its nature such in vain, and therefore that good or evil in the life that is next will be the lot of all.

CHAPTER III.

OF THE NATURAL KNOWLEDGE OF GOD AND HEAVEN.

Q. 1. You have told me how we know the things which we see and feel, without us and within us; but how can we know any things which we neither see nor feel, but are quite above us?

A. By certain effects and signs which notify them: how little else did man differ from a beast, if he knew no more than he seeth and feeleth! Besides what we know from others that have seen; you see not now that the sun will rise to-morrow, or that man must die; you see not Italy, Spain, France; you see no man's soul: and yet we certainly know that such things are and will be.

Q. 2. How know you that there is any thing above us, but what we see?

A. 1. We see such things done here on earth, which nothing doth, or can do, which is seen. What thing, that is seen, can give all men and beasts their life, and sense, and safety? And so marvellously form the bodies of all, and govern all the matters of the world? 2. We see that the spaces above us, where sun, moon, and stars are, are so vast, that all this earth is not so much to them, as one inch is to all this land. And we see that the regions above us excel in the glory of purity and splendour: and when this dark spot of earth hath so many millions of men, can we doubt whether those vast and glorious parts are better inhabited. 3. And we find that the grossest things are the basest, and the most invisible the most powerful and noble; as our souls are above our bodies: and therefore the most vast and glorious worlds above us must have the most invisible, powerful, noble inhabitants.

Q. 3. But how know you what those spirits above us are?

A. 1. We partly know what they are, by what they do with us on earth. 2. We know much what they are, by the knowledge of ourselves. If our souls are invisible spirits, essentiated by the power of life, understanding, and will, the spirits above us can be no less, but either such or more excellent. And he that made us must needs be more excellent than his work.

Q. 4. How know you who made us?

A. He that made all things must needs be our Maker, that is, God.[a]

Q. 5. What mean you by God? and what is he?

A. I mean the eternal, infinite, glorious Spirit, and Life, most perfect in active power, understanding, and will, of whom, and by whom, and to whom, are all things; being the Creator, Governor, and

[a] Rom. i. 19—21.

End of all. That is that God whom all things do declare.

Q. 6. How know you that there is such a God?

A. By his works (and I shall afterwards tell it you more fully by his word). Man did not make himself; beasts, birds, fishes, trees, and plants, make not themselves; the earth, and water, and air, make not themselves: and if the souls of men have a maker, the spirits next above them must have a maker: and so on, till you come to a first cause, that was made by none. There must be a first cause, and there can be but one.

Q. 7. Why may not there be many gods, or spirits, that were made by none, but are eternally of themselves?

A. Because it is a contradiction; the same would be both perfect and imperfect: perfect, because he is of himself eternally, without a cause, and so dependent upon none; and yet imperfect, because he hath but a part of that being that is said to be perfect: for many are more than one, and all make up the absolute, perfect Being, and one of them is but a part of all; and to be a part, is to be imperfect. However many subordinate created spirits may unfitly be called gods, there can be but one uncreated God, in the first and proper sense.

Q. 8. How know you that God is eternal, without beginning?

A. Because else there was a time when there was nothing, if there were a time when there was no God. And then there never would have been any thing; for nothing can make nothing.

Q. 9. But how can man conceive of an eternal, uncaused Being?

A. That such a God there is, is the most certain, easy truth, and that he hath all the perfection before described: but neither man nor angel can know him comprehensively.

Q. 10. What mean you by his infiniteness.

A. That his being and perfection have no limits or measure, but incomprehensibly comprehend all places and beings.

Q. 11. What is this God to us?

A. He is our Maker, and therefore our absolute Owner, our supreme Ruler, and our chief Benefactor, and ultimate End.

Q. 12. And how stand we related to him? What duty do we owe him? And what may we expect from him?

A. We are his creatures, and all that we are, and have, is of him; we are his subjects, made with life, reason, and free-will, to be ruled by him: he is the infinite good, and love itself. Therefore we owe him perfect resignation, perfect obedience, and perfect complacency and love: all that we are, and all that we have, and all that we can do, is due to him in the way of our obedience; to pay which, is our own rectitude and felicity, as it is our duty: but all this you may much better learn from his word, than nature alone can teach it you. Though man's nature, and the frame of nature about us, so fully proveth what I have said, as leaveth all the ungodly without excuse.

CHAPTER IV.

OF GOD'S KINGDOM, AND THE GOVERNMENT OF MAN, AND PROVIDENCE.

Q. 1. I PERCEIVE that nothing more concerneth us, than to know God, and our relation and duty to him, and what hope we have from him: therefore, I pray you, open it to me more fully, and first tell me where God is?

A. God being infinite, is not confined in any place, but all place and things are in God; and he is absent from none, but as near to every thing as it is to itself.

Q. 2. Why then do you say that he is in heaven, if he be as much on earth, and every where?

A. God is not more or less in one place, than another, in his being, but he is apparent and known to us by his working, and so we say he is in heaven, as he there worketh and shineth forth to the most blessed creatures in heavenly glory. As we say the sun is where it shineth: or, to use a more apt comparison, the soul of man is indivisibly in the whole body, but it doth not work in all parts alike; it understandeth not in the foot, but in the head; it seeth not, heareth not, tasteth not, and smelleth not, in the fingers or lower parts, but in the eye, the ear, and other senses in the head; and therefore when we talk to a man, it is his soul that we talk to, and not his flesh, and yet we look him in the face; not as if the soul were no where but in the face or head, but because it only worketh and appeareth there by those senses, and that understanding which we converse with: even so, we look up to heaven, when we speak to God; not as if he were no where else, but because heaven is the place of his glorious appearing and operation, and as the head and face of the world, where all true glory and felicity is, and from whence it descendeth to this earth, as the beams of the sun do from its glorious centre.

Q. 3. You begin to make me think that God is the soul of the world, and that we must conceive of him in the world, as we do of the soul of man in his body.

A. You cannot better conceive of God, so you will but take in the points of difference, which are very great; for no creature known to us doth resemble God without vast difference.

The differences are such as these. First, the soul is part of the man, but God is not a part of the world, or of being: for to be a part is to be less than the whole, and so to be imperfect. Secondly, we cannot say that the soul is any where out of the body, but the world is finite, and God is infinite, and therefore God is not confined to the world. 3. The soul ruleth not a body, that hath a distinct understanding and free-will of its own to receive its laws, and therefore ruleth it not by proper law, but by despotical motion: but God ruleth men that have understanding and free-will of their own, to know and receive his laws, and therefore he ruleth them partly by a law. 4. The soul doth not use another soul under it to rule the body, but God maketh use of superior spirits to move and rule things, and persons below them, so that there is a great difference between God's ruling the world, and the soul's ruling the body.

But yet there is great likeness also. 1. God is as near every part of the world, as the soul is near the body. 2. God is as truly and fully the cause of all the actions and changes of the world, (except sin, which free-will, left to itself, committeth,) as the soul is the cause of the actions and changes of the body. 3. The body is no more lifeless without the soul than the world would be without God. Yea, God giveth all its being to the world, and without him it would be nothing; and in this he further differeth from the soul, which giveth not material being to the body.

So that you may well conceive of God as the soul of the world, so you will but put in that he is far more.

Q. 4. Is it not below God to concern himself with these lower things? Doth he not leave them to those that are under him?

A. It is below God to be unconcerned about any part, even the least of his own works. Men are narrow creatures, and can be but in one place at once, and therefore must do that by others which they cannot do themselves, at least without trouble: but God is infinite, and present with all creatures; and as nothing is in being without him, so nothing can move without him.

Q. 5. By this you make God to do all things immediately, whereas we see he works by means and second causes: he giveth us light and heat by the sun; he upholdeth us by the earth, &c.

A. The word immediate sometimes signifieth a cause that hath no other cause under it; so the sun is the immediate cause of the emanation of its beams of light: and so God is not always an immediate cause; that is, he hath other causes under him. But sometimes immediate signifieth that which is next a thing, having nothing between them: and so God doth all things immediately; for he is, and he acteth, as near us as we to ourselves, and nothing is between him and us: he is as near the person and the effect, when he useth second causes, as when he useth none.

Q. 6. But is it not a debasing God, to make his providence the cause of every motion of a worm, a bird, a fly, and to mind and move such contemptible things; and so to mind the thoughts of man?

A. It is a debasing God to think that he is like a finite creature, absent, or insufficient for any of his creatures. That there is not the least thing or motion so small as to be done without him, is most certain to him that will consider, 1. That God's very essence is every where: and wherever he is, he is himself, that is, most powerful, wise, and good: and if such a God be as near to every action, as the most immediate actor is, so that in him they all live, and move, and be, how can he be thought to have no hand in it, as to providence or causality?

2. And it is certain that God upholds continually the very being of every thing that moveth, and all the power by which they move: for that which had no being but from him can have none continued but by him: that which could not make itself cannot continue itself: should not God by his causality continue their being, every creature would turn to nothing. For there can be nothing without a cause, but the first cause, which is God.

2. And it is all one to infiniteness, to mind every creature and motion in the world, and to cause and rule the least, as it is to cause and rule but one.

God is as sufficient for all the world, even every fly and worm, as if he had but one to mind. Seeing, then, that he is as present with every creature as it is with itself, and it hath not the least power but what he continually giveth it, and cannot move at all but by him, and he is as sufficient for all as for one, it is unreasonable to think that the least thing is done without him. Is it a dishonour to the sun, that every eye, even of flies, and ants, and toads, and snakes, as well as men, do see by the light of it; or that it shineth at once upon every pile of grass, and atom? This is but the certain effect of God's infiniteness and perfection.

Q. 7. How doth God govern all things?

A. He governeth several things, according to their several natures which he hath made: lifeless things by their natural inclinations, and by moving force; things that have sense by their sensitive inclinations, and by their objects, and by constraint; and reasonable creatures by their principles, and by laws and moral rules; and all things by his infinite power, wisdom, and will, as being every one parts of one world, which is his kingdom: especially man.

Q. 8. What is God's kingdom? And why do you call him our King?

A. I call him our King, because, 1. He only hath absolute right, power, and fitness, to be our supreme Ruler: 2. And he doth actually rule us as our Sovereign. And in this kingdom, 1. God is the only supreme King and Head. 2. Angels, or glorified spirits, and men, are the subjects. 3. All the brutes and lifeless creatures are the furniture, and goods, and utensils. 4. Devils and rebellious, wicked men, are the enemies, to be opposed and overcome.

Q. 9. How doth God govern man on earth?

A. The power of God our Lord, Owner, and Mover, moveth us, and disposeth of us as he doth of all things, to the fulfilling of his will. 2. The wisdom of God our King doth give us sound doctrine, and holy and just laws, with rewards and penalties, and he will judge men, and execute accordingly. 3. And the love of our heavenly Father doth furnish us with all necessary blessings, help us, accept us, and prepare us for the heavenly kingdom.

Q. 10. Why is man ruled by laws, rather than beasts and other things?

A. Because man hath reason, and free-will, which maketh them subjects capable of laws, which beasts are not.

Q. 11. What is that free-will which fits us to be subjects?

A. It is a will made by God, able to determine itself, by God's necessary help, to choose good, and refuse evil; understood to be such, without any necessitating predetermination by any other.

CHAPTER V.

OF GOD'S LAW OF NATURE, AND NATURAL OFFICERS.

Q. 1. By what laws doth God govern the world?

A. How he governeth the spirits above us, whether by any law besides the immediate revelation of his will, seen in the face of his glory, or how else, is not much known to us, because it doth not concern us. But this lower world of man he governeth by the law of nature, and by a law of supernatural revelation, given by his Spirit or by messengers from heaven.

Q. 2. What is it that you call the law of nature?

A. In a large and improper sense, some call the inclinations, and forcing or naturally moving causes of any creatures, by the name of a law: and so they say that beasts and birds are moved by the law of their nature; and that stones sink downward, and the fire goeth upward, by the law of nature. But this is no law in the proper sense which we are speaking of, whatever you call it.

Q. 3. What is it then that you call a law?

A. Any signification of the will of the ruler, purposely given to the subject, that thereby he may know and be bound to his duty, and know his reward or punishment due. Or any signification of the ruler's will for the government of subjects, constituting what shall be due from them, and to them. A rule to live by, and the rule by which we must be judged.

Q. 4. What, then, is God's law of nature, made for man?

A. It is the signification of God's governing will, by the nature of man himself, and of all other creatures known to man, in which God declareth to man his duty, and his reward or punishment.

Q. 5. How can a man know God's will, and our duty, by his nature, and by all other works of God about us?

A. In some things as surely as by words or writings; but in other things more darkly. I am sure that my nature is made to know and love truth and goodness, and to desire and seek my own felicity. My nature tells me that I was not made by myself, and do not live by myself, and therefore that I am not my own, but his that made me. All things show me that there is a God who must needs be greater, wiser, and better, than all his creatures, and therefore ought to be most honoured, feared, loved, and obeyed. I see multitudes of persons of the same nature with me, and therefore obliged to the same duty to God; I see much of God's work in them which is good, and therefore to be loved; and I see that we are all parts of one world, and made to be useful to one another. These, and many such things, the reason of man may discern in himself and other works of God.

Q. 6. But I thought the law of nature had been every man's natural temper and disposition, which inclineth him to action, and you make it to be only a notifying sign of duty.

A. Figuratively, some call every inclination a law, but it is no such thing that we are speaking of, only a man's natural inclination, among other signs, may notify his duty. But I hope you cannot think that a man's vicious inclination is God's law: then you would make original sin, and the work of the devil, to be God's law. One man's sinful distemper of soul, and another man's bodily distemper, (the fruit of sin,) inclineth him to wrath, to lust, to idleness, to sinful sports, or drinking, or gluttony; and these are so far from being God's law of nature, that they are the contraries, and the law of Satan in our members, rebelling against the law of God. And though the good inclinations of our common nature (to justice, peace, temperance) be by some called the law of nature, it is not as they are inclinations, but as from them we may know our duty.

Q. 7. Hath God any natural officers under him in governing man? I pray you tell me how far man's power is of God?

A. God hath set up divers sorts of human governing powers under him in the world, which all have their place and order assigned them; some by nature as entire; some by the law of nature, since the fall; and some by supernatural revelation, which is not to be here spoken to, but afterward.

Q. 8. Because I have heard some say that God made no government, but men do it by consent for their necessity, I pray you show me what government God made by nature, and in what order?

A. 1. Next to God's own governing right, which is the first, God hath made every man a governor of himself. For God made him with some faculties which must be ruled, (as the appetite, senses, and tongue, and other bodily members, yea, and passions too,) and with some which must rule the rest, as the understanding by guidance, and the will by command. And this self-governing power is so necessary and natural, that no man can take it from us, or forbid us the due exercise of it, any more than they can bind us to sin or to self-destruction.

Q. 9. Which is the next human power in order?

A. 2. The governing power of the husband over the wife, whose very nature, as well as original, shows that she was made to be subject, though under the law of love.

Q. 10. But is not this by consent, rather than by nature?

A. It is by consent that a woman is married; but when she hath made herself a wife, nature maketh her a subject, unless madness, or disability, make the man unmeet for his place?

Q. 11. Which is the next sort of natural government?

A. 3. The parents' government of their children: nature maketh it the duty of parents to rule, and of children to obey. And though some have been so unnatural as to deny this, and say that children owe nothing but reverence and gratitude, yet there is no danger of the common prevalency of such a heresy, which the nature of all mankind confuteth, save that licentious youth will take advantage of it, to disobey their parents, to please their lusts.

Q. 12. What is the human government which God's law of nature hath instituted to man, since his fall and corruption?

A. 4. That is to be afterwards explained: but magistracy, or civil government, is certainly of natural institution, though it is uncertain how God would have governed man in such societies by man, if they had not sinned. The law of nature teacheth man the necessity of civil society, and of government therein, and therefore obligeth man thereto.

Q. 13. This seemeth to be but the effect of men's own perceived necessity, and so to be but their arbitrary choice.

A. Their necessity is natural, and the notice of it is natural, and the desire of remedy is natural, and the fitness of magistracy to its use is natural: therefore it is the law of God in nature that bindeth them to choose and use it: and if any country should choose to live without magistracy, they would sin against the law of nature, and their own good.

Q. 14. But I have heard that God hath made no law what form of civil government shall be used, but left it to every country's choice.

A. God hath, by nature, made it necessary that there be magistracy; that is, some men in power over societies, to enforce the obedience of God's own common laws, and to make their subordinate laws about undeterminate, mutable matters to that end, for the honour of God, and the good of the society.

But, 1. Whether this government shall be exercised by one or many; 2. And who shall be the persons; God's law hath left undetermined to human liberty: the form and the persons are chosen, neither by the said persons, nor by the people only, but by the mutual consent and contract of both. 3. And also by this contract, the degree of power, and order of the exercise, may be stated and limited; but for all that, when human consent hath chosen the persons, the essential power of governing in subordination to God's laws, floweth, not from man, but immediately from God's law of nature.

Q. 15. But what if these sorts of government prove cross to one another, and reason commandeth one thing, a husband another, a parent another, and the magistrate another, which must be obeyed?

A. Each have their proper work and end, which none of the other can forbid. Self-government is the reasonable management of our own faculties and actions in obedience to God, for our own salvation, and no king, or other, can take this from us: and if they forbid us any necessary duty to God, or necessary means of our salvation, they do it without authority, and are not to be therein obeyed.

A husband's power to govern his wife is for the necessary ends of their relation, which the king hath no power to forbid. A parent's power to rule his children is for the necessary education of them, for the welfare of soul and body, and the king hath no power to forbid it. Should he forbid parents to feed their children, or teach them God's laws, or to choose for them orthodox, fit tutors, pastors, and church communion where God is lawfully worshipped, and should he command the children to use the contrary, it is all null and powerless.

But it belongeth to the magistrate only (though not to destroy any of the three former governments, which are all before his in nature and time, yet) to govern them all, by directing the exercise of them in lawful things to the common good.

Q. 16. How far doth the law of nature assure us of God's rewards and punishments?

A. As it assureth us that perfect man owed God perfect obedience, trust, and love, so it certifieth us, 1. That this performed, must needs be acceptable to God, and tend to the felicity of the subject, seeing God's love is our felicity. 2. And that sinning against God's law deserveth punishment. 3. And that governing justice must make such a difference between the obedient and the sinner as the ends of government require. 4. And seeing that before man's obedience, or sin, God made man's soul of a nature not tending to its own mortality, we have cause to expect that man's rewards and punishments should be suitable to such immortal souls. For though he can make brutes immortal, and can annihilate man's soul, or any creature, yet we see that he keeps so close to his natural establishments, that we have no reason to think that he will cross them here, and annihilate souls to shorten their rewards or punishments.

Q. 17. But doth nature tell us what kind of rewards and punishments men have?

A. The faculties of the soul being made in their nature to know God in our degree, to love him, to please him, and to rest and rejoice herein, and this in the society of wise, and good, and blessed, joyful fellow-creatures, whom also our nature is made to love, it followeth that the perfection of this nature, in these inclinations and actions, is that which God did make our nature for, to be obtained by the obeying of his laws.

And sin being the injurious contempt and forsaking of God, and the most hurtful malady of the soul, and of societies, and to others, it followeth that those that have finally forsaken God, be without the happiness of his love and glory, and under the sense of their sin and his displeasure; and that their own sin will be their misery, as diseases are to the body; and that the societies and persons that by sin they injured or infected, will somewhat contribute to their punishment. Happiness to the good, and misery to the bad, the light and law of nature teacheth man to expect, but all that I have taught you is much more surely and fully known by supernatural revelation.

CHAPTER VI.

OF SUPERNATURAL REVELATION OF GOD'S WILL TO MAN, AND OF THE HOLY SCRIPTURES, OR BIBLE.

Q. 1. WHAT do you call supernatural revelation?

A. All that revelation of God's mind to man, which is made by him extraordinarily, above what the common works of nature do make known: though, perhaps, God may use in it some natural second causes, in a way unknown to us.[a]

Q. 2. How many ways hath God thus revealed his will to man?

A. Many ways. 1. By some voice and signs of his presence, which we do not well know what creature he used to it, whether angels, or only at present caused that voice and glory. So he spake to Adam and Eve, and the serpent, and to Moses in the mount, and tabernacle, and in the cleft of the rock, Exod. xxxiv. And to Abraham, Jacob, &c.[b]

2. By angels certainly appearing, as sent from God; and so he spake to Abraham, Isaac, Jacob, Lot, Moses, and to very many.[c]

3. By visions and dreams in their sleep, extraordinary.[d]

4. By the vision of some signs from heaven in their waking; as Saul (Acts ix.) saw the light that cast him down.[e]

5. By visions and voices in an ecstasy; as Paul saw paradise, and heard unutterable things; whether in the body, or out of the body, he knew not. And it is like in such a rapture Daniel and John had their revelations.

6. By Christ's own voice, as he spake to men on earth, and Paul from heaven.

7. By the sight of Christ and glory, as Stephen saw him.

8. By immediate inspiration to the minds of prophets.

9. By these prophets sent as messengers to others.

10. By certain uncontrolled miracles.

11. By a convincing course of extraordinary works of God's providence; as when an angel killed the armies of enemies, or when they killed one another in one night or day, &c.

12. By extraordinary works of God on the souls of men; as when he suddenly overcometh the strongest vicious habits and customs, and maketh multitudes new and holy persons, by such improbable but assigned means, by which he promised to do it.

Q. 3. These are all excellent things, if we were sure that they were not deceived, nor did deceive. But how shall we be sure of that?

A. It is one thing to ask how they themselves were sure that they were not deceived, and another thing to ask how we are, or others may be, sure of it. As to the first, they were sure, as men are of other things which they see, hear, feel, and think. I am sure, by sense and intellectual perception, that I see the light, that I hear, feel, think, &c. The revelation cometh to the person in its own convincing evidence, as light doth to the eye.[f]

Q. 4. They know what they see, hear, feel; but how were they sure that it was of God, and not by some deceiving cause?

A. 1. God himself gave them the evidence of this also in the revelation, that it was from him, and no deceit. But it is no more possible for any of us, that never had such a revelation ourselves, to know sensibly and formally what it is, and how they knew it, than it is for a man born blind to know how other men see, or what seeing is. 2. But, moreover, they also were sure that it was of God, by the proofs by which they make us sure of it. And this leads us up to the other question.[g]

Q. 5. And a question of unspeakable moment it is, how we can be sure of such prophetical revelations

[a] Matt. xi. 25, 27; Luke x. 22; Deut. xxix. 29; Matt. xvi. 17; 1 Cor. ii. 10.
[b] Eph. iii. 5; 1 Pet. i. 12; Dan. ii. 47, 22, 28, 29; Amos iii. 7; Gal. i. 12; ii. 2.
[c] Eph. iii. 3.
[d] 1 Cor. xiv. 6, 26.
[e] 2 Cor. xii. 1, 7.
[f] 1 John i. 1—3.
[g] Heb. ii. 3, 4.

delivered to us by others; viz. that they were not deceived, nor deceive us.

A. It is of exceeding consequence, indeed, and therefore deserveth to be understandingly considered and handled.

And here you must first consider the difference of revelation. Some were but made or sent by prophets to some particular persons, about a personal, particular business; as to Abraham, that he should have a son, that Sodom should be burnt; to David, that his son should be his punishment, his child die; to Hezekiah, that he should recover, &c. These none were bound to know and believe but the persons concerned, to whom they were revealed and sent, till they were made public afterwards. But some revelations were made for whole countries, and some for all the world, and that as God's laws, or covenants, which life and death dependeth on; and these must, accordingly, be made known to all.

Q. 6. I perceive, then, that before we further inquire of the certainty, I should first ask you of the matter; what things they be that God hath supernaturally revealed to man, especially for us all?

A. The particular revelations to and about particular men's matters, are many of them recorded to us for our notice; but there may be many thousands more in the world that we know not, nor are concerned to know. What revelation God ever made to any persons throughout the world, as what should befall them, when they should die, what wars, or plagues, or famine, should come, &c. little do we know; but what is recorded by God we know.

2. But as for his laws and promises, which we are all concerned to know, I shall now but name, and afterward open what God hath revealed.

I. He revealed to Adam, besides the law of nature, which was perfecter and clearer to him than it is now to us, a trying prohibition to eat of the fruit of the tree of knowledge, adding the penalty of death to restrain him.[h]

II. He judged him after his fall to some degree of punishment, but declared his pardoning mercy, and promised victory to and by the woman's seed, in the war which they now engaged in with Satan, the serpent, and his seed; and he instituted sacrificing to typify the means.[i]

III. He renewed this covenant with Noah, after the flood.

IV. He made a special promise to Abraham, to be the God of his seed, as a peculiar people chosen to him out of all the world, and that all nations should be blessed in his seed: and he instituted the sacrament of circumcision to be the seal and symbol.[k]

V. When his seed were multiplied in Egypt, he brought them out, and in performance of this promise, made them a holy commonwealth, as their sovereign, and gave them at large a law and subgovernors, which, as political, was proper to that people.[l]

VI. In the fulness of time God sent his Son to reconcile man to God, to reveal his love and will most fully, and to make and seal the covenant of grace in its last and best edition, and, as King, to rule and judge the redeemed, and sanctify, justify, and glorify the faithful. These are the public laws and covenants supernaturally revealed.[m]

Q. 7. Is it equally necessary to us to believe every word in the Bible? or is every word equally certain to us?

A. All truths are truths, which is to be equally true in themselves: and so, if by certainty you mean nothing but infallible truth, every truth is so certain; and all God's words are true. But if by certain you mean that which is so evident to us, that we may ourselves be fully certain of the truth, so the parts of God's word have different degrees of certainty. We suppose false translations and false printings are none of God's work; nor the words of Satan, or fallible men, recited in the Bible, save only the historical assertion that such words were spoken by them. But that which is God's word indeed, is none of it so far void of proof but that we may come to a certainty that it is true: and if we had equal evidence that every word is God's word, we should have equal evidence that all is true; for that God cannot lie is the foundation truth of all our certainty. But God did not reveal every truth in the Bible with equal evidencing attestation from heaven. Some of them much more concern us than others, and therefore were more fully sealed and attested.[n]

Q. 8. How are we sure of the law that was given to Adam, and that he sinned, as is written, and had after a pardoning law?

A. 1. The law of nature given him is yet God's common law to the world, saving the strictness of it as a condition to life. 2. The fall of man hath too full proof in all the pravity of mankind from the birth. 3. The pardoning act is evident in the execution: God giveth all men mercy, contrary to their deserts, and useth none in the utmost rigour. 4. The notorious enmity, between Christ and Satan, and their seeds, through all ages and places of the world, doth prove the sentence, and the law of grace. 5. The universal curse, or punishment, on mankind, showeth somewhat of the cause. 6. The tradition of sacrificing was so universally received over all the world, as confirmeth to us that God delivered it to Adam, as a symbol and a type of the grace then promised. 7. But our fullest proof of all that history, is that which after proved the word that revealed it to us.[o]

Q. 9. How are we certain that the law of Moses was God's law?

A. 1. By a course of wonderful miracles wrought to prepare them to receive it, and to attest it. The ten marvellous plagues of Egypt; the passage through the Red sea; the opening of the rock to give them water; feeding them with manna; raining twice quails upon them; the sight of the flaming mount, with the terrible concomitants; the sight of the pillar of fire by night, and cloud by day, which conducted them; the sight of the cloud and symbol of God's presence at the door of the tabernacle; the miraculous destruction of the rebellious, even by the opening of the earth; and the performance of God's promises to them: all these were full proofs that it was of God. 2. But we have yet fuller proof in Christ's latter testimony, which confirmeth all this to us.

Q. 10. These were full proofs to those that saw them. But are we certain that the records of them in the Scripture are true?

A. 1. Consider that they were written, by Moses, to that very people who are said to see them.[p] And if one should now write to us Englishmen, that God brought us out of another land by ten such public

[h] Gen. ii. 16, 17; iii. 15. [i] Gen. iv. 4; ix. 1, 2—8.
[k] Gen. xii. 2, 3; xvii. 1, 2, 4, 6—11.
[l] Exod. ii. &c. xx. &c.
[m] John i.; iii. 16; Gal. iv. 4—6; i. 4; Matt. xxviii. 19, 20.
[n] Heb. vii. 22; ix. 15—18; ix. 13; viii. 10; x. 16; Matt. iv.

[o] Psal. xiv.; Rom. iii.; Psal. cxlv. 9; Acts xiv. 17; 1 John iii. 8; Rom. iii. 21, 23; iv. 12, 15—17; 2 Kings x. 19; Acts xiv. 13, 18; 1 Cor. x. 20.
[p] Deut. i. 31; iii. 21, 22; iv. 3, 9; v. 24; x. 21; xi. 7; xxix. 3; Josh. xxiv. 7.

miracles, as the frogs, the flies, the lice, the darkness, the waters turned blood, the death of their cattle, and of all their first-born; that he opened the sea, and brought us through it on foot; that he opened rocks; fed us with manna; rained quails for a month's food; spake from a flaming mount, and opened the earth to swallow up rebels, &c. When we know all this to be false, would not all men deride and abhor the reporter? Would any of us receive a law, and that of such operous, numerous, costly services, by the motive of such a report as this?

2. Consider that this law so delivered was on this ground entertained, and unchangeably kept by them from generation to generation, it being taken for a heinous crime to alter it in one word.[q]

3. Consider that practised, sacramental symbols, from the first day, were so uninterruptedly kept, as was a fuller proof of the fact than the bare writings. 1. All their males, from the promise to Abraham, were constantly circumcised, (save in the wilderness travels,) and are to this day. 2. From the very night that the first-born were killed in Egypt, and they driven hastily out, they yearly continued the eating of the passover with unleavened bread, as in a hasting posture. 3. Since the law given in the wilderness, they constantly used the sacrifices, the oblations, the tabernacle, the priesthood and ceremonies, as that law prescribed them. And the national, constant use of these was, an ascertaining tradition of the matters of fact which were their cause. 4. Yea, so tenacious were they of this law, that (as they taught the very syllables of it to their children, and kept in the ark the very tables of stone that had the ten commandments, so) they were enemies to christianity, because the christians were against the gentiles' observation of their law, and for its abrogation.

4. Consider again, that the matter of fact, and the divine institution, is since made certain to us by Christ's testimony.

Q. 11. But seeing this law doth not bind us now, nor the particular messages of the prophets were sent to us, is it any of our concern now to know or believe them? It belongeth to those that they were made for, and sent to; but what are they to us?

A. There is not the same necessity to know them, and so to be such that they were all of God, as there is to know and believe the gospel: but it is greatly our duty and concern to believe them; 1. Because they were preparatory to the gospel, and bore an antecedent testimony to it. 2. Because the gospel itself beareth witness of their truth, which therefore, if we believe it, we must believe. 3. Because by the Holy Ghost's direction all now make up our books of sacred records, which is the certain word of God, though not all of the same necessity and evidence.

And here I must tell you a great and needful truth, which ignorant christians, fearing to confess, by overdoing, tempt men to infidelity. The Scripture is like a man's body, where some parts are but for the preservation of the rest, and may be maimed without death: the sense is the soul of the Scripture, and the letters but the body, or vehicle. The doctrine of the creed, Lord's prayer, and decalogue, and baptism, and Lord's supper, is the vital part, and christianity itself. The Old Testament letter (written as we have it about Ezra's time) is that vehicle which is as imperfect as the revelation of those times was; but as after Christ's incarnation and ascension the Spirit was more abundantly given, and the revelation more perfect and sealed, so the doctrine is more full, and the vehicle or body, that is, the words, are less imperfect, and more sure to us; so that he that doubts of the truth of some words in the Old Testament, or of some small circumstantials in the New, hath no reason, therefore, to doubt of the christian religion, of which these writings are but the vehicle, or body, sufficient to ascertain us of the truth of the history and doctrine. Be sure, first, that Christ is the very Son of God, and it inferreth the certainty of all his words, and enforceth our whole religion.

Q. 12. I perceive, then, that our main question is, both as to necessity and evidence, how we are sure that the gospel is true, and the records of it the very word of God?

A. It is so: and as it is this that must rule and judge the church, so we have to us fuller proof of this than of the Old Testament; because, that the narrowness of the Jews' country, in comparison of the christian world, and the many thousand years' distance, and a language whose phrase and proverbial speeches, and the very sense of the common words of it, must needs make it more unknown to us, than the language that the gospel is recorded in. And it is not the least proof of the truth of the Old Testament, that it is attested and confirmed by the New.

Q. 13. Will you first tell me, how the apostles, and that first age, were sure that the gospel of Christ was the very word of God?

A. Here I must first tell you, that the great mystery of the blessed Trinity, Father, Son, and Holy Ghost being one God, is made necessary to us to be believed, not only as to the eternal, unsearchable Inexistence, but especially for the knowledge of God's three great sorts of works on man: that is, as our Creator, and the God of nature; as our Redeemer, and the God of governing and reconciling grace; and as our Sanctifier, and the applier and perfecter of all to fit us for glory. And as the Son, as Redeemer, is the way to the Father, (to know him and his love, and be reconciled to him,) and the Holy Ghost is the witness of the Son. The proof, therefore, of the gospel of Christ, in one word, is the Holy Ghost; that is, the certain testimony of God's Spirit. And this testimony consisteth of these several parts. I. The foregoing testimony of the Spirit by all the prophecies of the Old Testament, and the typical prefigurations, which became a fuller proof than before, when they were seen all to be fulfilled in Christ; yet many were fulfilled before. When Abraham had no child, he was promised the multiplication of his seed, and that all nations should be blessed therein, Gen. xii. 2; xiii. 16; xv. 5; xvii. 2; xviii. 11, 12. The four hundred years of their abode in Egypt and Canaan before were foretold, and punctually fulfilled, Gen. xv. 13, 14; Exod. xii. 31, 32. So was Jacob's prophecy of Judah's sceptre, Gen. xlii. 8—10, and Joseph's dreams: and verily Balaam's last prophecy was marvellous; who, when he had blessed Israel, and foretold their victories, foretold also the sceptre of David and Christ, and the success of the Assyrians; and after that of Chittim against the Hebrews themselves, Numb. xxiv. And who seeth not the fulfilling of the terrible prophecy of Moses against the Jews? Deut. xxxi. Josiah by name, and his deeds, were foretold three hundred years before he was born, 1 Kings xiii. 2; 2 Kings xxiii. 15. Oft was the captivity of the Jews foretold, and the destruction of Babylon; and the Jews' return, by Cyrus, named long before he was born, and the very time foretold. From the beginning Christ was promised, and the circumstances of his coming foretold, Gen. iii. 15; xxvi. 4; xlix. 10; Deut. xviii. 15; Psal. ii.; xxvii.; lxxxix.; cx.; Isa. liii.; xi. 1; Jer. xxxiii. 15; Mic. v. 2; that he should be born of a virgin, (Isa. vii. 14,) in Bethlehem, (Mic. v. 2,) and then the infants killed, Jer. xxxi. 15; that he should

q Deut. xii. 32.

come into the temple, as the angel of the covenant whom they desired, but they should not endure therein when he came, because he came as a refiner, Mal. iii. 1, 3; that he should go into Egypt, and return thence, Isa. xix. 1; Hos. xi. 1; that one should go before him to prepare the way, Mal. iii. 1; that he should do wonders for the people, Isa. xxxv. 5; that a familiar should betray him, and that for thirty pieces of silver, (Psal. xli. 9; lv. 13, 14; Zech. xi. 12, 13,) and a potter's field be bought with them. All his persecution, and abuse, and sufferings, are foretold, (Isa. l. 6; liii.; Psal. lxix. 21; xxii. 18; cxviii. 22; Isa. vi. 9,) even to the circumstances of giving him vinegar, casting lots for his garments, suffering as a malefactor; yea, the very time is foretold, Dan. ix. 25, 26; and that then the second temple should be destroyed.

II. The second part of the Spirit's testimony, or the certain proof of christian truth, is, the inherent constitutive proof or testimony in the inimitable excellency of the person and gospel of Christ, which is the image and superscription of God. The person of Christ was of such excellency of wisdom, goodness, and power, apparent in his doctrine, works, and patience, all sinless, and full of holy love to God and man, as is not consistent with being the deceiver of the world. His gospel, in the very constitution of it, hath the impress of God. He that hath the Spirit of God, will find that in the gospel, which is so suitable to the divine nature, as will make it the easier to him to believe it. Angels preached the sum of it, Luke ii. 14. It is all but the fore-promised and prefigured redemption of man historically delivered, and the doctrine,[r] laws, and promises of saving grace most fully promulgated; it is the wonderful revelation of the power, wisdom, and goodness, the truth, justice, and holiness of God, especially his love to man; and of his marvellous design for the recovery, sanctifying, and saving of sinners, and removing all the impediments of their repentance and salvation; it is so wholly fitted to the glorifying of God, and the reparation of depraved nature, and the purifying and perfecting of man's soul to the guidance of men's lives in the ways of true wisdom, godliness, righteousness, soberness, mutual love and peace, that men may live profitably to others, and live and die in the sense of God's love, and in a safe and comfortable state; that we may be sure so good a thing had a good cause: for had it been the device of men, they must have been very bad men that would put God's name to it, and tell so many lies from generation to generation, to deceive the world; and it is not to be imagined, that from Moses' time to the writing of John's Revelation, there should arise a succession of men of such a strange, self-contradicting constitution, as should be so good as to devise the most holy, and righteous, and self-denying doctrines, for the great good of mankind, and yet all of them so odiously wicked as to belie God, and deceive men, and do all this good in so bad a manner, with so bad a heart.

And if any blasphemer would father it upon evil spirits, what a contradiction would he speak! As if Satan would promote the greatest good, for the honour of God and benefit of man, while he is the greatest hater of God and man; and as if he would devise a doctrine to reproach himself, and destroy his own kingdom, and bless mankind; and so were at once the best and the worst.

Indeed the holy Scriptures do bear the very image and superscription of God in their ends, matter, and manner, and prove themselves to be his word: for God hath not given us external proofs that such a book or doctrine is his, which is itself no better than human works, and hath no intrinsic proof of its divine original;[s] but the intrinsic and extrinsic evidences concur. What book, like the sacred Scriptures, hath taught the world the knowledge of God; the creation of the world; the end, and hope, and felicity of man; what the heavenly glory is, and how procured, and how to be obtained, and by whom; how man became sinful and miserable; and how he is recovered; and what wonders of love God hath shown to sinners, to win their hearts in love to him? What book hath so taught men to live by faith, and the hopes of glory, above all the lusts of sense and flesh, and to refer all things in this world to spiritual, holy, and heavenly ends; to love others as ourselves, and to do good to all, even to our enemies; to live in such union, and communion, and peace, as is caused by this vital grace of love, and not like a heap of sand, that every spurn or blast of cross interest will separate? What book so teacheth man to love God above all, and to pray to him, praise him, and absolutely obey him with constant pleasure, and to trust him absolutely with soul, body, and estate, and cast all our care upon him; and, in a word, to converse in heaven while we are on earth; and to live as saints, that we may live as angels?[t]

Q. 14. But how few be there that do all this?

A. 1. I shall further answer that anon: none do it in perfection, but all sound christians do it in sincerity. 2. But at present, it is the perfection of the doctrine of Christ, and of the sacred Scriptures, that I am proving; and it is not men's breaking the law that will prove that God made it not.

Q. 15. You have told me of the foregoing testimony of the Spirit of Christ and the gospel, and of the inherent constitutive testimony, or proof; is there any other?

A. Yes, III. There is the concomitant testimony, by the works of Christ. Nicodemus could say, "We know that thou art a teacher come from God, for no man can do the works that thou doest, except God were with him," John iii. 2. He cleansed the lepers with his word; he cast out devils; he healed the lame, the deaf, the blind, yea, those that were born blind; he healed palsies, fevers, and all manner of sicknesses, with a touch, or a word; he turned water into wine; he fed twice many thousands by miracle; he walked on the sea, and made Peter do the same; the winds and sea obeyed his command; he raised the dead. This course of miracles was the most evident testimony of God.

And he was brought into the world by miracle: born of a virgin; foretold and named Jesus by an angel; preached to shepherds by angels from heaven; a star conducting the eastern wise men to the place; John, his foregoer, named by an angel, and Zacharias struck dumb for not believing it; prophesied of by Anna and Simeon; owned at his baptism by the visible descent of the Spirit, in the shape of a dove, and by a voice of God from heaven, and the like again at his transfiguration, when Moses and Elias appeared with him, and he did shine in glory; and at his death the earth trembled, the sun was obscured, and the air darkened, and the veil of the temple rent; but the fullest evidence was Christ's

[r] Col. i. 15—19; Prov. xxx. 5; Heb. iv. 12; 1 Pet. i. 23; 1 John ii. 14; John viii. 48; xii. 48; xiv. 25; xv. 3; Acts xiv. 3; xx. 32; Rom. x. 8; Eph. v. 26; Phil. ii. 16; 1 Thess. i. 5; James i. 2; Matt. xii 26; Mark iv. 15; Luke x. 18; Acts xxvi. 18; Rom. xvi. 20; Rev. xx. 2, 3.

[s] 2 Pet. i. 20; 2 Tim. iii. 15, 16; Matt. v. 16, 44, 45.

[t] John iii. 3, 5; Tit. ii. 14; 1 Pet. ii. 9; Rom. viii. 9; Matt. v. 20; Heb. xii. 14; Matt. xviii. 3; 2 Cor. v. 17; Rom. viii. 14.

own resurrection from the dead, his oft appearing to his disciples after, and conversing with them at times for forty days, and giving them their commission, and promising them the Spirit, and ascending into heaven in their sight. And all this was the fuller testimony, in that he had oft over and over foretold them of it, that he must be put to death, and rise again the third day, before he entered into his glory; and the Jews knew it, and were not able to prevent it, angels terrifying the soldiers on the watch; yea, the disciples understood it not, and, therefore, believed it not, and Peter dissuaded him from such talk of his sufferings, till Christ called him Satan, (doing like Satan that had tempted him, when he fasted forty days,) to show that the disciples were no contrivers of a deceit herein.

Q. 16. Is there yet any further witness of the Holy Ghost?

A. Yes, IV. There was the consequent testimony of the Spirit by the apostles, and other first publishers of the gospel. Christ bid them wait at Jerusalem for this gift, and promised them that when he was ascended he would send that Paraclete, Advocate, or Comforter, that should be better than his visible presence, and should lead them into all truth, and bring all things to their remembrance, and teach them what to say; that is, to enable them to perform the work to which he had commissioned them, which was to go into all the world, and preach the gospel, and disciple the nations, baptizing them, and teaching them to observe all things that he had commanded them; which they performed partly by word, and partly by writing, and partly by practice, baptizing, gathering churches, establishing offices and officers; and he promised to be with them to the end of the world; that is, with their persons for their time, and with their doctrine, ordinary successors, and the whole church ever after.[u]

On the day of Pentecost, even the Lord's day, when they were assembled, this promise was so far performed to them, that the Holy Ghost suddenly fell on all the assembly, in the likeness of fiery, cloven tongues, after the noise as of a rushing wind, and they were filled with the Spirit, and spake in the tongues of all the countries near them, the praises and wondrous works of God. After which they were endued with the various miraculous gifts of the Spirit; that is, the use of the tongues which they had never learned; the interpretation of them, prophesying, miracles, healing all diseases, insomuch that those that came but under the shadow of Peter, and those that had but clothes from the body of Paul, were all healed; the lame and blind cured, devils cast out, the dead raised, some enemies struck blind, some sinners struck dead; and, which was yet greater, by their preaching, or praying, or laying on of hands, God gave the same miraculous gift of the Spirit to others; and that not to a few, but ordinarily to the faithful, some having one such gift, and some another.

And as Christ had promised that when he was lifted up he would draw all men to him, so he blessed the labours of the apostles, prophets, and evangelists, accordingly; many thousands being converted at a sermon, and multitudes still added to the church. And when the preachers were forbidden and imprisoned, Christ strengthened them, and angels miraculously delivered them. When Peter was in prison, designed for death, the angel of God loosed his bolts, and opened the doors, and led him forth. When Paul and Silas had been scourged, and were in the stocks in the prison, an earthquake sets them free, and prepareth for the conversion of the jailer and his house. And Christ himself had before appeared to Paul in glory, when he was going on in persecution, and struck him down in blindness, and preached to him with a voice from heaven, and converted him, and sent him as his apostle into the world. By these miracles was the world converted.

And as Christ had promised them that they should do greater works than those which he himself did, so indeed their miracles did more to convert the world than the works of Christ in person had done. For, 1. Those which were wrought by one man would leave suspicious men more doubtful of the truth than that which is done by many, at a distance from each other, and in several places. 2. And that which was done but in one small country would be more doubted of than that which is done in much of the world. Sometimes, indeed, thousands, but usually twelve men, were the witnesses of what Christ said and did; but what these witnesses said and did to prove their testimony, thousands in many lands did see and hear.

Q. 17. But why was it that Christ forbade some to declare that he was the Christ?

A. Because the time was not come, till the evidences were given by which it must be proved; it was not a matter to be rashly believed, and taken upon the bare word of himself or any other. That a man living in a mean condition was the Son of God, and Saviour, and Lord, and Teacher of the world, and the Judge of all men, was not to be believed without good proof: and the chief proof was to be from all Christ's own miracles, and his resurrection, and ascension, and the great gift of the Holy Ghost, and the tongues and miracles of the apostles and other disciples; and these were not all done or given then: yet because the Jews received Moses and the prophets, he sometimes showed how they prophesied of him; yea, his very doctrine, whose frame had a self-evidencing light, was not fully revealed till it was done by the Spirit in the apostles.[x]

Q. 18. But though all these miracles were wrought, how could it be certain that they were the attestation of God, when it is said that magicians, false prophets, and antichrist may do such things?

A. 1. I shall first mind you, that though we were never so uncertain of the nature of a miracle, whether it be wrought by any created cause, yet we are agreed that, by miracles, we mean such works which were wrought quite out of and against the common course of second courses, called nature; and we are sure that as no work can be done without God's promotion, or permission, at least, so especially the course of nature cannot be altered and overruled but by God's knowledge, consent, and execution; whatever second cause unknown to us may be in it, certainly God is the first cause.

2. And it is most certain that the most perfect Governor of the world is not the great deceiver of the world, and is not so wanting in power, wisdom, and goodness, as to rule them by a lie; yea, and an unresistible and remediless deceit: this is rather the description of Satan.

3. And man must know the will of God by some signs or other, or else he cannot do it; and what signs can the wit of man devise, by which they that would fain know the will of God may come to be certain of it, if such a course of miracles may deceive

u John xvi.; Acts ii.; Matt. xxviii. 20. The whole book of the Acts of the Apostles is the history of these miracles. Gal. iii. 1—4; John vii 3, 9; Rom. i. 4; 1 Cor. xii. 4, 7—9, 11, 13.

x Luke iv. 22; xxiv. 27, 32, 45; John v. 39; Acts xvii. 2, 11; xviii. 28; Rom. i. 2; xvi. 26; 1 Cor. xv. 3, 4; 2 Pet. i. 19, 20; Heb. ii. 3, 4; Rom. iii. 4; John iii. 2; 1 John v. 10; Tit. ii. 2.

us? Would you believe if some came from the dead as witnesses? or, if an angel, or many angels, came from heaven? All these could give you no more certainty than such miracles may do.[y]

4. And you must note, that the proof of miracles lieth not on this, that angels, or other spirits, or second causes, can do no such things, but that they cannot do it without God, and that God will not do it to confirm a lie, or any thing which he would not have man believe; for then either man must believe nothing sent from God, though it were by a host of angels, or else he must say, I am unavoidably deceived by God himself, for I have no possible means left to know the fallacy.

5. Therefore you must note, that whenever God permitteth a magician, or false prophet, to do any wonder, or unusual thing, he never leaveth man without a remedy against the deceit, but doth control and confute the words of the deceiver; and usually he doth it but first to try the faith and stedfastness of men, and then to bring truth into the clearer light. And he controlleth false miracles these ways.

1. He sealeth up the truth which the deceiver denieth, with a stream of most unquestionable miracles, and so showeth us that it cannot be a truth, and of God, which is said against such sealed verity, while all his miracles confute theirs. 2. Or, if it be a truth known to man by the common light of nature, that light confuteth the pretender's miracle. 3. If he do it to confirm a false prediction, it is confuted by the thing not coming to pass. 4. In the case of Egyptian[z] magicians' wonders, God permitted them, that his power might triumph over them, and confute them; as he may permit a sophist to talk against the truth, that he may be silenced and shamed. In none of all this doth God become the world's deceiver. But the miracles of Christ, and his apostles and disciples, were never controlled by the light of nature, by more prevalent miracles, or any such means; but were the fullest signification of God's attestation that man can have to save him from deceit.

Q. 19. I confess if I had seen all these things myself, I should have made no doubt, but God and reason bound me to believe; but how can we at this distance be sure that all these words of Christ were spoken, and these works done?

A. Let us first consider how they were sure of it that lived in that age with the apostles, and then how we may be also sure. And, I. That age, 1. Had the common evidences of the best credibility of men. 2. They had most infallible perception of it by their senses. And, 3. They had an immediate testimony from God themselves. Of these let us consider in order.

Q. 20. I. What credible human testimony do you mean they had?

A. It is supposed that some persons are to be believed much above others,[a] else all human trust and conversation would cease. He that will believe nobody, cannot expect to be himself believed.

And, 1. The witnesses of Christ's words and works were not strangers to him, that took it by report, but those that had accompanied him, and heard and seen them.

2. They spake to men of the same generation, time, and country, and mentioned things done before multitudes of spectators; so that had it been a false report, it had been most easy to confute it, and turn it all, as a lie, unto their scorn.

3. They sharply reproved the rulers and teachers for rejecting Christ, and provoked all their rage against them; so that no doubt they would do their best to have searched out all deceit in the reprovers.

4. They were men of no carnal interest, to tempt them into a deceiving plot; but were foretold that they must be hated, persecuted, and killed for their testimony.

5. They were purposely chosen from among the meaner unlearned sort, that there might be no suspicion that it was a work of carnal craft or power.

6. Though they heard and saw, so far were they from plotting it, that they understood it not themselves, nor believed that Christ must die for sin, rise the third day, and ascend into heaven, and gather a catholic church, and reign spiritually, till the time that Christ was risen, and the Holy Ghost came down upon them. And yet Christ over and over foretold it them.

7. They taught not one another, nor came to it by study and degrees; but, in the main, by sudden, common inspiration, and such as Christ had before promised them.[b]

8. Paul was called by a glory and a voice of Christ from heaven, in the sight of other persecuting company.

9. Their testimony all agreed, and all spake the same truth.

10. Their enemies never wrote a confutation of them, nor decried most of the matters of fact, but imputed it to Beelzebub.

11. None of them ever repented of his testimony; whereas had they confederated to deceive the world, some one's conscience, living or dying, would sure have forced him to confess it.

12. Yea, they sealed it with their great labour, sufferings, and blood.

13. When false teachers turned some of their followers to heresies, and to forsake them, they still appealed for the matters of fact, even to those dissenters or opposers.[c]

14. Their doctrine, by its fore-described light and goodness, testified of itself that it was of God; and that those men that at so dear a rate divulged it, in design to sanctify and save mankind, were no such wicked knaves as to plot the world's delusion. These were evidences of more than human credibility.

II. And the disciples in Judea heard and saw Christ and his miracles, and so had as much certainty of the matter of fact as sense could give them.

III. And they had God's immediate testimony in themselves; even his Spirit's internal revelation, illumination, and sanctifying work; and the wonderful gifts of healing, tongues, miracles, by which they convinced others.

Q. 21. Proceed to show me how their followers were certain?

A. 1. They were persons present, and, therefore, their senses assured them what was said and done; they were the men that heard the use of languages given by inspiration; that heard the triumphant praises of God; that saw them that were miraculously healed, and some raised from the dead. Could those doubt of the miracles that saw the lame man that begged at the temple cured by Peter and John; and that saw multitudes cured by the very shadow and clothes of the apostles; when they that saw the lame man healed, (Acts xiv.) would have sacrificed to Paul and Barnabas as gods?[d]

2. They kept constant church meetings; and the use of languages, and other extraordinary gifts of the Spirit, were the ordinary exercises of those assemblies; so that they could not be unknown.[e]

[y] 2 Cor. xi. 4; Mark xvi. 17; Exod. iv. 5, 8; xix. 9.
[z] Acts viii.; Simon Magus's case.
[a] John xix. 35; xx. 31; 1 John v. 13; 1 Cor. xv. 6.

[b] Gal. i.; ii.
[c] Gal. iii. 3, 5.
[d] Acts ii.; iii.; iv.
[e] 1 Cor. xiv.; xii.; Rev. i. 9, 10.

3. It was not a few apostles only that had this extraordinary spirit, but in one sort or other the generality of the persons converted by them; sometimes as the apostles were preaching, the Spirit came upon the hearers, as it did on Cornelius and his assembly, Acts x. Usually by the laying on of the apostles' hands the Holy Ghost was given; and this not only to the sincere christians, but to some unsound ones that fell away; all that did miracles in Christ's name were not saved.

4. Yea, those that accused Christ, as casting out devils by devils, might have seen their own children cast them out, Matt. xii. And those that were seduced, and quarrelled with the apostles, could not deny but they themselves had received the Spirit, by their preaching. Paul appealeth to themselves when the Galatians were perverted: "O foolish Galatians! who hath bewitched you, that you should not obey the truth, before whose eyes Jesus Christ hath been evidently set forth crucified among you. This only would I learn of you: received ye the Spirit by the works of the law, or by the hearing of faith? Are ye so foolish, having begun in the Spirit, are ye now made perfect by the flesh? He that ministereth to you the Spirit, and worketh miracles among you, doth he it by the works of the law, or by the hearing of faith?" Gal. iii. 1—3.

If these Galatians had not the Spirit, and such as worked miracles among them, would not this argument have turned to Paul's reproach, rather than to their conviction? Even Simon Magus was so convinced by the Spirit falling on the Samaritans, that he was baptized, and would have bought the power of giving the Holy Ghost with money, Acts viii. Their sense convinced them, and they that had the Spirit themselves must needs be sure of it.

Q. 22. Now tell me, how we may be certain that all this history is true, and that these things are not misreported by the Scripture?

A. I will speak first of the gospel as such, and then of the book.

1. You must first know, that the gospel, in the strict sense, is the history and doctrine of Christ, necessary to be believed to our salvation; which is summarily contained in the baptismal covenant. For men were christians when they were baptized; and they were not adult christians till they believed the gospel.

2. You must know, that this gospel was long preached and believed before it was written. St. Matthew began and wrote eight years after Christ's resurrection; and the Revelation of St. John was written about ninety-four years after Christ's birth; Luke's gospel, about fifty; and Mark's, about fifty-nine; and St. John's, about ninety-nine from the birth of Christ.[f]

3. You must know, that all the aforesaid miracles were wrought to confirm this gospel preached before it was written.

4. And that while the apostles lived, their preaching had as much authority as their writing. But they being to die, were moved by the Spirit to write what they had preached, that it might be, certainly without change, delivered to posterity to the end of the world; for had it been left only to the memory of man, it would soon have been variously reported and corrupted.

5. And you must know, that this Scripture is so far from being insufficient, as to the matter of our faith, as that it containeth not only the essentials, but the integrals, and useful accidents of the gospel; as a complete body hath every part, and the very ornament of hair and colour. So that a man may be a christian, that knoweth not many hundred words in the Scripture, but not unless he know and believe the essentials of the gospel.

6. And you must note, therefore, that the foresaid miracles were wrought primarily, to confirm the gospel; and that they do confirm all the accidental passages in the Bible but by consequence, because the same persons, by the same Spirit, wrote them.

Q. 23. Proceed now to show me the proof, which you promised.

A. 1. That there have been, from that time, christians in the world, is, past all doubt, acknowledged by the history of their enemies that persecuted them. And all these christians were baptized, for baptism was their solemn christening. And every one that was baptized at age did openly profess to receive this same gospel; even to believe in God the Father, the Son, and the Holy Ghost, renouncing the devil, the lusts of the flesh, and the vanities of the world.[g]

2. Yea, all that were baptized, were before taught this gospel by teachers or catechisers, who had all but one gospel, one faith, and baptism.

3. And they were all tried how they understood the foresaid general words; and therefore they were opened in more words, which we call the creed: which, in substance and sense, was still the same, though two or three words be added since the first forming of it. So that every christian, being instructed by the gospel, and professing the essence of it in the creed and baptism, we have as many witnesses that this gospel was then delivered, as there have been christians.

4. And no man doubteth but there have been ministers as long. And what was a minister but a preacher of this same gospel, and a baptizer and guide of them that believe it?

5. And none can doubt but there have been christian assemblies from that time; and what were those assemblies, but for the preaching, professing, and practising this gospel?

6. And none doubteth but they celebrated the Lord's supper in those assemblies: and the celebration of that sacrament containeth practically the profession of all the gospel of Christ.

7. And none can doubt but that the Lord's day hath ever since been constantly kept by christians, in commemoration of Christ's resurrection, and in the performance of the foresaid exercises. And therefore the very use of that day assureth us, that the gospel hath been certainly delivered us.

8. And all grant that these churches had still the use of discipline, which was, the censuring of such as corrupted this sacred doctrine by heresy, or sinned against it by wicked lives. And this could not have been, if the gospel had not been then received by them.

9. Yea, the numbers and opinions of heretics then are left on record; and they tell us what the gospel then was, by telling us wherein they departed from it.

10. Yea, the history of the persecutors and enemies tell us, that this gospel was then extant which they persecuted.

11. The Old Testament was long before in the common possession and use of the Jews. They read it every sabbath day. And in that we see Christ foretold, and abundance of prophecies, which in him are since fulfilled.

12. Lastly, the sacred Scriptures, which contain all that God thought needful to be transmitted to posterity for history and doctrine, have been most certainly kept and delivered to us; so sure and full is our tradition.

[f] Mark xvi. 20; Acts iv. 16, 22; vi. 8; viii. 6, 13; xv. 12; xix. 11.

[g] The Acts of the historical tradition of the gospel.

Q. 24. That christianity hath been propagated, none can doubt; but how are we sure that those christians of the first age did indeed see, or believe that they saw and heard those miracles?

A. 1. To be a christian, was to be one that believed them. It was half their belief in Christ, and in the Holy Ghost, and so the very essence of christianity, to believe that Christ wrought his miracles and rose again, and that the apostles, by the Holy Spirit, did work theirs, and that believers received the Spirit by their ministry.

2. They had not been made christians but by these miracles. They all professed that it was the gifts of the Spirit that convinced and converted them.

3. All the forementioned professions of their christianity contained a profession that they believed these miracles: as the use of the Lord's day, baptism, the eucharist, showed their belief of Christ's life, death, and resurrection.

4. They suffered persecution and martyrdom, in the profession of that belief.

5. They pleaded these miracles in all their defences against their adversaries.

6. The writings of their adversaries commonly acknowledge this plea; yea, and deny not the most of the miracles themselves.

7. But most fully their receiving the sacred Scriptures as the word of God, as indited by the Holy Ghost in the apostles, showeth that they believed the miracles recorded in that book.

Q. 25. You are come up to the last part of the doubt in the history: how are we sure that these christians then commonly believed the book as now we have it, and that it is the very same?

A. We have for this, full, infallible, historical proof, premising that some parcels of the book (the Revelations, the Epistle of Jude, the Second of Peter, the Epistle to the Hebrews, and that of James) were longer unknown to some particular churches than the rest.

1. The constancy of christian assemblies and public worship is a full proof, seeing that the reading, expounding, and applying of these books was a great part of their public work, as all history of friends and enemies agree.

2. The very office of the ministry is full proof, which lay most in reading, expounding, and applying these same books. And therefore they were as much by office concerned to keep them, as judges and lawyers are to keep the statute-book.

3. These ministers and churches, which so used this book, were dispersed over a great part of the world. If therefore they had changed it by adding or diminishing, they must have done it by confederacy, or by single men's error or abuse. It was impossible that all countries should agree in such a confederacy, but the meeting, motives, and treatises, would have been known. But no history of friend or foe hath any such thing, but the clean contrary. And that it should be done by all single persons in the christian world, agreeing by chance in the same changes, is a mad supposition.

4. And it is the belief of all christians, that it is a damnable sin to add or alter in this book; and the book itself so concludeth. Therefore if some had agreed so to do, the rest would have detected and decried it.

5. They took this book to be the charter for their salvation, and therefore would never agree to alter it; when men keep the deeds, evidences, leases, and charters of their estates and worldly privileges unaltered.

6. When a few heretics rose up, that forged some new books as apostolical, and rejected some that were such indeed, the christian churches condemned and rejected them, and appealed to the churches that had received the apostles' own epistles, and kept them.

7. The many heresies that rose up did so divide men, and set them in cross interests and jealousies against each other, that it was impossible for any one sect to have altered the Scripture, but the rest would have fallen upon them with the loudest accusations. But all sorts of adversaries are agreed. that these are the same books.

And though the weakness and negligence of scribes have made many little words uncertain, (for God promised not infallibility to every scribe or printer,) yet these are not such as alter any article of faith or practice, but show that no corruption hath been designedly made, but that the book is the same.

For instance, let it be questioned, whether our statute-book contained really the same statutes that are there pretended? and you will see that the historical certainty amounteth even to a natural certainty, the contrary being a mere impossibility. For, 1. They are the king's laws, and the king would not bear a fraudulent alteration. 2. Parliaments would not bear it. 3. Judges that successively judge by these laws would soon discover it. 4. So would all justices and magistrates. 5. Men's lives and estates are held by them, and therefore multitudes would decry the fraud. 6. Enemies have daily suits, which are tried by these laws, and each party pleads them for himself; and their advocates and lawyers plead them against each other, and would soon detect the forgery. So that to suppose such a change is, 1. To suppose an effect that hath no cause in nature. 2. And that is against a stream of causes moral and natural, and so impossible.

And to feign such forgeries in the book that all christians have taken for God's laws, is just such another case, and somewhat beyond it. That is but moral evidence, which dependeth only on men's honesty, or any free unnecessary acts of man's will. But man's will hath also of natural necessity, such as the love of ourselves, and our felicity, &c. And it is a natural impossibility that all men, or many, should agree in a lie, which is against these acts of natural necessity. But so they must do, if all men of cross interests, principles, and dispositions, should knowingly agree; e. g. that all our statutes are counterfeit, that there is no such place as Rome, Paris; or other such lies. And so the gospel history hath such testimony of necessary truth.

Q. 26. You have made the case plainer to me than I thought it had been. But you yet seem to intimate that some words, yea, some books of Scripture, have not the same evidence as the rest: can a man be saved that believeth not all the Scripture?

A. All truth is equally true, and so is all God's word; but all is not equally evident. He that taketh any word to be God's word, and yet to be false, believeth nothing as God's word; for he hath not the formal, essentiating act and object of faith. If God could lie, we had no certainty of faith. But he that erroneously thinketh that this or that word, yea, epistle, or text, or book in the Bible, is not God's, but came in by mistake, may be saved, if he believe that which containeth the essentials of christianity. A lame faith may be a saving faith; and he may see how miracles sealed the gospel, that cannot see how they sealed every book, text, or word, in the Bible.[h]

Q. 27. Though we have been long on this, it is of so great importance to us living or dying, to be sure

[h] Rom. xiv.; xv.

of the foundations of our faith, that I will yet ask you, have you any more proof?

A. I have told you of four proofs already: I. The antecedent testimony of the Spirit in the Old Testament. II. The inherent constitutive testimony in Christ and the gospel. III. The concomitant testimony of miracles. IV. The consequent testimony of the Spirit to, and by, the apostles' miracles and gifts. But there is yet that behind which to us is of the greatest moment; and that is,

V. The sanctifying testimony of the Holy Spirit in all true christians, in all ages and places on the earth.[i]

Here you must remember, 1. That the common experience of the world assureth us, that man's nature is greatly vitiated, inclined to known evil for some inferior good, and averse to the greatest good by the prevalency of the lesser; hardly brought to necessary knowledge, and more hardly to the love, delight, and practice of that which is certainly the best. And that hence the world is kept in confusion and misery by sin.[k]

2. Experience assureth us that there is no hope of any great cure of this, by the common helps of nature and human reason; for it is that reason that is diseased, and blinded, and therefore unapt to cure itself, as an infant or fool is to teach himself. And as philosophers are a small part of the world, (for few will be at the cost of getting such knowledge,) so they are woefully dark themselves in the greatest things, and of a multitude of sects, contradicting one another, and few of them have hearts and lives that are answerable to that which they teach others; and the wisest confess that they must expect few approvers, much less followers. And every man's own experience tells him, how hard it is to inform the judgment about holy things, and to conform the will to them, and to reform the life to a holy and heavenly state.[l]

3. The multitude of temptations makes this the more difficult, and so doth the nature of a vicious habit, and the privation of a good one; the self-defending and propagating nature of sin, and the experience of the world, tell us how wicked the world is, and how little the labours of the wisest philosophers, divines, or princes, do to reform it, and to make men better; and especially how hard it is to get a heavenly mind, and joy, and conversation: and all this being sure, it is as sure that the renovation of souls is a great work, well beseeming God. 4. And it must be added, that this is the most necessary work for us, and the most excellent: Paul tells us but what reason tells us in that, 1 Cor. xiii. how much holy love (which is the divine nature and real sanctity) excelleth all knowledge, gifts, and miracles: this is the soul's health and well-being: no man can be miserable so far as he is good and holy; and no man can choose but be miserable that is not so: many shall lie in hell that cast out devils and wrought miracles in Christ's name; but none that loved God, and are holy. Christ wrought miracles but in order to work holiness (as St. Paul, 1 Cor. i. 14, tells them, that strange languages are below edifying plainness); his work, as a Saviour, is to destroy the works of the devil. Holiness is incomparably better than the gift of working miracles.[m]

This being considered, further think, 1. That all true christians are saints: hypocrites have but the name and image: no one soundly and practically believeth in Christ, and consenteth to his covenant, but he is renewed by the Holy Ghost.

2. Consider how great and excellent a work this is; to set a man's hope and heart on heaven; to live by faith on an unseen world; to place our chiefest love and pleasure on God, holiness, and heaven; to mortify fleshly lusts, and be above the power of the love of the world, and natural life; to love others as ourselves in the measure that God appeareth in them; to love our enemies, and to make it the work of our lives to do the most good we can in the world; to bring every true believer to this in all ages and countries, which neither princes nor persuasion alone can do; this is above all miracles. And this is a standing witness which every true christian hath in himself.[n]

3. And note, also, that it is by the foresaid gospel or sealed word of Christ, that all this is wrought on all true christians; and the divine effect proveth a divine cause. God would never bless a lie, to be the greatest means of the holiness, reformation, and happiness of the world. And were not the cause fitted to it, it would never produce such effects.

Q. 28. Is this it that is called, the witness of the Spirit in us?

A. Besides all the foresaid witnessings of the Spirit without us, the Spirit within us, 1. Causeth us to understand and believe the Scripture. 2. Maketh it powerful to sanctify us. 3. And therein giveth us a connaturality and special love to it, and sense of its inherent, divine excellency; which is writing it in our hearts. 4. And causeth us to live by it. 5. And confuteth the objections made against it. 6. And causeth us to fetch our comfort from it; in a word, imprinteth the image of it on us; and this is the inward witness.

Q. 29. But when we see so much ignorance, wickedness, confusion and cruelty, pride, lust, and worldliness among christians, and how they live in malicious tearing one another, how can we know that their goodness is any proof of the truth of christianity?

A. I told you, hypocrites have but the name, and picture, and art of christianity. If custom, prosperity, laws, or carnal interest, bring the world into the visible church, and make men say,[o] they believe, when they do not, is christianity to be judged of by dissemblers and enemies? Mark any that are serious believers, and you will find them all seriously sober, just, and godly; and though weak believers have but weak grace, and many failings, they are sincerely, though imperfectly, such as I have described. And though the blind, malignant enemies can see no excellency in a saint, he that hath either known faith and holiness in himself, or hath but impartially observed mankind, will see that christians indeed are quite another sort of men than the unbelievers, and that Christ maketh men such as he teacheth them to be, and the sanctifying Spirit is the sure witness of Christ, dwelling in all true christians, (Rom. viii. 9,) as Christ's agent and advocate, witnessing that he is true, and that we are his, interceding from Christ to us, by communicating his grace, and in us toward Christ, by holy love and desires; and is God's name and mark on us, and our pledge, earnest, and first-fruits of life eternal: and though we were in doubt of old historical proofs, yet,

[i] Rom. iii. 10—12.
[k] Rom. viii. 5—9; John xii. 39, 40; Acts xxviii. 26, 27.
[l] Luke xviii. 34; 1 Cor. ii. 14; xiii. 11; Isa. xvii. 11; Jer. xiii. 23.
[m] 1 John iii. 24; iv. 12, 15, 16; Matt. vii. 21, 22, 25, 26; Heb. xii. 14.
[n] Ezek. xxxvi. 26; 1 John v. 10; 2 Tim. i. 7; Rom. viii. 3, 4, 13, 15, 26, 33; 1 Cor. ii. 10—12; vi. 10, 11, 17; xii. 11, 13; 2 Cor. iii. 3, 17; Gal. iv. 6; v. 5, 16—18, 25; Eph. ii. 18, 22; iv. 3, 4, 23; v. 9; 2 Thess. ii. 13; 1 Pet. i. 2, 3; 1 John iii. 24; iv. 13.
[o] 1 Cor. i. 1, 2; Acts xx. 32; xxvi. 18.

1. The Old Testament fulfilled in the New; 2. The divine impress discernible on the gospel; 3. And the most excellent effect of sanctification on all true believers; are evidences of the truth of christianity and the Scriptures, which all true christians have still at hand.[p]

Q. 30. But there are things in the Scripture of exceeding difficulty to believe; especially that God should become man.

A. 1. It is folly to be stalled at the believing of any thing, which we once are sure that God revealeth, considering how unmeet our shallow wit is to judge of the things of infinite wisdom, to us unseen.[q]

2. To holy, illuminated, prepared souls, belief is not so hard: it is blindness and vice that make it difficult.

3. God did not become man by any change of his Godhead, nor by confining his essence to the manhood of Christ: but, 1. by taking the human nature into a special aptitude for his operations. 2. And so relating it nearly to himself; and operating peculiarly in and on it, as he doth not on any other creature. And when all are agreed that God is essentially every where, and is as near us as we are ourselves, and more the cause of all good which we do than we ourselves are; it will be harder to show, that he is not hypostatically united to every man, than that he is so to Christ (though the foresaid aptitude of Christ's human nature, and the relation and operation of the divine, indeed, make that vast difference). If God can so peculiarly operate in and by our human nature, where lieth the incredibility?

Q. 31. But it is so transcendently above all the works of nature, that such condescension of God is hard to be believed?

A. Great works best beseem the infinite God: is not the make of the whole world as wonderful, and yet certain? God's love and goodness must have wonderful products, as well as his power.

But is it not very congruous to nature and reason, that God should have mercy on lapsed man? And that he should restore depraved human nature? And that he should do this great work like his greatness and goodness, and above man's shallow reach? And that polluted souls should not have immediate access to the Most Holy, but by a holy Mediator? And that mankind should have one universal Head and Monarch in our own nature? And that when even heathens are conscious of the great need of some divine revelations, besides the light of nature, and therefore consult their oracles and augurs, that God should give us a certain messenger from heaven to teach us necessary truth? Many such congruities I have opened in the "Reasons of the Christian Religion," Part II. Chap. 5.

The sum of all that is said, is this: I. If any history in the world be sure, the history of the gospel is sure. II. And if the history be sure, the doctrine must needs be sure. III. The continued evidences: 1. In the holiness of the doctrine; and, 2. In the holiness of all true, serious believers; are a standing proof of both, as the miracles were to all the beholders, who did not blaspheme the Holy Ghost.

Q. 32. But how comes it to be so hard then to the most to become serious believers and godly, when the evidence is so clear?

A. A blind, dead, worldly, fleshly heart doth undispose them, and they will not consider such things, nor use the means.

Yea, they so wilfully sin against knowledge and conscience, and will not obey that which they know, that they forfeit further grace. I will name you briefly many things, which every man's natural reason might know, and ask you whether you ever knew any unbeliever that was not false to this light of nature.

1. Doth not sense and reason tell men, how vile a thing that flesh is which they prefer before their souls? 2. Doth it not certify them that they must die, and so that fleshly pleasure is short? 3. Doth it not tell them of the vanity and vexation of this world? 4. And that greatest prosperity is usually parted with with greatest sorrow? 5. Doth it not tell them, that man's nature can hardly choose but fear what will follow after death? 6. Doth it not tell them, that there is a God that made them, and ruleth all? 7. And that he is infinitely great, and wise, and good, and therefore should be obeyed, loved, and trusted above all? 8. And that their lives, and souls, and all, are his, and at his will? 9. And that man hath faculties which can mind a God and life to come, which brutes have not; and that God doth not make such natures in vain? 10. Doth not experience tell them, that human nature seeth a vast difference between moral good and evil, and that all government, laws, and converse show it; and no man would be counted false and bad? 11. And that good men are the blessing of the world, and bad men the plagues? 12. And that there is a conscience in man, that condemneth sin, and approveth goodness? 13. And that most men when they die, cry out against that which worldly, fleshly men prefer; and wish that they had lived the life of saints, and might die their death? Are not these easily knowable to all? And yet all the ungodly live as if they believed none of this: and can you wonder, if all such men understand not, or believe not, the heavenly things; have no experience of the[r] sanctifying work and witness of the Holy Spirit, and have no delight in God and goodness, no strength against sin and temptations, no trust in God in their necessity, no suitableness to the gospel, nor the heavenly glory; but as they lived in sin, do die in a stupid or despairing state of soul?

p John xvii. 17, 19; Eph. v. 26; 1 Thess. v. 23; Heb. ii. 11; x. 10, 14.

q Prov. viii. 9; xiv. 6.

r John iii. 7, 8; Rom. i. 19, 20; Acts xiv. 17.

CHAPTER VII.

OF THE CHRISTIAN RELIGION, WHAT IT IS, AND OF THE CREED.

Q. 1. Now you have laid so good a foundation, by showing the certain truth of the gospel, I would better know what christianity is? And what it is to be a true christian.

A. First I must tell you what religion is in general, and then what the christian religion is. Religion is a word that signifieth either that which is without us, the rule of our religion, or that which is within us, our conformity to that rule.

The doctrinal, regulating religion, is the signification of God's will, concerning man's duty to God, and his hopes from God. The inward religion of our souls is our conformity to this revealed, regulating will of God, even our absolute resignation to God, as being his own; our absolute subjection to him, as our absolute, sovereign Ruler; and our prevailing chief love to him, as our chief Benefactor, and as love and goodness itself. Thus religion is our duty to God, and hope from God.

Q. 2. Now what is the christian religion?

Obj. A. The christian religion, as doctrinal, is, the revelation of God's will concerning his kingdom, as our Redeemer; or the redeeming and saving sinful, miserable man by Jesus Christ.

Subj. And the christian religion as it is in us, is the true conformity of our understanding, will, and practice, to this doctrine, or the true belief of the mind, the thankful love and consent of the will, and the sincere obedience of our lives to God, as our reconciled Father in Christ, and to Jesus Christ, as our Saviour, and to the Holy Ghost, as our Sanctifier, to deliver us from the guilt and power of sin, from the flesh, the world, and the devil, from the revenging justice of God, and from everlasting damnation, giving us here a union with Christ, the pardon of our sins, and sanctifying grace, and hereafter everlasting, heavenly glory. [a]

Q. 3. Is there any other religion besides the christian religion?

A. There be many errors of men, which they call their religion.

Q. 4. Is there any true religion, besides christianity?

A. There be divers that have some part of the truth, mixed with error. 1. The heathens acknowledge God, and most of his attributes and perfections, as we do; but they have no knowledge of his will, but what mere nature teacheth them; and they worship many idols, if not devils, as an under sort of gods.

2. The Jews own only the law of nature, and the Old Testament, but believe not in Jesus Christ our Redeemer.

3. The Sadducees, and all brutists, worship God as the Governor of man in this world, but they believe not a life to come for man.

4. The Pythagorean heathens look for no reward or punishment after death, but by the passing of the soul into some other body on earth, in which it shall be rewarded or punished.

5. The Mahometans acknowledge one God, as we do: but they believe not in Jesus Christ, as man's Redeemer, but only take him for an excellent, holy prophet; and they believe in Mahomet, a deceiver, as a prophet greater than he.

6. The mere deists believe in God, but not in Jesus Christ, and have only the natural knowledge of his will, as other heathens, but worship not idols, as they do.

Q. 5. Is there but one christian religion?

A. No: true christianity is one certain thing.

Q. 6. How then are christians said to be of divers religions?

A. Sound christians hold to christian religion alone, as Christ did institute it; but many others corrupt it: some by denying some parts of it, while they own the rest; and some by adding many corrupting inventions of man, and making those a part of their religion, as the papists do.

Q. 7. Where is the true christian religion, doctrinal, to be found, that we may certainly know which is it indeed?

A. The christian religion containeth, I. The light and law of nature, and that is common to them with others, and is to be found in the nature of all things, as the significations of God's will. II. Supernatural revelation, clearing the law of nature, and giving us the knowledge of the Redeemer, and his grace. [b]

And this is contained, 1. Most fully in the holy Bible. 2. Briefly and summarily in the creed, Lord's prayer, and commandments. 3. Most briefly of all in the sacraments of baptism and the Lord's supper, and the covenant made and sealed by them.

Q. 8. But are not the articles of our church, and the confessions of churches, their religion?

A. Only God's word is our religion as the divine rule; but our confessions, and books, and words, and lives, show how we understand it.

Q. 9. What is the protestant religion?

A. The religion of protestants is mere christianity: they are called protestants but accidentally, because they protest for mere Scripture christianity, against the corruptions of popery.

Q. 10. What sorts of false religions are there among christians?

A. There are more corruptions of religion than can easily be named. The chief of them are of these following sorts:

I. Some of them deny some essential article of faith or practice, as the immortality of the soul, the Godhead, or manhood, or offices of Christ, or the Holy Ghost, or the Scripture, &c.

II. Some of them pretend new revelations falsely, and set their pretences of the Spirit's inspirations against the sealed word of God.

III. Some of them set up a usurped power of their own, against the office, authority, or sufficiency of the said sealed Scriptures, pretending that they are successors to the apostles, in the power and office of making laws for the universal church, and being the judges of the sense of Scripture; yea, and what is to be taken for God's word, and what not, and judges of all controversies about it. Of these, the papists pretend that the pope and a general council are supreme, visible governors under Christ of all the christian world, and that none may appeal from them to God, to Christ, to the Scripture, or to the day of judgment. Others pretend to such a power in every patriarchal, national, or provincial church. And all of them, instead of a humble, helping, guiding ministry, set up a church leviathan, a silencing Abaddon, and Apollyon, a destroying office, setting up their usurped power above, or equal in effect with, God's word.

Q. 11. How come the Scriptures to be God's word, when the bishops' canons are not; and to be so far above their laws?

A. You must know, that God hath two different sort of works to do for the government of his church: the first is legislation, or giving new doctrines and laws; the other is the teaching and guiding the church by the explication and application of these same laws. God is not still making new laws for man, but he is still teaching and ruling them by his laws. [c]

Accordingly, God hath had two sorts of ministers: one sort for legislation, to reveal new doctrines and laws; and such was Moses under the old administration, and Christ and his commissioned apostles under the new. These were eminent prophets inspired by God infallibly to record his laws, and God attested their office and work by multitudes of evident, uncontrolled miracles. But the laws being sealed, the second sort of ministers are only to teach and apply these same laws and doctrines, and not to reveal new ones. And such were the priests and Levites under Moses, and all the succeeding ministers and bishops of the churches under Christ and the apostles, who are the foundation on which the church is built. And though all church guides may

[a] John i. 11, 12; iii. 16, 21; Acts xxvi. 18; Matt. xxviii. 19, 20; John xiv. 5; xv. 10; 1 John ii. 3; v. 2, 3; Rev. xiv. 12.

[b] Matt. v. 17; xxiii. 23; Rom. ii. 14; viii. 4, 7; xiii. 8, 10.

[c] Isa. viii. 20; Isa. xxxiii. 22; Jam. iv. 12; Mal. ii. 7, 8; Matt. xxviii. 20.

determine of the undetermined circumstances of holy things, by the general laws which God hath given therein, yet to arrogate a power of making a new word of God, or a law that shall suspend our obedience to his laws, or any law for the universal church, whether it be by pope or council, is treasonable usurpation of a government which none but Christ is capable of: and as if one king or council should claim the civil sovereignty of all the earth, which is most unknown to them.

Q. 12. But I pray you tell me how the creed comes to be of so great authority, seeing I find it not in the Bible?

A. It is the very sum and kernel of the doctrine of the New Testament, and there you may find it all, with much more: but it is older than the writing of the New Testament, save that two or three words were added since.

I told you before, 1. That Christ himself did make the nature and terms of christianity, commissioning his apostles to make all nations his disciples, baptizing them into the name of the Father, the Son, and the Holy Ghost: this is the sum of the creed first made by Christ himself.

2. The apostles were inspired and commissioned to teach men all that Christ commanded, Matt. xxviii. 19, 20.

3. To say these three words, I believe in the Father, Son, and Holy Ghost, without understanding them, was easy, but would make no true christians; therefore, if we had never read more of the apostles' practice, we might justly conclude that those inspired teachers, before they baptized men at age, taught them the meaning of those three articles, and brought them, accordingly, to confess their faith, and this is the creed. And though a man might speak his profession in more or various words, the matter was still the same, and the words made necessary must not be too many, nor left too much at men's liberty to alter, lest corruption should creep into the common faith. For the baptismal confession was the very symbol, badge, or test by which all christians were visibly to pass for christians; and as christianity must be a known, certain thing, so must its symbol be.

4. And infallible historical tradition assureth us, that accordingly, ever since the apostles' days, before any adults were baptized, they were catechised, and brought to understand and profess these same articles of the faith. And if the Greeks and the Latins used not the same words, they used words of the same signification (two or three words being added since).

Q. 13. Do you not by this set the creed above the Bible?

A. No otherwise than I set the head, heart, liver, and stomach of a man above the whole body, which containeth them and all the rest; or than I set the ten commandments above the whole law of Moses, which includeth them; or than Christ did set loving God above all, and our neighbour as ourselves, above all that law of which they were the sum. We must not take those for no christians, nor deny them baptism, who understand and believe not particularly every word in the Bible; as we must those that understand not and believe not the creed.

CHAPTER VIII.

OF BELIEVING, WHAT IT SIGNIFIETH IN THE CREED.

Q. 1. I UNDERSTAND by what you have said, that as man's soul hath three powers, the understanding, the will, and the executive, so religion, being but the true qualifying and guidance of these three powers, must needs consist of three parts: I. Things to be known and believed. II. Things to be willed, loved, and chosen. And, III. Things to be done in the practice of our lives. And that the creed is the symbol or sum of so much as is necessary to our christianity, of the first sort; and the Lord's prayer the rule and summary of the second; and the ten commandments of the third.[a]

I entreat you, therefore, first to expound the creed to me, and first the first word of it, "I believe," as it belongs to all that followeth.

A. You must first know what the word signifieth in common use. To believe another, signifieth to trust him as true or trusty; and to believe a thing, signifieth to believe that it is true, because a trusty person speaketh it. The things that you must believe to be true, are called the matter, or material object, of your faith. The person's trustiness that you believe or trust to, is called the formal object of your faith, for which you trust the person, and believe the thing. The matter is as the body of faith, and the form as its soul. The matter which the church hath believed, hath by God had alterations, and to this day more is revealed to some than to others. But the formal reason of your faith is still and in all the same, even God's fidelity, who, because of his perfection, cannot lie.[b]

Q. 2. How may I be sure that God cannot lie, who is under no law?

A. His perfection is more than a law. 1. We see that God who made man in his own image, and reneweth them to it, making lying a hateful vice to human nature and conversation: no man would be counted a liar, and the better any man is, the more he hateth it.[c]

2. No man lieth but either for want of wisdom to know the truth, or for want of perfect goodness, or for want of power to attain his ends by better means. But the infinite, most perfect God hath none of these defects.

Q. 3. But God speaketh to the world by angels and men, and who knows but they may be permitted to lie?

A. When they speak to man as sent by God, and God attesteth their credibility by uncontrolled miracles or other evidence, if then they should lie, it would be imputable to God, that attesteth their word: of which I said enough to you before.

Q. 4. Proceed to open the formal act of faith, which you call trust?

A. As you have noted, that man's soul hath three powers, understanding, will, and executive, so our affiance, or trust in God, extendeth to them all: and so it is in one an assenting trust, a consenting trust, and a practical trust. By the first, we believe the word to be true, because we trust the fidelity of God. By the second, we consent to God's covenant, and accept his gifts, by trusting to the truth and goodness of the promiser. By the third, we trustingly venture on the costliest duty.[d]

---

[a] Heb. xi. 6. [b] Tit. i. 2; Rom. iii. 4; Numb. xxiii. 29. [c] Prov. xii. 22; vi. 17; xix. 5, 9; xiii. 5; John viii. 44, 55; 1 John v. 10; Rev. xxi. 8; Prov. xiv. 5; Col. iii. 9; Heb. vi. 18.

[d] Psal. cxii. 7; Matt. xxvii. 43; Heb. xi.; Eph. i. 12, 13; 2 Tim. i. 12; 1 Tim. iii. 16; Tit. iii. 8; 1 Pet. i. 21; Heb. xi. 39; Acts xxvii. 25.

Q. 5. I pray you open it to me by some familiar similitude?

A. Suppose you are a poor man, in danger of a prison, and a king from India sends his son hither, proclaiming to all the poor in England, that if they will come over with his son, he will make them all princes. Some say, he is a deceiver, and not to be believed: others say, a little in hand with our old acquaintance is better than uncertainty in an unknown land: another saith, I know not but a leaky vessel, storms, or pirates, may prevent my hopes. Here are now three questions: 1. Do you believe that he saith true? 2. Do you so far trust him as to consent to go with him? 3. When it comes to it, do you so far trust him as to venture on all the difficulties, and go?

Again, suppose you have a deadly sickness. There are many unable and deceitful physicians in the world; there is one only that can cure you, and offereth to do it for nothing, but with a medicine made of his own blood. Many tell you he is a deceiver; some say others can do it as well; and some say the medicine is intolerable, or improbable. Here are three questions: 1. Do you trust his word by believing him? 2. Do you trust him so as to consent and take him for your physician? 3. Do you trust him so as to come to him, and take his medicine, forsaking all others? I need not apply it; you can easily do it.

Trust, then, or affiance, is the vital, or formal, act of faith; and assenting, consenting, and practice, are the inseparable effects, in which, as it is a saving grace, it is always found.

Q. 6. But is all this meant in the creed?

A. Yes: 1. The creed containeth the necessary matter revealed by God, which we must believe. 2. And it mentioneth him to whom we must trust, in our assent, consent, and practice, even God the Father, the Son, and the Holy Ghost.

Q. 7. But is this the faith by which we are justified? Are we justified by believing in God the Father and the Holy Ghost, and the rest of the articles? Some say it is only by believing in Christ's righteousness as imputed to us.

A. Justification is to be spoken of hereafter. But this one entire christian faith, is it which God hath made the necessary qualification, or condition, of such as he will justify by and for the merits of Christ's righteousness.

Q. 8. Doth not "I believe," signify that I believe that this God is my God, my Saviour, and my Sanctifier, in particular?

A. It is an applying faith. It signifieth, 1. That you believe his right to be your God. 2. And his offer to be your God. 3. And that you consent to this right and offer, that he may, by special relation, be yours. 4. But it doth not signify that every believer is sure of the sincerity of his own act of believing, and so of his special interest in God, though this is very desirable and attainable.

CHAPTER IX.

OF THE FIRST ARTICLE—"I BELIEVE IN GOD THE FATHER ALMIGHTY, MAKER OF HEAVEN AND EARTH."

Q. 1. SEEING you before proved that there is a God, from the light of nature, and heathens know it, why is it made an article of faith?

A. The understanding of man is so darkened and corrupted now by sin, that it doth but grope after God, and knoweth him not as revealed in his works alone, so clearly and surely as is needful to bring home the soul to God, in holy love, obedience, and delight: but he is more fully revealed to us in the sacred Scripture by Christ and his Spirit, which, therefore, must be herein believed.[a]

Q. 2. What of God doth the Scripture make known better than nature?

A. That there is a God, and what God is, and what are his relations to us, and what are his works, and what are our duties to him, and our hopes from him.[b]

Q. 3. That there is a God, none but a mad-man, sure, can doubt: but what of God is so clearly revealed in Scripture?

A. 1. His essential attributes; and, 2. The Trinity in one essence.

Q. 4. Which call you his essential attributes?

A. God is, essentially, life, understanding, and will, or vital power, wisdom, and goodness, or love, in one substance, and this in absolute perfection.[c]

Q. 5. But are not all the rest of his attributes essential?

A. Yes; but they are but these same named variously, from their various respects to the creatures: such are his truth, his justice, and his mercy, as he is our Governor; his bounty, as our Benefactor; and his self-sufficiency, eternity, immensity, or infiniteness, his immutability, immortality, invisibility, and very many such respective names, are comprehended in his perfection.[d]

Q. 6. I have oft heard of three persons and one God, and I could never understand what it meant, how three can be but one?

A. It is like that is, because you take the word "person" amiss, as if it signified a distinct substance, as it doth of men.

Q. 7. If it do not so, doth it not tend to deceive us that never heard of any other kind of person?

A. The Scripture tells us that there are three, and yet but one God;[e] but it giveth us not a name which may notify clearly so great a mystery, for it is unsearchable and incomprehensible. We are to be baptized into the name of the Father, Son, and Holy Ghost, Matt. xxviii. 29. And there are three that bear record in heaven, the Father, the Word, and the Holy Spirit, and these three are one, 1 John v. 7. But the custom of the church having used the word "person," having none that clearly expresseth the mystery, it is our part rather to labour to understand it, how a divine person differs from a human, than to quarrel with an improper word. God is one infinite, undivided Spirit; and yet that he is Father, Son, and Holy Ghost, must be believed.

And God hath made so marvellous an impression on all the natures of active beings, of three in one, as to me doth make this mystery of our religion the more easy to be believed; so far is it from seeming a contradiction.

Q. 8. I pray show me some such instances?

A. I. The sun and all true fire is one substance, having three essential powers, the moving power, the enlightening power, and the heating power. Motion is not light, light is not heat, and heat is not motion or light, yet all are one substance, and, radically, one virtue or power, and yet three as operative.

II. Every plant hath one vegetative principle, which hath essentially a power discretive, as discerning its own nutriment; appetitive, desiring or

[a] John xvii. 3.
[b] Heb. xi. 6; 1 Tim. ii. 5.
[c] John xiv. 24; Psalm xc. 2.
[d] Mal. iii. 6; Psalm lxxxvi. 5; cxlv. 17; Prov. xv. 3; Psalm cxxxix. 4, 5, 12, 23; Jer. xxiii. 24; Deut. xxxii. 4.
[e] Matt. xxviii. 19; 1 John v. 7.

drawing it in; and motive, and so digestive and assimilative.

III. Every brute hath one sensitive soul, which essentially hath a power of vital, sensitive motion, perception, and appetite.

IV. Every man hath one soul in substance, which hath the powers of vegetation, sense, and intellection, or reasoning.

V. The soul of man, as intellective, hath essentially a three-fold power, or virtue, mental life for motion and execution, understanding, and will. All active beings are three virtues in one substance.

Q. 9. But these do none of them make three persons?

A. 1. But if all these be undeniable in nature, and prove in God active life, understanding, and will, it shows you that three essentials in one substantial essence is no contradiction. And why may not the same be as true of the divine persons.

2. And in God, who is an infinite, undivided Spirit, little can we conceive what personality signifieth, and how far those school-men are right or wrong, who say that God's essential self-living, self-knowing, and self-loving, are the Trinity of the persons as in eternal existence; and that the operations and appearances in power, wisdom, and love in creation, incarnation for redemption, and renovation in nature, grace and initial glory, or communion, are the three persons in the second notion as outwardly operative. And how much more than this soever there is, it is no wonder that we comprehend it not; yea, I believe there is yet more in the mystery of the Trinity, because this much is so intelligible.

Q. 10. But is it not strange that God will lay our salvation on the belief of that which we cannot understand; yea, is it not on the bare saying of a word, whose meaning none can know?

A. The doctrine of the Trinity in unity is the very sum of all the christian religion, as the baptismal covenant assureth us; and can we think that christianity saveth men as a charm, by words not understood? No; the belief of the Trinity is a practical belief. Far be it from us to think that every plain christian shall be damned, who knoweth not what a person in the Trinity is, as eternally inexistent, when all the divines and school-wits as good as confess, after tedious disputes with unintelligible words, that they know not: it is the Trinity, as related to us, and operative, and therein notified, that we must necessarily understand and believe, even as our Creator, Redeemer, and Sanctifier; that the love of God the Father, and the grace of the Son, and the communion of the Holy Ghost, may be believed, received, and enjoyed: as there are diversities of gifts, but the same Spirit; and differences of administrations, but the same Lord; and diversities of operations, but the same God which worketh all in all, 1 Cor. xii. 4—6; 2 Cor. xiii. 14. Even as it is not our understanding the essence of the sun, but our reception of its communicated motion, light, and heat, that our nature liveth by.[f]

Q. 11. But how can any man love him above all, of whom we can have no true conception? I cannot conceive what God is?

A. It may be you think that you know nothing but what you see or feel by sense; for so men's long use of bodies and sense is apt to abuse them: or you think you know nothing, which you know not fully; and so no angel knoweth God by an adequate, comprehensive knowledge. How far are we from knowing fully what sun, and moon, and stars are, and what is in them, and how they are ordered, and move! And yet nothing is more easily and surely known, than that there is a sun and stars, and that they are substances that have the power of motion, light, and heat. Yea, philosophers cannot yet agree what light and heat are; and yet we know enough of them for our necessary use. And can it be expected, then, that man give a proper definition of the infinite God? And yet nothing is more certain than that there is a God, and that he is such as I have before described: and we may know as much of him as our duty and happiness requireth.[g]

Q. 12. But what is the best conception I can have of God?

A. I partly told you in the third chapter, and the second. I now tell you further, that we see God here but as in a glass: his image on man's soul is the nearest glass: how do you conceive of your own soul? You cannot doubt but you have a soul, while you perceive its constant acts; yet you see it not: you find clearly that it is a spiritual substance, that hath essentially the power of vital activity, understanding, and will. By this you perceive what a spirit is; and by this you have some perception what God is. All the world is far less to God than a body to a soul; and God is infinitely more than a soul to all the world; but by the similitude of a soul you may most easily conceive of him.

CHAPTER X.

OF GOD'S ALMIGHTINESS AND CREATION.

Q. 1. WHY is God here called "the Father," in whom we believe?

A. 1. As he is the first person in the eternal Trinity, and so called the Father of the eternal Word, or Wisdom, as his Son.

2. As he is the Father of Jesus Christ, as incarnate.[a]

3. As he is the Maker of the whole creation, and, as a common Father, giveth being to all that is.

4. As he is our reconciled Father by Christ; and hath adopted us as his sons, and bound us to love, and trust, and obey him, as our Father. But the two first are the chief sense.

Q. 2. What is God's "almightiness?"

A. His infinite power, by which he can do all things which are works of power: he cannot lie, nor die, nor be the cause of sin, for these are no effects of power, but of impotency.

Q. 3. Why is his almightiness to be believed by us?

A. We do not else believe him to be God: and we cannot else reverence, admire, trust him, and obey him as we ought.[b]

Q. 4. Why is his almightiness only named, and no other properties?

A. All the rest are supposed when we call him God; but this is named, because he is first to be believed in as the Creator; and his creation doth eminently manifest his power. And though the Son

[f] Psal. xvi. 8; cxxv. 2; Matt. xxviii. 19; 1 John v. 7, 10; 1 Cor. xii. 4—6; 2 Cor. xiii. 14. The doctrine of the Trinity is ever proposed relatively and practically to our faith.

[g] John xvii. 3; 2 Tim. i. 12; 1 John iv. 6, 7; John viii. 19; xiv. 7, 9; x. 14; 1 Cor. viii. 3; Gal. iv. 9; 1 John ii. 13, 14.

[a] 2 Cor. i. 3; xi. 31; 1 Cor. viii. 6; xv. 24; Gal. i. 1, 3, 4; Eph. i. 3, 17; iv. 6; vi. 23; Phil. ii. 11; Col. ii. 2; iii. 17; 2 Tim. i. 2; James iii. 9.

[b] Gen. xvii. 1; Rev. i. 8; 2 Cor. vi. 18; Psal. xci. 1, 2; Matt. viii. 2.

and the Holy Ghost are almighty, the Scripture eminently attributeth power to the Father, wisdom to the Son, and love and perfective operations to the Holy Ghost.

Q. 5. Is the creation named to notify to us God's almightiness?

A. Yes; and it is a great part of our duty when we look up to the heavens, and daily see so far as our short sight can reach, of this wonderful world, to think, with most reverend admiration, Oh what a God have we to serve and trust![c]

Q. 6. How did God make all things?

A. He gave them all their being, order, and well-being, by the power of his will and word.[d]

Q. 7. When did he make all things?

A. It is not yet six thousand years since he made this world, even as much as belongs to us to know.

Q. 8. How long was God making this world?

A. It pleased him to make it the work of six days; and he consecrated the seventh day, a sabbath, for the commemoration of it, and for the solemn worshipping him as our Creator.

Q. 9. For whom, and for what use, did God make the world?

A. God made all things for himself; not as having need of them, but to please his own will, which is the beginning and the end of all his works; and to shine in the glory of the greatness, order, and goodness of the world, as in a glass to understanding creatures, and to communicate goodness variously to his works.[e]

Q. 10. What did God with the world when he had made it?

A. By the same power, wisdom, and will, he still continueth it; or else it would presently return into nothing.[f]

Q. 11. What further must we learn from God's creating us?

A. We certainly learn that he is our Owner, our Ruler, and our Benefactor, or Father, and that we are his own, and his subjects, and his benefited children.

Q. 12. What mean you by the first, that he is our Owner?

A. He that maketh us of nothing, must needs be our absolute Lord or Owner; and therefore may do with all things what he will, and cannot possibly do any wrong, however he useth us. And we must needs be wholly his own, and therefore should wholly resign ourselves to his disposing will.[g]

Q. 13. What mean you by the second, that God is our Ruler?

A. He that by creation is our absolute Owner, and hath made us reasonable, and with free-will, must needs have the only right and fitness to be our Ruler by his laws and doctrine: and we are bound, as his subjects, to obey him absolutely in all things.[h]

Q. 14. How gather you that he is our Father, or Benefactor?

A. If we have our very being from him, and all the good that the whole creation enjoyeth is his free gift, then as he is love itself, so he is the great Benefactor of the world, but specially to his chosen, faithful people: and no man or angel hath any thing that is good by way of merited exchange from God, but all is of free gift: and we owe him our superlative love, and thanks, and praise.

Q. 15. Why are heaven and earth named as the parts of his creation?

A. They are all that we are concerned to know: we partly see the difference between them, and God's word tells us of more than we see: earth is the place of our present abode in our life of trials in corruptible flesh; heaven is the place where God doth manifest his glory, and from whence he sendeth down those influences which maintain nature, and which communicate his grace, and prepare us for the glory which we shall enjoy in heaven. By heaven and earth is meant all creatures, both spirits and corporeal.[i]

Q. 16. Were there no more worlds made and dissolved before this? It seems unlikely that God, from all eternity, should make nothing till less than six thousand years ago; when he is a communicative good, and delighteth to do good in his works?

A. It is dangerous presumption so much as to put such a question with our thought or tongue, and to pry into God's secrets, of which we are utterly uncapable (unless it be to shame it, or suppress it). God hath, by Christ and the Holy Ghost, in Scripture, set up a ladder, by which you may ascend to the heaven that you are made for; but if you will climb above the top of the ladder, you may fall down to hell.[k]

CHAPTER XI.

OF THE PERSON OF JESUS CHRIST, THE ONLY SON OF GOD.

Q. 1. WHO is Jesus Christ?

A. He is God and man, and the Mediator between God and man.[l]

Q. 2. When did he begin to be God?

A. He is the eternal God that had no temporal beginning?

Q. 3. When did he begin to be a man?

A. About one thousand six hundred and eighty-one years ago.[m]

Q. 4. If he be God, why is he called the Son of God? Are there more Gods than one? And how doth God beget a son?

A. There is but one God: I before opened to you the mystery of the Trinity in unity, to which you must look back. Begetting is a word that we must not take carnally; and a son in the Deity signifieth not another substance. If the sun be said to beget its own light, that maketh it not another substance.

But Christ is also, as man, begotten of God, in a virgin's womb.[n]

Q. 5. Was Christ God in his low condition on earth?

A. Yes, but the Godhead appeared not as in heavenly glory.

Q. 6. Is Christ a man now he is in heaven?

A. Yes, he is still God and man; but his glorified manhood is not like our corruptible flesh, and narrow souls.[o]

Q. 7. Hath Christ a soul besides his Godhead?

A. Yes, for he is a perfect man, which he could not be without a soul.

[c] Gen. xvii. 31; Rev. iv. 11; x. 6; Isa. xl. 28; xlii. 5; xlv. 12, 18; Psalm viii. 1, 3; xix. 1; lxxxix. 5, 11; civ. 1, 2; cxv. 16.

[d] Gen. i. 2, 3.

[e] Prov. xvi. 4; Rev. iv. 11.

[f] Heb. i. 3; Ezek. xviii. 4; 1 Cor. vi. 20; Psal. x. 16.

[g] Psalm cxix. 94; Acts xxvii. 23; 1 Cor. vi. 19; John xvii. 6, 9, 10; Isa. lxiii. 19; 1 Chron. xxix. 11.

[h] Psalm lix. 13; lxvi. 7; ciii. 19; Dan. iv. 17, 25, 32; 1 Tim. vi. 15; i. 17; Rev. xvii. 14; xix. 6.

[i] Gen. i. 1.

[k] Deut. xxix. 29.

[l] 1 Tim. ii. 5; Heb. xii. 24; viii. 6; ix. 15.

[m] John i. 1—3, &c.; 1 Tim. iii. 16; Rom. ix. 5; Tit. ii. 13.

[n] Phil. ii. 7—10.

[o] Acts iii. 21; John ii. 17; vi. 62; Eph. iv. 8—10.

Q. 8. Then Christ hath two parts: one part is God, and the other man?

A. The name of part, or whole, is not fit for God: God is no part of any thing, no, not of the universe of being; for to be a part is to be less than the whole, and so to be imperfect: and every whole consisteth of parts; but so doth not God.[p]

Q. 9. Is Jesus Christ one person or two, viz. a divine and human?

A. It is dangerous laying too great a stress on words, that are either not in Scripture, or are applied to God as borrowed from similitude in man: as the word person signifieth the eternal Word, the second in the Trinity, Christ is but one person. And though his human soul and body assumed be substances, they are not another person, but another nature united to his eternal person; yet not as a part of it, but by a union which we have no proper words to express. Christ hath two natures, and but one person. But if you take the word person only for a relation, (as of a king, a judge, &c.) so Christ, as Mediator, is a person distinct from the same Christ, as the eternal, second person in the Trinity.[q]

Q. 10. It seems then Christ had three natures, a divine, a soul, and a body?

A. This is a question about mere names, he hath only the nature of God and of man. But if you go to anatomize man, you may find in him on earth, perhaps, more natures than two, spirit, fire, air, water, and earth: but this is a frivolous dispute.

Q. 11. In what nature did Christ appear of old before his incarnation?

A. If it were not by an angel, as his agent, it must be by some body, light, or voice, made or assumed for that present time.

Q. 12. I hear some say, that Christ is not one God with the Father, but a kind of under God, his first creature, above angels.

A. The Scriptures fully prove Christ to be God, and one God with the Father: the form of baptism proveth it. There be some learned men that to reconcile this controversy say, that Christ hath three natures, 1. The divine: 2. A super-angelical: 3. A human. And that God, the Eternal Word, did first of all produce the most perfect of all his creatures, above angels, like a universal soul; and the Godhead uniting itself to this, did, by this, produce all other creatures; and, at last, did in and by this unite itself hypostatically to the human nature of Christ. They think divers texts do favour this threefold nature; and that the Arians erred only by noting the super-angelical nature, and not noting the divine united to it. But I dare not own so great a point, which I find not that the universal church ever owned; nor do I see any cogent proof of it in the Scripture.[r]

Q. 13. But God doth all his works in order: and he made angels far nobler than man: and is it like then that he setteth a man so far above all angels as personal union doth import?

A. It is not like, if we might judge by the conjectures of our reason: but God's lower works are none of them perfectly known here to us; much less the most mysterious, even the glorious person of the Son of God. If God will thus glorify his mercy to man, by setting him above all the angels, who shall say to him, What doest thou? And if there be in Jesus Christ a first created super-angelical nature, besides the divine and human, we shall know it when we see as face to face. In the mean time, he will save those that truly believe in him as God and man.[s]

Q. 14. Why is Christ called "our Lord?"

A. Because he is God; and also, as Mediator, all power in heaven and earth is given him, and he is made Head over all things to his church, Matt. xxviii. 28; Eph. i. 22, 23.

Q. 15. What do his names "Jesus Christ" signify.

A. Jesus signifieth a Saviour, and Christ, anointed of God. He being anointed by God to the office of a Mediator, as the great Prophet, Priest, and King of the church.

[p] Gal. iii. 20.
[q] 1 John v. 7; 1 Tim. ii. 5; Eph. iv. 5, 6; Rom. v. 17, 18.
[r] John i. 1, 2; Matt. xxviii. 19; Col. i. 15—18; Heb. i. 2—4; Rev. i. 5, 8.
[s] Heb. i.; ii.

CHAPTER XII.

HOW CHRIST WAS CONCEIVED BY THE HOLY GHOST, AND BORN OF THE VIRGIN MARY.

Q. 1. DOTH it not seem impossible, that Christ should be begotten on a virgin without a man?

A. There is no contradiction in it: and what is impossible to him that made all the world of nothing?[a]

Q. 2. But it seemeth incredible that God should be made man?

A. God was not at all changed by Christ's incarnation. The Godhead was not turned into flesh or soul, but united itself thereto.[b]

Q. 3. But it seemeth an incredible condescension in God to unite the nature of man to himself, in personal union.

A. When you understand what it is, it will not seem incredible to you, though wonderful. Consider, 1. That it doth not turn the human nature into divine. 2. Nor doth it give it any of that part or work which was proper to the divine nature, and second person in the Trinity, from eternity. 3. The divine nature is united to the human, only to advance this to the excellent office of mediation, and that Christ in it may be Head over all things to the church. 4. And it will abate your wonder if you consider, that God is as near to every creature as the soul is to the body: in him we live, move, and have our being. And he is more to us than our souls are to our bodies.

Q. 4. You now make me think that God is one with every man and creature, as well as with Christ. I pray you wherein is the difference?

A. God's essence is every where alike; but he doth not appear or work every where alike: as he is more in heaven than on earth, because he there operateth and appeareth in glory, and as he is more in saints than in the ungodly, because in them he operateth his grace; so he is in Jesus Christ, otherwise than he is in any other creature: 1. In that he by the divine power qualified him as he never did any other creature. 2. And designeth him to that work which he never did any other creature. 3. And fixeth him in the honourable relation to that work. 4. And communicateth to him, by a uniting act, the glory which he doth not to any other creature: and though it is like there is yet more unknown and incomprehensible to us, yet these singular operations express a singular, operative union. The sun, by shining on a wall, becomes not one with it: but by its influence on plants, it becometh one with them, and is their generical life.

[a] Matt. viii. 20; Luke i. 35.
[b] Rom. i. 3; John i. 14; 1 Tim. iii. 16; Gal. iv. 4.

Q. 5. But how is the second person in the Trinity more united to the human nature, than the Father and the Holy Ghost? Are they divided?

A. You may as well ask, why God is said to make [c] the world by his word, and by his Son: though the persons are undivided in their works on the creature, yet creation is eminently ascribed to the Father, incarnation and redemption to the Son, and sanctification to the Holy Ghost. The sun's power of motion, light, and heat are inseparable; and yet it is the light, as such, that with our eye doth cause the same act of light, as united to it. But the perfect answer to this doubt is reserved for heaven.

Q. 6. But how was he conceived by the Holy Ghost, the second person by the third, when it is only the second that was incarnate?

A. The Holy Ghost is not said to operate on the second person in the Trinity, or the Godhead, for Christ's conception, but on the virgin's body, and by miraculously causing a human soul and body, and their union with the eternal Word. God's perfecting operations are usually ascribed to the Holy Ghost: but the Father and Son are still supposed operating by the Holy Spirit.

Q. 7. Was Christ's flesh made of the substance of his mother?

A. Yes: else how had he been the Son of man? [d]

Q. 8. Was Christ's soul begotten by his mother?

A. It is certain that man begetteth man; but how souls are generated is not fully known by man: some say they are not generated, but created: some say, that they are not created, but generated: and I think that there is such a concurrence of God's act and man's, as may be called a conjunction of creation and generation; that is, that as the sunbeams by a burning-glass may light a candle, and that candle light another, and another; yet so that the light and heat that doth it, is only from the sun's continual communication; but will not light another, but as contracted and made forcible by the burning-glass, or the candle. So all the substance of new souls is from the divine efflux, or communication of it, which yet will not ordinarily beget a soul, but as it is first received in the generative, natural faculty, and so operateth by it, as its appointed natural means. Thus it seemeth all human souls are caused (pardon the defects of the similitude). But the soul of Christ miraculously, not without all operation of the mother's, (for then he had not been the Son of man,) but without a human father; the Holy Ghost more than supplying that defect.

Q. 9. If Christ was Mary's son, how escaped he original guilt?

A. By being conceived by the Holy Ghost, and so in his human nature made the Son of God, and not generated, as other men are.

Q. 10. Had Mary any children after Jesus Christ?

A. It goes for a tradition with most, that she had none: but it is uncertain, and concerneth not our faith or salvation. [e]

Q. 11. Why was Christ born of a Jew?

A. God had made a special promise to Abraham first, that [f] Christ should be his seed, in whom all nations should be blessed: and to David after, that he should be his offspring, and everlasting King.

Q. 12. Why was not Christ born till about four thousand years after the fall?

A. It is dangerous asking reasons of God's councils, which he hath not revealed. But this much we may know, that Christ was man's Redeemer, by undertaking what he after did, before his incarnation. And that he revealed the grace of redemption, by promises, types, and prophecies, and so saved the faithful: and that God's works are usually progressive to perfection, and ripest at last: and therefore when he had first sent his prophets, he lastly sent his Son to perform his undertaking, and bring life and immortality more fully to light, and bring in a better covenant, and gather a more excellent, universal church.

Q. 13. Were any saved by Christ before he was made man?

A. Yes: they had the love of the Father, the grace of Christ, and the necessary communion of the Holy Ghost, and the promise. And in every agė and nation, he that feared God, and worked righteousness, was accepted of him.[g]

CHAPTER XIII.

"SUFFERED UNDER PONTIUS PILATE, WAS CRUCIFIED, DEAD, AND BURIED; HE DESCENDED INTO HELL."

Q. 1. WHY is there nothing said in the creed, 1. Of Christ's overcoming the temptations of the devil and the world?[h] Or, 2. Of his fulfilling the law, his perfect holiness, obedience, and righteousness? 3. Nor of his miracles?

A. 1. You must know that the creed at first, when Christ made it the symbol of christianity, had but the three baptismal articles:[i] to be baptized into the name of the Father, Son, and Holy Ghost. 2. And that the rest were added, for the exposition of these three. 3. And that the errors that rose up occasioned the additions. Some denied Christ's real humanity, and some his death, and said, that it was another in his shape that died: and this occasioned these expository articles. 4. But the apostles, and other preachers, expounded more to those whom they catechised than is put into the creed: and more is implied in that which is expressed: and had any heretics then denied Christ's perfect righteousness, and victory in temptation, it is like it would have occasioned an article for these. 5. But Christ would not have his apostles put more into the creed than was needful to be a part of the test of christianity. And he that understandingly, consentingly, and practically believeth in God the Father, Son, and Holy Ghost, shall be saved. 6. And as to Christ's miracles, yea, and his holiness, they are contained in the true meaning of believing in the Holy Ghost, as I shall after show.

Q. 2. But why is none of Christ's sufferings mentioned before that of his being crucified?

A. This, which is the consummation, implieth the humiliation of his life: his mean [k] birth and education, his mean estate in the world, his temptations, accusations, reproaches, buffeting, scourging, his agony, his betraying, his condemnation as a malefactor, by false witness, and the people's clamour, and the rulers' malice and injustice: his whole life was a state of humiliation, finished in his crucifixion, death, and burial.

Q. 3. What made the Jews so to hate and crucify him?[l]

A. Partly a base fear of Cæsar, lest he should de-

[c] John i. 3, 10.
[d] Gal. iv. 4.
[e] Heb. vii. 26; Matt. xii. 46; Mark iii. 31; John ii. 12; vii. 3, 5, 10; Gal. i. 19.

[f] Gen. xxii. 18; xxvi. 4; Psalm lxxxix. 29, 36; Rom. i. 3; iv. 16; 2 Tim. ii. 8.
[g] See Heb. xi. [h] Matt. iv. [i] Matt. xxviii. 19.
[k] Phil. ii. 7—9; Heb. xii. 2—4. [l] John xi. 48, 50.

stroy them, in jealousy of Jesus, as a king: and having long revolted from sincerity in religion, and become ceremonious hypocrites, God left them to the blindness and hardness of their hearts, resolving to use them for the sacrificing of Christ, the redemption of the world, and the great enlargement of his church.

Q. 4. Why is Pontius Pilate named in the creed?

A. Historically, to keep the remembrance of the time when Christ suffered: and to leave a just shame on the name of an unjust judge.[m]

Q. 5. Why was crucifying the manner of Christ's death?

A. 1. It was the Romans' manner of putting vile malefactors to death. 2. And it was a death especially cursed by God; and Christ foretold it of himself.

Q. 6. Was it only Christ's body that suffered, or also his soul and Godhead?

A. The Godhead could not suffer; but he that was God suffered in body and soul.[n]

Q. 7. What did Christ's soul suffer?

A. It suffered not by any sinful passion, but by natural, lawful fear of what he was to undergo, and feeling of pain, and especially of God's just displeasure with man's sin, for which he suffered; which God did express by such withholdings of joy, and by such inward, deep sense of his punishing justice, as belonged to one that consented to stand in the place of so many sinners, and to suffer so much in their stead.[o]

Q. 8. Did Christ suffer the pains of hell, which the damned suffer?

A. The pains of hell are God's just punishment of man for sin, and so were Christ's sufferings, upon his consent. But, 1. The damned in hell are hated of God, and so was not Christ. 2. They are forsaken of God's Holy Spirit and grace, and so was not Christ. 3. They are under the power of sin, and so was not Christ. 4. They hate God and holiness, and so did not Christ. 5. They are tormented by the conscience of their personal guilt, and so was not Christ. Christ's sufferings and the damned's vastly differ.

Q. 9. Why must Christ suffer what he did?

A. 1. To be an expiatory sacrifice for sin. God thought it not meet, as he was the just and holy Ruler of the world, to forgive sin, without such a demonstration of his holiness and justice as might serve as well to the ends of his government as if the sinners had suffered themselves. 2. And he suffered to teach man what sin deserveth, and what a God we serve, and that we owe him the most costly obedience, even to the death, and that this body, life, and world are to be denied, contemned, and forsaken, for the sake of souls, and of life everlasting, and of God, when he requireth it. The cross of Christ is much of the christian's book.[p]

Q. 10. What sorts of sin did Christ die for?

A. For all sorts, except men's not performing those conditions which he requireth of all that he will pardon and save.

Q. 11. For whose sins did Christ suffer?

A. All men's sins were instead of a meritorious cause of Christ's sufferings; he suffered for mankind as the Saviour of the world: and as to the effect, his suffering purchased a conditional gift of free pardon and life to all that will believingly accept it, according to the nature of the things given. But it was the will of the Father and the Son not to leave his death to uncertain success, but infallibly to cause the elect to believe and be saved.[q]

Q. 12. Was it just with God to punish the innocent?

A. Yes, when it was Christ's own undertaking, by consent, to stand as a sufferer in the room of the guilty.

Q. 13. How far were our sins imputed to Christ?

A. So far as that his consent made it just that he suffered for them. He is said to be made sin for us, who knew no sin, which is, to be made a curse or sacrifice for our sin. But God never took him to be really, or in his esteem, a sinner: he took not our fault to become his fault, but only the punishment for our faults to be due to him. Else sin itself had been made his own, and he had been relatively and properly a sinner, and God must have hated him as such, and he must have died for his own sin when ours was made his own: but none of this is to be imagined.[r]

Q. 14. How far are Christ's sufferings imputed to us?

A. So far as that we are reputed to be justly forgiven and saved by his grace, because he made an expiation by his sacrifice for our sins: but not so as if God mistook us to have suffered in Christ, or that he or his law did judge that we ourselves have made satisfaction or expiation, by Christ.[s]

Q. 15. Was not that penal law "In the day that thou eatest thereof, thou shalt die," and "The soul that sinneth shall die," fulfilled by execution for us all in Christ, and now justifieth us as so fulfilled?

A. No: that law condemneth none but the sinner himself, and is not fulfilled unless the person suffer that sinned. That law never said, "Either the sinner, or another for him, shall die." Christ was given us by God as above his law, and that he might justly and mercifully forgive sin, though he executed not that law: that law did but make punishment our due, and not Christ's, but not bind God to inflict it on us, when his wisdom knew a better way. It is not that law as fulfilled that justifieth us, but another, even the law of grace. Satisfaction is not the fulfilling of the penal law.[t]

Q. 16. Did not Christ fulfil the commands of the law for us by his holiness and perfect righteousness? What need was there that he suffer for us?

A. The law, or covenant, laid on him by his Father was, that he should do both; and therefore both is the performance of that condition on which God gave us to him to be pardoned and saved by him. If he had fulfilled the commands of the law by perfect holiness and righteousness, in our legal persons, so as that God and his law would have reputed us to have done it by him, then, indeed, being reputed perfect obeyers, we could not have been reputed sinners, that needed suffering or pardon. But Christ's habitual, active, and passive righteousness, were (all the parts of his one condition) performed by him, to be the meritorious cause of our justification.[u]

Q. 17. Why is Christ's death and burial named besides his crucifixion?

A. Those words have been since added, to obviate their error who thought Christ died not on the cross.

Q. 18. What is meant by his descending into hell?

A. Those words were not of some hundred years

[m] 1 Tim. vi. 13; Col. i. 20; ii. 14; Eph. ii. 16; Gal. iii. 13.
[n] Matt. xxvi. 38; John xii. 27. [o] Luke xxii. 44.
[p] Heb. ix. 26; x. 12; 1 Cor. v. 7; Luke xiv. 33; 1 Cor. ii. 2; Gal. ii. 2; iii. 1; v. 24; vi. 14; Phil. ii. 8; iii. 7—9.
[q] Rom. v. 6, 8; xiv. 9, 15; 2 Cor. v. 14, 15; Heb. ii. 9; 1 Tim. ii. 6; 1 John ii. 2; John i. 29; iii. 16, 18, 19; iv. 42; vi. 51.
[r] 1 Pet. ii. 22. [s] 1 Pet. iii. 18; Acts xxvi. 18.
[t] Rom. iii. 19, 20, 21, 28; iv. 13, 15; x. 4; Gal. ii. 16, 21; iii. 11, 13, 18, 19, 24.
[u] Matt. iii. 15; v. 17; Isa. liii. 11; 1 Cor. i. 30; 2 Cor. v. 21.

in the creed, and since they were put in, have been diversely understood. There is no more certain nor necessary to be believed, but that, 1. Christ's soul was, and so ours are, immortal, and remained when separated from the body. 2. And that as death (being the separation of soul and body) was threatened by God, as a punishment to both, so the soul of Christ submitted to this penal separation, and went to the place of separated souls, as his body did to the grave.[x]

Q. 19. Of what use is this article to us?

A. Of great and unspeakable use. 1. We learn hence what sin deserveth. Shall we play with that which must have such a sacrifice?[y]

2. We learn hence that a sufficient expiatory sacrifice is made for sin, and therefore that God is reconciled, and we need not despair, nor are put to make expiation ourselves, or by any other.

3. We learn that death and the grave, and the state of separate souls, are sanctified, and Satan conquered, as he had the power of death, as God's executioner; and therefore that we may boldly die in faith, and commit soul and body into the hand of him that died for them.

Q. 20. But did not Christ go to paradise, and can that be penal?

A. Yes, and so do faithful souls. But the soul and body are a perfect man, and nature is against a separation: and as the union of Christ's soul and glorified body now in heaven is a more perfect state than that was of his separated soul, so the deprivation of that union and perfection was a degree of penalty, and therefore it was the extraordinary privilege of Enoch and Elias not to die.

CHAPTER XIV.

"THE THIRD DAY HE ROSE AGAIN FROM THE DEAD."

Q. 1. How was Christ said to be three days in the grave?

A. He was there part of the sixth day, all the seventh, and part of the first.[a]

Q. 2. Is it certain that Christ rose from the dead the third day?

A. As certain as any article of our faith. Angels witnessed it. Mary first saw him, and spake with him. Two disciples, going to Emmaus, saw him, to whom he opened the scriptures concerning him. Peter, and others fishing, saw him, and spake, and ate with him. The eleven assembled saw him. Thomas, that would not else believe, was called to see the print of the nails, and put his finger into his pierced side. He was seen of above five hundred brethren at once. He gave the apostles their commission, and instructions, and his blessing, and ascended bodily to heaven in their sight; and afterwards appeared in glory to Stephen and Paul. But I have before given you the proof of the gospel, and must not repeat it.[b]

Q. 3. Was it foreknown that Christ would rise?

A. Yes; it was foretold by the prophets, and expressly and often by himself to his apostles and the Jews; and therefore they set a sealed stone, with a guard of soldiers, on the sepulchre, to watch it.[c]

Q. 4. It is a wonder that the Jews then believed not in him.

C. The rulers were now more afraid than before that Christ would by the people be proclaimed their King, and then the Romans destroy their city and nation, for they feared men more than God: and withal they had put him to death on that account, as if his making himself a King had been rebellion against Cæsar, and "King of the Jews" was written, as his crime, by Pilate on his cross, and so they were engaged against him as a rebel, though he told them his kingdom was not a worldly one: and they seemed to believe that he did all his miracles by the devil as a conjurer, and therefore that he was raised by that devil:[d] which was the blasphemy against the Holy Ghost. And as for the common people, they deceived them by hiring the soldiers to say, that his disciples stole his body while they slept.[e]

Q. 5. But why would Christ appear to none but his disciples?

A. We are not fit to give God a law: his works are done in infinite wisdom. But we may see, 1. That they who had hardened their hearts against all his doctrine, and the miracles of his life, and maliciously put him to death as a blasphemer, a conjurer, and a traitor to Cæsar, were unworthy and unmeet to be the witnesses of his resurrection: and it is like it would but have excited their rage to have tried a new persecution. His resurrection being the first act of his triumphant exaltation, none were so fit to see him as those that had followed him in his sufferings: even as wicked men are not meet (as Paul was) to be rapt up into paradise and the third heavens, and hear the unutterable things.[f]

2. The witnesses whom he chose were enow, and fit persons for that office, being to be sent abroad to proclaim it to the world.

And God confirmed their testimony by such abundant miracles, of which you heard before.[g]

3. And yet he left not the infidels without convincing means: as he before told them that he would raise in three days the temple of his body, when they destroyed it, so they saw the earth quake, the sun darkened, the veil of the temple rent at his death, and their soldiers saw the angels that terrified them, and told the rulers what they saw: and, after all, it was to Paul, a persecutor, (and partly to his company,) that Christ appeared.[h]

Q. 6. Why must Christ rise from the dead?

A. You may as well ask why he must be our Saviour?

1. If he had not risen, death had conquered him, and how could he have saved us that was overcome and lost himself?[i]

2. He could not have received his own promised reward, even his kingdom and glory: it was for the joy that was set before him, that he endured the cross and despised the shame; therefore God gave him a name above every name, to which every created knee must bow.[k]

3. His resurrection was to be the chief of all those miracles by which God witnessed that he was his Son, and the chief evidence by which the world was to be convinced of his truth,[l] and so was used in their preaching by the apostles. That Christ rose from

[x] 1 Cor. xv. 4, 5; Psalm xvi. 9, 10; 1 Pet. iii. 18—21.
[y] Heb. ix. 21; Col. i. 20; Eph. i. 7; 1 Pet. i. 19; Rom. iii. 25; Heb. ii. 14; 1 John ii. 1—3; iv. 10; Heb. ix. 14; Eph. ii. 13; Rev. i. 5; v. 9; vii. 14; xiv. 20.
[a] Matt. xii. 39, 40; xvi. 4; John xx.; Matt. xxviii.
[b] 1 Cor. xv. 5, 6.
[c] Acts xxvi. 23; Matt. xx. 19; Mark viii. 31; ix. 31; x. 34; Luke xxiv. 7, 46; John xx. 9; Rom. xiv. 9; 1 Thess. iv. 14.
[d] Matt. xii.
[e] Matt. xxviii. 3.
[f] Acts x. 41; i. 2—5, 22; iv. 2, 33; xvii. 18; Heb. vi. 2.
[g] 1 Cor. xv. 4, 6; Heb. ii. 3—5.
[h] Matt. xxvi.; xxvii.; Luke xxiii.; Acts ix.
[i] 1 Cor. xv. 13, 14, 20.
[k] Heb. xii. 3, 4; Phil. ii. 7, 8
[l] Rom. i. 4; 1 Pet. i. 3, 4; iii. 21; John xi. 24, 25.

the dead, is the chief argument that makes us christians.

4. The great executive parts of Christ's saving office were to be performed in heaven, which a dead man could not do. How else should he have interceded for us, as our heavenly High Priest? How should he have sent down the Holy Ghost to renew us? How should he, as King, have governed and protected his church on earth unto the end? How should he have come again in glory to judge the world? And how should we have seen his glory (as the Mediator of fruition) in the heavenly kingdom? [m]

Q. 7. I perceive, then, that Christ's resurrection is to us an article of the greatest use. What use must we make of it?

A. You may gather it by what is said. 1. By this you may be sure that he is the Son of God, and his gospel true. 2. By this you may be sure that his sacrifice on the cross was accepted as sufficient. 3. By this you may be sure that death is conquered, and we may boldly trust our Saviour, who tasted and overcame death, with our departing souls. 4. By this you may be sure that we have a powerful High Priest and Intercessor in heaven, by whom we may come with reverent boldness unto God. 5. By this we may know that we have a powerful King, both to obey and to trust with the church's interest and our own. 6. By this we may know that we have a Head still living, who will send down his Spirit to gather his chosen, to help his ministers, to sanctify and comfort his people, and prepare them for glory. 7. By this we are assured of our own resurrection, and taught to hope for our final justification and glory. 8. And by this we are taught that we must rise to holiness of life.[n]

CHAPTER XV.

"HE ASCENDED INTO HEAVEN, AND SITTETH ON THE RIGHT HAND OF GOD, THE FATHER ALMIGHTY."

Q. 1. How long was it between Christ's resurrection and his ascension?

A. Forty days: he rose on the day which we call Easter day, and he ascended on that which we call Ascension day, or Holy Thursday.[a]

Q. 2. Did Christ stay all this while among his disciples visibly?

A. No; but appeared to them at such seasons as he saw meet.[b]

Q. 3. Where was he all the rest of the forty days?

A. God hath not told us, and therefore it concerneth us not to know.

Q. 4. He showed them that he had flesh and blood, how then was he to them invisible the most part of the forty days?

A. The divine power that raised Christ, could make those alterations on his body which we are unacquainted with.

Q. 5. How was Christ taken up to heaven?

A. While he was speaking to his apostles of the things concerning the kingdom of God, and answering them that hoped it would presently be, and had given their commission, and the promise of the Holy Ghost, and commanded them to wait for it at Jerusalem, he was taken up as they gazed after him, till a cloud took him out of their sight: and two angels, like two men in white, stood by them, and asked them why they stood gazing up to heaven, telling them that Jesus, who was taken up, should so come again.[c]

Q. 6. Had it not been better for us that he had staid on earth?

A. No: he is many ways more useful to us in heaven.[d] 1. He is now no more confined, in presence, to that small country of Judea, above the rest of the world, as a candle to one room, but, as the sun in his glory, shineth to all his church on earth. 2. He is possessed of his full power and glory (by which he is fit to protect and glorify us). 3. He intercedeth for us where our highest concerns and interest are. 4. He sendeth his Spirit on earth to do his work on all believer's souls.

Q. 7. What is meant by his sitting on the right hand of God?

A. Not that God hath hands, or is confined to a place as man is. But it signifieth that the glorified man, Jesus, is next to God in dignity, power, and glory; and, as the lieutenant under a king, is now the universal Administrator, or Governor, of all the world, under God, the Father Almighty.[e]

Q. 8. I thought he had been only the Lord of his church?

A. He is Head over all things to his church. All power and things in heaven and earth are given him; even the frame of nature dependeth on him; he is Lord of all; but it is his church that he sanctifieth by his Spirit, and will glorify.

Q. 9. If Christ have all power, why doth he let Satan and sin still reign over the far greatest part of the earth?

A. Satan reigneth but over volunteers that wilfully and obstinately choose that condition; and he reigneth but as the jailer in the prison, as God's executioner on the wilful refusers of his grace.[f] And his reign is far from absolute; he crosseth none of the decrees of God, nor overcometh his power, but doth what God seeth meet to permit him to do. He shall destroy none of God's elect, nor any that are truly willing of saving grace. And as for the fewness of the elect, I shall speak of it after, about the catholic church.

Q. 10. But is not Christ's body present on earth, and in the sacrament.

A. We are sure he is in heaven, and we are sure that their doctrine is a fiction contrary to sense, reason, and Scripture, that say the consecrated bread and wine are substantially turned into the very body and blood of Christ, and are no longer bread and wine. But how far the presence of Christ's soul and body extendeth, is a question unfit for man's determination, unless we better knew what glorified souls and bodies are: we see that the sun is eminently in the heaven; and yet, whether its lucid beams be a real part of its substance, which are here on earth, or how far they extend, we know not; nor know we how the sun differeth, in greatness or glory, from the soul and body of Christ; nor know when an angel is in the room with us, and when not: these things are unfit for our inquiry and decision.[g]

[m] 1 Pet. i. 3, 4; iii. 21; Phil. iii. 10, 11, 19, 20, 21; Rom. vi. 5; Heb. iv. 14, 15; vi. 20; vii. 16—18; viii. 1—3; x. 21, 22.

[n] Rom. viii. 34; Col. ii. 12, 15; Col. iii. 1—5.

[a] Acts i. 3, 4; Matt. xxviii.

[b] John xx. and xxi.

[c] Acts i. 4, 5.

[d] Acts i. 10, 11; John xvi. 17; xv. 26; xiv. 16, 26; Gal. iv. 4, 6.

[e] Matt. xxvi. 64; Acts vii. 55, 56; Rom. viii. 34; Eph. i. 20—23; Col. iii. 1; Heb. i. 3, 13; viii. 1; x. 12; Eph. i. 23; Matt. xxviii. 18.

[f] Rev. xii. 9; xiii. 14.

[g] Acts iii. 21; 1 Cor. xv. 44, 45.

CHAPTER XVI.

"FROM THENCE HE SHALL COME AGAIN TO JUDGE THE QUICK AND THE DEAD."

Q. 1. WHAT is meant by the quick and the dead?

A. Those that are found alive at Christ's coming, and those that were dead before.[a]

Q. 2. Are not the souls of men judged when men die?

A. In part they are: but as it is soul and body that make a man, so it is the judgment upon soul and body which is the full judgment on the man. God's execution is the principal part of his judgment; and as souls have not the fulness of glory or misery, till the resurrection, so they are not fully judged till then; and societies must be then judged, and persons in their sociable relations, together.[b]

Q. 3. Whither is it that Christ will come, and where will he judge the world?

A. Not in heaven, for the wicked shall not come thither: but Paul tells us, 1 Thess. iv. 16, "That the Lord himself shall descend from heaven with a shout, with the voice of the archangel, and with the trump of God, and the dead in Christ shall rise first, and then they that are alive and remain shall be caught up together with them in the clouds, to meet the Lord in the air; and so shall we ever be with the Lord." By which it appeareth that the place of judgment will be in the air, between heaven and earth.

Q. 4. In what manner will Christ come to judgment?

A. Christ tells us, Matt. xxv. 31, "That the Son of man (that is, Christ as man) shall come in his glory, and all the holy angels with him, and shall sit on the throne of his glory, and before him shall be gathered all nations, and he shall separate them one from another, as a shepherd divideth his sheep from the goats." And St. Paul saith, 2 Thess. i. 7, 8, "The Lord Jesus shall be revealed from heaven, with his mighty angels, in flaming fire, taking vengeance on them that know not God, and that obey not the gospel of our Lord Jesus Christ; who shall be punished with everlasting destruction from the presence of the Lord, and from the glory of his power, when he shall come to be glorified in his saints, and to be admired in all them that believe."

Q. 5. Where are the souls of the dead before the day of judgment?

A. The souls of the faithful are with Christ in heaven, and the souls of the wicked are with devils in misery.

Q. 6. Where is it that the devils and wicked are in misery.

A. They are shut out from the glory of God; and wherever it be that they are, it is as God's prison, till the judgment of the great day. But the Scripture calleth the devil, "the Prince of the power of the air," Eph. ii. 2. Yet is he on earth, "for he worketh in the children of disobedience," and is ready with his temptations with all men: and he is said to "go to and fro in the earth," Job i. 7; ii. 2. And he is said to "walk in dry places, seeking rest, and dwelling in the wicked," Matt. xii. 43, 44.

Q. 7. But are the souls of the wicked in no other hell than the devils are?

A. The Scripture tells us of no other; but it tells us not of their tempting and possessing men as devils do, but of their suffering.

[a] 1 Thess. iv. 15—17.
[b] Matt. xxv.; 2 Thess. i. 6, 7, 10, 11; John v. 22, 25.
[c] Luke xvi. 9, 22.

Q. 8. Are devils and wicked souls in the same hell that they shall be in after the day of judgment, and have they the same punishment?

A. Whether there shall be any change of the place, it is not needful for us to know; but the punishment is of the same kind, but it will be greater after judgment; were it but because the body joined to the soul, and the multitude of the damned joined in the suffering, will make every one more receptive of it.

Q. 9. Is there no middle place between heaven and hell? or a middle state of souls that are in hope of deliverance from their pain?

A. Hell itself is not all one place,[c] seeing devils are both in the air and in the earth, and where else we know not. And in Job i. 11, 12, "Satan was among the sons of God." But as for any hope of deliverance to them that die unpardoned, the Scripture tells us of none; but saith, that "the night cometh when none can work;" and that "This is the accepted time, this is the day of salvation;" and that "every man shall be judged according to what he had done in the body, whether it be good or evil." It is therefore mad presumption for any one to neglect this day of salvation, upon a hope of his own making, that they that die the slaves of the devil may repent and be delivered in their airy life, and be made the children of God; or that any purgatory fire shall refine them, or any prayers of the saints in heaven or earth deliver them.[d]

Q. 10. But it seems by their pleading, described by Christ, that they will not be past hope till the sentence be passed on them, Matt. xxv.

A. But the same text tells you what sentence certainly shall pass; and, therefore, that if they keep any hope, it is not of God's making, but their own, and will be all in vain; but indeed those words seem rather to express their fervent desire to escape damnation than their hope. The wicked may cry for mercy when it is too late, but shall not obtain it. Dives (Luke xvi.) may beg for a drop of water, but not get it.

Q. 11. But will it not be a long work to judge all that ever lived, from the beginning of the world unto the end?

A. God's judgment is not like man's, by long talk and wordy trial, though Christ open the reasons of it after the manner of men: God's judgment consisteth of full conviction and execution. And he can convince all men in a moment by his light, shining at once into every one's conscience; as the sun can enlighten at once the millions of eyes all over the earth. And God's execution (casting all the wicked into utter darkness and misery) needs no long time, though its continuance will be for ever.[e]

Q. 12. May we know in this life what judgment Christ will then pass on us?

A. All men, or most men, do not know it. Nor will it be known by a slight and sudden thought; nor by blinded or self-flattering sinners; nor by the worser sort of true believers, that sin as much as will stand with sincerity; nor yet by such ignorant christians who understand not well the terms of the covenant of grace, or have true grace, and know it not to be true; nor yet by such timorous christians, whose fear doth hinder faith and reason. But there is no doubt but we may know, and ought to use all diligence to know, what sentence Christ will pass upon us.[f]

For, 1. The difference between heaven and hell is

[d] Matt. v. 25, 26; Mark ix. 43—46. [e] 2 Tim. iv. 1.
[f] John xii. 47, 48; Rom. ii. 12, 13; Acts xvii. 31; Mark xvi. 16.

so great that there must needs be a great difference between them that shall go to each; and therefore it may be known. Christ's Spirit is not an undiscernible mark and pledge to them that have it. 2. And we are commanded to search and try ourselves; and many marks of difference are told us, and the persons plainly described that shall be justified and condemned; and they are already here justified and condemned by that law by which they shall be judged. 3. And what comfort could we have in all the redemption and grace of Christ, and all the promises of salvation, if we could not come to know our title by them?[g]

Q. 13. Who be they that Christ will then justify, or condemn?

A. I must not here answer that question, because its proper place is afterward, under some of the following articles.

Q. 14. But I find some scriptures saying, "That we are not justified by works, but by faith in Christ;" and yet, in Matt. xxv. Christ passeth the sentence upon men's works as the cause; and it is said, "We shall be judged according to our works."

A. By works, Paul meaneth[h] all works that are conceived to make the reward to be, not of grace, but of debt; all works which are set in competition, or opposition, to justification by faith in Christ. The question between him and the Jews was, whether the divine excellency of Moses' law was such as that it was given to justify the doers of it as such; or whether it was but an index to point them to Christ, the end of the law, by whom they must be justified. But it is not believing in Christ, nor begging his grace, nor thankfully accepting it, that Paul meaneth by works in his exclusion: it is this that he sets against these works. And as we are here made justified persons by mere grace, giving us repentance and faith in Christ, (that is, making us christians,) so this obligeth us to live and die as christians, if we will be saved. And therefore, the final, justifying sentence at judgment, doth pass on us according to such works only as are the performance of our covenant with Christ, without which we shall not be saved, and therefore not then justified: our justification then being the justifying of our title to salvation, and therefore hath the same conditions.

Q. 15. What may we further learn by this article of Christ's coming?[i]

A. 1. We must learn to fear and obey him, that must judge us, and to live as we would then hear of it, and to make it all the work of our lives to prepare for that day and final doom; and diligently to try our hearts and lives, that we may be sure to be then justified.

2. We must not be discouraged that we see not Christ, but remember that we shall shortly see him in his glory: in the sacrament, and all his worship, let us do it, as expectants of his coming.

3. We have no cause to be dismayed at the prosperity of the wicked, nor at our persecutions, or any sufferings, while we foresee, by faith, that glorious day.

4. We should live in the joyful hopes of that day when he that died for us, and sanctified us, shall be our Judge, and justify us, and finally judge us to endless life: and we must love, and long, and pray for this glorious coming of Christ. Come, Lord Jesus, come quickly. Amen.

[g] Mal. iii. 17, 18; Matt. xiii.; xxv.; Rom. viii. 30; John xvii. 2, 3; Heb. vi. 2; ix. 27; 2 Cor. v. 10.

[h] Acts xxiv. 25; James ii. 13; Acts xvii. 31; Rom. iii. 27; Gal. ii. 16, 17; iii. 2, 5, 10; Eph. ii. 7; Titus iii. 5, 6; Rom. iv. 4; ii. 2, 3, 5; Eccl. xii. 24.

[i] Rom. xiv. 10; Rev. xx. 12, 13; xxii. 14; James ii. 14, &c.; Matt. xii. 36, 37; 2 Pet. iii. 11, 12.

CHAPTER XVII.

III. "I BELIEVE IN THE HOLY GHOST."

Q. 1. WHAT is meant by believing in the Holy Ghost?[a]

A. It meaneth our believing what he is, and what he doth; and our trusting to himself, and to his works.

Q. 2. What must we believe of himself?

A. That he is God, the third person in the Trinity, one in essence with the Father and the Son.

Q. 3. What must we believe of his works?

A. We must believe, 1. That the Holy Ghost is the great Agent and Advocate of Jesus Christ on earth, by his works to be his witness, and to plead his cause, and communicate his grace.

2. That the Holy Ghost was the author of those many uncontrolled miracles by which the gospel of Christ was sealed to the world; and therefore that those miracles were the certain attestation of God.[b]

3. That the Holy Ghost was given by Christ to his apostles and evangelists, to enable them to perform the extraordinary office to which they were commissioned, to teach the nations to observe all things that Christ had commanded, and to lead them into all truth, and bring all things to their remembrance.

4. That therefore the doctrine of the said apostles and evangelists, first preached by them, and after recorded in the sacred Scriptures, for the use of the church to the end of the world, as the full doctrine and law of Christ, is to be received as the word of God, indited by the Spirit.

5. That it is the work of the Holy Ghost to sanctify all God's elect; that is, to illuminate their understandings, to convert their wills to God, and to strengthen and quicken them to do their duty, and conquer sin, and save them from the devil, the world, and the flesh; and to be in them a Spirit of power, and love, and a sound mind; and so that the Holy Ghost is an Intercessor within us, to communicate life, light, and love, from the Father and the Son, and excite in us those holy desires, thanks, and praise, which are meet for God's acceptance. All this is contained in our believing in the Holy Ghost.

Q. 4. If all this be in it, it seemeth a most necessary part of faith?

A. The perfective works of God are used to be ascribed to the Holy Ghost. This is so weighty and necessary a part of faith, that all the rest are insufficient without it. Millions perish that God created, and that Christ, in a general sort, as aforesaid, died for; but those that are sanctified by the Holy Ghost are saved. It is the work of the Holy Ghost to communicate to us the grace of Christ, that the work of creation and redemption may attain their ends.

Q. 5. How is it proved that the Holy Ghost is God?

A. In that we are baptized into the belief of him, as of the Father and the Son; and in that he doth the works proper to God, and hath the attributes of God in Scripture, which also expressly saith, "There are three which bear record in heaven, the Father, the Word, and the Holy Spirit; and these three are one," 1 John v. 7.

[a] Matt. xii. 31, 32; xxviii. 19; 1 John v. 7; Acts v. 3.

[b] John xiv. 15—17, 26; xv. 26; xvi. 7—11, 13—15; Mark i. 8; Acts i. 5, 8; ii. 4, 33, 38; iv. 31; vi. 3, 5; viii. 17; x. 44, 45; xi. 15, 16; xix. 2, 6; Rom. xv. 13, 16; 1 Cor. xii.; vi. 11, 19; 2 Cor. xiii. 14; Tit. iii. 5, 6; Heb. ii. 3, 4; 2 Pet. i. 21; Rom. viii. 9, 15, 16; Jude 20; Luke xi. 13; Eph. i. 13; iv. 30; 1 Thess. iv. 8.

Q. 6. I have oft marvelled that the creed left out, 1. The authority of the apostles. 2. And their miracles and Christ's. 3. And the authority of the Scriptures. And, now, I perceive that all these are contained in our believing in the Holy Ghost.

A. No doubt but it is a practical article of faith,[c] in which we profess to believe in the Holy Ghost, in his relation and works on man; and therefore, as Christ's agent in gathering his church, by the apostolical power, preaching, writings, and miracles; and in the sanctifying and helping all true believers.

Q. 7. By this it seems there are many ways of denying the Holy Ghost?

A. Yes; 1. They deny him, who deny his Godhead as the third person in the blessed Trinity.

2. They deny him, who deny that the miracles of Christ and his apostles were God's testimony to Christ, being convinced of the truth of the facts.

3. They deny him, who deny the extraordinary qualifications of the apostles, and suppose them to have had but the prudence of ordinary honest men.

4. They deny the Holy Ghost, who deny the sacred Scriptures to be indited by him, and to be true.

5. They deny him, who deny him to be the Sanctifier of God's elect, and feign holiness to be but conceit, deceit, or common virtue.

Q. 8. But are all these the unpardonable sin against the Holy Ghost?

A. The unpardonable sin is called "the blasphemy against the Holy Ghost," Matt. xii. And it is when men are convinced that those miracles were done, and those gifts given, which are God's attestation to Christ and his gospel; but they fixedly believe, and say, that they were all done by the power of the devil, by conjuration, and not by God; and therefore, notwithstanding them, Christ was but a deceiver. And this sin is unpardonable, because it rejecteth the only remedy, the Spirit's witness to the truth of Christ. He that will not believe this witness shall have no other.

Q. 9. But how may we know that we are sanctified by the Spirit?

A. By that holiness which he causeth. 1. When our understandings so know and believe the truth and goodness of the gospel and its grace, as that we practically esteem and prefer the love of the Father, the grace of the Son, and the communion of the Holy Ghost, and the heavenly glory, before all the pleasures, profits, and honours of this world, that stand against them, and before life itself.

2. When our wills do, with habitual inclination and resolution, love and choose the same, before all the said things that stand in competition.

3. When in the course of our lives, we seek them first, and hold them fastest in a time of trial, forsaking the flesh, the world, and the devil, so far as they are against them, and living in sincere, though not perfect, obedience to God.[d]

Q. 10. Is the Spirit, or the Scripture, higher than the rule of faith and life?

A. The Spirit, as the Author of the Scripture, is greater than the Scripture; and the Scripture, as the word of the Spirit, is the rule of our faith and lives, and greater than our spiritual gifts. The Spirit in the apostles was given them to write (when they had preached) that doctrine which is our rule: but the Spirit is not given to us to make a new law, or rule, but to believe, love, and obey that already made. As under the law of Moses, God, that made the law, was greater than the law. But when God had made that law their rule, he did not, after that, teach good men to make another law, but to understand and obey that.

Q. 11. There are many that boast of the Spirit and revelations. How shall we try such, whether their spirits be of God?

A. 1. If they pretend to do that which is fully done by the Spirit already, that is, to preach or write another gospel, or make a new law for the universal church, seeing this was the prophetical extraordinary office of Christ, and the Spirit in the apostles, such imply an accusation of insufficiency on Christ's and the Spirit's law, or rule, and arrogate a power never given them, and so are false prophets.

2. If they contradict the written word of God, which is certainly sealed by God's Spirit already, it must needs be by an evil spirit; for God's Spirit doth not contradict itself.[e]

Q. 12. But had not the priests, under the law, the Spirit of God, as well as Moses, that gave them the law?

A. Moses only, and Aaron under him, had God's revelation to make the law; and the priests only to keep it, to teach it, and rule by it. And so it is as to the apostles of Christ, and the succeeding ministry.

Q. 13. But might not kings, then, make religious laws?

A. Yes; to determine such circumstances as God had only given them a general law for, and left to be determined by them, but not to make new laws of the same kind with God's, nor to add to or alter them.

Q. 14. But were there not prophets, after Moses, that had the Spirit?

A. Yes; but they were not legislators, but sent with particular mandates, reproofs, or consolations, save only David and Solomon, who had directions from God himself, not to make a new law of God, but to order things about the temple and its worship.

So if any man now pretend to a prophetical revelation, it must not be legislative to the catholic church, nor against Scripture, but about particular persons, acts, and events; and it must be proved by miracle, or by success, before another is bound to believe him.

Q. 15. Must I take every motion in me to be by the Holy Ghost, which is agreeable to the word of God, or for doing what is there commanded?

A. Yes; if it be according to that word, for the matter, end, manner, time, and other circumstances. But Satan can transform himself into an angel of light,[f] and mind us of some text or truth to misapply it, and put us on meditation, prayer, or other duty, at an unseasonable time, when it would do more hurt than good; or in an ill manner, or to ill ends. He can move men to be fervent reprovers, or preachers, or rulers, that were never called to it, but are urged by him, and the passion and pride of their own hearts: and good men, in some mistakes, know not what manner of spirit they are of.

CHAPTER XVIII.

"THE HOLY CATHOLIC CHURCH."

Q. 1. How is this article joined to the former?

A. This article hath not been always in the creed,

[c] John xvi. 13.

[d] Acts xxvi. 18; Eph. i. 18; Col. i. 9, 10; 2 Cor. v. 17; Matt. xviii. 3; John iii. 3, 5, 6; Heb. xii. 14; Matt. vi. 33; 2 Thess. ii. 13; 1 Pet. i. 1, 2; 2 Thess. ii. 2; 1 John iv 1—3.

[e] Gal. ii. 7, 8

[f] 2 Cor. xi. 14.

in the same order and words as now. But the belief of a holy church was long before it was called "catholic;" and it is joined as part of our belief of the work of the Holy Ghost, and the redemption wrought by Christ. Christ, by his death, purchaseth, and the Holy Ghost gathereth, the "holy catholic church." It were defective to believe Christ's purchase, and the Holy Ghost's sanctification, and not know for whom, and on whom, it is done. To sanctify, is to sanctify some persons; and so to make them the holy society, or christian church.

Q. 2. What is a church?

A. The name is applied to many sorts of assemblies which we need not name to you; but here it signifieth the christian society.

Q. 3. Why is it called catholic?

A. Catholic is a Greek word, and signifieth universal. It is called catholic, because, 1. It is not, as the Jews' church, confined to one nation, but comprehendeth all true christians in the world: and, 2. Because it consisteth of persons that have every where in the world the same essentiating qualifications summed up, Eph. iv. 3—6, one body, one spirit, one hope of our calling, one Lord, one faith, one baptism, one God and Father of all, though in various measures of grace. And so the concordant churches of Christ through the world were called the catholic church, as distinct from the sects and heresies that broke from it.

Q. 4. How comes the pope of Rome to call only his subjects catholics?

A. The greatest part of the church on earth, by far, was long in the Roman empire, and when emperors turned christians, they gave the churches power, for the honour of christianity, to form the churches much like the civil state: and so a general council of all the churches in that empire was their supreme church power. And three patriarchs first, and five after, were in their several provinces, over all the rest of the archbishops and bishops: and so the orthodox party at first were called the catholics, because they were the greater concordant part; but quickly the Arians became far greater, and carried it in councils, and then they called themselves the catholics. After that, the orthodox, under wiser emperors, got up again, and then they were the greater part called catholics. Then the Nestorians a little while, and the Eutychians after, and the Monothelites after them, got the major vote in councils, and called themselves the catholic church: and so, since then, they that had the greatest countenance from princes, and the greatest number of bishops in councils, claimed the name of the catholic church: and the pope, that was the first patriarch in the empire, first called himself the head of the catholic church in that empire; and when the empire was broke, extended his claim to the whole christian world, partly by the abuse of the word "catholic church," and partly by the abuse of the name "general councils;" falsely pretending to men that what was called catholic and general, as to the empire, had been so called as to all the world. And thus his church was called catholic.

Q. 5. Why is the catholic church called holy?

A. 1. To notify the work of our Saviour, who came to save us from our sins, and gather a peculiar people, a holy society, who are separated from the unbelieving, ungodly world.

2. To notify the work of the Holy Ghost, who is given to make such a holy people.

3. Yea, to notify the holiness of God the Father, who will be sanctified in all that draw near him, and hateth the impure and unholy, and will have all his children holy as he is holy.

4. And to tell us the fitness of all God's children for his favour and salvation.

Q. 6. Wherein consisteth the holiness of the church?

A. 1. Christ their Head is perfectly holy. 2. The gospel and law of Christ, which is our objective faith and rule, are holy. 3. The founders of the church were eminently holy. 4. All sincere christians are truly holy, and marked out as such for salvation. 5. The common ministers have a holy office. 6. The church worship, as God's ordinances, are holy works. 7. All that are baptized, and profess christianity, are holy as to profession, and so far separated from the infidel world, though not sincerely to salvation.

Q. 7. What is it now that you call the holy catholic church?

A. It is the universality of christians, headed by Jesus Christ.

Or, it is a holy kingdom, consisting of Jesus Christ,[a] the Head, and all sincere christians, the sincere members, and all professed christians, the professing members; first founded and gathered by the Holy Ghost, eminently working in the apostles and evangelists, recording the doctrine and laws of Christ for their government to the end, and guided by his ministers, and sanctifying Spirit, according to those laws and doctrine in various degrees of grace and gifts.

Q. 8. What is it that makes all churches to be one?

A. 1. Materially their concord in their same qualifications, which is called, Eph. iv. 3, "the unity of the Spirit." They are all that are sincere, sanctified by the same Spirit, and have the same essentials of faith, hope, baptismal covenant, and love:[b] and the hypocrites profess the same.

2. Formally their common union with, and relation to, God the Father, Son, and Holy Ghost, that is, to Jesus Christ their Head, bringing them home to God the Father by the Spirit.

Q. 9. Is there no one ministerial head of all the church on earth?

A. No: neither one man, nor one council, or collection of men. For, 1. None are naturally capable of being one supreme pastor, teacher, priest, and ruler over all the nations of the earth, nor can so much as know them, or have human converse with them. And a council gathered equally out of all the world, as one such supreme, is a more gross fiction of impossibles than that of a pope.

2. And Christ, that never so qualified any, never gave any such power. But all pastors are like the judges, justices, and mayors that rule subordinately under one king, in their several precincts, and not like a universal viceroy, lieutenant, or aristocracy, or parliament.

Q. 10. But is not monarchy the best form of government, and should not the church have the best?

A. 1. Yes: and therefore Christ is its Monarch, who is capable of it.

2. But a human, universal monarchy of all the world is not best. Nor was ever an Alexander, a Cæsar, or any man, so mad, as soberly to pretend to it. Who is the man that you would have to be king at the antipodes, and over all the kings on earth?

3. Yea, the case of the church is liker that of schools and colleges, that rule volunteers in order to teaching them. And did ever papist think that all the schools on earth of grammarians, philosophers,

[a] Eph. i. 22, 23; v. 23, 24; Col. i. 18, 19, 24; Matt. xvi. 18; 1 Cor. xii. 28—30; Acts ii. 47.

[b] John xvii. 21, 23; 1 Cor. xii. 5, 27—29; Eph. iv. 5—7; Matt. xxviii. 19.

physicians, &c. should have one human, supreme schoolmaster, or a council or college of such to rule them?

Q. 11. But Christ is not a visible Head, and the church is visible?

A. We deny not the visibility of the church, but we must not feign it to be more visible than it is.[c] 1. It consisteth of visible subjects. 2. Their profession is visible, and their worship. 3. They have visible pastors in all the particular churches, as every school hath its schoolmaster. 4. Christ was visible in the flesh on earth. 5. He was after seen of Stephen and Paul. 6. He is now visible in heaven, as the king in his court. 7. And he will come in glorious visibility shortly, to judge the world. 8. And his laws are visible by which he ruleth us and will judge us. If all this visibility will not satisfy men, Christ will not approve of usurpation for more visibility.

Q. 12. Of what use is this article to us?

A. 1. To tell us that Christ died not in vain, but will certainly have a holy church which he will save.[d]

2. To show us, in the blessed effect, that the sanctification of the Spirit is not a fancy, but a holy church is renewed and saved by it.

3. To tell us that God forsaketh not the earth, though he permit ignorance, infidelity, and wickedness to abound, and malice to persecute the truth: still God hath a holy church which he will preserve and save. And though this or that church may apostatize, and cease, there shall be still a catholic church on earth.

4. To mind us of the wonderful providence of God, which so continueth and preserveth a holy people, hated by open enemies, and wicked hypocrites, by Satan and all his instruments on earth.

5. To teach us to love the unity of christians, and carefully maintain it, and not to tear the church by the engines of proud men's needless snares, nor to be rashly censorious of any, or excommunicate them unjustly, nor to separate from any, further than they separate from Christ; but to rejoice in our common union in christian faith and love, and not let wrongs, or infirmities of christians, or carnal interests, or pride or passion, nor different opinions about things not necessary to our unity, destroy our love or peace, or break this holy bond.

CHAPTER XIX.

"THE COMMUNION OF SAINTS."

Q. 1. How is this article joined to the former?

A. As it belongs to our belief in the Holy Ghost, it tells us the effect of his sanctification: and as it belongs to our belief of the holy catholic church, it tells us the end of church relation, that saints may live in holy communion.

Q. 2. What is it to be a saint?

A. To be separated from a common and unclean conversation unto God, and to be absolutely devoted to him, to love, serve, and trust him, and hope for his salvation.

Q. 3. Are all saints that are members of the catholic church?

A. Yes, by profession, if not in sincerity: all that are sincere and living members of the church, are really devoted to God by heart consent; and the rest are devoted by baptism, and outward profession, and are hypocrites, pretending falsely to be real saints.[e]

Q. 4. Why then doth the church of Rome canonize some few, and call them saints, if all christians be saints?

A. By saints they mean extraordinary saints: but their appropriating the name to such, much tendeth to delude the people, as if they might be saved though they be not saints.[f]

Q. 5. What is meant by the communion of saints?

A. Such a frame and practice of heart and life towards one another as supposeth union, such as is between the members of the body.

Q. 6. Wherein doth this communion consist?

A. 1. In their common love to God, faith in Christ, and sanctification by the Spirit. 2. In their love to one another as themselves.[g] 3. In their care for one another's welfare, and endeavour to promote it as their own:[h] and when love makes all their goods so far common to all christians within their converse, as that they do to their power supply their wants in the order and measure that God's providence, and their relations and acquaintance, direct them; preferring the relief of others' necessities before their own superfluity or fulness. 4. In their joining, as with one mind and soul and mouth, in God's public worship, and that in the holy order under their respective pastors, which Christ, by his Spirit in the apostles, hath instituted.[i]

Q. 7. Why is our joining in the Lord's supper called our communion?

A. Because it is a special symbol, badge, and expression of it instituted by Christ, to signify our communion with him and one another.

Q. 8. Is that to be only a communion of saints?

A. Yes, that in a special manner is appropriated to saints: other parts of communion, (as eating together, relieving each other, duties of religion, &c.) are so far to be used toward unbelievers, that they are not so meet to be the distinguishing symbols of christians: but the two sacraments, baptism for entrance, and the Lord's supper for continuance of communion, Christ hath purposely appointed for such badges or signs of his people as separate from the world.[k]

Q. 9. By what order are others to be kept from church communion?

A. Christ hath instituted the office of the sacred ministry for this end, that when they have made disciples to him, they may be intrusted with the keys of his church, that is, especially the administration of these sacraments, first judging who is fit to be entered by baptism, and then who is fit for continued communion.[l]

Q. 10. May not the pastors, by this means, become church tyrants?

A. We must not put down all government for fear of tyranny; else kingdoms, armies, colleges, schools,

[c] 1 Cor. xi. 3; Eph. v. 23; Col. ii. 10, 18; ii. 19; Acts xiv. 23; Tit. i. 5; Eph. ii. 20; Acts viii. 36; ix.; xxii. 14; Rev. i. 7; Matt. xxv. 40.

[d] Eph. v. 27; Acts ii. 47; xx. 28; 1 Cor. x. 32; Eph. iii. 10; Col. i. 18, 24; Eph. iii. 21; Heb. ii. 12; 1 Thess. v. 12, 13; Eph. iv. 16; 1 Tim. iii. 15.

[e] 1 Cor. i. 1, 2; Rom. i. 7; xii. 15; xv. 25, 26, 31; 1 Cor. xiv. 33; xvi. 1, 15.

[f] 2 Cor. i. 1; Eph. i. 1; v. 3; vi. 18; Phil. i. 1; Col. i. 2; Heb. xiii. 24; Acts iv.

[g] Col. i. 4; 1 Pet. i. 22. [h] Heb. xiii. 2, 3; 1 Tim. vi. 18.

[i] 1 Cor. x. 16; 2 Cor. vi. 14; Heb. x. 22, 24; John xiii. 34, 35; 1 Thess. v. 12, 13.

[k] Matt. xxvi. 26; 1 Cor. xi. 21, 22, 24, &c.; Acts xx. 7; 1 Cor. x. 16; Acts ii. 42, 46.

[l] Matt. xvi. 19; xxiv. 45, 46; 1 Cor. iv. 1, 2; Acts xx. 20, 28; 1 Thess. v. 12, 13; Heb. xiii. 7, 17, 24.

must be all dissolved, as well as churches: somebody must be trusted with this power; and who is fitter than they who are called to it as their office, and therefore supposed best qualified for it.

Q. 11. What if none were trusted with it, and sacraments left free to all?

A. Then sacraments would be no sacraments, and the church would be no church: if any man or woman that would, might baptize whom, and when, they would, they might baptize Turks and heathens, and that over and over, who come in scorn; and they might baptize without a profession of true faith; or upon a false profession. And if every man might give the Lord's supper to another, it might be brought into ale-houses and taverns, in merriment, or as a charm, or every infidel or enemy might in scorn profane it: do you think that if baptism and the Lord's supper were thus administered, that they would be any symbols or badges of christianity, or of a church, or any means of salvation? No christians ever dreamt of such profanation.

Q. 12. But why may not the pastors themselves give them to all that will?

A. Either you would have [m] them forced to do so, or to do it freely. If forced, they are no judges who is fit; and who then shall be judge? If the magistrate, you make him a pastor; and oblige him to teach, examine, hear, and try all the people's knowledge, faith, and lives, which will find them work enough; and this is not to depose the ministers' power, but to put it on another that hath more already than he can do: and a pastor then that delivereth the sacrament to every one that the magistrate bids him shall be a slave, and not a free performer of the acts of his own office, unless that magistrate try and judge, and the minister be but a deacon, that must give account for no more than the bare delivering it. But if it be the receivers of baptism, or the Lord's supper, that shall be judges, and may force the pastor to give it them; I have showed you already the profanation will make it no sacrament nor church.

And if pastors, that are judges, shall freely give them to all, they will be the profaners, and such ministration will confound the church and the world.

Q. 13. I do not mean that they should give them to heathens, but to all that profess the christian faith.

A. Therefore they must judge whether they profess the christian faith or not; and whether they speak as parrots, or understand what they say: and withal, christian love and a christian life must be professed, as well as christian faith.

Q. 14. What are the terms on which they must receive men to communion?

A. They must baptize them and their infants, who, with competent understanding, and seeming seriousness, profess a practical belief in God the Father, Son, and Holy Ghost, and consent to that covenant, as expounded in the creed, Lord's prayer, and ten commandments. And they must admit all to communion in the Lord's supper, who continue in that profession, and nullify it not by proved apostasy, or inconsistent profession or practice.[n]

Q. 15. May not hypocrites make such professions, that are no saints?

A. Yes; and God only is the judge of hearts, not detected by proved contrary words or deeds: and these are saints by profession.

Q. 16. But it is on pretence of being the judge of church communion, that the pope hath got his power over the christian world.

A. And if tyrants, by false pretences, claim the dominions of other princes, or of men's families, we must not therefore depose our kings or fathers.

Q. 17. But how shall we know what pastors they be that have this power of the keys, and judging men's fitness for communion?

A. All pastors, as such, have power, as all physicians have in judging of their patients, and all schoolmasters of their scholars. But great difference there is, who shall correct men's injurious administrations: whether the magistrate do it himself, or whether a bishop over many pastors do it, or many pastors in a synod do it, is no such great matter as will warrant the sad contentions that have been about it, so it be done. Or if none of these do it, a people intolerably injured may right themselves, by deserting such an injurious pastor. But the pastors must not be disabled, and the work undone, on pretence of restraining them from misdoing it.[o]

Q. 18. What is the need and benefit of this pastoral discipline?

A. 1. The honour of Christ (who, by so wonderful an incarnation, &c. came to save his people from their sins) must be preserved: which is profaned, if his church be not a communion of saints.[p]

2. The difference between heaven and hell is so great, that God will have a visible difference between the way to each, and between the probable heirs of each. The church is the nursery for heaven, and the womb of eternal happiness. And dogs and swine are no heirs for heaven.

3. It is necessary to the comfort of believers.

4. And for the conviction and humbling of the unbelievers, and ungodly.

Q. 19. What further use should we make of this article?

A. 1. All christians must carefully see that they be not hypocrites, but saints indeed, that they be meet for the communion of saints.

2. All that administer holy things, and govern churches, should carefully see that they be a communion of saints, and not a swine-sty: not as the common world, but as the garden of Christ: that they promote and encourage holiness, and take heed of cherishing impiety.

3. We must all be much against both that usurpation, and that neglect of necessary discipline, and differencing saints from wicked men, which hath corrupted most of the churches in the world.[q]

Q. 20. But when experience assureth us that few christians can bear church discipline, should it be used when it will do hurt?

A. It is so tender, and yet so necessary, a discipline which Christ hath appointed, that he is unfit for the communion of saints who will not endure it. It is not to touch his purse or body: it is not to cast any man out of the church for small infirmities: no, nor for gross sin, that repenteth of it, and forsakes it: it is not to call him, magisterially, to submit to the pastor's unproved accusation or assertions: but it is, with the spirit of meekness and fatherly love, to convince a sinner, and draw him to repentance, proving from God's word,[r] that the thing is a sin, and proving him guilty of it, and telling him the evil and danger of it, and the necessity of repentance, and confession, and amendment. And if he be stubborn, not making unnecessary haste, but praying for

[m] 1 Cor. v.; 2 Thess. iii.; Tit. iii. 10; 2 Cor. vi. 16, 17; 1 Cor. i. 1, 2; 2 Cor. i. 1; Eph. i. 1, 2.
[n] Matt. xxviii. 19; Rev. xxii. 17.
[o] Phil. i. 15—18.
[p] Tit. ii. 14; Eph. i. 22, 23; v. 25—29; Col. i. 18, 24; Eph. iv. 14, 16.
[q] Matt. xxii. 21, 22; xiii. 39, 41; vii. 21, 22; Luke xiii. 27.
[r] Matt. xviii. 21, 22; Luke xvii. 3; 2 Cor. ii. 7, 10; vii. 8; John xx. 23.

his repentance, and waiting a competent time, and joyfully absolving him upon his repentance: and if he continue impenitent, only declaring him unfit for church communion, and requiring the church accordingly to avoid him, and binding him to answer it at the bar of God, if he repent not.

Q. 21. But if men will not submit to public confes ion, may not auricular, private confession to the priest serve turn?

A. In case the sin be private, a private confession may serve; but when it is known, the repentance must be known, or else it attaineth not the ends of its appointment: and the papists' auricular confession, in such cases, is but a trick to delude the church, and to keep up a party in it of wicked men, that will not submit to the discipline of Christ: it pretendeth strictness, but it is to avoid the displeasure of those that are too proud to stoop to open confession. Let such be never so many, they are not to be kept in the church on such terms: he that hath openly sinned against Christ, and scandalized the church, and dishonoured his profession, and will by no conviction and entreaty be brought to open confession, (in an evident case,) doth cast himself out of the communion of saints, and must be declared such by the pastors.

CHAPTER XX.

"THE FORGIVENESS OF SINS."

Q. 1. WHAT is the dependence of this article on the former?

A. It is part of the description of the effects of Christ's redemption, and the Holy Ghost's application of it: his regeneration maketh us members of the holy catholic church, where we must live in the communion of saints, and therewith we receive the forgiveness of sins: the same sacrament of baptism signifying and exhibiting both, as washing us from the filth or power of sin, and from the guilt of punishment.[a]

Q. 2. What is the forgiveness of sin?

A. It is God's acquitting us from the deserved punishment.[b]

Q. 3. How doth God do this?

A. By three several acts, which are three degrees of pardon: the first is, by his covenant, gift, promise, or law of grace, by which, as his instrument or act of oblivion, he dissolveth the obligation to punishment which we were under, and giveth us lawful right to impunity, so that neither punishment by sense or by loss shall be our due.[c]

The second act is by his sentence as a Judge, pronouncing us forgiven, and justifying this our right against all that is or can be said against it.

The third act is by his execution, actually delivering us from deserved punishment of loss and sense.[d]

Q. 4. Doth not God forgive us the guilt of the fault as well as the dueness of punishment?

A. Yes: for these are all one in several words; to forgive the sin, and to acquit from dueness of punishment for that sin, are the same thing. God doth not repute or judge us to be such as never sinned, for that were to judge falsely; nor doth he judge that our sin is not related to us as the actors, for that is impossible; nor doth he judge that our sin did not deserve punishment; but only that the deserved punishment is forgiven, for the merits of Christ's righteousness and sacrifice.

Q. 5. Is not justification and forgiveness of sin all one?

A. To be justified, 1. Sometimes signifieth to be made just and justifiable in judgment; and then it sometimes includeth both the gift of saving faith and repentance, and the gift of pardon, and of right to life everlasting; and sometimes it presupposeth faith and repentance given, and signifieth the annexed gift of pardon and life.

2. Sometimes it signifieth God's justifying us by his sentence in judgment, which containeth both the justifying of our right to impunity and salvation, and the justifying our faith and holiness as sincere, which are the conditions of our right.[e]

3. And sometimes to justify us, is to use us as just men. And as long as we understand the matter thus signified by pardoning and justifying, we must not strive about words so variously used.[f]

Q. 6. But if Christ's perfect righteousness, habitual and actual, be our own righteousness by God's imputation, how can we need a pardon of sin, when we were perfectly obedient in Christ?

A. We could not possibly be pardoned as sinners, if God reputed us to have fulfilled all righteousness in Christ, and so to be no sinners; therefore it is no such imputation that must be affirmed. But God justly reputeth Christ's holiness and righteousness, active and passive, dignified by his divinity, to be fully meritorious of our pardon, justification, and salvation. And so it is ours, and imputed as the true meritorious cause of our righteousness, which consisteth in our right to pardon and salvation.[g]

Q. 7. Is pardon perfect in this life, and all punishment remitted at once?

A. No: 1. The punishment denounced in God's sentence of Eve and Adam is not wholly forgiven; the curse on the ground, the woman's sorrows, the pain and stroke of death. 2. Temporal, correcting punishments are not all forgiven. 3. Some measure of sin is penally permitted in us. 4. The want of more holiness, and help of God's Spirit, and communion with God, is to all of us a sore punishment. 5. The permission of many temptations from devils and men are punishments, specially when they prevail to heinous sinning. 6. To be so long kept out of heaven, and to lie after in the grave, are punishments. Sure few men believe that pardon is here perfect, that feel any of these. 7. And it is not perfect, till we are justified before the world, and put in possession of salvation: that is the perfect pardon.[h]

Q. 8. But some say, that chastisements are no punishments.

A. They are not damning, destructive punishments, but they are chastising punishments; for they are evil to nature, inflicted by fatherly, correcting justice, for sin.

[s] Mark iii. 6; Luke xiii. 3, 5; xvii. 3; Acts ii. 37, 38; iii. 19; Luke xxiv. 47; James v. 16; 1 John i. 9; Prov. xxviii. 13; Acts xix.

[a] 1 John i. 9.

[b] Matt. ix. 2, 5—7; Mark ii. 7, 10.

[c] Psalm xxxii. 1, 2; lxxxv. 2; Luke v. 20; vii. 48, 50; James v. 15; Eph. iv. 32; Heb. i. 3; 2 Cor. v. 18, 19; Psalm cxxx. 4.

[d] Acts v. 31; xiii. 38; xxvi. 18.

[e] Isa. liii. 11; xlv. 25; 1 Cor. vi. 11; Tit. iii. 5, 7; Rev. xxii. 12; Rom. iv. 2, 5; ii. 13; iii. 20; Gal. ii. 16, 17; Rom. viii. 33; Jam. ii. 21, 24.

[f] Isa. l. 8; 1 Kings viii. 32; Deut. xxv. 1; Isa. v. 23.

[g] Rom. iii. 22, 25, 26; Gal. iii. 6; Rom. iv. 5, 9, 22; v. 17—19; vi. 13, 16, 18; viii. 4, 10.

[h] I think no man that felt what I feel, at the writing of this, in my flesh, and for my friends, can possibly think that pardon is perfect in this life. Jam. v. 15; Luke vi. 37; Matt. xii. 31; Josh. xxiv. 19; Matt. vi. 12, 14; 2 Kings xxiii. 26, 27; Matt. xviii. 32.

Q. 9. Is that an evil which always bringeth greater good.

A. It is no such evil as sinners should repine at. But ask any of that opinion, under the stone, or other tormenting disease, or if he must die as a malefactor, whether it be not a natural evil? If there be no evil in it, why doth he groan under it, why doth he pray against it, or use physic, or other remedies? Why is he offended at those that hurt him? Had he not rather have his holiness and salvation without torment, prisons, &c. than with them.

2. But it is not true, that all the punishments of such as are saved make them better; some are permitted to fall into heinous sin, and to decline in their faith, love, and obedience, and to die worse than once they were; and so to have a less degree of glory, when they have been hurtful scandals in the world. And is there no harm in all this? Nothing is perfect in this imperfect world.[i]

Q. 10. But how are Christ's merits and satisfaction perfect then?

A. That is perfect which is perfectly fitted to its use; it was not a use that Christ ever intended, to pardon all temporal, correcting punishment, nor to make each believer perfect the first hour. That our greatest sins should go unpunished is against Christ's will and kingly government, and the nature of his salvation: and his righteousness and satisfaction are not intended against himself.[k]

Q. 11. What sins are pardoned? Is it all, or but some?

A. All sin is pardoned, though the pardon be not perfect at first, to all true penitent believers. But final impenitence, unbelief, and unholiness, never had a pardon purchased or offered; but that which is not final is forgiven: yea, no sin is actually forgiven, as to the everlasting punishment, to final impenitents and unbelievers.[l]

Q. 12. Are sins pardoned before they are committed?

A. If you call the mere purpose or purchase a pardon unfitly, or you speak but of the general act of oblivion, which pardoneth all men on condition that they penitently and believingly accept it, so sins to come are pardoned: but (not to strive about words) no one hath any actual, proper pardon for any sin before it is committed; for it is no sin, and so no pardoned sin.[m]

Q. 13. When is it that sin is pardoned?

A. God's purpose is eternal; the conditional pardon was made when the covenant of grace was made; some degrees of punishment God remitteth by common and preparatory grace. But saving pardon none receive (at age) till they believe, nor are they justified.[n]

Q. 14. Why do we pray for pardon daily, when sin is already pardoned?

A. 1. I told you, sin is not pardoned when it is no sin; we sin daily, and, therefore, must have daily pardon. And this also proveth, that pardon and justification are not perfect before death, because there are more sins still to be pardoned. 2. And we pray for the continuance of the pardon we have, and for removal of punishments.

Q. 15. Is this the meaning of this article, that "I believe my own sins are actually forgiven," as a divine revelation?

A. The meaning is: 1. That by Christ a certain degree of punishment is taken off from all mankind, and they are not dealt with according to the rigour of the law of innocent nature. 2. And that a conditional pardon is given to all in the new covenant so far as it is revealed. 3. And that this pardon becometh actual to every one when he penitently and believingly consenteth to the (baptismal) covenant with Christ.[o] 4. And that this pardon is offered to me as well as others, and shall be mine if I be a sincere believer; this is all that the article containeth. 5. But while I profess to believe, it is supposed that I hope I do it sincerely, and, therefore, have some hope that I am pardoned. 6. But because a man may sincerely believe, and yet doubt of the sincerity, and God hath no where said in Scripture, that I or you are sincere believers, or are pardoned; therefore to believe this is no divine faith, save by participation; nor is it professed by all that profess the creed. But it is an effect of two acts: 1. Of our faith; 2. And of the conscience of our sincerity in believing: it is a conclusion that all should labour to make sure, though it be not the proper sense of the article.

Q. 16. Seeing all true believers are at first justified and pardoned as to the everlasting punishment, doth it not follow, that all God's children have afterward none but temporal chastisement to be forgiven?

A. 1. I told you that sin is not forgiven, even to stated believers, before it is committed: and when it is committed, the qualifying condition must be found in us; and though our first true faith and repentance qualify us for the pardon of all sin past, yet when more is committed, more is required in us to our pardon, that is, that we renew repentance and faith as far as sin is known, and that we beg pardon and forgive others. 2. Yet the future punishment is not so much unforgiven to the faithful as to others, before renewed repentance; for they have the main qualification, and want but an act for which they are habituated, and have God's Spirit to assist them. 3. And though sins unknown, which are ordinary infirmities, are forgiven without express, particular repentance, yet, in order of nature, the desert of punishment goeth before the forgiveness; the very law of nature maketh durable punishment due to durable souls, till the dueness be remitted by forgive-ness.[p]

Q. 17. Is my sin forgiven, as long as I believe it not forgiven?

A. If you believe not that God is a merciful, pardoning God, and Christ a pardoning Saviour, whose sacrifice and merits are sufficient, and God's promise of pardon to the penitent believer is true, and to be trusted, you are not pardoned; but if you believe this, and consent to Christ's pardoning covenant, you are pardoned, though you doubt of your own forgiveness.

Q. 18. How may I be sure that I am forgiven?

A. The everlasting punishment is forgiven, when you are one that God by his covenant pardoneth, and that is, when by true faith and repentance you consent to the covenant terms, and give up yourself to God, as your God, and Saviour, and Sanctifier. And when temporal punishments are remitted in soul or body, experience of their removal may tell you.[q]

Q. 19. What keepeth up doubts of forgiveness of sin?

A. 1. Ignorance of the terms of the pardoning

[i] 2 Sam. vii. 14; Psal. lxxiii. 14; cxviii. 18; 1 Cor. xi. 32; Jer. xxxi. 18; Heb. xii. 8—10; 2 Cor. ii. 6; Lam. iii. 39; Job xxxi. 11; Amos iii. 2; Matt. xvi. 23.

[k] Phil. iii. 12, 13; 1 Pet. v. 10; 1 Cor. xiii. 10; 2 Cor. vii. 1; Prov. viii. 36; 1 John i. 8; v. 17.

[l] Matt. xii. 32; Exod. xxxiv. 6, 7; Luke xiii. 3, 5; John iii. 16; Mark xvi. 16.

[m] Matt. xviii. 32; 2 Cor. v. 19; Matt. vi. 12.

[n] Heb. i. 3; John iii. 16, 18, 25; Rom. iv. 2; v. 1.

[o] 2 Sam. xii. 12, 13; Psal. l.; xxxii.

[p] Psal. xxxii; xxv.; li.; Matt. xviii. 32; vi. 14, 15; 1 John i. 9; Acts viii. 22.

[q] John iii. 16; Rom. x. 14.

covenant. 2. And ignorance of ourselves and our own sincerity. 3. Especially renewing our guilt by sin, and being so defective in our repentance, and other grace, as that we cannot be sure of our sincerity; above all, when frequent sinning after promises makes us not credible to ourselves.

Q. 20. But is not the cure of a doubting soul to believe, though he find no evidence in himself; and that because he is commanded to believe, and so believing will be his evidence?

A. Believing is a word that signifieth divers acts. As I told you, it is every man's duty to believe God's mercy, and Christ's redemption and sufficiency, and the truth of the conditional promise,[r] and to accept pardon, as offered on the terms of that promise, and then not to cherish doubts of his sincerity. But it is not every man's duty to believe that he is sincere, or that his sin is pardoned; else most should be bound to believe an untruth that it may after become true. Presumption destroyeth far more than despair; for an ungodly, impenitent person to believe that he is godly, and justified by Christ, is to believe himself, who is a liar, and not to believe Christ; yea, it is to believe himself against Christ, who saith the contrary.

Q. 21. What is the use of this article of the forgiveness of sin?

A. The use is exceeding great; not to imbolden us in sin, because it is pardonable, nor to delay repentance and forsaking sin, for that were to cast away pardon by contempt. But, 1. To show us what a merciful God we serve. 2. And what a mercy it is to have a Redeemer,[s] and a pardoning Saviour. 3. And what a comfort to be under a pardoning covenant of grace. 4. And it tells us that the review of the sins of our unregenerate state, though they must keep us humble, should yet be still used to raise our hearts to joyful thankfulness to God, for the grace of a Redeemer. 5. And it should keep us from despair and discouragement in all our weaknesses, while we have the evidence of daily pardon. 6. Yea, it should make us hate sin the more, which is against so good a God. 7. We may come with reverent boldness to God, in meditation, prayer, and sacraments, when we know that sin is pardoned. 8. And we may taste the sweetness of all our mercies, when the doubt of our forgiveness doth not imbitter them. 9. And we may much the easilier bear all afflictions when the everlasting punishment is forgiven. 10. And we may die when God calls us, without horror, when we believe that we are pardoned through Christ. Nothing but sin can hurt or endanger us at Christ's tribunal; when that is forgiven, and there is no condemnation to us, being in Christ, how joyfully may we think of his appearing! 11. What peace of conscience may we have continually, while we can say that all our sins are forgiven us! For, as Psal. xxxii. 1, "And blessed are they whose transgression is forgiven, whose sin is covered, to whom the Lord imputeth not iniquity, and in whose spirit there is no guile."

CHAPTER XXI.

"THE RESURRECTION OF THE BODY."

Q. 1. I HAVE oft wondered why there is nothing in the creed of the immortality of the soul, and its state before the resurrection.

[r] Mark iii. 28; Acts v. 31.

A. 1. The article of Christ's descent tells us, that his soul was among the separated souls, while his body was in the grave; as he told the thief, that he should be that day with him in paradise.

2. The resurrection of the body is a thing not known at all by nature, but only by supernatural revelation, and therefore is an article of mere belief. But the immortality, or future life of souls, is a point which the light of nature revealeth, and therefore was taken, both by Jews and sober heathens, as a truth of common notice. Even as the love of ourselves is not expressed in the ten commandments, but only the love of God and others, because it was a thing presupposed.

3. The immortality of the soul is included in the article of the resurrection of the body; for if the soul continue not, the next at the resurrection would be another soul, and a new-created one, and not the same. And then the body would not be the same soul's body, nor the man the same man, but another. Who was so unwise to think that God had so much more care of the body than of the soul, as that he would let the soul perish, and raise the body from the dust alone, and join it with another soul?

4. Very learned and wise expositors think, that the Greek word, *anastasis*, used for resurrection, indeed signifieth the whole life after this, both of soul first, and body also after, oft in the New Testament. It is a living again, or after this life, called a standing up again. And there is great probability of it in Christ's argument with the Sadducees, and some passages of Paul's, 1 Cor. xv.

Q. 2. What texts of Scripture do fully prove that the soul liveth when it is separated from the body?

A. Very many: 1. God breathing into man the breath of life, and making him a living soul, is said thereby to make him in the image of God, who is the living God; and so the soul is essentially life.

2. God's calling himself the God of Abraham, Isaac, and Jacob, is by Christ expounded, as proving that he is the God of living Abraham.

3. None ever dreamed that Enoch and Elijah had no company of human souls in heaven. For (Matt. xvii.) Moses also appeared with them on the mount, and showed that his soul did live.

4. When Saul himself would have Samuel raised to speak with him, it plainly implieth that it was then the common belief of the Jews, that separated souls survive.

5. When (1 Kings xvii. 22) Elijah raised the dead child of the widow of Zarephath; and (2 Kings iv.) Elisha raised the Shunammite's child; and (2 Kings xiii. 21) a dead man was raised; all these proved that the soul was the same that came again, else the persons had not been the same.

6. When Christ raised Lazarus, and Jairus' daughter, (Mark v. 41, 42; Luke viii. 55,) and another, (Luke vii. 12, 14, 15,) the same souls came into them.

7. Many of the dead rose and appeared at Christ's death. And Peter raised one from death, which was by a re-union of the same living soul to the same body.

8. Christ tells us (Luke xii. 4) that men cannot kill the soul.

9. He tells us, (Luke xvi. 9,) that as the wise steward, when he was put out, was received by the persons whom he had obliged; so if we make us friends of the mammon of unrighteousness, when these things fail us. which is at death, we shall be received into the everlasting habitations.

10. The parable of the sensual rich man and Laza-

[s] Jer. xxxi. 34; xxxvi. 3; Luke vii. 12, 13; Acts xxvi. 18; Eph. i. 7; Col. i. 14.

rus, one going presently to hell, and the other to the bosom of Abraham in paradise, fully prove that Christ would have this believed, and would have all men warned accordingly to prepare; and that Moses and the prophets were so sufficient for such notice, as that one from the dead would have been less credible herein. Though it be a parable, it is an instructing, and not a deceiving, parable, and very plain in this particular. The name of Abraham's bosom was according to the common sense of the Jews, who so called that state of the blessed, not doubting but that Abraham was then in happiness, and the blessed with him.

11. Herod's thought, that John had been risen from the dead, and the Jews' conceit that Christ had been one of the old prophets risen, and the Pharisees' approbation of Christ's argument with the Sadducees, do put it past doubt, that it was then taken for certain truth, that the souls of the faithful do survive, by all, except such as the heretical Sadducees.

12. Christ saith, "This is life eternal, to know thee the only true God, and Jesus Christ whom thou hast sent," John xvii. 3. How is it eternal, if it have as long an interruption as from death till the day of judgment?

13. It is the sum of God's gospel, that "Whosoever believeth in Christ shall not perish, but have everlasting life," John iii. 16. Therefore they perish not till the day of judgment.

14. Christ hath promised, that whoever drinketh of the water which he will give him, (the Spirit,) "it shall be in him a well of water springing up to everlasting life," John iv. 14. But if the soul perish, that water perisheth to that soul.

15. To be born again of the Spirit fitteth a man to enter into the kingdom of God. But if the soul perish, all that new birth is lost to that soul, and profiteth the dust only.

16. "He that believeth on the Son, hath everlasting life," John iii. 36. "He is passed from death to life," John v. 24. "He giveth meat, which endureth to everlasting life," John vi. 27. "He shall never hunger or thirst (that is, be empty) that cometh to Christ," ver. 35. "Of all that cometh to him he will lose nothing;" therefore will not lose all their souls, ver. 39. "They have everlasting life," ver. 40, 47. "He dwelleth in Christ, and Christ in him," and therefore is not extinct, ver. 54, 56, 58. "Verily, verily, I say unto you, If a man keep my sayings, he shall never see death," John viii. 51. "I give unto them eternal life, and they shall never perish, neither shall any pluck them out of my hand," John x. 28.

17. "Whosoever liveth and believeth in me shall never die," John xi. 26.

18. "The Comforter shall abide with you for ever," John xiv. 16. "For he dwelleth with you, and shall be in you," ver. 17.

19. "I will that they whom thou hast given me, be with me where I am, that they may behold my glory," John xvii. 24. If the soul perish, it is not they that shall be with him, but others.

20. "To-day shalt thou be with me in paradise," Luke xxiii. 43.

21. "Father, into thy hands I commend my spirit," Luke xxiii. 46.

22. "Where I am, there shall my servant be," John xii. 26. But Christ is not perished.

23. "Stephen called on God, saying, Lord Jesus, receive my spirit," Acts vii. 79. Therefore it perished not.

24. "If children, then heirs," Rom. viii. 17. "We groan, waiting for the adoption," ver. 23. "Whom he justified, them he glorified," ver. 30. In short, all the whole gospel, that promiseth life to the sanctified, doth prove the immortality of the soul: for if the soul perish, no man that lived upon earth is saved: for if the soul be not the man, it is most certainly the prime, essential part of the man. The dust of the carcass is not the man; and if another soul, and not the same, come into it, it will be another man, and so all the promises fail.

25. So all the texts that speak of resurrection, judgment, that we shall all be judged according to our works, and what we did in the body. If it be another soul that must be judged, which never was in that body before, nor ever did any thing in that body, how shall it be judged for that which it never did? All the texts that threaten hell, or future punishment, and promise heaven, prove it. "I was hungry and ye fed me, naked and ye clothed me," &c. Matt. xxv. Ye did it, or did it not, to me: might they not say, We never did it, nor ever lived till now? "The angels shall gather out of his kingdom all things that offend, and them that work iniquity, and cast them into the lake of fire," Matt. xiii. And all the Scripture which threateneth damnation to them that obey not the truth, and promiseth salvation to the faithful; which is never performed, if all be done on another soul, 2 Thess. i. 6—10, and ii. 12.

26. And all the texts that speak of God's justice and mercy hereafter. Is it justice to damn a new-made soul that never sinned?

27. Paul knew not whether he were in or out of the body, when he was in paradise, 2 Cor. xii. 2—4. The separated soul then may be in paradise.

28. How can the hope of unseen things make affliction and death easy to that soul that shall never be saved? And how can we be comforted or saved by such hope? 2 Cor. iv. 16—18.

29. "We know that if our earthly house of this tabernacle were dissolved, we have a building of God," 2 Cor. v. 1. "For in this we groan, earnestly desiring to be clothed upon with our house which is from heaven," ver. 2. "He that hath wrought us for the self-same thing is God, who also hath given us the earnest of the Spirit," ver. 5. "Therefore we are always confident, knowing that, whilst we are at home in the body, we are absent from the Lord; we are confident, and willing rather to be absent from the body, and present with the Lord. Wherefore we labour, that, whether present or absent, we may be accepted of him. For we must all appear before the judgment-seat of Christ, that every one may receive the things done in his body, whether it be good or bad," ver. 6—10.

30. "To me to live is Christ, and to die is gain. What I shall choose I know not: for I am in a strait between two, having a desire to depart and be with Christ, which is far better," Phil. i. 21—23.

31. "Blessed are the dead that die in the Lord," &c. Rev. xiv. 13.

32. "We are come to mount Zion, the city of the living God, &c. the spirits of the just made perfect," Heb. xii. 22, 23.

Abundance more might be added. And I have been so large on this, because it is of most unspeakable importance, as that which all our comfort and our religion lieth on; and though the light of nature have taught it philosophers, and almost all the world in all ages, yet the devil is most busy to make men doubt of it, or deny it.

Religion lieth on three grand articles. 1. To believe in God; and this is so evident in the whole frame of nature, that there is a God, that he is worse than mad that will deny it. 2. To believe the immortality of the soul, and the life hereafter. And, 3. To believe in Christ. And though it be this third that is known only by supernatural revelation, yet to him that believeth the immortality of the soul, and the life hereafter, christianity will appear so exceeding congruous, that it will much the more easily be believed. And experience tells us, that the devil's main game, for the debauching and damning of fleshly, worldly, ungodly men, and for troubling and discomforting believers, lieth in raising doubts of the soul's immortality, and the future life of reward and punishment.

Q. 3. But what good will a resurrection of the body do us, if the soul be in happiness before?

A. 1. It will be for God's glory to make and bless a perfect man. 2. It will be our perfection: a whole man is more perfect than a soul alone. 3. It will be the soul's delight.[a] As God that is perfectly blessed in himself, yet made and maintaineth a world, of which he is more than the soul, because he is a communicative good, and pregnant, and delighteth to do good; so the soul is made like God in his image, and is communicative, and would have a body to act on. As the sun, if there were nothing in the world but itself, would be the same that it now is; but nothing would receive its motion, light, or heat, or be the better for it. And if you did imagine it to have understanding, you must think it would be much more pleased to enlighten and enliven so many millions of creatures, and cause the flourishing of all the earth, than to shine to nothing. So may you think of the soul of man; it is by God inclined to actuate a body.

Q. 4. If that be so, it is till then imperfect, and deprived of its desire, and so in pain and punishment.

A. It is not in its full perfection; and it is a degree of punishment to be in a state of separation. But you cannot call it a pain as to sense, because it hath an unspeakable glory, though not the most perfect. Nor hath the will of the blessed any trouble and striving against the will of God, but takes that for best which God willeth. And so the separated state is best, while God willeth it, though the united state will be best (as more perfect) in its time.

Q. 5. But the dust in a grave is so vile a thing, that one would think the raising it should not be very desirable to the soul.

A. It shall not be raised in the shape of ugly dust, or filth, nor of corruptible flesh and blood; but a glorious and spiritual body, and a meet companion for a glorified soul. And even now, as vile as the body is, you feel that the soul is loth to part with it.[b]

Q. 6. But there are so many difficulties and improbabilities about the resurrection, as make the belief of it very hard.

A. What is hard to God, that made heaven and earth of nothing, and maintains all things in their state and course? What was that body a while ago? Was it not as unlikely as dust to be what it now is?

It is folly to object difficulties to omnipotency.

Q. 7. But the body is in continual flux, or change; we have not the same flesh this year that we had the last; and a man in a consumption loseth before death the mass of flesh in which he did good or evil; shall all that rise again, which every day vanisheth? And shall the new flesh be punished for that which it never did?

A. It is a foolish thing, from our ignorance and uncertainties, to dispute against God, and certain truth: will you know nothing, unless you know all things? Will you doubt of the plain matter, because, in your darkness, you understand not the manner or circumstances of it? The soul hath a body consisting of various parts; the fiery part in the spirits is its most immediate vehicle or body; the seminal, tenacious humour, and air, is the immediate vehicle of the fiery part; whether the spirits do any of them depart, as its vehicle or body, with the soul; or, if not, whether they be the identifying part, that the soul shall be re-united to first; or what, or how much, of the rest, even the aqueous and earthy matter, which we had from our birth, shall be re-assumed, are things past our understanding. You know not how you were generated in the womb, and yet you know that you were there made; and must God teach you how you shall be raised before you will believe it? Must he answer all your doubts of the flesh that is vanished, or the bodies eaten by other bodies, and teach you all his unsearchable skill, before you will take his word for true?

He that maketh the rising sun to end the darkness of the night, and the flourishing spring to renew the face of millions of plants, which seemed in the winter to be dead, and the buried little seed to spring up to a beautiful plant and flower or a strong and goodly tree, hath power and skill enough to raise our bodies, by ways unknown to foolish man.

Q. 8. What should a man do that he may live in a comfortable hope of the resurrection, and the soul's immortality, and the life to come?

A. We have three great things to do for this end. 1. To get as full a certainty as is possible, that there is such a life to come. And this is done by strengthening a sound belief. 2. To get a suitableness of soul to that blessed life; and this is by the increase of love and holiness, and by a spiritual, heavenly conversation. And, 3. To get and exercise a joyful hope and assurance that it shall be ours; and this is done by a life of careful obedience to God, and the conscious notice of our sincerity and title, and by the increase and exercise of the foresaid faith and love; daily dwelling on the thoughts of God's infinite goodness, and fatherly love; of Christ's office and grace, and the seals of the Spirit, and the blessed state of triumphant souls, in the heavenly Jerusalem, and living as in familiarity with them.

Q. 9. But when doubting thoughts return, would it not be a great help to faith if you could prove the soul's immortality by reason?

A. I have done that largely in other books; I will now say but this: if there be no life of retribution after this, it would follow that not only Scripture, but religion, piety, and conscience, were all the most odious abuses of mankind: to set a man's heart and care upon seeking, all his days, a life which he can never obtain, and to live honestly, and avoid sin, for fear of an impossible punishment, and to deny fleshly pleasure and lust, upon mere deceit, what an injury would religion, conscience, and honesty be! Men that are not restrained by any fear or hopes of another life, from tyranny, treason, murder, perjury, lying, deceit, or any wickedness, but only by present interest, would be the wisest men. When yet God hath taught nature to abhor these evils, and bound man to be religious and conscionable by common reason, were it but for the probability of another life. And can you believe that wickedness is wisdom, and all conscionable goodness is folly and deceit?

---

[a] Rev. xxi.; xxii. [b] 1 Cor. xv.

CHAPTER XXII.

OF THE "LIFE EVERLASTING."

Q. 1. WHERE is it that we shall live when we go hence?

A. With Christ in heaven, called paradise, and the Jerusalem above.

Q. 2. How is it, then, that the souls of men are said sometimes to appear on earth? Is it such souls, or is it devils?

A. Either is possible: for souls are in no other hell than devils are, who are said to be in the air, and to go to and fro, and tempt men, and afflict them here on earth: but when it is a soul that appeareth, and when a devil, we have not acquaintance enough to know. But though God can for just causes let a blessed soul appear, as Moses and Elias did on the mount, and perhaps Samuel to Saul, yet we have reason to suspect, that it is the miserable souls of the wicked that oftenest appear.

Q. 3. But how come devils or souls to be visible, being spirits?

A. Spirits are powerful, and dwell in airy and other elementary matter, in which they can appear to us as easily as we can put on our clothes. Fire is invisible in its simple unclothed substance, and yet when it hath kindled the air, it is visible light.

Q. 4. Why then do they appear so seldom?

A. God restraineth evil spirits, and keepeth them within their bounds, that they may not either deceive or trouble mankind: and the spirits of the just are more inclined to their higher, nobler region and work: and God will have us here live by faith, and not by seeing either the heavenly glory, or its inhabitants.

Q. 5. But it seems that we shall live again on earth; for it is said that the new Jerusalem cometh down from above, and we look for a new heaven, and a new earth, wherein dwelleth righteousness?

A. It greatly concerneth us to difference certainties from uncertainties. It is certain that the faithful have a promise of a great reward in heaven, and of being with Christ, and being conveyed into paradise by angels, and are commanded to lay up a treasure in heaven, and there to set their hearts and affections, and to seek the things that are above, where Christ is at God's right hand; and they desire to depart and be with Christ, as far better than to be here; and to be absent from the body, and be present with the Lord; so that the inheritance of the saints in heavenly light and glory is certain. But as to the rest, whether the new earth shall be for new inhabitants, or for us; and whether the descending Jerusalem shall be only for a thousand years, before the final judgment, or after for perpetuity; or whether it shall come no lower than the air, where it is said that we shall be taken up to meet the Lord, and so shall ever be with him; or whether earth shall be made as glorious to us as heaven, and heaven and earth be laid together in common, when separating sin is gone: these matters being to us less certain, must not be set against that which is certain. And the new Jerusalem coming down from heaven, doth imply that it was first in heaven; and it is said that it is now above, and we are come to it in relation and foretaste, where are the perfected spirits of the just, as it is described, Heb. xii. 22—24.

Q. 6. But some think that souls sleep till the resurrection, or are in an unactive potentiality, for want of bodies?

A. Reason and Scripture confute this dream. The soul is essential life, naturally inclined to action, intellection, and love or volition, and it will be in the midst of objects enow on which to operate: and is it not absurd to think that God will continue so noble a nature in a state of idleness, and continue all its essential faculties in vain, and never to be exercised? As if he would continue the sun without light, heat, or motion. What then is it a sun for? and why is it not annihilated? The soul cannot lose its faculties of vitality, intellection, and volition, without losing its essence, and being turned into some other thing. And why it cannot act out of a body, what reason can be given? If it could not, yet that it taketh not hence with it a body of those corporal spirits which it acted in, or that it cannot as well have a body of light for its own action, as it can take a body (as Moses on the mount) to appear to man, is that which we have no reason to suspect.

2. But Scripture puts all out of doubt, by telling us, that to die is gain, and that it is better to be with Christ, and that Lazarus was comforted in Abraham's bosom, and the converted thief was with Christ in paradise, and that the souls under the altar and in heaven pray and praise God, and that the spirits of the just are there made perfect; and this is not a state of sleep. It is a world of life, and light, and love, that we are going to, more active than this earthy, heavy world, than fire is more active than a clod. And shall we suspect any sleepy unactivity there? This is the dead and sleepy world; and heaven is the place of life itself.

Q. 7. What is the nature of that heavenly, everlasting life?

A. It is the perfect activity and perfect fruition of divine communicated glory, by perfected spirits and spiritual men, in a perfect glorious society, in a perfect place, or region, and this everlasting.

Q. 8. Here are many things set together, I pray you tell them me distinctly?

A. 1. Heaven is a perfect, glorious place, and earth to it is a dungeon. The sun which we see is a glorious place in comparison of this.

2. The whole society of angels and saints will be perfect and glorious. And our joy and glory will be as much in participation by union and communion with theirs, as the life and health of the eye or hand is, in and by union and communion with the body: we must not dream of any glory to ourselves, but in a state of that union and communion with the glorious body of Christ. And Christ himself the glorified Head, is the chief part of this society, whose glory we shall behold.

3. Angels and men are themselves there perfect. If our being and nature were not perfect, our action and fruition could not be perfect.

4. The objects of all our action are most perfect: it is the blessed God, and a glorious Saviour and society, that we shall see, and love, and praise.

5. All our action will be perfect: our sight and knowledge, our love, our joy, our praise, will be all perfect there.

6. Our reception and fruition will all be perfect. We shall be perfectly loved by God, and one another, and perfectly pleasing to him, and each other; and he will communicate to us and all the society as much glorious life, light, and joyful love, as we are capable of receiving.

7. And all this will be perfect in duration, being everlasting.

Q. 9. Oh what manner of persons should we be, if all this were well believed! Is it possible that they should truly believe all this, who do not earnestly desire and seek it, and live in joyful, longing hope to be put into possession of it?

A. Whoever truly believeth it, will prefer it before all earthly treasure and pleasure, and make it the chief end, and motive, and comfort of his soul and life, and forsake all that stands against it, rather than forsake his hopes of this. But while our faith, hope, and love, are all imperfect, and we dwell in flesh, where present and sensible things are still diverting and affecting us, and we are so used to sight and sense that we look strangely towards that which is above them, and out of their reach, it is no wonder if we have imperfect desires and joy, abated by diversions, and by griefs and fears, and if in this darkness unseen things seem strange to us; and if a soul united to a body be loth to leave it, and be unclothed, and have somewhat dark thoughts of that state without it, which it never tried.

Q. 10. But when we cannot conceive how souls act out of the body, how can the thought of it be pleasant and satisfying to us?

A. 1. We that can conceive what it is to live, and understand, and will, to love and rejoice in the body, may understand what these acts are in themselves, whether out of a body, or in a more glorious body: and we can know that nothing doth nothing, and therefore that the soul that doth these acts is a noble substance, and we find that it is invisible. But of this I spake in the beginning.

2. When we know in general all before mentioned, that we shall be in that described blessedness with Christ and the heavenly society, we must implicitly trust Christ with all the rest, who knoweth for us what we know not, and stay till possession give us that clear, distinct conception of the manner, and all the circumstances, which they that possess it not can no more have than we can conceive of the sweetness of a meat or drink which we never tasted of, and we should long the more for that possession which will give us that sweet experience.

Q. 11. Is not Gód the only glory and joy of the blessed? Why then do you tell us so much of angels and saints, and the city of God?

A. God is all in all things; of him, and through him, and to him are all things, and the glory of all is to him for ever. But God made not any single creature to be happy in him alone, as separate from the rest, but a universe, which hath its union and communion. I told you, as the eye and hand have no separated life or pleasure, but only in communion with the whole body, so neither shall we in heaven. God is infinitely above us, and if you think of him alone, without mediate objects for the ascent and access of your thoughts, you may as well think to climb up without a ladder. We are not the noblest creatures next to God, nor yet the most innocent: we have no access to him but by a Mediator, and that Mediator worketh and conveyeth his grace to us by other subordinate means. He is the Saviour of his body, which is the fulness of him that filleth all. If we think not of the heavenly Jerusalem, the glorious city of God, the heavenly society and joyful choir that praise Jehovah and the Lamb, and live together in perfect knowledge, love, and concord, in whose communion only we have all our joy; to whom in this unity God communicateth his glory; and if we think not of the glorious Head of the church, who will then be our Mediator of fruition, as he was of acquisition; nay, if we think not of those loving, blessed angels, that rejoiced at our conversion, and were here the servants, and will be for ever the companions of our joy; and if we think not of all our old, dear friends and companions in the flesh, and of all the faithful who, since Adam's days, are gone before us; and if we think not of the attractive love, union, and joy of that society and state; we shall not have sufficient familiarity above, but make God as inaccessible to us. Delight and desire suppose attractive suitableness: inaccessible excellency draws not up the heart. I thank God for the pleasure that I have in thinking of the blessed society, which will shortly entertain me with joyful love.

Q. 12. But may not "everlasting" signify only a long time, as it oft doth in the Scripture, and so all may be in mutable revolutions, as the stoics and some others thought?

A. 1. What reason have we to extort a forced sense against our own interest and comfort, without any warrant from God? 2. The nature of the soul being so far immortal as to have no inclination to its own death, why should we think it strange that its felicity should be also everlasting. 3. It can hardly be conceived how that soul can possibly revolt from God and perish, who is once confirmed with that sight of his glory, and the full fruition of his love. Whether nature be so bad as to allow such a revolt. If the devils had been as near God, and as much confirmed in the sight and sense of his love and glory, as the blessed shall be, I can hardly conceive how they could possibly have fallen.

Q. 13. How may I be sure that I shall enjoy this everlasting life?

A. I told you before, 1. If you so far believe the promise of it as made by God, and purchased by Christ's righteousness and intercession, as to take this glory for your chief felicity and hope, and to prefer it before all worldly vanity, pleasure, profit, honour, or life, to the flesh, and to make it your chief care and business to seek it, and rather let go all than lose it, and thus patiently wait and trust God's grace in Christ, and his Spirit, in the use of his appointed means unto the end, it shall undoubtedly be yours for ever.

CHAPTER XXIII.

WHAT IS THE TRUE USE OF THE LORD'S PRAYER.

Q. 1. What is prayer?

A. It is holy desires expressed, or actuated, to God, (with heart alone, or also with the tongue,) including our penitent confession of sin, and its deserts, and our thankful acknowledgment of his mercies, and our praising God's works and his perfections.

Q. 2. What is the use of prayer? Seeing God cannot be changed and moved by us, what good can it do us, and how can it attain our ends?

A. You may as wisely ask, what good any thing will do towards our benefit or salvation, which we can do, seeing nothing changeth God. As God, who is one, maketh multitudes of creatures; so God, who is unchangeable, maketh changeable creatures; and the effect is wrought by changing us, and not by changing God. You must understand these great philosophical truths, that, 1. All things effect according to the capacity of the receiver. 2. Therefore, the various effects in the world proceed from the great variety of receptive capacities. The same sunbeams do cause a nettle, a thorn, a rose, a cedar, according to the seminal capacity of the various receivers. The same sun lighteneth the eye, that doth not so by the hand or foot, or by a tree, or stone: and it shineth into the house whose windows are open, which doth not so when the windows are shut;

and this without any change in itself. The boatman layeth hold on the bank, and pulls as if he would draw it to the boat, when he doth but draw the boat to it. Two ways prayer procureth the blessing without making any change in God. First, by our performing the condition on which God promiseth his mercy. Secondly, by disposing our souls to receive it. He that doth not penitently confess his sin, is unmeet for pardon; and he that desireth not Christ and mercy, is unmeet to be partaker of them: and he that is utterly unthankful for what he hath received, is unmeet for more.

Q. 3. Who made the Lord's prayer?

A. The Lord Jesus Christ himself, as he made the gospel; some of the matter being necessary yet before his incarnation.

Q. 4. To whom and on what occasion did he make it?

A. To his disciples, (to whom also he first delivered his commands,) upon their request that he would teach them to pray.

Q. 5. To what use did Christ make it them?

A. First, to be a directory for the matter and method of their love, desires, hope, and voluntary choice and endeavours; and, secondly, to be used in the same words when their case required it.

As man hath three essential faculties, the intellect, will, and vital, executive power; so religion hath three essential parts, viz. to direct our understandings to believe, our will to desire, and our lives in practice.

Q. 6. What is the matter of the Lord's prayer in general?

A. It containeth, first, what we must desire as our end: and, secondly, what we must desire as the means; premising the necessary preface, and concluding with a suitable conclusion.

Q. 7. What is the method of the Lord's prayer?

A. I. The preface speaks, 1. To God, as God. 2. As our reconciled Father in Christ, described in his attributes, by the words "which art in heaven," which signify the perfection of his power, knowledge, and goodness; and the word "Father" signifieth that he is supreme Owner, Ruler, and Benefactor.

2. The word "our" implieth our common relation to him, as his creatures, his redeemed and sanctified ones, his own, his subjects, and his beneficiaries, or children.

II. The petitions are of two sorts (as the commandments have two tables): the first proceed according to the order of intention, beginning at the highest notion of the ultimate end, and descending to the lowest. The second part is according to the order of execution and assecution, beginning at the lowest means, and ascending to the highest.

III. The conclusion enumerateth the parts of the ultimate end by way of praise, beginning at the lowest, and ascending to the highest. The method throughout is more perfect than any of the philosophers' writings.

Q. 8. Why do we not read that the apostles after used this prayer?

A. It is enough to read that Christ prescribed it them, and that they were obedient to him. We read not of all that the apostles did.

2. This is a comprehensive summary of prayer, and therefore must needs be brief in the several parts: but the apostles had occasion sometimes for one branch, and sometimes for another, on which they particularly enlarged, and seldom put up the whole matter of prayer all at once.

3. They formed their desires according to the method of this prayer, though they expressed those desires as various occasions did require.

Q. 9. Is every christian bound to say the words of the Lord's prayer?

A. The same answer may serve as to the last. Every christian is bound to make it the rule of his desires and hopes, both for matter and order; but not to express them all in every prayer. But the words themselves are apt, and must have their due reverence, and are very fit to sum up our scattered, less ordered requests.

Q. 10. But few persons can understand what such generals comprehend?

A. 1. Generals are useful to those that cannot distinctly comprehend all the particulars in them. As the general knowledge, that we shall be happy in holy and heavenly joy with Christ, may comfort them that know not all in heaven that makes up that happiness, so a general desire may be effectual to our receiving many particulars. 2. And it is not so general as "God be merciful to me a sinner," an accepted prayer of the publican, by Christ's own testimony. There are six particular heads there plainly expressed.

CHAPTER XXIV.

"OUR FATHER WHICH ART IN HEAVEN," EXPOUNDED.

Q. 1. WHO is it that we pray to, whom we call "our Father?"

A. God himself.

Q. 2. May we not pray to creatures?

A. Yes, for that which it belongeth to those creatures to give us upon our request, supposing they hear us: but not for that which is God's, and not their own to give; nor yet in a manner unsuitable to the creature's capacity or place. A child may petition his father, and a subject his prince, and all men one another.

Q. 3. May we not pray to the Son, and the Holy Ghost, as well as to the Father?

A. As the word "Father" signifieth God as God, it comprehendeth the Son, and the Holy Ghost: and as it signifieth the first person in the Trinity, it excludeth not, but implieth the second and the third.

Q. 4. What doth the word "Father" signify?

A. That as a father, by generation, is the owner, the ruler, and the loving benefactor to his child, so is God, eminently and transcendently, to us.

Q. 5. To whom is God a Father, and on what fundamental account?

A. He is a Father to all men by creation; to all lapsed mankind, by the price of a sufficient redemption; but only to the regenerate by regeneration and adoption, and that effective redemption which actually delivereth men from guilt, wrath, sin, and hell, and justifieth and sanctifieth them, and makes them heirs of glory.

Q. 6. What is included, then, in our child-like relation to this Father?

A. That we are his own, to be absolutely at his disposal, his subjects, to be absolutely ruled by him, and his beloved to depend on his bounty, and to love him above all, and be happy in his love.

Q. 7. What is meant by the words "which art in heaven?"

A. They signify, I. God's real substantiality: he is existent.

II. God's incomprehensible perfection in power, knowledge, and goodness, and so his absolute sufficiency and fitness to hear and help us. 1. The vastness, sublimity, and glory of the heavens tell us, that he who reigneth there over all the world, must needs be omnipotent, and want no power to do his will, and help us in our need.

2. The glory and sublimity tell us, that he that is there above the sun, which shineth upon the earth, doth behold all creatures, and see all the ways of the sons of men, and therefore knoweth all our sins, wants, and dangers, and heareth all our prayers.

3. Heaven is that most perfect region whence all good floweth down to earth; our life is thence, our light is thence; all our good and foretaste of felicity and joy is thence: and therefore the Lord of heaven must needs be the best; the fountain of all good, and the most amiable end of all just desire and love. Yet heaven is above our sight and comprehension; and so much more is God.

III. And the word "art" signifieth God's eternity in heavenly glory: it is not "who wast," or "who wilt be." Eternity is indivisible.

Q. 8. Is not God every where? Is he more in heaven than any where else?

A. All places and all things are in God; he is absent from none; nor is his essence divisible or commensurate by place, or limited, or more here than there; but to us God is known by his works and appearances, and therefore said to be most where he worketh most: and so we say, that God dwelleth in him who dwelleth in love; that he walketh in his church; that we are his habitation by the Spirit; that Christ and the Holy Spirit dwell in believers, because they operate extraordinarily in them; and so God is said to be in heaven, because he there manifesteth his glory to the felicity of all the blessed, and hath made heaven that throne of his Majesty, from whence all light, and life, and goodness, all mercy, and all justice, are communicated to, and exercised on, men. And so we that cannot see God himself, must look up to the throne of the heavenly glory in our prayers, hopes, and joys: even as a man's soul is undivided in all his body, and yet it worketh not alike in all its parts, but it is in the head that it useth reason, sight, &c. and doth most notably appear to others in the face, and is almost visible in the eye: and therefore when you talk to a man, you look him in the face; and as you talk not to his flesh, but to his sensitive and intellectual soul, so you look to that part where it most apparently showeth its sense and intellection.

Q. 9. Is there no other reason for the naming of heaven here?

A. Yes: it teacheth us whither to direct our own desires, and whence to expect all good, and where our own hope and felicity is. It is in heaven that God is to be seen and enjoyed in glory, and in perfect love and joy: though God be on earth, he will not be our felicity here on earth: every prayer, therefore, should be the soul's aspiring and ascending towards heaven, and the believing exercise of a heavenly mind and desire. For a man of true prayer to be unwilling to come to heaven, and to love earth better, is a contradiction.

Q. 10. But do we not pray that on earth he may use us as a Father?

A. Yes: that he will give us all mercies on earth, conducing to heavenly felicity.

Q. 11. What else is implied in the words, "our Father?"

A. Our redemption and reconciliation by Christ, and, to the regenerate, our regeneration by the Holy Ghost, and so our adoption; by all which, of enemies and the heirs of hell, we are made the sons of God, and heirs of heaven. It is by Christ and his Spirit that we are the children of God.

Q. 12. Why say we "our Father," and not "my Father?"

A. 1. To signify that all christians must pray as members of one body, and look for all their good, comfort, and blessedness, in union with the whole, and not as in a separate state. Nor must we come to God with selfish, narrow minds, as thinking only of our own case and good, nor put up any prayer or praise to God but as members of the universal church in one choir, all seen and heard at once by God, though they see not and hear not one another; and therefore that we must abhor the pregnant, comprehensive sin of selfishness; by which wicked men care only for themselves, and are affected with little but their personal concerns, as if they were all the world to themselves, insensible of the world's or the church's state, and how it goeth with all others. 2. And therefore that all christians must love their brethren and neighbours as themselves, and must abhor the sin of schism, much more of malignant enmity, envy, and persecution, and must be so far from disowning the prayers of other christians, on pretence of their various circumstances and imperfections, and from separating in heart from them on any account for which God will not reject them, as that they must never put up a prayer or praise, but as in concord with all the christians on earth, desiring a part in the prayers of all, and offering up hearty prayers for all: the imperfections of all men's prayers we must disown, and most of our own; but not for that disown their prayers, nor our own. They that hate, or persecute, or separate from God's children, for not praying in their mode, or by their book, or in the words that they write down for them, or for not worshipping God with their forms, ceremonies, or rites, or that silence Christ's ministers, and scatter the flocks, and confound kingdoms, that they may be lords of God's heritage, and have all men sing in their commanded tune, or worship God in their unnecessary, commanded mode, do condemn themselves when they say "our Father." And to repeat the Lord's prayer many times in their liturgy, while they are tormenting his children in their prisons and inquisitions, is to worship God by repeating their own condemnation.

Q. 13. It seems this particle "our," and "us," is of great importance.

A. The Lord's prayer is the summary and rule of man's love and just desires; it directeth him what to will, ask, and seek. And therefore must needs contain that duty of love which is the heart of the new creature, and the fulfilling of the law: the will is the man; the love is the will. What man wills and loves, that he is in God's account, or that he shall attain. And therefore the love of God, as God, and of the church, as the church, and of saints, as saints, of friends, as friends, and of neighbours, as neighbours, and of men, (though enemies and sinners,) as men, must needs be the very spring of acceptable prayer, as well as the love of ourselves, as ourselves. And to pray without this love, is to offer God a carrion for sacrifice, or a lifeless sort of service. And love to all makes all men's mercies and comforts to be ours, to our great joy, and that we may be thankful for all.

CHAPTER XXV.

"HALLOWED BE THY NAME."

Q. 1. WHY is this made the first petition in our prayers?

A. Because it containeth the highest notion of our ultimate end; and so must be the very top or chief of our desires.

Q. 2. What is meant by God's name here?

A. The proper notices or appearances of God to man; and God himself as so notified and appearing to us. So that here we must see that we separate not any of these three: 1. The objective signs, whether words or works, by which God is known to us.

2. The inward conceptions of God received by these signs.

3. God himself so notified and conceived of.

Q. 3. And what is the hallowing of God's name?

A. To use it holily; that is, in that manner as is proper to God as he is God, infinitely above all the creatures: that is sanctified which is appropriated to God by separation from all common use.

Q. 4. What doth this hallowing particularly include?

A. First that we know God, what he is. 2. That our souls be accordingly affected towards him. 3. That our lives and actions be accordingly managed. 4. And that the signs which notify God to us be accordingly reverenced, and used to these holy ends.

Q. 5. Tell us now, particularly, what these signs or names of God are, and how each of them is to be hallowed?

A. God's name is either, 1. His sensible or intelligible works objectively considered. 2. Or those words which signify God, or any thing proper to God. 3. And the inward light or conception, or notice of God, in the mind. And all these must be sanctified.

Q. 6. What are God's works which must be so sanctified, as notifying God?

A. All that are within the reach of our knowledge. But especially those which he hath designed most notably for this use, and most legibly, as it were, written his name or perfections upon.[a]

Q. 7. Which are those?

A. First, the glorious, wonderful frame of heaven and earth.

2. The wonderful work of man's redemption by Jesus Christ.

3. The planting of his nature, image, and kingdom in man, by his Spirit.

4. The marvellous providence exercised for the world, the church, and each of ourselves, notifying the disposal and government of God.

5. The glory of the heavenly society, known by faith, and hoped for.

Q. 8. How must the first, God's creation, be sanctified.

A. When we look on, or think of, the incomprehensible glory of the sun, its wonderful greatness, motion, light, and quickening heat;[b] of the multitude and magnitude of the glorious stars, of the vast heavenly regions, the incomprehensible, invisible spirits or powers that actuate and rule them all; when we come downward and think of the air and its inhabitants, and of this earth, a vast body to us, but as one inch or point in the whole creation; of the many nations, animals, plants of wonderful variety, the terrible depths of the ocean, and its numerous inhabitants, &c.—all these must be to us but as the glass which showeth somewhat of the face of God, or as the letters of this great book, of which God is the sense; or as the actions of a living body by which the invisible soul is known. And as we study arts for our corporeal use, we must study the whole world, even the works of God, to this purposed use, that we may see, love, reverence, and admire God in all: and this is the only true philosophy, astronomy, cosmography, &c.

Q. 9. What is the sin which is contrary to this?

A. Profaneness; that is, using God's name as a common thing:[c] and, in this instance, to study philosophy, astronomy, or any science, or any creature whatsoever, only to know the thing itself, to delight our mind with the creature knowledge, and to be able to talk as knowing men, or the better to serve our worldly ends, and not to know and glorify God, is to profane the works of God. And, alas, then, how common is profaneness in the world!

Q. 10. What is it to sanctify God's name as in our redemption?

A. Redemption is such a wonderful work of God, to make him known to sinners for their sanctification and salvation, as no tongue of man can fully utter. To think of God, the Eternal Word, first undertaking man's redemption, and then taking the nature of man, dwelling in so mean a tabernacle, fulfilling all righteousness for us, teaching man the knowledge of God, and bringing life and immortality to light, dying for us as a malefactor, to save us from the curse, rising the third day, commissioning his apostles, undertaking to build his church on a rock, which the gates of hell should not prevail against; ascending up to heaven, sending down the wonderful and sanctifying Spirit, interceding for us, and reigning over all; who receiveth faithful souls to himself, and will raise our bodies, and judge the world. Can all this be believed and thought of, without admiring the manifold wisdom, the unconceivable love and mercy, the holiness and justice of God? This must be the daily study of believers.

Q. 11. How is this name of God profaned?

A. When this wonderful work of man's redemption is not believed, but taken by infidels to be but a deceit: or, when it is heard but as a common history, and affecteth not the hearer with admiration, thankfulness, desire, and submission to Christ; when men live as if they had no great obligation to Christ, or no great need of him.

Q. 12. How is God's name, as our Sanctifier, to be hallowed?

A. Therein he cometh near us, even into us, with illuminating, quickening, comforting grace, renewing us to his nature, will, and image, marking us for his own, and maintaining the cause of Christ against his enemies; and therefore must, in this, be specially notified, honoured, obediently observed, and thankfully and joyfully admired.

Q. 13. But how can they honour God's Spirit and grace, who have it not; or they that have so little as not well to discern it?

A. The least prevailing sincere holiness hath a special excellency, turning the soul from the world to God, and may be perceived in holy desires after him, and sincere endeavours to obey him; and the beauty of holiness in others may be perceived by them that have little or none themselves, if they be not grown to malignant enmity. You may see, by the common desire of mankind to be esteemed wise and good, and their impatience of being thought and called foolish, ungodly, or bad men, that even corrupted nature hath a radicated testimony in itself for goodness and against evil.

Q. 14. Who be they that profane this name of God?

A. Those that see no great need of the Spirit of holiness, or have no desire after it, but think that nature and art may serve the turn with it. Those that think that there is no great difference between

[a] Exod. ix. 16; Psal. viii. 1.
[b] Psal. xix. 1, &c.; Rom. i. 19, 20.
[c] Psal. xiv. 1, 2; l. 21; lxxviii. 19; Tit. i. 16.

man and man, but what their bodily temperature and their education maketh, and that it is but fanatic delusion, or hypocrisy, to pretend to the Spirit. Those that hate or deride the name of spirituality and holiness, and those that resist the Holy Ghost.

Q. 15. How is God known and honoured in his providence?

A. By his providence he so governeth all the world, and particularly all the affairs of men, as shows his omnipotence, his omniscience, and his goodness and love, ordering them all to his holy end, even the pleasing of his good-will in their perfection.[d]

Q. 16. How can we see this while the world lieth in madness, unbelief, and wickedness, and the worst are greatest, and contention, and confusion, and bloody wars, do make the earth a kind of hell, and the wise, holy, and just, are despised, hated, and destroyed?

A. 1. Wisdom, and holiness, and justice, are conspicuous and honourable by the odiousness of their contraries, which, though they fight against them, and seem to prevail, do but exercise them to their increase and greater glory: and all the faithful are secured and purified, and prepared for felicity, by the love and providence of God.

2. And as the heavens are not all stars, but spangled with stars, nor the stars all suns, nor beasts and vermin men, nor the earth and stones are gold and diamonds, nor is the darkness light, the winter summer, or sickness health, or death life; and yet the wonderful variety and vicissitude contributeth to the perfection of the universe, as the variety of parts to the perfection of the body; so God maketh use even of men's sin and folly, and of all the mad confusions and cruelties of the world, to that perfect order and harmony, which he that accomplisheth them doth well know, though we perceive it not, because we neither see the whole, nor the end, but only the little particles and the beginnings of God's unsearchable works.

3. And this dark and wicked world is but a little spot of God's creation, and seemeth to be the lowest next to hell, while the lucid, glorious, heavenly regions are incomprehensibly great, and no doubt possessed by inhabitants suitable to so glorious a place: and as it is not either the gallows or the prison that is a dishonour to the kingly government, so neither is hell, or the sins on earth, a dishonour to the government of God.

4. And as every man is nearest to himself, it is the duty of us all carefully to record all the mercies and special providences of God to ourselves, that we may know his government and him, and use the remembrance of them to his glory.

Q. 17. How is the heavenly glory as a name of God to us that see it not?

A. We see vast lucid bodies and regions above us; and, by the help of things seen, we may conceive of things unseen, and by divine revelation we may certainly know them. We have in the gospel, as it were, a map of heaven, in its description, and a title to it in the promises, and a notifying earnest and foretaste in our souls, so far as we are sanctified believers.

Q. 18. How must we hallow this name of God?

A. 1. Firmly believing the heavenly glory, not only as it shall be our own inheritance, but as it is now the most glorious and perfect part of God's creation, where myriads of angels and glorious spirits, in perfect happiness, love, and joy, are glorifying their most glorious Creator; and as the saints with Christ, their most glorious Head, shall for ever make up that glorious society, and the universe itself be seen by us in that glorious perfection, in which the perfection of the Creator will appear.

2. And in the constant delightful contemplation of this supernal glorious world, by heavenly affections and conversation, keeping our minds above while our bodies are here below, and looking beyond this prison of flesh, with desire and hope. As heaven is the state and place where God shineth to the understanding creature in the greatest glory, and where he is best known, so it is this heavenly glory, seen to us by faith, which is the most glorious of all the names or notices of God to be hallowed by us.

Q. 19. What is the profaning of this name of God?

A. The minding only of earthly and fleshly things, and not believing, considering, or admiring the heavenly glory; not loving and praising God for it, nor desiring and seeking to enjoy it.

Q. 20. So much of God's works which make him known. Next, tell us what you mean by the words which you call his name?

A. 1. All the sacred Scripture, as it maketh known God to us, by history, precepts, promises, or penal threats; with all God's instituted means of worship. 2. More especially the descriptions of God by his attributes. 3. And, most especially, his proper name, God, Jehovah, &c.[e]

Q. 21. I will not ask you what his attributes are, because you have told us that before; but how is this name of God to be hallowed?

A. When the soul is affected with that admiration, reverence, love, trust, and submission to God, which the meaning of these names bespeaks; and when the manner of our using them expresseth such affections, especially in public praises with the churches.[f]

Q. 22. How is this name of God profaned?

A. When it is used lightly, falsely, irreverently, without the aforesaid holy regard and affections.

Q. 23. III. What is that which you call God's name imprinted on man's mind?

A. God made man very good at first, and that was in his own image; and so much of this is either left by the interposition of grace in lapsed nature, or by common grace restored to it, as that all men, till utterly debauched, would fain be accounted good, pious, virtuous, and just, and hate the imputation of wickedness, dishonesty, and badness; and on the regenerate the divine nature is so renewed, as that their inclination is towards God, and "holiness to the Lord" is written on all their faculties; and the Spirit of God moveth on the soul, to actuate all his graces, and to plead for God and our Redeemer, and bring him to our remembrance, to our affections, and to subject us wholly to his will and love. And thus, as the law was written in stone, as to the letter, which is written only on tender, fleshy hearts, as to the spirit and holy effect and disposition; so the name of God, which is in the Bible in the letter, is, by the same Spirit, imprinted on believers' hearts, that is, they have the knowledge, faith, fear, and love of God.[g]

Q. 24. How must we hallow this inward name of God?

A. 1. By reverencing and loving God, that is, God's image and operations in us; not only God as glorified in heaven, but God as dwelling by grace in holy souls, must be remembered and reverenced by us. 2. By living as in habitual communion and

[d] Mal. ii. 2.

[e] Exod. iii. 15; vi. 3; Psalm lxxxiii. 18; Acts ix. 15.

[f] Exod. xxxiv. 5—7; xxxiii. 19; Acts xxi. 13; 1 Tim. vi. 1; Tit. ii. 5; Rom. ii. 24; Psalm xxii. 22; Heb. ii. 12; Neh. ix. 5; Psalm l. 23; lxvi. 2; Micah iv. 5; Rev. xi. 15.

[g] Psalm xxix. 2; xlviii. 10.

conversation with that God who dwelleth in us, and who hath made us his habitation by the Spirit. 3. And by ready obeying the moving operations of the Spirit for God.

And to contemn or resist these inward ideas, inclinations, and motions, is to profane the name of God.

Q. 25. But what is all this to the sanctifying of God himself?

A. The signs are but for him that is signified. It is God himself that is to be admired, loved, and honoured, as notified to us by these signs or name, otherwise we make idols of them. In a word, God must be esteemed, reverenced, loved, trusted, and delighted in, transcendently as God, with affections proper to himself; and this is to sanctify him, by advancing him in our heart, in his prerogative above all creatures; and all creatures must be used respectively to this holy end, and especially those ordinances and names which are especially separated to this use: and nothing must be used as common and unclean, especially in his worship and religious acts.[h]

CHAPTER XXVI.

"THY KINGDOM COME."

Q. 1. WHY is this made the second petition?

A. To tell us, that it must be the second thing in our desires. We are to begin at that which is highest, most excellent, and ultimate in our intentions, and that is, God's glory shining in all his works, and seen, admired, honoured, and praised by man, which is the hallowing of his name, and the holy exalting him in our thoughts, affections, words, and actions, above all creatures. And we are next to desire that in which God's glory most eminently shineth, and that is his kingdom of grace and glory.

Q. 2. What is here meant by the kingdom of God?

A. It is not that kingdom which he hath over angels, and the innumerable glorious spirits of the heavenly regions, for these are much unknown to us, and we know not that there is any rebellion among them which needeth a restoration. But man, by sin, is fallen into rebellion, and under the condemnation due to rebels:[a] and by Christ, the reconciling Mediator, they are to be restored to their subjection to God, and so to his protection, blessing, and reward. And because they are sinners, corrupt and guilty, they cannot be subjects as under the primitive law of innocency: and therefore God hath delivered them to the Mediator, as his Vicegerent, to be governed under a law of healing grace, and so brought on to perfect glory. So that the kingdom of God now is his reign over fallen man by Christ the Mediator, begun on earth by recovering grace, and perfected in heavenly glory.[b]

Q. 3. But the Scriptures sometimes speak of the kingdom of God as come already when Christ came, or when he rose and ascended to his glory, and sometimes as if it were yet to come at the great resurrection day.

A. In the first case, the meaning is, that the King of the church is come, and hath established his law of grace, and commissioned his officers, and sent forth his Spirit, and so the kingdom of healing grace is come; but in the second case, the meaning is, that all that glorious perfection which this grace doth tend to, which will be the glory of the church, the glory of Christ therein, and the glorification of God's love, is yet to come.

Q. 4. What is it, then, which we here desire?

A. That God will enlarge and carry on the kingdom of grace in the world, and bear down all that rebels, and hindereth it, and particularly in ourselves, and that he would hasten the kingdom of glory.

Q. 5. Who is it, then, that is the King of this kingdom?

A. God, as the absolute supreme, and Jesus Christ, the Son of God and man, as the supreme Vicegerent and Administrator.[c]

Q. 6. Who are the subjects of this kingdom?

A. There are three sorts of subjects. 1. Subjects only as to obligation,[d] and so those without the church are rebellious, obliged subjects. 2. Subjects by mere profession, and so all baptized, professing christians, though hypocrites, are the church visible, and his professed subjects. 3. Subjects by sincere heart consent, and so all such are his subjects as make up the church mystical, and shall be saved. So that the kingdom of God is a word which is sometimes of a larger signification than the church, and sometimes, in a narrower sense, is the same. Christ is Head over all things to the church, Eph. i. 23.

Q. 7. What are the acts of Christ's kingly government?

A. Law-making, judging according to that law, and executing that judgment.[e]

Q. 8. What laws hath Christ made, and what doth he rule by?

A. First, He taketh the law of nature now as his own, as far as it belongeth to sinful mankind. And, 2. He expoundeth the darker passages of that law. And, 3. He maketh new laws, proper to the church since his incarnation.

Q. 9. Are there any new laws of nature since the fall?

A. There are new obligations and duties arising from our changed state: it was no duty to the innocent to repent of sin, and seek out for recovery, and beg forgiveness, but nature bindeth sinners not yet under the final sentence to all this.

Q. 10. What new laws hath Christ made?

A. Some proper to church officers, and some common to all.

Q. 11. What are his laws about church officers?

A. First, He chose himself the first chief officers, and he gave them their commission,[f] describing their work and office; and he authorized them to gather and form particular churches, and their fixed officers or pastors, and necessary orders, and gave them the extraordinary conduct and seal of his Spirit, that their determinations might be the infallible significations of his will, and his recorded law to his universal church to the end of the world, his Spirit being the Perfecter of his laws and government.

Q. 12. How shall we be sure that his apostles, by the Spirit, were authorized to give laws to all future generations?

[h] Acts i. 15; iv. 12; Rev. iii. 4; xi. 13; Joel ii. 23; Deut. xxviii. 58; Exod. xxxiii. 19; xxxiv. 5—7; 1 Kings v. 3, 5; Lev. x. 3; Numb. xx. 12, 13.

[a] Col. i. 13; Matt. xii. 28; xxi. 31, 43; Mark i. 45; iv. 26, 30; xii. 34; x. 14, 15, 23; xv. 43.

[b] Luke vii. 28; viii. 1, 10; x. 9; xi. 20; xiii. 18, 20, 28, 29; xvi. 16; xvii. 21; xviii. 3, 17, 29.

[c] Rev. i. 9; Luke ix. 27; xiv. 15; xxii. 16, 18; xxiii. 51.

[d] Acts xiv. 22; Gal. v. 21; Eph. v. 5; 2 Thess. v.; Rev. xii. 10; Matt. xvi. 28; 2 Tim. iv. 1; 1 Thess. ii. 12.

[e] Heb. vii. 12; Isa. ii. 3; viii. 16, 20; xlii. 4, 21; li. 4; Mic. iv. 2; Rom. iii. 27; viii. 2, 4; Gal. vi. 2; Isa. li. 7; Jer. xxxi. 33; Heb. viii. 10, 16.

[f] Matt. xxviii. 19; Eph. iv. 6—9, 16; Acts xiv. 23; xv.

A. Because he gave them such commission, to teach men all that he commanded.[g] 2. And promised them his Spirit to lead them into all truth, and bring all things to their remembrance, and to tell them what to say and do. And, 3. Because he performed this promise, in sending them that extraordinary measure of the Spirit. And, 4. They spake as from Christ, and in his name, and as by his Spirit. And, 5. They sealed all by the manifestation of that Spirit, in its holy and miraculous, manifold operation.[h]

Q. 13. Have not bishops and councils the same power now?

A. No: to be the instruments of divine legislation, and make laws which God will call his laws, is a special, prophetical power and office, such as Moses had in making the Jewish laws, which none had that came after him. But when prophetical revelation hath made the law, the following officers have nothing to do, but, 1. To preserve that law. 2. And to expound it and apply it, and guide the people by it, and themselves obey it. 3. And to determine undetermined, mutable circumstances. As the Jewish priests and Levites were not to make another law, but to preserve, expound, and rule by Moses' law, so the ordinary ministers, bishops, or councils are to do as the laws of God, sufficiently made by Christ, and the Spirit in his apostles.[i]

Q. 14. What are the new laws which he hath made for all?

A. The covenant of grace in the last edition is his law,[k] by which he obligeth men to repent and believe in him as incarnate, crucified, and ascended, and interceding and reigning in heaven, and as one that will judge the world at the resurrection; as one that pardoneth sin by his sacrifice and merit, and sanctifieth believers by his Spirit: and to believe in God as thus reconciled by him, and in the Holy Ghost as thus given by him. And he promiseth pardon, grace, and glory, to all true believers, and threateneth damnation to impenitent unbelievers. And he commandeth all believers to devote themselves thus to God the Father, the Son, and the Holy Ghost, by a solemn vow in baptism, and live in the communion of saints, in his church and holy worship, and the frequent celebration of the memorial of his death in the sacrament of his body and blood, especially on the first day of the week, which he hath separated to that holy commemoration and communion by his resurrection, and the sending of his Spirit, and by his apostles. And he hath commanded all his disciples to live in unity, love, and beneficence, taking up the cross, and following him in holiness and patience, in hope of everlasting life.[l]

Q. 15. But some say that Christ was only a teacher, and not a lawgiver.

A. His name is King of kings, and Lord of lords, and all power in heaven and earth is given him, and all things put into his hands; the government is laid on his shoulders, and the Father (without him) judgeth no man, but hath committed all judgment to the Son. For this end he died, rose, and revived, that he might be Lord of the dead and of the living; he is at God's right hand, above all principalities and powers, and every name, being head over all things to the church.[m]

Q. 16. May not this signify only his kingdom as he is God, or that which he shall have hereafter only at the resurrection?

A. 1. It expressly speaketh of his power as God, and man the Redeemer. 2. And he made his law in this life, though the chief and glorious part of his judgment and execution be hereafter. How else should men here keep his law, and hereafter be judged according to it?

He that denieth Christ to be the Lawgiver, denieth him to be King; and he that denieth him to be King, denieth him to be Christ, and is no christian.

Q. 17. Hath Christ any vicegerent, or universal governor, under him on earth?

A. No: it is his prerogative to be the universal Governor; for no mortal man is capable of it: as no one monarch is capable of the civil government of all the earth, nor was ever so mad as to pretend to it; much less is any one capable of being a universal church teacher, priest, and governor over all the earth; when he cannot so much as know it, or send to all, or have access into the contending kingdoms of all the world: to pretend to this is mad usurpation.[n]

Q. 18. But had not Peter monarchical government of all the church on earth in his time?

A. No: he was governor of none of the eleven apostles, nor of Paul; nor ever exercised any such government: no, nor it seems, so much as presided at their meeting, Acts xv.

Q. 19. But is not a general council the universal governor?

A. No: 1. Else the church would be no church, when there is no general council, for want of its unifying government. And, 2. There indeed never was a general council of all the christian world: but they were called by the Roman emperors, and were called general as to that empire (as the subscriptions yet show). 3. And there never can be a universal council: it were madness and wickedness to attempt it: to send for the aged bishops from all nations of the christian world, (when none is empowered to determine whither or when,) even from the countries of Turks, and other infidels, or princes in war with one another, that will not permit them: and what room shall hold them, and what one language can they all speak? And how few will live to return home with the decrees! And will not the country where they meet, by nearness, have more voices than all the rest? And what is all this to do? To condemn Christ, as not having made laws sufficient for the universal part of government, but leave such a burden on uncapable men: and to tell the church that christian religion is a mutable, growing thing, and can never be known to attain its ripeness, but, by new laws, must be made still bigger, and another thing.

Q. 20. But the bishops of the world may meet by their delegates?

A. Those delegates must come from the same countries and distance: and how shall the whole world know that they are truly chosen? and that all the choosers have trusted them with their judg-

[g] Acts x. 42; xiii. 47; Matt. xxviii. 19, 21; John xiv. 16, 17, 26; xv. 26, 27; xvi. 7, 13—15; Rev. ii. 7, 11, 16, 17, 29; iii. 6, 13, 22; 1 Pet. i. 11.

[h] Acts ii. 4; Gal. i.; ii.; Mark xiii. 11; Luke xii. 12; Isa. xxxiii. 22.

[i] Jam. iv. 12; Acts i. 5, 8; ii. 4, 33; xv. 28; 1 Cor. ii. 13; 2 Pet. i. 21; 1 Cor. vii. 25; Acts i. 2; 1 Cor. xiv. 37; Col. ii. 22; Matt. xv. 9.

[k] John i. 9—11; iii. 16; Matt. xxviii. 19, 20; 1 Cor. xv. 3—5; xi. 28; Acts xiii. 47; x. 42; John xiv. 21.

[l] John xiii. 34; Rev. i.; Matt. xxviii. 18; John xiii. 2; xvii. 3; v. 22; Isa. ix. 6; Rom. xiv. 9; Col. i.; Heb. i.; vii.

[m] Eph. i. 22; Luke xvii. 9, 10; xix. 15, &c; Rev. xxii. 14; 1 John ii.; iii. 24; v. 3.

[n] 1 Cor. xii. 5, 18, 20, 27—29; iii. 4—6, 11, 22, 23; Matt. xxiii. 7, 8, 10, 11; Eph. iv. 5, 7, 8, 11—16; v. 23, 24; Matt. xviii. 1, 4; Mark ix. 34; Luke ix. 46; xxii. 24—26; 1 Pet. v. 2—4.

ments, consciences, and salvation, and will stand to what they do?

Q. 21. But if the universal church be divided into patriarchates, and chief seats, those can govern the whole church when there is no general council; even by their communicatory letters.

A. 1. And who shall divide the world into those chief seats, and determine which shall be chief in all the kingdoms of infidels, and christian kings, in the world? and which shall be chief when they differ among themselves? How many patriarchs shall there be, and where? There were never twelve pretenders to succeed the twelve apostles: the Roman empire had three first, and five after, within itself: but that was by human institution, and over one empire, and that is now down; and those five seats have many hundred years been separated, and condemning one another: so far are they from being one unifying aristocracy to govern all the world: and if they were so, then Europe is schismatical, that now differs from the major vote of those patriarchs.

Q. 22. But did not the apostles, as one college, govern the whole church?

A. 1. I proved to you before, that the Holy Ghost was given the apostles to perfect universal legislation, as Christ's agent and advocate, and that in this they have no successors. 2. And it was easy for them to exercise acts of judicial determination over such as were among them, and near them, when the church was small. 3. And yet we read not that ever they did this in a general council, or by the authority of a major vote. For that meeting in Acts xv. was no general council, and the elders and brethren joined with them that belonged to Jerusalem: and they were all by the same Spirit of the same mind, and none dissenters. Every single apostle had the Spirit of infallibility for his proper work: and they had an indefinite charge of the whole church, and in their several circuits exercised it. Paul could by the Spirit deliver a law of Christ to the world, without taking it from the other apostles, Gal. ii. The apostles were foundation-stones, but Christ only was the head corner-stone. They never set up a judicial government of all the churches under themselves as a constitutive, unifying aristocracy, by whose major vote all must be governed. When they had finished the work of universal legislation, and settled doctrine and order, for which they staid together at Jerusalem, they dispersed themselves over the world; and we never find that they judicially governed the churches, either in synods or by letters, by a major vote, but settled guides in every church as God by Moses did priests and Levites, that had no legislative power.[o]

Q. 23. But hath not Christ his subordinate, official governors?

A. Yes: magistrates by the sword, and pastors by the word and keys. These are rulers in their several circuits, as all the judges, and justices, and schoolmasters of England are under the king: but he that should say that all these judges and justices are one sovereign aristocracy, to make laws and judge by them by vote, (as one person political, though many natural,) would give them part of the supreme power, and not only the official: all the pastors in the world guide all the churches in the world by parts, and in their several provinces, and not as one politic person.

Q. 24. But how is the universal church visible, if it have no visible, unifying head and government under Christ?

A. It is visible, 1. In that the members and their profession are visible. 2. And Christ's laws are visible, by which he ruleth them. 3. And their particular pastors are visible in their places. 4. And Christ was visible on earth, and is now visible in his court in heaven, and will visibly judge the world ere long: and God hath made the church no further visible, nor can man do it.

Q. 25. But should not the whole church be one?

A. It is one: it is one body of Christ, having one God, and one Head, or Lord, one faith, one baptism, one Spirit, one hope of glory.[p]

Q. 26. But should they not do all that they do in unity and concord?

A. Yes, as far as they are capable. Not by framing a new, universal, legislative power in man, or making a universal head under Christ, but by agreeing all in the faith and laws that Christ hath left us: and synods may well be used to maintain such union as far as capacity reacheth, and the case requireth. But a universal synod, and a partial or national, a governing synod, and a synod for concord of governors, differ as much as doth a monarch, or governing senate, over all the world, and a diet, or an assembly of christian princes, met for mutual help and concord, in the conjunction of their strength and councils.

Q. 27. What is the pastoral power of the church keys?

A. It is the power of making christians by the[q] preaching of the gospel, and receiving them so made into communion of Christ and his church, by baptism, and feeding and guiding them by the same word, and communicating the sacrament of Christ's body and blood in his name, declaring pardon and life to the penitent, and the contrary to the impenitent, and applying this to the particular persons of their own charge on just occasion, and so being the stated judges who shall by them be received to church communion, or be rejected, and this as a presage of Christ's future judgment.

Q. 28. But have not pastors or bishops a power of constraint by the sword, that is, by corporeal punishments, or mulcts?

A. No: that is proper to magistrates, parents, and masters, in their several places. Christ hath forbidden it to pastors, (Luke xxii.) and appointed them another kind of work.[r]

Q. 29. But if bishops judge that civil magistrates are bound to destroy or punish heretics, schismatics, or sinners, are not such magistrates thereby bound to do it?

A. They are bound to do their duty, whoever is their monitor: but if prelates bid them sin, they sin by obeying them. Nor may a magistrate punish a man merely because bishops judge him punishable, without trying the cause themselves.

Q. 30. But if it be not of divine institution that all the church on earth should have one governing, unifying head, (monarchical or aristocratical,) is it not meet as suited to human prudence?

A. Christ is the builder of his own church or house, and hath not left it to the wit or will of man[s] to make him a vicegerent, or a unifying head or ruler of his whole church, that is, to set up a usurper against him under his own name, which is naturally uncapable of the office.

Q. 31. But sure unity is so excellent that we

[o] Eph. ii. 20; 1 Cor. iii. 11; i. 11, 12; iii. 21, 22; Gal. ii. 9; 2 Cor. xi. 5; xii. 11.

[p] Eph. iv. 1, 3, 6, 7, 14—16; 1 Cor. xii.

[q] Matt. xxviii. 19, 20; 1 Thess. v. 12, 13; Heb. xiii. 17, 24; Tit. iii. 10, 11; i. 13; 1 Pet. v. 1—5; 1 Tim. iii. 5; Isa. xxii. 22; Luke xi. 52; Rev. iii. 7; i. 18; Matt. xvi. 19.

[r] Luke xxii. 24—26; 1 Pet. v. 3, 4; 2 Tim. ii. 24; Tit. i. 7

[s] Heb. iii. 2, 5, 6.

may conceive that God delighteth in all that promoteth it?

A. Yes: and therefore he would not leave the terms of unity to the device of men, in which they will never be of a mind; nor would he have usurpers divide his church, by imposing impossible terms of unity. Must God needs make one civil monarch, or senate, to be the unifying governor of all the earth, as one kingdom, because he is a lover of unity? The world is politically unified by one God and Sovereign Redeemer, as this kingdom is by one king, and not by one civil, human, supreme ruler, personal or collective: men so mad as to dream of one unifying, church-governing monarch, or aristocracy, are the unfittest of all men to pretend to such government.[t]

Q. 32. At least, should we not extend this unifying government as far as we can, even to Europe, if not to all the world?

A. Try first one unifying, civil government (monarchical or aristocratical) for Europe, and call princes schismatics (as these men do us) for refusing to obey it, and try the success. 2. And who shall make this European church sovereign? and by what authority; and limit his kingdom? 3. And what is all this to do? To make better laws than Christ's? When were any so mad as to say, that all Europe must have one sovereign person, or college of physicians, schoolmasters, philosophers, or lawyers, to avoid schism among them? 4. Is not agreement by voluntary consent a better way to keep civil and ecclesiastical unity in Europe, than to have one ruling king, senate, or synod, over all? Councils are for voluntary concord, and not the sovereign rectors of their brethren.

Q. 33. But are not national churches necessary?

A. No doubt but Christ would have nations discipled, baptized, and obey him; and kings to govern them as christian nations; and all men should endeavour that whole nations may be christians, and the kingdoms of the world be voluntarily the kingdoms of Christ. But no man can be a christian against his will; nor hath Christ ordained that each kingdom shall have one sacerdotal head, monarchical or aristocratical. But princes, pastors, and people, must promote love, unity, and concord in their several places.

Q. 34. So much for God's public kingdom on earth: but is there not also a kingdom of God in every christian's soul?

A. One man's soul is not fitly called a kingdom; but Christ, as King, doth govern every faithful soul.

Q. 35. What is the government of each believer?

A. It is Christ's ruling us by the laws which he hath made for all his church, proclaimed, and explained, and applied by his ministers, and imprinted on the heart by his Holy Spirit, and judging accordingly.

Q. 36. What is the kingdom of glory?

A. It hath two degrees: the first is the glorious reign of our glorified Redeemer over this world, and over the heavenly city of God before its perfection; which began at the time of Christ's ascension, (his resurrection being the proem,) and endeth at the resurrection. 2. The perfect kingdom of glory, when all the elect shall be perfected with Christ, and his work of redemption finished, which begins at the resurrection, and shall never end.

Q. 37. What will be the state of that glorious kingdom?

A. It containeth the full collection of all God's elect, who shall be perfected in soul and body, and employed in the perfect obedience, love, and praise of God, in perfect love and communion with each other, and all the blessed angels, and their glorified Redeemer; and this is in the sight of his glory, and the glory of God, and in the continual, joyful sense of his love and essential, infinite perfection. All imperfection, sin, temptation, and suffering, being for ever ceased.

Q. 38. But some think this kingdom will be begun on earth a thousand years before the general resurrection; and some think that after the resurrection it will be on earth.[u]

A. This very prayer puts us in hope that there are yet better things on earth to be expected than the church hath yet enjoyed. For when Christ bids us pray that "his name may be hallowed, his kingdom come, and his will done on earth, as it is done in heaven," we may well hope that some such thing will be granted; for he hath promised to give us whatever we ask, according to his will, in the name of Christ: and he hath not bid us pray in vain.

But whether there shall be a resurrection of the martyrs a thousand years before the general resurrection, or whether there shall be only a reformation by a holy magistracy and ministry, and how far Christ will manifest himself on earth, I confess are questions too hard for me to determine: he that is truly devoted to Christ, shall have his part in his kingdom, though much be now unknown to him, of the time, place, and manner.[x]

And as to the glory after the general resurrection, certainly it will be heavenly, for we shall be with Christ, and like to the angels. And the new Jerusalem, being the universality of the blessed now with Christ, may well be said to come down from heaven, in that he will bring all the blessed with him, and, in the air with them, will judge the world: but whether only a new generation shall inhabit the new earth, and the glorified rule them as angels now do; or whether heaven and earth shall be laid common together, or earth made as glorious as heaven, I know not.

But the perfect knowledge of God's kingdom is proper to them that enjoy it: therefore even we who know it but imperfectly, must daily pray that it may come, that we may perfectly know it when we are perfected therein.

CHAPTER XXVII.

"THY WILL BE DONE ON EARTH, AS IT IS IN HEAVEN."

Q. 1. WHY is this made the third petition?

A. Because it must be the third in our desires. I told you this prayer in perfect method beginneth at that which must be the first in our intention; and that is, God's interest as above our own, which is consistent, and expressed in these three gradations. 1. The highest notion of it is, the hallowing and glorifying of his name, and resplendent perfections. 2. The second is, that in which this is chiefliest notified to man, which is his kingdom. 3. The third is the effect of this kingdom in the fulfilling his will.

Q. 2. What will of God is it that is here meant?

A. His governing and beneficent will, expressed in

[t] John xvii. 22—24; Eph. iv. 3—5, 7, 8, 16.

[u] Rev. xx.; 2 Pet. iii. 12, 13.

[x] Matt. vi. 20, 21; v. 12; xix. 21; Eph. i. 3; 2 Tim. iv. 18; Heb. xi. 16; xii. 22, 23; 1 Cor. xv. 49; Phil. iii. 20; Col. i. 5; 1 Pet. i. 4; Heb. x. 34.

his laws and promises, concerning man's duty, and God's rewards and gifts.[a]

Q. 3. Is not the will of his absolute dominion expressed in the course of natural motion, here included?

A. It may be included as the supposed matter of our approbation and praise: and as God's will is taken for the effects and signs of his will, we may and must desire that he will continue the course of nature, sun, and moon, and stars, earth, winds, and waters, &c. till the time of their dissolution, and mankind on earth: for these are supposed as the subject, or accidents, of government. But the thing specially meant is God's governing will, that is, that his laws may be obeyed, and his promises all performed.[b]

Q. 4. But will not God's will be always done, whether we pray or not?

A. 1. All shall be done which God hath undertaken or decreed to do himself, and not laid the event on the will of man; his absolute will of events is still fulfilled. But man doth not always do God's will; that is, he doth not keep God's laws, or do the duty which God commandeth him, and therefore doth not obtain the rewards or gifts which were but conditionally promised. 2. And even some things, decreed absolutely by God, must be prayed for by man: for he decreeth the means as well as the end: and prayer is a means which his commands and promises oblige us to.

Q. 5. Why is it added, "as it is done in heaven?"

A. To mind us, 1. Of the perfect, holy obedience of the glorified. 2. That we must make that our pattern, and the end of our desires. 3. And to keep up our hopes and desires of that glorious perfection; and strive to do God's will understandingly, sincerely, fully, readily, delightfully, without unwillingness, unweariedly, concordantly, without division, in perfect love to God, his work, and one another; for so his will is done in heaven. And these holy, heavenly desires are the earnest of our heavenly possession.

Q. 6. What is it that we pray against in this petition?

A. Against all sin, as a transgression of his law, and against all distrust of his promises, and discontentedness with his disposals; and so against every will that is contrary to the will of God.

Q. 7. What will is it that is contrary to the will of God?

A. 1. The will of Satan, who hateth God and holiness, and man, and willeth sin, confusion, calamity, and who is obeyed by all the ungodly world.

2. The will of all blind, unbelieving, wicked men, especially tyrants, who fill the world with sin, and blood, and misery, that they may have their wills without control or bounds.

3. Especially our own sinful self-willedness, and rebellious and disobedient dispositions.[c]

Q. 8. What mean you by our self-willedness?

A. Man was made by the creating will of God, to obey the governing will of God, and rest and rejoice in the disposing, rewarding, and beneficent will of God, and his essential love and goodness: by sin he is fallen from God's will to himself and his own will, and would fain have all events in the power and disposal of his own will, and fain be ruled by his own will, and have no restraints, and would rest in himself, and the fulfilling of his will: yea, he would have all persons and things in the world to depend on his will, fulfil and please it, and ascribe unto it; and so would be the idol of himself, and of the world: and all the wickedness, and stir, and cruelty of the world is but that every selfish man may have his will.

Q. 9. What then is the full meaning of this petition?

A. That earth, which is grown so like to hell by doing the will of Satan, of tyrants, and of self-willed, fleshly, wicked men, may be made liker unto heaven, by a full compliance of the will of man with the will of God, depending submissively on his disposing will, obeying his commanding will, fearing his punishing will, trusting, rejoicing, and resting in his rewarding and beneficent will, and renouncing all that is against it.[d]

Q. 10. But if it be God's will to punish, pain, and kill us, how can we will this when it is evil to us; and we cannot will evil?

A. As God himself doth antecedently or primarily will that which is good without any evil to his subjects, and but consequently will their punishment on supposition of their wilful sin, and this but as the work of his holiness and justice for good; so he would have us to will first and absolutely, next his own glory and kingdom, our own holiness and happiness, and not our misery; but to submit to his just punishments, with a will that loveth (not the hurt, but) the final good effect, and the wisdom, holiness, and justice of our chastiser. Which well consisteth with begging mercy, pardon, and deliverance.[e]

Q. 11. But is not heaven too high a pattern for our desires?

A. No: though we have much duty on earth which belongs not to them in heaven, and they have much which belongeth not to us, yet we must desire to obey God fully in our duty, as they do in theirs; and desiring and seeking heavenly perfection is our sincerity on earth.[f]

Q. 12. What sin doth this clause specially condemn?

A. 1. Unbelief of the heavenly perfection. 2. Fleshly lusts and wills, and a worldly mind. 3. The ungodliness of them that would not have God have all our heart, and love, and service, but think it is too much preciseness, or more ado than needs, and give him but the leavings of the flesh.

CHAPTER XXVIII.

"GIVE US THIS DAY OUR DAILY BREAD."

Q. 1. WHY is this the fourth petition?

A. I told you that the Lord's prayer hath two parts: the first is for our end, according to the order of intention, beginning at the top, and descending; the second part is about the means, according to the order of execution, beginning at the bottom, and ascending to the top. Now this is the first petition of the second part, because our substance and being is supposed to all accidents; and if God continue not our humanity, we cannot be capable of his blessings.[g]

Q. 2. What is meant by bread?

A. All things necessary to sustain our natures, in a fitness for our duty and our comforts.[h]

Q. 3. It seems, then, that we pray that we may not want, or be sick, or die, when God hath foretold us the contrary events.

[a] John iv. 34; vi. 39, 40.
[b] Acts xxi. 14; Matt. vii. 21; xii. 50; xviii. 14; xxi. 31.
[c] John i. 13; v. 30; vi. 38; Luke xxii. 42; Acts xiii. 22; Heb. xiii. 21.
[d] Luke xii. 47; John vii. 17; Acts xxii. 14; Rom. ii. 18; Col. i. 9.
[e] Matt. xxvi. 42. [f] Psal. iv.; lxxx.
[g] Luke xii. 23. [h] Jer. xlv. 5; 1 Tim. iv. 8; 2 Pet. i. 3.

A. We justly show that our nature is against death, and sickness, and wants, as being natural evils; and God giveth us a discerning judgment to know natural good from evil, and an appetite to desire it accordingly: but because natural good and evil are to be estimated, as they tend to spiritual and everlasting good or evil, God giveth us reason and faith to order our desires accordingly: and because our knowledge of this is imperfect, (when and how far natural good or evil conduceth to spiritual and eternal,) it is still supposed that we make not ourselves, but God, the Judge; and so desire life, health, and food, and natural supplies, with submission to his will, for time and measure, they being but means to higher things.

Q. 4. Why ask we for no more than bread?

A. To show that corporeal things are not our treasure, nor to be desired for any thing but their proper use; and to renounce all covetous desires of superfluity, or provision, for our inordinate, fleshly lusts.[i]

Q. 5. Some say that by bread is meant Jesus Christ, because there is no petition that mentioneth him?

A. Every part of the Lord's prayer includeth Christ: it is by him that God is our Father; by him that the holy name of God is hallowed: it is his kingdom that we pray may come; it is his law or will which we pray may be done: it is he that purchaseth our right to the creature, and redeemed nature: it is by him that we must have the forgiveness of sin, and by his grace that we are delivered from temptations, and all evil, &c.

Q. 6. Why ask we bread of God, as the Giver?

A. To signify that we are and have nothing but by his gift, and must live in continual dependence on his will, and begging, receiving, and thanksgiving are our work.[k]

Q. 7. But do we not get it by our labour, and the gift of men?

A. Our labours are vain without God's blessing, and men are but God's messengers to carry us his gifts.[l]

Q. 8. What need we labour, if God give us all?

A. God giveth his blessings to meet receivers, and in the use of his appointed means: he that will not both beg and labour as God requireth him, is unmeet to receive his gifts.[m]

Q. 9. Why do we ask bread from day to day?

A. To show that we are not the keepers of ourselves, or our stock of provisions, but, as children, live upon our Father's daily allowance, and continually look to him for all, and daily renew our thanks for all, and study the daily improvement of his maintenance in our duties.[n]

Q. 10. But when a man hath riches for many years, what need he ask daily for what he hath?

A. He hath no assurance of his life or wealth an hour, nor of the blessing of it, but by God's gift.[o]

Q. 11. Why say we "give us," rather than "give me?"

A. To exercise our common love to one another, and renounce that narrow selfishness which confineth men's regard and desires to themselves; and to show that we come not to God merely in a single capacity, but as members of the world, as men, and members of Christ's body or church, as christians; and that in the communion of saints, as we show our charity to one another, so we have a part in the prayers of all.

Q. 12. May we then pray against poverty, and sickness, and hurt?

A. Yes, as aforesaid, so far as they are hurtful to our natures, and thereby to our souls, and the ends of life.[p]

Q. 13. Doth not naming bread before forgiveness and grace, show that we must first and most desire it?

A. We before expressed our highest desire of God's glory, kingdom, and will; and as to our own interests, all the three last petitions go together, and are inseparable; but the first is the lowest, though it be first in place. Nature sustained is the first, but it will be but the subject of sin and misery without pardon and holiness: I told you that the three last petitions go according to the order of execution, from the lowest to the highest step. God's kingdom and righteousness must be first sought in order of estimation and intention, by all that will attain them.

Q. 14. But if God give us more than bread, even plenty for our delight, as well as necessaries, may we not use it accordingly?

A. Things are necessary to our well-being, that are not necessary to our being. We may ask and thankfully use all that, by strengthening and comforting nature, tendeth to fit the spirit for the joyful service of God, and to be helpful to others. But we must neither ask nor use any thing for the service of our lusts, or tempting, unprofitable pleasure.

Q. 15. What if God deny us necessaries, and a christian should be put to beg, or be famished, how then doth God make good his word, that he will give us whatever we ask through Christ, and that other things shall be added, if we seek first his kingdom and righteousness, and that godliness hath the promise of this life and that to come.[q]

A. Remember, as aforesaid, 1. That the things of this life are promised and given, not as our happiness, but as means to better. 2. And that we are promised no more than we are fit to receive and use. 3. And that God is the highest Judge, both how far outward things would help or hinder us; and how far we are fit to receive them. Therefore, if he deny them, he certainly knoweth that either we are unmeet for them, or they for us.[r]

Q. 16. When should a man say, he hath enough?

A. When having God's grace and favour, he hath so much of corporeal things, as will best further his holiness and salvation, and as it pleaseth the will of God that he should have.

Q. 17. May not a man desire God to bless his labours, and to be rich?

A. A man is bound to labour in a lawful calling that is able, and to desire and beg God's blessing on it: but he must not desire riches, or plenty, for itself, or for fleshly lusts; nor be over-importunate with God to make him his steward for others.[s]

Q. 18. What if God give us riches, or more than we need ourselves?

A. We must believe that he maketh us his stewards, to do all the good with it that we can to all, but specially to the household of faith. But to spend no more in sinful lust and pleasure than if we were poor.[t]

Q. 19. What doth daily bread oblige us to?

[i] 2 Cor. ix. 10; 1 Tim. vi. 8.
[k] Matt. vi. 25—27, &c.; Psal. cxxxvi. 25.
[l] Psal. cxxvii. 1; Matt. iv. 3, 4.
[m] 2 Cor. ix. 10; Prov. xii. 11; xxviii. 19; Psal. viii. 13; Prov. xxxi. 27.
[n] Matt. vi. 24, &c.; Luke xii. 19—21.
[o] 1 Cor. xii.
[p] Prov. xxx. 8.
[q] Matt. vi. 19, 20, 33; John v. 40.
[r] 1 Sam. ii. 29—31; Jam. iv. 3; Phil. iv. 10, 11; Heb. xiii. 5.
[s] Prov. x. 22: Psal. cxxix. 8; Deut. xxviii. 8, 9, &c.; xxxiii. 11.
[t] 1 Pet. iv. 10; Luke xii. 21, 24.

A. Daily service, and daily love, and thankfulness to God, and to mind the end for which it is given, to be always ready, at the end of a day, to give up our account, and end our journey.

Q. 20. What is the sin and danger of the love of riches?

A. The love of money, or riches, is but the fruit of the love of the flesh, whose lust would never want provision; but it is the root of a thousand further evils. As it shows a wretched soul, that doth not truly believe and trust God for this life, much less for a better, but is worldly, and sensual, and idolatrous, so it leadeth a man from God, holiness, heaven, yea and from common honesty, to all iniquity: a worldling, and lover of riches, is false to his own soul, to God and man, and never to be much trusted.[u]

CHAPTER XXIX.

"AND FORGIVE US OUR TRESPASSES, AS WE FORGIVE THEM THAT TRESPASS AGAINST US." (OR, AS WE FORGIVE OUR DEBTORS.)

Q. 1. WHY is this made the fifth petition, or the second of the first part?

A. Because it is for the second thing we personally need. Our lives and natural being supposed, we next need deliverance from the guilt and punishment which we have contracted. Else to be men, will be worse to us than to be toads or serpents.[a]

Q. 2. What doth this petition imply.

A. 1. That we are all sinners, and have deserved punishment, and are already fallen under some degree of it.[b]

2. That God hath given us a Saviour, who died for our sins, and is our Ransom and Advocate with the Father.

And, 3. That God is a gracious, pardoning God, and dealeth not with us on the terms of rigorous justice according to the law of innocency, but hath brought us under the Redeemer's covenant of grace, which giveth pardon to all penitent believers: so that sin is both pardonable, and conditionally pardoned to us all.[c]

Q. 3. What, then, are the presupposed things which we pray not for?

A. 1. We pray not that God may be good, and love itself, or a merciful God, for this is presupposed. 2. We pray not that he would send a Saviour into the world, to fulfil all righteousness, and die for sin, and that his merit and sacrifice may procure a conditional universal pardon and gift of life, viz. to all that will repent and believe, for all this is done already.[d]

Q. 4. Is it to the Father only, or also to the Son, that we pray for pardon?

A. To the Father primarily, and to the Son as glorified, for now the Father without him judgeth no man, but hath committed all judgment to the Son, John v. 22. But when Christ made this prayer, he was not yet glorified, nor in full possession of his power.

Q. 5. What sin is it whose forgiveness we pray for?

A. All sin, upon the conditions of pardon made by Christ; that is, for the pardon of all sin to true penitent believers. Therefore we pray not for any pardon of the final non-performance of the condition, that is, to finally impenitent unbelievers.[e]

Q. 6. Sin cannot hurt God; what need, then, is there of forgiveness?

A. It can wrong him by breaking his laws, and rejecting his moral government, though it hurt him not: and he will right himself.

Q. 7. What is forgiving sin?

A. It is by tender mercy, on the account of Christ's merits, satisfaction, and intercession, to forgive the guilt of sin, as it maketh us the due subjects of punishment, and to forgive the punishment of sin, as due by that guilt and the law of God, so as not to inflict it on us.[f]

Q. 8. What punishment doth God forgive?

A. Not all: for the first sentence of corporeal punishment and death is inflicted. But he forgiveth the everlasting punishment to all true believers, and so much of the temporal, both corporeal and spiritual, as his grace doth fit us to receive the pardon of: and so he turneth temporal, correcting punishments to our good.[g]

Q. 9. Doth he not pardon all sin at once, at our conversion?

A. Yes, all that is past, for no other is sin. But not by a perfect pardon.

Q. 10. Why must we pray for pardon, then, every day?

A. 1. Because the pardon of old sins is but begun, and not fully perfect till all the punishment be ceased: and that is not till all sin and unholiness, and all the evil effects of sin, be ceased. No, nor till the day of resurrection and judgment have overcome the last enemy, death, and finally justified us.[h]

2. Because we daily renew our sins by omission and commission, and though the foundation of our pardon be laid in our regeneration, that it may be actual and full for following sins, we must have renewed repentance, faith, and prayer.

Q. 11. God is not changeable, to forgive to-day what he forgave not yesterday; what, then, is his forgiving sin?

A. The unchangeable God changeth the case of man. And, 1. By his law of grace, forgiveth penitent believers who were unpardoned in their impenitence and unbelief. And, 2. By his executive providence, he taketh off and preventeth punishments both of sense and loss, and so forgiveth.

Q. 12. How can we pray for pardon to others, when we know not whether they be penitent believers, capable of pardon?

A. 1. We pray as members of Christ's body for ourselves, and all that are his members, that is, penitent believers.

2. For others, we pray that God would give them faith, repentance, and forgiveness. As Christ prayed, "Father, forgive them, for they know not what they do;" that is, qualify them for pardon, and then pardon them; or give them repentance and forgiveness.

Q. 13. Why say we, "as we forgive them that trespass against us?"

A. To signify that we have this necessary qualification for forgiveness; God will not forgive us fully till we can forgive others; and to signify our obligation to forgive; and as an argument to God to forgive us, when he hath given us hearts to forgive others.

[u] Luke xviii. 23, 24; Mark x. 24; 1 Tim. vi. 10; 1 John ii. 15.

[a] Psal. xxxii. 1—3. [b] Rom. iii. throughout.

[c] 1 John ii. 1, 2; John iii. 16; Psal. cxxx. 4; Acts v. 31; xiii. 38; xxvi. 18.

[d] Luke xxiii. 34; Matt. ix. 6; xii. 31, 32.

[e] Luke xv. 3, 5.

[f] Col. ii. 13; Jam. v. 15; Matt. xviii. 27, 32; Luke vii. 42, 43; Rom. vi. 21, 23; 1 Cor. xv. 22.

[g] Psal. ciii. 3; 1 John i. 9;

[h] 1 Cor. xi. 30—32; Matt. xviii. 27; Psal. lxxxv. 2—4, &c.; Luke vi. 37; Jam. v. 15.

But not as the measure of God's forgiving us, for he forgiveth us more freely and fully than we can forgive others.[i]

Q. 13. Are we bound absolutely to forgive all men?

A. No; but as they are capable of it. 1. We have no power to forgive wrongs against God. 2. Nor against our superiors, or other men, or the commonwealth, or church, further than God authorizeth any man by office. 3. A magistrate must forgive sins, as to corporeal punishment, no further than God alloweth him, and as will stand with the true design of government and the common good; and a pastor no further than will stand with the good of the church; and a father no further than will stand with the good of the family: and so of others. 4. An enemy that remaineth such, and is wicked, must be forgiven by private men, so far as that we must desire and endeavour their good, and seek no revenge; but not so far as to be trusted as a familiar, or bosom friend. 5. A friend that offended, and returneth to his fidelity, must be forgiven and trusted as a friend, according to the evidence of his repentance and sincerity, and no further.

The rest about forgiveness is opened in the exposition of that article in the creed, "The forgiveness of sins." Still remembering that all forgiveness is by God's mercy, through Christ's merits, sacrifice, and intercession.

CHAPTER XXX.

"AND LEAD US NOT INTO TEMPTATION, BUT DELIVER US FROM EVIL."

Q. 1. WHY is this made the sixth petition?

A. Because it is the next in order to the attainment of our ultimate end. Our natures being maintained, and our sin and punishment forgiven, we next need deliverance from all evils that we are in danger of for the time to come, and then we are saved.

Q. 2. What is meant by temptation?

A. Any such trial as may overcome us or hurt us, whether by Satan, or by the strong allurements of the world and flesh, or by persecutions or other heavy sufferings, which may draw us to sin, or make us miserable.[a]

Q. 3. Doth God lead any into temptation?

A. 1. God placeth us in this world in the midst of trials, making it our duty to resist and overcome. 2. God permitteth the devil, by his suggestions, and by the world and flesh, to tempt us. 3. God trieth us himself by manifold afflictions, and by permitting the temptations of persecutors and oppressors.[b]

Q. 4. Why will God do and permit all this?

A. It is a question unmeet for man to put. It is but to ask him why he would make a rank of reasonable creatures below confirmed angels? And why he would make man with free-will? And why he would not give us the prize without the race, and the crown without the warfare and victory? And you may next ask why he did not make every star a sun, and every man an angel, and every beast and vermin a man, and every stone a diamond.[c]

Q. 5. Doth God tempt a man to sin?

A. No: sin is none of God's end or desire. Satan tempts men to sin; and God tempteth men to try them whether they will sin, or be faithful to him, to exercise their grace and victory.[d]

Q. 6. Is it all that we need that God lead us not into temptation?

A. The meaning is, that God, who overruleth all things, will neither himself try us beyond the strength which he will give us, nor permit Satan, men, or flesh, to over-tempt us unto sin.

Q. 7. But are we not sure that this life will be a life of trial and temptation, and that we must pass through many tribulations?

A. Yes: but we pray that they may not be too strong and prevalent to overcome us, when we should overcome.[e]

Q. 1. What be the temptations of Satan which we pray against?

A. They are of so many sorts that I must not here be so large as to number them. You may see a great number with the remedies, named in my "Christian Directory:" but, in general, they are such by which he deceives the understanding, perverteth the will, and corrupteth our practice; and this is about our state of soul, or about our particular actions, to draw us to sins of commission, or of omission, against God, ourselves, or others. The particulars are innumerable.[f]

Q. 9. What is the evil that we pray to be delivered from?

A. The evil of sin and misery, and from Satan, ourselves, and men, and all hurtful creatures, as the causes.

Q. 10. What is the reason of the connexion of the two parts of this petition, "Lead us not into temptation, but deliver us from evil?"

A. Temptation is the means of sin, and sin the cause of misery. And they that would be delivered from sin, must pray and labour to be delivered from temptation; and they that would be delivered from misery, must be delivered from sin.[g]

Q. 11. May not a tempted man be delivered from sin?

A. Yes, when the temptation is not chosen by him, and cannot be avoided, and when it is not too strong for him, grace assisting him.

Q. 12. What duty doth this petition oblige us to, and what sin doth it reprehend?

A. 1. It binds us to a continual, humble sense of our own corrupt dispositions, apt to yield to temptations, and of our danger, and of the evil of sin; and it condemneth the unhumbled that know not, or fear not, their pravity, or danger.

2. It binds us all to fly from temptations, as far as lawfully we can; and condemneth them that rush fearlessly on them, yea, that tempt themselves and others. The best man is not safe that will not avoid such temptations as are suited to his corrupt nature, when he may. While the bait is still near unto his senses, he is in continual danger.[h]

3. It binds us to feel the need of grace and God's deliverance, and not to trust our corrupted nature, and insufficient strength.

Q. 13. How doth God deliver us from evil?

A. 1. By keeping us from over-strong temptations. 2. By his assisting grace. 3. By restraining Satan and wicked men, and all things that would hurt us, and, by his merciful providence, directing, preserving, and delivering us from sin and misery.

[i] Matt. vi. 14, 15; xviii. 35; Mark xi. 25, 26.
[a] 2 Pet. ii. 9; Rev. iii. 10; Mhtt. xxvi. 41; Luke viii. 13.
[b] 1 Pet. i. 6; Matt. iv.; Gen. xxii. 1.
[c] Jam. i. 2, 12; 1 Cor. x. 13. [d] Jam. i. 13—15.
[e] 1 Cor. x. 13; Heb. ii. 18.
[f] 1 Thess. iii. 5; Eph. vi. 11.
[g] Prov. iv. 14, 15; 1 Thess. v. 22; Prov. vii. 23; 2 Tim. iii. 7; vi. 9; 1 Cor. vii. 35; Matt. v. 29—31.
[h] Matt. xviii. 6—9; xvi. 22—24; 1 Cor. viii. 9; Rom. xiv. 13; Rev. ii. 14.

CHAPTER XXXI.

"FOR THINE IS THE KINGDOM, THE POWER, AND THE GLORY, FOR EVER. AMEN."

Q. 1. WHAT is the meaning of this conclusion, and its scope?

A. It is a form of praise to God, and helps to our belief of the hearing of our prayers.

Q. 2. Why is it put last?

A. Because the praise of God is the highest step next heaven.[a]

Q. 3. What is the meaning of kingdom, power, and glory here?

A. By kingdom is meant that it belongeth only to God to rule all the creatures, dispose of all things; and by power is meant that, by his infinite perfection and sufficiency, he can do it; and therefore can give us all that we want, and deliver us from all that we fear. And by glory is meant that all things shall be ordered so as the glory of all his own perfections shall finally and everlastingly shine forth in all, and his glory be the end of all for ever.[b]

Q. 4. What is the reason of the order of these three here?

A. I told you that the last part ascendeth from the lowest to the highest step. God's actual government is the cause of our deliverances and welfare. God's power and perfection is it that manageth that government. God's glory shining in the perfected form of the universe, and especially in heaven, is the ultimate end of all.

Q. 5. But it seems there is no confession of sin, or thanksgiving, in this form of prayer.

A. It is the symbol or directory to the will's desire: and when we know what we should desire, it is implied that we know what we want, and what we should bewail, and what we should be thankful for: and praise includeth our thanksgiving.[c]

Q. 6. Why say we, "for ever?"

A. For our comfort and God's honour, expressing the everlastingness of his kingdom, power, and glory.

Q. 7. Why say we "Amen?"

A. To express both our desire, and our faith and hope, that God will hear the desires which his Spirit giveth us through the mediation of Jesus Christ.

CHAPTER XXXII.

OF THE TEN COMMANDMENTS IN GENERAL.

Q. 1. ARE the ten commandments a law to christians, or are they abrogated with the rest of Moses' law?

A. The ten commandments are considerable in three states: 1. As part of the primitive law of nature. 2. As the law given by Moses, for the peculiar government of the Jews' commonwealth. 3. As the law of Jesus Christ.[d]

1. The law of nature is not abrogate, though the terms of life and death are not the same as under the law of innocency.[e]

2. The law of Moses to the Jews as such, never bound all other nations, nor now bindeth us, but is dead and done away, 2 Cor. iii. 7, 9, 10, 11; Rom. ii. 12; xiv. 15; iii. 19; vii. 1—3; Heb. vii. 12; 1 Cor. ix. 21. But seeing it was God that was the Author of that law, and by it expressly told the Jews what the law of nature is, we are all bound still to take those two tables to be God's own transcript of his law of nature, and so are, by consequence, bound by them still. If God give a law to some one man, as that which belongs to the nature of all men, though it bind us not as a law to that man, it binds as God's exposition of the law of nature when notified to us.

3. As the law of Christ, it binds all christians.

Q. 2. How are the ten commandments the law of Christ?

A. 1. Nature itself, and lapsed mankind, is delivered up to Christ as Redeemer, to be used in the government of his kingdom. And so the law of nature is become his law.[f]

2. It was Christ, as God Redeemer, that gave the law of Moses; and as it is a transcript of the common law of nature, he doth not revoke it, but suppose it.

3. Christ hath repeated and owned the matter of it in the gospel, and made it his command to his disciples.

Q. 3. Is there nothing in the ten commandments proper to the Israelites?

A. Yes: 1. The preface, "Hear, O Israel;" and "that brought thee out of the land of Egypt, out of the house of bondage." 2. The stating the seventh day for the sabbath, and the strict ceremonial rest commanded as part of the sanctifying of it.

Q. 4. How doth Christ and his apostles contract all the law into that of love?

A. God, who, as absolute Lord, owneth, moveth, and disposeth of all,[g] doth, as sovereign Ruler, give us laws, and execute them, and, as Love and Benefactor, giveth us all, and is the most amiable object and end of all: so that as to love and give is more than to command, so to be loved is more than as a commander to be obeyed; but ever includeth it, though it be eminently, in its nature, above it. So that, 1. Objectively, love to God, ourselves, and others, in that measure that it is exercised wisely, is obedience eminently, and somewhat higher. 2. And love, as the principle in man, is the most powerful cause of obedience, supposing the reverence of authority and the fear of punishment, but is somewhat more excellent than they. A parent's love to a child makes him more constant and full in all that he can do for him,[h] than the commands of a king alone will do. In that measure that you love God, you will heartily and delightfully do all your duty to him; and so far as you love parents or neighbours, you will gladly promote their honour, safety, chastity, estates, rights, and all that is theirs, and hate all that is against their good. And as parents will feed their children, though no fear of punishment should move them; so we shall be above the great necessity of the fear of punishment, so far as God and goodness is our delight.[i]

[a] Psalm cxix.; clxiv.; lxxi. 6, 8; lxxviii. 13.

[b] Psalm ciii. 19; cxlv. 12; Dan. iv. 3, 34; Matt. xvi. 28; Psal. cxlv. 11, 13; Heb. i. 8; Luke ii. 14; Matt. xvi. 27; xxiv. 30; Acts xii. 23.

[c] Psalm cxlv. 4, 10; cxlviii.; lxvi. 2, 8; cxlvii. 1, 7; cvi. 2, 47; Phil. iv. 20; Jude 25; Rev. v. 13; vii. 12; Rom. xi. 36; xvi. 27.

[d] Exod. xv.; xxxiv. 28; Deut. v.

[e] Luke i. 6.

[f] Matt. v. 18, 19; xxiv. 40; Mark x. 19; xii. 29, 30; John xiv. 21; 1 Cor. vii. 19; xiv. 37; 1 John ii. 4; iii. 24; v. 3; John xv. 12.

[g] Mark xii. 30, 33; Rom. xiii. 9, 10; 1 Cor. xiii.; Tit. iii. 4; Rom. v. 5; viii. 39; 1 John iv. 16; John xiv. 23.

[h] 2 Tim. i. 7; 1 John iv. 17, 18; Gal. v. 14.

[i] Psalm i. 2, 3; cxix.

Q. 5. How should one know the meaning and extent of the commandments?

A. The words do plainly signify the sense: and according to the reasonable use of words, God's laws, being perfect, must be thus expounded.[k]

1. The commanding of duty includeth the forbidding of the contrary.

2. Under general commands and prohibitions, the kinds and particulars are included which the general word extendeth to.

3. When one particular sin is forbidden, or duty commanded, all the branches of it, and all of the same kind and reason, are forbidden or commanded.

4. Where the end is commanded or forbidden, it is implied that so are the true means as such.

5. Every commandment extendeth to the whole man, to our bodies and all the members, and to the soul and all its faculties respectively.

6. Commands bind us not to be always doing the thing commanded. Duties be not at all times duty: but prohibitions bind us at all times from every sin, when it is indeed a sin.

7. Every command implieth some reward or benefit to the obedient, and every sin of omission or commission is supposed to deserve punishment, though it be not named.[l]

8. Every command supposeth the thing commanded to be no natural impossibility (as to see spirits, or to dive into the heart of the earth, to know that which is not intelligible, &c.); but it doth not suppose us to be morally or holily disposed to keep it, or to be able to change our corrupt natures without God's grace.

9. So every command supposeth us to have that natural freedom of will which is a self-determining power, not necessitated or forced to sin by any; but not to have a will that is free from vicious inclinations, nor from under God's disposing power.[m]

10. The breach of the same laws may have several sorts of punishment: by parents, by masters, by magistrates, by the church; on body, on name, on soul, in this life, by God; and, finally, heavier punishment in the life to come.

11. The sins here forbidden, are not unpardonable, but by Christ's merits, sacrifice, and intercession, are forgiven to all true penitent, converted believers.

CHAPTER XXXIII.

OF THE PREFACE TO THE DECALOGUE.

Q. 1. WHAT are the parts of the decalogue?

A. 1. The constitution of the kingdom of God over men described. And, 2. The administration, or governing laws of his kingdom.

Q. 2. What words express the constitution of God's kingdom?

A. "I am the Lord thy God, which brought thee out of the land of Egypt, out of the house of bondage."

Q. 3. What is the constitution here expressed?

A. 1. God, the Sovereign. 2. Man, the subject. 3. The work of God, which was the next foundation or reason of the mutual relation between God and man, as here intended.[a]

Q. 4. What is included in the first part, of God's sovereignty?

A. 1. That there is a God, and but one God in this special sense. 2. That the God of Israel is this one true God, who maketh these laws. 3. That we must all obey him.

Q. 5. What is God, and what doth that word here mean?

A. This was largely opened in the beginning. Briefly, to be God is to be a spirit, infinite in being, in vital power, knowledge, and goodness, of whom, as the efficient cause, and through whom, as the Governor, and to whom, as the end, are all things else; related to us as our Creator, and as our absolute Owner, our supreme Ruler, and our greatest Benefactor, Friend, and Father.

Q. 6. What words mention man as the subject of the kingdom?

A. "Hear, O Israel," and "Thy God that brought thee," &c.

Q. 7. What relations are included?

A. That we, being God's creatures and redeemed ones, are, 1. His own. 2. His subjects, to be ruled by him. 3. His poor beneficiaries, that have all from him, and owe him all our love.

Q. 8. What do the words signify, "that brought thee out of the land of Egypt?"

A. That besides the right of creation, God hath a second right to us as our Redeemer. The deliverance from Egypt was that typical one that founded the relation between him and the commonwealth of Israel. But as the decalogue is the law of Christ, the meaning is, I am the Lord thy God, who redeemed thee from sin and misery by Jesus Christ.[b] So that this signifieth the nearest right and reason of this relation between God and man. He giveth us his law now, not only as our Creator, but as our Redeemer, and as such we must be his willing subjects, and obey him.

Q. 9. Are all men subjects of God's kingdom?

A. 1. All are subjects as to right and obligation.

2. All that profess subjection as professed consenters.

3. And all true hearty consenters are his sincere subjects, that shall be saved.

God the Creator and Redeemer hath the right of sovereignty over all the world, whether they consent or not. But they shall not have the blessing of faithful subjects without their own true consent, nor of visible church members without professed consent. But antecedent mercies he giveth to all.

Q. 10. Why is this description of God's sovereignty, and man's subjection, and the ground of it, set before the commandments?

A. Because, 1. Faith must go before obedience.[c] He that will come to God and obey him, must believe that God is God, and that he is the rewarder of them that diligently seek him, Heb. xi. 6. And he that will obey him as our Redeemer, must believe that we are redeemed by Jesus Christ, and that he is our Lord and King. 2. And relations go before the duties of relation: and our consent foundeth the mutual relation. The nature and form of obedience is, to obey another's commanding will, because he is our rightful Governor. No man can obey him formally whom he taketh not for his Ruler. And subjection, or consent to be governed, is virtually all obedience.

Q. 11. But what, if men never hear of the Redeemer, may they not obey God's law of nature?

A. They may know that they are sinners, and that the sin of an immortal soul deserveth endless punish-

[k] Matt. vii. 12; Phil. ii. 14; iii. 8; 1 Cor. xiv. 26.
[l] Mal. iii. 14. [m] Rom. viii. 6–8; Jer. xiii. 23.
[a] Mal. ii. 10; Matt. xix. 17; Mark xii. 32; Jer. vii. 23; John xx. 17.
[b] Matt. xxviii. 19; Rom. xiv. 9; John v. 22; xvii. 2, 3.
[c] John xvii. 3; xiv. 1, 2; Gal. iii. 16; Josh. xxiv. 18; John xx. 28.

ment: and they may find, by experience, that God useth them not as they deserve, but giveth many mercies to those that deserve nothing but misery; and that he obligeth them to use some means in hope for their recovery, and so that he governeth them by a law (or on terms) of mercy: and being under the first edition of the law of grace, though they know not the second, they ought to keep that law which they are under, and they shall be judged by it.

Q. 12. How, then, doth the christian church, as Christ's kingdom, differ from the world without, if they be any of his kingdom too?

A. As all the world was under that common law of grace which was made for them to Adam and Noah, and yet Abraham and his seed were only chosen out of all the world as a peculiar, holy nation to God, and were under a law and covenant of peculiarity, which belonged only unto them; so, though Christ hath not revoked those common mercies given to all by the first edition of the law of grace, nor left the world ungoverned and lawless, yet he hath given to christians a more excellent covenant of peculiarity than he gave the natural seed of Abraham, and hath elected them out of the world to himself, as a "chosen generation, a royal priesthood, an holy nation, a peculiar people, to show forth the praises of him that hath called them out of darkness into his marvellous light," 1 Pet. ii. 9.

Q. 13. It seems, then, we must take great heed that we make not Christ's kingdom either less or greater than it is?

A. To make it greater than it is, by equalling those without the church, or church hypocrites, with the sincere, doth dishonour God's holiness, and the wonderful design of Christ in man's redemption, and the grace of the Spirit, and the church of God; and obscureth the doctrine of election, and God's peculiar love, and tendeth to the discomfort of the faithful, and even to infidelity.

And to make Christ's kingdom less than it is, by denying the first edition of the law of grace made to all, and the common mercies given to all, antecedently to their rejection of them, doth obscure and wrong the glory of God's love to man, and deny his common grace and law, and feigneth the world either to be under no law of God, or else to be all bound to be perfectly innocent at the time when they are guilty,[d] and either not bound at all to hope and seek for salvation, or else to seek it on the condition of being innocent, when they know that it is impossible, they being already guilty: and it maketh the world, like the devils, almost shut up in despair; and it leaveth them as guiltless of all sin against grace, and the law of grace, as if they had none such: and it contradicteth the judgment of Abraham, the father of the faithful, who saw Christ's day; for he thought that even the wicked city of Sodom had fifty persons so righteous as that God should have spared the rest for their sakes, to say nothing of Job, Nineveh, &c. In a word, the ungrounded extenuating the grace of Christ, and the love of God, hardeneth infidels, and tempteth christians to perplexing thoughts of the gospel, and of the infinite goodness of God, and maketh it more difficult than indeed it is, to see his amiableness, and consequently to glorify and love him, as the essential love, whose goodness is equal to his greatness. It is Satan, as an angel of light and righteousness, who, pretending the defence of God's special love to his elect, denieth his common mercies to mankind, to dishonour God's love, and strengthen our own temptations against the joyful love of God.

Q. 14. Is government and subjection all that is here included?

A. No: God's kingdom is a paternal kingdom, ruling children by love, that he may make them happy. "I am the Lord thy God," signifieth I am thy greatest Benefactor, thy Father, who gave thee all the good thou hast, and will give to my obedient children grace and glory, and all that they can reasonably desire, and will protect them from all their enemies, and supply their wants, and deliver them from evil, and will be for ever their sun and shield, their reward and joy, and better to them than man in flesh can now conceive, even love itself.[e]

CHAPTER XXXIV.

OF THE FIRST COMMANDMENT.

Q. 1. What are the words of the first commandment?

A. "Thou shalt have no other gods before me," Exod. xx. 3.[f]

Q. 2. What is the meaning of this commandment?

A. It implieth a command that we do all that is due to God; which is due to God from reasonable creatures, made by him, and freely redeemed by him from sin and misery. And it forbiddeth us to think there is any other God, or to give to any other that which properly belongs to him.[g]

Q. 3. Doth not the Scripture call idols and magistrates gods?

A. Yes; but only in an equivocal, improper sense: idols are called gods, as so reputed falsely by idolaters; and magistrates only as men's governors under God.[h]

Q. 4. What are the duties which we owe to God alone?

A. 1. That our understandings know, believe, and esteem him as God. 2. That our wills love him, and cleave to him as God. 3. That we practically obey and serve him as God.

Q. 5. When doth the understanding know, believe, and esteem him as God?

A. No creature can know God with an adequate, comprehensive knowledge: but we must in our measure know, believe, and esteem him to be the only infinite, eternal, self-sufficient Spirit, vital Power, Understanding, and Will, or most perfect Life, Light, and Love; Father, Son, and Holy Ghost, of whom, and through whom, and to whom, are all things; our absolute Owner, Ruler, and Father, reconciled by Christ; our Maker, our Redeemer, and Sanctifier.

Q. 6. When doth man's will love and cleave to him as God?

A. When the understanding believing him to be best, even infinitely good in himself, and best to all the world, and best to us, we love him as such; though not yet in due perfection, yet sincerely above all other things.[i]

Q. 7. How can we love God above all, when we never saw him, and can have no idea or formal conception of him in our minds?

A. Though he be invisible, and we have no corporeal idea of him, nor no adequate or just formal

[d] Psal. cxlv. 9.
[e] 2 Cor. vi. 16, 18; John xx. 28.
[f] Deut. v. 7; x. 21.
[g] Deut. xxvi. 27; Dan. vi. 16; Isa. xvi. 19.
[h] Gal. iv. 8; 1 Cor. viii. 5; John x. 34, 35; xvii. 3; xiv 1, 2; Deut. x. 12; xxx. 16, 20; Mic. vi. 8.
[i] Psal. lxxiii. 25; cxix. 68; cxlv. 9; Matt. xxii. 37.

conception of him, yet he is the most noble object of our understanding and love, as the sun is of our sight, though we comprehend it not. We are not without such an idea or conception of God, as is better than all other knowledge, and is the beginning of eternal life, and is true in its kind, though very imperfect.[k]

Q. 8. How can you know him that is no object of sense?

A. He is the object of our understanding; we know in ourselves what it is to know and to will, though these acts are not the objects of sense (unless you will call the very acts of knowing and willing, an eminent, internal sensation of themselves). And by this we know what it is to have the power of understanding and willing; and so what it is to be an invisible substance with such power. And as we have this true idea or conception of a soul, so have we more easily of him, who is more than a soul to the whole world.[l]

Q. 9. How doth the true love of God work here in the flesh?

A. As we here know God, so we love him: as we know him not in the manner as we do things sensible, so we love him not in that sort of sensible appetite, as we do things sensible immediately. But as we know him as revealed in the glass of his works, natural and gracious, and in his word, so we love him as known by such revelation.[m]

Q. 10. Do not all men love God, who believe that there is a God, when nature teacheth men to love goodness as such, and all that believe that there is a God, believe that he is the best of beings?

A. Wicked men know not truly the goodness of God, and so what God is indeed. To know this proposition, God is most good, is but to know words and a logical, general notion: as if a man should know and say that light is good, who never had sight; or sweetness is good, who never tasted it. Every wicked man is predominantly a lover of fleshly pleasure, and therefore no lover, but a hater, of all the parts and acts of divine government and holiness, which are contrary to it, and would deprive him of it. So that there is somewhat of God that a wicked man doth love, that is, his being, his work of creation, and bounty to the world, and to him in those natural good things which he can value: but he loveth not, but hateth God as the holy governor of the world and him, and the enemy of his forbidden pleasure and desires.[n]

Q. 11. What be the certain signs, then, of true love to God?

A. 1. A true love to his government, and laws, and holy word; and that as it is his, and holy; and this so effectual, as that we unfeignedly desire to obey that word as the rule of our faith, and life, and hope; and desire to fulfil his commanding will.

2. A true love to the actions which God commandeth (though flesh will have some degree of backwardness).

3. A true love to those that are likest God in wisdom, holiness, and doing good; and such a love to them as is above the love of worldly riches, honour, and pleasure; so that it will enable us to do them good, though by our suffering or loss in a lower matter, when God calls us to it. For if we see our brother have need, and shut up the bowels of compassion, so that we cannot find in our hearts to relieve his necessities by the loss of our unnecessary superfluities, how dwelleth the love of God in us?

4. True love to God doth love itself. It is a great sign of it, when we so much love to love God as that we are gladder when we feel it in us, than for any worldly vanity; and when we take the mutual love of God and the soul to be so good and joyful a state, as that we truly desire it as our felicity, and best in heaven, to be perfectly loved of God, and perfectly to love him, joyfully express it in his everlasting praises. To long to love God as the best condition for us, is a sign that we truly love him.[o]

Q. 12. But must not all the affections be set on God as well as love?

A. All the rest are but several ways of loving or willing good, and of nilling, or hating and avoiding, evil.

1. It is love that desireth after God, and his grace and glory. 2. It is love that hopeth for him. 3. It is love that rejoiceth in him, and is pleased when we and others please him, and when his love is poured out on the sons of men, and truth, peace, and holiness prosper in the world. 4. It is love that maketh us sorrowful, that we can please him no more, nor more enjoy him; and that maketh us grieved that we can no more know him, love him, and delight in him, and that we have so much sin within us to displease him, and hinder our communion of love with him. 5. And love will make us fearful of displeasing him, and losing the said communion of love. 6. And it will make us more angry with ourselves, when we have most by sin displeased God, and angry with others that offend him.[p]

Q. 13. What is the practical duty properly due from us to God?

A. To obey him in doing all that he commandeth us, either in his holy worship, or for ourselves, or for our neighbour; and this by an absolute, universal obedience, in sincere desire and endeavour, as to a Sovereign of greatest authority, and a Father of greatest love, whose laws and works are all most wise, just, and good.[q]

Q. 14. What if our governors command or forbid us any thing, must we not take our obeying them to be obeying God, seeing they are his officers whom we see, but see not him?

A. Yes; when they command us by the authority given them of God: but God's universal laws are before and above their laws; and their power is all limited by God; they have no authority but what he giveth them; and he giveth them none against his laws: and therefore if they command any thing which God forbiddeth, or forbid what God commandeth, you must obey God in not obeying them. But this must never be made a pretence for disobedience to their true authority.[r]

Q. 15. What is the thing forbidden in the first commandment?

A. 1. To think that to be God which is not God, as the heathens do by the sun. 2. To ascribe any part of that to creatures which is essential and proper to God; and so to make them half gods.

Q. 16. How are men guilty of that?

A. 1. When they think that any creature hath that infiniteness, eternity, or self-sufficiency, that power, knowledge, or goodness, which is proper to God alone. Or that any creature hath that causality which is proper to God, in making and maintaining,

k Matt. xix. 17; John xvii. 3.

l 1 Cor. xiii. 12; ii. 3, 8, 18; John i. 18.

m Exod. xx. 6; Prov. viii. 17, 21; John xiv. 15, 23.

n 1 Cor. viii. 3; Rom. viii. 28; Jam. i. 12; ii. 5; 1 John iii. 16, 17; iv. 20; v. 3; John xiv. 23; Jude 21.

o Luke xi. 42; John v. 42; xv. 10; 1 John ii. 5; iii. 17; Psal. xlii. 1—4, &c.

p Deut. v. 29; xi. 13; xiii. 3; xxvi. 16; xxx. 2, 6, 10; Josh. xxii. 5; 1 Sam. xii. 24; Matt. vi. 21; xxii. 37.

q John xiv. 15, 23; 1 John v. 3.

r Rom. xiii. 2, 3; Acts iv. 19, 24; v. 29, 32; Dan. iii.; vi.

or governing the world, or being the ultimate end. Or that any creature is to be more honoured, loved, or obeyed, than God, or with any of that which is proper to God.[s]

2. When the will doth actually love and honour the creature, with any of that love and honour which is due to God as God, and therefore to God alone.

3. When in their practice men labour to please, serve, or obey any creature against God, before God, or equal with God, or with any service proper to God alone. All this is idolatry.[t]

Q. 17. Which is the greatest and commonest idol of the world?

A. Carnal self: by sin man is fallen from God to his carnal self, to which he giveth that which is God's proper due.

Q. 18. How doth this selfishness appear and work as idolatry?

A. 1. In that such men love their carnal self, and pleasure, and prosperity, and the riches that are the provision for the flesh, better than God: I mean not only more sensibly, but with a preferring, choosing love; and that which as best is most loved, is made a man's god. The images of heathens were not so much their idols as themselves; for none of them loved their images better than themselves; nor than a worldling loveth his wealth, power, and honour.[u]

2. In that such are their own chief ultimate end, and prefer the prosperity of carnal self before the glorifying of God in perfect love and praise in the heavenly society for ever. And so did idolaters, by their images, or other idols.

3. In that such had rather their own will were done than God's; and had rather God's will were brought to theirs than theirs to God's. Their wills are their rule and end; yea, they would have God and man, and all the world, fulfil their wills; even when they are against the will of God: self-will is the great idol of the world: all the stir, and striving, and war, and work of such, is but to serve it.[x]

4. Selfish men do measure good and evil chiefly by carnal self-interest: they take those for the best men that are most for them herein; and those for the worst that are against their interest in the world: and their love and hatred is placed accordingly. Let a man be never so wise and good, they hate him if he be against their interest.[y]

5. And as holy men live to God in the care and endeavour of their lives, so do selfish men to their carnal selves: their study, labour, and time is thus employed, even to ruin the best that are but against their carnal interest: and if they be princes or great men in the world, the lives and estates of thousands of the innocent, seem not to them too dear a sacrifice by bloody and unlawful wars or persecutions, to offer to this grand idol self.

6. And when it cometh to a parting choice, as the faithful will rather let go liberty, honour, estate, and life, than forsake God and the heavenly glory; so selfish men will let go their innocency, their Saviour, their God and all, rather than part with the interest of carnal self.[z]

7. And in point of honour, they are more ambitious to be well thought and spoken of, and praised themselves, both living and dead, than to have God, and truth, and goodness honoured; and they can more easily bear one that dishonoureth God, and truth, and holiness, yea, and common righteousness and honesty, than one that (though justly) dishonoureth them.

So that all the world may easily see that carnal self, and specially self-will, is the greatest idol in the world.[a]

Q. 19. But is not that a man's idol which he trusteth most? and all men are so conscious of their own insufficiency, that they cannot trust themselves for their own preservation?

A. I say not that any selfish man[b] is a perfect idolater, and giveth all God's properties to himself. He must know, whether he will or not, that he is not infinite, eternal, almighty, omniscient, self-sufficient; he knoweth he must suffer, and die. But self hath more given it that is due only to God, than any other idol hath. And though such men know their own insufficiency, yet they have so little trust in God, that they trust their own wits and the choice of their own wills, before the wisdom and choice of God; and had far rather be at their own wills and choice if they could; and indeed had rather that all things in the world were at their will and choice, than at the will and choice of God. And therefore they like not his laws and government, but make their wit, will, and lust, the governors of themselves, and as many others as they can.

Q. 20. Is there not much selfishness in all? By this you will make all men, even the best, to be idolaters. But a man cannot be saved that liveth in idolatry.

A. It is not every subdued degree of any fault that denominateth the man, but that which is predominant in him: every man hath some unbelief, some backwardness to God and goodness, some hypocrisy, pride, &c., and yet every man is not to be called an infidel, an enemy to God and goodness, a hypocrite, &c. So every man hath some idolatry and some atheism remaining, and yet is not an idolater or atheist. If a man could not be saved till he were perfectly healed of every degree of these heinous sins, no man could be saved. But God's interest is predominant in holy souls.

Q. 21. Doth not Paul say of all, save Timothy, that all seek their own, and not the things that are Jesus Christ's?

A. He meaneth not that they predominantly do so, except those among them who were hypocrites: but that all did[c] too much seek their own, and too little the things that are Jesus Christ's, and were not so self-denying as Timothy, who, as it were, naturally cared for the good of the church: as Demas forsook Paul in his suffering, and went after his own worldly business; but yet did not forsake Christ and prefer the world before him (for aught we find of him).

Q. 22. You make this first commandment to be the sum of all.

A. It is the summary of all, and our obedience to it is virtually (but not actually) our obedience to all the rest. This is it which Christ calleth the first and greatest command, "Thou shalt love the Lord thy God with all thy heart, and soul, and might." This is the foundation of all the rest of the commandments, and the root of all: the rest are but branches from it. When we are obliged to love God and obey him, we have a general obligation to keep all his commandments. But as this general command doth not put the special, particular commands in existence, so neither doth it oblige us to obey them till they exist: and then, as the genus and species

[s] Isa. ii. 22; xlii. 8; Acts xii. 22, 23; Mic. ii. 9.
[t] Rev. xvi. 9; 1 Chron. xvi. 28, 29; 1 Cor. x. 31; Gal. i. 10.
[u] Rom. xii. 3; xiv. 7; Matt. xvi. 24; xviii. 4; xxiii. 12; Mark xii. 33; Phil. ii. 4, 21.
[x] Tit. i. 7; 2 Pet. ii. 10.
[y] 1 Kings xxii. 8; 2 Chron. xviii. 7.
[z] Luke xiv. 26, 33.
[a] 2 Tim. iii. 2, 3; Prov. xxi. 4; Psalm x. 2, 4.
[b] Mark x. 24; 1 Tim. vi. 17; Psalm xx. 7; cxviii. 8; Prov. iii. 5.
[c] Jer. xlv. 4, 5; Mic. vi. 8.

constitute every defined being; so the general and special obligation concur to make up every duty. He that sincerely obeyeth this first command, is a true subject of God, and in a state of salvation, and will sincerely obey all particular commands in the main course of his life, when they are revealed to him.[d]

CHAPTER XXXV.

OF THE SECOND COMMANDMENT.

Q. 1. WHAT are the words of the second commandment?

A. "Thou shalt not make to thyself any graven image, or any likeness of any thing that is in heaven above, or that is in the earth beneath, or that is in the water under the earth: thou shalt not bow down thyself to them nor serve them. For I, the Lord thy God, am a jealous God, visiting the iniquity of the fathers upon the children unto the third and fourth generation of them that hate me, and showing mercy to thousands of them that love me, and keep my commandments."

Q. 2. How prove you against the papists, that this is not part of the first commandment?

A. 1. By the matter, which is different from it.

2. And by the Scripture, which saith there were ten, and without this there are but nine. 3. And by historical tradition, which we can prove that the papists falsify.

Q. 3. What is the true meaning of the second commandment, and wherein doth it differ from the first?

A. The first commandment bindeth us to give God his own, or his due as God, both in heart and life, and to give it to no other. The second commandeth men to keep so wide a difference between God and heathen idols, as not to worship him as the heathens do their idols, nor yet to seem by their bodily action to worship an idol, though they despise it in their thoughts, and pretend to keep their hearts to God. Corporeal, and outward, and seeming idolatry is here forbidden. For though a man renounce in heart all other gods, yet if he be seen to bow down before an image, 1. He seemeth to the beholder to mean as idolaters do, while he symbolizeth with them. And as lying and perjury with the tongue is sin, though a man's inward thoughts do own the truth, so bowing as worshippers do before an image, is idolatry, though the mind renounce all idols. And God is the God of the body as well as of the soul: and God would not have others encouraged to idolatry by so scandalous an example. 2. And if it be the true God that such profess to worship, it is interpretative blasphemy; as if they told men that God is like to that creature whose image they make. So that scandal, and bodily idolatry, and blasphemy, are the things directly forbidden in this commandment, as the real choosing and worshipping a false god is in the first.[e]

Q. 4. By this, it seems that scandal is a heinous sin?

A. Scandal is enticing, tempting, or encouraging others to sin, by doing or saying that which is like to be abused by them to such an effect; or laying a stumbling-block in the way of blind or careless souls. If they will make our necessary duty the occasion of sin, we may not therefore omit our duty, if indeed it be an indispensable duty at that time: but if it be no duty, yea, or if it be only a duty in other seasons and circumstances, it is a heinous sin to give such scandal to another, much more to multitudes or public societies.

Q. 5. Wherein lieth the evil of it?

A. 1. It is a countenancing and furthering sin.

2. It is uncharitableness and cruelty to men's souls.

3. And therefore it is the devil's work.[f]

Q. 6. But if our rulers command us to do a thing indifferent, which others will turn to an occasion of sin and damnation, must we disobey our lawful governors, to prevent men's sin and fall?

A. If the thing in its own nature tended to so great and necessary good as would weigh down the contrary evil to the scandalized, we must do our duty to help them some other way. But supposing it either indifferent or of so small benefit as will not preponderate against the sin and danger of the scandalized, we are soul-murderers if we do not forbear it. For, 1. God hath given no rulers power to destruction of souls, but to edification; no power to command us that which is so contrary to the indispensable duty of love or charity. If an apothecary, or physician, or king, command his servant to sell arsenic to all that will buy it, without exception, the servant may not lawfully sell it to such as he knoweth mean to poison themselves or others by it. If the commander be a sober man, the servant ought to suppose that he intended such exceptions, though he expressed them not. But if he expressed the contrary, he commanded contrary to God's command, without authority, and is not to be obeyed. 2. But God himself dispenseth with his own commands about rituals, or smaller matters, when greater good or hurt stands on the other side. The disciples did justly pluck and rub the ears of corn, and the priests in the temple break the rest of the sabbath, and an ox or an ass was to be watered or pulled out of a pit on that day. If the king or priest had made a law to the contrary, it had been null: if God's laws bind not in such cases, man's cannot. God bids us preach, and pray, &c. and yet to quench a fire, or save men's lives, we may or must at that time forbear preaching, or sacraments, or other public worship.[g]

Q. 7. But what if as many will be scandalized, or tempted to sin, on the other side, if I do it not?

A. No duty being a duty at all times, much less a thing indifferent, though commanded, every christian must prudently use the scales, and by all the helps of wise men that he can get, must discern which way is like to do most good or hurt, considering the persons, for number, for quality, and probability of the effect. God binds us to charity and mercy, and no man can disoblige us from that. And he that sincerely desireth to do the greatest good, and avoid the greatest hurt, and useth the best means he can to know it, shall be accepted of God, though men condemn him.[h]

Q. 8. But is nothing here forbidden but symbolizing with idolaters, in seeming to mean as they by doing as they?

A. That is it that is directly forbidden. But by consequence it is implied that all doctrines are forbidden that falsely represent God, and all worship or acts pretended to be religious, which are unsuitable

[d] Hos. ix. 1, 2; iv. 6; xii. 2.

[e] Deut. iv. 16, 17; vii. 5; xvi. 22; Lev. xxvi. 1, 2; Dan iii.; Isa. xl. 18, 25; xlvi. 5.

[f] Matt. xviii. 6—9, &c.; xiii. 41; 1 Cor. viii. 13; Lev. xix. 14; Ezek. xiv. 3, 4, 7; Rom. xiv. 13; Rev. ii. 14.

[g] Rom. xiv. 15, 17, 20; 2 Cor. x. 8; xiii. 10.

[h] 1 Cor. x. 33; vi. 12, 13; ix. 22; xiv. 26.

to God's holy nature, attributes, will, or word, as being profanation, and an offering to God that which is unclean.[i]

Q. 9. What is the command which is here implied?

A. That we keep our souls chaste from all outward and seeming idolatry; and that we worship him who is the infinite, almighty, holy Spirit, with reverence, holiness, in spirit and truth, according to his blessed, perfect nature, and his holy will and word.[k]

Q. 10. Hath God given us a law for all things in his worship?

A. The law of nature is God's law, and obligeth man to that devotion to God and worship of him which is called natural: and the sacred Scripture prescribeth both that and also all those positive means or ordinances of God's worship, which are made necessary to the universal church on earth: and as for the mere accidents of worship, which are not proper parts, as time, place, words, methods, gesture, vesture, &c. God's laws give us general precepts, only telling us how to order them, leaving it to human prudence, and church guides, to order them according to those general rules.

Q. 11. Is all use of images unlawful?

A. God did so much hate idolatry, and the neighbourhood of idolaters made it so dangerous to the Israelites, that he did not only forbid the worshipping of images, but all such making or using of them as might become a snare or temptation to any. So that though it be lawful to make images for civil uses, and, when they are made, to fetch holy thoughts or meditations from them, as from all other creatures or things in the world; yet, in any case when they become a snare or danger, being not necessary things, they become a sin to those that so use them as a snare to others or themselves.[l]

Q. 12. Is it lawful to make any picture of God?

A. No; for pictures are the signs of corporeal things, and it is blasphemy to think God like a bodily substance: but it is lawful to make such pictures, (as of a glorious light,) from which occasion may be taken of good thoughts concerning God.[m]

Q. 13. Is it lawful to make the picture of Christ as man, or as crucified?

A. The doing it as such is not forbidden, nor the right use of it when done: but the abuse, that is, the worshipping of it, or of Christ by it, is forbidden, and the making or using such, when it tendeth to such abuse, and hath more of snare than profit.

Q. 14. Why is God's jealousy here mentioned?

A. To make us know that God doth so strictly require the great duty of worshipping him as the true God, and hate the sin of idolatry, or giving his glory to another, or blaspheming him, as if he were like to painted things, that he would have us accordingly affected.

Q. 15. Why doth God threaten to visit the iniquities of the fathers on the children, in this command, rather than in the rest?

A. God hath blessings and curses for societies, as well as for individual persons; and societies are constituted and known by the symbols of public profession. And as God's public worship is the symbol of his church which he will bless, so idolatrous worship is the symbol of the societies which he will curse and punish: and it was especially needful that the Israelites should know this, who could never else have been excused from the guilt of murdering man, woman, and child, of all the nations which they conquered, had not God taken it on himself as judging them to death for their idolatry and other crimes, and making the Israelites his executioners.[n]

Q. 16. But doth not God disclaim punishing the children for the fathers' sins, and say the soul that sinneth shall die?

A. Yes; when the children are either wholly innocent of that sin, or else are pardoned through Christ upon their true repentance, and hating and renouncing their fathers' sins; but not else.

Q. 17. Are any children guilty of their parents' sins?

A. Yes; all children are guilty of the sins which their parents committed before their birth, while they were in their loins. Not with the same degree and sort of guilt as the parents are, but yet with so much as exposeth them to just penalties.

Q. 18. How prove you that?

A. First by the nature of the case; for though we were not personally existent in them when they sinned, we were seminally existent in them, which is more than causally or virtually; and it was that semen which was guilty in them, that was after made a person, and so that person must have the same guilt. 2. From the whole history of the Scripture, which tells of the children of Cain, the old world, Sodom, Ham, the Canaanites, Saul, David, (as an adulterer,) Achan, Gehazi, and others, punished for their parents' sins, and the Jews cast off and cursed on that account to this day. 3. And our common, original sin from Adam proveth it.

Q. 19. But our original sin from Adam had another cause; God decreeing that Adam should stand or fall for all his posterity?

A. We must not add to God's word, much less blaspheme him, as if it were God himself that, by a decree or covenant, made all the world sinners, save Adam and Eve. If Adam had not sinned, it would not have saved all or any of his posterity unless they also had continued innocent themselves. Nor did God make any promise to continue and keep innocent all Adam's posterity, in case he sinned not. We sinned in Adam, because we were seminally in him, and so are our children in us; and who can bring a clean thing out of an unclean, if it were essentially in it?

Q. 20. If we are guilty of all nearer parents' sin, will not our guilt increase to the end of the world, and the last man have the greatest guilt?[o]

A. 1. No; because all guilt from Adam, and from our nearer parents too, is pardoned by Christ, when we were baptized as sincere believers, or their seed. But it is true that we are so far more guilty as to have the more need of a Saviour's grace. 2. And guilt is considerable, either as more obligations to the same punishment, or as obligation to more or greater punishment. It is true that impenitent persons, who are the seed of a line of wicked ancestors, have more obligations to the same punishment, but not obligation to greater punishment; because as great as they were capable of was due before.

Q. 21. But many say that for nearer parents' sins no punishments but temporal are due?

A. 1. If any at all are due, it proveth an answerable guilt. 2. To say that Adam's sin deserveth our spiritual and eternal punishment, and all other parents' sin only temporal, is to speak without and against Scripture, and the nature of the case. The

[i] Psal. l. 21—23.

[k] 1 John v. 21; 2 Cor. vi. 16; 1 Cor. viii. 10, 11; x. 19, 20, 27, 28; Rev. ii. 14, 20; Isa. ii. 18.

[l] Exod. xxxiv. 13—15; Numb. xxxiii. 52; Deut. vii. 5; 2 Kings xi. 18; xxiii. 14, 24.

[m] Exod. xxv. 18—20; 1 Sam. iv. 4; Psal. xviii. 1; Ezek. x. 2.

[n] Jer. x. 25; Deut. ii. 34; iii. 6; iv. 26; vii. 2, 23, 24; xii. 2, 3; xx. 17, 20; Numb. xxxiii. 50—52.

[o] On this I have written a peculiar Treatise of Original Sin.

case of the seed of the old world, the Sodomites, the Canaanites, and the present heathens, speaks much more. 3. It is clear that nearer parents' sin is a cause that many of their posterity are more sinful, in lust, pride, fornication, heresy, and ignorance, than others: and sin, as well as grace, hath a tendency to perpetuity, if not cured and remitted.

Q. 22. Why doth God name only the third and fourth generation?

A. To show us, that though he will punish the sins of his enemies on their posterity who imitate their parents, yet he sets such bounds to the execution of his justice, as that sinners shall not want encouragement to repent and hope for mercy.

Q. 23. Who be they that be called here haters of God?

A. All that have a predominant hatred to his servants, his service, and his holy laws. But the text specially meaneth those societies of infidels, heathens, and malignants, who are the professed enemies of his church and worship. As I said before, the outward symbols of idolatry were the professing signs by which his church's enemies were openly noted in the world; as baptism and the Lord's supper were the badges of his church and servants.[p]

Q. 24. What is the meaning and extent of the promise of mercy to thousands of them that love him and keep his commandments?

A. 1. As to the subject, it must be noted, that such a belief in God as causeth men to love him and keep his commandments, is the qualification of them that have the promise of God's saving mercy: faith working by love and obedience.

2. The words signify God's wonderful mercy, and his delight to do good to those that are qualified to receive it.

3. And they signify, that God will not only love and bless a godly offspring for their own sake, but also for the sake of their godly ancestors; and while they succeed them in true piety, God will increase his blessings on them.

4. And though those forfeit all, that prove ungodly when they come to age, yet the infant seed of the faithful, while such, are in covenant with God, on the account of their relation to those godly parents who dedicate themselves and theirs to him.

Q. 25. How doth God perform this promise, when many godly parents have wicked and miserable children?

A. This promise doth not say that God will keep all the children of the faithful from sinning against him, and casting away his mercy and salvation. But if men be sincerely godly, and dedicate themselves and their children to God, and enter them into his covenant, and perform their own part promised by them, God will accept them into his family, and pardon their original sin, and give them the necessary helps for their personal faith and obedience when they come to the use of reason.[q] And if the children keep their covenant according to their capacity, and do not violate it, and reject his grace, God will accept and save them, as actual, obedient believers.

Q. 26. Will he not do so also by the children of unbelievers?

A. If such at age see their parents' sin, and forsake it, and devote themselves to God, he will accept them. But as infidels and wicked hypocrites have no promise of God's acceptance of them and theirs, so such do not dedicate themselves and their children to God; he that will devote his child to God, must do it, as it were a part of himself; and cannot do it sincerely if he first devote not himself to God.

Q. 27. But may not others do it for his children?

A. In infancy they are considered in the covenant of grace but as infants, that is, appurtenances to another. As the infidels' infants they have neither capacity nor promise; but if any other adopt them, and take them truly as their own, I am in hope that God accepteth such so devoted to him.

CHAPTER XXXVI.

OF THE THIRD COMMANDMENT.

Q. 1. WHAT are the words of the third commandment?

A. "Thou shalt not take the name of the Lord thy God in vain, for the Lord will not hold him guiltless that taketh his name in vain."

Q. 2. What is it that is specially here forbidden?

A. Profaneness; that is, the unholy using of God's holy name, and holy things; especially by perjury, or any other entitling him to falsehood, or to any of the sins of men, as if he were the author or approver of them.

Q. 3. What is meant by the name of God?

A. Those words, or other signs, by which he is described, denominated, or otherwise notified to man; which I opened so fully on the first petition of the Lord's prayer, that to avoid repetition I must refer you thereto.

Q. 4. What is meant by taking the name of God in vain?

A. Using it profanely, and specially falsely. It is contrary to the hallowing of God's name, which is mentioned in the Lord's prayer.

In the Scripture, 1. The creature is called vanity, as being but a shadow, and untrusty thing; and to use God's name and holy things in a common manner, as we use the creature's, is to profane his name, and take it vainly.

2. And falsehood and lies are usually called vanity; for vanity is that shadowyness which seemeth something and is nothing, and so deceiveth men. A lie is that which deceiveth him that trusteth it: so idols are called vanity and lies, for their falsehood and deceit; and all men are said to be liars, that is, untrusty and deceitful.

Q. 5. What is an oath?

A. I have said heretofore, as others, that it is but an appeal to God as the witness of the truth, and the avenger of a lie; but, on further thoughts, I find that the common nature of an oath is to pawn some greater thing in attesting of the truth of our words; or to take some grievous thing on ourselves as a penalty if we lie; or to make some certain truth a pledge of the truth of what we say. And to swear by our faith, or truth, or honesty, by the temple, the altar, the fire, the sun, is as much as to say, If this be not true, then I have no faith, truth, honesty; there is no temple, altar, fire, sun: or, Let me be taken for one that denieth that I have any faith, that there is any sun, fire, &c.: or, It is as true as that this is fire, sun, &c. So to swear by God is to say, It is as true as that there is a God, or as God liveth, &c.; or, If I lie, take me for one that denieth God to be God; and consequently it is an appeal to him as the

[p] Deut. xxxii. 41; Psalm lxxxi. 15; Rom. i. 30; Luke xix. 27.

[q] Prov. xx. 7; Psalm xxxvii. 28, 29; Matt. xix. 13, 14; Acts ii. 39; 1 Cor. vii. 14; Isa. xlv. 25; lxv. 23; Mal. ii. 15; Rom. iv. 16; ix. 8.

Avenger: so, By the life of Pharaoh, was, As true as Pharaoh liveth: or, Else take me for one that denieth the life of Pharaoh. So that there is somewhat of an imprecation, or self-reproach, as the penalty of a lie, in every oath, but more dreadfully of divine revenge when we swear by God, and of idolatry when men swear by an idol, as if it were a god.

Q. 6. Which be the chief ways of taking God's name in vain?

A. 1. Fathering on him false doctrine, revelations, or laws; saying as false prophets, God sent me, and, Thus saith the Lord, when it is false; saying, This doctrine, or this prophecy, God's Spirit revealed to me, when it is not so. Therefore all christians must be very fearful of false revelations and prophecies, and see that they believe not every spirit, nor pretend to revelations; and to take heed of taking the suggestions of Satan, or their crazed, melancholy fancies, for the revelations of God.

2. So also gathering false doctrines out of Scripture by false expositions, and fathering these on God. And therefore all men should, in dark and doubtful cases, rather suspend their judgments till they have overcome their doubts by solid evidence, than rashly to conclude, and confidently and fiercely dispute for error. It is a great profanation to father lies on God, who is the hater of them, when lying is the devil's work and character.

3. The same I may say of a rash and false interpretation of God's providences.

4. And also of fathering false laws on God, and saying that he either commandeth or forbiddeth what he doth not; to make sins and duties which God never made, and say he made them, is to father falsehood on him, and corrupt his government.

5. Another way is by false worship. 1. If men say that God commanded such worship, which he commanded not, it is the sin last mentioned. 2. If they worship him with their own inventions without his command, (particular or general,) they profane his name, by offering him that which is unholy, common, and unclean.

6. Another way is by false pretending that God gave them that authority which he never gave them; like counterfeiting a commission from the king. If princes should pretend that God gave them authority to oppose his truth, to persecute godliness, unjustly to silence faithful ministers of Christ, to raise unnecessary wars, to oppress the innocent; this were a heinous taking of God's name in vain. If priests shall pretend that God gave them authority to make themselves pastors of the flocks that are unwilling of them, without a just call, or to make laws for any that are not rightfully their subjects, and to impose their dictates, words, and forms, and unnecessary inventions, as conditions of ministration or communion, without true right, and to make themselves the rule of other men's words and actions by usurpation; this is all taking God's name in vain. And so it is, if they preach false doctrine in his name, and if they pronounce false excommunications and absolutions, and justify the wicked, and condemn, reproach, and slander the just, and brand unjustly the servants of Christ as hypocrites, schismatics, or heretics, and this as by ministerial power from Christ: especially if they silence Christ's ministers, impose wolves or incompetent men, scatter the flocks, and suppress serious godliness, and all this in the name of Christ. Much more if any pretend, as the pope or his pretended general councils, to be Christ's vicar-general, or head, or supreme, unifying governor over all the church on earth, and to make laws for the whole church: or if they corrupt God's worship with imposed superstitions, falsehood, or profanations, and say God hath authorized them to do this; it is heinous profaning God's name by a lie: such doing brought up the proverb, *In nomine Domini incipit omne malum:* when all their abuses began with, "In the name of God, Amen."

And they that make new church forms which God made not, either papal, universal aristocracy, patriarchal, and such like, and either pretend that God made them, or gave them, or such other, power to make them, must prove what they say, lest they profane God's name by falsehood.

But the highest profanation is, when they pretend that God hath made them absolute governors, and set them so far above his own laws, and judgment, and himself, as that whatever they say is the word of God, or the sense of the Scripture, though never so falsely, must be taken for such by all; and whatever they command or forbid, they must be obeyed, though God's word command or forbid the contrary; and that God hath given power (to popes or councils) to forbid men the worship which God commandeth; yea, to interdict whole kingdoms, and excommunicate and depose kings; and that from these, as a supreme power, no man must appeal to the Scripture, or to God and his final judgment. This is, by profane lying, to use God's name to the destroying of souls, the church, and the laws and government of God himself.[a]

7. Another way of taking God's name in vain is, by heresies; that is, imbodying in separated parties or churches, against the church and truth of God, for the propagating of some dangerous false doctrine which they father on God, and so militate in his name against his church. If men, as aforesaid, do but promote false doctrine in the church without separation, it is bad; but to gather an army against the truth and church, and feign Christ to be the leader of it, is worse.[b]

8. Another way is by perjury, appealing to God, or abusing his name, as the witness and owner of a lie.

9. Another way is by false vows made to God himself. When men either vow to God to do that which he abhorreth, or hath forbidden; or when they vow that which is good, with a false, deceitful heart, and, as Ananias and Sapphira, with false reserves; or when they vow and pay not, but wilfully break the vows which they have made. The breach of covenants between princes, or between them and subjects, or between husband and wife, confirmed by appeal to God, is a dreadful sin; but the violation of the great baptismal vow in which we are all solemnly devoted and obliged to God, is one of the heinousest sins in the world. When it is not about a lesser duty, but even our oath of allegiance to God, by solemn vow taking him for our God, our Saviour, and Sanctifier, and giving up ourselves to him accordingly, renouncing the contrary, and laying on this covenant all our hopes of grace and glory, pardon and salvation, what can be more heinous than to be false to such a vow and covenant?[c]

10. And hypocrisy itself is a heinous taking God's name in vain. When we offer God the dead carcass of religious acts without the life and soul, and present him with ceremony, self-exalting pomp, mere heartless words, an artificial image of religion, that hath not the spiritual nature, life, or serious desire of the heart; this is seeking to mock God, or making

[a] Jer. xiv. 14; xxiii. 32; xxxvii. 14; Mark xiii. 22; 2 Cor xi. 13; 2 Pet. ii. 1; Jer. xxvii. 15; xxix. 9, 10, 31; 1 John iv. 1, 2.

[b] Acts xx. 30; Rom. xvi. 16, 17; Eph. iv. 14.

[c] Jer. iv. 2; v. 2; vii. 9; xxiii. 10; Mal. iii. 5; Psalm xv. 4; Zech. v. 3, 4; Hos. iv. 2; x. 4.

him like an idol that seeth not the heart, and knows not what is offered him. Alas! how much of the preaching, hearing, praying, and sacraments of many is a taking God's name in vain, as if he did accept a lie!

11. Another way of this profanation is making God's name and acts of religion an engagement to wickedness: as when men bind themselves to treason, murder, or any sin, by taking the sacrament. As many, alas! (which I unwillingly name,) have done in a blind zeal for the Roman usurpation, being told, that it pleaseth God and Saint Peter, and meriteth salvation, to destroy the enemies of the church, that is, of the pope and his clergy. And those that bound themselves with an oath to kill Paul, thought God accepted the oath indeed. And the general council at Lateran, under Innocent III. which bound temporal lords to take an oath to exterminate such as they called heretics, fathered the work on God by that oath. And the pope and council of Trent, which hath brought in on all the clergy a new oath to many new and sinful things, by that oath make God the approver of all. And the Mahometans, that give liberty of religion, yet think it pleaseth God and meriteth heaven, to kill the enemies of Mahomet. And Christ saith, "They that kill you, shall think they do God good service." And is it not profaning the name of God, to make him the author of the murder of his servants?

12. Another way of taking God's name profanely, and pleading it for vanity and lies, is by making God the determining first cause of all the acts of men in the world, as specified by their objects and circumstances; that is, of all the lies, and all the other sins that are done in the world: as if God had given no such free-will to men or devils, by which they can lie, murder, hate God, or commit any sin, till God move their wills, tongues, and hands to do it, by an unavoidable, predetermining efficacy. This is so much to profane and take in vain God's name, as that it maketh him the chief cause of all the devil's works.

13. Another way of vain abuse, and profanation of God's name, is by blasphemy, and contempt, and scorn of God, or of the word or ways of God: and, alas! who would think that this should be so common among men, when even the devils believe and tremble! I hope posterity will account it so odious as hardly to believe that ever there were men, and so many men, even in England, who used to deride the name, word, providence, and worship of God, and make serious regard of God and religion the common scorn; and familiarly to wish, by way of imprecation, as a by-word, "God damn me," and to swear by the name, the wounds, and blood of God.

14. Lastly, another way of taking God's name in vain, is by an unholy, irreverent tossing of it in common talk, in jest, and on every ludicrous occasion. Plays and play books use it; it is made an ordinary accident to all common and profane discourse; beggars profanely beg by it; children cry by it; O God, and O Lord, is become an interjection.

Q. 7. Why do we take ordinary, light swearing, specially by God, or by sacred things, to be a sure sign of a wicked man?

A. Because it showeth a predominant habit of profaneness; that the man liveth without the reverence of God's holiness, majesty, knowledge, and presence, and is hardened into a senselessness or contempt of God, and of his dreadful judgment, as if he derided God, or dared him; or as if he did believe that there is no God that heareth him. To live in the fear of God, and subjection to his government, is the property of every godly man.

Q. 8. What is meant by the words, "The Lord will not hold him guiltless?"

A. God will not leave him unpunished, nor account this as a small offence: he himself will be revenged for this sin.

Q. 9. Why is this threatening annexed more to this commandment than to others?

A. Because this sin is, 1. An immediate injury to God; while it expressly fathereth lies and other sin on him, it doth, as we may say, engage him to vindicate himself. When rulers or usurpers pretend that God authorizeth them to do mischief, and fight against himself; when persecutors and corrupters of religion pretend God's interest and will for all, that it is for order, unity, government, and obedience for the church, that they corrupt, destroy, silence, and tyrannize; they invite God to cast the lie and cruelty back on them, which they would father upon him, and to turn their canons, prisons, and inquisitions, and other devilish plagues of the world, upon the author, in disowning them himself.

2. And they that by perjury, hypocrisy, false doctrine, and the rest of the forementioned sins, do appeal to God, and make him openly the author of all, do thereby, as it were, summon God to revenge. As they said to Paul, "Hast thou appealed to Cæsar? to Cæsar shalt thou go:" so it may be said to the perjured, the hypocrite, the usurper, the false judge, &c. Hast thou appealed to God, and do you father on him your lies, cruelties, tyrannies, and usurpations, and false doctrines? to God shall you go, who will undertake the cause which you cast upon him, and will judge the secrets of men's hearts, as he did Ananias and Sapphira's. If men sin under the laws of men, God requireth magistrates to judge them: but if they appeal to God, or, by falsehood, escape the judgment of man, they more immediately cast themselves on the justice of God: and it is a fearful thing to fall into his hands who is a consuming fire: God is the avenger especially on such.[d]

Q. 10. Is it meant of God's vengeance in this life, or in the next?

A. In both: usually profanation of God's name and holy things, especially by perjury, and by fathering cruelty and wickedness on God, is more notably punished by him in this life. Though such may seem to prosper for a while, God usually overtaketh them here, and their sins do find them out: but if they escape such bodily punishment here they are usually more dreadfully forsaken of grace than other men, and heap up wrath against the day of wrath.

I will only add, in the conclusion, that even true christians should take great care lest their very thoughts of God, and their prayers and speaking of him, should be customary and dead, and like their thoughts and talk of common things, and in some degree of taking of God's name in vain.

CHAPTER XXXVII.

OF THE FOURTH COMMANDMENT.

Q. 1. WHAT are the words of the fourth commandment?

A. "Remember the sabbath day, to keep it holy. Six days shalt thou labour, and do all thy work: but

[d] Deut. xxxii. 43; 1 Thess. iv. 6; Rom. xii. 19; Heb. x. 30; xii. 29; Isa. xxxv. 4; xlvii. 3; lxi. 2; lxiii. 4; i. 24; Luke xviii. 7, 8.

the seventh day is the sabbath of the Lord thy God; in it thou shalt not do any work, thou, nor thy son, nor thy daughter, thy man-servant, nor thy maid-servant, nor thy cattle, nor thy stranger that is within thy gates: for in six days the Lord made heaven and earth, the sea, and all that in them is, and rested the seventh day: wherefore the Lord blessed the sabbath day, and hallowed it."[a]

Q. 2. Why doth Deut. v. repeat it in so different words?

A. Because the words are but for the sense, and they being kept in the ark as written in stone, and safe from alteration, Moses, in Deut. v. gave them the sense, and added some of his own explication; and nothing is altered to obscure the sense.[b]

Q. 3. Which day is it which was called the sabbath in this commandment?

A. The seventh, commonly called, from the heathen custom, Saturday.

Q. 4. Why was that day made the sabbath?

A. God having made the world in six days' space, seeing all good, and very good, rested in his own complacency; and appointed the seventh day every week to be separated as holy, to worship and praise him the great Creator, as his glorious perfections shine forth in his works.

Q. 5. What is meant by God's resting from his work?

A. Not that he had been at any labour or weariness therein; but, 1. That he finished the creation. 2. That he was pleased in it as good. 3. And that he would have it be a day of holy, pleasant rest to man.

Q. 6. What is meant by keeping holy the sabbath day?

A. Separating it to the holy worship and praise of the Creator, and resting to that end from unnecessary, bodily labour.

Q. 7. What doth the word "remember" signify?

A. 1. First, it is an awakening *caveat*, to bid us take special care that we break not this commandment. 2. And then that we must prepare, before it comes, to avoid the things that would hinder us in the duty, and to be fit for its performance.

Q. 8. Why is "remember" put before this more than before the rest of the commandments?

A. Because, 1. Being but of positive institution, and not naturally known to man, as other duties are, they had need of a positive excitation and remembrance. And, 2. It is of great importance to the constant and acceptable worship, and the avoiding of impediments, to keep close to the due time which God hath appointed for it: and to violate it, tendeth to atheistical ungodliness.

Q. 9. Why is it called "the sabbath of the Lord thy God?"

A. Because, 1. God did institute and separate it. 2. And it is separated to the honour and worship of God.

Q. 10. When and how did God institute and separate it?

A. Fundamentally by his own resting from the work of creation: but immediately by his declaring to Adam his will for the sanctifying of that day, which is expressed Gen. ii. 3.

Q. 11. Some think that the sabbath was not instituted till man had sinned, and Christ was promised, and so God rested in Christ?

A. When the text adjoineth it close to the creation, and giveth that only as the reason of it, (that God ended his works which he had made, and rested from them,) this is human, corrupting presumption.

[a] Exod. xx. 10, 11; xxxi. 17; Heb. iv. 4. [b] Gen. ii. 2, 3.
[c] 1 Thess. iv. 11; 2 Thess. iii. 10—12; Prov. xviii. 9; Matt. xxv. 26; Rom. xii. 11.

Q. 12. But some think the sabbath was first instituted in the wilderness, when they were forbid to gather manna?

A. It is not there mentioned as newly instituted, and it is mentioned Gen. ii. 2, 3, and then instituted with the reason of it: "And God blessed the seventh day, and sanctified it, because in it he rested from all his works which God created and made." And the same reason is repeated in the fourth commandment.

Q. 13. Is this commandment of the law of nature as are the rest?

A. It was more of the law of nature to Adam than to us; his nature knowing otherwise than ours, both when God ended his works, and how beautiful they were before the curse. It is now of the law of nature, (that is, known by natural light without other revelation,) 1. That God should be worshipped. 2. That societies should assemble to do it together. 3. That some set time should be separated, statedly, to that use. 4. That it should be done with the whole heart, without worldly diversions or distractions.

But I know nothing in nature alone from whence a man can prove that, 1. It must be either just one day in seven. 2. Or, just what day of the seven it must be. 3. Nor just what degree of rest is necessary. Though reason may discern that one day in seven is a very convenient proportion.

Q. 14. Are the words "Six days shalt thou labour," &c. a command, or only a license?

A. They are not only a license, but a command to man,[c] to live in an ordinary calling, or lawful course of labour, according to each one's ability and place, and diligently to exercise it, and not spend time in idleness: and the ordinary time is here assigned thereto.

Q. 15. Then how can it be lawful to spend any of the week days in religious exercises, any more than to spend any part of the sabbath day in labour?

A. All labours are to be done as the service of God, and as a means to holy and everlasting ends; and therefore it is implied still that God be sought, and remembered, and honoured in all; as our eating and drinking is our duty, but to be done to the glory of God, and therefore with the seeking of his blessing, and returning him our thanks.[d]

Q. 16. But is it lawful, then, to separate whole days either weekly, or monthly, or yearly, to religious exercises, when God hath commanded us to labour on them?

A. As God's command of resting on the sabbath is but the stating of the ordinary time, supposing an exception of extraordinary cases; (as in time of war, of fire, of dispersing plagues, of hot persecution, &c.; as circumcision was omitted in the wilderness forty years;) so this command to labour six days doth state our ordinary time, but with supposed exception of extraordinary occasions for days of humiliation and thanksgiving. And all God's commands suppose that when two duties meet together, and cannot both be then done, the greater must ever be preferred: and therefore saving the life of a man, or a beast, yea, feeding and watering beasts, labouring in temple service, &c. were to be preferred before the rest of the sabbath: and so when our necessity or profit make religious exercises more to our good, and so a greater duty, (as lectures, fasts, &c.) we must prefer them to our ordinary labour. For as the sabbath was made for man, and not man for the sabbath, so were the other days.[e]

[d] Prov. xxxi. 27; Ezek. xvi. 41; 1 Tim. v. 13; Matt. xx. 6.
[e] Esth. ix. 26, 28, 31

Q. 17. May not rich men, that have no need, forbear the six days' labour?

A. No; if they are able. It is part of God's service, and riches are his gift: and to whom he giveth much, from them he expecteth not less, but more. Shall servants work less because they have more wages? It is not only for their own supplies that God commandeth men to labour, but also for the public good, and the benefit or relief of others, and the health of their bodies, and the suitable employment of their minds, and that none of their short, precious time be lost in sinful idleness.[f]

Q. 18. But it will seem sordid for lords, and knights, and ladies to labour?

A. It is swinish and sinful not to labour; but they must do it in works that are suitable to their places. As physicians, schoolmasters, and church ministers labour not in the same kind of employment as ploughmen and tradesmen do; so magistrates have their proper labour in government, and rich persons have families, children, and servants to oversee, their poor neighbours and tenants to visit, encourage, and relieve, and their equals so to converse with as tendeth to the greatest good; but none must live idly.[g]

Q. 19. Was rest on the sabbath absolutely commanded?

A. It was always a duty to break it, when a greater duty came in which required it, as Christ hath told the Pharisees, in the case of feeding man or beast, healing the sick, and doing such necessary good; for God preferreth morals before rituals; and his rule is, "I will have mercy, and not sacrifice."[h]

Q. 20. Why, then, was bodily rest commanded?

A. That body and mind might be free from diversion, weariness, and distraction, and fit with pleasure wholly to serve God in the religious duties of his worship.

Q. 21. Why doth God mention not only servants but beasts?

A. As he would not have servants enslaved and abused by such labour as should unfit them for sabbath work and comfort, so he would have man exercise the clemency of his nature, even towards the brutes; and beasts cannot labour, but man will be put to some labour or diversion by it: and God would have the whole place where we dwell, and all that we have to do with, to bear an open signification of our obedience to his command, and our reverence to his sanctified day and worship.

Q. 22. Is this commandment now in force to christians?

A. So much of it materially is in force as is of the law of nature, or of Christ by supernatural revelation, and no more. Therefore the seventh-day sabbath of corporal rest is changed by Christ into the Lord's day, appointed for christian worship.

Q. 23. Was not all that was written in stone of perpetual obligation?

A. No; nor any as such; for as it was written on those stones it was the law of Moses for the Jews, and bound no other nations, and is done away by the dissolving of their republic, and by Christ.

Q. 24. How prove you all this?

A. 1. As Moses was ruler, or mediator, to none but the Jews, the words of the decalogue are appropriate to them as redeemed from Egyptian bondage; so the tables were delivered to no other, and a law cannot bind any without promulgation. All the world was not bound to send to the Jews for revelation, nor to be their proselytes.

2. The Scripture expressly affirmeth the change, 2 Cor. iii. 3, 7, 11, "If the ministration of death written and engraven in stones was glorious, so that the children of Israel could not stedfastly behold the face of Moses for the glory of his countenance, which was to be (or is) done away," &c. "For if that which is done away was glorious, (or, by glory,) much more that which remaineth is glorious (or, in glory)." Here it is evident that it is the law written on stone that is mentioned, and that it is not, as some say, the glory only of Moses' face, or the flaming mount, which is done away, for that was done away in a few days; but it is the law, which is called "glorious," that is said to be done away. The words can bear no other sense. It is too tedious to cite all. The texts following fully prove it; Heb. vii. 11, 12, 18; ix. 18, 19; Eph. ii. 15; John i. 17; Luke xvi. 16; Rom. ii. 12, 14—16; iii. 19—21, 27, 28, 31; iv. 13—16; v. 13, 20; vii. 4—8, 16; ix. 4, 31, 32; x. 5; Gal. ii. 15, 16, 19, 21; iii. 2, 10—13, 19, 21, 24; iv. 21; v. 3, 4, 14, 23; vi. 13; Phil. iii. 6, 9; 1 Cor. ix. 21.

3. And the sabbath itself is expressly said to be ceased with the rest; "Let no man judge you in meat or in drink, or in respect of an holy day, (or feast,) or of the new moon, or of the sabbaths, which are a shadow of things to come; but the body is of Christ," Col. ii. 16. It was the weekly sabbath that was the chief of sabbaths, and therefore included in the plural name, there being no exception of it.

4. And to put all out of doubt, Christ (who commandeth not two weekly sabbaths) hath appointed and sanctified the first day of the week, instead of the seventh day, sabbath; not calling it the sabbath, but the Lord's day.

Q. 25. How prove you that?

A. If you will search the Scripture, you shall see it proved by these degrees. I. Christ commissioned his apostles to teach the churches all his doctrines, commands, and orders, and so to settle and guide them; Luke vi. 13; x. 16; Matt. x. 40; xvi. 19; xxviii. 18—20; John xiii. 16, 20; xvii. 18; xx. 21; xxi. 15—17; Acts i. 2, 24, 25; ii. 42; x. 5; xxvi. 17; 1 Cor. iv. 1, 2; xi. 23; xii. 28, 29; xv. 3; Gal. i. 1, 11, 12; Eph. ii. 20; iv. 11—16; 2 Pet. iii. 2.

II. Christ promised his Spirit to them, to enable them to perform their commission, and lead them into all truth, and to bring them all to their remembrance, and to guide them as his church's guides, and so as the promulgators of his commands. For this see Jer. iii. 15; Isa. xliv. 3; Joel ii. 28, 29, &c.; Luke xxiv. 49; John xv. 26, 27; xvi. 7, 12—15; xvii. 18; Matt. xxviii. 20; Acts i. 4, 8.

III. Christ performed this, and gave them the infallible Spirit accordingly to perform their commissioned work. See Heb. x. 23; Tit. i. 2; 1 John v. 10; John xx. 22; Acts ii.; xv. 28; Heb. ii. 4; 1 Pet. i. 12; Rom. xv. 19, 20, &c.

IV. Christ himself laid the foundation, by rising that day (as God did of the sabbath by ceasing from his work). He appeared to his disciples congregate on that day; he sent down the Holy Ghost (his agent, and the perfecter of his work) on that day: the apostles settled that day as the stated time for constant church assemblies and communion; and all the churches in the world have constantly called it the Lord's day, and kept it as thus appointed, and used by the apostles, from their days till now with one consent. And because I must not here write a volume on this point, instead of a catechism; he that doubteth may see all this fully proved in my book, called "The Divine Appointment of the Lord's Day," and in Dr. Young's book, called "The Lord's Day Vindicated."

[f] See Prov. xxxi. 27, &c.

[g] Ezek. xvi. 49.

[h] Matt. xii. 5; Mark ii. 27, 28; Luke xiii. 15.

Q. 26. Is rest as necessary now as under Moses' law?

A. It was then commanded, both as a means to the holy work of the day, and also as a ceremony which was made a duty in itself, as a shadow of the christian rest. In the first respect, we are as much (or more) obliged to forbear labour, even so far as it hindereth holy work, as they were then; but not in the second respect.[i]

Q. 27. When doth the Lord's day begin and end?

A. It is safest to judge of that according to the common estimation of your country, of the measure of all other days: remembering that it is not now, as the Jewish sabbath, to be kept as a ceremony, but as the season of holy works. As therefore you allow on other days a stated proportion of twenty-four hours for labour, and the rest for sleep or rest, do so by the Lord's day, and you need not further be scrupulous as to the time.

But remember, 1. That you avoid scandal. 2. That even the sabbath (and so the Lord's day) was made for man, and Christ is the Lord of it, who will have the greatest works preferred.

Q. 28. Doth not Paul tell us that all days are alike, and we must not judge one another for days? Why then should christians make a difference, and not serve God equally every day?

A. Paul tells you that Christ hath taken away the Jewish ceremonial difference of days; for neglect of which none is to be judged: but it followeth not that Christ hath made no difference himself, and hath not stated a day for christian work in communion above the rest. One hour of the day doth not in itself now differ from another. And yet every wise master of a family will keep the order of stated hours, for dinner and for prayer. And so will a congregation for lectures, and other ordinary occasions. I told you in the beginning, that the light and law of nature tells us, that God's public worship should have a stated day; in which, as free from diversions and distractions, we should wholly apply ourselves thereto. And that all the christians in the world assemble for the same work on the same day, hath much of laudable concord, harmony, and mutual help. And therefore it concerned him who only is the King and Lawgiver to the universal church, to make them a law for the determination of the day, which he hath done.

Q. 29. But is it not more spiritual to make every day a sabbath?

A. It is most christian-like to obey Christ our King. Thus the same men pretend to make every meal a sacrament, that they may break the law of Christ, who instituted the sacrament. Satan's way of drawing men from Christ's laws, is sometimes by pretending to do more and better. But to keep every day a sabbath, is to keep none. It is not lawful to cast off our outward labour all the six days: nor can mind or body bear it to do nothing but religious worship. These men mean no more but to follow their earthly business with a spiritual mind, and at some seasons of the day to worship God solemnly: and this is but what every good christian should do every day. But who knoweth not that the mind may, with far more advantage, attend God's instructions, and be raised to him in holy worship, when all worldly diverting businesses are laid by, and the whole man employed towards God alone?

If men will regard, 1. The experience of their own souls; 2. And of all others in the world; they might soon be resolved how mischievous a thing the neglect of the Lord's day is, and how necessary its holy observation. 1. That man never knew what it is to attend God's worship seriously, and therein to receive his special blessing, who hath not found the great advantage of our separation from all common business, to attend holy work only on the Lord's day. He that feeleth no miss or loss of it, sure never knew what communion with God is. 2. And servants would be left remediless under such masters, as would both oppress them with labour, and restrain them from God's service. It is therefore the great mercy of the universal King to secure the liberties of the servants, and to bind all men to the means of their own felicity.

3. And common reason will tell us, that a law, obliging all men to spend one day of seven in learning God's word, and offering him holy worship, must needs tend abundantly more to the increase of knowledge and holiness, than if all men were left to their own or to their rulers' wills herein.

4. And common experience puts the matter of fact out of doubt, that where the Lord's day is most conscionably spent in holy exercises, there knowledge, piety, charity, and all virtue, do most notably prosper; and where the sanctifying of the Lord's day is neglected, ignorance, sensuality, and worldliness abound. Oh how many millions of souls hath grace converted, and comforted, and edified on the Lord's days! When men are obliged to hear, read, pray, and praise God, and to catechise their children and servants, as that which God requireth, is it not liker to be done, than if they be left to their own erroneous, backward, sluggish minds, or to the will of rulers perhaps worse than they?

Q. 30. How is it that the Lord's day must be spent and sanctified?

A. Not in diverting, worldly thoughts, words, or deeds; much less in idleness, or vain pastimes; and, least of all, in such sinful pleasures as corrupt the mind, and unfit a man for holy work, such as gluttony, drunkenness, lasciviousness, stage plays, romances, gaming, &c. But the Lord's day is specially separated to God's public worship in church communion; and the rest to private and secret holy exercises. The primitive christians spent most of the day together: and the public worship should not be only preferred, but also take up as much of the day as we can well spend therein.[k]

Q. 31. What are the parts of the church service to be used on the Lord's day?

A. The reading of the sacred Scriptures, by the teachers, and expounding them to the people: their preaching the doctrine of the gospel, and their applying it to the case and consciences of the hearers. Their guiding them in the solemn exercise of God's praise, special worship, celebrating the sacraments, especially that of communion of the body and blood of Christ, and that with such conjunction of praises to God, as that it may be fitly called the eucharist, speaking and singing joyfully of God's perfections, and his mercies to man; but specially of the wonderful work of our redemption, and therein chiefly of the resurrection of Jesus Christ. For the day is to be spent as a day of thanksgiving, in joyful and praising commemoration of Christ's resurrection.

Q. 32. On days of thanksgiving men use to feast: may we labour on the Lord's day in providing feasts?

A. Needless cost and labour, and sensual excess, must be avoided, as unsuitable to spiritual work and rejoicing. But such provision as is suitable to a festival, for sober, holy persons, is no more to be scrupled, than the labour of going to the church, or

[i] Exod. xxxi. 15; xxxv. 3; Numb. xv. 32; Neh. xiii. 16, 17; Jer. xvii. 21, 22, 24, 27.

[k] Isa. lviii. 13—15; Luke iv. 16, 18; vi. 1, 6; xiii. 10; Acts xiii. 27, 42, 44; xv. 21; xvi. 13; xx. 7; 1 Cor. xiv.; xvi. 1; Psal. c. 1—3, &c.

the minister's preaching. And it is a laudable use for men to wear their best apparel on that day.

Q. 33. What are the private duties on the Lord's day?

A. Principally speaking and singing God's praises for our redemption in our families, and calling to mind what we were publicly taught, and catechising children and servants, and praying to God, and meditating on God's word, and works of nature, grace, and glory.[l]

Q. 34. Seeing the Lord's day is for the commemoration of Christ's resurrection, must we cease the commemoration of the works of creation, for which the seventh-day sabbath was appointed?

A. No: the appointing of the Lord's day is accumulative, and not diminutive, as to what we were to do on the sabbath. God did not cease to be our Creator and the God of nature, by becoming our Redeemer and the God of grace; we owe more praise to our Creator, and not less. The greater and the subsequent and more perfect work comprehendeth the lesser, antecedent, and imperfect. The Lord's day is to be spent in praising God, both as our Creator and Redeemer; the creation itself being now delivered into the hands of Christ.[m]

Q. 35. But is it not then safest to keep two days; the seventh to honour the Creator, and the first to commemorate our redemption?

A. No; for when the world was made all very good, God delighted in man, and man in God, as his only rest. But upon the sin of man God is become a condemning Judge, and displeased with man, and the earth is cursed; so that God is so far now from being man's rest, that he is his greatest terror, till he be reconciled by Christ. No man cometh to the Father but by the Son. So that now the work of creation must be commemorated with the work of redemption, which restoreth it to its proper use.[n]

Q. 36. But what if a man cannot be satisfied that the seventh day is repealed, is it not safest for him to keep both?

A. God hath laid no such task on man, as to dedicate to religious duties two days in seven; and he that thinketh otherwise, it is his culpable error. But if he do it conscionably, without contentious opposing the truth, and dividing the church for it, good christians will not despise him, but own him as a brother. Paul hath decided that case, Romans xiv. and xv.

Q. 37. Why is mention here made of all within our gates?

A. To show that this commandment is not only directed to private persons, but to magistrates, and masters of families as such, who, though they cannot compel men to believe, they may restrain them from violating the rest of the sabbath, and compel them to such external worship of God as all men are immediately obliged to; even all within the gates of their cities or houses.

Q. 38. What if one live where are no church meetings, or none that he can lawfully join with?

A. He must take it as his great loss and suffering, and with the more diligence improve his time in private.[o]

Q. 39. What preparation is necessary for the keeping holy that day?

A. 1. The chief part of our preparation is the habitual holiness of the soul, a love to God, and his word, and grace, and a sense of our necessities, and heart full of thankfulness to Christ, which relisheth sweetness in his gospel, and in God's praise, and the communion of saints. 2. And the other part is our endeavour to prevent all distracting hinderances, and the greatest helps that we can in the most sensible means; and to meditate before of the great mercy of our redemption, of Christ's resurrection, the giving of the Holy Ghost, and the everlasting, heavenly rest which this prepareth for; and to pray for God's assistance and blessing.

l Psal. xcii.; xcv.; xcvi.; cxviii. 21—24; Col. iii. 16.
m James v. 14; Rev. iv. 11; x. 6; Col. i. 16.
n Col. ii. 16.
o Rev. i. 10.

CHAPTER XXXVIII.

OF THE FIFTH COMMANDMENT.

Q. 1. WHAT are the words of the fifth commandment.

A. "Honour thy father and thy mother, that thy days may be long in the land which the Lord thy God giveth thee."

Q. 2. Doth this commandment belong to the first table, or the second?

A. No man knoweth which of the two tables of stone it was written in by God: but if we may judge by the subject, it seemeth to be the hinge of both, or belong partly to each. As rulers are God's officers, and we obey God in them, it belongs to our duty to God; but as they are men, it belongs to the second.[a]

Q. 3. Why is father and mother named, rather than kings?

A. 1. Parents are our first governors, before kings. 2. Their government is deeplier founded, even in nature, and not only in contract. 3. Parents give us our very being, and we are more obliged to them than to any. 4. They have a natural love to us, and we to them; so that they are justly named first.

Q. 4. Is it only parents that are here meant?

A. No; all true governors are included. But so far as the commandment is part of the law of nature, it bindeth us but to natural rulers antecedently to human contract and consent, and to those that rule us by contract but consequently.[b]

Q. 5. What is the power of parents and rulers, which we must obey?

A. They are of various ranks and offices; and every one's power is special, in that which belongeth to his own place and office. But in general they have power first to command inferiors to obey God's laws: and, 2. To command them such undetermined things in subordination to God's laws, which God hath left to their office to determine of; as corporations make by-laws, by virtue of the king's law.

Q. 6. What if parents or princes command what God forbids?

A. We must obey God, rather than men.[c]

Q. 7. Are we not then guilty of disobedience?

A. No, for God never gave them power to contradict his laws.

Q. 8. But who shall be judge when men's commands are contrary to God's? Must subjects and children judge?

A. While children are infants naturally uncapable of judging, we are ruled as brutes by our parents. But when we grow up to the use of reason, our obligation to govern ourselves is greater than to be

a Prov. i. 8; vi. 20; xiii. 1; xv. 5; xx. 20; xxiii. 22, 25; xxx. 17; Heb. xii. 9; Eph. vi. 1, 2; Mark vii. 10, 11; Deut. xxi. 18, 19; xxvii. 16; Lev. xix. 3; xx. 9; Exod. xxi. 15, 17; Gen. ix. 23; Col. iii. 20, 22; Jer. xxxv. 8, 10.
b Rom. xiii. 1—3; Prov. v. 13; Tit. iii. 1, 2; 1 Pet. ii. 13; iii. 1, 5; v. 5; 1 Tim. ii. 11; Heb. xiii. 7, 17; 1 Cor. xvi. 16.
c Acts v. 29.

governed by others.[d] God's government is the first in order of nature; and self-government is the next, though we are not capable of it till we come to some ripeness. A man is nearer to himself than his parents are, and his happiness or misery depends more on himself than on them. And indeed children's or men's obedience to others is but an act of self-government. It is a man's self-governing reason and will which causeth him to obey another; nor can a child perform any act of proper obedience differing from a brute, unless by a self-governing act. But parents' government is the next to self-government, and the government of husbands, princes, and masters, which are by contract, is next to that. Every subject, therefore, being first a subject of God, and next a self-governor, is to obey as a reasonable creature, and to understand what is his duty and what not. And because all is our duty which God commandeth, but not all that man commandeth, God's power being absolute, and all men's limited; therefore we have nothing to do with the laws of God but to know them, and love them, and obey them. But as to man's commands, we must know also, that they are not contrary to God's laws, and that they belong to the office of the commander.[e] If a parent or prince command you to blaspheme God, or worship idols, or deny Christ, or renounce heaven, or not to pray, &c. you must obey God by disobeying him. And if a king command you not to obey your parents, or will choose for you your wife, your diet, your physic, the words you shall say to God in your secret prayers, &c. these are things which belong not to his office, no more than to a captain's, to become judge of the Common Pleas. Subjects, therefore, must judge what they must or must not obey, as rulers must judge what they must or must not command; or else they act not as men.

Q. 9. But what confusion will this cause, if every subject and child become judge whether their prince's or parents' commands be lawful! Will they not take all for unlawful which their folly or corrupt wills dislike, and so cast off all obedience?

A. It is not finding inconveniences in the miserable state of lapsed mankind that will cure them. Were there any avoiding error, sin, and confusion, by government, some would have found out the way before now. But while man is bad, he will do accordingly. In avoiding these evils, we must not run into far greater. Are they not greater, if men must not discern who is their lawful governor, but must fight for a usurper in power against his prince or parents, if commanded by him? And if every child and subject must renounce God, Christ, and heaven, that is commanded; and men become gods and anti-gods.[f]

Q. 10. But is there no remedy against both these confusions?

A. Yes, the remedies are these: 1. Rulers, that should have most reason, must give us the first remedy, by knowing God's laws, and taking care that they command and forbid nothing contrary to them, and not put on subjects a necessity of disobeying them.

2. Children and subjects must be instructed also to know the laws of God, that they may not take that for his law which is not. It is not keeping them ignorant of God's laws, lest they pretend them against the laws of man, that is the way; no more than keeping them ignorant that there is a God, lest they obey him against man.

3. They must be taught betimes the difference between the capacity of children and of men at age, and of young unfurnished wits and those that study and experience have ripened. And they must be taught the duty of self-suspicion, humility, and submission: and that as learning is necessary to knowing, so believing our teachers, with a human belief, is necessary to learning of them.[g] Who can learn, that will believe nothing which his teacher saith? But this is not taking him for infallible, nor resolving only to be ruled still by his knowledge, but in order to learn the same evidence of truth which our teachers themselves discern it by.[h]

4. They must be taught to know, that if they mistake God's laws, and erroneously pretend them against their rulers, their error and abuse of the name of God is their sin, and will not excuse their disobedience; and therefore they must try well before they disobey.

5. All the churches near them should agree publicly of all the necessary articles of divine faith and obedience, that the authority of their concord may be some awe to the minds of commanders and obeyers.

6. Rulers are not to suspend the executive part of their government upon every conscientious error of the child or subject. If they will pretend God's law for intolerable sin or injury, they must nevertheless be restrained by punishment.

7. But, lastly, the conscience of subjects' duty to God must be tenderly used and encouraged, and their mistakes through infirmity must be tolerated in all tolerable cases. Some differences and disorders in judgment and practice must be borne with by them that would not bring in greater.[i] Gentle reasoning, and loving usage, must cure as much of the rest as will be cured; and our concord must be placed in the few plain and necessary things. The king hath more wit and clemency, than to hang all ignorant, erroneous, faulty subjects, or else he would have none left to govern. And if pastors have not more wit and clemency than to excommunicate all such, they would be no pastors, as having no flocks. But heinous is their sin that can tolerate multitudes of the ignorant and ungodly in their communion, who will but be for their power and wealth, and can tolerate none of the wise and conscionable if they do but differ from them in tolerable cases, or dislike them. Yet there goeth more to make a tolerable christian and church member than a tolerable subject. And consent to the relation is necessary to both.

Q. 11. What duty doth the word honour contain and command?

A. 1. The first and chief of honouring them is to acknowledge their relation to God as his appointed officers, and the authority which God hath given them, that they may be obeyed reverently, and God in them.

2. The next, is to take all their laws and commands, which God hath authorized them to make, to be the rule of our duty in subordination to God's laws, and so far to obey them for conscience' sake, believing it a sin to resist or disobey them.

3. Another is to maintain them honourably, so far as we are able, and they need: though parents provide for children in youth, children must maintain parents if they need it, when they come to age; and so must people their princes and pastors, and pay tribute to whom it is due.[k]

[d] 1 Pet. i. 14; 1 John v. 21; Jude 20, 21; Mark xiii. 9; Prov. xxv. 28; xvi. 37; ix. 12; 2 Tim. ii. 15; 1 Tim. iii. 15; iv. 7, 15, 16; v. 22; vi. 5.
[e] Dan. iii; vi.
[f] Isa. ix. 6, 7; Job xxxiv. 17; Neh. v. 14, 18.
[g] Eph. vi. 1—3.
[h] Eph. v. 21; 1 Thess. v. 12, 13; 1 Pet. v. 5; 2 Pet. ii. 10.
[i] Rom. xiv. 1, 2, &c.
[k] Mal. i. 6, 7; Matt. xv. 5, 6; xxi. 30, 31; Eph. v. 33; vi. 2; 1 Pet. ii. 17; 1 Tim. v. 17; Rom. xiii. 6, 7; Heb. xii. 9; 2 Sam. ix. 6; 1 Kings i. 31.

4. Also they ought to speak reverently to them, and honourably of them, and not use any unjust, dishonouring thoughts, words, or deeds, against them, specially which would disable them for government.

5. Lastly, they ought to do their best to defend them against injuries.

Q. 12. But seeing parents are named, and not princes, must we defend our parents against our king, if he be their enemy?

A. If their cause be just, we must defend them by all lawful means; that is, by prayer to God, by argument, by petition to the king, and by helping their flight, or hiding them: and if a king would ravish or murder your mother or wife, you may hold his hands while they escape; as you may do if he would kill himself in drunkenness or passion. But you may not, on such private accounts, raise a war against him, because war is a public action, and under the judgment of the public governor of the commonwealth, and not under the judgment of your parents, or any private person.[l]

Q. 13. But if the king command me one thing, and my parents another, which of them must I prefer in my obedience?

A. Each of them have their proper office, in which they must be preferred and obeyed. Your mother must be obeyed before the king, in telling you when to suck or eat. Your parents must be obeyed before the king in matters proper to family government; as what daily food you shall eat, and what daily work for them you shall do, and what wife to choose, &c. But the king is to be obeyed before your parents in all matters belonging to national government.

Q. 14. But what if it be about religious acts, as what pastor I shall choose; what church I shall join with; how I shall spend the Lord's day, &c.; must I prefer the king, or my parents, in my obedience?

A. While you are in your minority, and understand not the king's laws, you must obey your parents, and if they command you any thing contrary to the king's commands, they must be answerable for it as the case shall prove: some commands about your religion belong to your parents, and some to the king, and they are accordingly to be obeyed. It is not the king's, but your parents', to catechise you, to teach you to read and pray; to choose your schoolmaster or tutor; in these, therefore, your parents are first to be obeyed: and it is your parents' office to choose where you shall dwell, and, consequently, to what pastor you shall commit the conduct of your soul; and also how in the family, and in private, you shall spend the Lord's day. But the determination of all those public circumstances, which are needful to be imposed on all christians in the land, belongs not to your parents, but to the supreme power.[m]

Q. 15. But what if the king and the bishops, or pastors, differ about matters of religion to be believed or done, which of them must I obey?

A. If it be in things belonging to the king's determination, (as what translation shall be used in all the churches; when synods shall meet; who shall have the tithes, glebe, and temples; what national fasts or thanksgivings shall be kept, and such like,) you must obey the king. But if it be in things proper to the pastoral office, as who shall be judged capable of baptism, or of the Lord's supper and church communion; who shall be admonished, excommunicated, or absolved by the pastors; what text the minister shall preach on, and on what subject, in what method, and in what words; what he shall say to troubled consciences, or to the sick, or to others; what words he shall use in exhortation, prayer, or thanksgiving; all these being part of the pastor's work, you are to obey him in them all. But neither prince nor pastor have power against God.[n]

Q. 16. But what if the bishops or pastors be divided, which of them must we obey?

A. 1. Those that obey God's laws. 2. Those that impose the safest course, where the matter on one side is no sin, when on the other we fear it is. 3. All other things being equal, those that are most unanimous and concordant with the universality of christians and the primitive church; and our own pastors rather than others; and the godly and eminently wise, before the ignorant and ungodly.[o]

Q. 17. But what if the bishop or pastor who is over us, differ from most in the nation? And if the national bishops and ministry differ from most other foreign churches, as England from France, Spain, Italy, Germany, Muscovy, the Greeks, Armenians, Abyssinians?

A. The things in which the difference is supposed, must not be thus confounded: either they are necessary points of faith or practice to all christians in order to salvation; 2. Or else they are controverted opinions not so necessary; 3. Or else they are matters of local, occasional, mutable practice.

1. As to the first, all true christians are agreed in all things necessary to our common salvation: if any oppose these, and draw men from the church on that account, he is a heretic. In this case God's law must be known to us, to which we must stick, whoever gainsay it.[p]

2. In the second case, (of disputable, less necessary opinions,) we must suspend our judgments till evidence determine them; but judge them most probably to be in the right, who are in those matters discerned commonly to have greatest skill and sincerity. But the ignorant cannot subscribe to any of them in the dark.

3. In the third case, (as what time and place we shall meet at; what subject we shall hear; what catechism questions we shall answer when we shall communicate, and with what individual persons, in what words the assembly shall pray and praise God, &c.) we are to obey our own pastors, and not strangers: as every wife is to be governed by her own husband, and every child by his own parents, and every servant by his own master. I scarce think our papists (monarchical or aristocratical) would have a universal husband, parent, or master, or a council of husbands, parents, or masters of all the world, or all the kingdom, set up for such acts as these.

Q. 18. But is there no command to parents, princes, and pastors for their duty, as well as to children and subjects for theirs?

A. The commandments written on stone were necessarily brief, and the duty of rulers is here implied and included.

Q. 19. What is the duty of parents for their children?

A. 1. To take due care of their lives, health, and necessary maintenance.[q] 2. To teach them when they are capable to know God and his word, his doctrine, laws, promises, and penalties; to know themselves, their souls, their relation to God, their

[l] 1 Sam. xix. 1, 4, 7, 11—13, 17; xx. 16, 30, 42; xiv. 44, 45.
[m] Deut. vi.; xi. 19.
[n] 2 Chron. xxix. 27. See all the examples of David, Solomon, Jehoshaphat, Hezekiah, Josiah, and Nehemiah.

[o] Rom. xvi. 16, 17; 1 Thess. v. 12, 13; Heb. xiii. 7, 17.
[p] Gal. i. 8; ii. See the case of Paul and Peter.
[q] Deut. vi. 11; xi. 19; xxxiii. 46; Josh. iv. 6, 7, 22; Eph. vi. 3, 4; 1 Tim. iii. 12; Prov. xxii. 6; xxiii. 13; xxix. 15.

duty to him, their original pravity, and guilt, and danger. To know Jesus Christ, his person, life, doctrine, death, resurrection, ascension, glory, kingdom, intercession, and judgment. To know the Holy Ghost as sent by Christ, to indite and seal the Scripture, qualify the apostles and evangelists to deliver infallibly Christ's commands, and record them to all after-ages, and accordingly settle the churches; to confirm their ministry by miracles, and to sanctify all true christians to the end of the world. To know the use of the ordinary ministry, and of the communion of saints. To know the covenant of grace, and the grace of pardon, adoption, and sanctification, which we must here receive, and the glory which we shall receive hereafter, at death, and at the general resurrection; and the great duties of faith and repentance, of obedience and love to God and man, and renouncing the lusts of the flesh, the world, and the devil, which must be done by all that will be glorified by and with Jesus Christ.[r]

This is the catechism which parents must teach their children.

Q. 20. Alas! it will be a hard and long work to teach children all this; or servants either, that are at age.

A. All this is but the plain meaning of the creed and ten commandments, which the church requireth all to learn; and no more than in their baptism the parents should, and the godfathers do, solemnly promise to see them taught. It is these things for which God hath given them life, and time, and reason, and on which their present safety and comfort, and their everlasting life dependeth. And will you set them seven years apprentice to a trade, and set them seven and seven to schools, and universities, and inns of court, where study must be their daily business; and will you think it too much to teach them the sense of the creed, Lord's prayer, and ten commandments, needful to far greater and better ends?[s]

Q. 21. In what manner must parents teach their children?

A. 1. Very plainly, by familiar talk. 2. Gently and lovingly, to win them, and not discourage them. 3. Beginning with the history and doctrine which they are most capable to receive. 4. Very frequently, that it be not neglected or forgotten, Deut. vi. and xi. 3. Yet a little at a time, that they be not overwhelmed. 6. Praising them when they do well. 7. Doing all with such holy reverence that they may perceive it is the work of God, and not a common matter. 8. Teaching them by an answerable life.

Q. 22. What else, besides teaching, is the parents' duty?

A. 3. To use all just means to make religion pleasant to them, and win their hearts to love it; and therefore to tell them the Author, the excellency, the certainty, and profit of it here and hereafter. 4. To possess them with necessary fear of God, of death, of hell, and of sin. 5. To make a great difference between the good and the bad; rewarding good children, and correcting the bad, disobedient, and stubborn. 6. To choose safe and godly schoolmasters for them, if they teach them not all themselves. 7. To keep them out of ill company, and from temptations, especially to know their vices, and watch against all occasions of their sin. 8. To choose meet trades or callings for them, and faithful masters, ever preferring the welfare of their souls before their bodies. 9. To choose meet husbands or wives for them, if they are to be married.[t] 10. To settle them under a faithful pastor in the real communion of saints. And all this with constant, serious diligence, praying to God for his grace and blessing.

Oh! how happy were the church and world, if parents would faithfully do all this needful, certain duty, and not perfidiously and cruelly break the promise they made in baptism, and by negligence, worldliness, and ungodliness, betray the souls of their own children to sin and Satan! The happiness or misery of families, churches, cities, kingdoms, and of the world, lieth most eminently on parents' hands.

Q. 23. What is the duty of children to their parents in special?

A. To honour their judgment and authority; to be thankful to them for their being, love, and education; to love them dearly; to learn of them willingly and diligently; to obey them faithfully; and to requite them as they are able; and what is included in the general duty of subjects opened before.[u]

Q. 24. What if the father be a papist and the mother a protestant, and one commandeth the child to read one book, and go to one church, and the other another, which must be obeyed?

A. Either the child is of age and understanding to try and judge which of them is contrary to God's law, or not. If he be, he must obey God first, and therefore not obey any thing that is contrary to his law; but if not, then he is one that will not put such questions, nor do what he doth out of conscience to God, but perform mere human obedience to man: and if his ignorance of God's law be through his own negligence, it will not excuse his sin if he mistake; but if it be from natural incapacity, he is ruled like a brute, and no doubt the father is the chief governor of the house, and will and must be obeyed before the mother, when obedience to God doth not forbid it, which this child understandeth not.

Q. 25. What if children be rebellious in wickedness, as drunkenness, stealing, &c. must the parents cause them to be put to death, as Moses' law commanded, or what must they do with them?

A. Moses' law had some special severities, and was peculiar to that nation, and is abrogate. Whether the common good and safety require the death of such a son, or any, the Supreme Power is judge, and not the parents: nor is it meet, though some think otherwise, that parents have the power of putting to death their children; for the commonwealth, which is better than the family, is concerned in all the subjects' lives: and experience proveth it, that were this granted, whores, beggars, and raging, passionate persons would be common murderers of their children.

But if the magistrate would appoint one house of correction in every county for children that will not be ruled by parents, where they may be kept in labour till they are humbled and subdued, it would be an excellent work.

Q. 26. But what shall such sorrowful parents do?

A. First, use all means by wisdom, love, and patience, while there is hope; and next, if they are past their correction, send them to the house of correction; and, lastly, disinherit them, or deny them all maintenance for their lust.

Q. 27. Is it a duty to disinherit an incorrigible, wicked son, or to deny such filial maintenance and portions?

A. Supposing it to be in the father's power, it is a duty to leave them no more than will maintain their lives in temperance; for all men are God's stewards, and must be accountable for all that he doth trust

[r] 1 Tim. iii. 16; 1 Cor. xv. 3—6; Heb. v. 11, 12; vi. 1—3.
[s] 2 Tim. iii. 15.

[t] Deut. vi. 11; xi. 19, 20; Eph. vi. 3, 4; 2 Tim. iii. 15; 1 Thess. ii. 7.
[u] Eph. vi. 1, 2; Col. iii. 20, 21.

them with; and they ought not to give it to be the fuel of lust and sin, when they have reason to believe that it will be so used: that were to give God's mercies to the devil, to be turned against him. Nor are parents bound to give those children the necessary maintenance for their lives and health, or any thing at all, who, by obstinate rebellion, utterly forfeit it. Nature is not so strong a bond but that some sin may dissolve it, and forfeit life itself, and therefore forfeit fatherly maintenance. The rebellion and ingratitude of an incorrigible child is far more heinous than a neighbour's injuries. And though Moses' law, and its rigours, be ceased, the reason of it still remaineth, as directive to us. When thousands of good people want food, and we cannot give all, it is a sin to prefer an incorrigible, wicked son before them.[x]

Q. 28. But God may change them when the parents are dead?

A. It is supposed that the parents have tried to the utmost of their power; and parents cannot judge of what unlikelihoods God may bring to pass when they are dead. If God change them, God will provide for them. If parents have any hope, they may leave somewhat in trusty hands to give them when they see them changed. If not, such may work for themselves.

Q. 29. But what if a son be not deboist, but civil; but be of a corrupt understanding, inclined to ill opinions, and averse to serious piety, and like to use his estate to the hurt of the church or commonwealth, what shall parents do by such?

A. The public interest is to be preferred before a son's. If parents have good hopes that such a son may do more good than harm with his estate, they must trust him as far as reason requireth, rather than to trust a stranger. But if they have reason to believe that he will do more harm than good with it, they should settle it in trust to do all that good which he should do, and not leave it to do hurt, if it be in their power, allowing him necessary maintenance.

Q. 30. Should not parents leave all their estates to their children? or what proportion must they give them?

A. Nature makes children so near their parents, that no doubt they must be specially careful of their corporeal and spiritual welfare above others; and the Israelites, being tied to keep their possessions in their families and line, were under an extraordinary obligation in this matter. But, to all christians, the interest of God and the common good is the chief, and to be preferred.[y] All they that sold their possessions, and laid down the money at the apostles' feet, did not scruple alienating them from their heirs. In this case, children are to be considered, 1. As mere receivers of their own due. 2. Or, as their parents' trustees for doing good. If they be like to prove faithful, their parents should rather trust them than others with their estates to do good when they are gone. But if not, they should secure a due proportion for good works.

And, however, all men should in their life do all the good that regularly they can do; for who can expect that his son should do that good with his estate which he had not a heart to do himself? And who would not rather secure a reward to himself than to his son?

Q. 31. Do you disallow of the common course, which is to give all that men can get to their children, save some small droppings now and then to the poor?

A. I take it to be the effect of that selfishness which is the grand enemy to the love of God and man. A carnal, selfish man doth live to his flesh and carnal self, for which he gathers all that he can get: and when he must needs die, and can no longer enjoy it, he takes his children to be as parts of himself, and what they have he thinks he almost hath himself; and so out of mere self-love, doth love them and enrich them. But a holy person thinks all is God's, and that it is best used which is best improved to his will and kingdom.

But, alas! what have selfish, carnal worldlings to account for, when the best they can say of the use of God's talents is, that they pampered the flesh with as much as it craved, and the rest they gave their children to make them rich, that their flesh also might be pampered, and their lust might want no fuel or provision, nor their souls want temptation! Hundreds or thousands given to daughters, and lands purchased for their sons, and now and then a farthing or a penny given to the poor. And though the hypocrites take on them to believe Christ, that it is harder for a rich man to enter into the kingdom of God than for a camel to go through a needle's eye, yet they live as if nothing were the desire and business of their lives, but to make their own and their children's salvation by riches thus next to impossible.[z]

Q. 32. Is it well, as is usual, to give the eldest son all the inheritance?[a]

A. Nature and Scripture tell us of some pre-eminence of the eldest: this birth-right Jacob thought worth the buying of Esau: Christ is called the first-born of every creature, because the first-born have the pre-eminence of rule, wealth, and honour: and the heavenly society are called "The general assembly of the first-born whose names are enrolled in heaven," Heb. xii.; because they are in honour and power above others. But yet, 1. The younger also are sons, and must have their part: and it pleased God to leave on record how oft he hath preferred the younger; even an Abel before Cain; a Seth before his seniors; a Shem before Japhet and Ham; Isaac before Ishmael; Jacob before Esau; David and Solomon before their elder brethren.

2. But to the faithful, though nature be not disregarded, yet grace teacheth us what to prefer. And Christ and his members are dearer to us than our sons or natural members.[b] In cases where we must deny ourselves for Christ and the public good, we may also deny our natural kindred: for they are not nearer to us than ourselves. And if an eldest son be wicked or unprofitable, a believing parent should give him the less, and more to a younger (yea, to a stranger) that will do more service to God and his country; and not prefer a fleshly difference and privilege before a spiritual, and his Master's service.

Q. 33. What is the duty of husbands to their wives?

A. To love them as themselves, and live with them in conjugal chastity, as guides and helpers, and provide for them and the family; to endeavour to cure their infirmities and passions, and patiently bear what is not cured; to preserve their honour and authority over inferiors, and help them in the education of their children, and comfort them in all their sufferings.[c]

Q. 34. What is the duty of wives to their husbands?

A. To live with them in true love and conjugal chastity and fidelity; to help them in the education of children, and governing servants, and in worldly affairs; to learn of them and obey them; to provoke

[x] Luke xv. 16; Deut. xxi. 18—21; xvii. 11, 12; 2 Thess. iii.
[y] Acts iv.; v. 1—3; 1 Cor. iv. 2; 1 Pet. iv. 10; Psalm xvii. 14; Job xxi. 11; Luke xix. 8.

[z] Psal. xlix. 9—15.
[a] Gen. xxv. 31.
[b] Matt. xix. 21; Mark x. 21; Luke xii. 33; xviii. 22.
[c] Eph. v. 25; Col. iii. 19; 1 Pet. iii. 7.

them to duties of piety and charity, and to bear with their infirmities, and comfort and help them in their sufferings: and both must live as the heirs of heaven, in preparation for the life to come.[d]

Q. 35. What is the duty of masters to their servants?

A. To employ them suitably, not unmercifully, in profitable labour, and not in sin or vanity: to allow them their due wages, and maintenance, keeping them neither in hurtful want, nor in idleness, or sinful fulness: to teach them their duty to God and man, and see that they join in public and family worship, and live not in any wilful sin: and as fellow-christians (if they are such) to further their comfortable passage to heaven.[e]

Q. 36. But what if we have slaves that are no christians?

A. You must use them as men that are capable of christianity, and do your best, with pity, to cure their ignorance, and unbelief, and sin, and to make them christians, preferring their souls before your worldly commodity.

Q. 37. Is it lawful to buy and use men as slaves?

A. It is a great mercy accidentally for those of Guinea, Brazil, and other lands, to be brought among christians, though it be as slaves; but it is a sin in those that sell and buy them as beasts, merely for commodity, and use them accordingly: but to buy them in compassion to their souls, as well as for their service, and then to sell them only to such as will use them charitably like men, and to employ them as aforesaid, preferring their salvation, is a lawful thing, especially such as sell themselves, or are sold as malefactors.

Q. 38. What is the duty of servants to their masters?

A. To honour and obey them, and faithfully serve them, as part of their service of Christ, expecting their chief reward from him: to be trusty to them in word and deed, not lying, nor stealing, or taking any thing of theirs without their consent, nor wronging them by idleness, negligence, or fraud. Learning of them thankfully, and sincerely, and obediently, joining with them in public and family worship of God.[f]

Q. 39. Doth God require family teaching, and daily worship?

A. Yes, both by the law of nature and Scripture. All christian societies must be sanctified to God: christian families are christian societies: they have, as families, constant dependence on God, constant need of his protection, help, and blessing, and constant work to do for him, and therefore constant use of prayer to him: and as nature and necessity will teach us to eat and drink every day, though Scripture tell us not how oft, nor at what hour, so will they tell us that we must daily ask it of God. And stated times are a hedge to duty, to avoid omissions and interruptions: and Scripture commandeth parents to teach and persuade their children constantly, lying down and rising up, &c.[g] Deut. vi. and xi.; and to bring them up in the nurture and admonition of the Lord. Cornelius, Crispus, and others converted, brought in their households with them to Christ. Daniel prayed openly daily in his house. The fourth commandment requireth of masters that all in their house do sanctify the sabbath. Reason and experience tell us, that it is the keeping up religion and virtue in families, by the constant instruction, care, and worship of God, by the governors, that is the chief means of the hopes and welfare of the world, and the omission of it the great cause of all public corruption and confusion.[h]

Q. 40. What must children, wives, servants, and subjects do that have bad parents, husbands, masters, and magistrates?

A. Nature bindeth children in minority so to their parents, and wives to their husbands, (except in case of lawful divorce,) that they must live in patient bearing with what they cannot amend: and so must such servants and subjects as by law or contract may not remove, nor have legal remedy. But those that are free may remove under better masters and princes when they can.

Q. 41. But whole nations cannot remove from enemies and destroyers?

A. It is God, and not I, that must answer such cases. Only I say: 1. That there is no power but of God.

2. That governing power is nothing but right and obligation to rule the people in order to the common good.[i]

3. That destroying the common good is not ruling, nor any act of power given by God.

4. That all man's power is limited by God, and subordinate to his universal government and laws, and he hath given none authority against himself or his laws.

5. That so far as God's laws have not determined of the species and degrees of power, they must be known by the human contracts or consent which found them.

6. Nations have by nature a right to self-preservation against destroying enemies and murderers.

7. And when they only seek to save themselves against such, they resist not governing authority.

8. But particular persons must patiently bear even wrongful destruction by governors; and whole nations tolerable injuries, rather than by rebellions and wars to seek their own preservation or right, to the hurt of the commonwealth.[k]

9. They are the great enemies of government who are for perjury, by which mutual trust is overthrown.

CHAPTER XXXIX.

OF THE SIXTH COMMANDMENT.

Q. 1. What are the words of the sixth commandment?

A. "Thou shalt do no murder."

Q. 2. What is murder?

A. Killing unjustly a reasonable creature. And all that culpably tends to it bringeth an answerable degree of guilt.

Q. 3. Why is this command the first that forbiddeth private wrongs?

A. Because a man's life is more precious than the accidents of his life; death depriveth him of all further time of repentance and earthly mercies, and depriveth all others of the benefit which they might receive by him. They rob God and the king of a subject. Therefore God, who is the Giver of life, is a dreadful Avenger of the sin of murder: Cain was

[d] Eph. v. 22, 24; Col. iii. 18; Tit. ii. 4, 5; 1 Pet. iii. 1—3.
[e] Eph. vi. 9; Col. iv. 1.
[f] 1 Pet. ii. 18; Tit. ii. 9; 1 Tim. vi. 1, 2; Eph. vi. 5—7; Col. iii. 22.
[g] Acts x. 2, 3; 1 Cor. i. 16; Gen. xviii. 10; 2 Sam. vi. 11, 20; Exod. xii. 3, 4.
[h] Acts ii. 46; v. 42; xii. 12; Prov. iii. 33.
[i] Rom. xiii. 2—7; 2 Cor. x. 8; xiii. 10; 1 Pet. iii. 11—14.
[k] Matt. xvii. 25, 26; xxii. 19, 20.

cast out with terror for this sin; for it was the devil's first service, who was a murderer from the beginning. Therefore God made of old the law against eating blood, lest men should be hardened to cruelty, and to teach them his hatred of blood-guiltiness.[a] And it was the murder of the prophets, and of Christ himself, and his apostles, that brought that dreadful destruction on the Jews, when wrath came upon them to the uttermost.[b]

Q. 4. If God hate murder, why did he command the Israelites to kill all the Canaanites, men, women, and children?

A. Justice done by God, or his authority, on capital malefactors, is not murder. You may as well ask why God will damn so many in hell, which is worse than death. The curse was fallen on Ham's posterity. They were nations of idolaters, and murderers of their own children, offering them to idols, and so drowned in all wickedness that God justly made the Israelites his executioners, to take away their forfeited lands and lives.[c]

Q. 5. When is killing murder, or unlawful?

A. When it is done without authority from God, who is the Lord of life.

Q. 6. To whom doth God give such authority to kill men?

A. To the supreme rulers of commonwealths, and their magistrates, to whom they communicate it.[d]

Q. 7. May they kill whom they will?

A. No, none but those whose crimes are so great as to deserve death by the law of God in nature, and the just laws of the land; even such whose crimes make their death the due interest of the republic, and needful to its good and safety.

Q. 8. What if a prince think that the death of an innocent man is accidentally necessary to the safety of himself or the commonwealth, through other men's fault, may he not kill him?[e]

A. No; he is a murderer if he kill the innocent, or any whose fault deserveth not death: should God permit killing on such pretences, no men's lives would be safe. In factions there be other ways of remedy; and such wicked means do but hasten and increase the evil which men would so prevent.[f]

Q. 9. May not parents have power to kill bad children?

A. No; I have given you the reason under the fifth commandment.

Q. 10. May not a man kill another in the necessary defence of his own life?

A. In some cases he may, and in some not; he may, in case it be his equal or inferior, as to public usefulness, and he have no other means, being assaulted by him, to save his life from him. But he may not, 1. If by flight, or other just means, he can save his own life. 2. Nor if it be his king, or father, or any public person, whose death would be a greater loss to the commonwealth than his own.[g]

Q. 11. How prove you that?

A. Because the light of nature tells us, that seeing good and evil are the objects of our willing and nilling; therefore the greatest good should still be preferred, and the greatest evil be most avoided; and that the good or hurt of the commonwealth is far greater than of a single, private person.

Q. 12. But doth not nature teach every creature to preserve its life, and rather than die to kill another?

A. The nature of man is to be rational, and above brutish nature, and to choose by reason, though against sensitive inclination.[h] Why else must martyrs choose to die rather than to sin? and soldiers choose their own death before their captain's, or their king's, in which God and reason justify them?

Q. 13. But by this rule an army should kill their general, rather than to be killed or betrayed to death by him; because all their lives are better than one man's.

A. If they be but some part of an army, and the general's life be more useful to the rest, and to their king and country, and the public good, than all theirs, they should rather die, as the Theban legion did. But if the general be a traitor to his king and country, and would destroy all, or part, of the army to the public loss and danger, it is no murder if they kill him when they have no other way to save their lives.

Q. 14. How many sorts of murder are there, and which are the worst?

A. I. One of the worst is persecution; killing men because they are good, or because they will not break God's laws. And lower degrees of persecution by banishment, imprisonment, mulcts, participate of guilt against this command.[i]

II. A second sort of heinous murder is by massacres, and unlawful wars, in which multitudes are murdered, and that studiously, and with greatest industry, and countries ruined and undone. The multitude of heinous crimes that are contained in an unlawful war are hardly known but by sad experience.

III. Another sort of heinous murder is, when parents kill their own children, or children their parents.

IV. Another is, when princes destroy their own subjects, whom by office they are bound to protect; or subjects their princes, whom they are bound to obey, and defend, and honour.

V. Another sort of heinous murder is, when it is committed on pretence of justice, by perjured witnesses, false accusers or false judges, or magistrates:[k] as Naboth was murdered by Jezebel and Ahab, and Christ by the Jews, upon false accusations of blasphemy and treason. For in this case the murder is fathered on God, and on justice, which must abhor it, and the best things which should preserve the peace of the innocent are used to the worst ends, even to destroy them. And a man hath no defence for himself, as he may have against murderers, or open enemies; and he is destroyed by those that are bound to defend him. And the most devilish, wicked, perjured men, are made the masters of men's lives, and may conquer subjects by perverting law.

VI. One of the most heinous crimes is, soul-murder, which is done by all that draw or drive men into sin, or from their duty to God and the care of their salvation, either by seducing, false opinions, opposing necessary truth and duty, or by scorns, or threats. But none here sin so grievously as wicked rulers, and wicked teachers and pastors of the churches. Others kill souls by one and one, but these by hundreds and thousands. And therefore it is the devil's main endeavour, through the world,

[a] Deut. xix. 10, 13; 1 Kings ii. 31; 2 Kings xxi. 16; xxii. 4; Prov. vi. 17; xxviii. 17; Gen. iv. 10, 11; ix. 4—6; xxxvii. 26; xlii. 22; Hos. iv. 2.

[b] Matt. xxiii. 31; xxvii. 4, 25; Luke xi. 50; Rev. xvi. 6; Acts xxii. 20.

[c] Deut. xxvii. 15; xviii. 9, 12; xxix. 17; 2 Kings xvi. 3; Lev. xviii. 26, 27.

[d] Gen. xxvi. 11; Exod. xix. 12; xxi. 12, 15—17; Deut. xvii. 6, 7; xxi. 22; xxiv. 16; Josh. i. 18.

[e] John xviii. 14.

[f] 1 Sam. xiv. 43—45.

[g] So David to Saul.

[h] 1 Chron. xi. 19; 1 John iii. 16; Rev. xii. 11.

[i] Prov. xxix. 10; Rev vi. 10, 12; xviii. 24; xix. 2; Matt. xxiii. 35.

[k] 1 Kings xxi. 19.

to get rulers and teachers on his side, and turn the word and sword against him that did ordain them. All the idolatrous world that know not Christ are kept under the power of the devil, principally by wicked rulers and teachers. And so is the infidel and Mahometan world. When the Turks had once conquered the Eastern empire, how quickly did those famous churches and large nations forsake Christ, and turn to the grossest of deceivers! Oh, how many millions of souls have been since hereby destroyed! And what wicked, deceitful, and contentious teachers have done to the murdering of souls, alas! the whole christian world is witness. Some by heresy, and some by proud tyranny, and some by malignant opposition to the serious practice of that holy law of God which they preach; and some by ignorance, and some by slothful, treacherous negligence, and some by church divisions, by their snares, or contentiousness. Such as Paul speaks of, Phil. i. 15, 16; ii. 3. And some, in envy, malign and hinder the preaching of the gospel, by such as they distaste, 1 Thess. ii. 16.

VII. But of all soul-murder, it is one of the greatest which is done by wicked parents on their own children, who breed them up in ignorance, wickedness, and profane neglect, if not hatred and scorn, of serious holiness,[l] and teach them malignant principles, or hinder them from the necessary means of their salvation; that by example teach them to swear and lie, and be drunken or profane. For parents to be the cruel damners of their own children, and this when in false hypocrisy they vowed them in baptism to God, and promised their godly education, is odious cruelty and perfidiousness.

VIII. And it is yet a more heinous sin to be a murderer of one's own soul, as every ungodly and impenitent sinner is: for nature teacheth all men to love themselves, and to be unwilling of their own destruction. And no wonder that such are unmerciful to the souls of wives, children, and servants, who will damn themselves, and that for nothing; and that, after all the importunities of God and man to hinder them.[m]

Q. 15. When may a man be accounted a soul-self-murderer, seeing every man hath some sin?

A. Every sin (as every sickness to the body) is an enemy to life, though it destroy it not: and as wounding a man, yea, or injurious hurting him, or desiring his hurt, is some breach of this command, as Christ tells us, (Matt. v.) so every sin is as hurtful to the soul. But those are the mortal, murdering sins, which are inconsistent with the predominant habitual love of God and holiness, and are not only from the imperfection of this divine nature and image, but from the absence of it: such as are the sins of the unbelievers and impenitent.

Q. 16. But he shall not be hanged for killing another that doth it against his will: and no man is willing to damn himself.

A. But a man will himself be a dead man if he kill himself unwillingly: and all wicked men do willingly murder their own souls. They be not willing to burn in hell, but they are willingly ungodly, worldly, sensual; and unholiness is the death or misery of the soul: and the departing of the heart or love from God, and choosing the world and fleshly pleasure before his grace and glory, is the true soul-murdering.[n] When God maketh poison destructive to man's nature, and forbids us taking it, and tells a man that it will kill him; if this man will yet take the poison because it is sweet, or will not believe that it is deadly, it is not his being unwilling to die that will save him. When God hath told men that unholiness and a fleshly mind is death, he destroyeth his soul that yet will choose it.[o]

And it is a heinous aggravation that poor sinners have so little for the salvation which they sell. The devil can give them nothing that is to be put into the balance against the least hope or possibility of the life to come; and for a man to sell his own soul and all his hopes of heaven, for a base lust, or a transitory shadow, as profane Esau sold his birthright for a morsel, is self-murder of a most odious kind.

Q. 17. But you make also our friends that love us to be murderers of us, if they draw us to sin, or neglect their duty?

A. As the love of his own flesh doth not hinder, but further, the drunkard's, fornicator's, and idle person's murder of his own soul; so your friend's carnal love to you may be so far from hindering, that it may further your destruction. They that draw each other to fornication, to gaming, to time-wasting plays, to gluttony and drunkenness, may do it in love. If they give you poison in love, it will kill you.[p]

And if parents that are bound to feed their children do famish them, do you think they do not murder them by omission? So may they, and so may ministers, murder the souls that they are by nature or office intrusted to instruct and diligently govern.

Q. 18. Are there any other ways of murder?

A. So many that it is hard to number them. As by rash anger, hatred, malice, by drunkenness disposing to it; by magistrates not punishing murderers; by not defending the lives of others when we ought, and abundance more, which you may read in Bishop Downam's tables on the commandments.

Q. 19. Must I defend my parents or children against the magistrate, or any one that would kill them by his commission?

A. Not against justice, no doubt; what you must do against subjects who pretend an illegal commission to rob or kill yourself, parents, or children, or destroy cities and countries, is partly touched on under the fifth commandment, and partly matter unmeet for a catechism, or private, unlearned men's unnecessary discourse.

Q. 20. Are there more ways of self-murder?

A. Among others, excess of meat and idleness destroy men's health, and murder millions.

CHAPTER XL.

OF THE SEVENTH COMMANDMENT.

Q. 1. WHAT are the words of the seventh commandment?

A. "Thou shalt not commit adultery."

Q. 2. What is the sin here forbidden?

A. All unlawful, carnal copulation, and every evil inclination, or action, or omission, which tendeth thereto, or partaketh of any degree of unchastity or pollution.

Q. 3. Is all lust or inclination to generation a sin?

A. No: for, 1. Some is natural to man, and that not as corrupt; but as God said, "Increase and multiply," before the fall, so no doubt he inclined nature thereto.[a] 2. And the regular propagation of mankind is one of the noblest, natural works that man

[l] Deut. xii. 31; Psal. cvi. 37, 38.
[m] Prov. xiii. 13; xxix. 1; vi. 32; xxi. 15.
[n] Rom. ii. 5, 6, 8; 1 Cor. vi. 9, 10; Eph. v. 5—7.

[o] Heb. xii. 14, 16; Mark viii. 36.
[p] Gal. iv. 17, 18.
[a] Heb. xiii. 4; Gen. i. 22, 28; ix. 7; xxii. 17; xxvi. 4, 24.

is instrumental in; a man being a more excellent thing than a house or any work of art. 3. And God hath put some such inclination into nature, in great wisdom and mercy to the world: for if nature had not some considerable appetite to generation, and also strong desire of posterity, men would hardly be drawn to be at so much care, cost, and labour, to propagate mankind; but especially women would not so commonly submit to all their sickness, pain, danger, and after-trouble which now they undergo. But if a few self-denying persons did propagate mankind only as an act of obedience to God, the multitude of the ungodly would not do it.

Q. 4. If it be so, why is any carnal act of generation forbidden? especially when it is an act of love, and doth nobody any harm?

A. God hath in great wisdom and mercy to man made his laws for restraining men from inordinate lust and copulation.

1. The noblest things are basest when corrupted. Devils are worse than men, because they were higher and better before. A wicked man is incomparably worse and more miserable than a beast or a toad, because he is a nobler nature depraved. And so human generation is worse than that of swine or dogs, when it is vicious.

2. Promiscuous, unregulated generation, tends to the utter ruin and vitiating of mankind, by the overthrow of the just education of children, on which the welfare of mankind doth eminently depend. Alas, all care and order is little enough, and too little, to keep corrupted nature from utter bestiality and malignity, much more to make youth wise and virtuous, without which it had been better never to have been born! When fathers know their own children, and when mothers have the love, and encouragement, and household advantage of order, which is necessary, some good may be done. But lawless exercise of lust will frustrate all. 1. Women themselves will be slaves, or their advantage mutable and uncertain; for such lust will serve its turn of them but for novelty, and will be still for change; and when a younger or a fairer comes, the mother is cast off and hated.[b] And then the next will hate her children, or at least not love them as a necessary education doth require. And when the father hath forsaken the mother, it is like he will forsake the children with her. And when women's lusts are lawless as well as men's, men being uncertain what children are their own, will be regardless both of their souls and bodies: so that confusion would destroy religion and civility, and make the world worse than most of the American savages are, who are taught by nature to set bounds to lust.

And besides all this, the very lust itself, thus increased by lawless liberty, would so corrupt men's minds, and fantasies, and affections, into a sordid, beastly sensuality, that it would utterly indispose them to all spiritual and heavenly, yea, and manly, employments of heart and life; men would grow sottish and stupid, unfit to consider of heavenly things, and uncapable of holy pleasures.

Q. 5. But if these evil consequents be all, then a man that can moderately use fornication, so as shall avoid these evils, sinneth not?

A. Sin is the breach of God's law: these mischiefs that would follow lawless lust show you that God made this law for the welfare of mankind. But God's own wisdom and will is the original reason of his law, and must satisfy all the world. But were there none but this forementioned, to avoid the world's confusion and ruin, it was needful that God set a law to lust; and when this is done for the common good, it is not left to man to break God's law, whenever he thinks he can avoid the consequents, and secure the end of the law. For if men be left to such liberty, as to judge when they may keep God's law, and when they may break it, lust will always find a reason to excuse it, and the law will be in vain. The world needed a regulating law, and God's law must not be broken.

Q. 6. Which are the most heinous sorts of filthiness?

A. Some of them are scarce to be named among christians. 1. Sodomy. 2. Copulation with brutes. 3. Incest; sinning thus with near kindred. 4. Rapes, or forcing women. But the commonest sorts are, adultery, fornication, self-pollution, and the filthiness of the thoughts and affections, and the words and actions, which partake of the pollution.[c]

Q. 7. Why is adultery so great a sin?

A. Besides the aforesaid evils that are common to it and fornication, it is a perfidious violation of the marriage covenant, and destroys the conjugal love of husband and wife, and confoundeth progeny, and, as is aforesaid, corrupteth family order and human education.[d]

Q. 8. Why may not a man have many wives now, as the Jews had?

A. As Christ saith of putting away, from the begining it was not so, but it was permitted for the hardness of their hearts; that their seed might be multiplied, in which they placed their chief prosperity. And (that we may not think worse of them than they were) as God hath taught the very brutes to use copulation no oftener than is necessary to generation, so it is probable, by many passages of Scripture, that it was so ordinarily then with men; and, consequently, that they that had many wives, used them not so often as now too many do one; and did not multiply wives so much for lust as for progeny.[e]

Q. 9. But is no oftener use of husband and wife lawful than for generation?

A. Yes, in case of necessitating lust; but such a measure of lust is to be accounted inordinate, either as sin, or a disease; and not to be causelessly indulged, though this remedy be allowed it.[f]

Q. 10. But why may not many wives be permitted now, as well as then?

A. 1. No man can either dispense with God's laws, or forgive sin against them, but God himself. If he forbear men in sin, that doth not justify it. 2. If a few men and many women were cast upon a wilderness, or sent to plant it by procreation, the case were liker the Israelites, where the men were ofter killed by wars and God's judgments than the women: but with us there is no pretence for the like polygamy, but it would confound and disquiet families.

If one should make a difficult case of it, whether a prince that hath a barren wife may not take another for the safety of a kingdom, when it is in notorious danger of falling into the hands of a destroyer, (as Adam's own sons and daughters lawfully married each other, because there were no others in the world,) this would be no excuse, where no such public notorious necessity can be pleaded.

Q. 11. Why must marriage be a public act?

A. Because else adultery and unlawful separations cannot be known or punished, but confusion will come in.

[b] Acts xv. 20, 29; Rom. i. 29, 30; 1 Cor. v. 11; vi. 13, 18; vii. 2; x. 8; Gal. v. 19; Eph. v. 3, 4; Col. iii. 5; 1 Thess. iv. 3; Rev. ii. 14, 20; Matt. xv. 19; Heb. xii. 16.

[c] Gen. xviii.; 1 Cor. v.; Lev. xviii.

[d] Matt. v. 32; xix. 6; Mal. ii. 13.

[e] Gen. xxix. 30, 34; xxx. 15, 18, 20; Deut. xxv. 6, 7.

[f] 1 Cor. vii. 9.

Q. 12. But is it not adultery that is committed against secret marriage, which was never published or legally solemnized?

A. Yes: secret consent makes a marriage before God, though not before the world; and the violation of it is adultery before God.

Q. 13. May not a man put away his wife, or depart from her, if she seek his death, or if she prove utterly intolerable?

A. While he is governor, he hath divers other remedies first to be tried: a Bedlam must be used as a Bedlam: and no doubt but if he have a just cause to fear poisoning or other sort of murder, he may secure his life against a wife as well as against an enemy. Christ excepted not that case, because nature supposeth such exceptions.

Q. 14. But if utter unsuitableness make their cohabitation an insuperable temptation, or intolerable misery, may they not part by consent for their own good; seeing it is their mutual good, which is the end of marriage?

A. 1. The public good is a higher end of all men's worldly interests and actions than their own: and when the example would encourage unlawful separaters, they must not seek their own ease to the public detriment. 2. And if it be their own sinful distempers which maketh them unsuitable, God bindeth them to amend, and not to part: and if they neglect not his grace, he will help them to do what he commandeth: and it is in his way, and not their own, by the cure of their sin, and not by indulging it, that they must be healed: but, as the apostle saith in another case, if the faulty person depart, and the other cannot help it, a brother or sister is not left in bondage, but may stay till the allay of the distemper incline them to return.[g]

Q. 15. What is inward heart fornication, or uncleanness?

A. 1. Inordinate filthy thoughts are some degree. 2. Inordinate desires are a higher degree. 3. Inordinate contrivance and consent are yet a higher. And when such thoughts and desires become the ordinary inhabitants of the soul, and pollute it when they lie down and when they rise, and shut out holy and sober thoughts, and become a filthy habit in the mind, then the degree is so great as that an unclean devil hath got great advantage, if not a kind of possession, of the imagination and the soul.[h]

Q. 16. Which way are the other senses guilty of this sin?

A. 1. When an ungoverned eye is suffered to fetch in lustful thoughts and desires into the mind. 2. Much more when to such immodest or unchaste looks there is added immodest actions and dalliance, unfit to be named. 3. And when fleshly appetite and ease do bring in fuel to unchaste inclinations. 4. And when the ear is set open to ribald and defiling words.

Q. 17. How is the tongue guilty of uncleanness?

A. By the aforesaid filthy or wanton talk, reading alluring books, using alluring words to others; but, worst of all, by defending, extenuating, or excusing any filthy lusts.

Q. 18. What are the chief causes of this sin?

A. It is supposed that God put into nature an ordinate governable appetite to generation in mankind: but that which rendereth it inordinate, and unruly, and destructive, is, 1. Over-much pampering the flesh by pleasing meats and drinks. 2. Idleness; not keeping under the body by due labour, nor keeping the mind in honest employment about our callings, and the great matters of our duty to God, and of our salvation, which leave no room for filth and vanity. 3. Want of a sanctified heart and tender conscience to resist the first degrees of the sin. 4. Specially wilful running into temptation.[i]

Q. 19. By what degrees do persons come to fornication?

A. 1. By the aforesaid cherishing the causes, appetite and idleness.

2. By this means the lustful inclinations of the flesh grow as strong and troublesome in some as a violent itch, or as a thirst in a fever.[k]

3. Then an ungoverned eye must gaze upon some tempting piece of flesh.

4. And if they get opportunity for frequent privacy and familiarity, and use it in immodest sights and actions, they are half overcome.

5. For then the devil, as an unclean spirit, gets possession of the imagination, and there is a strong inclination in them to think of almost nothing else but fleshly filth, and the pleasure that their sense had in such immodest brutishness. When God should have their hearts morning and night, and perhaps at church and in holy actions, this unclean spirit ruleth their thoughts.

6. Then conscience growing senseless, they fear not to feed these pernicious flames with ribald talk, and romances, and amorous foolish plays, and conversing with such as are of their own mind.

7. After this, where their fancy is infected, they study and contrive themselves into further temptation, to get that nearness, opportunity, and secrecy which may encourage them.

8. And from thence Satan hurrieth them, usually against conscience, into actual fornication.

9. And when they are once in, the devil and the flesh say, Twice may be pardoned as well as once.

10. And some, at last, with seared consciences, grow to excuse it as a small sin; and sometimes are forsaken to fall into utter infidelity or atheism, that no fear of judgment may molest them. But others sin on in horror and despair; of whom, of the two, there is more hope, as having less quietness in their sins to hinder their repentance.

Q. 20. What are the best remedies against all unchastity and uncleanness of mind and body?

A. 1. The principal is the great work of renewing grace, which taketh up the heart of man to God, and maketh him perceive that his everlasting concerns are those that must take up his mind and life; and this work still mortifieth the flesh, with the affections and lusts thereof.

2. Another is, to make it seriously a great part of our religion to subdue and destroy all fleshly, sinful lusts: and not to think a bare conviction or wish will do it; but that it requireth more labour than to kill weeds in your ground, or to tame unruly colts or cattle.[l]

3. Another means is, to resolve upon a constant diligence in a lawful calling. Poor labouring men are seldom so vicious in lust as idle gentlemen are.[m]

4. Temperance and fasting, when there is need, and avoiding fulness, and flesh-pleasing meats and drinks. Gluttons and drunkards are fitted to be boars and stallions.

5. To keep a conscionable government of the eye,

[g] Matt. v. 32; xix. 6.

[h] Matt. v. 28, 29; Eph. v. 4, 5; Jam. i. 21; 2 Pet. ii. 18; 1 John ii. 16; Job xxxi. 1.

[i] Deut. vi. 21; Ezek. xvi. 49.

[k] Eph. ii. 3; Judg. xii. 7, 8; 2 Pet. ii. 14, 16, 18; 1 John ii. 16; Gal. v. 19, 20.

[l] Rom. viii. 1, 5, 7, 12, 13; 2 Pet. ii. 10; Gal. v. 13, 17, 24.

[m] Jude 23; 1 Cor. ix. 17; Rom. xiii. 13, 14; Prov. v. 8; Gen. xxxiv.

and thoughts, and call them off as soon as Satan tempteth them.

6. Above all, to be sure to keep far enough from tempting persons. Touch them not; be not private with them. There is no safety when fire and gunpowder are long near, and in an infectious house. Distance is the greatest means of safety.

7. Another means is to foresee the end, and think what will follow: specially think of death and judgment. Consider what the alluring flesh will be when the small-pox shall cover it with scabs, or when it shall have lain a few weeks stinking in a grave. This must be. But oh, the thoughts of the judgment of God, and the torment of a guilty conscience, should be more mortifying helps. To go to the house of mourning, and see the end of all men, and see what the dust and bones of men are when they are cast up out of the grave, and to think where the souls are and must be for ever, methinks should cure the folly of lust.

Q. 21. Is it unlawful for men and women, especially the unmarried, to set out themselves in such ornaments of apparel as may make them seem most comely and desirable?

A. 1. The common rule is to be clothed with decent, but modest apparel, such as shows the body without deceit to be what it is, which is neither loathsome nor alluring. 2. And persons must be invited to conjugal desires by truth, and not by deceit, and by the matters of real worth, such as wisdom, godliness, patience, and meekness, and not by fleshly snares; for marriages so contracted are like to turn to continued misery to both, when the body is known without the ornaments, and deceit and diseases of the soul become vexatious.

3. But there is much difference to be made of the time, and ends.[n] A young woman that hath a suitor, and intendeth marriage, may go further in adorning herself to please him that chooseth her, and a wife to please her husband's eye, than they may do to strangers, where there is no such purpose or relation. To use a procacious garb to be thought amiable to others, where it may become a snare, but can do no good, is the act of one that hath the folly of pride, and some of the disposition of a harlot; even a pleasure and desire to have those think them amiable, desirable persons, in whom it may kindle concupiscence likelier than good.

Q. 22. But may not a crooked or deformed person hide their deformity by apparel, or other means?

A. Yes, so far as it only tends to avoid men's disdain in a common conversation; but not so as to deceive men in marriage desires, or purposes, or practice.

Q. 23. What if one's condition be such that marriage is like to impoverish them in the world, and cast them into great straits and temptations, and yet they feel a bodily necessity of it?

A. God casteth none into a necessity of sinning. Fornication must not be committed to avoid poverty. If such can by lawful means overcome their lust, they must do it; if not, they must marry, though they suffer poverty.

Q. 24. What if parents forbid their children necessary marriage?

A. Such children must use all lawful means to make marriage unnecessary to them. But if that cannot be done, they must marry whether their parents will or not. For man hath no power to forbid what God commandeth.

Q. 25. Is that marriage void which is without the consent of parents, and must such be separate as adulterers?

[n] Jer. ii. 32; 1 Pet. iii. 3, 4; Gen. xxxviii. 15; Prov. vii. 10.

A. Some marriage, as aforesaid, is lawful without their consent; some is sinful, but yet not null, nor to be dissolved, which is the most usual case; because all at age do choose for themselves, even in the matters of salvation; and though they ought to be ruled by parents, yet when they are not, their own act bindeth them. But if the incapacity of the persons make it null, that is another case.

Q. 26. How shall men be sure what degrees are prohibited, and what is incest, when Moses' law is abrogated, and the law of nature is dark and doubtful in it, and Christ saith little of it?

A. I. Those passages in Moses' laws, which are but God's explication of a dark law of nature, do still tell us how God once expounded it, and consequently how far it doth extend, though Moses' law as such be abrogated.

2. The laws about such restraint of marriage are laws of order; and therefore bind when order is necessary for the thing ordered, but not when it destroyeth the good of the thing ordered, which is its end. Therefore incest is unlawful out of such cases of necessity; but to Adam's sons and daughters it was a duty: and all the children of Noah's three sons must needs marry either their own brothers and sisters, or the children of their father's brethren, which moved Lot's daughters to do what they did.

3. In these matters of order some laws of the land must be obeyed, though they restrain men more than the laws of God.

Q. 27. Is marriage in every forbidden degree to be dissolved?

A. Not if it be a degree only forbidden by man's laws; or if it were in such foresaid cases of absolute necessity: but that which God doth absolutely forbid, must not be continued but dissolved; as the case of Herod, and him, 1 Cor. v. tells us.

CHAPTER XLI.

OF THE EIGHTH COMMANDMENT.

Q. 1. WHAT are the words of the eighth commandment?

A. "Thou shalt not steal."

Q. 2. What is the stealing here forbidden?

A. All injurious getting or keeping that which is another's.

Q. 3. When is it injurious?

A. When it is done without right: and that is, when it is done without the owner's consent, or by a fraudulent and forcible getting his consent, and without just authority from a superior power, who may warrant it.

Q. 4. What power may allow one to take that which is another's?

A. 1. God, who is the only absolute owner of all, did allow the Israelites to take the Egyptians' and Canaanites' goods; and so may do by whom he will. 2. And a magistrate may take away the goods of a delinquent who forfeiteth them; and may take from an unwilling subject such tribute as is his due, and as much of his estate as the law alloweth him to take for the necessary defence of the commonwealth, and may force him to pay his debts: and a father may take from his child, who is but a conditional sub-proprietor, what he seeth meet.

Q. 5. But what if it be so small a matter, as will be no loss to him? Is it sinful theft to take it?

A. Yes; if there be none of his consent, nor any

law to warrant you, it is theft, how small soever the thing be. But if the common sense of mankind suppose that men would consent if they knew it; or if the law of God, or the just law of man, enable you to take it, it is no theft. And so God allowed the Israelites to pluck the ears of corn, or eat fruit as they passed through a vineyard in hunger, so be it that they carried none away. And a man may gather a leaf of an herb for a medicine in another man's ground, because humanity supposeth that the owner will not be against it.[a]

Q. 6. But what if he can spare it, and I am in great necessity, and it be his duty to relieve me, and he refuseth?

A. You are not allowed to be your own carver; the common good must be preferred before your own. And if every one shall be judge when their necessity alloweth them to take from another, the property and right of all men will be vain, and the common order and peace be overthrown. And while you may either beg, or seek to the parish or magistrate for relief, there is no place for a just plea of your necessity.

Q. 7. But should a man rather die by famine, than take from another that is bound to give, and will not?

A. If his taking will, by encouraging thieves, do the commonwealth more hurt than his life will do good, he is bound rather to die than steal. But I dare not say that it is so, where all these following conditions concur. 1. If it be so small a thing as is merely to save life (as God allowed the foresaid taking of fruit and corn). 2. If you have first tried all other means, as begging, or seeking to the magistrate. 3. If by the secrecy, or by the effect, it be no hurt to the commonwealth, but good. As for instance, if to save life, one take an apple from a tree of him that is unwilling, or eat pease or corn in the field; if children have parents that would famish them; if a company in a ship should lose all their provision save one man's, and he have enough for them all, and would give them none, I think the law of nature alloweth them to take as much as will save their lives, against his will. If David, the Lord's anointed, and his six hundred men, want bread, they think they may take it from a churlish Nabal.[b] If an army, which is necessary to save a kingdom from a foreign enemy, should want money and food, and none would give it them, it seemeth unnatural to say, that they should all famish, and lose the kingdom, rather than take free quarter, or things absolutely necessary, from the unwilling. The commonwealth's right in every subject's estate is greater than his own, as the common good is better than his. But these rare cases are no excuse for the unjust taking of the least that is another's without his consent.

Q. 8. But may not a child, or servant, take that meat or drink which is but meet, if the parents and masters be unwilling?

A. No, unless, as aforesaid, merely to save life. If children have hard parents, they must patiently bear it. If servants have hard masters, they may leave them, or seek remedy of the magistrate for that which they are unable to bear. But the world must not be taught to invade other men's property, and be judges of it themselves.

Q. 9. But what if he owe me a debt and will not pay me, or keep unjust possession of my goods, may I not take my own by stealth or force, if I be able?

A. Not without the magistrate, who is the preserver of common order and peace, when your taking it would break that order; and such liberty would encourage robbery. If you take it, you sin not against his right, but you sin against the greater right and peace of the commonwealth.

Q. 10. But what if I owe him as much as he oweth me, may I not stop it, and refuse to pay him?

A. Yes, if the law and common good allow it, but not else; for you must rather lose your right, than hurt the commonwealth, by breaking the law which keeps its peace.

Q. 11. What if I win it by gaming, or a wager, when he consented to run the hazard?

A. Such gaming as is used in a covetous desire of getting from another, without giving him any thing valuable for it, is sinful in the winner and the loser; and another's covetous, sinful consent to stand to the hazard, maketh it not lawful for you to take it. You forfeit it on both sides, and the magistrate may do well to take it from you both. But if a moderate wager be laid, only to be a penalty to the loser for being confident in some untruth, it is just to take his wager as a penalty, and give it to the poor. But the just law of exchanging rights by contract is, to take nothing that is another's, without giving him for it that which is worth it.

Q. 12. Is it lawful to try masteries for a prize or wager; as running of men, or horses, cockfights, fencing, wrestling, contending in arts, &c.?

A. It is not lawful to do it, 1. Out of covetousness, desiring to get another man's money, though to his loss and grief. 2. Nor by cruelty, as hazarding men's lives by over-striving, in running, wrestling, fencing, &c. But if it be used as a manly recreation, and no more laid on the wager than is meet to be spent on a recreation, and may be justly spared without covetousness, or hurting another, I know not but it may be lawfully done.

Q. 13. What are the rules to avoid sinful injury, in buying and selling?

A. 1. That you give the true worth, that is, the market price, for what you buy, and desire not to have it cheaper, unless it be of a rich man that abateth you the price in kindness or charity, or one that, having bought it cheaper, can afford to sell accordingly.[c] And that you neither ask nor desire more than the said true worth for what you sell, unless it be somewhat that you would not otherwise part with, which is worth more to some one man than to others, or one that in liberality will give you more.

2. That you do as you would be done by, if you were in the same circumstances with the other, supposing your own desires just.

3. That you work not on the ignorance or necessities of another, to get more or take less than the worth.

4. And, therefore, that you deceive him not by hiding the fault of what you sell, nor by any false words or wiles.

5. That if a man be overseen, you hold him not to his bargain to his loss, if you can release it without a greater loss. Yet that you stand to your own word to him if he will not discharge you. More I omit.[d]

Q. 14. Is it lawful to take usury, or gain, for money lent?

A. The great difference of men's judgments about usury, should make all the more cautelous to venture on none that is truly doubtful. I shall give my judgment in some conclusions.

1. It is evident that usury of other things, as well as of money, was forbidden the Jews, Deut. xxiii. 19, 20; Lev. xxv. 36, 37; Exod. xxii. 25. And by

[a] Deut. xxiii. 25; Matt. xii. 1; Luke vi. 1.

[b] Even king Ahab might not take Naboth's vineyard.

[c] Lev. xxv. 14; Prov. xx. 14.

[d] Amos viii. 6.

usury is meant any thing more than was lent taken for the use of it.

2. It is manifest, the word "nesheck" signifying biting usury, that it is unmerciful hurting another that is here meant.

3. It is manifest, that it was to the poor that this manner of lending was not to be used; and that only to a brother or Israelite, who also might not be bought as a forced servant; but to a stranger it was lawful.

4. The Israelites then used no merchandise, or buying and selling for gain. They lived on flocks, herds, and vineyards, and fig-trees. So that it is only taking usury of any thing that was lent to the needy, when charity bound them to relieve them by lending, that is here meant.

5. To exact the principal, or thing lent, was as truly forbidden, when the poor could not pay it. And so it was to deny to give him freely in his need.

6. All this plainly showeth that this supposeth a case in which one is bound to use mercy to another in want, and that it is mere unmercifulness that is here forbidden.

7. The law described the sin, and the prophets, when they speak against usury, do but name it; making no new law, but supposing it described in the law before.

8. The law of Moses, as such, bound not the rest of the world, nor bindeth christians now, 2 Cor. iii.

9. Therefore there is no usury forbidden but what is against the law of nature, or the supernatural revelation of Christ.

10. The law of nature and of Christ forbid all injustice and uncharitableness, and therefore all usury which is against justice or charity. Every man must in trading, lending, and giving, keep the two grand precepts; "Do as you would (justly) be done by," and "Love your neighbours as yourselves."

11. To take more for the use than the use of the money, horse, goods, or any thing, was really worth to the user, is injustice. And to take either use or principal when it will do more hurt to him that payeth it, than it is like to do good to ourselves, or any other to whom we are more obliged, is contrary to charity: and so it is not to give where we are obliged to give.

12. Merchandise, or trading by buying and selling for gain, is real usury. They that lay out money on goods, and sell them for more than they gave for them, do take use or increase for their money of the buyer: which was forbidden the Israelites to poor brethren. And it is all one to make a poor man pay one shilling in the pound for the use of the money to buy cloth with, as to make him pay one shilling more than was paid for the cloth. And if a draper be bound to lend a poor man money to buy cloth, without use, he is as much bound to sell him cloth without gain.

13. Merchandise, or trading for gain, is not unlawful, being used without injustice and uncharitableness.

14. Every one that hath money is not bound to lend it at all: and not to lend it at all is as much against the good of some borrowers, as to lend it and take but what the use of it was worth to them.

15. No more must be taken for use than the user had real profit by it; unless it be when the rich are willing to pay more, or run the hazard, or what a man loseth by one bargain he gets by another.[e]

16. Some usury is an act of great charity: viz. a landlord offereth to sell his tenant his land for much less than the worth: the tenant hath not money to buy it; a rich neighbour told him, The land is also offered to me; but if you will, I will lend you money on use to buy it, and pay me when you can. It was wood land: the tenant borrows the money; and in two years sells the wood, which paid it all, and had the land for almost nothing. Was not this charitable usury?[f]

I know a worthy person that, trading in ironworks, did, partly for himself and partly in charity, take to use the monies of many honest, mean people, that knew not else how to live or to use it: and from a small estate he grew to purchase at least seven thousand pounds per annum to himself and his sons. Was there any uncharitableness in this usury?[g]

17. It is great uncharitableness in some not to give use for money, and cruelty to set it out without use: as when poor orphans are left with nothing but a little money to maintain them, and abundance of poor widows that have a little money, and no trade to use it in, and must beg if they presently spend the stock; if they lend it the rich, or those that gain by it in trading, the gainers are unmerciful if they pay not use for it, as well as unjust.

18. They that say, We must not lend to make men rich, but only to the needy, do put down all common trading; and forbid most young men to marry: for that which will maintain a single man plentifully will not maintain a wife and children, and provide them necessary portions: and if he must not endeavour to grow richer than he is, how shall he maintain them, who had but enough for himself before? And how shall he be able to relieve the poor, or do any such good works, if he may not endeavour to grow richer?

Q. 15. If a merchant find that it is usual to deceive the custom-house, or poor men think chimney money or other legal taxes to be an oppression, may they not, by concealment, save what they can?

A. No; the law hath given it the king; if you like not to be his subjects on the terms of the law, remove into another land; if you cannot, you must patiently suffer here. It is no more lawful to rob the king than to rob another man.

Q. 16. Is it necessary to restore all that one hath wrongfully got?

A. Yes, if he be able.[h]

Q. 17. What if he be not able?

A. If he can get it by his friends, he must; if not, he must humble himself to him that he wronged, and confess the debt, and bind himself to pay him if ever he be able.

Q. 18. But what if it be a malicious man, that will disgrace or ruin him if he know it, is he bound to confess it?

A. Humanity itself will tell a man, that repentance is the greatest honour, next to innocence; and that a repenting person, that will do it at so dear a rate, is unlike to wrong him any more: and, therefore, we may suppose that there are few so inhuman as to undo such a penitent. But if he that knoweth him have good cause to judge that the injured person will make use of his confession, 1. To the wrong of the king or the commonwealth, or the honour of christianity; 2. Or to a greater hurt of the confessor than the confession is like to prove a good to any; he may then forbear such a confession to the person injured, and send him secretly his money by an unknown hand: or, if he cannot pay him, confess it to God and his spiritual guide.

Q. 19. What if a man can restore it, but not without the wrong or ruin of his wife and children, who knew not of his sin?

e Deut. xxiii. 20.
f Matt. xxv. 27; Luke xix. 23.
g Prov. xxii. 16.
h Exod. xxii. 5, 6, 12; Lev. vi. 4; Luke xix. 8.

A. His wife took him with his debts, as he did her; and this is a real debt: she can have no right by him in that which he hath no right himself to; and he cannot give his children that which is none of his own.

Q. 20. What if I wronged a master but in some small matter in marketing, which is long since gone?

A. The debt remaineth: and if you have the value, you must offer satisfaction; though it is like, that for small things few will take it: but you must confess the fault and debt; and forgiveness is equal to restitution.

Q. 21. What if those that I wronged be dead?

A. You owe the value to those that they gave their estate to: or, if they be dead, to the next heirs: and if all be dead, to God, in some use of charity.

Q. 22. What if any father got it ill, and left it me?

A. He can give you no right to that which he had none to himself; sinful keeping is theft, as well as sinful getting.

Q. 23. What if the thing be so usual as well as small, as that none expect confession or restitution: as for boys to rob orchards?

A. Where you know it would not be well taken, restitution is no duty; but if you have opportunity, it is safest to confess.

Q. 24. Is it thievery to borrow and not pay?

A. Deceitful borrowers are of the worst sort of thieves, against whom one cannot so well save his purse as against others: and they would destroy all charitable lending, by destroying mutual belief and trust. Many tradesmen that after break, do steal more, and wrong more, than many highway robbers that are hanged. But it is not all breakers that are so guilty.[i]

Q. 25. What borrowing is it that is theft?

A. 1. When you have no intent to pay. 2. When you know that you are not able to pay, nor like to be able. 3. When there is a great hazard and danger of your not paying, with which you do not acquaint the lender, and so he consenteth not to run the hazard.[k]

Q. 26. What if it would crack my credit, and ruin my trade, if I should reveal the hazard and weakness of my estate?

A. You must not rob others for fear of ruin to yourself. If you take his money without his consent, you rob him. And no man that is ignorant is said to consent: if you hide that which would hinder him from consenting if he knew it, you have not really his consent, but rob him.

Q. 27. What is the duty required in this eighth commandment?

A. To further the prosperity or estate of your neighbour as you would do your own, that is, with the same sincerity.

Q. 28. Must a man work at his trade for his neighbour as much as for himself; or as much use his estate for others?

A. I said, with the same sincerity, not in the same manner and degree. For there are some duties of beneficence proper to ourselves as the objects, and some common to others. And as nature causeth the eye to wink for itself, and the gust to taste for itself immediately, and yet also consequently for every member's good, and principally for the whole man; so every man must get, possess, and use, what he can immediately for himself. But as a member of the body which hath a due regard to the good of every member, and is more for the whole than for himself.[l]

Q. 29. Who be the greatest breakers of this commandment?

A. 1. They that care for nobody but themselves, and think they may do with their own as they list, as if they were absolute proprietors, whereas they are but the stewards of God: and it is the pleasure of the flesh which is the use they think they may put all their estates to.

2. Those that see their brother have need, and shut up the bowels of their compassion from him;[m] that is, relieve him not when it is not for want of ability, but of compassion and will; or that drop but some inconsiderable pittance to the poor, like the crumbs or bones to the dogs, the leavings of the flesh, while they please their appetites and fancies with the rest, and live as he (Luke xvi.) who was clothed in purple and silk, and fared sumptuously or deliciously daily, while the poor at the door had but the scraps. That make so great a difference between themselves and others, as to prefer their own superfluities and pleasures before the necessities of others, even when multitudes live in distressing poverty.

3. Those that live idly, because they are [n] rich or slothful, and think they are bound to labour for none but themselves; whereas God bindeth all that are able to live in some profitable labour for others, and to give to them that need. So also they that by prodigality, drunkenness, gaming, luxury, or other excess, disable themselves to relieve the poor.

4. Those that out of a covetous, worldly mind heap up riches for themselves and their children,[o] to leave a name and great estate behind them; (that their children may as hardly be saved as themselves;) as if all that they can gather were their children's due, while others better than they are utterly neglected.

5. Those that give with grudging, or make too great a matter of their gifts, and set too high a price upon them, and must have it even extorted from them.

6. Those that neglect to pay due wages to them that labour for them, and would bring down the price below its worth, so that poor labourers cannot live upon it: and that strive in all their bargainings to have every thing as cheap as they can get it, without respect to the true worth or the necessities of others.[p]

7. Those that help not to maintain their own families and kindred as far as they are able.

Q. 30. Who are the greatest robbers, or breakers of both parts of this command, negative and preceptive?

A. 1. Emperors, kings, and other chief rulers, who oppress the people, and impoverish them, while they are bound by office to be God's ministers for their good.[q]

2. Soldiers who, by unjust wars, destroy the countries, or, in just war, unjustly rob the people. Oh, the woeful ruins that such have made! So that famine hath followed the poverty and desolation, to the death of thousands.

3. Unrighteous judges, who for bribes or partiality, or culpable ignorance, do fine righteous men, or give away the estates of the just, and do wrong men by the pretence of law, right, and justice, and deprive the just of their remedy.

4. Perfidious patrons, who simoniacally sell, or

[i] Rom. xiii. 8, 9.
[k] Psal. xxxvii. 21.
[l] 1 Cor. xii. 21; Eph. iv. 28.
[m] Deut. xv. 8, 11; Eph. iv. 28; Jam. ii. 16; 1 John iii. 17; Matt. xxv.; Prov. xxxi. 20; Psal. lxxii. 13; Ezek. xvi. 49.
[n] Prov. xxxi.; 2 Thess. iii.
[o] Nabal.
[p] 1 Tim. v. 8; Jam. v. 4, 5.
[q] Exod. iii. 9, 10; Psal. xii. 5, 6; lxxiii. 8; Prov. xxviii. 16; Eccl. iv. 1, 2; 1 Sam. xii. 3, 4.

sacrilegiously alienate, the devoted maintenance of the church.

5. Much more those rulers and prelates who factiously, maliciously, or otherwise culpably, silence and cast out faithful ministers, sacrilegiously alienating them from the work of Christ, and the church's service, to which they were consecrated and devoted, and casting them out of their public, ministerial maintenance.[r]

6. All persecutors who unjustly fine men, and deprive them of their estates, for not sinning against God by omission or commission, especially when they ruin multitudes.

7. Cruel, oppressing landlords, who set their poor tenants such hard bargains as they cannot live on.[s]

8. Cruel lawyers, and other officers, who take such fees as undo the clients; so that men that have not money to answer their covetous expectations, must lose their right.

9. Unmerciful physicians, who consider not the scarcity of money with the poor, but by chargeable fees, and apothecaries' bills, put men to die for want of money.[t]

10. Unmerciful usurers and creditors, that will not forgive a debt to the poor, who have it not to pay.

11. People that rob the ministers of their tithes.

12. Cheaters, who by gaming, false plays, and tricks of craft, or false writings, concealments, or by quirks in law that are contrary to equity, do beguile men of their right.[u] And especially the poor, who cannot contend with them; yea, and some their own kindred.

CHAPTER XLII.

OF THE NINTH COMMANDMENT.

Q. 1. What are the words of the ninth commandment?

A. "Thou shalt not bear false witness against thy neighbour."

Q. 2. What is it which is herein forbidden?

A. All falsehood injurious to the innocency, right, or reputation of another; especially in witness-bearing, accusations, or judgments, contrary to public justice. The act forbidden is falsehood; the object against which it is done is our neighbour's good or right of any sort; whether his good name, or estate, or life, especially as it perverteth the hearer's judgment and love, or public justice.[a]

Q. 3. Is all lying here forbidden, or only injurious lying?

A. All lying is injurious, and forbidden.[b]

Q. 4. What injury doth a jesting lie do to any one? or a lie which only saveth the speaker from some hurt, without hurting any other? Yea, some lies seem to be profitable and necessary. As if a parent, or physician, tell a lie to a child or patient, to get them to take a medicine to save their lives; or a subject tell a lie to a traitor, or enemy, to save the life of the king; tell me, I pray you, why God forbiddeth all such lies.

A. 1. You must consider, that God is the Author of order; and order is to the world its useful disposition to its operations and ends. Just as it is to a clock, or watch, or a coach, or ship, or any such engine; disorder the parts, and it is good for nothing. A kingdom, army, church, or any society, is essentiated by order, without which it is destroyed. And the world of mankind being made up of individual persons, the ordering of particular men is the chief thing to the order of the human world. As we die, when disorder of parts or humours maketh the body uncapable of the soul's operations, so a man's soul is vitiated and dead to its chief ends, when its order is overthrown. All godliness and morality is nothing but the right order of the dispositions and acts of man, in our subordination to the governing will of God, which is our law. It is not another substance that grace maketh in us, but another order. And all sin is nothing but the contrary disorder; and that man's words be the true and just expression of his mind is a great part of the order of his words, without which it were better man were speechless.

And, 2. You must consider, that God hath made man a sociable creature, and each one a part of the world, which is one kingdom of God, the universal King. And that each part is more for the whole than for itself, because the common welfare of the whole is better than of any part, as being a higher end of government, and more illustriously showing the glory of God.

And, 3. You must consider, that because God only knoweth the heart, there can be no society and conversation but by words, and other signs. And that without mutual trust there can be no society of love, concord, or mutual help. But utter distrust is a virtual war. There can be no prince and subjects, no husband and wife, no pastor and flocks, without some trust. And trustiness is truth-telling. So far as a man is taken for a liar, he is not believed or trusted.[c]

4. You must consider, that if God should leave it to man's discretion in what cases to lie, and in what not, and did not absolutely forbid it, selfishness, interest, and folly, would scarce leave any credibility or trustiness in mankind; for how can I know whether your judgment now bid you not lie, for some reason that I know not?

5. So that you see that leave to lie when we think it harmless would be but to pluck up a flood-gate of all deceit, untrustiness, and utter confusion, which would shame, and confound, and ruin societies and the world. And then it is easy to know that it is better that any man's commodity or life miscarry, (which yet was scarce ever done merely for want of a lie,) than that the world should be thus disordered and confounded. As men sick of the plague must be shut up rather than go about to infect the city; and some houses must be blown up rather than the fire not be stopped; and as soldiers burn suburbs to save a city, &c.; so no man's private good must be pretended for the corruption and misery of the world.[d]

6. And remember that lying is the devil's character and work, and so the work and character of his servants. And truth is the effect of God's perfection, and his veracity so necessary to mankind, that without it we could have no full assurance of the future blessedness which he hath promised. If God could lie, our hopes were all shaken; for we should be still uncertain whether his word be true. And God's laws and his image must signify his perfection.[e]

Q. 5. Wherein doth the truth of words consist?

A. In a threefold respect: 1. In a suitable significancy of the matter. 2. In an agreeable significancy of the mind of the speaker. 3. And both these, as suited to the information of the hearer.

[r] 2 Cor. vii. 2. [s] Isa. v. 7; Jer. vi. 6.
[t] Isa. iii. 12; xvi. 4; xix. 20.
[u] Lev. xix. 13; 1 Cor. vi. 7, 8; 1 Thess. iv. 6.
[a] Lev. xix. 11; Prov. xv. 4.

[b] Col. iii. 9; Rev. xxi. 17; xxii. 15.
[c] Prov. vi. 17; xii. 19, 22; xiii. 5; xvii. 7; 1 Tim. i. 10.
[d] Rom. iii. 7.
[e] 1 Kings xxii. 22; John viii. 44; Tit. i. 2; Heb. vi. 18.

Q. 6. What is false speaking?

A. 1. That which is so disagreeable to the matter as to represent it falsely. 2. That which is so disagreeable to the speaker's mind as to represent it falsely to another. 3. That which speaketh the matter and mind aptly as to themselves and other hearers, but so as the present hearer, who we know takes the words in another sense, will by our design be deceived by them.[f]

Q. 7. Is all false speaking lying, or what is a lie?

A. Lying properly signifieth a culpable speaking of falsehood; and it hath divers degrees of culpability. When falsehood is spoken without the speaker's fault, it is not morally to be called a lie. Though improperly the Hebrews called any thing a lie which would deceive those that trust in it; and so all men and creatures, though blameless, are liars to such as overtrust them.[g]

Q. 8. Which are the divers degrees of lying, or culpable false speaking?

A. 1. One is privative; when men falsely represent things by diminutive expressions. Things may be falsely represented by defective as well as by excessive speeches. He that speaks of God, and heaven, and holiness, faintly as good, saith a grammatical truth; but if he speak not of them as best, or excellent, it is, morally, a false expression through defect. He that saith coldly, "To murder, to be perjured, to silence Christ's ministers unjustly, is not well," as Eli said of his sons' wickedness; or only saith, "I cannot justify it," or, "It is hard to justify it;" saith a grammatical truth, but a moral falsehood, by the extenuating words, as if he would persuade the hearer to think it some small or doubtful matter, and so to be impenitent.

2. He that speaketh falsely through rashness, heedlessness, neglect of just information, or any ignorance which is culpable, is guilty of some degree of lying; but he that knowingly speaketh falsely, is a liar in a higher degree.

3. He that by culpable forgetfulness speaks falsely, is to be blamed; but he that remembereth and studieth it, much more.

4. He that lieth in a small matter, which seemeth not to hurt, but perhaps to profit, the hearer, is to be blamed; but he that lieth in great matters, and to the great hurt of others, much more.

5. He that speaketh either contrary to his mind, or contrary to the matter, culpably, lieth; but he that speaketh both contrary to his mind and the matter, lieth worse.

6. He that by equivocation useth unapt and unsuitable expressions, to deceive him that will misunderstand them, is to be blamed; but he that will stand openly, bold-faced, in a lie, much more.

7. It is sin to speak untruths of our own, which we might avoid; but it is much worse to father them on God, or the holy Scripture.[h]

8. It is sin, by falsehood, to deceive one; but much more to deceive multitudes, even whole assemblies, or countries.

9. It is sin in a private man to lie to another about small things; but much more heinous for a ruler, or a preacher, to deceive multitudes, even in matters of salvation.

10. It is a sin rashly to drop a falsehood; but much greater to write books, or dispute for it, and justify it.

11. It is a sin to lie from a good intent; but much more out of envy, malice, or malignity.

12. It is a sin to lie in private talk; but much more to lie to a magistrate or judge who hath power to examine us.

13. It is a sin to assert an untruth as aforesaid; but much greater to swear it, or offer it to God in our profession or vows.

Q. 9. Is all deceiving of another a sin?

A. No; there is great difference, 1. Between deceiving one that I am bound to inform, and one that I am not bound to inform. 2. And between deceiving one to his benefit or harmlessly, and to his hurt and injury. 3. And between deceiving him by just means, and by unjust, forbidden means.

I. I am under no obligation to inform a robber, or an usurping persecutor, as such; but to others I may be obliged to open the truth.

II. I may deceive a patient, or child, to profit him, when I may not do it to hurt him.

III. I may deceive such as I am not bound to inform, by my silence, or my looks or gestures, which I suppose he will misunderstand, when I may not deceive him by a lie.

Q. 10. Is it not all one to deceive one way or another?

A. No; 1. I am not bound to open my mind to all men. What right hath a thief to know my goods or heart; or a persecutor to know where I hide myself?

2. But I have before largely showed you that lying is so great an evil against common trust and society in the world, as is not to be used for personal commodity or safety.

3. And other signs, looks, and gestures, being not appointed for the natural and common indications of the mind, are more left to human liberty and prudence, to use for lawful ends. As Christ, Luke xxiv. made by his motion as if he would have gone further; and even by words about Cæsar's tribute, and other cases, concealed his mind, and oft denied the Pharisees a resolution of questions which they put to him. Stratagems in a lawful war are lawful, when by actual shows and seemings an enemy is deceived.

Q. 11. But the Scriptures mention many instances of equivocation and flat lying, in the Egyptian midwives, in Rahab, in David, and many others, without blame, and some of them with great commendation and reward, Heb. xi.

A. 1. It is God's law that tells us what is sin and duty, when the history oft tells us but what was done, and not how far it was well or ill done.

2. It is not the lie that is commended in the midwives and Rahab, but their faith and charity.

3. That which God pardoneth, as he did polygamy and rash divorce, to godly men that are upright in the main, and especially such as knew it not to be sin, is not thereby justified; nor will it be so easily pardoned to us, who live in the clearer gospel light.

Q. 12. But when the Scripture saith that all men are liars, and sad experience seemeth to confirm it, what credit do we owe to men, and what certainty is there of any history?

A. History, by writing or verbal tradition, is of so great use to the world, that Satan maketh it a chief part of his work, as he is the deceiver and enemy of mankind, to corrupt it: and false history is a most heinous sin, and dangerous snare, by which the great deceiver keeps up his kingdom in the world. Heathenism, Mahometanism, popery, heresy, and malignity, and persecution, are all maintained by false tradition and history. Therefore we must not be too hasty or confident in believing man; and yet denying just belief will be our sin and great loss.

[f] Rom. iii. 4.

[g] Prov. xii. 17; Psalm lii. 4; cxvi. 11; cxx. 7; Eph. v. 6.

[h] 1 Cor. xv. 15; 1 John v. 10.

Q. 13. How then shall we know what and whom to believe?

A. 1. We must believe no men that speak against God or his word; for we are sure that God cannot lie; and the Scripture is his infallibly sealed word.

2. We must believe none that speak against the light of nature and common notices of all mankind; for that were to renounce humanity; and the law of nature is God's first law. But it is not the sentiments of nature, as depraved, which is this law.

3. We must believe no men against the common senses of mankind, exercised on their duly qualified objects. Faith contradicteth not common sense, though it go above it. We are men before we are christians, and sense and reason are presupposed to faith. The doctrine which saith there is no bread nor wine, after consecration, in the sacrament, doth give the lie to the eyes, taste, and feeling, and intellectual perception of all sound men, and therefore is not to be believed; for if sense be not to be trusted, we know not that there is a church, or a man, or a Bible, or any thing in the world, and so nothing can be believed. Whether all sound senses may be deceived or not, God hath given us no surer way of certainty.

4. Nothing is to be believed against the certain interest of all mankind, and tending to their destruction. That which would damn souls, or deny their immortality and future hope, or ruin the christian world or nations, is not to be believed to be duty or lawful; for truth is for good, and faith is for felicity, and no man is bound to such destructive things.[i]

5. Nothing is to be believed as absolutely certain, which depends on the mere honesty of the speakers; for all men are liable to mistake, or lie.

6. The more ignorant, malicious, unconscionable, factious, and siding any man, the less credible he is; and the wiser and nearer to the action any man is, and the more conscionable, peaceable, and impartial he is, the more credible he is. An enemy speaking well of a man, is far more credible than a friend: multitudes, as capable and honest, are more credible than one.

7. As that certainty which is called moral, as depending on men's free-will, is never absolute, but hath many degrees, as the witness is more or less credible; so there is a certainty by men's report, tradition, or history, which is physical, and wholly infallible: as that there is such a place as Rome, Paris, &c.; and that the statutes of the land were made by such kings and parliaments to whom they are ascribed; and that there have been such kings, &c. For proof of which know, 1. That besides the free acts, the will hath some acts as necessary as it is to the fire to burn, viz. to love ourselves and felicity, and more such. 2. That when all men of contrary interest, friends and foes, agree in a matter that hath sensible evidence, it is the effect of such a necessitating cause. 3. And there is no cause in nature that can make them so agree in a lie. Therefore it is a natural certainty. Look back to the sixth chapter.

Q. 14. Why is false witness in judgment so great a sin?

A. Because it containeth in it all these odious crimes conjunct: 1. A deliberate lie. 2. The wrongful hurting of another contrary to the two great principles of converse, justice and love. 3. It depriveth the world of the benefit of government and judicatures. 4. It turneth them into the plague and ruin of the innocent. 5. It blasphemeth or dishonoureth God, by whose authority rulers judge, as if he set up officers to destroy us by false witness, or knew it not, or would not revenge injustice. 6. It overthroweth human converse and safety, when witnesses may destroy whom they please, if they can but craftily agree.[k]

Q. 15. Is there no way to prevent this danger to mankind?

A. God can do it. If he give wise and righteous rulers to the world they may do much towards it; but wicked rulers use false witness as the devil doth, for to destroy the just, as Jezebel did.

Q. 16. How should good rulers avoid it?

A. 1. By causing teachers to open the danger of it to the people. 2. Some old canons made invalid the witness of all notorious wicked men: how can he be trusted in an oath, that maketh no conscience of drunkenness, fornication, lying, or other sin?

Q. 17. How, then, are so few destroyed by false witnesses?

A. It is the wonderful providence of God, d claring himself the Governor of the world; that when there are so many thousand wicked men who all have a mortal hatred to the godly, and will daily swear and lie for nothing, and any two of these might take away our lives at pleasure, there are yet so few this way cut off. But God hath not left himself without witness in the world, and hath revenged false witness on many, and made conscience a terrible accuser for this crime.[l]

Q. 18. What is the positive duty of the ninth commandment?

A. 1. To do justice to all men in our places.

2. To defend the innocent to the utmost of our just power. If a lawyer will not do it for the love of justice and man, without a fee when he cannot have it, he breaketh this commandment.

3. To reprove backbiters, and tell them of their sin.

4. To give no scandal, but to live so blamelessly that slanderers may not be believed.

5. On all just occasions especially to defend the reputation of the gospel, godliness, and good men, the cause and laws of God, and not silently for self-saving, to let Satan and his agents make them odious by lies, to the seduction of the people's souls.[m]

i 1 John iv. 1, 2.

k Matt. xxvi. 62; xxvii. 13; Mark xiv. 55, 56; Numb. xxxv. 30; Acts vi. 13; Deut. xix. 16—18; Prov. vi. 19; xii. 17; xxi. 28; xxv. 18; Psal. xxxv. 11.

l Prov. xix. 5, 9.

m Prov. xxv. 23; Psal. xv. 3, 5.

CHAPTER XLIII.

OF THE TENTH COMMANDMENT.

Q. 1. WHAT are the words of the tenth commandment?

A. "Thou shalt not covet thy neighbour's house; thou shalt not covet thy neighbour's wife, nor his man-servant, nor his maid-servant, nor his ox, nor his ass, nor any thing that is thy neighbour's."

Q. 2. What is forbidden here, and what commanded?

A. 1. In some, the thing forbidden is selfishness, and the thing commanded is to love our neighbour as ourselves.

Q. 3. Is not this implied in the five foregoing commandments?

A. Yes; and so is our love to God in all the nine last. But because there are many more particular instances of sin and duty that can be distinctly named and remembered, God thought it meet to make two general, fundamental commandments, which should contain them all, which Christ called the first and second commandment; "Thou shalt love the Lord thy God with all thy heart," &c; and "Thou shalt love thy neighbour as thyself." The first is the summary and root of all the duties of the other nine, and especially of the second, third, and fourth. The other is the summary of the second table duties; and it is placed last, as being instead of all unnamed instances: as the captain leads the soldiers, and the lieutenant brings up the rear.[a]

Q. 4. What mean you by the sin of selfishness?

A. I mean that inordinate self-esteem, self-love, and self-seeking, with the want of a due, proportionable love to others, which engageth men against the good of others, and inclineth them to draw from others to themselves: it is not an inordinate love of ourselves, but a diseased self-love.[b]

Q. 5. When is self-love ordinate, and when is it sinful?

A. That which is ordinate, 1. Valueth not a man's self blindly above his worth. 2. It employeth a man in a due care of his own holiness, duty, and salvation. 3. It regardeth ourselves but as little members of the common great body, and therefore inclineth us to love others as ourselves, without much partial disproportion, according to the divers degrees of their amiableness, and to love public good, the church and world, and, much more, God above ourselves. 4. It maketh us studious to do good to others, and rejoice in it as our own, rather than to draw from them to ourselves.[c]

II. Sinful selfishness, 1. Doth esteem, and love, and seek self-interest above its proper worth: it is over-deeply affected with all our own concerns. 2. It hath a low, disproportionable love and regard of others' good. 3. And when it groweth to full malignity, it maketh men envy the prosperity of others, and covet that which is theirs, and desire and rejoice in their disgrace and hurt, when they stand against men's selfish wills, and to endeavour to draw from others to ourselves: selfishness is to the soul like an inflammation or imposthume to the body; which draweth the blood and spirits to itself from their due and common course, till they corrupt the inflamed part.

Q. 6. What mean you by loving others as ourselves?

A. Loving them as members of the same body or society (the world or the church as they are) impartially, with a love proportionable to their worth, and such a careful, practical, forgiving, patient love, as we love ourselves.[d]

Q. 7. But God hath made us individual persons, with so peculiar a self-love, that no man can possibly love another as himself?

A. 1. You must distinguish between sensitive natural love, and rational love. 2. And between corrupt and sanctified nature.

1. Natural sensitive love is stronger to oneself (that is, more sensible of self-interest) than to all the world. I feel not another's pain or pleasure, in itself: I hunger and thirst for myself: a mother hath that natural sensitive love to her own natural child (like that of brutes) which she hath not for any other.[e]

2. Rational love valueth, and loveth, and preferreth every thing according to the degree of its amiableness, that is, its goodness.

3. Rational love destroyeth not sensitive; but it moderateth and ruleth it, and commandeth the will and practice to prefer, and desire, and seek, and delight in higher things (as reason ruleth appetite, and the rider the horse); and to deny and forsake all carnal or private interests, that stand against a greater good.

4. Common reason tells a man, that it is an unreasonable thing in him that would not die to save a kingdom; much more that when he is to love both himself and the kingdom inseparably, yet cannot love a kingdom, yea, or more excellent persons, above himself. But yet it is sanctification that must effectually overcome inordinate self-love, and clearly illuminate this reason, and make a man obey it.[f]

5. To conquer this selfishness is the sum of all mortification, and the greatest victory in this world: and therefore it is here perfectly done by none: but it is done most where there is the greatest love to God, and to the church and public good, and to our neighbours.

Q. 8. What is the sinfulness and the hurt of selfishness?

A. 1. It is a fundamental error and blindness in the judgment: we are so many poor worms and little things; and if an ant or worm had reason, should it think its life, or ease, or other interest, more valuable than a man's, or than all the country's?

2. It is a fundamental pravity and disorder of man's will: it is made to love good as good, and therefore to love most the greatest good.

3. Yea, it blindly casteth down, and trampleth on, all good in the world which is above self-interest. For this prevailing selfishness taketh a man's self for his ultimate end, and all things else but as means to his own interest: God and heaven, and all societies and all virtue, seem no further good to him than they are for his own good and welfare. And selfishness so overcometh reason in some, as to make them dispute for this fundamental error as a truth, that there is nothing to be accounted good by me but that which is good to me as my interest or welfare: and so that which is good to others is not, therefore, good to me.[g]

4. And thus it blasphemously deposeth God in the mind of the sinner; making him no further good to us than as he is a means to our good; and so he is set quite below ourselves: as if he had not made us for himself, and to love him as God, for his own goodness.

5. I told you before (of the first commandment) how this maketh every man his own idol, to be loved above God.

6. Yea, that the selfish would be the idols of the world, and have all men conformed to their judgment, wills, and words.

7. A selfish man is an enemy to the public peace of all societies, and of all true unity and concord: for whereas holy persons as such have all one centre, law, and end, even God and his will, the selfish have as many ends, and centres, and laws as they are persons. So that while every one would have his own interest, will, and lust, to be the common rule and centre, it is by the wonderful, over-ruling power of God that any order is kept up in the world; and because when they cannot be all kings, they agree to make that use of kings which they think will serve their interest best.

8. A selfish man so far can be no true friend; for

[a] Matt. xix. 19; Luke x. 27; Rom. xiii. 9; Lev. xvi. 24; Mark viii. 34.
[b] Jer. xlv. 5; Matt. xvi. 22, 23; Luke xiv. 26, 29, 32, 33.
[c] Phil. ii. 4, 21; 1 Cor. xii.; x. 24.
[d] Col. iii. 12, 13; 1 Cor. xiii.; Eph. iv. 1, 2.
[e] Prov. xiv. 10.
[f] 1 Cor. x. 33; Tit. i. 8; Jam. iii. 15, 17; Col. i. 24.
[g] Prov. iii. 5; xx. 6; xxiii. 4; xxv. 27; xxvi. 5, 12, 16; xxvii. 2; xxviii. 11.

he loveth his friend but as a dog doth his master, for his own ends.

9. A selfish person is so far untrusty, and so false in converse and all relations; for he chooseth, and changeth, and useth all, as he thinks his own interest requireth. If he be a tradesman, believe him no further than his interest binds him; if he be a minister, he will be for that doctrine and practice which is for his carnal interest; if he be a ruler, woe to his inferiors! And therefore it is the highest point in policy, next conscience and common obedience to God, to contrive, if possible, so to twist the interest of princes and people, that both may feel that they are inseparable, and that they must live, and thrive, or die, together.[h]

10. In a word, inordinate selfishness is the grand pravity of nature, and the disease and confusion of all the world: whatever villanies, tyrannies, rebellions, heresies, persecutions, or wickedness you read of in all history, or hear of now on earth, all is but the effects of this adhering by inordinate self-love to self-interest. And if Paul say of one branch of its effects, "The love of money is the root of all evil," we may well say it of this radical, comprehensive sin.

Q. 9. Alas! who is it that is not selfish? How common is this sin! Are there then any saints on earth; or any hope of a remedy?

A. It is so common and so strong, as that, 1. All christians should most fear it, and watch, and pray, and strive against it. 2. And all preachers should more open the evil of it than they do, and live themselves as against it and above it.

1. How much do most over-value their own dark judgments and weak reasonings, in comparison of others![i]

2. How commonly do men measure the wisdom or folly, goodness or badness, of other men, as they are for or against their selfish interest, opinions, side, or way!

3. How impatient are men if self-will, reputation, or interest, be crossed!

4. How will they stretch conscience in words, deeds, or bargaining for gain!

5. How soon will they fall out with friends or kindred, if money or reputation come to a controversy between them!

6. How little feeling pity have they for another in sickness, poverty, prison, or grief, if they be but well themselves!

7. How ordinarily doth interest of body, reputation, wealth, corrupt and change men's judgments in religion! so that selfishness and fleshly interest chooseth not only other conditions and actions of life, but also the religion of most men, yea, of too many teachers of self-denial.[k]

8. And if godly people find this and lament it, how weakly do they resist it, and how little do they overcome it!

9. And though every truly godly man prefer the interest of his soul above that of his body, how few get above a religion of caring and fearing for themselves; to study more the church's good, and, more than that, to live in the delightful love of God, as the infinite good!

10. And of those that love the church of God, how many narrow it to their sect or party, and how few have a universal impartial love to all true christians, as such![l]

Q. 10. Where then are the saints, if this be so?

A. All this sin is predominant in ungodly men; (saving that common grace so far overcometh it in some few, that they can venture and lose their estates and lives for their special friends, and for their country;) but in all true christians it is but in a subdued degree.[m] They hate it more than they love it: they all love God and his church with a far higher estimation than themselves, though with less passion. They would forsake estate and life, rather than forsake Christ and a holy life.[n] They were not true christians if they had not learned to bear the cross, and suffer. They seek and hope for that life of perfect love and unity, where selfishness shall never more divide us.

Q. 11. What is it that maketh the love of others so great a duty?

A. 1. It is but to love God, his interest and image, in others. No man hath seen God; but rational souls, and especially holy ones, are his image, in which we must see and love him. And there is no higher duty than to love God.

2. Love maketh us meet and useful members in all societies, especially in the church of God. It maketh all to love the common good above their own.

3. It maketh all men use their utmost power for the good of all that need them.

4. It overcometh temptations to hurtfulness and division; it teacheth men patiently to bear and forbear; it is the greatest keeper of peace and concord. As one soul uniteth all parts of the body, one spirit of love uniteth all true believers. It is the cement of individuals; the vital, healing balsam which doth more than art to cure our wounds.[o]

If all magistrates loved the people as themselves, how would they use them? If bishops and teachers loved others as themselves, and were as loth to hurt them as to be hurt, and to reproach them as be reproached, and to deliver them from poverty, prison, or danger, as to be safe themselves, what do you think would be the consequent?

How few would study to make others odious, or to ruin them! How few would backbite them, or censoriously condemn them, if they loved them as themselves! If all this city and kingdom loved each other as themselves, what a foretaste would it be of heaven on earth! how delightfully should we all live together! every man would have the good of all others to rejoice in as his own, and be as ready to relieve another as the right hand will the left. We can too easily forgive ourselves our faults and errors, and so should bear with others.[p]

Love is our safety: who is afraid of any one who he thinks loveth him as himself? Who is afraid that he should persecute, imprison, or destroy himself, unless by ignorance or distraction? Love is the delight of life, when it is mutual, and is not disappointed: what abundance of fears, and cares, and passions, and law-suits, would it end! It is the fulfilling of the preceptive part of the law; and as to the penal part, there is no use for it where love prevaileth. To such, saith Paul, there is no law; they are not without it, but above it, so far as it worketh by fear.[q]

5. Love is the preparation and foretaste of glory. Fear, care, and sorrow, are distantly preparing works; but it is joyful love, which is the immediate preparation and foretaste. There is no war, no persecution, no hatred, wrath, or strife in heaven; but

[h] Phil. ii. 4, 21.
[i] 1 Kings xxii. 8; 2 Chron. xviii. 7.
[k] 1 John ii. 15.
[l] Col. i. 4, 8.
[m] 2 Tim. iii. 2.
[n] Luke xiv. 26, 27, 33; 1 Cor. xiii.
[o] 1 Cor. xii.; Eph. iv. 1—3, 16; Rom. xii. 9, 10.
[p] 2 Cor. ii. 4, 8; viii. 7, 8, 24.
[q] Rom. xiii. 10; Gal. v. 6, 13, 22; Phil. i. 15, 17; ii. 1—3; 1 Thess. iv. 4; 1 Tim. vi. 11; Heb. xiii. 1, 2; 1 John iv. 7, 18; Eph. iv. 16.

perfect love, which is the uniting grace, will there more nearly unite all saints, than we that are in a dividing world and body can now conceive of, or perfectly believe.

Q. 12. Is there any hope that love should reign on earth?[r]

A. There is hope that all the sound believers should increase in love, and get more victory over selfishness. For they have all that spirit of love, and obey Christ's last and great command, and are taught of God to love one another; yea, they dwell in love, and so in God, and God in them; and it will grow up to perfection.

But I know of no hope that the malignant seed of Cain should cease the hating of them that are the holy seed, save as grace converteth any of them to God. Of any common or universal reign of love, I see no prognostics of it in rulers, in teachers, or any others in the world; prophecies are dark; but my greatest hope is fetched from the three first petitions of the Lord's prayer, which are not to be put up in vain.

Q. 13. What should we do toward the increase of love?

A. 1. Live so blamelessly, that none may find just matter of hatred in you.[s]

2. Love others, whether they love you or not. Love is the most powerful cause of love.

3. Do hurt to none, but by necessary justice or defence; and do as much good as you can to all.

4. Praise all that is good in men, and mention not the evil without necessity.

5. Do all that you can to make men holy, and win them to the love of God; and then they will love each other by his Spirit, and for his sake.

6. Do all that you can to draw men from sinful, worldly love; for that love of the world which is enmity to God, is also enmity to the love of one another. Further than you can draw men to centre in Christ, and in holy love, there is no hope of true love to others.

7. Patiently suffer wrongs, rather than provoke men to hate you, by unnecessary seeking your right or revenge.

Q. 14. Is all desire of another man's unlawful?

A. All that is to his hurt, loss, and wrong. You may desire another man's daughter to wife, by his consent; or his house, horse, or goods, when he is willing to sell them; but not else.[t]

Q. 15. But what if in gaming, betting, or trading, I desire to get from him, though to his loss?

A. It is a covetous, selfish, sinful desire: you must desire to get nothing from him to his loss and hurt.

Q. 16. But what if he consent to run the hazard, as in a horse race, a game, a wager, &c.? It is no wrong to a consenter.

A. The very desire of hurtful drawing from him to yourself is selfish sin: if he consent to the hazard, it is also his covetous desire to gain from you, and his sin is no excuse for yours; and you may be sure it was not the loss that he consented to; but if he do it as a gift, it is another case.[u]

Q. 17. What be the worst sorts of covetousness?

A. 1. When the son wisheth his father's death for his estate.

2. When men that are old, and near the grave, still covet what they are never like to need or use.

3. When men that have abundance, are never satisfied, but desire more.

4. When they will get it by lying, extortion, or other wicked means, even by perjury and blood, as Jezebel and Ahab got Naboth's vineyard.

5. When princes, not content with their just dominions, invade other men's, and plague the world with unjust wars, blood, and miseries, to enlarge them.[x]

Q. 18. How differ charity and justice?

A. Charity loveth all, because there is somewhat in them lovely; and doth them good without respect to their right, because we love them. Justice respecteth men as in the same governed society, (under God or man,) and so giveth every man his due.

Q. 19. Is it love or justice that saith, "Whatever you would that men should do to you, do ye also to them?"

A. It is both. Justice saith, Do right to all, and wrong to none, as you would have them do to you. Charity saith, Love, and pity, and relieve all to your power, as you would have them love, pity, and relieve you.

Q. 20. Hath this law no exceptions?

A. It supposeth that your own will, for yourselves, be just and good; if you would have another make you drunk, or draw you to any sinful or unclean pleasure, you may not therefore do so by them. But do others such right and good as you may lawfully desire they should do to you.

Q. 21. What are those foundations on which this law is built?

A. 1. That as God hath made us individual persons, so he is the free distributor of his allowance to every person, and therefore we must be content with his allowance, and not covet more.

2. That God hath made us for holiness, and endless happiness in heaven: and therefore we must not so love this world as to covet fulness, and desire more of it than God alloweth us.[y]

3. That God hath made every man a member of the human world, and every christian a member of the church, and no one to be self-sufficient, or independent, as a world to himself. And therefore, all men must love themselves but as members of the body, and love the body, or public good, above themselves, and love other members, as their place and the common interest doth require.[z]

4. That we are not our own, but his that did create us and redeem us: and therefore must love ourselves and others, as his, and according to his will and interest; and not as the selfish, narrow interest tempteth us.

5. That the faithful are made spiritual by the sanctifying Spirit, and therefore savour the things of the Spirit, and refer all outward things thereto; and therefore must not so overvalue provision for the flesh, as to covet and draw from others for his pleasure.[a]

So that, 1. As the first greatest command engageth us wholly to God, as our Creator, Redeemer, and Sanctifier, against that selfishness, which is the idol enemy to God, including the privation of our love to him, and against the trinity of his enemies; the flesh, which would be first pleased; the world, which it would be pleased by; and the devil, who deceiveth and tempteth men by such baits of pleasure; even so this tenth (which is the second summary command) engageth us to love God in our brethren, and to love them according to his interest in them, as members of the same society, with an impartial

r Jam. ii. 8.
s 1 Pet. ii. 17; iii. 8.
t Psal. x. 3; 1 Cor. v. 10, 11; vi. 10; Eph. v. 5; Luke xii. 15.
u Acts xx. 33; 1 Tim. vi. 10.
x Josh. vii. 21; Mic. ii. 2; Prov. xxi. 26; xxviii. 16; Hab. ii. 9; Exod. xviii. 21.
y Heb. xiii. 5; 1 Tim. vi. 8; Phil. iv. 11; 1 John ii. 15; Psal. cxix. 36; Ezek. xxxiii. 31.
z 1 Cor. xii.; vi. 20; vii. 23.
a Rom. viii. 6—8; xiii. 13; Luke xii. 21; Matt. vii. 22.

love, against that selfishness, which is the enemy of impartial love, and common good; and against the lusts of the flesh, which would be first pleased; and the world, which is the provision which it coveteth; and the devil, who would, by such worldly baits, and fleshly pleasure, deceive mankind into ungodliness, sensuality, malignity, mutual enmity, contention, oppression, persecution, perfidiousness, and all iniquity; and finally into endless misery, in separation from the God of love, and the heavenly, perfected, united society of love.[z]

And this is the true meaning of the tenth commandment.

CHAPTER XLIV.

OF THE SACRED MINISTRY, AND CHURCH, AND WORSHIP.

Q. 1. Though you have opened the doctrine of the catholic church and the communion of saints before, in expounding the creed, because the sacraments cannot be understood without the ministry and church, will you first tell us what the ministerial office is?

A. The sacred ministry is an office instituted by Christ, in subordination to his prophetical office, to teach; and to his priestly office, to intercede in worship; and to his kingly office, to be key-bearers of his church, to try and judge of men's title to its communion: and this for the converting of the infidel world, the gathering them into the christian communion, and the helping, guiding, and edifying them therein.[a]

Q. 2. Are they ministers in office to any but the church?

A. Yes: their first work is upon the world, to make them christians, and gather them into the church by teaching and baptizing them.[b]

Q. 3. Is not that the common work of laymen, that are no officers?

A. Laymen must do their best in their capacity and station; but, 1. Officers do it as separated to this work, as their calling. 2. And accordingly do it by a special commission and authority from Christ. 3. And are tried, chosen, and dedicated thereto, as specially qualified.

Q. 4. What must Christ's ministers say and do for the world's conversion?

A. Luke xiv. and Matt. xxii. tell you: they must tell men of the marriage-feast, the blessed provision of grace and glory by Christ, and, by evidence and urgency, compel them to come in. More particularly:

1. They must speak to sinners as from God, and in his name, with a "Thus saith the Lord." They must manifest their commission, or at least that the message which they bring is his; that men may know with whom they have to do; and that he that despiseth, despiseth not men, but God.[c]

2. They must make known to sinners their sinful, dangerous, and miserable state, to convince them of the necessity of a Saviour. As if they should say, He that hath no sin, that is no child of Adam, that shall not die and come to judgment, that needs no Saviour, pardon, and deliverance, let him neglect our invitation: but sin and misery are all men's necessity.

3. They are to tell men what God hath done for them by Christ; what a Saviour he hath given us; what Christ hath done and suffered for us.[d]

4. They are to tell men what grace and glory is purchased for them, and offered to them, and what they may have in Christ, and by him.

5. They are to tell men how willing God is of men's recovery, so that he beseecheth them to be reconciled to him, and ministers are sent to entreat them to accept his grace, who refuseth none that refuse not him.

6. They are to acquaint men with God's conditions, terms, and expectations: not that they give him any satisfying or purchasing price of their own, but that they accept his free gift according to its proper nature and use, and come to Christ that they may have life; but that they come in time, and come sincerely and resolvedly, and believe, and penitently return to God, for which he is ready to assist them by his grace.[e]

7. They must acquaint men with the methods of the tempter, and the hinderances of their faith and repentance, and what opposition they must expect from the flesh, the world, and the devil, and how they must overcome them.

8. They must acquaint men what great assistances and encouragements they shall have from Christ: how good a Master, how perfect a Saviour and Comforter, how sure a word, how sweet a work, how good and honourable company, and how many mercies here, and how sure and glorious a reward for ever; and that all this is put in the balance for their choice, against a deceitful, transitory shadow.[f]

9. They must answer the carnal objections of deceived sinners, and show them clearly that all is folly that is said against Christ and their conversion.

10. They must make men know how God will take it, if they unthankfully neglect or refuse his grace, and that this will leave them without remedy, and greatly add to their sin and misery, and that there is no more sacrifice for sin, but a fearful looking for of judgment, from that God who to such is a consuming fire; and that it will be easier for Sodom in the day of judgment than for such.[g]

Q. 5. In what manner must Christ's ministers preach all this?

A. 1. With the greatest gravity and holy reverence; because it is the message of God.

2. With the greatest plainness; because men are dull of understanding.

3. With the greatest proof and convincing evidence, to conquer prejudice, darkness, and unbelief.

4. With powerful, winning motives, and urgent importunity, because of men's disaffection and averseness. And oh what powerful motives have we at hand, from self-love, from God, from Christ, from necessity, from heaven and hell![h]

5. With life and fervency, because of the unspeakable importance of the matter, and the deadness and hardness of men's hearts.

6. With fervency, in season and out of season, because of men's aptness to lose what they have heard and received, and their need still to be carried on.

[z] Eph. v. 3; Col. iii. 5.

[a] Matt. xvi. 19; xxii. 3, 4; xxiv. 45; xxviii. 19, 20; Acts ii. 42; Rom. i. 1, 2; 1 Cor. iv. 1, 2.

[b] Acts xiv. 23; xx. 28; Tit. i. 5; 1 Tim. iii.

[c] Acts xxvi. 17, 18; Luke x. 16; xxiv. 47; 1 Thess. iv. 8; Matt. ix. 13.

[d] John iii. 16; Heb. x. 14; Rom. iii. 1, 10; Tit. ii. 14.

[e] 2 Cor. v. 19, 20; Luke xiv. 17.

[f] 1 Thess. iii. 5; Eph. vi. 11; 2 Cor. ii. 11; iv. 16, 18; Heb. xi.; xii. 28, 29.

[g] 2 Tim. ii. 25; Tit. ii. 8; Heb. ii. 3; x. 22, 23.

[h] Tit. ii. 6—8; Heb. v. 10, 11; 1 Cor. i. 17, 18; Matt. vii. 29; Acts ii. 37.

7. With constancy to the end, that grace may be preserved and increased by degrees.

8. With seemly and decent expressions, because of captious, cavilling hearers, and the holiness of the work.

9. With concord with all the church of Christ, as preaching the same faith and hope.

10. By the example of holy practice, doing what we persuade them to do, and excelling them in love, and holiness, and patience, and victory over the flesh and world, and winning them, not by force, but by light and love.[i]

Q. 6. What is it that all this is to bring men to?

A. 1. To make men understand and believe what God is to them; what Christ is; what grace and glory are; as is aforesaid in the christian faith.

2. To win men's hearts to the love of these, from the love of sinful, fleshly pleasure, and to fix their wills in a resolved choice.

3. To engage them in the obedient practice of what they love and choose, and help them to overcome all temptations to the contrary.[k]

Q. 7. Why will God have all this and the rest which is for the church, to be an office, work of chosen, separated, consecrated persons?

A. 1. It is certain that all men are not fit for it; alas! too few. The mysteries of godliness are deep and great. The chains of sinners are strong, and God useth to work according to the suitableness of means. Great abilities are requisite to all this: and God would not have his cause and work dishonoured by his ministers' unfitness. Alas! unfit men have been the church's great calamity and reproach![l]

2. God would have his work effectually done; and, therefore, by men that are wholly devoted to it. Were they never so able, if they have avocations, and do it by the halves, dividing their labours between it and the world, this will not answer the necessity and the end: even a Paul must do it publicly, and from house to house, night and day, with tears, Acts xx. 20, 28. It must be done in season and out of season, 2 Tim. iv. 1, 2. Timothy must meditate on these things, and give himself wholly to them, 1 Tim. iv. 15. Paul was separated to the gospel of God, Rom. i. And ministers are stewards of his mysteries, to give the children their meat in season.

3. It is much for the comfort of the faithful to know that it is by God's own ordained officer that his message of invitation, and his sealed covenant, pardon, and gift of Christ and grace, are delivered to them.[m]

4. The very being of an ordered church requireth a guiding official part. It is no ruled society without a ruler; no school without a teacher. Men must know to whom to go for instruction: the law was to be sought from the mouth of the priest, as the messenger of the Lord of hosts, Mal. ii. 7. Read Acts xiv. 73; Tit. i. 5; Eph. iv. 14—16; 1 Thess. v. 12, 13; Luke xii. 42, 43.

5. The safety and preservation of the truth requireth the ministerial office. As the laws of England would never be preserved without lawyers and judges, by the common people; so the Scriptures, and the faith, sacraments, and worship, would never have been brought down to us as they are, without a stated ministry, whose interest, office, and work it is continually to use them. See 1 Tim. v. 20; Eph. iv. 14; Rom. xvi. 16, 17; 1 Tim. iii. 15; Heb. xiii. 7, 9, 17. None have leisure to do this great work as it must be done, but those that by office are wholly separated thereto. Will you leave it to magistrates, or to the people, who, if they were able, have other work to do? Deny the office, and you destroy the church and work.

Q. 8. How are men called and separated to the sacred ministry?

A. There are many things concur thereto. The first ministers were called immediately by Christ himself, and extraordinarily qualified; but ever since all these things must concur.

1. A common obligation on all men to do their best in their places to propagate the gospel and church, and to save men's souls, is presupposed, as a preparatory antecedent.

2. There must be necessary qualifying abilities: 1. Natural wit and capacity. 2. Acquired improvement, and so much knowledge as must be exercised in the office. 3. If apt to teach and able signified no more than to read what is prescribed by others, a child, fool, or an infidel, were apt and able. Ability for competent utterance and exercise. 4. And to his acceptance with God and his own salvation, saving faith and holiness is necessary. If you would know the necessary degrees of ability, it is so much without which the necessary acts of the office cannot be done. "The things that thou hast heard of me among many witnesses, the same commit thou to faithful men, who shall be able to teach others also," 2 Tim. ii. 2.

3. The approving judgment of other senior ministers is ordinarily necessary; for men are not to be the only judges themselves where the public interest is concerned. And the investing ordination of such is the orderly solemnizing of their entrance, and delivery of Christ's commission; and is that to the general office of the ministry which baptism is to christianity, and solemn matrimony to marriage, or coronation to a king. This is not done by the election of the people; it is not their work to choose ministers to the general office, or men to call the world.[n]

4. To make a man the pastor of a particular church or flock, the consent both of the man and of the flock is necessary; and to the well-being also, the consent of the neighbour pastors; and to peace and liberty, the prince's. This is an ordination or relation, which may be often renewed and changed; but the ordination to the general office is to be but once: to license a physician, and to choose him for my physician, are divers things: and so it is here.

Q. 9. What laws or canons have pastors power to make for the church?

A. 1. None to the universal church, for that hath no ruler, or law-maker, or judge, but Christ; man being utterly uncapable of it.

2. None which shall cross the laws of Christ, in nature or Scriptures.

3. None which are of the same kind and use with Christ's own universal laws, and no more needful to one place or age than to all: for this will accuse Christ, as if he had been defective in his own legislation, when more must be added of the same kind.[o]

4. Taking the word "laws" strictly, pastors, as such, have no legislative power. But taking it laxly for mandates, or directions given by just power, such as a parent or tutor hath, they may make such laws as these: 1. Such as only enjoin the obeying of Christ's own laws. 2. And such as only determine of such mere accidents of doctrine, worship, and discipline, as Christ hath commanded in general, and virtually,

[i] 1 Cor. xiv.; 2 Tim. ii. 15; 1 Pet. iii. 16; Acts xx. 25, 29, 31, 32.

[k] Acts xx. 21.

[l] 1 Tim. iii. 16; iv. 15; 2 Tim. ii. 2, 15; Tit. i. 6, 9.

[m] 2 Cor. v. 19.

[n] 2 Tim. ii. 2; Tit. i. 5; Acts xiv. 23; ix.; xiii. 2.

[o] Isa. xxxiii. 22; Jam. iv. 12; 1 Tim. iv. 6; 1 Cor. iii. 5; iv. 1.

and left the particular sort to human determination of governors (as time, place, utensils, &c.) 3. Such as are not extended beyond the churches of which they are pastors, to others of whom they are no rulers. 4. Such as, being indifferent, are not made more necessary than their nature and use requireth; nor used to the church's destruction or hurt, but to its edification. 5. Such as, being mutable in the reason or cause of them, are not fixed. And continued when the reason of them ceaseth.[p]

Christ maketh us ministers that we may not think we are lords of his heritage: our work is to expound and apply his laws, and persuade men to obey them, and not to make laws of our own of the same kind, as if we were his equals, and lords of his church. It is true he hath bid us determine of circumstances to the church's edification, and the pastor is judge for the present time and place, what chapter he shall read, what text he shall preach on, and in what method; what psalm shall be sung, and in what tune, and such like: but who made him lord of other churches, to impose the like on them? or, how can he prove that the very same circumstances are necessary to all, when a day may alter the case with himself, which depends on mutable causes? If all the world or land be commanded on such a day to read the same psalm and chapter, and occurrents make any subject far more suitable, who hath power to deprive the present pastor of his choice, and to suppose ministers unable to know what subject to read or preach on, unless it be they that make such men ministers, that they may so rule them?

Q. 10. Why must there be stated worshipping congregations?

A. 1. For the honour of God and our Redeemer, who is best honoured in united, solemn assemblies, magnifying him with one mind, and heart, and mouth.[q]

2. For the preservation of religion, which is so best exercised, honoured, and kept up.

3. For the benefit and joy of christians, who, in such concordant societies, receive encouragement, strength, and comfort.

4. For the due order and honour of the particular churches and the whole.

Q. 11. Is every worshipping congregation a church?

A. The name is not much worthy of a debate: there are divers sorts of christian assemblies, which may be called churches. 1. There are occasional, accidental assemblies that are not stated. 2. There are stated assemblies, like chapels, which have only curates, and are but parts of the lowest political, governing churches. 3. Christians statedly associated under such pastors as have the power of the church keys for personal communion in holy doctrine, worship, and conversation, are the lowest sort of political, governing churches. 4. Synods, consisting of the pastors and delegates; these may be called churches in a lax sense. 5. And so may a christian nation under one king. 6. And all the christian world is one catholic church as headed by Jesus Christ. 7. And the Roman sect is a spurious church, as it is headed by a human, uncapable sovereign, claiming the power of legislation and judgment over all the churches on earth.

Q. 12. But how shall I know which is the true church, when so many claim the title, and the papists say it is only theirs?

A. I have fully answered such doubts on the article of the "holy catholic church, and communion of saints," in the creed. Either you speak of the whole church, or of a paticular church, which is but a part. If of the whole church, it is a foolish question, How shall I know which is the true church? when there is but one. If of a particular church, every true christian society (pastors and flocks) is a true church, that is, a true society, as a part of the whole.

Q. 13. But when there are divers contending churches, how shall I know which of them I should join with?

A. 1. If they are all true churches, having the same God, and Christ, and faith, and hope, and love, you must separate from none of them, as churches, though you may separate from their sins; but must communicate with them in all lawful exercises, as occasion requireth. 2. But your fixed relation to a particular pastor and church peculiarly, must be chosen, as your own case and benefit, all things considered, doth require. When you can have free choice, the nearest, and ablest, and holiest pastor and society should be chosen: when violence interposeth, a ruler's will may do much to turn the scales for a tolerable pastor and society, if it make it most for the common good, and your edification.

Q. 14. May men add any thing to the prescribed worship of God?

A. Worship is a doubtful word; if you will call mere mutable accidents and circumstances by the name of worship, man may add to them, such as is putting off the hat, the metre and tune of psalms, and such like. But men may do nothing which implieth a defect in the law of Christ, and therefore may make no new articles of faith, or religion, or any thing necessary to salvation, or any sacraments or ordinances of worship of the same kind with Christ's, much less contrary thereto.

Q. 15. May we hold communion with a faulty church and worship?

A. Or else we must have communion with none on earth: all our personal worship is faulty: we join with them for christian faith and worship. If the minister say or do any thing contrary, it is his sin, and our presence maketh it not ours. Else we must separate from all the world. But we may not by false professions, subscribing, swearing, or practice, commit any sin ourselves for the communion of any church on earth.[r]

[p] Matt. xx. 27, 28; 2 Cor. i. 24; iii. 6; 1 Pet. v. 1—3; iv. 9—11.
[q] 1 Cor. xiv; Heb. x. 21, 22; Acts xiv. 23.
[r] Luke iv. 16; vi. 6; Matt. viii. 4.

CHAPTER XLV.

OF BAPTISM.

Q. 1. WHAT is baptism?

A. It is a sacred action, or sacrament, instituted by Christ, for the solemnizing of the covenant of christianity between God and man, and the solemn investing us in the state of christianity, obliging us to Christ, and for his delivering to us our relation and right to him as our Head, and to the gifts of his covenant.[a]

Q. 2. Why did Christ institute such a ceremony as washing in so great and weighty a work as our christening?

A. 1. A soul in flesh is apt to use sense, and needs some help of it. 2. Idolaters had filled the world with images and outward ceremonies, and the Jews

[a] Matt. xxviii. 19; Acts ii. 38, 41; viii. 12, 13, 16, 37, 38; xix. 5; xxii. 16; Rom. vi. 3, 4; 1 Cor. xii. 13; Gal. iii. 27; Eph. iv. 5; Col. ii. 12; 1 Pet. iii. 21.

had been long used to abundance of typical rites; and Christ being to deliver the world from these, and teach them to worship in spirit and truth, would not run into the extreme of avoiding all sensible signs and helps, but hath made his sacraments few and fitted to their use, to be instead of images, and men's vain inventions, and the Jewish burdens, as meet and sufficient helps of that kind to his church, that men might not presume to set up any such things of their own, on pretence of need, or usefulness.

Q. 3. What doth this great sacrament contain?

A. 1. The parties covenanting and acting. 2. The covenant as on both parts, with the benefits given of God, and the duty professed and promised by man. 3. The outward signs of all.

Q. 4. Who are the parties covenanting and acting?

A. God and man; that is, 1. Principally God the Father, Son, and Holy Ghost; and, ministerially under him, the baptizing minister. 2. The party baptized; and if he be an infant, the parent or owner on his behalf.

Q. 5. In what relation is God a covenanter with man?

A. 1. As our Creator and Governor, offended by sin, and reconciled by Christ, whom his love gave to be our Saviour. 2. As Christ is our Redeemer and Saviour. 3. As the Holy Ghost is our Regenerator and Comforter; sent by the Father and the Son.

Q. 6. In what relation stands the person to be baptized?

A. As a sinner, miserable by guilt and pravity, and loss of his blessed relation to God, but redeemed by Christ, and called by him, and coming to receive him and his saving grace.

Q. 7. What is it that God doth as a covenanter with the baptized?

A. You must well understand that two covenanting acts of God are presupposed to baptism, as done before. I. The first is God's covenant with Jesus Christ, as our Redeemer, by consent, in which God requireth of him the work of man's redemption as on his part, by perfect holiness, righteousness, satisfactory suffering, and the rest: and promiseth him, as a reward, to be Lord of all, and the saving and glorifying of the church, with his own perpetual glory.[b]

II. A promise and conditional covenant, or law of grace, made to lost mankind by the Father and the Son, that whoever truly believeth, that is, becometh a true christian, shall be saved.[c]

Now baptism is the bringing of this conditional promise, upon man's consent, to be an actual mutual covenant.[d]

Q. 8. And what is it that God there doth as an actual covenanter?

A. First he doth by his minister stipulate, that is, demand of the party baptized whether he truly consent to his part. And next, on that supposition, he delivereth him the covenant gifts, which at present are to be bestowed.[d]

Q. 9. What be those?

A. 1. The relation of a pardoned, reconciled sinner and adopted child of God, or that God will be his God in love through Christ.

2. A right and relation to Christ as his actual Saviour, Head, Teacher, Intercessor, and King.

3. A right and relation to the Holy Ghost, to be to him the illuminating, sanctifying, quickening Spirit of light and love, and holy life; and deliverance from the devil, the world, and flesh, and from the wrath of God.[e]

Q. 10. What is it that God requireth of man, and he professeth?

A. That he truly believe in this God the Father, Son, and Holy Ghost, and presently and resolvedly consenteth to be his in these relations, taking him as his God and Father, his Saviour, and his Sanctifier, repenting of his sins, and renouncing the contrary government of the devil, world, and flesh.[f]

Q. 11. What are the outward signs of all this?

A. 1. The water. 2. And the actions of both parties. I. The action of the minister on God's part is to wash the body of the baptized with the water, which, in hot countries, was by dipping them overhead, and taking them up: to signify, 1. That they are washed from the guilt of sin by the blood of Christ. 2. And are as dead and buried to sin and the world and flesh, and risen to a new and holy life and heavenly hope. 3. And that by this act we are solemnly bound by God to be christians.

II. The action of the baptized is, to be a willing receiver of this washing, to signify his believing and thankful receiving these free gifts of Christ, and his solemn self-engagement to be henceforth a christian.

Q. 12. Are infants capable of doing all this?

A. No: they are personally capable of receiving both the sign and the grace, even right to Christ and life, but not themselves of actual believing and covenanting with Christ.

Q. 13. Why then are they baptized who cannot covenant?

A. That you may understand this rightly, you must know, 1. That as children are made sinners and miserable by their parents without any act of their own; so they are delivered out of it by the free grace of Christ, upon a condition performed by their parents; else they that are visibly born in sin and misery should have no visible or certain way of remedy: nature maketh them as it were parts of the parents, or so near as causeth their sin and misery: and this nearness supposed, God, by his free grace, hath put it in the power of the parents to accept for them the blessings of the covenant; and to enter them into the covenant of God, the parents' will being instead of their own, who yet have none to choose for themselves.[g]

2. That baptism is the only way which God hath appointed for the entering of any one into the christian covenant and church.

3. That the same sacrament hath not all the same ends and uses to all, but varieth in some things, as their capacities differ. Christ was baptized, and yet not for the remission of sin: and the use of circumcision partly differed to the old and to the infants.

4. It is the will of God that infants be members of the christian church, of which baptism is the entrance. For, 1. There is no proof that ever God had a church on earth in any age, of which infants were not members.

2. The covenant with Abraham, the father of the faithful, was made also with his infant seed, and sealed to them by circumcision. And the females who were not circumcised, were yet in the church and covenant: and when the males were uncircumcised forty years in the wilderness, they were yet members of the Jewish church: and (Deut. xix.) the parents entered their little ones into the renewed covenant: and Christ came not to cast all infants out of the church who were in before.

3. Christ himself saith, that he would have gathered Jerusalem as a hen gathereth her chickens, and

[b] John xvii. 1—3; iii. 35; v. 22, 27; vi. 39.
[c] John iii. 16; 2 Cor. v. 19, 20; 1 John v. 11, 12.
[d] 1 Pet. iii. 21, 22.
[e] Gal. iii. 27; 1 Cor. 12, 13.
[f] Matt. xxviii. 19, 20; 1 John v. 7, 11, 12.
[g] 1 Cor. vii. 14; Isa. lxv. 23; Psalm xxxvii. 26; Acts ii. 39.

they would not: so that he would have taken in the whole nation, infants, and all that were in before.[h]

4. And in Rom. xi. it is said, that they were broken off by unbelief: therefore, if their parents had not been unbelievers, the children had not been broken off.

5. And Christ himself was Head of the church in his infancy, and entered by the sacrament then in force, though, as man, he was not capable of the work which he did at age: therefore infants may be members.[i]

6. And he rebuked his disciples that kept such from him, because of such is the kingdom of God: he would have them come as into his kingdom.

7. And plainly the apostle saith to a believing parent, that the unbeliever is sanctified to the believing, (for the begetting of a holy seed,) else were your children unclean, but now they are holy; mere legitimation is never called holiness, nor are heathens' children bastards.[k]

8. And most plainly, Christ, when he instituteth baptism, saith, "Go, disciple me all nations, baptizing them." Which fully showeth that he would have ministers endeavour to disciple and baptize nations, of all which infants are a part.[l]

9. And accordingly many prophecies foretell, that nations shall come in to Christ; and christians are called "A holy nation." And it is said, "The kingdoms of the world are become the kingdoms of the Lord and of his Christ."

Q. 14. But though infants be church members, is it not better that their baptism be delayed till they know what they do?

A. Christ knew what is best: and he hath told us of no other door of entrance into the visible church regularly, but by baptism. And if he had intended so great a change to the believing Jews as to unchurch all their infants, he would have told it. And the apostles would have had more ado to quiet them in this, than they had for casting off circumcision: but we read of no such thing, but the constant baptizing of whole households.

Q. 15. But infant baptism seems to let in all the corruption of the churches, while infants receive they know not what, and are all taken after for christians, how bad soever, or without knowing what christianity is: whereas, if they staid till they understood it, it would engage them to be resolved christians indeed?

A. This is not long of infant baptism, but of unfaithful parents and ministers. For, 1. If the parents were told their duty, and also what a blessing it is to have their children in Christ's church and covenant, it would awaken them better to do their part, and comfort them in their children's state of grace.

2. And if infants were not betimes engaged, the usage would tempt multitudes to do as some did of old, even sin on as long as they durst, that baptism might wash it away at last.

3. And doubtless, with unfaithful ministers, baptism at age also would be made but a ceremony, and slubbered over as confirmation is now, and as customary going to the church and sacrament is.

4. But that which should be done is, that at age every baptized person, before he is admitted among adult communicants, should be as diligently catechised, and as solemnly own and renew his baptismal vow and covenant, as if it were now to be first done. The full nature of baptism is best to be understood by the case of the adult, who were capable of more than infants are. And no adult person must be baptized without serious, deliberate understanding, profession of faith, repentance, and holy obedience to Christ. Infants cannot do this; though they must not do that again which they did and could do, viz. receive baptism; yet they must do that which they did not nor could do.

I confess to you, of the two evils, I think the church is more corrupted for want of such a solemn, serious renewing of the baptismal covenant at age, and by turning confirmation into a ceremony, than by those anabaptists, who call people to be seriously re-baptized, as the Afric council did those that had been baptized by heretics.

Q. 16. Do you think that anabaptists should be tolerated, or that all should not be forced to bring their children to baptism?

A. 1. Infant baptism is no such easy controversy or article of faith, as that no one should be tolerated that receiveth it not.

2. The ancient church, which we most reverence, left all men to their liberty to be baptized only when they pleased, and compelled none for themselves or their children. Tertullian was for the delay till they understood. Gregory Nazianzen was for staying some years. Augustine, and other of the fathers, were baptized at age.

3. Baptism giveth so great a gift, even Christ, and pardon, and adoption, and right to life eternal, on condition of thankful acceptance and believing consent, that undoubtedly the unwilling have no right at all to it. The ancient church baptized none till they desired and sought it for themselves or children. Yea, they must be willing of it on self-denial terms, forsaking the flesh, the world, and the devil, and taking God instead of all. So that to force any to be baptized by mulcts and penalties, and baptize those so forced, is to deceive souls, defile Christ's church, and profane the sacred ordinance of God.

Q. 17. I have oft wondered what harm twice baptizing doth, that it should be accounted a heresy and intolerable?

A. It is a fault, because it is contrary to Christ's appointed order: baptism is the sacrament of our new birth, and we are born but once. To be baptized again implieth an untruth, that we were not baptized before: but I suppose none do it but through ignorance. And Cyprian, and the bishops of many countries in many councils, were so ignorant as to be guilty of re-baptizing all that heretics baptized. The great fault of the anabaptists is their schism, that they cannot be contented when they are re-baptized to live in love and communion with others, but grow so fond of their own opinion as to gather into separated churches, and avoid communion with all that are not of their mind, and spend their time in contentious endeavours to draw men to them.

Q. 18. What the better are infants for being baptized?

A. The children of the faithful are stated by it in a right to the foresaid benefits of the covenant, the pardon of their original sin, the love of God, the intercession of Christ, and the help of the Holy Ghost, when they come to age, and title to the kingdom of heaven, if they die before they forfeit it.

Q. 19. But how can we judge all such in a state of salvation, when we see many at age prove wicked, and enemies?

A. This is a point of so great difficulty, that I may but humbly propose my opinion to trial. 1. There is a degree of grace or goodness, which doth only give a man a power to believe or obey God, but not

h Matt. xxiii. 37. i Matt. xix. 13, 14; xviii. 3. k 1 Cor. vii. 14. l Matt. xxviii. 19, 20; Rev. xi. 15.

give a rooted, habitual determination to his will. Such the fallen angels had, and Adam before his fall, who was thereby in a state of life, till he fell from it by wilful sin: and so it may be with the baptized infants of believers. But when the special, sanctifying gift of the Holy Ghost is given them, and they are habitually rooted in the love of God, as the seed sown in good ground, they fall not totally away. 2. As parents and children are covenanters for their several duties, if parents will perfidiously neglect their promised duty for the holy education of their children, or children rebelliously sin against that power and measure of grace which they received, they may perish by apostasy, as the angels did; or need, as Adam, a renewing by repentance. All Christ's grace is not confirming: as the best may lose much, and fall into foul sin, and grow worse than they once were, so common grace, and I think this middle infant grace which children have, as related to their parents, may be lost.

Q. 20. But is it not safer to hold that baptism puts none but the elect, who never lose it, into a title to salvation?

A. 1. Then it would be little comfort to parents, when their children die, who know not whether one of ten thousand be elect. 2. And it would be little satisfaction to the minister to baptize them, who knoweth not the elect from others. 3. It is plain that it is not another, but the same covenant of grace which is made with infants and adult; and that the covenant giveth pardon of sin, and right to life, to all that have the requisite qualification; and as that qualification in the adult is faith and repentance, so in infants it is nothing but to be the children of the faithful dedicated to God. God never instituted any baptism which is not for remission of sin. If I thought infants had no visible right to remission in which baptism should invest them, I durst not baptize them. I think their holiness containeth a certain title to salvation.

Q. 21. But is it not enough to know that they are of the church visible?

A. All at age that are of the visible church are in a state of salvation, except hypocrites. Therefore all infants that are of the visible church, are also of the mystical church, except such as had not the requisite qualification, and that is such as were not the children of the faithful.

All the world are in the kingdom of the devil, who are not in the kingdom of God; and if there be no visible way of salvation for them, what reason have we to hope that they are saved?

Q. 22. Some say we must leave their case to God as unknown to us, and that he will save such of them as he electeth?

A. True faith and hope is grounded on God's promise. What reason have we to believe and hope that any are saved whom God never promised to save? This would teach wicked men to presume that God will save them too, though he do not promise it: and this giveth no more comfort to a christian than to an infidel. How know we, but by his promise, whether God elect one of ten thousand, or any at all: but God hath promised a special blessing to the seed of the faithful, above all others.

Q. 23. You make the mercy so very great, as maketh the denial of it seem a heinous sin in the anabaptists?

A. There are three sorts of them, greatly differing. 1. Some say that no infants have original sin, and so need no baptism nor pardon: or, if it be sin, it is done away by Christ's mere death, and all infants in the world are saved.

2. Others say that infants have original sin, but have no visible remedy; nor are any in covenant with Christ, nor members of his church, because no pardon is promised but to believers.

3. Others hold that infants have original sin, and that the promise is to the faithful and their seed, and that parents ought thankfully to acknowledge this mercy, and devote them to Christ as infant members of his church; but that baptism is not for infant members, but only, as the Lord's supper, for the adult. This last sort are they whom I speak of as such whom I would not separate from, if they separate not from us; but the other two sorts are dangerously erroneous. When God hath made so many plain promises to the seed of his servants, and, in all ages before Christ, hath taken infants for church members, and never made a covenant but to the faithful and their seed, to say that Christ, the Saviour of the world, came to cast all infants out of the visible church, into the visible kingdom of Satan, and give them no greater mercy instead of it, seemeth to me very great ingratitude, and making Christ too like to Satan, as coming to do much of his destroying work.

Q. 24. But every where salvation is promised only to believers.

A. The promise is to them and their seed, keeping covenant. The same text that saith, "He that believeth shall be saved," saith, "He that believeth not shall be damned." Which showeth that it is only the adult that it speaketh of; or else all infants must be damned for unbelief. It shuts them no more out of baptism than out of heaven.

Q. 25. But the Scripture speaks of no infants baptized.

A. 1. No infants are to be baptized but the infants of the faithful; therefore the parents were to be made believers first. 2. The Scripture speaks of baptizing divers households. 3. No Scripture mentioneth that ever any child of a believer was baptized at age. 4. The Scripture commandeth it, and that is enough: "Disciple nations, baptizing them," Matt. xxviii. 19.[m]

Q. 26. How can infants be disciples that learn not?

A. 1. Did Christ mistake when he sent them to disciple nations, of which infants are a part? 2. Cannot infants be disciples of Christ, if Christ, an infant, can be the Master and King of his church? Christ was our Teacher, Priest, and King, in his infancy, by right, relation, and destination, and undertaking, and obligation to what he was after to do; and so may infants be his subjects and disciples. May not an infant be a king that cannot rule? And are not infants the king's subjects, though they cannot obey? May not they be knights and lords, and have right to inheritances? 3. Yea, are not infants called God's servants? Lev. xxv. 42; yea, and Christ's disciples? Acts xv. 10. Peter saith, those that would have imposed circumcision would put a yoke on the neck of the disciples; but it was infants on whom they would have put it.

Q. 27. We are all by nature children of wrath, and none can enter into heaven that is not regenerate, and born of the Spirit?

A. But we are all the children of God, we and our seed, by the grace of Christ; and infants are capable of being regenerate by the Spirit; or else they would not be called holy, 1 Cor. vii. 14.

Q. 28. The apostle only giveth a reason why a believing husband may lawfully live with an unbelieving wife.

A. True; but what is the reason which he giveth? The doubt was not whether it be fornication: that

[m] Acts xvi. 15, 33; xviii. 8.

was past doubt: but the faithful must, in all their relations, be a peculiar, holy people, and the doubt was, whether their conjugal society became not such as infidels, common and unholy; and Paul saith, no. To the pure all things are sanctified. The unbeliever is not holy in herself, but sanctified to the husband for conjugal society; else, saith he, "your children were unclean," not bastards, but unholy, as those without are; "but now are they holy," as the Israelites, adult and infants, were a holy people, separated from the world to God, in the covenant of peculiarity, and not common and unclean.

Q. 29. Is it the infants of all professed christians and hypocrites, or only the infants of sincere christians, who have the promise of pardon and salvation delivered and sealed by baptism?

A. As the church is to receive all the adult who make a credible profession, so are they to receive all their infants, for God only knoweth the heart. But it is with the heart that man believeth to righteousness, Rom. x. And as adult hypocrites are not pardoned by God, who knoweth the heart, so neither is there any promise of pardon to their seed. No text of Scripture giveth any pardon but to sincere believers and their seed. And the child is in the covenant as the child of a believer devoted to God. And that faith which qualifieth not the parent for pardon, cannot qualify the child for it. I know no more promise of pardon and life to a hypocrite's than to a heathen's child.

Q. 30. But what if the godfather, or grandfather, be a true christian, or the ancestors, and the parents both infidels, may not the child be baptized and pardoned?

A. The further you go from the parent the darker is the case. We are all the offspring of righteous Noah, and yet that maketh not the infants of heathens baptizable or pardoned. But the case of Abraham's covenant maketh it probable, that whoever is the true owner of the child by nature, purchase, or adoption, may devote it acceptably to God in baptism; because the infant having no choosing power, the will of his owner goeth for his own, in accepting the mercies of the covenant, and obliging him to such conditions as are for his good; which, if he like them not, he may renounce when he comes to age. But if the grandfather or godfather be no owner of the child, I know no proof that their causing him to be baptized helps him to pardon and salvation. If we dream that baptism giveth pardon to all infidels, and heathen's children, whose owners were not in the covenant themselves, we make a gospel, which, as far as I can find, Christ never made.

Q. 31. May not any man take an infant out of the street, and give him food and raiment, much more offer him to baptism, which is an act of greater charity?

A. The first God alloweth: but pardon and salvation is none of ours to give, but God's; and we can ministerially deliver the investing signs to none that have no title to which God hath promised the gift. If, as some think, bare redemption hath given a right to all the world, then all infidels and heathens shall be saved, if baptized. If they say it is to all infants in the world, then, whether they have godfathers or no, they may be baptized. And if all that are baptized are saved, it is irrational to think that want of baptism without their fault shall hinder their salvation. But though God offer to all men pardon and life for themselves and their infants, yet no scripture giveth it to either without acceptance and consent of the adult. We must not make a gospel of our own.

Q. 32. Some say, that so much faith will serve for a title to baptism, as taketh Christ for a teacher, and maketh us disciples, that we may after attain to saving holiness; but that it is not special, saving faith that must needs be then professed.

A. This is to make a new baptism and christianity to vie with that which alone Christ made. No adult person is a christian, in Scripture sense, who believeth not in Christ as Christ. Which is as Saviour, as Prophet, Priest, and King. The essentials of Christ's office and gifts, as offered, are essential to that accepting faith which makes us christians. A disciple and a christian were words of the same importance, Acts xi.[n] Christ made no baptism but for the remission of sin, and giving men a relation right to Father, Son, and Holy Ghost: baptism saveth by the answer of a good conscience to God. "Arise and wash away thy sins," was the word to Saul. We are sacramentally buried and risen with Christ, as dead to sin, and made new creatures, when we are baptized, Rom. vi. Therefore it is called "The laver of regeneration," Tit. iii. 5. All the church of Christ, from the apostles, taught that baptism put away the guilt of sin, to all that were truly qualified for that sacrament. And they required the profession of a saving faith and repentance; and all the form of baptism used in England, and the whole christian world, so happily agreeth in expressing this, that whoever will bring in the opinion, That the profession of a faith short of that which hath the promise of pardon and life, entitleth to baptism, must make a new baptismal form.

Q. 33. But many divines say, that baptism is not administered to infants on the title of a present faith, nor to give present pardon; but on a promise that they shall believe at age, and so have the benefits of baptism at age.

A. None dare say so of the adult. If they say, We repent not, nor believe now, but we promise to do it hereafter, no wise man will baptize them. It is present believing, and not a mere promise to believe, that is their title. An infant's title is the parent's faith and dedication. By this doctrine infants of christians are not in the same covenant or baptism as their parents, nor are they any more pardoned than heathens.[o]

Q. 34. What use are we to make of our baptism ever after?

A. It is of great and manifold use. 1. We must live under the humble sense of that miserable state of sin from which christianity doth deliver us.[p]

2. We must live in the thankful sense of that grace of God in Christ which did deliver us, and in the exercise of our belief of that truth and love which was then sealed to us.

3. We must live in the faithful remembrance of that covenant which we sealed, and that obedience which we promised, and in that war against the devil, the world, and the flesh, in which we then engaged ourselves.

4. It is the knowledge of the baptismal covenant which tells us what christianity is, and who we must take and love as christians, while sects and dividers, by narrow, false measure, do limit their christian love and communion, and hate or cast off the disciples of Christ.

5. Accordingly it is the baptismal covenant that must tell us what true faith is; viz. such a belief as causeth us truly to consent to that covenant: and

[n] Mark xvi. 16; Rom. x. 10, 14.
[o] Acts ii. 39.

[p] Rom. iii.; vi. 1—3; Rev. i. 5; vii. 14; 1 Cor. vi. 10—12; Heb. x. 22.

what true conversion is; viz. such a change as containeth a true consent to that covenant. And so it tells us how to judge of our sincerity of grace; viz. when we unfeignedly consent to that covenant; and tells us what sin is mortal, that is, inconsistent with true grace and title to salvation; viz. all sin which is not consistent with an unfeigned consent to the covenant of grace.[q]

6. It tells us what the catholic church is; viz. visibly all that profess consent to the baptismal covenant, and forsake it not; and mystically all that sincerely do consent to it.

And, 7. So it tells us how to exercise church discipline, that we cast not out those as none of Christ's members, for their infirmities, who are not proved by sufficient witness to have done that which cannot stand with the sincere keeping of that covenant.

And thus baptism, not as a mere outward washing, but as including the grace which it signifieth, and the covenant and vow which it sealeth, is the very kernel of the christian religion, and the symbol, or livery, of the church and members of Christ.

Q. 35. Are all damned that die unbaptized?

A. Baptism is the solemn devoting men in covenant to Christ. All that hear the gospel are condemned that consent not to this covenant. But the heart consent for ourselves and children is our title condition before God, who damns not men for want of an outward ceremony, which, by ignorance or necessity, is omitted. Believers' children are holy, because they and theirs are devoted to God before baptism. Baptism is to christianity what public matrimony is to marriage, ordination to the ministry, enlisting to a soldier, and crowning to a king.

q John xiii. 8; Eph. iv. 26; Tit. iii. 5; Acts xxii. 16.

CHAPTER XLVI.

OF THE SACRAMENT OF CHRIST'S SACRIFICED BODY AND BLOOD.

Q. 1. WHAT is the sacrament called the Lord's supper, or eucharist?

A. It is a sacred action in which, by bread and wine consecrated, broken, and poured out, given and taken, and eaten and drunk, the sacrifice of Christ's body and blood for our redemption is commemorated, and the covenant of christianity mutually and solemnly renewed and sealed, in which Christ, with the benefits of his covenant, is given to the faithful, and they give up themselves to Christ, as members of his church, with which they profess communion.[a]

Q. 2. Here are so many things contained, that we must desire you to open them severally: and first, what actions are here performed?

A. 1. Consecration. 2. Commemoration. 3. Covenanting and communication.

Q. 3. What is the consecration?

A. It is the separating and sanctifying the bread and wine to this holy use; by which it ceaseth to be mere common bread and wine, and is made sacramentally, that is, by signification and representation, the sacrificed body and blood of Christ.

Q. 4. How is this done, and what action consecrateth them?

A. As other holy things are consecrated, as ministers, utensils, church maintenance, oblations, the water in baptism, &c. which is by an authorized devoting it to its proper holy use.

Q. 5. But some say it is done only by saying these words, "This is my body;" or by blessing it.

A. It is done by all that goeth to a dedication or separation to its holy use; and that is, 1. By declaring that God commandeth and accepteth it, (which is best done by reading his institution,) and that we then accordingly devote it. 2. By praying for his acceptance and blessing. 3. By pronouncing ministerially that it is now, sacramentally, Christ's body and blood.

Q. 6. Is the bread and wine the true body and blood of Christ?

A. Yes, relatively, significantly, representatively, and sacramentally: that is, it is consecrated bread and wine, on these accounts so called.

Q. 7. But why do you call it that which it is not really, when Christ saith, "This is my body," and not, This signifieth it?

A. The name is fitly taken from the form; and a sacramental form is a relative form. If you see a shilling of the king's coin, and the question be, whether this be a shilling, or the king's coin, or silver? You will answer, it is all three; the matter of it is silver; the general relation is money or coin; the special relative form is, it is a shilling. And this is the fittest name, when the value is demanded. So the question is, whether this be bread and wine, or a sacrament, or Christ's sacrificed body and blood. It is all these, and the answer must be according to the meaning of the question.

It is usual to say of pictures, this is the king, and this is such a one, and this is my father, &c. Certainly the two parts of the sacrament must be understood alike. And of one, Christ saith, "This cup is the new testament in my blood which is shed for you," Luke xxii. 20; 1 Cor. xi. 25. Where none can deny, that by "cup," is meant the wine, and by "is the new testament," is meant, is the exhibition and sealing of the new testament, and not the very testament itself.

And it is known that Christ's common teaching was by parables and similitudes, where he saith, (Matt. xxi. 28,) "A certain man had two sons," &c. v. 33, "A certain householder planted a vineyard," &c. And so frequently, Matt. xiii. 21—23, 37—39, "He that soweth is the Son of man; the field is the world; the good seed are the children of the kingdom; the tares are the children of the wicked one; the enemy is the devil; the reapers are the angels:" that is, they are signified. This is ordinary in the gospel: John xv. 1, "I am the vine, and my Father is the husbandman." John x. 7, 9, 14, "I am the Door; I am the good Shepherd." As David, Psal. xxii. 6, "I am a worm, and no man." Matt. xv. 13, 14, "Ye are the salt of the earth, the lights of the world;" that is, ye are like these things.

Yea, the Old Testament useth "is" for "signifieth," most frequently, and hath no other word so fit to express it by.

Q. 8. Why then do the papists lay so much stress on the word "is;" yea, why do they say, that there is no bread and wine after the consecration, but only Christ's body and blood, under the show of them?

A. The sacrament is exceeding venerable, being the very eating and drinking Christ's own sacrificed body and blood, in similitude or representation. And it was meet that all christians should discern the Lord's body and blood in similitude, from common bread and wine. And in time, the use of the name, when the church was drowned in ignorance, was taken (about one thousand years after Christ) for the thing signified without the sign; as if they

a Matt. xxvi. 26—28; Luke xxii. 19; 1 Cor. x. 16, 17; xi. 23—26, 28.

had said, This is the king; therefore it is not a picture, nor is it cloth, or colours. And it being proper to the priests to consecrate it, they found how it exalted them to be judged able to make their Maker, and to give or deny Christ to men by their authority; and so they set up transubstantiation, and by a general council made it heresy to hold that there is any bread or wine left after consecration.

Q. 9. Wherein lieth the evil of that opinion?

A. The evils are more and greater than I must here stay to recite. In short, 1. They feign that to be Christ's body and blood, which was in his hand, or on the table, when he spake the words, as if he had then two bodies.

2. They feign his body to be broken, and his blood shed, before he was crucified.

3. They feign him to have flesh and blood in heaven, which two general councils have condemned; his body being a spiritual body now.

4. They feign either himself to have eaten his own flesh and drunk his own blood, or at least his disciples to have done it while he was alive.

5. They feign him to have been the breaker of his own flesh, and shedder of his own blood, and make him to do that which was done only by the Jews.

6. They contradict the express words of the Scripture, which three times together call it bread, after the consecration, in 1 Cor. xi.[b] When yet they say, it is not bread.

7. They condemn the belief of the soundest senses of all men in the world, as if it were heresy. All our eyes, touch, taste, &c. tell us that there is bread and wine, and they say there is none.

8. Hereby they deny all certainty of faith, and all other certainty; for if a man may not be certain of what he seeth, feeleth, and tasteth, he can be certain of no sensible thing: for we have no faculties but sense to perceive things sensible as such: nor any way to transmit them to the intellect but by sense. And we can no otherwise know that there is a Bible, a church, a council, a pope, a man, or any thing in the world, and therefore much less can believe any of them. So that all human and divine faith are thus destroyed; yea, man is set below a beast that hath the benefit of sense.

9. Hereby they feign God to be the grand deceiver of the world; for things sensible are his works, and so is sense; and he makes us know no supernatural revelation but by the intromission of some sense; and if God may deceive all men by the way of sense, we can never be sure but he may do it otherwise.

10. They set up men, who confess their own senses are not to be credited, to be more credible than all our senses, and to be the lords of the understandings of all princes and people in despite of sense; and he that is to be believed before our senses is an absolute lord.

11. They deny it to be a sacrament, for if there be no sign there is no sacrament.

12. They feign every ignorant, drunken priest, every time he consecrateth, to work greater miracles than ever Christ wrought, and so to make miracles common, and at the wills of thousands of wicked men. I must not here stay to handle all this, but in a small book called "Full and Easy Satisfaction which is the True Religion," I have showed thirty-one miracles with twenty aggravations, which all priests are feigned to work at every sacrament.

Q. 10. What is it that is called the mass, which the papists say that all the fathers and churches used in every age, and we renounce?

A. In the first ages, the churches were gathered among heathens, and men were long instructed and catechised hearers before they were baptized christians; and the first part of the day was spent in public, in such common teaching and prayer as belonged to all, and then the deacon cried, *Missa est;* that is, dismissed the unbaptized hearers, and the rest that were christians spent the rest of the time in such duties as are proper to themselves, especially the Lord's supper and the praises of God. Hereupon all the worship following the dismission of the unchristened and suspended, came to be called barbarously the mass or dismission. And this worship hath been quite changed from what it was in the beginning, and the papists, by keeping the name mass or dismission, make the ignorant believe, that the worship itself is the same as of old.

Q. 11. What be the changes that have been made?

A. More than I may now stay to number. Justin Martyr and Tertullian describe it in their time to be just such as the Scripture mentioneth, and we now commonly perform, that is, in reading the Scripture, opening and applying it, praying as the minister was able, praising God, baptizing, and administering the Lord's supper. After this, ministers grew less able and trusty, and they decreed that they should pray and officiate in set forms; yet so that every bishop might choose his own, and every presbyter must show it to the bishops and have their approbation; the creed, Lord's prayer, and commandments, and the words of baptism, and delivery of the Lord's supper, were always used in forms before. After this, they grew to use the same forms called a liturgy in whole provinces: some ceremonies were so ancient, that we cannot find their original, that is, the anointing of the baptized, the giving them milk and honey to taste; dipping them thrice; clothing them in a white garment after; to worship with their faces toward the east; and not to kneel in prayer or adoration any Lord's day in the year, nor any week-day between Easter and Whitsuntide; and especially to observe those two yearly festivals, and Good Friday's fast.

And quickly after, the encouraging of persecuted christians to suffer, drew them to keep a yearly day at the place where a martyr was killed or buried, to honour their memories, and give God thanks for them. After this, they built altars over them, and they built their churches where their graves or some of their bones were laid, and in honour of their memory, called the churches by their names. Next, they brought their names daily into the church liturgies, and next they added to the names of such bishops of those particular churches as had left an honourable memorial behind them. And the Lord's supper was celebrated much like as it is in our English liturgy (save these names). And thus far the changes were then accounted laudable, and were not indeed such as should discourage any christians from communion, nor do we read of any that were against them. Besides which they overvalued the use of crossing.

But quickly (though by degrees) a flood of ceremonies came in, and popes and prelates added at their pleasure, till God's public worship was made quite another thing.

I. God who is a Spirit, and will be worshipped in spirit and truth, is by mass priests and papists worshipped by such a mass of ceremonies, as makes it like a stage play, and representeth God so like the heathen idols, delighted in mummeries and toyish actions, as is greatly to the dishonour of religion and God.[c]

[b] So 1 Cor. x. 15; xi. 25—28; Acts xx. 7 11; ii. 42, 46.

[c] John iv. 20, 22—24; v. 39; Acts xvii. 11, 23, 25; Phil. iii. 3; 1 Cor. xiv. 2—27; Luke xi. 52; 2 Tim. iii. 15.

II. They have brought in the worshipping of God, in a language which the people understand not, and praying for they know not what.

III. They have locked up the very Scriptures from the people, and forbid all to use it in their known tongue translated, but those that get a special license for it.

IV. They abolish all substantial signs in the sacrament, as is aforesaid, and say, there is no bread or wine, and so make it no sacrament.

V. They give the laity the bread only, without the cup.

VI. They call the consecrated bread by the name of their Lord God, and taking it to be no bread, but Christ's body, worship it with divine worship, which seemeth to me flat idolatry.

VII. They reserve is as their God, long after the sacrament, to adore and to work pretended miracles by.

VIII. They solemnly celebrate a sacrament before the congregation, where none communicate but the priests, and the people look on.

IX. They say these masses by number, to deliver souls out of the flames of purgatory.

X. They have many prayers for the dead as in purgatory, for their ease and deliverance.

XI. They pray to the dead saints to intercede for them, and help them, and to the virgin Mary, for that which is proper to Christ.

XII. They worship God by images, and adore the images as the representations of saints and angels; yea, and of God: and some profess that the cross, and the images of the Father, Son, and Holy Ghost, are to be worshipped with honour participatively divine.[d]

These, with abundance more, and many false doctrines on which they depend, are brought into God's public worship, and called the mass, and are added by degrees to that sounder worship, which was called the mass at first.

Q. 12. You have spoken much about the consecration in the sacrament; what is it which you call the commemoration?

A. It containeth the signal representation of the sacrificing of Christ, as the Lamb of God, to take away the sins of the world. Where the signs are, 1. The materials, the bread and wine. 2. The minister's breaking the bread and pouring out the wine. 3. The presenting them to God, as the commemoration of that sacrifice in which we trust; and declaring to the people, that this is done to this commemoration?

The things signified, are, 1. Christ's flesh and blood, when he was on earth. 2. The crucifying of Christ, the piercing of his flesh, and shedding his blood. 3. Christ's offering this to God as a sacrifice for man's sin. And this commemoration is a great part of the sacrament.

Q. 13. What think you of the name sacrifice, altar, and priest, here?

A. The ancient churches used them all, without exception from any christian that ever I read of. I. As the bread is justly called Christ's body, as signifying it, so the action described was of old called a sacrifice, as representing and commemorating it. And it is no more improper than calling our bodies, and our alms, and our prayers sacrifices, Rom. xii. 1; Eph. v. 2; Phil. ii. 17; iv. 18; Heb. xiii. 15, 16; 1 Pet. ii. 5.[e]

II. And the naming of the table an altar as related to this representative sacrifice is no more improper than that other. "We have an altar whereof they have no right to eat," Heb. xiii. 10, seems plainly to mean the sacramental communion. And the Scripture (Rev. vi. 9; viii. 3, 5; xvi. 7) oft useth that word.

III. And the word "priest," being used of all christians that offer praise to God,) 1 Pet. ii. 5, 9; Rev. i. 6; v. 10; xx. 6,) it may sure as well be used of those whose office is to be sub-intercessors between the people and God, and their mouth to God, in subordination to Christ's priesthood: causeless scruples harden the papists. We are not offended that the Lord's day is called the sabbath, though the Scripture doth never so call it; and a sabbath in Scripture sense was a day of ceremonial rest: and the ancient church called it the christian sabbath, but by such allusion as it (more commonly) used the word sacrifice and altar.

Q. 14. But we shall too much countenance the papists' sacrifice by using the same names.

A. We can sufficiently disclaim their turning a commemoration of Christ's sacrifice into the feigned real sacrificing of his flesh and blood, without renouncing the names. Else we must, for men's abuse, renounce the name of a sabbath too, and a temple, &c. if not also of a church and bishop.

Q. 15. You have spoken of the sacramental consecration, and commemoration; what is it which you call the covenanting part and communication?

A. It containeth the signs, and the things signified, as communicated. The signs are, 1. The actual delivering of the consecrated bread and wine (first broken and poured out) to the communicants, with the naming what it is that is given them. 2. Bidding them take, eat, and drink. 3. Telling them the benefits and blessings given thereby: and all this by a minister of Christ, authorized thus to act in his name, as covenanting, promising, and giving what is offered.[f]

And on the receiver's part the signs are, 1. Freely taking what is offered (the bread and wine). 2. Eating and drinking. 3. Vocal praise and thanksgiving to God, and professed consent to the covenant.

Q. 16. What are the things signified and given?

A. I. 1. On God's part, the renewed giving of a sacrificed Saviour to the penitent believer.

2. The will and command of Christ, that as sacrificers feasted on the sacrifice, so the soul by faith should thankfully and joyfully feast on Christ by hearty acceptance of the free gift.[g]

3. The actual applicatory gift of the benefits of Christ's sacrifice; which are, 1. Our confirmed relation to Christ as our Head and Saviour, and to God as our Father reconciled by him, and to the Holy Ghost as our Sanctifier, and to the church as his kingdom or body. 2. The pardon of our sins by his blood. 3. Our right confirmed to everlasting life. 4. The strengthening of our faith, hope, love, joy, patience, and all grace.[h]

4. Christ's promise and covenant for all this sealed to us.

II. On the receiver's part is signified, 1. That in the sense of his own sin, misery, and need, he humbly and thankfully receiveth his part in Christ as sacrificed. 2. That he endeavoureth by faith to feast on him. 3. And that he thankfully receiveth the blessings purchased, to wit, his relation to Christ as his Head, to God as his Father, and to the Holy Ghost as his Sanctifier and Comforter, with the pardon of sin, the sealed promise, and right to heaven, and all the helps of his faith and other graces. 4. That he

[d] Col. ii. 18.
[e] Luke xxii. 19; 1 Cor. xi. 24, 26, 27.
[f] Matt. xxvi. 26; John vi. 53, 54, 57, 58.
[g] Zech. ix. 11; Heb. x. 29; xiii. 20.
[h] 1 Cor. x. 16; 2 Cor. xiii. 14; Luke xxii. 20; Heb. ix. 15—18.

resolvedly reneweth the dedication of himself to God the Father, Son, and Holy Ghost, as thus related to these ends; covenanting fidelity in these relations, and renouncing the contraries. 5. Doing all this as in communion with all the church of Christ, as being united to them in the same Head, the same faith, and hope, and love. 6. Thankfully praising God and our Redeemer for this grace.

Q. 17. Should not one prepare for the Lord's supper by fasting and humiliation before? Or how should we prepare?

A. We must always live in habitual preparation, and special fasts are not ordinarily necessary thereto: the primitive church did communicate not only every Lord's day, but on other days when they met to worship God; and therefore used not every week to spend a day in fasting for preparation. But as christians must use fasting on just occasions, so must they do before this sacrament in case that any heinous sin, or heavy judgment or danger, call for it; and preparing considerations and prayers are necessary.

Q. 18. May one communicate who is uncertain of the sincerity of his faith?

A. By faith you mean either objective or active faith.

1. One that is so far uncertain that the gospel is true, and that there is a life to come, as that he dare not say, I have no wavering or doubt of it, may yet be a true believer and may communicate, if his persuasion be but so prevalent, as to resolve him to consent to the covenant of grace, and take God for his God, and Christ for his Saviour, and the Holy Ghost for his Sanctifier, God's law for his rule, his promise for his security, and heaven for his happiness, and here to place his hope and trust, forsaking all that stands against it. A weak and doubting faith may bring a man to martyrdom and to heaven, if it bring him to trust Christ with soul and body in the way of obedience to him.[i]

2. If by faith you mean the act of believing and consenting, God hath made the sincerity of our faith necessary to our salvation, but not the certainty that it is sincere. Every man must do his best to discern the trust, consent, and choice of his own heart: and he that truly believeth, and yet is not sure of it, if he can say, As far as I am able to know my own heart by trial, I seriously think that I resolvedly consent to the covenant of grace, and prefer Christ, holiness, and heaven, before all this world, and trust to Christ and his promises for my felicity; ought to come to the table of the Lord, notwithstanding his uncertainty.[k]

Q. 19. Whence is it that so many christians are more terrified than comforted by the Lord's supper?

A. 1. Some of them, by an excess of reverence to this above all other ordinances of God, which, by degrees, brought in the papists' transubstantiation and adoration; and by a dread lest, by unworthy receiving, they should eat and drink their own damnation; and so coming thither with a deeper sense of the danger than of the benefit, and mistaking their imperfections for this unworthy receiving. 2. And some come with too high expectations that God must suddenly give them joy, or all the grace that is signified by the sacrament, while they have not the holy skill to fetch in comfort by the exercise of their faith: and when they miss of what they expected, they are cast down. 3. And too many, by wilful sin or negligence, deal falsely with God, and break their covenant, and renew their wounds of conscience, and deprive themselves of the comforts of the love of God, and the grace of Christ, and the communion of the Holy Spirit.[l]

Q. 20. Is not the Lord's supper a converting ordinance, which therefore should be used by the unbelievers, or ungodly?

A. Many things may accidentally, by God's grace, convert a man, which are not to be chosen and used to that end. Plagues, sickness, death approaching, may convert men; falling into a heinous sin hath affrighted some to leave their sin. But these are not means to be chosen for such ends, and the fear and care of preparing for a sacrament hath converted some, when it was not the receiving that did it. It is so evident as not to need long proof that God never appointed the Lord's supper to be chosen and used by infidels, or impenitent, ungodly persons, as a means to convert them. 1. Because it is presupposed that they be baptized who communicate: and I have proved that baptism to the adult presupposed the profession of faith and repentance, and that it delivereth pardon and title to salvation.

2. Because faith, and repentance, and covenant consent renewed, are also to be professed by all before they communicate.

3. Because it was ever an ordinance proper to the church, which consisteth of professors of faith and holiness.

4. And the communicants are said to be one bread and one body, and to eat Christ's flesh, and drink his blood, and Christ to dwell in them by faith, and to have eternal life hereby.

And as for them that say it is not saving faith, but some commoner, preparatory sort, which is necessarily to be professed in baptism and the Lord's supper, I have at large confuted them in a treatise of "Right to Sacraments," and the reasons before and now named confute it. I add, that their opinion is destructive to true christian love; for by them no one should be taken for a child of God, and in a state of salvation, for being baptized, and communicants, and so not loved as such. And how poor a charity is it to love all visible church members, but as the children of the devil must be loved!

Q. 21. Must we love all as true christians who are baptized, and communicate, and profess christianity?

A. Yes, with these three exceptions; 1. That it is not as a certain truth, that we must judge them as sincere, but as probable. 2. That there be divers degrees of probability as there be of profession. Some, we are almost sure, are sincere; and some we have more fear than hope of: and we must measure our love and trust accordingly. 3. If men by word or life apostatize, or plainly contradict and destroy their profession of christianity, thereby they nullify our obligation to take them for christians: but till men render their profession incredible by contrary profession or practice, we are, by the rules of christian and human charity, to take all professed, baptized, communicating christians to be sincere, but only in various degrees of probability.[m]

Q. 22. How must the Lord's supper be improved after the receiving?

A. By a serious remembering with joy and thankfulness, how great mercies we have received of God; and, with cheerful obedience, what a covenant we have made, and what duty we have most solemnly promised; and in how near a relation and bond we

[i] Acts viii. 37; Mark ix. 24; Matt. vi. 30; viii. 26; xiv. 31; xvi. 8; Luke xvii. 5.
[k] John xx. 25; Matt. xxviii. 17; Acts xiii. 39.
[l] 1 Cor. xi. 20, 30, 31.

[m] Acts xi. 26; ii. 38, 41, 42, 44—46; iv. 32, 34; Mark xvi. 16; 1 Cor. x. 16, 17; xii. 8, 11, 13; 2 Cor. xi. 2; Gal. iii. 28; Eph. iv. 3, 5; John iv. 1; xiii. 35; Rom. vi. 3, 5; Matt. x. 42; Luke xiv. 26, 33.

are tied to the whole church of Christ, and to all our fellow-christians: and frequently to plead these great receivings and great obligations, to quicken our faith, and hope, and joy, and to overcome all temptations to the world and flesh, to unbelief, disobedience, and despair.[n]

Q. 23. Some say that no man should be kept from the sacrament, or excommunicated, because it is the food of their souls, &c.

A. 1. If none be kept from baptism, heathens, and infidels, and professed deriders of christianity, might be baptized to make a mock of baptism. We must make men Christ's disciples before we baptize them, Matt. xxviii. 19. And then baptism would be no baptism, nor the ministry no ministry, the specifying end and use being changed. 2. Then the church would be no church, but lie common with the world. 3. And then Christ would be no King, and Head, and Husband of his church, that is, no Christ.[o] 4. If all may not be baptized, all may not communicate; for baptism entereth them into a state of communion, else the unbaptized, and all infidels, might communicate. 5. Some baptized persons turn atheists, sadducees, or infidels after; and these are worse than common infidels that never were baptized. The church is no church if it be common to these. 6. Some that continue a nominal christianity, openly hate and persecute the practice of it, and live in common adultery, perjury, murder; and the church is holy, and a peculiar people, a holy nation, a royal priesthood:[p] and repentance and obedience are necessary to the church as well as faith. If, therefore, these notorious, flagitious, impenitent persons, must be members in communion with the church, it will be a swine sty, and not a church; a shame to Christ, and not an honour. If his church be like the rest of the world, Christ will not be honoured as the Saviour of it, nor the Spirit as its Sanctifier. It is the unity of the spirit that all christians must keep in the bond of peace.[q] But these have none of his Spirit, and therefore are none of Christ's.

The sacraments are symbols of the church as differenced from the world; and Christ will have them be a visibly distinct society. 7. Communicants come to receive the greatest gift in the world, pardon, justification, adoption, right to heaven. The gospel giveth these to none but penitent believers. To say that Christ giveth them to flagitious, impenitent rebels, whose lives say, "We will not have him reign over us," is to make a new gospel, contrary to Christ's gospel, which Paul curseth, were it done by an angel, Gal. i. 7, 8. They are not yet capable of these precious gifts.

8. The objectors take no notice of 1 Cor. v. 2; 2 Thess. iii.; Rom. xvi. 16, 17; Tit. iii. 10; Rev. ii.; iii.; where the churches are reproved for suffering defilers: nor Heb. xiii. 7, 17, 24; Luke xii. 42, 43; 1 Thess. v. 12, 13; which describe the office of church guides: nor 1 Tim. iii.; iv., &c. where the governing of the church, and avoiding communion of the impenitent, are described.

9. In a word, Christ's office, works, and law, the nature of the church and sacrament, the office of the ministry, the frequent precepts of the apostles, and the constant practice of the church in its greatest purity, down from the apostles' days, do all speak so plainly for keeping and casting out infidels and impenitent, wicked men, and for keeping the church as a society of visible saints, separated from the world, that I can take him for no better than a swine or an infidel, who would have the church keys cast away, and the church turned common to swine and infidels.

Q. 24. But it will make ministers lords and tyrants to have such power?

A. 1. Somebody must be trusted with the power, if the work must be done. The church must be differenced from the world. Therefore some must try and judge who are fit to be baptized, and to have its communion; and who are fitter than those whom Christ, by office, hath thereto appointed. Would you have magistrates, or the people do it? Then they must be prepared for it by long study and skill, and wholly attend it, for it will take up all their time.[r]

Q. 25. Must ministers examine people before they communicate?

A. They must catechise and examine the adult before they baptize them, and, consequently, those who were baptized in infancy, before they number them with adult communicants; or else atheists and infidels will make up much of the church, who will come in for worldly interest. This examination should go before confirmation, or the public owning of their baptism; but there is no necessity of any more examination before every sacrament, except in case of scandal, or when persons need and crave such help.

Q. 26. Who be they that must be excommunicated, or refused?

A. Those who are proved to be impenitent in gross, scandalous sins, after sufficient admonition and patience. And to reject such, is so far from tyranny, that it is necessary church justice, without which a pastor is but a slave, or executioner of the sinful will of others: like a tutor, philosopher, or schoolmaster, who is not the master of his own school, but must leave it common to all that will come in, though they scorn him, and refuse his conduct. But no man must play the pastor over other men's flocks, nor take the guidance of a greater flock than he can know and manage, much less be the only key-bearer over many score or hundred churches; and, least of all, take upon him to govern and judge of kings and kingdoms, and all the world, as the Roman deceiving tyrant doth.

CHAPTER XLVII.

OF PREPARATION FOR DEATH AND JUDGMENT.

Q. 1. How must we prepare for a safe and comfortable death?

A. I have said so much of this in my "Family Book," that to avoid repetition I must refer you thither: only in brief; 1. Preparation for death is the whole work of life, for which many hundred years are not too long, if God should so long spare and try us. And all that I have hitherto said to you, for faith, love, and obedience, upon the creed, Lord's prayer, and commandments, is to teach you how to prepare for death. And though sound conversion at last may tend to pardon and salvation, to them that have lived a careless, wicked life, yet the best, the surest, the wisest preparation, is that which is made by the whole course of a holy, obedient, heavenly life.[a]

[n] 1 Cor. xii. 16, 20—22.
[o] Matt. xxviii. 19; Mark xvi. 16; 1 Cor. xi. 27—30; Eph. i. 22, 23.
[p] Tit. ii. 14; 1 Pet. ii. 9.
[q] Eph. iv. 3, 16; Rom. viii. 9.
[r] 1 Cor. iv. 1, 2; Matt. xxiv. 45—47; 1 Thess. v. 12.
[a] Phil. ii. 12; Heb. v. 9; xii. 28; Tit. ii. 11, 12; Luke xix. 9; xiv. 26, 33; Rom. x. 10, 11; 2 Pet. iii. 11, 12; 1 Pet. i. 9.

Q. 2. What life is it that is the best preparation?

A. I. When we have so well considered of the certain vanity of this world, and all its pleasures, and of the truth of God's promises of the heavenly glory, as that by faith we have there placed our chiefest hopes, and there expect our chief felicity, and make it our chief business in this world to seek it, preferring no worldly thing before it, but resolved, for the hopes of it, to forsake them all when God requireth it: this is the first part of our preparation for death.[b]

II. When we believe that this mercy is given by Christ, the Mediator between God and man, and trust in his merits and intercession with the Father, and take him for our teacher also, and our ruler, resolving to obey his word and Spirit. This is the second part of our preparation for death.[c]

III. When the Holy Spirit hath shed abroad God's love upon our hearts, and turned their nature into a habit of love to God and holiness, and given us a victory over that love of the world, and fleshly prosperity, and pleasure, which ruleth in the hearts of carnal men, though yet our love show itself but in such mortification, and endeavour, and grief for what we want, we are prepared for a safe death.[d]

But if the foretastes of heavenly glory, and sense of the love of God, do make our thoughts of heaven sweeter to us than our thoughts of our earthly hopes; and cause us, out of love to God and our glorified Redeemer and his church, and out of love to a life of perfect knowledge, love, and joy, to long to depart and be with Christ; then we are prepared not only for a safe but a joyful death.[e]

Q. 3. Oh! but this is a great and difficult work.

A. It is not too hard for the Spirit of Christ, and a soul renewed by it. It is our great folly and naughtiness that maketh it hard: why else should it be hard for a man that loveth himself, and knoweth how quickly a grave, and rotting in the dark, must end all his pleasures in this world, to be earnestly desirous of a better after it? And why should it be hard for one that believeth that man's soul is immortal, and that God hath sent one from heaven, who is greater than angels, to purchase it for us, and promise it to us, and give us the first-fruits by his Holy Spirit; to rejoice that he dieth not as an unpardoned sinner, nor as a beast, but shall live in perfect life, and light, and love, and joy, and praise, for ever? What should rejoice a believing, considerate man like this?[f]

Q. 4. Oh! but we are still apt to doubt of things unseen.

A. 1. You can believe men for things unseen, and be certain by it; for instance, that there is such a place as Rome, Paris, Venice; that there have been such kings of England as Henry VIII. King James, &c. You know not, but by believing others, whether ever you were baptized, nor who was your father or mother. 2. You see not your own soul, nor any one's that you talk with; and yet you feel and see such things as may assure any sober man that he hath a soul. God is not seen by us, yet nothing is more certain than that there is a God.

3. We see plants, flowers, fruits, and all vital acts, produced by an unseen power; we see vast, lucid, glorious regions above us, and we see and feel the effects of invisible powers: therefore, to doubt of things because they are unseen, is to doubt of all the vital, noblest part of the world, and to believe nothing but gross and lowest things, and to lay by reason, and become brutes. But of this I have said more near the beginning.

Q. 5. What should we do to get the soul so familiar above as to desire to be with Christ?

A. I. We must not live in a foolish forgetfulness of death, nor flatter our souls into delays and dulness, by the expectations of long life on earth; the grave must be studied till we have groundedly got above the fears of it.

II. We must not rest quiet in such a human belief of the gospel and the life to come, as hath no better grounds than the common opinion of the country where we live, as the Turks believe Mahomet, and his Alcoran; for this leaveth the soul in such doubts and uncertainty as cannot reach to solid joy, nor victory over the world and flesh. But the true evidences of the gospel, and our hopes, must be well digested, which I have opened to you in the beginning, of which I give you a breviate in two sentences.

1. The history of the gospel of Christ's life, miracles, death, resurrection, ascension, sending down the Spirit, the apostles' miracles, and preaching, and writing, and sufferings, is a true history: else there is none sure in the world, for none of such antiquity hath greater evidence.

2. And if the history aforesaid be true, the doctrine must needs be true; for it is part of the history, and owned and sealed certainly by God.[g]

III. We must not be content to be once satisfied of the truth of the life to come, but we must mentally live upon it and for it, and know how great business our souls have every day with our glorified Lord, and the glorified society of angels, and the perfected spirits of the just, and with the blessed God of love and glory: we must daily fetch thence the motives of our desires, hopes, and duties, the incentives of our love and joy; the confutation of all temptations from the flesh and the world, and our supporting patience in all our sufferings and fears. Read oft John xvii. 22—24; xx. 17; Heb. xii. 22—24; Matt. vi. 19—21, 33; Col. iii. 4, 5; 2 Thess. i. 10, 11; Heb. xi.; 2 Cor. iv. 16, 17; v. 1—3, 5, 7, 8; Phil. i. 21, 23; iii. 18—20. They that thus live by faith on God and glory will be prepared for a joyful death.

IV. We must take heed that no worldly hope or pleasure vitiate our affections, and turn them down from their true delight.[h]

V. We must live wholly upon Christ, his merit, sufficiency, love, and mediation; his cross and his kingdom must be the sum of our learning, study, and content.[i]

VI. We must take heed of grieving the Spirit of consolation, and wounding our consciences by wilful sin of omission or commission.

VII. We must faithfully improve all our time and talents to do God all the service, and others all the good, that we can in the world, that we may be ready to give an account of our stewardship.

VIII. We must be armed against temptations to unbelief and despair.

IX. We must, while we are in the body, in our daily thoughts fetch as much help from sensible similitudes as we can, to have a suitable imagination of the heavenly glory. And one of the most familiar is, that which Christ calleth the coming of the kingdom of God, which was his transfiguration with Moses and Elias in glorious appearance in the holy mount, (Matt. xvii. 1,) which made Peter say, "It is good to be here."[k] Christ purposely so appeared to them to give them a sensible apprehension of the

[b] Matt. vi. 33. [c] 2 Cor. iv. 16, 18; John iii. 16.
[d] 2 Cor. v. 17; Heb. xii. 14; Rom. viii. 9, 13.
[e] 2 Cor. v. 1, 3, 8; Phil. i. 21, 23.

[f] 1 Pet. i. 6, 8; 1 Thess. v. 16; Phil. ii. 16—18; iv. 4; Heb. iii. 6.
[g] Phil. iii. 18—20; Col. iii. 1—3; Heb. xii. 22—24.
[h] Eph. iii. 17, 18. [i] Eph. iv. 30. [k] Matt. xvii. 4.

glory which he hath promised. And Moses, that was buried, appeared there in a glorified body.

And we must not think only of God, but of the heavenly society, and even our old acquaintance, that our minds may find the more suitableness and familiarity in their objects and contemplations.

X. We must do our best to keep up that natural vivacity and cheerfulness, which may be sanctified for spiritual employment; for when the body is diseased with melancholy, heaviness, or pains, and the mind diseased with griefs, cares, and fears, it will be hard to think joyfully of God, or heaven, or any thing.

XI. We must exercise ourselves in those duties which are nearest akin to the work in heaven. Specially labouring to excite hope, love, and joy, by faith, and praising God, especially in psalms in our families and the sacred assemblies, and using the most heavenly books and company.

XII. We must not look when all is done to have very clear conceptions of the quality and acts of separated souls, or the world of spirits, but must be satisfied with an implicit trust in our Father and our glorified Lord, in the things which are yet above our reach: and, giving up soul and body to him, we should joyfully trust them with him as his own, and believe that while we know as much as may bring us well to heaven, it is best for us that the rest is known by Christ, in whose hand and will we are surer and better than in our own.

As for the special preparations in sickness, I refer you to the "Family Book."

Q. 6. What shall one do that is tempted to doubt, or to think hardly of God, because he hath made heaven for so few?

A. 1. Those few may be assured that he will never forsake them whom he hath so chosen out of all the world, and made his jewels and his treasure.

2. It is improbable rashness to say, heaven is but for few: all this earth is no more to the glorious world above us (even so far as we see) than one inch is to all the earth; and what if God forsake one inch or molehill? See Heb. xii. 23, 24.

Again I say, I take hell to be as the gallows, and this earth to be as Newgate gaol, where some prisoners are that shall die, and some shall live; and the superior world to be like the city and kingdom. Who will say that the king is unmerciful, because malefactors have a prison and a gallows, if all else in the kingdom live in peace?

And though this world seems almost forsaken as the prison-way to hell, yet, while the elect are saved, and the superior, lucid, glorious world is many thousand, and thousand, and thousand times greater than all this earth, I doubt not but experience will quickly tell us, that the glory of God's love is so unmeasurably manifested in heaven, as that the blindness, wickedness, confusions, and miseries of this earth and hell shall be no eclipse or dishonour to it for ever.

Finitur, Jan. 10, 1681-2.

THE

POOR MAN'S FAMILY BOOK.

I. TEACHING HIM HOW TO BECOME A TRUE CHRISTIAN.

II. HOW TO LIVE AS A CHRISTIAN TOWARDS GOD, HIMSELF, AND OTHERS, IN ALL HIS RELATIONS; ESPECIALLY IN HIS FAMILY.

III. HOW TO DIE AS A CHRISTIAN IN HOPE AND COMFORT, AND SO TO BE GLORIFIED WITH CHRIST FOR EVER.

IN PLAIN FAMILIAR CONFERENCE BETWEEN A TEACHER AND A LEARNER.

WITH A FORM OF EXHORTATION TO THE SICK; TWO CATECHISMS; A PROFESSION OF CHRISTIANITY; FORMS OF PRAYER FOR VARIOUS USES, AND SOME PSALMS AND HYMNS FOR THE LORD'S DAY.

A REQUEST TO THE RICH.

THIS book was intended for the use of poor families, which have neither money to buy many, nor time to read them: I much desired therefore to have made it shorter; but I could not do it, without leaving out that which I think they cannot well spare. That which is spoken accurately, and in few words, the ignorant understand not: and that which is large, they have neither money, leisure, nor memory to make their own. Being unavoidably in this strait, the first remedy lieth in your hands: I humbly propose it to you for the souls of men, and the comfort of your own and the common good, on the behalf of Christ, the Saviour of your souls and theirs, that you will bestow one book (either this or some fitter) upon as many poor families as you well can. If every landlord would give one to every poor tenant that he hath, once in his life, out of one year's rent, it would be no great charge in comparison of the benefit which may be hoped for, and in comparison of what prodigality consumeth. The price of one ordinary dish of meat will buy a book: and to abate, for every tenant, but one dish in your lives, is no great self-denial. If you, indeed, lay out all that you have better, I have done. If not, grudge not this little to the poor, and to yourselves; it will be more comfortable to your review, when the reckoning cometh, than that which is spent on pomp and ceremony, and superfluities, and fleshly pleasures. And if landlords (whose power with their tenants is usually great) would also require them seriously to read it, (at least on the Lord's days,) it may further the success. And I hope rich citizens, and ladies, and rich women, who cannot themselves go talk to poor families, will send them such a messenger as this, or some fitter book, to instruct them, seeing no preacher can be got at so cheap a rate. The Father of spirits, and the Redeemer of souls, persuade and assist us all to work while it is day, and serve his love and grace for our own and other men's salvation. Amen.

Your humble Monitor,

Aug. 26, 1672. RICHARD BAXTER.

TO THE READER.

MR. ARTHUR DENT's book, called "The Plain Man's Pathway to Heaven," was so well accepted, because it was a plain, familiar dialogue, that about forty years ago I had one, said to be of the thirtieth impression. While I was thinking to endeavour the reprinting of it, those reasons that hindered me, did persuade me to do somewhat like it to the same ends. Accordingly I began in the three or four first days' conference, to speak as much as I could in the language of the vulgar, though I thought it not best so to hold on to the end; 1. Because it would have made the book too big, or else have necessitated me to leave out much that cannot (in order to practice) be well spared. 2. Because I may suppose, that riper christians need not so loose a style, or method, as the ignorant or vulgar do: and the latter part of the book supposeth the reader to be got above the lowest form, though not to be a learned, accurate man. The title of the book is rough, according to the design. In the conference with the malignant, I have brought in only such objections as are now most commonly used, and therefore which the ignorant most need our help against.

I have two things which some readers will think need an excuse. I. That I have put in the sixth day's conference two sheets of instructions published heretofore; which I did because such small things alone are cast away, and lost; and because I would neither write oftener than is needful the same things, nor yet omit so necessary a part.

II. That I have published forms of prayer and catechising: but I have not now so little to do as to confute their conceits, who think such forms to be unlawful or unuseful. But that they are not better done, I confess doth need more excuse than I can give you. I expect that the catechism should satisfy bu few; for neither it, nor any that I ever saw, doth fully satisfy myself. It is harder than most think, to suit the words both to the matter and to the learners. Had I used fewer words, I must have left out some of the necessary matter. Had I used more, I had overmatched the memories of the weaker sort. The more ignorant any one is, the more words his understanding needeth, and the fewer words his memory needeth: and who can give the same man few and many? I have therefore put but few into the catechism to be remembered, and put the rest in the exposition to be read. Those that think that so short a summary as the creed, Lord's prayer, and decalogue, with the baptismal covenant, which make up the first catechism, is unuseful, are not of my judgment, nor of the ancient churches', who made these the test of men's christianity, and fitness for christian communion. I know that the exposition of the longer catechism is too hard for the ignorant that have no instructer to open it further to them, and that the first part (about God) is harder than the rest: but that is from the incomprehensibleness of God, with whom yet order requireth us to begin; and it is so in most systems of theology: and the reader that understandeth it not at first, must come back, and study it again; for he that is the first and the last, must be first and last of all these studies. I had thought to have done as others, and have added another catechism, with numerous and shorter answers; but I was afraid of overdoing. The hard passages which the younger do not reach, are not unuseful to the riper, who must have their parts. The Lord be your teachers, and bless (when we are dead and gone) the instructions which we leave you, according to his word and will!

THE FIRST DAY'S CONFERENCE.

THE CONVICTION OF AN UNCONVERTED SINNER.

SPEAKERS.—Paul, a pastor; and Saul, an ignorant sinner.

PAUL. WHEN I saw you last, neighbour, I told you, that both my love to you, and my office, do bind me, besides my public preaching, to watch over every person of my flock, and to instruct and help them, man by man, as far as I am able, and they consent: thus Christ himself instructed sinners, and thus must we. You know we cannot speak so familiarly, and come so close to every one's case, in a common sermon, as we may do by conference: and in conference it is not a little rambling discourse upon the by that is fit for so great a business; and therefore I entreated you to allow me now and then an hour's set and sober talk with you, when all other matters might for that time be laid by: and I am now come to claim it, as you promised.

SAUL. You are welcome, sir. I confess to you that, being ignorant and unlearned, I am loth to talk with such a man as you about high matters and things of religion, which I do not well understand. But because you desired it, I could not say you nay.

P. You shall see that I come not to dispute with you, or to cavil, or to do you any harm, nor to pose you with any needless questions, nor to try your learning; but only to help you, before you die, to make sure of everlasting life.

S. I have so much reason myself as to know, that Christ's ministers are like nurses, that must cut every child his meat as it is fit for him; and that if I were sick, it is not a long speech of my physician that will serve to cure me; but he must come and see me, and feel my pulse, and find out my disease, and then tell me what will do me good, and how to take it. But to tell you the truth, sir, there are so many busy fellows that love to meddle with other folk's matters, and censure others, and do but trouble men, either to draw them to their own opinions, or else to make themselves teachers, and to seem better than they are themselves, that I was at first unwilling you should trouble me with such matters; till I thought with myself that I am one of your charge; and till I heard how discreetly, and tenderly, and well you speak to those that have been with you. And now I am ready to receive your instruction.

P. But I have this one request to you before we begin, that we may do all with reverence, as in the presence of God, and beg his blessing; and that you will not be offended with me if I speak freely, and come close to you, as long as you know that I have no ends of my own, but only, in love, to seek the salvation of your soul: and it is not flattery that will cure diseases, or save souls.

S. I confess man's nature loveth not to be shamed, or galled, or troubled; but yet God forbid that I should be offended with you for seeking my own good: for I know you are wiser than I, and know by your life and labour that it is nothing but all our salvation that you seek.

P. I pray you[b] tell me what case do you take your soul to be in for another world; and what do you think would become of you if you should die this day?

[a] John iv.; iii. 1, 2, &c.

[b] 1 Pet. iii. 15.

S. God knows what he will do with us all, I know not. But we must hope the best, and put our trust in the mercy of God.

P. No doubt but God knows; but do you think that we may not[c] know ourselves? May not a man know certainly whether he shall be saved or not?

S. I think not. We can but hope well, but not be sure, for who can tell the secrets of God?

P. Cannot a man know it, if God should tell him?

S. Yes, but God tells nobody his mind.

P. Do you not think the[d] holy Scripture is God's word; and that whatever it tells us, God tells us?

S. Yes, I cannot deny that.

P. Do you believe that there is[e] another life after this, and that man dieth not like a dog, but that his soul goeth either to heaven or hell?

S. Yes, that must not be denied.

P. Seeing heaven is an unconceivable glory, and hell the most unexpressible misery, do you not think but there must needs be a[f] very great difference between those that go to heaven, and those that go to hell?

S. Yes, no doubt; God is not unjust: he would not take one to heaven, and send another to hell, if they were both alike.

P. And do you think that there is so great difference, and yet that it cannot be known? Is a godly man and a wicked man so like that they cannot be known asunder by themselves, if they will?

S. Nobody knoweth the heart but God.

P. Another cannot infallibly know it, further than the life declareth it. But cannot you[g] know your own? Cannot you know what you love and what you hate?

S. No doubt but a man may know his own mind.

P. Very good. And you hear the Scriptures read at church, where there are abundance of promises made to the godly, both for this life and that to come, and terrible threatenings to the ungodly? To what use and purpose were all these, if no one could know whether he were godly or ungodly? Who could take any comfort in the promises, if he could not know that they belong to him?

S. Not unless he have some guess, or hope.

P. And do you not hear, that "We must give all diligence to make our calling and election sure?" 2 Pet. i. 10. And "Examine yourselves, whether you be in the faith or no. Prove yourselves. Know you not your own selves, that Jesus Christ is in you except ye be reprobates?" 2 Cor. xiii. 5. Do you think God would bid men try and examine, and make sure, if it were impossible?

S. No, sure, we must do our best. But who can tell who are elected and who are reprobates, which are God's secrets?

P. You cannot know, before they are converted, whom God will convert and whom not. But when he converteth a sinner, he sets his name and mark upon him; not outwardly only, as you do on your sheep, or goods; but inwardly,[h] as the parents convey their own nature and likeness to their children. That is, he regenerateth and sanctifieth them: he putteth into them a holy nature, a new mind, and a new will, and turneth them to a new life. And may not all this be known? Cannot God's elect be known to themselves, when he hath given them the Spirit of Christ, and made them new creatures, and set his certain mark upon them? Did you never hear, "The foundation (or obligation) of God standeth sure, having this seal, The Lord knoweth them that are his; and, Let every one that nameth the name of Christ depart from iniquity?" 2 Tim. ii. 19. God knoweth whom he will convert and save from eternity. But when men believe in Christ, and depart from iniquity, then they have his seal of election on them, and by it they may know themselves that they are his.

S. I cannot deny what you say, for it is plain.

P. I pray you tell me further, have you not read, or heard, that one sort are called in Scripture the children of God, and said to[i] have his nature and his image? and therefore are said to be regenerated and born again, and born of God, and begotten by incorruptible seed to a lively hope, and a never-fading crown in heaven, and are made holy as he is holy? And the other sort are called[k] the children of the devil, and said to be of him, and to be ruled as captives by him, and to do his works and will? And dare you think that God and the devil are so like, as that their image, and nature, and works, and children, cannot be known one from another?

S. I dare not think so. God forbid!

P. And have you not heard in Scripture abundance of particular marks laid down, by which we may know whether we are the children of God? And can you think they are all laid down in vain?

S. No; none of the word of God is in vain.

P. And do you not hear expressly, that by these marks we may know that we[l] are the children of God? And that, knowing it, we may rejoice, even with unspeakable glorious joy; and that believers are commanded to rejoice in the Lord, yea, always to rejoice? And God's word cannot be false, nor doth it command the [m]ungodly thus to rejoice. Therefore, certainly a man may know whether he is the child of God or not.

S. I never thought of so much before as you have told me: I cannot deny it. But I must confess that I have no such knowledge of myself.

P. Be not offended with me, if I freely proceed upon your own confession. Have you no assurance of your salvation? no certain knowledge what case your soul is in? Tell me truly, what care, what[n] diligent labour have you used to have made all sure? Is it because you could not get assurance? or because you would not do your part? Can you truly say that you have set your heart upon the matter, and made it the greatest of your care and labour in this world, and left nothing undone which you were able to do, to make sure of everlasting life?

S. I would I could say so, but I confess I cannot. God forgive me! I have had some shallow thoughts of these matters upon the by, but I never laid out such serious thoughts, such earnest labours, upon them as you speak of.

P. Have you not? I am sorry to know it. But I pray you tell me what is it that hath hindered you?

S. Alas, sir, many things have[o] hindered me. One is the cares, and business, and crosses of this world, which have taken up my mind and time: and another is the vain pleasures of the flesh, the delights of sense, and a daily contentedness in the

[c] 2 Cor. xiii. 5.
[d] John v. 39; Matt. xiv. 49; xii. 24; 2 Tim. iii. 16.
[e] Matt. xxv.; Heb. ix. 27.
[f] Matt. xxv.; Psal. i.; Mal. iii. 17, 18; Rom. viii. 5—7, 9.
[g] 2 Cor. i. 5; 1 John iii. 14, 24; iv. 13; v. 19, 20.
[h] John iii. 3, 5; Rom. viii. 9; Matt. xiii. 3; Tit. ii. 13, 14; 2 Cor. v. 17
[i] 2 Pet. i. 4; 1 Pet. i. 3, 4, 15—17.
[k] John viii. 48; 2 Tim. ii. 25, 26; 1 John iii. 8—10; Acts xiii. 10.
[l] 2 Cor. i. 12; Gal. iv. 4; Heb. iii. 6; Phil. iii. 1; iv. 4; Psal. xxxiii. 1; Rom. v. 2; 1 Thess. v. 16; 1 Pet. i. 6, 8.
[m] Hos. ix. 1.
[n] 2 Pet. i. 10; Isa. lv. 1, 6, 10; Matt. vi. 33; John vi. 27.
[o] Matt. xiii. 22; Luke viii. 14; xxi. 34; Rom. viii. 6—8; Phil. iii. 19; Psal. x. 3, 4.

particulars of my prosperity. Something or other so took me up, that my mind hath no leisure, nor room, for God.

P. And do you think you have done well and wisely? Will this course serve your turn for ever? What have you now to show of all the pleasures that sin afforded you ever since you were born? What now are you the[p] better for every merry hour that is past; for every sweet, delicious dish; for every pleasant, merry cup; for every playful day, or company; for every wanton lust and dalliance? Tell me now, what good, what sweetness, what inward comfort, is left behind? What the better are you now for all?

S. You need not ask me such a question. The pleasure is gone of all that is past, but I am still in hope of more.

P. And how long will that endure which you hope for? Are you sure to live another week, or day, or hour? And are you not sure that an end will come, and[q] shortly come, and irresistibly come? And where then are all your delights and merriments? Do you think that death is made more safe and comfortable, or more dangerous and terrible, by the remembrance of all the sinful pleasures of a fleshly life? Go, try if you can comfort a dying man, that is not mad, by telling him that he hath had a life of sport and pleasure; or that he had his cups, and feasts, and whores, and honours, for so long a time; and that he[r] hath had his good things here; and that this world hath done for him all that it can do, and now he must part with it for ever. Go, try whether death be more comfortable to Dives, who is clothed in purple and silk, and fareth sumptuously or deliciously every day, than to a Lazarus that waiteth in patient poverty for a better life.

And as for all your possessions and wealth, what will they do for you, more than to be the fuel of these transitory delights, that your fleshly lusts may not lack provision? Will you carry any of it with you? Will it make your death more safe or easy? Or, do you not know that unsanctified wealth and pleasures do all leave nothing but their sting behind, and prepare for everlasting woe?

S. I know all this. And yet this world hath a marvellous power to blind men's minds, and take up their hearts, and turn their thoughts from better things.

P. It is true with those that are blind already, and never had spiritual wisdom, or holy inclination, to mind God, or any thing truly good. But if men were well in their wits, could the beastly pleasures of the flesh for a moment be preferred before holy, everlasting pleasures? Could they be quieted in all their misery with the pride and pelf of a few days, and which they know they must shortly leave for ever? Could a life, that is posting so speedily to its end, make men forget an endless life?

But tell me, neighbour, did you not know all this while that you must die; you must certainly die; you must shortly die? And did you not know, that when death cometh, time is gone, for ever gone, and all the world cannot recall it? Did you not know that your[s] business in this world was to prepare for heaven, and to do all that ever must be done for your everlasting hope and happiness? And that it must go with all men in heaven and hell as they have prepared here?

S. I have heard all this, but it was with a dull and sleepy mind; it did not stir me up to sober consideration, because I hoped still for longer life.

P. But you know that the longest life must have an end: where now are all that lived before us? And, alas! what are a hundred years when they are gone? What now is all your time that is past? But tell me further: what shift make you all this while with your conscience? Did you never think of the[t] end of all your prosperity, and of your soul's appearing in another world? Do you not pass through the churchyard, and see the graves, and tread upon the dust of those that have lived in the pleasures of the world before you? Have you not seen the graves opened, and the carcasses of your neighbours left there in the silent darkness, to rot into ugly loathsomeness and dust? Have you not seen the bones, the skulls of your forefathers, and the holes where meat and drink went in? And did you not know that all this must be your own condition? And is such a life better than heaven? And such a corruptible body fit to be pampered with all the care and labour of our lives, whilst our souls are almost forgotten and neglected?

S. God forgive us! we forget all this, though we have daily and hourly remembrancers, till death is just upon us, and then we do[u] perceive our folly. I was once sick, and like to die, and then I was troubled for fear what would become of me; and I was fully resolved to amend my life; but when I was recovered, all wore off, and the world and the flesh took place again.

P. But you are a man, and have the use of reason. When you confess that you are unready to die, and have done no more to make sure work for your soul, tell me, what shift make you to lie down quietly to sleep, lest you should die, and be past hope, before the morning? Are you not afraid in the morning lest you should die before night, and never have time of repentance more? What shift make you to forget that, if you die unready and unconverted, you are a lost and miserable man for ever? Are you sure at[x] night to live till morning? Are you sure in the morning to live till night? Are you not sure that it will not be long? Do you not know by what a wonder of providence we live? how many hundred veins, and arteries, and sinews, and other parts, our bodies have, which must every one be kept in order? so that if one break, or be stopped, or if our blood do but corrupt or sour, or our other nourishing moisture be distempered, or our spirits be quenched, how quickly are we gone! And dare you wilfully or negligently live one day unprepared for death in so slippery and uncertain a life as this?

S. You say well: but, for all this uncertainty, I thank God I have lived until now.

P. And will you turn God's patience and mercy into presumption, to the hardening of your heart, and the delaying of your repentance? Will he always wait your leisure? As long as you have lived, will not death come, and shortly come? And where are you then? And what will you do next? Have you ever soberly bethought you what it is for a soul to take its farewell of this world, and presently to appear in another world, a world of spirits, good or bad, and to be[y] judged according to our preparation in this life, and to take up a place in heaven or hell, without any hope of ever changing?

S. You trouble me and make me afraid by this talk: but death will not be prevented; and why

p Eccl. i. 2, 3, &c. "All is vanity and vexation."
q Luke xii. 19, 20.
r Luke xvi. 25.
s Matt. vi. 19, 20, 33.
t 1 Pet. iv. 7; Luke xii. 19, 20; 2 Pet. iii. 11; Psal. xxxvii. 37, 38, &c.; Rom. vi. 21, 22; 2 Cor. xi. 15; Phil. iii. 19.
u Psal. lxxviii. 33—35, &c.
x Prov. xxvii. 1; Matt. xxiv. 44; Luke xii. 19, 20, 40.
y Matt. xxv.

then should we begin our fears too soon? They will come time enough of themselves. The fear of death is a greater pain than death itself.

P. Alas! is dying all that you look at? Though death cannot be prevented, damnation may be prevented. Dying is a small matter, were it not for what cometh next. But can hell be escaped without fear, and care, and serious diligence? Or had you rather be condemned for ever, than be frightened to your duty, and from your sin and danger? Is hell easier than a little necessary fear and care? If you were either a beast or a devil, there were some sense in what you say. For if you were a beast, you had nothing after death to fear; and therefore the fear of death beforehand would do no good, but increase your sorrow: and if you were a devil, there were no hope; and therefore you might desire not to be tormented before the time, for it will come time enough at last. But, God be thanked, neither of these is your case: you must live for ever; and you may live in heavenly joys for ever if you will. And are not these things, then, to be forethought of?

S. Really, sir, I am afraid if I should but set myself to think of another world, and the state of my soul, as seriously as you talk of it, it would frighten me out of my wits; it would make me melancholy or mad. I have seen some people moped and melancholy with being so serious about such things; and therefore do not blame me to be afraid of it.

P. God be thanked that you have yet your reason; and seeing you have it, will you study these few questions following?

1. What did God give you your reason for, and difference you from a beast, but to use it in preparation for an endless life? And is it madness to use our reason for that which it was given us for, and which we are made and live for?

2. Is not that man actually mad already, who hath a God to serve, and a soul to save, and a heaven to get, and a hell to escape, and a death to prepare for, and spends his life in worldly[z] fooleries that all perish in the using, and leaveth all this work undone? Is he not mad, and worse than mad, that setteth more by these trifles than by his God? and setteth more by a little meat and drink, and beastly pleasure, for a few days, than by an endless, heavenly glory? That careth more for a body, that must rot in the earth, than for a never-dying soul? That spareth no pains to avoid shame, and poverty, and sickness; and will do little or nothing to avoid everlasting shame, and pain, and horror, in hell? Tell me, if your wife and child should behave themselves but half as madly about the things of this world, would you not send them to Bedlam, or to a physician, presently, or bind them, and use them as the mad are used? And is it not a pitiful hearing, to hear one that is thus mad for his poor soul, to neglect it still, and cast it away, and say he doth it for fear of being mad? More pitiful a thousand times, than to hear one in Bedlam say, I dare not take physic, lest it make me mad. Were such madness a disease, it were but like a fever, or another sickness, for which God would not punish us, but pity us: if you should fall into diseased madness, or melancholy, though it is a sad disease, it would not damn you; for it is no sin. But when men have reason for trifles and none for their salvation, and are wise in nothing but unprofitable vanities, and cunning to cheat themselves out of all their hopes of heaven, and to go to hell with ease and honour; God bless us from such wit as this!

3. But I ask you further, What is there in God, in Christ, in heaven, or in a holy life, that should make a man mad to think of it? I beseech you, neighbour, consider what we are talking of. Is not[a] God better than your house, and land, and sports? Is he not a better friend to you than any you have in the world? And will it make you mad to think of your house, or land, or pleasures? Do not all men confess that we should love God above all? And if it make you not mad to love your friend, or your riches, or yourself, why should it make you mad to live in the love of God? Is not love, and the noblest love, the sweetest delight? And will delight, and the highest delight, distract you? Tell me, do you think that heaven is a desirable place, and better than this miserable world, or not? If you say No, you bear witness against yourself; that you are unfit for heaven, who do not love it, or desire it; and God will deny you but that which you had no mind of. But if you say Yea, then tell me why the hopes of everlasting, heavenly joys, and the forethoughts thereof, should make one mad? Alas! man, we have no other cordial against all our calamities in this world, but the hopes and forethoughts of the joys of heaven. What have I to keep me from being melancholy, or mad, but the promise and belief of endless glory? If God and heaven be not our best, what are we but beasts, or worse? And what do we live for in the world? And what have we, for one day, to keep up our hearts under all our crosses, but the comfortable forethought that we shall for ever be with the Lord, and all his holy ones? Take away this, and you will kill our comforts. Our hearts would sink and die within us. And do men use to go mad for fear of their felicity, and with delightful thoughts of the only good?

S. All this is true, if a man were sure of heaven: but when he must think of hell too, and his fears are greater than his hopes, the case is otherwise.

P. Now you say something. But I pray you consider, that it is one thing to think of hell despairingly, as those that have little or no hopes to escape it: this might make a man mad indeed; but this is not your case. But it is another thing to fear hell as that which you[b] may most certainly avoid, and withal attain eternal life, if you will but consent to the offers of that Saviour who will freely save you. No man shall be damned that is truly willing to be saved: to be saved, I say, from sin and hell.

S. I pray you tell me, then, what maketh the thoughts of the world to come so terrible to us? And what maketh so many that are troubled in conscience to be melancholy, or to live so sad a life?

P. I will tell you what. I have had to do with as many melancholy, conscientious persons as any one that I know of in England; and I have found that, 1. There is not one of many of them, but it is some[c] worldly cross which makes them melancholy; and then it turneth to matters of conscience afterwards, when they have awhile had the disease. 2. And for the most part it befalleth very few, but either weak-spirited, tender women, whose brains are so weak, and their fancies and passions so strong and violent, that they can bear no trouble, nor serious thoughts, but their reason is presently disturbed and borne down; or else some men, that by natural distempers of body, either from their parents, or contracted by some disease, are specially inclined to it.

2. And when I have known it befall some few in their first repentance, it hath usually been some

[z] Luke xii. 20; Psalm xiv. 1; xcii. 6; Jer. xvii. 11; Prov. xiv. 9; Eccl. v. 1, 4; Luke xxiv. 25.

[a] Psalm iv.; lxxiii. 25, 26, 28; xciii. 3; Phil. iii. 7, 8.

[b] Isa. lv. 1—3, 6, 7; Matt. xi. 28; Rev. xxii. 17; Mark xvi. 10; John iii. 16, 18, 19.

[c] 2 Cor. vii. 10, 11.

very heinous sinners, who have lived so debauchedly in drunkenness or whoredom, or committed perjury, or murder, that conscience did more terrify them than they were able to bear. But this was not from any harm that they apprehended in a godly life, but because they had been so ungodly. This was but the fruit of their former wickedness, and partly God's justice, that will not pardon heinous sinners till he hath made them perceive sin is evil, and that they must indeed be beholden to his mercy, and to Christ. But, usually, when God hath broken the hearts of such men by his terrors, he tenderly binds them up with comforts, and maketh those terrors very profitable to them as long as they live. Oh how precious is Christ to such! How sweet are the promises of pardon and salvation! How odious is sin to them all their lives after! But if it should fall out, that such a wicked man, repenting, should never recover from his melancholy sadness, it is a thousand times better, and a more hopeful state, than he was in before, when he went on in sin with presumption and delight.

3. And there is another case too common; like the case of some women that, in travail, are hurt by an unskilful midwife. Every poor, repenting sinner is not so happy as to fall into the hands of a wise, experienced counsellor to direct him: but some do distract men's minds about different opinions in religion, and talk to a poor sinner for this side, and against that side, or about matters that are past their understandings. And some do not clearly and fully open the nature of the covenant of grace, which giveth Christ and life to all true consenters; nor seek sufficiently, by opening the riches of grace and glory, to win men's hearts or love to God; but bend themselves much more to raise men's fears, and tell them more of what they deserve, and what they are in danger of, if they repent not, than of what they shall enjoy with God, through Christ, when they come home. The first must, in its time and place, be done; but the [d] latter is the great work that must save the soul. For a man is not converted and sanctified indeed, by any change that is made by fear alone, till love come in, and win his heart, and repair his nature.

S. You have said so much as doth convince me that I must not, for fear of the trouble, cast away the thoughts of my soul and eternity; but truly, sir, I have thought of these things so little, that I am but puzzled and lost, and know not what to do. And, therefore, you must help to guide my thoughts, or I can do nothing with them.

P. You have now hinted yourself another cause that so many are puzzled about religion, and turn it to a melancholy life. When a sinner hath lived ignorantly, carelessly, and sinfully, all his days, and cometh at last, by the mercy of God, to see his misery, it cannot be expected that he should presently be acquainted with all those great mysterious things which he never did seriously mind before. And so is like a man that hath a way to go that he never went, and a book to learn that he never learned before. And all young scholars do find the easiest lessons hard, till they have time to be acquainted with them. They are like a man that was born and bred in a dungeon, where he had only candle-light; who, when he first cometh into the open world, and seeth the sun, is astonished at the change, but must have a time before (by all that light) he can be acquainted with all the things and persons which he never before saw. Long ignorance [e] will not be cured in a day: and darkness naturally feedeth fears; but time and patience in the light will overcome them.

But to answer your desire, I will direct your thoughts: and I think that now the next thing you have to think on is to look into your heart, and look back upon your life, and come to a clear resolution of this question, whether you are yet a truly converted sinner, and are forgiven and reconciled to God, or not? and whether you are yet in the way to heaven or no? I pray you tell me now what you think of yourself. If you die this night in the case you are now in, do you think you shall be saved, or not?

S. God knows; I told you that I do not know, but I hope well, for no man must despair.

P. To despair of ever being converted and saved, is one thing that you must not do. And to know that a man is not yet converted, and to despair of being saved without conversion, is another thing; that is your duty, if you are yet unrenewed. But as for your hoping well, I must tell you that there is a hope of God's giving, and there is a hope of your own, and of the devil's making. And you [f] must not think that God will make good the devil's word, nor our word, but only his own word. To a repenting believer, God promiseth forgiveness and salvation; and such a one must hope for it; and God will never disappoint his hopes. But to unbelievers, ungodly, impenitent persons, the devil and their own deceitful hearts only do promise forgiveness and salvation. And they that do promise it must perform it, if they can; for God will not. Do you think that God hath promised that all men should be saved, any where in his word?

S. No; I dare not say so.

P. Do you think, then, that if all men shall hope to be saved, that this would save them ever the more?

S. No; but yet there is some comfort in hoping well.

P. But how little a while will deceitful comfort last! Do you not know that there are some men that God hath told us that he will not save? As Luke xiii. 3, 5, "Except ye repent ye shall all perish." "Except ye be converted, and become as little children, ye shall not enter into the kingdom of heaven." Matt. viii. 13. "If ye live after the flesh, ye shall die." Rom. viii. 13. The text is plain, you cannot deny it. Tell me, then, if any of these shall hope to be saved, in such a condition in which God saith, that no man shall be saved, should a man do well to hope for the contrary? Is not this to hope that God's word is false? And should a man hope that God will lie? Or will God go contrary to his word?

S. But may we not hope that God will be better than his word? There is no harm in that.

P. That which you call better is not better, but worse. The king hath made laws for the hanging of murderers: if he should pardon them all, they would call it better to them; but the commonwealth would call it worse. For no man could have any security for his life: but every one that had a mind of his money, or that hated him, would kill him if he could. And where, then, were justice? What is the law made for, but to be the rule of the subject's life, and of the judge's sentence, and to tell men what they must expect? And if it be not fulfilled, it is vain and deceitful, and showeth that the lawmaker either had not wit enough to make it well, or had not power enough to execute it. A benefactor

[d] Tit. iii. 3—5; Rom. v. 5; viii. 28; 1 Pet. i. 8, 9; read Luke xv.; John v. 42; 1 Cor. xvi. 22; ii. 9; Eph. vi. 24; Jam. i. 12; ii. 5.

[e] John iii. 4, 6—8; Heb. v. 11—14; Acts viii. 30, 31.

[f] 1 Cor. vi. 9; iii. 18; Gal. vi. 7; Eph. v. 6; 1 John i. 8; Jam. i. 22, 26.

or friend, indeed, may give more than he hath promised, if he see cause; but a [g] righteous governor must rule according to his laws, or else he deceiveth men by them, which is not to be imputed to God. At least, he will not [h] lie, and falsify his word.

S. But for all that, the king may pardon an offender.

P. That is, because that weak man can make no law so perfect, but on some occasions there will be need of a dispensation. But it is not so with God. And a righteous king will never pardon crimes, but in some rare, extraordinary case, which shall be no disparagement to his law, nor hurt to his subjects; which is no comfort to all the rest of the malefactors.

But I doubt you do not understand that God did at first make a perfect [i] law, which forbade all sin on pain of death: and man did break this law, and we all still break it from day to day, by every sin; and God, being merciful, hath given us a Saviour, and by him the forgiveness of all our sins. But how? not absolutely; but he pardoneth us all by an act of oblivion, a pardoning law: and this law maketh our faith and true repentance (or conversion) to be the condition of pardon. And in it God affirmeth and protesteth, that he will pardon and save [k] all that believe and are converted; and that he will never pardon or save them that continue unconverted in their sin and unbelief. God hath already given out a pardon to all the world, if they will but take it thankfully on his terms, and cease their rebellion, and turn to him: and hath resolved, that they that continue to refuse this pardon and mercy shall be doubly punished, first for their common sins, and then for their base unthankfulness and contempt of mercy. And now bethink you whether it be not foolishness for any to say, I hope God will forgive me, and be better than his word? He hath already forgiven you, if you repent and turn to him; but if you will not, it is impudence for a man, at the same time, to refuse forgiveness and yet to hope for it; to despise mercy, and say, I hope for mercy.

What if the king make an act of pardon to the Irish rebels, forgiving them all, on condition they will thankfully take his pardon, and lay down their rebellious arms, were it not impudency in them to continue in arms, and refuse these conditions, and yet say, We hope the king will pardon us?

There are two things that may fully resolve you that God will pardon and save no unconverted sinner: the first is, because that, in his pardoning law itself, (that is, the gospel,) he hath said and protested that he will not; and it is impossible for God to lie. The second is, that the thing itself is incongruous and unfit for the wise, holy, and righteous God to do. For a pardoned person is reconciled to God, and hath communion with him. And what communion hath light with darkness, or God with the devil and his works? It is blasphemy to say, that God can be actually reconciled to ungodly souls, and take them into his complacency and kingdom. Yea, what if I said, that it is a thing impossible, and a contradiction for a man to be forgiven and saved, that is unholy and unconverted? If you knew what sin is, you would know that it is a self-punishment, and the sorest evil; the sickness and misery of the soul: and to forgive a man is to deliver him from this misery; and to save him, is to [l] save him from his sin. For it is, as it were, a spark of hell-fire kindled in the soul, which is not saved till it be quenched. And what is heaven itself but the perfect light and love of God? And to say that a man is saved, that loveth not God above his sin, and is not holy, is to say that he is saved and not saved.

S. I understand these things better than I did; but I can hardly digest it, that you thus seem to drive men to despair.

P. You greatly mistake; I am driving you from despair. There is no hope of the salvation of a sinner that continueth unconverted; flatter not yourselves with foolish hopes of the devil's making; as sure as God's word is true, there is no hopes of it. Everlasting despair in hell is the portion of all that die unconverted and unsanctified. They will then cry out for ever, All our [m] hope is past and gone; we had once hope of mercy, but we refused it, and now there is no hope. This thought, that there is no more hope, will tear the sinner's heart for ever. This is the state that I would keep you from, and do I not then seek to keep you from despair?

Suppose you met a man riding post towards York, and thinketh verily he is in the way to London, and tells you, I ride for life, and must be at London at night. You tell him that he must turn back again, then, for he is going the quite contrary way, and the further he goeth, the further he hath to go back again. He answereth you, Alas! I hope I have not lost all this time and travel; I hope I may come this way to London. Will not you tell him that his hopes will deceive him? there is no hope of coming to London that way, but he must needs turn back; and if he answer you, You would drive me to despair; I will hope well, and go on; what would you say to this man? Would you not take him for a fool? and tell him, If you will not believe me, ask somebody else, and know better, before you go on any further?

So say I to you, if you are out of the way to heaven, you must despair of ever coming thither,[n] till you turn; but that is not to despair of conversion and salvation, but despair of being saved in the devil's way, that you may be saved in God's way, and not despair for evermore. Changing false hopes for sound hopes is not to cast away all hope. There is nothing more hindereth men from repenting and being saved, than hoping to be saved without true repentance. For who will ever [o] turn to God, that still hopeth to be saved in the worldly, ungodly way that he is in? who will turn back again that hopeth he is right and safe already?

Tell me, I pray you, must not every wise man have some ground and reason for his hope? And should a man's soul and everlasting state be ventured upon unsound and uncertain hopes?

S. No, if we can have better.

P. Tell me freely, then, what are the grounds and reasons of your hopes? Heaven is not for all men. What have you to show that will truly prove your title to it?

S. I ground my hope on the great mercy of God.

P. But God's mercy saveth none but by conversion; devils nor [p] unconverted men are not saved by it. It is the refusing and abusing of mercy that condemneth men: the question is, whether this mercy will save you?

[g] Job viii. 3; Psal. lxxxix. 14; Heb. xii. 28, 29.
[h] Tit. i. 2; Heb. vi. 18; Rom. iii. 4; 1 John v. 10.
[i] Rom. iii. 21, &c.; v. throughout.
[k] Mark xvi. 16; John iii. 16, 18, 19; 2 Thess. ii. 7—10, Heb. ii. 3, 4; iv. 1; xii. 27—29.
[l] Matt. i. 21; Tit. iii. 3, 5.
[m] Job viii. 13, 14, xi. 20; xxvii. 8; Prov. xi. 7; xiv. 32; Isa. lvii. 10; 1 Pet. i. 3, 21; iii. 15; 1 John iii. 3.
[n] Luke xiii. 3, 5.
[o] Jam. iii. 40; Ezek. xxxiii. 9, 11, 49; xviii. 21, 30, 32; xiv. 6.
[p] Isa. xxvii. 11; 2 Thess. i. 7, 8, &c.; ii. 10, 12; Rom. i. 20, to the end.

S. I place my hope in Jesus Christ, who is my Saviour.

P. I say as before, Christ saveth not all men: what hope have you that he will save you more than others?

S. Is it not said, that he is the Saviour of all men, and that he is the Lamb of God, that taketh away the sins of the world?

P. That is, because saving is his office, for which he is all-sufficient, and by his sacrifice he hath pardoned all the world, on condition that they believe and turn to God, but till they believe and repent they are not actually pardoned. He may be the physician of all the city or hospital, who undertaketh to cure all in the city or hospital that will trust him, and take his remedies; and yet all may die that will not trust him, and be ruled by him.

S. But I do believe in Christ, and believers are forgiven.

P. If you truly believe, you have good reason for your hopes: but I am loth you should be mistaken in so great a business. I must first tell you, therefore, what true believing is: every true believer doth at once believe in God the Father, the Son, and the Holy Ghost. And he believeth all God's word to be true, and he heartily consenteth that God be his only God, and that Christ be his only Saviour, and the Holy Ghost his Sanctifier, and he trusteth himself wholly to God alone, for happiness, and for justification, and sanctification, and salvation. Do you do this?

S. I hope I do; I believe in God, and trust him.

P. Let us a little consider all the parts of faith, and try whether you thus believe or not. 1. Do you truly believe that without regeneration, repentance, conversion, and holiness, none can be saved and see God? John iii. 3, 6; Luke xiii. 3, 5; Matt. xviii. 3; Heb. xii. 14. And that if any man have not the Spirit of Christ, he is none of his, Rom. viii. 9. If you do not, you believe not the word of God.

2. Do you take the[r] love of God and the heavenly glory to be your only happiness, and trust to nothing in this world, neither health, life, wealth, or pleasure, for your daily comfort, and greatest content.

3. Do you desire and trust that Christ will save you from all your sins, and will teach you all the will of God: and that he will sanctify you by the Holy Ghost, that you may live a[s] holy and heavenly life in the love of God; and may forsake, not only lust, and wantonness, and gluttony, and drunkenness, and pride and ambition, and deceit and covetousness, but also mortify all fleshly desires, and destroy all your own will, which is against the will of God, and bring you up to the greatest holiness?

S. You put me hard to it now. I know not what to say to this.

P. You may know whether you believe and trust in God and Christ, or not, if you will but consider these three things. 1. What you must believe and trust him for. 2. What word of his it is that you believe. 3. What are the effects which are always brought forth by a serious faith.

And, I. You must trust in God for that which he hath promised to give, and you must take all together, or else it is not trusting God: as you trust a physician to cure you, and trust a schoolmaster to teach you, and trust a lawyer to counsel you in his way, and so you trust every man in his own undertaken work; so must you trust in God to be your only everlasting joy, and better to you than all the world, and to be the Lawgiver and Ruler of your life: and you must trust[t] Christ to justify you, and save you from your sins, and you must trust the Holy Ghost to kill your sins; and to illuminate, sanctify, and quicken you, and, by degrees, to make you perfectly holy: for these are the things that God is to be trusted for. But, if any should trust God to save them from hell and not from sin, or from the guilt of sin, and not from the power of it; or to let them keep their fleshly lusts while they live, and then to give them heaven at death; this is not to trust God, but to abuse him, nor to trust his mercy, but to refuse it. How doth he trust in Christ to save him, that is not willing to be saved by him? And he that will not be saved from his sin, will not be saved by Christ. And how can he trust the Holy Ghost to sanctify him, who is not willing to be sanctified, but thinketh a holy life to be an intolerable toil and misery?

II. To believe God is to believe his word. And what word of God have you to believe, but that he will save converted believers, and condemn all ungodly unbelievers? If now you will believe that God will save any unconverted, ungodly sinners, this is to believe the devil and yourselves, and not God; for God never said any such word in all the Bible, but protesteth the contrary. And what a self-deceit is it to hope to be saved for believing a lie, and fathering it upon God! And what blasphemy is it to call it a believing God, when you believe the devil that contradicteth him!

III. Believing and trusting will be seen in their effects. Is it possible for a man truly to believe that he shall have a life of joys in heaven for ever, if he will turn from the flesh and the world to God, and value and seek heaven more than earth, and yet not do it, but be a carnal worldling still? Is it possible truly to believe that the wicked shall be turned into hell, (Psal. ix. 17,) and yet to go on still in wickedness?

If you were a beggar or a slave in England, and the king should promise you a kingdom in the Indies, if you will but trust yourself in the ship with his own son, who undertaketh to bring you thither, I pray you tell me now, what is the meaning of this trusting his son, and how may it appear whether you trust the king's promise and his son's conduct, or not? If you trust him, you will pack up and be gone; you will leave your own country, and all that is in it, and on ship-board you will go, and venture[u] all that you have in the voyage, in hope of the kingdom which is promised you. But if you fear that the king deceiveth you, or that his son wanteth either skill, or will, or power, to bring you to the promised place, and that the ship is unsafe, or the waves and tempests like to drown you, then you will stay at home, and will not venture.

So when God offereth you a heavenly kingdom, if so be you will, in heart, forsake the world, and all its pomp and pleasures, and all the sinful desires of the flesh; if now you trust this promise of God, you will forsake all and follow a crucified Saviour as a cross-bearer; you will take shipping with Christ and his servants, and let go all in hope of heaven. But if you do not forsake all (in heart) and follow him, resolving to take heaven instead of all, you do not trust him, whatever you may pretend.

S. I cannot deny but what you say is the plain truth.

P. Suppose that you were sick, and only one physician could cure you, and he offereth to do it freely if you trust him, that is, will trust your life to his skill and care: and some give out that he is but a

[q] John iii. 16; 2 Cor. v. 19, 20.
[r] Psal. lxxiii. 25; lxiii. 3; iv. 6, 7.
[s] Rom. viii. 1, 6—8, 13; Heb. xi. 6; 2 Tim. ii. 4; 1 Thess. iv. 1; Isa. lvi. 4; Col. i. 10.

[t] Acts xxvi. 18; Tit. ii. 14.
[u] Luke xi. 22, 23; xiv. 26, 33; Matt. xiii. 45, 46.

deceiver, and not to be trusted, and others tell you that he never failed any that he undertook. If you trust him now, you will commit yourself wholly to his care, and follow his counsel, and take his medicines, and forsake all others. But if you distrust him you will neglect him. And if any should say, I trust this physician with my life, and yet stay at home, and never come near him, nor take any of his counsel, or at least, none of his medicines, would you not count him mad that looked to be cured by such a trust?

S. I confess this helpeth me better to understand what trusting in God, and believing in Christ, is. I doubt many[x] say they trust him, that keep their sins, and hold fast the world, and never dreamt of forsaking all for the hopes of heaven.

But I thought, sir, that this command of forsaking all, and taking up our cross, had been spoken only to such as lived in times of persecution, when they must deny Christ or die, and not to us that live where christianity is professed. God forbid that none should be saved but martyrs.

P. But do you not find, 1. That it is the very covenant and common law of Christ, imposed on all that will be saved, that they deny themselves, and forsake all, and take up the cross, and follow him, or else they cannot be his disciples? Matt. x. 37, &c.; Luke xiv. 24, to the end; and xviii. 21, 22, &c. 2. And doth not every one that is baptized covenant and vow to forsake the world, the flesh, and the devil; and to take God for their only God, which is their all? For if he be not enough for them, and taken as their portion, and loved above the world, he is not taken for their God. But it is well that you confess that you[y] must forsake life and all for Christ rather than deny him: for if a man must do this actually in persecution, then he must do it before, in affection and resolution. Can you die for Christ, then, unless your heart be prepared for it now? Can you, then, leave all this world for God and heaven, unless you beforehand love God and heaven better than all the world, and resolve to forsake it when you are called to do it?

S. No man is like to do that which his heart is not disposed to before, and which he is not purposed to do.

P. Why then you see the case is plain, that every one that will be Christ's disciple must forsake the world in heart and resolution, and be a martyr in true preparation and disposition, though no one must cast away his estate or life, nor be a martyr, by suffering, till God call him to it. "He that loveth the world, the lôve of the Father is not in him," 1 John ii. 15.

By this time you may perceive, if you are willing, whether your faith in Christ, and trust in God, have been true or false: and now tell me what else you have to prove that you are a justified christian, and that your hope of salvation is built on God?

S. My next proof is, that I repent of my sins; and God hath promised to forgive them that repent.

P. Repentance is a good evidence, as well as faith. But here, also, you must take heed of that which is counterfeit; and therefore you must be sure to understand well what true repentance is.

S. Repentance is to be sorry for my sins when I have committed them, and to wish I had never done them.

P. If you know repentance no better than so, you may be undone by the mistake. True repentance is the same with true conversion;[z] and it is such a settled change of the mind, will, and life, from fleshly, worldly, and ungodly, to spiritual, heavenly, and holy, as maketh us hate all the sin which we loved, and heartily love a holy life, and all those duties to God and man which before our hearts were set against. And this change is so firmly rooted in us, as that it is become as a new nature to us; so that all the same temptations which before prevailed with us, would not draw us to the same sins again, nor turn us from a holy life, if we were exposed to them as we were.

S. There is a great deal in this. I pray you open it to me more fully in the particulars.

P. By this you may see what goeth to make up true repentance, and how many sorts of repentance are counterfeit.

1. True repentance is a change of the whole soul,[a] the judgment, the will, and the life, and not of any one of these alone. It is a counterfeit repentance which changeth only a man's opinion, and not his heart and his conversation: and it is counterfeit repentance when men pretend that their wills are changed, and they are willing to live a godly life, when they do it not, and their lives are not changed.

2. True repentance doth not only turn a man's heart and life from this or that particular sin, but from a fleshly, worldly, ungodly state;[b] so that he that before did seek, above all, to fulfil the desires of his flesh, and to prosper in the world, doth now strive as hard to kill those desires as he did to satisfy them, and now taketh the world for vanity and vexation, and turneth it out of his heart. It is counterfeit repentance which reformeth only some open, shameful sin, as drunkenness, prodigality, fornication, deceiving, or the like, and still keepeth up a worldly mind, and the pleasing of the flesh in a cleanlier way. No one sin is rightly killed, till the love of every sin be killed.

3. True repentance is a turning to God, and setting of our hearts and hopes on heaven;[c] so that we now love holiness, and seek God's kingdom above this world. It is counterfeit repentance, or mere melancholy, when men, by affliction, or conviction, cry out of the vanity of this world, and set not their hearts upon a better, and seek not after the heavenly felicity.

4. True repentance is a settled and an effectual change. It maketh a man[d] love that which is good, as if it were now natural to him, and not only to do some good for fear, which he had rather leave undone; nor only to forbear some sins for fear, which he had rather he might keep: and therefore the very heart and love being changed, temptations, even the same that before prevailed, would not now prevail again, if he were under them. It is but a counterfeit repentance, when men are sorry for sinning, but amend not, or are sorry to-day and sin again to-morrow; and that by such gross and wilful sin, which they might forsake, if they were truly willing.[e] By this time, then, you may try whether you have repented indeed, as you supposed.

S. But (Luke xvii. 4) Christ bids us forgive those that seven times in a day trespass, and seven times in a day return and say they repent: and will not God then do so?

x Tit. i. 16.

y Rom. viii. 16—18; 2 Tim. ii. 12; Matt. x. 33; xvi. 24—26; Luke ii. 9.

z Matt. xviii. 3; 1 Cor. vi. 11; 2 Cor. vii. 10, 11; Tit. iii. 3, 5.

a 2 Cor. v. 17; Acts xxvi. 18; Rom. viii. 30.

b John iii. 6; 1 John ii. 15; Rom. viii. 1, 8, 13; xiii. 12—14.

c Phil. iii. 18—20; Col. iii. 1, 3—5; Matt. vi. 21, 33.

d Psal. i. 2, 3; xix. 7—9; cxix. &c.

e Matt. vii. 20—23; 2 Tim. ii. 19.

P. 1. Christ speaketh of true repentance, as far as we can judge, and not of saying, I repent, when it is an apparent lie, or mockery. 2. And he speaketh of such trespasses, the oft committing of which is consistent with true repentance: for instance, it is possible that a man may seven times a day think a vain thought, speak a vain word, or, if he pray seven times a day, he may have, every time, some coldness or imperfections in his prayers; and such like infirmities oft returning, may stand with true repentance, because the sinner would fain overcome them if he could. And so, if a man often wrong you through infirmity, and oft repent, you must forgive him. But, tell me truly, if one of your own servants or children should, seven times a day, or but once a week, or once a month, spit in your face, and beat and buffet you, or wound you, and set your house on fire, and as oft come and say, I repent of it, would you take this for true repentance, or think that this is it that Christ here meant? Or, if your servant should every night come to you and say, Master, I have done no work to-day, but I repent; I wish I had done it; and so hold on from day to day, will you take this for repentance? Do you think it possible for an ungodly, worldly, fleshly man, to repent truly of such a life to-day, and turn to it again to-morrow, and so on? It cannot be. A man may repent of an angry look, or a vain word, to-day, and through infirmity, commit the same to-morrow; but a man cannot repent of an ungodly, sensual life, and turn to it again to-morrow.

I do not think that there is one wicked man of many, but when he hath been guilty of fornication, drunkenness, or any such sin of sensual pleasure, doth repent of it when the pleasure is gone, and wisheth that he had not done it, when yet he goeth on, and is a lover of such beastly pleasure more than of God; for there needeth no saving grace to such a kind of repentance; sense and experience may serve the turn. For when the pleasure of the sin is gone, it is nothing: and therefore is no matter for the sinner's love (unless it be the fanciful remembrance of it, which is another thing). But it is the future pleasure which is still desired. When the drunkard is sick, and findeth the next day the sweetness all gone, and nothing left but shame, or poverty, or a wounded conscience, no thanks to him to say, I am sorry, and wish I had been sober: but still he loveth the sin, and will not leave it, and therefore hath no true change of heart and life, which is the true repentance. And now consider well what I have said, and judge yourself whether you have ever truly repented of a worldly, a fleshly, and an unholy heart and life.

S. You put me so hard to it that I know not what to say. I know not well what to think of myself: and therefore, sir, as you have examined my case, I shall entreat you to help me to pass a right judgment of it, for you are wiser in these things than I. And though the patient feel the pains, yet the physician can better judge of the cause, and nature, and danger of the disease.

P. You say well: but then the patient must tell what he feeleth, and you must answer me these few questions.

I. Hath your soul and everlasting state had your more deep and[f] serious thoughts and regard than your body and your worldly welfare?

S. I cannot say so, though I have often thought of it.

P. 2. Do you verily believe that your sins are so odious, as that if God should condemn you to hell,[g] he should do no worse by you than you deserve?

S. I know you would not have me lie. I have been taught, indeed, that so it is; but my heart never perceived my sins to be so great as to deserve hell. I should think it unjust to be so used as I would not use my greatest enemy.

P. 3. Have you not only heard, but believed, and perceived that you have as much need of Christ to be your Saviour, as a condemned malefactor hath of a pardon; and is Christ more precious[h] to you than all the riches of the world, his ransom and mediation being your hope, and his grace your earnest desire?

S. I know that we cannot be saved without Christ; but I cannot say that I have so much desired him.

P. 4. Have you perceived at the heart, that the love and favour of God is far[i] better than all the treasures and pleasures of this world? And do you verily believe that all the blessed shall see his glory in heaven, and perfectly love, and praise, and serve him, and be filled with perfect joy for ever, in this blessed sight and love of God? And do you set more by the hope of this heavenly glory than by your life and all this world? And do you prefer heaven before earth, in your esteem, your desire, and heartiest labour and diligence to make it sure?

S. I would I could say so: I doubt there be but few that reach so high as that.

P. 5. Have you truly believed, that all[k] that will come to heaven must be a regenerate, sanctified people, in mind, and will, and life; and that this must be done by the Holy Ghost? And have you earnestly desired that he would sanctify you thoroughly, and kill all your sins, and make you fervently in love with God, and all that is good, and fully obedient to his will? And have you given up yourself to Jesus Christ, in a well-considered, resolved covenant; consenting to be taught and governed by him, and willing to imitate him, and to receive his Spirit?

S. I cannot say so; though I desire to amend.

P. 6. Do you feel the[l] evil and odiousness of a worldly, carnal, unrenewed heart, and of an unholy life? yea, of your own want of faith and love to God, as well as of outward, shameful sins? And are these sins of heart and practice the greatest trouble and burden to you in the world?

S. I would it were so; but I do not find it so.

P. 7. Can you truly say that you[m] live not wilfully in any known gross sin, and that you have no sin, no, not the least known infirmity, which you had not rather leave than keep? And that you had rather be perfectly holy (in perfect knowledge, love, and obedience) than to have all the riches, and pleasures, and honours of this world?

S. I should dissemble if I should say so.

P. 8. Can you truly say, that when a temptation cometh to your most beloved sin, God's authority, which forbiddeth it, is more[n] powerful to keep you from it than the temptation and your lust to draw you to it?

[f] Matt. vi. 23—25.

[g] Rom. vi. 23; iii. 23; vii. 24; viii. i; Eph. ii. 3; 1 Thess. i. 10.

[h] Phil. iii. 7—9; 1 Pet. ii. 4, 6, 7.

[i] Matt. vi. 20, 21, 33; Col. iii. 1, 3, 4, &c.; Psalm lxxiii. 25; lxiii. 3; Phil. iii. 20, 21; John vi. 27; 2 Pet. i. 10; iii. 11.

[k] 2 Cor. v. 19, 20; Matt. xxviii. 19, 20; xi. 28, 29; Rom. viii. 9; Gal. v. 17, 21; Acts iii. 22; vii. 37; Luke xix. 27; Heb. xii. 14.

[l] Rom. vii. 14, 24; Ezek. vi. 9; xx. 43; xxxvi. 31.

[m] 1 John iii. 4, 8, 9; Mal. vii. 21; Psalm v. 5; Rom. vii. 17, 24; Luke xiv. 26.

[n] Gen. xxxix. 9; Rom. xii. 21; 2 Pet. ii. 19, 20; 1 John v. 4, 5; Rev. ii. 7, 11, &c.

S. I would it were: I should then sin less.

P. 9. Are you truly willing to[o] wait on God to obtain his grace, in the constant use of hearing, prayer, meditation, and the company and counsel of the godly; even in the strictest means which God appointeth you to use for your salvation?

S. I think they are happy that can do so; but I cannot.

P. 10. Can you truly say that you are at a[p] point with all this world, resolving to let go estate, honour, liberty, and life, rather than let go your faith and obedience; or, by wilful sin, to turn from God?

S. I know I should do so; but I am not come to that.

P. In a word: if you were now to be[q] baptized first, and understood what you did, would you take God for your only God and Father, and Christ for your only Saviour, and the Holy Ghost for your Sanctifier; to save you from lust, and sin, and hell, and to bring you to perfect holiness and glory; forsaking the world, the flesh, and the devil, and totally giving up yourself to God: and this by a solemn, sacred vow; which, if you keep not, you are lost for ever? Would you thus considerately be baptized, if it were to do again?

S. I should promise, and be baptized; but whether I should consent to all this heartily, I doubt.

P. By all these answers set together, you have enabled me how to judge of your condition. If all this be so as you have answered, I must needs tell you, that I think you are yet unconverted and unjustified, and under the guilt and power of your sins, even in the gall of bitterness and bond of iniquity, and that if you should die as you are, without conversion, you are lost for ever: you must be made a new creature, or you are undone. I know this judgment may possibly seem harsh, and be displeasing to you, but it is foolish to flatter our friends or ourselves, when we stand so near the world of light.

But withal I tell you, 1. That your case is not remediless, and that you may be saved from it whenever you are truly willing. 2. And that you are not so far from grace and recovery, as many hardened sinners are, for I perceive that you deal openly, and are not so desperately set against conviction and conversion as too many are.

S. I thank you for dealing plainly with me: but what makes you judge so hardly of my case?

P. Out of your own mouth I pass my judgment; for you confess that it is not yet with you as it is with all that have the Spirit of Christ. And if any man have not the Spirit of Christ, he is none of his, Rom. viii. 9.

And I will here take the boldness to add some observations of my own, which have long made me fear that yet you have not the Spirit of Christ, nor true repentance unto life. For, 1. I have never perceived that you did seriously mind the case of your soul. One might be often in your company, and hear nothing but of common, worldly things, (which may be talked of in due time and measure,) not a word of heaven, nor that savoured of any care of your salvation. And sure one cannot truly believe, and mind, and regard so great a matter as life everlasting, and never show it, by any serious inquiries, or[r] discourse.

2. And I have observed that you were very indifferent for your company,[s] and were more with ignorant, worldly men, or merry sensualists, than with those that set their hearts on heaven, and might have helped you thitherward, by their counsel and example.

3. And I never heard that you[t] set up the worship of God in your family. You seldom prayed with them at all, unless now and then that you said over hastily a few cold words, without any fervency. You never[u] instructed or catechised them, nor took care of the souls of children or servants, but only used them like your beasts, to eat and drink, and do your work. And you are often from the church assemblies, and seem not much moved with what you hear; and neither neighbours or your family hear a word of it from you, when you are once out of the church.

4. And you can now and then drop a petty oath, and curse when you are angry. And you spend the Lord's day almost all in common talk and business, except just while you are at church. And though I never took you for a drunkard, nor whoremonger, nor heard you scorn and rail at godliness, you can sit by them that do it, and easily bear it, as if it were but a small matter. And I heard of one that you once overreached by an unconscionable bargain, but you never made him any restitution. And I perceive that you are all for yourself, though you are a quiet and good neighbour. You speak best of those that do you any good, be they what they will in other respects: and you have always an ill word for those that you are fallen out with, and that you think have wronged you, or that think ill or meanly of you, let them be never so honest in all other respects. In a word, the love of God, and a heavenly mind, is a thing that will, in some measure, show itself, by preferring God and heaven still before all; and I could never perceive any such thing by you, which made me fear your case was as bad as you now confess it.

I do not name these things as if each one of them by itself were a certain sign of an ungodly person. How far an honest-minded man may be carried in a passion to a curse, or railing speech, or an oath, or, through disability, may omit any family duty, or, through a wrong opinion of it, may neglect the Lord's day, I am not now determining. But sure I am, that God saveth none but those that love, honour, and obey him above all others, and make him their trust, and hope, and happiness; and that Christ saveth none but those that value him as their Saviour, and give up themselves to be taught and ruled by him, and sanctified by his Spirit; and that heaven is a place for no carnal worldling, that loveth the world above it, and seeketh this world before it, and that mindeth most the things of the flesh, and had rather[x] satisfy than mortify his sinful lusts and will. And as far as I could perceive by your conversation, this is your case, though you are not so grossly wicked and unconscionable as the debauched sort.

S. I confess I never made the saving of my soul so much of my care, and so serious a business as you talk of; nor hath my heart been so sensible of the need that I have of Christ, or of the greatness of God's love and mercy to sinners in our redemption; nor have I had such believing and serious thoughts of the life to come, as to make it seem more desirable to me than this world; nor can I say, and not lie, that I loved God better than my money, and estate, and fleshly pleasure; nor that I ever made so great a matter of sinning as to avoid it at the rate of any great suffering or loss; or that ever I was very desirous to lead a holy and a heavenly life; nor that I had any great delight in the thoughts or prac-

[o] Psalm i. 1, 2; Matt. vii. 13; Prov. ii. 1—4; Luke x. 42.
[p] Luke xiv. 26, 33; xviii. 22, 23; Matt. x. 38, 39.
[q] Matt. xxviii. 18—20; Mark xvi. 16; Luke xiv. 29, 30.
[r] Psal. xxxvii. 30—32.
[s] Psalm i. 1, 2; xv. 4.
[t] John xxi. 15.
[u] Deut. vi. 7, 8; xi.
[x] John viii. 34.

tice of such things, much less that ever I made the pleasing of God, and the obtaining of perfect and everlasting holiness and happiness with him in heaven, to be the chief care, and end, and labour of my life. But yet I thought that all being sinners, and God being merciful, I might be saved if I believed in Christ, and put my trust in him alone. But now you have made me better to understand what it is to believe and trust in Christ, I perceive that I did not indeed believe and trust in him when I thought I had.

P. I pray you tell me, do you not think there are such sins as presumption, carnal security, false believing, and false hope, whereby the devil undoeth souls?

S. Yes; I have heard preachers often say so.

P. What do you think presumption is?

S. Presuming or thinking that God doth accept us,[y] and we are in a state of grace, when it is not so.

P. What do you think carnal security is?

S. To be [z] careless about the state of our souls, when our danger calleth for our greatest care.

P. What is false believing?

S. To believe ourselves, or [a] bad men, or the devil, against God, or instead of God; or to believe that God hath promised that which he hath not promised; or to trust that Christ will give heaven to such as he hath told us shall not have it.

P. And what is false hope?

S. To hope for heaven or mercy [b] without any such ground, upon terms that God never promised to give it on, or hath plainly said, he will not give it.

P. You have answered very well and truly. And do you not think that all these have been your sins?

S. I am now afraid so: but I am loth to think that it is so bad with me, and therefore I would fain hope still that it is better. But if it should be so, I pray you tell me, what would you yet advise me to do?

P. God knoweth, I have no desire to trouble you, nor to put you into any needless fears, much less to drive you into despair; nor would I have you conclude that your state is bad, upon my word alone: but I will here cite you some texts of Scripture, by which you may certainly judge yourself; and I will entreat you, when you come home, to bestow a few hours in secret, as in God's presence, in a true and impartial examination of yourself by them, and tell me when I next see you how you find the case yourself.

S. But if I do find it bad, I pray you tell me now what I must do to be pardoned and saved?

P. I will now only tell you these generals. 1. That you must well consider how bad and sad an unconverted man's condition is, that you may not delay to seek for mercy, and to come out of such a miserable state. 2. That yet you need not despair or be discouraged, for Christ is a sufficient Saviour and remedy.

And for the first, believe it, till you repent and are converted, you are void of the holy image of God, and have the image of the devil in ignorance, unbelief, and averseness or enmity to God and holiness, in pride, sensuality, worldliness, disobedience, and carnal selfishness. Your heart is against the holy laws and ways of God: you have a fleshly will and concupiscence of your own, which is your idol, and the great rebel against God, which will still be striving against his will, and will draw you to be still pleasing it, though it displease God. You will be a slave to the devil, by your slavery to this fleshly mind and appetite; and you will spend your little time in the world, in pleasing that[c] flesh, if God convert you not. You will never truly love God and heaven, nor make him your end, nor take him for your God, and so you will live in enmity and rebellion against him: you are yet unreconciled, unpardoned, unjustified, unsanctified: all your sins that ever you committed are yet upon you in their guilt. And, in a word, (pardon my plain dealing,) if you die as you are, you will be certainly damned; and as you have departed from God's grace, he will judge you to depart for ever from his glory also. And it will go much the worse with you in hell, because that you might have had the grace of a Redeemer, and you refused Christ, and resisted his Spirit, and neglected his great salvation. So that to deal freely with you, I would not be in your case one day for all the riches in the world, for you have no assurance of your life a minute, and you are certain it cannot be long, and you are still in the power of that God whom you offend: and if you thus die before a true and sound conversion, you are lost for ever, and all your time, your mercies, your comforts, and your hopes, are gone for ever, past all remedy. This is sure the state of every unregenerate, unholy, impenitent sinner, as the [d] word of God is true. And, therefore, as you love yourself, and as ever you care what becomes of your soul, when it must shortly leave your body, go presently try, and throughly try, whether you are a penitent, regenerate, person or not?

S. Alas! sir, I know not how to do it, for I have left my soul hitherto carelessly to a venture, thinking that this had been trusting Christ with it, and now I am unskilful in such matters, and know not how to examine myself. Therefore, I pray you give me your directions.

P. With all my heart, if you will but promise me to do your best. Will you set yourself some time apart for the business, and do it as a man would cast up an account, with your most serious thoughts? And will you examine yourself as you would do another man, with an unfeigned willingness to know the truth, be it better or be it worse?

S. Alas! what good will it do me to flatter and deceive myself, when God knoweth all, and will not be deceived? I desire to know what case I am in, and that I may know what course to take hereafter.

P. Indeed, till you know that, you know not well whether comfort or sorrow best become you, nor whether the promises or threatenings should be first applied by you, nor how well to use any text you read, or sermon you hear. And methinks that a mere uncertainty, what shall become of you when you die, and whether you shall be in heaven or hell for ever, should mar your mirth, and make you sleep with little quietness, till at least you had done your best to make your calling and election sure, and got some good, well-grounded hopes.

I will put you to no longer work than is necessary. 1. Take the Scriptures, especially these texts here transcribed, and set them before you, and well consider them as the word of God. 2. Fall down on your knees, and earnestly beg God's help and mercy to convince you, and show you the truth of your condition. 3. Look back upon all your life, and look into the inwards of your soul, and let conscience compare your heart and life with the word of God, and urge it to speak plainly, and to judge you truly as you are. 4. Do not only try and judge yourself

[y] John viii. 39, 41, 44; ix. 40.
[z] Matt. xxiv. 39; 1 Thess. v. 3.
[a] Matt. xxiv. 23, 26; 1 John iv. 1.
[b] Prov. xi. 7.
[c] Gal. v. 21, 22; Rom. viii. 5, 6, 8, 9; Eph. ii. 1—3, &c.; Mark iv. 12.
[d] John iii. 3, 5; Heb. xii. 14.

by some few actions which have been extraordinary with you; but by the main design, and scope, and tenor of your heart and life: for there is some good in the worst of men, and some evil in the best; and if you will judge of a good man by his worst actions, or of a bad man by his best, you will be unrighteous and misjudge them. Simon Magus, when he was professing his faith at his baptism, seemed better than Simon Peter when he was denying Christ. And judge not your heart by some good thoughts, or some bad thoughts, which have been rare; but judge it by that which hath had your chief esteem, your chief love, or choice, and been the main design which you have driven on, and had your chiefest care and diligence in seeking it. Be sure find out what it is, whether God or the flesh, that hath been uppermost, that hath had your heart and life, and been that to which the other hath stooped and subserved.

These are all the directions that I will trouble you with, saving that I would have you, 5. To follow on the search till you know the truth; and what you cannot do at once, come to it again, till you are resolved. And come and tell me how you have found the case to stand with you; and the Lord assist you.

The texts which I set before you are these.

"Verily, verily, I say unto thee, Except a man be born of water and of the Spirit, he cannot enter into the kingdom of God. That which is born of the flesh is flesh, and that which is born of the Spirit is spirit," John iii. 3, 5, 6.

"God so loved the world, that he gave his only begotten Son, that whosoever believeth in him should not perish, but have everlasting life.—He that believeth on him is not condemned; but he that believeth not is condemned already.—And this is the condemnation, that light is come into the world, and men loved darkness rather than light, because their deeds were evil. For every one that doeth evil, hateth the light, neither cometh to the light, lest his deeds should be reproved. But he that doeth truth cometh to the light, that his deeds may be made manifest, that they are wrought in God," John iii. 16, 18—21.

"Go and teach (or disciple) all nations, baptizing them in the name of the Father, and of the Son, and of the Holy Ghost; teaching them to observe all things, whatsoever I have commanded you," Matt. xxviii. 19, 20. So Mark xvi. 16.

"Verily I say unto you, Except ye be converted, and become as little children, ye shall not enter into the kingdom of heaven," Matt. xviii. 3.

"To open their eyes, and turn them from darkness to light, and from the power of Satan unto God; that they may receive forgiveness of sins, and an inheritance among the sanctified, by faith that is in me," Acts xxvi. 18.

"Except ye repent, ye shall all likewise perish," Luke xiii. 3, 5.

"There is no condemnation to them that are in Christ Jesus, who walk not after the flesh, but after the Spirit.—For they that are after the flesh, do mind the things of the flesh, but they that are after the Spirit, the things of the Spirit. For to be carnally minded is death; but to be spiritually minded is life and peace. Because the carnal mind is enmity against God: for it is not subject to the law of God, neither indeed can be. So then, they that are in the flesh cannot please God. But ye are not in the flesh, but in the Spirit, if the Spirit of God dwell in you. Now if any man have not the Spirit of Christ, he is none of his.—For if ye live after the flesh, ye shall die; but if by the Spirit ye mortify the deeds of the body, ye shall live: for as many as are led by the Spirit of God, are the sons of God.—Ye have received the Spirit of adoption, whereby we cry, Abba, Father. The Spirit itself beareth witness to (or with) our spirit, that we are the children of God," Rom. viii. 1, 2, &c.

"Now the works of the flesh are manifest, which are, adultery, fornication, uncleanness, lasciviousness, idolatry, witchcraft, hatred, variance, emulations, wrath, strife, seditions, heresies, envyings, murders, drunkenness, revellings, and such like.—They which do such things shall not inherit the kingdom of God. But the fruit of the Spirit is love, joy, peace, long-suffering, gentleness, goodness, faith, meekness, temperance: against such there is no law; and they that are Christ's have crucified the flesh, with the affections and lusts thereof," Gal. v. 19, &c. "God forbid that I should glory, save in the cross of our Lord Jesus Christ, by whom the world is crucified to me, and I unto the world," Gal. vi. 14.

"Now if any man be in Christ, he is a new creature: old things are passed away; behold, all things are become new," 2 Cor. v. 17. "Know ye not the unrighteous shall not inherit the kingdom of God? Be not deceived, neither fornicators, nor idolaters, nor adulterers, nor effeminate, nor abusers of themselves with mankind, nor thieves, nor covetous, nor drunkards, nor revilers, nor extortioners, shall inherit the kingdom of God. And such were some of you, but ye are washed, but ye are sanctified, but ye are justified, in the name of the Lord Jesus, and by the Spirit of our God," 1 Cor. vi. 9—11; so Eph. v. 3—11.

"Follow peace with all men, and holiness, without which no man shall see the Lord," Heb. xii. 14.

"For the grace of God, which bringeth salvation, hath appeared to all men, teaching us that, denying ungodliness and worldly lusts, we should live soberly, righteously, in this present world; looking for that blessed hope, and the glorious appearing of the great God and our Saviour Jesus Christ: who gave himself for us, that he might redeem us from all iniquity, and purify to himself a peculiar people zealous of good works," Tit. ii. 11—14.

"Love not the world, nor the things that are in the world; for if any man love the world, the love of the Father is not in him," John ii. 15.

"Ye cannot serve God and mammon," Luke xvi. 13.

"Whatsoever is born of God overcometh the world. —And this is the victory that overcometh the world, even your faith," 1 John v. 4, 5.

"The foundation of God standeth sure, having this seal, The Lord knoweth who are his. And, Let him that nameth the name of Christ depart from iniquity," 2 Tim. ii. 19.

"By this the children of God are manifest, and the children of the devil: whosoever doeth not righteousness is not of God, neither he that loveth not his brother. We know that we have passed from death to life, because we love the brethren. He that loveth not his brother abideth in death," 1 John iii. 10, 14.

"Blessed is the man that walketh not in the counsel of the ungodly, nor standeth in the way of sinners, nor sitteth in the seat of the scornful: but his delight is in the law of the Lord, and in his law doth he meditate day and night," Psalm i. 1, 2.

"Let us walk honestly, as in the day; not in rioting and drunkenness, not in chambering and wantonness, not in strife and envying; but put ye on the Lord Jesus Christ, and make no provision for the flesh, to fulfil the lusts (or wills) thereof," Rom. xiii. 13, 14.

"He shall be called Jesus, for he shall save his people from their sin," Matt. i. 21.

"If any man come to me, and hate not his father, and mother, and wife, and children, and brethren, and sisters, yea, and his own life also, (that is, love them not so much less than me, that he can cast them by, as we do things hated, when they stand against me,) he cannot be my disciple. And whosoever doth not bear his cross, and come after me, cannot be my disciple.—Whosoever he be of you that biddeth not farewell to, or forsaketh, all that he hath, he cannot be my disciple," Luke xiv. 26, 33.

"Him that overcometh will I make a pillar in the temple of my God, and he shall go no more out," Rev. iii. 12.

"He that overcometh shall inherit all things; and I will be his God, and he shall be my son. But the fearful, and unbelieving, and the abominable, and murderers, and whoremongers, and sorcerers, and idolaters, and all liars, shall have their part in the lake that burneth with fire and brimstone; which is the second death," Rev. xxi. 7, 8.

"There is laid up for me a crown of righteousness, which God the righteous Judge will give me, and to all them that love his appearing," 2 Tim. iv. 8. Read Matt. xxv.

THE

SECOND DAY'S CONFERENCE.

OF THE CONVERSION OF A SINNER, WHAT IT IS.

SPEAKERS.—Paul, a teacher; and Saul, a learner.

PAUL. Well, neighbour, have you examined yourself by the word of God, since I saw you, as I directed you?

SAUL. I have done what I can in it.

P. And what do you think now of your case, upon trial?

S. I think it is much worse than I had hoped it was, and as bad as you feared. When I first read the promises to all that believe in Christ, I was ready again to hope that I was safe; but when I read further, I found that it was as you had told me; and that I had none of Christ's Spirit, and therefore am none of his; and that I am not a penitent convert, and am not in a state of life. But I now beseech you, sir, upon my knees, as you pity a poor sinner, tell me[a] what I must do to be saved.

P. Are you willing and resolved to do it if I tell it you, and prove it to you fully by the word of God.

S. By the grace of God I am resolved to do it, be it what it will, for I know it cannot be so bad as sin and hell.

P. You say well. I will first tell you this again in the general, 1. That your case is[b] not remediless, but a full and sufficient salvation is purchased, and tendered in the gospel to you as well as to any others.

2. That Christ and his grace is this remedy; and[c] that God hath given us eternal life, and this life is in his Son. He that hath the Son hath life, and he that hath not the Son hath not life, but remaineth in his guilt and sin.

3. That Christ having already made himself a sufficient sacrifice for sins, and merited our reconciliation, pardon, and salvation, to be given in his way,[d] hath made a covenant of grace (conditional) with sinful man, by the promise of which he forgiveth us all our sins, and giveth right to everlasting life.

4. That Christ's way of saving men from sin is by sending his[e] ministry and word to call them, and giving his[f] Spirit within to sanctify them. And this Spirit is Christ's advocate to plead his cause, and do his work, and prepare us by holiness for the heavenly glory.

5. That all the condition required of you, that you may have all these blessings of the covenant of grace, is but sincerely to[g] believe and consent, and give up yourself in covenant to God the Father, Son, and Holy Ghost, and continue true to the covenant which you make.

Read over these five points well, and consider of them; and then tell me whether this be not glad tidings to an undone, miserable sinner? Have you read them over.

S. I have read them, and I perceive that they are glad tidings of hope indeed. But truly, sir, I have heard the gospel so carelessly, that I do not thoroughly understand these things; and therefore entreat you to open them to me more fully and plainly.

P. I know you were baptized in your infancy; which was your privilege, being entered by your parents into the covenant of God. But their consent and dedication will serve your turn no longer than till you come to age and natural capacity to consent and covenant for yourself. Tell me, then, have you ever soberly considered what your baptism was, and what covenant was then made between God and you? And have you seriously renewed that covenant yourself, and so given up yourself to God?

S. Alas! I never either seriously considered or renewed it; but I thought I was made a christian by it, and was sufficiently regenerated, and my sins done away, and that I was a child of God, and an heir of heaven.

P. And how did you think all your sins, since your baptism, were forgiven you?

S. I confessed them to God, and some of them to the minister, and I received the Lord's supper; and I thought that then I was forgiven, though I never had the true sense and power thereof on my heart and life.

P. What if you had never been baptized, and were now first to be baptized, what would you do?

S. I would understand and consider better of it, that I might not do I know not what.

P. Why truly, baptizing is well called christening; for baptism is such a covenant between God and man, as maketh the receiver of it a visible christian; and if you had sincerely renewed and kept this same covenant, you had needed no new conversion or regeneration, but only particular repentance for your particular following sins. Baptism is to our christianity what matrimony is to a state of marriage; or like the enlisting and oath of a soldier to his captain, or of a subject to his prince. And therefore I will put you upon no other conversion than to review your baptism, and understand it well, and after the most serious deliberation to make the same covenant with God over again, as if you had never yourself made it before, or rather as one that hath not kept the covenant which once you made.

Now, if you were to be baptized presently, there are these three things which you must do: 1. Your understanding must know the meaning of the covenant, and[h] believe the truth of the word of God,

[a] Acts ii. 37; xvi. 30. [b] Matt. xi. 28.
[c] 1 John v. 11, 12. [d] Matt. xxviii. 19, 20; John iii. 16.
[e] Acts xxvi. 16—18; Rom. x. 8—10, 14, 15.
[f] Rom. viii. 9.
[g] Matt. xxviii. 19, 20; Mark xvi. 16; Rev. xxii. 17.
[h] John xviii. 12; Acts i. 37; xvi. 31; 2 Cor. viii. 5.

which is his part. 2. Your will must heartily desire and accept of the benefits of God's covenant offered you, and resolvedly consent to the conditions[i] required of you. 3. And you must presently oblige yourself to the faithful practice of them, and to continue true to your covenant, from the time of your baptism till death.

S. Truly, if conversion be no more than to do what I vowed to do, and to be a christian seriously which before I was but by name and hypocritical profession, I have no more reason to stick at it than to be against baptism and christianity itself. First, then, will you help my understanding about it?

P. 1. You must understand and believe the articles of the christian faith, expressed in the common creed, which you hear every day at church, and profess assent to it.

S. Alas! I hear it, and say it by rote, but I never well understood it, or considered it.

P. The christian belief hath three principal parts: that is, our believing in[k] God the Father, and in God the Son, and in God the Holy Ghost. And each of these hath divers articles. I. In the first part all these things must be understood and believed. 1. That there is[l] one only God, in three persons, the Father, Son, and Holy Ghost; who is an infinite, eternal, perfect Spirit; a perfect life, understanding, and will; perfectly powerful, wise, and good; the first efficient, chief governing, and final Cause, or End, of all; of whom, and through whom, and to whom, are all things; the Creator, and therefore the Owner, the Ruler, and the Benefactor, and End, especially of man.

2. That this God made Adam and Eve, in his own[m] image, under a perfect law of innocency, requiring perfect obedience of them on pain of death.

3. That they[n] broke this perfect law by wilful sin, and thereby fell under the sentence of death, the displeasure of God, the forfeiture of his grace, and of all their happiness.

4. That all of us having our very beings and natures from them, (and their successors,)[o] derive corruption or pravity of nature also from them, and a participation of guilt: and these corrupted natures are disposed to all actual sin, by which we should grow much worse, and more miserable.

5. That God, of his mercy and wisdom, took advantage of man's sin and misery to glorify his grace, and[p] promised man a Redeemer, and made a new law or covenant for his government and salvation, forgiving him all his sins, and promising him salvation, if he believe and trust in God his Saviour, and repent of sin, and live in thankful, sincere obedience, though imperfect.

6. In the[q] fulness of time, God sent his Son, his eternal Word, made man, to be our Redeemer; who was conceived in a virgin by the Holy Ghost, and, by perfect obedience, fulfilled God's law, and became our example, and conquered all temptations, and gave himself a sacrifice for our sins, in suffering, after a life of humiliation, a cursed, shameful death upon the cross; and being buried, he arose again the third day, and having conquered death, assured us of a resurrection; and after forty days' continuance upon earth, he ascended bodily, in the sight of his disciples, into heaven, where he is the Teacher, the King, and the Intercessor for the church with God; by whom alone we must come unto the Father, and who prepareth for us the heavenly glory, and us for it.

7. Before he ascended, he made a more full and plain edition of the aforesaid law or covenant of grace; and he gave[r] authority to his chosen ministers, to go and preach it to all the world, and promised them the extraordinary gift and assistance of his Holy Spirit: and he ordained baptism to be used as the solemn initiation of all that will come into his church, and enter into the covenant of God. In which covenant God the Father[s] consenteth to be our reconciled God and Father, to pardon our sins for the sake of Christ, and give us his Holy Spirit, and glorify us in heaven for ever: and God the Son consenteth to be our Saviour, our King and Head, our Teacher and Mediator, to bring us reconciled to his Father, and to justify us, and give us his Spirit, and eternal life: and God the Holy Ghost consenteth to[t] dwell in us as the Agent and Advocate of Christ, to be our quickener, our illuminator, and sanctifier, the witness of Christ, and the earnest of our salvation. And we, on our part, must profess unfeigned belief of this gospel of Christ, and repentance for our former sins, and consent to[u] receive these gifts of God, giving up ourselves, soul and body, to him, as our only God, our Saviour and our Sanctifier, as our chiefest Owner, Ruler, and Benefactor; resolving to live as his own, as his subjects and his children, in true resignation of ourselves to him, in true obedience and thankful love:[x] renouncing the world, the flesh, and the devil, that would tempt us to the contrary: and this is the end; but not in our own strength, but by the gracious help of the Spirit of God.

This is the baptismal covenant, the manner of whose outward administration you have often seen.

By this covenant, as it is God's law and act on his part, all that truly consent and give up themselves thus absolutely to God the Father, Son, and Holy Ghost, are presently pardoned all the sins that ever they were guilty of, as by God's instrumental act of oblivion: and in it they have the gift of their right to the Spirit, and to everlasting life, and of all the mercies necessary thereunto.

8. The[y] Holy Ghost, in a peculiar manner, is given to all that thus truly believe and consent to the holy covenant; to dwell and work in them, and regenerate them more fully to the nature and image of God: working in them, 1. A holy liveliness and activity for God. 2. A holy light and knowledge of God. 3. A holy love and desire after God, and all that by which God is manifested unto man. And they that have not this renewing Spirit of Christ, are none of his: and by this the temptations of the flesh, the world, and the devil, must be overcome.

9. At death men's souls are judged particularly, and[z] enter into joy or misery; and, at the end of this world, Christ will come in glory, and raise the

i Matt. xxviii. 19, 20. k Matt. xxviii. 19, 20.

l 1 Cor. viii. 4, 6; 1 John v. 7; 1 Tim. i. 17; Psal. cxxxiv. 7—9; cxlvii. 5; xlvii. 7; cxlv. 9; Isa. xl. 17; Neh. ix. 6; Rev. iv. 8; xv. 3; Ezek. xvii. 4.

m Gen. i. 27; ii. 16, 17; Eccl. vii. 29.

n Gen. iii.; Rom. iii. 23; vi. 23.

o Rom. v. 12, 18; iii. 9, 19; Gen. ii. 16, 17; Eph. ii. 2, 3; Heb. ii. 14; John viii. 44.

p Gen. iii. 15; John iii. 16.

q Gal. iv. 4; John i. 1—3; xiv. 2, 3; iii. 16; 1 John ii.; John x. 30; 1 Tim. ii. 5; Matt. i. 20, 21; Heb. ii. 14, 15; iv. 15; vii. 26; ix. 26; viii. 2; x. 21; 1 Cor. xv. 3, 4; Luke xxiii. 43; i. 27, 31; 2 Tim. i. 10; Acts ii. 9; iii. 21; ii. 36; x. 36.

r Matt. xxviii. 19, 20; Mark xvi. 16; Rom. x. 10.

s 2 Cor. v. 18—20; 1 John v. 9—12; John vi.

t Gal. iv. 6; Tit. iii. 3, 5.

u John i. 10—12; Rom. xii. 1, 2.

x Rom. viii. 13; Luke xiv. 26; Acts xxvi. 18.

y 1 Cor. xii. 12, 13; Rom. viii. 9, 16, 26, 30; Gal. iv. 6; v. 17, 24; John iii. 6—8; Eph. ii. 1, 2; Tit. iii. 3, 5; Acts xxvi. 18; 2 Tim. v. 7; 1 John ii. 15.

z Luke xxiii. 43; xvi. 22, 26; 2 Cor. v. 18; Phil. i. 23; Acts i. 11; 1 Cor. xv.; John v. 22, 29; xvii. 24; Matt. xxv. xiii. 41—43; 2 Tim. iv. 8, 18; 2 Thess. i. 8—10; ii. 12.

dead, and judge all the world according to their works. And they that have sincerely kept this covenant (according to the several editions of it, which they were under) shall be openly justified and glorified with Christ; where they shall be made perfect themselves in soul and body, and perfectly know, love, praise, and please the most blessed God for evermore, among the blessed saints and angels: and those that have not performed this covenant shall be for ever deprived of this glory, and suffer in hell everlasting misery, with devils and ungodly men.

These nine points must all be competently understood by you; or else you cannot understand what baptism, repentance, conversion, christianity, is; and you consent to you know not what.

S. Alas! sir, when shall I ever be able to understand and remember all this?

P. It is all but your common catechism; yea, it is all but the creed which you daily repeat, a little opened. But if you do not remember all these words; if yet you remember the sense and matter of them, it will suffice.

S. But you told me, that besides understanding and belief, the [a] will's true consent is also necessary.

P. II. That is the second part of religion and holiness, and, indeed, the very heart of all: for what the will is, that the man is. But I need not here many words to tell you, that when you have considered the terms of the baptismal covenant, your hearty, resolved, full consent to it, is the condition of your present right, upon which Christ taketh you as his own.

S. But hath my will no more to do but to consent to that covenant?

P. That implieth that your consent must still continue, and that it reach to the particular means and duties which Christ shall appoint you. And the Lord's prayer is given as the more particular rule of all the desires of your will. Wherefore you must well study the meaning of that prayer.

S. You told me also that practice is the third part of religion: how shall I know what that must be?

P. III. You must here know, 1. The rule of your practice. 2. That your practice must be according to that rule. The foundation and end of all your practice is laid down already in what is said.

I. The foundation and root of all is your relation to God, according to this covenant. 1. You are devoted to him as being totally his own;[b] and therefore you must live to him, and seek his glory, and rest in his disposals. 2. You are related to him as his subject,[c] and therefore must endeavour absolutely to obey him above all the world. 3. You are related to him, when you are a true believer, as his child and friend;[d] and therefore must live in faithfulness and love. And this is the foundation and sum of all your holy life.

II. And the ends of all your practice must be, 1. That you may be fully delivered from all sin and misery, be made more holy and more serviceable to God and profitable to men,[e] and may glorify your Father, Redeemer, and Sanctifier, by the glory of his image on you, and so may be more pleasing to him; and, 2. That you may be perfectly holy and glorious, and happy in heaven, and may with saints and angels dwell with Christ, and know, and love, and praise, and serve the Lord in glory, in perfect joy for evermore. These ends being all most excellent and sure, must be still in your eye, as the great and constant poise and motive of all your practice.

III. As you are a subject, your obedience hath its rule; and the rule is the law of your Redeemer and Creator.[f] This law is the law of nature, and the commands of Christ superadded in the gospel, set together. The law of nature [g] is the whole nature and order of all things in the world, and especially of man himself, as it signifieth the will of God about man's duty, and his reward or punishment.

The special superadded commands of Christ are, that we [h] believe in him as our Saviour, and believe all the added articles of faith, and hope for life by his purchase and promise, and love God as his goodness appeareth in his Son and gospel, and love Christ's members for his sake; that we pray for the Spirit of Christ, and obey him; and that we observe that church order, as to ministry, church assemblies, the Lord's day, the two sacraments, public worship, and discipline, which Christ, by himself, or his Spirit in his apostles, hath commanded us.

And yet you must understand, 1. That the law of nature itself is much [i] more plainly described and opened in the holy Scripture than you are able to read it in itself. 2. That even these gospel superadded laws have somewhat of natural obligation in them, supposing but foregoing matters of fact, that Christ did all that indeed he did. So much for your rule.

IV. The degree of obedience, which is your duty, is indeed [k] perfection without further sin: but your daily infirmities have a pardon; and therefore the degree of obedience necessary to your salvation is but that it be sincere, that is, that as to the predominant bent of your heart and life, you truly obey your Creator and Redeemer, and make this the chief trade or business which you live for and manage in the world.

V. I must also add that, in all this, you must still remember that, 1. The devil; and, 2. The world; 3. But, above all, your own [l] fleshly mind and appetite, will be the great enemies of all this holiness and obedience; and therefore you must understand their enmity, and the danger of it, and resolve, by God's grace, to renounce them and resist them, as your enemies, to the last.

And though only sincerity is necessary to salvation, yet, 1. You have not sincerity, unless you have a desire and endeavour after perfection.[m] 2. And a greater degree of holiness is necessary to a great degree of glory.

S. Alas! sir, I shall never remember all this.

P. You may see, then, how foolishly you have done, to lose your time in childhood and youth, which you should have spent in learning the will of God, and the way to your salvation. If you had, morning and night, desirously meditated on these things, and read God's word, and asked counsel of your teachers, and learned catechisms, and read good books, and if you had marked well what you heard at church, and had spent all the Lord's days in such work as this, which you spent in play and idleness,

[a] Exod. xx. 3; Josh. xxiv. 16, 25; 2 Cor. viii. 5; Mark xvi. 16; 1 Pet. iii. 21; Rev. xxii. 17; Matt. xi. 29; xxviii. 24; John xiv. 8; Luke v. 14; xiv. 26, 33; Acts ix. 6, 7; Eph. ii. 18, 22; iii. 5, 16.

[b] Cor. vi. 19; Psal. c. 2—5.

[c] Psal. v. 2; x. 16; xlvii. 6, 7.

[d] Gal. iii. 26; iv. 6; John xi. 52; Rom. viii. 16, 17, 26.

[e] Tit. ii. 14; iii. 3, 5, 6; 1 Cor. vi. 20; vii. 32; John xv. 8; 1 Pet. iv. 11; 1 Thess. iv. 1; 2 Tim. ii. 3, 4, 12; 2 Thess. i. 9, 10; Col. iii. 1, 4, 5; Luke xii. 32; Jam. ii. 5; 2 Pet. i. 11.

[f] Psal. i. 2; Matt. xi. 29; xxviii. 20.

[g] Psal. xix. 1, 2, &c.; Rom. i. 19, 20; ii.

[h] John xiv. 1; i. 12; vi. 29; xvi. 27; xvii. 1—3; 1 John iii. 16, 17; iv. 9; Tit. iii. 4; Luke xi. 13; x. 16; Heb. xiii. 7, 17; 1 Thess. v. 12; 1 Cor. xvi. 16.

[i] Psal. xix. 7—10; John i. 8—10; iii. 19—21.

[k] Matt. v. 48; Psal. xix. 7; xxxii. 1, 2; 2 Cor. vii. 1; Eph. iv. 12; Matt. vi. 33.

[l] Rom. viii. 5—8, 13; Gal. v. 17.

[m] Psal. cxix. 1—5; Matt. xxv. 20, 21, 23.

and vain talk, you might have been acquainted familiarly with all this, and more. But that which is past cannot be recalled. If you cannot remember all this, 1. Labour to understand it well. 2. And remember that which is the sum of all.

S. What is that?

P. 1. The shortest sum is the baptismal covenant itself, to believe in[n] and give up yourself to God the Father, the Son, and the Holy Ghost, as your Creator, Redeemer, and Sanctifier, your Owner, Ruler, and chief Good and End; renouncing the flesh, the world, and the devil.

2. The next summary, explaining this more largely, is, 1. The creed,[o] as the sum of what you must believe. 2. The Lord's prayer,[p] as the sum of what you must desire. 3. And the sum of the law of nature is in the ten commandments;[q] and the church laws of Christ, about ministry, communion, sacraments, and other worship, you will be taught in the church by sense and use, and daily teaching. Cannot you say the creed, Lord's prayer, and ten commandments?

S. Yes, I learned the words, but I never laid the sense and substance of them to heart.

P. All that I have said to you is but the sense of those three. Understand the exposition, and remember the forms or words themselves. But even your duty is yet shortlier summed up in love,[r] which is the fulfilling of the law; for justice is comprehended in love, which will teach you to do as you would be done by.

S. What love is it that you mean?

P. The love of God, the love of yourself, and the love of your neighbour, is the sum of all your duty.

S. This is but reasonable duty, which no man can deny or speak against: and one part of it I shall easily keep, which is to love myself.

P. Alas, poor man! have you kept it hitherto? What enemy have you had in all the world comparable to yourself?[s] All that your enemies could do against you is but as a flea-biting. What if they slander you, oppress you, imprison you, or otherwise abuse you? Wrong not yourself, and all this cannot hinder your salvation, nor make God love you ever the less, nor make death ever the more terrible; nor will it ever be your sorrow in heaven to think of it. All your enemies in the world cannot force you to commit one sin, or make you a jot displeasing unto God. But you yourself have committed thousands of sins, and made yourself an enemy to God. Oh the folly of ungodly men! They can hardly forgive another if he do but beat them, or slander them, or impoverish them: and yet they can go on to abuse, undo, and destroy their souls, and run towards hell, and easily forgive themselves all this; yea, take it for their benefit,[t] and will not be restrained,[u] nor persuaded to forbear, nor show any mercy to their own miserable souls. I tell you, though the devil hate you, yet all the devils in the world have not done so much against you as you have done against yourself. The devils did but tempt you to sin, but never did nor could compel you; but it is you that have wilfully sinned yourself, and sold your soul, as Esau his birthright, for a morsel, for a pleasant cup or game, or for a lust or filthy pleasure, and for a thing that is worse than nothing.

Was it not you, even you yourself, that forgot your God, neglected your Saviour, resisted the Holy Spirit, refused sanctifying grace, despised heaven, and set more by this dirty world? Was it not you yourself that loved not holiness, nor a holy God, nor the holy Scriptures, nor holy persons, nor holy thoughts, or words, or ways, that lost your precious time, and omitted almost all your duty, and ran into a multitude of sins? And if the devil studied his worst to hurt you, what could he do more than to tempt you unto sin? If you had been a sworn enemy to yourself, and plotted how to do yourself the greatest mischief, what could you do worse than to sin and run on God's displeasure? Which is the way to the gallows, but by breaking the law, by murder, felony, or the like; and which is the way to hell, but loving sin, and refusing grace? And yet are you a lover of yourself?

S. All this is too true, and yet I am sure that I love myself: how then comes all this to pass?

P. You love yourself with a sensitive love, that goeth all by sense, and little by reason, much less by faith. As a swine loveth himself when he is bursting his belly with whey, or a rat when he is eating ratsbane. You love your appetite, but you have little care of your soul. You love yourself, but you love not that which is good for yourself: as a sick man loveth his life, but abhorreth his meat and medicine.

Indeed, God hath planted a love to yourselves so deep in nature, that no man can choose but love himself: and, therefore, in the commandments, the love of God and our neighbour only are expressed, and the love of ourselves is presupposed. But Christ, knowing what destroyers men are of themselves, and forsakers of their own salvation, doth call upon sinners to love, care, and labour, for their own souls.

These things conjunctly make up man's enmity against his own salvation. 1. The soul hath lost much of the knowledge of its own excellency in its higher faculties. 2. Its love to itself, as rational, is dulled, and wanteth stirring up. 3. It is inordinately fallen in love with itself as sensitive, and its lower faculties. 4. It doteth on all sensual objects that are delightful. 5. It is as dead and averse to those noble, spiritual, higher objects in which it must be happy. And in this sense man is his own greatest enemy.

I the rather speak all this to you on this point, because your very repentance consisteth in being angry with yourself, and falling out with, and even loathing, yourself, for your sins, and your self-undoing. And till you come to see what you have done against yourself, you will never come to that true humiliation and self-distrust as is needful to your salvation. And also because that it is here, and here only, that your safety and happiness is like to stick for the time to come. Do but as a man that loveth himself, and you are safe. God entreateth you to have mercy on yourself. He hath resolved on what terms he will have mercy upon sinners: they are unchangeably set down in his gospel. And sinners will not yield unto his terms. Though they be no harder than to receive his gifts according to their nature, men will not be entreated to receive them. They would have fleshly and worldly prosperity, but deliverance from sin, and holy communion with God, they will not have. Here is the only stop of their salvation. All men[x] might be holy and happy if they would, but most men will not. This is the woeful state of sinners. They will cry to God for mercy, mercy, when judgment cometh, and

[n] Matt. xxviii. 19; Mark xvi. 16.
[o] 1 Cor. xv. 2—5. [p] Matt. vi. 6.
[q] Matt. ix. 17, 18; Rom. xiii. 8, 9.
[r] Rom. xiii. 8, 9; Mark xii. 30, 33; Matt. xxii. 37, 39.
[s] Hos. xiii. 9; Prov. xxix. 24; viii. 36.
[t] Tit. iii. 2—5. [u] 2 Cor. v. 19, 20.
[x] Josh. xxiv. 15; Isa. lv. 1—4.

it is too late, and yet now no counsel, no reason, no entreaty, will persuade them to accept it. It is a pitiful thing to hear Christ's ministers, in his name, beseech men to accept of sanctifying, saving mercy, from day to day, and all in vain, and to think how these same men will cry for mercy when mercy hath done with them, and the door is shut. Yea, how they still say, We hope to be saved because God is merciful, while they will not have his saving mercy. As if mercy stuck in the hand of God as an unwilling giver, while it is they that refuse it as unwilling to receive it. Like a thief that is entreated by the judge to give over in time, and to have mercy on himself, and not to cast away his life, and will not hear nor be persuaded; and yet at the bar or gallows will cry out for mercy. What would you say to a famished beggar that should stand begging for an alms, and will not take it? Would it not be a strange sight at once to hear the beggar say, I pray you give me money or bread, and the giver offering it, and say, I entreat thee to take it, and have pity on thyself, and do not famish, and cannot prevail?

S. It is a sad and mad condition that you describe, and it is too true: but methinks it were a fitter comparison if you likened them to a sick man that begs for health of the physician, but will take no physic; while the physician begs of him in vain, to take physic that he may have health. For it is not the health that men are unwilling of, but the physic. It is not salvation, but the strait gate and narrow way.

P. There is some truth in what you say, (that they are against the means,) but you are mistaken in the rest. For holiness, which they refuse, is not only a means, but it is much of[y] salvation itself. Holiness is the soul's health, and not only its medicine: and perfect holiness, which is the perfect knowledge and love of God, will be heaven itself. And to refuse holiness is to refuse health and heaven.

S. The Lord knoweth that this hath been my case. I have been my own most hurtful enemy, and done more against myself than all the world hath done, and while I loved myself carnally, I undid myself foolishly: and I understand now that it is not so easy a matter to love one's own soul aright as I had thought. But he that will not love God, it is pity he should live, for God is all goodness.

P. Alas! man, it is far harder to[z] love God truly than yourself: I tell you, that your want of love to God is the greatest sin that ever you were guilty of, and the very sum of all your sins. And were the true love of God more common, salvation would be more common, for no true lover of God shall be condemned. I know that there is something of God that all men love. They love him as he is the Maker and Maintainer of the world, and of their own lives and bodily prosperity; and as he giveth them food and raiment, and all the mercies which they abuse, to gratify their lusts. But they love him not as he is holy and a righteous Governor, forbidding sin, requiring holiness, hating and punishing the ungodly, restraining fleshly lusts, and not forgiving nor saving the impenitent.

If you had loved God all this while indeed, would you not have loved his word, and loved to praise him, and call upon his name, and loved what he loveth, and delighted to do his will and please him? Did you love God when you broke his laws, and hated holiness, and could not abide an obedient, holy, heavenly life, and loved not to think or talk much of him, nor to call upon him? You may as well say that he loveth the king who spits in his face, and rebelleth against him.

As long as you think you have been a lover of God in your[a] sinful state of life, and think it is so easy still to love him, you know not God, you know not yourself, you know not the need or the nature of true conversion, nor can you repent of this greatest sin while you know not that you are guilty of it. Do you not know that you have all this while been an enemy to God, and a hater of him?

S. I have been an enemy to myself, but sure nobody can hate God.

P. Where there is enmity, loathing, aversation of mind, and unwillingness, there is hatred. The carnal mind is enmity against God; for it is not subject to the law of God, nor indeed can be, Rom. viii. 5—7. If there were no enmity between God and man, what need was there of a Mediator, or Reconciler? And will you think so ill of the most gracious God, and so well of yourself, a naughty sinner, as to think that the enmity is[b] only in God, and not in you? Is he an enemy to any man that is not first an enemy to him? "He hateth all the workers of iniquity," (Psal. v. 5,) because they are all enemies to him, and contrary to his holiness as darkness is to light. It is the very case of all ungodly persons, that their hearts are turned away from God to this[c] world, and the pleasures of the flesh; and being in love with these, they[d] love not that God, nor that holy word, which calls them off, and condemneth them for their sinful minds and pleasures. Let your conscience speak plainly; had not the world more of your heart than heaven? Were you not a lover of pleasure more than of God? Were not your thoughts, lying down, and rising up, and all the day, more forward and ready to think of your worldly and fleshly concernments, than of God? And were not those thoughts more sweet and welcome to you? Was not your heart so loth and backward to think of God with pleasure, that you never did seriously set yourself one hour together, in your life, to meditate of him and of the heavenly glory? Nay, in sermons and prayer you could not keep your thoughts upon him. You know what it is to love your friend, to love your money, lands, and pleasure; do you know, by as good experience, what it is to love God? And if you love him not above all, you love him not indeed as God. Were you not more weary of holy thoughts, or holy conference, or prayer, than of your worldly business and discourse? Was not your heart against the holiness and strictness of God's word and of his servants? In a word, if you had no[e] enmity to a holy and heavenly mind and life, why did you not choose it? And why could not all God's mercies invite you to it? nor all teaching and entreaties ever persuade you to it? Why are you yet so backward to it? Is this no enmity? And if you were an enemy to holiness, and to the holy word and government of God, was not this to be an enemy to God? I tell you, we are all enemies to God till Christ have reconciled us, and the Holy Ghost renewed us, and turned the enmity into love.

S. I never laid this state of enmity to heart till now. I knew that I was a sinner; but I knew not that I was an enemy to God, even when I began to fear that he was for my sin an enemy to me. But I find now that it hath been with me just as you say; and I perceive that all sin hath some enmity to God in it.

P. Where God is not loved as God, he is in some

[y] Matt. i. 21; Tit. ii. 14; Eph. v. 27; Col. i. 22; 1 Pet. i. 16.
[z] Luke xviii. 22—24; xiv. 26, 33; Rom. viii. 8.
[a] Eph. ii. 1—3; Rom. v. 9, 10.
[b] Zech. xi. 8; Eph. iii. 18, 19.
[c] Phil. iii. 18, 19; Col. i. 21.
[d] Heb. x. 13; Luke xiv. 27; Isa. i. 24; Psalm xxxvii. 30.
[e] Gen. iii. 15; Jam iv. 4; Rom. viii. 7.

sort[f] hated; and between love and enmity there is in man no middle state. For none in this are perfect neuters, or indifferent. Have you not heard that enmity between the seed of the woman and of the serpent was put from the beginning of the covenant of grace? And how this was presently manifested in Cain and Abel, the two first men and brothers that were born into the world: "Cain was of that wicked one (the devil) and slew his brother. And wherefore slew he him? Because his own works were evil and his brother's righteous," 1 John iii. 12. If you have read the Scripture, and other history, and have but heeded what is done about you in the world, you might easily perceive that the world hath ever consisted of two contrary sorts of men, who, as two armies, are still to this day in constant opposition to each other. The wicked are the[g] devil's seed and army; and the godly are the army of Christ, and the regenerate seed of God. Whence is all the hatred of godliness on the earth, all the scorns, and slanders, and cruel persecutions and butcheries of holy persons, and the number of martyrs and sufferers, but from this inbred enmity? This is Christ's meaning when he saith, that he came not to send peace, but a sword; because he came to cause that holiness which the wicked will still hate and persecute. Look about you, and see whether we may not yet truly say with St. Paul, "But as then he that was born after the flesh persecuted him that was born after the Spirit, even so it is now," Gal. iv. 29. And we are all of this malignant disposition in some degree till grace recover us; "When we were enemies, we were reconciled to God by the death of his Son," Rom. v. 10. So "He that will be a friend of the world is an enemy to God. The friendship of the world is enmity to God," Col. i. 21; James iv. 4. I will mind you of no other proof, more than Christ's own sentence, which is not unjust. "Those mine enemies that would not I should reign over them, bring them hither, and slay them before me," Luke xix. 27. Those that would not have Christ reign over them, and subdue their worldly minds, and fleshly lusts, and make them holy, are his enemies. And hath not this been your case?

S. I cannot deny it; the Lord forgive me, and have mercy on me. I see now that it is not so easy a matter, nor so common, to love God truly, as I thought it was.

P. To[h] love God as God, with all our mind, and heart, and might, is the sum of holiness, the proper fruit of the Spirit, the certain mark of God on the soul, and the surest evidence of his love to us, and the very beginning and foretaste of heaven. It is that which Christ came into the world to effect, by the most wonderful demonstration of God's love to sinners, as the fittest means to win their love. Faith in Christ is but the bellows to kindle in us the love of God; and faith working by love is all our religion in a few words. Therefore, if love to God were easy and common, all goodness would be so, and salvation would be so.

But having said thus much of the love of your soul, and the love of God, what think you next of the love of others? Is that also easy to you?

S. I am sometimes angry when I am wronged, or provoked, but I know no one in the world that I wish ill to.

P. So far it is well. But, 1. Do you love men more for God and his image on them than for yourself? 2. Do you[i] love your neighbour as yourself? I pray you understand the matter aright. 1. God must be first and principally loved, as the chief and infinite good: he must be loved for himself, as being goodness itself, and most amiable in himself, and that unlimitedly with all the soul. The creature must be loved only for God, as bearing his image, or the marks of his perfection, and as a means to know, and please, and glorify him. Those must be most loved who have most of the image of God, in wisdom, righteousness, and holiness. The godly must be loved as godly, with a special love. Professed christians must be beloved as such. All men, even our[k] enemies, must be loved as men, with a common love; and all this for God's work upon them, and his interest in them.

But a selfish, carnal man, loving his carnal self more than God, doth make himself the standard and reason of his love to others. He loveth not those best who are best, and most holy, or serviceable to God and the public good, but those that love and honour him most, and those that are most of his opinion, and those that will be ruled by his will, and never cross it; and those that do most for him, and are most profitable to him. A true christian loveth his neighbour, as you love the children of your dearest friend, for the parents' sake. But a carnal man loveth his neighbour partly as a dog loveth his master for feeding him, and partly as all creatures, birds, and beasts, do love their companions, for likeness of kind, and from sociableness and acquaintance. Have you not loved an ignorant worldling, a profane swearer, a derider of holiness, who loved you and spoke well of you, and took your part, and did you many friendly offices, better than a wise and godly person, that never did any thing for you, or that had low thoughts of your wit and honesty, though no worse than indeed you did deserve?

S. I cannot deny but you describe me rightly.

P. And did you never dishonour your governors, prince, or parents? Did you never seek to hurt another, nor desire revenge? Did you never deceive your neighbour, nor wrong him any way in his estate? Did you never belie nor slander him, or backbite him, nor falsely accuse him, nor seek to make him odious or contemptible to others? Did you never envy him, nor covet his estate, or honours, nor seek to draw any thing from him to yourself? If you did, what love was in all this but self-love?

Nay, what labour and cost have you been at to save the souls of miserable sinners, or to relieve their bodies? "And he[l] that seeth his brother hath need, and shutteth up the bowels of his compassion from him, how dwelleth the love of God in him?" At what rates, and with what condescension, self-denial, and diligence have you showed your neighbours that you love them?

2. At least hath it been with any such love as you love yourself? How easily can you bear your neighbour's wrongs, reproaches, slanders, poverty, sickness, in comparison of your own! You can aggravate his faults, and extenuate your own; and judge him very culpable, and censurable, and punishable, for that which you make nothing of in yourself.

S. I must confess I have sinned against the love of God, of myself, and of my neighbour. And I see

[f] Rom. i. 30; Psalm lxxxi. 15; lxviii. 1; xxi. 8; Command. ii; Deut. vii. 10; 2 Chron. xix. 2.
[g] John viii. 44.
[h] 2 Thess. iii. 5; Luke xi. 42; Rom. v. 5; Gal. v. 6; Jude 21.
[i] Gal. v. 6, 13, 14, 22; Jam. ii. 8; 1 Pet. ii. 17; iii. 8; Rom. xii. 9, 10; xiii. 9, 10; 2 Cor. xiii. 11; Col. i. 4; 1 Thess. iv. 9; 1 Pet. i. 22; 1 John iv. 7, 8, 11, 12, 20, 21; v. 2; John xiii. 34; xv. 12, 17; 2 John 5; Col. ii. 2; Eph. iv. 2, 15 16; v. 2.
[k] Lev. xix. 18, 34; Matt. v. 44, 46.
[l] 1 John iii. 17; iv. 12.

that I must have a better heart, before I can truly love God, myself, and my neighbour, for the time to come.

P. I have plainly opened to you the nature of true conversion, even[m] faith and repentance; that is, the nature of the covenant which your parents in your baptism made in your name, or entered you into, and which at age you must sincerely make yourself, if you will be saved. What say you now to it upon consideration of the whole? Can you heartily consent to it, and thus give up yourself to God and to Jesus Christ, or not?

S. O sir, it is a great business: I must have many a thought of it yet before I shall understand it well; and many a thought more to overcome all the backwardness of my heart: such a work is not to be rashly done.

P. I like your answer, so be it that it come not from unwillingness, nor imply not a purpose to delay: that which must needs be done, or you are for ever[n] undone, cannot be done too soon, so it be done well. But tell me, were you never confirmed by a bishop, by the laying on of his hands?

S. Yes, to tell you the truth, I was; though none of all the parish went to him but I myself.

P. And what was it that he did to you? And what did you?

S. He said a short prayer, and laid his hand on my head, which I took to be his blessing; but what he said I know not. But I said not a word to him.

P. Did he not examine you of your knowledge, and faith, and repentance; and whether you have kept your baptismal covenant, and now consent to it?

S. Not a word: we were all children that kneeled down to him, and had his blessing, and we knew no more. Only now you remember me, I heard him tell one at age that went before us, that we must stand to the covenant that we made in baptism: but little did I know or consider what that covenant was; nor could I have given any other account if I had been examined, but only that I could say the creed, the Lord's prayer, and the ten commandments; though I understood them not.

P. If you will read the church liturgy about confirmation, you will see that, 1. You should have been able to say all the church catechism. 2. And that you should have had the curate's certificate thereof. 3. And that being come to years of discretion, and having learned what was promised for you in baptism, you should yourself, with your own mouth and consent, ratify and confirm the same; and also promise that, by the grace of God, you will evermore endeavour yourself faithfully to observe it. And the bishop, I suppose, though you understood him not, did put this question to you; "Do you here in the presence of God and this congregation renew the solemn promise and vow that was made in your name at your baptism, ratifying and confirming the same in your own persons, and acknowledging yourselves bound to believe, and to do all those things which your godfathers and godmothers then undertook for you?" And you were to say, "I do." And it is ordered, that "none shall be admitted to the holy communion, till such time as he be confirmed, or be ready and desirous to be confirmed." I confess these covenanting words are only in the New Common Prayer Book, 1662, and therefore it is like you heard no such thing; but there was yet more in the old rubric of the reasons of it.

So that you see, that if the bishops and pastors would faithfully manage this great work, none should communicate at the Lord's table till he professed all this covenant consent, in which your true conversion doth consist.

S. I would it were so; it would make a great reformation in the church. I had learned the church catechism at about seven years of age, but I knew little more than a parrot what I said, and soon forgot it, and never dreamt of such a solemn covenant with God as you describe, on which my whole salvation doth depend, which needeth the best understanding and deliberation.

P. I am so much the more of your mind, because it was the wisdom of all Christ's churches for many hundred years, to keep those that desired baptism at age a sufficient time in the order of catechised persons, long teaching them the meaning of christianity and baptism before they baptized them. And because the Bereans (Acts xvi.) are commended for searching the Scripture, to see whether that which was taught them was so or not: but especially because Christ himself (Luke xiv. 28—30) would have all that come to him sit down first and count what it is like to cost them to be his true disciples, and to consider well of the work, and how they shall go through with it, before they engage themselves to him.

S. But why then did Peter[o] baptize thousands in the day that he had converted them?

P. 1. They were Jews, that had been instructed in the law, and known the true God, and had been solemnly entered into his covenant before, and so wanted no necessary knowledge, except only about the true Messiah, whom they themselves expected. So that their case much[p] differed from that of the gentiles, or any that are found in utter ignorance. 2. And though the time was short, yet they gave sufficient evidence of their conversion, in their humiliation, confession, and penitent desires of being acquainted with the way of salvation in Christ; and no doubt but they openly professed the christian faith with their repentance at their baptism. If you are just now truly acquainted with the meaning of the baptismal covenant, and fully resolved to consent to it, and perform it, I would have you renew it without delay: but else take time to be instructed and resolved.

S. Seeing I must make just the same preparation, and profession, and covenant, as if I were newly to be baptized, had it not been better to have forborne my baptism till now, than to be baptized in infancy, when I knew not what was done? What warrant is there for being baptized before we believe?

P. You are not now capable of disputes: when you are, read my book for infants' baptism. In the mean time I shall only tell you, 1. That all that are to be entered into Christ's church, as its members and his disciples, must enter by baptism; which is proved, 1. Matt. xxviii. 19, 20, "Disciple me all nations, baptizing them:" baptism is made the door of entrance into the gospel church, and there is neither a word of command, nor example of entering any other way.

2. But the infants of believers are to be entered into Christ's church, as its infant members and disciples; which is proved, 1. Because infants were members of the church before Christ's incarnation: and Christ came not to destroy the church's privileges, but to enlarge them. Circumcision entered the Jews' children: and the Ishmaelites and Edomites, and the posterity of Keturah, used circumcision, as well as the Jews: and though circumcision cease, infants' church membership ceaseth not; for these two were separable before. In the wilderness, for forty years, all the Jews' children were uncircum-

m. Acts xx. 21; xxvi. 18.
n Luke xiii. 3, 5; Matt. xviii. 3.
o Acts ii. 38, 39, &c.
p Rom. ii. 12—14, &c.

cised, and yet they ceased not to be church members; yea, (Deut. xxix.) they were expressly entered into the covenant of God.

2. It appeareth, therefore, that the institution of circumcision proveth not that infants' church membership was then instituted; yea, it is plain that it continued from Adam's time. 1. Because there is not one word of intimation in the Scripture else when it began. 2. The word "seed," Gen. iii. 15, in the new covenant, is extensive to all ages; for though it be meant of Christ, as the Head and Captain, it is meant of all the holy seed as his members. 3. God did still join the children with the parents, in promises and threats, blessings and cursings, in all ages, before circumcision. 4. There is no proof that ever God had any church on earth of which infants were not members.

3. God hath, by nature and institution, (Deut. xxix. 10—12; Gen. xvii. 13,) made it the duty of parents to enter their children into the covenant of God, which is no where reversed; but under the gospel there is no appointed way of entering them into covenant but by baptism. If God command us to dedicate them to him, he will sure receive them.

4. Scripture telleth us that Christ would not have cast off the Jewish nation, and consequently their children, from their church state, if their own unbelief and rejecting him had not done it. Matt. xxiii. 37, "O Jerusalem! how oft would I have gathered thy children, as a hen gathereth her chickens under her wings, and ye would not." Rom. xi. they were broken off for unbelief. Therefore, but for unbelief, they had not been broken off; and the gentiles are grafted into the same olive, or church state. And, mark it, it is plain here, that the believing part of the Jews were not broken off from a church state, though they ceased to be a kingdom and national church; and therefore their children lost their church and covenant right: and if the children of believing Jews had it, all had it, when the church was one.

5. He tells us that nations are capable of being discipled, Matt. xxviii. 19; and the kingdoms of the world are to be the kingdoms of the Lord and of his Christ; but there is no nation or kingdom which infants are not a part of.

6. And Christ himself was angry with his disciples that would have kept little children from him, and said, "Forbid them not to come unto me, for of such is the kingdom of heaven;" and therefore he is still ready to receive them, when dedicated to him, though he then baptized them not, because the common use of christian baptism was to begin after his death.

7. And the apostle (1 Cor. vii. 14,) tells us, that our children are holy, which must needs signify more than legitimate, for so are heathen's children.

8. And the apostles still baptized whole households.

9. And the universal church, in all ages, hath observed it.

10. And infants have a visible way of sin and misery by generation, and if there were no visible way of their recovery by forgiveness, that is, if there were no promise or covenant of pardon which they had a certain part in, Christ's remedy would be so narrow as to exclude the age that is first miserable; and what hope could we have of the salvation of any of our infants without a promise?

S. But they believe not.

P. Nor they sin not, and yet they are guilty of original sin, and need a Saviour. Though they believe not actually, they are the infants of believers; and their parents' faith is as far imputed to them for their reception as the unbelief of the wicked is imputed to their children for their rejection and greater punishment, which is plain in Scripture. Indeed, while they have no reason and will of their own, their parents' reason and will hath the disposal of them, they being in their members.

S. But what good doth it to those that understand not?

P. Is it no good to have a solemn delivery of a sealed pardon of original sin, and a covenant relation to God the Father, Son, and Holy Ghost; and a visible title to the blessings of the covenant; and to be no more strangers, but fellow-citizens of the saints, and of the church or household of God; and if they die, to have right to life eternal; when it is the dogs that are without the doors? The benefit is the child's, and the comfort is the parents'. Is it not a privilege that you may take a lease of lands for your child's life as well as your own, and make him a party in the covenant, and bind him to pay the rent, though he understand it not? And if at age he thinks he is wronged, he may quit his part in Christ and heaven whenever he pleases.

S. But I perceive by my own case, we should do it more sensibly, if we stay till we understand what we do.

P. 1. Your parents should be as sensible when they dedicate you to God, though you could not. 2. And your former baptism hindereth not your personal covenanting now as understandingly and sensibly as if you never had been baptized before. All men are prone to outsideness and formality, even about God's own institutions. Too great stress is laid by many sorts upon the outward washing,[q] who weigh not enough the nature of the covenant. Though you may not be baptized again, you may as seriously and solemnly again covenant with God, even the same covenant which you made in baptism; and it is the same which is still renewed in the Lord's supper: so that it did you no harm to be baptized in infancy; though you have been so sinful as to neglect the due consideration of it, you may, nevertheless, upon your repentance, renew the same covenant; and the same covenant will give you the same benefits, though you be not re-baptized. Therefore now set to it, not only as if you had never done it before, but with double humiliation and seriousness, as beseemeth one that made and broke it.

S. Have you any more to say to me about it?

P. Yes. I must before let you know in what manner it is that this covenant must be made, if you will be a christian indeed, and have the benefits. 1. You must consent to the whole covenant of God, and not only to some part. You must be devoted[r] to your Creator, your Redeemer, and your Sanctifier: you must take him for your Owner, your Ruler, and your Saviour: you must be willing to be sanctified as well as pardoned, and to be saved from sin, and not only from punishment.

2. You must understand all the terms well, and count your costs, and reckon upon taking up the cross, and denying yourself, and forsaking all this world, in heart and resolution, for Christ, and take God and heaven for your whole portion, and resolve to stick to God if you have nothing else; and if you meet with never so much tribulation in the world, you must believe that heaven is as sure as if you saw it, and take that and the necessary means thereto for

[q] 1 Pet. iii. 21; Mark xvi. 16; John iii. 16; Jam. v. 20; 1 John ii. 1.

[r] Matt. xxviii. 19, 20; xi. 28; Luke xix. 27; Rom. xiv. 9; Eph. i. 22; Luke xiv. 26, to the end; Rom. viii. 17; Matt. xiii. 46; vi. 19, 20.

all your part, and not reckon upon ease, pleasure, profit, or safety to the flesh.

3. You must covenant absolutely, without any secret exceptions or reserves.[s] If you secretly keep a reserve in your heart that you will come to Christ but upon trial, and that you will be religious as far as will stand with your prosperity and safety in the world, and so you may not be undone; if you except secretly either honour, estate, or life, which you resolve not to lay down if Christ require it; you then play the hypocrite and lose all.

4. You must consent to a present change, and at present thus wholly give up yourself to God, and not only that you will do it some time hereafter. As he that will not take up christianity and a holy life till hereafter should not be baptized till hereafter, when he will do it; so, if you do but consent to repent and be converted till some time hence, this is at present no repentance, conversion, nor true covenanting with God. All this you must understand and do.

And now I will give you time to learn and resolve of all this that I have said to you. Read over and over the exposition of the covenant which I have written; and what you understand not, ask the meaning of it. And when you have done all, come to me, and tell me your resolution.

THE

THIRD DAY'S CONFERENCE.

THE CONFUTATION OF UNGODLY CONTRADICTERS.

SPEAKERS.—Paul, a Teacher; Saul, a Learner; Sir Elymas Dives, a malignant Contradicter.

PAUL. Welcome, neighbour. You are come sooner than I expected you. Are you well resolved of what we talked of?

SAUL. Since I saw you, I opened my case to my landlord, Sir Elymas Dives; and he is accounted a man of wit and learning; and he saith so much against all that you persuade me to, that I am perplexed between both, and know not what to say or do; but, at last, I got him to come to you, and say that to you which he said to me, that I may hear which seemeth in the right.

P. You did very wisely; and I have the more hope of your conversion and salvation, because you are diligent, and deal faithfully with yourself, and do not let deceivers carry you away quietly, without hearing what can be said against them. Desire him to come in.

Sir Elymas Dives. Good-morrow, Mr. Paul. I perceive you have troubled the mind of my poor tenant, here; so that he can scarce sleep. You precise preachers make such a stir with your religion in the world, that you will not let men live in quiet by you.

P. Sir, he that is called and consecrated to this office, to declare, from the word of God himself, things[a] great, and necessary, and true, concerning the everlasting state of their souls, must needs call men to sober and serious thoughts. And if there be some trouble in these thoughts, to those that have foolishly neglected their own happiness, it is no wonder.

El. The man hath been all his time an honest, painful, labouring man. I never heard that he said or did any man harm; but hath followed his business, and gone to church, and received the sacrament, and lived in love and peace with his neighbours. I never saw him drunk, nor any harm by him; and now you will make him doubt of his salvation.

P. Sir, I would have no man doubt of his salvation without cause; nor no man presume of salvation without cause. The saving or losing of the soul, for ever, is a great business, and not to be cast upon presumptuous and blind hopes. I would but have him[b] make sure of heaven; and can any man, think you, make too sure? It is not you, nor I, that are the judge of souls, but God; and his laws are the rule of his judgment. His word tells us who it is that he will save. If I tell any man that Christ will not save him, to whom the gospel promiseth salvation, condemn me, and spare not. But if you tell any man that God will save him, to whom God hath spoken no such thing, but the contrary, what wrong can be greater to God and him? And as to his good life, which you talk of; faith and repentance, and the love of God, and a holy life, are matters of another nature than all that you have said. Pardon me for telling you, that you speak out of your element, like an unlearned man about law, or physic, and not like one that had made divinity the study of his life, as we have done. I have but inquired of the man himself how the case standeth with his soul, and set the word of God before him, and directed him how to judge himself. Ask him whether he hath lived by faith, or sense; after the Spirit, or after the flesh; whether he hath[c] loved God or pleasure better; whether he hath sought heaven, or earthly prosperity, with the greater care and diligence. If he have, I will assure him that he is in a state of grace. It is he that must answer you.

El. Are you a preacher, and think that to frighten men, and cast them into terrors, is the way to mend them? It is believing well, and hoping well, that is the way to salvation.

P. Believing and hoping falsely, is not the believing and hoping well. He that knoweth not and feareth not a danger, will not sufficiently labour to escape it. Did you never read, that "The[d] fear of God is the beginning of wisdom: a good understanding have all they that do hereafter?" Doth not Christ say, "Fear him that is able to destroy both soul and body in hell?" Yea, I say unto you, (whosoever saith the contrary,) "Fear him!" Matt. x. 28; Luke xii. 5. "Seeing we receive a kingdom that cannot be moved, let us have grace whereby we may serve God acceptably, with reverence and godly fear; for our God is a consuming fire," Heb. xii. 28, 29. "Having a promise left us of entering into his rest, let us fear, lest any of you come short of it," Heb. iv. 1. The Scripture is full of such like passages.

Suppose I am a physician, and have a medicine that infallibly cureth all dropsies and consumptions in time; and I see the signs of a dropsy or consumption on one of your servants, and I tell him my opinion of his case and danger, that he will die, unless he presently take this certain remedy; and you come, and chide me for frightening and discomforting him; and tell him that there is no danger. Which of us is the more comfortable friend to the

[s] Luke xiv. 26, 33.
[a] Psalm iv. 5—7; li.; cxix. 59; Acts ii. 37.
[b] 2 Cor. xiii. 5; 2 Pet. i. 10; Isa. iv. 5, 6.
[c] 2 Tim. iii. 4; Matt. vi. 20, 21, 23.
[d] Psal. cxi. 10; Prov. i. 10; xv. 33.

man? I assure him of recovery, if he will use the means: you flatter him with false hopes, to keep him from using them: and I am a physician, and you are none. Which of us may he wiselier believe?

El. When you should draw men to believe, you drive them to unbelief and doubting.

P. Faith is not merely to believe that we are already forgiven, and shall be saved. If it would prove a man good, to believe that he is good; or prove that a man shall be saved, to believe that he shall be saved; and that he hath true grace when he hath none; then all the heathens and wicked men in the world may be saved, by believing it shall be so. Then let your tenant believe that he hath money when he hath none; and believe that he hath paid your rent when he hath not. Believing God, supposeth some word of his to be believed. And what word of his promiseth salvation to the ungodly? We must believe the gospel, that Christ pardoneth and saveth all that truly[e] believe in him: that is, take him practically for their Teacher, their Saviour, and Lord; to sanctify them by his Spirit, and mortify their worldly, fleshly lusts, and make them a holy and heavenly people. To take Christ for such a Physician and Saviour of your soul, is truly to believe; and to doubt of the truth of his word, is the doubting of unbelief; but so is not every doubting of our own sincerity. A drunkard may doubt he is not sober, and yet not thereby doubt of the gospel of Christ.

El. If poor men have no more wit than to hearken to all that you would put into their heads, you will drive them all into despair at last.

P. We do but teach them how to prevent everlasting despair. There is no hope of being saved in despite of God, or against his will. And to cherish such[f] hopes (of being saved without holiness) till time be past, is the way to hellish desperation. What if the king tell his subjects, If you murder, there is no hope of your lives; I will not pardon you; will you say to them, Go on, and kill men; do not despair; the king doth ill to put you upon desperation? What, if you had been with Paul in the shipwreck, when he said, "There shall not a hair of your head perish; but if these stay not in the ship, ye cannot be saved;" would you have said, "He preacheth despair; go forth, and fear not? What, if you had heard Christ himself say, "Verily I say unto thee, Except a man be born again, of water and the Spirit, he cannot enter into the kingdom of God," John iii. 3, 5; and "Except ye be converted, and become as little children, ye cannot enter into the kingdom of heaven," Matt. xviii. 3; or "Except ye repent, ye shall all perish," Luke xiii. 3, 5; would you have said, Believe him not; he preacheth desperation? What, if you say to your servant, If thou do not work, thou shalt have no wages; shall he say, I will not despair; but I will hope well, though I work not? What do you by this talk, but the same that the devil did to Eve? God said, "In the day that thou eatest, thou shalt die:" the devil said, "Ye shall not surely die." Did God preach despair, and the devil preach better? Till men despair of being saved without holiness, they will never seek holiness, and so never be saved. I do despair that ever the devil should make good his word, and save any souls that God hath said shall not be saved.

El. Christ came to abolish the law, and set up the gospel; and you preach nothing but the law, when mercy better beseemeth the mouth of a gospel preacher.

P. Do I preach either the law of innocency, which giveth no pardon, or the Jewish law? It was these that Christ abolished, (in a sort,) and not his own law of grace. Doth not he preach mercy, who proclaimed pardon to all that will truly repent, and turn to God by faith in Christ? Repentance and conversion are gospel mercies. The law knoweth no place for repentance: but, Sin and die, is all that it saith. Is it all our work, from year to year, to magnify the mercy of God in Christ, and[g] to entreat men to accept of mercy, and not to refuse it, or abuse it? And yet must it be said, that we preach not mercy? I pray you, tell me, sir, what is the doctrine of mercy that you would preach, if you were in our stead?

El. I would tell them of the mercy of God, and that it is greater than our sins; and that Christ died for sinners; and that they that believe in him and trust God, shall be saved.

P. What it is to believe in Christ, and trust God, I have opened to Saul already, and must not oft repeat the same things. We doubt not but God's mercy is greater than our sins; but no unholy soul shall be saved by it. For this merciful God hath said, that "without holiness none shall see God," Heb. xii. 14. The sun is brighter than our eyes, and yet the blind cannot see by it. We tell them of the exceeding mercy of God, and of the sufficiency of the sacrifice and merits of Christ; but we tell them withal, that the rejecting of this Christ and mercy will increase their misery, and be the food of the never-dying worm, the torment of their conscience to remember it for ever. Read Heb. iii.; vi.; x.; xii.; and see whether we say true or not. Would you tell the people that all men shall be saved; or that any other faith and repentance would save them, than such as I described?

El. I would tell them that a quiet and sober religion will be accepted better than all the stir you make; and that all this ado, and noise about religion, to trouble men's minds, instead of making them better, is but the work of a few hot-brained coxcombs, that can neither let themselves nor other men live quietly.

P. Oh, sir, that you had but tried what[h] quietness there is in the conscience of a renewed, justified person, in comparison of what is in the galled, ulcerous conscience of the ungodly. Oh! it is a proud, a worldly, a fleshly heart and life, which is the sting, that will give the sinner no rest; and the defiled, guilty conscience which will never let the soul be quiet; which hath a life of unpardoned sin to look back upon; a life of sensuality and ungodliness, of pride, fulness, and idleness; abundance of oaths, curses, lies, contempt of God! These are they that will not let the world be quiet, nor suffer the consciences of the wicked long to give them any rest. Twice God protesteth by the prophet, "There is no peace to the wicked," Isa. xlviii. 22; lvii. 21. "The way of peace they know not. There is no judgment in their goings: they have made them crooked paths: whosoever goeth therein shall not know peace," Isa. lix. 8. "God hateth all the workers of iniquity," Psal. lv. And what peace is there, then, to such? "Because they have seduced my people; saying, Peace, and there was no peace: and one built up a wall, and others daubed it with untempered mortar: say unto them, that it shall fall. Lo, when the

[e] John i. 6—12; iii. 16, 19; Luke xix. 27; Matt. vii. 21—23.

[f] Isa. xlviii. 18, 22; lvii. 21; lix. 8; Jer. iv. 10; vi. 14; viii. 11; xxviii. 9; Ezek. xiii. 10, 16; 1 Thess. v. 3.

[g] Matt. xxviii. 19; 2 Cor. v. 19.

[h] Hab. iii. 18; Psal. iv. 7, 8; Rom. xiv. 17; Heb. x. 34.

wall is fallen, shall it not be said unto you, Where is the daubing wherewith ye have daubed it?" Ezek. xiii. 11, 12. "When they shall say, Peace and safety; sudden destruction cometh upon them, as travail on a woman with child, and they shall not escape," 1 Thess. v. 3.

I pray you tell me truly, do you think that he that hath truly repented of his careless, ignorant, worldly, proud, fleshly life, and hath forsaken it; or he that hath yet all this sin unrepented of to answer for; is like to live the quieter life? If sin be the way of peace, how did it drown the world? How did it kill Christ? How doth it cause hell? Then you may say also, that poison, and wounds, and breaking our bones, and sickness, are the way to the body's ease.

I pray you, sir, yet answer me these two questions. 1. Do you not believe, in your conscience, that a truly penitent, godly man, that hath spent his days chiefly in laying up a treasure in heaven, is liker to die in hope and peace than a careless, fleshly, worldly man? 2. And may not he live in the greatest peace, who will die in the greatest peace? Is not that course the fittest to give us peace in health which is fittest to give us peace in sickness?

And will you tell me what is the quiet and sober religion which you are for yourself?

El. It is to love God and my neighbour, and do as I would be done by, and to go to church, and say my prayers, and, when I have sinned, repent, and cry God mercy, and trust in Christ, and so be quiet, and trouble myself no further.

P. You have said a great deal in a few words. But I hope you do not think that saying this will save them that do it not. Give me leave, then, to go over all particularly. 1. If you love God, you will love his [i] laws, and his government, and his service, and his servants, and you will love to please him, and you will long to be with him, and you will love him better than fleshly pleasure, or all this world. Will you think he loveth you, that loveth the dirt in the streets better than you? or that careth not how far he is from you, nor how little he hath to do with you? that loveth not much to hear, or think, or speak of you? If you love God, you will make him your delight, and not think his word and service the trouble of the world; and you will keep his commandments, and not think sin your greatest pleasure, and obedience to God your greatest pain.

2. And if you love your neighbour as yourself, you will not let Lazarus lie in hunger at your doors, nor your poor tenants and neighbours feel cold and want, while you are clothed in purple and silk, and fare sumptuously and deliciously every day. You will not lay out hundreds by the year on hounds, and sports, and idle gentlemen servants, and on feasting and gallantry, and excess of bravery [k] and furniture, while your poor tenants live in toil and misery. You will not rack your rents so as poor men, with all their care and labour, cannot live. You will not see your brother have need, and shut up the bowels of your compassion from him, and then say that you love God and your neighbour. You will not hate, and scorn, and persecute God's servants that are most careful to please him, and still say you love both God and them. You will not think that to love your riotous companions and play-fellows, is to love your neighbour as yourself.

3. And for your repenting when you have sinned, and crying God mercy, I hope you do not mean a mocking of God, with saying that you repent when you do not. I hope it is not only to be sorry and wish you had not sinned, when you have got all that sin can give you, and still to go on and do the same: to cry God mercy for a worldly, fleshly, voluptuous life of pride, fulness, and idleness, (the sins of Sodom, (Ezek. xvi. 49,) and of too many gentlemen,) and [l] to continue it still, and hate those that are against it; nor to repent of oppressing the poor, and racking your tenant, and to do so still. Repentance is a true change of mind, will, and conversation: true repentance is all that I persuade this man to, when you say that I trouble him, and break his peace.

El. You are an arrogant, saucy fellow. What have you to do to meddle with my bravery, or sports, or tenants' rents? You think your priestly calling may warrant all your incivilities and insolence. Were it not for the reverence of your coat, I would kick you out of doors, or lay you by the heels. It was never a good world since such fellows as you were suffered to prate your pleasure against your betters, under pretence of reproving sin.

P. I knew, sir, on what disadvantage I should discourse with such a one as you, but I do it for this poor man's sake, who desired it. If I were discoursing with you about common things, I would keep such a distance as should no way offend you. If any submissiveness would excuse me, I would not seem insolent or uncivil. I would not stand covered before you. I would not press into your presence, nor expect honour from you, but would be content to stand with your poorest servants. But when it is a business that God's truth and holiness, and men's salvation, and my ministerial fidelity, lieth on, it is cowardice and base treachery, and not civility, to desert the truth for want of [m] plain dealing. I hope you know that not only the prophets and apostles, but Basil, Chrysostom, Ambrose, and such others, have dealt much plainer with emperors than I have done with you: and Gildas spake homelier of the British princes and nobility. As long as you may use us at your pleasure, you may give us leave to speak according to our Master's pleasure. For we do not fear but at last he will bear us out.

El. It is the trick of you all to claw the vulgar by accusing the gentry and nobility of oppression, yea, and you would say as much by the king himself, if you durst.

P. The worst I wish you, sir, is but that you would go now and then into the houses of the poor, and see how they live; and that you would read over Luke xii. and Luke xvi. and James iv. and v. and Matt. xxv. and try to write yourself a commentary on them. And that you would remember how you must leave this world, and what comes next.

El. It is such as you that set up levellers; you would have rich and poor live all alike, and we must fare and go no better than they, nor live at more ease.

P. No, sir: but death will shortly play the leveller with you, and call away your soul, and turn your flesh to corruption and common earth: and then [n] whose are those things that you possessed? I would have all honour done to magistrates, though I reverence not riches so much as I do magistracy. And I would not have you put yourself into any of the afflicting or hindering cases of the poor, in your food, raiment, or employment: but I must needs tell you, that in your place and way, you must labour as diligently, and live a mortified, self-denying life, as well as the poor. And [o] riches will excuse no man for idleness, or voluptuous living, nor allow you to waste one groat in vain.

i John xiv. 15, 23; 1 John v. 3.
k 1 John iii. 16, 17; Jam. ii. 14—16; v. throughout.
l 1 Cor. vi. 9, 11; Tit. iii. 3, 5; Acts xviii. 26.

m Isa. lviii. 1; vii. 4; li. 7, 8; Matt. xvi. 26, 28, 31; Heb. xiii. 6.
n Luke xii. 18—21.
o Jam. v.

El. The poor live in their way as well as we in ours: their diet and their labour is as suitable to them as our plenty and ease is to us.

P. It is but from use, then, for their flesh is of the same kind with yours: and if so, I hope if you be put to it, you can use yourself to live so too. And if so, methinks a due abatement of excesses and voluptuousness should be much more easy to you.

But, sir, it is not the mere labour of the poor that I pity them for, nor the unpleasantness of their diet. I am persuaded the minds of many of them are quieter, and that their meat and sleep is sweeter than yours, but, pardon me for telling you that I am much among them, and I find, 1. That some of them drink nothing but water, or beer that is little better, and use a diet so unwholesome, that it breedeth dropsies, consumptions, and deadly sicknesses, having not fire and clothes to keep them warm. 2. That many are so full of cares how to pay their rents and debts, that they have no heart to think of the greater business of their souls; and many are so tired with their excessive labour, that when they should pray, or read a chapter, or instruct their families, either they have no time, or they are presently, with weariness, asleep; yea, tired on the Lord's days with the week days' labour. 3. And worst of all, they cannot spare their children from work while they learn to read, though I offer them to pay the schoolmaster myself, much less have they time to catechise and teach them. So that poverty causeth a generation of barbarians in a christian, happy land. You would forgive my boldness, if you understood the sadness and sinfulness of all this, and that some rich men, that have caused such things as these, do now want themselves a drop of water to cool their tongues.

But all this is by a digression. I pray you tell me next what that is which you accuse me of as over-troublesome to my neighbour, or to the world, in my doctrine?

El. I have told you: it is disquieting men's consciences.

P. But what is it that I say amiss to disquiet them?

El. You would make them believe that God made us to damn us, and make his mercy as narrow as your conceits.

P. Do you not think that[p] some shall be damned for their sins; and that God best knoweth who? and that he best knoweth how to use his own mercy? and that we must believe his word? If you think that all shall be saved, speak out, and let us hear your proof. If not, tell me to whom I deny salvation that God hath promised it to?

El. You make strict laws and opinions of your own brains, and then damn all who do not keep them.

P. What be those laws and opinions of ours?

El. What! more than a good many. If a man go finer than yourselves; if he be not of your fashion; if a woman wear black spots, or go with bare breasts; if we play at cards or dice, or go to a play-house; if the people set up a may-pole, or dance on Sundays; if one drink a cup, and be but merry; Oh, these are profane people; they are not precise enough to be saved.

P. There is nothing so small in which a true servant of God would not be obedient: and great sin is oft committed in[q] small things. And their signification, and the omissions which they import, are oft sadder than the things themselves. If your harvest were out, or your house were on fire, and your servant should let all alone, and go to cards, or a play-house, the while, and say, How precise is my master to think that there is any harm in this! you know how to answer him. Truly, sir, our lives are short; our souls are precious; our work is great, and much undone; time makes haste; we have lost much already; hell is terrible; heaven is glorious; God is just; and all that ever must be done for our souls must be now done. And in this case, he that hath time to cast away on stage-plays, and cards, and idleness, let him do it; for my part, I have not. As strict as you think me, God knoweth that my work is yet so much to do, that I have no time to spare for such things as these. He that liveth by faith, foreseeth heaven open all the way, and such a sight doth cool my appetite to sports. O precious time! how fearful am I lest thou wilt be gone, before my faith be strengthened, my hope confirmed, my love to God increased, and my preparation made for death and judgment! Oh what hearts are in those men that can see time passing, death coming, God present, judgment and eternity at hand, and yet sit needlessly at dice or cards, or idle recreations! Have we no more to do with time? I speak not against needful recreations, which fit us for an ordinary, laborious calling, as whetting doth the mower's scythe. But woe to them that cast away so short and precious time in fooleries and idleness, which is all that ever they shall have to prepare for their everlasting state!

And I must tell you too, sir, that I need not such pleasures: the word of God and the foresight of eternal glory, afford me better; so much better, that these stink in comparison of them.

But yet, sir, it is not my custom to talk first or much of such things as these. Here stands your tenant; ask him whether I once named any such matters to him? I remember old Mr. Dod's saying to one that would have him preach against long hair, "Win their hearts to Christ, and they will cut their hair themselves." I remember a person of great estate yet living, that in youth was ignorant, vain, and gaudy, and being oft persuaded to leave some gaudy fashions, long despised all that was said; but at last, by a sermon, being convinced of greater matters, and humbled, and suddenly changed to a godly life, all the beloved vanities and fashions were in two days cast away, and never taken up again, without any talk about such things, to the marvel of spectators.

O sir, could I but persuade you to that due sense of things eternal, as their truth and greatness do bespeak even of reason itself; could I prevail with you to engage your heart and life to such care and[r] diligence for God and your salvation, and the common good, as God will require of you, I would leave you to pass away as much time as this work can reasonably spare.[s] One thing is necessary; do that, and then go to play.

El. But you are the most censorious generation of men in the world. You make a sect and party for religion, of precise and self-conceited people, and then none must be saved but your precise party; and how empty will heaven be, if none be there but puritans!

P. 1. I suppose you will grant, that if we should never so much flatter ungodly persons with the hopes of salvation, their case might be the worse, but it could be never the better. God's will, or word, will not change with ours; he will never save an unholy soul. If all the prelates and preachers in the world should agree to tell them that they shall be saved, they would stand before God never the more justified for all this; it would but keep them

[p] 2 Thess. i. 7—10; ii. 11, 12.
[q] Heb. xii. 16; Matt. v. 19.
[r] John vi. 27.
[s] Luke x. 42.

from repentance, and consequently from being saved indeed. 2. And you cannot but know that all mankind is proner to security, presumption, self-flattery, and impenitence, than to over-much fear, unless it be some persons that are melancholy. 3. And you cannot but know that false hopes are far more dangerous, though unjust fears be the more troublesome; for presumption keepeth them more from repentance. 4. And if I may judge of others by myself, we ministers are more prone to be too tender of troubling people, than too terrible; for naturally we all love our own ease and quiet, and the love of our neighbours;[t] and we know that it is flattery that gets love, and plain dealing hatred; and we long not to be hated. And most ministers have need of their neighbours' bounty; and hatred is not the way to procure that, especially with the rich. Therefore you should rather charge us to deal plainly, and to take heed lest poverty, or cowardliness, or lukewarmness, tempt us to daubing flattery, or silence.

2. But, sir, what is the sect or party of puritans that you say we confine salvation to? I pray you let us not spend time in mere words. If you mean that we confine salvation to any that agree with us in by-matters, circumstances, doubtful opinions, or any thing not essential to christianity and godliness, it is a sin which we detest. Prove it by me, if you can: ask Saul, whether I spake a word to him of any doubtful controversy in religion.

But, if the party you talk of be that which Christ calleth believers, penitent, regenerate, sanctified, godly persons, do you not believe yourself that God in Scripture hath confined salvation to such only? All the world is of[u] two parties; the seed of the woman and of the serpent; the godly and the ungodly. Do you believe Christ himself, or not? If you do, doth he not most expressly and vehemently confine salvation to them that are born again of the Spirit, John iii. 3, 5; to them that are converted, Matt. xviii. 3; to them that are new creatures, 2 Cor. v. 17; to them that have the Spirit of Christ, and mind the things of the Spirit, and live after the Spirit, and mortify the lusts of the flesh, Rom. i. 5—9, 13, 14; to them that have a heart in heaven, Matt. vi. 21, and a heavenly conversation, Phil. iii. 20, 21; to them that seek first God's kingdom and righteousness, Matt. vi. 33. Are these the words of man, or of God? Are they ours, or Christ's? Are we censorious for believing our Saviour, and for preaching his word, and persuading others to believe it?

Oh, how much better were it for men to judge themselves by the word of God, and not by their self-flattering, fleshly mind, before God judge them; rather than to call God, or his holy word, or his ministers that speak it, censorious.

El. Do you allege God's word against his goodness, and merciful nature? It is contrary to God's goodness to save none but a few puritans and precisians, and to condemn all the rest of the world to hell. Would you have us to believe things utterly incredible, as well as undesirable?

P. Your scornful names of puritans and precisians are but words of your own, thrust in to vent your spleen, and to darken the question. If you mean any other than repenting, sanctified believers, it is nothing to our case, I talk for no other. But, sir, we will not be mocked out of our duty and salvation: heaven were little worth, if it were not worth the bearing of derision, from poor souls that are hastening themselves to hell. But to the matter.

1. As to the number of those that God will save, I never presumed to determine of it. I only tell you, that none are saved but those that are sanctified by the Spirit of Christ: remember, I pray you, that this is all that I say. How many are sanctified I know not, but I would advise you, instead of such inquiries, as you love yourself, to make sure that you are one of them. But experience may help to make some conjectures: if all the world, or most of the world, be truly holy, that is, do love God and heaven better than fleshly pleasure and worldly prosperity, then all, or most of the world, shall be saved. But if there be few such, there are few that will be saved. This is the truth, if God's word be true; and instead of being offended at it, you had best to lay your hand upon your heart, and see whether or not it be so with you; for God will not save you for your riches, nor high looks, nor for contending against his word.

2. Do you think that God doth not know his own nature and goodness, and what is consistent with it, better than you? Will you tell him, that he hath made a law, or given us a word, which is[x] contrary to his own nature and goodness? If you will teach God to know himself better, or to amend his word, he will convince you, ere he hath done with you, that you should rather have known yourself and God better.

3. Is it contrary to the goodness of God to shut men out of heaven who will have none of it, or who hate it, or who prefer a swinish lust before it? Attend a little, sir, and I shall show you your unrighteous censure of God. If you can but forgive God for making you a man, you may perceive that it is you that damn yourself, and then quarrel with God for it. Is it not man himself that loveth the world and fleshly pleasure more than God; that committeth all the sin that is committed; that[y] turneth away his heart, his love, his delight, his thoughts from God, and from all that is heavenly and holy? Are not your lusts your own, and your passions your own? Is it not yourself that maketh yourself ungodly, and contrary to the holy nature of God and heaven? and yourself that resist and refuse the Spirit and grace of God? Do you know how much of hell is in sin itself, and of your own making, as well as of your own deserving? To be saved, is to know God and love him, and delightfully serve him: this in perfection is heaven. And doth God deny you this when you truly desire it; or do you not[z] deny it to yourself? Is it not you that delight not in God and his service; and that rather choose your fleshly pleasure? And is it not you, then, that put yourself out of heaven? Heaven is a state of perfect holiness; and you will not have holiness, and yet you say you would have heaven. God setteth before you a feast of holy joys; and your appetite is against it: you loathe it, you refuse it; no entreaty will persuade you to taste it; you deride it as preciseness; and when you have done, you blame God because you have it not. If you would have a Mahometan heaven of lechery, and wine, and sports; a heaven of cards, and dice, and plays, and jesting; a heaven of proud domination over your brethren, or of money, and great estates, and pomp, you are mistaken; there is none such in another world. All this heaven was[a] here on earth; and here you chose

[t] 1 Kings xxii.; Amos ii. 12; Mic. ii. 11; Job xxxii. 21, 22; 1 Thess. v.; Prov. xxviii. 23; xx. 19, 20; xxvi. 28; Ezek. xii. 24.

[u] Gen. iii. 15; Mal. iii. 17, 18; Matt. xxv.; 2 Thess. i. 9, 10; John iii. 3, 5.

[x] Rom. iii. 3, 4, &c.

[y] Job xxviii. 28; Prov. xiii. 14; xiv. 27; xv. 24.

[z] Job xxi. 14; xxii. 17.

[a] Luke xvi. 25.

it; and here you had it. Hereafter there is no heaven but the sight and delightful love of God, and perfection of holiness. Would you have this, or would you not? If you will, then refuse it not, deride it not, neglect it not; presently begin, and spit out your filthy, fleshly pleasures, and[b] seek the Lord, and he will assist you and accept you; but if you will not, remember who put you out of heaven.

And when death hath opened your eyes, and showed you what it is that you refused, and have[c] lost, and what it is that you preferred before it, your own conscience will tear you with perpetual torments, to think what a glory you might have had and would not; what a God you departed from; and what all the fleshly pleasures were which you preferred; and what is now become of all. I tell you, if God should no further meddle with you, your[d] conscience in the remembrance of this would torment you.

You see, then, that besides what they deserve from the hand of divine justice, what it is that sinners execute upon themselves. You cannot both refuse heaven and make yourself uncapable of it, and yet have it; and you cannot lose it, and not for ever feel the loss.

4. And is not God just? and injustice contrary to his nature? Is it contrary to the goodness of the king or judge to hang a thief or murderer? And what if they be many? Must they, therefore, be[e] unpunished? If many should beat you or abuse you, doth not that rather aggravate the wrong than extenuate it? You scruple not killing a nest of wasps or hornets, though they be many. Millions of men are not so much to God as a swarm of flies are unto man.

5. And I would know whether you think it contrary to God's goodness to condemn any at all, or not? If not, what numbers proportionably will you impose upon him to save? What if he saved a thousand or ten thousand for one that he condemneth; would that seem to you consistent with his goodness? And are you sure it is not so? We are sure that this earth is to the rest of the universe, but as one inch is to the whole earth; and how small a part is that! And you know not but[f] angels and pure inhabitants may possess all the rest, except what is allotted to the devils and the damned. And if so, if ten thousand to one in this wicked world (which is next to hell) were damned, it would not all be one to many millions of the pure and blessed ones in the rest of the creation. I only say that men that are ignorant of such matters, as we all are, are unfit to quarrel with God about them.

El. You have said much, I confess; but it is all no justification of your own arrogance, that lay claim to heaven before your neighbours. All we are profane and ungodly people; and you only are the holy brethren and the[g] children of God. You say, Stand by, I am holier than thou? and as the Pharisee, I thank thee, Lord, that I am not as other men, nor as this publican.

P. 1. Who do you mean by us and by you? Speak plainly, that you may be understood. If any arrogate the name of holy or godly that is not so, he is a hypocrite. Do you hear me say that such shall be saved? And either you and the rest of our neighbours are really godly, sanctified persons, or you are not. If you are, we say you are the children of God, and the heirs of heaven as well as we or any others. Did you ever hear me say that any godly man is ungodly? or is not the child of God? Name the man that I have said so by. If your own conscience tell you that you love God better than the world, and[h] seek first his kingdom and righteousness, and if your conversation prove it, you have then the witness in yourself that you are sanctified, and need not care what others say of you; but if your conscience tell you that it is not so, but that you are a lover of the world and pleasure more than of God, silence not your conscience, and desire not that we should flatter you with lies, when your own conscience knoweth that the case is otherwise.

2. But, sir, do you think that there is no difference among men? Are the good and bad, the godly and wicked, all alike? Then, indeed, there would be no difference hereafter. But if there be a difference, may it not be known? And must he that hath God's grace be unthankful, and falsely say that he hath none? Those are like the unhumbled Pharisees, who thank God for that grace which they have not; and not they that humbly thank him for what they have. Would you have a temperate, chaste, and just person think himself to be a drunkard, a fornicator, a thief, when it is not so, and all for fear of being proud? Then why are you angry with those that count you ungodly, if humility bind all men to think themselves ungodly? God neither desireth that we should think with the Pharisee, that we are sanctified when we are not, nor that we deny the grace which we have. Unthankfulness for the greatest mercy is no virtue.

El. You are the true offspring of the Pharisees; a pack of godly hypocrites; a generation that are pure in your own eyes, but are not cleansed from your filthiness. In secret you are as bad as any others.

P. Who do you mean, sir?

El. I mean all, or the most of you, that take on you to be so godly and religious above other men.

P. 1. Would you have men profess ungodliness? Would you have us be drunkards, swearers, fornicators, covetous, for fear of being hypocrites? or would you have us say that we are such when we are not? Is this your confession of Christ? Would you have no man profess himself a christian or a servant of God? What, then, must we profess the service of the flesh and the devil?

2. Do not you take on you to be a christian, and to be godly? Why else are you angry with them that count you ungodly? Else you are an infidel and an atheist. But if you profess christianity and godliness yourself, are you therefore a hypocrite? If not, profession makes not others to be hypocrites. I pray you tell me, what do you profess less than I do? You profess christianity and godliness, and I profess no more. But which of us is the hypocrite our consciences and lives must tell. I hope you will not renounce God and Christ, for fear of being a hypocrite.

3. But alas! sir, too many people fearing God are so far from being pure in their own eyes, that the greatness of their sins overwhelmeth them; and we can hardly keep them from concluding that they have no grace at all, and are as ready to call themselves hypocrites in their fears, as you are in your spleen against them. And why do you at once accuse us for over-terrifying them, and driving them to despair, and yet of puffing them up with a conceit of godliness?

4. But how is it that you come to know our hypocrisy, and what we are in secret? If you know it, it is no secret: if it be a secret, you know it not. If our

[b] John v. 40; Rev. xxii. 17; Jos. xxiv. 15.
[c] Matt. xxv. 6—8. [d] Rom. xxi. 15.
[e] Psal. i. 5, 6; 1.; Matt. xxv.

[f] Heb. xii. 22, 23, an innumerable company of angels, or myriads.
[g] 1 John v. 19, 20. [h] Matt. vi. 33.

lives be vicious, prove it, and reprove us: if they be not, how know you that our hearts are so? Is not God only the searcher of hearts?

5. I am glad if, indeed, you hate hypocrisy. The hypocrite is he that professeth to be that which indeed he is not. You and I do both profess the same christianity: now the question is, which of us is the hypocrite? If one man live according to his profession, and be serious in his religion, and hate all known sin, great and small, and seek God diligently, and use all the means that God commandeth him; and if another, making the same profession of christianity, do live in open worldliness and sensuality, in gluttony, drunkenness, gaming, idleness, fornication, and deride holy living, and all that are serious in the religion which he himself professeth, and counteth the practice of Christ's own commands to be needless preciseness; do I need to ask you, which of these is like to be the hypocrite? I have admired to hear debauched persons call serious christians hypocrites, when the want of seriousness in professed christianity is the very nature of hypocrisy. Do not all these railers call themselves christians? Is not[i] holiness essential to christianity? Is not a drunken christian, a worldly christian, a fornicating christian, a sensual, voluptuous christian, a very self-contradicting stigmatized hypocrite? Every gross sin which such wilfully live in, is the brand of a hypocrite.

El. Are not all men sinners? And he that saith he hath no sin, deceiveth himself. Why then make you such differences between yourselves and others.

P. You may try whether by that trick you can deceive the king and the judges first: go to the bar and to the gallows, and say, Why should these poor men be hanged rather than all you? Are not all sinners? If one of your servants beat you, excuse him, because all are sinners. But, sir, do you not know that there are[k] sinners that shall be saved in heaven, and sinners that shall go to hell; sinners that are pardoned, and sinners that are not pardoned? And why so? But that there are sinners that are penitent, contrite, and truly converted, and sinners that are not so. There are[l] sinners that are ungodly, and sin wilfully, and love their sin: and there are sinners that are godly, and sin only of infirmity, and hate their sins, and make it the care of their lives to avoid them. Some make provision for the flesh to satisfy its desires or lusts; and some make it their work to mortify such lusts, and not to please them. If you will not difference between these two sorts of sinners, God will; and you shall shortly see it. They that stand on Christ's right hand and on his left in judgment, and hear, "Come, ye blessed," and "Go, ye cursed," were all sinners: but read Matt. xxv. whether Christ maketh no difference?

El. The difference is, that you are the Pharisees, and we are the publicans: you justify yourselves, and we smite on our breasts, and cry, "God be merciful to me a sinner!" And which of these was justified of God?

P. I pray you speak truly, sir; do you think that Christ meant a dissembling publican, that took on him to repent and did not? Doth God justify wicked hypocrites? Or was it not a truly penitent publican, that confessed his sins with true repentance, and went home with a changed mind and life? And is not this all that I persuade your tenant to? And are not these the persons that we say shall be saved? If you be this publican, go, and do likewise: repent, confess, and be converted to a holy life.

And I will make bold this once to paint out the Pharisee to you in Christ's own words, and then you shall be judge yourself, who is the Pharisee. The Pharisees were a sect that set up the traditions of the elders against God's word, Matt. xv. 3. They were all for ceremony in religion, washing before meat, and washing cups, and formal, set fasting often, Matt. ix. 14; Luke xi. 39. They worshipped God in vain, teaching for doctrines the commandments of men, Matt. xv. 9. They drew near to God with their lips, saying over certain prayers, when their hearts were far from him, Matt. xv. 8. They were the rulers of the Jewish church, Matt. xxiii. 2; John vii. 45, 47, 48. They were called by high titles, and were set in the highest seats, and went in pomp and state, with the formalities of broad phylacteries, and such like, Matt. xxiii. 5—7. They were strict for tithing mint, annise, and cummin: they were tyrants and extortioners, and oppressors of the poor: they strained at a gnat, and saw the mote in another's eye, condemning Christ and his apostles for not observing their ceremonies, while they saw not the beam of malignity and persecution in their own eye, but could swallow a camel, even these heinous sins: for their way was to honour the memorials of the martyrs, and to make more; to erect monuments for the dead saints whom their forefathers persecuted, and to go on to do the like by the living, Matt. xxiii. 24, to the end. They were the deadliest enemies of Christ, the silencers of his apostles, as far as they could, and the persecutors of christians. And now I pray you tell me, who are the Pharisees?

El. But you leave out that which is against you: they devoured widows' houses, and, for a pretence, made long prayers; and so do you.

P. I pray, sir, tell me what widow's house I have devoured, and I promise you to restore it quickly. Do I oppress my tenants, as I before described to you? Have I any house but a mean one that I dwell in? Am I not fain to take up with the common jail, when your worship sends me thither for preaching?

And as for long prayers, I have two questions to put to you. 1. Was it the length of prayer, or the false pretence, which Christ reproved? If the length, why did he continue all night in prayer himself, who had less need than I? Luke vi. 12. Why are we bid pray continually, and continue instant in prayer? 1 Thess. v. 17; Rom. xii. 12; Col. iv. 2.

El. No: it was the false pretence that was blamed.

P. Was it not a proof that long prayer is a thing very good and laudable, when sincerely used? Else it would not have made a cloak for sin; for one evil is not a fit covering for another. My second question is, whether the Pharisees' long prayers were free prayers, uttered from the habits of the mind, or forms of liturgy?

El. I think they were such as your extemporate prayers.

P. Then you will wound the cause of liturgies, which I would not have you do; for if the Pharisees, that were so ceremonious, used none, it will scarce be probable that any were used in the Jewish church.

El. Well, then, suppose them to be set liturgies.

P. It is they, then, that are likest to the Pharisees, who by long liturgies cloak their oppressions and covetousness.

El. You are noted to be as covetous a sort of people as any: you will cheat a man in bargaining, and you will not swear; but you will lie like devils.

P. I assure you, sir, if we do so, it is contrary to our doctrine: for we profess that such persons are no

[i] 2 Cor. v. 17; Rom. viii. 8, 9, 13, 30; Acts xxvi. 18; Luke xiv. 26, 27, 33.

[k] 1 John i. 7, 8; iii. 8, 9; v. 16, 17; John v. 14; 1 Cor. vi. 10, 11.

[l] Rom. vi. 16; xiii. 13; Gen. xxxix. 9.

children of God, nor can be saved in such a state. Therefore you must prove it against the particular persons whom you accuse. For if we know of such, we number them with wicked men, and bring them to repentance and restitution, or excommunicate them.

And for those ministers that are called puritans by you, whether they are in the right or wrong, I meddle not. But, 1. If they be so covetous, how come they these many years to live in pinching poverty, (except a few that have something of their own, or live in other men's houses,) and all to avoid that which they think is sin? 2. And if they are such liars, why do they not escape all their sufferings? If they durst but once lie under their hands, and say that they assent and consent to what they do not, they might be as free as others.

El. There are as many villanies committed secretly among you as among others. Our faults are open, and known to all; but you are as bad in corners, as demurely as you carry it. Did you not hear lately of a great professor near you that was drunk, and another that got his servant-maid with child? This is your profession. If the truth might be known, on my conscience you are all alike.

P. Your[m] own tongue still confuteth you, and honoureth those whom you would fain reproach, If you sin openly, it seemeth you are not ashamed of it; you tell us that it is no wonder among you, as if it were your profession. If we sin secretly, how do you know it? Your naming one or two defamations, implieth that with such as you mean, it is a rarity and strange thing. And slanders are so common against such persons, that when it is examined, it is two to one but it proves false. But if it be true, either the acts you mention are marvels, committed by one of a hundred, once perhaps in all their life-time since their change; or else they are such as you describe that live secretly in such sin. If it be the latter, they are hypocrites, and such as we call to repentance and conversion, as being in the gall of bitterness and bond of iniquity; and all that I desire of you and your tenant here is, that you will not be such. If you like such, why do you blame them? If you dislike them, why will you be such yourselves? If you say that you make no profession of religion, I answer again; unless you renounce Christ, you profess as much as the hypocrites named by you, for you profess christianity, and they profess no more.

But if they were the falls of serious christians, I ask you, which is the likelier sort of men to be true christians, they that live impenitently and commonly in gross sin, and hate those that reprove them and live better; or they that live blamelessly in the fear of God, save that[n] one among many of them doth once in his life commit some heinous sin, which layeth him in such shame and brokenness of heart, that ofttimes such never well recover their comforts again while they live? If Noah was once drunk in his life; if there were one Ham in his family; if Lot was twice tempted to drunkenness and incest; if David once was guilty of odious sin; if Peter once, or thrice at once, denied his Master; if there were one Judas in the family of Christ himself; will any but the malicious thence conclude that they are all alike, or that one sin repented of is as bad as a life of sin never truly repented of?

And do you know what your slanderous inference doth import? No less than that Christ is no Christ, and that all the world shall be damned; for mark, I pray you, that we are certain that open unconverted sinners[o] are not saved from their sins by Christ; and that so dying they are lost for ever. Now you come in and say that the rest that profess repentance and obedience are in secret, and at the heart, as bad as they. And if so, they are all certainly lost men, for without holiness none shall see God; and the ungodly shall not stand in judgment, Heb. xii. 14; Psal. i. 6; and God hateth all the workers of iniquity.[p] Now, to say that all are such, either openly or secretly, is to say that either God is a liar, or that no one shall be saved; and yet you are the man that cannot believe that many are damned: and if Christ sanctify and save none from their sins,[q] he is no Saviour, and so no Christ.

But, sir, if you will search after such scandals, and bring such sins to open shame and punishment wheresoever they be found and proved, you shall have all our help and thanks, and you shall not cry down hypocrisy and scandal more heartily than we will do.

El. Fain would you seem pure and perfect, without sin, as the old Catharists pretended themselves to be.

P. Did you never hear any of us pray? If you had, you would have heard that we are more large and earnest in confessing and lamenting our sins, even in public, before God and the congregation, than any others ordinarily are. In truth, every godly man is so humbled in the sense of his sins,[r] that he is a greater burden and trouble to himself than all the world is besides, and he loatheth himself for all his sins. We confess ourselves sinners, with daily grief and shame; and if, indeed, the Catharists did otherwise, they were no kin to us, nor any of our acquaintance. Why do we exhort others so much to contrition and repentance, if we are not for the same ourselves? Would not all men make others of their own mind?

El. Come, come, when you have prated never so long, you must confess that you are a pack of rebels, and seditious rogues, the firebrands of your country, that would destroy the king and all of us, if we were in your power. The world hath had experience enough of you. You have learned to cant and talk smoothly in your way, and have God, and Christ, and heaven, and Scripture in your mouths; but, on my conscience, the devil and treason is in your hearts.

P. Whom do you mean, sir?

El. I mean all of you that pretend so much to godliness and preciseness, and make such ado with Scripture and religion. You will not swear, nor drink, nor whore, nor go to a play, but you are traitors all.

P. Doth not every man profess godliness, who professeth to be a christian? Doth not the king himself, and his council, and nobles, and judges, and all the magistrates of the land almost, and all the bishops and clergy, profess christianity, and godliness, and to believe the Scripture, and to hope for heaven? Do not they all pray in the Common Prayer, that the rest of our life hereafter may be pure and holy, that at the last we may come to eternal joy; and that we may live a godly, righteous, and sober life; and that we may fall into no sin; and that we may serve him without fear, in holiness and righteousness before him all the days of our lives; with many more such passages? Are you good friends to your king and country, that would make men believe that it is a sign of a bad subject to be religious, and that to "fear God and honour the king" may not stand together? What! will you charge the king and all his magistrates with treason? Are they all traitors who obey him and defend him?

m Isa. iii. 9; Jer. vi. 15; viii. 12.
n Psal. li.
o Luke xiii. 3, 5; xv.
p Psal. v. 5.
q Matt. i. 21; Tit. ii. 14.
r Rom. viii. 16, 17, 24; Psal. li; Acts xxvi.; Tit. iii. 2, 3.

El. You know who I mean well enough. I mean you puritans, all the pack of you.

P. A puritan is a word of so arbitrary interpretation, that sure it is too large to found a charge of treason upon. Mr. Robert Bolton, and Bishop Downame, and Bishop Robert Abbot, and many such, will tell you that it is commonly used in the mouths of the profane for any man that feareth God, and liveth holily, and avoideth wilful sin, and will not be debauched as sensualists are: and sometimes it is taken for one that is against the prelacy and ceremonies. In the first sense, as a puritan signifieth a serious christian, and a godly man, dare you say that the king, nobles, judges, and bishops are not such? I am not acquainted with them: but our religion teacheth us to judge all men to be what they profess themselves to be, till the contrary be certain and notorious. Dare you say that all the magistrates, prelates, citizens, and subjects of the land are either ungodly men, or traitors? Sure this cannot be your meaning.

El. You are loth to know my meaning. I mean all the pack of the precisians that are for so much strictness, and preaching and praying, and talking of Scripture.

P. Dare you say that neither the king, nor his nobles, nor judges, nor bishops, nor clergy, are for Scripture, and for much preaching and praying, and for strict, precise obedience to God, and for strictness of justice, temperance, and sobriety? What, will you say that all are traitors to the king, that will not be rebels against God, and perfidious traitors against Christ and christianity?

El. I mean your second sort of puritans, the nonconformists, if you are willing to understand.

P. Now I understand you, sir, but it is but in part. But what is conformity or nonconformity to our case? What, if all nonconformists were as bad as you make them, will you, therefore, plead for nonconformity and rebellion against God? What an argument is this! Nonconformists are rebels. Therefore an ungodly man needeth no repentance and conversion, or we may be saved without a holy heart and life. Do you think this is wise reasoning? Do not conformists plead for holiness? Be you but a godly conformist, and I shall rejoice in your felicity. But, because I must love my neighbour as myself, I have three or four questions further to ask you. 1. Is it they that conform in nothing, or they that conform not in every thing? Such a one was Chillingworth; and I thought you had not taken the papists to be all traitors, who are nonconformists too.

3. Is it their doctrine that is traitorous? Or is it their hearts and practice contrary to their doctrine? For the former, they defy their slanderers, and challenge them to cite one confession of any reformed church that hath in it any disloyal doctrine. Bishop Andrews, in "Tortura Torti," will tell you that in this the puritans are belied, and that they take the same oaths of allegiance and supremacy, and profess the same loyalty with others. But if it be their hearts and practices, as contrary to their own doctrine, are you not a slanderer if you charge such dissembling on any one that you cannot prove it by? Such charges must fall on particular persons, and be proved, and not on parties; for what shall notify any man's mind but his own profession, or his practice? When they readily swear allegiance and loyalty, are they not to be believed till some proof confute them? And if, in civil wars, you gentlemen, lawyers, and statesmen, say this is law, and that is law, and entangle poor men's consciences, will you afterwards conclude that no man's conscience will be true to his oath of allegiance, which scrupleth ecclesiastical oaths or subscriptions? Another man would think it a more probable arguing to say, He that scrupleth one oath or subscription is like to make conscience of another; for if he dare break an oath when he hath taken it, why should he not venture as far to take it?

3. But, sir, all this is Satan's ordinary course, to endeavour to engage the interest of princes seemingly on his side, to make religion odious. Christ must be accused as forbidding to pay tribute to Cæsar, and as a usurper of the kingdom. Pilate must condemn him, lest he seem not Cæsar's friend. Paul goes for a pestilent fellow, and a mover of sedition among the people, that taught things contrary to Cæsar and the law.

But again, sir, what is all this to the case here that you come to treat about? Did I persuade your tenant to be a nonconformist? Did I speak one syllable to him of any such matter? Did I put any scruple into his mind against any orders of the church? Ask him whether I did? When I had nothing to say to him but to exhort him to repentance and the love of God, and a holy and heavenly life and conversation, and quickly to forsake his sins, how cometh nonconformity to have any thing to do here? What is that to the question in hand? Pray you, Saul, mark your landlord's argument: nonconformists are all traitors and rebels, if you will believe him; therefore, forsake not your sins, and turn not to God and a holy life by true repentance: or, other men are, saith he, rebels against the king, therefore continue you a rebel against God. Have not you natural logic enough to perceive the deceit of such an argument?

For my part, I here give you my plain profession, that all that fear God, must honour the king, and not resist the higher powers, and that for conscience' sake, lest they receive damnation; and that rebellions and treasons against king or kingdom are the works of the devil and the flesh, which all true christians must abhor.

El. However, you cannot deny but you are a pack of schismatics, that, for a ceremony, will tear the church, and set up conventicles of your own; and schism is kin to rebellion.

P. You shall not thus draw us away from the business in hand. I will not now dispute with you what schism is, who seem not to understand it, because it is impertinent, and tendeth but to divert us from our business. I ask you, 1. Do I persuade your tenant here to schism, or only to repentance and a holy life? 2. Are not conformists and nonconformists agreed in that? You know not what I am in those matters myself; but send for one able minister that is a conformist, and another that is a nonconformist, and try whether both agree not in the truth of all that I am persuading him to believe or practise.

El. The truth is, you are of so many sects and so many opinions, that he may sooner grow a Bedlam among you, than a good christian. You are of as many minds as men. One tub-preacher saith, This is the word of God, and another saith, That is the word of God; scarce a whole house is of one religion; and if he must turn to any of you, how shall he know which party it must be? Must he be a presbyterian, or an independent, or a Brownist, or an anabaptist, or what? How shall he be sure which of all these is in the right, that he may rest?

P. Saul, you hear this terrible objection of your landlord. Will you but mark my answer in these three parts, and if it be not reason, spit in my face, and take your course.

1. Every different opinion[s] is not a different religion. Our religion is but one thing, which is simple christianity; and every by-opinion is not essential to christianity. No two men in the world, I think, are, in every thing, of one opinion. He that will not take a journey which is for his estate or life, till all the clocks in London strike together, is as wise a man as he that will not turn from his sin to God till all christians are of one opinion in all the difficult points in religion.

2. My earnest advice to you, Saul, is, that you become not a[t] sectary of any party whatsoever. Become a true christian, and love the unity, peace, and concord of believers; and, for opinions, follow the right, as far as you can know it, but not to engage for doubtful things in any divisions, sects, or parties: but if men will needs quarrel, stand by, and pray for the church's peace.

3. Try whether christians of all opinions do not agree in all that I exhort you to. If I have taught you, or persuaded you to, any one thing, but what the conformists and nonconformists, episcopal, presbyterian, independent, yea, and the papists, are all of a mind in, and will all bear witness to the certain truth, then let your conscience judge whether you be not a most inexcusable man, that will not be persuaded to that which even all differing christians are agreed in; and whether this objection of sects and different religions condemn not you the more, that will not agree with them where they all agree? and I leave it also to Sir Elymas's conscience.

El. You would make me seem a fool, or an atheist; as if I persuaded him from all religion. By —— you are a set of the insolentest rogues in the world. I will stand talking with you no more. But for you, Saul, I tell you; if you hearken to such fellows, and turn a puritan, I will turn thee, and thy wife and children, out of doors the next week after it. And you, sir preacher, I will take another course with you, if you cease not thus to trouble my neighbours. I doubt not but I shall cause the bishop to trounce you; but if he do not, I will once more send you to the common jail, for all your sick night-cap, and there you shall lie among rogues like yourself.

P. I beseech you, let not loose your passion, sir: remember that you said you love your neighbour as yourself. Poverty, and a[u] prison, are as near and sure a way to heaven as riches, and earthly prosperity, and pleasure. I must shortly die; and whether at home, or in a jail, or with Lazarus at your doors, among your dogs, it is not my interest or care: God is the Lord of your life and mine. Boast not of to-morrow; for who knoweth "what a day may bring forth?" Prov. xxvii. 1.

But, sir, seeing you are not against all religion, I beseech you, in the conclusion, yet, make us to understand what it is that you are against?

El. I am against being righteous over-much; and making men believe that they cannot be saved without being so holy and so strict; and so frightening poor people out of their wits. A puritan is nothing but such a frightened protestant. Cannot you go to church, and sometimes say your prayers; and so be quiet, and be moderate in your religion? It is these bigots, and zealots, that trouble all the world; and will neither let men live nor die in peace. Cannot you live as your neighbours do, and your forefathers have done? What, are they all damned? and will you be wiser than all the world? Moderation is good in all things.

P. Your speech hath many parts which must be distinctly considered. I. To be righteous over-much, in Solomon's sense, is to be stricter than God would have us; by a preciseness, or a devised righteousness of our own: where righteousness is not taken formally, but materially, for a rigid preciseness and pretended exactness, which is not commanded; and, indeed, is no duty, but a great hinderance of duty, and that which I use to call over-doing. As some men will be so accurate in their expressions in preaching and praying, as that over-curiousness in words destroyeth the life and use. And some will pretend that every thing must be done better, and mended still, till nothing be done, or all be marred. As in household affairs, over-curiosity about every little thing is accompanied with the neglect of greater things; because we are not sufficient for all: so in religion, some, upon pretence of strictness, lay out so much of their zeal, and talk, and time, about many lesser or doubtful points of church order, discipline, and modes, and circumstances of worship, and about controverted opinions, that thereby they neglect the great substantials. This[x] tithing of mint, anise, and cummin, and omitting the weighty matters of the law, faith, judgment, and mercy, and preferring sacrifice before mercy, is at once to be unrighteous, and to be righteous over-much, even with an unrighteous righteousness; that is, a strictness of our own devising. Do I persuade any one to this?

II. We would make men believe nothing but God's own word. If that word say not, that "If any man have not the Spirit of Christ, he is none of his," (Rom. viii. 9,) let it not be believed. But if it do, what are we to preach for, but to persuade men to believe God's word, and obey it? And will it save men's souls to be unbelievers? Believing God is the way which he hath appointed for salvation: and will you say, that not to believe him is the way?

III. We would affright stupid sinners into their wits, and not out of them. When the prodigal came to himself, he returned to his father, Luke xv. 17. We take that man to be much worse than mad, that will sell his soul for so base a price as a little worldly pelf, or fleshly pleasure; and having but one short, uncertain life, in which he must win or lose salvation, will cast it away upon the fooleries of sin. And if you would have such a man to go quietly to hell for fear of being made mad, I wish that none may fall into the hands of such a physician for mad-men. "Wisdom is justified of her children," Matt. xi. 19. He that sets less by heaven and his soul, than by lust and vanity, can scarce (in that) be madder than he is. And if that be your wit, we envy you not the honour of it. We are no friends to melancholy, because it is no friend to the holy, joyful life of a believer. We wish men so much[y] fear of God, and of sin, and hell, as is necessary to keep them out of these; and we would encourage no more. The kingdom of God consisteth in "righteousness, and peace, and joy in the Holy Ghost," Rom. xiv. 17. We would have no tormenting fear, which is contrary to love, but only that which doth prepare for it, and promote it, or subserve it. To call men from a life of brutes, to seek and hope for a life with angels in heavenly glory, is not the way to frighten them out of their wits. The derisions of self-destroyers are easy trials to us, and cut not so deep as an offended God, or a guilty conscience.

IV. Moderation is a good effect of prudence; and

[s] Read Rom. xiv.; xv.
[t] Rom. xvi. 17, 18; 1 Thess. v. 12, 13; 1 Cor. i. 10, 11; ii.; iii.; Tit. iii. 10.
[u] Matt. v. 10—12.

[x] Matt. xxiii. 23, and per totum; ix. 13; xii. 7; xvi. 3—6; Col. ii. 19, 20, &c.
[y] Luke xii. 4, 5.

we are greatly against imprudence and irregular zeal. But because I perceive that this is the very point of all our difference, and that you think that a godly, righteous, and sober life is more ado than needs, and an excess in religion; and would take us down to some dead formality, under pretence of being moderate; I entreat your patient consideration of these questions following:

Quest. 1. Is it possible to[z] love God too much; and is not love an active, operative principle?

2. Is it possible to please God too well, and obey him too exactly?

3. Is it not blasphemy against God to say so? For God made all his laws: and he chargeth God's laws with folly and iniquity, who saith that any of them are such as should not be obeyed.

4. Do you think that you can[a] give God more than his own, and more true service than he deserveth?

5. Are you afraid of paying[b] too dear for heaven? Do you think it is not worth more than it will cost the most serious, laborious believers?

6. Are such men as you and I fit to be pulled back and dissuaded from loving and serving God too much? Do you not say that we are all sinners? And what is a sinner, but one that obeyeth not God enough? And is sin a thing to be justified? Are not we all such as we are sure shall do[c] too little, and come far short of our duty, when we have done our best? Do you need to entreat lame men to run towards heaven too fast? If the best are imperfect, and do too little, why will you persuade even an ignorant sinner to do less? If you had servants that would do but a day's work in a week, or scholars that would learn but a lesson in a month, you would think that he abused you, that should exclaim against their working or learning too much.

7. Can that man be sincere, who desireth not to be perfect? Doth he love holiness, that would not have more?

8. Doth not all God's word call us up still to higher degrees of obedience, and to cleanse ourselves from all filthiness of flesh and spirit, perfecting holiness in the fear of God? 2 Cor. vii. 1. And did not God know what he said? Are you wiser than he? And doth not the devil every where call men off from holiness, and make them believe that it is needless, or too troublesome? And whose work is it, then, that you are doing?

9. Doth too much holiness trouble any man when he is[d] dying, or too little, rather? Had you rather yourself have too little, yea, none, or have much, when you come to die?

10. Did you ever know any man so holy, and obedient, and good, that did not[e] earnestly desire to be better? Nothing in the world doth half so much grieve the holiest persons that ever I knew, as that they can know, and love, and serve God no more. And if there were no excellency in it, or if they had enough already, why should they desire more?

11. Is not sin the only plague of the world, the troubler of souls, and churches, and kingdoms, that will not suffer the world to have peace? And were it not better if there were none? Would not the world be then like a heaven, a blessed place? And should men be then blamed for sinning too little? which is your sense who blame them for being religious too much.

12. What have you in this world to mind, which is worthier of your greatest care and labour than the pleasing of God and the saving of your soul? If doing nothing be the best condition, sleeping out your life is better than waking, and death is better than life. But if any thing at all should be[f] minded and sought, should it not be that first and most which is most worth? And have you found out any thing that is more worthy of your love and labour than heaven, or the everlasting fruition of God in glory? I pray you, sir, what do you set your heart upon, yourself? What do you seek with your greatest diligence? Dare you say it is any thing better than God? If one come to you at death, will you say then that it is better? I beseech you think whether I may not much wiselier say to you, and to all that are of your minds, Why make you such a[g] stir for nothing? Is a few nights' lodging in a wicked world, in the way to the grave, and hell, worth all this ado? than you can say to others, What need all this ado for your salvation? Do you know ever a one of us whom you account too religious, that in his love and service of God doth seem much to exceed the[h] ungodly in their love and service of the flesh? How early rise your poor labouring tenants! How much toil and patience have your servants to please you! and the husbandman, for a poor living! and almost all men for provision for the body, till it be cast into a grave! Is not all this too much ado? And is our poor, dull labour too much for heaven? They think of the world as soon as they are awake. They speak of it the first words they say. They hold on thinking, and talking, and labouring, till they go to bed again. In company and alone, they forget it not: and thus they do from year to year. And yet men say, that this is good husbandry; and who blameth them for it, and asketh them whether their maintenance be worth all this ado? Yea, God saith, "Six days shalt thou labour." What if we should, as early and late, as constantly and unweariedly, in company and alone, still think and talk of our God and Saviour, and labour as hard in all appointed means for salvation? Had we not a thousand times greater motives for it? And yet who is it that doth so much? And are we puritans, and precisians, and such as trouble ourselves and others with doing too much, when we let every worldling overdo us? yea, when a drunkard, or ambitious seeker of preferment, will run faster and more unweariedly towards hell, than most of us dullards do towards heaven? O Lord, pardon our slothfulness for doing so little! and we will bear these gentlemen's scorns and hatred for doing so much. O may we but escape thy deserved wrath for loving thee so little, and let us bear from persecutors what thy wisdom shall permit, for loving thee so much! My God, thou knowest, who knowest my heart, if thou wilt but make me believe more strongly, and hope for heaven more confidently and confirmedly, and love thee more fervently, and serve thee more faithfully, and successfully, and bear the cross more patiently, I ask for no other reward nor happiness in this world, for all that I shall do or suffer! I will not call thee too hard a master; nor say that thy service is a toil; nor such a life a tedious trouble. O let me have this feast, these sweet delights, these restful labours, and let worldlings take their dirt and shadows, and Bedlams call me mad or foolish! Thou art my portion, my first and last, my trust and hope, my desire, my all! O do not forsake me, and leave me to a dead and unbelieving heart, to a cold, unholy, disaffected heart, to a fleshly, worldly, selfish mind, to live or die a stranger to my God, and the heavenly society, Christ and his triumphant church, and then I will never join with the accusers of thy pleasant

[z] Matt. xxii. 37; 2 Tim. ii. 4; 1 Thess. iv. 1; ii. 4; Col. i. 10.
[a] 1 Cor. iv. 7.
[b] Luke xii. 32, 33; Matt. xvi. 26.
[c] Luke xvii. 10, 49.
[d] Numb. xxiii. 10; Hos. v. 15.
[e] Rom. vii. 24.
[f] Matt. vi. 19, 20.
[g] Isa. v. 11; Zech. iii. 7.
[h] Luke xvi. 8.

service, nor crave one taste of the beastly, deceitful pleasures of sin!

El. O holy soul! No doubt you were in a rapture now! Were you not in the third heaven? Those tears were sanctified! Would not that holy water work miracles! Sure this was the breathing of the Spirit! Were you not fanatics, how could you think that God is pleased with your weeping and whining, and speaking through the nose, and cutting faces, and such like hypocritical shows?

P. Sir, I have no weapons to use but reason and God's word, and scorning is like sense and appetite, a thing that reason hath nothing to do with but rebuke, nor do I purpose to answer you in that dialect. I doubt you cannot undertake that you will not weep or whine on your death-bed: but if not, it may be worse.

El. Come, sir, when you have all done, who made the way to heaven so long? Why lead you the people so far about? What need so many sermons, and so long prayers, as if God were moved or pleased with our talk? I can say all that is in your sermons and volumes in three words. All is but think well, and say well, and do well.

P. That is quickly said, sir; but if I desire you to spend all or half your life in thinking well, and saying well, and doing well, will you not say that I am a puritan, and ask what need all this ado? Is it any thing else that I have persuaded your tenant to, and that you are opposing all this while? See still how unhappily you confute yourself. Let us but agree of this, that we must labour faithfully to think well, and say well, and do well, and repent unfeignedly that ever we did otherwise, and trust in Christ for pardon and for help, and we will so conclude, and differ no more.

But you must know that well and ill do differ; and what thoughts, words, and deeds are well indeed. And that is well which God commandeth, whether you like it or not.

But if you mean that our sermons need to be no[i] longer, will you try first this art of short in a scrivener? Let him tell his boys, You have nothing to do but to make your letters well, and set them together well. Let a schoolmaster say no more to his scholar but, You must know your letters and syllables, words and sentences, matter and method, and there needs no more. Let a carpenter tell his apprentice, There is nothing to do but frame the house and rear it; and in rearing, nothing but lay the foundation and erect the superstructure, and cover, and ceil it. Why do men set boys so many years to schools, and to apprenticeships, when two or three words may serve the turn?

But as for long prayers, sir, we know that God is not moved by words; but we are ourselves. And, 1. The exercise of holy desires exciteth them: as all habits are increased by act, and all acts further us by excitation of the faculties. And our fervent desires are our receptive disposition: and if you have any philosophy, you know that *recipitur ad modum recipientis*, and what a wonderful variegation of effects there is in the world, from the same beams or influxes of the sun, by the great variety of receptive dispositions. Two ways prayer maketh us receptive of the blessing: by physical disposition, (as appetite maketh our food sweet and effectual,) and by[k] moral disposition, as we are in the way where mercy cometh, and in the use of the means which God will bless. What if you offer your children money, or what else you see best, and bid them ask it first, and thank you after, and one of them doth so, and the other saith, My father is not so childish, mutable, or unloving, as to be moved with my asking or thanking. What good doth this do to him? Will you not say, No; but it is good for you to do your duty, without which you are unworthy of my gift; and it is not wisdom in me to encourage your disobedience, nor to give you what you think not worth the asking. We cannot have God's mercies against his will, and prayer is one of his conditions. And what can be more reasonable than ask and have? He that valueth not mercy, will neither relish it well, nor use it well.

There is a sweet and admirable co-operation between the bountiful communications of God, and the holy and constant desires of the soul. The heavenly influx cometh down on the soul and exciteth those desires; and desires arise, and by receptive disposition cause us more plenteously to receive that influx; even as the influx of the sun, and the fiery spirits in the eye, concur to our sight. We are receiving grace all the while we are desiring it. Therefore the constant excitation of holy desires, by fervent prayer, is the constant way of our reception and heavenly benediction.

2. And also it is part of the due[l] homage that we owe to the great Benefactor of the world. The eyes of all things look up to him, and all things praise him in their kind; but man must do it as man, understandingly and freely. What else have we reason for, but to know the original and end of all the good that we receive? What have we tongues for, but to glorify our Creator and Redeemer, and to speak his praise? This is the use of our faculties; this is our duty, and our honour, and our joy. God made all his creatures for himself; even for the pleasure of his holy will; therefore he made our reason and tongues for himself. And can we have a nobler, sweeter theme for our thoughts, our affections, or our words? Oh! what is there in our blessed Saviour, our glorious God, and the heavenly joys, that we should ever be backward to think or speak of them; or ever count such work a toil; or ever be weary of it? Would you have us think that heaven is a place of weariness? or have us afraid lest it be a house of correction? As no papist can rationally ever be willing to die, who believeth he shall go to the pains of purgatory, which is sharper, they say, than their sufferings here; so you would have none at all willing to die, if you would make them believe that long praising God is a wearisome employment to a well-disposed soul. If you do not think that an hour is too long for dinner and supper at your plenteous tables; if you can feast long, and talk long, and play long, and game long, and read romances, and see plays long, I pray you pardon us for praying long. And I would whisper this word to your conscience: ask Sir Elymas, on his death-bed, when time is[m] ending, whether he could then wish it had been spent in longer feasting, and dressing, and playing, or in longer praying?

Sir, the worst I wish you is, that you had felt but one hour what some of God's servants have felt in prayer, and in the joyful praise of their glorious Lord, and then our dispute about the troublesomeness of religion would be at an end; as feasting would end the controversy, whether it would be a toil for a hungry man to eat?

El. This hath ever been the custom of hypocrites, to place all their religion in words and strictness; but where are your good works? You will call good works a piece of popery; you are as covetous and griping as any men in the world; you will cut a

[i] Acts xx. 9—11, &c. [k] Luke xviii. 1—8. [l] Psal. lxv. [m] Luke xvi. 25—27.

man's throat for a groat, rather than give a poor man a groat. This is the precisian's holiness and religion.

P. You say as you are taught; you are not their first accuser. But, sir, men's religion must be known by their doctrine and principles: if a christian be an[n] adulterer, or murderer, or malignant, will you say that the christian religion is for adultery, murder, or malignity. I will tell you our doctrine: it is that we must love our neighbours as ourselves, and must[o] honour God with our substance, and with the first-fruits of our increase; and that we must devote all that ever we have to God; and that we are[p] created in Christ Jesus to good works, and[q] redeemed and purified, to be zealous of good works; and that we must do[r] good to all men, but especially to the household of faith; and that what we[s] do, or deny, to his members, is as done or denied to Christ himself; and that[t] to do good and communicate we must not forget, for with such sacrifice God is well pleased. In a word, that we must even pinch our own flesh, and[u] labour hard, that we may have wherewith to relieve the needy; and that, as God's stewards, we must not waste one farthing in sensuality, or superfluous pomp, or pleasure, because, if we do, we rob the poor of it; and that we must give God an[x] account of every farthing, whether we used it according to his will; and that we must lay out all, as we would hear of it at last; and that he that[y] seeth his brother have need, and shutteth up the bowels of his compassion from him, the love of God dwelleth not in him; and that we must be judged according to our works; without which pretended faith is dead. Is this the doctrine which you or the papists do reproach?

El. These are good words, if your deeds were answerable.

P. 1. If men live not as they profess, blame not their profession, but their lives. 2. But then you, that are a justice, must be so just as to hear men speak for themselves, and condemn no man till it is proved by him: and condemn no more than it is proved by, and not precisians in the general. 3. He that liveth contrary to his profession doth, by his profession, but make a rack for his conscience, and a proclamation of his own shame to the world. If you like our doctrine, why do you blame us for persuading others to it? If you like it not, why do you blame us for not practising it?

But come, sir, you and I live near together; I pray you name me the men that are such covetous villains as you describe, and compare the rest of your neighbours with them.

El. You would put me upon odious work; I will not defile my mouth with naming any of you.

P. Am I one of them whom you mean?

El. I confess you have got you a good report, for a charitable man, but on my conscience it is but to be seen of men.

P. Nay, then, there is no ward against your calumnies. Before, you denied our good works; and now it is but our hearts and hypocrisy that you accuse, which God only knoweth. If you gave half your revenue to the poor, should I do well to think that you did it in hypocrisy?

But come, sir, I will do that for you which you avoid: you know in our county there are few gentlemen of estate called precisians, but Mr. T. F. and you know he hath built an hospital, and endowed it with many hundred pounds per annum.

You know Mr. N. N. in another county, who is called a precisian, and I have credibly heard, that he giveth five hundred pounds a year to charitable uses these sixteen years at least: and both of them go plain, and forbear pomp and gallantry, that they may have to do it with.

I used to lodge but in two houses in London, and therefore am not acquainted with many men's secrets of this kind. One of them is a godly man of no great estate, and is readier to offer me money to any good use than I am (for shame) to receive it. The other is a tradesman also, not reputed now worth very many hundreds by the year; and he giveth in one county a hundred pounds a year to charitable uses; and I do not think that it is another hundred that excuseth him at home. I will offend them all by telling you this, because of the text, Matt. v. 16.

But why do I mention particulars: I here seriously profess to you and the world my ordinary experience, that if I have at any time a collection or contribution to motion for any poor widow, or orphans, or any real work of charity, those that you call precisians do usually give their[z] pounds more freely than most others give their crowns, and freelier give a crown, than most others a shilling, proportionable to their estates. Yea, they do now in London give many pounds, where men of far greater estates will give next nothing. Not but there are great men of great estates, that in gallantry, it is like, will sometimes be liberal. And I doubt not but there are some men that have liberal minds, who have little religion. But I tell you only my own experience. But still remember, that I speak not of men of any sect as such, but of such serious holy men as you call precisians, of what side soever.

And these things more I desire you to remember: 1. That you know not other men's estates, and therefore know not what they are able to give. 2. That such men as you and others will keep many of them poor enough whom you call precisians, that they shall have more cause to receive than to give. 3. That Christ hath[a] charged them to give their alms in secret, and not to let the right hand know what the left hand doth; and therefore you are no competent judge of their charity. 4. That the great covetousness of abundance that we have to do with maketh them think that they have never enough; and they accuse all of covetousness that satisfy not their covetous desires. 5. That no man hath enough to satisfy all men: and if we give to nine only, the tenth man that hath none will call us cruel, as if we had never given to any. 6. That the malignant enmity of the world to godliness doth dispose men to[b] slander all godly persons, without proof or reason, and to carry on any lie which they hear from others. 7. That there are more and greater good works than giving alms. A poor minister, that saith with Peter and John,[c] "Silver and gold have I none, but such as I have I give thee," shall be accepted for what he[d] would have given if he had had it. And if he[e] convert souls, and turn many to righteousness, and help men to heaven, and all the year long doth waste himself in study and labour to do it, and liveth a poor despised life, and suffereth poverty, scorn, and wrath, from the ungodly, which, if he would change his calling, he might escape; doth not this man do more and greater good works, at a dearer rate, than he that should glut his flesh, and gratify his pride, and lust, and ease, with a thousand or six hundred pounds a year, and give as much more to

[n] 1 Cor. vi. 9, 10. [o] Prov. iii. 9. [p] Eph. ii. 10. [q] Tit. ii. 14. [r] Gal. vi. [s] Matt. xxv. [t] Heb. xiii. [u] Eph. iv. 28. [x] Matt. xxv. [y] 1 John iii. 17; Rom. xiv. 10; Jam. ii.

[z] Luke xix. 8; Acts iv. [a] Matt. vi. 1—5. [b] Matt. v. 10—12. [c] Acts iii. 6. [d] 2 Cor. viii. 12. [e] Jam. v. 20

charitable uses? Though I never knew such a one that did so.

And because you have said so much for good works, I take the boldness to entreat you to do more. We that are your neighbours see nothing that you do, but only give Lazarus a few scraps at your door; but we see that you are clothed in purple and silk, and that not only you, but your children and servants, fare sumptuously and deliciously every day. How much you spend in taverns, and pomp, and state, and feasting, and gaming, and visits, and on your pride and pleasure, the country talks of; but we hear little of any impropriations that you buy in for the church, or of any free-schools, or hospitals, that you settle, or of any poor children that you set to school, or apprenticeships, or the like. The sins of Sodom are your daily business; pride, fulness of bread, and idleness, and want of compassion to the poor, make them up, Ezek. xvi. 49. Oh what a dreadful account will you have, when all this comes to be reckoned for, as is foretold, Matt. xxv.; when it is found, on your accounts, so many pounds on visits, and needless entertainments, and pomp; so many on sports, and on superfluities of horses, dogs, and furniture; so many to tempt all in your house to gluttony, to say nothing of other wasteful lusts; and to pious and charitable uses, alas, how little! The Lord convert you, lest you hear, "Take the slothful and unprofitable servant, and cast him into outer darkness;" and lest you want a drop of water for your tongue. At least, O do less hurt, if you will do no good.

El. I will talk no longer with you, lest you think to make me tremble, with Felix, or to say, Almost you persuade me to be a precisian, you put such a face of reason upon your religion.

P. Sir, I beseech you let me end all our controversy with one question more. You profess yourself a christian. Had you denied the Scripture, or the life to come or the immortality of the soul, I had proved them, and talked to you at another rate. I ask you, then, if Saul had never been baptized till now, would you advise him to be baptized or not?

El. Yes; do you think I would not have him a christian?

P. And would you have him do it understandingly? or ignorantly to do he knoweth not what?

El. Understandingly; or else why is he a man?

P. And would you have him do it seriously, or hypocritically; dissemblingly, or in jest?

El. Do you think I am for hypocrisy and jesting about our christianity?

P. I have done, sir. Saul, mark what your master saith. He would advise you to be baptized, if you had not been baptized before; and, therefore, now to stand to your baptism (for I will never ask him whether he would have you renounce it as an apostate). He would have you do it understandingly and seriously: I desire no more of you. Remember that we are agreed of your duty. I call you to no other conversion nor holiness, than understandingly and seriously to renew your baptismal vow and covenant with God the Father, Son, and Holy Ghost. Whatever you hear scorners talk of puritans, and preciseness, and troublesome religion, and of our many sects and many religions, of conformity and nonconformity, of a hundred controversies, remember that the serious renewing and faithful keeping your baptismal covenant is all that I preach to you and persuade you to. I will therefore write you out this covenant, desiring you to take it home with the exposition of it which I gave you, and consider of it with your most serious thoughts; and when you are resolved, come and tell me.

THE HOLY COVENANT.

I do[f] believe in God, the Father, the Son, and the Holy Ghost, according to the particular articles of the christian faith; and heartily repenting of my sinful life, I do personally, absolutely, and resolvedly give up myself to him, my Creator and reconciled God and Father in Christ, my Saviour and my Sanctifier; renouncing the devil, the world, and the sinful desires of the flesh: that, taking up my cross, and denying myself, I may follow Christ, the Captain of my salvation, to the death, and live with him in endless glory.

Read but our church liturgy, yea the papists' liturgies, and you will see that here is not a word but what is in the sense of baptism, and what papists, and protestants, and all christians, are agreed on.

I pray you, Sir Elymas, read it, and tell him here whether there be any word that you except against.

El. I cannot deny it without denying christianity. God make us all better christians; for I perceive we are not what we promised to be. It was you that I talked against, I thought, all this while; but I begin to perceive that it is christianity itself (in the[g] practice, though not in the name) which my heart is against. I cannot like this godliness, and self-denying, and mortification, and cross-bearing; and yet I perceive that I vowed it, when I was baptized; and if I renounce it, I must renounce my christianity itself. I would I had not talked with you, for you have disquieted my mind; and I find that it is serious religion itself that is against my mind and course of life, and my mind against it, and that I must be either a saint or an atheist; and which I shall prove I cannot tell. But if I must repent, there is no haste.

THE

FOURTH DAY'S CONFERENCE.

THE RESOLVING AND ACTUAL CONVERSION OF A SINNER.

SPEAKERS.—Paul, a Teacher; and Saul, a Learner.

PAUL. Welcome, neighbour; you have been longer away than I expected; what was the matter with you?

SAUL. O sir, I have seen and felt the heavy hand of God since I saw you. We had a violent fever common among us, and my landlord, Sir Elymas, is dead, and so is his servant that was with him when you talked with him; and I narrowly escaped with my life myself.

P. Alas! is he dead? I pray you tell me how he took our conference, and how he died?

S. He told me that you were too bold and saucy with him; but he thought you were an honest man, and that you had more reason for your religion than he thought any of you had: and that the truth is, you had the Scripture on your side; and while he disputed with you on Scripture principles, you were too hard for him. But though he was loth to tell you so, he liked the papists better, who set not so much by Scripture; and when a man hath sinned, if he confess to the priest, they absolve him. Yea, rather than believe that none but such godly people

[f] Matt. xxviii. 18—20; Mark xvi. 15, 16; Luke xiii. 3, 5; xiv. 26, 33; Rom. viii. 8, 9, 17, 18.

[g] Prov. iii. 18, 19.

could be saved, and rather than live so strict a life, he would not believe that the Scripture was the word of God.

P. Alas, how the rebellious heart of man stands out against the law and grace of God! As for the papists, I assure you they confess all the Scriptures to be the word of God, and of certain truth, as well as we; and they will deny never a word of that which I persuaded you to consent to. They differ from us in this, that they take in more books into the canonical Scripture than we do; and they say, that all that is in their Scripture and ours, is not religion enough for us; but we must have a great deal more, which they call tradition. See, then, the ignorance of these men: that because they think we make them too much work, they will run to them that make them much more. Though I confess their additions consist so much in words, and ceremonies, and bodily exercise, that flesh and blood can the more easily bear it. When the papists dispute with us, they would make men believe that our religion is too loose and favoureth the flesh, and that theirs is far more strict and holy; and yet our sensualists turn papists to escape the strictness of our religion.

And as for their pardons and absolutions, I assure you, their own doctrine is, that they profit and save none but the truly penitent. And even their Gregory VII. called Hildebrand, (and the firebrand of the church and empire,) and that in a council at Rome, professeth, that neither false penitence, nor false baptism, is effectual: though some of them make attrition, without contrition, or bare fear without love, to serve the turn. And if their priests do flatter the presumption and false hopes of fornicators, drunkards, and such grosser sinners, by absolving them as oft as they confess their sin, without telling them that it is all ineffectual, unless, by true conversion, they forsake it, they do this but as a mere cheat for worldly ends; to increase their church, and win the great and wealthy of the world to themselves; quite contrary to their own knowledge and professed religion.

But as for his not believing the Scriptures, the truth is, there lieth the core of all their errors. There are abundance amongst us, that call themselves christians, because it is the religion of the king and country, who are no christians at the heart, which made me say so much of the hypocrisy of ungodly men. And I cannot see how a man, that truly believeth the Scripture, can quiet himself in a fleshly and ungodly life, but his belief would either convert him or torment him.

S. But I am persuaded he had some convictions upon his conscience, which troubled him. When he was taken first with the fever, they all put him in hopes that there was no danger of death; and so he was kept from talking at all of his soul, or of another world, till the fever took away his understanding; but twice or thrice he came to himself for half an hour, and Mr. Zedekiah, his chaplain, advised him to lift up his heart to God, and believe in Christ; for he was going to a place of joys, and angels were ready to receive his soul. And he looked at him with a direful countenance, and said, Away, flatterer! You have betrayed my soul! Too late! too late! And he trembled so that the bed shook under him.

P. And how died his servant, Malchus?

S. O, quite in another manner! He heard, in the next room, all the talk between his master and you, and, doubtless, it convinced him; but he went on in his former course of life, till [a] sickness took him, and then he was greatly terrified in conscience, especially when he heard that his master was dead. And he would often talk of you, and wish that he could have spoken with you; but none would endure to hear of sending for you. Oh! if you had but heard how he cried out toward the last: Oh, my madness! Oh, my sinful, wicked life! Oh, what will become of my miserable soul? Oh that I had the time again which I have lost! Would God but try me once again, I would lead another life than I have done; I would make nothing of all the scorns of fools, and all the temptations of the world! His groans did strike me as a dagger at the heart: methinks I still hear them which way ever I go.

P. And what hath been your own condition since I saw you? And what thought you of your master's conference?

S. O sir, I would not, for a great deal, but I had heard it. I thought, till I heard you answer him, that there had been some sense in the talk of these revilers at a godly life; but then I soon saw that it is all but a foolish scorn and railing; any scolding woman could talk as wisely. His superiority, and confidence, and contempt, was all his wisdom.

P. It is no wonder if he talk foolishly, who talketh against the God of wisdom, and his holy word, and against the interest, health, and happiness of his own soul. He that can live so far below reason as to sell his salvation for the short and swinish pleasures of sin, may talk with as little reason as he liveth.

S. But how could I be any longer in doubt, when you constrained him, in the conclusion, to yield you all the cause?

P. And what course did you resolve upon, and take?

S. Alas! sir, my own naughty heart did hinder me much more than his objections did. I went home, convinced that your words were true, and that I must become a [b] new creature, or be undone. And I perused the baptismal covenant which you wrote down, and the articles of the creed, the Lord's prayer, and the commandments. I studied the meaning of them, with that exposition which you gave me. My ignorance so darkened my mind, that all seemed strange and new to me, though I used to rote them over in the church from day to day. And being very unskilful in such matters myself, I went oft to my neighbour, Eusebius, as you advised me; and, I thank him, he gladly helped me to understand the words and things which were too hard for me. But when I had done all this, my worldly business took up my thoughts so, and the cares of my family were so much at my heart, and my old companions so often tempted me, and my flesh was so loth to let go all my sinful pleasures, and the matters of religion were so strange to me, that I delayed my resolution, and continued still purposing that I would shortly turn; but while I was purposing, and delaying, the fever took me. And having seen the death of Sir Elymas, and of Malchus, and then received the sentence of death in myself, God, by his terrors, did awaken me out of my delays.

P. Oh what an unreasonable thing is it to delay, when you are once convinced! What! delay to come out of the bondage of the devil; the guilt of sin; the flames of Sodom; the wrath of God! If death take you in an unconverted state, you are lost for ever! What, if you had died formerly in your sin? What, if you die this night? What assurance have you to live an hour? Alas! how brittle and corruptible a thing is the body of a man! And by what a wonder of providence do we live! Is sin so

[a] Eccl. vii. 2—6.

[b] 2 Cor. v. 17.

good? Is the state of a sinner so safe, or comfortable, that any should be loth to leave it? Is God, and Christ, and heaven, so bad, that any should delay, and be loth to be godly? Can you be happy too soon; or too soon be a child of God; or too soon get out of the danger of damnation? Is God hateful? Is sin and misery lovely, that you are so loth to change? If sin be best, keep it still. If God and heaven be worst, never think of turning to him. But if best, do you not presently desire the best? Must Christ, and his Holy Spirit, wait on you, while you take the other cup; and stay your leisure, while you are destroying yourself? How know you, but the Spirit of God may [c] forsake you, and leave you to your own will, and lust, and counsel; and say, Be hardened, and be filthy still. What a forlorn, miserable creature would you be! Do you not know that every sin, and every [d] delay, and every resistance of the Spirit, doth tend to the greater hardening of your heart, and making your conversion less hopeful, and more hard? Do you hope for pardon and mercy from God, or do you not? If not, desperation would begin your hell: if you do, is it ingenuous to desire to commit more of that sin, which you mean to repent that ever you committed, and to beg for pardon of from God? Dare you say, in your heart, Lord, I have abused thee, and thy Son, and Spirit, and mercy, long; I will abuse thee yet a little longer, and then I will repent, and ask forgiveness? Do you love to spit a little longer in the face of that Saviour, and that mercy, which you must fly to, and trust to, at the last? Do you not purpose to love him, and honour him, afterward, and for ever; and yet would you a little longer despise and injure him? would you gratify and please the devil a little longer; and root and strengthen sin a little more, before you pull it up; and kindle a greater flame in your house, before you quench it? Must you needs give yourself a few more stabs before you go to the physician? Is your life too long; and hath God given you too much time, that you are desirous to lose a little more? Are you afraid of too easy an assurance of forgiveness, that you would make it harder, and would invite despair, by sinning wilfully against knowledge and conviction? What will you delay for? Do you think ever to find the market fall, and Christ come down to lower terms; and change his law and gospel, to excuse you for not changing your heart and life? Do you ever look to find conversion an easier work than now? Do you know how much more you have to do, when you are converted; what knowledge, faith, hope, assurance, and patience, and comfort, more to get; how many temptations to overcome, and how many duties to perform; and what a work it is to prepare for immortality? And are you afraid of having too much time, and beginning so great a work too soon? Believe it, Satan doth not loiter; time stands not still; sun, and moon, and all the creatures, delay not to afford you all their service. Delay is a denial: God needs not you, but you need him. You would not have him delay to help you, in the time of your pain and great extremity. Patience will not be abused for ever. Behold, this is the [e] accepted time! Behold, this is the [f] day of salvation! We, that are Christ's servants, are apt to be weary of calling and warning you in vain ourselves; and, usually, when the preacher hath done, God hath done his invitation; because he worketh by his appointed means. Oh that you knew what others are enjoying, and what you are losing, all the time that you delay, and on how slippery ground you stand; and what after-sorrows you are preparing for yourself?

S. Sir, I thank you for your awakening, convincing reasons. But I was telling you, how God hath already, I hope, resolved me against any longer delay. When I thought I must presently die, all my sins, and all your counsels, came into my mind; and the fear of God's displeasure did overwhelm me. I thought I had but a few days to be out of hell; and, oh what would I not have given for assurance of pardon by Jesus Christ; and for a little more time of preparation in the world, before my soul did enter upon eternity! Oh, I never saw the face of sin, the truth of God's threatenings, the need of a Saviour, the preciousness of time, the madness of delaying, thoroughly, until then! And now, sir, the great mercy of God having restored me, I come presently to you, to profess my resolution, and to take your further good advice.

P. You see that God is merciful to us, when we think that he is destroying us.[g] Afflictions are not the least of God's mercies, which our dull and hardened hearts make necessary: such fools we are, that we will not understand without the rod. My advice is, that you read over here, again, the doctrine of christianity, which I gave you in our second day's conference; and the covenant of baptism, which I wrote you the third day; and let me see whether you understand and believe it, and consent thereto. [Here Saul readeth it over.]

S. You would have me understand what I do. I desire you, here, to answer me these few doubts, that I may clearlier proceed, and make my covenant with God in [h] judgment.

Question I. What must I trust to for the pardon of my sin; and which way, and on what terms, may I be sure of it?

P. The prime cause is God's mercy: this mercy hath given Jesus Christ to be our Redeemer. Christ hath, by perfect holiness and obedience, and by becoming a sacrifice to God for our sins, deserved and purchased our pardon and salvation. So that you must trust to the sacrifice and meritorious righteousness of Christ alone, as the purchasing, meritorious cause of your forgiveness, and of your reconciliation, justification, sanctification, and salvation. But the way that God, our Father and Redeemer, doth take to give us a right unto these blessings, is by making with man a law and [i] covenant of grace. By this law he commandeth us to become christians; that is, to believe in God the Father, the Son, and the Holy Ghost; and to give up ourselves to him in the covenant of baptism, repenting of sin; and thus turning to God by Jesus Christ. To all that do this, he giveth right to [k] Christ himself, first as their Head and Saviour, and with him right to pardon, to the Spirit, and salvation: so that God is the giver of Christ to redeem us. Christ is our Redeemer, and the Meriter of our life: the new law, or covenant, is the instrumental donation of life; like an act of oblivion. Your own covenanting, or giving up yourself to God in Christ, which is by a repenting, practical [l] faith, or (which is all one) your accepting the gift of the covenant as it is offered, according to its nature, is that condition, or duty, on your part, upon which the covenant giveth you right. So that God's covenant, gift, or grant, is your title, or the foundation of your right, (as Christ is the Meriter and Maker of the covenant,) and your practical faith is the condition on your part. And to every one of

[c] Psal. lxxxi. 11, 12. [d] Psal. cxix. 60.
[e] 2 Cor. vi. 2. [f] Heb. iii. 7, 13, 15; iv. 7.
[g] Psal. cxix. 61, 71, 75; 1 Thess. i. 6.
[h] Jer. iv. 2; Hos. ii. 19.

[i] Heb. ix. 15—17; vii. 22; Matt. xxviii. 19; xxvi. 28; 2 Cor. iii. 6; Mark xvi. 16; John iii. 16.
[k] 1 John v. 9—12.
[l] John i. 10—12.

these, to [m] God's mercies, to Christ's sacrifice, merits, and intercessions, to the covenant, or gift of God, and to your own sincere faith, consent, and acceptance, you must trust for its own proper part. And you must understand what the part of each one is, and not trust to any one of these for the other's part. The mercy of God as the fountain; the blood and righteousness of Christ as the merit and purchase; the covenant of Christ, or donation, as the instrument and title; and your faith and consent as the condition of your title: as thankful acceptance usually is, of all free gifts.

And then the gift itself, or benefit given, is Christ and life, 1 John v. 11, 12. By life I mean, 1. Pardon. 2. The Spirit. 3. Right to glory, or justification, sanctification, adoption, and future glory. I have repeated things that I might make them as plain to you as I can.

S. *Quest.* II. Are all my sins pardonable whatsoever? I have been a greater sinner than you know of. I must here confess to you in secret what I did not before confess: I minded not my soul; I prayed not once in a week; I have been in the ale-house when I should have been at church; I have been drunken more than once or twice. When I was a servant, I robbed my master; I sold for more than I gave him, and I bought for less than I told him I paid. I was oft guilty of immodest carriage with women, and, to confess my shame, I was guilty of actual fornication. I made little conscience of a lie: alas! my sins have been so many and so great, that I can hardly think that God will pardon them!

P. The covenant of grace [n] forgiveth all sins without exception, which consist with the performance of the condition of pardon after them; that is, all sins are pardoned to the penitent believer; but to the impenitent unbeliever no sin is pardoned (except conditionally); and final impenitence and unbelief are pardoned to none. So that a true christian is not to doubt of the pardon of any of his former sins, any further than he doubteth of his faith and christianity.

S. *Quest.* III. But I shall sin again, in some degree: how then must I have pardon of my sins hereafter? I have heard that baptism washeth away all sin: but it is long since I was baptized; and I am yet imperfect.

P. Baptism is said to wash away sin, because that God's covenant, celebrated in baptism, giveth pardon of all sin through the blood of Christ, to all that truly receive it, and consent, on their part, to the covenant. Now this covenant on God's part is a standing law and pardoning act; and it pardoneth all sin to our death to them that still repent and believe. But it is said to pardon all at baptism, because then there it is supposed that we have no more to be pardoned. But if any be ungodly after baptism, God's law or covenant pardoneth all that it findeth us guilty of, whenever we truly turn to God, by faith and repentance. But afterward it pardoneth daily our daily sins of infirmity only; and to the lapsed their extraordinary falls upon their extraordinary repentance: because the faithful [o] have no other afterward to be forgiven. For being sanctified, they no more live an ungodly, sensual, worldly life. So that you must hereafter, for your particular sins, have a particular repentance, and recourse to Christ.

[m] Rom. iv. 16, 22, 24, 25.
[n] Acts v. 31; xiii. 38, 39; xxvi. 18; Jam. v. 15; Eph. i. 7; Col. i. 14; Matt. xii. 31, 32; Luke vii. 47.
[o] 1 John i. 6—9; Rom. vi. 1—3, 16, &c.; 1 John iii. 9.
[p] John xv. 5.
[q] Rom. viii. 4, 9.

S. *Quest.* IV. How must I do for grace and strength to keep my covenant when I have made it?

P. [p] Of yourself you can do nothing that is good. Your heart is so corrupted with sin, till it be sanctified, that you will not be willing; and your mind so blind that you will not well understand your duty nor your interest; and your soul so dead and impotent, that you will have no life or strength to practise what you know. But if the [q] Spirit of Christ do once give you faith, and repentance, and consent, by this you have right to him as an indwelling principle; and you are then entered into covenant relation to the Holy Ghost: and that which he will do in you is to sanctify your three faculties. 1. Your vital power, with spiritual [r] life, strength, and activity. 2. Your understanding, with spiritual light, that is, knowledge and faith. 3. Your will, with holy love and willingness. And when he hath planted these in you, he will be ready still to preserve, excite, actuate, and increase them. So that it is the Holy Ghost that must be your life, light, and love. But you must know how to obey his motions, and not resist him.

S. *Quest.* V. What must I do to get, keep, and obey the Spirit, that I lose it not, and miss not of these benefits?

P. You must know that God hath first possessed Christ's human glorified nature with the Spirit, that he may have it as the head, and from him it is to come to us as his members. Therefore I said that the whole gift of the covenant is [s] Christ and life. Now Christ giveth us his Spirit, both as a Saviour, freely, and as a Ruler, according to his law of grace, as to the order of conveyance. Therefore, as the first gift of the indwelling Spirit is on condition of your faith, so the continuance of it is on condition of your continuing in the faith. (For all that you neither had faith at first, nor in continuance, without the antecedent work of the Spirit.) And the increase and actual helps and comfort of the Spirit are given you on condition of your dependence on Christ your Head for the daily communication of it.

Therefore you must remember, 1. That the giving or denying the helps of the Spirit to our souls, are the greatest rewards and punishments which Christ, as our King, doth exercise and administer on us in this world. And therefore look much at this in yourself, whether God's Spirit help you or forsake you.

2. That your means is to wait on Christ in the daily exercise of faith, and use of all his instituted ordinances, and to attend his Spirit, and not resist it.

S. But I am afraid I have sinned against the Holy Ghost, the unpardonable sin; for I have joined with profane persons in deriding the Spirit. Especially when I heard many young students, and ministers themselves, do the same, it imboldened me to imitate them. I have mocked at them that did but talk of the Spirit, or speak of the necessity of the Spirit: I have said, These be the spiritual men, the holy brethren, that pray by the Spirit, and preach by the Spirit, and whine by the Spirit, and cheat, and lie, and dissemble by the Spirit. These are the gifted brethren! with many such foolish scorns. And is not this the sin against the Holy Ghost?

P. The sin was very great, and the case of those that encouraged you, fearful; and no doubt but it was a sin against the Holy Ghost. But it is not

[r] Eph. ii. 1—3, 5, 11; i. 18, 19; Acts xxvi. 18; Rom. v 3—6, 10; 2 Tim. i. 7.
[s] John vi. 51, 52, &c.; lvii. 58; xiv. 19; Gal. ii. 20; iii. 3, 14; iv. 6; v. 17, 21—23; 1 Thess. v. 19; Heb. x. 29; Neh. ix. 20; Prov. i. 23; Luke xi. 13; Eph. iv. 30; Psal. li. 11; Col. i. 23.

every sin against the Holy Spirit which is unpardonable; but only the blasphemy of infidels described Matt. xii.; which is, that when they cannot deny the miracles of Christ, they will rather hold and maintain that he[t] wrought them by the power of the devil, than they will believe in him. So that it is none but infidels, and but few of them, that have this blasphemy of the Holy Ghost.

S. *Quest.* VI. How shall I do to know the operations and motions of the Spirit from delusions, and how shall I know whether I have the Spirit or not?

P. I. The Spirit is from God and our Saviour, and leadeth to them. I told you its operations are, 1.[u] Holy life, or vivacity toward God. 2. Holy light, to know and believe God. 3. Holy love, to love God, and his government, and children. If you have these, you have God's Spirit; for it is nothing else. These are God's restored image on the soul, and the new divine nature of his regenerate, adopted children.

II. The motions of the Spirit are, 1. Always fitted to God and holiness, as the end. 2. And always actuate the three foresaid habits, of holy life, light, and love. 3. And they are always agreeable to the holy Scriptures, and by them must be tried.

S. What is the reason of that.

1. Because God giveth the same Spirit indeed,[x] but not in the same measure to all. Now, to the apostles and evangelists he gave it in the greatest extraordinary degree, purposely to plant his churches, and to indite an infallible Scripture, the records of that gospel, and to confirm it by miracles, and leave it to the world, as the rule of our faith and life; so that as a man first engraveth a seal, and then sets it on the wax, so the Holy Ghost first inspired the apostles to write us the infallible word and rule; and then he is given to all others, in a smaller degree, only[y] to help us to understand, believe, and obey that word. Therefore the lower operations of the Spirit in us are to be tried by the higher operations in the apostles recorded.

S. *Quest.* VII. What then is the law and rule that I must live by, according to the covenant that I make?

P. 1. God is the universal King, and Christ, our Redeemer, as man, his Administrator. God's law is written, as I told you, 1. In nature. 2. In Scripture, where also the law of nature is contained, in the main. This is God's law which you must live by.

2. But God hath officers under him in the world.[z] 1. Parents and masters in families. 2. Pastors in the churches. 3. Kings in kingdoms. These are to promote the execution of God's laws; and, to that end, to make subordinate laws or commands of their own, about things subordinate, undetermined in God's universal law, and left to their determination. Like as are the by-laws of corporations under the laws of the king: and all these, under God, must, in their places, be obeyed.

S. *Quest.* VIII. What church must I join myself unto?

P. You were baptized only into Christ's universal church; and to be a christian and to be a member of that church is all one.[a] That church is nothing but, spiritually, all heart covenanters, or believers, and, visibly, all baptized, visible covenanters, or professors, united to, or with, Christ the Head: and no pope or general council is the head of it, supreme or official.

But you must join with that part of this church where you live, and God giveth you opportunity to worship him and learn his will, with the best advantage to your own soul, not violating the common good, and peace. But you must join actually with none that will not receive you unless you sin.

S. *Quest.* IX. What are the institutions or means which I must use, in attendance on Christ and his Spirit?

P. 1. The reading and[b] hearing of God's word, and its explication and application by your teachers.

2. Prayer, thanksgiving, praises to God, and the Lord's supper, in communion with his church.

3. Holy discipline, in submission to your guides, in obedience, penitent confessing sins when necessary, and the like; if you live where such discipline is exercised.

S. *Quest.* X. What must I do with my calling, and labour, and estate in the world: must I forsake it or not?

P. Adam was to labour in innocency. Six days must you labour and do all that you have to do, Exod. xx. He that will not labour,[c] if able, is unworthy to eat. Idleness was one of Sodom's sins; religion must be no pretence for slothfulness. You must not love the world as your felicity,[d] or for itself, or for your fleshly lust; but you must make use of the world in the service of your Creator, yea, and love it as a sanctified means of your salvation, and as a wilderness-way to your promised inheritance, as the mariner loveth not the sea for a dwelling, but as a passage to his desired port. Good husbandry is not unbeseeming a good christian. You must labour for your daily bread, as well as pray for it: yea, for the maintenance of your family, and that you may have things decent, and give to him that needeth, Rom. xii. 17; 2 Cor. viii. 21; Eph. iv. 28; 1 Tim. v. 8.

But this is the thing that you must principally remember, That God and the heavenly glory is your end,[e] which must still be desired for itself and before all; and the world, and all things in it, are but means to help you to that end; and only as they are such must be valued, loved, desired, and sought; and whenever they oppose God and your heavenly interest, must be forsaken, and used as we do hated things.[f]

And when common, worldly things thus further your obedience, and are devoted to God, and referred to his will and service, then they are sanctified to you,[g] which else will be but common, unclean, and your mortal enemy.

S. *Quest.* XI. What, if I am now uncertain whether my heart be sincere in this covenant which I make with God when I renounce all, and profess to prefer him before all? May I venture to covenant and profess that consent whose sincerity I am uncertain of? Will not this be a kind of lying unto God?

[t] Matt. xii.
[u] John iii. 5, 6; Col. iii. 10; 2 Tim. i. 7; 2 Cor. v. 17; Tit. iii. 3, 5; Gal. iv. 6.
[x] 1 Cor. xii. 11—13, &c.; Eph. iii. 3, 4, 7, 9, 11, 13, 15, 16; Matt. xxviii. 20.
[y] 2 Tim. iii. 16; John xvi. 13.
[z] Deut. xi. 19; Rom. xiii. 3—5; 1 Thess. v. 2, 13; Eph. vi. 1, &c.
[a] Eph. i. 22; iv. 3, 4, 15; 1 Cor. xii. 12, 13, 27—29; we never find in Scripture two churches in one city, Acts ii. 42; xiv. 23; xx. 7, 8.
[b] 2 Tim. iv. 1, 2; 1 Tim. iv. 13, 14; 1 Thess. v. 12, 13; Acts ii. throughout; 1 Cor. xi.; xiv.; Heb. xiii. 7, 17; James v. 16.
[c] 2 Thess. iii. 10.
[d] 1 John ii. 15, 16.
[e] Matt. vi. 19, 20, 33; John vi. 27; Col. iii. 3—5.
[f] Luke xiv. 26, 33; Tit. i. 15.
[g] Acts ii. 38; xxii. 16; John iii. 5, 6; Mark xvi. 16; Eph. iv. 5; Col. ii. 12; 1 Pet. iii. 21; Rom. vi. 3, 4; Gal. iii. 27.

P. If your heart be false, it will be lying; but if it be not, it will be no lying, though you are uncertain. The truth of your consent is one thing, and your certainty of it is another. That it be true is necessary to your salvation; but not that you be sure that it is true. But there is much difference between, 1. One that flattereth himself with conceits that he consenteth, when he doth not. Such an one sinneth in professing a lie. 2. And one that is but yet deliberating, and is unresolved what to choose and do. This person must not covenant till he feel the scales turn by a true resolution. 3. And one that truly consenteth and resolveth, but is afraid lest his deceitful heart is not sincere in it: this person must covenant in this uncertainty, because all that can be expected from us is, that we speak our own minds, according to the best acquaintance with them that we can get; otherwise we must forbear all thanksgiving for special mercies, and a great part of our worship of God, till we are certain of the sincerity of our own hearts, which too many are not.

S. But some think that baptism is not to enter us into this special covenant which presently pardoneth; but only to enter us into Christ's school, as our teacher, that by him we may learn how to be regenerate and sincere, that we may then be pardoned. If this would serve, I could easilier consent.

P. I may not stand at large to show you the falseness of that opinion. The best is, baptism hath these sixteen hundred years been kept unchanged by the church in one form; and the church never knew any baptism but, 1. Such as was joined with a present profession of present faith and repentance, and renunciation of the devil, the world, and the flesh, and a total devotedness to God in Christ. 2. Such as had the promise of present pardon of sin to all sincere receivers of baptism. 3. Such as stated the receiver in a visible membership to Christ, and right to glory; so that in charity we are bound to take, and love, and use such as sincere, till they show the contrary. 4. The church never baptized any whom they took not thereby to be made visible christians; and they took no man for a christian that took not Christ presently for his Saviour, Priest, and King, as well as for his Teacher, yea, and God for his God, and the Holy Spirit for his Sanctifier. 5. And so much as you talk of maketh a man but one of the catechised, prepared for christianity, whom the church never took for christians till they were baptized. 6. And the few that are of the opinion which you mention yet confess that you cannot be saved till you consent sincerely to the covenant of grace itself.

S. *Quest.* XII. What if it prove that my heart is not sincere? or what if I should fall away again hereafter?

P. I. If your heart be not[h] sincere in your consent to the covenant, you will remain unpardoned in your sin and misery, till it be sincere.

II. If you fall into a particular sin, I have told you how you must be restored, by renewed repentance for it, through faith in Christ. But as you love God and your soul, take heed of wilful sinning. But if (which God forbid) you should fall quite away from Christ, renouncing him, as if you believed him not to be the Messiah; I say, if you thus totally and settledly renounce Christ by unbelief, I cannot see but you must either be guilty of the blasphemy of the Holy Ghost, or come so near it as that, according to Heb. vi. 6—8, your recovery will be utterly improbable.

S. I am much afraid lest, when temptation cometh, I should turn again to my former folly (though God forbid I should renounce my Saviour). I am so entangled in ill company, and in a custom of sinning, and have so bad a nature, and so many temptations and worldly snares, that though I am now resolved, I am afraid lest I should yield, and lose my resolutions.

P. It becometh you to[i] fear it, that so you may prevent it. But this fear should not hinder you from resolving and consenting. For, 1. You know that sin is odious, and its pleasures are poison and deceit; and, therefore, that this world affordeth nothing to stand in competition with God and your salvation. If you will take this world for your part, you are undone; if you will not,[k] resolve accordingly. But dream not of joining sin and holiness, or the worldly and the heavenly felicity into one, and dividing your heart and service between[l] God and mammon; for that is the damning self-deceit of hypocrites.

2. You shall not only have that which is a hundred-fold better than all that you forsake; but you shall have the world itself, refined and sanctified to your greater good. You would have it as your fleshly felicity: God would have you renounce it in that sense; but he will give it you as your daily provision for his service, and as a blessed means to further your salvation, that you may see God in every creature, and thank him for it, and serve him by it. And one mercy thus sanctified is worth a thousand abused: ten pounds, or ten shillings, a year, used for God to further your salvation, is better than lordships and kingdoms, used to serve the flesh and the devil, and to prepare men for damnation. Read Jam. v.

3. When you are once entered well into the service of God, you will find the light which will shame all temptations, and that sweet experience of greater pleasures, which will make you loathe what formerly you loved. The comforts of faith, and hope, and love, will make you spit out the filthy pleasures of the flesh.

4. And you will have the direction, encouragement, and example of those that fear God; and the help of all his holy ordinances.

5. And, which is more, you will be planted into Christ, and receive the communications of his Spirit, and his strength will be magnified in your weakness. You are not to trust in your own strength, but in the love of God, the grace of Christ, and the communion and operation of the Holy Ghost.

6. And your resolution is a matter of absolute necessity: you must resolve, or perish for ever; you must consent, or be condemned as a rejecter of salvation. God sets before you Christ, and holiness, and heaven; the devil sets before you the[m] pleasures of sin for a moment, and everlasting damnation in the end. Take which you will; for one you must have. There is no middle way; nor no reconciling both together.

The truth is, it is that shameful folly which you must lament, that in so great, so necessary, so plain a case, you should be unresolved to this day! That a man in his wits should live twenty years so, as if he had been resolved to be damned; and after that, stay so long delaying before he can resolve, whether he were best be saved or no! What! is it yet a hard question to you whether God or the devil be your owner, and the better friend and master; and whether heaven or hell be the better dwelling; and whether sin or holiness be the better life; and whether you should consent that Christ and his Spirit save you from your sins or not? Have you

[h] Psal. xxxii. 1—3. [i] Heb. iv. 1. [k] Matt. vi. 24. [l] Matt. xiii. 46. [m] Heb. xi. 25, 26, &c.

so long taken on you to be a christian; and are you yet unresolved, whether it be best be a christian indeed, or not? Certainly you have had leisure enough, and reasons enough set before you, to have[n] resolved you long ago. Till you firmly resolve, you are not a christian and convert indeed. If you did well know what a case you stand in till you are resolved, and what a scorn and indignity you put upon your God, and Saviour, and heaven, to make a question of it, whether the filth of sin, and the dreaming profits and pleasures of this world, be not better than they, and whether your Redeemer, after all his love, should be preferred before a fleshly lust, you would fear and blush to make such a question any more.

S. But I have been used so long to a looser life, that I am afraid I shall be weary of a strict, religious, godly course, and shall never be able to hold out.

P. I tell you again, that if you think of the life that you must turn to, as a tedious, melancholy, grievous state, you know it not; and are not well informed what it is you have to do. It is the only honourable, the only profitable, the only safe, and the only pleasant life in the world, as to manly pleasure.

I will give you but a taste of it in some particulars.

1. You must, indeed,[o] repent of sin with shame and godly sorrow, and loathing of yourself; but it is no further than fitteth you for the comfort of pardoning and healing grace.

2. You must believe all the comfortable promises of the gospel; all the love that Christ hath manifested; all the wonderful history of his life, and death, and resurrection, and ascension, and heavenly glory; the certainty of his word and gracious covenant.

3. You must believe the wonderful[p] love of the Father, in giving us his Son, and reconciling us to himself, and adopting us as his sons, and undertaking to secure us as his peculiar treasure, and giving us his Holy Spirit.

4. You must live under the helps and consolations of the Holy Ghost, still drawing you to God, and making you more holy, and helping your infirmities against your sins.

5. You must live in the hopes and desires of everlasting glory, verily to see Christ glorified, with all the saints and blessed angels, and to see the glory of God, and with the perfected soul and body, perfectly to feel his love, and perfectly to love and praise him to eternity.

6. In all your sickness, wants, persecutions, and[q] death itself, you have all these comforts, and this hope of glory, to be a constant cordial at your heart; and when others fear death for fear of hell, you must welcome it as the door to endless life.

7. You must live in the church, in the communion of saints, where all God's ordinances must be your helps for the daily exercise of all these graces and delights. And your chiefest exercises of piety must be the hearing these glad tidings in the gospel opened to you; begging for more grace; joyful thanksgiving for all these mercies; singing forth, and speaking the praises of Jehovah; and, with joy and thankfulness, feasting upon Christ's flesh, and blood, and Spirit in the sacrament thereof, and there, in the renewing of this your covenant, receiving a renewed, sealed pardon and new degrees of life and strength.

Tell me now, what trouble is in all this, that a man should be afraid or weary of it? Unless you take it for a trouble to be safe and happy; to have the greatest mercies, the greatest hopes, and to live in the love of your dearest friend, and in the foretastes of everlasting joys. In a word, "Godliness is profitable to all things, having the promise of the life that now is, and of that which is to come," 1 Tim. iv. 7.

S. You tell me of another kind of godliness than I thought of. And I was the more afraid it had been a melancholy, tedious life, because I saw many that professed it live so.

P. I told you the reasons of that before, which I must not repeat. And, moreover, to young beginners, that come new out of another kind of life, and whose souls are not by grace yet suited to the work, it may seem strange and troublesome. And the truth is, many converts, in the beginning, are moved at a sermon, and stifle their own convictions, and open not their case to their teachers, or else fall not into the hand of a judicious guide, who will clearly open to them the true nature of conversion; and so they set on they know not well what; which maketh me lay all these matters so plainly and distinctly before you; because it will be a wonderful prevention of your troubles and dangers after, if you do but set out well instructed in the beginning.

But the worst and common cause of all is, that people are so exceeding ignorant and dull, (together with their undisposedness,) that one must be whole months, if not years, before we can make them understand these few, plain things which here I have opened to you. But yet we must take up with a dark and general understanding, rather than delay too long, or be too strict with them.

S. I thank God for your counsel, and his grace; I am resolved, and ready to subscribe my resolution to be the Lord's, entirely upon his covenant terms.

P. I will go home with you to your house, and I will try whether you and I can instruct all your family that need it, and bring them to the same resolution. For as it is your duty to endeavour it, so God useth to bless his believing servants, with the conversion of their household with them; as the case of the jailer, and Lydia, (Acts xvi.) Zaccheus, Stephanus, and others, show us. You shall therefore delay your open profession of your resolved conversion till you do it in the presence of them all. And it will be a great mercy to you, if God give you but a family willing to go along with you in the way to heaven; and daily to worship the same God and obey him. Then your house will be part of the family of God, and under his continual blessing and protection. [Here Paul goeth home with Saul, and openeth such things to his family as he did to him, and convinceth them: and they promise him to take time, as Saul did, to learn the true knowledge of the covenant of grace, that so they may consent to it themselves: and Saul before them all lamenteth his sinful life, and openly professeth his consent to the covenant, and they pray together for his confirmation.]

S. I bless the Lord for this day of grace. What would you yet advise me do?

P. One thing more, to God's glory and your comfort; that you will the next Lord's day communicate with the church in the sacrament of the Lord's supper, which is appointed to be the renewal of the baptismal covenant before the church; where God will set his seal to your pardon, and to his covenant part.

But withal, seeing you have been a known offender,

n Josh. xxiv. 15; 1 Cor. xv. 58.
o Luke xiii. 3, 5; xv., throughout; 2 Cor. xi.
p John iii. 16; 1 John iii. 1

q 1 Cor. xv. 55, &c; 1 Thess. iv. 13, 15—18; 1 Tim. v. 8; Phil. i. 21, 23; 2 Cor. v. 1, 3, 5—9; iv. 16—18.

that you will freely, before the congregation, confess your sinful life, and profess your repentance, and resolution, for a new and holy course; and crave their prayers to God for your pardon and strength, and their loving reception of you, and give God the glory, and warn others to take heed of sinning against God and their baptismal vows.

S. This is sweet and bitter; I shall be glad to be admitted to the sacrament of communion; but I shall be ashamed to make so public a confession.

P. It is a shame to sin, but it is an honour to confess it and repent. I persuade you not to confess your secret sins before the church; but only those which are commonly known, and therefore are your shame already: and how will that shame be removed, till men have notice of your repentance? And you must not be ashamed of your duty, if you would not have Christ be ashamed of you.

S. But where doth God require such confession?

P. 1. Those that were baptized by John, confessed their sins, Matt. iii. 6; Mark i. 5; Acts ii. 37. The Jews confessed their killing of Christ, by being pricked at the heart, and crying out for help when it was charged on them, Acts xix. 18. The converts confessed their sinful deeds, and publicly testified it to their cost, Jam. v. 16. "Confess your faults one to another," Prov. xxviii. 13. "Whoso confesseth, and forsaketh them, shall have mercy." See further Lev. v. 5; xvi. 21; xxvi. 40; Numb. v. 7; Neh. i. 6; 1 John i. 9; Ezra x. 11; Neh. ix. 2, 3; Josh. vii. 19; 2 Chron. xxx. 22.

2. You were publicly baptized, and you have openly sinned against that covenant; therefore, if you will be openly taken for a penitent into church communion, you must openly profess repentance. Unless you would have us take all impenitent persons to communion.

3. You are obliged to be more tender of[r] God's honour than of your own; and therefore to honour him publicly, as you have publicly dishonoured him, and stick at nothing that tendeth to his glory, as this will do.

4. You are bound to cast the greatest shame that you can on sin; it is the shameful thing that hath deceived and defiled you: if you have set it up above God, and now refuse to cast it down, by open shame, how do you repent of it?

5. You owe all possible help to others, to save them from the sin which hath deceived you. You have encouraged men to sin, and, for aught you know, some of them may be in hell for ever, for that which you have drawn them to; and should you not do your best now to save the rest, and to undo the hurt that you have done? See, therefore, that you tell them, with deep repentance, how sin deceived you, and warn them, and beseech them to take warning by you, and to repent with you, as they sinned with you. Your companions that are not there, may hear of this and be convinced.

6. You owe this to the church and[s] godly christians, that they may rejoice in your conversion, and may see that you are indeed a due object of their special love.

7. You owe this to yourself, 1. That you may remove your public shame, and have the comfort of christians' special love: as God cannot delight in an impenitent sinner, no more should his servants. 2. That your conscience may have the comfort that your repentance is sincere; which it will justly be still doubting of, if you cannot repent at as dear a rate as open confession. How will you forsake all, and die for Christ, if you cannot so far deny your pride as to confess your sin?

8. Lastly, you owe this to me, that the church may not take me for a polluter of its communion by admitting the impenitent thereto.

S. You have said more than ever I heard of this, and it fully satisfies me. But would you have all that are converted and repent do thus?

P. Some have lived with some kind of religiousness from their childhood, though with many ordinary sins, and have, by undiscerned degrees, grown up unto true godliness. These are uncertain when they first had special grace, and were not open scandalous violators of their baptismal vow; and, therefore, I can lay no such injunction on them.

But I would have all do thus, that have thus broken that vow, and are converted afterward to true repentance, for all the reasons which I now mentioned: and the universal church hath ever been for such public repentance in such a case; yea, and for particular gross lapses afterward. And the papists to this day call it the sacrament of penance, though they corrupt it by auricular confession, when it should be open; and by many unwarrantable adjuncts and formalities.

S. What would you have me do after that?

P. I will record your name in the church book among the church communicants, and we will all pray for your confirmation and perseverance; and you must live as a member of the holy catholic church of Christ, in the communion of saints, and return no more to your ungodly, sinful life: and come to me again, and I shall give you further counsel. In the mean time, you may do as the converted eunuch did, (the lord treasurer of the queen of Ethiopia, Acts viii. 39,) even go on your way rejoicing in this, that you are united to Christ, and are justified from all your former sins, and are sincerely entered into the covenant and family of God, and are made a[t] fellow-citizen with the saints, and an heir of certain, endless glory.

THE

FIFTH DAY'S CONFERENCE.

DIRECTIONS TO THE CONVERTED AGAINST TEMPTATION.

SPEAKERS.—Paul, a Teacher; and Saul, a Learner.

PAUL. Welcome, neighbour. How go matters with your soul?

SAUL. I thank God and my Redeemer, and you, his minister, since I publicly repented, renounced my sin, and gave up myself to my God, and Saviour, and Sanctifier. I find myself as in a new world. My[u] hopes revive, and I have had already more comfort in believing, and in seeking God, than ever I had in my life of sin. I am grieved and ashamed that I stood off so long, and have spent so much of my life in wickedness, and in wronging God, who gave me life. I am ashamed that ever such trifles and fooleries possessed my heart, and kept me so long from a holy life, and that I delayed after I was convinced. I could wish, from my very heart, that I had spent all that time of my life in beggary, slavery, or a gaol,

[r] Paul frequently confesseth his sinful life, Acts xxii.; xxvi.; Tit. iii. 3—5; 1 Tim. i. 13—15; Luke xxii. 32.

[s] Jam. v. 15, &c.

[t] Eph. ii. 12; Rom. viii. 16—18, 30, 32.

[u] Rom. v. 1—6, 10.

which I have spent in a fleshly, sinful course. Oh had I not now a merciful God, a sufficient Saviour, a pardoning covenant of grace, and a comforting Sanctifier, which way should I look, or what should I do? It amazeth me to think what a dangerous state I so long lived in. Oh what if God had cut off my life, and taken away my unsanctified soul, what would have become of me for ever! Oh that I had sooner turned to my God, and sooner cast away my sins, and sooner tried a holy life! But my soul doth magnify the Lord, and my spirit doth rejoice in God my Saviour, that he hath pitied a self-destroying sinner, and at last his mercy hath [b] abounded where my sin did abound.

P. It is but little of his goodness which as yet you have tasted of, in comparison of what you must find at last. But that you may yet make sure work, I shall spend this day's conference in acquainting you what temptations you have yet to overcome, and what dangers to escape, for yet you have but begun your race and warfare.

S. Your counsel hath hitherto been so good, that I shall gladly hear the rest.

P. I. The first temptation that you are like to meet with, is a seeming [c] difficulty and puzzling darkness in all or many of the doctrines and practices of godliness. You will think strange of many things that are taught you, and you will be stalled at the difficulties of understanding and believing, of meditating and praying, of watching against sin, and of doing your duty. And by reason of this difficulty, Satan would make God's service seem wearisome, uncomfortable, and grievous to you, and so turn back your love from God.

And all this will be, because you are yet but as a stranger to it; like a scholar that entereth upon books and sciences, which he never meddled with before; or like an apprentice that newly learneth his trade; or like a traveller in a strange way and country. To an ignorant and unexperienced person, that never meddled with such things before, but hath been used to a contrary course of life, all things will seem strange and difficult at first.

S. What course must I take to escape this temptation?

P. 1. When you meet with any difficulty, you must still remember that it is your own dark mind, or backward heart, that is the cause, and never suspect God's word or ways, no more than a sick man will blame the meat, instead of his stomach, if he loathe a feast. But take occasion to renew your repentance, and think, All this is long of myself, who spent my youth in sin and folly, which I should have spent in hearing the word of God, and practising a godly life. What need have I now to double my labour to overcome all this!

2. Resolve to wait patiently on God in the use of all his means, and teaching, time, and use, and grace will make all more plain, and easy, and delightful to you. Do not expect that it should come all on a sudden, without time, and diligence, and patience.

3. Keep still as a humble disciple of Christ, in a learning mind and way, and turn not, in self-conceitedness, to cavil against what you do not understand. This is the chief thing in which conversion maketh us like little children, Matt. xviii. 3. Children are conscious of their ignorance, and are teachable, and set not their wits against their teachers, till they grow towards twenty years of age, and then they grow wise in their own conceits, and begin to think that their tutors are mistaken, and to set their wits against the truth which they should receive. But of this more anon.

[b] Rom. v. 12, 13, to the end.
[c] John vi. 60; Heb. v. 11, 12; 2 Pet. iii. 16.

II. The second temptation will be, upon these difficulties and your mistakes in religion, to grow so perplexed as to be overwhelmed with doubts and fears, and so to turn melancholy, and ready to despair.

The devil will strive to lose you, and bewilder you in some mistakes, or to make you think that your conversion was not true, because you had no more brokenness of heart for sin, or because you know not just the time when you were converted. Or he will make you think that all religion lieth in striving to weep and break your heart more; or that you have no grace, because you have not such a lively sense of things invisible, as you have of the things that are seen. Or he will tell you that now you must not think nor talk of the world, but all your thoughts and talk must be of God, and his word and holy things, and that all other is idle thoughts and talk; and that you must tie yourself to longer tasks of meditation and prayer than you have time and strength to carry on.

S. Sir, you make me admire to hear you. Can such motions of holiness come from the devil. If I did not know you, I should suspect some carnal malignity against holiness in your speeches.

P. Did not the devil plead Scripture with Christ in his temptations? Matt. iv. And doth he not [d] transform himself into an angel of light to deceive? When he cannot keep you in security and profaneness, he will put on a visor of godliness: and whenever the devil will seem religious and righteous, he will be religious and righteous over-much.

S. What getteth he by this? Would he make us more religious?

P. You little know what he hopeth to get by it. Overdoing is undoing all; he would destroy all your religion by it. If you run your horse till you tire him or break his wind, is not that the way to lose your journey? Nothing over-violent is durable. If a scholar study so hard as to crack his brains, he will never be a good scholar, or wise man, till he is cured. Our souls here are united to our bodies, and must go on that pace that the body can endure. If Satan can tempt you into longer and deeper musing (especially on the sadder objects in religion) than your body and brain can bear, you will grow melancholy before you are aware, and then you little know how ill a guest you have entertained.

For when once you are melancholy, you will be disabled then from secret prayer and from meditating at all: it will but confound you; you cannot bear it: and so by overdoing, you will come to do nothing of that sort of duty. And you will then have none but either fanatic whimsies, and visions, and prophesyings, or else (more usually) sad despairing thoughts in your mind: all that you hear, and read, and see, you will think maketh against you; you will believe nothing that soundeth comfortably to you; you can think none but black and hideous thoughts. The devil will tell you a hundred times over, that you are a hypocrite and unsanctified, and all that ever you did was in hypocrisy, and that none of your sins are yet forgiven; and that you shall as sure be in hell as if you were there already; that God is your enemy; that Christ is no Saviour for you; that you have sinned against the Holy Ghost, or that the day of grace is past; that the Spirit is departed, and God hath forsaken you; that it is now too late, too late to repent and find mercy; and that you are undone for ever. These black thoughts will be like a beginning of hell to you.

And it is not yourself only that will be the sufferer by this; but many of the ignorant and wicked will,

[d] 2 Cor. xi. 14, 15.

by seeing you, be hardened into a love of security and sensuality, and will fly from religion as a frightful thing which doth not illuminate men, but make them mad, or cast them into desperation. And so Satan will use you as some papists have drawn the picture of a protestant like a devil, or an ass, to affright men from religion; or as we set up maukins to frighten birds from the corn; as if he had written on your back for all to read, See what you must come to, if you will be religious.

S. You describe to me so sad a case, as almost makes me melancholy to hear it, and it tempts me to be afraid of religion itself, if it tend to this: but what would you have me do to escape it?

P. Religion itself, as God commandeth it, tendeth not to this. It is a life of holy faith, and hope, and joy: but it is errors about religion that tend to it. And especially when any great cross or disappointment in the world becometh an advantage to the tempter to cast you into worldly discontents and cares, and trouble and perplexity of mind: this is the most usual beginner of melancholy; and then it turneth to religious trouble afterwards.

And I the rather tell you of it now, because you are capable, through God's mercy, of preventing it: but it is a disease which, when it seizeth on you, will disable you to think, or believe, or do any thing that much tendeth to your cure; words are usually in vain; it overcometh the freedom of the will.

The prevention is this: 1. Set not too much by any thing in the world, that so the losing of it may not be able to reach your heart. Take the world as nothing, and it can do nothing with you. Take it for dung, and the loss of it will not trouble you.

2. Keep true apprehensions of the nature of religion, that it lieth in faith, hope, and love;[e] in righteousness, peace, and joy in the Holy Ghost; in the forethoughts of everlasting glory; and in comforting yourself and one another, with remembering that you shall for ever be with the Lord, in thanksgiving to your bountiful God, and in his joyful praises: let these be your thoughts, your speeches, your exercise, publicly and secretly. Set yourself more to the daily exercise of divine praises and thanksgiving, to actuate love and joy, than to any other part of duty. Not that you have done repenting; but that these are the chief, the life, the top, the end of all the rest.

3. When you feel any scruples or troubles begin to seize upon you, open them presently to a judicious minister or friend, before they fasten and take rooting in you. Remember and observe these things.

III. A third temptation that will assault you will be, to be in continual doubt of your own sincerity; so that though you be not melancholy before, Satan would bring you to it, by a life of continual doubts and fears.

And here he hath very great advantage, because man's heart is so dark and deceitful, and because our grace is usually very little and weak; and a little is hardly discerned from none; and because that the greatest assurance of sincerity is a work that requireth much skill, great diligence, and clear helps.

S. I easily believe that this will be my case: I feel some beginnings of it already: but what would you advise me to do to prevent it?

P. I have written a small book on this point alone, called "The Right Method for Peace of Conscience," &c. to which I must refer you: but briefly now I say,

1. You must still keep by you in writing the baptismal covenant of grace, with the explication of it, which I gave you, and never mistake the nature of that covenant and of true religion: and on all occasions of doubting, renew your part, that is, your consent; and go no further for marks of godliness and true conversion, if you can truly say, that you still consent to that same covenant: for this is your faith and repentance, and your certain evidence of your right to the benefits of God's part. Find still your true consent, and never doubt of your sincerity.

2. But because he that consenteth to learn will learn, and he that[f] consenteth to obey will obey, your life must also testify the truth of your consent. Therefore, instead of over-tedious trying and fearing whether you truly consent and obey or not, set yourself heartily to your duty; study to please God, and to live fruitfully in good works; resolve more against those sins which make you question your sincerity; and the practice of a godly life, and the increase of your grace, will be a constant discernible evidence; and you will have the witness in yourself, that you are a son of God.

S. I thank you for this short and full direction. I pray go on to the next temptation.

P. IV. If you escape these sadder thoughts, Satan will tempt you to security, and tell you, that now you are converted, all is sure, and you never need to fear any more: those that have true grace can never lose it; and sins once pardoned, are never unpardoned again; and therefore now all your danger is past. And if he can thus take off all your fear and care, he will quickly take off your zeal and diligence.

S. Why; is not all my fear and danger past?

P. No; not as long as you are on earth: tormenting fear you must resist; but preventing[g] fear, and repenting fear, will be still your duty. You are but entered into the holy war. You have many a temptation yet to resist and conquer; temptations from Satan and from men, and from your flesh; temptations of prosperity and adversity. You have constant and various duties to perform, which require strength, and skill, and willingness. You have remaining corruptions yet to mortify, which will be striving to break out against and to undo you. You know not how many burdens you have to bear, where flesh, and heart, and friends may fail you. I tell you, all the rest of your life must be the practice of what you have promised in your covenant; a labour, a race, a warfare: and you must defend yourself with one hand, as it were, while you build with the other: and all the way to heaven must, step by step, be carried on by labour and victory conjunct. Will you reward a man merely for promising to serve you? Will you excuse a soldier from fighting and watching, because he is enlisted, and engaged to do it? The two first articles of religion are, that God is, and that he is [h] the rewarder of them that diligently seek him. If you receive the immovable kingdom, you must[i] serve God acceptably with reverence and godly fear, as knowing that our God is a consuming fire. And though it be God that giveth you to will and to do, you must [k] work out your salvation with fear and trembling. You must be[l] "stedfast, unmovable always abounding in the work of the Lord, as knowing that your labour is not in vain in the Lord." You must fight a good fight, and finish your course, and love the appearing of Jesus Christ, if you will expect the crown of righteousness. You must overcome, if you will inherit, and [m] be faithful to the

[e] Rom. xiv. 17; 1 Cor. xii. 31; xiii.; 1 Thess. iv. 17, 18.
[f] Tit. i. 16; Jam. ii. 14, &c.; Matt. 21, 30—33.
[g] Heb. iv. 1; xii. 1, 2. [h] Heb. xi. 6.
[i] Heb. xii. 28, 29. [k] Phil. ii. 12, 13.
[l] 1 Cor. xv. 58; 1 Tim. iv 8
[m] Rev. ii.; iii.

death, if you will receive the crown of life. Do you think that you come into Christ's army, vineyard, and family to be careless?

S. But if I cannot fall from grace, nor be unjustified, though there be duty, there is no danger, nor cause for fear.

P. Controversies of that kind are not yet fit for your head, much less to build security upon: it is certain that God's grace will not forsake you, if you [n] forsake it not first; and it is certain that none of his elect shall fall away and perish. But it is certain that Adam lost true grace, and that such apostasy may be not only possible, but too easy in itself, which yet shall never come to pass. The church of Christ lived in joy and peace, without meddling much with that controversy, till Pelagius and Augustin's disputations: and Augustin's opinion was, that all the elect persevere, but not all that are truly sanctified and love God. But this is enough to the present case; that as you have no cause to distrust God, so it is certain that God doth not decree to save men without danger, but to save them from danger; and that your fear and care to escape that danger (of sin and misery) is the means decreed and commanded for your escape; and that God hath no surelier decreed that you shall escape, than he hath decreed that you shall fear it, and so escape by rational care, excepting some unknown dangers which he puts by: Heb. iv. 1, "Let us therefore fear, lest a promise being left of entering into his rest, any of you should seem to come short of it." The sum of all this is instanced in Heb. xi. 7, "By faith Noah, being warned of God of things not seen as yet, moved with fear, prepared an ark to the saving of his house, by which he condemned the world, and became heir of the righteousness which is by faith."

Go on, therefore, with faith, and hope, and joy; but think not that all the danger is past till you are in heaven.

V. The most dangerous temptation of all will be the stirring up the remnants of your own corruption, of sensuality, and pride, and covetousness, to draw you back to your former pleasant sins, especially by appetite and fleshly lust.

1. If you be addicted to your appetite, though you be poor, you will not want a bait, especially to excess of drinking. And the tempter will tell you, that because you fare hardly, and have small drink at home, you may lawfully comfort your heart with a cup of extraordinary abroad. And so from one cup to two, and so to three, you shall be tempted on, till your appetite become your master, and your love to the drink doth become so strong, that you cannot easily restrain it.

S. God forbid that ever I should again become a swine!

P. If you should but once be overtaken with this sin, you are in great danger of committing it again and again: for the remembrance of the pleasure in your fancy will be a continual temptation to you; and when Satan hath deceived any man into sin, usually God leaveth that man proportionably to his power, and he gets that advantage of which he is very hardly dispossessed: as he ruleth by deceiving, so where he hath deceived once, he hath double advantage to deceive again.

And then I will foretell you, besides the danger of damnation, and the odious ingratitude to your Saviour, &c. you will live in a kind of hell on earth: the devil and the flesh will draw you one way, and God's Spirit and your conscience will draw you another way. The terrors of God will be upon you; and no sooner will the pleasure of your sin be over, but conscience will be God's executioner upon you, and some sparks of hell will fall upon it; so that you will think that the devil is ready to fetch you; unless you sin yourself into stupidity, and then you are undone for ever.

S. I pray you tell me how to prevent such a misery.

P. Be not confident of your own strength: keep away from the tavern and ale-house: come not within the doors, except in cases of true necessity: keep out of the company of tipplers and drunkards. Let not the [o] tempting cup be in your sight: or if you be unwillingly cast upon temptation, let holy fear renew your resolution.

And so as to the case of fleshly lusts; if your bodily temper be addicted to it, as you love your soul, keep at a sufficient distance from the bait. If you feel your fancy begin to be infected towards any person, whose comeliness enticeth you, be sure that you never be with them alone without necessity, and that you never be guilty of any immodest looks, or touch, or words; but keep at such a distance that it may be almost impossible for you to sin. You little know what you have done, when you have first broken the bounds of modesty: you have set open the door of your fancy to the devil; so that he can, almost at his pleasure, ever after, represent the same sinful pleasure to you anew: he hath now access to your fancy to stir up [p] lustful thoughts and desires; so that when you should think of your calling, or of your God, or of your soul, your thoughts will be worse than swinish, upon the filth that is not fit to be named. If the devil here get in a foot, he will not easily be got out. And if you should be once guilty of fornication, it will first strongly tempt you to it again, and the devil will say, If once may be pardoned, why not twice? and if twice, why not thrice? And next, the flames of hell will be hotter in your conscience than the flames of lust were in your flesh: and if God do not give you up to hardness of heart, and utterly [q] forsake you, you will have no rest till you return from sin to God: which, if you be so happy as to do, you little think how dear it may cost you; what terrors, what [r] heart-breaking, and, perhaps, a sad and disconsolate life, even to your death.

And you will not suffer alone: oh what a grief will it be to all the godly, that know or hear of you! What a reproach to religion! What a hardening to the wicked, to make them hate religion, to their damnation! The malignant will triumph, and say, No doubt, they are all alike: these are your puritans, your precisians, your holy brethren! And if you thus wound religion, God will wound your conscience and reputation at the last.

S. You make me tremble to hear of such a horrid state. And the rather because, to confess the truth to you, my nature is not without some lustful inclinations: I entreat you, therefore, to tell me how to subdue and mortify them, and prevent such sin?

P. You are married already, and therefore I need not advise you to that lawful remedy; but I charge you to take heed of all quarrels and fancies which would make your own wife distasteful to you. 2. And, above all, be sure that you be not idle in mind or body. You that are a poor labourer, are in tenfold less danger than rich men and gentlemen are. When a man is idle, the devil findeth him at leisure for filthy thoughts, and immodest dalliance; but if you will labour hard in your calling from morning to night, so that your business may necessarily take up

[n] Josh. xxiv. 26, 40; 1 Chron. xxviii. 9; xv. 2; Isa. i. 28; Jer. xvii. 13; Matt. xxiv. 24; Rom. viii. 21, 29, 30.

[o] Matt. vi. 13; xxvi. 41; Luke viii. 13.
[p] Jam. i. 13, 14. [q] 1 Thess. iii. 7. [r] Psalm li

your thoughts, and also weary and employ your body, you will neither have a mind to filthiness, nor time of dalliance. 3. And be sure that you fare hard for quantity and quality: the fire of lust will go out, if it be not fed with idleness, fulness, and pride. Gluttons and drunkards are still laying in fuel for filthy lusts. And great lustful inclinations must have great fasting. And physic and diet will do much (as eating much cold herbs, and drinking cold water). But to have a body still employed in business and labour, and a mind never idle, but still taken up with your calling, or with God, together with a spare diet, is the sum of the cure, with keeping far enough from the baits, and casting out filthy thoughts before they fasten in the mind.

The story is commonly reported of a lord keeper in our time, who near Islington, as he passed by, saw a man that had newly hanged himself; and, causing him to be cut down, recovered him to health. And, upon examination, found that he hanged himself for love, as lust is called. He sent him to Bridewell, and gave orders that his labour should be hard, and his usage severe: till at last, the man being cured of love, came and thanked him for the healing of his soul, as well as for the saving of his life.

You will be tempted also to pride and ambition, to seek preferment and domination over others; and to a worldly mind, to thirst after [s] riches and great matters for yourself and your children after you in the world. And this pride and worldliness are the most mortal sins of all the rest, as possessing the very heart of love, which is the seat that God reserveth for himself. But, against these you must have daily instructions in the public ministry. I will now say no more to you but this: that he that thinketh on the grave, and what man's flesh must shortly turn to, and of the brevity of this life, which every hour expecteth its end; and thinketh how dreadful a thing it will be for a soul to appear in the guilt of pride or worldliness before the holy God, one would think should easily detest these sins, and [t] use the world as if he used it not.

S. Proceed, I pray you, to the other temptations.

P. VI. The controversies and differences which you will hear about religion, and the many sects, and parties, and divisions which you will meet with, together with their speeches and usage of one another, will be a great temptation to you.

I. In doctrinals, you will hear some on one side, and some on the other, hotly contending about predestination and providence, and universal redemption, and free-will, and man's merits, and in what sense Christ's righteousness is imputed to us, and about justification, and the law, and the covenants of works and of grace; and of the nature of faith and repentance, of assurance of salvation, and whether any fall away from grace, with many such like.

II. In matters of church government and God's worship, you will meet with some that are for prelacy, and some against it; some for government by the pastors in equality, some for the people's power of the keys, and some for a universal government of all the world by the pope of Rome. And you will find some against all praying by the book, or a set form of words; and some against all other praying save that, at least, in public; some for images, and many symbolical ceremonies of men's making, in God's public worship, and some against them; some for keeping all from the sacrament, of whose conversion or holiness the people are not satisfied, and some for admitting the scandalous and ignorant, and some for a middle way: with many other differences about words, and gestures, and manner of serving God.

III. And it will increase your temptation to hear all these called by several names, some Greeks, some papists, some protestants; and of them, some Lutherans, and Arminians, some Calvinists, some antinomians, some libertines, some prelatical, some Erastians, some presbyterians, some independents, some anabaptists, besides seekers, quakers, familists, and many more that are truly heretic; and some (especially the papists) would make you believe that all these are so many several religions, of which none but one (that is, their own) is true and saving.

IV. But the greatest part of your temptation will be to see how all these do use one another, and to hear what language they give to one another. You shall find that the papists make it a part of their religion or church laws, that those whom they account heretics must be burnt to death and ashes; and that inquisitions, by torments, must force them to confess and detect themselves and others; and that [u] temporal lords that will not exterminate all such from their dominions, are to be excommunicated first, and next deprived by the pope of their possessions, and their dominions given to others that will do it: and that preachers are to be silenced and cast out, that swear not, subscribe not, and conform not, as their church canons do require them. Others, in all countries almost, you will find, inclining to the way of force in various degrees, and saying, that without it the church cannot stand, and discipline would be of no effect, and no union or concord would be maintained: these will call those that do not obey them schismatics, factious, seditious, and such like. Others you will find pleading for liberty of conscience, some for all, and some for many, and some for themselves only; some crying out against the prelates as antichristian persecutors, and formalists, and enemies to all serious, godly men; some will separate from them as no churches, not fit for christians to hold communion with. One party will charge you, as you would escape schism and damnation, not to join with the protestants, or nonconformists or separatists: another will charge you, as you would not be guilty of false worship, idolatry, popery, persecution, &c. not to hold communion with the conforming churches. And the anabaptists will tell you, that your infant baptism was nothing but a sin and a mockery, and that you must be baptized again if you will be saved, say some, or if you will be capable of church communion, say others. The antinomians will tell you, that if you turn not to their opinions, you are a legalist, and a stranger to free grace, and set up a righteousness of your own, against the righteousness of Christ, and are fallen from grace by adhering to the law. The Arminians, and Jesuits, and Lutherans will tell you, that if you are against them, you blasphemously make God a tyrant, a hypocrite, and the author of sin. The Dominicans and anti-arminians will tell you, that if you be of the opinion which they oppose, you make man an idol, and ascribe to him that which is proper to God, and are enemies to God's grace and providence, and near to Socinianism. These, and such other temptations, you must meet with from disputers, who account themselves, or are accounted by their party, the best, the wisest, and learnedest men.

S. You greatly perplex me to hear such unexpected things as these: what then shall I do if I come to see them, and should be thus assaulted? Is religion no plainer and surer a way; or are christians no wiser and better people than to live in such uncertainties,

[s] 1 Tim. vi. 9, 10; Luke xxii. [t] 1 Cor. vii. 29—31.

[u] Concil. Later. sub Innoc. 3. Can. i. 3.

contentions, and confusions? I thought that their warfare had been only against the world, the flesh, and the devil. Do they live in such a war against each other? I am almost utterly discouraged to hear of such a war as you describe.

P. I had rather you knew it beforehand, that you may be prepared for it, than to be overthrown hereafter by an unexpected surprise. I. Religion, you must know, is a thing which consisteth of several parts; as a man's body hath, 1. A head, and a heart, and a liver, and a stomach. These we call essential parts; without which it is not a human body. 2. It hath arms, and hands, and legs, and feet, which we call integral parts; without these it may be a body, but not a whole body. These are, some of them, great and few, and some of them are exceeding small and almost innumerable; there are hundreds, or thousands, of capillary veins, arteries, nerves, and fibres, so small as that the curiousest anatomists in the world, that open men's bodies, cannot see them while they are before their eyes; much less the true nature and causes of all the humours, and their motions and effects. 3. There are also nails, and millions of hairs, which are no parts of the body at all, but accidents; even so religion hath, 1. Its essential parts, which I have opened to you in the baptismal covenant. These all true christians know, and are agreed in. 2. It hath its integral parts, which are next to these. The greater sort of these, some erroneous christians wanting, are like men that are without a leg or an arm; but the smaller parts are so many that no christian on earth is so perfect as to know and have them all.

1. Of difficulties in divinity.

Is not all plain and sure which I have opened to you, and engaged you in? And yet there are a thousand texts of Scripture, and hard points in divinity, which the most learned are disagreed about. All that without which a man cannot be a good and holy christian and be saved, is plain and easy in itself. And Christ did choose, therefore, to speak to the capacity of the meanest, though it offend some subtle, curious wits, who expected that God should have sent from heaven a philosopher to resolve their doubts about unprofitable creature speculations, rather than a Redeemer to save their souls. Believe and repent, and love God above all, and heaven above earth, and your neighbour as yourself, and mortify the lusts of the flesh by the Spirit, and deny yourself, and suffer patiently, and forgive your enemies, &c. All these are doctrines harder to be practised than to be understood.

But yet the subtlest wits shall not complain for want of work, for God hath put many things into the Scriptures to[x] exercise them. And the nature of the matter doth of itself make multitudes of the lesser things in divinity to be difficult.

II. And as for christians themselves, you must know, 1. That there are[y] among them abundance of worldly hypocrites, such as you were before your repentance; for such men are of that opinion and side which is uppermost, and maketh most for their advantage and honour in the world. And these strive to get into places of wealth and power, to be the masters of all others. And it is not mere learning, nor a doctor's habit, or pastor's chair, or power to hurt others, that will make a holy, mortified man. And what wonder is it if such as these be troublers of the church, and revilers or persecutors of good men; and if they use their religion to serve their pride, and passion, and worldly interest, and ends?

2. Of the differences of christians.

2. And among those that are sincerely devoted to God, there are abundance of lamentable imperfections. 1. Some are yet young and[z] raw of understanding, and never had time, and hard study, and helps sufficient to acquaint them with all these difficult, controverted points. 2. And then it is the common disease of mankind, to be too little distrustful of our own understandings, and to be too confident of our first apprehensions; whereas, alas! the understanding of man is a poor, dark, slippery, fumbling thing; and most men's first conceptions of doctrinal matters are very lame, if not false: because, at first, we come strangers to the matters, and we always leave out one half, at least, that is to be known. And a half knowledge hath half ignorance with it, if not error; because truths are like the parts of a clock, or watch, in such connexion that the ignorance of one part may make us err about the use of all, or many of the rest. And the truth is, wise and judicious christians are very few; for it is but few that are born with strong natural wits, and few that fall into the hands of right teachers, and few that are patient, diligent students; all which, besides the special helps of God's Spirit, are necessary to make a judicious man.

3. And there are in most of us too much of our inordinate pride, and selfishness, and passion unmortified, according to the various degrees of grace. Most christians are weak and[a] infants; and weak grace hath strong corruptions; and strong corruptions will be great troublers of the church and family, as they are great troublers of the soul that hath them.

Do you not hear in prayer what large and sad confessions all christians make, both pastors and people, of their many and great corruptions, of their ignorance, pride, passion, and the like? And do you not hear, by their complaints, that they are their own grievous trouble, and make their own lives a burden to them? And do you think that they dissemble, and mean not as they speak? And do you not think that those corruptions which disturb themselves will disturb the church? It is strange if a church, which consisteth of a thousand self-troublers, have not some hundreds of church-troublers.

You will be apt, at your first conversion, to think that true christians are nearer to perfection than they are; as if the godly had nothing but godliness in them: but when you have tried them longer you will find that grace is weak; and men's faults are many, and very stiff, and hardly cured; and your over-high estimation of the best may, by experience, receive a check, and you will see that men are still but men.

S. But I shall never be able to keep up that fervent love to the brethren which is my duty, if I find them as bad as you describe them. It will tempt me to think that grace itself is less excellent than I thought it, if it do no more, and make men no better. I feel already your very discourse abate my great estimation of religious persons; what then will such experience do?

P. If your estimation be erroneous, and you think them perfecter than they are, the abatement of it is your duty; for God would not have us judge falsely of them, nor ground our love to them upon mistake. But the excellency of holiness, and the true worth of the godly, may be discerned through all these troublesome faults. The use that you must make of all this is such as followeth:

1. You must consider how great God's[b] mercy is to man that will bear with so much faultiness in the

x 2 Pet. iii. 16. y John xiii. 10, 11.
z Heb. v. 11—14. a 1 Cor. iii. 1—4; Gal. iii. 1, 2, &c.

b Matt. xviii. 32; Exod. xxxiv. 7; Col. iii. 13; Psalm ciii. 3; Eph. iv. 32.

best; and how tender a Physician we have who endureth all these stinking corruptions which we can scarce endure in one another, and the humble can scarce endure in themselves.

2. What constant need we have of a Saviour and a[c] Sanctifier, and how much we must still live upon the healing grace of Christ.

3. How bad our case was before conversion, when it is so bad still; and what wretches we should have been if God had left us to ourselves; and what church troublers the ungodly are, when the better sorts have such troublesome faults.

4. What an excellent thing grace is, that doth not only keep alive under so much sin, but daily work it out, till at last it perfectly overcome it.

5. How[d] tender we must be of judging one another to be ungodly, for such faults as are too common among some of the penitent. Though sin be never the better, because we are all so bad, yet we are the unfitter to be hasty censurers of one another.

6. It is a help to the hope and comfort of a penitent burdened sinner, that yet Christ will[e] pardon him and heal him at the last, when he seeth how much God beareth with and pardoneth in all; as it is a comfort to the sick man to hear that thousands do live that have had the same disease. If almost all God's servants were perfect, it would be hard for the[f] imperfect to believe that they are his servants.

7. It showeth you what need we have all to bear with one another, if ever we will have love and peace; and what a[g] self-condemning course it is of persecutors, to ruin the godly upon an accusation of some tolerable error or fault, when all men have such like.

8. It will tell you how little cause any of us have to be[h] proud, and how needful[i] humility and renewed repentance is to those that are still so bad.

9. It will tell you how little reason we have to be[k] secure and idle, and to think that our mortifying work is done, when still we have all so much sin to overcome.

10. It will keep us from too contemptuous and unmerciful carriage towards those that are unconverted, or that are lapsed into sin; and teach us to pity them and pray for them, rather than revile them, when we find so much faultiness among the better sort of christians. And it will keep us from that[l] over-rigid, and censorious, and magisterial expectation or execution of church discipline, when faults are so common under high professions.

11. It will make those[m] few christians the more amiable in your eyes, whose great wisdom, piety, sobriety, peaceableness, and patience, not only keep them from joining with the church troublers, but also make them both the supporters and healers of the rest. For through God's great mercy many such judicious, wise, humble, blameless, charitable, and peaceable men there are, who are to the ordinary weak professors what the healthful are in a hospital or family to the sick, and the aged to the children; that bear with the rest, and help to cure them by degrees, and keep the peace which they would break, and reconcile the differences which others make, and rid out of the church the excrements of reviling, and hatred, and divisions, wherewith the others do defile it. And[n] blessed are these peacemakers, who have the[o] pure and peaceable wisdom from above, for they are eminently the children of God.

12. Lastly, This must teach you to remember the difference between earth and heaven, and to look up with honour and desire to the perfect harmony of holy souls, united in one flame of love to God; and to say, Come, Lord Jesus! When shall I be in that peaceable, perfect world, where no ignorance, no sin, no pride, no passion, no carnal domination, troubleth the holy triumphant church? And it must quicken your prayers, that God's will may be done on earth, as it is in heaven. These are the true uses to be made of all our differences, contentions, scandals, persecutions, and church divisions.

S. Oh how great a mercy is a wise and seasonable monitor and guide! I was ready to think the scandal described to be so great, as might even warrant, if not necessitate my offence, and the abatement of my liking of godly men, if not of godliness itself. And you have showed me abundance of fruitful uses to be made of it; and that with undeniable evidence of reason.

P. To think ill of Christ or christianity, of God or godliness, for the errors or faults of any man in the world, is a mad and a most disingenuous thing. For, 1. What is all sinfulness but a want of godliness, or that which is its contrary? And will you vilify health, because many are sick; or ease, because many have pain; or life, because many die; or light, because many are blind, or in darkness; when, on the contrary, it is pain and sickness that best teacheth men to value ease and health? And should not the sinful confusions in the world, then, and the miscarriages of christians, cause us to value wisdom, holiness, and peace, the more? It is not godliness, but want of more godliness, that maketh men do all this amiss. There is nothing in the world but more wisdom, and more true godliness, that can cure it; and when there is none, the world is so much worse, that it is almost like hell.

2. And is it not God that forbiddeth and condemneth all this? Is it not his law that every sinner breaketh? Is there any one in the world, or all the world, so much against all sin as God is? What would you have him do more to signify his dislike of it? He forbids it; he caused his Son to die for sin; he yet chastiseth the godly themselves for it; and he will cast the impenitent into hell for it; and he will never suffer any sin in his heavenly kingdom. And is it not madness of blasphemy, then, if any will lay the blame of men's sins on God, or on his holy laws?

3. And it is God that is most abused and injured by sin, and displeased with it: and for you to think hardly of him, or of those that please him, because that others, by sin, do injure him, is as unreasonable, and unrighteous, as if many of your neighbours should rob you and beat you; and, therefore, the rest should rob and beat you again, because the first did so, and should beat all that will not beat you. It is no more equal dealing, to think the worse of God, and godliness, and godly men, because that scandalous persons do offend him.

S. But could not God make men better, and cure all this, if he would? Why, then, is the world so bad?

P. God, who, in himself, is infinitely good, in his infinite wisdom, seeth it best to make his creatures in great variety, and not to communicate the same degrees of excellency to them all. As you see that every star is not a sun, nor all stars equal; nor the clouds like the stars; nor the earth and water so pure as the air, nor so active as the fire. As you see a difference between men, and beasts, and birds, and worms, and trees, and plants, and stones, in wonderful variety. And it is folly to accuse God for not making every worm a man, or every man an angel,

[c] John i. 9; Eph. v. 26. [d] Gal. vi. 1—3; Matt. vii. 1—3.
[e] 1 John ii. 1, 2. [f] 1 John i. 7—9.
[g] Matt. xviii. 32; John viii. 6—8. [h] Isa. lxii. 5.

[i] Matt. xviii. 3; xi. 28, 29.
[k] Heb. xii. 28, 29; Phil. ii. 12. [l] 2 Tim. ii. 25, 26.
[m] Phil. ii. 21. [n] Matt. v. [o] Jam. iii. 17.

or every stone a star or sun. Because he is a free Creator and Benefactor, and may make or not make, give or not give, as he pleaseth; and knoweth well why he doth what he doth, which we poor worms are unfit to know. Even so some reasonable creatures he hath made so glorious in holiness and perfection, that they cannot sin; that is, they never will sin; I mean the angels. And some he hath made such as may please him, and be happy, if they will; (assisting them by abundance of instructions, and mercies, and afflictions;) and yet[p] may sin, and perish, if they will not be persuaded. And among these, even mortal men, he freely giveth more mercy to some than he doth to others: but, to all, so much, as that nothing can undo them, if they do not wilfully, obstinately, and impenitently, refuse and abuse the mercy which is given and offered them, even to the last.

Now, it is true, that God could make every man an angel, and every wicked man a saint: and all those to whom he hath left a possibility either to stand or fall, as themselves shall choose, he could have made such, as that to sin should have been impossible to them. But it pleaseth him to do otherwise, and he well knoweth why.

S. VII. You have brought to my mind, and almost here answered already, another temptation, which I have sometimes felt myself. It hath posed me to think that God, who is so good, should make hell for any, and damn men to such torments as I would not have my greatest enemy feel; much more that the far greatest part of the world should all be damned. For if Scripture had never said that few are saved, yet, as long as it saith that none but the holy and obedient are saved, it is all one; for I see that very few are holy; few love God, and his word, and heaven, above this world. Upon these thoughts I have sometimes been tempted to doubt whether God be good and merciful; and sometimes to doubt whether the Scripture, that saith these things, be true. For he that is good will do good: therefore, if God save but one of many, where is the abundance of his goodness?

P. That you may understand these matters well, you must begin at the bottom with the clearest certainties, and so proceed to the rest. And, 1. I ask you, Is it not absolutely certain that God is good; yea, better than all the world? If not, how came all that goodness into the whole world, which we find in nature and virtue, if God did not make it? And he cannot make that which is better than himself.

S. This is not to be questioned, else he were not God.

P. *Quest.* 2. Is it not certain that there is pain and misery found in the world, even on some creatures that never sinned? What toil do you put your ox and horse to! You beat and abuse them; they have painful diseases, and sometimes broken bones: and you take away the lives of multitudes of harmless creatures at your pleasure; yea, they torment and kill one another; the cat the mouse, and the dog the hare, and the hawk the birds, &c. Doth not all this stand with the goodness of God?

S. Yes, experience telleth us that.

P. *Quest.* 3. Doth not a wilful sinner deserve to feel more than an innocent creature?

S. Yes, no doubt of that.

P. *Quest.* 4. Do not many feel great torments in this world by gout and stone, and many diseases, by poverty, and cares, and sorrows, and injuries from men? And yet God is good.

S. Yes, there needs no proof of that.

P. *Quest.* 5. Might not God take away the life of an innocent man if he had pleased, as well as of a bird or beast?

S. Yes, no doubt of it. They are all his own.

P. *Quest.* 6. Might not God freely have made you a labouring horse, a toad, a serpent, when he made you a man?

S. No doubt, if he would.

P. *Quest.* 7. Might he not then turn you to be a toad if you had never sinned; or lay on you such pain as any of the brutes do undergo?

S. That cannot be denied. It is no more contrary to his goodness to do it to me than unto them.

P. *Quest.* 8. How much pain would you choose to undergo for ever rather than be made a toad, or to be turned into nothing?

S. Just so much as might not be greater than the pleasure of living as a man.

P. *Quest.* 9. If God make man an immortal soul, and man afterwards sin, is God bound to change this immortal nature, and to end man's being; may he not continue our natures, when we have depraved them?

S. No doubt of that.

P. *Quest.* 10. If a man turn his own heart from God, and neither loveth him nor delighteth in him, but is troubled to think of him, who is the cause of this?

S. Himself that did it, and continueth it.

P. *Quest.* 11. If heaven be the joyful perfection of souls in the love and praise of God, and delight in him, who is it that depriveth this man of heaven?

S. Himself, by depriving himself of joyful love.

P. *Quest.* 12. If a man turn his own heart to the love of riches and honours, and sensual delights, of meat and drink, and ease and lust, may not God take away from man the things that he abuseth? Or when such a man dieth, is God bound to supply him with wine and women, with sensual pleasures in another world?

S. No, he is not; but I have heard that after death the sensitive powers cease, and the rational only continue.

P. You have heard men talk of that which they cannot prove, nor is likely. The sensitive soul, or faculties, is totally distinct from the body, which now it worketh in, and will be the same thing when separated. At least, I ask,

Quest. 13. Is God bound to separate a sinner's sensation from his soul?

S. No doubt but he may continue it; and I confess I think it likely that sinners who have subjected their reason to sense, should rather, after death, be less reasonable, than less sensitive.

P. *Quest.* 14. Will not a vehement desire of meat, drink, women, ease, honour, riches, turn to a continual torment, if they cannot have the things desired?

S. No doubt of that. What else is hunger and thirst, and shame and grief, or scorn and disappointment?

P. *Quest.* 15. If the very nature of God be to hate all sin, and to be displeased with sinners, who is it that maketh any man hated of God, and displeasing to him?

S. He himself that maketh himself a sinner. As a weed or dunghill stinketh when the sun shineth on it, because it is a weed or dunghill.

P. *Quest.* 16. If a reasonable creature know that he hath brought himself into such a case, in which he hath lost both heaven and all his sensual pleasures, and made himself hateful to God, and angels, and good men, and all this for a little transitory pleasure, which he knew would quickly end, and when he was often told what it would cost him, and

[p] Prov. i. 20—25. &c.

might have been happy for ever if he would, is it not likely or certain that the thoughts of this will be a torment to his mind?

S. Yes, no doubt, unless he have great command of himself.

P. *Quest.* 17. Is it likely that he who lost the power of his own reason here, by a wilful subjecting it to sense, should, by God's grace, or his own strength, recover the power of it hereafter, so as to be able to restrain his own tormenting conscience or passions?

S. I think that too late they may be wiser by experience, as knowing good and evil, but not to their own benefit.

P. *Quest.* 18. If an immortal soul hath thus cast out God and holiness from itself, besides whom there is no true heaven and happiness; and if it have kindled hell-fire in its own nature, in wicked, self-tormenting lusts, passions, and enmity to God, how do you think that it should ever be recovered, or this fire quenched? God pitied his enemies once, and did redeem them; but is he obliged to interpose, and save the final enemies of his grace from their own doings, when the time of grace is past? And no man can expect that such a wicked and enthralled nature should then change, and deliver itself. Therefore their everlasting misery is the everlasting self-tormenting of the wicked: and is God bound to hold all men's hands from cutting their own throats; or to cure every man as oft as he will wound himself; or to build every man's house as oft as he will burn it wilfully, when he is entreated to forbear; or to shut men's mouths for fear lest they should gnaw their own flesh?

S. I perceive that man is his own tormenter, and his very sin is a hell for ever to the sinner.

P. *Quest.* 19. If all this damnation be not only deserved, but executed by sinners on themselves, who will not be entreated to have mercy on themselves, is it not impudency to turn the accusation against God, and charge him with cruelty against these cruel and obstinate self-destroyers?

S. All that is to be said is, that it pleased not God to make their misery impossible, and to save them from themselves.

P. *Quest.* 20. Seeing that human government is necessary to the peace and order of the world, and justice as necessary as government, is not divine government, laws, and justice more necessary? else all the sovereigns of the world would be ungoverned, and all powerful wickedness be unpunished, and all heart sins, which are the roots of all the rest, and all secret villanies, would be as free as piety itself; and no universal order could be maintained without a universal governor: and if all governors inflict more punishment on offenders than they are willing of themselves, must not God do so? Sin is voluntary, but punishment is most involuntary: and if sin against man deserve the gallows, or temporal death, sure sin against God deserveth more, even a punishment as durable as the sinner's soul, which is immortal.

S. You have silenced my murmuring thoughts as to the being of hell; but what say you of the numbers that are damned?

P. 1. Remember that it is proved to you that God doth, before their sin, no worse to any than as a free benefactor to give his own benefits, in various degrees: and that, in the lowest degree, he giveth to all men pardon and salvation, if they will have it, and will not finally and obstinately reject it?

2. Remember that none are damned but those that wilfully damn themselves, and refuse salvation.

3. Consider that man is as nothing to God, and therefore there is no reason that he should spare sinners for their numbers' sake, when the number maketh the sin the greater, as many fire sticks make the greater flame. Millions of men are not so much to God as two or three flies or wasps to us, who yet never stick to destroy a thousand of them.

I ask you, *Quest.* 1. If God damned but one of a million, or of a kingdom, and that only for obstinacy and impenitency in sin, would it much offend you?

S. No; for I should see then that his mercy is greatest.

P. 2. If he damned none but the devils, and saved all mankind, would it offend you?

S. Not much; because their malice is so great.

P. 3. Do you not grudge sometimes that God doth not punish the wicked, especially the persecutors of his church? And are not good men ready sometimes to call for fire from heaven, and sometimes to marvel that God doth no more show his hatred against them? And yet will you grudge at him, because he will do it fully and seasonably in hell?

S. The Lord pardon us! we are hardly pleased with his judgments.

P. 4. Do you not know that all this earth is no bigger, in comparison of all the world, than one inch of ground is to all the earth? And how many thousand, thousand, thousand times is all the earth greater than one inch! And are not all the rest of the vast and glorious parts of the world as like to be fully inhabited as this? How know you but those unmeasurable regions have a thousand thousand millions of blessed angels and spiritual inhabitants for one wicked man or devil that is damned? Are you sure it is not so?

S. How should I be sure? God only knoweth. I confess it is likely enough, if we may judge by the different spaces as you compare them.

P. 5. If, when you come to heaven, you shall find that hell was the sinful place of devils, and earth, by sin, was one spot of God's world, made next like hell; and that millions of millions of angels, and holy spirits, and inhabitants, are glorified, for one wicked man or devil that is damned; will you not be ashamed of murmuring at God?

S. I see that it is unfit for poor, dark sinners to judge the Judge of all the world, or to presume to quarrel with his judgments, when we know no better what we say.

P. The uses which you should rather make of the numbers that are condemned, are such as these: 1. To consider how mad a creature an ungodly man is, when so great a number will by no warnings be kept from damning their own souls for ever.

2. That man hath exceeding need of a Saviour and a Sanctifier, who is such a pernicious enemy to himself.

3. How much you are beholden to God, who hath made you, by his grace, to be one of those few that shall be saved.

4. How foolish and unsafe it is to think, and speak, and do as the most do, unless you would speed as the most do for ever: and how unmeet it is for them to be conformed to this world, who hope to be for ever separated from them.

5. How excellent a people those few should be, above the common rates of men, whom God hath called out of so great a number to himself. How fervently should they love him, and how holily and heartily should they serve him.

S. Oh that we could be such as this mercy doth deserve!

P. Two things more I will conclude with, for your satisfaction. 1. That hell is not to be thought of as a mere furnace of fire, where sinners are fried, as abiding in one place; but the state of the devils, who are now at once tormented in hell, and yet[q] rule in the air under one Beelzebub, or prince, and night and day compass the earth, as seeking whom to deceive and devour. This, I say, showeth us, that hell is a state of sin and misery, continued partly by the voluntary pravity of the damned, and consistent with a kind of active and political life. And the greatest resemblance of it is the case of wicked men in deep melancholy, who can neither cease to be wicked nor to torment themselves; or of rogues in irons in the gaol, compared with the state of the angels in heaven.

2. That all great excellences are rare: there is but one sun (that we know of). The number of men on earth is small, to the number of flies, and worms, and fishes, &c. Gold is not so common as iron, or clay; nor diamonds, or other jewels, so common as pebble-stones. The woods are covered with thorns and briers, and the commons with heath, and furze, and weeds, without any care and labour of man; but orchards and gardens must have greater care, and lie in a much narrower room. Kings, and nobles, and judges, and doctors, are but a small part of mankind. And if God will have but few of us come to heaven, one of those few shall be of more worth than thousands of the wicked reprobates that perish.

S. But, sir, the chief matter is yet behind. You have told me before of the scandals, errors, and sects, and temptations by them, which will be in the church; and you have told me now of the multitudes that are wicked; but you have not told me how I may escape either of these temptations. What shall such an ignorant sinner as I do, when I not only see the ill example of the multitude, high and low, but also hear men that seem learned and godly, condemning one another; when one saith, This is the true church, and another saith, Nay, but they are heretics, or antichristian; one saith, You are damned if you be not of our way, and another saith, You are damned if you be not of our way? Alas! I am not able to judge which of them is in the right; I know not what a Socinian, a quaker, a papist, an antinomian, or any of these parties are, nor what they hold: how, then, shall I answer them, or know whether they be in the right? what will you advise me to do in this difficulty?

P. 1. I will first remember you, that all this is no more than Christ foretold us of, and warned all his disciples to prepare for; that false Christs and false prophets should arise, who should deceive, were it possible, the very elect, Matt. xxiv. 24. When they say, Here is Christ, and there is Christ, go not after them, ver. 26. That of our own selves men should arise, speaking perverse things, to draw away disciples after them, Acts xx. 30. That it must be that heresies must arise, that they which are approved may be made manifest, 1 Cor. xi. 19. That Satan would transform himself into an angel of light, and his ministers into ministers of righteousness, to deceive, 2 Cor. xi. 14. That some would cause divisions and offences contrary to the apostles' doctrine; even such as serve not the Lord Jesus, but their own bellies, and by good, fair speeches, deceive the hearts of the simple, Rom. xvi. 16, 17. Among the Corinthians, how quickly did the more carnal sort of christians fall into factions and divisions, some being of Paul, and some of Apollos, and some of Cephas! And the Galatians so followed the Jewish teachers, that Paul was afraid of them, lest he had laboured in vain. And in many of the churches, the Nicolaitans and deceivers (called the woman Jezebel) did teach and seduce the people from the truth, Rev. ii. and iii.

But your safety in this great danger must be thus maintained:

I. You must [r] hold fast to your baptismal covenant, as explained in the creed, Lord's prayer, and commandments; and take all for christians who are true to that; and take all such christians for the true catholic church: for that which maketh a man a christian, maketh him a member of the body politic of Christ, which is his church. So that if any man teacheth you any thing contrary to that, you must reject it; for your baptismal covenant is your christianity. And if any call him a heretic that owneth this christian covenant, as opened in the creed, Lord's prayer, and commandments, believe him not, but take him for a slanderer of your brother; except he prove it, 1. By some proved, contrary profession, which will prove that he doth not indeed believe as he professeth to believe. 2. Or by some impenitent wickedness of life. So that the same covenant which your own christianity consisteth in, will serve both for a test to try men's doctrines by, and also to try which is the true church, and who are the members of it, with whom you must have communion, and who are heretics, whom you must avoid.

II. Adhere to those truths wherein all christians are [s] agreed. Papists, and protestants, and Greeks, and all sorts truly christian, are agreed in the points forenamed, of the baptismal covenant, the creed, the Lord's prayer, and the ten commandments: and they all confess, that all which we receive for canonical Scripture, is the true, infallible word of God. In all this our divisions are no temptation to you, because we are all of a mind in these.

III. The holy [t] Scripture then being acknowledged by all for the word of God, you must receive no doctrine which contradicteth it; nor refuse any doctrine which is asserted in it: but try all by this divine and certain rule.

IV. Because that the doubtful sense of many texts is the occasion of men's different opinions, you may well take up with that sense which hath either of these two marks: 1. That which is so plain and frequently repeated, that to an impartial, sober man it is past controversy; and if any pervert it, the plainness of the text will certainly shame him. 2. That which all christians (unless some inconsiderable dotards) are agreed in, as the proper sense in all the commentaries of their learned men. And if you hold fast all the texts which are thus plain, and all which papists, Greeks, protestants, &c. do give the same exposition of, you will have a great stock of saving truths.

V. Be sure that you faithfully love and [u] practise this much forementioned, which all are agreed in. And then, 1. The very love and practice will help you to such a lively, experimental kind of knowledge as will certainly save your soul, and keep you from every damning error; yea, and will greatly advantage you in all practical, and many doctrinal, controversies. 2. And God will bless you with [x] more of his illuminating help. Whereas false hypocrites, that have no religion but opinion, and talk, and proud self-conceit, and contending zeal, deserve to be forsaken of God, and given up to believe many falsehoods, and to lose the truth which they perfidiously abused. Holy souls have great advantage of worldly

[q] Eph. ii. 2; Job i. 6—8; 1 Pet. v. 8; Rom. ii. 10; Heb. ii. 14.
[r] 2 Tim. i. 13; Eph. iv. 3—7, 14, 15; 1 Cor. xii. 12, 13, &c.; Mark xvi. 16.
[s] 1 Tim. iv. 6; vi. 3; Rom. xvi. 16, 17.
[t] John v. 39.
[u] John vii. 17; xiii. 17; xv. 14; Matt. vii. 22—24.
[x] John xv. 3—9; Matt. xxviii. 20; John xiv. 21.

or opinionative hypocrites, in times of differences and contentions. At least[y] these souls shall certainly be saved.

VI. Learn all that you yet understand not,[z] in the same humble teachableness from the ministers of Christ in which you first entered into his church. Think not that you grow too wise to [a] need their further teaching. When you once grow proud of your own understanding, and think that you can judge of all things at the first hearing, and that all is false which crosseth your first conceits, and that ministers can add but little to what you know already, then you are as bad as perverted already: for this is the root of a multitude of errors.

VII. The [b] judgment of the generality of able, godly, self-denying, impartial ministers, should prevail more with you than the judgment of any partial sect, whether it be great or small, either such as stand for worldly interest, or such as run into parties by division. For the church of Christ hath ever suffered by these two sorts, and therefore they are still both to be suspected.

1. Ungodly, carnal men, that thrust themselves into the sacred ministry for preferment, will teach you such doctrine as tendeth to their worldly ends, to magnify themselves, and [c] keep the world in subjection to them, that all may honour them, and be ruled by their wills. Domination is evidently their work and end; and no wonder if they fit their doctrine to it.

2. On the other side, the raw, injudicious sort of christians, if once they grow into an over-high esteem of their own understandings and godliness, are exceeding apt to fasten with confidence upon their own first undigested notions, and publish them as saving truths, when, after twenty years' experience, they will be ashamed of them themselves. And they are as apt to desire to be made conspicuous for their godliness in the world, and to that end to separate from ordinary christians, as below them, and unworthy of their communion; as among the papists the religious must separate themselves from others, into religious houses and societies, which are accounted holier than the rest. These sects have ever been the nest of errors; and divisions have still tended to sub-divisions; and all to the ruin of love, peace, and godliness, and consequently of the church.

So that the generality of divines and godly people, who you plainly perceive to avoid both these extremes, and to live in concord among themselves, in a self-denying, sober, holy life, neither seeking worldly honours and preferments, nor running from concord into[d] proud, self-opinionated sects, are they whom you may best trust with the resolution of your doubts, and the conduct of your soul, so far as ministers must be trusted.

For, 1. God is not so likely to guide by his Spirit falsehearted, worldly hypocrites,[e] whose god is their belly and mammon, as the humble, holy, faithful pastors of his churches. And Christ himself hath given you this direction, Matt. vii. "By their fruits ye shall know them." For though a bad man may be in the right, and a good man in the wrong, yet, if in a practical controversy you see the generality of bad men go one way, and the generality of good men go the other way, the far greater probability of truth is on the good men's side.

2. But yet it is not so likely that God should reveal his mind to a few good men, and those of the rawer, injudicious sort, and such as are most infected with proud overvaluing their own wisdom and godliness, and such as have had least time, and study, and means to come to great understanding, and such as show themselves the proudest censurers of others, and least tender of the church's peace and concord, and such as are aptest to break all to pieces among themselves. I say, it is not so likely that these are in the right, as the main body of agreeing, humble, godly, peaceable, studious ministers, who have had longer time and better means to know the truth: and the body of christians, even the church, hath more promises from Christ than particular, dividing persons have.

VIII. The light and law of nature is the primitive, original light and law of God: therefore, receive nothing from any teachers which is certainly against it.

IX. Pray earnestly to God to preserve you from error, and when conscience and experience tell you that any opinion or party would lead you to plain sin, (as to dishonour your superiors, to favour persecution or idolatry, to divide christians, and set them against each other, to destroy christian love, to favour loose and fleshly living, to neglect God's ordinances, or the like,) be sure so far it must needs be false.

X. Wait still as a doubting learner, where you cannot yet reach to a divine belief.

If you understand but these two lines, it will help you to escape all the cheats of the papists, and the chief perplexities of mind which all our sects would draw you into.

1. Remember that the christian faith and religion is of God, and if you believe the same articles merely upon the word of men, (whether few or many,) it is not formally true faith and religion in you, because it is human only, and not divine. If you believe the priest only, or the church, that there is a resurrection of the body, and a life everlasting, this is not a believing God.

2. Therefore the use that you must make of the teachers of the church is, to help you to know what God hath revealed, what is his word, and so to believe and practise it, and not merely to believe the priests themselves.

3. Yet a certain belief of them in their places is needful towards the promoting of your belief of God. As he that cannot read, and is unlearned, must believe that what is read is in the Bible, and that the translation in the main agreeth with the original, and that this Bible is the same which the church received from the apostles, and such like. He that will believe his teacher in nothing, can learn nothing of him.

4. But this human faith is another thing, quite different from the belief of God, and it is but a subordinate help to it, and no part of it. If man be not God, to believe man is not to believe God. Therefore, if you should believe all the creed, and all the volumes of councils and canons, merely as the testimony of the church, or whatsoever else you take only on the teacher's word, remember that it is no part of your divine faith or religion, but only an appurtenance to it (good or bad, as the matter is). So far as you learn of, and believe, your teachers, you are a learner and disciple of theirs, and by them may be taught to know what is the word and will of[f] Christ, which must be known by its proper evidence, which they must show you, and not upon their bare word alone: for to be a teacher, is to show you that truth and reason of believing which they have learned themselves. But to be an authoritative[g] lord of your faith, is another thing; and such say,

[y] Rev. xxii. 14 [z] Matt. xviii. 3.
[a] 1 Thess. v. 12, 13; Heb. xiii. 7, 17, 24.
[b] Rom. xvi. 16—18; 1 Cor. i. 10; Eph. iv. 14—16.

[c] 1 Pet. v. 3, 4. [d] 1 Tim. iii. 6; Acts xx. 30.
[e] Phil. iii. 18, 19; Tit. i. 9, 10. [f] 1 Pet. i. 21.
[g] 2 Cor. i. 24; x. 15

Believe, because we speak it. But so far as you have learned by your teachers, what is the word and will of Christ,[h] and believe and obey it because it is his word, so far you are indeed a christian, and religious.

5. Therefore, if any tell you this or that is the word of God, or this is the true meaning of the word of God, this is my counsel, and this is your duty: 1. If they be such as you are obliged to hearken to, as being your teachers, or men of credit in such things, hear what they can say, as one that is willing to learn the truth, and hear what others say against it, for it is hard to judge in controversies where both sides are not heard, if the difficulty be considerable. 2. Be not hasty to conclude off or on, that it is true or false; but continue merely as a learner, till you know by all their teaching that the thing is true. And tell them in the mean time, I know not whether it be so or not. I will not pretend to be wiser than I am. I will be a learner, that so I may come to be a believer of it as a truth of God, as soon as I have learned it to be so.

Either the thing is true or false, before you believe it. If it be false, no teachers or church can make it true, nor can show you the real evidence of truth in it: therefore, if you believe it, whoever tell it you, you are guilty of believing a falsehood fathered upon God, when it had no evidence. If you say that their evidence seemed good to you, that was because you were sinfully rash and hasty in receiving falsehood, and not staying till you had time to[i] try it to the full. But if the thing prove true, yet it cannot be expected that you receive it till you have time sufficiently to[k] try it. Nor can it be said, that your delay being dangerous, you must presently receive it on your teacher's word; for that is but to be a believer of a man: and which a man cannot know to be God's word without time to try and see the evidence, it is in vain to say, he must do it. And when a man hath first received both all the essentials of the christian religion before mentioned, and all the doctrines, and all the expositions of Scripture, which the generality of christians in all ages have agreed in, together with all the light and law of nature, the controversies which remain can be of no such necessity, as that we must needs make haste to believe men that tell us they are God's truth, before we have time to prove and learn it to be so indeed.

Whoever, therefore, be your teachers, or whatever church pretendeth to inform you, call nothing God's truth, or word, till you have sufficient evidence to prove it so; but continue as learners in that doubt which you cannot overcome, till you can be[l] divine believers: and if you do believe any thing merely on your teacher's word, say plainly, I believe you as a man in this; but it is no part of my religion and belief of God, till I find, indeed, that it is his word.

Follow these ten directions, and you will be safe against all the divisions and clamours of contenders, that say, Here is the church and truth, and there is the church and truth. And when sects and reasonings make others at their wits' end, your way will be sure and plain before you.

S. How clear have you made that case to me which I thought would have utterly bewildered and confounded me!

P. VIII. The eighth temptation which I must forewarn you of, is this; you will be in danger to mistake the nature of the christian religion, by minding only some parts of it, and overlooking the rest, and perhaps the greatest, and taking up with the separated parts alone.

[h] 1 Cor. ii. 5; 1 Thess. i. 8. [i] 1 Thess. v. 21.
[k] Gal. vi. 4. [l] 1 Thess. ii. 13.

God's word is large, and man's mind is narrow: and we are apt, when we observe something, to think that it is all. So some are so intent on duty, that they have poor thoughts of grace and mercy; and some think that the magnifying of grace obligeth them to vilify inherent holiness, and performed duty. And nothing is now more common than to set truth against truth, and duty against duty; when they are such as God conjoineth. But the instance that I will now warn you of, is this; the true nature of religion is nothing else, but faith turning the soul by repentance from the flesh and world, to the love, and praise, and obedience of God, in the joyful hope of the heavenly glory. Read this over and over again. Now the too common case of christians is to live so much in the use of mere self-love and fear, as that almost all the notable exercise of their religion is but a timorous care to be saved; and an inquiring after marks, or other ways, by which they may know that they shall be saved; and a performing of duty, as a heavy, but necessary task, that they may be saved: but that which you must aim at is, to study much God's wondrous love in Christ, and the certainty and greatness of the heavenly glory; and so far to mourn for sin as it tendeth to magnify grace, and to cleanse and preserve the heart and life; and to live in the constant delights of divine love, and joyful thanksgiving and praises to our Creator, Redeemer, and Sanctifier, and in the belief and hopes of life everlasting; and, out of love to God and man, to delight in constant obedience to God, and in doing all the good that we can do in the world; and in this way to trust God quietly and gladly with body and soul.

This is true religion; and weeping for sin, and particular ordinances, must not be neglected, but esteemed only as lower parts, which are but stepping-stones to this ascent, and never to be set against it, nor our chiefest care to be spent upon them.

S. I thank you for this warning; for I perceive by this that true religion is a very noble and a pleasant life. But most good people that I have known do but ask what they shall do to be saved, and beg for a softer heart that can weep for sin, and keep on in hearing, prayer, and sacraments. And the praises of God do take up but a little room in their devotions (except some that do it by way of erroneous opposition to humiliation, and confession of sin). And divine love, and the joys of faith, and hope, and holiness are little seen.

P. IX. Your next and sore temptation will be, to[m] abate your zeal and diligence by degrees, and to grow to a customary coldness and formality, and lose all the life of your religion. All your spiritual vigour will die away into a carcass and image, if you be not careful to prevent it.

S. What would you have me do to prevent it?

P. 1. Let your first and chief labour be every day about your heart; stir up your soul when you find it sluggish. Learn how to preach to it in your meditations, and to[n] chide it, and urge it to its work.

2. Live under the liveliest ministry, and in the most serious christian company you can get; or if that may not be, supply that want by reading the most lively, serious books.

3. Take heed of turning your religion and zeal to by-opinions and parties, instead of the life and practice of faith, hope, and love. For a factious, wrangling, contentious zeal is as destructive of true, holy zeal as a fever is of natural heat and life.

4. Take heed of growing in love with the world; for, as the thoughts of riches, and rising, grow sweet

[m] Rev. ii. 4, 5; iii. 15, 16; Matt. xxiv. 12.
[n] Psalm xlii. 5, 11; xliii. 5.

to you, the thoughts of God and heaven will grow lifeless and unpleasant.

5. Take heed of sinning wilfully; for all such sin doth harden the heart, and forfeit the quickening help of the Spirit.

6. Hold on in the use of all God's ordinances; for intermissions and unconstancy tendeth to a total neglect; and a contented course of lifeless duty tendeth to spiritual death itself.

P. X. Your next temptation is the dreadfullest of all the rest: you may be tempted at last to doubt whether the Scripture be the word of God, and whether Christ be indeed the Son of God, and whether there be a heaven and hell, an immortality of the soul. And this may befall you, 1. Either by the company or books of infidels or atheists, who prate against the Scripture and the life to come. 2. Or else by the malicious suggestions of Satan, stirring up in you unbelieving thoughts. 3. But especially in case of melancholy, which is a disease of the body, which giveth him great advantage to molest the mind with blasphemous temptations; so that he will draw you to doubt whether there be a God, or whether he be the Governor of the world, or whether Christ be true, or Scripture be God's word: and here he will set before you the texts which you understand not, and persuade you that they are contradictory, and ask you, Is it likely that this or this should be true. And thus will your very foundation be assaulted: and the consequent may be either very troublesome or very dangerous to you. If you do abhor these suggestions, it will be a torment to you to be followed with such odious, hideous motions; though as long as you abhor them, they will not condemn you. But if you patiently hearken to them, then your danger will be great.

S. I pray you open the danger to me, that I may the more dread it and avoid it.

P. If God do not, by his grace, stir up your soul to detest and cast away such thoughts, or show you, by his light, the falseness of them, they may bring you to atheism or infidelity itself; and your latter end will be worse than your beginning.

But if you do not turn professed infidel, yet if your doubts or unbelief be the stronger party in you, they will make you a hypocrite, which is a secret infidel. For while you prevalently doubt of the life to come, and whether the Scripture be God's word, you will take this life as your surest portion, and you will secretly resolve to save your life and worldly prosperity, and put the matters of the life to come upon a venture; you will never die nor be undone for Christ, nor ever win heaven for the loss of earth; but only take up that religion which is most in fashion, or which may best quiet your conscience in a fleshly, worldly life: and you will hope, that if there be a heaven, you may have it as a reserve when you can keep the world no longer; but because it seemeth so uncertain to you, you will hold fast what you have in present as long as you can. Therefore, in all controversies and matters of religion you will have an indifferency, covered with the name of moderation; for he that doubteth of all religion, can, in case of danger, be of any, while indeed he is heartily of none: and he that doubteth whether there be a heaven will not much stick with you about the way to it; and he that heartily believeth not in Christ will not be very scrupulous about his doctrines or commands. Thus secret unbelief, or prevalent doubting of the christian truth, will make men miserable infidel hypocrites.

S. I tremble to think of so great a danger; and the more, because that I find not myself able to defend the faith against a subtle adversary and deceiver. But what if I should be brought into doubting, will all doubting have such sad and damnable effects?

P. No: the question will be, whether your faith or your unbelief be the stronger and more prevalent. If your doubting be stronger than your belief, then you will be an infidel hypocrite, and will have no religion but what shall give place to your worldly interest, and will never forsake all for Christ; and God, and Christ, and heaven, must come under the world and the flesh; and while, lest it should prove true that there is a life to come, you will think it necessary to have some religion, it will indeed be none; because it maketh God no God, and Christ no Christ, and heaven no heaven, by putting them after or below the world.

But if your belief be stronger than your unbelief or doubting, then it will not only resist such temptations, but it will still keep up the interest of God, and heaven, and Christ, and holiness in your heart; and your faith, though weak, will[o] overcome the world; your resolutions to forsake all for Christ and heaven will be firm and constant; you will go on in the serious use of all the means of your salvation; you will forsake the gainfullest and sweetest sins; you will perform the hardest and the dearest duties; and though your graces will be all the weaker, and your life the worse for the weakness of your faith, yet you will rather die, or let go all, than forsake your Master, or hazard your hopes of life eternal. And as long as your doubts or unbelief are thus overcome by a faith that is weak, but stronger than they, though you cannot say, I am certain that there is another life, or that the Scripture is the word of God, yet Christ will take you for a true believer.

S. This is comfortable; but methinks, then, all men should be saved, though they have no belief but the mere discerning of a possibility of another life. For all men are most certain that they must die; and a little time is even as nothing; and all the pleasures of this little time are but a doting dream; and vanity and vexation shameth them all. If, then, we are most certain that there is no true felicity here, and that by seeking a better we have nothing here to lose that is worth the keeping, common reason will tell any man that he should let go all for the smallest hope or possibility of an endless, heavenly glory: for no man in the world can say, I am sure that there is no heaven or hell; and all can say, We are sure there is nothing but a very short dream of vanity here. And what need faith, then, for the determining of so plain a case?

P. You speak a great deal of reason; but you must consider, 1. That reason in all[p] carnal men is much enslaved to their sense, and cannot rightly do its office. Do you not see it in drunkards, fornicators, gluttons, and all voluptuous persons, how they daily go against the plainest reason, yea, and their own knowledge, through the violence of sense? And reason itself, also, is oft bribed and[q] blinded to take part with sensuality. As vain as this world is, it hath the heart of every carnal man; and that reason which shall turn it out of his heart must show him a better in a powerful manner, and that must be with a certainty, or with so strong a probability as seemeth to him near to certainty; yea, and this must be powerfully presented to his mind by God's Spirit within, (to heal his blindness and sensual violence,) as well as by the word without.

2. And this apprehension of reason must be by[r] faith, which is a rational act. How far the natural

[o] 1 John v. 4; Heb. xi.

[p] Rom. viii. 5—9.

[q] 1 Cor. ii. 14.

[r] Heb. xi. 6; Matt. xi. 27.

evidence of a life to come may carry those that have not the gospel, I now pass by; but we that have both natural and supernatural revelation of it do find all little enough: and that without a prevalent belief of the gospel the heart will not be turned from this world to God, nor sensuality be truly turned into holiness, or overcome.

S. But I heard a learned man say, that if infidels were turned loose, to dispute with professors against christianity and the Scriptures, they would silence most of the very ministers themselves; and find us far harder work than anabaptists, antinomians, or separatists, or any other sect. And if so, what shall such ignorant persons as I do, and what certainty or stability of faith can I expect to have and keep?

P. 1. It is the merciful providence of God which commonly so ordereth it, that weak and young christians have but weak temptations to unbelief. Their temptations at first are strongest unto sensuality and the love of the world, and not to infidelity itself. And then they are more troubled with doubtings about their own sincerity, than about the truth of the word of God. You see somewhat like it in every tree that groweth in the earth: whether do you find more young plants and little trees, or more old and great ones, overturned by the winds?

S. More of the old and great ones.

P. And what is the cause of it?

S. Because the great ones more resist the wind, and it hath the fuller stroke at them.

P. And yet the young and little ones have so little rooting, that if they felt the tenth part of the force which falleth on the bigger, it would overthrow them. But the wise God so ordereth it, that the roots and the top shall equally grow together, that so the winds may assault the top no stronglier than the roots can bear. And so he dealeth with young believers. But those hypocrites that grow all in the top of outside actions and professions, and not at all in the roots of inward faith and love, are they that fall in times of trial.

2. And then you must know that it is not the most [s] subtle wit, but the most sanctified heart, which hath the best advantage against temptations to unbelief; and therefore young [t] christians, that have but little learning, may stand, when learned doctors [u] fall and perish. And God hath not so ordered the evidences of christianity as that the finest wits must always make the best believers.

S. I pray you tell me then, how I must be established against all temptations to unbelief, and how I must prove the truth of Christ and the gospel to be indeed the word of God, so as that I may stand fast against the subtlest reasonings of unbelievers, and may trust God's word to the forsaking of life and all.

P. This case is of itself so great and weighty, as that I cannot sufficiently speak to it in this short discourse; but I advise you seriously to read of it what I have written in a book, called The Life of Faith, Part 2. And if that do not satisfy you, read thoroughly what I have written in four books more: 1. In one called, The Reasons of the Christian Religion. 2. One called, More Reasons for the Christian Religion. 3. One called, The Unreasonableness of Infidelity. And, 4. In the Second Part of The Saints' Rest.

But yet I shall now tell you enough to establish you, if you can but understand much in few words.

You must know, therefore, what your baptismal profession doth contain, when you believe in the Father, the Son, and the Holy Ghost.

S. I think you will make the baptismal covenant serve for all things, from first to last?

P. As the Father reconcileth us to himself by the Son, who came as his Messenger from heaven, to make known God, and life eternal, to mankind; so the Father and the Son do send the Holy Ghost into the souls of men to be Christ's Advocate, Agent, and Witness, in the world. So that in one word it is [x] the Holy Spirit that is the proof of the truth of Christ, and of the gospel.

S. But I have heard preachers speak much against this argument, and say, that, 1. Thus no man can know that Christ and the gospel are true, but he that hath the Spirit. And what then shall we say to infidels to convince them? 2. And that thus every fanatic that thinks he hath the Spirit will make himself the only judge. 3. And that few godly men do feel such a testimony of the Spirit in themselves, as to tell them what is, and what is not, God's word. 4. And if they did, how shall they prove that it is indeed God's Spirit, and no delusion? So that when our catechisms say, that only the witness of the Spirit can assure us that the gospel is the word of God, many learned men cry shame upon that assertion.

P. That is, because that those catechisms have not made them understand the matter, one side or both not knowing what is meant here by the testimony of the Spirit; or else they speak of another thing.

Fanatics mean, an inward impulse, or actual word, or suggestion of the Spirit within them, saying, or persuading their minds, that this is the word of God. But this is not the thing that I am speaking of. But I will better tell you how the Holy Spirit is the advocate and witness of Christ.

The Holy Spirit is sent by the Father and the Son, to do that on souls which none but God can do, and which God doth not do by any other means but by Christ, his servants, and his doctrine. This work of the [y] Spirit is the extraordinary expression and impression of God's three-fold perfections, his power, his wisdom, and his goodness. This way the Spirit is witness of Christ.

I. Before his coming, in the [z] prophets, and the first edition of the covenant of grace, where, 1. Many miracles; 2. A word of divine wisdom and prophecies fulfilled; 3. And the mercy and holiness of God, were all expressed.

II. In Christ's own [a] person, and his life, appeared the same divine impressions and expressions of the Holy Spirit. 1. In the [b] power which he exercised in working abundance of uncontrolled miracles; healing all diseases by his word, raising the dead, and finally rising from the dead himself, and, after forty days' abode on earth, ascending visibly up to heaven, while his disciples gazed after him. 2. The wisdom of God was notably imprinted on all that holy doctrine, by which he brought life and immortality to light, and taught men to know God and life eternal. 3. Love and goodness were most conspicuous in his wonderful work of man's redemption, his condescension, his sufferings, his covenant of grace, with all the rest of his declarations of the Father's love and holiness. And thus the Spirit on Christ himself (which also in a visible shape fell upon him at his baptism) was his witness.

III. In the persons and lives of Christ's [c] apostles

[s] Matt. xi. 25; xvi. 17.
[t] Eph. iii. 17—19; Col. ii. 7.
[u] Matt. xiii. 6, 21.
[x] Heb. x. 15; 1 John v. 10.
[y] 2 Tim. i. 7; 1 Pet. i. 2.
[z] 1 Pet. i. 11; Isa. lix. 21.
[a] John iii. 34; i 32, 33; Isa. xlii. 1; Matt. xii. 18; Isa. xi. 2.
[b] Rom. i. 4; Heb. iii. 3, 4; Acts vii. 22.
[c] Rev. xix. 10; Acts ii. 4, 16, 18; vi. 10; v. 3, 5; Joel ii. 28; Gal. iii. 2, 3; Zech. iv. 6; 1 Cor. iv. 10, 12; xii. 4, 7—9, 11; xiv. 2; v. 4, 5; Eph. iii. 5.

and chief disciples, who were the witnesses and reporters of his own words and miracles, the same impressions and expressions of the Holy Spirit appeared as the witness of the truth of Christ. 1. While they declared his word and miracles, they wrought abundance themselves, (or rather God by them,) to prove that they were true witnesses of Christ. They healed the sick, and raised the dead, and judged and destroyed some obstinate enemies of Christ, by the mere power of God. 2. The wisdom of God did notably appear in the light and harmony of their doctrine and lives. 3. The goodness and love of God appeared in their wonderful holiness, self-denial, and love to souls.

IV. All the same impressions of the Holy Spirit appeared on the christians who were converted by the apostles, and received their testimony of Christ, and delivered it downwards to us. 1. Miracles of one kind or other were common among them long; even among such culpable churches as the Galatians, Gal. iii. 1, 3, and the Corinthians, 2 Cor. xiii. 1, 5. 2. Prophets, and teachers of eminent wisdom, without universities, or much previous study, were suddenly made such by the Holy Ghost, 1 Cor. vii.; xii. 13. Their love and holiness were wonderful, God was all to them, and the world and life itself was as nothing; so that they stand yet as patterns of love, and goodness, and patience, to this day.

V. The sacred[d] gospel and doctrine itself, delivered by Christ and his apostles, doth to this day visibly bear this image and superscription of God. 1. In the works of power there recorded, and in the powerful truths of it, which conquer the world, the flesh, and the devil. 2. In its wonderful wisdom, and prophecies fulfilled, and clear directions for man's salvation. 3. In the goodness of itself and its design, being the glass in which we see God's face, the immortal Seed, the Sanctifier of souls, the most wonderful declaration of God's love and amiableness, and his deed of gift of life eternal. So that God's deep imprinted image and superscription telleth us that it is the word of God.

IV. Lastly, The same [e] Holy Spirit doth, by this same word, imprint the same image of God on every believer, from Adam to this day; but in a greater degree since the ascension of Christ, and promulgation of the gospel: so that if any man have not the Spirit of Christ, it is because he is none of his, Rom. viii. 9. All that are saved have, 1. The spirit of power, which quickeneth them to God, as from the dead, and enableth them to overcome the world and the flesh, and to forsake their dearest sins. 2. They have all the spirit of wisdom, or a sound mind, by which they practically, and powerfully, and savingly know God, and Christ, and heaven, and the beauties and mysteries of holiness, and the evil of sin, the vanity of the world, and the madness and misery of the wicked: in a word, they are wise to God and to salvation, though, in their generation, the men of this world may be wiser than they.

3. They have the spirit of holy love, to God and man, and to themselves for God's sake, 2 Tim. i. 7. They love God above all, and love him in his works, and especially in his word and saints, and love to do good to all they can, and think not life too dear to exercise and manifest this love.

Now this holy image of God is first printed on the gospel as a seal; and by it, as the instrument, and by the Spirit, as the hand, it is imprinted on the souls of all believers. And how is it possible for God to set a plainer mark of his approbation on Christ's gospel, and to tell the world that it is his own, more clearly than by the Holy Spirit, thus witnessing to Christ by all these six particular instances? 1. The Spirit on the prophets and covenant that foretold Christ. 2. The Spirit on Christ himself. 3. The Spirit on the apostles. 4. The Spirit on the first churches. 5. The impress of the Spirit on the gospel itself. And, 6. The Spirit on all believers, in all generations.

And now you may see why I told you, that by the Spirit, as Christ's advocate, agent, and witness, I mean another thing, than an inward suggestion of the Spirit, telling us that this is the word of God; that by witness, I mean especially evidence. Even as the being of a rational soul in all men, having the faculties of vital action, understanding, and free-will, do prove by evidence, that a God who hath life, understanding, and will, is their Creator; so the regenerating of (not one or few, but) all true believers, by the quickening, illuminating, and converting work of the word and Spirit conjunct, powerfully giving us a new vital activity, wisdom, and love to God and holiness, doth in the same sort prove, by way of evidence, that God is the author of the new creature, and consequently the owner of the gospel that is used thereunto.

And also hence you may see why I told you, that it is not only the subtle wit of the learned, but much more the holiness of every regenerate soul, that best helpeth men to a confirmed belief of the gospel. If you are truly sanctified, you have the witness in yourself, 1 John v. 7—11. You have Christ's sanctifying Spirit, which is his mark, his advocate, and agent in you, and your earnest, and pledge, and first-fruits of eternal life. By this you may know that Christ is true, and that you are the child of God, even by the Spirit which he hath given you, 1 John iii. 24; Rom. viii. 9, 16, 26; Gal. iv. 6. As the likeness of the child to the father is his evidence, so is the divine nature and image on the regenerate. None but God can thus regenerate souls: and God would not do it by a doctrine that is false, to honour it and to deceive the world. And this love to God and holy nature which is in you is the seed of God, which will not suffer you to deny your Father, your Saviour, and your Regenerator. You see now how the weakest may prove Christ and his gospel to be true, and may stand fast against all the assaults of the devil, even by the great witness of the Holy Spirit, and not in any fanatic sense or feigned operations.

S. The Lord help me to understand and remember it. You have said that which already I see to be the light itself, and feel it give some strength to my belief. And though I was ready to ask you, how I shall be sure that the history of all these things and miracles is true; yet now I am answered by this continued evidence, which is not far off, but is in me, and, down to the end of the world, is continually at hand to answer doubts.

P. The history of these miracles, and other facts, is also delivered down to us with as great advantage as our acts of parliament, and that there were such men as Alexander, Cæsar, and Constantine in the world, which are most easily proved true.

[d] 1 Pet. i. 23; ii. 2; John vi. 63; Acts xi. 14; Rom. x. 8; Col. i. 5; Heb. iv. 12; Prov. xxx. 5; Psalm xii. 5, 6; xix. 7—9; 1 John v. 9—12.

[e] 2 Thess. ii. 13; 1 John iii. 24; iv. 13; v. 6, 9, 10; Rom. viii. 1, 9, 13, 16, 23, 26; xii. 11; ii. 29; Gal. iv. 6; iii. 14; v. 5, to the end; Phil. i. 19, 27; ii. 1; iii. 3; Ezek. xxxvi. 26, 27; xxxvii. 14; xxxix. 29; xi. 19; xviii. 31, &c.; Eph. i. 13, 17; ii. 18, 22; iii. 16; iv. 3, 4; v. 9, 18; John iii. 5, 6; vii. 39; 1 Cor. vi. 11, 17; xii. 12, 13; 2 Cor. iii. 3, 17.

S. But have none of the heathens had the Spirit, who knew not Jesus Christ?

P. In what measure they had it, and whether to their salvation, I pass by. But as it is the light of the sun itself, which appeareth before sunrising, so was it the Spirit of Christ himself, which illuminated good men before Christ's incarnation, under the first edition of the covenant of grace; and also which gave the heathens that measure of wisdom and virtue which they had. But all was much less than what true christians commonly have, since the sun is risen.

S. But you have not yet told me, how they that have not the Spirit shall be convinced of the truth of Christ?

P. Do you not see that the works of the Spirit, which I have opened to you, are such as a stander-by, that is rational and true to his own conscience, cannot deny? Might not an unregenerate man have seen the miracles of the prophets, and Christ, and the apostles, and been convinced of them, and of Christ's resurrection, by historical, certain evidence? May he not be convinced of God's image on the gospel itself, and of the holiness and wisdom of the godly, and plainly see that the righteous is more excellent than his neighbour, and perceive the Spirit by its fruits? Doubtless he may, if malignity blind him not?

S. I perceive by this, that it greatly concerneth all Christ's servants to cherish and obey the Spirit, and to grow in grace, and live very holy and heavenly, and especially loving and fruitful lives, when their holiness is to be the standing witness for Christ and the gospel to the world, from age to age? And that the sins of christians are a greater wrong to Christ than ever I before imagined.

P. I will give you one proof of that from the words of Christ himself. Christ prayeth for them that shall believe on him by the word, "that they all may be one, as thou Father art in me, and I in thee, that they also may be one in us, that the world may believe that thou hast sent me: and the glory which thou gavest me I have given them, that they may be one, even as we are one: I in them, and thou in me, that they may be made perfect in one; and that the world may know that thou hast sent me, and hast loved them, as thou hast loved me," John xvii. 21—23.

S. This text is so vehement, and layeth so much of the glory of christians, and so much of the convincing evidence of christianity to convert the world, upon the unity of believers, that it stirreth up in me a greater fear of schisms, and divisions, and sects, than I had before. I pray you, therefore, add a short character of each sect, telling me what that evil is in each one which I must avoid.

P. That I must not do now, 1. Lest I be tedious. 2. And what I give you in writing will not be read by any of those sects, if they find a word against themselves.

I will now conclude with these five graces and duties, which must be your general helps against all temptations whatsoever.

I. You must [f] grow in holy knowledge: children and fools are easilier cheated than the wise.

II. You must come to a full resolution. Resolve rather to die than wilfully sin. An unresolved person encourageth the tempter, and is more than half overcome already.

III. Be fearful of sinning, as conscious of your badness, and the multitude of temptations; and let watchfulness be your constant work.

IV. Be sure that your heart and life be wholly given up to God, and filled with good, and still employed in his service; and then the tempter will never find you disposed, or at leisure, for his turn. An empty heart (much more a carnal) and an idle life, is ready to entertain any motion unto sin.

V. Look still by faith to Christ and his Spirit, as your only strength. And trust not to your own understanding, goodness, or resolutions: for man, of himself, is very mutable. The Lord that hath converted you, confirm you, and preserve you.

[f] 1 Pet. ii. 2; 2 Pet. iii. 18; 2 Thess. i. 3; Eph. i. 17, 18; Phil. i. 9; Col. i. 9; iii. 10; Prov. xiv. 16.

THE

SIXTH DAY'S CONFERENCE.

INSTRUCTIONS FOR A HOLY LIFE.

I. THE NECESSITY, REASON, AND MEANS OF HOLINESS.
II. THE PARTS AND PRACTICE OF A HOLY LIFE.
 1. FOR PERSONAL DIRECTION.
 2. FOR FAMILY INSTRUCTION.

SPEAKERS.—Paul, a Teacher; Saul, a Learner.

PAUL. Come, neighbour, methinks by this time you should so well understand your own condition, as to know yourself what further instructions to desire. What would you have me teach you next?

SAUL. You have already, in your familiar conference, made known to me what is the nature of christianity and holiness, and what are the temptations which must be resisted. And I truly approve your wisdom in rather acquainting me with them beforehand, that I may be prepared, or may prevent them, than (as many do) to stay till I come to you in a temptation for resolution to help me out. For I know it is easier and cheaper to prevent the kindling of this fire than to quench it. And sometimes it falls among stubble, or gunpowder, and hath done its work before the sinner cometh to a minister for help. They are strange physicians who choose rather to cure diseases at the height, than to teach men how to prevent them. But I would yet entreat you to give me in writing some distinct instructions for a holy life. My reasons are, 1. I am afraid I shall not well set together what you gave me in conference, nor well remember it; and therefore would have it orderly before my eyes. 2. I would have somewhat to instruct my family with; and therefore desire you to write it me so as I may oft read it to them.

P. What is it particularly that you would have?

S. I. I would have you distinctly to write me down the true reasons and means of conversion and a holy life; for I know that it is the same reasons which made me a christian which must keep me one. And, therefore, I would oft review them, as if I had never been converted; for if I forget what moved and turned my heart to God by Christ, I shall be ready to lose the effect, and to turn back. And I would read the same reasons often to my family.

II. I would desire you to set before me all the duties of a christian life, that I may see them together, and have the sum of them imprinted on my mind, and know how to conjoin them in my practice. And this summary, also, I would read often to my family.

P. Your desires are reasonable and seasonable; and both these are done in the two sheets which I published for families, some years ago. It is them, therefore, that I shall give you in answer to your desires.

But I must tell you, that the necessity of brevity constrained me to bring much into so narrow a room, that the style is too close and concise for your ignorant family; unless you will read it very often over to them, and remember that every word is to be marked, and explain it to them in more words as you go. For once reading, especially if it be carelessly, will not serve for the understanding of so short and close a style. Ignorant hearers cannot receive much in few words; but must have a little matter in many words, oft and oft repeated, that their wits may have leisure to work upon it. And this will serve you instead of a catechism, while, in one discourse, all the heads of the catechism are delivered in a plain and practical manner. So that if you will read it over once a month to your family, and make them learn the heads of the second part by memory, it will help them unto a practical knowledge. But yet that you may have the same thing several ways, for fear of losing it, I will hereafter give you a catechism for your family besides; but this shall serve for this day's work.

I. *The Necessity, Reason, and Means of Holiness.*

1. To keep up the resolutions of the converted; and,
2. To instruct those in families that need them.

Though the[a] saving of souls be a matter of unexpressible importance, yet (the Lord have mercy upon them) what abundance are there that think it not worthy of their serious inquiry; nor the reading of a good book one hour in a week. For the sake of these careless, slothful sinners, I have here spoken much in a little room, that they may not refuse to read and consider so short a lesson, unless they think their souls worth nothing. Sinner, as thou wilt shortly answer it before God, deny not to God, to thyself, and me, the sober pondering, and faithful practising, these few directions.

I. Begin at home, and know thyself: consider what it is to be a[b] man. Thou art made a nobler creature than the brutes: they serve thee, and are governed by thee; and death ends all their pains and pleasures. But thou hast reason to rule thyself and them; to know thy God, and foresee thy end, and know thy way, and do thy duty. Thy reason, and free-will, and executive power, are part of the image of God upon thy nature; so is thy dominion over the brutes, as (under him) thou art their owner, their ruler, and their end. But thy holy wisdom, and goodness, and ability, is the chief part of his image, on which thy happiness depends. Thou hast a soul, that cannot be satisfied in knowing, till thy[c] knowledge reach to God himself; nor can it be disposed by any other; nor can it (or the societies of the world) be well governed, according to its nature, without regard to his sovereign authority, and without the hopes and[d] fears of joy and misery hereafter; nor can it be[e] happy in any thing, but seeing, and loving, and delighting in this God, as he is revealed in the other world. And is this nature given thee in vain? If the nature of all things be fitted to its[f] use and end, then it must needs be so with thine.

II. By knowing thyself, then, thou must needs know that there is a God;[g] and that he is thy Maker, and infinite in all perfections; and that he is thy Owner, thy Ruler, and thy felicity, or end. He is mad that seeth not that such creatures have a cause, or maker, and that all the power, and wisdom, and goodness of the world is caused by a power, and wisdom, and goodness, which is greater than that of all the world. And who can be our owner, but he that made us? and who can be our highest governor but our owner; whose infinite power, wisdom, and goodness, maketh him only fit thereto? And if he be our governor, he must needs have laws, with rewards for the good, and punishments for the bad, and must judge and execute accordingly. And if he be our chiefest benefactor, and all that we have is from him, and all our hope and happiness is in him, nothing can be more clear than that the very nature of man doth prove that, in hope of future happiness, he should absolutely resign himself to the will and disposal of this God, and that he should[h] absolutely obey him, and that he should love and serve him with all his powers; it being impossible to love, obey, and please that God too much who is thus our cause, our end, our all.

III. By knowing thus thyself and God, it is easy to know what primitive holiness and godliness is. Even this hearty, entire, and absolute resignation of the soul to God, as the infinite power, wisdom, and goodness, as our Creator, our Owner, Governor, and felicity, or end; fully submitting to his disposals, obeying his laws, in hope of his promised rewards, and fear of his threatened punishments; and loving and delighting in himself, and all his appearances in the world; and desiring and seeking the endless sight and enjoyment of him in heavenly glory, and expressing these affections in daily prayer, thanksgiving, and praise. This is the use of all thy faculties, the end and business of thy life, the health and happiness of thy soul. This is that holiness or godliness which God doth so much call for.

IV. And by this it is easy to know what a state of sin and ungodliness is;[i] even the want of all this holiness, and the setting up of carnal self instead of God. When men are proudly great, and wise, and good, in their own eyes, and would dispose of themselves, and all their concernments, and would rule themselves, and please themselves, according to the fleshly appetite and fancy; and therefore love most the pleasures, and profits, and honours of the world, as the provision to satisfy the desires of the flesh; and God shall be no further loved, obeyed, or pleased, than the love of fleshly pleasure will give leave; nor shall have any thing but what the flesh can spare. This is a wicked, a carnal, an ungodly state, though it break forth in various ways of sinning.

V. By this, experience itself may tell you that most men,[k] yea, all, till grace renew them, are in this ungodly, miserable state, though only the Scripture tells us how this came to pass. Though all are not fornicators, nor drunkards, nor extortioners, nor persecutors, nor live not in the same way of sinning; yet selfishness, and pride, and sensuality, and the love of worldly things, ignorance, and ungodliness, are plainly become the common corruption of the nature of man; so that their hearts are turned to the world from God, and filled with impiety, filthi-

[a] Mark viii. 36; Matt. vi. 33; Job xxi. 14; xxii. 17; Psalm i. 2, 3; xii.; xiv.
[b] Psal. viii. 4—6; Gen. i. 26, 27; ix. 6; Col. iii. 10.
[c] John xvii. 3; iv. 6, 7; Jer. ix. 21.
[d] Luke xii. 4, 5. [e] Psal. xvi. 5—11. [f] Isa. xlv. 18.
[g] Psal. xiv. 1; xlvi. 10; ix. 10; c.; xxiii.; xix. 1—3; xlvii. 7; Gen. i. 1; xviii. 25; Rev. i. 8; Rom. i. 19, 20; Ezek. xviii. 4; Mal. i. 6.
[h] Matt. xxii. 37; vi. 20, 21; Jer. v. 22; 2 Cor. v. 8, 9; viii. 5; vi. 16—18; iv. 17, 18; Tit. ii. 14; 1 Pet. ii. 9; Psal. x.; xxxvii. 4; xl. 8; Col. iii. 1, 2.
[i] Psal. i.; xiv.; Heb. xii. 14; Rom. viii. 13, 19; xiii. 14, 15; vi. 16; John iii. 3, 5, 6; 1 John ii. 15, 16; Luke xviii. 23; xiv. 26, 33.
[k] Rom. iii.; v. 12, 17, 19; Psal. xiv.; Eph. ii. 2, 3; John iii. 6.

ness, and injustice; and their reason is but a servant to their senses; and their mind,[l] and love, and life is carnal; and this carnal mind is enmity to the holiness of God, and cannot be subject to his law. This corruption is hereditary, and is become, as it were, a nature to us, being the mortal malady of all our natures. And it is easy to know that such an unholy, wicked nature must needs be loathsome to God, and unfit for the happy enjoyment of his love,[m] either here, or in the life to come; for what communion hath light with darkness?

VI. Hence, then, it is easy to see what grace is needful to a man's salvation. So odious a creature, such an unthankful rebel, that is turned away from God, and set against him, and defiled with all this filth of sin, must needs be both renewed and reconciled,[n] sanctified and pardoned, if ever he will be saved. To love God, and be beloved by him, and to be delighted here in the sight of his glory, is the heaven and happiness of souls; and all this is contrary to an unholy state. Till men have new and holy hearts, they can neither see God, nor love him, nor delight in him, nor take him for their chief content, for the flesh and world have their delight and love: and till sin be pardoned,[o] and God reconciled to the soul, what joy or peace can it expect from him whose nature and justice engageth him to loathe and punish it?

VII. And experience will tell you how insufficient[p] you are for either of these two works yourselves, to renew your souls, or to reconcile them unto God. Will a nature that is carnal resist and overcome the flesh, and abhor the sin which it most dearly loveth? Will a worldly mind overcome the world? When custom hath rooted your natural corruptions, are they easily rooted up? Oh! how great and hard a work is it, to cause a blind, unbelieving sinner to set his heart on another world, and lay up all his hopes in heaven, and to cast off all the things he seeth, for that God and glory which he never saw; and for a hardened, worldly, fleshly heart, to become wise and tender, and holy and heavenly, and abhor the sin which it most fondly loveth! And what can we do to satisfy justice, and reconcile such a rebel soul to God?

VIII. Nature and experience having thus acquainted you with your sin and misery, and what you want, will further tell you, that God[q] doth not yet deal with you according to your deserts. He giveth you life, and time, and mercies, when your sin had forfeited all these. He obligeth you to repent and turn unto him. And, therefore, experience telling you that there is some hope, and that God hath found out some way of showing mercy to the children of wrath, reason will command you to inquire of all that are fit to teach you, what way of remedy God hath made known. And as you may soon discover, that the religion of heathens and Mahometans is so far from showing the true remedy, that they are part of the disease itself; so you may learn, that a[r] wonderful person, the Lord Jesus Christ, hath undertaken the office of being the Redeemer and Saviour of the world, and that he, who is the eternal Word and Wisdom of the Father, hath wonderfully appeared in the nature of man, which he took from the Virgin Mary, being conceived by the Holy Ghost, that we might have a teacher sent from[s] heaven, infallibly and easily to acquaint the world with the will of God, and the unseen things of life eternal; how God[t] bare witness of his truth, by abundant, open, uncontrolled miracles;[u] how he conquered Satan and the world, and[x] gave us an example of perfect righteousness, and underwent the scorn and cruelty of sinners, and suffered the death of the cross, as a sacrifice for our sins, to reconcile us unto God; how he rose again the third day, and conquered death, and lived forty days longer on earth, instructing his apostles, and giving them commission to preach the gospel to all the world, and then ascended bodily into heaven while they gazed after him; how he is now in heaven, both God and man in one person, the Teacher, and King, and High Priest of his church. Of him must we learn the way of life; by him must we be ruled, as the Physician of souls. All power is given him in heaven and earth. By his sacrifice, and merit, and intercession, must we be pardoned, and accepted with the Father; and only by him must we come to God. He hath procured and established a covenant of grace, which baptism is the seal of, even that God will in him be our God and reconciled Father, and Christ will be our Saviour, and the Holy Ghost will be our Sanctifier, if we will unfeignedly consent; that is, if penitently and believingly we give up ourselves to God the Father, Son, and Holy Ghost, in these resolutions. This covenant, in the tenor of it, is a deed of gift of Christ, and pardon and salvation to all the world, if, by true faith and repentance, they will turn to God. And this shall be the law according to which he will judge all that hear it at the last; for he is made a Judge of all, and will raise all the dead, and will justify his saints, and will judge them unto endless joy and glory, and condemn the unbelievers, impenitent, and[y] ungodly, unto endless misery. The soul alone is judged at death; and body and soul at the resurrection. This gospel the apostles preached to the world; and that it might be effectual to men's salvation, the[z] Holy Ghost was first given to inspire the preachers of it, and enable them to speak in various languages, and infallibly agree in one, and to work many great and open miracles to prove their word to those they preached to; and by this means they[a] planted the church, which ordinary ministers must increase, and teach, and oversee, to the end of the world, till all the elect be gathered in. And the same[b] Holy Spirit hath undertaken it, as his work, to accompany this gospel, and by it to convert men's souls, illuminating and sanctifying them; and, by a secret[c] regeneration, to renew their natures, and bring them to that knowledge, and obedience, and love of God, which is the primitive holiness for which we were created, and from which we fell. And thus, by a Saviour and a Sanctifier, must all be reconciled and renewed, that will be glorified with God in heaven. All this you may learn from the sacred Scriptures, which were[d] written by the inspiration of the Holy Spirit, and sealed by multitudes of open[e] miracles, and contain the very image and superscription of God, and have been received and preserved by the church, as the certain oracles of God, and blessed by him through all generations, to the sanctifying of many souls.

[l] Rom. viii. 5—7. [m] Psal. iv. 3; 2 Cor. vi. 14, 17.
[n] Psal. xxxii. 1, 2; 1 Cor. vi. 11; Tit. ii. 14; iii. 5—7; Heb. xiv. 14; Matt. v. 8.
[o] Rom. v. 1—3.
[p] Psal. xlix. 7, 8, 15; 1 Cor. ii. 11; Luke xi. 21; Heb. xiv. 12; 2 Pet. i. 3.
[q] Acts xiv. 27; xvii. 24, 27, 28; Rom. i. 19, 20; ii. 4; Job xxxiii. 14—25; Matt. xii. 42, 43.
[r] Isa. ix. 6, 7; liii.; John iii. 16, 19; i. 1, 3, 4; iii. 2.
[s] John i. 18. [t] Acts ii. 22; Heb. ii. 3, 4.
[u] Matt. iv.
[x] 1 Pet. ii. 22—25; Matt. xxvi. 27, 28; xxv.; Acts i.; Heb. iv.; viii. 9, 13; viii. 6, 7; vii. 25; Eph. i. 22, 23; Rom v. 1, 3, 9; 1 John v. 10, 12; John v. 22; iii. 18, 19.
[y] Luke xvi. [z] Acts ii.; John xvii. 23.
[a] Matt. xxviii. 19, 20; Acts xiv. 23; xx.; xxvi. 17, 18.
[b] Rom. viii. 9. [c] Tit. iii. 5, 6; John xiii. 5, 6.
[d] 2 Tim. iii. 16. [e] Heb. ii. 3, 4.

IX. When you understand all this, it is time for you to[f] look home, and understand now what state your souls are in. That you were made capable of holiness and happiness, you know; that you and all men are fallen from God, and holiness, and happiness, unto self, and sin, and misery, you know; that you are so far redeemed by Christ, you know, as to have a pardoning and saving covenant tendered you, and Christ and mercy offered to your choice. But whether you are truly penitent believers, and renewed by the Holy Ghost, and so united unto Christ, this is the question yet unresolved; this is the work that is yet to do, without which there is no salvation; and if thou die before it is done, woe to thee that ever thou wast a man! Except a man be[g] regenerate by the Spirit, and converted, and made a new creature, and of carnal be made spiritual, and of earthly be made heavenly, and of selfish and sinful be made holy and obedient to God, he can never be saved, no more than the devil himself can be saved. And if this be so, (as nothing is more sure,) I require thee now, who readest these words, as thou regardest thy salvation, as thou wouldst escape hell-fire, and stand with comfort before Christ and his angels at the last, that thou soberly consider whether reason command thee not to try thy state, whether thou art thus[h] renewed by the Spirit of Christ or not; and to[i] call for help to those that can advise thee, and follow on the search till thou know thy case; and if thy soul be a stranger to this sanctifying work, whether reason command thee not, without any delay, to make out to Christ, and beg his Spirit, and cast away thy sins, and give up thyself entirely to thy God, thy Saviour, and Sanctifier, and enter into his covenant with a full resolution never to forsake him; to deny thyself, and the desires of the flesh, and this deceitful, transitory world, and lay out all thy hopes on heaven, and speedily, whatever it cost thee, to make sure of the felicity which hath no end. And darest thou refuse this, when God and conscience do command it? And, further, I advise you,

X. Understand how it is that Satan hindereth souls from being sanctified, that you may know how to resist his wiles. Some he deceiveth by[k] malicious suggestions, that holiness is nothing but fancy or hypocrisy! (And if God, and death, and heaven, and hell were fancies, this might be believed.) Some he debaucheth by the power of fleshly appetite and lust, so that their sins will not let their reason speak; some he keepeth in utter ignorance, by the evil education of ignorant parents, and the negligence of[l] ungodly, soul-murdering teachers; some he deceiveth by worldly hopes, and keepeth their minds so taken up with worldly things, that the matters of eternity can have but some loose, uneffectual thoughts, as bad as none; some are entangled in[m] ill company, who make a scorn of a holy life, or feed them with continual diversions and vain delights; and some are so[n] hardened in their sin, that they are even past feeling, and neither fear God's wrath, nor care for their salvation, but hear these things as men asleep, and nothing will awake them. Some are discouraged with a conceit that godliness is a life so[o] grievous, sad, and melancholy, that, rather than endure it, they will venture their souls, come on it what will, as if it were a grievous life to love God and hope for endless joys, and a pleasant life to love the world and sin, and live within a step of hell! Some that are convinced, do[p] put off their conversion with delays, and think it is time enough hereafter, and are purposing and promising till it be too late, and life, and time, and hope be ended; and some that see there is a necessity of holiness, are[q] cheated by some dead opinions, or names, or shows and images of holiness, either because they hold a strict opinion, or because they join with a religious party, or because they are of that which they think is the true church, or because they are baptized with water, and observe the outward parts of worship; and perhaps because they offer God a great deal of lip-service, and lifeless ceremony, which never savoured of a holy soul. Thus deadness, sensuality, worldliness, and hypocrisy do hinder millions from sanctification and salvation.

XI. If ever thou wouldst be saved, oppress not reason by sensuality or diversions; but sometimes[r] retire for sober consideration. Distracted and sleepy reason is unuseful; God and conscience have a great deal to say to thee, which in a crowd of company and business thou art not fit to hear. It is a[s] doleful case, that a man who hath a God, a Christ, a soul, a heaven, a hell to think of, will allow them none but running thoughts, and not once in a week bestow one hour in manlike, serious[t] consideration of them! Sure thou hast no greater things to mind. Resolve, then, sometimes to spend half an hour in the deepest thoughts of thy everlasting state.

XII. [u]Look upon this world and all its pleasures as a man of reason, who foreseeth the end, and not as a beast, that liveth but by sense or present objects. Do I need to tell thee, man, that thou must die? Cannot carcasses, and bones, and dust instruct thee to see the end of earthly glory, and all the pleasures of the flesh? Is it a controversy whether thy flesh must shortly perish? and wilt thou yet provide for it before thy soul? What a sad farewell must thou shortly take, of all that worldlings sell their souls for! And oh how quickly will this be! Alas, man, the day is even at hand. A few days more, and thou art gone! And darest thou live unready, and part with heaven for such a world as this?

XIII. And then think soberly of the[x] life to come. What it is for a soul to appear before the living God, and be judged to endless joy or misery. If the devil tempt thee to doubt of such a life, remember that nature, and Scripture, and the world's consent, and his own temptations, are witnesses against him. O man! canst thou pass one day, in company or alone, in business or in idleness, without some sober thoughts of everlastingness? Nothing more showeth that the hearts of men are asleep or dead, than that the thoughts of endless joy or pain, so near at hand, constrain them not to be holy, and overcome not all the temptations of the flesh, as toys, and inconsiderable things.

XIV. Mark well what mind most men are of, when they come to[y] die. Unless it be some desperate, forsaken wretch, do they not all speak well of a holy life; and wish that their lives had been spent

[f] 2 Cor. xiii. 5; Psal. iv. 4; 2 Pet. i. 10.
[g] John iii. 5; 2 Cor. v. 17; Rom. viii. 7, 9; Phil. iii. 18, 20.
[h] Acts xvi. 14.
[i] Acts ii. 37; xvi. 30; xi. 23; 2 Cor. vi. 1, 2; Rev. ii. 7.
[k] Acts xxiv. 14; xxviii. 22; xxiv. 5, 6.
[l] Mal. ii. 7, 9; Hos. iv. 9.
[m] Prov. xiii. 20.
[n] Eph. iv. 18, 19.
[o] Mal. i. 13.
[p] Matt. xxv. 3, 8, 12; xxiv. 43, 44.
[q] John viii. 39, 42, 44; Rom. iii. 1, 2; Gal. iv. 29; i. 14; Matt. xiii. 19—22; xv. 2, 3, 6.
[r] Psalm iv. 4; Hag. i. 5; Deut. xxxii. 7, 29.
[s] Isa. i. 3.
[t] Job xxxiv. 27; Jer. xxiii. 20; Psal. cxix. 59.
[u] 2 Cor. iv. 18; Deut. xxxii. 29; 1 John ii. 17; 1 Cor. vii. 31; Luke xii. 19, 20; John xiv. 1, 2; 1 Thess. v. 13.
[x] Luke xii. 4; Eccl. xii. 7; 2 Pet. iii. 11; 2 Cor. iv. 18; Phil. iii. 18, 20.
[y] Numb. xxiii. 10; Matt. xxv. 8; vii. 21, 22; Prov. i. 28, 29.

in the most fervent love of God, and strictest obedience to his laws? Do they then speak well of lust and pleasures, and magnify the wealth and honours of the world? Had they not then rather die as the most mortified saints, than as careless, fleshly, worldly sinners? And dost thou see and know this, and yet wilt thou not be instructed, and be wise in time?

XV. Think well what manner of men those were, whose[z] names are now honoured for their holiness. What manner of life did St. Peter, and Paul, St. Cyprian, St. Augustine, and all other saints and martyrs live? Was it a life of fleshly sports and pleasures? Did they deride or persecute a holy life? Were they not more strictly holy than any that thou knowest? And is he not self-condemned that honoureth the names of saints, and will not imitate them?

XVI. Think what the difference is between a christian and a[a] heathen. You are loth to be heathens or infidels, but do you think a christian excelleth them but in opinion? He that is not holier than they, is worse, and shall suffer more than they.

XVII. Think what the difference is between a[b] godly christian and an ungodly. Do not all the opposers of holiness among us yet speak for the same God, and Christ, and Scripture, and profess the same creed and religion, with those whom they oppose? And is not this Christ the Author of our holiness, and this Scripture the commander of it? Search and see, whether the difference be not this, that the godly are serious in their profession, and the ungodly are hypocrites, who hate and oppose the practice of the very things which themselves profess; whose religion serveth but to condemn them, while their lives are contrary to their tongues.

XVIII. Understand what the devil's policy is, by raising so many[c] sects, and factions, and controversies about religion in the world; even to make some think that they are religious, because they can prate for their opinions, or because they think their party is the best, because their faction is the greatest, or the least, the uppermost, or the suffering side; and to turn holy, edifying conference into vain jangling, and to make men atheists, suspecting all religion, and true to none, because of men's diversity of minds: but remember that christian religion is but one, and a thing easily known by its ancient rule; and the universal church, containing all christians, is but one. And if carnal interest or opinions so distract men, that one party saith, "We are all the church," and another saith, "It is we," (as if the kitchen were all the house, or one town or village all the kingdom,) wilt thou be mad with seeing this distraction? Hearken, sinner. All these sects, in the day of judgment, shall concur as witnesses against thee, if thou be unholy, because, however else they differed,[d] all of them, that are christians, professed the necessity of holiness, and subscribed to that Scripture which requireth it. Though thou canst not easily resolve every controversy, thou mayst easily know the true religion. It is that which Christ and his apostles taught; which all christians have professed; which Scripture requireth; which is first[e] pure, and then peaceable; most spiritual, heavenly, charitable, and just.

[z] Matt. xxiii. 29—31, 33; Heb. xi. 38; John viii. 39.
[a] Matt. x. 15; Rom. ii.; Acts x. 34, 35.
[b] Rom. ii. 12, 28, 29; Matt. xxv. 28; Luke xix. 22; Acts xxiv. 15; Gal. iv. 29.
[c] Eph. iv. 3, 14, &c.; Acts xx. 30; 1 Cor. xi. 19; xii.; 2 Tim. iv. 3; ii. 14, 16; 1 Tim. i. 5, 6; Tit. iii. 9; Matt. xii. 25; Rom. ii. 12, 27—29.
[d] Gal. i. 7, 8; Matt. xxviii. 20. [e] James iii. 17.

XIX. Away from that[f] company which is sensual, and an enemy to reason, sobriety, and holiness; and consequently to God, themselves, and thee. Can they be wise for thee, that are foolish for themselves? or friends to thee, that are undoing themselves? or have any pity on thy soul, when they make a jest of their own damnation? Will they help thee to heaven, who are running so furiously to hell? Choose better familiars, if thou wouldst be better.

XX. Judge not of a holy life by hearsay, for it cannot so be known.[g] Try it awhile, and then judge as thou findest it. Speak not against the things thou knowest not. Hadst thou but lived in the love of God, and the lively belief of endless glory, and the delights of holiness, and fears of hell, but for one month or day, and with such a heart hadst[h] cast away thy sin, and called upon God, and ordered thy family in a holy manner, especially on the Lord's day, I dare boldly say experience would constrain thee to[i] justify a holy life. But yet I must tell thee, it is not true holiness, if thou do but try it with[k] exceptions and reserves. If, therefore, God hath convinced thee that this is his will and way, I adjure thee, as in his dreadful presence, that thou[l] delay no longer, but resolve, and absolutely give up thyself to God, as thy heavenly Father, thy Saviour, and thy Sanctifier, and make an everlasting covenant with him, and then he and all his mercies will be thine. His grace will help thee, and his mercy pardon thee. His ministers will instruct thee, and his people pray for thee and assist thee. His angels will guard thee, and his Spirit comfort thee: and when flesh must fail, and thou must leave this world, thy Saviour will then receive thy soul, and bring it into the participation of his glory: and he will raise thy body, and justify thee before the world, and make thee equal to the angels: and thou shalt live in the sight and love of God, and in the everlasting pleasures of his glory. This is the end of faith and holiness. But if thou harden thy heart, and refusest mercy,[m] everlasting woe will be thy portion, and then there will be no remedy.

And now, reader, I beg of thee, and I beg of God, on my bended knees, that these few words may sink into thy heart, and that thou wouldst read them over and over again, and bethink thee, as a man that must shortly die, whether any deserve thy love and obedience more than God; and thy thankful remembrance more than Christ; and thy care and diligence more than thy salvation? Is there any felicity more desirable than heaven? or any misery more terrible than hell? or any thing so regardable as that which is everlasting? Will a few days' fleshly pleasures pay for the loss of heaven and thy immortal soul? or will thy sin and prosperity be sweet at death, and in the day of judgment? As thou art a man, and as ever thou believest there is a God, and a world to come, and as thou carest for thy soul, whether it be saved or damned; I beseech thee, I charge thee, think of these things; think of them once a day at least! think of them with thy most sober, serious thoughts! Heaven is not a May-game, and hell is not a flea-biting: make not a jest of salvation or damnation. I know thou livest in a distracted world, where thou mayst hear some laughing at such things as these, and scorning at a holy life, and fastening odious reproaches on the godly, and mer-

[f] Eph. v. 11; Prov. xxiii. 20; 2 Cor. vi. 17, 18; Psalm xv. 4; Deut. xiii. 3.
[g] John v. 40; vi. 35, 37, 45; Luke xiv. 29, 30.
[h] Isa. lv. 6, 7. [i] Matt. xi. 19. [k] Luke xiv. 33.
[l] Rev. xxii. 17; ii.; iii.; John i. 12; 1 John v. 12; Psalm xxxiv. 7; lxxiii. 26; Matt. xxv.; Luke xx. 36; Heb. ii. 3; 1 Thess. ii. 12.
[m] Luke xix. 27; Prov. xxix. 1; i. 25.

rily drinking, and playing, and prating away their time, and then saying that they will trust God with their souls, and hope to be saved without so much ado! But if all these men do not change their minds, and be not shortly down in the mouth, and would not be glad to eat their words, and wish that they had lived a holy life, though it had cost them scorn and suffering in the world, let me bear the shame of a deceiver for ever: but if God and thy conscience bear witness against thy sin, and tell thee that a holy life is best; regard not the gainsayings of a Bedlam world, which is drunk with the delusions of the flesh: but give up thy soul and life to God, by Jesus Christ, in a faithful covenant! Delay no longer, man, but resolve; resolve immediately, resolve unchangeably; and God will be thine, and thou shalt be his for ever. Amen. Lord, have mercy on this sinner! and so let it be resolved by thee and him.

II. *The Parts and Practice of a Holy Life; for Personal and Family Instruction.*

All is not[n] done when men have begun a religious life. All trees that blossom prove not fruitful; and all fruit comes not to perfection. Many fall off, who seemed to have good beginnings: and many dishonour the name of Christ, by their scandals and infirmities. Many do grieve their teachers' hearts, and lamentably disturb the church of Christ, by their ignorance, errors, self-conceitedness, unruliness, headiness, contentiousness, sidings, and divisions: insomuch that the[o] scandals and the feuds of christians are the great impediments of the conversion of the infidel and heathen world, by exposing christianity to their contempt and scorn, as if it were but the error of men, as unholy, and worldly, and proud as others, that can never agree among themselves: and many, by their passions and selfishness, are a trouble to the families and neighbours where they live; and more by their weaknesses and great distempers, are snares, vexations, and burdens to themselves. [s] Whereas christianity in its true constitution is a life of such holy[p] light and love, such purity and peace, such fruitfulness and heavenliness, as, if it were accordingly showed forth in the lives of christians, would command admiration and reverence from the world, and do more to their conversion than swords or words alone can do: and it would make christians useful and amiable to each other; and their lives a feast and pleasure to themselves. I hope it may prove some help to those excellent ends, and to the securing men's salvation, if, in a few sound, experienced directions, I open to you the duties of a christian life.

I. Keep still the true[q] form of christian doctrine, desire, and duty, orderly printed on your minds; that is, understand it clearly and distinctly, and remember it. I mean the great points of religion contained in catechisms: you may still grow in the clearer understanding of your catechisms, if you live a hundred years: let not the words only, but the matter, be as familiar in your minds as the rooms of your house are. Such[r] solid knowledge will establish you against seduction and unbelief, and will be still within you a ready help for every grace, and every duty, as the skill of an artificer is for his work: and for want of this, when you come among infidels or heretics, their reasonings may seem unanswerable to you, and shake, if not overthrow, your faith: and you will easily err in lesser points, and trouble the church with your dreams and wranglings. This is the calamity of many professors; that while they will be most censorious judges in every controversy about church matters, they know not well the doctrine of the catechism.

II. Live daily by faith on [s] Jesus Christ, as the Mediator between God and you: being well grounded in the belief of the gospel, and understanding Christ's office, make use of him still in all your wants. Think on the fatherly love of God, as coming to you through him alone; and of the Spirit, as given by him, your Head; and of the covenant of grace, as enacted and sealed by him; and of the ministry, as sent by him; and of all time, and helps, and hope, as procured and given by him. When you think of sin, and infirmity, and temptations, think also of his sufficient pardoning, justifying, and victorious grace. When thou thinkest of the world, the flesh, and the devil, think how he overcometh them. Let his doctrine, and the pattern of his most perfect life, be always before you as your rule. In all your doubts, and fears, and wants, go to him in the Spirit, and to the Father by him, and him alone. Take him as the root of your life and mercies, and live as upon him and by his life. And when you die, resign your souls to him, that they may be with him where he is, and see his glory. To live on Christ, and use him in every want and address to God, is more than a general, confused believing in him.

III. So believe in the Holy Ghost as to [t] live and work by him, as the body doth by the soul. You are not [u] baptized into his name in vain; but too few understand the sense and reason of it. The Spirit is sent by Christ for two great works: 1. To the apostles (and prophets) to [x] inspire them infallibly to preach the gospel, and confirm it by miracles, and leave it on record for following ages in the holy Scriptures. 2. To all his [y] members, to illuminate and sanctify them, to believe and obey this sacred doctrine; beside his common gift to many to understand and preach it. The Spirit, having first indited the gospel, doth by it first regenerate, and after govern, all true believers. He is not now given us for the revealing of new doctrines, but to understand and obey the [z] doctrine revealed and sealed by him long ago. As the sun doth, by its sweet and secret influence, both give and cherish the natural life of things, sensitive and vegetative, so doth Christ, by his [a] Spirit, our spiritual life. As you do no work but by your natural life, you should do none but by your spiritual life. You must not only believe, and love, and pray by it, but manage all your calling by it; for "Holiness to the Lord" must be written upon all. All things are sanctified to you, because you, being sanctified to God, devote all to him, and use all for him; and, therefore, must do all in the strength and conduct of the Spirit.

IV. Live wholly upon God,[b] as all in all; as the first efficient, principal dirigent, and final cause of all things. Let faith, hope, and love, be daily feeding on him. Let "Our Father which art in

[n] Col. i. 23; Heb. iv. 1; 2 Pet. ii. 20; 1 Cor. iii.; Gal. iii.; iv.; Matt. xiii. 41; xviii. 7.
[o] Phil. iii. 18, 19; Acts xx. 30.
[p] Matt. v. 16; 1 Pet. iii. 1; ii. 15; i. 8; 2 Cor. i. 12.
[q] 2 Tim. i. 13; iii. 7; Heb. v. 12; Phil. i. 9; Rom. xv. 14.
[r] Eph. iv. 13, 14; Col. i. 9; ii. 13; iii. 10; 1 Tim. vi. 4.
[s] John xvii. 3; xvi. 33; Eph. iii. 17, 18; i. 22, 23; iv. 6, 16; Matt. xxviii. 19; Rom. v.; 2 Cor. xii. 9; 1 John v. 4; Heb. iv. 14, 16; Col. iii. 3, 4; Acts vii. 59.
[t] Gal. v. 16, 25.
[u] Matt. xxviii. 19.
[x] John xvi. 13; Heb. ii. 3, 4.
[y] 1 Cor. xii. 12, 13; Rom. viii. 9, 13; John iii. 5, 6.
[z] 2 Tim. iii. 15, 16; Jude 19, 20.
[a] Ezek. xxxvi. 27; Isa. xliv. 3; Rom. viii. 1, 5; 1 Cor. vi. 11; Zech. xiv. 20.
[b] 1 Cor. x. 31; Rom. xi. 36; v. 1, 3; 2 Cor. v. 7, 8, 19; 1 John iii. 1; Matt. xxii. 37; Eph. i. 6; Gal. iv. 4—6.

heaven," be first inscribed on your hearts, that he may seem most amiable to you, and you may boldly trust him, and filial love may be the spring of duty. Make use of the Son and Spirit to lead you to the Father; and of faith in Christ, to kindle and keep alive the love of God. The love of God is our primitive holiness, and specially called, with its fruits, our sanctification, which faith in Christ is but a means to. Let it be your principal end, in studying Christ, to see the goodness, love, and amiableness of God in him: a condemning God is not so easily loved as a gracious, reconciled God. You have so much of the Spirit as you have love to God; this is the proper gift of the Spirit to all the adopted sons of God, to cause them, with filial affection and dependence, to cry "Abba, Father." Know not, desire not, love not any creature, but purely as subordinate to God. Without him, let it be nothing to you but as the glass without the face, or scattered letters without the sense, or as the corpse without the soul. [c] Call nothing prosperity, or pleasure, but his love; and nothing adversity, or misery, but his displeasure, and the cause and fruits of it. When any thing would seem lovely and desirable, which is against him, call it [d] dung. And hear that man as [e] Satan, or the serpent, that would entice you from him; and count him but vanity, a worm, and dust, that would affright you from your duty to him. Fear him much, but love him more. Let [f] love be the soul and end of every other duty; it is the end and reason of all the rest; but it hath no end, or reason, but its object. Think of no other heaven, and end, and happiness of man, but love, the final act, and God, the final object. Place not your religion in any thing but the love of God, with its means and fruits. Own no grief, desire, or joy, but a mourning, a seeking, and a rejoicing love.

V. Live in the belief and hopes of heaven, and [g] seek it as your part and end; and daily delight your souls in the forethoughts of the endless sight and love of God. As God is seen on earth but as in a glass, so he is proportionably enjoyed. But when mourning, seeking love hath done, and sin and enemies are overcome, and we behold the glory of God in heaven, the delights of love will then be perfect. You may desire more on earth than you may hope for. Look not for a kingdom of this world, nor for mount Zion in the wilderness. Christ reigneth on earth, as Moses in the camp, to guide us to the land of promise: our perfect blessedness will be, where the kingdom is delivered up to the Father, and God is all in all. A doubt, or a strange heartless thought of heaven, is water cast on the sacred fire, to quench your holiness and your joy. Can you travel one whole day to such an end, and never think of the place that you are going to? which must be intended in every righteous act, either notedly, or by the ready, unobserved act of a potent habit. When earth is at the best, it will not be heaven. You live no further by faith like christians, than you either live for heaven in seeking it, or else upon heaven, in hope and joy.

VI. Labour to make religion your pleasure and [h] delight. Look oft to God, to heaven, to Christ, to the Spirit, to the promises, to all your mercies. Call over your experiences, and think what matter of high delight is still before you, and how unseemly it is, and how injurious to your profession, for one that saith he hopeth for heaven, to live as sadly as those that have no higher hopes than earth. How should that man be filled with joy, who must live in the joys of heaven for ever! Especially rejoice when the messengers of death do tell you that your endless joy is near. If God and heaven, with all our mercies in the way, be not reason enough for a joyful life, there can be none at all. Abhor all suggestions which would make religion seem a tedious, irksome life. And take heed that you represent it not so to others; for you will never make them in love with that which you make them not perceive to be delectable and lovely. Not as the hypocrite, by forcing and framing his religion to his carnal mind and pleasure; but bringing up the heart to a holy suitableness to the pleasure of religion.

VII. Watch, as for your souls, against this flattering, tempting [i] world; especially when it is represented as more sweet and delectable than God, and holiness, and heaven. This world, with its pleasure, wealth, and honours, is it that is put in the balance by Satan, against God, and holiness, and heaven; and no man shall have better than he chooseth and preferreth. The bait taketh advantage of the brutish part, when reason is asleep; and if, by the help of sense, it get the throne, the beast will ride and rule the man, and reason become a slave to sensuality. When you hear the serpent, see his sting, and see death attending the forbidden fruit. When you are rising, look down and see how far you have to fall. His reason, as well as faith, is weak, who for such fool-gauds as the pomp and vanities of this world, can forget God, and his soul, and death and judgment, heaven and hell, yea, and deliberately command them to stand by. What knowledge or experience can do good on that man who will venture so much for such a world, which all that have tried it call vanity at the last? How deplorable, then, is a worldling's case! O fear the world, when it smileth, or seems sweet and amiable. Love it not, if you love your God, and your salvation.

VIII. Fly from temptations, and crucify the [k] flesh, and keep a constant government over your appetite and senses. Many who had no designed, stated vice, or worldly interest, have shamefully fallen by the sudden surprise of appetite or lust. When custom hath taught these to be greedy, and violent, like a hungry dog, or a lusting boar, it is not a sluggish wish or purpose that will mortify or rule them. How dangerous a case is that man in, who hath so greedy a beast continually to restrain, that if he do but neglect his watch one hour, is ready to run him headlong into hell! Who can be safe, that standeth long on so terrible a precipice? The tears and sorrows of many years may, perhaps, not repair the loss which one hour or act may bring. The case of David, and many another, are dreadful warnings. Know what it is that you are most in danger of; whether lust and idleness, or excess in meat, or drink, or play; and there set the strongest watch for your preservation. Make it your daily business to mortify that lust; and scorn that your brutish sense or appetite should conquer reason. Yet trust not purposes alone, but away from the temptation;

[c] Psal. xxx. 5; lxiii. 3.
[d] Phil. iii. 7, 8.
[e] Matt. xvi. 23.
[f] 2 Thess. iii. 5; 2 Cor. xiii. 14.
[g] Col. iii. 1, 2, 4; Matt. vi. 19—21, 33; 2 Cor. iv. 17, 18; v. 7; Luke xii. 20; Heb. vi. 20; 1 Cor. xv. 28; Eph. iv. 6; i. 2, 3; Phil. iii. 18, 20; Psal. lxxiii. 25, 26; John xviii. 36.
[h] Psal. i. 2, 3; xlviii. 2, 10; lxiii. 3, 5; xxxvii. 4; ix. 19; cxix. 48, 70; cxii. 1; xxxii. 11; Isa. lviii. 14; Rom. xiv. 17; v. 1, 3, 5; 1 Pet. i. 8; Matt. v. 11, 12.
[i] Gal. vi. 14; i. 4; 1 John ii. 15, 16; v. 4, 5; Jam. i. 27; iv. 4, 5; i. 11; v. 1, 2, 4; Rom. xii. 2; Tit. ii. 12; Matt. xix. 24; Luke xii. 16, 21; xvi. 25; viii. 14; Heb. xi. 26.
[k] Rom. viii. 1, 13; xiii. 14; Gal. v. 17, 24; Jude 8, 23; 2 Pet. ii. 10; Eph. ii. 3; 1 Pet. ii. 11; Matt. vi. 13; xxvi. 41; Luke viii. 13.

touch not, yea look not on, the tempting bait; keep far enough off, if you desire to be safe. What miseries come from small beginnings: temptation leads to sin, and small sins to greater, and those to hell. And sin and hell are not to be played with. Open your sin or temptation to some friend, that shame may save you from danger.

IX. Keep up a constant, skilful government over your [l] passions and your tongues. To this end, keep a tender conscience, which will smart when in any of these you sin; let holy passions be well ordered, and selfish, carnal passions be restrained; let your [m] tongues know their duties to God and man, and labour to be skilful and resolute in performing them; know all the sins of the tongue, that you may avoid them, for your innocency and peace do much depend on the prudent government of your tongues.

X. Govern your [n] thoughts with constant, skilful diligence. In this, right habits and affections will do most by inclining them unto good; it is easy to think on that which we love. Be not unfurnished of matter for your thoughts to work upon; and often retire yourselves for serious meditation. Be not so solitary and deep in musings as to overstretch your thoughts, and confound your minds, or take you off from necessary converse with others; but be sure that you be considerate, and dwell much at home, and converse most with your consciences and your God, with whom you have the greatest business. Leave not your thoughts unemployed or ungoverned; scatter them not abroad upon impertinent vanities: oh that you knew what daily business you have for them! Most men are wicked, deceived, and undone, because they are inconsiderate, and dare not, or will not, retiredly and soberly use their reason; or use it but as a slave in chains, in the service of their passion, lust, and interests. He was never wise, or good, or happy, who was not soberly and impartially considerate. How to be good, to do good, and finally enjoy good, must be the sum of all your thoughts. Keep them first holy, then charitable, clean, and chaste; and quickly check them when they look towards sin.

XI. Let [o] time be exceeding precious in your eyes, and carefully and diligently redeem it. What haste doth it make, and how quickly will it be gone! and then how highly will it be valued, when a minute of it can never be recalled! Oh what important business have we for every moment of our time, if we should live a thousand years! Take not that man to be well in his wits, or to know his God, his end, his work, or his danger, who hath time to spare. Redeem it, not only from needless sports, and plays, and idleness, and curiosity, and compliment, and excess of sleep, and chat, and worldliness, but also from the entanglement of lesser good, which would hinder you from greater. Spend time as men that are ready to pass into another world, where every minute must be accounted for; it must go with us for ever as we lived here. Let not health deceive you into the expectation of living long, and so into a senseless negligence; see your glass running, and keep a reckoning of the expense of time; and spend it just as you would review it when it is gone.

XII. Let the [p] love of all, in their several capacities, become, as it were, your very nature, and doing them all the good you can be very much of the business of your lives. God must be loved in all his creatures his natural image on all men, and his spiritual imag on his saints. Our neighbour must be loved as our natural selves; that is, our natural neighbour as our natural self, with the love of benevolence; and our spiritual neighbour as our spiritual self, with a love of complacence. In opposition to complacence, we may hate our sinful neighbour as we must ourselves; (much more;) but, in opposition to benevolence, we must neither hate ourselves, our neighbour, or our enemy. Oh that men knew how much of christianity doth consist in love and doing good! With what eyes do they read the gospel, who see not this in every page. Abhor all that selfishness, pride, and passion, which are the enemies of love; and those opinions, and factions, and censurings, and backbitings, which would destroy it. Take him that speaketh evil of another to you, without a just cause and call, to be Satan's messenger, entreating you to hate your brother, or to abate your love; for to persuade you that a man is bad, is directly to persuade you so far to hate him. Not that the good and bad must be confounded; but love will call none bad without constraining evidence. Rebuke backbiters; hurt no man, and speak evil of no man, unless it be not only just, but necessary to some greater good. Love is lovely; they that love shall be beloved. Hating and hurting makes men hateful. "Love thy neighbour as thyself," and "Do as thou wouldst be done by," are the golden rules of our duty to men, which must be deeply written on your hearts. For want of this, there is nothing so false, so bad, so cruel, which you may not be drawn to think, or say, or do, against your brethren. Selfishness, and want of love, do as naturally tend to ambition and covetousness, and thence to cruelty, against all that stand in the way of their desires, as the nature of a wolf to kill the lambs. All factions, and contentions, and persecutions, in the world, proceed from selfishness, and want of charity. Devouring malice is the devilish nature. Be as zealous in doing good to all as Satan's servants are in hurting: take it as the use of all your talents, and use them as you would hear of it at last. Let it be your business, and not a matter on the by, especially for public good and men's salvation; and what you cannot do yourselves, persuade others to. Give them good books, and draw them to the means which are most like to profit them.

XIII. Understand the right terms of church communion; especially the unity of the universal church, and the universal communion which you must hold with all the parts; and the difference between the church as visible and invisible. For want of these, how woeful are our divisions! Read oft 1 Cor. xii.; Eph. iv. 1—17; John xvii. 21—23; Acts iv. 32; ii. 42; 1 Cor. i. 10, 11, 13; iii. 3; Rom. xvi. 17; Phil. ii. 1—4; 1 Thess. v. 12, 13; Acts xx. 30; 1 Cor. xi. 19; Tit. iii. 10; Jam. iii.; Col. i. 4; Heb. x. 25; Acts viii. 37; xii. 13; 1 Cor. i. 2, 12, 13; iii. 3, 4; xi. 18, 21. Study these well. You must have union and communion, in faith and love, with all the christians in the world; and refuse not local communion when you have a just call, so far as they put you not on sinning. Let your usual meeting be with the purest church, if you lawfully may, and still respect the public good; but sometimes occasionally communicate even with defective, faulty churches,

[l] Jam. i. 19; iii. 13, 17; 1 Pet. iii. 4; Matt. v. 5; Eph. iv. 2, 3; Col. iii. 12.

[m] Jam. i. 26; iii. 5, 6; Psal. xxxiv. 13; Prov. xviii. 21.

[n] Deut. xv. 9; xxxii. 29; 2 Cor. x. 5; Gen. vi. 5; Psal. x. 9; xciv. 19; cxix 59, 113; Prov. xii. 5; xv. 26; xxx. 32; Jer. iv. 14.

[o] Eph. v. 16; John xiv. 1, 2; ix. 4; Acts xvii. 21; 1 Cor. vii. 29; 2 Cor. vi. 2; Luke xix. 42, 44; Psalm xxxix. 4; Matt. xxv. 10, 12.

[p] 1 Tim. i. 5, 6; Matt. xix. 19; v. 44, 45; Rom. xiii. 10; xv. 1, 3; 1 John i. 16; Eph. iv. 2, 15, 16; Col. ii. 2; i. 4; 1 Tim. vi. 11; Jam. iii. 17; iv. 11; Phil. ii. 1, 2; ii. 20, 21; 1 Thess. iv. 9; John xiii. 35; 1 Cor. xiii.; Gal. vi. 10; Tit. ii. 14.

so be it they are true christians, and put you not on sin; that so you may show that you own them as christians, though you disown their corruptions. Think not your presence maketh all the faults of ministry, worship, or people, to be yours, for then I would join with no church in the world. Know, that as the mystical church consisteth of heart covenanters, so doth the church, as visible, consist of verbal covenanters, which make a credible profession of consent. And that nature and Scripture teach us to take every man's word as credible, till perfidiousness forfeit his credit; which forfeiture must be proved, before any sober profession can be taken for an insufficient title. [q] Grudge not, then, at the communion of any professed christian in the church visible; though we must do our part to cast out the obstinately impenitent by discipline, which, if we cannot do, the fault is not ours. The presence of hypocrites is no hurt, but oft a mercy, to the sincere: how small else would the church seem in the world! Outward privileges belong to outward covenanters, and inward mercies to the sincere. [r] Division is wounding, and tends to death. Abhor it, as you love the church's welfare, or your own. The wisdom from above is first pure, and then peaceable: never separate what God conjoineth. It is the earthly, sensual, devilish wisdom, which causeth bitter envying, and strife, and confusion, and every evil work. "Blessed are the peace-makers."

XIV. Take heed of [s] pride and self-conceitedness in religion. If once you overvalue your own understandings, your crude conceptions and gross mistakes will delight you as some supernal light; and, instead of having compassion on the weak, you will be unruly, and despisers of your guides, and censorious contemners of all that differ from you; and persecutors of them, if you have power; and will think all intolerable, that take you not as oracles, and your words as law. Forget not, that the church hath always suffered by censorious, unruly professors on the one hand, (and oh what divisions and scandals have they caused! as well as by the profane and persecutors on the other: take heed of both. And when contentions are afoot, be quiet and silent, and not too forward, and keep up a zeal for love and peace.

XV. Be faithful and conscionable in all your [t] relations. Honour and obey your parents, and other superiors. Despise not, and resist not, government. If you suffer unjustly by them, be humbled for those sins which cause God to turn your protectors into afflicters; and, instead of murmuring and rebelling against them, reform yourselves, and then commit yourselves to God. Princes and pastors I will not speak to: subjects, and servants, and children, must obey their superiors as the officers of God.

XVI. Keep up the government of God in your [u] families: holy families must be the chief preservers of the interest of religion in the world. Let not the world turn God's service into a customary, lifeless form. Read the Scripture and edifying books to them; talk with them seriously about the state of their souls and everlasting life; pray with them fervently; watch over them diligently; be angry against sin, and meek in your own cause; be examples of wisdom, holiness, and patience; and see that the Lord's day be spent in holy preparation for eternity.

[q] Matt. xiii. 29, 41.
[r] John xvi. 2; 1 Cor. i. 10; Rom. xvi. 17; Jam. iii. 14—18.
[s] 1 Tim. iii. 6; vi. 4; Col. ii. 18; 1 Cor. viii. 1; iv. 6; 1 Pet. v. 5; Jam. iii. 1, 17.
[t] Eph. v.; vi.; Col. iii.; iv.; Rom. xiii. 1, 7; 1 Pet. ii. 13, 15.
[u] Command. iv.; Josh. xxiv. 15; Deut. vi. 6—8; Dan. vi.
[x] Heb. xiii. 5; Command. iv.; 2 Thess. iii. 10, 12; 1 Thess. iv. 7; 1 Tim. v. 13; Prov. xxxi.; 1 Cor. vii. 29.

XVII. Let your [x] callings be managed in holiness and laboriousness. Live not in idleness: be not slothful in your work. Whether you be bound or free, in the sweat of your brow you must eat your bread, and labour the six days, that you may have to give to him that needeth. Slothfulness is sensuality, as well as filthier sins. The body (that is able) must have fit employments as well as the soul; or else body and soul will fare the worse. But let all be but as the labour of a traveller, and aim at God and heaven in all.

XVIII. Deprive not yourselves of the benefit of an able, faithful [y] pastor, to whom you may open your case in secret; or at least of a holy,[z] faithful friend; and be not [a] displeased at their free reproofs. Woe to him that is alone! how blind and partial are we in our own cause! and how hard is it to know ourselves without an able, faithful helper! you forfeit this great mercy, when you love a flatterer, and angrily defend your sin.

XIX. [b] Prepare for sickness, sufferings, and death. Overvalue not prosperity, nor the favour of man: if selfish men prove false and cruel to you, even those of whom you have deserved best, marvel not at it, but pray for your enemies, persecutors, and slanderers, that God would turn their hearts, and pardon them. What a mercy is it to be driven from the world to God, when the love of the world is the greatest danger of the soul! Be ready to die, and you are ready for any thing: ask your hearts seriously, what is it that I shall need at a dying hour? and let it speedily be got ready, and not be to seek in the time of your extremity.

Understand the true method of peace of conscience, and judge not of the state of your souls upon deceitful grounds. As presumptuous hopes do keep men from conversion, and imbolden them in sin; so causeless fears do hinder our love and praise of God, by obscuring his loveliness: and they destroy our thankfulness, and our delight in God, and make us a burden to ourselves, and a grievous stumblingblock to others. The general grounds of all your comfort, are, 1. The [c] gracious nature of God; 2. The [d] sufficiency of Christ; and, 3. The truth, and [e] universality of the promise, which giveth Christ and life to all, if they will accept him: but this acceptance is the proof of your particular title; without which, these do but aggravate your sin. Consent to God's covenant is the true condition and proof of your title to God as your Father, Saviour, and Sanctifier, and so to the saving blessings of the covenant. Which consent, if you survive, must produce the duties which you consent to. He that heartily consenteth that God be his God, his Saviour, and Sanctifier, is in a state of life. But this includeth the [f] rejection of the world. Much knowledge, and memory, and utterance, and lively affections, are all very desirable: but you must judge your state by none of these; for they are all uncertain. But, 1. If God, and holiness, and heaven, have the highest estimation of your practical judgment, as being esteemed best for you; 2. And be preferred in the choice and resolution of your wills, and that habitually, before all the pleasures of the world; 3. And be first and chiefly sought in your endeavours; this is the infallible proof of your sanctification.

[y] Mal. ii. 7. [z] Eccl. iv. 10, 11.
[a] Prov. xii. 1; xv. 5, 10, 31; Heb. iii. 13.
[b] Luke xii. 40; 2 Pet. i. 10; Phil. i. 21, 23; Jer. ix. 4, 5; Matt. vii. 4, 5; 2 Cor. v. 1, 2, 4, 8.
[c] Exod. xxxiv. 6. [d] Heb. vii. 25.
[e] John iii. 16; iv. 42; 1 Tim. iv. 10; ii. 4; Matt. xxviii. 19, 20; Rev. xxii. 17; Isa. lv. 1—3, 6, 7.
[f] Luke xiv. 26, 33; 1 John ii. 15; Matt. vi. 19—21, 33; Col. iii. 1, 2; Rom. viii. 1, 13.

Christian, upon long and serious study and experience, I dare boldly commend these directions to thee, as the way of God, which will end in blessedness. The Lord resolve and strengthen thee to obey them.

This is the true constitution of christianity; this is true godliness; and this is to be religious indeed; and all this is no more than to be seriously such, as all among us, in general words, profess to be. This is the religion which must difference you from hypocrites; which must settle you in peace, and make you an honour to your profession, and a blessing to those that dwell about you. Happy is the land, the church, the family, which doth consist of such as these! These are not they that either persecute or divide the church; or that make their religion servant to their policy, to their ambitious designs, or fleshly lusts; nor that make it the bellows of sedition, or rebellion, or of an envious, hurtful zeal; or a snare for the innocent; or a pistol to shoot at the upright in heart; these are not they that have been the shame of their profession, the hardening of ungodly men and infidels, and that have caused the enemies of the Lord to blaspheme. If any man will make a religion of or for his lusts, of papal tyranny, or pharisaical formality, or of his private opinions, or of proud censoriousness, and contempt of others, and of faction, and unwarrantable separations and divisions, and of standing at a more observable distance from common professors of christianity than God would have them; or yet of pulling up the hedge of discipline, and laying Christ's vineyard common to the wilderness; the storm is coming, when this religion, founded on the sand, will fall, and great will be the fall thereof. When the religion, which consisteth in faith and love to God and man, in mortifying the flesh, and crucifying the world, in self-denial, humility, and patience, in sincere obedience and faithfulness in all relations, in watchful self-government, in doing good, and in a divine and heavenly life, though it will be hated by the ungodly world, shall never be a dishonour to your Lord, nor deceive or disappoint your souls.

THE

SEVENTH DAY'S CONFERENCE.

OF A HOLY FAMILY; AND HOW TO GOVERN IT, AND PERFORM THE DUTY OF ALL FAMILY RELATIONS, AND OTHERS.

SPEAKERS.—Paul, a Teacher; and Saul, a Learner.

PAUL. Welcome, neighbour: how do you like the new life which you have begun? You have taken home instructions already which will find you work: but what do you find in the practising of them?

SAUL. I find that I have foolishly long neglected a necessary, noble, joyful life; and thereby lost my time, and made myself both unskilful and undisposed to the practice of it: I find that the things which you have prescribed me are high and excellent, and doubtless must be very sweet to them that have a suitable skill and disposition; and some pleasure I find in my weak beginnings: but the greatness of the work, and the great untowardness and strangeness of my mind, doth much abate the sweetness of it, by many doubts, and fears, and difficulties: and when I fail, I find it hard both to repent aright, and, by faith, to fly to Christ for pardon. And if you had not forewarned me of this temptation, I should have thought by these troubles, that my case is worse in point of ease (though not of safety) than it was before. But I foresee that better things may yet be hoped for; and I hope I am in the way.

P. Where is your great difficulty that requireth counsel?

S. I find a great deal of work to do in my family, to govern them in the fear of God, to do my duty to them all; especially to educate my children, and daily to worship God among them. And I am so unable for it, that I am ready to omit all. I pray you help me with your advice.

P. My first advice to you is, that you resolve, by God's help, to perform your duty as well as you can: and that you devote your family to God, and take him for the Lord and Master of it, and use it as a society sanctified to him. And I pray you let these reasons fix your resolution.

1. If God be not master of your family, the devil will; and if God be not first served in it, the flesh and the world will. And I hope I need not tell you how bad a master, work, and wages, they will then have.

2. If you devote your family to God, God will be the Protector of it. He will take care of it for safety and provision as his own. Do you not need such a Protector; and can you have a better, or better take care for the welfare and safety of you and yours? And if your family be not God's, they are his enemies, and under his curse as rebels. Instead of his blessings of health, peace, provision, and success, you may look for sickness, dangers, crosses, distresses, unquietness, and death; or, which is worse, that your prosperity shall be a curse and snare to you and yours.

3. A holy family is a place of comfort, a church of God. What a joy will it be to you to live together daily in this hope, that you shall meet and live together in heaven; to think that wife, children, and servants, shall shortly be fellow-citizens with you of the heavenly Jerusalem! How pleasant is it to join with one heart and mind in the service of God, and in his cheerful praises! How lovely will you be to one another, when each one beareth the image of God! What abundance of jars and miseries will be prevented, which sin would daily bring among you; and when any of you die, how comfortably may the rest be about their bed, and attend their corpse unto the grave, when they have good hopes that the soul is received to glory by Christ. But if your family be ungodly, it will be like a nest of wasps, or like a jail, full of discord and vexation: and it will be grievous to you to look your wife or children in the face, and think that they are like to lie in hell; and their sickness and death will be tenfold the more heavy to you to think of their woeful and unseen end.

4. Your family hath such constant need of God, as commandeth you constantly to serve him. As every man hath his personal necessities, so families have family necessities, which God must supply, or they are miserable. Therefore family duty must be your work.

5. Holy families[a] are the seminaries of Christ's church on earth, and it is very much that lieth upon them to keep up the interest of religion in the world. Hence come holy magistrates, when great men's children have a holy education. And, oh, what a blessing is one such to the countries where they are! Hence spring holy pastors and teachers to the

[a] 1 Tim. iii. 12; Deut. vi. 7; xxx. 2; Psal. cxlvii. 13; Acts ii. 39; Eph. vi. 4—6; Prov. xxii. 6, 15; xxix. 15; xxiii. 13

churches, who, as Timothy, receive holy instructions from their parents, and grace from the Spirit of Christ in their tender age. Many a congregation that is happily fed with the bread of life, may thank God for the endeavours of a poor man or woman, that trained up a child[b] in the fear of God, to become their holy, faithful teacher. Though learning be found in schools, godliness is oftener received from the education of careful parents. When children and servants come to the church with understanding, godly, prepared minds, the labours of the pastor will do them good; they will receive what they hear with faith, love, and obedience. It will be a joy to the minister to have such a flock: and it will be joyful to the people that are such, to meet together in the sacred assemblies, to worship God with cheerful hearts: and such worshippers will be acceptable to God. But when families come together in gross ignorance, and with unsanctified hearts, there they sit like images, understanding little of what is said, and go home little the better for all the labours of the minister: and the motions of their tongue and bodies is most of the worship which they give to God; but their hearts are not offered in faith and love as a sacrifice to him, nor do they feel the power and sweetness of the word, and worship him in spirit and truth.

6. And in times when the churches are corrupted, and good ministers are wanting, and bad ones either deceive the people, or are insufficient for their work, there is no better supply to keep up religion than godly families. If parents and masters will teach their children and servants faithfully, and worship God with them holily and constantly, and govern them carefully and orderly, it will much make up the want of public teaching, worship, and discipline. Oh that God would stir up the hearts of people thus to make their families as little churches, that it might not be in the power of rulers or pastors that are bad to extinguish religion, or banish godliness from any land! For,

7. Family teaching, worship, and discipline, hath many advantages which churches have not. 1. You have but a few to teach and rule, and the pastor hath many. 2. They are always with you, and you may speak to them as seasonably and as often as you will, either together, or one by one, and so cannot he. 3. They are tied to you by relation, affection, and covenant, and by their own necessities and interest, otherwise than they are to him. Wife and children are more confident of your love to them than of the minister's; and love doth open the ear to counsel. Children dare not reject your words, because you can correct them, or make their worldly state less comfortable. But the minister doth all by bare exhortation; and if he cast them out of the church for their impenitence, they lose nothing by it in the world: and unless it be in a very hot persecution, families are not so restrained from holy doctrine, worship, and discipline, as churches and ministers often are. Who silenceth you and forbiddeth you to catechise and teach your family? Who forbiddeth you to pray or praise God with them, as well and as often as you can? It is self-condemning hypocrisy in many rulers of families, who now cry out against them as cruel persecutors, who forbid us ministers to preach the gospel, while they neglect to teach their own children and servants, when no man forbiddeth them; so hard is it to see our own sins and duty, in comparison of other men's.

8. You have greater and nearer obligations to your family than pastors have to all the people. Your wife is as your own flesh; your children are, as it were, parts of yourself. Nature bindeth you to the dearest affection, and therefore to the greatest duty to them. Who should more care for your children's souls than their own parents? If you will not provide for them, but famish them, who will feed them? Therefore, as ever you have the bowels of parents, as ever you care what becometh of your children's souls for ever, devote them to God, teach them his word, educate them in holiness, restrain them from sin, and prepare them for salvation.

S. I must confess that natural affection telleth me that there is great reason for what you say: and my own experience convinceth me; for if my parents had better instructed and governed me in my childhood, I had not been like to have lived so ignorantly and ungodlily as I have done: but, alas! few parents do their duty. Many take more pains about their horses and cattle than they do about their children's souls.

P. Oh that I could speak what is deeply upon my heart to all the parents of the land; I would be bold to tell them that multitudes are more cruel than bears and lions to their own children. God hath committed their souls as much to their trust and care as he hath done their bodies. It is they that are at first to devote them to God, in the covenant of baptism: it is they that are to teach them,[c] and to exhort them to keep the covenant which they made, to catechise them, and to mind them of the state of their souls, their need of Christ, the mercy of redemption, the excellency of holiness, and of everlasting life. It is they that are to watch over them with wisdom, love, and diligence, to save them from temptation, Satan, and sin, and to lead them by the example of a holy life.

But, alas! instead of this, they bring their children hypocritically to make that covenant in baptism with God, which they never heartily consented to themselves. They turn all into a mere ceremony, and know no more of it, than to have godfathers and godmothers as ignorant and ungodly as themselves, to promise and vow that in the name of the child, which they never understood, nor intended to perform their promise for his holy education, the child being none of their own, nor ever instructed by them. And when they think that the water, and the gossips, and the words of the priest, have thus made a christian of their child, they afterward as formally teach him at age to go to church, and at last to receive the Lord's supper: and this is almost all that they do for his salvation. They never teach him the meaning of the covenant which he was entered into. If they teach him to say the creed, the Lord's prayer, and the ten commandments, they never teach him to understand them. They never seriously mind him of his natural corruptions, or of the need and use of a Saviour and a Sanctifier, nor of the danger of sin and hell, nor of the way of a holy life, or of the joyful state of saints in glory. They teach him his trade and business in the world, but never how to serve God, and be saved. They chide him for those faults which are against themselves, or against his prosperity in the world, but those that are against God and his soul only, they regard not. If they do not by their own example teach him to be prayerless, and to neglect God's word, to curse, to swear, to speak filthily, and to deride a holy life, (which in baptism he vowed to live,) yet they will bear with him in all this wickedness. The Lord's day they are content that he spend in idleness and sports, instead of learning the word of God, and practising his holy

[b] 2 Tim. iii. 15.

[c] Deut. vi. 6—8; xi. 19, 20.

worship, that so he may be the willinger to do their work the week following. In a word, they treacherously teach their children to serve the flesh, the world, and the devil, which in their baptism they renounced, and to neglect, if not despise, God, the Creator, Redeemer, and Sanctifier of souls, to whom by vow and covenant they were dedicated. So that their education is but a teaching or permitting them to break and contradict their baptismal vow, and, under the name of christians, to rebel against God and Jesus Christ.

And is not this greater treachery and cruelty than if they famished their bodies, or turned them naked into the world? Yea, or if they murdered them, and ate their flesh? If an enemy did this, it were not so bad as for a parent to do it. Nay, consider whether the devil himself be not less cruel, in seeking to damn them, than these parents are? The devil is not their parent; he hath no relation to them, no charge of them to educate and save them. He is a known, renounced enemy, and what better could be expected from him? But for father and mother thus to neglect, betray, and undo their children's souls for ever! for them to do it, that should love them as themselves, and have the tenderest care of them! oh worse than devilish, perfidious cruelty!

Repent, repent, O you forsworn, unmerciful murderers of your children's souls! Repent for your own sakes! Repent for their sakes! And yet teach them and remember them of the covenant which they made, and tell them what christianity is. You have conveyed a sinful nature to them: help yet to instruct them in the way of grace. But how can we hope that you should have mercy upon your children's souls, that have no mercy on your own? or that you should help them to that heaven which you despise yourselves? or save them from sin, which is your own delight and trade?

S. Your complaint is sad and just: but I find that men think that the teaching of their children belongeth to the schoolmaster and the minister only, and not to them.

P. Parents, schoolmasters, and pastors, have all their several parts to do, and no one's work goeth on well without the rest. But the parents' is the first and greatest of all. As when the lower school is to teach children to read, and the grammar school to teach them grammar, and then the university to teach them the sciences. If now the first and second shall omit their parts, and a boy shall be sent to the university before he can read, yea, or before he hath learned his grammar, what a scholar do you think that he is like to make? If you have a house to build, one must fell and square the timber, and another must saw it, and another frame it, and then rear it, but if the first be undone, how shall the second and third be done? A minister should find all his hearers catechised and holily educated, that the church may be a church indeed; but if a hundred or many hundred parents and masters will all cast their work upon one minister, is it like, think you, to be well done? Or is it any wonder if we have ungodly churches of christians that are no christians, who hate the minister, and his doctrine, and a holy life; and the physician that would heal their souls is beholden to them, if they do not deride him, and lay him not in the gaol?

I know that all this will not excuse ministers from doing what they can for such. If you will send your children and servants ignorant and ungodly to him, he must do his best; but oh how much more good might he do, and how comfortable would his calling be, if parents would but do their parts!

We talk much of the badness of the world, and there are no men (except bad rulers and pastors) that do more to make it bad, than bad parents and family governors. The truth is, they are the devil's instruments, (as if he had hired them,) to betray the souls of their families into his power, and to lead them to hell with a greater advantage than a stranger could do, or than the devil in his own name nd shape could do.

Many call for church reformation, and state reformation, who yet are the plagues of the times themselves, and will not reform one little family. If men would reform their families, and agree in a holy education of their children, church and state would be soon reformed, when they were made up of such reformed families.

S. I pray you set me down such instructions together, as you think best, concerning all my duty to my children, that I may do my part; and if any of them perish, their damnation may not be long of me.

P. I. Be sure that you do your part in entering them at first into the baptismal covenant. That is, 1. See that you be true to your covenant yourself, for the promise is made to[d] true christians and their seed. No man can sincerely and rightly consent to the covenant for his child, that doth not consent to it for himself. 2. Do not think that his[e] bare being the child of godly parents is his full condition of right to the benefits of the covenant. That is but the fundamental part: but you must also actually dedicate him to God in baptism, when it may be had: and when it cannot, yet in the same covenant which baptism solemnizeth. As you are a believer, he and all that you have are virtually devoted to God; but besides that, there must be an actual dedication of him. The child of a believer, actually offered or dedicated to God, is a rightful receiver of baptism and its benefits. 3. Understand well the covenant, and what you do: and first humble yourself for your own sins against the holy covenant; and then with the greatest seriousness and thankfulness, enter your child into the same covenant.

II. Understand, that as his first condition of right is upon your faith and consent, and not upon his own, so the continuance of his right, while he is an infant short of the use of reason, cannot be upon any condition to be performed by him, but by you, which is the continuance of your own[f] fidelity, with your faithful endeavours for his holy education. And, therefore, if you should send a baptized child to be educated as the janissaries among infidels, he falleth, as I think, from his covenant right by your perfidiousness. And what forfeiture parents' gross neglect at home may make, I leave to further consideration.

III. [g]Teach them, therefore, to know what covenant they have made, and do by them just as I have done by you. Cease not till you have brought them heartily to consent to it at age themselves; and then bring them to the pastor of the church, that they may seriously and solemnly own the covenant, and so may be admitted into the number of adult communicating members, in a regular way.

IV. Let your teaching of them to this end be jointly of the words, the sense, the due affections, and the practice. That is, 1. Teach them [h]the words of the covenant, and of the creed, the Lord's prayer,

[d] Rom. v. 12, 16—18; Eph. ii. 13; Gen. xvii. 4, 13, 14.
[e] Deut. xxix. 10—12; Rom. xi. 17, 20; John iii. 3, 5; Matt. xix. 3, 14; xxviii. 19, 20; 1 Cor. vii. 14.
[f] Mark through all the Scriptures, how God useth the children as related to their faithful or faithless parents.
[g] Josh. xxiv. 15—18; Deut. xxix. 10, 11.
[h] 1 Tim. iv. 6; vi. 3; 2 Tim. i. 13.

and commandments, and of a catechism, and also the words of such texts of Scripture as have the same sense. 2. Teach them the meaning of all these words. 3. Join still some familiar, earnest persuasions and motives, to stir up holy affections in them. 4. And show them the way of practising all.

No one or two of these will serve without all the rest. 1. If you teach not the forms of wholesome or sound words, you will deprive them of one of the greatest helps for knowledge and soundness in the faith. 2. If you teach them not the meaning, the words will be of no use. 3. If you excite not their affections, all will be but dead opinion, and tend to a dreaming and prating kind of religion, separated from the love of God. 4. And if you lead them not on to the practice of all, they will make themselves a religion of zealous affections corrupted by a common life, or quickly starved for want of fuel. Therefore be sure you join all four. When you teach them the words of Scripture and catechism, make them plain, and oft mix familiar questions and discourse about death, and judgment, and eternity, and their preparations. Many professors teach their children to go in a road of hearing, reading, and repeating sermons, and joining in constant prayer, when all proveth but customary formality, for want of some familiar, serious, wakening speech or conference interposed now and then.

To this end, 1. Labour to possess them with the greatest reverence of God and the holy Scriptures; and then show them the word of God, for all that you would teach them to know or do; for till their consciences come under the fear and government of God, they will be nothing. 2. Never speak of God and holy things to them but with the greatest gravity and reverence, that the manner, as well as the matter, may affect them; for if they are used once to slight, or jest, or play with holy things, they are hardened and undone. 3. Therefore avoid such kind of frequencies and formality in lifeless duties, as tendeth to harden them into a customary deadness and contempt. 4. Oft take an account of what they know, and how they are affected and resolved; and what they do, both in their open and their secret practice. Leave them not carelessly to themselves, but narrowly watch over them.

V. Use all your skill and diligence, by word and deed, to make a holy life appear to them as it is, the most honourable, profitable, safe, and pleasant life in the world, that it may be their constant delight. All your work lieth in making good things pleasant to them; and keep them from feeling religion as a burden, or taking it for a disgraceful, needless, or unpleasant thing. To which end, 1. Begin with, and intermix, the easiest parts, such as the Scripture history. Nature is pleased sooner with history than with precept, and it sweetly insinuateth a love of goodness into children's minds, which maketh the Roman fathers of the oratorian order make church history one part of their exercise to the people. Let them read the lives of holy men, written by Mr. Clark, and his Martyrology; and the particular lives of Mr. Bolton, Mr. Joseph Allein, Dr. Beard's Theatre of God's Judgments, Mr. Janeway's Life, &c.

2. Speak much of the praise of ancient and later holy men; for the due praise of the person allureth to the same cause and way. And speak of the just disgrace that belongs to those sots and beasts, who are the despisers, deriders, and enemies of godliness.

3. Overwhelm them not with that which for quality or quantity they cannot bear.

4. Be much in opening to them the riches of grace, and the joys of glory.

5. Exercise them much in psalms and praise.

VI. Let your conference and carriage tend to the just disgrace of sensuality, voluptuousness, pride, and worldliness. When fools commend fineness to their children, do you tell them how pride is the devil's sin; teach them to desire the lowest room, and to give place to others. When others tell them of riches, and fine houses, and preferments, do you tell them that these are the devil's baits, by which he stealeth men's hearts from God, that they may be damned. When others pamper them, and please their appetites, do you oft tell them how base and swinish a thing it is to eat and drink more by appetite than by reason; and labour thus to make pride, sensuality, and worldliness, odious to them. Make them oft read Luke xii.; xvi.; xviii.; James iv. 5.; Rom. viii. 1, 2, &c.; Matt. v. 1—21; vi.

VII. Wisely break them from their own wills, and let them know that they must obey and like God's will and yours. Men's own wills are the grand idols of the world, and to be given up to them is next to hell. Tell them how odious and dangerous self-willedness is. In their diet let them not have what they have a mind to, nor yet do not force them to what they loathe; but use them to stand to your choice. And let them have that in temperance which is wholesome, and not loathsome, and rather of the coarser, than of the finer, or the sweeter sort. A corrupted appetite, strengthened by custom, is hardly overcome by all the teaching and counsel in the world: especially use them not to strong drink, for it is one of the greatest snares to youth. I know that some wise parents (wise to further the everlasting ruin of the children's souls) do still say, that the more they are restrained, the more greedily they will seek it when they are at liberty. Unhappy children that have such parents! As if the experience of all the world had not told us long ago, that custom increaseth the rage of appetite, and temperance by custom turneth to a habit. And in those years of youth, while they are restrained, we have time to tell them the reason of all, and so settle their minds in a right government of themselves; so that custom and teaching, till they come to age, is the means on our part to save them from sensuality and damnation. When they that will teach them sobriety with the cup at their noses, or temperance at a constant feast or full table of delicious food, and this in their injudicious youth, deserve rather to be numbered with the devil's teachers than with God's.

So if their fancies be eagerly set upon any vanity, deny it them, and tell them why. Use them not to have their wills, and let them know that it is the chief thing that the devil himself desireth for them, that they may have all their own carnal will fulfilled. But they must pray to God, "Thy will be done," and deny their own.

VIII. As you love their souls, keep them as far from temptations as you can. Children are unfit persons to struggle against strong temptations. Their salvation or damnation lieth very much on this; therefore my heart melteth to think of the misery of two sorts: 1. The children of heathens, infidels, heretics, and malignants, who are taught the principles of sin and wickedness from their infancy, and hear truth and godliness scorned and reproached. 2. The children of most great men and gentlemen, whose condition maketh it seem necessary to them to live in that continual fulness, or plainly, pomp and idleness, which is so strong a temptation daily to their children, to the sins of Sodom, (Ezek. xvi. 49,) pride, fulness of bread, and idleness, as that it is as hard for them to be godly, sober persons, as for those that are bred up in play-houses, ale-houses, and taverns. Alas, poor children, that must have your salvation made as hard as a camel's passage through a needle's eye! No wonder if the world be no better than it is, when the rich must be the rulers of it, of whom [i] Christ and James have said what they have done.

Be sure, therefore, 1. To breed your children to a temperate and healthful diet; and keep tempting meats, but specially drinks, from before them.

2. Breed them up to constant labour, which may never leave mind or body idle, but at the hours of necessary recreation which you allow them.

3. Let their recreations be such as tend more to the health of their bodies, than the humouring of a corrupted fancy; keep them from gaming for money, from cards, dice, and stage-plays, play-books, and love-books, and foolish wanton tales and ballads. Let their time be stinted by you; and let it be no more than what is needful to their health and labour, as whetting to the mower.

4. Let their apparel be plain, decent, and warm, but not gaudy; neither such as useth to signify pride, or to tempt people to it.

5. Be sure when they grow towards ripeness, that you keep them from opportunity, nearness, or familiarity, with tempting persons of another sex.

I am sure this is the way to your children's safety. If presumptuous, self-conceited persons, especially the rich, will despise such counsel, as they use to do, let them take what they get by it: if the gentry be debauched, if their children be everlastingly undone, if the whole country, church, and state, must suffer by it, and if their own hearts at last be broken by such children, it is not long of me; let them thank themselves.

IX. Be sure that you engage your children in good company, and keep them as much as possible out of bad. Wicked children, before you are aware, will infect them with their wicked tongues and practices; they will quickly teach them to drink, to game, to talk filthily, to swear, to mock at godliness and sobriety: and, oh, what tinder is in corrupted nature!

But the company of sober, pious children and servants will use them to a sober, pious language, and will further them in knowledge and the fear of God, or at least will keep them from great temptations.

X. Do all that you do with them in love and wisdom: make them not so familiar with you as shall breed contempt; and be not so strange to them as shall tempt them to have no love to you, or pleasure in your company. But let them perceive the tender bowels of parents, and that, indeed, they are dear to you, and that all your counsel and government is for their good, and not for any ends or passions of your own. And give them familiarly the reason of all which they are apt to be prejudiced against. For love and reason must be the means of most of the good that you do them.

XI. Keep a special watch upon their tongues, especially against ribaldry and lying; for dangerous corruptions do quickly this way obtain dominion.

XII. Teach them highly to value time: tell them the preciousness of it, by reason of the shortness of man's life, the greatness of his work, and how eternity dependeth on these uncertain moments. Labour to make time-wasting odious to them. And set death still before their eyes; and ask them oft, whether they are ready to die.

XIII. Use them much to the reading of the most suitable books: such as Mr. Richard Allen's, Mr. Joseph Allen's, Mr. Whateley's New Birth, and Redemption of Time; Mr. Gurnal, Mr. Bolton, Dr. Preston, Dr. Sibbes, Mr. Perkins, Dod, Hildersham; of which more anon.

XIV. Let correction be wisely used, as they need it; neither so severely as to disaffect them to you, nor so little as to leave them in a course of sin and disobedience. Let it be always in love; and more for sin against God, than any worldly matters: and show them Scripture gainst the sin, and for the correction.

XV. Pray earnestly for them, and commit them by faith to Christ, into whose covenant you did engage them.

XVI. Go before them by a holy and sober example, and let your practice tell them what you would have them be, specially in representing godliness delightful, and living in the joyful hopes of heaven.

XVII. Choose such trades and callings for them as have least dangerous temptations, and as tend most to the saving of their souls, and to make them most useful in the world, and not those that tend most to the ease of the flesh, or worldly ends.

XVIII. When they are marriageable, and you find it needful, provide such for them as are truly suitable, and stay not till folly and lust insnare them.

These are the counsels which I earnestly recommend to you in this important work. But you must know that your children's souls are so precious, and the difference between the good and bad so great, that all this must not seem too much ado to you: but as you would have ministers hold on in the labour of their places, so must you in yours, as knowing that a dumb and idle parent is no more excusable, than an unfaithful, dumb, and idle minister. The Lord give you skill, and will, and diligence, to practise all; for I take the due education of children for one of the needfullest and excellentest works in the world, especially for mothers.

S. I pray you, next tell me my duty to my wife, and hers to me.

P. I. The common duty of husband and wife is, 1. Entirely to [k] love each other; and therefore choose one that is truly lovely, and proceed in your choice with great deliberation; and avoid all things that tend to quench your love.

2. To dwell together, and [l] enjoy each other, and faithfully join as helpers in the education of their children, the government of the family, and the management of their worldly business.

3. Especially to be helpers of each other's salvation: to stir up each other to faith, love, and obedience, and good works: to warn and help each other against sin, and all temptations: to join in God's worship in the family, and in private: to prepare each other for the approach of death, and comfort each other in the hopes of life eternal.

4. To avoid all dissensions, and to bear with those infirmities in each other which you cannot cure: to assuage, and not provoke, unruly passions; and, in lawful things, to please each other.

5. To keep conjugal chastity and fidelity, and to avoid all unseemly and immodest carriage with any other, which may stir up jealousy; and yet to avoid all jealousy which is unjust.

6. To help one another to bear their burdens (and not by impatience to make them greater). In poverty, crosses, sickness, dangers, to comfort and support each other. And to be delightful companions in holy love, and heavenly hopes and duties, when all other outward comforts fail.

S. II. What are the special duties of the husband?

P. They are, 1. To exercise love and authority

[i] Luke xii. 19; xvi.; Jam. v.

[k] Eph. v. 25, &c.; Col. iii. 19.

[l] 1 Cor. vii. 29.

together (never separated) to his wife. 2. To be the chief teacher and governor of the family, and provider for its maintenance. 3. To excel the wife in[m] knowledge and patience, and to be her teacher and guide in the matters of God, and to be the chief in bearing infirmities and trials. 4. To keep up the wife's authority and honour in the family over inferiors.

S. III. What are the special duties of the wives?

P. 1. [n]To excel in love. 2. To be obedient to their husbands, and examples therein to the rest of the family. 3. Submissively to learn of their husbands, (that can teach them,) and not to be self-conceited, teaching, talkative, or imperious. 4. To subdue their passions, deny their own fancies and wills, and not to tempt their husbands to satisfy their humours and vain desires in pride, excess, revenge, or any evil, nor to rob God and the poor by a proud and wasteful humour (as the[o] wives of gentlemen ordinarily do). 5. To govern their tongues, that their words may be few, and grave, and sober; and to abhor a running and a scolding tongue. 6. To be contented in every condition, and not to torment their husbands and themselves with impatient murmurings. 7. To avoid the childish vanity of gaudy apparel, and following vain fashions of the prouder sort; and to abhor their vice that waste precious time in curious and tedious dressings, gossipings, visits, and feasts. 8. To help on the maintenance of the family by frugality, and by their proper care and labour. 9. Not to dispose of their husband's estate without his consent, either explicit or implicit. 10. Above all, to be constant helpers of the holy education of their children. For this is the most eminent service that women can do in the world; and it is so great that they have no cause to grudge at God for the lowness of their place and gifts, for mean gifts (with wisdom and godliness) may serve to speak to children. The mother is still with them, and they are still under her eye; her love must chiefly work towards their salvation. She must be daily catechising them, and teaching them to know God, and speaking to them for holiness and against sin, and minding them of the world to come, and teaching them to pray. Godly mothers may educate children for magistracy, ministry, and all public services, by helping them to that honest and holy disposition, which is the chief thing necessary in every relation to the common good; and so they may become chief instruments of the reformation and welfare of churches and kingdoms, and of the world.

S. I pray you tell me, also, the duty of children?

P. I. The duty of[p] children to their parents is, 1. To love them dearly, and to be thankful for all their love and care, which they can never requite. 2. To learn of them submissively, especially the doctrine of salvation. 3. To obey them diligently in all lawful things, and that for conscience' sake, in obedience to God. 4. To[q] honour them in thought, and words, and actions; and avoid all appearance of slighting, dishonour, or contempt. 5. To be contented with their parents' allowance and provisions, and willing and ready to such labour or employment as they command them. 6. To take patiently the reproofs and corrections of their parents, and to confess their faults with humble penitence, and amend. 7. To use such company as their parents command them, and not to run into the company of vain and tempting persons. 8. To be content with such a calling as their parents choose for them. 9. To marry by their parents' choice or consent only. 10. To relieve their parents, if they need.

S. What is the duty of children towards God?

P. II. 1. To learn what they are by nature, and what that covenant was which in baptism they were entered into; what are the duties, and what the benefits; and to renew that covenant with[r] God themselves, and understandingly, seriously, and resolvedly to give up themselves absolutely and entirely to God the Father, Son, and Spirit, their Creator, Redeemer, and Sanctifier. 2. To remember that the corruption of their nature must be more and more healed, and their sins forgiven; and, therefore, daily, by faith and obedience, to make use of the justifying, teaching, and sanctifying grace of Christ. 3. To remember that they are not here entering upon a life of rest, or sinful pleasure, but upon a short, uncertain life of care, and labour, and sufferings, in which they must do all that ever must be done, for an everlasting life that followeth; and that to make sure of heaven is their work on earth. 4. To love and learn the word of God, and to delight in all that is good and holy, especially on the Lord's days. 5. To see that they love not fleshly pleasures more than God and holiness, and that they fly from[s] youthful lusts, from excess of eating, drinking, and sports; that they avoid wantonness, and immodesty of speech or action, cards or dice, gaming, pride, love-books, play-books, loss of time by needless recreation. 6. That they use their tongues to sober and godly speech, and abhor lying, railing, ribaldry, and idle, foolish talk. 7. To subdue their wills to the will of God and their superiors, and not to be eagerly set on any thing which is unnecessary, or which God or their superiors forbid them.

S. What is the duty of masters towards their servants?

P. 1. To[t] rule them with such gentleness as becometh fellow-christians; and yet, with such authority as that they be not encouraged to contempt. 2. To restrain them from sinning against God. 3. To instruct them in the doctrine of salvation, and pray with them, and go before them by the example of a sober, holy life. 4. To keep them from evil company, and temptations, and opportunities of sinning. 5. To set them upon meet labours; to keep no idle serving-men, nor yet to over-labour them to the injury of their health, nor command them any unlawful thing. 6. To provide them such food and lodging as is wholesome and meet for them; and to pay them what wages is due to them by promise or desert. 7. Patiently to bear with daily infirmities, and such frailties as must be expected in mankind.

S. What is the duty of servants towards their masters?

P. 1. [u]To honour and reverence them, and obey them in all lawful things belonging to their places to command; and to avoid all words and carriage which savour of dishonour, contempt, or disobedience. 2. Willingly to perform all the labour which they undertake and is required of them, and that without grudging; and to be as faithful behind their master's back as before his face. 3. To be trusty in word and deed; to abhor lying and deceit; not to

[m] 1 Pet. iii. 7.
[n] 1 Tim. iii. 11, 12; Zech. xii. 14; 1 Pet. iii. 1; Col. iii. 18; Eph. v. 22, 24; Tit. ii. 4, 5; 1 Cor. vii. 16.
[o] Jer. xliv. 9.
[p] Eph. vi. 1—3; Col. iii. 20; Prov. i. 8, 9; xiii. 1; xxiii. 22.
[q] Gen. ix. 22, 25; Prov. xxx. 17; xiii. 24; xxii. 15; xxix. 15; xxiii. 13, 14; xix. 18.

[r] Eccl. xii. 1.
[s] 2 Tim. ii. 22; Prov. vii. 7, 8; Luke xv. 12, &c.
[t] Eph. vi. 9, 10; Col. iv. 1—3.
[u] 1 Pet. ii. 18; Tit. ii. 9; 1 Tim. vi. 1, 2; Col. iii. 22—25 Eph. vi. 5—8; Matt. x. 24.

wrong their masters in buying or selling, or by stealing, or taking any thing of theirs, no not meat or drink, against their will; but being as thrifty and careful of their master's profit as if it were their own. 4. Not to murmur at the meanness of food that is wholesome, nor to desire a life of fulness, ease, and idleness. 5. To be more careful to do their duty to their masters than how their masters shall use them; because sin is worse than suffering. 6. Not to reveal the secrets of the family abroad, to strangers or neighbours. 7. Thankfully to receive instruction, and to learn God's word, and observe the Lord's day, and seriously join in public and private worshipping of God. 8. Patiently to bear reproof and due correction, and to confess faults, and amend. 9. To pray daily for a blessing on the family, on their labours, and on themselves. 10. And to do all this in true obedience to God, expecting their reward from him.

S. What is the duty of children and servants to one another?

P. 1. To provoke one another to all their duty to God, and to their parents and masters. 2. To help one another in knowledge, and all the means of salvation, especially by godly, profitable conference, when they are together. 3. To save each other from sin and temptation, by loving advice; and to take heed that they be not tempters to each other, either to lust, and wanton dalliance, and unchaste speech or actions, or to excess of meat or drink, or idleness, or deceiving their master, or, by passionate words, provoking wrath; but that they assuage the passions of each other, and keep peace in the family. 4. To love each other as themselves, and do as they would be done by; and not to envy one another, nor strive who shall have the most, or who shall be highest, but humbly to submit to one another, and be helpful to each other in their labour and every way they can. 5. To bear patiently with little injuries to themselves; and open none of the faults of each other, when it tendeth but to stir up strife, and do no good. 6. But conceal not those faults which by concealment will be cherished, and whose concealment hindereth the right government of the family, or tendeth to the master's wrong. But in sins against God, first admonish each other privately; if that prevail not, reprove it before others; if that prevail not, acquaint your master with it.

S. Now you have gone so far, tell us our duty to our neighbours.

P. Your duty to your neighbours lieth in love and justice. 1. To love them as yourself. 2. To do as you would be done by; for which the six last commandments are your rule. Your love must be exercised, 1. Towards their souls, in furthering their salvation, by drawing them to hear God's word, helping them to good books, giving them seasonable, wise, and serious exhortations, and by the example of a holy, blameless life. 2. Towards their bodies, by doing them all the good you can, and doing them no wrong, nor speaking evil of them, nor provoking or scandalizing them, but patiently bearing and forgiving injuries from them.

S. And what is the duty of subjects to magistrates?

P. 1. To reverence and honour them as the officers of God, and speak not dishonourably of them. 2. To pay them due tribute, and to protect them to your power in your place. 3. To obey them in all lawful things,[x] which it belongeth to their several powers, places, and offices to command. 4. To provoke others to the same obedience. 5. To avoid all conspiracies, seditions, treasons, and rebellions, and resistance of the higher powers;[y] and patiently to suffer where God forbiddeth us to obey. 6. To approve and further the execution of true justice. 7. To detect and resist all treasons, conspiracies, and rebellions in others. 8. To do all this for conscience' sake, in obedience to God, and for the common good.

S. Must I not obey all the laws and commands of rulers?

P. No: you must obey none which command you any thing which God forbiddeth; or which forbid you any thing which is at that time and place your duty by God's command; nor that which certainly and notoriously tendeth to the destruction of the common good, unless, accidentally, any obedience of yours, to a particular command, be like to do more good than hurt, as to that end.

S. Will you next lay me down distinct directions how to spend every day in my family and by myself?

How to spend every day in a family.

P. I will not set you upon too much, nor upon any unnecessary task, lest I hinder you while I seem to help you. 1. Let the time of your sleep be so much only as health requireth,[z] for precious time is not to be wasted in unnecessary sluggishness.

2. Let your heart be so disposed God-ward, that your waking thoughts may make out towards him.[a] Lift up a thankful heart for your night's rest unto him, and think what a blessed rest you shall have in the presence of his glory, and how great a privilege it is to be in his love, and under his protection; and, if you have company, speak these thoughts to others.

3. Quickly dress you, and use no vain attire that shall steal your time:[b] but if sickness or other necessity make it long, either let one of your children read a chapter to you till you are ready, or let some suitable meditation or discourse take up the time.

4. If you have leisure, go presently to prayer by yourself, or with your wife. If you have not, at least put in the same requests in your family prayer, especially if you be the family's mouth.

5. Let family worship be kept up twice a day, unless some extraordinary necessity hinder it, at the most convenient hours of the day.

6. Do all your business as the work of God more than your own, and do nothing but what it is his will that you should do, that you may expect from him both protection and reward; and oft renew your devotion of yourself, and all your business, to him, and your actual intending to please and glorify him.

7. Highly value all your time, and follow your labours with constant diligence, believing that it is part of your service of God; six days must you labour and do all that you have to do. Idleness is the ruin of soul, body, and estate.

8. Be well acquainted with your special corruptions, and the special temptations of every day; and never intermit your watch against them.

9. If you labour alone, take in such seasonable meditations as you need, and your business will permit, but turn it to good conference if you are in company: not so as to think and talk of nothing else, to turn all to weariness or affected formality, but at seasonable times, and in a serious manner; and talk not of small matters, but of heart and heaven affairs.

10. Crave God's blessing upon your food, and return him thanks for it. Receive it, not chiefly to please your appetite, but to strengthen you as a servant of God, for your duty; and for quality and quantity avoid[c] flesh-pleasing curiosity and excess,

[x] Rom. xiii. 1—7. [y] Tit. iii. 1, 2; 1 Tim. ii. 2. [z] Prov. vi. 9, 10; John xvi.

[a] Psalm cxxxix. 18. [b] 1 Pet. iii. 3. [c] Prov. xxxi. 4, 6.

and make your health and reason, and not your appetite, the measure of both. Write over your table, "Behold, this was the iniquity of Sodom; pride, fulness of bread, and abundance of idleness was in her; neither did she strengthen the hand of the poor and needy," Ezek. xvi. 49. And, "There was a certain rich man who was clothed in purple and silk, and fared sumptuously every day." "Son, remember that thou, in thy life-time, receivedst thy good things," &c. Luke xvi. 12, 25. "Make no provision for the flesh, to fulfil the lusts (or desires) thereof," Rom. xiii. 14.

11. At evening, return to your food, and to God's worship in your family; and in secret, if you have time, as was directed you in the morning.

12. At night, look back how you have spent the day: not to waste time in writing down all sins and mercies which are ordinary (for the same coming daily to be repeated will turn all to formality); but to have a special thankfulness for special mercies, and a special repentance for great or aggravated sins, yea, for all that you remember. And quickly rise, by free confession, repentance, and faith, where you have fallen: and so betake yourself to rest,[d] with a holy confidence in God's protection, and delightful meditation of him.

S. You tell me of family worship twice a day. I pray you tell me how I must perform it.

Directions for family worship.

P. 1. With a composed, reverent mind, having all your family together that can come, briefly crave God's assistance and acceptance. 2. Then read a chapter, and, if you have leisure, some leaves of some other good book, or else bid them mark such passages as most concern them as they go. 3. Before or after sing a psalm, if you have a family that can sing; if not, read some psalms of praise. 4. Then, in faithful, fervent prayer, call on God through Jesus Christ, in his Spirit: and so at evening.

S. I pray you resolve me these few questions. *Quest.* 1. How oft in a day must I pray in my family?

P. God hath not punctually determined just how oft; therefore you must not superstitiously feign more commands than he hath made. But the general commands of praying continually, and in all things, with the final law, "Do all to edification," and the nature of families, and their necessities and opportunities, and Scripture examples, do fully prove that, ordinarily, twice a day is a duty; which, because I must not here stay to prove, read the full proof in the second part of my "Christian Directions." Keep up the life of grace within, and sense of your necessity, and of the worth of mercy, and keep up the experience what lively prayer and thanksgiving is, and it will preserve you against the libertines' opinion, who cry down constant worship in families as superstition.

S. 2. At what hours must I pray?

P. God hath not tied you to an hour by Scripture; but his providence will direct you. Usually, early and late are fittest; but if all families have not the same employments nor leisure, that hour must be chosen which family occasions, and bodily temper, and company, do make most fit.

S. 3. Must I pray in secret with my wife, and in my family too, twice every day?

P. Only the general rule of edification, with your conveniences and opportunities, must here also direct you. Family prayer is of greatest necessity; because there each person is contained. But secret prayer hath great advantages; the heart is there more free to open its particular sins and wants; and they that can do all, must do them. But if you cannot, you must rather take up with family prayer alone, than secret alone.

S. What do you mean by "cannot?" Must not all business give place to secret prayer?

P. No. There are businesses of greater obligation which must be preferred. Learn what this meaneth, "I will have mercy, and not sacrifice." A physician, in case of necessity, may omit all prayer, to go help to save a sick man's life. So may any man, to relieve the poor and miserable when it cannot be put off to another time; so may a magistrate to do justice; and so may a pastor to preach to the congregation, when he hath not time to do both. And poor men, that cannot spare time from their labour, are not bound to spend as much time in reading and prayer as rich men are, who have fuller opportunities.

2. But the case of those who are the speakers in family prayer, much differeth from the case of them that join; for he that speaketh may put up all the same requests in the family as he may do in secret; and therefore a greater duty may oftener dispense with his secret prayer: for it is not to be used as a formality. But he that joineth with the speaker hath not the choice of his own matter, nor can so easily keep up a praying mind, without distractions, as he can do when he speaketh himself. Therefore, (avoiding superstitious conceits, and making laws to ourselves, as God's, which he hath not made,) secret prayer is so great a duty, that every man must use it as oft as other duties at that time are not to be preferred, but will give leave. And some can find time for it (with meditation) in their labour, and travel, when they are alone.

S. 4. Is long or short prayer to be preferred?

P. The general rule, also, must direct you in this. It varieth the case, as times, and persons, and occasions vary. When no greater duty (at that time) putteth you off, you can scarce be too long, if you continue fit for it in mind and expression; but when other duties call you off, or you cannot be long without unmeet expressions and repetitions before others, or without your own or the family's dulness and unfitness, shorter, at that time, may be the best. But see that formal affectation be not the lengthener of your prayers, nor carnal weariness the shortener of them; at least, do not justify either of these.

S. 5. Is it better to pray by a set form, or book, or without, as I am able to express my desires?

P. God hath not made you a law against either, but left every man the way that is fittest for him.

S. How shall I know which is fittest for me?

P. 1. In secret, usually, it is best to use yourself oftest to pray freely, from the present sense of your condition, that you may be able to do it; and vary as occasion serveth. For the best man's mind is apt to grow dull in using the same words a hundred times over: as a music lesson played too oft, doth become less pleasing; and it will not cure us, to say that it should not be so.

2. Therefore, also, you should learn to pray freely, from a habit, before others also, as soon as you can.

3. But till you can do it without disgraceful expressions, repetitions, and disorders, it is better in your family to use a book or form.

4. If in public, or secret, any one find that a form, having more fit, large, and lively expressions than he can have himself without it, doth quicken and enlarge him, he may best use it; but if it more bind and straiten him, he may forbear it.

I will add these two advices here. 1. Settle not yourself in such a calling and way as will not stand with family worship. 2. Take heed of growing in customariness and dead formality, which may too easily befall you, even under extemporate prayers.

[d] Psalm iv. 7—9.

S. Have you any more counsel for me, for the good and order of my family?

P. At this time I will add no more but these. 1. Watch against your worldly business, that it eat not out the life and seriousness of holy duties. Alas! in most families the world is all that they have any sense of: though yet your calling must be followed.

S. Truly, landlords are so hard, and people so very poor, that necessity is a constraint and great temptation to them.

P. I know it is. But if landlords be cruel, shall men be more cruel to themselves? If they keep you poor, will you therefore keep your soul ungodly and miserable? The less comfort you have here, and the harder this world useth you, the more careful should you be, in reason, to make sure of a better world. Poor men have souls to save, and a heaven to win, and a hell to escape, and a Christ to believe in, and a God to love and serve, as well as the rich. And I tell you that your temptations are less than theirs.

2. Do all that you can to keep up, in yourself and family, the joy of believing, and a delight in God and all his service; and therefore, let your daily duty have much in it of thanksgiving and praise.

3. You, that are a farmer, and sit by your servants in the long winter nights, get a good book, and [e] read to them while they are with you. I will not discourage your own exhortations; but few husbandmen can discourse so profitably, so closely, soundly, and searchingly, as many such books will do, if you choose aright. But more of this in the next day's conference.

THE

EIGHTH DAY'S CONFERENCE.

HOW TO SPEND THE LORD'S DAY IN CHRISTIAN FAMILIES, IN THE CHURCH, AND IN SECRET DUTIES.

Speakers.—Paul, a Teacher; and Saul, a Learner.

PAUL. Welcome, neighbour. How go matters between you and your family; yea, and your God?

SAUL. O sir, you have set me a great deal of work, which my conscience telleth me is good and necessary, and better than any else that I can spend my time in. But my heart is bad and backward; and it is not so soon learned as heard, nor so soon done as learned; and yet I come to you for more. For I am resolved to take God and heaven for my all, and, therefore, to be true to the covenant I have made. I desire you now, to instruct me about the right observation of the Lord's day; and, first, tell me our obligation to it.

P. I have published a treatise only on that subject, to which I must refer you now, as to the obligation and the disputing part; only giving you this brief intimation: 1. Christ gave his apostles commission to acquaint the world with his will, and to settle the orders of the gospel churches. 2. To this end he promised and gave them the infallible conduct of the Holy Ghost; who is now the Author of what they did in obedience to their commission. 3. As Christ rose from the dead on the [a] first day of the week, so he oft on that day appeared to his disciples, and on that day (Whitsunday) he sent down the Holy Ghost; so that the new world was begun on that day. And on that day the apostles constantly celebrated the holy assemblies, and appointed the churches to do the like, separating that day to the holy worship of God. 4. All the churches in the world from the apostles' times, till a few years ago, did unanimously keep the Lord's day as holy, or separated to holy worship; no one church, no one person, no, not a heretic, that I remember, who confessed Christ's resurrection, ever once excepting against it, or dissenting; and this is as ordained by the apostles in their times.

S. You need say no more: he that will contradict such proof as this, hath an evil spirit of contradiction. But that which is questioned is, whether it be a sabbath, and come in the place of the seventh-day sabbath?

P. Trouble not your brains about mere names: it is enough for you that it is a day separated by Christ and the Holy Ghost to holy worship, and called the Lord's day. If by a sabbath be meant a day of Jewish ceremonial rest, (which is the Scripture sense of that word,) then we confess that it is no sabbath, but that all such sabbaths are abolished, as types of better things.

S. I am the more easily satisfied by reason and experience for the holy keeping of the day: for, 1. I know that one day in seven is as due a proportion now as when Moses' law was made. 2. I am sure it is a great mercy and benefit to man, to be obliged every seventh day to rejoice in God, and lay by our care and labour, and learn the way to everlasting life. Alas! what would servants and poor men do without it! 3. It is a hedge, and great engagement to the holy employments of the soul, when every seventh day is separated to that use alone. 4. And I feel by experience the great benefit of it to myself. 5. And I see that religion most prospereth where the Lord's day is conscionably kept, and falls where it is neglected. But I pray you set me down directions for the right spending of the day, both general and particular.

P. I. The general instructions which you must take are these.

1. That the chiefest use of the day is for the [b] public worshipping of God, our Creator and Redeemer; and therefore the church worship is to be preferred before all that is more private.

2. That the chief work which it is to be spent in, is learning the doctrine of the gospel, and praising, and giving thanks to our heavenly Father, our Redeemer, and Sanctifier: the rest cometh under this.

3. Therefore the manner of it, and the frame of our hearts, should be holy joy, and gratitude, and love, stirred up by the exercise of faith and hope: and it should be spent as a day of thanksgiving for the greatest mercy.

4. Therefore the positive part of duty is the main, viz. that heart and tongue be thus employed towards God. And the negative part (our abstaining from other thoughts and words, and labours and sports) is so far our duty, as they are any hinderance to this holy work; and not on a mere ceremonial account.

S. Now set me down all my duty in its order.

The order of the duties of the Lord's day.

P. I. Make due preparation for the day beforehand. Let your six days' labour be so despatched, that it may not hinder you: cast off worldly thoughts, and remember the last Lord's-day instructions; and repent of all the sins of the week past: and go in season to your rest.

2. Let your first thoughts be suitable to the day. Remember with joy the resurrection of your Saviour,

[e] Deut. xvii. 19; Acts viii. 28, 30.

[a] John xx. 1, 19. 26; xvi. 13—15; Acts ii. 1; 1 Cor. xvi. 1, 2; Rev. i. 10; Matt. xxviii. 19, 20; 2 Thess. ii. 15.

[b] Acts ii. 4, 5; 1 Cor. xvi. 1, 2.

which begun the triumphant, glorious state, as you awake in the beginning of this holy day: and let your heart be glad to think that a day of the Lord is come.

3. Rise full as early on that day as on your labouring days; and think not that swinish sloth is your holy rest.

4. Let your dressing time be short, and spent as aforesaid, in hearing a chapter read, or in good thoughts, or suitable speech to those about you.

5. If you can, go first to secret prayer; and let servants despatch their necessary business about cattle, that it stand not after in their way.

6. Then call your servants to family worship, and if you can have time, without coming too late to the assembly, read the Scripture, sing a psalm of praise, and call on God with joyful thanksgiving, for our redemption and the hopes of glory: or so much of this as you can do. But do all with seriousness and alacrity: and tell your servants and children what it is that they go to do at the church.

7. Go to the beginning of public worship; and let none be absent that can be spared to go. Your duty there I must show you by itself, anon.

8. After your return, while dinner is preparing, is a seasonable time for secret prayer, or meditation on the great business of the day, and to consider of what you heard in public.

9. If company allow you opportunity, let your time at meat be seasoned with some cheerful mention of the mercies of our Redeemer, or what is suitable to the hearers and the day.

10. After dinner, if there be time, call your family together, and sing a psalm of praise, and help them to remember what was taught them.

11. Then take them again (in time) to the assembly.

12. When you come home, call them all together, and after craving God's assistance, and acceptance through Christ, sing a psalm of praise, and repeat the sermon, or cause it to be repeated, not tediously, but so much as the time may bear. Or if there were no sermon, or one unsuitable to your family, read near an hour to them in some suitable and lively book. (Of which anon.) And conclude with prayer and praise to God; and all with seriousness, alacrity, and joy.

13. Between that and supper, both you, and such children and servants as can possibly be spared, betake yourselves to secret prayer and meditation.

14. At supper do as beforesaid at dinner. (Still remember that though it be a day of thanksgiving, yet not of sensuality, gluttony, or excess.)

15. When they have supped, examine your children and servants what they have learned that day, unless you appoint an hour on the week day for it: and so for catechising them. Then sing a psalm of praise, and so conclude with prayer and thanksgiving. Catechising must not be neglected; but if you can do most of it on week days or holidays, it will be best that it take not up the Lord's day, which is for holy praise.

16. When you go to rest, review briefly the special occurrences of the day; repent of failings; give thanks for mercies; and comfortably compose yourself to rest, as trusting in the protection of your gracious God, and so let your thoughts be such as are meet to shut up such a holy day.

These directions are soon given and heard; but, oh happy you, if you sincerely practise them!

S. You talk of reading to my family at nights, and on holidays, and the Lord's days: what books be they which you would have me read?

P. Were you not a poor man, I would name many to you: because you are one of my charge, I will bestow some of my own upon you. 1. Here are, The Call to the Unconverted, Directions for a Sound Conversion, A Treatise of Conversion, A Sermon against making light of Christ, A Treatise of Judgment, A Saint or a Brute, and Now or Never, with this present book. Read these to them in the order that I have named, as much at a time as you have leisure. And here is the Saints' Rest; on the Lord's days read oft in that: and when you have done those, here is a Treatise of Self-denial, and one of Crucifying the World, and one of Self-ignorance: I will trouble you with no more. But if you have my Christian Directory, you may choose still what subject you think most seasonable.

What books to read to the family.

For other men's works, I would you had Mr. Joseph Allen's book of Conversion, and his Life, and all Mr. Richard Allen's books; and Mr. Dod on the Commandments, and Mr. Perkins on the Creed and the Lord's Prayer, that you might read, as an exposition of the catechism, one article, one petition, one commandment, expounded at a time; which will be a great help to yourself and them. And the Practice of Piety, and Mr. Scudder's Daily Walk, and Mr. Reyner, and Mr. Pinke's sermons, are very good books. But I dare name you no more, lest I overset you.

S. What catechism would you have me use?

P. There are so many that I know not which to prefer: at present I commend you to Mr. Gouge's, or Mr. Rawlet's; the lesser of the Assembly's first, and the larger after. But because you are one of my charge, I will here write you two in the end, a shorter for beginners, and a longer for proficients.

S. I pray you next instruct me how to worship God in public: you have before told me what church I must join with; have you more to say of that?

P. Yes: 1. I advise you to hear the best teacher that you can have: for experience telleth us that the bare office worketh not without meet abilities; and that there is a very great difference to the hearer,[c] between man and man: therefore be not indifferent herein.

What church and teacher to choose.

S. Whom am I to account the best teacher?

P. Not he that is most[d] learned, elegant, and rhetorical, nor he that speaketh the loudest and most earnestly; but he that hath all the three necessary abilities conjunct: 1. A clear explication of the gospel, to make the judgments of the hearers[e] sound. 2. He that hath the most convincing and persuading reasons to resolve the will. 3. He that doth this in the most serious, affectionate, lively manner, together with practical directions, to quicken up the soul to practice, and direct it therein. But when you cannot have one that is excellent in all these, you must take the best that you can have.

S. But what if the minister of the parish be not such?

P. If he be intolerable, through ignorance, heresy, disability, or malignity, forsake him utterly: but if he be tolerable, though weak and cold, and if you cannot remove your dwelling, then public order and your soul's edification must both be joined as well as you can. In London, or other cities where it is usual, you may go ordinarily to another parish church: but in the country, and where it would be a great offence, you may one part of the day hear in your own parish, and the other at the next, if there be a man much fitter within your reach: but communicating with the church you dwell with.

[c] Matt. vii. 29; 2 Cor. iii. 6; 2 Tim. i. 12; Rom. xv. 14.

[d] 1 Cor. i.; ii.; iii.; and iv.

[e] 2 Tim. i. 7.

2. I advise you, that if there be parish churches orderly settled under the magistrates' countenance, whose teachers are sound, and promote the power of godliness in concord, though an abler minister should gather a separated church in the same place, out of that and other neighbour parishes, and should have stricter communicants and discipline, be not too forward to join yourself to that separated church; till you can prove that the hurt that will follow by discord, offence, division, encouraging schism and pride, is not like to be greater than your benefit can compensate. But where liberty is such as these mischiefs are not like to follow, take your liberty, if your benefit require it.

3. But if this separated church be a [f] factious anti-church, set up contentiously against the concordant churches, though on pretence of greater purity; and if their meetings be employed in contention and reviling others, and making them odious that are not of their mind, and in killing the love of christians to each other, and in condemning other churches as no churches, or such as may not lawfully be communicated with, and, in puffing up themselves with pride, as if they were the only churches of Christ; avoid such separated churches, as the enemies of love and peace.

4. If a church, in other respects sound, shall [g] require of you any false subscriptions, promises, or oaths, or require you to do any unlawful thing, you must not do it: but hold communion with them in other lawful things, if they will allow you. If not, be content to have spiritual communion with them at a distance, in the same faith and love, and kind of worship, and join with others.

5. Though your ordinary communion should be with the best minister and church that you can have without scandal and public hurt, yet sometimes, if it be expected, communicate with more [h] imperfect churches, so far as they force you not to sin, that you may keep up love, and show that you are for universal peace.

S. Will you instruct me how to hear with profit?

How to hear.

P. You must have distinct helps for four particular uses: 1. To understand what you hear. 2. To be duly affected with it. 3. To remember it. 4. To practise it.

S. I. What are the helps for [i] understanding?

P. 1. A plain, clear, convincing teacher. 2. Reading the Scripture and good books to prepare you; especially catechisms. 3. Careful attending. 4. Specially marking the doctrine, design, and drift of the preacher. 5. Laying the several parts together. 6. Meditating after, and asking the meaning of what you doubt of. 7. Prayer, and conscionable practice of what you know.

S. II. What are the helps for the will and affections?

P. 1. A lively preacher. 2. Remember with whom you [k] have to do, and of how great importance the business is which you are upon. Go to church as one that is going to hear a message from the God of heaven, concerning your everlasting salvation. 3. Remember that you have but a little time to hear, and then you must be laid in the dark, with those that are under your feet, who lately sat where you now sit; and your soul must speed as sermons did speed with you in hearing. 4. Observe how nearly the matter doth concern you; and stir up your minds from sloth and wandering. 5. Remember that God, who sends the message, doth wait for your resolution and your answer; whether you will yield to him or reject him; whether you will have his grace or not? And remember how you will shortly cry to him for mercy in your extremity, and wait for his answer to your cries. Resolve now as you would speed then; and answer God as you would be answered by him. If you would have mercy then, receive it and obey it now. If you deny God but this once, you know not but he may leave you to yourself, and never make you such an offer more. 6. Bethink you how the [l] miserable souls in hell were like to hear such offers of mercy, if they might be tried here again, and sit in your places. 7. Lift up a secret request to Christ for his quickening Spirit. 8. When you come home, preach over the doctrine again to your own heart, and urge it on yourself. 9. And pray it all over to God, by begging his grace to make it powerful. 10. And pressing it on your family will quicken yourself.

S. III. What are the helps for memory?

P. 1. A thorough understanding. 2. And a deep affection: we easily remember that which we well understand, and are much affected with. 3. Method is a great help to memory; therefore observe the preacher's method, at least the doctrine, or subject, and somewhat of the explication, proof, and use. 4. Number much helpeth memory. Mark how many the several heads are. 5. Fasten upon some one significant word of every head, which will bring in all the rest. 6. Grasp not at more than you can hold, lest you lose all; but choose out so much of the chief matter, which concerneth you, as you find your memory can bear. 7. In the time of hearing, you may oft run over that one significant word of each head which you heard first, to settle it in your memory, without turning your attention from that which followeth, which is a singular help. 8. Writing is the easiest help for memory. 9. If you forget the words, yet remember the main drift and matter. 10. Review it, or hear it repeated by others, when you come home.

S. 4. What are the helps for practice?

P. 1. If you speed well in the three first, especially if the word take hold upon your heart, the practice will the more easily follow. 2. Be acquainted with the corruptions of your heart, which need a cure, and the wants that need supply, and go with a desire to get that cure and that supply; as you go to the market to buy what you want, or to the physician to be healed. An intent of practice prepareth for practice. 3. Mark the uses and the practical directions, and let conscience urge them on yourself as you are hearing them; resolve to obey whatever God maketh known to be his will. 4. When you come home consider what you heard which doth concern your practice, and there let conscience drive it home, and revive your resolutions. 5. Especially labour to get your radical graces strengthened, the belief of the life to come, the hope of glory, and the love of God; and these will carry you on to practice. 6. Take heed of those preachers that stifle practice. I mean, 1. Libertines, called antinomians, who, under pretence of extolling Christ and free grace, destroy the principles of practice. 2. [m] Factious disputers, who fill men's heads with little but controversy. 3. Wordy orators, who, like sounding brass and tinkling cymbals, make but a lifeless noise of words. 4. Malignants, who jeer at holy practice as hypocrisy. 5. Pharisees, that set up the

[f] Rom. xvi. 17; 1 Cor. i. 10; 1 Thess. v. 12, 13; Tit. iii. 10; Acts xx. 30.
[g] Gal. ii. 3—5, 14; iii.; and iv.
[h] Luke iv. 16; v. 14; John xviii. 20; Matt. xxiii. 2
[i] Matt. xiii. 14, 15; iv. 3; vii. 14, 16; xv. 10; Rev. i. 3; ii. 7, 11, 17, 29; iii. 6.
[k] Heb. iv. 13.
[l] Luke xvi. 24, 26, 27.
[m] Phil. i. 15; ii. 3; 1 Tim. vi. 3, 4; 2 Tim. ii. 14, 24; Tit. iii. 9.

practice of their own ceremonies,[n] traditions, and superstitions, instead of the practice of the commands of God. 6. Live, if you can, with practising christians. 7. Lastly, keep a daily account how you practise what you know.

S. How must I hear and read the Scriptures themselves?

Of reading the Scriptures.

P. 1. Be sure you come to them with a[o] believing, reverent, spiritual mind, as to the word of the living God, by which you must be ruled and judged, and which you must fully resolve to obey; as a humble learner of heavenly mysteries from the Son and Spirit of God, and not as a proud and arrogant[p] caviller, or judge; nor as expecting philosophy, or curious words, instead of the laws of God for our salvation. 2. Read most the New Testament, and the most suitable parts of Scripture. 3. Expound the dark and rarer passages by the plain and frequent ones. 4. Read some commentary, or annotations, as you go, if you can. 5. [q]Ask your pastor of that which you understand not.

S. What must I do in public prayer, praises, and thanksgiving?

Of public prayer, &c.

P. 1. [r]Join in them earnestly with the desires and praises of your heart; and be not a bare hearer, for that is to be a hypocrite, and to seem to pray when indeed you do not.

2. Do not peevishly pick quarrels with the prayers of the church, nor come to them with humoursome prejudice. Think not that you must[s] stay away, or go out of the church, for every passage that is disorderly, unmeet, yea, or unsound, or untrue; for the words of prayer are the work of man; and while all men are fallible, imperfect, and sinful, their prayers, and praises, and preaching will be like themselves. And he that is the highest pretender, and the peevishest quarreller, hath his own failings. If I heard him pray, it is ten to one I could tell you of much immethodicalness, at least, and sometimes falsehoods, in his words. We must join with no church in the world if we will join with nothing that is faulty. Nor is every fault made mine by my presence: I profess to come thither to worship God according to the gospel, and to own all that the pastor saith which is agreeable thereto; but not to own all that he saith, whether in preaching or in prayer, in God's name, or his own, or ours.

Yet I would not have you indifferent with what words you join: for if the words, or actions, be such as so corrupt the worship of God as that he himself will not accept it, you must not offer it.

3. In all the lawful orders, gestures, and manner of behaviour in God's worship, affect not to differ from the rest, but conform yourself to the use of the church which you join with; for in a church singularity is a discord.

S. How must I receive the sacrament of Christ's body and blood?

How to communicate in the Lord's supper.

P. You must, 1. Have a due preparation; 2. A due performance.

S. 1. What is the due preparation?

P. 1. To understand what you do; and, 2. To be what you must be, viz. a true christian; and, 3. To do what you must do, in particular preparation.

S. 1. What is it that I must understand?

P. What the ends of the sacrament are, and what are the parts and nature of it.

S. What are the ends of it?

P. Not really to[t] sacrifice Christ again; nor to turn [u]bread into no bread, and wine into no wine; which, if every priest can do, he might consecrate all the bread and wine in the baker's shop, and vintner's, or any other cellar, and so famish men. But the papists themselves say, without his intention it is not done; but no man knoweth the priest's intention, therefore no man knoweth whether he take bread or the body of Christ. And if all the sound men's senses in the world be not to be trusted whether bread be bread, and wine be wine, then we can know nothing; no, not that there is a Bible, or that ever God revealed his will to man, or that there is a man in the world, and therefore cannot possibly be believers. Nor is the use of the sacrament to confirm men's wicked confederacies, nor to flatter wicked men in their presumption, nor to save them by the outward act alone.

But the end of the sacrament is, 1. To be a solemn[x] commemoration of the sacrifice of Christ by his death, until he come. That the church may, as it were, see his body broken and his blood shed, and behold the Lamb of God, who taketh away the sins of the world.

2. To be a solemn renewing of the covenant of grace, on Christ's part and on ours; even the same which you made in baptism, and at conversion, but with some addition: the one being the sacrament of our new birth and entrance; the other of feeding, nourishment, continuance, and growth. Here Christ for life is delivered to us, and we accept him; and man delivereth up himself to Christ, and Christ accepteth him.

3. To be a lively means for Christ's Spirit and our souls to work by, to stir up faith, desire, love, thankfulness, hope, joy, and new obedience, besides repentance. By showing us the doleful fruits of sin, the wonderful love of God in Christ, the firmness of the promise or covenant, the greatness of the gift, and our grateful obligations. Thus we must here have communion with God and Jesus Christ, in the exercise of all these graces; and receive more grace through our sacrificed Redeemer.

4. It is a symbol or badge of the church, and a public profession of our continued faith, hope, thankfulness, and obedience.

5. It is a sign and means of the union, love, and communion of the saints, and their readiness to communicate to one another.

S. What are the parts of the sacrament, and their nature?

P. I. It hath three general parts: I. The parties covenanting; which are, 1. Christ, or God the Father, Son, and Holy Ghost, as the principal Giver; 2. His minister as his agent; 3. The receivers.

II. The signs; that is, I. The signifying matter: 1. Bread, 2. Wine. II. The manner: 1. Broken bread; 2. Wine poured out; 3. Both delivered, or given. III. The signifying actions: 1. Taking and breaking the bread; 2. Pouring out the wine; 3. Giving both; 4. Receiving both; 5. Eating and drinking both.

III. The things signified. I. As the means: 1. The sacrificing of Christ's body and blood on the cross for our sins; 2. The giving of them to believ-

[n] Matt. xv.; Col. ii. 22, 23.
[o] Heb. iv. 2; Matt. xii. 3, 5; xxi. 16; xxiv. 15; 1 Tim. iv. 13; Neh. viii. 8; Eph. iii. 4.
[p] Matt. xviii. 3.
[q] Acts viii. 28—31.
[r] 1 Chron. xvi. 36; Neh. v. 13; viii. 6; Psalm cvi. 48.
[s] Luke iv. 16; John xviii. 29; 1 Cor. xiv.; xi. 16, 25, &c.; xiv. 33, &c; Rev. ii.; iii.
[t] Heb. x. 12; ix. 16; vii. 27. [u] 1 Cor. xi. 26—29.
[x] 1 Cor. xi. 24—26, 28—30; x. 16, 24; Matt. xxvi. 28; Mark xiv. 24; Luke xxii. 20; Heb. ix. 15—18; John vi. 32, 35, 51, 58.

ers; 3. The receiving them by the believers, and improving them unto life.

II. As the ends. 1. The contracted union and mutual relation between God and Creator, Redeemer and Sanctifier, and the receiver. 2. The soul's receiving from Christ, 1. Pardon, reconciliation, and adoption of right to the heavenly inheritance; 2. More of the Holy Ghost to sanctify, seal, and comfort us; 3. The soul's dedication of itself to God in Christ, for future love and obedience; 4. And God's acceptance of him.

S. What are the special parts of the whole sacrament?

P. II. They are three: I. The consecration. II. The commemoration. III. The communion, or communication and participation.

S. I. What is the consecration?

P. Not the bare pronouncing of the words, as the papists think; nor the turning of the bread into Christ's natural body; but it is the [y] separation of the bread and wine to the sacramental use, and making it to be no longer mere or common bread and wine, but the very body and blood of Christ representative. This is done by the dedicating or offering this bread and wine to God, and by God's acceptance and benediction, of which the minister is his agent; which is fitliest consummate and declared by Christ's words, "This is my body, and this is my blood;" though it is so by the separation and benediction, before it is so called and pronounced.

As Christ was the true Messiah, incarnate before he was sacrificed to God, and was sacrificed to God before that sacrifice was given to man for life and nourishment, so here consecration first maketh the bread and wine to be the body and blood of Christ representative; and then the sacrificing of Christ to God must be represented and commemorated; and lastly, a sacrificed Christ communicated to the receivers, and accepted by them.

S. II. What is the commemoration?

P. It is the [z] visible representation of the sacrificing of Christ upon the cross to the Father, for the sins of man; to keep up the remembrance of it, and lively affect the church thereby, and to profess our confidence in a crucified Christ, for the acceptance of our persons and all our performances with God, as well as for the pardon of our sins.

S. III. What is the communication and participation?

P. It is the [a] giving of Christ himself really for life, or with his covenant benefits, to the believing receiver, by the investing sacrament of the bread and wine ministerially delivered by the pastor in Christ's name, together with the acceptance of the receiver.

S. You hint to me that which seemeth to reconcile the controversy, about the real presence; but I would entreat you to make it plainer to me. What is the gift and the donation?

P. Suppose that a king should, under his hand and seal, make a grant of his son, and the son of himself, to a poor woman beyond sea, to be her husband, and send an ambassador with this instrument, and with the espousing signals, his effigies, the ring, or the like, as his proxy or agent, to marry her to the prince in his name; the words of the instrument run thus: "I do give thee my son, to be thy husband, and he thereby giveth himself to thee, with thy due interest in his estate, if thou consent and give thyself to him as a wife; and have sent this my ambassador with the signals of matrimony to espouse thee in my son's name." Hereupon she consenteth, and the agent in the celebration delivereth to her the effigies or image of the prince as the signal, and saith, "This is the prince, who hereby giveth himself to thee as a husband." And he delivereth her a key, and saith, "This is such a house, which he endoweth thee with."

Now you can easily [b] expound all this: 1. It is the very prince himself in person, and not only the effigies, that is now given her, but how? Not into present, sensible, physical possession or contact; but in the true right of relation as a husband. 2. The image is the prince representative, not real, physically considered; and is physically an image of him still. 3. The image, which is the prince representative, or signal, is a means or instrument of conveying right and relation to the prince real. But it is only the secondary instrument, viz. of investiture. 4. Another instrument, and in part a representer, is the agent or ambassador. 5. The chief instrument is the written donation, which he is to read at the marriage.

Just so, 1. It is very Christ himself, and not only the signs, that is given to the believer by means of the signs; that is, he is given, not to contact, but in right and relation as a Head and Saviour, by contract. But, 2. The signs are physically but signs still, though representatively they are the very body and blood of Christ; that is, it is the very body and blood which is represented and given by him. 3. And the gospel covenant on God's part is his chief instrument of this right and relation as conveyed. 4. And the minister and the sacrament are the two subservient instruments. All this is not only plain in itself, but that doctrine which Christ's church hath ever held. And Paul (1 Cor. xi.) calleth it bread three times after the consecration.

So that the minister is the ministerial instrument; the promise, or covenant, is the donative or entitling instrument; the sacramental signs and actions are the investing instruments, by which Christ himself, with all his covenant benefits, are given and delivered to the believing receiver, in relation and true right; and by which Christ's Spirit confirmeth the soul. This is the true and plain doctrine of that sacrament; study it till you understand it.

S. II. You have told me what I must understand: now tell me what I must be, that I may be prepared to receive.

P. You must be a true christian; that is, a penitent believer already in covenant with God, by consent.

S. May every christian come, how weak soever?

P. Yes; if there be nothing to hinder him but weakness, and not some particular let, or unpreparedness, which I am next to speak to you of.

S. But what if he be in doubt whether he be sincere?

P. He must do his best to be satisfied, and, when he hath done, must do according to the best judgment that he is able to make of himself. As now I tell you that your consent to the covenant is your christianity, I ask you whether you consent unfeignedly? If you do, you may somewhat perceive that you do; and if you say, I am not sure that I consent sincerely, but as far as I can know my heart I think I do, you must then communicate; for it is the being of sincerity, and not the assurance of it, which is

[y] Luke xxii. 16—19; 1 Cor. xi. 23—26.

[z] John i. 29, 36; 1 Pet. i. 19; 1 Cor. v. 7; xi. 23—25; Heb. ix. 26; x. 8, 12.

[a] 1 John v. 9—12; vi. 33, 35, 41, 50, 51; 1 Cor. x. 16, 17.

[b] That this is the true sense, see these texts: 1 Cor. xi. 23—28; x. 4, 15, 16; Matt. xxvi. 29; v. 13, 14; Mark xiv. 25; Luke xxii. 20, compared with Exod. xii. 11, 27; John vi. 53, 63; xv. 1; Isa. xl. 17; Psal. xxii. 6; Acts xx. 7, 11; ii. 42, 46.

necessary. And we are all so unacquainted with our own hearts, that if we must not speak according to our best discerning of them without assurance, we must lay by our thanksgiving, and a great part of our other duty.

S. But what if I prove mistaken, and be not sincere?

P. If you are not[c] sincere, and yet think you are, it is your great sin that you are not so, and will not consent to the covenant and mercy offered you; and it is your sin to think that you consent when you do not. And there is a greater weight lieth upon this than your respect to the sacrament; for you are an heir of hell till you truly consent, whether you receive the sacrament or not.

S. But what if I find it a work too hard for me, to try myself?

Of pastoral help.

P. Go to your pastor, or to some other able divine, or friend, and[d] open your case fully to them, and take their help.

S. Can any one else tell what is in me, if I cannot tell myself?

P. You can best tell what you feel; but another may better tell you what that signifieth, and also by what rules and signs you must proceed in judging. The patient knoweth better than the physician what he feeleth, and must first tell that to the physician; but the physician, then, can better tell him what cause it cometh from, and what is the nature of the disease, and what is like to come of it, and how it must be cured. Many know not that covenant consent is that christianity and faith which they are to try, but think that godliness is some other thing than indeed it is: what wonder, then, if they lie in doubtings?

S. But may not an unregenerate man come, that thinketh he is sincere, and doth mistake?

May the unregenerate communicate.

P. He may not lawfully come; for, 1. He is a refuser of Christ and his benefits; and the work there to be done is to profess that he accepteth him, and truly consenteth to his covenant; and should he falsely come and profess acceptance and consent, who doth it not indeed, nor will not be persuaded to it? The question is, whether it be lawful solemnly to lie? He that is truly willing to have God for his God, and Christ for his Saviour, Teacher, and Lord, and the Spirit for his Sanctifier, is a true christian, and may come; and he that[e] will not, must not lie, by taking Christ in representation, when he refuseth him in heart and deed; nor may he outwardly take the signs of those benefits, pardon and life, which, indeed, he is uncapable of.

S. Then, it seems, the pastor must not receive such.

P. The pastor must receive[f] hypocrites that are unknown to him to be such; for it is only God and conscience that know the heart. It may be my duty to receive a hypocrite when it is his sin to come and claim it.

S. But what if the open profane shall come?

P. The[g] pastors have the church keys, and are its guides; and they are to keep out all that are not baptized and professed covenanters with Christ, and to cast out all who are obstinate and impenitent in a wicked life, which is contrary to the essence of the covenant; but they must do this in a regular course of church justice, upon due proof and trial, after due admonition, and exhortation, and patience with the impenitent; and not upon common report, without this proceeding.

[c] Josh. ii. 4, 15; Matt. xvi. 15, 16; 1 John v. 10—12; Rev. xxii. 17.
[d] Acts ii. 37, 38; John iii. 20, 21.
[e] 1 Cor. xi. 28—30. [f] Acts viii. 13.

S. But what if either by bad men's intrusion, or the pastor's negligence, many such come in, may I join with such?

Of joining with the scandalous. Many churches are blamed in Scripture, but none required to separate from them.

P. If you do not your part, by wise advice, to bring them to repentance, and after, by accusation and proof, to cast out the impenitent, this will be your sin; but the fault of the sinner or of the pastor shall not be imputed to you if you be innocent. It is the church's duty to cast out the uncapable; but it is a sin to go from the church and God's ordinance because they are there, if they be not cast out. You must do your best to promote true church discipline; but must not separate from the church because it is neglected. But yet, for your own edification and comfort, you may remove to a better church and pastor, if some greater reason, as public hurt, &c. hinder it not.

S. III. What is the particular preparation which is necessary?

P. 1. To renew our meditations of the nature and use of the sacrament, and how holy a work it is to transact so great a business with God and our Redeemer, before the congregation, that so we may come with holy and reverent, and not with common and regardless, minds.

2. To [h]examine ourselves, both whether we continue our unfeigned consent to the covenant of God, and also whether we live according to our covenant, in a godly, sober, righteous, and charitable life, and live not in any wilful sin; and what falls we have been guilty of; and, accordingly, to humble ourselves to God, and to man where the case requireth it, by true repentance; and to ask them forgiveness whom we have wronged, and to forgive them that have wronged us, that we may be fit to receive forgiveness from God, and for loving communion with him and his church.

3. To consider beforehand what we are to do when we come to the sacrament, and what we are to receive.

S. II. You have told me what the preparation must be; will you now tell me what I must do at the sacrament?

P. In general, you must renew your covenant with God in Christ, and receive renewed mercies from him.

In particular, I. You must stir up and exercise, 1. A firm belief of the doctrine of the gospel, the truth of Christ, and the world to come. 2. A lively sense of your sin and misery, your need of Christ, his blood, and Spirit; a loathing of yourself and sins, and a high esteem of him and of his grace. 3. A hungering and thirsting after him and his grace, and communion with God. 4. A thankful sense of the wonderful love of God in our redemption. 5. The exercise of love to him that hath thus loved us, and of joy in the sense of so great salvation. Love and joy are the life of our sacramental communion. 6. A quieting confidence in Christ and his covenant now sealed to us. 7. A renunciation of all other love and hopes, and carnal, worldly pleasures and felicity; forsaking all in heart for Christ, and ready to suffer for him whose sufferings save us. 8. A hearty love to one another, and great desire of the unity of believers, and readiness to communicate to their wants. 9. You must renew the devoting and giving up yourself to God, your Father, Redeemer, and Sanctifier, with a firm resolution, sincerely to cleave unto him, and obey him to the death. 10.

[g] 1 Cor. v.; Matt. xviii. 15—18; 1 Thess. v. 12, 13; Heb. xiii. 7, 17.
[h] 1 Cor. xi. 26—30.

You must do all in hope of Christ's second coming, and of everlasting life. All these graces must be exercised in the sacrament.

S. What have I there to move me to all this?

P. 1. You bring with you a sinful soul to humble you. 2. You have God's truth there sealed, and Christ crucified, represented, and freely offered you, to exercise your faith; and all his benefits and salvation given you, to exercise your desires, thankfulness, love, and joy. 3. You have the Bread of life there broken to you, and the Spirit of Christ there given you, with his body and blood, to stir up your appetite after holiness. 4. You have the odiousness of sin, and the justice of God, presented to you in the commemoration of the sacrificed Lamb of God. 5. You have a sealed pardon of sin given you, to teach you thankfulness and resolution of new obedience. 6. You have a commemoration of Christ, till he come in glory, to keep up your hope and desire of that glory which he purchased, and prepareth for you. 7. You have the most wonderful demonstration of the love of God; giving his Son, and all his mercy, to his enemies; and promising you life eternal by him, to win your heart to the love of God. 8. You have a sight of him that despised all the riches, and honours, and pleasures of the world, and willingly hung upon the cross, as if he had been a malefactor. And all this to please God, condemn sin, and save souls; to show you how the flesh, and world, and life itself, is to be forsaken and contemned; and at what rates God must be pleased, and how highly souls must be valued. 9. You have the church before you, as one body partaking of one bread, one cup, one Christ, to show you how love and unity must be valued. 10. And you there are a receiver of the signs, and give up yourself to him that giveth them to you, to show that you receive Christ and his salvation, and are obliged, and absolutely devoted to him, to serve him in thankful, obedient love.

S. Direct me when and how to do all this.

P. 1. When you are [i] called, and going up to the table, remember, with humble thankfulness, to what a feast God's mercy freely inviteth such an unworthy sinner.

2. When the minister is confessing sin, cast down your soul in penitent confession of your own sins.

3. When you see the bread and wine provided for this use, remember that it is the Creator of all, by whom we live, whom we have offended.

4. When you hear the words of the institution read, remember that [k] love which prepared and gave us a Redeemer.

5. When you look on the consecrated bread and wine, [l] discern and reverence the representative body and blood of Christ, and take it not profanely now for common bread and wine.

6. When you see the bread broken, and the wine poured out, remember the sacrificed Lamb of God, [m] that loved us to the death, and taketh away the sins of the world.

7. When the minister prayeth to God for the efficacy of the sacrament, join heartily with him, and beg for that pardon, peace, and Spirit, which is here offered.

8. When the minister delivereth you the bread and wine, look on him as the [n] messenger of Christ, appointed to deliver to you Christ himself, his sacrificed [o] body and blood, to be your Saviour; and with him the sealed covenant of grace, pardoning all your sins, and giving you right to justification, sanctification, and glory; and, accordingly, with thankful faith receive him.

9. When you see the communicants receiving the same Christ with you, let your heart be [p] united in love to all believers, and long for their union, and think how perfectly we shall be one in Christ the heavenly glory.

10. When the minister returneth [q] thanks and praise to God, stir up your soul to love and joy; and suppose you saw the heavenly society, who are saved by Christ, how vigorously they thank and praise him, that you may endeavour to imitate them in your degree.

11. When the minister telleth you what you have done, and received, and what you must [r] do for the time to come, consent, and resign yourself to Christ, and resolve to live in thankful, obedient love.

12. When you are going away, remember, Thus we are ready to go out of the world, and church on earth, where our mercies are much in signs and means, and are hastening to the place where we shall [s] see and enjoy the things now signified, and know, face to face, as we are known, and have higher joys than faith can raise.

S. What must I do when I come home?

P. 1. Continue to love and praise him that hath feasted you with [t] such salvation; and keep up a life of thanks and joy. 2. Continue in the [u] use of all other means, to keep up the life and resolution which you here obtained. 3. See that you live as you have covenanted.

S. How oft should I communicate?

P. As oft as the church doth in which you live. In old time, it was done at least [x] every Lord's day.

S. I pray you, next, teach me how to meditate profitably in private on all occasions.

Of meditation.

P. I. Choose such matters to [y] meditate on as you have greatest use for on your heart: which is above all. 1. truth of the gospel, and of the life to come, to confirm your faith and hope. 2. The infinite goodness and love of God in Christ, and the joyful state of the blessed in heaven, to inflame your love, and heavenly desires and joys. 3. The sufficiency of Christ, in all cases, to exercise your communion with him by faith. 4. The operations of the Spirit, that you may know how to receive and improve them. 5. The nature of all duties, that you may know how to do them. 6. The evil and nature of every sin, and the ways of all temptations, that you may know how to avoid or overcome them. 7. The nature of all mercies, that you may thankfully improve them. 8. The use of afflictions, and the nearness of death, and what will be then necessary, that you may be prepared with faith and patience, and all may be your gain.

II. For the time and length of meditation, let it be, whether at your work, or when you do nothing else, at your best opportunity and leisure. And let it be as long as your time will allow you, without neglecting any other duty, and as your head can well bear it. For solid, sober men can carry on long and regular meditations; but ignorant, weak men must take up with short and broken thoughts, like short

[i] Matt. xxii.; Luke xiv.; Cant. v. 1; Isa. lv. 1—3; Rev. xxii. 17.
[k] John iii. 16; 1 John ii. 1.
[l] 1 Cor. xi. 28, 29.
[m] Rev. i. 5; 1 John iv. 19.
[n] 2 Cor. v. 19—21.
[o] 1 Cor. x. 16, 17.
[p] John xvii. 23, 24; 1 Cor. i. 10; 1 John iv. 11.
[q] Luke ii. 13, 14; Heb. viii. 5; xii. 22, 23; Rev. v. 5—7, 11, 14.
[r] John v. 15.
[s] 1 Cor. xiii. 12.
[t] Rom. v. 1—3.
[u] Phil. ii. 12.
[x] Acts xx. 7, 11.
[y] Gen. xxiv. 63; Josh. i. 8; Psal. i. 2; lxiii. 6; civ. 34; cxix. 15, 97, 99, 23, 48, 78, 149; cxliii. 5; lxxvii. 12; 1 Tim. iv. 15.

prayers; and melancholy people are unfit for any musings or meditation at all. For to do that which they cannot do, will but make them worse.

III. As for the work itself; observe how profitable ministers preach; and even so in meditation do you[z] preach to your own heart. 1. Consider of the meaning of the matter, and understand it. 2. Consider of the truth of it, and believe it. 3. Consider how it is most useful to you. And there convince your conscience by evident reasons: disgrace your sins by odious aggravations: invite your soul to God, and Christ, and goodness, by spreading the amiableness of all before it. Chide yourself sharply for the sins you find: stir up yourself earnestly by all the powerful motives that are before you. Comfort your soul, by spreading before it the present and the everlasting joys; support it by thinking on the grounds of faith; and direct it into the right way of duty, and drive it to resolve and promise obedience for the time to come.

And in all this, let clearness and liveliness concur: for as it is those that make a good preacher, so it is those that make a profitable meditation. Preach not coldly and drowsily to your hearts, but even as you would have a minister preach.

I tell you, the benefits of such meditation are very great: few men grow very wise, or very good, that use it not. We are full of ourselves, and near ourselves, and know our hearts better than others do: and many will hear and learn of themselves that will hardly hear and learn of others. And secret duties have usually most sincerity.

S. I would next entreat you to teach me how to pray in secret.

Of secret prayer.

P. I told you in part before. I now only add, I. Understand well what it is that you must desire in your heart, and in what order; and then you will have a habit of prayer in you when you have got a habit of those desires. For desire is the life of prayer. To this end study well the true meaning of the [a] Lord's prayer; for that is the platform, and the very seal that should imprint the same matter and order of desires on your soul. I have elsewhere opened that prayer at large.[b]

II. When you have got this impression of holy desires on your heart, you are then a christian indeed; let the expressing or wording them be according to occasions: you are not always to speak them just in the order as they are in your heart and in the Lord's prayer; for [c] particular occasions may call you oft to mention some particular sins, wants, or mercies, without then mentioning the rest; or to mention them more largely than the rest; as there is cause.

III. Think not that you have prayed, when your tongue hath gone [d] without your heart: therefore, get the deepest sense of your sins, wants, and mercies, and labour more with your hearts than with your tongues: and out of the abundance and treasure of a feeling, fervent heart, the tongue will be able so to speak as that God will accept it.

IV. Go to God only in the [e] name of Christ, in trust upon his merits and intercession: put all your prayers as into his hands, to offer them to God; and expect every mercy from God as by his hands. For since sin defiled us, man can have no happy communion with God in himself, but by a Mediator.

V. [f] Live as you pray, and think not that confessing sin to God will excuse you for continuing in it. And labour for what you pray for: and think not that praying is all that you have to do, to get God's grace, any more than to get your food and raiment; but you must labour, and beg, for God's blessing thereon.

About forms and family prayer I spoke before.

S. I pray you briefly direct me for good conference.

Of conference.

P. 1. Be [g] furnished for it, by a good understanding and a zealous soul; for as a man is, so will he speak; the inward disposition is all in all.

2. When you are with those that can teach you, be much forwarder to hear than to speak. Pride maketh men of a teaching, talkative disposition.

3. Yet if such be silent as can teach you, set them on work by some seasonable question. For the best aıe too dull and backward to good. And many are silent for want of occasion, opportunity, or invitation.

4. When you speak to the ignorant and sinful, do it not in a contemptuous, proud, magisterial way; but with clear, convincing reason, and with great love and gentleness. Let instruction and sweet exhortation be instead of reproof, for the most part. And when you must reprove them, do it usually in secret, and not before others; for disgrace will provoke them, and hinder from repentance.

4. Drive home all your holy conference to some practical issue, for your own affection and resolution when you learn of others, and to affect the hearers at the very heart, and bring them to resolve on that which is their duty, when it is your lot to be as a teacher to others.

5. Avoid two pernicious destroyers of good discourse: 1. Choosing [h] little things, though good, to talk of. As some small [i] controversy, word, or text, less pertinent to men's present necessities. 2. An ignorant, unskilful manner of talking of weighty matters. Abundance of good people breed scorn and contempt in the wittier sort of hearers, by their imprudent manner of speech.

6. Because the ignorant and unlearned cannot well avoid this, when they talk with those that are more witty and learned than themselves, I advise them to say little to such, unless to name some plain text of Scripture which may convince them: and, instead of the rest, 1. To get them to read some fit books: 2. And to get them to discourse with some ministers or others that can overwit them, and silence all their cavils.

S. I have but one thing more to desire now: that you will teach me how to keep days of humiliation and thanksgiving in private and in public.

Of days of humiliation and thanksgiving.

P. I would not overwhelm you with precepts: a little may serve for both these, besides what is said on other subjects. 1. In public, the pastors must choose the time of humiliations and fasts, with the order, and words, and circumstances of performance. But in private, your discretion must be chooser. And it must be, 1. After some great sin. 2. Or in some great danger or judgment, private or public. 3. Or when some great mercy is desired, or work to be done. And so thanksgivings are for great mercies and deliverances.

[z] Psal. xvi. 2, 3; xlii. 1, 2, 4, 5, 11; xliii. 5; lxii. 1, 5; lxiii. 8; lxxxvi. 4; ciii. 1, 2, 22; civ. 1, 35; cxvi. 7, &c.; cxlvi. 1; Gen. xlix. 6.

[a] Matt. vi. 6, 9; Rom. viii. 26.

[b] In my Christian Directory.

[c] So did the apostles oft. Acts i. 24; iv. 31; vi. 6, 8, 15; ix. 40; xxviii. 8.

[d] Psal. cxlii. 2; xlii. 4; lxii. 8; Lam. ii. 19; Matt. xv. 5.

[e] 1 John ii. 12; John xiv. 13, 14; xv. 16; xvi. 23, 24, 26; 1 Tim. ii. 5; Heb. vii. 25; Rom. viii. 34; 2 Tim. iv. 16.

[f] Luke xxii. 40, 46; xxi. 36.

[g] Matt. xii. 34—36; xiii. 52; Psal. cxix. 46; cxlv. 5, 6.

[h] John iv. 20, 22.

[i] Tit. iii. 9.

2. The manner of humiliation is, by due[k] fasting, and confession, and prayer, to humble the soul penitently for sin, and beg the mercy which we want: and the manner of thanksgiving, to[l] rejoice soberly and spiritually, with moderate feasting, when that is convenient, and give God thanks for his mercy, and beg the grace to improve it, and renew our devotion and resolutions of obedience.

3. The outward parts (fasting and feasting) must not be made a form or ceremony of, nor judged to be pleasing to God merely in and for themselves; but must be chosen only as means which help us to their proper ends, humiliation and thanksgiving; and may be varied as men's cases and bodies differ. The weak may be humbled[m] without fasting, or with less; and the poor and the sickly may give thanks without feasting, or with little. And all must take heed of offering God a sacrifice of the sin of sensuality and excess.

4. [n] True repentance in humiliation, and increased love to God in thanksgiving, and true reformation of life by both, is the great end to be aimed at; and all that attaineth not, or truly intendeth not, that end, is vain. But so much for this present conference.

THE

NINTH DAY'S CONFERENCE.

DIRECTIONS FOR A SAFE AND COMFORTABLE DEATH.

SPEAKERS.—Paul, a Teacher; and Saul, a Learner.

SAUL. Sir, I have been, since I saw you, with divers of my neighbours at their death; and I see that weakness and pain of body, and the terrors of death, and the stir of friends and physicians, are so great impediments to men's preparation then, that I earnestly entreat you to help me to make ready while I am in health. For I am loth to leave so great work to so weak a state, and so sad and short, uncertain time.

Awakening thoughts of death.

PAUL. It is God's great mercy to make you so wise. There is nothing in which the folly of ungodly men doth more appear than in delaying their serious preparations for death. Is there any man so brutish as not to know that he must die? And he is scarce a man, much less a christian, who believeth not that death will pass him into another state of life. There is no man can doubt but this change is sure, and very near; and no man knoweth how near, or when; and oh how great a change will it be! The body, which was spruced up and pampered, which must now be honoured, and pleased, and preferred, must then become a loathsome corpse: the pleasant cups, the delicious food, the adorned rooms, the gay attire, the soft beds, the delightful gardens, walks, and fields, the honour and precedency, power and command, are all at an end, and turned into a dark and silent grave. The flesh that must be daily pleased, and nothing is too good for it, must be an ugly, black, and stinking carcass, many years rotting out of sight and smell, lest it should annoy the living, and mar their mirth, before it can come to be dry and less abominable dust, and equal with the common earth. [a] House and lands, wealth and honour, greatness and vain-glory, sports and worldly pleasures, are wholly at an end, and will follow them no further, but be to them as if they had never been. And the soul must appear in another society, among the spirits that have finished their course on earth, and are gone before to receive their doom: there it must see what before we heard of; either the hellish misery of undone souls, which have cast away all their hopes for ever, and the wicked devils which deceived them; or the perfected spirits of the just, the glorious angels, our glorified Redeemer, and the most glorious God. There they will soon see the truth of that word and that world which they doubted of; and quickly feel what they must trust to for evermore. Oh what a change is it suddenly to pass from our company, our dwellings, our business, our pleasures, and from all this world, and to see a world which we never saw before, and to enter presently upon the joys or sorrows which must never, never end or change! Oh what a stone is a hardened heart! What a senseless thing is an ungodly man! that can either forget such a day, and such a change as this, or can think of it without awakened resolutions, presently, and with their utmost diligence, to prepare! If they believe not God's word, and the life to come, why do they not come and debate the case with us, and hear what we can say, till they are resolved, upon the best inquiry, whether it be so indeed or not? Do they think that we can give them no better proof of it, than what their unstudied brains lay hold on; or no better than the devil giveth them against it? But if they do believe it, oh what self-condemning wretches are they! What! believe such a change as sure and near, and not prepare for it? Believe that they must be in heaven or hell for ever, and yet live as if they cared not which of them it be?

S. I confess it is an evident truth and duty which you urge, and an undeniable madness in men to forget so great, and sure, and near a change; for death is a thing past all dispute. It is no controversy whether we must die. And a man that loveth himself should think, then, whither we must go next.

P. If we tell men, in preaching, of things which they never knew before, they understand us not; and, instead of learning, they cavil and question whether they are true; and when we tell them of such things as they know already, and all the world knoweth, they despise it, and say, Who knoweth not this? But, by this, you may see that we have need to preach nothing more than that which all men's tongues confess. It is a shame, either for the preachers or hearers, that so many sermons are preached of death. If there be no need of it, the shame is ours; but if there be, the shame is theirs. O man! what a dark, and dead, and sottish thing art thou become, that hast need to be told that thou must die; and need to be told it at every funeral; yea, every day; and all too little: as if the place which we meet in did not tell it us, where we tread on the dust of so many generations, and, within a yard or two of our feet, some carcasses lie in black and loathsome rottenness, and the skulls and bones of others forget what once they were pleased with on earth. Our diseases and pains of body forewarn us; our weariness in our labours tells us that we have a body that must break at last; our grey hairs will tell us, as the golden leaves on the trees in autumn, that our fall is at hand; our children tell us that others are rising up in our steads, while we are going off

[k] Esth. iv. 16; Joel i. 14—16; Ezra viii. 21, &c.
[l] Esth. ix. 17, 18; Psalm lxxxi. 3.
[m] Matt. ix. 13; xii. 7.

[n] Rom. xiv. 17; 1 Cor. viii. 8; Isa. lviii. 2, &c.; Psalm l. 14, 15, 23; xvi.; 1 Cor. v. 8.
[a] Luke xvi.

the stage. Every bit that we eat, and cup that we drink, doth tell us what bodies we have, that can be no longer upheld than new reparations are daily made of their decays; our every night's sleep warneth us to prepare for that sleep from which the resurrection only will awake us; all the poor beasts, and birds, and fishes, whose lives must go to keep up ours, do tell us that our own will not be long, and that we must die as well as they, and that a life maintained by so many lives, at so dear a rate, should be well spent for his service that giveth us these, and all. When we plough up and dig the earth for our seed, and cast it in, where it must corrupt before it spring up again, we do but represent the digging of our graves, and the burial of this body till the rising day. Every time that the sun setteth at night and riseth again the next morning, it warneth us how our lives must set and rise again; and so doth every fall and spring. Every bell that tolleth or ringeth for the dead, is our call to prepare to follow them; yea, every bell that calleth to the church doth tell us that the same bells must shortly be tolled for our burial. Every clock that striketh, every watch that moveth, every hour-glass that runneth, hath a voice to call senseless sinners. See and hear, O man or woman, how thy time passeth away; how quickly will thy last[b] hour come! Yea, every breath that we fetch ourselves, and every stroke that our pulse both beat, doth call to sinners, Your days are numbered; it is determined how many more breaths you must breathe, and how many times more your pulse must beat; your last pulse and your last breath is near at hand! Oh what abundance of preachers have we to tell us that we must die! and yet men live as if they did not believe it, or never had been warned to prepare.

S. But sure, sir, it is a thing that men know so well, that they need not be told that they must die; but only be told better how to prepare for it.

P. I tell you, to the shame of corrupted nature, that men have need to be told, and told again, a thousand times, with the loudest voice, that they must die. It was not a vain lesson which the philosopher taught the great emperor, Remember that thou art mortal. Oh had I a voice that could be heard all over the land, to cry to all men, Remember that you must die; and could I speak it to their hearts, it would awaken the secure, it would unbefool the dreaming world, who are playing away their lives for nothing. I tell you, the preacher that doth but thunder this in the ears of a sleepy, worldly congregation, O sinners, you must die, you must die, as sure as you are alive you must die, doth not preach an unsuitable or unprofitable sermon. If you believe me not, answer me these few questions:

Quest. 1. Why else are men so surprised with the fears of death when it is just coming? They knew, all their lives before, that it would come, and yet they live merrily and carelessly till it is just upon them; and then when the physician tells them there is no hope, oh what heart-sinking terror are they in, as if they had never known that they must die till now! Sure there is a way to make death less terrible; and why is not this way used in time?

Quest. 2. And what maketh such a difference between their healthy and their dying thoughts? Now nothing doth relish with them but the world and the flesh; and then they cry out, the world is vanity. Now nothing is so unwelcome to them as the motions of a holy life; but then they cry out, with Balaam, "Oh that I might die the death of the righteous, and my last end might be as his," Numb. xxiii. 10.

[b] Matt. xxiv. 44; xxv. 10; Luke xii. 40.

Now praying wearieth them; but then they cry for mercy, mercy, and learn to pray without book, and without a teacher. Now they cannot bear him that telleth them of their sins; but then they can cry out, as Judas, "I have sinned." Now they must not be stopped nor troubled in their sins; but then they trouble themselves more, and cry out, Oh that I had the time again which I have lost! Oh that God would try me once again! I would be a new man; I would lead a new life; I would never do as I have done. Then they can be serious in thinking of their change, and the dread of it amazeth them; and oh that they could make sure of heaven! But now they regard it as little almost as if it did not much concern them, while they have time, and helps, and warning to make sure. Either this change is wise, or not. If not, why will they do it then? if it be, why not now? That which is best then is best now. Death should be the comfortable ending of a well-spent life; and they make it either the terrible or the senseless conclusion of a loser's game, or a doleful tragedy; and all because they be not awakened to learn to die in the time of health.

Quest. 3. Why is it that their teachers never hear them once seriously inquire, How shall I make ready; and how shall I know where I must dwell for ever? If we can afford them no help herein at all, why do they desire us to counsel them on their death-bed? if we can, why do we not hear this sooner from them? Do you understand Christ's parable of the unjust steward? Luke xvi. 4, 5. His wit is commended, that when he was to be turned away, he seriously bethought him whither to go next, and provided himself of another habitation. Nature taught him to make some provision for his change. But we cannot get men that know, past doubt, that shortly they must leave this world for ever, to bethink them carefully, whither they must go next; and how their poor souls may find a comfortable entertainment with God.

S. I pray you name some of the benefits that would come to men, by the serious warnings and thoughts of death; otherwise we shall think that it is but troubling us before the time, with the fears of that which cannot be prevented, and so the increasing of our sorrows.

P. O friend! I tell you death is a powerful preacher; it teacheth many men that to the quick which we have preached twenty years in vain. We preach them asleep; but the sentence of death doth awaken them to purpose. I will begin with myself, and the rest of my profession:

1. The serious thoughts of death do teach ministers how to preach, and the people how to hear. I am sure, through God's mercy, it hath been the expectation of death these thirty-four years which hath been a great means to help me to that little, too little, seriousness in preaching which I have had. Who is so dull that, if he thought that this were the last day that he should preach and live, would not importunately beg of his hearers to receive the gospel, and repent of sin, and turn to God, and save their souls? But when men think that they have forty years more to live yet, and preferments to get, and prosperity to enjoy, they make the public assembly a stage, to set out themselves, and act the part of a servant of Christ, to win the prize and reward of a worldling; they play with Scripture, and talk of heaven and hell in jest, and jingle out a few canting words, contrived by hypocrites to beget hypocrisy, and, from a senseless heart, to make men more senseless, and teach them to take christianity for a stage-play, and the service of God for a common thing. For all things would generate their like;

the spirit of slumber as well as the Spirit of sanctification.

But death awakeneth the preacher to awaken the hearers. We are dying while we are speaking, and you while you are hearing. The breath which we speak by, is measuring out our time. We have but so many breaths to breathe, and we have done. We shall all be shortly silenced in the grave. It is your mercy and our mercy that yet we have tongues to speak, and you have ears to hear. But we preach and you hear as men in a boat, which is all the while swiftly carried down the stream, and will be quickly in the ocean of eternity. No wonder if Paul adjure Timothy to most constant and importunate preaching, 2 Tim. iv. 1, 2; and if Christ so often call out to sinners, "He that hath an ear to hear, let him hear." All that we have to say must be quickly said, and all that you will learn must be quickly learned; even now, or never. Oh how many a hundred times have I risen off my knees with shame and consternation, to think that a dying man, in so great necessity, could pray no harder at the door of eternity! and how many a time have I come down from the pulpit with shame and grief, to think that I could speak with no more affection to men that are so near another world; that my heart did not melt over miserable sinners, and that I did not, with tears and importunity, entreat them; that I could so easily and quietly go away without a grant of that which I came for, when I knew not that ever I should speak to them more. Methinks death should make us all better preachers, and you better hearers, were it well foreseen. It stirred up Peter to stir up his flock, knowing that speedily he must put off his tabernacle, 2 Pet. i. 13, 14. It stirred up Paul to rouse up Timothy, to think that the time of his departure was at hand, 2 Tim. iv. 1, 2, 6. It moved him, and melted his hearers, when he told them that they must see his face no more, Acts xx. 38.

S. What other benefit doth foreseen death bring?

P. 2. It teacheth us the wisest estimate of all the wealth, and honour, and greatness of this world; for it showeth them all to us in their final state, and what they will prove to us in our greatest needs. If all the congregation were sure that they were to die to-morrow, or the next week or month, how easily could we preach them into a contempt of the world! Though it changed not their love to it, (for they would still keep it if they could,) it would make them confess that all is vanity. Then, what is riches worth? what are lands and sumptuous houses worth? what are honours and places of command worth? Now, are these, think you, better than a Christ; or worthy the purchasing with the loss of heaven? Would not assurance of salvation now be better? Suppose the preacher that cometh to comfort a dying man, should come to him only with worldly comforts; suppose he say, Sir, be of good comfort; you have had many a merry cup, many a sumptuous feast, many a gallant entertainment; you have lived in honour, and wealth, and ease: would he not say, O but it is all past and gone, and I must never more enjoy it! If the priest shall say, You have fair houses, and a great estate, to comfort you, will he not say, O that is my sorrow, for I must leave them all for ever! If it be told him, Your children shall enjoy it all when you are gone, will he not say, But they must leave it as I do; and whither shall my soul go; and what comfort will their pleasure be to me; when the[c] rich worldling in hell would have had one to warn his brethren on earth, lest they should follow him to the place of torment? The church-yard is that market-place where the things of this world are duly rated. If they will purchase you a pardon from God, or open heaven to you, or make your bones and dust more happy, value them, and spare not; seek them, and keep them, and use them as far as furthereth the service of God and your salvation, and will give true comfort to a dying man. But if all your plenty prepare but for this farewell,[d] "Thou fool, this night thy soul shall be required of thee, and then whose shall all these things be which thou hast provided?" such a parting is not worth so dear a price. Read Psal. xlix. 6, 7, 13, 14.

S. What other benefit can you get by the thoughts of death?

P. Death is the great disgracer of pride. It will tell you whether it be seemly for him to look big, and boast, and domineer to-day, who must shortly be buried in the society of bones and dust, in darkness. Oh! can that man be proud that is going to answer for all his sins before that God that hateth pride, and must leave his beloved body in the earth, swelling with haughtiness to-day, and in the grave, and perhaps in hell, to-morrow? Is it congruous to dress that body with needless cost and curiosity, and spend precious time in adorning that flesh, which must so quickly rot and stink? The grave is the looking-glass which will teach proud gallants how to dress them. If they saw but what is now within them, they would think that such dung and guts did scarce well suit with such curious coverings. If you did but now see and smell one of your neighbour's carcasses, which was buried a year or two ago, would you think it suitable for him to be proud that must come to this? That skull and those bones retain no signs of the proud man's glory. O foolish mortals! if you know not, and remember not, that you must come, and quickly come to this.

S. What else learn you by the foresight of death?

P. 4. It teacheth men how to value their mirth and sensual delight. All the pleasure of meat, drink, plays, of lust, and all your fleshly accommodations, are now past and gone, and never shall return. There you may see the skull and hole where the meat and drink did once go in, but the delight is ended. And must all come to this? And yet will not men seek more durable delights? Your swine and ox is fed for your own table, and therefore it is worth the cost. But is it worth the wasting of your estate, and the loss of your soul too, to feed and pamper a corpse for the worms or grave? Is it more comfortable to a dying man to hear, You have lived a merry life in the world, or to know that he shall live in the heavenly joys with his Redeemer?

S. What other lesson will death teach us?

P. 5. It will teach us how to spend our time. O precious time! how basely art thou esteemed by idle, voluptuous, and ungodly men! Now they can play it away, and prate it away, and idle it away in a hundred vanities, as if God had made their lives too long, and they knew not what to do with it. But when they hear, You are past recovery, Oh then for more time! Oh that we might live one year longer! Oh that we had now all that time to repent in, and make sure of heaven, which we spent in sports, and idleness, and worldliness! Oh that we had lived as obediently to God, and as holy lives, as the strictest saints, so we had but their safety and hopes of heaven! O time, time, how art thou past away and gone, and all the world cannot call back one day or moment! Oh what a hateful word is pastime! O happy men, that have hearts to use it for the ends that God created and redeemed them, before it be

[c] Luke xvi. 26, 27.

[d] Luke xii. 20.

too late, and time, and soul, and heaven be lost! It is death that teacheth men the worth of time.

S. Have you any more to say of this?

P. 6. Death teacheth men how to behave themselves to each other. How peaceably do those bones and that dust lie together! There is no striving, no cruelty, no domineering or abusing others. On a death-bed you will say that you forgive all the world. You dare not desire revenge then, lest God be revenged on you. And will you be worse living than dead? Doth oppression, and persecution, and treading down the poor and low, beseem them that must so soon be levelled with the lowest, and be unable to stir away a worm that feedeth on their heart or face?

7. I will add but one more; death teacheth us whether we should rather fly from sufferings or from sin. Die we must, whether we will or no; and is it not better to die for Christ, if he require it, than die without any such advantage? Will it comfort us at death to think what sufferings we escaped by sin?

S. I have oft marvelled why God would not save us from dying, seeing Christ died for us; but now you have partly satisfied my doubt.

P. Though God's great day of judgment be to come, yet he will have some justice done upon sinners in this world: and though Christ have suffered for us, there is a necessity both to our own and the common good, that even sinning christians suffer something themselves. But God doth so moderate it, by his wisdom and mercy, that even this punishment becometh a cure to the sin that causeth it, and a great means to our good. Were it but an uncertain thing whether we should die or not; did but some die, and some not die; yea, did men live but as many hundred years as before the deluge, oh what a wicked world would this be!

1. Covetousness then would have no restraint. How dearly would men love this world! Oh what a striving then would be for it! They that would live in sin, and sell heaven for a few years' uncertain commodity here, what would they do for a thousand years' riches, or for the hopes of living here for ever? But when this is written on all the worldling's doors, on his houses, on his wealth, on his flesh, Thou must die, thou must certainly and shortly die! this is it that mars the markets of the world. A sober look on a skull and coffin, or a grave, doth blast all the beauty of this world, and telleth reason itself it is but a dream. It writeth vanity upon all. Who would say,[e] "Soul, take thine ease, eat, drink, and be merry," how rich soever he were, if he looked not to possess it many years, but expected to hear, "Thou fool, this night shall thy soul be required of thee, and then whose shall all these things be which thou hast provided?" Now take thy houses, and lands, and money with thee if thou canst. At least take so much as will buy thee a drop of water to cool thy tongue. If death did not preach to worldlings, no other preachers could be heard. It crieth out to them, What mean you, sinners, to bestow all this labour for a few days' vanity? Is it worth all this stir to make your salvation more doubtful, and more difficult, as a camel's passage through a needle's eye? to increase your load, and double your temptations, and all for the pleasures of so short a life? If death did not preach with us, we should preach to little purpose.

2. And were it not for death, ambition would have no bounds. If Alexanders and Cæsars are such plagues to mankind while they are posting to the grave, what would they be if they had any hope of an earthly immortality! Then the great ones of the world would be great indeed. How big would they look; how insolently would they lord it over the poor; and how cruelly would they oppress and persecute the innocent! No wonder, then, if their flatterers were so many and so base as to make them think they were gods, and to require a divine obedience and honour. But foreseen death doth curb this arrogance, and standeth like Haman's gallows before their own doors. As he was highest, he had the honour to be hanged highest. When Satan hath brought them to the pinnacle of the temple, they see how low they have to fall. When he hath brought them to the exceeding high mountain, and showed them the kingdoms and glory of the world, if they accept them as his gift, and on his dreadful terms, it is a wonder that without terror they are able to look down so low, as death assures them they must be cast. If you had the greatest entertainments on the battlements of the steeple, and were sure that shortly you must be cast down, it would spoil the pleasure of them all. It is a brave thing for Absalom to be a king, and for Ahithophel to be his chief counsellor, but had they both foreseen their hanging, it would have made them sooner hang down the head. Poor men and preachers may thank God that the ungodly great ones of the world must die, and that they are constrained to foreknow it; or else earth would be like hell, and oppression and persecution would be the state of mankind. For man, being in honour, would have no understanding; if now both they and their posterity go on in the folly of their way, when they abide not, but are as the beast that perish, (Psal. xlix. 12, 13, 20,) what would they do, if death were not their instructor?

3. Were it not for death, sensuality would have no restraint. Voluptuous swaggerers would scorn reproof. The fornicator would not be ashamed by the light, nor the drunkard fear what is in the bottom of the cup. Who would not be[f] clothed with purple and fine linen, and fare sumptuously and deliciously every day, that could? O but this death! this death is it that marreth all the mirth. When Belshazzar seeth the hand-writing on the wall, in all his jollity, his joints do tremble. "Rejoice, O young man, in thy youth, and let thy heart cheer thee. Walk in the way of thy heart, and in the sight of thine eyes; but know thou that for all these things God will bring thee into judgment," Eccl. xi. 9. This is it that spoileth all the sport. Remember that thou dancest about the grave, and death must end the game at last. I tell you, except the promise of the life to come, there is nothing that so much marreth the devil's markets, and spits so much shame in the face of sin, as certain, foreseen, approaching death; and therefore the devil is wiser than to come with the ordinary bait to a dying man. Should he then offer him cards and dice, and tempt him to fornication or to drunkenness, yea, or offer him lands and dignities, he knows they would do nothing. What is this to a man that must die to-morrow? I conclude, therefore, "It is better to go to the house of mourning, than to the house of feasting; for that is the end of all men, and the living will lay it to his heart. The heart of the wise is in the house of mourning, but the heart of fools is in the house of mirth," Eccl. vii. 2—6.

S. It is a wonder of stupidity, that reasonable men can so much forget so great, and near, and sure a change; and that so few do bethink them whither

[e] Luke xii. 19, 20.

[f] Luke xvi.

their souls must go, and where they must dwell next.

P. Some would have no funeral sermons, and I would have almost no other. All our religion is but a continual preparation for death; to learn to die well, by learning and practising to believe, and love, and live well. Every sermon must teach men this. Men would have a funeral sermon when they are dead, that will not hear the same doctrine while they live; as if they had more care of the souls of those that survive them than of their own. Look on their tombs, and you shall see them almost all in a praying posture, with hands lifted up, who prayed but seldom and coldly while they lived; which showeth what conscience telleth men will be best at last. On their death-beds they desire us to pray for them to God. And now God sendeth us to pray to them for themselves, and they will not hear us, and yet think God must hear us for them then. God denieth us nothing which he hath promised; but if we beg never so hard of themselves, but to care for the salvation of their own souls, we cannot prevail with them; no, not soberly to remember that they must die, and to live as men that do believe it.

S. It is terrible to them, and they are loth to be troubled.

P. 1. If you were to be turned out of your house at the quarter's end, and I should advise you to provide another, would you say, "I would not think of going out, because it is troublesome?" We must go, whether we will or not; and shall we not care whither? 2. Is it troublesome to think of living for ever with Christ in glory? What then is pleasant? or what more comfortable thoughts will they choose? Is it better to die like a beast, and to live no more? If this miserable world seem better than heaven to them, yet, methinks, seeing they must leave it, whether they will or not, they should be glad to hear how they may be next provided for, and should never be at rest till they had made sure of the everlasting, holy, heavenly rest.

S. Well, sir, I pray you lay me down those directions by which I may in health prepare for a safe and comfortable death.

How to make ready for death.

P. It will be needful that I first tell you, I. Wherein your readiness doth consist. II. And how much it is your interest to be ready. III. How much it is your work and duty to make ready. And then, IV. To tell you how you must do it.

S. I like your order well; I pray you open the first.

I. There are two degrees of readiness for death: the first is for a safe death, that you may be saved when you die. The second, for a comfortable death, that you may die also in peace and joy.

P. All those, and only those, die safely and go to heaven, who are pardoned by Christ's blood, and sanctified by his Spirit. The Spirit of Christ is your preparation. If you have that Spirit you are justified, and shall be saved; for it is given you on purpose to fit you for heaven, and to be God's seal upon you, and the pledge, and the earnest, and first-fruits of your celestial happiness. "Blessed are the[g] pure in heart; for they shall see God."

2. But that, besides safety, you may have comfort in your death, it is also necessary, 1. That you have some certainty or knowledge that indeed you have the Spirit. 2. That you have faith, hope, and love, the graces of the Spirit, in suitable exercise. 3. And that the great impediments of your comfort be removed.

[g] Matt. v. 8.

S. Wherein is this readiness to die our interest?

P. II. Nature itself may tell you much of that, and faith more. 1. He that is not ready for a safe death, is in a state of damnation. If he so die, he is lost for ever. His endless state of joy or misery dependeth on it. Where then can a man's interest be so much concerned; especially considering that our flesh is frail, and liable to many hundred diseases every hour, and no man hath assurance to live another day or night. Oh what a madness is it for such a person to live one day in an unprepared state, if he can possibly get out of it (as if he will he may)! It is one of the most notorious evidences how much man's nature is enslaved by the devil, that when they are sure to die ere long, and know not but each hour or day may be their last, and hear from God's word, that as they are found at death it must go with them for ever, and that without holiness none shall see the Lord; yet they can sleep quietly, and rise carelessly, as if all were well with them, while they live in an unregenerate, unsanctified state. If such a person did indeed believe God's word, and were not dead or asleep in sin, surely his heart would meditate terrors; he would think that he even saw hell ready to receive him; he would dream of it in the night; he would find pleasure in nothing in the world till he were converted, and made holy, and prepared for heaven by the Spirit of God; he would, morning and evening, yea, night and day, cry earnestly to God in prayer for that grace which must prepare him for so great a change; he would go to ministers or godly friends, and ask them how he must make ready for death. 2. And he that is thus unready to die is unready for all duty, for suffering, for every thing; and is but losing the time that he liveth; and till he prepare for death he is preparing for hell. No business, therefore, no other cares, should hinder or delay men; no profit, honours, or pleasure, should quiet them till they have got their souls into a safe condition, and are ready to die.

S. Of what moment is it to die comfortably?

P. 2. The knowledge of your safety is the ground of your comfort. And it must needs be a terror to a man that hath any faith and sensibility, to be utterly uncertain what shall become of his soul for ever: to believe that there is a hell for all the unholy, and not to know but it may prove to be his lot: to believe that none but the holy shall be glorified, and not to know at all whether he be such or not: to know that he must shortly be in heaven or hell, and never more have a change of the place which he first possesseth, and not to know which of these it will be! This must needs be an amazing, dreadful thought. When the body is languishing in pain, and all worldly help and comforts fail, to be then utterly doubtful of everlasting comforts, must needs be a most uncomfortable state. To think, I must now go to my long home, and take my unchangeable possession, either of heaven or hell, but I know not whether it will be, is a sad thought to a dying man.

Yea, all a man's life must needs be uncomfortable till he be prepared for a comfortable death; for it is not the perishing trifles of this world that can suffice to comfort a wise man that still foreseeth their end. If, therefore, he cannot fetch comfort daily from heaven, he can have none that is worth the having. How can a wise man live comfortably till he can die comfortably, when he knoweth still that death is even at hand?

Yea, till we have some good preparations even for a comfortable death, we live in continual danger of very heinous sin. If we be called to martyrdom for Christ, the terrors of death may sorely tempt us to deny him. How can a man be saved that [h] loveth his life better than Christ and life eternal? And how can a man be willing to go out of this life, that hath not some considerable hopes of a better?

But if a man be ready to die well, he is ready to live well, and ready to suffer, and ready for any thing. When he can [i] fetch comfort from the thoughts of his being for ever with the Lord, what need such a man to fear? What is there that should much trouble him? How quietly may he sleep! how easily may he suffer! how joyfully may he live!

Nothing can be more evident than that to be in a continual readiness to die is the great interest of man; in comparison of which nothing else is worthy to be minded, or to be named.

S. III. What mean you by saying that it is also our chiefest work?

P. He that knoweth that it is his chief interest, must needs know that it is his chief work, as long as self-love is so deep a principle in nature, and interest so much acteth and ruleth all mankind. As a man, when he beginneth his life, doth begin his journey or race towards death and life everlasting, so God doth give him all his time to do this work, and his life is nothing but the time allotted him to prepare for death and a better life; and every hour that is not spent in such preparation is cast away and lost. All the time and work of a christian's life must be holy and religious; though not all spent in acts of worship, all must be a seeking of God and glory, by the conduct of Christ, his Spirit, and word. And all religion is nothing else but a preparing ourselves and others for death. Many trouble the world, and cheat themselves, with a religiousness which rather unfitteth men for death; even a religion made up of unprofitable opinions, contentions, and disputes. But when they have wearied themselves, and corrupted others, with their opinionative, wrangling zeal, they will find that one day spent in learning to die well would have tended more to solid comfort than such a dreaming kind of life. I know that sound doctrine maketh sound christians; but it is practical doctrine that must do it. And all christian practice is but a due preparation for death. Christ is the only way; but heaven, that is, God in the heavenly glory, is the only end. And Christ came from heaven, and is ascended to heaven, and sendeth his Spirit into our hearts from heaven, to call up our hearts, and prepare us for it. Death, therefore, which is our passage into heaven, must be in our eye in all the exercises of our religion, and all the businesses of our lives. Away with those opinions and practices, whatsoever, which no way tend to prepare you for a safe and comfortable death.

S. IV. Now tell me how this preparation must be made.

P. I. The chief part of it must be done in your health. II. And the rest in the time of your sickness.

How to prepare for death in health.

I. In your health, it must be the main business of your life to prepare for death. Particularly bestow much care and diligence to strengthen your belief of the truth of God's word, of the immortality of the soul, and of the life to come. Nothing more perniciously strengtheneth temptations, killeth all hope, desire, and endeavour, than secret doubtings whether God's word be true, and whether there be another life indeed for man or not. Uncertainties will hardly prevail against sense, and present things; uncertainties will hardly sufficiently comfort a departing soul, when all worldly comforts must be parted with for ever. Every doubt here is as water cast upon the fire; it quencheth all our desires and joys.

Now, the strengthening of our faith about the world to come is a thing that is not done with a wish: there must be due and constant endeavours used. I desire you to read the directions I have given you in the second part of my "Life of Faith;" and if that seem not enough, read my "Treatise against Infidelity," and my "Reasons of the Christian Religion," and "More Reasons." Now, I only advise you,

1. Never forget the miracles, resurrection, and ascension of Christ.

2. Forget not the miracles wrought by his apostles and evangelists in all the countries where they came.

3. Forget not the spirit of miracles given to all the first-planted churches.

4. But, above all, forget not the Spirit of holiness, which, in its effects, is apparent in all that are serious christians, in all ages and countries; especially [k] since the Spirit is Christ's standing Witness and Advocate in us, and a certain proof that he is the Saviour of souls. Forget not that by this Spirit, the living image of God's vital power, his wisdom, and his goodness, is printed on the sacred Scriptures; and the same image, by the Spirit and the Scriptures, is printed on all true believers' souls; which makes a notable difference between them and the rest of the world, and is the certain, present, common evidence that Christ is true, and that he is preparing for everlasting life.

5. Remember that God hath not given man, in vain, a soul which is capable of thinking on our Maker and another world; of desiring and seeking an endless home. The wise Creator fitteth all his creatures to their uses.

6. Look up, and think whether all those vast and glorious spaces which are above us are likely to be without inhabitants, when we see every corner of this lower world, both earth and water, are inhabited.

7. And when we find by experience that the invisible spirits are our helpers, and disdain not to regard and serve our interests, is it not like that our souls, being intellectual spirits, as well as they, shall have communion with them hereafter? Nothing is annihilated; much less such noble and spiritual beings as men's souls.

8. And mark but the common experience of the world, which telleth us that certainly there are evil spirits, by the temptations which we feel to evil, the hinderance of good, the strange power they have upon corrupted fantasies, and the common war which is maintained against Christ and godliness by all the wicked in the world. And you may thus learn, from the devil himself, that all this malice is not against nothing.

9. And the certain histories of witches will serve to confirm this evidence.

10. And so will the certain histories of apparitions; for instance, see one in a little book, called, "The Devil of Mascon."

11. And the common testimony of all men's consciences, the consent of almost all the world.

12. And that God doth actually govern the world, even among heathens and infidels, principally by the hopes and fears of a life to come: and God cannot need a lie to rule us. These and many such reasons help to confirm our faith: but it is the sacred impressions of the Spirit, first, on the Scripture, and next on your own hearts, and all the holy change which it hath made upon you, which is the near, the sure, the constant [l] witness in yourself and with you,

[h] Matt. x. 37—39; Luke xiv. 26, 33.
[i] 1 Thess. iv. 17, 18; 1 Cor. xv. 58; 2 Pet. iii. 10—12; Phil. i. 17, 21—23; 2 Cor. iv. 16—18; v. 1—4, 6—8.

[k] John xvi.; Rom. viii. 16, 26; 2 Tim. ii. 7; Heb. xii. 22—24.
[l] 1 John v. 10, 11.

that Christ is true, and that he is preparing us here for a better life.

These things must all be daily thought of, and all suggestions to the contrary first confuted, and then abhorred and cast away, till the soul grow up to such a habit of believing as will serve[m] instead of sight itself; and we can say that we are sure that there is an everlasting life for souls.

To all which must be added a cherishing of the Spirit, which is the author of faith, 1. By earnest prayer for his grace; 2. And by obeying and improving it.

II. Be sure that you truly repent of your known sin;[n] for nothing makes death so frightful to us as our guilt. Nothing else can make us reasonably fear whether God will save or damn our souls, but unpardonable sin. And the mercy of God is so great, and his promise so sure, that nothing can reasonably make us doubt of pardon, but that which maketh us doubt of the sincerity of our repentance, and faith in Christ. Spare not sin, then, but repent presently; repent deeply; confess it plainly; forsake it resolutely; and then it will not leave such fears in the soul, as shall make the sentence of death to be dreadful to us as sin but half repented of will do. Sin is the sting of death; and true repentance hath the promise of forgiveness.

III. Put your souls, with all their sins, and dangers, and all their interests, into the hand of Jesus Christ your Saviour; and trust them wholly with him by a resolved faith. It is he that hath purchased them, and therefore loveth them. It is he that is the owner of them, by the right of redemption. It is now become his own interest, even for the success and honour of his redemption, to save them. Be not too thoughtful about things unknown to you, as how separated souls do act, with what manner of intellection and sense, &c. what idea to have of spiritual bodies, of heaven, &c. But implicitly trust Christ with all these things, remembering that he knoweth what you know not: and as he possesseth heaven for you till he bring you to possess it, so he knoweth all these things unrevealed, for you, till he bring you to see and know them. If your most faithful friend were in the Indies, and invited you thither with the promises of the greatest wealth and pleasure, you would trust him, though you see it not yourselves, nor know the particulars distinctly. It is a great comfort to us that we have a Head and Saviour in heaven, and that heaven and earth are in his power. He that saved you[o] from sin and Satan's power will save you from hell's and Satan's torments. If angels rejoice at our conversion, Christ and angels will joyfully entertain victorious souls into the heavenly society, and welcome them to heaven with dearest love. Read oft, and meditate on, his special promises. "If any man serve me, let him follow me; and where I am, there shall also my servant be," John xii. 26; and he is at the "right hand of the Majesty on high," Heb. i. 3. "If I go to prepare a place for you, I will come again and receive you to myself, that where I am there you may be also," John xiv. 2, 3. "Father, I will that they also whom thou hast given me, be with me where I am, that they may behold the glory which thou hast given me," John xvii. 24. "For we know that if our earthly house of this tabernacle were dissolved, we have a building of God, an house not made with hands, eternal in the heavens: for in this we groan, earnestly desiring to be clothed upon with our house which is from heaven, that mortality may be swallowed up of life. We are confident, and willing rather to be absent from the body and present with the Lord," 2 Cor. v. 1, &c. "To depart and to be with Christ, is far better," Phil. i. 23. "Blessed are the dead which die in the Lord," Rev. xiv. 13. "This day shalt thou be with me in paradise," Luke xxiii. 43. "To the spirits of the just made perfect," Heb. xii. 23. "And so shall we ever be with the Lord: wherefore comfort one another with these words," 1 Thess. iv. 17. "We receive a kingdom that cannot be moved," Heb. xii. 28. "Receiving the end of our faith, the salvation of our souls," 1 Pet. i. 9. "Lord Jesus, receive my spirit," Acts vii. 59. "Him that overcometh will I make a pillar in the temple of my God, and he shall go no more out," Rev. iii. 12, 21.

But, above all, those words of our risen Lord I would have written over my sick bed, and on my heart: "Go to my brethren, and say to them, I ascend to my Father, and your Father, and to my God, and your God," John xx. 17.

Boldly, then, and quietly deliver up thy soul to the care of Christ. There is all things in him which thou needest. Are you afraid of guilt, and the law, and the wrath of God, and hell? Remember that he is "the Lamb of God that taketh away the sins of the world, in whom the Father is well pleased: that he hath, by once offering of himself, perfected for ever them that are sanctified: that he was made sin for us who knew no sin, that we might be made the righteousness of God in him. He is made of God unto us wisdom, righteousness, sanctification, and redemption. If any man sin we have an Advocate with the Father, Jesus Christ the righteous; and he is the propitiation for our sins, and not for ours only, but for the sins of the whole world."[p] "For God so loved the world that he gave his only begotten Son, that whosoever believed in him should not perish, but have everlasting life."[q] "Having, therefore, boldness to enter into the holiest by the blood of Jesus, by a new and living way which he hath consecrated for us, through the veil, that is to say, his flesh, and having an High Priest over the house of God, let us draw near with a true heart, in full assurance of faith."[r] "God willing more abundantly to show to the heirs of promise the immutability of his counsel, interposed himself by an oath; that by two immutable things, in which it is impossible for God to lie, we might have strong consolation, who have fled for refuge to lay hold on the hope set before us; which hope we have as an anchor of the soul both sure and stedfast, and which entereth into that within the veil, whither the Forerunner is for us entered, even Jesus, made an High Priest for ever."[s] "Seeing, then, we have a High Priest that is passed into the heavens, Jesus, the Son of God, let us hold fast our confession; for we have not an High Priest that cannot be touched with the feeling of our infirmities, but was in all points tempted like as we are, without sin. Let us, therefore, come boldly to the throne of grace, that we may obtain mercy, and find grace to help in time of need."[t] "O death! where is thy sting? O grave! where is thy victory? The sting of death is sin, and the strength of sin is the law; but thanks be to God who giveth us the victory through our Lord Jesus Christ."[u] "Who, by death, destroyeth him that had the power of death, that is, the devil, and delivereth them who, through fear of death, were all their lifetime subject to bondage."[x]

[m] Heb. xi. 1. [n] Luke xiii. 3, 5.
[o] Acts xxvi. 18; Rom. viii. 34—36.
[p] John i. 29; Heb. x. 14; 2 Cor. v. 21; i. 21; 1 Cor. i. 30; 1 John ii. 1, 2.
[q] John iii. 16. [r] Heb. x. 19, 20.
[s] Heb. vi. 17—19. [t] Heb. iv. 14—16.
[u] 1 Cor. xv. 55—57.
[x] Heb. ii. 14, 15.

Trust boldly your soul into the hand of such a Saviour, and distract not your mind with unbelieving fears.[m] He wanteth neither power, nor wisdom, nor love. You may boldly and quietly trust him with his own. He hath testified his love at so dear a rate that we should not question it, Gal. ii. 20; Rev. i. 5. To save us is his proper office and work, 1 John iv. 14; Eph. v. 23. It is his covenant to save his body, Heb. ix. 15; 1 Tim. iv. 18; Heb. x. 36; Jam. i. 12. He is our Judge himself, John v. 22. He hath the keys of hell and death, Rev. i. 17, 18. His work in heaven is to prepare a glorious receptacle for us; and there he is interceding for us to that end, Heb. ii. 10, and vii. 25; John xiv. 1—3. When you were received into the state of grace and reconciliation, you were entered into the outer part of the [n] kingdom of heaven. Here you were made [o] heirs, co-heirs with Christ; and here you had God's pledge and earnest, and the first-fruits: and will he not give us that which he hath already given us so much right to? Our near relation to him assureth us that he will not condemn his friends, his flesh, John xv. 14, 15; Eph. v. 29, 30; 2 Cor. vi. 17, 18. Is his love, his promise, his oath, his seal as nothing to us? He would never have given us a heavenly mind and desire, nor set us on seeking it, if he would not have given it us, Matt. vi. 20, 21, 33; John iv. 14; vi. 27; Matt. vii. 7, 8; 1 Cor. xv. 58; Psal. lxxiii. 24. It is faith in Christ which we must live and die by, if we will live and die in a well-grounded peace.

IV. Devote yourself entirely to God, and make it your trade of life to please him, doing all the good that you can to others for soul and body; that so your conscience may bear you witness at death, that notwithstanding your infirmities, the very business for which you lived in the world, was to serve your Lord, and to do good, and not to pamper the flesh, nor to grow rich, nor to get into honour and applause with men.

Though our good works give nothing unto God, nor can men or angels merit any thing of him, in commutative justice, as to the value of the thing, but only in point of governing, paternal justice, as to the order of free donation, it being impossible that any creature should have any thing from God, but by his gift, under what covenant soever; yet God, who is holy, is the lover of holiness, and the [p] rewarder of them that diligently seek him. And nothing can reasonably make a dying man question his salvation but the doubtfulness of his own sincerity in his covenant with God, and of his true repentance and sanctification. And no man can well judge his faith or repentance to be sincere, who liveth not as absolutely devoted to God. Therefore, though you must abhor all thoughts of ascribing any thing to your own faith or repentance, or holiness and sincerity, which is proper to God the Father, or to our Saviour, or to the Holy Ghost,[q] yet, without holiness none shall see God; for he [r] hateth all the workers of iniquity. And conscience will be conscience still; and its office is not to question whether God be God, and Christ be Christ, but whether we be christians. And he that never so fully believeth in Jesus Christ, must find himself to be indeed a believer, and to be sanctified by his [s] Spirit, before he can comfortably die, or have any assurance of his own salvation. If we are over the temptations to infidelity itself, the rest of our fears and troubles will be raised by the doubts of our own sincerity, and by the discerning of that they must be resolved.

And there is no such full and satisfying evidence of that as this [t] testimony of our conscience, that in simplicity and godly sincerity, and not in fleshly wisdom, we have had our conversation in the world. That is, that we really lived not to the flesh, but unto God, and how weakly soever, our main business in the world was to serve and please him with all the powers and estate he gave us. And that we did not principally live to the world, and put God off with the leavings of the flesh, nor made his service our secondary business, and seek him and heaven but in the second place. Oh that we knew well how much a life of total resignation, devotedness, and serviceableness to God, doth tend to a quiet and comfortable death! We should live otherwise than most do.

S. But I have oft heard that we must put no confidence in any works or holiness of our own, and that it is legal, and pharisaical, and popish, to fetch any of our comfort from them.

Of trusting in our own holiness.

P. 1. We must not dream that any works or holiness of ours can justify us if we are judged by the law of works, or innocency, in whole or in part. Because nothing but perfect, sinless holiness will so justify. But when Christ hath fully satisfied for our violation of that law, and made us a law of grace by which we must be judged, that [u] law of grace doth justify or condemn men, as they perform or not perform its conditions, giving free justification against the curse of the former law, through Christ alone, to all true believers.

2. I told you before that nothing must be ascribed to our own holiness or works that is proper to God the Father, or to Christ, or to the Spirit. And can you desire any more? If nothing, under Christ's person or thing, be a means of our salvation, then no person or thing must be loved or trusted, as a means. But who is it that dare say so?

3. When any thing of our own is put in competition with Christ, or opposition to him, and the question is, whether Christ or that is to be trusted, or to be our comfort, it must not only be distrusted, but rejected as dung.

4. Did Paul sin in the rejoicing before cited? 2 Cor. i. 12.

5. Do you think that no sin of our own should trouble us? Is there no sin which is just cause of doubting of our justification? What! not unbelief, nor impenitence, nor malignity, nor a fleshly or ungodly life? Shall not all perish that continue such? And is it not part of our comfort to see that we are free from that cause of discomfort? If there be any damning sin in the world, or any difference of the wicked from the righteous, must not our dying comfort lie much in finding that this is not our case?

Quench not the Spirit.

V. Take heed of quenching the Spirit of grace. He is our life from Christ, our Head. Whatever good we do in health or sickness, it must be by his gracious operations. You may think of Christ, and read over the promises, and think of the joys of heaven, and all will have little power upon you, if the Spirit help you not. You will but strive and come off with discouragement, and say, I cannot

[m] Ezek. xvi. 8; xviii. 4; 1 Cor. vi. 19; Psal. cxix. 49.
[n] Matt. iii. 2; x. 7; xiii. 11, 24, 31, 33, 44, 45, 47.
[o] 1 Pet. i. 3, 4; Rom. viii. 17, 18; v. 8—11; viii. 16; Gal. iv. 6; Eph. ii. 19; i. 13, 14; iv. 30; John xvii. 3; 2 Cor. i. 22; v. 5.

[p] Heb. xi. 6.
[q] Heb. xii. 14.
[r] Psal. v. 5.
[s] Rom. viii. 1, 8—13.
[t] 2 Cor. i. 12.
[u] John iii. 16, 18—20.

get assurance with all my examination. I cannot believe, I cannot reach to any powerful apprehensions of God, or heaven. I cannot choose but fear and doubt, even with the most evident arguments before my eyes. There is no effectual light in any knowledge, no holy love and delight in God, no spiritual life in any of our thoughts, but what is wrought by the illuminating, sanctifying, quickening Spirit. Oh, therefore, tenderly cherish and preserve this heavenly guest, as ever you would have joy in health or sickness, for it must be the joy of the Holy Ghost!

S. What is the cherishing, and what the quenching, of the Spirit?

P. It is a great truth, not sufficiently considered by the wiser sort of christians, that God, in his course of government over the souls, even of the justified, doth exercise great rewards and great punishments here; and these are much more upon the soul within, than upon the body without; even the giving of more of the operations of his Spirit, is his great reward, and the withholding, the withdrawing, or denying its operations, is his great punishment. The sin which provoketh him is unthankful neglect of convictions and holy persuasions of the Spirit, and much more wilful resistance of them. When we sin, it is not the bare sin that is all, as to the act itself, but especially the resisting of the Spirit, which in that sin we were guilty of, which we pay dearest for, when the Spirit convinceth us, reproveth us, and striveth with our hearts, and we will not yield, but overcome it. And the punishment of withdrawing the Spirit's operations is the more dangerous by how much the less perceived and lamented. Usually the signs of this judgment are, for men to lose their life and love to goodness by degrees, and to grow indifferent in the matters of God. To grow formal in meditations, exhortations, and prayer, and to keep up only an affected fervency. To grow stranger to God and the life to come, and more bold with sin, and more worldly wise; to prove duty to be no duty, and sin no sin, and to plead for every fleshly interest. Many a true christian, that loseth not all grace, yet comes to so low a state of faith, that faith doth but live, but acteth not with the conquering and quickening vigour as it ought.

And alas! I must tell you, that one gross sin, or many wilful lesser sins, may so quench the Spirit as that many a year's time doth not recover it; nay, with some it is never recovered in the same degree to their death. Oh if we knew what one hour's sin may lose us this way, we would not commit it for a world!

S. Alas! but what if I have quenched the Spirit, is there no way to recover it? What must I do?

P. You must deal faithfully with yourself, by deep repentance, and free confessions. You must mark what sinful lust or affection hath got possession of your heart, instead of holy, spiritual affections: and you must set upon the mortifying of those lusts resolvedly; especially you must get far enough away from the temptations which have prevailed with you. You must note what declining you have made in duty, for matter or fervour, and you must set yourself to all that duty you have omitted. You must be much in meditating on the greatest quickening truths, and plead them oft and earnestly with your soul. You must use, if possible, the converse of lively spiritual christians; and, in a word, the same means must be used again which God blessed to your quickening at first; especially earnest prayer that God would restore that measure of his Spirit's operations which you have lost: and you must mark by what ways of omission or commission you quenched the Spirit, and by the contrary must it be restored to you. And then in health and sickness you will have in you that heavenly fire which will carry up your heart to God; and that divine nature which will make heaven and holiness connatural, and suitable, and desirable to you.

S. But how shall I know whether I have the Spirit? or whether I have more or less of it?

P. By the love of God and holiness, and by the love of man, and a desire to do good: for these are its proper works.

S. But how shall I know that I love God truly?

How to know the Spirit, and love of God.

P. [x] When God's holy word, and the holy practice of it, and the thoughts of your perfect holiness and heaven, with Christ and his holy angels, in the perfect love, praise, and service of the most holy God, are all most pleasing to your mind; and more desired by you than the riches, honours, and fleshly pleasures of this world; and when you long for the holiness of the world, and the prosperity of the church, and the good of the souls and bodies of all men; and heartiliest pray for the hallowing of God's name, and the coming of his kingdom, and the doing of his will on earth as it is in heaven; and when doing all the good you can in the world is your daily trade and pleasure: this is the sure evidence of the love of God, and of his Spirit.

S. I have heard far different signs of it from some, as if it lay in impulses, raptures, and revelation of more than is in the Scripture: and I have heard others mock at all mention of the Spirit, as if there were no such thing, besides the effects of nature, art, industry, and imagination.

P. Between these two malefactors the church of Christ, in all ages, hath been crucified. But do you bless God who hath given you that in[y] possession and experience which others that have it not can hardly know. And yet it were easy for them, were they considerate, to discern that the foresaid love of God and man is the true excellence of human nature; and that some have it as I described it, though not in perfection: and that no men are brought to it, but by the gospel and God's special blessing on it; which is by the operation of his Spirit.

VI. The sixth direction to prepare for death is, that you make it your chief care to dwell continually in the sense of God's love; and be daily employed in studying the greatness of it, in the nature of God, and the mercies of the gospel, and in all your own particular experiences; and that praise and thanksgiving be your daily work.

Distinctly note the parts of this direction:

1. If you can but keep the sensible apprehension of God's[z] love continually upon your heart, it must needs make heaven desirable to you: and the drawings of God's love will overcome the fears of death.

2. Think much of the infinite perfection of God. Remember that his goodness is equal to his greatness; and what that is, look up to the heavens, and think of all the world, and you may see. Therefore he is called love itself. And shall it be hard for a soul that desireth to please God, to believe that love itself doth love him, and that infinite goodness will be pleased with him in Christ.

3. The Son of God incarnate, in his whole work of redemption, is so wonderful a glass to reveal to man

[x] Rom. v. 5; viii. 39; John xiv. 15, 23; 1 John ii. 5; iii. 14, 16, 17; v. 3; iv. 12, 16; Eph. iii. 17; iv. 2, 15, 16; v. 2; ii. 10.

[y] 1 John v. 10, 11; Rom. viii. 1, 9, 13.

[z] 2 Tim. i. 7; Gal. iv. 6; Rom. v. 5; viii. 17, 39; Psal. xix. 1, 2; ciii. 3, 8, 11, 17; 1 John iv. 7, 8; John xvi. 27.

the love of God, that[a] the studying of Christ doth as aptly tend to acquaint the soul with divine love, and loveliness, as the greatest beneficence of the greatest friend doth tend to convince us of his friendship.

4. The[b] remembering all the great mercies of your lives, to your souls and bodies, in every place, state, and company, will help to convince you that he that hath done all this for you, loveth you. And you may trust that God of love at death, who hath filled up your lives with the benefits of his love.

5. And if you make[c] praise and thanksgiving to be half your prayers every day, and employ your heart and tongue still in them, this exercise of love to God will keep on your soul a sweet apprehension of his love to you, and make both health and sickness easy, if not full of delight.

To live in the sense of God's love, and so in the exercise of love to God, by praise and holy desires and good works, is the very first-fruits and foretaste of heaven on earth, and is a fruit of believing more excellent than belief itself, and comforteth the soul, and draweth it to God by the most powerful way, even by experimental taste of his love and goodness. And he will easiliest believe that there is a heaven for him, who hath the beginning and foretastes of it already.

VII. And a great part of your preparation lieth in this, that you daily live as in heaven while you are on earth, by faith, hope, and love, exercised in heavenly contemplation.

If you live as a stranger to heaven in health, you will be strange to it, it is like, in sickness; and the soul will rather have terror than pleasure in thinking of going to a strange place, a strange God, strange company, and strange employment. Therefore Christ calleth us to "lay up our treasure in heaven," Matt. vi. 20; that is, to make it the work of our lives, so to use all our present time, and means, and mercies, as may best make sure of the heavenly reward: and where our treasure is our hearts will be, Matt. vi. 21. If you believe that you have a far greater happiness reserved for you with God than this world affordeth, nature will teach you to desire your own happiness: and we are commanded, (Col. iii. 1—4,) as being risen with Christ, to seek the things that are above, where Christ sitteth on the right hand of God: to set our minds or affections on things above, and not on things on earth, because we are dead to the world, and our life, that is, our felicity, is hid, or out of sight, with Christ in God, in the sight and fruition of God in heaven; and when Christ, who is our life, (causally and radically,) shall appear in his glory to the sight of man, then shall we also appear with him in glory. Our happiness will be visible to all. And (Phil. iii. 20) it is said "our conversation," or burgesship, or city converse, "is in heaven."

Remember, daily, that there is your Father, your Saviour, your Comforter, your home, your happiness, your glory, your friends, your interest, and your great business. You are already[d] heirs, and must quickly be possessors. [e] "You are come to mount Zion, and to the city of the living God, the heavenly Jerusalem, and to an innumerable company (or ten thousands) of angels, to the general assembly and church of the first-born, which are enrolled in heaven, and to God the Judge of all, and to the spirits of just men made perfect, and to Jesus the Mediator of the new covenant, and to the blood of sprinkling, which speaketh better things than Abel's."

Therefore, let me advise and entreat you, that you do all that you do in the world, with heaven still in your eye. Hear, and read, and pray, as if heaven were open still before you. Resist temptations; trade, and follow your business in the world, as if heaven were still in sight, as a traveller holdeth on his journey in remembrance of the end.

And especially use often to set yourself purposely at seasonable hours, as you are able, to meditate on the heavenly glory: and though we must form no image in our minds of God himself, but think of him as an infinite Spirit, infinitely powerful, wise, and good, yet we may and must think, by the help of imagination, of the glorified human nature of Christ, and the glorious state of heaven itself. And as, intuitively, we here know our own souls in act, our vitality, understanding, and wills; so, by knowing ourselves, we may know, in part, what God, and angels, and holy souls are. And as our bodies shall be glorified, so we may have answerable apprehensions of them: and where we may not think of imagined glories, as of the light of the sun, or shining bodies, as if the glory of spirits were just the same, yet we may think of them as resemblances or similitudes:[f] as the new Jerusalem is described, Rev. xxi.; xxii.: and, from the sense and thoughts of all the delights of man on earth, we may aggravate the unconceivable joys of heaven.

Set, therefore, oft before your eyes the certainty, the nearness, the greatness of that glory. Think how many millions of holy souls are there in joy, while we are here in fears and cares; think of the excellent servants of God, who have passed thither through a world of trials, and were lately compassed with such infirmities as ours, and passed through death as we must do. Remember that we go not an untrodden path; but are followers of all the spirits of the just. Think how much better it is with them than with us; how they are freed from all our sins and sufferings, doubts and fears. Oh think what it is for a perfected, holy soul to see the glorified Redeemer, and all the holy company of saints and angels; yea, to see the glory of God himself, and to have the knowledge of all his glorious works; to feel his love poured out unto us, and to be rapt up in loving and praising him for ever, in the most transcendent joy and pleasure of the soul. Think of your holy acquaintance that are gone before you, and frequently fetch, as it were, a walk in the streets of the city of God; suppose you saw their glory, and heard their concordant praises of their Creator, Redeemer, and Sanctifier. Let these kind of thoughts be so oft and serious that they may be your daily work and pleasure, and the daily conversation of your minds with God above.

And because your heart will be backward, drive it on; and, as I told you about meditation, you must use to preach, as it were, to yourself. Let heaven be your subject; convince your heart with evidence, urge it with heavenly motives, solace it with heavenly comforts; and when it is dull, turn your thoughts, by petition, to God, and beg his helps. Sometimes speak to yourselves, and sometimes reverently to God; and thus keep a holy communion and familiarity above; and this will make heaven desirable to you at a dying hour.

But the fuller directions for the practice of this duty I must refer you to in the fourth part of my "Saint's Rest."

VIII. The next direction to prepare for death is, that you mortify the flesh in time of health, and

[a] Eph. iii. 17—19; Tit. iii. 3—5; 1 John ii. 1, 2.
[b] Psal. ciii. 1—5; lxvi.; cxvi.
[c] Psal. cxlv.; cix. 30; lxxi. 8, 15; lxiii. 3—6; xxxiv. 1—3; cxlviii.; cxlix.; cl.
[d] Rom. viii. 15, 17, 18.
[e] Heb. xii. 22—24.
[f] 1 Cor. iii. 11, 12; 2 Cor. iii. 18.

see that nothing in this world be too dear and pleasing to you; and let not sense and imagination rule you.

If you be in love with any thing here, you will be the lother to leave it; and if the flesh be too dear to you, its sufferings will be the more grievous, and you will be the lother to lay it to rot in the earth. And if you use to live too much by sight and sense, you will grow so familiar with things sensible, and so strange to things unseen, that you will scarce be able to see any further with the mind than you can see with your eyes; and scarce any thing will seem certain to you, or be effectual with you, which you see not.

But if you get your affections loosed from the world, and mortify the [g] flesh with its affections and desires, and become indifferent to the things of sense, and use to overrule your sense by faith, and live most upon unseen things, there will be little to entangle and hinder the willingness of your departing souls.

IX. Next, I advise you to settle well the state of your soul, by examination and self-acquaintance, in a good assurance of your own sincerity; for, as I told you, when you have overcome the doubts of the truth of God's promises and the life to come, it will be the doubts of your own sincerity then which will be your fear, and make you unwilling to die.

How you may do this I have told you oft, and fully, in a book called "The Method for Peace of Conscience." At the present I shall add these brief instructions.

1. By what evidence or signs to judge, I have here before oft told you,[h] even by faith working by love to God and man, or by your true consent to the covenant of grace, expressed in a holy, obedient life: particularly, 1. If God, to be seen and loved in the joys of the heavenly glory, be the chief end of your heart and life. 2. If Christ be taken for your only Saviour. 3. If you are desirous that, by his Spirit, he should perfectly sanctify you. 4. If you have no sin but what you had rather leave than live in. 5. If you love the word and means which should sanctify you, and love a holy life, and had rather have more holiness than have all the wealth and pleasure of the world. 6. If you are willing to use God's means hereto. 7. If the main desire of your heart and drift of your life be to please God. 8. If you love God's servants for their holiness, and desire the increase of holiness in the world, and labour to do good to the souls and bodies of others, in your place, as you are able: all these will prove the truth of your consent to the covenant of God, and that you have his Spirit.

2. And having these certain marks before you, examine your state impartially by them, as one that is going to the judgment of God: and what you cannot do at one time do at another; and cease not till you are able to conclude that your soul is sincerely devoted to God, and trusteth on Christ for the pardon of your sins. And if you cannot satisfy your conscience without help, advise with some able, faithful minister.

3. And when you see God's graces evident in you, give him thanks for them, and rejoice in his love, and watchfully study to keep, and exercise, and increase the grace which he hath given you; and let not Satan make you still question all again at his pleasure.

4. Two extremes you must here carefully avoid. 1. Be not presumptuous and partial, and blinded by self-love, to think, without proof, that all is well with you, merely because you would have it so. 2. Keep not up a timorous, scrupulous disposition, like a childish servant, who, instead of doing his work as well as he can, doth nothing but cry, because he cannot do it to please his master: as if, when you sincerely desire to please God before your flesh, and do your best, or truly endeavour it, you could not believe that in Christ he will accept you; but are still thinking of God as an enemy, or cruel, that nothing can please but the death of sinners.

When you have thus settled the state of your soul, and can say, I know that I am passed from death to life, you are fortified then against most of your temptations to sinful fears, and unwillingness to come to God.

X. The last part is more easily done; that is, settle your worldly affairs so, as one should do that is ready to depart. Make your will, that none may contend about your estate when you are dead. If you have wronged any, make them restitution. If you are fallen out with any, be quickly reconciled, and forgive them.

To these I would have added, that you learn beforehand what temptations are like to assault you in sickness, and get particular defensatives against them. But this I have spoken to before.

S. You have told me how to prepare for death in health. I pray you tell me next how to prepare further in sickness?

Preparation in sickness.

P. I must not here overwhelm you with multitudes of directions, nor set you upon long and hard tasks of meditations, for, usually, nature, through pains and weakness, is unable for much work. It is the time of health which is the working time: yet because something is then to be done, especially by them that have longer sicknesses, which destroy not their reason, I shall briefly advise such.

1. By the unconverted.

I. If it be one that is unconverted and unprepared before, alas! what shall I say? The time is short, and the body weak, and it is hard to know that their repentance is not the fruit of mere fears, rather than of a changed heart. They are many things that such a man hath to learn and think on, and a great change to be made before he can be saved. And is a little time of sickness fit for all this? But yet there is some hope, and while there is life and hope we must do our best. To such, therefore, I say, Be it never so late, these three things must be done, or you are lost for ever.

1. You must be convinced not only that you are sinners, but that you are ungodly, unconverted sinners, and that God's[i] displeasure and damnation is your due, till your humbled souls do feel the need of a Saviour and Sanctifier.

2. When you feel that you are lost in misery by sin, you must believe that Christ is a sufficient Saviour, who hath died for our sins, and is risen and glorified, and is our Intercessor with the Father, and hath made a covenant, that whoever truly believeth in the Father, Son, and Holy Ghost,[k] and repenteth of his sinful life, and turneth to God by his Son and Spirit, shall be pardoned and saved: and this covenant is offered to you as well as others; and nothing but your obstinate refusal of Christ, and his sanctifying Spirit, word, and grace, can deprive you of pardon and salvation. Therefore you must presently and absolutely consent, and give up yourself, soul and body, to God

[g] Rom. viii. 13; xiii. 13, 14; Gal. v. 24; 2 Cor. iv. 16, 18; v. 7; Col. iii. 5, 6.

[h] Matt. xxviii. 19; v. 3—9; vi. 20, 33; Mark xvi. 16; John iii. 16, 18—22; Gal. v. 5, 13, 22—24; Rom. xiii. 10; viii. i. 9, 13; 2 Cor. v. 8; 1 John iii. 14.

[i] John iii. 18, 36; Mark xvi.

[k] John iii. 15, 16; Acts xx. 18.

the Father, to your Saviour and Sanctifier, to justify, adopt, sanctify, and save you, resolving, if you recover, to live to God in a holy life, and not to the world, the flesh, and the devil, even as if you were newly to be baptized and vowed unto God.

3. You must think next of the infinite goodness of God, the love which he hath showed us in Christ for soul and body, the mercifulness of his nature, the riches and certainty of his promises, and the unspeakable glory which you shall have in heaven with God and your Redeemer, and his holy angels and saints, if you refuse it not. O think what a blessed life it is to be for ever full of joy in the sight, and love, and praises of God, in comparison of this life of sin and misery. Think of this goodness and kingdom of God till your heart, your love itself, be changed, and till you had rather have God in heaven than to have all the pleasures of this world; for till then you are not sanctified, nor in a state of salvation. All that is done by fear alone (till the heart and love be turned from sin to God and holiness) will not save you.

And seeing these three things must needs be had, or you are utterly undone, pray hard for such a renewed heart yourselves, and get others to pray for you; and know that if your late repentance have truly converted your hearts from the love of the world and sin, to the love of God, and heaven, and holiness, and you be such as would hold out if you should recover, you shall be saved, how late soever it be. But if it be only the resolution of a frightened conscience, which would not bring forth a holy life if you did recover, it will not save you.

2. By the converted.

II. But if it be the converted that I must direct for their further preparations, their duty is as followeth.

1. Mistake not sickness and death, as if there were more harm in it than there is indeed. Believe not flesh and sense in this, which cannot see into the [l] love and wisdom of God, which ordereth it; nor unto that quiet fruit of righteousness, which is the end. Sickness is (though in its pains a fruit of sin, yet) now an ordinance of God, on which you may as confidently expect his blessing, as on his word and sacraments. Labour, therefore, to get the benefit of it, to find out your sin, and repent of it, and abhor it, and see more effectually the vanity and vexation of the world; and remember what a mercy it is that man, who is so loth to die, should end his days in such pain and weakness, as make him weary of himself, and make him the more willing to be dissolved. For though this alone, without faith and love, will draw no man's heart to heaven, or save him, yet such a help against the sinful love of life, and fear of death, is no small mercy. Get but the benefit of sickness, and experience will reconcile you to the providence of God, and prevent repining.

2. [m] Beg of God, for the sake of your Redeemer, such assistance and operations of his Spirit, as your low and weak condition needeth, and as are suitable to a dying man. He hath great help and grace for great necessities.

3. Renew your repentance and confessions of sin, and warn all about you to learn by your experience, and to set their hopes and hearts on heaven, and to make it the work of all their lives to prepare for such a change. O tell them what deceit and mischief you have found in sin; what vanity and vexation you have found in the world; what goodness you have found in God and holiness; what comfort you have found in Christ and his promises, and the hopes of endless glory; and what a miserable case you had now been in if you had had no better a portion than this world, and nothing to comfort you but the pleasures of sin, which now are all your shame and discomfort. Advise them to live as they would die, and tell them how little all the world doth signify to a dying man; call on them not to be deceived by such baits, as all dying men, since Adam, have confessed to be but vanity; call on them to turn without delay, and not to pamper a body for the worms, but to set themselves presently, with all their hearts, to receive their Saviour, and to obey his Spirit and word, and to live to God, and to make much of their short, uncertain time, and to make sure of everlasting joys, whatever become of the flesh and world.

4. Renew your believing thoughts of God's love, and of all the mercies of your life, which he hath given you. Instead of sorrowing that they are at an end, rejoice with thankfulness for what you have had: O think what a mercy it is to be brought forth in a land and age of light; to have had all the teaching, and means, and warnings, and deliverances, which you have had; and to have had that effectual assistance of God's Spirit which opened your eyes, and turned you from darkness to light, and from the power of Satan unto God; that all your sins are pardoned through Christ, and that you are reconciled to God, and adopted through him, and led by the Spirit to the heavenly inheritance. O triumph in that love that hath thus delivered you, and brought you so near your journey's [n] end, and saved you from so many temptations of Satan, and from the flesh, and this deceitful world. Think of God's goodness and love, as exceeding the goodness and love of the best of creatures, infinitely more than the sun exceedeth a candle in light and heat. And shall a poor servant of his, who hath endeavoured, in sincerity, though in sinful weakness, to do his will, and hath a High Priest interceding for him in heaven, be afraid to go to such a God? What can encourage and draw up a soul, if infinite goodness cannot do it? If God were but as loving as my dearest friend; if he were but as good and amiable as the sun is light and glorious, as the heavens are spacious, as the earth is firm, as the sea is deep; should I not joyfully give up my soul into his hands; and confidently yield to his disposal; and fearlessly come to him at his call? Oh that we knew the goodness of God! What a full content and satisfaction would it be to us; and to turn our fears into fervent love, and earnest longings for his glory!

5. Now steep your souls in the believing thoughts of the heavenly glory, to which you are going. O now remember that the time is but short, till you shall sin no more, and fear no more, and suffer no more; till you shall know God and his works, not only as much as you can now desire, but as much as then your heart can wish, and your enlarged capacity receive; till you shall love him more than now you can desire to love him; and your joy shall be greater than now you can conceive and wish: when God shall be more to your soul for ever than the sun is to your eyes, or your soul is to your body! Oh what an hour will it be, when you shall be newly entered into the city of God, the heavenly society, and sing your first song of joyful praise, in the blessed choir, to God and to the Lamb! Oh what an enemy, what an unreasonable thing, is unbelief, that can make us stand trembling without the doors, and afraid to enter, while millions of our brethren are rapt up in triumphant joys within; while our Lord prepareth us our place, and, with all his holy angels, is desirous

[l] Heb. xii. 8—12; 1 Cor. xi. 31, 32.
[m] Psalm xli. 3; 2 Kings xx. 1, &c.; Isa. xxxviii. 1, &c.
[n] 2 Tim. iv. 7, 8; 2 Cor. v. 1—8.

of our presence, and the heavenly host will welcome us with joy!

6. Now confidently deliver up your souls into the hand of your Father and your Redeemer, and give over distrustful caring for yourselves.

1. Will you not trust the God and Father of your spirits, who is love itself? Will you not trust your Saviour, that hath saved you so far already, and hath saved so many millions before you? Trust him with his own: believe it, he loveth you better than you love yourself. He is as loth that you should be damned as you are to be damned, and more willing to save you than you are to be saved! O, woe to you, if, through all your life, he had not showed himself more willing than you! Trust him against all the accusations of the law; trust him as the Satisfier of God's legal justice; trust him as the Meriter of life eternal; as the Justifier of those that could not be justified by the law of innocency, and their righteous works; as the Mediator of the new covenant, sealed by his blood, by which free forgiveness and life is given to all true believers. Trust him as the King and Judge of all; and as the Advocate of the faithful, and our great High Priest who intercedeth for us, and hath himself possession of the glory to which he hath promised to bring us!

And, 2. Trust him implicitly and absolutely, and give over Eve's desire of knowing good and evil for yourself. We little consider how much that desire did let in at once of corruption and calamity upon the nature of mankind! When Adam and Eve should have only desired to know God's perfection of power, wisdom, and goodness, as the first and last, the fountain and end of all our good, and to know their own relation to him and their duty, expecting his love, which is better than life, upon their love and obedience; they were tempted to selfishness and independency, and to leave their trust and rest in God, and to desire to be their own carvers, and as gods to themselves: like a child that, instead of trusting his father for his food and raiment, must become judge what is best for himself; or like a patient who, instead of trusting his physician, and obediently taking what he giveth him, must needs know the ingredients of his medicines, and the reasons of them all. Thus foolish man fell from God to himself, and, not putting all his trust in God, would fain be his own guide, and judge, and carver, and take that care of his own affairs which belonged not to himself, but unto God. And as this misguideth all our lives, so this tormenteth us with cares and fears in life at death.

But Christ came to recover us from ourselves to God. Care, then, how to know your Creator and Redeemer; his power, wisdom, and love; care how to trust him with soul and body, and to do your duty; and then [o] care for no more; but leave soul and body more quietly and comfortably to his love and will, than if they were absolutely at your own will, to be, and do, and have, what you would wish. For God is fitter to choose for you, and to dispose of you, than you.

Take not, then, one careful thought of the corruption of your flesh, or of any of the amazing unsearchable difficulties of the nature of spirits, and the things unseen, which overwhelm and bewilder those that must know good and evil themselves. But rest your soul in the will of God through your Redeemer; in that will which is infinitely good, and which is the beginning, guide, and end of all things, and the only felicitating rest of souls.

7. Let all these holy affections be exercised in your expressions, if your disease allow you an expressing strength. Magnify God's goodness, and speak good of his name, and word, and ways; not by a dissembled affectation, but from your heart: make others to see that there is a reality in the comforts of faith and hope; and that the death of the righteous is so desirable, as maketh their lives desirable also. Your tongues are given you to praise the Lord; they have but a little while more to speak; let their last work be done to his glory, as strength will bear. Tell men what you have found him, and speak of the glory of his kingdom which you expect, that the hopes and desires of others may be excited.

And turn your last words to God himself in prayer and praises, beginning the work which you must do in heaven. Imitate your dying Lord, "Father, into thy hands I commend my spirit," Luke xxiii. 46; and his first martyr, "Lord Jesus, receive my spirit," Acts vii. 59.

The Prayer of a dying Believer.

Thy mercy brought me into the world; thy mercy chose my parentage, education, and habitation; it brought me up; it kept me from a thousand dangers; it attempered my body, and furnished my mind; it gave me teachers, books, and helps; yea, it gave me a Redeemer, and a promise of life, and the word of salvation! It gave me all the operations of thy Spirit, which touched and turned my sinful heart. All my repenting and resolving thoughts; all the forgiveness of my manifold sins; all the sweet meditations of thy love, and the experience of thy good and pleasant service; the comfortable hours which I have had in secret thoughts, in public worship, on thy holy days, at thy holy table, among thy people; all these have been the dealings of thy love. All my deliverances from temptation and sin; from enemies, death, and danger; all my preservations from the deceits of the world, and from its troubles; from errors against thy sacred truth, and from backsliding; all my recoveries from my too frequent falls, and pardon of my daily sins; the quietness thou hast given my troubled conscience; and the tranquillity of my life, notwithstanding my sins: all the use which it hath freely pleased thee to make of me, an unworthy wretch, for the good of any, for soul or body: all these are the pledges of thy wondrous love; and shall I be afraid to come to such a God? Hath mercy filled up all my life, and brought me now so near the end, and shall I not trust it after so much trial? It is heaven that thou madest me for; and heaven that Christ did purchase for me; it is heaven that thou didst promise if I would be thine; and it is heaven which I consented to take for my portion,[p] and for which I did covenant to forsake the world: and oh that I had more entirely done it! for I now find how little reason I have to repent of my covenant. It is heaven which thy Spirit of grace, and merciful providences, have all this while been preparing me for; and shall I now be fearful and unwilling to possess it?

O thou that knowest how deadly an enemy unbelief is to thy honour and my soul, I beseech thee, show that thou takest not me but it for thy foe. O send that heavenly light to my mind, which may banish and confound it; let it not blaspheme thy truth, and imprison, blind, and torment my soul. O thou that givest the world, the Saviour, the heaven, which I must believe, deny me not that faith by which I must believe them: earth and flesh are dungeons of darkness and despair: there is with us no sun to show us thy face. It must be thy glory whose reflections must reveal thy glory to us; and a light from heaven which must show us heaven! O send

[o] Matt. vi. 25–27, 31, 34; Luke xii. 22; 1 Pet. v. 7; Phil. iv. 6.

[p] Luke xviii. 22, 23; Matt. vi. 20, 21, 33; Col. iii. 2, 4.

one beam, one beam, Lord, of that heavenly light into this darkened, sinful soul; that, with Stephen, I may see in my passage the glory of my blessed Lord, to whom I go! and, with Simeon, may gladly say, "Lord, now let thy servant depart in peace, for mine eyes have seen thy salvation!" One beam of thine will drive away the powers of darkness, and banish all these doubts and fears, and let in somewhat of heaven into my soul, before it is let into heaven. O blessed Spirit, the illuminator of dark, imprisoned souls, remember not all my resistances of thy grace, and forsake me not in this last necessity of my life, and leave me not to the power of darkness and unbelief! Though glory be not openly seen till it is enjoyed, let me now, when I am so near it, have such a sight of it by faith, as is suitable to this low and darker state. O thou that art the Spirit of life, so quicken and actuate this sluggish soul, that the last part of my race may be run with vigour, and the last act of my life may be done in evidence of the heavenly influence, and may be liker to the heavenly employment than all the rest hath been! O thou that art the Sanctifier and Comforter of souls, now kindle the fire of heavenly love in me, and give me some taste of the celestial joys, which may feelingly tell me that there is a heaven indeed; and may be the witness within me, and the pledge and earnest that I shall live with Christ! My flesh and my own heart now fail: the world and all therein is nothing to me; I am taking my everlasting farewell of them all: but one beam of his face, and one taste of his love, who is my portion for ever, will be strength and joy to my departing soul, and[q] better than this life and all its pleasures. Come, Lord, with these seasonable comforts into my soul, that my soul may comfortably come to thee! My life had been but death, and darkness, and disaffection to God, if thou hadst not been in me, a Spirit of life, and light, and love; the tempter had else been still too strong and subtle for me; and how then shall I deal with him myself, when the languishing of my body disableth my soul? Thou despisest not art and reason: I thank thee for the use I had of them in their season. But one beam of thy light, and spark of thy love, one motion of thy heavenly life, will better confute the enemy of faith than my disputes can do: the divine nature, incited by divine inspiration, must do much more than human art. Teach me, effectually, but to love and praise thee, and it shall powerfully prove to me that there is a heaven, where I shall joyfully love and praise thee for ever.

Alas, dear Lord, I am ashamed that to love and praise thee should be to my soul a work of difficulty! that it is not more natural and easy to me, than to love and praise any created thing or person whatsoever! What shall I love, if not goodness and love itself, which made me purposely to love him; who redeemed me, that by love he might win my love; and sanctified me, to dispose my soul to love him? What shall I praise, if not infinite perfection; the glory of whose power, wisdom, and goodness, doth shine forth in the whole creation? Heaven and earth praise thee; and am I no part of heaven or earth? The whole creation doth proclaim thy glory; and am I none of thy creation? Thy very enemies, when redeemed, reconciled, and forgiven, do praise the love and grace of their Redeemer; and am I not one of these? The great Teacher of the church is the schoolmaster of love and praise; and have I not learned them yet, who have so long had so excellent a Teacher? Thy saints all love thee; for it is the essence of a saint: they praise thee; for it is the work of saints: and am I none of these? I am less than the least of all thy mercies. But it is not the least of thy mercies which I have received: and if a life full of mercies have not brought forth a life full of love and praise; O yet let it end in a loving and a praising death!

Glory be to God in the highest; on earth, peace; and good will towards men! Holy, holy, Lord God Almighty, who was, and is, and is to come; of thee, and through thee, and to thee are all things; thine is the kingdom, the power, and the glory. For thou hast created all things, and for thy pleasure they are and were created. Blessing, and honour, and glory, and power, be to him that sitteth on the throne, and to the Lamb for ever and ever; even to our Redeemer who washeth us in his blood, and maketh us kings and priests to God. Great and marvellous are thy works, Lord God Almighty! Just and true are thy ways, thou King of saints! Who shall not fear thee, O Lord, and glorify thy name; for thou art holy. Amen; Hallelujah! For the Lord God omnipotent reigneth. Praise our God, all ye his servants; and ye that fear him both small and great. Praise ye the great Redeemer of the world, who is our wisdom, righteousness, sanctification, and redemption: the beloved Son, in whom we are reconciled and adopted, and in whom the Father is well pleased; who will smite the nations with the sword of his mouth, and rule them with a rod of iron, and treadeth the wine-press of the wrath of God; who hath the keys of death and hell, and is King of kings, and Lord of lords. My soul doth magnify the Lord, and my spirit rejoiceth in God my Saviour; who hath redeemed me from my low and lost estate; for his mercy endureth for ever. Bless the Lord, O my soul; and all that is within me, bless his holy name. Bless the Lord, O my soul, and forget not all his benefits: who forgiveth all thine iniquities, and hath often healed thy diseases. Who redeemed thy life from destruction, and crowneth thee with love and tender mercies. Whom have I in heaven but thee? And what is there on earth desirable besides thee? The Lord taketh pleasure in his people; he will beautify the meek with salvation. In thy light we shall see light; thou shalt make us drink of the rivers of thy pleasure. In thy presence is fulness of joy, and at thy right hand are pleasures for evermore. Goodness and mercy have followed me all my days, and thou hast showed me the path of life. Let my heart, therefore, be glad, and my glory rejoice; and let me leave this flesh to rest in hope. Let the heavens rejoice; and oh that the earth were taught to imitate them in thy praise! Thy angels and the triumphant church do glorify thee: O train up this militant church on earth, in love and concord, to this joyful work! And let all flesh bless thy holy name for ever and ever! Let every thing that hath breath praise the Lord! And so let me breathe out my departing soul! And thou wilt not cast away the soul that cometh unto thee in love and praise. Father, into thy hands I commend my spirit; who art the Father of spirits, and my Father in Christ! Lord Jesus, receive my spirit; and present it justified and spotless to the Father! And O, our Forerunner, take me to thyself! who, being risen, sentest this message even to sinners: "Say to my brethren, I ascend to my Father, and your Father; to my God, and your God." Amen.

Short instructions for the Sick, to be read by the Master of the Family to them, or by themselves; the unprepared.

THOSE happy persons who have made it the chief care and business of their lives to be always ready

[q] Psalm lxxiii. 25, 26; lxiii. 3.

for a dying hour, have least need of my present counsel. It is, therefore, those unhappy souls who are yet unprepared whom I shall now instruct. And oh that the Lord would bless these words, and persuade them yet, ere time be gone.

If sin had not bewitched men, and made them monsters of senselessness and unbelief, it could not be that an endless life, so sure, so near, could be so sottishly made light of all their lives, as is by most, till they perceive that death is ready to surprise them. But, poor sinner, if this have been thy case, supposing that thou art unwilling to be damned, I earnestly entreat thee, in the name of Christ, for the sake of thy immortal soul, that thou wilt presently lay to heart these instructions, before time and hope are gone for ever.

I. At last, bethink thee what thou art; and for what end and work thou camest into the world. Thou art a man of reason, and not a brute; and hast a soul which was made to know, and [r] love, and serve the Maker; and that not in the second place, with the leavings of the flesh, but in the first place, and with all thy heart and might. If this had been, indeed, thy life, God would have been thy Portion, thy Father, and thy Defence; and thou mightest have lived in peace and comfort with God, and then have lived with God for ever. And, should not a creature live to the ends and uses which it was made for? Must God give thee all thy powers for himself, and wilt thou turn them from him, to the service of the flesh, and that when thou hadst vowed the contrary in thy baptism? How wilt thou answer for such treacherous ungodliness?

II. It is time for thee now to have serious thoughts of the life thou art going to. If thou couldst sleepily forget it all the way, it is time to awaken when thou comest almost there. When thy friends are burying that flesh in the earth which thou didst more regard than God and thy salvation, thy soul must appear in an [s] endless world, and see those things which God foretold thee of, and thou wouldst not believe, or set thy heart upon. As soon as death hath opened the curtains, oh what a sight must thou presently behold! A world of angels, and of holy souls, adoring, and praising, and admiring that God whom thou didst refuse to mind, and love, and serve; a world of devils and damned souls, in torment and despair, bewailing their contempt of Christ and grace, their neglect of God and their salvation, their serving the flesh and loving the world, and wilfully losing the time of mercy, and all the means which God vouchsafed them. Believe it, sinner, there is an endless joy and glory for the saints, and an [t] endless misery for all the ungodly; and one of these must quickly be thy case. Thy state is changeable while thou art in the flesh; if thy soul be miserable, there is yet a remedy; it is possible Christ may renew and pardon it: but as soon as thou goest hence, thou enterest into a state of joy or torment, which must never change; no, not when millions of years are past. And dost thou not think now, in thy conscience, that such an endless misery should have been prevented with greater care and diligence than all the sufferings of this life; and that the attaining of such an endless glory had been worth thy greatest care and labour; and that it is far better to see the glory of God, and be filled with his love, and joyfully praise him with his saints and angels for evermore, and, by a holy life, to have prepared for this, than to please the flesh and follow the world a little while, and be undone for ever? Hast thou got more by the world and sin than heaven is worth? Thou art almost at the end of worldly pleasures, and hast all that ever they will do for thee; but if God had had thy heart and service, he would not thus have cast thee off; and his rewards and joys would have had no end. Oh how much happier are the blessed souls in heaven than we!

III. And seeing you are so near to the judgment of God, where your soul must receive its final sentence, it is high time now to [u] judge yourself, and know what [x] estate your soul is in; whether in a state of justification or of damnation; for this may be certainly known if you are willing. And, first, you must know who they be whom Christ will justify, and whom he will condemn; and this the word of God will tell you, for he will judge them by that word. In a word, "all those whom Christ will justify, and save, are made new [y] creatures, by the renewing work of the Holy Ghost; their [z] eyes are opened to see the vanity of this world, and the certainty and excellency of the glory of heaven, and to see the odiousness of sin, and the goodness of a holy life, and to believe that Christ is the [a] only Saviour to cleanse them from their sins, and bring them to that glory. And therefore they forsake the sinful [b] pleasures of the flesh, and set their [c] hearts on the everlasting blessedness, and seek it before all things; and lamenting and hating their former sins, they give themselves sincerely to their God and Father, their Saviour and their sanctifier, to be [d] taught and ruled, justified, [e] sanctified, and saved by him; resolving, whatever it [f] cost the flesh, to stand to this choice and covenant to the death." This is the case of all that Christ will justify and save: the rest who never were thus renewed and sanctified will be [g] condemned, as sure as the gospel is true. Therefore, let it be speedily your work to try whether this be your case or not. Have you been thus enlightened, convinced, and renewed to believe in Christ, and the life to come, and to give up yourself in a faithful covenant to God your Father, your Saviour, and Sanctifier, to hate your sin, and to live and love a holy life, in mortifying the flesh, and seeking heaven before the world? If this be not your case, I should but flatter and deceive you to tell you of any hope of being saved, till you are thus renewed and justified. Never imagine a lie to quiet you till help is past. No one that is unregenerate, or unholy, shall ever dwell with God. Yet you may be saved, if yet you will be truly converted and sanctified; but without this, assuredly there is no hope.

IV. Therefore I counsel you, in the name of Christ, to look back upon your [h] sinful life with sorrow; not only because of the danger to yourself, but also because you have offended God. What think you now of a sinful, and of a holy life? Had it not been better that you had valued Christ and grace, and lived in the love of God, and in the joyful hopes of the life to come, and denied the sinful desires of the flesh, and been ruled by the law of God, and spent your time in preparing for eternity? Do you not heartily wish that this had been your course? Would you take this course if it were to do again, and God recover you? Repent, repent, from the bottom of your heart, of the time you have lost, the mercy

[r] Deut. vi. 5; x. 12; xi. 1, 13.
[s] Deut. xxxii. 2; Matt. vi. 19, 20, 33; xxv.; Rom. ii.; 2 Cor. iv. 18; v. 1, 7—9; Phil. iii. 18, 20.
[t] 2 Thess. i. 9, 10; 1 Pet. iv. 18.
[u] 1 Cor. xi. 31; 2 Cor. xiii. 5.
[x] 2 Pet. i. 10.
[y] John iii. 3, 5; 2 Cor. v. 17.
[z] Eph. i. 18.

[a] John iii. 16, 19.
[b] Gal. v. 24; Rom. viii. 9.
[c] Matt. vi. 21, 23.
[d] Matt. xxviii. 20.
[e] Heb. xii. 14.
[f] Rev. ii. 7, 10.
[g] Prov. xi. 7; Job viii. 13, 14.
[h] Luke xiii. 3, 5; xv.; Matt. xviii. 3.

you have abused, the grace you have resisted; of all your fleshly, worldly desires, words, and deeds; and that you gave not up your soul and life to the love of God, and life eternal.

V. And now resolvedly[i] give up yourself in a hearty covenant to God: though it be late, he will yet accept and pardon you, if you do it in sincerity. Take God for your God, your portion, and felicity, to live in his love and praise for ever; take Christ for your Saviour, to teach, and rule, and justify you, and bring you unto God; and the Holy Spirit for your Sanctifier; and certainly he will take you for his child. But see that you be truly willing of his grace, and resolved never to forsake him more. O happy soul! if at last the Lord will make this [k] change upon thee: and I will tell you certainly how to know whether this late repentance will serve for your salvation or not. If it be but fear only that causeth your repentance, and the heart and will be not renewed, but you would turn again to a fleshly, worldly, and ungodly life, if you be recovered, then it will never save your soul; but if your heart, your will, your love be changed, and this change would hold if God recovered you to health again, then doubt not of pardon and salvation.

VI. And if God have thus changed your heart, and drawn it to himself, be thankful for so great a mercy. Oh! bless him for giving you a Redeemer and a Sanctifier, and the pardoning covenant of grace. And now be not afraid or loth [l] to leave a sinful world, and come to God. Pray harder for grace and pardon than for life. Commit and trust your souls to Christ; he had never done so much for souls, if he had not loved them and been willing to receive them. How wonderfully came he down to man, to bring up man to the sight of God! He is gone before, to [m] prepare us a mansion in the city of God; and hath promised to take us to himself, that we may dwell with him and see his glory. The world which you are going to is [n] unlike to this: there is no pride, or lust, or cruelty, oppression, deceit, or any sin; no wicked men to scorn or persecute us; no vanity to allure us; no devil to tempt us; no corruption of our own to burden or endanger us; no fears, or cares, or griefs, or discontents; no poverty, sickness, pain, or death; no doubtings of the love of God, or our salvation; but the sight of God, and the feelings of his love, and the fervent flames of our love to him, will be the everlasting pleasure of the saints. These will break forth into triumphant and harmonious thanks and praise in the presence of our glorified Redeemer, and in concord with all the heavenly host, the blessed angels, and the spirits of the just. This is the end of faith and holiness, patience and perseverance; when hell is the end of unbelief, ungodliness, sensuality, and hypocrisy. How justly are they condemned who sell their part of endless joys for a shadow, and dream of transitory pleasures; and can delight more in the filth of sin, and in fading vanity, than in the love of God, and the forethoughts of glory! What love can be too great; what desires too fervent; what prayer and labour can be too much; what sufferings too dear, for such a blessedness?

VII. Lastly, because there are many cases of the sick which require the presence of a[o] judicious divine; if it be possible, get the help of such; if not, remember that God is just in denying of men that mercy in their distress which in time of their health and prosperity they rejected with scorn and contempt; and [p] cleave to him whom you may enjoy for ever.

[i] 2 Cor. viii. 5; Acts xi. 23.
[k] Psal. lxxviii. 34—37; Heb. viii. 10; x. 16; Jer. xxxii. 40.

The Shortest Catechism.

Quest. 1. WHAT is the christian religion?

Answ. The christian religion is the baptismal covenant made and kept: wherein God the Father, Son, and Holy Ghost, doth give himself to be our reconciled God and Father, our Saviour, and our Sanctifier; and we believing, give up ourselves accordingly to him, renouncing the flesh, the world, and the devil: which covenant is to be oft renewed, specially in the sacrament of the Lord's supper.

Quest. 2. Where is our covenant part and duty fullier opened?

Answ. 1. In the creed, as the sum of our belief. 2. In the Lord's prayer, as the sum of our desires. 3. And in the ten commandments, as given us by Christ, with the gospel explications, as the sum of our practice. Which are as followeth:

The Creed.

I BELIEVE in God, the Father Almighty, Creator of heaven and earth. And in Jesus Christ, his only Son, our Lord; who was conceived by the Holy Ghost, born of the Virgin Mary, suffered under Pontius Pilate, was crucified, dead, and buried. He descended into hell: the third day he rose again from the dead; he ascended into heaven, and sitteth on the right hand of God, the Father Almighty: from thence he shall come to judge the quick and the dead. I believe in the Holy Ghost, the holy catholic church, the communion of saints, the forgiveness of sins, the resurrection of the body, and the life everlasting. Amen.

The Lord's Prayer.

OUR Father, who art in heaven; hallowed be thy name: thy kingdom come: thy will be done on earth, as it is in heaven. Give us this day our daily bread. And forgive us our trespasses, as we forgive them that trespass against us. And lead us not into temptation; but deliver us from evil. For thine is the kingdom, the power, and the glory, for ever. Amen.

The Ten Commandments.

I. I AM the Lord thy God, who have brought thee out of the land of Egypt, out of the house of bondage. Thou shalt have no other gods before me.

II. Thou shalt not make unto thee any graven image, or any likeness of any thing that is in heaven above, or that is in the earth beneath, or that is in the water under the earth. Thou shalt not bow down thyself to them, nor serve them. For I the Lord thy God am a jealous God, visiting the iniquity of the fathers upon the children, unto the third and fourth generation of them that hate me, and showing mercy unto thousands of them that love me, and keep my commandments.

III. Thou shalt not take the name of the Lord thy God in vain; for the Lord will not hold him guiltless who taketh his name in vain.

IV. Remember the sabbath day to keep it holy. Six days shalt thou labour and do all thy work; but the seventh day is the sabbath of the Lord thy God: in it thou shalt not do any work; thou, nor thy son, nor thy daughter, thy man servant, nor thy maid servant, nor thy cattle, nor thy stranger that is within thy gates: for in six days the Lord made heaven and earth, the sea, and all that in them is, and rested

[l] Phil. i. 21, 23; 2 Cor. v. 8; Rev. xiv. 13; Acts vii. 9.
[m] John xvii. 24; xii. 26. [n] Rev. xxi.; xxii.
[o] Mal. ii. 7; Jam. v. 14. [p] Psal. lxxiii. 26.

the seventh day: wherefore the Lord blessed the sabbath day, and hallowed it.

V. Honour thy father and thy mother, that thy days may be long upon the land which the Lord thy God giveth thee.

VI. Thou shalt not kill.

VII. Thou shalt not commit adultery.

VIII. Thou shalt not steal.

IX. Thou shalt not bear false witness against thy neighbour.

X. Thou shalt not covet thy neighbour's house; thou shalt not covet thy neighbour's wife, nor his man servant, nor his maid servant, nor his ox, nor his ass, nor any thing that is thy neighbour's.

Quest. 3. Where is the christian religion most fully opened, and entirely contained?

Answ. In the holy Scriptures, especially of the New Testament; where, by Christ, and his apostles, and evangelists, inspired by his Spirit, the history of Christ and his apostles is sufficiently delivered, the promises and doctrine of faith are perfected, the covenant of grace most clearly opened, and church offices, worship, and discipline established. In the understanding whereof the strongest christians may increase whilst they live on earth.

The explained Profession of the Christian Religion.

The Assent.

I. I BELIEVE that there is one God, an infinite Spirit of life, understanding, and will, perfectly powerful, wise, and good; the Father, the Word, and the Spirit; the Creator, Governor, and End of all things; our absolute Owner, our most just Ruler, and our most gracious Benefactor, and most amiable Good.

II. I believe that man, being made in the image of God, an embodied spirit of life, understanding, and will, with holy vivacity, wisdom, and love, to know, and love, and serve his Creator, here and for ever, did, by wilful sinning, fall from his God, his holiness, and innocency, under the wrath of God, the condemnation of his law, and the slavery of the flesh, the world, and the devil; and that God so loved the world that he gave his only Son to be their Redeemer, who, being God, and one with the Father, took our nature, and became man; being conceived by the Holy Ghost, born of the Virgin Mary, called Jesus Christ, who was perfectly holy, sinless, fulfilling all righteousness, overcame the devil and the world, and gave himself a sacrifice for our sins, by suffering a cursed death on the cross, to ransom us, and reconcile us unto God, and was buried and went among the dead: the third day he rose again, having conquered death. And he fully established the covenant of grace, that all that truly repent and believe, shall have the love of the Father, the grace of the Son, and the communion of the Holy Spirit; and if they love God, and obey him sincerely to the death, they shall be glorified with him in heaven for ever; and the unbelievers, impenitent, and ungodly, shall go to everlasting punishment. And having commanded his apostles to preach the gospel to all the world, and promised his Spirit, he ascended into heaven; where he is the glorified Head over all things to the church, and our prevailing Intercessor with the Father; who will there receive the departed souls of the justified, and at the end of this world, will come again, and raise all the dead, and will judge all according to their works, and justly execute his judgment.

III. I believe that God, the Holy Spirit, was given by the Father and the Son to the prophets, apostles, and evangelists, to be their infallible guide in preaching and recording the doctrine of salvation, and the witness of its certain truth, by his manifold divine operations; and to quicken, illuminate, and sanctify all true believers, that they may overcome the flesh, the world, and the devil. And all that are thus sanctified are one holy catholic church of Christ, and must live in holy communion, and have the pardon of their sins, and shall have everlasting life.

The consent or covenant.

Believing in God the Father, Son, and Holy Spirit, I do presently, absolutely, and resolvedly, give up myself to him, my Creator and reconciled God and Father, my Saviour and Sanctifier; and, repenting of my sins, I renounce the devil, the world, and the sinful desires of the flesh; and, denying myself, and taking up my cross, I consent to follow Christ, the Captain of my salvation, in hope of his promised grace and glory.

A Short Catechism, for those that have learned the First.

Quest. 1. WHAT do you believe concerning God?

1. Assent.

Answ. There is one only God, an infinite Spirit of life, understanding, and will, most perfectly powerful, wise, and good; the Father, the Word, and the Spirit: the Creator, Governor, and End of all things; our absolute Owner, our most just Ruler, and our most gracious and most amiable Father.

The word "God" signifieth both the nature and the relations.

I. God's nature or essence is not known to us in itself immediately, but in the glass of the creatures, as the cause in the effects, and especially by God's image on our own souls. Therefore we have no name, or words of God, but such as are borrowed from creatures, as the first things signified in our use of them; though God only be signified by them in this our application. Therefore we are fain to describe God in terms, 1. Of generical notion. 2. Of formal or specifical notion. 3. Of accidental notion. Though God is not properly matter or form, genus or species, nor accident.

1. The generical notion is that he is a Spirit, which includeth the more general notions of a substance and being, as distinct from accidents and nothing. A spirit chiefly signifieth, not only negatively that which is no body, but also positively a pure substance, transcending our sensitive conception or apprehension, which some call metaphysical matter: but before we think what form or virtue a spirit is possessed of, we think of it as something substantial, though not corporeal. But of the substance of a spirit, as different from a body, before we come to the formal virtues, we can have no satisfying conception but its purity, and transcending the most perfect sense. Whatsoever some say of penetrability and indivisibility, which are also considerable, if any say that the true nature of fire is a spirit, and so that a spirit is sensible, as far as motion, light, and heat are, I only say, if that were true, yet motion, light, and heat are not sensed by us in pure fire, but only as from fire incorporate in air at least. But the word "spirit" also includeth the formal special notion of it, by which we most clearly discern it from a body, called matter; which is, that it is formally a life, or an active nature; in which is included the three notions of power, force (*vis*), and inclination, and, all together, may be called a virtue; so that to be a pure substance, transcending sense, not accidentally having, but naturally being, an active, vital virtue, is to be a spirit.

2. But though this formal notion be included in the word "spirit," yet it is of distinct conception from essence and substance: and this one formal virtue in God is wonderfully, yet certainly, three in one, that

is, 1. Vital, active virtue. 2. Intellective virtue. 3. Volitive or willing virtue. This spiritual virtue is not an accident in God, but his essence; not his essence as essence, but his essence in its formal or specific notion as distinct from other essences. It is one substantially and formally. It is three, as active on a three-fold object, or by connotation of the object, at the least. All this we certainly gather from our souls, which are God's image, of which anon; and yet the word "spirit," understanding, will, and life of man, signify that which is not at all of the same kind or sort with that which the same words signify of God: but yet there is in us an image of what is in God.

And when I speak of active virtue, it must be remembered that it is another property of spirit, that it is not passion from a body, or any inferior nature; for all action proceedeth orderly from the first active cause, and so down. God worketh upon all things. An intellectual spirit can operate on a sensitive, and that on a vegetative, and that, as the rest, on passive matter or bodies, but not contrarily.

3. Though we are fain to use names of God, which signify but modes or qualities in men, and so mention powerful, wise, and good; yet these, in God, are his very essence, under the notion of modal perfection.

4. As we think of creatures, in respect of quantity and degrees, as well as kind, so we are fain to mention God's attributes: and I comprehend a multitude in one, which is infiniteness, or perfection, which have the same signification, saving that one soundeth better as applied to essence, and the other as to quality. When I say that God is infinite, it respecteth, 1. Duration, or time, and so it is his eternity. 2. Or space and extension, by analogy to which, it is his immensity; and perfection of power, wisdom, and goodness, excludeth all imperfection, and includeth that which to man is incomprehensible, though certainly known. This one God is three persons, the Father, the Word, (or Son,) and the Spirit, (or Holy Ghost,) whose properties are to beget, to be begotten, and to proceed. The mystery is fulliest opened in Athanasius's Creed; and we have no reason to think it contradictory or incredible, when the aforesaid trinity of principles, life, understanding, and will, in one spiritual virtue and essence, is so clear and sure in our own souls, and so in God.

II. The relations of God respect his creatures: 1. In their being, and so he is, 1. Fundamentally their Creator. 2. And thence their Owner. 2. Or in their well-being, and so he is their Benefactor, or the first cause of all their good. 3. Or their action, and so he is, 1. The Mover, 2. The Ruler, and, 3. The end of every thing in its kind; but of man, in a special manner, agreeable to his intellectual nature. But the moral relations which we have here reason practically to note, are all comprehended in the word Father, which signifieth that he is fundamentally our Creator; and thence, 1. Our Owner; 2. Our Ruler; 3. Our most amiable Good. For a father giveth being to his child; and thence, by nature, the child is his own, and being uncapable of self-government, it is the father who hath, 1. That authority, 2. Wisdom, 3. And love which make him meet to be the ruler; and nature teacheth the child to love his father, as the cause of his very being. But in this last consideration God is more than a father, and is to be loved more than ourselves, and more for his own goodness, which is his amiableness, than for ourselves. I had put the word Friend for the third relation, as being most short and full to the sense intended, but that it will be thought to sound too familiarly; though Abraham and Christ's disciples have that title.

The attribute of God, as our Owner, is absolute; and as our Ruler, he is just, in which his truth, which is the justness of his sayings, is included; and as our Father or Friend, he is doubly considered: 1. As good to us; and so he is gracious, or loving and merciful. 2. As good in himself; and so he is our ultimate end, and the ultimate object of our love, where the soul resteth in the perpetual act of loving him, and in feeling his love. And this is the highest notion of God's relation to us, and of all relation.

Note, that the attributes of God must not be cast together on a heap, but distinctly laid down. First, the attributes of his essence, that he is one, eternal, immense, necessary, independent, immutable, &c. Then the attributes proper to each person, and those proper to each active principle, which, summarily, are perfection: and then the attributes of God's relations, which are so many that I may not here stay to name any more.

The proof that there is a God, is so evident in nature, that he is well called a fool in Scripture (Psal. xiv. 1) who denieth it. All things which we see in the world preach God to us, telling us that they have a cause above them and in them which must needs be able to make and uphold the world, because we see that it is made and upheld, while every part is sufficient for itself; and he must have as much wisdom as is visible in the effects, in the order of the universe; and more goodness than all the world hath, because it hath none but from its first cause. So that one most powerful, wise, and good first-cause, that is, God, is so notorious to reason, that he is mad that questioneth it.

And this God can be but one, because two Infinites, two Almighties, most wise, most good, and first causes, &c. it is a contradiction. For if there be two, one is but half, and so not infinite or perfect; and that one is not the cause of the other, nor his end, &c.

That God is immense, is evident, because all the world must be contained in him, else he had made that which is greater than himself, and operateth where he is not: and he can have no bounds who hath nothing to bound him, and hath no proper locality. And he that is infinite in duration, must be so in degree or essence.

That God is eternal, is most evident, because, else, there was a time imaginable before there was a God, and so before any thing; and then there never would have been any thing; for nothing can make nothing. The rest I pass by.

I must tell the reader here, that though this first lesson, what God is, be the hardest and highest in divinity, yet order commandeth us to set it first; and till God be known, nothing is well known. Therefore I advise you to read this over, and understand as much of it as you can, and then pass on to the rest; and when you have gone through all, come back again and learn this better: for God is as the sun, most certainly known, but least comprehended, and still most unknown. He is the first and last: you must begin and end with him. You must know something from him, that you may know Christ and Scripture; and then you must know Christ and the Scriptures, that you may know more of God; for all other knowledge is but a means to help you to know, love, and serve him, in which you must still grow to the last, till you come to the world of true perfection.

Quest. 2. What believe you of the creation, and the nature of man, and the law which was given to him?

Answ. God created all the world; and made man in his own image, an embodied spirit of life, understanding, and will, with holy liveliness, wisdom, and love, to know, and love, and serve his Maker, here and for ever; and gave him the inferior creatures for his use; but forbade him to eat of the tree of knowledge, upon pain of death.

1. To create, is to make of nothing, in the first notion; and so God created only spirits, and the elements, fire, air, water, and earth; but all the rest of his works he made of these, as the sun, and moon, and stars, &c. which is creating in the second notion, because they never were before.

2. The whole world which God made is to us incomprehensible. It is like that it is but a small part of it which we see; we know not how much more is unseen; and no part is perfectly known by mortals. But we have so much knowledge of all, as is needful to the ends of our own creation in this imperfect state. And to spend our days in searching after more, is but to lose and neglect things possible and profitable, while we seek things impossible and unprofitable, and to trouble ourselves and the world with pretensions and contentions, mere names. But all the true knowledge of God's works which we can really attain is useful to us, though in great diversity of degrees.

3. When I call man an embodied spirit, I determine not that this body is not a part of him; but only that the soul or spirit is so noble a part, as that the body is but a habitation and servant to it, though a part of the man, being made of the common, passive elements.

4. The image of God on man is threefold, or hath three parts: 1. Natural; the image of God's being and nature. 2. Moral; which is the image of God's perfection or holiness. 3. Dominion; which is the image of God's dominion over all.

I. In God's natural image, man's soul hath a notable trinity in unity: 1. In one soul there are the vegetative, sensitive, and intellective powers. 2. In one superior, intellectual soul, as such, there is the virtue of superior life, or vital activity, and the virtue of understanding, and of free will. The will is not the understanding, nor the understanding the will, nor the vital power either understanding or will; nor is any one of these a part of the soul: but the whole soul is life, the whole is understanding, and the whole is will; yet not wholly; that is, no one of these words express all that is essential to the soul.

II. The moral image of God on the soul is nothing but the rectitude or health of these three faculties, which is their holiness: that is, 1. The holy liveliness of the vital faculty, when it is lively towards God. 2. The holy wisdom of the understanding, to know God. 3. The love of God and goodness, which is the holiness of the will.

III. Our dominion over other creatures is the image of God's dominion, by which we are, 1. Their owners, under God; and they are our own. 2. Their governors, under God, according to their capacities; and they are ordered by us. 3. Their benefactors under God; we provide for them, feed them, manure the ground; and their end, under God; they are given us for our use.

5. The end of man's nature, evident in the faculties' aptitude thereto, is, as, (1. In general, God, who is the end of all things, so, 2. specially,) holiness, living to God; that is, 1. To know God practically; 2. To love him; 3. To serve him. God maketh nothing in vain; much less the nobler natures. When he made man's nature capable and apt to know, love, and serve him, it plainly telleth us that he made him for that use. Those, therefore, who deny this to be natural to Adam, deny humanity, and make man a brute by nature, and suppose a supernatural grace to come after, and make Adam as of another species; as if grace only made him a man. And they that deny man to have such faculties know not what a man is.

6. Man's soul being made apt for perpetual duration, is truly said to be immortal; for God having made it a simple spirit, it is not liable to dissolution of parts and corruption of substance. Therefore if it perish, it must be by annihilation, or by turning it into another species of being; both which being operations or effects, which must be contrary to the established course of nature, it is not to be supposed that God will do them, though he can.

7. But man, consisting of soul and body, was not so immortal as his soul is, yet God could have perpetuated his life; yea, and would have done it, so far as that he should not have died, had he not sinned. But it is most probable that he should, at a certain period of time, have been changed, as Enoch and Elias were, and Christ, at his ascension; and the saints shall be, who are found alive at Christ's coming; and, it is like, the bodies that rose and appeared at Christ's death were so in their ascension.

8. Seeing the soul, yea, Adam, was to be thus far immortal, his felicity must be so too: which is no other than the perfecting of his knowledge, love, and service of God, in his perfected state. And, therefore, briefly I sum up all in "here and for ever."

9. It pleaseth God to try and exercise Adam's obedience, by forbidding him the fruit of one tree, on pain of death. But this positive law presupposed the law of nature, which is not mentioned as spoken to man, because it was in the very nature of him and the creatures compared together, which objectively signified to him what was God's will as to his duty; from which signification his duty did result.

10. Why it is called the tree of knowledge of good and evil, is very hard to know. It is said by most, because by it he was to have the sad experimental knowledge of good by the loss of it, and of evil by the feeling of it. Others hold, that Adam had before all holy necessary knowledge of God and his own duty, with which, had he been content, he had been happy, but that God had really made this fruit apt to breed in man a subtle, inquisitive wit, and that kind of needless, troublesome knowledge which multiplieth sin and sorrow still in the world. Such as is a great deal of the present philosophy, and vain formalities of sciences, and wordy, wrangling craft, and the presumptuous, distrustful search into God's secrets, and into that which is not our part but his; as if the patient must needs know all that the physician giveth him, and why: and it seemeth that some addition of knowledge sin brought them; and doubtless it was not of the good of duty, nor a holy knowledge, but an inflicting unnecessary apprehension of natural good and evil.

11. Death threatened is all that penal evil that man's nature was capable of: which is, 1. The desertion of the sinful soul. 2. The pain and dissolution of the body. 3. The perpetuity of the soul's suffering, at least, it being a capable subject, without a resurrection.

Quest. 3. What believe you of man's fall into sin and misery?

Answ. Man, being tempted by Satan, did by wilfully sinning fall from his holiness, his innocency, and his happiness, under the justice of God, the condemnation of his law, and the slavery of the flesh, the world, and the devil. When sinful, guilty, and miserable natures are propagated to all mankind, and no mere creature is able to deliver us.

1. It was Satan in the serpent that tempted Eve; and Satan by Eve, having by her sin got power to use her as his instrument, that tempted Adam.

2. Man sinned not till he was tempted. But he was but tempted, and not forced to sin, much less was he forced or necessitated to it by God himself. 3. God could have made man indefectible, or prevented his fall; but he is no more bound to tell us why he did not, than to tell us why he made not all men angels, or all beasts men. But we know that he will be no loser by it, but equally be glorified and pleased in the way of recovering grace. 4. God gave man free will, which was mutable, and not unchangeable in holiness, for he would have such a free will to be the subject of his earthly government, which is but preparatory to a perfect and unchangeable state. Not that an undetermined, mutable will is our perfection, but fitted on this life and work which God would have to be a lower degree and way to perfection. And free will was the first cause of sin, by an omission of its duty, and then by an ill determination of itself; though objects and temptation, and the understanding's and senses' apprehensions, were antecedents and occasions.

5. The very act of sin was a departing from holiness, from innocency, and from happiness. Sin itself becoming man's unholiness, his guilt, and misery.

6. Hereupon without any change, yea, or act of God, 1. The justice of God stood related to the sinner, as to one to whom death by right was due. 2. And the law, without any change in it, did virtually condemn him. 3. And by God's bare permission and desertion, the flesh, world, and devil, which had tempted him and overcome him, obtained a greater power to tempt and overcome him more, till the Spirit of God should recover and deliver him.

7. The three fore-mentioned evils, which Adam contracted to himself, are all propagated by him to his posterity. By natural propagation infants are, 1. Polluted with a sinful pravity. 2. Guilty both of that, and, in their kind, of Adam's sin. 3. And miserable by this sin and guilt, and the fore-mentioned penal consequents. To all which it is wonderful to consider well how much is done by the sinner himself, and how little by God, either as to the sin or punishment.

8. They that deny original sin go against plain Scripture, reason, and the experience of mankind; and do make infants saved without a Saviour, either pardoning or purifying them.

9. It is an error to lay our guilt of Adam's sin upon any such supposed covenant, will, or arbitrary imputation of God, which chargeth more on us than we were naturally guilty of. God doth neither make men sinners by imputation, who are not so in themselves, nor judge them falsely that men did what they did not. Adam was a public person, first naturally, and then reputatively. We were not then in him as persons, and therefore sinned not in him as distinct persons, nor are reputed by God so to have done, but we were in him virtually and seminally; not as a house is in the workman, as its cause by art, but as those whose essence is generated by his essence. And as all of us, that were then in him, were guilty then, so when we become persons, those persons are then guilty, as becoming now personal subjects of it; and all our personality is derived from a defiled, guilty, and miserable sinner, who can generate no essence or person better than he was himself. But yet the due difference between the principal agent and his offspring must be still acknowledged.

10. The guilt which, from our nearest parents, we contract also, with such additional pravity and penalty as our natural capacity, and the tenor of the new covenant allow, is too sadly overlooked by most divines, contrary to the whole scope of Scripture, from the days of Cain to the rejection of the Jews, and contrary to the second commandment: which matter deserveth a larger explication.

11. If we dream of any other deliverer or saviour, we fall from Christ.

Quest. 4. What believe you of man's redemption by Jesus Christ?

Answ. God so loved the world, that he gave his only Son to be their Saviour: who being God, and one with the Father, took our nature, and became man; being conceived by the Holy Ghost, born of the Virgin Mary, and called Jesus Christ: who was perfectly holy, without sin, fulfilling all righteousness; and overcame the devil and the world; and gave himself a sacrifice for our sins, by suffering a cursed death on the cross to ransom us, and reconcile us unto God; and was buried, and went among the dead: the third day he rose again, having conquered death. And having sealed the new covenant with his blood, he commanded his apostles and other ministers to preach the gospel to all the world; and promised the Holy Ghost; and then ascended into heaven, where he is God and man, the glorified Head over all things to his church, and our prevailing Intercessor with God the Father.

1. God's free love, without either merit, suit, or condition on man's part, gave Christ for a Saviour to the world. It is not possible for any good to befall a creature, which cometh not from the free gift of God.

2. God is said to love men, either when he willeth some good to them, or when he is pleased or delighted in them: with the first (called a love of benevolence) he loveth man, not because he is good, but to make him good: but this is less properly called one when it goeth alone. With the other more proper love (of complacence) he loveth every thing so far only as it is good and lovely. Both these concurred to lost mankind; but the first most eminently: the good which remained in fallen man, as lovely, was his nature, which was God's work, and partly his image; and therein his capacity of that grace, and all that holy duty, and that heavenly perfection, in which he would be fully amiable.

3. Christ is called the Saviour of the world, with different respects to the several parts of the world, not as if he were equally the Saviour of all. So far as he saveth any, he is their Saviour: he hath so far saved all men, as to make so sufficient a satisfaction to the justice of God for their sins, that none of them shall perish for want of such a satisfaction made; and so far as to make a universal gift of free pardon, justification, adoption, and the Spirit to all mankind, on condition of acceptance; so that nothing but their ungrateful refusing it, can deprive them of it: and hath commanded his ministers to publish and offer this to all the world. And he giveth men various degrees of help, towards the winning of their own consent. But the consent of some he effectually and insuperably procureth; and actually justifieth, sanctifieth, and glorifieth them. So that "he is the Saviour of all men, especially of those that believe:" when yet those that had a Saviour as to the antecedent satisfaction, the covenant offer and common helps only, will perish for ever, for unthankfully refusing the salvation offered them, together with their other sins: for none are forgiven, where the Forgiver and his grace are not accepted.

4. That Christ is both God and man is evident in Scripture: God, and therefore one substance with the Father, from eternity; but man in the fulness of time, about four thousand years after the creation of the world. Because he is God, he is of perfect suf-

ficiency for all the work of our redemption, and his sacrifice, merit, and intercession of full force: because he is man, he was fit to be the Head of the church, and to be a messenger from God, familiarly to teach men, and to show them a perfect example of holiness, and to suffer for us in our stead, and to possess heaven in our nature, and to intercede for us as the Mediator between God and man. So that there is nothing wanting in Christ's person, as to sufficiency, or compassionate condescension and nearness, to the consolation of penitent believers.

5. That God, the eternal Word of the Father, should take to him the nature of man, is the most astonishing wonder of all God's works: but having given us full proof of it by his Spirit, in his doctrine, miracles, and the sanctifying of believers, it is the grand article of our certain faith, yea, he giveth us to believe it, as well as commandeth it. That God is most intimately near to all men, and specially all saints, is no wonder; for he is more than the soul of the world: but his union with the manhood of Christ is an extraordinary conjunction for an extraordinary work; though the manner of it is above our reach. It was not by turning the Godhead into man, nor the manhood into the Godhead; nor doth the divine nature lose by it any of his perfection, or honour. And he that seeth how the same sun doth insinuate itself into some creatures as their very life, and yet leave others lifeless, will not think it incredible that God should more nearly unite himself to Christ's humanity than to others. We can hardly keep some philosophers from believing that all men's souls are parts of God; and yet as hardly get others to believe that God is so united to one man as to make one person.

6. Yet we must, in this mystery, take heed what notions we use: we must not say that the Godhead is a part of the person of Christ, for God cannot be part of any thing, for he is infinite; and a part is less than the whole, and therefore not infinite. Nor yet must we say that the Godhead is the whole person; part and whole are not words to be here used; but God and man are one Christ; as God and creatures are one universe of being, and yet God is not to be called the whole or part of that universe.

7. Nor must we think that the Godhead is instead of a human soul to Christ's flesh, and that he had no other soul; for he was perfect man, having human soul and body, which the Godhead assumed into personal union, and was as a soul to his soul. Much less was the Godhead turned into humanity, or any way altered.

8. Christ was not generated as other men are, but, without man, was conceived by the Holy Ghost; that is, by the Godhead operating outwardly by the divine effectual will or love, and eminently by the third person in the Trinity. Yet is Christ rather called the Son of the Father than of the Holy Ghost, because the Father is the first in order of operation.

Adam's soul was created, and not generated. Our souls are generated, and not merely created of nothing; that is, God, as the fountain of natural being, giveth multiplied essences wholly from himself, yet not as he first created things of nothing, but by an incomprehensible influence on, and use of, the generating soul, which, under God, have a causality in the multiplication: but Christ's soul was neither merely generated nor merely created, but was principally created so far as it was conceived by the Holy Ghost; and yet there was a participation of generation, so far as there was a concourse of the Virgin's soul. And by this wonderful conception Christ was free, both from the guilt and corruption of original sin; for though he be called the Son of David and of man, totally as a man, and not as to his flesh alone, yet was he not so by a proper and full generation, as others are; but the Spirit's creative conception made him, even as to his humanity, more eminently the Son of God than the Son of man.

9. The name "Jesus" signifieth his office, even "A Saviour;" and the name "Christ," signifieth the appointment of God, his mission and authority, and qualification for this office, "The Anointed of God."

10. Christ's perfect holiness and righteousness was both habitual in his perfect nature, and active in his perfect actions; that is, in perfect resignation, obedience, and love to God. The perfection of his divine nature advanced the merit of his human perfection two ways: 1. Causally, as it had the chief causality in producing it. 2. Relatively, as it was the perfection of the same person. The active righteousness of Christ consisted in his conformity to the divine will, as signified in that law which was given to himself by God; which was, 1. That he should fulfil the law of nature as a man; 2. And the Mosaical law as a Jew; 3. And a proper law of mediation by his proper mediatory works, doctrine, miracles, sufferings, justifications, &c. So that the perfection or righteousness of Christ, by which we were justified and saved, as the meritorious cause, is all this in one, even his perfect, habitual, and actual holiness, caused and relatively dignified by his divine perfection. Not as if one part merited one benefit for us, and another part another; but all entirely merited all for us; for all together was, that one condition required of Christ by the law or covenant of mediation; upon which condition performed, he had right to all the promised fruits of that mediation, as to give us the pardoning and saving covenant, &c.

11. Christ's conquering the devil and the world, as tempters, and the flesh, so far as without sin its natural desires were to be denied, as in the love of life, &c. was a great and needful part of his work, that he might deliver us from the tempters that had overcome us, and might confound God's enemies, and break the serpent's head, and vindicate the truth and holiness of God's law, by demonstration.

12. The reason of Christ's sufferings were, as a sacrifice to expiate our sins by his suffering in our stead, to demonstrate the holiness of God, his justice and truth, and the authority and equity of his law, that God and his laws may not be despised, nor the world encouraged by impunity to unbelief and sin. By suffering, he fulfilled that law which required him to suffer, but he did not fulfil that law which made suffering due to us; for it was not the punishment of another for him, but of every sinner himself, which was due by that law. But it was satisfaction to the Lawgiver, which he made by his sufferings, by giving him that which was equivalent to all our sufferings: not that same thing, by which the threatening of the law is properly and fully performed, for that is nothing but our destruction; but it is something in its stead. Not altogether of the same kind neither; for our great punishment is to be left in our sin itself, which is the misery of the soul, and to be denied the Spirit of life, and to be hated of God as unholy creatures, and deprived of that love of his which all holy souls are the proper objects of, and to be tormented of our guilty consciences for each sin, and to be tormented by devils in hell, and to despair of deliverance: all which Christ was never capable of, nor did undergo; but he suffered the cursed death of the cross, after a life of humiliation; and sensible sorrows, also, in his soul;

and not a little in his intellectual nature, so far as was consistent with perfect holiness, and its necessary consequences.

And Christ's sufferings are satisfactory to divine justice, not because they are the very same, in subject, matter, or duration, with what was due to us; but because they better attained the ends of the Governor and Lawgiver aforesaid, than the damnation of all the world would have done. Their aptitude to that end, was their satisfactory and meritorious dignity.

13. Christ suffered for our sins, and in our stead, because it was to free us from sufferings; and it freeth us as certainly (supposing us believers) as if we had made satisfaction ourselves; but yet he suffered in the person of a Mediator, who, indeed, is one that undertook to suffer in the sinner's stead; but never was, nor consented to be, esteemed the very sinner himself. If a man pay a debt by his servant, it is imputed to him as his own act and payment: because the law alloweth him to do it by a servant; and the servant is but his instrument. But this is not our case. Christ suffered in our stead; but not as our delegate, nor in our name and person properly, but as a voluntary Mediator, who may use us after as he pleaseth, and give us the benefits as he will. We did not pay our own debt by him: his sufferings were not ours in deed, nor in law: we were not crucified in him; we did not satisfy God's justice by him; and, therefore, the effects are not ours till he after give them us; and that in the degree that pleaseth him. It is not the suffering in itself which he giveth us, (that were a sad gift,) nor the first effect in itself, (satisfaction,) for that is made to God for us, and not to us; but it is the fruits hereby procured of God.

14. Much less can it be truly and properly said, that Christ in our person, and we in and by Christ, did fulfil the law of works, by perfect habitual holiness, and outward obedience and love, and this dignified by a divine perfection. The same habits, and acts, or righteousness, being accidents, cannot be in divers subjects. We are not justified by the precept and promise of the law of works, as if we had fulfilled it all by Christ, but by the law of grace. Had we fulfilled all the law of innocency by Christ, we could have no need of his death, or any pardon; because we should have no sin to pardon, either of omission or commission from birth to death. To forgive all our sins, and to repute us to have neither sinned, but perfectly obeyed by another, are contradictory; and God judgeth not falsely; nor supposeth us to do what we never did; therefore, we have not present right to all the benefits of Christ's merits or righteousness. Our punishments are no wrong to us, while he correcteth us. He giveth us pardon and life, on condition that we be penitent believers; and doth not tell us, that we repented, believed, and persevered in and by him, which shall be imputed to us; nor that we need it not because we are innocent in him. Nor did Christ by his death only save us from punishment, and by his perfection only merit our justification and salvation. For to be acquit from all punishment of sense and loss, is to have right to life; and to be innocent from all sin of omission and commission, is to be just. But we are not justified by Christ against this charge, Thou art a sinner, simply; but against this charge, Thou art to be condemned for thy sin: not by imputation of innocency in itself to us, and reputing us innocent; but by pardoning our sins, and giving us right to life, and so accepting us. And so Christ is the Lord our righteousness; and as he was made sin for us, not in deed, nor did God so repute him, but as one that was to suffer for sinners, so are we made the righteousness of God in him; being righteous by God's gift of pardon and life, purchased by his righteousness, demonstrating God's righteousness.

15. God is said to be reconciled to the world in general upon Christ's death, in that he is no more obliged in justice to punish them as mere sinners by the law of works; but hath granted a conditional pardon to all mankind, and that free, upon condition of meet acceptance of Christ and life.

God is said to be reconciled actually to believers, in that he is not at all obliged by justice to condemn them, but hath, as it were, obliged himself by a covenant of grace to forgive and save them. So that it importeth no real change in God, but in us, and in God's covenant, and a change in God's relation to us. Yea, 2. Though also he judge us now just, and love us as just, who before judged us unjust, and loathed us as such, this change is in us, and not any other in God than in relation and denomination.

16. Christ was buried, that he might be at the lowest before he was exalted; death seemed to have conquered him before he showed his conquest of it. So is it with us. The word translated hell in English, in the Greek and Latin ancient creeds is ᾅδης and *inferi*, and signifieth not necessarily the place of the damned. But it is more than his burial that is here meant, and respecteth his soul; and signifieth that his soul went among the souls of the dead, without determining it to heaven or hell: the very separating it from the body being part of Christ's humiliation. To paradise it went, but whither else, or what it did, we are necessarily ignorant. But hence it is plain that the soul liveth itself when it is separated from the body. And believers may joyfully follow Christ to the grave, and the state of separation.

17. Christ's resurrection was the great victory over death, the beginning of his triumph, and of the eminent church state under the Messiah, and the great proof of his truth as the Son of God, and is the great comfort of believers, assuring them that they have a victorious and a living Saviour, and that his word is true, and that they shall rise again.

18. The making of the new covenant sealed with Christ's blood, and commissioning a ministry to publish it to the world, was the great ordained means, by which Christ would give out the fruits of his merits and sacrifice with himself, for men's justification and salvation; of which more anon.

19. Christ's ascension was the second step of his exaltation. His bodily presence was more necessary in heaven than on earth; there he is still God and man, his body and soul being glorified, and natural flesh and blood changed into an incorruptible, spiritual body; for so it will be with believers, for flesh and blood cannot enter into the kingdom of God. So absurdly do they err who say that bread is no bread, but Christ's flesh, and wine is no wine, but his blood, when his glorified body hath no flesh and blood at all. It is unspeakable joy to believers, that we have a Head in heaven that is over all. 20. The apostle distinguishes Christ's headship as it is "over all," and as it is to "the church." For to this end he died, and rose, and revived, that he might be Lord of the dead and living.[q] He hath dominion over the uncalled to call them, and over believers to defend and glorify them, and over rebels to destroy them.

21. The intercession of Christ is a great article of the christian faith, and signifieth not only that he prayeth for us, but that he is the heavenly High Priest and Mediator with God. And that when

[q] Eph. i. 22, 23; John xvii. 2, 3; Rom. xiv. 9; John v. 22.

once sin hath defiled us there is no coming to God, but by a Mediator; no, not in our thoughts, or hopes, or affections. We must expect no acceptance of our persons, or prayers, or duties, but through Christ. We must put all into his hands, that he may present them to God: we cannot so much as love God but by him, as the glass and revealer of God's love and goodness. And also we must look for nothing from God now but through him, and by his hands; that is, by his merits and his administration. The Spirit and special grace are given by him even as Mediator; ministers and ordinances are by him; magistrates, and the rule of the natural world, for the ends of redemption, are by him; for all power is given him, and he judgeth all.

Quest. 5. What is the new testament, or covenant, or law of grace?

Answ. God, through Jesus Christ, doth freely give to all mankind himself to be their reconciled God and Father, his Son to be their Saviour, and his Holy Spirit to be their Sanctifier, if they will believe and accept the gift, and will give up themselves to him accordingly; repenting of their sins, and consenting to forsake the devil, the world, and the flesh, and sincerely, though not perfectly, to obey Christ and his Spirit to the end, according to the law of nature, and his gospel institutions, that they may be glorified in heaven for ever.

1. It is the same thing which in several respects is called Christ's new testament, law, and covenant. It is his testament, because he established it by and at his death; and it contained a free gift, or legacy to man. It is his covenant, because God on his part bindeth himself by promise to do all that is there offered; and requireth men to consent and covenant accordingly with him, if they will have the benefit. It is his law, in that it containeth his established terms on which men shall obtain remission and salvation, or miss of it and be condemned, if they refuse; and by which men shall be judged to heaven or hell.

2. This law hath two parts: 1. The first is a presupposed part, which is the law of nature, as to its obligation to duty; which Christ doth not new-make, but find made, and taking nature itself and man as his own, upon the title of redemption, that law also falleth into his hand. And as he doth not destroy, but perfect our nature; so he doth not destroy the law of nature, but superadd his remedying law. 2. Which is the second part, newly made by the Redeemer, and called the law of grace: the first being now as a part or appurtenance to this, as used to our sanctification, and yet the obedience of it part of the end of this. This special law and covenant of grace containeth, 1. A free deed of gift, though conditional, of God himself, the Father, Saviour, and Sanctifier, as aforesaid, with pardon of all sin, and right to the love of the Father, the grace of the Son, and the communion of the Holy Ghost, and to the heavenly glory. 2. The imposed condition of this free gift, which is sincere belief and consent by covenanting accordingly with God as is expressed. 3. The preceptive part, which is to be the rule of sincere obedience, as it is in gospel institutions (the law of nature supposed). 4. The penal part, as it leaveth men unsaved, and threateneth a sorer punishment to all impenitent and unbelieving refusers of the offered grace. And this is now the law and covenant by which we must live and be judged. And which is God's instrument, like an act of oblivion, and a deed of gift, by which the benefits of Christ are, with himself, to be regularly conferred on mankind, and on which we must trust as our title to Christ and life.

Quest. 6. What believe you of the Holy Ghost?

Answ. God the Holy Spirit was given by the Father and the Son to the prophets, apostles, and evangelists, to be their infallible guide in preaching and recording the doctrine of salvation; and the witness of its certain truth by his manifold divine operations; and he is given to quicken, illuminate, and sanctify all true believers, and to save them from the devil, the world, and the flesh.

1. The Holy Spirit is God, the third person in the Trinity. To him, in Scripture, is oft ascribed eminently, 1. The love of God, and the gift of love to man; as to the Son is ascribed the wisdom of God, and the word of wisdom. 2. The exterior operations of God on the creature; as the sun operateth on the earth by its motive, enlightening, and heating beams, which are indeed itself. 3. The perfecting of God's operations especially; and so, though the three persons are undivided, and all work together on the creature; yet eminently the Father is called the Creator and the Original of nature; the Son is called the Redeemer and the Giver of grace; the Holy Spirit is called the Sanctifier and the Beginner of glory; or, the nature of man is of the Father, his medicine of the Son, and his health of the Holy Ghost given by the Father and the Son.

2. The Holy Ghost is given in several measures to men, and for several uses, for the church's edification. When any new law or doctrine was revealed to the world, God gave the Spirit of miracles to prove it to be of him. So it was when Moses gave the law, and sometimes to the prophets, when they brought any new message; and as they prophesied of Christ, so they had the Spirit of Christ to inspire them. But the great and wonderful measure of the Spirit was given to the apostles, and other christians in the first age of the gospel church, to enable them infallibly to preach and record the history, and doctrine, and commands of Christ, and to seal it with miracles, by healing the sick, raising the dead, speaking various languages, &c. Therefore the Scripture written by the Spirit in them is left as the rule of our faith and life; and all the motions or revelations that seem to come from the Spirit now, are to be tried by the Scripture, because we have not the same gifts or measure of the Spirit as the apostles had; so that to try the Spirit by the Scripture, is but to try our doubtful and smaller gifts of the Spirit by the apostles' certain and greater gifts of the Spirit. The belief of the Scriptures, indited by the Spirit, belongeth to this article of our belief in the Holy Ghost.

3. The ordinary renewing work of the Holy Spirit is the accessory beginning of our salvation; and without holiness none can see God. So great a work is this on man, that Christ's own death and resurrection, and mediation in heaven, is the means to procure and give us this Spirit; and its work is God's image on us, and called the divine nature. There are three parts of this operation on us. 1. Its quickening work to make us alive to God, who were dead and dull to all holy acts. 2. Its illumination to open the eye of our darkened understanding, by knowledge and faith, curing our ignorance and unbelief. 3. Its converting or sanctifying work on the will, turning us from the love of sensual and worldly pleasures to the love of God and holiness, which, because it is the perfective act, love is taken in Scripture for the sum of all sanctification; and to give the Spirit of adoption, and to give us the love of God, is the same thing; to which faith in Christ is the means: and yet the Spirit worketh also that faith in us. But when he worketh faith in us, he is but opening the door and entering, that, by love, he

may dwell and work within us. As one compareth it to a bird that first maketh her nest, and then layeth her eggs and hatcheth them. Faith in Christ is as the bellows by which the Spirit kindleth in us the love of God; and faith kindling love, and love kindled by faith, and working by holy, fruitful obedience, is all the Spirit's work and all our religion: for mortification, and conquest of the flesh, the world, and the devil, is here comprised.

This work of the Spirit is a certain proof that Christ is the true Saviour of the world, and his gospel true; for none but God can thus renew souls, and God would not do it by false doctrine.

This article, therefore, of our belief in the Holy Ghost, is of grand importance to be understood and well considered; for while Christ is in heaven, his Spirit is his advocate and agent in the souls of men on earth, and his witness in all true believers, to plead Christ's cause, and prove his truth, and finish his saving works, and fit men for the love of God, and for glory: and this Spirit is to our souls as our souls to our bodies, in some sort; without which we can do nothing holily: it is our life, light, and love; it is our earnest, pledge, and first-fruits of heavenly glory, giving us the foretastes of it by love, and so our witness or evidence, that we are the children of God.

But it is a dangerous error to think that this Spirit is given us to do all at once, or to do all absolutely, however we use it. It worketh the love of God in us by degrees, and is to be working it in us while we live. It worketh it by means, even by the gospel understood, believed, and considered; and we may no more look for the Spirit without the word and means used by us, than for health without food and physic. Though he worketh insuperably when and where he please, yet men may, by resistance, forfeit and quench his operations. And, mark it well, the greatest rewards for obedience and punishments for sin, which God, as judge, doth execute in this life, are by giving men more of the Spirit, or by denying or withholding its operations on men's abuse, which is more to be feared than all other judgments in this world.

Quest. 7. What believe you of the holy catholic church, the communion of saints, and the forgiveness of sins?

Answ. All that truly consent to the baptismal covenant, are one sanctified church or body of Christ, and have communion in the same spirit of faith and love, and have the forgiveness of all their sins: and all that by baptism visibly covenant, and that continue to profess christianity and holiness, are the universal visible church on earth; and must keep holy communion with love and peace in the particular churches, in the doctrine, worship, and order instituted by Christ.

1. The world is Christ's kingdom by right, and governed by his wisdom and power. The church is Christ's consenting kingdom, ruled by wisdom and special love. He is Head over all things to the church: it is his body political, relatively, yet really quickened by his Spirit: it is his office to be both the constitutive, governing, and quickening Head. The form of the church is its relation to him as its Head. He giveth it laws, and judgeth and executeth them; and appointeth officers to it by his word and grace. He, as a mediating Head, is the conveyer of the Spirit from God to us.

The church hath no universal head but Christ. None else hath right; none else is capable or able, either as principal or vicar under him. He hath commissionated none to such an office. "Ye are the body of Christ, and members in particular. And God hath set some in the church, first apostles, secondarily prophets, &c. Are all apostles? are all prophets?" &c. 1 Cor. xii. 27—29. Here Christ only is the Head; the church is only his body. Apostles are but chief members, and not the head; and apostles are the first rank of members, who were twelve at least; therefore there is no one as a head over them. Peter never governed the apostles; they were never bid obey him. It was one of the Corinthians' schisms for some to make him a head, as others did Paul, and others Apollos; and to say, We are of Cephas. The schism was not cured by calling them all to take Peter for the head. The pope is no more Peter's successor than the bishop of Antioch is, and others: if he had, he had not been either constitutive or governing head of the church. He that is head, as Christ's vicar, must be a universal prophet, universal priest, and universal king of the church. The church is not the pope's body or kingdom; he is a usurper of much of Christ's prerogative, by a false pretence of being a vicar-head; and so will any general council be that shall claim the same office. The church of Rome materially, so far as they are christians, are a part of the catholic church, though a corrupt part; but formally, as they are a body headed by the pope, they are a sinful policy, and no church of Christ at all; for he commandeth not, but condemneth such a policy.

This church of Rome is a sect or schism from the catholic church; it is but about the fourth part of the christians in the world, who all make up the universal church. The Abyssines, Coptics, Syrians, Armenians, Indians, the Greeks, and Moscovites, with all the reformed churches, are as many; calculate four parts of five, but, at the least, two parts in three, of the church. The cutting off of all these as none of Christ's church, and making none in the world to be christians but the subjects of the pope, and contending for this with fire and sword, and false, railing volumes, is the grand schism in the world, and that which still keepeth open the wounds of the church, and the scandalous, pernicious contentions of christendom.

The pope had the same original with the patriarchs, being but the first of them, which all confess was human. Had not the Greek church (then far bigger than the Latin) thought his primacy to be human, they could never have claimed that right to Constantinople, which they knew had none but human right. The truth is, the pope was at first, and for many hundred years, but the chief bishop in one empire, as the archbishop of Canterbury is in England; and it was the churches of that empire that made up the councils called general, being called by the emperors, who had no power any where else through the world; and in time, his usurpation turned the Roman world into the whole world, and his kingdom must be the whole circumference of the earth, which is most unknown, and, but three or four times, was never so much as compassed by sea. And seeing it is the apostolic office to convert souls as well as rule them, and he undertaketh that universal headship, which never any apostle did, what a world of people in Tartary, India, the Turkish empire, Africa, at the antipodes, and the unknown world, hath this desperate undertaker to answer for! A true catholic must be of a greater church than that of Rome; even the universal church containeth all christians. He must be of no sect or schism, and therefore no papist, for they are but a sect.

The true consenters to the baptismal covenant are, the church in the first sense, truly holy; but the baptized, not apostatized, who are visible consenters and professors of christianity, are the church, as visible, and are holy by visible separation to God, and dedication to him. The confounding of the church, mystical and visible, tempteth some to separate from the church visible, as if it were not holy; and the papists have made a church visible, of their own invention, which is a body politic, headed by a pretended human head: some call it The Church Congregate, to insinuate that it is such a policy. But the grand point in which we renounce popery is this; and we hold, that there is no such political church on earth, that hath any universal, constitutive, or governing head besides Christ, who is visible in heaven, and was once visible on earth, where his church is still visible.

3. The unity of the spirit of faith and love is the chief part of the communion of saints; and the second is in the exercise of that faith and love in external communion, which is in doing all the good they can for each other, and communicating for the relief of those that need, as men will do who love others as themselves; and also in a concordant, holy worshipping of God; for which end particular churches are appointed by Christ, who are to be guided by their several pastors, who are ministers under Christ, in his teaching, priestly, and ruling office. And that worship is instituted by Christ in which this communion must be exercised, saving that the ordering and circumstances are much left to the church guides: and the Lord's day is separated for this solemn, holy communion. And discipline is to keep clean the church, that it may be a communion of saints.

4. The remission of sins is the other part of the salvation of the church; the fruit of Christ's blood, and the gift of his covenant, as sanctification is the work of his Spirit. Remission of sin is our justification, including the gift of right to life: and it hath three degrees, or is of three sorts: 1. Constitutive, which giveth us right to impunity, and dissolveth our guilt or obligation to punishment: this is God's act as legislator and donor by the new covenant, which is the gift of our right. 2. Sentential, by which God, as Judge, pronounceth us pardoned and just. 3. Executive, by which God actually freeth us from punishment, of sense and loss, and giveth us life.

Remission is, 1. Universal of all sins past; and this is given at once: really, by God at the time of our true believing and consenting to the covenant; but by solemn ministerial delivery in baptism visibly; in which Christ with pardon is solemnly delivered by God's appointment to true believers and their seed, that by them are dedicated to God. 2. Particular, of every sin after baptism and conversion: for, upon particular repentance God giveth us the pardon of particular sins from day to day. Sin may be said to be virtually forgiven before it is committed, because the causes of forgiveness are existent: but that is not properly actual forgiveness; for that which is not yet sin, cannot be forgiven sin.

The condition of pardon and justification is sometimes called faith simply, sometimes also repentance, and indeed is a penitent believer's consent to the covenant of grace, which is the condition of his title to this and the other rights of the covenant at once: it being a free gift purchased by Christ's sacrifice and meritorious righteousness, and by this covenant made ours. This is the plain and full doctrine of remission and justification; beyond which a good christian need not trouble his head with the invented words, and niceties, and controversies of these times. The sentential and executive justification or remission is begun on earth, but perfected at the final judgment; and both pass according to our constitutive remission and justification by the covenant. Adoption addeth some further dignity to believers, above what is in bare remission and justification, which cometh from the same merits and gift of Christ.

Quest. 8. What believe you of the resurrection and everlasting life?

Answ. At death the souls of the justified go to happiness with Christ, and the souls of the wicked to misery. And at the end of this world, Christ will come to glory, and will raise the bodies of all men from death, and will judge all according to their works. And the righteous shall go into everlasting life, where, being made perfect themselves, they shall see God, and perfectly love and praise him with Christ, and all the glorified church; and the rest into everlasting punishment.

1. The souls of the righteous go presently at death to Christ, in paradise or heaven; and the wicked to misery, which is hell.

2. Christ's second glorious coming is the day of our great deliverance and joy, which all true believers love and should long for.

3. The doctrine of the resurrection is fully opened by Christ, John v. and by Paul, 1 Cor. xv. of which Christ's own resurrection is our pledge.

4. The last judgment is that which endeth all controversies, and finally and perfectly justifieth believers, who are but initially and preparatorily justified before. Christ will be both judge and our advocate. The law of grace, and not innocency, is it that we must be judged by; but according to the divers editions of that law which men lived under. And the works that they shall be judged by, are the performance or not performance of the conditions of this law of grace. For by the works of the law of Moses, or of innocency, none can be justified. Nor yet by any commutative merits of his faith, love, or gospel obedience; but only as they are the terms on which God giveth the life, which is purchased by the death and perfect righteousness of Christ, which in the thing itself and value is a mere gift, though the order of giving it is by the law of grace, by which we must be judged. So that Christ justifieth by his own merits, satisfaction, and free gift thereon, against the charge of our deserving damnation for sin, as sin against the law of innocency and works, so be it we be otherwise justifiable against the charge of being infidels, impenitent, and ungodly. For Christ did not repent and believe for us, nor was holy to excuse us from being holy; but we must believe, repent, and be holy ourselves by his grace; and by these themselves be justified against the false accusation that we are unbelievers, impenitent, and unholy.

Christ doth not take away the faultiness of our actions, or the guilt of sin, as sin simply in itself, so as that we shall be reputed innocent or sinless; but he taketh away the guilt of punishment, and the guilt of sin, respectively as binding to punishment, and no more.

5. The glory of saints will be, 1. In the full perfection of their own souls and bodies; 2. In the perfect knowledge, love, and praise, and service of God, for his own sake, as the infinite good, and object of love and praise; 3. And in the full reception and joyful sense of God's love to us, and to all the church; 4. And in the fruition of Christ in glory; 5. With the blessed society of all the glorified angels and saints; and this to all eternity. This faith foreseeth, love foretasteth, and we must joyfully expect by hope and seek in obedience.

6. The wicked shall be miserable with the devil and his servants in their own sin, and the loss of the favour of God, and the tormenting sense of both on their consciences, and in bodily misery, and despair of all remedy for ever.

II. Consent. *Quest.* 9. You have told me what you believe; tell me now what is the full resolution and desire of your will, concerning all this which you believe.

Answ. Believing in God the Father, Son, and Holy Spirit, I do presently, absolutely, and resolvedly give up myself to him, my Creator, and reconciled God and Father, my Saviour, and my Sanctifier; and, repenting of my sins, I renounce the devil, the world, and the sinful desires of the flesh; and denying myself, and taking up my cross, I consent to follow Christ the Captain of my salvation, in hope of the grace and glory promised; which I daily desire and beg, as he hath taught me, saying, "Our Father which art in heaven," &c.

1. The will is the man, and, according to the will, we are esteemed of God. Knowledge and belief is but the entrance of grace to the heart and will, where love is the heart of the new creature. The hour when we truly make this heart covenant and consent we are converted, sanctified, justified, and adopted; and not till then.

But children are as parts of their parents; who are bound to enter them into the covenant of God; and whose will chooseth for them till they have natural reason and will to use themselves.

It is faith in God the Father, Son, and Holy Ghost, which is only saving, and not in one alone; even a consenting practical faith, which is our true christianity itself; nor are we justified by any other.

2. The Lord's prayer, being the sum of our desires, belongeth to this head; [r] it being but the will's prosecution of that good which it consented to, and hopeth for.

Quest. 10. What is this practice which, by this covenant, you are obliged to?

Answ. According to the law of nature, and Christ's institutions, I must (desiring perfection) sincerely obey him, in a life of faith, and hope, and love: loving God as God, for himself, above all; and loving myself as his servant, especially my soul, and seeking its holiness and salvation; and loving my neighbour as myself: I must avoid all idolatry of mind or body, and must worship God according to his word; by learning and meditating on his word; by prayer, thanksgiving, praise, and use of his sacrament: I must not profane, but holily use his holy name: I must keep holy the Lord's day, especially in communion with the church assemblies: [s] I must honour and obey my parents, magistrates, pastors, and other rulers: I must not wrong my neighbour in thought, word, or deed, in his soul, his body, his chastity, estate, right, or propriety; but do him all the good I can, and do as I would be done by; which is summed up in the ten commandments, "God spake all these words, saying," &c.

Because the ten commandments are plain themselves, and parents yet must read fuller expositions of them to their families, than I must here lay down, I shall give no other expositions of them but only, 1. That every commandment both forbiddeth evil, and commandeth the contrary good. 2. That every commandment reacheth to thoughts and affections, words and actions. 3. That the things commanded are not to be done always, but in their proper seasons; but nothing absolutely forbidden must ever be done; but things forbidden only in some cases, may be done out of those cases. 4. That the commandments must be understood by Christ's exposition with the addition of his gospel institutions: and obeyed as Christ's, joined to the new covenant; and not as given by Moses, as belonging to the covenant of works made with the Jews, or as part of the covenant of innocency made with Adam at the first.

Forms of Prayer, Praise, and Catechism, for the use of ignorant Families that need them.

Reader, I purposely avoid overdoing and preparing thee too much work, lest my intended help should prove a hinderance. But because all have not the same leisure, I have given you both longer and shorter forms, that you may use that which is fittest for the time and persons.

I. When you awake, let your hearts thus move towards God:

Thou, Lord, who art the life of all the world, hast mercifully preserved me in life this night, when I could do nothing to keep myself. I thank thee for my health, and rest, and peace. O now let thy mercies to me be renewed with the day: and let me spend this day in thy protection, by the help of thy Spirit, in love and faithful service to thee, and in watchfulness against my corruptions and temptations; for the sake of Jesus Christ. Amen.

II. Those that have opportunity to pray secretly before family prayer, should speak freely, without book, from the feeling of their own wants, if they are able: if not, they may use the same prayer which is for families, so far as their wants and cases are the same.

III. *A Morning Prayer for a Family.*

O almighty, all-seeing, and most gracious God, who hast created us and all things for thy glory! we, sinful worms, encouraged by thy own command and promise, and the mediation of Jesus Christ our Redeemer, do humbly cast down ourselves before thee, to acknowledge thy mercies, to confess our sins, to beg thy grace, and to tender thee our praise and service.

We thank thee that thou hast made us reasonable creatures, to know, and love, and serve our Creator, and capable of everlasting happiness in thy glory. We thank thee that we, who were born in sin, and were thy enemies in our fleshly state, were not forsaken by thee in our sins, nor left with the devils to helpless desperation; but have a sufficient Saviour given us by thy love, who hath redeemed us by his blood, and given a free pardon and title to life, in his covenant of grace, to all that heartily accept him as their Lord and Saviour. We thank thee for his holy gospel, for his holy example, for his Holy Spirit, given to his apostles, ministers, and all true believers. We thank thee for our birth, our education, our friends, our health, our peace and liberty, and all our comforts of this life. We thank thee for our public teaching and our private helps, the comfort of thy holy worship, and all the means of our salvation; but especially that thou hast blessed any of it to our good, and didst not forsake our sinful souls, and give us over to the blindness of our own minds, and the hardness of our hearts, and the slavery of our fleshly desires and wills. How great was that mercy, which did not only spare our lives, and keep us out of hell while we were sinning, but at last convinced any of us of our sin and misery, and awakened our sleepy souls unto repentance, and made us know the vanity of this world, and the certainty and glory

[r] The foregoing prayers expound the Lord's prayer.

[s] The Lord's supper and other church ordinances, are opened in the eighth day's conference, and more fully in my "Universal Concord."

of the life to come, that we might know thee and seek thee, our end and happiness! How great was thy mercy, which opened to us the mysteries of thy gospel, and drew us to thy Son, as the way to thee!

But, alas, we have ill requited thee for thy love; our original sin hath been too fruitful in our sinful lives; our childhood and youth was spent in too much folly, and fleshly sensuality! How long did we forget our God and our souls, our death and our everlasting state, as if we had no life to live but this, and we had been made to live and die like beasts! How long did we live in ignorance and unbelief, and little knew the nature and office, our want, and the worth and riches of Christ! How long did we live before thy love in Christ did melt us; and before we knew the life of faith; and before we were brought to the hatred of sin, and love of holiness; and before that ever we loved thee, our God, and the heavenly kingdom, above this world! Alas! we were deceived by the vanities here below, and followed the sinful desires of the flesh, and resisted thy Spirit which moved us to repent and turn to thee. And since we consented to thy holy covenant, we have too often yielded to temptations, and loved thee so coldly, and served thee so slothfully, and lived so unfruitfully, and made so ill a use of thy mercies, and of our afflictions, that thou mightest justly have taken thy Spirit from us, and suffered us to return to our former misery.

But O do not enter into judgment with us; forgive us for his sake, who is the sacrifice and propitiation for our sins. Charge not upon us the sins of our corrupted nature, or of our lives; of our childhood, youth, or riper age; our sins of omission or commission, of knowledge or of ignorance, of rashness or negligence, of sinful lust, passion, or of sloth. Wash us in the blood, and accept us for the merits of the perfect holiness and sufferings of our Redeemer. We dare not come to thee, but in his name, nor expect any pardon or mercy from thee, but for his sake, and by his hand. Let our hearts be sincere in consenting to his covenant by a lively faith, that we may be one with him, our blessed Head, and may receive the continual communications of his Spirit. Our souls are by corruption dead to God, and dark through ignorance, error, and unbelief, and disaffected to thee and to thy holy ways, till that Spirit do quicken, illuminate, and sanctify us. O give us this Spirit, the greatest of thy gifts on earth! Let him dwell by a new and holy nature in us; let him fill our hearts with holy life, that we may live to thee and die to sin; and with holy light, that we may know thee in Christ, and know thy word, and believe thy truth; and with holy love, that our whole desire may be to thee, and our delight be in thee; and being pleased in thee, we may, through Christ, be pleasant to thee for ever. O let not our ignorance and unbelief prevail! Let not our love to thee be still so cold, our desire so dull, nor our endeavours so slothful; nor our hopes of heaven so faint and weak! Let not the pleasures, or riches, or honours of this world ever steal our hearts away from thee; nor our fleshly desires overcome thy Spirit: govern our affections, thoughts, words, and actions, our senses, our appetites, and our passions by thy grace. Deliver us from selfishness, and teach us to love our neighbours as ourselves, and to wrong no man in our thoughts, or words, or deeds; but to do all the good that we can to others, to their souls and bodies. Save us from the devilish sin of pride, and all the fruits of it; and make us humble and low in our own eyes, and to loathe ourselves for all our sins; and to be patient, if we are vile in the eyes of others. Save us from temptations, and confirm our wills, that they may not easily be drawn to sin. Especially save us from those great heart distempers which are most powerful in us, and which we least hate and resist. Give us such public and private helps for our souls, as we most need; and bless them to us. Make us faithful in all the duties of our relations, in kingdom, church, and family, as we are superiors, inferiors, or equals; that we may have the comfort of them all. Mercifully dispose of our persons, our friends, and affairs. Provide for and protect our bodies, and make us contented with our daily bread, and patient if, for our sins, we want it. Be merciful to the afflicted, and give such seasonable deliverance to the sick, the poor, the oppressed, and the broken-hearted, as is most for their own and others' good, and for thy glory. Continue thy gospel to these and all the rest of the churches; furnish them all with skilful, holy, and diligent pastors; and bless their labours to the increase of holiness, love, and peace. Rebuke the ignorance, pride, and uncharitableness which do still divide us; and give us the knowledge, humility, and love, which must unite and heal us. Bless the queen, and all in authority, with the wisdom, holiness, and justice, which are necessary to the welfare of themselves and us. Teach them to govern, and us to obey, as the subjects of thee the King of kings. Revive knowledge and holiness in all the churches through the world, and lead them into the way of peace and concord, and save them from their sins and enemies! Deliver all deceived and oppressed nations, especially christians, from the tyranny, seduction, and malignity of their deceivers and oppressors. Pity the many kingdoms of the world that are drowned in heathenism, infidelity, and Mahometanism. Subdue the powers that rebel against thee, and let the kingdoms of the world be the kingdoms of Christ. Open a way for the gospel to them; and send them meet teachers for so great a work; that thy name may be hallowed, and thy kingdom come, and thy will be done on earth as it is in heaven. Give us this day our daily bread. Forgive us our trespasses, as we forgive them that trespass against us. Lead us not into temptation, but deliver us from evil; for thine is the kingdom, the power, and the glory, for ever. The world and all therein are thine: whatever pleaseth thee thou dost. Thy enemies and ours are in thy power; thou givest life to all the living; and thy mercies are over all thy works. Heaven and earth are continued by thy power and will; and all things in them are ordered by thy wisdom. Great art thou, O Lord, and greatly to be feared; wise art thou, and absolutely to be obeyed. Good art thou, and unmeasurably to be loved. The image and glory of thy perfection shineth in thy wonderful works. But above all in our glorified Redeemer and his triumphant church, where thy light enlighteneth, thy love inflameth, and thy glory glorifieth the blessed spirits of that glorious world, where angels and saints in beholding, and loving, and praising thy glory, are filled with everlasting joy: for of thee, and through thee, and to thee, are all things. To thee be the glory for ever. Amen.

A short Prayer for the Morning, in the method of the Lord's Prayer, being but an Exposition of it.

MOST glorious God, who art power, and wisdom, and goodness itself, the Creator of all things, the Owner, the Ruler, and the Benefactor of the world, but specially of thy church and chosen ones: though by sin original and actual we were thy enemies, the slaves of Satan and our flesh, and under thy displeasure and the condemnation of thy law, yet thy children redeemed by Jesus Christ thy Son, and regenerated by thy Holy Spirit, have leave to call thee their reconciled Father: for by thy covenant of grace thou hast given them thy Son to be their Head, their Teacher, and their Saviour: and in Him thou hast pardoned, adopted, and sanctified them, sealing and preparing them, by thy Holy Spirit, for thy celestial kingdom, and beginning in them that holy life, and light, and love, which shall be perfected with thee in everlasting glory. Oh with what wondrous love hast thou loved us, that of rebels we should be made the sons of God! Thou hast advanced us to this dignity, that we might be devoted wholly to thee as thine own, and might delightfully obey thee, and entirely love thee, with all our heart, and so might glorify thee here and for ever.

O cause both us, and all thy churches, and all the world, to hallow thy great and holy name, and to live to thee as our ultimate end; that thy shining image on holy souls may glorify thy divine perfection.

And cause both us and all the earth to cast off the tyranny of Satan and the flesh, and to acknowledge thy supreme authority, and to become the kingdoms of thee and thy Son Jesus, by a willing and absolute subjection. O perfect thy kingdom of grace in ourselves and in the world, and hasten the kingdom of glory!

And cause us and thy churches, and all people of the earth, no more to be ruled by the lusts of the flesh, and their erroneous conceits, and by self-will, which is the idol of the wicked; but by thy perfect wisdom and holy will, revealed in thy laws, make known thy word to all the world, and send them the messengers of grace and peace; and cause men to understand, believe, and obey the gospel of salvation, and that with such holiness, unity, and love, that the earth, which is now too like to hell, may be made liker unto heaven, and not only thy scattered, imperfect flock, but those also who in their carnal and ungodly minds do now refuse a holy life, and think thy word and ways too strict, may desire to imitate even the heavenly church where thou art obeyed, and loved, and praised, with high delight, in harmony and perfection.

And because our being is the subject of our well-being, maintain us in the life which thou hast here given us, until the work of life be finished. And give us such health of mind and body, and such protection and supply of all our wants, as shall best fit us for our duty. And make us contented with our daily bread, and patient if we want it. And save us from the love of the riches, and honours, and pleasures of this world, and the pride, and idleness, and sensuality which they cherish. And cause us to serve thy providence by our diligent labours, and to serve thee faithfully with all that thou givest us. And let us not make provision for the flesh, to satisfy its desires and lusts.

And we beseech thee, of thy mercy, through the sacrifice and propitiation of thy beloved Son, forgive us all our sins, original and actual, from our birth to this hour; our omissions of duty, and committing of what thou didst forbid; our sins of heart, and word, and deed; our sinful thoughts and affections; our sinful passions and discontents; our secret and our open sins; our sins of negligence, and ignorance, and rashness; but especially our sins against knowledge and conscience, which have made the deepest guilt and wounds. Spare us, O Lord, and let not our sin so find us out as to be our ruin; but let us so find it out as truly to repent and turn to thee. Especially, punish us not with the loss of thy grace! Take not thy Holy Spirit from us, and deny us not his assistance and holy operations. Seal to us by that Spirit the pardon of our sins, and lift up the light of thy countenance upon us, and give us the joy of thy favour and salvation: and let thy love and mercy to us fill us, not only with thankfulness to thee, but with love and mercy to our brethren, and our enemies, that we may heartily forgive them that do us wrong, as through thy grace we hope we do.

And for the time to come, suffer us not to cast ourselves wilfully into tempations, but carefully to avoid them, and resolutely to resist and conquer what we cannot avoid: and oh, mortify those inward sins and lusts, which are our constant and most dangerous temptations; and let us not be tempted by Satan or the world, or tried by thy judgments, above the strength which thy grace shall give us. Save us from a fearless confidence in our own strength; and let us not dally with the snare, nor taste the bait, nor play with the fire of thy wrath, but cause us to fear and depart from evil, lest, before we are aware, we be entangled and overcome, and wounded with our guilt and with thy wrath, and our end should be worse than our beginning: especially, save us from those radical sins of error, and unbelief, pride, hypocrisy, hardheartedness, sensuality, slothfulness, and the love of this present world, and the loss of our love to thee, to thy kingdom, and thy ways.

And save us from the malice of Satan and of wicked men, and from the evils which our sins would bring upon us.

And as we crave all this from thee, we humbly tender our praises with our future service to thee. Thou art the King of all the world, and more than the life of all the living. Thy kingdom is everlasting: wise, and just, and merciful is thy government. Blessed are they that are thy faithful subjects; but who hath hardened himself against thee, and hath prospered? The whole creation proclaimeth thy perfection; but it is heaven where the blessed see thy glory, and the glory of our Redeemer; where the angels and saints behold thee, admire thee, adore thee, love thee, and praise thee with triumphant, joyful songs, the holy, holy, holy God, the Father, Son, and Holy Ghost, who was, and is, and is to come; of thee, and through thee, and to thee, are all things: to thee be glory for ever. Amen.

IV. *A Prayer for Morning or Evening in Families.*

O God, the Infinite, Eternal Spirit, most perfect in power, wisdom, and goodness; though mortal eyes cannot behold thee, nor any created understanding comprehend thee, thou art present with us, and seest all the secrets of our hearts; our sins and wants are known to thee: but thou requirest our confessions as the exercise of our repentance, and our petitions as the exercise of our desires and filial dependence upon thee. And oh that our souls were more fit for thy holy presence, and for this great and holy work! O thou whose mercy inviteth miserable sinners to come unto thee by the new and living way, meet us not in thy justice as a consuming fire, but accept us in thy righteous and beloved Son, in whose mediation is our trust.

Thou, who art the great Creator of all things, didst make us in thine image, to know thee, to love thee, and to serve thee. But sin hath corrupted all our powers, and turned them from thee, and against those holy ends and uses for which thou didst create us. In sin we were conceived, and in sin we have lived, increasing our original guilt and misery. Though we knew that thou art our Owner, we have lived as if we were at our own disposal. We have called thee our King and Ruler, but we have rebelled against thee, and obeyed our carnal wills and appetites. Thou art goodness and love itself, and the Author of all that is good and amiable in all the world, and our souls should have loved thee with fervency and delight; but our hearts have been estranged from thee, and have sought delight in worldly vanities, and in the pleasing of our fleshly minds and lusts. This deceitful world hath had our love, our care, our thoughts, our words, our time, our labour, as if it had been our home and portion, and we had been to continue here for ever, whilst our God and our immortal souls have been neglected. Thou hast made us capable of endless glory, and called us to seek it, and to set our hearts above on thee; but we have lived as if we believed not thy word, and have despised the joys of heaven, which thou hast offered us, and preferred our short and sensual pleasures. We have trifled in thy worship, and served thee hypocritically with our lips alone. We have taken thy dreadful name in vain. We have mispent thy holy day, we have dishonoured our superiors, and neglected our inferiors. Our family, which should have been ordered in holiness, as a church of God, hath been a house of vanity, worldliness, and discontent. Our thoughts have been guilty, not only of vanity, folly, and confusion, but of malice, and of unclean and filthy lusts. Our tongues have been guilty, not only of idle and foolish talk, but also wrathful words and railings, of filthy and immodest speech, and of evil speaking and backbiting others, and of many a lie. We have not loved our neighbours as ourselves, nor done by all others as we would have had them done by us; but we have been all for our carnal selves, proudly desiring our own exaltation and commodity, and sensually desiring pleasure to ourselves, whilst we have too little cared for the corporal or spiritual good of others. We have been very backward to love our enemies, and heartily to forgive a wrong. We have been unprofitable abusers of thy talents, and have wasted our precious time in vanity, and done but little good in the world.

And though thy wonderful mercy hath given us a Redeemer, and in him a sufficient remedy for our sins; and thou hast posed the understandings of men and angels in this strange expression of thy wisdom and thy love; yet have we staggered at thy word in unbelief, and stupidly neglected this great salvation. How carelessly have we heard and read thy gospel! How little have we been affected with all the love and sufferings of our Saviour! We could have been thankful to one that had saved our lives, or enriched us in the world; but how unthankful have we been to him, who hath done so much to save our souls from endless misery? Alas, our hard, unhumbled hearts do make light of our sins and of thy just displeasure, and therefore make light of Christ and grace. And it is just with thee to deny us for ever the mercy which we set so light by.

But deal with us, O Lord, according to thy goodness, and according to our great necessity, and not according to our deserts. We have sinned as men, but be thou merciful as God. Where our sin aboundeth, O, let thy grace abound much more. Thou gavest mankind a Saviour when we were thine enemies, and thou wast in Christ reconciling the world unto thyself: and it is thy great design to glorify thy wonderful love and mercy, by the advantage of our great unworthiness and misery, and to forgive much, that we may love thee much; and if, after all this, we should doubt of thy willingness to forgive believing, penitent souls, we should greatly wrong the riches of thy grace. Thou soughtest us, when we sought not after thee; and it is by thine own command that we seek thee, and beg thy mercy; and thou givest us the very desires which we pour out before thee: thou beseechest us to be reconciled, and to receive thy grace; and shall we question then whether thou art willing to give it. There is enough in the sacrifice and merits of thy Son to expiate our sins, and justify penitent believers in thy sight. Thou hast made him the infallible Teacher of thy church: he is a King most fit to rule us, to defend and justify us. Thy Spirit is the Sanctifier of souls; and thy love is sufficient to be our everlasting felicity and rest. We therefore humbly give up ourselves to thee our God; to thee our Father, our Saviour, and our Sanctifier; beseeching thee to receive us upon the terms of thy covenant of grace. Remember not against us our youthful folly, ignorance, and lusts: forgive our secret and open sins; our sins of negligence, rashness, and presumption; especially those sins which we have deliberately and wilfully committed, against our knowledge and the strivings of thy grace. Renew and sanctify us thoroughly by the Spirit: take from us the old and stony hearts, and give us hearts more tender and tractable; and give us the divine and heavenly nature; and make us holy in the image of thy holiness. Cause us to resign and devote ourselves, and all that thou givest us, entirely to thee as being thine own. Bring all the powers of our souls and bodies into a full subjection to thy government. O show us thine infinite goodness and perfections, and the wonderful mercy which thou hast given us in Christ; and shed abroad thy love upon our hearts, by the Holy Ghost, that we may be constrained by thy love to love thee above all things, with all our heart, and soul, and might. Let the beams of thy love so fire our hearts, that we may love thee fervently, and delight to love thee, and taste the beginning of the heavenly felicity and pleasures in thy love, and may perceive that we can never love thee enough; but may still be longing to love thee more. We dare not say, Oh that we could love thee as thou art worthy! for that is above both men and angels: but oh that we could love thee as much as we would love thee; till we come to that most blessed state, where we shall love thee more than now we can desire! If we had never sinned in word or deed, the want and weakness of our love to thee is a sin which we can never sufficiently lament; and the very shame of our corrupted natures, and a burden that we cannot bear. We crave no other felicity in this life, than to know thee better and to love thee more. Give us the spirit of adoption, which may possess us with all child-like affections to thee, as our reconciled God and Father in Christ. Cause us to make thee our ultimate end, and to seek thy glory in all that we do. Let it be our chiefest study in all things to please thee, to promote thy kingdom, and to do thy will. Set up thy glory above the heavens, and let thy name be sanctified in all the earth. Convert the heathen and infidel world, and let their kingdoms become the kingdoms of thy Son. Give wise and holy rulers to the nations; and let the gospel of Jesus go forth as the sun, to the enlightening of all the quarters of the earth. Oh that the world which is ruled by the malicious prince of darkness might receive and obey thy holy laws; and in the beauty and harmony of holiness be made more like the saints in heaven. Reform the churches which are darkened and defiled, and cast down that tyranny, ungodliness, heresy, and schism, which keep out knowledge, holiness, and peace. Preserve and bless the reformed churches; especially in these kingdoms where we live. Bless the queen, and all in authority; teach our teachers, and give both able and faithful pastors to all the congregations of these lands. And give the people obedient, pious, and peaceable minds. Cause us to seek first thy kingdom and righteousness; and let all other things be added to us. Give us all necessaries for the sustaining of our natures; and make us contented with our daily bread; and patient, if for our sins we want it. Teach us to improve our precious time, and not to spend it in idleness, or sin; but despatch the work upon which our endless life dependeth; and to live as we shall wish at last that we had lived. Let our daily sins be daily and unfeignedly repented of; and be daily pardoned through Jesus Christ: and let us live in the belief of his mediation, according to our continual necessities. Let thy exceeding love and pardoning mercy teach us to love our neighbours as ourselves: and to love our enemies, and to pardon wrongs, and to do good to all according to our power. Strengthen us in our warfare against the flesh, the world, and the devil, that we may not only resist, but overcome. Keep us from the baits and snares of sin; and let us not thrust ourselves into temptations. Save us from ignorance and unbelief, from ungodliness and hypocrisy, from pride, and worldliness, and slothfulness, and all sinful pleasing of the flesh. Cause us to worship thee in holiness, and reverently to use thy dreadful name, and to remember the keeping holy of thy day. Keep us from sinful disobeying our superiors; and all unfaithful neglecting our inferiors; and from injuring any in thought, word, or deed. Keep us from sinful wrath and passions; from all unchastity in thoughts, desires, words, or actions. Keep us from stealing and defrauding others, from lying, slandering, and backbiting; and mortify that selfishness, which would set us against our neighbour's welfare: keep us from the judgments which we deserve; and let all afflictions work together for our good. O help us to spend this transitory life in a faithful preparation for our death, and let our hearts and conversation be in heaven; and forsake us not in the time of our extremity; but take our departing souls to Christ.

Add in the Morning.

Protect, direct, and bless us this day, in all our lawful ways and labours, that in the evening we may return thee joyful thanks, through Jesus Christ, our only Saviour: in whose words we sum up all our prayers. Our Father, which art in heaven, hallowed be thy name. Thy kingdom come. Thy will be done on earth, as it is in heaven. Give us this day our daily bread; and forgive us our trespasses, as we forgive them that trespass against us. And lead us not into temptation, but deliver us from evil. For thine is the kingdom, the power, and the glory, for ever. Amen.

Add in the Evening.

Preserve us this night, and give us such rest of body and mind, as may fit us for the labours of the following day, for the sake of Jesus Christ, our Saviour: in whose words we sum up our requests. Our Father which art in heaven, &c.

Another Prayer for Families: for Evening, or Morning.

O ETERNAL God, infinitely great, and wise, and good, our reconciled, merciful Father in Christ; reject not us vile and miserable sinners, who, constrained by our necessities, and invited by thy goodness, cast down ourselves in the humble confession of our sins, and thankful acknowledgment of thy manifold mercies, and earnestly beg thy further grace.

We were born with corrupted, sinful natures, which from our childhood we increased by actual sin. And though thy great mercy had given us a sufficient Saviour and a covenant of grace, and betimes engaged us to thee in that covenant by our baptismal vow, and gave us the great mercy of the gospel, and christian education, yet did we sinfully forget our Creator, unthankfully neglect our Redeemer, and rebelliously resist the Holy Ghost. How blindly, how wilfully, and how long did we follow our fleshly minds and lusts, and loved pleasure more than God, and lived brutishly by sense and appetite, and minded little but the vanities of this world! Yet all this while didst thou preserve our lives, and supply our wants, and save us from many a danger and calamity, when thy justice might have cut us off in our sins, and sent us to hell as we deserved. But we abused thy patience, and all thy mercies, and wasted our precious time in sin, and refused or delayed to repent, and hearkened not to the voice of thy Spirit and word, thy ministers or our consciences, but hardened our hearts against them all. We knew that we must die, but we prepared not for it, nor seriously thought of the life that followeth. We did not, by a changed heart and life, prepare for the great change which death will make, nor consider, that except we are born again of the Spirit, we cannot enter into the kingdom of heaven. We were never sure one day, or night, or hour, to see another, and we knew our time could not be long; and we were oft told, that as we lived here, we must speed in heaven or hell for ever: and yet, alas! how senselessly have we heard and known all this! And how little care have we taken for our souls, that they might be saved from sin and hell, and live with Christ in the heavenly glory, in comparison of the care that we have taken for our bodies, which we know must turn shortly to dust! Alas! pride and folly, and the vanities of this world, and examples of sinners, and the sloth, and appetite, and lusts of our own flesh, have deceived us, and turned away our hearts from thee. And while we quieted our conscience with the name of christianity, and a dead and outside show of worship, we were strangers to a holy and heavenly heart and life, and drew near thee with our lips, while our hearts were far from thee. And those of us, whom thy grace hath turned from this sin and vanity to thyself, did too long stand out and delay our conversion, and resist thy Spirit. And since we have served thee, alas! how poorly, how coldly, how unconstantly, with what wavering and divided hearts, as if we were loth to leave the world and sin. And by how many failings have we quenched thy Spirit, and wronged thy glory, and our brethren's souls, and hindered our own comfort and increase of grace! We have too little differed in heart and life from the ungodly, and from our former state of sin, and no wonder if our faith, hope, and love be weak, and if we have little of the joys of thy love and our salvation.

But, O thou, the merciful Father of spirits, have mercy upon us; forgive our great and manifold sins! Woe to us that ever we were born, if thou deal with us as we deserve! How quickly then shall we be in hell, past all remedy, in endless pain and desperation! where we shall have time to lament that sin in vain, which we would not forsake in the day of our visitation. But we appeal from the justice of thy law of innocency, to the blood and merits of Jesus our Redeemer, and to thy law and covenant of grace, which for his propitiation freely pardoneth all penitent, true believers. We are sinners, but he is righteous, and hath satisfied for our sins: we are worthy of misery; but he is worthy for whom thy mercy should forgive our sin! Oh! wash us in his blood; justify, adopt, and accept us in him. O take possession of our souls by that Spirit which is the advocate and witness of Christ, and which may dwell in us as a principle of spiritual life, and may form us fully to thy will and image, and overcome in us the flesh, the world, and the devil, and be our seal, and pledge, and earnest, and first-fruits of everlasting life. Let his quickening virtue heal our deadness, and make us lively and strong for thee. Let his illuminating virtue heal our ignorance, error, and unbelief, and fill our minds with faith and wisdom. Let his converting, sanctifying virtue kill in us the love of the pleasures, honours, and riches of this world, and give us a settled hatred of all sin, and fill our hearts with a fervent love to thee, thy word, thy ways, and servants, and to all men in their several capacities; and cause us to delight our souls in thee. Leave us not to serve thee outwardly and unwillingly from fear alone; but make thy love and service to be our food and our feast, our business and our recreation. O make thy ways so pleasant to us, that we may have no need to beg pleasure at the devil's door, nor to steal the forbidden pleasures of sin. Let the thoughts of thy precious love in Christ, of our pardon and peace with thee, and of the heavenly endless joys with Christ which thou hast promised us, be the readiest and sweetest thoughts of our minds; and a daily cordial at our hearts, to rejoice them under all the crosses and vexations of this world, and the pains of our flesh, and the foresight of death, and to comfort us at a dying hour. O cause us all the days of our lives to comfort ourselves and one another with these words, That we shall for ever be with our glorified Lord; more than with the possession or hopes of life, or health, or wealth, or any thing which earth affordeth. Teach us to redeem our short and precious time, and to cast away no part of it on vanity; but to lay up our treasure in heaven, and first to seek thy kingdom and its righteousness, and to give all diligence to make our calling and election sure, and to work out our salvation with fear and trembling, remembering that we must be adjudged according to our works. Teach us to worship thee spiritually and acceptably through Christ: to reverence thy name, and word, and ordinances, and to sanctify thy holy day: to honour our superiors, and behave ourselves aright to our equals and inferiors: to wrong none in their bodies, chastity, estates, or names; but to do as we would be done by: to love our neighbours as ourselves; to love and forgive our enemies, and those that do us wrong. Cause us to hate and overcome our selfishness, pride, sensuality, worldliness, hypocrisy, and all our fleshly lusts, which fight against the Spirit, and are odious in thy sight. Help us to govern our thoughts, affections, senses, appetites, words, and actions, by thy word and Spirit; to labour faithfully in our callings, to fly from idleness, and yet to be contented with our daily bread. Prepare us for all sufferings, with faith, hope, and patience. Cause us to overcome in all temptations, and to persevere unto the end; that having lived soberly, righteously, and godly in this world, we may joyfully receive the sentence of death; and that may be the day of our entrance into the heavenly joys, which is the terror of the wicked, and the beginning of their endless misery.

O send the word of life to the dark and miserable nations of the earth; call the kingdoms of heathens and infidels to the saving knowledge of Jesus Christ; let every knee bow to him, and every tongue confess him to thy glory. Subdue the proud and rebellious tyrants of the earth, who keep out the gospel, and keep up wickedness, and set up their interest against the kingdom and interest of Christ. Deliver the churches from all their oppressors and deceivers; and reform them to such wisdom, holiness, and concord, that their light may shine to Mahometans and other infidels, and do more to win them to Christ, than the scandal of their ignorance, wickedness, and divisions, hath done to hinder the world's conversion and salvation. O show to partial, blind, uncharitable, and contentious christians, the true way of peace, in returning to the ancient simplicity and purity of doctrine, worship, discipline, and conversation. Save all the churches from their sins and enemies. Bless these kingdoms, and never take thy gospel from us! Bless the queen, with all her nobles, judges, and magistrates; that they may rule as being ruled by thy laws and Spirit, promoting knowledge, holiness, and peace; and suppressing deceivers, ungodliness, and injustice; that we may live a quiet and peaceable life in all godliness and honesty. Be merciful to all christian congregations, and give them able, holy, and laborious pastors, who will guide the flocks in the way of life with the wisdom from above, which is first pure, and then peaceable and gentle; even by sound doctrine, and holy living, and by love and concord among themselves, according to the blessed example of our Lord. Be merciful to the afflicted, by sickness, pains, wants, dangers, or distress of soul: bless their sufferings to their sanctification and salvation, and relieve them in the time and way as is most for thy glory and their good. Save the prosperous from the temptations of prosperity. Be merciful to this family, and let there be no ignorant, ungodly, fleshly, worldly persons in it; that shall serve the flesh and the devil, instead of serving thee, and sell their souls for the pleasures of sin. Keep us all in holiness, love, and peace, and in our duties to one another; and let thy blessing be on all our souls and bodies, and on our labours and affairs · and let not thy judgments seize upon us.

Add this at Night.

We thank thee for all the mercies of our lives to soul and body, and particularly for preserving us this day. We have had another day's time of repentance, to prepare for our last day: but, alas, how little good have we got or done! Forgive all our sins of omission and commission: and protect us this night from the evils that we deserve. Refresh us with safety, rest, and sleep: and let our meditations of thee be sweet, and thy comforts still delight our souls. Prepare us for the mercies and duties of the day following; and teach us to live in thy service and praise, that we may live with thee for evermore, through Jesus Christ our Lord and Saviour; in whose name and words we sum up our prayers, as he hath taught us to say,—

Our Father, which art in heaven, hallowed be thy name. Thy kingdom come. Thy will be done on earth as it is in heaven. Give us this day our daily bread; and forgive us our trespasses, as we forgive them that trespass against us. And lead us not into temptation; but deliver us from evil: for thine is the kingdom, the power, and the glory, for ever. Amen.

Add this in the Morning.

We thank thee for all thy mercies to our souls and bodies this night, and all our days and nights; for our rest and safety, and this morning's light. Cause us to spend this day in thy fear and faithful service. Preserve our souls from sin, and our bodies from all dangers or hurt which would hinder us from thy service. Cause us to live as in thy presence, and let us do all to please thee, and to thy glory, and to the good of our own souls and one another: and let thy love, and praise, and service, be our continual delight; for Jesus Christ's sake, our Saviour and Intercessor at thy right hand: in whose name and words we sum up our imperfect prayers, as he hath taught us to say,—

Our Father, &c.

V. *A Prayer before Meat.*

Most bountiful God, who maintainest us and all the world; we thank thee for our life, health, peace, and food, and all thy mercies given to us in Christ. Bless these thy creatures, to nourish our bodies, and fit them for thy service. Cause us to receive them soberly, and to serve thee holily, cheerfully, and diligently: devoting ourselves and all our receivings to thy glory, through Jesus Christ our Lord and Saviour. Amen.

A Thanksgiving after Meat.

Merciful Father, we thank thee for Christ, and all the blessings which thou hast given with him; for pardon, and grace, and peace, and the hopes of life eternal, and all the means which tend thereto. We thank thee for feeding our bodies at this time. Oh! let us not turn thy mercies into our sin, nor use them against ourselves and thee, by gratifying any sinful desire; but cause us to use them to the increase of our love, and thankfulness, and obedience; and to relish and labour for the food that perisheth not, but endureth to everlasting life: for Jesus Christ's sake. Amen.

VI. *A Prayer for converting Grace, to be used by the unconverted which are convinced of their sinful, miserable state.*

O most holy, just, and dreadful God, yet gracious and ready to receive poor sinners, who penitently return unto thee by faith in Christ. Pitifully behold this miserable sinner, who is prostrate as at thy feet, and fleeth with fear from thy terrible justice, in hope of thy pardoning and saving mercy. I hear from thy word that thou hast redeemed the world by Jesus Christ, and he hath satisfied thy justice as a propitiation for our sins, and hath merited thy pardoning, saving grace for all that truly believe and repent, and heartily accept of Christ for the saving work and benefits of his mediation. But I hear that except we repent we shall all perish, and that he that believeth not shall be damned; and that except we be born again of the Spirit, and be converted, and become as little children, we cannot enter into the kingdom of God; and that without holiness none shall see thee; and that if any man have not the Spirit of Christ he is none of his; and that all that are in Christ are new creatures, old things are passed away, and all things are become new; and that the carnal mind is enmity, and neither is nor can be subject to thy law; and that if we live after the flesh we shall die; and that Christ is the Author of eternal salvation to all them that obey him.

I am convinced, O Lord, that thou art my Creator, and therefore my Owner; and that I, and all that I have, and can do, should be used to thy glory as thine own. As also that thou art the rightful Governor of the world; that thy laws are holy, and just, and good; that my baseness, and folly, and corrupted will, do make me unfit to rule myself. I am convinced that thou art best, and best to me, and that I should love thee with all my heart, and vilify all the pleasures, and riches, and honours of this world, in comparison of thee. I am convinced that this world is vanity, and that heaven alone, where thou art seen, and perfectly loved and praised, is the only felicity of souls, and should be sought before all transitory things. I am convinced that thou art the first and last, of whom, and through whom, and to whom, both I and all things are. And I am convinced that my forsaking thee and turning to my carnal self, and this deceitful world, and all my sins, deserve thy wrath and my destruction; and that I have no hope but in penitent sincere conversion to thee, by faith in Christ the only Reconciler.

But alas, the hardness of my heart, the power of unbelief and fleshly lusts, prevaileth against all this conviction! I fear lest all my knowledge will but condemn me to be beaten with many stripes! When I know that I should do good, evil is present with me; and the will of the flesh prevaileth against thy holy will. The custom of sinning hath increased my sinful inclination; and I have not a will which hateth my pleasant and grateful sins; I forbear them oft through fear, while I love them, and wish that thou didst not forbid them. Long have I been wishing and purposing to repent, and come to thee; but alas, how many purposes have I changed, and how many promises have I broken, and how many wishes have come to nothing! My corrupted will, enslaved by my sense, will not change itself, nor forsake the pleasant vanities which it loveth.

Oh that I had a heart, a will, to love thee as much above all the world, as I know I should love thee! And to delight in thee, and in thy holy ways, in thy grace, and in the hopes of glory, as much as I know thou art more delectable than all the pleasures of the world and sin! Oh that I had a heart that would enlargedly run the way of thy commandments, and did delight to do thy will, O God; and did still obey thee from the power of love! Oh that the new nature did more strongly incline me to thee, and to thy service, than my corrupted nature inclineth me to the interest of carnal self and sense! Oh that I had a heart to believe in Christ, as strongly as I know I should believe in him, and to hate sin as much as I am convinced that I should hate it; and to live by faith, and not by sight!

And though these desires may be but from the power of self-love, and the fears of hell, oh that I had more spiritual and sincere desires!

I have corrupted this heart, O Lord, but I cannot renew it. I have defiled it, but I cannot cleanse it. I have kindled in it the fire of sinful lusts, but I cannot quench it. I have undone myself, and rejected that Saviour, and resisted that Holy Spirit, which should have sanctified and saved me. And I have not a thought, nor a desire, a will, nor an endeavour, for my own recovery, but of thy gift. Nor shall I so much as forbear my own sin and destruction, unless thy mercy turn me or restrain me. I have none to fly to now, or in the hour of my last extremity, but that God whom I have so heinously offended! I have none to trust in but the Saviour whom I have so unthankfully neglected! I have none to regenerate and make clean my soul but the same Spirit whom I have so long resisted!

Have mercy upon me, O God, according to the greatness of thy mercy. I have sinned like a frail and foolish man; but do thou have mercy on me, as a gracious God. As my sin hath abounded, let thy grace much more abound. When I hear of the wonderful design of thy love in saving lost sinners by Jesus Christ, and at what a rate he hath redeemed souls, it reviveth my hope, and fainting heart! When I think, that it is not the way of thy providence to bring men by innocency to heaven, but by healing and recovering grace; and that all men's souls, save Christ's, that are now in heaven, were once sinners on earth, as I now am: and that thou hast glorified none, but such as were first condemned by thy law, and had deserved everlasting death; it imboldeneth me to hope for mercy and salvation. Create in me a clean heart, O God, and renew a right spirit within me. I am dead in sin, and almost past feeling! O when wilt thou quicken me, and cure my stupidity! I have a heart as hard as stone itself; it feeleth not sin: it feareth not thy judgments as it ought: it relisheth not aright thy mercy: it trembleth not to think of death, and hell, though I have no assurance to be thence one day. O when wilt thou turn this stone into a new and tender heart! I have a presumptuous and self-flattering heart, that will hardly fear what it would not feel. I have a careless, sottish heart, which little regardeth the things of everlasting consequence; as if it cared not where I dwell for ever. O when wilt thou give me a necessary care of my own salvation! The spirit of slumber hath seized on me! I see my sins, and cannot forbear them! I see my duty, and have not a heart to do it! I see my danger, and yet run upon it! I foresee the dreadful awakening day of death and judgment, when the most senseless sinners shall feel and fear: and yet I have not a heart to stir, and cry for grace, and strive as for the life of a miserable soul, nor fly to Christ, and improve the day of my visitation. I know that this is the accepted time, and this is the day of salvation! and that all that ever must be done for heaven, must be quickly done! I know that I must now be saved from sin, or else I shall never be saved from hell! And yet, alas, my slumbering, senseless soul awaketh not! I see time is swiftly posting away, my glass is almost run out: the frailties of my decaying, corruptible flesh are daily warning me to prepare! But I cannot; I cannot, alas! Lord, I cannot! There is not a heart in me to believe and feel, and to set on duty, and to do my part. My time is going! O precious time! It is going, Lord, and almost gone! Many that have gone to the grave before me have been my warnings! I have but a few breaths more to breathe, and I am gone from hence for ever; and yet, alas! my work is undone! my soul is unready! If I die this night, oh where shall I awake, and where must I take up my endless dwelling! It is thy wonderful mercy which hath kept me alive and from hell so long! The time that is past will never return! It is in vain to call it back. When I am once gone hence, there is no returning to live better or die better, and make a better preparation for eternity. It must be now or never: and yet my senseless, sluggish soul scarce feeleth or stirreth at all this. O thou that art the living God, and raisedst Jesus Christ from the dead, revive and raise this stupid soul. Lord Jesus, raise me by thy quickening Spirit, which hath raised millions that were dead in sin. O speak effectually that word of life, Awake thou that sleepest, and stand up from the dead, and Christ shall give thee light. Awake me by thy grace, lest the thunder of thy wrath and the fire of hell too late awake me!

And, Lord, I have a dark, an ignorant, a prejudiced, and an unbelieving heart. It staggereth at thy word; it questioneth the Scriptures; it looketh strangely upon Christ himself; it looketh doubtingly and amazedly towards the world to come. I am so captivated in flesh, and used to live by sight and sense, that I can scarce believe or apprehend the things unseen, though thou hast revealed them with certain evidence. Oh for one beam of thy heavenly illumination! Pity a dark and unbelieving soul! Alas, if unbelief prevail, Christ will be as no Christ to me, and the promise as no promise, and heaven as no heaven. O, heal this evil heart of unbelief, which hath neglected Christ, his sacrifice, merits, doctrine, example, his covenant, and his intercession, and hath departed from the living God. A promise is left us of entering into rest; O let me not fall short by unbelief! Let me be taught, by the inward light of thy Spirit, to understand the light of thy holy word, and leave me not in the power of the prince of darkness.

And, Lord, my will is as sinful as my mind. It is biassed by sense, and followeth the rage of lust and appetite. O how little is it inclined to thee, and to heaven, and to any holy work! I can love my flesh, I can love my food, and ease, and wealth, I can love my friend; yea, wretch that I am, I can love my sin, my brutish, God-provoking sin. But oh that I could say, I love my Saviour, and love my God, and love the place of glorious perfection above all these! O touch this heart with the loadstone of thy love! O kindle in it this heavenly fire! Nothing will do it but the holy Spirit of love, working with the revelation of thy wonderful love in Jesus Christ. Hold the eye of my soul upon my Saviour; upon my humbled, crucified Saviour; upon my ascended, glorified, interceding Saviour! And let me never cease gazing on this glass of love, and hearing this heavenly messenger of thy love, till thy blessed co-operating Spirit of love have turned my heart into love itself; even into that love which is the living image of thy love. And then, in Christ, I shall be lovely to thee.

As ever thou hadst mercy on a miserable sinner, have mercy on me, and renew this soul! Of all mercies in the world, O give me thy Holy Spirit, through the mediation of my dear Redeemer! even the Spirit of life, and light, and love. And let this be Christ's advocate and witness in me, and the witness, earnest, and pledge of my salvation. Of all plagues, O save me from the plague of a heart forsaken by thy Spirit, and left in death, and darkness, and disaffection! Is it not thy will that I should pray for grace? Hast thou not said, that thou wilt give thy Holy Spirit to them that ask it? I hope it is not without thy Spirit that I beg thy Spirit, though I know not whether it be his common or special grace. Had I asked for riches, and honours, and the pleasures of sin, no wonder if my prayer had been denied, or granted with a curse. But wilt thou deny me the grace which thou hast bid me ask? the holiness which thou lovest? without which I cannot love or serve thee, but shall serve thine enemy to my own destruction? O thou that hast sworn that thou hast not pleasure in the death of the wicked, but that he turn and live, have mercy upon me; sanctify this sinful, miserable soul, that I may live in the fruitful and delightful exercise of thy grace unto thy glory here, and may live in the delights of thy glorious love for evermore, through the merits and intercession of my blessed Saviour, who hath encouraged me with the publican to hang down this ashamed face, and smite upon this guilty breast, and in hope through his name to cry unto thee, "God be merciful to me a sinner!" Amen, Amen.

VII. *A Confession and Prayer for a penitent Sinner.*

O most great, most wise, and gracious God, though thou hatest all the workers of iniquity, and canst not be reconciled unto sin; yet, through the mediation of thy blessed Son, with pity behold this miserable sinner, who casteth himself down at the footstool of thy grace. Had I lived to those high and holy ends for which I was created and redeemed, I might now have come to thee with the boldness and confidence of a child, in assurance of thy love and favour. But I have played the fool and the rebel against thee. I have wilfully forgotten the God that made me, and the Saviour that redeemed me, and the endless glory which thou didst set before me. I forgot the business which I was sent for into the world, and have lived as if I had been made for nothing but to pass a few days in fleshly pleasure and pamper a carcass for the worms. I wilfully forgot what it is to be a man, who hath reason given him to rule his flesh, and to know his God, and to foresee his death, and the state of immortality. And I made my reason a servant to my senses, and lived too like the beasts that perish. Oh the precious time which I have lost, which all the world cannot call back! Oh the calls of grace which I have neglected; and the teachings of God which I have resisted; the wonderful love which I unthankfully rejected, and the manifold mercies which I have abused, and turned into wantonness and sin! How deep is the guilt which I have contracted, and how great are the comforts which I have lost! I might have lived all this while in the love of thee, my gracious God, and in the delights of thy holy word and ways; in the daily sweet foresight of heaven, and in the joy of the Holy Ghost; if I would have been ruled by thy righteous laws. But I have hearkened to the flesh, and to this wicked and deceitful world; and have preferred a short and sinful life before thy love and endless glory.

Alas! what have I been doing since I came into the world? Folly and sin have taken up my time. I am ashamed to look back upon the years which I have spent, and to think of the temptations which I have yielded to. Alas! what trifles have enticed me from my God! How little have I had for the holy pleasures which I have lost! Like Esau, I have profanely sold my birthright for one morsel. To please my fancy, my appetite, and my lust, I have set light by all the joys of heaven: I have unkindly despised the goodness of my Maker; I have slighted the love and grace of my Redeemer: I have resisted thy Holy Spirit, silenced my own conscience, and grieved thy ministers and my most faithful friends, and have brought myself into this woeful case, wherein I am a shame and burden to myself, and God is my terror, who should be my only hope and joy.

Thou knowest my secret sins, which are unknown to men.: thou knowest all their aggravations. My sins, O Lord, have found me out; my fears and sorrows overwhelm me. If I look behind me, I see my wickedness pursue my soul, as an army ready to overtake me and devour me: if I look before me, I see thy just and dreadful judgment, and I know that thou wilt not acquit the guilty: if I look within me, I see a dark, defiled heart: if I look without me, I see a world still offering fresh temptations to deceive me: if I look above me, I see thine offended, dreadful Majesty: and if I look beneath me, I see the place of endless torment, and the company with which I deserve to suffer. I am afraid to live, and more afraid to die.

But yet when I look to thine abundant mercy, and to thy Son, and to thy covenant, I have hope. Thy goodness is equal to thy greatness. Thou art love itself, and thy mercy is over all thy works. So wonderfully hath thy Son condescended unto sinners, and done and suffered so much for their salvation, that if yet I should question thy willingness to forgive, I should but add to all my sins, by dishonouring that matchless mercy which thou dost design to glorify. Yea, more: I find upon record in thy word, that through Christ thou hast made a covenant of grace, an act of oblivion, in which thou hast already conditionally, but freely, pardoned all, granting them the forgiveness of all their sins, without any exception, whenever, by unfeigned faith and repentance, they turn to thee by Jesus Christ. And thy present mercy doth increase my hope, in that thou hast not cut me off, nor utterly left me to the hardness of my heart, but showest me my sin and danger before I am past remedy.

O, therefore, behold this prostrate sinner, which, with the publican, smiteth on his breast, and is ashamed to look up towards heaven. O God, be merciful to me a sinner! I confess not only my original sin, but the follies and fury of my youth, my manifold sins of ignorance and knowledge, of negligence and wilfulness, of omission and commission, against the law of nature, and against the grace and gospel of thy Son. Forgive and save me, O my God, for thy abundant mercy, and for the sacrifice and merit of thy Son, and for the promise of forgiveness which thou hast made through him; for in these alone is all my trust. Condemn me not, who condemn myself. O thou that hast opened so precious a fountain for sin and uncleanness, wash me throughly from my wickedness, and cleanse me from my sin. Though thy justice might send me presently to hell, let thy mercy triumph in my salvation. Thou hast no pleasure in the death of sinners, but rather that they repent and live. If my repentance be not such as thou requirest, O soften this hardened, flinty heart, and give me repentance unto life. Turn me to thyself, O God of my salvation, and cause thy face to shine upon me. Create in me a clean heart, and renew a right spirit within me. Meet not this poor returning prodigal in thy wrath, but with the embracements of thy tender mercies. Cast me not away from thy presence, and sentence me not to depart from thee with the workers of iniquity: thou who didst patiently endure me when I despised thee, refuse me not now I seek unto thee, and here in the dust implore thy mercy. Thou didst convert and pardon a wicked Manasseh, and a persecuting Saul, and there are multitudes in heaven who were once thine enemies. Glorify also thy superabounding grace in the forgiveness of my abounding sins.

I ask not for liberty to sin again, but for deliverance from this sinning nature. O give me the renewing Spirit of thy Son, which may sanctify all the powers of my soul. Let me have the new and heavenly birth and nature, and the Spirit of adoption to reform me to thine image, that I may be holy as thou art holy. Illuminate me with the saving knowledge of thyself, and thy Son, Jesus Christ. O fill me with thy love, that my heart may be wholly set upon thee, and the remembrance of thee may be my chief delight. Let the freest and sweetest of my thoughts run after thee, and the freest and sweetest of my discourse be of thee, and of thy glory and kingdom, and of thy word and ways. O let my treasure be laid up in heaven, and there let me daily and delightfully converse. Make it the great and daily business of my devoted soul to please thee and to honour thee, to promote thy kingdom, and to do thy will. Put thy fear into my heart, that I may never depart from thee. This world hath had too much of my heart already. Let it now be crucified to me, and I to it, by the cross of Christ. Let me not love it, nor the things which are therein, but, having food and raiment, cause me therewith to be content. Destroy in me all fleshly lusts, that I may not walk after the flesh, but the Spirit. Keep me from the snares of wicked company, and from the counsel and ways of the ungodly. Bless me with the helpful communion of the saints, and with all the means which thou hast appointed to further our sanctification and salvation. Oh that my ways were so directed that I might keep thy statutes! Let me never return again to folly, nor forget the covenant of my God. Help me to quench the first motions of sin, and to abhor all sinful desires and thoughts; and let thy Spirit strengthen me against all temptations, that I may conquer and endure to the end. Prepare me for sufferings, and for death, and judgment, that when I must leave this sinful world, I may yield up my departing soul with joy into the faithful hands of my dear Redeemer; that I be not numbered with the ungodly who die in their unpardoned sin, and pass into everlasting misery, but may be found in Christ, having the righteousness which is of God by faith, and may attain to the resurrection of the just. That so the remembrance of the sin and miseries from which thou hast delivered me, may further my perpetual thanks and praise to thee, my Creator, my Redeemer, and my Sanctifier.

And oh that thou wouldst call and convert the miserable nations of idolaters and infidels, and the multitudes of ungodly hypocrites who have the name of christians, and not the truth, and power, and life. O send forth labourers into thy harvest, and let not Satan hinder them! Prosper thy gospel, and the kingdom of thy Son; then sinners may more abundantly be converted to thee, and this earth may be made liker unto heaven: that when thou hast gathered us all into unity in Christ, we may all with perfect love and joy ascribe to thee the kingdom, the power, and the glory, for ever and ever. Amen.

VIII. *Prayer and Praise for the Lord's Day.*

Glorious Jehovah! thou art infinitely above the praise of angels, much more of such sinful worms as we are: far be it from us to think that thou needest any thing that we can do, or that all our praise can add unto thy blessedness! But thy love and mercy hath advanced us to this honour, and made our own felicity our duty: for all that are far from thee shall perish; but it is good for us to draw near to thee. And lest the vanities and business of this world should hinder us, thou hast appointed us this thy special day, that our composed minds might be taken up with thy love and praise, and might attend upon thee without distraction, and might foretaste our everlasting rest. O be thou now to thy servants' souls the Spirit of life, the Spirit of light, and love, and power, that the heavenly life may quicken us to this holy and heavenly work; that by faith we may see thee in thy own communicated light; and that our love may rise with fervour and delight through the sweet communication of thy love; and that all within us which doth resist, may be overpowered by thy strength, which is manifested in our weakness; that so the sacrifice of our persons and of our praises, which we humbly offer at thy command, may be such as are fit for thine acceptance, through Jesus Christ.

Thou, and thou alone, art God, the immortal and invisible Spirit; eternal and infinite in being and perfections! Before the forming of the world, from everlasting to everlasting, thou art God. Thy understanding is infinite. Thou perfectly knowest thyself and all things; but art comprehended by none. Thy will is good, yea, goodness itself, and perfect love; loving thyself and all thy works. Thou art the Almighty, and nothing is too hard for thee. Thou art the Creator of all the world: thou broughtest all things out of nothing! Thou spakest the word, and they were made. Thou gavest their being to the glorious angels, and all the intellectual spirits! All the heavens were made by thee. Thou saidst, Let there be light, and there was light. Thou madest the sun and all the stars: thou gavest them their wonderful powers, and their offices; that by their light, and heat, and motion, they might be for life and action, and for times and seasons here below. How glorious art thou, O God, in these thy wondrous works! the greatness, the glory, and the virtues whereof are so far beyond our dark apprehensions. The higher spirits who better know them, and possess the high and glorious mansions, do better praise thee, the great Creator, whose word did form that noble frame, when the morning stars did sing together, and all the sons of God did shout for joy. Thou madest the earth, the land and sea, and all the creatures that dwell therein. All fowls, and fishes, beasts, and plants; in wonderful variety, beauty, and virtue hast thou made them all. The air and clouds, the thunder and lightning, rain and snow, the winds and earthquakes, the marvellous motions of the sea, are all thy great unsearchable works. The smallest worm or flower doth far surpass our knowledge. How, then, should mortals comprehend the greatness and harmonious order of the world? how thou hast founded the earth upon nothing; and what is in the depths thereof: how thou movest, and maintainest, and preservest the order of the universal frame, and causest the sweet and powerful influences of the fiery and celestial parts upon the things below: how thou shuttest up the sea with sandy doors, and makest the clouds to be its garments, and the darkness as its swaddling-bands, and sayest, Hitherto, and no further, shalt thou come. How great, O Lord, and manifold are thy works! In perfect wisdom, goodness, and power thou hast made them all.

But it is man whom thou hast made the noblest inhabitant of this lower world. Thou breathedst into his body the breath of life, and he became a living soul. Thou madest him little lower than the angels that thou mightest crown him with glory and honour. Thou gavest him dominion over the works of thy hands, and hast put all things below, as under his feet. Thou madest him in thine image, with an understanding mind, and an unforced will, and executive power, to know, and love, and serve thee, his most wise, and good, and great Creator. Thou placedst him in this lower world, that he might pass through it to the blessed presence of thy glory. Thou becamest a Father to him, being his Owner, his Ruler, and his chiefest good; even his great Benefactor, and his ultimate end; that he might live in absolute resignation, subjection, and love to thee. Thou gavest him in nature, and in thy precept, a law which was holy, just, and good, that, by following thy conduct, he might please thee, and attain to full felicity. Thou didst furnish him with all things necessary to his obedience, and oblige him thereto by the abundance of thy blessings. But he quickly fell from his innocency and honour, by turning from his God. He believed the false and envious tempter, even when he accused thee of falsehood and envy, as if all thy wondrous works and mercies had not proved thee to be true and good. Thus did man foolishly requite the Lord, and forsook the Rock of his salvation. And by one man sin entered into the world, and death by sin. But mercy rejoiced against judgment, and thou didst not let out all thy wrath; but with the sentence of death thou didst join the promise of a Redeemer. Oh that men would praise the Lord for his goodness, and for his wonderful works for the children of men!

As thou gavest the mercies of the promise to the fathers; so in the fulness of time thou didst send thy Son. He came and took our nature to his Godhead; being conceived by the Holy Ghost; made of a woman, under the law; born of a virgin. He made himself of no reputation; but took upon him the form of a servant, and was made in the likeness of man. Oh wonderful, condescending love! Angels proclaimed it; and angels admire it, and search into it, and in the church's glass they still behold the manifold wisdom of God: how low, then, should redeemed sinners fall, in the humble admirations of this grace! how high should they rise in the thankful praise of their Redeemer!

He came on earth and conversed with men, to make known to men the invisible God, and the unseen things of the world above. He came as the Light and Saviour of the world, to bring to light immortality and life. He was holy, harmless, and undefiled, separated from sinners, and fulfilling all righteousness, that he might be a meet High Priest and effectual Saviour of sinners. He taught us, by his perfect doctrine and example, to be humble and obedient, and to contemn this world; to deny ourselves, and bear the cross, that we may attain the everlasting crown of glory. He humbled himself to the false accusations and reproach of sinners, and to the shameful and bitter death of the cross, to make himself a sacrifice and propitiation for our sins, and a ransom for our guilty souls, that we might be healed by his stripes. Oh matchless love, which even for enemies, did thus lay down his precious life! He hath conquered and sanctified death and the grave to all believers. He, therefore, took part of flesh and blood, that he might by death destroy the devil that had the power of death, and deliver them who, through the fear of death, were all their lifetime subject unto bondage. He hath procured for mankind a covenant of grace, and sealed it as his testament with his blood. And now there is forgiveness with thee, that thou mightest be cheerfully feared and obeyed in hope. It was thine own love to the world, O Father, which gave thine only begotten Son, that whosoever truly believeth in him should not perish, but have everlasting life. Thou wast in Christ reconciling the world unto thyself, and not imputing their sins unto them. Thou hast committed the word of reconciliation to thy ministers, to beseech sinners, even in thy name, and in the stead of Christ, to be reconciled to thee. Thou commandest them to offer thy mercy unto all, and, by importunity, to compel them to come in, that thy house may be filled, and thy blessed feast may be furnished with guests.

Thou refusest none that come to thee by Christ. Thou deniest thy mercy to none but the obstinate and final rejecters of it. Thou givest eternal life to them who were the sons of death; and this life is in thy Son; for he is able to save to the uttermost all that come to thee by him. To as many as receive him thou givest power to become the sons of God. Thou givest them also the Spirit of thy Son, even the Spirit of adoption, to renew them to thy holy image, that they may be like their heavenly Father; to sanctify them to thyself, and by shedding abroad thy love upon their hearts, to draw up their hearts in love to thee. Thou makest them a peculiar people to thyself, and zealous of good works, for which thou dost regenerate them. Thou givest them all repentance unto life; and crucifiest their flesh, and all its lusts; thou teachest them to live soberly, righteously, and godly, and savest them from this present evil world, and mortifiest their sinful love thereof, that thou mayst have their love, and be their felicity. Oh, with what love hast thou loved poor rebellious sinners, that they should be converted and made the sons of God, yea, heirs of heaven, and co-heirs with Christ; that when we have suffered with him, we may also be glorified with him!

Thou dost build thy church upon the Rock, the blessed Mediator; that the power of hell may not prevail against it. Thou hast made him its Teacher, Priest, and King: of him we learn to know thee and thy will. By him we have our peace, our acceptance, and access to thee. He is the Lord, both of the dead and living. Thou hast delivered all things into his hands, and made him Head over all things to the church. When he ascended up on high he appointed his ministers to gather, and order, and edify this universal church, which is his body. He gave his apostles the infallible Spirit, to lead them into all truth; and the Spirit of power, to be his witness, by miracles, to the world. They have taught us all things whatsoever he commanded them, and committed that doctrine in the sacred Scriptures to those pastors and teachers whom thou hast appointed to preserve and preach it, and to feed thy flock to the end of the world: and though sin, alas, hath woefully defiled, and schism divided, these thy churches, yet art thou still amongst them, and bearest with their infirmities, and givest them thine oracles, and callest them to holiness, love, and peace, and knowest thy wheat among the chaff.

Oh that men would praise the Lord for his goodness, and for his wondrous works for the children of men! How glorious art thou, O Lord, in holiness, to be reverenced in the assemblies of the saints, and honoured of all that are about thee! Holiness becometh thy house for ever: in thy temple shall every man speak of thy glory. We bless thy name, O our great Creator; we bless thy name, our gracious Redeemer; we bless thy name, most Holy Spirit. Oh that our souls could, with greater thankfulness, magnify the Lord, and our spirits rejoice in God our Saviour! who hath pitied us in our lost estate; for thy mercy endureth for ever. We thank thee for our being; we thank thee that thou hast redeemed us from sin and hell; we thank thee that thou hast brought us, by baptism, into thy covenant and church. We thank thee for these high and sacred privileges, that we are not foreigners or strangers among the heathen and infidel world, but fellow-citizens with the saints, and of the household of God; that we may stand in the presence of thy holiness, and praise thee in the assemblies of believers, and are not banished from these sacred societies and works. A day in thy courts is better than a thousand. We had rather be door-keepers in the house of God, than to dwell in the palaces of wickedness. Blessed are they that know the joyful sound, and fruitfully live under the dews of heaven. They shall walk, O Lord, in the light of thy countenance; in thy name shall they rejoice all the day, and in thy righteousness shall they be exalted: for thou art their glory and their strength; and in thy favour they shall be safe, and glad, and great.

But especially those whom thou hast brought into the invisible church of the regenerate can never sufficiently magnify thy grace. When we lived as without thee in the world, and never sincerely loved or desired thee, but followed our fleshly lusts, and the deceitful vanities of the world; when God was not in all our thoughts, and we had no pleasure in thy holy ways; when we despised grace, and resisted thy Spirit, and went on adding sin to sin; then didst thou pity us in our blood. Thou sentest us thy word; thou madest it powerful on our hardened hearts; thou broughtest us to consider of our state and ways, and gavest us some relenting and contrition. It is comfortable to us to review the stirrings and victories of thy grace, the meltings of thy mercy, and the comforts of thy love. When we feared lest our sins would have been our damnation, and that thou wouldst never receive such wretched rebels, how freely didst thou pardon all! how graciously didst thou embrace us; delighting to show mercy, and overcoming our hearts with the greatness of thy love! Oh how many sins didst thou forgive! what work had thy Spirit to do upon these ignorant, proud, and selfish minds; upon these carnal, worldly, disobedient hearts! how many mercies, preservations, comforts, hast thou since that time vouchsafed to us; how many desires hast thou first given us, and then accepted from us; how many afflictions hast thou shortened or sanctified; how many joyful or profitable hours have we had with thee alone in secret, and with thee and thy people in the communion of saints! Many, O Lord, are thy wondrous works, and thy thoughts of mercy towards thy servants; if we would reckon them in order, and declare them before thee, they are more than can be numbered. And after all these, as priests to God, we are here to offer thee the sacrifice of praise; rejoicing in thee, our portion and salvation.

And when this short and troublesome life is ended, we have thy promise that we shall rest with thee for ever. If in this life only we had hope, we should be of all men most miserable. But thou wilt conduct us through this wilderness, and guide us by thy counsel, and bring us in season to thy glory. For thou hast not given us these faculties to see thee, and know thee, and love thee, and delight in thee in vain: thou wilt surely perfect nature and grace, and cause them to attain their end. The great undertaking, work, and sufferings of our Redeemer, shall not be in vain. Thy sealed promise shall not be broken. Thy Spirit hath not in vain renewed us, and sealed us to that blessed day; nor shall thy pledge, and earnest, and witness within us, prove deceits. These desires and groans shall not be lost; and these weak beginnings of light and love, do foreshow our full fruition and perfection. This seed of grace portendeth glory; and the foretastes of love do tell us that we shall be happy in thy love for ever. Our hope in thy goodness, thy Son, and thy covenant, will never leave us frustrate and ashamed.

We therefore bless thy name, O Lord, as those that are redeemed from death and hell; as those who are advanced to the dignity of sons; as those whom thou savest from all their enemies, but especially from ourselves, and from our sins! We bless thy name, as those who are entering into glory; and hope to be with Christ for ever; where sin and sorrow, enemies and fears, shall be shut out, and shall molest our souls no more for ever.

We foresee, by faith, that happy day. We see, by faith, the new Jerusalem; the innumerable angels; the perfect spirits of the just; their glorious light; their flaming love; their perfect harmony. We hear, by faith, their joyful songs of thanks and praise. Lately they were as low and sad as we; in sins and sorrows, in manifold weaknesses, sufferings, and fears; but by faith and patience they have overcome; and in faith and patience we desire to follow our Lord and them. The time is near; this flesh will quickly turn to dust, and our delivered souls shall come to thee: our life is short, and our sins and sorrows will be short; then we shall have light: we shall no more groan, and cry out in darkness, Oh that we could know the Lord! then shall we love thee with pure, unmixed, perfect love; and need no more to groan and cry, Oh that our souls were inflamed with thy love! then shall we praise thee with thankful alacrity and joy, which will exceed our present apprehensions and desires.

O blessed streams of light and love, which will flow from thy opened, glorious face, upon our souls for ever! How far will that everlasting sabbath, and those perfect praises, excel these poor and dull endeavours, as far as that triumphant city of God excelleth this imperfect, childish, discomposed church.

Quicken, Lord, our longing for that blessed state and day! O come, Lord Jesus, come quickly, and fulfil thy word, that we may be with thee where thou art, and may behold thy glory! Stay not till faith shall fail from the earth. Stay not till the powers of darkness conquer all the remnant of thine inheritance, and make this world yet like unto hell; nor till the godly cease, and the faithful fail, from among the children of men! O when shall the world acknowledge their great Creator and Redeemer, and abhor their idols, and cease from their unbelief? When shall the rest of the heathens and infidels be thy Son's inheritance, and the kingdoms of the world become his kingdom? O when shall heaven be made the pattern of this earth, and men delight to do thy will? When shall the proud, the worldly, and the sensual, renounce their deceits, and walk humbly and holily with their God; and the fool, whose heart denieth the Lord, and calleth not upon thee, but eateth up thy people as bread, return unto thee, and fear thy name, and fight no more against his Maker? Hasten, O Lord, the salvation of thy people, and keep them in uprightness and patience to the end. Have mercy upon all the ignorant and unreformed churches in the world: deliver them from the eastern and western tyranny, which keepeth out the means of knowledge and reformation, and restore them to the primitive purity, simplicity, and unity, that their light may shine forth, to the winning of the heathen and infidel world, whom now their pollutions drive from Christ. Preserve and repair the churches which are reformed, and revive among them knowledge, holiness, and peace. Bless these kingdoms with the light and power of the gospel, and with peace. O bless the queen, and all in authority, with the wisdom, holiness, and prosperity, which are needful to their own and the common good; and keep the subjects in their duty to thee and their superiors, that we may live a quiet and peaceable life, in all godliness and honesty. Let all the congregations be blessed with burning, shining lights; and let the buyers and sellers be cast out of thy temple; and let not the malice of Satan, or the sacrilege of men, be able to hinder the gospel of thy kingdom, nor alienate thy devoted, faithful labourers from thy harvest work.

Give us the necessaries of this present life, and a contented mind with what thou givest us; and kill in us our worldly love, and fleshly lusts.

Teach us to live daily by faith on our Redeemer: and by him let us have continual access to thee; and the daily pardon of our daily sins; and a heart to love and pardon others.

O save us from all the suggestions of Satan, and from the snares of this world, and the allurements of sinners, and from all the corrupt inclinations of the flesh; and give us not up to sin, nor to our own concupiscence, nor to the malice of Satan or ungodly men, nor to any destructive punishment which our sin deserves.

O teach us to know the work of life, and the preciousness of our short and hasty time, and to use it as will most comfort us at our last review. Teach us so to number our days that we may apply our hearts to wisdom, and not like fools, to waste in vain those precious hours on which eternity dependeth, and which all the world cannot call back. Let us do thy work with all our might, especially in our particular callings and relations. Let us make our calling and election sure, and spend our days in the delightful exercise of faith, hope, and love. Keep us still watchful, and in a continual readiness for death and judgment, and longing for the coming of our Lord. Let our hearts and conversations be in heaven, from whence we look for our glorious Redeemer; in whose words we sum up all our prayers.

Our Father which art in heaven, hallowed be thy name. Thy kingdom come. Thy will be done on earth, as it is in heaven. Give us this day our daily bread; and forgive us our trespasses, as we forgive them that trespass against us. And lead us not into temptation; but deliver us from evil: for thine is the kingdom, the power, and the glory, for ever. Amen.

A shorter Form of Praise and Prayer for the Lord's Day.

Glorious Jehovah! while angels and perfected spirits are praising thee in the presence of thy glory, thou hast allowed and commanded us to take our part in the presence of thy grace. We have the same most holy God to praise; and though we see thee not, our Head and Saviour seeth thee, and our faith discerneth thee in the glass of thy holy works and word. Though we are sinners, and unworthy, and cannot touch these holy things without the marks of our pollution, yet have we a great High Priest with thee, who was separate from sinners, holy, harmless, and undefiled, who appeareth for us in the merits of his spotless life and sacrifice, and by whose hands only we dare presume to present a sacrifice to the most holy God; and thou hast ordained this day of holy rest as a type and means of that heavenly rest with thy triumphant church, to which we aspire, and for which we hope. Thou didst accept their lower praise on earth, before they celebrated thy praise in glory. Accept ours also by the same Mediator.

Glory be to thee, O God, in the highest; on earth peace; good-will towards men. Holy, holy, holy Lord God Almighty, who wast and art to come; eternal, without beginning or end; immense, without all bounds or measure; the infinite Spirit, Father, Word, and Holy Ghost; the infinite life, understanding, and will, infinitely powerful, wise, and good: of thee, and through thee, and to thee, are all things; to thee be glory for evermore. All thy works declare thy glory, for thy glorious perfections appear on all; and for thy glory, and the pleasure of thy holy will, didst thou create them. The heavens, and all the hosts thereof; the sun, and all the glorious stars; the fire, with its motion, light, and heat; the earth, and all that dwell thereon, with all its sweet and beauteous ornaments; the air, and all the meteors; the great deeps, and all that swim therein: all are the preachers of thy praise, and show forth the great Creator's glory. How great is that power which made so great a world of nothing; which, with wonderful swiftness, moveth those great and glorious luminaries which in a moment send forth the influences of their motion, light, and heat, through all the air, to sea and earth. Thy powerful life giveth life to all; and preserveth this frame of nature, which thou hast made. How glorious is that wisdom, which ordereth all things, and assigneth to all their place and office, and by its perfect laws maintaineth the beauty and harmony of all! How glorious is that goodness and love, which made all good, and very good!

We praise and glorify thee, our Lord and Owner; for we, and all things, are thine own. We praise and glorify thee, our King and Ruler; for we are thy subjects, and our perfect obedience is thy due. Just are all thy laws and judgments; true and sure is all thy word. We praise and glorify thee, our great Benefactor; in thee we live, and move, and are: all that we are, or have, or can do, is wholly from thee, the cause of all; and all is for thee, for thou art our end. Delightfully to love thee is our greatest duty, and our only felicity; for thou art love itself, and infinitely amiable.

When man, by sin, did turn away his heart from thee, believed the tempter against thy truth, obeyed his sense against thy authority and wisdom, and forsaking thy fatherly love and goodness, became an idol to himself; thou didst not use him according to his desert. When we forsook thee, thou didst not utterly forsake us. When we had lost ourselves, and, by sin, became thine enemies, condemned by thy law, thy mercy pitied us, and gave us the promise of a Redeemer, who in the fulness of time did assume our nature, fulfilled thy law, and suffered for our sins, and, conquering death, did rise again, ascended to heaven, and is our glorified Head and Intercessor. Him hast thou exalted to be a Prince and Saviour, to give us repentance and remission of sins. In him thou hast given pardon and justification, reconciliation and adoption, by a covenant of grace, to every penitent believer. Of enemies and the heirs of death, thou hast made us sons and heirs of life.

We are the brands whom thou hast plucked out of the fire; we are the captives of Satan, whom thou hast pardoned! We praise thee, we glorify thee, our merciful God and gracious Redeemer! Our souls have now refuge from thy revenging wrath. Thy promise is sure; Satan, and the world, and death, are overcome; our Lord is risen; he is risen, and we shall rise through him. O death! where is thy sting? O grave! where is thy victory? Our Saviour is ascended to his Father and our Father, to his God and our God, and we shall ascend! To his hands we may commit our departing souls! Our Head is glorified, and it is his will and promise that we shall be with him where he is, to see his glory. He hath sealed us thereunto by his Holy Spirit. We were dead in sins, and he hath quickened us. We were dark in ignorance and unbelief, and he hath enlightened us. We were unholy and carnal, sold under sin, and he hath sanctified our wills, and killed our concupiscence. We praise and glorify this Spirit of life, with the Father and the Son, from whom he is sent, to be life, and light, and love to our dead, and dark, and disaffected souls. We are created, redeemed, and sanctified, for thy holy love, and praise, and service: O let these be the very nature of our souls, and the employment and pleasure of all our lives! O perfect thy weak and languid graces in us, that our love and praise may be more perfect! We thank thee for thy word and sacred ordinances; for the comfort of the holy assemblies, and communion of the saints, and for the mercy of these thy holy days. But let not thy praise be here confined, but be our daily life, and breath, and work.

Fain we would praise thee with more holy and more joyful souls! But how can we do it with so weak a faith, and so great darkness and strangeness to thee; with so little assurance of thy favour and our salvation? Can we rightly thank thee for the grace which we are still in doubt of? Fain we would be liker to those blessed souls who praise thee without our fears and dulness. But how can it be, while we love thee so little, and have so little taste and feeling of thy love; and whilst this load of sin doth press us down, and we are imprisoned in the remnant of our carnal affections? O kill this pride and selfishness, these lusts and passions! Destroy this unbelief and darkness, and all our sins, which are the enemies of us, and of thy praise. Make us more holy and more heavenly; and O bring us nearer thee in faith and love, that we may be more suitable to the heavenly employment of thy praise!

Vouchsafe more of thy Spirit to all thy churches and servants in the world; that as their darkness, and selfishness, and imperfections, have defiled, and divided, and weakened them, and made them a scandal and hardening to infidels, so their knowledge, self-denial, and impartial love, may truly reform, unite, and strengthen them; that the glory of their holiness may win the unbelieving world to Christ. O let not Satan keep up still so large a kingdom of tyranny, ignorance, and wickedness in the earth, and make this world as the suburbs of hell. But let the earth be more conformable to heaven in the glorifying of thy holy name, the advancing of thy kingdom, and the doing of thy just and holy will. Let thy way be known upon earth, and thy saving health among all nations. Let the people praise thee, O God, let all the people praise thee! Yea, give thy Son the heathen for his inheritance, and let his gospel enlighten the dark, forsaken nations of the earth. Let every knee bow to him, and every tongue confess that he is Christ, to their salvation and thy glory. Provide and send forth the messengers of thy grace through all the earth. Deliver all the churches from sin, division, and oppression. Let thy holy word and worship continue in these kingdoms, whilst this world endureth. Bless the queen, and all in authority, with all that wisdom, justice, and holiness, which are needful to her own and her subjects' safety, peace, and welfare. Let every congregation among us have burning and shining lights, that the ignorant and ungodly perish not for want of teaching and exhortation. And open men's hearts to receive thy word, and cause them to know the day of their visitation. Be merciful to the afflicted in sickness, dangers, wants, or sorrows, according to thy goodness and their necessities. Let all the prayers and praises of the faithful throughout the world, sent up this day in the name of our common Mediator, by him be presented acceptable unto thee, notwithstanding the imperfections and blemishes that are on them, and the censures, divisions, and injuries, which in their frowardness they are guilty of against each other! Let them centre as one in Christ, our Head, who are too sadly and stiffly distant among themselves. Prepare us all for that world of peace where the harmony of universal love and praise shall never be interrupted by sins, or griefs, or fears, or discord, but shall be everlastingly perfect, to our joy and to thy glory, through our glorified Mediator; who taught us when we pray to say, Our Father which art in heaven, hallowed be thy name. Thy kingdom come. Thy will be done on earth, as it is in heaven. Give us this day our daily bread. And forgive us our trespasses, as we forgive them that trespass against us. And lead us not into temptation; but deliver us from evil. For thine is the kingdom, the power, and the glory, for ever. Amen.

IX. *A Form of Prayer for the Sick, who are unready to die.*

Merciful God, reject not this sad, unworthy sinner, who in pain and sorrow fleeth to thy grace in Jesus Christ! Though I have trifled away too much of the day of my salvation, and sinfully neglected thy Son, and his saving grace; O say not that it is now too late, for thy promise through Christ is large and free, forgiving all without exception, who in the time of this life are penitent believers. Oh that I had better found out my sin, before it found me out; and that it had been more my grief before it was so much my pain; and that I had better known the evil of it by thy word and grace, before my flesh and bones had felt it! But pity my misery, and forgive my sin, through the propitiation which thy mercy hath provided and accepted. Remember not the iniquities of my youth, nor the sins which I have since committed against thy great and manifold mercies, the motions of thy Spirit, and the reproofs of my own conscience. I have sinned foolishly as a man, but do thou forgive me mercifully as a gracious God. If the suffering of my flesh do seem so grievous, how should I bear thy burning wrath for ever on my soul? O give me true repentance unto life! Let not pain and fear only make me purpose to amend, but let thy Spirit of grace renew my soul, by the powerful sense of thy love in Christ. Let this be the fruit of my affliction, through his grace, to purge and take away my sin, and to make me partaker of thy holiness. And have mercy on this weak and pained flesh. O spare a little, and give me space to make a better preparation for my change, before I go hence, and am seen no more! O let not my fearful soul appear before thee, the holy, dreadful God, in an unpardoned or unrenewed state! Renew my time, and renew my soul, that I may live to thee, before I die. I have abused thy long-suffering: I have forfeited both health, and life, and hope: I have foolishly and sinfully lost many an hour of precious time, which never can be called back! I foresaw this day, and was oft forewarned of it by thy servants and by my conscience, but I took not warning, and now, alas! how unready is my soul to appear before thee! My sins affright me; thy justice and holiness affright me; eternity, eternity doth amaze my soul. I have no assurance to escape thy wrath and everlasting misery! I have not set my heart on heaven, nor lived in a heavenly conversation, as to desire to depart that I may be with Christ, and to come with boldness and comfortable hope before the Judge of all the world; forgive my sin through the sacrifice and intercession of my Redeemer. O try me once more with opportunities and means of grace! Return, O Lord, deliver my soul! O save me for thy mercies' sake. Kill me not till my sin be killed. End not this life till thou hast prepared me for a better. Though it be a life of vanity and vexation, it is all the space that ever I shall have to prepare for the endless life which followeth. Cut not off my time till I am ready for eternity. Let me not die in my sins, nor fall into the hands of thy revenging justice. I condemn myself; do not thou condemn me. If thou wilt renew my days, it is the resolution of my soul to hearken to thy Spirit, to obey my Saviour, to study thy wondrous love in Christ, to seek the things that are above with him, and to forsake my sin, and live to thee: but because I know that without thy grace I cannot do it, O give me yet both time and grace! Or, if thou wilt try me no longer here on earth, now, Lord, before my soul departeth, sanctify it by thy Spirit, and wash it in the blood of Jesus Christ, and shed abroad thy love upon it, and give me such a sight of the heavenly glory, that in the lively exercise of faith, hope, and love, my soul may willingly forsake this world, and come to thee. Though I have departed from thee, and delighted not to know thee, refuse not to know me, and bid me not depart with workers of iniquity. And if this be all the time that ever I shall have, to beg thy saving grace and mercy, though it be short, let it be an accepted time. Have mercy, mercy, mercy, Lord, upon a sinful, undone soul, and let me not be the firebrand of thy hot displeasure. Now glorify thy grace in Jesus Christ, who is an all-sufficient Saviour, to whom I fly, and on whom I cast my miserable soul. Merciful Saviour, receive it as thine own! Refuse it not as unworthy, but for thy worthiness justify it, and let thy Spirit now renew it, and let thy grace abound where my sin aboundeth. It is thy promise, that him that cometh unto thee thou wilt in no wise cast out. Let this enemy by thee be reconciled to the Father, and adopted as a son and heir of life, and present me spotless and acceptable to God. Whether I live or die, I desire to be thine: and though I have broken my covenant with thee, I here again renew it. I give up myself to thee, my reconciled God and Father, my Saviour and my Sanctifier. Accept me, and assure me of the blessings of thy covenant. And then, though I deserve to dwell with devils, I shall see thy glory, and be filled with thy love, and with saints and angels shall joyfully praise my Creator, Redeemer, and Sanctifier for ever. Amen, Amen.

X. *A Prayer for the Faithful before Death, is the end of the ninth day's Conference.*

A short Prayer for Children and Servants.

Ever-living and most glorious God, Father, Son, and Holy Ghost. Infinite is thy power, thy wisdom, and thy goodness. Thou art the Maker of all the world, the Redeemer of lost and sinful man, and the Sanctifier of the elect. Thou hast made me a living, reasonable soul, placed a while in this flesh and world to know, and love, and serve thee my Creator, with all my heart, and mind, and strength; that I might obtain the reward of the heavenly glory. This should have been the greatest care, and business, and pleasure of all my life. I was bound to it by thy law: I was invited by thy mercy: and, in my baptism, I was devoted to this holy life, by a solemn covenant and vow. But, alas! I have proved too unfaithful to that covenant; I have forgotten and neglected the God, the Saviour, and the Sanctifier, to whom I was engaged, and have too much served the devil, the world, and the flesh, which I renounced. I was born in sin, and sinfully I have lived: I have been too careless of my immortal soul, and of the great work for which I was created and redeemed: I have spent much of my precious time in vanity, in minding and pleasing this corruptible flesh. And I have hardened my heart against those instructions, by which thy Spirit, and my teachers, and my own conscience, did call upon me to repent and turn to thee.

And now, O Lord, my convinced soul doth confess that I have deserved to be forsaken by thee, and given over to my lust and folly, and to be cast out of thy glorious presence into damnation. But seeing thou hast given a Saviour to the world, and made a pardoning and gracious law, promising forgiveness and salvation through his merits, to every true penitent believer, I thankfully accept the mercy of thy covenant in Christ: I humbly confess my sin and guiltiness: I cast my miserable soul upon thy grace, and the merits, and sacrifice, and intercession of my Saviour. O, pardon all the sins of my corrupted heart and life; and, as a reconciled Father, take me to be thy child: and give me thy renewing Spirit, to be in me a principle of holy life, and light, and love, and thy seal and witness that I am thine. Let him quicken my dead and hardened heart: let him enlighten my dark, unbelieving mind, by clearer knowledge and firm belief: let him turn my will to the ready obedience of thy holy will: let him reveal to my soul the wonders of thy love in Christ, and fill it with love to thee and my Redeemer, and to all thy holy word and works; till all my sinful carnal love be quenched in me, and my sinful pleasures turned into a sweet delight in God. Give me self-denial, humility, and lowliness, and save me from the great and hateful sins of selfishness, worldliness, and pride. O set my heart upon the heavenly glory, where I hope, ere long, to live with Christ, and all his holy ones, in the joyful sight, and love, and praise of thee the God of love for ever. Deny me not any of those helps and mercies which are needful to my sanctification and salvation. And cause me to live in a continual readiness for a safe and comfortable death: for what would it profit me to win all the world, and lose my soul, my Saviour, and my God?

Additions for Children.

Let thy blessings be upon my parents and governors: cause them to instruct and educate me in thy fear, and cause me with thankfulness to receive their instructions; and to love, honour, and obey them, in obedience to thee. Keep me from the snares of evil company, temptations, and youthful pleasures; and let me be a companion of them that fear thee. Let my daily delight be to meditate on thy law; and let me never have the mark of the ungodly, to be a lover of pleasures more than of God. Furnish my youth with those treasures of wisdom and holiness, which may be daily increased and used to thy glory.

Additions for Servants.

And as thou hast made me a servant, make me conscionable and faithful in my place and trust, and careful of my master's goods and business, as I would be if it were my own. Make me submissive and obedient to my governors; keep me from self-will and pride, from murmuring and irreverent speeches, from falsehood, slothfulness, and all deceit; that I may not be an eye-servant, pleasing my lust and fleshly appetite; but may cheerfully and willingly do my duty, as believing that thou art the revenger of all unfaithfulness; and may do my service not only as unto man, but as to the Lord; expecting from thee my chief reward.

All this I beg and hope for, on the account of the merits and intercession of Jesus Christ, concluding in the words which he hath taught us;—Our Father which art in heaven, hallowed be thy name. Thy kingdom come. Thy will be done on earth, as it is in heaven. Give us this day our daily bread. And forgive us our trespasses, as we forgive them that trespass against us. And lead us not into temptation; but deliver us from evil. For thine is the kingdom, the power, and the glory, for ever. Amen.

A plain and short Prayer for Families for Morning and Evening.

Almighty, all-seeing, and most gracious God! the world and all therein is made, maintained, and ordered by thee. Thou art every where present, being more than the soul of all the world. Though thou art revealed in thy glory to those only that are in heaven, thy grace is still at work on earth to prepare men for that glory. Thou madest us not as the beasts that perish, but with reasonable, immortal souls, to know, and seek, and serve thee here, and then to live, with all the blessed, in the everlasting sight of thy heavenly glory, and the pleasures of thy perfect love and praise. But we are ashamed to think how foolishly and sinfully we have forgotten and neglected our God and our souls, and our hopes of blessed immortality; and have over-much minded the things of this visible, transitory world, and the prosperity and pleasure of this corruptible flesh, which we know must turn to rottenness and dust.

Thou gavest us a law which was just and good, to guide us in the only way to life; and when by sin we had undone ourselves, thou gavest us a Saviour, even thy eternal Word made man, who by his holy life and bitter sufferings reconciled us to thee, and both purchased salvation for us, and revealed it to us, better than an angel from heaven could have done, if thou hadst sent him to us sinners on such a message. But, alas! how light have we set by our Redeemer, and by all that love which thou hast manifested by him, and how little have we studied, and understood, and less obeyed that covenant of grace which thou hast made by him to lost mankind.

But, O God, be merciful to us, vile and miserable sinners! Forgive the sins of our natural pravity, and the follies of our youth, and all the ignorance, negligence, omissions, and commissions of our lives; and give us true repentance for them, or else we know that thou wilt not forgive them. Our life is but as a shadow that passeth away; and it is but as a moment till we must leave this world, and appear before thee to give up our account, and to speed for ever as here we have prepared. Should we die before thou hast turned our hearts from this sinful flesh and world to thee by true faith and repentance, we shall be lost for evermore. Oh, woe to us, that ever we were born, if thou forgive not our sins, and make us not holy, before this short, uncertain life be at an end! Had we all the riches and pleasures of this world, they would shortly leave us in the greater sorrows. We know that all our life is but the time which thy mercy allotteth us to prepare for death; therefore we should not put off our repentance and preparation to a sick bed. But now, Lord, as if it were our last and dying words, we earnestly beg thy pardoning and sanctifying grace, through the merits and intercession of our Redeemer. O thou that hast pitied and saved so many millions of miserable sinners, pity and save us also, that we may glorify thy grace for ever; surely thou delightest not in the death of sinners, but rather that they return and live: hadst thou been unwilling to show mercy, thou wouldst not have ransomed us by so precious a price, and still entreat us to be reconciled unto thee. We have no cause to distrust thy truth or goodness; but we are afraid lest unbelief, and pride, and hypocrisy, and a worldly, fleshly mind, should be our ruin. O save us from Satan and this tempting world, but especially from ourselves! Teach us to deny all ungodliness and fleshly lusts, and to live soberly, righteously, and godly in this world. Let it be our chiefest daily work to please thee, and to lay up a treasure in heaven, and to make sure of a blessed life with Christ, and quietly to trust thee with soul and body. Make us faithful in our callings, and our duties to one another, and to all men; to our superiors, equals, and inferiors. Bless the queen, and all in authority, that we may live a quiet and peaceable life in all godliness and honesty. Give wise, holy, and peaceable pastors to all the churches of Christ, and holy and peaceable minds to the people. Convert the heathen and infidel nations of the world; and cause us and all thy people to seek, first, the hallowing of thy name, the coming of thy kingdom, and the doing of thy will on earth as it is done in heaven. Give us our daily bread, even all things necessary to life and godliness, and let us be therewith content. Forgive us our daily sins, and let thy love and mercy constrain us to love thee above all; and for thy sake to love our neighbours as ourselves, and in all our dealings to do justly and mercifully, as we would have others do by us. Keep us from hurtful temptations, from sin, and from thy judgments, and from the malice of our spiritual and corporeal enemies; and let all our thoughts, affections, passions, words, and actions, be governed by thy word and Spirit, to thy glory. Make all our religion and obedience pleasant to us, and let our souls be so delighted in the praises of thy kingdom, thy power, and thy glory, that it may secure and sweeten our labour by day, and our rest by night, and keep us in a longing and joyful hope of the heavenly glory: and let the grace of our Lord Jesus Christ, and the love of God our Father, and the communion of the Holy Spirit, be with us now and for ever. Amen.

The Prayer of a Penitent Sinner, collected out of the Psalms.

LORD, from the horrid deep my cries Psal. cxxx. 1.
Ascend unto thine ear;
Do not my mournful voice despise,
But my petition hear.
I do confess that I receiv'd li. 5.
My very shape in sin:
In it my mother me conceiv'd,
And brought me forth therein.

Numberless evils compass me, xl. 12.
My sins do me assail:
More than my very hairs they be,
So that my heart doth fail.
But there is mercy to be had cxxx. 4.
With thee, and pardoning grace,
That men may be encouraged
With fear to seek thy face.

Have mercy, Lord, and pity take li. 1.
On me in this distress;
For thy abundant mercies' sake,
Blot out my wickedness.
My youthful sins do thou deface, xxv. 7.
Keep them not on record;
But after thine abundant grace
Remember me, O Lord.

If thou the failings shouldst observe cxxx. 3.
Ev'n of the most upright,
And give to them as they deserve,
Who should stand in thy sight?
O blessed is the man to whom xxxii. 1.
Are freely pardoned
All the transgressions he hath done;
Whose sin is covered.

Blessed is he to whom the Lord 2.
Imputeth not his sin;
Whose heart hath all deceit abhorr'd,
And guile's not found therein.
Lord, hide thy face from all my sins, li. 9, 10.
And my misdeeds deface.
O God, make clean my heart within,
Renew it by thy grace.

O then let joy and gladness speak, li. 8.
And let me hear their voice;
That so the bones which thou didst break
May feelingly rejoice!
Oh that my ways thou wouldst direct, cxix. 5, 6.
And to thy statutes frame!
Which when entirely I respect,
Then shall I know no shame.

What mortal man can fully see xix. 12.
The errors of his thoughts?

Then cleanse me, and deliver me
From all my secret faults.
From every presumptuous crime
Thy servant, Lord, restrain;
And let them not at any time
Dominion obtain.

Thou art my God; thy Spirit is good; Ps. cxliii. 10.
Thy servant's soul instruct
In thy commands, and to the land
Of uprightness conduct;
With upright heart I'll speak thy praise, cxix. 7, 8.
When I have learn'd thy word.
Fain would I keep thy laws always;
Forsake me not, O Lord.

A Psalm of Praise to our Redeemer: especially for the Lord's Day.

THE FIRST PART.

Bless thou the living Lord, my soul; Psal. ciii. 1.
His glorious praise proclaim:
Let all my inward powers extol
And bless his holy name.
Forget not all his benefits; 2.
But bless the Lord, my soul:
Who all thy trespasses remits, 3.
And makes thee sound and whole.

Who did redeem and set thee free 4.
From death's infernal place;
With loving-kindness crowneth thee,
And with his tender grace.
As far as is the sun's uprise 12.
In distance from its fall;
So far our great iniquities
He sep'rates from us all.

Behold what wondrous love on us 1 John iii. 1.
The Father hath bestowed!
That we should be advanced thus,
And call'd the sons of God.
Because thy loving-kindness is Psal. lxiii. 3.
Better than length of days,
And preciouser than life itself,
My lips shall speak thy praise.

Thus will I bless thee all my days,
And celebrate thy fame:
My hands I will devoutly raise
In thy most holy name.
With marrow and sweet fatness fill'd,
My thankful soul shall be;
My mouth shall join with joyful lips
In giving praise to thee.

For whom have I in heaven but thee? lxxiii. 25.
Nor is there any one
In all the world desir'd of me
Besides thyself alone.
My flesh consum'd, my heart as broke, 26.
I feel do fail me sore:
But God's my heart's unshaken rock,
And portion evermore.

For they shall all destroyed be 27.
That far from Thee are gone:
They that a whoring go from thee
Shall all be overthrown.
Neverthless I do remain 23.
Continually with Thee:
By my right hand thou dost sustain
And firmly holdest me.

And in the crowd and multitude Psal. xciv. 19.
Of troubling thoughts that roll
Within my breast, thy comforts rest,
And do delight my soul.
With the just counsels of thy word lxxiii. 24.
Safely thou wilt me guide;
And wilt receive me afterwards,
In glory to abide.

THE SECOND PART.

O God, how doth thy love and grace xxxvi. 7.
Excel all earthly things!
Therefore the sons of men do place
Their trust under thy wings.
With fatness of thy house on high
Thou wilt thy saints suffice,
And make them drink abundantly
The rivers of thy joys.

Because the spring of life most pure 9.
Doth ever flow from thee:
And in thy light we shall be sure
Eternal light to see.
Therefore the gladness of my heart xvi. 9.
Is by my tongue express'd;
And when I must lie down in dust,
My flesh in hope shall rest.

The path of life thou wilt show me; 11.
Where there are all the treasures
Of joy, and at thy right hand be
The everlasting pleasures.
Goodness and mercy all my days xxiii. 6.
Shall surely follow me;
And in the house of God always
My dwelling-place shall be.

O still draw out thy love and grace xxxvi. 10.
To them that have thee known!
And with thy righteousness embrace
The upright-hearted one.
That so my tongue may sing thy praise, xxx. 12.
And never silent be.
O Lord my God, ev'n all my days
Will I give thanks to thee!

THE THIRD PART.

Glory to the eternal God, Luke ii. 14.
In his transcendent place!
Let peace on earth make her abode:
Let men receive his grace.
Praise ye the Lord! sing unto him Psal. cxlix. 1.
A song not sung before:
In the assemblies of his saints,
With praises Him adore.

The holy God his great delight 4.
Doth in his people place:
And the Most High will beautify
The meek with saving grace.
Therefore let God's redeemed saints 5.
In glory joyful be;
And let them raise in his high praise 6.
Their voice continually.

Lord, all thy works do speak thy praise, cxlv. 10.
And Thee thy saints shall bless:
They shall proclaim thy kingdom's fame,
And thy great power express!
To make known to the sons of men 12.
His acts done mightily;
And of his kingdom powerful,
The glorious majesty.

Thy kingdom everlasting is, Psal. cxlv. 13.
Its glory hath no end:
And thine alone dominion
Through ages doth extend.
The elders and the blessed saints, Rev. iv. 8.
Who do thy throne surround,
Do never cease by night or day
These praises to resound.

O holy, holy, holy Lord,
Almighty God alone!
Who ever hath been, and still is,
And ever is to come.
Worthy art thou, Lord, to receive 11.
Glory and honour still.
For all the world was made by Thee,
To please thy blessed will.

The song of Moses and the Lamb, xv. 3.
They sing with one accord;
Great are thy works and marvellous,
Almighty God our Lord:
Just are thy ways, thou King of saints,
And true is all thy word.
Who would not fear and glorify 4.
Thy holy name, O Lord?

The Lamb is worthy, that was slain, v. 12.
Of power and renown,
Of wisdom, honour, and to wear
The royal, glorious crown.
For thou our souls redeemed hast, 9.
By thy most precious blood,
And made us kings, and sacred priests, 10.
To the eternal God.

THE FOURTH PART.

Oh that mankind would praise the Lord, Psal.
For his great goodness then; cvii. 8.
And for his works most wonderful
Unto the sons of men!
And let them offer sacrifice 22.
Of praise unto the Lord,
And with the shouts of holy joys
His wondrous works record.

Sing to the Lord, and bless his name; xcvi. 2.
His boundless love display:
His saving mercies to proclaim
Cease not from day to day.
O worship ye the world's great Lord, xxix. 2;
In beauteous holiness! xcvi. 9.
Let all the earth, with one accord,
With fear his name confess.

Let the exalted heav'ns rejoice, xcvi. 11.
And let the earth be glad;
The sea, with its applauding noise,
Triumphant joys shall add
Before the Lord; for he doth come, 13.
He comes the earth to try;
The world and all therein to doom,
With truth and equity.

O, all his angels, bless the Lord! ciii. 20.
Ye that in strength excel!
That hearken to his holy word,
And all his laws fulfil.
O bless the Lord, all ye his hosts, 21.
And ministers of his;
And all his works, through all the coasts 22.
Where his dominion is.

Bless thou the Lord, my soul; my mouth
His praises shall proclaim. cxlv. 21.
Bless him, all flesh; all that hath breath, Psal.
Praise ye the Lord's great name. cl. 6.

A Psalm of Praise, to the Tune of Psalm cxlviii.

THE FIRST PART.

Ye holy angels bright, Angels.
Which stand before God's throne,
And dwell in glorious light,
Praise ye the Lord each one!
You there so nigh,
Fitter than we
Dark sinners be,
For things so high.

2 You blessed souls at rest, The glorified saints.
Who see your Saviour's face,
Whose glory, ev'n the least,
Is far above our grace,
God's praises sound
As in his sight
With sweet delight,
You do abound.

3 All nations of the earth, The world.
Extol the world's great King:
With melody and mirth
His glorious praises sing;
For he still reigns,
And will bring low
The proudest foe
That him disdains.

4 Sing forth Jehovah's praise, The church.
Ye saints, that on him call!
Him magnify always
His holy churches all!
In him rejoice,
And there proclaim
His holy name
With sounding voice.

5 My soul, bear thou thy part, My soul.
Triumph in God above;
With a well-tuned heart,
Sing thou the songs of love.
Thou art his own,
Whose precious blood
Shed for thy good
His love made known.

6 He did in love begin,
Renewing thee by grace;
Forgiving all thy sin,
Show'd thee his pleased face.
He did thee heal
By his own merit;
And by his Spirit
He did thee seal.

7 In saddest thoughts and grief,
In sickness, fears, and pain,
I cried for his relief,
And did not cry in vain.
He heard with speed,
And still I found
Mercy abound
In time of need.

8 Let not his praises grow
On prosp'rous heights alone;
But in the vales below
Let his great love be known!

Let no distress
Curb and control
My winged soul,
And praise suppress.

THE SECOND PART.

9 Let not the fear or smart
Of his chastising rod,
Take off my fervent heart
From praising my dear God.
Still let me kneel,
And to him bring
This offering,
Whate'er I feel.

10 Though I lose friends and wealth,
And bear reproach and shame;
Though I lose ease and health,
Sill let me praise God's name:
That fear and pain,
Which would destroy
My thanks and joy,
Do thou restrain.

11 Though human health depart,
And flesh draw near to dust,
Let faith keep up my heart
To love God, true and just;
And all my days
Let no disease
Cause me to cease
His joyful praise.

12 Though sin would make me doubt,
And fill my soul with fears;
Though God seem to shut out
My daily cries and tears:
By no such frost
Of sad delays
Let thy sweet praise
Be nipp'd and lost.

13 Away, distrustful care!
I have thy promise, Lord:
To banish all despair,
I have thy oath and word:
And therefore I
Shall see thy face,
And there thy grace
Shall magnify.

14 Though sin and death conspire
To rob thee of thy praise,
Still tow'rds thee I'll aspire;
And thou dull hearts canst raise.
Open thy door;
And when grim death
Shall stop this breath,
I'll praise thee more.

15 With thy triumphant flock,
Then I shall number'd be;
Built on th' eternal Rock,
His glory we shall see.
The heav'ns so high
With praise shall ring,
And all shall sing
In harmony.

16 The sun is but a spark
From the eternal Light;
Its brightest beams are dark
To that most glorious sight.
There the whole choir,
With one accord,
Shall praise the Lord
For evermore.

CONFIRMATION AND RESTAURATION,

THE NECESSARY MEANS OF

REFORMATION AND RECONCILIATION,

FOR THE

HEALING OF THE CORRUPTIONS AND DIVISIONS OF THE CHURCHES.

SUBMISSIVELY, BUT EARNESTLY TENDERED TO THE CONSIDERATION OF THE SOVEREIGN POWERS, MAGISTRATES, MINISTERS, AND PEOPLE, THAT THEY MAY AWAKE, AND BE UP AND DOING IN THE EXECUTION OF SO MUCH AS APPEARETH TO BE NECESSARY AS THEY ARE TRUE TO CHRIST, HIS CHURCH, AND GOSPEL, AND TO THEIR OWN AND OTHERS' SOULS, AND TO THE PEACE AND WELFARE OF THE NATIONS; AND AS THEY WILL ANSWER THE NEGLECT TO CHRIST, AT THEIR PERIL.

"For I will pour water upon him that is thirsty, and floods upon the dry ground: I will pour my Spirit upon thy seed, and my blessing upon thine offspring: and they shall spring up as among the grass, as willows by the water-courses. One shall say, I am the Lord's; and another shall call himself by the name of Jacob; and another shall subscribe with his hand unto the Lord, and surname himself by the name of Israel."—ISA. xliv. 3—5.

TO THE READER.

CHRISTIAN READER,

HAVING in divers writings moved for the restitution of a solemn transition, of all that pass from an infant state of church membership into the number of the adult, and are admitted to their privileges, and the associated ministers of this county having made it an article of their agreement, at last came forth an excellent Exercitation on Confirmation, written by Mr. Jonathan Hanmer, very learnedly and piously endeavouring the restoration of this practice. Being very glad of so good a work, upon an invitation, I prefixed an epistle before it; which hath occasioned this following disputation. For when the book was read, the design was generally approved, as far as I can learn, and very acceptable to good men of all parties. But many of them called to me, to try whether some more Scripture proofs might not be brought for it, that the preceptive, as well as the mediate necessity might appear. At the desire of some reverend godly brethren, I hastily drew up this which is here offered you; partly to satisfy them in the point of Scripture evidence; but principally to satisfy my own earnest desires after the reformation and healing of the churches, to which I do very confidently apprehend this excellent work to have a singular tendency. Here is a medicine so effectual to heal our breaches, and set our disordered societies in joint, (being owned in whole by the episcopal, presbyterian, congregational, and Erastian, and in half, by the anabaptists,) that nothing but our own self-conceitedness, perverseness, laziness, or wilful enmity to the peace of the churches, is able to deprive us of a blessed success. But, alas! our minds are the subjects of the disease; and are so alienated, exulcerated, and so selfishly partial and uncharitable, that when the plaster is offered us, and peace brought to our doors, I must needs expect that many should peevishly cast it away, and others betray it, by a lazy commendation, and so disable the few that would be faithful, practical, and industrious, from that general success, which is so necessary and desirable.

As for them that lay all our peace on episcopacy and liturgy, I intend, if God will, to send them after this, some healing motions on those subjects also. And if they have no better success, than presently to satisfy my own conscience, in the faithful performance of so great a duty, and to awaken the desires, endeavours, and prayers of the more moderate and impartial, I shall not think my labour lost. Pray for the peace of Jerusalem; they shall prosper that love it. Let us seek it of God, as well as men; which is the daily, though too defective, practice of

The most unworthy servant
of the King of peace,
RICHARD BAXTER.

April 7, 1658.

If magistrates or others, who are obliged to promote the work, which is here commended to them, do want leisure or patience to read the whole, I desire them to peruse the contents of this book, and those parts of the work in which they are most unsatisfied.

QUEST. *Whether those that were baptized in infancy, should be admitted to the privileges proper to adult church members, without Confirmation or Restauration, by an approved profession of personal faith and repentance? Neg.*

THOUGH the distempers of the churches of Christ in England are not so great as the popish adversaries, or some discontented brethren, do pretend, nor as some inconsiderate lamenters of our condition do imagine, who observe less our enjoyments than our wants, and that have not the faculty of discerning our true agreements, where there is any difference, but think that many things are wanting that are not, because they cannot find them; yet is our discomposure such as the wisest have cause to mourn for, and all of us should contribute our endeavours to redress. And for the accomplishment of this blessed work, two things must be done: the first is, to discover the principles that must reform and heal us, if ever we be healed; and to acquaint the world with the necessary means. The second is, to concur for the execution, in the application and use of the remedy, when it is discovered. The first is a work, that is usually done best by a few at first; though the more receive and approve of the discovery, the better it will be brought into use. But it is here, saith Pemble, as in discerning a thing afar off, where one clear eye will see further than many that are dim, and the greatest conjunction of unfurnished intellects, affords not so much assistance for the discovery, as the greater sight of a few may do. But in the executive part there must be many hands to the work. If the pastors and people do not consent, it cannot be accomplished; and if they barely consent, and be not up and doing, discoveries will lie dead, and nothing will go on: and if the christian magistrate afford not his assistance, his guilt will be great, and the work will go the more heavily on. Though all the body be not an eye, and therefore be not as good at discovering as the eye is; yet must each member perform its own office, and none be idle, or withdraw its help, because it is not an eye, but all must execute by the guidance of the eye.

In order to the discovery of the healing means, among others, this rule is worthy our observation:—If any church order, or administration, seem offensive to you, before you wholly cast it out, consider whether there be not somewhat that is necessary and excellent either in the substance, or in the occasion and reason of it; and you will find, that reformation is to be accomplished more by restoration of ordinances and administrations to their primitive nature and use, than by the utter abolition of them.—Satan found it easier to corrupt the ordinances of Christ, and to cause them to degenerate into somewhat like them, than to introduce such of his own as were wholly new, and as Christ had given no occasion of. I could give you very useful instances in many of the popish administrations, which require a restoration, rather than an abolition, lest that which is Christ's part be cast out with that which is man's, and we should throw away the apple which should be but pared; and lest we cast away our necessary food, and most precious jewels, because they have fallen into Romish dirt. But my present business is to instance only in confirmation and penitence, so far as is requisite to the decision of the question now before us.

I know you will easily excuse me from the needless labour of explaining any terms in the question which you understand already: I think the best method to lay the matter naked before your understandings, will be by approaches and degrees in the opening and confirming of these propositions:—

PROP. 1. *It is here supposed, that the infants of believers should by baptism be admitted into the church, and so be partakers of infant privileges.*

Their sin and misery is come upon them without any actual consent of their own, by the will of others; and the remedy must be applied to them accordingly; not by any actual consent of their own, which is as impossible, but by the will of others, as the condition, and by the gift of God as the cause. In his dealing with mankind, God is not so much more prone to wrath and vengeance than to mercy, as to put infants into the comminatory terrible part of the covenant, with their parents, and not into the remedying part; and to condemn them for their first father's covenant breaking, and give them no help from their gracious parents' covenant keeping; and to fetch weight from parents' sins to weigh down the scale of vindictive justice, and to put nothing from the gracious parents into the other end. Yet is it not to infants, as the mere natural issue of godly parents, that God extendeth this grace. But, (1.) As they are naturally their own, the parents have a power of them to dispose of them for their good. (2.) Every man that is sanctified, hath devoted himself, and in general, all that he hath, to God, according to the several capacities of what he hath, that every thing may be for God in its proper capacity. (3.) Virtually then the children of the godly, even in the womb, are thus devoted unto God. (4.) It is the revealed will of God, that infants should be actually dedicated and devoted to him. (5.) He that requireth us to make this dedication, doth imply therein a promise of his acceptance of what is dedicated to him by his command; for his precepts are not vain or delusory. (6.) He hath also expressly signified this in Scripture promises, extending his covenant to the seed of the faithful, and telling us that his kingdom is of such. (7.) This dedication is to be made by baptism, the ordinance which God hath appointed to that end; and in which he is ready to signify his acceptance, that so there may be a mutual, solemn covenant.

The servants of God, before Christ's coming, were enabled and required to enter their infants into the covenant of God, sometimes and ordinarily in circumcision, and sometimes, as in the wilderness, Deut. xxix. without it. And they have the same natural interest, and as large a discovery that it is the will of God, for the dedicating of their children to God, and choosing for them, and entering them into the holy covenant, now as then. If then a child that had no exercise of its own will, might by the will of his parents choose the Lord, and be entered into the covenant with him, it is then so still. God hath no where reversed or abrogated that command which obliged parents to enter their children into covenant with God, and devote them to him. Nay, Christ chided those that would keep them from him, because his kingdom, that is, his church, is of such. A place that doth purposely and plainly express the continuance of his love to infants, and that the gospel entertaineth them as readily as the law or promise before did. Oft and again doth Christ signify to the Jews that he would have gathered them wholly to his church, and not have broken them off, if they had not by unbelief been broken off, and in the same olive hath he engraffed the gentile church. Infants are members of all commonwealths on the face of the earth, though they know not what a commonwealth is, nor yet what sovereignty or subjection mean; and he that should say they are no members, because they are imperfect members, would but be laughed at: and Christ hath not cast them out of his family or commonwealth, nor shut the door against them.

And that in this infant state they are capable of many privileges is apparent: they have original sin, which must be pardoned, or they are lost. Most of the anabaptists, that I hear of, do hold that all the infants in the world are pardoned by Christ, and shall be saved if they die in infancy, and run in the downright Pelagian road. But this is not only utterly unproved, but contrary to Scripture, which telleth us, that sin is not pardoned by the bloodshed of Christ, till men be brought into union with him, and participation of him; and for all his bloodshed, no man shall have pardon by it till it be given him by the act of pardon in the gospel. Now the gospel no where gives out pardon to every infant in the world; nay, it frequently and plainly makes a difference. The parents' will doth accept the offer, and choose for them that cannot choose for themselves; for others, whatever God will do with them, doubtless they have no promise of mercy. And it is strange that they should deny baptism to infants that deny not salvation to them; yea, that think, though ungroundedly, that they are all in a state of salvation. For either infants have original sin, or not: if they have none, then they need no Saviour, and must be saved without a Saviour; for the whole need not the physician, but the sick. If they have original sin, and that it is pardoned to them by Christ, then how can men deny them the sign and seal of pardon, or the solemn investing means? If they are sure that they are washed with Christ's blood, how can they deny to wash them with that water, that is appointed to signify and invest?

Moreover, infants are capable of many other privileges; and of being the adopted sons of God, the members of Christ, the heirs of heaven, as having right thereto; and being the members of the church, and being under the special protection and provision of God, and in an especial sort partakers of the prayers of the church, with divers more. As in the commonwealth, an infant is capable of having honour and inheritance in right, though not actually to use them; and of the protection of the laws for life, reputation, and estate; and of being tenant, and obliged to pay a certain rent and homage when he comes to age, and in the mean time to have provisions from the estate that he hath title to.

But all this I have more fully expressed elsewhere. And I have lately read Mr. Tombes's last, and large Reply, to part of my book, and many others; and must needs say that it leaves me still persuaded that it is the will of Christ, that the infants of his servants should be dedicated to him in baptism, and members of his visible church; and though upon the review of my arguments I find that I have used too many provoking words, for which I am heartily sorry, and desire pardon of God and him, yet I must say, that I am left more confident than before, that the cause is God's which Mr. Tombes opposeth. Of which, if God will, I intend yet to give some further account: in the mean time I deal with this but as a supposition that is already sufficiently proved, though all men, yea, all good men, see not the sufficiency of the proof.

Prop. 2. *There are many privileges belonging to the adult members of the church, which infant members are not capable of.*

This is true both of natural and moral capacities. The privileges which I mean are, the pardon of many actual sins, committed since they are adult; the exercise of all holy graces; knowing God; loving him; trusting him; serving him; the communion that we have with God herein, as particularly in prayer, in holy praises and thanksgivings, in heavenly meditations; the peace and joy that followeth believing, and the hopes of everlasting life; the communion which we have with the church of Christ in hearing, praying, praises, the sacrament of the body and blood of Christ; in distribution by giving and receiving, and an endearing holy love within. These and many more privileges are proper to the adult.

That infants are not naturally capable of these, is as needless to prove, as that they are infants: and then that they are not morally capable, as an inseparable consequent. For though natural capacity may be without moral; yet moral cannot be without natural. In point of duty, infants are not bound to the work; as to hear, pray, praise, &c. beyond the natural capacity of their intellects and bodies. And so in point of benefit we must have more sobriety than to suppose God to make over any benefit to them which they are not capable of: all this is plain.

Prop. 3. *The continuation of privileges received in infancy, is part of the privileges of the adult; or the restoration of them if they be lost.*

If the cause discontinue, the effect will cease. Adult privileges comprehend the infant privileges, partly as that which is perfect comprehendeth the imperfect, and partly as the whole comprehendeth the parts, and partly as the thing continued is the same with the thing begun. Infant privileges would all cease with infancy, if the causes or conditions cease, and there be no other cause for their continuance. God never took infants into his church and covenant, with a purpose so to continue them, without any other condition than that upon which they were admitted. This is past denial, and will be more cleared in the next.

Prop. 4. *The title condition of infant church membership and privileges is not the same with the title condition of the church membership and privileges of the adult; so that if this new condition be not performed when men come to age, their former title ceaseth, and there is no other that ariseth in its stead.*[a]

1. We are agreed, I think, that our title (which is *Fundamentum Juris)* is God's covenant, grant, or gift.[b] As it is his precept that constituteth our duty, so it is his promise or deed of gift which is our title to the benefit.

2. And we are agreed, I hope, that this promise, or grant from God, is conditional; for if church-membership and privileges be absolutely given, then it is to all, or but to some: not to all; for then the church and the world are all one; and then it is not *Ecclesia cœtus evocatus;* and then heathens and infidels have right; which are things that no christian,

[a] See the Rubric of the Common Prayer Book before Confirmation, after cited.

[b] G. Gassander Consult. de Confirm. Hujusmodi sane Institutionem seu Catechismi explicationem in pueris fieri debere, et Veteres præcipiunt, et Recentiores quoque ex utraque parte consentiunt. Vide August. Serm 116. in Ramis palmarum, et Wallafridum de rebus Ecclesiast. cap. 26. et quæ scripsit Ruardus Tappenus Lovan. tom. ii. ad illud Calvini Instit. c. 17.

I think, will grant. If it be but some that have title, then there must be some note to know them by: or else the some will be equal to all, or to none. And if they be marked out, then it must be by name or by description: not by name; for we find the contrary. Scripture doth not name all that have title to church privileges. If it be by description, it is either by mere physical or by moral qualifications that they are described: the former, none doth imagine, that I hear of. If they are moral qualifications, then either they are such as are prerequisite to our right and privileges, or not: that they are prerequisite all must confess that read the promise, and all do confess that they are prerequisite to all the following privileges; and if prerequisite, then either as means or no means. The latter none can affirm, without going against so much light, as ordinary christians have still ready at hand to confute them with: and if they are required as means, then either as causes or conditions. And I think you will sooner yield them to be conditions than causes, though either concession sufficeth to the end that is before us.

But of this we need to say no more, both because it is commonly confessed, and because that the words of the promises are so plain, and undeniable, being uttered in conditional terms.

Nor is this either inconsistent with, or any way unsuitable to, an absolute decree; for as a threatening, so the conditionality of a promise, are instruments admirably suited to the accomplishment of an absolute purpose or decree. He that is fully resolved to save us, or to give us the privileges of his church, will deal with us as men, in bringing us to the possession of the intended benefits; and therefore will by threats and conditional promises excite us to a careful performance of the condition; and that grace which is resolved to effect the very condition in us, is also resolved to make a conditional promise, yea, and a threatening, the instrument of effecting it.

3. Note, that the great question, Whether all the infants of true believers are certainly justified, or whether some of them have but lower privileges, is not here to be determined, but in a fitter place: and therefore I determine not what privileges they are that will cease, if our infant title cease; but that according to the tenor of the promise, the continuance of them, with the addition of the privileges proper to the adult, are all laid upon a new condition.

4. Note also, that when I call it another or different condition, I mean not that it is different in the nature of the act, but in the agent or subject. It is the same kind of faith which at first is required in the parent, for the child's behoof, and that afterward is required in ourselves. But the condition of the infant's title is but this,—that he be the child of a believer, dedicated to God; but the condition of the title of persons at age is, that they be themselves believers, that have dedicated themselves to God. The faith of the parent is the condition of infant title; and the faith of the person himself, is the condition of the title of one at age.

That their own faith is not the condition of an infant's title, I think I need not prove: for, (1.) They are uncapable of believing without a miracle. (2.) If they were not, (as some Lutherans fondly think,) yet it is certain that we are uncapable of discerning by such a sign. I think no minister that I know, will judge what infants do themselves believe, that he may baptize them. (3.) And I think no man that looks on the command, or promise, and the person of an infant, will judge that he is either commanded then to believe, or that his believing is made the condition of his infant title.

But that a personal believing is the condition of the title of them at age, is as far past doubt; and it is proved thus:—

Arg. 1. The promise itself doth expressly require a faith of our own, of all the adult that will have part in the privileges; therefore it is a faith of our own that is the condition of our title. " He that believeth and is baptized shall be saved, and he that believeth not, shall be damned," Mark xvi. 16. " And the eunuch said, See here is water, what doth hinder me to be baptized? And Philip said, If thou believest with all thy heart, thou mayest," Acts viii. 36, 37. " Repent, and be baptized every one of you in the name of Jesus Christ for the remission of sins, &c. Then they that gladly received his word were baptized," Acts ii. 38, 41; x. 44, 47, 48; xvi. 14, 15, 32, 33; Rom. x. 13, 14, with many other texts, do put this out of doubt.

Arg. 2. We were engaged in our infant baptismal covenant to believe and repent, when we came to age, as a means to our reception of the benefits of the covenant, proper to the adult; therefore we must perform our covenant, and use this means, if we will have the benefits.

Arg. 3. If another condition were not of necessity to the aged, beside the condition that was necessary to them in infancy, then Turks, Jews, and heathens, should have right to church membership, and privileges of the adult; but the consequent is notoriously false, therefore so is the antecedent.

The reason of the consequent is evident; because a man that hath believing parents may turn Turk, (as is known in thousands of janizaries,) or Jew, or pagan; and therefore, if it were enough that he was the child of a believer, his title to church privileges would still continue. And so among professed christians, the child of a believer may turn heretic, or notoriously profane and scandalous, and yet have title to church privileges, if his first title still hold, and a personal faith be not a necessary condition of his right. Add to these, the many arguments tending to confirm the point in hand, which I have laid down on another occasion in my " Disputations of Right to Sacraments." But I think I need not spend more words to persuade any christians, that our parents' faith will not serve to give us title to the church privileges of the adult, but we lose our right even to church membership itself, if when we come to age, we add not a personal faith, or profession at least, of our own.

I only add, that this is a truth so far past doubt, that even the papists and the Greeks have put it into their canons. For the former; you may find it in the Decrees, part 3, dist. 3, p. (mihi) 1241, cited out of Augustine in these words, *Parvulus qui baptizatur, si ad annos rationales veniens, non crediderit, nec ab illicitis abstinuerit, nihil ei prodest, quod parvulus accepit.* That is, an infant that is baptized, if, coming to years of discretion, he do not believe, nor abstain from things unlawful, that which he received in infancy doth profit him nothing.

And for the Greeks; that this is according to their mind, you may see in Zonaras in Comment. in Epist. Canon. Can. 45, cited ex Basilii Mag. Epist. 2, ad Amphiloch. thus, *Siquis accepto nomine christianismi, Christum contumelia afficit, nulla est illi appellationes utilitas:* that is, If any one having received the name of christianity, shall reproach Christ, he hath no profit by the name. On which Zonaras added, *Qui Christo credidit, et christianus appellatus est, cum ex Divinis præceptis vitam instituere oportet, ut hac ratione Deus per ipsum glorificetur, quemadmodum illis verbis præcipitur, sic luceat lux vestra coram hominibus, &c. Siquis autem nominatur quidem chris-*

tianus, Dei vero præcepta transgreditur, contumeliam irrogat Christo, cujus de nomine appellatur, nec quicquam ex ea appellatione utilitatis trahit: that is, Seeing he that believed in Christ, and is called a christian, ought to order his life by the commandments of God, that so God may be glorified by him; according to that, "Let your light so shine before men, &c." If any one that is called a christian, shall transgress God's commands, he brings a reproach on Christ, by whose name he is called; and he shall not receive the least profit by that title, or name. This is somewhat higher than the point needs, that I bring it for.

And indeed it were a strange thing, if all other infidels should be shut out of the privileges of the church, except only the treacherous covenant breaking infidel; (for such are all that being baptized in infancy, prove no christians when they come to age;) as if perfidiousness would give him right.

PROP. 5. *As a personal faith is a condition before God of title to the privileges of the adult; so the profession of this faith is the condition of his right before the church; and without this profession, he is not to be taken as an adult member, nor admitted to the privileges of such.*

This proposition also, as the sun, revealeth itself by its own light, and therefore commandeth me to say but little for the confirmation of it.

Arg. 1. The church cannot judge of things unknown: *non entium, et non apparentium eadem est ratio:* not to appear, and not to be, is all one as to the judgment of the church. We are not searchers of the heart, and therefore we must judge by the discoveries of the heart, by outward signs.

Arg. 2. If profession of faith were not necessary *coram ecclesia* to men's church membership and privileges, then infidels and heathens would have right, as was said in the former case, and also the church and the world would be confounded, and the church would be no church; but these are consequents that I hope no christians will have a favourable thought of; and therefore they should reject the antecedent.

Arg. 3. It is a granted case among all christians, that profession is thus necessary. The apostles and ancient churches admitted none without it; nor no more must we. Though all require not the same manner of profession, yet that profession itself is the least that can be required of any man, that layeth claim to church privileges and ordinances proper to adult members; this we are all agreed in, and therefore I need not add more proof, where I find no controversy.

But yet as commonly as we are agreed on this, yet because it is the very point which most of the stress of our present disputation lieth on, it may not be amiss to foresee what may possibly be objected by any new comers hereafter.

Object. Perhaps some may say, 1. That we find no mention of professions required in Scripture: 2. It is not probable that Peter received a profession from those thousands whom he so suddenly baptized: 3. Our churches have been true churches without such a profession, personally and distinctly made; therefore it may be so still. To these briefly, yet satisfactorily:

1. The Scripture gives us abundant proof that a plain profession was made in those times by such as were baptized at age, and so admitted, by reason of their ripeness and capacity, into the church, and to the special communion and privileges of the adult at once. To say much of the times of the Old Testament, or before Christ, would be but to interrupt you with less pertinent things; yet there it is apparent, that all the people were solemnly engaged in covenant with God, by Moses, more than once; and that this was renewed by Joshua, and other godly princes; and that Asa made the people not only "enter into a covenant to seek the Lord God of their fathers, with all their hearts, and with all their souls; but that whosoever would not seek him should be put to death, whether small or great, man or woman: and they sware to the Lord with a loud voice, and with shoutings, and with trumpets, and with cornets," 2 Chron. xv. 12—14. So following princes called the people to this open covenanting. But this is not all; to take "the Lord only to be their God," (with the rest of the law,) was the very essence of an Israelite's religion, which they did not only openly profess, but excessively sometimes glory in. As circumcision sealed the covenant, and therefore supposed the covenant, to infants and aged whoever were circumcised, so had they many sorts of sacrifice, and other worship, in which they all were openly to profess the same religion and covenant. Many purifications also, and sanctifyings of the people, they had; and many figures of the covenant. "I am the Lord thy God," &c. "Thou shalt have no other gods before me," &c. was the tenor of the covenant which every Israelite expressly, and by frequent acts, professed to consent to. The law is called a covenant, which all were to own, and avouch the Lord to be their God, and themselves his people. See Deut. xxvi. 17, 18; xxix. 10, 11, 14, &c.; 2 Kings xxiii. 3; 2 Chron. xxiii. 3, 16; xxix. 10; Ezra x. 3; Neh. ix. 38; Psal. l. 5; Ezek. xx. 37; Jer. l. 5; Isa. lvi. 4, 5; Exod. xxxiv. 27; Psal. ciii. 18; xxv. 10; xviii. 10, &c.

And yet I hope no christian would wish that we should deal no more openly and clearly with God, the church, and ourselves, in days of gospel light and worship, than the Jews were to do in their darker state, under obscure types and shadows.

We find that when John Baptist set up his ministry he caused the people to "confess their sins," Matt. iii. 6. And "if we confess our sins, God is faithful and just to forgive us our sins," 1 John i. 19. And whereas some say, that John baptized them that he calleth "a generation of vipers," I answer, (1.) We will believe that when they prove it. It seems rather that he put them back. (2.) If he did baptize them, it was not till they "confessed their sins" (before that all did); and it seems by his charge, till they promised to "bring forth fruits meet for repentance," Matt. iii. 8.

Christ would not have so instructed Nicodemus in the nature and necessity of regeneration, before he was a disciple, if a professed or apparent preparation had not been necessary; nor would he ordinarily have taught men the necessity of denying themselves, and forsaking all for a treasure in heaven, with such like, if they would be his disciples, if the profession of so doing had not been necessary to their visible discipleship.

I grant that so full a profession was not made before Christ's resurrection as after: for many articles of our belief were afterwards made necessary; and the apostles themselves were unacquainted with what the weakest christian did afterwards believe. But still the essentials of faith, then necessary in existence to men's justification, were necessary in profession to men's visible christianity in church membership.

2. As to those Acts ii. 37, &c. it is plain, that they made an open profession, if you consider, (1.) That they were openly told the doctrine which they must be baptized into, if they did consent. (2.) It is said, They that gladly received that word, were baptized.

(3.) It is certain therefore that they first testified their glad reception of the word. (4.) We may not imagine that Peter was God, or knew the hearts of all those thousands, and therefore he must know it by their profession, that they gladly received the word. (5.) Their own mouths cry out for advice in order to their salvation. (6.) It had been absurd for the apostles to attempt to baptize men, that had not first professed their consent. (7.) The Scripture gives us not the full historical narration of all that was said and done in such cases, but of so much as was necessary. (8.) The institution and nature of the ordinance tells us, that baptism could not be administered without a profession, to the adult; for they were to be "baptized into the name of Father, Son, and Holy Ghost," and therefore were to profess that they "believed in Father, Son, and Holy Ghost." Yea, the very receiving of baptism was an actual profession. (9.) The constant practice of the universal church hath given us, by infallible tradition, as full assurance of the order of baptism, and in particular of an express profession and covenant then made, as of any point that by the hands of the church can be received by us. (10.) And it was in those days a more notorious profession to be so baptized, and to join in the holy assemblies, than now it is. When the profession of christianity did hazard men's liberties, estates, and lives, to be openly then baptized upon covenanting with God the Father, Son, and Holy Ghost, and openly join with a hated, persecuted sort of men, was an eminent sort of profession. It being also usually private in houses, as separated from the main body of the people, and not in public places like ours, where men are justly driven to come as learners for instruction.

Moreover, it is said of all that were baptized, being then at age, that they first believed; and how could the baptizers know that they believed, but by their profession? Yea, it is said of Simon Magus, that he believed and was baptized; which (though he might really have some historical faith, yet) implieth, that he openly professed more than he indeed had, or else he had scarce been baptized: which hath caused interpreters to judge that by *faith* is meant a *profession of faith.* And if so, then sure a profession was still necessary.

Yea, Christ in his commission directeth his apostles to make "disciples," and then "baptize them;" promising, that "he that believeth and is baptized shall be saved." And who can tell whether a man be a disciple, a believer or an infidel, but by his profession?

How was it known but by their profession, that "the Samaritans believed Philip, preaching the things concerning the kingdom of God, and the name of Jesus Christ," before they were "baptized, both men and women?" Acts viii. 12.

Philip caused the eunuch to profess, before he would baptize him, that he "believed that Jesus Christ is the Son of God;" which upon his teaching the rest, did import the rest, if it were not more fully (as is likest) professed, Acts viii. 37, 38.

Saul had more than a bare profession before baptism, Acts ix. 5, 15, 17.

Cornelius and his company had a profession, and more, for they had the Holy Ghost poured on them, "speaking with tongues, and magnifying God;" that use of the gift of tongues importing more than the gift itself, Acts x. 46. Yea, the Spirit bid Peter "Go and not doubt," Acts xi. 12. And it was such a gift of the Spirit, as caused the apostles to conclude, that "God had granted the gentiles repentance unto life," Acts xi. 18.

How was it known but by their profession, that that "great number believed and turned to the Lord," and the "grace of God" was such as Barnabas saw, Acts xi. 21, 23.

And when Saul after his baptism "assayed to join himself to the disciples at Jerusalem," they so suspected him, that they would not receive him, till Barnabas took him and brought him to the apostles, and declared to them how God had dealt with him, and how boldly at Damascus he had preached in the name of Jesus; which shows that they admitted not men to their communion, till their profession seemed credible to them; for no doubt but Saul told them himself that he was a believer, before he was put to make use of the testimony of Barnabas.

The converted gentiles (Acts xiii. 48) showed their belief and gladness, and openly glorified the word of the Lord. How but by a profession did it come to pass, that the great multitude at Iconium, both Jews and Greeks, were known to be believers? Acts xiv. 1. The same I may say of the jailer, (Acts xvi.) who by works, as well as words, declared his conversion. And the Bereans, Acts xvii. 12; and the Athenians, Acts xvii. 34; and Crispus, with the Corinthians, Acts xviii. 8.

The believing Ephesians "confessed and showed their deeds, and many of them burnt as many of their books of ill arts as came to fifty thousand pieces of silver," Acts xix. 18.

In a word, it is the standing rule, that "If thou confess with thy mouth the Lord Jesus, and believe in thy heart that God raised him from the dead, thou shalt be saved; for with the heart man believeth unto righteousness, and with the mouth confession is made unto salvation." He that bids us "receive him that is weak in the faith, but not to doubtful disputations," implieth, that we must not receive them that profess not at least "a weak faith." Heb. v.; vi. 1—3, show that the "principles of the doctrine of Christ" were first laid as the foundation before baptism. And who received those principles could not be known but by a profession.

To this let me add, that *pœnitentiam agere* was judged by the ancient doctors the repentance that was prerequisite to baptism; and that is, a manifested, professed repentance.

God's order is, to the adult, first to send preachers to proclaim the gospel; and when by that men are brought so far, as to profess, or manifest, that "their eyes are opened, and that they are turned from darkness to light, and from the power of Satan unto God," then must they be "baptized for the remission of their sins, and to receive the inheritance among the sanctified by faith in Christ," Acts xxvi. 17, 18.

As their sins are not forgiven them till they are converted, (Mark iv. 12,) so they must not be baptized for the forgiveness of sins, till they profess themselves converted, seeing to the church *non esse, et non apparere*, is all one. "Repentance towards God, and faith towards our Lord Jesus Christ," is the sum of that preaching that maketh disciples, (Acts xx. 21,) and therefore, both these must by profession seem to be received, before any at age are baptized.

"If as many as are baptized into Christ, are baptized into his death, and are buried with him by baptism into his death; that like as Christ was raised from the dead, so we also should walk in newness of life," (Rom. vi. 4, 5,) then no doubt but such as were to be baptized, did first profess this mortification, and a consent to be buried and revived with Christ, and to live to him in newness of life. For Paul was never so much for the *opus operatum* above the papists, as to think that the baptizing of an infidel might effect these high and excellent things.

And he that professeth not faith, nor ever did, is to the church an infidel.

In our baptism "we put off the body of the sins of the flesh, by the circumcision of Christ, being buried with him, and rising with him through faith—quickened with him, and having all our trespasses forgiven," Col. iii. 11—13. And will any man, yea, will Paul, ascribe all this to those that did not so much as profess the things signified, or the necessary condition? Will baptism, in the judgment of a wise man, do all this for an infidel, or one that professeth not to be a christian?

Baptism is said to save us, (1 Pet. iii. 21,) and therefore they that will be baptized must profess the qualifications necessary to be saved.

"The keys of the kingdom of heaven" are put into the church's hands; and they that are loosed on earth shall be loosed in heaven (if the key do not err); and therefore pastors of the church must absolve none, by baptism, that do not by profession seem to be absolvable in heaven. They must profess to have "the old man crucified with Christ, that the body of sin might be destroyed, that henceforth they might not serve sin," Rom. vi. 5—8.

"As many as have been baptized into Christ, have put on Christ, and are all one in Christ Jesus, and are Abraham's seed, and heirs according to the promise," Gal. iii. 27—29. Thus speaks the apostle of the probability grounded on a credible profession; and therefore it is clear, that the profession was presupposed, that might support this charitable judgment. Our baptism is the solemnizing of our marriage with Christ; and it is a new and strange kind of marriage, where there is no profession of consent.

The baptized are in Scripture called men "washed, sanctified, justified," &c. 1 Cor. vi. 11; xiv. 33. They are all called "saints, and churches of saints," 1 Cor. i. 2. All christians are called "sanctified ones, or saints;" therefore it is certain that they professed themselves such.

But why should I go any further in this, when the main substance of my "Dispute of Right to the Sacraments" proves it? I entreat the reader that would have more, to prove not only the necessity of a profession, but also of the profession of a saving faith, to peruse that book, or at least the second Disputation, where are twenty arguments for it; and the sense of all the ancient churches there cited out of Mr. Gataker's Collections. See also Dr. Hammond's many testimonies to prove the use of the Abrenunciation, Paraenes. p. 18—20. I love not needlessly to recite what others have already cited; but he that knows not that the universal church, from the days of the apostles, hath baptized the adult upon a personal profession of faith, and repentance, and vow, or promise, or covenant for obedience, knows little of what the church hath practised. And I hope few sober men will be found that will be so singular and self-conceited, as to contradict the practice of the universal church in such a case as this, and set up their own private judgment against it, and go about to persuade us to a new way of church entrance and admission, now in the end of the world. Blame me not to be confident with you, where I have so good ground as Scripture, and so good company as the primitive universal church.

To this let me add, that most, or too many, that we are to receive to the privileges of adult members, have violated their baptismal covenant, and proved ungodly after baptism, and that by open, notorious scandals. Now Scripture, and the practice of the universal ancient church, direct us to require of these an open confession of sin; for they need an absolution, and not a mere confirmation. It is past all controversy, that such have both an open confession and profession to make. Yea, how scrupulous the ancient church was of receiving and absolving such violators of the baptismal covenant, and on how severe terms they did it, is known to all, that know any thing of those times. I pray amongst others see what Grotius, (Discus. Apol. Rivet. p. 221, 222,) citeth from Irenæus, Tertullian, Pacianus, Jerom, &c. ad p. 235. n.

3. And as to the last objection, that our churches were true churches, when we made no particular professions, I answer, (1.) Without some profession of true christianity, our churches could not have been true churches. And therefore against those that would prove them no churches, we plead, and justly, that a profession was made by them. (2.) But I pray you mark, that that will prove a church to be a true church, which will not prove every person in the parish to be a true member of that church. (3.) And he that thinks it enough, that our churches have a mere metaphysical verity, (such as Bishop Hall, and multitudes of learned protestants, allow the church of Rome itself,) is as good a friend to it, as he is to his wife or child, that will let them go naked; yea, and be contented that they catch the plague, or leprosy; yea, and plead for it too; and all because they have still the truth of human nature.

I know that any thing that may truly be called a profession, will, in that point, seem to prove the being of the church. But as it will not seem to prove the well-being; so an obscure profession doth but obscurely prove the being of it, which an open, plain profession doth more clearly prove. Let us not befriend either the kingdom of darkness, or the separatists, so much, as to leave our churches so open to their exceptions, and so apt to cherish and befriend their ignorance, and infidelity of the world. If coming to church, and sitting there, be somewhat a probable argument that men do implicitly believe as that church believes; yet it is a very dark proof, that they understand what the church believes; especially when experience hath acquainted us with the contrary of many of them.

But now I have said this much for a personal and plain profession, I would fain know what any man hath against it. The church, through the great mercy of God, hath yet liberty to use it; and we see how many thousands make a blind kind of show of christianity,[c] going from one public duty to another, and knowing not what they do. And is there not need that they should be brought out into the open light, and see their way? If covenanting with God the Father, Son, and Holy Ghost, be the essence of our christianity; in the name of God, I desire you to consider whether it be a thing to be huddled up in the dark? Unless it be men's design to hide the nature of christianity, and keep people in destructive ignorance, and delude their souls with a name and show of a religion which they understand not; they will surely be willing that men should know the covenant that they make, and understand what they do, before they enter into a marriage bond with Christ, if at age, or own it, if they have been entered in infancy. Why should we choose darkness rather

[c] Albaspin. in Tertul. de Præscript. c. 43. p. 308. Non nisi magna cum deliberatione quenquam in societatum et communionem ecclesiarum venire patiebantur—Ait igitur diu multumque orthodoxos deliberare, quorum sententiis subscribere, quosve in societatem ejusdem ecclesiæ et corporis recipere debeant: contra vero hæreticos ullo discrimine cum omnibus hæreticis pacem miscere.

than light? Why should an implicit covenant and profession be pleaded for, when the being of a profession is *palam fateri*, openly to make known; and when we know by sad experience, that when we have all done the best we can, to make our ignorant people understand, we shall find enough to do to accomplish it? Ignorance hath no need of friendship; especially from ministers it deserveth none; especially in so great a point as the covenant that men make with Christ. We have wares that deserve the light, and need not a dark shop. We have a Master that we need not be afraid, or ashamed, explicitly and publicly to confess. It beseems not so high and honourable a profession as that of a christian, to be wrapped up in obscurity. Such a glorious state as sonship to God, to be an heir of heaven, &c. should be entered into with great solemnity, and owned accordingly at our first rational acceptance and acknowledgment. Kings are crowned more solemnly, than poor men take possession of their cottages. Christ will be ashamed of them before the angels, that are ashamed of him before men; and will confess them before his Father, that confess him before men. Christianity is not a game to be played underboard. Why then should any be against an open professing and covenanting with Christ? If it be needful that we covenant, certainly the plainest and most explicit covenanting is the best. And what will be his portion that hath a male in his flock, and offereth the worst, yea, the halt and blind, to God?

Let us therefore deal as openly, plainly, and understandingly in the covenant of God as we can, and not contrive it in the greatest darkness that is consistent with the essence of a church. Nay, let us not tempt men to unchurch us, or separate from us, by leaving our cause to such arguments as this, Such a man sitteth among other hearers in the congregation, therefore he maketh a profession of the christian faith; lest they think it followeth not, therefore he seemeth to understand the christian faith, much less, he professeth it; especially when it is known that so many understand it not; and that the papists in their writings maintain it lawful for them to be present at our assemblies; and infidels tell us, that they can hear any man, and do come thither.[d]

Nehemiah caused the Jews "to subscribe the covenant, and seal it," Neh. ix. 38. Even under the law it was the character of visible "saints, to make a covenant with God by sacrifice," Psal. l. 5. At least, now God "hath caused us to pass under the rod," let us yield to be "brought under the bond of the covenant," Ezek. xx. 37; and let us, as weeping Israel and Judah, "seek the Lord our God, and ask the way to Zion, with our faces thitherward, saying, Come and let us join ourselves to the Lord, in a perpetual covenant, that shall not be forgotten," Jer. l. 4, 5. Let us "take hold of his covenant, and choose the things that please him, that he may bring us into his holy mountain, and make us joyful in his house of prayer, and our sacrifices may be accepted on his altar," Isa. lvi. 4, 6, 7. Are not these the days of which it is said, "I will pour out water upon him that is thirsty, and floods upon the dry ground: I will pour my spirit upon thy seed, and my blessing upon thine offspring; and they shall spring up as among the grass, as willows by the water-courses. One shall say, I am the Lord's; and another shall call himself by the name of Jacob; and another shall subscribe with his hand unto the Lord, and surname himself by the name of Israel," Isa. xliv. 3—5. I would have as little covenanting for doubtful, or needless, or mutable things, in church or state, as is possible: but in the great thing of our salvation, even the essence of christianity, we cannot be bound too fast, nor deal too understandingly and openly with God.

d Vid. Thom. a Jesu de Convers. Omn. Gentium de hac quæst.

PROP. 6. *It is not every kind of profession, that is the condition, or necessary qualification, of those that are to be admitted to the privileges of adult members; but such a profession as God hath made necessary, by his express word, and by the nature of the object, and the uses, and ends, to which he doth require it.*

The negative is not controverted among us. If any were so quarrelsome or ignorant, it is easily proved. And I shall do it briefly, but satisfactorily, in the opening of the affirmative.

I have proved in my first "Disputation of Right to Sacraments," (which I desire the reader, that would have further satisfaction, to peruse,) the necessity of these following qualifications of this profession.

1. In general, as to the *object* of our faith, it must be a profession of true christianity, and no less. It must be a profession of our entertainment, both of the truth of the gospel, and of the good therein revealed and offered. More particularly, it must be a profession that we believe in God the Father, Son, and Holy Ghost, as to the nature, persons, and works, which they have done and undertaken for us. Yet more particularly, and explicitly; it must be a profession, (1.) That we believe in God the Father, and so the pure Deity, as our Creator, Sovereign, and chief good, who gave us the law of nature, by breaking of which, we have lost ourselves, and all our part in everlasting life. (2.) That we believe in Jesus Christ, God and man, that taking our nature, fulfilled the law, overcame the devil, died as a sacrifice for our sins, rose again, and conquered death, ascended into heaven, where he is Lord of all, and the King, Prophet, and Priest of his church, in glory with the Father. That he hath offered himself with pardon and eternal life, to all that will accept him on his terms; and that he will come again at last to raise us from death, and judge the world, and justify his saints, and bring them to eternal glory, and cast the wicked into utter misery. (3.) That we believe in God the Holy Ghost, that inspired the prophets and apostles to deliver and confirm the word of God, and who is the Sanctifier of all that shall be saved, illuminating their understandings, and changing their hearts and lives, humbling them for their sin and misery, causing them to believe in Christ, the remedy, and heartily and thankfully accept him; possessing them with a hearty love of God, a heavenly mind, a hatred of sin, a love of holiness, and turning the principal bent of their hearts and lives to the pleasing of God, and the attaining of eternal life. This much must be believed, and the belief of this much must be somehow professed.

2. As to the *acts* of the thing professed, it must be, not only the naked assent of the understanding; but both this assent that the gospel is true, and a consent of the will, to take God the Father, Son, and Holy Ghost, to the fore-mentioned ends, in the fore-mentioned relations; and to give up ourselves unfeignedly to him, renouncing the flesh, the world, and the devil.

3. As to the nature of the profession itself, (1.) It must in general be credible; for no man is bound to believe that which is incredible. The words are the signs of the mind, and as such they are to be uttered and received. If they be contrary to the mind they are false; and if wilfully contrary, they

are a lie: and God doth not make a lie to be the condition of church membership, or privileges; nor doth he bind his ministers, or church, to believe a known lie: nothing but real or seeming truth is to be believed.[e] (2.) More particularly, the profession which we speak of must have these qualifications.

[1.] It must be, or seem to be, *understanding*. *Ignorantis non est consensus.* If a parrot could say the creed, it were not a credible profession of faith. Therefore the ancient church was wont, by catechists, to prepare them to understand the doctrine which they were to believe, and profess. This is past controversy. I think no minister would take that man's profession, that seemeth not to understand what he saith.

[2.] No profession is credible, but that which is, or seems to be, *serious*. He that speaks in scorn, or jest, is not to be believed, as one that speaks his mind; nor is it to pass for a profession.

[3.] No profession is credible or sufficient, but that which is, or seems to be, free and voluntary. Though some force, or outward urgencies, in some cases may help to incline the will, yet *willing* it must be; or it is not a credible profession. He that professeth himself a christian, when a sword or pistol is at his breast, is not to be credited, if he continue it not when he is free. And also, that which is done in a mere passion, without deliberation, is not to be taken as the act of the man, and a true expression of the bent of his mind; unless he afterwards stand to it upon deliberation.

[4.] It must be a profession not nullified by a contradiction in word or deed. Though there may an obscure contradiction, not understood, consist with it; or a contradiction only in degree: as, "Lord, I believe, help thou my unbelief;" yet there must be no contradiction of the essentials of our profession, that nullifieth it, by showing that we lie, or speak against the bent of our hearts. If a minister can by contrary words or deeds disprove the profession of the party, he is not to believe it, or accept it; for we are not to believe without evidence of credibility, much less against it. I have given instances of this in the foresaid "Disputation of the Sacrament."

[5.] When by covenant breaking, and perfidiousness, or often lying, a man is become incredible, having forfeited the credit of his word with wise and charitable men, this man must give us a practical, as well as verbal profession, before we can again admit him to the privileges of the church. For though we are not to be so strict, as some old fathers seem to have been, and the Novatians were, that would not admit such penitents again into the church at all, but leave them to God's own judgment; yet must we not go against reason and Scripture, and the nature of the thing, in believing that which is not to be believed; nor to cast by all order and discipline, and prostitute God's ordinances to the lusts of men, and make them a scorn, or level the church of Christ with the world.

The testimonies cited by me on another occasion, in the foresaid disputations, show the judgment of protestants in these points, and somewhat of the judgment of antiquity. I shall recite but those on the title-page of the third Disputation.

Tertullian Apologet. cap. 16. *Sed dices etiam de nostris, excedere quosdam a regulis disciplinæ. Desinunt tum christiani haberi penes nos: philosophi vero illi cum talibus factis, in nomine et honore sapientiæ perseverant:* that is, But you will say, that even of ours, some swerve from, or forsake, the rules of discipline.

Answ. They cease then to be counted christians with us: but your philosophers, with such deeds, do keep the name and honour of wisdom.

The judgment of the French professors at Saumours, you have in these words: Thes. Salmuriens. vol. 3. p. 39. *Sacramenta non conferuntur nisi iis, qui vel fidem habent vel saltem eam præ se ferant, adeo ut nullis certis argumentis compertum esse possit, eam esse ementitam:* that is, Sacraments are conferred on none, but those that either have faith, or at least pretend, or profess, to have it, so that it cannot by any certain arguments be proved to be feigned.

The judgment of the Scottish divines may be much discovered in these two testimonies following: Gillespie, "Aaron's Rod Blossoming," p. 514. "I believe no conscientious minister would adventure to baptize one, who hath manifest and infallible signs of unregeneration. Sure we cannot be answerable to God, if we should minister baptism to a man whose works and words do manifestly declare him to be an unregenerated, unconverted person. And if we may not initiate such a one, how shall we bring him to the Lord's table."

Rutherford, "Due Right of Presbyteries," p. 231, n. 2. "But, saith Robinson, most of England are ignorant of the first rudiments and foundations of religion; and therefore cannot be a church."

Answ. Such are materially not the visible church, and have not a profession; and are to be taught; and if they will fully remain in that darkness, are to be cast out.

If you would have the testimonies of protestants, you may read above threescore of them, expressly maintaining that it is a profession of saving faith, that is prerequisite to our right of sacraments, cited in my forementioned second Disputation. To which I add thirty-three more, cited to a like purpose in my fifth Disputation of Sacraments. And to these add the large testimony of Davenant, with his many arguments, on Col. i. 18, too large to recite.

And for the latter sort of episcopal divines, that they also agree in the same, I will satisfy you from an eminent man among them, Mr. Herbert Thorndike, in his "Discourse of the Right of the Church," p. 31, 32, where he saith, "And hereby we see how binding and loosing sins is attributed to the keys of the church: which being made a visible society, by the power of holding assemblies, to which no man is to be admitted, till there be just presumption that he is of the heavenly Jerusalem, that is above." I shall add more from him anon.

Somewhat I have elsewhere cited, of the fathers' judgments in this point, and more anon I shall have occasion to produce. But in a point that we are agreed on, that is, not every profession, but only a credible profession of true christianity, even of faith and repentance, that must be taken as satisfactory by the church, I hope I may spare any further proof.

PROP. 7. *The profession of those that expect the church-state and privileges of the adult is to be tried, judged, and approved by the pastors of the church, to whose office it is, that this belongeth.*

This proposition hath two parts: 1. That it is not a profession untried, and unapproved, that must serve the turn. 2. That the trying and approving of

[e] Therefore it is to be made at years of understanding. The papists themselves say in their catechism, composed for the Armenians, translated by Peter Paulus, p. 194. Tum recipiendum est sacramentum hoc, quando ad usum rationis pervenit homo, fidemque profiteri incipit, et ut confirmetur, et stabiliatur in gratia opus habit.

it, belongeth to the office of the pastors of the church.

The *first* is owned by almost all christians that I know of, and therefore need not many words.

(1.) If every man should be the sole judge of the soundness and validity of his own profession, then heretics, and heathens, and infidels may all crowd into the church; for when there is any outward advantage, or other common motive to induce them to it, they would all join with the church, as if they were christians. And we see that it is the custom of heretics to intrude: and who shall say to any of them, why do you so, if themselves are the only judges? We meet daily among our own neighbours with abundance that know not whether Christ be God or man; nor who he is, nor what he hath done for us, nor why he came into the world, and are ignorant of almost all the essentials of the christian faith; and with abundance more that live in common drunkenness, scorning at holy duties, and at a godly life, and hating those that use it, and giving up themselves wholly to the flesh and the world: and yet all these men are so confident of the soundness and validity of their own profession, that they will hate that minister, that shall make any question of their right to the privileges of the church. I speak not by hearsay, or conjecture, but by sad experience. And if they be their own judges, all these will be approved, and admitted; and, indeed, what man would not be admitted where christianity is in credit, or hath any worldly advantages? So that it is certain, that this would pluck up the hedge, and lay open the vineyard of Christ unto the wilderness. For self-love is such a powerful, blinding thing, that it will make every man almost, especially of the worser sort, approve of that which is their own.

(2.) If every man should be the sole judge of his own profession, and fitness for church privileges, then there could be no communion of saints: for all the most ignorant and impious persons would intrude into our communion; and it would be a communion not only of actual, but of professed impious men. But the consequent is intolerable, as being contrary to an article of our belief, and a principal part of christian practice.

(3.) If each man were the only judge of his own profession, then there could be no exercise of church discipline, nor keeping or casting out the wicked: but the consequent is insufferable; therefore,

(4.) If each man be the only judge of his own profession, then the church is an unguided, ungoverned society: but the consequent is false; therefore so is the antecedent.

2. And now I prove that it belongeth to the office of the ministers to judge of and approve the profession of such as expect admission, or the privileges of the church.

Arg. 1. If persons are not the sole judges themselves, then it must belong to the minister to judge: but the antecedent is before proved. The consequence is proved thus: It must belong either to the pastors, or the magistrate only, or the people only; or to all, or some of these conjunctly. Not to the *magistrate only;* for, 1. No man that I know of affirmeth it. 2. It is another man's office. Not to the *people only:* for, 1. None that I know of affirmeth this; they all include the pastors. 2. As I said, it is made part of the pastor's office. If you say that it belongs to *magistrates, people,* and *pastors jointly,* then you include the pastors: and I grant that in some sort it belongs to them, but in a different sort, as I shall tell you under the next proposition.

Arg. 2. It is to ministers, as such, that the keys of the kingdom of heaven are committed; but to approve of the profession of such as are to be admitted into the church, or to its privileges, is part of the exercise of the keys of the kingdom: therefore it is ministers, to whom it belongeth thus to judge and approve.

I have proved in another place, (and so have many others, more at large,) that the keys were not given to Peter, or to the apostles, as to private men; for so they were not; nor as to a church of private christians; for so they were not; nor the representatives of any such: nor yet as to apostles only; for then they should have belonged to none but themselves; the contrary whereof is certain: nor as to fixed diocesan bishops; for such they were not; and it is generally granted that the keys belong also to presbyters, either wholly, or the chief of them, and particularly, that in question: nor yet were the keys given them only as a synod, or presbytery; for Peter was not such: and this in question hath ever been exercised by such ministers.

Arg. 3. The rulers of the church are the lawful judges or approvers of the profession of those that come into the church, or demand the privileges of it: but it is the ministers of Christ that are the rulers of the church, as is expressed, 1 Thess. v. 12; Acts ii. 28; Heb. xiii. 7, 17, 24; 1 Tim. v. 17; therefore,

Arg. 4. Those that are by office the stewards of the mysteries of God, and rulers over his household, to give them meat in due season, which they must do as faithful and wise servants, till their Lord cometh, are the men that must judge of and approve the qualifications of those that come under their stewardship, government, and administration, of these mysteries; but such are the ministers of Christ, 1 Cor. iv. 1; Matt. xxiv. 45—47; therefore,

Arg. 5. To whom it belongeth, to receive men at age into the church; to restore by absolution them that fall off, and to administer Christ's ordinances to those that are within; to them doth it belong to try, judge, and approve of them, that are to be thus received, absolved, or that expect the privileges of the church. But it belongeth to Christ's ministers to receive men, absolve them, and administer the ordinances to them: therefore the antecedent is commonly granted, and plain Scripture. The consequence hath reason so evident, as needs no confirmation.

Arg. 6. If all that enter into the church, or that are restored by absolution, or are stated in a right to church privileges of the adult, are therewithal engaged into a mutual, voluntary relation to Christ's ministers, then must their profession be judged of and approved by Christ's ministers: but the antecedent is certain; therefore so is the consequent. The antecedent is clear, because, 1. All that enter into the universal church, do enter under the hand of the ministry, and thereby acknowledge their relation to them, and authority to admit them. 2. Because all such do engage themselves to be Christ's disciples, and learn of him as their master, not as coming down from heaven, to teach them personally, but as teaching them by his word, Spirit, and ministers conjunctly, saying, "He that heareth you, heareth me; and he that despiseth you, despiseth me," Luke x. 16. 3. Because they all engage themselves to take Christ for their king, who ruleth them by his laws and officers; and his ministers are his ruling officers, 1 Tim. v. 17; Heb. xiii. 7, 17, 24; 1 Thess. v. 12. 4. Because they are all engaged to take Christ for the great High Priest of the church, who hath appointed his ministers to officiate under him, in leading them in public worship of the church; and in offering up the praises of God, and blessing the people, and praying for them, and celebrating the commemoration and representation of Christ's sacrifice on the cross. 5. Because they that enter into a particular church, where only the constant stated use of holy ordinances and privileges are to be had, (though occasionally elsewhere,) do enter into a relation to the pastors of that particular church, as members of their flock and church, whom they must oversee and watch over: all this is past controversy.

And then for the consequent of the major proposition, that therefore ministers must approve of their profession, I prove it thus: Ministers are naturally freemen, as well as others; and therefore no man can become a member of their charge, and put them upon so great a duty as the relation doth require, against their wills, without their consent, and contrary to their judgment and consciences. It is an exceeding great burden that lieth on us, and a great deal of work that is required of us, to each particular soul. In our charge we must exhort, instruct, admonish, in season and out of season, publicly and privately, and watch over and govern them, visit them in sickness, comfort, strengthen them, &c. Oh what a mountain lieth on me, and how should I bear it, if God did not support me! And if every man that will, shall make me more work, and put himself under my care, without my consent, then I am so far from being a freeman, as all others are, that I am enslaved, and undone in slavery. For, 1. They may oppress me, when they will, with number; and so many may flock into my charge, in despite of me, as shall nullify the particular church, and by the magnitude make it another thing, by making it uncapable of its ends. 2. And hereby they may force me to leave undone my duty, both to them and others, by oppressing me with work; for when I have ten times more than I can teach and oversee, I must needs neglect them all or most. 3. And they may abuse the church and me with the evil qualities, as well as the excessive quantity of members; and we shall be obliged to give that which is holy to dogs, and to use those as church members, that are enemies to the church; and to administer sacraments to any, that will have them, how unfit soever; and to profane all God's ordinances, and turn them to a lie. 4. And by this means, the church will be utterly ruined, and made a den of thieves, and a sty of swine; for besides that all the worst may at pleasure be members of it, all men that are faithful, or most at least, will run away from the ministry, and sooner turn chimney-sweepers than pastors. For what man dare venture his soul on so great a charge, for which he knows he must give an account, when he is certain to leave undone the work of his office, in so great a measure, and when he knows he may be thus oppressed in soul and body, and so undone by wicked men, whenever they please; yea, if they purposely do it to despite him.

Arg. 7. That which belongeth to all other superiors, in voluntary relations, is not to be denied to ministers in theirs; but a free consent and approbation of them, that they are related to, belong to all other superior, voluntary relations: therefore to us.

A schoolmaster is to approve the capacity of his scholars; and a physician is to judge of the fitness of a person to be his patient, and his fitness for this or that medicine in particular. Not only a master would take it ill, if he may not have the approbation of his own servants, but have as many and as bad thrust on him as shall please; but a husband would think it hard, if he might not have the approbation and choice of his own wife, but that any might force him to take them that they please. And are the pastors of Christ's church the only slaves on earth? How improbable a thing is this!

Arg. 8. That relation which must be rationally, regularly, and faithfully managed, must be rationally, regularly, and freely entered, for otherwise we cannot so manage it: but the relation of a minister to each member of his charge must be thus managed; therefore,

Arg. 9. It is plainly expressed in the minister's commission, that he is to approve of the profession of disciples; therefore it belongeth to his office, "Go, disciple of all nations, baptizing them—teaching them to observe all things," Matt. xxviii. 19. Which plainly manifesteth, that it is they that must judge when a man is made a disciple, and when not; or else how can they either baptize them as such, or teach them the precepts of Christ as such? So when he giveth to his servants the keys of the kingdom, (Matt. xviii. &c.) it showeth that they are to judge who is to be admitted, and who not, as is aforesaid; or else he would never have set them at the door, and made them the porters and key-bearers of his church, to let men in.

Arg. 10. No man in the administration of holy ordinances, is ordinarily to renounce his own reason and conscience, and to act against them; but thus it would be if we have not the approving of the profession or qualification of those that we must administer them to: therefore—He that is to execute here, is to judge: for, (1.) Else you will force ministers to go against their reason and conscience in all administrations. (2.) You will deny them so much as *judicium discretionis*, which you allow to every christian, much more *judicium directionis*, which belongeth to their office. Every man must judge and understand what he doth, and why he doth it. You will not force the people to participate of sacraments against their consciences, why then should ministers be forced to give them against their consciences? Administering is their work; and therefore they must know why they do it, and on what grounds: else you will make them but like hangmen, or worse, if they must do execution against their judgments, because it is another's judgment. And whose judgment is it that we must follow, when we go against our own?

Arg. 11. If it belong to Christ, to pass an open approbation of the qualification of such as are to be admitted into his church, or to his special ordinances or church privileges, then doth it belong to the ministers of Christ, as his instruments; but it doth belong to Christ. (1.) For all that enter either into an infant or adult church state, do join themselves into a near relation to Christ: and will Christ have men married to him, and made his children, and members, and servants, without his approbation of them, or against his particular will? (2.) All that thus come into the church, or are restored, and claim church privileges, do expect and claim the benefits of Christ, and the greatest benefits in the world. And shall any man have Christ's great and precious benefits against his will, and without his approbation? It may be, you will say, that he hath already expressed his consent in the free promise of the gospel to all believers. I answer, he hath so to believers: but he hath done it only to believers, and he hath not said in the gospel that you are a believer.

Object. But it is sufficient, that my own conscience bear me witness.

I answer, It is so; as to all matters of conscience that are to be transacted only between God and you, as about your justification, and glorification, &c.

[f] It is before proved, that men are not here their own judges.

And yet, in this case, ministerial absolution is a great means to help the peace of your consciences. But where the minister hath to do with you by administrations, and the church hath to do with you in the way of communion, there they must know what they do, and why, and must have some expression of what you say your conscience testifieth to you.

And the consequence of the major is plain, that if it belongs thus to Christ to approve, then it belongs to his ministers; (1.) Because he appointeth not personally on earth, nor useth or approveth any other way, to signify his own approbation of you in particular, for a church state, and privileges. (2.) Because he hath expressly intrusted his ministers with this power, as to speak to men in Christ's stead, 2 Cor. v. 19, so to espouse them to Christ their husband, that we may present them a chaste virgin to Christ, 2 Cor. xi. 2; yea, and hereupon they are to give up themselves to the Lord first, and to us by the will of God, 2 Cor viii. 5. Christ's ministers are his agents, or ambassadors, as to solicit men in his name to be reconciled to him, so to approve them in his name, and tell them that he is reconciled to them. And therefore they are to deliver himself, his body, and blood, in his name to them in the Lord's supper; and to bind and loose in his name; and whatsoever they loose on earth, according to his promise, shall be loosed in heaven: so much of his work doth Christ by his officers.

And even men's first faith is a believing the preacher, and Christ by them. Acts viii. 12, "They believed Philip preaching," &c.

Arg. 12. To whomsoever the labour belongeth, to them the power of doing it belongeth; but it is to ministers that the labour of trying and judging of such professions, and qualifications, belongeth; therefore it is to ministers that the power belongeth.

The major is undoubted; for else we must be bound by God to do that which we have no power or authority to do, and others must have power to do it, and not be bound to it, which are both senseless. The minor I prove,

(1.) From the frequent commands of Scripture, that lay this burden on the ministers, but not magistrates or people, in the way that is now in question. All the directions and canons which Paul giveth to Timothy, Titus, to the elders of Ephesus, Acts xx. and other pastors, together with the exhortations to performance, and terrible charges given them to be faithful, do show that it is they that must do the work.

(2.) From common consent: all would have the honour and power; but who besides the pastors would have the work, and care, and severe obligations to perform it? Will magistrates, or all the people, undertake it to try, and judge of the professions of every man that enters upon adult church membership or privileges, or such as are to be restored? They that will undertake this work must attend it, and give themselves wholly to it, and confer with the persons, and do so much work as our people would be hardly brought to do, if they were able. It is unexperienced rashness and perverseness, that makes them so jealous of the minister's power in such cases, and some of them to reproach us for it. Ah blind, unthankful souls! do you know what the ministry and this power is? It is a power to be the servants of all; a power to spend and be spent, even for the unthankful. It is a power to do the most toilsome and displeasing work to flesh and blood, one of them, in the world; such as flesh calls a very drudgery. I profess unfeignedly, that if God had left it to my choice, and I should consult with flesh and blood, I had rather preach twice or thrice a week for nothing, and do no more, than to have this power, a duty of guiding and governing this one parish, though I had for it many hundred pounds a year. Nothing doth bring so much trouble upon us, as that power which unthankful persons scorn at. I had rather, if I might consult with flesh and blood, be advanced to the power of holding or driving plough for you, if not of sweeping your streets: though yet because of God's interest, and the ends of the work, I count it the happiest life in the world. And do you grudge us such a power as this? Would you grudge me the power of thrashing your corn; or will you grudge a physician the power of judging of your disease, and the remedy to save your life; or a schoolmaster the power of examining and teaching your children? Do the work, and take the power, if you are able, and can go through with it, and spare not.

Arg. 13. It is only the ministers of Christ that are able and capable to receive the power and do the work: and therefore it is they only that have authority thereto.

Nothing but the antecedent needs proof. And that I prove by three several enablements, which ministers have, and others want. (1.) Ministers only have ability of mind for the work of this trial and approbation. Here I speak of them ordinarily; and I have these grounds for it. [1.] God hath commanded that the most knowing, able, faithful, holy men, shall be destinated to this work, 1 Tim. iii.; Titus i. &c.; and therefore it is supposed that usually they are such, or else it is the shame of the magistrate that should see to it. [2.] It is they only that set themselves apart to the work, and study from their youth for the accomplishments that are requisite (unless here and there one of other sorts); and men are likeliest to be understanding in that which they have all their days set themselves to study. [3.] We see by experience that they are the most able, unless it be (alas, how few!) here and there a godly, studious gentleman, or other person; who are most of them to blame, that they become not ministers, I think.

(2.) It is only the ministers, who being separated to the gospel and work of God, do lay by all other business, and give themselves wholly to these things. Gentlemen (much less all the people of the church) cannot lay by their callings to attend this business of trying and judging of men's professions as ministers must do, if they will be faithful. Should private members have so much church governing work as some cut out for them, and should they bear such a burden, as some would lay upon them, under the name of power and privileges, it would undo them soul or body, or both; they would find time little enough for it in some places, if they all cast off their outward callings.

And, (3.) The pastors only are capable, because of unity: for should the people have this work, as some would have it, the multitude would hinder execution, and they would turn all to wrangling. [1.] Such bodies move slowly. [2.] Multitude with that diversity of parts and minds that is among them, would set them by the ears; and the church would be always in a flame. If every man that is to make profession of his faith, on this or the like occasion, must be tried and judged by all; some would approve, and others would disapprove and reject, in most or very many cases. Whereas the pastors being single, or not many, and more experienced, and able, and vacant for a full inquiry, have less reason to be partial, injurious, or disagreed.

Arg. 14. The practice of the apostles, evangelists, and the pastors of Christ's church in all ages, doth put us quite out of doubt, that it is not only belonging to the ministerial office, to judge and approve of such professions, but that it is a very great part of that office.

John Baptist received, and judged of the profession of his penitents, before he did baptize them. The twelve apostles, (Matt. x. 13, 14,) were to judge of the worthiness, or unworthiness, of those that they were to abide with, Mark vi. 11. Who were the judges or approvers of the profession of the three thousand converts, (Acts ii. 41,) but the apostles that baptized them, or judged them to be baptized? Who else approved of all the believers that were added, (Acts v. 14,) even multitudes both of men and women? They that continued in the apostles' doctrine and fellowship, (Acts ii. 42,) and under their government, no doubt entered at first under their conduct. Philip was the judge of the eunuch's profession, Acts viii. 37, 38. Ananias was scrupulous of admitting Paul; but as God himself approved of him to Ananias, (Acts ix. 13—15,) so Ananias also must ministerially approve him, ver. 17. Who judged of Lydia's profession, and the jailer's, (Acts xvi.) but the apostles, or other ministers of Christ? What need we instance any more, when we all know, that no convert entered at age into the church but under the hand of some minister of Christ, that did baptize him, or appoint him to be baptized?

Object. But this is not our case, for we were baptized in infancy, and are in the church already.

Answ. You entered not into the number of adult and more perfect members in your infancy; nor did you make any personal profession in your infancy: that is yet to be done. Your parents' profession will serve you no longer than your infant state. These being not in the gospel church before, were at once baptized, and entered thereby into the number of the adult members. So would we do if we converted those that were the seed of heathens or infidels. But though this be not your case in respect of baptism, and an infant church state, yet this is your own case in regard of personal profession, and adult church state.

If the ministers of Christ in Scripture times admitted none into an adult church state, and to the privileges of such, but upon a personal profession, approved by the said ministers, then neither must we do so now: but the antecedent is past doubt; therefore—

The reasons of the consequence is, because the Scripture is our rule, and the reasons of the cases are the same. If you say with the anabaptists, that I may as well argue from the apostles' example, for the baptizing of the aged: I answer, so I will, when the case is the same: when they are converted from infidelity, or are not born and baptized into the gospel church before. The apostles did not baptize at age any person that was born of believing parents in the gospel church, after baptism was instituted.

Anabap. object. answ.

As to them that say, that Mary was a christian, and yet Christ was not baptized till full age; I answer, (1.) That Mary was not a baptized person. (2.) That baptism into the name of Father, Son, and Holy Ghost, was not instituted in Christ's infancy: how should he be baptized in infancy, when there was no such ordinance of God in the world, as gospel baptism, or John's baptism? If you think baptism, and profession, or church membership, so inseparable, that we must not require such a profession, but in order to baptism, 1. You speak without proof. 2. You speak even contrary to the experience of the Jewish church, where in the wilderness circumcision was separated from profession and church membership, both of infants and adults; the latter being without the former. 3. If we may be baptized in infancy, without a personal profession, then they are separable; but the antecedent is proved in due place. 4. No man denieth, that I know of, but that personal profession approved by the ministers, is necessary in several cases, after baptism. But all the examples of the baptized adult in the New Testament, will fully prove, that all men should enter into the state and number of adult church members, upon a personal profession approved by the ministers of Christ; for so did all in the Scripture times, on reasons common to them and us; and no man can put by the obligation of the example, by any pretence of an imparity of reason, but what will be as strong to evacuate almost all Scripture example, and much of the commands. But as to the baptizing persons at age, we will do the same, when the persons are such as the apostles baptized: and that they baptized none others was never yet proved; but more said for the affirmative.

And ever since the apostles' days, it hath been the constant practice of the church, that the profession and claim of the adult should be tried by the ministers of Christ. (1.) In case of infant baptism, the minister was to receive and approve the parents' profession. (2.) In case of the baptism of the aged, they always entered under the trial, approbation, or hand of the minister. (3.) In case of the confirming of those at age, that were baptized in infancy, it was always done under the hand and judgment of the minister. (4.) In case of absolution of those that fell after either infant or adult baptism, it was always upon a profession approved by the minister. To prove these things is vain, it being the subject of so many canons, and so commonly known, both by record and practice.

Mr. Herbert Thorndike, in his forecited "Discourse of the Right of the Church," is full upon it. P. 32, he saith, "As the power of judging who is and who is not thus qualified presupposes a profession; so that an instruction, obliging the obedience of them, which seek remission of sins, by the gospel, and therefore confidently assuring it to them, which conform themselves. In a word, because admitting to and excluding from the church is, or ought to be, a just and lawful presumption of admitting to or excluding from heaven, (N. B.) it is morally and legally the same act, that entitleth to heaven and to the church; that maketh an heir of life everlasting and a christian; because he that obeyeth the church, in submitting to the gospel, is as certainly a member of the invisible as of the visible church." You see here in his judgment, both what kind of profession it must be, and who is the judge of it (of which he is more large). And surely, they that see confirmation, and penance, or absolution, grown up to the reputation of proper sacraments, and understandeth how they came to it, will never question whether the universal church hath still taken the pastors for the lawful judges and approvers of that confession and profession, which in such cases was requisite.

And that it was a profession, both of saving faith and repentance, that was expected by the church, which the pastors were to judge of, I mentioned some plain testimonies of antiquity, Apol. p. 95, to which I shall add some more.

Justin Martyr, Apol. 2, expressing how baptism was then administered to the adult, saith, "As many as being persuaded, do believe these things to be true which we teach, and to promise to live according to them, they first learn, by prayer and fasting, to beg pardon of God for their former sins, ourselves also joining our prayer and fasting; then they are brought to the water, and born again, in the same way as we ourselves were born again." And of the

Lord's supper he saith, "This food we call the eucharist, to which no man is admitted, but he that believeth the truth of our doctrine, being washed in the laver of regeneration, for the remission of sin, and that so liveth as Christ hath taught."

Nazianzen, Orat. 40, vol. 1, p. 641. "The force and faculty of baptism is nothing else but a covenant entered with God for a second (or new) life, and a more pure course of living. And therefore that we should all exceedingly fear, and with all diligence keep our souls, lest we be found to have violated this covenant." Basil's words, and many more to the like purpose there recited, I forbear.

And that a man baptized is not so much as to be taken for a christian, if by word or deed he nullify that profession, much more when he never made a personal profession, when he is at age, the ancients commonly agree. Some I cited before: Tertullian again saith, Apol. cap. 44, speaking of the jailer, *Nemo illic christianus, nisi plane tantum christianus, aut se et aliud, jam non christianus.*

Athenagoras, in Legat. pro Christ. p. 3. *Nullus christianus malus est nisi hanc professionem simulaverit.*

Damascene Orthodox. fid. lib. 4, cap. 11, p. 303. *Qui enim secundum traditionem catholicæ ecclesiæ credit, sed communicat operibus diabolo, infidelis est.*

Salvian. de Gubern. lib. 4, in the beginning: *Nam cum hoc sit hominis christiani fides, fideliter Christi mandata servare: fit absque dubio ut nec fidem habeat, qui infidelis est, nec Christum credat qui Christi mandata conculcat. Ac per hoc totum in id resolvitur, ut qui christiani nominis opus non agit, christianus non esse videatur. Nomen enim sine actu, atque officio suo nihil est.*

Cyprian, de dupl. Mart. *Frustra miscetur cœtui sanctorum, in templo manufacto, si submotus est ab universo corpore mystico Christi.*

August. de Baptis. cont. Donatist. lib. 4, cap. 2. *Ad ecclesiam non pertinet omnes qui sunt intus, sed qui sunt in ea pie viventes.* Et cap. 4. *In corpore unicæ columbæ, nec hæretici, nec improbi nominantur.*

See the like passages of the ancient schoolmen, cited by Davenant in Col. i. 18, p. 118.

And thus I have showed you the necessity of a profession, and of what sort of profession, and that the pastors of the church are by office appointed by Christ, to try, approve, and receive it.

PROP. 8. *Though it belong to the pastor's office to judge of the profession of such expectants, yet are they bound up by the laws of Christ what profession to accept, and what to refuse; and if by breaking these laws they shall dangerously or grossly wrong the church, it belongeth to the magistrate to correct them, and to the people to admonish them, and to disown their sin.*

In sum, as is aforesaid, it is a credible profession of true christianity, which they must accept. And as that which seemeth not to be understanding, serious, voluntary, and deliberate, is not credible; nor that which is nullified by verbal or actual contradiction; nor that which is made by one that hath forfeited the credit of his word; so on the other side, a credible man's profession is his title condition, in the judgment of the church, or that evidence of the condition that we must take up with. And if a man produce the positive evidence of his title, we must be able to disprove and invalidate it, before we reject him: so that it is a profession of true christianity, which we cannot prove to be false, at least by a violent presumption, (as the lawyers speak,) which we must accept.

By this it appears, 1. That a grossly ignorant person, that knoweth not the essentials of christianity, is not to be taken for a professed christian. For trial of such, the Ordinance of Parliament, of October 20, 1645, doth give us satisfaction (recited in the Form of Church Government, of March 29, 1648). 2. Nor one that denieth any of the said essentials heretically. 3. Nor one that speaketh ludicrously, and jestingly. 4. Nor one that speaks in a passion, not deliberately. 5. Nor one that is manifestly forced and unwilling. 6. Nor one that saith and unsaith. 7. Nor one whose life doth prove his profession to be incredible. 8. Nor one that hath perfidiously been a breaker of covenant with God already, till his reformed life shall recover the credit of his word. So that with a credible person, his bare profession is evidence before the church of his right; and we must prove him a liar, or false in his profession, before we can reject him. But a man that hath been wicked, after open covenanting with God or profession of christianity, hath forfeited his credit, and therefore must show us a new life, as well as a verbal profession, before he is to be restored to his privileges. In the first case, with a credible person, we must prove his profession false, before we reject him: but in the second case, with an incredible person, he must evidence his profession to be true, by probable evidences, that shall make it credible. If I thought that the very light and law of nature, joined with the known general rules of Scripture, did not put this past controversy, with most judicious christians, I should stand to prove all this by parts.

But on the other side, it is hence manifest, 1. That the pastors of the church must refuse no man that hath the least degree of grace, or makes a credible profession of the least. 2. And that we must not require as a matter of necessity, such ripe, or clear and judicious expressions from the ignorant, bashful, or such as, for want of us and good breeding, are unable to express their minds, as we may from others. If a man or woman be unable in good sense to express their faith, in the very essentials, or to reveal the grace of God within them, yet if upon our interrogations, and helping them, they can do it in any intelligible manner, so that we do but perceive that it is a sound profession in the essentials, which they mean, though they cannot handsomely utter it, we may not reject any such as these. 3. Note also, that defects in knowledge must be indeed exceeding gross, where the person is willing to be taught, and ruled by Christ, and use his means, and thus seems to love God and holiness, before they will warrant us to reject them. Should the judgments of such persons seem unacquainted with some fundamentals, about the Trinity, and the like mysteries, I should search them better; and I should plainly tell them presently of the truth, and if they received information, I should not reject a willing soul. The very apostles of Christ had the sacrament administered to them by himself, when they did not understand and believe the death and resurrection of Christ. I know that this will not warrant us to give such persons the eucharist now; because that those great truths were not then of such great necessity, as after Christ's death and resurrection they did become; as being not so fully revealed, nor the actual belief of them so peremptorily imposed. But yet it shows us thus much, that even in persons admitted to the Lord's supper, if there be but a belief in God the Father, Son, and Holy Ghost, and the points of absolute necessity, though in rude and imperfect conception, and a love to Christ, and a willingness to learn of him and obey him, a great deal of lamentable ignorance may be borne with, in those that have wanted either means of knowledge, and clear discoveries of the truth, or natural ripeness of understanding to receive it. You see then that pastors are not arbitrary, nor merely left to their own wills.

Prop. 9. *It is most evident, that ministers, people, and magistrates, have each a power of judging; but different, as they have different works.*

1. When the question is, to whom the sacraments, and other ordinances, and church relations and privileges, are to be ministerially delivered as from Christ, and to whom not? here the ministers of Christ are the judges. And so are they, when the question is, Whom must we teach, direct, and persuade, and in Christ's name command the people to avoid or to hold communion with? for those two are our own work in the execution. And if either magistrate, people, or any other must be judge, where ministers must execute and work; then, 1. We have not that common *judicium discretionis* to guide our own actions, which is allowed, and necessary, to every christian. 2. Then the rulers of the church are not only degraded, and made no rulers, but are put into that slavery, and subjection to them, that are commanded to obey them, which no pastor must desire the people, or any one of them, to be in; for we must not deny them a judgment of discretion, about their own actions. 3. And by this course, ministers that are the eyes of the body, must not only be guided by other parts, but they must execute against their own knowledge, and conscience, when other men misjudge. 4. And if so, either God commandeth us to sin, whenever people or magistrates bid us, (which none dare say,) or else it is no sin, when it doth but get their vote; and so we may warrantably do what the magistrate bids us, (as Hobbs thinks,) or what the people bids us (as others as unreasonably think). As if it would be a sufficient excuse for me, to say, Lord, I did what the magistrate, or the major vote of the people, bid me, though it was that which thou forbiddest. 5. If the people have no such power over one another, then they have none over their rulers or guides: but they have none such over one another. Indeed, in order to unity, a major vote may (not effectually oblige) but occasion an obligation: but as to government, let them show us if they can from Scripture, where the major vote of a church hath the government of the lesser part; or that the lesser may go against their own judgment and conscience, merely because the greater part requireth it. This governing vote is as strange a thing to the Scripture as a pope is. 6. Pastors, or general, unfixed ministers, may receive persons into the universal church sometimes, without receiving them into any particular church: and what have any people there to do with the trial or approbation of their profession or qualifications? One can lay no more claim to it than another: and sure all the world must not have the trial of them. 7. What people did Philip advise with before he baptized the eunuch? or who but Philip alone was judge of his profession? What vote approved of the three thousand converts, Acts ii.; or of Paul, Acts ix.; or of Lydia, or the jailer, Acts xvi.; or any other that ever were admitted by the ministers of Christ in Scripture times? And what magistrates were the approvers for three hundred years after Christ? no, nor after. 8. If in this part of our office we must obey men, against God, (whether magistrate or people,) then in other parts: and so if the vote of the church, or magistrate, forbid me to pray or preach against pride, covetousness, or drunkenness, I must obey them; that is, I must obey men before God, and please men, and be no longer the minister of Christ. 9. What can be more plainly contrary to Scripture, than for the people, by a major vote, to rule those whom God commandeth to obey, as their rulers? Heb. xiii. 7, 17, 24; 1 Tim. v. 17; 1 Thess. v. 12; Acts xx., &c.

Object. Pastors have but a ministerial ruling power.

Answ. Who doubts of that? But is a ministerial rule no rule? No man on earth hath more than a ministerial power; for all are under God, and the Redeemer. All judges, justices, and other officers in the commonwealth, have but a ministerial rule as officers: but is that no rule? or shall the people therefore rule these rulers? We are Christ's ministers for the people: we are theirs finally, but have our power from Christ only efficiently. If the people are the rulers, who are the ruled? It is a strange society, when the ruling and ruled part is the same; where all the body is a head and an eye. 10. If people or magistrates will oblige the ministers by their power, whom they shall baptize, confirm, or absolve, and what profession they shall accept; then must the people and magistrates undertake to answer it before God, and to bear all the blame and punishment, if we miscarry in obedience to them. And truly, if they dare undertake this, we should gladly accept of the condition, with a thousand thanks, if we could but be sure that God would give us leave, and thus acquit us, and accept of our service on these terms. Oh then how easy a thing were it to obey, rather than to rule! So much for the power of the ministers in this, and other such like work.

2. When the question is, Whether such a professor be fit for our own communion or not, and whether it be our duty to avoid him or not, then the people have a judgment of discretion; not a governing judgment, as the pastors have, but a judgment that must be the immediate guide of their actions. Yet this is to be thus exercised: they are to look to God's word as the rule, and to trust that with a divine faith: they are also to look at the judgment and directions of the pastors, that are their authorized guides; and to trust them as the officers of Christ. For the word is their regulating guide; and the pastors are their authorized directing guides; and their own understandings are their immediate discerning guides. So that they must not be wise in their own conceits, nor lean to their own understanding, without the use of Scripture, and ministry; but use their understandings for the improvement of these. So that if they know not that the pastors of the church do mislead them, contrary to the word of God, they cannot deny them obedience, for the command to obey them is unquestionable. Or if they have not a grounded strong presumption, or probability of it, they may not suspend their obedience; but must leave the pastors to the work of their office, and trust them in it, and avoid those whom they reject, and hold communion with those whom they accept, and introduce, confirm, or restore. But in case they know that a pastor leadeth them into sin, they are not to follow him; and if they have just ground for a strong suspicion of it, they must suspend, and consult with other pastors, and get full information; for christian people are not to be ruled as beasts, but as the children of God; and must understand what they are required to do, and why, as being free subjects (though subjects) in the kingdom of Christ, and to be governed accordingly.

3. When the question is, Whether ministers are to be punished for abusing their power, receiving or

rejecting men to the injury of the church, and contrary to the word of God; here the magistrate is the judge. For as forcing, or punishing corporally, is his work, so he must be the judge where he is the executioner, or else he should be forced to go against his own judgment, and to be a mere servile executioner, which were to him an insufferable injury.

But here, 1. The magistrate must not give the minister a law to govern the church by, unless the determination of circumstantial appendants; but must see that we govern it according to the word of God, our only and sufficient rule. 2. And he must not be over-busy, nor unnecessarily intermeddle in the works of another's office, nor be too confident of his own understanding in the matters of the pastor's work, as if he knew better than they. 3. But he must correct or cast out those ministers that will not obey the word of God; punishing us for breaking the old rule, and not making new rules for us, is their work, so be it he can procure a better supply. 4. In this case, if the magistrate's judgment be right, he doth his duty, and ministers must obey him; if he err, he may be guilty of persecution, in hindering good, under pretence of punishing evil. If his error tend not to the destruction, or great and certain hurt, of the church, the ministers whom he casteth out are bound to obey him, and give place to others, and bestow their labours in some other country, or in some other kind at home; but if his error lead him to destructive persecution, we must passively submit, but not actively or negatively obey him, but must preach as long as we are able, and do our duty, till by prison or death he stop us in the exercise.

PROP. 10. *To this ministerial approbation of the profession, and qualification of the expectant, there is to be adjoined a ministerial investiture, or delivery of the benefit expected.*

This is the proper work of the ministers of Christ. He that is himself in the heavenly glory, hath left his Spirit within to draw men to him, and his ministers without, to deliver up the counter-covenant on his part, in his name, and to espouse them to Christ, and to accept them in his name and stead. And this investiture is one of the principal parts of the nature and use of sacraments, which all have not fully considered of. The papists tell us of seven sacraments, baptism, confirmation, penance, orders, the eucharist, matrimony, and extreme unction. Calvin sticks not to yield them three. The name *sacrament* being not in Scripture, but of mere ecclesiastic use, and being a word that will stretch, I distinguish between three sorts of sacraments. (1.) For any divine institution which notably signifieth spiritual grace; and so, though I think extreme unction none, as being now no duty, yet I doubt not but there are more than seven. (2.) For any solemn investiture of a person by ministerial delivery, in a state of church privileges, or some special gospel mercy. And so I grant that there are five sacraments; baptism, confirmation, absolution, the Lord's supper, and ordination. As a man that delivereth possession of a house, doth deliver the key to him that enters; and as we are invested in the possession of land, by the delivery of a twig or turf; and as ministers were wont to be invested, or have induction into the churches, by giving them the books, and the bell-ropes; and as women were wont to be married with a ring; and as a prince doth knight a man by a sword; so Christ, by his ministers, doth first by baptism invest us in our church state, and infant privileges; and by confirmation, confirm us in our church state, and invest us with a right to the privileges of the adult; and by absolution, reinvest us in the privileges that we had forfeited; and by the Lord's supper, deliver to us Christ and his benefits, for our ordinary nourishment, and growth in grace; and by ordination he investeth the person ordained with ministerial power. (3.) But taking the word sacrament in that strictest sense, as our divines define a sacrament, as it is an outward sign of Christ's institution, for the obsignation of the full covenant of grace, betwixt him and the covenanter, and a delivery, representation, and investiture of the grace, or benefits of that covenant; thus we have only two sacraments, baptism, and the Lord's supper. But truly, I would not quarrel with them for the mere name, as to the five which I mentioned.

PROP. 11. *The solemn ministerial investiture of professors, into the right of the church privileges of the adult, is either, 1. Of the unbaptized, who are now first entered. 2. Or of the baptized in infancy, that never proved ungodly, nor violated that first covenant. 3. Or of those baptized, whether in infancy or at age, that have since proved wicked, and broke that covenant. The first of these investitures is to be by baptism: the second by confirmation; and the third by absolution. So that the solemn investiture that I am pleading for, is by confirmation to one sort, that never proved ungodly since their baptism, and by absolution to the other sort, that broke their covenant.*

The baptism of the adult, we have not now to do with. Of those that are baptized in infancy, some do betimes receive the secret seeds of grace, which by the blessing of a holy education, (and some among the profane,) is stirring within them, according to their capacity, and working them to God by actual desires, and working them from all known sin, and entertaining further grace, and turning them into actual acquaintance with Christ, as soon as they arrive at full natural capacity; so that they never were actual ungodly persons. To these their investiture in the state of adult members upon their personal, approved profession, is a confirmation of the mutual covenant that it findeth them under, and of them in that covenant.

But there are others, (I doubt the most,) that since their infant baptism have proved actual wicked and ungodly persons; if not openly flagitious and scandalous, yet at least unacquainted with any special sanctifying work, till after they attain to the full years of discretion. These break their covenant made with God in baptism,[g] in which they were devoted to him, and engaged to live to him, forsaking the flesh, the world, and the devil. And therefore these must come in as penitents, even as if they had proved wicked after an adult baptism they must do; and therefore it is first an absolution which they must receive; not only a particular absolution from an act of heinous sin, which afterwards may be renewed upon particular penitence, but a general absolution from a state of sin. Yet this doth consequently participate of the nature of the former, and hath a confirmation in it, or with it; not a confirmation in the wicked state that such have lived in, but a renewal, and solemn confirming of the covenant, between God and them, which in baptism was made. So that to such it is as an absolution and confirmation conjunct.

[g] De Exhomologes. vide Albaspin. in Tertul. de Pœnit. c. 10. p. 297. et Observ. passim.

Prop. 12. *This solemn investiture on personal profession, being thus proved the ordinance of God, for the solemn renewing of the covenant of grace, between God and the adult covenanter, it must needs follow, that it is a corroborating ordinance, and that corroborating grace is to be expected in it from God, by all that come to it in sincerity of heart; and so it hath the name of confirmation upon that account also.*

The papists quarrel with us, and curse us in the council of Trent, for denying their ends of confirmation, and making it another thing. But they falsely describe our opinion: we do not take it to be a mere catechising, or receiving the catechised to the Lord's supper, or to a higher form; but we take it to be the approbation of the personal profession of them that claim a title to the church state, and privilege of the adult, and an investing them solemnly therein, upon the solemn renewal (and personal adult entrance) into covenant with God. Now in this renewed covenant, as they give up themselves to Christ afresh, and personally engage themselves to him, and renounce his enemies, owning their infant baptism, when this was done by others in their names; so God is ready on his part to bless his own ordinance, with the collation of that corroborating grace, which the nature of the renewed covenant doth import. Otherwise God should appoint us means in vain, and fail them in the use of his own ordinances, that use them as he hath appointed; which is not to be imagined. Though the unsound hypocritical receivers may miss of this blessing; and though as the degrees of corroborating grace, God is free to give it out as he pleaseth. So that the papists shall have no cause to say, that we needlessly, or erroneously, do deny either the name of confirmation, or the true use and ends of it, or the notional title of a sacrament to it in a larger, yet not the largest, sense. We affect not to fly further from them than we needs must; much less to fly from the ancient practice of the universal church. But we must crave their pardon, if we introduce not their anointing, though ancient, seeing when it was used of old but as an indifferent ceremony, they have turned it now into a proper, necessary, sacramental sign: and if we give not the confirmed a box on the ear, as they do, for a holy sign, or abuse it not as they in many respects, and turn it not into a mere deceiving formality, in this also we must needs crave their pardon. So much of the name and ends of confirmation.

Prop. 13. *Ministerial imposition of hands in confirmation, and the fore-described sort of absolution, is a lawful and convenient ceremony, and ordinarily to be used, as it hath been of old by the universal church. But yet it is not of such necessity, but that we must dispense in this ceremony with scrupulous consciences, that cannot be satisfied to submit to it.*

Thus must we take heed of both extremes; either of rejecting a ceremony that hath so much to be said for it as this hath; or of making it more necessary than it is, to the wrong of tender consciences that are not yet ripe enough, to be well informed of it, and to answer the objections that they have heard against it; nor yet to receive your answers.

[h] I. For the first part of the proposition, I think it may suffice, (1.) That imposition of hands was used in Scripture times, and so used, as may invite us to imitation, but not deter us from it at all. (2.) And that it hath been since of ordinary use in the universal church, in this very case, so that no other original of it can be found, but apostolical; yea, we have exceeding probable evidence, that the use of it was never interrupted, from the days of the apostles down to the Reformation. (3.) Nor is it laid aside in many of the reformed churches. So that you will find, that as it is easy to prove it *lawful*, so it is more likely to be a Divine institution, necessary *necessitate præcepti*, than to be *unlawful*. I shall purposely say the less of it, because Mr. Hanmer hath said so much already as to the judgment of the ancients; and my intent is to pretermit that part, or say less to it, which he hath performed. But that it is lawful and fit, if not of some necessity, I shall prove by the fore-mentioned evidence.

1. Imposition of hands is allowed in Scripture to be used generally by spiritual superiors, to signify their will and desire, that the blessing may fall on the inferior, or the gift or power be conferred on him, for which they have a call to mediate: so that it is not confined to any particular blessing, power, or ordinance; and therefore if there had been no example of the use of it in this particular case, (of confirmation, or absolution,) yet hence it is proved to be lawful and meet, because it hath this general use and allowance. The lifting up of hands in prayer was used to signify from whom and whence they did expect the blessing; even from our Father which is in heaven: and the laying of hands on the head of the person, in or after prayer, was used as an applicatory sign, to signify the *terminus ad quem* of the blessing desired, or the person on whom they would have it bestowed. And as you will not cast away the use of lifting up of hands, though it be for such mercies as you read no Scripture instance that hands were lift up for, because the general warrant is sufficient; so you have as little reason to scruple or cast away the laying on of hands, though in such cases as you read not that the sign was used for in Scripture; because the unlimited general use is sufficient warrant, in such particular cases. God showed that the very outward sign of lifting up of the hands was not to be despised, when Amalek had the better when Moses' hands fell down, though but through weakness, so that Aaron and Hur were fain to underset them, Exod. xvii. And I think we have no reason to contemn the laying on of hands, which in grounds and nature is so near akin to the other. And as spreading forth the hands doth not cease to be good and meet, for all that God hath said he will "not hear them" that spread forth hands that are full of blood, Isa. i. 15; so the laying on of hands doth not cease to be good and meet, though in some cases the blessing do not follow it. Still we must every where "lift up holy hands" in prayer, "without wrath and doubting," 1 Tim. ii. 8. Though the

[h] Grotius Epist. 154. p. 377, 378. Mihi legendo compertum est manuum impositionem ceremoniam fuisse judaicam, usurpatam, non lege ulla divina, sed moribus, ubicunque precandi pro aliqua causa quædam emerserat. Tunc enim Judæi orabant ut sic Dei efficacia esset super illum, sicut manus, efficaciæ symbolum, ei imponebantur. Hunc quemque morem ut synagogæ pleraque secutus est Christus, sive pueris benedicendum fuit, sive ægrotis adhibenda sanatio addita, ut semper honos Patri haberetur, prece, Eodem more non ex ullo præcepto est quod apostoli manus imposuere iis, quibus ignoto ante hac jure dona conspicua Sancti Spiritus precando conferebant: quod presbyteri eundem ritum adhibuere non tantum in allegendis presbyteris, puta Timotheo, 1 Tim. iv. 15. Sed et ipsis apostolis, ubi novi aliquid opus aggrederentur, Acts xiii. 2. Ita ut si quotiens manus imponitur toties sacramentum est, jam nulla futura sit ad precandum pro aliquo occasio, quæ non eo nomine veniat; quod nec vocis origo, nec veterum in ea usus repudiat. Et ex una hac non imperata sed usitata Judais christianisque ceremonia, existitere illa, quæ dicuntur sacramenta confirmationis, ordinationis, pœnitentiæ, extremæ unctionis, imo et matrimonii.

sign be not of absolute necessity in every prayer, yet it is very meet, and too much neglected among us: and so I may say of the other. When Solomon prayed in the temple, he "spread forth his hands towards heaven," 1 Kings viii. 22; and so he supposed all would do, that look to be heard by the God of heaven, when (verse 38) he prayeth for the people thus: "What prayer and supplication soever be made by any man, or by all thy people Israel, which shall know every man the plague of his own heart (that was their prayer-book) and spread forth his hands towards this house, then hear thou in heaven thy dwelling-place, and forgive, and do," &c. See verse 54; 2 Chron. vi. 12, 13. We must "lift up our hearts with our hands to God in the heavens," Lam. iii. 41. We must prepare our hearts, and stretch out our hands towards him," Job xi. 13. Praying "to a strange God" is signified by stretching out the hand to him, Psal. xliv. 20. Even in praises the people were to lift up their hands towards heaven, Neh. viii. 6; yea, and in blessing, lifting up the hands was used to signify whence the blessing came, Luke xxiv. 50. Now this being so commonly applied, the other that is so near akin to it, may without scruple be used in any case that falls under the fore-described general case. Indeed every man must lift up hands, because every man must pray; and it is an engagemenl, that those hands that are lifted up to God, be not used in wicked works; but laying on of hands is ordinarily the act of a superior, to the ends above said.

Thus Jacob, Gen. xlviii. 14, 15, laid his hands on the sons of Joseph in blessing them. Moses laid his hand on Joshua, when he ordained him his successor, Numb. xxvii. 18, 23; Deut. xxxiv. 9. Yea, even in the execution of evil they lay on hands, as an applicatory sign, as in sacrificing; as if they should say, Not on me, but on this substitute let the evil of punishment be. See Lev. xvi. 21, 22; Exod. xxix. 10, 15; Lev. iv. 15; viii. 14, 22; Numb. viii. 12. Yea, in putting a blasphemer and curser to death, they first laid their hands on his head, as an applicatory sign, in whom the fault was, and to whom the punishment did belong, Lev. xxiv. 14. In the ordination or consecration of the Levites, the people were to lay their hands on them, Numb. viii. 10; not to give them authority, but to consecrate, and give them up to God. By laying on of the hands, as an applicatory sign, did Christ and his disciples heal diseases, &c. Mark v. 23; where note, that the ruler of the synagogue, Jairus, took this as an ordinary sign of conferring blessings from a superior, and therefore he mentioneth it with the blessing desired, Mark vi. 5; viii. 23, 25; Luke xiii. 13; iv. 40. So you may see also the apostles did; yea, and other believers, as the promise runs, Mark xvi. 18; Acts xxviii. 8. Also by laying on of hands, as an applicatory sign, they invested the seven deacons in their office, Acts vi. 6. And the prophets, and teachers in the church of Antioch, separated Barnabas and Paul to the work that God appointed them, (Acts xiii. 2, 3,) by fasting, and prayer, and imposition of hands. And Timothy received his ministerial gift, by the laying on of Paul's hands, and the hands of the presbytery, 1 Tim. iv. 14; 2 Tim. i. 6; if this last text be understood of the ministerial ordination and gift, which I rather think is meant of the apostolical imposition of hands, after baptism, for giving of the Holy Ghost. So that this sign was used upon several occasions, and is not at all forbidden in this, directly or indirectly, and therefore it is undoubtedly lawful; seeing that without doubt the less is blessed of the greater, Heb. vii. 7; and the duty and power of the pastor to bless the person in this case is unquestionable, and this imposition of hands is an allowed sign in blessing, as lifting up the hands is in praying; here is Scripture enough to prove it lawful, and very meet.

2. But let us inquire yet whether the Scripture lay not some kind of obligation on us, to use this ceremony in confirmation. To which end let these several things be well considered.[i]

(1.) We find in Scripture a blessing of church members with laying on of hands. (2.) We find in Scripture, that the Holy Ghost is in a special manner promised to believers, over and above that measure of the Spirit, which caused them to believe. (3.) We find that prayer with laying on of hands, was the outward means to be used by Christ's ministers, for the procuring of this blessing. (4.) We find that this was a fixed ordinance to the church, and not a temporary thing. Lay all this together, and you will see as much as my proposition doth affirm. Let us try the proof of it.

I. Though the proof of the first be not necessary to the main point, yet it somewhat strengtheneth the cause. Mark x. 16, Christ took the children up in his arms, put his hands upon them, and blessed them: so Matt. xix. 15. This is not I confess a confirmation upon personal profession, which I am now pleading for; but this is a benediction by laying on of hands: and the subjects of it were such children as were members at least of the Jewish church, being before circumcised.

II. But to come nearer the matter; let us inquire what this gift of the Holy Ghost was, that is promised to believers. Whatsoever the Pelagians say, the Scripture assureth us, that faith and repentance, which go before baptism in the adult, are the gifts of the Holy Ghost; and yet for all that the Holy Ghost is to be given afterward; and though very often this after-gift is manifested by tongues, and prophecy, and miracles, yet that is not all that is meant in the promise of the Holy Ghost. God hath not tied himself by that promise to any one sort of those extraordinary gifts, no, nor constantly to give any of them; but he hath promised in general to give believers the Spirit; and therefore there is some other standing gift, for which the Spirit is promised to all such. And indeed, the Spirit promised is one, though the gifts are many; and the many sorts of gifts make not many Spirits. If any man therefore shall ask, whether by the promised Spirit be meant sanctification, or miracles, or prophecy, &c. I answer with Paul, "There are diversities of gifts, but the same Spirit, as there are differences of administrations, but the same Lord, and diversities of operations, but the same God," 1 Cor. xii. 4—6. It is therefore no wiser a question to ask, whether by the Spirit be meant this gift, or that, when it is only the Spirit in general that is promised, than to ask, whether by the Lord be meant this or that administration; and whether by God be meant this or that operation. "To one is given the word of wisdom by the Spirit, and to another the word of knowledge, by the same Spirit, to another faith by the same Spirit," &c. ver. 8—10. Now I confess, if any man can prove that this promise of the Spirit to the faithful is meant only of the extraordinary gift of miracles, then he would weaken the argument that I am about. But I prove the contrary, 1 Cor. xii. 12, 13. It is the gift of the Spirit, by which we are one body, which is called Christ's, by which we are all baptized into this one body; and such members as have a lively fellow-feeling on each other's state, ver. 26, 27; yea, such as giveth to the elect the excellent, durable grace of charity, ver. 31, and chap. xiii.

[i] Leg. Albaspin. Observat. 31. lib. 2. p. 166—168.

Gal. iv. 6, "And because ye are sons, God hath sent forth the Spirit of his Son into your hearts, crying, Abba, Father." Note here, that it is not only the gift of miracles, but the Spirit of adoption, that is here mentioned; and that it is given to believers, because they are sons. And all the first part of Rom. viii. to verse 29, do show, that it is the Spirit of adoption, supplication, and that by which we mortify the flesh, that is given to believers.

2 Cor. i. 21, 22, "Now he which stablisheth us with you in Christ, and hath anointed us, is God, who hath also sealed us, and given the earnest of the Spirit in our hearts." It is not the common gifts of the Spirit only that are here spoken of, nor is it the first gift of faith, but it is confirmation, or inward establishment in Christ, and that Spirit, which is the Father's seal upon us, and the earnest of the inheritance. I believe not that it is outward anointing, or sealing with the sign of the cross, that is here mentioned, as many papists dream; but inward unction, seal, earnest, and confirmation by the Spirit, are here expressed. So, 2 Cor. v. 5; Zech. xii. 10. It is the Spirit of grace and supplication that is promised to the church. And see the pattern in Christ our Head, on whom after baptism the Spirit descended, and to whom it is promised, Matt. xii. 18.

Ephes. i. 13, 14, "In whom also after ye believed, ye were sealed with the Holy Spirit of promise, which is the earnest of our inheritance." Here it is evident, that it is such a gift of the Spirit, which is an earnest of heaven, that is given to men, after they believe.

John vii. 39, "For the Holy Ghost was not yet given them, because that Jesus was not yet glorified." Yet the apostles had saving faith then. And that it is not meant only of the apostles' extraordinary gifts of miracles, the foregoing words show: "He that believeth on me, out of his belly shall flow living waters: but this he spake of the Spirit, which they that believe on him should receive."

By all this it is evident, that there was an eminent gift of the Holy Ghost promised to them that had already the grace of faith, repentance, and love to Christ, wrought in them by the Holy Ghost: and that though this eminent gift did very much consist in gifts of languages, prophecy, and mighty works for the confirmation of Christ's doctrine, which was then to be planted in the world; yet it was not only in those gifts, but as some had only those common, though extraordinary, gifts for the good of the church; so some had an eminent addition of special gifts, to seal them up to the day of redemption, and be the earnest of the inheritance, to the saving of the soul. If you ask, Wherein these special eminent gifts of the Holy Ghost do consist, I answer, 1. In a clearer knowledge of Christ, and the mysteries of the gospel: not an uneffectual, but a powerful, affecting, practical knowledge. 2. In a fuller measure of love, agreeable to this knowledge. 3. In joy and peace, and sweet consolation. 4. In establishment and corroboration, and firmer resolution for Christ and everlasting life.

For the understanding of which we must know, that as the doctrine is the means of conveying the Spirit, so the Spirit given is answerable to the doctrine and administration that men are under. It is a very great question, whether Adam in innocency had the Spirit or not? But as the administration, according to the mere light, and law of nature, is eminently in Scripture attributed to the Father; so Adam certainly may be well said to have had the Spirit of the Father, to enable him with gifts that were answerable to the law that he was under, and the state that he was in. But we cannot fitly say that he had that which the Scripture calleth the Spirit of the Son, as not being under the administration of the Son. But after the promise, till the coming of Christ, as the administration was mixed of law and promise, nature and grace, as the dawning of the day before sun-rising doth partake of darkness and of light; so the Spirit that was then given, was answerable to the administration and doctrine. And therefore, as there was somewhat of the gospel in those times, though yet God hath not thought it meet to call it (at least usually) by that name, but rather by the name of the promises, and prophecies of Christ; so there was somewhat of the Spirit of Christ, though it be not usually so called; but when it appeared in some eminent servants of Christ, as the prophets were, in whom the Spirit of Christ is said to have been, 1 Peter i. 11. Now as it was part of that work ascribed to the Father, to send and give the Son, and to give men to the Son; so commonly those gifts are ascribed to him which are contained in these expressions, and are the accomplishment of this work; and that not only in the Old Testament, but in the New: and therefore it is called the giving and the drawing of the Father, by which we are brought to believe in the Son; though yet the grace of faith is a special saving grace, and not common to the wicked, as the papists dream, because they find an uneffectual assent to be common.

But now, as Christ at his coming doth bring to the world a clearer light, and fuller revelation of himself, and the mysteries of redemption, and bring life and immortality to light in the gospel; and as the rising sun dispelleth the remnants of legal darkness, and his doctrine is fully called, the gospel, the Testament of Jesus Christ, so answerably he doth, by and with this doctrine, give out such a measure of the Spirit to the church, as is eminently called, the Spirit of Jesus Christ: which carrieth us higher than the first grace of faith and repentance, to those fuller degrees which were not ordinary; no not to the godly in the time of the law. And as this Spirit of Christ did extrinsically shine in the glory of tongues and wondrous works, while those were necessary to the church, and Christ's service; so both then and ever after it doth work, but in various degrees, for the sanctifying of believers, and conforming their hearts and lives to Christ, in his humiliation, patience, self-denial, meekness, contempt of the world, obedience, &c. till at last we be conformed to him in his glory.

III. I have cleared the second point, That there is an eminent gift of the Holy Ghost to be expected after our first believing, even such as ceased not with miracles: I now come to the third point, which is, That ministerial prayer, with laying on of hands, was the Scripture way for the giving of this eminent gift of the Spirit.

For the understanding of this, observe these things:—1. How sacraments, and investing signs, confer grace.—2. How the Spirit is given in baptism.—3. How far God hath, as it were, tied himself to ordinances for conferring grace.—4. What proof the Scripture yields us of the proposition.—5. What aptitude there is in ministerial confirmation, for the attainment of these ends.

1. We find in Scripture, that sacraments are not appointed (nor to be used according to the intent of the institutor) for the conferring of that grace which men have not in any degree already: but they are, (1.) Partly a solemn investiture in that which before we had a fundamental right to; as the enlisting of a soldier, or the solemnization of marriage after a firm contract; the crowning a king; the delivering possession by a key, a twig, a turf; the knighting a man by a sword, &c. This is as to relative benefits, and

right to physical benefits. (2.) And withal they are by actual excitation of grace, to increase the inherent grace received, and so to give us more. All this is evident in baptism itself, where we are to receive both remission of sins, with right to everlasting life, and also an increase of grace in the adult: and yet no man at age is to come to baptism, to require it, that is not a penitent believer already; and consequently that hath not the beginning of special saving grace, and somewhat of Christ, and the Holy Ghost, and title to forgiveness, and everlasting life. For he is under the promise, that "whosoever believeth shall not perish, but have everlasting life." And a papist will grant, that the *votum baptismi* may serve to his salvation, if he die without it. And the case of infants is the same, as to these mercies which are necessary to their state of life. Their parents must be believers, before they dedicate them to God, and consequently the child hath the covenant right before it is sealed. And it is ridiculous in the papists to damn all infants for want of baptism, and not the aged; and to make the *votum* to serve for the parent, and yet not for his child, when yet the parents' faith must serve to prove his title to baptism itself. But to leave these corrupters and innovators; we see now what is to be expected by confirmation: not that men that have no signs of corroborating grace, should come thither first to receive it; but that such as appear initially resolved, confirmed, and corroborated, may be (though not by a full and proper sacrament, yet) ministerially; 1st, Invested into the state of the confirmed, and their privileges, which is a higher form in the school of Christ: 2d, And may receive yet further confirmation, and corroboration by God's approbation and ordinance.

2. But hath not baptism done all this already, seeing we are baptized into the name of the Holy Ghost? This is our second point to be resolved. I answer, It is a great error, to think that adult persons that have nothing of the Holy Ghost, may demand baptism, and that baptism doth not give the Holy Ghost: but yet it is one thing to give the Holy Ghost in relation, and fundamental right, and another thing to give the graces of the Spirit; and it is one thing to seal and increase the initial, special grace of the Spirit, and another thing to invest in a stablishing degree: and so it is evident, that baptism, as such, is appointed but for the two first: that is, (1.) As we must have some faith and repentance, before a person at age may come to baptism, and so must have fundamental right by promise, to Christ, and pardon, and life; so this is sealed in baptism, and we are solemnly invested in it, and our grace excited for increase: but is it not requisite that a man have a further degree of grace before he come. (2.) In baptism, it is our very relation to God, as our Father and God, to Christ as our Saviour, and to the Holy Ghost as our Sanctifier, that is sealed to us, and we are invested with; which is the foundation of all that afterward from the Spirit is given us. As in marriage the persons in relation are given to each other for marriage ends; so in baptism, God the Father, Son, and Holy Ghost, one God in three persons, are solemnly given to us in relation to themselves, for christian baptismal ends. But as after marriage, the man takes home his wife, and delivereth her a possession of his house first, and after admits her to bed and board, according to his covenant; so Christ doth after baptism take home the christian into his church, and admit him to the several privileges of it, in the season and manner as he seeth meet: so that as all the good that we do after baptism is but the fulfilling of our baptismal covenant, and yet we did not the good when we covenanted to do it; so all the after-mercies, that God giveth us by promise (at least) on his part, are but the fulfilling or fruits of his baptismal covenant; and that he did not give them in our baptism. So that confirmation is no full and proper gospel sacrament, as baptism is, but a particular subsequent investiture in some of the fruits of baptism itself, in the season of them.

3. But have we any certainty that this ordinance shall prove effectually confirming to us? If not, it will be but an idle, empty ceremony. This is our third question: to which I answer, (1.) Ordinances are duties, which we must use, and in which we must wait on God for his blessing if we will have it: and therefore in the way of duty we must be found. (2.) What if you have not a certainty that your prayer shall be granted, will you not therefore pray? or if you are not certain that a sermon shall profit you, will you not hear it? or that reading shall profit you, will you not read? or that the Lord's supper shall increase your grace, will you not use it? (3.) But I may say more: if you come prepared, you may be sure of a blessing in some degree: as it is not every one that prayeth, and heareth, and receiveth the Lord's supper, that shall certainly have the blessing, but the prepared soul that is the subject of the promise, which is annexed to that ordinance; so it is not every one that is externally confirmed by prayer, and imposition of hands, that shall be sure of the blessing, but the soul that is prepared as afore described. (4.) But yet the several degrees of blessing God hath kept in his own hand, and not affixed them by promise to any person, in any ordinance. He may bless the word, prayer, the Lord's supper, &c. to one true christian more than to another, and yet perform his promise to them all; and so he may this outward confirmation.

4. But what proof is there in Scripture of such an ordinance, or practice? That is our fourth question: to which I answer, (1.) For the main point in question, it is already proved, beyond all controversy; viz. the necessity of a personal profession, and covenant, before men be admitted to the church privileges of the adult, and that it belongeth to the office of Christ's ministers to judge of and approve this profession, &c. It is none of this we have now to prove, but only the manner of admission hereupon, whether it be to be done by prayer, with benediction, and imposition of hands. And it is not the lawfulness of this, for that is proved before; but whether this manner and solemnity be a thing which ordinarily we should observe? And that it is so, this seems to me to prove, as beyond controversy it belongeth to spiritual superiors, even the ministers of Christ, to pray for the people, and bless them, so this must be in a special manner exercised upon great and special occasion: but the admission of the adult upon their personal covenanting and profession, is a great and special occasion. This is as good an argument as any we have for stated family prayer, that I remember; and it is clearly good for both.

1. I should but trouble you to prove the general part of the major, that it belongeth to the pastors to pray for and bless the people ministerially. 2. And the application to this reason is proved thus: 1. "All things are sanctified by the word and prayer;" therefore this. 2. If the great and special works and changes of our lives be not thus to be sanctified, much less the smaller; and so the whole command would be void. We agree, that at marriage, at our investiture in the ministerial office, &c. there must be ministerial prayer, and benediction, usually, to sanctify it to the faithful: but here there is as great,

if not greater, reason for it, the change and blessing being in some sort greater.[k]

And as this is plain for ministerial prayer and benediction, so it seems that the weight and nature of the work doth determine us to the sign of imposition of hands, seeing God hath not tied it to any one or two particular cases, but made it a sign of general use, in spiritual benediction, and collations of authority, from a superior, or great and special occasions.

(2.) But we have yet a more clear proof from Scripture example, Acts viii. 15—17. Peter and John were sent to Samaria, when they heard that they believed, and "when they were come down, they prayed for them, that they might receive the Holy Ghost; for as yet he was fallen on none of them; only they were baptized in the name of the Lord Jesus: then laid they their hands on them, and they received the Holy Ghost." So Acts xix. 5, 6, "When they heard this, they were baptized in the name of the Lord Jesus: and when Paul had laid his hands upon them, the Holy Ghost came on them, and they spake with tongues, and prophesied." And Acts ix. 17, Ananias laid his hands on Saul (before converted by a voice from heaven, though not baptized) that he might receive his sight and the Holy Ghost at once.

And this was the gift that Simon Magus would have bought with money. And it seemeth to me most probable, that this was the gift that Timothy received by laying on of Paul's hands (which being for the service of the church, 1 Cor. xii. 7, he was to stir up, and exercise in his ministry, 2 Tim. 1, 6.) And that the laying on of the hands of the presbytery, (1 Tim. iv. 14,) was at another time. That the Holy Ghost was then given by prayer, with imposition of hands, is thus evident.

IV. But the last point remaineth, whether this were not temporary, and now ceased: where I shall take in the fifth particular, before named, about the aptitude of the means now. And when I have proved it once appointed, it lieth on the contrary-minded, to prove it changed or ceased; that is the task of them that affirm it ceased. If I show them an obligation once laid, they must prove it taken off. Their only argument is, that the persons and occasion were only extraordinary, and are ceased, and therefore so is the sign and means. To which I answer, 1. By the denying the antecedent; both as to persons and occasion: they were not only extraordinary. 2. By the denying the consequence, as it is inferred from the persons; for extraordinary persons were our patterns for ordinary, durable works.

But I prove the negative: 1. The use and ends of the ancient imposition of hands do still continue: therefore we are to judge that the sign and means is not to cease. For the proof of the antecedent, remember that I have before proved, that it was not only (though very eminently) the gift of tongues and miracles, that was then meant by the Holy Ghost that was given, but also corroborating grace. And the necessity and actual collation, and use of this, doth still continue.

2. There is still a discernible aptitude in the means to these necessary ends. The baptized believer may yet want the joy of the Holy Ghost, and boldness of access to God, and the shedding abroad of fuller love in the heart, Rom. v. 5; and that consolation which is much of the work of the promised Spirit, which therefore is called the Comforter; and that corroboration and stability which he needeth. Now to have a messenger of Christ that hath received a binding and loosing power, in the name of Christ to encourage us in our profession, and to put up solemn prayers for us, and as it were take us by the hand, and place us in the higher form, at least to place us at our first personal profession among adult believers, and make particular application of the promise to us, and bless us in the name of Christ, by virtue of their ministerial office; this must needs tend much to confirm, and comfort, and encourage the weak. Though still further ministerial confirmation by praying and exhortation will be necessary to the end, Acts xiv. 22; xv. 31, 32.

3. The Scripture signifieth to us, that imposition of hands was of standing use in the church, and therefore not to cease with miracles. In Heb. vi. 2, we find it named among the parts of the foundation, "laying on of hands." Now all the doubt is, what imposition of hands is there mentioned. 1. For them that think the apostle meaneth Jewish imposition, when he mentioneth the christian foundation points, I think their opinion saveth me the labour of confuting it. 2. Either then it is imposition of hands, in case of ordination, or in case of confirmation, or in case of absolution, or for working miraculous cures. The last alone it cannot be, because we find it among foundation points, and find it a continued thing; and because there is no evidence to lead us to such a restrained exposition. And if it be in the case of absolution, or ordination, that imposition is to continue, it will by consequence be proved, that it no more ceaseth here than there. And usually, they that question the use of it in one case, question it in the rest. 3. For my part, I think that it is no one of these cases alone, that the Scripture here speaketh of, but of the power and use of it in general, for the ministers of Christ to be his instruments, in conferring evangelical gifts and power, by imposition of hands. We must not limit and restrain the sense of Scripture, without evident cause. It is as if the apostle had said, You are long ago taught the necessity of repenting, and forsaking the works of death, and of believing in the true God, and of being dedicated and engaged to Father, Son, and Holy Ghost in the baptismal covenant, in which you yourselves have been consecrated unto God, and received the remission of sin; and you have seen the power that is given to the ministers of Christ, that by their prayers and imposition of hands, miracles have been wrought to confirm their doctrine, and grace is given to confirm the soul, and absolution and peace is given to the penitent, and ministerial power delivered to others, &c. But however you understand this imposition of hands, without apparent violence, you must confess either imposition in the case that we are speaking of, or that which will warrant it, and stands on the same ground, to be here meant.

So, 1 Tim. v. 22, "Lay hands suddenly on no man, neither be partaker of other men's sins." Some think that here is meant imposition of hands in ordination, and some that it is meant only of confirm-

[k] As some doubt whether conversion, or building up, be the greater work, and give it to the latter, that they may conclude the latter only to be the work of pastors, and the former but of gifted private men, so the doubt in this case is, on the same ground, whether baptizing and confirming be not as great as ordaining; and some give it to the latter, lest presbyters be thought to have power to ordain. But I answer both, as Aquila in Scotell. in Sent. 4 Des. 7, 8. et 2. p. 816. In the case of confirmation. Quando bene sit comparatio harum gratiarum: hæc potest fieri dupliciter. Uno modo sine præcisione; et sic omnino major est gratia confirmationis, quam baptismalis; sicut bene et perfecte vivere, est melius quam vivere: si autem fiat comparatio harum gratiarum cum præcisione, sic major est gratia baptismalis quam confirmationis, quia majoris virtutis est mortuum vivificare, quam vivificatum fortificare. So I say between initiating a christian and initiating a minister.

ation, and some of absolution; but however, it will help us in the following argument.

4. Scripture fully proveth that laying on of hands is a thing to be continued to other uses, where the reason of continuance is the same: therefore we are not to judge it ceased as to this use. This text last named shows that it is a standing or continued thing; and if for absolution, then for confirmation; and if for ordination, then for both the other. So, 1 Tim. iv. 14, showeth, that the presbytery did lay hands on Timothy in ordination: and if it cease not to this, it ceaseth not to other continuing uses.

Thus much from Scripture, for imposition of hands is more than nothing; though it may not be so full as you expected: but on the contrary, nothing is brought to prove it unlawful, that is worth the mentioning.

The last thing that I have to do, is to argue from the practice of the church, as the exposition of these texts of Scripture. If the universal church of Christ have used confirmation by prayer and laying on of hands, as a practice received from the apostles, and no other beginning of it can be found; then have we no reason to think the ceremony to be ceased, or to interpret the forementioned scripture contrary to this practice of the universal church. But the antecedent is true, as I now come briefly to prove, supposing what Mr. Hanmer hath said. It is commonly known, that the ancientest canons of the church do speak of this as the unquestioned practice and duty of the church: so that to recite canons were loss of time in so known a case. And if any say, that anointing and crossing were ancient; I answer, 1. That "they were as ancient in the popish use, as the matter of a sacrament, or as necessary signs," is not true, nor proved, but disproved by our writers against the popish confirmation frequently. 2. Nor can it be proved that they were as ancient as indifferent things. 3. We prove the contrary, because they were never used in Scripture times, there being no mention of them. 4. So that we bring antiquity but to prove the continuance of Scripture practice, and so to clear the sense of it; but the papists plead the fathers, for that which Scripture is a stranger to.[l]

If Ignatius ad Heronem Diaconum be genuine, there is this testimony, *Nihil sine episcopis operare. Sacerdotes enim sunt: tu autem diaconus Sacerdotum: Illi baptizant, sacrificant, manus imponunt, tu autem ipsis ministra.* I recite it out of Usher's Latin copy, as supposed the most pure.

Tertullian, lib. de Proscript. cap. 36, appealing to the practice of the apostle John, in the African churches, mentioneth, as his faith that he taught; one God the Creator, and Jesus Christ the Son of God, and the resurrection of the body; and that he joined the law and prophets, with the evangelical and apostolic writings, and thence drunk this faith. And of his practice he saith, *Aqua signat, Sancto Spiritu vestit, Eucharistia pascit;* as three distinct ordinances, Lib. de Baptismo, cap. 8, having mentioned baptism, and the unction joined to that, and not then to confirmation, he addeth, *Dehinc manus imponitur, per benedictionem advocans, et invitans Spiritum Sanctum.*

Idem de Resur. Carn. cap. 8. *Sed et caro abluitur, ut anima immaculetur: Caro unguitur, ut anima consecratur: Caro signatur, ut et anima muniatur. Caro manus impositione adumbratur, ut et anima Spiritu illuminetur.*

Cyprian ad Stephan. Epist. 72, et ad Jubaian, is too much for it. I will not trouble you in citing any writers since general councils were in use, because their testimony is enough. He that would see such may read Baronius ad An. 35, at large. So much for the proof of the fitness of imposition of hands in confirmation.

I come now to the second part of my proposition, viz. That this ceremony is not of such necessity, as that such as scruple it, should be denied liberty of forbearing the reception of it, if they submit to the ministerial trial and approbation of their profession, and admission, and reception to church privileges.

[m] For proof of this consider, 1. That we do not find that God any where instituted this sign, as a matter of necessity still, without interruption, to be used; but only that by holy men it was applied as a convenient sign, or gesture to the works, in which they used it. Even as lifting up of hands in prayer was ordinarily used as a fit gesture, not wilfully to be neglected without cause, and yet not of flat necessity; or as kneeling in prayer is ordinarily meet, but not always necessary. We find no more Scripture for the one than for the other; which indeed showeth on one side, how causeless it is to question the lawfulness of it, any more than of lifting up the hands, or kneeling; and yet how little reason there is on the other side, to make it a matter of flat necessity.

2. As we find that kneeling in prayer, and lifting up the hands, were oft omitted, so we find that sometimes the Holy Ghost is given before baptism, or imposition of hands, Acts x.; and we find not that the apostles used it to all. Though I confess the negative arguing is infirm, yet it seems not probable that this was always done.

3. It is somewhat suspicious to find in Justin Martyr's description of the christian churches' practices, no mention of this, nor any sacrament, but baptism, and the Lord's supper; nor any of these Roman ceremonies. And Irenæus and some others are silent in it.

4. God maketh no ceremonies under the gospel so necessary, except the two sacraments; nor layeth so great a stress on them, as under the law; and therefore we are not to interpret the gospel as laying men's salvation, or the peace of the church, on any ceremonies; unless we find it clearly expressed.

5. For all that I have said from Scripture for imposition of hands in confirmation, though the lawfulness of it is proved past doubt, yet the proof of the duty of using it is liable to so many objections, as that I must needs conclude, that the gospel tenderness, and the sense of our mutual infirmities, and our care of tender consciences, and of the church's peace, should restrain all the sons of piety and peace from making it a matter of flat necessity, and forcing them that scruple it to submit to it.

And now having said thus much of imposition of hands, and confirmation, as grounded on the apostles'

[l] Greg. M. in Epist. ad. Quirin. (Leg. inter Usserii Hybernic. Epist. 2. p. 6.) Et quidem ab antiqua Patrum institutione didicimus, ut qui apud hæresin in Trinitatis nomine baptizantur, cum ad sanctam ecclesiam redeunt, aut unctione chrismatis, aut impositione manuum, aut sola professione fidei, ad sinum matris ecclesiæ revocentur.

[m] The ancient church also used it so variously, as that it is plain they fixed it to no one case alone. Of the divers cases, in which they imposed hands, (on the catechumens, and four times on the penitents, and divers other,) you may see in Albaspinæus Observationes, Obs. 31, 32. et passim. Grotius Epist. 154. p. 379. Manus impositas baptizatis, nisi ab iis, qui jus haberent conferendi cælestia illo dona, primis temporibus non apparet. Serius id introductum est in episcoporum honorem, quo magis in apostolicum jus successisse crederentur. Nec causa aberat, quam ceremoniæ illi, velut naturalem diximus, precandi, scilicet, Deum, ut ei qui baptizatus jam fidem erat professus, ea largiri vellet, quæ ad præstandum in fide, maxime in periculis gravibus, sunt necessaria.

example; I must again and again remember you, that this is in a manner but *ex abundanti*, and that the cause that I am pleading doth not at all need it; but that I did before most clearly manifest the truth of my position upon other grounds, upon which I shall proceed; and having showed the necessity of ministerial judging of men's profession, and the personal covenanting of the adult, and the lawfulness of imposing hands therein, I go on as to the manner.

PROP. 14. *Though in receiving adult persons out of infidelity by baptism into the church, a sudden profession, without any stay to see their reformation, may serve turn; yet in the receiving those that were baptized heretofore, into the number of adult members, or to the privileges of such, their lives must be inquired after, which must be such as do not confute their profession.*

We find in Scripture, that the converted were suddenly baptized, and they staid not for any reformation of life to go before. Indeed, the ancient churches afterwards kept their catechumens long in expectation; but that was not to see their lives first reformed, but that they might have time to teach them the doctrine of Christ, which they must know before they could be converts indeed. The apostles did suddenly baptize converted Jews and proselytes, because they had so much preparatory knowledge, as that a shorter teaching might acquaint them with the christian doctrine. But the heathens must be long in learning so much as the Jews knew before conversion.[n]

Yet if the catechumens did fall into gross sin, in time of their expectation and learning, they were so much the longer delayed, because it signified, that their first professed desires of entering into the church, upon Christ's terms, were not right.

But the baptized stand upon other terms: for, 1. They are already in covenant with God the Father, Son, and Holy Ghost; and have renounced the flesh, the world, and the devil, and promised obedience to God, and to live according to their covenant. And this the church hath still required of them, as I showed out of Justin Martyr, and others before.[o] Dionysius, (or whoever else,) in lib. de Hierarch. Eccles. saith, *Ipse autem se omnino ea quæ tradentur, sequuturum esse pollicetur;* and *Ex eo præterea quærit, num ita instituat vivere, cum promisit asseverationibus*, &c.: upon which saith Albaspinæus, *Qui scilicet, fidem christianam, christianumque vivendi genus, et mores, sese complexos persequuturosque jurabant, antequam baptizarentur.* (in Tertul. de Pœnit. p. 289.) *et postea. Non accedebant ad baptismum nisi de rebus fidei plane instructi, id est, de Dei magnitudine, et potestate, rebusque quæ in evangeliis continentur, uno excepto, eucharistiæ mysterio; neque baptizabantur, nisi postquam ea omnia se credere jurassent, quorum fides a fide pœnitentiæ incipiebat*, &c. *Et in sequ. Jurabant in baptismo solennibus verbis, se nunquam*[p] *peccaturos; deinde renunciabant diabolo et pompis ejus. Denique censura si peccarent post baptismum coercebantur.* So that men that are engaged in covenant with God, must keep covenant, or manifest themselves penitent, for the violation of it, before they are admitted to further privileges. There is a long time, in which they grow up from an infant state to an adult; and how they live in that time, must be inquired after.

2. Otherwise the apostate would have equal acceptance and privileges with the faithful.

3. And so penitence and absolution would be excluded and confounded with mere confirmation.

4. Moreover the baptized are obliged to be responsible for their lives, being under the government of Christ's ministers, and among his saints.

5. For the sake of their own souls, and of the church and ordinances, we must endeavour to preserve them from corruption, which lying professions would introduce; and therefore must not overlook or neglect such evidence as is within our reach.

6. Else ministers that are by office to judge of their profession, would be unfaithful judges, and forfeit their trust, if they shall wilfully neglect any evidence within their cognizance, by which they may be enabled to judge.

But yet it is not the certainty of inward, saving grace, that we must find out by men's lives; for no man can have such certainty of another; but only that their lives be not such, as null, and invalidate, and confute their profession, and they live not in the perfidious violation of their baptismal covenant.

PROP. 15. *It is not of flat necessity that the profession of the expectant be made in the open congregation, or before many, in order to his confirmation and admittance.*

Proved, 1. It is not of necessity, that converted infidels be admitted by baptism into the state of adult members, upon a public profession in a congregation; therefore it is not of necessity, that others be so admitted in confirmation. The antecedent is proved by the instance of the eunuch, (Acts viii.) whom Philip baptized in their way, and the jailer and his household, (Acts xvi.) baptized in the night at home. The consequence is proved by the propriety and reason of the case.

2. If a man may by confirmation be admitted into the number of adult christians, in the church universal, without being admitted into a particular church, then his profession and admission need not, in that case, to be before the congregation: but the antecedent is true; as I prove thus. A man may, by adult baptism, be admitted first into the universal church only; as was the eunuch, the jailer, Lydia, Sergius Paulus, and every first convert in any city, where the apostles came; therefore a man may, by confirmation, be admitted into the number of the adult, in the catholic church only: for the reason is the same, and the former admitteth them into the same number.

The consequence of the major is plain. For no one congregation more than another, can claim the cognizance of the admission of a member into the universal church, or confirming them in it.

3. Scripture hath no where made such public admission to be of constant necessity; therefore it is not so.

4. Else none could be admitted, or confirmed, when persecution hindereth church assemblies.

5. The church is to believe and trust the pastors, to whom it doth by office belong to try and admit them.

6. General, unfixed ministers may thus try, approve, and confirm, who are not pastors of any particular church, such as apostles, evangelists, and others were; therefore they are not always to do it

[n] Lege quæ habet Grotius, Discus. Apol. Rivet, p. 235. cum antecedentibus ex Antiq. et de suis.

[o] Read the whole order of Baptism in Dionysius, ibid. c. 4.

[p] That is, not to turn to an ungodly life, but to endeavour and perform sincere obedience. Albaspin. in Tertul. de Pœnitent. cap. 7. Sexcentis locis, non dicam hoc capite; unam ait tantum a lavacro veniam superesse, neque ullum primis illis temporibus inter privatum aut publicum graviorum criminum discrimen invenient. Vide cætera.

before a particular church; nor indeed did they always do so.

PROP. 16. *When a person is admitted among the adult members of a particular church, as well as the universal, his profession and admission must be either before the church, or satisfactorily made known to the church at least, who must approve of it by a judgment of discretion, in order to their communion with him; and this among us is the ordinary case; because it is the duty of all that have opportunity, to join themselves to some particular church; and it is in such churches that communion in public worship and order must be had, either statedly, or transiently and temporarily.*

1. The solemnity itself of our transition into the number of adult members, and their communion, is of very great advantage, as I shall manifest more anon.

2. We that are commonly against the private admission of infants, (at least except in some urgent case,) have less reason to be for the private transition and admission of men among the adult, and that into a particular governed church.[q]

3. The whole society among whom such a person is entered, do owe him much duty and brotherly assistance. They must love him with a special love: they must live, though not in a levelling, yet in a charitable community with him, not shutting up the bowels of compassion from him, when they see him in want, but relieving him, as if they suffered with him; they are not only to love him, and relieve him as a man, but as one of Christ's little ones, or friends; yea, as his brethren; yea, as loving and relieving Christ in them, Matt. xxv. 35, to the end. They must receive and relieve a disciple in the name of a disciple. Besides this, they must have church union and communion with him, as one body; and must pray for him, rejoice with him in God's praises, and the Lord's supper, and watch over him, and admonish and reprove him in sin, for his recovery; and avoid him if he walk disorderly, and be impenitent in scandalous sin, &c.

Now, 1. No man can perform all this duty, to a man that he knoweth not to be thus related to him. If he know not that he owes him this duty, any more than to any one else in the world, how shall he pay it to him? To say that we are bound to take all men that converse with us to be such, is to say, that christians must renounce their wits, and turn the church into Bedlam.

2. And as this proves, that the church members must be made known to one another, so it proves that they must have a judgment of discretion in receiving them; though the pastors have the judgment of governing direction. For God hath not left the pastors at liberty, to take in whom they please; but hath described what profession they shall accept, or what persons they shall admit, and whom they shall reject. If therefore the pastors go against the word of God, then this following is the people's duty: (1.) If they know not the error, or the case be doubtful, they are to rest in obedience to their pastors, (for that is undoubtedly their duty,) the work being the pastor's, and not theirs. (2.) But if the case be plainly contrary to the Scripture, as if he would admit an impenitent drunkard, fornicator, &c. they must disown his sin, that it lie not upon them, and refuse private familiarity with that person; but not withdraw from public ordinances, because of his presence; for when they have done their duty, and rid themselves of the guilt by a dissent, the person is to them as morally absent, though locally and physically present; and the ordinance is not defiled to them by his corporal presence; but the guilt will lie on the rulers of the church; otherwise all churches should be broken in pieces, if the people must separate, when every one that they are confident is unworthy is introduced; and the governed will become the governors. (3.) But if it be not a few that the pastors thus introduce against the certain word of God, but so many and such as will corrupt the substance of the church, and make it an uncapable matter for the form, and so to become another thing, and destroy the very ends of church association, so that it is no longer a communion of saints; then the people fearing God, are bound to stop this before it have quite corrupted the church, by admonishing the pastors, and advising with neighbour churches to admonish them; and if that prevail not, by rejecting them: and if they cannot do so, by reason of a major vote of uncapable persons, they ought to withdraw themselves, and worship God in such a church as is truly capable of the name and ends. And this is a lawful and necessary separation; of which as it is a duty, God is the cause; and as it is a forsaking of the rest, the culpable cause is only in themselves. I can easily prove all this, but that I think it needless tediousness.[r]

(4.) And indeed, it would be very hard measure, if at the corrupt administration of a carnal, or careless, or erroneous pastor, all the church must be under an obligation to give their estates by way of relief to every one, that he will put the name of a christian and church member upon unworthily: then may he force them to maintain all the beggars and rogues about them, though they were infidels and impious men. I speak not of the common relief of the needy; for that I know they owe to an infidel; but of a special community, which charity must make among the disciples of Christ. It is against all reason, that an erring or careless pastor shall thus command all the people's estates, by introducing such without their consent, whom they are bound thus to maintain.

(5.) Yea indeed, the Spirit of God is, in the saints, a spirit of discerning; so that it is not possible that all the church should in their affections obey such a corrupt administrator, by loving all the notorious, ungodly men, as saints, with the special love of brethren, whom he will carelessly or erroneously put in the place of saints. I cannot possibly love that man as a saint, or disciple of Christ, that I am certain is his enemy, and none such.

I conclude therefore, that though the people be not church governors by a vote, (that is a great error,) yet they have a judgment of discerning, according to which they must obey, or reject, their pastor's administrations. And he that denieth this, and would have them yield an absolute obedience, without trying, choosing, and refusing, would not

[q] Read Dr. Hammond's Prac. Catech. l. 5. sect. 4. p. 298, 299. Of the Communion of Saints.

Albaspinæus in Tertul. de Pœnitent. cap. 8, 9. p. 291. Cum pro foribus templi starent pœnitentes, prætereuntibus sacerdotibus, cæterisque fidelibus omnibus, omnino dolentis animi signis pœnitentiam suam testabantur, lacrymis non parcebant, precibus instituebant, volvebantur, et si quæ alia habet pœnitentia, quæ misericordiam movere possint; non omittebant, ut pacem recuperarent. Primum ante sacerdotes procumbebant, martyribus deinde adgeniculabantur, cæteris denique fratribus et viduis, ut ait Pacianus, enixe supplicabant, ut a Deo et ab ecclesia veniam pro se impetrarent.

[r] Albaspin. ubi sup. Animadvertendum est, pœnitentes non solum hæc et similia egisse, ut cum Deo in gratiam redirent, verum etiam ut sacerdotes, et cæteros fratres æquiores haberent, in quorum arbitrio et judicio nonnunquam erat, eos in ecclesia revocare.

I cite this to show what cognizance the people were to have of such affairs.

only make the pastors of the papal strain, but would give them a Jesuitical obedience, above what the moderate papists give the pope. And therefore seeing that *ad finem* there is a necessity that the people consent, or else they cannot obey, nor hold communion with the person, therefore there is also the same necessity *ad finem* that they have satisfaction offered them, and have either the cognizance of the profession, and admission of the person, or that they be satisfied in the fidelity of their pastors in administration, and that he seek their consent; or, which is best, that some chosen persons do represent them, and be present at such professions with the pastors; and the pastors, and their own delegates together, do acquaint the congregation of all that are admitted, and of their satisfactory profession, that they may hold communion with them. This I speak of those (which are very many) that are fit for church communion, and yet through bashfulness, or want of utterance, are unable to make a public profession before all. (The choicest christians that I have known, have been such.) But those that are able, should rather in public make their own profession.

Object. But what if one part of the congregation approve of the person and profession, and the other disallow it?

Answ. 1. They are to be governed by the pastors. 2. And consult with the pastors of neighbour churches, in cases of great weight and danger. 3. And the lesser part of the church, in doubtful cases, and tolerable differences, is to yield to the greater part: not as if a major vote had the government of the rest, much less of their governors; but in order to unity the fewer must submit.

Quest. But what if the people would have the pastor baptize, confirm, or introduce an open heretic, or wicked person in his impenitency?

Answ. The pastor must obey God, and refuse to obey them.

Quest. And what if the people think a man unfit, whom the pastor would approve and introduce?

Answ. 1. He may admit him into the universal church, notwithstanding their unjust refusal. 2. He hath power to admit him into that particular church, against their unjust dissent, as he is the ruler of the church, and the administrator of the ordinances. 3. He hath authority to persuade and command them from Christ, to hold communion with the person, and do their duty to him; which if they do not, they commit a double sin; one of injustice and uncharitableness, in a causeless rejecting of a member of Christ; and another of disobedience, against the fifth commandment. 4. But yet the pastors cannot force the people to obey their advice and command, nor effectually procure it perhaps. 5. And therefore their fore-mentioned power is not always to be exercised; for it is in vain to use a means, that will rather hinder the end than attain to it; and so is, at that time, no means. Sometimes the pastor may see just cause to exercise all this power, and execute his part of church communion with the person, in administering the ordinances to him, and leave the people answerable to God, for refusing their part; but this is not a usual case: usually, if he see the people resolve against communion with that person, how fit soever, he is publicly to clear himself by disallowing them in their sin, and reproving them for it, and leaving the blame on them; and then in prudence to forbear the intruding of the person; because no duty is at all times a duty to be performed; and especially when the hurt that will follow upon it, in the divisions of the church, is like to be far greater than the good, if it be done. 6. But if the church should be so corrupted, as that the major vote doth set against faith and godliness as such, and so will not admit a sound member to be added to them, the pastor, with the minor part, may, after due admonition and patience, as justly reject the guilty and obstinate, as if they were but one man, and not a major part.

What is said of this case of admission, holds also of rejection by excommunication, and of other antecedent acts of discipline.

(4.) Lastly, If excommunication must usually be done in public, before the whole church, that they may know whom to avoid, and know the reason of it; then admission must usually be done in public, the person or the pastor opening the case to the people, that they may know whom to have communion with; and know the reason of it: but the antecedent is confessed by almost all. And it is proved plainly by Paul's practice and direction, 1 Cor. v. throughout: and it was the custom of the christian churches in Tertullian's days, Apolog. cap. 39. There also (in the christian meeting for worship) are exercised exhortations, castigations, and the divine censure: for judgment is passed with great deliberation, or weight, as with men that are assured of the presence or sight of God: and it is the highest representation of the judgment to come, if any one so offend, as that he be discharged, or banished from communion of prayer, and of the assembly, and of all holy commerce, or fellowship.

Abundance more out of Cyprian, and others, might be easily produced, to prove that this which I have spoken, was the ancient interest of the people in these church affairs, yea, in the choice of their pastors: yea, and in rejecting unworthy pastors, Cyprian saith, they had a chief interest; not by ruling power, but by a prudent exercise of obedience, choosing the good, and refusing the evil. Self-preservation is natural to every body, where it is not by evil means, and to the hurt of the public state. It is hard if a natural body may not lawfully refuse or cast up poison, if a governor should give it them. God bindeth none to the perdition of their souls; nor any holy society to destroy itself, or suffer itself to be destroyed, or corrupted by others, without the use of all just means to resist the bane. But of this I shall desire the reader, that would know the judgment and practice of the ancient church, to peruse Dr. Blondel's "de Jure plebis in Regimine Ecclesiast." adjoined to that excellent piece of Grotius "de Imperio summarum Potestatum circa Sacra."[s]

This much may satisfy you, that it should not be usually a secret, but a solemn transition from an infant state of membership, into an adult state; and that by a public profession or notification of it, the particular church should have satisfaction herein.

PROP. 17. *It is convenient, though not of necessity, that every church do keep a register of all that are admitted thus into the number of the adult members.*

As we were wont to keep a register of the infants baptized, so have we as much reason of the adult, approved and confirmed, or restored. Corporations of old were wont to keep a book of the names of their burgesses or citizens; in respect to which, God is said to have a book of life, wherein he writes men's names, and out of which he blots them, speaking after the manner of men. The church hath great reason for this practice, the business being of so great weight; that we forget not who are of our

[s] To recite more after all those of Blondel, is but to do a needless work. There is enough to satisfy all that are moderate for popular interest.

communion, which without a register, in great congregations, must needs be done. If any be so vain, as to demand a Scripture proof of this; let him first bring me a Scripture proof, that he may read with spectacles, or write a sermon from the preacher's mouth, or use notes in the pulpit, or print, &c. and then I will give him proof of this: in the mean time, if this do not satisfy him, he shall have liberty to disuse it.

Prop. 18. *Those that were never thus ministerially and explicitly approved, confirmed, or absolved, (after an ungodly life,) but have been permitted without it to join ordinarily with the church in prayer and praises, and have been admitted to the communion of the church in the Lord's supper, are approved and confirmed, eminently though not formally; though, in so doing, both the pastors and themselves did sin against God, by the violation of his holy order. So that such may be a true church, though much corrupted or disordered.*

This I add for two reasons: 1. To confute them that say our churches are no true churches, for want of an explicit profession. 2. And to acquaint you who it is among us that are, or are not, to be called to confirmation.

1. It is not the degree of clearness and openness in our profession, or in the ministerial approbation or admission, that is essential to a church member. An obscure profession may be truly a profession. Some obscure profession hath been ordinarily made by our people in this land heretofore, by their ordinary hearing the word, and standing up at the recital of the creed; and joining with the church in prayer and praise, and confessing the Scriptures to be the word of God, and acknowledging the ministry: and a further profession they made, by actual receiving the Lord's supper, which is a silent profession of their faith in Christ. And though they were not solemnly approved and confirmed, (except that one of many had a ceremonious confirmation from the bishop in their childhood,) yet were they actually admitted to daily communion with the church, and the special part of communion in the Lord's supper. And though this profession and admission was lamentably defective, (of which more anon,) yet it is such as may prove our ordinary assemblies to have been true churches.

2. And I do not think it fit, that any that have been already admitted to church communion in the Lord's supper, should be now called out to confirmation, by imposition of hands; though where there is just cause to question their knowledge, faith, or lives, they may by the pastor be called to give an account of them; and put upon a clearer profession than they have yet made: but sure when they have been admitted to the Lord's supper by any regular ministry and church, they are to be taken for adult members till they are justly cast out, or do cast out themselves. For the more perfect doth include the less perfect in it. If a man be ordained a presbyter, that was never ordained deacon, he is not to be called back again and made a deacon. If you make a man free of your trade, before he was ever bound apprentice, you cannot call him back again, and bind him apprentice after this. If the university give a man the degree of doctor of divinity, or master of arts, that never took degree of bachelor of divinity, or of arts, they cannot afterwards call him back to take his bachelor's degree. If you have irregularly admitted the untried, unapproved, unconfirmed to the Lord's supper, you have *eminenter*, though not *formaliter*, confirmed and approved him, though irregularly. Of this more anon.

Prop. 19. *So exceeding great and many are the mischiefs that have befallen us, by the neglect of a solemn, meet transition from an infant into the adult church state, and which undoubtedly will continue, till this be remedied, that all magistrates, ministers, and people, that dissemble not, in professing themselves to be christians, should with speed and diligence attempt the cure.*

Let us here take a view of the case of our nation, and congregation, and then consider the effects and consequents.

All the people of our parishes, except anabaptists, do bring their children to be baptized; which, if it were faithfully done, were a happy means of an early engagement unto Christ, and a happy entrance upon further mercy. Multitudes of those know not what baptism is, nor to what use and end it is appointed, nor what benefit their children may receive by it. I speak upon too sure and large experience; nor do they know what christianity is, nor who Jesus Christ is, nor what it is they are to do in baptism; but there they make a promise customarily, as they are bid, in words not understood, that they will acquaint their children at age with the covenant there made, which they never understood themselves, and that they will educate them in godliness, when they hate godliness at the heart. And when they come home, they perform their promise accordingly: they teach them nothing of the doctrine of christianity, and the life to come, but they give them up to the flesh, and the world, which there in words they did renounce; and they teach them by their daily examples to curse, and swear, and rail, and to be proud, and covetous, and voluptuous, serving their bellies instead of God; and hatefully reproaching a godly life, instead of teaching it their children. These children are customarily brought to the assemblies, where they hear the plainest teaching, without understanding or regarding it, and grow hardened under daily reproofs and exhortations; living as their parents taught them, some in gross ignorance and worldliness, without any signs of godliness, further than to come to church; some in drunkenness, some in whoredom, abundance in a malignant hatred of a holy life, making them that use it the common scorn, and taking them for the hatefullest persons in the parish or country where they live. For custom sake, and to quiet their conscience in their sin, they will come to the Lord's table, if they be admitted by the pastor, and may have it in their mode and way: and if a minister shall desire them to come to him first, that he may understand their knowledge and profession, they scorn it; and ask him by what authority he would examine them, and what proof he hath that men must be examined, before they be admitted to the Lord's supper? And some self-conceited, half-witted writers have taught them this lesson, and made ministerial trial and approbation odious to them. But because they were once baptized, and have since come to hear and join with us in the assembly, therefore they think that they have right to all ordinances, and are true christians and adult members of the church; and also exempt from the government of the pastors, that require them to submit to the means of their own good. In the bishops' days, some few of them were confirmed: in the country where I lived, about one of ten or twenty; and what that was, and how it was done, I can tell you, by what I once made trial of. When I was a schoolboy, about fifteen years of age, the bishop coming into the country, many went in to him to be confirmed. We that were boys, ran out to see the bishop among the rest, not knowing any thing of the meaning of the business. When we came thither, we met about thirty or forty in all, of our own stature and temper, that had come for to be *bishopped,* as then it was called. The bishop examined us not all in one article of the faith; but in a church-yard, in haste, we were set in a rank, and he passed hastily over us, laying his hands on our head, and saying a few words, which neither I nor any that I spoke with understood; so hastily were they uttered, and a very short prayer recited, and there was an end. But whether we were christians or infidels, or knew so much as that there was a God, the bishop little knew, nor inquired. And yet he was esteemed one of the best bishops in England. And though the canons require that the curate or minister send a certificate that children have learned the catechism; yet there was no such thing done, but we ran of our own accord to see the bishop only; and almost all the rest of the county had not this much: this was the old, careless practice of this excellent duty of confirmation. Some few, perhaps half a parish in the best places, will send their children to church, to be catechised yet; but even those few that learn the words, for the most part understand not what they say, and are as ignorant of the matters, as if they never learned the words. This is the common way, by which our parishes come to be churches, and our people to be christians; supposing some to be mixed among them, that are more faithfully devoted to God in baptism, and better educated in the fear of God.

Now let us see what are the real, visible, undeniable fruits of this defective, sinful course. Because men build upon this fundamental falsehood, that infant baptism, upon the parents' profession, doth give them right to the church state and privileges of the adult, without any personal profession and covenanting with God, when they come to the use of reason, which the church must have cognizance of; and so they that entered somewhat more regularly into an infant church state, do become adult members secretly, unobservedly, and nobody well knows how. Hereupon it followeth,

1. That our churches are lamentably corrupted and diseased, though they are true churches, and have life in them, while they are made so like the unbelieving and ungodly world; and the garden of Christ is made too like the common wilderness: for heathens, and impious persons, and all sorts of the unclean (almost) are the members of them, where parishes, or parish-meetings, are made convertible with churches. I would make the case never worse nor better than it is. Till within these few years, I knew but very imperfectly how it is, and I thought the case had been better with some and worse with others than I have found it upon trial. And had I not set upon the duty of personal instruction, I should never have known the state of the people: but now we have dealt with them almost all in private personally, I shall truly tell you the state of this parish, by which you may conjecture at the rest of the nation. I know not a congregation in England that hath in it proportionably so many that fear God: and yet our whole parish consisteth of all these sorts following: (1.) Among eight hundred families, there are about five hundred persons such as the vulgar call precise, that are rated to be serious professors of religion, or perhaps are somewhat more. These live in unity, and seem to me to seek first the kingdom of God and his righteousness, and are of as peaceable, harmless, humble spirits, and as unanimous, without inclination to sects, or ostentation of their parts, as any people I know. (2.) Besides these, there are some of competent knowledge and exterior performances, and live so blameless, that we can gather from them no certain proof, or violent presumption, that they are ungodly, or that their profession is not sincere. So many of these joining with the rest, as make about six hundred, do own their church membership, and consent to live under so much of church order and government, as unquestionably belongeth to presbyters to exercise, and to be my pastoral charge. (3.) Besides these, there are some that are tractable and of willing minds, that by their expressions seem to be ignorant of the very essentials of christianity; which yet I find to have obscure conceptions of the truth, when I have condescendingly better searched them, and helped them by my inquiries. These also (as weak in the faith) we receive. (4.) Some there are that are of competent understandings, and of lives so blameless, that we durst not reject them; but they hold off themselves, because they are taught to question, if not to disown, our administrations; for all that, we give liberty to all that in tolerable things do differ.[t] (5.) Some there are that are secret heathens, believing with Aristotle, that the world was from eternity; making a scorn of Christ, and Moses, and heaven, and hell, and Scripture, and ministers, and all religion; thinking that there is no devil, no immortality of the soul, or everlasting life: but this they reveal only in secret, to those that they find capable by viciousness, unsettledness, or any malignity, or discontent against the godly, or the orders of the church: and yet for the hiding of their minds, they will hear, and urge us to baptize their children, and openly make the most orthodox confessions, and secretly deride it when they have done, as I can prove. And this is the only differing party among us in judgment and design, that is in danger of leavening many, that God forsaketh. (6.) Many more there are that have tolerable knowledge, and live in some notorious, scandalous sins: some in gross covetousness, and these will not be convinced: some in common drunkenness, and those will confess their faults, and promise amendment a hundred times over, and be drunk within a few days again; and thus have spent the most part of their lives: some in as constant tippling, drinking as great a quantity, but bearing it better away: some in ordinary swearing, cursing, ribaldry, whoredoms sometime: many in neglect of all family duties, and the Lord's day: and some in hateful, bitter scorns at prayer, holy conference, church order, and holy living, and the people that use it; sometimes rising up in tumults against the officers that endeavour to punish a drunkard or sabbath-breaker, and rescuing them, and seeking the ruin of the officers.[u] (7.) Some there are that are of more tractable dispositions, but really know not

[t] Of this fourth sort I hope are many that truly fear God, that, some on one pretence and some on another, forbear to join with us in the communion of the church, in the Lord's supper; but yet hear, and live in love and peace with us. And some do join with us (on the grounds as godly strangers may be admitted) sometimes in the Lord's supper, that yet expressly own not a membership in the particular church.

[u] As I would not have mentioned the faults of any of my parishioners, but on this necessity of opening the state of the nation *de facto,* so they have no reason to take it ill of me. For, 1. I accuse none by name, much less the generality. 2. The innocent do themselves know, and bewail the sins that I mention. 3. I am so far from making them worse than other parishes, that I unfeignedly profess, that I do not know any other in England of so much godliness and tractableness; which testimony is true, and more to their honour, than the mentioning of the remnants of ignorance and ungodliness is to their dishonour. If it be thus here, how much worse is it in most parts of the land '

what a christian is; that hear us from day to day, yea, and some few of them learn the words of the catechism, and yet know not almost any more than the veriest heathen in America. They all confess, that we must mend our lives, and serve God; but they know not that God is eternal, or that Christ is God, or that he is man, but say, he is a Spirit; some say neither God nor man; some say God and not man; some say man and not God; abundance say, he was man on earth, but now he is not: abundance know not what he came to do in the world; nor that there is any satisfaction made for sin, but what we must make ourselves; and they tell me, they trust to nothing for pardon and salvation, but God's mercy, and their good serving him (which is only saying every night and morning in bed, or as they undress them, the Lord's prayer, and the creed for a prayer, and coming to church). They say openly, they do not know of any surety that we have, or any that hath borne the punishment of our sin, or suffered for us: and when I repeat the history of the incarnation, life, death, and resurrection of Christ to them, they stand wondering, and say, they never heard it before. What the Holy Ghost is, they know not; nor what sanctification, faith, or justification is; nor what baptism is; nor the Lord's supper; nor to what use, but in general, for our salvation. What a church is, they know not; nor what is the office of pastor or people, save only to preach and hear, and give and receive the sacraments. If I ask them what christianity is, the best answer is, that it is a serving God as well as we can, or as God will give us leave. So that there is scarce an article of the creed, or very few, that they tolerably understand. Nay one of above fourscore years of age (now dead) thought Christ was the sun, that shineth in the firmament; and the Holy Ghost was the moon. (8.) Many there be, that join this heathenish ignorance and wicked obstinacy together; hating to be instructed; scorning to come near me, to be taught, and to be told of their sin, when they come. They will rail at us bitterly behind our backs, if we will not let them have their own will and way about the sacraments, and all church affairs; but they will not submit to that teaching, that should bring them to know what Christ or christianity is. (9.) Some there be that are of tolerable knowledge, and no drunkards, nor whoremongers, that the world knoweth of, but of more plausible lives, and have some forms of prayer in their families; but yet live in idle or tippling company, or spend their lives in vanity, and hate more a diligent serving of God, and heavenly life, than the open drunkards do:[x] these make it their work to possess people with a hatred of strict professors, and of our churches and administrations, and to that end get all the books that are written for admitting all to the Lord's table, that they can light of; and contrary to the authors' meanings, they make them engines to harden others in their impiety, and hatred of reformation. The like use they make of the writings of many dissenting divines, about church government; or any from whence they may fetch matter of reproach against the pastors and ordinances among us. (10.) Another sort there are, that are deeply possessed with a conceit, that God having determined before we are born, whether we shall be saved or not, it is in vain to strive; for if we be predestinated, we shall be saved, whatever we do; and if we be not, we shall not, whatever we do; and that we can do nothing of ourselves, nor have a good thought, but by the grace of God: and if God will give it us, we shall have it, and the devil cannot prevail against us; but if he will not give it us, it is in vain to seek it; for it is not in him that willeth, nor in him that runneth, but in God that showeth mercy; and therefore they give up themselves to security and ungodliness, because they can do nothing of themselves. And thus by misunderstanding some texts of Scripture, and abusing some truths of God, they are hardened in ungodliness, thinking that all is long of God; and they will not so much as promise reformation, nor promise to use the means, because they say, they cannot tell whether God will put it into their hearts, and it is all as he will.[y] (11.) Besides these, there is one or two honest, ignorant professors that are turned anabaptists, and join with the church of them in the next parish. (12.) And some papists are among us; and whether only those that stay from the assemblies, I cannot say.[z]

Of these twelve sorts of people this parish is composed; which I therefore mention, that the state of our parishes may be truly known; while others are compared with this: for every one hath not had the opportunities which I have had, to know all their people, or the most.

And now if all these are fit to go for christians, then must we make a new kind of christianity, and a new gospel, and a new Christ. And if all these are fit to be church members, then we must make a new kind of churches.

And why then may not those be christians and church members, that never heard of the name of Christ, as well as many of these?

2. By this untried entrance of all sorts into our churches, we bring a dishonour on the very christian name, and so on the Lord Jesus himself, and on his gospel and holy ways. Christianity is not a matter of mere opinion: Christ came not into the world only to persuade men to have high thoughts of him, but to save his people from their sins, and to destroy the works of the devil. And when the church of Christ shall be turned into a den of thieves, or a sty of swine, what a great dishonour is it to the Lord! as if we would persuade the world that his servants are not holier than others, and differ but in an opinion from the world. Christ needeth not disciples, and therefore will not take in all that refuse to come upon his terms; but hath fixed his terms; and will have only those that will yield to them. Though I abhor the rigour of the contrary extreme, that would make the church narrower than it is, and pin it up in so small a number, as would tempt men to doubt of christianity itself; and teacheth men to exclude their brethren merely because they are themselves uncharitable judges, when they are not able to disprove their profession; yet must I also detest this horrible dishonouring of the Lord, as if his body were no better than the army of the devil.

3. And by this means the heathens, Jews, Mahometans, and all infidels, are exceedingly hindered from believing in Christ; when they can say as the Turks, when men question their fidelity, *What!*

[x] I have but very few of these; but I know neighbour parishes that have too many, to the grief of their godly ministers.

[y] This tenth sort are some of them infected by the infidels, (who are all for Hobbs's necessity,) but most of them have got it I know not how: but so many are possessed by these conceits, that I little thought that never so many of the ungodly vulgar had so abused the doctrine of predestination and grace; as if they had been hired to disgrace it.

[z] Our papists are but few; but if the rest of them be such as ours, their church hath small reason to boast of its holiness.

Besides, if all these were fit to be members, yet we must know their own consent, which mere living in the parish, or coming to church, doth not signify *dost thou think I am a christian?* He that knows any thing of religious affairs, knoweth that commonly the first thing that draweth men to any party, is the liking of the persons and their practices; from whence they grow to inquire with inclination into their doctrines. The ancient christians that lived before the days of Constantine, did bring christianity into reputation by their *holiness*, and God was then more eminently seen among them. But when the countenance of the emperor, and worldly advantages, had drawn in all men to the church, and the bishops did set the door too wide open, christianity looked like another thing, and that inundation of wickedness overspread the church, which Salvian and so many more complain of. Our likeliest way to win the Jews and all infidels to the church, is by showing them the true nature of christianity in the church members.

4. Hereby also we confound the ancient order of catechumens, or expectants, with the true members of the church, and lay the church and the porch, yea, and the church-yard, if not the commons, all together. By which also our preaching and administrations are confounded: so that whereas the ancient churches had their common sermons (and some prayers) which were fitted to the unconverted or expectants, and had also both doctrine, prayers, praises, and other worship, proper to the church, especially on the Lord's days, we must now speak to all, and join with all; and the church, and the enemies of the church, must sing the same praises, as if they were one body. And God is not the God of confusion, but of order, in the churches. He that put two sorts of preaching and doctrine into the apostles' commission, (Matt. xxviii. 19, 20,) one for making disciples, and another for the edifying and guidance of disciples, did never intend that these should be confounded.

5. And then by this means, the souls of millions of poor people are deprived of the great benefits of the ordinances and administrations suitable to their state. The begetting word goeth before the feeding, strengthening word, even before the milk for babes. The laying of the foundation must go before our building thereon. Every one will thrive best in his own element and place. A fish will not prosper on dry land, nor a man under water. The womb is the only place for the embryo and unborn child, though not for those that have seen the sun. If you will break the shell before the chicken be hatched, that you may hasten its production, or honour it with a premature association with the rest that see the sun, your foolish charity will be the death of it. And so deal abundance of mistaken zealots with the souls of men; who cry out against the wisest and most conscionable ministers, as if they were unchristianing the people, and undoing the world, because they would feed them with food convenient for them, and will not be such hasty midwives, as to cast the mother into her throes, if not rip her up, that she may have the child at her breasts, which should yet be many days or months in the womb. Moreover they thus cause our people to lose all that benefit of preparations, and solemn engagement to Christ: of which more anon among the benefits.

6. By this means also, the souls of our poor people are deluded, and they are made believe that they are christians when they are not, and in a state of salvation when it is no such thing. As Mr. Thorndike saith, as afore-cited, "No man is to be admitted to the assemblies, or visible societies of christians, till there be just presumption that he is of the heavenly Jerusalem that is above:——And admitting to and excluding from the church is, or ought to be, a just and lawful presumption, of admitting to or excluding from heaven: it is morally and legally the same act that entitleth to heaven, and to the church, that maketh an heir of life everlasting and a christian:[a]——" And if so, then what greater mischief can we do the soul of an ungodly man, than so to delude him, by our admitting him into the church; and make him believe he is in a state of salvation, when it is no such thing? False faith, and false hopes, are the things that fill hell, and are the common undoing of the world; and all that ever we can do, is too little to cure it. When I bend all my studies and labours but to make a wicked man know that he is wicked, I cannot procure it. I can make him believe that he is a sinner, but not that he is an unconverted, ungodly sinner, and in a state of condemnation. Oh the power of blinding self-love, that will not suffer them to see themselves miserable, when they see themselves sinful, and all because they would not have it so, when yet it is most visible to others! And shall we all join to strengthen this potent enemy? and lay this snare, and thrust men headlong to hell, that are running down-hill so fast already; and all under pretence of charity and compassion?

7. We shall put them by this means into a way, not only of losing the fruit of ordinances, but of misapplying all to the increasing of their deceit: when we preach peace to the believer, the wicked will misapply it, and say, it belongs to them; when we speak against the unbelievers and ungodly, they will think that this is not their part, but bless themselves because they are christians. In our praises they are tempted with the Pharisee to thank God, and perhaps for mercies which they never had, as justification, adoption, sanctification, &c. The sacraments by misapplication will confirm them in presumption; and thus as they enter by deceit among adult believers, so will they turn all the ordinances of God, and the privileges of the church, to feed that deceit, more effectual than among the expectants it would have been.

8. But the greatest mischief that troubleth me to think of, is this; that by this hastening and admitting all the unprepared into the number of adult christians, and members of the church, we do either put a necessity upon ourselves to throw away church discipline, or else to be most probably the damnation of our people's souls, and make them desperate, and almost past all hope, or remedy. I must confess, that what I am saying now, I was not sensible of, till lately that experience made me sensible. While I meddled not with public reproofs or censures, I disputed of these things, without that experience, which I now find is one of the greatest helps to resolve such doubts; which makes me bold to tell the church, that the practice of so much discipline, as we are agreed in, is a likelier way to bring us all to agreement in the rest, than all our disputings will do without it; and that I resolve hereafter, to take that man for an incompetent judge, and unmeet disputer about church discipline, that never exercised it, or lived where it was exercised; and I shall hereafter suspect their judgments, and be almost as loth to follow such, as to follow a swimmer that never was before in the water, or a pilot that was never before at sea, or a soldier that never saw wars before, but have only learned their skill by the book. Our case stands thus: If we take all our parishes according to the old church constitution, to be particular churches, and all parishioners to be mem-

[a] Mr. Thorndike: see Dr. Hammond's Practic. Catech. lib. 2. sec. 2. p. 103, and l. 6. sec. 82. p. 311, 313, 314, 319—323, &c.

bers; then either we must exercise the discipline which Christ hath commanded, or not. If not, then we disobey our Lord and Master, and own such a church as is utterly uncapable of church ends, and consequently of the essence, seeing that it is a relative being. For it is supposed that it is not for any unusual accident, that we cannot exercise this discipline, but from the very church constitution, or incapacity of the matter. And then, (1.) We shall be traitors to Christ, under the name of pastors, if we will wilfully cast out his ministerial, kingly government. (2.) We shall betray the church to licentiousness. And, (3.) We shall set up a new church-way, which is contrary to that which hath been practised in all ages, from the apostles' days, till impiety had overspread the christian world. He that dare take on him to be an overseer and ruler of the church, and not to oversee and rule it, and dare settle on such a church state, as is uncapable of discipline, is so perfidious to Christ, and ventureth so boldly to make the church another thing, that I am resolved not to be his follower.

But if we shall exercise the discipline of Christ upon all in our ordinary parishes, what work shall we make? I will tell you what work, from so much experience, as that no reasonings can any more persuade me to believe the contrary, than that wormwood is not bitter, or snow is not cold.

(1.) We shall have such a multitude to excommunicate, or reject, that it will make the sentence grow almost contemptible by the commonness. (2.) We shall so extremely enrage the spirits of the people, that we shall go in continual danger of our lives: among so many that are publicly reproved, and cast out, it is two to one but some desperate villains will be studying revenge.[b] But all this is nothing; but that which sticks upon my heart is this: (3.) We shall be the cruellest enemies to the souls of our poor people in the world; and put them the very next step to hell. For as soon as ever we have rejected them, and cast them under public shame, they hate us to the heart, and either will never hear us more, or hear us with so much hatred and malice, or bitterness of spirit, that they are never like to profit by us. If you say that doubtless discipline will have better fruits, if it be an ordinance of God: I answer, 1. It is no time now in the end of the world, to question whether that be an ordinance of God, which Scripture speaks for so fully, and so plainly; and which the catholic church hath so long practised, and that with such severity as it hath done. 2. I know that discipline is of excellent use, and is likely to have excellent effects; but upon whom? upon such as are fit to come under discipline, and with such I have seen the usefulness of it; but with the rest it makes them next to mad. They that before would patiently hear me, in the plainest, sharpest sermons that I could preach, and would quietly bear any private admonition, when once they are publicly admonished and cast out, are filled with the gall of malice and indignation, and never more likely to profit by a sermon. Nay, they set themselves with malice to reproach and oppose, and stir up others; and fall in to any party that will receive them, that are enemies to the ministry; so that I look upon some of them, when once they are cast out, almost as if they were already in hell: for they are desperately hardened against any further means of their recovery. 3. Yea, I am persuaded, that if we exercise Christ's discipline according to the Scripture rule, upon all in the parishes in England, it would endanger a rebellion; and the rage of the people would make them ready to take any opportunity to rise up against the sovereign power that doth maintain and protect us; and if we were not protected, we should soon have enough of it.

Object. Perhaps you will say, That public admonitions, and church censures, are not to be easily exercised, nor upon any but notorious, scandalous sinners, and that in case of obstinate impenitency.

Answ. I am as much against a rash, unnecessary censure, or use of the severity of discipline, as another: I know that a fly must not be killed with a beetle. Let it be exercised but according to the parliament's ordinance, called The Form of Government, to be used in the Church of England and Ireland, Aug. 29, 1648. Or let it be exercised but with one half, or the sixth part, of the severity of the ancient canons of the church; and you shall certainly see the effects that I tell you of. Do you think to use it but with few, when impenitent scandalous sinners are so many? But perhaps you think to use it only *in terrorem*, or now and then one, and let others alone that are in the same case. But, 1. That is the same disobedience to God, as to use it upon none at all. He that hath commanded us to reject a heretic, to have no company with the disorderly livers, to turn away from scandalous, ungodly men, and not to enter with drunkards, railers, &c. hath not bid us do thus by some, but by all. 2. God condemneth partiality. 3. Your partiality will presently be so noted by men, that it will turn to your reproach, and make both you and your discipline odious, when they can say, He casteth out one, and forbeareth others in the same case.

Object. But were there not more offenders than the incestuous man at Corinth? And yet Paul casteth out but him.

Answ. 1. How can you tell how many Paul cast out? 2. Doth he not give the church a flat command to cast out and avoid the rest? 1 Cor. v. 11, 12, When will you make us believe, that Paul at that time commanded them to do that which he would not have them do? 3. Corinth had many offenders, whom Paul in that epistle reprehendeth; but can you prove that any of them were obstinately impenitent, after admonition? I know you cannot.

But perhaps you will think, that you should by the preparatory, private admonition so bow them, and work upon them, that few of them should be so obstinate as to fall under censure.

I answer, You speak this because you never tried, and know not, the world. I must presume to tell you, (though to tell you the reasons be unmeet,) that there are but few men in England must expect more advantage for interest in their people, than I have in mine; and yet all is nothing, when I come to exercise discipline, and cross their selfish, sensual inclinations. Those that will tell me, they are beholden to me for their lives, yet will not hear me when I persuade them to any humbling confession. Those that cannot hide their sin, will confess it, and commit it over and over: will you accept of their private confession for satisfaction, that will publicly slander their neighbours, and be drunk openly every week or month, or swear every day? But many of them will not so much as confess before a few ministers or officers of the church, that they have sinned, but will stand impenitently in it to the last. Let me entreat them with all the submissiveness and earnestness that I can, when one hath beat or slandered another, or in the like cases, if I would kneel to them, I cannot get many of them once (hypocritically) to say, I am sorry, or I did amiss; and those that do say so, in a cold, hypocritical, heartless manner, will join with it such bitter words

[b] This is no dishonour to the discipline; for we find it hath great effect on such as are capable of it.

against the accuser or reprover, and show such hatred to those that admonish them, that declareth their impenitency.[c] If you have such extraordinary abilities, to melt and mollify hardened sinners, more than we have, you are the more unexcusably unfaithful to God and man, that will not use them. And all are not so happy as to have your conquering parts. For my part, I can say in uprightness of heart, that I do what I can, (abating those neglects which are the consequents of my frailty,) and if I knew how to do more, I would, with study, preaching, conference, labour or estate; and yet with abundance I am not able to prevail so much as to make them capable of discipline. So that I see plainly by unquestionable experience, that either we must have churches without the discipline of Christ, and be rulers without ruling it; or else we must utterly undo our people, body and soul for ever, and plunge them into a desperate state, and make all our following labours in vain to multitudes of them: or else we must take another course, than to admit all our parishes to adult church membership, as was formerly done, without preparation, and fitness for such a state.

And yet in their blindness, gentlemen, ministers, and all that plead for common church membership, pretend to be charitable to the people's souls, when they are exercising this grievous cruelty. It is just as if in mercy to the schoolboys, you should set them that cannot read English in the highest form, where they must make orations in Latin and Greek, or else be whipped: would they thank you for such advancement? It is as if you should put an ignorant, unexercised, cowardly soldier, or one that is but learning to use his arms, into the front of the battle, for his honour: or as if you should prefer a pupil to be a tutor, or put a freshman in the doctor's chair, or admit a new baptized novice to be a pastor of the church, where the blood of the people shall be required at his hands: or as if to honour him, you should admit any common mariner to the pilot's place, or any apothecary to play the physician to other men's ruin, and his own shame. If you set such children on horseback, while you pretend their good, you will break their necks. No man is safe out of his own rank and place. If the husbandman know that every sort of plants and grain must have their proper soil and season, and the gardener knoweth that several herbs and flowers must be variously manured, or else they will not prosper; why should we be less wise in the work of God? As country schools are seminaries to the academies, so the state of catechumens or expectants is the seminary to the church, and the state of infant church membership the seminary to the state of the adult, into which they must be seasonably and solemnly transplanted, when they are ripe and ready, and not before. Truly our merciful hastlings do but yoke untamed bullocks, that are fitter to strive and tire themselves than to plough; and do but saddle such wild, unbroken colts, as are liker to break their own and their riders' necks, than to go the journey which they are designed for. In the state of expectants, these men may profit by preparing ordinances, and the season may come, when they may fitly be transplanted: but if we put them *inter fideles*, that are infidels, among actual believers and adult church members, that are not such, nor prepared for the station, we bring them under a discipline which will exasperate them, and turn them to be malignant enemies, and undo them for ever. The disposition of the matter must go before the reception of the form; for undisposed matter will not receive it. As the operation followeth the being, and the disposition, so we must employ every person and thing, in such operations only, as their being and qualification is capable of, and suited to. A due placing of all according to their qualifications, is the chiefest part of our government. Misplace but one wheel in your watch, and try how it will go. If any person or thing be not good in his own place, he will be much worse out of it, in the place of his superior. Fire is better in the chimney than in your bed, or upon your table: a good clerk may make but a sorry counsellor; and a good subject may make but an ill magistrate; and many a man becomes the seat of a justice, that would not become the prince's throne. If you would not undo men's souls by a discipline which they cannot bear, let them stay in the seminary of expectants, till they are ripe for it.

Object. But how do the churches of France, Holland, Geneva, and Scotland, that have exercised discipline upon all?

Answ. 1. Must I be sent to another nation to know that which I have made trial of, and attained the certain knowledge of, at home? I was never in France, nor at Geneva, and therefore I know not what number of obstinate, impenitent, scandalous persons are there; nor how many that know who Jesus Christ is, nor what a christian or a church is; but I have been in England, and I partly know what store of these are there, and what usage they will bear, and what not. 2. Either other churches have such materials as our parishes, or not. If not, their cause is none of ours: if they have, then either they exercise Christ's discipline on them faithfully and impartially, or not. If not, then they are not to be imitated by us in their negligence, unfaithfulness, or partiality: if they do, and yet do not undo the people, they have not such a people as ours, or else they have other means to further their ends. 3. The truth is, as in France, they are but a people gathered from among the papists, whose church doth drink up most of the scum; so the other churches, 1. Are too lamentably careless, partial, or defective, in executing their own discipline:[d] and if I should come to think it lawful to forbear the execution of it upon nineteen, I should soon think it lawful to forbear the twentieth; and then what should we think of Scripture, and the canons of the universal church? 2. By this neglect it is, that reformed churches have contracted the greatest dishonour that is upon them, while they are sound in doctrine, and have learned pastors, able to confound the Romish adversaries; but, alas! too many unmeet church members. 3. They have (and Scotland had till lately) the magistrate's sword to drive men on, and force them to submit to discipline, which is not our case, nor was the case of the primitive church. It is not there the church's censure that doth the work,

[c] I desire those that are over rigid and uncharitable in censuring others, not to extend these complaints to more than I extend them; nor to take it as an occasion for the unchurching of whole parishes, or any one particular person, without sufficient evidence. For I must profess that I meet with hundreds in my parish, that I can comfortably hold communion with, that some men of stricter principles, or more censorious dispositions would reject; yea, and I take abundance for truly godly men, that are not noted for any eminency of religion, perhaps their parts, or callings, or opportunities, being such as to keep them much from the knowledge of others.

[d] Melancthon Epist. (Impres. Lugdun. 1648.) ad Dominum Schleupnerum, saith, 1. Quia in tanta multitudine vix pauci sunt christiani, et apti qui sacramento fruantur, cavendum est ne vulgus invitetur ad prophanandum Corpus Domini.

Lege Calvin. Institut. lib. 4. cap. 12. sect. 1, 2; Zanch. de Ecclesia, vol. 3. fol. 123, 124, 134, 135; and others cited in the preface of my "Reformed Pastor."

but the magistrate's sword, no more than it was with our bishops in England. 4. And yet what work a little exercise of discipline made, may appear in the case of Calvin, at Geneva, when for suspending the sacrament, when the people were in enmity, he was banished Geneva, and their dogs called by the name of Calvin; and when the suspending of one Bertelerius could put them all into such a flame.

Object. But, *fiat justitia, et ruat cœlum;* let us trust God with his own ordinances: we must do our duty, whatever come of it.

Answ. This doth but beg the question: God's ordinances are not for destruction, but edification; at least as to the multitude of the ungodly, they tend to their conversion, and not to their perdition. Is that likely to be God's ordinance, which certain experience telleth us will put such multitudes of men into a hopeless case, or next to hopeless? Ministers are appointed to make disciples, and gather men to Christ, and further their conversion, and not plunge them into a remediless state, and to hurry them all unprepared into church communion, that they may be thrust out again, and brought to hate the church. It is another's work to advance them to the pinnacle of the temple, that he may cast them down headlong. And yet I never knew the man, or saw his face, that practised what this objection pleads for; and exercised discipline faithfully on a whole parish. Nor do I believe that any man can do it that would; unless the magistrate do it for him. For he cannot do it without the people's consent: and if he sentence such to be avoided by the people, they will despise his sentence, and hold communion with them the more, and do as our drunkards do, when one of their companions is put in the stocks, bring him ale and good cheer, and eat, and drink, and make merry with him, if the magistrate restrain them not.

Object. But excommunication must not be used, till all other remedies will do no good; and when all will do no good, what good will it do such to be kept under other means?

Answ. To do good for the bringing a man out of that sin, for which he is admonished, is one thing; and to do good, for his information and conversion in the main, is another thing: it is the use of discipline, to cure men of the particular sins that they are reproved for, rather than to convert them from a state of wickedness in general. 2. Nor is excommunication to be deferred, as long as there is any hope by other means; but only till we have used other means in vain, for such a season as is meet; that the ends of discipline be not frustrated: for else there should never man be excommunicated: for there is some hope that preaching against his sin may do him good at last; though he come drunk to the Lord's table twenty years together, you cannot say that his conversion is impossible: and yet we must not hereupon defer the casting out of such a member. But in his expectant state, or among the catechumens, we may bear with him lawfully in his wickedness, without excluding him from among our hearers; and if he hear us seven and seven years in vain, there is yet some hope of his conversion, while he waiteth in his own place and way.

And yet I yield this much to the objectors freely, That when fit persons are taken into the church, (yea, or unfit, by negligence,) we must wait with all patience that is consistent with the ends of government, and cutting off must be the last remedy; and that when it is necessary, it must be used, though we see that it is ten to one it will plunge the person (occasionally) into a worse condition. For the public ends of discipline, the credit of christianity, the preservation of the church, and abundance more, are to be preferred before the good of that man's soul: and as *Pœna debetur Reipublicæ*, and we cut not off malefactors for their own good, so much as the commonwealth's, which by their hurt must be promoted, so is it as to the church. But this must be done but upon a few, for example; and therefore but few that will need this severity, are supposed to be in our communion. And I cannot believe that way to be of God, that would bring such multitudes into this miserable state.

Object. Your very keeping them from the communion of the church, and not approving or confirming them, would as much exasperate them.

Answ. It is no such matter. Much it may, but not near so much, as I certainly know by experience: those not admitted, hear with hope; but to the rejected I speak as almost hopeless, except such as were fit to live under discipline, on whom it may have its due effect.

9. And by this admitting all men, without trial and confirmation, to come unobservedly into the state of adult christians, we breed and feed continual heart-burnings against the ministers of Christ; while we are necessitated to do our work upon such unprepared souls. And how much the hatred and contempt of ministers doth conduce to the destruction of the people, Satan is not ignorant, who is the diligent promoter of it.

10. By this means also we frustrate our own studies, and ministerial labours, to abundance of our people; partly by deluding them actually, in the reception of them among christians, that really are no christians, and partly by this provocation of their hatred.

11. By this means also we breed and feed abundance of controversies in the church; for when once we displace any parts of the frame, we shall find almost all in pieces, and one error draweth on so many, that controversies grow numerous, and will never be reconciled by mere words and writings, till we actually set the church in joint again.

12. By this course also, we lay open the ordinances of God to a continual profanation, while abundance that know not who Christ is, nor what christianity is, are admitted as christians, to our christian communion; and so themselves are involved in more sin, and God's own worship turned into provocation; so that we may fear lest God should frown upon our assemblies, and withdraw the tokens of his presence, and deny his blessing to those profaned ordinances. Though the innocent may still have their share in the blessing, yet may the pastors and the guilty majority deeply suffer by this great abuse of holy things.

13. By this means also it is that so many scruples are cast in our way, about administrations, and reception of ordinances; and the comfort of ministers and people in them, is much abated.

14. And I doubt it is a hinderance to the conversion of many sects about us, and of many ungodly ones among us, who if they saw the primitive holiness of churches might be drawn in.

15. And it much corrupteth the communion of saints, and turneth it to another thing; when this holy communion is so much of our duty and our comfort, and such a representation of heaven itself.

16. And if it be not a practical denial of some of the articles of our faith, it is well. We say there, That we believe the catholic church to be holy; and that it is a communion of saints, that is by the parts of it to be exercised. And shall we deny this in our works, which in words we profess?

17. By this means also we dishonour the work of reformation, when we hinder the fruits of it that

should be visible to the world; and make men believe that it lieth but in a change of bare opinions. They that see no great difference between the reformed and the Romanists in their lives, will think it is no great matter which side they are joined to. It is noted by some protestant writers, that when Luther opposed popery in Germany, abundance of the common, licentious people, that were weary of popish confessions, and penances, did join with those that were truly conscientious, and dishonoured the Reformation by their lives, though they increased the number, and did the service as Erasmus' gospeller, that used to carry a bottle of wine, and Erasmus' New Testament, with great brass bosses, and when he disputed with a papist, knocked him about the pate with the Bible, and so confuted him.

18. And by this means we give the papists more room than they should have, to reproach our churches, and glory comparatively of the holiness of theirs. Though I know that their glory is exceeding unreasonable, and that our impurities are no more to theirs than a few boils to a leprosy; yet we do ill to give them so much occasion, as we do, who are ready to make the worst of all.

19. By this means also we leave all sects to quarrel with us, and dispute against us, even whether we be true churches of Christ or not; because our adult profession and covenant is no more express and discernible than it is. And though we have enough to prove ourselves a church, yet do we leave them under their temptations, and ourselves under the obloquy. And indeed we perversely maintain our own dishonour, while we think it a condition to be rested in, if we can but prove ourselves true churches; when our learned divines do give as much to the Romanists themselves, though not as papal, yet as christian. A leper is a true man, and yet his cure is a thing to be desired.

20. Lastly, By this means we tempt many well-meaning people among us to endanger their separation from us, and to fly from our churches, as if they would fall on their heads; and we too much harden those that are already separated, and all because we will not yield to the healing of our own diseases, or will do little or nothing to procure it. I know these men have no just ground for their hard conclusions, and censures of us; but we have little reason to give them this occasion, and cast a stumblingblock in the way of so many precious souls.

To what is here briefly thrust together, if the reader will add the twelve reasons in my "Christian Concord," p. 11—14, and what is said in my book "of Right to Sacraments," where these matters, or those that sustain them, are handled more at large; I suppose he may easily be convinced, that the former church governors, in England, have been lamentably negligent, and ours by their means are much disordered; and that the present ministers should be more forward, and diligent, and unanimous for the cure; and that the magistrate, if he love the church of Christ, and the souls of men, should speedily afford his help, and all too little to remedy these great and many evils, which we have let in, by suffering such a loose, unobserved transition from the state of infant church members, or from apostasy, into the number of adult members, without approved profession and confirmation.

PROP. 20. *So many and great are the benefits, that would follow the general practice of this duty, of trying, approving, and confirming (or absolving) all those that enter into the number of adult christians, that it should mightily provoke all christian magistrates, ministers, and people, to join in a speedy and vigorous execution of it.*

1. One excellent fruit of this practice, will be the great increase of knowledge, and godliness, and the destruction of ignorance, and notorious impiety. This is an effect most apparent in the causes. When men are made to understand, that by the law of God, seconded by the common consent of the church, and the most learned, godly pastors, and, if it may be, by the law of the land; no man is to be accounted or numbered with adult christians, but those that make a sober, serious, understanding profession of christianity, renouncing the flesh, the world, and the devil; and not contradicting and nullifying this profession by a wicked life; this will engage parents to teach their children, and children themselves to learn what christianity is, when they cannot have the name, or the honour, and the privileges of christians, without some credible appearance of the thing. For doubtless while christianity is in credit, the same motives that now prevail with the multitude to seem christians, and to desire the baptism of their children, will continue then, to make them desire to be numbered with christians, when they are at age; and so will provoke them to do that, without which they know they cannot be esteemed christians. And as it is now a common thing to be baptized in infancy, so will it be then a common thing, for our young people to learn the principles of christianity, yea, and to reform their lives, (I hope with the most,) when they understand, that else they must be taken to be no christians. And if it were but the making of the understanding, profession, and outside of christianity, to be commoner among us, it would be a precious fruit of our endeavours. But much more, when true christianity itself, in the life and power of it, would also be more common. As no doubt but it would; for the knowledge of the letter, is the way to the receiving of the Spirit; and among the multitudes that have the outside of true religion, there will be far more that have the life and soul of it, than among those that have not so much as the outside. Any man in reason may foresee, that if we be openly agreed, and it be publicly enacted, or declared, That none be taken into the number of adult christians, nor admitted to their privileges, till they have made an approved profession of christianity, and so be received by Jesus Christ himself, acting by his ministers, it will set all that care for the name, or hopes or privileges of christians, to learn, and be, and do, that which they know will be required of them. Whereas, as things go now in most places, they may bring their children to baptism, without understanding what baptism is; and those children may slide into the state of the adult christians, and possess the name, and place, and outward communion, and other honours and privileges of such, without knowing whether Christ were a man or a woman, or who he is, or what business he came about into the world. And when no outward necessity is laid upon them by the church, to know more, or to seem better, no wonder if so many heathens do sit among christians, and if the multitude look not much after knowledge or godliness.

2. And moreover, it will be a very great help to their consciences, in order to the convincing them of their sin and misery, and of the insufficiency of that condition which multitudes do now rest in; and so to waken them to look after a safer state, and to be what they must seem to be, if they will be taken to be christians. It is a great help to the deceiving of the multitude of the ungodly, to be currently esteemed christians, when they are not: and self-

love is such a blinding thing, that a little help will go far with it, in the promoting of such deceits. Naturally men are very easily brought to think well of themselves, and hardly brought to confess their misery. Every man almost will easily confess himself a sinner, and a very great sinner, so you will but allow him to be a christian, and a pardoned sinner. For this is a common confession, and brings no very terrible conclusion and message to the soul. But when a man must confess himself no true christian, but unsanctified, unpardoned, and a slave of Satan, this is as much as to confess himself in a state of damnation, in which if he die he is lost for ever, and men are hardly drawn to believe so terrible a conclusion; when yet it is so necessary where it is true, that we can scarce imagine how a man can be saved without it. He that knoweth not himself to be out of his way, will hardly be persuaded to turn back; and he that knows not himself to be unpardoned, will hardly value or seek a pardon; and he that thinks he is sanctified, and a true christian already, will not seek to be made what he takes himself already to be. And how much reputation doth to help or hinder men, even in self-judging, is easily perceived. Now here is a threefold reputation, of very great moment, to concur, either for men's deception or conversion. (1.) The reputation of prince and parliament, and so of law-givers and rulers of the nation, who by their laws do manifest whom they esteem good christians, and this the people very much look at. (2.) The reputation of all the pastors of the church, which is to be manifested in their agreements, confessions, or declarations and practices. (3.) The common consent of christian people, which is to be manifested by their actions, according to the laws of Christ, and the direction of their guides. If magistrates, ministers, and people do concur, to repute all the infidels, and utterly ignorant, wicked men among us to be christians; how many thousand souls may this deceive, and undo for ever! Whereas if the magistrates, ministers, and people that fear God, would all agree according to the laws of Christ, to esteem none adult christians, but those that by a credible profession of christianity do seem to be such, it would abundantly help to convince them of their misery, and the need of Christ, and grace, and the absolute necessity of a change. We see even among good men, in the case of a particular sin, how much common reputation doth help to hinder the work upon their consciences; among the reformed churches beyond the sea, what conscience is troubled for these actions or omissions on the Lord's day, which in England would much trouble men of the same temper in other things. Among several sects it troubleth them not, freely to revile the servants of Christ that are against them, because they find it rather go for commendable, than much condemnable, by those whom they most esteem. Among the papists, the believing in a Vice-Christ, and the worshipping of his image and cross with divine worship, and also the consecrated host, and the condemning all the churches of Christ that do it not, do go for virtues, and christian practices, though they are most heinous, odious sins; and what is it but common reputation of princes and priests, and multitudes of people, that could make so many, yea, and such persons as some of them are, to continue in such sins, as if they were a part, yea, an essential part of holiness, and one generation to succeed another in them? Were these sins but commonly reputed to be as odious as indeed they are, what a change would it make on millions of souls! So that it is strange to see the power of reputation.

3. Moreover, this course would be an excellent help to the labours of the ministers of Christ, for men's salvation. They would better understand and apply our sermons; whereas now, they lose the benefit by misapplying them. Now we must labour all our lives, and with most in vain, to make unbelievers and ungodly persons understand what they are, and no means will serve to convince many people, that they are not truly christians, that know not what it is to be a christian, or that hate it and fight against it. When they all go together under the name of christians, whatever comforts they hear offered to believers, they take them to themselves, or mistake them as offered to them; and all the threatenings that are uttered against unbelievers, they put by and think it is not they that they are spoken against. But if once we could but get men to stand in their own places, and to know themselves, how easily then would our message work! Methinks the devil should not be able to keep one man of a hundred in his power, if they knew themselves to be in his power; nor one of a hundred in a state of ungodliness and condemnation, if they knew that they are in such a state. At least, I am sure men will not so numerously nor easily run into hell, when they know they are going into it, as when they are confident that they are good christians, and in the way to heaven.

4. If this fore-described confirmation be practised, it will more powerfully oblige our people to Christ, than a secret sliding into the number of adult christians will do. And doubtless solemn engagements and obligations have some force upon conscience, to hold men to Christ, and restrain them from sin; or else baptism itself would be much frustrate, and the Jews should not have been so often called by Moses, Joshua, Asa, and other princes, to renew their covenant with God. But with us, men feel no such bonds upon them; and many question whether they are bound at all by their parents' promises for them in baptism.

5. The profiting of our people will be much greater in their own place, when those that are not yet fit for adult membership and privileges are kept in the place of catechumens or expectants. Every thing doth thrive and prosper best in its own place: if you tear them not out of the church's womb, till they are ready for the birth, they will prosper there, that else may perish. Your corn will best prosper in the cold earth, where it seems to be dead and buried, till the springing-time shall come. And you should not violently unhose the ears, till nature put them forth. The first digestion must be wrought before the second, and nature must have time allowed it, and the stomach must not too hastily let go the food, if you would have good sanguification and nutrition follow. Men think they do a great kindness to grossly ignorant or impious men, to take them into the church before they are capable of such a station, and the work or privileges thereto belonging; but, alas! they do but hurry them to perdition, by thrusting them out of the state where they might have thriven in preparation to a church state, into a state which will set them abundance of work, which they are utterly unfit for, and under the pretence of benefits and privileges, will occasion abundance of aggravations of their sins. A boy in his A B C will learn better in his own place, among his fellows, than in a higher form, where he hath work set him which he is uncapable of doing.

6. By this means also church discipline will attain its ends; it will awe and preserve the church, and terrify and reduce offenders, and help them to repentance, and preserve the order of the church

and gospel, when it is exercised upon such as are capable of it; that know the nature of it, and either are habitually disposed to profit by it, or at least understand what it was that they were engaged to, and understandingly consent to live under such a discipline; and when it is exercised upon few, and we have not such multitudes to sweep out of the church.

7. By this means both church associations and ordinances may attain their ends; and people will be capable of doing the duty of christians one to another, when others are capable of receiving it. Church members are bound to "exhort one another daily, while it is called to-day, lest any be hardened by the deceitfulness of sin," Heb. iii. 13; and to "teach and admonish one another," Col. iii. 16. But before "swine we must not cast such pearls, nor give that which is holy to dogs," Matt. vii. 6. Therefore it necessarily followeth, that dogs and swine should be kept out of the church, and cast out if they be crept in. Nothing hath more destroyed that charitable community, which should be among the members of the church, and that loving and relieving Christ in church members, than the crowding of such into the place, as indeed are Satan's members, and appear not capable of that special love, nor are capable of returning it to others.

8. This will make easy the minister's work, and free him from abundance of hatred, trouble, and disadvantage, when, like a workman's tools in his shop, that all are in their place, and so at hand when he should use them, so his hearers are in order, and each one looks for his portion, and none are snatching at our fingers for the children's bread, that belongs not to them, and men be not drawn to hate and rail at ministers, for not fulfilling their desires.

9. By this means also the ordinances will be more purely administered, agreeably to their nature, and the institution; and so God will bless them more to his church, and own his people with the fuller discoveries of his presence, and take pleasure in the assemblies and services of his saints.

10. By this means also the communion of the saints, and the holy ordinances of God, will be abundantly more sweet to his servants, when we have it in the appointed way, and it is not imbittered to us, by the pollutions of infidels, and notorious ungodly men. Though yet I know, that in a negligent, polluted church, God's servants may have their share of comfort, in his ordinances, when they have done their own duty for reformation, without success.

11. By this means the church, and the christian religion, will be more honourable in the eyes of the world, who judge by the members' and professors' lives, before they can judge of the thing as in itself; and as Christ will be thus honoured, and the mouths of adversaries of all sorts stopped, so it will do much to further their conversion, when they have such a help to see the beauty of the church and christian faith. Many more such benefits I could name, but that you may gather some of them from what was said of the contrary incommodities: only I add,

12. Lastly, it is a way that is admirably suited both to reformation and reconciliation; to unity, as well as purity; which removeth many of the impediments that else would trouble us in the way. For as all wicked men will agree against it, as they will against any holy practice; so all parties considerable among us, do in their doctrine and professions own it; and it will suit the principles or the ends of all that fear God, either wholly or very far. I shall here distinctly show you, 1. That the episcopal; 2. Presbyterians; 3. Independents; 4. Anabaptists; 5. Yea, and I may put in, the papists themselves, have no reason to be against this practice; but all of them have great reason to promote it, supposing them to be what they are.

1. That this is so far agreeable with the doctrine of the church of England, that our episcopal party have reason to be for it, appeareth, (1.) By the Rubric for Confirmation, in the Common Prayer Book,[e] which saith as followeth: "The curate of every parish, or some other at his appointment, shall diligently upon Sundays and holydays, half an hour before evening prayer, openly in the church, instruct and examine so many children of his parish, sent unto him, as the time will serve, and as he shall think convenient, in some part of this catechism. And all fathers, mothers, masters, and dames, shall cause their children, servants, and apprentices (which have not learned their catechism,) to come to the church at the time appointed, and obediently to hear, and be ordered by the curate, until such time as they have learned all that is appointed here for them to learn. And whensoever the bishop shall give knowledge, for children to be brought before him, to any convenient place, for their confirmation, then shall the curate of every parish either bring, or send in writing, the names of all those children of his parish which can say the articles of the faith, the Lord's prayer, and the ten commandments, and also how many of them can answer to the other questions, contained in this catechism. And there shall none be admitted to the holy communion till such time as he can say the catechism, and be confirmed."

So that you see we must not admit any but the confirmed to the sacrament. And I suppose in common reason, they will extend this to the aged, as well as unto children, seeing ignorance in them is more intolerable: and indeed the words themselves exclude the unconfirmed, and that cannot say the catechism, from the sacrament, of what age soever. (2.) And I may take it for granted, that it is not bare saying the catechism that they expect, but also a profession that they own their baptismal covenant to God the Father, Son, and Holy Ghost.[f] And also that it be a profession somewhat understood; and not barely to say the words which they understand not, as a parrot doth. And this I prove to be their meaning, yea, and also that they live a christian life, from the prayer in confirmation, adjoined, which is this; "Almighty and Everlasting God, who hast vouchsafed to regenerate these thy servants by water and the Holy Ghost, and hast given unto them forgiveness of all their sins; strengthen them, we beseech thee, O Lord, with the Holy Ghost the Comforter, and daily increase in them the manifold gifts of grace, the spirit of wisdom and understanding, the spirit of counsel and ghostly strength, the spirit of knowledge and true godliness." So that here you see that the church of England supposeth all those that are to be confirmed, to have already the Holy Ghost, and the spirit of wisdom, understanding, counsel, knowledge, and true godliness, which they beg of God, as to an increase only, for the confirmed. And sure they do not think that every notorious ungodly man hath the spirit of true godliness if he can but say the catechism; or that every ignorant person or infidel hath the spirit of knowledge, wisdom, &c. as soon as he can speak the words which he understands not. And in the following prayer they say, "We have laid our hands on them, to certify them (by this sign) of thy favour and gracious good-

[e] The rest of the Rubric see after.

[f] The first part of the Rubric anon cited, also proves this.

ness towards them." And sure they will not think to certify men that know not what christianity is, or that live not christian lives, for this favour of God towards them, merely because they say the words which they do not understand. So that if they will but let men understand what they do, and make good what is here expressed, we are agreed with them that stand for common prayer, that such as are unconfirmed be not admitted to the holy communion. And as for the person confirming, I shall speak to that anon.

[g]2. I will next speak of the papists, because in their words I shall have opportunity to recite some more of our own, even those of the Canons. Convocat. London, An. 1603, c. 60. I will pass by Frans. de S. Clara, and such reconcilers, lest you say, that is not the common judgment of the papists: and at this time it may suffice to instance in one, that most petulant, insolent Jesuit, Hen. Fitz-Simon, in his Britanomach. lib. 3, cap. 4, p. 289—291; where he reciteth the words of our canon, that "seeing it was a solemn, ancient, laudable custom in the church of God, observed even from the days of the apostles, that all bishops laying hands on those that were baptized in infancy, and are instructed in the catechism of the christian religion, should pray over them, and bless them, which we commonly call confirmation,—we will and ordain, that every bishop, or his suffragan, do in their proper person, diligently observe this rite and custom, in their ordinary visitation." To which saith the Jesuit, "What do I hear? ——All this is very orthodox, very catholic, if uttered in good sadness——" And citing the Rubric before mentioned, he mentioneth the conference at Hampton Court, p. 10, 11, 32, 33. "That the doctrine of confirmation was part of the apostles' catechism, rashly rejected by some churches, but in Calvin's judgment to be taken up again, and is ungrateful to the puritans only, because they may not themselves administer it." And p. 64, he would persuade us, that most certainly the bishops borrowed this passage from the Rhemist's Test. Annot. in Heb. vi. 2, against the puritans. More he adds from Resp. Oxon. ad Libel. supplic. Covel, &c. and concludes, "All this the formalists (as he constantly calls that party) do freely grant us, than which the catholics themselves, as to the sound of the words, seem scarce able to think or speak any thing more honourable of confirmation." And that you may see how far he accepts also of Calvin's concession, he doth with ostentation cite the words of Calvin, in Acts ii.; and Instit. lib 4, cap. 19, sect. 28; that "it is incredible that the apostles should use imposition of hands, but by Christ's command; and that it was not an empty sign, and that it is to be accounted for a sacrament." So that these two parties cannot be against us, in the matter of confirmation, though I know that the papists are against us for laying by their ceremonies and abuse of it.

3. And as for the presbyterians they cannot be against it: for, (1.) The most eminent divines of that judgment have written for it, of whom I could cite abundance. But Calvin, Hyperius, and others, cited by Mr. Hanmer already, sufficiently declare their desires after the restoring of confirmation: and Chemnitius, a Lutheran, is large for it, and others of that way. (2.) And it is so clearly useful and necessary to the reforming of distempers in the church, and the quiet of the ministry, and the safe and successful exercise of discipline, that I know they will heartily consent to it.

4. And for the congregational party, (1.) Some of them have declared their judgments for it, in the approving or promoting Mr. Hanmer's book. (2.) And I have spoke with some of the most eminent of that mind, that are for it. (3.) And the solemn covenant or profession, which they require of all that enter among them, as church members, doth show that they are for it in the substance, though how far they like or dislike the sign of imposition of hands I know not. It is the want of this, that they are so much offended with in our parish church, and therefore doubtless they will consent.

5. And for anabaptists, though we cannot expect their full consent, because they admit not infants into the visible church; and therefore baptize those whom we confirm or restore, yet, doubtless, they will like this as next to that which they suppose to be the right; and because we come as near to them as is fit and lawful for us to do, it is the likeliest way to abate their censures, and procure with them so much peace, as in reason may be expected, with men that differ from us in the point of infant baptism.[h] Three sorts of them I suppose we may meet with: 1. Some that grant that infants are Christ's disciples, christian, and visible church members, but yet think that baptism is not for their admission, but only for the adult. I confess I know of none so moderate, nor am I sure there are any such, but by hearsay, or conjecture; but if there be, our differences with these men would be most in the external sign. If they do but as much by infants, as the express words of the gospel do commend, and Christ chid his disciples for opposing, that is, if they yield that they shall be offered unto Christ, and that the minister of Christ do in his name receive them, lay his hands on them, and bless them, because of such is the kingdom of God; and then baptize them, when at age they make a personal profession; and if we on the other side offer them to Christ, and the minister in his name accept them by baptism, and at age confirm them, upon their personal covenanting or profession; the difference here would be most, that they change the outward sign, and they use imposition of hands when we use baptism; and we use baptism when they use imposition. And with such it were easy for moderate men to hold brotherly love and peace. 2. Some we shall meet with, that deny infants to be visible church members, and yet think the infants of believers to have some promises more than the rest of the world, or at least that they are *candidati christianissimi*, expectants of a church state, and are, as soon as they understand any thing, to be bred up as catechumens in the church seminaries, and to be baptized as soon as they are actual believers. And as far as I understand them, some of them will consent that they be offered and dedicated to God in infancy, and solemnly received, by ministerial imposition of hands, into the state of expectants. If these men be of peaceable, moderate spirits, and agree with us in other matters of religion, in the substance at least, they must needs acknowledge, that in the fore-described practice of confirmation, we come so near them, that they cannot deny us brotherly love and peace. For I hope they will not think, that they may lawfully deny these, yea,

[g] De hoc dissidium nullum futurum sperem, &c. De tempore confirmationis, Video bonis viris utriusque partis non displicere, si ejus usus ad ætatem paulo adultiorem differatur, —ut parentibus, susceptoribus, et ecclesiarum præfectis occasio detur, pueris de fide quam in baptismo professi sunt, diligentius instituendi et admonendi. (Georg. Cassander, in Consult. de Confirmatione.)

[h] Some few also there are, that are antipædobaptists (against baptizing infants) and yet not anabaptists (as not judging it a nullity, nor to be iterated); and these one would think we might live at peace with.

or their communion, to all that be not punctually of their opinion, against the church membership and baptism of infants. 3. And as for all the rest of the anabaptists, that hold also the doctrine of Pelagianism, or Socinianism, or libertinism, or familism, or quakers, or heathenism, they are not in a capacity for us to treat with about accommodation, or christian peace.

But yet as to all the intemperate, dividing, unpeaceable anabaptists, that will but reproach us for our drawing so near them, at least we shall have this advantage against their reasonings, that we shall be far better able to manifest the vanity of them, than otherwise we could do. For whereas their common argument against infant baptism is, that it defileth the church, by letting in all the children in the nation, which must be cast out again, or the most will be openly vile; and that it defraudeth the adult of the benefits of solemn engagement to Christ; all this will be taken off by confirmation, and will lie no more on us, than on themselves, seeing by this means we can as faithfully hold the church door against the adults, that are unfit to enter into the number, as they can.

And here I shall entreat the moderate, godly persons among us, that are of the episcopal, presbyterian, congregational, or Erastian judgment, yea, and the first and second sort of anabaptists, to consider how nearly we are all agreed, or how near to an agreement, when we are not aware of it, or live at such a distance as if we were not aware of it; and whether it be not our duty to close upon this practice, at least much nearer than we are? It is a sad and fearful case, when men professing godliness, and all pretending to a love of unity, peace, and holiness, shall hate or oppose each other, and separate from each other, upon a pretence that we differ in things that we are agreed in; and when such shall persuade the common enemies, and the ignorant people, that we differ where we do not: as if the enemy had not already matter enough of reproach against us, nor the ignorant matter enough of temptation and offence, but we must falsely give them more, by seeming to differ when there is no such thing! And if this be caused by any men's hating their own principles, when they see them in another's hand, or yet by hating the practice of their own principles, I leave it to the consideration of sober men, whether such are liker to the ministers of Christ, or Satan.

Give me leave here a little, by way of application, to review what I said concerning our accord.

1. How much many brethren of the episcopal judgment do censure other men's attempts for reforming their congregations, is too open to be hid. But how little cause they have to be offended with any moderate attempts, let their own forecited principles be judge. I know that it is the administration of government of the churches that seems, by the noise of opposition among us, to be the greatest point of differences; but as far as I can discern, it is not so. The constitution of our churches is the great difference: it is a shame to speak it; we differ most where we are agreed. I have so much experience of the minds of godly ministers, and private men in England, that I dare boldly say, would we but all agree in practice, in the constituting our churches of due materials, where, for aught I know, we are almost all agreed in principles, there were no probability that all the rest of our disagreements would keep us at a quarter of the distance as we are. Truly the common, honest, godly people, stick not much on the difference in formalities, and extrinsic modes of government. If they hear a minister pray heartily, preach soundly, judiciously, and powerfully, live holily, and righteously, and charitably, and beat down sin, and set himself to promote true piety, they are, commonly where I am acquainted, if not indifferent what forms of government he is for, yet at least can easily bear with him, though he differ from them. Let us have the work of God well done, and we shall care the less who it is that doth it. The greatest offence, that commonly is taken against episcopacy, is, 1. The former viciousness, negligence, and persecution, that men of that way were guilty of; and, 2. Because men know that a diocesan bishop hath so much work upon his hands, that he will certainly leave the far greatest part undone. So that the question is not so much who shall do the work, as whether it shall be done or not.

But now if this principle were practised, in which we are agreed, about confirmation, or at least, a public profession, that so our churches might be constituted of fit materials, and not be pestered with so many infidels, or persons so ignorant as that they know not Christ; or persons so notoriously vicious, as that they are openly brutish and profane, and make a very scorn of honesty and godliness; this would do much to heal all the rest of our divisions. The country knows that the reason why the multitude of ignorant, ungodly people are for episcopacy, is principally because they think that government will do as it did, and rather curb the precisians, as they call them, than them; and will not trouble them with a differencing discipline or administrations, nor urge them so hard to labour for knowledge, and live a godly life. Take away this conceit from them, by the faithful practice of your own principles, and they will hate you as much as others. What great satisfaction would you give to all that fear God among us, if you would practise but that which the Rubric of the Common Prayer Book requireth of you, in this one point? For it requireth not only a learning of the catechism, but also a public owning of their baptismal covenant in the face of the congregation, and a solemn promise to live a holy, obedient life, and this at full age; and after this they must be confirmed, before they be admitted to the sacrament of the eucharist. That it may appear how fully we are agreeable in this point, I shall transcribe some more of the Rubric of Confirmation, which is as followeth:

The reasons given why none shall be confirmed, till they can answer such questions of the catechism, as they shall be apposed in, are these: "1. Because that when children come to the years of discretion, and have learned what their godfathers and godmothers promised for them in baptism, they may then themselves with their own mouth, and with their own consent, openly before the church ratify and confirm the same; and also promise, that by the grace of God they will evermore endeavour themselves faithfully to observe and keep such things as they by their own mouth and confession have assented unto. 2. Forasmuch as confirmation is ministered to them that be baptized, that by imposition of hands, and prayer, they may receive strength and defence against all temptations to sin, and the assaults of the world and the devil, it is most meet to be admitted, when children come to that age, that partly by the frailty of their own flesh, partly by the assaults of the world and the devil, they begin to be in danger, to fall into sundry kinds of sin. 3. For that it is agreeable with the usage of the church in times past; whereby it was ordained, that confirmation should be ministered to them that were of perfect age; that they being instructed in Christ's religion, should openly profess their own faith, and promise to be obedient to the will of God."

This, with what was before cited, shows, that in this main point we are agreed with the brethren of the episcopal judgment, and therefore may expect their concurrence: and to that end, we desire them to promote the practice of their own principles: and let us not leave the work of God undone, while we strive who shall do it, or rather who shall not do it. If the canons allow the bishop's suffragan to do it, you may bear with others of the same order to do it, rather than leave it undone.

2. And for the presbyterians, I entreat them to consider, (1.) How much the faithful practice of this duty will put by all the offence and mistaken reasons of the Erastians, who ask them so earnestly, How they can prove that people must be examined by the minister, in order to the Lord's supper, any more than in order to a day of thanksgiving? I know it is an easy matter to prove that a pastor may call his people to private, personal instruction, at any fit season; and therefore before a sacrament when he sees just cause; and they are bound to obey him, ordinarily, by virtue of the general precept, "Obey them that rule over you," &c. Heb. xiii. 17. But if you make this the season and use of your examination, to admit men out of a state either of catechumens, or infant members, into the number of adult members, and never trouble them afterward with examinations, unless upon some special occasion, or in your ordinary course of personal instruction, this would put by the opposition of gainsayers; and I think, satisfy all of them that have any sober considerations and love to the prosperity of the church.

(2.) And consider also how much this way would facilitate your course of discipline; you would be much more clearly satisfied, who are your church members, and of your special charge, and on whom you are specially bound to exercise discipline, and to whom you owe your special care and labour; and your people will be better satisfied than now they are, both of the quality, and regular reception of members, and who they be, to whom they owe the special duty of members, and whom they are more especially bound to communicate their worldly goods in their necessity. How much uncertainty, confusion, dissatisfiedness, and neglect of duty remaineth in those congregations, where this work is quite omitted, is obvious to common observation.

(3.) And if any should have a jealousy of this design, as seeming to set up the congregational way of covenanting; I entreat such to remember, 1. What an enemy to the unity of the church, and how unbeseeming a charitable christian, a spirit of causeless jealousy is. 2. That it should be the more grateful to you, because it is acceptable to your brethren. If you are lovers of unity and peace, you will be far from avoiding a practice, because those hold it with whom you would be united, that is, because it tends to unity; but rather you will be glad of such a healing means. 3. Consider that it is no more the congregational men's principle, than the episcopal presbyterians' and the Erastians'. It is our common principle, let us therefore make it our practice; an easy, a reasonable way of agreement. The not practising of this hath cast us into confusions; and the practice of it must be it that must restore our church order, and heal most of our divisions. I know it is agreeable to your judgments. I move you not to forsake your principles, but to practise them. Do but enrol those only for your adult church members, that are confirmed, or approved, upon a personal credible profession of true christianity, and consent to live under your ministerial discipline; and it will do more than you can easily now apprehend for a union with your brethren, and for the closing of the sad and long-continued divisions of the churches.

3. And to the congregational brethren, I may boldly say, it is a practice so suitable to your own practice already, (although I think it is a more regular performance of it that I propound, than most have used,) that in reason we may expect your approbation and concurrence. Perhaps you will fear that some of your brethren may slubber over the work, and make but a ceremony of it: but so may some of your own mind, if they be personally remiss and negligent, as well as others. And perhaps others will fear lest *you* should use it over-rigorously, and make it a pretence for excluding many that are not to be excluded. But this will be according to the prudence and charity of particular pastors; and is nothing to those principles, in which we are all agreed: only I beseech you in the fear of God, take heed of giving just occasion of this offence. Be not righteous over-much: remember how tender Christ is of his little ones; and how he is displeased with those that keep them from him; and will not break the bruised reed. If he carry the lambs in his arms, and gently drive those that are with young, it beseems not us to turn them out of the fold, or to disown them. We are commanded to "receive him that is weak in the faith, though not to doubtful disputations," Rom. xv. 1. It is a conjunction of impiety, injustice, and uncharitableness, to thrust back those that Christ would have admitted. It is *impiety*, to rob Christ of his church members, and diminish his visible flock, and wrong those whom he values as his jewels, and is tender of as the apple of his eye. It is great *injustice*, to defraud men of their due, in so great a matter as his church privileges and helps to heaven. It is greater injustice than to turn them out of their houses and lands; for the benefits are greater. It is *uncharitableness*, to deal so cruelly with us, in matters of such consequence. And it is the greater, 1. Because it is none of our own, but our Master's treasure which we deny them. 2. And because we are conscious, if we are christians indeed, of so much sin and unworthiness ourselves, as should provoke us to deal the more tenderly and compassionately with others. I would not have you blind under pretence of charity, nor to let in known swine, for fear of keeping out the sheep. But remember, that when the case is but so doubtful and difficult, that you cannot know certainly the tares from the wheat, or cannot make a separation without a danger of pulling up the wheat with the tares, it is better let both alone till harvest. We will not be wilfully guilty of men's lying, or hypocritical professions; but if they be guilty of them, we may yet believe that God hath much service for hypocrites in his church. And the number shall be some honour to him; and some encouragement to some that are yet without, to draw nearer us. Though it be the intention of Christ in instituting his ordinances, and the intention of the church, that men be truly penitent believers before they are baptized at age, or admitted into the number of adult church members, and to the Lord's table; and so never made the eucharist an ordinance which is primarily and directly intended for conversion of the unregenerate, and which known ungodly men may seek, and be admitted to, in order to their conversion: Bellarmine himself confessing that such come into the church *præter intentionem ecclesiæ*. Yet Christ, that knew abundance of unsound professors would thrust themselves into the church, hath provided those ordinances there, which conduce much to their regeneration: and even the Lord's supper, though instituted primarily for another use, may be

a means of this, to those that yet unworthily drew near it. However, if we be commanded to invite, yea, and compel men to come into the church, that the house of Christ may be filled, we must not be too scrupulous in admitting them, nor too busy in keeping them back. If any where, it is here that Christ is like to say, *Odi servum nimis diligentem.* If men make a credible profession, I dare not refuse them: nor dare I by my uncharitable incredulity, take that for incredible, which I cannot prove to be so. His profession is the evidence of his title with the church. If I will deny him when he seeks admittance, I must disprove that profession, and show it to be invalid. Truly much experience hath taught me, that many that were never commonly noted for godliness, and that through bashfulness, or want of expressions, or the hinderance of carnal friends, and worldly affairs, have lived as strangers to those that are eminent for the fear of God, have yet at last disclosed themselves to me, to have been humble, serious christians many years, as far as I was able to judge. Especially take heed how you slight or reject people for want of parts, or gifts, or utterance. I have known excellent christians, that through bashfulness are not able to give an account of their knowledge of the very fundamentals of religion, to a person whom they much reverence, and are in awe of. And I meet with many ignorant people, that in answer to many of my questions, do seem to be ignorant of Christ himself, who yet show the contrary, when by other words I have caused them better to understand me. If people be but desirous, and willing, and diligent, it must be very gross ignorance indeed, that must warrant us to refuse them. Many thousands are guilty of wrong intruding into the church, when the ministers and church were not guilty of wrong admitting them, but had been culpable if they had refused them.

I speak all this to the congregational brethren, rather than the rest, because they are most suspected to be over-strict in their admissions; and because I would entreat them to avoid all just occasions of offence and disunion in their practice, when we are all so happily agreed in our principles, in this great point, of the necessity of an approved profession.

4. And for the Erastians, as in the point of discipline, they commonly contend with us upon a mere mistake, thinking we claim a proper imperium or magisterial power, whenas we claim but the power of an ambassador, with such a kind of power as a physician hath over his patients, or as Plato or Zeno had in their schools, (besides the ministerial power in worshipping,) so their principal quarrel with us will be removed by the practice of confirmation. You talk much of the sacraments being converting ordinances, and against examining men in order to the Lord's supper, and keeping men away. But are you not agreed with us, That a personal understanding, serious profession of christianity, even of faith and repentance, which containeth a renouncing the flesh, the world, and the devil, is necessary to those that will, either by baptism or confirmation, be admitted into the number of adult members of the church? And do you not grant that the adults, whether before baptism or confirmation, are to be tried and approved by the pastors, before they baptize or confirm them? Grant us but this, and that the ancient discipline should be exercised in the church, which the Scriptures and all the church canons do record, and we shall be agreed with you in a moment. For baptism we are no stricter than the Common Prayer Book, that required that the party, by himself or others, did promise and vow, 1. To forsake the devil and all his works, the pomps and vanities of the wicked world, and all the sinful lusts of the flesh. 2. To believe all the articles of the christian faith. 3. To keep God's holy will and commandments, and walk in the same all the days of his life. That so it may be truly said of the baptized, that he is made a member of Christ, a child of God, and an inheritor (or heir) of the kingdom of heaven. And of the confirmed, we expect but that which is here said to be given, and assured in baptism, viz. a death unto sin, and a new birth unto righteousness; that being by nature born in sin, and the children of wrath, we are hereby made the children of grace: yea, we expect but what is required of persons to be baptized; viz. repentance, whereby they forsake sin; and faith, whereby they stedfastly believe the promises of God made to them in that sacrament. All these are the words of the catechism in the Common Prayer Book. Yea, we expect but that open profession before the congregation, which the fore-cited Rubric of Confirmation requireth; no, nor always so much as that. So that I may well suppose, that no godly, moderate man of the Erastian way, can dissent from us in this point of confirmation: and a consent in this, will be next to a consent in all, between us and them.

5. And for the anabaptists themselves, though we expect not their consent, yet we may well expect their moderation, and non-opposition, and that as we thus draw as near them as possibly (in our present judgment) we can, so they would lay by all bitterness and reproach, and divisive carriage, and come as near us as they can. And as now with the more moderate of them, our difference appeareth less than many of them imagined, so it may appear, that the distance in affection and communion shall be no greater than there is cause. The odium of division and unpeaceableness hath so long lain upon their party, that methinks they should be willing to have it taken off. And there is no way to take it off, but their visible amendment; by becoming lovers and promoters of union, communion, and peace among the churches of Christ. Men will never take your opinion to be of God, while general experience shall show them, that it will not stand with that love, union, and communion of the saints, but engageth almost all that receive it, in divisions, opposition, and reproach of the servants of Christ and his churches. Though you think your own opinion right, let it not so far dispossess you of charity and reason, as to unchurch all the churches of Christ that think otherwise, or to cast off communion with the godly that are not of your opinion; as long as we come so near you, as to take none into the number of adult church members, but those that are confirmed, or approved by Christ's ministers, upon their personal, credible profession of faith and holiness.

Lay all this together, and we may well conclude, that this practice of ministerial approbation and confirmation, or restoration of all that are admitted into the number of adult christians, or visible church members, and to their privileges, is so necessary, and so admirably fitted, both for reformation and reconciliation of the episcopal, presbyterian, independent, Erastian, and moderate anabaptists, and to stop the mouths of the intemperate, and of the papists, that all magistrates, ministers, and people, that love the church's purity and people, and long to see it cleansed and healed, should gladly embrace it, and vigorously promote it.

I have two things yet more to do upon this subject: 1. To answer some objections; and, 2. To give some directions to all sorts, for the effectual putting it in execution. The objections are these.

Object. 1. You will tempt the anabaptists to say, that this is but a shift of our own devising, instead of baptism, lest we should yield to them, when we are convinced of the necessity of a personal covenanting with the adult.

Answ. There is no ordinance or truth of God that will not be spoken against by mistaken men, and yet we must not therefore cast them away. Nor is it the way to vindicate a truth or ordinance from reproach, to disclaim it, and so to reproach it actually ourselves. Nor is it the way to get advantage of an adversary, to fly from him too far into the contrary extreme, but rather to come as near him as the truth will give us leave. And to the anabaptists' objection, we shall give them our reasons against their way, in a fitter place, and have already done it. We are most certain that the servants of God of old, both with circumcision and without it, (Deut. xxix.) did enter their children into covenant with God, as well as themselves. And if it be the express word of God, that both infants and aged should be entered and engaged to him in covenant, we will obey his word, and do both, though the anabaptists will do but the one. He must have a hard face, that will deny that it was once the duty of parents to offer their children to God, and enter them into covenant with him; and when they have proved that this duty or power is recalled, (which I never yet saw done, no not in Mr. Tombes' last voluminous review,) then we will forbear it; but till then it is not men's talk and confident words that must make a tender conscience yield, to omit so great and plain a duty, or give up so great a mercy as this is. I am sure that infants were then no more able to believe themselves, nor enter themselves in covenant with God, than now; and I am sure parents, by God's appointment, did it for them, offering and engaging them to God, and that God hereupon is called their God, and they his people, and that usually the sign of the covenant was annexed. And I am sure that parents have as much natural interest in their children now as then: and I never yet saw where God had acquit us of this duty, or withdrawn this mercy from us and our seed.

Object. 2. The proof which you bring for this confirmation is so obscure, that it is not like to be generally received.

Answ. 1. It was generally received in almost all the churches on earth, till lately: and as far as I plead for it, it is yet, doctrinally at least, owned and maintained, even by those churches that practically have disused it. Of all the christians on earth, I suppose there is a thousand, if not ten thousand, for it, (doctrinally or dogmatically,) for one that is against it, if we judge by the laws, confessions, and writings of their guides. Though the Greeks I know do not own the popish confirmation, nor have it so formally as they should, and the papists have corrupted it by their abuse; yet the thing in substance is owned dogmatically by almost all the christian world; and they must be very singular persons that disown it. 2. And I think the proof that hath been given you is clearer, than you have for the morality of the Lord's-day, for constant family prayer, for infant baptism, and many a holy duty, which yet we have sufficient proof for. What would you have plainer? Is there the least doubt of it, whether a personal profession and covenanting with God, be necessary to him that will be taken into the number of adult christians, and possess their privileges and communion? or whether this profession must be approved by the pastor of the church, and known to them that must hold communion with him? Prove, if you can, that ever one man was admitted among adult christians to enjoy communion with them, without such a personal profession. You cannot prove it. If infant covenanting were enough for the adult, then infidels are believers.

Object. 3. But this will make ministers to be lords of the church; when no man can be taken into the church, or possess the privileges of a christian, till he be approved by them. This will put a tyrannical power into their hands.

Answ. 1. Such a tyrannical power as every physician hath, who may choose or refuse his patients; or every schoolmaster hath, that may choose or refuse his scholars, if he engage not himself to the contrary, as Plato, Zeno, and every philosopher did in his school.

2. It is such a tyranny as Christ hath unquestionably set up; and to accuse him of setting up tyranny, is an unkind part of them that look to be saved by him.

3. It is a power that hath constantly been exercised by the officers of Christ; and did not men smell out the tyranny of it till now? What prince did govern the church doors, and judge who should be admitted, from the days of Christ till Constantine's days, when the church was at the purest; yea, or ever after so many hundred years? Did not all the apostles, and every preacher of the gospel, baptize those that they converted, and judge of them whether they were baptizable? and did not the bishops confirm the baptized, without consulting another power? Half that were admitted into the church by baptism, (and more,) for some hundred years after Christ, were the adult; and of these the pastor required a personal covenant and profession. The other half were their infants; and for them they required the parents' profession, and entering them into covenant: but still the pastors were the judges, who were the administers.

4. If you think it too much power for us, I beseech you think it too much work for us: and dream not that we have a work, and not power to do it, or discern what we do. Set others to do it, that you can better trust.

5. Who would you have trusted with this power? Somebody must have it. I have proved to you fully, that every man must not be the sole judge of his own fitness for baptism or church privileges; and that the people or magistrates are not the sole or chief judges: and who should it be but they to whom it is committed by Christ in their call to the office of the ministry?

6. Ministers, as I before showed, have no tyrannical or arbitrary power; for Christ hath tied them by a law whom to admit, and whom to reject; and if they disobey this law, the magistrate may correct them: so that in the exercise of this tyrannical power, every minister is under the lash of the magistrate's violence, if he grossly offend; whereas none of the people are under any violence, or force from us to obey us; but if all of them disobey us and rebel, it is their own loss, and we have no remedy. This is the tyranny.

7. Lastly, if you think it (as it is) so great a power, for us to judge of men's profession and fitness for church privileges, let it awaken you the more, to get the wisest, ablest men you can for the ministry, that are fit for so great a trust. If the best that are to be got are not in the office, beshrew our governors, and the choosers. And if you do not cast us all out, if you can put fitter men into the place, that are meeter for the trust, beshrew you for your negligence: we give you no thanks for it. But if you have no fitter for this work and trust, will you cast it upon unfitter, or on none? It is a great trust for a physician to be trusted with your lives, and a schoolmaster and tutor with your children: but what of that? will you

therefore trust the good women, or common neighbours about you with them; yea, or the magistrate himself? Or will you have no tutors or physicians? Or rather will you not be the more careful to keep out empirics and unworthy persons, and get the ablest and faithfullest that you can? O unthankful men! that grudge us the power of labouring and spending ourselves for their salvation, and judging, where we must act!

Object. 4. Is it not the use of the Lord's supper to confirm us; and do not men there renew their covenant and profession? What need is there then of any more?

Answ. 1. You would think much, if at the Lord's supper we should openly call each man to a personal explicit profession of his faith, and covenanting with God: and indeed it would be a tedious as well as unseasonable work. It is but a general or joint profession of all together, that there is renewed; and notwithstanding that, there may, for aught we know, be many a one there that is an infidel, and knoweth not what christianity is. 2. The Lord's supper is the food of the soul, confirming by way of nutrition and augmentation; and therefore you must show that you are alive, before you may partake of it. It is a feasting upon Christ, and with him in his family, and at his table; it is a work of communion with Christ and with his saints; it is one of the highest privileges of the church: and therefore you must produce your title, before you can lay claim to it. If a man must be admitted to the Lord's supper, without any precedent personal profession or covenanting with God, upon supposition that by the act of receiving he doth all this; then men that know not whether there be a Christ, or what he is, may be admitted: for multitudes of such there are, that in infancy were baptized: and I know not by seeing him receive, whether he know or believe any thing of christianity. If a man converted at age from heathenism, may not be admitted to the Lord's table without a personal profession in baptism, then neither may such as are baptized in infancy, be admitted without a personal profession in confirmation, or such as is without any other baptism. Our parents' profession will not serve our turn, instead of our own, when we come to age. And therefore this objection is vain, unless infidels may be admitted to communion, and all be common. But I need not speak much of this, because I shall have few such objectors to deal with: even the papists themselves are many of them against promiscuous communion, though the Jesuits of late have fitted almost all their work to their man-pleasing design: (see Joh. Thauleri flores. cap. 23, 24. p. 257, &c.; an old puritan, among the papists:) and they make confession also prerequisite.

Object. 5. According to your arguing, confirmation is not necessary to those that were baptized at full age; and therefore it is not necessary to any, if not to all.

Answ. I have given some reasons why it should be used with all that have opportunity after baptism; but I have proved it more necessary to those that were baptized in infancy: and if it were necessary to no other, it would not follow, that it is not necessary at all, because not to all.

Object. 6. Is it not better take up with an implicit profession and covenanting, than make so great a trouble to ourselves, and disturbance among the people, as this will make?

Answ. 1. Methinks, not only the face of the Roman church, but of our own, might by this time have afforded us satisfying experience, what implicit faith and implicit professions are, and to what they tend. Peruse the forementioned evils of this course, and look upon the state of our people, where you may see them in existence, and then judge whether this objection be answered.

2. An implicit profession is the lowest and least that in any case of extremity or necessity can be thought tolerable, and accepted by God, and consistent with the life and being of a church. And shall we deliberately choose to offer God the worst, the least, the lowest that is possible to find acceptance? Nay, he will have the best, as he deserves the best, or he will not accept it, when we have it to give. Shall we think that in a case of freedom, the same will be accepted, which necessity only can excuse? Or shall we be content that our churches have as many diseases as will consist with life and being?

3. An implicit profession makes or proves men but implicitly christians. Such dumb, uncertain signs, do leave us in so great uncertainty of the thing signified, that it seems but a very mocking of God, (that will not be mocked,) when we have opportunity for an open, intelligible profession, and will not use it, or require it.

4. It is against nature, for a man that hath a tongue in his head, to refuse to utter his mind any otherwise than by dumb shows, and yet expect to be understood and accepted. What is the tongue made for but to express the mind? Indeed if a man be dumb, and can neither speak nor write, it is more tolerable to take an uncertain sign from such a man, than from another that hath the use of tongue or pen.

5. It is a very implicit denying of Christ, which many call an implicit profession. If a man that hath a tongue in his mouth, shall refuse to profess the christian faith, and quarrel with the minister that calls him to it, and say, We shall have no other profession from him than to come to church, and put the bread and wine into his mouth, and not to deny Christ expressly, I leave it to any reasonable man, whether there be not so much of an implicit denying Christ in this refusing to confess him, when they are called to it by their pastors, whom God hath commanded them to obey, and that in a case and season, when all the church hath required it, or taught it to be due.

6. It is contrary to the honour of Christ, and the very nature of christianity, for men to take up with implicit, uncertain professions, when we have opportunity of more open, free professions. He is not a Master to be ashamed of: and he will have no servants that will not confess him before men, even in the hazard of life; much more in days of the freedom of the gospel. As "with the heart men must believe to righteousness, so with the mouth confession is made unto salvation," Rom. x. 10. What reason have we to whisper or draw back in a cause of such a nature and weight as this?

7. Shall we thus teach our people to esteem christianity, as an unobservable thing, by no more observing it? The solemnity of men's transition into the adult state of actual believers, doth make it more observable in the eyes of men; and they will see that there is more in it, than commonly is now esteemed. I find by experience that our people hate no preaching more, than differencing preaching, which leaves or shuts them out from the number of the sanctified, and sets them as on the left hand, in the face of the congregation, and judgeth them before the time; but fain they would have ministers confound and jumble all together; and then you may make them as great sinners as you will, so you will make them no worse than the justified, that are forgiven, and shall be saved: and so in practice, they love no differencing ways. But shall we so far gratify

the devil and the flesh? No; we must labour to make the difference between Christ's servants and the world as conspicuous as we can, that the consciences of poor sinners may rather be awakened, than cheated by us; and therefore we should choose the most solemn transition, and record the names of the confirmed, and let the people be brought to a public observation of the necessity of faith and holiness, while the covenant and profession of it is made so necessary.

8. That is the best means, that is fittest to attain the end; the end of a covenant is to oblige, and the end of a profession to declare the mind: and I pray you which is fittest for these ends; an express profession and covenant, or a dumb uncertain sign, by coming to church, paying tithes, &c.

9. Such dumb professions are less tolerable now, because we have many in our assemblies that we know to be no christians. I know of many that will hear, that believe no life to come, and secretly make a scorn of Christ and Scripture, and many more that know not what christianity is, as is aforesaid. Now shall we take up with such signs of christianity, as we see and know are commonly used by infidels, when we may have better?

10. It is essential to a profession to be in some measure explicit; for *proficeri* is but *palam vel publice fateri;* it is no profession if it be not, or pretend not to be, an expression of the mind; and therefore to be implicit and not express, is so far to be against the very nature of the profession: in that measure as your profession is implicit, as it is called, and not express, in that measure it is no profession at all.

Object. 7. But when you have the most express covenant or profession, you are not sure that it is true, and that the man is a believer at the heart.

Answ. 1. I am sure that it is truly a profession, that is, a pretended sign of the mind, though I am not sure that it is true profession, that is, a true infallible sign of the mind: I can know the metaphysical though not the moral truth of it. And then I can be sure that I do my duty, and take up according to the directions of Christ. It is his work to judge the heart immediately, as being his prerogative to know it; but it is my work to judge of the credibility of the profession. 2. And what if I have no infallible certainty? Must I therefore throw up all, and make the pastoral church government to be void, and cast open the vineyard of Christ to the wilderness, and not so much as require a credibility, because we cannot have an infallibility? This may not be.

Object. 8. But this will encourage the anabaptists and congregational, in their express covenantings, by our coming so near them?

Answ. 1. I may better say, you will make men anabaptists, and drive them too far by your looseness, and wilfully shunning plain duty. How can weak professors be drawn to think well of that party, which they see do shun so needful a work of God? 2. Love and peace will teach all christians to say, that it is the best for unity and healing of our breaches, to come as near dissenting brethren as we may, and not to fly the further from them. At least we may not run from truth and duty, that we may be unlike our dissenting brethren. 3. And I take it to be my duty to tell this aloud to the christian world, that after long contest with the anabaptists, and opposition of their ways, I am grown, as I confidently think, to this discovery of the mind of God in suffering them among us; that he had this great truth and duty, to which he saw it necessary to awaken us; the church having been so lamentably defiled, discipline made an impossible thing, and men's salvation grievously hindered, by the common *secret, unobserved* transition of all people into the name, number, and privileges of adult christians; therefore did God permit these men to step too far on the other side, that the noise might be the greater, and his call the more observable; so that they are his messengers, calling aloud to England, and all other christian churches in Europe, to keep the door, and repair the hedge, and no more to take an infant baptism, and profession of our parents, as a sufficient evidence of the title of the adult, to the name, or place, or privileges of christians; but to give them infant privileges upon the parents' profession; but to require of them a sober, serious profession and covenanting by themselves, in owning their baptismal covenant, before we number them with adult christians. And that God hath suffered the anabaptists to make such a stir among us, will prove a mercy to us in the end, if we have the wit and grace to learn this, upon this troublesome occasion; and then the reformation will do us more good, than ever the anabaptists did us harm. But if we will not learn, nor obey God's call, we must yet look to be molested by them more, or else to do and suffer worse.

Object. 9. But if you will not take a non-renouncing of Christ and infant baptism as sufficient, without a personal covenant and profession, you may on the same grounds call men every week to such a profession, because that the former profession shows not what they afterwards are, but what then they are.

Answ. 1. The case is quite another: in your instance, it is but the continuance of the same profession and condition that is requisite; and I am bound to take it as continued, while I have no evidence to question it, and see the performance of it, as far as belongeth to my cognizance. But in my case, the conditions and the professions are not the same; a new condition of right is necessary to the adult, which they had not at all in their infant baptism. Then they entered upon their parents' faith or profession; but at age they must necessarily have a faith or profession of their own, or else they actually cease to be christians.

2. And yet, let me add, that frequent professions of faith, and renewing covenant with God, hath ever been used in the church; both before Christ's incarnation and since, and indeed, the Lord's supper doth import it; and for my part, I think it a very convenient, edifying course, to have the articles of our faith every day repeated, as the belief of that church, and the people to stand up at it, to signify their consent: so be it, you will not take up with this silent profession alone, and exclude a more explicit one, when it is requisite. But this fitly signifieth our standing to the first.

Object. 10. But this will cast you upon the same difficulties which you object to the anabaptists; you will not know at what age to take men for adult christians.

Answ. 1. We shall not accept them for their age, but for their profession; and we can easily tell when they offer themselves to trial and profession, and desire the communion of the church; as the ancient churches could tell when their catechumens were to be baptized.

2. And for the time when we must judge their infant church state to cease, if they own not the covenant personally, we cannot set a certain year, nor is it necessary; but when their infancy ceaseth, then their infant state ceaseth; that is, when they come to the full or competent use of reason. But then observe, (1.) That if they be called at such a time to profess their faith, and own their covenant, and refuse it, then we must judge them refusers of chris-

tianity, unless the reason of the refusal allows another judgment. (2.) Or, if they wilfully neglect, for a considerable space, to own their baptismal covenant, and to seek a standing among the adult christians, it is a strong presumption that they are backsliders. (3.) If they only suspend their personal profession at age, we must only suspend our judgment, till we have some light to discern the cause; and cannot be sure that they are deserters or apostates. (4.) But we are sure that they are not to be numbered by the church among adult christians, till they have produced the evidence of their title, which is no other than *a credible, personal profession.* So that it is easy to know when any such person is to be admitted, and publicly owned as an actual believer, though it be not so easy to discern of all, before that time, whether they are to be reckoned as deserters or not. He that wilfully neglecteth to come among the adult christians, long after he hath the full use of reason, which is not with all at the same age, is to be much suspected, at least; and commonly about sixteen, or seventeen, or eighteen years of age, is the time when we have reason to expect that they should seek the communion and privileges of the adult; for about that age they have a competent use of reason.

Object. 11. But if you admit them into the church in infancy, say the anabaptists, you will be obliged to excommunicate them all, that prove ungodly when they come to age, and not to let them silently pass out of the church again.

Answ. Excommunication is either an excluding them from all relation of members to the catholic church, or from the actual communion of the church, or from both. The former we can do but declaratively. In the latter we also adjoin the charge of God, for the execution of the sentence. But those that were never personal professors of faith, nor admitted into the communion of adult christians, are not fit to be cast out of it; and this is the common use of excommunication, to remove those, as unfit, from the communion of the adult, that once were in it, and forfeit that communion; which cannot belong to them that never were in it. And for our declaring them deserters, or apostates, we may do it upon just occasion, but we are not bound to do it publicly by all that are guilty; this being not the excommunication that is so enjoined in the Scriptures. Where do you find that the church, in Scripture times, or after, was wont to excommunicate apostates? And yet apostates were formerly of the church. It is those that hang on, and pretend still to be of the church, and intrude into the actual communion of it, that we must cast out, when they deserve it.

Object. 12. But if they cease to be christians, you must baptize them again, if you will receive them.

Answ. No such matter; the anabaptists themselves will not rebaptize an apostate, when he returneth to the church. He is to be received by confession and absolution, and not by baptism. If a christian turn Turk, and afterward return, he is not to be rebaptized.

Object. 13. But by this means you will unchristian the people, and they will be exasperated, and turn heathens, or hearken to any seducers that will mislead them.

Answ. 1. No: we will unchristian no man; but do that honour to christianity, and that right to the church and the souls of men, as to make a difference between christians and infidels, and that somewhat wider than the bare names. He that is a christian shall be more encouraged by this course, and he that is not cannot be unchristianed by us. If men will not unchristian themselves, they need not fear lest the just trying and approving of their christianity should unchristian them. 2. How little honour it is to Christ and the church, to have the number made up by such as we would disallow, I have showed you before, and also what a mischief that is to themselves, which some would give them as a benefit. 3. If magistrates and ministers do their duty, yea, or but ministers alone, they will better be kept from heathenism, or other evils, in the state of expectants and catechumens, than in the state of church members, where discipline will make them mad.

Object. 14. But at least your design looks as if you would keep the children of all such unchristianed; and what work would that make!

Answ. I meddle not with that question, but leave every man to his own judgment. And if I did myself keep off such children, I think it would prove but very few. For, 1. I would refuse none of the parents that had *aliquid Christi*, that made but a credible profession of christianity. 2. I am persuaded that this practice would bring almost all the people to a tolerable profession, when they know it is expected, and what lieth on it. 3. Upon experience now I find, that both the parents are seldom so bad as to be uncapable of offering their child to God, in the judgment of the church. Nay, commonly here, the more one of the persons is in scandalous sin, the more the other hates it; and they are seldom both grossly ignorant. And those that were delayed on these terms, would receive no wrong by it. God's way is the best. The children of unbelievers must not be inchurched in ways of our devising, nor respected before the honour of Christ, and the common good of the church of God. But of this I say again, I interpose not my judgment, but leave each man to his own.

Object. 15. But though confirmation be a duty, yet none but bishops have power to do it; and therefore it is not a lawful thing for presbyters to attempt it.

Answ. 1. What mean you by bishops?[i] It is a word that hath, by men's application, got so many significations, that we may well expect that you give us the definition of a bishop, before you make him the matter of your dispute. And yet I have read so many books that dispute for episcopacy, and so few that tell us what they mean by it, that I must needs say, that most of them lose their labour, with such as I. If by a bishop you mean such as our English were, or any fixed pastor of many particular churches, I deny that such were ever instituted by Christ, much less have they the sole power of such administrations.

2. Do you mean that it is by God's law, or the laws of men, that diocesan bishops only may confirm?[k] If by God's laws, prove it, and we shall quickly yield. But that it is very unlikely you should do. If you say that only the apostles had this power, I answer, (1.) That then fixed diocesan bishops had none of it; for the apostles were none such. (2.) Then Timothy, Titus, Epaphroditus, &c. whom they pretend to have been bishops, had it not. (3.) Ananias was no apostle, that laid hands on Paul, that he might receive the Holy Ghost. Of

[i] Leg. Grotii, Epist. 162. ad Bignon. p. 397. Clem. Roman. against a lower episcopacy than ours.

[k] Petav. himself saith, Dissert. Eccles. lib. 1. cap. 3. p. 35. Ignorare non potuit Hieronimus quibusdam in locis absente episcopo presbyteros idem illud sacramentum confirmationis, dedisse: quod de Ægypto testatur commentarius, &c. And p. 36, he saith, Constat olim solos episcopos ordinario jure tam baptismum, quam pœnitentium reconciliationem administrasse. So that they may then as well forbid presbyters to baptize.

this more anon. But if you say, that this power is given to the bishops merely by the laws of men; then either by the laws of magistrates or of bishops. For the former we know of none in force with us, to that purpose; and if it were, it is a work out of their line, which Christ hath done before them, and not left to them, to describe the offices of the church. And for bishops' canons, we know no power that any bishops ever had, to make standing laws for the universal church; nor of any such laws that are obligatory to us: and the opponents themselves do violate the canons of general councils without scruple, (as the 20th of 1 Con. Nic. and abundance more,) and how can they oblige us more than them?

3. Presbyters have the keys of the kingdom; therefore they may take in and confirm thereby.

4. Presbyters may, by baptism, take in members into the universal church, and judge of their fitness in order thereto; therefore much more may they confirm them, and judge of their fitness in order thereto.

5. It is granted, that presbyters may absolve, which was ordinarily by imposition of hands; yea, saith Bishop Usher, the deacons were sometimes allowed it: therefore presbyters may confirm; or if you yielded but absolution, you would yield much of what we contend for, seeing so many violate their baptismal covenant, that absolution for restoring of them will be as necessary as confirmation.

6. Jerom, that makes presbyters and bishops by God's law to be the same, doth yet according to the custom of the church say, that "What doth the bishop, except ordination, which the presbyter doth not?" Therefore he supposed that presbyters might confirm.

7. The same Jerom expressly saith, that "Imposition of hands was reserved to the bishop, for the honour of priesthood, rather than by divine ordination:"[1] therefore it is but a human institution.

8. The episcopal divines and other writers of their side, do commonly maintain the validity of presbyters' ordination, viz. that in case of necessity it is lawful, and where there is no flat necessity, it is not a nullity where it is irregular. I cited "Christian Concord," p. 53, 54, &c. Many bishops and their defenders, that thus justify the protestant churches, that have no bishops; as Dr. Field, Bishop Downame, Bishop Jewel, Saravia, Bishop Alley, Bishop Pilkington, Bishop Bridges, Bishop Bilson, Grotius, Lord Digby, Mr. Chisenhal, Bishop Davenant, Bishop Prideaux, Nowel, Bishop Andrews, Mr. Chillingworth: to whom I add, (to make up twenty,) Bishop Bramhal, of Schism; and Dr. Steward, in his Answer to Fountaine's letter; Dr. Ferne; and Bishop Usher, in his Judgment, lately published. Abundance more might be easily added; but Mr. Mason's book in Vindication of the Ordination of the Foreign reformed Churches, may serve instead of more.

9. We have no bishop to do it, and therefore it must be done by presbyters: or we have none that we know of; and *non esse, et non apparere*, are to us all one.

10. Presbyters may impose hands in ordination, and ever did here in England: therefore much more in absolution and confirmation.

11. King Charles, by the advice of his doctors in the Isle of Wight, reserved only ordination, and not confirmation and absolution, to the bishops.

12. Presbyters are governors of the churches, which are their pastoral charge; and are called rectors: (see Bishop Usher's Reduction of Episcopacy, &c. proving it:) therefore they may do this, which is an act of government or guidance of the particular church.

13. Presbyters must teach and oversee the people as their charge, and deliver them the sacrament: therefore they must judge to whom they must do it.

14. A diocesan bishop is uncapable of doing it faithfully. Could one man try, approve, and confirm faithfully, all the souls in two or three hundred churches? It is known that here they did not; and it is plain they cannot. If they lay hands on them without trial, upon the presbyters' words, then, (1.) This yieldeth all, save the ceremony, which we require. (2.) And it is a venturing their practices on the judgment and fidelity of other men; who may send them infidels to be confirmed for aught they know. But if they try themselves, they are never able to do for so many, in season: some will be old men, before the bishop will have leisure to confirm them; and many a hundred die without it. Nor do they know the people as their pastors do.

15. The doctrine and practice of the church of England, under the bishops, is for the power of presbyters herein as far as we desire: for, (1.) The presbyters of curates had, by the rubric, the trial and approbation of those that were sent to the bishop for confirmation. (2.) The bishops accordingly took them on their words, with a certificate, and used not to try them themselves, but only to impose hands with prayer and blessing. (3.) And this, by the canon, their suffragan also might do; which yieldeth that a presbyter may do it.

16. The pope himself doth yield that presbyters may do it. And Gregory's Epist. to that end, is put into their canon law, Dist. 95. 1. part. *Baptizatos etiam Chrismate eos tangere conceditur;* and Gregory's Epist. to Januar. Calaritan. is annexed. By which it appeareth that they took his former prohibition so ill, that he was fain to reverse it. And though (c. 11.) he be forbidden *Infantes signare*, in the presence of the bishop, without his command, yet so he was forbidden also to administer the eucharist; yea, and the rural presbyters might not give the cup or bread in the presence of the city presbyters, (c. 12. ex Concil. Neocæsar. 1. c. 13.) But certainly this proveth neither the one nor the other out of their power.

17. The papists commonly confess, that presbyters may *ex dispensatione*, confirm by imposition of hands; so Bellarmine himself. And the schoolmen ordinarily make it an act of the presbyter's power.

18. If it be proper to bishops, that is, either because of their order or jurisdiction. Not of order; for they are of the same order with presbyters, as is frequently confessed by bishops and papists them-

[1] Hier. cont. Lucifer. Ad honorem potius sacerdotii, quam ad legis necessitatem. Alioqui si ad episcopi tantum imprecationem Sp. Sanctus defluit, lugendi sunt, qui in vinculis, aut castellis, aut in remotioribus locis, per presbyteros et diaconis baptizati, ante dormierunt, quam ab Episcopis inviserentur.

Clem. Alexand. Pedagog. 3. Cui imponet presbyter manus.

Ambros. in Eph. 4. Apud. Ægyptum presbyteri consignant, si præsens non sit episcopus.

Grotius Epist. cordes. 154. p. 382. Si recte expendantur quæ ipse Aurelius, de rebus nec vetitis, nec prohibitis disserit, non mirum si in iis alibi atque alio tempore alii fuerint mores; non erat causæ satis, cur tantis animis, tam odiosis illationibus ista quæstio tractaretur. Nam etiamsi aut baptizatus nunquam ungeretur, aut ungeretur tantum baptismi tempore, baptizante etiam presbytero. Adde etiam si nulla subsequeretur manuum impositio, donis illis quæ per manuum impositionem conferebant apostoli pridem cessantibus, non ideo periret honor præsidentiæ episcopalis, quæ tunc etiam in ecclesia fuit cum episcopi et presbyteri nomen indiscriminatim usurparetur, et cum præsidentia illa, non electione, quæ Alexandriæ primum fieri cepit, Marco mortuo, sed participati consensus gradu deferetur.

selves, and differ but in degree. Not of jurisdiction; for it is no more an act of jurisdiction to confirm, than to baptize or give the eucharist.

19. Protestant divines are commonly agreed, that confirmation is not proper to bishops, but may be used by presbyters. For, (1.) France, Belgia, Helvetia, Denmark, Saxony, Sweden, the Palatinate, the countries of the Duke of Brandenburg, the Duke of Brunswick, the Landgrave of Hessia, with the rest of the Protestant princes of Germany, and also Hungary, Transylvania, the protestants in Poland, &c. besides Scotland, and so many in England, are all without bishops, having put them down. And though three or four of these countries have superintendents, yet they make not confirmation proper to them. (2.) The English bishops ordinarily maintain against the papists, that presbyters may confirm; and therefore we have their concurrence, as in Dr. Field, Bishop Downame, Mason, and many others, is apparent.

20. If all this will not satisfy you, for peace sake, we will forbear imposition of hands, which you suppose to be the bishop's prerogative; and we will be content to do no more than presbyters always did in baptizing the adult; even to judge and approve of the capacity of those whom they baptized; and so will we only judge of the profession and capacity of those that we take charge of, and own as adult christians, and must administer the Lord's supper to: and this common reason cannot deny us.

Object. 16. But if presbyters may do it, yet so cannot you: for you are no presbyters, as wanting episcopal ordination; or else schismatical, as having cast them off to whom you were sworn.

Answ. 1. In my "Second Sheet for the Ministry," and my "Christian Concord," I have answered already. And for fuller answer, I refer you to "The London Ministers' Vindication," to "Mr. Mason's Vindication of the Ordination of the Protestant Churches," &c. If Bishop Bancroft himself, as Dr. Bernard mentions, in Bishop Usher's judgment, and the rest of the prelates, were against the reordination of the Scots ministers, methinks few should be so much more intemperate, than that intemperate prelate, as to judge their ordination null. And if the papists in the canon law do judge that in some cases an excommunicate man's ordination is valid, methinks protestants should not be worse to the church than they: especially those that are for the necessity of an uninterrupted succession of justly ordained pastors; who must (I dare boldly say) derive their succession from unmeeter and more uncapable hands than English pastors.

2. No more is necessary to the authority and just ordination of a pastor, but that he enter according to the laws of God; which laws require us to submit to the trial of our rulers and brethren, magistrates (in some cases) and pastors; and to come in according to the best means, for election and approbation, that are then to be had and used: but they bind us not to come in by ways impossible, nor to see that our antecessors through all generations have been lawfully ordained.

3. I have showed already, and, God willing, shall more fully do it, in a Disputation on that subject, that our English episcopacy was not that which God established, but intolerably inconsistent with it: and therefore neither are men the less ministers for being without their ordinations, nor are they schismatics for consenting to their deposition.

4. As for breaking oaths of canonical obedience to them, I think but few among us did take any such oath, and therefore broke none.

5. Many among us were ordained by bishops, and some that were ordained took not that oath; and others that did, yet obeyed them while they stood: and what could they do more?

6. The younger of ministers had no hand in taking down the bishops, and therefore are not schismatical thereby: and that their ordination is no nullity, Bishop Usher and other twenty prelatical witnesses forecited will testify.

Object. 17. But on the contrary side it will be said, that you would set up the popish sacrament of confirmation again.

Answ. The papists have made another thing of it: they use it to infants, and so will not we: they make a proper sacrament of it: they make the visible signs to be anointing and crossing, in the name of the Father, Son, and Holy Ghost; and they make imposition of hands no part of it, but cast it off, though in words they own it. They adjoin a box on the ear, to signify the opposition that Christ's soldiers must expect.[m] They make it to imprint I know not what indelible character, and to give grace *ex opere operato*. They make it to be an entering of us into Christ's militia, abusing baptism, as being but an entering us into his family, and not his warfare. All this is nothing to that which I am pleading for, and which the protestant writers do wish for.

Object. 18. At least you will revive the prelatical confirmation again, which the old nonconformists were against.

Answ. We will revive nothing of it but what was good: the corruption we shall omit. They did it but on a few, contrary to their own laws, but we would have it used to all. They confirmed children that understood not what they said: but we shall expect an understanding profession of faith. They did it in a hurry, as an idle ceremony: we would have it done deliberately and with great reverence. The bishop only did it with them, that knew not whom he did confirm, but ventured on other men's words, or without: but we will have the pastor do it, that knoweth the persons, and hath time to try them, having one parish, and not two hundred, to oversee.

Object. 18. But, at least, the papists and prelates will be hardened or encouraged by your coming so near them.

Answ. I will not cast off the work of God, because that any will make it an occasion of sin. And I take it to be the more my duty and not the less, because it tends to peace with all. I take it not to be any part of my religion, to study how to cross my brethren, or forbear a practice, yea, so necessary a duty, because they like it. I detest that principle and spirit. I rather fear, lest their own self-conceitedness, interest, prejudice, and discontent, will make them dislike it.

Object. 19. What have we to do with the sign, when the thing that occasioned the use of it is ceased? Imposition of hands was at first only for the gift of miracles.

Answ. 1. It was much for the gift of miracles, but not only. And if the giving of one sort of the gifts of the Holy Ghost be ceased, yet the other more excellent and necessary gifts continue; and therefore no reason the sign should cease, because it was not appropriated to the gift of miracles. But, 2. If any man scruple either the sign of imposing hands, or the name of confirmation, we desire him his liberty; these are not the things that we contend for. Let him but yield us that which I have showed to be most certain, and most useful to the church: that is, a solemn transition out of an infant church state into

[m] Vid. Chamier, l. 4. de Sacram. cap. 10, 11.

an adult, under approbation of the pastors, and the just cognizance of the church, and let him call it what he will, I shall not much contend with him about the name, or sign of imposition.

Object. 20. Abundance of ministers are raw, imprudent young men, and not fit to manage so great a trust: and so it will mar all; while some are so strict, that they will refuse all that seem not godly to their censorious minds; and some will be loose man-pleasers, and let in all, and turn it but to an unprofitable formality.

Answ. 1. While men are men, they will act as men. If we shall have no church ordinances and administrations, till you are secured from human abuse of them, you must shut up the church doors, and give up all; and shut up your Bibles, till papists and infidels can find no matter of cavilling at the translation. 2. As I said before, this indeed should provoke the magistrate to set a faithful guard on the church doors, that seeing the pastors have so great a trust, and the danger of abusing it is so great, the worthiest should be chosen that can be had. And if it be not so, you reproach yourselves, that are choosers and pastors, and have the rule. Why choose you not better, if you know where to find them? 3. This objection is as much against our judging of those that are to be baptized, which yet the ministers that did baptize have ever done; and were you not baptized already, we must admit you, and judge who is to be admitted, as the ancient preachers of the gospel did. 4. The episcopal brethren had no more wit, than to be against confirmation, because one man may use it too strictly, and another too loosely. The congregational men are not against church covenants or professions, because one pastor or church may be too strict, and another too loose in judging of men's piety. The presbyterians are not against trying men before admission to the Lord's supper, nor against discipline, because one eldership may be too strict, and another too loose. The anabaptists are not against rebaptizing men at age, because one minister may refuse the fit, and another may take in all that come. Why then should a possibility of ministers' miscarriage cause you to be more against this, than all the rest? 5. If ministers be associated, they will be accountable for such miscarriages; and the advice and admonition of their brethren may do much to prevent or reform such abuses: and the faithful people of their charge will somewhat observe them, and "bid Archippus take heed to the ministry that he hath received in the Lord, that he fulfil it," Col. iv. 17. 6. As long as you are not forced into our charge, but have your liberty to choose your pastor, as now it is, you have the less reason for this complaint. If the laws of Zeno or Plato be thought too strict in their schools, as long as the scholars may choose to come there, and all volunteers they may the better bear it. 7. As I said before, the trust must be put in some or other to judge: and where can it be fitter than in them, who by study are prepared, and by office appointed by Christ hereunto? 8. If you will give a presbytery, or one eminent minister in every market-town, or visiters of your own appointment, a special care to oversee the rest in doing this, and such like works, I shall be no gainsayer, so the work be but done: the more inspection and circumspection the better. 9. If one minister refuse the fit, there be many more that will not. 10. Your commissioners may have power moderately to correct the ministers' abuses in their work.

But because I perceive that rulers are unreasonably jealous lest the pastors of the church will do too much, rather than lest they do too little, and are more solicitous to use the bridle of restraint, than the spur of instigation; I entreat them to consider these things:—

1. That most certainly there is no part of all our ministry that stirs up near so much ill-will, passion, malice, yea and persecutions against us, as this part, about taking in and casting out, and exercising the keys of the kingdom; in which you are so jealous of us.

2. And alas! ministers are flesh and blood, as well as others; and all of them too tender of their interest, of profit, of reputation, and ease; which are all contradicted notably by this work. Do you think ministers will be so hot on it, to have their neighbours hate them and revile them, and to live as owls in the places where they live, and to put themselves on a great deal of trouble? Surely it is a very self-displeasing thing to the very nature of man, unless he be a monster, to displease his neighbours, and be hated and baited by them. And it will provoke them not only to forbear all acts of kindness or bounty, but to deny them their due maintenance, as far as ever they can: and many, if not most, ministers have no great mind to be so used; nay, had rather lose, than go to law for all their dues; the trouble, and cost, and odium of it is so great. So that our parliaments have been too much afraid lest ministers should cease to be men, or to be sinners, and to be man-pleasers, and to indulge their flesh; and lest we should run into the fire, and lie down among the thorns, and choose a life of trouble and sufferings.

3. And methinks, experience should satisfy men of this. Do you not see how backward ministers are to church reformation, and discipline in the exercise, when they have been most forward for the power? How little is yet done in it, for all our liberty, after all our prayers, and petitions, and writing for it! Do you find in most parishes that ministers are prone to overdo? certainly you do not.

4. Do you not know that all the work of God is so much against nature, and hath such abundance of enemies and difficulties in the way, that few men are like to be guilty of overdoing? Why be you not as careful to hinder men from overdoing in sanctifying the Lord's day, in teaching and praying with their families, &c. but because you see that few need your curb. I am confident, should parliaments do their best to drive on ministers to such works as these, and make laws upon laws to spur them to the practice, they would not be able to bring one half of us, nor the tenth man, to reach so far as Christ hath bound us; no, nor one man of us, in all respects.

And yet I again say, that if any rash men are over-rigid and abuse their trust, (which is likeliest to be those whose maintenance no whit cometh from the people; for in the rest there is more danger of the contrary,) we desire not that they should be exempted from the magistrate's, minister's, or people's due means for their amendment. But let the spur be most used, seeing there is most need; and let us see some severe laws, to drive us on to those duties, that flesh and blood, and all the world, are so much against.

I come now to the last part of my task, which is to give some brief directions for the most effectual practice of this excellent, needful work. And I shall, *first*, speak of the duty of ministers in order to it; and, *secondly*, of the people's duty; and, *lastly*, of the magistrate's. The duty of the pastors I judge to consist in these particulars:—

Direct. 1. Let the pastors in each county meet together, and agree as one man, in faithfulness and self-denial, to do their duty; that the most conscionable may not be liable to the reproach of singularity, because the rest betray them, and the church, and cause of Christ, by withdrawing, and leaving the work undone: so long hath the church already suffered, the neglect, even of godly ministers, that in such a time of leave and help, we still hold off, and dare not venture on a little displeasure of the people, when our ancestors ventured on the flames; I grieve to think what a shame it will be to our names, and to the reformed churches, and what a confusion it may bring upon our faces, before our righteous Judge. And it is a grief to me, if I were sure of magistrates' assistance, that all our enemies shall say, and that the histories of this age shall tell posterity, that the ministers of England, after fasting, prayers, wars, and vows pretended for reformation, would yet do little or nothing toward it but preach, even in times of liberty and encouragement, till the magistrate did it; and that it must be the work of the magistrate, after our unworthy, lazy, or treacherous desertion of it. Had we no more help than we have, we might do much, were we willing and unanimous.

Direct. 2. Let us take heed of extending these agreements to any unnecessary circumstances, so as to lay the stress of the business on them, or to make that necessary, which is unnecessary: but let us agree on the general certain points, and leave particular men to their liberty, in modes and circumstances, not judging each other, if we differ herein: or if one be more or less strict than another in the execution.

Direct. 3. Let us yet all be very careful, that in point of trial and judging men's profession, we avoid extremes: on one side let us not be righteous overmuch, by keeping out any that make the most broken, intelligible profession of faith and repentance, and a godly life, that may be taken for credible: and remember that we are not searchers of the heart, and that charity judgeth not evil of any that are capable of a better judgment. And certainly a humble soul that is conscious of its own infirmities and unworthiness, will be very tender of condemning another, without very satisfying evidence. Of this I refer you to my first dispute, of "Right to Sacraments."

On the other side, let us take heed of turning this duty into a mere formality, and making nothing of it, but mocking the church and God. Let us not take up with a profession of any other kind of faith, but the true christian faith; nor with any profession of this faith, which we are able to prove to be incredible.

Direct. 4. None of the aged that have already been admitted to the communion of the church in the Lord's supper, may be brought under confirmation by imposition of hands, as we have before showed. But all that were yet never admitted to this special part of communion, nor have made any solemn approved profession, should yet be called to it, be they young or old, when they demand church communion.

If you ask me what will be done with the rest, seeing they were admitted irregularly, without any profession of the faith? I answer, 1. Acquaint them plainly with the nature of christianity, and what a church is, and what is the office of a pastor, and what the duty of the flock to God, to him, and themselves, and one to another. 2. Then tell them, that you resolve to proceed according to these rules in the government of your flock; and to exercise this discipline. Tell them plainly (that they be not deceived) both what are the benefits of a church state and discipline, and what are the difficulties that unprepared men are like to grudge at; and how hardly they will take it to be followed, and not suffered to rest in sin, and openly reproved and cast out with shame, if they will not be penitent and reform. And then tell them, that if there be any that have slipped into a church state, in show, and knew not what christianity was, or what they did, and find themselves as yet unfit for it, if they do forbear the privileges of the church, till they are better prepared, and acquainted with them, and can use them to their profit, you shall in the mean time be ready to teach them publicly and privately, till they are prepared: and those that are fit to continue, and use such privileges, advise not to forbear them. But let them know, that you can neither take all the parish, as such, for members of the universal church, or of your charge; and therefore must have some better evidence, especially after such a confusion that negligence hath brought into the church: and you cannot take any man to be of your charge against his will, and therefore you must know their minds. 3. Give them notice, that all that own their church membership, and will have communion with that church, under your ministry and pastoral oversight, are desired by you to signify their desires, by giving in their names to the clerk of the parish, or some other fit person; or if they refuse that, by coming to you. 4. For when you have their names, keep them some time, while you get information of the persons' lives. And then give notice to all, (if it may, to avoid imputation of partiality; or at least, of all that you have reason to suspect of gross ignorance or impiety,) by streets, villages, or houses, to come to speak with you, on some appointed days; where you may discern the fitness of some; and such as you find to be grossly ignorant or scandalous, advise them to stay till they are prepared, offering them your help; because else you must do that in a way of discipline, that they are unfit to bear. 5. All that disown their own standing and church membership, or present right to privileges, and withdraw into the order of catechumens, as being ignorant in what they did before, you may safely teach them as catechumens, and are not bound to enrage them by church discipline, which they consent not to, and are not capable of. 6. All those that you find tolerable, that have owned their church-membership, and not withdrawn themselves, you ought to keep their names in a church book for memory, and to call them solemnly (at some days of humiliation, or other fit season) to own their relation publicly; their names being read, that all may know with whom they are to hold communion. And if there be need, you may justly require them there openly to renew their profession and covenant with God. 7. Your flock being then reformed and known, you need not call them again to examination before particular sacraments, or other parts of church-communion. 8. When any members are after added, they should, if unconfirmed, and such as never did communicate, be received solemnly by prayer and benediction; and if they be such as have been admitted to communion, let them be only approved upon renewing their profession. For the one sort are confirmed in their relation to both catholic and particular church; but the other only enter then into the particular church, being solemnly received into the catholic church before, and perhaps into some other particular church, or into that from which they departed.

Direct. 5. If any come in that hath violated his baptismal covenant, by a wicked life, he is, before you receive him, to give some open testimony of his repentance, if his sin were open, that so he may be ministerially absolved, and the church receive him, not merely as an adult believer, but as a convert, with prayers and rejoicing. And the fuller confession he makes of his ungodly life, and of the way and love of God in his recovery, and the fuller warning he giveth others of the sins that he was guilty of, and the fuller he communicateth to them the satisfying reasons that caused him to turn, the better it is, and more suitable to the state of a penitent; as also the fuller he professeth his resolution to stick close to Christ, by the help of his grace, for the time to come.

Direct. 6. For the execution of this, because all the people cannot be still ready, nor attend, because it is fit they have some cognizance of these things; let some of the most sober, judicious persons be chosen by the church, not into office, but as their delegates, or trustees, to meet with the pastors monthly in some convenient place, where all persons may first address themselves that seek the privileges of the church, and where matters of discipline may be first transacted, before we bring them to the assembly, yet not forbidding any other of the church to be there present that will. And either in that meeting may members after be admitted, and their names made public at the next communion; or else some meetings publicly appointed, four times a year or more, for admitting such in public, as shall be found fittest, which may be at a fast before a sacrament: and let any of the church, at that preparative meeting, have leave to put in what exceptions they have against the person for his profession or conversation.

Direct. 7. Let the pastors and churches that live within the reach of any communion, be as many as is possible, associate and meet for the maintaining of communion of churches, by their officers and delegates. And those that differ in such tolerable matters, as may not hinder their christian or church communion, and yet are not satisfied to join in synods with the rest, let them agree upon such terms of communion and christian correspondence as their principles will admit. And let no stranger be admitted to our church communion, that bringeth not a certificate, (called of old *Communicatory Letters*,) or some sufficient testimony from one of these sorts, either from the churches nearly associated, or those that we agree to take for brethren. And those that bring such certificates must be admitted by us, without any further trial or confirmation; unless there be some notable cause of suspicion. But for those who live in heretical or impious societies, or such as refuse all church order and communion with neighbour churches, or are justly disowned by the associated churches, we should not admit them to our communion, without a particular trial, or a better certificate than those churches can give them. And thus should all the churches be concatenated, and their communion settled.

Direct. 8. Above all, let every minister see that he wisely and diligently carry himself to the rest of his parish; avoiding, indeed, the excommunicate as heathens: but for all that are willing to learn in an expectant state, let us deal lovingly, gently, and tenderly with them, denying them nothing that lawfully we can yield them, in matters of burial, marrying, praying, preaching, or the like. And be sure to carry on the necessary duty of catechising, and personal conference and instruction with them, family by family, by which you may the better know them, and prepare them for church communion, and have opportunity to quiet them, and answer their objections; and they may see that you cast them not off as heathens, but only prepare them for the state and privileges which they are yet unfit for.

And especially, let us by all possible condescension, meekness, and loving carriage, blameless lives, and charitable contribution to the utmost of our abilities, endeavour to win them, and take off that offence, or at least abate it, or hinder the success of the reproaches of those, that will undoubtedly be offended by our reformation and discipline. And let us have a vigilant eye upon any seducers, especially infidels and papists, that may creep in among them, to take advantage of their discontents; that we may prudently and effectually counterwork them. This much faithfully done by ministers, might be an admirable mercy to the church.

Secondly, The people's duty in order to this reformation before mentioned is—1. Of the godly, and such as are fit for church communion.—2. Of the grossly ignorant and ungodly that are unfit.

1. The duty of the first sort lieth in these particulars. (1.) They must highly value the benefit of pastoral oversight and church communion, and therefore be ready to promote any work of reformation that is necessary, to their more fruitful and comfortable enjoyment of them. (2.) They must so behave themselves as may honour and further the work, and take heed of that by which it may be hindered; lest they weaken our hands and be a stumblingblock to others. For what can a minister do himself, if the church assist him not; much less if they hinder him? Especially, [1.] They must take heed of scandalous sins, which may be a shame to their profession, and open the mouths of the enemies of the church. [2.] They must take heed of sects and divisions, and quarrellings among themselves, which will break them in pieces, or hinder their edification, and make them a stumblingblock to the weak and a laughingstock to the wicked. [3.] They must take heed of surliness, and pride, and domineering carriage towards those that are yet without: and must be as eminent in meekness, humility, patience, forbearance, and self-denial, as they are in the profession of religion. For a proud, domineering spirit, or strangeness and unnecessary distance, doth lose these ungodly, whom you should be a means to win. [4.] They must study to do all the good they can to those without; be as little as may be in executing penalties on them, and as much as may be possible in speaking kindly and familiarly to them, and relieving them in wants, and visiting them in sickness; and think it not much to purchase their love, in order to their salvation, with the loss of your right, or with the price of much of your worldly goods. For all men love those, or at least will less dislike them, that do no hurt to any, but do good to all, or as many as they can. To be the servants of all, is the highest christian dignity, and the way to win them. [5.] Take heed of falling out or contending with any of them, or of giving them any harsh, provoking words, to their faces, or behind their backs. But put up any wrong that is merely your own, and is in your power to forgive, for the sake of peace, and your own neighbour's good. [6.] Be not men of common spirits, or common speech, or a common conversation; but as we must make a difference between you and others in our communion and church administrations, so let the rest see that it is not without cause. For if you be but like other men, we shall seem to be partial in making a difference between you and other men. Let your light therefore shine before men to the glory of your heavenly Father. Let them see that you despise the world, and live above it, and can easily part with it; that you can forgive and bear a wrong; that your heart is in heaven, and your treasure there; and that you are the heirs of another world: let all

men hear and see by you, that you have a higher design in your eye than the ungodly, and that you are driving on another trade than the men that have their portion in this life. Heaven is your real glory; and to be heavenly is your true reputative glory, not only in the eyes of the wise, but of the common earthworms of the world. [7.] Set yourselves in the most diligent and faithful improvement of all your parts and interests to help on the work of God on men's souls. Though you preach not, you have work enough in your own places to do, to further the preacher's work. Speak to poor people prudently, seasonably, and seriously about the state of their souls, and everlasting life; and consult with the ministers, how to deal with them. Tell them in what state you find the people, and take their advice in further dealing with them. Oh, if our neighbours would but help us in private, and do their parts, and not cast all the burden on the minister, there would much more be done than is! Nay, alas, to our grief and hinderance, some of our professing people are so hot, and self-conceited, and proud, that unless we will outrun our own understandings, and be ruled by them that shut out abundance that the word of God allows us not to shut out, and be righteous over-much, and shut up the church of Christ as in a nut-shell; they presently murmur, and rebel, and separate, and must betake themselves to a stricter congregation. And others of them must have us cast off discipline, and cut up the hedge, and admit all to the communion and privileges of the church, and all under a blind pretence of charity; and some learned gentlemen, by words and writings, do enrage our ignorant and ungodly neighbours against us, and make them believe that we do them some grievous wrong, because we will not indeed deceive them and undo them, and set up new church orders (or disorders) now in the end of the world, so contrary to all the ancient canons and orders of the church. I honour and dearly love the names of many of these studious, pious gentlemen; but seriously, I must tell them, that they want humility, and in their good meanings do the church a world of wrong. And though they may be more learned, even in theology, than we, yet it is a great matter to have or to want experience. They have not been so much in church administrations as we, nor had so much to do with ignorant souls. And verily I must say again, that the bare theory maketh but a bungler in this work: I must much suspect the judgment of that man in matters of church government, or dealing with poor souls, that wants experience. Let these gentlemen but turn ministers, (be it known to their faces, there's none of them too good for it, nor too great,) and let them but try our life a little while, and I shall set more by their judgments than now I do. I read many a physician's writings, before I was fit to attempt a cure. It is a raw, deceitful kind of knowledge in these practical affairs, that is not furthered by experience.

2. And as for the duty of the ignorant, ungodly people, I shall say little of it, because I suppose they are not like to read or regard what I say. Only in general, it is their first duty to become truly godly persons, and so to live in communion with the church. But upon supposition that they will not yet be such, their next choice should be to live in quiet submission to their teachers, and patiently stay among the catechumens and expectants, till they are fit for a higher place and privileges. And with the reasonableness of this motion, and how it conduceth to their good, we should labour to acquaint them, and make them sensible of it, that they may be patient in their station.

Thirdly, Our last work is to tell you, what is the magistrates' part, for the promoting of this work. And I shall urge them here to no great matters, because they shall not say that we would either drive them in the dark upon questionable things, or put them upon that, which any reason can call persecution, or make them think that we can do nothing but by their sword. And therefore whether they should force people to be church members, or christians, or to come under discipline, are questions that at this time I shall not meddle with: but,

[n] *Direct.* 1. It is a great part of the magistrate's duty to cause the people that are yet unfit for church communion, to keep in their visible station, and to behave themselves as expectants, and submit to that instruction of their teachers, which is necessary to prepare them for the privileges of the church; and to this end the magistrate should, by laws and proclamations, own this ministerial reformation. Alas! how little knew they what they did, that have so long been jealous of us, lest we would do too much, and under pretence of discipline inflame, or abuse them by severity! Whenas it is a work that casteth on us so much rage and hatred, of rich and poor, and calls for such abundance of faith and zeal, and diligence and self-denial, when we have so little, and are commonly, like other men, addicted too much to man-pleasing, and to save ourselves, that if we had all the help that magistrates can give us, it is ten to one but we should leave the most of this work undone. Preaching is a very cheap and easy work, in comparison of church government. They have taken great pains to stop poor, lazy, short-winded men from running up the steepest hill, and carrying the heaviest burden, and passing through the greatest sufferings, that in those prosperous times we can expect. And indeed I know it to be true, that for all the countenance of authority, he that will faithfully execute the pastoral oversight and discipline, shall live a persecuted life, which by mere preaching he might avoid.

Therefore the chief governors of the nation ought to make laws, and cause them to be executed, for the constraining of the grossly ignorant and ungodly, to hear the word preached publicly, and to submit to be privately catechised, and instructed by the ministers, and to command them patiently to wait, as learners, in this condition, till they are fit to be approved members of the church. These carnal people look more at the sword and will of the magistrate, in matters of religion, than others do; because they understand no other argument, and can savour nothing but the things of the flesh. Did but the rulers of the nation hear how they daily inquire what religion shall be owned and settled by them, they would sure think it their duty to lend them a little more of their help. We desire you not to drive them to christianity, nor to sacraments, or church

[n] In Tertullian's days, saith Albaspinæus in Tert. de Prescrip. c. 41. p. 306. the catechumeni being somewhat instructed at home, cum cæteris tandem in ecclesia primis concionibus, quæ in gratiam catechumenorum habebantur, intererant; quibus peractis rursus omnes idem ipsi catechumeni ex templo discedere jubebantur, ne scilicet Divina mysteria rudium conscientia polluerentur. So that it seems they had then in the morning a sermon fitted for the catechumens, and all the after-part of their worship was more eucharistical, fitted to the communion of saints.

In the ancient churches the catechumeni were not suffered to sit with the church members, but had a separated place by themselves; and Tertullian accuseth the heretics for breaking this order, ut vid. Albaspin. in Tertul. de Præscription. c. 41. p. 306. He blames them also, that they suffered them to join with the church in prayers, and other holy worship; ut Albaspin. ibid.

communion; only drive them to hear, and learn, and be instructed, that the light of truth may do the rest. Surely none can reasonably suspect, that this is against the liberty of their consciences, unless the slavery of Satan be their liberty, and it be their liberty to be free from Christ, and righteousness, and heaven. It is hard to believe that governor to be a christian, that will not do this much to help his subjects to be christians.

Direct. 2. And as the magistrate should constrain such people to submit to be instructed, so should he constrain the ministers to instruct them, both by public preaching, and by private conference and catechising, if they be able: and if through the greatness of the place, one minister is not able to perform it, there should be so many maintained proportionably, to the number and necessities of souls, as may be able. The reason why ministers themselves should be compelled by penalties are, (1.) Because some are so dull, that they need the spur. (2.) Because our performances will be the less resisted by the people, when they know we are forced by the magistrate. (3.) Because the magistrate's judgment puts much authority and honour on the work, in the people's eyes. Compel us, therefore, as well as them.

Direct. 3. The magistrate should also impose a penalty upon all that undertake to be pastors of a church, and administer the Lord's supper, and yet will not make any necessary trial of the knowledge, faith, and lives of those, to whom they do administer it, nor exercise any church discipline on the scandalous; but utterly neglect that oversight and church government, which is as much a part of the pastoral work, as public preaching is. They that will undertake to be pastors, and meddle with sacraments, must be compelled to do the work of pastors, and to dispense the sacraments in a tolerable order. Though yet we are not for compulsion in any doubtful points, of lesser moment, where a difference among the godly may be tolerated: but that pastors should act as no pastors, and rectors of the churches be as no rectors, and should cherish all ignorance, infidelity, and impiety, and profane God's ordinances, and subvert the communion of saints, and lay the garden of Christ open to the common wilderness, and thereby make all seem singular to the people, that will not do as wickedly as these; this is not to be tolerated; but the commissioners for ejecting scandalous ministers with the advice of the assistants, should have power to correct them, and in case of obstinate unreformedness, to eject them: not to silence them from preaching to the catechumens or any; but to prohibit them from the actions proper to church rulers or pastors, till they will perform them more agreeably to the Scripture rule.

And this compulsion also of the ministers, we desire especially for the people's sake, who we are content should be excused themselves from any such penal laws, to restrain them from sacraments; but when they know that ministers are under such penalties, they will bear it at their hands, and take it the better, when we deal with them as the word of God requireth. I hear it with my ears, to the grief of my heart, how some of my neighbours' ministers are spoken against with bitterness by their people, because they give not the Lord's supper to all, even to the most ignorant and ungodly, that refuse to be instructed, or so much as to take themselves for any members of the minister's charge: and that which they say is, that though bishops and common prayer be taken down, yet the giving of the sacrament to all the parish is not taken down. And they that now submit so quietly to the diffusing of many other things, because ministers are punishable if they use them, would also do the like in this case. And yet if you are jealous, that ministers will go as far on the other hand in refusing the people that are not to be refused, (though with one of a hundred, there is little fear of that,) we are contented that you look to us also in this: to which end these two things will be sufficient. (1.) Let the magistrate join with the pastors and delegates of the church in their meetings, where church affairs are transacted, that he may see what we do. If there be no justice of peace in the parish, let every church have a church magistrate purposely chosen by the chief magistrate; or some agent on his behalf deputed hereunto. (2.) And let the magistrate's agent acquaint the commissioners how things are transacted in cases of complaint; and let them, by the advice of the assistant ministers, correct us as we deserve, if you should imagine this to be necessary.

Direct. 4. The magistrate should promote, encourage, countenance, yea, command the pastors to associations and brotherly correspondences, for the more cautelous, and vigorous, and effectual management of these works; and for the concatenation and communion of churches, and the right understanding of each other's affairs; that he that hath communion in one church, may, by communicatory letters, have communion in any of the rest; and he that is cast or kept out of one may not be received by the rest, till it be proved that he is excluded unjustly. And those that join not so fully as the rest, may yet be provoked to own one another as far as we can; that so we may maintain brotherly love, with all that differ from us by tolerable differences; and may own them as churches, though we cannot own their different opinions or ways; may have such communion with them, as we may, and upon their letters may admit their members to our communion. This the magistrate should at least openly provoke, and encourage the churches and pastors to; seeing no man can doubt whether it be for the edification of the church.

Direct. 5. For the better promoting of this necessary work, I conceive it would be a very ready and unquestionable way, for the magistrate to appoint an able, godly, moderate minister to be a visiter in each county, or rather in each half or quarter of a county, to see the churches thus reformed, and provoke the several pastors to their duty, and assist them in it, where there is need; but not to have any episcopal power to punish or cast out any minister, or excommunicate them, suspend them, or the like: but let every visiter have an agent of the magistrate joined with him, armed with authority to convene the ministers, and examine witnesses, and do what more the chief magistrate shall see meet, so that still these two visiters go together, but have not the same authority or work: but let the ministers only inquire, direct, exhort, and give account and advice to the civil visiter; and let the civil visiter have all the coercive power; and let both of them transmit such causes as are exempt from their determination, to the commissioners for ejecting scandalous ministers, who, by the advice of the assistant ministers, may determine them. These visiters did very much to the first and great reformation of Scotland, when popery had overrun all; nor did they scruple the using of them, for all that they were against prelacy.

Direct. 6. It is one of the chief and unquestionable parts of the magistrate's duty, in order to the reformation and peace of the churches, and the saving of men's souls, to see that dangerous seducers be restrained from infecting and carrying away the ignorant, ungodly, discontented people, that are kept under ministerial teaching, as expectants. I do not move to have men driven into our churches; nor do I move to have an unnecessary restraint laid upon men's tongues or pens, in case of tolerable differences, among the servants of Christ. In this case I only desire now, that the dissenting godly brethren would agree together, to meddle with their differences no more than needs, and to manage their disagreements with such cautions, and in such manner, and season, and measure, as may least hinder their success in the common work, viz. the promoting of the common fundamental verities, and the converting and saving of the ignorant and ungodly, and getting down the reigning sins of the world. And then they will find, (1.) That if there be any truth in the private opinions, which they would propagate, it will far easier be received, when the minds of their brethren are sedate and peaceable, than when they are alarmed to the conflict, by unseasonable preaching for the said opinions. (2.) And that the errors, of this lower nature among brethren, which some fear a toleration of, will sooner die of themselves for want of fuel in such peaceable deportment, than when the bellows of opposition, contradiction, reproach, and violence are blowing them up, and putting life continually into them. For most dividers are proud and selfish, and must needs be noted for somewhat extraordinary; and you take the principal way to animate them, when you make so much ado with them: whereas a few years' neglect, and not observing them, as if there were no such men in the world, (unless when they impose a necessity on us,) would more happily extinguish them. I speak but what I have seen and tried. This therefore is not the matter of my present request, that magistrates would use rigour and violence with godly men, about tolerable differences; which the power of greater light and love in the contrary-minded, is the principal means to reconcile.

But the thing requested now of magistrates is, That they would keep out the wolves, while we are feeding the sheep, or help us in it. That they suffer not damnable deceivers, or any that plainly go about to subvert men's souls, or the state of the church, to fall in with our ignorant, ungodly people, in the time of their learning and expectancy. And as I shall be ready against any libertine, infidel, or papist in the world, to prove this to be in the magistrate's power, and his flat duty, of which I hope no sober christian doubteth, so I shall here lay before the magistrate the reasons that shall evince the need of his help, in the present case.

Reason 1. The people that we now speak of are so utterly ignorant, that it is easy to deceive them. It is no dishonour to truth, that a fool or a child may be deluded; but such are not to be left to the malice and craft of juggling enemies.

Reason 2. So wicked are the hearts of those that we now speak of, or many of them, that they are prepared for deceit, and willing of it materially, though not formally, as such. It is easy drawing men from that which they hate, or their hearts are bent against, and to that which they love, and their hearts are set upon: such gunpowder will soon take fire.

Reason 3. Our people, by the afore-mentioned work of reformation, will undoubtedly be cast into *discontents;* they will be sorely displeased with their teachers; which is a small matter, were it not that it hindereth their own salvation. They have so long been used to have their own will, and to be admitted even in heathenish ignorance and impiety to the communion of the saints, and all the outward privileges, without any considerable exercise of discipline over them, that now it will be a strange provoking thing to them, when their custom shall be altered. So that in the discontent and hatred of their minds, if infidels or papists, or any such malignant adversaries, shall come among them, their own malignity and discontent will drive them by multitudes into their nets; and they will turn to the first that comes with any plausible though pernicious doctrine. With half an eye we may easily see this; and therefore, if the magistrate will not help us to quiet and secure the people, and keep off deceivers, while we are catechising and instructing, and preparing the grossly ignorant and ungodly, it will be to the hazard of many thousand souls, and a temptation to many faint-hearted ministers again to cast open the hedge, and lay the church's communion common, for fear of the ill consequence, that will follow to the people by displeasing them.

And yet I may well conclude, that though still the church will have need of some of the magistrate's help in this same way, yet nothing so much hereafter as at first. (1.) It is custom that most holdeth the people now, and enrageth them against the breakers of it. And when once the custom is broken and turned, they will be much more quiet. (2.) We now find the churches in the rubbish, and have the harshest work at first to do, which will soon be over, and the churches and minds of men more settled. (3.) A few years' practice of confirmation, in the fore-described way, I hope, will introduce such abundance of knowledge, and so increase the face of godliness, that we shall have little need of the magistrate's help, in this kind as now we have. But now at first our necessity is very great.

Reason 4. Moreover, our doctrine and practice is most contrary to men's sins, and carnal interest, and therefore, though it be true, yet it is provoking, and seemeth to be against them; as bloodletting, fasting, and bitter medicines to a child, or a foolish patient. And therefore no wonder if tolerated seducers can draw them from it, by sense or nonsense, in such a case. A little reason seems to take men off from that which seems against them, or which they hate.

Reason 5. On the contrary, the doctrine and practice of deceivers is suited to their nature, and purposely sugared for them by art. For instance: if papists fall in with them in the depth of their discontent, and first rail at us as no ministers, but liars and heretics; and then revile us for receiving maintenance, (which is their way, though their clergy receive so exceedingly much more,) and then tell them of all their ancestors, and then set them upon an easy outside piety, which, *ex opere operato,* will certainly confer grace, and shall take up at the strictest with an auricular confession, instead of necessary humiliation and true church discipline; and shall make those venial and improper sins, which we make damnable; and shall send many but to purgatory, that according to Scripture we send to hell: in a word, when they shall comply with carnal hearts and interests but as much as Montalte, the Jansenian, sheweth us that the Jesuits do; what wonder if our ignorant, discontented people do greedily swallow such baits as these, and turn to such a kind of religiousness! And this makes the Jesuits glad of our reformation, and stand by us as the crows by the sheep, that they may have our leavings, or all that we cut off: for it is number that they regard; and, if they will but believe in the pope, they shall be welcome to them; yea, be catholics and be saved, though they believe not in Christ and the Holy Ghost, nor know what christianity is. He that thinks I wrong them, (1.) Let him look on millions and millions in their churches. (2.) Let him but read Fr. a Sancta Clara, Problem 15 and 16.[o]

Reason 6. The adversaries also are very industrious, and have many advantages of us from without. In most churches they will meet, though with godly, yet with young, unexperienced disputers; because our ministry is but reviving, and the young ones must have time to grow. And the Jesuits, friars, and other missionaries, have a pope and cardinals, and bishops, and princes, and lords, and revenues, and wealth, and seminaries, and trained soldiers in abundance, at their backs beyond sea, to furnish them with continual supply. And how eager and busy they are, the christian world hath had long experience; so that if such be let loose on ignorant souls, what wonder if they prevail?

Reason 7. And for the event, if the magistrates shall refuse us this reasonable and unquestionably lawful aid, it may be the means of the damnation of many thousand souls. I suppose I speak to christians, that believe that sin is the poison of the soul, and believe that faith in Christ is necessary, and that there is a heaven and a hell; and if so, they must needs understand what it is to suffer men to draw their subjects from Christ, from Scripture, from the means of grace, and a holy life; and to draw them into sin. That this is but to give men leave to do their worst, to undo and damn as many as they can; and to take them at the greatest advantage in their ignorance and discontent, to trip up their heels, and entice them into hell: how dreadful a thing is this to a magistrate, once to think of, that hath but any belief of Scripture, and pity on the souls of men! And therefore, as long as we do not now call upon them so much as to force papists or infidels, either to be of our religion, or to profess that they are so, or join in communion with us, but only desire that they may keep their venom to themselves, and may not be suffered to take the advantage of our people's ignorance and discontent, undoubtedly the rulers that are friends to Christ and the souls of men, will never find in their hearts to deny this assistance.

Reason 8. And if they should deny it, in reason they must needs see, that they will fully give up the churches of Christ, that are under their government, to distraction and confusion. They know well enough what would come of it, if every man have but liberty to persuade their armies into mutinies and rebellion; or to persuade the subjects against themselves that rule them; or to entice men's children or servants to lewdness, or their wives to unchastity. And will they, under pretence of mercy or liberty, permit men to do that against Christ, and the church, and the souls of many that are bad enough already, which they would not, they durst not permit against men's bodies, or against themselves, or against the peace of the commonwealth.

And what a dishonour will it be to Christ and the church, and reformation, and religion; and what a joy to all the enemies of these; to see that our reformation shall breed such confusion, and bring upon us such inconveniences; and all because the magistrate shall refuse his help!

Reason 9. And, perhaps, the magistrates will quickly find, that the distractions of the church will breed and feed such distractions in the commonwealth, as may make them wish they had quenched the fire, while it was yet quenchable. Our unity is not only our strength, but their strength, especially if they promote it: our divisions weaken us as well as them. What will the magistrate do, if he help us not in this case? Ministers cannot in conscience always forbear their duty, but will set about it. Either the rulers will suffer us to do it, or not. If they suffer us and assist us, it will be our peace, and theirs, and our people's good. If they suffer us, and assist us not, as is now desired, we shall exasperate so many of their subjects by our reformation, and shutting them from church communion, that will shake the peace of the commonwealth, and the odium will fly on the governors, for setting up a ministry that so provoketh them, and so the people will be still in discontents, and prepared for rebellion, or any violent change. And the fire that began in the church, if it be let alone, may reach the court. But if to mend this, they will put down or hinder ministers, their persecution will bring down God's judgments on them, and turn the hearts of honest, sober men against them. They have seen what deformation and persecution have done, before their eyes.

Reason 10. Lastly, it will bring a most heavy guilt on the magistrate's soul, which he will never be able to stand under, before the King of all the world. To be guilty of the neglect of an office so divine, received from God, that it might be used for him; and to be guilty of the frustrating of much of our ministerial work; and of grieving the hearts of so many that fear God, and frustrating such hopes as we lately had, to say nothing of the prayers, tears, hazards, blood, and ruin of so many thousands, and the promises, oaths, and covenants to God; to be guilty of the sins of so many thousands, and of their everlasting condemnation; to be guilty of the distractions, and betraying of the church, and cause, and people of the Lord, and to be guilty of the insultings of so many enemies; all this and much more, that would certainly follow the denial of this moderate necessary help, would be a burden intolerable.

Direct. 7. But because both the magistrates and many others are afraid, lest by going too far in such assistance, they may be guilty of persecution, by restraining men from preaching, or private persuasion, or by keeping the ignorant and wicked from church communion, or by compelling them to come to hear, and to be personally instructed, I humbly propound these following things, for such a regulation of their granted liberty, as may free them from all danger of persecuting, without depriving us of their principal help.

1. If you compel not the ignorant and ungodly to hear, and be personally instructed by the minister of the parish where they live, yet at least compel them thus to submit to some minister; and let that minister certify under his hand, that he takes care of him as a catechumen, or expectant, by public and private instruction.

2. Let not every man that will, be tolerated either to teach, persuade, or hold assemblies; but let your toleration be regulated, as well as your approbation is. To which end, (1.) Let such persons as are thought meet for such a work, be appointed as commissioners, to approve or judge of such as shall be tolerated through the land, as the commissioners now approve of such as shall have the public maintenance. For there is no reason, that the tolerated should not go under trial, as well as the allowed. And indeed without some such course to keep the door of toleration, as well as the door of public, allowed teachers, you cannot put any reasonable laws of toleration in execution; but any will come in, whatever your laws say. (2.) Let these commissioners for trying the tolerated have rules given them by the lawgivers, whom to license or tolerate, and whom not. (3.) Let all that will gather assemblies, or administer sacraments, or preach, have an instrument of toleration, under the hands and seal of these

[o] In his "Deus, Natura, Gratia;" where abundance more are cited of his side.

commissioners, and let them be hindered that have no such instrument. Otherwise if you stay till they are convict of blasphemy, they may do more mischief first, (for who will persecute them,) than ever the magistrate can comfortably be accountable to God for suffering.

3. When a man hath a sealed toleration to preach, or hold assemblies, let him yet be as liable to any just accusation, before the commissioners for ejection, as the approved, public ministers are: that so if he be proved to be wicked and scandalous, or to preach any thing excepted from toleration, by the legislators, the said commissioners may be authorized to deprive them of their toleration, as they do others of their public station and maintenance. And this is a most reasonable and necessary thing.

(1.) For else the public ministers will be hardlier dealt with than they. It is supposed that there is so much difference in the soundness of their doctrine, that one deserveth the public encouragement, as well as the other deserveth a toleration: or else the lawgivers would make no difference. And that being supposed, if they shall not be questionable, as well as we, nor their right forfeitable, as well as ours, they are more cherished proportionably than others.

(2.) And if you do not this, it is as good do nothing, but openly license heathens, and papists, and all blasphemers: for they will make a fair confession, till they have got their sealed toleration, and then preach contrary to that profession. Two sorts we know this to be true by: 1. Papists, that are for equivocation, and mental reservation, in their professions and oaths; or for the popes to dispense with them. 2. Heathens and infidels, that believe not that there is any sin, or devil, or hell, or heaven; and therefore care not what they swear. And indeed these are the two sects that now are up; and all other are like to fall into these. Alas! by sad experience I speak it; those that will openly, and to my face, make an orthodox confession, do secretly harden many poor souls, by making a scorn of Scripture, as a fable, and of the immortality of the soul, and of Christ and the Holy Ghost, and heaven and hell, and say all these are nothing but the inventions of men; and that the knave-priests do persuade men that there are devils and hell, as a bugbear, to make them do what they would have them; and all religion is but deceit. Such heathens are the predominant sect in many places, and higher in England than once I thought to have seen them. And if all such perfidious infidels and Jesuits shall have leave to blaspheme God, Christ, and Scripture, because they once made an orthodox profession, then let hell be turned loose upon our people, and the devil that was bound up from deceiving the nations, have a toleration from the magistrate to do his worst.

Thus I have showed that magistrates, if they will, may help the church without any danger of persecuting the truth, if they take not popery, damnable heresy, and heathenism for truth. 1. If the approvers keep the door of toleration, as well as of public maintenance and ministry. 2. If a church justice, or civil agent, do keep the church's peace. 3. If the civil visiter do purposely take cognizance of the state of parishes, and see the laws put in execution. 4. If the commissioners for ejections have power of judging all seducers and blasphemers, as well as the public ministers. And if these only have the coercive power; but some able, chosen, godly ministers be joined with them for advice and exhortation: as magistrates and ministers sat together before the days of William the Conqueror.

"If ye know these things, happy are ye if ye do them," John xiii. 17. "And the servant which knew his Lord's will, and prepared not, nor did according to his will, shall be beaten much," Luke xii. 47.

Finitur February 13, 1648.

POSTSCRIPT.

Reader,

As great and needful a duty as this is, that I have here proposed, and commonly agreed on by all the parties before mentioned; I am yet far from expecting, that all men should acknowledge it and obey it; or that no person of contrary apprehensions or intentions, should rise up against it as an enemy, with all the strength that the measure of his wit and passions can prepare. We cannot speak for God himself, for Christ, for Scripture, for men's own salvation, but we meet with contradiction and resistance, even from them that we would save. And were it not for this, what blessed work would the gospel make! and why might we not hope, that all our people should be saved? No wonder then, if whenever we attempt reformation or reconciliation, we meet with learned, reverend brethren that come against us, armed with plausible cavils and contempts, and cast away the medicine as dangerous, or ungrateful, and strenuously vindicate the disease that should be healed.[a] And were it not that the church hath many, very many such, what would have kept us unhealed so long? and who could have continued our deformities and divisions, and frustrated such means as have been used for our cure? Satan is not so poor a politician, as to be without his agents in our ecclesiastic armies, and councils, and pulpits, to speak for his cause and do his work, and resist and frustrate that which would displease him; and all this under pretence of enmity to Satan, and friendship to Christ, and a better doing of his work. As the names of the chiefest of Christ's servants were not cast out as holy, but as evil, (Luke vi. 22,) so their doctrine was not cast out as truth, nor as saving, but as deceit. And his means will not be openly resisted, (at least by those that are building with us,) as reforming or reconciling, but as groundless or unreproved, or troublesome or unseasonable, or as suspected of some ill design or event. Some will say, It is mere prelacy, or a prelatical design; and some, that it is independency, or an independent design; and some, that it is but presbyterian examination. Whereas they might know, that it is proper to none of them, which is common to them all. If it be prelacy, how comes it to be found with independents? If it be independency, how comes it to be approved by prelates and presbyterians? Is it not rather like christianity itself, and the truths and duties which we commonly own; and therefore not to be appropriated to any?

[p] I humbly propound it to the consideration of the sovereign rulers, whether it be not fit that the testimonies of these two sorts of men, in any weighty case, against another be invalid. And is it not a pitiful case that the lives of the godly people whom they hate, shall be at the mercy of any two of these wretches, that make no more of an oath than of another word.

[a] Nunquam enim, ait Lutherus, periclitatur ecclesia nisi inter reverendissimos.

By all that I have heard and read of late, concerning this subject, I understand that the principal objections that are likely to be used against the doctrine of this treatise are these following:—

Object. We were all baptized in our infancy, and therefore are church members, and have right to the privileges of the adult, when we are adult, without any new title or condition: our first right continueth, though we never make profession of the christian faith, nor personally renewed the covenant with God that we made in baptism. And therefore, though in some cases such an approved profession be a duty, yet is not any more neccessary to our church state, and right to the communion of the adult, than that we were born church members, and so baptized. Nothing but heresy, schism, or apostasy can cut us off. And therefore all that were baptized, and are not thus cut off, are still church members, and have right to all the ordinances in the church.

Answ. I have said enough to this already to satisfy the considerate, impartial reader; proving the necessity of personal faith before God, and of some profession of it *ecclesia judice,* before the church, to the being of the said title of the adult, as its condition; and that all Scripture examples do make for the confirmation of this truth. Moreover let me add, to answer the new or foreseen assaults,

1. If there be no word of promise in the Scripture, that giveth the privilege of adult communion to any, upon their infant title condition only, nor any example in the gospel, or the ancient church, that any possessed or used that privilege upon that title condition only, then are we not to imagine that the infant title condition alone is sufficient to the said privilege: but the antecedent is true; as hath in part been manifested, and will be more, when the dissenter shall bring forth his pretended evidences, by which his title should be proved.

2. The title condition of infants is not sufficient to make any morally capable of the ends of adult communion; therefore it is not sufficient to make them capable of a proper plenary right to such communion. For the right and relation are for these ends; if a natural incapacity may consist with a plenary title, so cannot a moral. No man can really possess and exercise the communion of the adult intrinsically without faith, or extrinsically without profession of faith; therefore no man without faith, or profession of faith, can have a plenary right to that communion. For a man to have a plenary right to please God, and celebrate with the church the memorial of our redemption, and participate of the Redeemer, and his benefits, that believeth not in him, is a palpable absurdity.

3. If the mere title-condition of infants will serve *in foro ecclesiæ,* for the adult, then it will serve also *in foro Dei:* for the church looks but to the outward appearance, or visibility of that, whose reality and sincerity God expecteth. And it is God's covenant that giveth us our right; and therefore if the church find us to have true right, it must find us receiving it from God's covenant; and therefore find us the heirs of the promise. The reason why the church takes our birth privileges for a sufficient title condition, is because God is supposed so to take it. But that this will not serve the adult *in foro Dei* is manifest; because God will not own such infidels, as neither have faith, nor a profession of it.

4. If the title condition of infidels may serve them when adult, then is there no personal difference in acts, or qualities; no not so much as in profession, required on our parts, to distinguish christians from infidels and atheists: (required I mean as necessary conditions:) but the consequent is absurd; therefore so is the antecedent. If no differencing character between actual believers and infidels or atheists, be made thus necessary, then the church and the infidel world are laid together; and the body of Christ, and consequently Christ himself, is dishonoured and blasphemed, as common and unclean. But if any personal difference be necessary, it must be the personal profession of christianity, or nothing less than this can be it. For our birth privilege cannot be it. Atheists and infidels are born of christian parents. Much of the Turkish army of janizaries have their birth privileges to show, as well as we. It is a probable argument, Such an infant is born of christian parents; therefore he will be an actual believer. But it is not a probable argument, Such a man at age, that professeth not christianity, had christian parents; therefore he is a believer: much less, therefore he had right to the benefits of the covenant, whether he be an actual believer or not. If christians have no visible note, by which they must be known from infidels, then either the church is not visible, or infidels may be the visible church, without so much as disowning their infidelity.

5. If the title condition of infants may suffice the adult for church right and communion, then heretics and apostates have such right: but the consequent is denied by them that I now dispute with. They confess that heresy, and some schism, and apostasy, do cut off from the church, and so from this right. But it is plain that such heretics and apostates have that which was their infant condition: as they were the seed of believers in infancy, so they are since apostasy: they cease not to be the seed of believers, by their renouncing Christ. If this therefore would prove a right in silent infidels, it will prove a right in professed apostates.

Object. The apostates cast away their right; and therefore have it not.

Answ. 1. Either it dependeth on their own wills when they come to age, or not. If it do not, then they cannot cast it away. They may refuse to use their right, but they cannot cast it away, or nullify it; for they cannot make themselves not to be the children of christian parents. The foundation stands whether they will or no: and therefore so must the relation. But if the relation or right do now depend upon their own wills, then our cause is granted; for from their wills then must the condition or evidence be fetched. 2. Yea, such persons, ordinarily as we have now in question, are actual apostates, and are so to be taken by the church; and therefore not to be taken as church members, having right to sacraments. He that being engaged to God the Father, Son, and Holy Ghost, in his infancy, doth make no profession of actual faith at full age, is ordinarily to be taken for an apostate; but such are the persons in question. I say ordinarily, because I except them that have been cast upon natural impossibilities or impotency, or wanted a call and opportunity: that is, all persons that prove idiots, or deaf and dumb, or otherwise destitute of natural capacity; such come not to the use of reason and free-will, and therefore are not bound to actual belief. Such also as have their tongues cut out, are separated from human society, or otherwise disabled from profession. But for the common case of mankind, (1.) It is plain that they have their tongues given them by nature to express their minds. And, (2.) That Christ commandeth confession with the tongue, and professing him before men. (3.) That much of his worship lieth in holy profession, and all of it containeth answerable profession. (4.) That we have constant calls from God, even to profess our christianity:

the godly and the wicked that live among us call us to it: we have daily invitations to profess our christianity, one way or other. And among all these occasions of profession, he that professeth not, is to be taken for an infidel and apostate. For the business is so exceeding great and weighty, and the object so glorious, and the duty so incumbent, and the very life of christianity so inconsistent with a non-profession, that we have just reason to conclude, that he that professeth not himself a christian, ordinarily is to be taken for none by the church.

Object. But though at the first admitting of a foreigner into a commonwealth, you require an oath of fidelity, or profession of subjection, yet when we are born subjects, we must be supposed to continue such, till we rebel, and so declare the contrary; and our fidelity is not to be questioned.

Answ. 1. The case doth exceedingly differ from ours in hand. Princes vary their commands as their affairs require. If you are born in the midst of a peaceable republic, you may perhaps have no oath of fidelity imposed, because the peace of the commonwealth requireth it not: for while there is no enemy near you, to solicit you to rebellion or treason, or with whom you may conjoin, it is supposed, that you have either no mind or no power to it. And it is only the common peace that is concerned in the cause. But our case is otherwise; for we live among devils and wicked men, and are known to have hearts ourselves, that are naturally treacherous, and at enmity to God. So that we are still among enemies, that would seduce us, and with whom we are inclined to take part. And besides that, our profession is not only necessary to the common safety, but to our personal performances, and daily communion with the saints, and worship of God. 2. If it be in a garrison that is near the enemy, or in a country that is inclined to rebellion, or where rebellion is on foot, and the enemy hath a party, there princes use to cause all their subjects to take an oath of fidelity; and ordinarily also in peaceable kingdoms this is practised. At such an age all persons are to take an oath of allegiance, or fidelity, or to make profession of their subjection, in many places; and in other places they do it, before they enter upon any office. And if you will come nearer the case, and suppose that men were born in a school, or an army, as well as a republic, I think you would yield, that when they come to age, it is necessary that they have more than their birth privilege to show, to prove them scholars or soldiers. We are Christ's disciples and soldiers, as well as his subjects; and one is as essential to our christianity as the other. We may be initiated into his school and army in our infancy, and so stand related to him; but sure we are apostates, if when we come to age, we have nothing to show but our mere infant condition; and to more we must be called. 3. The case also differeth in this; princes do make known to all in their laws, that no man that is an enemy, yea, or that is not *pro tempore* a subject, shall dwell on their soil, among their subjects: they suffer not subjects and enemies to live promiscuously together in their dominions; and therefore it is supposed that a man's very abode and residence in their land, is a profession of subjection; much more when they live in obedience to the laws, and hold their estates by them. But Christ dealeth not thus: he suffereth believers and infidels to live together, and his flock to be but little in the world; so that it cannot be the least presumption, that a man is a christian, because he liveth among christians. 4. At least let us not teach Christ what he should have done, when we find he hath done otherwise: we find that he requireth personal faith and profession of all at age, that are naturally capable; and therefore we must perform it, and not give reasons why we should not do it. No good subject that is called to profess his fidelity will refuse, and say, you have no reason to question me, and put such a trial or obligation upon me.

So that I may conclude, that an adult person not professing christianity is not a visible christian, notwithstanding his birth privileges; and therefore not a visible church member; and therefore an apostate, seeing he was once engaged in covenant to Christ (though not an apostate from actual faith); and therefore such as hath no proper right to church communion and privileges.

Object. If his infant title be cut off, it is either by ignorance, wickedness, heresy, schism, or apostasy: but ignorance and wickedness do not cut him off; and heresy, schism, or apostasy, he is not guilty of; therefore, &c.

Answ. 1. His infant-title will cease of itself without any other cutting off, if it be not continued by his personal actual believing, when he comes to capable age. His birth privileges alone, or his parents' dedicating him to God in baptism, will serve no longer of itself. It is therefore for want of personal faith, *coram Deo*, and of the profession of faith, *coram ecclesia*, that his right doth cease.

2. Ignorance, where it proveth infidelity, must needs prove a cessation of the infant title, when they come to a capable age, and ignorance is privative. He that knoweth not that there is a God, a Christ, or what he hath done for us, or what a christian is, can have no faith in God, or Christ; and therefore is an atheist, and an infidel privatively, if at a capable age, among means at least. It is not only he that denieth Christ that is an infidel, but he that never heard of him, negatively at least; and he that having heard of him, understood not what he heard, and therefore believeth not in him, because he knoweth not. And it is not only he that denieth God, that is an atheist, but he that knoweth not that there is a God. And therefore if ignorance cut not off, then infidelity and atheism cut not off. And if neither of these cut not off, then no particular heresy can; nor any such apostasy, as men are capable of, that had but an infant church state: gross ignorance at a capable age, proveth gross ungodliness and apostasy. For if men's hearts had been towards God, they would have sought to know him; and if they know him not, their hearts are atheistical, and without him.

3. Wickedness is either such as may consist with habitual adhering to God in Christ; or such as shows a separation or renunciation; the one being ungodliness partial, and *quoad actum particularem*, (as Peter's denial,) and the other being ungodliness *quoad statum*. He that saith the former cutteth not off from the church, will scarcely say, that it doth not meritoriously suspend the offender from the communion of the church, till he appear penitent. And he that saith the latter cuts not off from the church meritoriously, must say that nothing doth it; for this is apostasy, and comprehendeth the greatest heresy. Such heretics hold that the pleasure of sin for a season is to be chosen before a life of holiness, with the hopes of everlasting life; and the flesh to be pleased before the Lord: and I think this is heresy. But whether these be cut off from the church or not, either they bring the person under the guilt of excommunication, or else there is no excommunication to be used. And if they be excommunicated, we shall not much contend with you about their rights. As long as you grant that they have no such right as that they may have the use of church communion, we are satisfied.

And yet I must say, that it is a blind conclusion, that the excommunicate are church members, without distinguishing of excommunication. If a man shall openly declare that he believeth not in Jesus Christ that died at Jerusalem, nor that there is any life to come; but yet he believeth in a Christ within him, and a heaven and hell within men (as the ranters, familists, &c. did); and yet this man, that he may pervert the souls of others, will hold communion with the church, and declare that he takes the Scripture in his sense; I doubt not but this man, though a professed infidel and apostate, is yet to be excommunicated, while he pretendeth to communion; and if this excommunicate man be not out of the catholic church, then no man is out of it; and you may next question whether the devil be not a member, that believeth much more than he.

But when I say that infidelity, impiety, heresy, do cut off or cast out, I mean it but meritoriously. Either these crimes are private and unknown, or provable. If not provable, then they merit this, and more *coram Deo*, but not *ecclesia judice*, that is, though there be guilt or demerit, yet we are no capable judges of it. But if the crime be provable, then it is either such as needs a judgment, or not. If it need a judgment, the person is only *de jure* cast out before the sentence, (which is *terminus diminuens*, and is not actual casting out,) and he is actually cast out by the sentence, and the execution: so that his sin cast him out meritoriously, the law obligatorily, the pastors of the church sententially, and the whole church, pastors and people, executively in avoiding him. But if there need no judgment, then he is excommunicate actually *ipso jure*, by the law alone, without a judge, which may be in many a case; as if he be a notorious infidel, atheist, blasphemer, or notoriously, beyond all doubt or controversy, one of those that the law commands us to avoid; we must execute this law, though there be no sentence pronounced. The want of a man's sentence will not excuse us from obeying God's laws. And where there is no controversy through the notoriousness of the case, there needs no judge.

6. If birth privilege will serve alone for the adult to prove their title to the church state and privileges of the adult, then no man that is born of christian parents can be obnoxious to excommunication, or justly excommunicate; for he is still a child of believing parents; and no sin will make them otherwise. And therefore if that were enough, he hath a good title still. Nay, it would follow that he cannot apostatize; for he cannot fall away from this. But the consequence is absurd, therefore so is the antecedent.

7. If infant title only be sufficient to the adult, then no parent is necessarily obliged to profess himself a christian, or actual believer, in order to prove the interest of his child to baptism (nor any that offer him in the parent's stead). For it is sufficient if the parents, or susceptors, say, We were infant members and baptized, and therefore our child must be so; but whether we are actual believers now, it is not necessary that we tell you. But the consequent is so absurd, that whoever shall have offered a child to baptism on these terms in the ancient church, (or any church that I know of, till very lately,) would have been rejected. The acceptance and baptism of our infants, is one of the privileges of believers; but no one hath right to this privilege, that his children be thus accepted into the church, upon a bare infant title, without the profession of a personal actual faith. Therefore, &c.

8. If the opposed doctrine should hold good, then all the world hath right to church communion, or millions of infidels, at least: but the consequent is false; therefore so is the antecedent. The reason of the consequence is plain; because Noah was a church member, and all the world came out of his loins; and the men of Thracia, Bithynia, and most of Asia, where Mahomet is worshipped, may say, Our ancestors were christians: therefore the birth privileges still going down from generation to generation, even to the thousandth generation, it must follow that the present generation of Mahometans and other infidels are church members still; for they lost not their natural relation to their parents.

9. It will not prove a society of adult persons to be a christian church, if they have no more but their infant condition; therefore it will not prove a single person to be a member of the church. That which is necessary to make a society a christian society, is necessary to make a person a christian person. But I hope none will deny, but that some kind of profession is necessary, to make or prove a company of men to be a christian church; therefore some profession is necessary to make or prove a man to be a church member.

10. If infant conditions will suffice to the adult for church membership and common privileges, then will they serve for justification and salvation, that are special privileges: but the consequent is false; therefore so is the antecedent. The reason of the consequence is, because though the benefits be various, yet the covenant and conditions are the same, by which we have a right to one and to the other. It is the appearance of the same faith, by profession before men, that gives title *coram ecclesia*, whose inward sincerity giveth right *coram Deo*, as was aforesaid. And God giveth title to all the blessings of the covenant, *coram Deo*, on the same conditions. And there is also a parity of reason. For if it be enough to prove our right to adult communion to praise God, and have all his ordinances and helps in the church, &c. that we had christian parents, then must it be enough to prove our title in all the rest of our benefits. The ancient fathers and churches thought that baptism did as certainly give the infant, rightly baptized, a right to pardon of original sin, and eternal life, as to outward church privileges. And if the same covenant give both on the same condition, then he that hath the condition of one, hath of both. I have proved in another disputation, that God hath not two covenants of grace on his part, one of spiritual or inward mercies, and another of outward ordinances; and that he giveth not these inward benefits and the outward signs of them, upon various conditions, but on the same.

11. Faith, or the profession of it in the adult, is either necessary to church communion, or unnecessary; if unnecessary, then christians have no more to do in the church than heathens; if necessary, then either as a mere duty, or as a condition, or other means. Not as a mere duty; for then still the infidels should be equally received, though not applauded; it must be therefore necessary as a means. And the very words of the promise tell us what sort of means it is, that makes faith to be its condition.

12. I would know of my adversary, what he would do with the son of a believer that were unbaptized at forty or fifty years of age? Would he baptize him without a profession of actual faith of his own, or not? If he would, then he would make new-fashioned christians and churches; and might baptize all the posterity of the apostates, or the ancient christians in the world, that would consent. Yea, he could not indeed baptize them; for baptism essentially containeth a profession of consent unto the

covenant, which therefore others make for infants that have the disposal of them. But if he would not baptize such without profession, then it seems he takes not their birth privileges to be a sufficient condition of their title thereunto.

13. A covenant breaker can claim no right to the benefits of the covenant (supposing him to violate the main conditions on which the benefits are suspended): but all those at capable age that have nothing but their infant condition to show, are covenant breakers; therefore they have no right to the benefits of the covenant. They therefore were engaged personally to believe in God the Father, Son, and Holy Ghost, when they came to the use of reason; as we have cause therefore to see whether they have broke or kept this covenant; and if they have broke it, they can at present claim no title to the benefits.

14. He "that cometh to God must believe that God is, and that he is a rewarder of them that diligently seek him:" therefore those that profess not this belief, cannot come to God, and consequently not have communion with the church. "Without faith it is impossible to please God," Heb. xi. 5, 6; therefore, without a profession of faith, it is impossible to have right to just communion, which is purposely for the pleasing of God.

Object. But it is said infants have faith; that is, a relative faith, and a federal faith, as well as a relative federal holiness: their right is not only in their parents, but in themselves; and therefore their faith is in themselves; and this continueth with the aged till heresy and schism cut it off.

Answ. Call any thing under heaven by the name of faith, so you will but explain your meaning, and we will quarrel as little as may be with you about words: but little know we what you mean by relative or federal faith, unless it be plainly, to be *semen fidelium*, the seed of believers. That there is a relative and federal holiness, is Scripture doctrine, and good sense; for the formal nature of the thing is a relation which commonly is expressed by the name of holiness, and which in that phrase is implied. But I remember not that Scripture ever speaks of a relative or federal faith; for I believe not that it was infants, that Christ calls the "little ones that believe in him." And faith being an act or habit, you must mean some other species of faith, which consisteth in relation. I know it not, nor will I use your language; though I think it more tolerable to call the infant relatively a believer, than to say he hath relative faith; for in so saying, no more is meant, but that he is a disciple of Christ, or belongs to him as he is the seed of a believer in covenant. But let this word of federal relative faith be used by you as you please; if the thing signified by it be any more than I have expressed, you should tell us what you mean; if it be no more but to be the seed of a believer, then we doubt not but this continueth when they come to age; but it doth them no good at age, as to the continuing of their title to church membership before God, without a faith of their own, nor before the church without a profession of it. That the infant himself is the subject of his own right, is a thing that no man, that I know, makes doubt of, that believeth him to have any right; but the active main condition of that right is not to be performed by himself, but by the parent; and only the passive condition is to be found in himself, that he be the seed of that parent. If he must be a believer's seed, it is the parent that must believe; but that will not serve his turn at age, if he do not also believe himself.

15. It is granted by the dissenters, that the ignorant, for all their infant title, have no immediate right to the communion of the church. And we will not contend about names: this satisfieth us in the main. It is not actual right, if it be not immediate plenary right: that which they call a remote right, is properly no actual right, but a term of diminution, as to it: when right hath two conditions, you may call it right, when the first and greatest is performed; but actually it is none, till all be performed; for it is still but conditional, while any part of the condition is unperformed. Saith learned Mr. Fullwood, p. 274, "The rule, to give all their due, is of indispensable obligation; but seeing ignorant persons have no such immediate right in the supper, what injury or wrong is there done them?"

Object. But ignorance doth not wholly cut a man off from the church; for such a knowledge goeth not to the essence of the church; for its form is society or community.

Answ. 1. It is sufficient to our present purpose, that it excludeth men meritoriously from immediate right to the communion of the adult. 2. Ignorance *qua talis* materially is no sin, as in idiots, paralytics, &c. and therefore cuts not off.[b] But ignorance in a subject, where knowledge should be found, is culpable, and complicate always with infidelity, or not believing; and therefore doth declare the person to be matter uncapable. If you choose to say, it cuts not off, I easily can prove, that it manifesteth that he is not in the invisible, and ought not to be esteemed of the visible church, by reason of his incapacity; his former title ceasing, for want of the condition of its continuation. 3. Knowledge in the capable adult, is an essential to the church as a society. A church is a society of christians: as it is a society, christianity is not essential to it, and so not knowledge; for there are societies of heathens and infidels enough. But as it is a christian society, knowledge is essential to it; and therefore, as it is a church. It is essential to a field of wheat, that there be wheat in it; or to a heap of wheat, that it be of wheat. And yet not as a field, or as a heap; for there are heaps of dirt also. The aggregation of a number of individuals makes it a community, and the form of the body aggregated, as to the mutual relation of the parts, makes it a body politic or society. But the essential qualification of the individuals, viz. christianity, is essential to that society in specie, as a christian church. And faith in the adult is essential to christianity, and knowledge is essential to faith, or inseparable from it.

Object. Then one should not take another to be a church member, till he is satisfied of his knowledge, which were a stranger thing.

Answ. Not so strange as true: supposing him an adult person capable of knowledge. For he cannot be satisfied of his faith without being satisfied of knowledge, nor of his christianity without his faith; for we are yet unacquainted with the christian infidels. But then consider, what must be satisfactory to other men concerning their brother's knowledge. It must satisfy them, that he is by the pastors of the church, who are to judge, approved and enumerated with believers; and that he professeth himself to be a believer, which cannot be without knowledge. This must satisfy them, till he nullify this evidence, by a clean bewraying of his infidelity.

Object. But the Scripture saith not that ignorant persons cannot be church members, or so much as that they ought merely for their ignorance to be excommunicate.

Answ. Doth not the Scripture exclude visible un-

[b] It is total ignorance that the objection extendeth to, or ignorance of the christian faith.

believers, and take in only visible believers, of the adult, and make the church a society of believers separated from unbelievers? Such ignorance therefore as is essential to, or inseparable from, infidelity, is in Scripture made the very brand of them that are without, excluded from the church. "If our gospel be hid, it is hid to them that are lost, in whom the god of this world hath blinded the minds of them that believe not, lest the light of the glorious gospel of Christ," &c. 2 Cor. iv. 3, 4. That preaching which discipleth men, Matt. xxviii. 19, doth give them knowledge, or else it could not give them faith; for it "openeth their eyes, and turneth them from darkness to light," &c. Acts xxvi. 18. And surely we are "translated out of the power of darkness into the kingdom of Christ," Col. i. 14. "Those that in time past were not a people, but now are the people of the living God, are called out of darkness into his marvellous light," 1 Pet. ii. 9, 10. "And what communion hath light with darkness, righteousness with unrighteousness, Christ with Belial, the believer with the infidel," 2 Cor. vi. 14—16.

Object. If knowledge, as such, were necessary to membership, then none could be a member without it: but that is not so.

Answ. 1. Knowledge, as such, is necessary no otherwise than faith as such, and all one; you may therefore as well plead thus against the necessity of faith. 2. And we grant that neither knowledge, nor faith, are necessary to uncapable subjects, that is, in themselves. You know faith in infants (such as we call faith) is not necessary to their justification: and yet will you say, it is not necessary to the adult? The promise hath made it necessary to the capable. 3. And we grant that neither knowledge, nor faith, (justifying or dogmatical,) are necessary to the being of a visible member, that is merely such: God only seeth the heart. But yet the appearance or profession of faith, and so of knowledge, in the essentials of christianity, is of necessity. 4. But though a personal faith, or knowledge, in truth or in profession, be not necessary to an infant, either for membership or justification, yet their parents' faith or profession is necessary; or else the promise is to more than believers and their seed, *quod restat probandum.*

Object. But a negative consent is sufficient to continue such in covenant, as before were admitted in infancy, or at age: and this negative consent is but non-actual dissent, or a non-renouncing of the gospel: and therefore, as positive consent, so actual faith and knowledge, are not necessary.

Answ. A dangerous doctrine![c] A negative consent is no consent. Why then should the ears of men be abused by the name, when there is nothing to answer it? A negative faith, in English, is infidelity, or not believing. Is not this a delusory teaching of the church, to call unbelief by the name of negative faith or negative consent? If a block, a brute, or a subject otherwise naturally uncapable, be the subject; then indeed it is inculpable, and your negative consent or faith is properly but a negative dissent, or unbelief. But if a capable, obliged person be the subject, (which is our case,) then your negative consent is in English privative not consenting, and privative unbelief, or rejecting Christ. What a means is here to convey flat infidels into the church, or continue them there, under the cloak of an abusive name! even by calling a non-dissenting conjunct with their infidelity, or not consenting to the covenant of grace, by the name of *negative consent.* Were it a person that had entered at age, yet if he have afterwards but your negative consent, (which is neither to consent or dissent,) he is an apostate: and if he refuse consent, when called to it by his lawful governors, he gives occasion to be suspected of apostasy, much more when he continueth to refuse consent, when so much of the life and practice of christianity consisteth in it, and in the manifestation of it; but especially when persons were baptized in infancy, and never yet professed a faith or consent of their own. If that man that had no faith but his parents', (and his being a believer's seed, which you call federal faith,) shall be continued at age a member of the church, by a not-actual dissenting or renouncing Christ, by express words, then let us talk no more of a church, nor abuse poor heathens and infidels so much as to question their salvation, or set them below us. But again, I answer you, that not consenting is dissenting in the inward act; it is undoubted, that he that for one year, or month, doth not consent, doth certainly dissent. There is no middle state between believers and infidels, consenters and refusers. How shall they escape that neglect so great salvation? Neglecting and not consenting in a capable, invited subject, is certain infidelity; and therefore in the external profession, we must judge accordingly. He that will not confess Christ, even in a christian church, and a peaceable age, deserves not to be called a christian: he that is not for him is against him.

Object. But God's covenant people under the law were not only admitted without their voluntary consent or knowledge, but commanded to renew their covenant in such a manner, as that they that were absent, and not in place to express consent, were included in those that were present.

Answ. 1. None but infants were admitted without consent: nor they without the consent of their parents, natural or civil, that had the power of disposing of them. 2. Those that were admitted upon others' consent, were not continued at age without their own. 3. The covenant, Deut. xxix. 11, 12, 15, was no mutual covenant to the absent or unborn there mentioned; but only a covenant offered to the nation, and conditionally made on God's part as a promise, to them and their posterity, even to many generations: but those unborn generations were not in covenant on their parts, as promisers in the stipulation.

Object. Wickedness itself doth not put a man out of the visible church. For a man is said to be cut off, but either *de jure,* or *de facto,* meritoriously, or effectually: the former is improperly called cutting off, being but the desert of it: therefore if those baptized in infancy prove afterwards wicked, they are not thereby cut off.

Answ. 1. Such persons as we have in question, lose their right and title by a cessation, for want of that personal condition, which the covenant made necessary to its continuance; so that we need not prove any other cutting off. 2. If he be but meritoriously cut off, it is the church's duty to do it sententially and executively; it being of indispensable obligation, to give to all their due. 3. It is granted that heresy cuts off; but how doth heresy cut off any otherwise than meritoriously? If therefore wickedness do as much as heresy, then thus far they are equal.

[c] Should a man never think of God, Christ, or heaven, and so never have actual dissent, he were yet an atheist and infidel. Much more when he heareth, and therefore must needs think of them: for then it is impossible the will should neither dissent nor consent. Faith is a positive being, and therefore must have a positive discovery: perhaps many a janizary never renounced Christ in words, nor many another child of christians, that is carried away, where they never heard of Christ.

4. Either wickedness signifieth some actual crime, like David's or Peter's, when the church knoweth not whether it be joined with habitual impenitence; or else it signifieth habitual, stated wickedness with impenitency. The first sort requireth but an exclusion from actual church communion, (called suspension by some,) as it is but actual sin that deserveth it. The second sort must have an exclusion from their state and church relation, as it is a state of impenitency, that deserveth it. The first sort of excommunication leaveth a man in the church, *quoad statum et relationem*, but out of it *quoad actum et usum*. The second sort leaves him out of it, both in state and act. Not that the excommunication puts him out of the church, as invisible: for that he did first himself meritoriously, and so efficiently, even by the efficiency of his demerits; as the law of Christ did it, by its obligatory efficiency. But when he hath put himself out of the church invisible, and plainly declared this to the church by his impenitent courses, the church further declareth it by their sentence, and puts him out of the church visible executively, when he had before put out himself meritoriously. 5. As I said before, the person's wickedness is either notorious and out of question, (as if a man be an open persecutor of godliness, or daily blaspheme God in the open streets, or congregation, and many lower cases,) or else it is controvertible, needing proof, and not notorious. In the latter case a wicked man is not actually cast out of the communion of the visible church, or cut off from it, by his demerits, till his fault be proved, and sentence be passed. But in the former case he is excommunicate *ipso jure*, which is more than *de jure*. We call him excommunicate *de jure*, who ought to be excommunicate *de facto;* but we call him excommunicate *ipso jure*, which is actually excommunicated by the law, without any further sentence of a judge, the law itself sufficing to enable men to the execution: so the law of Christ commanding us to avoid and have no company with drunkards, adulterers, heretics, &c. if any be notoriously such, past doubt, every man is obliged by this law to avoid them in their several capacities, after the due admonitions given them, which the law requireth, whether the pastors censure them or no; but his censure layeth on them a double obligation.

Object. If wickedness cut off a man, excommunication cannot do it, because it is done already.

Answ. If wickedness being not notorious do only cut him off meritoriously, and *de jure* only he be excommunicate, then actual excommunication must do that which was not actually done, but ought to be done. But if by the notoriety of the crime he be cut off *ipso jure*, the sentence yet may do the same thing, by adding a second obligation to the first. A traitor in actual prosecution of the sovereign, seeking his life, is condemned *ipso jure*, and any subject may kill him without sentence: and yet he may be proclaimed or sentenced a traitor for all that.

Object. It is proved by some writers, that such persons as have neither grace indeed, nor in show, may yet have both a real and visible interest in the covenant and church; and the arguments for this are yet unanswered: therefore persons baptized in infancy are in the church and covenant at age, though they never by profession made so much as a show of grace.

Answ. It was never proved by any writer, nor ever will be, that any person at age, and natural capacity, ought to be a member of the church of Christ, under the gospel, (no, nor under the law neither,) without a show of grace, even of faith by his profession of consent to the holy covenant. It is the arguments against them that remain unanswered: but that all their arguments, that I remember, are sufficiently answered, I shall take for granted, till I see a reply.[d] And for them that tell us of the church membership of the adult, considered without respect to saving grace, I shall regard them, when they have proved, either that faith and repentance are no saving graces; or that profession of faith hath no respect to faith; or that men may have title to church membership, without respect to profession of faith; even of their parents' if they are infants; or their own if at age. All these three points are yet unproved.

If any think the learned Mr. Fullwood to be of another mind, let them judge by his own words: of the Visible Church, cap. 28, p. 180. Saith he; "However, I humbly conceive though more than a bare historical faith should be requisite, yet less than a faith that justifieth (I do not say less than the profession thereof) may truly entitle to visible church membership," &c.; mark the parenthesis. And in his Epist. Propos. 3 and 4. "From the promises it seems at least probable to me, that the church is to have some kind of respect unto the saving condition of the person she is about to admit into communion, &c. 4. Yet I humbly conceive that more than a bare outward profession is requisite, to give real interest in the visible church, and the privileges thereof, before God; though no more is requisite to give visible interest before men," &c. And for immediate right to the communion of the church in the Lord's supper, he saith, p. 270, "Where there is want of knowledge, (whether naturally or morally,) there, we are sure, the condition of right is wanting; and consequently admission is to be denied, when all is done." And for the main design of this book, he saith, Append. p. 1, 2, (mentioning Mr. Hanmer's book,) "Some happily may be willing to surmise that our two propositions are irreconcilable, and interpret me an enemy to that most ancient, useful, and desirable ordinance. Wherefore, if I may possibly prevent so scandalous a censure, I shall not venture to hold my reader in so long suspense, till he come to the pages, where confirmation is considered in the book; nor yet barely to acknowledge my allowance of it under my hand; but after my humble thanks heartily tendered to our worthy author, for this excellent pains, in so seasonable a subject, I do also presume earnestly to beseech my reverend brethren, that what Mr. Baxter hath so smartly pressed upon the ministry about it, may be speedily and seriously considered, and undertaken by us." And many pages after he adds: 7. "Yea, though after all due pains and endeavours used, we should not be able to reconcile our principles in every point, yet if we can meet in the same practice about confirmation, though on some small differing grounds, why may not the church be happily edified, and the peace thereof in a measure obtained, by such a unity, uniformity in practice, while the persons differing but in lighter matters, may wait upon the Lord in this good service, for the great blessing of unanimity, promised also?"

Object. But he addeth the proviso, that confirmation be not thought to have any ingrediency into the nature or being of our membership; and that the temper of the people be found such, as will admit of such a change.

Answ. We shall easily grant, that confirmation, as it is a solemn reception of the person by imposition of hands, or without imposition in a purposed solemnity, commonly known by that name, is not of

[d] I would fully answer such kind of writings, but that judicious readers are weary of such contending, and think it not worth the reader's time or mine.

necessity to the being of our membership: and that all those that are received upon profession of faith may be church members; and that the ordinary use of christian assemblies, and exercises of worship, is a profession, though obscure; and that a baptized person that never was called to a verbal profession may be taken for a christian, or church member, upon such a practical sort of profession, joined with a not denying of Christ in word or life. But yet we are far from thinking that the infant title condition of such a one serveth to prove his present church state and title, now he is at capable age. The infant title ceaseth, if he continue it not by a personal profession at age. And as there is no middle between believers and unbelievers, so there is no such thing in a capable subject, as non-dissenting, in a moral sense, but true consenting. It is not possible for the soul to be neuter, when the thing is offered to our consent, but we must either will or nill, consent or dissent; though if it were, yet not willing, or not consenting, is infidelity and rebellion in such a subject. And accordingly we maintain, and must maintain, that profession of some sort or other is a necessary condition of the title and church state of the capable adult, and of right to the privileges; and as an obscure kind of profession may serve, when a man is called to no more, to prove his right, so a clearer sort of profession is necessary to the clearer proof, and *ad bene esse ecclesiæ*. And I have showed what great and weighty reasons we have, to require an open, clear, intelligible profession; and he that is justly called to for such, giveth cause to the church to question him of apostasy, if he refuse without cause. So that of the three conditions in question, the first, which is our infant condition, is utterly insufficient to the capable adult; and the second, which is an obscure signification of our mind, by our christian practices, may serve *ad esse*, at least when no more is required; and the third, which is an open approved profession by word or subscription, is necessary ordinarily *ad bene esse*.

Thus far we are agreed: but what if we were not? Must we therefore refuse to agree in the practice of the aforesaid confirmation? Will any good and peaceable man refuse to join with those that think it necessary to adult church membership? If this opinion, of the said non-necessity, had been an article of faith, and among the necessary *credenda* of the church, we should have had it in some creed, or heard more of the necessity of it than we have done, from the ancient churches. If we meet about the *agenda* in our practice, let them take heed how they divide from such as differ in the reasons of their practice, till they can prove that they deny some article of the faith, which is of necessity to be believed.

And as for the people's unfitness, or any disturbance that will follow thereupon: 1. If there be such a thing, it will be much long of the ministers: let them unanimously agree, and they may do well enough with the people, or much the better. But when ministers themselves are the bellows of faction, and think they can never sufficiently vilify dissenters, and so have themselves taught the people to take such a practice for a prelatical foppery, or formality, or for an independent rigidity and extremity; no wonder, if when they come to practise their duty, they meet with such reproaches from the people, as they have taught them. 2. But suppose that people would disturb us, that may in some cases excuse us, as to the mode of confirmation, or profession; but no unfitness of the people can excuse us, as to the substance of the duty, the requiring and approving their profession. We are false to our trust, and the church of God, if to avoid disturbance, we will confound believers and infidels, and destroy the nature of the church and ordinances, under pretence of the people's good.

Object. But it would be your only sure and happy course to exercise discipline upon all that are baptized in their infancy; whether at age they consent or no; and finding them in the church, you must do so.

Answ. I have said enough to this before. Have they that talked thus tried this course, or have they not? If they have not, we will bear with them as well-meaning men, that talk of what they never tried; as we would do with a confident man, that would condemn the actions of soldiers and seamen, that himself was never in the wars, nor at sea. But if they have tried it, what kind of discipline do they exercise? Would they make us believe, that they are able in a parish of four, five, or six thousand souls, to exercise the discipline mentioned in Scripture, and the canons of the ancient churches, and that upon such persons as our parishes commonly consist of? I know they cannot do it. I have had trial to tell me what a man can do. With the help of divers ministers, and many hundred godly people, to watch over others, and promote this work, I am not able to do it on all this parish, if I might. There are so many offenders weekly to be dealt with, and so much time required to hear witnesses, and admonish them, that it is more than I could possibly do. How bishops deal with dioceses, let them see themselves. And if we could do it, yet the people will not consent; if you send for them, they will not come near you; if you admonish them in the congregation by name, they will have an action at law against you, if they can. However, you will have such a multitude enraged by the exercise of discipline, if it be faithfully, though never so tenderly, done, that the church will be in a flame, and your ministry hated, and the people undone, as I have before declared. So that it is but a name of discipline, to the destruction of discipline, that this objection pleadeth for; or else it dishonoureth itself and the authors.

And as they do by discipline, so they do by christian charity, which is a greater thing. Of old, the visible members of the church were the objects of brotherly, christian love; and so as they seemed to them to be believers and penitent persons, the living members did love all the body with that special love, that was the matter of the new commandment, and proved them to be Christ's disciples. No man knew the hearts of others, and therefore knew not whom to love as christians infallibly discerned. But the profession of saving faith and holiness, being then (and ever) the test of adult members, they took all the members of the visible church as credibly of the invisible; though with different degrees of credibility. And accordingly they loved them all, with a christian, special love, of the same species, though with different degrees of that love. Whereas this popish, new-found trick, of making a new common sort of faith, and visible membership, that hath no respect to saving faith, doth teach all christians to love the members of the visible church but with a common love; and relieve and help them but with a common charity. And so the device is to confine our special, brotherly love and charity to a corner of the visible church; to a few, whom we will please to think to be godly.

I have oft marvelled in observing some learned divines, that bend that way, that they think compassion, and christian charity, is on their side. What charity can their doctrine glory of? They will be so merciful to infidels, that are uncapable of a church state, as to plead them into the church; and when they are there, they leave them under the curse, and in a state of damnation in their own judgments; teaching us to judge uncharitably of the visible church in general for their sakes; and to look on them as without respect to any saving grace, and so without any special love. A cold comfort! to bring them into no more capacity of God's mercy nor of our charity; but into much more capacity of aggravated damnation, which they might better have prevented by being kept in their proper station till they were capable of more. I confess, though my belief of men's profession have different degrees, as I see in them different degrees of credibility, yet I have charitabler thoughts of the members of the visible church, than these that make so low and miserable a description of them. And though I know that there are abundance among them that are hypocrites and unsanctified, yet know I none but saints and hypocrites that are tolerable in the church; nor will I accuse particular persons of hypocrisy, till I have cause. Neither in my secret or open censures, will I pluck up the tares upon any such terms, as will not stand with the safety of the wheat, but rather let them grow together in my esteem and in the church, till the time of harvest. And that I may think charitably of the church, and walk charitably in and towards it, therefore I would not have it consist of such notorious, ungodly, or heretical men, as are uncapable objects of christian brotherly love. For heresy, the aforesaid learned brother tells us, that it cuts men off from the church. I say so too, meritoriously at least, if by heresy be meant the exclusion of any essential article of the christian faith: but p. 199, where he saith, "the controversy may be easily ended, by parting stakes: viz. that some heresy, which absolutely denieth some particular fundamental truth, and taketh up some one or few stones thereof, is consistent with church interest; and other heresy, which razeth up the very foundation of religion, denying most, or the most chief, if not all of the articles of our christian faith, is inconsistent therewith." I most humbly but very confidently say, that this answer will not serve the turn. If by fundamentals, be meant (as commonly) the essential articles of christian faith, then the absolute denying of any one article doth prove that person to be no christian, nor capable of a church state; for the form is wanting, where any essential part is wanting. But if any thing else be meant by fundamentals, no man can decide the controversy by it, till it be known what it is; and it will be hard to fasten it to any thing, where the absolute denial of many points shall unchurch, and the absolute denial of one or two points of the same rank and kind not do it. Saith he, p. 198, "The Jews held that an heretical Israelite had no communion with the church of Israel: and why? but because communion supposeth union; and union with Israel, or the true church, is lost without faith: they also held, (as Selden noteth,) than an Israelite turning an heretic, i. e. denying any of the thirteen fundamental articles, to be as an heathen man." And a few lines before, he saith, that "historical faith, which hath the doctrine of faith for its object, none do doubt to be an essential, requisite to a true church member." Yet that with me is a visible member, that hath not this much, which is said to be essential, no man doubting of it. If they profess true faith, though they are stark atheists at the heart, and have not so much as historical faith, I shall believe them, till they nullify their own profession: but if they profess not also to consent to have Christ to be their Saviour, I shall not take it for a profession of christianity.

Certain I am, that ancient doctors with one consent did look on the baptized generally as pardoned, justified, and adopted; and therefore thought that visible church membership did imply a credibility at least of a state of saving grace. Saith Cyprian, Epist. 76, Magn. *In baptismo unicuique peccata sua remittuntur*. And upon this supposition run the arguments of the Council of Carthage, and Firmilian, Epist. ibid.

Saith Augustine, De Catechizandis rudibus, cap. 26, *His dictis interrogandus est, an hæc credat, atque observare desideret? Quod cum responderit, solemniter utique signandns est, et ecclesiæ more tractandus.* Obedience itself was promised, and a consent to it professed before baptism then, and ever since christian baptism was known.

Idem Epistol. 119, Ad Januar. cap. 2. *Secundum hanc fidem et spem et dilectionem, qua cœpimus esse sub gratia, jam commortui sumus cum Christo, et consepulti per baptismum in morte*, &c. Baptism then supposeth credibly faith, hope, and love.

Idem Epist. 23. Having showed why parents' faith profiteth infants, and yet their after-sins hurt them not, saith, *Cum autem homo sapere cœperit, non illud sacramentum repetit, sed intelliget, ejusque veritati consona etiam voluntate coaptabitur. Hoc quamdiu non potest* (N. B.) *valebit sacramentum ad ejus tutelam adversus contrarias potestates; et tantum valebit, nisi ante rationis usum ex hac vita emigraverit, per ipsum sacramentum ecclesiæ charitate ab illa condemnatione, quæ per unum hominem intravit in mundum, christiano adjutorio liberetur. Hoc qui non credit, et fieri non posse arbitratur, profecto infidelis est, et si habeat fidei sacramentum, longeque melior est ille parvulus, qui etiamsi fidem nondum habeat in cogitatione, non ei tamen obicem contrariæ cogitationis opponit, unde sacramentum ejus salubriter percipit.*

And saith the Synod of Dort, Artic. 1. 8. 17. *Quandoquidem de voluntate Dei ex verbo ipsius nobis est judicandum, quod testatur liberos fidelium, esse sanctos, non quidem natura, sed beneficio fœderis gratuiti, in quo illi cum parentibus comprehenduntur, pii parentes de electione et salute suorum liberorum, quos Deus in infantia ex hac vita evocat, dubitare non debent.* And if there be such certainty of the election and salvation of all such infants of the godly, as ought to exclude all doubting, surely the visible church state of the adult also hath some respect to saving grace, so far as that it is credible *fide humana*, that such have saving faith.

And saith Mr. Fullwood, Append. p. 6, "I conceive that such a one's personal profession in his general owning the true faith, and usual attending God's public worship, doth superadd a kind of new right, and mingle it with such a person's former right, had by his birth privilege." And if the *new right* be not a necessary right, I think it will prove no right.

I will contend with no man whether the approved profession which I have pleaded for in this book be the very same thing with the ancients' confirmation. I have given you my thoughts of it, and I am sure the thing in question is our duty, and the name not unfit, and that it is the same with the confirmation owned by the divines of the Reformed churches, and particularly with that established and recommended in the Book of Common Prayer, here in England, for the substance.

I shall conclude with this serious request to my brethren, seconded with weighty reasons. Even that they would take heed of both extremes in their judging of church members, and managing the discipline and ordinances of Christ. 1. Should we be so loose as to cast out discipline, or settle the churches either with such materials for quality, or quantity, as that it shall be uncapable of discipline, we shall never be able to answer it to Christ. And should we make a new qualification of adult church members, even their infant title condition alone, or the profession of a faith that is not saving, we should come too near the making of a new baptism, and church. And truly if we do but slubber over the business, and to avoid offence or trouble to ourselves, should take up with a profession utterly incredible,[e] especially in these times when we have so much liberty and countenance from the magistrate for a fuller reformation, we shall be guilty of so much injury to the church, and the christian name, and our people's souls, as is little considered by many that have their eye only on the contrary extreme, as if there were no danger but on one side.

2. On the other side, if we go so rigidly and unrighteously to work, as some men are bent to do, we may accomplish those ends that we are endeavouring to overthrow, and frustrate our own which we think to attain. If we reject the Scripture ancient character or evidence of title to church privileges, even a credible profession of christianity, we shall confound ourselves, and trouble the church, and be at a loss for a certain evidence, and never know what ground to rest upon. And we shall injure the souls of multitudes of true believers, and keep out those that Christ will entertain. For there are no other terms, besides taking men's profession by a human faith, on which we can admit persons, without excluding multitudes that should not be excluded. I doubt many ministers, that have had a more ingenuous education themselves, are not sufficiently sensible of the great disadvantage that country people are under, by their want of such education. Many that are bred where holy discourse is strange, and never were used to any thing of that nature, no, nor to common urbanity of speech or behaviour, may be brought to hearty sorrow for sin, and desires after Christ and grace, long before they can express their knowledge or desires, in any such manner as some men do expect. Many gracious souls (as far as I can discern) I have met with, that never were noted for any thing extraordinary in religion, though they lived among such. I had rather let in many that are unregenerate into the church, than keep out one that is a true believer, if there be no other remedy. The Lord Jesus that died for them, and sent the ministry for them, and will at last admit them into heaven, will give us little thanks, for excluding his weakest members from the church, and from the use of the sacrament and communion of saints, who have most need of them of any that have right to them. For my part, I desire not, nor dare be guilty of, that way of government in the church, as shall grieve those that Christ would not have grieved, and exclude the weak, and turn or keep out the infants in grace, from the family of the Lord. A compassionate minister is likest to Christ, that will not break the bruised reed. How dealt he with the woman taken in adultery! How tenderly excuseth he the sluggishness of his disciples, that could not watch nor pray with him one hour in his last extremity, with "the spirit is willing, but the flesh is weak!" when many now that think well of themselves would almost excommunicate men for as small a fault: we know not, in such cases, what spirit we are of.

But this is not all; I must confess, brethren, (which I beseech you patiently to hear,) these three things very much stick upon my thoughts. 1. I cannot but observe, how many eminent professors of piety have miscarried, and grievously miscarried, of late, when some of lower professions have stood fast. And I think God suffers the falls of many of his own, to let them know the frailty of our natures, and cause them to be compassionate to others. And some censorious men's hearts might smite them, if they had heard from their Master, "Let him that is faultless cast the first stone."

2. And it sticks very much upon my thoughts, how small a handful the censorious way would reduce the catholic church of Christ to. When it is but about the sixth part of the world that are at all baptized christians; and scarce the sixth part of them, that are protestants; and of the protestants, so few, except in England, that are so qualified for holiness, as in your admissions you expect;[f] and in England how small is the number that you would admit; I am deeply afraid lest you heinously injure the cause of Christ, by your excessive rigour: and lest confining even the visible church into so exceeding small a compass, should tempt men to infidelity. For he that to-day can believe that Christ died not for one of a hundred thousand in the world, may tomorrow believe that he died for none at all. I hope the little flock of the elect is not so little as some would have the visible church of the called.

3. We are deeply sensible of the increase of infidels here in England. They are too thick about us, under several garbs, especially under the mask of seekers; and are persuading people against the christian faith, and truth of Scripture, and the life to come: and so much do these apostates now abound, that we have reason to be jealous of them. And if any of you should strike in with good men, that are of this censorious, over-rigorous way, consider how far they may make use of such to accomplish their designs. If by you they can get almost all the world unchurched in estimation; and fifty for one, if not a hundred for one, in England, actually unchristianed, and their children after them left unbaptized; what will follow? I doubt this, if God should not save us from your miscarriages; when there is but one of a hundred in all the land that is a christian, the rest will want neither malice, nor power, to put an end here to the christian name; or at least to the liberty and glory of christianity. They may choose our parliaments for us, and in a word, do with us what they list, when they are exasperated to the greatest hatred of us; and cut off our liberties, and set up infidelity or heathenism by a law. I trust God will never suffer this; but let us take heed of gratifying infidels, and casting all our safety upon miracles, lest we be found to be but foolish builders, and tempters of God: still you may find that over-doing is the most effectual undoing. And if you would find out the most dangerous enemies of the gospel, look for them among those that seem over-zealous against the enemies of the gospel, and seem to overdo in the work of the gospel. I desire to bring no party of godly men into suspicion or odium by this; but indeed I desire to countermine the apostates; and it would be the most amazing, confounding thing, that could befall us in this world, if we should see the church of God betrayed into the hands of infidels, and the gospel lost by the indiscreet and inconsiderate over-doing of those well-

[e] I am sensible also how the arguments for both extremes do either drive or draw the reader to the anabaptists.

[f] The most experienced holy of my flock are very tender of the scandalous themselves, and would not have me to cast them out while there appeareth any present hope; remembering the condition that once they were themselves in, and their failings after convictions, and what had become of them if then they had been cast out.

meaning men, that did the work of infidels and ungodly men for them, while they thought that none were so much against them. If the neck of religion be broken among us, I am afraid the imprudent will be some cause, that would lead us above the top of the ladder.

Sure I am, between you both, you have the easiest way to the flesh, that run into extremes. Durst I cast off discipline, and only preach, and please all the parish in sacraments and other ordinances, how easy a life should I have to the flesh! And if I durst take out one of a hundred, that are eminent in piety, that will scarce ever call me to any penal acts of discipline, I should have a much more easy life than the former. But they are both so easy, that I the more suspect them to be the fruit of the wisdom of the flesh. Indeed, both the extremes do cast off discipline for the most part, whatever they pretend. One sort never mean to exercise it; and the other sort extol it; and when they have done, they separate a few of the best that are like to have no need of the troublesome part of it, and so sit down without the exercise of it; pretending to be physicians, but refusing to receive the sick into their hospitals. Brethren, I speak not as an accuser, but a monitor, and shall continue to pray for the church's purity and peace, while I am

R. B.

July 30, 1658.

Dr. H. Hammond, in his View of the Direct. sec. 41. p. 45, 46. "For confirmation, which being so long and so scandalously neglected in this kingdom, (though the rulers have also been severe, and careful in requiring it,) will now not so easily be digested, having those vulgar prejudices against it; yet must I most solemnly profess my opinion of it; That it is a most ancient christian custom, tending very much to edification: which I shall make good by giving you this view of the manner of it. It is this; that every rector of any parish, or curate of charge, should by a familiar way of catechising, instruct the youth of both sexes within his cure in the principles of religion, so far, that every one of them, before the usual time of coming to the Lord's supper, should be able to understand the particulars of that vow, made in baptism, for the *credenda* and *facienda*, yea, and *fugienda* also; what must be believed, what done, and what forsaken; and be able to give an intelligent account of every one of these: which being done, every such child, so prepared, ought to be brought to the bishop for confirmation. Wherein the intent is, that every such child, attained to years of understanding, shall singly and solemnly before God, the bishop, and the whole congregation, with his own consent, take upon himself the obligation to that, which his godfathers and godmothers in baptism promised in his name; and before all those reverend witnesses, make a firm, public, renewed promise that by God's help he will faithfully endeavour to discharge that obligation in every point of it, and persevere in it all the days of his life. Which resolution and promise, so heightened with all those solemnities, will in any reason have a mighty impression on the child, and an influence on his actions for ever after. And this being thus performed by him, the bishop shall severally impose his hands on every such child, (a ceremony used to this purpose by Christ himself,) and bless and pray for him, that now, that the temptations of sin begin more strongly in respect of his age to assault him, he may receive grace and strength against all such temptations or assaults, by way of prevention and special assistance; without which, obtained by prayer from God, he will never be able to do it. This is the sum of confirmation; and were it rightly observed, (and no man admitted to the Lord's table, that had not thus taken the baptismal bond from the sureties into his own name; and no man after that suffered to continue in the church, which break it wilfully; but turned out of those sacred courts by the power of the keys in excommunication,) it would certainly prove, by the blessing of God, were it begun, a most effectual means to keep men, at least within some terms of christian civility, from falling into open, enormous sins: and that the defaming and casting out of this so blameless, gainful order, would be necessary or useful to any policy, save only to defend the devil from so great a blow, and to sustain and uphold his kingdom, I never had yet any temptation or motive to suspect or imagine. Instead of considering any objections of the adversary against this piece, whether of apostolical or ecclesiastical discipline, (which I never heard with any colour produced,) I shall rather express my most passionate wish unto my friends, those who sincerely wish the good of this national church, that they will endeavour their uttermost to revive these means of regaining of purity and exemplary lives of all its members, when God, by restoring our peace, shall open a door for it."

GILDAS SALVIANUS.

THE

REFORMED PASTOR;

SHOWING

THE NATURE OF THE PASTORAL WORK; ESPECIALLY IN PRIVATE INSTRUCTION AND CATECHISING: WITH AN OPEN CONFESSION OF OUR TOO OPEN SINS.

PREPARED FOR

A DAY OF HUMILIATION KEPT AT WORCESTER, DECEMBER 4, 1655, BY THE MINISTERS OF THAT COUNTY, WHO SUBSCRIBED THE AGREEMENT FOR CATECHISING AND PERSONAL INSTRUCTION, AT THEIR ENTRANCE UPON THAT WORK.

THE PREFACE.

TO MY REVEREND AND DEARLY BELOVED BRETHREN, THE FAITHFUL MINISTERS OF CHRIST, IN BRITAIN AND IRELAND, GRACE AND PEACE IN JESUS CHRIST, BE INCREASED.

REVEREND BRETHREN,

THE subject of this treatise so nearly concerneth yourselves and the churches committed to your care, that it persuadeth and imboldeneth me to this address, notwithstanding the imperfections in the manner of handling it, and the consciousness of my great unworthiness to be your monitor.

Before I come to my principal errand, I shall give you that account which I suppose I owe you, of the reasons of this following work, and of the freedom of speech which to some may be displeasing.

When the Lord had awakened his ministers in this county, and some neighbouring parts, to a sense of their duty in the work of catechising, and private instruction of all in their parishes that would not obstinately refuse their help, and when they had subscribed an Agreement, containing their resolutions for the future performance of it, they judged it unmeet to enter upon the work without a solemn humbling of their souls before the Lord, for their so long neglect of so great and necessary a duty: and therefore they agreed to meet together at Worcester, December 4, 1655, and there to join in such humiliation, and in earnest prayer to God for the pardon of our neglects, and for his special assistance in the work that we had undertaken, and for the success of it with the people whom we are engaged to instruct: at which time, among others, I was desired by them to preach. In answer to their desires, I prepared the following discourse; which though it proved longer than could be delivered in one or two sermons, yet I intended to have entered upon it at that time, and to have delivered that which was most pertinent to the occasion, and to have reserved the rest to another season. But before the meeting, by the increase of my ordinary pain and weakness, I was disabled from going thither. To recompense which unwilling omission, I easily yielded to the requests of divers of the brethren, forthwith to publish the things which I had prepared, that they might *see* that which they could not *hear*. If now it be objected, that I should not have spoken so plainly or sharply against the sins of the ministry, or that I should not have published it to the view of the world; or at least that I should have done it in another tongue, and not in the ears of the vulgar, especially at such a time when quakers and papists are endeavouring to bring the ministry into contempt, and the people are too prone to hearken to their suggestions: I confess I thought the objection very considerable; but that it prevailed not to alter my resolutions is to be ascribed to the following reasons: 1. It was a purposed solemn humiliation that we were agreed on, and that this was prepared and intended for. And how should we be humbled without a plain confession of our sins?—2. It was principally our own sins that the confession did concern; and who can be offended with us for confessing our own, and taking the blame and shame to ourselves, which our consciences told us we ought to do?—3. I have excepted in our confessions those that are not guilty: and therefore hope that I have injured none. 4. Having necessarily prepared it in the English tongue, I had no spare time to translate it.—5. Where the sin is open in the sight of the world, it is in vain to attempt to hide it.—6. And such attempts will but aggravate it, and increase our shame.—7. A free confession is a condition of a full remission; and when the sin is public, the confession must be public. If the ministers of England had sinned only in Latin, I would have made shift to have admonished them in Latin, or else have said nothing to them. But if they will sin in English, they must hear it in English. Unpardoned sin will never let us rest or prosper, though we be at never so much care and cost to cover it: our sin will surely find us out, though we find not it. The work of confession is purposely to make known our sin, and freely to take the shame to ourselves: and if he that confesseth and forsaketh be the man that shall have mercy, no wonder then if he that covereth it prosper not, Prov. xxviii. 13. If we be so tender of ourselves, and loth to confess, God will be less tender of us, and will indite our confessions for us. He will either force our consciences to confession, or his judgments shall proclaim our iniquities to the world. Know we not how many malicious adversaries are day and night at work against us? Some openly revile us, and some in secret are laying the designs, and contriving that which others execute, and are in expectation of a fuller stroke at us, which may subvert us at once. What is it but our sins that is the strength of all these enemies? Is not this evil from the ordering of the Lord? Till we are reconciled unto him we are never safe: he will never want a rod to scourge us by. The tongues of quakers and papists, and many other sorts, are all at work to proclaim our sins, because we will not confess them ourselves: because we will not speak the truth, they will speak much more than the truth. Yet if we had man only to plead our cause with, perhaps we might do much to make it good; but while God accuseth us, how shall we be justified? and who shall hide our sins, when he will have them brought to light? And God is our accuser till we accuse ourselves: but if we would judge ourselves, he would not judge us.—8. The fire is already kindled which revealeth our sin: judgment is begun at the house of God. Hath the ministry suffered nothing in England, Scotland, and Ireland? and have there been no attempts for their overthrow? Hath it not been put to the vote in an assembly that some called a parliament of England, Whether the whole frame of the established ministry, and its legal maintenance, should be taken down? And were we not put to plead our title to that maintenance, as if we had been falling into the hands of Turks, that had thirsted for our subversion, as resolved enemies to the christian cause? And who knows not how many of these men are yet alive; and how high the same spirit yet is, and busily contriving the accomplishment of the same design? Shall we think that they ceased their enterprise, because they are working more subtlely in the dark? What are the swarms of railers at the ministry sent abroad the land for, but to delude, exasperate, and disaffect the people; and turn the hearts of the children from their fathers, that they may be ready to promote the main design? And is it then not our wisest course to see that God be our Friend, and to do that which tendeth most to engage him in our defence? I think it is no time now to stand upon our credit, so far as to neglect our duty and befriend our sins, and so provoke the Lord against us. It rather beseems us to fall down at the feet of our offended Lord, and to justify him in his judgments, and freely and penitently to confess our transgressions, and to resolve upon a speedy and thorough reformation, before wrath break out upon us, which will leave us no remedy. It is time to make up all breaches between us and heaven, when we stand in such necessity of the Divine protection! For how can an impenitent, unreformed people expect to be sheltered by holiness itself? It is a stubborn child, that under the rod will refuse to confess his faults; when it is not the least use of the rod to extort confession. We feel much, we fear more, and all is for sin; and yet are we so hardly drawn to a confession?—9. The world already knows that we are *sinners;* as none suppose us perfect, so our particular sins are too apparent to the world: and is it not meet then that they should see that we are *penitent* sinners? It is sure a greater credit to us to be penitent sinners, than impenitent sinners; and one of the two we shall be while we are on earth. Certainly as repentance is necessary to the recovery of our peace with God, so it is also to the reparation of our credit with wise and godly men: it is befriending and excusing our sin that is our shame indeed, and leadeth towards everlasting shame; which the shame of penitent confession would prevent.—10. Our penitent confession and speedy reformation are the means that must silence the approaching adversaries. He is impudently inhuman, that will reproach men with their sins that bewail and penitently charge them upon themselves. Such men have a promise of pardon from God; and shall men take us by the throat when God forgiveth us? Who dare condemn us, when God justifies us? Who shall lay that to our charge, which God hath declared that he will not charge us with? When sin is truly repented of, by gospel indulgence it ceaseth to be ours. What readier way then can we imagine to free us from the shame of it, than to shame ourselves for it in penitent confessions, and to break off from it by speedy reformation?—11. The leaders of the flock must be exemplary to the rest; and therefore in this duty as well as in any other. It is not our part only to teach them repentance, but to go before them in the exercise of it ourselves. As far as we excel them in knowledge and other gifts, so far should we also excel them in this and other graces.—12. Too many that have set their hand to this sacred work do so obstinately proceed in self-seeking, negligence, pride, division, and other sins, that it is become our necessary duty to admonish them. If we could see that such would reform without reproof, we could gladly forbear the publishing of their faults. But when reproofs themselves do prove so ineffectual, that they are more offended at the reproof than at the sin, and had rather that we should cease reproving, than themselves should cease sinning, I think it is time to sharpen the remedy. For what else should we do? To give up our brethren as incurable, were cruelty, as long as there are further means to be used. We must not hate them, but plainly rebuke them, and not suffer sin upon them, Lev. xix. 17. And to bear with the vices of the ministers, is to promote the ruin of the church. For what speedier way is there for the depraving and undoing of the people, than the pravity of their guides? And how can we more effectually further a reformation, (which we are so much obliged to do,) than by endeavouring the reforming of the leaders of the church? Surely, brethren, if it be our duty to endeavour to cast out those ministers that are negligent, scandalous, and unfit for the work, and if we think this so necessary to the reformation of the church, (as no doubt it is,) it must needs be our duty to endeavour to heal the sins of others, and to use a much gentler remedy to them that are guilty of a less degree of sin. If other men's sin deserve an ejection, sure ours deserve and require plain reproof. For my part, I have done as I would be done by; and it is for God and the safety of the church, and in tender love to the brethren, whom I do adventure to reprehend: not (as others) to make them contemptible and odious, but to heal the evils that would make them so; that so no enemy may find this matter of reproach among us. But especially because our faithful endeavours are of so great necessity to the welfare of the church, and the saving of men's souls, that it will not consist with a love to either (in a predominant sort) to be negligent ourselves, or silently to connive at and comply with the negligent. If thousands of you were in a leaky ship, and those that should pump out the water and stop the leaks should be sporting or asleep, yea, or but favour themselves in their labours, to the hazarding of you all, would you not awake them to their work, and call out on them to labour as for your lives? And if you used some sharpness and importunity with the slothful, would you think that man were well in his wits that would take it ill of you, and accuse you of pride, self-conceitedness, or unmannerliness, to presume to talk so saucily to your fellow-workmen? or should tell you, that you wrong them by diminishing their reputation? Would you not say, The work must be done, or we are all dead men: is the ship ready to sink, and do you talk of reputation? or had you rather hazard yourself and us, than hear of your slothfulness? This is our case, brethren! The work of God must needs be done: souls must not perish while you mind your worldly business, or observe the tide and times, and take your ease, or quarrel with your brethren: nor must we be silent while men are hastened by you to perdition, and the church to greater danger and confusion, for fear of seeming too uncivil and unmannerly with you, or displeasing your impatient souls. Would you be but as impatient with your sins as with reproofs, you should hear no more from us, but we should be all agreed! But neither God nor good men will let you alone in such sins. Yet if you had betaken yourselves to another calling, and would sin to yourselves only, and would perish alone, we should not have so much necessity of molesting you, as now we have: but if you will enter into the office which is for the necessary preservation of us all, so that by letting you alone in your sins, we must give up the church to apparent loss and hazard; blame us not if we talk to you more freely than you would have us do. If your own body be sick, and you will despise the remedy; or if your own house be on fire, and you will be singing or quarrelling in the streets; I can possibly bear it, and let you alone (which yet in charity I should not easily do). But if you will undertake to be the physician of an hospital, or to all the town that is infected with the plague; or will undertake to quench all the fires that shall be kindled in the town; there is no bearing with your remissness, how much soever it may displease you. Take it how you will, you must be told of it; and if that will not serve, you must be yet closelier told of it; and if that will not serve, if you be rejected as well as reprehended, you must thank yourselves. I speak all this to none but the guilty. —And thus I have given you those reasons, which forced me, in plain English, to publish so much of the sins of the ministry, as in the following treatise I have done. And I suppose the more penitent and humble any are, and the more desirous of the truest reformation of the church, the more easily and fully will they approve such free confessions and reprehensions.

The second sort of objections against this free confession of sin, I expect to hear from the several parties whose sins are here confessed. Most of them can be willing that others be blamed, so they might be justified themselves. I can truly say, that what I have here spoken, hath been as impartially as I could, and not as a party, nor as siding with any, but as owning the common christian cause, and as somewhat sensible of the apparent wrongs that have been offered to common truth and godliness, and the hinderances of men's salvation, and of the happiness of the church. But I find it impossible to avoid the offending of guilty men; for there is no way of avoiding it, but by our silence, or their patience: and silent we cannot be, because of God's commands; and patient they cannot be, because of their guilt and partiality, and the interest that their sin hath got in their affections. I still except those humble men that are willing to know the worst of themselves, and love the light that their deeds may be made manifest, and long to know their sins that they may forsake them, and their duty that they may perform it.

Some, it is like, will be offended with me, that I blame them so much for the neglect of that discipline which they have disputed for so long. But what remedy? If discipline were not of God, or if it were unnecessary to the church, or if it were enough to dispute for duty, while we deliberately refuse to perform it; then would I have given these brethren no offence.

Some, it is like, will be offended that I mention, with disallowance, the separatists or anabaptists; as I understand some are offended much that I so mentioned them in an epistle before the Quakers' Catechism, as if they opened the door to the apostasy of these times; and they say that by this it appeareth that while I pretend so much zeal for the unity of the church, I intend and endeavour the contrary. To which I answer: 1. Is it indeed a sign that a man loveth not the unity of the saints, because he loveth not their disunion and division? Who can escape the censure of such men but he that can unite the saints by dividing them? 2. I never intended, in urging the peace and unity of the saints, to approve of any thing which I judged to be a sin; nor to tie my own tongue or other men's from seasonable contradicting it. Is there no way to peace but by participating of men's sin? The thing I desire is this: (1.) That we might all consider how far we may hold communion together, even in the same congregations, notwithstanding our different opinions; and to agree not to withdraw where it may possibly be avoided. (2.) But where it cannot, that yet we may consult how far we may hold communion in distinct congregations: and to avoid that no further than is of mere necessity. And (3.) and principally, to consult and agree upon certain rules for the management of our differences, in such manner as may be least to the disadvantage of the common christian truths which are acknowledged by us all. Thus far would I seek peace with Arminians, antinomians, anabaptists, or any that hold the foundation. Yea, and in the two last, I would not refuse to consult an accommodation with moderate papists themselves, if their principles were not against such consultations and accommodations: and I should judge it a course which God will better approve of, than to proceed by carnal contrivances to undermine their adversaries, or by cruel murders to root them out, which are their ordinary courses. I remember that godly, orthodox, peaceable man, Bishop Usher, (lately deceased,) tells us in his sermon at Wansted, for the unity of the church, that he made a motion to the papist priests in Ireland; that, because it was ignorance of the common principles that was like to be the undoing of the common people, more than the holding of the points which we differ in; therefore both parties should agree to teach them some catechism containing those common principles of religion which are acknowledged by us all: but jealousies and carnal counsels would not permit them to hearken to this motion.

3. And as concerning that epistle before my paper to the quakers, I further answer, that by *separatists* there I plainly mean church dividers; even all that make unnecessary divisions in or from the churches of Christ, whom the apostle so earnestly beseecheth us to mark and avoid, (Rom. xvi. 17,) and which he calleth them carnal for, and so earnestly contendeth against, 1 Cor. i. ii. iii.; and in many other places in his epistles. And if this be a tolerable sin, then the unity of the church is not a necessary thing; and then the apostles would never have condemned this sin as they have done. Do we all so sensibly smart by the effects of these sins, and is the church of Christ among us brought into such a torn and endangered condition by them, so that we are in no small danger of falling all into the hands of the common adversaries? Is so hopeful and chargeable a reformation so far frustrated by these men, and yet must we not open our mouths to tell them of it? May we not tell them of it, when we are bleeding by their hands? Is it tolerable in them to cut and wound, and let out our blood, and is it unpeaceableness in us to tell them that we suffer by them, and to beseech them to repent and to have compassion on the church of Christ? Must we be patient to be ruined by them, and have they not the patience to hear of it? What remedy? Let them be silent that dare; for I profess I dare not. I must tell them that this height of pride hath been in their ancestors a concomitant of schism. A poor drunkard or swearer will more patiently hear of his sin, than many that we hope are godly will of theirs, when once they are tainted with this sin. But godliness was never made to be the credit of men's sins: nor is sin to be let alone, or well thought of, when it can but get into a godly man. Shall we hate them most, whom we are bound to love best? and shall we show it by forbearing our plain rebuke, and suffering their sin upon them? It must not be: however they take it in their sick distemper, it must not be. No man that erreth doth think that he erreth: these men are confident themselves that they are in the right. But the sober, prudent servants of Christ, that have escaped their disease, do see their error; and England feeleth it, and that at the very heart: what! must we die by their hand, and our very heart blood be let out, and the gospel delivered up to the adversaries, before they will believe that they have done us wrong? or before they will endure to hear us tell them of it? If the ages to come do not say more against the ways of these mistaken men, than I have done in that epistle, and if either mercy or judgment do not bring them one day to think or speak more sharply of themselves, then I must confess myself quite out of my prognostics.

Another sort that will be offended with me, are some of the divines of the prelatical way, whom I had no mind to offend, nor to dishonour: but if necessary duty will do it, what remedy? If they cannot bear with just admonition, I must bear with their impatience. But I must tell them, that I spoke not by hearsay, but from sight and feeling. It is more tolerable in an Englishman to speak such things, that hath seen the sad work that was made in England, the silencing of most godly, able men, the persecution even of the peaceable, the discountenance of godliness, and the insulting scorn of the profanest in the land, than for a foreigner that hath known of this but by hearsay. When we remember what a sort of ministers the land abounded with, while the ablest and most diligent men were cast out, (of which matters we cannot be ignorant, if there were no records remaining of their attested accusations,) we must needs take leave to tell the world that the souls of men and the welfare of the church were not so contemptible in our eyes, as that we should have no sense of these things, or should manifest no dislike of them, nor once invite the guilty to repent. And if you think my language harsh, I will transcribe some words of a far wiser man, and leave it to your consideration how far they concern the present case, or justify my free and plain expressions.

Gildas de Excid. Britan. edit. Polid. Virgil. sub fine. *Quid plura? Fertur vobis in medium Matthiæ in confusionem vestram, exemplum, sanctorum quoque apostolorum electione, vel judicio Christi, non propria voluntate sortiti, ad quod cæci effecti non videtis, quia longe a meritis ejus distatis, dum in morem et affectum Judæ traditoris sponte corruitis. Apparet ergo eum qui vos sacerdotes sciens ex corde, dicit non esse eximium christianum. Sane quod sentio proferam. Posset quidem lenior fieri increpatio, sed quid prodest vulnus manu tantum palpare, unguentove ungere quod tumore jam vel fœtore sibi horrescens cauterio, et publico ignis medicamine eget? Si tamen ullo modo sanari possit, ægro nequaquam medelam quærente et ob hoc medico longius recedente. O inimici Dei, et non sacerdotes; o licitatores malorum, et non pontifices; traditores, et non sanctorum apostolorum successores; impugnatores, et non Christi ministri. Auscultastis quidem secundæ lectionis apostoli Pauli verborum sonum, sed nullo modo monita virtutemque servastis, et simulachrorum more, quæ non vident, neque audiunt, eodem die alteri astitistis, licit ille tunc et quotidie vobis intonaret. Fratres, fidelis sermo est, et omni acceptione dignus. Ille dixit, fidelem, et dignum, vos ut infidelem et indignum sprevistis. Si quis episcopatum cupit, bonum opus cupit. Vos episcopatum magnopere avaritiæ gratia, non spiritualis profectus obtentu, cupitis, et bonum opus illi condignum nequaquam habetis. Oportet ergo hujusmodi irreprehensibilem esse: In hoc namque sermone lachrymis magis, quam verbis opus est, ac si dixisset apostolus eum esse omnibus irreprehensibiliorem debere. Unius uxoris virum. Quid ita apud nos, quoque contemnitur, quasi non audiretur vel idem dicere. Et virum uxoris sobrium, prudentem? Quis etiam ex vobis hoc aliquando in esse sibi saltem optavit. Hospitalem? Id forte casu evenerit, popularis auræ potius, quam præcepti gratia factum. Non prodest, Domino salvatore ita dicente. Amen dico vobis, receperunt meredem suam. Ornatum, non vinolentum, non percussorem, sed modestum, non litigiosum, non cupidum? O feralis immutatio, o horrenda præceptorum cœlestium conculcatio; nonne infatigabiliter ad hæc expugnanda, vel potius obruenda actuum verborumque arma corripitis, pro quibus conservandis, atque firmandis, si necesse fuisset, et pœna ultro subeunda, et vita ponenda erat? Sed videamus et sequentia. Domum suam (inquit) bene regentem, filios habentem subditos in omni castitate. Ergo imperfecta est patrum castitas, si non item et filiorum accumuletur? Sed quid erit, ubi nec pater, nec filius, mali genitoris exemplo privatus, conspicitur castus? Si quis autem domui suæ præesse nescit, quomodo ecclesiæ Dei diligentiam adhibebit? Hæc sunt verba quæ indubitatis affectibus approbantur. Diaconos similiter pudicos, non bilingues, non vino multo deditos, non turpe lucrum sectantes, habentes ministerium fidei, in conscientia pura. Hi autem probentur primum, et sic ministrent nullum crimen habentes. His nimirum horrescens diu immorari, unum veridice possum dicere. Quin hæc omnia in contrarios actus mutantur, ita ut clerici quod non absque dolore cordis, fateor, impudici, bilingues, ebrii, turpis lucri cupidi, habentes fidem, et ut verius dicam, infidelitatem, in con-*

scientia impura, non probati in bono, sed in malo præsciti ministrantes, et innumera crimina habentes, sacro ministerio adsciscantur. Audistis etiam illo die, quo multo dignius, multoque rectius erat, ut ad carcerem vel catastam pœnalem quam ad sacerdotium traheremini domino scitante, quem se esse putarunt discipuli, Petrum respondisse. Tu es Christus filius Dei, eique dominum pro tali confessione, dixisse. Beatus es Simon Barjona, quia caro et sanguis non revelavit tibi, sed Pater meus, qui in cœlis est. Ergo Petrus a Deo Patre doctus recte Christum confitetur. Vos autem moniti a patre vestro diabolo inique, salvatorem malis actibus denegatis. Vero sacerdoti dicitur: Tu es Petrus, et super hanc petram, ædificabo ecclesiam meam. Vos quidem assimilamini viro stulto, qui ædificavit domum suam, super arenam. Notandum vero est, quod insipientibus in ædificando domo, arenarum pendulæ mobilitati Dominus non co-operatur, secundum illud. Fecerunt sibi reges; et non per me. Itidemque quod sequitur eadem sonat dicendo. Et portæ inferi non prævalebunt, ejusque peccata intelliguntur. De vestra quidem exitiabili factura pronunciantur. Venerunt flumina, flaverunt venti, et impegerunt in domum illam, et cecidit, et fuit ruina ejus magna. Petro ejusque successoribus dicit Dominus, et tibi dabo clavis regni cœlorum. Vobis vero; non novi vos, discedite a me, operarii iniquitatis, ut seperati sinistræ partis hœdi eatis in ignem æternum. Itemque omni sancto sacerdoti promittitur: Et quæcunque solveris super terram, erunt soluta et in cœlis; et quæcunque ligaveris super terram, erunt ligata et in cœlis. Sed quomodo vos aliquid solvetis, ut sit solutum, et in cœlis, a cœlo ob scelera adempti, et immanium peccatorum funibus compediti? Ut Solomon quoque ait, funiculis peccatorum suorum unusquisque constringitur. Qua ratione aliquid in terra ligabitis, quod supra mundum etiam ligetur, propter vosmetipsos, qui ita ligati iniquitatibus, in hoc mundo tenemini, ut in cœlis nequaquam ascendatis, sed in infausta tartari ergastula non conversi in hac vita ad dominum, decedatis. Nec sibi quisquam sacerdotum de corporis mundi solum conscientia supplaudat, cum eorum quibus præest, si propter ejus imperitiam, seu desidiam, seu adultationem, perierin in die judicii de ejusdem manibus veluti interfectoris animæ exquirantur. Quia nec dulcior mors, quam quæ infertur ab unoquoque homineque malo, alioquin non dixisset apostolus velut paternum legatum suis successoribus derelinquens. Mundus ego sum ab omnium sanguine, non enim subterfugi, quo minus annuntiarem vobis omne ministerium Dei. Multum namque usu ac frequentia peccatorum inebriati, et incessanter irruentibus vobis scelerum cumulatorum, ac si undis quassati unum veluti post naufragium, in qua ad vivorum terram evadatis, pœnitentiæ tabulam toto animi nisu exquirite, ut avertatur furor Domini a vobis, misericorditer dicentis, Nolo mortem peccatoris, sed ut convertatur et vivat. Ipse omnipotens Deus totius consolationis et misericordiæ paucissimos bonos pastores conservet ab omni malo, et municipes faciat civitatis Hierusalem cœlestis, hoc est, sanctorum omnium congregationis, Pater, et Filius, et Spiritus Sanctus, cui sit honor, et gloria in secula seculorum. Amen.

If the English translation of this book (for translated it is long ago) do fall into the hands of the vulgar, they will see what language the British clergy received from one that was neither a censorious railer, nor schismatically self-opinionated.

Perhaps some will say, That the matter is not much amended, when in former times we were almost all of a mind; and now we have so many religions that we know not well whether we have any at all.

Answ. 1. Every different opinion is not another religion.—2. This is the common popish argument against reformation, as if it were better that men believed nothing *fide divina*, than inquire after truth, for fear of misbelief: and as if they would have all ungodly, that they might be all of a mind. I am sure that the most of the people in England wherever I came, did make religion, and the reading of the Scripture, or speaking of the way to heaven, the matter of their bitter scorn and reproach. And would you have us all of that mind again, for fear of differences? a charitable wish!—3. If others run into the other extreme, will that be any excuse to you? Christ's church hath always suffered between profane unbelievers and heretical dividers, as he suffered himself on the cross between two thieves. And will the sin of one excuse the other?—4. And yet I must say, (lest I be impiously blind and ungrateful,) that through the great mercy of God, the matter is so far amended, that many hundred drunken, swearing, ignorant, negligent, scandalous ministers are cast out; and we have many humble, godly, painful teachers in a county for a few that we had before. This is so visibly true, that when the godly are feasted, who formerly were almost famished, and beaten for going abroad to beg their bread, you can hardly by all your arguments or rhetoric persuade them that the times are no better with them than they were; though men of another nation may possibly believe you in such reports. I bless God for the change that I see in this county; and among the people, even in my own charge, which is such as will not permit me to believe that the case is as bad with them as formerly it hath been. I say, with Minutius Fœlix, p. 401, (mihi,) *Quid ingrati sumus? quid nobis invidemus? Si veritas divinitatis nostri temporis ætate maturuit. Fruamur nostro bono: Et vecii sententiam temperemus: cohibeatur superstitio: impietas expietur: religio servetur.* It is the sinful unhappiness of some men's minds, that they can hardly think well of the best words or ways of those whom they disaffect; and they usually disaffect those that cross them in their corrupt proceedings, and plainly tell them of their faults. And they are ready to judge of the reprover's spirit by their own, and to think that all such sharp reproofs proceed from some disaffection to their persons, or partial opposition to the opinions which they hold; and therefore they will seldom regard the reproofs of any but those of their own party, who will seldom deal plainly with them, because they are of their party. But plain dealers are always approved in the end; and the time is at hand when you shall confess, that those were your truest friends. He that will deal plainly against your sins in uprightness and honesty, will deal as plainly for you against the sins of any that would injure you: for he speaks not against sin, because it is *yours*, but because it is *sin*. It is an observable passage that is reported by many, and printed by one, how the late King Charles, who by the bishops' instigation had kept Mr. Prynne so long in prison, and twice cropt his ears, for writing against their masks and plays, and the high and hard proceedings of the prelates, when he read his notable, voluminous speech for an acceptance of the king's concessions, and an agreement with him thereupon, did, not long before his death, deliver the book to a friend that stood by him, saying, Take this book; I give it thee as a legacy; and believe it, this gentleman is the Cato of the age. The time will come when plain dealing will have a better construction than it hath, while prejudice doth turn the heart against it.

I shall stand no longer on the apologetical part: I think the foregoing objections being answered, there is no great need of more of this. The title of the book itself is apologetical, which if I tell you not, I may well expect that some of my old ingenious interpreters should put another sense upon it. I pretend not to the sapience of *Gildas*, nor to the sanctity of *Salvian*, as to the degree; but by their names I offer you an excuse for plain dealing. If it was used in a much greater measure by men so wise and holy as these, why should it in a lower measure be disallowed in another? At least from hence I have this encouragement, that the plain dealing of Gildas and Salvian being so much approved by us now they are dead, how much soever they might be despised or hated while they were living, by them whom they did reprove, at the worst I may expect some such success in times to come.

But my principal business is yet behind. I must now take the boldness, brethren, to become your monitor, concerning some of the necessary duties of which I have spoken in the ensuing discourse. If any of you should charge me with arrogancy or immodesty, for this attempt, as if hereby I accused you of negligence, or judged myself sufficient to admonish you, I crave your candid interpretation of my boldness, assuring you that I obey not the counsel of my flesh herein, but displease myself as much as some of you; and had rather have the ease and peace of silence, if it would stand with duty and the church's good. But it is the mere necessity of the souls of men, and my desire of their salvation, and the prosperity of the church, which forceth me to this arrogancy and immodesty, if so it must be called. For who that hath a tongue can be silent, when it is for the honour of God, the welfare of his church, and the everlasting happiness of so many persons?

And the *first* and main matter which I have to propound to you is, Whether it be not the unquestionable duty of the generality of ministers, in these three nations, to set themselves presently to the work of catechising, and personal instructing all that are to be taught by them, who will be persuaded to submit thereunto? I need not here stand to prove it, having sufficiently done it in the following discourse. Can you think that holy wisdom will gainsay it? Will zeal for God, will delight in his service, or love to the souls of men gainsay it? (1.) That people must be taught the principles of religion, and matters of greatest necessity to salvation, is past doubt among us. (2.) And that they must be taught it in the most edifying, advantageous way, I hope we are agreed. (3.) And that personal conference, and examination, and instruction, hath many excellent advantages for their good, is beyond dispute, and afterward manifested. (4.) As also that personal instruction is commended to us by Scripture, and the practices of the servants of Christ, and approved by the godly of all ages, so far as I can find, without contradiction. (5.) It is past all doubt that we should perform this great duty to all the people, or as many as we can: for our love and care of their souls must extend to all. If there be a thousand or five hundred ignorant people in your parish, it is a poor discharge of your duty now and then occasionally to speak to some few of them, and let the rest alone in their ignorance, if you are able to afford them help. (6.) And it is as certain that so great a work as this is, should take up a considerable part of our time. (7.) And as certain is it, that all duties should be done in order, as far as may be, and therefore should have their appointed times. And if we are agreed to practise according to these commonly acknowledged truths, we need not differ upon any doubtful circumstances.

Object. We teach them in public; and how then are we bound to teach them man by man besides?

Answ. You pray for them in public: must you not also pray for them in private? Paul taught every man, and exhorted every man, and that both publicly, and from house to house, night and day with tears. The necessity and benefits afterward mentioned prove it to be your duty. But what need we add more, when experience speaks so loud? I am daily forced to admire how lamentably ignorant many of our people are, that have seemed diligent hearers of me these ten or twelve years, while I spoke as plainly as I was able to speak! Some know not that each person in the Trinity is God; nor that Christ is God and man; nor that he took his human nature into heaven; nor many the like necessary principles of our faith. Yea, some that come constantly to private meetings are grossly ignorant; whereas in one hour's familiar instruction of them in private, they seem to understand more, and better entertain it, than they did in all their lives before.

Object. But what obligation lieth on us to tie ourselves to certain days for the performance of this work?

Answ. This is like the libertines' plea against family prayer. They ask, where are we bound to pray morning and evening? Doth not the nature and end of the duty plainly tell you that an appointed time conduceth to the orderly successful performance of it? How can people tell when to come if the time be not made known? You will have a fixed day for a lecture, because people cannot else tell when to come without a particular notice for each day: and it is as necessary here, becase this must be a constant duty, as well as that.

Object. But we have many other businesses that sometimes may interrupt the course.

Answ. Weightier business may put by our preaching, even on the Lord's day, but we must not therefore neglect our constant observance ordinarily of that day: and so it is here. If you have so much greater business, that you cannot ordinarily have time to do the ministerial work, you should not undertake the office: for ministers are men separated to the gospel of Christ, and must give themselves wholly to these things.

Object. All the parish are not the church, nor do I take the pastoral charge of them, and therefore I am not satisfied that I am bound to take this pains with them.

Answ. I pass by the question, whether all the parish be to be taken for your church; because in some places it is so, and in others not. But let the negative be supposed: yet, (1.) The common maintenance which most receive, is for teaching the whole parish; though you be not obliged to take them all for a church. (2.) What need we look for a stronger obligation, than the common bond that lieth on all christians, to further the work of men's salvation, and the good of the church, and the honour of God, to the utmost of their power; together with the common bond that is on all ministers, to further these ends by ministerial teaching, to the utmost of their power? Is it a work so good, and apparently conducing to so great benefits to the souls of men, and yet can you perceive no obligation to the doing of it?

Object. But why may not occasional conference and instructions serve the turn?

Answ. I partly know what occasional conferences are, compared to this duty, having tried both. Will it satisfy you to deal with one person of twenty or forty, or a hundred, and to pass by all the rest? Occasional conferences fall out seldom, and but with few; and (which is worst of all) are seldom managed so thoroughly as these must be. When I speak to a man that cometh to me purposely on that business, he will better give me leave to examine him, and deal closely with him, than when it falls in on the by: and most occasional conferences fall out before others, where plain dealing will not be taken so well. But so much is said afterward to these and several other objections, that I shall add no more.

I do now, in the behalf of Christ, and for the sake of his church and the immortal souls of men, beseech all the faithful ministers of Christ, that they will presently and effectually fall upon this work. Combine for a unanimous performance of it, that may more easily procure the submission of your people. But if there should be found any so blind or vile as to oppose it, or dissent, God forbid that other ministers should because of that, forbear their duties. I am far from presuming to prescribe you rules or forms, or so much as to motion to you to tread in our steps, in any circumstances where a difference is tolerable; or to use the same catechism or exhortation as we do: only fall presently and closely to the work. If there should be any of so proud and malicious a mind, as to withdraw from so great a duty, because they would not seem to be our followers, or drawn to it by us, as they would have approved it if it had risen from themselves; I advise such, as they love their everlasting peace, to make out to Christ for a cure of such cankered minds; and let them know that this duty hath its rise neither from them nor us, but from the Lord; and is generally approved by the church: and for my part, let them, and spare not, tread me in the dirt, and let me be as vile in their eyes as they please, so they will but hearken to God and reason, and fall upon the work, that our hopes of a more common salvation of men, and of a true reformation of the church, may be revived. I must confess I find by some experience that this is the work that must reform indeed; that must expel our common prevailing ignorance; that must bow the stubborn hearts of men; that must answer their vain objections, and take off their prejudice; that must reconcile their hearts to faithful ministers, and help on the success of our public preaching; and must make true godliness a commoner thing, through the grace of God, which worketh by means. I find that we never took the rightest course to demolish the kingdom of darkness till now. I do admire at myself, how I was kept off from so clear and excellent a duty so long. But I doubt not but other men's case is as mine was. I was long convinced of it, but my apprehensions of the difficulties were too great, and my apprehensions of the duty too small; and so I was hindered long from the performance. I thought that the people would but have scorned it, and none but a few that had least need, would have submitted to it. And the thing seemed strange, and I staid till the people were better prepared; and I thought my strength would never go through with it, having so great burdens on me before; and thus I was long detained in delays, which I beseech the Lord of mercy to forgive. Whereas, upon trial, I find the difficulties almost nothing, save only extraordinary bodily weakness, to that which is imagined; and I find the benefits and comforts of the work to be such, as that I profess, I would not wish that I had forborne it for all the riches in the world (as for myself). We spend Monday and Tuesday from morning to almost night in the work; besides a chapelry, catechised by another assistant; taking about fifteen or sixteen families in a week, that we may go through the parish, which hath above eight hundred families, in a year; and I cannot say yet, that one family hath refused to come to me, nor but few persons excused and shifted it off. And I find more outward signs of success with most that come, than of all my public preaching to them. If you say, it is not so in most places: I answer, 1. I wish that be not much long of ourselves. 2. If some refuse your help, that will not excuse you for not affording it to them that would accept it. If you ask me what course I take for order and expedition; I have after told you: In a word, at the delivery of the catechisms, I take a catalogue of the persons of understanding in the parish; and the clerk goeth a week before to every family to tell them when to come, and at what hour; (one family at eight o'clock, the next at nine, and the next at ten, &c.) And I am forced by the number to deal with a whole family at once; but admit not any of another to be present (ordinarily).

Brethren, do I now invite you to this work without God, without the consent of all antiquity, without the consent of the reformed divines, or without the conviction of your own consciences? See what our late assembly speak occasionally, in the Directory, about the visitation of the sick: "It is the duty of the minister, not only to teach the people committed to his charge in public, but privately and particularly to admonish, exhort, reprove, and comfort them upon all seasonable occasions, so far as his time, strength, and personal safety will permit. He is to admonish them in time of health to prepare for death; and for that purpose, they are often to confer with their minister about the state of their souls, &c. Read this over again, and consider it. Hearken to God, if you would have peace of conscience. I am resolved to deal plain with you, if I displease you. It is an unlikely thing, that there should be a heart that is sincerely devoted to God in the breast of that man, that after advertisements and exhortations, will not resolve on so clear and great a duty as this is. As it is with our people in hearing the word, so it is with us in teaching. An upright heart is an effectual persuader of them to attend on God in the use of his ordinances; and an upright heart will as effectually persuade a minister to his duty: as a good stomach needs no arguments to draw it to a feast, nor will easily by any arguments be taken off: and as a child will love and obey his parents, though he could not answer a sophister that would persuade him to hate them; so I cannot conceive that he that hath one spark of saving grace, and so hath that love to God, and delight to do his will, which is in all the sanctified, should possibly be drawn to contradict or refuse such a work as this; except under the power of such a temptation as Peter was when he denied Christ, or when he dissuaded him from suffering, and heard a half excommunication, "Get thee behind me, Satan, thou art an offence unto me: for thou savourest not the things that be of God, but those that be of men," Matt. xvi. 22, 23. You have put your hand to the plough of God; you are doubly sanctified and devoted to him, as christians, and pastors; and dare you after this draw back and refuse his work? You see the work of reformation at a stand; and you are engaged by many obligations to promote it; and dare you neglect that means by which it must be done? Will you show your faces in a christian congregation, as ministers of the gospel, and there pray for a reformation; and pray for the conversion and salvation of your hearers, and the prosperity of the church; and when you have done, refuse to use means by which it must be done? I know that carnal wit will never want words and show of reason to gainsay that truth and duty which it abhors; it is easier now to cavil against duty than perform it; but stay the end before you pass your final judgment. Can you possibly make yourselves believe that you shall have a comfortable review of the neglects, or make a comfortable account of them unto God? I dare prognosticate, from the knowledge of the nature of grace, that all the godly ministers in England will make conscience of this duty, and address themselves to it; except those that by some extraordinary accident are disabled, or those that are under such temptations as aforesaid. I do not hopelessly persuade you to it; but take it for granted it will be done: and if any lazy, or jealous, or malicious hypocrites, do cavil against it, or hold off, the rest will not do so; but they will take the opportunity, and not resist the warnings of the Lord. And God will uncase the hypocrites ere long, and make them know to their sorrow what it was to play fast and loose with God. Woe to them, when they must be accountable for the blood of souls! The reasons which satisfy them here against duty, will then be manifested to be the effects of their folly, and to have proceeded radically from their corrupted wills and carnal interest. And (unless they be desperately blinded and seared to the death) their consciences will not own those reasons at a dying hour, which now they seem to own. Then they shall feel to their sorrow, that there is not that comfort to be had for a departing soul, in the review of such neglected duty, as there is to them that have wholly devoted themselves to the service of the Lord. I am sure my arguments for this duty will appear strongest at the last, whatever they do now. And again I say, I hope the time is even at hand, when it shall be as great a shame to a minister to neglect the private instructing and oversight of the flock, as it hath been to be a seldom preacher; for which men are justly sequestered and ejected. And if God have not so great a quarrel with us, as tendeth to a removal of the gospel, or at least to the blasting of its prosperity and success in the desired reformation, I am confident that this will shortly be. And if these lazy, worldly hypocrites were but quickened to their duty by a sequestering committee, you should see them stir more zealously than all arguments fetched from God and Scripture, from the reward or punishment, or from the necessity and benefits of the work, can persuade them to do. For even now, these wretched men, while they pretend themselves the servants of Christ, are asking, What authority we have for his work? And if we could but show them a command from the lord protector or council, it would answer their scruples, and put the business beyond dispute; as if they had a design to confirm the accusation of the papists, that their ministry only is divine, and ours dependeth on the will of men. Well! for those godly, zealous ministers of Christ, that labour in sincerity, and, denying their worldly interest and ease, do wholly devote themselves to God, I am confident there needs not much persuasion; there is somewhat within that will presently carry them to the work: and for the rest, let them censure this warning as subtlely as they can, they shall not hinder it from rising up against them in judgment, unless it be by true repentance and reformation.

And let me speak one word of this to you that are my dear fellow-labourers in this county, who have engaged yourselves to be faithful in this work. It is your honour to lead in sacred resolutions and agreements; but if any of you should be unfaithful in the performance, it will be your double dishonour. Review your subscribed Agreement, and see that you perform it with diligence and constancy. You have begun a happy work; such as will do more to the welfare of the church than many that the world doth make a greater stir about. God forbid now, that imprudence or negligence should frustrate all. For the generality of you, I do not much fear it; having so much experience of your fidelity in the other parts of your office. And if there be any found among you, that will shuffle over the work, and deal unfaithfully in this and other parts of your office, I take it for no just cause of reproach to us, that we accept of your subscription, when you offer to join with us. For catechising is a work not proper only to a minister; and we cannot forbid any to engage themselves to their unquestionable duty: but in our association for discipline we must be somewhat more scrupulous with whom we join. I earnestly beseech you all in the name of God, and for the sake of your people's souls, that you will not slightly slubber over this work; but do it vigorously and with all your might; and make it your great and serious business. Much judgment is required for the managing of it. Study therefore how to do it beforehand, as you study for your sermons. I remember how earnest I was with some of the last parliament, to have had them settle catechists in our assemblies; but truly I am not sorry that it took no effect, unless for a few of the larger congregations. For I perceive that all the life of the work, under God, doth lie in the prudent, effectual management in searching men's hearts, and setting home the saving truths: and the ablest minister is weak enough for this, and few of inferior place or parts would be found competent. For I fear nothing more, than that many ministers that preach well, will be found too unmeet for this work; especially to manage it with old, ignorant, dead-hearted sinners: and indeed if the ministers be not reverenced by the people, they will rather slight them and contest with them, than humbly learn and submit; how much more would they do so by inferior men! Seeing then the work is cast upon us, it is we that must do it, or else it must be undone; let us be up and doing with all our might, and the Lord will be with us. I can tell you one thing for your encouragement: It is a work that the enemies of the church and ministry do exceedingly vex at, and hate, and fear more than any thing that yet we have undertaken. I perceive the signs of the papists' indignation against it. And methinks it hath the most notable character of a work extraordinarily and unquestionably good; for they storm at it, and yet they have nothing to say against it. They cannot blame it, and yet they hate and fear it, and would fain undermine it, if they knew how. You know how many false rumours have been spread abroad this country, to deter the people from it: as that the lord protector and council were against it; that the subscribers were to be rejected; that the Agreement was to be publicly burnt, &c. And when we have searched after the authors, we can drive it no higher than the quakers, the papists' emissaries; from whom we may easily know their minds. And yet when a papist speaks openly as a papist, some of them have said that it is a good work; but that it wants authority, and is done by those that are not called to it: forsooth, because we have not the authority of their pope or prelates: and some that should be more sober have used the same language; as if they would rather have thousands and millions of souls neglected, without commission from a prelate. Yea, and some that differ from us about infant baptism, I understand repine at it; and say that we will hereby insinuate ourselves into the people, and hinder them from receiving the truth. A sad case, that any that seem to have the fear of God should have so true a character of a partial, dividing, and siding mind; as to grudge at the propagation of christianity itself, and the common truths which we are all agreed in, for fear lest it should hinder the propagation of their opinions. The common cause of christianity must give place to the cause of these lower controverted points; and they grudge us our labour and suffering for the common work, though there be nothing in it which meddleth with them, or which they are able with any show of reason to gainsay. I beseech you, brethren, let all this, and the many motives that I have after given you, persuade you to the greater diligence herein! When you are speaking to your people, do it with the greatest prudence and seriousness, and be as earnest with them as for life or death; and follow it as close as you do your public exhortations in the pulpit. I profess again, it is to me the most comfortable work, except public preaching, (for there I speak to more, though yet with less advantage to each one,) that ever I yet did set my hand to; and I doubt not but you will find it so to you, if you faithfully perform it.

Secondly. My second request to the reverend ministers in these nations is, that at last they would, without any more delay, unanimously set themselves to the practice of those parts of christian discipline which are unquestionably necessary, and part of their work. It is a sad case that good men under so much liberty, should settle themselves so long in the constant neglect of so great a duty. The common cry is, *Our people are not ready for it; they will not bear it.* But is not the meaning, that *you will not bear* the trouble and hatred which it will occasion? If indeed you proclaim our churches uncapable of the order and government of Christ, what do you but give up the cause to them that withdraw from them, and encourage men to look out for better societies where that discipline may be had? For though preaching and sacraments may be omitted in some cases, till a fitter season, and accordingly so may discipline be; yet is it a hard case to settle in a constant neglect, for so many years together as we have done, unless there were a flat impossibility of the work: and if it were so, because of our uncapable materials, it would plainly call us to alter our constitution, that the matter may be capable. I have spoke plainly afterward to you of this, which I hope you will bear, and conscionably consider of. I now only beseech you that would make a comfortable account to the chief Shepherd, and would not be found unfaithful in the house of God, that you do not wilfully or negligently delay it, as if it were a needless thing; nor shrink not from the duty because of trouble to the flesh that doth attend it: for as that is too sad a sign of hypocrisy, so the costliest duties are usually the most comfortable; and be sure that Christ will bear the cost. I could here produce a heap of testimonies, of fathers and reformed divines, that charge this duty with great importunity. I shall only now give you the words of two of the most godly, laborious, judicious divines, that most ever the church of Christ had since the days of the apostles.

Calvin. Institut. lib. 4. cap. xii. sec. 1, 2. *Sed quia nonnulli in odium disciplinæ ab ipso quoque, nomine abhorrent, hi sic habeant: Si nulla societas, imo nulla domus quæ vel modicam familiam habeat, contineri in recto statu sine disciplina potest: Eam esse multo magis necessariam in ecclesia, cujus statum quam ordinatissimum esse decet. Proinde quemadmodum salvifica Christi doctrina anima est ecclesiæ, ita illic disciplina pro nervis est: qua fit ut membra corporis, suo quæque loco inter se cohæreant. Quamobrem quicunque vel sublatam disciplinam cupiunt, vel ejus impediunt restitutionem, sive hoc faciant data opera, sive per incogitantiam, ecclesiæ certe extremam dissipationem quærunt. Quid enim futurum est, si unicuique liceat quod libuerit? Atqui id fieret nisi ad doctrinæ prædicationem accederent privatæ monitiones, correctiones, et alia ejusmodi adminicula quæ doctrinam sustinent et otiosam esse non sinunt. Disciplina igitur veluti frænum est, quo retineantur et domentur qui adversus Christi doctrinam ferociunt: vet tanquam stimulus quo excitentur parum voluntarii: interdum etiam velut paterna ferula, qua clementer et pro Spiritus Christi mansuetudine castigentur, qui gravius lapsi sunt. Quum ergo jam imminere cernamus initia quædam horrendæ in ecclesia vastitatis, ex eo quod nulla est cura, nec ratio continendi populi, ipsa necessitas clamat remedio opus esse. Porro hoc unicum remedium est quod et Christus præcipit, et semper usitatum inter pios fuit. 2. Primum disciplinæ fundamentum est, ut privatæ monitiones locum habeant: hoc est, siquis officium sponte non faciat aut insolenter se gerat, aut minus honeste vivat, aut aliquid admiserit reprehensione dignum, ut patiatur se moneri: atque ut quisque fratrem suum, dum res postulabit, monere studeat. Præsertim vero in hoc advigilent pastores ac presbyteri, quorum partes sunt non modo concionari ad populum, sed per singulas domos monere et exhortari, sicubi universali doctrina non satis profecerint: quemadmodum docet Paulus, quum refert se docuisse privatim et per domos: et se munaum a sanguine omnium attestatur, quia non cessaverit cum lachrymis nocte et die monere unumquemque.* See the rest. And sec. 4, he adds of the necessity; *Sine hoc disciplinæ vinculo qui diu stare posse ecclesias confidunt, opinione fallantur: nisi forte carere impune possimus eo adminiculo, quod Dominus fore nobis necessarium providit.* Et sec. 5. *Atque hic quoque, habenda est cœnæ Dominicæ ratio, ne promiscua exhibitione profanetur. Verissimum est enim eum, cui comissa est dispensatio, si sciens ac volens indignum admiserit quem repellere jure poterat, proinde reum esse sacrilegii acsi corpus Domini canibus prostituerit.*

Hier. Zanchius de Ecclesia, vol. 3. fo. 123, 124. *(Disciplina) est actio qua ecclesia, secundum facultatem sibi a Christo traditam fideles suos non solum publice, sed etiam privatim, tam in vero Dei cultu quam in bonis moribus, idque tum doctrina, tum correctionibus, tum ecclesiasticis pœnis et censuris, tum etiam si opus sit excommunicationibus instituit et institutos retinet.* Fol. 124. *Primo habet privatam doctrinam. Habet enim ecclesia potestatem, si publica doctrina in publico templo non sufficiat, privatas fidelium domos ingrediendi; atque ibi eos privatim docendi, ac in vera doctrina ac religione christiana instituendi: et fideles pati debent ut pastor suas ædes ingrediatur, et eos privatim instituat. Hujus exemplum est,* in Acts xx. &c. *Idem fecerunt reliqui apostoli. 2. Habet privatas admonitiones, correctiones, objurgationes, &c.* This is for private teaching: now for the sacrament, hear what he saith, ibid. fol. 79. *Obj. Manebimus in ecclesia, audiemus verbum, &c. sed qui possumus in cœna communionem vobiscum habere, cum ad eam admittantur multi impuri, ebrii, avari, &c. Resp.* 1. *Quantum ad hos peccatores, eos intelligi posse bifariam; vel qui ante fuerunt ebrii, &c. Sed postea resipuerunt. Hos dicimus secundum verbum Domini non esse excludendos a mensa Domini, quandoquidem vera penitentia et fide præditi sunt: vel eos qui etiamnum ebrietati student, aliisque vitiis, et talis sine pœnitentia et fide accedunt: hos dicimus simpliciter non esse admittendos. Quod autem admittantur plerumque hoc contingere potest bifariam: vel ex ignorantia ministrorum, eo quod non agnoverint tales esse, quales sunt: Et hanc certe ignorantiam, non probamus, quoniam debet minister agnoscere, qualesnam sint illi quibus cœnam Domini administrat: quod si ignorat, non potest non accusari supinæ et reprehendæ negligentiæ, &c. Aut cum sint omnibus noti qualesnam sint, non student tamen eos arcere præ timore, vel aliquo alio humano respectu. Hoc damnamus in ministro vitium timiditatis. Debet enim minister Christi esse cordatissimus et heroicus. Sed hic non est spectandum quid unus aut alter vilis minister agat* (mark the title) *sed quæ sit ecclesiæ institutio, quæque communis in omnibus ecclesiis consuetudo: in omnibus autem ecclesiis nostris antequam cœna ministretur, omnibus hujusmodi, interdicitur, &c. Et certo magnum est probrum, quod inter filios Dei locum habeant et porci et canes: Multo vero magis, si illis prostituuntur sacro-sancta cœnæ Dominicæ symbola, &c. Quare ecclesiæ Christi non debent hujusmodi sceleratos in sinu suo ferre, nec ad sacrum cœnam dignos simul et indignos promiscue admittere: id quod plerumque sit in ecclesiis nostris.*" (How many were then the *viles ministri!)*

But the principal is behind, of the necessity of discipline: and I desire both magistrates and ministers, into whose hands these lines shall fall, to read and consider it.

Ibid. fol. 134, 135. *Videant igitur principes et magistratus qui hanc disciplinam in ecclesiam restitutam nolunt, quid agant. Hæc instituta est à Christo, ut perpetuo in ecclesia tanquam singularis thesaurus conservetur: ergo qui eam exulare volunt, sciant se velle Christum exulare. Hæc pars est evangelii Jesu Christi. Ergo qui hanc restitutam nolunt, sciant eo nolle evangelium Christi, sicut debet, restitutum. Quomodo igitur gloriamur restitutum esse evangelium in ecclesiis nostris, si hanc eamque non postremam partem evangelii restitutam nolumus? Hac vitia corriguntur; virtutes promoventur: Ergo qui hanc disciplinam restitutam nolunt, quomodo audent dicere se vitia odisse, virtutum vero amantes esse, pietatis promotores, impietatis osores. Hac conversatur et regitur ecclesia, singulæque ecclesiæ membra sua quæque loco cohærent: ergo quomodo qui hanc expulsam, volunt dicunt se velle Christi ecclesiam bene rectam, siquando sine hac bene regi non potest. Si nulla domus, nullum oppidum; nulla urbs, nulla respublica, nullum regnum, imo ne exiguus quidem ludus literarius, sine disciplina regi potest, quomodo poterit ecclesia?* I would magistrates would read the rest, which is purposely to them.

Et fol. 135. *At timetur seditio et tumultus. Resp. Ergo neque evangelium est prædicandum, &c. Quid: Annon vident principes et magistratus nostri quantum malum in ecclesia oriatur, et intus et foris ex neglectu contemptuve hujus disciplinæ? Foris nulla res est, quæ magis papistas et alios arceat, vel saltem retrudet amplectendo evangelio, atque hæc disciplinæ ecclesiasticæ destitutio, quæ est in ecclesiis nostris. Intus, nihil quod magis alat vitia, hæreses, &c. Annon vident ecclesias suas principes plenas sectis hæreticorum, et impurorum hominum? Ad has confluit omne genus hominum fanaticorum, impurorum, &c. tanquam ad asylum. Quare? Quia ibi nulla disciplina.*

Sciant ergo principes, et quicunque illi sint qui disciplinam ecclesiasticam in ecclesiis restitutam nolunt, sed ei adversantur, eamque proscribunt, se Christo adversari: Qui ministros impediunt ne eam exerceant, se Christum et Deum impedire, ne sua fungantur potestate. Quid enim agunt ministri cum excommunicant? Pronunciant sententiam Domini. Ait enim Christus: Quicquid ligaveritis in terris, &c. Quid igitur agunt qui impediunt ecclesiam ne sententiam Domini pronunciet? Peccant contra Christum, et rei sunt læsæ Divinæ Majestatis. Annon reus esset læsæ majestatis Cesareæ, siquis ejus judicem ne sententiam Cæsaris pronunciet impediat? Videant igitur quid agant. Hactenus Christus rexit ecclesiam suam hac disciplina; et ipsi principes, imo et ministri aliqui, nolunt eam sic regi? Viderint ipsi. Pronuncio, proclamo, protestor, eos peccare, qui cum possint et debeant eam restituere, non restituunt.

I hope both magistrates and ministers that are guilty, will give me leave to say the like with Zanchy; if not to call them traitors against the majesty of God, that hinder discipline, and adversaries to Christ, yet at least to pronounce, proclaim, protest that they sin against God, who set it not up when they may and ought. But what if the magistrate will not help us? Nay, what if he were against it? So he was for about three hundred years, when discipline was exercised in the primitive church. To this Zanchy adds, ib. *Ministri ecclesiæ quantum per consensum et pacem ecclesiæ licet hanc disciplinam exercere debetis. Hanc enim potestatem vobis dedit Dominus, neque quispiam auferre eam potest: nec contenti esse debetis ut doceatis quid agendum, quid fugiendum sit, utut quisque pro sua libidine vivat nihil curantes, sed urgenda disciplina.* Vid. August. de Fide et Operib. c. 4. *Obj. At impedimur per magistratum. Resp. Tunc illi significate quam male agat*, &c. Read the rest of the solid advice that Calvin and Zanchy in the forecited places do give both to ministers and people, where discipline is wanting.

The great objection that seemeth to hinder some from this work is, because we are not agreed yet who it is that must do it? whether a prelate, or whether a presbytery, or a single pastor, or the people?

Answ. Let so much be exercised as is out of doubt. 1. It is granted that a single pastor may expound and apply the word of God: he may rebuke a notorious sinner by name. He may make known to the church that God hath commanded them, with such a one, no not to eat! and require them to obey this command, &c. I shall say no more of this now, than to cite the words of two learned, godly, moderate divines, impartial in this cause. The one is Mr. Lyford, a maintainer of episcopacy, in his "Legacy of Admission to the Lord's Supper;" who, page 55, saith,

"*Quest.* 1. In which of the ministers is this power placed?

"*Answ.* Every minister hath the power of all Christ's ordinances to dispense the same in that congregation or flock, over which the Holy Ghost hath made him overseer; yet with this difference: he may preach the word, baptize, and administer the holy supper alone of himself without the assistance or consent of the people; but not excommunicate alone *(he means not without the people, though of that more must be said);* because excommunication doth presuppose an offence to the congregation, a conviction and proof of that offence, and witnesses of the party's obstinacy: and therefore hereunto is required the action of more than one, &c. Excommunication compriseth several acts: admonition, private, public: the last act is, the casting out of a wicked, obstinate person from the society of the faithful. (1.) By the authority of Christ. (2.) Dispensed and executed by the ministers of the gospel. (3.) With the assistance and consent of the congregation, &c. 2. If you ask by whose office and ministry this sentence is denounced? I answer, By ministers of the gospel; we bind and loose doctrinally, in our preaching peace to the godly, and curses to the wicked: but in excommunication, we denounce the wrath of God against this or that particular person (thou art the man! thou hast no part with us): and that not only declaratively, but judicially. It is like the sentence of a judge on the bench, &c. 3. If you ask whether this be done by the minister alone? I answer, No; it must be done by the assistance and consent of the congregation, 1 Cor. v. 4. Excommunication must not be done in a corner, by the chancellor and his register, &c. But whosoever doth, by his offences, lose his right to the holy things of God, he must lose it in the face of the congregation; and that after proofs and allegations, as is abovesaid: the people hear and see the offence, complain of it, and are grieved at his society with them, and judge him worthy to be cast out. This concurrence and consent being supposed, every minister is *episcopus gregis*, a bishop in his own parish, (N. B.) "To all the flock over which the Holy Ghost hath made you ἐπισκόπους, *overseers*," Acts xx. 28. And, "Remember them which have the rule over you, who have spoken to you the word of God," Heb. xiii. 17. Where note, (1.) That they who preach the word of God, must rule and govern the church; and every preacher is a ruler, unto whom the people must submit, ver. 17. Besides, every minister is vested with this authority at his ordination: Whose sins thou dost forgive, they are forgiven: whose sins thou dost retain,' &c. (2.) Every minister is vested with this authority by the laws of this land. The words of the Rubric for the Administration of the Lord's Supper, which do enable us thereto, are these: 'If any of those which intend to be partakers of the holy communion, be an open, notorious evil liver, so that the congregation by him is offended, or have done wrong to his neighbours by word or deed, the curate having knowledge thereof, shall call him, and advertise him in any wise not to come to the Lord's table, until he have openly declared himself to be truly repented and amended of his former naughty life; that the congregation may thereby be satisfied, which afore was offended; and that he have recompensed the parties whom he hath done wrong to; or at least, declare himself to be in full purpose so to do as soon as he conveniently may.' Besides this, our authority in this particular is confirmed by an ordinance of the Lords and Commons in Parliament," &c. So far Mr. Lyford's words.

The other is of Mr. Thomas Ball, of Northampton, in his late book for the ministry; where (part iii. chap. 4) he bringeth many arguments to prove it the minister's duty to exercise discipline as well as to preach; and the seventh argument is this:

"What was given by the bishops unto such ministers as they ordained, and laid their hands upon, should not be grudged or denied them by any body: for they were never accounted lavish or over liberal to them, especially in point of jurisdiction; that was always a very tender point, and had a guard and sentry always on it. For conceiving themselves the sole possessors of it, they were not willing to admit partners. Whatever they indulged in other points, as Pharaoh to Joseph, 'Only in the throne I will be greater than thou;' yet bishops granted to all that they ordained presbyters, the use and exercise of discipline as well as doctrine; as appears in the book of Ordering Bishops, Priests, and Deacons, whereof the interrogatories propounded to the party to be ordained is, 'Will you then give your faithful diligence always so to minister the doctrine and sacraments, and the discipline of Christ, as the Lord hath commanded, and as this realm hath received the same according to the commandments of God, so that you may teach the people committed to your care and charge, with all diligence to keep and observe the same:' which a reverend and learned brother not observing, would confine all jurisdiction to diocesan bishops, &c. *Arg.* 8. What is granted and allowed to ministers, by the laws and customs of this nation, cannot reasonably be denied: for the laws of England have never favoured usurpation in the clergy, &c. But the laws and customs of this nation allow to the ministers of England the use and exercise of discipline as well as doctrine; for such of them as have parsonages or rectories, are in all processes and proceedings called rectors," &c.

2. And as to the points of the people's interest, the moderate seem to differ but in words. Some say the people are to govern by vote: I confess if this were understood as it is spoken, according to the proper sense of the words, and practised accordingly, it were contrary to the express commands of Scripture, which command the elders to rule well, and the people to obey them as their rulers, in the Lord: and it seems to me to be destructive to the being of a political church, whose constitutive parts are the *ruling* and the *ruled* parts; as every school consisteth of master and scholars, and every commonwealth of the *pars imperans et pars subdita:* and therefore those that rigidly stick to this, do cast out themselves from all particular political churches' communion of Christ's institution. (Which because I have formerly said, or somewhat to that purpose, a late nameless writer makes me cruel to his party, while I seem for them, and so self-contradicting: as if it were sin to tell a brother of his sin, and not to leave him; or, as if I understood not myself, because he understands me not!) But I perceive the moderate mean not any such things as these words, in their proper sense, import. They only would have the church ruled as a free people, (as from unjust impositions,) and in a due subordination to Christ. And we are all agreed that the pastors have the *judicium directionis*, the teaching, directing power, by office; and that the people have *judicium discretionis;* and must try his directions, and not obey them when they lead to sin: and therefore we cannot expect that the people should execute any of our directions, except their judgment lead them to execute them. (Though if their judgment be wrong, God requireth them to rectify it.) And as for the *judicial decisive power*, about which there is so great contending, in the strictest sense, it is the prerogative of Christ, and belongeth to neither of them: for only Christ is proper lawgiver and judge of the church, whose law and judgment is absolute, of itself determinative, and not subjected to our trial of its equity or obligation. So that we must as much conclude, that there is no final judge of controversies in a particular church, as we do against the papists, that there is none in the church in general. And therefore the church's judicial decisive power is but improperly such, reducible to the former; which seeing we are agreed in, we are as far in sense agreed in this. A pastor is judge, as a physician in an hospital, or as Plato or Zeno was in his school, or any tutor in a college of voluntary students. For any more, it belongeth to Christ, and to the magistrate. Why then do we stand quarrelling about the name? One saith, *the people have a power of liberty, and the ministers only the power of authority.* And what is this more than we yield them; viz. That the guiding authority being only in the guides, and the people commanded to obey them in a due subordination to Christ, there is a liberty belonging to all the saints; from any other kind of ministerial rule, that is, from a *sic volo, sic jubeo*, a rule without divine authority: and therefore the people must first try and judge, whether the direction be according to God, and so obey: and this in church censures as well as in other places. So that, (1.) As the people ought not to dissent or disobey their guides, unless they lead them to sin; (and therefore must see a danger of sin before they suspend obedience;) so, (2.) The guides cannot bring the people to execute their censures or directions, but by procuring their consent. And therefore though he must do his duty, and may pass his directive censure though they dissent, and ministerially require them in the name of the Lord, *e. g.* to avoid a notorious, obstinate offender, and so to obey the command of God; that is, though we may charge them in the name of the Lord to consent and obey, and do their duty; yet, if their judgments remain unconvinced in a case which is to them obscure, we have no more to do, but satisfy ourselves that we have done our duty. So that when we have quarrelled never so long, what is it but the people's *consent* that the moderate men on one side require? and *consent* the other side requireth also. Call it what else you will, whether a government, or an authority, or a liberty; consent is the thing which both require! And are we not then in the matter agreed? Peruse for this Mr. Lyford's words before cited. See also what the leading men for presbyterian government do not only acknowledge, but maintain as effectually as others: as Dav. Blondel-

lus de Jure plebis in Regim Eccles. Calvin. Institut. lib. 4. cap. xii. sec. 4. *Ne quis tale judicium spernat, aut parvi æstimet se fidelium suffragiis damnatum, testatus est Dominus*, &c. Ita Zanchius ubi sup. and many more. Indeed this consent of the people is not *sine qua non* to the pastor's performance of his own part; viz. Charging the church in Christ's name to avoid the communion of such a notorious, obstinate offender, and suspending his own acts towards him; and so charging them to receive the innocent or penitent. (For, if the people consent not to avoid such, and so would exclude all discipline, yet the pastor must charge it unto them, and do his part.) But it is *sine qua non* to their actual rejecting and avoiding that offender. In a word, we must teach them their duty, and require it; and they and we must obey and do it: and neither they nor we may oblige any to sin.

Object. But we are not agreed about the matter of the church that must be governed.

Answ. Peruse the qualifications required in church members in the writings of the moderate on both sides, and see what difference you can find! Are both agreed, that professors of true faith and holiness, cohabiting and consenting, are a true church? And when they contradict that profession by wicked actions, (doctrine or life,) they are to be dealt with by discipline. Though I confess in our practice we much differ; most that I know running into one of the extremes of looseness or rigour.

Thirdly, My third and last request is, that all the faithful ministers of Christ would, without any more delay, unite and associate for the furtherance of each other in the work of the Lord, and the maintaining of unity and concord in his churches. And that they would not neglect their brotherly meetings to those ends; nor yet spend them unprofitably: but improve them to their edification, and the effectual carrying on the work. Read that excellent letter of Edmond Grindal, archbishop of Canterbury, to Queen Elizabeth, for ministerial meeting and exercises (such bishops would have prevented our contentions and wars): you may see it in Fuller's New History of the Church of England.

And let none draw back, that accord in the substantials of faith and godliness; yea, if some should think themselves necessitated, I will not say to schism, lest I offend them; but to separate in public worship from the rest: methinks if they be indeed christians, they should be willing to hold so much communion with them as they can, and to consult how to manage their differences to the least disadvantage to the common truths and christian cause; which they profess to own and prefer.

And here I may not silently pass by an uncharitable slander, which some brethren, of the prelatical judgment, have divulged of me far and near; viz. That while I persuade men to accommodation, it was long of me that the late proclamation or ordinance was procured for silencing all sequestered ministers, viz. by the late Worcestershire petition, which they say was the occasion of it; and they falsely report that I altered it after the subscription. To which I say, (1.) It was the petition of many justices, and the grand jury, and thousands of the country, as well as me. (2.) There is not a word in it, nor ever was, against any godly man; but only that the notoriously insufficient and scandalous should not be permitted to meddle with mysteries of Christ (especially the sacraments); which we desire should have impartially extended to all parties alike. And so much of this as was granted, we cannot but be thankful for, whosoever grudge at it; and wish it had been fully granted. (3.) I desire nothing more, than that all able, godly, faithful ministers, of what side soever, in our late state differences, may not only have liberty, but encouragement; for the church hath not any such to spare, were they ten times more. In a word, I would have those, of what party soever, to have liberty to preach the gospel, whose errors or miscarriages are not so great, as that probably they will do as much hurt as good.

Brethren, I crave your pardon for the infirmities of this address; and earnestly longing for the success of your labours, I shall daily beg of God, that he would persuade you to those duties which I have here requested you to perform, and would preserve and prosper you therein, against all the serpentine subtlety and rage that is now engaged to oppose and hinder you.

Your unworthy fellow-servant,

April 15, 1656. RICH. BAXTER.

TO THE LAY-READER.

THE reason why I have called this volume *the first part* of the book is, because I intend, if God enable me, and give me time, a *second part;* containing the duty of the people in relation to their pastors; and therein show, 1. The right and necessity of a ministry. 2. The way to know which is the true church and ministry; and how we justify our own calling to this office; and how false prophets and teachers must be discerned. 3. How far people must assist pastors in the gospel, and the pastors put them on, and make use of them to that end. And, 4. How far the people must submit to their pastors, and what other duty they must perform in that relation. But because my time and strength are so uncertain, that I know not whether I may live to publish my yet imperfect preparations on this subject; I dare not let this first part come into your hands, without a word of caution and advice, lest you should misunderstand or misapply it.

The caution that I must give you, is in two parts.

1. Entertain not any unworthy thoughts of your pastors, because we here confess our own sins, and aggravate them in order to our humiliation and reformation. You know it is men and not angels that are put by God in the office of church guides; and you know that we are imperfect men: let papists and quakers pretend to a sinless prefection; we dare not do it; but confess that we are sinners. And we should heartily rejoice to find the signs of imperfect sincerity, in them that so confidently pretend to sinless perfection: yea, if in some of them we could find but common honesty, and a freedom from some of the crying abominations of the ungodly, such as a cruel bloodiness, lying, slandering, railing, &c. If it would make a man

perfect, to say he is perfect; and if it would deliver a man from sin, to say, I have no sin; I confess this were an easy way to perfection.

There is one Richard Farnworth, called a quaker, that hath lately published a pamphlet against our Agreement for Catechising; and the substance of it is this: because we confess, that by neglecting that work of the Lord, we have sinned, and do beg pardon of our miscarriages; and say, that by nature we are children of wrath, and prone to do evil, &c.; therefore he will prove us deceivers, and no ministers of Christ; as from our own confession. As if they that are dead by nature, may not be made alive by grace! And as if *are* is not as proper a term as *were*, when we speak of the state of mankind in their natural condition, wherein the most do still abide! And as if the confessing our sin would prove us to be ungodly! O shameless men! God saith, He that confesseth and forsaketh his sin shall have mercy. And the quaker maketh it a matter of his reproach. John saith, if we confess, he is faithful and just to forgive: and the quaker maketh it a sign that we are not forgiven. God will not forgive us, if we refuse to confess; and the quaker makes us unpardoned, because we do it. What would this wretch have said to David, Ezra, Nehemiah, Daniel, &c. if he had lived in their days, who made such full confessions of their sins? God hit them not in the teeth with them, but the quakers will! Christ did forgive even Peter's denial of him; but it seems the quaker would have condemned him for the penitent lamenting of it. Is Paul damned for confessing himself the chief of sinners? ("of whom I am chief," 1 Tim. i. 15.) And that formerly he was a persecutor, blasphemer, &c.? Or because he saith, Eph. iii. 8, "Unto me who am less than the least of saints? Or for crying out, "O wretched man that I am! who shall deliver me from the body of this death? What I would that I do not, and what I hate that do I. I find a law that when I would do good, evil is present with me," &c.? Rom. vii. 24, 15, 21. Or is Isaiah a wicked man, and no prophet of God, for saying, Woe is me! I am undone, because I am a man of unclean lips," &c.? Isa. vi. 5. Or Jacob, for saying, Gen. xxxii. 10, "I am not worthy of the least of all thy mercies," &c.? Or Job, for abhorring himself in dust and ashes? Job xlii. 6. It irketh me to spend words upon such impudent revilers! But in this much you have sufficient reply to his book.

But for our parts we believe, that he that saith he hath "no sin, deceiveth himself, and the truth is not in him," 1 John i. 8. "And that in many things we offend all," Jam. iii. 2. And we profess to know but in part, and to have our treasure in earthen vessels, and to be insufficient for these things. And therefore see that you love and imitate the holiness of your pastors, but take not occasion of disesteeming or reproaching them for their infirmities.

2. I take it to be my duty as a watchman for your souls, to give you notice of a train that is laid for your perdition. The papists, who have found that they could not play their game here with open face, have masked themselves, and taken the vizards of several sects; and by the advantage of the licence of the times, are busily at work abroad this land, to bring you back to Rome. What names or garb soever they bear, you may strongly conjecture which be they by these marks following: (1.) Their main design is to unsettle you, and make you believe that you have been all this while misled, and to bring you to a loss in a matter of religion; that when they have made you dislike or suspect that which you had, (or seemed to have,) you may be more respective of theirs. (2.) To which end their next means is to bring you to suspect first, and then to contend and reject your teachers. For, saith Rushworth, one of their writers, "Not one of ten among the people, indeed, do ground their faith on the Scripture, but on the credit of their teachers," &c. therefore they think, if they can bring you to suspect your teachers, and so to reject them, they may deal with the sheep without the shepherds, and dispute with the scholars without their teachers, and quickly make you say what they list. To this end their design is partly to cry them down as false teachers; (but how are they baffled when it comes to the proof!) and partly to persuade you that they have no calling to the work; and urge them to prove their calling; (which how easily can we do!) and partly to work upon your covetous humour, by crying down tithes, and all established maintenance for the ministry. And withal they are busy yet in contriving to procure the governors of the nation, to withdraw their public countenance and maintenance, and sacrilegiously to deprive the church of the remnant that is devoted to it for God, and to leave the ministry on equal terms with themselves or all other sects (which in Spain, Italy, France, &c. they will be loth to do). And time will show you, whether God will suffer them to prevail with the governors of this sinful land, to betray the gospel into their hands, or not? But we have reason to hope for better things. (3.) Their next design, is to diminish the authority and sufficiency of Scripture; and because they dare not yet speak out, to tell us what they set up in its stead: some of them will tell you of new prophets and revelations; and some of them will tell you, that in that they are yet at a loss themselves, that is, they are of no religion; and then are no christians. I shall now proceed no further in the discovery; but only warn you, as you love your souls, keep close to Scripture and a faithful ministry; and despise not your shepherds if you would escape the wolves. If any question our calling, send them to our writings, where we have fully proved them; or send them to us, who are ready to justify them against any papist or heretic upon earth. And let me tell you, that for all the sins of the ministry which we have here confessed, the known world hath not a more able, faithful, godly ministry than Britain hath at this day. If at the Synod of Dort the Clerus Anglicanus was called *stupor mundi*, before all those ignorant and scandalous ones were cast out; what may we now call it? Brethren, let me deal free with you! The ungrateful contempt of a faithful ministry is the shame of the faces of thousands in this land! And if thorough repentance prevent it not, they shall better know in hell whether such ministers were their friends or foes, and what they would have done for them, if their counsel had been heard. When "the messengers of God were mocked, and his words despised, and his prophets abused, the wrath of the Lord arose on the Israelites themselves; and there was no remedy," 2 Chron. xxxvi. 16. Shall ministers study, preach, and pray for you, and shall they be despised? When they have the God of heaven and their conscience to witness, that they desire not yours but you, and are willing to spend and be spent for your sakes; and all the wealth in the world would not be regarded by them in comparison of your salvation, and that all their labours and sufferings are for your sake; if they will be requited with your contempt, or scorn, or discouraging unteachableness, see who will prove the losers in the end. When God himself shall justify them with a *Well done, good and faithful servant;* let those that reproached, despised, and condemned them, defend their faces from shame, and their consciences from the accusations of their

horrid ingratitude, as well as they can! Read the Scriptures and see, whether they that obey God's messengers, or they that despise and disobey them, speed best. And if any of the seducers will tell you that we are not the ministers of Christ; leave them not till they tell you which is his true church and ministry, and where they are? and by that time they have well answered you, you may know more of their minds.

3. My last advice to you is this: See that you obey your faithful teachers, and improve their help for your salvation while you have it; and take heed that you refuse not to learn when they would teach you. And in particular, see that you refuse not to submit to them in this duty of private instruction, which is mentioned in this treatise. Go to them when they desire you, and be thankful for their help. Yea, and at other times when you need their advice, go to them of your own accord, and ask it. Their office is to be your guides in the way of life: if you seek not their direction, it seems you despise salvation itself, or else you are so proud as to think yourselves sufficient to be your own directors. Shall God in mercy send you leaders to teach you and conduct you in the way to glory; and will you stoutly send them back, or refuse their assistance, and say, We have no need of their direction? Is it for their own ease or gain that they trouble you, or is it for your own everlasting gain? Remember that Christ hath said to his messengers, "He that despiseth you, despiseth me." If your obstinate refusal of the instruction do put them to bear witness against you in judgment, and to say, Lord, I would have taught these ignorant sinners, and admonished these impenitent wretches, but they would not so much as come to me, nor speak with me! look you to it, and answer it as you can: for my part, I would not be in your case for all the world! But I shall say no more to you on this point, but only desire you to read and consider the exhortation, which is published in our Agreement itself, which speaks to you more fully; and if you read this book, remember the duty which you find to belong to the ministers doth show also what belongs to yourselves: for it cannot be our duty to teach, catechise, advise, &c. if it be not yours to hear, learn, and seek advice. If you have any temptation to question our office, read the London ministers' Jus Divinum Minister. Evang.; and Mr. Thomas Ball's book for the ministry. If you doubt of the duty of learning the principles, and being catechised, read the London ministers' late exhortation to catechising; and Mr. Zach. Crofton's book for Catechising (now newly published).

April 16th, 1656. RICHARD BAXTER.

Dr. H. Hammond, Of the Power of the Keys, cap. 4. sect. 104. p. 113.

"Nay, thirdly, there will be little matter of doubt or controversy, but that private, frequent, spiritual conference betwixt fellow-christians, but especially (and in matters of high concernment and difficulty) between the presbyter and those of his charge, even in the time of health; and peculiarly that part of it which is spent in the discussion of every man's special sins, and infirmities, and inclinations, may prove very useful and advantageous (in order to spiritual directions, reproof, and comfort) to the making the man of God perfect. And to tell truth, if the pride and self-conceit of some, and wretchlessness of others, the bashfulness of the third sort, the nauseating and instant satiety of any good in a fourth, the follies of men, and the artifices of Satan, has not put this practice quite out of fashion among us, there is no doubt but more good might be done by ministers this way, than is now done by any other means separated from the use of this particularly, than by that of public preaching, (which yet need not be neglected the more when this is used,) which hath now the fate to be cried up, and almost solely depended on; it being the likelier way, as Quintilian saith, (comparing public and private teaching of youth,) to fill the narrow-mouthed bottles, (and such are the most of us,) by taking them single in the hand, and pouring in water into each, than by setting them all together, and throwing never so many bottles of water on them."

Mr. William Gurnal, in his excellent book, called, The Christian in Complete Armour, p. 235.

"The ignorant soul feels no such smart: if the minister stay till he sends for him to instruct him, he may sooner hear the bell go for him, than any messenger come for him. You must seek them out, and not expect that they will come to you. These are a sort of people that are more afraid of their remedy than their disease, and study more to hide their ignorance, than how to have it cured; which should make us pity them the more, because they can pity themselves so little. I confess it is no small unhappiness to some of us, who have to do with a multitude, that we have neither time nor strength to make our addresses to every particular person in our congregations, and attend on them as their needs require; and yet cannot well satisfy our consciences otherwise. But let us look to it, that though we cannot do to the height of what we should, we be not found wanting in what we may. Let not the difficulty of our province make us like some, who when they see they have more work upon their hands than they can well despatch, grow sick of it, and sit down out of a lazy despondency, and do just nothing.——Oh! if once our hearts were filled with zeal for God, and compassion to our people's souls, we would up and be doing, though we could lay but a brick a day; and God will be with us. May be, you who find a people rude and sottishly ignorant, like stones in the quarry and trees unfelled, shall not bring the work to such perfection in your days as you desire! Yet, as David did for Solomon, thou mayst by thy pains in teaching and instructing them, prepare materials for another, who shall rear the temple."

Read the rest.

ACTS XX. 28.

TAKE HEED THEREFORE UNTO YOURSELVES, AND TO ALL THE FLOCK, OVER THE WHICH THE HOLY GHOST HATH MADE YOU OVERSEERS, TO FEED THE CHURCH OF GOD, WHICH HE HATH PURCHASED WITH HIS OWN BLOOD.

CHAPTER I.

SECTION I.

Reverend and dearly beloved Brethren,

THOUGH some think that Paul's exhortation to these elders doth prove him their ruler, we hope, who are this day to speak to you from the Lord, that we may freely do the like without any jealousies of such a conclusion. Though we teach our people as officers set over them in the Lord, yet may we teach one another as brethren, in office as well as in faith. If the people of our charge must teach, and admonish, and exhort each other daily, (Col. iii. 16; Heb. iii. 13,) no doubt teachers may do it to one another without any supereminency of power or degree. We have the same sins to kill, and the same graces to be quickened and corroborated, as our people have: we have greater works than they to do, and greater difficulties to overcome, and no less necessity is laid upon us; and therefore we have need to be warned and awakened, if not to be instructed, as well as they. So that I confess, I think such meetings should be more frequent, if we had nothing else to do together but this. And as plainly and closely should we deal with one another, as the most serious among us do with our flocks; lest if only they have the sharp admonitions and reproofs, they only should be sound and lively in the faith. That this was Paul's judgment, I need no other proof, than this rousing, heart-melting exhortation to the Ephesian elders:—a short sermon, but not soon learned. Had the bishops and teachers of the church but thoroughly learned this short exhortation, though with neglect of many a volume which hath taken up their time, and helped them to greater applause in the world, how happy had it been for the church and them!

Our present straits of time will allow me to touch upon no part of it but my text; which, supposing Paul the speaker, and the Ephesian elders his hearers, containeth, 1. A twofold duty. 2. A fourfold motive to enforce it.

The first duty is, *to take heed to themselves;* the second is, *to take heed to all the flock.* And the main work for the flock which is thus heedfully to be done, is expressed, even *to feed them, or play the shepherd for them.*

The motives closely laid together are these;—1. From their engagement and relation; they are overseers of the flock; it is their office.—2. From the efficient cause, even the authority and excellency of him that called them to it; which was the Holy Ghost.—3. From the dignity of the object, which is the matter of their charge: it is the church of God, the most excellent and honourable society in the world.—4. From the tender regard Christ has of his church, and the price it cost him: he purchased it with his own blood. This motive is particularly subordinate to the former.

The terms of the text have no such difficulty as to allow me the spending of much of our little time for their explication. Προσέχειν, here is, *maxima cura et diligentia animum adhibere:* ποίμνιον, as Jansenius and others of note, a *little flock.* It signifieth not here the whole church, which elsewhere is called ποίμνιον, in reference to Christ the great Shepherd; but it signifieth that particular church which these elders had a special charge of. Whether that was one or many, we shall inquire anon. What is meant by Ἐπισκόπους, *bishops* or *overseers,* here, is thus far agreed on, that they were officers appointed to teach and guide those churches in the way to salvation; and that they are the same persons that are called elders of the church of Ephesus before, and bishops here: of whom more anon. The verb ἔθετο, seemeth here to import both the qualification, ordination, and particular designation of these elders or bishops to their charge; for we must not limit and exclude without necessity. The Holy Ghost did by all these three ways make them overseers of their flocks. (1.) By qualifying them with such gifts as made them fit for it. (2.) By directing the minds of those that ordained to the ministry. (3.) By disposing both their own minds, and the ordainers', and the people's, for the affixing them to that particular church, rather than another. *Dicit eos constitutos a Spiritu Sancto,* saith Grotius, *quia constituti erant ab apostolis plenis Spiritu Sancto, quanquam approbante plebe.* But no doubt, in those times the Holy Ghost did give special directions, as by internal oracle, for the disposal of particular teachers, as we read in the case of Saul and Barnabas, and for the provision of particular congregations.

Ποιμαίνειν τὴν ἐκκλησίαν, is by some translated barely to *feed,* as ours here; by others only to *rule;* but indeed as Gerhard, Jansenius, and others note, it is not to be restrained to either, but containeth in it all the pastoral work. In one word, it is *pastorem agere,* to do the work of a pastor to the flock. Whether it be the Ephesian congregation, before called ποίμνιον, that is here called ἐκκλησίαν τοῦ Θεοῦ, or whether it be the universal church which they may be said to feed and rule, by doing their part towards it, in their station, (as a justice of peace may be said to rule the land,) is not a matter of much moment to be stood upon; but the former seems most likely to be the sense: περιεποιήσατο, is both *acquisivit et asseruit et in suam vindicavit.* It is said to be done by the blood of God, by a communication of the names of the distinct natures: and it affords us an argument against the Arians, seeing Christ is here expressly called God.

SECTION II.

But it is necessary before we proceed to instruction and application, that we be resolved more clearly who those elders or bishops be that Paul doth here exhort. I am desirous to do all that lawfully I may to avoid controversy, especially in this place, and on such occasions; but it is here unavoidable, because all our following application will much depend upon the explication: and if you shall once suppose that none of this exhortation was spoken to men in your office and capacity; no wonder if you pass it over and let it alone, and take all that I shall hence gather for your practice, as impertinent. This text was wont to be thought most apt to awaken the ministers of the gospel to their duty; but of late the negligent are gratified with the news, (for news it is,) that only bishops in a supereminent sense, whom we usually call prelates, are spoken to in this text; and not only so, but no other text of Scripture doth speak to any other church presbyters (certainly) but them; yea, that no other were in being in Scripture times. Here are two questions before us to be resolved. 1. Whether the elders here mentioned, were the elders of one church of Ephesus, or all that part of Asia, that is, of every church one? This is but in order to the second, which is, Whether these elders were only prelates, or such bishops as among us have carried that name?

The reasons that may be brought to prove these to be prelates of the several cities of Asia, and that the πᾶν τὸ ποίμνιον, is those many cities, are these following. 1. The affirmation of Irenæus. To which we say, (1.) There might be many elders of Ephesus present, though some from the nearest cities were there also; which is all that Irenæus affirms. (2.) We oppose to the saying of Irenæus the ordinary exposition of the ancients: the most singular is of least authority, *cæteris paribus*.

2. It may be said that Paul calls them to remember how he had been among them three years, not ceasing to warn every one, &c. But he was not three years at Ephesus only, but in Asia, &c. *Answ.* He may be said to be where his chief place of abode is. He that resideth ordinarily at Ephesus, though he thence make frequent excursions to the neighbour parts, may well be said to abide so long at Ephesus. And the Ephesian elders might well be acquainted with his industry round about them, though here is no certainty that he mentioneth any more than what he did with them. For what he did in Ephesus he did in Asia, as that which is done in London is done in England.

Object. 3. But it is meant in all Asia; for he saith, "among whom I have gone," &c. *Answ.* (1.) As though Paul might not go preaching the gospel in Ephesus. (2.) If he went further, the Ephesian elders might accompany him. *Object.* 4. Ephesus was the metropolis, and therefore all Asia might be thence denominated. *Answ.* (1.) It must be proved that it was so denominated. All France is not called Paris, nor all England London. (2.) It is not whole countries, but a church that, Paul speaks of: and it is yet unproved that the church of one city had then any such dependence on the church of another city, as lesser cities had upon the metropolis.

Our reasons that make us think that either all or many of these elders or bishops were over the particular church of Ephesus, are these: 1. It is expressly said in the text, that they were elders of the church, referring to Ephesus next before mentioned; "He sent to Ephesus, and called the elders of the church." And it cannot be proved in all the New Testament, that the bishops of other churches and cities are called bishops of a great city, because it is the metropolis. 2. Here is mention but of one church and one flock, in the singular number, and not of many; when yet, it is acknowledged that he speaketh not of the universal church, (for then that language were not strange,) but of a particular church. And it is the use of the apostles to speak still in the plural number, when they mention the particular churches of many cities, and not to call them all one church or flock. 3. And it may seem else that the elder of each one of these cities hath a charge of all the rest. For they are required to take heed of all the flock: which though it may possibly be by taking every one his part, yet if one should fail, the rest seem to have his charge upon them, which is more than they can do. 4. Paul was now in so great haste in his journey to Jerusalem, that Luke measureth it out by the days. And it is not like that Paul could in such haste call the elders from the several cities of Asia. If he had passed through the British seas in such haste, and lodged at Plymouth, and had thence called to him the elders of Paris, he must have staid many days or weeks before he could have gathered also the bishops of Rheims, Arles, Orleans, and the rest of France. 5. The numbers of prophets and gifted men in those times, and the state of other particular churches, doth give us sufficient reason to conjecture that Ephesus was not so scant of help, as to have but one presbyter. Grotius thought that Timothy with his co-presbyters made this appearance; but others have given very probable reasons that Timothy was none of them. 6. The judgment of expositors, ancient and modern, running so commonly the other way, commandeth some respect from us.

But I confess the matter seemeth but conjectural on both sides, and neither part to have a certainty; but if probability may carry it, there seems to be many of the elders of Ephesus, though possibly some of the neighbouring cities might be with them. But let this go how it will, it maketh not much to the main matter in hand. What if Ephesus and each other city, or church, had then but one presbyter, will it follow that he was a prelate? No; but the contrary: it will prove that there were none such at all, if there were no subject presbyters. For there is no king without subjects; nor master without servants. 1. The stream of ancient and modern expositors do take this text to speak of presbyters in the common sense. And we must be cautelous, before we be singular in the expounding of so many texts as speak the same way. 2. If men be put now, in the end of the world, to find out a new foundation for prelacy, suppose that it hath been amiss defended till now, and all these texts (except by one or two) amiss expounded, it will occasion the shaking of the frame itself. 3. But the best is, we begin to be pretty well agreed, at least about the whole government that *de facto* was in being in Scripture times. For, (1.) It is at last confessed, that the word presbyter is not certainly taken any where in the New Testament, for one that is subject to a bishop, having not power of ordination or jurisdiction; and that no such presbyters were in being in Scripture times. And by what authority they are since erected, let them prove that are concerned in it. (2.) We are agreed now that they were the same persons who in Scripture are called bishops and presbyters. (3.) And that these persons had the power of ordination and jurisdiction. (4.) And that these persons were not the bishops of many particular churches, but one only: they ruled not many assemblies ordinarily meeting for church communion: for there could no such meetings be kept up without a bishop or presbyter to administer the ordinances of Christ in each. And if there were in a diocess but one bishop, and no other presbyters in Scripture times, then it must needs be that a diocess contained but one ordinary church assembly, and that *de facto* no bishop in Scripture times had under him any presbyters, nor more such assemblies than one: that is, they ruled the particular churches just as our parish pastors do. So that we are satisfied that we go that way that the apostles established, and was used *de facto* in Scripture times. And if any will prove the lawfulness of latter mutations, or will prove that the apostle gave power to these particular pastors to degenerate into another sort of officers hereafter, according to the cogency of their evidence, we shall believe it. In the mean time, desiring to be guided by the word of God, and to go upon sure ground, and take only so much as is certain, we hold where we are, and are glad that we are so far agreed. Yet not presuming to censure all superior episcopacy, nor refusing to obey any man that commandeth us to do our duty, but resolving to do our own work in faithfulness and peace.

For my own part, I have ever thought it easier to be governed than to govern; and I am ready, as the British told Austin, to be obedient to any man in and for the Lord. Nor can I think that any government can be burdensome, which Christ appointeth, but all beneficial to us; as making our burden lighter and not heavier, and helping and not hindering us in the way to heaven. Were Christ's work but thoroughly done, I should be the backwardest in contending who should have the doing of it. Let us agree but on this one thing which is plain here in my text, That the churches or flocks should be no greater than the pastors can personally oversee, so that they may "take heed to all the flock;" and then let but able, faithful men be the overseers, that will make the word of God the rule, and lay out themselves for the saving of men's souls, and I am resolved never to contend with such about the business of superiority; but cheerfully to obey them in all things lawful, if they require my obedience. If the difference were not more about the matters commanded, and the work itself to be done, than who should command it, methinks humble men should be easily agreed. Would they but lay by all needless human impositions and obtrusions, and be contented with the sufficient word of God, and not make new work to necessitate, new canons and authorities to impose it, but be content with the gospel simplicity, and let us take that for a way to heaven that Peter and Paul went thither in; I think I should not disobey such a bishop, though I were satisfied of his differing order or degree. Yea, if he were addicted to some encroaching usurpation of more power than is meet, would he but forbear the *Ecce duo gladii*, and come to us only with the sword of the Spirit, which will admit of fair debates, and works only upon the conscience, I know no reason much to fear such power, though it were undue. But enough of this.

SECTION III.

The observations which the text affordeth us are so many, that I may not now stay so much as to name them; but shall only lay down that one which containeth the main scope of the text, and take in the rest as subordinate motives in the handling of that in the method in which the apostle doth here deliver them to us.

Doct. The pastors or overseers of the churches of Christ, must take great heed both to themselves, and to all their flocks, in all the parts of their pastoral work.

The method which we shall follow in handling this point, shall be this: I. I shall briefly open to you the terms of the subject: what is meant by pastors and churches. II. I shall show you, what it is to take heed to ourselves, and wherein it must be done. III. I shall give some brief reasons of that part of the point. IV. I shall show you, what it is to take heed to all the flock in our pastoral work, and wherein it must be done. V. I shall make some application of all.

SECTION IV.

I. What the words, pastor, bishop, and church, do signify, I will not waste time to tell you, they being so well known. As for the things signified: By a pastor or bishop here is meant, an officer appointed by Christ for the ordinary teaching and guiding a particular church and all its members, in order to their salvation, and the pleasing of God.

Christ appointed the office itself by his laws. The person he calleth to it by his qualifying gifts, providential disposal, secret impulses, and ordinarily by the ordination of his present officers, and the acceptance of the church.

Teaching and guidance contain the main parts at least of the work to which they are designed. The particulars we shall further stand upon anon.

A particular church is the object of their work; by which they are distinguished from apostolical, unfixed, itinerant ministers.

They are the stated, ordinary teachers of such a church; by which they are differenced, both from private men, who do occasionally teach, and from the foresaid itinerant ministers, and do but *in transitu*, or seldom, teach a particular church. The subject is the matters of salvation and obedience to God, and the end is salvation itself, and the pleasing of God therein; by which work and ends the office is distinguished from all other offices, as magistrates, schoolmasters, &c.; though they also have the same remote or ultimate ends.

By the flock and church is meant that particular society of christians of which these bishops or elders have the charge, associated for personal communion in God's public worship, and for other mutual assistance in the way to salvation. Exact definitions we may not now stand on; we have more fully made some attempts that way heretofore.

SECTION V.

II. Let us next consider, What it is to take heed to ourselves, and wherein it must be done. And here I may well, for brevity sake, adjoin the application to the explication, it being about the matter of our practice, that I may be put to go over, as little as may be, of the same things again. Take therefore I beseech you all this explication, as so much advice and exhortation to the duty, and let your hearts attend it as well as your understandings.

1. Take heed to yourselves, lest you should be void of that saving grace of God which you offer to others, and be strangers to the effectual workings of that gospel which you preach; and lest while you proclaim the necessity of a Saviour to the world, your own hearts should neglect him, and you should miss of an interest in him and his saving benefits! Take heed to yourselves, lest you perish, while you call upon others to take heed of perishing! and lest you famish yourselves while you prepare their food. Though there be a promise of shining as the stars to those that turn many to righteousness, (Dan. xii. 3,) that is but on supposition that they be first turned to it themselves: such promises are meant *cæteris paribus, et suppositis supponendis*. Their own sincerity in the faith is the condition of glory simply considered, though their great ministerial labours may be a condition of the promise of their greater glory; many a man hath warned others that they come not to the place of torment, which yet they hasted to themselves: many a preacher is now in hell, that hath a hundred times called upon his hearers to use the utmost care and diligence to

escape it. Can any reasonable man imagine that God should save men for offering salvation to others, while they refused it themselves; and for telling others those truths which they themselves neglected and abused? Many a tailor goes in rags, that maketh costly clothes for others; and many a cook scarce licks his fingers, when he hath dressed for others the most costly dishes. Believe it, brethren, God never saved any man for being a preacher, nor because he was an able preacher; but because he was a justified, sanctified man, and consequently faithful in his Master's work. Take heed therefore to yourselves first, that you *be* that which you persuade your hearers to *be*, and believe that which you persuade them daily to believe; and have heartily entertained that Christ and Spirit which you offer unto others. He that bid you love your neighbours as yourselves, did imply that you should love yourselves, and not hate and destroy yourselves and them.

SECTION VI.

2. Take heed to yourselves, lest you live in those actual sins which you preach against in others; and lest you be guilty of that which daily you condemn. Will you make it your work to magnify God, and when you have done, dishonour him as much as others? Will you proclaim Christ's governing power, and yet contemn it, and rebel yourselves? Will you preach his laws, and wilfully break them? If sin be evil, why do you live in it? if it be not, why do you dissuade men from it? if it be dangerous, how dare you venture on it? If it be not, why do you tell men so? If God's threatenings be true, why do you not fear them? if they be false, why do you trouble men needlessly with them, and put them into such frights without a cause? Do you know the judgment of God, that they that commit such things are worthy of death, and yet will you do them? Rom. i. 32. Thou that teachest another, teachest thou not thyself? Thou that sayest a man should not commit adultery, or be drunk, or covetous, art thou such thyself? Thou that makest thy boast of the law, through breaking the law dishonourest thou God? Rom. ii. 21—23. What, shall the same tongue speak evil, that speaketh against evil? Shall it censure and slander, and secretly backbite, that cries down these and the like in others? Take heed to yourselves, lest you cry down sin and not overcome it; lest while you seek to bring it down in others, you bow to it, and become its slaves yourselves. "For of whom a man is overcome, of the same is he brought into bondage," 2 Pet. ii. 19. "To whom ye yield yourselves servants to obey, his servants ye are to whom ye obey, whether of sin unto death, or of obedience unto righteousness," Rom. vi. 16. It is easier to chide at sin, than to overcome it.

SECTION VII.

3. Take heed also to yourselves, that you be not unfit for the great employments that you have undertaken. He must not be himself a babe in knowledge, that will teach men all those mysterious things that are to be known in order to salvation. Oh what qualifications are necessary for that man that hath such a charge upon him as we have! How many difficulties in divinity to be opened! yea, about the fundamentals that must needs be known! How many obscure texts of Scripture to be expounded! How many duties to be done, wherein ourselves and others may miscarry, if in the matter, and end, and circumstances they be not well informed! How many sins to be avoided, which without understanding and foresight cannot be done! What a number of sly and subtle temptations must we open to our people's eyes, that they may escape them! How many weighty and yet intricate cases of conscience we have daily to resolve! Can so much work, and such work as this, be done by raw, unqualified men? Oh, what strong holds have we to batter, and how many of them! What subtle, and diligent, and obstinate resistance must we expect at every heart we deal with! Prejudice hath blocked up our way; we can scarce procure a patient hearing. They think ill of what we say while we are speaking it. We cannot make a breach in their groundless hopes and carnal peace, but they have twenty shifts and seeming reasons to make it up again; and twenty enemies that seeming friendly are ready to help them. We dispute not with them upon equal terms: but we have children to reason with, that cannot understand us; we have distracted men (in spirituals) to reason with, that will bawl us down with raging nonsense: we have wilful, unreasonable people to deal with, that when they are silenced, they are never the more convinced; and when they can give you no reason, they will give you their resolution; like the man that Salvian had to deal with, (lib. iv. de Gubernat. p. 133,) that being resolved to devour a poor man's means, and being entreated by Salvian to forbear, told him, he could not grant his request, for he had made a vow to take it; so that the preacher *audita religiosissimi sceleris ratione* was fain to depart. We dispute the case against men's wills and sensual passions, as much as against their understandings; and these have neither reason nor ears: their best arguments are, I will not believe you, nor all the preachers in the world, in such things. I will not change my mind or life: I will not leave my sins; I will never be so precise, come on it what will. We have not one, but multitudes of raging passions and contradicting enemies to dispute against at once, whenever we go about the conversion of a sinner; as if a man were to dispute in a fair or tumult, or in the midst of a crowd of violent scolds; what equal dealing, and what success, were here to be expected? Why, such is our work, and yet a work that must be done.

O, dear brethren, what men should we be in skill, resolution, and unwearied diligence, that have all this to do! Did Paul cry out, "Who is sufficient for these things?" 2 Cor. ii. 16; and shall we be proud, or careless and lazy, as if we were sufficient? As Peter saith to our great approaching change, 2 Pet. iii. 11, "What manner of persons ought we to be in all holy conversation and godliness?" so may I say to every minister, Seeing all these things do lie upon our hands, what manner of persons ought we to be in all holy endeavours and resolutions for our work! This is not a burden for the shoulder of a child. What skill doth every part of our work require, and of how much moment is every part! To preach a sermon I think is not the hardest part; and yet what skill is necessary to make plain the truth, to convince the hearers; to let in the unresistible light into their consciences, and to keep it there, and drive all home; to screw the truth into their minds, and work Christ into their affections; to meet every objection that gainsays, and clearly to resolve it; to drive sinners to a stand, and make them see there is no hope, but they must unavoidably be converted or condemned: and to do all this so for language and manner as beseems our work, and yet as is most suitable to the capacities of our hearers: this, and a great deal more that should be done in every sermon, should sure be done with a great deal of holy skill. So great a

God, whose message we declare, should be honoured by our delivery of it! It is a lamentable case, that in a message from the God of heaven, of everlasting consequence to the souls of men, we should behave ourselves so weakly, so unhandsomely, so imprudently, or so slightly, that the whole business should miscarry in our hands, and God be dishonoured, and his work disgraced, and sinners rather hardened than converted, and all this much through our weakness or neglect! How many a time have carnal hearers gone jeering home, at the palpable and dishonourable failings of the preacher! How many sleep under us, because our hearts and tongues are sleepy; and we bring not with us so much skill and zeal as to awake them!

Moreover, what skill is necessary to defend the truth against gainsayers, and to deal with disputing cavillers according to their several modes and cases! and if we fail through weakness, how will they insult! but that is the smallest matter: but who knows how many weak ones may be perverted by the success to their own undoing and the trouble of the church?

What skill is there necessary to deal in private with one poor soul for their conversion! (Of which more in the end.)

O brethren, do you not shrink and tremble under the sense of all this work? Will a common measure of holy skill and ability, of prudence, and other qualifications, serve for such a task as this? I know necessity may cause the church to tolerate the weak; but woe to us if we tolerate and indulge our own weakness! Doth not reason and conscience tell you, that if you dare venture on so high a work as this, you should spare no pains to be fitted to perform it? It is not now and then an idle snatch or taste of studies that will serve to make a sound divine. I know that laziness hath lately learned to pretend the lowness of all our studies, and how wholly and only the Spirit must qualify and assist us to the work: and so, as Salvian saith in another case, (lib. iv. p. 134,) *authorem quodammodo sui sceleris Deum faciunt:* as if God commanded us the use of the means, and then would warrant us to neglect them! As if it were his way to cause us to thrive in a course of idleness; and to bring us to knowledge by dreams when we are asleep, or to take us up into heaven, and show us his counsels, while we think of no such matter, but are rooting in the earth. Oh that men should dare so sinfully by their laziness to quench the Spirit; and then pretend the Spirit for the doing of it! *Quis unquam,* (saith he before mentioned,) *crederet usque in hanc contumeliam Dei, progressuram esse humanæ cupiditatis (ignaviæ) audaciam? ut id ipsum in quo Christo injuriam faciunt, dicant se ob Christi nomen esse facturos? O inestimabile facinus et prodigiosum!* God hath required of us that we be "not slothful in business, but fervent in spirit, serving the Lord," Rom. xii. 11. Such we must provoke our hearers to be, and such we must be ourselves. O therefore, brethren, lose no time: study, and pray, and confer, and practise; for by these four ways your abilities must be increased. Take heed to yourselves, lest you are weak through your own negligence, and lest you mar the work of God by your weakness. "As the man is, so is his strength," Judg. viii. 21.

SECTION VIII.

4. Moreover, take heed to yourselves, lest your example contradict your doctrine, and lest you lay such stumblingblocks before the blind, as may be the occasion of their ruin; lest you may unsay that with your lives, which you say with your tongues; and be the greatest hinderers of the success of your own labours. It much hindereth our work, when other men are all the week long contradicting to poor people in private, that which we have been speaking to them from the word of God in public; because we cannot be at hand to manifest their folly: but it will much more hinder, if we contradict ourselves, and if your actions give your tongue the lie, and if you build up an hour or two with your mouths, and all the week after pull down with your hands! This is the way to make men think that the word of God is but an idle tale, and to make preaching seem no better than prating. He that means as he speaks, will sure do as he speaks. One proud, surly, lordly word, one needless contention, one covetous action, may cut the throat of many a sermon, and blast the fruit of all that you have been doing. Tell me, brethren, in the fear of God, do you regard the success of your labours, or do you not? Do you long to see it upon the souls of your hearers? If you do not, what do you preach for, what do you study, and what do you call yourselves the ministers of Christ for? But if you do, then sure you cannot find in your heart to mar your work for a thing of nought! What, do you regard the success of your labours, and yet will not part with a little to the poor; nor put up an injury, or a foul word, nor stoop to the meanest, nor forbear your passionate or lordly carriage, no not for the winning of souls, and attaining the end of all your labours? You much regard the success indeed, that will sell it at so cheap a rate, or will not do so small a matter to attain it!

It is a palpable error in those ministers that make such a disproportion between their preaching and their living, that they will study little or not at all to live exactly: all the week long is little enough to study how to speak two hours; and yet one hour seems too much to study how to live all the week. They are loth to misplace a word in their sermons, or to be guilty of any notable infirmity; (and I blame them not, for the matter is holy and of weight;) but they make nothing of misplacing affections, words, and actions in the course of their lives. Oh how curiously have I heard some men preach, and how carelessly have I seen them live! They have been so accurate as to the wordy part in their own preparations, that seldom preaching seemed a virtue to them, that their language might be the more polite; and all the rhetorical jingling writers they could meet with, were pressed to serve them for the adorning of their style, and gauds were oft their chiefest ornaments. They were so nice in hearing others, that no man pleased them that spoke as he thought, or that drowned not affections, or dulled not or distempered not the heart by the predominant strains of a fantastic wit. And yet when it came to matter of practice, and they were once out of church, how incurious were the men, and how little did they regard what they said or did, so it were not so palpably gross as to dishonour them! They that preached precisely, would not live precisely! What difference between their pulpit speeches and their familiar discourse! They that are most impatient of barbarisms, solecisms, and paralogisms in a sermon, can easily tolerate them in their conversations.

Certainly, brethren, we have very great cause to take heed what we do, as well as what we say: if we will be the servants of Christ indeed, we must not be tongue servants only, but must serve him with our deeds, "and be doers of the work, that in our deed we may be blessed," James i. 25. As our people must be "doers of the word, and not hearers only;" so we must be doers and not speakers only, lest we be "deceivers of ourselves," James i. 22. A practical doctrine must be practically preached. We must study as hard how to live well, as how to preach well. We must think and think again, how to compose our lives as may most tend to men's salvation, as well as our sermons. When you are studying what to say to them, I know these are your thoughts, or else they are naught and to no purpose: How should I get within them? and what shall I say that is most effectually to convince them, and convert them, and tend to their salvation? And should you not diligently bethink yourselves, How shall I live, and what shall I say and do, and how shall I dispose of all that I have, as may most probably tend to the saving of men's souls? Brethren, if saving souls be your end, you will certainly intend it as well out of the pulpit as in it! If it be your end, you will live for it, and contribute all your endeavours to attain it: and if you do so, you will as well ask concerning the money in your purse, as the words of your mouth, Which way should I lay it out for the greatest good, especially to men's souls? Oh that this were your daily study, how to use your wealth, your friends, and all you have for God, as well as your tongues! And then we should see that fruit of your labours that is never else like to be seen. If you intend the end of the ministry in the pulpit only, then it seems you take yourselves for ministers no longer than you are there; and then I think you are unworthy to be esteemed such at all.

SECTION IX.

III. Having showed you in four particulars how it is that we must take heed to ourselves, and what is comprised in this command; I am next to give you the *reasons* of it, which I entreat you to take as so many motives to awaken you to your duty, and thus apply them as we go.

1. You have a heaven to win or lose yourselves, and souls that must be happy or miserable for ever; and therefore it concerneth you to begin at home, and take heed to yourselves as well as unto others. Preaching well may succeed to the salvation of others without the holiness of your own hearts or lives; it is possible at least, though less usual; but it is impossible it should serve to save yourselves: many shall say at that day, "Lord, have we not prophesied in thy name?" Matt. vii. 22, who shall be answered with, "I never knew you; depart from me, ye that work iniquity," ver. 23. O sirs, how many men have preached Christ, and perished for want of a saving interest in him! How many that are now in hell, have told their people of the torments of hell, and have warned them against it! How many have preached of the wrath of God against sinners, that are now feeling it! Oh what sadder case can there be in the world, than for a man that made it his very trade and calling to proclaim salvation, and to help others to attain it, yet after all to be himself shut out! Alas! that ever we should have many books in our libraries that tell us the way to heaven; that we should spend so many years in reading those books, and studying the doctrine of eternal life, and yet for all this to miss of it! that ever we should study and preach so many sermons of salvation, and yet fall short of it!—so many sermons of damnation, and yet fall into it! And all because we preached so many sermons of Christ while we neglected him; of the Spirit, while we resisted it; of faith, while we did not heartily believe; of repentance and conversion, while we continued in the state of flesh and sin; and of a heavenly life, while we remained carnal and earthly ourselves. If we will be divines only in tongues and title, and have not the divine image upon our souls, nor give up ourselves to the divine honour and will, no wonder if we be separated from the divine presence, and denied the fruition for ever. Believe it, sirs, God is no respecter of persons: he saveth not men for their coats or callings; a holy calling will not save an unholy man. If you stand at the door of the kingdom of grace, to light others in, and will not go in yourselves, when you are burnt to the snuff, you will go out with a stink, and shall knock in vain at the gates of glory, that would not enter at the door of grace. You shall then find that your lamps should have had the oil of grace as well as of ministerial gifts; of holiness as well as of doctrine; if you would have a part in the glory which you preached. Do I need to tell you that preachers of the gospel must be judged by the gospel; and stand at the same bar, and be sentenced on the same terms, and dealt with as severely as any other men? Can you think to be saved then by your clergy; and to come off by a *legit ut clericus*, when there is wanting the *credidit et vixit ut christianus?* Alas, it will not be; you know it will not! Take heed therefore to yourselves for your own sakes; seeing you have souls to save or lose as well as others.

SECTION X.

2. Take heed to yourselves, for you have a depraved nature, and sinful inclinations, as well as others. If innocent Adam had need of heed, and lost himself and us for want of it, how much more need have such as we! Sin dwelleth in us, when we have preached never so much against it: and one degree prepareth the heart to another, and one sin inclineth the mind to more. If one thief be in the house, he will let in the rest, because they have the same disposition and design. A spark is the beginning of a flame; and a small disease may bring a greater. A man that knows himself to be purblind, should take heed to his feet. Alas! even in our hearts, as well as in our hearers, there is an averseness to God, a strangeness to him, unreasonable and almost unruly passions. In us there is at the best the remnants of pride, unbelief, self-seeking, hypocrisy, and all the hateful, deadly sins. And doth it not concern us to take heed? Is so much of the fire of hell yet extinguished, that at first was kindled in us? Are there so many traitors in our hearts, and is it not time for us to take heed? You will scarce let your little children go themselves while they are weak, without calling upon them to take heed of falling. And alas! how weak are those of us that seem strongest! How apt to stumble at a very straw! How small a matter will cast us down, by enticing us to folly; or kindling our passions and inordinate desires, by perverting our judgments, or abating our resolutions, and cooling our zeal, and dulling our diligence! Ministers are not only sons of Adam, but sinners against the grace of Christ, as well as others, and so have increased their radical sin. Those treacherous hearts will one time or other deceive you, if you take not heed. Those sins that seem to lie dead will revive: your pride and worldliness, and many a noisome vice, will spring up, that you thought had been weeded out by the roots. It is most necessary therefore, that men of such infirmities should take heed to themselves, and be careful in the dieting and usage of their souls.

SECTION XI.

3. And the rather, also, take heed to yourselves, because such works as ours do put men on greater

use and trial of their graces, and have greater temptations, than many other men's. Weaker gifts and graces may carry a man out in a more even and laudable course of life, that is not put to so great trials. Smaller strength may serve for lighter works and burdens. But if you venture on the great undertakings of the ministry; if you will lead on the troops of Christ against the face of Satan and his followers; if you will engage yourselves against principalities and powers, and spiritual wickednesses in high places; if you undertake to rescue captivated sinners, and to fetch men out of the devil's paws; do not think that a heedless, careless minister is fit for so great a work as this. You must look to come off with greater shame, and deeper wounds of conscience, than if you had lived a common life; if you will think to go through such things as these with a careless soul. It is not only the work that calls for heed, but the workman also, that he may be fit for business of such weight. We have seen by experience, that many men that lived as private christians, in good reputation for parts and piety, when they have taken upon them either military employment, or magistracy, where the work was above their parts, and temptations did overmatch their strength, they have proved scandalous, disgraced men. And we have seen some private christians of good note, that having thought too highly of their own parts, and thrust themselves into the ministerial office, they have been empty men, and always burdens to the church, and worse than some that we have endeavoured to cast out. They might have done God more service in the station of the higher rank of private men, than they do among the lowest of the ministry. If you will venture into the midst of the enemies, and bear the burden and heat of the day, take heed to yourselves.

SECTION XII.

4. And the rather, also, take heed to yourselves, because the tempter will make his first or sharpest onset upon you. If you will be the leader against him, he will spare you no further than God restraineth him. He beareth you the greatest malice, that are engaged to do him the greatest mischief. As he hateth Christ more than any of us, because he is the General of the field, and the "Captain of our salvation," and doth more than all the world besides against the kingdom of darkness; so doth he hate the leaders under him, more than the common soldiers, on the like account (in their proportion); he knows what a rout he may make among the rest, if the leaders fall before their eyes. He hath long tried that way of fighting, neither against great or small comparatively, but these; and of smiting the shepherds, that he may scatter the flock; and so great hath been his success this way, that he will follow it on as far as he is able. Take heed therefore, brethren, for the enemy hath a special eye upon you. You shall have his most subtle insinuations, and incessant solicitations, and violent assaults. As wise and learned as you are, take heed to yourselves lest he overwit you. The devil is a greater scholar than you, and a nimbler disputant; he can transform himself into an angel of light to deceive: he will get within you and trip up your heels before you are aware: he will play the juggler with you undiscerned, and cheat you of your faith or innocency, and you shall not know that you have lost it; nay, he will make you believe it is multiplied or increased when it is lost. You shall see neither hook nor line, much less the subtle angler himself, while he is offering you his bait: and his bait shall be so fitted to your temper and disposition, that he will be sure to find advantages within you, and make your own principles and inclinations to betray you; and whenever he ruineth you, he will make you the instruments of your own ruin. Oh what a conquest will he think he hath got, if he can make a minister lazy and unfaithful! if he can tempt a minister into covetousness or scandal, he will glory against the church, and say, These are your holy preachers: you see what their preciseness is, and whither it will bring them. He will glory against Jesus Christ himself, and say, These are thy champions! I can make thy chiefest servants to abuse thee; I can make the stewards of thy household unfaithful. If he did so insult against God upon a false surmise, and tell him he could make Job to curse him to his face, (Job i. 11,) what would he do if he should indeed prevail against us? And at last he will insult as much over you, that ever he drew you to be false to your great trust, and blemish your holy profession, and to do him so much service that was your enemy. O do not so far gratify Satan! do not make him sport: do not suffer him to use you as the Philistines did Samson, first to deprive you of your strength, and then to put out your eyes, and so to make you the matter of his triumph and derision.

SECTION XIII.

5. Take heed to yourselves also, because there are many eyes upon you, and therefore there will be many observers of your fall. You cannot miscarry but the world will ring of it. The eclipses of the sun by day time are seldom without witnesses. If you take yourselves for the lights of the churches, you may well expect that men's eyes should be upon you. If other men may sin without observation, so cannot you. And you should thankfully consider how great a mercy this is, that you have so many eyes to watch over you, and so many ready to tell you of your faults, and so have greater helps than others, at least for the restraining of your sin. Though they may do it with a malicious mind, yet you have the advantage by it. God forbid that we should prove so impudent, as to do evil in the public view of all, and to sin wilfully while the world is gazing on us! He that is drunk, is drunk in the night; and he that sleepeth, doth sleep in the night, 1 Thess. v. 7. What fornicator so impudent as to sin in the open streets while all look on? Why, consider that you are still in the open light; even the light of your own doctrine will disclose your evil doings. While you are as lights set upon a hill, look not to lie hid, Matt. v. 14. Take heed therefore to yourselves, and do your works as those that remember that the world looks on them, and that with the quicksighted eye of malice, ready to make the worst of all, and to find the smallest fault where it is, and aggravate it where they find it, and divulge it, and make it advantageous to their designs; and to make faults where they cannot find them. How cautiously then should we walk before so many ill-minded observers!

SECTION XIV.

6. Take heed also to yourselves; for your sins have more heinous aggravations than other men's. It is noted among King Alphonsus' sayings, That a great man cannot commit a small sin: we may much more say, that a learned man or teacher of others cannot commit a small sin; or at least, that the sin is great, as committed by him, which is smaller in another.

(1.) You are likelier than others to sin against knowledge, because you have more than they. At least you sin against more light or means of knowledge. What! do you not know that covetousness and pride are sins? Do you not know what it is to be unfaithful to your trust, and by negligence, or self-seeking, to betray men's souls? You know your Master's will, and if you do it not, shall be beaten with many stripes. There must needs, therefore, be the more wilfulness, by how much there is the more knowledge. If you sin, it is because you will sin.

(2.) Your sins have more hypocrisy in them than other men's, by how much the more you have spoken against them. Oh what a heinous thing it is in us, to study how to disgrace sin to the utmost, and make it as odious to our people as we can; and when we have done, to live in it, and secretly cherish that which we openly disgrace! What vile hypocrisy is it, to make it our daily business to cry it down, and yet to keep it; to call it publicly all to naught, and privately to make it our bed-fellow and companion; to bind heavy burdens for others, and not to touch them ourselves with a finger! What can you say to this in judgment? Did you think as ill of sin as you spoke, or did you not? If you did not, why would you dissemblingly speak it? If you did, why would you keep it and commit it? O bear not that badge of the miserable Pharisees, "They say, but do not," Matt. xxiii. 3. Many a minister of the gospel will be confounded, and not able to look up, by reason of this heavy charge of hypocrisy.

(3.) Moreover, your sins have more perfidiousness in them than other men's. You have more engaged yourselves against them. Besides all your common engagements as christians, you have many more as ministers. How oft have you proclaimed the evil and danger of sin, and called sinners from it! How oft have you declared the terrors of the Lord! All these did imply that you renounced it yourselves. Every sermon that you preached against it, every private exhortation, every confession of it in the congregation, did lay an engagement upon you to forsake it. Every child that you have baptized and entered into the covenant with Christ, and every administration of the supper of the Lord, wherein you called men to renew their covenant, did import your own renouncing of the flesh and the world, and your engagement unto Christ. How oft and how openly have you been witness of the odiousness and damnable nature of sin! and yet will you entertain it against all these professions and testimonies of your own? Oh what treachery is it to make such a stir in the pulpit against it, and after all to entertain it in the heart, and give it the room that is due to God, and even prefer it before the glory of the saints!

Many more such aggravations of your sins might be mentioned; but as we haste over these, so we must pass them by through our present haste.

SECTION XV.

7. Take heed to yourselves; for the honour of your Lord and Master, and of his holy truth and ways, doth lie more on you than on other men. As you may do him more service, so always more disservice than others. The nearer men stand to God, the greater dishonour hath he by their miscarriages; and the more will they be imputed by foolish men to God himself. The heavy judgment was threatened and executed on Eli and on his house, because they "kicked at his sacrifice and offering," 1 Sam. ii. 29. "For therefore was the sin of the young men great before the Lord, for men abhorred the offering of the Lord," ver. 17. It was that great aggravation of "causing the enemies of the Lord to blaspheme," which provoked God to deal sharplier with David than else he would have done, 2 Sam. xii. 11—14. If you are indeed christians, the glory of God is dearer to you than your lives. Would it not wound you to the heart to hear the name and truth of God reproached for your sakes! To see men point to you, and say, There goes a covetous priest, a secret tippler, a scandalous man; these are they that preach for strictness, when themselves can live as loose as others; they condemn us by sermons, and condemn themselves by their lives: for all their talk they are as bad as we. O brethren, could your hearts endure to hear men cast the dung of your iniquities in the face of the holy God, and in the face of the gospel, and of all that desire to fear the Lord? Would it not break your hearts to think on it, that all the godly christians about you should suffer reproach for your misdoings? Why, if one of you that is a leader of the flock should but once be insnared in a scandalous crime, there is scarce a man or woman that seeketh diligently after their salvation, within the hearing of it, but besides the grief of their hearts for your sin, they are likely to have it cast in their teeth by the ungodly about them, though they never so much detest and lament it. The ungodly husband will tell the wife, and the ungodly parents will tell their children, and neighbours and fellow-servants will be telling one another of it, and saying, These are your godly preachers: you may see what comes of your stir; are you any better than others? you are even all alike. Such words as these must all the godly in the country perhaps hear for your sakes. "It must needs be that offences come; but woe to that man by whom the offence cometh!" Matt. xviii. 7. O take heed, brethren, in the name of God, of every word that you speak, every step that you tread; for you bear the ark of the Lord, you are intrusted with his honour, and dare you let it fall, and cast it in the dirt? If you "that know his will, and approve the things that are more excellent, being instructed out of the law, and being confident that you yourselves are guides of the blind, and lights to them that are in darkness, instructers of the foolish, teachers of babes," &c.; if you, I say, should live contrary to your doctrine, and "by breaking the law, dishonour God, the name of God will be blasphemed among the ignorant and ungodly through you," Rom. ii. 19—24. And you are not unacquainted with that standing decree of heaven, "Them that honour me I will honour: and they that despise me shall be lightly esteemed," 1 Sam. ii. 30. Never did man dishonour God, but it proved the greatest dishonour to himself. God will find out ways enough to wipe off all that can be cast upon him; but you will not easily remove the shame and sorrow from yourselves.

SECTION XVI.

8. Take heed to yourselves; for the souls of your hearers, and the success of your labours, do very much depend upon it. God useth to fit men for great works before he will make them his instruments in accomplishing them. He useth to exercise men in those works that they are most suited to. If the work of the Lord be not soundly done upon your own hearts, how can you expect that he bless your labours for the effecting it in others? He may do it if he please, but you have much cause to doubt whether he will. I shall here show you some particular reasons under this last, which may satisfy you, that he who would be a means of saving others,

must take heed to himself, and that God doth more seldom prosper the labours of unsanctified men.

(1.) Can it be expected that God should bless that man's labour (I still mean comparatively, as to other ministers) who worketh not for God, but for himself? Why this is the case of every unsanctified man. None but the upright do make God their chief end, and do all or any thing heartily for his honour: they choose it rather than another calling, because their parents did destinate them to it, and because it is a pleasant thing to know; and it is a life wherein they have more opportunity to furnish their intellects with all kind of science; and because it is not so toilsome to the body, to those that have a will to favour their flesh; and because it is accompanied with some reverence and respect from men; and because they think it a fine thing to be leaders and teachers, and have others depend on them, and receive the law at their mouth; and because it affordeth them a competent maintenance. For such ends as these are they ministers, and for these do they preach; and were it not for these, and such as these, they would soon give it over. And can it be expected that God should much bless the labour of such men as these? It is not him they preach for, but for themselves, and their own reputation or gain: it is not him, but themselves, that they seek and serve; and therefore no wonder if he leave them to themselves for the success, and if their labours have no greater a blessing than themselves can give them, and the word reach no further than their own strength is able to make it reach.

(2.) Can you think that he is likely to be successful as others, that dealeth not heartily and faithfully in his work, and never soundly believeth what he saith, and never is truly serious when he seemeth to be most diligent? And can you think that any unsanctified man can be hearty and serious in the ministerial work? It cannot be. A kind of seriousness indeed he may have, such as proceedeth from a common faith, or opinion that the word is true, and is actuated by a natural fervour, or by selfish ends; but the seriousness and fidelity of a sound believer, that ultimately intendeth the glory of God and men's salvation, this he hath not. O sirs, all your preaching and persuading of others will be but dreaming and trifling hypocrisy, till the work be thoroughly done upon yourselves. How can you set yourselves day and night to a work that your carnal hearts are averse from? How can you call out with serious fervour upon poor sinners to repent and come to God, that never repented or came in yourselves? How can you heartily follow poor sinners with importunate solicitations, to take heed of sin, and to set themselves to a holy life, that never felt yourselves the evil of sin, or the worth of holiness? I tell you, these things are never well known till they are felt, nor well felt till they are possessed; and he that feeleth them not himself, is not so like to speak feelingly to others, nor to help others to the feeling of them. How can you follow sinners with compassion in your hearts, and tears in your eyes, and beseech them in the name of the Lord to stop their course and return and live, that never had so much compassion on your own soul, as to do thus much for yourselves? What! can you love other men better than yourselves? and have pity on them, that have none upon yourselves? Sirs, do you think they will be hearty and diligent to save men from hell, that be not heartily persuaded that there is a hell? or to bring men to heaven, that do not soundly believe that there is such a thing? As Calvin saith on my text; *Neque enim aliorum salutem sedulo unquam curabit, qui suam negligit.* He that hath not so strong a belief of the word of God, and the life to come, as will take off his own heart from the vanities of this world, and set him upon a resolved diligence for salvation, I cannot expect that he should be faithful in seeking the salvation of other men. Sure he that dare damn himself, dare let others alone in the way to damnation: and he that will sell his Master, with Judas, for silver, will not stick to make merchandise of the flock; and he that will let go his hopes of heaven rather than he will leave his worldly and fleshly delights, I think will hardly leave these for the saving others. In reason we may conceive, that he will have no pity on others, that is wilfully cruel to himself; and that he is not to be trusted with other men's souls, that is unfaithful to his own, and will sell it to the devil for the short pleasures of sin. I confess that man shall never have my consent to have the care and charge of others, and to oversee them in order to their salvation, that takes not heed to himself, but is careless of his own (except it were in case of absolute necessity, that no better could be had).

(3.) Do you think it is a likely thing that he will fight against Satan with all his might, that is a servant of Satan himself? And will he do any great harm to the kingdom of the devil, that is himself a member and subject of that kingdom? And will he be true to Christ that is in covenant with his enemy, and Christ hath not his heart? Why this is the case of every unsanctified man, of what cloth soever his coat be made. They are the servants of Satan, and the subjects of his kingdom; it is he that ruleth in their hearts; and are they like to be true to Christ that are ruled by the devil? What prince chose the friends and voluntary servants of his enemy to lead his armies in war against him? That is it that hath made so many preachers of the gospel to be enemies to the work of the gospel which they preach. No wonder if such be secretly girding at the holy obedience of the faithful; and while they take on them to preach for a holy life, if they cast reproaches on them that use it! Oh how many such traitors have been in the church of Christ in all ages, that have done more against him under his colours, than they could do in the open field; that have spoken well of Christ, and Scripture, and godliness in the general, and yet slily and closely do what they can to bring it into disgrace, and make men believe that those that set themselves to seek God with all their hearts, are but a company of hypocrites, or self-conceited, fantastical fellows: and what they cannot for shame speak that way in the pulpit, they will do it in secret amongst their companions. How many such wolves have been set over the sheep, because they had sheep's clothing; pretending to be christians, and as good as others! If there were a traitor among the twelve in Christ's family, no marvel if there be many now. It cannot be expected that a slave of Satan, "whose god is his belly, and who mindeth earthly things," should be any better than "an enemy to the cross of Christ." What though they live civilly, and preach plausibly, and have the outside of an easy, cheap religiousness? They may be as fast in the devil's snares by worldliness, pride, a secret distaste of a diligent godliness, or by an unsound heart that is not rooted in the faith, nor unreservedly devoted to God in Christ, as any others by drunkenness, uncleanness, and such disgraceful sins. Publicans and harlots do sooner come to heaven than Pharisees, because they are sooner convinced of their sin and misery.

And though many of these men may seem excellent preachers, and cry down sin as loud as others, yet it is all but an affected fervency, and too commonly but a mere uneffectual bawling. For he that cherisheth it in his own heart, doth never fall upon it in good sadness in others. I know that a wicked man may be more willing of another's reformation than his own, and may thence have a kind of real earnestness in dissuading them from it; because he can preach against sin at easier rates than he can forsake it, and another man's reformation may stand with his own enjoyments of his lusts. And therefore many a wicked minister, or parent, may be earnest with his people or family to mend, because they lose not their own sinful profits or pleasures by another's reformation, nor doth it call them to that self-denial as their own doth. But yet for all this, there is none of that zeal, resolution, and diligence, as is in all that are true to Christ. They set not against sin as the enemy of Christ, and as that which endangereth their people's souls. A traitorous commander, that shooteth nothing against the enemy but powder, may cause his guns to make as great a sound or report, as some that are laden with bullets; but he doth no hurt to the enemy by it. So one of these men may speak loud, and mouth it with an affected fervency; but he seldom doth any great execution against sin and Satan. No man can fight well but where he hateth, or is very angry; much less against them whom he loveth, and loveth above all. Every unrenewed man is so far from hating sin to the purpose, that it is his dearest treasure; though not as sin, yet the matter of it is, as it affordeth delight to his sensual desires. So that you may see, that an unsanctified man is very unfit to be a leader in Christ's army, who loveth the enemy; and to draw others to renounce the world and the flesh, who cleaveth to them himself as his chiefest good.

(4.) And it is not a very likely thing that the people will regard much the doctrine of such men, when they see that they do not live as they preach. They will think that he doth not *mean* as he speaks, if he *do* not as he speaks. They will hardly believe a man that seemeth not to believe himself. If a man bid you run for your lives, because a bear, or an enemy, is at your backs, and yet do not mend his pace himself in the same way, you will be tempted to think that he is but in jest, and there is really no such danger as he pretends. When preachers tell people of a necessity of holiness, and that without it no man shall see the Lord, and yet remain unholy themselves, the people will think they do but talk to pass away the hour, and because they must say somewhat for their money, and that all these are but words of course. Long enough may you lift up your voices against sin, before men will believe that there is any such harm or danger in it as you talk of, as long as they see the same man that reproacheth it, to put it in his bosom and make it his delight. You rather tempt them to think that there is some special good in it, and that you dispraise it as gluttons do a dish which they love, that they may have it all to themselves. As long as men have eyes as well as ears, they will think they see your meaning as well as hear it; and they are apter to believe their sight than their hearing, as being the most perfect sense. All that a preacher doth is a kind of preaching: and when you live a covetous or a careless life, you preach these sins to your people by your practice. When you drink, or game, or prate away your time in vain discourse, they take it as if you told them, Neighbours, this is that life that you should all live; you may venture on this course without any danger. If you are ungodly, and teach not your families the fear of God, nor contradict the sins of the company you come into, nor turn the stream of their vain talking, nor deal with them plainly about the matters of their salvation, they will take it as if you preached to them that such things are needless, and they may boldly do so as well as you. Yea, and you do worse than all this, for you teach them to think ill of others that are better. How many a faithful minister and private man is hated and reproached for the sake of such as you! What say the people to them? You are so precise, and tell us so much sin, and dangers, and duty, and make so much a stir about these matters; when such or such a minister that is as great a scholar as you, and as good a preacher as you, will be merry and jest with us, and let us alone, and never trouble themselves or us with such discourse. The busy fellows can never be quiet, but make more ado than need, and love to frighten men with talk of damnation; when sober, learned, peaceable divines can be quiet, and live with us like other men. This is the very thoughts and talk of people, which your negligence doth occasion. They will give you leave to preach against sins as much as you will, and talk as much for godliness in the pulpit, so you will but let them alone afterwards, and be friendly and merry when you have done, and talk as they do, and live as they, and be indifferent with them in your conference, and your conversation. For they take the pulpit to be but as a stage; a place where preachers must show themselves and play their parts; where you have liberty to say what you list for an hour: and what you say, they much regard not, if you show them not by saying it personally to their faces, that you were in good earnest, and indeed did mean them. Is that man likely therefore to do much good, or fit to be a minister of Christ, that will speak for him an hour, and by his life will preach against him all the week besides; yea, and give his public words the lie?

And if any of the people be wiser than to follow the examples of such men, yet the loathsomeness of their lives will make this doctrine the less effectual. Though you know the meat to be good and wholesome, yet it may make a weak stomach rise against it, if the cook or the servant that carrieth it have pocky, or leprous, or dingy hands. Take heed therefore to yourselves, if ever you mean to do good to others.

(5.) Lastly, consider whether the success of your labours depend not on the grace and blessing of the Lord: and where hath he made any promise of his assistance and blessing to the ungodly men? If he do promise *his church* a blessing even by such, yet doth he not promise *them* any blessing. To his faithful servants he hath promised that he will be with them, that he will put his Spirit upon them, and his word into their mouths, and that Satan shall fall before them as lightning from heaven. But where is there any such promise to the ungodly, that are not the children of the promise? Nay, do you not rather by your abuse of God, provoke him to forsake and blast your endeavours? at least as to yourselves, though he may bless them to his chosen? For I do not all this while deny but that God may often do good to his church by wicked men, but not so ordinarily nor eminently as by his own.

And what I have said of the wicked themselves, doth hold in part of the godly while they are scandalous and backsliding, proportionably according to the measure of their sin. So much for the *reasons*.

CHAPTER II.

SECTION I.

IV. HAVING showed you what it is to take heed to ourselves, and why it must be done; I am next to show you what it is to "take heed to all the flock," and wherein it doth consist and must be exercised. It was first necessary to take into consideration, *what we must be*, and *what we must do for our own souls*, before we come to that which must be done for others: *Ne quis aliorum vulnera medendo ad salutem, ipse per negligentiam suæ salutis intumescat, ne proximos juvando, se deserat; ne alios erigens, cadat*, saith Gregor. M. de cur. past. l. 4. Yea, lest all his labours come to nought, because his heart and life is naught that do perform them. *Nonnulli enim sunt qui solerti cura spiritualia præcepta perscrutantur, sed quæ intelligendo penetrant, vivendo conculcant: repente docent quæ non opere sed meditatione dedicerunt: et verbis prædicant, moribus impugnant; unde fit ut cum pastor per abrupta graditur, ad præcipitium grex sequatur.* Idem ib. li. 1. cap. 2. When we have led them to the living waters, if we muddy it by our filthy lives, we may lose our labour, and yet they be never the better. *Aquam pedibus perturbare, est sancta meditationis studia male vivendo corrumpere,* inquit. Idem ibid.

Before we speak of the work itself, we must begin with somewhat that is implied and presupposed.

And, 1. It is here implied, that *every flock should have their own pastor, (one or more,) and every pastor his own flock.* As every troop or company in a regiment of soldiers must have their own captain and other officers, and every soldier know his own commanders and colours; so it is the will of God, that every church have their own pastors, and that all Christ's disciples "do know their teachers that are over them in the Lord," 1 Thess. v. 12, 13. The universal church of Christ must consist of particular churches guided by their own overseers; and every christian must be a member of one of these churches; except those that upon embassages, travels, or other like cases of necessity, are deprived of this advantage. "They ordained them elders in every church," Acts xiv. 23; so Tit. i. 5. And in many places this is clear. Though a minister be an officer in the universal church, yet is he in a special manner the overseer of that particular church which is committed to his charge. As he that is a physician in the commonwealth, may yet be the *Medicus vel Archiater cujusdam civitatis,* and be obliged to take care of that city, and not so of any other: so that though he may and ought occasionally to do any good he can elsewhere, that may consist with his fidelity to his special charge (when an unlicensed person may not); yet is he first obliged to that city, and must allow no help to others that must occasion a neglect of them, except in great extraordinary cases, where the public good requireth it: so is it betwixt a pastor and his special flock. When we are ordained ministers without a special charge, we are licensed and commanded to do our best for all, as we shall have a call for the particular exercise: but when we have undertaken a particular charge, we have restrained the exercise of our gifts and guidance so specially to that, that we may allow others no more than they can spare of our time and help, except where the public good requireth it, which must be first regarded. From this relation of pastor and flock, arise all the duties which mutually we owe. As we must be true to our trust, so must our people be faithful to us, and obey the just directions that we give them from the word of God.

2. When we are commanded "to take heed to all the flock," it is plainly implied, that *flocks must be no greater regularly and ordinarily than we are capable of overseeing or taking heed of;* that particular churches should be no greater, or ministers no fewer, than may consist with a taking heed to *all;* for God will not lay upon us natural impossibilities. He will not bind men on so strict account as we are bound, to leap up to the moon, to touch the stars, to number the sands of the sea. If it be the pastoral work to oversee and take heed to all the flock, then sure there must be such a proportion of pastors assigned to each flock, or such a number of souls in the care of each pastor, as he is able to take such heed to as is here required. Will God require of one bishop to take the charge of a whole county, or of so many parishes or thousands of souls, as he is not able to know or to oversee? yea, and to take the sole government of them, while the particular teachers of them are free from that undertaking? Will God require the blood of many parishes at one man's hands, if he do not that which ten or twenty, or a hundred, or three hundred men can no more do than I can move mountains? Then woe to poor prelates! This were to impose on them a natural or unavoidable necessity of being damned. Is it not therefore a most doleful case that learned, sober men should plead for this as a desirable privilege; or draw such a burden wilfully on themselves; and that they tremble not rather at the thoughts of so great an undertaking? Oh happy had it been for the church, and happy for the bishops themselves, if this measure that is intimated by the apostle here had been still observed; and here the diocess had been no greater than the elders or bishops could oversee and rule, so that they might have taken heed to all the flock! Or that pastors had been multiplied as churches multiplied, and the number of overseers proportioned so far to the number of souls, that they might not have let the work be undone, while they assumed the empty titles, and undertook impossibilities! And that they had rather prayed the Lord of the harvest to send forth more labourers, even so many as had been proportioned to the work; and not to have undertaken all themselves! I should scarce commend the prudence or humility of that labourer, (let his parts in all other respects be never so great,) that would not only undertake to gather in all the harvest in this county himself, and that upon pain of death, yea of damnation, but would also earnestly contend for this prerogative.

Object. But there are others to teach, though one only have had the rule.

Answ. Blessed be God it was so; and no thanks to some of them. But is not government of great concernment to the good of souls, as well as preaching? If not, then what matter is it for church governors? If it be, then they that nullify it by undertaking impossibilities, do go about to ruin the churches, and themselves. If only preaching be necessary, let us have none but mere preachers: what need there then such a stir about government? But if discipline (in its place) be necessary too, what is it but enmity to men's salvation to exclude it? and it is unavoidably excluded when it is made to be his work that is naturally uncapable of performing it. He that will command an army alone, may as well say, it shall be destroyed for want of command: and the schoolmaster that will oversee or govern all the schools in the county alone, may as well say plainly, they shall all be ungoverned: and the physician who will undertake the guidance of all the sick people in a whole nation or county, when he is not able to visit or direct the hundredth man of them, as well say, *Let them perish!*

Object. But though they cannot rule them by themselves, they may do it by others.

Answ. The nature of the pastoral work is such as must be done by the pastor himself. He may not delegate a man that is no pastor to baptize, or administer the Lord's supper, or to be the teacher of the church: no more may he commit the government of it to another. Otherwise by so doing he may make that man the bishop, if he make him the immediate ruler and guide of the church: and if a bishop may make each presbyter a bishop, so he do but derive the power from him, then let it no more be held unlawful for them to govern, or to be bishops. And if a prelate may do it, it is like Christ or his apostles might, and have done it; for as we are to preach in Christ's name, and not in any man's, so it is likely that we must rule in his name. But of this somewhat more anon.

Yet still, it must be acknowledged, that in case of necessity, where there are not more to be had, one man may undertake the charge of more souls than he is able well to oversee particularly. But then he must only undertake to do what he can for them, and not to do all that a pastor ordinarily ought to do. And this is the case of some of us that have greater parishes than we are able to take that special heed to as their state requireth. I must profess for my own part, I am so far from their boldness that dare venture on the sole government of a county, that I would not for all England have undertaken to have been one of the two that should do all the pastoral work that God enjoineth to that one parish where I live, had I not this to satisfy my conscience, that *through the church's necessities more cannot be had, and therefore I must rather do what I can, than leave all undone, because I cannot do all.* But cases of unavoidable necessity are not to be the standing condition of the church; or at least, it is not desirable that it should so be. O happy church of Christ, were the labourers but able and faithful, and proportioned in number to the number of souls; so that the pastors were so many, or the particular flocks or churches so small, that we might be able to take heed to all the flocks!

SECTION II.

Having told you these two things that are here implied; I come next to the duty itself that is expressed. And this taking heed to all the flock in general is, *a very great care of the whole and every part, with great watchfulness and diligence in the use of all those holy actions and ordinances which God hath required us to use for their salvation.*

More particularly, this work is to be considered,

1. In respect to the subject matter of it.
2. In respect to the object.
3. In respect to the work itself, or the actions which we must do.

And, 4. In respect to the end which we must intend. Or it is not amiss if I begin at first with this last, as being first in our intention, though last as to the attainments.

I. The ultimate end of our pastoral oversight, is that which is the ultimate end of our whole lives; even pleasing and glorifying of God, to which is connexed the glory of the human nature also of Christ, and the glorification of his church, and of ourselves in particular: and the nearer ends of our office are, the sanctification and holy obedience of the people of our charge; their unity, order, beauty, strength, preservation, and increase; and the right worshipping of God, especially in the solemn assemblies.

By which it is manifest, that before a man is capable of being a true pastor of a church, according to the mind of Christ, he must have so high an estimation of these things, that they may be indeed his ends.

1. That man, therefore, that is not himself taken up with the predominant love of God, and is not himself devoted to him, and doth not devote to him all that he hath and can; that man that is not addicted to the pleasing of God, and maketh him not the centre of all his actions, and liveth not to him as his God and happiness; that is, that man that is not a sincere christian himself, is utterly unfit to be a pastor of a church.

And if we be not in a case of desperate necessity, the church should not admit such, so far as they can discover them; though to inferior common works (as to teach the languages, and some philosophy, to translate Scriptures, &c.) they may be admitted. A man that is not heartily devoted to God, and addicted to his service and honour, will never set heartily about the pastoral work: nor indeed can he possibly (while he remaineth such) do one part of that work, no, nor of any other, nor speak one word in christian sincerity; for no man can be sincere in the means, that is not so in his intentions of the end. A man must heartily love God above all, before he can heartily serve him before all.

2. No man is fit to be a minister of Christ that is not of a public spirit as to the church, and delighteth not in its beauty, and longeth not for its felicity: as the good of the commonwealth must be the end of the magistrate, (his nearer end,) so must the felicity of the church be the end of the pastors of it. So that we must rejoice in its welfare, and be willing to spend and be spent for its sake.

3. No man is fit to be a pastor of a church that doth not set his heart on the life to come, and regard the matters of everlasting life above all the matters of this present life; and that is not sensible in some measure how much the inestimable riches of glory are to be preferred to the trifles of this world. For he will never set his heart on the work of men's salvation, that doth not heartily believe and value that salvation.

4. He that delighteth not in holiness, hateth not iniquity, loveth not the unity and purity of the church, and abhorreth not discord and divisions, and taketh not pleasure in the communion of saints, and the public worship of God with his people, is not fit to be a pastor of a church: for none of all these can have the true ends of a pastor, and therefore cannot do the work. For of what necessity the end is to the means, and in relations, is easily known.

SECTION III.

II. The subject matter of the ministerial work is, in general, *spiritual things*, or matters that concern the pleasing of God, and the salvation of our people. It is not about temporal and transitory things. It is a vile usurpation of the pope, and his prelates, to assume the management of the temporal sword, and immerse themselves in the businesses of the world; to exercise the violent coercion of the magistrate, when they should use only the spiritual weapons of Christ. Our business is not to dispose of commonwealths, nor to touch men's purses or persons by our penalties; but it consisteth only in these two things:

1. In revealing to men that happiness, or chief good, which must be their ultimate end.

2. In acquainting them with the right means for the attainment of this end, and helping them to use them, and hindering them from the contrary.

1. It is the first and great work of the ministers of Christ, to acquaint men with that God that made them, and is their happiness; to open to them the treasures of his goodness, and tell them of the glory that is in his presence, which all his chosen people shall enjoy: that so by showing men the certainty and the excellency of the promised felicity, and the perfect blessedness in the life to come, compared with the vanities of this present life, we may turn the stream of their cogitations and affections, and bring them to a due contempt of this world, and set them on seeking the durable treasure: and this is the work that we should lie at with them night and day. Could we once get them right in regard of the end, and set their hearts unfeignedly on God and heaven, the chiefest part of the work were done; for all the rest would undoubtedly follow.

2. Having showed them the right end, our next work is to acquaint them with the right means of attaining it; where the wrong way must be disgraced, the evil of all sin must be manifested, and the danger that it hath brought us into, and the hurt it hath already done us, must be discovered. Then have we the great mystery of redemption to disclose; the person, natures, incarnation, perfection, life, miracles, sufferings, death, burial, resurrection, ascension, glorification, dominion, intercession of the blessed Son of God. As also the tenor of his promises, the conditions imposed on us, the duties which he hath commanded us, and the everlasting torments, which he hath threatened to the final impenitent neglecters of his grace. Oh what a treasury of his blessings and graces, and the privileges of his saints, we have to unfold! What a blessed life of holiness and communion therein have we to recommend to the sons of men! And yet how many temptations, difficulties, and dangers to disclose, and assist them against! How many precious spiritual duties have we to set them upon, and excite them to, and direct them in! How many objections of flesh and blood, and cavils of vain men, have we to refute! How much of their own corruptions and sinful inclinations to discover and root out! We have the depth of God's bottomless love and mercy, the depth of the mysteries of his designs, and works of creation, redemption, providence, justification, adoption, sanctification, glorification; the depth of Satan's temptations, and the depth of their own hearts, to disclose. In a word, we must teach them, as much as we can, of the *word* and *works* of God. Oh what two volumes are there for a minister to preach upon! How great, how excellent, how wonderful, and mysterious! All christians are disciples or scholars of Christ; the church is his school; we are his ushers; the Bible is his grammar: this is that we must be daily teaching them. The papists would teach them without book, lest they should learn heresies from the word of truth; lest they learn falsehood from the book of God, they must learn only the books or words of priests. But our business is not to teach them without book, but to help them to understand this book of God. So much for the subject matter of our work.

SECTION IV.

III. The object of our pastoral care is, *all the flock;* that is, the church, and every member of it. It is considered by us, 1. In the whole body or society. 2. In the parts or individual members.

1. Our first care must be about the whole: and therefore the first duties to be done are public duties, which are done to the whole. As our people are bound to prefer public duties before private, so are we much more. But this is so commonly confessed, that I shall say no more of it.

2. But that which is less understood or considered of, is, that *all* the flock, even each individual member of our charge, must be taken heed of, and watched over by us in our ministry. To which end it is to be presupposed necessary, that (unless where absolute necessity forbiddeth it, through the scarcity of pastors, and greatness of the flock) we should *know* every person that belongeth to our charge; for how can we take heed to them if we do not know them? Or how can we take that heed that belongeth to the special charge that we have undertaken, if we know not who be of our charge, and who not, though we know the persons? Our obligation is not to all neighbour churches, or to all stragglers, so great as it is to those whom we are set over. How can we tell whom to exclude, till we know who are included? Or how can we refel the accusations of the offended, that tell us of the ungodly or defiled members of our churches, when we know not who be members and who not? Doubtless the bounds of our parish will not tell us, as long as papists, and some worse, do there inhabit. Nor will bare hearing us certainly discover it, as long as those are used to hear that are members of other churches, or of none at all. Nor is mere participation of the Lord's supper a sure note, while strangers may be admitted, and many a member accidentally be kept off. Though much probability may be gathered by these, or some of these, yet a fuller knowledge of our charge is necessary where it may be had, and that must be the fittest expression of consent, because it is consent that is necessary to the relation.

All the flock being thus known, must afterward be heeded. One would think all reasonable men should be satisfied of that, and it should need no further proof. Doth not a careful shepherd look after every individual sheep? and a good schoolmaster look to every individual scholar, both for instruction and correction? and a good physician look after every particular patient? and good commanders look after every individual soldier? Why then should not the teachers, the pastors, the physicians, the guides of the churches of Christ, take heed to every individual member of their charge? Christ himself, the great and good shepherd, and Master of the church, that hath the whole to look after, doth yet take care of every individual. In Luke xv. he tells us, that he is as the Shepherd that "leaveth the ninety and nine sheep in the wilderness, to seek after one that was lost;" or, as the "woman that lighteth a candle, and sweepeth the house, and searcheth diligently to find the *one* groat that was lost; and having found it, doth rejoice, and call her friends and neighbours to rejoice." And Christ telleth us, that "even in heaven there is joy over *one* sinner that repenteth." The prophets are oft sent to single men. Ezekiel is made a watchman over individuals; and must say to the wicked, "Thou shalt surely die," Ezek. iii. 18, 19; xviii. And Paul taught them "publicly, and from house to house;" which was meant of his teaching particular families; for even the public teaching was then in houses; and *publicly*, and *from house to house*, signify not the same thing. The same Paul "warned every man, and taught every man, in all wisdom, that he might present every man perfect in Christ Jesus," Col. i. 28. Christ expoundeth his public parables to the twelve apart, Mark iv. 34. Every man must "seek the law at the mouth of the priest," Mal. ii. 7. We must give an account of our watching for the souls of all that are bound to obey us, Heb. xiii. 7. Many more passages in Scripture assure us that it is our duty to take heed of every individual person in our flock. And many passages in the ancient councils do plainly tell us, it was the practice of those times, till churches began to be crowded, and to swell so big that they could not be guided as churches should be, when they should rather have been multiplied, as the converts did increase. But I will pass over all these, and mention only one passage in Ignatius (or whoever it was, I matter not much, seeing it is but to prove what was the custom of the church) ad Polycarp. *Πυκνότερον συναγωγαὶ γενέσθωσαν· ἐξ ὀνόματος πάντας ζήτει δοῦλȣς καὶ δούλας μὴ ὑπερήφανει.* i. e. Let assemblies be gathered, seek after (or inquire of) all by name: despise not servant-men or maids. You see it was then taken for a duty to look after every member of the flock by name; though it were the meanest servant-man or maid. The reasons of the necessity of this I shall pass over now, because some of them will fall in when we come to the duty of catechising and personal instruction in the end.

Object. But the congregation that I am set over is so great that it is not possible for me to know them all, much less to take heed of all individuals.

Answ. 1. Is it necessity, or not, that hath cast you upon such a charge? If it be not, you excuse one sin with another. How durst you undertake that which you knew yourself unable to perform, when you were not forced to it? It seems then you had some other ends in your undertaking, and never intended to make it good, and be faithful to your trust. But if you think that you were necessitated to it, I must ask you, 1. Might not you possibly have procured some assistance for so great a charge? Have you done all that you could with your friends and neighbours to get maintenance for another to help you? 2. Have you not so much maintenance yourself as might serve yourself and another? What though it will not serve to maintain you in fulness? Is it not more reason that you should pinch your flesh and family, than undertake a work that you cannot do, and neglect the souls of so many men? I know it will seem hard to some what I say; but to me it seems an unquestionable thing: that if you have but a hundred pounds a year, it is your duty to live upon part of it, and allow the rest to a competent assistant, rather than the flock that you are over should be neglected. If you say, that this is hard measure, your wife and children cannot so live. I answer, (1.) Do not many families in your parish live on less? (2.) Have not many able ministers in the prelates' days been glad of less, with liberty to preach the gospel? There are some yet living (as I have heard) that have offered the bishops to enter into bond to preach for nothing, so they might but have the liberty to preach. (3.) If still you say, that you cannot live so nearly as poor people do, I further ask, can your parishioners better endure damnation than you can endure want and poverty? What! do you call yourselves ministers of the gospel, and yet are the souls of men so base in your eyes, that you had rather they did eternally perish, than yourselves and family should live in a low and poor condition? Nay, should you not rather beg your bread, than put such a thing as men's salvation upon a hazard or disadvantage? yea, or hazard the damnation but of one soul? O sirs, it is a miserable thing when men study and talk of heaven and hell, and the fewness of the saved, and the difficulty of salvation, and be not all this while in good sadness. If you were, you could never sure stick at such matters as these, and let your people go to damnation, that you might live at higher rates in the world! Remember this, the next time you are preaching to them, *that they cannot be saved without knowledge;* and hearken whether conscience do not conclude, *It is likely they might be brought to knowledge, if they had but diligent instruction and exhortation privately, man by man;* and then, *were there another minister to assist me, this might be done:* and then, *if I would live nearly and deny my flesh, I might have an assistant:* and then it must conclude, *Dare I let my people live in ignorance, which I myself have told them is damning, rather than put myself and family to a little want?*

And I must further say, that indeed this poverty is not so sad and dangerous a business as it is pretended to be. So you have but food and raiment, must you not therewith be content? and what would you have more than that which may enable you for the work of God? And it is not purple and fine linen, and faring deliciously every day, that you must expect, as that which must content you. "A man's life consisteth not in the abundance of the things that he possesseth." So your clothing be warm, and your food be wholesome, you may as well be supported by it to do God service, as if you had the fullest satisfaction to your flesh: a patched coat may be warm, and bread and drink is wholesome food. He that wanteth not these, hath but a cold excuse to make for hazarding men's souls, that he may live on a fuller diet in the world.

Object. If this doctrine be received, then it will discourage men from meddling with great places; and so all cities, market-towns, and other great parishes, will be left desolate.

Answ. It will discourage none but the carnal and self-seeking, and not those that thirst after the winning of souls, and are wholly devoted to the service of God, and have taken up the cross and follow Christ in self-denial. And for others, they are so far from being good ministers, that they are not his disciples or true christians. Christ would not forbear to tell the world of the absolute necessity of self-denial, and resigning up all, and bearing the cross, and mortifying the flesh, for fear of discouraging men from his service; but contrarily telleth them that he will have no other servants but such, and those that will not come on those terms, may go their ways, and take their course, and see who will lose by it, and whether he do want more their service, or they want his protection and favour.

Object. But I am not bound to go to a charge which I cannot perform, and take a greater place, when I am fit but for a less.

Answ. 1. If you would undertake it but for want of maintenance, then it is not unfitness, but poverty that is your discouragement; and that is no sufficient discouragement.

2. We are bound to dispose of ourselves to the greatest advantage of the church, and to take that course in which we may do God the greatest service: and we know that he hath more work for us in greater congregations than in lesser, and that the neglect of them would be the greatest injury and danger to his church and interest; and therefore we must not refuse, but choose the greatest work, though it be accompanied with the greatest difficulties and suffering. It must be done, and why not by you as well as others?

Object. But no man must undertake more than he can do.

Answ. I will add the rest of my inquiries, which

will answer this objection. 3. Would the maintenance of the place serve two others, that have less necessity or smaller families than you? If it will, try to get two such as may accept it in your stead. 4. If this cannot be done, nor addition be procured, and there be really so little that you cannot have assistance, then these two things must be done. (1.) You must take the charge with limitation, with a profession of your insufficiency for the whole work, and your undertaking only so much as you can do; and this you do for the necessity of the place that cannot otherwise be better supplied. (2.) You must not leave off the work of personal oversight, nor refuse to deal particularly with any, because you cannot do it with all: but take this course with as many as you are able; and withal put on godly neighbours, and special parents and masters of families, to do the more. And thus doing what we can will be accepted.

And in the mean time, let us importune the rulers of the commonwealth, for such a proportion of maintenance to great congregations, that they may have so many ministers to watch over them, as may personally as well as publicly instruct and exhort them. It may please God at last to put this into the hearts of governors, and to give them a love to the prosperity of his church, and a conscience of their duty for the promoting of men's salvation.

Some more of these objections we shall answer anon, under the uses. So much for the distribution of the work of the ministry, drawn from the object materially considered.

We are next to consider of it in reference to the several qualities of the object. And because we here speak somewhat of the acts with the object, there will be the less afterward to be said of them by themselves.

1. The first part of our ministerial work lieth in bringing unsound professors of the faith to sincerity, that they who before were christians in name and show, may be so indeed. Though it belong not to us, as their pastors, to convert professed infidels to the faith, because they cannot be members of the church while they are professed infidels; yet doth it belong to us as their pastors, to convert these seeming christians to sincerity, because such seeming christians may be visible members of our churches. And though we be not absolutely certain that this or that man in particular is unsound, and unsanctified; yet as long as we have a certainty that many such are usually in the church, and have too great probability that it is so with several individuals whom we can name, we have therefore ground enough to deal with them for their conversion. And if we be certain by their notorious impiety that they are no christians, and so to be ejected from the communion of christians; yea, if they were professed infidels, yet may we deal with them for their conversions, though not as their pastors, yet as ministers of the gospel. So that upon these terms we may well conclude that the work of conversion is the great thing that we must first drive at, and labour with all our might to effect.

Alas! the misery of the unconverted is so great, that it calleth loudest to us for our compassion! If a truly converted sinner do fall, it will be but into sin, which will sure be pardoned, and he is not in that hazard of damnation by it as others be. Not, as some unjustly accuse us to say, that God hateth not their sins as well as others, or that he will bring them to heaven let them live never so wickedly; but the Spirit, that is within them will not let them live wickedly, nor to sin as the ungodly do; but they hate sin habitually, when through temptation they commit it actually; and as they have a general repentance for all, so have they a particular repentance for all that is known; and they usually know all that is gross and much more, and they have no iniquity that hath dominion over them. But with the unconverted it is far otherwise: they are in the gall of bitterness and bond of iniquity, and have yet no part nor fellowship in the pardon of their sins, or the hopes of glory. We have therefore a work of greater necessity to do for them, even "to open their eyes, and turn them from darkness to light, and from the power of Satan unto God; that they may receive forgiveness of sin, and inheritance among the sanctified by faith in Christ," Acts xxvi. 18. To soften and open their hearts to the entertainment of "the truth, if God, peradventure, will give them repentance to the acknowledging of it, that they may escape out of the snares of the devil, who are taken captive by him at his will," 2 Tim. ii. 25. That so "they may be converted, and their sins may be forgiven them," Mark iv. 12. He that seeth one man sick of a mortal disease, and another only pained with the tooth-ache, will be moved more to compassionate the former, than the latter, and will sure make more haste to help him, though he were a stranger, and the other a son. It is so sad a case to see men in a state of damnation, wherein if they should die they are remedilessly lost, that methinks we should not be able to let them alone, either in public or private, whatever other work we have to do. I confess, I am forced frequently to neglect that which should tend to the further increase of knowledge in the godly, and may be called stronger meat, because of the lamentable necessity of the unconverted. Who is able to talk of controversies, or nice unnecessary points, how excellent soever, while he seeth a company of ignorant, carnal, miserable sinners before his face, that must be changed or damned? Methinks I even see them entering upon their final woe! Methinks I even hear them crying out for help, and speediest help! Their misery speaks the louder, because they have not hearts to seek, or ask for help themselves. Many a time have I known, that I had some hearers of higher fancies, that looked for rarities, and were addicted to despise the ministry, if he told them not somewhat more than ordinary; and yet I could not find in my heart to turn from the observation of the necessities of the impenitent, for the humouring of these, nor to leave speaking to the apparently miserable for their salvation, to speak to such novelists, for the clawing of their ears; no, nor so much as otherwise should be done, to the weak for their confirmation, and increase in grace. Methinks as Paul's spirit was stirred within him, when he saw the Athenians so addicted to idolatry, Acts xvii. 16; so it should cast us into one of his paroxysms, to see so many men in great probability of being everlastingly undone; and if by faith we did indeed look upon them as within a step of hell, it should more effectually untie our tongues, than they tell us that Crœsus' danger did his son's. He that will let a sinner go to hell for want of speaking to him, doth set less by souls than the Redeemer of souls did, and less by his neighbour than rational charity will allow him to do by his greatest enemy. O therefore, brethren, whomsoever you neglect, neglect not the most miserable! Whatever you pass over, forget not poor souls that are under the condemnation and curse of the law, and may look every hour for the infernal execution, if a speedy change do not prevent it. O call after the impenitent, and ply this great work of converting souls, whatever else you leave undone!

2. The next part of the ministerial work, is for the building up of those that are already truly converted. And according to the various states of these, the work is various. In general, as the persons are either such as are young and weak, or such as are in danger of growing worse, or such as are already declining, so our work is all reducible to these three, *confirmation and progress, preservation* and *restoration.*

(1.) We have many of our flock that are young and weak; though of long standing, yet of small proficiency or strength, Heb. v. 11, 12. And indeed it is the most common condition of the godly: most of them stick in weak and low degrees of grace; and it is no easy matter to get them higher. To bring them to higher and stricter opinions, is very easy; that is, to bring them from the truth into error, on the right hand as well as on the left: but to increase their knowledge and gifts is not easy; but to increase their graces is the hardest of all. It is a very troublesome thing to be weak: it keepeth under dangers, it abateth consolation and delight in God, and taketh off the sweetness of his ways, and maketh us go to work with too much backwardness, and come off with little peace or profit. It maketh us less serviceable to God and man, to bring less honour to our Master and profession, and do less good to all about us. We find but small benefit by the means we use; we too easily play with the serpent's baits, and are insnared by his wiles. A seducer will easily make us shake, and evil may be made appear to us as good, truth as falsehood, sin as a duty, and so on the contrary. We are less able to resist and stand an encounter; we soon fall; we hardlier rise, and are apt to prove a scandal and reproach to our profession. We less know ourselves, and are more apt to be mistaken in our own estate, not observing corruptions when they have got advantage; we are dishonourable to the gospel by our very weakness, and little useful to any about us; and, in a word, though we live to less profit to ourselves or others, yet are we unwilling and too unready to die.

And seeing the case of weakliness is comparatively so sad, how diligent should we be to cherish and increase their grace! The strength of christians is the honour of the church. When men are inflamed with the love of God, and live by a lively, working faith, and set light by the profits and honours of the world, and love one another with a pure heart fervently, and can bear and heartily forgive a wrong, and suffer joyfully for the cause of Christ, and study to do good, and walk inoffensively and harmlessly in the world, as ready to be servants of all men for their good, becoming all things to all men to win them, and yet abstaining from the appearances of evil, and seasoning all their actions with a sweet mixture of prudence, humility, zeal, and heavenly spirituality; oh what an honour are such to their profession! what ornaments to the church! and how excellently serviceable to God and man! Men would sooner believe that the gospel is indeed a word of truth and power, if they could see more such effects of it upon the hearts and lives of men. The world is better able to read the nature of religion in a man's life than in the Bible. They that obey not the word, may be won by the conversations of such as these, 1 Pet. iii. 1. It is therefore a necessary part of our work, to labour more in polishing and perfecting of the saints, that they may be strong in the Lord, and fitted for their Master's use.

(2.) Another sort of converts that need our special help, are those that labour under some particular distemper, that keeps under their graces, and maketh them temptations and troubles to others, and a burden to themselves. For, alas! too many such there are! Some that are specially addicted to pride, and some to worldliness, and some to this or that sensual desire; and many to frowardness and disturbing passions. It is our duty to set in for the assistance of all these, and partly by dissuasions and clear discoveries of the odiousness of the sin, and partly by suitable directions about the way of remedy, to help them to a fuller conquest of their corruptions. We are leaders of Christ's army against the powers of darkness, and must resist all the works of darkness wherever we find them, though it be in the children of light. We must be no more tender of the sins of the godly than the ungodly, nor any more befriend them or favour them. By how much more we love the persons above others, by so much the more we must express it in the opposition of their sins. And yet must look to meet with some tender persons here, especially when iniquity hath got any head, and made a party, and many have fallen in love with it: they will be as pettish and impatient of a reproof as some worser men, and interest piety itself into their faults, and say that a minister that preacheth against them, doth preach against the godly:—a most heinous crime, to make God and godliness accessory to their sins; when all the world besides hath not the thousandth part of that enmity and opposition against them. But the ministers of Christ must do their duties for all men's peevishness; and must not so far hate their brother, as to forbear the plain rebuke of him, or suffer sin to lie upon his soul, Lev. xix. 17. Though it must be done with *much* prudence, yet done it *must* be.

(3.) Another sort that our work is about, is declining christians, that are either fallen into some scandalous sin, or else abate their zeal and diligence, and show us that they have lost their former love! As the case of backsliders is very sad, so our diligence must be great for their recovery. It is sad to them to lose so much of their life, and peace, and serviceableness to God; and to become so serviceable to Satan and his cause! It is sad to us to see that all our labour is come to this, and that when we have taken so much pains with them, and had so much hopes of them, all should be so far frustrate. It is saddest of all to think that God should be so abused by those that he hath loved, and done so much for; and that the enemy should get such advantage upon his graces, and that Christ should be so wounded in the house of a friend, and the name of God evil spoken of among the wicked through such, and all that fear God should be reproached for their sakes. Besides, that partial backsliding hath a natural tendency to total apostasy, and would effect it, if special grace prevent it not.

The sadder the case of such christians is, the more lieth upon us for their effectual recovery, "to restore those that are but overtaken with a fault by the spirit of meekness," Gal. vi. 1, 2; and yet to see that the sore be throughly searched and healed, and the joint be well set again, what pain soever it cost; and especially to look to the honour of the gospel, and to see that they rise by such free and full confessions and significations of true repentance, that some reparation be thereby made to the church and their holy profession, for the wound of dishonour that they had given it by their sin. Much skill is required to the restoring of such a soul.

(4.) Another part of ministerial work is about those that are fallen under some great temptation. Much of our assistance is needful to our people in such a case; and therefore every minister should be a man that hath much insight into the tempter's wiles. We should know the great variety of them, and the cunning craft of all Satan's instruments that lie in wait to deceive, and the methods and devices of the grand deceiver. Some of our people lie under temptations to error and heresy, especially the young, unsettled, and most self-conceited; and those that are most conversant or familiar with seducers. Young, raw, ungrounded christians are commonly of their mind that have most interest in their esteem, and most opportunity of familiar talk to draw them into their way. And as they are tender, so deceivers want not the sparks of zeal, to set them in a flame. A zeal for error and opinions of our own, is natural and easily kindled and kept alive: but it is far otherwise with the spiritual zeal for God. Oh what a deal of holy prudence and industry is necessary in a pastor to preserve the flock from being tainted with heresies, and falling into noxious conceits and practice; and especially to keep them in unity and concord, and hinder the rising or increase of divisions. If there be not a notable conjunction of all accomplishments, and a skilful improvement of parts and interests, it will hardly be done; especially in such times as ours, when the sign is in the head, and the disease is epidemical. If we do not publicly maintain the credit of our ministry, and second it by unblamable and exemplary lives, and privately meet with seducers, and shame them; if we be not able to manifest their folly, and follow not close our staggering people before they fall; how quickly may we give great advantage to the enemy, and let in such an inundation of sin and calamity, that will not easily be again cast out.

Others lie under a temptation to worldliness; and others to gluttony or drunkenness; and others to lust; some to one sin, and some to another. A faithful pastor therefore should have his eye upon them all, and labour to be acquainted with their natural temperament, and also with their occasions and affairs in the world, and the company that they live or converse with, that so he may know where their temptations lie; and then speedily, prudently, and diligently to help them!

(5.) Another part of our work is to comfort the disconsolate, and to settle the peace of our people's souls, and that on sure and lasting grounds. To which end, the quality of the complainants, and the course of their lives, had need to be known; for all people must have the like consolations that have the like complaints. But of this I have spoken already elsewhere; and there is so much said by many, especially Mr. Bolton in his "Instructions for Right Comforting," that I shall say no more.

(6.) The rest of our ministerial work is upon those that are yet strong; for they also have need of our assistance; partly to prevent their temptations and declinings, and preserve the grace they have; partly to help them for a further progress and increase; and partly to direct them in the improving of their strength for the service of Christ, and the assistance of their brethren. As also to encourage them, especially the aged, the tempted, and afflicted, to hold on, and to persevere that they may attain the crown. All these are the objects of the ministerial work, and in respect to all these we must take heed to all the flock. Abundance more distributions of our work, with directions how to perform it to rich and poor, young and old, &c. you may find in Gregor. M. de cura pastorali, worth the reading. You may have the book by itself, of Mr. Jer. Stephen's edition.

SECTION V.

IV. Having done with our work in respect of its objects, I am next to speak of the *acts themselves*. But of this I shall be brief, 1. Because they are intimated before; 2. And because they are so fully handled by many; 3. And because I find I have already run into more tediousness than I intended.

1. One part of our work, and that the most excellent, because it tendeth to work on many, is the public preaching of the word: a work that requireth greater skill, and especially greater life and zeal, than any of us bring to it. It is no small matter to stand up in the face of a congregation, and deliver a message of salvation or damnation, as from the living God, in the name of our Redeemer. It is no easy matter to speak so plain, that the ignorant may understand us; and so seriously, that the deadest hearts may feel us; and so convincingly, that the contradicting cavillers may be silenced. I know it is a great dispute whether preaching be proper to the ministers or not? The decision seems not very difficult. Preaching to a congregation as their ordinary teacher, is proper to a minister in office; and preaching to the unbelieving world, (Jews, Mahometans, or pagans,) as one that hath given up himself to that work, and is separated and set apart to it, is proper to a minister in office; but preaching to a church, and infidels occasionally, as an act of charity extraordinarily; or upon special call to that act, may be common to others. The governor of a church, when he cannot preach himself, may in a case of necessity appoint a private man, *pro tempore*, to do it, that is able, as Mr. Thorndike hath showed. But no private man may obtrude without his consent, who by his office is the guide and pastor of that church. And a master of a family may preach to his own family, and a schoolmaster to his scholars, and any man to those whom he is obliged to teach; so be it, he goes not beyond his ability, and do it in a due subordination to church teaching, and not in a way of opposition and division. A man that is not of the trade, may do some one act of a tradesman in a corporation for his own use, or his family or friend; but he may not addict or separate himself to it, or set up and make it his profession, nor live upon it, unless he had been an apprentice and were free. For though one man of ten thousand may do it of himself as well as he that hath served an apprenticeship, yet it is not to be presumed that it is ordinarily so: and the standing rule must not bend to rarities and extraordinaries, lest it undo all; for that which is extraordinary and rare in such cases, the law doth look upon as a *non ens*.

But the best way to silence such usurping teachers, is for those to whom it belongeth to do it themselves so diligently, that the people may not have need to go a begging; and to do it judiciously, and affectingly, that a plain difference may appear between them and usurpers, and that other men's works may be shamed by theirs; and also by the adding of holy lives and unwearied diligence to high abilities, to keep up the reputation of their sacred office, that neither seducers nor tempted ones may fetch matter of temptation from our blemishes or neglects. But I shall say no more of this duty.

2. Another part of our pastoral work is to administer the holy mysteries, or seals of God's covenant, baptism and the Lord's supper. This also is claimed by private usurpers: but I will not stand to discuss their claim. A great fault it is among ourselves, that some are so careless in the manner, and others do reform that with a total neglect, and others do lay such a stress on circumstances, and make them a matter of so much contention, even in that ordinance where union and communion is so professed.

3. Another part of our work is to guide our people, and be as their mouth in the public prayers of the

church, and the public praises of God; as also to bless them in the name of the Lord. This sacerdotal part of the work is not the least, nor to be so much thrust into a corner as by too many of us it is. A great part of God's service in the church assemblies was wont, in all ages of the church till of late, to consist in public praises and eucharistical acts in holy communion: and the Lord's day was still kept as a day of thanksgiving, in the hymns and common rejoicings of the faithful, in special commemoration of the work of redemption, and the happy condition of the gospel church. I am as apprehensive of the necessity of preaching as some others: but yet methinks, the solemn praises of God should take up much more of the Lord's day than in most places they do. And methinks, they that are for the magnifying of gospel privileges, and for a life of love and heavenly joys, should be of my mind in this; and their worship should be evangelical as well as their doctrine pretendeth to be.

4. Another part of the ministerial work is, to have a special care and oversight of each member of the flock. The parts whereof are these that follow:

(1.) We must labour to be acquainted with the state of all our people as fully as we can; both to know the persons, and their inclinations and conversation; to know what are the sins that they are most in danger of, and what duties they neglect for the matter or manner, and what temptations they are most liable to. For if we know not the temperament or disease, we are like to prove but unsuccessful physicians.

(2.) We must use all the means we can to instruct the ignorant in the matters of their salvation; by our own most plain familiar words; by giving or lending, or otherwise helping them to books that are fit for them; by persuading them to learn catechisms; and those that cannot read, to get help of their neighbours; and to persuade their neighbours to afford them help, who have best opportunities thereto.

(3.) We must be ready to give advice to those that come to us with cases of conscience, especially the great case which the Jews put to Peter, and the jailer to Paul and Silas, (Acts xvi.) "What must we do to be saved?" A minister is not only for public preaching, but to be a known counsellor for their souls, as the lawyer is for their estates, and the physician for their bodies; so that each man that is in doubts and straits, should bring his case to him and desire resolution. Not that a minister should be troubled with every small matter, which judicious neighbours can give them advice in as well as he, no more than a lawyer or physician should be troubled for every trifle or familiar case, where others can tell them as much as they: but as when their estate or life is in danger they will go to these; so when their souls are in danger, they should go to ministers: as Nicodemus came to Christ, and as was usual with the people to go to the priest, whose lips must preserve knowledge, and at whose mouth they must ask the law, because he is the messenger of the Lord of hosts. And because the people are grown unacquainted with the office of the ministry, and their own necessity and duty herein, it belongeth to us to acquaint them herewith, and to press them publicly to come to us for advice in such cases of great concernment to their souls. We must not only be willing of the trouble, but draw it upon ourselves by inviting them hereto. What abundance of good might we do, could we but bring our people to this! And doubtless much might be done in it, if we did our duties. How few have I ever heard that heartily pressed their people to their duty in this! A sad case, that people's souls should be so injured and hazarded, by the total neglect of so great a duty, and ministers scarce ever tell them of it, and awaken them to it: were they but duly sensible of the need and weight of this, you should have them more frequently knocking at your doors, and open their cases to you, making their sad complaints, and begging your advice. I beseech you put them more on this for the future, and perform it carefully when they seek your help. To this end it is very necessary that we be acquainted with practical cases, and especially that we be acquainted with the nature of true grace, and able to assist them in trying their states, and resolve the main question that concerns their everlasting life or death. One word of seasonable prudent advice given by a minister to persons in necessity, hath done that good that many sermons would not have done.

(4.) We must also have a special eye upon families, to see that they be well ordered, and the duties of each relation performed; the life of religion, and the welfare and glory of church and state, depending much on family government and duty. If we suffer the neglect of this, we undo all. What are we like to do ourselves to the reforming of a congregation, if all the work be cast on us alone, and masters of families will let fall that necessary duty of their own, by which they are bound to help us! If any good be begun by the ministry in any soul in a family, a careless, prayerless, worldly family is like to stifle it, or very much hinder it. Whereas, if you could but get the rulers of families to do their part, and take up the work where you left it, and help it on, what abundance of good might be done by it! (as I have elsewhere showed more at large). I beseech you, therefore, do all that you can to promote this business, as ever you desire the true reformation and welfare of your parishes! To which end let these things following be performed.

[1.] Get certain information how each family is ordered, and how God is worshipped in them; that you may know how to proceed in your carefulness for their further good.

[2.] Go now and then among them when they are like to be most at leisure, and ask the master of the family whether he pray with them, or read the Scripture, or what he doth? And labour to convince the neglecters of their sin. And if you can have opportunity to pray with them before you go, and give them an example what you would have them do, and how; and get a promise of them that they will be more conscionable therein for the future.

[3.] If you find any unable to pray in tolerable expressions, through ignorance and disuse, persuade them to study their own wants, and get their hearts affected with them, and so go oft to those neighbours who use to pray, that they may learn, and in the mean time persuade them to use a form of prayer rather than none. Only tell them, that it is their sin and shame that they have lived so negligently, as to be now so unacquainted with their own necessities, as not to know how to speak to God in prayer, when every beggar can find words to ask an alms; and therefore tell them that this form is but for necessity, as a crutch to a cripple, while they cannot do as well without it: but they must not resolve to take up there, but to learn to do better as soon as they can, seeing prayer should come from the feeling of the heart, and be varied both according to our necessities and observations. Yet it is necessary to most unaccustomed, ill-bred people, that have not been brought up where prayer hath been used, that they begin at first with a form, because they will else be able to do nothing at all, and in sense of their disability will wholly neglect the duty, though they desire to perform it. For many disused persons can mutter out some honest requests in secret, that be not able before others to speak tolerable sense. And I will not be one of them that had rather the duty were wholly neglected, or else profaned and made contemptible, than encourage them to the use of a form, either recited by memory or read.

[4.] See that they have some profitable, moving book (beside the Bible) in each family: if they have not, persuade them to buy some of small price, and great use; such as Mr. Whately's "New Birth," and Dod "on the Commandments," or some smaller, moving sermons. If they be not able to buy them, give them some if you can: if you cannot, get some gentlemen, or other rich persons that are willing to good works, to do it; and engage them to read in it on nights when they have leisure, and especially on the Lord's day.

[5.] By all means persuade them to procure all their children to learn to read English.

[6.] Direct them how to spend the Lord's day; how to despatch their worldly businesses, so as to prevent encumbrances and distractions; and when they have been at the assembly, how to spend the time in their families. The life of religion lieth much on this, because poor people have no other free considerable time; and therefore if they lose this, they lose all, and will remain ignorant and brutish. Specially, persuade them to these two things: 1. If they cannot repeat the sermon, or otherwise spend the time profitably at home, that they take their family with them, and go to some godly neighbour that spends it better, that by joining with them they may have the better help. 2. That the master of the family will every Lord's day at night cause all his family to repeat the catechism to him, and give him some account of what they have learned in public that day.

[7.] If there be any in the family that are known to be unruly, give the ruler a special charge concerning them, and make them understand what a sin it is to connive at them, and tolerate them.

Neglect not therefore this necessary part of your work. Get masters of families to their duties, and they will spare you a great deal of labour with the rest, or further much the success of your labours. If a captain can get his lieutenant, cornet, and other inferior officers, to their duties, he may rule the soldiers with less trouble, than if all should lie upon his hands alone. You are like to see no general reformation till you procure family reformation. Some little obscure religion there may be in here and there one; but while it sticks in single persons, and is not promoted by these societies, it doth not prosper, nor promise much for future increase.

(5.) Another part of the work of our private oversight consisteth in a vigilant opposing of seducers, and seeking to prevent the infection of our flock, and speedy reclaiming those that begin to itch after strange teachers, and turn into crooked paths. When we hear of any one that lies under the influence of their temptation, or that is already deceived by them, we must speedily with all our skill and diligence make out for their relief. The means I shall show in the directions in the end.

(6.) Another part of this oversight lieth in the due encouragement of those that are humble, upright, obedient christians, and profit by our teaching, and are an honour to their profession. We must in the eyes of all the flock put some difference between them and the rest by our praises, and more special familiarity, and other testimonies of our approbation, and rejoicing over them; that so we may both encourage them, and incite others to imitate them. God's graces are amiable and honourable in all, even in the poorest of the flock, as well as in pastors; and the smallest degrees must be cherished and encouraged; but the highest more openly honoured and propounded to imitation. They that have slighted or vilified the most gracious, because they were of the laity, while they claimed to themselves the honour of the clergy, though adorned with little or none of that grace, as they showed themselves to be proud and carnal, so did they take the next way to debase themselves by self-exaltation, and to bring the office itself into contempt. For if there be no honour due to the real sanctity of a christian, much less to the relative sanctity of a pastor: and he that vilifieth the person, cannot well plead for the honouring of robes and empty titles; nor can he expect that his people should give him the honour of a pastor, if he will not give them the love and honour that is due to christians, and the members of Christ. As the orator said to Domitius, *Cur ego te habeam ut principem, cum tu me non habeas ut senatorem.* It was an unchristian course therefore, which our prelates and their agents took, who discountenanced none so much as the most godly, whom they should have rejoiced in and encouraged; and made them not only the common scorn, but also the objects of their persecuting rage, as if they had fed their flock for the butcher, and called them out for suffering as they came to any maturity. This vilifying and persecuting the most diligent of the flock, was neither the note of christian shepherds, nor the way to be so esteemed. As Jerom saith, *Quid de episcopis, qui verberibus timeri volunt, canones dicant, bene fraternitas vestra novit. Pastores enim facti sumus, non percussores. Egregius prædicator dixit; Argue, obsecra, increpa in omni patientia et doctrina: nova vero atque inaudita est illa prædicatio, quæ verberibus exigit fidem.* Much more might he have said, *quæ verberibus castigat pietatem.*

(7.) Another part of our oversight lieth in visiting the sick, and helping them to prepare either for a fruitful life or a happy death. Though this be the business of all our life and theirs, yet doth it at such a season require extraordinary care both of them and us. When time is almost gone, and they must be now or never reconciled to God, and possessed of his grace, oh how doth it concern them to redeem those hours, and lay hold upon eternal life! And when we see that we are like to have but a few days' or hours' time more to speak to them, in order to their endless state, what man that is not an infidel or a block, would not be with them, and do all that he can for their salvation in that short space!

Will it not awaken us to compassion to look upon a languishing man, and to think that within a few days his soul will be in heaven or in hell? Surely it will much try the faith and seriousness of ministers and others, to be about dying men; and they will have much opportunity to discern whether they are themselves in good sadness about the matters of the life to come. So great is the change that is made by death, that it should awaken us to the greatest sensibility, to see a man so near it, and should provoke us in the deepest pangs of compassion, to do the office of inferior angels for the soul before it is departed from the flesh, that it may be ready for the convoy of superior angels, to transmit it to the prepared glory when it is removed from sin and misery. When a man is almost at his journey's end, and the next step puts him into heaven or hell, it is time for us to help him if we can, while there is hope. As Bernard saith, The death of the righteous is *bona propter requiem, melior propter novitatem, optima propter securitatem: sed mors peccatorum est mala in mundi amissione, pejor in carnis separatione, pessima in vermis ignisque duplici contritione.* Could they have any hope that it would be their *ultima linea rerum*, and that they have no more to suffer when that dismal day is past, they might have such abatements of their terror to die as brutes, who fear no sorrow after death. But it is so far otherwise, that death itself is the smallest matter that they need to care for: *Sed moriendo quo ire cogantur*, ut August. It is not the *prima mors quæ animam pellit violenter e corpore*, that is the most terrible, *sed secunda quæ animam nolentem tenet in corpore*, inquit idem.

And as their present necessity should move us to take that opportunity for their good, so should the advantage that sickness and the foresight of death affordeth. There are few of the stoutest hearts but will hear us on their death-bed, that scorned us before. They will then let fall their fury, and be as tame as lambs, that were before as untractable as wasps or madmen: a man may speak to them then, that could not before. I find not one of ten of the most obstinate, scornful wretches in the parish, but when they come to die, will humble themselves; confess their fault, and seem penitent, and promise, if they should recover, to do so no more. If the very meditations of death be so effectual in the time of health, that it is, saith Augustinus, *quasi clavis carnis omnes motus superbiæ ligno crucis affigens*, (l. 2. de Doct. Christ.) much more when it comes in, as it were, at the window, and looks men in the face. Cyprian saith to those in health, *Qui se quotidie recordatur moriturum esse, contemnit præsentia, et ad futura festinat:* much more *qui sentit se statim moriturum. Nil ita revocata peccato*, saith Austin, *quam frequens mortis meditatio.* Oh how resolvedly will the worst of them seem to cast away their sins and promise a reformation, and cry out of their folly, and of the vanity of this world, when they see that death is in good sadness with them, and away they must without delay! Perhaps you will say, that these forced changes are not cordial, and therefore we have no great hope of doing them any saving good. I confess that it is very common to be frighted into uneffectual purposes, but not so common to be at such a season converted to fixed resolutions: and as Austin saith, *Non potest male mori, qui bene vixerit; et vix bene moritur, qui male vixit.* Yet *vix* and *nunquam* are not all one. It should make both them and us the more diligent in the time of health, because it is *vix:* but yet we should bestir us at the last, in the use of the last remedies, because it is not *nunquam.*

And it will not be unuseful to ourselves, to read such lectures of our own mortality: it is better to go into the house of mourning, than into the house of feasting: for it tendeth to make the heart better, when we see the end of all the living, and what it is that the world will do for those that sell their salvation for it. When we see that it will be our own case, and there is no escape;

("Scilicit omne sacrum mors importuna prophanat,
Omnibus obscuras injicit illa manus;")

it will make us talk to ourselves in Bernard's language, *Quare, O miser, non omni hora ad mortem te disponis? Cogita te jam mortuum, quem scis necessitate moriturum: distingue qualiter oculi vertentur in capite, venæ rumpentur in corpore, et cor scindetur dolore.* When we see that (as he saith) death spareth none: *inopiæ non miseretur, non reveretur divitias; non sapientiæ, non moribus, non ætati denique parcit; nisi quod senibus mors est in januis, juvenibus vero in insidiis;* it will excite us the better to consider the use of faith and holiness; that it is not to put by death, but to put by hell; not that we may not die as certainly as others, but that we may die better, and be certainly happy after death.

Because I intend no such thing as a directory for the whole ministerial work, I will not stand to tell you particularly what must be done for men in that last extremity; but only choose out these three or four things to remember you of, passing by all the rest.

[1.] Stay not till strength and understanding be gone, and the time so short that you scarce know what you do; but go to them as soon as you hear that they are sick, whether they send for you or not.

[2.] When the time is short, that there is no opportunity to endeavour the change of their hearts in that distinct way, as is usual with others, nor to press truths upon them in such order, and stay the working of it by degrees, we must therefore be sure to ply the main, and dwell upon those truths which must do the great work: showing them the certainty and glory of the life to come, and the way by which it was purchased for us, and the great sin and folly of their neglecting it in time of health; but yet the possibility that remaineth of obtaining it, if they but yet close with it heartily as their happiness, and with the Lord Jesus, as the way thereto; and abhorring themselves for their former evil, can now unfeignedly resign up themselves to him, to be justified, sanctified, ruled, and saved by him. Three things must be chiefly insisted on.

1. The end: the certainty and greatness of the glory of the saints in the presence of God, that so their hearts may be set upon it.

2. The sufficiency and necessity of the redemption by Jesus Christ; and the fulness of the Spirit which we may and must be made partakers of. This is the principal way to the end, and the nearer end itself.

3. The necessity and nature of faith, repentance, and resolutions for new obedience according as there shall be opportunity. This is the subservient way, or the means that on our part must be performed.

[3.] Labour, upon conviction and deliberation, to engage them by solemn promise to Christ, and new obedience according to their opportunity; especially if you see any likelihood of their recovery.

[4.] If they do recover, be sure to mind them of their promises. Go to them purposely to set it home, and reduce them into performance. And whenever after you see them remiss, go to them then, and mind them of what they formerly said. And because it is of such use to them that recover, (and hath been a means of the conversion of many a soul,) it is very necessary that you go to them whose sickness is not mortal, as well as to them that are nearer death; that so we may have some advantage to move them to repentance, and engage them to newness of life; and may afterward have this to plead against their sins. As a bishop of Colen is said by Æneas Silvius to have answered the emperor Sigismund, when he asked him, what was the way to be saved; that he must be what he purposed or promised to be, when he was last troubled with the stone and gout: so may we hereafter answer these.

(8.) Another part of our ministerial oversight consisteth in the right comforting the consciences of the troubled, and settling our people in a well-grounded peace. But this I have spoken of elsewhere, and others have done it more at large.

(9.) Another part of this oversight is in reproving and admonishing those that live offensively, or impenitently, and receiving the information of those that have admonished them more privately in vain. Before we bring such matters to the congregation, or to a representative church, it is ordinarily most fit for the minister to try himself what he can do more privately to bow the sinner to repentance, especially if it be not a public crime. A great deal of skill is here required; and difference must be made, according to the various tempers of offenders; but with the most it will be necessary to fall on with the greatest plainness and power, to shake their careless hearts, and make them see what it is to dally with sin; to let them know the evil of it, and its sad effects, and the unkindness, unreasonableness, unprofitableness, and other aggravations; and what it is they do against God and themselves. For the matter, the following directions may be applied.

(10.) The next part of our oversight consisteth in the use of church discipline: and this consisteth, after the foresaid private reproofs, 1. In more public reproof. 2. And persuading the person to meet expressions of repentance. 3. And praying for them. 4. In restoring the penitent. 5. And excluding and avoiding the impenitent.

[1.] And for reproof, these things must be observed. 1. That the accusations of none (no not the best in the church) be taken without proof, nor rashly entertained; nor that a minister should make himself a party before he have a sufficient evidence of the case. It is better let many vicious persons go unpunished, or uncensured, when we want sufficient evidence, than to censure one unjustly; which we may easily do, if we will go upon too bold presumptions; and then it will bring upon the pastors the scandal of partiality, and unrighteous and injurious dealing, and make all their reproofs and censures become contemptible.

2. Let there be therefore a less public meeting of chosen persons (as the officers and some delegates of the church on their behalf) to have the hearing of all such cases before they be made more public; that once a month, at a set place, they may come together to receive what charge shall be brought against any member of the church, that it may be considered whether it be just, and the offender may be dealt with then first: and if the fault be either less public or less heinous, so that a less public profession of repentance may satisfy, then if the party shall there profess repentance, it may suffice.

3. But if it be not so, or if the party remain impenitent, he must be reproved before all, and there again invited to repentance. This duty is never the less, because our brethren have made so little conscience of the practice of it. It is not only Christ's command to *tell the church*, but Paul's to *rebuke such before all;* and the church hath constantly practised it till selfishness and formality caused them to be remiss in this and other duties together; and the reformers have as much stood up for it as the rest; and as deeply are we engaged by vows, covenants, prayers, and other means, for the executing of it: of which more in the application. Austin saith, *Quæ peccantur coram omnibus, coram omnibus corripienda, sunt, ut omnes timeant: Qui secreto peccant in te, secreto corripe; nam si solus nosti, et eum vis coram aliis arguere, non es corrector sed proditor.* Greg. Mag. in Registro, saith, *Manifesta peccata non sunt occulta correctione purganda: sed palam sunt arguendi qui palam nocent; ut dum aperta objurgatione sanantur, hi qui eos imitando delinquerant, corrigantur. Dum enim unus corripitur, plurimi emendantur, et melius est ut pro multorum salute unus condemnetur, quam ut per unius licentiam multi periclitentur.* Isidore saith, *Qui admonitus secrete de peccato corrigi negligit, publice arguendus est, ut vulnus quod occulte sanari nescit, manifeste debeat emendari.* If any shall say, that we shall thus be guilty of defaming men by publishing their crimes; I answer, in the words of Bernard sup. Cantic. *Cum carpuntur vitia, et inde scandalum oritur, ipse sibi scandali causa est, qui fecit quod argui debet; non ille qui arguit. Non ergo timeas contra charitatem esse, si unius scandalum multorum recompensaveris pace. Melius est enim ut pereat unus quam unitas.* There is no room for a doubt, whether this be our duty, nor any to doubt whether we are unfaithful as to the performance of it. I doubt many of us that would be ashamed to omit preaching or praying half so much, have little considered what we do in the wilful neglect of this duty, and the rest of discipline, so long as we have done. We little think how we have drawn the guilt of swearing, and drunkenness, and fornication, and other crimes upon our own heads, for want of using God's means for the cure of them. As Greg. Mag. saith in Reg. *Qui non corrigit resecanda, committit: et facientis culpam habet, qui quod potest corrigere, negligit emendare;* saith the Comedian. *Si quid me scis fecisse inscite aut improbe, si id non accusas, tuipse objurgandus es.* Plaut.

If any say, there is little likelihood that public, personal reprehension should do good on them, because they will be but enraged by the shame, I answer:—

1. Philo, a Jew, could say, (de Sacrif. Abel et Cain,) "We must endeavour, as far as we are able, to save those from their sins that shall certainly perish; imitating good physicians, who when they cannot save a sick man, do yet willingly try all means for cure, lest they seem to want success through their own neglects.

2. I further answer, It ill beseems the silly creature to implead the ordinances of God as useless, or to reproach his service instead of doing it, and set their wits against their Maker. God can make use of his own ordinances, or else he would never have appointed them.

3. The usefulness of this discipline is apparent to the shaming of sin, and humbling of the sinner; and manifesting the holiness of Christ and his doctrine and church before all the world.

4. What would you have done with such sinners? give them up as hopeless? That were too cruel. Would you use other means? Why it is supposed that all other have been used without success; for this is the last remedy.

5. The church of Christ hath found reason enough to use this course, even in times of persecution, when our carnal reason would have told them that they should then above all have forborne it, for fear of driving away all their converts.

6. The principal use of this public discipline is not for the offender himself, but for the church. It tendeth exceedingly to deter others from the like crimes, and so to keep pure the congregations, and their worship. Seneca could say, *Vitia transmittit ad posteros, qui præsentibus culpis ignoscit.* And elsewhere, *Bonis nocet, qui malis parcit.* If you say, that it will but restrain them as hypocrites, and not convert them: I answer, 1. As I said, it may preserve others. 2. Who knows how God may bless his ordinance even to them? 3. The restraint of sin is a benefit not to be contemned. *Audebo peccanti mala sua ostendere: vitia ejus si non excidero, inhibebo. Non desinent; sed intermittent: fortasse autem desinent, si intermittendi consuetudinem fecerint,* said the Moralist. Sen. Epist. 40. The scorns that I have heard from many against the Scottish ministers, for bringing offenders to the stool of repentance, as if it were mere formality and hypocrisy, to take such a thing as satisfactory, when true repentance is absent, hath discovered more of the accuser's error than of theirs. For no doubt, it is

true repentance that they exhort men to; and it is true repentance which offenders do profess; and whether they truly profess it, who can tell but God? It is not nothing that sin is brought to so much disgrace, and the church doth so far acquit themselves of it. But of this next.

[2.] Next to the duty of public reproof must be joined an exhortation of the person to repentance, and to the public profession of it for the satisfaction of the church. For as the church is bound to avoid communion with impenitent, scandalous sinners, so when they have had the evidence of their sin, they must see some evidence of their repentance; for we cannot know them to be penitent without evidence. And what evidence is the church capable of, but their profession of repentance first, and their actual reformation afterwards? both which must be expected.

[3.] To these may most fitly be joined the public prayers of the church, and that both for the reproved before they are rejected, and for the rejected (some of them at least) that they may repent and be restored. But we are now upon the former. Though this is not expressly affixed to discipline, yet we have sufficient discovery of God's will concerning it in the general precepts. We are commanded to *pray always;* and in *all things*, and for *all men*, and *in all places:* and *all things* are said to be *sanctified by it*. It is plain therefore, that so great a business as this should not be done without it! And who can have any just reason to be offended with us, if we pray to God for the changing of their hearts, and the pardon of their sins? It is therefore in my judgment a very laudable course of those churches, that use for the three next days together to desire the congregation to join in earnest prayer to God for the opening of the sinner's eyes, and softening of his heart, and saving him from impenitency and eternal death! And though we have no express direction in Scripture just how long we shall stay to try whether the sinner be so impenitent, as to be necessarily excluded, yet we must follow the general directions, with such diversity as the case and quality of the person and former proceeding shall require; it being left to the discretion of the church, who are, in general, to stay so long till the person manifest himself obstinate in his sin: not but that a temporary exclusion, called suspension, may oft be inflicted in the mean time; but before we proceed to an exclusion *a statu*, it is very meet (ordinarily) that three days' prayer for him and patience towards him should antecede.

And indeed, I see no reason but this course should be much more frequent than it is; and that not only upon those that are members of our special charge, and do consent to discipline, but even to those that deny our pastoral oversight and discipline, and yet are our ordinary hearers. For so far as men have christian communion or familiarity with us, so far are they capable of being excluded from communion. Though the members of our special charge have fuller and more special communion, and so are more capable of a fuller and more special exclusion; yet all those that dwell among us, and are our ordinary hearers, have some communion. For as they converse with us, so they hear the word, not as heathens, but as christians, and members of the universal church, into which they are baptized; and they join with us in public prayers and praises in the celebration of the Lord's day. From this therefore they are capable of being excluded, or from part of this, at least morally, if not locally. For the precept of *avoiding*, and *withdrawing from*, and *not eating with* such, is not restrained to the members of a governed church, but extended to all christians that are capable of communion.

When these ungodly persons are sick, we have daily bills from them to request the prayers of the congregation: and if we must pray for them against sickness, and temporal death, I know no reason but we should much more earnestly pray for them against sin and eternal death. That we have not their consent, is no dissuasive: for that is their disease, and the very venom and malignity of it; and we do not take it to be sober arguing, to say, I may not pray for such a man against his sickness, because he is sick; or, if he were not sick, I would pray against his sickness. No more is it to say, If he were not impenitent, so as to refuse our prayers, I would pray that he might be saved from his impenitency. I confess I do not take myself to have so strict a charge over this sort of men, that renounce my oversight, as I do over the rest that own it; and that is the reason why I have called no more of them to public repentance, because it requireth most commonly more time to examine the matter of fact, or deal with the person first more privately, that his impenitency may be discerned, than I can possibly spare from the duties which I owe to my special charge, to whom I am more indebted; and therefore may ordinarily expend no more on the rest (who are to me but as strangers, or men of another parish, and of no governed, particular church) than I can spare when I have done my main duty to my flock. But yet though I cannot use any such discipline on all that sort, nor am so much obliged to do it, yet some of them that are most notoriously and openly wicked, where less proof and short debates are requisite, I intend to deal thus with hereafter, having found some success in that kind already. But especially to all those whom we take for members of that particular church which we are pastors of, there is no question but this is our duty, and therefore where the whole parish are members, discipline must be exercised on the whole.

I confess much prudence is to be exercised in such proceedings, lest we do more hurt than good; but it must be such christian prudence as ordereth duties, and suiteth them to their ends, and not such carnal prudence as shall enervate or exclude them. It may be fit therefore for younger ministers to consult with others, for the more cautelous proceeding in such works. And in performance of it, we should deal humbly, even when we deal most sharply, and make it appear that it is not from any contending or lordly disposition, nor an act of revenge for any injury; but a necessary duty which we cannot conscionably avoid: and therefore it will be meet we disclaim all such animosities, and show the people the commands of God obliging us to what we do.

E. G. Neighbours and brethren, sin is so hateful an evil in the eyes of the most holy God, how light soever impenitent sinners make of it, that he hath provided the everlasting torments of hell for the punishment of it; and no lesser means can prevent that punishment than the sacrifice of the blood of the Son of God, applied to those that truly repent of it and forsake it, and therefore God that calleth all men to repentance, hath commanded us to exhort one another daily, while it is called to-day, lest any be hardened through the deceitfulness of sin, Heb. iii. 13; and that we do not hate our brother in our heart, but in any wise rebuke our neighbour, and not suffer sin upon him, Lev. xix. 17; and that if our brother offend us, we should tell him his fault between him and us; and if he hear not, take two or three, and if he hear not them, tell the church; and if he hear not the church he must be to us as a heathen or a publican, Matt. xviii. 17; and those that sin, we must rebuke before all, that others may fear, 1 Tim. v. 20; and rebuke with all authority, Tit. i. 15. Yea, were it an apostle of Christ that should openly sin, he must be openly reproved, as Paul did Peter, Gal. ii. 11, 14; and if they repent not, we must avoid them, and with such not so much as eat, 2 Thess. iii. 6, 12, 14; 1 Cor. v. 11, 13. According to these commands of the Lord, having heard of the scandalous practice of N. N. of this church, (or parish,) and having received sufficient proof that he hath committed the odious sin of ——; we have seriously dealt with him to bring him to repentance; but, to the grief of our hearts, do perceive no satisfactory success of our endeavours; but he seemeth still to remain impenitent, or still liveth in the same sin, though he verbally profess repentance. We do therefore judge it our necessary duty to proceed to the use of that further remedy which Christ hath commanded us to try; and hence we desire him in the name of the Lord, without any further delay, to lay by his obstinacy against the Lord, and to submit to his rebuke and will, and to lay to heart the greatness of his sin, the wrong he hath done to Christ and to himself, and the scandal and grief that he hath caused to others; and how unable he is to contend with the Almighty, and prevail against the holy God, who to the impenitent is a consuming fire! or to save himself from his burning indignation! And I do earnestly beseech him for the sake of his own soul, that he will but soberly consider, what it is that he can gain by his sin or impenitency, and whether it will pay for the loss of everlasting life? And how he thinks to stand before God in judgment, or to appear before the Lord Jesus one of these days, when death shall snatch his soul from his body, if he be found in this impenitent state? When the Lord Jesus himself, in whose blood they pretend to trust, hath told such with his own mouth, that except they repent they shall all perish, Luke xiii. 3, 5. And I do beseech him for the sake of his own soul, and require him as a messenger of Jesus Christ, as he will answer the contrary at the bar of God, that he lay by the stoutness and impenitency of his heart, and unfeignedly confess and lament his sin before God and this congregation! And this desire I here publish, not out of any ill will to his person, as the Lord knoweth, but in love to his soul, and in obedience to Christ that hath made it my duty; desiring, that if it be possible, he may be saved from his sin, and from the power of Satan, and from the everlasting burning wrath of God, and may be reconciled to God and his church, and therefore that he may be humbled by true contrition, before he be humbled by remediless condemnation.

Thus, or to this purpose, I conceive our public admonition should proceed; and in some cases where the sinner taketh his sin to be small, the aggravation of it will be necessary, and specially the citing of some texts of Scripture that do aggravate and threaten it.

And in case he either will not be present, that such admonition may be given him, or will not be brought to a discovery of repentance, and to desire the prayers of the congregation for him, it will be meet that with such a preface as this afore expressed, we desire the prayers of the congregation for him ourselves; that the people would consider what a fearful condition the impenitent are in, and have pity on a poor soul that is so blinded and hardened by sin and Satan, that he cannot pity himself; and think what it is for a man to appear before the living God in such a case; and therefore that they would join in earnest prayer to God, that he would open his eyes, and soften and humble his stubborn heart, before he be in hell beyond remedy: and accordingly let us be very earnestly in prayer for them, that the congregation may be provoked affectionately to join with us; and who knows but God may hear such prayers, and the sinner's heart may more relent, than our own exhortation could procure it to do. However, the people will perceive that we make not light of sin, and preach not to them in mere custom or formality. If ministers would be conscionable in thus carrying on the work of God entirely and *self-denyingly*, they might make something of it, and expect a fuller blessing. But when we shrink from all that is dangerous or ungrateful, and shift off all that is costly or troublesome, they cannot expect that any great matter should be done by such carnal, partial use of means; and though some may be here and there called home to God, yet we cannot look that the gospel should prevail, and run, and be glorified, where it is so lamely and defectively carried on.

[4.] When a sinner is thus admonished and prayed for, if it pleased the Lord to open his eyes and give him remorse, before we proceed to any further censure, it is our next duty to proceed to his full recovery; where these things must be observed.

1. That we do not either discourage him by too much severity, nor yet by too much facility and levity make nothing of discipline, nor help him to any saving cure, but merely slubber and palliate it over. If therefore he have sinned scandalously but once; if his repentance seem deep and serious, we may in some cases restore him at that time, that is, if the wound that he hath given to the credit of the church, be not so deep as to require more ado for satisfaction, or the sin so heinous as may cause us to delay. But if it be so, or if he have lived long in the sin, it is most meet that he do wait in penitence a convenient time before he be restored.

2. And when the time comes, whether at the first confession or after, it is meet that we urge him to be serious in his humiliation, and set it home upon his conscience till he seem to be truly sensible of his sin; for it is not a vain formality, but the recovery and saving of a soul that we expect.

3. We must see that he beg the communion of the church, and their prayer to God for his pardon and salvation.

4. And that he promise to fly from such sin for the time to come, and watch more narrowly and walk more warily.

5. And then we have these things more to do.

1. To assure him of the riches of God's love, and the sufficiency of Christ's blood to pardon his sins, and that if his repentance be sincere, the Lord doth pardon him, of which we are authorized as his messengers to assure him.

2. To charge him to persevere and perform his promises, and avoid temptations, and continue to beg mercy and strengthening grace.

3. To charge the church that they imitate Christ in forgiving, and retaining; or if he were cast out, receive the penitent person in their communion; and that they never reproach him with his sins, or cast them in his teeth, but forgive and forget them as Christ doth.

4. And then to give God thanks for his recovery so far, and to pray for his confirmation, and future preservation.

[5.] The next part of discipline, is the rejecting and removing from the church's communion, those that after sufficient trial do remain impenitent; where note,

1. That if a man have sinned but once (so scan-

dalously) or twice, it is but a profession of repentance that we can expect for our satisfaction; but if he be accustomed to sin, or have oft broke such promises, then it is an actual reformation we must expect. And therefore he that will refuse either of these, to reform, or to profess and manifest repentance, is to be taken by us as living in the sin: for a heinous sin, but once committed, is morally continued in till it be repented of; and a bare forbearing of the act is not sufficient.

2. Yet have we no warrant to rip up matters that are worn out of the public memory, and so to make that public again that is ceased to be public: at least in ordinary cases.

3. Exclusion from church communion, commonly called excommunication, is of divers sorts or degrees, more than two or three, which are not to be confounded; of which, I will not so far digress as here to treat.

4. That which is most commonly to be practised among us is, only to remove an impenitent sinner from our communion, till it shall please the Lord to give him repentance.

5. In this exclusion or removal, the minister or governors of that church are authoritatively to charge the people in the name of the Lord to avoid communion with him; and to pronounce him one, whose communion the church is bound to avoid; and the people's duty is obedientially to avoid him, in case the pastor's charge contradict not the word of God. So that he hath the guiding or governing power; and they have, 1. A discerning power, whether his charge be just. 2. And an executive power; for it is they that must execute the sentence in part by avoiding the rejected, as he himself must execute it by denying him those ordinances and privileges not due to him, whereof he is the administrator.

6. It is very convenient to pray for the repentance and restoration, even of the excommunicate.

7. And if God shall give them repentance, they are gladly to be received into the communion of the church again. Of the manner of all these I shall say no more, they being things that have so much said of them already. And for the manner of other particular duties, of which I have said little or nothing, you have much already, as in other writings, so in the Directory of the late Assembly.

Would we were but so far faithful in the practice of this discipline, as we are satisfied both of the matter and manner; and did not dispraise and reproach it by our negligence, while we write and plead for it with the highest commendations. It is worthy our consideration, who is like to have the heavier charge about this matter at the bar of God? Whether those deluded ones that have reproached and hindered discipline by their tongues, because they knew not its nature and necessity; or we, that have so vilified it by our constant omission, while with our tongues we have magnified it? If hypocrisy be no sin, or if the knowledge of our masters will be no aggravation of the evil of disobedience, then we are in a better case than they. I will not advise the zealous maintainers, and obstinate neglecters and rejecters of discipline, to unsay all that they have said, till they are ready to do as they say; nor to recant their defences of discipline, till they mean to practise it; nor to burn all the books that they have written for it, and all the records of their costs and hazards for it, lest they rise up in judgment against them to their confusion; nor that they recant their condemnation of the prelates in this, till they mean a little further to outgo them: but I would persuade them without any more delay, to conform their practices to these testimonies which they have given, lest the more they are proved to have commended discipline, the more they are proved to have condemned themselves for neglecting it.

I have often marvelled, that the same men who have been much offended at the books that have been written for free admissions to the Lord's supper, or for mixed communion in that one part, have been no more offended at as free permission in a church state, and as free admission to other parts of communion; and that they have made so small a matter at as much mixture in all the rest: I should think that it is a greater profanation to permit an obstinate, scandalous sinner, to be a stated member of that particular church, without any private (first) and then public admonition, prayer for him, or censure of him; than for a single pastor to admit him to the Lord's supper, if he had no power to censure him; as these suppose. I should think that the faithful practice of discipline in the other parts, would soon put an end to the controversy about free admission to the Lord's supper, and heal the hurt that such discourses have done to the rebellions of our people. For those discourses have more modesty than to plead for a free admission of the censured or rejected ones; but it is only of those that have yet their standing in that church, that are not censured. And if, when they forfeit their title to church communion, we would deal with them in Christ's appointed way, till we had either reclaimed them to repentance, or censure them to be avoided; it would be past controversy then, that they were not to be admitted to that one act of communion in the supper, who are justly excluded from the whole. But as long as we leave them uncensured members, and tell a single pastor that he hath no power to censure them, we tempt him to think that he hath no power then to deny them that communion with the body which is the common privilege of uncensured members.

And as we thus ourselves oppose discipline by parts, or cherish church corruption by parts, one party being for the free admission of them, while members to the sacraments; and the other as freely permitting them in church state, and other parts of communion, while they exclude them from the sacrament; so some have learned to tie these ends together, and by holding both, to set open the doors of church and chancel, and pluck up the hedges, and lay the vineyard common to the wilderness. It hath somewhat amazed me to hear some that I took for reverend godly divines, to reproach as a sect, the sacramentarians and disciplinarians! And when I desired to know whom they meant, they tell me, they mean them that will not give the sacrament to all the parish, and them that will make distinction by their discipline. I had thought the tempter had obtained a great victory if he had but got one godly pastor of a church to neglect discipline, as well as if he had got him to neglect preaching; much more if he had got him to approve of that neglect: but it seems he hath got some to scorn at the performers of the duty which they neglect. As the impure were wont to reproach the diligent by the name of puritans, so do they reproach the faithful pastors by the name of disciplinarians. And I could wish they would remember what the ancient reproaches were both symptomatically, and effectively, and accordingly judge impartial of themselves, and fear a participation of the judgment that befell them. Sure I am, if it were well understood how much of the pastoral authority and work consisteth in church guidance, it would be also discerned, that to be against discipline is *tantum non* to be against the ministry;

and to be against the ministry, is *tantum non* to be absolutely against the church; and to be against the church, is near to being absolutely against Christ. Blame not the harshness of the inference, till you can avoid it, and free yourselves from the charge of it before the Lord. Prelates would have some discipline; and other parties would have some. Yea, papists themselves would have some, and plead only against others about the form and manner of it. But these are so much worse than all, that they would have none. Was not Christ himself the leader of these disciplinarians, who instituted discipline, and made his ministers the rulers or guiders of his church, and put the keys of the kingdom into their hand, and commanded the very particular acts of discipline, and required the people to submit to them, and obey them in the Lord? What would these men have said, if they had seen the practice of the ancient church for many hundred years after Christ, who exercised a discipline so much more rigorous than any among us do, and that even in the heat of heathen persecutions; as if they read but the ancient canons, and Cyprian's Epistles, they may soon see, though they look no further. And it was not then (no nor after, under christian magistrates) taken to be a useless thing; nor would it appear such now, if it were showed in its strength and beauty by a vigorous practice: for it is a thing that is not effectually manifested to the ear, but to the eye; and you will never make men know well what it is by mere talking of it—till they see it they will be strangers to it. As it is in the military art, or in navigation, or in the government of commonwealths, which are so little known till learned by experience. And that will tell us that, as Cyprian saith, *Disciplina est custos spei, retinaculum fidei, dux itineris salutaris, fomes ac nutrimentum bonæ indolis, magistra virtutis; facit in Christo manere semper, ac jugiter Deo vivere, ad promissa cœlestia, et divina præmia pervenire: Hanc et sectari salubre est, et aversari ac negligere lethale:* as he begins his book de Discip. et Hab. Virg. p. (mihi) 265. When the martyrs and confessors would, upon others' persuasions, have had some offenders restored before they had made confession, and manifested openly repentance for their sin, and been absolved by their pastor; Cyprian resisteth it, and tells them that they that stand so firmly to the faith, should stand as firmly to Christ's law and discipline: *Sollicitudo loci nostri, et timor Domini compellit, fortissimi ac beatissimi martyres, admonere vos literis nostris, ut a quibus tam devote et fortiter servatur fides Domino, ab iisdem lex quoque et disciplina Domini reservetur,* &c. Epist. 11. p. 32. Upon which Goulartius puts this note, *Locus de necessitate disciplinæ in Domo Dei, quam qui tollunt, et manifeste impios ac sceleratos ad mensam Christi, sine censura ecclesiastica, et acta pœnitentia pro delictorum ratione recipiunt, ii videant quam de gregibus sibi commissis pastori summo rationem reddituri sint; vel quid commune habeant in ecclesiarum regimine cum beato illo Cypriani et aliorum vere episcoporum christianorum seculo.* And Cyp. Ep. 67, p. 199, mentioning God's threatenings to negligent pastors, addeth, *Cum ergo pastoribus talibus per quos Dominicæ oves negligantur et pereant, sic Dominus comminetur, quid nos aliud facere oportet, quam colligendis et revocandis Christi ovibus exhibere diligentiam plenam, et curandis lapsorum vulneribus paternæ pietatis adhibere medicinam?* In Epist. 61, 28, 38, 41, 49, 53, 55, and many other places of Cyprian, you may see that they were then no contemners of discipline. Vide etiam, eundem de Orat. Dominic. p. 313, in Pet. 4.

Saith Augustine, *Ibi superbia, ubi negligitur disciplina: Nam disciplina est magistra religionis et veræ pietatis, quæ nec ideo increpat ut lædat, nec ideo castigat ut noceat,* &c. Saith Bernard, Ep. 113, *O quam compositum reddit omnem corporis statum, nec non et mentis habitum disciplina! Cervicem submittit, ponet supercilia, componit vultum, ligat oculos, moderatur linguam, frænat gulam, sedat iram, format incessum.*

I know that when the church began to be tainted with vain inventions, the word discipline began to have another signification, for their own various rules of life and austere impositions, *touch not, taste not, handle not;* but it is the ancient and truly christian discipline that I am contending for. So much for the acts of pastoral oversight.

From what hath been said, we may see that the pastoral office is another kind of thing than those men have taken it to be, who think it consisteth in preaching and administering sacraments only; much more than they have taken it for, that think it consisteth in making new laws or canons to bind the church: as if God had not made us laws sufficient; and as if he had committed the proper legislative power over his church to ministers or bishops, whose office is but to expound, and apply, and execute in their places the laws of Christ.

Object. But will you deny to bishops the power of making canons? What are all those articles that you have agreed on among yourselves about catechising and discipline, but such things?

Answ. 1. I know pastors may teach, and expound Scripture, and deliver that in writing to the people, and apply the Scripture generals to their own and the people's particular case, if you will call this making canons. 2. And they may and ought to agree among themselves for a unanimous performance of their duties, when they have discovered it; that so they may excite one another, and be more strong and successful in their work. 3. And they must determine of the circumstances of worship in special, which God hath only determined in general; as what time and place they shall meet in, what chapter read, what text preached on, what shape the table, cups, &c. shall be; where the pulpit, when each person shall come to be catechised or instructed, and whither, &c. But these are actions that are fitter to be ordered by them that are in the place, than by distant canon-makers: and to agree for unity in a necessary duty, as we have done, is not to make laws, or arrogate authority over our brethren. Of this I refer you to Luther de Conciliis, at large; and to Grotius de Imper. sum. pot. that canons are not properly laws.

CHAPTER III.

SECTION I.

HAVING spoken of the matter of our work, we are next to speak a little of the manner; not of each part distinctly, lest we be too tedious, but of the whole in general; but specially referring to theprincipal part.

1. The ministerial work must be managed purely for God and the salvation of the people, and not for any private ends of our own. This is our sincerity in it. A wrong end makes all the work bad, as from us, how good soever in itself. It is not a serving God, but ourselves, if we do it not for God, but for ourselves. They that set upon this as a common work, to make a trade of it for their worldly livelihood, will find that they have chosen a bad trade, though a good employment. Self-denial is of abso-

lute necessity in every christian, but of a double necessity in a minister, as he hath double sanctification or dedication to God. And without self-denial he cannot do God an hour's faithful service. Hard studies, much knowledge, and excellent preaching, is but more glorious hypocritical sinning, if the ends be not right. The saying of Bernard (Serm. in Cant. 26.) is commonly known; *Sunt qui scire volunt eo fine tantum ut sciant, et turpis curiositas est; et sunt qui scire volunt, ut scientiam suam vendant: et turpis quæstus est: sunt qui scire volunt ut sciantur ipsi: et turpis vanitas est: Sed sunt quoque, qui scire volunt ut ædificent; et charitas est; et sunt qui scire volunt ut ædificentur; et prudentia est.*

2. This work must be managed laboriously and diligently; as being of such unspeakable consequence to others and ourselves. We are seeking to uphold the world, to save it from the curse of God, to perfect the creation, to attain the end of Christ's redemption, to save ourselves and others from damnation, to overcome the devil, and demolish his kingdom, and set up the kingdom of Christ, and attain and help others to the kingdom of glory. And are these works to be done with a careless mind, or a lazy hand? O see then that this work be done with all your might. Study hard, for the well is deep, and our brains are shallow; and (as Cassiod.) *Decorum hic est terminum non habere: hic honesta probatur ambitio; omne si quidem scientificum quanto profundius quæritur, tanto gloriosius invenitur.* But especially be laborious in practice and exercise of your knowledge. Let Paul's words ring in your ears continually, "Necessity is laid upon me, and woe unto me if I preach not the gospel!" Still think with yourselves, what lieth upon your hands. If I do not bestir me, Satan may prevail, and the people everlastingly perish, and their blood be required at my hand. And by avoiding labour and suffering, I shall draw on me a thousand times more than I avoid: for as Bernard saith, *Qui in labore hominum non sunt, in labore profecto Dæmonum erunt,* whereas by present diligence you prepare for future blessedness. For, as Gregor. in Mor. saith, *Quot labores veritati nunc exhibes, tot etiam remunerationis pignora intra spei tuæ cubiculum clausum tenes.* No man was ever a loser by God.

3. This work must be carried on prudently, orderly, and by degrees. Milk must go before strong meat: the foundation must be first laid before we build upon it. Children must not be dealt with as men at age. Men must be brought into a state of grace, before we can expect from them the works of grace. The work of conversion, and repentance from dead works, and faith in Christ, must be first, and frequently and thoroughly, taught. The stewards of God's household must give to each their portion in due season. We must not go beyond the capacities of our people ordinarily, nor teach them the perfection, that have not learned the principles. As August. saith, li. 12, de Civit. *Si pro viribus suis alatur infans, fiet ut crescendo plus capiat: si modum suæ capacitatis excedat, deficit antequam crescat:* and as Gregor. Nyssen saith, Orat. de Pauper. amand. "As we teach not infants the deep precepts of science, but first letters, and then syllables, &c.; so also the guides of the church do first propound to their hearers certain documents, which are as the elements, and so by degrees to open to them the more perfect and mysterious matters." Therefore did the church take so much pains with their catechumeni, before they baptized them, and would not lay unpolished stones into the building; as Chrysost. saith, Hom. 40. imperfect. operis, (or whoever else it be, p. (mihi) 318,) *Ædificatores sunt sacerdotes, qui——domum Dei componunt, sicut enim ædificatores, nodosos lapides et habentes torturas, ferro dolant, postea vero ponunt eos in ædificio, alioqui non dolati lapides lapidibus non coherent: Sic et ecclesiæ doctores vitia hominum quasi nodos acutis increpationibus primum circumcidere debent, et sic in ecclesiæ ædificatione collocare: alioquin vitiis manentibus christiani christianis concordare non possunt.*

4. Through the whole course of our ministry, we must insist most upon the greatest, most certain, and necessary things, and be more seldom and sparing upon the rest. If we can but teach Christ to our people, we teach them all. Get them well to heaven, and they will have knowledge enough. The great and commonly acknowledged truths are they that men must live upon, and which are the great instruments of raising the heart to God, and destroying men's sins; and therefore we must still have our people's necessities in our eyes. It will take us off gauds, and needless ornaments, and unprofitable controversies, to remember that *one* thing is necessary. Other things are desirable to be known, but these *must* be known, or else our people are undone for ever. I confess, I think necessity should be a great disposer of a minister's course of study and labours. If we were sufficient for every thing, we might fall upon every thing, and take in order the whole Encyclopædia: but life is short, and we are dull; and eternal things are necessary, and the souls that depend on our teaching are precious. I confess necessity hath been the conductor of my studies and life; it chooseth what book I shall read, and tells when and how long; it chooseth my text, and makes my sermon for matter and manner, so far as I can keep out my own corruption. Though I know the constant expectation of death hath been a great cause of this, yet I know no reason why the most healthful man should not make sure of the necessaries first, considering the uncertainty and shortness of all men's lives. Xenophon thought, "there was no better teacher than necessity, which teacheth all things most diligently." Curtius saith, *Efficacior est omni arte necessitas.* Who can in study, preaching, or life, *aliud agere,* be doing other matters, if he do but know, that this must be done? Who can trifle or delay, that feeleth the spurs of hasty necessity: as the soldier saith, *Non diu disputandum, sed celeriter et fortiter dimicandum ubi urget necessitas.* So much more must we, as our business is more important. And doubtless this is the best way to redeem time, and see that we lose not an hour, when we spend it only on necessary things: and I think it is the way to be most profitable to others, though not always to be most pleasing and applauded; because through men's frailty, it is true that Seneca complains of, that *Nova potius miramur quam magna.*

Hence it is, that a preacher must be oft upon the same things, because the matters of necessity are few. We must not either feign necessaries, or fall much upon unnecessaries, to satisfy them that look after novelties: though we must clothe the same necessaries with a grateful variety in the manner of our delivery. The great volumes and tedious controversies, that so much trouble us and waste our time, are usually made up more of opinion than necessary verities. For, as Marsil. Ficinus saith, *Necessitas brevibus clauditur terminis: opinio nullis.* And as Greg. Nazianz. and Seneca often say, "Necessaries are common and obvious: it is superfluities that we waste our time for, and labour for, and complain that we attain them not." Ministers therefore must be observant of the case of their flocks, that they may know what is most necessary for them, both for matter and for manner: and usually matter is first to be regarded, as being of more concernment than the manner. If you are to choose what authors to read yourselves, will you not rather take those that tell you what you know not, and speak the needful truth most evidently, though it were with barbarous or unhandsome language, than those that will most learnedly, and elegantly, and in grateful language tell you that which is false or vain, and *magno conatu nihil dicere?* I purpose to follow Austin's counsel, (li. de Catech.) *Præponendo verbis, sententiam, ut animas præponitur corpori: ex quo fit, ut ita mallem veriores quam discretiores invenire sermones, sicut mallem prudentiores quam formosiores habere amicos.* And sure as I do in my studies for my own edification, I would do in my teaching for other men's. It is commonly empty, ignorant men that want the matter and substance of true learning, that are over-curious and solicitous about words and ornaments; when the ancient, experienced, most learned men, abound in substantial verities, usually delivered in the plainest dress. As Aristotle makes it the reason why women are more addicted to pride in apparel than men, because being conscious of little inward worth and ornament, they seek to make it up with borrowed ornaments without; so is it with empty, worthless preachers, who affect to be esteemed that which they are not, and have no other way to procure esteem.

5. All our teaching must be as plain and evident as we can make it; for this doth most suit to a teacher's ends. He that would be understood, must speak to the capacity of his hearers, and make it his business to make himself understood. Truth loves the light, and is most beautiful when most naked. It is a sign of an envious enemy to hide the truth; and a sign of a hypocrite to do this under pretence of revealing it: and therefore painted, obscure sermons, (like the painted glass in the windows that keep out the light,) are too oft the marks of painted hypocrites. If you would not teach men, what do you in the pulpit? If you would, why do you not speak so as to be understood? I know the height of the matter may make a man not understood when he hath studied to make it as plain as he can; but that a man should purposely cloud the matter in strange words, and hide his mind from the people whom he pretendeth to instruct, is the way to make fools admire his profound learning, and wise men his folly, pride, and hypocrisy. And usually, it is a suspicious sign of some deceitful project and false doctrine that needeth such a cloak, and must walk thus masked in the open daylight. Thus did the followers of Basilides and Valentinus, and others among the old heretics; and thus do the Behmenists and other Paracelsians now; who, when they have spoken that few may understand them, lest they expose their errors to the open view, they pretend a necessity of it, because of men's prejudice, and the unpreparedness of common understandings for the truth. But truth overcomes prejudice by mere light of evidence, and there is no better way to make a good cause prevail, than to make it as plain, and commonly and thoroughly known as we can; and it is this light that will dispose an unprepared mind. And at best it is a sign that he hath not well digested the matter himself, that is not able to deliver it plainly to another. I mean, as plain as the nature of the matter will bear, in regard of capacities prepared for it by prerequisite truths. For I know that some men cannot at present understand some truths, if you speak them as plainly as words can express them: as the easiest rules in grammar most plainly taught, will be no whit understood by a child that is but learning his alphabet.

6. Our whole work must be carried on in a sense of our insufficiency, and in a pious, believing dependence upon Christ. We must go to him for light, and life, and strength, who sends us on the work: and when we feel our own faith weak, and our hearts grown dull, and unsuitable to so great a work as we have to do, we must have recourse to the Lord that sendeth us, and say, Lord, wilt thou send me with such an unbelieving heart to persuade others to believe? Must I daily and earnestly plead with sinners about everlasting life and death, and have no more belief and feeling of these weighty things myself? O send me not naked and unprovided to the work; but as thou commandest me to do it, furnish me with a spirit suitable thereto. As Austin saith, (de Doct. Christ. l. 4,) "A preacher must labour to be heard understandingly, willingly, and obediently, *et hoc se posse magis pietate orationum, quam oratoris facultate non dubitet: ut orando pro se ac pro aliis, quos est allocuturus, sit prius orator quam doctor; et in ipsa hora accedens, priusquam exeat, proferat linguam ad Deum, levet animam sitientem, &c.*" Prayer must carry on our work as well as preaching: he preacheth not heartily to his people, that will not pray for them. If we prevail not with God to give them faith and repentance, we are unlike to prevail with them to believe and repent. Paul giveth us frequently his example, of praying night and day for his hearers. When our own hearts are so far out of order, and theirs so far out of order, if we prevail not with God to mend and help them, we are like to make but unsuccessful work.

7. Our work must be managed with great humility; we must carry ourselves meekly and condescendingly to all; and so teach others, as to be as ready to learn of any that can teach us, and so both teach and learn at once: not proudly venting our own conceits, and disdaining all that any way contradict them, as if we had attained to the top of knowledge, and we were destinated for the chair, and other men to sit at our feet. Not like them that Gregory M. mentioneth in Moral. l. 24, par. 5, c. xii. *In quorum verbis proditur, quod cum docent, quasi in quodam sibi videntur summitatis culmine residere, eosque quos docent, ut longe infra se positos, velut in imo respiciunt, quibus non consulendo loqui, sed vix dominando dignantur.* Pride is a vice that ill beseems them that must lead men in such a humble way to heaven. And let them take heed, lest when they have brought others thither, the gate should prove too strait for themselves. For, as Hugo saith, *Superbia in cœlo nata est, sed velut immemor qua via inde cecidit, istuc postea redire non potuit.* God that thrust out a proud angel, will not entertain there a proud teacher, while such. Methinks we should remember at least the title of a minister, which though the popish priests disdain, yet so do not we. It is indeed this pride at the root that feedeth all the rest of our sins: hence is the envy, the contention, and unpeaceableness of ministers, and hence the stops in all reformation. All would lead, and few will follow or concur; yea, hence are the schisms and apostasies, as hence have been former persecutions, and arrogant usurpations and impositions: as Gregory M. saith, in Mor. *Latet plerumque superbia, et castitas innotescit, atque ideo tentata diu castitas, circa finem vitæ perditur; quia cooperta superbia usque ad finem, in correcta retinetur.* And the same may be said of other vices, which oft revive when they seemed dead, because pride was unmortified, which virtually contains them all. Hence also is the non-proficiency of too many ministers, because they are too proud to learn; unless it be as Jerom's adversaries, *publice detrahentes, legentes*

in angulis; and scarcely will they stoop to that. But I may say of ministers as Augustine to Jerom, even of the aged of them, *Etsi senes magis decet docere quam discere: magis tamen decet discere quam ignorare;* humility would teach them another lesson: ut Hugo, *Ab omnibus libenter disce quod tu nescis: quia humilitas commune tibi facere potest, quod natura cuique proprium fecit, sapientior omnibus eris, si ab omnibus discere volueris: qui ab omnibus accipiunt, omnibus ditiores sunt.*

8. There must be a prudent mixture of severity and mildness both in our preaching and discipline; each must be predominant according to the quality or the person, or matter that we have in hand. If there be *no* severity, there will be contempt of our reproofs. If *all* severity, we shall be taken as usurpers of dominion, rather than persuaders of the minds of men to the truth, as Gregory M. saith, Moral. li. 20. *Miscenda est lenitas cum severitate, et faciendum ex utraque quoddam temperamentum, ut nec multa asperitate exulcerentur subditi, nec nimia benignitate solvantur.*

9. We must be sincerely affectionate, serious, and zealous in all our public and private exhortations. The weight of our matter condemneth coldness, and sleepy dulness. We should see that we be well awakened ourselves, and our spirits in such a plight as may make us fit to awaken others. As Gregory saith, Mor. l. 30. c. v. We should be like the cock, that, *Cum edere cantus parat, prius alas solerter excutit, et seipsum feriens vigilantiorem reddit: ita prædicatores cum verbum prædicationis movent, prius se in sanctis actionibus exercent, ne in se ipsis torpentes opere, alios excitent voce, sed ante se per sublimia facta excutiunt, et tunc ad bene agendum alios sollicitos reddunt. Prius sua punire fletibus curant, et tunc quæ aliorum sunt punienda, denuntiant.* If our words be not sharpened, and pierce not as nails, they will hardly be felt by stony hearts. To speak coldly and slightly of heavenly things, is near as bad as to say nothing of them.

10. All our work must be managed reverently; as beseemeth them that believe the presence of God, and use not holy things as if they were common. The more of God appeareth in our duties, the more authority will they have with men: and reverence is that affection of the soul, which proceedeth from deep apprehensions of God, and signifieth a mind that is much conversant with him. To manifest irreverence in the things of God, is so far to manifest hypocrisy, and that the heart agreeth not with the tongue. I know not what it doth by others, but the most reverend preacher, that speaks as if he saw the face of God, doth more affect my heart, though with common words, than an unreverend man with the most exquisite preparations. Yea, if he bawl it out with never so much seeming earnestness, if reverence be not answerable to fervency, it worketh but little. Of all preaching in the world, (that speaks not stark lies,) I hate that preaching which tendeth to make the hearers laugh, or to move their mind with tickling levity, and affect them as stage-players use to do, instead of affecting them with a holy reverence of the name of God. Saith Jerom, (in Ep. ad Nepotian, p. (mihi) 14,) *Docente in ecclesia te, non clamor populi, sed gemitus suscitetur; Lacrymæ auditorum laudes tuæ sunt.* We should as it were suppose we saw the throne of God, and the millions of glorious angels attending him, that we might be awed with his majesty, when we draw near him in his holy things, lest we profane them, and take his name in vain.

To this I annex, that all our work must be done spiritually, as by men possessed by the Holy Ghost and acted by him, and men that savour the things of the Spirit. There is in some men's preaching a spiritual strain, which spiritual hearers can discern and relish; and in some men this sacred tincture is so wanting, that even when they speak of spiritual things the manner is such as if they were common matters. Our evidence also and ornaments must be spiritual, rather from the holy Scripture, with a cautelous, subservient use of fathers, and other writers, than from Aristotle or the authorities of men. The wisdom of the world must not be magnified against the wisdom of God; philosophy must be taught to stoop and serve, while faith doth bear the chiefest sway: and great scholars in Aristotle's school must take heed of too much glorying in their master, and despising those that are there below them; lest themselves prove lower in the school of Christ, and *least* in the kingdom of God, while they would be *great* in the eyes of men. As wise a man as any of them, would glory in nothing but Him crucified. They that are so confident that Aristotle is in hell, should not too much take him for their guide in the way to heaven. It is an excellent memorandum that Gregory M. hath left in his Moral. l. 33. *Deus primo collegit indoctos; post modum philosophos; et non per oratores docuit piscatores, sed per piscatores subegit oratores."* The learnedest men should think of this.

Let all writers have their due esteem, but compare none of them with the word of God. We will not refuse their service, but we must abhor them as competitors. It is a sign of a distempered heart that loseth the relish of Scripture excellency. For there is a connaturality in a spiritual heart to the word of God, because this is the seed that did regenerate him: the word is that seal that made all holy impressions that be in the hearts of true believers, and stamped the image of God upon them. And therefore they must needs be like that word, and highly esteem it as long as they live. Austin tells us, (in his lib. 10, de Civit. Dei, c. xxix.) *Quod initium Sancti Evangelii, cui nomen est secundum Joannem, quidam Platonicus (sicut a sancto sene Simpliciano, qui postea Mediolanesi Ecclesiæ præsedit Episcopus, solebamus audire) aureis literis conscribendum, et per omnes Ecclesias in locis eminentissimis proponendum esse dicebat.* If he could so value that which suited with his Platonism, how should we value the whole which is suitable to the christian nature and interest! God is the best teacher of his own nature and will.

11. The whole course of our ministry must be carried on in a tender love to our people: we must let them see that nothing pleaseth us but what profiteth them; and that which doth them good doth us good; and nothing troubleth us more than their hurt. We must remember as Jerom saith, ad Nepotian, "That bishops are not lords but fathers," and therefore must be affected to their people as their children; yea, the tenderest love of a mother should not surpass theirs: we must even "travail in birth of them till Christ be formed in them." They should see that we care for no outward thing, not money, not liberty, not credit, not life, in comparison of their salvation; but could even be content, with Moses, to have our names wiped out of the book of life, i. e. to be removed *e numero viventium;* rather than they should perish, and not be found in the Lamb's book of life, *in numero salvandorum.* Thus should we, as John saith, be ready to lay down our lives for the brethren, and with Paul, not to count our lives dear to us, so we may but finish with joy, in doing the work of God for their salvation. When the people see that you unfeignedly love them, they will hear any thing, and bear any thing, and follow you the more easily. As Austin saith, *Dilige, et dic quicquid voles.*

We will take all things well ourselves from one that we know doth entirely love us. We will put up a blow that is given us in love, sooner than a foul word that is given us in anger or malice. Most men use to judge of the counsel, as they judge of the affection of him that gives it; at least so far as to give it a fair hearing. O therefore, see that you feel a tender love to your people in your breasts, and then let them feel it in your speeches, and see it in your dealings. Let them see that you spend and are spent for their sakes; and that all you do is for them, and not for any ends of your own. To this end the works of charity are necessary, as far as your estate shall reach; for bare words will hardly convince men that you have any great love to them. *Amcitia a dando et accipiendo nascitur.* Chrysost. But when you are not able to give, show that you are willing to give if you had it, and do that sort of good that you can; *Si potes dare, da, si non potes, affabilem te fac. Coronat Deus intus bonitatem, ubi non invenit facultatem. Nemo dicat, non habeo, Charitas non de sacculo erogatur.* August. in Psal. ciii. But be sure to see that your love prove not carnal, flowing from pride, as one that is a suitor for himself, rather than for Christ, and therefore doth love because *he is* beloved, or that he *may be*, pretendeth it. And therefore take heed that you do not connive at their sins under pretence of love; for that were to cross the nature and ends of love: *Amici vitia si feras, facis tua.* Senec. Friendship must be cemented by piety: *Primum exhibe te bonum, et quæ alterum similem tibi.* Sen. A wicked man can be no true friend; and if you befriend their wickedness, you show that you are such yourselves. Pretend not to love them, if you favour their sins, and seek not their salvation. *Soli sancti, et Dei sunt, et inter se amici.* Basil. *Improborum et stultorum nemo amicus.* Id. By favouring their sin you will show your enmity to God, and then how can you love your brother? *Amicus esse homini non potest, qui Deo fuerit inimicus.* Ambros. If you be their best friends, help them against their worst enemies. *Amicus animæ custos.* And think not all sharpness inconsistent with love: parents will correct their children; and God himself will chasten every son that he loveth. *Melius est cum severitate diligere, quam cum lenitate decipere.* Aug.

Besides this, the nature of love is to excite men to do good, and to do it speedily, diligently, and as much as we can. *Alios curat ædificare, alios contremiscit offendere, ad alios se inclinat, cum aliis blanda, aliis severa, nulli inimica, omnibus mater.* August. de Catech. *Ecce quem amas Domine infirmatur: Non dixerunt veni; Amanti enim tantum nunciandum fuit: sufficiet ut noverit: Non enim amat, et deserit.* August. in Joan. So will it be with us.

12. Another necessary concomitant of our work is patience. We must bear with many abuses and injuries from those that we are doing good for. When we have studied for them, and prayed for them, and beseeched and exhorted them with all condescension, and spent ourselves for them, and given them what we are able, and tendered them as if they had been our children, we must look that many should requite us with scorn, and hatred, and contempt, and cast our kindness in our faces with disdain, and take us for their enemies, because we tell them the truth; and that the more we love, the less we shall be beloved. And all this must be patiently undergone, and still we must unweariedly hold on in doing good: "in meekness instructing those that oppose themselves, if God peradventure will give them repentance," &c. If they unthankfully scorn and reject our teaching, and bid us look to ourselves, and care not for them, yet must we hold on. We have to deal with distracted men, that will fly in the face of their physician, but we must not therefore forsake the cure. He is unworthy to be a physician that will be driven away from a frenetic patient by foul words, καθάπερ οἱ μαινόμενοι καὶ τὸν ἰατρὸν, i. e. *Sicut insani etiam medicum impetere conantur, ita et illi,* saith Chrysostom of the Sodomites. Hom. 43. in Gen. *Et alibi, Medici ferant ægrotum calcibus ferientem, incessentem contumeliis, et conviтiis, nec offenduntur: quia nihil aliud quam salutum ægroti quærentes, licet facientis indecora, non ideo a cura desistant, sic concionator licet mala patiatur ab auditoribus,* &c. If we tell them that natural men savour not the things of the Spirit, and are beside themselves in matters of salvation, we must measure our expectations accordingly, and not look that fools should make us as grateful a return as the wise. These are things that all of us can say, but when we come to the practice with sinners that reproach and slander us for our love, and are readier to spit in our faces, than to give us thanks for our advice, what heart-risings will there be, and how will the remnants of old Adam, pride and passion, struggle against the meekness and patience of the new man! And how sadly do many ministers come off in this part of their trial!

Having given you these twelve concomitants of our ministerial labour, singly to be performed by every minister, let me conclude with one other that is necessary to us as we are conjoined, and fellow-labourers in the work; and that is this: We must be very studious in union and communion among ourselves, and of the unity and peace of the churches that we oversee. We must be sensible how needful this is to the prosperity of the whole, the strengthening of our common cause, the good of the particular members of our flock, and the further enlargement of the kingdom of Christ. And therefore ministers must smart when the church is wounded, and being so far from being the leaders in divisions, that they should take it as a principal part of their work to prevent and heal them. Day and night should they bend their studies to find out means to close such breaches. They must not only hearken to motions for unity, but propound them and prosecute them. Not only entertain an offered peace, but even follow it when it flieth from them. They must therefore keep close to the ancient simplicity of the christian faith, and the foundation and centre of catholic unity. They must abhor the arrogancy of them that frame engines to rack and tear the church of God, under pretence of obviating errors, and maintaining the truth. The Scripture sufficiency must be maintained, and nothing beyond it imposed on others; and if papists, or others, call to us for the standard and rule of our religion, it is the Bible that we must show them, rather than any confessions of churches, or writings of men. We must learn to difference well between certainties and uncertainties, necessaries and unnecessaries, catholic verities (*quæ ab omnibus, ubique et semper sunt retentæ,* as Vincent, Licen. speaks), and private opinions; and to lay the stress of the church's peace upon the former, and not upon the latter. We must therefore understand the doctrine of antiquity, that we may know what way men have gone to heaven by in former ages, and know the writings of later divines, that we may partake of the benefit of their clearer methods and explications; but neither of them must be made the rule of our faith or charity. We must avoid the common confusion of speaking for those that difference not between verbal and real errors, and hate that *rabies quorundam theologorum,* that tear their brethren as heretics, before they understand them. And we must learn to see the true state of controversies, and reduce them to the very point where the difference lieth, and not to make them seem greater than they are. Instead of quarrelling with our brethren, we must combine against the common adversaries; and all ministers must associate and hold communion, and correspondency, and constant meetings to those ends; and smaller differences of judgment are not to interrupt them. They must do as much of the work of God in unity and concord as they can; which is the use of synods: not to rule over one another, and make laws; but to avoid misunderstandings, and consult for mutual edification, and maintain love and communion, and go on unanimously in the work that God hath already commanded us. Had the ministers of the gospel been men of peace, and of catholic rather than factious spirits, the church of Christ had not been in the case as it is now; the notions of Lutherans and Calvinists abroad, and the differing parties here at home, would not have been plotting the subversion of one another, nor remain at that distance, and in that uncharitable bitterness, nor strengthen the common enemy, and hinder the building and prosperity of the church, as they have done.

CHAPTER IV.

SECTION I. USE.

REVEREND and dear brethren, our business here this day is to humble our souls before the Lord for our former negligence, especially of catechising and personal instructing those committed to our charge; and to desire God's assistance of us in our undertaken employment for the time to come. Indeed, we can scarce expect the latter without the former. If God will help us in our future duty and amendment, he will sure humble us first for our former sin. He that hath not so much sense of his faults, as unfeignedly to lament them, will hardly have so much more as may move him to reform them. The sorrow of repentance may go without the change of heart and life, because a passion may be easier wrought than a true conversion; but the change cannot go without some good measure of the sorrow. Indeed, we may justly here begin our confessions: it is too common with us to expect that from our people, which we do little or nothing in ourselves. What pains take we to humble them, while ourselves are unhumbled! How hard do we squeeze them by all our expostulations, convictions, and aggravations, to wring out of them a few penitent tears, (and all too little,) when our own eyes are dry, and our hearts too strange to true remorse, and we give them an example of hard-heartedness, while we are endeavouring by our words to mollify and melt them. Oh, if we did but study half as much to affect and amend our own hearts, as we do our hearers, it would not be with many of us as it is! It is a great deal too little that we do for their humiliation; but I fear it is much less that some of us do for our own. Too many do somewhat for other men's souls, while they seem to forget that they have any of their own to regard. They so carry the matter, as if their part of the work lay in calling for repentance, and the hearers' in repenting; theirs in speaking, tears, and sorrow, and other men's only in weeping, and sorrowing; theirs in preaching duty, and the hearers' in performing it; theirs in crying down sin, and the people's in forsaking it.

But we find that the guides of the church in Scripture did confess their own sins as well as the sins of the people; and did begin to them in tears for their own and the people's sins. Ezra confesseth the sins of the priests as well as of the people, weeping and casting himself down before the house of God, Ezra ix. 6, 7; x. 1. So did the Levites, Neh. ix. 32—34. Daniel confesseth his own sin, as well as the people's, Dan. ix. 20; and God calleth such to it, as well as others, Joel ii. 15—17. When the fast is summoned, the people gathered, the congregation sanctified, the elders assembled, the priests the ministers of the Lord are called to begin to them in weeping, and calling upon God for mercy. I think if we consider well of the duties already opened, and withal how we have done them; of the rule, and of our unanswerableness thereto; we need not demur upon the question, nor put it to a question, whether we have cause of humiliation. I must needs say, though I judge myself in saying it, that he that readeth but this one exhortation of Paul in Acts xx. and compareth his life with it, is too stupid and hard-hearted, if he do not melt in the sense of his neglects, and be not laid in the dust before God, and forced to bewail his great omissions, and to fly for refuge to the blood of Christ, and to his pardoning grace. I am confident, brethren, that none of you do in judgment approve of the libertine doctrine, that crieth down the necessity of confession, contrition, and true humiliation; yea, and in order to the pardon of sin! Is it not pity then, that our hearts are not more orthodox as well as our heads? But I see our lesson is but half learned when we know it, and can say it. When the understanding hath learned it, there is more ado to teach it our wills and affections, our eyes, our tongues, and hands. It is a sad thing that so many of us do use to preach our hearers asleep; but it is sadder if we have studied and preached ourselves asleep, and have talked so long against hardness of heart, till our own grow hardened under the noise of our own reproofs. Though the head only have eyes, and ears, and smell, and taste, the heart should have *life*, and *feeling*, and *motion*, as well as the head.

And that you may see that it is not a causeless sorrow that God calleth us to, I shall take it to be my duty to call to remembrance our manifold sins, or those that are most obvious, and set them this day in order before God and our own faces, that God may cast them behind his back; and to deal plainly and faithfully in a free confession, that he who is faithful and just, may forgive them; and to judge ourselves, that we be not judged of the Lord: wherein I suppose I have your free and hearty consent, and that you will be so far from being offended with the disgrace of your persons, and of others in this office, that you will readily subscribe the charge, and be humble self-accusers; and so far am I from justifying myself by the accusation of others, that I do unfeignedly put my name with the first in the bill; for how can a wretched sinner, of so great transgressions, presume to justify himself with God? or how can he plead guiltless, whose conscience hath so much to say against him? If I cast shame upon the ministry, it is not on the office, but on our persons, by opening that sin which is our shame. The glory of our high employment doth not communicate any glory to our sin, nor will afford it the smallest covering for its nakedness; for "sin is a reproach to any people," or persons, Prov. xiv. 34. And it is myself as well as others on whom I must lay the shame: and if this may not be done, what do we here to-day? Our business is to take shame to ourselves, and to give God the glory; and faithfully to open our sins, that he may cover them; and to make ourselves bare by confession, as we have done by transgression, that we may have the white raiment that clotheth none but the penitent; for be they pastors or people, it is only he "that confesseth and forsaketh his sins, that shall have mercy; when he that hardeneth his heart shall fall into mischief." Prov. xxviii. 13.

And I think it will not be amiss, if in the beginning of our confession we look behind us, and imitate Daniel, and other servants of God, who confess the sins of their fore-fathers and predecessors. For, indeed, my own judgment is so far from denying original sin, even the imputed part, with the ancient opposers of it, or those of the new edition, that it doth not so much excuse me from the guilt of my later progenitors' offences, as most other men's do seem to excuse them. Let us fetch up then the core of our shame, and go to the bottom, and trace the behaviour of the ministers of the gospel, from the days of Christ till now, and see how far they have been from innocency.

When Christ had chosen him but twelve apostles, who kept near his person, that they might be acquainted with his doctrine, life, and miracles; yet how ignorant did they long remain, not knowing so much as that he must die, and be a sacrifice for the sins of the world, and be buried, and rise again, and ascend into glory; nor what was the nature of his spiritual kingdom! So that it puts us hard to it to imagine how men so ignorant could be in a state of grace; but that we know that those points were after of absolute necessity to salvation, that were not so then. [a] How oft doth Christ teach them publicly and apart, (Mark iv. 34,) and rebuke them for their unbelief and hardness of heart! and yet after all this, so strange were these great mysteries of redemption to them, and these (now) articles of our creed, that Peter himself dissuadeth Christ from suffering, and goeth so far in contradicting his gracious thoughts for our redemption, that he is called *Satan*, and *tantum non* excommunicated: and no wonder; for if his counsel had been taken, the world had been lost for ever. And, as there was a Judas among them, so the twelve are before Christ's face contending for superiority; so early did that pride begin to work in the best, which afterwards prevailed so far in others, as to bring the church so low as we have seen. What should we say of their joint forsaking Christ, of their failings even after the pourings out of the Spirit; of the dissension and separation between Paul and Barnabas; how strange Peter made of the calling of the gentiles; of his compliance with the Jews to the endangering the liberties of the gentiles, Gal. ii.; of the dissimulation of Barnabas; and the common desertion of Paul in his suffering. When he had found one Timothy, he saith, he "had no man like-minded, that would naturally care for their estate; for all seek their own, and not the things of Jesus Christ," Phil. ii. 20, 21. A sad charge of self-seeking in that glory of the church for faith and purity! And what charges are against most of the angels of the seven Asian churches is expressed, Rev. ii.; iii. And it is likely that Archippus was not the only man that had need to be warned to look to his ministry, Col. iv. 17; nor Demas the only man that forsook a persecuted partner, and turned after the things of the world; nor Diotrephes the only man that loved to have the pre-eminence, and made quarrels, and dealt unjustly and unmercifully in the church upon that account!

And even while the churches were frying in the flames, yet did the pride and dissensions even of godly pastors do more than the fire of persecution could do, to turn all to ashes. How sad a story is it that Policrates with all the Eastern churches should be arrogantly excommunicated by Victor with his Romans, upon no higher crime than mischoosing of Easter day, which our Britains also long after were guilty of! Who would think that so great weakness, and presumptuous usurpation, and uncharitable cruelty, and schismatical zeal, could have befallen the pastors of the church in the strongest temptations of prosperity; much less in the midst of heathenish persecutions? What toys and trifles did the ancient reverend fathers of the church trouble their heads about, and pester the church with; and what useless stuff are many of their canons composed of! Yet these were the great matter and work of many of their famous consultations. How quickly did they seem to forget the perfection of holy Scripture, the non-necessity and burdensomeness of ceremonious impositions: and by taking upon them an unnecessary and unjust kind of jurisdiction, they made the church so much more work than ever Christ made it, and so clogged religion with human devices, that the christian world hath groaned under it ever since, and been almost brought to ruin by it; and the reverence of their persons hath put so much reputation on the crime, and custom hath so taught it to plead prescription, that when the lacerated, languid churches will be delivered from the sad effects of their presumption, God only knoweth. It would make an impartial reader wonder, that peruseth their canons and the history of the church, that ever men of piety, charity, and sobriety, could be drawn to perplex and tear in pieces the churches by such a multitude of vanities, and needless determinations (to say no worse). And that the preachers of the gospel of peace, which so enjoineth humility, unity, and love, should ever be drawn to such a height of pride, as to think themselves meet to make so many laws for the whole church of Christ, and to bind all their brethren through the world to the obedience of their dictates, and practice of the histrionical, insnaring ceremonies; and that upon the penalties of being accounted no less than damned heretics or schismatics. Though Paul had told them betimes, that he was afraid of them, lest as the serpent deceived Eve, so they should be deceived, and drawn from the simplicity that was in Christ, 2 Cor. xi. 3; yet quickly was this caution forgotten, and the thing that Paul feared soon befell them; and instead of the simplicity of doctrine, they vexed the churches with curious controversies; and instead of the simplicity of discipline and government, they corrupted the church with pomp and tyranny, and varieties of new orders and rules of religions; and instead of the simplicity of worship, they set up such a train of their own inventions, of which the church had no necessity, that the bishops were become the masters of ceremonies, who should have been the humble and faithful observers of the pure laws and ordinances of Christ. Though their councils were useful for the churches' communion, had they been rightly ordered, yet so unhappily did they manage them for the most part, that Gregory Nazianzen purposed to come at them no more, as having never seen any that did not more harm than good. And so bold and busy were they in additions and innovations, even in making new creeds, that Hilary sadly

[a] If any one about the time of Moses offering sacrifice according to the law, were not instructed in the doctrine of the death of our Redeemer, but only believed that God, through the means which he knoweth to be most agreeable and convenient, will forgive us our trespasses, it were rashness to go about to exclude such a man from salvation. Pet. Molinæus de Tradition. c. 19. p. 251, 252.

complains of it, not sparing the council of Nice itself, though their creed were allowable, because they taught others the way, and set the rest a work. And Luther showeth us at large in his book "De Conciliis," what thoughts he had of those assemblies. Three lamentable vices did the prelates of the church then commonly abound in, *pride* the root, *contention*, and *vain impositions* and *inventions*, the fruits. No charity that is not blind can hide this guilt. We had never else had the christian world so plagued with their quarrels about superiority and vain traditions, after such warnings, and lessons, and examples as Christ had given his own apostles. When once the favour of a christian prince did shine upon the churches, what self-exhortation and contention of the prelates did ensue! So that if they had not been restrained and kept in quiet by the emperor, how soon would they have made a sadder havoc than they did! Perhaps in their first general council itself. And though that council had a good occasion, even to suppress the Arian heresy, yet had not Constantine committed their mutual accusations to the flames, and shamed them from their contendings, it had not had so good an end. And yet as good as it was, Luther saith, p. 226, de Concil. *Arianæ hæresis jocus fuit ante Nicænum concilium, præ illa confusione quam ipsi post concilium excitaverunt.* Augustine's sad complaint of the loading of the church with ceremonies, and comparing them to Judaism, is commonly known: of which see Luther's Comment. ib. p. 55, 56. And so strange did it seem to Luther, that the learned prelates of those better times should so scold *circa nænia et nugas*, about pre-eminence and ceremonies, and things of nought, that he is again and again taken up in admiring it. Read that treatise throughout.

Is it not sad to think of the heat of an Epiphanius, and Theophilus Alexand. against Chrysostom, and of Chrysostom against them! of Jerom against Ruffinus, Chrysostom, and many others; and if Austin had not been more peaceable than he, one of them must have been a heretic, or schismatic at least. How many more such sad examples have we!

And for their damnatory sentences, they were more presumptuous than their laws: few men could stand in another's way, or fall out, but one of them must be a heretic before they had made an end. Small differences were named damnable heresies: though they had enough among them that were such indeed, whereof some of the clergy were almost always the causes and fomenters; yet did they so multiply them by their imputation, that their catalogues swelled beyond the credit of charity. And he that had the highest reputation, was usually safest from the blot, and had power to make others heretics almost at his pleasure; and if a man had once got the vote and fame, it was dangerous gainsaying him: had Vigilantius or Jovinian had Jerom's name, some of their heresies might possibly have been articles of faith.

And, as they were dangerously forward on one side, to make every small mistake a heresy, and cause divisions in the church by their unjust condemnations; so many on the other hand were as forward to provoke them, by novelties or false conceits, especially about the Trinity, and the person and natures of Christ: so that unquiet spirits knew not when or where to rest; and multitudes of them did turn cheaters and deluders of the vulgar, by pretending to miracles, and revelations, and visions, and drawing the people deeper into superstition; by such means as Bonifacius Moguntinus wrote to the Pope Zachary about the hypocritical Saint Aldebert: and in that age especially, when few learned men, as Erasmus complaineth, did escape the suspicion of heresy, and he that was a mathematician was counted a magician, it had been more wit to have silenced some unnecessary verities, than to have angered impatient ignorance. Virgilius might have talked more of the world above us, and let the world below us alone, rather than to force the learned Pope Zachary to say to his brother Boniface of Mentz: *De perversa et iniqua doctrina, quam contra Deum et animam suam locutus est* (a high crime) *; si clarificatum fuerit ita eum confiteri, quod alius mundus et alii homines sub terras sint, hunc accito concilio, ab ecclesia pelle, sacerdotii honore privatum.* Vid. Usher. syllog. Hibernic. Epistol. p. 49, 50. But to mention the twentieth part of the proud usurpation, innovations, impositions, and sentences of those following times, especially among the Romanists, is fitter for large volumes, than a cursory lamentation of the church's sins. I will not meddle with the errors and cruel bloodshed of the popish clergy of late, against the Waldenses, and protestants; nor yet with the sad condition of the rest of the clergy through the christian world, in Ethiopia, Muscovia, Greece, &c.; for you will think that this is less to us that do disclaim them: but let us come nearer ourselves, and we shall find yet matter of further lamentation. And I will purposely say nothing of any of the sins of our foreign reformers, nor meddle with any of those sad contentions, which have brought the reformed churches into two such exasperated parties, *Lutherans* and *Calvinists*, as they are commonly called, and hindered their reconciliation, and frustrated all means that have been used to that end till this day; to the exceeding shame of the pastors of these churches, and the publishing of our darkness, pride, and selfishness to all the world. But my present business lieth only at home, and that only with the reformed pastors of our churches. For though, through the great mercy of God, they are far from the papal cruelty, which made bonfires of their brethren better than themselves throughout the land, and as far from the worst of their errors and false worship; yet have we been so far from innocency, that all posterity is bound to lament the miscarriages of their predecessors.

Is it not a very sad history of the troubles at Frankfort, to read that so many godly, learned men that had forsaken all for the reformed profession, and were exiles in a foreign land, even in a city where they had but borrowed the liberty of one church, should even then fall in pieces among themselves, and that about a liturgy and ceremonies, so far as to make a division; and after many plotting, and counter-plotting, and undermining one another, one part of them must leave the city and go seek another for their liberty! What! had not those few exiles that left their native country, lands, and friends, and all for the gospel, that fled so far for the liberty of God's worship, and had as great advantage as most men in the world to be sensible of the excellency of reformation and liberty; had these, I say, no more christian love and tenderness, no more esteem of what they suffered for, than to fall out with one another, and almost fall upon one another, for such things as these? Would not suffering abate their pride and passions, and close their hearts, nor yet make them so far patient as to tolerate each other in so small a difference? even when their dearest friends and fellow-servants were frying in the flames at home, and the prisons filled with them, and they had daily news of one after another that was made a sacrifice to the fury of the papists, could they yet proceed in their own dissensions, and that to such a height? Oh what is man, and the best of men! Yea, before this, in King Edward's days, what rigour was used against

Bishop Hooper about such ceremonies! But the prison abated Bishop Ridley's uncharitableness, and they then learned more charity when they were going to the flames.

From Frankfort the sad division at the death of Queen Mary was transported into England; and the seeds that were sown, or began to spring up, in the exiled congregation, did too plentifully fructify in the land of their prosperity. No sooner doth the sun shine upon them, but contentious spirits begin to swarm: and the prison doors are no sooner open, and their bolts knocked off, but they contrive the suppressing of the brethren, as if they had been turned loose as fighting cocks to fall upon one another, and to work for Satan when they had suffered for Christ. The party that was for prelacy and ceremonies, prevailed for the countenance of the state, and quickly got the staff into their hands, and many of their brethren under their feet; and so contrived the business, that there was no quiet station to be had in the ministry, for those that would not be of their mind and way. And many of them endeavoured to have a brand of ignominy set upon their names, who desired the discipline and order of other reformed churches; that all might be accounted schismatics that would not be ruled by them even in ceremonies. The contrary-minded, also, were some of them too intemperate, and impatient, and unpeaceable; and some few of them turned to flat separation, and flew into the faces of the prelates with reviling. For their sakes many wise and peaceable men were the worse used; and they that were got into the chair, began to play the scorners, and the persecutors, and thought meet to impose upon them all the nickname of puritans, as knowing how much names of reproach and scorn could do with the vulgar for the furthering of their cause: some of these puritans (as now they had named them) were imprisoned, and some put to death, and some died in and by imprisonment: they are all made uncapable of being preachers of the gospel in England, till they would change their minds, and subscribe to the lawfulness of prelacy, and the liturgy and ceremonies, and use these accordingly when they use their ministry. Oh how much did many good men rejoice that the Lord had visited their native country with deliverance, and the light of the glorious gospel of his Son! How much did they long to lay out themselves for the saving of their dear countrymen, and to improve the present freedom for the most effectual propagation of the truth! When, alas! their own friends, some of their fellow-sufferers, animated and assisted by many temporizers, did suddenly disappoint their hopes, and shut them out of the vineyard of the Lord, and would suffer none to labour in it, but themselves and theirs. Alas, that persecution should be so soon forgotten! And that they should have no more sense of the cruelty of the papists, to have moved them to some more tenderness of the consciences and liberties of their brethren. That they had no more compassion on the church of Christ, than to deprive it of the labours of so many choice and worthy men; and that at such a time of necessity. When popish priests were new cast out, and multitudes of congregations had no preachers at all, but some silly readers, yet might not these men be allowed to preach. If the judgments of these prelates were never so absolute for the divine right of their own government, yet could it not be so for the absolute necessity of the cross, surplice, and every part of the forms in their liturgy. Had they but countenanced most their own party, and silenced all that did speak against their government and ceremonies, and only allowed them to preach the gospel with subscription to the lawfulness of these things, and with a silent forbearance of the use of the ceremonies, they might have better secured their own power and way, and have exercised some sense of brotherly love and compassion on the necessitous state of the church, and in all likelihood, might have stood safe themselves to this day. A wonderful thing it seems to me, that wise and good men, for such I doubt not but many of them were, should think it better that many hundred congregations in England (to say nothing of Ireland or Scotland) should be without any preaching at all, to the apparent hazard of the damnation of men's souls, who were so deep in popish ignorance before, than that a man should preach to them that durst not use the cross or surplice! Were these of more worth than so many souls? It was lawful in the apostles' days to baptize without the cross, and to pray and praise God without the surplice. And why might not the prelates of England have tolerated that in the church's necessities, at least as a weakness in well-meaning brethren, which the apostolical churches used not at all? What if they were lawful? They that thought so might have them. Were they now become more necessary than the preaching of the gospel, when in the apostles' times they were of no necessity or use at all? If it were obedience to the prelates that was necessary, they might have required obedience to undoubted and necessary things, and they should soon have found it. Had they contented themselves to be as officers under Christ, and to see the execution of his laws, and to meddle at least with no needless new legislation, I think few would have questioned obedience to them but the ungodly. But it was sadly contrived to have such impositions on men's consciences in needless or indifferent things, as the most tender-conscienced men were likest to disobey, and as might be snares to those that desired to please God; when the business of church governors should be to promote the obedience of Christ's laws, and to encourage those that are most fearful to disobey them, and to do as the law-makers, Dan. vi. 5, "We shall not find any occasion against this Daniel, except we find it against him concerning the law of his God."

But thus it came to pass that the enemy of the church did too much attain his ends; such excellent men as Hildersham, Brightman, P. Bayn, Parker, Ames, Bradshaw, Dod, Nicolls, with multitudes more, were laid aside and silenced; and multitudes of them that petitioned for liberty in Lincolnshire, Devonshire, and other parts, suppressed; and the nation in the mean-time abounding with gross ignorance, was brought by observing the countenance of the times to like their own readers better than painful preachers, and to hate and scorn the zealous obedience to the laws of Christ, and all diligence for salvation, because they observed, that those men that were such, were so many of them hated and persecuted by the rulers, though on the occasions before mentioned. And here was the foundation of our greatest misery laid; while some of the rulers themselves began to turn their hatred against practical godliness, (which corrupted nature hates in all,) and the common people took the hint, and no longer confined the word puritan to the nonconformists, but applied it commonly through all parts of the land, to those that would but speak seriously of heaven, and tell men of death and judgment, and spend the Lord's day in preparation thereto, and desire others to do the like; that did but pray in their families, and keep their children and servants on the Lord's day to learn the way to salvation, instead of letting them spend it in gaming or revelling: they that did but reprove a swearer or a drunkard, these were become the puritans and the precisians, and the hated ones of the time; so that they became a by-word in all the towns and villages in England that ever I knew, or heard of, as to these things. And thus when the prelates had engaged the vulgar in their cause, and partly by themselves, and partly by them, had so far changed their cause, as that all serious christians that feared sin, and were most diligent for salvation, were presently engaged among their adversaries, and they were involved with the rest, though they did nothing against the government or ceremonies, and the most ignorant and impious became the friends and agents of the times, and every where made the most pious and sedulous christians a common scorn, to the dishonour of God, and the hardening of the wicked, and discouraging of the weak, and filling men with prejudice against a godly life, and hindering many thousands from the way of salvation; then did God himself appear more evidently as interested in the quarrels, and rose against them, and shamed them that had let in scorn and shame upon his ways. And this, even this, was the very thing that brought them down.

Besides this, there was scarcely such a thing as church government or discipline known in the land, but only this harassing of those that dissented from them. In all my life I never lived in the parish where one person was publicly admonished, or brought to public penitence, or excommunicated, though there were never so many obstinate drunkards, whoremongers, or vilest offenders. Only I have known now and then one for getting a bastard, that went to the bishop's court and paid their fees; and I heard of two or three in all the country, in all my life, that stood in a white sheet an hour in the church; but the ancient discipline of the church was unknown. And indeed it was made by them impossible, when one man that lived at a distance from them, and knew not one of many hundreds of the flock, did take upon him the sole jurisdiction, and executed it not by himself, but by a lay-chancellor, excluding the pastors of the several congregations, who were but to join with the churchwardens and the apparitors in presenting men and bringing them into their courts; and an impossible task must needs be unperformed. And so the controversy, as to the letter and outside, was, *Who shall be the governors of all the particular churches?* but as to the sense and inside of it, it was, *Whether there should be any effectual church government or not?* Whereupon those that pleaded for discipline were called by the new name of the disciplinarians; as if it had been a kind of heresy to desire discipline in the church.

At last, the heat began to grow greater, and new impositions raised new adversaries. When conformable puritans began to bear the great reproach, there being few of the nonconformists left, then must they also be gotten into the net; altars must be bowed to, or towards; all must publish a book for dancing and sports on the Lord's day, disabling the masters of families, and parents, though they had small time on the week days, by reason of their poverty or labour, to keep in their own children or families from dancing on that day, that they might instruct them in the matters of God. If a man, as he read a chapter to his family, had persuaded them to observe and practise it, and with any reasons urged them thereto, this was called *expounding*, and was inquired of in their articles, to be presented together with adultery, and such like sins; so also was he used that had no preaching at home, and would go hear a conformable preacher abroad. So that multitudes have I known exceedingly troubled or undone for such matters as these, when not one was much troubled for scandalous crimes. Then lectures were put down, and afternoon sermons, and expounding the catechism or Scripture in the afternoons. And the violence grew so great, that many thousand families left the land, and many godly, able ministers, conformists as well as others, were fain to fly and become exiles, some in one country, and some in another, and most in the remote American parts of the world. Thither went Cotton, Hooker, Davenport, Shepherd, Allen, Cobbet, Noyes, Parker, with many another that deserved a dwelling-place in England.

Yet I must profess, I should scarce have mentioned any of this, nor taken it for so heinous a crime, had it been only cruelty to the persons of these men, though they had dealt much hardlier with them than they did, and if it had not been greater cruelty to the church, and if they had but had competent men for their places when they were cast out. But, alas! the churches were pestered with such wretches as are our shame and trouble to this day. Abundance of mere readers, and drunken, profane, deboist men, were the ministers of the churches; so that we have been these many years endeavouring to cleanse the church of them, and have not fully effected it to this day. And many that had more plausible tongues did make it their chief business to bring those that they called puritans into disgrace, and to keep the people from being such: so that I must needs say, that I knew no place in these times, where a man might not more safely have been drunken every week, as to their punishment, than to have gone to hear a sermon if he had none at home. For the common people readily took the hint and increased their reproach, as the rulers did their persecution; so that a man could not, in any place of England that I came in, have said to a swearer or a drunkard, O do not sin against God, and wound or hazard your own soul, but he should have been presently hooted at as a puritan: he could not have said to an ignorant or careless neighbour, Remember your everlasting state; prepare for death and judgment; or have talked of any Scripture matters to them, but he was presently jeered as a puritan or precisian; and Scripture itself was become a reproach to him that talked of it, and they would cry out, What! we must have talk of Scripture now! You will preach to us! We shall have these preachers ordered ere long. So that it was become commonly in England a greater reproach to be a man truly living in the fear of God, than to live in open profaneness, and to rail at godliness, and daily scorn it, which was so far from being a matter of danger, that many took it up in expectation of preferment; and the preachers of the times were well aware that the rising way was to preach against the precise puritans, and not to live precisely themselves: and thus both ministry and people grew to that sad pass, that it was no wonder if God would bear no longer with the land.

Even as it was in the Western churches before the inundation of the Goths and Vandals, as Salvian, among others, tells us; indeed I know not a writer that more fitly painteth out the state of our times: I shall therefore borrow some of his words to express our case, which it seems had been then the church's case.

Ipsa Dei ecclesia, quæ in omnibus esse debet placatrix Dei, quid est aliud quam exacerbatrix Dei? aut præter paucissimos quosdam qui mala fugiunt, quid est aliud pene omnis cœtus christianorum quam sentina vitiorum? Quotum enim quemque invenies in ecclesia non aut ebriosum aut helluonem, aut adulterum, &c.—immo facilius invenias qui totum sit quam qui nihil: et quod diximus nihil nimis forsitan gravis videatur esse censura; plus multo dicam, facilius invenias reum malorum omnium quam non omnium; facilius majorum criminum quam minorum, id est, facilius qui et majora crimina cum minoribus, quam qui minora tantum sine majoribus perpetrarint. In hanc enim morum probrositatem prope omnis ecclesiastica plebs redacta est, ut in cuncto populo christiano genus quodammodo sanctitatis sit, minus esse vitiosum. Itaque, ecclesias vel potius templa atque altaria Dei minoris reverentiæ quidem habent quam cujuslibet minimi ac municipalis judicis domum. Siquidem intra januas non modo illustrium potestatum, sed etiam præsidum et præpositorum, non omnes passim intrare præsumunt, nisi quos aut judex vocaverit, aut negotium traxerit, aut ipsa honoris proprii, dignitas introire permiserit: ita ut, si quispiam fuerit insolenter ingressus, aut cædatur, aut propellatur, aut aliqua verecundiæ atque existimationis suæ labe mulctetur. In templa autem vel potius in altaria atque sacraria Dei passim omnes sordidi ac flagitiosi sine ulla penitus reverentia sacri honoris irrumpunt, non quia non omnes ad exorandum Deum currere debent: sed quia qui ingreditur ad placandum, non debet egredi ad exacerbandum. Neque enim ejusdem officii est indulgentiam poscere et iracundiam provocare: novum siquidem monstri genus est; eadem pæne omnes jugitur faciunt, quæ fecisse se plangunt: et qui intrant in ecclesiasticam domum, ut mala antiqua defleant, exeunt; et quid dico exeunt? in ipsis pene hoc orationibus suis moliuntur. Salv. de Gubern. l. 3, p. 86, 87.

Et p. 180. *O miseriam lacrymabilem, O miseriam luctuosam! Quam dissimilis nunc a seipso est populus christianus, id est, ab eo qui fuit quondam!—Ecce in quid reducti sumus, ut beatam fore ecclesiam judicemus, si vel tantum in se boni habeat quantum mali. Nam quomodo non beatam arbitremur, si mediam plebis partem haberet innoxiam, quam pene totam nunc esse plangimus criminosam—superflue unius scelera deflevimus; aut omnes enim, aut pene omnes flendi atque lugendi sunt.*

Et. p. 195, 196. *Omnia amamus, omnia colimus; solus nobis in comparatione omnium Deus vilis est? Siquando enim veniret, (quod sæpe evenit) ut eodem die et festivitas ecclesiastica et ludi publici agantur, quæso ab omnium conscientia, quis locus majores christianorum virorum copias haberet? Caveo ne ludi publici, an atrium Dei! Et templum omnes magis sectentur, an theatrum? Dicta evangeliorum magis diligant an Thymelicorum? Verba vitæ, an mortis? Verba Christi, an mimi? Non est dubium quin illud magis amemus quod anteponimus.*

Too like to these, here described, were our times grown, through the fault of those that professed themselves to have the oversight of their souls. A most sad thing it was to see those men that undertook to guide men in the ways of life, to be the chief means of discouraging them; and to hear them make a mock at holiness, that should have devoted their doctrine and life thereto. The accusation may seem harsh to those of after-times that knew not this; or that by the patrons of iniquity are persuaded of the contrary. But I say as Salvian, l. 6, p. 197, *Sed gravis est forsitan hæc atque iniqua congestio. Gravis profecto, si falsa.*

Yet through the mercy of God, it was not all the prelates of the church that thus miscarried; we have yet surviving our Usher, our Hall, our Morton, learned, godly, and peaceable men; whose names are as dear to us as any men's alive. And oh that it had been the will of God that all had been such! Then had we not been like to have seen those days of blood that we have seen; nor those great mutations in church and state! But so far were these good men from being able to do the good that they would, that they were maligned for their piety and soundness in the faith, and many a time have I heard them despised as well as others, and scorned as puritans for all they were prelates.

And yet, it were well if all the guilt had lain upon that party! But, alas! it was not so. Those pious and painful divines that were oppressed, and much more that part of the people that joined with them, were too impatient under their suffering; and bent themselves, some of them, more than was meet against the persons of those that they suffered by; and too much endeavoured to make the prelates odious with the people, as persecutors of the church of God; and were ready to go too far from them on the other hand, and to think the worse of some things because they commanded them. Doubtless, had we all suffered with more patience, and carried ourselves with meekness and gentleness to those that we differed from, and given them so much commendation as was their due, and put the best constructions on their actions that we could, and covered their infirmities with the most charitable interpretations, we might have done more to mollify their minds; or at least, to have maintained our own innocency. But as there was no room on their part to a motion for peace, or a petition for liberty, in the time of their prosperity; so when advantages did seem to appear to us of vindicating our liberties, we looked upon them as unreconcilable, and too inconsiderately rushed on, and were wanting in those peaceable endeavours that were our duty. We did not in our assembly invite them to a free consultation, that their cause might have the fullest and fairest hearing, before it had been condemned. Proposals that had any tendency to healing and accommodation, had never that entertainment from us that they did deserve. What moderate proposals were made to one party by Bishop Usher, which both parties did dislike! How many pacificatory motions and excellent treatises came from that heavenly, peaceable Bishop Hall, especially his "Peacemaker," his "Pax Terris," and his "Modest Offer!" But how little did they effect! Certainly some of the men were so venerable for their admirable learning and piety, that they deserved to have been heard, and consulted with too, as wise and most judicious men. And prelacy was not so young a plant in the church, nor had it in former and latter ages had so few or mean persons to adorn and credit it, but that it well deserved the fairest hearing and debate.

But thus have we all showed our frailty, and this is the *heed* that we have *taken to ourselves, and to all the flock.* The Lord open our eyes at last, that we may all fuller see our own miscarriages; for surely they lie as mountains before us, and all the world about us may see them, and yet we will hardly see them ourselves.

A man would think that now if the heart of man be curable, we should by this time be all brought to the sense of our miscarriages, and be prepared to a closure on any reasonable terms. Who would think but after all the smart of our divisions, we should long ere this have got together, and prayed, and consulted ourselves into peace! But, alas! there is no such matter done; and few do I find that mind the doing of it. We continue our quarrels as hot as ever: as Salvian saith in another case, *Miseri jam sumus: et nec dum nugaces (discordes) esse cessamus!* l. 6, p. 202. Et p. 200. *Mala incessabiliter malis addimus, et peccata peccatis cumulamus: et cum maxima nostri pars jam perierit, id agimus ut pereamus omnes.*

——*Nos non vicinos nostros tantum ardere vidimus, sed ipsi jam ex maxima nostrorum corporum parte arsimus. Et quid hoc, proh nefas, mali est? Arsimus, arsimus, et tamen flammas quibus jam arsimus non timemus. Nam quod non ubique agantur quæ prius acta sunt, miseriæ est beneficium, non disciplinæ. Facile hoc probo. Da enim prioris temporis et statum ubique sunt quæ fuerunt.*

The minds of many are as much exasperated or estranged as ever. Three sorts I meet with, that all are too backward to any accommodation.

1. The violent men of the prelates' side, especially those of the new way, who are so far from reconciliation and healing of our breaches, that they labour to persuade the world that the contrary-minded are schismatics, and that all the ministers that have not episcopal ordination are no ministers, nor any of the churches that have not prelates are true churches (at least, except it can be proved to be through unavoidable necessity). And they say, to agree with such, were to strike a covenant with Schism itself.

2. Some on the other side say, Do you not see, that except an inconsiderable number, the prelatical party are all empty, careless, if not scandalous, ungodly men? Where are almost any of them whose communion is desirable? that set themselves to the winning and saving of souls, and are serious men in the matters of salvation, in whom you can perceive a heavenly conversation? Hath God brought down these enemies of godliness, and persecutors and depopulators of his church, and would you make a league with them again? Do you not see that they are as bitter and implacable as ever? And have not some of them the faces to justify all the former impositions and persecutions, and draw or continue the guilt of it upon their heads? and would make the world believe that they are wrongfully ejected, when so many accusations in parliament before the division, so many centuries of horrid, scandalous ones published by Mr. White, and so many more centuries, that lie on record under depositions in the several counties of the nation where the committees ejected them, will be perpetual witnesses of the quality of these men.

3. Others there be that are peaceable men on both sides, that will not justify the former miscarriages, nor own the present evils of any; but think, though there be too much truth in these latter accusations, yet the nature of the difference, and the quality of some of the persons, is such, as deserveth our desires and endeavours of reconciliation. But they think the work to be hopeless and impossible, and therefore not to be attempted.

And thus our breach is made; but how or when it will be well healed, the Lord knoweth. But this is not all: it behoveth us yet to come nearer home, and inquire into the ways of the present approved godly ministers, of what party soever; and doubtless, if we are willing to know ourselves, we may soon find that which will lay us very low before the Lord. I shall, in all, have an eye at my own corrupt heart, which I am so far from justifying in this common lamentation, that I take it as my necessary duty to cast the first stone at myself.

The great sins that we are guilty of, I shall not undertake to enumerate; and therefore my passing over any particular is not to be taken as a denial of it for our justification. But I shall take it to be my duty to give instances of some few, that cry loud for humiliation and speedy reformation.

Only I must needs first premise this profession; that for all the faults that are now among us, I do not believe that ever England had so able and faithful a ministry since it was a nation as it hath at this day; and I fear that few nations on earth, if any, have the like. Sure I am the change is so great within these twelve years, that it is one of the greatest joys that ever I had in the world to behold it. Oh how many congregations are now plainly and frequently taught, that lived then in great obscurity! How many able, faithful men are there now in a county in comparison of what were then! How graciously hath God prospered the studies of many young men, that were little children in the beginning of the late troubles; so that now they cloud the most of their seniors! How many miles would I have gone twenty years ago, and less, to have heard one of those ancient, reverend divines, whose congregations are now grown thin, and their parts esteemed mean, by reason of the notable improvement of their juniors! And in particular, how mercifully hath the Lord dealt with this poor county of Worcestershire, in raising up so many of these, that credit their sacred office, and self-denyingly and freely, zealously and unweariedly, do lay out themselves for the good of souls! I bless the Lord that hath placed me in such a neighbourhood, where I may have the brotherly fellowship of so many able, humble, unanimous, peaceable, and faithful men. Oh that the Lord would long continue this admirable mercy to this unworthy county! And I hope I shall rejoice in God while I have a being for the common change in other parts, that I have lived to see; that so many hundred faithful men are so hard at work for the saving of souls, *frementibus licet et frendentibus inimicis;* and that more are springing up apace. I know there are some men, whose parts I reverence, who being in point of government of another mind from them, will be offended at my very mention of this happy alteration; but I must profess, if I were absolutely prelatical, if I knew my heart, I could not choose for all that but rejoice. What! not rejoice at the prosperity of the church, because the men do differ in opinion about its order? Should I shut my eyes against the mercies of the Lord? The souls of men are not so contemptible to me, that I should envy them the bread of life, because it is broken to them by a hand that had not the prelatical approbation. Oh that every congregation were thus supplied! But all cannot be done at once. They had a long time to settle a corrupted ministry; and when the ignorant and scandalous are cast out, we cannot create abilities in others for the supply; we must stay the time of their preparation and growth; and then, if England drive not away the gospel by their abuse, even by their wilful unreformedness, and hatred of the light, they are like to be the happiest nation under heaven. For as for all the sects and heresies that are creeping in daily and troubling us, I doubt not but the free gospel, managed by an able, self-denying ministry, will effectually disperse and shame them all.

But you may say, this is not confessing sin, but applauding those whose sins you pretend to confess.

Answ. It is the due acknowledgment of God's graces, and thanksgiving for his admirable mercies, that I may not seem unthankful in confession, much less to cloud or vilify God's graces, while I open the frailties that in many do accompany them.

SECTION II.

Among the many things that are yet sadly out of order in the best, I shall touch upon these few particulars following:

1. One of our most heinous and palpable sins is *pride;* a sin that hath too much interest in the best, but is more hateful and unexcusable in us than in any

men. Yet is it so prevalent in some of us, that it inditeth our discourses for us; it chooseth us our company, it formeth our countenances, it putteth the accents and emphases upon our words: when we reason, it is the determiner and exciter of our cogitations; it fills some men's minds with aspiring desires and designs; it possesseth them with envious and bitter thoughts against those that stand in their light, or by any means do eclipse their glory, or hinder the progress of their idolized reputation. Oh what a companion, what a tyrannous commander, what a sly, and subtle, insinuated enemy is this sin of pride! It goes with men to the draper, the mercer, the tailor; it chooseth them their cloth, their trimming, and their fashion. It dresseth them in the morning, at least the outside. Fewer ministers would ruffle it out in the fashion in hair and habit, if it were not for the command of this tyrannous vice: and I would that were all, or the worst; but alas, how frequently doth it go with us to our studies, and there sit with us and our work! How oft doth it choose our subject, and more often choose our words and ornaments! God biddeth us be as plain as we can, for the informing of the ignorant, and as convincing and serious as we are able, for the melting and changing of unchanged hearts; and pride stands by and contradicteth all: and sometimes it puts in toys and trifles, and polluteth rather than polisheth, and under pretence of laudable ornaments, it dishonoureth our sermons with childish gauds; as if a prince were to be decked in the habit of a stage-player or a painted fool. It persuadeth us to paint the window that it may dim the light; and to speak to our people that which they cannot understand, to acquaint them that we are able to speak unprofitably. It taketh off the edge, and dulls the life of all our teachings, under the pretence of filing off the roughness, unevenness, and superfluity. If we have a plain and cutting passage, it throws it away as too rustical or ungrateful. When God chargeth us to deal with men as for their lives, and beseech them with all the earnestness that we are able, this cursed sin controlleth all, and condemneth the most holy commands of God, and calleth our most necessary duty a madness; and saith to us, What! will you make people think you are mad? Will you make them say you rage or rave? Cannot you speak soberly and moderately? And thus doth pride make many a man's sermons; and what pride makes the devil makes; and what sermons the devil will make, and to what end, we may easily conjecture. Though the matter be of God, yet if the dress, and manner, and end be from Satan, we have no great reason to expect success.

And when pride hath made the sermon, it goes with them into the pulpit; it formeth their tone, it animateth them in the delivery, it takes them off from that which may be displeasing, how necessary soever, and setteth them in a pursuit of vain applause: and the sum of all this is, that it maketh men, both in studying and preaching, to seek themselves and deny God, when they should seek God's glory and deny themselves. When they should ask, What should I say, and how should I say it, to please God best, and do most good? it makes them ask, What shall I say, and how shall I deliver it, to be thought a learned, able preacher, and to be applauded by all that hear me? When the sermon is done, pride goeth home with them, and maketh them more eager to know whether they were applauded, than whether they did prevail for the saving change of souls! They could find in their hearts, but for shame, to ask folks how they liked them, and to draw out their commendation. If they do perceive that they are highly thought of, they rejoice, as having attained their end; but if they perceive that they are esteemed but weak or common men, they are displeased, as having missed the prize of the day.

But yet this is not all, nor the worst, if worse may be. Oh that ever it should be spoken of godly ministers, that they are so set upon popular air, and of sitting highest in men's estimation, that they envy the parts and names of their brethren that are preferred before them, as if all were taken from their praises that is given to another; and as if God had given them his gifts to be the mere ornaments and trappings of their persons, that they may walk as men of reputation in the world, and all his gifts in others were to be trodden down and vilified, if they seem to stand in the way of their honour! What! a saint, a preacher for Christ, and yet envy that which hath the image of Christ, and malign his gifts for which he should have the glory, and all because they seem to hinder our glory! Is not every true christian a member of the body, and therefore partaketh of the blessings of the whole, and of each particular member thereof? And doth not every man owe thanks to God for his brethren's gifts, not only as having himself a part in them, as the foot hath the benefit of the guidance of the eye; but also because his own ends may be attained by his brethren's gifts as well as by his own? For if the glory of God and the church's felicity be not his end, he is not a christian. Will any workman malign another because he helpeth him to do his master's work? Yet alas, how common is this heinous crime among men of parts and eminence in the church! They can secretly blot the reputation of those that stand cross to their own: and what they cannot for shame do in plain and open terms, lest they be proved palpable liars and slanderers, they will do in generals and malicious intimations, raising suspicions where they cannot fasten accusations. And so far are some gone in this satanical vice, that it is their ordinary practice, and a considerable part of their business, to keep down the estimation of any they dislike, and defame others in the slyest and most plausible way. And some go so far, that they are unwilling that any one that is abler than themselves should come into their pulpits, lest they should be applauded above themselves. A fearful thing, that any man that hath the least of the fear of God, should so envy at God's gifts, and had rather that his carnal hearers were unconverted, and the drowsy not awakened, than that it should be done by another who may be preferred before them. Yea, so far doth this cursed vice prevail, that in great congregations that have need of the help of many teachers, we can scarce in many places get two in equality to live together in love and quietness, and unanimously to carry on the work of God! But unless one of them be quite below the other in parts, and content to be so esteemed, or unless one be a curate to the other, or ruled by him, they are contending for precedency, and envying each other's interest, and walking with strangeness and jealousy towards one other, to the shame of the profession and the great wrong of the congregation. I am ashamed to think of it, that when I have been endeavouring with persons of public interest and capacity to further a good work, to convince them of the great necessity of more ministers than one in great congregations, they tell me, they will never agree together! I hope the objection is ungrounded as to the most; but it is a sad case that it should be so with any. Nay, some men are so far gone in pride, that when they might have an equal assistant to further the work of God, they had rather take all the burden upon themselves, though more than they can bear, than that any should share with them in the honour; and for fear lest they should diminish their interest in the people.

Hence also it comes to pass, that men so magnify their own opinions, and are as censorious of any that differ from them in lesser things, as if it were all one to differ from them and from God; and do expect that all should be conformed to their judgments, as if they were the rulers of the church's faith! And while we cry down papal infallibility, and determination of controversies, we would, too many of us, be popes ourselves, and have all stand to our determination, as if it were infallible. It is true, we have more modesty than expressly to say so: we pretend that it is only the evidence of truth that appeareth in our reasons that we expect men should yield to, and our zeal is for the truth and not for ourselves: but as that must needs be taken for truth which is ours, so our reasons must needs be taken for valid; and if they be freely examined, and found to be infirm and fallacious, and so discovered, as we are exceeding backward to see it ourselves, because they are ours, so how angry are we that it should be disclosed to others! We so espouse the cause of our errors, as if all that were spoken against them were spoken against our persons, and we were heinously injured to have our arguments throughly confuted, by which we injured the truth and the minds of men! So that the matter is come to that pass through our pride, that if an error or fallacious argument do fall under the patronage of a reverend name, (which is no whit rare,) we must either give it the victory and give away the truth, or else become injurious to that name that doth patronize it. For though you meddle not with their persons, yet do they put themselves under all the strokes which you give their arguments, and feel it as sensibly as if you had spoken it of themselves, because they think it will follow in the eyes of men, that weak arguing is a sign of a weak man. If therefore you take it for your duty to shame their errors and false reasonings, by discovering their nakedness, they take it as if you shamed their persons; and so their names must be a garrison or fortress to their mistakes, and their reverence must defend all their sayings from the light.

And so high are our spirits, that when it becomes a duty to any man to reprove or contradict us, we are commonly impatient both of the matter and of the manner. We love the man that will say as we say, and be of our opinion, and promote our reputation, though he be less worthy of our love in other respects; but he is ungrateful to us that contradicteth us, and differeth from us, and that dealeth plainly with us in our miscarriages, and telleth us of our faults! Especially in the management of our public arguings, where the eye of the world is upon us, we can scarce endure any contradiction or plain dealing. I know that railing language is to be abhorred, and that we should be as tender of each other's reputation, as our fidelity to the truth will permit: but our pride makes too many of us to think all men contemn us that do not admire us, yea, and admire all that we say, and submit their judgments to our most palpable mistakes! We are so tender that no man can touch us scarce but we are hurt; and so stout and high-minded, that a man can scarce speak to us: like froward children, or sick folk, that cannot endure to be talked to; the fault is not that you speak amiss to them, but that you speak to them. So our indignation is not at men for writing or speaking injuriously or unjustly against our words, but for confuting them. And a man that is not versed in complimenting, and skilled in flattery above the vulgar rate, can scarce tell how to handle them so observantly, and fit their expectations at every turn, but there will be some word, or some neglect, which their high spirits will fasten, and take as injurious to their honour: so that a plain countryman that speaks as he thinks, must have nothing to do with them, unless he will be esteemed guilty of dishonouring them.

I confess I have often wondered at it, that this most heinous sin should be made so slight of, and thought so consistent with a holy frame of heart and life, when far lesser sins are by ourselves proclaimed to be so damnable in our people! And more have I wondered to see the difference between ungodly sinners and godly preachers in this respect. When we speak to drunkards, worldlings, or any ignorant, unconverted men, we disgrace them as in that condition to the utmost, and lay it on as plainly as we can speak, and tell them of their sin, and shame, and misery: and we expect, not only that they should bear all patiently, but take all thankfully, and we have good reasons for all this; and most that I deal with do take it patiently; and many gross sinners will commend the closest preachers most, and will say that they care not for hearing a man that will not tell them plainly of their sins. But if we speak to a godly minister, against his errors or any sin, (for too many of them,) if we honour them and reverence them, and speak as smoothly as we are able to speak, yea, if we mix commendations with our contradictions or reproofs, if the applause be not apparently predominant, so as to drown all the force of the reproof or confutation, and if it be not more an applause than a reprehension, they take it as an injury almost insufferable. That is railing against them, that would be no better than flattery in them to the common people; though the cause may be as great.

Brethren, I know this is a sad and harsh confession; but that all this should be so among us, should be more grievous to us than to be told of it. Could this nakedness be hid, I should not have disclosed it, at least so openly in the view of all. But, alas, it is long ago open in the eyes of the world: we have dishonoured ourselves by idolizing our honour; we print our shame, and preach our shame, and tell it unto all. Some will think that I speak over-charitably to call such persons godly men, in whom so great a sin doth so much prevail. I know where it is indeed predominant, not hated, and bewailed, and mortified in the main, there can be no true godliness; and I leave every man to a cautelous jealousy and search of his own heart. But if all are graceless that are guilty of any, or many, or most of the forementioned discoveries of pride, the Lord be merciful to the ministers of this land, and give us quickly another spirit; for grace is then a rarer thing than most of us have supposed it to be.

Yet I must needs say, that it is not all that I intend. To the praise of grace be it spoken, we have some among us here, and I doubt not but it is so in other parts, that are eminent in humility, and lowliness, and condescension, and exemplary herein to their flocks and to their brethren; and it is their glory, and shall be their glory, and maketh them truly honourable and amiable in the eyes of God and themselves: and oh that the rest of us were but such! But, alas, this is not the case of all.

Oh that the Lord would lay us at his feet, in the tears of unfeigned sorrow for this sin! Brethren, may I take leave a little to expostulate this case with my own heart and you, that we may see the shame of our sin and be reformed? Is not pride the sin of devils? the firstborn of hell? Is it not that wherein Satan's image doth much consist? And is it tolerable evil in a man that is so engaged against him and his kingdom as we are? The very design of the gospel doth tend to self-abasing; and the work of grace is begun and carried on in humiliation. Humility is not a mere ornament of a christian, but an essential part of the new creature. It is a contradiction to be a sanctified man, or a true christian, and not humble. All that will be christians must be Christ's disciples, and come to him to learn; and their lesson is, to be meek and lowly, Matt. xi. 28. Oh how many precepts and admirable examples hath our Lord and Master given us to this end! Can we once conceive of him as purposely washing and wiping his servants' feet, and yet be stout and lordly still? shall he converse with the meanest, and we avoid them as contemptible people, and think none but persons of riches and honour to be fit for our society? How many of us are oftener found in the houses of gentlemen, than in the poor cottages of those that have most need of our help! There are many of us that would think a baseness, to be daily with the most needy and beggarly people to instruct them in the matters of life, and supply their wants; as if we had taken charge only of the souls of the rich! Alas, what is it that we have to be proud of? Of our body? Why, are they not made of the like materials as the brutes, and must they not shortly be as loathsome and abominable as the dung? Is it of our graces? Why the more we are proud of them, the less we have to be proud of. And when so much of the nature of grace is in humility, it is a great absurdity to be proud of it. Is it of our learning, knowledge, and abilities and gifts? Why sure if we have any knowledge at all, we must needs know much reason to be humble; and if we know more than others, we must know more reason than others do to be humble. How little is it that the most learned know in comparison of that which yet they are ignorant of! And to know that things are past your reach, and to know how ignorant you are, one would think should be no great cause of pride! However, do not the devils know more than you? And will you be proud of that which the devils do excel you in? Yea, to some I may say, as Salvian, lib. 4, de Gubern. p. 98. *Quid tibi blandiris, O homo quisquis es, Credulitate, quæ sine timore atque obsequio Dei nulla est? aliquid plus Dæmones habent. Tu enim unam rem habes tantummodo; illi duas. Tu credulitatem habes; non habes timorem: illi et credulitatem habent pariter et timorem.* Our very business is to teach the great lesson of self-denial and humility to our people, and how unfit is it then that we should be proud ourselves! We must study humility, and preach humility, and must we not possess and practise it? A proud preacher of humility, is at least a self-condemning man.

What a sad case is it, that so vile a sin is no more easily discerned by us! But many that are most proud, can blame it in others, and take no notice of it in themselves. The world takes notice of some among us that they have aspiring minds, and seek for the highest rooms, and must be rulers, and bear the sway wherever they come, or else there is no standing before them. No man must contradict them that will not partake of the fruits of their indignation. In any consultations, they come not to search after truth, but to dictate to others that perhaps are fit to teach them. In a word, they have such arrogant, domineering spirits, that the world rings of it; and yet they will not see it in themselves.

Brethren, I desire to deal closely with my own heart and yours. I beseech you consider, whether it will save us to speak well of the grace that we are without; or to speak against the sin that we live in? Have not many of us cause to inquire once and again, whether sincerity will consist with such a measure of pride? When we are telling the drunkard that he cannot be saved unless he become temperate; and the fornicator, that he cannot be saved unless he become chaste (an undoubted truth); have we not as great reason if we are proud, to say of ourselves, that we cannot be saved unless we become humble? Certainly, pride is a greater sin than whoredom or drunkenness; and humility is as necessary as chastity and sobriety. Truly, brethren, a man may as certainly, and more slily and dangerously, make haste to hell in a way of profession, and earnest preaching of the gospel, and seeming zeal for a holy life, as in a way of drunkenness and filthiness. For what is true holiness but a devotedness to God, and a living to him? And what is a wicked and damnable state, but a devotedness to our carnal selves, and a living to ourselves? And doth any man live more to himself than the proud, or less to God? And may not pride make a preacher study for himself, and pray, and preach, and live to himself, even when he seemeth to outgo others in the work, if he therefore outgo them that he may have the glory of it from men? It is not the work without the principle and end that will prove us upright: the work may be God's, and yet we do it, not for God, but for ourselves. I confess I feel such continual danger in this point, that if I do not watch against it, lest I should study for myself, and preach for myself, and write for myself, rather than for Christ, I should soon miscarry; and after all, I justify not myself, when I must condemn the sin. Consider, I beseech you, brethren, what baits there are in the work of the ministry, to entice a man to be selfish; that is, to be carnal and impious, even in the highest work of piety! The fame of a godly man is as great a snare as the fame of a learned man: and woe to him that takes up with the fame of godliness instead of godliness! Verily I say unto you, they have their reward. When the times were all for learning and empty formalities, then the temptation of the proud did lie that way; but now through the unspeakable mercy of God, the most lively practical preaching is in credit, and godliness itself is in credit: and now the temptation to proud men is here, even to pretend to be zealous preachers and godly men. Oh what a fine thing doth it seem to have the people crowd to hear us, and to be affected with what we say, and that we command their judgments and affections! What a taking thing is it to be cried up as the ablest and godliest man in the country! and to be famed through the land for the highest spiritual excellences! Alas, brethren, a little grace will serve turn to make you to join yourselves with the forwardest of those men, that have these inducements or encouragements. To have the people plead for you as their felicity, and call you the pillars of the church of God; and their fathers, the chariots and horsemen of Israel, and no lower language than excellent men, and able divines; and to have them depend upon you and be ruled by you; though this may be no more than their duty; yet I must again tell you, that a little grace may serve to make you seem zealous men for this. Nay, pride may do it without any special grace. O therefore be jealous of yourselves; and in all your studies, be sure to study humility. "He that exalteth himself shall be brought low, and he that humbleth himself shall be exalted." I observe commonly, that almost all men, good and bad, do loathe the proud, and love the humble: so far doth pride contradict itself, unless it be where it purposely hideth itself, and, as conscious of its own deformity, doth borrow the homely dress of humility. And we have cause to be the more jealous, because it is the most radicated vice, and as hardly as any extirpated from the soul. *Nam sæpe sibi de se mens ipsa mentitur, et fingit se de bono opere amare quod non amat: de mundi autem gloria, non amare quod amat;* inquit Gregor. M. de cura Pastor. p. 1, c. 9. When it was a disgrace to a man to be a godly, zealous preacher, then had not pride such a bait as now. As the same Gregory saith, ibid. p. 21, c. 8. *Eo tempore quo quisquis plebibus præerat, primus ad martyris tormenta ducebatur; Tunc laudabile fuit episcopatum quærere, quando per hunc quemque dubium non erat ad supplicia majora pervenire.*"

But it is not so now, as he saith in another place, cap. 1, initio, *Sed quia authore Deo ad religionis reverentiam omne jam præsentis seculi culmen inclinatur, sunt nonnulli qui intra sanctam ecclesiam per speciem regiminis gloriam affectant honoris; videri doctores appetunt, transcendere cæteros concupiscunt, atque attestante veritate, primas salutationes in foro, primos recubitus in cœnis, primas cathedras in conventibus quærunt, qui susceptum curæ pastoralis officium ministrare digne tanto magis nequeunt, quanto ad cujus humilitatis magisterium ex sola elatione pervenerunt; ipsa quippe in magisterio lingua confunditur, quando aliud discitur, et aliud docetur. Hactenus Gregorius, et ipse nimis magnus.*

But I have stood longer upon this sin than is proportionable to the rest of my work; I shall be the shorter in the confession of some of the rest.

SECTION III.

2. Another sin the ministers of England, and much more of many other churches, are sadly guilty of, is, *an undervaluing the unity and peace of the whole church.* Though I scarce ever met with any that will not speak for unity and peace, or at least, that will expressly speak against it; yet is it not common to meet with those that are addicted to promote it: but too commonly do we find men averse to it, and jealous of it, if not themselves the instruments of division. The papists have so long abused the name of the catholic church, that in opposition to them, many do either put it out of their creeds, or fill up room with the name, while they understand not, or consider not, the nature of the thing; or think it enough to believe that there is such a body, though they behave not themselves as sensible members of it. If the papists will idolize the church, shall we therefore deny it, disregard it, or divide? It is a great and common sin through the christian world, to take up religion in a way of faction; and instead of a love and tender care of the universal church, to confine that love and respect to a party. Not but that we must prefer in our estimation and communion the purer parts before the impure, and refuse to participate with any in their sins; but the most infirm and diseased part should be compassionated and assisted to our utmost power; and communion must be held as far as is lawful, and no where avoided but upon the urgency of necessity. As we must love those of our neighbourhood that have the plague or leprosy, and afford them all the relief we can, and acknowledge all our just relations to them, and communicate to them, though we may not have local communion with them: and in other diseases which are not so infectious, we may be the more with them for their help, by how much the more they need it. Of the multitude that say, they are of the catholic church, it is too rare to meet with men of a catholic spirit; men have not a universal consideration of and respect to the whole church; but look upon their own party as if it were the whole. If there be some called Lutherans, some Calvinists, some among these of subordinate divisions, and so of other parties among us, most of them will pray hard for the prosperity of their party, and rejoice and give thanks accordingly, when it goes well with them; but if any party suffer, they little regard it, as if it were no loss at all to the church. If it be the smallest parcel that possesseth not many nations, no nor cities on earth, they are ready to carry it, as if they were the whole church, and as if it went well with the church in the Romish pale; and no doubt but this is an abominable schism: but alas, how many do imitate them too far while we reprove them! And as they foist the word *Roman* into their creed, and turn the catholic church into the Roman catholic church; as if there were no other catholics, and the church were of no larger extent; so it is with many others, as to their several parties. Some will have it to be the Lutheran catholic church, as if it were all reformed; some the anabaptist catholic church; and so of some others. And if they differ not among themselves, they are little troubled at differing from others, though it be from almost all the christian world. The peace of their party they take for the peace of the church: no wonder therefore if they carry it no further.

How rare is it to meet with a man that smarteth or bleedeth with the church's wounds, or sensibly taketh them to heart as his own; or that ever had solicitous thoughts of a cure! No, but almost every party thinks that the happiness of the rest consisteth only in turning to them; and because they be not of their mind, they cry, Down with them! and are glad to hear of their fall, as thinking that is the way to the church's rising; that is, their own. How few are there that understand the true state of controversies between the several parties; or that ever well discerned how many of them are but verbal, and how many are real! And if those that understand it do, in order to right information, and accommodation, disclose it to others, it is taken as an extenuation of their error, and a carnal compliance with them in their sin. Few men grow zealous of peace, till they grow old, or have much experience of men's spirits and principles, and see better the true state of the church, and several differences, than they did before. And then they begin to write their *Irenicons*, and many such are extant at this day. Paræus, Junius, and many more, have done their parts; as our Davenant, Morton, Hall, (whose excellent treatise called *The Peace-maker,* and his *Pax Terris*, deserve to be transcribed upon all our hearts,) Huttonus, Amyraldus also have done. But *recipiuntur ad modum recipientis;* as a young man in his heat of lust and passion was judged to be no fit auditor of moral philosophy; so we find that those same young men who may be zealous for peace and unity, when they are grown more experienced, are zealous for their factions against these in their youthful heat. And therefore such as these before mentioned, and Duræus, who hath made it the business of his life, do seldom do much greater good than to quiet their own consciences in the discharge of so great a duty, and to moderate some few, and save them from further guilt, and to leave behind them when they are dead a witness against a wilful, self-conceited, and unpeaceable world.

Nay, commonly it bringeth a man under suspicion either of favouring some heresy, or abating his zeal, if he do but attempt a pacificatory work: as if there were no zeal necessary for the great fundamental verities for the church's unity and peace, but only for parties and some particular truths.

And a great advantage the devil hath got this way, by employing his own agents, the unhappy Socinians, in writing so many treatises for catholic and arch-catholic unity and peace, which they did for their own ends, and would have done it on insufficient terms; by which means the enemy of peace hath brought it to pass, that whoever maketh motion for peace, is presently under suspicion of being one that hath need of it for an indulgence of his own errors. A fearful case, that heresy should be credited, as if none were such friends to unity and peace as they; and that so great and necessary a duty, upon which the church's welfare doth so depend, should be brought into such suspicion or disgrace!

Brethren, I speak not all this without apparent reason. We have as sad divisions among us in England, considering the piety of the persons, and the smallness of the matter of our discord, as most nations under heaven have known. The most that keeps us at odds is but about the right form and order of church government. Is the distance so great that presbyterian, episcopal, and independent might not be well agreed? Were they but heartily willing and forward for peace, they might—I know they might. I have spoken with some moderate men of all the parties, and I perceive by their confessions it were an easy work. Were men's hearts but sensible of the church's case, and unfeignedly touched with love to one another, and did they but heartily set themselves to seek it, the settling of a safe and happy peace were an easy work. If we could not in every point agree, we might easily find out and narrow our differences, and hold communion upon our agreement in the main; determining of the safest way for the managing of our few and small agreements, without the danger or trouble of the church. But is this much done? It is not done. Let each party flatter themselves now as they please, it will be recorded to the shame of the ministry of England, while the gospel shall abide in the christian world. What will be recorded? What? why this: That learned and godly ministers in England did first disagree among themselves, and head and lead on their people in those disagreements! That they proceeded in them for the space of fourteen years already; how much more will be, God knows; and in all that time had as great advantages and opportunities for agreement as any people in the world. They had the sad experience of the conflagration of the commonwealth, and were scourged to it by a calamitous war. They saw the fearful confusions of the church; and the perverting of multitudes of seduced souls, some to be seekers, some Socinians, some ranters, quakers, or infidels. They saw the continual exasperation of minds, and the jealousies and bitterness that their distance bred, and how it was the fuel of a daily course of sin: and yet for all these, they were moved little to them. They had magistrates that did not hinder them from the work; but gave them full liberty to have consulted and endeavoured a full agreement. They lived near together, and might have easily met together for the work: and if one or two, or a hundred meetings could not have accomplished it, they might have held on till it was done. And yet for all this there is no such thing done, nor any considerable attempt yet made. And oh what heinous aggravations do accompany this sin! Never men since the apostles' days, I think, did make greater profession of godliness: the most of them are bound by solemn oaths and covenants, for unity and reformations. They all confess the worth of peace; and most of them will preach of it, and talk for it, while they sit still and neglect it, as if it were not worth the looking after. They will read and preach on those texts that command men to follow peace with all men, and as much as in us lieth, if it be possible, to live peaceably with them: and yet we are so far from following it, and doing all that possibly we can for it, that too many will snarl at it, and malign and censure any that endeavour it, as if all zeal for peace did proceed from an abatement of our zeal for holiness; and as if holiness and peace were so fallen out, that there were no reconciling them; when yet they have found, by long experience, that concord is a sure friend to piety, and piety always moves to concord. We have seen how errors and heresies breed by discord, as discord is bred and fed by them. We have seen to our sorrow that where the servants of God should live together as one, of one heart, and one soul, and one lip, and should promote each other's faith and holiness, and admonish and assist each other against sin, and rejoice together in the hope of their future glory, we have contrarily lived in mutual jealousies, and drowned holy love in bitter contendings; and have studied to disgrace and undermine one another, and to increase our own parties by right or wrong; and we that were wont to glory of our love to the brethren, as the certain mark of our sincerity in the faith, have now turned it into a love of a party only, and those that are against that party have more of our spleen, and envy, and malice than love. I know this is not so with all, nor prevalently with any true believer, but yet it is so common, that it may cause us to question the sincerity of many that are thought by themselves and others to be most sincere. And it is not ourselves only that are scorched in this flame, but we have drawn our people into it, and cherished them in it, so that most of the godly in the nation are fallen into several parties, and have turned much of their ancient piety into vain opinions, and vain disputes, and envyings, and animosities; yea, whereas it was wont to be made the certain mark of a graceless wretch to deride the godly, how few be there now that stick at secret deriding and slandering those that are not of their opinion! A pious, prelatical man can reverently scorn and slander a presbyterian; and some of them an independent, and an independent both. And, which is the worst of all, the common ignorant people take notice of all this, and do not only deride us, but are hardened by us against religion; and when we go about to persuade them to be religious, they see so many parties, that they know not which to join with, and think that it is as good be of none at all as of any, when they are uncertain which is the right: and thus thousands are grown into a contempt of all religion by our divisions; and poor carnal wretches begin to think themselves in the better case of the two, because they hold to their old formalities, when we hold to nothing. Yea, and these pious contenders do more effectually plead the devil's cause against one another, than any of the ignorant people can do. They can prove one another deceivers and blasphemers, and what not; and this by secret slanders among all that they can handsomely vent them to; and perhaps, also, by public disputation, and printed slanderous books. So that when the obstinate drunkards are at a loss, and have nothing to say of their own, against a man that would drive them from their sin, they are prompted by the railing books or reports of factious, zealous malice; then they can say, I regard him not, nor his doctrine; such a man hath proved him a deceiver and a blasphemer; let him answer him if he can. And thus the lies and slanders of some, (for that is no news,) and the bitter, opprobrious speeches of others, have more effectually done the devil's service, under the name of orthodoxness and zeal for truth, than the malignant scorners of godliness could have done it. So that the matter is come to that pass, that there are few men of note of any party, but the reproaches of the other parties are so publicly upon them, that the ignorant and wicked rabble that should be converted by them, have learned to be orthodox, and to vilify and scorn them. Mistake me not: I do not slight orthodoxness, nor jeer at the name; but disclose the pretences of devilish zeal in pious or seemingly pious men. If you are offended with me for my harsh language, because I can tell you that I learned it of God, I dare be bold therefore to tell you further, that you have far more cause to be offended at your satanical practices. The thing itself is surely odious, if the name be so odious as to turn your stomachs. How should the presence and guilt of it terrify you, if the name make you start! I know that many of the reverend calumniators do think that they show that soundness in the faith, and love to truth, which others want. But I will resolve the case in the words of the Holy Ghost; "Who is a wise man and endued with knowledge among you? Let him show out of a good conversation his works with meekness of wisdom; but, if you have bitter envying (or zealousness) and strife in your hearts, glory not, and lie not against the truth: this wisdom descendeth not from above, but is earthly, sensual, devilish. For where envying (or zeal) and strife is, there is confusion, and every evil work. But the wisdom that is from above is first pure, then peaceable, gentle, easy to be entreated, full of mercy and good fruits, without partiality, without hypocrisy; and the fruit of righteousness is sown in peace of them that make peace," James iii. I pray you read these words again and again, and study them.

Oh doleful case to think of! that a while ago we were afraid of nothing, but lest papists and deboist persons should have swallowed up the gospel and our liberty, and destroyed us together; and now when the work hath been put into the hands of those men, that were joined in these fears, and are joined in the strictest profession of piety, and are of one judgment in all the articles of the faith, they cannot, or will not unanimously join in carrying on the work; but they either fall upon one another, or live at a distance, and cast their work upon a hundred disadvantages by the bitter disagreements that are among themselves. Oh what a nation might England have been ere now, if it had not been for the proud and obstinate contentions of godly ministers! What abundance of good might we have done! Nay, what might we not have done, if our perverseness had not marred our work! Did we but agree among ourselves, our words would have some authority with the people; but when they see us some of one mind, and some of another, and snarling and reviling at each other, they think they may well enough do so too. Why may not we call them sectaries or deceivers, say they, when they call one another so? Nay, if we were not all of a mind in some smaller matters, yet if we did but hold communion and correspondence, and join together in the main, and do as much of God's work as we can in concurrent unanimity, the people would far more regard us, and we might be in a greater capacity to do them good. But when we are single, they slight us; and when we disagree and divide, they despise us: and who can marvel at it, when we despise one another? What! must we be ruled by every singular man? Are you wiser than all the ministers in the country? Are not such and such as learned as you? But when we go hand in hand, it stops their mouths. They think either themselves may be wiser than one or two ministers, or at least other ministers may be wiser than they; but common modesty will not suffer them to think that they are wiser than all the ministers in the country, or in the world. I know that matters of faith are not to be received on credit alone; but yet our credit may do much to remove prejudice, and to unblock the entrance into men's minds, and procure the truth a more equal hearing, and therefore is necessary to our people's good.

Nay, more than all this—I know it—I see and hear it, that there are some ministers that are glad when they perceive the people despise their brethren that differ from them in some lesser things; they would have it so, and they foment it as far as they can for shame; and they secretly rejoice when they hear the news of it. This is next to prelatical silencing them, and casting them out of the church. And I confess, I cannot but suspect that such men would go near to silence them, if they had their will and way; for he that would have a minister under disgrace, would have him useless; which is next to silencing him, and tendeth to the same end. You will say, we do not desire that he should be disabled to do good, but to do hurt. I answer, but the question is, whether his error be so great, that the holding or propagating it doth more hurt, than all his preaching, and the labours of that whole party which you would disgrace, is like to do good? If so, then I think it is a desirable work to disgrace him, and silence him in a just measure, and by just means, and I would concur therein; but if it be otherwise, we are bound to keep up that reputation with others, which is necessary ordinarily to the success of their labours.

I may not here, without wrong to my conscience, pass over the late practices of some of our brethren of the new prelatical way; for those of the ancient prelacy are more moderate. I know it will be displeasing to them, and I have no mind to displease them; but yet I will more avoid the treacherous or unfaithful silence which may wrong them, than the words of faithful friendship which may displease them; and I will say no more to them, than, if I know myself, I should say, if I were resolved for prelacy. It is the judgment of these men that I now speak of, that a prelate is essential to a church, and there is no church without them; and that their ordinance is of necessity to the essence of a presbyter: and that those that are ordained without them (though some will except a case of necessity) are not ministers of Christ. Hereupon they conclude, that our congregations, here in England, are no true churches, except where the presbyter dependeth on some prelate, and the ministers ordained by presbyters only are no true ministers; and they will not allow men to hear them, or communicate with them, but withdraw from our congregations like separatists or recusants. And the same note many of them brand upon all the reformed churches abroad, that have no prelates, as they do on us: so that the church of Rome is admirably gratified by it; and instead of demanding where our church was before Luther, they begin to demand of us, where it is now? And indeed, had it been no more visible in the ages before Luther, than a reformed prelatical church is now, they would have a fairer pretence than now they have, to call upon us for the proof of its visibility. Suppose that the presbyters who rejected prelacy were guilty of all that schism and other sin, as they are ordinarily accused of; (for I will now go on such suppositions;) must the people therefore turn their back on the assemblies and ordinances of God? Is it better for them to have no preaching, and no sacraments, and no public communion in

God's worship, than to have it in an assembly that hath not a prelate over it, or from a minister ordained without his consent? I confess I would not for all the world stand guilty before God of the injury that this doctrine hath already done to men's souls, much less of what it evidently tendeth to. They lay out themselves faithfully for the healing of that ignorance, and common profaneness, which got so much head under their careless or drunken predecessors. They desire nothing more than the saving of souls; they preach sound doctrine; they live in peace; and it is the greatest of their grief that many of their hearers remain so ignorant and obstinate still. And see what a help these poor impenitent sinners have for their cure! They are taught to turn their backs upon their teachers; and whereas before they heard them but with disregard, they are now taught not to hear them at all; and if we privately speak to them. they can tell us, that it is the judgment of such and such learned men, that we are not to be heard, nor our churches to be communicated with, nor we to be at all regarded as Christ's ministers. And thus drunkards, and swearers, and worldlings, and all sorts of sensualists, are got out of gunshot, and beyond the reach of our teaching or reproof: and those that do not (for shame of the world) obey their doctrine to stay from the assembly, yet do they there hear us with prejudice and contempt, and from the communion of the church in the Lord's supper they commonly abstain. Were it only the case of those few civil persons, that conscientiously go this way, and address themselves to these kind of men for government and sacraments, I would never have mentioned the thing; for it is not them that I intend. For what care I what minister they hear or obey, so it be one that leadeth them in the ways of truth and holiness? Let them follow Christ, and forsake their sins, and go to heaven, and I will never contend with them for the forsaking of my conduct. But it is the common sort of profane and sensual men, that are every where hardened against the ministry, and they have nothing but the reputation of the prelatical divines to countenance it with. If their teachers do but differ in a gesture from these men, they vilify them and reject their guidance, having nothing but the authority of such men to support them. Fain would we reach our consciences to awaken them from their security; for it pitieth to see them so near unto perdition. But we can do no good upon them; for our ministry is in contempt because of the contrary judgment of these men. Not that the poor people care any more for a prelate, as such, than for an ordinary minister: for if prelates would have troubled them as much with their preaching, and reproofs, and discipline, they would have hated them as much as they do the ministers. But because they found by experience, that under their government they might sin quietly, and make a scorn of godliness without any danger or trouble, and that to this day the men of that way are so much against those precise ministers, that will not let them go quietly to hell, therefore are they all for prelacy, and make this the great shelter for their disobedience and unreformed lives. So that I confess I think that the hurt that separatists and anabaptists do in England at this day, is little to the hurt that is done by these men: for I count that the greatest hurt, which hardeneth the greatest number in the state and way of greatest danger. An anabaptist may yet be a penitent and godly person, and be saved; but the sensual and impenitent worldlings can never be saved in that condition. I see by experience, that if separation infect two or three, or half a score in a parish; or if anabaptistry infect as many, and perhaps neither of them mortally; this obstinate contempt of ministerial exhortation, encouraged by the countenance of the contrary-minded, doth infect them by the scores or hundreds. If we come to them in a case where they have no countenance from the ministry, how mute or tractable comparatively do we find them! But if it be a case where they can but say, that the prelatical divines are of another judgment, how unmovable are they, though they have nothing else to say! Try, when we come to set afoot this work that we are now upon of catechising, and private instruction, whether this will not be one of our greatest impediments; though in a work of unquestioned lawfulness and necessity: even because they are taught that we are none of their pastors, and have no authority over them. I know that some of these men are learned and reverend, and intend not such mischievous ends as these; the hardening of men in ignorance is not their design, but this is the thing effected. To intend well in doing ill, is no rarity. Who can, in reverence to any men on earth, sit still and hold his tongue, while he seeth the people thus run to their own destruction, and the souls of men be undone by the contendings of divines for their several parties and interests? The Lord that knows my heart, knows that, if I know it myself, as I am not of any one of these parties, so I speak not a word of this in a factious partiality, for one party, or against another, as such; much less in spleen against any person; but if I durst in conscience, I would have silenced all this, for fear of giving them offence whom I much honour. But what am I but a servant of Christ? and what is my life worth, but to do him service? and whose favour can recompense for the ruin of the church? and who can be silent while souls are undone? Not I, for my part, while God is my Master, and his word my rule, his work my business, and the success of it, for the saving of men, my end. Who can be reconciled to that which so lamentably crosseth his Master's interest, and his main end? Nor yet would I have spoken any of this, if it had been only in respect to my own charge; yet I bless God, the sore is but small, in comparison of what it is in many other places. But the observation of some neighbour congregations, and others more remote, methinks, should make the very contrary-minded divines relent, if they were present with them.

Would it be a pleasant hearing to them, to hear a crowd of scandalous men to reproach their ministers that would draw them to repentance, and to tell them they have no authority over them, and all this under the pretence and shelter of their judgments? Had they rather men went to hell, than be taught the way to heaven by presbyters that had not their imposition of hands? Is that point of order more necessary than the substance of the work, or the end itself? Nay, I must needs in faithfulness say yet more: that it is no credit to the cause of those reverend men, nor ever was, that the generality of the most wicked men, and haters and contemners of all devotion, are the great friends and maintainers of it; and the befriending of such a party did more to gain their love, than to save their souls; and the engaging such a party for them, hath not been the least cause of their fall. This is true, however it be taken.

And what a case would the churches of England be in, if we should yield to the motions of these reverend men! Supposing that men's judgments are not at their own wills, and therefore many cannot see the reasons for prelacy; must we all give up our charges as no true ministers, and desert the congregations as no true churches? Why, whom will they then set over them in our stead? First, it is known that they cannot, if they had fit men, procure them what liberty their way requires, because of the discountenance of authority; and it is known that they have not fit men for one congregation of very many. And had they rather that the doors were shut up, and God had no public worship, nor the people any public teaching or sacraments, than any but they should have a hand in the performance of it? Or if the ministers keep their places, can they wish all the congregation to stay at home, and live like heathens? Nay, are they not angry with us for casting out a grossly ignorant, insufficient, scandalous sort of ministers, who were the great means of the perdition of the people, whose souls they had taken charge of? As for the casting out of any able, godly men upon mere differences about the late troubles, and state affairs; I speak not of it, I approve not of it; if any such thing were done, let them maintain it if they can that did it, for I neither can nor will. But it is a very sad case, that any men of judgment and piety would not only be indifferent in matters of such moment, but should think it a persecution, and an injury to their party and cause, to have hundreds of unworthy wretches to be ejected, when it was a work of so great a necessity to the church.

And indeed, by all this they plainly show what a condition they would reduce this nation into again, if it were in their power. Sure they that would have the people disown and withdraw from them as being no ministers, and turn their backs on the word and sacraments, would silence them if they could: I think there is no doubt of that. And surely they that are so offended, that the insufficient and scandalous ones are cast out, would have them in again if they could. And if this be the change that they desire, let them not blame men that believe the Scripture, and value men's salvation, if they have no mind of their change. If it were a matter of mere opinion, we should be more indifferent with them: or, if the question were only whether men would be conducted in ways of holiness by a prelate, or by mere presbyters only, we should think it of less moment, than the matter that is before us: but when it comes to this pass, that the prince of darkness must be so gratified, and so much of the church of Christ delivered over-much into his power, and the people led by multitudes to perdition, and all for the upholding of our own parties, or interests, or conceits; we cannot make light of such matters as these: these are not mere speculations, but matters that are so obvious to sense and christian experience, that they must not think much that serious, experienced christians are against them.

But that I be not mistaken, it is far from my thoughts to speak what I have done of any peaceable man of the prelatical way, or to meddle in the controversy of the best way of government; nor do I speak to any of the new prelatical way, but only those who are guilty of the miscarriages which I have spoken of; and for them, I had rather bear their indignation, than the church should bear the fruits of their destructive, intemperate conceits.

The most common cause of our divisions and unpeaceableness, is men's high estimation of their own opinions. And it ordinarily worketh these two ways; sometimes by setting men upon novelties, and sometimes by a censorious condemning of all that differ from the party that they are of.

Some are as busy in their inquiries after new doctrines, as if the Scripture were not perfect, or Christ had not told us all that is necessary; or the way to heaven were not in all ages one and the same, from Christ to the end of the world; or the church were not still the same thing. And they look not only after new discoveries in lesser things, but they are making us new articles of faith, and framing out new ways to heaven. The body of popery came in at this door; their new fundamentals were received on these terms; their new catholic church, which their forefathers knew not, was thus set up. Before, it consisted of all christians through the world; and now it must consist of none but the pope's subjects. So is it with the anabaptists; they must now in the end of the world have a new church for Christ, even in the natural capacity of the matter! Never since the creation can it be proved that God had any where a church on earth where infants were excluded from being members, if there were any among them. They were members before the law, under the promise, under the law, and under the gospel through the christian world to this day; and yet they would needs make Christ a church now without them; as if Christ had missed it in the forming of his church till now! or as if he begun to be weary of infants in his church now at last! or as if the providence of God did now begin to be awakened to have a right-formed church in the conclusion of the world; and to eject those infants as incapable, who till now have been in the bosom of his family.

Yea, this disturbing vice doth also work by setting a higher rate of necessity upon some truths, than the church of Christ had ever done: when we will needs make that to be of absolute certainty, which hath been either not before received, or but as a dark and doubtful thing; and we will make that to be of necessity to salvation, which the former ages did hold but as a point of a far lower nature, which some were for, and some against, without any great disagreement or mutual censure. I confess, I do hold some points of doctrine myself to be true, which I cannot find that the church, or any in it, did hold of many ages after the apostles; but then I cannot lay such a stress on them, as to think them of flat necessity to the welfare of the church, and the saving of souls: as the doctrine of the certain perseverance of all the justified, and some few more. If I may think, that Austin, Prosper, and all the church in those ages, did err therein (as I think they did); yet to think that they erred fundamentally, were to think that Christ had no church. I will not take the judgment or practice of the church in any age since the apostles', as my rule of faith and life; but I will suppose, that they had all things in the most defiled age, that were of absolute necessity to salvation. I know that we must be justified in the same way as they were, and upon the same terms. Faith is the same thing now as it was then, and hath the same object to apprehend for our justification, and the same office in order to our justification. Many new notions are brought in by disputers, which must not be made matters of necessity to the soundness or integrity of the church's faith. We may talk of peace as long as we live, but we shall never obtain it but by returning to the apostolical simplicity. The papists' faith is too big for all men to agree upon; or all their own, if they enforced it not with arguments drawn from the fire, the halter, and the strappado. And many antipapists do too much imitate them in the tedious length of their subscribed confessions, and novelty of impositions, when they go furthest from them in the quality of the things imposed. I shall speak my mind to these in the words of Vincentius Lirinensis, cap. 26. *Mirari satis nequeo tantum quorundum hominum væsanium, tantam excœcatæ mentis impietatem; tantam postremo errandi libidinem, ut contenti non sint tradita semel et accepta antiquitus credendi regula; sed nova ac nova in diem quærunt, semperque aliquid gestant religioni addere, mutare, detrahere: quasi non cœleste dogma sit quod semel revelatum esse sufficiat, sed terrena institutio, quæ aliter perfici nisi assidua emendatione, immo potius reprehensione non possit.* When we once return to the ancient simplicity of faith, then, and not till then, we shall return to the ancient love and peace.

But the pride of men's hearts doth make them so overvalue their own conceptions, that they expect all men else should be of their mind, and bow down to those reasons which others can see through, while they were as confident as if there were no room for doubting. Every sect is usually confident in their own way, and as they value themselves, so they do their reasons. And hereupon arise such breaches in affections and communion as there are, while most men cry down the divisions of others, but maintain the like. Some will have no communion with our churches, because we have some members that they take to be ungodly, and do not pull up the tares in doubtful unproved cases, where we cannot do it without pulling up the wheat. Others are so confident that infants should be unbaptized, and out of the church, that they will be of no church that hath infant members, till these scandalous infants be (I say not excommunicated, for that supposeth a former right, but) taken as such that have no part or fellowship in the business; they will not join with such a society. Christ tells us, That except we become as little children, we shall not enter into his kingdom; and they say, Except little children be kept out of the church, they will not enter or abide in it. Is not this extreme height of spirit to be so confident, as to avoid communion upon it, in a case where the church hath been in all ages, or almost all, by their own confession, so much against them? Would they not have separated from the whole church on the same ground, if they had lived in these times? Others, as is before said, are so confident that we are no ministers or churches, for want of prelatical ordination and government, that they separate also, or deny communion with us. And thus every party, in the height of their self-conceitedness, is ready to divide, and condemn all others that be not of their mind.

And it usually falls out that this confidence doth but bewray men's ignorance, and that too many make up that in passion and wilfulness, which they want in reason. How many have I heard zealously condemning what they little understand? It is a far easier matter to say that another man is erroneous, or heretical, or rail at him as a deceiver or blasphemer, than to give a sound account of our belief. And as I remember twenty years ago, I have observed it the common trick of a company of ignorant, formal preachers, to get the repute of that learning which they wanted, by railing at the puritans, as being all unlearned: so is it now the trick of some that can scarce give a sound reason for any controverted part of their belief, (nor it may be of their fundamentals,) to use this as the chief remedy, to get the name of sound divines, by reproaching some that differ from them as unsound; and to be esteemed orthodox, by calling others erroneous or heterodox.

The truth is, most ministers in the world do take up their opinions in compliance with their several parties; and they look more who believeth it, than what is believed, and on what ground; or they have nothing but what is spoken by the men that they must concur with: and thus too many take up their religion in a faction; even the truth itself. And therefore they must speak against those that they hear that party speak against. As Prosper said of the detractors of Austin, Præf. ad capit. Gall. *Injustis opprobriis catholici prædicatoris memoria carpitur; in quod peccatum cadunt, qui aliena instigatione commoti; scriptorem celeberimi nominis promptius habent culpare, quam nosse.* And as Salvian saith in his Preface ad Salonium: ad Cathol. Eccles. *Tam imbecilia sunt judicia hujus temporis, ac pene tam nulla, ut qui legunt, non tam considerant quid legant, quam cujus: nec tam dictionis vim atque virtutem quam dictatoris cogitant dignitatem.* How many a hot dispute have I heard of several subjects, which the disputants have been forced to manifest that they understood not! And yet they will drive all to damnatory conclusions, when the parties understand not one another's meaning, and take not the subject of the dispute in the same sense, or at least not the several predications. One disputeth for free-will, another against it: and call them to give you their definition of free-will, and you shall see to what purpose it was. And so in many other cases.

And thus do we proceed in a contentious zeal to divide the church, and censure our brethren, and make our differences seem greater than they are, while we know not well what they are ourselves, who so eagerly manage them.

SECTION IV.

3. The next sin that I shall mention, that we are lamentably guilty of, is this: We do not so seriously, unreservedly, and industriously lay out ourselves in the work of the Lord, as beseemeth men of our profession and engagements. I bless the Lord that there are so many that do this work with all their might! But, alas! for the most part, even of those that we take for godly ministers, how reservedly and how negligently do we go through our work! How few of us do so behave ourselves in our office, as men that are wholly devoted thereto, and have devoted all that they have to the same ends! And because you shall see my grounds for this confession, I shall mention to you some of the sinful discoveries of it, which do too much abound.

(1.) It is common with us to be negligent in our studies. And few men will be at that pains that is necessary for the right informing of their understandings, and fitting them for their further work. Some men have no delight in their studies, but take only now and then an hour, as an unwelcome task which they are forced to undergo, and are glad when they are from under the yoke. Will neither the natural desire of knowing, nor the spiritual desire of knowing God and things divine, nor the consciousness of our great ignorance and weakness, nor the sense of the weight of our ministerial work, will none of all these keep us closer to our studies, and make us more painful in seeking after the truth? This diligence is now the more necessary for ministers, because the necessity of the church doth draw so many from the universities so young, so that they are fain to teach and learn together: and for my part, I would not discourage such young ones, so be it they be but competently qualified, and quickened with earnest desires of men's salvation, and are drawn out by the present necessities, sooner than they would go, if the church could longer wait for their preparation; and will but study hard in the country. For I know, that as theology is a practical science, so the knowledge of it thriveth best in a practical course. And laying out here is a means of gathering in; and a hearty endeavour to communicate and do good, is not the smallest help to our own proficiency. Many men have not been ashamed to confess how young and raw they were at their entrance, who yet have grown to eminent parts. Vigilius the martyr was made bishop of Trent at twenty years old. Ambrose de Offic. li. c. 1, saith thus; *Homines discunt priusquam docent, et ab illo accipiunt quod aliis tradant: Quod ne ipsum quidem mihi accidit: Ego enim de tribunalibus atque administrationis insulis ad sacerdotium captus, docere vos cœpi quod ipse non didici. Itaque factum est, ut prius docere inciperem quam discere. Discendum igitur mihi simul et docendum est, quoniam non vacavit ane discere. Et quantum libet quisque profecerit, nemo est qui doceri non egeat dum vivit.*

Oh what abundance of things are there that a minister should understand; and what a great defect is it to be ignorant of them; and how much shall we miss such knowledge in our work! Many ministers study only to compose their sermons, and very little more, when there are so many books to be read, and so many matters that we should not be unacquainted with. Nay, in the study of our sermons we are too negligent, gathering only a few naked heads, and not considering of the most forcible expressions by which we should set them home to men's hearts. We must study how to convince and get within men, and how to bring each truth to the quick, and not leave all this to our extemporary promptitude, unless it be in cases of necessity. Certainly, brethren, experience will teach you, that men are not made learned or wise without hard study, and unwearied labours and experience.

SECTION V.

(2.) If ministers were set upon the work of the Lord, it would be done more vigorously than by the most of us it is. How few ministers do preach with all their might; or speak about everlasting joy or torment in such a manner as may make men believe that they are in good sadness! It would make a man's heart ache to see a company of dead and drowsy sinners sit under a minister, and not have a word that is like to quicken or awaken them. To think with ourselves, Oh if these sinners were but convinced and awakened, they might yet be converted and live! And alas, we speak so drowsily or gently, that sleepy sinners cannot hear; the blow falls so light, that hard-hearted persons cannot feel it. Most ministers will not so much as put out their voice, and stir up themselves to an earnest utterance. But if they do speak loud and earnestly, how few do answer it with earnestness of matter; and then the voice doth little good; the people will take it but as mere bawling, when the matter doth not correspond. It would grieve one to hear what excellent doctrines some ministers have in hand, and let it die in their hands for want of close and lively application. What fit matter they have for convincing sinners, and how little they make of it; and what a deal of good it might do if it were set home; and yet they cannot or will not do it. O sirs! how plain, how close, and earnestly should we deliver a message of such a nature as ours is, when the everlasting life or death of men is concerned in it! Methinks we are no where so wanting as in this seriousness. There is nothing more unsuitable to such a business than to be slight and dull. What! speak coldly for God, and for men's salvation! Can we believe that our people must be converted or condemned, and yet can we speak in a drowsy tone? In the name of God, brethren, labour to awaken your hearts, before you come, and when you are in the work, that you may be fit to awaken the hearts of sinners. Remember that they must be awakened or damned; and a sleepy preacher will hardly awake them. If you give the holy things of God the highest praises in words, and yet do it coldly, you will seem in the manner to unsay what you said in the matter. It is a kind of contempt of great things, especially *so* great, to speak of them without great affection and fervency: the manner as well as the words must set them forth. If we are commanded, whatever our hand findeth to do, to do it with all our might, then certainly such a work as preaching for men's salvation should be done with all our might. But, alas, how few, how thin are such men! here one and there one, even among good ministers, that have an earnest, persuading, working way, or that the people can feel him preach when they hear him.

SECTION VI.

(3.) If we are all heartily devoted to the work of God, why do we not compassionate the poor, unprovided congregations about us, and take care to help them to able ministers; and in the mean time, step out now and then to their assistance, when the business of our own particular charge will give us any leave. A lecture in the more ignorant places purposely for the work of conversion, performed by the most lively working preachers, might be a great help where constant means is wanting.

SECTION VII.

(4.) The negligent execution of acknowledged duties, doth show that we be not so wholly devoted to the work as we should be. If there be any work of reformation to be set afoot, how many are there that will go no further than they are drawn! and it were well if all would do but that much.

If any business for the church be on foot, how many neglect it for their own private business! When we should meet and consult together for the unanimous and successful performance of our work, one hath this business of his own, and another that business, which must be preferred before God's business.

And when a work is like to prove difficult and costly, how backward are we to it, and make excuses, and will not come on! For instance: what hath been more talked of, and prayed for, and contended about, in England for many years past, than the business of discipline? And there are but few men (the Erastians) but they seem zealous in disputing for one side or other; some for the prelatical way, and some for the presbyterian, and some for the congregational. And yet when we come to the practice of it, for ought I see, we are most of us for no way. It hath made me admire sometimes to look on the face of England, and see how few congregations in the land have any considerable execution of discipline, and to think withal what volumes they have written for it; and how almost all the ministry of the nation is engaged for it—how zealously they have contended for it, and made many a just exclamation against the opposers of it; and yet for all this will do little or nothing in the exercise of it. I have marvelled what should make them so zealous in siding for that which their practice shows that their hearts are against: but I see a disputing zeal is more natural than a holy, obedient, practising zeal. How many ministers in England are there that know not their own charge, that plead for the truth of their particular churches, and know not which they are, or who are the members of them; and that never cast out one obstinate sinner; no, nor brought one to public confession, and expression of repentance and promise of reformation; no, nor admonished one publicly to call him to such repentance. But they think they do their duties if they give them not the sacrament of the Lord's supper, when it is perhaps avoided voluntarily by themselves, and thousands will keep away themselves without our prohibiting them; and in the mean time we have them stated members of our churches, and grant them all other communion with the church, and call them not to personal repentance for their sin. Read Albaspineus, a sober papist, in his Observat. 1, 2, 3, after his Annot. on Optatus, and see whether church communion in former times was taken to consist only in co-partaking of the Lord's supper. Either these hundreds that we communicate not with in the supper, are members of our churches, or not: if not, then we are separatists while we so much disclaim it; for we have not cast them out, nor have we called them to any profession, whether they own or disown their membership, but only whether they will be examined in order to a sacrament; nor do we use to let them know that we take their refusal of examination for a refusal of church membership, and exclusion of themselves. It follows therefore, that we have gathered churches out of churches before they were unchurched, or before we took God's way to cast any of them, much less all of them, out. But if they are taken for members, how can we satisfy our consciences to forbear all execution of discipline upon them? Is it not God's ordinance that they would be personally rebuked and admonished, and then publicly called to repentance, and be cast out if they remain impenitent? If these be no duties, why have we made such a noise and stir about them in the world as we have done? If they be duties, why do we not practise them? If none of all these persons be scandalous, why do we not admit them to the Lord's supper? If they keep away themselves, is not that a sin which a brother should not be permitted to remain in? Is it not a scandal for them to avoid the ordinances of God and the communion of the church for so many years together as they do? Yea, and many a one of them avoideth also the very hearing of the word. The ancient discipline was stricter, when the sixth general council at Trull, in Constantinople, ordained, Can. 80, that whosoever was three days together from the church, without urgent necessity, was to be excommunicated.

Brethren, for my part, I desire not to offend any party, nor to bring the least dishonour to them; but I must needs say, that these sins are not to be cloaked over with excuses, extenuations, or denials. We have long cried up discipline, and every party their several ways. Would you have people value your way of government or not? No doubt but you would: why, if you would have them value it, it must be for some excellency: show them then that excellency. What is it, and wherein doth it consist? And if you would have them believe you, show it them not only in paper, but in practice; not only in words, but in deeds. How can the people know the worth of bare notions and names of discipline, without the thing? Is it a name and a shadow that you have made all this noise about? How can they think that that is good which doth no good? Truly, I fear we take not the right way to maintain our cause, but even betray it while we are hot disputers of it. Speak truly; is it not these two things that keep up the reputation of the long-contended-for discipline among men; viz. with the godly, the *mere reputation of their ministers that stand for it;* and with many of the ungodly, *the non-execution of it,* because they find it to be toothless, and not so much troublesome to them? Verily, brethren, if we get the late prelates' carnal wisdom, and go their way to work, by ingratiating our way of government with the ungodly multitude, by the mere neglect of practice, and the befriending of their sins, we may well look for the same blessing and issue as the prelates had. If once our government come to be upholden by the votes of those who should be corrected or ejected by it, and the worst men be friends to it, because it is a friend to them in their ungodliness, we then engage it against the Lord, and he will appear as engaged against us. Set all the execution of discipline together that hath been practised in a whole county ever since it was so contended for, and I doubt it will not appear so observable as to draw godly people into a liking of it for the effects. How can you wonder if many that desired deeds and not words, reformation and not the mere name of reformation, do turn over to the separate congregations, when you show them nothing but the bare name of discipline in yours? All christians value God's ordinances, and think them not vain things; and therefore are unwilling to live without them. Discipline is not a needless thing to the church: if you will not difference between the precious and the vile by discipline, people will do it by separation. If you will keep many score or hundreds in your churches that are notoriously scandalous, and contemners of church communion, and never openly, nor perhaps privately, reprove them, nor call them to repentance, nor cast them out, you cannot marvel if some timorous souls do run out of your churches as from a ruinous edifice, that they fear is ready to fall upon their heads. I pray you consider, if you should do in the same manner with them in the sacrament, as you do in the discipline, and should only show the bread and wine, and never let them taste of it, could you expect that the name of a sacrament should satisfy them, or that they should like your communion? Why should you think then that they will be satisfied with the empty sound of the word, *church government?* And consider but what a disadvantage you cast your cause upon in all your disputations with men of another way. If your principles be righter than theirs, and their practice be righter than yours, the people will suppose that the question is, whether the name or the thing, the shadow or the substance, be more desirable? And they will take your way to be a mere delusory formality, because they see you but formal in the use of it, yea, that you use it not at all. I speak not against your government, but for it, all this while, and tell you, that it is you that are against it, that seem so earnest for it; while you more disgrace it for want of exercise, than you credit it by your bare arguments: and you will find before you have done, that faithful execution will be your strongest argument. Till then, the people will understand you, as if you openly proclaimed, We would have no public admonitions, confessions, or excommunications; our way is to do no good, but to set up the naked name of a government. Doubtless it was a fault more past all disputation, for the prelates to destroy discipline and do little or nothing in it, than for them to be prelates; and if they had but done the good that discipline is ordained for, prelacy might have stood to this day, for aught I know; I am sure it would have had no opposition from many hundred godly people that have opposed it; and again I say, if you will run into the error, you may expect their fate.

And what are the hinderances now that keep the ministers of England from the execution of that discipline which they have so much contended for? I hear not all speak; but I hear some, and see more. The great reason, as far as I can learn, is, the difficulty of the work, and the trouble or suffering that we are like to incur by it. We cannot publicly reprehend one sinner, but he will storm at it, and bear us a deadly malice. We can prevail with very few to make a public profession of true repentance. If we proceed to excommunicate them, they will be raging mad against us; they will be ready to vow revenge against us, and to do us a mischief: if we should deal as God requireth with all the obstinate sinners in the parish, there were no living among them; they would conspire in hatred against us to the hazard of our lives. We should be so hated of all, that as our lives would be uncomfortable, so our labours would become unprofitable; for men would not hear us when they are possessed with a hatred of us; therefore duty ceaseth to be duty to us, because the hurt that would follow would be greater than the good; and affirmatives bind not *ad semper*.

These are the great reasons for the non-execution of discipline, together with the great labour that private admonition of each offender would cost us. And to these I answer,

1. Are not these reasons as valid against christianity itself, in some times and places, as now against discipline? Christ came not to send us peace; we shall have his peace, but not the world's; for he hath foretold us that they will hate us. Might not Mr. Bradford, or Hooper, or any that were burnt in Queen Mary's days, have alleged more than this against duty? They might have said, It will make us hated, if we own the Reformation, and it will expose our lives to the flames. How is he concluded by Christ to be no christian, who hateth not all that he hath, and his own life, for him: and yet we can take the hazard of our life as a reason against his work! What is it but hypocrisy to shrink from suffering, and take up none but safe and easy works, and make ourselves believe that the rest are no duties? Indeed this is the common way of escaping suffering, to neglect the duty that would expose us thereunto. If we did our duty faithfully, ministers should find the same lot among professed christians, as their predecessors have done among the infidels. But if you could not suffer for Christ, why did you put your hand to his plough, and did not first sit down and count your costs? This makes the ministerial work so unfaithfully done, because it is so carnally undertaken; and men enter upon it as a life of ease, and honour, and respect from men, and therefore resolve to attain their ends, and have what they expected by right or wrong. They looked not for hatred and suffering, and they will avoid it, though by the avoiding of their work.

2. And as for the making yourselves uncapable to do them good: I answer, That reason is as valid against plain preaching, reproof, or any other duty which wicked men will hate us for. God will bless his own ordinances to do good, or else he would not have appointed them. If you admonish, and publicly rebuke, the scandalous, and call men to repentance, and cast out the obstinate, you may do good to many that you reprove, and possibly to the excommunicate: I am sure it is God's means; and it is his last means, when reproofs will do no good: it is therefore perverse to neglect the last means, lest we frustrate the foregoing means, whenas the last is not to be used but upon supposition that the former were all frustrate before. However, those within and those without may receive good by it, if the offender do receive none; and God will have the honour, when his church is manifestly differenced from the world, and the heirs of heaven and hell are not totally confounded, nor the world made to think that Christ and Satan do but contend for superiority, and that they have the like inclination to holiness, or to sin.

3. And I would know, whether on the grounds of this objection before mentioned, all discipline should not be cast out of the church, at least ordinarily; and so is not this against the thing itself, rather than against the present season of it? For this reason is not drawn from any thing proper to our times, but common to all times and places. Wicked men will always storm against the means of their public shame; and the use of church censures is purposely to shame them, that sin may be shamed, and disowned by the church. What age can you name since the days of the apostles wherein you would have executed the discipline that you now refuse, if you go these grounds, supposing that it had not been by magisterial compulsion? If therefore it be discipline itself that hath such intolerable inconveniences, why have you so prayed for it, and perhaps sought for it, and disputed for it, as you have done? What, must all dissenters bear your frowns and censures, and all for a work which yourselves judge intolerable, and dare not touch with one of your fingers? When do you look to see all these difficulties over, that you may set upon that which you now avoid? Will it be in your days? or will you wait till you are dead, and leave it as a part of your epitaph to posterity, that you so deeply engaged and contended for that which you so abhorred to the death, that you would never be brought to the practice of it? And doth not this objection of yours plainly give up your cause to the separatists; and even tell them that your contending is not for your way of discipline; but that there may be none, because it will do more harm than good? Certainly if this be true, it would have been better to speak it out at first, before all our wars, and tears, and prayers, and contentions, than now in the conclusion to tell the world, that we did all this but for a name or word, and that the thing is so far from being worth our cost, that it is not tolerable, much less desirable.

4. But yet let me tell you, that there is not such a lion in the way as you do imagine; nor is discipline such a useless thing. I bless God upon the small and too late trial that I have made myself of it, I can speak by experience, it is not vain; nor are the hazards of it such as may excuse our neglect.

But I know the pinching reason is behind. They say that, When we pleaded for discipline, we meant a discipline that should be established and imposed by the secular power; and without them what good can we do; when every man hath leave to despise our censures, and set us at nought; and therefore we will not meddle with it? (say they) without authority. To which I answer, 1. I thought it once a scornful indignity that some fellows attempted to put upon the ministry, that denied them to be the ministers of Christ, and would have had them called the ministers of the state, and dealt with accordingly. But it seems they did not much cross the judgments of some of the ministry themselves, who are ready to put the same scorn upon their own calling. We are sent as Christ's ambassadors, to speak in his name, and not in the prince's; and by his authority we do our work, as from him we have our commission: and shall any of his messengers question the authority of his commands? The same power that you have to preach without or against the magistrate's command, the same have you to exercise pastoral guidance and discipline without. And shall all ministers refuse preaching if the magistrate bid them not? yea, or if they forbid them? 2. What mean you, when you say, you will not do it without authority? Do you mean the *love*, or the *countenance* and approbation, or the *command* upon yourselves; or do you mean a *force* or *penalty* on the people to obey you? The magistrate's leave we have; who hindereth or forbiddeth you to set up discipline, and exercise it faithfully? Doth the secular power forbid you to do it, or threaten or trouble you for not doing it? No, they do not. To the shame of the far greatest part of the ministers of England it must be spoken, for we have so opened our own shame that it cannot be hid, we have had free liberty to have done the work of Christ which we have desired and pleaded for, and yet we would not do it. What might not the ministers of England have done for the Lord, if they had been but willing! They had no prohibition, nor any man to rise up against them, of all the enemies whose hearts are against their work; and yet they would not do it. Nay more, for aught you know, you have no approbation of authority. You have the commands of former powers yet not repealed. You have the protection of the laws and present governors: if any one seek revenge against you for the sake of discipline, you have not only laws, but as many willing magistrates to restrain and punish them, as ever you knew, I think, in England. And what would you have more? Would you have a law made to punish you if you will not do your duty? What! dare you tell God that you will not do this work unless the magistrate drive you to it with scourges? I confess if I had my will it should be so; and that man should be ejected as a *negligent* pastor, that will not rule his people by discipline, though yet I might allow him to be a preacher to the unchurched, as well as he is ejected as a negligent preacher that will not preach. For ruling is as essential a part of a pastor's office as preaching, I am sure. And therefore seeing these men would fain have the magistrate interpose, if he did eject them for unfaithful, negligent pastors, (were it not for the necessity of the church that hath not enough better,) I know not well how they could blame him for it. It is a sad discovery of our carnal hearts, when men can do so much more with us than God, that we would obey the commands of men, and will not obey the commands of Christ. Is he fit to be Christ's officer, that will not take his command as obligatory?

But I know the thing expected is, that all the people should be forced under a penalty to submit to our discipline. I confess, I think that the magistrate should be the hedge of the church, and defend the ministry, and improve his power to the utmost to procure a universal obedience to Christ's laws, and restrain men from the apparent breach of them, especially from being false teachers and seducers of others. How far I am against the two extremes of universal licence, and persecuting tyranny, I have frequently manifested on other occasions. But I shall now say but this: 1. Doth not this further discover the carnal frame of our hearts, when we will not do our duty unless the magistrate will do his to the full, and all we conceive may be his duty? What! will his neglect excuse yours? Hath Christ bid you use the keys of the kingdom, and avoid a scandalous sinner upon condition that the magistrate will punish him with the sword? Is not this your meaning, if you would speak it out, that you find a great deal of difficulty in your work, and you would have the magistrate, by terrifying offenders, make it easy to you? For if it be not safe, and cheap, and easy, you are resolved you will not do it; and of such servants Christ may have enough. Nay, is not your meaning, that you would have the magistrate to do your work for you? Just as your pious people have long cried and prayed for discipline, and called upon ministers to do it, but we cannot get them to reprove offenders, and deal with them seriously and lovingly for their good, and inform the church officers of them that are obstinate. So do we toward the magistrates: the word of God is so much beholden to us, that we would all have it done, but few will do it. We can easilier censure and talk against others for not doing it, than do it ourselves. Oh the guilt and hypocrisy of our hearts!

2. But further, What is it that you would have the magistrate to do? I pray you consider, how you will answer it before God, that you should wilfully neglect your own duty, and then make it your religion to quarrel with others. Is it not a fearful deceit of heart for a man to think himself a godly minister for finding fault with them that are less faulty than himself? I say less faulty; for tell me truly, whether the magistrate do more of his part in government, or you in yours? I am no more a flatterer of the magistrate than of you; nor was ever taken for such, that I could understand: but we must deal justly by all men. Would you have the magistrate to punish men *eo nomine*, because excommunicated, without any particular cognizance of the fact and case? 1. That were unjust; then he must do wrong whenever we mistake and do wrong. If an honest man were a hangman, he would be willing to know that he hanged not a man that was unjustly condemned. However, the magistrate is not the mere executioner of the ministers, but a judge; and therefore must be allowed the use of his reason, to know the cause, and follow his own judgment, and not punish men against it. 2. And excommunication is so great a punishment of itself, that I hope you do not think it nothing unless the magistrate add more. If so, then the temporal punishment might serve turn, and what need of yours? But I suppose that this is not your sense, but you are so just, that you would have the magistrate to punish a man as an offender, and not as excommunicate. And if so, I think it is nothing that he doth. Are all the penalties against swearers, cursers, drunkards, peace-breakers, sabbath-breakers, &c. nothing? Certainly the laws of the land do punish much sin against God. Well, what do you as church governors against these same sins? The magistrate fineth and imprisoneth them, that is his part. It is your part to bring them to open repentance, or to cast them out. Have you done this as oft as he hath done his part? Doth not the magistracy of England punish ten, twenty, what if I say a hundred swearers, drunkards, or sabbath-breakers by the sword, for one that the elders of the church do punish by censures, or bring to public repentance for the satisfaction of the church? Brethren, these things seem strange to me; that the case should stand thus as it doth, and yet that the deceit of our hearts should be so great, and that we should go on to account ourselves such blameless, godly men, whom magistrates and people are bound to reverence, and to speak against the magistrate so much as we do. I believe they are all slack and faulty; but are not we much more faulty? What if they should pay us in our own coin? What language might they give the ministers, that after so many years' talk of discipline will do nothing in it? I say, nothing in most places: to meet together for consultation, is no exercise of discipline, nor reformation of the church, which our meetings should conduce to.

3. And I give you this further answer: What had the church of Christ done till the days of Constantine the Great, if it had no better pastors than you, that will govern it without the joined compulsion of

the magistrate? Discipline, and severe discipline, was exercised for three hundred years together, where the prince did not give them so much as a protection, nor toleration, but persecuted them to death. Then was the church at the best, and discipline most pure and powerful; say not then any more for shame, that it is to no purpose without a magistrate, when it hath done so much against their wills! Oh, what an aggravation is it of our sin, that you cannot be content to be negligent and unfaithful servants, but you must also fly in the face of your Lord and Master, and obliquely lay the blame on him! What do you else, when you blame church censure as ineffectual, when you should blame your lazy, self-seeking hearts, that shift off the use of them? Hath Christ put a leaden sword into your hands, when he bids you smite the obstinate sinner? Or are you cowardly and careless, and then blame your sword instead of using it, as thinking that the easier task? Are the keys of Christ's kingdom so unmeet and useless, that they will not open and shut without the help of the sword; or are you unskilful and lazy in the use of them? If they have contracted any rust, by which they are made less fit for service, next to the prelates we may thank ourselves, that let them lie so long unused.

4. And I must tell you, that too much interposition of the sword with our discipline, would do more harm than good. It would but corrupt it by the mixture, and make it become a human thing. Your government is all to work upon the conscience, and the sword cannot reach that. It is not a desirable thing to have repentance so obscured by mere forced confessions, that you cannot know when men do mean as they speak; and so it will be the sword that doth all, by forcing men to dissemble, and you will not discern the power of the word and ordinance of Christ. I confess since I fell upon the exercise of some discipline, I find by experience, that if the sword interpose and force all those public confessions of sin, and professions of repentance, which I have persuaded men to by the light of the word of God; it would have left me much unsatisfied concerning the validity of such confessions and promises, whether they might indeed be satisfactory to the church. And I find that the godly people do no further regard it than they perceive it hearty and free; and if it were forced by magistrates, they would take him for no penitent person, nor be any whit satisfied, but say, He doth it because he dare do no otherwise.

And I must add this word of plainer dealing yet. You blame the magistrate for giving so much liberty; and is it not long of ourselves that he do so? You will scarce believe that such enemies to liberty of conscience are the causes of it: I think that you are; and that the keenest enemies have been the greatest causes. For you would run too far to the other extreme, and are so confident in every controversy that you are in the right, and lay such a stress upon many opinions of your own, as if life or death did lie upon them, (when perhaps the difference may prove more verbal than real, if it were searched to the quick,) that this occasioneth magistrates to run too far the other way; and if they look on such as ——— and dare not trust the sword in such hands, you may thank yourselves. Truly, brethren, I see by experience, that there is among many of the most injudicious of us, such a blind, confused zeal against all that is called error by their party, that without being able to try and make a difference, they let fly pell-mell at all alike, and make a great outcry against errors; when either we know not what they are, nor how to confute them, nor which be tolerable in the church and which intolerable, nor how far we may hold or break communion with the owners of them, and perhaps are the erroneous persons ourselves. The observation of this hath made the magistrates so over-jealous of us, that they think if they set in with a party in each contention, we shall never be without blood and misery. And I confess I see in some ministers so little of the fire of divine love, and christian charity, and compassion, nor heavenly-mindedness, nor humble sense of their own infirmities; and so much of the zeal that James describeth, (James iii. 14, 15,) which is kindled from another fire, that makes them full of suspicions and jealousies, and keen and eager against their brethren, censuring, defaming, and unconscionably backbiting them, and straining an ill sense out of their well-meant words and actions, and living towards them in plain envy and malice, instead of christian love and peace; I say, I see so much of this in many that affect the reputation of orthodox, while they are indeed factious, that I am the less sorry that the magistrate doth so little interpose. For were the sword in such envious, angry hands, there would be little quiet to the church; for there is no two men on earth but differ in something, if they know or believe any thing. And these men must square the world to their own judgments, which are not always the wisest in the world: they that dare so rail at others as blasphemers, when they know not what they say themselves, durst sure smite them as blasphemers, if they had power. This may possibly make the magistrate think meet (seeing we are so quarrelsome and impatient) to let us fight it out by the bare fists, and not to put swords into our hands till we are more sober, and know better how to use them: for if every passionate man, when he hath not wit enough to make good his cause, should presently borrow the magistrate's sword to make it good, truth would be upon great disadvantage in the world! Magistrates are commonly the most tempted and abused men, and therefore I know not why we should call so loud to have them become the arbitrators in all our quarrels, lest error have two victories where truth gets one. I could wish the magistrate did more; but if he do but give us protection and liberty, especially, if he will but restrain deceivers from preaching against the great unquestionable truths of the gospel, and give public countenance and encouragement to those master-truths, I shall not fear, by the grace of God, but a prudent, sober, unanimous ministry will ere long shame the swarm of vanities that we think so threatening.

But I have been too long on this. I shall only conclude it with this earnest request to my brethren of the ministry,—that they would speedily and faithfully put in execution at least all the unquestionable part of the discipline, that they have so much contended for. When we are so offended with the parliament for their enumeration of scandals, as too defective, and a protestation was published that we acted only on supposition that it was defective, sure we little thought then that we, that were so earnest to have had more power, would use none; and we that must need have authority to reject more than the parliament did enumerate, would censure so few even of them as we have done, since we have had more liberty to do it.

But one objection is common, which I forgot: they say, we are but single pastors, and therefore cannot excommunicate men alone, unless we should make every pastor a pope in his parish, or a bishop at least.

Answ. For my part I have no mind to obtrude my own opinion on such (for the power of a single person to excommunicate); I have sufficiently already proved myself a novelist, and singular with some, by asserting ancient and most common truths. But yet, 1. I could wish these men so much moderation, as to be sure that they are in this as much wiser than the contrary-minded, as their confidence doth import, before they proceed in calling them popes: lest as the cunning of the times is, by making many antichrists, to make none; so these men should, contrary to their intention, credit the pope, by making so many popes; and the prelates too, by making such kind of prelates.

2. A pope is the pretended head of the catholic church, and a universal bishop to govern it. Are single ruling pastors such? A diocesan bishop is the ruler of all the pastors and churches in a diocess: is such a pastor one of these?

3. Why do you in your disputes against the prelates, maintain that every minister is a bishop of his own church, and do you now abhor it?

4. What if you might not excommunicate; may you not therefore do the rest? May you not personally and publicly reprove them, pray for them, &c.?

5. Must not the people avoid a notorious drunkard, &c. whether you bid them or not? If not, why hath God commanded it? If yea, why may you not bid them do that which is their duty?

6. Have you none in your parish, not one or two to make ruling elders of, that by their conjunction you may be authorized to do more than now you do? I mean, according to your own principles; for I confess it is not according to mine.

7. And what hindereth but you may join together if you will? If it must needs be many pastors conjunct, that must exercise any act of discipline, why is it not so done? Doth any forbid them, or threaten them if they do it? If you say, I am alone because no neighbour minister will join with me. You speak hardly of all the ministers about you. What! are they all so negligent? Blame us not then to reprove them. But it is an incredible thing that they should be all so bad that are of your judgment, that no one or two will be persuaded to assist you. And I think you will confess that two or three may do it authoritatively, though no one else in the county do it. I could wish that the prelates had not such an argument given them as this; no one presbyter hath the power of the keys, by their own confession, therefore two or three have not; lest they go further in proving the consequence than you expect. But if it must be so, I could yet wish that no single pastor, for the excusing of himself, would lay such a reproachful charge upon all the ministers in the country that be of his own judgment, as to say, that discipline is cast aside, because they can get none to join with them in the execution; at least, till they have thoroughly tried whether it be so indeed, or not.

SECTION VIII.

(5.) Another sad discovery, that we have not so devoted ourselves and all we have to the service of God, as we ought, is, *The prevalency of worldly, fleshly interests too much against the interest and work of Christ.* And this I shall further manifest in these three instances following: 1. Our temporizing. 2. Our too much minding worldly things, and shrinking from duties that will hinder our commodity. 3. Our barrenness in works of charity, and in the improving of all that we have to our Master's use.

[1.] I would not have any to be thwart and contentious with those that govern them, nor to be disobedient to any of their lawful commands. But it is not the least reproach upon the ministry, that the most of them for worldly advantage do still suit themselves with the party that is most likely to suit to their ends. If they look for secular advantages, they suit themselves to the secular power; if for the air of ecclesiastical applause, then do they suit themselves to the party of ecclesiastics that is most in credit. This is not a private, but an epidemical malady. In Constantine's days, how prevalent were the orthodox! In Constantius's days, they almost all turned Arians, so that there were very few bishops at all that did not apostatize or betray the truth; even of the same men that had been in the council of Nice. And when not only Liberius, but great Osius himself fell, who had been the president or chief in so many orthodox councils, what better could be expected from weaker men! Were it not for secular advantage, or ecclesiastical faction and applause, how could it come to pass, that ministers in all the countries in the world, are either all, or almost all, of that religion and way that is in most credit, and most consistent with their worldly interest? Among the Greeks, they are all of the Greek profession: and among the Abassines, the Nestorians, the Maronites, the Jacobites, the ministers generally go one way. And among the papists, they are almost all papists. And in Saxony, Sweden, Denmark, &c. almost all Lutherans: in Holland, France, Scotland, almost all Calvinists. It is strange that they should be all in the right in one country, and all in the wrong in another, if carnal advantages and reputation did not sway much. When men fall upon a conscientious search, the variety of intellectual capacities causeth unavoidably a great variety of conceits about some hard and lower things: but let the prince and the stream of men in credit go one way, and you shall have the generality of ministers too often change their religion with the prince, at several times in this land. Not all, as our Martyrology can witness, but the most. I will purposely forbear the mention of any latter change. If the rulers of a university should but be corrupt, who have the disposal of preferments, how much might they do with the most of the students, where mere arguments would not take! And the same tractable distemper doth so often follow them into the ministry, that it occasioneth the enemies to say, that reputation and preferment is our religion, and our reward.

[2.] And for the second, How common is it with ministers to drown themselves in worldly business! Too many are such as the sectaries would have them be, who tell us that we should go to plough and cart, and labour for our living, and preach without so much study: and this is a lesson easily learned. Men take no care to cast off and prevent care, that their souls and the church may have their care.

And especially how commonly are those duties neglected, that are like, if performed, to diminish our estates! For example: Are there not many that dare not, that will not set up the exercise of any discipline in their churches; not only on the forementioned accounts, but especially because it may hinder the people from paying them their dues? They will not offend sinners with discipline, lest they offend them in their estates; yea, though the law secure their maintenance. I find money is too strong an argument for some men to answer, that can proclaim the love of it to be the root of all evil, and can make large orations of the danger of covetousness.—I will say no more now to these, but this: If it were so deadly a sin in Simon Magus to offer to buy the gift of God with money, what is it to sell his gifts, his cause, and the souls of men, for money; and what reason have such to fear lest their money perish with them!

[3.] But the most that I have to say is to the third discovery.—If worldly and fleshly interest did not much prevail against the interest of Christ and the church, surely most ministers would be more fruitful in good works, and would more lay out what they have to their Master's use. Experience hath fully proved it, that the works of charity do most potently remove prejudice, and open the ears to words of piety. If men see that you are addicted to do good, they will the easilier believe that you are good, and the easilier then believe that it is good which you persuade them to. When they see that you love them, and seek their good, they will the easilier trust you; and when they see that you seek not the things of this world, they will the less suspect your intentions, and the easilier be drawn by you to seek that which you seek. Oh how much good might ministers do, if they did set themselves wholly to do good, and would dedicate all their faculties and substance to that end! Say not that it is a small matter to do good to men's bodies, and that this will but win them to us, and not to God, nor convert the soul; for it is prejudice that is a great hinderance of men's conversion, and this will remove it. We might do men more good, if they were but willing to learn of us; and this will make them willing, and then our further diligence may profit them. Brethren, I pray you do not think that it is ordinary charity that is expected from you, any more than ordinary piety. You must, in proportion to your talents, go much beyond others. It is not to give now and then two-pence to a poor man: others do that as well as you. But what singular thing do you with your estates for your Master's use? I know you cannot give away that which you have not: but methinks, all that you have should be for God. I know the great objection is, We have wife and children to provide for: a little will not serve them at present, and we are not bound to leave them beggars. To which I answer, 1. There are few texts of Scripture more abused than that of the apostle, "He that provideth not for his own, and especially those of his family, hath denied the faith, and is worse than an infidel." This is made a pretence for gathering up portions, and providing a full estate for posterity, when the apostle speaketh only against them that did cast their poor kindred and family on the church to be maintained out of the common stock, when they were able to do it themselves. As if one that hath a widow in his house, that is his mother or daughter, and would have her to be kept on the parish, when he hath enough himself. His following words show that it is present provision, and not future portions, that the apostle speaketh of, when he bids "them that have widows administer to them, or give them what is sufficient." 2. You may so educate your children as other mean persons do, that they may be able to get their own livings, in some honest trade or employment, without other great provisions. I know that your charity and care must begin at home, but it must not end there. You are bound to do the best you can to educate your children, so as they may be capable of being most serviceable to God, but not to leave them rich, or a full estate; nor to forbear other necessary works of charity, merely for a larger provision for them. There must be some proportion kept between our provision for our families, and for the church and poor. A truly charitable, self-denying heart, that hath devoted itself and all that he hath to God, would be the best judge of the due proportions, and would see which way of expense is likely to do God the greatest service, and that way he would take. 3. I confess I would not have men to lie too long under endangering strong temptations to incontinency, lest they wound themselves, and their profession, by their falls: but yet, methinks, it is hard that men can do no more to mortify the concupiscence of the flesh, that they may live in a single, freer condition, and have none of these temptations from wife and children, to hinder them from furthering their ministerial ends by charitable works. If he that marrieth not doth better than he that doth, sure ministers should labour to do that which is best; and if he that can receive this saying, must receive it, we should endeavour after it. This is one of the highest points of the Romish policy, which they pretend to be a duty of common necessity, that all the bishops, priests, and other religious orders, must not marry, by which means they have no posterity to drain the church's revenues, nor to take up their care: but they make their public cause to be their interest, and they lay out themselves for it while they live, and leave all that they have to it when they die: so that their church's wealth doth daily increase, as every bishop, abbot, Jesuit, or other person doth gather more in their life-time, and usually add it to their common stock. It is pity that for a better cause we can no more imitate them in wisdom and self-denial, where it might be done. 4. But they that must marry, should take such as can maintain themselves and their children, or maintain them at the rate as their temporal means will afford, and devote as much of the church means to the church's service as they can.

I would put no man upon extremes; but in this case flesh and blood doth make even good men so partial, that they take their duties, and duties of very great worth and weight, to be extremes. If worldly vanities did not blind us, we might see when a public or other greater good did call us to deny ourselves and our families. Why should we not live nearlier and poorer in the world, rather than leave those works undone, which may be of greater use than our plentiful provisions? But we consult in matters of duty with flesh and blood; and what counsel it will give us, we may easily know. It will tell us we must have a competency; and many pious men's competency is but little below the rich man's rates. If they be not clothed with the best, and fare not deliciously every day, (Luke xvi.) they have not a competency. A man that preacheth an immortal crown of glory, must not seek much after transitory vanity; and he that preacheth the contempt of riches, must himself contemn them, and show it by his life; and he that preacheth self-denial and mortification, must practise these in the eyes of them that he preacheth to, if ever he would have his doctrine prosper. All christians are sanctified, and, therefore, themselves and all that they have are consecrated and dedicated to their Master's use; but ministers are doubly sanctified; they are devoted to God, both as christians and as ministers, and therefore they are doubly obliged to honour him with what they have.

O brethren, what abundance of good works are before us, and how few of them do we put our hands to! I know the world expecteth more from us than we have: but if we cannot answer the expectations of the unreasonable, let us do what we can to answer the expectations of God, and conscience, and all just men. It is the will of God that with well-doing we should put to silence the ignorance of foolish men. Especially those ministers that have larger maintenance, must be larger in doing good.

I will give but one instance at this time, which I mentioned before. There are some ministers that have 150*l.* or 200*l.* or 300*l.* per annum of church means; and have so great parishes that they are not able to do a quarter of the ministerial work, nor once in a year to deal personally with half their people for their instruction; and yet they will content themselves with public preaching, as if that were all that were necessary, and leave almost all the rest undone, to the everlasting danger or damnation of multitudes, rather than they will maintain one or two diligent men to assist them. Or, if they have an assistant, it is but some young man to ease them about baptizings, or burials, or such work, and not one that will faithfully and diligently watch over the flock, and afford them that personal instruction which is so necessary. If this be not a serving ourselves of God, and not a serving God, and a selling men's souls for our fuller maintenance in the world, what is? Methinks such men should fear lest while they are accounted excellent preachers and godly ministers by men, they should be accounted cruel soul-murderers by Christ; and lest the cries of those souls whom they have betrayed to damnation should ring in their ears for ever. Will preaching a good sermon serve the turn, while you never look more after them, but deny them that closer help that you find to be necessary, and alienate that maintenance to your own flesh, which should provide relief for so many souls? How can you open your mouths against oppressors, when yourselves are so great oppressors, not only of men's bodies, but their souls? How can you preach against unmercifulness, while you are so unmerciful? And how can you talk against unfaithful ministers, while you are so unfaithful yourselves? The sin is not therefore small, because it is unobserved, and not become odious in the eyes of men; nor because the charity which you withhold is such as the people blame you not for withholding. Satan himself, their greatest enemy, hath their consent all along in the work of their perdition. It is no extenuation, therefore, of your sin, that you have their consents; for that you may sooner have for their hurt than for their good.

I shall proceed no further in these confessions and discoveries, but beseech you to take what is said into consideration; and see whether this be not the great and lamentable sin of the ministers of the gospel, that *they are not fully devoted to God*, and give not up themselves and all they have to the carrying on of the blessed work which they have undertaken? And whether flesh-pleasing and self-seeking, and an interest distinct from that of Christ, do not make us neglect much of our duty, and walk too unfaithfully in so great a trust, and reservedly serve God in the cheapest and most applauded part of his work, and withdraw from that which would put us upon cost and sufferings? and whether this do not show that too many are earthly that seem to be heavenly, and mind the things below while they preach for the things above, and idolize the world while they call men to contemn it? And as Salvian saith, li. 4, ad Eccles. Cath. p. 454, *Nullus salutem plus negligit quam qui Deo aliquid anteponit.* Despisers of God will prove despisers of their own salvation.

SECTION IX.

And now, brethren, what remaineth, but that we all cry guilty, of too much of these forementioned sins, and humble our souls in the lamentation of our miscarriages before the Lord? Is this *taking heed to ourselves, and to all the flock?* Is this like the pattern that is given us here in the text? If we should prove now stout-hearted and unhumbled men, and snuff at these confessions, as tending to our disgrace, how sad a symptom would it be to ourselves and to the church! The ministry hath been oft threatened here, and is still maligned by many sorts of adversaries: though all this may show their impious malice, yet may it also intimate to us God's just indignation. Believe it, brethren, the ministry of England is not the least or last in the sin of the land. It is they that have encouraged the common profaneness; it is they have led the people into divisions, and are now so backward to bring them out; and as sin hath been found in them, so judgments have been found and laid upon them. It is time therefore for us to take our part of that humiliation which we have been calling our people to so long. If we have our wits about us, we may perceive that God hath been offended with us, and that the voice that called this nation to repentance, did speak to us as well as others. He therefore that hath ears, let him hear the voice of railing enemies of all sorts, the voice of them that cry, Down with us, even to the ground; all calling us to try our ways, and to reform. He that hath eyes to see, let him see the precepts of repentance written in so many admirable deliverances and preservations, and written in so many lines of blood. By fire and sword hath God been calling even us to humiliation; and as judgment hath begun at the house of God, so, if humiliation begin not there too, it will be a sad prognostic to us, and to the land. What! shall we deny, or excuse, or extenuate our sins, while we call our people to such free confessions? Is it not better to give glory to God by a full and humble confession, than in tenderness of our own glory to seek for fig-leaves to cover our nakedness; and to put God to it, to build his glory which we denied him, upon the ruins of our own, which we preferred before him; and to distrain for that by a yet sorer judgment, which we denied voluntarily to surrender to him? Alas! if you put God to get his honour as he can, he can get it to your greater sorrow and dishonour. If any of our hearers in a day of humiliation, when sin is fully confessed and lamented, should be offended at the confession, and stand up against it, and say, You wrong me; I am not so bad! You should have told me of this in private, and not have disgraced me before the congregation. What could we think of such a man but that he was a hardened, impenitent wretch, and as he would have no part in the confession, so he should have none in the remission. And shall we do that which we scarce ever see the most hardened sinner do? Shall we say, This should not have been spoken of us in the ears of the people, but we should have been honoured before them! Certainly sins openly committed are more dishonourable to us when we hide them, than when we confess them. It is the sin, and not the confession, that is our dishonour. And we have committed them before the sun, so that they cannot be hid. Attempts to cloak them, do increase the guilt and shame: there is no way to repair the breaches in our honour, which our sin hath made, but by free confession and humiliation. I durst not but make confession of my own; and if any be offended that I have confessed theirs, let them know, that I do but what I have done by myself. And if they dare disown the confession of their sin, let them do it at their peril. But as for all the truly humbled ministers of the gospel, I doubt not but they will rather be provoked more solemnly in the face of their several congregations, to lament their sins, and promise reformation.

CHAPTER V.

SECTION I.

The Use of Exhortation.

HAVING disclosed and lamented our miscarriages and neglects, our duty for the future lies before us. God forbid that we should now go on in the sin that we have confessed, as carelessly as we did before. Then would the exclamation of Salvian fall upon us, De Gubern. l. 3, p. 87, *Novum siquidem monstri genus est; eadem pene omnes jugiter faciunt, quæ fecisse plangunt. Et qui intrant ecclesiasticam domum, ut mala antiqua defleant, exeunt; et quid dico exeunt? In ipsis pene hoc orationibus suis ac supplicationibus moliuntur: Aliud quippe ora hominum, aliud corda agunt: Et dum verbis præterita mala plangunt, sensu futura meditantur: ac si oratio eorum rixa est magis criminum quam exoratrix; ut vere illa in eis Scripturæ maledictio compleatur, ut de oratione ipsa exeunt condemnati, et oratio eorum fiat in peccatum.*

Be awakened, therefore, I beseech you, brethren, by the loud and manifold voice of God, to set more seriously to the work of God, and to do it for the future with all your might, and to take heed to yourselves, and to all the flock. The reasons why you should take heed to yourselves, I gave you in the beginning. The reasons why you should take heed to all the flock, I shall give you now, as motives to enforce this exhortation; and the Lord grant that they may work with us according to their truth and weight.

I. The first quickening consideration which the text here affordeth us, is taken from our relation to all the flock. We are *overseers* of it. In this I shall further show you these subordinate particulars, which will manifest the force of this consideration.

1. The nature of the office requireth us to *take heed.* What else are we overseers for? *Episcopus est nomen quod plus oneris quam honoris significat,* saith Polid. Virgil. p. 240; and a father before him. To be a bishop or pastor is not to be set up as idols for the people to bow to, or as idle, slow bellies, to live to our fleshly delight and ease. The particulars of our duty we have somewhat touched before, and more shall do anon. It is a sad case that men should be of a calling that they know not the nature of, and undertake they know not what. Do these men know and consider what they have undertaken, that live at ease and pleasure, and have time to take their superfluous recreations, and to spend an hour and more at once in loitering and vain discourses, when so much work doth lie upon their hands? Why, brethren, do you consider where you stand, and what you have taken upon you? Why you have undertaken the conduct, under Christ, of a band of his soldiers, against principalities, and powers, and spiritual wickedness in high places. You must lead them on the sharpest conflicts; you must acquaint them with the enemies' stratagems and assaults; you must watch yourselves, and keep them watching. If you miscarry, they and you may perish. You have a subtle enemy, and therefore must be wise; you have a vigilant enemy, and therefore must be vigilant; a malicious, and violent, and unwearied enemy, and therefore you must be resolute, courageous, and unwearied. You are in a crowd of enemies, compassed with them on every side, and if you heed one and not all, you will quickly fall. And oh what a world of work have you to do! Had you but one ignorant old man or woman to teach, though willing to learn, what a tedious task is it; but if they be as unwilling as ignorant, how much more difficult is it! But to have such a multitude of these, as most of us have, what work will it find us! Who that ever tried it, that knoweth it not by experience? What a pitiful life is it to reason with men that have almost lost the use of reason, and to talk with obstinate, wilful people, that know what they will and resolve, but not why they do it; and to argue the case with them that neither understand themselves nor you, and yet think that no man hath understanding that contradicteth them; and that are confident they are in the right, when they can show nothing but that confidence to make them confident. Their will is the reason of their judgments and lives: it satisfies them, and it must satisfy you. O brethren, what a world of wickedness have we to contend against, even in one soul, and what a number of those worlds! What rooting have their sins! What disadvantage must truth come upon! How strange are they to the heavenly message that we bring them; and know not what you say when you speak in that only language that they understand! And when you think you have done something, you leave your seed among the fowls of the air; wicked men are at their elbows to rise up and contradict all that you have said. They will cavil, and carp, and slander you, that they may disgrace your message, and deride and scorn them away from Christ, and quickly extinguish the good beginnings that you hoped you had seen. They use indeed weaker reasons than yours, but such as come with more advantage, being near them, and familiarly and importunately urged, and such as are fetched from things that they see and feel, and which are befriended by their own flesh. You speak but once to a sinner, for ten or twenty times that the messengers of Satan speak to them. Moreover how easily do the cares and businesses of the world devour and choke the seed which you have sown! And if it had no enemy but what is in themselves, how easily will a frozen, carnal heart extinguish those sparks which you have been long in kindling! and for want of fuel and further help, they will go out of themselves. What abundance of distempers, and lusts, and passions do you cast your gracious words amongst! and what entertainment such companions will afford them, you may easily conjecture. And when you think your work doth happily succeed, and have seen men under troubles and complaints, confessing their sins, and promising reformation, and living as new creatures and zealous converts; alas, after all this, they may prove unsound and false at the heart, and such as were but superficially changed, and took up new opinions, and new company, without a new heart. How many are, after a notable change, deceived by the profits and honours of the world, and fallen away while they think they stand! How many are entangled again in their former sensuality! and how many do but change a disgraceful way of flesh-pleasing, for a way that is less dishonourable, and maketh not so great a noise in their consciences! How many grow proud before they reach to a settled knowledge, and greedily snatch at every error that is presented to them, under the name of truth; and in confidence of the strength of their unfurnished intellects, despise them that they were wont to learn of, and become the greatest grief to their teachers, that before rejoiced in their hopeful beginnings! and like chickens that straggle from the hen, they are carried away by that infernal kite, while they proudly despise the guidance and advice of those that Christ hath set over them for their safety. O brethren,

what a field of work is there before us! not a person that you can see but may find you work. In the saints themselves, how soon do their graces languish if you neglect them; and how easily are they drawn into scandalous ways, to the dishonour of the gospel, and their own loss and sorrow!—If this be the work of a minister, you may see what a life he hath to lead. Up then, and let us be doing with all our might. Difficulties must quicken, and not discourage in a possible and necessary work. If we cannot do all, let us do what we can; for if we neglect it, woe to us and them! Should we pass over all these needful things, and by a plausible sermon only think to prove ourselves faithful ministers, and to put off God and man with such a shell and formal visor, our reward would prove as superficial as our work.

2. Consider also, that it is your own voluntary undertaking and engagement, that all this work is laid upon you. No man forced you to be overseers of the church; and doth not common honesty bind you to be true to your trust?

3. Consider also, that you have the *honour*, to encourage you to the *labour;* and a great honour indeed it is, to be the ambassadors of God, and the instruments of men's conversion and salvation, "to save men's souls from death, and cover a multitude of sins," Jam. v. 20; indeed the honour is but the attendant of the work. To do therefore, as the prelates of the church in all ages have done, to strive for precedency, and fill the world with vile contentions about the dignity and superiority of their seats, doth show that they much forget the nature and work of that office which they strive about. I seldom see men strive so furiously, who shall go first to a poor man's cottage to teach him and his family the way to heaven; or, who shall first endeavour the conversion of a sinner; or first become the servant of all. Strange, that for all the plain expressions of Christ, men will not understand the nature of their office! If they did, would they strive who would be the pastor of a whole county and more, when there are ten thousand poor sinners in it that cry for help, and they are not so eager to engage for their relief; nay, when they can patiently live in the houses with riotous, profane persons, and not follow them seriously and incessantly for their change? They would have the name and honour of the work of a county, who are unable to do all the work of a parish; when the honour is but the appendix of the work? Is it names and honour, or the work and end, that these desire? Oh, if they would faithfully, humbly, and self-denyingly lay out themselves for Christ and his church, and never think of titles and reputation, they should then have honour whether they would or not: but by gaping after it, they lose it. For this is the case of virtue's shadow, *Quod sequitur fugio, quod fugit ipse sequor.*

4. Consider also, you have the many other excellent privileges of the ministerial office to encourage you to the work. If you will not therefore do the work, you have nothing to do with the privileges. It is something that you are maintained by other men's labours, and live on the commonwealth's allowance. This is for your work, that you may not be taken off it, but as Paul requireth, may wholly give yourselves to these things, and not be forced to neglect men's souls whilst you are providing for your own bodies. Either do the work then, or take not the maintenance.

But you have far greater privileges yet than this. Is it nothing to be bred up to learning, when others are bred at the plough and cart; and to be furnished with so much delightful knowledge, when the world lieth in ignorance? Is it nothing to converse with learned men, and talk of high and glorious things, when others must converse with almost none but silly ignorants?

But especially, what an excellent life is it to live in the studies and preaching Christ! to be still searching into his mysteries, or feeding on them; to be daily in the consideration of the blessed nature, or works, or ways of God! Others are glad of the leisure of the Lord's day, and now and then an hour besides, when they can lay hold of it: but we may keep a continual sabbath. We may do nothing else almost but study and talk of God and glory, and call upon him, and drink in his sacred, saving truths. Our employment is all high and spiritual! Whether we be alone, or with others; our business is for another world. Oh, were but our hearts more suitable to this work, what a blessed, joyful life should we live! How sweet would the pulpit be, and what a delight would our conference of these things afford! To live among so many silent, wise companions, whenever we please, and of such variety:—all these, and more such privileges of the ministry, bespeak our unwearied diligence in the work.

5. You are related to Christ as well as to the flock; he therefore being also related to you, you are not only advanced but secured by the relation, if you be but faithful in the work that it requireth. You are the stewards of his mysteries, and rulers of his household; and he that intrusted you will maintain you in his work. But then, "it is required of a steward that a man be found faithful," 1 Cor. iv. 2. Be true to him, and never doubt but he will be true to you. Do you feed his flock, and he will sooner feed you as he did Elias, than forsake you. If you be in prison, he will open the doors; but then you must relieve imprisoned souls. He will give you a tongue, and wisdom that no enemy shall resist; but then you must use it faithfully for him. If you will put forth your hand to relieve the distressed, and willingly put it to his plough, he will wither the hand that is stretched out against you. The ministers of England, I am sure, may know this by large experience. Many a time hath God rescued them from the jaws of the devourer. Oh, the admirable preservations and deliverances that they have had from cruel papists, from tyrannical persecutors, from malicious sectaries, and misguided, passionate men! Brethren, in the fear of God, consider why it is that God hath done all this? Is it for your persons, or for his church? What are you to him more than other men, but for his work and people's sake? Are you angels or men? Is your flesh of any better mettle than your neighbours? Are you not of the same generation of sinners, that need his grace as much as they? Up then, and work as the redeemed of the Lord; as those that are purposely rescued from ruin for his service. O, do not prepare a remediless overthrow for the English ministry, by your ingratitude, after all these deliverances. If you believe that God hath rescued you for himself, live to him then, as being unreservedly his that hath delivered you.

SECTION II.

II. The first motive mentioned in the text, we have spoken of, which is from the consideration of our office itself. The second is from *the efficient cause.* It is God by his Spirit that makes us overseers of his church, therefore it concerneth us to take heed to ourselves, and it. I did before show you how the Holy Ghost is said to make bishops or pastors of the church in three several respects: by qualifying them for the office; by directing the ordainers to discern their qualifications, and know the fittest men; and by directing them, the people, and themselves, for the affixing them to a particular charge. All these were done then in an extraordinary sort, by inspiration, at least very oft. The same are all done now by the ordinary way of the Spirit's assistance. But it is the same Spirit still; and men are made overseers of the church (when they are rightly called) by the Holy Ghost now as well as then. It is a strange conceit therefore of the papists, to think that ordination by the hands of the man, is of more absolute necessity in the ministerial office, than the calling of the Holy Ghost. God hath determined in his word, that there shall be such an office, and what the work and power shall be, and what sort of men, as to their qualifications, shall receive it. None of these can be undone by man, or made unnecessary. God also giveth men the qualifications which he requireth. So that all that the church hath to do, whether pastors or people, ordainers or electors, is but to discern and determine, which are men that God hath qualified, and to accept of them that are so provided, and upon consent to instal them solemnly in this office. But I purposely cut short the controvertible part.

What an obligation then is laid upon us by our call! If our commission be sent from heaven, it is not to be disobeyed. When Paul was called by the voice of Christ, he was not disobedient to the heavenly vision: when the apostles were called by Christ from their secular employments, they presently leave friends, and house, and trade, and all, and follow him. Though our call be not so immediate or extraordinary, yet is it from the same Spirit. It is no safe course to imitate Jonah, in turning our back upon the commands of God. If we neglect our work, he hath a spur to quicken us; and if we overrun it, he hath messengers enough to overtake us, and fetch us back, and make us do it; and it is better to do it at first than at last. This is the second motive.

SECTION III.

III. The third motive in the text is, from *the dignity of the object*. It is the church of God which we must oversee and feed. It is that church which the world is much upheld for, which is sanctified by the Holy Ghost, which is united to Christ, and is his mystical body; that church which angels are present with, and attend upon as ministering spirits, whose very little ones have their angels beholding the face of God in heaven. Oh what a charge is it that we have undertaken! And shall we be unfaithful to such a charge? Have we the stewardship of God's own family, and shall we neglect it? Have we the conduct of those saints that must live for ever with God in glory, and shall we neglect them? God forbid! I beseech you, brethren, let this thought awaken the negligent! You that draw back from painful, displeasing, suffering duties, and will put off men's souls with uneffectual formalities; do you think this is an honourable usage of Christ's spouse? Are the souls of men thought meet by God to see his face, and live for ever in his glory, and are they not worthy of your utmost cost and labour? Do you think so basely of the church of God, as if it deserved not the best of your care and help? Were you the keepers of sheep or swine, you might better let them go, and say, they be not worthy the looking after; and yet you would scarce do so if they were your own. But dare you say so by the souls of men, even by the church of Christ? Christ walketh among them. Remember his presence, and keep all as clean as you can. The praises of the most high God are in the midst of them. They are a sanctified, peculiar people, a kingly priesthood, a holy nation, a choice generation, to show forth the praises of him that hath called them, 1 Pet. ii. 9; and yet dare you neglect them? What a high honour is it to be but one of them, yea, but a door-keeper in the house of God! but to be the priest of these priests, and the ruler of these kings,—this is such an honour, as multiplieth your obligations to diligence and fidelity in so noble an employment.

SECTION IV.

IV. The last motive that is mentioned in my text is, from *the price that was paid for the church which we oversee.* God the Son did purchase it with his own blood. Oh what an argument is here to quicken the negligent; and what an argument to condemn those that will not be quickened up to their duty by it! Oh, saith one of the ancient doctors, if Christ had but committed to my keeping one spoonful of his blood in a fragile glass, how curiously should I preserve it, and how tender should I be of that glass! If then he have committed to me the purchase of his blood, should I not as carefully look to my charge? What, sirs, shall we despise the blood of Christ? shall we think it was shed for them that are not worthy of our utmost care? You may see here, it is not a little fault that negligent pastors are guilty of. As much as in them lieth, the blood of Christ should be shed in vain; they would lose him those souls that he hath so dearly bought!

O then let us hear those arguments of Christ, whenever we feel ourselves grow dull and careless: Did I die for them, and wilt not thou look after them? Were they worth my blood, and are they not worth thy labour? Did I come down from heaven to earth, to seek and to save that which was lost; and wilt not thou go to the next door, or street, or village to seek them? How small is thy labour or condescension as to mine! I debased myself to this, but it is thy honour to be so employed. Have I done and suffered so much for their salvation, and was I willing to make thee a co-worker with me, and wilt thou refuse that little that lieth upon thy hands? Every time we look upon our congregations, let us believingly remember, that they are the purchase of Christ's blood, and therefore should be regarded accordingly by us.

And think what a confusion it will be at the last day to a negligent minister, to have this blood of the Son of God to be pleaded against him, and for Christ to say, It was the purchase of my blood that thou didst so make light of, and dost thou think to be saved by it thyself? O brethren, seeing Christ will bring his blood to plead with us, let it plead us to our duty, lest it plead us to damnation.

SECTION V.

I have done with the motives which I find in the text itself: there are many more that might be gathered from the rest of this exhortation of the apostle; but we must not stay to take in all. If the Lord will set home but these few upon your hearts, I dare say we shall see reason to mend our pace; and the change will be such on our hearts, and in our ministry, that ourselves and our congregations will have cause to bless God for it. I know myself unworthy to be your monitor; but a monitor you must have; and it is better for us to hear of our sin and duty from anybody than from nobody. Receive the admonition, and you will see no cause in the monitor's unworthiness to repent of it; but if you reject it, the unworthiest messengers may bear that witness against you that will confound you. But before I leave this exhortation, as I have applied it to our general work, so I shall carry it a little further to some of the special parts and modes of our duty which were before expressed.

I. And first, and above all, *See that the work of saving grace be thoroughly wrought on your own souls.* It is a fearful case to be an unsanctified professor, but much more to be an unsanctified preacher. Doth it not make you tremble when you open the Bible, lest you should read there the sentence of your own condemnation? When you pen your sermons, little do you think that you are drawing up indictments against your own souls! When you are arguing against sin, you are aggravating your own; when you proclaim to your hearers the riches of Christ and grace, you publish your own iniquity in rejecting them, and your unhappiness in being without them. What can you do in persuading men to Christ, in drawing them from the world, in urging them to a life of faith and holiness; but conscience, if it were but awake, might tell you, that you speak all this to your own confusion! If you mention hell, you mention your own inheritance; if you describe the joys of heaven, you describe your misery that have no right to it. What can you devise to say, for the most part, but it will be against your own souls? O miserable life, that a man should study and preach against himself, and spend all his days in a course of self-condemning! A graceless, unexperienced preacher, is one of the most unhappy creatures upon earth; and yet is he ordinarily most insensible of his unhappiness; for he hath so many counters that seem like the gold of saving grace, and so many splendid stones that seem like the christian's jewel, that he is seldom troubled with the thoughts of his poverty; but thinks he is rich, and wanteth nothing, when he is poor, and miserable, and blind, and naked. He is acquainted with the holy Scripture; he is exercised in holy duties; he liveth not in open, disgraceful sin; he serveth at God's altar; he reproveth other men's faults, and preacheth up holiness both of heart and life; and how can this man choose but be holy? Oh what an aggravated misery is this, to perish in the midst of plenty, and to famish with the bread of life in our hands, while we offer it to others, and urge it on them! That those ordinances of God should be the occasions of our delusion, which are instituted to be the means of our conviction and salvation; and that while we hold the looking-glass of the gospel to others, to show them the true face of the state of their souls, we should either look on the backside of it ourselves, where we can see nothing, or turn it aside, that it may misrepresent us to ourselves. If such a wretched man would take my counsel, he should make a stand, and call his heart and life to an account, and fall a preaching awhile to himself, before he preach any more to others; he should consider whether food in the mouth will nourish that goeth not into the stomach; whether it be a Christ in the mouth, or in the heart, that will save men; whether he that nameth him should not depart from iniquity; and whether God will hear their prayers, if they regard iniquity in their hearts; and whether it will serve the turn at that day of reckoning to say, "Lord, we have prophesied in thy name," when they shall hear, "Depart from me, I know you not;" and what comfort it will be to Judas when he is gone to his own place, to remember that he preached with the rest of the apostles, or that he sat with Christ, and was called by him, Friend; and whether a wicked preacher shall stand in the judgment, or sinners in the assembly of the just? When such thoughts as these have entered into their souls, and kindly worked awhile upon their consciences, I would advise them next to go to the congregation, and there preach over Origen's sermon, on Psal. l. 16, 17, "But to the wicked saith God, What hast thou to do to declare my statutes, or that thou shouldest take my covenant into thy mouth, seeing thou hatest instruction, and hast cast my words behind thee?" And when they have read this text, to sit down, and expound, and apply it by their tears; and then to make a free confession of their sin, and lament their case before the assembly, and desire their earnest prayers to God, for pardoning and renewing grace: and so to close with Christ in heart, who before admitted him no further than into the brain, that hereafter they may preach a Christ whom they know, and may feel what they speak, and may commend the riches of the gospel by experience.

Verily, it is the common danger and calamity of the church, to have unregenerate and unexperienced pastors; and to have so many men become preachers before they are christians; to be sanctified by dedication to the altar as God's priests, before they are sanctified by hearty dedication to Christ as his disciples; and so to worship an unknown God, and to preach an unknown Christ, an unknown Spirit, an unknown state of holiness and communion with God, and a glory that is unknown, and like to be unknown to them for ever. He is like to be but a heartless preacher, that hath not the Christ and grace that he preacheth in his heart. Oh that all our students in the university would well consider this! What a poor business is it to themselves, to spend their time in knowing some little of the works of God, and some of those names that the divided tongues of the nations have imposed on them, and not to know the Lord himself, nor exalt him in their hearts, nor to be acquainted with that one renewing work that should make them happy. They do but walk in a vain show, and spend their lives like dreaming men, while they busy their wits and tongues about abundance of names and notions, and are strangers to God and the life of saints. If ever God waken them by saving grace, they will have cogitations and employments so much more serious than their unsanctified studies and disputations were, that they will confess that they did but dream before. A world of business they make themselves about *nothing*, while they are wilful strangers to the primitive, independent, necessary Being, who is all in all. Nothing can be right known, if God be not known; nor is any study well managed, nor to any great purpose, where God is not studied. We know little of the creature, till we know it as it standeth in its order and respects to God; single letters and syllables uncomposed are nonsense. He that overlooketh the Alpha and Omega, and seeth not the beginning and end, and Him in all who is the *all* of all, doth see nothing at all. All creatures are as such broken syllables; they signify nothing as separated from God. Were they separated *actually*, they would cease to be, and the separation would be an annihilation; and when we separate them in our *fancies*, we make *nothing* of them to ourselves. It is one thing to know the creatures as Aristotle, and another thing to know them as a christian. None but a christian can read one line of his physics so as to understand it rightly. It is a high and excellent study, and of greater use than many do well understand; but it is the smallest part of it that Aristotle can teach us. When man was made perfect, and placed in a perfect world, where all things were in perfect order, and very good, the whole creation was then man's book in which he was to read the nature and will of his great Creator; every creature had the name of God so legibly engraven on it, that man might run and read it. He could not open his eyes, but he might see some image of God, but no where so fully and lively as in himself: and therefore it was his work to study the whole volume of nature; but first and most to study himself. And if man had held on in this prescribed work, he would have continued and increased in the knowledge of God and himself; but when he would needs know and love the creature and himself, in a way of separation from God, he lost the knowledge of all, both of the creature, himself, and God, so far as it could beautify, and was worth the name of knowledge; and instead of it he hath got the unhappy knowledge which he affected, even the empty notions and fantastic knowledge of the creature and himself as thus separated. And thus he that lived to the Creator, and upon him, doth now live to and as upon the other creatures and himself; and thus "every man at his best estate (the learned as well as the illiterate) is altogether vanity.—Surely every man walketh in a vain show: surely they are disquieted in vain," Psal. xxxix. 5, 6. And it must be well observed, that as God laid not by the relation of a Creator by becoming our Redeemer, nor the right of his propriety and government of us in that relation, but the work of redemption standeth in some subordination to that of creation, and the law of the Redeemer to the law of the Creator; so also the duties that we owed God as Creator are not ceased, but the duties that we owe to the Redeemer, as such, are subordinate thereto. It is the work of Christ to bring us back to God, whom we fell from, and to restore us to our perfection of holiness and obedience; and as he is the way to the Father, so faith in him is the way to our former employment and enjoyment of God. I hope you perceive what all this driveth at, viz. that to see God in his creatures, and to love him, and converse with him, was the employment of man in his upright state; that this is so far from ceasing to be our duty, that it is the work of Christ by faith to bring us back to it: and therefore the most holy men are the most excellent students of God's works; and none but the holy can rightly study them, or know them. His "works are great, sought out of all them that have pleasure therein," Psal. cxi. 2; but not for themselves, but for him that made them. Your study of physics and other sciences is not worth a rush, if it be not God by them that you seek after. To see and admire, to reverence and adore, to love and delight in God appearing to us in his works, and purposely to peruse them for the knowledge of God, this is the true and only philosophy, and the contrary is mere foolery, and so called and called again by God himself. This is the sanctification of your studies, when they are devoted to God, and when he is the life of them all, and they all intend him as the end, and the principal object.

And therefore I shall presume to tell you by the way, that it is a grand error, and of dangerous consequence in the christian academies; (pardon the censure from one so unfit for it, seeing the necessity of the case commandeth it;) that they study the creature before the Redeemer, and set themselves to physics, and metaphysics, and mathematics, before they set themselves to theology; whenas, no man that hath not the vitals of theology is capable of going beyond a fool in philosophy; and all that such do is but doting about questions, and opposition of science, falsely so called, 1 Tim. vi. 20, 21. And as by suffering a separated creature-knowledge Adam fell from God, so those that mind these *βεβήλȢς κενοφωνίας, καὶ ἀντιθέσεις τῆς ψευδωνύμȢ γνώσεως*, they miss the end of all right studies, *περὶ τὴν πίστιν ἠστόχησαν*, while they will needs prefer these, they miss that faith which they pretend to aim at. Their pretence is, that theology being the end, and the most perfect, must be the last, and all the subservient sciences must go first. But, (1.) There is somewhat of natural knowledge indeed pre-requisite, and somewhat of art, before a man can receive theology; but that is no more than their mothers can teach them before they go to school. (2.) And it is true, that all right natural knowledge doth tend to the increase of theological knowledge; but that which is a means to its perfection, may be the effect or consequent of its beginning. (3.) The end must be first known, because it must be intended before the choice, or use of means. (4.) The Scripture revealeth to us the things of God himself in the most easy way, and therefore he must be first learned there. And, (5.) The book of the creatures is not to show us more of God than the Scripture doth; but by representing him to us in more sensible appearances, to make our knowledge of him the more intense and operative; and being continually before our eyes, God also would be continually before them, if we could aright discern him in them. It is evident, therefore, that theology must lay the ground and lead the way of all our studies, when we are once acquainted with so much of words and things as is needful to our understanding the sense of its principles. If God must be searched after in our search of the creature, and we must affect no separated knowledge of them, then tutors must read God to their pupils in all; and divinity must be the beginning, the middle, the end, the life, the all of their studies; and our physics and metaphysics must be reduced to theology; and nature must be read as one of God's books, which is purposely written for the revelation of himself. The holy Scripture is the easier book. When you have first learned God and his will there, in the necessary things, address yourselves cheerfully to the study of his works, that you may see there the creature itself as your alphabet, and their order as the composure of syllables, words, and sentences, and God as the subject matter of all, and the respect to him as the sense or signification; and then carry on both together, and never more play the mere scriveners; stick no more in your letters and words, but read every creature as a christian or a divine. If you see not yourselves and all things as living, and moving, and having being in God, you see nothing, whatever you think you see. If you perceive not in your perusals of the creatures, that God is all, and in all, and see not *ἐξ ἀυτοῦ, καὶ δί αὐτοῦ, καὶ εἰς αὐτὸν τὰ πάντα*, (Rom. xi. 36,) you may think perhaps that you know something, but you know nothing as you ought to know, 1 Cor. viii. 2. But he that seeth and loveth God in the creature, the same is known and loved of him, verse 3. Think not so basely of the works of God, and your physics, as that they are only a preparatory study for boys. It is a most high and noble part of holiness to search after, behold, admire, and love the great Creator in all his works. How much have the saints of God been employed in it! The beginning of Genesis, the books of Job and the Psalms, may acquaint us that our physics are not so little akin to theology as some suppose. I do therefore in zeal to the good of the church, and their own success in their most necessary labours, propound it to the consideration of all pious tutors, whether they should not as timely and as diligently read to their pupils, or cause them to read, the chiefest parts of practical divinity (and there is no other) as any of the sciences; and whether they should not go together from the very first? It is well that they hear sermons; but that is not enough. If they have need of private help in philosophy besides public lectures, much more in theology. If tutors would make it their principal business to acquaint their pupils with the doctrine of life, and labour to set it home upon their hearts, that all might be received according to its weight, and read to their hearts as well as to their heads, and so carry on the rest of their instructions, that it may appear they make them but subservient unto this, and that their pupils may feel what they drive at in all, and so that they would teach all their philosophy *in habitu theologico*, this might be a happy means to make happy souls, and a happy church and commonwealth. (The same I mean also along of the course of schoolmasters to their scholars.) But when languages and philosophy have almost all their time and diligence, and instead of reading philosophy like divines, they read divinity like philosophers, as if it were a thing of no more moment than a lesson of music, or arithmetic, and not the doctrine of everlasting life; this is it that blasteth so many in the bud, and pestereth the church with unsanctified teachers! Hence it is, that we have so many worldlings to preach of the invisible felicity, and so many carnal men to declare the mysteries of the Spirit; and I would I might not say, so many infidels to preach Christ, or so many atheists to preach the living God. And when they are taught philosophy before, or without religion, what wonder if their philosophy be all or most of their religion; and if they grow up in admirations of their unprofitable fancies, and deify their own deluded brains, when they know no other God; and if they reduce all their theology to their philosophy, like Campanella, White, and other self-admirers; or if they take christianity for a mere delusion, and fall with Hobbs to write Leviathans, or with Lord Herbert, to write such treatises, *de veritate*, as shall show the world how little they esteem of verity; or at best, if they turn Paracelsian Behmenists, and spin them a religion of their own inventions! Again therefore I address myself to all them that have the education of youth, especially in order to preparation for the ministry. You that are schoolmasters, and tutors, begin and end with the things of God. Speak daily to the hearts of your scholars those things that must be wrought into their hearts, or else they are undone. Let some piercing words fall frequently from your mouths, of God, and the state of their souls, and the life to come. Do not say, they are too young to understand and entertain them. You little know what impressions they may make which you discern not. Not only that soul of the boy, but a congregation, or many souls therein, may have cause to bless God for your zeal and diligence, yea, for one such seasonable word. You have a great advantage above others to do them good. You have them before they are grown to the worst, and they will hear you when they will not hear another. If they are destinated to the ministry, you are preparing them for the special service of God; and must they not first have the knowledge of Him whom they must serve? O think with yourselves, what a sad thing it will be to their own souls, and what a wrong to the church of God, if they come out from you with common and carnal hearts, to so holy, and spiritual, and great a work! Of a hundred students that be in one of your colleges, how many may there be that are serious, experienced, godly men? some talk of too small a number. If you should send one half of them on a work that they are unfit for, what bloody work will they make in the church, or countries! Whereas if you be the means of their thorough sanctification, how many souls may bless you, and what greater good can you do the church! When once their hearts are savingly affected with the doctrine which they study and preach, they will study it more heartily, and preach it heartily. Their own experience will direct them to the fittest subjects, and will furnish them with matter, and quicken them to set it home. And I observe, that the best of our hearers can feel and savour such experimental preachers, and usually do less regard others, whatever may be their accomplishments. See, therefore, that you make not work for sequestrators, nor for the groans and lamentation of the church, nor for the great tormenter of the murderers of souls.

SECTION VI.

II. My second particular exhortation is this: Content not yourselves to have the main work of grace, but *be also very careful that your graces be kept in life and action, and that you preach to yourselves the sermons that you study, before you preach them to others.* If you did this for your own sakes, it would be lost labour; but I am speaking to you upon the public account, and that you would do it for the sake of the church. When your minds are in a heavenly, holy frame, your people are likely to partake of the fruits of it. Your prayers, and praises, and doctrine, will be heavenly and sweet to them! They will likely feel when you have been much with God. That which is on your hearts most, is like to be most in their ears. I confess, I must speak it by lamentable experience, that I publish to my flock the distempers of my soul: when I let my heart grow cold, my preaching is cold; and when it is confused, my preaching will be so: and so I can observe too oft in the best of my hearers, that when I have a while grown cold in preaching, they have cooled accordingly; and the next prayers that I have heard from them hath been too like my preaching. We are the nurses of Christ's little ones. If we forbear our food, we shall famish them; they will quickly find it in the want of milk; and we may quickly see it again on them, in the lean and dull discharge of their several duties. If we let our love go down, we are not like to raise up theirs. If we abate our holy care and fear, it will appear in our doctrine. If the matter show it not, the manner will. If we feed on unwholesome food, either errors, or fruitless controversies, our hearers are like to fare the worse for it. Whereas if we could abound in faith, and love, and zeal, how would it overflow, to the refreshing of our congregations, and how would it appear in the increase of the same graces in others! O brethren, watch, therefore, over your own hearts! Keep out lusts and passions and worldly inclinations; keep up the life of faith and love; be much at home; and be much with God. If it be not your daily, serious business to study your own hearts, and subdue corruptions, and live as upon God; if you make it not your very work which you constantly attend, all will go amiss, and you will starve your auditors; or if you have but an affected fervency, you cannot expect such a blessing to attend it: be much, above all, in secret prayer and meditation. There you must fetch the heavenly fire that must kindle your sacrifices. Remember, you cannot decline and neglect your duty to your own hurt alone; but many will be losers by it as well as you. For your people's sakes, therefore, look to your hearts. If a pang of spiritual pride should overtake you, and you should grow into any dangerous or schismatical conceits, and vent your own overvalued inventions to draw away disciples after you, what a wound might this prove to the church that you are set over; and you might become a plague to them instead of a blessing, and they might wish they had never seen your faces. O, therefore, take heed of your own judgments and affections! Error and vanity will slily insinuate, and seldom come without fair pretences. Great distempers and apostasies have usually small beginnings. The prince of darkness doth frequently personate the angels of light, to draw children of light again into his darkness. How easily also will distempers creep into our affections, and our first love, and fear, and care abate! Watch therefore, for the sake of yourselves and others.

And more particularly: methinks a minister should take some special pains with his heart, before he is to go to the congregation: if it be then cold, how is it like to warm the hearts of the hearers? Go, therefore, then especially to God for life; and read some rousing, awakening book, or meditate on the weight of the subject that you are to speak of, and on the great necessity of your people's souls, that you may go in the zeal of the Lord into his house.

SECTION VIII.

III. My next particular exhortation is this, *Stir up yourselves to the great work of God, when you are upon it, and see that you do it with all your might.* Though I move you not to a constant loudness, (for that will make your fervency contemptible,) yet see that you have a constant seriousness; and when the matter requireth it, as it should do in the application at least of every doctrine, then lift up your voice, and spare not your spirits, and speak to them as to men that must be awakened either here or in hell. Look upon your congregations believingly, and with compassion, and think in what a state of joy or torment they must all be for ever; and then, methinks, it should make you earnest, and melt your heart in the sense of their condition. O speak not one cold or careless word about so great a business as heaven or hell! Whatever you do, let the people see that you are in good sadness. Truly, brethren, they are great works that are to be done, and you must not think that trifling will despatch them. You cannot break men's hearts by jesting with them, or telling them a smooth tale, or patching up a gaudy oration. Men will not cast away their dearest pleasures upon a drowsy request of one that seemeth not to mean as he speaks, or to care much whether his request be granted. If you say, that the work is God's, and he may do it by the weakest means; I answer, It is true, he may do so; but yet his ordinary way is to work by means; and to make not only the matter that is preached, but also the manner of preaching, to be instrumental to the work: or else it were a small matter whom he should employ that would but speak the truth. If grace made as little use of the ministerial persuasions as some conceive, we need not so much mind a reformation, nor cast out the insufficient.

A great matter also, with the most of our hearers, doth lie in the very pronunciation and tone of speech. The best matter will scarce move them, if it be not movingly delivered. Especially, see that there be no affectation, but that we speak as familiarly to our people as we would do if we were talking to any of them personally. The want of a familiar tone and expression, is as great a defect in most of our deliveries, as any thing whatsoever, and that which we should be very careful to mend. When a man hath a reading or declaiming tone, like a schoolboy saying his lesson, or an oration, few are moved with any thing that he saith. Let us, therefore, rouse up ourselves to the work of the Lord, and speak to our people as for their lives, and save them as by violence, pulling them out of the fire. Satan will not be charmed out of his profession. We must lay siege to the souls of sinners which are his garrisons, and find out where his chief strength lieth, and lay the battery of God's ordinance against it, and ply it close till a breach be made; and then suffer them not by their shifts to make it up again, but find out their common objections, and give them a full and satisfactory answer. We have reasonable creatures to deal with; and as they abuse their reason against truth, so they will accept better reason for it before they will obey. We must therefore see that our sermons be all convincing, and that we make the light of Scripture and reason shine so bright in the faces of the ungodly, that it may even force them to see, unless they wilfully shut their eyes. A sermon full of mere words, how neatly soever it be composed, while there is wanting the light of evidence, and the life of zeal, is but an image or a well-dressed carcass. In preaching there is intended a communion of souls, and a communication of somewhat from ours unto theirs. As we and they have understandings, and wills, and affections, so must the bent of our endeavours be to communicate the fullest light of evidence from our understandings unto theirs; and to warm their hearts by kindling in them holy affections, as by a communication from ours. The great things which we have to commend to our hearers, have reason enough on their side, and lie plain before them in the word of God; we should therefore be so furnished with all store of evidence, as to come as with a torrent upon their understandings, and bear down all before us, and with our dilemmas and expostulations to bring them to a nonplus, and pour out shame upon all their vain objections, that they may be forced to yield to the power of truth, and see that it is great, and will prevail.

SECTION VIII.

IV. Moreover, if you would prosper in your work, be sure to *keep up earnest desires and expectations of success.* If your hearts be not set on the end of your labours, and you long not to see the conversion and edification of your hearers, and do not study and preach in hope, you are not likely to see much fruit of it. It is an ill sign of a false, self-seeking heart, that can be content to be still doing, and see no fruits of their labour. So I have observed, that God seldom blesseth any man's work so much as his whose heart is set upon the success. Let it be the property of a Judas to have more regard to the bag than to his business, and not to care much for what they pretend to care; and to think if they have their tithes, and the love and commendations of the people, that they have enough to satisfy them. But let all that preach for Christ, and men's salvation, be unsatisfied till they have the thing they preach for. He had never the right end of a preacher, that is indifferent whether he do obtain them, and is not grieved when he misseth them, and rejoiced when he can see the desired issue. When a man doth only study what to say, and how with commendation to spend the hour, and looks no more after it, unless it be to know what people think of his own abilities, and thus holds on from year to year; I must needs think, that this man doth preach for himself, and drive on a private trade of his own, and doth not preach for Christ even when he preacheth Christ, how excellent soever he may seem to do it. No wise or charitable physician is content to be still giving physic, and see no amendment among his patients, but have them all to die upon his hands; nor will any wise and honest schoolmaster be content to be still teaching, though his scholars profit not; but either of them would rather be weary of the employment. I know that a faithful minister may have comfort when he wants success; and though Israel be not gathered, our reward is with the Lord; and our acceptance is not according to the fruit, but according to our labour; and as Greg. M. saith, *Et Æthiops etsi balneum niger intrat, et niger egreditur, tamen balneator nummos accipit.* If God set us to wash blackamoors, and cure those that will not be cured, we shall not lose our labour, though we perform not the cure. But then, 1. He that longeth not for the success of his labours, can have none of his comfort, because he was not a faithful labourer: this is only for them that I speak of, that are set upon the end, and grieved if they miss it. 2. And this is not the full comfort that we must desire, but only such a part as may quiet us, though we miss the rest. What if God will accept a physician though the patient die? He must work in compassion, and long for a better issue, and be sorry if he miss of it, for all that; for it is not only our own reward that we labour for, but other men's salvation. I confess for my part, I marvel at some ancient, reverend men, that have lived twenty, or forty, or fifty years with an unprofitable people, where they have seen so little fruit of their labours, that it was scarce discernible how they can with so much patience there go on. Were it my case, though I durst not leave the vineyard nor quit my calling, yet I should suspect that it was God's will I should go some whither else, and another come thither that might be fitter for them; and I should not be easily satisfied to spend my days n such a sort.

SECTION IX.

V. *Do well,* as well as *say well.* Be zealous of good works. Spare not for any cost, if it may promote your Master's work.

1. Maintain your innocence, and walk without offence. Let your lives condemn sin, and persuade men to duty. Would you have your people be more careful of their souls than you will be of yours? If you would have them redeem their time, do not you mispend yours. If you would not have them vain in their conference, see that you speak yourselves the things which may edify, and tend to minister grace to the hearers. Order your own families well if you would have them so do by theirs. Be not proud and lordly, if you would have them to be lowly. There is no virtue wherein your example will do more, at least to abate men's prejudice, than humility, and meekness, and self-denial. Forgive injuries, and be not overcome of evil, but overcome evil with good. Do as your Lord, who when he was reviled, reviled not again. If sinners be stubborn, and stout, and contemptuous, flesh and blood will persuade you to take up their weapons, and to master them by their carnal means; but that is not the way, further than necessary self-preservation or public good requireth it; but overcome them with kindness, and patience, and gentleness. The former may show that you have more worldly power than they, wherein yet they are ordinarily too hard for the faithful; but it is the latter only that will tell them that you overtop them in spiritual excellency, and in the true qualifications of a saint. If you believe that Christ was more imitable than Cæsar or Alexander; and that it is more glory to be a christian than to be a conqueror, yea, to be a man than a beast, who oft exceed us in strength, contend then with charity, and not with violence; and set meekness, and love, and patience against force, and not force against force; remember you are obliged to be the servants of all. Condescend to men of low estate; be not strange to the poor ones of your flock. They are apt to take your strangeness for contempt. Familiarity improved to holy ends, is exceeding necessary, and may do abundance of good. Speak not stoutly, or disrespectfully to any one; but be courteous to the meanest as your equal in Christ. A kind and winning carriage is a cheap way of advantage to do men good.

2. Remember what I said before of works of bounty and charity. Go to the poor, and see what they want, and show at once your compassion to soul and body. Buy them a catechism and some small books that are likeliest to do them good, and bestow them on your neighbours, and make them promise you to read them, and specially to spend that part of the Lord's day therein, which they can spare from greater duties. Stretch your purse to the utmost, and do all the good you can. Think not of being rich; seek not great things for yourselves or posterity. What if you do impoverish yourselves to do a greater good; will it be loss or gain? If you believe that God is your safest purse-bearer, and that to expend in his service is the greatest usury, and the most thriving trade; show them that you believe it. I know that flesh and blood will cavil before it will lose its prey, and will never want somewhat to say against that duty that is against its interest. But mark what I say, and the Lord set it home upon your hearts: *That man that hath any thing in the world so dear to him, that he cannot spare it for Christ, if he call for it, is no true christian.* And because a carnal heart will not believe that Christ calls for it, when he cannot spare it, and therefore makes that his self-deceiving shift; I say, furthermore, that *That man that will not be persuaded that duty is duty, because he cannot spare that for Christ which is therein to be expended, is no true christian;* for a false heart corrupteth the understanding, and that again increaseth the delusions of the heart. Do not take it therefore as an undoing, to make you friends of the mammon of unrighteousness, and to lay up a treasure in heaven, though you leave yourselves but little on earth. *Nemo tam pauper potest esse quam natus est; aves sine patrimonio vivunt, et in diem pecua pascuntur: et hoc nobis tamen nata sunt; quæ omnia si non concupiscimus possidemus,* inquit Minutius Felix, p. (mihi) 397. You lose no great advantage for heaven by becoming poor; *Quia viam terit, eo fælicior quo levior incedit.* Id.

I know where the heart is carnal and covetous, words will not wring their money out of their hands. They can say all this and more to others; but saying is one thing, and believing is another. But with those that are true believers, methinks such considerations would prevail. Oh what abundance of good might ministers do, if they would but live in a contempt of the world, and the riches and glory of it, and expend all they have for the best of their Master's use, and pinch their flesh that they might have wherewith to do good. This would unlock more hearts to the reception of their doctrine than all their oratory will do; and without this, singularity in religiousness will seem but hypocrisy, and it is likely that it is so. *Qui innocentiam colit, domino supplicat—qui hominem periculo surripit, opinam victimam cædit; hæc nostra sacrificia; hæc Dei sacra sunt; sic apud nos religiosior est ille qui justior*, inquit idem Minutius Felix, ib. Though we need not do as the papists, that will betake them to monasteries, and cast away propriety, yet we must have nothing but what we have for God.

SECTION X.

VI. The next branch of my exhortation is, That you would *maintain your christian and brotherly unity and communion, and do as much of God's work as you can in unanimity, and holy concord.* Blessed be the Lord that it is so well with us in this county, in this regard, as it is! We lose our authority with the people when we divide. They will yield to us when we go together, who would resist and contemn the best of us alone.

Two things, in order to this, I beseech you to observe: the first is, That you still maintain your meetings for communion; incorporate, and hold all christian correspondence; grow not strange to one another; do not say that you have business of your own to do, when you should be at any such meeting or other work for God. It is not only the mutual edification that we may receive by lectures, disputations, or conferences, though that is not nothing, but it is specially for consultations for the common good, and the maintaining of our communion, that we must thus assemble. Though your own person might be without the benefit of such meetings, yet the church and our common work requireth them. Do not then show yourselves contemners or neglecters of such a necessary work. Distance breedeth strangeness, and fomenteth dividing flames and jealousies, which communion will prevent or cure. It will be our enemies' chiefest plot to divide us, that they may weaken us. Conspire not with the enemies, and take not their course. And indeed, ministers have need of one another, and must improve the gifts of God in one another; and the self-sufficient are the most deficient, and commonly proud and empty men. Some there be that come not among their brethren to do or receive good, nor afford them any of their assistance in consultations for the common good, and their excuse is only, We love to live privately. To whom I say, Why do you not on the same grounds forbear going to church, and say you love to live privately? Is not ministerial communion a duty, as well as common christian communion; and hath not the church always thought so, and practised accordingly? If you mean that you love your own ease or commodity better than God's service, say so, and speak your minds. But I suppose there are few of them so silly as to think that is any just excuse, though they will give us no better. Somewhat else sure lieth at the bottom. Indeed some of them are empty men, and afraid their weakness should be known, whenas they cannot conceal it by their solitariness, and might do much to heal it by communion. Some of them are careless and scandalous men; and for them we have no desire of their communion, nor shall admit it, but upon public repentance and reformation. Some of them are so in love with their parties and opinions, that they will not hold communion with us, because we are not of their parties and opinions; whereas by communication they might give or receive better information, or at least carry on so much of God's work in unity as we are agreed in. But the mischief of schism is to make men censorious and proud, and take others to be unmeet for their communion, and themselves to be the only church, or pure church, of Christ.

The papists will have no catholic church but the Romans, and unchurch all besides themselves. The separatists, and many anabaptists, say the like of their parties. The new prelatical party will have no catholic church but prelatical, and unchurch all except their party, and so avoid communion with others; and thus turning separatists and schismatics, they imitate the papists, and make an opposition to schism their pretence. First, all must be accounted schismatics that be not of their opinion and party, (when yet we find not that opinion in the creed,) and they must be avoided because they are schismatics. But we resolve, by the grace of God, to adhere to more catholic principles and practices, and to have communion with all godly christians that will have communion with us, so far as they force us not to actual sin. And for the separating brethren, as by distance they are like to cherish misinformations of us, so if by their wilful estrangedness, and distance, any among us do entertain injurious reports of them, and think worse of them, and deal worse by some of them, than there is cause, they may partly thank themselves.

Sure I am, by such means as these, we are many of us grown so hardened in sin, that men make no great matter what they say one against another, but stand out of hearing and sight, and vent their spleen against each other behind their backs. How many jeers and scorns have they among their companions for those that are against their party! And they easily venture, be the matter never so safe. A bad report of such is easily taken to be true; and that which is true, is easily made worse; whenas Seneca saith, *Multus absolvemus si cœperimus ante judicare quam irasci: nunc autem primum impetum sequimur.* It is passion that tells the tale, and that receiveth it.

2. The second thing therefore, that I entreat of you, is, that you would be very tender of the unity and peace of the catholic church; not only of your own party's, but of the whole. And to this end these things will prove necessary: 1. Do not too easily introduce any novelties into the church, either in faith or practice: I mean not that which seems a novelty to men that look no further than yesterday; for so the restoring of ancient things will seem novelty to those that know not what was anciently; and the expulsion of prevailing novelties will seem a novelty to them that know not what is such indeed. So the papists censure us as novelists for casting out many of their innovations; and our common people tell us, we bring up new customs if we do not kneel at the receiving of the Lord's supper; a notorious novelty. Even in the sixth general council at Trull, in Constantinople, this was the ninth canon: *Ne Dominicis diebus genua flectamus, a divinis Patribus nostris Canonice accepimus: Quare post vespertinum ingressum Sacerdotum in Sabbato ad altare, ut more observatum est, nemo genu flectit usque ad sequentem vesperem post dominicam.* It is that which is indeed novelty that I dissuade you from; and not the demolishing of novelties. Some have already introduced such new phrases, at least, even about the great points of faith, justification, and the like, that there may be reason to reduce them to the primitive patterns.

A great stir is made in the world about the test of a christian and true church, with whom we may have communion, and about that true centre and cement of the unity of the church, in and by which our common calamitous breaches must be healed. And indeed the true cause of our continued divisions and misery is for want of discerning the centre of our unity, and the terms on which it must be done; which is great pity, when it was once so easy a matter, till the ancient test was thought insufficient! If any of the ancient creeds might serve, we might be soon agreed. If Vincentius Lirinens.' test might serve, we might yet make some good shift, viz. To believe (explicitly) all that *quod ubique, quod semper, quod ab omnibus creditum est.* For as he addeth, *hoc est etenim vere proprieque catholicum.* But then we must see, 1. that the first age may not be excluded which gave the rule to the rest; 2. and that this extend not to every ceremony which never was taken for unalterable, but to matters of faith; and that the acts and canons of councils which were not about such matters of faith, but mere variable order, and which newly constituted those things, which the apostolic age knew not, and therefore were not properly *credita*, much less *semper, et ab omnibus* may have no hand in this work. I say, if either the ancient Western or Eastern creed, or this catholic faith of Vincentius, might be taken as the test for explicit faith, or else rather all those Scripture texts, that express the *credenda* with a note of necessity, and the whole Scripture, moreover, be confessed to be God's word, and so believed (in other points) at least implicitly; this course might produce a more general communion and agreement: and more lines would meet in this centre, than otherwise are like to meet. And indeed, till men can be again content to make the Scripture the sufficient rule, in necessaries to be explicitly believed, and in all the rest implicitly, we are never like to see a catholic, christian, durable peace. If we must needs make the council of Trent, or the papal judgment, our test; or if we must make a blind bargain with the papists, to come as near them as ever we dare, and so to compose another Interim, and make that a test, (when God never made it so, and all christians will never be of a mind in it, but some dare go nearer Rome than others dare, and that in several degrees,) or if we must thrust in all the canons of the former councils about matters of order, discipline, and ceremonies into our test, or gather up all the opinions of the fathers for the three or four first ages, and make them our test; none of all these will ever serve to do the business, and a catholic union will never be founded in them. It is an easy matter infallibly to foretell this. Much less can the writings of any single man, as Austin, Aquinas, Luther, Calvin, Beza, &c.; or yet the late confessions of any churches that add to the ancient test, be ever capable of this use and honour.

I know it is said, that a man may subscribe the Scripture, and the ancient creeds, and yet maintain Socinianism, or other heresies. To which I answer, 1. So he may another test which your own brains shall contrive; and while you make a snare to catch heretics, instead of a test for the church's communion, you will miss your end, and the heretic by the slipperiness of his conscience will break through, and the tender christian may possibly be insnared. And by your new creed the church is like to have new divisions, if you keep not close to the words of Scripture. 2. In such cases, when heretics contradict the Scripture which they have subscribed, this calls not for a new or more sufficient test, but the church must take notice of it, and call him to account, and if he be impenitent, exclude him their communion. What! must we have new laws made every time the old ones are broken? as if the law were not sufficient because men break it! Or rather, must not the penalty of the violated law be executed? It is a most sad case that such reasons as these should prevail with so many learned men to deny the sufficiency of Scripture as a test for church communion, and to be still framing new ones that depart at least from Scripture phrase, as if this were necessary to obviate heresies! Two things are necessary to obviate heresies, the law, and good execution; God hath made the former, and his rule and law is both for sense and phrase (translated) sufficient; and all their additional inventions, as to the foresaid use, are as spiders' webs. Let us but do our part in the due execution of the laws of Christ, by questioning offenders in orderly synods, for the breaking of these laws, and let us avoid communion with the impenitent; and what can the church do more? The rest belongs to the magistrate, (to restrain him from seducing his subjects,) and not to us.

Well! this is the thing that I would recommend therefore to all my brethren, as the most necessary thing to the church's peace, that you *unite in necessary truths, and tolerate tolerable failings; and bear with one another in things that may be borne with; and do not make a larger creed, and more necessaries, than God hath done.* And to that end, let no man's writings, nor the judgment of any party, though right, be taken as a test, or made that rule. And, (1.) Lay not too great a stress upon controverted opinions, which have godly men, and especially whole churches, on both sides. (2.) Lay not too great a stress on those controversies that are ultimately resolved into philosophical uncertainties (as some unprofitable controversies are about free-will, and the manner of the Spirit's operation of grace, and the divine decrees, and predetermination). (3.) Lay not too great a stress on those controversies that are merely verbal, and if they were anatomized, would appear to be no more. Of which sort are far more, I speak it confidently upon certain knowledge, that now make a great noise in the world, and tear the church, than almost any of the eager contenders that ever I spoke with do seem to discern or are like to believe. (4.) Lay not too much on any point of faith which was disowned of, or unknown to, the whole church of Christ in any age since the Scriptures were delivered us. (5.) Much less should you lay too much on those which any of the more pure or judicious ages were wholly ignorant of. (6.) And least of all should you lay too much on any point which no one age since the apostles did ever receive, but all commonly hold the contrary. For to make such an error which all the church held, to be such as is damning, were to unchurch all the church of Christ; and to make it such, as must exclude them from our communion, 1. Doth make the whole church excommunicable, which is absurd: 2. And doth show that if we had lived in that age, you would it seems have separated from the whole church. To give an instance of the differences among errors: That any elect person shall fall away totally and finally, is a palpable condemned error, of dangerous consequence. But that there are some justified ones not elect, that shall fall away and perish, is an error of a lower nature; which may not break the communion of christians: for otherwise we must renounce communion with the catholic church in Augustine's days, and much more before, as is said before. What then? Shall I take this therefore for a truth which the church then held? Some will think me immodest to say no; as if I were wiser than all the church, and that in so learned an age, if not for so many: but yet I must be so immodest, as long as Scripture seemeth to me to warrant it. Why might not Augustine, Prosper, and all the rest, mistake in such a thing as that? but then I am not so immodest, nor unchristian, as to unchurch all the church on that account: nor would I have separated from Austin and all the church, if I had then lived; nor will do now from any man on that account. Both sides will be displeased with this resolution; one, that I suppose all the church to err, and ourselves to be in the right;

and the other, that I take it for no greater an error. But what remedy? It will and must be so: read Prosper's Resp. ad Capit. Gall. and you may quickly know both Austin's mind and his.

He that shall live to that happy time, when God will heal his broken churches, shall see all this that I am now pleading for reduced to practice, and this moderation take place of the new dividing zeal, and Scripture sufficiency take place, and all men's confessions and comments to be valued only as subservient helps, and not be the test of church communion, any further than they are exactly the same with Scripture. And till the healing age come, we cannot expect that healing truths be entertained, because there are not healing spirits in the leaders of the church. But when the work is to be done, the workmen will be fitted for it; and blessed will be the agents of so glorious a work!

But because the love of unity and verity, peace and purity, must be conjunctly manifested, we must avoid the extremes both in doctrine and communion. The extremes in doctrine are on one side by innovating additions; on the other side, by envying or hindering the progress of the light. The former is the most dangerous; of which men are guilty these ways.

1. By making new points of faith or duty.

2. By making those points to be fundamental, or necessary to salvation, that are not so.

3. By pretending of prophetical and other obscurer passages of the Scriptures, that they have a greater objective evidence, and we a greater certainty of their meaning, than indeed is so.

As I have met with some so confident of their right understanding of the revelation, (which Calvin durst not expound, and profess he understood it not,) that they have framed part of their confessions or articles of faith out of it; and grounded the weightiest actions of their lives upon their exposition; and could confidently tell in our late changes and differences, which side was in the right, and which in the wrong, and all from the revelation; and thence would fetch such arguments as would carry all, if you would but grant the soundness of their expositions; but if you put them to prove that, you marred all.

And these corruptions of sacred doctrine by their additions are of two sorts. Some that are the first inventors; and others that are the propagators and maintainers: and these when additions grow old, do commonly maintain them under the notion of ancient verities, and oppose the ancient verities under the notion of novelty, as is before said.

The other extreme about doctrine is by hindering the progress of knowledge: and this is commonly on pretence of avoiding the innovating extreme. It must be considered therefore, how far we may grow and not be culpable innovators. And, 1. Our knowledge must increase extensively *ad plura;* we must know more verities than we knew before, though we may not feign more. There is much of Scripture that will remain unknown to us when we have done our best. Though we shall find out no more articles of faith which must be explicitly believed by all that will be saved, yet we may find out the sense of more particular texts, and several doctrinal truths, not contrary to the former, but such as befriend them, and are connexed with them. And we may find out more the order of truths, and how they are placed in respect to one another, and so see more of the true method of theology than we did, which will give us a very great light into the matter itself, and its consectaries.

2. Our knowledge also must grow subjectively, intensively, and in the manner, as well as in the matter of it. And this is our principal growth to be sought after. To know the same great and necessary truths with a sounder and clearer knowledge than we did: which is done,

(1.) By getting strong evidence and reasons instead of the weak ones which we trusted to before, (for many young ones receive truths on some unsound grounds).

(2.) By multiplying our evidence and reasons for the same truth.

(3.) By a clear and deeper apprehension of the same evidence, and reasons, which before we had but superficially received: for one that is strong in knowledge seeth the same truth as in the clear light, which the weak do see but as in the twilight. To all this must be added also, the fuller improvement of the truth received to its ends.

I shall give you the sum of my meaning in the words of that great enemy of innovation, Vincent. Lirinens. c. 28. *Sed forsitan dicit aliquis: Nullusne ergo in ecclesia Christi profectus habebitur? Religionis habeatur plane, et maximus: Nam quis ille est tam invidus hominibus, tam exosus Deo, qui istud prohibere conetur? Sed ita tamen ut vere profectus sit ille fidei; non permutatio. Siquidem ad perfectum pertinet, ut in semetipsa unaquæque res amplificetur: ad permutationem vero ut aliquid ex alio in aliud transvertatur. Crescat igitur oportet et multum, vehementerque proficiat, tam singulorum quam omnium: tam unius hominis quam totius ecclesiæ ætatum ac seculorum gradibus intelligentia, scientia, sapientia; sed in quo duntaxat genere, in eodem scilicet dogmate, eodem sensu, eademque sententia.*

And more plainly, and yet more briefly, cap. 30. *Jus est etenim, ut prisca illa cœlestis philosophiæ dogmata recessu temporis excurentur, limentur, poliantur: sed nefas est, ut commutentur. Accipiant licet evidentiam, lucem, distinctionem; sed retineant necesse est plenitudinem, integritatem, proprietatem.* Let this mean then be observed if we would perform both truth and peace.

About church communion the common extremes are: on one side, the neglect or relaxation of discipline, to the corrupting of the church, the encouragement of wickedness, and confounding the kingdom of Christ and Satan: and on the other side, the unnecessary separation of proud men, either because the churches own not their own opinions, or because they are not so reformed and strict in discipline as they would have them, or as they should be. I have ever observed the humblest men very tender of making separations; and the proudest most prone to it. Many corruptions may be in a church, and yet it may be a great sin to separate from it; so that we be not put upon an owning of their corruptions, nor upon any actual sin. There is a strange inclination in proud men to make the church of Christ much narrower than it is, and to reduce it to almost nothing, and to be themselves the members of some singular society, as if they were loth to have too much company in heaven. And by a strange delusion, through the workings of a proud fancy, they are fuller of joy in their separated societies, than they were while they kept in the union of the church. At least such powers of ordinances, and presence of the Spirit, purity and peace, is promised to the weak by the leaders that would seduce them, as if the Holy Ghost were more eminently among them than any where else in the world. This hath ever been the boasting of heretics. As the aforesaid Vincentius saith, cap. 37. *Jam vero illis quæ sequuntur promissionibus miro modo incautos homines hæretici decipere consueverunt. Audent enim polliceri et docere.*

quod in ecclesia sua, id est, in communionis suæ conventiculo, magna et specialis ac plane personalis quædam sit Dei gratia, adeo ut sine ullo labore, sine ullo studio, sine ulla industria, etiamsi nec quærunt, nec petant, nec pulsant, quicunque illi ad numerum suum pertinent, tamen ita divinitus dispensentur, &c. But their consolations and high enjoyments being the effect of self-conceitedness and fancies, are usually so mutable and of short continuance, that either the heat of oppositions, or mutation to other sects, must maintain their life, or else they will grow stale and soon decay.

Having said thus much of the means, I return to the ends of this exhortation, beseeching all the ministers of Christ to compassionate the poor, divided church, and to entertain such catholic principles and charitable dispositions, as tend to their own and the common peace. Hath any thing in the world done more to lose our authority, and disable us for God's service, than our differences and divisions? If ministers could but be all of a mind, or at least concur in the substance of the work, so that the people that hear one might as it were hear all, and not have any of us to head a party for the discontented to fall into, or to object against the rest, we might then do wonders for the church of Christ. But if our tongues and hearts be divided, what wonder if our work be spoiled, and prove more like a Babel than a temple of God? Get together then speedily, and consult for peace, and cherish not heart-burnings, and continue not uncharitable distances and strangeness. If dividing hath weakened you, closing must recover your authority and strength. If you have any dislike of your brethren, or their ways, manifest it by a free debate to their faces, but do not unnecessarily withdraw from them. If you will but keep together, you may come to better understanding of each other, or at least may chide yourselves. Friends, especially quarrel not upon points of precedency, or reputation, or any interest of your own. No man will have settled peace in his mind, nor be peaceable in his place, that proudly envieth the precedency of others, and secretly grudgeth at them that seem to cloud their parts and name. One or other will ever be an eyesore to such men. There is too much of the devil's image on this sin for a humble servant of Christ to entertain. Moreover, be not too sensible of injuries; and make not a great matter of every offensive word or deed. At least do not let it interrupt your communion and concord in God's work; for that were to wrong Christ and his church because another hath wronged you. And if you be of this impatient humour, you will never be quiet; for we are all faulty, and cannot live together without wronging one another. *Ubique causæ supersunt nisi deprecator animus accessit*, saith Seneca. And these proud, over-tender men are often hurt by their own conceits; like a man that hath a sore that he thinks doth smart more when he conceits that some one hits it. They will think a man jeereth them, or contemneth them, or meaneth them ill, when it never came into his thoughts! Till this *self* be taken down, we shall every man have a private interest, and of his own, which will lead us all into several ways, and spoil the peace and welfare of the church. While every man is for himself and his own reputation, and all mind their own things, no wonder if they mind not the things of Christ.

And as for those opinions which hinder our union, (alas, the great dividers of the age!) methinks, if I cannot change their minds, I might yet rationally expect of every party among us that profess themselves christians, that they should value the whole before a part; and therefore not so perversely seek to promote their party as may hinder the common good of the church, or so to propagate their supposed truths as to hinder the work of the main body of divine truths. And methinks, a little humility should make men ashamed of that common conceit of unquiet spirits; viz. that the welfare of the church doth so lie upon their opinions, that they must needs vent and propagate them, whatever comes of it. If they are indeed a living part of the body, the hurt of the whole will be so much their own, that they cannot desire it for the sake of any party or opinion. Were men but impartial to consider in every such case of difference, how far their promoting their own judgment may help or hurt the whole, they might escape many dangerous ways that are now trod. If you can see no where else, look in the face of the church's enemies, how they rejoice and deride us. And as Seneca saith to demulce the angry, *Vide ne inimicis iracundia tua voluptati sit.* When we have all done, I know not which party of us will prove a gainer: so true are the old proverbs, *Dissensio ducum hostium succum*, and *Gaudent prædones, dum discordant regiones.* And is it not a wonder, that godly ministers, that know all this, how the common adversary derideth us all, and what a scandal our divisions are through the world, and how much the church doth lose by it, should yet go on, and after all the loudest calls and invitations to peace, go on still, and few, if any, sound a retreat, and seriously call to their brethren for a retreat? Can an honest heart be insensible of the sad distractions and sadder apostasies that our divisions have occasioned? *Sæpe rixam conclamatum, in vicino incendium solvit*, saith Seneca. What scolds so furious that will not give over, when the house is on fire over their heads? Well! if the Lord hath given that evil spirit, whose name is Legion, such power over the hearts of any, that yet they will sit still, yea, and quarrel at the pacificatory endeavours of others who hunger after the healing of the church, and rather carp, and reproach, and hinder such works than to help them on, I shall say but this to them: How diligently soever such men may preach, and how pious soever they may seem to be, if this way tend to their everlasting peace, and if they be not preparing sorrow for themselves, then I am a stranger to the way of peace.

SECTION XI.

VII. The next branch of my exhortation is, That *you would no longer neglect the execution of so much discipline in your congregations, as is of confessed necessity and right.* I desire not to spur on any one to an unseasonable performance of the greatest duty. But will it never be a fit season? Would you forbear sermons and sacraments so many years on pretence of unseasonableness? Will you have a better season for it, when you are dead? How many are dead already before they ever did any thing in this work, that were long preparing for it! It is now near three years, since many of us here present did engage ourselves to this duty: and have we been faithful in the performance of that engagement? I know some have more discouragements and hinderances than others; but what discouragements can excuse us from such a duty? Besides the reasons that we then considered of, let these few be further laid to heart.

1. How sad a sign do we make it to be in our preaching to our people, to live in the wilful, continued omission of any known duty! And shall we do so even year after year, and all our days? If excuses will take off the danger of this sign, what

man will not find them as well as you? Read Austin Medul. cap. 37, de Disciplin. Eccles. et Gelespi's Aaron's Rod, with Rutherford, and many more that are written to prove the need and dueness of discipline. Saith Ames. ib. sec. 5, *Immo peccat in christum authorem ac institutorem quisquis non facit quod in se est, ad hanc disciplinam, in ecclesiis Dei constituendam et promovendam.* And do you think it safe to live and die in such a known sin?

2. You gratify the present designs of dividers, whose business is to unchurch us and unchristian us; to prove our parishes no true churches, and ourselves no baptized christians. For if you take them for people uncapable of discipline, they must be uncapable of the sacrament of the Lord's supper, and other church communion: and then they are no church. And so you will plainly seem to preach merely as they do; to gather churches where there were none before. And indeed, if that be your case, that your people are not christians, and you have no particular churches, and so are no pastors, tell us so, and manifest it, and we shall not blame you.

3. We do manifest plain laziness and sloth, if not unfaithfulness in the work of Christ. I speak from experience; it was laziness that kept me off so long, and pleaded hard against this duty. It is indeed a troublesome and pitiful work, and such as calls for some self-denial, because it will cast us upon the displeasure of the wicked. But dare we prefer our carnal ease, and quietness, and the love or peace of wicked men, before our service to Christ our Master? Can slothful servants look for a good rewarder? Remember, brethren, that we of this county have thus promised before God in the second article of our Agreement, "We agree and resolve by God's help, that so far as God doth make known our duty to us, we will faithfully endeavour to discharge it, and will not desist through any fears or losses in our estates, or the frowns and displeasure of men, or any the like carnal inducements whatsoever." I pray you study this promise, and compare your performance with it. And do not think that you are insnared by thus engaging; for God's law hath laid an obligation on you to all the same duty, before your engagement did it. Here is nothing but what others are bound to, as well as you.

4. The ministry that are for the presbyterian government, have already by their common neglect of the execution, made those of the separating way believe, that they do it in a mere carnal compliance with the unruly part of the people, that while we exasperate them not with our discipline, we might have them on our side. And we should do nothing needless, that hath so great an appearance of evil, and is so scandalous to others. It was the sin and ruin of many of the clergy of the last times, to please and comply with them that they should have reproved and corrected, by unfaithfulness in preaching, and neglect of discipline.

5. The neglect of discipline hath a strong tendency to the deluding of souls; by making them think they are christians that are not: while they are permitted to live in the reputation of such; and be not separated from the rest by God's ordinance. And it may make the scandalous to think their sin a tolerable thing, which is so tolerated by the pastors of the church.

6. We do corrupt christianity itself in the eyes of the world; and do our part to make them believe, that to be a christian is but to be of such an opinion, and to have that faith which James saith the devils had, and to be *solifidians*, and that Christ is no more for holiness than Satan, or that the christian religion exacteth holiness no more than the false religions of the world: for if the holy and unholy are all permitted to be the sheep of the same fold, without the use of Christ's means to difference them, we do our part to defame Christ by it, as if he were guilty of it, and as if this were the strain of his prescripts.

7. We do keep up separation by permitting the worst to be uncensured in our churches, so that many honest christians think they are necessitated to withdraw. I must profess that I have spoke with some members of the separated (or gathered) churches, that were moderate men, and have argued with them against their way; and they have assured me, that they were of the presbyterian judgment, or had nothing to say against it, but they joined themselves with other churches upon mere necessity, thinking that discipline, being an ordinance of Christ, must be used by all that can, and therefore they durst no longer live without it when they may have it, and they could find no presbyterian churches that executed discipline, as they wrote for it; and they told me, that they did thus separate only *pro tempore*, till the presbyterians will use discipline, and then they would willingly return to them again. I confess I was sorry that such persons had any such occasion to withdraw, and the least ground for such a reason of their doings. It is not keeping them from the sacrament that will excuse us from the further exercise of discipline, while they are members of our churches.

8. We do too much to bring the wrath of God upon ourselves and our congregations, and so to blast the fruit of our labours. If the angel of the church of Thyatira was reproved for suffering the seducers in the church, we may be reproved on the same ground for suffering open, scandalous, impenitent ones, Rev. ii. 20.

9. We seem to justify the prelates, who took the same course in neglecting discipline, though in other things we differ.

10. We have abundance of aggravations and witnesses to rise up against us, which though I will purposely now overpass, lest I seem to press too hard in this point, I shall desire you to apply them hither, when you meet with them anon under the next branch of the exhortation.

I know that discipline is not essential to a church; but what of that? Is it not therefore a duty; and necessary to its well-being; yea, more. The power of discipline is essential to a particular political church; and what is the power for, but for the work and use? As there is no commonwealth that hath not *partem imperantem* as well as *partem subditam*, so no such church that hath not *partem regentem*, in one pastor or more.

SECTION XII.

VIII. The last particular branch of my exhortation is, That *you will now faithfully discharge the great duty which you have undertaken, and which is the occasion of our meeting here to-day, in personal catechising and instructing every one in your parishes that will submit thereto.* What our undertaking is you know, you have considered it, and it is now published to the world. But what the performance will be I know not: but I have many reasons to hope well of the most, though some will always be readier to say than to do. And because this is the chief business of the day, I must take leave to insist somewhat the longer on it. And, (1.) I shall give you some further motives to persuade you to faithfulness in the undertaken work, presupposing the former general motives which should move us to this as well as to any other part of our duty. (2.) I shall give to the younger of my brethren a few words of advice for the manner of performance.

CHAPTER VI.

SECTION I.

THE *first* reasons by which I shall persuade you to this duty are taken from the benefits of it. The *second* from the difficulty. And the *third* from the necessity, and the many obligations that are upon us for the performance of it. And to these three heads I shall reduce them all.

I. And for the first of these; when I look before me, and consider what, through the blessing of God, this work well managed is like to produce, it makes my heart to leap for joy. Truly, brethren, you have begun a most blessed work; and such as your own consciences may rejoice in, your parishes rejoice in, the nation rejoice in, and the child yet unborn; yea, thousands and millions, for aught we know, may have cause to bless God for it, when we have finished our course. And though it be our business here to humble ourselves for the neglect of it so long, as we have very great cause to do; yet the hopes of a blessed success are so great in me, that they are ready to turn it into a day of rejoicing. I bless the Lord that I have lived to see such a day as this, and to be present at so solemn an engagement of so many servants of Christ to such a work. I bless the Lord that hath honoured you of this country to be the beginners and awakeners of the nation hereunto. It is not a controverted business, where the exasperated minds of divided men might pick quarrels with us, or malice itself be able to invent a rational reproach; nor is it a new invention, where envy might charge you as innovators, or proud boasters of any new discoveries of your own; or scorn to follow in it because you have led the way. No; it is a well-known duty. It is but the more diligent and effectual management of the ministerial work, and the teaching of our principles, and the feeding of babes with milk. You lead indeed, but not in invention of novelty, but the restoration of the ancient ministerial work, and the self-denying attempt of a duty that few or none can contradict. Unless men do envy you your labours and sufferings, or unless they envy the saving of men's souls, I know not what they can envy you for in this. The age is so quarrelsome, that where there is any matter to fasten on, we can scarce explain a truth, or perform a duty, but one or other, if not many, will have a stone to cast at us, and will speak evil of the things which they do not understand, or which their hearts and interest are against. But here I think we have silenced malice itself: and I hope we may do this part of God's work quietly, as to them. If they cannot endure to be told what they know not, or contradicted in what they think, or disgraced by discoveries of what they have said amiss, I hope they will give us leave to do that which no man can contradict, and to practise that which all are agreed in. I hope we may have their good leave, or silent patience at least, to deny the ease and pleasure of our flesh, and to set ourselves in good earnest to help men to heaven, and to propagate the knowledge of Christ with our people. And I take it for a sign of a great and necessary work, which hath such universal approbation; the commonly acknowledged truths and duties being, for the most part, of greatest necessity and moment. A more noble work it is to practise faithfully the truths and duties that all men will confess, than to make new ones, or discover somewhat more than others have discovered. I know not why we should be ambitious of finding out new ways to heaven: to make plain, and to walk in the old way, is our work and our greatest honour.

And because the work in hand is so pregnant of great advantages to the church, I will come down to the particular benefits which we may hope for; that when you see the excellency of it, you may be the more set upon it, and the lother by any negligence or failing to destroy or frustrate it. For certainly he that hath the true intentions of a minister, will rejoice in the appearances of any further hopes of the attaining of his ends, and nothing can be more welcome to him than that which will further the very business of his life; and that our present work is such, I shall show you more particularly.

1. It will be the most hopeful advantage for the conversion of many souls that we can expect; for it hath a concurrence of those great things which must further such a work.

(1.) For the matter of it is about most needful things; the principles or essentials of the christian faith.

(2.) For the manner of exercise; it will be by private conference, where we may have opportunity to set home to the heart.

(3.) The common concord of ministers will do much to bow their hearts to consent. Were it but a meeting to resolve some controverted questions, it would not have so direct a tendency to conversion. Were it but occasional, we could not handsomely fall on them so closely; but when we make it the appointed business, it will be expected, and not strangely taken. And if most ministers had singly set upon this work, perhaps but few of the people would have submitted; and then you might have lost your chiefest opportunities, and those that had most needed our help, would have had least of it. Whereas now we may hope that when it is a general thing, few will refuse it; and when they see that other neighbours do it, they will be ashamed to be so singular or openly ungodly as to deny.

The work of conversion consisteth of two parts.

1. The well informing of the judgment of the necessary points.

2. The change of the will, by the efficacy of this truth. Now in this work we have the most excellent advantage for both. For the informing of their understandings, it must needs be an excellent help to have the sum of all christianity still in memory; and though bare words, not understood, will make change, yet when the words are plain English, he that hath the words is far liker to know the meaning and matter, than another; for what have we to make things known by, that are themselves invisible, but words and other subservient signs? Those, therefore, that will deride all catechisms and professions, as unprofitable forms, may better deride themselves for talking and using the form of their own words to make known their minds to others; and they may deride all God's word on the same account, which is a standing form for the guiding of preachers, and teaching all others the doctrine of eternal life. Why may not written words that are still before their eyes, and in their memories, instruct them, as well as the transient words of a preacher? These forms, therefore, of wholesome words are so far from being unprofitable, as some fantastic persons do imagine, that they are of admirable use to all.

And then we shall have the opportunity by personal conference to try them how far they understand it, and how far not; and so to explain it to them as we go; and to choose out and insist on those particulars which the persons that we speak to have most need to hear. So that these two conjunct, a form of words, with a plain explication, may do more than either of them could do alone.

Moreover, we have the best opportunity to imprint the same truths upon their hearts, when we can speak to each one's particular necessity, and say to the sinner, "Thou art the man;" and plainly mention his particular case, and set home the truth with familiar importunity. If any thing in the world is likely to do them good, it is this. They will understand a familiar speech, that hear a sermon as if it were nonsense, and they have far greater help for the application of it to themselves. And withal you shall hear their objections, and know where it is that Satan hath most advantage on them, and what it is that stands up against the truth; and so may be able to show them their errors, and confute their objections, and more effectually to convince them. We can better drive them to a stand, and urge them to discover their resolutions for the future, and to promise the use of means and reformation, than otherwise we could do. What need we more for this than our experience? I seldom deal with men purposely on this great business, in private, serious conference, but they go away with some seeming convictions, and promises of new obedience, if not some deeper remorse, and sense of their condition. And I hope your own experiences are the same.

O brethren, what a blow may we give the kingdom of darkness by the faithful and skilful managing of this work! If then the saving of souls, of your neighbours' souls, of many souls, from everlasting misery, be worth your labour, up and be doing! If the increase of the true church of Christ be desirable, this work is excellent, which is so likely to promote it. If you would be the fathers of many that shall be new-born to God, and would see the travail of your souls with comfort, and would be able to say at last, "Here am I, and the children that thou hast given me;" up then and ply this blessed work. If it will do you good, to see your holy converts among the saints in glory, and praising the Lamb before his throne; if you will be glad to present them blameless and spotless to Christ; be glad then of this singular opportunity that is offered you. If you are ministers of Christ indeed, you will long for the perfecting of his body, and the gathering in of his elect; and your hearts will be set upon it, and you will travail as in birth of them till Christ be formed in them. And then you will take such opportunities as your harvest time, and as the sunshine days in a rainy harvest, in which it is unreasonable and unexcusable to be idle. If you have any spark of christian compassion in you, it will sure seem worth your utmost labour to save so many souls from death, and to cover so great a multitude of sins. If you are indeed co-workers with Christ, set then to this work, and neglect not the souls for whom he died. O remember when you are talking with the unconverted, that now there is an opportunity in your hands to save a soul, and to rejoice the angels of heaven, and to rejoice Christ himself, and that your work is to cast Satan out of a sinner, and to increase the family of God. And what is your own hope, or joy, or crown of rejoicing? Is it not your saved people in the presence of Christ Jesus at his coming? Yea, doubtless, they are your glory and your joy, 1 Thess. ii. 19, 20.

2. The second happy benefit of our work, if well managed, will be the most orderly building up those that are converted, and the establishing them in the faith.

It hazardeth the whole work, or at least much hindereth it, when we do it not in the order that it must be done. How can you build if you first lay not a good foundation; or how can you set on the topstone while the middle parts are neglected? *Gratia non facit saltum*, any more than nature. The second order of christian truths have such dependence upon the first, that they can never be well learned till the first are learned. This makes so many deluded novices, that are puffed up with the vain conceits of knowledge while they are grossly ignorant, and itch to be preaching before they well know what it is to be christians; because they took not the work before them, but learned some lesser matters they heard most talk of, before they learned the vital principles. And this makes many labour so much in vain, and are still learning, but never come to the knowledge of the truth, because they would learn to read before they learn to spell, or to know their letters; and this makes so many fall away, and shaken with every wind of temptation, because they were not well settled in the fundamentals. It is these fundamentals that must lead men to further truths; it is these they must bottom and build upon. It is these that they must live upon, and that must actuate all their graces, and animate all their duties; it is these that must fortify them against particular temptations; and he that knows these well, doth know so much as will make him happy; and he that knows not these, knows nothing; and he that knows these best, is the best and most understanding christian. The most godly people, therefore, in your congregations will find it worth their labour to learn the very words of a catechism. And if you would safely edify them, and firmly establish them, be diligent in this work.

3. A third benefit that may be expected by the well-managing of this work, is this, It will make our public preaching to be better understood and regarded. When you have acquainted them with the principles, they will the better understand all you say. They will perceive what you drive at, when they are once acquainted with the main. This prepareth their minds, and openeth you a way to their hearts; when without this you may lose the most of your labour; and the more pains you take in accurate preparations, the less good you do. As you would not therefore lose your public labour, see that you be faithful in this private work.

4. And this is not a contemptible benefit, that by this course you will come to be familiar with your people, when you have had the opportunity of familiar conference; and the want of this with us, that have very numerous parishes, is a great impediment to the success of our labours. By distance and unacquaintedness, slanderers and deceivers have opportunity to possess them with false conceits of you, which prejudice their minds against your doctrine; and by this distance and strangeness abundance of mistakes between ministers and people are fomented. Besides that, familiarity itself doth tend to beget those affections, which may open their ears to further teaching. And when we are familiar with them, they will be more encouraged to open their doubts, and seek resolution, and deal freely with us. But when a minister knoweth not his people, or is as strange to them as if he did not know them, it must be a great hinderance to his doing them any good.

5. Besides, by the means of the private instructions, we shall come to be the better acquainted with

each person's spiritual state, and so the better know how to watch over them, and carry ourselves towards them, ever after. We may know the better how to preach to them, when we know their temper, and their chief objections, and so what they have most need to hear. We shall the better know wherein to be jealous of them with a pious jealousy, and what temptations to help them most against. We shall the better know how to lament for them, and to rejoice with them, and to pray for them to God. For as he that will pray rightly for himself, will know his own sores and wants, and the diseases of his own heart; so he that will pray rightly for others, should know theirs as far as he may, and as is meet. If a man have the charge but of sheep or cattle, he cannot so well discharge his trust, if he know them not, and their state and qualities. So is it with the master that will well teach his scholars, and parents that will rightly educate their children: and so with us.

6. And then this trial of and acquaintance with our people's state, will better satisfy us in the administration of the sacraments. We may the better understand how far they are fit or unfit. Though this give them not the state or relation of a member of that church whereof we are overseers; yet, because the members of the church universal, though they are of no particular church, may in some cases have a right to the ordinances of Christ in those particular churches where they come, and in some cases they have no right, we may by this means be the better informed how to deal with them, though they be no members of that particular church. And whereas many will question a minister that examineth his people in order to the Lord's supper, by what authority he doth it, the same work will be done this way, in a course beyond exception. Though I doubt not but a minister may require his flock to come to him at any convenient season, to receive instruction, and therefore he may do it in preparation to the sacrament; yet because ministers have laid the stress of that examination upon the mere necessity of fitness for that ordinance, and not upon their common duty to see the estate and proficiency of each member of their flock at all fit seasons, and upon the people's duty to submit to the guidance and instruction of the pastors at all times, they have therefore occasioned people ignorantly to quarrel against their examinations, and call for the proof. Whereas it is an easy thing to prove that any scholar in Christ's school is bound at any time to be accountable to his teachers, and to obey them in all lawful things in order to their own edification and salvation; though it may be more difficult to prove a necessity that a minister must so examine them in order to the Lord's supper, any more than in order to a day of thanksgiving, or a Lord's day, or the baptizing of their children.

Now by this course, we shall discern their fitness in an unquestionable way.

7. Another benefit will be this: We shall by this means be the better enabled to help our people against their particular temptations, and we shall much better prevent their entertainment of any particular errors or heresies; or their falling into schism to the hazard of themselves and the church. For men will freelier open their thoughts and scruples to us, and if they are infected already, or declined to any error or schism, they will be ready to discover it, and so may receive satisfaction before they are past cure; and familiarity with their teachers will the more encourage them to open their doubts to them at any other time. The common cause of our people's infections and heresies, is the familiarity of seducers with them, and the strangeness of their own pastors. When they hear us only in public, and hear seducers frequently in private unsaying all that we say, and we never know it, or help them against it, this settleth them in heresies before we are aware of it. Alas, our people are most of them so weak, that whoever hath, 1. Most interest in their estimations and affections; and, 2. Most opportunity in private frequent conferences to instil his opinions into them, of that man's religion will they ordinarily be. It is pity then that we should let deceivers take such opportunities to undo them, and we should not be as industrious, and use our advantages to their good. We have much advantage against seducers in many respects, if our negligence and their diligence did not frustrate them.

8. Another, and one of the greatest benefits of our work will be this: It will better inform men of the true nature of the ministerial office, or awaken them to better consideration of it, than is now usual. It is now too common for men to think that the work of the ministry is nothing but to preach well, and to baptize and administer the Lord's supper, and visit the sick; and by this means the people will submit to no more, and too many ministers are negligently or wilfully such strangers to their own calling, that they will do no more. It hath oft grieved my heart to observe some eminent able preachers, how little they do for the saving of souls, save only in the pulpit; and to how little purpose much of their labour is, by this neglect. They have hundreds of people that they never spoke a word to personally for their salvation; and if we may judge by their practice, they take it not for their duty: and the principal thing that hardeneth men in this oversight, is the common neglect of the private part of the work by others. There are so few that do much in it, and the omission is grown so common among pious, able men, that they have abated the disgrace of it by their parts; and a man may now be guilty of it, without any common observance or dishonour. Never doth sin so reign in a church or state, as when it hath gained reputation, or at least is no disgrace to the sinner, nor a matter of any offence to beholders. But I make no doubt through the mercy of God, but the restored practice of personal oversight will convince many ministers that this is as truly their work as that which they now do; and may awaken them to see that the ministry is another kind of business than too many excellent preachers do take it to be. Brethren, do but set yourselves closely to this work, and follow on diligently; and though you do it silently, without any words to them that are negligent, I am in hope that most of you here may live to see the day, that the neglect of private personal oversight of all the flock shall be taken for a scandalous and odious omission, and shall be as disgraceful to them that are guilty of it, as preaching but once a day was heretofore. A schoolmaster must not only read a common lecture, but take a personal account of his scholars, or else he is like to do little good. If physicians should only read a public lecture of physic, their patients would not be much the better for them; nor would a lawyer secure your estate by reading a lecture of law. The charge of a pastor requireth personal dealing as well as any of these. Let us show the world this by our practice; for most men are grown regardless of bare words.

The truth is, we have been occasioned exceedingly to wrong the church in this, by the contrary extreme of the papists, who bring all their people to auricular confession; for in the overthrowing of this error of theirs, we have run into the contrary extreme, and led our people much further into it than we are gone ourselves. It troubled me to read in an orthodox historian, that licentiousness, and a desire to be from under the strict inquiries of the priests in confession, did much further the entertainment of the reformed religion in Germany. And yet it is like enough to be true, that they that were against reformation in other respects, yet partly for the change, and partly on that licentious account, might join with better men in crying down the Romish clergy. But by this means, lest we should seem to favour the said auricular confession, we have too commonly neglected all personal instruction; except when we occasionally fall into men's company, few make it a stated part of their work. I am past doubt that the popish auricular confession is a sinful novelty, which the ancient church was unacquainted with. But perhaps some will think strange that I should say, that our common neglect of personal instruction is much worse, if we consider their confessions in themselves, and not as they respect their connexed doctrines of satisfaction and purgatory. Many of the southern and eastern churches do use a confession of sin to the priest, and how far Mr. Thomas Hooker in his "Soul's Preparation," and other divines, do ordinarily require it, as necessary or useful, is well known. If any among us should be guilty of this gross mistake, as to think when he hath preached, he hath done all his work, let us show him to his face by our practice of the rest, that there is much more to be done, and that taking heed to all the flock is another business, than careless, lazy ministers do consider of. If a man have the least apprehension that duty, and the chiefest duty, is no duty, he is like to neglect it, and be impenitent in the neglect.

9. Another singular benefit which we may hope for from the faithful performance of this new work, is, that it will help our people better to understand the nature of their duty towards their overseers, and consequently to discharge it better. Which were no matter if it were only for our sakes; but their own salvation is very much concerned in it. I am confident by sad experience, that it is none of the least impediments to their happiness, and to a true reformation of the church, that the people understand not what the work and power of a minister is, and what their own duty towards them is. They commonly think that a minister hath no more to do with them but to preach to them, and visit them in sickness, and administer sacraments, and that if they hear him, and receive the sacrament from him, they owe no further obedience, nor can he require any more at their hands. Little do they know that the minister is in the church, as the schoolmaster in his school, to teach and take an account of every one in particular, and that all christians ordinarily must be disciples or scholars in some such school. They think not that a minister is in the church as a physician in a town, for all people to resort to, for personal advice for the curing of all those diseases that are fit to be brought to a physician: and that the priest's lips must preserve knowledge, and the people must ask the law at his mouth, because he is the messenger of the Lord of hosts: and that every soul in the congregation is bound for their own safety, to have personal recourse to him for the resolving of their doubts, and for help against their sins, and for direction in duty, and for increase of knowledge and all saving grace: and that ministers are purposely settled in congregations to this end, to be still ready to advise and help the flock. If our people did but know their duty, they would readily come to us when they are desired, to be instructed, and to give an account of their knowledge, faith, and lives; and they would come themselves without sending for, and knock oftener at our doors, and call for advice and help for their souls; and ask, What shall we do to be saved? Whereas now the matter is come to that sad pass, that they think a minister hath nothing to do with them, and if he admonish them, they will bid him look to himself, he shall not answer for them: and if he call them to be catechised or instructed, or to be prepared for the Lord's supper, or other holy ordinances, or would take an account of their faith and profiting, they will ask him, by what authority he doth these things; and think that he is a busy and pragmatical fellow, that loves to be meddling where he hath nothing to do; or a proud fellow, that would bear rule over their consciences. When they may as well ask him, by what authority he preacheth, or prayeth for them, or giveth them the sacrament; or they may as well ask a schoolmaster, by what authority he calls his scholars to learn or say their lesson; or a physician, by what authority he enjoineth them to take his medicines. People consider not that all our authority is but for our work, even a power to do our duty, and our work is for them; so it is but an authority to do them good. And the silly wretches do talk no wiselier than if they should thus quarrel with a man that would help to quench the fire in their thatch, and ask him by what authority he doth it; or that would give his money to relieve the poor, and they should ask him, by what authority do you require us to take this money; or as if I offered my hand to one that is fallen to help him up, or to one that is in the water to save him from drowning, and he should ask me by what authority I do it. Truly, we have no wiser nor thankfuller dealing from these men; nay, it is worse, in that we are doubly obliged, both by christian charity and the ministerial office, to do them good. I know not of any simile that doth more aptly express the ministerial power and duty, and the people's duty, than these two conjunct: viz. Even such as a physician is in an hospital, that hath taken the charge of it, and such as a schoolmaster is in his school, especially such as the philosophers, or teachers of any science or art, whose schools have the aged and voluntary members, as well as children; Christ's hath all ages; even such is a minister in the church, and such is their work, and their authority to do it, and the duty of the people to submit thereto; allowing such differences as the subject requireth.

And what is it that hath brought people to this ignorance of their duty, but custom? It is long of us, brethren, to speak truly and plainly, it is long of us, that have not used them nor ourselves to any more than common public work. We see how much custom doth with the people. Where it is the custom, they stick not among the papists at the confessing of all their sins to the priest; and because it is not the custom among us, they disdain to be questioned, catechised, or instructed. They wonder at it as a strange thing, and say, Such things were never done before. And if we can but prevail to make this duty become as usual as other duties, they will much more easily submit to it than now. What a happy thing would it be if you might live to see the day that it should be as ordinary for people of all ages to come in course to their teachers for personal advice, and help for their salvation, as it is now usual for them to come to the church, or as it is for them to send their children thither to be catechised. Our diligence in this work is the way to do this.

10. Moreover, our practice will give the governors of the nation some better information about the

nature and burden of the ministry, and so may procure their further assistance. It is a lamentable impediment to the reformation of the church and the saving of souls, that in most populous congregations, there is but one or two men to oversee many thousand souls, and so there are not labourers in any measure answerable to the work. But it becomes an impossible thing to them to do any considerable measure of that personal duty which should be done by faithful pastors to all the flock. I have often said it, and still must say it, that this is a great part of England's misery, and a great degree of spiritual famine which reigns in most cities and great towns through the land, even where they are insensible of it, and think themselves well provided. Alas, we see multitudes of carnal, ignorant, sensual sinners, round about us! Here is a family, and there a family, and there almost a whole street or village of them, and our hearts pity them; and we see that their necessities cry aloud for our speedy and diligent relief, so that he that hath ears to hear must needs hear it: and if we would never so fain, we cannot help them; not only through their obstinacy, but also through our want of opportunity. We have experience, that if we could but have leisure to speak to them, and to open plainly to them their sin and danger, there were great hopes of doing good to many of them, that receive little by our public teaching. But we cannot come at them: more necessary work prohibits us: we cannot do both at once; and the public must be preferred, because there we deal with many at once: and it is as much as we are able to do, to perform the public work, or some little more. And if we do take the time when we should eat or sleep, besides the ruining of our weakened bodies by it, we shall not be able, after all, to speak to one of very many of them. So that we must stand by and see our people perish, and can but be sorry for them, and cannot so much as speak to them to endeavour their recovery. Is not this a sad case in a nation that glorieth of the fulness of the gospel? An infidel will say, no; but methinks no man that believes an everlasting joy or torment, should say so. I will give you the instance of my own case: We are together two ministers, and a third at a chapel, willing to bestow every hour of our time in Christ's work. Before we undertook this work that we are now upon, our hands were full, and now we are engaged to set apart two days every week from morning to night for private catechism and instruction; so that any man may see that we must leave undone all that other work that we were wont to do at that time: and we are necessitated to run upon the public work of preaching with small preparation, and so must deliver the message of God so rawly and confusedly, and unanswerably to its dignity, and the needs of men's souls, that it is a great trouble to our minds to consider it, and a greater trouble to us when we are doing it. And yet it must be so: there is no remedy. Unless we will omit this personal instruction, we must needs run thus unprepared into the pulpit; and to omit this we dare not, it is so great and necessary a work. And when we have incurred all the forementioned inconveniences, and have set two whole days a week apart for the work that we have now undertaken, it will be as much as we shall be able to do, to go over the parish but once in a year, being about eight hundred families; and, which is worse than that, we shall be forced to cut it short, and do it less effectually to those that we do it, having above fifteen families a week to deal with. And alas, how small a matter is it to speak to a man once only in a year, and that so cursorily as we must be forced to do, in comparison of what their necessities do require! Yet are we in hope of some fruit of this much; but how much more might it be, if we could but speak to them once a quarter, and do the work more fully and deliberately, as you that are in smaller parishes may do. And many ministers in England have ten times, if not more, the number of parishioners that I have; so that if they should undertake the work that we have done, they can go over the parish but once in ten years! So that while we are hoping for opportunities to speak to them, we hear of one dying after another; and, to the grief of our souls, are forced to go with them to their graves, before we could ever speak a word to them personally to prepare them for their change. And what is the cause of all this misery? Why our rulers have not seen a necessity of any more ministers than one or two in such parishes; and so they have not allowed any maintenance to that end. Some have alienated much from the church, (the Lord humble all them that consented to it effectually, lest it prove the consumption of the nation at last,) while they have left this famine in the chief parts of the land. It is easy to separate from the multitude; and gather distinct churches, and let the rest sink or swim, and if they will not be saved by public preaching, let them be damned; but whether this be the most charitable and christian course, one would think should be no hard question. But what is the matter that wise and godly rulers should be thus guilty of our misery, and that none of our cries will awaken them to compassion? What! are they so ignorant as not to know these things? Or are they grown cruel to the souls of men; or are they falsehearted to the interest of Christ, and have a design to undermine his kingdom? No; I hope it is none of these, but for aught I can find, it is even long of us, even of us the ministers of the gospel, whom they should thus maintain. For those ministers that have small parishes, and might do all this private part of the work, yet do it not, but very few of them, nor will not do it: and those in great towns and cities, that might do somewhat, though they cannot do all, will do just nothing but what accidentally falls in their way, or next to nothing; so that the magistrate is not wakened to an observance or consideration of the weight of our work. If it be not in their eyes, as well as in their ears, they will not regard it. Or if they do apprehend the usefulness of it, yet if they see that ministers are so careless and lazy that they will not do it, they think it in vain to provide them a maintenance for it—it would be but to cherish idle drones; and so they think that if they maintain ministers enough to preach in the pulpit, they have done their parts; and thus are they involved in heinous sin, and we are the occasions of it. Whereas if we do but heartily all set ourselves to this work, and show the magistrate to his face, that it is a most weighty and necessary part of our business, and that we would do it thoroughly if we could, and that if there were hands enough at it, the work might go on; and withal, when he shall see the happy success of our labours; then, no doubt, if the fear of God be in them, and they have any love to his truth and men's souls, they will set to their helping hand, and not let men perish because there is no man to speak to them to prevent it. They will one way or other raise a maintenance in such populous places for labourers proportioned to the number of souls, and greatness of the work. Let them but see us fall to the work, and see it prosper in our hands; as if it be well managed, through God's blessing, there is no doubt but it will do; and then it will draw our hearts to the promoting of it: and instead of laying parishes together to diminish the number of teachers, they will either divide them, or allow more teachers to a parish. But when they see that many carnal ministers do make a greater stir to have more maintenance to themselves, than to have more help in the work of God, they are tempted by such worldlings to wrong the church, that particular ministers may have ease and fulness.

11. Another benefit that is like to follow our work, is this: It may exceedingly facilitate the ministerial service to the next generation that shall succeed us, and prevent the rebellion of people against their teachers. As I said, custom is the thing that sways much with the multitude; and they that first break a destructive custom, must bear the brunt of their indignation. Somebody must do this. If we do it not, it will lie upon our successors; and how can we look that they should be more hardy, and resolute, and faithful than we? It is we that have seen the heavy judgments of the Lord, and heard him pleading by fire and sword with the land. It is we that have been ourselves in the furnace, and should be the most refined, Mal. iii. 23. It is we that are most deeply obliged by oaths and covenants, by wonderful deliverances, experiences, and mercies of all sorts; and if we flinch and turn our back, and prove false-hearted, why should we expect better from them, that have not been driven by such scourges as we, nor drawn by such cords. But if they do prove better than we, and will do it, the same odium and opposition must befall them which we avoid, and that with some increase, because of our neglect; for the people will tell them that we, their predecessors, did no such things. But if we would now break through, that are set in the front, and break the ice for them that follow us, their souls will bless us, and our names shall be dear to them, and they will feel the happy fruits of our labour every week and day of their ministry. When the people shall willingly submit to their private instructions and examinations, yea, and to discipline too, because we have acquainted them with it, and removed the prejudice, and broke the evil custom that our foregoers had been the cause of; and so we may do much to the saving of many thousand souls in all ages to come, as well as in the present age that we are working in.

12. Another benefit will be this: We shall keep our people's minds and time from much of that vanity that now possesseth them. When men are at work in their shops, almost all their talk is vanity; the children also learn foolish and ribald songs and tales; and with such filth and rubbish are their memories furnished. Many an hour is lost, and many a thousand idle thoughts and words are they guilty of. Whereas when they once know the catechisms must be learned, and that they must all give account, it will turn much of their thoughts and time that way.

13. Moreover, it will do much to the better ordering of families, and better spending of the Lord's day. When we have once got the master of the family to undertake it, that he will once every Lord's day examine his family, and hear them what they can say of the catechism, it will find them the most profitable employment; whereas otherwise, many of them would be idle, or ill employed; and many masters that know little themselves, may yet be brought to do this for others.

14. Moreover, it will do some good to many ministers that are apt to be too idle, and mispend their time in unnecessary discourses and businesses, as journeys, or recreations; and it will let them see that they have no time to spare for such things. And so when they are engaged in so much pressing employment, of so high a nature, it will be the best cure for all that idleness or loss of time; and withal, it will cut off that scandal which usually followeth thereupon: for people use to say, Such a minister can sit in an ale-house or tavern, or spend his time at bowls, or other sports, or vain discourse; and why may not we do so as well as he? Let us set close to this part of our work, and then see what time we can find to spare, and live idly, or in a way of voluptuousness, yea or worldliness, if we can.

15. And many personal benefits to ourselves are consequential to these. It will do much, 1. To exercise and increase our own graces; and, 2. To subdue our own corruptions. And, 3. Besides our safety, it will breed much peace to our own consciences, and comfort us when our time and actions must be reviewed.

(1.) To be much in provoking others to repentance, and heavenly-mindedness, may do much to excite them in ourselves.

(2.) To cry down the sin of others, and engage them against it, and direct them to overcome it, will do much to shame us out of our own; and conscience will scarce suffer us to live in that which we make so much ado to draw others from. And this very constant employment for God, and busying our minds and tongues against sin, and for Christ and holiness, will do much to habituate us, and to overcome our fleshly inclinations, both by direct mortification, and by diversion, leaving our fancies no room nor time for their old employment. I dare say, that all austerities of monks and hermits, who addict themselves to unprofitable solitude, and are the true imitators of the unprofitable servant, (Matt. xxv.) that hid his talent because his master was an austere man, and that think to save themselves by neglecting to show compassion to others, will not do near so much in the true work of mortification, as this fruitful diligence for Christ will do.

16. And it will be some benefit, that by this means we shall take off ourselves and our people from vain controversies, and from letting out our care and zeal and talk upon the lesser things in religion, which least tend to their spiritual edification: for while we are taken up in teaching, and they in learning, the fundamentals, we shall divert our minds and tongues, and have less room for lower things; and so it will cure much wranglings and contentions between ministers and people; for we do that which we need not and should not, because we will not fall closely to do that which we need and should.

And if we could handsomely contrive the more understanding sort of our people to assist us in private helping others, (though prejudice of others, and their own unripeness and unfitness, much hinder,) it would be the most effectual way to prevent their running into preaching distempers, or into schisms; for this employment would take them up, and content the teaching humour that they are inclined to. And it might make their parts more useful in a safe and lawful way.

17. Moreover, the very diligent practice of this work that we are upon, would do much to set men right about many controversies that now trouble the church, and so put an end to our differences. Especially most of those about the ministry, churches, and discipline, would receive more convincing light by practice, than all our idle talking or writing will afford us. We have fallen of late into parties, and troubled the church about many controversies concerning excommunication, in such and such cases, which perhaps will never fall out; or if they do, they cannot be so well decided by any man that is not engaged in the practice. It is like the profession of a physician, a soldier, a pilot, &c. who can never

be worth a straw at his work, by all the precepts in the world, without practice and experience. This will be the only course to make, (1.) Sound divines in the main, which bare studying will not do. (2.) And recover us again to the primitive simplicity, to live upon the substantial, necessary things. (3.) And to direct and resolve us in many of our quarrels that will no other way be well resolved. For example: If this work had been set on foot, and it had been but visible, what is it to have the oversight of souls? durst any prelates have contended for the sole oversight of two hundred, four hundred, or a thousand churches; and that the presbyters might be but their curates and informers? Durst they have striven with might and main, to have drawn upon themselves such impossibilities, and have carried such mountains on their back, and to answer God as overseers and pastors of so many thousand people, whose faces they were never like to see, much less were they ever like to speak one word to them for their everlasting life? Would they not have said, If I must be a bishop, let me be a parochial bishop, or have no more to oversee than I am capable of overseeing; and let me be such as the primitive bishops were, that had but one church, and not hundreds to take care of; and let me not be engaged to natural impossibilities, and that on pain of damnation, and to the certain destruction of the business that I undertake. Sure these would rather have been their strivings. I speak not this against any bishops that acknowledge the presbyters to be true pastors to rule and teach the flock, and take themselves only to be the chief or presidents among the presbyters, yea, or the rulers of presbyters, that are the rulers of the flock; but of them that null the presbyter's office, and the church's government and discipline, by undertaking it alone as their sole prerogative.

Many other disciplinary controversies I might instance in, that will be better resolved by this course of practice, by the abundant experience which it will afford, than by all the disputations or writings that have attempted it.

18. And when for the extent of the aforesaid benefits, which in the two next places shall now be considered, the design of this work is, the reforming and saving of all the people in our several parishes; for we shall not leave out any man that will submit to be instructed. And though we can scarce hope that every particular person will be reformed and saved by it, yet have we reason to hope, that as the attempt is universal, so the success will be more general or extensive than hitherto we have seen of our other labours. Sure I am it is most like to the spirit, and precept, and offers of the gospel, which requireth us to preach the gospel to every creature, and promiseth life to every man if he will accept it by believing. If God would have all men to be saved, and to come to the knowledge of the truth, that is, as Rector and Benefactor of the world, he hath manifested himself willing to save all men if they will themselves, though his elect he will also make willing; then sure it beseems us to offer salvation unto all men, and to endeavour to bring them to the knowledge of the truth: and if Christ tasted death for every man, it is meet we should preach his death to every man. This work hath a more excellent design, than our accidental conferences with now and then a particular person. And I observe that in such occasional discourses men satisfy themselves to have spoken some good word, but seldom set plainly and closely to the matter, to convince men of sin, misery, and mercy, as in this purposely appointed work we are now more like to do.

19. And further, it is like to be a work that shall reach over the whole land, and not stop with us that have now engaged in it. For though it be at the present neglected, I suppose the cause is the same with our brethren as it hath all this while been with us; who by vain expectations of the magistrates' interposition, or by that inconsiderateness, and laziness which we are bewailing here this day, have so much omitted it till now as we have done; but especially a despair of a common submission of the people hath been the hinderance. But when they shall be remembered of so clear and great a duty, and excited to the consideration of it, and see with us the feasibleness of it, in a good measure, when it is done by common consent, no doubt they will universally take it up, and gladly concur with us in so blessed a work. For they are the servants of the same God, as regardful of their flocks, and as conscientious as we, and as sensible of the interest of Christ, and as compassionate to men's souls, and as self-denying, and as ready to do or suffer for such excellent ends. Seeing therefore they have the same Spirit, rule, and Lord, I will not be so uncharitable as to doubt, whether all that are godly, or the generality of them, will gladly join with us through all the land. And oh what a happy thing it will be to see such a general combination for Christ; and to see all England so seriously called upon, and importuned for Christ, and set in so fair a way to heaven! Methinks the consideration of it should make our hearts rejoice within us, to see so many faithful servants of Christ all over the land, to fall in with every particular sinner with such industrious solicitations for the saving of their souls, as men that will hardly take a denial. Methinks I even see all the godly ministers of England even setting upon the work already, and resolving to take the opportunity that unanimity may facilitate it; which if they do, no doubt but God will succeed them. Is it not then a most happy undertaking that you are all setting your hands to, and desiring the assistance of Christ in this day?

20. Lastly, of so great weight and excellency is the duty that we are upon, that the chiefest part of church reformation that is behind, as to means, consisteth in it; and it must be the chiefest means to answer the judgment, the mercies, the prayers, the promises, the cost, the endeavours, and blood of the nation: and without this it will not be done; the ends of all these will never be well attained; a reformation to purpose will never be wrought; the church will be still low, the interest of Christ will be much neglected; and God will still have a controversy with the land, and above all, with the ministry that have been deepest in the guilt.

How long have we talked of reformation, how much have we said and done for it in general, and how deeply and devoutly have we vowed it for our own parts (of which more anon)! And after all this, how shamefully have we neglected it, and neglect it to this day! We carry ourselves as if we had not known or considered what that reformation was that we vowed. As carnal men will take on them to be christians, and profess with confidence that they believe in Christ, accept of his salvation, and may contend for Christ, and fight for him, and yet for all this would have none of him, but perish for refusing him, who little dreamed that ever they had been refusers of him; and all because they understood not what his salvation is, and how it is carried on; but dream of a salvation without flesh-displeasing, and without self-denying, and renouncing the world, and parting with their sins, and without any holiness or any great pains and labour of their own in subserviency to Christ and the Spirit: even so did too many ministers and private men talk, and write, and pray, and sigh, and long for reformation, and would little have believed that man, that should have presumed to tell them that for all this their very hearts were against reformation, and that they that were praying for it, and fasting for it, and wading through blood for it, would never accept it, but would themselves be the rejecters and destroyers of it. And yet so it is, and so it hath too plainly proved. And whence is all this strange deceit of heart, that good men should no better know themselves? Why, the case is plain: they thought of a reformation to be given by God, but not of a reformation to be wrought on and by themselves. They considered the blessing, but never thought of the means of accomplishing it. But as if they had expected that all things besides themselves should be mended without them; or that the Holy Ghost should again descend miraculously; or every sermon should convert its thousands; or that some angel from heaven, or some Elias, should be sent to restore all things; or that the law of a parliament, and the sword of a magistrate, would have converted or constrained all, and have done the deed. And little did they think of a reformation that must be wrought by their own diligence and unwearied labours, by earnest preaching, and catechising, and personal instructions, and taking heed to all the flock, whatever pains or reproaches it should cost them. They thought not that a thorough reformation must multiply their own work. But we had all of us too carnal thoughts, that when we had ungodly men at our mercy, all would be done, and conquering them was converting them, or such a means as would have frightened them to heaven. But the business is far otherwise; and had we then known how a reformation must be attained, perhaps some would have been colder in the prosecution of it. And yet I know that even foreseen labours seem small matters at a distance, while we do but hear or talk of them; but when we come nearer them, and must lay our hands to the work, and put on our armour, and charge through the thickest of opposing difficulties, then is the sincerity and the strength of men's hearts brought to trial, and it will appear how they purposed and promised before. Reformation is to many of us, as the Messiah was to the Jews. Before he came they looked and longed for him, and boasted of him, and rejoiced in hope of him; but when he came, they could not abide him, but hated him, and would not believe that he was indeed the person, and therefore persecuted and put him to death, to the curse and confusion of the main body of their nation. "The Lord whom we seek, shall suddenly come to his temple, even the messenger of the covenant, whom ye delight in. But who can abide the day of his coming, and who shall stand when he appeareth? For he is like a refiner's fire, and like fuller's soap: and he shall purify the sons of Levi, and purge them as gold and silver, that they may offer to the Lord an offering in righteousness," Mal. iii. 1—3. And the reason was, because it was another manner of Christ that the Jews expected, than Jesus was that did appear to them; it was one to bring them riches, and liberty, and to this day they profess that they will never believe in any but such. So it is with too many about reformation. They hoped for a reformation that should bring them more wealth and honour with the people, and power to force men to do what they would have them; and now they see a reformation that must put them to more condescension and pains than ever they were at before: this will not down with them. They thought of having the opposers of godliness under their feet; but now they see they must go to them with humble entreaties, and put their hands under their feet, if it would do them good, and meekly beseech even those that sometimes sought their lives; and make it now their daily business to overcome them by kindness, and win them with love. Oh how many carnal expectations are here crossed!

Hence also it is, that most men do lay so great a part of reformation in their private opinions or singular ways. The prelatical party think that the true reformation is to restore them to power; the presbyterians have thought, that if prelacy and independency were well down, and classes up, the work were much done; and the independents have thought, that if they had gathered a separated body of godly people under covenant, much of the reformation were wrought; and the anabaptists have thought, that if they could but get people to be baptized again, they had done a great matter for reformation. I am not now reproving any of these in the matter, though the last, especially, well deserve it, but that they lay so much upon their several orders and formalities as many of them do: when indeed if we had our will in all such matters of order, and had the rightest form of government in the world, it is the painful execution, and the diligent and prudent use of means for men's conversion and edification, by able, faithful men, that must accomplish the reformation. Brethren, I dare confidently tell you, that if you will faithfully perform what you have agreed upon, both in this business of catechising and personal instruction, and in the matter of discipline formerly, where we have well waved all the controverted part, which hath so much ascribed to it, you will do more for the true reformation, that is so desirable, and hath been so long prayed and eagerly contended for, are ever like to effect. If bishops would do this work, I would take them for reformers; and if presbyters will do it, I will take them for reformers; and it was those that neglected and hindered it, that I ever took for *deformers*. Let us see the work well done, that God hath made so necessary for men's conversion, preservation, restoration, and salvation, and the doers of it, whether prelates or presbyters, shall never have fierce opposition of mine. But it is not bare canons, and orders, and names, and shows, that any wise man will take for the substance of reformation. It is not circumcision or uncircumcision, to be a Jew or a gentile, bond or free, that availeth any thing, but a new creature, and faith that worketh by love. That is the reformation which best healeth the ignorance, and infidelity, and pride, and hypocrisy, and worldliness, and other killing sins of the land, and that most effectually bringeth men to faith and holiness. Not that I would have the least truth or duty undervalued, or any part of God's will to be rejected: but the kingdom of God consisteth not in every truth or duty; not in ceremonies or circumstances; not in meats or drinks; but in righteousness and peace, and joy in the Holy Ghost.

Dear brethren, it is you, and such as you, that under Christ must yet give this nation the fruit of all their prayers and pains, their cost and blood, and heavy sufferings. All that they have been doing for the good of the church, and for the true reformation for so many years, was but to prepare the way for you to come in and do the work which they desired. Alas, what would they do by fire and sword, by drums and trumpets, for converting of souls? The actions of armies and famous commanders which seem so glorious, and make so great a noise that the world rings with them, what have they done, or what can they do that is worth the talking on, without you? In themselves considered, all their victories and great achievements are so far from being truly glorious, that they are lamentable; and a butcher may as well glory that he hath killed so many beasts, or a hangman that he hath executed so many men, as they can glory in the thing considered in itself; for war is the most heavy temporal judgment; and far less cause would they have to glory, if their cause and end were wrong. And if their hearts, and end, and cause be right, and they mean as honestly as any men in the world, yet are these great commanders but your pioneers, to cut up the thorns that stand in your way, and to cast out the rubbish, and prepare you the way to build the house. Alas, they cannot with all their victories exalt the Lord Jesus in the soul of any sinner; and therefore they cannot set up his spiritual kingdom, for the hearts of men are his house and throne. If the work should stop with the end of theirs, and go no further than they can carry it, we should be in the end but where we were in the beginning; and one generation of Christ's enemies would succeed another, and they that take down the wicked would inherit their vices, as they possess their rooms, and the last would be far the worst, as being deeper in the guilt, and more engaged in evil-doing. All this trouble then, and stir of the nation, hath been to bring the work to your hands; and shall it die there? God forbid! They have opened you the door; and, at exceeding cost and sufferings, have removed many of your impediments, and put the building instruments into your hands; and will you now stand still and loiter? God forbid! Up then, brethren, and give the nation the fruit of their cost and pains. Frustrate not all the Preparer's works: fail not the long expectations of so many thousands that have prayed in hope of a true reformation; and paid in hope, and ventured in hope, and suffered in hope, and waited till now in hope. In the name of God, take heed that now you fail not of these hopes! Have they spent so long time of fencing the vineyard, and weeding and pruning it, and making it ready for your hands, and will you fail them that are sent to gather in the vintage, and lose their labours? When they have ploughed the field, will you sow it by halves? If they had known beforehand that ministers would have proved idle and unfaithful, how many hundreds would have spared their blood, and how many thousands would have sat still, and have let the old readers and formalists alone, and have said, If we must have dullards and unprofitable men, it is as good have one as another; it is not worth so much cost and pains to change one careless minister for another. The end is the mover and life of the agent in all the means. How many thousands have prayed, and paid, and suffered, and more upon the expectation of a great advantage to the church, and more common illumination and reformation of the nation by your means; and will you now deceive them all? Again I say, God forbid! Now it is at your hands that they are expecting the happy issue of all. The eyes of the nation are, or should be, all under God upon you, for the bringing in the harvest of their cost and labours. I profess, it maketh me admire at the fearful deceitfulness of the heart of man, to see how every man can call on others for duty, or censure them for the omitting it, and what excellent judges we are in men's cases, and how partial in our own! The very judicious teachers of the nation can cry out, and too justly, against one sect and another sect, and against unfaithful underminers of those that they thought would have done the work, and against the disturbers of the reformation that was going on, and say, These have betrayed the church, and frustrated the nation's cost and hopes, and undone all that hath been so long a doing. And yet they see not, or seem not to see, that it is we that are guilty of this, as much as they. It was not the magistrates' driving, but the ministers' drawing, that was the principal saving means that we have waited for. Brethren, it were a strange mistake, sure, if any of us should think, that the price of the nation's wealth and blood was purposed to settle us in good benefices, and to pull down the bishops, and give us the quiet possession of our livings which they would have deprived us of. Was this the reformation, that we might live in greater ease and fulness, and succeed the ejected ministers in their less disgraced sins? Why, sirs, what are we more than other men, that the people should do all this for us? that they should impoverish the whole nation almost to provide us a livelihood? What can they see in our persons, or countenances, for which they should so dote upon us? Are we not men, frail and corruptible flesh, unworthy sinners like themselves? Surely it was for our work, and the ends of our work, and not for our persons, but in order to our work, that they have done all this. What say you now, brethren? Will you deal faithfully with your creditors, and pay the nation the debt which you owe them? Shall all the blood and cost of this people be frustrated or not? You are now called upon to give your answer, and it is you that must give it. The work is now before you; and in these personal instructions of all the flock, as well as in public preaching, doth it consist. Others have done their part, and borne their burden, and now comes in yours. You may easily see how great a matter lies upon your hands, and how many will be wronged by your failing, and how much by the sparing of your labour will be lost. If your labour be more worth than all our treasures, hazards, and lives, and than the souls of men and the blood of Christ; then sit still, and look not after the ignorant or the ungodly; follow your pleasures or worldly business, or take your ease: displease not sinners, nor your own flesh; but let your neighbours sink or swim; and if public preaching will not save them, let them perish. But if the case be far otherwise, you were best look about you. But I shall say more of this anon.

SECTION II.

II. Having given you the first sort of moving reasons, which were drawn from the benefits of the present undertaken work, I come to the *second* sort, which are taken from the *difficulties;* which if they were taken alone, or in a needless business, I confess might be rather discouragements than motives; but taking these with those that go before and follow, the case is otherwise. For difficulties must excite to greater diligence in a necessary work. And difficulties we shall find many both in ourselves and in our people; which, because they are things so obvious, that your experience will leave no room for doubting, I shall take leave to pass them over in a few words.

1. In ourselves there is much dulness and laziness, so that there will be much ado to get us to be faithful in so hard a work. Like a sluggard in bed, that knows he should rise, and yet delayeth and would stay as long as he can; so do we by duties that our corrupt natures are against, and put us to the use of all our powers. Mere sloth will tie the hands of many.

2. We have also a base man-pleasing disposition, which will make us let men perish lest we lose their love, and let them go quietly to hell lest we should make them angry with us for seeking their salvation;

and we are ready to venture on the displeasure of God, and venture our people into everlasting misery, rather than get ill-will to ourselves. This distemper must be diligently resisted.

3. We have some of us also a foolish bashfulness, which makes us very backward to begin with them, and to speak plainly to them. We are so modest forsooth, that we blush to speak of Christ, or to contradict the devil, or to save a soul; when shameful works we are less ashamed of.

4. We are so carnal, that we are prone by our fleshly interests to be drawn to unfaithfulness in the work of Christ. Lest we lose our tithes, or bring trouble upon ourselves, or set people against us, and many such like. All these require diligence for their resistance.

5. The greatest impediment of all is, that we are too weak in the faith; so that when we should set upon a man for his conversion with all our might, if there be not the stirrings of unbelief within us, to rise up actual questionings of heaven and hell, whether the things that we should earnestly press be true; yet at least the belief of them is so weak, that it will hardly excite in us so kindly, resolute, and constant zeal: so that our whole motion will be but weak, because the spring of faith is so weak. Oh what need therefore have all ministers for themselves and their work, to look well to their faith, especially that their assent to the truth of Scripture, about the joy and torments of the life to come, be sound and lively.

6. And lastly, we have commonly a great deal of unskilfulness and unfitness for this work. Alas, how few know to deal with an ignorant, worldly man for salvation! To get within him, and win upon him, and suit all speeches to men's several conditions and temper, to choose the meetest subjects, and follow them with the holy mixture of seriousness, and terror, and love, and meekness, and evangelical allurements! Oh who is fit for such a thing! I profess seriously, it seems to me, by experience, as hard a matter to confer aright with such a carnal person in order to his change, as to preach such sermons as ordinarily we do, if not much more. All these difficulties in ourselves, should waken us to resolutions, preparations, and diligence, that we be not overcome by them, and hindered from or in the work.

Secondly, And for our people, we have as many difficulties to encounter with in them. 1. Too many of them will be obstinately unwilling to be taught; and scorn to come at us, as being too good to be catechised, or too old to learn, unless we deal wisely with them in public and private, by the force of reasons, and the power of love, to conquer their perverseness; which we must carefully endeavour.

2. And so great is the dulness of many that are willing, that they can scarce learn a leaf of a catechism in a long time, and therefore will keep away, as ashamed of their ignorance, unless we are wise and diligent to encourage them.

3. And when they do come, so great is their ignorance and unapprehensiveness, that you will find it a wonderful hard matter to get them to understand you; so that if you have not the skill of making things plain, you will leave them as strange to it as before.

4. And yet harder will you find it to work things upon their hearts, and set them so close to the quick, as to make that saving change, which is our end, and without which our labour is almost lost. Oh what a block, what a rock is a hardened, carnal heart! How stiffly will it resist the most powerful persuasions, and hear of everlasting life or death, as a thing of nothing! If you have not therefore great seriousness, and fervency, and working matter, and fitness of expression, what good can you expect? And when all is done, the Spirit of grace must do the work: but as God and men do use to choose instruments most suitable to the nature of the agent, work, or end, so here the Spirit of wisdom, life, and holiness, doth not use to work by foolish, dead, or carnal instruments, but by such persuasions of light, and life, and purity, as are likest to itself, and to the work that is to be wrought thereby.

5. And when you have made some desirable impressions on their hearts, if you look not after them, and have a special care of them when they are gone, their hearts will soon return to their former hardness, and their old companions and temptations will work off all again. I do but briefly hint these things which you so well know. All the difficulties of the work of conversion, which you use to acquaint the people with, are here before us in our present work; which I will forbear to enumerate, as supposing it unnecessary.

SECTION III.

III. The *third* sort of moving reasons are drawn from the *necessity* of the undertaken work: for if it were not necessary, the lazy might be discouraged rather than excited, by the forementioned difficulties, as is aforesaid. And if we should here expatiate, we might find matter for a volume by itself. But because I have already been longer than I did intend, I shall only give you a brief hint of some of the general grounds of this necessity.

And, 1. It is necessary by obligation, *Ut Officium, necessitate præcepti:* and, 2. It is necessary *ad finem;* and that, 1. For God; 2. For our neighbours; 3. And for ourselves.

1. For the first of these. (1.) We have on us the obligation of Scripture precepts. 1. General. 2. Special. And, (2.) The subservient obligation (or the first bound faster on us) by promise and threatenings. (3.) And these also second by executions; even, 1. By actual judgment. 2. And mercies. And lastly, we have the obligation of our own undertaking upon us. These all deserve your consideration, but may not be insisted on by me, lest I be over-tedious.

1. Every christian is obliged to do all that he can for the salvation of others: but every minister is doubly obliged, because he is separated to the gospel of Christ, and is to give up himself wholly to that work, Rom. i. 1; 1 Tim. iv. 15. It is needless to make any further question of our obligation, when we know that this work is needful to our people's conversion and salvation, and that we are in general commanded to do all that is needful to those ends, as far as we are able. That they are necessary to those ends hath been showed before; and shall be more anon. Even the ancient professors have need to be taught the principles of God's oracles, if they have neglected it or forgot it, saith the apostle, *πάλιν χρέιαν ἔχετε τοῦ διδάσκειν ὑμᾶς τίνα τά ϛοιχεῖα τῆς ἀρχῆς τῶν λογίων τοῦ Θεοῦ*, Heb. v. 12. Whether the unconverted have need of conversion, and the means of it, I hope is no doubt among us; and whether this be a means, and a needful means, experience may put us far out of doubt, if we had no more. Let them that have taken most pains in public, examine their people, and try whether many of them be not yet as ignorant and as careless almost as if they had never heard the gospel. For my part, I study to speak as plainly and movingly as I can; and next my study to speak truly these are my chief studies; and yet I frequently meet with those that have been my hearers this eight or ten years, who know not whether Christ be God or man, and wonder when I tell them the his-

tory of his birth, life, and death, and sending abroad the gospel, as if they had never heard it before; and that know not that infants have any original sin: and of those that know the history of the gospel, how few are they that know the nature of that faith, repentance, and holiness, that it requireth; or at least, that know their own hearts! But most of them have an ungrounded affiance in Christ, trusting that he will pardon, justify, and save them, while the world hath their hearts, and they live to the flesh; and this affiance they take for a justifying faith. I have found by experience, that an ignorant sot that hath been an unprofitable hearer so long, hath got more knowledge and remorse of conscience in half an hour's close discourse, than they did from ten years' public preaching. I know that preaching of the gospel publicly is the most excellent means, because we speak to many at once; but otherwise, it is usually far more effectual to preach it privately to a particular sinner, as to himself; for the plainest man that is, can scarce speak plain enough in public for them to understand; but in private we may much more. In public, we may not use such homely expressions, or repetitions, as their dulness doth require, but in private we may. In public our speeches are long, and we quite overrun their understandings and memories, and they are confounded and at a loss, and not able to follow us, and one thing drives out another, and so they know not what we said; but in private we can take our work *gradatim*, and take our hearers with us as we go; and by questions, and their answers, we can see how far they go with us, and what we have next to do. In public, by length and speaking alone, we lose the attention; but when they are interlocutors, we can easily cause them to attend. Besides that, we can, as we above said, better answer the objections, and engage them by promises before we leave them, which in public we cannot do. I conclude, therefore, that public preaching will not be sufficient; for though it may be an effectual means to convert many, yet not so many as experience and God's appointment of further means may assure us. Long may you study and preach to little purpose, if you neglect this duty.

2. And for instances of particular special obligations, we might easily show you many, both from Christ's own examples, who used this interlocutory preaching both to his disciples and to the Jews, and from the apostles' examples, who did the like; but that indeed it would be needless tediousness to recite the passages to those that so well know them, it being the most ordinary way of the apostle's preaching, to do it thus interlocutorily and discourse it out in the conclusion. Thus Peter preached to the Jews, (Acts ii.) and to Cornelius and his friends, (Acts x.) and thus Philip preached to the eunuch, (Acts ix.) and thus Paul preached to the jailer, (Acts xvi.) and to many others. It is plain that it was the commonest preaching of those times, which occasioneth the quakers to challenge us to show where any ever took a text, and preached as we do; (though they might have found that Christ did so, Luke iv. 18.) Paul preached privately to them of reputation, lest he should have run and laboured in vain, Gal. ii. 2; and that earnest charge, no doubt, includeth it, 2 Tim. iv. 1, 2, "I charge thee, therefore, before God and the Lord Jesus Christ, who shall judge the quick and the dead at his appearing and his kingdom; preach the word, be instant in season, and out of season; reprove, rebuke, exhort, with all long-suffering and doctrine." Both public preaching, and all sorts of reproofs and exhortations, are here required.

3. And how these precepts are seconded with promises and threatenings, is so well known, I shall pass it over with the rest.

2. There is a necessity also of this duty *ad finem.*

(1.) And first, to the greater glory of God, by the fuller success of the gospel: not simply to his glory, as if he could not have his glory without it; for so our salvation is not necessary to his glory: but to his greater glory, because he is most honoured and pleased when most are saved; for he hath sworn that he hath no pleasure in the death of a sinner, but rather that he return and live. And, doubtless, as every christian liveth to the glory of God as his end, so will he gladly take that course that may most effectually promote it; for what man would not attain his end? O, brethren, if we could generally set this work afoot in all the parishes of England, and get our people to submit to it, and then prosecute it skilfully and zealously ourselves, what a glory would it put upon the face of the nation, and what a glory would redound to God thereby! If our common ignorance were thus banished, and our vanity and idleness turned into the study of the way of life, and every shop, and every house, were busied in learning of catechisms, and speaking of the word and works of God, what pleasure would God take in our cities and countries! He would even dwell in our habitations, and make them his delight. It is the glory of Christ that shineth in his saints, and all their glory is his glory: that therefore which honoureth them, in number or excellency, that honoureth him. Will not the glory of Christ be most wonderful and conspicuous in the new Jerusalem, when the church shall have that shining lustre that is described in Rev. xxi.? It is he that is the sun and the shield of his church, and his light is it in which they shall have light; and the business of every saint is to glorify him. If therefore we can increase the number or strength of the saints, we thereby increase the honour of the King of saints; for he will have service and praise where before he had disobedience and dishonour. Christ also will be honoured in the fruits of his bloodshed, and the Spirit of grace in the fruit of his operations; and do not all these ends require that we use the means with diligence?

(2.) This duty also is necessary to the welfare of our people: how much it doth conclude to their salvation, is manifest. Brethren, can you look believingly on your miserable neighbours, and not perceive them calling for your help? There is not a sinner whose case you should not so far compassionate, as to be willing to relieve them at dearer rates than this comes to. Can you see them as the wounded man by the way, and unmercifully pass by? Can you hear them cry to you, as the man of Macedonia to Paul in his vision, "Come and help us;" and yet will you refuse your help? Are you intrusted with an hospital, where one languisheth in one corner, and another groaneth in another, and crieth out, O help me, pity me for the Lord's sake, and a third is raging mad, and would destroy himself and you; and yet will you sit idle, or refuse your help? If it may be said of him that relieveth not men's bodies, how much more of them that relieve not men's souls, that "if you see your brother have need, and shut up the bowels of your compassion from him, how dwelleth the love of God in you?" You are not such monsters, such hard-hearted men, but you will pity a leper—you will pity the naked, imprisoned, or desolate—you will pity him that is tormented with grievous pain or sickness; and will you not pity an ignorant, hard-hearted sinner? Will you not pity one that must be shut out from the presence of the Lord, and lie under his remediless wrath, if thorough repentance speedily prevent it not? Oh what a heart it is that will not pity such a one! What shall I call the heart of such a man? A heart of stone, or a very rock, or adamant, or the heart of a tiger, or rather the heart of an *infidel;* for sure if he believed the misery of the impenitent, it is not possible but he should have pity on him! Can you tell men in the pulpit, that they shall certainly be damned except they repent, and yet have no pity on them when you have proclaimed such a danger? and if you pity them, will not you do thus much for their salvation? What abundance round about you are blindly hastening to perdition; and your voice is appointed to be the means of reclaiming them! The physician hath no excuse, who is doubly bound to relieve the sick, when every neighbour is to help them. Brethren, what if you heard sinners cry after you in the streets, O sirs, have pity on me, and afford me your advice, I am afraid of the everlasting wrath of God! I know I must shortly leave this world, and I am afraid lest I shall be miserable in the next! Could you deny your help to such a sinner? What if they came to your study door, and cried for help, and would not away till you had told them how to escape the wrath of God; could you find in your hearts to drive them away without advice? I am confident you could not. Why, alas, such persons are less miserable than they that cannot cry for help. It is the hardened sinner that cares not for your help, that most needeth it; and he that hath not so much life as to feel that he is dead, nor so much light as to see his danger, nor so much sense left as to pity himself —this is the man that is most to be pitied. Look upon your neighbours round about you, and think what abundance need your help in no less a case than the apparent danger of damnation. And every impenitent person that you see and know about you, suppose that you hear them cry to you for help, As ever you pitied poor wretches, pity us, lest we should be tormented in the flames of hell; if you have the hearts of men, pity us! And do that for them that you would if they followed you with such complaints. O how can you walk and talk, and be merry with such people, when you know their cases? methinks when you look them in the face, and think how they must lie in perpetual misery, you should break forth into tears, as the prophet did when he looked upon Hazael, and then fall on with the most importunate exhortations! When you must visit them in their sickness, will it not wound your hearts, to see them ready to depart into misery, before you have ever dealt seriously with them for their recovery? O then, for the Lord's sake, and for the sake of poor souls, have pity on them, and bestir yourselves, and spare no pains that may conduce to their salvation.

(3.) And I must further tell you, that this ministerial fidelity is necessary to your own welfare, as well as your people's; for this is your work, according to which (among others) you shall be judged. You can no more be saved without ministerial diligence and fidelity, than they or you can be saved without christian diligence and fidelity. If you care not for others, at least care for yourselves. O what is it to answer for the neglect of such a charge; and what sins more heinous than the betraying of souls! Doth not that threatening make us tremble, "If thou warn not the wicked—their blood will I require at thy hands." I am afraid, nay, I am past doubt, that the day is near when unfaithful ministers will wish that they had never known that charge; but that they had rather been colliers, or tinkers, or sweepers of channels, than pastors of Christ's flock! when, besides all the rest of their sins, they shall have the blood of so many souls to answer for. O brethren, our death, as well as our people's, is at hand; and it is as terrible to an unfaithful pastor as to any! When we see that die we must, and there is no remedy, no wit or learning, no credit or popular applause, can put by the stroke, or delay the time; but willing or unwilling, our souls must be gone, and that into the world that we never saw, where our persons and worldly interest will not be respected. Oh then for a clear conscience, that can say, I live not to myself but to Christ, I spared not my pains, I hid not my talent; I concealed not men's misery, nor the way of their recovery. O sirs, let us take the time while we may have it, and work while it is day; for the night cometh when none can work. This is our day too; and by doing good to others, we must do good to ourselves. If you would prepare for a comfortable death, and a sure and great reward, the harvest is before you. Gird up the loins of your minds, and quit yourselves like men, that you may end your days with that confident triumph, "I have fought a good fight, I have kept the faith, I have finished my course; henceforth is laid up for me a crown of righteousness, which God the righteous Judge shall give me." And if you would be blessed with those that die in the Lord, *labour now,* that you may rest from your labours then; and do such works as you would wish should follow you, and not such as will prove your terror in the review.

SECTION IV.

Having found so great reason to move us to this work, I shall, before I come to the direction, 1. Apply them further for our humiliation and excitation. And, 2. Answer some objections that may be raised.

And, 1. What cause have we to plead before the Lord this day, that have neglected so great and good a work so long—that we have been ministers of the gospel so many years, and done so little by personal instructions and conference for the saving of men's souls! If we had but set a-work this business sooner, that we have now agreed upon, who knows how many more might have been brought over unto Christ, and how much happier we might have made our parishes, ere now: and why might we not have done it sooner, as well as now? I confess many impediments were in our way, and so there are still, and will be while there is a devil to tempt, and a corrupt heart in man to resist the light; but if the greatest impediment had not been in ourselves, even in our own darkness, and dulness, and undisposedness to duty, and our dividedness and unaptness to close for the work of God, I see not but much might have been done before this. We had the same God to command us, and the same miserable objects of compassion, and the same liberty from governors of the commonwealth; but we stood looking for changes, and we would have had the magistrate not only to have given us leave to work, but to have done our work for us, or at least to have brought the game to our hands; and while we looked for better days, we made them worse by the lamentable neglect of a chief part of our work. And had we as much petitioned parliaments for the interposition of their authority to compel men to be catechised and instructed by the minister, as we did for maintenance and other matters, it is like we might have obtained it long ago, when they were forward to gratify us in such undisputable things. But we have sinned, and have no just excuse for our sin; somewhat that may perhaps excuse *a tanto*, but nothing *a toto;* and the sin is so great, because the duty is so great, that we should be afraid of pleading excuse too much. The Lord in mercy forgive us, and all the ministry of England, and lay not this or any of our ministerial negligences to our charge. Oh that he would cover all our unfaithfulness; and by the blood of the everlasting covenant, would wash away our guilt of the blood of souls, that when the chief Shepherd shall appear, we may stand before him in peace, and may not be condemned for the scattering of his flock. And oh that he would put up his controversy which he hath against the pastors of his church, and not deal the hardlier with them for our sakes, nor suffer underminers or persecutors to scatter them, as they have suffered his sheep to be scattered! And that he will not care as little for them, as they have done for the souls of men; nor think his salvation too good for them, as they have thought their labour and sufferings too much for men's salvation. And as we have had many days of humiliation in England, for the sins of the land, and the judgments that have lain upon us; I hope we shall hear that God will more thoroughly humble the ministry, and cause them to bewail their own neglects, and to set apart some days through the land to that end, that they may not think it enough to lament the sins of others, while they overlook their own; and that God may not abhor our solemn national humiliations, because they are managed by unhumbled guides; and that we may first prevail with him for a pardon for ourselves, that we may be the fitter to beg for the pardon of others.

And oh that we might cast out the dung of our pride, contention, self-seeking, and idleness, lest God should cast our sacrifices as dung in our faces, and should cast us out as the dung of the earth, as of late he hath done many others for our warning! And that we might presently resolve in concord to mend our pace, before we feel a sharper spur than hitherto we have felt.

SECTION V.

2. And now, brethren, what have we to do for the time to come, but to deny our lazy, contradicting flesh, and rouse up ourselves to the business that we are engaged in. The harvest is great; the labourers are too few; the loiterers and contentious hinderers are many; the souls of men are precious; the misery of sinners is great, and the everlasting misery that they are near to is greater; the beauty and glory of the church is desirable, the joy that we are helping them to is unconceivable; the comfort that followeth a faithful stewardship is not small; the comfort of a full success also will be greater. To be co-workers with God and his Spirit, is not a little honour; to subserve the bloodshed of Christ for men's salvation, is not a light thing; to lead on the armies of Christ through the thickest of the enemies, and guide them safely through a dangerous wilderness, and steer the vessel through such storms, and rocks, and sands, and shelves, and bring it safe to the harbour of rest, requireth no small skill and diligence. The fields now seem even white unto harvest, the preparations that have been made for us are very great, the season of working is more warm and calm than most ages before us have ever seen: we have carelessly loitered too long already; the present time is posting away: while we are trifling men are dying; how fast are men passing into another world! And is there nothing in all this to awaken us to our duty, and to resolve us to speedy and unwearied diligence? Can we think that a man can be too careful and painful under all these motives and engagements? Or could that man be a fit instrument for other men's illumination, that were himself so blind? or for the quickening of others, that were himself so senseless? What, sirs, are you that are men of wisdom, as dull as the common people? And do we need to heap up a multitude of words to persuade you to a known and weighty duty? One would think it should be enough to set you on work, to show a line in the book of God to prove it to be his will; or to prove to you that the work hath a tendency to men's salvation; one would think that the very sight of your miserable neighbours should be motive sufficient to draw out your most compassionate endeavours for their relief. If a cripple do but unlap his sores, and show you his disabled limbs, it will move you without words; and will not the case of souls that are near to damnation move you? O happy church, if the physicians were but healed themselves; and if we had not too much of that infidelity and stupidity which we daily preach against in others! and were soundlier persuaded of that which we persuade men of, and deeplier affected with the wonderful things wherewith we would affect them! Were there but such clear and deep impressions upon our souls, of those glorious things that we daily preach, oh what a change would it make in our sermons, and in our private discourse! Oh what a miserable thing it is to the church and to themselves, that men must preach of heaven and hell, before they soundly believe that there are such things, or have felt the weight of the doctrines which they preach! It would amaze a sensible man to think what matters we preach and talk of! what it is for the soul to pass out of this flesh, and go before a righteous God, and enter upon unchangeable joy or torment! Oh with what amazing thoughts do dying men apprehend these things! How should such matters be preached and discoursed of! Oh the gravity, the seriousness, the uncessant diligence that these things require! I know not what others think of them, but for my part I am ashamed of my stupidity, and wonder at myself that I deal not with my own and other's souls, as one that looks for the great day of the Lord; and that I can have room for almost any other thoughts or words, and that such astonishing matters do not wholly take me up. I marvel how I can preach of them slightly and coldly, and how I can let men alone in their sins, and that I do not go to them and beseech them for the Lord's sake to repent, however they take it, and whatever pains or trouble it should cost me! I seldom come out of the pulpit, but my conscience smiteth me that I have been no more serious and fervent in such a case.

It accuseth me not so much for want of human ornaments or elegancy, nor for letting fall an unhandsome word; but it asketh me, How couldst thou speak of life and death with such a heart? How couldst thou preach of heaven and hell, in such a careless, sleepy manner? Dost thou believe what thou sayest? Art thou in earnest or in jest? How canst thou tell people that sin is such a thing, and that so much misery is upon them and before them, and be no more affected with it? Shouldst thou not weep over such a people, and should not thy tears interrupt thy words? shouldst not thou cry aloud, and show them their transgressions, and entreat and beseech as for life and death? Truly, this is the peal that conscience doth ring in my ears, and yet my drowsy soul will not be awakened. Oh what a thing is a senseless, hardened heart! O Lord, save us from the plague of infidelity and hard-heartedness ourselves, or else how shall we be fit instruments of saving others from it? O do that on our own souls, which thou wouldst use us to do on the souls of others! I am even confounded to think what difference there is between my sickness apprehensions, and my pulpit and discoursing apprehensions, of the life to come: that ever that can seem so light a matter to me now, which seemeth so great and astonishing a matter then; and I know will do so again when death looks me in the face, when yet I daily know and think of that approaching hour. And yet those forethoughts will not recover such working apprehensions. O brethren, sure, if you had all conversed with neighbour death as oft as I have done, and as often received the sentence in yourselves, you would have an unquiet conscience, if not a reformed life in your ministerial diligence and fidelity; and you would have something within you that would frequently ask you such questions as these: Is this all thy compassion on lost sinners? Wilt thou do no more to seek and to save them? Is there not such and such a one,—oh how many round about thee, that are yet the visible sons of death? What hast thou said to them, or done for their recovery? Shall they die, and be in hell, before thou wilt speak to them one serious word to prevent it? Shall they there curse thee for ever that didst no more in time to save them? Such cries of conscience are daily in mine ears, though the Lord knows I have too little obeyed them. The God of mercy pardon me, and awake me with the rest of his servants that have been thus sinfully negligent! I confess to my shame, that I seldom hear the bell toll for one that is dead, but conscience asketh me, What hast thou done for the saving of that soul before it left the body? There is one more gone to judgment; what didst thou to prepare them for judgment? And yet I have been slothful and backward to help the rest that do survive. How can you choose, when you are laying a corpse in the grave, but think with yourselves, Here lieth the body, but where is the soul, and what have I done for it before it departed? It was part of my charge, what account I give of it? O sirs, is it a small matter to you to answer such questions as these? It may seem so now, but the hour is coming when it will not seem so. If our hearts condemn us, God is greater than our hearts, and will condemn us much more, even with another kind of condemnation than conscience doth. The voice of conscience now is a still voice, and the sentence of conscience is a gentle sentence, in comparison of the voice and the sentence of God. Alas! conscience seeth but a very little of our sin and misery, in comparison of what God seeth. What mountains would those things appear to your souls, which now seem mole-hills; what beams would these be in your eyes, that now seem motes, if you did but see them with a clearer light! I dare not say, as God seeth them. We can easily make shift to plead the cause with conscience, and either bribe it, or bear its sentence; but God is not so easily dealt with, nor his sentence so easily borne. "Wherefore we receiving (and preaching) a kingdom that cannot be moved, let us have grace, whereby we may serve God acceptably with reverence and godly fear; for our God is a consuming fire," Heb. xii. 28, 29. But because you shall not say, that I affright myself or you with bugbears, and tell you of dangers and terrors when there are none, I will here add the certainty and sureness of that condemnation that is like to befall the negligent pastors, and particularly that will befall us that are here this day, if we shall hereafter be wilful neglecters of this great work. How many will be ready to rise up against us to our condemnation!

(1.) Our parents that destinated us to the ministry may condemn us, and say, Lord, we devoted them to thy service, and they made light of it, and served themselves.

(2.) Our masters that taught us, our tutors that instructed us, the schools and universities that we lived in, and all the years that we spent in study, may rise up in judgment against us, and condemn us. For why was all this, but for the work of God?

(3.) Our learning, and knowledge, and ministerial gifts will condemn us. For to what are we made partakers of these, but for the work of God?

(4.) Our voluntarily undertaking the charge of souls will condemn us; for all men should be true to the trust that they have undertaken.

(5.) All the care of God for his church, and all that Christ hath done and suffered for them, will rise up in judgment against us, if we be negligent and unfaithful, and condemn us; for that we did by our neglect destroy them for whom Christ died.

(6.) All the severe precepts and charges of holy Scripture, with the promises of assistance and rewards, and the threatenings of punishment, will rise up against the unfaithful and condemn them; for God did not speak all this in vain.

(7.) All the examples of the prophets and apostles and other preachers recorded in Scripture, will rise up against such and condemn them: even this pattern that is set them by Paul, Acts xx. and all the examples of the diligent servants of Christ in these later times, and in the places about them. For these were for their imitation, and to provoke them to a holy emulation, fidelity, and ministerial diligence.

(8.) The holy Bible that is open before us, and all the books in our studies that tell us of our duty, directly or indirectly, may condemn the lazy and unprofitable servant; for we have not all these helps and furniture in vain.

(9.) All the sermons that we preach to persuade our people to work out their salvation with fear and trembling, to lay violent hands upon the crown, and take the kingdom as by force, to strive to enter in at the strait gate, and so to run as that they may obtain, &c. will rise up against the unfaithful and condemn them. For if it so nearly concern them to labour for their salvation, doth it not concern us who have the charge of them to be also violent, laborious, and unwearied in striving to help on their salvation? Is it worth their labour and patience, and is it not also worth ours?

(10.) All the sermons that we preach to them to set out the danger of a natural state, the evil of sin, the need of Christ and grace, the joys of heaven, and the torments of hell, yea, and the truth of christian religion, will rise up in judgment against such and condemn them. And a sad review it will be to themselves, when they shall be forced to think, Did I tell them of such great dangers and hopes in public, and would I do no more to help them in private? What! tell them daily of threatened damnation, and yet let them run into it so easily? tell them of such a glory, and scarce speak a word to them personally to help them to it? Were these such great matters with me at church, and so small when I came home? All this is dreadful self-condemnation.

(11.) All the sermons that we have preached to persuade other men to such duties; as neighbours to exhort one another daily, and plainly to rebuke them, and parents and masters to do it to their children and servants; will rise up in judgment against such and condemn them. For will you persuade others to that which you will not do as far as you can yourselves? When you threaten them for neglecting it, you threaten your own souls.

(12.) All our hard censures of the magistrate for doing no more, and all our reproofs of him for permitting seducers, and denying his further assistance to the ministers, doth condemn ourselves if we refuse our own duty. What, must all the rulers of the world be servants to our slothfulness, or light us the candle to do nothing, or only hold the stirrup to our pride, or make our beds for us, that we may sleep by daylight? Should they do their part in a subordinate office to protect and further us, and should not we do ours, who stand nearest to the end?

(13.) All the maintenance that we take for our service, if we be unfaithful, will condemn us: for who is it that will pay a servant to take his pleasure, or sit still, or work for himself? If we have the fleece, it is sure that we may look to the flock; and by taking the wages, we oblige ourselves to do the work.

(14.) All the honour that we expect or receive from the people, and all the ministerial privileges before mentioned, will condemn the unfaithful; for the honour is but the encouragement to the work, and obligeth to it.

(15.) All the witness that we have borne against the scandalous, negligent ministers of this age, and the words we have spoken against them, and all the endeavours that we have used for their removal, will condemn the unfaithful; for God is no respecter of persons. If we succeed them in their sins, we spoke all that against ourselves; and as we condemned them, God and others will condemn us, if we imitate them; and though we be not so bad as they, it will prove sad to be too like them.

(16.) All the judgments that God hath executed on them in this age before our eyes, will condemn us, if we be unfaithful; hath he made the idle shepherds and sensual drones to stink in the nostrils of the people, and will he honour us, if we be idle and sensual? Hath he sequestered them, and cast them out of their habitations, and out of the pulpits, and laid them by as dead while they are alive, and made them a hissing and a by-word in the land; and yet dare we imitate them? Are not their sufferings our warnings? and did not all this befall them for our examples? If any thing in the world should awaken ministers to self-denial and diligence, one would think we had seen enough to do it. If the judgments of God on one man should do so much, what should so many years' judgment on so many hundreds of them do? Would you have imitated the old world, if you had seen the flood that drowned them? Would you have taken up the sins of Sodom, "pride, fulness of bread, idleness," if you had stood by and seen the flames of Sodom? This was God's argument to deter the Israelites from the nations' sins, because, "for all these things they had seen them cast out before them." Who would have been a Judas that had seen him hanged and burst? and who would have been a lying, sacrilegious hypocrite, that had seen Ananias and Sapphira die? and who would not have been afraid to contradict the gospel, that had seen Elymas smitten blind? And shall we prove self-seeking, idle ministers, when we have seen God scourging such out of his temple, and sweeping them away as dirt into the channels? God forbid! for then how great and how manifold will our condemnation be!

(17.) All the disputations and eager contests that we have had against unfaithful men, and for a faithful ministry, will condemn us, if we be unfaithful; and so will the books that we have written to those ends. How many scores if not hundreds of catechisms are written in England! and yet shall we forbear to use them? How many books have been written for discipline, by English and Scottish divines; and how fully hath it been defended! and what reproach hath been cast upon the adversaries of it through the land! and yet shall we lay it by as useless, when we have free leave to use it? Oh fearful hypocrisy! What can we call it less? Did we think when we were writing against this sect and that sect that opposed discipline, that we were writing all that against ourselves? Oh what evidence do the booksellers' shops, and their own libraries, contain against the greatest part, even of the godly ministers of the land! The Lord cause them seasonably to lay it to heart.

(18.) All the days of fasting and prayer that have been of late years kept in England for a reformation, will rise up in judgment against the unreformed, that will not be persuaded to the painful part of the work. And I confess it is so heavy an aggravation of our sin, that it makes me ready to tremble to think of it. Was there ever a nation on the face of the earth, that hath so solemnly and so long followed God with fasting and prayer as we have done? Before the parliament began, how frequent and fervent were we in secret! after that, for many years' time together, we had a monthly fast commanded by the parliament, besides frequent private and public fasts on the by. And what was all this for? Whatever was sometime the means that we looked at, yet still the end of all our prayers was church reformation, and therein, especially, these two things: *a faithful ministry; and exercise of discipline in the church.* And did it once enter then into the hearts of the people, yea, or into our hearts, to imagine, that when we had all that we would have, and the matter was put into our own hands, to be as painful as we could, and to exercise what discipline we would, that then we would do nothing but publicly preach; that we would not be at the pains of catechising and instructing our people personally, nor exercise any considerable part of discipline at all? It astonisheth me to think of it! What a depth of deceit is in the heart of man! What! are good men's hearts so deceitful? Are all men's hearts so deceitful? I confess I told many soldiers and other sensual men then, that when they had fought for a reformation, I was confident they would abhor it, and be enemies to it, when they saw and felt it: thinking that the yoke of discipline would have pinched their necks; and that when they had been catechised and personally dealt with, and reproved for their sin, in private and public, and brought to public confession and repentance, or avoided as impenitent, they would have scorned and spurned against all this, and have taken the yoke of Christ for tyranny. But little did I think that the ministers would have let all fall, and put almost none of this upon them, but have let them alone for fear of displeasing them, and have let all run on as it did before.

Oh the earnest prayers that I have heard in secret days heretofore, for a painful ministry, and for discipline! As if they had even wrestled for salvation itself! Yea, they commonly called discipline, The kingdom of Christ; or the exercise of his kingly office in his church; and so preached and prayed for it, as if the setting up of discipline had been the setting up of the kingdom of Christ: and did I then think that they would refuse to set it up when they might! What! is the kingdom of Christ now reckoned among the things indifferent?

If the God of heaven, that knew our hearts, had in the midst of our prayers and cries on one of our public monthly fasts, returned us this answer with his dreadful voice, in the audience of the assembly: You deceitful-hearted sinners, what hypocrisy is this, to weary me with your cries for that which you will not have if I would give it you, and thus to lift up your voices for that which your souls abhor! What is reformation, but the instructing and importunate persuading of sinners to entertain my Christ and grace as offered them, and the governing my church according to my word? And these, which are your work, you will not be persuaded to, when you come to find it troublesome and ungrateful. When I have delivered you, it is not me, but yourselves, that you will serve; and I must be as earnest to persuade you to reform the church in doing your own duty, as you are earnest with me to grant you liberty for reformation; and when all is done, you will leave it undone, will be long before you will be persuaded to my work. I say, if the Lord, or any messenger of his, had given us in such an answer, would it not have amazed us, and have seemed incredible to us, that our hearts should have been such as now they prove? And would we not have said as Hazael, "Is thy servant a dog, that he should do this thing?" or as Peter, "Though all men forsake or deny thee, yet will not I." Well, brethren, too sad experience hath showed us our frailty: we have denied the troublesome and costly part of the reformation that we prayed for: but Christ yet turneth back, and looketh with a merciful eye upon us. Oh that we had yet the hearts, immediately to go out and weep bitterly, and to do so as we have done no more, lest a worse thing come unto us; and now to follow Christ through labour and suffering, though it were to the death, whom we have so far forsaken.

(19.) All the judgments upon the nation, the cost, the labour, the blood, and the deliverances, and all the endeavours of the governors for reformation, will rise up against us, if we now refuse to be faithful for a reformation, when it is before us, and at our will.

I have said somewhat of this before. Hath God been hewing us out a way with his sword, and levelling opposers by his terrible judgments, and yet will we sit still or play the sluggards? Have England, Scotland, and Ireland, paid so dear for a reformation, and now shall some men treacherously strangle it in the birth, and others expose it to contempt, and overrun it? and others sit still and look on it as a thing not worth the trouble? How many thousand persons may come to the condemnation of such men! The whole countries may say, Lord, we have been plundered and ruined, or much impoverished, we have paid taxes these many years, and it was a reformation that was pretended, and that we were promised, in all; and now the ministers, that should be the instruments of it, do neglect it. Many thousands may say, Lord, we ventured our lives, in obedience to a parliament that promised reformation, and now we cannot have it. The souls of many, that have died in these wars, may cry out against us, Lord, it was the hopes of a reformation that we fought and suffered for, in obedience to those governors that professed to intend it; and now the pastors reject it by their idleness. The parliament may say, how long did we sit and consult about reformation, and now the ministers will not execute the power that is granted them. The nation may say, How oft did we beg of God, and petition the parliament for it, and now the ministers deny us the enjoyment of it. Yea, God himself may say, How many prayers have I heard, and what dangers have I delivered you from; how many, how great, and in what a wonderful manner; and what do you think it was that I delivered you for? Was it not that you should do my work? and will you betray it, or neglect it, after all this? Truly, sirs, I know not what others think; but when I consider the judgments that we have felt, and the wonders of mercy that my eyes have seen, to the frequent astonishment of my soul, as I know it is great matters that these things oblige us to, so I am afraid, lest they should be charged on me as the aggravations of my neglect. I hear every exasperated party still flying in the faces of the rest; and one saith, It was you that killed the king, and the other saith, It was you that fought against a parliament, and put them to defend themselves, and drenched the land in blood. But the Lord grant that it be not *we*, if we prove negligent in our ministry, and betray the reformation that God hath called us to, that shall have all this blood and misery charged on us, yea, though we had never any other hand therein; and that the Lord say not of us as of Jehu, even when he had destroyed the house of Ahab by his command, because he accomplished not the reformation which that execution tended to, "Yet a little while, and I will avenge the blood of Jezreel on the house of Jehu," Hosea i. 4. O sirs, can we find in our hearts to lose all the cost and trouble of the three nations, and all to save us a little trouble in the issue, and so to bring the guilt of all upon ourselves? Far be it from us, if we have the hearts of christians.

(20.) Lastly, If we should yet refuse a reformation in our instructing of the ignorant, or our exercise of Christ's discipline, how many vows and promises of our own may rise up in judgment against us, and condemn us! (1.) In the national covenant, those that entered into it did vow and promise most solemnly before the Lord and his people, that Having before our eyes the glory of God, and the advancement of the kingdom of our Lord and Saviour, Jesus Christ—we would sincerely, really, and constantly endeavour, in our several places and callings, the reformation of religion in doctrine, worship, discipline, and government;—and we did profess our true and unfeigned purpose, desire, and endeavour for ourselves and all others under our power and charge, and both in public and private, in all duties we owe to God and man, to amend our lives, and each one to go before another in the example of a real reformation. And this covenant we made as in the presence of God, the searcher of all hearts, with a true intention to perform the same, as we shall answer at the great day when the secrets of all hearts shall be disclosed. Oh dreadful case then, that we have put ourselves into, if infinite mercy help us not out! May we not say after the law, (2 Kings xxii. 13; 2 Chron. xxxiv. 21,) "Great is the wrath of the Lord that is kindled against us, because we have not done according to this covenant." Could a people have devised a readier way to thrust themselves under the curse of God, than by taking such a solemn, dreadful covenant, and when they have done, so long, so wilfully, so openly to violate it? Doth not this plainly bind us to the private as well as the public parts of this duty; and to a real reformation of discipline in our practice? Again, therefore, I must needs say, what a bottomless depth of deceit is the heart of man! Oh what heavy charges have we brought against many others of these times, for breaking this solemn vow and covenant, (from which I am far from undertaking to acquit them,) when yet we that led the way, and drew on others, and daily preached up reformation and discipline, have so horribly violated this covenant ourselves, that in a whole country it is rare to find a minister that hath set up discipline or private instruction. And he that can see much done towards it in England, hath more acquaintance or better eyes than I have.

(2.) Also in our frequent, solemn humiliation days in the time of our deepest distress and fear, how publicly and earnestly did we beg for deliverances, not as for our sakes, but for the church and gospel sake; as if we had not cared what had become of us, so that the reformation of the church might go on; and we promised if God would hear and deliver us, what we would do towards it. But oh how unfaithful have we been to those promises! As if we were not the same men that ever spoke such words to God! I confess it filleth my own soul with shame, to consider the unanswerableness of my affections and endeavours to the many fervent prayers, rare deliverances, and confident promises of those years of adversity! And such experiences of the almost incredible unfaithfulness of our hearts, is almost enough to make a man never trust his heart again; and consequently to shake his certainty of sincerity. Have we now, or are we like to have, any higher resolutions than those were which we have broken? And it tends also to make us question in the next extremity, even at the hour of death, whether God will hear and help us any more, who have forfeited our credit with him by proving so unfaithful. If so many years' public humiliation, spurred on by such calamities as neither we nor our fathers for many generations had ever seen, had no more in them than now appears, and if this be the issue of all, how can we tell how to believe ourselves hereafter? It may make us fear lest our cases be like the Israelites, (Psal. lxxviii. 34—37, 41, 42, 57,) who "when he slew them, then they sought him, and they returned, and inquired early after God; and they remembered that God was their Rock, and the high God their Redeemer. Nevertheless they did flatter him with their mouth, and they lied unto him with their tongues; for their heart was not right with God, neither were they stedfast in his covenant. They remembered not his hand, nor the day when he delivered them from the enemy.—But turned back and dealt unfaithfully like their fathers: they were turned aside like a deceitful bow."

(3.) Moreover, if we will not be faithful in duties that we are engaged to, our own agreements and engagements which remain subscribed by our hands, and are published to the view of the world, will rise up in judgment against us and condemn us. We have engaged ourselves under our hands near three years ago, that we will set up the exercise of discipline, and yet how many have neglected it to this day, without giving any just and reasonable excuse! We have now subscribed another agreement and engagement for catechising and instructing all that will submit. We have done well so far; but if now we should flag and prove remiss and superficial in the performance, our subscriptions will condemn us—this day of humiliation will condemn us. Be not deceived, God is not mocked; it is not your names only, but your hearts and hands also, that he requireth: there is no dallying with God by feigned promises; he will expect that you be as good as your word. He will not hold him guiltless, that by false oaths, or vows, or covenants with him doth take his holy name in vain. "When thou vowest a vow unto God, defer not to pay it; for he hath no pleasure in fools: pay that which thou hast vowed. Better is it that thou shouldst not vow, than that thou shouldst vow and not pay. Suffer not thy mouth to cause thy flesh to sin; neither say thou before the angel, that it was an error; wherefore should God be angry at thy voice, and destroy the work of thy hands?" Eccles. v. 4—6.

And thus I have showed you what will come on it if you shall not set yourselves faithfully to this work, to which you have so many obligations and engagements; and what an inexcusable thing our neglect will be, how great and manifold a condemnation it would expose us to. Truly, brethren, if I did not apprehend the work to be of exceeding great moment to yourselves, to the people, and to the honour of God, I would not have troubled you with so many words about it, nor have presumed to have spoken so sharply as I have done. But when it is for life and death, men are apt to forget their reverence, and courtesy, and compliments, commonly called good manners. For my part, I apprehend this as one of the best and greatest works that ever I put my hand to in my life. And I verily think that your thoughts of it are as mine; and then you will not think my words too many or too keen. I can well remember the time when I was earnest for the reformation of matters of ceremony; and if I should be cold in such a substantial matter as this, how disorderly and disproportionable would my zeal appear! Alas, can we think that the reformation is wrought, when we have cast out a few ceremonies, changed some vestures, and gestures, and forms? O no, sirs! it is the converting and saving of souls that is our business. That is the chiefest part of the reformation that doth most good, and tendeth most to the salvation of the people. Let others take it how they will, I will so far speak my conscience for your just encouragement, as to say again, that I am verily persuaded that as you are happily agreed and combined for this work, so if you will but faithfully execute this agreement, together with your former agreement for discipline, you will do much more for a true reformation, and that peaceably without meddling with controverted points, than I have heard of any part of England to have done before you, and yet no more than is unquestionably your duty.

SECTION VI.

I am next to answer some of those objections which backward minds may cast in our way. And, 1. Some may object, that this course will take up so much time that a man shall have no time to follow his studies: most of us are young and raw, and have need of much time to improve our abilities, which this course will prohibit us. To which I answer: (1.) We suppose them whom we persuade to this work, to understand the substance of the christian religion, and to be able to teach it others; and the addition of lower and less necessary things is not to be preferred before this needful communication of the fundamentals. I highly value common knowledge, and would not encourage any to set light by it; but I value the saving of souls before it. That work which is the next end must be done, whatever be undone. It is a very desirable thing for a physician to be thoroughly studied in his art; and to be able to see the reason of his experiments, and to resolve such difficult controversies as are before him; but if he had the charge of an hospital, or lived in a city that had the raging pestilence, if he would be studying *de fermentatione, de circulatione sanguis, de vesiculo chylo, de instrumentis sanguificationis*, and such like excellent, useful points, when he should be looking to his patients, and saving men's lives; and should turn them away, and let them perish, and tell them that he cannot have while to give them advice, because he must follow his own studies; I should take that man for a preposterous student, that preferred the remote means before the end itself of his studies, and indeed, I should think him but a civil kind of murderer. Men's souls may be saved, without knowing whether God did predominate the creature in all its acts; whether the understanding necessarily determines the will; whether God works grace in a physical or moral way of causation; what free-will is; whether God have *scientiam mediam,* or positive decrees, *de malo culpæ;* with a hundred such like, which are the things that you would be studying when you should be saving souls. Get well to heaven, and help your people thither, and you shall know all these things in a moment, and a thousand more, which by all your studies you can never know: and is not this the most expeditious and certain way to knowledge?

(2.) If you grow not extensively in knowledge, you will by this way of diligent practice obtain the intensive and more excellent growth. If you know not so many things as others, you will know the great things better than they; for this serious dealing with sinners for their salvation will help you to far deeper apprehensions of their saving principles, than will be got by any other means; and a little more of the knowledge of these is worth all the other knowledge in the world. Oh, when I am looking heavenward, and gazing towards the inaccessible light, and aspiring after the knowledge of God, and find my soul so dark and distant, that I am ready to say, I know not God—he is above me—quite out of my reach; this is the most killing and grievous ignorance! Methinks I could willingly exchange all other knowledge that I have for one glimpse more of the knowledge of God and the life to come. Oh that I had never known a word in logic, metaphysics, &c. nor known whatever schoolmen said, so I had but one spark more of that light that would show me the things that I must shortly see! For my part, I conceive that by serious talking of everlasting things, and teaching the creed and shorter catechism, you may grow more in knowledge, though not in the knowledge of more things, and prove much wiser men, than if you spent that time in common or curious, less necessary things.

(3.) Yet let me add, that though I count this the chief, I would have you to have more; because those subservient sciences are very useful: and therefore I say, that you may have competent time for both, lose none upon vain recreations and employments; trifle not away a minute; consume it not in needless sleep; do that you do with all your might, and then see whether you have not a competent time. If you set apart but two days in a week in this great work that we are agreed on, you may find some for common studies out of all the other five.

(4.) Duties are to be taken together; the greatest to be preferred, but none to be neglected that can be performed; not one to be pleaded against another, but each to know its proper place: but if there were such a case of necessity, that we could not read for ourselves in the course of our further studies, and instruct the ignorant both, I would throw by all the libraries in the world, rather than be guilty of the perdition of one soul; or at least I know that this is my duty.

Object. 2. But this course will destroy the health of our bodies, by continual spending the spirits, and allowing us no time for necessary recreations; and it will wholly lock us up from any civil friendly visitations; so that we must never stir from home, nor take our delight at home one day with our friends, for the relaxation of our minds; but as we shall seem discourteous and morose to others, so we shall tire ourselves, and the bow that is still bent will be in danger of breaking at last.

Answ. 1. This is the mere plea of the flesh for its own interest: the sluggard saith, There is a lion in the way; he will not plough because of the cold. There is no duty of moment and self-denial, but if you consult with flesh and blood, it will give you as wise reasons as these against it. Who would ever have been burnt at a stake for Christ, if this reasoning had been good? yea, or who would ever have been a christian?

(2.) We may take time for necessary recreation for all this. An hour, or half an hour's walk before meat, is as much recreation as is of necessity for the health of most of the weaker sort of students. I have reason to know somewhat of this by long experience. Though I have a body that hath languished under great weakness many years, and my diseases have been such as require as much exercise as almost any in the world, and I have found exercise the principal means of my preservation till now, and therefore have as great reason to plead for it as any man that I know alive, yet I have found that the aforesaid proportion hath been blessed to my preservation, though I know that much more had been like to have tended to my greater health. And I do not know one minister of a hundred, that needeth so much as myself. Yea, I know abundance of ministers that scarce ever use any exercise at all, though I commend it not in them. I doubt not but it is our duty to use so much exercise as is of necessity for the preservation of our health, so far as our work requireth: else we should for one day's work lose the opportunity of many. But this may be done, and yet the works that we are engaged in be done too. On those two days a week that you set apart for this work, what hinders but you may take an hour or two to walk for the exercise of your bodies, much more on other days.

But as for those men that limit not their recreations to their stated hours, but must have them for the pleasing of their voluptuous humour, and not only to study better the nature of christianity, and learn the danger of living after the flesh, and get more mortification and self-denial before they preach these things to others. If you must needs have your pleasures, you should not have put yourselves into that calling that requireth you to make God and his service your pleasure, and restraineth you so much from fleshly pleasures. Is it your baptismal engagement to fight against the flesh? and do you know that much of the christian warfare consisteth in the combat between the flesh and the Spirit; and that is the very difference between a true christian and a wicked wretch, that one liveth after the Spirit, and mortifieth the deeds and desires of the body, and the other liveth after the flesh? and do you know that the overcoming the flesh is the principal part of our victory, on which the crown of life depends? and do you make it your calling to preach all this to others, and yet for all this must you needs have your pleasures? If you must, then for shame give over the preaching of the gospel, and the profession of christian self-denial, and profess yourselves to be as you are; and as you sow to the flesh, so of the flesh shall you receive the wages of corruption. Doth such a one as Paul say, "I therefore so run, not as uncertainly: so fight I, not as one that beateth the air: but I keep under my body, and bring it into subjection, lest that by any means, when I have preached to others, I myself should be a cast-away," 1 Cor. iv. 26, 27; and have not such sinners as we need to do so? Shall we pamper our bodies, and give them their desires in the unnecessary pleasures, when Paul must keep under his body, and bring it into subjection? Must Paul do this, lest after all his preaching he should be a cast-away; and have not we cause to fear it of ourselves much more? I know that some pleasure itself is lawful; that is, when it is of use to the fitting us for our work. But for a man to be so far in love with his pleasures, as that he must unnecessarily waste his precious time in them, and neglect the great work of God for men's salvation, yea, and plead for this as if it must or might be done, and so to justify himself in such a course, is a wickedness inconsistent with the common fidelity of a christian, much more with the fidelity of a teacher of the church. And such wretches as are lovers of pleasure more than lovers of God, must look to be loved of him accordingly, and are fitter to be cast out of christian communion, than to be the chief in the church; for we are commanded from such to turn away, 2 Tim. iii. 5. Recreations for a student, must be especially for the exercise of his body, he having before him such variety of delights to his mind; and they must be as whetting is with the mower, that is only to be used so far as is necessary to his work. And we must be careful that it rob us not of our precious time, but be kept within the narrowest bounds that may be. I pray peruse well Mr. Wheatley's Sermon of Redemption of Time. And then the labour that we are now engaged to perform, is not likely much to impair our health. It is true, we must be serious; but that will but excite and revive our spirits, and not so much spend them. Men can talk all the day long of other matters without any abatement of their health; and why may not we talk with men about their salvation, without such great abatement of ours?

(3.) It is to be understood that the direction that we give, and the work which we undertake, is not for dying men, that are not able to preach or speak; but for men of some competent measure of strength, and whose weaknesses are tolerable, and may admit of such labours.

(4.) What have we our time and strength for, but to lay it out for God? What is a candle made for but to be burnt? Burnt and wasted we must be, and is it not fitter it should be in lighting men to heaven, and in working for God, than in living to the flesh? How little difference is there between the pleasure of a long life and of a short, when they are both at an end! What comfort will it be at death, that you lengthened your life by shortening your work? He that works much, lives much. Our life is to be esteemed according to the ends and works of it, and not according to the mere duration. As Seneca can say of a drone, *Ibi jacet, non ibi vivit; et diu fuit, non diu vixit.* Will it not comfort us more at death to review a short time faithfully spent, than a long time unfaithfully?

(5.) And for the matter of visitations and civilities, if they be for greater ends or use than our ministerial employments are, you may break a sabbath for them; you may forbear preaching for them, and so may forbear this private work. But if it be otherwise, how dare you make them a pretence to neglect so great a duty? Must God wait on your friends? What if they be lords, or knights, or gentlemen; must they be served before God? Or is their displeasure or censure a greater hurt to you, than God's displeasure? Or dare you think when God will question you for your neglects, to put him off with this excuse, Lord, I would have spent more of my time in seeking men's salvation, but that such a gentleman, and such a friend, would have taken it ill if I had not waited on them. If you yet seek to please men, you are no longer the servants of Christ. He that dares spend his life in flesh-pleasing and man-pleasing, is bolder than I am; and he that dares waste his time in compliments, doth little consider what he hath to do with it. Oh that I could but improve my time according to my convictions of the necessity of improving it! He that hath looked death in the face as oft as I have done, I will not thank him to value his time. I profess I admire at those ministers that have time to spare, that can hunt, or shoot, or bowl, or use the like recreations two or three hours, yea, whole days almost together; that can sit an hour together in vain discourses; and spend whole days in complimental visitations, and journeys to such ends. Good Lord, what do these men think on! when so many souls about them cry for their help, and death gives us no respite, and they know not how short a time their people and they may be together; when the smallest parish hath so much work that may employ all their diligence night and day! Brethren, I hope you are content to be plainly dealt with. If you have no sense of the worth of souls, and the preciousness of that blood that was shed for them, and of the glory that they are going to, and of the misery that they are in danger of; then are you no christians, and therefore very unfit to be ministers: and if you have, how can you find time for needless recreations, visitations, or discourses? Dare you, like idle gossips, chat and trifle away your time, when you have such works as these to do, and so many of them? O precious time! how swiftly doth it pass away!—how soon will it be gone! What are the forty years of my life that are past? Were every day as long as a month, methinks it were too short for the work of a day! Have we not lost enough already in the days of our vanity? Never do I come to a dying man that is not utterly stupid, but he better sees the worth of time! Oh then, if they could call time back again, how loud would they call! If they could but buy it, what would they give for it! And yet can we afford to trifle it away! Yea, and to allow ourselves in this, and wilfully cast off the greatest works of God! O what a foolish thing is sin, that can thus distract men that seem so wise! Is it possible that a man of any true compassion and honesty, or any care of his ministerial duty, or any sense of the strictness of his account, should have time to spare for idleness and vanity?

And I must tell you further, brethren, that if another might take some time for mere delight which were not necessary, yet so cannot you; for your undertaking binds you to stricter attendance than other men are bound to. May a physician in the plague time take any more relaxation or recreation than is necessary for his life, when so many are expecting his help in a case of life and death? As his pleasure is not worth men's lives, so neither is yours worth men's souls. Suppose your cities were besieged, and the enemy on one side watching all advantages to surprise it, and on the other seeking to fire it with grenadoes which are cast in continually. I pray you tell me now, if certain men undertake it as their office to watch the ports, and others to quench the fires that shall be kindled in the houses, what time will you allow these men for their recreation or relaxation? when the city is in danger, or the fire will burn on, and prevail if they intermit their diligence! Or would you excuse one of these men if he come off his work, and say, I am but flesh and blood, I must have some pleasure or relaxation? At the utmost, sure you would allow him none but of necessity.

Do not grudge at this now, and say, "This is a hard saying, who can bear it?" For it is your mercy; and you are well, if you know when you are well, as I shall show you in answering this next objection.

Object. 3. I do not think that it is required of ministers that they make drudges of themselves. If they preach diligently, and visit the sick, and do other ministerial duties, and occasionally do good to those they converse with, I do not think that God doth moreover require that we should thus tie ourselves to instruct every person distinctly, and to make our lives a burden and a slavery.

Answ. (1.) Of what use and weight the duty is, I have showed before; and how plainly it is commanded. And do you think God doth not require you to do all the good you can? Will you stand by and see sinners gasping under the pangs of death, and say, God doth not require me to make myself a drudge to save them? Is this the voice of ministerial or christian compassion, or rather of sensual laziness and diabolical cruelty? Doth God set you work to do, and will you not believe that he would have you do it? Is that the voice of obedience, or of rebellion? It is all one whether your flesh do prevail with you to deny obedience to acknowledged duty, and say plainly, I will obey no further than it pleaseth me, or whether it may make you wilfully reject the evidence that should convince you that it is a duty, and say, I will not believe it to be my duty, unless it please me. It is the true character of a hypocrite, to make a religion to himself of the cheapest part of God's service, which will stand with his fleshly ends and felicity; and to reject the rest, which is inconsistent therewith. And to the words of hypocrisy, this objection superaddeth the words of gross impiety. For what a wretched calumny is this against the most high God, to call his service a slavery and drudgery! What thoughts have these men of their Master, their work, and their wages? the thoughts of a believer or of an infidel? Are these men like to honour God, and promote his service, that have such base thoughts of it themselves? Do these men delight in holiness that account it a slavish work? Do they believe indeed the misery of sinners, that account it such a slavery to be diligent for to save them? Christ saith, that he that denieth not himself, and forsaketh not all, and taketh not up his cross and followeth him, cannot be his disciple; and these men count it a slavery to labour hard in his vineyard, and deny their ease, in a time when they have all accommodations and encouragements. How far is this from forsaking all! and how can these men be fit for the ministry, that are such enemies to self-denial, and so to true christianity? Still therefore I am forced to say, that all these objections are so prevalent, and all these carnal reasonings hinder the reformation; and in a word, hence is the chief misery of the church, *that so many are made ministers before they are christians.* If these men had seen the diligence of Christ in doing good, when he neglected his meat to talk with one woman, (John iv.) and when they had no time to eat bread, (Mark iii. 22,) would not they have been of the mind of his carnal friends, that went to lay hold on him, and said, "He is beside himself," ver. 21. They would have told Christ he made a drudge or a slave of himself, and God did not require all this ado. If they had seen him all night in prayer, and all day in preaching and healing, it seems he should have had this censure from them for his labour! I cannot but advise these men to search their own hearts, whether they unfeignedly believe that word that they preach? Do you believe indeed that such glory attends those that die in the Lord, and such torment attendeth those that die unconverted? If you do, how can you think any labour too much, for such weighty ends? If you do not, say so, and get you out of the vineyard, and go with the prodigal to keep swine, and undertake not the feeding of the flock of Christ.

Do you not know that it is your own benefit which you grudge at? The more you do, the more you receive: the more you lay out, the more you have coming in. If you are strangers to these christian paradoxes, you should not have taken on you to teach them to others. At the present our incomes of spiritual life and peace are commonly in way of duty; so that he that is most in duty hath most of God: exercise of grace increaseth it. And is it a slavery to be more with God, and to receive more from him, than other men? It is the chief solace of a gracious soul to be doing good, and receiving by doing, and to be much exercised about those divine things which have his heart. A good stomach will not say at a feast, What a slavery is it to bestow my time and pains so much to feed myself! Besides, that we prepare for fuller receivings hereafter. We set our talents to usury, and by improving them we shall make five become ten, and so be made rulers of ten cities. We shall be judged according to our works. Is it a drudgery to send to the utmost parts of the world to exchange our trifles for gold and jewels? Do not these men seek to justify the profane, that make all diligent godliness a drudgery, and reproach it as a precise and tedious life? They say they will never believe but a man may be saved without all this ado. Even so say these in respect to the works of the ministry; they take this diligence for ungrateful tediousness, and they will not believe but a man may be a faithful minister without all this ado! It is a heinous sin to be negligent in so great a business; but to approve of that negligence, and so to be impenitent, and to plead against duty as if it were none; and when they should lay out themselves for the saving of souls, to say, I do not believe that God requireth it; this is so great an aggravation of the sin, that, where the church's necessity doth not force us to make use of such, for want of better, I cannot but think them worthy to be cast out as the rubbish, and as salt that hath lost its savour, that is neither fit for the land, nor yet for the dunghill, but men cast it out. "He that hath ears to hear," saith Christ in these words, "let him hear," Luke xiv. 34, 35. And if such ministers become a by-word and reproach, let them thank themselves; for it is their own sin that maketh them vile, 1 Sam. iii. 13. And while they thus debase the service of the Lord, they do but debase themselves, and prepare for a greater abasement at the last.

Object. 4. But if you make such severe laws for ministers, the church will be left without: for what man will put himself upon such a toilsome life, or what parents will choose such a burden for their children? Men will avoid it both for the bodily toil, and the danger to their consciences if they should not well discharge it.

Answ. (1.) It is not we, but Christ, that hath made and imposed these laws which you call severe; and if I should silence them, or misinterpet them, or tell you that there is no such things, that would not relax them, nor disoblige or excuse you. He that made them, knew why he did it, and will expect the performance of them. Is Infinite goodness itself to be questioned or suspected by us, as making bad or unmerciful laws? Nay, it is mere mercy in him that imposeth this great duty upon us. If physicians be required to be as diligent in hospitals or pest-houses, or with other patients, to save their lives, were there not more mercy than rigour in this law? What! must God let the souls of your neighbours perish, to save you a little labour and suffering, and this in mercy to you? Oh what a miserable world should we have, if blind, self-conceited man had the ruling of it!

(2.) And for a supply of pastors, Christ will take care. He that imposeth duty, hath the fulness of the Spirit, and can give men hearts to obey his laws. Do you think Christ will suffer all men to be as cruel, unmerciful, fleshly, and self-seeking as you? He that hath undertaken himself the work of our redemption, and borne our transgressions, and been faithful as the chief Shepherd and Teacher of the church, will not lose all his labour and suffering for want of instruments to carry on his work; nor will he come down again to do all himself, because no other will do it: but he will provide men to be his servants and ushers in his school, that shall willingly take the labour on them, and rejoice to be so employed, and account that the happiest life in the world which you account so great a toil; and would not change it for all your ease and carnal pleasure; but for the saving of souls and the propagating of the gospel of Christ, will be content to bear the burden and heat of the day, and to fill up the measure of the sufferings of Christ in their bodies, and to do what they do with all their might, and to work while it is day, and to be the servants of all, and not to please themselves but others for their edification; and to become all things to all men, that they may save some; and to endure all things for the elect's sake; and to spend and be spent for men, though the more they love, the less they should be beloved, and should be accounted their enemies for telling them the truth: such pastors will Christ provide his people after his own heart, that will feed them with knowledge; as men that seek not theirs, but them. What! do you think Christ can have no servants, if such as you shall, with Demas, turn to the present world, and forsake him? If you dislike his service, you may seek you a better where you can find it, and boast of your gain in the conclusion: but do not threaten him with the loss of your service. He hath made such laws as you will call severe, for all who will be saved, as well as for his ministers, though he impose not on them the same employment; for all must deny themselves, and mortify the flesh, and be crucified to the world, and take up their cross, and follow Christ, that will be his disciples. And yet Christ will not be without disciples, nor will he hide his seeming hard terms from men, to entice them to his service, but will tell them of the worst, and then let them come or choose. He will call to them beforehand to count what it will cost them, and tell them that "foxes have holes, and the birds of the air have nests, but the Son of man hath not where to lay his head." He comes not to give them worldly peace and prosperity, but to call them to suffer with him, that they may reign with him; and in patience to possess their souls, and conquer, that they may be crowned with him, and sit down on his throne; and all this he will cause his chosen to perform. If you be at that pass with Christ as the Israelites were once with David, and say, "Will the son of Jesse give you fields and vineyards? Every man to your tents, O Israel." And if you say, "Now look to thy own house, O David," you shall see that Christ will look to his own house; and do you look to yours as well as you can, and tell me at the hour of death or judgment which is the better bargain, and whether Christ had more need of you, or you of him.

And for scrupling it in conscience for fear of failing; 1. It is not involuntary imperfections that Christ will take so heinously, but it is unfaithfulness and wilful negligence: 2. And it shall not serve your turn to run out of the vineyard or harvest, on pretence of scruples that you cannot do the work as you ought. He can follow you and overtake you as he did Jonas, with such a storm, as shall lay you out in the belly of hell: totally to cast off a duty, because you cannot endure to be faithful in the performance of it, will prove but a poor excuse at last. If men had but reckoned well at first, of the difference between things temporal and eternal, and of what they shall lose or get by Christ, and had that faith which is the evidence of things not seen, and lived by faith and not by sense, all these objections would be easily resolved; and all the pleas of flesh and blood for its interest, would appear to have no more reason, than a sick man's plea for cold water in a pestilential fever.

Object. 5. But to what purpose is all this, when most of the people will not submit? They will but make a scorn at your motion, and tell us they will not come to us to be catechised, and that they are too old now to go to school; and therefore it is as good to let them alone, as trouble ourselves to no purpose.

Answ. (1.) It is not to be denied, but too many people are obstinate in their wickedness, and too many simple ones love simplicity, and too many scorners delight in scorning, and fools hate knowledge, Prov. i. 22. But the worse they are, the sadder is their case, and the more to be pitied, and the more diligent should we be for their recovery.

(2.) I would it were not too much long of ministers, that a great part of the people are so obstinate and contemptuous. If we did shine and burn before them as we should, had we convincing sermons and convincing lives, did we set ourselves to do all the good we could, whatever it cost us; were we more humble and meek, more loving and charitable, and let them see that we set light by all the worldly things in comparison of their salvation; much more might be done than is, and the mouths of many would be stopped, and though still the wicked will do wickedly, yet more would be tractable, and the wicked would be fewer and calmer than they are. If you say, that the ablest and godliest ministers in the world have had as untractable and scornful parishioners as any others; I answer, that even able, godly men have some of them been too lordly and strange, and some of them too uncharitable and worldly, and backward to costly though necessary works; and some of them have done but little in private, when they have done excellently in public, and so have hindered the fruit of their labours. But where these impediments are absent, experience telleth us that the success is much greater, at least, as to the bowing of people to more calmness and teachableness; but we cannot expect that it should be brought to so much reason.

(3.) Their wilfulness will not excuse us from our duty. If we offer them not our help, how know we who will refuse it? Offering it is our part, and accepting is theirs. If we offer it not, we leave them excusable, (for then they refuse it not,) but it is we that are left without excuse; but if they refuse our help when it is offered, we have done our part, and delivered our own souls.

(4.) If some refuse our help, others will accept it; and the success with them may be so much, as may answer all our labour, were it more. It is not all that are wrought on by your public preaching, and yet we must not therefore give it over as unprofitable.

Object. 6. But what likelihood is there that men will be informed or converted by this means, that will not by the preaching of the word, when that is God's chief ordinance appointed to that end? Faith comes by hearing, and hearing by the word preached.

Answ. (1.) The advantages I have showed you before, and therefore will not stand to repeat them; only, lest any think that this will wrong them by hindering them from preaching, I add to the twenty benefits before mentioned, that it will be an excellent means to help you in preaching. For as the physician's work is held done when he fully knows the disease, so when you are acquainted well with your people's case, you will know what to preach on; and it will further you with matter to talk an hour with an ignorant or obstinate sinner, as much as an hour's study will do; for you will know what you have need to insist on, and what objections of theirs to refel.

(2.) I hope there is none so silly as to think this conference is not preaching. Doth the number we speak to make it preaching; or doth interlocution make it none? Sure a man may as truly preach to one as to a thousand; and, as is aforesaid, if you search, you will find, that most of the gospel preaching in those days, was by conference, or serious speeches to people occasionally, and frequently interlocutory; and that with one or two, fewer or more, as opportunity served. Thus Christ himself did most commonly preach. Besides, we must take account of our people's learning, if we mind the success of our work.

There is nothing therefore from God, from the Spirit, from right reason, to cause us to make any question of our work, or to be unwilling to it; but from the world, from the flesh, and the devil, we shall have much, and more perhaps than we yet expect. But against all temptations, if we have recourse to God, and look on his great obligations on one side, and the hopeful effects and reward on the other, we shall see that we have little cause to draw back, or to faint.

Let us set before us this pattern in the text, and learn our duty thence, and imitate it. From ver. 19, to serve the Lord, and not man or ourselves, with all humility of mind, and not proudly, and with many tears, &c.: ver. 20, to keep back nothing that is profitable to the people, and to teach them publicly and from house to house: ver. 21, that the matter of our preaching be repentance towards God, and faith towards our Lord Jesus Christ: ver. 22—24, that though we go bound in the spirit, not knowing particularly what shall befall us, but know that every where bonds and afflictions do abide us, yet none of these things should move us, neither should we count our life dear to ourselves, so that we may finish our course with joy, and the ministry which we have received of the Lord Jesus, to testify the gospel of the grace of God: from ver. 28, to take heed to ourselves and to all the flock, particularly against domestic seducers and schisms: from ver. 31, without ceasing to warn every one day and night with tears: ver. 33, to covet no man's silver, or gold, or apparel, as counting it more honourable to give than to receive. Oh what a lesson is here before us! but how ill is it learned by those that still question whether these be their duty! I confess some of these words of Paul have so often been presented before mine eyes, and stuck upon my conscience, that I have been much convinced by them of my duty and neglect: and I think this one speech better deserves a twelve month's study, than most things that young students do lay out their time in. O brethren, write it on your study doors, or set it as your copy in capital letters still before your eyes! Could we but well learn two or three lines of it, what preachers should we be! (1.) For our general business, "Serving the Lord with humility of mind." (2.) Our special work, "Take heed to yourselves, and to all the flock." (3.) Our doctrine, "Repentance towards God, and faith toward our Lord Jesus Christ." (4.) The place and manner of teaching, "I have taught you publicly and from house to house." (5.) The object and internal manner, "I ceased not to warn every one night and day with tears." This is it that must win souls and preserve them. (6.) His innocency and self-denial for the advantage of the gospel, "I have coveted no man's silver or gold." (7.) His patience, "none of these things move me, neither count I my life dear." (8.) And among all our motives, these have need to be in capital letters before our eyes. 1. We oversee and feed "the church of God which he hath purchased with his own blood." 2. "Grievous wolves shall enter in among you, not sparing the flock, and of your own selves shall men arise, speaking perverse things, to draw away disciples after them." Write all this upon your hearts, and it will do yourselves and the church more good than twenty years' study of lower things, which though they get you greater applause in the world, yet separated from these, will make you but sounding brass and tinkling cymbals.

The great advantage of a sincere heart is, that God and glory, and the saving of souls, are their very end; and where that end is truly intended, no labour or suffering will stop them, or turn them back; for a man must have his end, whatever it cost him. He still retains this lesson, whatever he forget, "One thing is necessary;" and "Seek first the kingdom of God:" and therefore says, "Necessity is laid upon me, and woe unto me if I preach not the gospel!" And this is it that will most effectually make easy all our labours, and make light all burdens, and make our sufferings seem tolerable, and cause us to venture on any hazard in the way. That which I once made the motto of my colours in another warfare, I desire may be still before my eyes in this, which yet, according to my intention, is not altogether another. On one side, *He that saveth his life shall lose it;* on the other, *Nec propter vitam vivendi perdere causas.* Which Doctor Jo. Reignolds thought had reason enough in it to hold him to his labours, though it cost him his life. He that knoweth that he serveth a God that will never suffer any man to be a loser by him, need not fear what hazard he runs in his cause; and he that knows that he seeks a prize, which if obtained, will infinitely overmatch his cost, may boldly engage his whole estate on it, and sell all to purchase so rich a pearl. Well, brethren, I will spend no more words in exhorting wise merchants to such a bargain, nor telling teachers themselves of such common truths; and if I have said more than needs already, I am glad. I hope now I may take it for granted, that you are resolved of the utmost diligence and fidelity in the work. On which supposition I shall now proceed.

CHAPTER VII.

DIRECTIONS FOR THE RIGHT MANAGING THIS WORK.

SECTION I.

It is so happy a work which we have before us, that it is a thousand pities it should be destroyed in the birth, and perish in our hands. And though I know that we have a knotty generation to deal with, and that it is past the power of any of us all to change a carnal heart without the effectual grace of the Holy Ghost; yet it is so usual with God to work by means, and to bless the right endeavours of his servants, that I cannot fear, but great things will be done, and a wonderful blow will be given to the kingdom of darkness by our undertaken work, if it do not miscarry through the fault of the ministers themselves. And the main danger is in these two defects. 1. Of diligence. 2. Of skill. Against the former I have spoken much already: as for the latter, I am so conscious of my own unskilfulness, that I am far from imagining that I am fit to give directions to any but the younger and unexperienced of the ministry; and therefore must expect so much justice in your interpretation, as that you will suppose me now to speak to none but such. But yet something I shall say, and not pass over this part in silence, because the number of such is so great, and I am so apprehensive that the welfare of the church and nation doth much depend on the management of this work.

The points wherein you have need to be solicitous are these two.

(1.) To bring your people to submit to this course of private catechising or instructing; for if they will not come at you, what good can they receive?

(2.) To do the work so as may most tend to the success of it, when they do come to you.

I. And for the *first*, the best directions that I can give are these following:

1. The chief means of all is, for a minister so to behave himself in the main course of his ministry and life, as may tend to convince his people of his ability, sincerity, and unfeigned love to them; for if they take him to be ignorant, they will despise his teaching, and think themselves as wise as he. And if they think him self-seeking, or hypocritical, and one that doth not mean as he saith, they will suspect all that he saith and doth for them, and will not be regardful of him. And if they think he intendeth but to domineer over their consciences, and to trouble and disgrace them, or merely to exercise their wits and memories, they will fly away from him as an adversary, and from his endeavours, as noxious and ungrateful to them. Whereas when they are convinced that he understandeth what he doth, and have high thoughts of his abilities, they will reverence him, and the easilier stoop to his advice. And when they are persuaded of his uprightness, they will the less suspect his motions; and when they perceive that he intendeth no private ends of his own, but merely their good, they will the sooner be persuaded by him. And because those that I write to are supposed to be none of the most able ministers, and therefore may despair of being reverenced for their parts; I say to such :—

(1.) You have the more need to study and labour for their increase.

(2.) You must necessarily have that which Amesius makes the lowest degree tolerable, viz. to be *supra vulgus fidelium;* and it will produce some reverence when they know you are wiser than themselves.

(3.) And that which you want in ability, must be made up in the other qualifications, and then your advice may be as successful as others.

If ministers are content to purchase an interest in their people at the dearest rates to their own flesh, and would condescend to them, and be familiar, and loving, and prudent in their carriage, and abound according to their ability in good works, they might do much more with their people than ordinarily they can do. Not that we should much regard an interest in them for our own sakes; but that we may be more capable of promoting the interest of Christ, and of furthering their own salvation. Were it not for their own sakes, it were no great matter whether they love or hate us: but what commander can do any great service by an army that hates him? And how can we think that they will much regard our counsel, while they abhor or disregard the persons that give it them! Labour therefore for some competent interest in your people's estimation and affection, and then you may the better prevail with them.

Object. But what should a minister do that findeth he hath quite lost his interest with them?

Answ. If they be so vile a people that they hate him not for any weakness, nor through misreports about particular things, but merely for endeavouring their good, though in prudence as well as zeal, and would hate any other that should do his duty; then must he in patience and meekness continue to instruct these that oppose themselves, if God peradventure will give them repentance to the acknowledgment of the truth. But if it be upon any weaknesses of his, or difference in lesser opinions, or prejudice merely against his own person, let him try first to remove the prejudice by all lawful means; and if he cannot, let him tell them, It is not for myself, but for you that I labour; and therefore seeing that you will not obey the word from me, I desire that you will agree to accept of some other that may do you that good, which I cannot: and so leave them, and try whether another man may not be fitter for them, and he fitter for another people. For an ingenious man can hardly stay with a people against their wills; and a sincere man can more hardly, for any commodity of his own, remain in a place where he is like to be unprofitable, to hinder the good which they might receive from another man, who hath the advantage of a greater interest in their estimation and affection.

2. Supposing then this general preparation; the next thing to be done is, to use the most effectual means to convince them of the benefit and necessity of this course, to their own souls. The way to win the consent of any man to any thing that you offer, is to prove it to be good for him, and to do this in evidence that hath some fitness and proportion with his own understanding; for if you cannot make him believe that it is good or necessary for him, he will never let it down, but spit it out with loathing or contempt. You must therefore preach to them some effectual convincing sermons to this purpose beforehand, which shall fully show them the benefit and necessity of the knowledge of divine truths in general, and of knowing the principles in special, and that the aged have the same duty and need as others, and in some respects much more: e. g. from Heb. v. 12, which affordeth us many observations suitable to our present business.

As, (1.) That God's oracles must be a man's lessons.

(2.) Ministers must teach these, and people must learn them of them.

(3.) The oracles of God have some principles or fundamentals, that all must know that will be saved.

(4.) These principles must be first learned: that is the right order.

(5.) It may be will expected that people thrive in knowledge according to the means or teaching which they possess; and if they do not, it is their great sin.

(6.) If any have lived long in the church under the means of knowledge, and yet be ignorant of these principles, he hath need to be taught them yet, how old soever he be. All this is plain from the text; whence we have a fair opportunity by twenty clear convincing reasons to show them; 1. The necessity of knowing God's oracles. 2. And more especially, of the principles. And, 3. Especially for the aged, that have sinfully lost so much time already, that have so long promised to repent when they were old, that should be teachers to the younger, whose ignorance is a double sin and shame, who have so little time to learn it, and are so near their judgment; and who have souls to save or lose as well as others, &c. Convince them how impossible it is to go the way to heaven without knowing it, when there are so many difficulties and enemies in our way; and when men cannot do their worldly business without knowledge, nor learn a trade without an apprenticeship. Who can love, or seek, or desire that which he knoweth not? Convince them what a contradiction it is to be a christian, and yet to refuse to learn. For what is a christian but a disciple of Christ? and how can he be his disciple that refuseth to be taught by him? And he that refuseth to be taught by his ministers refuseth to be taught by him. For Christ will not come down from heaven again to teach them by his own mouth, but hath appointed his ministers to keep school and teach them under him. To say therefore that they will not be taught by his ministers, is to say, they will not be taught by Christ; and that is to say, they will be none of his disciples, or no christians. Abundance of such undeniable evidences we have at hand to convince them of their duty. Make them understand that it is not an arbitrary business of our own devising and imposing, but necessity is laid upon us, and if we look not to every member of the flock according to our power, they may perish in their own iniquities, but their blood will be required at our hands: it is God, and not we, that is the contriver and imposer of the work; therefore they blame God more than us in accusing it. Would they be so cruel as to wish a minister to cast away his own soul knowingly and wilfully, for fear of troubling them in hindering their damnation? Especially acquaint them fully with the true nature of the ministerial office, and the church's necessity of it; how it consisteth in teaching and guiding all the flock; and that as they must come to the congregation as scholars to school, so must they be content to give account of their learning, and to be instructed man by man.

Let them know what a tendency this hath to their salvation, what a profitable improvement it will be of their time, and how much vanity and evil it will prevent; and when they once find that it is for their own good, they will the easilier yield to it.

3. When this is done, it will be very necessary, that according to our Agreement, we give one of the catechisms to every family in the parish, poor and rich, that so they might be so far without excuse. For if you leave it to themselves, perhaps half of them will not so much as get them. Whereas, when they have them put into their hands, the receiving is a kind of engagement to learn them; and if they do but read the exhortation, as it is likely they will do, it will perhaps convince them, and incite them to submit. And for the delivery of them, the best way is, for the minister first to give notice in the congregation that they shall be brought to their houses, and then to go himself from house to house and deliver them, and take the opportunity of persuading them to the work; and as they go, take a catalogue of all the persons at years of discretion in the several families, that they may know whom they have to take care of and instruct, and whom to expect when it cometh to the turns. I have formerly, in the distributing of some books among them, desired every family to fetch them; but I found more confusion and uncertainty in that way, and now took this as the better, but in small parishes either way may serve.

And for the charge of the books, if the minister be able, it will be well for him to bear it; if not, the best affected of his people of the richer sort should bear it among them: or at a day of humiliation in preparation to the work, let the collection that is wont to be for the poor be employed to buy catechisms, and the people be desired to be the more liberal, and what is wanting, the well-affected to the work may make it up.

And for the order of proceeding in small parishes, the matter is not great; but in greater it will be needful that we take them in order, family by family, beginning the execution a month or six weeks after the delivery of the books, that they may have time to learn; and thus taking them together in common, they will the more willingly come, and the backward will be the more ashamed to keep off.

4. Be sure that you deal gently with them, and take off all discouragements as effectually as you can. (1.) Tell them publicly, that if they have learned any other catechism already, you will not urge them to learn this, unless they desire it themselves; for the substance of all catechisms that are orthodox is the same; only our reasons for offering them this, was the brevity and fulness, that we might give them as much as we could in few words, and so make their work more easy. Or, if any of them had yet rather learn any other orthodox catechism, let them have their choice.

(2.) As for the old people that are of weak memories, and not like to live long in the world, and complain that they cannot remember the words; tell them that you expect not that they should over-much perplex their minds about it, but hear it oft read over, and see that they understand it, and get the matter into their minds and hearts, and then they may be borne with, though they remember not the words.

(3.) And let your dealing with those that you begin with be so gentle, convincing, and winning, that the report of it may be an encouragement to others to come.

5. If all this will not serve to bring any particular persons to submit, do not so cast them off; but go to them and expostulate the case with them; and know what their reasons are, and convince them of the sinfulness and danger of their contempt of the help that is offered them. A soul is so precious, that we should not lose one for want of labour; but follow them while there is any hope, and not give them up as desperate, till there be no remedy. Before we give them over as dogs or swine, let us try the utmost, that we may have the experience of their obstinate contempt or renting us, to warrant our forsaking them. Charity beareth and waiteth long.

SECTION II.

II. Having used these means to procure them to come in and submit to your teaching, the next thing to be considered is, how you should deal most effectually with them in the work: and again I must say, that I think it an easier matter by far, to compose and preach a good sermon, than to deal rightly with an ignorant man for his instruction in the necessary principles of religion. As much as this work is contemned by some, I doubt not but it will try the parts and spirits of ministers, and show you the difference between one man and another, more fully than pulpit preaching will do. And here I shall, as fitting to my purpose, transcribe the words of a most learned, orthodox, and godly man, Bishop Usher, in his sermon before King James at Wansted, on Ephes. iv. 13, p. 44, 45; (but impres. 3, p. 34, 35;) "Your Majesty's care can never be sufficiently commended, in taking order that the chief heads of the catechism should in the ordinary ministry be diligently propounded and explained unto the people throughout the land; which I wish were as duly executed every where, as it was piously by you intended. Great scholars possibly may think, that it standeth not so well with their credit, to stoop thus low, and to spend so much of their time in teaching these rudiments and first principles of the doctrine of Christ. But they should consider that the laying of the foundation skilfully, as it is the matter of greatest importance in the whole building; so is it the very masterpiece of the wisest builder, 1 Cor. iii. 10. According to the grace of God which is given to me, as a wise master-builder, I have laid the foundation, saith the great apostle. And let the learnedest of us all try it whenever we please, we shall find, that to lay this groundwork rightly, (that is, to apply ourselves to the capacity of the common auditory, and to make an ignorant man to understand these mysteries in some good measure,) will put us to the trial of our skill, and trouble us a great deal more, than if we were to discuss a controversy, or handle a point of learning in the schools. Yet Christ did give as well his apostles, and prophets, and evangelists, as his ordinary pastors and teachers, to bring us all, both learned and unlearned, unto the unity of this faith and knowledge: and the neglecting of this, is the frustrating of the whole work of the ministry. For let us preach never so many sermons to the people, our labour is but lost, as long as the foundation is unlaid, and the first principles untaught, upon which all other doctrine must be builded." So far the reverend bishop.

The directions which I think necessary to be observed in the managing of the work, for matter and manner, are these following:

Direct. 1. When your neighbours come to you, one family, or more, begin with a brief preface, to demulce their minds, and take off this offence, unwillingness, or discouragement, to prepare them to entertain your following instructions.

E. g. Neighbours, it may perhaps seem to some of you, as an unusual, so a troublesome business, that I put you upon; but I hope you will not think it needless; for if I had thought so, I should have spared you and myself this labour. But my conscience hath told me; yea, God hath told me in his word, so roundly, what it is to have the charge of men's souls, and how the blood of them that perish in their sins will be required at the hands of a minister that neglecteth them, that I dare not be so guilty of it as I have been. Alas, all our business in this world is to get well to heaven; and God hath appointed us to be guides to his people, to help them safe thither; if this be well done, all is done; and if this be not done, we are for ever undone! The Lord knows how little a while you and I may be together; and therefore it concerns us to do what we can for our own and your salvation, before we leave you, or you leave the world. All other businesses in the world are but toys and dreams in comparison of this. The labours of your calling are but to prop up the cottages of the flesh, while you are making ready for death and judgment, which God knows is near at hand. And I hope you will be glad of help in so needful a work, and not think much that I put you in this trouble, when the trifles of the world will not be got without greater trouble.

This, some of this, or somewhat to this purpose, may tend to make them more willing to hear you, and receive instruction, or give you an account of their knowledge or practice, which must be the work of the day.

Direct. 2. When you have (to spare time) spoken thus to them all, take then the persons one by one, and deal with them as far as you can in private, out of the hearing of the rest; for some cannot speak freely before others, and some will not endure to be questioned before others, because they think that it tendeth to their shame to have others hear their answers; and some persons that can make better answers themselves, will be ready when they are gone to twattle of what they heard, and to disgrace those that speak not so well as they, and so people will be discouraged, and backward persons will have pretences to forbear and forsake the work, and say, they will not come to be made a scorn or laughing-stock. You must therefore be very prudent to prevent all these inconveniences. But the main reason is, as I find by experience, people will better take plain close dealing about their sin, and misery, and duty, when you have them alone, than they will before others; and if you have not opportunity to set it home and deal freely with them, you will frustrate all. If therefore you have convenient place, let the rest stay in the room, while you confer with each person by themselves in another room; only for the necessary avoiding of scandal, we must speak to the women only in the presence of some others: and if we do lose some advantage by it of the success of our instructions, there is no remedy; it is better to do so, than by giving matter of reproach to the malicious, to destroy all the work. Yet we may so contrive it, that though some others be in the room, yet what passages are less fit for others' observance, may be spoken *submissa voce,* that others may be no hearers of it; and therefore they may be placed at the remotest part of the room. Or at least let none be present but the members of the same family, that be more familiar, and not so likely to reproach one another. And then, in your most rousing examinations and reproofs, deal most with the most ignorant, and secure, and vicious, that you may have the clearer ground for your closest dealing, and the hearing of it may awaken the standers-by, to whom you seem not so directly to apply it. These small things deserve observance, because they be in order to a work that is not small: and small errors may hinder a great deal of good.

Direct. 3. Let the beginning of your work be, by taking an account of what they have learned of the words of the catechism, receiving their answer to each question; and if they are able to recite but a little or none of it, try whether they can rehearse the creed and the decalogue.

Direct. 4. Then choose out some of the weightiest points, and try, by further questions, how they understand them. And therein be careful of these things following: (1.) That you do not begin with less necessary points, but these which themselves may perceive are of nearest concernment to them. As, e. g. What do you think becomes of men when they are dead? What shall become of us, after the end of this world? Do you believe that you have any sin? or that you were born with sin? And what doth every sin deserve? What remedy hath God provided for the saving of sinful, miserable souls? Hath any one suffered for our sins in our stead? Or must we suffer for them ourselves? Who be they that God will pardon? and who shall be saved by the blood of Christ? What change must be made on all that shall be saved? And how is it made? Where is our chief happiness? and what is it that our hearts must be most set upon? with such like as these.

(2.) Take heed of asking them nice, or needless, or doubtful and very difficult questions, though about those matters that are of greatest weight in themselves: specially be very cautelous how you put them upon the definition or description. Some self-conceited men will be busy with such questions which they cannot answer themselves, and as censorious of the poor people that cannot answer them, as if life and death depended thereon. You will ask them perhaps, What is God? and how defective an answer must you make yourselves! specially if it be the *quid*, and not the *qualis*, that you mean. You may tell what he is not, sooner than what he is. If you ask what is *faith?* or what is *repentance?* how sorrily would many very learned divines answer you! Or else they would not be at so great difference among themselves about them; not only disagreeing about the definitions of them, but so widely disagreeing? If you ask them what is *forgiveness of sin*, how many ministers may you ask before you have a right answer! or else they would not be so disagreed in the point. Much more may I say so about justification (though perhaps the same thing with remission). So if you ask them what *regeneration* is, what *sanctification* is? why divines are not agreed what they are themselves. But you will say, perhaps, If men know not what God is, what faith, repentance, conversion, sanctification, and pardon of sin, or justification be, how can they be true christians, and be saved? I answer, It is one thing to know exactly what they be, and another thing to know them in the nature of them in the main, though with a more general, indistinct, and undigested knowledge; and it is one thing to *know*, and another thing to *tell* what this or that is. The very name as commonly used doth signify to them, and express from them the thing without a definition; and they partly understand what that name signifieth, when they cannot tell it you in other words. As they know what it is to believe, to repent, to be forgiven; by custom of speech they know what these mean, and yet cannot define them, but perhaps put you off with the country answer, To repent, is to repent; and to be forgiven, is to be forgiven; or if they can say, It is to be pardoned, it is fair. Yet do I not absolutely dissuade you from the use of such questions; but do it cautelously, in case you suspect some gross ignorance in the point; specially about God himself. And, (which is the next part of this direction,)

(3.) In such a case, so contrive the predicate into your question, that they may perceive what you mean, and that it is not a nice definition, but a necessary solution, that you expect, and look not after words but things; and there leave them to a bare yea or nay, or the mere election of one of the two descriptions which yourself shall propound. As, e. g. What is God? is he made of flesh and blood as we are, or is he an invisible Spirit? is he a man or is he not? had he any beginning? can he die? What is faith? is it a believing all the word of God? What is it to believe in Christ? is it all one as to become a true christian; or to believe that Christ is the Saviour of the world, and to accept him for your Saviour, to pardon, teach, govern, and glorify? What is repentance? is it only to be sorry for sin, or is it the change of the mind from sin to God, or both?

(4.) And as you must do thus when you come to hard points, as definitions, or the like; so in all points where you perceive that they understand not the meaning and stress of your question, there you must first draw out their answer into your question, and demand but his yea or nay; yea, if it be never so easy a point that you are upon, you must do thus at last, in case by the first question you have an unsatisfactory answer: e. g. I have oft asked some very ignorant people, How do you think that your sins, so many and great sins, shall be pardoned? And they tell me by their repenting and mending their lives; and never mention Jesus Christ. I ask them further, But do you think that your amendment can make God any amends or satisfaction for the sin that is past? They will answer, We hope so, or else we know not what will. A man would think now that these men had no knowledge of Christ at all, in that they make no mention of him. And some I find have indeed none; and when I tell them over the history of the gospel, and what Christ is, did, and suffered, and why, they stand wondering at it as a strange thing that they had never heard before, and some say, they never heard this much before, nor knew it, though they came to church every Lord's day. But some, I perceive, do give such answers, because they understand not the scope of my question, but think that I take Christ's death as granted, and only ask them what shall make God satisfaction, as their part under Christ; though thus also they discover sad ignorance. And when I ask them whether their deeds can merit any thing of God? they say, No; but they hope God will accept them. And if I ask further, Can you be saved without the death of Christ? they say, No. And if I ask, What hath he done or suffered for you? they will say, He died for us, or shed his blood for us; and will profess that they place their confidence in that for salvation. Many men have that in their minds, which is not ripe for utterance, and through ill education and disuse, they are strangers to the expressions of those things which they have some conceptions of: and, by the way, you may here see the cause to deal very tenderly with the common people for matter of knowledge and defect of expression, if they are teachable and tractable, and willing to use means, and to live obediently; for many even ancient, godly persons, cannot speak their minds in any tolerable expressions; no, nor cannot learn when expressions are put into their mouths. Some of the most pious, experienced, approved christians that I know, (aged people,) complain exceedingly to me with tears, that they cannot learn the words of the catechism; and when I consider their advantages, that they have lived under the most excellent helps, in constant duty, and in the best company, for forty, or fifty, or sixty years together, it teacheth me what to expect from poor ignorant people, that never had such company and converse for one year or week, and not to reject them so hastily as some hot and too high professors would have us do. But this is on the by.

(5.) This also must be observed, that if you find them at a loss, and unable to answer your questions, drive them not on too hard or too long with question after question, lest they conceive you intend but to puzzle them and disgrace them: but presently, when you perceive them troubled that they cannot answer, then step in yourself and take the burden off them, and make answer to the question yourselves; and then do it thoroughly and plainly, and make a full explication of the whole business to them, that by your teaching they may be brought to understand it before you leave them. And herein it is commonly necessary that you fetch up the matter *ab origine*, and take it on in order till you come to the point in question.

(6.) And usually, with the grossly ignorant, it is flatly necessary that you do run over all the sum of our religion to them in the most familiar way that you can possibly devise. But this must be the next direction.

Direct. 5. When you have done what you see cause in the trial of their knowledge, proceed next to instruct them yourselves: and this must be according to their several capacities. If it be a professor that understandeth the fundamentals, fall upon somewhat which you perceive that he most needeth, either explaining further some of the mysteries of the gospel, or laying the grounds of some duty which he may doubt of, or showing the necessity of what he neglecteth, or meeting with his sins or mistakes, as may be most convincing and edifying to him. If it be one that is grossly ignorant, give him a plain familiar recital of the sum of the christian religion in a few words; for though it be in the catechism already, yet a more familiar way may better help them to understand it. As thus: You must know, that from everlasting there was one only God, that had no beginning, and can have no end, who is not a body as we are, but a most pure, spiritual Being, that knoweth all things, and can do all things, and hath all goodness and blessedness in himself. This God is but one, but yet three persons, the Father, the Son, and the Holy Ghost, in an incomprehensible manner, above our reach; yet we have somewhat in ourselves and other creatures that may give us some resemblance of it. As in a man, his power, and his understanding, and will, are but one soul, and yet they are not one faculty, but differ one from another; or as in the sun, the being or power, and the heat and the light, are not all one, and yet there is but one sun; so in a more incomprehensible manner it is in God. And you must know that this one God did make all the world by his word; the heavens he made to be the place of his glory, and made a world of holy angels to serve him, in his glory; but some of these did by pride or other sin fall from God, and are become devils that shall be miserable in torments for ever. When he had made the rest of this lower world, he made man, as his noblest creature here, even one man and one woman, Adam and Eve; and he made them perfect without any sin or fault, and put them into the garden of Eden, and forbid them to eat but of one tree in the garden, and told them that if they did, they should die. But the devil that had first fallen himself did tempt them to sin, and they yielded to his temptation, and by wilful sinning they fell under the curse of God's law, and fell short of the glory of God. But God of his infinite wisdom and mercy did send his own Son Jesus Christ to be their Redeemer, who as he was promised in the beginning, so in the fulness of time, sixteen hundred and fifty-five years ago, was made man, and was born of a virgin by the power of the Holy Ghost, and lived on earth among the Jews about thirty-three years; and he preached the gospel himself, and wrought many miracles to prove his doctrine, and bring men to believe in him; healing the lame, the blind, the sick, and raising the dead by the word of his mouth, by his divine power; and at the end by the malice of the Jews, and his own consent, he was offered upon the cross, as a sacrifice for our sins, to bear that curse that we should have borne; and when he was buried, he rose again the third day, and lived on earth forty days after: and before his departure he sent his apostles and other ministers to preach the gospel of salvation to the world, and to call home lost sinners by repentance, and to assure them in his name, that if they will but believe in him and take him for their Saviour, and unfeignedly lament their former sins, and turn from them to God, and will take everlasting glory for their portion, and be content to resign their carnal interests and desires, he will pardon freely all that is past, and be merciful to them for the time to come, and will lead them up into spiritual communion with God, and bring them to his glory when this life is ended. But for them that make light of their sins and of his mercy, and will not forsake the pleasures of this world for the hopes of another, they shall be condemned to everlasting punishment. This gospel Christ hath appointed his ministers to preach to all the world; and when he had given this in charge to his apostles, he ascended up into heaven before their faces, where he is now in glory with God the Father, in our nature, ruling all; and at the end of this world, he will come again in that nature, and will call the dead to life again, and set them all before him to be judged; and all that truly repented and believed in him and were renewed by his Spirit, and renounced this world for the hopes of a better, shall be judged to live with God in glory, and shall be like to his angels, and praise him for ever; and the rest that repented not, and believed not in him, but lived to the flesh and the world, shall be condemned to everlasting misery. So that you may see by this, that man's happiness is not in this world but in the next, and that all men have lost their hopes of that happiness by sin, and that Jesus Christ, the only Son of God and the Redeemer of the world, hath recovered it for us by the price of his blood shed, and hath made a new covenant with us, assuring us of life and salvation, if we repent and believe in him for that life, and mortify our fleshly desires. To which end he sendeth forth his Holy Spirit to convert all that shall be saved, and to turn their hearts from this world to God. If ever you mean to be saved, therefore, it must be thus with you: your former sins must be the grief of your soul, and you must fly to a crucified Christ as your only refuge from the deserved curse, and the Spirit of Christ must convert you, and dwell in you, and make you wholly a new creature; or there is no salvation. Some such short, plain rehearsal of the principles of religion, in the most familiar manner that you can devise, with a brief touch of application in the end, will be necessary when you deal with the grossly ignorant; and if you perceive they understand you not, go over it again, and ask them whether they understand it, and seek to leave it fixed in their memories.

Direct. 6. Whether they be grossly ignorant or not, if you suspect them to be ungodly, fall next upon a prudent inquiry into their states; and the best and least offensive way will be this: to take your occasion from some article of the catechism, as the fifth or seventh; and then to make way by a word that may demulce their minds, by convincing them of the necessity of it; as e. g. thus, or to this purpose: You see in the seventh article proved in Scripture, that the Holy Ghost doth by the word enlighten men's minds, and soften and open their hearts, and turn them from the power of Satan to God by faith in Christ, and so makes them a sanctified, peculiar people to God; and that none but these are made partakers of Christ and life. Now though I have no desire needlessly to pry into any man's secrets, yet because that it is the office of ministers to give advice to a people in the matters of salvation, and because it is so dangerous a matter to be mistaken where life or death everlasting doth lie upon it, I would entreat you to deal truly, and tell me whether you ever found this great change upon your own heart, or not? Did you ever find the Spirit of God by the word, come in your understanding with a new heavenly life, which hath made you a new creature? The Lord that seeth your heart doth know whether it be so or not; therefore I pray you, see that you speak the truth.

If he tell you, that he hopes he is converted—all are sinners—but he is sorry for his sins, or the like; then tell him more particularly in a few words of the plainest notes, or by a short description, what true conversion is, and so renew and enforce the inquiry; as thus: Because your salvation or damnation lieth upon it, I would fain help you a little in this, that you may not be mistaken in a business of such consequence, but may find out the truth before it be too late; for as God will judge us impartially, so we have his word before us, by which we may know now how God will judge us then; for this word tells us most certainly who they be that shall go to heaven, and who to hell. Now the Scripture tells us that the state of an unconverted man is this: he seeth no great matter of felicity in the love and communion of God in the life to come, which may draw his heart thither from this present world; but he liveth to his carnal self, or to the flesh, and the main bent of his life is, that it may go well with his body here, and that religion that he hath is but a little on the by, lest he should be damned when he can keep the world no longer; so that the world and flesh are highest in his esteem, and nearest to his heart, and God and glory stand below them and further off, and all their service of God is but a giving him that which the world and flesh can spare. This is the true case of every unconverted man; and all that are in this case are in a state of misery. But he that is truly converted, hath had a light shining into his soul from God, which hath showed him the greatness of his sin and misery, and made it a heavy load upon his soul; and showed him what Christ is, and hath done for sinners, and made him admire at the riches of God's grace in him! Oh what glad news is it to him, that yet there is hope for such lost sinners as he; that so many and so great sins may be pardoned; and that this is offered to all that will accept it! How gladly doth he entertain this message and offer: and for the time to come he resigneth himself and all that he hath to Christ to be wholly his, and disposed of by him, in order to the everlasting glory which he hath promised. He hath now such a sight of the blessed state of the saints in glory, that he despiseth all this world as dross and dung in comparison of it, and there he layeth up his happiness and his hopes, and takes all the matters of this life but as so many helps or hinderances in the way of that; so that the very bent and main care and business of his life is to be happy in the life to come. This is the case of all that are truly converted, and shall be saved. Is this your case or not? Have you found such a change or work as this upon your soul? If he say, he hopes he hath, descend to some particulars distinctly: e. g. I pray you then answer me to these two or three questions. (1.) Can you truly say, that all the known sins of your life past are the grief of your heart, and that you have felt that everlasting misery is due to you for them, and that in the sense of this heavy burden, you have felt yourself a lost man, and have gladly entertained the news of a Saviour, and cast your soul upon Christ alone for pardon by his blood? (2.) Can you truly say, that your heart is so far turned from your former sins, that you hate the sins that formerly you loved, and love that holy life that you had no mind to before, and that you do not now live in the wilful practice of any known sin? Is there no sin which you are not heartily willing to leave, whatever it cost you, and no duty which you are not willing to perform? (3.) Can you truly say, that you have so far taken the everlasting enjoyments of God for your happiness, that it hath the most of your heart, of your love, desire, and care; and that you are resolved by the strength of grace to let go all that you have in the world rather than hazard it; and that it is your daily principal business to seek it? Can you truly say that, though you have your failings and sins, yet your main care and the bent of your whole life is to please God and enjoy him for ever; and that you give the world God's leavings, as it were, and not God the world's leavings, and that your worldly business is but as a traveller seeking for provision in his journey, and heaven is the place that you take for your home?

If he say yea to the first and third, tell him how great a thing it is for a man's heart to abhor his sin, and to lay up his happiness unfeignedly in another world, and to live in this world for another that is out of sight; and therefore desire him to see that it be so indeed. If he say yea to the second question, then turn to the ninth, tenth, eleventh, or twelfth articles of the catechism, and read over some of those duties which you must suspect him to omit; and ask him, whether he performs such or such a duty, especially prayer, (in family or private,) and the holy spending of all the Lord's day; because these are of so great moment (of which anon).

Direct. 7. When you have, either by former discovery of gross ignorance, or by these latter inquiries into his spiritual state, discerned an apparent probability that the person is yet in an unconverted state; your next business is to fall on with all your skill and power to bring his heart to the sense of his condition: e.g. Truly, neighbours, I have no mind, the Lord knows, to make your condition worse than it is, nor to put any causeless fear or trouble in your mind: but I suppose you would take me but for a flattering enemy, and not a faithful friend, if I should daub with you, and not tell you the truth. If you sought to a physician in your sickness, you would have him tell you the truth, though it were the worst: much more here; for there the knowledge of your disease may by fears increase it, but here you must know it, or else you can never be recovered from it. I much fear that you are yet a stranger to the new life of all them that Christ will save; for if you were a christian indeed, and truly converted, your very heart would have been set on God and the life to come, and you would have admired the riches of grace in Christ, and you would have made it your business to prepare for everlasting, and you durst not, you would not, live in any wilful sin, nor in the neglect of such duties. Alas, what have you done, how have you spent your time till now! Did you know that you had a soul to save or lose, and that you must live in heaven or hell for ever, and that you had your life and time in this world for that purpose, to prepare for another? Alas, what have you been doing all this while that you are so ignorant, or so unprepared for death if it should now find you? If you had but had as much mind of heaven as of earth, you would have known more of it, and done more for it, and inquired more diligently after it than you have done! You can learn how to do your business in the world, and why could you not have learned more of the will of God if you had but minded it? You have neighbours that could learn more, that have had as much to do in the world as you, and as little time. Do you think that heaven is not worth your labour, or that it is like it can be had without any care or pains, when you cannot have the trifles of the world without, and when God hath bid you first seek his kingdom and the righteousness thereof? Alas, neighbours, what if you had died before this hour in an unconverted state; what had become of you, and where had you now been? Why you did not know all this while that you should live a day to an end! Oh that ever you would be so cruel to yourselves as to venture your everlasting state so desperately as you have done! What did you think of? Did you not all this while know that you must shortly die, and be judged as you were then found?

Had you any greater work to do, or any greater business to mind, than your salvation? Do you think that all that you can get in this world will comfort you at a dying hour, or purchase your salvation, or ease the pains of hell-fire?

Set these things home with a more earnest voice than the former part of your conference was managed with; for if you get it not to the heart, you do little or nothing, and that which affecteth not is soon forgotten.

Direct. 8. Next this, conclude the whole with a practical exhortation, which must contain two parts: First, The duty of the heart in order to a closure with Christ, and that which is contained in that closure; and, secondly, The use of external means for the time to come, and the avoiding of former sins:—e. g. Neighbour, I am heartily sorry to find you in so sad a case, but I should be more sorry to leave you in it; and therefore let me entreat you, for the Lord's sake, and for your own sake, to regard what I shall say to you, as to the time to come. It is the Lord's great mercy that he did not cut you off in your unconverted, natural state, and that you have yet life and time, and that there is a sufficient remedy provided for your soul in the blood of Christ; and he is yet offered with pardon and life to you as well as any others; God hath not left sinful man to utter desperation, for want of a ransom by a Redeemer, as he hath done the devils; nor hath he made any exception in the offer or promise of pardon and life against you, any more than against any others. If you had yet but a bleeding heart for sin, and could come to Christ believingly for recovery, and resign yourselves to him as your Saviour and Lord, and would be a new man for the time to come, the Lord would have mercy on you, in the pardon of your sins, and the saving of your soul; and I must tell you that as it must be the great work of God's grace to give you such a heart, so if ever he mean to pardon and save you, he will make this change upon you, that I have before mentioned: he will make you feel your sin as the heaviest burden in the world, as that which is most odious in itself, and hath laid you open to the curse of God; he will make you see that you are a lost man, and that there is no way but one for you, even everlasting damnation, unless you are pardoned by the blood of Christ, and sanctified by his Spirit; he will make you see the need you have of Christ, and how much you are beholden to him for his bloodshed, and how all your hope and life is in him: he will make you see the vanity of this world and all that it can afford you, and that all your happiness is with God, in that everlasting life, where with saints and angels you may behold his glory, and live in his love and praises, when those that reject him shall be tormented with the devils; and because it is only Christ the Redeemer that can bring you to that glory, and deliver you from that torment, he will make you look to him as your hope and life, and cast your burdened soul upon him; and give up yourselves to be saved, and taught, and ruled by him: and he will possess you with the Spirit of holiness, that your heart shall be set upon God and heaven as your treasure, and the care of your mind, and the business of your life, shall be to obtain it; and you shall despise this world, and deny your fleshly interests and desires, and cast away the sin with abhorrence which you delighted in; and count no pains too great, nor no suffering too dear, for the obtaining of that everlasting life with God. Let me tell you that till this work be done upon you, you are a miserable man; and if you die before it is done, you are lost for ever. Now you have hope and help before you, but then there will be none. Let me therefore entreat these two or three things of you, and do not deny them me, as you love your soul. (1.) That you will not rest in this condition that you are in: be not quiet in your mind, till you find a true conversion to be wrought. Think when you rise in the morning, Oh what if this day should be my last, and death should find me in an unrenewed state! Think when you are about your labour, Oh how much greater a work have I yet to do, to get my soul reconciled to God and possessed of his Spirit! Think when you are eating, or drinking, or looking on any thing that you possess in the world, what good will all this do me, if I live and die an enemy to God, and a stranger to Christ and his Spirit, and so must perish for ever. Let these thoughts be day and night upon your mind, till your soul be changed. (2.) The thing that I would entreat of you is, that you would bethink you seriously what a vain thing this world is, and how shortly it will leave you to a cold grave, and everlasting misery, if you have not a better treasure than this. And bethink you what it is to live in the sight of the face of God, and to reign with Christ, and be like the angels; and that this is the life that Christ hath procured you, and is preparing for you, and offereth you if you will accept it in and with himself upon his easy, reasonable terms. Bethink yourself whether it be not madness to slight such an endless glory, and to prefer these fleshly dreams and earthly shadows before it. Use yourself to such considerations as these, when you are alone, and let them dwell upon your mind. (3.) The thing that I would entreat of you is, that you will presently, without any more delay, accept of this felicity, and this Saviour: close with the Lord Jesus that offereth you this eternal life. Joyfully and thankfully accept his offer, as the only way to make you happy; and then you may believe that all your sins shall be done away by him. (4.) My request to you is, that you will resolve presently against your former sins; find out what hath defiled your heart and life, and cast it up now by the vomit of repentance as you would do poison out of your stomach, and abhor the thought of taking it in again. (5.) My request to you is, that you will set yourselves close to the use of God's means till this change be wrought, and then continue his means till you are confirmed, and at last perfected. 1. Because you cannot of yourselves make this change upon your heart and life, betake yourself daily to God for it by prayer, and beg earnestly as for your life that he will pardon all your former sins, and change your heart, and show you the riches of his grace in Christ, and the glory of his kingdom, and draw up your heart to himself. Follow God day and night with these requests. 2. That you will fly from temptations and occasions of sin, and forsake your former evil company, and betake yourselves into the company of those that fear God, and will help you in the way to heaven. 3. That you will especially spend the Lord's day in holy exercises, both public and private, and lose not one quarter of an hour of any of your time, but especially of that most precious time, which God hath given you purposely that you may set your mind upon him, and be instructed by him, and to prepare yourself for your latter end. What say you? Will you do this presently? At least so much of it as you can do, if you will. Will you promise me to think of these things that I before mentioned, and to pray daily for a changed heart till you have obtained it, and to change your company and courses, and fall upon the use of God's means in reading or hearing the Scriptures, meditating on them, especially on the Lord's day?

And here be sure, if we can, to get their promise,

and engage them to amendment, especially to use means, and change their company, and forsake actual sinning, because these are more in their reach, and in this way they may wait for the accomplishing of that change that is not yet wrought. And do this solemnly, remembering them of the presence of God that heareth their promises, and will expect the performance. And when you have afterward opportunity you may remember them of that promise.

Direct. 9. At the dismissing of them, do these two things: (1.) Again lenify their minds by a deprecation of offence in a word: e. g. I pray you take it not ill that I have put you to this trouble, or dealt thus freely with you. It is as little pleasure to me as to you. If I did not know these things to be true and necessary, I would have spared this labour to myself and you. But I know that we shall be together here but a little while; we are almost at the world to come already; and therefore it is time for us all to look about us, and see that we be ready when God shall call us.

(2.) Because it is but seldom that we ourselves shall have opportunity to speak with the same persons, set them in a way for perfecting of what is begun. 1. Engage the governor of each family to call his family to account every Lord's day before they go to bed, what they can rehearse of the catechism, and so to continue till they have all learned it perfectly; and when they have done so, yet still to continue to hear them recite it, at least once in two or three Lord's days, that they may not forget it; for, even to the most judicious, it will be an excellent help to have still in memory a sum of the christian doctrine, for matter, method, and words. 2. As for the rulers of families themselves, or those that are under such rulers as will not help them, if they have learned some small part of the catechism only, engage them either to come to you, though before their course, when they have learned the rest, or else to some able, experienced neighbour, and recite it to them, and take their assistance when you cannot have time yourself.

Direct. 10. Have all the names of your parishioners by you in a book; and when they come and recite the catechism, note in your book who come, and who do not; and who are so grossly ignorant as to be utterly uncapable of the Lord's supper and other holy communion, and who not. And as you perceive the necessities of each, so deal with them for the future. But for those that are utterly obstinate, and will not come to you, nor be instructed by you, remember the last article of our Agreement, to deal with them as the obstinate despisers of instruction should be dealt with, in regard of communion, and the application of sealing and confirming ordinances; which is, to avoid them, and not hold holy or familiar communion with them, in the Lord's supper or other ordinances: and though some reverend brethren are for admitting their children to baptism, and offended with me for contradicting it, yet so cannot I be, nor shall dare to do it upon any pretences of their ancestors' faith, or of a dogmatical faith of the rebellious parents, supposing them both to be such as in that article we have mentioned. To these particulars I add this general:—

Direct. 11. Through the whole course of your conference with them, see that the manner as well as the matter be suited to the end. And concerning the manner, observe these particulars:

(1.) That you make a difference according to the difference of the persons that you have to deal with. To the dull and obstinate you must be more earnest and sharp; to the tender and timorous that are already humbled, you must rather insist on direction and confirmation; to the youthful you must lay greater shame on sensual voluptuousness, and show them the nature and necessity of mortification; to the aged you must do more to disgrace this present world, and make them apprehensive of the nearness of their change, and the aggravations of their sin, if they should live and die in ignorance or impenitency; to inferiors and the younger you must be more free; to superiors and elders more reverend; to the rich this world must be more disgraced, and the nature and necessity of self-denial opened, and the damnableness of preferring the present prosperity to the future, with the necessity of improving their talents in well-doing; to the poor we must show the great riches of glory which is propounded to them in the gospel, and how well the present things may be spared, where the everlasting may be got. Also those sins must be most insisted on which each one's age, or sex, or temperature of body, or calling and employment in the world, doth most incline them to: as in females, loquacity, evil speeches, passion, malice, pride, &c. Of all which, and abundance more differences, calling to us for different carriage, see Gregor. Mag. de Officio Pastor.

(2.) Be as condescending, familiar, and plain as is possible, with those that are of the weaker capacity.

(3.) Give them the Scripture proof, the light of full evidence and reason of all, as you go, that they may see that it is not you only, but God by you, that speaketh to them.

(4.) Be as serious in all, but specially in the applicatory part, as you can. I scarce fear any thing more than lest some careless ministers will slubber over the work, and do all superficially and without life, and destroy this as they do all other duties, by turning it into a mere formality; putting a few cold questions to them, and giving them two or three cold words of advice, without any life and feeling in themselves, nor likely to produce any feeling in the hearers. But sure he that valueth souls, and knoweth what an opportunity is before him, will do it accordingly.

(5.) To this end, I should think it very necessary that we do both before and in the work, take special pains with our own hearts; especially to excite and strengthen our belief of the truth of the gospel, and the invisible glory and misery that is to come. I am confident this work will exceedingly try the strength of our belief; for he that is but superficially a christian, and not sound in the faith, will likely feel his zeal quite fail him, specially when the duty is grown common, for want of a belief of the things which he is to treat of to keep it alive. An affected fervency and hypocritical stage action, will not hold up in such kind of duties long. A pulpit shall have more of them, than a conference with poor ignorant souls; for the pulpit is the hypocritical minister's stage. There, and in the press, and in public acts, where there is room for ostentation, you shall have his best, and almost all. It is other kind of men that must effectually do the work now in hand.

(6.) It is therefore very meet that we prepare ourselves to it by private prayer; and if time would permit, and there be many together, if we did begin and end with a short prayer with our people, it were best.

(7.) Carry on all, even the most earnest passages, in clear demonstrations of love to their souls, and make them feel through the whole, that you aim at nothing but their own salvation, and avoid all harsh, discouraging passages, throughout.

(8.) If you have not time to deal so fully with each one particularly as is here directed, then, 1. Omit not the most necessary parts. 2. Take several of them together that are friends, and will not seek to divulge each other's weaknesses, and speak to them in common as much as concerneth all; and only the examinations of their knowledge and state, and convictions of misery and special directions, must be used to the individuals alone: but take heed of slubbering it over, upon an unfaithful laziness, or being too brief, without a real necessity.

Direct. 12. Lastly, if God enable you, extend your charity to those of the poorest sort, before they part from you: give them somewhat towards their relief, and from the time that is thus taken from their labours, especially for encouragement of them that do best; and to the rest, promise them so much when they have learned the catechism. I know you cannot give what you have not; but I speak to them that can.—And so much shall serve for directions to the younger ministers, in their dealing with the more ignorant or carnal sort of persons.

As for them that are under fears and troubles of mind, who yet give us hopes of the work of saving grace on their souls, though it deserve a full discourse to direct us in dealing with them, yet I shall not meddle with it now. 1. Because I intended this discourse for another end. 2. Because divines being at some variance about the methods of comforting and confirming troubled minds, are many of them so impatient of reading any thing which is not cut out according to their present opinions, that I perceive it my duty, as far as I can, to avoid points controverted. 3. Because I have done so much as I think necessary already in my "Directions for Peace of Conscience."

CHAPTER VIII.

SECTION I.

ANOTHER sort there are, that we may have occasion of conference with, though they will scarce stoop to be catechised; and that is, opinionative questionists, that being tainted with pride and self-conceitedness, are readier to teach than to be taught, and to vent their own conceits, and quarrel with you, as being ignorant or erroneous yourselves, than to receive instruction; and if they are tainted with any notable error or schismatical disposition, they will seek to waste time in vain janglings, and to dispute, rather than to learn. I am not now directing you what to do with those men at other times (of that I shall give a touch anon); but only if they come to you at this time which is appointed for catechising and edifying instruction: nor is it my thought to presume to direct any but the weaker sort of ministers in this, any more than in the former.

It is like you will have some come to you amongst the rest, that when they should give an account of their faith, will fall into a teaching and contentious discourse: and one will tell you, that you have no true church, because you have such bad members; another will ask you, by what authority you baptize infants; another will ask you, how you can be a true minister, if you had your ordination from prelates; and another will tell you, that you are no true minister, because you had not your ordination from prelates; another will ask you, what Scripture you have for praying or singing psalms in a mixed assembly; and another will quarrel with you, because you administer not the Lord's supper to them in the gesture and manner as they desire, and were wont to receive it; or because you exercise any discipline among them. If any such person should come to you, and thus seek to divert your better discourse, I should think it best to take this course with them:—

1. Let them know that this meeting is appointed for another use, that is, for the instructing of the people in the principles of religion, and you think it very unmeet to pervert it from that use; it being a sin to do God's work disorderly, or to be doing a lesser work when you should be doing a greater: and therefore as you durst not turn God's public worship on the Lord's day into vain or contentious disputing, which discompose men's minds, and spoil a greater work; so neither do you think it lawful to abuse these times to lower uses, which are appointed for higher.

2. Yet let him know that you do not this to avoid any trial of the truth; and that he may know so much, you will at any other fit season, when he will come on purpose to that end, endeavour to give him full satisfaction; or you will as willingly receive instruction from him, if he be able, and have the truth, as you desire he should receive instruction from you: and if it must be so, you will yield to his desire before you part, if there be but time when you have despatched the greater work; but upon condition only that he will submit to the greater first.

3. Then desire him first to give you some account of the principles in the catechism: and if he deny it, convince him before all of the iniquity of his course.

(1.) In that it is the principles that salvation most dependeth on, and therefore being of greatest excellency and necessity, are first to be taken into consideration.

(2.) In that it is the appointed business of this day.

(3.) It is orderly to begin with the fundamentals, because they bear up the rest, which suppose them, flow from them, and cannot be understood without them.

(4.) It is the note of a proud, vain-glorious hypocrite, to make a flourish about lesser things, and yet either to be ignorant of the greater, or to scorn to give that account of his knowledge, which the people, whom he despiseth, refuse not to give.

If he yield to you, ask him only such questions as seem to be of great weight, and yet strain him up a peg higher than you do the common people; and especially keep out the predicate usually from your question, and put him most upon defining or distinguishing, or expounding some terms or sentences of Scripture, &c. As such questions as these may be put to him, which call for definitions, wherein it is ten to one but you will find him ignorant: e. g. What is God? What is Jesus Christ? What is the Holy Ghost? What is person in the trinity? How many natures hath Christ? Was Christ a creature before his incarnation or the creation? Is he called the firstborn of all creatures as God, or as man? Is he called the image of the invisible God, and the express image of the Father's person or subsistence, as a creature, or as God? Was Adam bound to believe in Christ? Was one or two covenants made with Adam before his fall? Did the first covenant of nature make any promise of everlasting celestial glory? Did it threaten hell-fire or temporal death? Did it threaten eternal torment to the soul only, or to the body also? Should there have been any resurrection of the body, if Christ had not come to procure it? Should Christ have come, or have been our Head, or have brought us to glory, if man had not fallen? What is the first covenant? What its conditions? What the second covenant, and its conditions? What was the difference between the covenant with Adam and that by Moses? Was it a covenant of works or of grace, that was made by Moses? What were the conditions of salvation before Christ's incarnation? What is forgiveness of sin? What is justification? How are we said to be justified by faith? How by works? What is faith? What repentance? What sanctification, vocation, regeneration? Is the covenant of grace made with the elect only, or with all; or with whom? What is free-will? Is there any conversion without the word? What is the true nature of special grace; and what is the proper difference of a regenerate man from all others? What is the catholic church? How will you know the true church? How know you the Scripture to be the word of God? What is Christ's priestly, prophetical, kingly office? Be they three offices, or but one; and be they all?—with abundance the like.

And if it be sacrament controversies which he raiseth, tell him it is necessary that you be first agreed, what baptism is, (what the Lord's supper is,) before you dispute who should be baptized, &c.; and it is twenty to one he is not able truly to tell you what the sacrament itself is.

A true definition of baptism or the Lord's supper is not so commonly given, as pretended to be given.

4. If he discover his ignorance in the cases propounded, endeavour to humble him in the sense of his pride and presumption; and let him know what it is, what it signifieth to go about with a teaching, contentious, proud behaviour, while he is indeed so ignorant in things of greater moment.

5. But see that you are able to give him better information yourselves in the points wherein you find him ignorant.

6. But specially take care that you discern the spirit of the man; and if he be a settled, perverse schismatic, or heretic, so that you see him peremptory, and resolved, and quite transported with pride, and have no great hopes of his recovery; then do all this that I have before said openly before all that are present, that he may be humbled or shamed before all, and the rest may be confirmed. But if you find him godly and temperate, and that there is any hope of his reduction, then see that you do all this privately, between him and you only; let not fall any bitter words, nor that tend to his disparagement. And thus I advise, both because we must be as tender of the reputation of all good men, as fidelity to them and to the truth will permit; we must bear one another's burdens, and not increase them; and we must restore those with a spirit of meekness that fall through infirmity, remembering that we ourselves also may be tempted; and also because there is small hope that you should ever do them good, if once you exasperate them, and disaffect them towards you.

And therefore, 7. See that to such erring persons as you have any hopes of, you carry yourselves with as much tenderness and love as will consist with your duty to the church of God: for most of them, when they are once tainted this way, are so selfish and high-minded, that they are much more impatient of reproof than many of the profaner sort of people.

This way did Musculus take with the anabaptists, visiting them in person, and relieving them, even while they railed at him as antichristian, and so continued without disputing with them, till they were convinced that he loved them, and then they sought to him for advice themselves, and many of them were reclaimed by him.

8. Either in the conclusion of your meeting, or at another appointed time, when you come to debate their controversy with them, tell them, That seeing they think you unable to teach them, and think themselves able to teach you, it is your desire to learn: you suppose disputing, as tending usually to exasperate men's minds, rather than to satisfy them, is to be used as the last remedy; therefore you are here ready, if they are able to teach you, to learn of them, and desire them to speak their minds. Which if they refuse, tell them you think it the humblest and most christian edifying way for him that hath most knowledge to teach, and the other to learn; and therefore your purpose is to be either a learner or teacher, and not be a disputant, till they make it to be necessary. When they have declared their minds to you in a teaching way, if it be nothing but the common pleas of the seduced, as it is like it will not, tell them, That this is no new thing to you; it is not the first time that you have heard it, or considered of it, and if you had found a divine evidence in it, you had received it long ago: you are truly willing to receive all truth, but you have received that which is contrary to this doctrine, with far better evidence than they bring for it, &c. If they desire to hear what your evidence is, tell them, if they will hear as learners, you shall communicate your evidence in the meetest way you can; which if they promise to do, let them know that this promise obligeth them to impartiality, and a humble, free entertainment of the truth, and that they do not turn back in rash carping and contention, but take what shall be delivered into sober consideration: which if they promise, 1. If you are so far versed in the point in hand, as to manage it well *ex tempore*, or the person be temperate and fit for such debates, then come in with your evidence in a discursive way, first showing your reasons against the grossest imperfections of his own discourse, and then giving him your grounds from Scripture; not many, but rather a few of the clearest, best improved. And, 2. When you have done, (or without verbal teaching if you find him unfit to learn that way,) give him some book that most effectually defendeth the questioned truth, and tell him, That it is a vain thing to say that over so oft, which is so fully said already, and a man may better consider of what he hath before his eyes, than of that which slideth through his ears, and is mistaken or forgotten: and therefore you desire him as a humble learner to peruse that book with leisurely consideration; because there are the same things that you would say to him, and desire him to bring you in a sober and solid answer to the chief strength of it, if after perusal he judge it to be unsound, but, if it may be, fasten some one of the most sticking evidences on him before you leave him. If he refuse to read the book, endeavour to convince him of his unfaithfulness to the truth and his own soul: doth he think that God's truth is not worth his study? or, will he venture his soul, as the ungodly do, and the church's peace with it, and all to save himself so small a labour? Is it not just with God to give him over to delusion, that will not be at a little pains to be informed, nor afford the truth an equal hearing?

9. But above all, before you part, yea, or before you debate the controversy, see that you do sum up the precedent truths wherein you are both agreed. (1.) Know whether he agree to all that is in the catechism, which you teach the people? (2.) Whether he suppose that you may attain salvation, if you be true to so much as you are agreed in? (3.) Whether they that are so far agreed as you are, should not live in love and peace, as children of the

same God, and members of the same Christ, and heirs of the same kingdom? (4.) Whether you are not bound, notwithstanding your smaller differences, to be helpers in the main work of the gospel for the conversion and saving of souls? (5.) Whether they are not bound to manage the private differences so, as they may not hinder the main work, and therefore to let the lesser stoop to the greater? (6.) Whether they ought not to hold communion in public worship, and church relation, with those that are so far agreed, and walk in the fear of God? (7.) And whether it be not schism to separate from them, for the sake of that small disagreement, themselves being not necessitated by communion to any actual sin?

I speak all this only of the tolerable differences that are among men fearing God; and in that case, if the person be sober and understanding, he must needs yield to the affirmative of these questions: which if he do, or to any of them, let him subscribe it, or openly aver it; and then let all the standers-by be made apprehensive, that none of the great matters that you deal with them about are questioned, but all yielded unquestionable; and the affixed scripture leaves them so; therefore there is no cause for them to receive the least discouragement in their way.

I confess it is past doubt, that differing brethren may well join in recommending the truth that they are agreed in to the ignorant people! Bishop Usher told King James, in his sermon at Wansted, on the church's unity, that he made this motion even to the papist priests themselves, that they might join in teaching the people of that barbarous nation the common principles that both were agreed in: a motion too christian for sullen, factious zeal to entertain. I will repeat his own words, page 33, "The danger then of this ignorance being, by the confession of the most judicious divines of both sides, acknowledged to be so great; the woeful estate of the poor country wherein I live is much to be lamented, where the people generally are suffered to perish for want of knowledge, (he meant the papists,) the vulgar superstitions of popery not doing them half that hurt that the ignorance of those common principles of the faith doth, which all true christians are bound to learn. The consideration whereof hath sometimes drawn me to treat with those of the opposite party to move them, that however in other things we differ one from another, yet we should join together in teaching those main points, the knowledge whereof was so necessary to salvation, and of the truth whereof there was no controversy betwixt us. But what for the jealousies which these distractions in matters of religion have bred among us, and what for other respects, the motion took small effect; and so betwixt us both, the poor people are kept still in miserable ignorance, neither knowing the grounds of the one religion, nor of the other." So far this learned christian bishop.

And what wonder if popish priests refuse this motion, when now among us it is so rare a matter to find any in England, though he differ only in the point of infant baptism, that will calmly and without fraudulent designs of secret promoting his own opinions by it, entertain and prosecute such a motion from the common good; as if they had rather that christianity were thrust out of the world, or kept under, than infants should be admitted into the church! Well, let any party or person pretend what they will of zeal or holiness, I will ever take the *dividatur* for an ill sign: the true mother abhors the division of the child; and the true christian doth prefer the common interest of christianity before the interest of a faction, or an opinion, and would not have the whole building endangered, rather than one peg should not be driven in as he would have it; he had rather a particular truth, if we suppose it a truth, should suffer than the whole or the main.

And having given you this advice, what to do with this kind of men in your conference on the occasion now in question, so I shall add a word or two of advice, how to carry yourself towards them at other times; for the preservation of the unity and peace of your congregations doth much depend on your right dealing with such as these. For, alas, for grief and shame, it is most commonly men that profess more than ordinary religiousness, that are the dividers of the church.

1. I must premise, that the chief part of your work to preserve the church from such, doth consist in the prevention of their fall; seeing when they are once thoroughly infected, be the error what it will, they are but seldom recovered; but if they be beaten out of the error, which they first fell into, they go to another, and perhaps thence to another; but through a just excecation, they seldom return to the truth.

2. To which end, it is most desirable that the minister should be of parts above the people, so far as to be able to teach them, and awe them, and manifest their weaknesses to themselves, or to all. The truth is, for it cannot be hid, it is much long of the ministers, that our poor people are run into so many factions; and particularly the weakness of too many is not the least cause. When a proud seducer shall have a nimble tongue, and a minister be dull or ignorant, so that such a one can baffle him, or play upon him in the ears of others, it brings him into contempt, and overthrows the weak; for they commonly judge him to have the cause, that hath the most confident, plausible, triumphant tongue. But when a minister is able to open their shame to all, it mightily preserveth the church from their infection.

3. It is necessary also to this end, that you frequently and thoroughly possess your people with the nature, necessity, and daily use of the great unquestionable principles of religion, and of the great sin and danger of a perverse zeal about the lower points before the greater are well laid, and let them be made sensible how it is the principles, and not their smaller controversies, that life or death doth depend upon.

4. Make them sensible of the mischiefs of schism, and the great and certain obligations that lie upon us all to maintain the church's unity and peace.

5. When a fire is kindled, resist it in the beginning, and make not light of the smallest spark; and therefore go presently to the infected person, and follow him by the means hereafter mentioned, till he be recovered.

6. Especially use a fit diversion. When a small controversy begins to endanger the church, raise a greater yourself, which you have better advantage to manage, and which is not like to make a division; that is, let them know that there are far greater difficulties than theirs to be first resolved, such as some of the questions before mentioned, and so give them a catalogue of them, and set them at work upon them, that they be matter of avocation from that sore, where the humours begin their conflux, and also that they may be humbled in the sense of their ignorance, and their proud self-conceits may be somewhat abated.

7. See that you preach to such auditors as these some higher points, that stall their understandings, and feed them not with all milk, but sometimes with stronger meat; for it exceedingly puffs them up with pride, when they hear nothing from ministers but what they know already, or can say themselves.

This makes them think themselves as wise as you, and as fit to be teachers; for they think you know no more than you preach: and this hath set so many of them on preaching, because they hear nothing from others but what they can say themselves; and ministers do not set them such patterns as may humble them, and deter them from that work. Not that I would have you neglect the great fundamental verities, or wrong the weak and ignorant people, while you are dealing with such as these; but only when the main part of your sermons is as plain as you can speak, let some one small part be such as shall puzzle these self-conceited men: or else have one sermon in four or five of purpose for them; not by heaping up citations of fathers, nor repeating words of Latin or Greek, unless when you are convincing them of the difficulty of a text of Scripture, for they will but deride all this; but take up some profound question, such as the schools voluminously agitate, and let them see that it is not your obscure manner of handling, but the matter itself that is too hard for them, and so may see that they are yet but children that have need of milk, and that you would be more upon such higher points, if it were not that their incapacity doth take you off.

8. See that you preach as little as may be against them in the pulpit, in any direct manner, opposing their sect by name, or by any reproachful titles; for they are exceeding tender, proud, passionate, and rash, ordinarily, that are entangled in a schism; and they will but hate you, and fly from you as an enemy, and say you rail. The way therefore is, without naming them, to lay the grounds clearly and soundly, which must subvert their errors; and then the error will fall of itself; and when you are necessitated to deal with them directly, do it not by short, unsatisfactory applications, and toothed snatches, or angering reproaches; but, without naming them, take up the controversy, and handle it thoroughly, peaceably, and convincingly, and so let them alone in public: yet be not too long upon it neither; but give them your fullest evidence in a few sermons, not saying all that may be said, but choosing out that which they can have least pretence to quarrel with, and passing over that which they may say more against, or will require more ado to clear and defend.

9. Be sure to keep up some private meetings, and draw them in among you, and manage them prudently. By this means you may keep them from dividing meetings among themselves, where they may say what they will behind your back without control; for most professors are addicted to private meetings, and, well ordered, they are of great use to their edification; and if they have not the opportunity of such as they should have, they will gather to such as they should not have. In the managing of them, as to the present purpose, observe these things:

(1.) Be sure to be still with them yourselves.

(2.) Let not the main exercises of the meeting be such as tend to contention, or to private men's proud ostentation of their parts, but such as tend to the edification of the people; not for private men to preach or expound Scripture, nor, as some do, to let every one of them speak to questions of their own propounding; but to repeat the sermons that you have preached, and to call upon God, and sing his praise.

(3.) Yet let there be some opportunity for them to speak, and appear in a learning way. To which purpose, when you have done repeating, let all that are present know, that if they doubt of any thing that was delivered, or would have any thing made plainer to them, or would be resolved in any thing else that concerneth the subject in hand, or any other case of need, you desire them to propound their doubts: and so let them have the liberty of questioning as learners, while you remain the teacher, and resolve all the doubts yourselves; and do not set them on disputing, by leaving it to them to make the answer. And if you have not competent abilities *ex tempore* to resolve their doubts, you were much better let pass this too; but if you have, it will be of very great use, both for their edification, and the maintaining of order and their necessary dependence on you.

(4.) But if you perceive them so set upon the exercise of their own parts for ostentation, that they are like to divide, if they have not opportunity to do it, be not too stiff against them; but mildly let them know that it is for their good that you dislike it, both because it is an ill sign of a proud heart, that had rather teach than learn, especially where a teacher by office is in place, and where there is no necessity; and also because you fear it will not tend to the best edification of the flock, but to vain janglings, or to excite others that are unable to an imitation. Desire also to know of them, whether they have any truth of God to reveal to them, that you do not reveal. If they have not, why should they desire needlessly to tell them what they are daily told by you? If they have, it is necessary that you know it and consider of it, before you consent that it should be taught to your flock. But if this mild resistance satisfy not, let them take their course awhile, rather than separate from you, unless they be already perverse and subtle heretics, and when they have done their exercises, tell them, that as you give liberty to all to propound their doubts about what you have delivered, so you must take the like liberty that you give: and so propound, first, Whether the understandings of people are like to be more edified by such vain obtrusions of vanity, or by a fastening well upon their memories the things that they have lately heard? and so whether such exercises or repetitions be more necessary? and then open the weaknesses of their discourse; the mis-expounding of Scriptures, the errors in matter, in method, and in words; and that not in a contemptuous or disgraceful way, but as the points wherein you remain unsatisfied. By such means as these you will quickly shame them out of their way of ostentation, and make them give it over.

10. Make use of your people's parts to the utmost, as your helpers, in their places, in an orderly way, under your guidance; or else they will make use of them in a disorderly, dividing way in opposition to you. It hath been a great cause of schism, when ministers would contemptuously cry down private men's preaching, and withal desire not to make any use of the gifts that God hath given them for their assistance; but thrust them too far from holy things, as if they were a profane generation. The work is like to go poorly on, if there be no hands employed in it but the minister's. God giveth not any of his gifts to be buried, but for common use. By a prudent improvement of the gifts of the more able christians, we may receive much help by them, and prevent their abuse, even as lawful marriage preventeth fornication. And the uses you must specially put them to, are these:—(1.) Urge them to be diligent in teaching and praying with their own families, especially catechising them, and teaching them the meaning of what they learn, and whetting it on their affections; and there if they have a mind to preach to their children and servants, so they undertake not more than they are able to do, I know no reason but they may. —(2.) Urge them to step out now and then to their poor ignorant neighbours, and catechise and instruct them in meekness and patience, from day to day; and that will bring them more peace of conscience, than

contemning them.—(3.) Urge them to go oft to the impenitent and scandalous sinners about them, and deal with them with all possible skill and earnestness, yet also with love and patience, for the converting, reforming, and saving of their souls.—(4.) Acquaint them with their duty of watching over each other in brotherly love, and admonishing and exhorting one another daily; and if any walk scandalously, to tell them their fault before two or three, after the contempt of private reproof; and if that prevail not, to tell the officers of the church, that they may be further proceeded with, as Christ hath appointed. —(5.) At your private meetings, and on days of humiliation or thanksgiving in private, employ them in prayer, and in such learning questions as is aforesaid.—(6.) If there be any very ignorant or scandalous sinner that you know of, and you cannot possibly have time yourselves to speak to them at that season, send some of those that are able and sober, to do it in your stead, to instruct the ignorant, and to admonish the offenders, as far as a private man on a message from a minister, and in discharge of his own duty, may go.—(7.) Let some of them be chosen to represent the church; or to see that they have no wrong, and to be their agents to prepare all cases of discipline for public audience, and to be present with the church officers at appointed meetings, to hear the evidences that are brought in against any scandalous, impenitent sinners; and to discern how far they are valid, and how far the persons are obliged to make satisfaction, and give public testimony of repentance, or to be further proceeded against.—(8.) Let such as are fit be made subservient officers, I mean deacons; and then they may afford you help in a regular way, and will by their relation discern themselves obliged to maintain the unity of the church, and authority of the ministry, as they have some participation of the employment and honour; and so by a complication of interests you will make them firmer to the church: but then see that they be men competently fit for the place.

I am persuaded, if ministers had thus made use of the parts of their ablest members, they might have prevented much of the divisions, and distractions, and apostasy that have befallen us; for they would have then found work enough upon their hands for higher parts than theirs, without invading the ministry, and would rather have seen cause to bewail the imperfection of their abilities to that work which doth belong to them. Experience would have convinced and humbled them more than our words will do. A man may think he can stir such a block, or pluck up a tree by the roots, that never tried; but when he sets his hand to it he will come off ashamed. And see that you drive them to diligence in their own works, and let them know what a sin it is to neglect their families, and their ignorant, miserable neighbours, &c.; and then they will be kept humble, and have no such mind to be running upon more work, when they feel you spurring them on to their own, and rebuking them for the neglect; nor will they have any leisure for schismatical enterprises, because of the constancy and greatness of their employment.

11. Still keep up christian love and familiarity with them, even when they have begun to warp and make defection; and lose not your interest in them, while you have any thoughts of attempting their recovery.

12. If they do withdraw into separated meetings, follow them, and be among them, if it may be, continually. Enter a mild dissent as to the lawfulness of it; but yet tell them that you are willing to hear what it is that they have to say, and to be among them for their good, if they will give you leave, for fear lest they run to further evil, and be not easily removed; but hold on, unless they resolvedly exclude you; for, 1. You may thereby have the opportunity of a moderate, gentle opposing their errors, and so in time may manifest the vanity of their course. 2. And you will prevent much of that impudent reviling, and grosser venting of further error, which they will do more freely where there is no contradicter. They may say any thing when there is none to gainsay them; and make it seem good in the eyes of the weak. 3. And by this means, if any seducers from abroad come in to confirm them, you will be ready to oppose them; and so at the least you will do much to prevent the increase of their party. It hath been a very great cause of the schisms in England, that ministers have only (too many) contemned them, and when they have withdrawn into private separated meetings, have talked against them to others, or reproved them in the pulpit, and in the mean time fled away from the faces of them, or been strangers to them, while they have given seducers opportunity to come among them, and be familiar with them without contradiction, and to have the advantages of deceiving them, and even doing what they list. Oh that the ministry had been more guiltless of those errors and schisms that they talk against! But it is easier to chide a sectary in the pulpit, and to subscribe a testimony against them, than to play the skilful physician for their cure, and do the tenth part of the duty that lieth upon us to prevent and heal such calamitous distempers. I am not finding fault with the prudent reprehensions of them in public, or testimonies against them; but I think too many of us have cause to fear, lest we do but publicly proclaim our own shame in the guilt of our negligence, or imprudent weaknesses; and lest in condemning them, and testifying against them, we testify against and condemn ourselves.

13. If you be not well able to deal with them, do as I before advised; give them the best book on that subject to peruse.

14. If all this will not do, get the fittest neighbour minister that you know, to come over and help you; not in public, nor as a set disputation (without necessity); but let him come as occasionally, and, *ex improviso*, come upon them in one of their private meetings, as desirous to see and hear them, and so take the opportunity to deal with them. And if after that there be any disputations appointed, be sure to observe the old rule, fight with them on their own ground, and keep up the war in their quarters, and let it come as little as you can into your own: and therefore go to their assemblies, but let them not come into yours. For with them you can lose little, and may gain much; but at home you can gain little, but it is two to one will lose some, let the error be never so gross. The sectaries commonly observe this course themselves, and therefore you will have much ado to get their consent to bring your disputations into their own assemblies.

15. Let not the authors of the schism outdo you, or go beyond you in any thing that is good: for as truth should be more effectual for sanctification than error; so if you give them this advantage, you give them the day, and all your disputations will do but little good: for the weaker people judge all by the outward appearance, and by the effects, and are not so able to judge of the doctrine itself. They think that he hath the best cause whom they take to be the best man.

I extend this rule both to doctrine and life: e. g. If a libertine preach for free grace, do you preach it up more effectually than he: be much upon it, and make it more glorious on right grounds, than he can do on his wrong. If, on the like pretences, he magnify the grace of love, and, in order to cry down fear and humiliation, be all for living in pure love to God; do not contradict him, in the assertive, but only in the negative and destructive part; but outgo him, and preach up the love of God, with its motives and effects, more fully and effectually than he can do on the corrupt grounds on which he doth proceed: or else you will make all the silly people believe that this is the difference between you, that he is for free grace and the love of God, and you are against it; for if you dwell not upon it in your preaching as well as he, they will not take notice of a short concession or profession. So, if an enthusiast do talk all of the Holy Ghost, and the light, and witness, and law within us; fall you upon that subject too, and do that well which they did ill; and preach up the office of the Holy Ghost, his indwellings and operations, and the light, and testimony, and law within us, better than they. This is the most effectual way of settling your people against their seduction. So if you be assaulted by the Pelagians, if they make a long story to prove that God is not the author of sin, do you fall upon the proof of it too. If they plead for free-will, do you plead for that free-will which we have, (the natural liberty, which none deny, consisting in a self-determining power, and supposing actual indetermination,) and deny only that liberty which the will hath not; that is, 1. Either a freedom from God's government; 2. Or from the necessary guidance of the intellect, and moral force of the object; 3. Or that true spiritual, ethical freedom from various inclinations, which consisteth in the right disposition of the will: though the sanctified indeed have this in part, and that predominantly. So if any Pelagian or Semi-Pelagian will go about industriously to prove man's power, or rather impotency, to will or do evil, do it as effectually as he: for this is indeed but to prove a man a sinner, under pretence of proving him free, or at least to prove him defectible, if it be not the ill inclination, but the possibility of sinning, that they defend; in which case we can say more than they. So if they go about laboriously to prove that Christ died for all, I would endeavour to do it as effectually as they, that it might appear to the people, that the difference between us is not in this, That they would magnify the riches of grace above me, or that I would leave sinners hopeless and remediless, and without an object for faith, any more than they; nor that I abase or reject express scriptures, when they own them in their proper sense: but I would let them know, that the controversy lieth elsewhere; viz. Whether Christ, in offering himself a sacrifice for sin, had not a special intention or resolution, in compliance with his Father's predestinating will, infallibly and effectually to save his chosen, even such and such by name, in making his blood applied effectually to the pardon of all their sins, and to give them his Spirit to seal them unto glory; having no such will, intention, resolution in dying (no more than his Father had in predestinating) as to the rest of the world. So if one that is for private men's preaching, come and inveigh against ministers for inhibiting them to use the gifts of God for the edification of the church, I would not presently set to thwart him; but I would rather fall a persuading private men to use their gifts in all the ways that I even now mentioned; and sharply chide them for using them no more; and then among my cautions or reprehensions meet with his desired abuse in the end. And what I have said by way of instance in these few points, I mean in all others. Preaching truth is the most successful way of confuting error; and I would have no seducer to have the glory of outgoing us in any good, and so not in befriending or defending any truth. Once more, e. g. If a Socinian should fall a pleading for the church's peace, and for unity upon the ancient simplicity of faith, I would labour to outgo him in it; and then would show that the ancient simple faith condemned him. If he would plead reason for Scripture, or the christian religion, I would endeavour to outgo him in it, and he should not have opportunity to glory that he only had reason for what he held, and I had none. But I would show, that as I have reason to believe the Scriptures, so that Scripture condemneth his errors. If a separatist will plead for the necessity of church order and discipline, so would I as well as he; and show him that it is only disorder and confusion, inconsistent with right order and discipline, that I dislike in him or those of his way. And so would I do by others in this case.

And you should be as loth that they should outgo you in the practice of a holy and righteous life, any more than in sounder diligent teaching. Do any of them express a hatred of sin, and desire of church reformation? So must we do more. Do any of them use to spend their time when they meet together in holy discourse, and not in vain janglings? Let us do so much more. Are they unwearied in propagating their opinions? Let us be more so in propagating the truth. Will they condescend to the meanest, and creep into houses to lead captive the silliest of the flock? Let us stoop as low, and be as diligent to do them good. Are any of them loving to their party, and contemners of the world? Let us be lovers of all, and specially of all saints, and do good to all, as we have power; and specially to all the household of faith; and love an enemy; as well as they can do a friend. Let us be more just than they, and more merciful than they, and more humble, and meek, and patient than they; "for this is the will of God, that by well-doing we may put to silence the ignorance of foolish men." Let us excel them in a holy, harmless, righteous, merciful, fruitful, heavenly life, as we do in soundness of doctrine; that by our fruits we may be known, and the weaker sort of our people may see the truth in this reflection, that cannot see it in itself; and that our light may so shine before men, that they may see our conversation, and glorify our Father which is in heaven, and even they that obey not the word, may without the word be won by the conversation of their teachers, 1 Pet. iii. 1, 2. Oh how happy had England been, how happy had all the church been, if the ministers of the gospel had taken these courses! It would have done more against errors and schism, than all our chiding at them hath done, or than all the force can do which we desire from the magistrate.

Three sorts of persons that we may meet with in our conference, are now over: viz. (1.) The grossly ignorant and unconverted; (2.) The doubting, troubled believer; (3.) The cavilling questionist, or seduced schismatic. The fourth that I should speak of in this direction are, those that by a professed willingness to learn and obey, and by other signs, do give us some probability that they may have true repentance and faith, and yet by their ignorance, or lukewarmness, (being not noted for any special profession of godliness,) or by some uneven walking, do make our fears to be as great or greater than our hopes: so that we are between hope and fear of them; doubting the worst of their present safety, though we have not ground to charge them to be unconverted, impenitent, unsanctified persons. I think half that come to me are of this sort, and ten of this sort, if not forty, for one that I dare flatly say are unregenerate. Now it may be a great difficulty with some younger ministers what you should do with this sort of people, where they have no sufficient ground to determine of them as godly or ungodly, whatever their fears or hopes may be.

Of these I shall only briefly say this: 1. The first directions may suffice in the main, for dealing with these, and are as much fitted to these as to the worst. As we may tell a notorious, ungodly man, Your case is miserable, you are a child of death; so may we tell these, I much fear your case is sad—these are ill signs—I wonder how you dare so hazard your salvation: and so abating of the several degrees of the hopeful good that appeareth in them, we may see in the first case, how to deal in this.

2. And I would advise you to be very cautelous how you pass too hasty or absolute censures on any that you have to do with; because it is not so easy a matter to discern a man to be certainly graceless that professeth himself a christian, as many do imagine it to be: and you may do the work in hand as well without such an absolute conclusion as with it, as the former examples, which will serve all with a little alteration, do show.

3. The general descriptions of the ministerial work may supply the rest. I shall only add in a word: (1.) Keep them close to the use of private and public means. (2.) Be oft with the lukewarm, to awaken them rousingly, and with the careless, to admonish them. (3.) Take the opportunity of sickness, which will bow their hearts and open their ears. (4.) See that they spend the Lord's day, and order their families aright. (5.) Draw them from temptations, and occasions of sin. (6.) Charge them to come and seek help in all great straits, and open their temptations and dangers before they are swallowed up. (7.) Strike at the great radical sins, self-seeking, fleshly-mindedness, sensuality, pride, worldliness, infidelity, &c. 1. Keep them to the reading of Scripture and good books, and direct them to those that are likest to awake them. (8.) Engage their godly neighbours to have an eye upon them. (9.) Keep up discipline to awe them. (10.) Maintain the life of grace in yourselves, that it may appear in all your sermons to them; that every one that comes cold to the assembly may have warming helps before he depart.

I have done my advice, and leave you to the practice. Though the proud may receive it with scorn, and the selfish and slothful with some distaste and indignation, I doubt not but God will use it, in despite of the oppositions of sin and Satan, to the awakening of many of his servants to their duty, and promoting of the work of a right reformation: and that his much greater blessing shall accompany the present undertaking for the saving of many a soul, the peace of you that undertake and perform it, the exciting of servants through the nation to second you, and to increase purity and the unity of his churches.—Amen.

December 25th, 1655.

AN APPENDIX:

IN ANSWER TO SOME OBJECTIONS WHICH I HAVE HEARD OF SINCE THE FORMER EDITION.

TO THE REVEREND AND FAITHFUL MINISTERS OF CHRIST IN THE SEVERAL COUNTIES OF THIS LAND, AND THE GENTLEMEN AND OTHER NATIVES OF EACH COUNTY, NOW INHABITING THE CITY OF LONDON.

REVEREND AND BELOVED BRETHREN,

The whole design and business of this discourse, being the propagation of the gospel, and the saving of men's souls, I have thought it not unmeet to acquaint you with another work to that end, which we have set afoot in this county, and to propound it to your consideration, and humbly invite you to a universal imitation. You know, I doubt not, the great inequality in ministerial abilities, and that many places have ministers that are not qualified with convincing lenity and awakening gifts. Some must be tolerated, in the necessity of the church, that are not likely to do any great matters towards the conversion of ignorant, sensual, worldly men; and some that are learned, able men, and fitted for controversies, may yet be unfit to deal with those of the lower sort. I suppose, if you peruse the whole ministry of a county, you will not find so many, such lively, convincing preachers as we could wish. And I take it for granted, that you are sensible of the weight of eternal things, and the worth of souls; and that you will judge it a very desirable thing that every man should be employed according to his gifts, and the gospel in its light and power should be made as common as possible we can: upon these and many the like considerations, the ministers in this county resolved to choose out four of the most lively, yet sober, peaceable, orthodox men, and to desire them once a month to leave their own congregations, to the assistance of some other, and to bestow their labour in the places where they thought there was most need; and as we were resolving upon this work, the natives of this county, inhabiting the city of London, having a custom of feasting together once a year, and having at their feast collected some monies by contribution, for the maintaining of a weekly lecture in this county, besides other good works, did, by their stewards, desire us to set up the said lecture, and to dispose of the said monies in order thereto; and their judgments upon consultation did correspond with our design. So that the said money being sufficient to satisfy another that shall in their absence preach in their own places, we employ it accordingly, and have prevailed with some brethren to undertake this work.

I propound to your consideration, reverend brethren, and to you, the natives of each county, in London, whether the same work may not tend much to the edification of the church, and the welfare of souls, if you will be pleased speedily and effectually to set it afoot through the land? Whether it may not, by God's blessing, be a likely means to illuminate the ignorant, and awaken the secure, and countermine seducers, and hinder the ill success of Satan's itinerants, and win over many souls to Christ, and establish many weak ones in the faith? And not doubting but your judgments will approve of the design, I humbly move, that you will please to contribute your faculties to the work; viz. that the Londoners of each county will be pleased to manifest their benevolence to this end, and commit the monies to the hands of the most faithful, orthodox ministers, and that they will readily and self-denyingly undertake the work.

I hope the gentlemen, natives of this county, will be pleased to pardon my publishing their example, seeing my end is only the promoting of men's salvation, and the common good.

And that you may fullier understand the scope of our design, I shall annex the letters directed to the several ministers of the county which the lecturers send to the minister of the place, and receive his answer. before they presume to preach in any congregations.

TO ALL THE REST OF THE MINISTERS OF THE GOSPEL IN THIS COUNTY, OUR REVEREND AND BELOVED BRETHREN, GRACE AND PEACE IN OUR LORD JESUS CHRIST.

REVEREND BRETHREN,

THE communication of the heavenly evangelical light, for the glory of our Redeemer in the conversion, edification, and salvation of men's souls, is that which we are bound to by many obligations, as christians, and as ministers of Christ for his church, and therefore must needs be solicitous thereof; and it is that which the Spirit of grace, where it abideth, doth proportionably dispose the heart to desire: by convictions of the excellency and necessity of this work, and of our own duty in order thereto, and by the excitation of undeserved grace, our hearts are carried out to long after a more general and effectual illumination and saving conversion of the inhabitants of this county, in which we live; which, while we were but entering upon a consultation to promote, it pleased God, without our knowledge of it, to put the same thoughts into the hearts of others. The natives of this county of Worcester, who dwell in London, meeting at a feast, (as is their yearly use,) collected a sum of money for the setting of eight poor boys to trades, and towards the maintaining of a weekly lecture, and have committed the execution of this last to our care; and upon consultation with their stewards, and among ourselves, both they and we are satisfied, that a movable lecture, on the Lord's day, is the likeliest way for the improvement of their charity, to the attainment of their ends. For, 1. Many people through poverty cannot, and many through negligence will not, come to a week-day's lecture: experience telleth us, that such are usually attended but little by those that have the greatest need. 2. And thus the benefit may extend to more, than if it were fixed in one place.

We have therefore desired our reverend and dear brethren, Mr. Andrew Tristram, minister at Clent, Mr. Henry Oasland, minister at Bewdley, and Mr. Thomas Baldwin, minister at Wolverley, and Mr. Joseph Treble, minister at Lench, to undertake this work, and that each of them will be pleased every fourth Lord's day to preach twice in those places where they shall judge their labours to be necessary: and as we doubt not but their own congregations will so far consent for the good of others; so we do hereby request of you our brethren, that when any of them shall offer their labours for your congregations, in preaching the said lecture, you will receive them, and to your power further them in the work. For as we have no thoughts of obtruding their help upon you without your consent, so we cannot but undoubtedly expect, that men fearing God, and desiring their people's everlasting good, will cheerfully and gratefully entertain such assistance. And we hope that none will think it needless, or take it as an accusing the ministry of insufficiency; for the Lord doth variously bestow his gifts. All that are upright are not equally fitted for the work; and many that are learned, judicious, and more able to teach the riper sort, are yet less able to condescend to the ignorant, and so convincingly and fervently to rouse up the secure, as some that are below them in other qualifications; and many that are able in both respects, have a barren people, and the ablest have found by experience that God hath sometimes blessed the labours of a stranger to that which their own hath not done. We beseech you, therefore, interpret not this as an accusation of any, which proceedeth from the charity of our worthy countrymen in London, and from the earnest desires of them and us to further the salvation of as many as we can. And that you may have no jealousies of the persons deputed to this work, we assure you that they are approved men, orthodox, sober, peaceable, and of upright lives, happily qualified for their ministerial work, and zealous and industrious therein; and so far from being likely to sow any errors, or cause divisions, or draw the hearts of people from their own faithful pastors, that they will be forward to assist you against any such distempers in your flocks. Not doubting, therefore, but as you serve the same Master, and are under the same obligations as we, so as many as are heartily addicted to his service will readily promote so hopeful a work: we commend you and your labours to the blessing of the Lord.

Your brethren and fellow-labourers in the work of the gospel,

Kidderminster:

In the name, and at the desire of the ministers of this association, } RICHARD BAXTER, JOHN BORAGON, JARVIS BRYAN.

Evesham:

In the name of the ministers of this association, } GILES COLLIER, GEORGE HOPKINS, JOHN DOLPHIN.

IT is a hard case, that either so good a Master and work should have servants so bad, as will plead against their duty when they practise it; or that good men themselves should be so backward, and need so many words to draw them to so needful an employment! There is no sanctified man but hath virtually in him a love to the main work that is urged in this treatise: and it is hard that men should oppose, or stiffly refuse, the duties which as christians they love, and by their nature are inclined to! And it is harder, that those should be ministers of the gospel that have no such sanctified natures and inclinations! (Though I am thankful to God that useth even such for the service of his church.) If we are sanctified, we are devoted, separated, and resigned up to God as being wholly his. And if indeed we are absolutely resigned up to God, we shall have no time or labour that will seem too much and too good for his service. It is one of the clearest, surest differences between a damnable hypocrite and a truly sanctified man, that the hypocrite hath something, but the sanctified hath nothing so dear to him that he cannot spare it for God. If we love not our work for the end, and therefore the end more than the work, we are deceitful workmen; and if we do but value the success of our labour, methinks we should be willing of that sort of labour in which we have greatest probability of success, though it may be somewhat troublesome in the performance. If we are faithful servants, the work of God will be pleasant to us: and if it were pleasant, methinks we should not be drawn to it, as a bear to the stake; much less should we fly from it, and oppose it like enemies! Whatever a Jonas may do in a temptation against one particular act, methinks the ordinary discharge of such duties should neither be opposed nor wholly neglected by the faithful. Methinks while we live among the miserable, and see such multitudes near to hell, compassion should be argument enough to persuade us to do all that we can for their relief, and humanity should be enough to convince us of the duty, and stop our mouths from cavilling against it.

Though I seemed to myself even unmannerly bold with my brethren in this book, yet I must needs say, that conscience did not accuse me for it, but provoke me to it, and often asked me, Is there not a cause? Nor can I repent of this adventure, when I consider the necessity and the success. I bless God that I have lived to hear of so many faithful servants of Christ falling close to this work of *personal instruction*, not only in this county, but in many other parts of the land. Now I begin to hope that the pastoral office will be better understood, by some competent time of experience, both by our people and ourselves, and that they will come in time to understand what use they have of ministers, and what duty towards them they are obliged to perform: I hope now that misunderstandings between people and their teachers will be removed; and they will perceive what we aim at, and how far we are from intending their hurt, or lording it over them, when they see us take our greatness and dignity to consist in *being the servants of all*. Now I am in hopes that we shall get a more universal, effectual advantage against the common ignorance, and profaneness, and security that have discouraged and disappointed both us and our predecessors; and that we shall have more satisfactory acquaintance with the state of our hearers, to direct us in the several acts of administration and discipline. These and abundance more fruit we may expect, if the Lord will but give us hearts to proceed with a vigorous seriousness in the work, and not to faint and be weary of well-doing. The greatest thing that I fear next *unskilfulness*, is *laziness;* lest we begin to favour ourselves, and say, What a toil is this! and so the flesh pervert our reason, and make us say, I do not think that I am bound to all this stir and trouble; especially lest when we have gone once over the parish, we lazily say, I have done enough already, what need I do the same again? Though I hope experience of men's necessity, and the benefit, will do much to save us from the power of these temptations.

I have no great fear of any opposition from conscience or unbiassed reason; but only from unwillingness, and from reason biassed by the flesh. Most of the objections that I have heard of since the publishing of this book, are the same that are already answered in it, especially in the Preface; and yet I hear of no reply that they make to those answers. I shall not think it my duty to answer the same again, because men will not observe what is answered already; but shall answer now to the new objections only.

Object. 1. Some carry about this objection at a distance, that my whole book doth run upon a false supposition, viz. That discipline and personal instruction are essential to our ministry.

Answ. 1. I know of no such word that ever I

spoke or wrote. Nor do I build on any such supposition; otherwise I should have said, that all that perform not these duties are no ministers. But these words I did write indeed, *Ruling is as essential a part of the pastor's office as preaching, I am sure.* But then I difference the special office of a pastor from the general office of a minister; and secondly, I distinguish between the power and duty of ruling, and personal instructing, and the exercise of that power and performance of that duty; and I distinguish between the ministry or office, and the pastor. And so I conclude, 1. That it is essential to the office or ministry of a pastor of a particular church to have the power of ruling as well as of public preaching, and to be *obliged* on fit occasions to rule as well as to preach.

2. But actually to rule is not essential to his being a pastor; for to be a *pastor*, is to be *empowered* and *obliged:* these only are contained in the office, and the exercise followeth as an effect. A man is a pastor before ever he preach; and continueth to be so when he interrupteth his exercise.

3. Ruling taken for authoritative guidance in the way to heaven, (which is our ministerial kind of rule; even as a physician ruleth his patient, supposing him to be of divine institution,) is the general work of the ministry, and comprehendeth public preaching, and therefore is more necessary than a part alone.

4. A man may be a faithful minister, and yet never preach a sermon. If a great congregation have six or more pastors, and two or three of them be the ablest preachers, and the rest more judicious, and fit for discourse and private oversight, these latter may well employ themselves in such oversight, conference, and other ministerial works, and leave public speaking in the pulpit to them that are more able for it, and so they may divide the work among them according to their parts: and it will not now follow that they are no pastors, that preach not publicly. I think then that all this laid together, will warrant me to say, that *ruling is as much essential to a pastor's office as preaching.* At least, though methinks it should be enough to persuade us to our duty to know that it is commanded, without disputing whether it be essential to our office.

Object. 2. The same persons say, that they cannot agree with us, because we make a difference between the members of our flock, or church, and the rest of the parish, and so take not all the parish to be our church, as in the tenth article of our Agreement is expressed.

Answ. 1. The palpable vanity of this objection is a dishonour to the heads or the hearts of the objectors, and doth but open their own nakedness. What force is in this reason, or what show of force? If they take all their parish for their church, cannot they agree to catechise and instruct them personally, because we take not all our parishes for church members? They may as well give over preaching, and say, they cannot agree to preach to their own parish churches, because we take not all in our parishes to be of our churches. Who can believe that this is a reason to excuse them from their duty?

2. But, to give them also an account of our actions, I add, that we expressly there exclude none of our parishioners from our churches, but *such as have withdrawn themselves from our charges, and particular church, by refusing to own and profess their membership.* And for our parts, we have not the faculty of making men church members, whether they will or no, or discerning them to be such, whether they will signify it or no; much less when they disown it, and after many public invitations, and a year or two's waiting for their fuller information, do still refuse to profess themselves members. They that have this faculty, let them use it: in the mean time let them know, that their doctrine obligeth them to more duty than ours; and therefore will be no excuse to them for doing less. We shall endeavour to instruct and catechise men, whether they be members of our churches or not: but we take not ourselves bound to rule and watch over all those in our parishes that withdraw themselves from our pastoral oversight, with the same exactness and authority as we must guide and oversee the members of our charge. But you that take all in the parish to be of your churches, must see that you rule and oversee them accordingly.

Object. 3. Others object against the following words in the same article of our Agreement, "that we shall in regard of communion, and the application of sealing and confirming ordinances, deal with them as the obstinate despisers of instruction should be dealt with." And who are these that we must so deal with? Those that after sufficient admonition shall contemptuously and obstinately refuse to be either catechised or instructed thus personally by us, giving us no valuable reason of their refusal.

Answ. 1. It seems then, that these objectors first, either take not those for obstinate despisers of instruction, that after sufficient admonition shall contemptuously and obstinately refuse either to come to the minister, or to let the minister come to them, and be instructed by them, not giving any valuable reason of such refusal. By which it may appear what reformation they desire, and how they judge of the qualification of church members; and why cannot they also be as charitable to those that contemptuously and obstinately refuse to hear them preach, and will join only in sacraments and common prayer. I like not charity unreasonably large for the exempting of ourselves from the labour of duty: I would not choose such a charitable physician that would make his patients believe that they are in no danger, to save himself the labour of attending them for the cure. 2. Or else they think that we must not deal with such men, in regard of church communion and sacraments as they should be dealt with, which we agree to; but this sure can never be their sense. But I suppose they will say, that the thing offensive is the intimation, that such persons should be denied the sealing and confirming ordinances.

Answ. And indeed, would you not have it so? If people will neither come to you for instruction, nor let you come to them, nor give you any valuable reason, yea, contemptuously and obstinately refuse this, after sufficient admonition, would you yet have these admitted to communion in the sacraments? It seems then, either this is no scandalous sin with you, or you would have the garden of Christ lie common as the wilderness; and you would be their pastor in despite of them, that contemptuously and obstinately refuse to take you for their pastor. Or you will divide Christ and his ordinances, and give them one part at their will, that obstinately refuse the other.

But think as you please of this resolution of ours; and admit all the most obstinate refusers of your instruction to the sacrament, (which yet a papist will not do,) if you can make it good: but what is this to the business of catechising and instructing those that will submit? Cannot you agree with us in the rest, because of this clause? Cannot you agree to instruct them that will submit, because we resolve to deal with the obstinate refusers as we ought?

Object. 4. You cut us a shoe too narrow for our foot. You judge all our congregations by your own we have stubborn people that will not be instructed, nor come near us, and are not fit for church discipline. Had we a tractable people, we would yield to all.

Answ. 1. If I understand this, the meaning of it is, We are resolved not to suffer the hatred, ill-will, and railing of our neighbours: if we had a people that would take it well, and put us to no such suffering, but rather drive us on to duty, then we would do it. If this be the meaning, it sounds not well. 2. The worse your people are, the more need they have of instruction and help. 3. If a thousand refuse your help, will that excuse you from offering it them, and affording it a thousand others that will not refuse it? Sure all your people will not so refuse it. 4. Are your whole parishes fit to be church members, and to be admitted to communion in all ordinances, and yet are they unfit for discipline? This cannot ordinarily be: it is a contradiction. If indeed all your parishioners be infidels, or ungodly, and unfit matter to constitute a church, confess then that you are no pastors of a particular church, and give them no communion ordinances, but preach to them as infidels, to make them christians. But if indeed you take yourselves for pastors, and your parishes, or part of them, for churches, use them as churches, and rule as pastors are bound to rule, and take not an office which you constantly refuse to exercise; and choose not out that part of the work of your office, which is least costly, or distasteful to flesh and blood, but be true to your undertakings.

Object. 5. But you build much on Acts xx. 20, Paul's teaching from house to house, whereas, *κατ' οἴκους* and *κατ' οἶκον*, in the New Testament, is ever spoken of the houses where the churches did usually assemble for public worship.

Answ. 1. If I had misinterpreted Acts xx. 20, it is excusable to err with so good company. Mr. Mede confesseth, (p. 31,) that the most of the reformed writers, and some of the other side, are against him: and (p. 44) that the phrase, *κατ' οἶκον* is commonly expounded against his way. And Beza, on 1 Cor. xvi. 19, saith, *Apparet enim apostolum commendare Aquilæ et Priscillæ familiam quasi sit ecclesia quædam.* And he expounds, *κατ' οἶκον*, Acts v. 42, by *Privatim ubicunque opus erat, ut vere testatur de se Paulus infr.* xx. 20; and so gives us his sense of that place also. And, to let pass ordinary interpreters, and speak only of those critics that may be expected most to befriend Mr. Mede's opinion, Grotius, on Rom. xvi. 5, saith, *Eodem modo de illorum domo loquitur Paulus,* 1 Cor. xvi. 20. *Quia recens ab exilio redibant christiani, credibile est cum hæc Paulus scriberet nullos Romæ fuisse communes christianorum conventus, neque presbyteros quos alioqui salutaret Paulus. Tali autem tempore quæque domus ecclesia est, sicut Tertullianus ait, ubi tres, ecclesia est, licet laici.* And on Acts xx. 20, he saith, *καὶ κατ' ὄικους, singulos, occasione data;* and on Philem. 2, *In ejus domo complures erant christiani.* And 1 Cor. xvi. 20, *σὺν τῇ κατ' οἶκον αὐτῶν ἐκκλησία. Id est, cum tota familia sua quæ erat christiani. Quocunque illi ibant, secum ferebant ecclesiam.* So he expoundeth Col. iv. 15.

And Dr. Hammond (1 Cor. xvi.) saith, "It is evident what is meant by the church in their house, i. e. all the believers of their family; the same are called, *ἡ κατ' οἶκον ἀυτῶν ἐκκλησία*, (Rom. xvi. 4,) the church or christians belonging to their family. The prepositions *ἐν* and *κατὰ* being promiscuously used in the writings. And he expoundeth Acts xx. 20, thus: "Willing to use all opportunities of instructing any, both in the public synagogues, and in private schools, and in your several houses, whither I also came."

I confess myself somewhat inclinable to the exposition of the objectors, though I come not quite up to their sense; and I am somewhat stopped by this consideration, that there is mention of the church in the house of Aquila and Priscilla in several cities. And it is not probable that such movable persons coming as strangers to such places, should have the opportunity of making their house still the public meeting-place of the several churches where they come.

And moreover, besides the texts observed by some, that in Acts viii. 3, will hardly be proved to be spoken only of church houses; *Σᾶυλος δὲ ἐλυμαίνετο τὴν ἐκκλησίαν, κατὰ τοὺς οἴκους πορευόμενος.* I confess it was likely that he made his first assault on the assemblies, but improbable that this is all that is there meant.

The apostles then did preach to several sorts of auditors: 1. Sometimes to any multitude they could fitly, to speak for their conversion; either in the temple, in the market-place, or at the judgment-seat, or any place of concourse. 2. Sometimes in mixed assemblies of christians and infidels; admitting unbelievers to be their auditors in order to their conversion. So Paul admitted all that would come into his own hired house, Acts xxviii. 30, 31. And it was ordinary for the church to admit unbelievers to be present, as appears 1 Cor. xiv. 23—25. 3. Sometimes there were solemn assemblies of the church above, where they all came together into one place, that is, it was the place of their most public meeting; where the main body assembled, and no others with them, as in breaking bread, and feasting together, and such acts of special communion. 4. Sometimes there were occasional meetings of certain parcels of the church, as that was Acts xii. when they were praying for Peter. And such a meeting I suppose there was in almost every house where the apostles were known to come, among christians. It is not probable but that many would come in to them, if they did but go into any private house to visit or exhort the persons of that house. 5. Besides these, they ordinarily used to teach particular persons, as the gaoler, the eunuch, &c. as oft as they had opportunity. Now our question of Acts xx. 20, is, which of these three last senses it is taken in. And I agree not with the objectors, that it is taken in the first of the three only, though I will not exclude that: but understand it more comprehensively, as extending to all the three last sorts, and comprising all that house-teaching of christians that was then usual with the apostles, both first, teaching the churches in houses: and secondly, teaching such companies of christians as were in the houses where the apostles came, as Cornelius, Acts x. had gathered his friends to hear Peter, so christians would call their next friends when an apostle came to visit them: thirdly, and teaching the particular families where they had opportunity; especially the second.

Object. But this was not an orderly taking the houses of a parish or church before them, and going to every one.

Answ. Very true; I know of no such parishes that then were; nor do I make it a minister's duty absolutely to go up and down from house to house, to each house in his parish, or of his charge, I would not so much as advise you to do this without necessity; but first call the people to come to you, and learn of you at your own house, or the church house, or where you please, so you will but give them that personal instruction, upon necessary pre-inquiry into their states, which their conditions do require.

And then go to those that will not come to you, if they will not consent, and you are able. For my own part, I am not able to go from house to house; there being not one house of many among the poor people, where I can stand half an hour in the midst of summer, without taking cold, to the apparent hazard of my life; so that those few that will not come to me, I must send to. And I think it more to the people's benefit to accustom them to attend their pastor, than for him to go to hunt up and down after them, he scarce knows where and when. But men's obstinacy may make that necessary which is inconvenient.

2. But I have spoken all this but as on the by, as to this objection. My answer to it is this: It is not either only or chiefly on this text, or any like it, that I build my persuasions of you to this duty. In good sadness, can you find nothing but Acts xx. 20, in all these papers, that is urged to convince you of the duty in hand? If you have observed no more, read again, and save me the labour of recitals. If there were nothing but the general command of taking heed to all the flock, and no more but your very pastoral relation to each member, as a master to every servant, and a teacher to every scholar in his school, and a physician to every patient in his hospital, and a shepherd to every sheep in his flock, and a commander to every soldier in his regiment; what need there more to convince you that you should take care of them, and help every one particularly as effectually as you can. In a word, the sum of the question is, whether you are bound to do the best you can to save the souls of all your parishioners? Do this, and I desire no more. Do you think in conscience that you do the best you can, if you can exhort, instruct, or catechise them personally, and will not?

As to the objection, Where are we bound to spend two days a week in this, or one day, or to take the houses in course, or the like? I have answered it already in this book, whither I refer you. As if the general precept of Teaching every one, exhorting every man, doing good to all, taking heed to all the flock, &c. were not sufficient! What if God only bid you pray continually, or on all fit occasions, will you approve of those deluded ones that ask, Where am I bid pray morning and night, or in my family; or before and after meat, or before and after sermon? &c. Providence will direct you, and honest prudence will discern the season and other circumstances of your duty. What if God have not told us what day or hour our lecture shall be at, or what chapter I shall read, or what psalm I shall sing, or what text I preach on, or whether on any or not; or how the seals and utensils shall be ordered; must not we therefore determine these ourselves, as Providence shall lead us, and as may conduce to the end of our work? I do not think but you do as much, and justly do it, beyond God's particular Scripture determination, in your ordinary preaching, as we do in catechising, and personal instructing. But methinks with ministers I should not need to say so much to such a rustical objection as this, from the defect of particular precept.

Object. 6. If all ministers should bestow two days a week, they would have but a little time to study, and so the adversaries would have their will when our ministry comes to the unlearned, or unskilled in controversies.

Answ. 1. I have answered this already in the book. 2. I only add, these things are not objected to mere standers-by; we try the work, and can tell by some experience what it is. Is not four days a week, after so many years in the university, a fair proportion for men to study controversies and sermons? Though my weakness deprive me of abundance of time, and extraordinary works take up six if not eight parts of my time, yet I bless God I can find time to provide for preaching two days a week, notwithstanding the two days for personal instruction. Now for those that are not troubled with any extraordinary work, I mean writings, and conversations of several sorts, besides the ordinary work of the ministry, I cannot believe, but if they are willing, they may find two half days a week at least for this work.

3. And perhaps they will find before we have done, that this employment tends to make men able pastors for the church, much more than private studies alone. He shall be the ablest physician, and divine, and lawyer too, that addeth practice and experience proportionably to his studies; and that man shall prove a useless drone, that refuseth God's service all his life, under pretence of preparing for it; and lets men's souls pass on to perdition, while he pretendeth to be studying how to recover them, or to get more ability to help and save them.

Object. 7. The times that Paul lived in required more diligence than ours; the churches were but in the planting, the enemies many, and persecution great, but now it is not so.

Answ. This was the bishops' argument against so much preaching when they put it down. But it savours of a man locked up in study, and unacquainted with the world. Good Lord! are there such multitudes round about us that know not whether Christ be God or man, the first person in the Trinity or the second; whether he have taken his body to heaven, or left it on earth, nor what he hath done for them; nor what they must trust to for pardon and salvation? are there so many thousands round about us that are drowned in presumption, security, and sensuality, that break the hearts of preachers, and when we have done all, will neither feel us, nor understand us? are there so many wilful drunkards, worldlings, self-seekers, railers, haters of a holy life, that want nothing but death to make them remediless? are there so many ignorant, dull, and scandalous professors, so many dividers, seducers, and troublers of the church? and yet is the supineness of our times so great, that we may excuse ourselves from *personal instruction*, because of the less necessity of the times? What needs there but faith and experience, to answer this objection? Believe better within, and look more without among the miserable, and I warrant you you will not see cause to spare your pains for want of work, or of necessities to invite you: what conscionable minister finds not work enough to do, from one end of the year to another, if he have not an hundred souls to care for? Are ungodly men the less miserable, because they make profession of christianity, or the more?

Object. 8. You have here too confidently determined, that it is ministers' duties that have large congregations, to procure assistance, though they leave themselves by it but that low allowance to live upon, which you mention. We must not be wise above what is written. And you will scarce show us where this, or the *quota pars temporis* for catechising, or taking a set time, are written in the Scripture.

Answ. 1. Must I go turn to my Bible to show a preacher where it is written, that a man's soul is more worth than a world, much more than a hundred pounds a year; much more are many souls more worth? or that both we and that we have is God's, and should be employed to the utmost for his service? or that it is inhuman cruelty to let many souls go to hell, for fear my wife and children should live somewhat the harder, or live at lower rates; when, according to God's ordinary way of working by means, I might do much to prevent their misery, if I would but a little displease my flesh, which all that are Christ's have crucified with its lusts? Every man must give God the things that are God's, and that is all. How is all pure and sanctified to us but in the separation, dedication, and using them for God? Are not all his talents, and must be employed to his service? Must not every christian first ask, which way may I most honour God with my substance? Are not these things written? Do we not preach them to our people? Are they true to them, and not to us? Yea, more; is not the church maintenance devoted in a special manner to the service of God for that church; and should we not then use it for the utmost furtherance of the end? If any minister that hath two hundred pounds a year, can prove that a hundred pounds of it may do God more service if it be laid out on himself or wife and children, than if it maintain one or two meet assistants to help the salvation of the flock, I shall not presume to reprove his expenses; but where this cannot be proved, let not the practice be justified.

No wonder that we have so many sensual gentlemen that do little good with all their riches; but see their brother have need, and shut up the bowels of their compassion from him, rather than they will live at lower rates, or not fare deliciously every day; and that they can find no Scripture that commandeth them such things; when even the preachers of the Scriptures cannot see the wood for trees; they want a letter to express to them the common moral verities. No wonder if these gentlemen can find no Scripture that requireth them to buy in impropriations, to endow or build colleges, to give a common stock for the poor, or the like, or out of two thousand pounds or three thousand pounds portion to a daughter, to give one or two hundreds to some pious, charitable use, though the daughter have the less. How should gentlemen find any Scripture for self-denial, or preferring God before themselves, yea their flesh, or children's superfluities and snares, when some ministers of the gospel can find no such Scripture, when the case concerns themselves; or at least can meet with no expositor that can make them understand such difficult texts.

And for the other matters, of the stated time for catechising, and the *quota pars:* as I never presumed to impose an unnecessary task on any, nor should do, were it in my power, but leave it to their prudence that are on the place to determine of circumstances; so I know not why any man should be loth to tie himself to this duty, especially in order to a common reformation, and after so long and general a neglect, unless because he is loth to practise it. If set times be not needful for the constant performance of such a work as this, devise for us some way of doing it without a stated time; and do not keep a set time for your lectures, classical meetings, family duties, no nor your studies, or secret prayers. When you have showed me a written word for these, and for your preaching twice or once every Lord's day, then I will show you more than one text for the things in question.

Object. 9. The next objections made, are against my urging them to associate; and one is this: say they, Why cannot I do my duty to God and for my people at home, without travelling many miles to a meeting of ministers? What Scripture binds me to this labour?

Answ. Were I in a disputation, I would give you several formal arguments for all these things; but in this brief way of answering objections, I think it more profitable to them that are in love with truth, to take up with the general grounds of the duty, which may afford them matter for many arguments. And to the objection, can you find no Scripture that commandeth christians to be of one mind, and mouth, and way, and to keep the unity of the Spirit in the bond of peace? Cannot you prove from Scripture that God would have ministers to be one, in mind and heart, "as Christ and the Father are one?" (John xvii. 21.) Do you doubt whether you should do the work of God with as much unity and concord as is possible; and do you know that constant communion and correspondence is necessary to that end? You cannot be ignorant how the unity and consent of ministers is their honour, and much of their strength with the people; and takes off much prejudice and odium that would fall on single men; and that singular actions brings us into contempt with them. Doubtless, as many christians are bound to hold communion together in particular churches, so many particular churches, by their guides, are bound to maintain communion as far as nature makes them capable. And I hope few ministers are ignorant that these ministerial assemblies for concord among ourselves and the churches, have been the constant practice of the churches of Christ, as high as we have any history to acquaint us with their practice (I mean when the persecution made it not impossible.) And shall we now in the end of the world begin to be wiser; and one single pastor, and perhaps of no seraphical intellectuals, correct this practice of the universal church, as a needless thing, and say, Why may not I do my duty as well at home alone?

You owe duty to your neighbour ministers and churches, for communion, and in order to the common good, and the promoting of your common work. Are you humble men, and yet can you think that yourselves have no need of the advice and assistance of your brethren? I should hardly think you humble if you say so. But if you be so far above teaching, advice, or any other help to yourselves, your brethren have the more need of you, by how much the less need you have of them. There are many young raw ministers that very much need the helps that such communion may afford them, and the advice of more grave, experienced men for carrying on the work of their ministry; and many so humble and sensible of their need of such communion, that they would be loth to be deprived of it. One would think we should no more need such a stir to make ministers desire the communion of ministers, than to make christians desire the communion of christians, or to make men desire the society of men.

Object. 10. But we have observed in most associations where we have been, that some one, or two, or few more, do all, and the rest do but follow them: it is as good then to go to these men alone, if we need advice.

Answ. 1. There is no one that pretends to any authority over their brethren, in our association; neither civil coercive power, nor ecclesiastical directive power. You cannot say therefore, that any one doth either force the rest, or awe them by any pretended commission from Christ. So that if any have so much power as you speak of, it is like it is but the power of truth in them, and such as light hath against darkness; or, if it be from the strength of their parts and gifts, have not you need even of the gifts of your brethren? And are they not given for the body? It seems by this objection, that you justify our associations from all popular or factious prevalency of the multitude, or major part; and that they lay not the cause upon number and votes, but upon wisdom, and the prevailing power of evidence; and that one man that can bring more reason than others, shall be heard and regarded by all. What could you have said more to the honour of our associations, to vindicate them from all imputations of pride and faction, and clamorous running on with the most.

And where you say, It is as good to go to those men in private, I answer, those men themselves do not think so. Perhaps, they that you call the leaders of the rest, do find themselves more in need of the help of those whom you say they lead, than you do of theirs. Among many, that may be spoken by a man of inferior parts, that came not into the minds of wiser men: which of you are so wise that needs no addition or assistance; and what minister is so weak that may not sometimes add to the wiser? Moreover, among many, they that are of greater parts have the better opportunity to do the greater good with them, than with one in a corner. Would you have your neighbours say, What shall we do at the congregation—there is but one man that does all, and I can go as well to him at home: it is sooner done to speak to twenty or forty at once, than one by one.

But if indeed you think that these leading ministers do mislead the rest, there is the more need of the presence of such as you that discern it. Care you not that your brethren and the churches be misled? If you see it, you can give your reasons that may disclose it; and how know you what your light may do: seeing your brethren are not forced into error, but seduced; if it be so, why may not you do as much to undeceive them?

Object. 11. But, as I hear many say, under pretence of associating, you will but fall into a multitude of fractions! Not two counties can agree upon the same terms; but one company go one way, and another go another way; and why should we join with any of them till there be a greater likelihood of union among themselves?

Answ. 1. A self-condemning, unreasonable objection. Are they more divided where they associate, than you that are single, and every man goes on his own head? What if there were as many ways as counties? that is not so bad as to have as many ways as parishes. Have you no more modest a way to excuse your singularity and disunion, than by charging communion itself with singularity, and uniting with division?

2. But wherein is it that this diversity of ways consisteth, which you complain of? Tell us the particulars; for I see no such great diversity! Most counties that I hear of that have associated, do only agree to hold communion in stated meetings, and there to afford the best help they can to one another; and have not proceeded to any more particular agreements, unless perhaps to catechise, or personally instruct the people. And you cannot accuse them for diversity of ways, that descend to no more particular agreements. Indeed this county, (Worcestershire,) and the counties of Cumberland and Westmoreland, have published the articles of their associations and agreements: and I pray you compare them, and see whether one egg be liker another than they are in sense.

But it is like you mean, that our articles are not in the same words, and it is not the same forms *in terminis* that we agree upon.

Answ. And what of that? I think there be above a hundred catechisms now in England, that yet contain the very same principles of religion. Will you fall out with catechising, and use none, because we all agree not in one, for the terms? or should you not be more encouraged to it, because among so many there is such full agreement in sense, that they are all but as one? How many of the ancient councils of the church did determine only of the same canons; and yet this was not called a disagreeing diversity.

2. The truth is, this objection is commonly made by men that place the unity of the church in matters that God never placed it in. We must not be one, because we subscribe not the same form of words, and agree not in every circumstance and expression. Whereas, indeed, we shall never be one, while unity is placed in such indifferent things. There are no greater dividers of the church in the world, than they that overdo in their pretendings to unity, and lay the unity of the church upon that which will not bear it. The papists must needs centre all the churches in their pope, and by this means have made the agreement of the churches with them to be impossible; whereas, if they would have left out these false means of union, and the concomitants, we might have held our union and communion with them. So if formalists will lay the union of the church on this gesture, and that vesture, and this order, and these words in prayer, preaching, &c. they will presently make union with them impossible; for there is a possibility of bringing all true christians to uniting in the revealed will of God, but no possibility of bringing them all to be of every formalist's opinion, and to use every gesture or form of words that he and his like shall impose upon them. I speak not against agreement in circumstances, but against unnecessary impositions therein, much more against laying the church's unity and peace upon them. For example: at the reception of the Lord's supper all were forced to kneel: at the eucharistical action of singing psalms, when we speak to God in the highest worship that we can perform on earth, no man was forced to kneel, or to any one gesture. In the former we were altogether by the ears, and driven from communion; and to this day thousands do separate from assemblies because they may not kneel, as formerly some did because they might not have it any other way but kneeling: but in the other case, of singing, where all were left at liberty, I never heard of one contention about the gesture to this day; no nor of any offence that one took at another. So in reading that parcel, that was then peculiarly called *the gospel,* all were bound to stand; and this bred contention: but at the reading of the same words in the chapter, all had liberty to choose their gesture; and there I never heard of contention or offence. So I may say in our present case, we do not intend by associating to tie one another to new forms and ceremonies, nor make new terms of the union of the churches. In this county we only chose out so much of the unquestionable work of presbyters, about that government which had been long neglected, which episcopal presbyterians and congregational are agreed in, and resolved at present to practise that which all are for, rather than to neglect an acknowledged duty, because of by-circumstances in which we differ; so that all these parties may join with us, without deserting the principles of their parties: and I think this is no way of division or discord.

Object. 12. But if this be all, what need we subscribe to articles of agreement? Is it not enough that we have all subscribed to the Scriptures already, if you require no more but what is there?

Answ. We require no more, but that all agree to perform those duties which God's word doth command; and freely, without force, accord about those circumstances which Scripture hath not particularly determined, but given as general rules to discern according to providential changes, how to determine them ourselves. I mean only such circumstances in which an agreement may further us in our work, without agreeing in those where agreement is wholly unnecessary, and without laying the church's peace upon any of them. We associate, not to make new laws and duties, but to accord in obeying the laws of God; and therefore the articles which we agree upon are Scripture articles. And if any scruple subscribing to any that are not the very express words of Scripture, we will not differ with him, but will give him as much as is necessary in such Scripture words to subscribe. And the reason why we subscribe to these articles, though we have already subscribed to Scripture, is because they are matters long and generally neglected; and we do but hereby awaken ourselves to duty, and bind ourselves faster by renewing our obligations; and hereby manifest our repentance for our former neglects, and our resolution for new obedience. As the people did in Ezra, that had taken heathen wives, and as it was ordinary in the Old Testament, after some notable breach of covenant, to renew this covenant with God: and as we use to do at sacraments, and days of humiliation, though we have formerly taken the same covenant, yet we see cause to renew it again and again, especially as against those sins, and for those duties, where we have lately been most faulty.

And if it be no more than is your duty already; whether you subscribe or no, what reason have you to refuse an agreement or subscription to such duty, unless, as I said, because you are unwilling to perform it. He that is resolved to do it, is willing to be as much as may be obliged to it. When it must be done, the strongest bonds are surest.

Object. 13. But some associations do not only practise, but subscribe to such things that we cannot in conscience agree to: as the use of lay-elders, as the presbyterians do; the calling people to profess that they own us for their pastors, as you do.

Answ. 1. I hope you are not of such dividing principles, as that you cannot in conscience hold communion with men that differ from you in as great a matter as this, if they will but leave you free. Else, if you should plead conscience for such dividing, I would desire you to see that you can plead Scripture for it, as well as plead conscience for it; for an erring conscience, engaging men against the will of God, is a poor excuse for sin: it is no more than to say, When I sin, I think I do not sin. It is a very considerable answer that Mr. Lawson, in his book against Hobbs's Politics, doth give to the common question, Whether an erring conscience bind? He saith, that an erring conscience is not conscience; for conscience is a sort of science, and error is not science, or knowledge.

But if these brethren would force you to subscribe with them in such matters as you mention, which your judgment is against, or else they will hold no communion with you, then it is they that exclude you, and not you that exclude yourselves. But I hope no associations now with us, will be guilty of such a course. I hope they are not resolved to refuse communion with all that are not for lay-elders, or such like matters. Then they would be the dividers, that lay the church's unity and peace on such a doubtful point. But if they do themselves subscribe to that, may not you desire to join with them, with a modest excepting of that article alone in which you are unsatisfied? which, no doubt, if they be peaceable men they will admit.

And for the instance you give of our calling people to an express consent, viz. (1.) To christianity: (2.) To their membership in the churches where we are pastors: I answer, 1. It is a strange conscience that can find matter of scruple against this. When we are assured, that people cannot be members or christians against their wills, and their wills cannot be known to us but by the expressions of it, may we not call them to express it? Especially, since parish habitation is grown a less fit note than heretofore, and hearing is certainly no sufficient evidence; and people will take it to be a heinous injury to them if we should exercise discipline on them without their consent, and perhaps would have an action against us at law for it! And where consent must be necessarily signified, is not the most express signification more satisfactory to us, and obligatory to them, than an uncertain, implicit, dark signification, which our own consciences tell us, with abundance of them, is really no signification, nor intended by them to any such use, as not knowing what a church is, or what discipline is, but thinking that to be a church member, is no more than to be a parishioner, and come to church. Though we might well prove against the separatists that this much, with the professions of the rest that had more knowledge, was enough to prove the truth of our churches, when we could do no more; yet if we shall now (after so many years of fullest liberty, when we may reform if we will) proceed no further, but tolerate, yea, plead for all such defects as will but consist with the truth of the churches, yea, pretend conscience against them, it is just with God to lay upon us so much of his wrath, and withdraw from us so much of his mercy, as shall leave us no more to comfort us, but that still we are truly men, as our churches are truly churches.

But, 2. I must further tell you, that the objection is grounded on a mere mistake and wilful or careless oversight. For our Agreement to call our people to a profession of their christianity and church membership, is but with this exception: "Except any of us should judge that they can better exercise the forementioned discipline without calling their people to such a profession of consent, in which case we will declare our reasons to our brethren of the ministry, in our meetings, and hear their advice when the case is opened." If indeed you can and will exercise Christ's discipline on all in your parish, without their express consent, we shall not refuse communion with you: only let us see in good sadness that you do it. First privately, and at last openly, admonish all the scandalous, obstinate sinners in your parish; and if they do not repent and reform, reject them; and then we will not differ with you about calling them to this profession. But if you will not do this, you must pardon me, if I conclude, that whatever you pretend, it is not the calling your people to this profession that you scruple in conscience, but it is the trouble and opposition that discipline exercised would draw upon you, that makes your flesh scruple any thing that would engage you to it. And if this be so, faithfulness to God and you, commandeth me to tell you, that the searching day of God is at hand, when self-seeking hypocrites shall have their reward. If I may speak according to my experience of the state of our ordinary congregations, I must needs conclude, that if you did but perceive that you must exercise Christ's discipline impartially, we should need no other argument to bring you to call for your people's consent, than your own safety and self-love, and that very flesh would be for it that is now against it. For I imagine, that if you should exercise this discipline on all your parish, especially in great and bad congregations, you would hardly escape long from being knocked on the head, without a special preservation of God.

Object. 14. But some associations are forming canons, and putting laws upon us, which we know not that we are obliged to obey.

Answ. 1. Associations sometimes draw up articles of agreement, whereto the several members oblige themselves by consent: but I know of none with us that presume to impose any laws on others. 2. If the things you speak be made already your duty by God, either expressly by a particular command, or else by a general word determined by Providence, as about some necessary, variable circumstances, then it is no man, but God that imposeth on you, and it is not your refusing your consent that shall disoblige you or excuse you. But if they be things evil, that are imposed on you by men; put in the reasons of your dissent, and take the leave of differing in that one point without withdrawing unnecessarily from their communion. If it be but about indifferent circumstances, as I would not have any, no, not by an agreement, much less by imposition, make common determinations of such without any need; so if they did, I must tell you, that union and communion of churches is not indifferent but necessary; and therefore reject it not upon the account of such things as you say yourselves are but indifferent.

Object. 15. But we are not satisfied with their practice of suspending men from the Lord's supper, that are not excommunicated: nor do we know any warrant for it.

Answ. Suspension is either penal, or not penal. That which is not penal is of two sorts: (1.) Sometimes I deny to give men the sacrament, merely because I have no call or obligation on me to do it. In this case, the proof lies on you, viz. to prove my obligation. For example: I take not myself obliged to give the sacrament to all the county, if they require it; nor to any neighbour parish that have a pastor of their own; nor to any of this parish where I live that are separated members of another church; or, that through hatred of discipline will be members of no particular church; or, that will be members of no particular church, and yet will not come near me to acquaint me with their reasons. Nor am I bound to watch over or administer sacraments to any that will not take me for their pastor in an ordinary stated course: no, nor at all, when I have so much to do with my own flock, that I cannot do such offices for others without neglecting as great duties to those whom I am more especially related and obliged to. Thus I suspend from the sacrament many a thousand; that is, I do not give it them that I have nothing to do with, or no obligation to give it to. (2.) Sometimes we may forbear to give men the sacrament, while we are admonishing them of their sin, and calling them to repentance, or doing some necessary previous duty. As if the whole congregation would have the sacrament on Thursday, I may desire them to stay till the Lord's day, and in the mean time to humble themselves and prepare. If you will call this a suspending of the whole church, you may speak as you please. So if you know a man that hath offended his brother, you may persuade him, yea, require him ministerially, by authority from Christ, to leave his gift at the altar, and go first and be reconciled to his brother, and then come and offer his gift. Though if he disobey, I will not presently without further trial censure him.

These acts are but negative (a not giving the sacrament) and not properly privative, and therefore not properly suspension. Duties must be done in right order: no duty is at all times to be performed. I am not bound to give a man the sacrament when I meet him in an ale-house, nor when I am admonishing him about a scandal; nor when three, or four, or a dozen shall send to me to bring it them to a private house without any more ado. All things must be done decently, orderly, and to edification; and the forbearing a disorderly, indecent, unedifying administration, is no proper penal suspension.

And I am even ashamed that the church is troubled about this question voluminously, by good men, that are for discipline and excommunication: whenas the things that we make such a stir about, are cases that are not like to fall out in a congregation once (I think) in twenty years. For if a man have offended, and no man have admonished him, nor the fact by notoriousness or accusation be brought to the church or officers, we are not bound to take notice of it, so far as to suspend any; nor do any that I know of plead for such a thing. But if the case be duly brought to the pastors, cannot they go to the person, or send for him before the very hour of the sacrament? Cannot they try whether he be penitent or not? And if he be penitent, we yield that he is not to be penally suspended. If he be not after other admonition, and the case is brought to the church, how can the officers be bound at the same time to give the sacrament to an impenitent person, and also to avoid him for his impenitency, or to tell the congregation, in order to his recovery? If these men are for discipline, they must confess that I am bound either to tell the congregation of this offender, (and that I must do when he demandeth communion,) or else, if telling the officers be enough, I must require them to avoid him, if he be impenitent.

2. And so this brings us to the other sort of suspension, which is penal, and properly so called: and this is nothing but an avoiding of the communion of the offender, *pro hac vice*. Where note, that it is one thing to be unsatisfied of the fact, and another to be unsatisfied of the person's repentance. In case the fact be not manifest, we confess there must be no suspension, save what prudence requires on the first-mentioned grounds, as not properly penal. But if the fact be manifest any of these three ways, By notoriety; or violent presumption; or valid testimony; and yet the person express not his repentance; we are bound by God to avoid communion with him till he repent: and therefore though I cannot sentence him as habitually obstinate, and therefore shall yet stay longer in a course of admonition before we reject him, as from his church relation, or state of communion; yet on the proved act of sin, till he manifest his repentance, I must forbear the actual communion with him, and deny him actual communion with us: for I cannot take him to be penitent till he profess it (probably); and if I take him not to be penitent, I must take him to be yet in his sin, e. g. to be an adulterer, a drunkard, &c.; and so am frequently commanded to avoid him, and forbidden to have communion with him. And this suspension is nothing but initial, actual excommunication. Even exclusion from the act of communion, before (upon the proof of fixed obstinacy) we exclude from the state of communion. This is plain, and methinks is enough to end, or at least to quiet, this needless controversy.

But if this be all; if you would indeed excommunicate only, and not suspend, this need not hinder any association. If you will go further than others, you may: as I confess you have great cause to go further than the most.

Object. 16. But, say others, is not denying them the Lord's supper a sufficient exercise of discipline on the most? What do you more to those that join not with you?

Answ. Either your not giving them the sacrament is penal, or not. If not, it is no exercise of discipline at all. Do you exercise discipline on all the county, when you give them not the sacrament? If it be penal, it is irregular and harsh dealing to punish and initially excommunicate, for so it is, one half of a parish without an orderly trial, or calling them to speak for themselves, or without taking Christ's course of first admonishing them. So that it seems to me not very much to differ from them that gather churches irregularly, by casting off the most without a trial, as no church members. And it is absurd to deprive them of actual communion so many years, and yet to let them remain in a *state* of communion, without any question. And if it be not a penal suspension, but they keep away themselves, it is gross neglect to let them alone so many years in the omission of church communion, and God's ordinances, while they are members.

As to our case, and the second part of the objection, I answer, We take not ourselves to have a pastoral charge of those that separate from us, and wilfully refuse to be members of our charge. We cannot make them our flock against their wills. We cast not out men, that cast not out themselves, but only in an orderly, regular way of discipline: but if many hundreds will withdraw in hatred of discipline, that is not our fault, but their own.

And yet I must tell you, that I let not them all so pass: but though I think not that I have such a charge of them as the rest, yet I sometimes publicly admonish the most notorious, and pray for them, and require the church to avoid them, as to private familiarity, as they withdraw themselves from sacramental communion. For I think, if a man call himself a brother, that is, a christian, and yet live scandalously, I must avoid him, and warn my people so to do, though he never joined himself to any church. Though I know what Beza's conjectural observation is on Acts xxi. that they are called merely *disciples* as they are christians not yet under the church order and officers, and they are called brethren when they are under officers and order: the observation hath its use; but it is not so always, but oft otherwise.

Object. 17. But are not there seasons when discipline may be forborne?

Answ. Yes, no doubt, and preaching too; but that must not be ordinarily. It is hard that there was scarce ever yet a season in England to execute it. I marvel when it will be seasonable, if not now!

Object. 18. But why do you go without the magistrate, and lay his interest aside?

Answ. 1. We go not without his licence, for he grants us liberty. 2. Nor without his encouragement. 3. But if we had neither, for discipline, sacraments, preaching, or praying, should we not use them? Is not Christ our Master? Is not his authority sufficient? How did all christian churches till Constantine's days?

See our Agreement, Artic. 6, et Reg. 20, whether we go without or wrong the magistrate. Our monthly meeting in this church for matters of discipline consisteth of two or three justices of peace, two or three presbyters, three or four deacons, and about twenty-four delegates of the people, of the most wise and pious men, chosen yearly by themselves to represent them, not prohibiting any other to be there, disclaiming any proper office, but only looking that the church have no wrong, and doing that which private members may do.

Object. 19. But some of the prelatical men are offended at our leaving out the clause of *Christ's descent into hell* in our profession.

Answ. 1. The creed is part of our profession, and if these men cannot find it and that clause in our papers, it is not our fault.

2. The rest is about our exposition of the creed, for our people's understanding: and either that clause is plain and commonly agreed on, as to the sense, or not. If it be, then what need we expound it. If not, methinks they should rather commend our modesty that thought ourselves unmeet judges of so great a controversy, where the church is so divided.

3. It seems a late clause, that came not into this creed of some hundred years after Christ.

4. The word *hell* was never put into the creed by the Greek or Latin church, and if it were a full and plain translation of the Greek ᾅδης, or the Latin *inferi*, we should the easilier receive it without scruple; but if we should change this English word by a stricter translation, you would be offended much more. See Dr. Hammond in his Practical Catechism, p. 286, 287, against the local descent into hell at large. Or if you would see much more, read that learned Treatise of Sandford and Parker, "de Descensu Christi," and Bishop Usher, in his answer to the Jesuit "de Limbo, et Descensu Christi ad Inferos." Read well but those two discourses, and you will but pity the self-conceitedness and confidence of such dry and raw discoursers, as Mr. Ashwell, and many of his strain, that seem to place more hope of their success in reproaching the contrary-minded, and in bold pretences to antiquity and universality, than in any evidence that should compel assent.

If these men have the moderation of true protestants, let them hear the words of one of them, Bishop Usher, de Limbo, p. 417. "And to speak truth, it is a matter above the reach of the common people to enter into the discussion of the full meaning of this point of the descension into hell; the determination whereof dependeth upon the knowledge of the learned tongues, and other sciences that come not within the compass of their understanding——It having here likewise been further manifested, what different opinions have been entertained by the ancient doctors of the church.—— I leave it to be considered by the learned, whether any such controverted matter may fitly be brought in to expound the rule of faith, which being common both to the great and the small ones in the church, (August. Ep. 57, ad Dard.) must continue such verities only as generally are agreed on by the common consent of all true christians." Or if they have more respect to the judgment of a Jesuit, let them hear one of greatest name there cited. Suarez, tom. 2, in 3 part; Thom. Disp. 43, sect. 4. *Si nomine articuli.*——"If by an article of faith we understand, a truth which all the faithful are bound explicitly to know and believe; so I do not think it necessary to reckon this among the articles of faith; because it is not a matter altogether so necessary for all men; and because that, for this reason peradventure, it is omitted in the Nicene creed; the knowledge of which creed seemeth to be sufficient for fulfilling the precept of faith. Lastly, for this cause peradventure Augustine and other fathers expounding the creed, do not unfold this mystery to the people."

And, saith Bishop Usher, ibid. "That he descended not into the hell of the damned by the essence of his soul, or locally, but virtually only, by extending the effect of his power thither, is the common doctrine of Thomas Aquinas, and the rest of the schoolmen. Card. Bellarmine at first held it to be probable, that Christ's soul did descend thither, not only by his effects, but by his real presence also; but after having considered better of the matter, he resolved that the opinion of Thomas and other schoolmen was to be followed."

And whereas some of them do with confidence persuade us that this article was in the creed from the beginning, they might also from a Jesuit have learned more modesty; John Busæus, de Descensu Christi, Thes. 33, cited by Bishop Usher, de Limbo,

p. 309; who saith, "Saint Cyprian, or Ruffinus rather, in his exposition of the creed, denieth that this article is read in the creed of the church of Rome, or the churches of the East: and some of the most ancient fathers, while either they gather up the sum of the christian faith, or expound the creed of the apostles, have omitted this point of doctrine! But at what time it was inserted into the creed, it cannot certainly be determined.' So far the Jesuit. And yet I will not imitate Mr. Ashwell's royal authority on his title-page, and so believe it to be from the apostles, till another certain author is found out, as he saith, of the creed; but I will contrarily believe it is not by the apostles, because it cannot be proved by the affirmers to be by them, and because I can prove a time since them, when it was not in the common creed.

And, saith Bishop Usher, ib. p. 310, "The first particular church that is known to have inserted this article into her creed, is that of Aquileia; which added also the attributes of *invisible* and *impassible* unto God the Father Almighty, in the beginning of the creed, as appeareth by Ruffinus, who framed his Exposition of the Creed according to the order used in that church. But whether any other church in the world, for five hundred years after Christ, (mark this,) did follow the Aquileians in putting the one of these additions to the apostles' creed more than the other, can hardly, I suppose, be showed out of any approved testimony of antiquity." He goes on further to prove this by instances of many authors' recitals of the creed, and out of some ancient manuscripts, as is there to be seen, p. 310, 311. Mr. Ashwell thankfully confesseth some things that he learned of him; if he had had the patience to have learned these and many more, before he had so far exalted himself against those that are not of his opinion, he had not done amiss.

Whether the Arians first put it into the church creed, I leave men to conjecture as they see cause, when they have perused the said bishop's allegations, p. 308; but certainly, when the Nicene fathers had none of it, the symbols of the Eastern church, not knowing it, as Ruffinus tells us, these bastard fatherlings, the Arians, saith the bishop, did not only insert this clause, He descended to the places under the earth, but added for amplification, whom hell itself trembled at. The like did they in another and a third creed.

And as Ruffinus testifieth, that this article was neither in the Eastern nor Roman creeds, so he adjoined presently, as the bishop noteth, p. 339, Yet the force or meaning of the word seemeth to have been buried, which some, saith the bishop, think to be the cause why in all the ancient symbols that are known to have been written the first six hundred years after Christ, that of Aquileia only excepted, which Ruffinus followed, where the burial is expressed, there the descending into hell is omitted; as in that of Constantinople, for example, commonly called the Nicene creed; and on the other side, where the descent into hell is mentioned, there the article of the burial is passed over, as in that of Athanasius: and to say the truth, the terms of *burial* and *descending into hell*, in the Scripture phrase, tend much to the expressing of the self-same thing," &c. So he.

These good men, therefore, that (some of them over their pots in an ale-house) do learnedly reproach us, for not expounding the article of the descent to hell, or not twice expressing it, should have considered, that with us they more reproach the Nicene and twenty other creeds; yea, that of Marcellus in Epiphanius, which is nearest to that now called the Apostles' of any so ancient a form that I have met with; and they should have thought it enough in us to retain it in our creed, without presuming to expound it, till they can answer what Bishop Usher, Parker, and other protestants in this cause have delivered; or if they be of their mind, they should confess that it is expressed in the terms which we in our explication do retain.

But, as they must confess, the creed was not delivered by the apostles in English, and so the word *hell* was not in the original; so if we must stick to the creed indeed, we must translate it truly, and you must help us to some word that is of as comprehensive a signification as ᾅδης is; which, as is most largely proved by Usher and Parker, besides many more, signifieth the state of the dead in general; or as applied to souls, the invisible state of separated souls; whereas, whatever the etymology of the word *hell* be, yet we are sure that the common use (which is the master of language) hath among the vulgar appropriated it to the damned's place or state of torment. Saith Bishop Usher, p. 388, "Some learned protestants do observe, that in these words there is no determinate mention made either of *ascending* or *descending* either to heaven or hell, taking hell according to the vulgar acceptation; but of the general only, under which these contraries are indifferently comprehended; and that the words literally interpreted, import no more than this, HE WENT UNTO THE OTHER WORLD. Allow us but this translation, and we shall please you; and sure you will not say, that the apostles agreed on your translation.

If you say, Then the words are superfluous, as intimating no more than his death before expressed; I answer, that you may as well say, the apostles superfluously expressed Christ's reviving after his rising. Rom. xiv. 9, "For this end he both died, rose, and revived." When indeed his reviving expresseth not the first re-union of soul and body, for that was before his rising; but his state of life among the living after. So here, his death expresseth his entrance into that state; but ᾅδης signifieth the world of souls, or state itself of the dead, which dying he presently passed into. But of this Bishop Usher hath said enough in answer, ib. p. 407, 408, and forward.

But yet for my part, I shall further tell you, that as I take the controversy to be of no greater moment than Suarez, Usher, and others do express, so also I suppose our difference about it is not so great as many do imagine: lay but aside the metaphysical controversy about the locality of spirits, and the popish conceit of Christ's fetching the Old Testament fathers from hell, which Usher shows that Marcion in likelihood first hatched, and then our difference is but small; for what would you have that we do not grant you? Would you have us yield that Christ's body lay in the grave? Why, who denieth it? Would you have us yield that his soul was in the region of the dead, or in a state of separation from the body? Who is there that questions it? Would you have us yield that this state was penal both to soul and body? We easily grant it you. Not that Christ had the pain of sense, or the loss of heaven, but the penalty of death: the soul's being separated from the body was a penal state, as such. If any say, that Christ's soul was in paradise, and there is no pain, I answer, There may be somewhat penal, where there is not that which vulgarly is called pain: and what glory soever the separated soul of Christ did partake of, yet the separation from the body, as separation, was penal. There remaineth a desire in separated souls to be re-united to their bodies, and therefore it is a better state; and glory is not perfect till the man be perfect. Death is a penalty to the whole man, and not to the body alone; and thus far it is a most undoubted truth, that both to the separated soul of Christ, and now of the saints with Christ, there is something penal in this separation and imperfection remaining, though joined with exceeding glory. Saith Bishop Usher, p. 390, "Heaven itself may be comprised within the notion of ᾅδης: heaven, I say, not considered as it is a place of life and perfection, nor as it shall be after the general resurrection; but so far forth only as death, the last enemy that shall be destroyed, (1 Cor. xv. 26,) hath any footing therein; that is to say, as it is the receptacle of the spirits of dead men, held as yet dissevered from their bodies; which state of dissolution, though carried to heaven itself, is still a part of death's victory, (1 Cor. xv. 54, 55,) and the saints' imperfection," Heb. xi. 40. Thus he. And Peter plainly saith, "Whom God did raise up, loosing the sorrows of death, forasmuch as it was not possible that he should be holden of it," Acts ii. 24. And "Christ being raised from the dead, dieth now no more: death hath now no more dominion over him," saith Paul, Rom. vi. 9. So that he was, as to his whole man, under some power or dominion of death for a time. Of this penalty on Christ's separated soul, and ours, see most fully Parker, l. 2, sect. 46, ad 50.

What would you have yet more granted? Is it that Christ triumphed over Satan and hell, and convinced the unbelieving, impious, damned souls of their sin and remediless misery? Why, we do not deny it you; for as the damned man (Luke xvi.) is said to see Abraham and Lazarus in his bosom, and the wicked in hell have such a knowledge of God and heaven, as sufficeth to convince them of the loss and misery, and to torment them; so we deny not but they might have such a sight of Christ, and he might make such a manifestation of himself to them.

Would you have us grant that he went to ᾅδης, to procure the deliverance of the captives of ᾅδης? we deny it not: his humiliation is the cause of our exaltation; his death and going to ᾅδης was to purchase deliverance for all his members, dead and living, that the dead bodies might in time be raised, and the separated souls be re-united to the bodies, and the whole man perfected. Would you have us believe that he went to bring the glad tidings of this to the spirits of the just? we do believe it; so that they that believed in him before might intuitively behold their Lord in whom they believed, in their own present state, and might be the more comforted in the assurance of the resurrection of their bodies, and their final perfection.

But if besides all this, you would have us believe, that Christ's soul was locally in its essence in the hell of the damned; and that thence he fetched the souls of the old fathers out of the limbus, that is part of hell, here we must leave you: 1. Because that else we must be worse than the papists, whose schoolmen are content with a virtual presence, and deny a local: 2. Because we know not what locality of spirits is: and, 3. Because in the latter branch, we are loth to be either Marcionites, or papists, till we see more reason for it; especially, we have no mind of your speculations in our creed.

Object. 20. The last objection that I have been troubled with, is against the title that we put over the old creed, *the ancient Western creed.* And what is the matter here? Engagement to their opinion makes them jealous; and jealousy suspecteth the most innocent syllables. Was not this the *ancient Western creed?* Yes, no doubt, they mean not to deny it; but they think we intimate hereby a distinction between the Eastern creed and the Western; and consequently intimate, that this creed was not the universal creed of the church, and composed and delivered for that use by the apostles.

But our intimated distinction can be supposed necessary to intimate no more, than that the East and West did ordinarily make use of several creeds in baptism and other solemnities; and that this was it that the West made use of. So that whether the East also, and all churches, used this sometimes, or whether it were thus formed by the apostles, are questions that we never intended to decide.

But being called to it, I must give a further account of my own opinion. You cannot in modesty, sure, either deny the aforesaid ground of distinction from the use of the several churches, nor yet the antiquity of the terms of the distinction; much less can you think that learned and wise men have not used it, and brought it to our hands. He that is your chief author for the apostolic composure of it, doth give you himself the matter and terms of this distinction, I mean Ruffinus; and Bishop Usher useth it frequently in the aforesaid dispute, and his "Dissertatio de Symbolis," and in other writings, to say nothing of Pithæus, Vossius, or any others. Why then doth the quarrel begin with us?

I have read Mr. Ashwell, and others of his opinion, as impartially as I could, being as unwilling to believe that the apostles were the authors of this symbol as not, if I could see any evidence for it; but I must confess that the reading of such writings as his, do more confirm me in my former opinion, which is as followeth:

1. I do believe that Christ himself is the author of the ancient creed, expressly in Matt. xxviii. 19, "Baptizing them into the name of the Father, and of the Son, and of the Holy Ghost." And that the creed at first contained but these three articles: and that all that were baptized, at age, were to profess this belief, viz. that they believed in the Father, Son, and Holy Ghost. And I desire them that are confident of the contrary opinion, to confute what Parker hath so copiously brought for the proof of it; and learned Ludov. Crocius that followeth him.

2. And yet I do fully believe, that before the New Testament was written, the apostles taught their catechumens and persons admitted to baptism, the sum of the gospel or christian religion in a few distinct articles. For it is certain that they could not deliver all the history or doctrine of Christ to every convert; and as certain, that they must deliver all the essentials before they could make a christian, and that every christian that was converted by them, was made such by the power of these essential truths; for the essentials of subjective christianity are the image and effects of the essentials of objective christianity or faith; as the image in the wax is of that in the seal.

3. I am persuaded that the method of the apostles in delivering their creed, or essential verities, was according to Christ's platform; even to deliver the doctrine of the Trinity, and what was found necessary to the explication of any one of the three articles; and consequently, that they ordinarily taught the same doctrine that is now in our creed to all their converts; yet enlarging it, especially on the second article, which was it that the world did most resist.

4. I do believe that it cannot be proved, and therefore should not be affirmed, that the apostles did in any one precise form of words, explain the three articles laid down by Christ; but as they ordinarily preached the same truths, and that much in the same or like phrase, not affecting novelty; so they did not compose this into any precise form of words, but de-

livered the same great truth in such expressions as they found meetest for the persons with whom they had to do.

5. Thus I do believe that every christian and church was a living gospel, or book, in which the creed, and all essentials of christianity, doctrinal and practical, were written by the Spirit of God, through the instrumentality of the preaching of these fundamental truths; and this before the scripture of the New Testament was written.

6. This I believe was the great tradition of the essentials of religion, distinct from Scripture: baptism itself was a notable means to deliver down these truths.

7. Yet I am not against a strict agreement upon such a form of profession *in terminis* without liberty to change a word; but think that exactness is as necessary in this, both for the sake of truth and unity, as in most matters that are left to man.

8. The reasons why I cannot believe that this present form of words, as now in our hands, was either composed by the apostles, or the universal creed from the beginning, are these following, among many more.

(1.) Because of the no-proof that is brought by the affirmers that should prove it.

(2.) Because I find the fathers in the first ages constantly giving us the creed of that church in other words; and in forms all differing one from another, and not one of them giving us this very form of above three hundred years at least after Christ. Ignatius, Irenæus, Origen, Tertullian, thrice recite the church's faith, and so do many others; and all in several forms of words, and not one of them in this form. So that it would make a man shake the head to read such kind of proofs as Mr. Ashwell's, that this is the apostles' creed; he heaps up other forms to prove the apostolic composure of this form. What did he think of his readers when he offers them with highest confidence such proofs as most effectually disprove the thing he brings them for. Who can think that all these men would offer to give us the very symbol of christianity in forms of their own, and various forms, and none of them use the apostles' form, if such a thing in precise terms had then been by them commended to the churches. Those willing men that can make their own faith, may believe many such matters as these; but so cannot I. The first that I remember to have read, that is like the present form, though maimed, is that of Marcellus, in Epiphanius 72. Heresies, which are delivered with such expressions adjoined, as would make a man imagine that it was the matter and not the form of words which he professeth to have received from his ancestors; nor is there any one cited by Mr. Ashwell himself of those elder times, that seems the same form with ours, but only this of Marcellus, and that of the Latin Chrysostom and one of Tertullian's de Veland. Virg. seems to be part of this. And among such abundance of forms of words, it were strange if they could possibly miss sometimes of delivering these few principles in the terms we now use. And for that of Marcellus, it is in many things different from ours; and that of Tertullian is so different that no man can prove that ever the author had seen our form. And as for that of Chrysostom, if it were his, he was about four hundred years after Christ; but indeed there is no such matter in his works. No wonder if Mr. Ashwell could not find it in Sir H. Sevil's edition, of "Fronto Ducæus des," but only in the Latin edition of Erasmus, saith a far greater antiquary, Bishop Usher, de Limbo, p. 310, 311, "For as for the two Latin expositions thereof that go under the name of S. Chrysostom, the latter whereof hath it, the former hath it not, and the others that are found in the tenth tome of S. Austin's works, among the sermons *de tempore;* because the authors of them, together with the time wherein they were written, be altogether unknown, they can bring us little light in this inquiry."

And all the rest of the three first centuries at least, that Mr. Ashwell citeth, are set as if it were on purpose to make his reader wonder at his self-confutation.

(3.) Another of my reasons is, because I find so many clauses new in this form that we now have, and find withal that the arising of new heresies was an avowed reason of adding new clauses to the creed in those days, that it makes me much suspect that all the rest, except the three essential articles, were brought in by degrees, as heresies gave occasion, and never formed all at once.

That several new clauses were added to this, Bishop Usher may satisfy you in his "Dissertatio de Symbolis," and other writings, ibid. p. *Quo tamen hodie Romana ecclesia utitur symbolum, additamentis aliquot auctius legi, res ipsa indicat*——. The additions not found in any of the more ancienter copies are these: "Creator of heaven and earth," added to the first article; which in likelihood was against that rabble of heretics that feigned the world to be created by angels, yea, bad angels: also the word "conceived" is added; the oldest forms having it "born of the Holy Ghost and the Virgin Mary." Also the word "dead" is added, and "he descended into hell," and the name of "God" and the attribute "Almighty," to the article of Christ's sitting at the Father's right hand. Also the word "catholic" is added to the "holy church," and so is the "communion of saints," and "the life everlasting." All which are a considerable part of so short a form. And that clauses were used to be put into the creed upon occasion of heresy, is well known of other creeds; and Ruffinus confesseth of their Aquileian creed, thus, *His additur invisibilem et impossibilem: sciendum quod duo isti sermones in ecclesiæ Romanæ symbolo non habentur: constat autem apud nos additos hæreseos causa sabellii, illius perfecto quæ a nostris Patri passiana appellatur.——Ut ergo excluderetur talis impietas de Patre, videntur hæc addisse majores,* &c. Ruffin. in Symb. c. 7.

Saith Bishop Usher, in his sermon of the Church's Unity, p. 17, "This creed, though for *substance,* it was the same every where, yet for *form* was somewhat different, and in some places received more enlargements than in others. The Western churches herein applied themselves to the capacity of the meaner sort, more than the Eastern did; using in their baptism that shorter form of confession, commonly called the apostles' creed, which in the more ancient times was briefer also than now it is: as we may easily perceive by comparing the symbol recited by Marcellus Ancyranus, with the expositions of the apostles' creed written by the Latin doctors, wherein the mention of the Father's being 'Maker of heaven and earth,' the Son's 'death,' and 'descended into hell,' and the 'communion of saints,' is wholly omitted. All which, though they were of undoubted verity, yet——and need not necessarily be inserted into that symbol, which is the badge and cognizance whereby the believer is to be differenced and distinguished from the unbeliever. The creed which the Eastern churches used in baptism, was larger than this; being either the same, or very little different from that which we commonly call the Nicene creed.

"And he begins his Dissertation de Symb. thus, *Licet apud omnes tum orientis, tum occidentis ecclesias ut unus Dominus, et baptismus ita et una fides fuerit; una tamen et eadem verborum formula fidei symbolum, quo in cultus Domini professione, et baptismi susceptione, illæ sunt usæ, non fuisse conceptum, omniumque Romanum fuisse brevissimum, in symboli explicatione, Ruffinus æquileiensis presbyter jamdudum nos docuit: de additamentis etiam apud occidentales ad Romanum hoc oppositis in prooemio suo sic præfatus.*

"And he useth the distinction in his preface, *Meam de occidentalis et orientalis ecclesiæ symbolis sententiam*, &c." Et passim p. 13, 18, 19, 20, 21, 26, &c.

(4.) And it is enough to debilitate the force that some imagine to lie in the title apostolic, that the Nicene creed was as confidently, and for aught ever I yet saw proved, as anciently, called the apostles' creed, as this, and said to be delivered from the apostles. Saith Usher, Dissert. p. 16, *Sed et ab occidentalibus consimiliter ecclesiis longius istud symbolum et apostolicum habitum et Nicænum etiam nominatum fuisse, observare liceat. Sic enim habet ordo Romanus in præfatione symboli cujus recitationi præmissa, ante administrationem baptismi: Audite suscipientes evangelici symboli sacramentum, a Domino, inspiratum, ab apostolis institutum, cujus pauca quidem verba sunt, sed magna mysteria.—Et in cœnæ sacræ celebratione Latina Missa, quæ circa annum* DCC. *in usu fuit, de eodem adjicit finito symbolo apostolorum dicat sacerdos, Dominus vobiscum.*

And p. 17, he had before said, *Hanc fidei formulam, ut ab apostolis ecclesiæ traditum, et a Nicænis patribus promulgatum, laudat Epiphanius.* And Cyril, or John of Jerusalem, calls the Jerusalem creed by the name of Ἁγίας καὶ ἀποστολικῆς πίστεως, Catech. 18. Bishop Usher, de Limbo, p. 309, saith, that "The creed of the council of Constantinople, much larger than our common creed, was itself no less than the other (N. B.) heretofore both accounted and named the apostles' creed: and it is not to be thought it would leave out any article that was then commonly believed to have been any parcel of the creed received from the apostles." And he citeth for the title Epiphan. in Ἄγκυρ; p. 518, and the Latin ancient Missal before mentioned. And citing Epiphan. again to the same purpose in his sermon of Unity, he addeth that "Cassianus avoucheth as much, where he urgeth this against Nestorius, as the creed anciently received by the church of Antioch, from whence he came: and that the second general council at Constant. approved it as most ancient and agreeable to baptism," apud. Theod. lib. 5, cap. 9.

Many other reasons that stick with me are at large expressed in Parker de Descen. lib. 4; which whoever will read impartially with judgment, I dare venture him easily upon Mr. Ashwell's answer to them: the sum of which alloweth the fathers to make additions, as being but an explication; whenas our question is only of the form of words. If any of them may be altered, and additions made, who knows which of them be apostolical? and why may not others now do the like? What commission can those fathers show more than other pastors of the church?

Far am I from believing him, that none but by an apostolical spirit could have known by the Scriptures which were fundamental articles of faith: thus far to have summed them up. When Scripture so expressly tells men, which are the principles, and which life and death are laid upon.

And further am I from believing him that there is so much difference between the creed and the Scripture as he expresseth, as if there were no understanding nor keeping our religion for all the Scripture, were it not for the creed, but the whole frame of our religion would fall instantly to the ground; and the contempt which he spitteth in the face of the Scriptures, I must needs say, I do dislike, and think it most unseemly in a man that is so tender of having the nakedness of the fathers opened, and that hath no more sensible an answer to give to those testimonies of the church of France and of England, so valued by him, and of Cyril and Paschasius, who all take the creed on the authority of the Scripture from whence it is gathered. (See his p. 115, 168, 169, and 178, to Object. 9.) It is past my understanding, that the bare words that Christ "was crucified, dead, buried," &c. should teach a man more plainly to what end it was that Christ did all this, whether only for example, as the Socinians, or for ransom, sacrifice, propitiation, &c. than the Scriptures that at large set forth these ends. As plain as the creed is, he must needs reserve the undoubted exposition, and applying of this rule, to the church and ancient fathers, "in whose writings," he saith, "the apostles have left it us, these being their successors, to whose care and custody they not only committed the oracles of God in writing, and the creed by word of mouth, but the interpretation also of both, as they heard them expounded from their own mouths, while they preached and lived amongst them; for in vain had the apostles given them the words, if they had not given them the sense withal, to stop the mouths of heretics."——True, it were in vain, if the words themselves are nonsense. I know the apostles have successors so far, as to have the care of expounding this Scripture delivered to them, by the ordinary helps of grace, art, and nature; discerning the sense by the words: but oh that I knew where to find that church that could give me the sense of all God's oracles, by this undoubted tradition, as from the apostles themselves! or, that I knew the names or characters of those fathers that had this *depositum* (the sense of the Scriptures) by tradition from the apostles, and where I may find it left to us! Is it each Father individually, or is it the greater number together? And how shall we take the vote? or know which of them to account a father and which not? Surely when I read them telling us no more of the sense of the oracles, and so often erring, and disagreeing, I cannot believe that their memories were all so good, as to deliver down from father to son an exposition of the Bible, without writing; and if ever any of them had such a voluminous commentary in his brain, from the hand of an apostle, which was not thought meet to be given in writing, the issue by this time may convince us, that either it was intended only for themselves, or else that indeed such a world of matter would have been surelier kept in writing, than this tradition hath hitherto kept it. For I think most of us love our fleshly ease so well, that if we knew where the book or the church were that would give us such a certain exposition of Scripture as from the apostles, we would be glad of it, not only to the quieting of our minds, but also for the sparing our time and labour that we now bestow in studying.

Yet still I say as before, that I doubt not but the principles were preached before the gospel was written, and that thousands were made christians by the reception of those principles; and that all christians and churches of them, successively contained these principles written in their hearts; and that the great articles of the creed, believing in God the Father, Son, and Holy Ghost, were in terms imposed on the church by Christ himself: and that the meaning of them was still taught to the catechumens and the church. And that the churches did well to keep the sum of faith in certain forms of words; and I would they had made fewer, and changed them less: and I think it meet that they be still used in baptism, and on other occasions of public confession of faith in our congregations.

But yet I am not convinced that the apostles did compose this form of words, or any other to that use; nor that it was composed of some hundreds of years after Christ, though the same articles were then professed in several forms of words; and those articles were all delivered from Christ and his apostles: nor do I believe that the form now called the apostles' creed, was any more theirs, or more ancient, than some other forms; nor do we owe it any more belief or reverence, than we do the Jerusalem or the Nicene creed; and yet I truly much reverence both, and believe them all. Nor do I think that ever this creed was the form which the universal church did use above others; but think that in the third century, the Nicene was the more common. So much (and perhaps too much) to these objections.

THE

VAIN RELIGION OF THE FORMAL HYPOCRITE,

AND

THE MISCHIEF OF AN UNBRIDLED TONGUE,

AS AGAINST RELIGION, RULERS, OR DISSENTERS,

DESCRIBED IN SEVERAL SERMONS, PREACHED AT THE ABBEY IN WESTMINSTER, BEFORE MANY MEMBERS OF THE HONOURABLE HOUSE OF COMMONS, MDCLX.:

AND THE

FOOL'S PROSPERITY THE OCCASION OF HIS DESTRUCTION:

A SERMON PREACHED AT COVENT GARDEN.

BOTH PUBLISHED TO HEAL THE EFFECTS OF SOME HEARERS' MISUNDERSTANDINGS AND MISREPORTS.

TO THE READER.

THOUGH God be not the author of sin, he knows why he permitteth it in the world. He will be no loser, and Satan shall be no gainer, by it in the end. The malice of the devil and wicked men is, ordinarily, the destruction of the cause which they most desire to promote; and an advantage by accident to the cause and persons which they would root out from the earth. Were there no more to prove this than the instances of Joseph's brethren, of Pharaoh, and the murderers of our Lord, it were enough. We usually lose more by the flatteries of Satan and the world, than by their violence. If these hasty, coarse, unpolished sermons, shall prove beneficial to the souls of any, this also may come in among the lower rank of instances. If the devil had let me alone, they might have been cast aside, and no further molested him or his kingdom, for aught I know, than they did upon the preaching of them. But seeing he will needs, by malicious misreports and slanders, kindle suspicion, and raise offence, against them and the author, let him take what he gets by it. He hath never got much from me, by violence, or by his foul-mouthed slanderous instruments: no, not when the impudence or multitude of their slanders have forced me to be silent, lest I trouble the reader, or mispend my time.

The first of these discourses, being intended to undeceive the formal hypocrite, and to call men from a vain, to a saving, serious religion, and to acquaint them that cry out against hypocrisy, where the hypocrite is to be found, it seems, provoked the ignorant or the guilty; insomuch that the cry went, that I preached down all forms of prayer, and all government and order in the church: when there is not a syllable that hath any such sense; but it seems what I spoke against the carcass, was interpreted to be spoken against the body of religion.

The words of Mr. Bolton, and other divines, which I have cited against the reproachers of serious piety, are added since the preaching of the rest, as being more fit to be presented here to the eye, than in the pulpit to the ear.

The petulancy of men on both extremes constrained me to add "The Bridle of their Tongues."

The second discourse, I understand, offended some few of the gallants, that thought they were too roughly handled; let them here peruse it, and better concoct it, if they please.

I only add this observation to the heirs of heaven, that are above this world, and live by faith.

Few rich men are truly religious; it is as hard for them to be saved, as for a camel to go through a needle's eye. Yet rich men will every where be the rulers of the world, and so (as to outward protection or opposition) the judges in matters of religion. Judge, therefore, whether dominion and earthly reign be the portion of the saints (as Jewishly some of late imagine); and what usage we must ordinarily expect on earth; and what condition the church of Christ is like to be in to the end. As his kingdom, so ours, is not of this world. A low, despised, suffering state, is that believers must ordinarily expect, and prepare for, and study to be serviceable in. If better (may I call it better) come, take it as a feast, and grudge not when the table is withdrawn; and look not it should be our every day's fare. But yet, value the more highly those few of the rich, and great, and rulers, that are above this world, and devote their power and riches to the Lord, and are holy and heavenly in the midst of so great temptations and impediments.

The Lord teach us to use this transitory world as not over-using it, that we may never hear, " Remember that thou in thy life-time receivedst thy good things," Luke xvi. 25. How shortly will they find themselves everlastingly undone, that made not sure of a more enduring portion! Reader, that thou mayst savingly remember these common, but necessary, though much neglected, truths, is the end of these endeavours, and shall be the matter of my heart's desire and prayers, while the Lord continueth me

His servant for the promoting the increase
and edification of his church,

November 15, 1660. R. BAXTER.

Postscript. Readers, meeting, in his consideration of the liturgy, with these following words of the Rev. D. Gauden, " I cannot but commend the candour, justice, and integrity of Mr. Baxter, who lately professed to me, that he saw nothing in the liturgy, which might not well bear a good construction, if men looked upon it as became christians, with eyes of charity," I was sensible of the great respects of this learned and reverend man; but, lest you misunderstand both him and me, I think it best to tell you more fully what were my words. Speaking for reformation of the Common Prayer Book, and an addition of other forms in Scripture phrase, with liberty of choice, &c. I said, " That for the doctrine of the Common Prayer Book, though I had read exceptions against divers passages, I remembered not anything that might not receive a good construction, if it were read with the same candour and allowance, as we read the writings of other men." So that it was only the truth of the doctrine that I spoke of; against which I hate to be peevishly quarrelsome, when God hath blest this church so wonderfully, with a moderate and cautelous, yet effectual, reformation in matter of doctrine: the more pity is it that the very modes of worship and discipline should be the matter of such sharp and uncharitable discords, which must one day prove the grief of those that are found to have been the causes of it, and of the sufferings of the church on that occasion.

THE

VAIN RELIGION OF THE FORMAL HYPOCRITE, &c.

JAMES I. 26.

IF ANY MAN AMONG YOU SEEM TO BE RELIGIOUS, AND BRIDLETH NOT HIS TONGUE, BUT DECEIVETH HIS OWN HEART, THIS MAN'S RELIGION IS VAIN.

BELOVED hearers, I may suppose that we are all come hither to-day for the great end of our lives; and to labour in that work for which we are created, preserved, instructed, and furnished with the helps and means of grace; even to prepare for death that is coming to arrest us, and for the presence of our Judge, who stands at the door; and to make our calling and election sure, that the glory of the saints may be our lot, when the world of the ungodly are cast into endless misery and despair. And I hope I may suppose that in order to this end, you would gladly be acquainted with the causes of damnation, that you may avoid them; with your greatest dangers, that you may escape them; and with the hinderances of your salvation, that you may overcome them. When we read in the gospel, that salvation is to be offered unto all, and no man is excepted or shut out, but such as shut out and except themselves; and yet read that there are but few that find the " strait gate," and the " narrow way," and that the " flock is little " that shall have the " kingdom," and that " many shall seek to enter that shall not be able," (Matt. vii. 13, 14; Luke xii. 32, and xiii. 24,) we must needs conclude that some powerful enemy standeth in the way, that can cause the ruin of so many millions of souls; but when we go further, and find what rich preparations God hath made, and what means he hath used, and what abundant helps he offereth and affordeth to bring men to this blessed state of life, it forceth us to admire that any enemy can be so strong, as to frustrate so many and such excellent means. But when we yet go further, and find that salvation is freely offered, and that the purchase is made by a Saviour to our hands, and that hearty consent is the condition of our title, and nothing but our wilful refusal can undo us; when we find that salvation is brought down to men's wills, and also what motives, and convincing helps, and earnest persuasions, are appointed and used to make men willing; we are then surprised with yet greater admiration, that any deceiver can be so subtle, or the heart of man can be so foolish, as to be drawn (in despite of all these means) to cast away the immortal crown that else no enemy could have taken from him. And now we discern the quality of our enemy, of our snares, of our danger, and of our duty; it is not mere violence, but deceit, that can undo us; not force, but fraud, that we have to resist. And were not the mind of a carnal man exceeding brutish, (while he seemeth wise for carnal things,) it were a thing incredible that so many men could, by all the subtlety of hell, be drawn, in the day-light of the gospel, deliberately and obstinately to refuse their happiness, and to choose the open way of their damnation, and leave their friends lamenting their calamity, that might have mercy, and cannot be persuaded to consent.

That Satan is the great deceiver, and layeth the snare, and manageth the bait, we are all convinced; that the world and all our fleshly accommodations are the instrumental deceivers, the snare, the bait which Satan useth, is also a thing that we all confess. But that besides the devil and the world, a reasonable creature should be his own deceiver, and that in a business of unspeakable, everlasting consequence; and that religion itself (a seeming religiousness that indeed is vain) should be made by himself the means of his deceit; this is a mystery that is opened to you in my text, and requireth our most careful search and consideration.

When Satan and the world have wounded us by their deceits, religion is it that helpeth us to a cure. He that is deceived by pleasures and profits, and the vain glory of the world, must be undeceived and recovered by religion, or he must perish. But that religion itself should become his deceit, and the remedy prove his greatest misery, is the most stupendous effect of Satan's subtlety, and a sinner's fraudulency, and the saddest aggravation of his deplorable calamity. And yet, alas, this is so common a case, that where the gospel is preached, it seems to be Satan's principal game, and the highway to hell. There is no other name by which we can be saved, but by Jesus Christ, the only Mediator between sinful man and the offended Majesty; and yet, what is there in all the world that is more abused to the deceiving of men's souls, than the name and grace of Jesus Christ? Men that may be saved by an effectual faith, are cheated and destroyed by false faith and presumption. The merciful nature of God is the groundwork of all the comforts of the godly; and yet there is nothing that is more abused to the deceiving of men's souls; that will profess that they trust in the mercies of God, while they are labouring to be miserable by the refusing and resisting the mercy that would save them. The free promises of the gospel do support true believers, but are abused to the deceiving of the presumptuous world. And so the apostle telleth us that many do by their religion; they will have a religion to deceive themselves, but not to save them.

It is the hypocrite that is the subject in my text, who is described by his double property. 1. That he seemeth to be religious. 2. That his obedience answereth not this seeming or profession: the instance is given in the bridling of his tongue, because that was the point that the apostle had some special reason to insist on, with those to whom he immediately directed his epistle. Though it is plain, in verses 22, 23, &c. that it is the whole work of obedience that he implieth, where he instanceth in this particular. The sin of the tongue which he specially intendeth to reprove, was the bitter reproaching of their brethren, upon the account of their differences in matters of religion, and the vilifying of others, and uncharitable passionate contendings and censures, upon pretence of knowing more than others; as appeareth in the third chapter throughout.

The predicate is double; one by way of supposition, viz. that this hypocrite doth but deceive his own heart; the other by way of assertion, viz. that his religion is vain.

Whether θρῆσκος and θρησκεία be fetched as far as from Orpheus the Thracian, as Erasmus and many others imagine, is of no great moment to our understanding of the text, it being evident that it is the worshipping of God that is here meant by religion; and it is men addicted to his worship that are called religious. The seeming, here spoken of, refers both to himself and others; he that seemeth to himself to be religious, or is judged so by other men. By bridling the tongue, is meant, restraining it from evil speech. By deceiving himself, is meant the mistake of his judgment concerning the sincerity and acceptableness and reward of his religion, and the frustrating of his own expectation hereupon; his religion is said to be in vain, in that it shall not attain the ends of an unfeigned, true religion, of which more anon. The sense of the text, then, is contained in these two propositions:

1. There is a seeming religiousness which is but self-deceiving, and will prove in vain.

2. Where sincere obedience doth not accompany the profession of religion, and, in particular, when such men bridle not their tongues, their religion is but vain, and self-deceiving.

These two being contained in the text, the former comprised in the latter, I shall handle them together, and show you, I. What this seeming religion is, and how it differeth from true religion. II. Wherein this self-deceiving by a seeming religion doth consist. III. Whence it is that men are so prone to this self-deceit. IV. In what respects this religion is vain, and why. V. And then we shall consider how to improve these truths by a due application.

I. Concerning the first I must show you, 1. What this seeming religion is made up of. 2. And what it wants, which maketh it delusory and vain.

In general, this vain religion is made up sometimes of all that, 1. A laudable nature or temperature of body; 2. And good education, and excellent means; 3. Assisted by the common workings of the Spirit, can produce.

More particularly, 1. A vain religiousness may have a great deal of superficial, opinionative knowledge, and so may have the truest religion for its object: the true doctrines of faith may be believed by a faith that is not true; the hypocrite, as to the materials of his creed, may be orthodox; when ignorance aboundeth, he may be a knowing man, and pity the ignorance of others; when errors abound, he may be of the right opinion in religion, and speak much against the errors of the times, as one that is wiser than the giddy, heretical sort of people: he may "know the will of God, and approve the things that are more excellent, being instructed out of the law, and be confident that he himself is a guide of the blind, a light of them which are in darkness, an instructor of the foolish, a teacher of babes, which hath the form of knowledge, and of the truth of the law," Rom. ii. 18—20. He may know as much materially as the upright may, and be able to convince gainsayers, and be a notable champion for the defending of the truth against the many adversaries that oppose it; and so may be eminently useful in his generation.

2. He that is but religious in vain, may be frequent in the worshipping of God; and may "seek him daily, and delight to know his ways, and to approach him, and ask of him the ordinances of justice," as if he were one of the people that "did righteousness," and "forsook not the ordinances of

their God," Isa. lviii. 1, 2. He may be oft in fasting, and punctual in keeping holy days and ceremonies, as ver. 3, Isa. i. 12—15; Luke viii. 11—13, and exercise much severity on himself, "after the commandments and doctrines of men, in things that have a show of wisdom, in will-worship, and humility, and neglecting of the body, not in any honour to the satisfying of the flesh," Col. ii. 20—22, 13. Though he be slow-paced in the right way, he is swift in his mistaken paths. Though he liketh not preciseness, zeal, and forwardness, in the spiritual works that God prescribeth, yet, when it comes to his own, or other men's inventions, he will be religious and "righteous over-much," (Eccl. vii. 16.) and forward to offer the sacrifice of a fool, that considereth not that he is but doing evil, while he thinks to please God with the sacrifice of his services, though he turn away his ear from an obedient hearing the word that should direct him, Eccl. v. 1, 2; Prov. xxviii. 9.

3. He that is but religious in vain, may see the evil of discord and divisions, and inveigh much against schismatics, and see the excellency of unity and peace; and therefore may join himself with the visible catholic church, and with the christians and congregations that are most for unity. There have always been hypocrites in the most orderly peaceable societies of believers, and still will be.

4. The self-deceiving hypocrite is ofttimes very sensible of the evil of vertiginous mutability in religion; and therefore he may be much resolved to continue what he is, and may cast many a jeer at the weathercocks of the times, and the unconstancy and levity of ignorant or temporizing men; and may stand to his party and profession, against much opposition, as glorying in his constancy, and being ashamed to be thought a changeling, or such a turncoat as others whom he merrily derideth.

5. A hypocrite that hath no other religion but delusory and vain, may observe the weaknesses of persons that are of lower education and parts, and may loathe their indiscretion in conference and behaviour, and their unhandsome expressions in prayer and other duties, and shake the head at them, as silly, contemptible, self-conceited fellows; and his heart may rise against their disorder, tautologies, and affectations: and it is like enough that hereupon he will jest at conceived prayer, or extemporate, (as they call it,) and bless himself as safe in his parrot-like devotions, because the same Spirit teacheth not fine words and rhetorical language to all that it teacheth to pray with unutterable sighs and groans, Rom. viii. 26, 27; though the Searcher of hearts (who is not delighted with compliments and set speeches) doth well understand the meaning of the Spirit.

5. The self-deceiving hypocrite doth frequently pretend to be a man of moderation in matters of religion, as distasting the hair-brained zealots, as he counteth them, that cannot be content to have their faith and religion to themselves before God, and to live and talk as others do, but must be singular, and make a stir with their religion, and turn the world upside down. The true zeal of the godly is usually distasteful to him, and the corrupt zeal of schismatical persons doth cause him to bless himself in his lukewarmness, and to take his most odious indifferency, and want of fervent love to God and his holy ways, to be his virtue.

6. This self-deceiving hypocrite doth frequently pretend to an exceeding great reverence in the managing of the outward part of worship; and to an extraordinary zeal about the circumstantials of religion. He accounts them all schismatical and profane that place not as much of their religion as he doth in gestures and forms and other accidents of worship, acquainting us that the pharisaical temper in religion is natural, and will continue in the world.

7. If the temptation of the hypocrite lie on the other side, he can withdraw himself into some small or separating society, and place his religion in the singularity of his opinions, or in the strictness of the way and party that he owneth, and in his conceited ability in his conceived or ready expressions in prayer; and can cry out as much upon the formalist, as the formal hypocrite upon him, and glory in his zeal, as the other in his moderation. It is in the heart that hypocrisy hath its throne, from whence it can command the outward acts into any shapes that are agreeable to its ends; and can use materials of divers natures, as the fuel and nutriment of its malignity. And whatever party such are joined to, and whatever way they have been trained up to, whether formality, or schism, or more regular, sober, equal ways, in all of them their religion is but vain, and they do but deceive themselves by all.

8. The religion that is but delusory and vain, may be accompanied with much alms, and works of seeming justice and charity, Matt. vi. 1, 2; Luke xviii. 11, 12. He may have many virtues called moral; and be a man of much esteem with others, even with the best and wisest, for his seeming wisdom, and piety, and justice. He may be no extortioner, unjust, adulterer, but as to gross sins seem blameless, Luke xviii. 11, 12; Phil. iii. 6; and be much in reproaching the scandalous lives of others, and thank God that he is none such, Luke xviii. 11.

9. He that hath but a vain religion, may, in his judgment, approve of saving grace, and like the more zealous, upright, self-denying, heavenly lives of others; and wish that he might die their death, and wish himself as happy as they, so it might be had on his own terms; and he may have some counterfeit of every grace, and think that it is true, Numb. xxiii. 10; Jam. ii. 14, &c.; 1 Cor. xiii. 1—3; Mark vi. 20.

10. None will be more forward to call another hypocrite, than the hypocrite; nor to extol sincerity and uprightness of heart and life. And thus you see what this vain religion is made up with.

2. If you marvel what the hypocrite yet wants, that makes his religion delusory and vain, I shall now tell you, I hope, to your conviction and satisfaction.

1. For all his fore-mentioned religion, he wants the Spirit of Christ, to dwell as his sanctifier within him; and "if any man have not the Spirit of Christ, the same is none of his," Rom. viii. 9. But because this is known by the effects, I add,

2. He wants that spiritual new birth, by which he should be made spiritual, as his first birth made him carnal, John iii. 5, 6; Rom. viii. 6—8. He is born of the will of the flesh, and of man, but not of God, John i. 13. From the first man Adam he is become a living soul, but by the second man Christ, the Lord from heaven, he is not yet quickened in the spirit, 1 Cor. xv. 45, 46. He is not born again of the incorruptible seed, the word of God, that liveth and abideth for ever, 1 Pet. i. 23. He is not yet saved by the washing of regeneration (save only as to the outward baptism) and by renewing of the Holy Ghost, which is shed by Christ on all his members, that, being justified by his grace, they should be made heirs according to the hope of eternal life, Tit. iii. 5, 6. They are not new creatures, old things being not past away, and all things with them become new: and therefore it is certain that they are not in Christ, 2 Cor. v. 17. They have not put off the old man

with his deceitful lusts, and deeds, nor have put on the new man, which after God is created in righteousness, and true holiness, Eph. iii. 22—24; Col. iii. 9, 10. They have but patched up the old unsanctified hearts, and smoothed over their carnal conversations with civility and plausible deportment, and so much religion as may cheat themselves, as well as blind the eyes of others: but they are strangers to the life of God, Eph. iv. 18, and never were made partakers of the divine nature, which all the children of God partake of, 2 Pet. i. 4, nor of that holiness, without which none shall see the Lord, Heb. xii. 14.

3. Though he make a slight and customary confession of his sins, unworthiness, and misery, yet is he not kindly humbled at the heart, nor made truly vile in his own eyes, nor contrite and broken-hearted, nor emptied of himself, as seeing himself undone by his own iniquities, crying out, Unclean, and loathing himself for all his abominations, weary of his sin, and heavy-laden, as all must be that are fit for Christ. Read Isa. lvii. 15; lxvi. 2; Psalm li. 17; xxxiv. 18; Rev. xiii. 44, 45; Ezek. xxxvi. 31; xx. 43; vi. 9; Matt. xi. 28; Rom. vii. 24.

4. This man's religion must needs be vain, for he wanteth the life of faith itself, and heartily believeth not in Christ. He hath but an opinion of the truth of christianity, through the advantage of his education and company; and thereupon doth call himself a christian, and heartlessly talk of the mystery of redemption as a common thing; but he doth not with a humble, broken heart, betake himself to Christ as his only refuge from the wrath of God, and everlasting misery, as he would lay hold on the hand of his friend, if he were drowning. The sense of the odiousness of sin, and of the damnation threatened by the righteous God, hath not yet taught him to value Christ, as he must be valued by such as will be saved by him. These hypocrites do but talk of Christ, and turn his name as they do their prayers, into the matter of a dry and customary form. They fly not to him as the only physician of their souls, in the feeling of their festering wounds: they cry not to him as the disciples in the tempest, "Save, Master, we perish." They value him not practically, (though notionally they do,) as the pearl for which they must sell all, Matt. xiii. 44—46. Christ doth not dwell in his heart by faith, nor doth he long with all the saints to comprehend what is the breadth, and length, and depth, and height, and to know the love of Christ which passeth knowledge, Eph. iii. 17—19. He counteth not all things loss for Christ, and the excellency of his knowledge; nor doth he count them as dung, that he may win Christ, and be found in him, not having his own righteousness, but that which is through the faith of Christ, Phil. iii. 8—10; nor can he truly say, that he desireth to know nothing but a crucified Christ, 1 Cor. ii. 2, and that "the life that he now liveth in the flesh, he liveth by the faith of the Son of God, that loved him, and gave himself for him," Gal. ii. 20. He is not taken up with that admiration of the love of God in Christ, as beseems a soul that is saved by him from the flames of hell, and that is reconciled to God, and made an heir of life everlasting. He hath not understandingly, deliberately, seriously, and unreservedly, given up himself and all that he hath to Christ; and thankfully accepted Christ and life, as given on the gospel terms to him. This living effectual faith is wanting to the hypocrite, whose religion is vain.

5. This vain religion doth never practically show the soul the amiableness and attractive goodness of God, so far as to win the heart to a practical observation of him, and adhering to him, above all; nor so far as to advance him, above all the creatures, in the practical judgment, will, and conversation; nor doth he cause the soul to take him for its portion, and prefer his favour before all the world, and devote itself and all unto his interest and will, and give him the superlative and sovereign honour, both in heart and life, Psalm lxiii. 3; xxx. 5; iv. 6, 7; xvi. 5; xvii. 4; Matt. x. 37.

6. This vain religion is always without that serious belief of the life to come, which causeth the soul to take it for its happiness and treasure, and there to set its desires and its hopes, and to make it his principal care and business to attain it, and to make all the pleasures and profits and honours of the world to stoop to it, as preferring it before them all, Matt. vi. 20, 21, 33; Luke xviii. 22, 23; xiv. 33; Col. iii. 1—5; Phil. iii. 18—20. The hypocrite taketh heaven but for a reserve, and as a lesser evil than hell, and seeks it but in the second place, while his fleshly pleasures and interest have the pre-eminence, and God hath no more but the leavings of the world; and he serveth him but with so much as his flesh can spare.

7. This vain religion consisteth principally in external observances. If he be a formalist that hath it, his religion lieth in his beads and prayer-books, in going so oft to church, and keeping holy days and fasting days, and saying over such and such words, and using such and such gestures and ceremonies, and submitting to church orders, and crying down sectaries and preciseness, and jeering at the simplicity of plain-hearted christians that never learned the art of dissimulation. Their religion is but a pack of compliments, a flattering of God, as if they would mock him with cap and knee who will not be mocked, Gal. vi. 7; while they draw near to him with their lips, their hearts are far from him, Matt. xv. 7—9. They wash the outside, and pay tithe of all, and give some alms, and forbear disgraceful sins, which would make them be esteemed ungodly among men, Matt. xv. 2, 3; Mark vii. 4, 8; Matt. xxiii. 25, 26, &c.; vi. 1, 4, 6, &c.; Isa. i. 11—14; lviii. 1, 2. But these self-deceivers are strangers to the inward spiritual work of holiness: their hearts are not busy in the worship of God, by fervent desire and exercise of other graces, while their tongues are put into an artificial pace, and they are acting the part of men that seem to be religious.

If they be cast into the sectarian mould, they place their religion in the strictness of their principles and parties, and in contending for them, and in their affected fervour, and ability to speak and pray extempore: but the humble, holy, inward workings of the soul toward God, and its breathings after him, and the watch that it sets over the heart, this hypocrite is much a stranger to.

If he be brought up among the orthodox in well-ordered churches, he placeth his religion in the holding of the truth, and taking the right side, and submitting to right order, and using God's ordinances: but the most of an upright man's employment is at home, within him; to order his soul, and exercise grace, and keep down sin, and keep out the world, and keep under the flesh and carnal self, and do the inward part of duty; and he is as truly solicitous about this as about the outward works, and contenteth not himself to have said his prayers, unless, indeed, his heart have prayed; nor to have heard, unless he have profited, or heard with obediential attention: and he makes conscience of secret duties, as well as of those that are done in the sight of men; but this the hypocrite comes not up to, to trade in the internal, spiritual part.

8. The religion that is vain is without a universal hatred of known sin, and an actual conquering of it, so far as to live out of gross sin, which some call mortal, and to be weary of infirmities, and to be truly desirous to be rid of all; and to be willing to use God's means against it. Thus it is with the sincerely religious, but not with these hypocrites that deceive themselves, John iii. 19, 20; Rom. vii. 24; Luke xiii. 3, 5; Rom. viii. 1—14; Gal. vi. 7, 8. The hypocrite hath not only some particular sin, which all his religion makes him not willing to see to be a sin, or to forsake; but his very state is sinful in the main, by the predominancy of a selfish carnal interest and principle; and he is not willing of close plain dealing, much less of the diligent use of means himself to overcome that sin, because he loveth it.

9. This vain religion is not accompanied with an unfeigned love to a life of holiness, which every true believer hath; delighting to meditate in the law of God, with a practical intention to obey it, and delighting in the inward exercise of grace, and outward ordinances as advantages hereunto; desiring still more of the grace which he hath tasted, and grieving that he knoweth, and trusteth, and loveth, and feareth, and obeyeth God so little, and loving to reach higher, to know, and love, and fear him more, Psal. i. 2; cxix. 1—5, 9, 10, &c.; Heb. xii. 14; 2 Pet. iii. 11; Matt. vii. 13, 14. But the self-deceiver either hath a secret dislike of this serious diligence for salvation, and loving God with all the soul and might, (because he is conscious that he reacheth it not himself,) or, at least, he will not be brought to entertain any more than will stand with his carnal ends.

10. A vain religion doth not so far reveal the excellency of Christ's image in his servants, as to cause an entire love to them as such; and to delight in them above the most splendid and accomplished persons that are strangers to the life of grace, and so far to love them as, when Christ requireth it, to part with our substance, and hazard ourselves for their relief. Thus do the truly religious, Psal. xvi. 2; xv. 4; 1 John iii. 14; Matt. x. 40; xi. 42; xxv. 34, 35, 40, 42, 45, 46. But the hypocrite either secretly hateth a heavenly, holy life, and consequently the people that are such, because they seem to condemn him by overgoing him and differing from him; or, at least, he only superficially approveth of them, but will forsake both Christ and them in trial, rather than forsake his earthen god. I have now showed you what the self-deceiver wants, in which you may see sufficient reason why his religion is but vain.

II. We are next to show you how these hypocrites do deceive themselves, and wherein their self-deceit consisteth. It may seem strange that a man of reason should do such a thing as this, when we consider that truth is naturally the object of the understanding, and that all men necessarily love themselves, and therefore love what they know to be simply good for them. How then can any man that hath the use of reason be willing to be deceived, yea, and be his own deceiver, and that in matters of unspeakable consequence? But it is not as falsehood, nor as deceit, that they desire it, but as it appeareth necessary to the carnal ease and pleasure which they desire.

The way by which they deceive their own hearts consisteth in these following degrees:—

1. The hypocrite resisteth the Spirit of grace, and rejecteth the mercies offered in the gospel; and so, by his refusal, is deprived of a part in Christ, and of the life of grace, and the hopes of glory, which were tendered to him.

2. But withal, he is willing of so much of this mercy as consisteth with his sinful disposition and carnal interest: he is willing enough to be happy in general, and to be saved from hell-fire, and to be pardoned, and to have such a heaven as he hath framed a pleasing imagination of.

3. And therefore he maketh him up a religion of so much of christianity as will stand with his pleasures, profits, and reputation in the world, that so he may not be left in despair of being saved, when he must leave the world that he most loved. The cheap and easy parts of christianity, and those that are most in credit in the world, and that flesh and blood have least against, these he will cull out from among the rest, and make him a religion of, passing by the dearer and more difficult and spiritual parts.

4. Having gone thus far, he persuadeth his own heart that this kind of religion which he hath patched up and framed to himself is the true religion, the faith, the hope, the charity, the repentance, the obedience to which salvation is promised; and that he is a true christian, notwithstanding his defects; and that his spots are but such as are consistent with grace; and that his sins are but pardoned infirmities; and that he hath part in Christ, and the promises of life, and shall be saved though he be not of the preciser strain. When he committeth any sin, he confidently imagineth that his confession and his wishing it were undone again, when he hath had all the pleasure that sin can give him, is true repentance; and that, as a penitent, he shall be forgiven: and thus, while he thinketh himself something, when he is nothing, he deceiveth himself, Gal. vi. 3. He hath a counterfeit of every grace of God; a counterfeit faith, and hope, and love, and repentance, and zeal, and humility, and patience, and perseverance; and these he will needs take to be the very life and image of Christ, and the graces themselves that accompany salvation.

5. Having got this carcass of religion without the soul, he makes use of all those things to confirm him in his deceit, which are appointed to confirm true christians in their faith and hope. When he reads or thinks of the infinite goodness, love, and mercy of God, he thinks God could not be so good and merciful, if he should refuse to save all such as he. When he readeth of the undertaking and sacrifice of Christ, and how he is a propitiation for the sins of the whole world, he confidently hence concludeth that a Saviour so gracious, that hath done and suffered so much for sinners, cannot condemn all such as he. When he readeth of the extent and freeness of grace in the promises of the gospel, he concludeth that these promises belong to him, and that grace could not be so free and so extensive, if it did shut out all such as he. When he observeth the mercies of God upon his body, in his friends and health, and credit and prosperity, he concludeth that surely God loveth him as a child, in that he dealeth so fatherly with him. If he suffer adversity, he thinks that it is the fatherly chastisement of God, and therefore proveth him to be his son, and that he shall have his good things in the world to come, because he hath his evils here. If he suffer any thing for a good cause, or a cause that he taketh to be good, he taketh himself to be a confessor, and marked out for life eternal. If he give any considerable alms, he applieth all the promises to himself that are made to those that are truly charitable, though he giveth but the leavings of the flesh, and giveth but on common compassions, or for applause, or for some common end, and not as to Christ whom he honoureth in his members, as one that hath resigned

all unto him. If he pray from the lips only, or only for pardon, and such other mercies as flesh itself would be glad to have, without the unexpressible groans of the spirit for spiritual mercies, (Rom. viii. 26,) he presently applieth all the promises to himself that are made to the upright that call upon God: and thus love, mercy, and Christ himself, are abused by him, to this damning work of self-deceit.

6. Moreover, he makes use of all the ordinances of God, to the deceiving of his own heart. The outward part of baptism persuades him that he is inwardly regenerate. He receiveth the Lord's supper that he may confirm his presumption, and increase his self-deceit, as the godly receive it to confirm and increase their saving faith. He joineth with the church in those prayers and praises that are fitted to the true believer's state, that he may thence more confidently deceive his own heart, with the conceit that he is a true believer. And thus he turneth the bread of life, and all the helps and means of grace, to the strengthening of his sin, and the furthering of his perdition.

7. Moreover, this miserable self-deceiver doth usually get into such company as may further his self-deceit, and maketh use of them to that end. If he get into any holy, well-ordered church of christians, it is that, by his outward communion with the saints, he may seem to himself to have inward communion with them. If he get among able godly ministers, and other judicious christians, and finds that he is well esteemed of by them, he is confirmed hereby in his presumption and self-deceit: when, alas! we must, in charity, judge of men as they profess and seem, and leave the infallible judgment of the heart to God. Usually, this self-deceiving hypocrite doth associate with some carnal or factious men, with whom he makes himself a party: and such will smooth him up, and make a saint of him, either because they are as bad themselves, and dare not condemn him, lest they condemn themselves, or because they are flatterers and daubers, or men that were never themselves acquainted with those saving operations of the Spirit which he wants, or because they are partial to one of their own faction. And thus a formal hypocrite may be stroked by formalists, and a schismatical hypocrite may be soothed up by those of his own sect, (as lamentable experience telleth us that such do,) to the increase of their pernicious self-deceit.

Yet more than so; if these hypocrites fall in company with the notoriously profane, from them they will fetch some confirmation of their self-deceit: when they hear them swear, and curse, and rant, and see them drunk, they secretly with the Pharisee rejoice and say, " I thank thee, Lord, that I am not as this publican." And this is one reason why such hypocrites are well content to have some servants in their families, or some neighbours or company about them, that are notoriously profane, that their deluded consciences, considering that they are more civil and religious themselves, may hence gather comfort, that they are the servants of God, and in a state of grace.

Hence also it is, that those of them that go on the schismatical side, do purposely go into separated societies, that, by withdrawing from so many, and (as they speak) coming out from among them, they may seem to themselves to be fellow-citizens with the saints, and to be of the little flock that shall have the kingdom. This is the use that self-deceivers make of their companions.

8. Moreover, the hypocrite confirmeth his self-deceit, by observing the great numbers of ungodly persons, worse than he, that are in the world: this makes him think that God should be unmerciful, and heaven be empty, if all such as he should be shut out: the damnation of so many seemeth so incredible to him, that it much increaseth his confidence and self-deceit.

9. And he deceiveth himself also by a misobserving and misapplying the faults and infirmities of the servants of the Lord, and the scandalous lives of many hypocrites like himself. When he readeth of Noah's drunkenness, and Lot's drunkenness and incest, and David's adultery and murder, and Peter's denial of his Master with cursing and swearing, he considereth not how much these singular actions were contrary to the scope of their lives, nor by what serious repentance they did rise, and do so no more; but he hence concludeth that sure he is in a state of grace, that hath no such heinous sins as these: though indeed he hath more heinous continually within him, (even a love of the world and pleasure above God, a secret root of unbelief, a servitude to the flesh, &c.) When he seeth any about him that profess the fear of God, prove hypocrites or apostates, or fall into any scandalous sin, he strengtheneth his presumption by it, and concludeth that this profession of greater holiness than he himself hath, is but hypocrisy; and that he is as good as those that seem more devout, though he make not so much ado with his religion; or at least that such as he shall be saved, when those are so bad that are accounted better: if there be but a Ham in the ark and family of Noah, an Ishmael in Abraham's house, an Esau in Jacob's, an Absalom in David's, a Judas among the disciples of Christ, these self-deceivers will thence fetch matter for their own delusion and perdition, as if the rest were all as bad, or sanctification were not necessary to salvation.

10. The self-deceiver also is confirmed in his presumption, by taking to himself the comforts that ministers hold forth, for truly humbled, upright souls, that are apt to be too much disquieted and cast down. Our congregations are mixed of godly and ungodly, and broken-hearted and hard-hearted, dejected and self-confident sinners (besides all those that are well settled in their spiritual peace). And as we cannot tell how to tell the wicked of their misery, nor open the hypocrite's self-deceit, but the self-suspecting, humbled souls will misapply it to themselves, and be more dejected by it, and say, It is thus with me; so we cannot tell how to comfort the distressed, and clear up the evidences of a drooping soul, but the presumptuous hypocrite will lay hold upon it, and think that it belongs to him. Every comfortable book or scripture that he readeth, and every comfortable sermon or discourse which he heareth, is abused to increase his self-deceit.

11. It increaseth the hypocrite's self-deceit, when he findeth some partial reformation in himself, and that he hath mended many things that were amiss; this he takes for a true conversion, and thinks that the civilizing and smoothing of his life, the change of his opinion, and the taking up a form of godliness, are true sanctification; and that he is not the man that once he was, and therefore is in a safe condition. Though, alas! he hath never yet known by experience the new heart, the new ends, the new resolutions, affections, and conversation of a saint.

12. Lastly, he deceiveth himself by misunderstanding the nature of hypocrisy. Because he perceiveth not that he is a gross dissembler, but meaneth as he speaks, so far as he goes, therefore, he thinks that he is no hypocrite; whereas, besides the gross hypocrite that knoweth that he doth dissemble, and only deceiveth others, there are also close hypocrites, that know not they are hypocrites, but deceive themselves. And these are they that my text here speaks

of, when it saith, "He deceiveth his own heart." It is hypocrisy, (to seem better than one is, and to profess to be a sincere christian when he is none,) though he confidently think that he is what he professeth himself to be.

III. But what is it that can move a reasonable creature to be wilfully guilty of such self-deceit in the day-light of the gospel, when he hath so much help to see his way?

Answ. 1. They are first deceived by the vanities of the world, and the pleasures of sin, before they deceive themselves by their religion. Their religious self-deceiving is but subservient to their fleshly servitude, and the world's deceit. They are carnal from the birth, (for that which is born of the flesh only, is but flesh, John iii. 6,) and custom in sinning fixeth and increaseth their sinful disposition. Their hearts are engaged to their worldly accommodations, and to their vain glory, and the things that please the flesh; they are willing slaves to their concupiscence. And therefore they cannot admit of that religion which would deprive them of that which they most dearly love. Christ speaks too late to them. They tell him they are promised already. Their affections are pre-engaged: sin hath taken up the chiefest rooms: and the heart that loveth sensuality and prosperity best, cannot love God best too; for it can have but one best. The nature of true sanctification is to take down the darling of a carnal heart, and to cross it in its dearest loves, and to lay that at our feet that before was our treasure, and to tame that body, and bring it into subjection, which before was in the throne. The motions of such a change will not be acceptable, till they are made so effectual as to cause that change: the command will be unpleasant, till the heart be suited to the nature of the command. He that seeth what care and labour there is to gather a worldly treasure, and what a stir is made in the world about it, can never expect that all this should be vilified and despised at a word, and that any doctrine (how true and heavenly soever) can be welcome to these worldly men, that would debase their glory, and imbitter their delights, and make their idol seem but dung. The doctrine of Christ would take the old heart out of their bodies: and they will not easily leave their hearts. It doth not only command the drunkard to live soberly, and the glutton temperately, and the lascivious, filthy sinner chastely, and the proud person humbly, and the covetous to live contentedly and liberally; but it commandeth the hearty forsaking of all for the sake of Christ, (Luke xiv. 33,) and the accounting them but as loss and dung that we may win him, (Phil. iii. 7—9,) and mortifying of that flesh which before we daily studied to please, (Col. iii. 4, 5,) and the crucifying of its affections and lusts, (Gal. v. 24,) and the denial even of ourselves, Luke ix. 23, 24. And for a carnal mind to love and yield to such commands, were no other than to cease to be a carnal mind. All this is largely expressed by the apostle, Rom. viii. 1, &c. They that are in Christ Jesus, "walk not after the flesh, but after the Spirit.—For they that are after the flesh, do mind the things of the flesh; but they that are after the Spirit, the things of the Spirit. For to be carnally-minded is death, but to be spiritually-minded is life and peace. Because the carnal mind is enmity against God; for it is not subject to the law of God, neither indeed can be. So then they that are in the flesh cannot please God.—For if ye live after the flesh, ye shall die: but if ye through the Spirit do mortify the deeds of the body, ye shall live."

You see here why it is that the self deceiver will not entertain the power of godliness, nor be religious seriously according to the true intent of the gospel, and the nature of christianity, even because he is engaged to a contrary object, and hath another game in chase, which he will not leave, and which true religion requireth him to leave, and will not give him leave to follow. And therefore he parteth with the religion which would have parted him from that which he will not part with.

2. But withal, he is all this while under the threatenings of the law of God, and conscience is ready to bear witness against him; and betwixt law and conscience, the poor wretch is as the corn between two mill-stones; he would be ground to powder and tortured with terrors before his time, if he had not some opiate, or intoxicating medicine, to ease him by deceiving him, and to abate his fears, and to quiet his conscience as long as a palliate cure will serve turn. So that here are two things for which the self-deceiving hypocrite is fain to fall into his vain religion: the one is, that it may be a cloak to the sin which he will needs keep: the other is, that it may save him from the terrors and disquietments that for this sin his conscience would else afflict him with. A belief that he may be saved, for all his sin, is the relief that he hath against the terrors of the law of God. He therefore chooseth out such parcels of religion as may serve him for this use, and yet will not separate him from the sin that he delighteth in. The power of godliness will not consist with his covetous, proud, or fleshly life; but the form and outside will. And therefore this regeneration, and mortification, and self-denial, and subjection to the whole will of God, and this heavenly-mindedness, and watching the heart, and walking with God, and living above the trifles of this world, and making it the chief business to prepare for another; this kind of religion, which is religion indeed, he cannot (because he will not) entertain. This is the strait gate and narrow way, that few men find. Here he must be excused. God is no God for him upon these terms; (and he cannot and will not be his God upon any other terms;) Christ is no Christ for him unless he will excuse him from this trouble, and bear with him in his carnal course; that is, unless he will be indeed no Christ to him. Heaven is no heaven for him, unless he may pass to it through prosperity and sin; and unless he may have it without the trouble of a holy life; that is, unless God will be unjust or false, and heaven cease to be heaven, and God cease to be God.

But yet these men are convinced that God is their rightful governor, and that, indeed, they should love him and serve him with all their heart and might, and that without true religion and godliness there is no salvation. To be irreligious and profane, they know is a state that can afford no comfort, or shelter from the wrath of God; and therefore some religion they must have: they are not able to endure the thoughts of lying under the curse of God. To conclude themselves to be utterly graceless, and the children of the devil, and in a state of condemnation, is so terrible, that they are not able to endure it: then every sermon they hear would torment them, and every chapter they read would torment them; and their pleasures would all be imbittered to them, and nothing that they enjoy in all the world would quiet and content them. (No, nor shall do long.) And therefore they must needs take up some religion, to quiet them for a little while, and to make them hope, that for all their sins, they are not so bad, nor in so dangerous a case, as preachers tell them; some religion they must needs have for fear of being damned: a sound and serious religion they will not have, because they love the world and sin, which it would deprive them of; and therefore they patch up a vain religion, composed of so much truth and duty as will stand with their prosperity and pleasures; which will not save them, but sufficeth to deceive them.

Two parts make up this self-deceiving frame, as consistent with their sins: the one is the formal, outward, easy, cheap part of duty to God and man in their practice; leaving out the spiritual, inward, difficult, dear, self-denying part. The other is, the strictest parts of religion in bare opinion and notion, while they shut it out of their hearts and lives. For both these may stand with a sensual, worldly, selfish life. He may read or say his prayers, and be a worldling still: he may come to church, and, with the greatest ceremony and seeming reverence, receive the sacrament, and bow before the Lord his Maker, and yet be sensual or a worldling still. And he may be of the strictest party or opinion, and notionally condemn all sin, and justify the most holy life, and yet be sensual and worldly still. And therefore this much he may be persuaded to take up, to save himself from the lashes of his conscience. And so the use of the hypocrite's religion is to be a screen betwixt him and the flames of wrath, that would scorch him too soon, if he were of no religion: and to be to him as a tent or penthouse to keep off the storms that would fall upon him, while he is trading for the world, and working for the flesh. His religion is but the sheath of his guilty conscience, to keep it from wounding him, and cutting his fingers, while they are busy in the brutish service of his lusts. It is but as a glove to save his skin, when he hath to do with the nettles and thorns of the threatenings of God, and the thoughts of vengeance, that else would rack his guilty soul. It is but as his upper garment, to save him from a storm, and then to be laid by as an unnecessary burden, when he is at home. The hypocrite's religion is but as his shoe: he can tread it in the dirt, so it will but save his foot from galling. As a man that hath an unquiet, scolding wife, is fain to speak her fair by flatteries, lest he should have no rest at home; or as a thief is fain to cast a crust to the dog that barketh at him, to stop his mouth; so is an ungodly, sensual person fain to flatter his conscience with some kind of religiousness, and to stop its mouth with some kind of devotion and seeming righteousness, that may deceive him into a belief that he is a child of God. Religion is the sovereign in a gracious soul, and the master in an upright conscience, and ruleth above all worldly interests. But with the unregenerate, it is but an underling and servant, that must do no more than the flesh and the world will give consent to; and is regarded no further than for mere necessity; and when it hath done the work which the hypocrite appointed it, it is dismissed and turned out of doors. God is acknowledged and loved by the hypocrite, but not as God. Christ is believed in and accepted, but not as Christ, but as an underling to the world, and a journeyman to do some job of work for a distressed, wrangling conscience; or as an unwelcome physician to give them a vomit when they have taken some extraordinary surfeit of sensual delight. When they have fallen into great affliction, or into any foul, disgraceful sin, then, perhaps, they take up their prayer-books, or call upon Christ, and seem devout and very penitent. But their piety is blown over with the storm. The effect ceaseth with the cause. It was not the love of God, or of his holy ways and service, that set them upon their devotions, but some tempest of adversity, or shipwreck of their estates, or friends, or consciences; and when the winds are laid, and the waves are still, their devotion ceaseth with their danger.

3. Add hereunto, (to show you the reason of the hypocrite's self-deceit,) that he is one that never practically saw the amiableness of holiness in itself; and never had a heart that was touched with the love of it by the spirit of holiness; and therefore he taketh it but for mere necessity; and therefore he taketh up no more than he thinks is of necessity to save him from damnation, when he can live in the pleasures of the world no longer. God never had his heart. He had rather be about his sports or worldly business, if he durst, and thought he could be so excused. He loveth a pair of cards, or dice, or a harlot, or his ambitious designs and honours, better than he loveth the holy Scriptures, and the heavenly discourse or contemplation of the life to come. And therefore he will have no more religion than needs he must, because he taketh it not for love, but need. The matters of the world and the flesh are his diet, and his extraordinary successes and prosperity are his feast; and therefore he will take as much of them as he can and dare: but religion is but his physic, and therefore he will take it as little and seldom as he dare. Had he but seen the face of God by faith, and had he but the heart of a true believer, that is suited by holiness to the holy works that God commandeth, as the heart of a true friend is suited to the will of him whom he loveth, he would then be no longer religious against his will, and consequently in vain; but he would think the most pure and heavenly mind and life, and the highest degree of love and holiness, to be the best and most desirable state for his soul, as every true believer doth. Had this hypocrite any true love to God, as he deceitfully pretends to have, he would love his image, and word, and ways; and then he would love best that kernel and marrow of religion, that life and soul of worship and obedience, which now he favoureth not, but shifteth off as a needless, or tedious, or unattainable thing.

The nature and use of these hypocrites' religion, is to save them from religion: they carry an empty gilded scabbard, accusing the sword of a dangerous keenness, as a thing more perilous than necessary to their use. When they seem most zealous, they are but serving God that they may be excused from serving him; and they worship him on purpose to shift off his worship. They offer him the lips, that the heart may be excused; and compliment him with cap and knee, that they may excuse themselves from real holiness: they offer him the empty purse for payment, and tender him a sacrifice of husks and shells, and lifeless carcasses: they will abound in the shadow and ceremony, that they may be excused from the spiritual life and substance. Alas! that dead-hearted hypocrite that sits there, and heareth all this, is so great a stranger to the opening of the heart, and the deep entertainment of saving truth, and to the savoury relish of the searching, healing, quickening passages of holy doctrine, and to the thankful welcoming of an offered Christ, and to the lookings and longings of the soul after God, and to the serious desires, and hopes, and labours of a gracious soul for life eternal, that he is idle, asleep, and dead as to all this spiritual work, and if he had not some customary service to perform, and some ceremonies or external task to do, and some bodily worship to be employed in, he would find little or nothing to do in the assemblies, but might sit here as a brute, or as one of a strange language, that comes but to see and to be seen. And therefore if there be not somewhat more suitable to him than power and spirituality, it seemeth as no worship to the formal hypocrite. It is the pretty jingles and knacks of wit, and the merry jeers at the preciser sort, or some scraps of Greek and Latin authors, or shreds of fathers and philosophy, or at best an accurate, well-set speech, that makes the sermon acceptable to this hypocrite's ears. It is not spirit and life within him that brought him hither, nor is it spirit and life that he favoureth, and that he came for. And therefore it is that this sort of hypocrites are usually most impatient of a misplaced word, or of a worship performed in the primitive simplicity. If a man deliver the Lord's supper but as Christ did, and receive it but as the apostles did, or serve God but as the churches in their days, he will seem unreverent, and slovenly, and sordid, to these self-deceiving formalists. They are set upon excess of ceremonies, because they are defective in the vital parts, and should have no religion if they had not this. All sober christians are friends to outward decency and order; but it is the empty self-deceiver that is most for the unwarrantable inventions of men, and sticketh in the bark of God's own ordinances, that taketh the garments for the man, and useth the worship of God but as a masque or puppet-play, where there is great doings, with little life, and to little purpose. The chastest woman will wash her face; but it is the harlot, or wanton, or deformed, that will paint it. The soberest and the comeliest will avoid a nasty or ridiculous habit, which may make them seem uncomely, when they are not; but a curious dress, and excessive care, doth signify a crooked or deformed body, or a filthy skin, or, which is worst, an empty soul, that hath need of such a covering. Consciousness of such greater want, doth cause them to seek these poor supplies. The gaudiness of men's religion is not the best sign that it is sincere. Simplicity is the ordinary attendant of sincerity. It hath long been a proverb, "The more ceremony, the less substance; and the more compliment, the more craft."

And yet if it were only for want of inward true religion that the hypocrite setteth up his shows, it were bad enough, but not so bad as with most of them, or all, it is. For it is an enmity to religion that accompanieth their religion. As in lapsed man, the body, that was before the soul's obedient attendant, is become its master, and the enemy of its perfection and felicity; so, in the carnal religion of the hypocrite, the outside, which should be the ornament and attendant of the inward spiritual part, hath got the mastery, and is used in an enmity against the more noble part which it should serve; and much more are his human inventions and mixtures thus destructively employed. His bellows do but blow out the candle, under pretence of kindling the fire. He sets the body against the soul, and sometimes the clothing against both. He useth forms to the destruction of knowledge, and quenching of all seriousness and fervour of affection. By preaching, he destroyeth preaching, and prayeth till prayer is become no prayer, but the image or carcass of prayer at the best. And useth his words to the destruction of the due principle, sense, and ends. Having still his carnal self for his end, he preacheth, and prayeth, and serveth God in a manner that seems most suitable to his end; so that it is not God's means that he useth, when he useth them, but his own; nor doth he indeed worship God, while he seems to worship; nor is indeed religious, but seems religious. It is materially, perhaps, God's work that he doth, and his means he useth, but formally they are his own, and not God's at all: when we meet with abundance of our people that are most nimble in their accustomed forms, that know not what religion or christianity is, nor who Christ is, nor almost any of the substance of the gospel, it assures us that it is easy to be infidels with christian expressions in their mouths, and that it is easier to teach a parrot to speak, than to be a man. As their bodies are but the prisons or dungeons of their souls, so their formal words and ceremonies are used to be the prison and dungeon, or rather the grave, of true devotion. Their religion is excessively laced, but so scant of cloth, that it covereth not their nakedness, nor keeps them warm. It is always winter with the hypocrite in his formal, lifeless services, and yet sometimes his leaf doth never fall. He is like the box-tree that knows no fruit, and yet its leaves are always green. Wherever his heart is, the formalist's prayers are always ready, for his prayer-book or memory is still the same; he can say them between sleeping and waking in his bed, and as he is dressing or washing him; and the interposition of a friend, or some intervenient word or business, is so small a rub, that it seldom puts him out of his way. Though he cannot make spiritual his common business, he can make his spiritual business common. Though he have not the art, the heart, to manage his trade or worldly business with a holy and heavenly mind, yet he can manage his holiest businesses with such a mind as he doth his trade. If you would know whether he be praying or playing, preaching or prating, serving God or himself and the flesh, you must not search deep for an internal difference, but must discern it by the show and sound of words. He is not one of them that are above ordinances, as turning every day into a sabbath, and every thought into a prayer, and every morsel into a sacrament; but he can turn every sabbath into a common day, and every prayer into common thoughts, and every sacrament into common food; and therefore that which is holy to others, is to him unclean. Hypocrisy is a natural popery; it filleth the places of worship with images. Instead of prayer, there is the image of prayer; and instead of preaching, hearing, praising God, and other parts of worship, there is the image of worship; and instead of christians, believers, saints, (and I was going to say, of men,) there are so many images of these. Church images are usually handsomely adorned, and placed in a posture of reverence and devotion, and so are they. But life they have none, but merely natural. They are seeing, hearing, speaking images, but images they are. They have eyes, but see not; ears, but hear not; hearts, but understand not.

And they are enemies to the life and power of religion in others as well as in themselves. The publicans were not so bitter persecutors of Christ, as the scribes and Pharisees were. He can hate and reproach the faithful by the Spirit, though he cannot, or will not, pray by the Spirit; for he hath the spirit of malignity, though not the spirit of supplication. He can rail without book, though he cannot pray without book. Were it as natural and easy to be a saint, as to scorn a saint, and to worship God in spirit and in truth, as to hate such worship, the man might become a saint yet before he dies. But his vain religion changeth not his nature, and therefore destroyeth not his serpentine enmity against the holy nature and practice of believers, though perhaps the times may stop his hissing, or hinder him from putting forth his sting. These spiritual worshippers, and heavenly, diligent sort of christians, that make it the main business of their lives to honour God and save their souls, are usually the greatest eyesore of the formalist. Many a disdainful thought he hath of them, and many a bitter gird he gives them: forgetting that their Redeemer heareth all, who is coming "with ten thousand of his saints, to execute judgment upon all, and to convince all that are ungodly among them of all their ungodly deeds which they have ungodly committed, and of all their hard speeches which ungodly sinners have spoken against him," Jude 14, 15. The humble, spiritual, heavenly believers, are they that condemn the hypocrite by their lives; were it not for them, he could easily believe that he is a saint himself, and should undoubtedly be saved. He looketh on the openly ungodly but as the beauty-spots of the assemblies, that serve to set out the piety of such as he. If he saw no better than himself, he could easily take himself for one of the best. Every dotted post and glow-worm would be more resplendent and observable in the absence of all greater lights. They hate the sun for making their candle to be but a scarce-discerned flame. The life of a holy, heavenly person doth as much gall the conscience of the hypocrite, and proclaim his misery, and bear a terrible witness against him, as a searching, powerful sermon doth. And therefore, as it is a vexation to him to live under such a searching minister as is always rubbing on the galled place, and causing conscience to torment him before his time; so is it a trouble to him to live among these heavenly believers, and to be daily condemned by their lives, and galled by their reproving practices.

By this time you may see the reason and use of the hypocrite's religion: the self-denying part of religion he cannot abide; the life and power of it is above him, and seems against him; the fears of hell and gripes of conscience he cannot abide; some hopes of heaven he must have awhile to keep him from despair, and therefore he must have some religion to deceive his heart, and maintain his hopes. And therefore he fitteth his religion to these uses, and takes up with so much as will not much trouble him, or undo him in the world, or absolutely forbid his sinful pleasures. And though sometimes he be afraid lest the power and life of godliness will prove necessary to his salvation, yet he revives his fainting hopes by running for comfort to his lifeless form. The rest he hath no mind to, and therefore will hope to be saved without it, till his deceit have brought him to the place of desperation, where is no hope. As a merchant in a storm is loth to cast his goods into the sea, and therefore hopes he may save himself and them, till he and they are drowned together; or as a patient that abhors his physic, or loves some forbidden thing too well, is hoping still that he may escape, though he use the thing he loves, and forbear the medicine which he loathes, till he be past remedy, and he consents too late; so is it often with the self-deceiving hypocrite: he loves not this strict, and holy, and heavenly, and self-denying life, and therefore he will hope that God will save him without it, as long as he is religious in a way that he accounts more wise, and safe, and moderate, and comely, and suited to the nature and infirmity of man. These are his hopes; and to deceive his heart, by maintaining these, it is that he is religious, till either grace convert, or justice apprehend him, and his hopes and he are swallowed up by convincing flames and utter desperation.

IV. We are next to show you in what respect it is that this religion is called vain. And first, negatively, it is not vain to his own carnal ends, but to the true ends of religion.

1. He intendeth by it the quieting of his own accusing conscience, and the keeping up his hopes of salvation, and keeping off the terrors of the Lord, and so consequentially the deceiving of his own heart; and to these ends it is not in vain. Here he sitteth as quietly as if all were well between God and him, and heareth the threatenings as securely as if they concerned not him at all, and applieth the promises as boldly as if he were one of the heirs of promise; you would little think that this man must shortly be cast into utter darkness, from the presence of the Lord, and have "his portion with the hypocrites," Matt. xxiv. 51. His everlasting horrors appear not now to himself upon his heart, nor to others in his face: what sign can you see of the curse of the law, or the wrath of God, in that man's countenance? what sign of his spiritual captivity and slavery, and of the load of sin that lieth upon his soul, unless it be that he feels it not? what sign of a man in so great danger of eternal torment, unless it be that he little feareth it? Doth he sit there like a man that is within a step of hell, and shall shortly be there with the devil and his angels, as sure as he is here, unless he be saved by that grace and holiness which he now resists? No; he is as confident to be saved as the precisest of you all; he is as little troubled with the fears of hell or the wrath of God as those that are discharged from it by justification, and perhaps much less. For all this he is beholden to his vain religion, that in the point of self-deceiving is not vain. As solid evidences promote the comforts of true believers, so this superficial kind of religion promoteth the present peace of the presumptuous.

2. This religion is not vain as to the frustrating of all the means of grace, and hindering the conversion and salvation of the hypocrite. This is his armour of defence against the sword of the Spirit, that would pierce his heart, and let out his close corruption, and separate him from his beloved sin. What tell you him of repentance and conversion? He thinks he needeth no conversion, or is converted long ago? What! is he not a christian, a protestant, a religious man? Tell swearers, and cursers, and drunkards, and extortioners, and cruel landlords, and fornicators, of conversion; tell these that they are slaves of Satan, and under the wrath and curse of God, that are indeed so, past all controversy; but tell not him of it that makes no doubt but he is a member of Christ, a child of God, and an heir of heaven. He loveth to hear a minister rouse up the profane and grossly sensual offenders, and seems in pity to wish for their conversion, and perhaps will exhort them to turn and mend their lives himself. But he little thinks that he is faster in the prison of Satan than they, and that he is himself in the same condemnation.

Do you go about to tell him of the necessity of the fear of God, and of loving him above all, and of trusting him, and serving him as our only Lord? Why, all this he will confess, and perhaps is as forward to say as you, and verily thinks that he is one that doth it; you may as soon make him believe that he is not an Englishman, as that he is not a christian, and that he loveth not himself, as that he loveth not God; even while he loveth not to think of him, to speak of him, to call upon him, to obey him; while he loveth not his word, his ways, or servants, or while he loveth the world and the pleasures of sin more heartily, and seeketh them more eagerly, and cleaveth to them more tenaciously, yet if you would persuade him that he hath not a heart as true to God as any of you all, you will lose your labour.

Do you tell him of hypocrisy? he will tell you that it is the thing he hateth: who speaks against it more than he? And because the world shall see he is no hypocrite, he will call them all hypocrites that are faithful to God and to their souls, and will not sit down in his truly hypocritical vain religion, but will be more holy and diligent than he. What can you say to such a man in order to his conversion, which his self-deceiving religion will not frustrate? Do you tell him of hell-fire, and of the wrath of God against the ungodly? All this he can hear as calmly as another man; for he thinks that he is none of the ungodly, he hath escaped the danger; let them be afraid of it whom it doth concern. If you tell him of his sins, he can tell you that all men are sinners; we are here imperfect: and you shall never persuade him that his reigning, deadly sins are any other than such human frailties and infirmities as may stand with grace. Do you put him upon the inward practice of religion, and the fuller devoting of his soul to God, and the life of faith, and a heavenly mind? He will tell you, that in his measure he doth all this already; though none of us are so good as we should be; and his heart being unseen to you, he thinks you must believe him. Do you blame him for his slightness and formality in religion, and put him upon a more serious, diligent course, and to live as one that seeketh heaven with all his heart, and soul, and might? Why, he thinks you do but persuade him to some self-conceited, over-zealous party, and draw him from his moderation to be righteous over-much, and to make too much ado with his religion. Unless he be a hypocrite that falleth into the schismatical strain, and then he will make a greater bustle with his opinions and his outside services than you can desire. So that one with his mere book-prayers, forms, and ceremonies, and the other with his mere extemporate words, and affected, outside, seeming fervour, and both of them by a mere opinionative, lifeless, carnal kind of religion, subject to their fleshly ends and interests, do so effectually cheat their souls, that they are armed against all that you can say or do, and you know not how to get within them, or fasten any saving truths upon their hearts.

3. This vain religion is not vain as to the preserving of his reputation in the world. It saveth him from being numbered with the filthy rabble, and from being pointed at as notoriously vicious, or branded with the disgraceful characters of the scandalous. Men say not of him, There goeth a drunkard, a swearer, a curser, a fornicator, or a profane, ungodly wretch. He may be esteemed civil, ingenuous, discreet, and perhaps religious, and be much honoured by wise, religious men; though most commonly his formal, or opinionative, heartless kind of religion is discerned or much suspected by experienced, judicious christians, by his sapless, unexperienced, common, and carnal kind of discourse and duty, sticking most in opinions, parties, or some outside things, and by his temporizing, and reserved, and uneven kind of conversation; yet it is not always so; but sometimes he is as far unsuspected as the best: perhaps he may be esteemed a reverend preacher, or a discreet, religious, well-accomplished gentleman, and may be set in the head of church or commonwealth, as a leader of the saints on earth, that shall be thrust into the place of hypocrites, and not come near the meanest of the saints in heaven.

4. Lastly, (but better than all this,) his religion is not vain as to the good of others. He may, by the perfume and odour of his gifts, be kept from stinking to the annoyance of others, while he is dead in sin. He may be very serviceable in the church of God; a judicious, earnest expounder of the Scripture, and preacher and defender of the truth; in his place as a magistrate, or master of a family, he may be a severe corrector of profaneness, and promoter of godliness; it being much easier to drive others from their sin, than to forsake their own, and to drive on others to a godly life, than to practise it themselves: and by their owning godliness, and disowning sin, they persuade themselves the more effectually that they are truly godly. The church cannot well spare the gifts and services of hypocrites, and many ungodly men. As bad or sick physicians may be God's instruments to cure our bodies, and a wicked carpenter may make a good house; so a wicked minister may well expound and apply the Scriptures: and he that refuseth the grace of Christ, may prevail with others to accept it; the sign-post that stands out of door itself, may invite others into the house; and the hand upon a post that goes not one step of the way, may point it out to others. There is more self-denial required to the forsaking of their own sins, than to persuade others to forsake theirs; a covetous man cares not how liberal others be; nor a glutton, drunkard, or fornicator, how temperate and chaste his neighbours be. And hence it is that many of these that refuse a holy life themselves, are willing their children or servants should embrace it. The end of the balance that goeth down itself, doth cause the other to go up. Other men's souls are more beholden to hypocrites than their own. They are like the common mariners, that enrich the merchant by fetching home his treasure, when they have nothing but a poor maintenance themselves; or like tailors, who make garments for others which they never wear themselves; or like carpenters, that build fair houses which they never dwell in; or like the cook, that dresseth meat which he eateth not. God giveth hypocrites their usual gifts for the service of the church more than for themselves. He sometimes maketh those to be nursing fathers to his church that are butchers of their own souls, and makes those his instruments to undeceive others, that deceive themselves. And thus far their religion is not vain.

But, 1. It is vain as to God's special acceptation. True religion pleaseth God; but the self-deceiver's opinion he abhorreth. He hath no pleasure in fools, Eccles. v. 4. He asketh such, To what purpose is the multitude of their sacrifices? Isa. i. 11. and saith, he is full of their burnt-offerings, and delights not in them. When they come to appear before him he asketh them, Who required this at their hands, to tread in his courts? and bids them bring no more vain oblations; incense is an abomination to him; the calling of their assemblies he cannot away with, and their solemn meetings are iniquity, ver. 12, 13; their appointed feasts his soul hateth, they are a trouble to him, he is weary to bear them. When they spread forth their hands, he will hide his eyes; when they make many prayers, he will not hear; because they do not forsake their sins, ver. 14: because they turn away their ear from hearing his law, their prayer is abomination to him, Prov. xxviii. 9; xv. 8; xxi. 27. When they have sinned, instead of repenting and forsaking it, they think to please God by their religion, and stop the mouth of justice with their services; whenas they do but provoke him more, by adding hypocrisy to iniquity. Were they truly willing to let go their sins, and to please God by universal obedience, he would willingly accept them, and be pleased with their services. But when men's religion, their prayers, and other duties, are not used against their sins, but for them, not to kill them, but to cover them, not to overcome them, but as it were to bribe God to give them leave to sin, because they are not willing to forsake it, this is the self-deceiving religion of hypocrites, that is in vain.

2. And this religion is in vain, as to any promoting of a work of sanctification upon his soul. It weaneth him not from the world; it crucifieth not the flesh, with its affections and lusts; it doth not further his self-denial, nor driveth him to Christ, by a faith unfeigned; it never raiseth him to a heavenly life, nor kindleth the love of God within him: it is dead and ineffectual, and cannot produce these high

effects. Yea, on the contrary, it hardeneth him in sin and self-deceit; it hindereth his repentance; it imboldeneth him in his fleshly, worldly life, and quieteth him in the neglect of Christ and heaven.

3. Moreover this kind of religion is in vain as to any solid peace of conscience. It affordeth him none of the well-grounded, durable comforts of the saints; but, on the contrary, keeps out solid comfort by feeding him with airy, delusory conceits; and making him to be but his own comforter, upon fancies and confidence of his own, when the Spirit of Christ is not his comforter; nor doth the word of God speak any peace at all unto him.

4. Lastly, his religion is in vain as to his salvation. As he had but an image of true religion, so he shall have but an image of heaven. Some dreams and self-created hopes of happiness may accompany him to the door of eternity, but there they will leave him to everlasting horror.

V. *Use* 1. From what hath been said, you may see the reason why an outside, formal, seeming religiousness, is a thing so common in the world, in comparison of the life and power of godliness. It is an easier thing to bring men to the strictest opinion, than to bring them to the affectionate and deep reception and practice of the truth. A strict opinion may be held without any great cost and trouble to the flesh. It is the practice that bereaveth a sinner of the pleasure of his sin. It is the common trick by which most hypocrites cheat their souls, to turn to the side and opinion, and assemblies and company, which they think to be the best; that so they may persuade themselves the more easily, that they are as good as those opinions and that company doth import, and that they are truly such as those they join with. As men are taken by others for such as those they correspond with; so hypocrites take themselves for such. As if it would prove that a man is sound, because he dwelleth with them that are so; or as if it would prove a man rich or honourable, that he converseth with such. As God will not save any nations on earth because they are such nations; nor will he save men because they are of such or such a trade, or because they are skilled in this or that art or science; no more will he save men for being of this or that party or sect, in matters of religion. One thinks when he hath lived a fleshly life, he shall be saved for hearing or saying the common prayer, or because he is for prelacy and ceremonies; another thinks he shall be saved, because he can pray without a book, or form of words, or because he frequenteth the private meetings of those that more diligently redeem their time for spiritual advantages than others do; another thinks he shall be saved because he is mocked as a puritan or as too strict, as others are that are serious believers, and diligent in the things of God; and another thinks that he shall be saved because he is re-baptized, or because he joineth with some separating congregation, which pretendeth to be more strict than other. But none shall be saved on any such account as these. Cain could not be saved for being the first-born in the family of Adam; Ham could not be saved for being in the ark and family of Noah; nor Esau for being in the house of Isaac; nor Absalom for being the son of David; nor Judas for being a disciple in the family of Christ. Even Mary that brought him forth, could not have been saved by him, if she had not had a better title, and had not borne him in her heart. Mark iii. 34, 35, when they talk to him of his mother and his brethren, Christ looked upon those that sat about him, and told them, that whosoever shall do the will of God, the same is his brother, his sister, and his mother. It is not an outward badge and livery, but a heart title, that must prove you the heirs of heaven. You may be snatched out of the purest church on earth, and from the purest ordinances, and out of the arms of the most upright christians, and cast into hell, if you have no better evidences than such to show for your salvation. If ever you be saved, it must not be because you are papists, or protestants, Lutherans, or Calvinists, Arminians, antinomians, anabaptists, independents, presbyterian, or prelatical, formally and merely as such; but because you are true christians, that have the Spirit of Christ, Rom. viii. 9, and are conformed to him, in his sufferings, death, and resurrection, and live in sincere obedience to his will. But hypocrites that want the inward life and power of religion, and are conscious of their wilful sins, would fain borrow something from the parties which they join with, or the opinions which they take up, or the formal outward worship which they perform, or the alms which they give, to make up the want, and cheat their souls with a self-created confidence that they shall be saved.

But more specially you may hence observe the reason that popery hath so many followers, and that it is so easy a thing to make an infidel, or whoremonger, or drunkard, to turn a papist, when yet it is not easy to bring them to faith, and chastity, and temperance, much less to the unfeigned love of God, and to a holy, heavenly life. Though I doubt not but there are many sincere-hearted christians among the papists, yet popery itself is of a hypocritical stain, and is notably suited to the hypocrite's disposition. It is revived pharisaism: I marvel that they tremble not when they read themselves so lively characterized by Christ, with the addition of so many terrible woes, as in Matt. xxiii. and other places, frequently they are: "Woe to you scribes, pharisees, hypocrites!" They bind heavy burdens of external observances, to lay upon the consciences of their proselytes; they make broad their phylacteries; and in variety of holy vestures, they make ostentation of such a religion, as a peacock may have when he spreads his tail. They contend for superiority and titles, to be called rabbi, pope, cardinal, patriarch, primate, metropolitan, archbishop, diocesan, abbot, prior, father, &c. to the great disturbance of all the nations of the christian world. They must needs be the fathers and masters of our faith: they shut the kingdom of heaven against the people, forbidding all to read the Scriptures in their vulgar tongue, without a special licence from their ordinary; and commanding them to worship God in a strange tongue which they do not understand: by the numbers of their masses and prayers for the dead, they delude the souls, and devour the patrimony of the living. In temples, and altars, and images, and ornaments consisteth no small part of their religion: they make more of tithing mint, anise, and cummin, than of judgment, mercy, and faith, the weightier matters of the law. The outside they make clean, and appear as beautiful to men as ceremonies and outward pomp can make them. They make it a part of their religion to murder the living saints, and keep holy days for the dead; they build the tombs of the prophets, and garnish the sepulchres of the righteous, and say, If we had lived in the days of our fathers, we would not have been partakers with them in the blood of the prophets. Thus, Matt. xxiii. is their description. They have their Touch not, taste not, handle not, after the commandments and doctrines of men; their voluntary humility, and worshipping of angels, and other rudiments of the world, and things that have a show of wisdom in will-worship and humility, and neglecting of the body, not in any honour to the satisfying of the flesh, Col. ii. 19—23. How easy a thing is it to bring an ungodly man to be of a religion that consisteth in such things as these! in eating fish on certain days instead of flesh; and saying over so many Pater-Nosters, and Ave Marias, and naming so oft the name of Jesus; in worshipping a piece of consecrated bread with divine worship; in bowing and praying before an image; in praying to the souls of such as the pope tells them are saints in heaven; in crossing themselves, and being sprinkled with holy water, and using Agnus Dei's, and consecrated grains and annulets; in dropping of beads; in saying such words as a prayer at such a canonical hour, and such words the next canonical hour; in hearing a mass in Latin, and saying a mass in Latin; in being anointed with hallowed oil, and burning hallowed candles on the altars by daylight; in going so many miles to the chapel of a saint in pilgrimage; in carrying about them a bone, or some other supposed relic of a supposed saint; in confessing their sins so often to a priest, and doing penance, if he impose it on them. And so while they live in whoredom, or drunkenness, or swearing, or lying, or all these, and many other such, it is but confessing and doing penance, and to it again; on which account (whatever some of them say for the necessity of contrition) it is usual with them to venture upon the sins of whoredom, drunkenness, and the rest, because they have so easy and cheap a remedy at hand. And therefore I wonder not that among infidels, (who, after baptism, apostatize to deny the holy Scriptures, and the immortality of the soul, and the life to come,) and among common swearers, and cursers, and whoremongers, and drunkards, the papists find their labours most successful, and that no fish will so easily take their bait: nor do I wonder that it is a point of the popish faith that none but the children of the devil, that are void of the love of God, and are unjustified, can possibly turn papists. (For they tell us that all are such till they are papists; saving that they are many of them for the salvation of heathens.) A poor wretch that is captivated to his lusts, and goes under a galled, accusing conscience, will be content to take a popish cure, and quiet his soul with a few compliments and formalities. But to bring one of these men to a thorough conversion, to a true humiliation, to a deep hatred of all sin and a love of holiness, to close with Christ as his only refuge from the wrath of God, and to give up himself without any reservation, and all that he hath, to the will and service of the Lord; to love God as his portion, and the infinite, transcendent good; to take all the honour and riches of the world as loss and dung, and use all in due subserviency to everlasting happiness; to crucify the flesh, and mortify all his earthly inclinations, and live a life of self-denial; and to walk with God, and serve him as a Spirit, in spirit and in truth; and to keep a watch over thoughts, affections, words, and deeds; to live by faith upon a world and happiness that is to us unseen; and to live in preparation for their death, and wait in hope to live with Christ: this is christianity and true religion; and this is it that they will not so easily be brought to. It is easier to make a hundred papists than one true regenerate christian. Children can make them a baby of clouts; and the statuary can make a man of alabaster or stone: but none can give life, which is essential to a man indeed, but God. There needeth the Spirit of the living God, by a supernatural operation, and a kind of new creation, to make a man a real holy christian. But to bring a man to make such a congee, or wear such a vesture, or say such and such words, and make to himself a mimical religion, this may be done, without any supernatural work. O therefore take heed of cheating your souls by hypocritical formalities, instead of the life and power of religion.

Use 2. And now, oh that the Lord of life would help me so to apply this truth, and help you so to apply it to yourselves, that it might be as a light set up in the assembly and in all your consciences, to undeceive the miserable self-deceivers, and to bring poor hypocrites into some better acquaintance with themselves, and to turn their seeming, vain religion into that which is real, serious, and saving!

And now I am to search and convince the hypocrite, I could almost wish that all the upright, tender souls that are causelessly in doubt of their own sincerity, were out of the congregation, lest they should misapply the hypocrite's portion to themselves, and think it is their case that I am describing: as it is usual with ignorant patients, especially if they be a little melancholy, when they hear or read the description of many dangerous diseases, to think that all or some of them are theirs, because they have some symptoms very like to some of those which they hear or read of. Or lest their fearful souls should be too much terrified, by hearing of the misery of the hypocrite; as a fearful child, that is innocent, will cry when he sees another whipped that is faulty. But if thou wilt stay and hear the hypocrite's examination, I charge thee, poor humbled, drooping soul, that thou do not misunderstand me, nor think that I am speaking those things to thee, that are meant to the false-hearted enemies of the Lord; and do not imagine that thou art condemned in his condemnation; nor put thyself under the strokes that are given him; but rejoice that thou art saved from this state of self-deceit and misery. And that thou mayst have some shelter for thy conscience against the storm that must fall on others, look back on the foregoing description of the hypocrite, and thou mayst find that thou hast the saving graces, which I there discovered him to want. Let these at present be before thine eyes, and tell thee, thou art not the person that I mean.

1. Thou art humbled to a loathing of thyself for thy transgressions.

2. Thou art willing to give up thyself to Christ, without reserve, that, as thy Saviour, he may cure thy miserable soul, upon his own terms.

3. The favour of God is dearer to thee than the favour of the world, or the pleasures and prosperity of sinners; and thou longest more to love him better, and to feel his love, than for any of the honours and advancements that flesh and blood desire.

4. It is the life to come that thou takest for thy portion, and preferrest before the matters of this transitory life.

5. Thy religion employeth thee about thy heart, as much as about the outside and appearing part; it is heart sins that thou observest and lamentest, and a better heart that thou daily longest, and prayest, and labourest for.

6. Thou livest not in any gross and deadly sin; and thou hast no infirmity but what thou longest and labourest to be rid of; and goest on in the use of Christ's holy means and remedies for a cure.

7. Thou dislikest not the highest degree of holiness, but lovest it and longest after it, and hadst rather be more holy than be more honourable or more rich.

8. Thou unfeignedly lovest the image of Christ on the souls of all his servants where thou canst discern it; and seest a special excellency in a poor, humble, heavenly christian, though never so low or despicable in the world, above all the pomp and splendour of the earth; and thou lovest them with a

special love; and that the holier they are, the better dost thou love them.

9. Thou lovest the most convincing, searching sermons, and wouldst fain have help to know the worst that is in thy heart; and comest unto the light that thy heart and deeds may be made manifest.

10. All this is the bent and bias of thy soul; thy habituated, ordinary case: though there be not alway the same opportunity for the acts, nor the same degree of life in acting. It is not only a good mood that thou art frightened into by some affliction, and then returnest to thy carnal course of life again; but thou heartily continuest thy consent to the covenant which thou hast made with Christ, and wouldst not turn back to a worldly, carnal, or formal life, nor change thy Master, nor forsake the holy course which thou art engaged in, for all the world.

This is the truth of thy case, poor, doubting, troubled christian! thou canst not deny it without much injury to thyself and God. And therefore be not now troubled at that which I shall say to the self-deceivers.

And now I am to speak to the self-deceiver, I perceive my task to be exceeding difficult: to get within him that is so guarded; and to pierce his heart that is so armed; and to open his eyes that is willing to be blind; and to undeceive him that hath been so long deceived, and that studieth to deceive himself, and is engaged in that unhappy work, by such subtle enemies that further his deceit, and by so many allurements, and such strong corruptions, and by a seeming necessity for the quieting of his conscience; all this is not an easy work. But we must attempt it, and leave the success to grace. And, first, let me solemnly profess before you all, (for the removing of your prejudice, and the calming of your resisting hearts,) that it is none of my desire, by the discovery of your hypocrisy, to shame you before others, or to make you seem more miserable than you are, or to disturb and grieve you any more than is necessary to the escaping of your exceeding danger, and than your own salvation and comforts do require. But when we know that religion is your business in the world; and that an endless world shall presently receive you; and that Christ is coming; and your souls are ready to quit their residence, and take their leave of your flesh till the resurrection; and when we know that hypocrisy and self-deceit is the thing that you are most in danger of, and that you must be saved from it or be in hell for ever; and that the enemies of your souls will do all they can to keep their possession in peace, and to continue your deceit till you are past remedy; what would you have us do in such a case? would you wish us to be silent, and betray your souls, and damn our own for fear of disquieting and displeasing you? How hard are your hearts, if you would wish us to do thus!

Be awakened, therefore, O all ye self-deceivers! and know that hypocrisy, as the harlot's paint, is but a base and borrowed beauty; that will vanish away when you draw near the fire; and that self-deceit will quiet you so short a time, that it is as good let go your delusory peace and comfortable dream to-day as to-morrow; and it is better now to begin and examine yourselves, than stay till the dreadful Judge examine you, who is even at the door! The discovery of your case is the one half of your cure: and as you have been your own deceivers, let us in justice find you so equitable to yourselves, as to be willing of the light that must undeceive you; and to go along with us into your consciences, and help us in the search, and impartially pass a preventing judgment, that Christ may not pass a condemning judgment.

And in order to your conviction and recovery, I shall first acquaint you with your misery, that so it may awaken you to look about you, while there is time and hope. If it were God's way to work by ocular demonstrations, and the christian life were a life of sense, and you had heaven and hell this hour open to your sight, how little need should I have to plead this cause with you any further! you would then see and hear that vengeance that would awake you; and make you presently fly into your hearts, and charge conscience to deal impartially with you, lest self-deceit should bring you to those flames. But it is a life of faith that we are to call you to, and a word of faith that we have to preach; but of things that are as sure as if you saw them.

And, 1. If thy religion be vain, thy hopes and comforts, that are built upon it, are all but vain. How vain is that hope that will vanish when the enjoyment is expected, and will end in endless desperation! What though thou sit here with so great hopes and confidence of salvation as maketh thee even scorn the man that questions it, art thou ever the better when death awakeneth thee, and thy confident dream is at an end? When thou art dying wilt thou hope? Perhaps thou mayst: but when thou art burning wilt thou hope? When thou art tormented wilt thou hope? Desperation will then be essential to thy misery. The devils that now feed thy hope by their deceits, will then as readily keep awake thy conscience, and exasperate thy despairing soul. If now thou wilt hope under the threatenings of God, (that thou mayst be saved in thy present state,) wilt thou then hope under his execution? Thy flatterers and prosperity may cherish thy deceitful hopes for a time, but who will maintain them, when God commandeth desperation to torment thee? Job xxvii. 8, 9, "For what is the hope of the hypocrite, though he hath gained, when God taketh away his soul? Will God hear his cry when trouble cometh upon him?" As Sands turns it:

> "What hope hath the prevailing hypocrite,
> When God shall chase his soul to endless night?
> Will God relieve him in his agonies?
> Or from the depth of sorrows hear his cries?"

His worldly glory will then desert him, and leave him to the fruit of his deserts: his fruition will perish with his hopes. Job xxvii. 22, 23, "For God shall cast upon him and not spare: he would fain flee out of his hand. Men shall clap their hands at him, and shall hiss him out of his place." Or as Sands turneth it:

> "God shall transfix him with his winged dart;
> Though he avoid him like a flying hart.
> Men shall pursue with merited disgrace;
> Hiss, clap their hands, and from his country chase."

Hopes that are built by self-deceit have no foundation but sand and water, and in trial they will fall, and their fall will be great and terrible, Matt. vii. 23, 24. Job viii. 11—15, "Can the rush grow up without mire? Can the flag grow without water? Whilst it is yet in its greenness, and not cut down, it withereth before any other herb: so are the paths of all that forget God; and the hypocrite's hope shall perish: whose hope shall be cut off, and whose trust shall be a spider's web. He shall lean upon his house, but it shall not stand: he shall hold it fast, but it shall not endure." Or—

> "Can bulrushes but by the rivers grow?
> Can flags there flourish where no waters flow?
> Yet they, when green, when yet untouch'd of all
> That clothe the spring, first hang their heads, and fall
> So double-hearted hypocrites; so they
> Who God forget, shall in their prime decay.
> Their airy hopes, as brittle as the thin
> And subtle webs which toiling spiders spin;

> Their houses full of wealth and riot, shall
> Deceive their trust, and crush them in their fall," &c.

Job xxxvi. 13, "The hypocrites in heart heap up wrath: they cry not when he bindeth them." Or as the paraphrase:—

> "For the deluder hastens his own fall,
> Nor will in trouble on th' Almighty call.
> Who on the beds of sin supinely lie,
> They in the summer of their age shall die."

And what we say of the hypocrite's hope, we may say also of all his pleasures and delights. He may now be as merry as the most righteous of his neighbours, and seem the most happy, because the most jocund; and abound with medicines against melancholy, and all wise and sober consideration: even his business, his cups, his wantonness and uncleanness, or, at least, his less disgraceful pleasures and recreations, which fortify his mind against the fears of death and judgment, and all the threatenings of God—

> "As sleepy opium fortifies the brain
> Against the sense of sicknesses and pain."

And if this mirth could always last, how happy a man were the self-deceiver! But, saith Solomon, Eccles. vii. 6, "As the crackling of thorns under a pot, so is the laughter of the fool."

> "As thorns beneath a caldron catch the fire,
> Blaze with a noise, and suddenly expire;
> Such is the causeless laughter of vain fools;
> This vanity in their distemper rules."

And as Job xx. 4—9, "Knowest thou not this of old, since man was placed upon earth, that the triumphing of the wicked is short, and the joy of the hypocrite for a moment? Though his excellency mount up to the heavens, and his head reacheth to the clouds; yet he shall perish for ever like his own dung; they which have seen him shall say, Where is he? He shall flee away as a dream, and shall not be found; yea, he shall be chased away as a vision of the night. The eye also which saw him shall see him no more; neither shall his place any more behold him." Or as the aforesaid paraphrase:—

> "This is a truth which with the world began,
> Since earth was first inhabited by man;
> Sin's triumph in swift misery concludes,
> And flattering joy the hypocrite deludes.
> Although his excellence to heaven aspire;
> Though radiant beams his shining brows attire;
> He as his dung shall perish on the ground;
> Nor shall th' impression of his steps be found;
> But like a troubled dream shall take his flight,
> And vanish as a vision of the night;
> No mortal eye shall see his face again,
> Nor sumptuous roofs their builder entertain."

Thus as the hypocrite's religion is vain, so all his hopes and joys will be vain, and will deceive him, as he deceived himself. As Zophar concludeth of him, Job xi. 20, "But the eyes of the wicked shall fail, and they shall not escape, and their hope shall be as the giving up of the ghost."

Poor soul! thy religion is already so vain, that it giveth thee no solid satisfaction or delight: thou art fain to go to thy lands, or friends, or pleasures, or carnal accomodations for delight: thy religion, which should let thee into heaven, and there refresh thee with the foretastes of everlasting pleasures, and should daily fetch thee fresh delights from the face of God, alas! is an impotent, lifeless thing; acquainted with shadows, but strange to the invisible substance; acquainted with formal shows and ceremonies, but unacquainted with God; acquainted with the letter, but not with the spirit; familiar with the orders of the church, but strange to the foretastes of heaven. If thou hadst no other comfort but what thy dead religion brings thee from the face of God, thy pensive heart would be better disposed to consideration and recovery than it is. If thou hadst a faith that brought thee in any solid, stablishing content, what needest thou be hunting abroad the world among thy crowd of vanities and deceits, to beg or borrow some short delight, which thou must return with griping usury? and what needest thou so many pitiful shifts to muzzle thy conscience, and to keep that peace a little longer, which will end in sorrow, and will part with thee as the devil went out of the possessed person, (Mark ix. 26,) that rent him, and left him as a dead man? That religion is certainly vain, that is not sufficient to acquaint the soul with matter of solid comfort and content, but leaves that felicitating work to worldly, transitory things, while itself is used only as a screen, to keep hell-fire from scorching the conscience, or as children's rackets, to quiet them when they are apt to cry.

2. But the vanity of a superficial religion will most appear in the hour of extremity; when their help, as well as their hope and comfort, will to them prove vain. Prosperity will not always last: as sure as winter followeth summer, and as the darksome night succeeds the day, so sure will adversity take its turn: sickness will follow the longest health, and death succeed the longest life; and your house of darkness in the dust will hold you longer than your present habitations. And when thou seest all things fail, oh what wouldst thou give for a hope and help that will not fail, that thou mightest be received into the everlasting habitations! The conscience that is now asleep, will be shortly awakened in such a manner, that it will be utterly past the skill and power of thyself, and all the friends thou hast, to cast it asleep, or quiet it again. And then, what wouldst thou not give for a lenitive to pacify it! No wonder if thou sit here as senseless as if no harm were near thee: it is now in thy power not to believe that there is a hell for hypocrites, or that it is thy own inheritance; but the day is near, (if a supernatural change prevent it not,) when it shall no more be in thy power, but sight and feeling shall convince thee whether thou wilt or no. Now we must entreat thy own consideration, and solicit thee for thy own consent, to know thy grievous sin and misery, and yet leave thee unconvinced, because thou art unwilling to know the truth, and because we cannot show thee heaven and hell while we are speaking of them: but then God will not crave, but force thy consideration; nor will he ask thy consent to feel thy misery; but the less thou art willing, the more hast thou to feel. And which way then wilt thou look for help? which way ever it be, it will be all in vain, because thy religion was but vain. Wilt thou look to thy duties and supposed honesty, whose sincerity now thou art so confident of? alas, this is the vain religion that could deceive thee, but cannot save thee. Thou art like a man in a falling house, that hath nothing to lay hold on but that which is falling, and it is that will break him unto death. Or like a drowning man that hath nothing but a handful of water to lay hold upon; which is it that will choke him, but is vain to save him. It is thy superficial, hypocritical, complimental services that will fall with thee, and fall upon thee, that will thus both deceive thee, and choke thee in the time of thy distress. To be told now that thy religion is vain is a thing that thy dead, unbelieving heart can too easily bear; but to find then, when thou lookest for the benefit of it, that it is vain, is that which is not borne so easily, but will overturn the stoutest heart with terrors. If thou wert a man of no religion, and so hadst none to deceive and quiet thee,

thou couldst scarcely keep off thy terrors now: if thou hadst not thy hollow-hearted prayers, thy affected zeal, or forms, and shows, and tasks of duty, thy profession, with its secret exceptions and reserves, thy smoothed outside, with the good conceit thou hast of thyself, and the good esteem that other men have of thee; if thou hadst not these to flatter thy conscience and cloak thee from the storms of threatened wrath, thou wouldst perhaps walk about like another Cain, and be afraid of every man thou seest, and tremble at the shaking of a leaf, and still look behind thee as afraid of a pursuit. But, alas! it will be ten thousand times more terrible to find thy confidence prove deceit, and thy religion vain, when God is judging thee, when hell is before thee, and thou art come to the last of thine expectations! nay, then to find not only that thy superficial religion was vanity, and lighter than vanity, nothing, and less than nothing; but that it was thy sin, and that which will now torment thee, and the remembrance of it be to thee as the remembrance of drunkenness to the drunkard, and of fornication to the unclean, and of covetousness to the worldling, the rust of whose money will eat his flesh, and burn like fire. Oh what a doleful plight is this! when the sentence is ready to pass upon thee, and hell is gaping to devour thee, and thou lookest for help to thy vain religion, and criest out, Oh now or never help! help me, or I am a firebrand of unquenchable wrath: help me, or I must be tormented in those flames: help me now, or it will be too late, and I shall never, never more have help! Then to have thy self-deceit discovered, and thy seeming religion condemn thee and torment thee, instead of helping thee, what anguish and confusion will this cast thy hopeless soul into, such as no heart can here conceive! Thy guilty soul will be like a hare among a company of dogs; whichsoever of thy duties thou fliest for help to, that will make first to tear thee, and devour thee. Like a naked man in the midst of an army of his deadly enemies; whichsoever he flieth to for pity and relief, is like to be one of the first to wound him. Poor self-deceiver! what wilt thou then do, or whither wilt thou betake thy soul for help? The reason why thou canst now make shift with a lifeless shadow of religion is, because thou hast thy sports or pleasures, thy friends and flatterers, thy worldly business, to divert thy thoughts, and take thee up, and rock the cradle of thy security; and thy piety is not yet brought unto the fire, nor thy heart and duties searched by the all-discovering light: but when the light comes in, and when all thy fleshly contents are gone, and when thou comest to have use for thy religion, and seest that, if it prove unsound, thou art lost for ever, oh then it is not shadows, and shows, and compliments, that will quiet thee. That will not serve turn then, that serves turn now. Thou wilt find then that it was easier deceiving thyself than God. Gal. vi. 3—5, 7, "For if a man think himself to be something when he is nothing, he deceiveth himself. But let every man prove his own work: for every man shall bear his own burden. Be not deceived; God is not mocked: for whatsoever a man soweth, that shall he also reap. For he that soweth to the flesh, shall of the flesh reap corruption: but he that soweth to the Spirit, shall of the Spirit reap life everlasting."

But perhaps thou wilt say, It is not any duties, but Christ, that I must trust to: he will be my help, and he is sufficient, and will not deceive the soul that trusteth in him.

Answ. Undoubtedly he is sufficient, and will not deceive thee. But doth he deceive thee, if he give thee not the salvation which he never promised thee? He never promised salvation to a hypocrite (without conversion). It is the upright soul, devoted to him, that takes him for the absolute master of his life, and for his only portion and felicity, to whom Christ hath promised salvation: and his promise shall be made good, and the sincere shall find that Christ deceives them not. But where did he ever promise salvation to a superficial Pharisee? to such a seeming christian as thou? Show such a promise from him if thou canst; and then trust it and spare not. But thou dost not trust him, but thy own deceit, if he have given thee no such promise to trust on. Nay, rather, should he not deceive all the world, if he should save such superficial hypocrites, when he hath professed in his word that he will not save them? and if he should not condemn such heartless formalists, when he hath so often told us that he will condemn them? Sure he that breaks his word is liker to be a deceiver, than he that keepeth it. Be it known to thee therefore, (and oh that thou wouldst know it while there is a remedy at hand!) that if thou trust that Christ should save an unsanctified, false-hearted person, whose soul was never renewed and revived by the Holy Ghost, and absolutely given up to God, and that setteth not up God and his service above all the interest of the flesh, and the commodities and contentments of the world, thou dost not then trust Christ, but thy own deceits and lies; and it is not Christ that is the deceiver, but thou art a deceiver of thyself, that makest thyself a false promise, and trustest to it; and when thou hast done, sayest thou wilt trust to Christ: yea, trustest thyself against Christ, and trustest that he will break his word, and not that he will make it good. See whether he resolve not to condemn all such, Matt. x. 37, 38; Luke xiv. 27, 33; Matt. vii. 26, 27; James ii. 14; Heb. xii. 14; Rom. viii. 9, with the texts before cited, and abundance such. Christ will be a Saviour; but he is the Saviour of the body, and not of the affixed hypocrite, Eph. v. 23. And his body is the church which is subject to him, verse 24. "He will save to the utmost:" but whom? "even all that come to God by him," Heb. vii. 2, 5; but not those that make the world their god, and would put God off with a few running, heartless words and duties. It is the living, fruitful branches that he will save: but the withered branches he casteth forth, to be burned in the fire, John xv. 2—7. "No man can serve God and mammon;" nor live both to the Spirit and the flesh: he that hath two hearts, hath none that is acceptable unto God: he that hath two faces, (a face of devotion in his formal customary services, and a face that smiles on the world and fleshly pleasures when he hath done,) hath none that God will ever smile upon. The leaves of the barren fig-tree saved it not from the curse of Christ, Matt. xxi. 18, 19. "Hew it down and cast it into the fire," shall be the sentence of the most flourishing tree that is fruitless, Luke xiii. 7. "The earth which drinketh in the rain that cometh oft upon it, and bringeth forth herbs meet for them by whom it is dressed, receiveth blessing from God; but that which beareth thorns and briers is rejected, and is nigh unto cursing; whose end is to be burned," Heb. vi. 7, 8. So that if thy religion be vain, the blood of Christ, and all the treasures of his grace, will be vain to thee, that are saving unto others. An infidel may then as well expect to be saved by the Christ whom he rejected, as thou. Nay, it is Christ himself that will condemn thee: it is his own mouth that will say to such as thee, "Depart from me, ye that work iniquity." And though thou couldst say, "Lord, Lord, I have prophesied, or cast out devils, or done many wonderful works in thy name," he "will profess to thee that he never knew thee," or owned thee, Matt. vii. 22, 23. If crying would then serve, I know thou wouldst not spare thy cries. But he must so pray as to be accepted and heard on earth, that looks to be accepted and regarded then. When the miserable soul, with endless horrors in its eye, is looking round about for help, and findeth none; when all the creatures say, We cannot, and he that can shall say, I will not; who can apprehend the calamity of such a soul? what soul so sleepy and regardless now, that will not then cry, "Lord, Lord, open to us," when the door is shut, and it is too late? Matt. xxv. 10—12. Then if thou roar in the anguish of thy soul, and cry out to him that saveth others, Condemn me not, O Lord, but save me also! now, Lord, have mercy on a miserable sinner! save me, or I am lost for ever; save me, or I must burn in yonder flame; turn not thy heart against an undone, perishing soul; if thou cast me off, I have no hope! a thousand such cries would be in vain, because thou hadst but a vain religion. Prov. i. 24, &c. "Because I have called, and ye refused; I have stretched out my hand, and no man regarded; but ye have set at nought all my counsel, and would none of my reproof: I also will laugh at your calamity; I will mock when your fear cometh; when your fear cometh as desolation, and your destruction cometh as a whirlwind; when distress and anguish cometh upon you. Then shall they call upon me, but I will not answer; they shall seek me early, but they shall not find me.—Therefore they shall eat of their own way, and be filled with their own devices," saith the Lord.

And when hell hath once taken thee into its possession, if thou cry and roar there ten thousand millions of ages it will be all in vain. Thy strongest and thy longest cries cannot procure thee a drop of water to cool thy tongue, tormented in those flames, Luke xvi. 24—26.

In a word, if thy religion be vain, all is vain to thee. Thy life itself is vain, Eccles. vi. 12. Thou walkest in a vain show, Psalm xxxix. 6. Thou disquietest thyself in vain, in all thy labours, Psalm xxxix. 6, and cxxvii. 1, 2; and vanity and vexation is all that thou shalt possess, Eccles. i. 2, 14; Prov. xxii. 8. And if conscience, when thy day of grace is past, shall force thee upon the review to say, My piety was but seeming and self-deceit, and all my religion was vain; it will be the voice of utter desperation, and will stab the heart of all thy hopes. This, and no better, being the self-deceiver's case, is not conscience now at work within you, and asking, as each of the disciples did, (Matt. xxvi. 24, 25,) "Is it I?" If thou have a heart within thee beseeming a reasonable creature, by this time thou art afraid of self-deceit, and willing to be searched, and to know thy hypocrisy while it may be cured. For my part, I shall pronounce no one of you personally to be a hypocrite, as knowing that hypocrisy is a sin of the heart, which, in itself, is seen by none but God and him that hath it. But my business is only to help such to know and judge themselves. Could I name the man to you in the congregation that had none but a seeming, vain religion, I am persuaded you would all look upon him as a most unhappy, deplorable wretch. Alas! sirs, hypocrites are not so rare among us as some imagine. There are few, or none, but saints and hypocrites in this assembly, or in most of the assemblies in the land. I think here are none that make not a profession of the christian faith, and of love to God. All, therefore, that have not this faith and love, must needs be hypocrites, as professing to be what they are not. In your baptism you engaged and professed yourselves the disciples of Christ, and gave up yourselves in solemn covenant to God the Father, Son, and Holy Ghost. This covenant, you will say, you stand to yet; and none of you will be known to have renounced your christianity. As christians, you use to come to these assemblies, and here to attend God in the use of his ordinances, and some of you to renew your covenant with him in the sacrament of the Lord's supper. I meet with none that will say, I am no christian, nor a servant of the God of heaven; I am an infidel, and rebel against the Lord. I think there is none of you but would take it ill if I should call you such, or should deny you to be christians and men fearing God. If, therefore, you are not such indeed, you must needs be hypocrites. What say you? Is there any of you that profess yourselves to be ungodly, unbelievers, and servants of the devil; and will take this as your current title, disclaiming the love and service of the Lord? I think you will not. If you are such as you profess, you are all saints, and shall be saved. If any of you be not such, they can be nothing else but hypocrites.

Seeing, therefore, that you are all either saints or hypocrites, come now to the bar, and refuse not a trial that may prevent the terrors of another kind of trial that you cannot refuse.

And here let me set before you your profession, and then try yourselves whether you are such as you profess yourselves to be or not. And I think I may take it for granted that the articles of the creed and the baptismal covenant is the least that every one of you do profess; and that the desires implied in the petitions of the Lord's prayer, you all profess to be your own desires; and that you take the ten commandments for part of the rule of your obedience. Let us peruse them briefly in the several parts.

1. Do you not all say that you "believe in God the Father Almighty, Maker of heaven and earth," and that you will "have no other gods but him?" and are you not accordingly engaged in covenant with him? You will not deny it. And what is the meaning of this much of your profession? It is no less than to take God for the only infinite good, to be loved with the chiefest love, and to take him for your absolute Lord and Governor, the Owner of you and all you have, to whom you owe universal obedience; and that you are truly willing to love him above all, and fear him, and trust him, and obey him accordingly, though your flesh and all the world should be against it. He that meaneth not all this, doth dissemble or lie, when he saith he taketh God to be his God: for to be God, is to be this much to us.

And really is it thus with you as you profess? Speak but as men that dare not lie before the Lord that knows your hearts. Do you indeed love God as God, with your superlative love? Are your hearts set upon him? Do you make it your principal care to please him? Is it your delight to do his will? Is it sweeter to you to think and speak of him than of the world? Doth it grieve you most to offend him? In a word, you are not such strangers to nature but you know what love is; and you are not such strangers to your own hearts, but you know what it is to love your pleasure, your profit, your honour, and your friend. Can conscience say before the Lord that you love him better than all these? if not more passionately, yet more deeply, effectually, and resolvedly—with a love that will cause you to deny and part with all for him? If you thus truly love him as God, and above all, how comes it to pass that you seek the world more carefully and eagerly than him; and that you are more pleased with worldly thoughts, and speeches, and employments, than with divine? Were not the hypocrite justly blinded, and a wilful stranger to himself, he could not but know that he loveth not God as God, and above all. And to love him, in subordination to your flesh and its contents, is not at all to love him as God; as it is no degree of conjugal love to love a wife but as a servant; nor no degree of the love due to your sovereign, to love him as an equal or as a slave.

And if really you take God for your absolute Lord and Governor, why is it then that you take no pleasure in his laws, but count them too strict, and had rather be at your own dispose? Why is it that you obey your fleshly desires, before and against the God whom you acknowledge? Why will you not be persuaded to that holiness, justice, and charity, which you know his law commandeth you? Why do you wilfully continue in those sins which conscience tells you God forbids? Will you live in wilful disobedience, and love your sins, and loathe your duty, and obstinately continue thus, and yet profess that you take God for your God, and, consequently, for your Lord and Governor? and yet will you not confess that you are dissembling hypocrites?

2. Do you not all profess that you "believe in Jesus Christ;" and have you not, in covenant, taken him for your Saviour and Lord? and do you so, indeed, or do you not, play the hypocrites? If you believe in Christ, and take him for your Saviour, you then take your sins for the disease and misery of your souls; and you are so grieved for them, and weary of them, and humbled in the apprehension of your lost estate, that you fly to Christ as your only refuge from the wrath and curse of the offended Majesty, and value his justifying and healing grace before all the riches of the world; and you are willing to take his bitterest medicines, and use the means appointed by him for the destruction of your sin and the perfecting of his graces. And is it thus with you that have unhumbled hearts, that never felt the need of Christ, as condemned miserable men must do; and that love the sin that he would cure, and are unwilling to be mortified and sanctified by his grace? Unless a carcass be a man, such hypocrites as these are no true christians, and have but a seeming, self-deceiving faith.

3. Do you not all profess "to believe in the Holy Ghost;" and are you not engaged to him in covenant as your Sanctifier; and do you not grossly play the hypocrites here? If not, how comes it to pass that you stick in your natural state, as if you had no need of sanctification; and live as quietly without any acquaintance with true regeneration, and the Spirit to dwell and rule within you, as if you needed no such change? Or else, that you take up with a formal, an affected, or a forced kind of religion, instead of sanctification and spiritual devotion? And how comes it to pass that you distaste the highest degrees of holiness; and that you will not be brought to the mortification, self-denial, and unreserved obedience, which are the essence of sanctification? As for the more debauched, profane sort of hypocrites, that can make a common mock of godliness, and scorn at the very name of holiness and sanctification, and deride at all who pretend to have the Spirit, I had rather tremble at the thought of their misery than now stand to reprove that notorious hypocrisy, which professeth to believe in the Holy Spirit which they deride, and covenanteth with the Sanctifier, while they hate and mock, or, at least, do obstinately refuse, sanctification, when God himself tells us, (Rom. viii. 9,) "That if any man have not the Spirit of Christ, the same is none of his:" and therefore to deride a man for professing that he hath the Spirit, is to deride him for professing to be a christian.

4. Do you not all profess to "believe the holy catholic church;" that is, that Christ hath a people dispersed through the world, that are sanctified by his Spirit, and made a holy, peculiar people, whom he loveth as his spouse and as his own body, of which number you must be if you will be saved? And yet, at the same time, the members of this church you contemn, the holiness of it you secretly hate, and the faithful pastors in it you despise and disobey. Is not this hypocrisy?

5. You all profess to "believe the communion of saints;" that is, that the true members of the catholic church are all saints, that have one and the same Spirit, and walk by the same holy law or rule, and in holiness must converse together, and join together for the public worshipping of God, according to his own institution; and must purely and fervently love each other with such a charity as shall make one as ready to relieve another, when God calls for it, as if our riches did belong, in common, to the saints. This is the meaning of this article of your creed. And do I then need to ask you whether those that profess this are hypocrites, if they hate the saints and their inward spiritual communion; and if they love them but with that lifeless charity that James describeth? James ii. 14, 15, &c.; or if they despise or hate the discipline, ordinances, and holy communion of the church; and if they live in communion with drunkards, with harlots, with worldlings, or sensual, vain, or ambitious men, and fly from the "communion of saints?" What dost thou when thou sayest, "I believe the communion of saints," but say, I am a dissembling hypocrite, if it be thus with thee?

6. You all profess to "believe the forgiveness of sins;" that is, that through the blood of Christ all true repenting and believing sinners shall be forgiven, and are not shut up under remediless despair; and also I think you all profess that you do repent yourselves, that forgiveness may be yours: and yet you love your sin; you love not to be told of it; you will not believe it to be sin, as long as you can strive against conviction; and when you must needs confess it, you will not forsake it; but while you seem to reform by parting with so much as you can spare, your dearer sins, which pleasure and honour and profit are much engaged in, you will not forsake; though repentance do consist in turning from sin to God, and Christ hath assured you that "except ye repent, ye shall all likewise perish," Luke xiii. 3, 5. Is not this, therefore, palpable hypocrisy, to profess repentance for remission of sin, and still keep the sin which you say you repent of, as if you thought to mock God with names and shows.

7. You all profess to "believe the resurrection of the body, and that Christ shall come again to judge the quick and the dead;" but do you live as men that believe it indeed, that they are passing unto such a judgment? If you seriously expected to be judged for your lives, for the words you speak, the deeds you do, the time you spend, the means of grace which you neglect or use, and for all that you receive and do, is it possible you could so waste your time, and neglect the means of your salvation, and sin so boldly and obstinately as you do?

8. You all profess that you "believe the life everlasting," that the righteous shall go into their Master's joy, and the rest into everlasting punishment in hell, Matt. xxv. 13. But do you not play the hypocrites? Can you heartily believe that you stand so near to heaven or hell, to everlasting joy or torments, and make no greater a matter of it, nor make

no better preparation for it, nor bestir yourselves no more in a case of such unspeakable weight? If you believe sincerely the glory of heaven, you set your hearts on it more than upon earth, and take it for your portion, and most desirable felicity. But do I need to tell the worldly, fleshly hypocrite how far he is from this?

9. You profess, as the sum of the ten commandments, that you love God above all, and your neighbours as yourselves. But doth not your selfishness, and quarrelling with your neighbours, when they do but stand in the way of your honour or commodity, convince you of hypocrisy in this profession?

10. In the use of the Lord's prayer, what word do you speak that is not hypocrisy? Do you first and principally desire the hallowing of God's name, and coming of his kingdom, and the doing of his will, when you are far more tender of your own names than of God's, and more regardful of your own honour? and when you care more for your own prosperity than for the prosperity of the church and gospel, and do yourselves become the hinderers of his kingdom and government in the church and in the souls of men? and when you cannot abide to do his will, when it crosseth the interest of your flesh, but dislike it as too strict, and had rather the word and will of God were agreeable to yours, than you will conform your own to his?

Do you only desire your daily bread, and that in subordination to the honour, and kingdom, and will of God? Or rather do you not play the hypocrites in saying so, when it is not daily bread that will content you; but plenty and prosperity is sweeter to you than holiness?

When you pray for "the forgiveness of your sins, as you forgive others," you intimate that you are weary of your sins, and hate them, and would forsake them; and that you forgive all that have wronged you, out of the sense of your own transgressions, and of the love of Christ. But is all this so, or is it mere dissembling, when you forsake not your sin, nor are willing to forsake it, and when your consciences know that there be some that you forgive not?

You pray against "being led into temptation," and yet you love it, and cast yourselves into it; into tempting company, and tempting talk, and tempting employments. And for recreation, meat, drink, apparel, houses, attendants, estate, reputation, and almost all things else, you love and choose that which is most tempting.

You pray to be "delivered from evil," when the evil of your pride, flesh-pleasing, and worldliness, you so love, that indeed you would not be delivered from them. What can you say to excuse all this from palpable hypocrisy.

To conclude, you pretend to all that is necessary to salvation, but have you that in reality which you pretend to?

1. You think yourselves wise enough to be saved. But is it not folly that goes under the name of wisdom? When you should be converted, and lead a holy life, you are wise enough to give reasons for the contrary, and wise enough to confute the preacher, and prove him a fool, instead of obeying the call of God. You are wise enough to prove the physician to be ignorant, and to cast away the medicine that should heal you. And what if nobody could deal with you in subtlety of argument, but you could say that against the necessary means of your own salvation, that none can answer? When you die by your wisdom, and have disputed yourselves out of the reach of mercy, will you not bewail it then as folly? Is he wiser, that, being hungry, eats his meat, or he that gives such reasons for his refusing it, and pleadeth so learnedly against eating and drinking, that none can answer him? Is the condemned man wiser that makes friends for a pardon, or he that with unanswerable subtlety reasoneth against it, till the ladder be turned? Such is your vain and seeming wisdom. You are not wise enough to be cured, but to give reasons why you should continue sick. In the issue, it will prove that you were not wise enough to be saved, but notably wise to resist salvation, and plead yourselves into hell.

2. You pretend that you have a saving faith, when your hearts refuse that salvation from sin, and that rule of Christ which is the object of faith; and when you will not believe the doctrines, precepts, or threatenings that cross your own conceits; and when your belief of heaven will not carry your hearts from earth, nor work you to a holy, heavenly life.

3. You pretend to repentance, as I said before, while you hold fast the sin, and give not up yourselves to God; whenas if your neighbour, or master, or husband, should but beat one of you, and tell you when he hath done that he repenteth, and do this as oft as you commit your wilful sins, and say you repent, I am confident you would not take it for true repentance. You repent, but will not confess when it is to your disgrace, as long as you can hide your sin. You repent, but will not make restitution or reparation of injuries to your power. You repent, but your heart riseth against him that reproveth you. You repent, but you had rather keep your sins than leave them. What is this but to deceive your own hearts, and to mock yourselves with a seeming, vain, and mock repentance?

4. You pretend to love God above all, (as was before said,) when you love not his image, ways, or communion, but love that which he hateth, and still prefer the world before him.

5. You pretend that you have true desires to be godly, and what God would have you be; but they are such desires as the sluggard hath to rise, and as the slothful hath to work: that is, if it could be done with ease, and without labour; you lie still, and use not the means with diligence for all your desires. When you can sit and have your work done with wishes, and your families maintained and your necessities all supplied with wishes, you may think to come to heaven with wishes. The good desires that the poor may be warmed, and clothed, that James speaks of, (James ii. 15,) did neither relieve the poor, nor save the wisher. "The desire of the slothful killeth him; for his hands refuse to labour," Prov. xxi. 25. Up and be doing according to thy desires, or else confess that thy wishes are hypocritical, and that thou deceivest thy own heart by vain desires.

6. You also pretend to be sincere worshippers of God. You pray, and you read the Scripture and good books, and you hear the word, and receive the Lord's supper. But I have before shown you your hypocrisy in these: you pray against the sin that you love and would not leave; you pray for holiness, when you hate it, or desire it not in any degree to cross your flesh; you serve God with mere words, (whether of your own conceiving or of others' prescribing,) with some forced acknowledgment of that God that hath not your hearts or lives. Let Christ pass the sentence on you, and not I: Matt. xv. 7—9; "Ye hypocrites, well did Esaias prophesy of you, saying, This people draweth nigh unto me with their mouth, and honoureth me with their lips; but their heart is far from me. But in vain they do worship me, teaching for doctrines the commandments of men." You like that teaching that soothes

you in your own opinions, and galleth not your consciences in the guilty place. A minister you would have, that should stand like an adorned idol that hurts nobody, and toucheth not your sores; or that is but like a pair of organs, or a tinkling cymbal, to tickle your fancy, and make church worship to be as a kind of religious stage-play to you. But a true minister of Christ, to open to you the doctrine of the kingdom, and roundly to awaken you from security in sin, and to call you up to the most serious, holy, heavenly life, and follow you, and let you take no rest, till you yield and practise it; and to call you to open confession of your open scandalous sins, that you may make such reparation to the wronged honour of God and souls of men, as you are capable of; and accordingly to absolve you, or to bind you over to answer it at the bar of God, and charge the church to avoid communion with you, if you are impenitent and incorrigible; such a minister as this (which is the minister of Christ's appointment) you abhor; at least, when he comes to touch your sores. Then you are too proud to be taught and ruled by such as these, though you hypocritically profess to be ruled by Christ, who ruleth his church by his Spirit, word, and ministers, conjunct. Then you say, Who gave you authority to do thus and thus by me? As if you knew not that Christ in Scripture hath described, confirmed, and limited the ministerial office. Like condemned traitors, that should say to him that bringeth them a pardon, Who gave you authority to make so bold with me? or like a man that hath the plague or leprosy, that asketh the physician, Who gave you authority to tell me that I am sick, and put me to such medicines as these? or as the Israelite to Moses, (Exod. ii. 14,) "Who made thee a prince and a judge over us?" "not understanding that God by his hand would deliver them," saith Stephen, Acts vii. 25; or as the Jews to Christ, when he was teaching men the way to heaven, Matt. xxi. 23, "By what authority doest thou these things? and who gave thee this authority?" So because you hate the way of your recovery, you will not be saved without authority, nor be satisfied of their authority that would save you, but are like a beggar that should proudly refuse a piece of gold, and ask, By what authority do you give it me? A minister that agreeth with God's description you cannot abide, Acts xx. 18—36; Heb. xiii. 7, 17; 1 Cor. iv. 1; 1 Thess. v. 12, 13; 1 Tim. v. 17, 20, and 2 Tim. iv. 1. So that, indeed, it is but a mock-minister, a mock-sacrament, a mock-prayer, and so a seeming, vain religion which you desire.

7. Lastly, you pretend also to sincere obedience. If we ask you whether you are willing to obey God? you will say, God forbid that any should deny it. But when it comes to the particulars, and you find that he commandeth you that which flesh and blood is against, and would cost you the loss of worldly prosperity, then you will be excused: and yet, that you may cheat your souls, you will not professedly disobey; but you will persuade yourselves that it is no duty, and that God would not have you do that which you will not do. Like a countryman's servant, that promiseth to do all that his master bids him; but when he cometh to particulars, thrashing is too hard work, and mowing and reaping are beyond his strength, and ploughing is too toilsome; and in conclusion, it is only an idle life, with some easy chars, that he will be brought to. This is the hypocrite's obedience. He will obey God in all things, as far as he is able, in the general: but when it comes to particulars, to deny himself, and forsake his worldly prosperity for Christ, and to contemn the world, and live by faith, and converse in heaven, and walk with God, and worship him in spirit and truth, to love an enemy, to forgive all wrongs, to humble himself to the meanest persons, and to the lowest works; to confess his faults with shame and sorrow, and ask forgiveness of those he has injured; these and other such works as these he will not believe to be parts of obedience, or at least, will not be brought to do them.

Poor souls, I have stood here a great while to hold you the glass, in which, if you were willing, you might see yourselves. But if you will yet wink, and hate the light, and perish in your self-deceiving, who can help it?

Briefly and plainly, be it known to thee again, whoever thou art that hearest this, that if thou have not these five characters following, thy religion is all but vain and self-deceiving.

1. If God's authority, as he speaketh by his Spirit, word, and ministers, be not highest with thy soul, and cannot do more with thee than kings and parliaments, and than the world and flesh, Matt. xxiii. 8—10.

2. If the unseen everlasting glory be not practically more esteemed by thee, and chosen, and sought, than any thing or all things in the world, Matt. vi. 21; Col. iii. 2; John vi. 27; 2 Tim. iv. 8, 9; Matt. xxii. 5; Luke xviii. 22, 23; Phil. iii. 20.

3. If thou see not such a loveliness in holiness, as being the image of God, as that thou unfeignedly desirest the highest degree of it, Matt. v. 20; Psal. cxix. 1—3, &c.; Phil. iii. 12—14.

4. If any sin be so sweet and dear to you, or seem so necessary, that you consent not and desire not to let it go, Matt. xix. 22; Phil. iii. 8; Psal. lxvi. 18.

5. If any known duty seem so costly, dangerous, troublesome, and unpleasant, that ordinarily you will not do it, Matt. xvi. 24—26; Psal. cxix. 6.

In a word, God must be loved and obeyed as God; Christ must be entertained as Christ; heaven must be valued and sought as heaven; and holiness loved and practised as holiness; though not to the height of their proper worth, (which none on earth is able to reach,) yet so, as that nothing be preferred before them.

But yet there is one more discovery, which, if I pass by, you will think I balk a chief part of my text.

An unbridled tongue in a professor of religion is enough to prove his religion vain.

By an unbridled tongue is not meant all the sins of our speech. "If any man offend not in word, the same is a perfect man, and able also to bridle the whole body. For in many things we offend all," Jam. iii. 2. Every unwarrantable jest, or angry word, or hasty, rash expression, is not enough to prove a man's religion to be in vain. Though Christ says that we shall "answer for every idle word," he doth not say, "we shall be condemned for every idle word." But when the tongue is unbridled, and is not kept under a holy law, but suffered to be the ordinary instrument of wilful known sin, or of gross sin, which men might know and will not; this proves the person void of holiness, and, consequently, his religion vain.

It is true, every hypocrite hath not an unbridled tongue: some of them have the bridle of moral precepts, and some of religious education, and some of the presence and awe of persons whom they esteem; common knowledge, with natural mansuetude and moderation, doth bridle the tongues of many a hypocrite: but as every wicked man is not a drunkard or fornicator, and yet every drunkard or fornicator (that liveth in it) is a wicked man; so every hypocrite hath not an unbridled tongue, (his vice may be some other way,) but every man that hath an unbridled tongue is a hypocrite, if withal he profess himself a christian.

The sins of the tongue are of three sorts. 1. Such as are against piety. 2. Such as are against justice. 3. Such as are against charity.

1. Against piety, that is, directly against God, are blasphemy, perjury, rash swearing, swearing by creatures, light and unreverent using of God's name and attributes, and words and works; pleading for false doctrine, or false worship, disputing against truth and duty; scorning at godliness, or reasoning against it. These and such impieties of the tongue, are the evidences of profaneness in the speaker's heart; though some of them much more than others; and if the tongue is not here bridled, all is in vain.

2. Sinful speeches against justice and charity are these:—reproaching parents, or governors, or neighbours; railing and reviling, cursing, provoking others to do mischief, or commit any sin, disputing against and dissuading men from truth and duty; and hindering them by your speeches from a holy life, and the means of their salvation; calling good, evil, and evil, good; lying, slandering, false-witness bearing, backbiting; extenuating men's virtues, and aggravating their faults beyond the certain apparent truth; receiving, and reciting, and carrying on evil reports, which you know not to be true; endeavouring to cool men's love to others, by making them seem bad, when we cannot prove it; mentioning men's faults and failings without a call and just occasion; unchaste, immodest, ribald speeches; cheating and deceitful words to wrong others in their estates; with other such like.

But undoubtedly that sin of the tongue which the apostle here had particular respect to, was the reproaching of fellow-christians, especially upon the occasion of some differences of judgment and practice in the smaller matters of religion. The judaizing christians gave liberty to their tongues to reproach those that refused the use of those ceremonies which they used themselves, and placed much of their religion in; the quarrel was the same that was decided by the apostles, Acts xv. and by Paul, Rom xiv. and xv. and throughout the epistle to the Galatians. And this is the religion that James calls vain here, which was much placed in ceremonies, with a pretence of highest knowledge, and a censorious vilifying of all that would not do as they.

There are especially three sorts that use to reproach each other about the matters of religion.

1. Those that are hardened to that height of impiety, as to make a mock at seriousness and diligence in the practice of christianity itself, hating and reproaching them that dare not sell their souls at as base a price as they.

2. Those that have so far extinguished charity by faction and self-conceit, as to confine their love and honour to their party, and to speak evil of those that are not of their own opinions.

3. Those that give liberty to their tongues unseasonably, unmeasurably, or unwarrantably to speak hardly of those that they suffer by upon religious accounts; though, perhaps, they are their superiors whom they are bound to honour.

1. The first sort are arrived at such a measure of maliciousness and misery, that they are as mad men, the objects of compassion to all men save themselves. Their sin and misery is so notorious, that I need not say anything to discover it to others that have anything of reason and true religion; and for themselves, being so far forsaken of God, as to hate and reproach the means of their salvation, no wonder if withal they are given over to that blindness as not to understand the words that should convince them, and neither to see their shame, nor the light that would discover it; and to such impenitency, as not to feel or fear the wrath and threatenings of the Almighty; but boldly to rage on, till hell hath brought them to their wits. Prov. xiv. 16, "A wise man feareth, and departeth from evil; but the fool rageth, and is confident." Yet this much, briefly, I shall say to these, if any of them be this day my auditors, that I may not leave them as utterly past hope.

1. Thou art one of the most self-condemned, stigmatized slaves of Satan, in the world. Thou bearest openly so undoubted a brand of wickedness, that there is no room for any rational hope in thyself, or any of thy friends, that ever thou shouldst be saved, if thou die in such a state; some hope is left that yet thou mayst be converted, but none that thou shouldst be saved without conversion. It is possible with God that can do all things, that yet thy wilful blindness may be cured, and thy tongue may unsay all that thou hast said; and thou mayst cry out of thy folly, and cry shame against thyself, for that which now thou gloriest in. It is possible for God of such a stone to make a child of Abraham; and to melt that hardened heart of thine, and lay it bleeding at the feet of Christ; and to make thee wish with tears or groans, that such thoughts had never entered into thy heart, nor such words of malice proceeded from thy mouth. And happy art thou, if God will have so much mercy on thee, that hast derided mercy, as to vouchsafe thee such a change. And pray for it, and pray hard, and pray again, if thou love thy soul; for this is thy hope, and thou hast no other. For that ever such a wretch as thou shouldst be saved, in the state that now thou art in, is as impossible as for God to lie, and as impossible as for the devils to be saved. I wonder (but that such a forsaken soul is a senseless block, and as a lifeless carcass) that thou dost not quake with the fears of hell, which way ever thou goest; and that thou art not still thinking whither thou art going, and how the devils are ready to take thy soul as soon as death hath opened the door and let it out into eternity! As carelessly or scornfully as thou sittest here, I wonder that thou dost not tremble to consider, where it is that thou must shortly be, and where thou must abide for ever. It is one of the most notable discoveries of the powerful craft of Satan, that he is able to keep such a garrison as thy heart in so much peace, and to quiet a poor wretch that is uncertain to be one hour out of hell! that thy sleep is not broken with terrible dreams, and that thou dost not eat thy meat in terrors, and that ever a smile should be seen in thy face! that thy business, or company, or sports, or pleasures, should once put out of thy mind thy endless misery. While I am speaking, and thou art hearing, hell-fire is burning, and the devils are waiting, and thy blinded soul is posting on, and, for aught thou knowest, may be there this night. Poor sinner! for my part, I know thee not! and, therefore, cannot justly be suspected to bear thee any ill will, or to speak these words with a desire of thy hurt. I know this is language that the guilty do not love to hear. But I must tell thee, who reproachest or deridest a serious, holy life, that, except the blasphemers of the Holy Ghost, there are few in the world in more certain misery than thou. Other sinners, though miserable, may have some cloak to hide their misery. Though the drunkard shall not enter into heaven, he may flatter himself with the remembrance that Noah was once overtaken with that sin. Though the fornicator or adulterer shall not enter into the kingdom of God, (Eph. v. 5,) he may cheat himself awhile with the

remembrance of David's guilt. Though the false-hearted, temporizing, self-saving hypocrite shall not be saved, he may deceive himself by the instance of Peter's denying his Master, and his dissimulation, Gal. ii. But what cloak hast thou to hide thy misery? Did ever any true disciple of Christ either hate or reproach his servants and his ways? What godly man hath made a mock at godliness (unless it were when he was ungodly)? If any should think that an act of drunkenness or fornication might consist with grace, no man that understands himself can think that a scorner at a holy life hath himself the holiness which he scorneth! I would not for a world be in the case of that wretch, that speaks well of holiness in others, while he lives in fornication, luxury, or worldliness himself, though he think that he cuts scores by daily crying to God for mercy. But I would much less for a thousand worlds be in the case of him that neither is godly, nor can speak well of it; that is not only void of the Spirit of Christ, but speaks against it; that is not only void of the holy image of God, but hateth it, and reproacheth it in others. Oh rather let me have no tongue to speak, no soul to think, than ever I should speak or think thus maliciously of the image, and ways, and servants of the Lord! I had rather be a dog, or a toad, than one of those men that use to mock at serious, diligent serving of the Lord, or that maliciously reproach his servants, and bend their wits and tongues against them; so legibly is the mark of the devil upon them, that I must needs tell you that are true believers, you are much to be blamed that you look not on them with more compassion, and weep not for them, as for men that are within a step of hell, when you hear them rail at the laws or servants of the Lord. I mean those of whom the apostle saith, "For many walk, of whom I have told you often, and now tell you, even weeping, that they are the enemies of the cross of Christ, (that is, to the self-denying mortified state of christians, and following him even through sufferings,) whose end is destruction, whose God is their belly, and whose glory is in their shame, who mind earthly things," Phil. iii. 18, 19. "That not only do wickedly, but teach men so to do," Matt. v. 19; "and have pleasure in them that do it," Rom. i. 32; "and think it strange that we run not with them to the same excess of riot, speaking evil of us, who shall give account to him that is ready to judge the quick and the dead," 1 Pet. iv. 4, 5.

2. Thou bearest most eminently the image of the devil, and most expressly speakest his mind, and art most openly employed in his works. What is the devil but an apostate spirit, filled with enmity against God and his servants, and hating holiness; the malicious accuser of the brethren, slandering and reproaching them, and seeking their destruction! And shall a malicious, lying sinner live, that imitateth Satan in his enmity to God? Oh that thou knewest whom thou servest! and that thou knewest whom thou speakest against! Woe be to him that striveth with his Maker! Isa. xlv. 2. It is hard for thee to kick against the pricks, Acts ix. 5. Whoever hardened himself against him, and hath prospered? Job ix. 4. If Satan were to speak with open face, what would he say, but as the tongues of the malicious enemies of holiness do; even to speak evil of the ways and servants of the Lord? Might he appear and speak himself in the assemblies and councils of the great ones of the earth, he would speak against the same men, and to the same purpose, as those that I have described. Your tongues are his instruments. You speak what he secretly suggesteth, as verily as if he had written you your instructions, and you had read it in his words: he hateth holiness, and, therefore, he tempteth you to hate it. He would bring it into hatred in the world, and, therefore, he speaks disgracefully of it by your tongues. His will is your will; and your words are his words; and the pleasantest music that you could make him. Oh how it pleaseth him to make a reasonable creature reproach the word and ways of his Creator! How eager was he to have got Job to have spoken evil of God!

3. Be it known to thee, thou reviler, that if ever thou be saved thyself, it must be in that way that thou revilest. Thy hope lieth in it. As sure as thou livest, there is no other way to life eternal. Without holiness none shall see God, Heb. xii. 14. Blessed are the pure in heart, for they shall see God, Matt. v. 8. When thou hast done all, thou must come back, and go that way thyself, or burn for ever. Either thou must be such as those that thou dost speak against, or thou art everlastingly undone. And if thou think to be such a one thyself, and to come to heaven by the very way that now thou dost revile, canst thou yet revile it? And if thou perish in hell for want of holiness, thou shalt then have enough of thy rebellion. Then thou shalt cry out against thy own malicious reproaches a thousand times more than ever thou didst against the servants of the Lord. Though the very distinction between the godly and ungodly be now thy scorn, yet I shall be bold to tell thee, in the words of Enoch, yea of God, Jude 14, 16, "Behold, the Lord cometh with ten thousands of his saints, to execute judgment upon all, and to convince all that are ungodly among them, of all their ungodly deeds which they have ungodly committed, and of all their hard speeches which ungodly sinners have spoken against him." Now you have your day, and judgment must begin at the house of God. And if it first begin at us, what shall the end be of them that obey not the gospel of God? And if the righteous scarce be saved, where shall the ungodly and the sinner appear? 1 Pet. iv. 17, 18. "Blessed is the man that walketh not in the counsel of the ungodly, nor standeth in the way of sinners, nor sitteth in the seat of the scornful! But his delight is in the law of the Lord; and in his law doth he meditate day and night. The ungodly are not so: but like the chaff which the wind driveth away: therefore the ungodly shall not stand in the judgment, nor sinners in the congregation of the righteous; for the Lord knoweth the way of the righteous, but the way of the ungodly shall perish," Psa. i. This is Scripture distinction, which God will make good.

I make no question, but the worst of you will put by all this in your self-deceit, and say, It is not holiness that we speak against, but it is hypocrisy, or schism; or some such accusation that malice shall suggest will be your mask. But will you answer me these few questions.

Quest. 1. Why then do you not imitate them so far as they do well? Why are you not as much in works of holiness as they? in reading, and meditating on the word of God, in holy conference, and secret prayer, and instructing your families, &c.? And then leave them, and spare not where they do amiss.

Quest. 2. Why do you not hate as much the sins of the notoriously ungodly, who show them without shame? Nay, why do you make such men your companions?

Quest. 3. Why go you to the heart, that is unseen, and arrogate the prerogative of God, to censure men of hypocrisy, and such secret sins that are out of your discerning? If you know your heart by outward actions, insist upon your proofs.

Quest. 4. Why speak you not of their good as well

as of the supposed evil? Why are you not more in speaking well of what is well, than in speaking ill of what is ill?

Quest. 5. Why is it that you speak of men that you know not? and of others that are innocent, for the sake of those you imagine to be guilty? And why do you so greedily snatch at any matter of reproach, and take it by hearsay from the most ignorant, rash, or malicious mouths?

Quest. 6. If it be hypocrisy, or other vice, that you so hate, why do you not hate them in yourselves? Why live you so viciously while you profess obedience to the Lord? And why do you take on you to believe a heaven and hell hereafter, and to give up yourselves in covenant to God, and live so contrary to that professed belief and covenant?

Quest. 7. Do you not feel that it is partly malice, and partly the recrimination of a guilty galled conscience, that fain would steal a little peace by thinking others to be as bad as you?

I shall dismiss this unhappy sort of men with these two requests: 1. You are the men that of all others have the most notable advantage from your conviction, of the misery of your present state; and therefore, I beseech you, take that advantage. One would think it should be the easiest matter in the world, for such as you to know that you are ungodly, that hate godliness and oppose it. You have no plausible pretence for self-flattery or self-deceit. And therefore confess your misery, and look out to Christ for help and pardon, while there is hope and time.

2. For the time to come, will you but try a serious, holy life before you speak against it any more? For shame, speak not evil of the things you know not, as those brutes described, Jude 10. And holiness was never well known but by experience. Oh that you would be entreated but to yield this most equal motion! Away with your worldly, fleshly lives; and live in faith and holiness, a just, a spiritual, and a heavenly life, but one year, or one quarter, or one month, and then if, by experience, you find just cause for it, reproach a holy life, and spare not.

II. To the second sort, (that speak evil of men upon differences of opinion, especially while they profess the same religion, in all the essential, necessary parts,) I shall propose these aggravations of their sin, for their humiliation.

1. Consider, can you think it agreeable to the law of Christ, to reproach men behind their backs, and unheard, for that which you never soberly and christianly told them to their faces? Did you lovingly first admonish them, and impartially hear what they can say for themselves? What is your end in speaking against your brother? Is it to do him hurt, or good? If hurt, be sure you do him justice; and backbiting is not the way of justice. If good, you cross your own intention. For what good can it do him, that another hears evil spoken of?

2. If you are Christ's disciples, it must be known to all men by your special love to one another, John xiii. 25. And is reproach and evil-speaking the fruit or evidence of such love? Can you talk so of the friends that are most dear to you, or that you love indeed? How do our hearts rise against that man, that speaks reproachfully of our dearest friends! Love would scarce suffer you to endure such abuse of christians in another, without a serious reprehension; much less to be the abuser of them yourselves.

3. Your evil speaking of your brethren destroyeth love in others, as it proves the want of it in yourselves. And to destroy their love is to destroy their souls. You do your worst to quench the love, both of him that you speak evil of, and of them to whom you speak it. Good is the object of love; and therefore to speak well of men, and manifest them to be lovely, is the only way to make them loved. Evil is the object of hatred; and therefore to speak evil of them, is to make them seem hateful, and draw men to the guilt of hating them. To praise a man will do more to make him loved, than if you only entreat another to love him; and to dispraise a man will do more to make him hated, than if you directly persuade another to hate him. And what service you do the devil, and what disservice unto Christ, by destroying love, and sowing hatred among his servants, were you impartial you might easily discern.

4. Is it not shame and pity, that the followers of Christ should imitate the devil, and ungodly men, as by detraction and reviling words they do? You aggravate your brethren's faults; and find faults where there are none; and so do Satan and ungodly men. You have a secret desire to make them seem contemptible and vile; and so have Satan and ungodly men. And hereby you seem to justify the wicked, and encourage them in their reproaching. They think they may boldly speak such a language of you all, as they hear you speak of one another. Oh what pity is it to hear the professed children of the Lord, to use the hell-bred language of his enemies, as if they had gone to school to Satan!

5. Are there not tongues enough sharpened against us in the world, but we must wound each other with our own? Is it not enough, if we are the seed of Christ, that every where the serpent's seed do hate us; and that all manner of evil is falsely spoken of us, and that we are made as the scorn and the offscouring of all things, but we must also hate and reproach each other? Have you not load enough from the world? Have you not enemies enough to do the work of enemies, but friends must do it? And hath not Satan instruments and tongues enough of his own, but we must use those that are Christ's against himself?

6. If thou hate thy brother, yet sure thou dost not hate thyself. Why then dost thou hurt and shame thyself? His hurt is but to be defamed, which is little, if any thing at all (for it is much in himself whether it shall hurt him). But thy hurt that doeth it, is to provoke God against thee, and incur his wrath, and wound thy soul by the guilt of sin. And if another hurt thee in the heel, wilt thou therefore stab thyself to the heart? If another be bad, wilt thou become so by unjust defaming him? And how dost thou cross thine own intentions! The stone that thou castest at him, flies back in thy face. Thou proclaimest thy own transgression and shame, when thou art uncharitably proclaiming his. Is not a backbiter, a reviler, is not a malicious calumniator, a worse name (which thou takest to thyself) than that which thou canst fasten on him whom thou dost reproach?

7. Thy uncharitable speeches are a dangerous sign of an unhumbled and unpardoned soul. If thou canst not forgive, thou art not forgiven. Did you know yourselves, it would teach you to deal more compassionately with others. You would have the act of oblivion as extensive as you could, if you knew what danger you are in yourselves. Do you not know as much by yourselves as you have to reproach your brother with? Do you not then invite both God and man to take you at the worst, and use you as you use your brother? Methinks you should rather be desirous of a more tender and indulgent way, as knowing what need yourselves have of it.

If you say, O but he hath done thus and thus against me. Let conscience say what you have done yourselves against God and others. If you say, he is a schismatic, a hypocrite, or this or that; remember that malice is blind, and never wants matter of accusation or reproach, and innocency is no defence against it: else Christ and his prophets and apostles had been better used by the world. And ask conscience whether more than you can truly say of him, may not be said against yourselves. If all such must be defamed, how infamous will you be!

8. If you will speak ill, you must hear ill. You teach men how to use you. *Si mihi pergit quæ vult dicere, quæ non vult audiet.*

Benedictis si certasset, audisset bene, saith the comedian. And God usually in justice suffereth it to be. And as those that by violence trample down others, when they feel themselves on the higher ground, do oft live to be trampled on themselves; so those that take their advantages to insult and defame others, do usually live to be defamed. "For with what measure you mete, it shall be measured to you again. Judge not therefore, that ye be not judged," Matt. vii. 1, 2.

To which of these two former ranks you should refer the common names of scorn that religious persons have been most loaded with among us, you must judge by the particular occasion and person. It is not my intention or desire to plead for any faction, disobedience, irregularity, or hypocrisy; much less to palliate heresies or odious crimes that are cloaked with the name or profession of religion. It is the hypocrite that I am all this while detecting. But I must say that it hath been the highest brand or character of hypocrisy and impudent profaneness conjunct; and one of the most crying transgressions of this land, that men, baptized into the name of Christ, have made a scorn at the diligent serving of him, and lived in the hatred of that religion in the life and practice, which themselves profess. And that if upon some small circumstantial differences, any of their superiors have encouraged them to use any nickname of reproach against their most conscientious brethren, they have been glad of the occasion, and used those reproaches against the serious practice of religion, which others pretend to use only against men's different opinions, which they account their exorbitancies or mistakes. How the names of zealots, precisians, puritans, and such like, have been used in this land; and what sort of people have been made thereby (and by the discountenance of those that have cherished a diligent, holy life) to be the common scorn; and how great a hinderance this hath proved to the salvation of many thousand souls, is a thing that is much more sad to mention than difficult to prove. And when one nickname is grown out of use, the serpentine enmity watcheth for the opportunity that is afforded by differences and discountenance of the times, to take up another that may have a sharper sting. The dead form of religion, and as much as you will of words and shows, they can reverence or endure; but life, and seriousness, and practice, is the thing they hate. Just like a bear, or other ravenous creature, that will let their prey alone while it seems dead and stirs not; but if it stir, they leap upon it, and tear it into pieces. And therefore it is that the diligent, zealous exercise of religion among the papists, by images, and tautologies, and lifeless ceremonies and forms, is not half so much hated or reproached by the vulgar, as the serious exercise of unquestionable duties, that all are in words agreed in, is here with us. To pray in our families; to instruct our children or servants in the necessary points of faith and duty; to exhort a drunkard, a swearer, a covetous person, or other ungodly ones to repent, and to give up themselves to a holy life; to take up any serious speech of death and judgment, and the life to come, and the necessary preparations thereto; these and such like are the odious marks of a zealot, a precisian, or puritan, with the ungodly rabble: so that serving the great and glorious God is with them become a matter of scorn; while serving the devil is taken for their glory, if they can but do it in the plausible, less disgraceful mode.

But because some of the chief accusers of the brethren would needs persuade men, that the ordinary usage of the forementioned nicknames hath been less impious and more justifiable, against a sort of people only whom they feign to be unfit for human society, I shall only appeal now to the godly bishops, and conformable ministers, that mention it.

Bishop G. Downame, (who, though he hath written so much for bishops, hath written as much to prove the pope to be the antichrist,) in his sermon called Abraham's Trial, p. 72, saith: "And even in these times, the godly live among such a generation of men, as that if a man do but labour to keep a good conscience in any measure, though he meddle not with matters of state, or discipline, or ceremonies, (as for example, if a minister diligently preach, or in his preaching seek to profit, rather than to please, &c.; or if a private christian makes conscience of swearing, sanctifying the sabbath, frequenting sermons, or abstaining from the common corruptions of the time,) he shall straightway be condemned for a puritan, and consequently be less favoured, than either a carnal gospeller, or a close papist," &c. Such were the times then.

Dr. Robert Abbot, public professor of divinity in Oxford, and after bishop of Salisbury, in a sermon on Easter-day, 1615, saith: "That men under pretence of truth, and preaching against the puritans, strike at the heart and root of faith and religion, now established among us: that this preaching against the puritans was but the practice of Parson's and Campian's counsel, when they came into England to seduce young students; and when many of them were afraid to lose their places if they should professedly be thus, the counsel they then gave them was, that they should speak freely against the puritans, and that should suffice," &c. So he.

Of Archbishop Laud's tract of doctrinal puritanism, drawn up for, and presented to, the Duke of Buckingham, see Pryne, in his Tryal, p. 156. Divers bishops have affirmed that the Jesuits were the masters of this nickname here in England, and the promoters of it.

But of the common sense of this word, and the use of it, I shall now call in no more witnesses but Mr. Robert Bolton, a man that frequently published his judgment for conformity to prelacy and ceremonies; in his Discourse of Happiness, p. 163, he thus speaketh:

"I am persuaded there was never poor persecuted word, since malice against God first seized on the damned angels, and the graces of heaven dwelt in the heart of man, that passed through the mouths of all sorts of unregenerate men, with more distastefulness and gnashing of teeth, than the name of puritan doth at this day; which notwithstanding as it is now commonly meant, (N. B.) and ordinarily proceeds from the spleen and spirit of profaneness and good fellowship, as an honourable nickname, that I may so speak, of christianity and grace. And yet for all this I dare say, that there is none of them all, but when they shall come unto their beds of death, and are to grapple immediately with the painful terrors of the king of fears, and to stand or fall to the dreadful tribunal of the living God,—then (except the Lord suffer them to fall into the fiery lake with senseless hearts and seared consciences) would give ten thousand worlds, were they all turned into gold, pleasures, and imperial crowns, to change their former courses of vanity, &c. into a life of holy preciseness, strictness, sincerity, and salvation. Oh! when the heavens shall shrivel together like a scroll, and the whole frame of nature flame about their ears; when the great and mighty hills shall start out of their places like frighted men; and the fearful reprobate cry and call upon this mountain, and that rock, to fall upon him; when as no dromedary of Egypt, nor wings of the morning, shall be able to carry them out of the reach of thy revenging hand; no top of Carmel, no depth of sea, or bottom of hell, to hide them from the presence of him that sits upon the throne, and from the wrath of the Lamb; no rock, nor mountain, nor the great body of the whole earth, to cover them from that unresistible power that laid the foundations of them; no arm of flesh, or armies of angels, to protect them from those infinite rivers of brimstone which shall be kept in everlasting flames by the anger of God, when their poor and woeful souls shall infinitely desire, rather to return into the loathed darkness of not being, and to be hid for ever in the most abhorred state of annihilation, than now to become the everlasting objects of that unquenchable wrath, which they shall never be able to avoid or to abide, and to be chained up by the omnipotent hand of God among the damned spirits, in a place of flames and perpetual darkness, where is torment without end, and past imagination: I say, at that dreadful day (and that day will come) what do you think they would give for part in that purity which now they persecute? and for the comforts of true-hearted holiness that now they hate, and yet without which (as it will clearly appear, when matters are brought before that high and everlasting Judge) none shall ever see the Lord, or dwell in the joys of eternity? Nay, I verily think there are no desperate despisers of godliness, or formal opposites to grace, which do now hold holiness to be hypocrisy, sanctification singularity, practice of sincerity too much preciseness,—but when the pit of destruction hath once shut her mouth upon them, and they are sunk irrecoverably into that dungeon of fire, would be content, with all their hearts, to live a million of years as precisely as ever saint did upon earth—to redeem but one moment of that torment." So p. 159. "The common conceit of these men is, that civil, honest men are in the state of grace, and that formal professors are very forward, and without exception; but true christians indeed are puritans, irregularists, exorbitants, transcendants to that ordinary pitch of formal piety, which in their carnal comprehensions they hold high enough for heaven: they either conceit them to be hypocrites, and so the only objects for the exercise of their ministerial severity, and the terrors of God; or else, though the Lord may at last pardon perhaps their singularities and excesses of zeal, yet in the mean time, they dissweeten and vex the comforts and glory of this life, with much unnecessary strictness and abridgment.

"Now, of all others, such prophets as these are the only men with the formal hypocrite, exactly fitted and suitable to his humour; for however they may sometimes declaim boisterously (N. B.) against gross and visible abomination, (and that is well,) yet they are no searchers into, nor censurers of, the state of formality; and therefore do rather secretly encourage him to sit faster upon that sandy foundation, than help to draw him forward to more forwardness," &c.

See also his description of a puritan, p. 132.

So, in his Direction for Walking with God, p. 172. "Good-fellow meetings and ale-house revellings, are the drunkard's delight: but all the while he sits at it, he is perhaps in a bodily fear of the puritan constable."

Many such passages tell you how the word puritan was commonly interpreted in Oxford, Northamptonshire, and wherever learned and holy Mr. Bolton was acquainted.

And having mentioned his testimony of the use of the word, I shall add somewhat of his discovery of this spirit of malignity and detraction that worketh in the anti-puritans. In his Discourse of Happiness, p. 190, he saith:—

"The reverence and respectful carriage to godly ministers, which may sometimes be found in the formal hypocrite, doth grow towards distaste and disaffection, when they press them by the powerful sense, and piercing application of some quickening scriptures, to a fervency in spirit, purity of heart, preciseness in their walking, supernatural singularity above ordinary and moral perfections, excellency of zeal, and a sacred violence in pursuit of the crown of life; to a holy strictness, extraordinary striving to enter in at the strait gate, and transcendent eminency over the formal righteousness of the scribes and Pharisees, to a nearer familiarity with God by prayer, daily examination of conscience, private humiliations, meditation upon the endless duration in a second life; to a narrow watch over the stirrings and imaginations of the heart, and expression of holiness in all the passages of both their callings, &c.—Points and ponderations of which nature are ordinarily to him as so many secret seeds of indignation, and many times breed in his formal heart, cold affections, exasperation, and estrangement, if not meditation of persecution and revenge. Sanctification, preciseness, purity, holiness, zeal, strictness, power of godliness, spiritual men, holy brethren, saints in Christ, communion of christians, godly conferences, conceived prayers, sanctifying the sabbath, family exercises, exercise of fasting, and mortifying humiliations, and such like; are commonly to men of this temporizing temper, and luke-warm constitution, terms of secret terror and open taunting. And sometimes they villanously sport themselves with them, and make them the matter of their hateful and accursed jests, that so they may keep under as much as they can, in disestimation and contempt, the faithful professors and practisers thereof, whom naturally they heartily hate, and also seem thereby to bear out the heartless flourishes of their own formality with greater bravery. Hereupon it is, that if they take a child of God but tripping in the least infirmity, (against which too, perhaps, he strives and prays with many tears, &c.) slipping only in some unadvised precipitant passage of his negociations, &c.—O then they take on unmeasurably! then they cry out, These are your men of the Spirit; these are the holy brethren; these are your precise fellows; these are they which make such show of purity and forwardness! You see now what they are, when matters come out, and their dealings are discovered, when it comes to the trial indeed, or to a matter of commodity, &c. Are they not proud? are they not malicious? are they not hard-hearted and covetous as well as others? &c. When by the mercies of God (in their sense) they are neither so nor so; but such censures as these are very often the mere evaporations of pure malice, and the bitter ebullitions and overflowings of their gall," &c.

And p. 164. "The ordinary conceit which unregenerate men entertain of these (experimental ministers) is—that they are troublers of Israel, preachers of terror, transgressors of policy, unfit to prophesy at court, or in the king's chapel, pestilent fellows, seditioners, factionists, born only to disquiet the world and vex men's consciences.—In these days of ours especially, which are strangely profane, and desperately naught, in what man soever the power of grace, undaunted zeal, resolute sincerity, are more working, eminent, and remarkable, ordinarily the more and more implacable, outrageous, and inflamed opposites shall that man find, wheresoever he lives."

And p. 10. "The formal hypocrite is moved to think his state good, and the way of his life to be right, from a prejudice which he conceives from the imputations which the world layeth upon the children of God; such as are pride, hypocrisy, singularity, melancholy, simplicity," &c.

Page 38. "His form of godliness in his conceit is the only true state of salvation: whatsoever is short of him is profaneness; whatsoever is above him is preciseness. But, when upon his death-bed, he awaketh."

And Direct. for Walk. p. 131. "The more forward he is in the narrow way, the more furiously is he persecuted by the spite of tongues: the most resolute for God's glory, and in good causes, is ordinarily most railed against, and reviled. The foul spirit of good fellowship, as they call it, is still foaming out against God's chiefest favourites the foulest censures: that they are hypocrites, humorists, factionists, traitors, pestilent fellows, and all that is naught. —There is no creature that ever God made, not Satan himself excepted, which is more maliciously set against and censured than good men. Neither should any have so bad a name as they, could the hellish mists of virulent tongues obscure and stain the glory of their reputation."

And p. 43. "At this day, professors of the gracious way be in greatest disgrace with the most; and a drunkard, and swaggering good fellow, a usurer, a son or daughter of Belial, shall find more favour, applause, and approbation with the world, than a man which makes conscience of his ways," &c.

Page 350. "They cry, These forward professors will all turn fantastical, familists, anabaptists, Arians, any thing; which cry awakes the state of jealousy, and so, by an unworthy consequent, draws upon those who are true of heart, even God's best servants, and the king's best subjects, discountenance, suspicions, if not molestations, unnecessarily, causelessly."

And p. 351, 352, out of Austin's Epistles, 137, he shows, that it was so in his time. "They every way and infinitely labour, that when some professors of holiness have foully fallen indeed, or be only so slandered, the world would believe that they are all such; do you not think in his time the world did thus exult and exclaim, or in the like manner, upon Lot's fall? Here now you see puritan Lot, who could not endure the good fellowship of the Sodomites, he is now himself seized on by incest: they are all such, I warrant you:" citing Du Barta's translation by Silvester, p. 412,

> "Base, busy stranger! com'st thou hither thus
> Controller-like, to prate and preach to us?
> No, puritan, thou shalt not here do so," &c.

Thus you hear, from a conformable divine, how men calling themselves christians, and being (some of them) formally religious, do prove themselves self-deceiving hypocrites, by their unbridled tongues, in reviling at those as puritans, and too precise, that will not be self-deceiving formalists as well as they. I shall only add some of Bishop Hall's characters of a hypocrite, that you may see what formality is in the judgment of knowing men.

Page 169. "Walking early up into the city, he turns into the great church, and salutes one of the pillars on one knee; worshipping that God which at home he cares not for, while his eye is fixed on some window, or some passenger, and his heart knows not whither his lips go. He rises, and looking about with admiration, complains on our frozen charity, commends the ancient;—with the superfluity of his usury, he builds an hospital, and harbours them whom his extortion hath spoiled: so while he makes many beggars, he keeps some. He turneth all gnats into camels, and cares not to undo the world for a circumstance. Flesh on a Friday is more abomination to him than his neighbour's bed. He abhors more not to uncover at the name of Jesus, than to swear by the name of God," &c. So Bishop Hall.

But perhaps you will say, these persons whom you describe, that will make a mock of godliness itself, are not to be numbered with hypocrites, but with the openly profane.

To which I answer, 1. Even these profess themselves to be christians, and therefore are hypocrites when they are not what they do profess. 2. They persuade themselves that they are as truly godly as those that they reproach, and do not think that it is godliness indeed, for which they do reproach them, but for engrossing the name or reputation of godliness to themselves, and for some differing manner or way of worship. For this is one of the most notable cheats by which the devil undoes the empty, formal hypocrite; finding that this man doth own christianity in his opinion, but is void of the true spirit, and power, and life of christian religion, he raiseth some controversies between the serious christian and the hypocrite, about some controvertible points of doctrine, or about some modes or circumstances of discipline and external worship, and when they fall into two sides, the hypocrite thinks that it is but in these controversies that the difference lies. The question, thinks he, is not whether men should be regenerate, godly, and religious, but whether my way of religion or the puritan's and precisian's be better? And presently he hence concludes, that indeed it is he that is the more truly religious. For, saith he, my judgment is sound, and the puritan's is erroneous; I am of the judgment of the church, which he is against; the reverend prelates or doctors are more of my side than on his; I am for order, and he is for confusion and irreverence, and followeth the humours and fancies of his own brain. And thus the devil turneth his eye from the main difference, and makes him believe that it is these controversies that are all that sets them at a distance. But alas! man, thou overlookest the point that thy life and soul lieth on. Agree first in the serious hearty entertainment and practice of the substance of that holy truth which you are both in point of opinion agreed in, and do not condemn thyself in the things which thou allowest; contradict not thy creed and profession by thy fleshly, worldly, negligent, careless, and ungodly life, but love God with all thy heart and might, and first seek his kingdom and his righteousness, which thou confessest thou shouldst do; and then the principal difference is healed, and thou hast escaped the principal danger of thy soul, and then it is not a few circumstantial differences that will divide your hearts, or divide you from each other in the life to come. Men that differ about bishops, and ceremonies, and forms of prayer, may be all true christians, and dear to one another, and to Christ, if they be practically agreed in the life of godliness, and join in a holy, heavenly conversation. But if you agree in all your opinions and formalities, and yet were never sanctified by the truth, you do but agree to delude your souls, and neither of you will be saved for all your agreement.

III. The third sort to be spoken to, is those that let out their passion in hard speeches against superiors or others, that they think do wrong or persecute them on a religious account. At this time I will suppose the injury be real, and the complaint be just, it yet beseems not christians to revile.

1. Consider how contrary this is to the example of our Lord; and that he left us his example in this particular, with a special recommendation for our imitation. When he was falsely accused, and the high priest urged him to answer for himself, (Matt. xxvi. 62, 63,) he was silent, to show that he could bear a false accusation, without so much as vindicating his innocency by a just defence. O learn both the lesson and motives recommended to you, 1 Pet. ii. 18, to the end. "Servants, be subject to your masters with all fear, not only to the good and gentle, but also to the froward. For this is thankworthy, if a man for conscience toward God endure grief, suffering wrongfully. For what glory is it if, when ye be buffeted for your faults, ye shall take it patiently? but if, when ye do well, and suffer for it, ye take it patiently, this is acceptable with God. For even hereunto were ye called: because Christ also suffered for us, leaving us an example that we should follow his steps: who did no sin, neither was guile found in his mouth: who, when he was reviled, reviled not again; when he suffered, he threatened not, but committed himself to him that judgeth righteously." Here is the description of your duty, and your example. Are you used worse than Christ was used? Isa. liii. 7, 8, "He was oppressed, and he was afflicted, yet he opened not his mouth: he is brought as a lamb to the slaughter, and as a sheep before her shearers is dumb, so he openeth not his mouth." And if you will come to him and be his disciples, you must learn of him to be meek and lowly in heart, that you may find rest unto your souls, Matt. xi. 28, 29.

2. Consider, as our kingdom is not of this world, so we are not to strive for worldly pre-eminence, nor with carnal weapons, but must know that our greatness here is in being the least, and our dignity in being the servants of all; and our gain is by our loss, and our honour by evil reports and by disgrace, and our advancement by our debasement, and our preferment by being kept from worldly honour, and our joy by sorrow, and our exaltation by humiliation. And therefore it is contrary to our state of faith to murmur at them that deprive us of the pleasures of sense, or the ease and privileges of the flesh. Mark the description of christianity in the gospel, and see how much of it consisteth in contempt of the esteem and honours of the world, and of all the accommodations and pleasures of the flesh, because of the expectation of the unseen eternal pleasures; and in the forsaking all, and taking up our cross, and following a crucified Christ; and in patience, and meekness, and forbearing and forgiving; and rather than seek either verbal or actual revenge, to give the cloak also to him that takes away our coat, and turn the other cheek to him that smiteth us. Unmortified passion, and untamed nature, will not give some men leave to understand these passages of Christ, but they search for some such figure to expound them by as shall annihilate the plain and proper sense. Self-love so blindeth men, that when they read these gospel precepts, they feel not their consciences touched and bound by them, but they read them as if they read them not, and retain no more than if it were nonsense which they read. Had the commands aforesaid (of patience, forbearing, and forgiving) but as much force and efficacy upon the souls of most professors as the commandments have that are against swearing, and cursing, and drunkenness, and fornication; we should have much better maintained our innocency and our peace, and have more honoured our profession by showing the world christianity exemplified in its proper, genuine nature and effects.

3. Consider, it is not oppression, persecution, or hard usage that will exempt us from the obligation of the fifth commandment, which requireth us to honour our superiors, our natural, and civil, and ecclesiastical fathers. It is the evil and froward, and not only the good and the gentle, that we must honour and obey. And the reason is plain from their original end. It is not as our trustees, or agents, or friends only, that our rulers must be honoured, but as the officers of the God of heaven; nor is it only as they do good to us, but as they preserve order and justice in the world, and are the pillars of the commonwealth. If magistrates should deal never so hardly with you and me, yet still their office is of necessity to the common good. And if their office be necessary, their honour is necessary, for when they are dishonoured and despised, they are disabled. And therefore, for the common good, we must be careful to keep up the honour of our governors, even when we suffer by them ourselves. Princes were none of the best when the apostles commanded the churches to honour them, and obey them, and this not only for fear of their penalties, but for conscience' sake, Rom. xiii. 5. Of old it was they that walked after the flesh, in the lust of uncleanness, that were presumptuous and self-willed, and despised government, and were not afraid to speak evil of dignities; whereas the angels that are greater in power and might, bring not railing accusations against them before the Lord, 2 Pet. ii. 10, 11; Jude 8, 9.

4. Consider, that reviling is a tongue revenge; and revenge is God's, and he is engaged to repay, and hath commanded us not to avenge ourselves. As we must not step into the judge's tribunal whenever we think he is negligent in his administrations, so much less must we accuse God of negligence or injustice, by stepping into his throne. And though the railers of these times excuse their sin with the name of justice, they must show their commissions for the executing of that justice, before it will pass in heaven for an excuse. Is not God severe enough? will not his judgment be terrible enough? would you wish men to suffer more than he will inflict on the impenitent? what! more than hell? And will it not be soon enough? are you so hasty for so dreadful a revenge? can you not stay when the Judge is at the door? Mark both the usage and remedy of believers, in James v. 5—8. To the rich and great ones of the world he saith, "Ye have lived in pleasure on the earth, and been wanton; ye have nourished your hearts as in a day of slaughter! Ye have condemned and killed the just, and he doth not resist you." There is your usage. "Be patient, therefore, brethren, unto the coming of the Lord." There is the remedy. But must we stay so long? He thus repeateth his advice: "Be ye also patient: stablish your hearts; for the coming of the Lord draweth nigh. Let your moderation be known to all men; the Lord is at hand," Phil. iv. 5. "Shall not God avenge his own elect, that cry night and day unto him, though he bear long with them? I tell you that he will avenge them speedily," Luke

xviii. 7, 8. There is no contradiction between crying long and avenging speedily.

5. Consider what compassion, rather than reproach, you owe to those by whom you suffer. They do themselves much more hurt than they do you. Are they great? They have the more to answer for, and their fall will be the greater, James v. 1—3. If you are yourselves believers, go into the sanctuary, and ask the Scriptures what will be their end; and then deny them compassion if you can. Alas! consider they are, at the worst, but such as you were formerly yourselves as to the main. Paul makes a sad confession of his own persecution of the church, when he was before Agrippa, and doth not complain that he was himself so hardly used. "I verily thought," saith he, "with myself, that I ought to do many things contrary to the name of Jesus. Many of the saints I shut up in prison (little thinking that they were saints); I gave my voice against them, I punished them oft in every synagogue; and being exceedingly mad against them, I persecuted them," Acts xxvi. 9—12. He would not tell Agrippa that he was mad, but he might speak more freely of himself. O sirs, pity poor men who have the temptations of worldly greatness and prosperity, and must go through a camel's eye if they will come to heaven; who stand so high that sun and wind have the greatest force upon them; who see so much vanity, and little serious exemplary piety; who hear so much flattery and falsehood, and so little necessary truth, saith Seneca, *Divites cum omnia habeant, unum illis deest; scilicet, qui verum dicat: si enim in clientelam fœlicis hominis potentumque perveneris, aut veritas, aut amicitia perdenda est.* If you were in their places, you know not how far you might be prevailed against yourselves. If little temptations can make you miscarry in your places so oft and foully as you do, what would you do if you had the strongest baits of the world, and allurements of the flesh, and the most dangerous temptations that Satan could assault you with? Have you not seen of late before your eyes, how low some have fallen from high professions, and how shamefully the most promising persons have miscarried, that were lifted up and put to the trial of such temptations of prosperity as they had never been used to before? Oh! pity those that have such dangerous trials to pass through, and be thankful that you stand on safer ground; and do not cruelly envy them their perils, nor reproach them for their falls, but pray, and daily pray, for their recovery.

6. Consider this speaking evil of those by whom you suffer, hath too much of selfishness and corrupted nature in it to be good. If another suffered as you do, and you were advanced as another is, would not you speak more mildly then? Or, if not so, yet the proneness of nature to break out into reviling words, though it were for religion and for God, doth intimate to you that it hath a suspicious root. Do you find it as easy to be meek and patient, and forgive a wrong, and love an enemy? Take heed lest you serve Satan in vindicating the cause of God. It is an unfit way of serving God, to do it by breaking his commands. Read seriously the description of a contentious, hurtful, foul-tongued zeal, in James iii. and then tell me what thanks Christ will give you for it. The two great disciples, James and John, thought it would have notably honoured Christ, and curbed the raging spirit of the ungodly, if he would have let them call for fire from heaven, to consume a town that refused to receive him. But doth Christ encourage their destroying zeal? No; but he tells them, "Ye know not what spirits ye are of." They little knew how unlike to the tender, merciful, healing spirit of Christ that fiery hurting spirit was, that provoked them to that desire, nor how unpleasing their temper was to Christ. This is the very case of many thousand christians that are yet young, and green, and harsh, and have not attained to that mellowness, and sweetness, and measure of charity, that is in grown, experienced christians. They think their passions and desires of some plagues on the contemners of the gospel, are acceptable to God, and blame the charitable as too cold, when they little know what spirit it is that raiseth that storm in them, and how unlike and unacceptable it is to Christ. Were you as zealous to serve all others in love, and to stoop to their feet for their salvation, and to become all things lawful to all men, that you may win some, this saving zeal would be pleasing to your Lord; who comes to do the work of a physician, and not of a soldier, to save, and not to destroy, and therefore most approves of those that serve him most diligently in his saving work.

7. Lastly, consider, your passions and evil speakings will but increase your suffering, and make it seem just, if otherwise it were unjust. If you are not meek, you have not the promise of inheriting the earth, Matt. v. 5. If you honour not your parents or superiors, you have not the promise that your "days shall be long in the land." And your evil speaking will make men conclude that you would do evil if you could and durst; as it is said to be Zoilus's answer, when he was asked why he spoke evil of Plato, and such worthy men, *Quoniam malum facere cum velim non possum*—Because I would do them hurt and cannot. Give not occasion for such a charge.

"Finally, be ye all of one mind, having compassion one of another, love as brethren, be pitiful, be courteous: not rendering evil for evil, or railing for railing: but contrariwise blessing; knowing that ye are thereunto called, that ye should inherit a blessing. For he that will love life, and see good days, let him refrain his tongue from evil," 1 Pet. iii. 8—11. "But if ye suffer for righteousness' sake, happy are ye: and be not afraid of their terror, nor be troubled," ver. 14.

But I suppose you will here say, Is it not lawful to call a spade a spade? Is not a woe against them that call evil good? May not a man speak of the hurtful crimes of others? I answer, first, Yes, when, as a magistrate, a minister, or a brother, you have just cause to tell them of it lovingly, though plainly, to their places, in order to their recovery: secondly, and when you have a just call to speak of it to others, either in seeking justice, or in charity and mercy, for the preservation of those that else will be more hurt by the silencing of men's faults, than you do hurt by mentioning them.

But, 1. You may not slander men as guilty of what indeed they are not.

2. You may not make men's faults seem worse than they are.

3. You must endeavour the good of the person as much as you can, while you blame the sin.

4. You must not mention men's faults without a call; unless the good of himself or others do require it.

5. You must not do it with a revengeful mind, for personal injuries.

6. You must manifest love and compassion in all.

7. You must difference between reigning sins and human frailties; and between a course of sin and an unusual fall; and between a sin repented of and not repented of; and must censure but as you find God censure in his word.

8. You must be more ready to speak of the good that is in the same men as you have a call, than of the evil; and not maliciously stick only in the galled place.

9. Let it be as far as may be to his face.

10. Let it be according to the common rule of equity: Do as you would be done by. Not measuring your duty to others, by a corrupt impatience of bearing such yourselves; but speaking nothing for matter or manner to another, which you would think unmeet to be spoken to you, if you were in his case.

11. And especially be tender of the honour of superiors, yea, though they were evil, and do you wrong.

12. And foresee the consequence, whether your words are not like to do more hurt than good.

And if still you think that sufferings will justify reviling, contumelious complaints, consider these two causes of your mistake.

1. You make a great matter of a little one. As there is not so great good in the prosperity of the flesh, as worldlings think; so neither is there so great evil in the loss of it; what great harm is poverty, imprisonment, reproach, or death? Nay, you have a promise that all shall work together for your good, Rom. viii. 28.

2. You make a strange matter of that which is the ordinary condition of believers, to be hated of all men; to have all manner of evil spoken falsely of you; to be persecuted from one city to another; to be killed all the day long, and counted as sheep to the slaughter. Do these seem strange matters to you? Did you never read or hear the gospel? nor know the terms of Christ till now? Did you never read of forsaking all for Christ, if indeed you would be his disciples? Did you never count what it must cost you to be saved? Did you not renounce the world and the flesh in your baptismal, oft-renewed covenant? 1 Pet. iv. 12, 13, "Beloved, think it not strange concerning the fiery trial, as if some strange thing happened to you; but rejoice, inasmuch as ye are partakers of Christ's sufferings." And will you think so strange of smaller matters, as to think they excuse your impatience, and evil speeches?

By this time you may see, if you are willing to see, that all among us that are not real saints, are hypocrites, if they profess themselves christians and the servants of God; and that miserable, ungodly souls, that call such hypocrites as are more diligent than themselves for their salvation, do but discover their ignorance and malignity, and condemn themselves in betraying their hypocrisy, while they reproach the practice of the same christian religion which themselves profess; and the obedience to that Scripture which they confess, themselves, to be the word of God. All the profane and unsanctified among us, that call themselves christians, are certainly hypocrites. And for the godly, it is the very same religion that is professed by them and you; it is the same engagement and vow that you all made to God in baptism: and suffer but reason impartially to tell you, when two men have entered the same covenant, and one never mindeth it so as to keep it, and the other makes it his chiefest care, which of these is liker to be the dissembler in his covenant? When two men profess themselves the servants of God, and such as place their hopes in heaven, and one of them makes a jest of sin, and serveth the flesh and world which he hath renounced, and hates those that diligently serve the Lord; and the other maketh it the principal care and business of his life to serve and please him, insomuch as he is reproached for it, as making more ado about it than he needs; which of these are hypocrites, and which are serious, in the performing of their covenants, and living according to their profession? If two servants promise to do your work, and one labour as hard as he can, and the other sit down and deride him for making so much ado, which was it that played the hypocrite in his promise? If diligence in God's service be a sign of hypocrisy, then promise-keeping is hypocrisy, and promise-breaking is sincerity; and then you may transfer the case to God, who will be the rewarder of them only that diligently seek him, (Heb. xi. 6,) and say that it is his faithfulness to break his promises, and his unfaithfulness to keep them. But who will spend words on such impious absurdities? so gross, that the devil would have showed himself a fool to vent them, if he had not made his followers such fools as to believe them. But for the faithful servants of the Lord, let them know, that they must serve him on such terms; they must live above the judgment and reputation of this world; and be content that God, the searcher of hearts, shall be their judge, who knoweth both sincerity and hypocrisy; and will bring forth their righteousness as the light. Christians, you must not only be sincere, but also patiently expect to be accounted hypocrites, and pointed at as the only dissemblers of the world; you must not only be honest, but patiently expect to be accounted dishonest. You must not only be wise and sober, but patiently expect to be accounted fools and madmen. You must not be only liberal, charitable, and contemners of the world, but patiently expect to be called covetous, even though you give away all that you have. You must not only be chaste and temperate, but also patiently expect to be defamed as incontinent and licentious, and, as Christ was called, a wine-bibber, a friend of publicans and sinners. A minister must not only lay out himself wholly for the saving of men's souls, and spend himself and all that he hath on his Master's work; but also patiently expect to be accounted unfaithful, covetous, and negligent, and murmured at by almost all whose unreasonable desires he doth not answer, and be censured by almost all whose wills and humours he doth not fulfil; and that is, most, that have a self that ruleth at home, and, therefore, they think should be the idol of others, as it is their own; and that are but unacquainted with the reasons of those things that do displease them. It is little comfort to us to do good, if we cannot bear the estimation of doing evil, and cannot lose all the observation, acknowledgment, and applause of man, as if we had never done the good at all. It is far from christian perfection to be honest, and godly, and sincere, if we must needs be accounted to be as we are, and cannot patiently be esteemed dishonest, ungodly, and hypocritical; and be judged worst when we are best: what have the servants of Christ lost their lives for in flames, and by other sorts of torments, but for the best of their service, and greatest of their piety and fidelity? When dogs bark at passengers, commonly it signifieth but two things, namely, that they are persons they know not, or that they hate; but it is no sign that the persons are bad, or poor, or sick; for be they never so bad and miserable, if they know them, and love them, the dogs will not bark at them. See that thou be not a hypocrite, and then it must be accounted a small matter by thee to be called a hypocrite; yea, if persons that fear God themselves shall so esteem thee, it is no other affliction but what thou must be armed for, and patiently undergo. Even from the godly, through mistake, we oft suffer most for our greatest duties, and are censured most for that which God and conscience most approve us for; and lose our reputations for that which

God would be greatly offended with us if we did otherwise. As ever then you would not prove yourselves hypocrites, see that you look not for the hypocrite's reward, as Christ calls it, (Matt. vi. 2,) which is, to be approved of men; be they good or bad men, their overvalued applause may be but the hypocrite's reward. To be content and patient in doing well, and being judged to do ill, and in being good, and being judged to be bad, is the property of him that is sincere indeed; therefore, to be unthankfully requited, and reviled, and spit upon, and buffeted, and shamefully used and put to death, even by those whose lives and souls he had, with greatest care and condescension, pitied, this was the pattern of love and self-denial that was set us by our Lord. And though we cannot reach his measure, and distempered christians find much struggling before they can bring themselves to patience, under such ingratitude and unworthy usage from the world, especially from their mistaken froward brethren, yet, in some prevailing measure, it must be done. For he that cannot serve God without the hypocrite's reward, is but a hypocrite. If he will not be a christian, obedient, charitable, diligent, faithful, for heaven and the pleasing of God alone, he is not a christian indeed. And, alas, what a pitiful reward is it, to be thought well of and applauded by the tongues of mortal men! How few were ever the more holy by applause! But thousands have been hurt, if not undone, by it. Thou givest all thou hast to the poor; thou spendest thyself wholly, and all that thou hast, for the service of God and the good of others: it is well; it must be so. But, after all, thou art censured, slandered, vilified, and unthankfully and unmannerly used. And what of that? what harm dost thou fear by it? What advantage thy pride and selfishness might have taken, even by due applause and thankfulness, it is easy to perceive. But now the temptation is taken out of thy way; thou art occluded from all creature comforts; and so art directed, and almost forced, to look up to the love of God alone: now thou hast no other reward before thee, it is easier to look singly on the saints' reward. When God hath no competitor, to whom else canst thou turn thy thoughts? When all others abuse thee, it is easier to have recourse to him. When earth will scarce afford thee any quiet habitation, thou wilt surely look to heaven for rest.

Thus much I thought meet to interpose here for the confirmation of the sincere, on occasion of the world's unjust accusations; and so to persuade them to be satisfied in the portion of the sincere. I now return again to the self-deceiver.

And here I shall conclude all with these two requests to you, which, as one that foreseeth the approaching misery of self-deceivers, I earnestly entreat you, for the sake of your immortal souls, that you will not deny me. The first is, that you will be now but as willing to try yourselves, as I have been to help you; and as diligent and faithful when you are alone, in calling your own hearts to a close examination, as I have been to hold the light here to you. O refuse not, delay not, to withdraw yourselves sometimes from the world, and set yourselves as before the eye of God, and there bethink yourselves whether you have been what you have vowed and professed to be? And whether that God hath been dearest to your hearts, and obeyed in your lives, and desired as your happiness, who hath been confessed and honoured with your lips? Consider therefore, that God judgeth not as man; nor will he think ever the better of you, for thinking well of yourselves. And that there must go more to prove your approbation with God, than commonly goes to keep up your reputation in the world. The religion that serveth to honour you before men, and to deceive yourselves, will never serve to please the Lord and save your souls. And the day is at hand when nothing but God can give you comfort, and when self-deceivers will become, everlastingly, self-tormenters. O therefore go willingly and presently to the word, to your lives, and hearts, and consciences, and try yourselves, and try again, and that with moderate suspicion, that in so great a business you may not be deceived, and be self-deceivers.

2. My second request is, that if you do discover, or but justly suspect yourselves of hypocrisy and self-deceit, you would stick there no longer, but presently change your vain religion, your seemings and formalities, for the power of godliness and sincerity of heart.

But I suppose that some of you will say, there lies the difficulty. Oh that we could do it! But how should it be done?

I answer: If thou really be willing to be above hypocrisy, and a vain religion, the cure is half wrought, at least; and I will not tire thee now with many, but help and try thee by these few directions.

In general, be what thou hast promised and vowed to be in thy baptism, and what thou still dost profess to be, a christian, and it will serve thy turn: what that is, I have told you before.

More particularly: *Direct.* 1. Deliberately renew thy covenant with God: and with a grieved heart, bewailing that thou hast been a covenant-breaker, give up thyself presently to God the Father, Son, and Holy Ghost; as thy Creator, Redeemer, and Sanctifier, thy Owner, thy Ruler, and thy Father.

2. Renounce sincerely the devil, the world, and the flesh, and be at a point with all below; and quit all conceits and hopes of felicity, or rest, on earth; and absolutely devote and resign thyself, and all thou hast, to the will and service of thy Lord, without any secret exceptions or reserves. This is the property and plague of hypocrites, that secretly they have exceptions and reserves in giving up themselves to God. They will follow him, except it would disgrace them, or undo them, in the world; he shall have all, provided the flesh may not be too much pinched. That is, in plain English, they take him not for God, but for a second to themselves and the world, and will give him but what the flesh can spare.

3. Fix the eye of lively faith of God upon the everlasting joys, and there take up thy whole reward, and look for no other. Quit all expectations of a reward from men. Let it seem a small thing to thee, what any mortal man shall think or speak of thee; unless as God's honour or interest is concerned in thine. I have told you before, he is a hypocrite that will not be godly without the hypocrite's reward; and that can sail no further than he is moved by the wind of man's applause, or some other worldly end.

4. Stick not in any externals of religion, nor in notions, and barren, ineffectual opinions. So far art thou religious, as thy soul is engaged unto God, and thy life employed for him; and so far thou dost truly worship him as thy heart is drawn up to him in love, and as thou dost fear him, admire him, trust him, and take thy pleasure in him. Think not, that it is a saving religiousness, to be of such or such an opinion, or such a party, or such a church, or to say over so many words of prayer, or to keep a task of outward duties, or to be of a ready, voluble tongue, in preaching, prayer, or discourse; religion lieth in the heart and life.

5. Indulge not thyself in one known sin. Retain no gross or wilful sin. Plead for no infirmity, but make it the business of thy life to extirpate the relics of the body of death. Be willing of the most search-

ing word, and of the plainest reproof, and of the help thou canst get against so dangerous an enemy.

6. Stint not thyself in any low degrees of holiness; but love, and long, and strive after the highest. If thou bear a secret core of distaste against those that outgo thee, it is a mortal sign. Thou must be perfect in desire, or thou art not sincere.

7. Walk always as in the presence of the holy, dreadful, heart-searching God: remember that he seeth thy ends, thine affections, and all thy thoughts. Be the same, therefore, in secret as thou art in public. Sincerely search the word of God, and know what it is that he would have, and that resolve on, if all the world should be against it. Unresolvedness is hypocrisy; and temporizing, or following the greater side, for the security of the flesh, is no better. Never think thou canst be too holy or too obedient. But make it thy study to do God all the service that thou canst, whatever suffering or cost it put thee to. Be not ashamed openly to own the cause of Christ. In the presence of the greatest, remember that thy Master is so much greater, that they are worms and vanity to him. Take heed of culling out the easy and cheap part of religion, and laying by the difficult and dear. Thy religion must be as the heart in thy breast, which is always working, and by which thou livest; which cannot stop long, but thou wilt die. But the hypocrite's religion is like the hat upon his head, for ornament and shelter from the weather, and not for life; in the night when none seeth him he can lie without it; and in the day he can put it off for the sake of a friend, and perhaps stand bare in the presence of a greater person that expecteth it. So can the hypocrite too oft dispense with his religion.

8. Be hearty and serious in all thou doest. Hear, and read, and pray, as for thy life. Sincerity consisteth much in seriousness. Remember that thou art almost at another world! While I am speaking, and thou art hearing, we are both hastening to our endless state. Oh how should men live on earth, that must live here for so short a time, and must live for ever in heaven or hell! These things are true, and past all question: and therefore, for your souls' sake, lose not heaven by trifling. Pray not in jest, and resist not sin in jest, lest you be damned in good sadness. When you are at work for eternity, it is time to do it with all your might. Oh what unconceivable mercies are now offered to you! Oh what an excellent price is in your hands! And nothing is so likely to deprive you of the benefit, as dreaming, and dallying, when you should be up and doing; as if this were not your business, but your play; and salvation and damnation were matters of sport! Oh do but set yourselves to the pleasing of God, and the saving of your souls with all your might, and ply it with diligence as your chiefest work, and then you are out of the danger of the hypocrite! But if still you will give the world the pre-eminence, and your flesh must be pleased, and your prosperity secured, and God must have but compliments, or the leavings, your misery is at hand, and vengeance shall undeceive those hearts that would not be undeceived by the word. And you shall remember, to the increase of your anguish, that you were told this day, that your seeming, trifling religion would prove vain. But I beseech you, as you are men, as you love your souls, dismiss us with some better hopes; and now resolve to be downright christians. Which, as I have begged of you, I shall now beg of God

---

THE FOOL'S PROSPERITY;

A SERMON

PREACHED AT COVENT-GARDEN: PUBLISHED UPON OCCASION OF SOME OFFENCE AND MISREPORTS.

PROV. I. 32, 33.

FOR THE TURNING AWAY OF THE SIMPLE SHALL SLAY THEM, AND THE PROSPERITY OF FOOLS SHALL DESTROY THEM. BUT WHOSO HEARKENETH UNTO ME, SHALL BE QUIET FROM FEAR OF EVIL.

The bounteous offers and vehement exhortations of Christ, here in this chapter, were accompanied with a foresight and prediction of their rejection, by many; yet doth not that prevent the offers and exhortations; but occasion the prediction of the calamity of the refusers. God will not go out of his way, because the ungodly will not walk with him. He will do the part of a righteous Governor, though he foresee that men will not do the part of obedient subjects. But his primary end shall be attained upon the righteous, in the successes of his grace, as his secondary end shall be upon the disobedient, in the honour of his vindictive justice. This is the sense of the words which I have now read to you. Which, 1. Describe the ungodly. 1. By their present way of sin. 2. And by their future state of misery. Their sin is described by: 1. The occasion. 2. The act. 3. The habit. Prosperity and ease is the occasion; turning away from God, and rejecting his counsel, is the act; and folly, or simplicity, is part of the habit. Simplicity is here taken for sinful foolishness, and not, as it is often, for commendable sincerity. Whether you read it, the turning away, or the ease, of the simple, it is all one as to the scope and use that I shall now make of it, both being included as to the sense in the other words. Folly is mentioned both as the cause of their abuse of prosperity, and as the effect of prosperity so abused. Because they are fools, they turn God's mercies to their own destruction: and because they prosper, they are confirmed in their folly.

2. The words describe the godly. 1. By their

obedience; they "hearken unto Christ." 2. By their privilege or reward; they "shall dwell safely, and be quiet from fear of evil."

We shall begin with the first, and show you, 1. That it is so, that "the prosperity of fools destroyeth them." 2. How folly and prosperity concur to their destruction; or how prosperity befooleth and destroyeth them. 3. How we should all improve this truth to our best advantage.

I. Scripture and experience concur in proving the truth of the conclusion.

1. Though God tells us in his word of a difficulty that all must conquer that will be saved, yet it is a greater, extraordinary difficulty that he tells us of, as to the rich and prosperous in the world; such a difficulty as is pathetically expressed by this interrogation, (Luke xviii. 24,) "How hardly shall they that have riches enter into the kingdom of God!" Such a difficulty as is expressed by his proverbial comparison, (ver. 25,) "For it is easier for a camel to go through a needle's eye, than for a rich man to enter into the kingdom of God." Such a difficulty as cast the hearers into admiration, and made them ask, (ver. 26,) "Who then can be saved?" Such a difficulty as is to man an impossibility, (ver. 27,) and leaves only this hope, that "Things are possible to God, that are impossible to man."

2. And though it is said of men indefinitely, that it is but few that shall be saved; yet is it noted of the rich and prosperous, that it is few of them among those few, or few in comparison of other sorts of men, that shall be saved. John vii. 48, "Have any of the rulers or of the Pharisees believed on him?" 1 Cor. i. 26, "For ye see your calling, brethren, how that not many wise men after the flesh, not many mighty, not many noble are called. But God hath chosen the foolish things of the world to confound the wise; and God hath chosen the weak things of the world to confound the things which are mighty; and base things of the world, and things which are despised, hath God chosen; yea, and things that are not, to bring to nought things that are, that no flesh should glory in his presence." And therefore Scripture speaketh in such general language, as if salvation had been almost appropriated to the poor, and the rich had been excluded, because of the rarity of their salvation. Luke vi. 24, 25, "But woe unto you that are rich! for ye have received your consolation: woe unto you that are full! for ye shall hunger: woe unto you that laugh now! for ye shall mourn and weep." Jam. ii. 5, 6, "Hearken, my beloved brethren, Hath not God chosen the poor of this world rich in faith, and heirs of the kingdom which he hath promised to them that love him? But ye have despised the poor. Do not rich men oppress you, and draw you before the judgment-seats? Do they not blaspheme that worthy name by the which ye are called?" And therefore when Christ would describe a wicked, miserable man, he doeth it in these words, (Luke xvi. 19,) "There was a certain rich man which was clothed in purple and fine linen, and fared sumptuously every day." And Luke xii. 16, 19, "The ground of a certain rich man brought forth plentifully," &c. And when he would describe a godly, happy man, he doth it under the name of Lazarus, Luke xvi. 20. Judge now by the success, as it is discovered in the Scripture, what good prosperity doth to fools.

I might turn you to David's observations in Psal. xxxvii.; lxxiii.; and mind you why it is that Christ himself went before us in a state of chosen poverty, 2 Cor. viii. 9; and why his disciples followed him in this track; and why he called them so much to deny and forsake the riches of the world, and tried them so oft by selling all, and following him in hopes of a heavenly reward. But the point is evident in what is said in my text, and these annexed testimonies.

2. But yet to make you more apprehensive of it, I shall adjoin the testimony of experience: and tell me whether prosperity be not the destruction of fools, when you have noted the fruits of it in these few observations.

1. Where do you find less serious care and labour for salvation than among the prosperous great ones of the world? What abundance of them are dead-hearted, senseless, disregarders of everlasting things! What abundance of them are of no religion, but the custom of their country and the will of their superiors, which are their Bible, their law and gospel, and their creed! What abundance of them are addicted to that worship which Christ pronounceth vain, which is measured by the traditions of men, and consisteth merely in ceremonious shows! How few of them are acquainted with the spiritual worship of that God, who, being a Spirit, can accept no worship but what is spiritual. Alas! poor souls, they drown their reason in sensuality, and are fed as for the slaughter, and think not seriously whither they are going, till prosperity hath ceased to deceive them, and Satan is content to let them see that they have lost and he hath won the game. They are of the religion described by the apostle, (1 Tim. vi. 5,) that taketh gain for godliness; but if godliness must go for gain, they will have none. To oppress their tenants, and devour widows' houses, and cloak it with a long pharisaical lip-service, or wipe their mouths with some customary complimental prayers, and offer God to be a sharer in the prey, this is the commonest religion of the rich. But they cannot endure to be so pure as to devote themselves to God in that pure and undefiled religion which visiteth the fatherless and widows in their affliction, and keepeth men unspotted from the world, Jam. i. 27. What houses or company can you go into, where religion is more bitterly derided, more proudly vilified, more slanderously reproached, or more ingeniously abused and opposed, than among the rich and full-fed worldlings!

And if there be here and there a person fearing God among them, he passeth for a rarity or wonder. And a little religion goes a great way, and is applauded and admired as eminent sanctity, in persons of the higher rank. If a poor man or woman dwell, as it were, in heaven, and walk with God, and think, and speak, and live by rule, it is scarce regarded; poverty, or want of a voluble tongue, or the mixtures of unavoidable frailties, or some imprudent passages that come from the want of a more polishing culture and education, doth make their piety but matter of jesting and reproach to the Dives of the world; but if a lord, or knight, or lady, have but half their piety, humility, and obedience to God, how excellent are they in their orb! Nay, if they do but countenance religion, and befriend the servants of the Lord, and observe a course of cold performances, with the mixture of such sins for which a poor man should be almost excommunicate, what excellent religious persons are they esteemed?

2. What families are worse ordered, and have less of serious piety, than the rich? If our splendid gallants should be desired to call their families constantly to prayer; to instruct them all in the matters of salvation; to teach them the word of God with that diligence as is commanded, Deut. vi. 11; and to help all in their preparations for death and judgment; to catechise them, and take an account of their proficiency; to curb profaneness and excess; and to say with Joshua, (xxiv. 15,) "As for me and

my house, we will serve the Lord;" how strange and precise a course would it seem to them! Should they purge their families of ungodly servants, and imitate David, (Psal. ci.) that would not let the wicked dwell in his sight; should they spend the Lord's days in as serious endeavours for the spiritual benefit of their families and themselves, as poor men do that fear the Lord, what wonders of piety would they seem!

3. In their entertainments, visitations, and converse, how rare is serious, holy conference among them! How seldom do you hear them remembering their guests and companions of the presence of the holy God; of the necessity of renewing, confirming, and assisting grace; of the riches of Christ revealed in the gospel; of the endless life of joy or misery which is at hand! How seldom do you hear them seriously assisting each other in the examining of their hearts, and making their calling and election sure, and preparing for the day of death and judgment! A word or two in private with some zealous minister or friend, is almost all the pious conference that shall be heard from some of the better sort of them. Should they discourse as seriously of the life to come, and the preparation necessary thereto, as they do about the matters of this life, they would mar the mirth and damp the pleasure of the company, and be taken for self-conceited hypocrites, or men of an unnecessary strictness and austerity, inconsistent with the jocund lepidity and sensual kind of delight wherewith they expect to be entertained. The honest, heart-warming, heavenly discourse that is usual among poor serious christians, would seem, at the tables of most of our great ones, but an unseasonable interruption of their more natural and acceptable kind of converse.

4. What men do more carelessly cast away their precious time than these Dives do? They think they have a licence to be idle and unprofitable, because they are rich; that is, to abuse or hide their talents, because they have more than other men; forgetting that to whom much is given, of them shall much be required. Because they have no poverty or family necessities to constrain them to a laborious life, they think they may lawfully take their ease, and live as drones on other men's labours, as if they owed nothing to God or the commonwealth, but all to their own flesh. Their morning hours, which are most seasonable for meditation, and holy addresses unto God, and the works of their calling, are, perhaps, consumed in excess of sleep: the next are wasted in long attiring and curious adorning of their flesh: from thence they pass to vain discourse, to needless recreations, to eating and drinking, and so to their vain talk and recreations again, and thence to the replenishing of their bellies, and so to sleep: and thus the words of the fool, that Christ describeth in Luke xii. 19, are turned by them into deeds; and it is the language of their sensual lives, "Soul, thou hast much goods laid up for many years: take thine ease, eat, drink, and be merry." Sleeping, and sporting, and jesting, and idle talking, and eating and drinking, and dressing and undressing, with worldly cares and passions intermixed, are the very business and employment of their lives. Thus contemptuously do they waste their precious hours, while God stands by, and time makes haste, and death draws near, and their miserable souls are unprepared, and heaven or hell are hard at hand; and this is all the time of preparation that ever shall be allowed them. O do but look on these distracted, piteous souls, that have but a short, uncertain life to provide for a life that hath no end, and see how they forget or senselessly remember the matters of infinite concernment! See how they trifle away that time that never will return! How they sport and prate away those hours which shortly they would recall, were it possible, with the loudest cries, or recover with the dearest price! When they know not but, in a laughter, or a merry jest, their breath may be stopped by an arrest from heaven; or justice may surprise their miserable, unready souls with the cards in their hands, or the cup at their mouths; when they have not the least assurance of being out of hell an hour, and yet can sell this time for nothing, and basely cast it away on toys, which is all that ever they shall have to prevent everlasting misery, or to procure everlasting joy. Stand by a while, and hearken to the discourse of sensual gallants, and mark how days and weeks are spent; and then tell whether the prosperity of such fools be not made the occasion of befooling and destroying them?

5. What men in the world do live so sensual a life as rich and prosperous worldlings live? The difference between the sanctified and the unsanctified, the children of God and of the devil, is, that one of them liveth after the Spirit, and the other liveth after the flesh, as in Romans viii. to ver. 14, you may read at large. And how few of these Dives do think the damning sin of flesh-pleasing to be any sin in them at all! If they do not eat till they are sick, or drink till they are drunk, their consciences scarce control them in their voluptuousness: they never well understood the meaning of such passages as these; Rom. xiii. 14, "Make no provision for the flesh, to fulfil the (desires or) lusts thereof." Rom. viii. 13, "If ye live after the flesh ye shall die." 1 Cor. ix. 27, "I keep under my body, and bring it into subjection," &c. They understand not how far the flesh is their enemy; or else (as they have verbally renounced it) they would use it as an enemy.

6. In their prosperity these fools have not the wit to love or bear the means of their preservation or recovery. They have the sorest maladies, and are most impatient of the remedies. They are in the stream of temptations, and have greater need of help than others; and yet there is none that reject it with more contempt and pride. Plain-dealing preachers, which honest humble souls delight in, do seem intolerable saucy fellows to these sons of pride. If we tell them but of the sin that God hath most plainly condemned in his word, or of the judgment which he hath there denounced, and make the most prudent and modest application of it unto them, we stir up their pride and enmity against us, and provoke them to slanderous recriminations, or revenge. It troubles them not to commit it, or to keep it, but to hear of it; and they take us to be more faulty for admonishing them of it, than themselves for being guilty of it. Though we are by office the messengers of Christ, that will tell them of it shortly to their faces, and fear not the proudest son of Belial, yet are they too stout to be admonished by such as we, but reject our message with hatred and disdain. And, indeed, it is a wonder of mercy that the prevalency of this impatient guilt and malice hath not, ere this, turned plain and faithful preaching into some toothless formalities, or homilies, and silenced the preachers for the security of the offenders; and expelled the physicians lest they displease the sick. The Lord still prevent it. If we tell them with the greatest caution but of the necessary truths, without which a sinful soul is never like to be humbled or saved, we are taken to be turbulent, and injurious to the ease or honour of these auditors. They must hear of the necessity of

regeneration and holiness, and of the weight and worth of things eternal, and yet they cannot bear to hear it. They must have heart-searching and heart-breaking truths, in a searching, awakening manner, brought home to them, if ever they will be saved by them; but they cannot endure it. The surgeon is intolerable that would search their sores; and yet there is no other way to heal them. Alas! the heart of man is so hard, that all the skill and industry of the preacher can scarce sufficiently sharpen and set home the truth that it may enter; but nothing that is sharp can be endured by these tender souls. Such language as Christ and his prophets and apostles used, doth seem too rough for silken ears. Their honour must not be blotted with the mention of their odious sins and deplorable misery. To be a glutton, or a drunkard, or a wanton, or a filthy fornicator, or a malicious Cain, they can endure; but to be told, "Thou art the man," though it be secret, and with love and tenderness, they cannot bear. The minister is thought to wrong them that shall secretly and faithfully admonish them, and tell them truly what will be the end: but Christ will execute all his threatenings, and make them feel what now they hear, and yet constrain them to confess that he doth not wrong them. We wrong them now, if we tell a gentleman of his impiety, and sensuality, and pride, and of his vilifying precious time, and casting it away on cards, and idleness, and unprofitable talk; yea, though he be so far forsaken of common grace and reason, as to hate and deride the serious practice of his own profession, and the way that the God of heaven hath prescribed as flatly necessary to salvation, yet cannot he endure to hear of his enmity against the Lord, nor to be told that he beareth the image of the devil, while he is against the image and laws of Christ. Should we but privately read a text to them that condemneth them, they are as angry with us as if we made the Scripture which we read; and it were not the word of God, but ours. If we tell them that "Without holiness none shall see God," Heb. xii. 14; and that "Except they be regenerated, converted, and become as little children, (in humility beginning the world anew,) they cannot enter into the kingdom of heaven," Matt. xviii. 3; John iii. 3, 5, 6; that "If any man have not the Spirit of Christ, the same is none of his," Rom. viii. 6; or that "Whoremongers and aduterers God will judge," Heb. xiii. 4; and that "The unrighteous, the fornicators, effeminate, covetous, extortioners, drunkards, or revilers, shall not inherit the kingdom of God," 1 Cor. vi. 9—11; Eph. v. 3—6; they think we talk too precisely or presumptuously to them. You would think by their proud contempt of his threatenings, and their boldness and carelessness in sin, that these silk-worms did imagine they had conquered heaven, and the righteous God were afraid to meddle with them; or that he would reverse his laws, and pervert his judgment for fear of dishonouring or offending them. Little do they think how many Dives are now in hell. But methinks they might easily believe, that their honourable flesh is rotten, and turned to common earth; and that death will make bold to tell them, also, when their turn is come, that they have been pampering but a piece of clay; and that it was not worth the loss of heaven, nor the suffering of hell, to spend so much time, and care, and cost, to feed up a carcass for the worms. We must now submissively ask their leave, to tell them what God hath said against them. But God will not ask them leave to make it good upon the highest, the proudest, and securest of them all; "For God shall wound the head of his enemies, and the hairy scalp of such a one as goeth on still in his trespasses," Psal. lxviii. 21. "He is not a God that hath pleasure in wickedness; neither shall evil dwell with him. The foolish shall not stand in his sight; he hateth all the workers of iniquity," Psal. v. 3, 4. "The ungodly (that delight not in the law of the Lord) are like the chaff that the wind driveth away; they shall not sit in judgment, nor sinners in the assembly of the righteous," Psal. i. "The wicked shall be turned into hell, and all the nations that forget God," Psal. ix. 17. Cannot you endure to hear and consider of these things? How then will you endure to feel them? God will not flatter you. If all your greatness enable you not to repulse the assaults of death, nor to chide away the gout or stone; and all your honour and wealth will not cure a fever, or ease you of the tooth-ache; how little will it do to save you from the everlasting wrath of God! or to avert his sentence which must shortly pass on all that are impenitent! And yet prosperity so befooleth sensual men, that they must hear of none of this; at least not with any close and personal application. If you speak as Christ did to the Pharisees, Matt. xxi. 45, that they perceived that he spake of them, they take you for their enemy for telling them the truth, Gal. iv. 16, and meet our doctrine as Ahab did Elijah, 2 Kings xxi. 20, "Hast thou found me, O mine enemy?" and, 1 Kings xviii. 17, "Art thou he that troubleth Israel?" or as the same Ahab of Micaiah, 1 Kings xxii. 8, "There is one man (Micaiah) of whom we may inquire of the Lord; but I hate him: for he doth not prophesy good concerning me, but evil." Or as Amaziah the priest said of Amos to king Jeroboam, "He hath conspired against thee; the land is not able to bear all his words," Amos vii. 10; and ver. 13, "Prophesy not again any more at Bethel; for it is the king's chapel, and it is the king's court." They behave themselves to faithful ministers as if it were a part of their inviolable honour and privilege, to be mortally sick without the trouble of a physician, and to have nobody tell them that they are out of their way, till it be too late; or that they are in misery, till there be no remedy; and that none should remember them of heaven till they have lost it; nor trouble them in the way to hell, and seek to save them, lest he should but torment them before the time. And thus prosperity makes them willingly deaf and blind, and "turn away their ears from the hearing of the law," and then their prayers for mercy in their distress are rejected as abominable by the Lord, Prov. i. 24—33; xxviii. 9.

7. Yea, if there be any persecution raised against the church of Christ, who are the chief actors in it, but the prosperous, blinded, sensual great ones of the world? The princes make it their petition against Jeremiah to the king; "We beseech thee, let this man be put to death: for thus he weakeneth the hands of the men of war—and the hands of all the people in speaking such words unto them: for this man seeketh not the welfare of his people, but the hurt," Jer. xxxviii. 4. It was the presidents and princes that said of Daniel, "We shall not find any occasion against this Daniel, except we find it against him concerning the law of his God," Dan. vi. 5. Were it not lest some malicious hearer should misapply it, and think I sought to diminish the reputation of magistrates, while I show the effects of the prosperity of fools, I should give you abundance of such lamentable instances, and tell you how commonly the great ones of the world have in all ages set themselves, and taken counsel, against the Lord and against his Christ, Psal. ii.: and stumbled upon the corner-stone, and taken no warning by those that have been thus broken in pieces before

them. How ready is Herod to gratify a wanton dancer with a prophet's head! In a word, as Satan is called the prince of this world, no wonder if he rule the men of the world, that have their portion in this life, Psal. xvii. 14. And to command his armies, and engage them against the servants of the Most High that run not with them to the same excess of riot, 1 Pet. iv. 4. And as James saith, (as before cited,) "Do not the rich oppress you, and draw you before the judgment-seats? Do they not blaspheme that worthy name by which you are called?" Jam. ii. 6, 7.

8. And in all this sin and misery how senseless and secure are the prosperous fools! as merry within a year, or month, or week of hell, as if no harm were near! How wonderful hard it is to convince them of their misery! The most learned, wise, or godly man, or the dearest friend they have in the world, shall not persuade them that their case is such as to need a conversion and supernatural change. They cannot abide to take off their minds from their sensual delights, and vanities, and to trouble themselves about the things of life eternal, come on it what will; they are resolved to venture, and please their flesh, and enjoy what the world will afford them while they may, till suddenly God surpriseth them with his dreadful call, "Thou fool! this night shall thy soul be required of thee; then whose shall those things be which thou hast provided?" Luke xii. 20. "So is he that layeth up riches for himself, and is not rich towards God," ver. 21.

II. I shall next show you how it is that prosperity thus destroyeth fools. Briefly, 1. By the pleasing of their sensitive appetite and fancy, and so overcoming the power of reason. *Perit omne judicium cum res transit in affectum.* Violent affections hearken not to reason. The beast is made too headstrong for the rider. Deut. xxxii. 15, "Jerusalem waxed fat and kicked—then he forsook God that made him, and lightly esteemed the Rock of his salvation."

2. "The friendship of the world is enmity to God: and if any man love the world, the love of the Father is not in him," Jam. iv. 4; 1 John ii. 15. And undoubtedly, the more amiable the world appears, the more strongly it doth allure the soul to love it. And to the prosperous it appeareth in the most enticing dress.

3. And hereby it taketh off the soul from God. We cannot love and serve God and mammon. The heart is gone another way when God should have it. It is so full of love, and desire, and care, and pleasure about the creatures, that there is no room for God. How can they love him with all their hearts who have let out those hearts to vanity before?

4. And the very noise and bustle of these worldly things diverts their mind, and hindereth them from being serious, and from that sober consideration that requireth some retirement and vacancy from distracting objects.

5. And the sense of present ease and sweetness doth make them forget the change that is near. Little do they think what is necessary to comfort a departing soul, when they are in the heat of pride or lust, or taken up with their business and delights. In the midst of bravery and plenty, feasting and sporting, and such other entertainments of the senses, it is hard to hold communion with God, and to study the life to come in such a college or library as this. Prosperity and pleasure make men drunk; and the tickled fancy sports itself in abusing the captivated mind. And these frisking lambs and fattened beasts forget the slaughter; they think in summer there will be no winter, and their May will continue all the year. Little do they feel the piercing, griping, tearing thoughts, that at death or judgment must succeed their security and mirth. Oh how hard do the best men find it, in the midst of health and all prosperity, to have such serious thoughts of heaven, and of the change that death will shortly make, as they have in sickness and adversity, when death seems near, and deluding things are vanished and gone! The words of God have not that force on a sleepy soul in the hour of prosperity, as they have when distress hath opened their ears. The same truths that now seem common, lifeless, inconsiderable things, will then pierce deep, and divide between the joints and marrow, and work as if they were not the same that once were laughed at or disregarded. Eccles. vii. 2—4, "It is better to go to the house of mourning than to the house of feasting;" (do you believe this?) "for that is the end of all men, and the living will lay it to heart. Sorrow is better than laughter; for by the sadness of the countenance the heart is made better. The heart of the wise is in the house of mourning, but the heart of fools is in the house of mirth." I beseech you take patiently your character and name here from the word of God.

6. Moreover these fools are by prosperity so lifted up with pride, that God abhors them, and is as it were engaged to abase them. For "The Lord will destroy the house of the proud," Prov. xv. 25. "Every one that is proud in heart is an abomination to the Lord; though hand join in hand, he shall not be unpunished," Prov. xvi. 5. "He scattereth the proud in the imagination of their hearts: he hath put down the mighty from their seats, and exalted them of low degree: he hath filled the hungry with good things, and the rich he hath sent empty away," Luke i. 51, 52, 53. "In the things wherein they deal proudly, he is above them," Exod. xviii. 11. "For every one that exalteth himself shall be abased: and he that humbleth himself shall be exalted," Luke xviii. 14. "For God resisteth the proud, but giveth grace to the humble," 1 Pet. v. 5.

7. But no way doth their prosperity so desperately precipitate them, and make them the scorn of heaven, and the football of divine contempt, as by engaging them in opposition to the word, and ways, and servants of the Lord. When it hath drawn them to those sins which God condemneth and his ministers must reprove, and hath puffed them up with pride, which makes them impatient of his reproofs, and hath increased their worldly interest, and treasure, and fleshly provision, which he commandeth them to deny, this presently involveth them in a controversy with Christ before they are aware, and casteth them into the temptation of Herod when he was contradicted in his lust; and they think they are necessitated to stop the mouths that dare reprove them, and to keep under the people, and doctrine, and discipline of Christ, that are so contrary to them, and cross them, and dishonour them in their sin; and to pluck away this thorn out of their foot, and cast it from them. And thus their prosperity, and carnal wisdom that is employed to secure it, engageth the earthworms in a war with Christ; and then you may conjecture how long they can endure to kick against the pricks, and irritate the justice and jealousy of the Almighty, and presume to abuse the apple of his eye; and who will have the better in the end? The stubble is more able to resist the flames, and a fly to conquer all the world, than these daring lumps of walking clay to conquer God, or escape his vengeance. Isa. xxvii. 4, "Who would set the briers and thorns against me in battle? I I would go through them, I would burn them together." Isa. xlv. 9, "Woe to him that striveth with

his Maker! Let the potsherd strive with the potsherds of the earth." Job ix.4, "Who hath hardened himself against him and hath prospered?" They all imagine a vain thing, that set themselves and take counsel together against the Lord, and his anointed, to break his bonds and cast away his cords from them. "He that sitteth in heaven will laugh: the Lord will have them in derision. Then shall he speak to them in his wrath, and vex them in his sore displeasure.—He shall break them with a rod of iron, and dash them in pieces like a potter's vessel. Be wise now, therefore, O ye kings! be instructed, ye judges of the earth. Serve the Lord with fear, and rejoice with trembling. Kiss the Son, lest he be angry, and ye perish in the way, when his wrath is kindled but a little. Blessed are all they that put their trust in him," Psal. ii. They think it is but a few contemptible or hateful men that they set themselves against; forgetting Acts ix. 4, 5; Luke x. 16; 1 Thess. iv. 8, that tell them all is done to Christ: and Matt. xviii. 6 "Whoso shall offend one of these little ones which believe in me, it were better for him that a millstone were hanged about his neck, and that he were drowned in the depth of the sea." Matt. xxi. 44, "And whosoever shall fall on this stone shall be broken; but on whomsoever it shall fall, it will grind him to powder." I will conclude this with Amaziah's case, 2 Chron xxv. 16, "Art thou made of the king's counsel? Forbear; why shouldest thou be smitten? Then the prophet forbare, and said, I know that God hath determined to destroy thee, because thou hast done this, and hast not hearkened," &c.

III. Before I tell you what use to make of the doctrine of this text, I shall first tell you, by way of caution, what use you should not make of it.

1. Though the prosperity of fools destroy them, do not hence accuse God that giveth them prosperity. 2. Nor do not think to excuse yourselves. 3. Nor do not think that riches are evil: for the things are good, and mercies in themselves, and being rightly used, may further their felicity. But it is the folly and corruption of their hearts that thus abuse them, and make good an occasion of evil. I may allude to Paul's words concerning the law, Rom. vii. 7, 13. Are they sin? or is that which is good made death to them? "God forbid. But sin, that it might appear sin, working death by that which is good:" because they are carnally sold under sin.

4. Nor must you cast away your riches, or refuse them when offered by God. But take them as a faithful steward doth his master's stock, not desiring to be over-burdened or endangered with the charge, but bearing what is imposed on you, resolving to improve it all for God. Not loving nor desiring wealth, authority, or honour, nor yet so lazy, timorous, or distrustful as not to accept the burden and charge, when God may be served by it. To cast away or hide your talents, is the part of an unprofitable servant.

5. Take heed lest, under pretence of contemning riches and prosperity, you be tempted to contemn your governors, or to speak evil of dignities, or diminish the honour of those that are set over us, whose honour is necessary to the ends of government, and therefore to the people's good. Though James reproves the church for partiality in over-honouring a man for a gold ring, or gay apparel, yet doth he not go about to abate the honour of authority. Magistracy and riches must be here distinguished.

6. Take heed lest, while you declaim of the misery of the rich, you think to be saved merely for being poor; for, poor or rich, if you be ungodly, you must turn, or die. God doth not condemn men for their riches, but their sin; nor save any for their poverty, but their faith and piety, through Christ.

But the uses you should make of the text are these:—

1. Grudge not at the prosperity of ungodly men, but compassionate them in their danger and misery.

2. Be not afraid of the prosperity of the wicked, Psal. xlix. 16—19. It is they that should be afraid that have so low to fall.

3. Take heed that you desire not riches or prosperity, unless you desire that the way to heaven should be made harder to you, that is so hard already. Be contented with food and raiment. Desire but your daily bread, unless as it is needful for your Master's service, and the relief of others.

4. Honour those ever with a double honour, that are great and godly, that are rich and religious; not because they are rich, but because they are so strong and excellent in grace as to overcome such great temptations; and to be heavenly in the midst of earthly plenty, and to be faithful stewards of so much. Religious, faithful princes, and magistrates, cannot easily be valued and honoured too much. What wonders are they in the most part of the earth! What a blessing to the people that are ruled by them! Were they not strong in faith, they could not stand fast in such a stormy place. Where is there in the world a more lively resemblance of God than a holy prince or governor, that liveth no more to the flesh than the poorest, for all his abundance of fleshly accommodations, and that devoteth and improveth all his power, and honour, and interest, to the promoting of holiness, love, and concord?

5. Let great men have a double interest in your prayers. They have a double need of grace and help; and we have a double need that they should be gracious. Oh! think how hard it is to save their faith, their innocency, and their souls, and to save the gospel and the public peace in the midst of so many and great temptations; and, therefore, pray hard where prayer is so needful.

And oh that I were now able to speak such enlightening and awakening words to you, as might show you at once your worldly prosperity and the heavenly glory in their proper value! and that God would now open your eyes and hearts accordingly, to esteem and seek them! Gentlemen, will you give this once an impartial hearing, to one that envieth not your wealth, but foreseeth the end of it; and how it will forsake you, and in how deplorable a case you will then be found, if you have not laid up a treasure in heaven, and secured the everlasting riches. I grudge you not your prosperity, for God doth not grudge it you: yea, the devil himself can afford it you for a time, while you serve him by it, and are captivated to his will in these golden fetters. And say not that it is I that call such fools: you see here it is God, that knoweth what he saith, and feareth not to speak it. But let me, with due submission, propound to your sober consideration these questions, which your consciences are concerned to resolve.

Quest. 1. Can any thing prove him truly wise that directly contradicteth the wisdom of the Lord, and valueth most the things that are most vilified by the doctrine and example of Christ and his apostles, and vilifieth that which Christ extolleth?

Quest. 2. Can any thing prove that man to be wise that is not wise enough to be saved? Surely it altereth the case but little, whether Satan be served in English, or in Latin, Greek, or Hebrew, in Spanish, Italian, or French; or whether you go towards everlasting woe in leather or in silk; and a miserable unsanctified soul do dwell in a comely or deformed body, and in a stately building or a smoky cottage;

and be titled a lord, a knight, or a ploughman; and whether he feed on the most delightful or the coarsest food. Alas! all this will soon be nothing. "The belly for meats, and meats for the belly; but God will destroy both it and them," 1 Cor. vi. 13. It is the endless life that puts the estimate upon all things here.

Quest. 3. Is he wise that preferreth a feather to a kingdom; an hour to eternity; earth to heaven? If you say you do not so, let your thoughts, your desires, your delights, your cares, and your labour and diligence, be the witnesses, and conscience and God shall finally judge. A man of reason should never make such a matter of nothing, as if there were so great a difference between riches and poverty, honour and dishonour, and a man's life or happiness consisted in his abundance. As it is usually the badge of empty, childish, brain-sick women, to value a curiosity of attire, and to have mind and time for so many toys, and to make ostentation of their pride and folly, by their curled, spotted, gaudy vanity, as if they were afraid lest they should be unacquainted with it, and should think them wise; so it is but a more plausible deliration in those that are more taken up with names, and titles, and commands, with houses and lands, and pompous attendance; and yet more brutish, where lust, and sports, and meats, and drinks, are taken for felicity, while God and heaven stand by neglected, and men forget that they are called christians, and that they are men.

Quest. 4. Is it wisdom to esteem men by their prosperity and pomp, and to admire a gilded post, or an ignorant, adorned wanton; and yet to overlook the divine and heavenly nature of the sanctified, and the beauty of holiness, and the image of God upon a humble, gracious soul, when that which is highly esteemed among men is abomination in the sight of God? Luke xvi. 15.

Quest. 5. Is it wisdom to be feasting, and playing, and dancing, while the soul is under the wrath of God, and in the gall of bitterness, and bonds of its iniquity? and by the noise, and business, and pleasures of the world, to be diverted and hindered from the speedy settling and securing your everlasting state? Should not a man of reason, without delay, the first thing he doth, make sure of his title to eternal happiness, when he is not sure of another hour; and if he miscarry in this, he is undone for ever? Should that time be laughed and played away that hasteth so fast, and is all so short for so great a work as the securing our salvation? Should men and women be courting, and complimenting, and fooling away their precious time, when the work is undone for which they were born into the world, and for which they have their lives, and all their mercies.

Quest. 6. Should all this be done by those that sin against their knowledge, and confess all this while that the world is vanity, and know it will leave them, and that all this is true?

O sirs, it must needs be the grief of a foreseeing man to think, when you forget it, what a change is coming, and what a sad preparation you are making, and how little a while the music, the feast, the cards and dice, and filthy lusts and wanton dalliance, will continue! and what a damp of self-tormenting desperation will seize upon those careless, scornful hearts that now will not be awakened and warned, nor understand any further than they see or feel! In compassion to those that are passing hence to another world, I beseech you, sometimes withdraw yourselves from sensual divertisements, and soberly bethink you whether this be the place and company that you must be with for ever; how long this merry life will last; and whether this be the work that the God of heaven did send you about into the world; and whether it would be more comfortable to your review when time is gone, to think of your days of sensual delight, or of a holy, and humble, and heavenly conversation; and to hear with Dives, Luke xvi. 25, "Son, remember that thou in thy life-time receivedst thy good things, and Lazarus evil things; but now he is comforted and thou art tormented." Oh then you would wish that you had never heard those airy titles, and never possessed those sumptuous houses, nor never tasted those delicious feasts, nor never worn that gay attire, nor never known that deceiving company, nor been polluted and brutified with those beastly lusts! Then conscience will force the now befooled Dives to cry out, Oh that I had been the most despised man on earth while honour did befool me! Oh that I had lain in medicinal poverty and rags when I took this mortal surfeit of prosperity! Oh that I had lain in tears and sorrow, when I was infatuated by fleshly mirth and pleasure, and that I had been among the saints that foresaw and provided for this day, when I drowned the voice of Christ and conscience with the laughter of a fool and the noise of worldly business and delights! Oh then, how revengefully will you befool yourselves, that you had time and knew no better how to use it! and how sensibly will you justify the wisdom of believers who bent their care for things eternal! I am ashamed of my heart that melts not in compassion in the foresight of your woe; and that I beg not of you with tears and importunity to prevent it, and to have mercy on yourselves. Paul had a better heart than I, that ceased not to warn every one, day and night, with tears, (Acts xx. 31,) and speaketh thus of such as you; Phil. iii. 18, 19, "For many walk, of whom I have told you often, and now tell you even weeping, the enemies of the cross of Christ; whose end is destruction, whose God is their belly, and whose glory is in their shame, who mind earthly things;" when the conversation of believers is in heaven, from whence they look for the Lord their Saviour.

I suppose you are afraid of the austerities of religion; and the devil would persuade you that it is but a self-tormenting or hypocritical life that we commend to you under the name of godliness, especially when you see the sadness of some honest souls that are abused by Satan through the advantages of melancholy: but I must profess it is sorrow that I call you from, and would prevent: it is no unnecessary grief that I would persuade you to, but to a life of heavenly peace and joy. If Satan have abused any servants of Christ, by darkening, and troubling, and discomforting their minds, which is his ordinary endeavour when he can no longer keep men quiet, and careless, and presumptuous in their misery; this is clean contrary to the nature of religion and the commands of Christ, that chargeth them always to rejoice. Do you think that I cannot have more solid joy with my daily bread, in the apprehensions of the love of God, and the belief of his promises of eternal life, than foolish mirth comes to, that is likened to the crackling of thorns in the fire? Eccles. vii. 6. You are for mirth, and we are for mirth, but it is a hearty, solid, spiritual, grounded, lasting mirth that we invite you to; and it is a beastly, sensual pleasure that ungodly men desire. For my part, it is almost half my work to promote the joys of true believers, and to dissuade them from such causeless despondencies and troubles as would rob them of their comforts, and God of their love, and thanks, and praise. Had you but tasted once the difference between this inward feast and yours, I should need no more words with you to persuade you that godliness is a life of joy. Dare any of you say, and stand to it, that there is not greater matter for joy in the love of Christ than in the love of a harlot? in the assurance of salvation than in lands and lordships? in the foresight of heaven than in the company of light-headed, voluptuous people, that have not wit enough to be serious, nor faith enough to foresee that which will so sadly and speedily spoil the sport? To be foolishly merry in the midst of misery, doth but make you the objects of greater compassion. Be as merry as you can, so it be grounded, and durable, and caused by that which God, and faith, and solid reason will approve, and doth not tend to greater sorrows. Bethink you well whether Christ and his apostles lived not a more comfortable life than you; and imitate them in their way of mirth, and spare not.

But if you are unsanctified, sensual, worldly men, lay by your mirth till you are fitter for it, and take your portion from the apostle James, (v. 1—3, 5,) "Go to now, ye rich men; weep and howl for your miseries that shall come upon you. Your riches are corrupted, and your garments moth-eaten; your gold and silver is cankered, and the rust of them shall be a witness against you, and shall eat your flesh as it were fire. Ye have heaped treasure together for the last days. Ye have lived in pleasure on earth, and been wanton; ye have nourished your hearts as in a day of slaughter."

What pity is it to see men destroy themselves with the mercies of the Lord! What pity is it to see them so eager for prosperity, and so regardless of the proper use and benefit of it! O be not like the bee that is drowned in her own honey! And do not so greedily desire a greater burden than you can bear; and to have more to answer for, when you have been so unfaithful in a little. And if you believe Christ, who tells you how hardly rich men come to heaven, and how few of them are saved, long not for your danger, and grudge not if you have not these exceeding difficulties to overcome. You would be afraid to dwell in that air where few men escape infection; or to feed on that diet that most are killed by. It is evident by the effects that prosperity befooleth and undoeth the most; we find you on your sick beds in a more tractable frame.

1. Then a man may speak to you about the case of your immortal souls, with less contempt than now we meet with. You look not then for laced speeches, but will more patiently hear our plain discourses of eternal life. 2. Then you will seem serious yourselves, and speak almost like those that you called precisians and puritans, for remembering you of these things in your prosperity. 3. Then you have some better relish of truth and duty; and judge better of the matter and manner of exhortation and prayer than you do now. 4. Then you have more charity and moderation to others; and are not enraged to the destroying of those that are not of your opinions in all your formalities. 5. You would then shake the head at him that should offer you cards, or dice, or fleshly vanities; and you would tell others that it is wiser to be delighted in the law of God, and meditate in it day and night. 6. Then you will speak as contemptuously of the honour, and pleasures, and profits of the world, and of pleasing men before the Lord, as we do now. 7. And then you will confess the preciousness of time; the folly of mispending it; and that one thing is necessary, for which we can never (regularly) do too much. And why are you not now of the mind that you will be at death or judgment, but that your folly doth turn your prosperity to your bane? Once more I beseech you, for the Lord's sake, retire from the deceiving world to God; and if you care where you live to all eternity, choose your abode; and now set your heart upon it, and seek it as your happiness. If all these warnings are refused, conscience shall tell you when you would not hear it, that you were warned.

Had time allowed it, I should next have delivered my message to the humble, upright souls. All you "that hearken to the Lord, shall dwell in safety, and be quiet from the fear of evil." Isaiah iii. 10, "Say to the righteous, it shall be well with him.—Woe to the wicked! it shall be ill with him." Eccles. viii. 12, "Though a sinner do evil an hundred times, and his days be prolonged, yet surely I know it shall be well with them that fear God." Psalm lxxiii. 1, "Truly God is good to Israel; even to such as are of a clean heart." Psalm xxxvii. 5, 28, 34, 37, "Commit thy way unto the Lord; trust in him, and he shall bring it to pass. For the Lord loveth judgment, and forsaketh not his saints: they are preserved for ever.—Wait on the Lord, and keep his way——and when the wicked are cut off, thou shalt see it. Mark the perfect man, and behold the upright: for the end of that man is peace."

If you say, How are they safe that are so tossed by sufferings? I answer, 1. Is he not safe that hath the promise of God for his security, and is related to him as his child, and hath Christ for his Head and Saviour? 2. Is he not safe that is delivered from the wrath of God and the flames of hell, and dare look before him to eternity with hope and comfort? and shall live with Christ in joy for ever? 3. Is he not safe that hath no enemy, but what is in his Father's power? 4. And that hath no hurt but what shall certainly procure his good? 5. Nor any but what we may rejoice in; and is sure shall be the matter of his thanks when it is past? That shall lose nothing but what he hath already forsaken, and esteemeth but as dross and dung? How oft have we told God in our prayers, that we had rather have the light of his countenance in adversity, than be strange to him in prosperity? And that he would not refuse that state of suffering, that should be blest to the destruction of our sins, and the furthering our communion with God, and our assurance of salvation, and in which we might most serve and honour him in the world. Did we live by sense, we should misjudge of our estate: but seeing we live by faith, and in the way can see the end, we can say we are safe in the thickest of our enemies, and will not fear what man can do, while the Almighty is our rock and fortress: well may we be quiet from that fear of evil, when we are saved from the great everlasting evil! No evil shall follow us into heaven: no malice shall there defame us; nor virulent tongue blaspheme our holy profession or our Lord; for the mists of hellish blasphemies shall never ascend to blot the glory of Christ or of his saints. Who then shall take us out of his hands? Who shall condemn us? It is he that justifieth us; not only against the calumnies of malice, but also against the accusations of Satan for our sin. How safe and quiet are those millions of souls that are now with Christ! How little are they annoyed, or their joy or melody interrupted, by all the rage of earth or hell! The glory of the sun may sooner be darkened or blemished by obloquy, than their celestial glory; for they are glorified with the glory of their Lord; and rejoice with his joy, and live because he liveth. Be of good cheer, christians! the haven is within the sight of faith; we are almost there; adversity is our speediest and surest passage: and then let sin, and rage, and malice, do their worst.

CAIN AND ABEL MALIGNITY,

THAT IS,

ENMITY TO SERIOUS GODLINESS;

THAT IS,

TO A HOLY AND HEAVENLY STATE OF HEART AND LIFE;

LAMENTED, DESCRIBED, DETECTED, AND UNANSWERABLY PROVED TO BE THE DEVILISH NATURE, AND THE MILITIA OF THE DEVIL AGAINST GOD AND CHRIST, AND THE CHURCH AND KINGDOMS, AND THE SUREST SIGN OF A STATE OF DAMNATION.

READER,

THIS reprehensive lamentation of English malignity, or hatred, and scorn, and persecution of serious godliness, by them who profess to believe in God, and to be christians, was written in prison, (but without any provoking sense of my suffering,) in anno 1685, 1686. And by one that was not wholly ignorant, how much of the papists' counsel and power was causal in our change since the return of King Charles II. 1660. And therefore it grateth so much upon the papists, though they were professed protestants who were the open agents.

It was written by one who can remember, at least since 1627, that the serious practice of godliness was the common scorn of the vulgar rabble; and he that did but read the Scripture, and books of piety, and pray in his family, and catechise children or servants, to hear a sermon at the next parish church from a godly conformist, when he had none at home; yea, that did but seriously talk of Christ or Scripture, or the life to come, or preparation for death and judgment, when under the name of a puritan, which was a reproach in the mouth of drunkards, swearers, fornicators, and all the sensual, worldly sort, both high and low. And that conformable ministers (yea and gentlemen) that were but seriously religious, no more escaped this scorn than nonconformists (who were then so few, that they were in most places unknown). He sadly remembereth how greatly this malignant rabble triumphed in the bishop's visitation articles, and in the preaching and talk of many priests, who sharpened their sermons with invectives against puritans as dangerous hypocrites, though they had not a nonconformist within many miles. He heard the godly conformable ministers lament, that the bishops and ecclesiastical courts by their jealousy and heat against the nonconformable puritans, became the strength and encouragement of this malignant, vicious rabble; and that the young worldly ministers took it for the way to preferment, to preach against puritans, while they treated the multitude of profane, prayerless families that had no savour of serious religion, as their good and peaceable flocks. He lived to see the godly, learned conformists, so grieved for this, that they longed for a reformation; and many conformists (as Bishop Robert Abbot, Bishop Downame, and divers others) published their reproof and lamentation for it: and good Robert Bolton (in his Directions for Walking with God) thinks that since malice entered into the heart of man, there was never a word tossed with more malice in the mouths of drunkards and profane men, than the word puritan. Hundreds and thousands of these wicked scorners of religion, were either admitted (or driven) to the sacrament, or lived quietly in great parishes while they despised it, while these poor puritans were strictly hunted after! And if they fasted and prayed with a dying or sick friend, without getting a licence for it from the bishop, the church-warden must enter them into their inquisition, or be forsworn.

These puritans having the greatest averseness to popery, in some things were too suspicious of all that they thought smelled of it. And when they heard that in Ireland the papists had most barbarously murdered the protestants, (two hundred thousand,) and that they boasted that they rose by the king's commission, and threatened to invade England, and that the English papists were against the parliament; this made many think that the protestant religion was not safe, but in the parliament's part and care: upon which the next year, when our odious civil war began, many of them went into the parliament's armies; but the generality would fain have lived quietly at home, but the debauched rabble and their patrons would not suffer them; but they turned the name puritan into roundhead, and Down with the roundheads, was the common cry. I have myself by that cry been in present danger, in passing through a city where no man knew me, because I wore not long hair. If their neighbours did but pray, and sing a psalm in their houses, the rabble would (like the Sodomites at the door of Lot) set up a cry against them in the streets, and say, Down with the roundheads, the rebels, a Gowry, a conspiracy, &c. Even where I lived they assembled with weapons, and sought my life, and knocked down (mortality being the issue) even strangers in the streets that meddled not with them, because they were accounted friends to the puritans. By this means the parliament's garrisons and armies were filled with religious men, that were forced to fly from their houses by the malignant, ignorant drunkards, to save their lives: and this, even this was the ruin of King Charles, and his army, and of the persecuting bishops and clergy. Necessity made thousands to be soldiers that could not live at home: and most were moved by an argument that was not cogent, still saying, We cannot believe that God would suffer the generality of the most religious to choose the wrong side, and the generality of the papists and ignorant drunkards and malignants to be in the right.

Oh what shame and pity is it that the antipuritan clergy no better remembered from 1660 till now, by what means they fell; and that they no more understood, nor yet understand, what a torrent of sin, of danger, and of shame, is come upon them, by their strengthening themselves, by sheltering (to say no worse) the sensual, irreligious, malignant rabble, (rich and poor,) that they may tread down the puritans, that by their own doings are brought into a dislike of them. Will God ever bless a profane rabble (or gentry) to be the honour and strength of the church, against the religious that desire a reformation?

It is not their new foolish names and scorns, (as whigs, trimmers, presbyterians, &c.) that will prove that it is not serious piety that they hate. As long as the most filthy wicked livers are the enemies and accusers, and in their own party and companions, the vilest debauchery passeth for sufferable, and a small disgrace, and thousands of such live at ease, when preaching the gospel, and praying without their fetters or book, must cost men ruin, and imprisonment, and scorn. And Sulpicius Severus's sharp invective against Ithacius, Idacius, and the rest of the bishops in their synod, was that in prosecuting the Priscillian Gnostics, they brought the matter to that pass, that if godly men did but fast, and pray, and read Scripture, the bishops made them suspected as Priscillianists (even St. Martin himself). Woe to them that turn the sacred offices of magistracy and ministry against God that did ordain them, to be used as in his name, and in some representation of himself, sacrilegiously blaspheming him as an enemy to himself! Shall the throne of iniquity have fellowship with God, that frameth mischief by a law, to make sin common and allowed?

By this the reader may see that there is a double history needful to the full understanding of this book; and of the nature and causes of malignity: that is, 1. The history of Adam's fall, and the great depravation of human nature thence arising; and the true meaning of the enmity thence put between the woman's and the serpent's seed, exemplified in the two first brothers born into the world; as also in Ishmael and Isaac, Esau and Jacob; and frequently mentioned by Christ and his apostles.

2. The history of the advantages that malignity hath got into England since the Reformation; and especially since the return of Charles the Second. This must contain the sad differences begun at Frankfort in Queen Mary's days; the errors and extremes of both the differing parties; the biassing determinations of Queen Elizabeth; the difference between the first bishops that had been exiles, and their successors; the presbyterians' provocations by over-opposing episcopacy, and the bishops' design to root them out, and the making of the canons to that end; the rise of a new sort of bishops, began in Laud, Neil, Howson, Corbet, and Buckeridge, with Mountague, and their growth under Buckingham against the old churchmen; the design of a coalition with Rome, and the French and English attempts thereto; the interruption of this design by the long parliament, and the wars; the Scots forcing the parliament (that in their straits asked their help) to take their covenant; the imposing that covenant on the whole ministry, and making it a divided engine on pretence of unity; the parliament's casting out with a multitude of flagitious ministers) some doctors, for being against them, for the king, contrary to the desires of peace-makers; the presbyterians under Monk restoring King Charles the Second; the return and preferment of his doctors, and their revengeful resolutions; their design to get all church power, and preferment, and academic rule into the hands of them that most hated puritans, or would endeavour their extirpation, and would educate youth in bitter prejudice and hatred of them; the vulgar hatred of serious godliness in conformists and nonconformists, under the name of puritans; the power that a few returned doctors had with the king and chancellor in the disposal of preferments, and thereby to overrule the parliament, and to procure the acts of uniformity, corporation oaths, vestry and militia oaths, and the acts for banishments, confinements, imprisonments, fining, ejecting, silencing, and ruining such whose consciences pleaded God's law and authority against any of their oaths, impositions, and silencing prohibitions to preach the gospel; the great difference in the wars (I meddle not with the cause) between the adherents and soldiers of the king, (Charles I.) and the parliament's, in point of piety and sobriety; the animosity and implacable heat by which the before-conquered, and now ruling party, proceeded towards the ruin of those that they took for enemies to the cause, civil or ecclesiastic, which they had owned; the unhappiness of the then present ministry, that being young then, had never meddled with wars, that they must equally suffer as enemies, for fearing the imposed oaths, subscriptions, covenants, and practices; the rejoicing of the common sort of the luxurious drunkards, whoremongers, and infidels, that they had got so many of the religious into contempt, and scorn, and ruin; the woeful increase of whoredom, luxury, and impiety, and Sadduceeism hereupon; the great numbers of religious people, who before hoped for peace and a pious prelacy, that fell hereupon into a hatred of prelacy, and a great disesteem of the conforming ministry; and so our divisions are grown to a fixed factious enmity; and malice and worldly interest will hear no motions or petitions for peace; and yet madly plead all for love and peace, while they implacably fight against them, and accuse those as the enemies of peace, who beg peace of them, and cannot obtain it.

This is the sum of the doleful history which this book presupposeth: but should I write it, the rage would be increased. The foregoing narrative is as much as is fit for this brief discourse, which, if you will, you may style Acris Gorreptio, with Gildas; or Planctus Ecclesia, with Alv.; Pelag. or, The groans of the Church, with a late conformable divine. It hath been cast by four years, at first because it would not be endured, and after in a vain hope that our church reformation would make such a complaint less necessary. But now I perceive the devil will be the devil, and mankind will be born blind, sensual, and malignant, till there be a new heaven and earth in which dwelleth righteousness. Come, Lord Jesus.

August 24, 1689, *the fatal day of silencing in England in* 1662.

CHAPTER I.

A LAMENTATION FOR THE CASE OF THE DELUDED, MALIGNANT, MILITANT WORLD.

1. THE depraved and miserable condition of mankind hath long been the astonishing wonder of the sober and inquisitive part of the world: philosophers were puzzled with the difficult questions, whence it first came; and why it is no more remedied. Christians are taught by the sacred Scriptures how to answer both, by laying it on man's misusing of his free-will, supposing God's permission of his trial and temptations; and on his resistance and rejection of remedying grace, in the degree that it is vouchsafed or offered. But still there are difficulties, and our understandings are dark, and hardly satisfied. And whencesoever it comes, the case is doleful, and we cannot but think of it with astonishment and lamentation. When we saw a hundred thousand made dead corpses by the London plague, 1665, it did not take off the terror to know how it begun. And when we saw the city on a dreadful flame, which none could stop, it cured not the general astonishment to conjecture how it was kindled or carried on. No doubt but hell itself proclaimeth that God is holy, wise, and just, and devils and men are the cause of their own everlasting punishment; but yet if we had a sight of it, amazement and dread would overwhelm us. And, alas! what a map of hell is the greatest part of earth! Hell is a place of lying, malignant and murderous, hurtful spirits, miserable by and for their wickedness: and is not this, in a low degree, a true description of most of the earth?

2. Nineteen parts in thirty of the earth are idolaters and heathens. And do I need to say, how ignorant, wicked, and miserable they are? Many of them publicly worship the devil, as witches do with us; and he deludeth them, and appeareth in divers shapes to them, and ruleth them as he doth witches. And those that are more civil, are strangers or enemies to Christ. Six parts of the thirty are ignorant Mahometans, destroyers indeed of heathenish idolatry, and such as take Christ for a great and true prophet, but know him not as a Saviour, but equal to prefer a gross deceiver, and live under barbarous tyrants, who by violence keep them in the dark. The other five parts that are called christians, alas! consist most of people bred up in lamentable ignorance, mostly barbarous or debased by the oppression of tyrants, such as the Muscovites, most of the Greeks, the Abassines, Armenians, and many eastern sects and nations. What ignorance the vulgar papists are bred in in Italy, Spain, Germany, Poland, France, and other countries, and what an enmity to true reformation prevaileth in princes, priests, and people; and by what lying and cruelty they fight against truth, and what inquisitions, murders, and inhuman massacres have been their powerful means, I need not use many words to tell.

And are the protestant reformed churches free from fleshly, worldly, wicked men? from ignorant, malignant, cruel enemies to truth, and piety, and peace?

3. Our king's dominions are the best and happiest nations on earth. Here is most knowledge of the truth, and most proportionably that truly love it, and live in a holy obedience thereto, and fain would live a quiet and peaceable life in all godliness, honesty, and sobriety. But, alas! they must be contented with their own personal uprightness and reward, and the peace of their consciences in God's acceptance. But with men there seemeth to be no hopes of common wisdom, piety, love, and peace.

We are all baptized with one baptism; we all profess to be the servants of one God, and the faithful followers of one Christ, and to believe in one holy, sanctifying Spirit, and to believe the same canonical Scriptures as the word of God, indited by that Spirit; and to be of one holy catholic church, which is all the members of Christ on earth; and to hold the communion of saints. We mostly in England and Scotland agree in the protestant reformed doctrine, and sacraments; our concord in profession is so great, that if some men had not devised some oaths, professions, covenants, practices, knacks and engines of their own (which they dare not say God made) to become the matter of our unavoidable dissent, they hardly have known how to pretend any difference in religion among us, and hell would scarce have found any cloak for malicious accusations, enmity, and discord.

You shall scarce meet with a man that will not speak well of love and peace, and say that we must love God above all, and our neighbours as ourselves, and do as we would have others do to us. And yet is there any enmity or disagreement? Alas, how great, and how incurable!

4. Who would think that knew us not by our profession, but only by our actions, but that the three kingdoms consisted of the deadliest enemies to each other? of Turks and christians; of wolves and sheep; that I say not of devils and men? Yea, Turks and christians can live together in Hungary, and all the eastern countries. Orthodox and heretics can live together in Poland, Helvetia, Holland, &c. But protestants and protestants cannot live together in Britain. Cities and corporations, countries and churches, if not families also, are distracted in enmity and more than mental feuds and war. Guelphs and Gibelines, party against party, studying accusations against each other, as if they were scholars daily exercised in the school of him that is the accuser of the brethren. All their learning and wit is called up, and poured out, to render others as odious as they are able. All their power, interest, friends, and diligence, are used to ruin and destroy each other. No lies or perjury with some seem unlawful to accomplish so desired an effect. In all companies, the discourse and converse that should be to edify each other in love, and comfort each other by the hopes of dwelling together in heaven, is taken up

with slanders, backbitings, scorning, railing, and plotting the overthrow of the best of their neighbours. Innocency never wants odious or scornful names. As if they were acting their part that called Christ and his apostles, and the ancient christians, deceivers, blasphemers, enemies to Cæsar, ringleaders of sedition, that taught men to worship God contrary to the law. Every drunkard and wicked liver can as easily make his conscionable neighbour a rogue, or a traitor, or a schismatic, or a hypocrite, as he can open his mouth and speak.

And to justify all this malice is become a virtue; hating the most religious, is zeal for government and order; destroying Christ's members, is standing up for the church; hunting them as dogs do hares, or as hawks do the lesser birds, is a meritorious work, of supererogation no doubt, and will not finally lose its reward. God is served by hating and scorning them that are serious in his service. It is religion to make religion odious, and call it hypocrisy, and to be for that which is uppermost, and befriends their worldly interest, and to make him suspected of disloyalty who is for obedience to God. Conscience, and fear of sinning and of damnation, is the mortal enemy to be conquered or driven out of the land; as if there were no quietness to be expected in men's minds, no concord in the church, no obedience to the clergy or the laws, no safety from sedition, till conscience be silenced or banished, and men give over fearing God; or as if Christ and Cæsar could not both reign, but God or princes must be dethroned.

And oh that the sacred tribe were innocent, and none of them were the leaders in such hypocritical malignity! Their canons *ipso facto* excommunicate all (not excepting princes, parliaments, or judges) that do but say, that any of their ceremonies, liturgy, or officers in church government (not excepting the lowest, or laymen's power of the church keys by decreeing excommunications and absolutions) are repugnant to the word of God. And when they have *ipso facto* excommunicated them all, they call them separatists for not coming to their communion. Think not the contradiction and hypocrisy incredible. Read but the fifth, sixth, and eighth canons, and judge. They have a law, and by their law he is cut off from the church of Christ, that doth but call any of these the inventions of prelates sinful, or to say that God forbids them. And the gaol must be his dwelling till he die there, who in ten cases remaineth excommunicate, and doth not openly profess that he repenteth, and judgeth that to be sinless, which he is utterly unable so to judge. When we have preached seven and seven years, to persuade a drunkard, a liar, and profane swearer, or an atheist, to repent, he liveth quietly out of the gaol though he repent not. But if a man repent not (when he cannot) of judging that God forbids such human inventions and impositions in religion, take him jailer; he that will not be for our human offices, ceremonies, and impositions, shall not be of our church. And when we have cast him out, we will say he separateth. And if he be not of our church, he shall be in gaol. As if the church and the gaol would hold all the land, except his sin be such a peccadillo as atheism, Sadduceeism, bestiality, Hobbism, popery, manslaughter, adultery, drunkenness, swearing, &c. not aggravated by the crimes of breaking the canons in point of conformity; or if many thousands cannot or will not come within the doors of the parish church, so they will go to no unlicensed preacher, nor worship God in house or church at all, they live quietly out of prison. But if the mote of an oath or ceremony scrupled be in their eye, that eye must be pulled out, (if the mote cannot,) or else the whole body be cast into their hell. And if the preacher be but a candidate of domination, his way is oft to call to the magistrate to execute the law upon such as dare presume to worship God openly, till they hold all such imposed oaths, covenants, professions, and practices to be lawful. He is to make his auditory believe that such men are dangerous, intolerable persons, and that their meeting to worship God and learn their duty, is to cherish sedition, heresy, and schism, and that rebellion is in their hearts; and that the preachers that even to a thing indifferent are not of their mind and obedience, are deceivers, and factious, and it is no sacrilege, but a duty, to forbid them to preach the gospel. If the people dare not trust the parson, vicar, or curate of the parish, (be he what he will, whom a —— patron chooseth for them,) with the pastoral ordinary conduct of their souls, or if he preach not at all, if they go to the next parochial conformist for the sacrament, he is to be driven home, and used as disobedient.

Through the great mercy of God, while the Bible is licensed, a preacher in England knoweth not how to spend his hour, if he say not somewhat for faith and godliness, love and peace. And when they come down, none are so hated by some of them, as those that believe and do to their utmost what they for fashion' sake persuaded them to believe and do. Their neighbours who have not a word with the priest of any thing but this world, nor read a chapter or put up a prayer in their families, these are good and quiet neighbours. But if any seriously prepare for their everlasting state, and mind their salvation above the world; especially if they pray without book, and dislike the ignorant and scandalous lives of sorry priests, these are the dangerous troublers of the land: Away with them, and give us those that trouble us not with the talk of God and of death, and heaven or hell, of Scripture or of conscience, and that scruple nothing that we could have them say or do. If such pray, it is but in hypocrisy; if they go to hear any other preacher, it is in faction. If they speak any words to God which are not written down for them to read, they saucily prate to God, and speak but nonsense. If they be earnest as knowing what they pray for, they do but whine and cut faces, and speak through the nose, or are a pack of groaning hypocrites. It is confessed that the Spirit of adoption and supplication is God's gift; and that this Spirit taught the bishops and convocation in what words to pray to God. But if the most holy or learned men besides them pretend to it, and think that any may pray by the Spirit's help but the convocation, there are reverend men that will deride that Spirit, or that prayer. I would at least they would let men pray by reason and the sense of their soul's necessities, (as a child will beg pardon of an offended father,) if they will not give them leave to pray by that Spirit (which all must live by that will be saved).

Physicians use their patients with some humanity, and will not say to him that saith, My stomach cannot take down this potion, I shall cast it up, You shall take it or die, or go to prison. Or if one say, This pill is bigger than my throat can swallow, they will rather say, It shall be made less, than they will cut his throat wider to get it down. And sure the reason is because the law doth make them physicians to none but volunteers, and give them no compelling power. If it did, I know not what inhumanity they might come to. For I will not believe that there is any thing in divinity which tendeth to make men more inhuman than physicians. I have seen jews and others, that will eat no swine's flesh; and I have known many that a taste of cheese would cast into a swoon near death; and I never knew any say, You shall eat this or die; nor that ever motioned the making of a law that all men should be imprisoned, or forbidden all other meat, who refused to eat swine's flesh, for fear of tolerating Jews.

But we have priests too many, that will say, Take every oath, promise, or ceremony required of you, or preach not, nor worship God openly at all. Take me for your pastor, or you shall have none. Hear me, or hear no man. Receive the communion from me, or from none. Deny not the lawfulness of a ceremony, or be excommunicate.

4. And is it now any wonder that the people say as they are taught? And these are lessons easilier learnt than a catechism, or the creed, or the meaning of baptism. How quickly can a man learn to call his neighbour whig or tory! or to hate a godly man, or in a tavern or alehouse to scorn them, or drink and curse to their confusion, and to say, I hope to see them all hanged or banished out of the land! As a priest that knows not what divinity or the priestly office is, may, before he taketh many degrees, attain the ability learnedly to call his godly neighbours schismatics, or hypocrites, or worse; so no doubt a few such sermons, if not a tavern, can quickly teach them that never knew what religion is, yea, that can scarce speak sense, to revile the wisest and best men, as if they were sinners against the true religion, if they will be serious in any true religion at all.

5. O sinful! O miserable land! who kindled all the hellish flames of thy malignity and mad divisions? And who continueth them, and for what? What cloven foot hath entered, and expelled concord? What spirit ruleth thee? Were it the Spirit of Christ, it would be for healing, love, and concord; it would set men on studying to promote love to all, even unto enemies, but much more to the most holy. It would make men zealous of good works, and if it were possible, as much as in them lieth, to live peaceably with all men, to bless those that curse them, to pray for those that hate and persecute them, forbearing and forgiving one another, even as God for Christ's sake forgiveth us. It would teach them while they have time to do good to all men, but especially to them of the household of faith. Men's hearts would be constituted of love. It would become a nature in them. Their speech and converse would be the savoury breath of love. Their dealings towards all men would be the works of love. Their sharpest reproofs would be but to do the sinner good.

But alas, another spirit hath possessed thee, which rageth and teareth thee; and is blind and deaf. It calleth for fire from heaven, and it kindleth a fire of hell. And sure his name is Legion, for there are many. It passeth under the name of Wisdom, and Hatred of some evil. But it must needs be earthly, sensual, and devilish, for it is neither pure nor peaceable, gentle, or merciful and impartial, but foameth with bitter envy and strife, unto confusion and every evil work. And yet thou knowest not what manner of spirit thou art of.

Is it God that setteth rulers and people against each other? Doth he divide his own kingdom against itself, when he tells that the devil will not do so by his? Is it God that sets the parts of the same body in a hatred and war against each other; as if it were the interest of the nobler and the servile parts to weaken or destroy each other? and it were an addition to the health and welfare of the one, which is gotten by conquest from the other? Is it God that maketh people despise or dishonour their lawful governors, or any rulers to hate the best subjects, and desire more to be feared than to be loved, and rather to have power to do hurt, than actually to do good? Is it God that sets corporations, and churches, and neighbours, and families, in a state of malice, vexation, strife, and a kind of war against each other? Doth the Spirit of God indite the malicious pamphlets which exercise the utmost of wit and hatred, to destroy love, and to call the nation into the devil's camp, by mutual hatred to live as enemies, and fight against the Lord and the ways of peace? And if any endeavour a reconciling healing of our wounds, it is turned into scorn, and his healing motions are represented as the grand causes of division; and to beg for peace is heinous schism, and next rebellion against the church, and a crime sufficient to forfeit that man's peace and reputation: and he that tells men of the only possible terms of concord, is made the chiefest cause of discord. To serve and worship God no otherwise than Peter and Paul did, and than God prescribeth, is enough to render us unworthy to live on English earth; and if England may not suffer such, why should any other nation suffer them? There are men that keep holy days for St. Peter and St. Paul, and dedicate churches to them, and their bellies are maintained at divers rates, and their wealth, and revenues, and grandeur help up, by that which is dedicated to these churches; and to alienate any of this superfluity from their flesh were worse sacrilege than to cast out and silence a thousand faithful preachers: and yet if St. Paul were a preacher now in France, Spain, Italy, or England, and would worship God but as he did when he was on earth, and would not swear, say, and do as much more as the bishop's canons bid him, I think we should again hear those words, (Acts xxii. 22,) "Away with such a fellow from the earth, for it is not fit that he should live" (here); unless he wrought miracles to convince men: and whether those would prevail is a doubtful case; or whether he would not pass for a deceiver and fanatic.

6. As in times of war, all broken, beggarly, and idle fellows turn soldiers, as the easiest trade to live by, are never after good for any other trade, but to kill and rob men; so the love-killing regiments have forsaken other trades, and this is like to put down all. Booksellers complain that they can sell few books but news, and scorning or invective libels. And what is the subject of our (formerly weekly and now daily) news-books? Why, they tell us that such a city or corporation are altogether by the ears as enemies, some choosing one mayor and some another; some called whigs and others tories; some seeking the ruin and blood of others, and some hardly escaping the power of false witnesses and oaths! One jury acquitting a man whose life is sought, and another condemning him. In such a town or city so many fined, and so many distrained on, and so many crowded into gaols, and such and such preachers cast into prison, and such a one dead there, for praying to God, and openly worshipping him without book, or by no book but his own. In such and such a country the people prosecuting each other on such accounts, and some flying into other parts, and some into America to seek that peace among savages, and wolves, and serpents, in wildernesses, which they could not have under sacred protestant prelates and their clergy. In France the poor protestants hunted like hares, neither suffered to live at home, nor to fly naked to beg their bread in other lands: and all this for the concord and peace of the holy catholic church; a pattern so worthy of imitation, that even such excellent men as Grotius think, that it is worth all hazards, labour, and cost, to reduce England and the Lutherans to the French church

consistence, and to silence and ruin all as Calvinists that are against it. From Hungary we must read, how the persecuted protestants, after their utmost suffering and patience, are fain to call in Turks to save them from the cruelties of christians. And that those parts that are under the Turks have far more prosperity and freedom in religion, than those that are under the emperor and papists.

And protestants under them are kept in continual fear, as knowing that it is their law and doctrine, that princes are bound to do their best to exterminate or destroy them, on pain of excommunication, deposition, and damnation: and remembering the inquisitions, the Piedmont, French, Dutch, Irish, &c. massacres: so that they are brought to this hard dilemma, Choose whether you will be dead men, or be proclaimed rebels. If whole countries will not lie down and die patiently without self-defence, they are odious rebels.

These, and such other, are the subjects of our news-books, which have broken the poor booksellers, who were wont to live by selling books of learning, and of practical divinity. And too many preachers are fain to be short as well as formal in their sermons for christian love, because they spend so much time in preaching up hatred and destruction. Were there but an art that could devise any engine that could reach the heart, and turn it into the hatred of those that never did them wrong, (as they say some philters and charms will make men mad with love,) or if any apothecary had an effectual medicine against brotherly love, I doubt these would become the most accustomed shops and prosperous trades in all the city: but for want of such, some pulpits, printers, booksellers, clubs, drinking-houses, and play-houses, (to pass by fouler,) must serve the turn. But if God have not mercy on the land by restraining them, gunpowder-makers, gunsmiths, sword-sellers, soldiers, swearers, and executioners, will swallow up most other trades in the land. It is worth inquiry whether in foresight of this, they set not their sons to such trades as these, or apprentices to such lawyers as are best at preparative accusations, and have learned Tertullus's art; or to such schools and tutors as can teach them the learning of Zedekiah, and the four hundred prophets, 1 Kings xxii.

7. And all this is the more inexcusable and lamentable, because they came but lately out of the fire, which this same malignant spirit kindled; the very same causes cast the three kingdoms into dreadful flames and blood. The histories of the bloody murder of many hundred thousands called Albigenses, Waldenses, and Bohemians, in Piedmont, Germany, and elsewhere, and of the Netherland cruelties, the Spanish inquisitions and invasions, the murder of thirty or forty thousand at once in France, and of two of their kings, the powder plot here, as well as the bonfires in Queen Mary's days, and much more their councils and doctors defending and commanding such usage of protestants, did set all our parliaments one after another into a vehement unwillingness to be so used, and to fall into their hands that will do it if they can: and when the evil spirit had raised cross interests and distrusts between king and parliament, the papists seeming to be for the war and king, and suddenly murdering in Ireland no fewer than two hundred thousand, and pretending the king's commission, and threatening the like in England, frightened people into the army, after raised by the parliament. And though I think all that war in England killed not the fourth part so many as the papists had murdered in Ireland; yet so dismal and odious was it, and had so direful an end, as loudly told us how bad the causes and beginnings were. Few parts of the land were free from spoil, plunder, and poverty; yea, or from terrible sieges and fields of blood: Englishmen labouring to destroy each other, and some hiring foreigners to help them: and lads running from their parents to be as apprentices to the man-killing trade. Counties were against counties, cities against cities, neighbours against neighbours, single persons flying from men as from bears and tigers, as after in the plague-time, afraid of almost all that they met: and at last the very armies falling out among themselves; the first raised for the parliament, were mastered by a second party, that brought in (as auxiliaries) a new imposition; and that party after mastered and cast down by a third, that brought in a new cause; and that prevailing, pulling down their masters, a usurper odiously destroying the king, and setting up himself with another title, and subduing and ruining those that were against it, even both the parties that began the war; and yet when he was dead, to show the world what divisions can do, that same victorious, rebellious army fell all into pieces by its own discord, and was totally dissolved as by a miracle, without one drop of blood that ever I could hear of, and the victorious leaders many of them hanged, drawn, and quartered, and their heads and quarters hanged up on the city gates.

And would not one think that a nation of men in their wits, should after so long and sad experience of the mischiefs of hatred and division, be willing of the reviving of love and concord, and hate all motions of dividing any more? But alas, they hate them that would heal our wounds; and if any one lay on a healing plaster, there are hands too many, both lay and clergy, ready with rage to pull it off; and yet it is all on pretence of healing us, that they will not suffer us to be healed; for the way of peace they have not known. Unhappy surgeons, that know no balsam but corrosives and distilled vinegar, yea, no way of healing but by dismembering, even the usefullest members of the body. Having learned of the Romish leeches that live on blood, when they are for exhausting the vital stock, and cast the kingdom into a palsy or marasmus, they tell you it was all but corrupt or hæmorrhoidal blood, and the loss of it necessary to cure the madness of the land.

The beginning of some reconciliation between the first contending parties, began to flatter us with the hopes of restored love and quietness: secret consultations prepared the way: lords, knights, and gentlemen, print their protestations for oblivion and reconciliation, and against revenge. Hereupon those that by land and sea, in the three kingdoms, had fought against the king, restore him: the land rejoiceth in the smiling hopes of reviving charity and concord. The king chiefly causeth these hopes by his declarations and act of oblivion, and especially his healing gracious declaration about ecclesiastical affairs. The house of commons and the city ministers give him thanks for it. Who would have thought now but such experience, such protestations, such obligations, such authorities, should have put the whole kingdom into a longing desire to perfect the work of love and peace? But it proved clean contrary: some had other things in their heads and hearts; outlandish fashions, especially French, have long been the badge of English folly! There are men in Spain that trade much in the fire, and Queen Mary brought the trade into England: there are men in many other foreign lands, who are so devout, that their canons and religion rule their appetites; and they love no meat like a carbonadoed protestant, nor are pleased with any perfume or incense so much as with the smell of a roasted saint, first called a heretic or schismatic: like the Roman tyrant that gloried in the sweetness of the smell when he smelt the stink of the carcasses which he had laid to dung the field. And there were men abroad that learned these fashions, and contracted such a familiarity and love to foreigners, as that for obtaining union with them, all the divisions, distractions, and calamities of England and Scotland are not thought too dear a sacrifice: and as some sons of nonconformists must be doubly virulent to expiate the guilt of their original sin; so some Englishmen must, like Samson and David, bring double testimony of their real enmity to the Philistines, from their skins, before they can be trusted abroad as real reconcilers: and they say that there are some things that will be closely united by no cement so well as by human blood. Doubtless the gospel as used in English, and preached by true protestants, (such as the pseudo-bellamy in Philanax Anglicus hatefully calleth protestants off sincerity,) goeth not with many beyond sea for the same gospel which they believe. And therefore no wonder if the preachers of it be unpleasing to them; and he that will please them, and unite with them, must silence or oppose those that they would have to be silenced and disgraced. And some think that union with many kingdoms of christians, which call themselves the catholic church, is much to be preferred before the love and concord of a hated party in our island. And as Dr. Saywell (the master of a college, and bishop Gunning's chaplain) saith, (to prove that there is a universal legislative and judicial power in the clergy, over kingdoms as well as persons,) "If more persons or particular churches give offence by heresy, schism, &c. the CHURCH UNIVERSAL, or the rest of the bishops, may reprove them for it, and then there is no reason why one man should be censured and many should go free, and consequently our Saviour hath established the authority of his church over all christians, as well particular churches as private men: churches of kingdoms and nations have a SOVEREIGNTY over them to which they must yield obedience. 'The nation and kingdom that will not serve thee, shall perish: yea, those nations shall be utterly wasted,' Isa. lx. 12." p. 343.

Though kings have no civil universal sovereign over them but Christ, yet it seems all the world, both kings and kingdoms, have an ecclesiastical sovereignty over them all. Communion of equals and christian counsel and reproof is not enough, such as all neighbour princes may use towards one another; nor the denial of such communion to the uncapable: but all kings and kingdoms must be under church sovereignty, which hath a legislative and judicial power over them all, to excommunicate, absolve them, &c. And how much more *in ordine ad spiritualia*, the common exposition of ecclesiastical power, tells you: as experience long told many kingdoms what the excommunicating of a king, and interdicting a kingdom the worship of God, do signify towards their dethroning or invasion.

And all this must be done, not as for the pope, but under the name of a general council, and the poor pope shall have no power but, say some, to call that council, and call it general when there is no such thing, and preside in it, and rule us as chief patriarch and St. Peter's successor, in the intervals of general councils, (that is, continually,) and that not arbitrarily, but by the laws of the church or councils (and no mortal man can tell which those authorized legislative councils are, among the hundreds of erroneous or contradicting ones). So that popery in England is an abhorred thing; for it is nothing with some but the pope's absolute government of the whole church, as without or above laws and ecclesiastic parliaments.

And can you reconcile all this to our oath of supremacy and the canons that establish it, renouncing all foreign jurisdiction? Yea, easily, we have been told it meaneth only foreign civil jurisdiction which belongs to the king, and not foreign ecclesiastical jurisdiction, (which is all that the sober popes do claim, save indirectly *in ordine ad spiritualia.)* To command a nation on pain of excommunication and damnation, (according to divers councils,) to renounce their allegiance to their excommunicate prince, and to depose him, and set up another, is no act of civil, but of ecclesiastical jurisdiction, which yet hath dethroned emperors and overthrown dominions.

And saith Archbishop Laud, in Dr. Stillingfleet's defence of him, p. 540, "It doth not follow, because the church may err, therefore she may not govern. For the church hath not only a pastoral power, to teach and direct, but a pretorian also, to control and censure," &c. And for external obedience to general councils when they err, "Consider whether it be not fit to allow a general council that honour and privilege which all other great courts have." Stillingfleet, page 534.

So that instead of a council of equals for concord, (as princes use for peace with their neighbours,) we have a universal sovereign court set up with pretorian power, to make binding laws, and pass judgment to all the christian world, and (say some) they are schismatics that obey not these universal laws; and obedience to them, and suppressing all forbidden assemblies for God's worship, is the only way to christian concord.

And where this foreign jurisdiction is made of such absolute necessity, that without subjection to it by kings and kingdoms, there is no concord to be had, nor any avoiding of the guilt of schism, what wonder if some can wish that silencings, reproaches, ruins, and confusions may be thought no dear price to obtain a universal union; for which Christ and his law are sufficient. They that have read Grotius, Cassander, Baldwin, Hoffmeister, Erasmus, Archbishop Laud, Dr. Heylin of his Life, Bishop Sparrow, Archbishop Bromhal and the Prefacer Bishop Parker, Thorndike, Bishop Gunning and his chaplain Dr. Saywell, and such others, and against them all have read Dr. Isaac Barrow of the Supremacy against Thorndike, &c. may understand where our difference and danger lieth.

8. And is England's self-destroying disease uncurable? God hath in wonderful mercy given us peace from foreign enemies; and is there no hope of prevailing with Englishmen to live together in peace? Must that of Isa. xlix. 36, be our case, to eat our own flesh, and be drunk with our own blood as with sweet wine? Alas, no counsel, no petitions, no tears, no experience, no judgments of God by plagues and flames, have hitherto one jot prevailed; but the ulcer of men's minds grows more and more putrid and malignant!

Two ways are by some proposed: first, that all the conscientious worshippers of God in the kingdom, should bring their judgments to a full conformity, in every particular, to their rulers; when as first they cannot tell us who these must be: some say, to the king or law; some say, to the bishops in a national convocation; others say, to the aforesaid foreign universal sovereignty of general councils (with the patriarchs). If the first be the way, what kingdoms must it be in? Is it no where but in Britain? or also in France, Spain, Italy, Germany, Poland? And must there be as many religions as kings and laws will make? And how far must this go? And where must we stop? Must kings choose us a God? Or choose whether we shall have any God, any

Christ, any Bible, any worship of God, and so any heaven?

If it be the bishops that must be the common rule of our religion, what countries and ages doth this rule serve for? Was it the rule where princes and prelates were Arians, or Nestorians, or Eutychians, or Monothelites, or papists? Is it the rule now in France, Spain, Italy, &c.? Or was it so in the pope's catholic church from anno 700 till the Reformation?

If it be general councils, I am weary of repeating the proofs that there never was one, nor ever is like to be one, or ought to be. If it be a European council, who shall call them, and who shall judge whether it be equal, and so far general? And are not the greater number of European bishops known papists? And will they not then be the major vote? And so we must be as bad as they? And if the rest of the christian world be not bound by them (in Greece, Ethiopia, Armenia, Syria, &c.) why are we? Is it the council of Ariminum, Sirmium, Milan, &c.; or of Ephesus 2, Nice 2d, many at Constantinople, at the Lateran, at Lyons, at Florence, at Constance, at Basil, at Trent, that are our rule? Must all that will be catholics and saved, hold all the heresies, contradictions, and corruptions that councils have held, and obey all their load of canons? If the Italians, French, English, &c. are all disagreed, how many and which councils we must obey, can all poor people know which is the right? And hath Christ left religion so uncertain a thing? or so mutable that general councils of prelates may be still increasing it? If he was the maker of it, by himself and his apostles, we may know more certainly where to find it: most christians may say, Christ we know, and Peter and Paul, &c. we know; but your councils are too many, too voluminous, too uncertain for us to know. But if they are such an absolutely necessary rule as you pretend, why do not teachers preach them to us daily as they do the sacred Scriptures?

If any would come down to confine these universal laws only to things indifferent, alas, must the world be confounded and divided about things indifferent? Are not things indifferent variable as countries and ages are? And must the world have one sovereignty to make laws for them? Cannot we have life, liberty, peace, and love, without things indifferent? or without agreeing in them? Are there any two in the whole world that are not ignorant, and that differ not about many greater matters than things indifferent? Doth he know himself, or know what a man is, that thinks all tolerated christians must be so skilled in all things indifferent, which men may impose, as to know them to be such; when it is so hard to teach the people things necessary, few, and plain? Alas, Lord! why must the churches be left in such hands?

9. But some have found out another remedy for our divisions; and that is, that only the bishops shall be engaged to a foreign jurisdiction, or profess the necessity of obeying them (under the name of a general council, and in the intervals, of a college of the bishops of the whole world, as one aristocracy); and that this shall not be imposed on any lay-communicants, but their consciences shall be left at liberty; nor at the first on the inferior clergy, till they are prepared to receive it; but only that the people obey the priests and prelates, and the priests obey the prelates and all their governing officers, and the prelates only profess obedience to the pretorian court, called the catholic church. Bishop Gunning's chaplain tells us that the laity are not required in order to communion to declare for general councils. Whether they use the like moderation in France, Spain, Germany, I know not, viz. for the bishops only to profess obedience to the pope, and the priests to the bishops, and the people to the priests and bishops. I hear they go further.

And if conventicles (as they will call them) are also suppressed, we need not fear religious violence, murder, and ruin (upon a feared Roman successor). For saith the same bishop's chaplain, p. 283, "For matters may be so ordered, that all officers, ecclesiastical, civil, and military, and all that are employed in power or authority of any kind, be persons both of known loyalty to the crown, and yet faithful sons of the church, and firm to the established religion, and the laws that they act by may be so explained in the favour of those that conform to the public worship, and the discouragement of all dissenters, that we must reasonably be secure from all violence that the papists can offer to force our submission: for when all our bishops and clergy are under strict obligations and oaths, and the people are guided by them; and all officers civil and military are firm to the same interest, and under severe penalties if they act any thing to the contrary; then what probable danger can there be of any violence or disturbance to force us out of our religion, when all things are thus secured, and the power of external execution is generally in the hands of men of our own persuasion."

Answ. The Dr. says well; I am of his mind in this. When they have subdued and cast out all dissenters, (as they do in France,) and the bishops and clergy are settled under a foreign church-jurisdiction, and the people settled in obedience to them, and all offices, civil, military, and ecclesiastic, in their hands, I do not think they need to fear that the papists will use violence to change their religion, whoever reigneth.

But the question is, whether this supposes a union with all in England that are now against a foreign jurisdiction, or only the destruction of them, or else the forcing them to these terms? As to a destruction of them, or forcing them to such terms, surely violence must do this. And what though the subjects of foreign power fear no violence, are all the rest (that is, the protestants) of the kingdom inconsiderable? We suppose the old church of England, and all our parliaments since the Reformation, were against a foreign jurisdiction: and will it be no loss to England to destroy so many, that is, the body of the land?

But the question is, whether they may not be thus brought to concord by consent? I answer, No; unless you suppose them to be men that indeed have no religion, and therefore can easily part with the bare name. For they are sworn by the oath of supremacy against all foreign jurisdiction: and put the case that the pope and a council, or the king of France, would bring the emperor's or the king's army to serve him, and be at his command, and he would only desire that the general officers and colonels may be engaged to obey him, and the captains and lower officers to obey them, and the soldiers to obey the officers; but the common soldiers shall be bound to no more, than this obedience to their officers. Query, Whether all these soldiers be not traitors to the king or emperor? Cromwell's common soldiers took no commissions against king or parliament; they did but obey their officers that pulled down both. And were they therefore guiltless? Protestants will not thus follow such prelates against their oaths, and against the known truth, and against their duty to God and the king.

10. But though it be notorious that domination and jurisdiction be the things which cause the papal clergy to trouble and tear the christian world, what is it that makes the laity so mad, and getteth

this clergy such a militant crowd against their own tranquillity and salvation? It is as visible as any moral thing, that the church's divisions, and wars, and miseries have about a thousand years risen from Satan's thrusting such worldly, fleshly, unholy men into holy offices, who seek them but to serve their pride, and covetousness, and fleshly appetites, and ease, and who are enemies at the heart to the serious obedience to Christ, which formally they preach. Christ's own apostles, in their time of ignorance, began to strive which of them should be greatest; of which we have recorded his sharp rebuke; which St. Peter himself did after second, in 1 Pet. v. 1—3, in words so plain, that if his pretended successors had not first claimed a power (as the church) to be the determining expounders of all the Bible, they had lain under the condemnation of Christ and Peter, naked, without a defence or cloak: but this church-expounding authority sets them above all the word of God, which is now but what they please to make it, and an instrument to execute their wills. And indeed it is now rather the pope and his prelates and councils than Christ, that are the law-makers to the church; for it is not he that maketh the words only that makes the law, but he that giveth them their sense. The words are but as the body, and the sense is the soul of the law. The ministerial church now scorn the name of ministers; and being become pretorian and magisterial, they give Christ and his Spirit in the apostles leave to make the words and body of the Scripture or divine law, as God formed Adam's body of the dust, so that they may give it the breath of life, and also may make far more voluminous laws of their own, and cut off and condemn all the children of God, that cannot believe that it is lawful to obey them.

And though the ignorant think that the claim of universal legislation and judgment, in the universal church and general councils, be no service to the domination of particular clergymen, no, nor to any, (seeing there will never be a general council,) they understand not the mystery of iniquity, and mistake. We have English writers that have told them, 1. That indeed power is first given to the body, (fine doctrine for royalists,) but by the body it is given to the prelates to use for them. 2. That as a general council hath the supreme power, so the prelates under them have the inferior ruling power, and the executive in the intervals of councils. 3. That as councils represent the church in sovereignty, so every bishop is, by his office, the true representative of the clergy of his diocess, and every metropolitan the representative of his province, and every patriarch of his patriarchate; and then are not the patriarchs (at least with the metropolitans) universal rulers in such intervals? 4. And the pope is the patriarch of the West, and hath a primacy in the church universal, and must be confessed to be *principium unitatis catholicæ*, and say some, to be the president of councils. 5. To which others add, that it belongs only to the president to call councils, and to judge which are lawful, without whose call they are so far from binding us, that they are themselves but unlawful routs. And what would you have more?

But what is all this to the poor priests? What? Why, 6. The people know not what the volumes of councils say, and it is the priests (or nobody) that must tell it them, (both what their exposition of Scripture is, and what their own additional laws are,) without which they cannot be obeyed. So that indeed the people's faith is ultimately resolved into the authority of the priest, who tells them what the bishop saith, who tells them what the metropolitan and his synod saith, who tells them what the chief patriarch and a general council saith, who tell them determinatively what Christ and the Scripture saith and meaneth.

But what is this to councils when there are none? Yes, 7. Those that are past and gone, have left all those binding laws by which the present bishops as an aristocracy must govern all the christian world.

But are not they for monarchy in the state? How come they then to plead for a sovereign aristocracy over the catholic church, and how come even the French clergy to be for the power of a church parliament above the pope? I cannot answer that; let the pope and they debate it.

But I wonder that Archbishop Laud should be for the derivation of all power from the body, as Richard Hooker is. See Dr. Stillingfleet's Defence on him, p. 544, 545, &c. "No body collective, whensoever it assembled itself, did ever give more power to the representing body of it, than a binding power upon itself and all particulars; nor ever did it give this power, otherwise than with this reservation in nature, that it would call again and reform, and, if need were, abrogate any law or ordinances upon just cause made evident, that the representing body had failed in trust or truth. And this power no body collective, ecclesiastical or civil, can put out of itself, or give away to a parliament or council, or call it what you will, that represents it.——The power which a council hath to order, settle, and define differences arising concerning faith, it hath not by any immediate institution of Christ, but it was prudently taken up by the church from the apostles' example."

I confess that the generality of politicians and lawyers, heathens, papists, and protestants, go much this way, as to civil government, and say that the *majestas personalis* is in the king or senate, but the *majestas realis* in the body which giveth the organical power, and on just cause may take it away. It is no honour to be singular in politics, and I have said enough of this elsewhere, (Christ. Direct. p. I.) But if it be the body of the whole church on earth that must give church officers and councils their power, and recall it when there is cause, if ever the whole christian world meet together to vote it, when it cometh to polling, we will give both the monarchical and the aristocratical conciliary papists three for one, to try who hath the power given by the body. But while two or three parts do already disown almost all their councils, the case is decided. But if an old council's heresies, errors, or tyranny can be invalidated only by a new one that is truly general, or a new one as papal as the last, we confess that Trent canons are like to be the law to the end of the world.

11. But again, what is it that maketh so many of the laity serve the popish prelate's universal claim, or keep up the destructive enmity and divisions of the christian world? A stranger would think that it were chiefly caused by some great contrariety of real interests, or that one party adhered to some principles or practices, which were already hurtful to the other's rights; while both were serious for christianity. But it is become by long experience notorious, that all the christian world's calamitous divisions are principally from the old enmity between the woman's and the serpent's seed, and that all is but the prosecution of that which their first patriarch Cain began; exemplified after in the discrimination of the children of men and the sons of God, and in Esau and Jacob, Ishmael and Isaac, and so down to the days of the apostles. And saith Paul, "As he that was born after the flesh persecuted him that was born after the Spirit, even so it is now." Among us it is notorious, that if we knew how to

cure men of the radical enmity of the flesh against the Spirit, and of a carnal mind's averseness to God and serious godliness, the rest of our differences were never like to continue our wounds and cruel factions.

In families you may hear that this is the fundamental difference. Husband and wife, parents and children, masters and servants, upon the mere account of serious godliness, do live like enemies, that are impatient of each other. If the husband be ungodly, the wife, children, or servants, that have but a care of their salvation, are still under his restraints, or frowns, or scorns. This praying, (especially if it be without book,) so much preaching and hearing, yea, any serious talk of God, or heaven, or Scripture, is a troublesome weariness to him; and he tells them it is but hypocrisy, or more ado than needs. If any compassionately tell him of the evil of his swearing, or tippling, or profaneness, he tells them they are precise puritans or fanatics, and worse than he. If they will needs hear sermons, he will have them go but to some cold or ignorant preacher, or one that will please him with a calumny or scorn at puritans, or that will say as he doth, that this stir for salvation, and meddling so much with Scripture and religion, is but proud, self-conceited fanaticism. In a word, it is serious preaching, and hearing, and reading God's word; serious praying, and preparation for the sacrament; serious discourse of the state of their souls, and preparation for death, judgment, and eternity; serious fearing and avoiding sin, and speaking against the sin of others; that is the common eyesore and troubler of the world, which they secretly hate, and cannot bear with in their families, in their neighbours, in magistrates, in ministers, or people.

And because it easeth their minds by vent, and by keeping up some hopes that they may be saved without this serious godliness themselves, they cherish a conceit that the persons that herein differ from them are as bad, if not much worse than others; and gladly hear those that slander and deride them. Such company, such pamphlets, such sermons please them. And to make them odious, they have for them some contemptuous, scornful nickname; which, though it be of no signification, is as effectual as the truest charge. Among the Roman sects, do but call a man a heretic or schismatic, a Lutheran, a Calvinist, a Zuinglian; and elsewhere do but call him a sectary, a schismatic, a puritan, a Calvinist, a nonconformist, an independent, a presbyterian, a roundhead, a fanatic, a whig; and it serveth the turn as well as if you had proved him a proud hypocrite, or a rebel. And there be among the real schismatics also some persons, that if you do but call a man episcopal, a conformist, an Arminian, a church-of-England man, that goeth to the common prayer, they think that he must needs be a temporizer, graceless or dangerously unsound.

And thus the miseries of the land are continued and increased. But because the Spirit of Cain is the grand incendiary, and the enmity against serious holiness throughout all the world is the principal cause of divisions, hatred, wars, and bloodshed, I will here annex many reasons which, with men that have any reason left them, should cure this malignant enmity to holiness, if men will but soberly consider them.

I have said so much to such already, especially in my "Saints' Rest," "Now or Never," my "Family Book," and "A Saint or a Brute," that I cannot do this work again without repeating much that is said. But seeing all that doth not serve, and the ulcer breaketh out more dangerously than ever, till it come to a *noli me tangere*, we must continue some hope and use of means; and if we lay on fresh plasters of the old materials, while only new books are by such regarded, we are bound to do our best. It is but so much labour lost; and it is not utterly lost to ourselves, while we have peace of conscience in God's acceptance.

But being sure to be misreported when I have done my best to be understood, that I be not guilty of it, I will first show what I mean by serious godliness, and next what I mean by malignity or enmity to serious godliness.

CHAPTER II.

WHOM I MEAN BY GODLY PERSONS, AND WHOM BY MALIGNANT ENEMIES TO GODLINESS.

I. By godliness I do not mean, 1. Any superstition, or making religions or religious duties which God never made, and extolling these, and the party that are for them. God hath made us religious work enough. Could we do that well, we need no more. Religion, so far as it is made by men, is no religion, but a contradiction or equivocation; for religion is our obligation and duty to God, and conscience of it. Could I be for superstition, or more religion than God hath made us, I might be for all the new religions of Rome, Franciscans, Dominicans, Carthusians, Jesuits, Oratorians, and all the rest. And I might be for their works of supererogation, their massings, worshipping bread, angels, dead saints, images, their pilgrimages, relics, and all their pretended traditions and councils, their new-made church laws, and I should know no end.

And, 2. By godliness I mean not any singular, odd opinion differing from the Scripture, and making a sect, or any error whatsoever; nor any opinion which is contrary to any thing which the whole church on earth did ever hold as necessary to salvation or communion.

Nor, 3. Do I mean any truth or duty of inferior moment, which only makes to the well-being of a christian, though this be an inferior part of godliness; at least not that which a godly, willing person knows not to be his duty.

Much less, 4. Do I mean any proud, false conceit of a man's own godliness, and becoming one of an unwarrantable sect, that he may be conspicuous to others, or cherish this presumption in himself, and say to others, "Stand by, I am holier than thou;" or as the Pharisee, "I thank thee, Lord, that I am not as this publican." (Though yet all that will be saved must greatly differ from the ungodly, and must with thankfulness own God's grace.)

Nor, 5. Do I mean any unlawful practice, which on the pretence of godliness may be done, whether unjust censures, backbiting, unwarrantable separations from others, divisions, disobedience to authority, sedition, rebellion, &c. These are all contrary to godliness and true religion. Christ is the strictest condemner of them, and godliness the best cure. If any godly or religious person be guilty of any one of these, 1. It cannot be as known and in a predominant degree. 2. And it is his disease (as a leprosy to a man) and not his godliness.

But by godliness I mean only the serious consent to and performance of the covenant which we made with God in our baptism. That we seriously believe that there is one only God, of most perfect power, knowledge, and goodness, our Creator, Maintainer, Governor, and end, whom we must obey, and serve, and love, above all creatures whatsoever; and that he is the "Rewarder of them that diligently seek him," and will give everlasting blessedness to the faithful, and everlastingly punish the ungodly. That we seriously believe that Jesus Christ is the Redeemer and Saviour, who teacheth, ruleth, pardoneth, sanctifieth, and saveth all true penitent believers; who is our Intercessor, Head, and Judge. That we seriously believe that the Holy Ghost indited and sealed by his gifts and miracles the doctrine and writings of the prophets and apostles, now recorded in the Scriptures; and that he is sent from the Father and the Son to regenerate, sanctify, comfort, and strengthen those that shall be saved.

And that we seriously consent to love and obey God our Father, Saviour, and Sanctifier, as his creatures, subjects, and children in these relations, that we may be pardoned and saved by him. And that we be willing to forsake the devil and his works, and the world and flesh, so far as they would tempt us to break this covenant against God, and our obedience and salvation.

And lastly, That we seriously or sincerely (though not perfectly) endeavour in our lives to keep his covenant; preferring God in our love and obedience, and our hopes of life everlasting, before all the pleasures and treasures of this world; and resisting the temptations of the devil, world and flesh, which would turn us from him, and from our obedience and hope. And that we truly (though not perfectly) trust God and our Redeemer for the heavenly glory which he hath promised.

This is plainly, distinctly, and fully what I mean by godliness or holiness. And such are the persons (though all imperfect, and of divers degrees) which I call saints or godly. He that feigneth me to mean any thing else, doth but abuse himself and me. If there be none such, there are no christians, and all the word of God is vain.

But every duty commanded by God is a part of the matter of our obedience and religion; viz. As, according to the first commandment, to take God for our God, to be absolutely obeyed, loved, and trusted, and to renounce all idols, and neither to obey, love, or trust ourselves or any other creatures before him; so also, according to the second commandment, to renounce all scandalous symbolizing with idolaters, in the outward worship of God in their sinful way, especially by images, and other appearances of idolatry. And that we worship God according to his word.

And according to the third commandment, that we avoid all profanation of holy things; all perjury, false vows, and fathering falsehoods upon God or his words, and rash swearing, and irreverent using of God's name, and turning his worship into a lifeless form.

And according to the fourth commandment, that we worship God publicly in solemn assemblies, and devote the Lord's day to holy exercises; that we search the Scriptures, pray for what God hath promised, or commanded; meditate and confer of holy things, and celebrate the sacraments in the communion of saints.

And so, according to the second table, that we honour and obey our parents, and (as far as their right of government reacheth) all others that God sets over us. And dishonour them not; nor obey civil, ecclesiastical, or domestical usurpers against them.

That we do our best to save our neighbour's life and bodily welfare, against murderers or usurpers; and hurt no man's life or health, either violently, or by Jezebel's pretence of justice.

That we keep our senses, thoughts, affections, passions, and actions, from all unchastity and immodest lasciviousness.

That we wrong no man in his estate, but to our power help them.

That we avoid all injustice, lying, false witness, false judgment, and oppressive, unrighteous government; and promote truth and justice to our power.

And lastly, that we love our neighbour as ourselves, and take his welfare and his sufferings as our own, and do as we would have others do by us, and covet not to draw from him to ourselves.

So that he that pretendeth to love God and godliness, and obedience to Christ, and yet loveth not such a life as this, he lieth, or says he knows not what.

And he that hateth men or opposeth them, for any one of all these duties, (for reading or hearing God's word, for praying for things promised, for holy conference and meditation, for sanctifying the Lord's day, for desiring a shepherd and not a wolf, for abhorring profaneness and other great sins,) doth thereby declare that it is so much of godliness or obedience which he abhorreth; and it is through ignorance doubtless if he seriously love and practise the rest of God's commands.

II. By malignant enemies of godliness, 1. I do not mean every one that hath any backwardness to any duty, which he overcometh in the practice; nor every one that is guilty of some omissions. The spirit is willing, and the flesh is weak.

2. I mean not those that are godly in the main so far as they can know, but through education or otherwise are ignorant of some integral truths or duties, and have an opposing, contentious zeal against them by mistake; and by factious company are taught therefore to speak evil falsely of those from whom they differ. I hear some revile all even with terms of enmity and unchristian threatenings, yea, seeking their ruin, who do not swear, say, and practise all that is required to English conformity. I do not conclude them therefore malignant enemies of godliness, if they live soberly, righteously, and godly in their way, and prefer God before men, heaven before earth, the soul before the body, and a holy life before the pleasures and profits of the flesh. If they are uncharitable against all that are not for diocesans, lay-chancellors, excommunications, symbolical crossing of children as a covenanting sign of christianity, and all the rest, I wish them more charity, but I call them not malignant enemies.

I find Bishop Gunning's chaplain thinks that he doth say well, when he saith, that "not only murderers, adulterers, drunkards, but such schismatics as disturb the peace, and weaken the authority of the church's disciples, (theirs,) are to be excommunicated and reckoned among heathens and publicans, and enemies to the gospel of Christ, (if they preach it without a diocesan's licence,)" p. 214. And "that it is already our case, that it is a very difficult matter to find a jury and witnesses, especially among the dissenters, upon whose credit we may rely." All this signifieth how little blind faction is to be believed; and how far it conquereth even human modesty and veracity. But yet I differ it from the enmity to godliness which I speak of. And that you may see that he is no papist, though for a foreign jurisdiction, he tells you of Cromwell, that "there is too great a reason to suspect that he intended to settle popery in the nation, when matters had been ripe to go through with it." I confess this is news to me. I have roundly told him to his face of his disloyalty in deposing our English monarchy, and told the world then of his treacherous usurpation; but it never came into my thoughts that he intended to settle popery in the nation. But if these words come from clergy truth and modesty, they are very considerable. I hope the old royalists will be against popery the more if Cromwell was for it. And the papists I hope will be more angry with Dr. Moulin, that answereth Philanax Anglicus, for making the king's death to be caused and concluded by the papists, if Cromwell was for them. But faction will face men down, that snow is black.

So on the other side, I hear some that are against infant baptism, sharply censure all that are not of their mind. And some over-sharply censure the prelatists and conformists; and almost all the christian world is divided into parties, that too little stick at the injurious censuring of others; the papists, Greeks, Abassines, Armenians, Nestorians, Jacobites, &c. And among the papists, the Dominicans, and Molinists, and Jansenians, &c. And among the protestants, too many. This is no small sin, but it is not that enmity to godliness itself which I mean.

3. And I mean not by malignity, men's differences in civil and political controversies. Though I take popery to be half a civil controversy, and to be unsufferable by such princes and people whom they bind themselves to depose and destroy. And that to subject all the christian world to the legislative, judicial, and executive government of one pope, or one pretorian court, is no better than to proclaim such a pope or court to be public enemies and usurpers to all christian princes and states. But yet abundance of political differences may consist with serious piety. My reason is, because God hath not made political controversies so clear as that all good christians can resolve them. Neither the light of nature, nor the Bible, nor tradition, endeth them. Nor hath he put them into our creed, or the ten commandments; nor laid men's salvation on them, as he hath done on the essentials of religion. Nor commanded all men to be so well skilled in statute-books and common law, as to be able to know which party is in the right. And therefore I join not with those clergy or lay gentlemen, who damn all that are not of their mind and side, in differences of that nature.

I often hear some say that kings and states do all receive their authority from the body of the nation, who are the chief seat of it. So Hooker, so Laud, and indeed, as aforesaid, so heathen, papist, and protestant politicians ordinarily hold. I call not all these malignants, though I am fully satisfied, 1. That God is the institutor of magistracy in general. 2. And that he hath so far specified it as to determine of its unchangeable essentials (that they shall as his officers promote obedience to the ten commandments). 3. And that he never gave this governing power to the people. 4. But that all that the people do is, 1. To specify it as to the number of persons (a monarchy, aristocracy, or mixed of these and some democracy). 2. To limit it by determining of the degrees of power, about property and liberty, and all things which God's law hath left undetermined and mutable. 3. And to determine of the persons and families that shall receive the immutable power from God and the mutable from men.

I often hear some most magnify democracy, and some aristocracy, and some monarchy, and some a mixture; and some English clergymen are for a civil monarchy subject to a catholic clergy aristocracy. I call none malignants for any such differences.

I find some papists and protestants political writers saying, that when it proveth hurtful to the commonwealth, the people may retract the power given the prince, and change the government; and Hooker saith, No doubt in such a case a prince will part with it. And Archbishop Laud, before cited, saith of the like, and abrogating laws, this power no body collective, ecclesiastical or civil, can put out of itselt and give away. And I find many that extol Hooker and Laud call this a principle of rebellion. It is neither of them that I call malignants.

I find most writers of politics agreed that the law of nature alloweth and commandeth kingdoms and commonwealths self-defence against any public enemies that seek to destroy them. And that no man on pretence of right to a crown hath any right to destroy the body of the people, or the *bonum publicum*, which is the essentiating end of government, nor can be *simul rex et publicus hostis*. I hear others take this for an unchristian doctrine of rebellion, and say, that if a king would destroy all the people of a kingdom, (in revenge, or in siding with another kingdom of his own or another's,) they ought not to resist him, or any that he commissioneth to do it. And that if he should commission a few men to kill all the parliament as they sit, or to burn the city, it is rebellion to resist by self-defence. I hear lawyers themselves at great difference on such matters, some for more power, and some for less. I find the great defenders of monarchy, such as Barclay and Grotius de Jure Belli, naming many cases in which kings may be resisted, yea, and forfeit all. And I find others among us of a contrary mind. Yea, I find the conformable and diocesan pillars quite differ in such cases. Bishop Bilson naming many cases in which resistance is no rebellion, " To subject his kingdom to a foreign realm, or to change the form of the commonwealth from impery to tyranny, or neglect the laws established by common consent of prince and people, to execute his own pleasure; in these and other such cases which might be named, if the nobles and commons join together to defend their ancient and accustomed liberty, regiment, and laws, they may not well be counted rebels," saith he, " of Obedience," page 520. But I hear many now say the contrary, and condemn such doctrine as disloyal.

I find some join with the papists in accusing the reformation as caused by rebellions in Germany, Geneva, France, Belgium, &c. And I find Bishop Jewel, Bilson, and other bishops defending the French defence, and Dr. Peter Moulin of Canterbury, in his answer to Philanax Anglicus, contradicting their accusers, as false in point of history.

Abundance of such political controversies are now lately agitated, some charging their adversaries with rebellion, and some with tyranny. Some saying, they are guilty of treason against the king; and others, they are traitors against the kingdom. And too ordinarily damning one another; as if these matters were articles of our creed.

What a dismal difference is there now about those words in the declaration in the corporation act: " There is no obligation on me or any other person, from the oath, called the Solemn League and Covenant. Some say there are none but rebels will refuse; and that if any obligation had been granted to things lawful or necessary, some would have extended it to rebellion or schism. And therefore all obligation is to be renounced. Others say, that national perjury is a forerunner of national calamity or ruin; and that where oaths bind not, there can be no trust; and no trust, no commerce. And they think as Dr. Sanderson, and casuists, papists and protestants, do, that though an oath or vow be unlawfully imposed, and sinfully taken, and part of the matter of it be unlawful, and the imposers and takers are bound to repent, and no one is bound by it to the unlawful part, yet the taker is bound to that part of the matter which is lawful or necessary. And they take it to be lawful and necessary to repent of sin, to oppose profaneness, schism, heresy, and popery, to defend the king, and therefore that it obligeth them to these.

I meddle not with the Roman opinion, that it is the Henrician heresy to say that kings have a power of investing bishops, and disobeying the pope's excommunication; and of such as Cardinal Perron, that dare not question or deny the power of the pope and councils to excommunicate and depose kings, because then they must condemn approved general councils, which are their religion itself, and (saith he) must grant that the pope is antichrist, and the church erroneous that hath so long used this.

I name all these political controversies,

1. To tell you that it is not factious and passionate enmity to each other on such accounts, which I mean by enmity to religion.

2. And to remember men, that if in so many and great points of politics and government, the learned and christian world have so great difference, what reason is there that we should damn, or excommunicate, or hate each other about a hard opinion in religion, or a ceremony.

3. And to tell the popish church, that if it were a good argument that there must be one pretorian court or church to oblige all the world by a universal determination in what sense to expound the Scripture, because it is abused to error by men's mistake, and there must be an end of controversies; by the same reason there must be a universal pretorian court to expound all human laws, and end the controversies of lawyers; yea, and to master all men's reason: for Scripture is no more commonly controverted and abused than law itself; and not half so much as reason is, which is pleaded for almost all the falsehood and wickedness in the world.

Moreover, it is not personal feuds between man and man that I mean by enmity to godliness. No; though any such be against an innocent and godly man, where it is not for his godliness, but some other difference.

I will say more, though some dislike it; it is not a papist as such that I mean by a malignant enemy of godliness. I know that education, and temptation, and want of hearing the confutation of their errors judiciously made, may cause godly persons to think that the universal church must be united in some human head or sovereign power; and that there is no other way to end controversies and schisms, and that (as Dr. Saywell saith) there must be some over kingdoms or national churches, as well as over particular persons, that many may not escape while a few are punished. It is easy to be deceived by the pretences of unity and concord, while men see the divisions and discords of others. And the false pretences of antiquity are so confidently uttered by their clergy, that men unacquainted with the history may verily believe them. And the plea for an uninterrupted succession of ministerial ordination, and that a superior must give power to the inferiors, deceiveth many. If there must be a diocesan to ordain and rule all presbyters, and a metropolitan to ordain or rule the diocesans, and a patriarch to rule them, from whom shall the patriarchs receive their power or commands, but from a pope? The poor reasoning which the French now use with the protestants, puzzleth unskilful persons; viz. Was there any church before your reformation? If yea, where was it? And had not you your ministerial power from it? It was Rome or none. And if it was the true church then, it is so now. We answer them, There was and is one only catholic church. Of this Christ only is the Head or universal Governor, and no man or men. Of this all lawful pastors are his official guides in their several provinces, as many justices and mayors of corporations under one king. That all these having one King, (Jesus,) and one law, (of Christ,) and one Spirit, and one faith and hope, are to keep the unity of the Spirit in the bond of peace, and to use synods when needful to that end, but not as a pretorian or regent aristocracy or court. That the church before Luther was all over the world wherever there were christians. In Ethiopia, Egypt, Syria, Armenia, Georgia, Circassia, Asia, and wherever the Greek christianity is in Muscovy, and in all Europe where there were true christians. That the envious man having sowed tares, this church is unhappily fallen into many corruptions, diseases, and factious sects, almost all censuring one another. No part of it is perfect. That the papal part is in doctrine, worship, and government, one of the most corrupted parts! Yet so far as their diseases or errors nullify not their profession of christianity, they are parts, though leprous. And therefore though they are the most uncharitable and schismatical part, as they cut off or unchurch all the christian world save themselves, yet being as christians united to the rest in the common faith, their baptism and ordinations are not nullities as they invest men in the christian society and christian ministry; though that part of them is a nullity which engageth men in schism and in sin. That the ministerial power is not the gift of man, but only of Christ, who by the charter of his recorded word, giveth the power and the obligation to that person who is duly chosen and called thereto; as the king's charter giveth the power to the mayor of a corporation duly qualified and chosen. That the ordainers are but partly judges of due qualification, and partly ministerial investers, and not at all the donors of the power. That ordination is for order's sake needful, when it may be had, to keep men from being judges of their own sufficiency. But order being only for the thing ordered, (as the sabbath was made for man, and not man for the sabbath,) is not necessary against the end. That there is no necessity that a superior must ordain. But as the college of physicians, philosophers, &c. make physicians and philosophers, as approved, so may equals in the ministry. Do not bishops make or consecrate bishops. If this were not so, who makes the pope? If he did not pretend that his power is given him immediately from Christ, he must grant that there are some men above him to give it him, and so he is not the sovereign. If they say that the power of popes (and kings) is given by the whole body, (the church,) he is then no pope. For it is known that three parts of the christian world are against him. If he will say, none are the church but those that are his party, any sect or rebels may say the like, and appropriate authority to themselves.

Nothing more cheateth the ignorant, than ambiguous words and confusion. And explaining those words, and needful, plain distinction, would save the writing of many volumes, and would make truth easily meet the seeker, and unravel all the spider webs of deceivers.

Do but well use these few distinctions, and all popery vanisheth into smoke: 1. Distinguish between a catholic church as headed by Christ, (this we are all members of,) and a pretended catholic church, headed by the pope or any men. This is another church as to the denominating form, having another informing, unifying head. And this is it which we deny.

2. Distinguish visibility. Christ's church is so far visible as to have a Head who was visible on earth, is visible in heaven, and will visibly come to judg-

ment, and visibly reign for ever. It hath visible laws, protection, and officers. The subjects' bodies and their profession are visible; and it is not further visible; no, not as to the souls or real faith of the subjects. The papists' church hath a usurping, visible, human head on earth.

3. Distinguish of baptism and ordination as into Christ's catholic church, and done by papists as christians; and as into the pope's catholic church, and done by papists as papists.

4. Distinguish of subjection and communion. We owe communion when we owe no subjection, and where men have no right to be our governors.

5. Distinguish between communion in christianity, and that in essentials, integrals, or accidents; and communion in errors and corruptions, or defects. We have communion with papists and all christians in christianity (if they be christians indeed). But we renounce communion to the errors and sins of them and all others, as far as we are able to avoid them. All christians have union and communion in the essentials of christianity. No christians have union and communion in all the integrals, (on earth,) all being imperfect. But the more such union and communion the better. No christians have, or ought to have, communion in all the accidents. All should avoid communion in sin.

6. Distinguish between communion of hearts, communion of profession, and communion in local presence. We have heart communion in one essential faith, hope, and love, with all true christians on earth. We profess all one faith in the essentials. We have nearer communion, or fuller, with the reformed churches which are soundest in the integrals, than we have with the more faulty and corrupt. But we have local presence but in one place at once; and we ought to avoid local presence where we cannot have it without sin, though we have communion in faith, love, and profession with the same men. If a reformed church will not admit our local presence without subscribing some one untruth, we must be absent, when we may be present with a worse church which excludeth us not by any such imposition.

7. Accordingly distinguish of separation. We separate not at all from union or communion with papists as they are christians, or as they hold any truth. But, 1. We separate from subjection and obedience to them, which we never owed them, or any other church. 2. We separate from communion with their church, as it is a policy informed by a usurping human king or head. 3. We separate from all their sins so far as we know them. 4. We deny local presence in their mass worship, because of the sin imposed on us, both before it and in it. 5. We are uncapable of communion in all accidents, or mutable indifferent things.

Understand and use well these few plain distinctions, and you need little more to answer all the papists.

And I fear not to add, that were the papists in my power, (as I never did,) I never would use any inhumanity or cruelty towards them; yea, I would use no offensive, but only defensive, force against them; nor hurt one of them, further than they made it necessary for the defence of the land, or those whom they would hurt.

I knew not till a book, called the "Liberties of England," lately told me, how many severe laws are against them. I am no judge of the times that they were made in, nor of their occasions. But I think that of late they have done more hurt than good. For, 1. Some of them seem too severe. 2. Some I cannot prove to be justifiable; viz. those which would compel them to come to our sacramental communion, when many a good minister would not receive them if they came. And that which excommunicateth them that never were of our communion. And that which layeth the excommunicate as such in prison, &c. 3. It greatly tendeth to misinform foreigners, who seeing these laws, think they are all put in execution; and so believe those that tell them, that the catholics here are under constant cruelties and frequent martyrdoms; whenas I never in all my life knew of one papist that suffered so much for his religion, as I have done myself, within these few years past, though my sufferings are so small as to be no meet matter of very great complaint. 4. These laws being a continual danger to them (should there be governors that would execute them) doth put them on continual plotting and striving against them. Sufferings, or great dangers, put men by fear upon self-defence, and the utmost endeavours for deliverance, who would be more quiet if they found themselves in safety; and though their clergy would be still plotting the recovery of the papal power, to subject king and kingdom to the sacred king of Rome, yet the laity would be less against the common peace, when they found that it was their own peace.

I have told you what I mean not by malignant enmity to godliness. I tell you now what I mean by it; viz.

When the blindness and ungodliness of corrupted nature, increased by practice into serpentine enmity, and turning men's hearts by unbelief and disaffection from God and heaven, doth possess them with a deep dislike of a holy, heavenly, and spiritual life; first as to their own practices, and then as it is in others: and because it is against their worldly hopes and fleshly lusts, they hate it and reject it themselves, and then hate and maliciously oppose it in others; yea, though law, custom, and worldly interest draw them formally to profess christianity and obedience to God's laws, and to vow that in baptism, they hate the serious performance of their own profession and vows; and would be glad to drive it out of the world, and to set up hypocrisy and ceremony, or a stage religion and mummery, or the toothless mass and formalities in its stead. And if custom or shame hinder them from persecuting or scorning truth and godliness in its proper name, they will show their mind by these things following:

1. They will set up some worldly, fleshly interest (like the papal kingdom) which is contrary to the christian and holy interest; and then they will persecute christians, not as christians, nor as godly in name, but as such indeed, by pleading conscience and obedience to God, against their inconsistent interest and ways.

2. Among all that are against their carnal, false interest, they will cull out the more serious, godly persons to afflict.

3. Among all the faithful, they will cull out those who do Christ more service in the world; because Christ's service is it that is their disservice, and opposite to their sin.

4. They will make a scorn of their very religious duties, and take up mimical derisions, to make them ridiculous or contemptible.

5. When they can charge them with no crimes, they will purposely make nets to catch them, as the enemies of Daniel did by him, Dan. vi.; and as the spider makes her curious web to catch and kill the flies.

6. Yea, they will make faults by slander and lies, if not by perjuries, if they can find none.

7. Yea, their virtue, piety, and innocence shall be all called hypocrisy; and when they cannot accuse

their actions, they will accuse their hearts and secret thoughts, and judge them as if they had a casement into their breasts.

8. Yea, if their innocency cannot be so stained, they will hate them so much the more, because they cannot tread down their reputation.

9. They will search after and aggravate all the failings of religious people, and turn them into crimes.

10. If any one of them, or a hypocrite that is like them, be guilty of any notable fall, they will persuade men that all the rest of their lives is like that crime; yea, and that all that profess much seriousness in godliness, are as bad as they: that all the rest of the life of Noah, Lot, David, Solomon, &c. was as bad as the criminal part; and that all the servants of Christ are Peters and Judases.

11. That it is not their sins, but their piety, which they hate, you will see in that they live in far greater sin themselves, and take it to be no great harm, but hate those that reprove them.

12. And they make light of the common crimes of others. They can bear with an atheist, an infidel, a drunkard, a profane swearer, a derider of godliness; yea, a persecutor, a fornicator, a man of no religion; if he will but be for them, and serve their interest, and will not scruple communion with such. But men never so sober, just, and godly, that cross their wills and carnal ways, they cannot endure. And if they be such clergymen, as the world hath too many, such serious, godly men, for disliking their ungodliness, are made the common objects of their pulpit and discoursing scorn or accusations, and perhaps are excommunicate *ipso facto*, for dissenting from their opinions or wills.

13. Such usually in former ages have been the chief instigators of princes and rulers, to hate men of serious religion, and to stir up persecution against them, and to render such odious to the world as heretics or intolerable villains. Oh what difference is there between the true narratives of the lives of Luther, Calvin, Beza, and abundance such, and the odious lies and defamations written of them by some others. Yea, those who commend Melancthon, Bucer, and many such for learning and moderation, hate their doctrine of reformation and serious piety.

14. And you may note, that in any slander of a godly man, they will sooner believe one or two ignorant, malicious drunkards against them, that never knew them, than the testimonies of hundreds of most faithful persons who praise and vindicate them, though they better knew them.

15. They seldom give the accused leave to speak for themselves before they believe accusations against them; but conclude that they are as bad as backbiting malice reporteth them behind their backs.

16. They are glad to hear of any infamy of religious persons, and loth to hear them praised without contradiction; and are glad to hear of any suffering that befalls them.

17. If there be any public differences in a church, city, or land, they are usually against that side which most favoureth serious godliness, be they who they will. If the king, parliament, bishops, will be for the persons and ways of soberness, justice, and serious godliness, they will be on the other side; and they will cry up any that will cry them down, or would oppress them.

18. Lastly, The quality of the enemies may help with the rest to tell what it is that they are against; when it is the generality of the worldlings, proud, ambitious men, sensual drunkards, gluttons, fornicators, profane and irreligious, who hate godliness so far as to drive it from themselves and families, and rather venture on hell-fire, than be truly godly; it is easy to know what these hate in others.

I have told you who I mean by malignant enemies of godliness, that the mistakers and slanderers of my words may have no excuse. Could we now but prevail against this Cainism, or devilism, it would do much to recover the peace of many nations of the earth: but Christ hath told us, that enmity between the seed of the woman and the serpent, of which Cain and Abel were the first specimen since the fall, will never cease till Christ come, as is terribly described, 2 Thess. i. 6, 10—12, and Matt. xxv. But yet some Sauls may become Pauls, and for the hope of the recovery of such, I will adjoin such reasons as should convince any that have the use of reason left.

CHAPTER III.

UNDENIABLE REASONS AGAINST MALIGNANT ENMITY TO SERIOUS GODLINESS.

1. To deny that there is a God who is the Supreme Governor of man, is to be mad in despite of the whole world which proveth it; and it deposeth all kings, who claim their authority as given them by God, and as his officers; for if there be no God, there is none to give them authority: and to grant that there is a God, and yet deny him our love, honour, and obedience, is to speak gross contradiction, or else profess open malice against God himself. If he be God, he is perfectly wise; and should not perfect wisdom govern us? If he be God, he is perfectly good, and man's chief Benefactor; and should he not then have our chiefest love? If he be God, he is of absolute power; and should he not then be obeyed? If he be God, he made us, and still maintaineth us, and we live continually by his will, and have all that we have of his bounty, and we and all we have are wholly his own; and are not then all our thanks and service due to him? If he be God, he is our Judge, and will be just in punishing and rewarding; and should we not then serve him with the greatest fear, and with the highest hopes? These things are undeniable.

Dare any man that believeth there is a God, say, that man can love him too much, or too much honour him or obey him? Can we return him more than his due? It is therefore no less than practical atheism, or else a rebellious defiance of God, to blame or hate men for loving, honouring, and serving him to the very utmost of their power. And to deny God, or defy him, is a thousand-fold more damnable sin and treason, than to deny and defy the king, or your own parents.

2. God hath himself commanded man to love him with all his heart, and soul, and might; and to obey him with his greatest fidelity and diligence, and to fear him more than any creature, and to place our chiefest hopes on his promised rewards, and to seek first his kingdom and righteousness, and not to sin wilfully to save our lives, or gain all the world, Deut. vi. 5—7; xx. 12; xi. 12—14; Matt. xxii. 37; Heb. xi. 6; 1 Cor. xv. 58; Luke xi. 4; Heb. xii. 28, 29; Matt. x. 39, 42; xvi. 25, 26; vi. 33; Luke xvi. 26, 33; Matt. v. 19, 20. And the law of nature speaks no less. And if God command it, and you condemn it, do you not condemn God? If you command your son, or servant, or subject any thing, he that blames him for obeying you, blames you more than him. If it be a fault or folly to love and serve God with all our heart, and mind, and might, the fault or folly

would be God's that requireth it, and not ours. And is such a blasphemer meet for human society, who will accuse his Maker? If God be blameworthy, he is not perfect; and if he be not perfect, he is not God: and so to be against our utmost obedience, doth amount to no less than blasphemy or atheism.

3. Do you think that man is a creature that needs to be blamed for loving or obeying God too much? Do you not know that nature is vitiated by sin, and man is now backward to God, and all that is good and holy? You may as well blame a lame man for running too fast, as a sinful man for obeying God too much. It is more foolish than to blame a sick man for working or eating too much, that can do neither; or to hold a man in a consumption from going up the hill too fast. Do you find your own heart so forward to a holy life, as that you need pulling back or hinderance, when no exhortation or necessity will persuade you to it? And if you need no such reproof or stop, why should you think others need it? Do you not use to say that all men are sinners? And do sinners need to be blamed for obedience? Do you not daily confess that you have done the things which you ought not to have done, and left undone the things that you ought to have done, and there is no health in you; and yet will you blame men for too much obedience? It seems then, that your confessions of sin are professions of it; and while you tell what you have done, you do but tell what you mean to do, and what you would have all others do; or else you blame yourselves for sinning, and hate your neighbours for not sinning.

4. If you hate men for holiness and avoiding sin, you hate Jesus Christ most; for he was most holy, and free from all sin: and you hate the angels and all in heaven, for they are holy, and void of all transgression.

5. Have you any better master to serve than God? Or any better work to do than he commandeth, or any better thing to seek and hope for than he hath promised? If not, should not the best be preferred? What do you love and seek yourselves? Is money or fleshly pleasure better than God and heaven? Is sin and sensuality a better employment than his service? Is your flesh and lust a better master? Compare them, and we are content that the best be preferred.

6. Why do you take on you to believe in Christ, if you be against holiness, and for sin? Christ came into the world to die for sin, to show God's hatred of it; and would you have us wilfully to commit it, and to despise his blood? He came to destroy the works of the devil; and will you plead for them? He came by his doctrine, example, and grace, to bring man to holy obedience; and do you hate men for the same, and yet call yourselves christians?

7. How dangerously do you draw towards the sin against the Holy Ghost, if you hate or blame men for being holy, or seeking to be such; when it is all the work of the Holy Ghost on men's souls to make them holy! It is a dangerous thing to hate the work of the Holy Ghost, and as it were defy him, and do despite to him.

8. Are you not yourselves in your baptism vowed and devoted to God the Father, Son, and Holy Ghost, renouncing the world, the flesh, and the devil? And do you hate men for being such as you have vowed to be yourselves? And do you think that God will not severely reckon with you for such perjury and base perfidiousness?

9. Do you not in your daily hypocritical devotions condemn yourselves by your own tongues? Do you not pray that the rest of your lives may be pure and holy? and at the same time hate purity and holiness? Do you not pray that God's will may be done on earth as it is in heaven? And can we have a higher, purer pattern? Do you know any that doth God's will better than it is done in heaven? Or is it not damnable hypocrisy to pray for that which you hate, and hate all men that desire and endeavour it? When you say or hear all the ten commandments, you pray, "Lord, have mercy upon us, and incline our hearts to keep this law;" and do you hate men for endeavouring to keep it? If you come to the Lord's table, you confess your sins, and bind yourselves in covenant to forsake them, and to live a holy life, and you take the sacrament upon it; and the liturgy warneth you to take heed that you dissemble not, nor be hinderers of God's holy word, lest the devil enter into you as he did into Judas, and fill you with all unrighteousness. And if you hate or oppose that holy obedience to God which you profess, after all this, what must be the portion of such hypocrites? And in your creed you profess to believe in God the Father, Son, and Holy Ghost, and to hold a holy catholic church, and the communion of saints; and yet do you hate saints that obey the Father, Son, and Holy Ghost, and hate their communion?

10. Hath not God printed on man's nature such a sense of the difference between good and evil, as that all laws and government are founded in that sense? And no man loveth to be counted or called a bad, or ungodly, or unconscionable man; a liar, a knave, a perjured man, or a wicked man; and yet do you hate men for avoiding wickedness?

11. Do not you use to accuse religious men of some sin or other, (truly or falsely,) and think by that to make them odious? And yet do you accuse them, and hate them most for not sinning? To be sober, just, and godly, is but to avoid sins of omission and commission; and do you at once accuse them as sinners, and hate them for obeying God, and sinning no more?

12. Doth it never affright you to find the devil's nature in you, as hating the divine or holy nature which is in faithful, godly men, and to think how openly you serve the devil, and do his work? No man that believeth there are devils, can doubt, but that the hatred of God as holy, and the hatred of his holy word, and work, and servants, is the devil's malignity, and the opposing of them his work. If he were to write you his commandments, they would be contrary to God's, and the chief of them should be, Thou shalt not love God, nor serve him with all thy heart, and soul, and might, nor love them that do so; but hate, deride, oppose, and persecute them. And is it honourable openly to serve the devil? Christ tells such men, (John viii.,) that the devil is their father, because they have his nature; and that his work they do, for he was from the beginning a liar, and a malignant murderer, and turned man from obeying God; and can you think that he loveth you, or that his service against God is better than God's, or his reward better?

13. Doth it never touch your consciences to consider that you are the children and followers of cursed Cain; and how punctually his case against Abel, and yours against God's servants, is the same? By faith Abel offered to God a more excellent sacrifice than Cain, by which he obtained witness that he was righteous, God testifying of his gifts; and by it he being dead, yet speaketh, Heb. xi. 4. Cain hated him because God more accepted him and his offering. "In this the children of God are manifest, and the children of the devil: whoever doeth not righteousness is not of God, nor he that loveth not his brother. For this is the message that ye heard from the beginning, that we should love one another. Not as Cain, who was of that wicked one, and slew his brother. And wherefore slew he him? Because his

own works were evil, and his brother's righteous," 1 John iii. 10—12.

14. Is it possible that any man can unfeignedly believe a heaven as the reward of holy obedience, and yet think we can do too much to obtain it, or be too careful to make it sure? Is not everlasting glory worth the cost of a holy life, or can it be too dearly bought?

15. Or is it possible to believe God's judgment, and hell's punishment, and yet to hate those that do their best according to God's own counsel to escape it?

16. What monstrous cruelty is it in you to wish poor souls to do that which God hath told us they shall be damned for! God saith, "Without holiness none shall see God," Heb. xii. 14. "Except your righteousness exceed the righteousness of the scribes and Pharisees, you shall in no wise enter into the kingdom of heaven," Matt. v. 20. "Blessed are the pure in heart, for they shall see God," Matt. v. 8. "If ye live after the flesh ye shall die; but if by the Spirit ye mortify the deeds of the body, ye shall live," Rom. viii. 7, 8, 13. "What manner of persons ought ye to be in all holy conversation and godliness?" 2 Pet. iii. 11. "We receiving a kingdom that cannot be moved, let us serve God acceptably, with reverence and godly fear; for our God is a consuming fire," Heb. xii. 28, 29. "Be stedfast, unmovable, always abounding in the work of the Lord, forasmuch as you know that your labour is not in vain in the Lord," 1 Cor. xv. 58. This is the very tenor of the gospel: and would you wish men to damn their souls for nothing? to lose heaven, and suffer in hell for ever, and all to avoid a pure and holy life? What a bloody motion is this; worse than if you entreated us all to cut our own throats! Let us try first whether you will do far less at our request. Will you give the poor all your lands and estates? Will you run into fire or water, or set your houses on fire, when any will but desire it? It is like you have heard of the woman who being tempted to adultery, desired the tempter first to hold his finger in the fire for her; which, when he refused, she told him it was less reason she should burn in hell to satisfy his lust. If you will not part with your life or estate when another desires you, why should we part with heaven for ever, and choose hell at your desire?

Yea, we see that you will not leave an ill-gotten gain, or a sport, or a whore, or a drunken cup, for all the love of God, the blood of Christ, and the hope of heaven; and shall we part with God, and heaven, and Christ to humour you?

And what is it that you offer us instead of all that we must part with, and to ease the pain that we must undergo? Nothing, or worse than nothing. If we should renounce God and our hope of heaven, you cannot give us health or wealth for it; much less can you secure these or life to us till to-morrow. And will any thing that you can give us be better than heaven to us, or will it make hell tolerable?

Will you undertake to answer for it at the bar of God, if we are charged with an ungodly, fleshly life, or omitting our necessary duty? You cannot answer for yourselves but by trembling confession: you cannot save yourselves; nor will all your wealth and honour get you one drop of water to cool your tongues. And shall we trust that you can answer for us, or save us? When you would have any man wilfully to neglect that holy life which God enjoineth, you would have him to be madder than one that would burn his house, and kill himself, if you did but require it: and what horrid cruelty is this! You are worse than man-eating cannibals! But the best is, you cannot force us to it; and if you think to hire or flatter us into hell, you must have somewhat more to say and to offer us than we yet ever heard of; much less are we so much below Bedlams, as to forsake our salvation, lest you should call us precisians, or puritans, or any such nickname or word of scorn, as doth but show the folly and misery of the speaker. You will not be laughed or mocked out of your estates or lives; nor we out of our salvation. In short, nature is not willing to lie in hell, and grace maketh us desire heaven; and we never yet found that any thing else was more desirable.

17. And what is there amiss in the word or work of God, and in a serious, godly life, that should make us be against it? Doth God make bad laws? Are your wills, and lusts, and appetites a better law? Or could you have taught God to amend the Bible, or to govern better? God needs us not: his laws are all made for our good. All his ways are pleasantness, and all his paths are peace. Speak true reason. Is it a better life to love a whore, or to please lust and appetite, than to love God? What is there in love and obedience to God, that should make it detestable, or make us miserable? Is it a greater trouble to live in hope of heavenly glory, than to live in the despair either of a Sadducee or a rebel? You may wiselier tempt us to fall out with our food, or friends, or health. We know that faith and godliness are not only man's duty, but his interest, much more than health is to our bodies, food to our natures, and the converse of dearest friends to our delight.

18. We have had experience of both ways, and would you have us mad against our experience? We tried the world and sin too long, and found nothing in it but brutish pleasure and luscious poison; nothing that will save soul, life, or health: and some trial God in mercy hath given us of his love, and the life of obedience, faith, and hope; and the more we try it, the better we find it: only we can reach to so small a degree as doth but tell us how good it is, and make us long for more. And whether the devil would persuade, scorn, or affright us from it, by his own mouth or by yours, we hope it shall be all in vain.

19. And who or what are you that would reason, mock, or affright us from a life of obedience to God? Are you wiser than God, and dare you give him the lie, that we should believe you before him? Or are you better than God, that you can make a better choice for yourselves and us? Are you more merciful than God, and would save us from some hurt that he would do us? Are you truer than God, and more to be believed? Are you greater than God, and more to be feared? Or are you not the most foolish, ignorant, and damnably yourselves deluded by the devil? And shall the words or mocks of such drive us to forsake our souls and God? Should we obey you and lie in hell for it for ever, it would be no small part of the torment of our consciences, to think that we came thither by regarding the threats or scorns of worms and fools before all the word and love of God and our Redeemer.

20. And before we change our obedience to God for another course, let us know what we shall change it for, and whether it be for something better: hath your course made you better or happier than the faithful are? Do we not see and feel with sorrow, that the worldly, fleshly, ungodly sort, are in all nations the plagues of the earth, and worse to mankind than wolves and serpents? They will not let the world live in peace; striving and fighting for dominion and mastership, and more of the world, they are like dogs about their carrion, worrying and tearing one another: they turn man into a more odious creature than swine or toads, by filthy lusts, and horrid profaneness: they make their countries worse

than Bedlam, raving against that which the God of heaven hath commanded and made necessary to salvation. And are these such good and pleasant fruits as should entice us to change our Master, work, and hopes, for this, and worse that followeth it?

And who shall be our rule, if we forsake God and his word? If princes, how many minds are they of through the world! and are they all in the right? or how shall we know which is right but by the word of God? or must all men be for the God and religion of his king? If it were prelates, of how many minds are they through the world, and how bitter in condemning one another! If it must be the major part, how shall obscure men know who those be that can have no just cognizance of the state of the earth, whether papists, Greeks, Jacobites, Nestorians, &c. be the major part? And how shall we know that the major part of the clergy are the best and soundest, when we see that the major part of the laity is usually the worst; or is it certain that the papist bishops are sounder than our protestant bishops, because they are more? If we forsake our concord in God and his word, we can have none.

21. What mean you to do with conscience, your own, and ours, and other men's? Conscience is God's officer in us, and judgeth of men and actions as they stand subject to God and his judgment. To drive conscience out of the world, and to drive all reverence and obedience to God out of the world, is all one. To subject conscience to lust or man, is to subject God to lust or man in our estimation and practice. And is God so easily deposed? and will he give up his sceptre to a scorner, a drunkard, or a persecutor?

And what shift will you make at home to quiet conscience in yourselves? You little know how deep it biteth, and how hardly it is quieted, when it is awaked, as shortly and certainly it will be: then Judas will bring back his price, and say, "I have sinned in betraying innocent blood;" and all the comfort his companions will give him is, "See thou to that: what is that to us?" And hanging or precipitating himself is next. It is like he before thought as you do, that he could have better mastered his conscience: but you may as wisely think to conquer pain and death.

But whatever you do with your own, if we should leave our obedience to God, to obey you or any men, we know not what we should do with our own consciences, nor how to quiet them. God hath brought us out of the darkness and lethargy which quieted them in sin heretofore: and we cannot now be ignorant of that duty to God, that self-interest, that danger to wilful sinners, and that evil of sin, which would begin hell in us here: and are not your scorns and threatenings easier than this?

22. Do not most men at death see the madness not only of enmity, but of neglect of a holy life, and wish that they might die the death of the righteous, and that their last end might be like his? Had you rather die a Dives or a Herod, or a Lazarus or a Paul? Is it not a shame to your devilish cause and you, to see men live in one mind and die in another? and scorn, hate, and persecute serious godliness till the sentence of death is passed upon them, and then to wish they were such themselves? Or if you be more hardened to the last, you are the more hopeful; but how quickly did such another change his note, and cry, "Father Abraham, send one to my five brethren to warn them, that they come not to the place of torment!" If you mock at these words, you mock at Christ that spake them; and sure you look not to be saved by a derided Christ. And it is base hypocrisy to deride him, and yet call yourselves christians, and go to church as if you served him. Live as you would die and be judged, for you shall be judged as you live and die. Either hold to the mind that you will never change, or change it quickly before it be too late.

23. If you know what a man is, you know that his soul is better than his corruptible flesh; and if you think your throats, and guts, and fancies worth all the cost, and care, and labour, which you bestow on them in the world, shall not we think our souls worth more? What godly man that you think makes too much ado for heaven, doth bestow more time, and words, and labour for it, than you do for the flesh and world? Do we not see how men will labour at land, and venture through dangerous seas, and fight in wars, and plot against all that stand in their way, and this is all day, from year to year, and all for provision for flesh and fancy. And do those that you accuse do more for their salvation? If you know not now, you will shortly know, which makes the better choice and bargain.

24. What harm doth godliness and conscience do you in other men? Had you not rather have a son that takes disobedience, whoredom, gaming, and drunkenness for sin, than one that makes no conscience of them? Had you not rather have a wife whose conscience restrains her from scolding and adultery, and a servant that makes conscience of robbing or deceiving you, than one that doth not? Sure unconscionable servants and debtors are more troublesome than they that fear God, and believe that injustice is a damning sin. But the truth is, most wicked men are for so much conscience and religion in others, as restrains them from wronging or hurting them, but no more, nor for that much in themselves which may restrain them from hurting others.

But if you resolve rather to be damned than to be sober, just, and godly, and obey God against the flesh; why cannot you bear with other men that make a wiser choice? What hurt doth their praying do you, or their preaching, while they are responsible for any ill doctrine? What if they be reading the Scripture, or hearing directions for a holy life, while you are drinking, or gaming, or reading a romance or railing libel, doth their piety hurt you? What if they dare not swear and drink as you do, doth this do you any harm? What is it but the serpentine enmity that maketh you hate those that never hurt you?

25. If you will believe God, it is for the sake of godly men that God preserves the world from ruin; he would have saved Sodom had there been but ten such persons in it; he will not destroy the world, till he hath gathered all his chosen out of it; and do they deserve to be most hated?

26. How exceeding dear a love hath God and our Redeemer expressed, to all holy, obedient believers! God calls them his jewels, his treasure, in whom he delighteth; he gave Christ especially for them. He sealeth them to salvation by his Spirit. He justifieth them, and will glorify them in heaven. Christ calls them flesh of his flesh, his friends, his spouse, they are united to him, he washeth them in his blood, and feedeth them with his flesh, and will make them equal to the angels, which will condemn their enemies. And are not you devilish enemies to God and Christ, who cull out those for your malice and enmity, whom God chooseth out to magnify the wonders of his love on them for ever?

27. The angels of heaven rejoice at the conversion of a sinner, Luke xv. 10; and rejoice to be Christ's servants for their defence continually: and is it not devils then and their servants and soldiers that are against them? Take heed; God's angels that smote a Herod, may do execution on you ere long.

28. The Holy Ghost saith, (1 Cor. vi.) that the saints shall judge the world, and even the angels, that is, the evil ones. Did you believe this, you would be afraid to hate and persecute them now.

29. Even heathens are for much honouring and worshipping their gods; yea, many offer them too costly sacrifice. What praises doth Julian give to the sun, and what strictness of life doth he command his priests! What great contempt of the body and the world did the Platonists, the stoics, and the cynics profess! And shall professed christians hate those that are obedient to the true God? Yea, to show that the war between good and evil goeth on in all the world, even among heathens those that were for true virtue were despised and hated by the sensual.

30. And is it not a self-condemning thing in those that accuse God's servants as making too much ado in obeying the law of God, and yet make (as the church of Rome doth) abundance more laws or canons of their own, and require precise obedience to them all? yea, will burn men at a stake for breaking their laws? Doth God make too much work in the judgment of them that think it not enough without much more, as if God's law were too narrow and insufficient? Yea, learn by the church of England, whose canons, (5—8,) *ipso facto*, excommunicate them that do but affirm any thing to be repugnant to God's word in their liturgy, ceremonies, or church-governing offices. And can you think that obeying God deserveth hatred, when disobeying men deserveth excommunication? Learn of our late laws, which account all the ministers of England worthy to be cast out and silenced if they dare not take the imposed declarations, oaths, and subscriptions, and do what the act of uniformity imposeth; and do you think it worthy of reproach to be as strict in obeying God's known laws, as is required to the act of uniformity and the canons?

31. Even the church of Rome applaudeth great rigour and strictness of life, in such as will obey the pope; and they have allowed orders of friars whose rulers tie them to great abstinence, to much praying, and some to much preaching, so that religion is all their calling. And shall the strict obeying of God's known laws render men odious among professed protestants? Yea, the papists honour the very bones and relics of their dead saints. And you yourselves keep holy-days for many saints: and will you at the same time hate and hurt those that endeavour to imitate them? Will you imitate those Pharisees whom Christ pronounceth woe against, who at once honoured the dead prophets with building them monuments or tombs, and murdered the living that succeeded them?

32. You can never come to heaven, or be saved from hell yourselves, without serious holiness, justice, and sobriety; and will you hate that without which you cannot be saved?

33. Scarce any sin doth more certainly prove you to be ungodly, than hating godliness: whatever hope there may be of those that sin against conscience, and wish to be better, and purpose repentance, that man cannot be a truly godly man, that is an enemy to godliness; so that this is a dreadful death's mark on you.

34. You would extirpate the principle of self-love, which God hath made inseparable from us. There is somewhat in our nature which we cannot lay by, which makes us unwilling to be damned. If you that believe no hell dare venture into it, we cannot do so who do believe it. If you say that it is our folly to believe that none shall be saved without holiness, and mortifying the deeds of the body by the Spirit, bear with that folly which doth you no harm: it is not men or devils that we had it from, but the Holy Ghost in Scripture. If it be your wisdom to give God the lie, and believe a drunken sot, or the devil, before him, it shall be none of ours. Speed as you choose, and let us speed as we choose. We shall meet your souls shortly in another mind and tune. Strive not to make us choose damnation now our eyes are open; we were once too easily befooled: but cannot now so hate ourselves.

35. Moreover, he that would not have a man live a life of holy obedience to God, would have him lay by that which he was made for, and that which God continueth his life for, and that which he hath his reason and all his daily mercies for. What else have we to do in the world? Have men going to the grave and eternity nothing to do but eat, and drink, and laugh, and play, and run up and down like ants with sticks and straws, and then die, and call all vanity and vexation too late? If we may not spend our time in making sure of a better world, we had rather we had never been born, or had died in infancy, or that we had a dose of opium that would make us sleep out the rest of our lives in quietness, rather than spend it as you do, and then give a sad account of all. We had rather we had been birds or beasts, dogs or swine, than men, were it not for that life which you hate, and the hopes which depend on it. It had been a greater kindness to us to have murdered us at the birth, than to tempt us to live for our damnation.

36. What do you think it is that is God's image on man's soul? You know that it is said in Scripture that God made man at first in his own image, and that Christ by his Spirit reneweth them to that image. What is it, think you? God hath not hands, and feet, and bodily parts, as we have: it is the soul that hath his image. And do you think it is the love of money, and lust, and sport, or gluttony, or drunkenness that is his image? Scripture saith, (Eph. iv. 23, 24; Col. iii. 10,) it is holiness; and this is called the divine nature, as coming from God, and inclining nature unto God. Either holiness, wisdom, and righteousness are God's image, or else there is none such on man; and then you make God's word to be false. And if this be it, and this it which you hate, are not you haters of God? And is not that to be devilish and hated by God?

37. While you are angry at them that say few are saved, or that none but saints, or serious, godly, obedient men are saved, you would sink all the world into utter despair, and make none or next to none to be saved. One part of the haters of godliness believe no life to come; and these would have all men despair. For if there be none, there is none to be hoped for; and they that think men die but as dogs and swine do, must be expected to live like dogs and swine. The other part of you labour by all means to make themselves and others believe that the profession of more godliness than worldly, carnal men have, is but hypocrisy, and that such are at the heart as bad as others; and if this be so, what is the consequence, but that none are saved? For unless you will give God the lie, or be saved in spite of him, you must believe that none are saved that are not sanctified by the Spirit of Christ, and live not after the Spirit, mortifying the flesh, John iii. 3, 5; Heb. xii. 14; Rom. viii. 6—9, 13; 2 Cor. v. 17. And that no man can be saved that loveth the world more than God and heaven, and fleshly pleasure more than holiness. And therefore if there be none such, then none are saved. Hypocrisy will not save men: God tells us that drunkards, fornicators, covetous, thieves, extortioners, revilers, effeminate, idolaters, cannot enter into the kingdom of God, 1 Cor. vi. 9, 10; Ephes. v. 5. "And if any man love the world (best) the love of the Father is not in him," 1 John ii. 5.

And if all that pretend to be better are hypocrites, then none at all are saved.

It may be you have the kindness to except some few. But if those few be all that be not either carnal men, (described Rom. viii. 5—7, 9,) or hypocrites, how few then do you make to be saved, if God be true!

38. Who do you think it is that Christ meaneth, when he saith, "I send you as lambs among wolves. Ye shall be hated of all men for my name's sake. Blessed are they that suffer persecution for righteousness' sake. When they say all manner of evil of you falsely for my sake. The world will hate you as it hated me, because you are not of the world, but I have chosen you out of the world. Marvel not if the world hate you. As many as will live godly in Christ Jesus shall suffer persecution," &c.? Who do you think all this is spoken of? It is not of you that are fleshly, worldly, ungodly men. Who persecuteth you for righteousness' sake? Who hateth, revileth, or imprisoneth, or fineth you, for living godly in Christ Jesus? Do you suffer as much for reviling preachers, as we have done for preaching? What suffer you for all the oaths that be sworn daily in streets and taverns, and the horrid profaneness, atheism, Sadduceeism, infidelity, that men are guilty of? If you did suffer for whoredom, drunkenness, or blasphemy, is that for Christ or righteousness? When the Holy Ghost saith, "As he that was born after the flesh persecuted him that was born after the Spirit, even so it is now;" it is such as you that he meaneth. When Peter saith, "They speak evil of you, and falsely accuse your good conversation in Christ," (1 Pet. iii. 16,) whom meaneth he? When he saith, (1 Pet. iv.) "They think it strange that you run not with them to all excess of riot, lasciviousness, lusts, excess of wine, revellings, banquetings, and abominable idolatry," who do you think he meaneth? And when he saith, (1 Pet. ii. 9,) "Ye are a chosen generation, a royal priesthood, a holy nation, a peculiar people, that ye should show forth the praises of him that hath called you out of darkness into his marvellous light," who is it that he meaneth? You will say, It is christians: true; but is it hypocrites? Is it those that will say at last, Lord, we have prophesied in thy name, and ate and drunk in thy presence, to whom Christ will say, Depart from me, ye workers of iniquity, I know you not? Sure false christians are worse than heathens.

39. The way which you take against religious persons doth show who it is that sets you on work, and what it is that is the root of your enmity. As God's image is in the understanding, will, and executing power of man, so is Satan's; and he is accordingly described by Christ to be, 1. A liar and deceiver. 2. A malignant hater of goodness or holiness, and a cause of sin. 3. A hurtful murderer or destroyer. And these are the three ways by which godly people are prosecuted in the world. 1. Belying them is grown so common with their enemies, that there is nothing scarcely so notoriously false which they will not affirm of them, and it is well if some will not preach it, print it, or swear it: and they make one another easily believe it. Till experience proved it, I did not think that human nature had been liable to such impudent, monstrous lying.

2. The daily business of many is, by wit and diligence to draw men to hate religious men on false pretences. As plainly as Christ preacheth and urgeth love, as his great commandment; so plainly do these press and urge men to hatred: but of this before.

3. And hatred tends to hurtfulness. What plotting and labouring is there in the world, to ruin and destroy each other! The malignant spirit is bloodthirsty. It is strange how the unclean devils thirst to draw or suck some blood from witches. Nothing more alienates me from the papal kingdom, than that it lives like leeches upon blood. To read over the history of the inquisition, and of their massacres, would make men take toads, and adders, and mad dogs, and wolves, for harmless things in comparison of some men. If any would requite them (or others) with the like, I hate it in protestant or papist. The Turks conquered the Greek empire, partly by the mutinous divisions of the christians, and partly by promising them liberty of religion. And when the christians thought they should have that, they yielded up the empire with the less resistance. And that which was so advantageous to the infidels, might, well used and limited, be more advantageous to the christian truth and church.

But though good things may be used in an ill cause, it is a sign of a bad cause which needeth bad means. That cause which is carried on by lying, perjury, and deceit, by malignant, love-killing endeavours, and by cruelty, and hurtfulness, and blood, is thereby made suspicious to all wise men. It is a wonder of impudence in Baronius, Binnius, and other papists, to justify Martin, a canonized saint, for renouncing communion to the death with the synods and bishops who persuaded the emperor to draw the sword against the Gnostic Priscillianists; and themselves to defend a thousandfold greater cruelties and murders in their own church on the account of religion. But sin is mad self-contradiction.

4. I conclude with this great truth: they that hate and oppose godly men's obedience to God, do seek to silence the chief witness of Christ, and to cast out christianity from the earth. Christianity cannot be proved to be true, but by the Spirit, which is its seal and witness. This witness of the Spirit was not only extraordinary in languages and numerous miracles, but also ordinary in the work of sanctification. This seal is set on all that shall be saved in all times and places, "The Lord knoweth who are his. And, Let him that nameth the name of Christ depart from iniquity." "He redeemed us to purify to himself a peculiar people zealous of good works; teaching us, that denying ungodliness and worldly lusts, we should live soberly, righteously, and godly in this present world: looking for that blessed hope, and the glorious appearing of the great God and our Saviour Jesus Christ," Tit. ii. 12—14. By this healing work Christ is known to be indeed our Physician, the Saviour that saveth his people from their sins. As man generateth man, and the father is known by the similitude of the child; and as he is known to be a good artist that can make others such. This is Christ's standing witness in all times and places. And when you would turn this into scorn, and cloud it with slanders, or the charge of hypocrisy, and would have such judged an odious people, and have them driven out of the world, what do you in effect but spit in the face of Christ, and crown him with thorns, and call him a deceiver, and crucify him afresh, and seek to expel christianity from the earth? What reasonable man could believe Christ to be Christ, the Saviour of the world, if he did not sanctify men, and make them much better and fitter for heaven than other men?

So that in this you directly militate for the devil, the world, and the flesh, against God the Father, Son, and Holy Ghost, against the holy catholic church, and the communion of saints, and the hope of resurrection and life everlasting; which if you did openly under the name of infidels or heathens, or rather as the professed soldiers of the devil, it were less disingenuous and hypocritical, than to do it in the church, and under Christ's colours, and in the christian name.

And you must be sure that you are stronger than God and our Saviour, if you will prevail to the last. God hath undertaken the defence of the just: Christ hath undertaken to present them triumphant before his Father, and cast their enemies into hell. Are you sure you can overcome him? Vile worms, that cannot fetch a breath without him! when began you to be stronger than God? Was it in the womb? or in infancy, when you could not go? Or was it when the devil and the flesh made you mad or drunken in ignorant malice? If so, the drunken fit will soon be over, and God will awake a tormenting wit. If you can conquer God, try your strength first on his works: stop the sun; change night and day; turn the tide of the sea; live without meat or air; resolve that you will never die; save all your friends from death. Can you do none of this, and yet will you venture a war against God? Or do you think to fight against his servants, and bribe him to be on your side, and forsake them to your rage? Did Christ take man's nature, and die to save them, and will he now turn on Satan's side against them? He overcame the devil's temptation on earth; yea, called Peter Satan, (Matt. xvi.) when he would have tempted him not to die for his chosen. Let men or devils go try him in his glory, whether he will change his mind, and take your part against his own holy truth and servants.

CHAPTER IV.

OBJECTIONS AND FALSE ACCUSATIONS ANSWERED.

BUT I know that as Christ and his apostles were not hated nor killed without pretended cause and reason, nor the martyrs murdered without accusation; so none will now justify the scorning or persecuting an innocent person, or a saint, as such, but they will first make them odious, and seem worthy of all that is done against them. They will say, It is not godly men, but wicked hypocrites, that we hate and prosecute; a false and odious sort of persons, who are unruly, and set up their own wit and will against the laws and governors of the several kingdoms where they live: they are the very worst of men.

Answ. If they are so indeed, they are none of the men that I am pleading for, nor you the men that I reprove. But before we come to particular accusations, it is your wisdom to answer these few questions.

1. Have you particular matter against them to make good this charge? or is it only a general malicious accusation?

2. Is it individual persons that you mean, by whom it is proved? or do you thus accuse whole companies of men? What if one said of papists, Jews, or Turks, They are murderers, adulterers, perjured, &c.; do you think he were not an odious slanderer, to speak that of all or most, or the whole party, which he can prove but by some few?

3. Do you know all the persons whom you accuse? And have you heard it proved? Or do you not say this of the whole congregations assembled to worship God, of whom you know not one of many? If this be so, it is inhuman calumny.

4. Have the particular persons been heard speak for themselves, and give the reason of their actions? And were they proved insufficient? Or were they condemned unheard? Or was God's word derided, and taken for no reason?

5. Do you not know that the devil is the great accuser of the brethren? And that he hath malice and craft enough to say as bad as you can say, by the best of men? And must he be believed?

6. Are you sure you can make God believe you, that these men are as bad as you affirm? If not, and if he find a man in prison for obeying his word, and ask who laid him there, will you undertake to prove that he was laid there for some crime? If God own him, and say, He is my servant, will you confute him, and say, No; but he is a schismatic? God knoweth a saint from a schismatic better than you do. Sheep-stealers use to shear the sheep, and cut out the mark. But they have to do with men. God's mark is where man cannot take it away; and the foundation of God standeth sure. The Lord knoweth who are his.

7. Know you not that Christ, and his apostles, and all the martyrs, were as deeply charged, and put to death as malefactors? We must then have better proof than accusation.

8. If they prove faithful christians whom you thus accuse, Christ hath undertaken their justification: it is his office. And do you think to baffle him? Can he not answer you? Rom. viii. 32, 33, 35. Who shall lay any thing to the charge of God's elect? It is God that justifieth: who is he that will condemn them?

9. Have you not greater sins yourselves than those whom you accuse? If so, you condemn yourselves. Would you have God judge of them as you do? If so, do you not tell him how to judge of you, and even crave him to condemn you?

10. Doubtless you know that you are sinners: and how think you to be justified at the bar of God? Is there any but Christ to judge and justify you? And do you think he will justify his enemies, that hated, accused, and condemned his servants?

11. Those that dwell near godly christians and should know them, are more inexcusable for their malice and slanders than foreigners and strangers are. Men of another land or age may be deceived by lying fame or history; but you that are their neighbours are without excuse. I speak for none but persons fearing and obeying God: and you might easily have known that they are neither fornicators, drunkards, perjured, swearers, liars, oppressors, thieves, nor suffer for any such crimes as these.

12. And if they are as wicked as you say, why do you not prosecute them for such wickedness? What are the French protestants now prosecuted and ruined for? Have any judicatures proved them guilty of any such crimes against God or man? Or is it not only for worshipping God contrary to the king's and prelates' laws? And how is that? As Christ's apostles did: they refuse nothing in God's worship which God commanded, or any of Christ's apostles used, or any churches in their days, or long after. And did the apostles offer God so odious a worship as deserved hatred and destruction? When Daniel's enemies designed his ruin, they said, "We shall find no matter against this Daniel except it be concerning the law of his God," Dan. vi.; and so they got a law made against praying to any God but the king for a certain time. Daniel must be cast to the lions for breaking the king's law. The poor flies deserve death for coming into the spider's web; but did not the venomous worm spin it of purpose out of her own bowels, or condensate air, to take and kill the flies by craft? In England there are many

that worship God as the French protestants do, and no better than Christ's apostles did: if this be their horrid wickedness that makes them unworthy to live out of prison, say so, and pretend no other. But if it be heresy, false doctrine, perjury, fornication, robbing, treason, sedition, or any other crime, why are they not accused of these before the judges? And why are those charged with them that never were so accused and proved guilty? Will not all wise men take those persons for malicious liars, who by their published accusations thus odiously charge multitudes, and never offer to prove it against them at the judicatures? Their accusations show they want not will, therefore their not prosecuting them for any such sort of crimes, shows that it is truth that is wanting.

13. And if they be such wicked persons, whence is it that they are charged merely with hypocrisy, by such as say that they live soberly, and justly, and demurely, but they are at the heart as bad as others. Their accusers commonly confess that they are most free from all immoralities, and have an outward show of righteousness, but these heart-searchers see that their hearts are bad. And do they not by this confute their own accusations?

14. And why is it that they that know them best can see none of the wickedness which you accuse them of (beyond those human infirmities of which they most accuse themselves). As I have oft done, I again solemnly profess, as one that cannot be far from my account before the Judge of all the world, that having now lived to the sixty-eighth year of my age, and been most familiar since the age of sixteen or seventeen, with that sort of men whom the vulgar then called puritans, (described by Mr. Bolton and such other conformists,) though I have met with many that had their mistakes, and frailties, and troublesome differences in lesser things, and some hypocrites intruded among them, yet I never knew any other sort of men comparable to them in christian knowledge, faith, obedience to God, hatred of sin, care of their duty to God and man, sobriety, temperance, chastity, truth, heavenly desires, endeavours, and hopes: and that they so far excelled the rest of my acquaintance, as made their grace amiable to me and confirmed my belief of the sacred Scripture: yea, more, if I had not had the happiness of knowing such a sort of men that in holiness, justice, and love excelled the rest of my acquaintance, or at least, credibly heard of such, I could not have believed in Christ, as a Saviour of men whom he made no better than Turks and infidels; nor could I have believed a heaven for men no better prepared for it. And that now near my end, I see so great a difference in holiness, justice, and charity, between those commonly reviled for worshipping God but as the apostles did, and those that hate and persecute them, as greatly helps me in believing that there is a Saviour, and Sanctifier, and heaven for the faithful, and a devil that deceives the rest, and a hell that will receive them, which is even visibly begun on earth.

Accus. But (say they) it is not for their godliness or sobriety that we accuse them, but for their sin and wickedness.

Answ. Still this is but general, and signifieth nothing. But, 1. What is that odious sin? 2. It is God's merciful providence that keeps sin in general under such shame, as that the actors of it speak against it, even in their slanders. 3. But if this be the true cause, why do you cull out those that have least sin, to fasten your accusations of sin upon? If there be a conformable minister that is more holy, charitable, and zealous against sin than the rest, he is one of those that is called a puritan, and accused of sin. Why do we hear none of your furious charges against the common drunkards, revellers, gamesters, whoremongers, persecutors, profane blasphemers, liars, and the families that call not upon God, show no serious regard of any religion at all? You can live among these, and swear, and drink, and play with them, and never cry out against them as bad men.

Accus. But religion being the best thing, the corrupters of that are worse than drunkards, and swearers, and adulterers.

Answ. Such corrupters there may be, as are worse indeed: but what is it that they corrupt religion in? They subscribe to all the Bible, and the ancient creeds; and if need be, to the English articles of religion. Is not all that enough? Their many large published writings tell the world their judgment in religion: such as Mr. Arthur Hildersham's, Mr. Perkins's, Mr. Greenham's, Dod's, Anthony Burgess's, Richard Alleine's, and abundance such. What errors are in these?

2. Why are not they these twenty years accused of preaching false doctrine, and proved guilty, and punished for it, if they are such?

3. If it be not in doctrine, what is it?

Accus. They worship God contrary to the law, in not using the Common Prayer Book.

Answ. 1. Those that constantly join in the parish churches in the Common Prayer are as much hated, reviled, and prosecuted as the rest. Therefore this charge is but hypocrisy.

2. What do they that for matter or manner is positively contrary to law in God's worship? They read Scripture, pray, preach, praise God with psalms, communicate in the Lord's supper: doth the law forbid any of this?

3. Not using the rest of the liturgy is a negation, and no act at all, and therefore no act of worship, and therefore no unlawful act, no more than silence is: he that is silent, and he that omits the rest of the liturgy, worships not God by using it; but he doth nothing contrary to it, or forbidden by it.

4. If Peter and Paul were unknown in England, and worshipped God but as they did on earth, would you therefore call them rogues or rebels, or lay them in gaol? Did they worship God in an odious, intolerable manner? Did the Holy Ghost by them write an infallible rule for all things necessary in religion; and yet are they unsufferable rogues that worship God but according to that rule?

5. Are they wiser men than they that have made us another rule or worship? or have they more of God's Spirit, and more authority in religion?

6. Do not the imposers say, that all which they add is no part of religion, but things indifferent? And are they odious corrupters of religion, who omit no part of religion, but only human indifferent things?

7. Do you not reverence the church for some hundred years after Christ, which imposed no liturgies, but left every pastor to use his own prayers?

8. Do you not harden the papists that call our religion new, and ask where it was two hundred years ago, if you make the liturgy, as now formed and imposed, our religion, when it is not two hundred years old.

9. The godly bishops of England have ever owned the other protestant churches, and their communion, who have none of our liturgies, nor any like it.

10. If this be odious crime, why do you never revile or prosecute the atheists, infidels, Sadducees, Hobbists, and those many thousands that seldom, if ever, go to any church, or worship God publicly at

all? Is the worship that Peter and Paul used worse than irreligiousness and infidelity?

11. Who can believe that you are sincerely zealous against mis-worshipping God, when you can ordinarily yourselves be in a drinking house or playhouse, at the time of public worship? And when so few of you never so much as worship God in your families, by prayer, or read the Scripture, or catechise your families?

12. Is it not a strange thing to hear men accuse others for not using the liturgy in God's worship, and at the same time would have them that refuse it, to be forbidden all public worshipping of God at all? Doth this signify any dislike of their omitting God's worship? Which is the more ungodly omission, to omit all worship of God, and live like atheists, or to omit only so much of the liturgy as the apostles used not? I have known many that could not eat cheese, as is said before (nor scarce smell it without danger of death). If you would have a law made that such shall eat no other meat, few wise men will believe that it is their health and life that you desire. If a man fail in paying his landlord some odd act of service, will you make a law that he shall pay nothing at all? If a subject neglect paying some excise, or using bow and arrows, will you forbid him paying any thing, or serving the king at all? Sure they that forbid men all public worship, be offended at somewhat else than that men do not rightly worship God, unless they think that not to worship him at all is better than doing it without their book.

Object. But he shall be compelled to better worship.

Answ. How? When he lieth in gaol he cannot publicly worship God at all. Is that better worship? I know it is banishment that some would have executed. And will men worship God any better among heathens or infidels, or others? Or why should other countries endure them, if they be not to be endured in their own?

Are not Englishmen that worship God only by their own book, as much nonconformists when they are in other lands, France, Spain, Italy, Germany, Holland, &c. as those are here that do not use it? And are they there intolerable and worthy of ruin?

Did the apostles or first churches banish any on such accounts? Will Christ banish them from his kingdom? Hath he made any such laws? And is not he the absolute Sovereign? Hath he left his servants to the will of man, to use them how they will, or cast out of his church whom they will? Are you sure these are none of the number of whom Christ saith, "I was hungry, and ye fed me not," &c. "Inasmuch as ye did it not to one of the least of these my brethren, you did it not to me," Matt. xxv.

Accus. But they are schismatics, and separate from the church; and is not that a damnable sin?

Answ. 1. Being speaking only to malignant enemies of serious godliness, I say, It is not only separatists that you hate, but godly conformists, yea perhaps most of all, because you are more restrained from hurting them. How oft hear we curses and revilings against conforming puritans, or as some call them, church whigs. If they are not haters of their brethren, but friends to love and peace, you nickname them trimmers. And cursing those whom Christ blesseth, when he saith, "Blessed be the peace-makers, for theirs is the kingdom of heaven," you say, Cursed be the trimmers, and would the kingdom were rid of them. It is any that are for a holy life, and obedience to God, that you abhor.

2. As I said before, you spare those that come to the parish churches no more than others. The old nonconformists wrote more against separation than any else in England did; and yet were hated as intolerable. The reconcilers who are since made nonconformists, did publicly offer to be subject to archbishops and bishops, to use the liturgy themselves if reformed, and if it were not, yet never pleaded for separation; and yet are never the more endured.

But who is it that they separate from? Do they not profess union and communion with the whole catholic church on earth? What separation do you mean? Is it their local absence? And are not you such separatists from all the world, saving the assembly where you meet? One cannot be in two places at once.

Or is it that they dislike somewhat in your forms of worship? So they in other forms, with whom yet they may profess communion. And in what is it that they show dislike or separation? They hold communion with you as christians, and as reformed from popery. They separate not from papists as christians. And from you it is only for that which you say is no part of your worship or religion, but things indifferent, which they think to be sin. And are those separatists from your church, who only separate from that which is no part of your church worship?

3. Are the French and Dutch churches in London schismatics or separatists, who profess communion with our churches, though they use not our oaths, subscriptions, or liturgy? Liking their own mode better, and preferring it, is no separation. If I like your liturgy better than any in the Bibliotheca Patrum, is that separating from all churches that use the rest?

4. Who are the schismatics in France, Italy, Poland, &c.; those that are called so, and persecuted as such; or those that impose on them the things which they judge sinful?

What if you were in a presbyterian land, where the liturgy and prelacy are forbidden, and another form set up by law; and you should contrary to that law use the liturgy and ceremonies; or at least refuse subscribing against prelacy, and for lay elders? If they excommunicated or ruined you for this, who do you think were guilty of the schism?

5. Do they forsake the assemblies before they are excommunicated? Or is it not an odd thing for to excommunicate men first, and then accuse them for not coming to church? I have known ministers stop in the midst of pulpit worship, and refuse to go on till an excommunicate person went out. The whole representative church of England do, in their fifth, sixth, seventh, and eighth canons, *ipso facto*, without trial or sentence, excommunicate all in England, who affirm any thing to be sinful or repugnant to God's word in the church-governing offices whatsoever, in the liturgy, ceremonies, or articles. And shall they after this be called separatists for not coming in? Doth not the canon show that the church would not have them come in when they cast them out?

Object. But the church and canon bid them repent of that their wicked error, and publicly confess it, and so come in.

Answ. 1. Is a man's judgment absolutely in his power? Can a man believe a thing to be a wicked error merely because the canon saith so? He that can believe what he list, believeth nothing truly. If this belief be necessary to church communion, and to escape damning schism, it is necessary to salvation. Why then is it not in the creed, ten commandments, or Bible? Do you call them the things indifferent, and then call it a wicked error to hold them sinful? Is not this to make it necessary to salvation or communion, to have so much learning or knowledge, as to know all indifferent words and things in the world to be indifferent which men will impose? I would all church members with yours and others knew all necessary things. Do you believe in your heart that all or half the parishioners do know these things to be lawful, or understand any more of them than those that think otherwise; when thousands cannot answer a necessary question of the creed or catechism, nor know who Christ is, and how he saveth us?

Why is there not a catechism made containing the sound proof that lay-chancellor's power of the keys, and diocesan bishops that have no bishops under them, and our present court-church discipline, and all the rubric, ceremonies, and forms, are lawful, if all must be excommunicate that think and say otherwise?

Object. If they are so ignorant that they cannot know church orders to be lawful, they are not fit to communicate with the church.

Answ. Make no church orders necessary to communion, but what Christ and his apostles have made necessary to it; and then cast out and spare not all as ignorant that refuse them.

2. But again, do you believe that most or all that you keep in, are wiser and more knowing than those that you cast out? How shall such as I believe you, who know that in all the parishes which my cohabitation alloweth me to know, it is the most knowing and religious part that most dissent, and the generality of the grossly ignorant, that understand few articles of the creed, do conform. As ignorant as I am, and hundreds of my calling and mind, I would I were not only silenced and imprisoned, but put to death, on condition that all that you now receive as members of the church, had no more ignorance than we have. But it is our lot to tire ourselves with teaching poor people to understand their baptism, christianity, creed, Lord's prayer, and ten commandments, and leave most ignorant when all is done, and yet ourselves, after our hardest and longest study, to be judged so ignorant about some indifferent things, as to be unfit for ministry or communion.

Accus. If men will not obey church governors and laws, they are rebels, and unfit for christian society. If every man shall follow his own fancy, what order will there be? Do not all churches require obedience to their orders?

Answ. 1. The church hath one universal King, who hath made universal laws for all; which must be first obeyed, and against which no man hath power. And yet his own laws have things necessary to all, in which they must unite, and integrals and accidents which all know not; in which they must bear with one another. No man understandeth all the Bible. And are many laws and books more necessary than God's?

2. Whoever depraveth the necessary points of religion by his own fancies, should be rejected. But all men living err in many lesser things.

3. In what countries is it that your rule holds, that rulers must be thus far obeyed in religion? Is it in China, or Pegu, or Hindostan, or Turkey? Or is it in Italy, Spain, Poland, Silesia, Bavaria, or France? Or is it at Geneva, Holland, or the presbyterian countries? Or is it only in England, Scotland, and Ireland? And was it so here before Henry the Eighth, or only since? And how shall any know where it is, unless he try and judge his ruler's commands by the laws of God? Will you follow this rule in France or Spain? Or shall all subjects judge of kings' capacities?

Accus. But they hold unlawful assemblies of their own, and worship God contrary to law, and yield not so much as passive obedience.

Answ. 1. You know the ministers are forbidden their office, unless they will take those oaths, subscriptions, professions, and practices, which they dare not take, for fear of sin and damnation. And they would be thankful if their reasons may be heard, and if any will instruct them better. And they are confirmed in their opinion by the answers, or no answers rather, made to the reasons already given in. And they are devoted or vowed to the sacred ministry in their ordination. And if there be such a sin as sacrilege in the world, they are confident it were sacrilege in them to alienate themselves from the office which they have undertaken. As it is apostasy from christianity to violate our baptismal vow, though men should command it, they doubt not but it is perfidious apostasy from the sacred ministry, to violate the ordination vow, though bishops silence them. As it is adultery to violate the conjugal contract, though a bishop should require it; seeing he that married them hath no power to unmarry them, unless they do it first themselves, and prove deserters or adulterers.

2. And the people that are excommunicate, or forbidden to worship God publicly, unless they will do that which they think is sin, are still under God's command to worship him, and not to forsake church assembling for his worship. What would you have these ministers and people do? They study and pray to God to convince them, if they take these oaths, subscriptions, professions, and practices to be sin, and they be no sin. They resolve to be ruled by God's word. They are willing to hear any thing that may better inform them. They wonder that men accuse them that have no more to say to change them. If they desert the ministry, they fear God's vengeance. If these poor people give over all God's public worship, and live like atheists, conscience living or dying will torment them. If they do that which they are persuaded is sin, when the imposers call it but indifferent, Paul hath antedated their sentence; "He that doubteth is damned if he eat, because he eateth not of faith. For whatsoever is not of faith is sin," Rom. xiv. Change their judgment they cannot. Sin they dare not. To give over worshipping God is to renounce salvation. Change the law or canon men will not. It seems to me a strange penalty to forbid men to worship God at all, because they think some subscriptions or forms to be sin: more strange than to say, all that will not wear crape shall go naked; or all that will not eat anchovies shall eat nothing. If a man think the use of a crucifix in worship sinful, sure to give over all worship is more sinful. But men have their ways.

3. What worship is it that they offer God contrary to law? They are willing to do all required in Scripture by Christ and his apostles. And were they rebels and rogues? Or is their worship intolerable?

4. What harm will it do their neighbours, or any, if they only read the Scripture, and praise God with psalms, and preach and pray as God prescribeth, without subscriptions or ceremonies? Are any hurt by this? Doth the same liberty to the Dutch here hurt any body, or break peace? Doth the difference of cathedral and parish worship break peace? or of those churches that have organs and altars, and those that have none?

The papists are the greatest pretenders to unity, and most cry down schism; and yet if all will but be servants to the pope, he will license multitudes of orders that more differ from one another than we from you; Jesuits, Benedictines, Dominicans, Carthusians, and abundance more.

5. Dare any man of self-knowledge and conscience say, that all your worship is not more faulty than

is the omission of a form or ceremony? Will not all the world be forbidden to worship God, if all as bad as this be forbidden? And how many worshippers of God, think you, will be left in England, if all must give over that have greater faults than the omission of a thing called but indifferent?

6. As to what you talk of passive obedience, though the phrase be a contradiction, yet the thing meant is a mere cheat of one that hath devised that absurd phrase; and calls omissive obedience by the name of passive: omitting an action is not suffering. Daniel was forbid to pray, and the apostles to preach. They would not yield this omissive obedience, but they yielded that which is commonly called passive. They patiently suffered.

7. Do you not know that about two hundred thousand in and near London cannot come within the doors of the parish churches (nor hundreds hear that can crowd in); shall all these be made atheists, or taken for rebels if they will not forbear to worship God?

8. I suppose you know that many thousands stay at home in their houses, shops, taverns, in sin or idleness. Are these thought worthy of a gaol or banishment? or is their course better than to worship God as Peter and Paul did? Oh the difference between God's judgment and some men's! But God's judgment shall determine all.

9. Are there no unfaithful and unskilful ministers? Will no patrons choose such? Is not the minister's skill and faithfulness of great importance to men's salvation? What if bishops or laws imposed an unskilful or untrusty physician on you, and forbade you to choose a better; would you die obediently, or rather say, No one hath power so to betray my life? No, nor your soul neither.

10. If you have the hearts of christians, consider this undeniable consequence. If you will have no union or concord among christians till they agree in all things that are of no greater weight and evidence than your forms and ceremonies are, you would have no concord in the world, no not between any two persons. And you may as well say, none shall be endured that are not just of the same visage and complexion. And then all the doubt will be, who is the man that will be the strongest and longest liver, to possess all England himself alone.

Accus. But they show that they are perjured, false, unconscionable rogues, that took on them to scruple oaths and our church communion till now, and now can do all rather than be out of places of trust.

Answ. 1. As to your church communion, can you blind men's eyes, that they shall not read what the old nonconformists have written to persuade men to it? See Messrs. Hildersham, Bradshaw, Gifford, Paget, Ball, and abundance more. And did not the present nonconformists show the same judgment, in 1660, and 1661, in their treaty? And do not many come to your assemblies? And would they not all that are ministers preach there if they could have leave? And have you not, as is afore proved, excommunicated them by your canons, 5—8? And is the Oxford act (which imprisoneth them all six months if they be seen within five miles of a corporation or any place where they have preached within twenty years) an invisible thing? Do you lay men in gaol by it, and yet think it must be unknown? And he that knows it, knows that it sentences all such to gaol if they be seen in your churches. And it is the course of human converse to say, If you come into any church within five miles, &c. you shall lie in gaol six months; and if you do not, you are rogues, and shall lie in gaol for not coming. Just when the ministers agreed to come more frequently than before, this act came out, and drove them back. You will say, they can appear in their own assemblies. *Answ.* 1. His Majesty encouraged them by granting them liberty by his declaration. 2. They have more hope there of escaping out of your hands, than they have in your own churches.

And do you not see in print what Mr. Tombes the anabaptist wrote long ago to persuade his followers to your communion? And what Mr. Nye wrote to persuade the independents to come to your churches? What great change is here of their judgments?

Object. But why did not the people do so all this while?

Answ. Because their own teachers did, as they thought, more profit them. Many a man thinks it lawful to wear rags that yet had rather wear whole and comely clothes; and lawful to eat brown bread, and drink water, that will fare better when they can, and yet take these when they cannot. The people that had good houses before the fire, did without any change of their judgments get into any poor rooms or cottages after it.

2. But suppose they lately change their judgments, (as many no doubt have,) you that think it is for the better are strange christians that reproach men for repenting and amending. Do you call them to church, and reproach them for not coming, and seek to ruin them for it, and now accuse them for coming? Doth not this show that some men desired the present impositions, not for concord of all, but to drive some away, lest they should come in, and the land have concord? And doth not this show what men we have to do with; and that it is somewhat else than nonconformity which such men hate? Your justice is, Come to church, or lie in gaol as schismatics. And if you come you are perfidious rogues. Whether they do or do not, all is one to such judges, who have some other hateful matter in their eye.

Object. But their doing it just now to keep their charter, and keep from suffering, proveth that they are perfidious rogues.

Answ. 1. I pray tell men of brains and sense, for what it is that you would have men excommunicated, and laid in gaol or fined, if they conform not. Do you do all this without any purpose or hope to drive them to conformity? And do you do it only to make them perfidious rogues. If suffering may not alter them, why do you use it on them?

2. But who knows not that some things are lawful to avoid suffering which else would not be lawful. It is lawful to cast your goods into the sea to save the ship and men's lives; which else were a sin. It is lawful to give a thief your purse to save your life, which else were unlawful. It is lawful to blow up neighbours' houses to stop a fire. Christ proved it lawful to break the sabbath in cases of necessity; he withdrew into the wilderness and far from Jerusalem, to avoid the Pharisees' persecution. And Paul was let down by the wall in a basket; and which, without danger of suffering, had not been lawful. Though no sin must be done to avoid suffering, yet that may and must be done, which self-preservation makes no sin, but a duty: to kill a man that assaults you in your own defence, is not the same crime as unnecessarily to kill him.

But as to the other case of taking the corporation oath and declaration, if you know the case, (as you should do before you accuse men,) you know that it is the true sense of them that is all the controversy. Nobody scruples swearing loyalty, and renouncing rebellion and sedition, and unlawful means of reformation. That which makes it difficult is that, on one side, the proper universal sense of the words seems to them unlawful, and oaths must be taken in the usual sense, unless our rulers give another; yet on the other side, learned sober conformists profess that they take such words in the limited sense, or else they would not take them; and they argue subtly to prove that to be the true sense; and our law-makers to whom it belongs will not end the controversy by an exposition. And can you wonder here if men fluctuate in uncertainty? And a late writer having given subtler arguments for the limited sense than were published before, did persuade many. And in that limited sense twenty nonconformist ministers took the oath long ago in London at one time.

But I justify none that mistake in so great a matter. And doubtless if they sinned God will not bless it to their good; it will prove their snare. And I am glad that we are agreed that perjury is a heinous sin. I beseech you then to consider, 1. Whether those men are fit to accuse them who drive them to it, and say to ministers, Swear or lie in gaol. 2. Or those who are of the mind of Grotius, Bishop Taylor, and such others, that lying is lawful when it saves ourselves, and wrongs no other; and of those divines that say, It is as lawful to defend myself from pernicious imposers with my tongue as with my hands.

3. Let us all with fear (who believe there is a God) avoid the dreadful crime of perjuring the whole land. This whole kingdom is sworn against all foreign jurisdiction in the oath of supremacy; and against all endeavours to alter the government of church or state, by, 1. The corporation act. 2. The vestry act. 3. The militia act. 4. The Oxford act of confinement. 5. And obliged by the act of uniformity. Is it not perjury then to endeavour any alteration of it? 1. What shall we then think of them that would bring in popery? Would they not perjure the kingdom? 2. What shall we say of them that write for a foreign church jurisdiction, under the name of general councils, or a college of bishops, or of foreign patriarchs, of whom the pope is chief, and the *principium unitatis* to the universal church. Is it no change of our church government to bring us under a foreign jurisdiction? Is it no change of state government to make the king and kingdom subject to that foreign jurisdiction, who may excommunicate him, and so bring on him all the evil that excommunication inferreth? And what man in his wits knoweth not that prelates and priests are much at the will and power of the princes under whom they live? Doth not our king expect that his bishops obey him? And those that must have this universal jurisdiction over our king and us, are the subjects of other princes, of which the far greatest part are papists, Mahometans, infidels, heathens, or such as are called heretics; and if our king and we be made subject to the subjects of the Turk, the pope, the kings of Spain, France, Poland, the emperor, the Muscovite, the dukes of Bavaria, Tuscany, and such like, is he not made a subject to their lords and masters, and much worse? Will not this project perjure England?

3. Whether it be any alteration of government by them that would change the power and use of parliaments, I leave to lawyers.

4. But I would fain be satisfied of another case. These kingdoms of England and Scotland took a covenant and vow, some voluntarily, some at their compositions, who had been sequestered for the king. This vow contained divers matters, of which some are notorious duties, as to repent of their sins, to oppose popery, schism, and profaneness, to defend the king, &c. It is not denied by most that I meet with, that this oath or vow was unlawfully imposed, and unlawfully taken, and many think some of the matter was unlawful, viz. to oppose prelacy, &c. But seeing casuists are agreed, that an oath unlawfully both imposed and taken, bindeth to that part of the matter which is lawful and necessary, notwithstanding the conjunction of the rest; and the corporations of England are all formed by a declaration taken by all in power and trust, that "There is no obligation (without the least exception) on me or any other person from the oath called the Solemn League and Covenant;" the doubt is, whether every man may declare that, of all the thousands of three kingdoms (whom he never knew) no one is bound by that oath, or vow, to repent of his sins, or in his place and calling to oppose schism, popery, or profaneness, or to defend the king. And whether all may declare that the Londoners and ministers, and the restored old parliament, and General Monk's army who restored the king, as supposing they were bound to it by that oath, were all deceived, and were under no such obligation thence. And whether I am not bound in charity to think that the sequestered royalists put a good sense on it when they took it. And so whether all the corporations of England are free from —— And for what it is that God hath singled them out for judgment.

If you be agreed with us (and with mankind) against so great a sin as perjury, especially national, let us help one another with love and patience to resolve such doubts.

Accus. But they have been guilty of rebellion in a civil war, and therefore are justly suspected to preach or hold rebellious doctrine.

Answ. 1. Are those men lovers of love and concord who purposely make use of pardoned acts to keep the kingdom's wounds still open? Did not the king tell you in his declarations and act of oblivion, that the putting up of all, (save to the excepted persons,) and closing for the future in mutual love, was the only way to the nation's peace? You would tempt men to think that you desire to see such days again, by trying whether destroying men will tempt nature to a self-defence.

2. But you have oft had it proved, (by Henry Fowlis, Bishop Barlow, and abundance more,) that no protestants come near the principles and practices of the papists, as to king-killing and rebellion. And if yet you know not that the war began between two parties of episcopal conformists here among the English, you are unfit to judge of that which you know not. And by reading Rushworth, Whitlock, or any true histories of such times and matters, you may be better informed. As you may of their different principles if you read Jewel, Bishop Bilson, and Richard Hooker on one side, and Mainwarning and Sibthorp on the other.

3. But how few men are alive that had any hand in those miserable wars! You have oft been offered a thousand thanks if you will silence and hunt no other that are as innocent as you, and more than many of their accusers. And shall thousands suffer for other men's deeds? 4. What will wise men think of such a sort of men, as charge multitudes in general with rebellious and seditious doctrine, and have accused so few of any such these twenty years, that I know not of one publicly accused, tried, and proved guilty, of all called presbyterians in all this land? If they are guilty prove it, and let the guilty suffer, and not the innocent; only had I my wish I would bar perjury, and condemning men unheard.

Accus. They are an unpeaceable sort of people.

Answ. That is soon said. Who hath these twenty-two years manifested most desires of peace? They that have begged for it again and again; pleaded and written for it; offered their oaths that they would obey any lawful commands for it, and do any thing which they did not believe that God forbids? Or those bishops that would not have one form, or ceremony, or needless subscription forborne, to save thousands of ministers from being silenced and laid in common gaols, nor to save many thousands of the people from suffering, and to heal the divisions of the church. One would think this should be as easy a controversy, as when soldiers are plundering the country, and the people on their knees entreating for their goods and lives, to determine which of them is most against war.

Accus. But what need they make such a stir with their religion. What need they any more than go to church and live obediently and be quiet? Why will they be righteous over-much; will no less ado bring men to heaven? Why do they differ from their neighbours, and judge all carnal that be not as scrupulous as they? God is merciful; and will he save none but puritans, or precise zealots?

Answ. Now you come to the real matter of your distaste. I did not meddle with the case of nonconformity as it is a controversy between godly men, but only as you make a pretence of it to exercise your enmity against serious godliness, and a handle to lay hold on many whom Christ will justify and save. To all before-said I add,

1. If you think they do too much, search the Scriptures, and see whether it be not less than God commandeth? And if so, is it not God whom you accuse and reproach?

2. If they do too much in obeying God, why do canon-makers impose such abundance on them, as if God had not imposed enough?

3. Why do you never find fault with men for being too strong, too healthful, too rich, too great, but only for being too obedient to God? When Christ saith, if we did all that God commandeth we must say, We are unprofitable servants, we have done no more than was our duty, and the best on earth came short of duty. But this, which is the core, I answered before: and conclude, that all that be in their right wits can easilier bear all your accusations and persecutions of us, as if we did too much in obedience to God, than the accusation of conscience and the displeasure of God for doing too little; which, alas! when we have done our best would sink us into despair, had we not the merits of Christ's suffering and perfect righteousness to trust to.

CHAPTER V.

A HUMBLE EXPOSTULATION WITH THE ENGLISH PAPISTS WHO BY INFORMATION AND PROSECUTION SEEK OUR RUIN.

THOUGH it be not popery as such that I am here reasoning against, the course that many papists take in seeking our destruction, giveth me cause of this humble expostulation; and I speak now of no other but of them. I mean, 1. Those that write so hotly and ragingly to provoke superiors to ruin us. 2. Those that make a trade of being delators against us for worshipping God as we do. 3. Those of them that break in upon us with greatest haughtiness and fury, to take away all our goods, and seek our imprisonment. 4. Those that seek to ruin us by those laws which were made against themselves. 5. Those that would make superiors believe that our doctrine is more rebellious than theirs. To these I offer a few modest questions.

Quest. 1. There are some among you that profess great spirituality and strictness in religion. Serenus Cressy wrote to me, (commending Baker's book which he published,) that he forsook the church of England because he found no spiritual contemplation and devotion among us. Such as Nerius, Sales, Kempis, Gerson Borromæus, Renti, &c. are really the chief honour of your church. Much of that for which I am hated by the enemies of serious godliness, I acknowledge to God's praise, I was first chiefly awakened to a book written by one whom Watson and others of your party grievously accuse, I mean Parson's book of Resolution corrected by Bunny. True christianity and godliness is the same thing in all that have it. Your priest, Mr. Hutchinson, alias Berry, writeth that the most of serious godliness among protestants is found among those called puritans: so that I was fain to defend the conformists against his charge. All this being so, is it the Spirit of God that engageth and enrageth you with the most destructive bitterness against those men whom you confess to be the most religious, merely because they are stiffest against your church government and way of worship? And do you not know that it tendeth more sensibly than disputes, to persuade the people whom you thus hate and prosecute, that your religion is malignity, and enmity to real godliness?

Quest. 2. Do you think it is prudent for you, as soon as ever you get up, and before you dare openly own your name and cause, to begin with malice, rage, and cruelty, and that against the most religious (as you say)? Will not this persuade the people that all is true that is said of your intended cruelty, and make them fear you, as so many leopards or wolves? Will they not say, if the young serpents can so easily sting, what will the old ones do? And if your infancy here begin with such destructive zeal, what will you do when you are at full growth?

Quest. 3. You cannot be ignorant what cause to accuse your church with cruelty and blood hath been given the world by your church laws and practices; by the council at the Lateran under Innocent III. the council for damning Henrician heretics, even kings that claim investiture of bishops, and those that decree the burning of all that you call heretics; by the murder of so many thousand Albigenses, Waldenses, Bohemians, &c.; by the inquisition's more inhuman cruelties in Belgium, and Spain, &c.; by the massacres in France, and the murder of Henry III. and IV.; by Queen Mary's flames; by the two hundred thousand murdered in Ireland. And there be many among you who disown all this, and say it is not from the principles of your religion (when yet general councils approved are your religion itself). This being copiously opened, (as I said before by Henry Fowlis, Bishop Barlow, &c.) had it not been more prudent for you to have begun with lenity and love, to have drawn men to think that you are better minded, than to persuade them that you are of your rulers' and forefathers' mind, and mean to imitate them?

Quest. 4. Have you not observed that all parties have fallen by forcing multitudes to be their enemies by seeking to destroy or hurt them? Most men love quietness, and will live in peace if others will give them leave; but when they see they must offend others, or not defend themselves, it sets all their wit and power to work against their intolerable enemies. There are few creatures in the world that have not some power and inclination to hurt others for their own defence. The bee hath a sting to defend her hive and honey. And do you not remember that your sufferings in England came by Queen Mary's flames, and the Spanish invasion, and the many treasons against Queen Elizabeth, and by the powder plot? And how the French massacre and murders of kings, and the horrid inquisition, set all our parliaments against you? And how the murder of 200,000 in Ireland drove many thousands into the parliament's army that else would not have gone? And will you yet stir up the land to fear and hate you?

Quest. 5. Is it not both imprudence and unrighteousness for you of all men to turn those laws against us, which were made against you, and have so much slept, and little troubled you? You will by this call people to take notice of them that did not before. For my own part, as I never hurt any of you, so I know not that any of the ministers did, whose ruin you endeavour. We hear of none of your sufferings by any such: indeed these late years many have died as for the plot so much talked of; but by whom did they die? Was it not by the accusation and witness of papists? Were not Oates, Bedlow, Dugdale, Turbervile, Prance, Dangerfield, Jenison, Smith, alias Barry, the Yorkshire witnesses, and the rest, besides the Irish, all men of yourselves, that came out of your own bosoms? Whether the men died justly or unjustly I leave to God; but sure it was men of your own selves that did it. And will you be revenged for this on such protestants that meddled not in it?

And you should remember that you and we have a protestant king, who hath sworn all his kingdom against all foreign jurisdiction, and all endeavour of any alteration of government in church or state, and so much abhors popery that he hath made a law severely to punish all that shall but raise any suspicion that he is a papist. And you must in reason take heed of dishonouring and defaming him, by defaming protestants in general.

And sure since Queen Elizabeth's days we have had no kings whom you can justly accuse of cruelty towards you. No not King James when the powder plot had provoked him, if half be true that the bishop of Ambrun saith of his conference with him, or that Rushforth and others say of the oath of the king, prince, and council for toleration, you are disingenuous if you accuse them of cruelty or rigorous severity.

In your Philanax Anglicus (as formerly in the Image of both Churches) you make all called protestants of sincerity, to be of rebellious principles, and their religion introduced by it; and yet profess that you honour the king, as if you would have men doubt whether he be a protestant of sincerity or else were as bad as you describe. Had the severe laws been executed against you, especially for mere religion, no one could wonder if you desired relief; but while you live quietly, and words and paper hurt you not, (that I hear of,) to begin with so much hurtfulness to them that meddled not with you, will disserve your cause.

Quest. 6. And is it consistent with reasonable modesty to go about to make the world believe that the protestant doctrine is less loyal than yours? Do you think your books are invisible, and all your practices forgotten. It is none of the business of this writing to accuse you herein, of any thing but falsely accusing others, and seeking to destroy us on such accusation. Though you may thus deceive the ignorant that know no more of you than what you tell them, that will but turn to your dishonour at last. Are not your foresaid council canons, which are your religion, visible? Have not the forecited writers truly cited them and multitudes of your doctrines which may better inform men? Are all the wars of Italy, Germany, &c. against princes and emperors, for the pope, forgotten? Was it not a council of your bishops that decreed that all the carcasses of those bishops that were for the Henrician heresy (that is, for the emperor's power of investing bishops, and his exemption from being excommunicated and deposed by the pope) should be digged out of their graves, and burnt? Was it not a council that deposed Ludovicus Pius? How many more such acts have they done? And are not your most learned doctors allowed to publish the justification of the pope's power to excommunicate and depose kings if they deserve it (in his judgment)? Do not your public writers, casuists, and divines, ordinarily hold that the people give kings their power, and may take it away when they forfeit it, and that tyranny is such a forfeiture? And that the people should not suffer a heretic to reign? And that subjects may be absolved from their oaths of allegiance, according to the foresaid Lateran and Greg. 7. Roman councils? But too much is said of this by many, and the case is past a modest denial.

Even those protestants that were in arms for the parliament, and restored the king, were so far from thinking that their oaths of allegiance may be dispensed with, that if I knew any thing of those men and times, it was principally the conscience of two oaths (the oath of allegiance, and the oath called the covenant) that by them overcame the opposition of the other army, and brought home the king. It was this that engaged the ministers of England against both Cromwell and a commonwealth: and the ministers were followed by most of the religious people of the land, which broke the adversary's strength. It was this that engaged the excluded members of the (then) long parliament. It was this that engaged the city of London. It seems it was this that engaged General Monk's army, when they say in their address to him, (see it in England's Triumph for King Charles II. p. 85,) "We hope to evince to his Majesty and all the world, that we and all those that have been engaged in the parliament's cause, are his Majesty's best and most real subjects, and that your Excellency and the armies under your command have complied with the obligations for which they were first raised, for the preservation of the true protestant religion, the honour and dignity of the king, the privileges of parliament, the liberty and property of the subjects, and the fundamental laws of the land."

I am not justifying all that I recite. I doubt not but they were much mistaken. But if they had then been told that shortly all the corporation offices and trusts in England shall be constituted by a personal declaration of every one, that "There is no obligation on any person from the oath called the Solemn Covenant," to restore the king, oppose schism, or any thing whatever, the effect would have been such, as makes me wonder that the royalists (as then called) should be very eager to make all such declare, that all these soldiers, ministers, parliament, and citizens that restored the king as bound to it by that oath, were therein mistaken, and no such obligation thence was on them.

Quest. 7. I need not name to you the sorry fellows out of the gaols, where they lay for inhuman villanies, that have been our zealous, ranting, tearing prosecutors. And do you think such actions are in honour to your cause? If it be good, use good men in it.

Quest. 8. Why do you play your game under-board, and behind the curtain? If you are not ashamed of your cause, openly own it. Is falsehood, lying, and dissembling becoming them that say they are of a church out of which none can be saved? I remember when Terret, alias Johnson, had seduced the eldest daughter of the countess of Balcarres, (whom they stole away and made a nun in France,) and she was afterwards asked, why she did so long go to our churches, join in family worship, read protestant books, and talk against the papists, and deride them after she was a papist herself; she answered that they had leave to do all that as long as they did not openly profess their religion, and were not detected. But when once they were discovered and openly professed themselves Roman catholics, they must then suffer any thing rather than conform to us.

God's cause needeth not such juggling and lying.

Quest. 9. Why do you not ingenuously plead your cause against us, so as may satisfy an understanding conscience, before you seek our destruction? 1. Your arguings are commonly fitted only to cheat the ignorant by ambiguities, and confusion, and equivocal terms; your queries or methods to the French sufferers, are only a formed cheat, by confounding, 1. Subjection to governors, and communion with neighbour churches. 2. Communion with your church in christianity and communion with its sins. 3. A catholic church informed only by the sovereignty of Christ, and a pretended universal church informed by the sovereignty of man (a monarch of a church parliament). 4. The office of keeping, delivering, and teaching men God's laws, and an absolute power to judge of their sense, and to make more as a supplement to their defects, obliging all the world on pain of excommunication and death; and more such.

2. Any writings which undeniably open your frauds, you take no notice of, nor vouchsafe to answer upon the importunity of Mr. Johnson, and divers others. I have lately written, 1. A reply to Johnson. 2. A small book in answer to one of your papers, to prove that we have a certainty of christianity without popery. 3. In answer to another, a small book called, "Full and Easy Satisfaction which is the True Religion." None of them will you answer, nor those before written. But instead of a sober investigation of the truth, some of you raise odious slanders of my life, and threaten and seek my destruction. I never hurt any of you, as I said before, nor ever persuaded any to severity against you. I have long ago publicly proposed terms on which we might live together as neighbours in peace. But destruction and misery are in your way, (that I have observed,) and the way of peace you have not known.

There are three things which alienate common christians from you more than all other disputes. 1. That you can go so openly against the plainest words of God, (as in blotting out the second commandment, in notoriously contradicting 1 Cor. xii.; Rom. xiv. and xv. about the terms of church union and communion, about Latin prayers and worship to the ignorant, denying the cup to the laity, denying sense in transubstantiation).

2. That you befriend ignorance so much, by the said Latin worship, forbidding most to read the Scripture translated, and accuse God's Spirit of writing obscurely, to cover this.

3. That your religion liveth by cruelty and blood, and cannot stand without it. Which at least in prudence you should hide as long as you can; or at least not design to make the ignorant and vicious protestants, your proselytes and agents, conjunctly to ruin those whom your consciences know to be the most conscientious and seriously religious.

By which already the flock of Christ do (under your sheep's clothing) so judge of you by your fruits, that if any man that is called a protestant clergyman, do but write and preach for cruelty and ruin towards serious conscionable christians, people by this very mark do presently suspect that he is either a papist, or so near them as that he is ready to pass over to them, whom he so assisteth in destructive work.

Quest. What must be the cure of malignity?

Answ. When the heel of the holy seed is sufficiently bruised, the serpent's head must be broken. 1. The war in heaven which formerly cast down the dragon, must break the supreme serpentine head. 2. Then his heads military on earth will be broken. 1. The usurping universal head called ecclesiastical. 2. The national serpentine heads. 1. Exterior; Mahometan and heathen. 2. Interior; called falsely christian. 1. Serpentine monarchs, that war against Christ. 2. Serpentine prelates and their patrons, that fight against Christ as in his own name, and by his pretended commission.

And all this by Christ, and not by sinful means.

Reformation is begun *a minoritis*, at the lowest, for personal salvation of the elect. But *a majoritis*, at the heads, for public welfare. And God must raise reforming princes and pastors to that end.

A TREATISE

OF

KNOWLEDGE AND LOVE COMPARED.

IN TWO PARTS:

I. OF FALSELY PRETENDED KNOWLEDGE.
II. OF TRUE SAVING KNOWLEDGE AND LOVE.

I. AGAINST HASTY JUDGING, AND FALSE CONCEITS OF KNOWLEDGE; AND FOR NECESSARY SUSPENSION.

II. THE EXCELLENCY OF DIVINE LOVE, AND THE HAPPINESS OF BEING KNOWN AND LOVED OF GOD.

WRITTEN AS GREATLY NECESSARY TO THE SAFETY AND PEACE OF EVERY CHRISTIAN, AND OF THE CHURCH: THE ONLY CERTAIN WAY TO ESCAPE FALSE RELIGIONS, HERESIES, SECTS, AND MALIGNANT PREJUDICES, PERSECUTIONS, AND SINFUL WARS; ALL CAUSED BY FALSELY PRETENDED KNOWLEDGE, AND HASTY JUDGING, BY PROUD, IGNORANT MEN, WHO KNOW NOT THEIR IGNORANCE.

TO THE RIGHT WORSHIPFUL

SIR HENRY ASHHURST, AND THE LADY DIANA HIS WIFE.

SIR,

YOUR name is not prefixed to this treatise, either as accusing you of the sin herein detected, or as praising you for those virtues which good men are more pleased to possess and exercise, than to have proclaimed, though they be as light that is hardly hid: but it is to vent and exercise that gratitude which loveth not the concealment of such friendship and kindness, as you and your lady eminently, and your relatives and hers, the children of the Lord Paget, have long obliged me by; and it is to posterity that I record your kindness, more than for this age, to which it hath publicly notified itself, during my public accusations, reproaches, sentences, imprisonments, and before and since: who knoweth you that knoweth not hereof? And it is to renew the record of that love and honour which I owed to your deceased father, (formerly, though too slenderly recorded,) to be the heir and imitator of whose faith, piety, charity, patience, humility, meekness, impartiality, sincerity, and perseverance, is as great an honour and blessing as I can wish you, next to the conformity to our highest Pattern. And though he was averse to worldly pomp and grandeur, and desired that his children should not affect it, yet God that will honour those that honour him, hath advanced his children, I believe partly for his sake: but I entreat you all (and some other of my friends whom God hath raised as a blessing to their pious and charitable parents and themselves) to watch carefully lest the deceitful world and flesh do turn such blessings into golden fetters, and to be sure to use them as they would find at last on their account.

And as you are a member of the present house of commons, I think the subject of this treatise is not unnecessary to your consideration and daily care: that when proof, and notorious and sad experience, telleth us what distractions have befallen church and state, by men's self-conceited, erroneous rushing upon sin and falsehood, as if it were certainly good and true, and how little posterity feareth and avoideth this confounding vice, though history tell us that it hath been the deluge that in all ages hath drowned the peace and welfare of the world; you may be wary, and try before you venture, in doubtful cases; especially where the sacred and civil interest of this and many other lands doth probably lie on the determination. Do you think all that ventured upon the actions and changes, that have tossed up and down both churches and kingdoms, by divisions, persecutions, and wars, had not done better to suspend their judgments, till they could have more certainly determined? *Who* should proceed more cautiously than *bishops?* and *where* rather than in *councils?* and in *what* rather than about *faith* and *public government* and *order?* And had bishops and councils torn the church, and empires, and kingdoms, as they have done by aspiring after superiority, and by contentious writings, and condemning each other, and by contradictory, and erroneous, and persecuting canons; or by raising wars and deposing princes, ever since four, five, or six hundred years after Christ, if not sooner, if they had known their ignorance, and suspended in such dangerous cases till they were sure?

I know you are none of them who dare pretend to a certain knowledge, that all those oaths, declarations, covenants, practices, imposed by laws and canons on ministers and people in this land, in the act of Uniformity, the Corporation Act, the Vestry Act, the Militia Act, the Five-Mile Act of Banishment, &c. are so good and lawful, as will justify the execution of them, and the silencing, ejecting, ruining, and judging to lie from six months to six in the common gaols till they die, two thousand as faithful ministers of Christ as any nation hath under heaven, unless they forbear to preach the gospel to which they are vowed, or venture their souls on that which they fear to be sins so great as they are loth to name: when Christ will sentence them to everlasting punishment, who did not visit, feed, clothe him in the least of them whom he calls his brethren. Before men silence conditionally the whole ministry of such a kingdom, and actually two thousand such, while the wounding, dividing consequents may be so easily foreseen, and before men deliberately and resolutely continue and keep up such battering engines on pretence of uniformity and obedience to men, and before they venture to own this to that Lord who hath made other terms of church unity and peace, it nearly concerneth them to think, and think on it a thousand times: a suspended judgment is here safer than prefidence and confident rage.

And also they that desire an abolition of episcopacy, should a thousand times bethink them first what true and primitive episcopacy is, and whether the *episcopi gregis*, or *eorum præsides*, or true evangelists, or apostolical general bishops, disarmed and duly chosen, be any injury to the church? And whether the Jews had not been a national christian church under the twelve apostles and seventy, if they had not rejected Him that would have gathered them as the hen gathereth her chickens under her wings?

They that cannot deny that Christ settled a superior rank of ministers, appointing them, besides their extraordinaries, the work of gathering and overseeing many churches, promising therein to be with them to the end of the world, and that only Matthias must make up the national number of such, though Justus had been with Christ as well as he, must be the provers that this rank and imparity was reversed by him that did institute it, if they affirm it; and not without proof charge Christ with seeming levity and mutability, as settling a form of ministry and government, which he would have continue but one age; much less must they impose such an unproved affirmation as the terms of church concord.

Woe, woe, woe! how effectually hath Satan almost undone the christian world, by getting in naughty ministers and magistrates, where he could not utterly extirpate christianity by arms! thereby making rulers and preachers the captains of the malignant enemies of seriousness in that religion which they profess and preach themselves; and if in such hypocrisy they convert a soul, they hate him as an enemy for believing them; and thereby tempt religious men to mistake the crime of the naughty preacher, as the fault of the office, and to oppose the office for the person's sake; and so ministry and christianity are despised by too many.

The shutting of their church doors, and condemning to scorn, and beggary, and gaols, those that were as wise and faithful as themselves, (unless fearing heinous sin made them worse,) should have been by the persecutors long and deeply thought on, twenty-eight years ago; and ever since, by them that believe that Christ will judge them. And so should all doctrines and practices that tend to unwarrantable separations and divisions by others. Things of this moment should not be ventured on, nor papists made both lords and executioners by our distracted combats with each other, and the miserable nation and undone church left to no better a remedy than a *non putaremus;* and to hear the worldly tyrants and the tempted sufferers accusing each other, and disputing when the house is burnt who was in the fault.

I think he was most faulty that could most easily have helped it, and would not: but if great and rich men will be the strength of the factious, as they have most to lose, they may be the greatest losers.

All this hath been said, to tell you how nearly the doctrine of this book, for necessary doubting, and a humble understanding, and for christian love, and against pretended knowledge and rash judging, doth concern the duty and safety of this nation, church and state.

My late book of the "English Nonconformity" fully evinceth this, and more; but blinding prejudice, worldliness, and faction, give leave to few of the guilty to read it.

I rest your much obliged servant,

July 31, 1689. RICHARD BAXTER.

TO THE READER.

READER,

UPON the review of this book, written long ago, I find, 1. That it is a subject as necessary now as ever; experience telling us that the disease is so far from being cured, that it is become our public shame and danger, and if the wonderful mercy of God prevent it not, is like to be the speedy confusion and ruin of the land. 2. As to the manner of this writing, I find the effects of the failing of my memory, in the oft repeating the same things, with little diversification: but I will not for that cast it away; considering, 1. That perhaps often repeating may make the matter the better remembered; and if it do the work intended, no matter though the author be not applauded. 2. And men may think justly that what is oft repeated dropped not from the author inconsiderately, nor is taken by him to be small and useless; but is that digested truth which he would most inculcate. 3. And those who blame their weakness who accuse the church liturgy of too much repetition, I suppose will not be much offended with it in our writings, while the dulness and forgetfulness of many readers maketh it needful.

R. B.

August 3, 1689.

PART I.

OF FALSELY PRETENDED KNOWLEDGE.

1 CORINTHIANS viii. 2, 3.

AND IF ANY MAN THINK THAT HE KNOWETH ANY THING, HE KNOWETH NOTHING YET AS HE OUGHT TO KNOW. BUT IF ANY MAN LOVE GOD, THE SAME IS KNOWN OF HIM.

CHAPTER I.

THE SCOPE AND TEXT OPENED; WHAT PHILOSOPHY OR WORLDLY WISDOM PAUL DEPRESSETH; AND WHY.

THE calamitous divisions of the churches of Christ, and the miscarriage and contentions of too many particular brethren, having been sad upon my thoughts above forty years, by this time, without imputation of hastiness and rash judging, I may take leave to tell the world, what I have discovered to be the principal cause,[a] which is *falsely* PRETENDED KNOWLEDGE OF IGNORANCE OF IGNORANCE, or proud, unhumbled understanding, confident that it knoweth that which it knoweth not. And consequently what must be the cure, if our calamity be here curable, viz. To know as much as we can; but withal to know how little we know, and to take on us to know no more than we do know, nor to be certain of our uncertainties.

The text which I have chosen to be the ground of my discourse, is so plain, notwithstanding some little difficulties, that did not the nature of the disease resist the clearest remedy, so many good people had never here often read their sin described, as insensibly as if they read it not.

The chapter hath so much difficulty, as will not stand with my intended brevity to open it; I refer you to expositors for that. Whether they were the Nicolaitans, or any other sort of heretics, that the apostle dealeth with, I determine not. It is plain that they were licentious professors of christianity, who thought that it was the ignorance of others that made them judge it unlawful to eat things offered to idols; and that their own greater knowledge set them above that scruple. A mixture of Platonic philosophy with christianity, made up most of the primitive heretics, and for want of a due digestion of each, too much corrupted many of the Greek doctors of the church. The unlearned sort of christians were so much despised by some of the philosophical heretics, that they were not thought worthy of their communion; for as Jude saith, they "separated themselves, being sensual, having not the Spirit," but more affected philosophical fancies: which made Paul warn them to take heed lest any seduced them by vain philosophy; not using the name of philosophy for that solid knowledge of God's works which is desirable, but for the systems of vain conceits and precepts which the word was then used to signify, as every sect derived them from their masters. And so the apostle taketh knowledge in this text; not for solid knowledge indeed, but for Gnosticism or philosophical presumptions; such as even yet most philosophers are guilty of, who take a multitude of precepts, some useful, some useless, some true, and some false, and all but notionally, or to little purpose, and joining these do call them philosophy. And Paul tells them, that opinionative and notional knowledge (were it true, like the devil's faith) is of no such excellency as to cause them to shelter their sins under the confidence and honour of it, and despise unlearned conscionable christians; for such knowledge by inflation oft destroyeth the possessors, or becomes the fuel of the devilish sin of pride, when love buildeth up ourselves and others to salvation. And to conceit that a man is wise because of such knowledge, and so to overvalue his own understanding, is a certain sign that he is destitute of that knowledge in which true wisdom doth consist; and knoweth nothing with a wise and saving knowledge, as every thing should be known: and indeed a man's excellency is so far from lying in vain philosophical speculations, that the use of all true knowledge is but to bring us up to the love of God, as the highest felicity, to be approved and beloved by God: and those unlearned christians that have the spirit of sanctification, without your vain philosophy, have knowledge enough to bring them to this love of God, which is a thing that passeth all your knowledge, or rather to be known of God as his own, and loved by him. For our felicity lieth in receiving from God, and in his loving us, more than in our loving him; but both set together, to love God, and so to be loved of him, are the ultimate end and perfection of man;

[a] Had I been supposed to have written this book to hide my sloth and ignorance, men would not have neglected my "Methodus Theologiæ, and Catholic Theology," through mere sloth, and saving that it is too high and hard for them.

and all knowledge is to be estimated but as it tendeth to this.

This being the plain paraphrase of the text, I shall stay no longer on it, but thence deduce and handle these two observations.

Doct. I. Falsely pretended knowledge is often pernicious to the possessor, and injurious to the church. And overvaluing one's own opinions and notions, is a certain mark of dangerous ignorance.

Doct. II. A man is so far truly wise, as he loveth God, and consequently is approved or loved by him, and as he loveth others to their edification.

I. The first is but the same that Solomon thus expresseth, "Seest thou a man wise in his own conceit; there is more hope of a fool than of him," Prov. xxvi. 12. And Paul elsewhere, "Be not wise in your own conceits," Rom. xii. 16; xi. 25; Prov. xxvi. 5, 16. For it is certain that we are all here in great darkness, and it is but little that the wisest know; and therefore he that thinks he knoweth much, is ignorant both of the things which he thinks he knoweth, and of his ignorance. Therefore "Let no man deceive himself. If any man among you seemeth to be wise in this world, let him become a fool, that he may be wise," 1 Cor. iii. 18. To be "wise in this world," is the same with that in the words following, "The wisdom of this world is foolishness with God." And 1 Cor. i. 19—22, "It is written, I will destroy the wisdom of the wise," &c. "Where is the wise? where is the scribe? where is the disputer of this world? hath not God made foolish the wisdom of this world? For after that in the wisdom of God the world by wisdom knew not God, it pleased God by the foolishness of preaching to save them that believe. For the Jews require a sign, and the Greeks seek after wisdom," &c. So chap. ii. 4—8, "And my speech and my preaching was not with enticing words (or probable discourses) of man's wisdom, but in demonstration of the Spirit and of power: that your faith should not stand in the wisdom of men, but in the power of God. Howbeit we speak wisdom among them that are perfect: yet not the wisdom of this world, nor of the princes of this world that come to nought: but we speak the wisdom of God in a mystery, even the hidden wisdom, which God ordained before the world unto our glory (even Christ the wisdom of God, chap. i. 24): which none of the princes of this world knew.——"

In all this, note,—1. That there is a wisdom which Paul placeth christianity itself in.—2. That this is to know God in Christ objectively, and to be taught of God by Christ and his Spirit efficiently.—3. That there is a wisdom which Paul comparatively vilifieth.—4. This is called the "wisdom of this world" (or age).—5. That most plainly he meaneth by it, that which then was called learning and philosophy; which the Greeks did value, and by which they judged of the gospel; which comprehended the methods of all the sects, Epicureans, academics, peripatetics, and stoics; but not their true morals, but their physics, and logic, and metaphysics; which Laertius and others tell us how variously they held. —6. That Paul doth not absolutely prohibit such studies, nor yet despise any true knowledge.—7. But he vilifieth this philosophy on these accounts. (1.) Because it was the exercise of a poor, low, insufficient light: they did but grope after God in the dark, as Acts xvii. 27. (2.) Because it was mostly taken up with inferior things, of small concernment comparatively: as things corporeal are good in themselves, and when sanctified and made subservient to things spiritual; so the knowledge of physics is to be esteemed: but as things corporeal yet are objectively the snare and ruin of those that perish, and therefore the world to be renounced and crucified, as it is our temptation, an enemy or competitor with Christ; just so it must be with natural philosophy. (3.) Because it was greatly overvalued by the world, as if it had been the only wisdom, when indeed it is of itself but an indifferent thing, or fit but to make a by-recreation of, till it be made to serve to higher ends; even as riches, honour, and pleasure are overvalued by worldlings, as if they were the only felicity; when in themselves they are but more indifferent things, and prove beneficial or hurtful as they are used. Therefore Paul was to take down the pernicious esteem of this kind of philosophy, as preachers now must take down men's esteem of worldly things, however they are the works and gifts of God. And as Christ would by his actual poverty and sufferings, and not by words only, take down the esteem of worldly wealth and pride; so Paul by neglecting and forbearing the use of artificial logic, physics, and metaphysics, would depress their rate. (4.) Because that there was abundance of falsehood mixed with the truth which the philosophers held; as their multitude of different sects fully proves. (5.) Because the artificial, organical part was made so operous, as that it drowned real learning instead of promoting it; and became but like a game at chess, a device rather to exercise vain, proud wits by, than to find out useful truth. As to this day, when logic and metaphysics seem much cultivated and reformed, yet the variety of methods, the number of notions, the precariousness of much, the uncertainty of some things, the falsehood of many, maketh them as fit for boys to play with in the schools, and to be a wood into which a sophister may run, to hide his errors, as to be a means of detecting them. And therefore a knavish cheater will often bind you strictest to the pedantic part of the rules of disputation, that when he cannot defend his matter, he may quarrel with your form and artifice, and lose time by questioning you about mood and figure. (6.) Because by these operous diversions the minds of men were so forestalled or taken up, as that they had not leisure to study great and necessary saving truth: and if men must be untaught in the doctrines of life, till they had first learned their logic, physics, and metaphysics, how few would have been saved! When at this day so many come from our universities after several years' study, raw smatterers in these, and half-witted scholars, whose learning is fitter to trouble than to edify: and if Scripture had been written in the terms and method of Aristotle, how few would have been the better for them! But great good must be common.

And as Paul on all these accounts sets light by this philosophy, so he calls it, the wisdom of this world:—1. Because this world was its chief object; —2. And the creatures were its only light;—3. And it led but few to any higher than worldly ends;— 4. And it was that which worldly men, that were strangers to heavenly light and holiness, did then most magnify and use.

Yet as Christ, when he said how hard it was for a rich man to be saved, did not make riches absolutely unlawful, nor to have no goodness nor usefulness at all; but teacheth men, if they are wise, not to overvalue them, and to be too eager for them; so is Paul to be interpreted about philosophy, or the wisdom of this world. (For it is not only craftiness for worldly ends that he so calls.)

And as God, when he denieth his servants riches and worldly fulness, doth it not because he taketh it to be *too good* for them, but because it is not *good enough*, and therefore he will give them better; even the heavenly riches, and honour, and delights: even so when Paul comparatively vilifieth philosophy, it is not as being really a wisdom too high for christians, but too low; nor doth he depress reason, or extol ignorance; but would lead men to the truest learning, the highest knowledge and improvement of reason, the only wisdom, from trifling, pedantic, unprofitable notions, and ludicrous loss of time and studies.

It is not therefore for want of wisdom that the Scripture is not written according to the philosophers' art. Though Erasmus overvalued his grammaticisms, it was not for want of learning in philosophy, that he so much despised the philosophical schoolmen; so that speaking of the bishop of London, who maligned Dr. Colet, and was a subtle Scotist, he saith of *such;* That he had known some of them whom he would not call knaves, but he never knew one of them whom he could call a christian. Vid. Mr. Smith's Life of Dr. Colet, by Erasmus. A smart charge: I suppose he meant it of them rather as *Scotists* than as *bishops*.

And therefore the apostle aptly joineth both together, 1 Cor. i. 26, "Not many wise men after the flesh, not many mighty, not many noble are called;" seeming to equal worldly wealth and greatness, with worldly wisdom or philosophy, as to the interest of religion and salvation. And the foolish wits that think he spake against learning, because he had it not, may as truly say, that he spake against worldly wealth and greatness because he had it not; for the possession, use, and knowledge of worldly things, are near of kin. But they knew not Paul so well as Festus, who thought him not unlearned, though he thought him mad. Nor was it the way of worldly wealth and greatness which he chose.

Doubtless neither Christ, nor Paul, did speak against any real knowledge; but, (1.) Against nominal, pretended knowledge, which was set up to divert men from real knowledge, and was full of vanities and falsehoods. (2.) And against the overvaluing of that learning, which is of little use, in comparison of the knowledge of great, and excellent, and necessary things. For knowledge is valuable according to its object and its use.

The knowledge of trifles for trivial ends, is itself a trifle. The knowledge of things great and necessary for great and necessary ends, is the great and necessary knowledge. And therefore how unmeasurably must the knowledge of God and our eternal happiness, excel the pedantic philosophy of the gentiles; however christians may sanctify and ennoble this by making it a help to higher knowledge! And therefore the Platonists and the stoics were the noblest philosophers; because the former studied the highest things, and the other the necessary means of felicity, amending of men's hearts and lives.

But in the present text the thing which the apostle reprehendeth is, the esteeming of a man's self to be wiser than he is; and taking himself to be a wise man because of his trifling philosophical knowledge. And he would have them know that till they knew nobler things than those, and were guided by a nobler light, they were very fools.[b]

I have looked over Hutten, Vives, Erasmus, Scaliger, Salmasius, Casaubon, and many other critical grammarians, and all Gruterus's critical volumes. I have read almost all the physics and metaphysics I could hear of: I have wasted much of my time among whole loads of historians, chronologers, and antiquaries: I despise none of their learning. All truth is useful; mathematics, which I have least of, I find a pretty manlike sport. But if I had no other kind of knowledge than these, what were my understanding worth! what a dreaming dotard should I be! Yea, had I also all the codes and pandects, all Cujacius, Wesenbechius, and their tribe at my fingers' ends; and all other volumes of civil, national, and canon laws, with the rest in the Encyclopædia, what a puppet-play would my life be, if I had no more!

I have higher thoughts of the schoolmen than Erasmus and our other grammarians had: I much value the method and sobriety of Aquinas, the subtlety of Scotus and Ockam, the plainness of Durandus, the solidity of Ariminensis, the profundity of Bradwardine, the excellent acuteness of many of their followers; of Aureolus, Capreolus, Bannes, Alvares, Zumel, &c.; of Mayro, Lychetus, Trombeta, Faber, Meruisse, Rada, &c.; of Ruiz, Pennatus, Suarez, Vasquez, &c.; of Hurtado, of Albertinus, of Lud. a Dola, and many others: but how loth should I be to take such sauce for my food, and such recreations for my business! The jingling of too much and too false philosophy among them, often drowns the noise of Aaron's bells. I feel myself much better in Herbert's Temple; or in a heavenly treatise of faith and love. And though I do not, with Dr. Colet, distaste Augustine above the plainer fathers, yet I am more taken with his Confessions, than with his grammatical and scholastic treatises. And though I know no man whose genius more abhorreth confusion instead of necessary distinction and method; yet I loathe impertinent, useless art, and pretended precepts and distinctions, which have not a foundation in the matter.

In a word, there is a divine knowledge, which is part of man's felicity, as it promoteth love and union; and there is a solid knowledge of God's word and works, a valuable grammatical knowledge, and a true philosophy, which none but ignorant persons will despise. But the vain philosophy, and pretended wisdom or learning of the world, hath been, and is, the cheat of souls, and the hinderer of wisdom, and a troubler of the church and world.

CHAPTER II.

WHAT WISDOM, AND ESTEEM OF IT, ARE NOT HERE CONDEMNED.

THE order which I shall observe in handling the first doctrine shall be this: I. I will tell you negatively what wisdom, and esteem of our own wisdom, is not here condemned. II. What it is that is here condemned. III. What are the certainties which we must hold fast, and make our religion of. IV. What degrees of these certainties there are. V. What are the uncertainties, which we must not pretend to be certain of; and the unknown things which we must not pretend to know. VI. What are the mischiefs of falsely

[b] A countryman having sent his son to the university, when he came home asked him what he had learned. He told him he had learned logic. He asked him what that logic was, and what he could do with it: and it being supper time, and the poor people having but two eggs for supper, he told them that he could prove that those eggs were three: This is one, saith he, and that is two, and one and two are three. The father gave him the better, and told him that his art was useful, for he had thought himself to have gone without his supper, but now, saith he, I will take one egg, and your mother the other, and take you the third. Such kind of logic the world hath gloried in as learning.

pretended knowledge. VII. What are the degrees or aggravations of this sin. VIII. What are the causes of it. IX. What are the remedies. X. What are the uses which we should make of this doctrine.

I. What wisdom, and what esteem of our wisdom, is not here condemned?

Answ. 1. Not any real useful knowledge at all, whilst every thing keepeth its proper place and due esteem, as is said.

2. That which of itself primarily is of so small use, as that it falleth under the contempt of the apostles, yet by accident, through the subtlety of Satan, and the viciousness of the world, may become to some men in some measure necessary. And here cometh in the calamity of divines. Of how little use is it to me in itself to know what is written in many hundred books, which yet by accident it much concerneth me to know! And if God restrain him not, the devil hath us here at so great an advantage, that he can make our work almost endless, and hath almost done it already; yea, can at any time divert us from greatest truth and works, by making another at that time more necessary.

If he raise up Socinians, our task is increased; we must read their books, that we may be able to confute them; so must we when he raiseth up libertines, familists, seekers, quakers, and such other sects. If he stir up controversies in the church, about government, worship, ceremonies, circumstances, words, methods, &c. &c. we must read so much as to understand all, that we may defend the truth against them. If papists will lay the stress of all their controversies on church history, and the words of ancients; we must read and understand all, or they will triumph. If schoolmen will build their theology on Aristotle, all men have not the wit with the Iberian legate at the Florentine council in Sagyrophilus, to cry against the preacher, What have we to do with Aristotle? But if we cannot deal with them at their own weapons, they will triumph. If cavillers will dispute only in mood and figure, we must be able there to overtop them, or they will insult. If the plica, pox, scurvy, or other new diseases do arise, the physician must know them all, if he will cure them. And hence it is that we say, that a lawyer must know the law; and a physician must know physic, medicine, &c. But a divine should know all things that are to be known; because the diseased world hath turned pretended knowledge into the great malady, which must be cured; but is the thing itself of any great worth; is it any great honour to know the vanity of philosophical pedantry; and to be able to overdo such gamesters, any more than to beat one at a game at chess, or for a physician to know the pox or leprosy?

3. Yet indeed, as all things are sanctified to the holy, and pure to the pure; a wise man may and must make great use of common, inferior kinds of knowledge: especially the true, grammatical sense of Scripture words, the true precepts of logic, the certain parts of real physics and pneumatology: for God is seen in his works as in a glass; and there to search after him and behold him, is a noble, pleasant work and knowledge. And I would that no Israelite may have need to go down to the Philistines for instruments of this sort.

4. It is not forbidden to any man to know that measure of wisdom which he truly hath; God bindeth us not to err, nor to call light darkness, or truth error, or to belie ourselves, or deny his gifts. 1. It is desirable for a man absolutely to know as much as he can, preferring still the greatest things, and to know that he knoweth them, and not to be sceptical, and doubt of all. 2. It is a duty for a converted sinner comparatively to know that he is wiser than he was in a sinful state, and to give God thanks for it. 3. It is his duty who groweth in wisdom, and receiveth new accessions of light, to know that he so groweth, and to give God thanks, and to welcome each useful truth with joy. 4. It is the duty of a good and wise man comparatively to know that he is not as foolish as the ungodly; nor to think that every wicked man, or ignorant person, whom he should pity and instruct, is already wiser than he; every teacher is not to be so foolish as to think that all his flock are more judicious than himself. In a word, it is not a true estimate of the thing, or of ourselves, that is forbidden us; but a false. It is not belying ourselves, nor ingratitude to God, nor a contradiction, to know a thing, and not to know that I know it, nor an ignorance of our own minds, which is commanded us under the pretence of humility; but it is a proud conceit, that we know what we do not know, that is condemned.

CHAPTER III.

II. WHAT PRETENDED KNOWLEDGE IS CONDEMNED, AND WHAT PHILOSOPHY AND LEARNING IT IS THAT PAUL DISLIKED.

MORE distinctly, 1. It is condemnable for any man to think himself absolutely or highly wise; because our knowledge here is so poor, and dark, and low, that compared with our ignorance it is little: we know not what, or how many, or how great the things are which we do not know; but in general we may know that they are incomparably more and greater than what we do know; we know now but as children, and darkly, and in a glass or riddle, 1 Cor. xiii. 11, 12. In the sense that Christ saith, none is good but God, we may say that none is wise but God. For a man that must know (unless he be a very sot) that he knoweth nothing perfectly in the world; that he knoweth but little of any worm, or fly, or pile of grass which he seeth, or of himself, his soul or body, or any creature; for this man to assume the title of a *wise man*, is arrogant, unless comparatively understood, when he is ignorant of ten thousandfold more than he knoweth, and the predominant part denominateth. The old inquirers had so much modesty, as to arrogate no higher name than philosophers.

2. It is very condemnable for any man to be proud of his understanding; while it is so low, and poor, and dark, and hath still so much matter to abase us. He knoweth not what a dungeon poor mortals are in, nor what a darkened thing a sinful mind is, nor what a deplorable state we are in, so far from the heavenly light, no, nor what it is to be a man in flesh, who findeth not much more cause of humiliation than of pride in his understanding. Oh how much ado have I to keep up from utter despondency under the consciousness of so great ignorance, which no study, no means, no time doth overcome. How long, Lord, shall this dungeon be our dwelling? and how long shall our foolish souls be loth to come into the celestial light?

3. It is sinful folly to pretend to know things unrevealed and impossible to be known. "The secret things belong unto the Lord our God, but those things which are revealed belong to us, and to our children for ever, that we do them," Deut. xxix. 29.

"For who hath known the mind of the Lord? or who hath been his counsellor?" Rom. xi. 34. And how many such compose the theology of some, and the philosophy of more!

4. It is sinful folly to pretend to know that which is impossible or unrevealed to him, though it be possible and revealed to others. For as the eye, so the understanding, must have its necessary light and due constitution and conditions of the object, and of itself; or else it cannot understand.

5. It is sinful folly to pretend to certainty of knowledge, when either the thing is but probable, or at best we have but doubtful opinions or conjectures of it, and no true certainty.

6. It is sinful folly to pretend that we know or receive any thing by divine faith (or revelation,) when we have it but by human faith, or probable conjecture from natural evidence. As soon as men are persuaded by a sect, a seducer, or a selfish priest, to believe what he saith, abundance presently take such a persuasion for a part of their religion, as if it were a believing God.

7. It is sinful folly to take on us that we know what we know not at all; because we do but know that it is knowable, and that wise men know it, and as soon as we understand that it should be known, and that wise men conclude it to be true, therefore to pretend that we know it to be true.

8. And it is sinful folly to pretend that we truly know or apprehend the thing or matter, or incomplex object, merely because we have got the bare words, and second notions of it, which are separable from the knowledge of the thing. All these are false and sinful pretences of knowledge which men have not.

But because Paul so warneth us to take heed of vain philosophy, and atheists and infidels deride him for speaking against the wisdom of the world, as if he spake against learning because he had it not; and because the disease which he attempted to cure remaineth among scholars to this day, and instead of a cure, many contemn the physician; and dislike Christ himself and the gospel, as defective of the learning which they overvalue; I will once again, and that more distinctly, tell you some few of the faults of our common learning, even now that it is cultivated and augmented in this age, that you may see that Paul did not injuriously accuse it, or Christ injuriously neglect it.[a]

I. Natural imperfection layeth the foundation of our common calamity; in that it is so long before sense and reason grow up to a natural maturity, through the unripeness of organs and want of exercise, that children are necessitated to learn words before things, and to make these words the means of their first knowledge of many of the things signified; so that most furnish themselves with a stock of names and words, before ever they get any true knowledge of the matter.

II. And then they are exceeding apt to think that this treasury of words and second notions is true wisdom, and to mistake it for the knowledge of the thing: even as in religion we find almost all children and ignorant people will learn to say by rote the creed, and Lord's prayer, and commandments, and catechism, and then think that they are not ignorants; when it is long after before we can get them to understand the sense of the words which they can so readily speak; yea, though they are plain English words, which they use for the most part in ordinary discourse.

III. When children come to school, also their masters teach them as their parents did, or worse; I mean that they bestow almost all their pains to furnish them with words and second notions: and so do their tutors too oft at the university. So that by that time they are grown to be masters of a considerable stock of words, grammatical, logical, metaphysical, &c. and can set these together in propositions and syllogisms, and have learned *memoriter* the theorems or axioms, and some distinctions which are in common use and reputation, they are ready to pass for Masters of the Arts, and to set up for themselves, and leave their tutors, and to teach others the like sort and measure of learning, which they have thus acquired. Like one that sets up his trade as soon as he hath gotten a shop full of tools.

IV. And indeed the memories of young men are strong and serviceable so many years sooner than their judgments, that prudent teachers think it meet to take that time to furnish them with words and organical notions, while they are unmeet to judge of things; even as pious parents must teach them the words of the catechism, that when they grow riper, their judgments may work upon that which their memories did before receive. And in this they are in the right upon two suppositions. 1. That distinguishing things obvious and easily understood from things remote, abstruse, and difficult, they would teach them those of the first sort with the words, though not the second: and while they make haste with the languages, they would not make too much haste with the notions and theorems of the arts and sciences. 2. That they still make them know that words as to matter are but as the dish to the meat, and all this while they are but preparing for wisdom and true learning, and not getting or possessing it; and that unless they will equalize a parrot and a philosopher, they must know how little they have attained, and must after learn *things*, or not pretend to know any thing indeed. As children learn first to speak, and then learn what to speak of.

V. And the great mischief is, that multitudes of those notions that are taught us are false, not fitted to the things, but expressing the conceptions of roving, uncertain, erroneous, bewildered minds. Words are the instruments of communication of thoughts. And when I hear a man speak, I hear, perhaps, what he *thinketh* of things, but not always what they are. Our universal notions are the result of our own comparing things with things. And we are so woefully defective in such comparings, that our universal notions must needs be very defective, so that they abound with error.

VI. And the penury and narrowness of words is a great impediment to the due expressing of those poor confused conceptions which we have; for a man can think more aptly and comprehensively than he can speak. And hence it cometh to pass, that words and universal notions are become like pictures or hieroglyphics, almost of arbitrary signification and use, as the speaker pleaseth. And, as a multitude of school-distinctions tell us, you can know little by the grammatical use or etymology of the words, what the meaning of them is in a theorem or distinction, till the speaker tell it you by other words.

VII. And the conceptions of men being as various as their countenances, the same words in the mouths of several men have several significations. So that when tutors read the same books to their scholars,

[a] M. Antonine, l. 1. sect. 17, doth thank God that he made no greater progress in rhetoric, poetry, and such-like studies, which might have hindered him from better things, if he had perceived himself to have profited in them. And, (in fine,) quod cum philosophandi cupiditas incessisset, not in sophistam aliquem inciderim, nec commentariis evolvendis, vel syllogismis resolvendis, vel meterologicis discutiendis tempus deses contriverim.

and teach them the same notions, it is not the same conceptions always that they thus communicate.

VIII. And when all is done, *recipiter ad modum recipientis*. It is two to one but the learner receiveth their notions with a conception somewhat different from them all. And when he thinks he hath learned what was taught him, and is of his teacher's mind, he is mistaken, and hath received another apprehension.

IX. And the narrowness of man's mind and thoughts is such, that usually there must go many partial conceptions to one thing or object really indivisible: so that few things, or nothing rather in the world, is known by us with one conception, nor with a simplicity of apprehensions answerable to the simplicity of the things: and hereby it cometh to pass that inadequate conceptions make up a great part of our learning and knowledge. And, yet worse, our words being narrower than our thoughts, we are fain to multiply words more than conceptions, so that we must have ten conceptions perhaps of one thing, and twenty words perhaps for those ten conceptions. And then we grow to imagine the things to be as various as our conceptions, yea, and our words: and so learning is become confused error, and the great and noble actions of the fantastical world, are a pitiful, confused agitation of phantasms, and, whether fortuitous or artificial, a congress of atoms, sometimes digladiating, and sometimes seeming by amicable embraces to compose some excellent piece of art. And things seem to us to be multiplied and ordered as our conceptions of them are. And the Scotists may yet write as many more treatises *de formalitatibus*, before men will understand indeed what a *conceptus formalis* with them is, and whether diverse formalities be diverse realities, or only *ejusdem conceptus inadequati*. But thus learning is become like a puppet-play, or the raising of the dust.

X. The *entia rationis* being thus exceeding numerous, are already confounded with objective realities, and have compounded our common systems of logic, metaphysics, and too much of physics: so that students must at first see through false spectacles, and learn by seducing notions, and receive abundance of false conceptions, as the way to wisdom; and shadows and rubbish must furnish their minds under the name of truth, though mixed with many real verities. For young men must have teachers; they cannot begin at the foundation, and yet every one learn of himself, as if none had ever learned before him: he is like to have but a slow proficient, that maketh no use of the studies and experience of any that ever learned before him. And he that will learn of others, must receive their notions and words as the means of his information.

XI. And when they grow up to be capable of real wisdom, oh! what labour is it, to cleanse out this rubbish, and to unlearn all the errors that we have learned! so that it is much of the happiest progress of extraordinary successful studies, to find out our old mistakes, and set our conceptions in better order one by one: perhaps in one year we find out and reform some two or three, and in another year one or two more, and so on. Even as when at my removal of my library, my servant sets up all my books, and I must take them half down again to set them in their right places.

XII. And the difficulty of the matter is our great impediment, when we come to study things. For, 1. Their matter, 2. Their composure, 3. Their numbers, 4. Their order and relations, 5. And their action and operation, are much unknown to us.

XIII. 1. The substance of *spirits* is so little known, as tempteth Sadducees to dream that there are none. The notion of a spirit to some, through ignorance, is taken to be merely negative, as if it signified no more but *not corporeal*. The notion of *immateriality* is lubricous, and he that knoweth not the true bounds of the signification of *materia*, knoweth not what it is to be immaterial. The purest spirit is known only by many inadequate conceptions: one must answer the similitude of matter, in fundamental substantiality; another must be answerable to that of forms of simple elements; and another answerable to accidents. And though nothing be so notorious of spirits as their operations, and from the acts we know the virtues or powers, yet that these virtues are not accidents, but the very essential form, and that they are (in all spirits) one in three, and many other things concerning their essentiality, are quite overlooked by the greater part of philosophers; and those few that open it, do either, with Campanella, lose it again in a wood of mistaken, ill-gathered consequences; or with Lullius, drown it in a multitude of irregular, arbitrary notions; or with Commenius, give us a little undigested, with the mixture of crudities and mistakes; or with our learned Dr. Glisson, de Vita Naturæ, confound spirits and bodies, and make those spirits which are the vital constitutive principle of compounds, to be but the inadequate conception of bodies, as if they were all simply and formally vital of themselves, and for a body to be inanimate were a contradiction, or impossible. And they that treat more nobly of spirits, (as Mr. Got and many Platonists,) do it so immethodically and confusedly, as greatly disadvantageth the learner.

And yet to treat of bodies without treating of the spirits that animate or actuate them, is a lame, deluding, unedifying thing. As it is to treat of a kingdom, an army, a school, without mentioning a king, a captain, or a school-master; or as to describe a gun, without any mention of gunpowder or shooting; or a clock or watch, without the poise or spring, or motion; or a book, or words, without the sense; and so of a man without a soul or reason, or a brute without any life or sense. I mean when we speak of compound beings, and not merely of corporeity in the notion, as abstracted from all vital moving principles.

XIV. 2. And what the true notion of matter or corporeity itself is, it is but darkly and uncertainly known, how confidently soever some decantate their moles or quantity, divisibility or discerptibility, and impenetrability: whether fire be material, and divisible and impenetrable, and how far fire and spirits herein differ, and so spirits and bodies, and how far sensible must enter the definition of *corpus*, is not easily known.

XV. 3. Nor do we well know the nature of the simple corporeal elements; whether they agree only in materiality, quantity, and divisibility, and impenetrability; and whether they differ only in magnitude, shape, sight, and contexture of parts; or by any essentiating formal virtues, or both; or (as Mr. Got thought) by a differencing proper spirit.

XVI. 4. How little of the divine artifice is known in the composition of mixed bodies! (And we know of no existent simples in the world, that are not found only in compositions.) All men confess that every plant, every worm, or fly; every sensitive, yea, every sensible being, is so little known to us, as that the unknown part far exceedeth the known.

XVII. 5. And we are not agreed of late of the number of the very elements themselves; much less of compounds; of which, while we know so few, that which we do know is the more defectively known; because (as in knowing of letters and syllables) the knowledge of one thing is needful to the true and useful knowledge of another.

XVIII. But the order and relations of things to one another is so wonderfully unsearchable, and innumerably various, as quite surpasseth all human understanding. Yea, though ORDER and RELATION constitute all morality, policy, literature, &c. so that it is as it were that world which human intellects converse in, and the business of all human wills and actions, yet few men know so much as what ORDER and RELATION is; nay, nor whether it be any thing or nothing. And though health and sickness, harmony and discord, beauty and ugliness, virtue and vice, consist in it, and heaven and hell depend upon it, and law and judgment do make and determine it; yet is it not easy to know what it is by a universal notion; nor whether it be truly to be called any thing at all. We doubt not but ORDER should be a most observable predicament in the series of human notions or *nominanda;* but yet I doubt not much but that Gassendus, who would make *tempus* and *spatium* two of his predicaments, doth describe to them that entity which they have not.

XIX. And though undoubtedly action is a noble predicament, and, whatever the Cartesians say, requireth more causation than *non agere* doth, yea, is itself the causation of the mutations in the world; yet men scarce know what to call it. Some say it is *res;* others, it is but *accidens rei;* and others, *modus rei:* some say, it is *in passo;* some say it is *in agente;* some say it is neither, but is *agentis:* some say immanent acts are qualities, as Scotus, &c.

XX. And, which is yet worse, the very name, accident, mode, and quality, are but general, unapt notions, not well understood by any that use them, nor suited meetly to the severals contained under them. And when we call a thing, or nothing, a quality, accident, or mode, we are little the wiser, and know not well what we have said. Sure I am that they are exceedingly *heterogenea* which Aristotle compriseth in the very predicament of quality. And Gassendus thought all accidents may be as well called qualities or modes.

XXI. And, which is yet worse, all human language is so woefully ambiguous, that there is scarce a word in the world that hath not many senses; and the learned world never came to agreement about the meaning of their common words, so that ambiguity drowneth all in uncertainty and confusion.

XXII. And, which is yet worse, the certain apprehension of sense and reason, is commonly, by men called learned, reduced to, and tried by, these dreaming, ambiguous names and universal notions; and men are drawn to deny their certain knowledge, because they know not by what universal term to call it: e. g. I know as far as is useful to me, by *seeing* what light is; but whether it be *substantia, accidens, modus,* &c. or what to call it universally, few know! And no wonder, for their universal notions are their own works or *entia rationis,* fabricated by the imperfect comparing of things with things, by ignorant understandings; but the sensibility of objects, and the sensitive faculty and the intellect, are the works of God. I know much better what light is by seeing it, than I know what an accident or a quality is.

So I know by *feeling* what heat is, I know what motion or action is, I know what pain and pleasure is, I know what love and hatred is, I know partly what it is to think, to know, to will, choose, and refuse; but what is the right universal notion of these, what true definition to give of any one of them, the learnedest man doth not well know; insomuch, as I dare boldly say, that the vulgar ordinarily know all these better without definition, than the most learned man living can know them by definitions alone.

And here I will presume to step aside, to say as in the ears of our over-doing separatists, who can take none into christian communion, that cannot tell you how they were converted, or at least give them a fair account of their understanding all the articles of the faith, in words that are adapted to the matter: I tell you, 1. That the knowledge of words, and second notions and definitions, is one thing, and the knowledge of matters or things is another. 2. And it is the knowledge of the things, and not of the words, that is primarily and absolutely necessary to salvation. 3. And that many an illiterate, ill-bred person understand things long before they can utter their understandings in any intelligible words. 4. And therefore if any man do but these two things: 1. By yea or nay, do signify to me, that he understandeth the truth, when I put the matter of nothing but the baptismal covenant into my questions; 2. And do manifest serious willingness accordingly, by avoiding evil, and using God's means; I dare not, I will not refuse that person from the communion of the church; though I would do as much as the most rigid censurer to bring such up to greater knowledge.

XXIII. And on the other side, men are made to think that they know the things because they know the names and definitions; and so that they are learned and wise, when they know little the more by all their learning. For to be able to talk over all the critical books, and lexicons, and grammars, all the logical notions and definitions, is nothing but organical knowledge; like the shoemaker that hath a shop full of lasts, (and that most of them unmeet for any man's foot,) but never made a shoe by any of them. And false and confused and idle names and notions, fill the learned world with false, confused, and vain conceptions, which common country people escape, so that it costeth many a man twenty years' study to be made more erroneous than he would have been, by following an honest trade of life.

XXIV. Nay, our very articles of faith and practice, which salvation lieth on, are commonly tried by these arbitrary organical notions: whole loads of school volumes are witnesses of this. Though the schoolmen, where our grammarians deride them as barbarians, have often done well in fitting words to things, and making the key meet for the lock: yet old terms and notions and axioms too often go for current; and overrule disputes, when they are not understood, nor are proper or univocal. What work doth Aristotle make with *actus* and *potentia,* and the schoolmen after him! What abundance of darkness do these two words contain in all their writings! And for want of other words to supply our needs, what abundance of distinctions of *actus* and *potentiæ* are the Scotists and other schoolmen fain to use! What abundance of disputes are kept up by the ambiguity of the word *cause,* while it is applied to things so different, as *efficience, constitution,* and *finality!* The like may be said of many more. And then when it cometh to a dispute of the divine nature, of the soul, of the most weighty things; these confounding notions must overrule the case. We must not have an argument for the soul's immortality, but what these notions check or vitiate; no, nor scarce for an attribute of God.

XXV. And it is so hard a thing to bring men to that self-denial and labour, as at age thoroughly and impartially to revise their juvenile conceptions, and for them that learned words before things, to proceed to learn things now as appearing in their proper evidence; and to come back and cancel all their old notions, which were not sound, and to build up a new frame, that not one of a multitude is ever master of so much virtue as to attempt it and go through with it. Was it not labour enough to study so many years to know what others say, but they must now undo much of it, and begin a new and harder labour? who will do it?

XXVI. And indeed none but men of extraordinary acuteness and love of truth, and self-denial and patience, are fit to do it. For, 1. The common dullards will fall into the ditch when they leave their crutches. And will multiply sects in philosophy and religion, while they are unable to see the truth in itself. And indeed this hath made the protestant churches so liable to the derision and reproach of their adversaries. And how can it be avoided, while all must pretend to know and judge, what indeed they are unable to understand?

2. Yea, the half-witted men, that think themselves acute and wise, fall into the same calamity.

3. And the proud will not endure to be thought to err, when they plague the world with error.

4. And the impatient will not endure so long and difficult studies.

5. And when all is done, as Seneca saith, they must be content with a very few approvers, and must bear the scorn of the ignorant-learned crowd; who have no way to maintain the reputation of their own wisdom, orthodoxness, and goodness, but by calling him proud, or self-conceited, or erroneous, that differeth from them by knowing more than they. And who but the truly self-denying can be at so much cost and labour for such reproach, when they foreknow that he that increaseth knowledge increaseth sorrow?

XXVII. By these means men's minds, that should be taken up with God and his service, are abused and vilified, and filled with the dust and smoke of vain, and false, and confused notions. And man's life is spent (as David saith) in a vain show. And men dream waking with as great industry as if they were about a serious work. Alas, how pitifully is much of the learned world employed!

XXVIII. By this means also men's precious time is lost; and he that had time little enough to learn and do things necessary, for the common good, and his own salvation, doth waste half of it on he knoweth not what. And Satan, that findeth him more ingenious than to play it away at cards or dice, or than to drink and revel it away, doth cast another bait before him, and get him learnedly to dream it away about unprofitable words and notions.

XXIX. And by this means the practice of goodness is hindered in the world; yea, and holy affections quenched. While these arbitrary notions and speculations (being man's own) are his more pleasant game; and studies and pulpits must be thus employed, and heart and life stolen from God. Yea, it is well if godliness grow not to be taken by such dreamers for a low, dull, and unlearned thing; yea, if they be not tempted by it to infidelity, and to think (not only the zealous ministers and christians, but even) Christ and his apostles to be unlearned men, below their estimation.

XXX. And by the same means the devilish sin of pride will be kept up, even among the learned; yea, and by the preachers of humility: for what is that in the world (almost) that men are prouder of, than that learning which consisteth in such notions and words as are afore-described? and the proudest man, I think, is the worst.

XXXI. And by these means the sacred chairs and pulpits will be possessed by such men, whose spirits are most contrary to a crucified Christ, and to that cross and doctrine which they must preach. And when Christ's greatest enemies are the pastors of his churches, all things will be ordered and managed accordingly; and the faithful hated and abused accordingly. Though I must add, that it is not this cause alone, but many more concurring to constitute a worldly, wicked mind, which use to procure these effects.

XXXII. And by false and vain learning contentions are bred and propagated in the churches. None are instruments so apt, and none have been so successful, as all church history recordeth, and the voluminous contentions of many such learned parties testify.

XXXIII. And this is an increasing malady; for new books are yearly written, containing the said arbitrary notions of the several authors. And whereas real and organical learning should be orderly and conjunctly propagated, and *things* studied for themselves, and *words* for *things*, the systems of arts and sciences grow more and more corrupted, our logics are too full of unapt notions, our metaphysics are a mere confused mixture of pneumatology and logic; and what part hath totally escaped?

XXXIV. And the number of such books doth grow so great, that they become a great impediment and snare; and how many years' precious time must be lost, to know what men say, and who saith amiss, or how they differ!

XXXV. And the great diversity of writers and sects increaseth the danger and trouble, especially in physics; by that time a man hath well studied the several sects, the Epicureans and Somatists, the Cartesians, with the by-parties, (Regius, Berigardus, &c.) the Platonists, the Peripatetics, the Hermetics, Lullius, Patricius, Telesius, Campanella, White, Digby, Glisson, and other novelists; and hath read the most learned improvers of the currenter sort of philosophy, (Scheggius, Wendeline, Sennertus, Hoffman, Honorat. Faber, Got, &c.) how much of his life will be thus spent! And perhaps he will be as far to seek, in all points saving those common evident certainties, which he might have learned more cheaply in a shorter time, than he was before he read them. And will wish that Antonine, Epictetus, or Plutarch had served instead of the greater part of them. And will perceive that physics are much fuller of uncertainties, and emptier of satisfying usefulness, than morality and true theology.

XXXVI. By such false methods and notions men are often led to utter scepticism, and when they have found out their own errors, they are apt to suspect all the substance of sciences to be error. And he speeds well that cometh but with Sanchez to a *nihil scitur*, and he better that cometh but with Cornelius Agrippa, to write vanity and vexation upon all the sciences: for many come to infidelity itself, and some to atheism; and, as Dr. Thomas Jackson noteth, by such distrust of men and human things, are tempted into a distrust or unbelief of Christ; or perhaps with Hobbes grow to cry down all learning besides their own, which is worse than the worst that they decry.

XXXVII. And by all this, princes and states are tempted to hate learning itself, and banish it as a pernicious thing; as the case of the Turkish, Muscovian, and some other empires testify.

All this I have said, not to dishonour true learning, which I would promote with all my power; but to show the corruption and vanity of that philosophy and human false learning, which Paul and the ancient writers did decry; and why the council of Carthage forbad the reading of the gentiles' books, and reproached Apollinarius, and other heretics, for their gentile learning.

Of the great uncertainty of our physics and metaphysics, almost all the chief authors themselves make free confessions. See Suarez, Metaph. disp. 35, p. 219, 221, 237; Fromondus de Anim. p. 63; Gassendus often; and who not.

Pious Bonaventure hath written a tract de Reductione Artium ad Theologiam; and another de non frequentandis Quæstionibus; Cornel. Agrippa de Vanitate Scientiarum, is well worth the reading beforehand to prevent men's loss of time.

CHAPTER IV.

III. WHAT ARE THE CERTAINTIES THAT MUST BE KNOWN AND HELD FAST, AND WHY.

It is none of the apostle's meaning that men should be mere sceptics: nor am I seconding Sanchez's Nihil Scitur, unless you take science for adequate science, or in a transcendent notion, as it signifieth that which is proper to another world, and therefore may be denied of this. He can neither play the part of a christian or of a man, who doubts of all things, and is assuredly confident of nothing.

That our discourse of this may be orderly and edifying, it is of great use that I first help you rightly to understand what *certainty* is. The word is ambiguous, and sometimes is applied to the object, and sometimes to the act and agent. The former is called *objective certainty*, the latter *subjective* certainty.

The objective is either certainty of the thing, or certainty of evidence, by which the thing is discernible or perceptible to us; and this either sensible evidence, or rational; and the latter is either self-evidence of principles, or derived evidence of consequences.

Subjective certainty is also either considered in the nature of it, or in the degree; and as to the nature, it is either the senses' certainty, or the intellect's; and this either of incomplex objects, or complex: the first is either of sensed objects, or purely spiritual; the second of principles, or of conclusions. Of all these there are certainty.

The degrees are these: It being first supposed that no human apprehension here is absolutely perfect; and therefore all our certainties subjective are imperfect; the word therefore signifieth not only a perfect apprehension, but it signifieth *non falli*, not to be deceived, and such an apprehension of the evidence as giveth us a just resolving and quieting confidence. And so, 1. The due objects of sense, and, 2. The immediate acts of the soul itself, are certain in the first and highest degree. I know certainly what I see clearly, so far as I see it; and I know certainly that I think, and know, and will. The next degree of certainty is of rational principles, and the next of consequents.

It is like in a scheme you will easilier understand it.

CERTAINTY being an ambiguous word, is either,

I. *Objective:* which is,
- I. Of *Being* of the Things; which is nothing but *Physical Verity.*
- II. Of Evidence; which makes Things *Perceptible;* and it is Evidence,
  - 1. Sensible; *viz.*
    - 1. To the External Senses.
    - 2. To the Internal Senses.
  - 2. Intelligible,
    - 1. Of the Being of Things, *viz.*
      - 1. *Quod sint,*
      - 2. *Quid sint,*
      - 3. *Qualia sint,*
        - 1. Things sensed and imagined, as colours, light, heat, &c.
        - 2. The Acts of Intellection and Will.
    - 2. Of Complex Verity, which is,
      - 1. Of self-evident Principles.
      - 2. Derivative Evidence of Conclusions.

I. Subjective *Certainty;* by which I am certain of the Object; Considerable,
- I. In its Nature; *viz.* Certainty,
  - 1. Of Sense.
    - 1. Of the Outward Senses, when they are not deceived.
    - 2. Of the Inward Sense and Imagination.
  - 2. Of the Intellect; which is,
    - 1. Of Beings,
      - 1. Sensed and imagined.
      - 2. Of the Acts of the Soul.
        - 1. *Quod sint.*
        - 2. *Quid sint.*
        - 3. *Qualia sint.*
    - 2. Of the Complex Verities,
      - 1. Of self-evident Principles.
      - 2. Of Conclusions.

  N. Qu. Whether there be not a third sort of *Certainty* both *Objective* and *Subjective; viz. Goodness* not sensible, *Certainty* apprehended by the Intellectual Soul, not only *sub ratione Veri, sed et Boni?* And whether the *Will* by its *Natural Gust* have not a Complacential *Perception* of it as well as the Intellect? *(Vid. Pemble Vindic. Grot.)*
- II. In the Degrees of Certainty; which are in the Order following:
  1. Sense perceiving the *Object* and *itself*, is the first perceiver; and hereof the surest.
  2. Imagination receiving from Sense, hath more requisites to its Certainty.
  3. Intellection about things sensible, hath yet more requisites to its Certainty; *viz.* 1. That the Object be true; 2. The Evidence sensible; 3. That the Sense be sound, and the Medium and other Conditions of Sense be just; 4. That the Imagination be not corrupt; 5. That the Intellect itself be sound.
  4. But Intellection about *itself* and *Volition* hath the highest Certainty.
  5. We are surer of the *Quod*, than the *Quid* and *Quale;* as that *we Think*, than *What* and *How.*
  6. We are certainer of self-evident Principles than of the Consequences.
  7. Consequences have various degrees of Evidence and Certainty.

A few propositions may further help your understandings.

I. All things in the world have their certainty physical of being; that is, it is a certainty, or a truth, that this thing is.

II. The thing which is most commonly called *objective certainty*, is such a degree of perceptibility or evidence as may aptly satisfy the doubting intellect.

III. Evidence is called infallible; 1. When he that receiveth it is never deceived; and so all truth is infallible truth; for he is not deceived who believeth it: 2. Or when a man cannot err about it. And there is no such evidence in the world, unless you suppose all things else agreeable.

IV. The perception is called infallible, 1. Either *quia non falsa*, because it is not deceived; and so every man is infallible in every thing which he truly perceiveth: 2. Or because it cannot or will not err. And so absolute infallibility is proper to God; but *secundum quid*, in certain cases, upon certain objects, with certain conditions, all sound men's senses and intellects are infallible.

V. Certainty of evidence consisteth in such a position of the thing evident, as maketh it an object perceptible to the faculty perceiving; to which many conditions are required. As, 1. That the thing itself have such intrinsic qualifications, as make it fit to be an object. 2. That it have the due intrinsic conditions concomitant.

1. To the nature of an object of perception it is necessary, 1. That it be a thing which in its nature is within the reach of the perceiving faculty; and not (as spirits are to sense) so above us, or alien to us, as to be out of the orb of our perception. 2. That they have a perceptible quantity, magnitude, or degree. 3. That, if it be an incomplex term and object, and not a universal of the highest notion, it be *hoc aliquid*, and have its proper individuation. 4. That it have some special distinct conformity to the distinct perceiving faculty. In sum, that it be *ens, unum, verum, bonum, vel hisce contraria reductive et per accidens cognita.*

2. To the extrinsic conditions, it is necessary, 1. That the object have a due site or position. 2. And a due distance; neither too near nor too far off. 3. And that it have a due medium, fitted to it and the faculty. 4. And that it have a due abode or stay, and be not like a bullet out of a gun, imperceptible through the celerity of its motion.

VI. That the perception of sense be certain, it is necessary, 1. That the organ be sound, in such a measure as that no prevalent distemper undispose it. 2. That it be not oppressed by any disturbing adjunct. 3. That the sensitive soul do operate on and by these organs; for else its alienation will leave the organ useless: as some intense mediations make us not hear the clock. 4. That it be the due sense and organ which meeteth with the object; as sounds with the ear, light with the eye, &c. besides the aforesaid necessaries.

VII. Common *notitiæ* or *principles* are not so called, because men are born with the actual knowledge of them; but because they are truths, which man's mind is naturally so disposed to receive as that, upon the first exercises of sense and reason, some of them are understood, without any other human teacher.

VIII. Even self-evident principles are not equal, but some of them are more, and some less evident; and therefore some are sooner, and some later known. And some of them are more commonly known than others.

IX. The self-evidence of these principles ariseth from the very nature of the intellect which inclineth to truth, and the nature of the will which essentially inclineth to good, and the nature and posture of the objects, which are truth and goodness in the most evident position, compared together, or conjunct; some call it instinct.

X. It is not necessary to the certainty of a principle, that it be commonly known of all or most. For intellects have great variety of capacities, excitation, helps, improvements; and even principles have various degrees of evidence, and appearances to men.

XI. Man's mind is so conscious of its own darkness and imperfections, that it is distrustful of its own inferences, unless they be very near and clear. When by a long series of *ergos* any thing is far-fetched, the mind is afraid there may be some unperceived error.

XII. He therefore that holdeth a true principle as such, and at once a false inference which contradicteth it, is to be supposed to hold the principle first and fastest, and that if he saw the contradiction he would let go the consequent, and not the principle.

XIII. He that denieth the certainty of sense, imagination, and intellective perception of things sensed as such, doth make it impossible to have any certainty of science or faith about those same objects, but by miracle. And therefore the papists denying and renouncing all these, (sense, imagination, and intellective perception,) when they say, that there is no bread or wine in the sacrament, do make their pretended contrary faith impossible. For we are men before we are christians, and we have sense and intellects before we have faith; and as there is no christianity but on supposition of humanity, so there is no faith but on supposition of sense and understanding. How know you that here is no bread and wine? Is it because Scripture or councils say so? How know you that; by hearing or reading? But how know you that ever you did hear or read, or see a book or man? By sense or no way. If sense be infallible here, why not there? You will say that sense may be fallible in one case, and not in others. I answer, either you prove it infallible from nature, even by sense, and intellective perception of and by sense, or else by supernatural revelation. If only by this revelation, how know you that revelation? How know you that ever you heard, read, or saw any thing which you call revelation? If by a former revelation, I ask you the same question *in infinitum.* But if you know the certainty of sense by sense and intellective perception, then where there is the same evidence and perception there is the same certainty. But here is as full evidence and perception as any other object can have. 1. We see bread and wine. 2. We taste it. 3. We smell the wine. 4. We hear it poured out. 5. We feel it. 6. We find the effects of it; it refresheth and nourisheth as other bread and wine. 7. It doth so by any other creature as well as by man. 8. It corrupteth. 9. It becometh true flesh and blood in us, and a part of our bodies; even in the worst: yea, part of the body of a mouse or dog. 10. It is possible for a mouse or dog to live only upon consecrated bread and wine. Is his body then nothing but Christ? 11. In all this perception the objects are not rare, but commonly exhibited in all ages; they have all the conditions that other sensible, evident objects have, as to sight, magnitude, distance, medium. 12. And it is not one or two, but all men in the world of the soundest senses, who sense and perceive them to be bread and wine. So that here is as full evidence as the words which you read or hear can have to ascertain us.

Object. But if God deny sense in this case and not in others, we must believe sense in others and not in this.

Answ. But again I ask you, how you know that God biddeth or forbiddeth you any thing, if sense be not first to be believed?

Object. But is it not possible for sense to be deceived? Cannot God do it?

Answ. 1. It is possible for sense to be annihilated, and made no sense; and it is possible that the faculty, or organ, or medium, or object be depraved, or want its due conditions, and so to be deceived. But to retain all these due conditions, and yet to be deceived, is a contradiction; for then it is not the same thing; it is not that which we call now formally sense and intellect, or sensation and intellection. And contradictions are not things for Omnipotency to be tried about. God can make a man to be no intellectual creature; but thereby he maketh him no man: for to be a man, and not intellectual, is a contradiction. And so it is to be men, and yet to have no sense nor intellect, that can truly perceive sensible objects as before qualified: therefore they unman all the world, on pretext of asserting the power of God.

2. But suppose that all sense be fallible, and intellection of things sensible, yet it is the first and only entrance of all things sensible into the mind or knowledge of man; and therefore we must take it as God hath given it us, for we can have no surer: no sensible thing is in the intellect which was not first in the sense. Whether my eyes and ears and taste be fallible or not, I am sure I have no other way to perceive their objects; but by them I must take them and use them as they are. All the words and definitions in the world will not give any man, without sensation, a true conception of a sensible object.

3. Such absurd suppositions therefore are not to be put, What if God should tell you by his word, that all the senses of all men are deceived, in one thing, or in all things? would you not believe him? It is not to be supposed that God will give us all our senses, and intellective perception by them, to be our discerner of things sensible, and then bid us not believe them, for they are false; unless he told us, that all our perceptions are false; and our whole life is but deceit. And I further answer, if God tell me so, it must be by some word or writing of man or angel, or himself; and how should I know that word, but by my sense?

But the great answer which seemeth to satisfy Bellarmine and the rest, is, that sense is no judge of substances, but of accidents only; therefore it is not deceived.

But, 1. It is false, that sense perceiveth not substances: it is not only colour, quantity, figure, which I see; nor only roughness and smoothness which I feel; nor only sweetness which I taste; but it is a coloured, extended, figured substance which I see; a rough or smooth substance which I feel; and a sweet substance which I taste: and if the accident were the only primary object, the substance is the secondary and certain. Else no one ever saw a man, a tree, a bird, a plant, the earth, a book, or any substance; but only the colour, quantity, or figure of them. No man ever felt or touched a body, but only the accidents of it.

2. And I pray you, tell me how substances come to the understanding, if they were never in the sense: prove a substance without sensation as a medium, if you can. Do you perceive any substances intellectually or not? If not, why pretend you that there are any? If yea, it must be either as conclusions, or as intellectual principles, (which are both logical complex objects, and therefore not substances,) or as the immediate immaterial objects of intellection, (which is only the soul's own acts,) or what is by analogy gathered from them; or else the objects of sense itself. It can be none of the former; therefore it must be the latter: and how can the understanding find that in sense which was never there?

If it be said that it is there but by accidents; I answer, 1. That is false, though said by many: I do as immediately touch substance as accidents, though not substance without the accidents. 2. Whether it be there by the mediation of the accidents, or immediately itself, we are sure that the understanding no otherwise receiveth it, than as the sense transmitteth it; we must know material substance as it is sensed, or not at all.

We see then what a pass this Roman religion bringeth the world to. That they may be christians, they must believe (and swear by the Trent oath) that they are not men; and that they may have faith, they must renounce their senses; and that they may be sure God's word is true, (and the church's decrees,) they must be sure that they are sure of nothing; and how then are they sure of that? And while they subvert all the order of nature in the world, they pretend that God can do it; and therefore we are to believe that he doth it, merely because these doctors can call themselves the church, and then can so expound the Scripture. When it is God's settled order in nature, that a man as an animal shall have sense to perceive things sensibly by, and as a man shall have understanding to receive from the imagination and sense these objects, we must now suppose that God hath quite overturned the course of nature, either by making sense no sense, or the object no object, or the medium no fit medium; and yet this is to be believed by men that have nothing but the same senses to tell their understandings that it is written or spoken, or that there is a man in the world.

Suppose we grant it to be no contradiction, and therefore a thing that God can do, no man can question but that he must do it as a miracle, by altering and overturning nature's course. And shall we feign, 1. Miracles to become ordinary things, through all the churches in the world, and every day in the week, or every hour to be done? 2. And miracles to be made a standing church ordinance? 3. And every one in the church, even all the wicked, and every mouse that eateth the host, to be partaker of a miracle? 4. Yea, that every such man and mouse may all the week long live on a continued miracle, while accidents without substance do nourish them, and turn to flesh and blood? 5. And all this ordinary course of miracles to be wrought at the will of every priest, be he never so ignorant or wicked a man? 6. And yet the same words spoken by the holiest of the protestant pastors will not do the miracle. 7. But if a papist priest should be unduly ordained, or forge his own orders, so be it the church think him truly ordained, he can do the miracle. All this must be believed.

And the plague of all is, all men must be burnt as heretics, or exterminated, that cannot believe all this, and disbelieve their senses. And yet worse, all temporal lords must be dispossessed of their dominions, who will suffer any such to live therein, and not exterminate them.

An epicure and a sensual infidel, who think man is but of the same species of brutes, do but unman us, and leave us the honour of being animals or brutes. But the papists do not leave us this much, but must reduce us to a lower order, and teach us to deny our sense itself; and torment and kill them that will not do it.

And what is it that must persuade us to all this? Why merely a *hoc est corpus meum*, as expounded by the councils of Lateran and Trent. And is not David's "I am a worm and no man," (Psal. xxii. 6,) as plain; yea, and that in a prophecy of Christ? Must we believe therefore that neither David nor Christ was a man, but a worm? Is not "I am the vine, and ye are the branches," (John xv. 1, 2,) as plain? Must sense be renounced and ordinary miracles believed for such words as these?

And doth not Paul call it bread, (1 Cor. xi.) after consecration three times in the three next verses? And is not he as good an expositor of Christ's words as the council of Trent?

And when did God work miracles which were

mere objects of belief against sense? Miracles were done as sensible things, thereby to confirm faith, and that which no sense perceived was not taken for a miracle.

To conclude, when the apostle saith, that "flesh and blood cannot enter into the kingdom of God," (plainly speaking of them formally as now called, and not as they signify sin,) and consequently that Christ's body is now in heaven a spiritual body and not formally flesh and blood, yet must the bread and wine be turned into his flesh and blood on earth, when he hath none in heaven?

And by their doctrine no baker nor vintner is secured, but that a priest may come into his shop or cellar, and turn all the bread and wine in it into Christ's body and blood: yea, the whole city or garrison may thus be deprived of their bread and wine, if the priest intend it; and yet it shall not be so in the sacrament itself, if the priest intend it not. But I have staid too long in this.

XIV. Next to the act of cogitation and volition itself, and to the most certain objects of sense, there is nothing in all the world so certain, that is, so evident to the intellect, as the being of God: he being that to the mind which the sun is to the eye, certainliest known, though little of him be known, and no creature comprehend him.

XV. That God is true, is part of our knowing him to be perfect, and to be God; and therefore is most certain.

XVI. That man is made by God and for God; that we owe him all our love, obedience, and praise; that we have all from him, and should please him in the use of all, with many such like, are *notitiæ communes*, certain verities, received by nature, some as principles, and some as such evident conclusions as are not to be doubted of.

XVII. That the Scripture is the word of God, is a certain truth, not sensible, nor a natural principle; but an evident conclusion drawn from that seal or testimony of the Spirit, antecedent, concomitant, impressed, and consequent; which I have oft opened in other treatises.

XVIII. That the Scripture is true, is a certain conclusion drawn from the two last-mentioned premises, viz. That God is true, *verax*, and that the Scripture is his word.

XIX. Those doctrines or sayings which are parts of Scripture, evidently perceived so to be by sense and intellective perception, are known to be true, by the same certainty as the Scripture in general is known to be true.

XX. To conclude, then, there are two sorts of certain verities in theology: 1. Natural principles with their certain consequents. 2. Scripture in general, with all those assertions which are certainly known to be its parts. And all the rest are to be numbered with uncertainties, except prophetical certainty of inspiration, which I pass by.

CHAPTER V.

IV. OF THE SEVERAL DEGREES OF CERTAINTY.

1. As certainty is taken for truth of being, it admitteth of no degrees: all that is true, is equally true.

2. But certainty of evidence hath various degrees: none doubteth but there are various degrees of evidence: all the doubt is whether any but the highest may be called certainty.

And here let the reader first remember that the question is but *de nomine*, of the name, and not the thing. And next, the evidence is called certain, because it is certifying aptitudinally. It is apt to certify us.

3. And then the question will be devolved to subjective certainty, whether it have various degrees. For if it have so, then the evidence must be said to have so, because it is denominated respectively from the apprehensive certainty.

And here *de re* it must be taken as agreed, 1. That certainty is a certain degree of apprehension. 2. That there are various degrees of apprehension. 3. That no man on earth hath a perfect intellectual apprehension, at least, of things moral and spiritual; for his apprehension may be still increased, and those in heaven have perfecter than we.

4. That there are some degrees so low and doubtful, as are not fit to be called certainty.

5. That even these lowest degrees with the greatest doubting, are yet often true apprehensions; and whenever they are true they are infallible, that is, not deceived: therefore this infallibility, which is but not to be deceived, is indeed one sort of certainty, which is so denominated relatively from the natural truth or certainty of the object; but it is not this sort of certainty which we inquire after.

6. Therefore it followeth that this subjective certainty containeth this infallible truth of perception, and addeth a degree which consisteth in the satisfaction of the mind.

7. But if the mind should be never so confident and satisfied of a falsehood, this deserveth not the name of certainty, because it includeth not truth. For it is a certain perception of truth which we speak of; and confident erring is not certainty of the truth.

8. As therefore the degrees of doubting are variously overcome, so there must needs be various degrees of certainty.

9. When doubting is so far overcome, as that the mind doth find rest and satisfaction in the truth, it may be called certainty. But when doubting is either prevalent, or so troublesome as to leave us wavering, it is not called certainty.

10. It is not the forgetting or neglect of a difficulty or doubt, nor yet the will's rejecting it, which is properly called certainty. This quieteth the mind indeed, but not by the way of ascertaining evidence. Therefore ignorant people that stumble upon a truth by chance with confidence, are not therefore certain of it. And those that take it upon trust from a priest or their parents, or good people's opinion, are not therefore certain of it. Nor they that say as some papists, Faith hath not evidence, but is a voluntary reception of the church's testimony, and meritorious, because it hath not evidence; therefore though I see no cogent evidence, I will believe, because it is my duty. Whether this man's faith may be saving or no, I will not now dispute; but certainly it is no certainty of apprehension. He is not certain of what he so believeth. This is but to cast away the doubt or difficulty, and not at all by certainty to overcome it.

11. When a man hath attained a satisfying degree of perception, he is capable still of clearer perception. Even as when in the heating of water, after all the sensible cold is gone, the water may grow hotter and hotter still. So after all sensible doubting is gone, the perception may grow clearer still.

12. But still the objective certainty is the same; that is, there is that evidence in the object which is *in suo genere* sufficient to notify the thing to a prepared mind.

13. But this sufficiency is a respective proportion;

and therefore, as it respecteth man's mind in common, it supposeth that by due means and helps, and industry, the mind may be brought certainly to discern this evidence. But if you denominate the sufficiency of the evidence, from its respect to the present disposition of men's minds, so it is almost as various as men's minds are. For *recipitur ad modum recipientis;* and that is a certifying, sufficient evidence of truth to one man, which to a thousand others is not so much as an evidence of probability. Therefore mediate and immediate sufficiency and certainty of evidence must be distinguished.

From all this I may infer, 1. That though God be the original and end of all verities, and is ever the first *in ordine essendi et efficiendi*, and so *a Jove principium, in methodo synthetica;* yet he is not the *primum notum*, the first known, *in ordine cognoscendi*, nor the beginning *in methodo inquisitiva* (though in such analytical methods as begin at the ultimate end, he is also the first). Though all truth and evidence be from God, yet two things are more evidence to man than God is, and but two: viz. 1. The present evident objects of sense; 2. Our own internal acts, of intellective cogitation and volition. And these being supposed, the being of God is the third evident certainty in the world.

2. If it be no disparagement to God himself, that he is less certainly known of us, than sensibles, and our internal acts, *de esse*, it is then no disparagement to the Scripture, and supernatural truths, that they are less certainly known; seeing they have not so clear evidence as the being of God hath.

3. The certainty of Scripture truths is mixed of almost all other kinds of certainty conjunct. 1. By sense and intellective perception of things sensed, the hearers and seers of Christ and his apostles knew the words and miracles. 2. By the same sense we know what is written in the Bible, and in church history concerning it, and the attesting matters of fact; and also what our teachers say of it. 3. By certain intellectual inference I know that this history of the words and fact is true. 4. By intellection of a natural principle I know that God is true. 5. By inference I know that all his word is true. 6. By sense I know (intellectually receiving it by sense) that this or that is written in the Bible, and part of that word. 7. By further inference therefore I know that it is true. 8. By intuitive knowledge, I am certain that I have the love of God, and heavenly desires, and a love of holiness, and hatred of sin, &c. 9. By certain inference I know that this is the special work of the Spirit of Christ by his gospel doctrine. 10. By experience I find the predictions of this word fulfilled. 11. Lastly, By inspiration the prophets and apostles knew it to be of God. And our certain belief ariseth from divers of these, and not from any one alone.

4. There are two extremes here to be avoided, and both held by some, not seeing how they contradict themselves.

I. Of them that say that faith hath no evidence, but the merit of it lieth in that we believe without evidence. Those that understand what they say, when they use these words, mean that things evident to sense, as such, that is, incomplex sensible objects, are not the objects of faith. "We live by faith and not by sight." God is not visible: heaven and its glory, angels and perfected spirits, are not visible. Future events, Christ's coming, the resurrection, judgment, are not yet visible: it doth not yet appear (that is, to sense) what we shall be: our life is hid (from our own and others' senses) with Christ in God. We see not Christ when we rejoice in him with joy unspeakable, and full of glory, 1 Pet. i. 8. Thus faith is the evidence of things not seen, or evident to sight, Heb. xi. 1; but ignorant persons have turned all to another sense; as if the objects of faith had no ascertaining intellectual evidence: when it is as impossible for man's mind to understand and believe any thing to be true, without perceiving evidence of its truth, as it is for the eye to see without light. As Richard Hooker saith in his Ecclesiastical Polity, "Let men say what they will, men can truly believe no further than they perceive evidence." It is a natural impossibility; for evidence is nothing but the perceptibility of the truth: and can we perceive that which is not perceptible?

It is true, that evidence from divine revelation is oft without any evidence *ex natura rei;* but it may be nevertheless a fuller and more satisfying evidence.

Some say there is evidence of credibility, but not of certainty. Not of natural certainty indeed. But in divine revelations (though not in human) evidence of credibility is evidence of certainty, because we are certain that God cannot lie.

And to say, I will believe, though without evidence of truth, is a contradiction or hypocritical self-deceit; for your will believeth not; and your understanding receiveth no truth but upon evidence that it is truth. It acteth of itself *per modum naturæ*, necessarily further than it is *sub imperio voluntatis;* and the will ruleth it not despotically; nor at all *quoad specificationem*, but only *quoad exercitium*. All therefore that your will can do, (which maketh faith a moral virtue,) is to be free from those vicious habits and acts in itself which may hinder faith, and to have those holy dispositions and acts in itself which may help the understanding to do its proper office, which is to believe evident truth on the testimony of the revealer, because his testimony is sufficient evidence. The true meaning of a good christian, when he saith, I *will believe*, is, I am truly willing to believe, and a perverse will shall not hinder me, and I will not think of suggestions to the contrary. But the meaning of the formal hypocrite, when he saith, I will believe, is, I will cast away all doubtful thoughts out of my mind, and I will be as careless as if I did believe, or I will believe the priest or my party, and call it a believing God. Evidence is an essentiating part of the intellect's act. As there is no act without an object, so there is no object *sub formali ratione objecti*, without evidence. Even as there is no sight but of an illustrated object, that is, a visible object.

II. The other extreme (of some of the same men) is, that yet faith is not true and certain if it have any doubtfulness with it. Strange! that these men can only see what is invisible, believe what is inevident as to its truth, that is, incredible, but also believe past all doubting, and think that the weakest true believer doth so too! Certainly there are various degrees of faith in the sincere: all have not the same strength! Christ rebuketh Peter in his fears, and his disciples all at other times, for their little faith. When Peter's faith failed not, it staggered, which Abraham's did not, Rom. iv. 20. "Lord, increase our faith," and, "Lord, I believe, help my unbelief," were prayers approved by Christ. I will call a prevalent belief, which can lay down life and all this world for Christ and the hopes of heaven, by the name of certainty, which hath various degrees. But if they differ *de nomine*, and will call nothing certainty but the highest degree, they must needs yet grant that there is true, saving faith, that reacheth to no certainty in their sense. Yea, no man on earth then attaineth to such a certainty, because that every man's faith is imperfect.

To conclude. Though all Scripture in itself (that

is indeed the true canon) be equally true, yet all is not equally certain to us, as not having equal evidence that it is God's word. But of that in the next chapter of the uncertainties.

CHAPTER VI.

V. WHAT ARE THE UNKNOWN THINGS, AND UNCERTAINTIES, WHICH WE MUST NOT PRETEND A CERTAIN KNOWLEDGE OF.

SOMEWHAT of this is said already, chap. iii. But I am here to come to more particular instances of it. But because that an enumeration would be a great volume of itself, I shall begin with the more general, that I may be excused in most of the rest; or mention only some particulars under them as we go.

I. A very great, if not the far greatest, part of that part of philosophy called physics, is uncertain (or certainly false) as it is delivered to us in any methodist that I have yet seen; whether Platonists, peripatetics, Epicureans, (the stoics have little, but what Seneca gives us, and Barlaam collecteth, I know not whence, as making up their ethics, and what in three or four ethical writers is also brought in on the by, and what Cicero reporteth of them,) or in our novelists, Patricius, Telesius, Campanella, Thomas White, Digby, Cartesius, Gassendus, &c.; except those whose modesty causeth them to say but little, and to avoid the uncertainties, or confess them to be uncertainties. To enumerate instances would be an unseasonable digression. Gassendus is large in his confessions of uncertainties. I think not his brother Hobbes, and his second Spinosa, worth the naming. Nor the Paracelsians and Helmontians, as giving us a new philosophy, but only as adding to the old. There needs no other testimony of uncertainty to a man that hath not studied the points himself, than their lamentable difference, and confutation of each other, in so many things, even in the great principles of the science.

Yet here, no doubt, there are certainties, innumerable certainties, such as I have before described. We know something certainly of many things, even of all sensible objects. But we know nothing perfectly and comprehensively; not a worm, not a leaf, not a stone, or a sand, not the pen, ink, or paper which we write with; not the hand that writeth, nor the smallest particle of our bodies; not a hair, or the least accident. In every thing nearest us, or in the world, the uncertainties and *incognita* are far more than that which we certainly know.

II. If I should enumerate to you the many uncertainties in our common metaphysics, (yea, about the being of the science,) and our common logic, &c. it would seem unsuitable to a theological discourse. And yet it would not be unuseful, among such theologians as the schoolmen, who resolve more of their doubts by Aristotle than by the holy Scriptures; doubtless, as Aristotle's predicaments are not fitted to the kinds of beings, so many of his distributions and orders, yea, the precepts, are arbitrary. And as he left room and reason for the dissent of such as Taurellus, Carpenter, Jacchæus, Gorlæus, Ritchel, and abundance more, so have they also for men's dissent from them. Even Ramus hath more adversaries than followers. Gassendus goeth the right way, by suiting *verba rebus*, if he had hit righter on the nature of things themselves. Most novel philosophers are fain to make new grammars and new logics, for words and notions, to fit their new conceptions, as Campanella, and the Paracelsians, Helmontians, (and if you will name the Behmenists, Rosicrucians, Weigelians, &c.) Lullius thought he made the most accurate art of notions; and he did indeed attempt to fit words to things; but he hath missed of a true accomplishment of his design, for want of a true method of physics in his mind, to fit his words to.[a] As Cornelius Agrippa, who is one of his chief commentators, yet freely confesseth in his lib. de Vanitate Scientiarum, which now I think of, I will say no more of this, but desire the reader to peruse that laudable book, and with it to read Sanchez's Nihil Scitur, to see uncertainty detected, so he will not be led by it too far into scepticism. As also Mr. Glanvile's Scepsis Scientifica.

As for the lamentable uncertainties in medicine, the poor world payeth for it. Anatomy, as being by ocular inspection, hath had the best improvement; and yet what a multitude of uncertainties remain! Many thousand years have millions yearly died of fevers, and the medicating them is a great part of the physicians' work; and yet I know not that ever I knew the man that certainly knew what a fever is. I crave the pardon of the masters of this noble art for saying it; it is by dear experience that I have learned how little physicians know; having passed through the trial of above thirty of them on my own body long ago, merely induced by a conceit that they knew more than they did; and most that I got was but the ruin of my own body, and this advice to leave to others:—*Highly value those few excellent men, who have quick and deep conjecturing apprehensions, great reading and greater experience, and sober, careful, deliberating minds, and had rather do too little than too much: but use them in a due conjunction with your own experience of yourself. But for the rest, how learned soever, whose heads are dull, or temper precipitant, or apprehensions hasty or superficial, or reading small, but especially that are young, or of small experience*, love and honour them, but use them as little as you can, and that only as you will use an honest, ignorant divine, whom you will gladly hear upon the certain catechistical principles, but love not to hear him meddle with controversies. So use these men in common, easy cases, if necessary, and yet there the less the better, lest they hinder nature that would cure the disease. If you dislike my counsel, you may be shortly past blaming it; for though their successes have tongues, their miscarriages are mostly silent in the grave. Oh how much goeth to make an able physician! but enough of such instances.

III. But though errors in politics the world payeth yet much dearer for, I must not be too bold in talking here. But I will confess that here the uncertainties are almost all in the applicatory part, and through the incapacity of the minds of men: for the truth is, the main principles of policy are part of the divine law, and of true morality, and in themselves are plain, and of a satisfying certainty, could you but get men's heads and hearts into a fitness duly to consider and receive them.

IV. But to come nearer to our own profession, there is much uncertainty in those theological conclusions, which are built on such premises, where any one of these physical, metaphysical, or logical uncertainties are a part; yea, though it be couched in the narrowest room, even in one ambiguous term of art, and scarce discerned by any but accurate observers. With great pomp and confidence many proceed to their *ergos*, when the detection of the

[a] See a book written long since this, called "the Samaritan," of excellent use, by Mr. Jones of Suffolk.

fraud not only of an uncertain medium, but of one ambiguous syllable, will mar all. And the conclusion can be no stronger or surer than the more weak and doubtful of the premises.

V. When the subject is of small and abstruse parts, far from the principles and fundamentals of the matter, usually the conclusions are uncertain. Nature in all matters beginneth with some few great and master parts, like the great boughs or limbs of the tree, or the great trunks and master vessels in our bodies; and from thence spring branches, which are innumerable and small: and it is so in all sciences, and in theology itself. The great, essential, and chief integral parts are few, and easily discerned; but two grand impediments hinder us from a certain knowledge in the rest: one is the great number of particles, where the understanding is lost, and, as they say, seeketh a needle in a bottle of hay, or a leaf in a wood; and the other is the littleness of the thing, which maketh it undiscernible to any but accurate and studious minds. And therefore how much soever men that trade in little things, may boast of the sublimity of them, and their own subtlety, their perceptions usually are accompanied with uncertainty; though in some cases an uncertain knowledge, known to be so, is better than none.

VI. Yea, though the matters themselves may be more bulky, yet if in knowing and proving them, we must go through a great number of syllogisms and inferences, usually the conclusion is very uncertain to us, whatever it may be to an extraordinary accurate and prepared mind. For, 1. We shall be still jealous (or may be) lest in so many terms and mediums, some one of them should be fallacious and insufficient, and weaken all. And we are so conscious of our own weakness, and liability to forget, oversee, or be mistaken, that we shall or may still fear lest we have missed it, and be overseen in something, in so long a course and series of arguings.

VII. Those parts of history which depend merely on the credit of men's wisdom and honesty, and are so merely of human faith, must needs be uncertain. For the conclusion can be no surer than the premises. All men as such are liars, that is, untrusty, or such as possibly may deceive. 1. They may be deceived themselves. 2. And they may deceive others where they are not themselves deceived. Every man hath some passion, some ignorance, some error, some selfish interest, and some vice. This age, if we never had known another instance, is so sad a proof of this, that tears are fitter than words to express it. Most confident reporters totally differ about the most notorious matters of fact. I must not name them, but I pity strangers and posterity. If it come especially to the characterizing of others, how ordinarily do men speak as they are affected! And they are affected as self-interest and passion leadeth them: with Cochlæus, Bolseck, and such others, what villains were Luther, Zuinglius, Calvin, &c. with their faithfullest acquaintance! what good and holy men, saving Luther's animosity! If the inquisitors torment protestants, or burn them, is it not necessary that they call them by such odious names as may justify their fact? If they banish and silence faithful, holy, able ministers, they must accuse them of some villanies which may make them seem worthy of the punishment, and unworthy to preach the gospel of Christ! What different characters did Constantius and Valens, and their party on one side, and Athanasius and the orthodox on the other side, give of one another! What different characters were given of Chrysostom! How differently do Hunnerichus and Gensericus on one side, and Victor Uticensis and other historians on the other side, describe the bishops and christians of Africa that then suffered! They were traitors, and rebels, and rogues, and enemies to the king, and heretics, to Hunnerichus: but to others, they were holy, blameless men; and those were tyrants and heretics that persecuted them. What difference between the histories of the orthodox, and that of Philostorgius, and Sondius! What different characters do Eusebius and Eunapius give of Constantine; and Eunapius and Hilary, &c. give of Julian! What different characters are given of Hildebrand on one side, and of the emperors Henrys on the other side, by the many historians who followed the several parts! How false must a great number of the historians on one side be! I know that this doth not make all human faith and history useless: it hath its degree of credibility answerable to its use. And a wise man may much conjecture whom to believe: 1. A man that (like Thuanus) showeth modesty and impartiality, even towards dissenters. 2. A man that had no notable interest to bias him. 3. A man that manifesteth other ways true honesty and conscience. 4. Supposing that he was himself upon the place, and a competent witness.

But there is little or no credit to be given, 1. To a factious, furious railer. 2. To one that was a flatterer of great men, or depended on them for preferment, or lived in fear of speaking the truth, or that speaketh for the interest of his riches and honour in the world; or for his engaged personal reputation, or that hath espoused the interest of a sect or faction. 3. There is little credit to be given to any knave and wicked man. He that dare be drunk, and swear, and curse, and be a fornicator or covetous worldling, dare lie for his own ends. 4. Nor to the honestest man that taketh things by rumours, hearsay, and uncertain reports, and knoweth not the things themselves.

But how shall strangers and posterity know when they read a history, whether the writer was an honest man or a knave, a man of credit or an impudent liar? Both may be equal in confident asserting, and in the plausibility of the narrative. Mere human belief therefore must be uncertain.

From whence we see the pitiful case of the subjects of the king of Rome (for so I must rather call him than a bishop). Why doth a layman believe transubstantiation, or any other article of their faith? Because the church saith it is God's word. What is the church that saith so? It is a faction of the pope, perhaps at Lateran, or forty of his prelates at the conventicle of Trent. How doth he know that these men do not lie? Because God promised that Peter's faith should not fail, and the gates of hell should not prevail against the church; and the Spirit should lead the apostles into all truth. But how shall he know that this Scripture is God's word? And also that it was not a total failing, rather than a failing in some degree, that Peter was by that promise freed from? Or that the Spirit was promised to these prelates which was promised to the apostles? Why, because these prelates say so! And how know they that they say true? Why, from Scripture, as before.

But let all the rest go. How knoweth the layman that ever the church made such a decree? That ever the bishops of that council were lawfully called? That they truly represented all Christ's church on earth? That this or that doctrine is the decree of a council, or the sense of the church indeed? Why, because the priest tells him so. But how knoweth he that this priest saith true, or a few more that the man speaketh with? There I leave you; I can answer no further; but must leave the credit of Scripture, council, and each particular doctrine, on the credit of that poor single priest, or the few that are his companions. The layman knoweth it no otherwise.

Quest. But is not the Scripture itself then shaken by this, seeing the history of the canon and incorruption of the books, &c. dependeth on the word of man?

Answ. No: 1. I have elsewhere fully showed how the Spirit hath sealed the substance of the gospel. 2. And even the matters of fact are not of mere human faith; for mere human faith depends on the mere honesty of the reporter: but this historical faith dependeth partly on God's attestation, and partly on natural proofs. 1. God did by miracles attest the reports of the apostles and first churches. 2. The consent of all history since, that these are the same writings which the apostles wrote, hath a natural evidence above bare human faith. For I have elsewhere showed, that there is a concurrence of human report, or a consent of history, which amounteth to a true natural evidence, the will having its nature and some necessary acts; and nothing but necessary, ascertaining causes could cause such concurrence. Such evidence we have that King James, Queen Elizabeth, Queen Mary, lived in England: that our statute-books contain the true laws, which those kings and parliaments made whom they are ascribed to. For they could not possibly rule the land, and overrule all men's interests, and be pleaded at the bar, &c. without contradiction and detection of the fraud, if they were forgeries (though it is possible that some words in a statute-book may be misprinted). There is in this a physical certainty in the consent of men, and it depends not, as human faith, upon the honesty of the reporter; but knaves and liars have so consented, whose interests and occasions are cross: and so is it in the case of the history of the Scripture books, which were read in all the churches through the world, every Lord's day; and contenders of various opinions took their salvation to be concerned in them.

VIII. Those things must needs be uncertain to any man, as to a particular faith or knowledge, which are more in number than he may possibly have a distinct understanding of; or can examine their evidence whether they be certain or not. For instance, the Roman faith containeth all the doctrinal decrees, and their religion also all the practical decrees, of all the approved general councils, that is, of so much as pleased the pope, such power hath he to make his own religion. But these general councils, added to all the Bible, with all the Apocrypha, are so large, that it is not possible for most men to know what is in them. So that if the question be whether this or that doctrine be the word of God, and the proof of the affirmative is, because it is decreed by a general council, this must be uncertain to almost all men, who cannot tell whether it be so decreed or no; few priests themselves knowing all that is in those councils. So that if they knew that all this in the councils is God's word, they know never the more whether this or that doctrine, *e. g.* the immaculate conception of the Virgin Mary, &c. be the word of God. And if a heathen knew that all that is in the Bible is the word of God, and knew not a word what is in it, would this make him a christian, or saint him?

You may object, That most protestants also know not all that is in the Scripture. *Answ.* True; nor any one. And therefore protestants say not that all that is in the Scripture is necessary to be known to salvation; but they take their religion to have essential parts, and integral parts and accidents; and so they know how far each is necessary. But the papists deride this distinction, and because all truths are equally true, they would make men believe that all are equally fundamental, or essential to christianity. But this is only when they dispute against us; at other times they say otherwise themselves, when some other interest leads to it, and so cureth this impudency.

It were worthy the inquiry, whether a papist take all the Bible to be God's word, and *de fide*, or only so much of it as is contained particularly in the decrees of councils? If the latter, then none of the Scripture was *de fide*, or to be particularly believed, for above three hundred years, before the council of Nice. If the former, then is it as necessary to salvation to know how old Enoch was, as to know that Jesus Christ is our Saviour!

IX. Those things must needs be uncertain, which depend upon such a number of various circumstances as cannot be certainly known themselves. For instance, the common rule by which the papist doctors do determine what particular knowledge and faith are necessary to salvation, is that so many truths are necessary as are sufficiently propounded to that person to be known and believed. But no man living, learned nor unlearned, can tell what is necessary to the sufficiency of this proposal. Whether it be sufficient, if he be told it in his childhood only, and at what age? or if he be told it but once, or twice, or thrice, or how oft? Whether by a parent or layman that cannot tell him what is in the councils? or by a priest that never read the councils? And whether the variety of natural capacities, bodily temperaments, education, and course of life before, do not make as great variety of proportions to be necessary to the sufficiency of this proposal? And what mortal man can truly take the measure of them? And how then can any man be certain what those points are which are necessary for him to believe?

X. Those things are uncertain which depend upon an uncertain author or authority. For instance, the Roman faith dependeth on the exposition of the Scriptures by the consent of the fathers, and on the tradition of the church, and the decrees of an authorized council. And here is in all this little but uncertainties.

1. It is utterly uncertain, who are to be taken for fathers, and who not. Whether Origen, Tatianus, Arnobius, Lactantius, Tertullian, and many such, be fathers or not. Whether such a man as Theophilus Alexandrinus, or Chrysostom, was the father, when they condemned each other. Whether such as are justly suspected of heresy, (as Eusebius,) or such as the Romanists have cast suspicions on (as Lucifer Calaritanus called a heretic, Socrates, Sozomens, falsely called Novatians, Hilary, Arelatensis, condemned by the Pope Leo, and Claud. Turonens. Rupertus Tuitiens. and such others). When the ancients renounced each other's communion, (as Martin did by Ithacius and Idacius and their synod,) when they describe one another as stark knaves, as Socrates doth Theophil. Alexandrin. and Sulpitius Severus doth Ithacius, which of them were the fathers.

2. How shall we know certainly which were the true uncorrupted writings of these fathers among so many forgeries and spurious scripts?

3. How shall it be known what exposition the fathers consented on, when not one of a multitude, and but few in all, have commented on any considerable parts of the Scripture, and those few so much often differ?

4. When in the doctrine of the Trinity itself, Petavius largely proveth that most of the writers of the three first centuries after the apostles were unsound,

and others confess the same about the millennium, the corporeity of angels, and of the soul, and divers other things; doth their consent bind us to believe them? If not, how shall we know in what to believe their consent, according to this rule?

2. And as to the church, they are utterly disagreed among themselves, what that church is which hath this authority.

1. Whether the pope alone. 2. Or the pope with a provincial council. 3. Or the pope with a general council. 4. Or a general council without the pope. 5. Or the universality of pastors. 6. Or the universality of the people with them.

3. And for a council. 1. There is no certainty what number of bishops, and what consent of the comprovincial clergy, is necessary to make them the true representatives of any church. 2. And more uncertain in what council the bishops had such consent. 3. And uncertain whether the pope's approbation be necessary. (The great councils of Constance and Basil determining the contrary.) 4. And uncertain which were truly approved. 5. And most certain that there never was any general council in the world, (unless you will call the apostles a general council,) but only general councils of the clergy of one empire, with now and then a straggling neighbour, even as we have general assemblies and convocations in this kingdom. And who can be certain of that faith which dependeth upon all or any of these uncertainties?

XI. That must needs be an uncertainty which dependeth on the unknown thoughts of another man. For instance, with the papists, the priest's intention, which is the secret of his heart, is necessary to the being of baptism, and transubstantiation. And so no man can be certain whether he or any other man be baptized or not; nor whether it be bread or Christ's body which he eateth. We confess that it is necessary to the being of a sacrament, that the minister do seem or profess to intend it as a sacrament; but if the reality of his intent be necessary to the being of it, no man can be certain that ever he had a sacrament.

XII. It is a hard thing to be certain on either side, in those controversies which have multitudes, and in a manner equal strength of learned, judicious, well-studied, godly, impartial men for each part. I deny not but one clear-headed man may be certain of that which a multitude are uncertain of, and oppose him in. But it must not be ordinary men, but some rare illuminated person, that must get above a probability, unto a certainty, of that which such a company as aforesaid are of a contrary mind in.

XIII. There is great uncertainty in matters of private impulse. When a man hath nothing to prove a thing to be God's will, but an inward persuasion or impulse in his own breast, let it never so vehemently incline him to think it true, it is hard to be sure of it. For we know not how far Satan, or our own distempered fantasies, may go. And most by far that pretend to this, do prove deceived. That which must be certain, must be somewhat equal to prophetical inspiration; which indeed is its own evidence: but what that is, no man can formally conceive but he that hath had it. Therefore we are bid to "try the spirits."

XIV. It is a hard thing to gather certainties of doctrinal conclusion from God's providences alone. Providential changes have their great use, as they are the fulfilling or execution of the word; but they that will take them instead of the Scripture, do usually run into such mistakes, as are rectified to their cost, by some contrary work of Providence ere long: these times have fully taught us this.

XV. It is hard to gather doctrinal certainties from godly men's experience alone. Even our experimental philosophers and physicians find, that an experiment that hits ofttimes, quite misseth afterwards on other subjects, and they know not why. A course of effects may oft come from unknown causes. And it is no rare thing for the common prejudices, self-conceitedness, or corruption of the weaker and greater number of good people, which needeth great repentance and a cure, to be mistaken for the *communis sensus fidelium*, the inclination and experience of the godly; especially when consent or the honour of their leaders or themselves hath engaged them in it. In my time, the common sense of the strictest sort was against long hair, and taking tobacco, and other such things, which now their common practice is for. In one country the common consent of the strictest party is for Arminianism; in another they are zealously against it. In Poland, where the Socinians are for sitting at the sacrament, the godly are generally against it; in other places they are for it. In Poland and Bohemia, where they had holy, humble, persuading bishops, the generality of the godly were for that episcopacy, as were all the ancient churches, even the Novatians; but in other places it is otherwise. So that it is hard to be certain of truth or error, good or evil, by the mere consent, opinion, or experience of any.

XVI. But the last and great instance is, that in the holy Scriptures themselves, there is a great inequality in point of certainty, yea, many parts of them have great uncertainty; even these that follow:

I. Many hundred texts are uncertain, through various readings in several copies of the original. I will not multiply them on Capellus's opinion; though Claud. Saravius, who got the book printed, and other worthy men, approve it. I had rather there were fewer varieties, and therefore had rather think there are fewer; but these that cannot be denied must not be denied: nor do I think it fit to gather the discrepancies of every odd copy, and call them *various readings*. But it is past denial, that the world hath no one ancient copy which must be the rule or test of all the rest, and that very many copies are of such equal credit, as that no man living can say that this, and not that where they differ, hath the very words of the Holy Ghost. And that even in the New Testament alone, the differences or various readings, of which no man is able to say which is the right, are so great a number as I am not willing to give every reader an account of; even those that are gathered by Stephanus, and Junius, and Brugensis, and Beza; if you leave out all the rest in the Appendix to the Polyglot Bible. In all or most of which we are utterly uncertain which reading is God's word.

II. There are many hundred words in the Scripture that are ambiguous, signifying more things than one; and the context in a multitude of places determineth not the proper sense; so that you may with equal authority translate them, either *thus* or *thus:* the margin of your Bibles giveth you no small number of them. It must needs here be uncertain which of them is the word of God.

III. There are many hundred texts of Scripture, where the phrase is general, and may be applied to more particulars than one: in some places the several particulars must be taken as included in the general. (And where there is no necessity a general phrase should not be expounded as if it were particular.) But in a multitude of texts the general is put for the particular, and must be interpreted but of one sort, and yet the context giveth us no certain determination which particular is meant. This is one of the commonest uncertainties in all the Scriptures. Here it is God's will that we be uncertain.

IV. In very many passages of the history of Christ, the evangelists set both words and deeds in various orders; one sets this first, and another sets another first. (As in the order of Christ's three temptations, Matt. iv. and Luke iv. and many such like.) Though it is apparent that Luke doth less observe the order than the rest, yet in many of these cases it is apparent that it was God's will to notify to us the matter only, and not the order. And it must needs be uncertain to us, which was the first said or done, and which was last.

The same is to be said of the time and place of some speeches of Christ recorded by them.

V. Many of Christ's speeches are recorded by the evangelists in various words.[b] Even the Lord's prayer itself, Matt. vi. and Luke xi. Besides, that Matthew hath the doxology, which Luke hath not (which Grotius and many others think came out of the Greek liturgy into the text). And even in Christ's sermon in the mount, and in his last commission to his disciples, Matt. xxviii. 18—20; Mark xvi. Now in some of these cases (as of the Lord's prayer) it is uncertain whether Christ spake it once or twice (though the former is more likely). In most of them, it is plain that it was the will of God's Spirit to give us the true sense of Christ's sayings in various words, and not all the very words themselves: for the evangelists that differ do neither of them speak falsely, and therefore meant not to recite all the very words. If you say that one giveth us the true words, and another the true sense, we shall never be certain that this is so, nor which that one is. So that in such cases, no man can possibly tell which of them were the very words of Christ.

VI. There are many texts of the Old Testament recited in the New, where it is uncertain whether that which the penman intended was an exposition, or proof of what he said, or only an allusion to the phrase of speech; as if he should say, I may use such words to express my mind or the matter by. As Matt. ii. 23, "He shall be called a Nazarene." So ver. 16, 17; Rom. x. 6—8, 18, and others. I know the excellent Junius in his Parallels hath said much, and more than any other that I know, to prove them all, or almost all, to be expository and probatory citations: but withal confessing that the generality of ancient and modern expositors think otherwise, he thereby showeth a great uncertainty; when he himself saith not that he is certain of it; and few others thought it probable.

VII. There are many texts cited in the New Testament out of the Septuagint, where it differeth from the Hebrew: wherein it is utterly uncertain to us, whether Christ and his apostles intended to justify absolutely the translation which they use, or only to make use of it as that which then was known and used for the sake of the sense which it contained. If they absolutely justify it, they seem to condemn the Hebrew, so far as it differeth. If not, why do they use it, and never blame it? It seemeth that Christ would hereby tell us, that the sense is the gold, and the words but as the purse; and we need not be over-curious about them, so we have the sense. As if I should use the vulgar Latin, or the Rhemists' translation with the papist, because he will receive no other.

VIII. There are many enigmatical and obscure expressions, which a few learned men only can probably conjecture at, and few or none be certain of the full sense. If any certainly understand much of the prophecies in Daniel and the Revelation, it must needs be very few; when Calvin durst not meddle with the latter: and though most of the famous commentators on the Revelation are such as have peculiarly made it their study, and set their minds upon it above all other things, and rejoiced in conceit that they had found out the true sense which others had overseen, (as men do that seek the philosopher's stone,) yet how few of all these are there that agree! And if ten be of nine minds, eight of them at least are mistaken. Franc. du Jon, the Lord Napier, Brightman, Dent, Mede, and my godly friend Mr. Stephens, yet living, (since dead,) with many others, have studied it thus with extraordinary diligence, but with different successes; and Lyra with other old ones turn all quite another way. And then come Grotius and Dr. Hammond and contradict both sides, and make it all (saving a few verses) to have been fulfilled many ages since. And can the unlearned or the unstudied part of ministers, then, with any modesty pretend a certainty, where so many and such men differ?

I know it is said, Rev. i. 3, "Blessed is he that readeth and they that hear the words of this prophecy, and keep those things which are written therein:" but that proveth no more than, 1. That some of it (as chap. i—iii.) is plain and commonly intelligible. 2. That it is a desirable thing to understand the rest; and worthy men's endeavour in due time and rank; and he that can attain to certainty may be glad of it.

I pass by the darkness of many types and prophecies of Christ in the Old Testament, and how little the Jews or the apostles themselves, till after Christ's resurrection, understood them. With very many other obscurities, which yet are not written in vain, nay, which make up the true perfection of the whole.

IX. There are very many proverbial speeches in the Scripture, which are not to be understood as the words properly signify, but as the sense of those proverbs then was among the Jews. But disuse hath so totally obliterated the knowledge of the sense of many of them, that no man living can certainly understand them.

X. There are many texts, which have words adapted to the places, the animals, the utensils, the customs, the coins, the measures, the vegetables, &c. of that place and time, which are some hard, and some impossible now to be certainly understood: and therefore such as Bochart, Salmasius, Casaubon, Scaliger, &c. have done well to add new light to our conjectures; but leaving great uncertainty still.

XI. Because the Jewish law is by Paul plainly said to be ceased or done away, it remaineth very difficult to be certain of abundance of passages in the Old Testament, how far they are obligatory to us. For when they now bind no otherwise than as the continued law of nature, or as reassumed by Christ into his special law, where the latter is not found, in the former there is often insuperable difficulty. For most lieth upon the proof of a parity of reason, which puts us upon trying cases hardly tried, unless we knew more of the reason of all those laws. (As about vows and dispensations, Numb. xxx.; about prohibited degrees of marriage, and such like; which makes divines so much differ about the obligation of the Judicials, (of which see Junius, vol. 1, p. 1861, &c. de Polit. Mos. observ.) and about usury, priesthood, magistrates' power in religion, and many such.

[b] It is most probable that Christ and the apostles then spake in the Chaldee called Hebrew, and so that the four Gospels are but translations of Christ's words, and so not the words, but the sense was Christ's: and what wonder then if the translating evangelists use divers words?

XII. There are abundance of texts which only open the substance of the matter in hand to us, and say nothing about abundance of difficulties of the manner, and many circumstances, (as the manner of the divine influx, and the Spirit's operation on the soul, &c.) And here all that which is unrevealed must needs be unknown.

XIII. There are many precepts which were local, personal, particular, and so temporary, and bind not universally all persons, at all times afterwards: such as the Rechabites' precepts from their father, and such as the love-feasts, the kiss of love, women's veil and long hair, men's being uncovered, &c.[c] Now it is very hard to know in all instances, whether the precepts were thus temporary, or universal and durable: which makes divines differ about the anointing of the sick, the office of deacons and deaconesses, the power of bishops, and extent of their diocesses, the eating things strangled and blood (against which Chr. Beckman in his Exercit. hath abundance of shrewd arguments, though few are of his mind). In these cases few reach a certainty, and none so full a certainty as in plainer things.

XIV. It is very hard to be certain when, and how far, examples of holy men in Scripture bind us: though I have elsewhere proved that wherever the apostles' practice was the execution of their commission for settling church orders, in which Christ promised them the help of his Spirit, their practice was obligatory. Yet in many instances the obligation of examples is very doubtful: which occasioneth the controversies about imitating John Baptist's life in the wilderness, and Anna, and about Lent, and about baptizing by dipping over head, and about the Lord's supper, whether it should be administered to a family, or at evening only, or after supper, or sitting, or in a private house, &c. And about washing feet, and many church orders and affairs.

XV. There are many things in Scripture that are spoken but once or twice, and that but as on the by, and not very plainly: and we cannot be so certain of any doctrine founded on these, as on passages frequently and plainly written.

XVI. There are so many seeming differences in Scripture, especially about numbers, as that if they be reconcilable, few or none in the world have yet found out the way. If we mention them not ourselves, such paltry fellows will do it as Bened. Spinosa in his Tractatus Theolog. Polit. I will not cite any, but desire the learned reader to consider well of what that learned and godly man, Ludov. Capellus, saith in his Critic. Sacr. l. c. 10, and l. 6, c. 7, 8.[d] (I own not his supposition of a better Hebrew copy used by the Sept.) I think an impartial considerer of his instances will confess, that as God never promised all or any of the scribes or printers of the Bible any infallible spirit, that they should never write or print a word falsely; and as it is certain by the various lections, that many such there have been in many and most books; so there is no one scribe that had a promise above the rest, nor any one Hebrew or Greek copy, which any man is sure is absolutely free from such miswritings. For how should we be sure of that one above all the rest? And I wish the learned reader to consider Bibliander's Preface to his Hebr. Grammar, and Casaubon's Exercit. 1, s. 28, and Pellicanus's Preface to his Comment. on the Bible. Jerom on Mic. 5. 2, is too gross, de Matth. 2. *Quod Testimonium nec Hæbraico nec 70 Interpretibus convenire*, &c. Let him read the rest that will, which is harsher. He that will not confess miswritings of numbers, and some names and words heretofore, as well as some misprintings now, doth but by his pretended certainty tempt men to question the rest for the sake of that, and injureth the sacred word.

XVII. We have not the same degree of certainty of the canonicalness or divineness of every book of Scripture: though they are all God's word, they have not all the same evidence that they are so. The New Testament had a fuller attestation from heaven for its evidence to man, than most of the Old had. And of the New Testament, it was long before many churches received the Epistle to the Hebrews, the second of Peter, Jude, Revelation, &c. Even in Eusebius's days, in his Præpar. Evangel. he showed that they were not received by all. And of the Old Testament, Moses, and the Psalms and Prophets, have fuller attestation than the rest. And indeed, as it is probable that the Chronicles were written in or after Ezra's time at soonest; so they do in so many places differ in numbers from the book of Kings, where all would agree with the rest of the history, if those numbers were but reduced to those in the Kings, that if any man should doubt of the divine authority of that book, that thereby he may be the less tempted to question any others, I should not think his error inconsistent with salvation. Put but that man to prove what he saith, who asserteth that we have equal evidence of the divinity of the Chronicles, Canticles, Esther, as we have of Moses, the Prophets, the Psalms, and the New Testament, and you shall quickly find that he did but pretend an equal degree of certainty, which indeed he had not. The papists pretend that they are as certain of the divinity of the Apocrypha, as we are of the rest. But they do but pretend a certainty for interest and custom' sake.

XVIII. Though it be to be held, that certainly the holy writers had no falsehoods in doctrine or history, but delivered us the truth alone, yet no one of them delivereth us all the truth, no not of many particular histories and speeches of Christ which they mention: and therefore we must set them all together for the understanding of them (as in the instance of Christ's appearing and the angel's speeches after his resurrection). And when all is done we have not all that Christ said and did, but all that was necessary to our faith and salvation. For as Paul citeth Christ, saying, "It is more honourable to give than to receive," so John tells us, "that the world could not contain the books that should be written;" we must take heed therefore how far we go with negatives, of such unmentioned things.

XIX. Though all that the holy writers have recorded is true, (and no falsehood in the Scripture, but what is from the error of scribes and translators,) yet we are not certain that the writers had not human infirmities in the phrase, method, and manner of expression. It is apparent that their style, yea their gifts, were various, as Paul oft openeth them, 1 Cor. xii. &c. Therefore Paul rather than Barnabas was the chief speaker. And Apollos was more eloquent than others: hence some were of Paul, and some of Apollos, and some of Cephas; and Paul is put to vindicate his ministerial abilities to the Corinthians. Therefore though weaker men's gifts put no sinful imperfection into the Scriptures, yet a

[c] It is very hard to be sure what the apostles settled as a universal perpetual law, in church matters, and what they settled only as suited to that time and place by the common rule of doing all to edification: I will have mercy and not sacrifice, being a standing rule, it is hard to plead their use of any rites against common good: perhaps more is mutable than most think.

[d] Without approving all that is in it, I may wish the reader to peruse Father Simon's second book, now newly printed in London.

human natural imperfection of style and order might be more in some than others. It is certain that they were not all perfect in knowledge and holiness. And how far every sermon which they preached was free from all that imperfection, (any more than Peter's carriage, Gal. ii.) we are uncertain. And how far their writings had a promise of, being free from natural modal imperfections more than their preachings, we know not fully. And yet God turned this weakness of theirs to the confirmation of our faith; showing us that heavenly power, and not human wisdom and ability, did his work. As David's sling in conquering Goliath showed God's power. And out of the mouths of babes doth God ordain strength; and the weak things of the world are used to confound the strong.

XX. Lastly, though all be certainly true which they have recorded, yet we have not the same degree of certainty, that no writer erred through lapse of memory in some less material passage, as we have that they infallibly delivered us the gospel. But this I have said so much of already in a small book called "More Reasons for the Christian Religion," that I must now refer you thither for the rest.

Quest. But if there be so many things, either uncertain or less certain, what is it that we are or may be fully certain of?

Answ. 1. What you are or are not certain of yourself, you should know if you know yourself, without my telling you.

2. I deny not but you may come to a certainty of all those things which are never so difficult, that have any ascertaining evidence, if you live long enough, and study hard enough, and have an extraordinary measure of divine illumination: I do not measure others by myself: you may know that which I know not. God may bless your studies more, as being better men and fitter for his blessing: he may give you extraordinary inspirations, or revelations, if he please: but I am thankful for my low degree, and confess my ignorance.

3. But I have told you before what certainties we have. 1. We are certain of things sensible. 2. And of our elicit and imperate acts. 3. And of natural principles. 4. And of clear inferences thence. 5. And of the truth of all the certain holy Scriptures, which are evidently the word of God. 6. And particularly therein of the plain historical parts. 7. And of all which is the main design and scope of the text in any book or chapter. 8. And of all that which is purposely and often repeated, and not only obscurely once spoken on the by. 9. Therefore we may be certain of all that is necessary to salvation: of every article in the creed, of every petition in the Lord's prayer, and every necessary common duty: we may be certain of the truth and sense of all the covenant of grace concerning the Father, Son, and Holy Ghost, his relation to us, and our relation and duty to him; and of the benefits of the covenant, of the necessity and nature of faith, repentance, hope, love, obedience, patience, &c. It is tedious to recite all; in a word, all that is of common necessity, and all (how small soever) which is plainly revealed and expressed. 10. And you may be certain of the fulfilling of much of this holy word already by sufficient history and experience.

CHAPTER VII.

INFERENCE 1. THE TRUE REASON AND USEFULNESS OF THE CHRISTIAN SIMPLICITY, IN DIFFERENCING THE COVENANT, AND PRINCIPLES OF RELIGION, FROM THE REST OF THE HOLY SCRIPTURES.

It hath ever been the use of the church of God, to catechise men before they were baptized; and therein to teach them the true meaning of the baptismal covenant, by opening to them the creed, the Lord's prayer, and the decalogue: and when they understood this covenant they were admitted (upon consent) by baptism into the church, and accounted christians and members of Christ, without staying to teach them any other part of the Bible, no not so much as the sacrament of the Lord's supper.[a] (Though indeed the opening of baptism was the opening of the life of that; because it is the same covenant which is solemnized in both.)

By doing thus, the church notoriously declared that they took not all the Scripture to be equally necessary to be understood; but that the covenant of grace, and the catechism explaining it, is the gospel itself, that is, the essence of it, and of the christian religion, and that all the rest of the Scriptures contain but partly the integrals and partly the accidents of that religion. He is the wisest man that knoweth most and best; and every man should know as much of the Scriptures as he can. But if you knew all the rest, without this (the covenant of grace, and its explication) it would not make you christians, or save you. But if you know this truly, without all the rest, it will.

The whole Scripture is of great use and benefit to the church. It is like the body of a man; which hath its head, and stomach, &c.; and hath also fingers, and toes, and flesh; yea, nails and hair. And yet the brain and heart itself fare the better for the rest, and would not be so well seated separate from them: though a man may be a man that loseth even a leg or arm. So is it here. But it is the covenant that is our christianity, and the duly baptized are christians, whatever else they do not understand. These are the things that all must know, and daily live upon.

The creed is but the exposition of the three articles of the baptismal covenant: "I believe in God, the Father, Son, and Holy Ghost." Though the Jews that had been bred up to a preparing knowledge, were quickly baptized by the apostles upon their conversion, (Acts ii.) yet no man can imagine, that either the apostles, or other ministers, did use to admit the ignorant gentiles into the covenant of God, without opening the meaning of it to them; or baptize them as christians, without teaching them what christianity is. Therefore reason, and the whole church's subsequent custom, assure us, that the apostles used to expound the three great articles to their catechumens; and thence it is called the *Apostles' Creed.*

Marcus, bishop of Ephesus, told them in the Florentine council, (as you may see Sgyropilus,) That we have none of the Apostles' Creed, and Vossius de Symbolis, besides many others, hath many arguments to prove, that this so called was not formally made by the apostles. Bishop Usher hath opened the changes that have been in it. Sandford and Parker have largely, de Descensu, showed how it came in as an exposition of the baptismal articles. Others

[a] As Antonine saith, (in greater darkness,) l. 2. s. 5. ὁρᾷς πῶς ὀλίγα ἐστίν, &c. Vide quam pauca sint, quæ siquis tenuerit, prosperam ac divinam propemodum vitam degere detur: siquidem et dii ipsi nihil amplius exigent ab eo, qui ista observaverit.

stiffly maintain that the apostles made it; but the case seemeth plain. The apostles used to call the baptized to the profession of the same articles, (which Paul hath in 1 Cor. xv. 1—3, &c.) and varied not the matter. All this was but more particularly to profess faith in God the Father, Son, and Holy Ghost. Two or three further expository articles are put into the creed since: otherwise it is the same which the apostles used; not in the very syllables or forms of words, but in the same sense; and the words indeed being left free, but seldom much altered, because of the danger of altering the matter. Of all the ancientest writers, not one repeateth the creed in the same words that we have it; nor any two of them in the same with one another. Irenæus once, Tertullian twice hath it; all in various words, but the same sense. That of Marcellus in Epiphanius cometh nearest ours called the Apostles', and is almost it. Afterward, in Ruffinus and others, we have more of it. Yet no doubt but the Western churches, at least, used it with little variation still. The Nicene creed is called by some ancients the Apostles' creed too: and both were so; for both are the same in sense and substance: for it is not the very words that are truly fathered on the apostles.

About three hundred years ago, Mr. Ashwell having published a book for the necessity and honour of the creed, I wrote in the postscript to my "Reformed Pastor," edit. 2nd, a corrective of some passages, in which he seemeth to say too much for it, or at least to depress the Scripture too much in comparison of it. But long experience now telleth me that I have more need to acquaint men with the reasons and necessity of the creed; seeing I find a great part of ignorant religious people much to slight the use of it, and say it is not Scripture, but the work of man: especially taking offence at the harsh translation of that article, *He descended into hell;* which, from the beginning, it is like was not in. It is the kernel of the Scripture, and it is that for which the rest of the Scripture is given us, even to afford us sufficient help to understand and consent to the covenant of grace; that our belief, our desires, and our practice may be conformed principally to these summaries. It is not every child, or woman, that could have gathered the essential articles by themselves out of the whole Scripture, if it had not been done to their hands: nor that could have rightly methodized the rule of our desires, or gathered the just heads of natural duty; if Christ had not done the first in the Lord's prayer, and God the second in the decalogue.

Object. But I believe these only, because the matter of the creed, and the words also of the other two, are in the Scripture, and not on any other authority.

Answ. If you speak of the authority of the author, which giveth them their truth, it is neither Scripture nor tradition; but God, for whose authority we must believe both Scripture and them.

But if you speak of the authority of the deliverers, and the evidence of the delivery; be it known to you, 1. That the creed, Lord's prayer, decalogue, and the baptismal covenant, have been delivered down to the church from the apostles by a distinct tradition, besides the Scripture tradition; even to all the christians one by one, that were baptized, and admitted to the Lord's table, and to every particular church. So that there was not a christian or church, that was not even constituted by them.

2. Be it known to you, that the church was long in possession of them, before it had the Scriptures of the New Testament. It is supposed to be about eight years after Christ's ascension, before Matthew wrote the first book of the New Testament; and near the year of our Lord 100, before the Revelation was written. And do you think that there were no christians or churches all that while? Or that there was no baptism? Or no profession of the christian faith in distinct articles? No knowledge of the Lord's prayer and commandments? No gospel daily preached and practised? What did the church assemblies, think you, do all those years? No doubt, those that had inspiration used it by extraordinary gifts. But that was not all: those that had not, did preach the substance of the christian religion, contained in these forms; and did pray, and praise God, and celebrate the Lord's supper; provoking one another to love, and to good works.

3. Be it known to you, that these three summaries come to us with fuller evidence of certain tradition from God, than the rest of the holy Scriptures. Though they are equally true, they are not equally evident to us. And this I thus prove: 1. The body of the Scriptures were delivered but one way; but the covenant, creed, Lord's prayer, and decalogue, are delivered two ways. They are in the Scripture, and so have all the evidence of tradition which the Scriptures have: and they were, besides that, delivered to the memories of all christians. If you say, that the creed is not in the Scripture; or that the Scripture is not altered as it is: I answer, 1. That it is in the Scripture, as to the matter signified in as plain words, even of the same signification. 2. There is no alteration made, but a small addition, which is no disparagement to it; because the ancient substance of it is still known, and the additions are not new-made things, but taken out of Scripture. And if yet any heretic should deny that God is wise and good, and just and merciful; it were no dishonour to the creed, nor weakening of its certainty, to have these attributes yet added to it.

2. These summaries, as is said, were far ancienter than the rest of the New Testament, as written, and known, and used long before them.

3. These summaries being in every christian's mind and memory, were faster held than the rest of the Scriptures: therefore parents could and did teach them more to their children. You never read that the catechisers of the people did teach them all the Bible, nor equally ask them, who Jared, or Mehaleel, or Lamech was, as they did who Christ was. Nor put every history into the catechism, but only the historical articles of the creed.

4. Therefore it was far easier to preserve the purity of these summaries, than of the whole body of the Scriptures; for that which is in every man's memory, cannot be altered without a multitude of reprovers: which makes the Greeks since Photius keep such a stir about *filioque* as to think that the Latins have changed religion, and deserved to be separated from, for changing that word. But no wonder that many hundred various readings are crept into the Bible, and whole verses and histories (as that of the adulterous woman) are out in some that are in others. For it is harder to keep such a volume incorrupt, than a few words. Though writing, as such, is a surer way than memory, and the whole Bible could never have been preserved by memory; yet a few words might, especially when they had those words in writings also.

5. Add to this, that the catechistical summaries aforesaid, were more frequently repeated to the people, at least every Lord's day. Whereas, in the reading of the Scriptures, one passage will be read but seldom, perhaps once or twice in a year: and so a corruption not so easily observed.

6. And if among a hundred copies of the Scripture, ten or twenty only should by the carelessness of the scribes be corrupted; all the rest who saw

not these copies, would not know it, and so they might fall into the hands of posterity, when many of the sounder might be lost.

7. And lastly. The danger of depravation hath no end; for in every age the Scripture must be written over anew, for every church and person that would use it. And who that knoweth what writing is, could expect that one copy could be written without errors; and that the second should not add to the errors of the first, as printers now do, who print by faulty copies. And though this danger is much less since printing came up, that is but lately. And the mischiefs of wars and heretical tyrants, burning the truest copies, hath been some disadvantage to us.

Object. Thus you seem to weaken the certain incorruption of the Scriptures.

Answ. No such thing: I do but tell you the case truly as it is. The wonderful providence of God, and care of christians, hath so preserved them, that there is nothing corrupted which should make one article of faith the more doubtful. I assert no more depravation in them, than all confess; but only tell you how it came to pass, and tell you the greater certainty that we have of the essentials of religion, than of the rest. And whereas every man of brains confesseth, that many hundred words in Scripture by variety of copies are uncertain; I only say, that it is not so in the essentials. And I do not wonder that Virgil, Ovid, Horace, Cicero, &c. have not suffered such depravations. For, 1. It is not so easy for a scribe's error to pass unseen *in oratione ligaga*, as *in oratione soluta;* in verse as in prose. 2. And Cicero, with the rest, was almost only in the hands of learned men; whereas the Scriptures were in the hand of all the vulgar, women and children. 3. And the copies of these authors were comparatively but few: whereas every one almost got copies of the Scripture, that was able. And it is liker that some depravation should be found among ten thousand copies than among a hundred.

So that I have proved to you, that the creed, Lord's prayer, commandments, and covenant of baptism, are not to be believed only because they are in the Scripture; but also because they have been delivered to us by tradition, and so we have them from two hands, as it were, or ways of conveyance; and the rest of the Scriptures but by one, for the most part.

I will say yet more, because it is true and needful. If any live among papists, that keep the Scripture from the people; or among the poor Greeks, Armenians, or Abassines, where the people neither have Bibles commonly, nor can read; or if any among us that cannot read, know not what is in the Bible; yea, if through the fault of the priest, any should be kept from knowing that ever there was a Bible in the world: yet if those persons by tradition receive the baptismal covenant, the creed, Lord's prayer, and commandments, as God's word; and truly believe, and love and practise them; those persons shall be saved; for they have Christ's promise for it; and the very covenant itself is the gift of Christ, and life to consenters. Whereas, he that knoweth all the Scripture, can be saved only by consenting to and performing this same covenant: but having greater helps to understand it, and so to believe it and consent; he hath a great advantage of them that have not the Scripture; and so the Scripture is an unspeakable mercy to the church. And it is so far from being too little, without the supplement of the papists' traditions and councils, as that the hundredth part of it, as to the bulk of words, is not absolutely itself of necessity to salvation.

Yet I say more: if a man that hath the Scripture, should doubt of some books of it, whether they be the word of God (as of Ruth, Judges, Joshua, Chronicles, &c.); yea, if he doubted of all the Old Testament, and much of the New; yet if he believe so much as containeth all the covenant of grace, and the aforesaid summaries, though he sin, and lose much of his helps, yet he may and will be saved, if he sincerely receive but this much. The reason is before given. Though no man can believe any thing truly, who believeth not all that he knoweth to be God's word; yet a man may doubt, whether one thing be God's word, who doubteth not of another, by several occasions.

And here you see the reason, why a particular or explicit belief of all the Scripture itself was never required of all that are baptized, nor of all or any man that entered into the ministry. For the wisest doctor in the world doth not attain so high. For no man hath a particular, explicit belief of that which he doth not understand. For it is the matter or sense that we believe; and we must first know what that sense is, before we can believe it to be true. And no man in the world understandeth all the Scripture.

Yea, more, it is too much to require as necessary to his ministry, a subscription in general, that he implicitly believeth all that is in that Bible which you shall shew him. For, 1. Many faults may be in the translation, if it be a translation. 2. Many errors may be in the copy, as aforesaid.

Nay, such a subscription should not, as absolutely necessary, be required of him as to all the real word of God. For if the man by error should doubt whether Job, or the Chronicles, or Esther were canonical, and none of the rest, I would not be he that should therefore forbid him to preach Christ's gospel. I am sure the ancient church imposed no such terms on their pastors, when part of the New Testament was so long doubted of; and when some were chosen bishops before they were baptized; and when Synesius was chosen a bishop before he believed the resurrection. I would not have silenced Luther, Althamer, or others that questioned the Epistle of James.

What then shall we say of the Roman insolence, which thinketh not all the Scripture big enough, but ministers must also subscribe to many additions of their own, yea, and swear to traditions and the expositions of the fathers, and take whole volumes of councils for their religion? No wonder if such men do tear the churches of Christ in pieces.

1. By this time, I hope, you see to what use baptism, and the summaries of religion, are. 2. And of how great use catechising is. 3. And that christianity hath its essential parts. And how plain and simple a thing true christianity is, which constituteth the church of Christ; and how few things, as to knowledge, are necessary to make a man a christian, or to salvation. Multitudes of opinions have been the means of turning pastors and people from the holy and diligent improvement of these few truths in our practice; where we have much to do, which might take up all our minds and time.

CHAPTER VIII.

INFERENCE 2. OF THE USE OF CATECHISING.

THOUGH it be spoken to in what is said, I would have you more distinctly here note the use of catechising.

1. It collecteth those few things out of many, which the ignorant could not themselves collect.

2. It collecteth those necessary things which all must know and believe that will be saved. 3. It containeth those great practical things which we have daily use for, and must still live upon, which are as bread and drink for our food. Other things may be well added, the more the better, which God hath revealed. But our life, our comfort, and our hope, are in these. 4. And it giveth us the true method or order of holy truths; which is a great advantage to understand them. Not but that the things themselves have the same orderly respect to one another in the Scripture, but they are not delivered in the same order of words.

Therefore, I. Catechisms should be very skilfully and carefully made. The true fundamental catechism is nothing else but the baptismal sacramental covenant, the creed, the Lord's prayer, and the commandments, the summaries of our belief, desires, and practice. And our secondary catechism must be nothing else but the plain expositions of these: The first is a divine catechism: the second is a ministerial expository catechism. And here, 1. Oh that ministers would be wiser at last, than to put their superfluities, their controversies and private opinions, into their catechisms, and would fit them to the true end, and not to the interest of their several sects! But the Roman Trent catechism (and many more of theirs) must needs be defiled with their trash, and every sect else must put their singularities into their catechisms; so hard is it for the aged, decrepit body of the diseased church, for want of a better concoction of the common essentials of christianity, to be free from these heaps of unconcocted crudities, and excrementitious superfluities, and the many maladies bred thereby.

I deny not but a useful controversy may be opened by way of question and answer: but pretend it not then to be what it is not, milk for babes. "Him that is weak in the faith receive, but not to doubtful disputations," Rom. xiv. 1. The servant of the Lord must be apt to teach, but must not strive.

2. And it is not commonly believed how great skill is needful to make a catechism, that the method may be true, and that it may neither be too long for the memory, nor too short for the understanding; for my part, it is the hardest work, save one, (which is the full methodizing and explaining the whole body of divinity,) that ever I put my hand to; and when all is done, I cannot satisfy myself in it.

II. Why is not catechising more used both by pastors and parents? I mean not the bare words unexplained without the sense, nor the sense in a mere rambling way without a form of words; but the words explained.[a] Oh how much fruit would poor souls and all the church receive by the faithful performance of this work, would God but cure the profaneness and sloth of unfaithful pastors and parents which should do it. But I have said so much of this in my "Reformed Pastor," that I may well forbear more here.

CHAPTER IX.

INFERENCE 3. THE TRUE PRESERVATIVE OF PUZZLED CHRISTIANS, FROM THE ERRORS OF FALSE TEACHERS WHO VEHEMENTLY SOLICIT THEM TO THEIR SEVERAL PARTIES.

IT is the common outcry of the world, How shall we know which side to be on? And who is in the right among so many, who all with confidence pretend to be in the right?

Answ. Your preservative is obvious and easy; but men usually bestow more labour and cost for error and hell, than for truth and heaven. *Pretend not to faith or knowledge before you have it,* and you are the more safe. SUSPEND your judgments till you have true evidence to establish them. 1. It is only christians that I am now instructing; and if you are christians, you have already received the essentials of christianity, even the baptismal covenant, the creed, the Lord's prayer, and decalogue. And I need not tell you, that moreover you must receive all those truths in nature and Scripture, which are so plain, that all these dissenting sects of christians are agreed in them. And when you have all these, and faithfully love and practise them, you are sure to be saved, if you do not afterward receive some contrary doctrine which destroyeth them. Mark then which is the *safe religion.* As sure as the gospel is true, he that is meet for baptism before God, is meet for pardon of sin; and he that truly consenteth to the baptismal covenant, and so doth dedicate himself to God, is made a member of Christ, and is justified, and an heir of heaven. Your church catechism saith truly of all such, that in baptism each one is made a member of Christ, a child of God, and an heir of heaven. So that as sure as the gospel is true, every true baptized christian, whose love and life doth answer that faith, shall certainly be saved.

Ask all parties, and few of them but impudent designers can deny this. Well then, the baptismal covenant, expounded in the creed, Lord's prayer, and commandments, is your christian religion. As a christian you may and shall be saved: that a true christian is saved, all confess. But whether a papist be saved, is questioned by the protestants; and so is the salvation of many other sects by others. You are safe then if you take in nothing to endanger you. And is it not wisdom then to take heed how you go further, and on what grounds, lest you overrun your safe religion?

Object. But then I must not be a protestant; for the papists say, that they cannot be saved.

Answ. A protestant is either one that holdeth to the ancient, simple christianity without the papists' manifold additions; or one that positively also renounceth and opposeth those additions. In the first sense, a protestant and a mere christian is all one; and so to say, that a protestant cannot be saved, is to say, that a christian as such cannot be saved. If it be the mere name of a protestant that the papist accounteth damnable, tell him that you will not stick with him for the name: you are contented with the old name of christian alone.

But protestantism in the second sense is not your religion, but the defensative of your religion; as flying from the plague is not my humanity or life, but a means to preserve it. And so protestants are of many sizes; some oppose some points, and some others, some more, some less, which the papists have brought in; and yet they are not of so many religions.

But whoever condemneth you, if Christ save you, he doth but condemn himself as uncharitable. Christianity is certainly a state of salvation; but whether popery be, or whether the Greek opinions be, or whether this or that difference and singularity stand with salvation, is the doubt. Cast not yourself then needlessly into doubt and danger.

Object. But then you will have us be still but infants, and to learn no more than our catechisms, and not to learn and believe all that God hath revealed in his word.

[a] Since this I have published a book called the "Catechising of Households."

Answ. No such matter. This is the sum of what I advise you to.

1. Hold fast to your simple christianity as the certain terms of salvation.

2. Receive nothing that is against it.

3. Learn as much more as ever you can.

4. But take not men's words, nor their plausible talk, for certifying evidence; and do not think if you believe a priest, that this is believing God; nor if his reasons seem plausible to you, and you are of his opinion, that this is divine knowledge. If you do incline to one man's opinion more than another, tell him that you incline to his opinion, but tell him that you take not this for divine knowledge, or any part of your religion. If you will needs believe one side rather than another, about church history, or the matters of their parties' interest, tell them, I believe you as fallible men; but this is none of my divine faith or religion. To learn to know, is to learn scientifical evidence, and not to learn what is another man's opinions, nor whether they are probable or not; much less to read a council's decrees, or the propositions of a disputing system, and then for the men's sake to say, this is orthodox; nor yet because it hath a taking aspect. To learn of a priest to believe God, is one thing; and to believe him, or his party, church, or council, is another thing. Learn to know as much as you can; and especially to know what God hath revealed to be believed: and learn to believe God as much as you can: and believe all your teachers, and all other men, as far as they are credible in that case, with such a human belief as fallible men may justly require. And where contenders do consent, suspect them the less. But where they give one another the lie in matters of fact, try both their evidences of credibility before you trust them, and then trust them not beyond that evidence.

But still difference your divine faith and religion from your opinion and human faith; and let men solicit you never so long, take not on you to know or believe till you do; that is, not beyond the evidence. I do but persuade you against presumption and hypocrisy. Shall I say, SUSPEND TILL YOU HAVE TRUE EVIDENCE, and you are safe? Why if you do not, you will know never the more, nor have ever the more divine faith: for I can mean no more than SUSPEND YOUR PRESUMPTIONS, and do not foolishly or hypocritically take on you to know what you do not, or to have a faith which you have not. If you can know truly, do it with fidelity, and be true to the truth, whoever offer it, or whatever it cost you. But suspend your profession or hasty opinions and conceits of what you know not.

Object. But every side almost tells me that I am damned if I do not believe as they do.

Answ. 1. By that you may see that they are all deceived, at least save one, (whichever it be,) while they differ, and yet condemn each other. 2. Thereby they do but give you the greater cause to suspect them, for by this shall all men know Christ's disciples, if they love one another. Right christians are not many masters, as knowing that themselves shall have the greater condemnation else; for in many things we offend all. And the wisdom which hath envy and strife, is not from above, but from beneath, and is earthly, sensual, and devilish, introducing confusion and every evil work, James iii. 1, 15, 16. Christ's disciples judge not, lest they be judged.

3. By this you may see that unless you can be of all men's minds, you must be damned by the censures of many. And if you can bear it from all the sects save one, why not from that one also?

4. But I pray you ask these damning sectaries, is it believing your word, and being of your opinion, that will save me? Or must I also know by scientific evidence that you say true, and that God himself hath said what you say: if he say that believing him and his party (though he call it the church) is enough to save you, you have then less reason to believe him: for unless he can undertake himself to save you, he cannot undertake that believing him shall save you? If he say, God hath promised to save you if you believe me, believe that when he hath proved it to you.

But if it be knowledge and divine faith which he saith must save you, it is not your believing his word or opinion that will help you to that. I would tell such a man, help me to knowledge and faith, by cogent or certifying evidence, and I will learn and thank you with all my heart. But till I have it, it is but mocking myself and you to say that I have it.

Object. But the papists herein differ from all other sects: for they will say, that if I believe the church concerning divine revelations, and take all for divine revelation which the church saith is so, and so believe it, then I have a divine faith.

Answ. 1. And is this to you a certifying evidence that indeed God revealed it, because their church saith so? If their church agree with Greeks, Armenians, Syrians, Coptics, Abassines, protestants, and all other christian churches, then it will be no part of the contest in question; and it is a stronger foundation of the two, to believe it, because *all* say it, than because *they* say it. But if they differ from the rest, know their proof that their church can tell God's mind, and not the rest of the christian world. And that about a third part of the christians in the world have such a promise which all the rest have not. 2. And how doth their church know that it is God's word? Is it by any certifying evidence, or by prophetical inspiration? If by evidence, let it be produced. Is it not revealed to others as well as to them? Must not we have a faith of the same kind as the church hath? If so, we must believe by the same evidence as that church believeth. And what is that? It is not their own words: doth a pope believe himself only? or a council believe themselves only? Or hath God said, You shall be saved if you will believe yourselves, and believe that I have said all that you say I have said? Where is there such a promise? But if pope and council be not saved for believing themselves, how shall I know that I shall be saved for believing them, and that one kind of faith saveth me, and another them?

I ask it of each particular bishop in that council, is he saved for believing himself or the rest? If no man be saved for believing himself, why should another be saved for believing him? And the faith of the council is but the faith of the individual members set together.

Object. But they are saved for believing themselves as consenters, and not singly.

Answ. All consenters know nothing as consenters, but what they know as individuals. And what is the evidence by which they know, and are brought to consent? Must not that evidence convince us also?

Object. But the present church are saved for believing not themselves but the former church.

Answ. Then so must we: it is not the present church then that I must believe by a saving faith: but why then was the last age saved, and so the former? and so on to the first? Is any thing more evident than that all men must be saved for believing God, and that his word must be known to be his word by the same evidence, by one man and another? And that evidence I have proved in several treatises to be another kind of thing than the decree of a pope, and his council.

But if it be not evidence, but prophetical inspiration and revelation, by which the council or church knoweth God's word, I will believe them when by miracles or otherwise they prove themselves to be true prophets; till then I shall take them for fanatics, and hear them as I do the quakers.

Should I here stay to bid you ask them, as before, how you shall be sure that their council was truly general, and more authentic and infallible than the second at Ephesus, or that at Ariminum, or that at Constance and Basil, &c.? And whether the more general dissent of all the other christians from them be not of as great authority as they that are the smaller part? And how you shall be sure of that? And also how but on the word of a priest you can know all that the church hath determined? with abundance such questions, of the meaning of each council, the ambiguity of words, the error of printers, the forgery of publishers, &c. I should help you to see, that saying as a priest saith, is not knowing the thing, nor believing God.

Stop therefore till you have evidence: follow no party as a party in the dark; or if probability incline you more to them than to others, call not this certainty, religion, divine faith. Thus your faith will be faith indeed, and you will escape all that would corrupt and frustrate it. The business is great. God requireth you to refuse no light: but withal he chargeth you to believe no falsehood, nor put darkness for light; much less to father men's lies, or errors, or conceits on God, and to lay your salvation on it, that they are all God's word. How dreadful a thing is this if it prove false! Is it not blaspheming God?[b]

No man in his wits then but a partial designer can look that you should make haste, or go any further than you have assuring or convincing evidence. If you know that any sect doth err, you need no preservative: if you do not, tell them, I am ignorant of this matter, I will learn as fast as I can, not neglecting greater matters; and I will be neither for you, nor against you, further than I can know.

And as to the former objection, of being still infants, I further answer, that as feigned knowledge is no knowledge, so manhood consisteth not in being of many uncertain opinions; no, not so much in knowing many little controverted things, as in getting a clearer, more affecting, powerful, practical knowledge and belief of our christianity, and the great and sure things which we know already; and in love and obedience practising of them. He is the strongest christian who loveth God best, and hath most holiness; and he knoweth God better than any others do.

By this much you may see that the world is full of counterfeit faith, and knowledge, and religion; even fancy and belief of men, and their own opinions, which go under these names. One turneth an anabaptist, and another a separatist, and another an antinomian, and another a Pelagian, and another a papist, when if you try them you shall find that they neither understand what they turn to, nor what they are against: they do but turn to his side, who hath the best advantage to persuade them, either by insinuating into their affections, or by plausible reasonings; they talk for one doctrine, and against another, when they understand neither; much less discern true evidence of their truth. And as for the papists, what wonder is it, when their religion is to believe as the church believeth? And what the church believeth, they know not perhaps but by believing a priest: and then though they know not what the church believeth, some say they are catholics; and others, that this implicit faith is that in the virtue of which all the explicit must proceed. And if God may but be allowed to be equal herein with their church, and so that all should be saved who implicitly believe that all that he saith is true, though they know not what he saith at all, then I think few infidels would perish that believe there is a God.

Reader, I advise thee therefore as thou lovest thy soul, 1. Not to neglect or delay any true knowledge that thou canst attain. 2. But not to be rash and hasty in judging. 3. Nor to take shows and men's opinions, or any thing below a certifying or notifying evidence of truth, to make up thy christian faith and knowledge. 4. And till thou see such certain evidence, suspend, and tell them that solicit thee, that thou understandest not the matter, and that thou art neither for them nor against them; but wilt yield as soon as truth doth certainly appear to thee.

If an anabaptist persuade thee, yield to him as soon as thou art sure that God would not have believers' children now to be infant members of his church, as well as they were before Christ's coming; and that the infants of believing Jews were cut off from their church state; and that there is any way besides baptism appointed by Christ, for the solemn initiating of church members with the rest, which in my "Treatise of Baptism" I have produced.

If thou art solicited to renounce communion with other churches of Christ as unlawful, either because they use the Common Prayer and ceremonies, or because that ministers are faulty, (if tolerable,) or the people undisciplined; before thou venture thy soul upon an uncharitable and dividing principle, make sure first that Christ hath commanded it. Try whether thou art sure that Christ sinned by communicating ordinarily with the Jewish church and synagogues, when the corruption of priests, people, and worship was so much worse than ours? Or whether that be now a sin to us, which (in the general) Christ did then? And whether Paul's compliance, and his precept, (Rom. xiv. and xv.) was an error? and Peter's separation (Gal. ii.) was not rather to be blamed? With much more the like. Are you sure that notwithstanding all this, God would have you avoid communion with the churches that in such forms and orders differ from you?

So if a papist solicit you, yield to him as soon as you are certain that the church is the body or church of the pope, and that none are christians that are not subject to him, and that therefore three or two parts of all the christian world are unchristianed; and that when the Roman emperor made patriarchs in his own dominion only, and there only called general councils, all the world must now take such as the church's heads, and must be their subjects: when you can be sure that all the senses of all the sound men in the world, are by a constant miracle deceived, in taking the consecrated bread and wine to be bread and wine indeed, and that it is none; and that the bread only without the cup must be used, though Christ's command be equal for both: when you are certain, truly certain of these and many other such things, then turn papist. If you do it sooner, you betray your souls by pretending to know and believe God's word, when you do but believe and embody with a faction.

---

[b] Fathering errors on God, and saying that he saith what he never said, and forbad or commanded what he doth not, is the most direct breach of the third commandment. To father lies on God, is the taking of his name in vain.

CHAPTER X.

INFERENCE 4. WHAT IS THE GREAT PLAGUE AND DIVIDER OF THE CHRISTIAN WORLD.

FALSELY PRETENDED KNOWLEDGE and FAITH are the great plague and dividers of the christian world.

I. As to the number of articles, and opinions, and precepts, what abundance of things go with many for certain truth of which no mortal man hath certainty! And abundance which some few rare wits may know, must go for evident certainties to all. It is not only our philosophy books, nor only our philosophical schoolmen's books, which are guilty of this. There is some modesty in their *Videtur's:* and indeed if they would not pretend to certainty, but profess only to write for the sport and exercise of wit, without condemning those that differ from them, a man might fetch many a pleasant vagary, if not in an over-subtle Cajetan, (who so oft feigneth notions and distinctions,) yet in a Scotus, Ockam, Ariminensis, with abundance of their disciples, and in Thomas and many of his learned followers. But their successors can hardly forbear hereticating one another. How many such a wound hath poor Durandus suffered! from many for his doctrine of Concourse; and by others for his pretty device to save the credit of our senses in transubstantiation; (that there is still the matter of bread, but not the form, as being informed by the soul of Christ, as digested bread in us is turned to flesh;) which, saith Bellarmine, is an heresy, but Durandus no heretic, because he was ready to be taught of the church.

But no where do these stinging hornets so swarm as in the councils and the canon law: so that, saith the preface to the Reformatio Legum Ecclesiast. Edward VI. (John Fox,) *In quo ipso jure, neque ullum modum tenet illius impudentia, quin leges legibus; decreta decretis, ac iis insuper decretalia, aliis alia, atque item alia accumulet, nec ullam pene statuit cumulandi finem, donec tandem suis Clementinis, Sixtinis, Intra et Extravagantibus, Constitutionibus Provincialibus et Synodalibus, Paleis, Glossulis, Sententiis, Capitulis, Summariis, Rescriptis, Breviculis, Casibus longis et brevibus, ac infinitis Rhapsodiis adeo orbem confarcinavit, ut Atlas mons quo sustineri cœlum dicitur, huic si imponeretur oneri, vix ferendo sufficeret.* Which made these two kings, Henry VIII. and Edward VI. appoint that compendium of ecclesiastical laws as their own. King Henry first abolishing the pope's laws, (whatever some say to the contrary,) his words being, *Hujus Potestatem huic cum divino munere sublatam esse manifestum est, ut quid superesset, quo non plane fractam illius Vim esse constaret, Leges omnes, decreta atque instituta, quæ ab authore Episcopo Romano profecta sunt Prorsus abroganda censuimus.*

Is it possible that all the clergy and nobles of the Roman kingdom can be so ignorant of their own and other men's ignorance, as to take all the decrees of the huge volumes of their councils for certain truths? Either they were certain in their evidence of truth, before they decreed them, or not: if they were so, 1. How came the debates in the councils about them to be so hard, and so many to be dissenters as in many of them there were. I know where Arians or other heretics make up much of the council, it is no wonder; but are the certainties of faith so uncertain to catholic bishops, that a great part of them know not certain truths, till the majority of votes have told them they are certain? Have the poor dissenting bishops in council nothing of certainty on which their own and all the poor people's faith and salvation must depend, but only this, that they are overvoted? As if the dissenters in the council of Trent should say, We thought beforehand the contrary had been true; but now the Italian bishops being so numerous as to over-vote us, we will lay our own and all men's salvation on it, that we were deceived, though we have no other reason to think so. Oh noble faith and certainty! It is possible one or two or three poor silly prelates may turn the scales and make up a majority, though as learned men as Jansenius, Cusanus, or Gerson were on the other side. And if the Jansenists' Articles were condemned, or Cusanus' antipapal doctrine, lib. de Concordia, or Gerson's for the Supremacy of Councils and de Auferibilitate Papæ, they must presently believe that they were certainly deceived.

But what is become then of the contrary evidence which appeared before to these dissenters? As suppose it were in the council of Basil about the immaculate conception of Mary; or the question whether the authority of the pope or council be greatest, decided there, and at Constance, and whereof at Trent the emperor and the French were of one opinion, and the pope of another: was it evidently true before, which is made false after by a majority of votes?

2. And if all these decreed things were evident truths before the said decrees, why have we not those antecedent evidences presented to us, to convince us?

3. But if they were not evident truths before, what made those prelates conclude them for truths? Did they know them to be such without evidence? This is grosser than a presumptuous man's believing that he shall be saved because he believeth it; or their doctrine that teach men to believe the thing is true, (that Christ died for them,) that thereby they may make it true; as if the object must come after the act. For then these prelates do decree that to be true, which before was false, (for *ex natura rei*, one party had evidence of its falsehood,) that so they might make it true, by decreeing that it is so.

A man might lawfully have believed his own and other men's senses, that bread is bread, till the council at Lateran sub Innoc. 3. decreed transubstantiation. And oh what a change did that council make! All Christ's miracles were not comparable to it, if its decrees be true. From that day to this, we must renounce sense, and yet believe; we must believe that by constant miracles all christians' senses are deceived: and so that this is the difference between christians, infidels, and heathens, that our religion deceiveth all men's senses, (even heathens' and all, if they see our sacrament,) and their religion deceiveth no man's senses, saith the grave author of the History of the Trent Council, (Ed. Engl. p. 474,) *a better mystery was never found, than to use religion to make men insensible.*

And what is the omnipotent power that doth this? Such a convention as that of Trent, while with our Worcester Pate, and Olaus Magnus, they made up a great while two-and-forty things called bishops; and after such a pack of beardless boys and ignorant fellows, created by and enslaved to the pope, as Dudithius Quinqueccles. one of the council, describeth to the emperor; and which Bishop Jewel, in his letter to Sign. Scipio, saith, he took for no council, called by no just authority, &c. where were neither the patriarchs of Constantinople, Alexandria, or Antioch, nor Abassines, nor Grecians, Armenians, Persians, Egyptians, Moors, Syrians, Indians, nor Muscovites, nor protestants, p. 133, 144. For, saith he after, p. 489, "Now-a-days (merciful God!) the intent or scope of councils is not to discover truth, or to confute falsehood: for these latter ages, this hath been the only endeavour of the popes, to establish the Roman tyranny; to set wars on foot, to set christian princes together by the ears, to raise money —— to be cast into some few bellies for gluttony and lust; and this hath been the only cause or course of councils for some ages last past." So he.

And can the vote of a few such fellows oblige all the world to renounce all their senses, who were never obliged to it before?

And all this consisteth in PRETENDED FAITH and KNOWLEDGE, when men must take on them to know what they do not know, and make decrees and canons, and doctrines suited to their conjectures, or rather to their carnal interests, and then most injuriously father them on God, on Christ, and the apostles.

II. And as the number of forgeries and inventions detecteth this public plague, so doth the number of persons that are guilty of it. How many such superfluities the Abassines,[a] (in their oft baptizings, and other trifles,) and the Armenians, Syrians, Georgians, Jacobites, Maronites, the Russians, &c. are guilty of, the describers of their rights and religion tell us. Some would have the state of the church in Gregory I.'s days to be the model of our Reformation: (that pope whom authors usually call the last of the good ones, and the first of the bad ones:) but is there either necessity or certainty in all the superfluities which the churches then had, and which that great prelate's writings themselves contain? Or were there not abundance of such things then used as things indifferent, (of which see Socrates and Sozomen in the chapters of Easter,) and must all their indifferents be now made necessary to the church's concord and communion? and all their uncertainties become certainties to us? Some will have the present Greek church to be the standard: but alas, poor men, how many of these uncertainties, crudities, and superfluities are cherished among them by the unavoidable ignorance which is caused by their oppressions! To say no more of Rome, oh that the reformed churches themselves had been more innocent! But how few of them unite on the terms of simple christianity and certainties! Had not Luther, after all his zeal for reformation, retained some of this leaven, he could better have endured the dissent of Zuinglius, Carolostadius, and Oecolampadius about the sacrament. And if his followers had not kept up the same superfluities, they had never so torn the churches by their animosities, nor resisted and wearied peaceable Melancthon, nor frustrated so many conventions and treaties for concord, as they have done. Bucer had not been so censured: agreement had not been made so impossible: all Dury's travels had not been so uneffectual. Schlusselbergius had not found so many heresies to fill up his catalogue with; nor Calovius so much matter for his virulent pen; nor so many equalled Calvinism with Turcism. Nor had Calixtus had such scornful satires written against him; nor the great peace-makers, Lud. Crocius, Bergh, Martinius, Camero, Amyraldus, Testardus, Capellus, Placæus, Davenant, Ward, Hall, and now Le Blanc, had so little acceptance and success. Had it not been for this spreading plague, (the overvaluing of our own understandings, and the accounting our crude conceits for certainties,) all these church wars had been prevented or soon ended; all those excellent endeavours for peace had been more successful, and we had all been one.

Had it not been for this neither Arminians nor anti-Arminians had ever so bitterly contended, nor so sharply censured one another, nor written so many confident condemning volumes against each other, which in wise men's eyes do more condemn the authors; and SELF-CONCEIT, OR PRETENDED KNOWLEDGE, should have been the title of them all. How far I am able to prove that almost all their bitter and zealous contentions are about uncertainties and words, the reader may perceive in my preface to the Grotian religion, and if God will, I shall fuller manifest to the world.[b] The synod of Dort had not had so great a work of it, nor the Breme and Britain divines so difficult a task, to bring and hold them to that moderation of expressions which very laudably they have done: one of the noblest successful attempts for peace, though little noted, which these ages have made.

In a word, almost all the contentions of divines, the sects and factions, the unreconciled feuds, the differences in religion, which have been the harvest of the devil and his emissaries in the world, have come from pretended knowledge, and taking uncertainties for certain truths.

I will not meddle with the particular impositions of princes and prelates; not so much as with the German Interim; nor the oaths which in some places they take to their synodical decrees: much less will I meddle at all with any impositions, oaths, subscriptions, declarations, or usages of the kingdom where I live. As the law forbiddeth me to contradict them, so I do not at all here examine or touch them, but wholly pass them by; which I tell the reader once for all, that he may know how to interpret all that I say. Nor is it the error of rulers that I primarily detect, but of human corrupted nature, and all sorts of men: though where such an error prevaileth, alas, it is of far sadder consequence in a public person, a magistrate, or a pastor, that presumeth to the hurt of public societies, than of a private man, who erreth almost to himself alone.

I profess to thee, reader, that (next to God's so much deserting so great a part of this world) there is nothing under the sun, of all the affairs of mankind, that hath so taken up my thoughts with mixtures of indignation, wonder, pity, and solicitude for a cure, as this one vice; A PROUD OR UNHUMBLED UNDERSTANDING, by which men live in PRETENDED KNOWLEDGE and FAITH, to the deceit of themselves and others, the bitter censuring and persecuting of dissenters, yea of their modest suspending brethren, tear churches and kingdoms, and will give no peace nor hopes of peace to themselves, their neighbours, or the world! Lord! is there no remedy, no hope from thee, though there is none from man?

1. Among divines themselves, that should not only have knowledge enough to know their own ignorance, but to guide the people of God into the ways of truth, and love, and peace, oh how lamentably doth this vice prevail! To avoid all offence, I will not here at all touch on the case of any that are supposed to have a hand in any of the sufferings

[a] And yet saith Zaga-Zabo in Damnian a Goes, p. 226. Nec Patriarcha nec episcopi nostri, per se, nec in conciliis putant aut opinantur ullas leges se condere posse, quibus ad mortale peccatum obligari quis posset. And p. 231. Indignum est peregrinos christianos tam acriter et hostiliter reprehendi ut ego de hac re (de delectu ciborum) et de aliis, quæ minime ad fidem veram spectabant reprehensus fui; sed multo consultius, fuerit, hujusmodi christianos homines sive Græcos, sive Armenos, sive Æthiopes; sive ex quavis Septem Christianarum ecclesiarum in charitate et Christi amplexibus sustinere, et eos sine contumeliis permittere, inter alios fratres christianos vivere ac versari; quoniam omnes filii baptismi sumus, et de vera fide unanimitur sentimus. Nec est causa cur tam acritur de ceremoniis disceptetur nisi ut unusquisque suas observet, sine odio et infectatione aliorum, nec commerciis ecclesiæ ob id excludendus est, &c. Learn of a ceremonious Abassine.

[b] Since done in "Catholic Theology."

of me and others of my mind; or of any that in points of conformity differ from me: remember that I meddle not with them at all. But even those that do no way differ among themselves as sect and sect, or at least, that all pretend to principles of forbearance, gentleness, and peace, yet are woefully sick of this disease.

And yet, that I may wrong none, I will premise this public declaration to the world, that in the country where I lived, God in great mercy cast my lot among a company of so humble, peaceable, faithful ministers and people, as free from this vice as any that ever I knew in the world; who, as they kept up full concord among themselves, without the least disagreement that I remember, and kept out sects and heresies from the people; so their converse was the joy of my life, and the remembrance of it will be sweet to me while I live; and especially the great success of our labours, and the quiet and concord of our several flocks, which was promoted by the pastors' humility and concord. Though we kept up constant disputations, none of them ever turned to spleen, or displeasure, or discord among us.

And I add, in thankfulness to God, that I am now acquainted with many ministers in and about London, of greatest note, and labour, and patience, and success, who are of the same spirit, humble and peaceable, and no confident troublers of the churches with their censoriousness, and high esteem of their own opinions: who trade only in the simple truths of christianity, and love a christian as a christian, and join not with backbiters nor factious, self-conceited men, but study only to win souls to Christ, and to live according to the doctrine which they preach: and both the former and these, have these ten[c] years since they were ejected, continued their humility and peaceableness, fearing God and honouring the king.

And I further add, that those private christians with whom I most converse, are many of them of the same strain, suspecting their own understandings, and speaking evil of no man so forwardly as of themselves.

So that in these ministers and people of my most intimate acquaintance, experience convinceth me, that this grand disease of corrupted nature is curable; and that God hath a people in the world, that have learned of Christ to be meek and lowly, who have the wisdom from above, which is first pure, and then peaceable, gentle, easy to be entreated, full of mercy and good fruits, (Jam. iii. 17,) and the fruit of mercy is sown in peace of these peacemakers. I see in them a true conformity to Christ, and a grand difference between them and the furious, fiery pretenders to more wisdom; and the two sorts of wise men and wisdom excellently described by James, chap. iii. I have seen in two sorts of religious people among us, most lively exemplified before our eyes. God hath a people that truly honour him in the world. But oh that they were more! And oh that they were more perfect! Alas! what a number are there that are otherwise!

Even among divines this plague is most pernicious, as being of most public influence. Take him that never had a natural acuteness of wit, nor is capable of judging of difficult points; if he be but of long standing, and grey hairs, and can preach well to the people, and have studied long; he is not only confident of his fitness to judge of that which he never understood, but his reputation of wisdom must be kept up among the people by his supercilious talking against what he understandeth not.[d] Yea, if he be one that never macerated his flesh with the difficult and long studies of the matter, without which hard points will never be well digested and distinctly understood; yet, if he be a doctor, and have lived long in a reputation for wisdom, his ignorant, flashy conjectures, and hasty, superficial apprehensions, must needs go for the more excellent knowledge. And if you put him to make good any of his contradictions to the truth, his magisterial contempt, or his uncivil wrath, and unmannerly interruptions of you in your talk, must go for reason: and if he cannot resist the strength of your evidence, he cannot bear the hearing of it; but like a scold, rather than a scholar, taketh your words out of your mouth before you come to the end; as if he said, Hold your tongue, and hear me who am wiser; I came to teach, and not to hear. If you tell him how uncivil it is, not patiently to hear you to the end, he thinks you wrong him, and are too bold to pretend to a liberty to speak without interruption: or he will tell you that you are too long; he cannot remember all at once. If you reply that the sense of the fore part of a speech usually depends much on the latter part, and he cannot have your sense till he have all; and that he must not answer before he understandeth you; and that if his memory fail, he should take notes; and that to have uninterrupted turns of speaking, is necessary in the order of all sober conferences, without which they will be but noise and strife: he will let you know that he came not to hear, or keep any laws of order or civility, but to have a combat with you for the reputation of wisdom or orthodoxness; and what he wants in reason and evidence, he will make up in ignorant confidence and reviling, and call you by some ill name or other, that shall go for a confutation.

But yet this is not the usual way: it is too great a hazard to the reputation of their wisdom, to cast it on a dispute. The common way is, never to speak to the person himself; but if any one cross their conceits, or become the object of their envy, they backbite him among those that reverence their wisdom; and when they are sure that he is far enough out of hearing, they tell their credulous followers, O such a man holdeth unsound or dangerous opinions! Take heed how you hear him or read his writings; this or that heresy they savour of. When the poor man knoweth not what he talketh of. And if any one have the wit to say to him, Sir, he is neither so sottish nor so proud as to be uncapable of instruction; if you are so much wiser than he, why do you not teach him? he will excuse his omission and commission together with a further calumny, and say, These erroneous persons will hear no reason: it is in vain. If he be asked, Sir, did you ever try? it is like he must confess that he did not, unless some magisterial rebuke once went for evidence of truth. If the hearers (which is rare) have so much christian wit and honesty, as to say, Sir, ministers above all men must be no backbiters, nor unjust: you know it is unlawful for us to judge another man, till we hear him speak for himself. If you would have us know whether he or you be in the right, let us hear you both together: his answer would be like Cardinal Turnon at the conference at Poisie, and as the papists' ordinarily is, It is dangerous letting heretics speak to the people, and it agreeth not with our zeal for God, to hear such odious things uttered against the truth.

In a word, there are more that have the spirit of a pope in the world than one, even among them that cry out against popery; and that would fain be

[c] Now it is above twenty-two years that they have been ejected, 1684.

[d] Yea, now it is also young, ignorant novices that are sick of the same feverish temerity.

taken for the dictators of the world, whom none must dissent from, much less contradict. And there are more idolaters than heathens, who would have their ignorant understandings to be instead of God, the uncontrolled director of all about them.

But if these men have not any confidence in their self-sufficiency, if they can but embody in a society of their minds, or gather into a synod, he must needs go for a proud and arrogant schismatic at least, that will set any reason and evidence of truth against their magisterial ignorance, when it is the major vote.

The very truth is, the great Benefactor of the world hath not been pleased to dispense his benefits equally, but with marvellous disparity. As he is the God of nature, he hath been pleased to give a natural capacity for judiciousness and acuteness in difficult speculations but to few. And as he is the Lord of all, he hath not given men equal education, nor advantages for such extraordinary knowledge; nor have all that have leisure and capacity, self-denial and patience enough for so long and difficult studies. But the devil and ourselves have given to all men pride enough, to desire to be thought to be wiser and better than we are; and he that cannot be equal with the wisest and best, would be thought to be so: and while all men must needs seem wise, while few are so indeed, you may easily see what must thence follow.

2. And it is not divines only, but all ranks of people, who are sick of this disease. The most unlearned, ignorant people, the silliest women, if they will not for shame say that they are wiser than their teachers in the general, yet when it cometh to particular cases, they take themselves to be always in the right: and oh how confident are they of it! And who more peremptory and bold in their judgments, than those that least know what they say? It is hard to meet with a person above eighteen or twenty years of age, that is not notably tainted with this malady.

And it is not only these great mischiefs in matters of religion which spring from self-conceitedness; but even in our common converse, it is the cause of disorder, ruin, and destruction: for it is the common vice of blinded nature, and it is rare to meet with one that is not notably guilty of it, when they are past the state of professed learners.

1. It is ordinary for self-conceited persons to ruin their own estates, and healths, and lives. When they are rashly making ill bargains, or undertaking things which they understand not, they rush on till they find their error too late; and their poverty, prisons, or ruined families, must declare their sin; for they have not humility enough to seek counsel in time, nor to take it when it is offered them. What great numbers have I heard begging relief from others, under the confession of this sin! And far more, even the most of men and women, overthrow their health, and lose their lives by it. Experience doth not suffice to teach them what is hurtful to their bodies; and as they know not, so you cannot convince them that they know not. Most persons by the excess in quantity of food, do suffocate nature, and lay the foundation of future maladies; and most of the diseases that kill men untimely, are but the effects of some former gluttony or excess. But as long as they feel not any present hurt, no man can persuade them but their fulness is for their health, as well as for their pleasure. They will laugh, perhaps, at those that tell them what they do, and what disease they are preparing for. Let physicians, if they be so honest, tell them, It is the perfection of the nutritive juices, the blood and nervous oil, which are the causes of health in man. Perfect concoction causeth that perfection. Nature cannot perfectly concoct too much, or that which is of too hard digestion. While you feel no harm, your blood groweth dispirited, and being but half concocted, and half blood, doth perform its office accordingly by the halves; till crudities are heaped up, and obstructions fixed, and a dunghill of excrements, or the dispirited humours, are ready to take in any disease, which a small occasion offereth; either agues, fevers, coughs, consumptions, pleurisies, dropsies, colics and windiness, headachs, convulsions, &c.; or till the inflammations or other tumours of the inward parts, or the torment of the stone in the reins or bladder, do sharply tell men what they have been doing. A clean body and perfect concoction, which are procured by temperance and bodily labours, which suscitate the spirits, and purify the blood, are the proper means which God in the course of nature hath appointed, for a long and healthful life.

This is all true, and the reason is evident; and yet this talk will be but despised and derided by the most; and they will say, I have so long eaten what I loved, and lived by no such rules as these, and I have found no harm by it. Yea, if excess have brought diseases on them, if abstinence do but make them more to feel them, they will rather impute their illness to the remedy, than to the proper cause: and so they do about the quality as well as the quantity. Self-conceitedness maketh men uncurable. Many a one have I known that daily lived in that fulness which I saw would shortly quench the vital spirits; and fain I would have saved their lives, but I was not able to make them willing. Had I seen another assault them, I could have done somewhat for them; but when I foresaw their death, I could not save them from themselves. They still said, they found their measures of eating and drinking between meals refresh them, and they were the worse if they forbore it; and they would not believe me against both appetite, reason, and experience. And thus have I seen abundance of my acquaintance wilfully hasten to the grave; and all long of an unhumbled, self-conceited understanding, which would not be brought to suspect itself, and know its error.

2. And oh how often have I seen the dearest friends thus kill their friends; even mothers kill their dearest children, and too oft their husbands, kindred, servants, and neighbours, by their self-conceit, and confidence in their ignorance and error! Alas, what abundance empty their own houses, gratify covetous landlords, and set their lands by lives, and bring their dearest relations to untimely ends, and a wise man knoweth not how to hinder them! How oft and oft have I heard ignorant women confidently persuade even their own children to eat as long as they have an appetite, and so they have vitiated their blood and humours in their childhood, that their lives have been either soon ended, or ever after miserable by diseases! How oft have I heard them persuade sick or weak, diseased persons, to eat, eat, eat, and take what they have a mind to, when, unless they would poison them, or cut their throats, they would scarce more certainly despatch them! How oft have these good women been persuading myself, that eating and drinking more would make me better, and that it is abstinence that causeth all my illness (when excess in my childhood caused it): as if every wise woman that doth but know me knew better what is good for me than myself, after threescore years' experience, or than all the physicians in the city! And had I obeyed them, how many years ago had I been dead!

How ordinary is it for such self-conceited women to obtrude their skill and medicines on their sick neighbours, with the greatest confidence, when they know not what they do! yea, upon their husbands and their children! One can scarce come about sick persons, but one woman or other is persuading them to take that or do that which is like to kill them. Many and many, when they have brought their children to the grave, have nothing to say, but I thought this or that had been best for them.

But you will say, They do it in love; they mean no harm. I answer, so false teachers deceive souls in love. But are you content yourselves to be killed by love? If I must be killed, I had rather an enemy did it than a friend; I would not have such have the guilt or grief. Love will not save men's lives, if you give them that which tends to kill them.

But you will say, We can be no wiser than we are: if we do the best we can, what can we do more?

I answer, I would have you not think yourselves wiser than you are: I would write over this word five hundred times, if that would cure you. About matters of diet, and medicines, and health, this is it that I would have you do to save you from killing yourselves and your relations: 1. Pretend not to know upon the report of such as yourselves, or in matters that are difficult and beyond your skill; or where you have not had long consideration and experience. Meddle with no medicining, but what in common, easy cases, the common judgment of physicians, and common experience, have taught you.

2. If you have not money to pay physicians and apothecaries, tell them so, and desire them to give you their counsel freely, and take not on you to know more than they that have studied and practised it all the riper part of their lives.

3. Suspect your understandings, and consider how much there may be unknown to you, in the secrecy and variety of diseases, difference of temperatures, and the like, which may make that hurtful which you conceit is good. Therefore do nothing rashly, and in self-conceited confidence, but upon the best advice ask the physician whether your medicines and rules are safe.

4. And be sure that you do rather too little than too much. What abundance are there, especially in the small-pox and fevers, that would have escaped, if women (yea, and physicians) would have let them alone, that die because that nature had not leave to cure them, being disturbed by mistaken usages or medicines. Diseases are so various and secret, and remedies so uncertain, that the wisest man alive, that hath studied and practised it almost all his riper days, (were it a hundred years,) must confess that physic is a hard, a dark, uncertain work, and ordinary cases, much more extraordinary, have somewhat in them which doth surpass his skill: and how then come so many medicining women to know more than they?

But you will say, We see that many miscarry by physicians, and they speed worst that use them most.

I answer, But would they not yet speed worse, if they used you as much? If they are too ignorant, how came you to be wiser? If you are, teach them your skill.

But I must add, that even physicians' guilt of the sin which I am reproving, doth cost many hundred persons their lives, as well as yours. Even too many physicians, who have need of many days' inquiry and observations, truly to discover a disease, do kill men by rash and hasty judging. (I talk not of the cheating sort, that take on them to know all by the urine alone, but of honester and wiser men.) It is most certain that old Celsus saith, that a physician is not able faithfully to do his office, for very many patients: a few will take up all his time. But they that gape most after money, must venture upon a short sight, and a few words, and presently resolve before they know, and write down their directions while they are ignorant of one half; which if they knew, would change their counsels! And such is man's body and its diseases, that the oversight and ignorance of one thing among twenty, is like enough to be the patient's death. And how wise, expedient, and vigilant must he be, that will commit no such killing oversight!

And as too many medicine a man whom they know not, and an unknown disease, for want of just deliberation; so too many venture upon uncertain and untried medicines, or rashly give that to one in another case, which hath profited others. In a word, even rash physicians have cause to fear lest by prefidence and hasty judging, more should die by their mistakes than do by murderers, that I say not by soldiers in the world; and lest their dearest friends should speed worse by them than their greatest enemies. For as seamen and soldiers do boldly follow the trade, when they find that in several voyages and battles they have escaped; but yet most or very many of them are drowned or killed at the last: so he that is tampering over-much with medicines, may escape well and boast of the success awhile; but at last one bloodletting, one vomit, one purge or other medicine may miscarry by a small mistake or accident, and he is gone! And there are some persons so civil, that if a rash or unexperienced physician be their kinsman, friend, or neighbour, they will not go to an abler man, lest they be accounted unfriendly, and disoblige him; and if such escape long with their lives, they may thank God's mercy, and not their own wisdom. Soldiers kill enemies, and unskilful, rash physicians kill their friends!

But you will say, They do their best, and they can do no more. I answer as before, 1. Let them not think that they know what they do not know; but sufficiently suspect their own understandings. 2. Let them not go beyond their knowledge. How little of our kind of physic did the old physicians (Hippocrates, Galen, Celsus, &c.) give? Do not too much. 3. Venture not rashly without full search, deliberation, counsel, and experience. Oh how many die by hasty judging, and rash mistakes! Physicians must pardon my free speaking, or endure it; for I conceive it necessary. It hath not been the least part of the calamity of my life, to see my friends and other worthy persons killed by the ignorance or hastiness of physicians. I greatly reverence and honour those few, that are men of clear, searching, judicious heads; of great reading, especially of other men's experiences; of great and long experience of their own; of present sagacity and ready memory to use their own experiments; of conscience and cautelousness to suspect, and know before they hastily judge and practise. I would I could say that such are not too few. But I must say to the people, as you love your lives take heed to all the rest: a highway robber you may avoid or resist with greater probability of safety, than such men. How few are they that are killed by thieves or in duels, in comparison of those that are killed by physicians; especially confident young men that account themselves wits, and think they may hit on such philosophical principles as will better secure both their practice and reputation than old physicians' doctrine and experience could do! Confident young men of unhumbled understandings, presently trust their undigested thoughts, and rashly use their poor, short experiments, and trust to their new conceptions of the reasons of all operations; and then they take all others for mere empyrics in comparison of them: and when all is done, their pretended reason, for want of full experience and judgment to improve it, doth but enable them to talk and boast, and not to heal; and when they have killed men, they can justify it, and prove that they did it rationally, or rather that it was something else, and not their error, that was the cause. They are wits, and men of rare inventions; and therefore are not such fools as to confess the fact. How oft have I seen men of great worth, such as few in an age arise to, who having a high esteem of an injudicious, unexperienced physician, have sealed their erroneous kindness with their blood! How oft have I seen worthy persons destroyed by a pernicious medicine, clear contrary to what the nature of the disease required, who without a physician might have done well! Such sorrows just now upon me, make me the more plain and copious in the case. And yet, alas, I see no hope of amendment probable! For, 1. Many hundred ministers being forbidden to preach the gospel, and cast out of all their livelihood, for not promising, asserting, swearing, and doing all that is required of them; many of these think that necessity alloweth them to turn physicians, which they venture on upon seven years' study; when seven, and seven, and seven, is not enough, though advantaged by the help of other men's experiments. 2. And others rush on practice in their youth, partly because they have not yet knowledge enough to discern uncertainties and difficulties in the art, or to see what is further necessary to be known; and partly, because they think that seeing skill must be got by experience, use must help them to that experience; and all men must have a beginning. 3. And when they do their best, they say, God requireth no more. 4. And they hope if they kill one, they cure many. But oh that they had the sobriety to consider, 1. That the physician is but one man; and will his maintenance or livelihood excuse him for killing many? 2. That even one man's life is more precious that one man's maintenance, or fuller supply. Is it not honester to beg your bread? 3. That killing men by virtue of your trade without danger to you, doth but hinder your repentance, but not so much extenuate your sin as many think: which is aggravated in that you kill your friends that trust you, and not enemies that oppose you or avoid you. 4. Your experience must not be got by killing men, but by accompanying experienced physicians till you are fit to practise: and if you cannot stay so long for want of maintenance, beg rather than kill men, or betake you to some other trade.

But if you be too proud or confident to take such counsel, I still advise all that love their lives, that they choose not a physician under forty years old at least, and if it may be, not under sixty, unless it be for some little disease or remedy, which hath no danger, and where they can do no harm if they do no good: old men may be ignorant, but young men must needs be so for want of experience, though some few rare persons are sooner ripe than others.

And whereas they say that they cure more than they kill; I wish that I had reason to believe them. I suppose that if more of their patients did not live than die, they would soon lose their practice; but it is like the far greatest part of those that live, would have lived without them, and perhaps have been sooner and easier cured, if nature had not by them been disturbed.

And what calling is there in which hasty judging and conceits of more knowledge than men have, doth not make great confusion and disappointment? If a fool that rageth and is confident be a pilot, woe to the poor seamen and passengers in the ship! If such a one be a commander in an army, his own and other men's blood or captivity must cure his confidence and stay his rage; for such will learn at no cheaper a rate. How often hear we such workmen, carpenters, masons, &c. raging confident that their way is right, and their work well done, till the ruin of it confute and shame them!

If this disease take hold of governors, who will not stay to hear all parties, and know the truth, but take up reports on trust, from those that please or flatter them, or judge presently before impartial trial, and hearing all, woe to the land that is so governed! The wisest and the best man must have due information and time, patience and consideration, to receive it, or else he may do as David between Mephibosheth and Ziba, and cannot be just.

What an odious thing is a partial, blind, rash, hasty, and impatient judge, that cannot hear, think, and know before he judgeth! Such the old christians had to do with among their persecutors, who knew not what they held, or what they were, and yet could judge them, and cruelly execute them. And such were Tacitus and other old historians, that from common prejudice spake words of contempt or reproach of them. The christians were glad when they had a Trajan, an Antonine, an Alexander Severus, &c. to speak to, that had reason and sobriety to hear their cause. Among the papists, the old reformers and martyrs took him for a very commendable judge or magistrate, that would but allow them a patient hearing, and give them leave to speak for themselves. Truth and godliness have so much evidence, and such a testimony for themselves in the conscience of mankind, as that the devil could never get them so odiously thought of, and so hardly used in the world, but only by keeping them unknown, which is much by expelling and silencing their defenders, (who speed well sometimes if an Obadiah hide them by fifties in a cave,) and by tempting their judges to hear but some superficial narrative of their cause, and to have but a glimpse of the outside as *in transitu*, and to see only the back parts of it, yea but the clothing; which is commonly such as are made by its enemies: good men and causes are too oft brought to them, and set out by them, as Christ with his scarlet robe, his reed and crown of thorns; and then they say, "Behold the man!" and when they have cried out, "Blasphemy, and an enemy to Cæsar!" they write over his cross in scorn, "The King of the Jews." Cain had not patience to hear his own brother, and weigh the case; no, not after that God had admonished him: but he must first hate and murder, and afterwards consider why, when it is too late. Judas must know his Master's innocency, and what he had done, in despair to hang himself. And so wise Ahithophel cometh to his end. If David would have pondered his usage of Uriah as much in time as he did when Nathan had awakened his reason, oh what had he prevented! If Paul had weighed before the case of christians, as he did when Christ did stop his rage, he had not incurred the guilt of persecution, and the martyrs' blood: but he tells us that he was exceedingly mad against them: and it is madness indeed to venture on cruelty and persecution, and not stay first to understand the cause, and consider why, and what is like to be the end.

How ordinary in the world are the excellentest men on earth, for wisdom and holiness, such as Ignatius, Cyprian, and the rest of the ancient martyrs, and such as Athanasius, Chrysostom, &c. reviled and used as if they were the basest rogues on earth, laid in gaols, banished, silenced, murdered; and all this by men that know not what they are, and have no true understanding of their cause! Men of whom the world was not worthy, wandered up and down in dens and caves, and suffered joyfully the spoiling of their goods, yea, and death itself, (Heb. xi.) from men that judged before they knew! Many a great man and judge that hath condemned Christ's ministers as heretics, false teachers, unworthy to preach the gospel, have been such as understand not their baptism, creed, or catechism, and have need of many years' teaching to make them know truly but those principles that every child should know. There needs no great learning, wisdom, sobriety, or honesty, to teach them to cry out, You are a rogue, a seducer, a heretic, a schismatic, disobedient, seditious; or, Away with such a fellow from the earth, it is not fit that he should live, Acts xxii. 22; xxi. 26; or, Away with him, crucify him, give us Barabbas; or to say, We have found this man a pestilent fellow, a mover of sedition, a leader of a sect, that teacheth contrary to the decrees of Cæsar, &c. But patience, till the cause were fully tried, and all things heard and equally weighed, would prevent most of this.

I know that ignorance and weakness of judgment is the common calamity of mankind; and there is no hope of curing us by unity in high degrees of knowledge. And though teachers are and must be a great stay to ignorant learners, yet, alas, how can they tell which are the wisest teachers, and whom to choose? When all pretend to wisdom, and no man can judge of that which he neither hath nor knoweth; and even the Roman sect, who pretend most to infallibility, have so exceeded all men in their error, as to make it a part of religion, necessary to our possessions, communion, dominion, and salvation, to maintain the falsehood of God's natural revelations to the senses of all sound men in the world. How shall one that would learn philosophy know in this age, what sect to follow, or what guide to choose? Hence is our calamity; and the remedy will be but imperfect till the time of perfection come.

But yet we are not remediless. 1. If men would but well lay in, hold fast, love, and faithfully improve the few necessary essential principles. 2. If they would make them a rule in trying what is built upon them; and receive nothing that certainly contradicteth them. 3. If they would stay, think, and try, till their thoughts are well digested, and all is heard, before they take in doubtful things. 4. If they will carry themselves as humble learners to those whose wisdom is conspicuous by its proper light, especially the concordant pastors of the churches. 5. And if they will not quarrel with truth for every difficulty which they understand not, but humbly, as learners, suspect their own wit, till their teachers have helped them in a leisurely and faithful trial: by such means the mischief of error and rashness might be much avoided.

In common matters, necessity and undeniable experience doth somewhat rebuke and restrain this vice. If children should set their wits against their parents, or scholars presently dispute with their masters, nature and the rod would rebuke their pride and folly. If they that never used a trade, should presently take themselves to be as wise as the longest practisers, who would be apprentices? And if an unskilful musician, painter, poet, or other such like, shall be confident that he is as good at his work as any, standers-by will not easily cherish his folly, as being not blinded by his self-love. A good workman shall have most praise and practice. Buyers will convince the ignorant boasters, by forsaking such men's shops: as it is with self-conceited, ignorant writers, who are restrained by the people, who will not buy and read their books. And usually good and bad judges, magistrates, lawyers, soldiers, pilots, artificers, are discerned by most that are capable of judging; because, 1. These are matters where the common sense and experience of mankind doth render them somewhat capable of judging, and save them from deceit. 2. And here is not usually such deep and long plots and endeavours to deceive, as in matters of speculation, and especially religion and policy, there is. And the devil is not so concerned and industrious to deceive men in matters of so low importance. 4. And if one be deceived, many are ready to rectify him. 5. And men's interest here is better understood in bodily matters, and they are not so willing to be deceived. A poor man can easily discern between a charitable man and an uncharitable; between a merciful and oppressing landlord. We discern between diligent and slothful servants; but in matters that are above our reach, which we must take on trust, and know not whom to trust, the difficulty is greater; where the errors and haste of either party will breed mischief, but much more of both. If the physician, or other undertaker, be confident in his error, and precipitant, he will impose ruin on men's health, as I have said: and if the patient be self-conceited and rash in his choice, he is like to suffer for it; but when both physician and patient are so, what hope of escape? And especially when through the great imperfection of men's understanding, not one of a multitude is clear and skilful in things that are beyond the reach of sense: and if one man, after great experience, come to be wiser than the rest, the hearer knoweth it not, and he must cast out his notions among as many assailing warriors, as there are ignorant, self-conceited hearers present, and that is usually as there are persons. And when every one hath poured out his confidence against it, and perhaps reproached the author as erroneous, because he will know more than they, and will not reverence their known mistakes; alas! how shall the person that we would instruct (be it for health or soul) be able to know which of all these to trust as wisest?

But the saddest work is that forementioned, in churches, kingdoms, families, and souls. I must expect that opening the crime will exasperate the guilty: but what remedy? 1. Should I largely open what work this maketh in families, I have too much matter for the complaint. If the wife differ from the husband, she seemeth always in the right; if the servant differ from the master, and the child from the parent, if a little past infancy, they are always in the right: what is the contention in families, and in all the world, but who shall have his way and will? If they are of several parties in religion, or if any be against religion itself; if they be foolish, erroneous, or live in any sin, that can without utter impudence be defended, still they are to make it good: and except children at school, or others that professedly go to be taught, whom can we meet with so ignorant or mistaken, that will not still think, when even superiors differ from them and reprove them, that they are in the right?

2. And what mischiefs doth it cause in churches! When the papal tyrannical part are so confident that they are in the right, that when they silence preachers, and imprison and burn christians, they think it not their duty so much as to hear what they have to say for themselves. Or if they hear a few words, they have not the patience to hear all, or impartially to try the cause: but they are so full of themselves and over-wise, that it must seem without any more ado a crime to dissent from them, or contradict them. And thus proud self-conceitedness smiteth the shepherds, scattereth the flocks, and will allow the church of Christ no unity or peace. And the popular crowd are usually or oft as self-conceited

in their way; and if they never so unreasonably oppose their teachers, how hard is it to make them know or once suspect that they are mistaken! Oh what mutinies in Christ's armies, what schisms, what confusions, what scandals, what persecutions in the church, what false accusations, what groundless censures, do proud, self-conceited understandings cause!

But scarce any where is it more lamentably seen than among injudicious, unexperienced ministers! What work is made in the christian world, by sect against sect, and party against party, in cases of controversy, by most men's bold and confident judging of what they never truly studied, tried, or understood! Papists against protestants, protestants against papists, Lutherans (or Arminians) and Calvinists, &c. usually charge one another by bare hearsay, or by a few sentences or scraps collected out of their writings by their adversaries; contrary to the very scope of the whole discourse or context. And men cannot have leisure to peruse the books, and to know before they judge. And then they think that seeing their reverend doctors have so reported their adversaries before them, it is arrogance or injury to think that they knew not what they said, or else belied them. And on such supposition the false judging doth go on. Of all the pulpits that oft trouble the people with invectives against this side or that, especially in the controversies of predestination, grace, and free-will, how few do we hear that know what they talk against!

Yea, those young or unstudied men, who might easily be conscious how little they know, are ready to oppose and contemn the most ancient studied divines; when if ever they would be wise men, they should continue scholars to such, even while they are teachers of the people.

I will not presume to open the calamities of the world, for want of rulers truly knowing their subjects' case, but judging hastily by the reports of adversaries: but that rebellions ordinarily hence arise I may boldly say; when subjects, that know not the reasons of their rulers' actions, are so over-wise as to make themselves judges of that which concerneth them not: and how few be they that think not themselves wiser than all their guides and governors!

And lastly, by this sin it is that the wisdom of the wisest is as lost to the world: for let a man know never so much more than others, after the longest, hardest studies, the self-conceitedness of the ignorant riseth up against it, or maketh them uncapable of receiving it, so that he can do little good to others.

I conclude again, that this is the plague and misery of mankind, and the cause of all sin, and shame, and ruin,—that ignorant, unhumbled understandings will be still judging rashly before they have thoroughly tried the case, and will not suspend till they are capable of judging, nor be convinced that they know not what they know not, but be confident in their first or ungrounded apprehensions.

CHAPTER XI.

THE SIGNS AND COMMON DISCOVERIES OF A PROUD, SELF-CONCEITED UNDERSTANDING, AND OF PRETENDED KNOWLEDGE.

BY such effects as these, the most of men do show their guilt of overvaluing their own apprehensions.

1. When they will be confident of things that are quite above their understandings, or else which they never thoroughly studied. Some are confident of that which no man knoweth; and most are confident of that which I think they are unlike to be certain of themselves, without miraculous inspiration, which they give us no reason to believe that they have. Things that cannot ordinarily be known, 1. Without the preparation of many other sciences, 2. Or without reading many books, 3. Or without reading or hearing what is said against it, 4. Or at least without long and serious studies; we have abundance that will talk most peremptorily of them, upon the trust of their teachers or party, without any of this necessary means of knowledge.

2. The hastiness of men's conclusions discovereth this presumption and self-conceit; when at the first hearing or reading, or after a few thoughts, they are as confident, as if they had grown old in studies. The best understandings must have long time to discern the evidence of things difficult, and a longer time to try that evidence by comparing it with what is brought against it; and yet a longer time to digest truths into that order and clearness of apprehension, which is necessary to distinct and solid knowledge: when without all this ado, most at the first lay hold of that which cometh in their way; and there they stick, at least till a more esteemed teacher or party tell them somewhat that is contrary to it. It is but few of our first apprehensions that are sound, and need not reformation; but none that are well-digested, and need not much consideration to perfect them.

3. Is it not a plain discovery of a presumptuous understanding, when men will confidently conclude of things, which their own tongues are forced to confess that they do not understand? I mean not only so as to give an accurate definition of them, but really not to know what it is that they talk of. Many a zealous anabaptist I have known, that knoweth not what baptism is. And many a one that hath disputed confidently for or against free-will, that knew not at all what free-will is. And many a one that hath disputed about the Lord's supper, and separated from almost all churches for want of sufficient strictness in it, and especially for giving it to the ignorant; who, upon examination, have not known the true nature of a sacrament, nor of the sacred covenant which it sealeth. Many a one forsaketh most churches as no churches, that they may be of a right-constituted church, who know not what a church is. What abundance will talk against an Arminian, a Calvinist, a prelatist, a presbyterian, an independent, that really know not what any of them are! Like a gentleman, the other day, that after long talk of the presbyterians, being urged to tell what a presbyterian was, could tell no more, but that he was one that is not so merry and sociable as other men, but stricter against sports, or taking a cup. And if I should tell you how few that can judge the controversies about predestination, do know what they talk of, it were easy to evince it.

4. May I not discern their prefidence, when men that hold contraries, five men of five inconsistent opinions, are yet every one confident that his own is right; when at best it is but one that can be right? When six men confidently expound a text in the Revelation six ways; when five men are so confident of five several ways of church-government, that they embody themselves into several policies or parties to enjoy them; is not here self-conceitedness in all, at least save one?

5. When men themselves, by turning from opinion to opinion, shall confess their former opinion was false; and yet made a religion of it, while they held it; was not this a presumptuous understanding? When a man shall be one year of one sect, and another of another, and yet always confident that he is in the right.

6. When men that are known to be ignorant in other parts of religion, shall yet in some one opinion which they have espoused, seem to themselves much wiser than their teachers, and make nothing of the judgments of those that have studied it many a year, is not this a presuming mind? Take the ablest divine that ever you knew living; suppose him to be Jewel, Andrews, Usher, Davenant, Calvin, Chamier, Camero, Amesius, Gataker, &c.; let him be one that all learned men admire, whose judgment is sent for from several kingdoms; who hath spent a long life in hard and very successful studies; every boy and silly woman, every ignorant, vicious clown, that differeth from him in any point, shall slight all the wisdom of this man, as if in comparison of himself he were a fool. Let it come but to the point of anabaptistry, separation, antinomianism, yea, the grossest opinions of the quakers, and what senseless fellow or wench is not much wiser than all these divines? And they will pity him as a poor, carnal, ignorant person, which hath not the teaching of God which they have. Yea, let him but seek to draw a sensualist from his voluptuousness, this poor sot doth presently take himself to be the wiser man, and can prove all his gaming, his idleness, his wantonness, his precious time wasted in plays and long feastings, his gluttony, his tippling, his prodigal wastefulness, to be all lawful things, whatever the learned pastor say.

But why do not such men suspect their understandings, and consider with themselves, what likelihood is there, that men as holy as I, that have studied it all their days, should not be wiser than I, that never searched as they have done? Doth not God say, "He that seeketh shall find;" and wisdom must be laboriously searched for, as a hidden treasure? And doth not God use to give his blessing on supposition of men's faithful endeavours?

7. Is it not palpable pride, when a few men, no wiser nor better than others, can easily believe that all the rest of the christian world, the most learned, godly, and concordant christians, are all deceived, ignorant souls; and they and their few adherents only are in the right, in some doubtful controversies, wherein they have no advantage above others, either for capacity or grace? I know that when the world is drowned in wickedness, we must not imitate them, be they never so many, nor "follow a multitude to do evil;" and I know that the certain truth of the gospel must be held fast, though most of the world be infidels; and that when the Arians were the most, they were not therefore the rightest; and that even among christians, carnal interests use to breed and keep up such corruptions, as must not for the number of the vicious be approved. But when those that truly fear God, and seek the truth, and faithfully serve him as self-denyingly as any others, shall agree in any part of holy doctrine or worship; for a few among them to rise us in a conceit of their own understandings, and separate from them as they separate from the world; and this upon less study than many of the rest have used to find out the truth; I am sure, none but a proud person will do this, without great jealousy of his own understanding and great fear of erring, and without long and serious search and deliberation at least.

8. Is it not pride of understanding, when we see men confident upon inconsiderable reasons? when they bring nothing that should move a man of any competent understanding; and yet they build as boldly on this sand, as if they built upon a rock?

9. And when they slight the strongest and clearest arguments of another; and in their prefidence disdain them, before they understand them, as not worthy of consideration, and as silly things?

10. When they obtrude all their conceits magisterially upon others, and expect that all men presently be of their mind, and say as they do; when they value men just as they agree with or disagree from their opinion, and all are dear to them that hold with them, and all are slighted that think they err; when a man that, without chewing, presently swalloweth their conceits, is taken for a sounder man, than he that will take nothing as sure till evidence prove it to him; is not this notorious pride of understanding? And oh how common is this imposing pride, even in them that cry out against it, and condemn it: they that will vilify one party, as imposing all their own conceptions, even in words, and forms, and ceremonies, on the churches of Christ, will yet themselves be rigid imposers: no man shall be of their communion, nor judged meet for the holy sacrament, who cometh not to their opinions in many of their singularities; nay, worse, that will not abstain from communion with other churches, whom their presumption separateth from.

11. And do not those people most value their own understandings, who choose teachers to please them, and not to teach them; and hear them as judges, or censurers, and not as learners? How ordinary is this! If they be to choose a pastor, they will rather have the most injudicious man who thinks as they think, than the wisest man that is able to teach them better. If they hear any thing which agreeth not with their former conceits, they go away magisterially censuring the preacher; he taught unsound doctrine, dangerous things; and neither understand him, nor endeavour to learn. I have seldom preached in strange congregations, nor seldom written on any subject, but among many learners some such hearers and readers I have had, that neither have understanding enough to teach, nor humility enough to know it, and to learn: but they go away prating among their companions of what they never understood; and if it fall out that I know of it, and answer them, they have nothing to say, but a *putaram*, or *non putaram;* I thought you had meant thus or thus, contrary to what I spoke; or, I noted not this or that word, which the sense depended on. Do but say as they would have you, and you are an excellent man! But if you tell them more than they knew, if it detect any error or ignorance which they had before, they condemn your teaching, instead of learning of you. Poor souls! if you are wise enough already, what need you a teacher? If you are not, why will you not learn? If you were wiser than he, why did you choose or take him for your teacher? If you are not, why will you not learn of him?

12. The deep and cruel censures which they pass against dissenters, doth show their self-conceitedness. None more censorious than raw, unexperienced persons, not only ignorant preachers, but women and boys. How readily and boldly, without any fear of God, doth one seek to make his brother odious as a schismatic and a fanatic, and worse than words can describe him; and another to reproach others as antichristian and carnal, whom he never understood! Nothing but pride could make men so ready, and bold, and fearless in their most foolish censures.

13. And it further showeth their proud presumption, when they dare do all this upon bare rumours and hearsay, and ungrounded suspicions. Were they not proud and presumptuous, they would think, Alas, my understanding is not so clear and sure, nor my charity so safe and strong, as that I should in reason venture to condemn my brother, upon uncertain rumours, and so slight reports! Have I heard him speak for himself? or is it charity or common justice to condemn a man unheard? What, though they

are godly men that report it? So was David, that committed adultery and murder, and hastily received a lie against Mephibosheth; and perhaps many of those Corinthians, against whose false censures Paul was put so largely to vindicate himself.

14. Yea, when they dare proceed to vend these false reports and censures upon hearsay, to the destruction of the charity of those that hear them; and so entangle them all in sin. As if it were not enough to quench their own love to their brother by false surmises, but they must quench as many others' also as they can.

15. Yea, when they dare venture so far as to unchurch many churches, yea, most in the world, and degrade most ministers, if not unchristian most christians, or at least themselves withdraw from the communion of such churches, and all for something which they never understood; about a doctrine, a form, a circumstance, where self-opinion or self-interest draweth them to all this bold adventure.

To say nothing of condemnations of whole churches and countries, the tyrannical, proud impositions, the cruel persecutions, which the papal faction hath been guilty of by this vice; judge now whether it be not too common a case to be guilty of an unhumbled understanding, and of pretended knowledge?

Object. If it be so, is it not best to do as the papists, and keep men from reading the Scriptures, or meddling with divine things which they cannot master, any further than to believe what the church believeth.

Answ. 1. It is best, no doubt, to teach men to know the difference between teachers and learners, and to keep in a humble, learning state, and in that state to grow as much in knowledge as they can; but not to cast away knowledge, for fear of overvaluing it, nor renounce their reason, for fear of error; no more than to put out their eyes for fear of mistaking by them, or choosing madness lest they abuse their wits: else we might wish to be brutes, because abused reason is the cause of all the errors and mischiefs in the world.

2. The popish clergy who give this counsel for the blinding of the vulgar, are worse themselves; and by their proud contendings, censures, and cruelties, show more self-conceitedness than the vulgar do.

3. The truth is, the cause is the common frailty of man, and the common pravity of corrupted nature; and it is to be found in persons of all ranks, religions, and conditions; of which more after in due place.

CHAPTER XII.

VI. OF THE MISCHIEVOUS EFFECTS OF THIS PROUD PRETENCE OF MORE KNOWLEDGE THAN MEN HAVE.

If the mischiefs of this sin had not been very great, I had not chosen this subject to treat of.

1. It is no small mischief to involve men's souls in the guilt of all the sins which I named in the last chapter, as the discovery of this vice. Sure all those disorders, censures, slanders, and presumptions, should not seem small in the eyes of any man that feareth God, and loveth holiness, and hateth sin.

2. Pretended knowledge wasteth men some time in getting it, and much more in abusing it: all the time that you study for it, preach for it, talk for it, write for it, is sinfully lost and cast away.

3. It kindleth a corrupt and sinful zeal; such as James describeth, James iii. 1, 15, which is envious and striving, and is but earthly, sensual, and devilish: a zeal against love, and against good works, and against the interest of our brother, and against the peace and concord of the church; a hurting, burning, devouring, excommunicating, persecuting zeal. And a fever in the body is not so pernicious as such a sinful zeal in the soul. Such a zeal the Jews had, as Paul bears them witness, Rom. xi. 1. Such a zeal, alas! is so common among persecuting papists on one side, and censorious sectaries and separatists on the other, that we must all bear the sad effects of it: and self-conceited knowledge is the fuel of this zeal, as James iii. fully manifesteth.

4. This pretended knowledge is the fixing of false opinions in the minds of men, by which the truth is most powerfully kept out. A child will not wrangle against his teacher, and therefore will learn; but these over-wise fools do presently set their wits against what you say to keep out knowledge. You must beat down the garrison of his pride, before you come within hearing to instruct him: he is hardlier untaught the errors which he hath received, than an unprejudiced man is taught to understand most excellent truths.

5. By this, the gifts of the most wise and excellent teachers are half lost: it is full bottles that are cast into these seas of knowledge, which have no room for more, but come out as they went in. If an Augustine, or an Aquinas, or Scotus were among them, yea, a Peter or Paul, what can he put into these persons that are full of their own conceits already? "Seest thou a man wise in his own conceit, there is more hope of a fool than of him."

6. Yea, they are usually the perverters of the souls of others. Before they can come to themselves, and know that they were mistaken, what pains have they taken to make others of their own erroneous minds, whom they are not able afterward to undeceive again!

7. It is a vice that blemisheth many excellent qualifications. To hear of a man that valueth his own judgment but according to its worth, and pretendeth to know but so much as he knoweth indeed, is no shame to him; though knowledge is a thing fitter to be used than boasted of: but if a man know never so much, and can never so well express it, if he think that he is wiser than he is, and excelleth others more than indeed he doth, and overvalueth that knowledge which he hath, it is a shame which his greatest parts cannot excuse or hide.

8. It exposeth a man to base and shameful mutability. He that will be hasty and confident in his apprehensions, is so oft mistaken, that he must as oft change his mind, and recant, or do much worse. I know that it cannot be expected, that any man should have as sound apprehensions in his youth as in his age, and that the wisest should not have need of mutations for the better, and retractations of some youthful errors; and he that changeth not, and retracteth nothing, it seems is in his childish ignorance and error still; but when natural frailty exposeth us all to much of this disgrace, we should not expose ourselves to so much more. A hasty judger, or prefident man, must be a very weathercock, or be defiled with a leprosy of error. Whereas if men would but be humble, and modest, and self-suspicious, and suspend their presumption, and not take on them to know before they know indeed, how safely might they walk, and how seldom would they need to change their minds, or either stick in the sink of error, or make many shameful retractations!

9. Prefidence and false judging engageth a man in a very life of sin. For when falsehood goeth for truth with him, it will infect his affections, and pol-

lute his conversation; and all that he doth in the obedience and prosecution of that error will be sin. Yea, the greatest sin that he can but think no sin may be committed; as was the persecution of Christ and christians, by the Jews and Paul, and others like them; and the papists' bloodiness for their religion throughout christendom.

10. It disturbeth the peace of all societies. This is the vice that disquieteth families: every one is wisest in his own eyes: the servant thinketh his own way better than his master's. What are all the contentions between husband and wife, or any in the family, but that in all their differences, every one thinketh himself to be in the right? His own opinion is right, his own words and ways are right; and when every one is wise and just, and every one is in the right, the effects are such as if no one were wise or in the right.

And in civil societies, seditions, rebellions, oppressions, tyranny, and all confusions come from this, that men pretend to be sure of what they are not. Rulers take up with false reports from idle, malicious whisperers and accusers against their inferiors, and have not the justice and patience to suspend their judgments till they have searched out the matter, and fully heard men speak for themselves. Subjects make themselves judges of the secrets of government, and of the councils and actions of their rulers, of which they have no certain notice, but venture to conclude upon deceitful suspicions. And the contentions and factions amongst nobles and other subjects, come from misunderstandings, through hasty and ungrounded judgings. But the woefullest effects are in the churches; where, alas, whilst every pastor will be wiser than another, and the people wiser than all their pastors, and every sect and party much wiser than all that differ from them, their divisions, their separations, their alienations, and bitter censurings of each other, their obtruding their own opinions, and rules, and ceremonies upon each other, their bitter envying, strife, and persecutions of each other, do make sober standers-by to ask, as Paul, "Is there not a wise man among you?" Oh happy the world, happy kingdoms, but most happy the churches of Christ, if we could possibly bring men but to know their ignorance! if the pastors themselves were not prefident and presumptuous overvaluers of their own apprehensions! and if the people knew how little they know! But now, alas, men rage against each other in their dreams, and few of them have the grace to awake before death, and find to repentance that they were themselves in error.

Hear me, with that remnant of meekness and humility which thou hast left, thou confident, bitter, censorious man! Why must that man needs be taken for a heretic, a schismatic, a refractory, stubborn, self-willed person, an antichristian, carnal, formal man, who is not of thy opinion in point of a controversy, of a form, of an order, of a circumstance, or subscription, or such like? It is possible it may be so; and it is possible thou mayst be more so thyself. But hast thou so patiently heard all that he hath to say, and so clearly discerned the truth on thy own side, and that this truth is made so evident to him as that nothing but wilful obstinacy can resist it, as will warrant all thy censure and contempt? or is it not an overvaluing of thy own understanding, which makes thee so easily condemn all as unsufferable that differ from it? Hath not pride made thy silly wit to be as an idol, to which all must bow down on pain of the heat of thy displeasure? Do not some of those men whom thou so magisterially condemnest, study as hard and impartially as thyself? Do they not pray as hard for God's assistance? Have they not the same books, and as good teachers? Do they not live as well, and show as much tenderness of conscience, and fear of erring and sinning, as thyself? Why then art thou so hasty in condemning them that are as fair for the reputation of wisdom as thou art?

But suppose them mistaken, hast thou tried that they are unwilling to be instructed? It may be you have wrangled with them by disputes, which have but engaged each other to defend his own opinion: but call them to thee in love, and tell them, You are ignorant, and I am wise; I will teach you what you know not; and open to them all the evidence which causeth your own confident apprehensions. Wish them to study it, and hear patiently what they have to say; and I am persuaded that many or most sober men that differ from you, will not refuse thus to become as your scholars, so far as to consider all that you have to offer to convince them, and thankfully receive as much of the truth as they can discern.

But, alas, no men rage so much against others as erroneous and blind, as the blind and erroneous; and no men so furiously brand others with the marks of obstinacy, factiousness, and schism, as the obstinate, factious, and schismatical. The prouder the obtruder of his own conceits is, the more he condemneth all dissenters as proud, for presuming to differ from such as he; and all for want of a humble mind.

11. Moreover it is this pretended knowledge which is the cause of all our false reformations. Men are so over-wise, that they presently see a beam in their brother's eye, which is but a mote; and they magnify all the imperfections of others, pastors and churches, into mountains of iniquity. Every mis-expression, or disorder, or inconvenient phrase in a prayer, or a sermon, or a book, is an odious, damning, intolerable evil. Oh! say such, what idolaters are they that use a form of prayer, which God did not command! What large consciences have they that can join with a parish church; that can communicate kneeling, and among bad men, or those whose conversion is not tried! What abundance of intolerable evils do such men find in the words, and forms, and orders, and circumstances of other men's worship, which God mercifully accepteth through Christ, taking all these but for such pardonable imperfections as he mercifully beareth with in all. And then the reformation must be presently answerable to the apprehension of the evil.

Yea, sometimes the very injudicious sort of zealous people make the cry of the greatness of this or that corruption, how antichristian and intolerable it is: and then the reformation must satisfy this vulgar error, and answer the cry and expectation of the people.

I would here give instances of abundance of misreformings, which all need a reformation, both in doctrine, discipline, and worship, but that I reserve it for another treatise, if I live to finish it, and can get it printed, called "Overdoing is Undoing."

12. Lastly, this voice of pretended certainty and knowledge hath set up several false terms of christian unity and peace, and by them hath done more to hinder the church's peace and unity than most devices ever did, which Satan ever contrived to that end. By this church-tearing vice, abundance of falsehoods, and abundance of things uncertain, and abundance of things unnecessary, have been made so necessary to the union and communion of the churches and their members, as that thereby the christian world hath been ground to powder by the names and false pretences of unity and peace. Just as if a wise statesman would advise his Majesty, that none may be his subjects that are not of one age, one

stature, one complexion, and one disposition, that so he might have subjects more perfectly concordant than all the princes on earth besides; and so might be the most glorious defender of unity and peace. But how must this be done? Why, command them all to be of your mind; but that prevaileth not, and yet it is undone. Why then they are obstinate, self-willed persons. Well, but yet it is undone. Why, lay fines and penalties upon them. Well, but yet it is undone: all the hypocrites that had no religion, are of the religion which is uppermost; and the rest are uncured. Why, require more bricks of them, and let them have no straw, and tell them that their religion is their idleness, stubbornness, and pride, and let your little finger be heavier than your father's loins. But hearken, young counsellors, Jeroboam will have the advantage of all this, and still the sore will be unhealed. Why then banish them, and hang them that obey not, till there be none left that are not of one mind. But, sir, I pray you, who shall do it; and who shall that one man be that shall be left to be all the kingdom? You are not such a fool as to be ignorant, that no two men will agree in all things, nor be perfectly of the same complexion. If there must be one king, and but one subject, I pray you who shall that one subject be? I hope not he that counselleth it; *Neque enim lex justior ulla est, quam necis artifices arte perire sua.* But hark you, sir, shall that one man have a wife or not? If not, the kingdom will die with him: if yea, I dare prognosticate he and his wife will not be in all things of a mind. If they be, take me for a mistaken man.

By this vice of pretended knowledge and certainty it is that the papacy hath been made the centre of the unity of the universal church. Unity we must have, God forbid else; there is no maintaining christianity without it. But the pope must be *principium unitatis:* and will all christians certainly unite in the pope? Well, and patriarchs must be the pillars of unity: but was it so to the unity of the first churches? or is it certain that all christians will unite in patriarchs? But further, all the mass of Gregory the too great, and all the legends in his dialogues, or at least all the doctrines and ceremonies which he received, and the form of government in his time, must be made necessary to church union. Say you so? But it was not all necessary in the apostles' times, nor in Cyprian's times, no nor in Gregory's own times; much of those things being used arbitrarily: and what was made necessary by canons of general councils in the empire, mark it, was never thereby made necessary in all the rest of the churches. And are you sure that mere christians will take all these for certain truths? Why, if they will not, burn and banish them. This is, as Tertullian saith, *solitudinem facere et pacem vocare.* But hark, sir, this way hath been tried too long in vain: millions of Albigenses and Waldenses are said by historians to be killed in France, Savoy, Italy, Germany, &c. The French massacre killed about thirty or forty thousand. The Irish massacre in that little island killed about two hundred thousand. But were they not stronger after all these cruelties than before? Alas, sir, all your labour is lost, and your party is taken for a blood-thirsty generation, and human nature, which abhorreth the blood-thirsty, ever after breedeth enemies to your way. This is the effect of false principles, and terms of unity and peace, contrived by proud, self-conceited men, that think the world should take their dictates for a supreme law, and obey them as the directive deities of mankind.

If all this be not enough to tell you what proud, pretended certainty is, read over the histories of the ages past, and you shall find it written in ink, in tears, in blood, in mutations, in subversions of the empires and kingdoms of the world, in the most odious and doleful contentions of prelates, lacerations of churches, and desolations of the earth. And yet have we not experience enough to teach us!

CHAPTER XIII.

THE ADVANTAGE OF A SUSPENDED JUDGMENT, AND HUMBLE UNDERSTANDING, WHICH PRETENDETH TO NO MORE KNOWLEDGE OR CERTAINTY THAN IT HATH.

THE advantages of a humble mind, which pretendeth not to be certain till he is certain, you may gather by contraries from the twelve forementioned mischiefs of prefidence; which to avoid prolixity, I leave to your collection.

Moreover I add: 1. Such a humble, suspended mind doth not cheat itself with seeming to have a knowledge, a divine faith, a religion, when it hath none. It doth not live on air and dreams, nor feed on shadows, nor is puffed up with a tympanite of vain conceits, instead of true, substantial wisdom.

2. He is not prepossessed against the truth, but hath room for knowledge; and having the teachableness of a child, he shall receive instruction, and grow in true knowledge, when the proud and inflated wits, being full of nothing, are sent empty away.

3. He entangleth not himself in a seeming necessity of making good all that he hath once received and entertained. He hath not so many bastards of his own brain to maintain, as the prefident, hasty judges have: which saveth him much sinful study and strife.

4. He is not liable to so much shame of mutability: he that fixeth not till he feel firm ground, nor buildeth till he feel a rock, need not pull down and repent so oft as rash presumers.

5. Unless the world be Bedlam mad in proud obtrudings of their own conceits, methinks such a wary, humble man should offend but few, and better keep both his own and the church's peace than others. Can persecutors for shame hang and burn men for mere ignorance, who are willing to learn, and will thankfully from any man receive information? What if in Queen Mary's days the poor men and women had told my lords of Winchester and London, We are not persons of so good understandings as to know what a spiritual body is, as Paul describeth it, 1 Cor. xv. And seeing most say that the sun itself is a body, and not a spirit; and late philosophers say that light is a substance, or body, which yet from the sun in a moment diffuseth itself through all the surface of the earth and air; we know not how far locality, limitations, extension, impenetrability, divisibility, &c. belong to the body of Christ, and consequently how far it may be really present; we can say nothing, but that we know not. Would my good lord bishops have burnt them for, I know not? Perhaps they would have said, You must believe the church. But which is the church, my lord? Why, it is the pope and a general council. But alas, my lord, I have never seen or heard either pope or council. Why, but we have, and you must believe us. Must we believe you, my lords, to be infallible; or only as we do other men that may deceive and be deceived? Is any infallible besides the pope and his council? Truly, my lords, we are ignorant people, and we know not what the pope

and councils have said; and we are uncertain whether you report them truly, and uncertain whether they are fallible or not; but we are willing to hear any thing which may make us wiser. Would their lordships have burnt such modest persons?

Suppose in a church where men are put to profess or subscribe to or against the opinions of free-will, or reprobation, or predetermination, or such like, a humble man should say, These are things above my understanding; I cannot reach to know what free-will is, nor whether all causes natural and free be predetermined by divine premotion, &c.; I can say neither it is so, nor it is not; they are above my reach: would they silence and cast out such a humble person, and forbid him to preach the gospel of Christ? Perhaps they would: but there are not so many hardened to such inhumanity, as there are men that would deal sharply with one that is as confident as they are on the other side. And those few that were thus silenced, would have the more peace, that they procured it not by self-conceited singularities; and the silencers of them would be the more ashamed before all sober persons that shall hear it. Other instances I pass by.

CHAPTER XIV.

VII. THE AGGRAVATION OF THIS SIN OF PREFIDENCE.

THOUGH there be so much evil in this sin of presumption, as I have noted, yet it is not in all alike culpable or unhappy, but differeth in both respects, as I shall tell you.

I. For culpability, it is worst in these sorts and cases following:

1. It is a great sin in those who have least reason to think highly of their own understandings, and greatest reason to distrust themselves: as, 1. In those that are young and unexperienced, and must be miraculously wise, if they are wiser than old experienced persons (*cæteris paribus*). 2. In the unlearned or half-learned, who have had but little time or helps for study, or at least have made but little use of them. 3. In duller wits, and persons that in other matters are known to be no wiser than others. 4. In those that take up their prefidence upon the slightest grounds, as bare surmises and reports from others that were uncertain. 5. In those that have been oft deceived already, and should by their sad experience have been brought to humble self-suspicion.

2. And it is an aggravated sin in those whose place and condition obligeth them to learn from others. As for the wife to be self-conceited of all her apprehensions against her husband, unless he be a fool: for the servant to set his wit against his master, where he should obey him: for children to think that their wits are righter than their parents' or masters'; and apprentices and learners to think that they know more than their teachers: and for the ignorant people to censure over-hastily the doctrine and practice of their pastors, as if they were wiser than they: perhaps they are; but it must be some rare person who is fit to be a teacher himself, or the teacher some sot that hath intruded into the office, or else it must be a wonder; for God usually giveth men knowledge according to the time, and means, and pains that they have had to get it, and not by miraculous infusions without means. Doth not the apostle expressly tell you this, Heb. v. 11, 12, "When for the time you ought to have been teachers," &c.? Men should be wise according to the time and means of wisdom which they have had.

3. It is the greater crime when men will seem wisest in other men's matters and concernments. When the subject will know best what belongeth to a king or governor; and the people will know best how the pastor should teach them, and when he faileth, and whom he should receive into the church, or exclude; when the servant will know best his master's duty, and every man his neighbour's, and least his own.

4. It is the greater crime when men will be the judges of their own understandings, and think highly of them in cases where they should be tried by others. As if an empyric, or woman, do think that they know better how to cure a disease than the ablest physicians; why do they not offer themselves to the trial, and before them make good their skill by reason? If an unexperienced young student think himself able to be a physician, he is not to be judge, but must be tried and judged by physicians: if a self-conceited professor, or a young student, think himself fit for the ministry, he must not presently contrive how to get in, and how to shift off examination, but freely offer himself to be tried by able, godly ministers, and then by the ordainers, who are to judge. But when such persons can think themselves sufficient if no body else do, or if but a few ignorant persons do, that are unfit to judge, this proves their pride and presumption to be a great and heinous sin.

5. And it is yet more heinously aggravated, when, to keep up the reputation of their own understandings, they use to depress and vilify the wiser, even those whom they never knew: as he that affecteth to be a preacher, and dare not pass the examination, hath no way to hide his shame, but, 1. By crying down the learning which he wanteth, as a human, carnal thing: and, 2. By reproaching those that should judge of him, and ordain him, as poor carnal persons, who understand not the things of the Spirit as he doth, and as proud, self-seeking men, that will approve of none but those that flatter them, and are of their way. Some such there may be; but sure all are not such. Why do you not desire the judgment of the wisest and most impartial men, but take up with the applause of unlearned persons that are of your own mind and way, and magnify you for humouring them?

So you shall hear empyrics and she-physicians, vilify doctors of physic, as men that have less knowledge than they, and are so proud, and covetous, and dishonest, that there is no trusting them. When pretended knowledge must have so base a cloak, it is the greater sin.

6. And it is the more heinous sin when they venture to do heinous mischief by it: as a papist, a quaker, or a separatist, will in his confidence be a perverter of others, and a condemner of the just, and a defamer of those that are against him, and a troubler of the church and world. He that in his self-conceitedness dare resist the wisest, and his teachers and rulers, and set countries on fire, is wickedly presumptuous.

So in the practice of physic, when people will be self-conceited, when the lives of others lie upon it; and a silly fellow or woman will venture to purge, to let blood, to give this or that, who know neither the disease nor proper cure.

7. It is therefore a heinous sin in rulers, who must judge for the life and death of others, or for the peace or misery of thousands about them. I mean pastors, and commanders in armies and navies, and other governors on whom the public welfare of the

church, or army or navy, or country doth depend. Oh how wise should that person be, whose errors may cost thousands so dear as their destruction! Or if their understandings be not extraordinary, how cautelous should they be in judging; upon hearing the wisest, and hearing dissenters, and not only flatterers or consenters; and hearing men of several minds, and hearing all witnesses and evidence, and hearing every man speak for himself: and after all considering thoroughly of it: especially of laws and wars, and impositions in religion, where thousands of consciences, say what you can, will expect satisfaction. When a woman called to Antigonus to hear her cause, and do her justice, he told her that he could not have leisure: she answered, You should not have while to be king then: whereupon he heard her, and did her right. Had it been to an inferior judge, she had spoken reason.

8. Lastly, pretended certainty is the greater sin when it is falsely fathered on God. But the pope and council dare pretend, that God hath promised them infallibility, and God hath certified them that the consecrated bread is no bread, and that our senses are all deceived; and God hath made the pope the universal ruler of the world or church, and made him and his council the only judges, by which all men must know what is the word of God. So, when fanatics will pretend, that by revelation, visions, or inspirations of the Spirit, God hath assured them that this or that is the meaning of a text which they understand not, or the truth in such or such a controversy. Alas! among too many well-meaning persons, God is pretended for a multitude of sinful errors; and they that preach false doctrine will do it, as the old prophet spake to the young, as from the Lord: and they that rail at godliness, and they that censure, backbite, cast out, or persecute their brethren, will do it as Rabshakeh; "Hath not God sent me," &c. Men will not make any snares for the church, or their brethren's consciences, but in the name of God: they will not divide the church, nor cast out infants, nor refuse communion with their brethren, but in the name of God. One man saith, God forbiddeth him all book prayers, or all imposed forms of prayer: and another saith, God forbiddeth him all but such. And all belie God, and add this heinous abuse of his holy word and name unto their sin.

CHAPTER XV.

SOME SPECIAL AGGRAVATIONS MORE OF THIS SIN, IN STUDENTS AND PASTORS, WHICH SHOULD DETER THEM FROM PRETENDED KNOWLEDGE OR PREFIDENCE.

To such, I will suppose, that to name the evils may suffice, on my part, without sharp amplifications. Though I have spoken to you first in what is said, I will briefly add,

1. That this sin will make slothful students. Few study hard, who are quickly confident of their first conceptions.

2. While you do study, it keepeth out knowledge: you are too full of yourselves, to receive easily from others.

3. It is the common parent of error and heresy. Ignorance is the mother and pride the father of them all; and prefidence and pretended knowledge is but proud ignorance in another name.

4. What a life of precious time will you waste in following the erroneous thoughts of your bewildered minds.

5. As food altereth the temperament of the body which it nourisheth, so the very temperament of your minds, and wills, and affections, will become vain, and frothy, and shadowy, or malignant and perverse, according to the quality of your error.

6. It is the common parent of superstition: it defileth God's worship with human inventions, with duties and sins of our own making. All such men's dreams will seem to them to be the laws of God.

7. It will entail a corrupt education of youth upon us, and consequently a corrupt, degenerate kind of learning, and so a degenerate ministry on the churches. When youths are possessed with abundance of uncertainties, under the name of learning and religion, it will grow the custom to teach, and talk, and live accordingly: do I say, it will do? If the schoolmen's error in this deserve but half as much as Faber, Valla, Hutten, Erasmus, charge upon them, you should hear and take warning; not to avoid the most accurate knowledge by the hardest studies, but to avoid pretending that you know what you do not.

8. And you will make vain strife and contention about vanity your very trade and business, when you come abroad in the world. They that make uncertainties or errors to be their studies and honourable learning, must keep up the honour of it by living as they learned, and talking vainly for the vanities of their minds.

9. And you are likely hereby to become the chief instruments of Satan, to trouble the church either with heresies, schisms, or persecutions.

10. And truly it should much turn your hearts against it, to know that it is a continual habit or exercise of pride. And pride, the devil's sin, is one of the most heinous and odious to God. If you hate any sin, you should hate pride. And it is one of the worst sorts of pride too. As nature hath three principles, active power, intellect, and will, and man three excellencies, greatness, wisdom, and goodness; so pride hath these three great objects: men are proud that they are greater, or wiser, or better than others; that is, they think themselves greater, or wiser, or better than they are, and they would have others think so too. As for pride of beauty, or clothing, or such like corporeal things and appurtenances; it is the vice of children, and the more shallow and foolish sort of women. But greater things make up a greater sort of pride. Oh what a number of all ranks and ages do live in this great sin of pride of wisdom, or an overvalued understanding, who never feel or lament it!

11. Moreover, your prefidence prepareth you for scepticism, or doubting of the most certain necessary truths: like some of our sectaries, who have been falsely confident of so many religions, till at last they doubt of all religion. He that finds that he was deceived while he was an anabaptist, and deceived when he was a separatist, and deceived while he was an antinomian or libertine, and deceived when he was a quaker; is prepared to think also that he was deceived when he was a christian, and when he believed the immortality of the soul and the life to come. When you have found your understandings oft deceive you, you will grow so distrustful of them, as hardly ever to believe them when it is most necessary. He that often lieth, will hardly be believed when he speaketh truth. And all this cometh from believing your first and slight apprehensions too easily, and too soon, and so filling up your minds with lies, which when they are discovered, make the

truth to be suspected. Like some fanciful, lustful youths, who hastily grow fond of some unsuitable, unlovely person, and when they know them, cannot so much as allow them the conjugal affection which they are bound to.

12. Lastly, consider what a shame it is to your understandings, and how it contradicteth your pretence of knowledge. For, how little knoweth that man, who knoweth not his own ignorance! How can it be thought that you are like to know great matters at a distance, the profundities, sublimities, and subtleties of sciences, who know not yet how little you know?

CHAPTER XVI.

PROOFS OF THE LITTLE KNOWLEDGE THAT IS IN THE WORLD, TO MOVE US TO A DUE DISTRUST OF OUR UNDERSTANDINGS.

If you think this sin of a proud understanding, and pretended knowledge, doth need for the cure a fuller discovery of its vanity, I know not how to do it more convincingly, than by showing you how little true knowledge is in the world, and consequently that all mankind have cause to think meanly of their understandings.

I. The great imperfection of all the sciences, is a plain discovery of it: when mankind hath had above five thousand years already to have grown to more perfection, yet how much is still dark, and controverted! and how much unknown in comparison of what we know! But above all, though nothing is perfectly known which is not methodically known, yet how few have a true methodical knowledge! He that seeth but some parcels of truth, or seeth them but confusedly, or in a false method, not agreeable to the things, doth know but little, because he knoweth not the place, and order, and respects of truths to one another, and consequently neither their composition, harmony, strength, or use. Like a philosopher that knew nothing but elements, and not mixed bodies, or animate beings: or like an anatomist that is but an atomist, and can say no more of the body of a man, but that it is made up of atoms, or at most can only enumerate the similar parts: or like a man that knoweth no more of his clock and watch, but as the pieces of it lie on a heap, or at best, setteth some one part out of its place, which disableth the whole engine: or like one that knoweth the chessmen only as they are in the bag, or at best in some disorder. Who will make me so happy as to show me one true scheme of physics, of metaphysics, of logic, yea of theology, which I cannot presently prove guilty of such mistake, confusion, misorder, as tendeth to great error in the subsequent parts? I know of no small number that have been offered to the world, but never saw one that satisfied my understanding. And I think I scarce know any thing to purpose, till I can draw a true scheme of it, and set each compounding notion in its place.

II. And the great diversity and contrariety of opinions, of notions, and of methods, proveth that our knowledge indeed is yet but small. How many methods of logic have we! how many hypotheses in physics! yea, how many contentious volumes written against one another, in philosophy and theology itself! What loads of *Videturs* in the schoolmen! How many sects and opinions in religion! Physicians agree not about men's lives. Lawyers agree not about men's estates; no nor about the very fundamental laws. If there be a civil war, where both sides appeal to the law, there will be lawyers on both sides. And doth not this prove that we know but little!

III. But men's rage and confidence in these contrarieties doth discover it yet more. Read their contentious writings of philosophy and theology; observe their usage of one another, what contempt, what reproach, what cruelties they can proceed to! The papist silenceth and burneth the protestant; the Lutheran silenceth and revileth the Calvinist; the Calvinist sharply judgeth the Arminians; and so round: and may I not judge that this wisest part of the world is low in knowledge, when not the vulgar only, but the leaders and doctors are so commonly mistaken in their greatest zeal; and that Solomon erred not in saying, "The fool rageth, and is confident?"

IV. If our knowledge were not very low, the long experience of the world would have long ago reconciled our controversies. The strivings and distractions about them, both in philosophy, politics, and theology, have torn churches, and raised wars, and set kingdoms on fire, and should in reason be to us as a bone out of joint, which by the pain should force us all to seek out for a cure: and sure in so many thousand years, many remedies have been tried: the issues of such disingenuous-ingenious wars, do furnish men with such experience as should teach them the cure. And yet after so many years' war of wits, to be so witless as to find no end, no remedy, no peace, doth show that the wit of man is not a thing to be proud of.

V. The great mutability of our apprehensions doth show that they are not many things that we are certain of. Do we not feel in ourselves how new thoughts and new reasons are ready to breed new conjectures in us, and that looketh doubtful to us, upon further thoughts, of which long before we had no doubt. Besides the multitudes that change their very religion, every studious person so oft changeth his conceptions, as may testify the shallowness of our minds.

VI. The general barbarousness of the world, the few countries that have polite learning, or true civility, or christianity, do tell us that knowledge in the world is low: when besides the vast unknown regions of the world, all that are of late discovery in the West Indies, or elsewhere, are found to be so rude and barbarous; some little differing from subtle brutes: when the vast regions of Africa, of Tartary, and other parts of Asia, are no wiser to this day: when the Roman Eastern empire so easily parted with christianity, and is turned to so much barbarous ignorance: this showeth what we are; for these men are all born as capable as we.

VII. Especially the sottish opinions which the heathen and Mahometan world do generally entertain, do tell us how dark a creature man is. That four parts of the whole world (if not much more, that is unknown) should receive all the sottish opinions as they do, both against the light of nature, knowing so little of God, and by such vain conceits of their prophets and petty deities: that above the fifth part of the known world should receive, and so long and quietly retain, so sottish an opinion as Mahometanism is, and build upon it the hopes of their salvation. If the Greek church can be corrupted into so gross a foolery, why may not the Latin, and the English, if they had the same temptations? Oh what a sad proof is here of human folly!

VIII. But in the Latin church (be it spoken without any comparing Mahometanism with christianity) the wonder is still greater, and the discovery of the fallaciousness of man's understanding is yet more clear: were there no proof of it, but the very being of popery in the world, and the reception of it by such and so many, it affordeth the strongest temptation that ever I thought of in the world, to the brutist, to question whether instinct advance not brutes above man! The brutes distrust not their right disposed senses; but the papists not only distrust them, but renounce them: bread is no bread, and wine is no wine with them, all men's senses are deceived that think otherwise: it is necessary to salvation to believe that God's natural revelations to sense here are false, and not to be believed. Every man that will be saved must believe that bread is no bread, that quantity, locality, colour, weight, figure, are the quantity, locality, colour, weight, figure of nothing:[a] and God worketh grand miracles by every priest, as frequently as he consecrateth in the mass: and if any man refuse to swear to this renunciation of human sense, and the truth of these miracles, he must be no priest, but a combustible heretic. And if any temporal lord refuse to exterminate all those from their dominions, who will believe their senses, and not think it necessary to renounce them as deceived, he must be excommunicated and dispossessed himself, his subjects absolved from their oaths and allegiance, and his dominions given to another: and this is their very religion, being the decree of a great general council, questioned indeed by some few protestants, but not at all by them, but largely vindicated: Later. sub. Innoc. 3. Can. 1. 3. The sum is, no man that will not renounce not only his humanity, but his animality, must be suffered to live in any one's dominions, and he that will suffer men in his dominions, must be himself turned out! This is plain truth: and yet this is the religion of popes, and emperors, and kings, of lords and counsellors, of prelates and doctors, universities, churches, and famous kingdoms; and such as men, all these wise men, dare lay their salvation upon; and dare massacre men by thousands and hundred thousands upon, and burn their neighbours to ashes upon; and what greater confidence of certainty can be expressed? And yet shall men be proud of wit? Oh what is man! How dark, how sottish and mad a thing! All these great princes, cardinals, universities, and kingdoms, are born with natures as capacious as ours. They are in other things as wise: they pity us as heretics, because we will not cease to be men. The infidel that denieth man's reason and immortality, would but level us with the brutes, and allow us the preeminence among them in subtlety; but all these papists forswear or renounce that sense which is common to brutes and us, and sentence us either below the brutes, or unto hell. Pretend no more, poor man, to great knowledge. As the sight of a grave and a rotten carcass may humble the fool that is proud of beauty, so the thought of the popish, Mahometan, and heathen world, may humble him that is proud of his understanding. I tell thee, man, thou art capable of that madness as to believe that an ox or an onion is a God; or to believe that a bit of bread is God; yea more, to believe as necessary to salvation, that thy own and all men's senses about their proper objects are deceived, and the bread which thou seest and eatest is no bread; yea, though it be three times in the three next verses (1 Cor. xi.) called bread after consecration by an inspired expositor of Christ's words.

IX. Moreover the poverty of man's understanding appeareth by the great time and labour that must be bestowed for knowledge. We must be learning as soon as we have the use of reason, and all our life must be bestowed in it. I know by experience, knowledge will not be got without long, hard, and patient studies. Oh what abundance of books must we read! what abundance of deep meditations must we use! what help of teachers do we need! And when all is done, how little do we obtain! Is this an intellect to be proud of?

X. And it is observable how every man slighteth another's reasons, while he would have all to magnify his own. All the arguments that in disputation are used against him, how frivolous and foolish are they! All the books that are written against him, are little better than nonsense, or heresy, or blasphemy: contempt is answer enough to most that is said against them. And yet the men in other men's eyes, are perhaps wiser and better than themselves. Most men are fools in the judgment of others! Whatever side or party you are of, there are many parties against you, who all pity your ignorance, and judge you silly, deceived souls. So that if one man be to be believed of another, and if the most of mankind be not deceived, we are all poor, silly, cheated souls: but if most be deceived, mankind is a very deceivable creature. How know I that I must believe you, when you befool twenty other sects, any more than I should believe those twenty sects, when they as confidently befool you, if no other evidence turn the scales?

XI. And verily I think that the wars, and contentions, and distractions of the kingdoms of the world, do show us that man is a pitiful, silly, deceivable thing. I am not at all so sharp against wars and soldiers as Erasmus was; but I should think that if men were wise, they might keep their peace, and save the lives of thousands, which must be dearly answered for. Were all the princes of christendom as wise as proud wits conceit themselves to be, how easy were it for them to agree among themselves, and equally to distribute the charge of two or three armies, which might quickly shake in pieces the Turk's dominions, and recover Constantinople, and free the Greek church from their captivity!

XII. And what need we more than every day's miscarriages to tell us of our folly? Do we not miss it in one degree or other in almost all that we take in hand? Hence cometh the ruin of estates, the ill education of children, the dissensions among neighbours and in families. Parents have scarce wit enough to breed and teach a child; nor husbands and wives to live together according to their relations; nor masters to teach their servants. If I write a book, how many can find folly and error in it! and I as easily in theirs. If I preach, how many faults can the silliest woman find in it! and I as many perhaps in other men's. Do we live in such weakness, and shall we not know it?

XIII. And the uncurableness of ancient errors is no small evidence of our folly. If our ancestors have but been deceived before us, though their error be never so palpable, we plead their venerable antiquity, for an honour to their ignorance and mistakes. The wisdom of wise ancestors almost dieth with them; but the errors of the mistaken must be successive, lest they be dishonoured. We will deny reason, and deny Scripture, and deny sense, for fear of being wiser for our souls than some of our forefathers were.

XIV. The self-destroying courses of mankind, one would think, should be enough to evince man's folly. Who almost suffer but by themselves? Few sicknesses befall us which folly brings not on us by excess of eating or drinking, or by sloth, or some unwise neglect! Few ruins of estates but by our own folly! Few calamities and relations but by our-

[a] Of this oft before.

selves? What churches distracted and ruined, but by the pastors and children of the church themselves! What kingdom ruined without its own procurement? It need not be said, *Quos perdere vult Jupiter hos dementat;* it is enough to say, *Insaniam eorum non curat:* If he cure not our madness, we shall certainly destroy ourselves. Whose hands kindled all the flames that have wasted the glory, wealth, and peace of England in state and church, except our own? Were they foreign enemies that did it, and still keep open our wounds, or is it ourselves? And yet are we wise men?

XV. But the greatest evidence in all the world of the madness of mankind, is the obstinate self-destruction of all the ungodly. Consider but, 1. The weight of the case; 2. The plainness of the case; 3. The means used to undeceive them; 4. And yet the number of the madly erroneous; and then bethink you what man's understanding is.

1. It is their souls and everlasting hopes that are cast away! It is no less than heaven and endless happiness which they reject: it is no better than hell and endless misery which they run into: and are these men in their wits?

2. It is themselves that do all this; neither man nor devils else could do it: they do it for nothing. What have the wretches for their salvation? a few cups of drink, a filthy whore, a little preferment or provision for a corruptible flesh, which must shortly lie and rot in darkness; the applause and breath of flatterers as silly as themselves! O profane persons, worse than Esau, who will sell their birth-right for so poor a morsel! Come see the madness of mankind! It is a doubt to them whether God or a filthy lust should be more loved and obeyed! It is a doubt with them whether heaven or earth be better worth their labour! Whether eternity or an inch of time, whether a soul or a perishing body, should be more cared for! Are these wise men? Did I say, It is a doubt? Yea, their choice and practice showeth that at the present they are resolved: vanity, and shadows, and dreams are preferred; heaven is neglected: "They are lovers of pleasure more than of God:" they set less than a feather in the balance against more than all the world, and they choose the first and neglect the latter. This is the wise world!

3. And all this they do against common reason, against daily teaching of appointed pastors, against the judgment of the learnedest and wisest men in the world; against the express word of God; against the obligation of daily mercies; against the warnings of many afflictions; against the experience of all the world, who pronounce all this vanity which they sell their souls for: even while men die daily before their eyes, and they are certain that they must shortly die themselves; while they walk over the churchyard, and tread on the graves of those that went before them; yet will they take no warning, but neglect God and their souls, and sin on to the very death.

4. And this is not the case only of here and there one; we need not go to Bedlam to seek them. Alas! in how much more honoured and splendid habitations and conditions may they be found! in what reverend and honourable garbs! and in how great numbers throughout the world! And these are not only sots and idiots, that never were told of better things; but those that would be accounted witty, or men of learning and venerable aspect and esteem. But this is a subject that we use to preach on to the people: it being easy, by a multitude of arguments, to prove the madness of all ungodly persons. And is this nothing to humble us, who were naturally like them, and who, so far as we are sinners, are, alas! too like them still?

XVI. And the fewness of wise men in all professions, doth tell us how rare true wisdom is. Among men whose wisdom lieth in speculation, where the effects of it do not openly difference it much from prefidence, the difference is not commonly discerned; a prating speculator goeth for a wise man; but in practicals the difference appeareth by the effects. All men see, that among physicians and lawyers, those that are excellent are few. And even among the godly preachers of the gospel, oh that it were more easy and common to meet with men suited to the majesty, mystery, greatness, necessity, and holiness of their works; that speak to God, and from God, like divines indeed, and have the true frame of sound theology ready in their heads and hearts; and that in public and private speak to sinners, as beseemeth those that believe that they and we are at the door of eternity, and that we speak, and they hear, for the life of souls, and that are uncertain whether ever they shall speak again. Alas! Lord, thy treasure is not only in earthen vessels, but how ordinarily in polluted vessels, and how common are empty, sounding vessels, or such as have dirt or air instead of holy treasure!

And as for philosophers and judicious speculators in divinity, do I need to say that the number is too small? of such as are able judiciously to resolve a difficulty, to answer cases of conscience, to defend the truth, to stop the mouths of all gainsayers, and to teach holy doctrine clearly and in true method, without confusion, or running into extremes? We bless God, this land, and the other reformed churches, have had a laudable degree of this mercy: the Lord restore it to them and us, and continue the comfortable measure that we possess.

XVII. And it is a notorious discovery of the common ignorance, that a wise man is so hardly known. And men that have not wisdom to imitate them, have not wit enough to value them; so that, as Seneca saith, He that will have the pleasure of wisdom, must be content with it for itself, without applause; two or three approvers must suffice him. The blind know not who hath the best eyesight. Swine trample upon pearls. Nay, it is well if, when they have increased knowledge, they increase not sorrow; and become not the mark of envy and hatred, and of the venom of malignant tongues and hands, yea, and that merely for their knowledge' sake. All the learning of Socrates, Demosthenes, Cicero, Seneca, Lucan, and many more; and all the learning and piety of Cyprian, and all the martyrs of those ages; of Boetius; of the African bishops that perished by Hunnerichus; of Peter Ramus, Marlorate, Cranmer, Ridley, Philpot, Bradford, and abundance such, could not keep them from a cruel death. All the excellency of Greg. Nazianzen, Chrysostom, and many others, could not keep them from suffering by orthodox bishops; no nor all the holiness and miracles of Martin. Insomuch that Nazianzen leaveth it to his people as a mark of the man whom he would have them value and choose when he was dead: "This one thing I require, that he be one of those that are envied, not pitied by others; who obey not all men in all things; but for the love of truth in some things incurreth men's offence." And of himself he professeth, that, "Though most thought otherwise than he did, that this was nothing to him, who cared only for the truth, as that which must condemn him or absolve him, and make him happy or miserable. But what other men thought was nothing to him, any more than what another dreameth." Orat. 27, p. 468. And therefore he saith, Orat. 26, p. 443, "As for me, I am a small and poor pastor, and to speak sparingly, not yet grateful, and accepted with other; pastors which whether it be done by right judgment and reason, or by malevolence of mind, and study of contention, I know not." And Orat. 32, p. 523, "I am tired, while I fight both with speech and envy, with enemies and with those that are our own. Those strike at the breast, and obtain not their desire; for an open enemy is easily taken heed of; but these come behind my back, and are more troublesome."

Such obloquy had Jerom, such had Augustine himself; and who knoweth not that envy is virtue's shadow? And what talk I of others, when all godly men are hated by the world, and the apostles and Christ himself were used as they were? and Christ saith, "Which of the prophets did not your fathers kill and persecute?" Matt. xxiii. If hating, persecuting, slandering, silencing, killing men that know more than the rest, be a sign of wisdom, the world hath been wise since Cain's age until this.

Even a Galilæus, a Savonarola, a Campanella, &c. shall feel it if they will be wiser than the rest: so that Solomon's warning (Eccl. vii. 16) concerneth them that will save their skin; "Be not righteous over-much, neither make thyself over-wise; why wilt thou destroy thyself?" But again I may prognosticate with Antisthenes in Laert. Then cities are perishing, when they are not wise enough to know the good from the bad. And with Cicero, Rhet. 1, That man's safety is desperate whose ears are shut against the truth, so that even from a friend he cannot hear it.

XVIII. And this leadeth me to the next discovery: How rare wisdom is in the world, in that the wisest men and learnedest teachers have so small success! How few are much the wiser for them! If they praise them, they will not learn of them, till they reach to their degree. Men may delight in the sweetness of truth themselves; but it is a feast where few will strive for part with them. A very few men that have first sprung up in obscure times have had great success: so had Origen at Alexandria, and Chrysostom at Constantinople, but with bitter sauce. Pythagoras, Plato, and Aristotle at Athens, and Augustine at Hippo, had the most that history maketh mention of, with Demosthenes and Cicero in oratory. Melancthon at Wirtemburg, with Luther, and Zuinglius in Helvetia, and Calvin at Geneva, prevailed much; and now and then an age hath been fruitful of learned, wise, and godly men: and when we are ready to expect, that each of these should have a multitude of scholars like themselves, suddenly all declineth, and ignorance and sensuality get uppermost again. And all this is because that all men are born ignorant and sensual; but no man attaineth to any excellency of wisdom, without so long and laborious studies, as the flesh will give leave to few men to perform. So that he that hath most laboriously searched for knowledge all his days, knoweth not how to make others partakers of it; no, not his own children of whom he hath the education: unless it be here and there one Scaliger, one Paræus, one Tossanus, one Trelcatius, one Vossius, &c. How few excellent men do leave one excellent son behind them! Oh what would a wise man give, that he could but bequeath all his wisdom to others when he dieth!

XIX. And it is evident that great knowledge is more rare than prefidence, in that the hardest students, and most knowing men complain more than others of difficulties and ignorance; when certainly other men have more cause. They that study a little, know little, and think they know much: they that study very hard, but not to maturity, oft become sceptics, and think nothing certain. But they that follow it till they have digested their studies, do find a certainty in the great and necessary things, but confess their ignorance in abundance of things which the presumptuous are confident in. I will not leave this out, to escape the carping of those that will say, that by this character I proclaim myself one of the wisest, as long as it is but the confession of my ignorance which is their occasion. But I will say as Augustin to Jerom, Epist. 29, *Adversus eos qui sibi videntur scire quod nesciunt, hoc tutiores sumus, quod hanc ignorantiam nostram non ignoramus.*

XX. Lastly, every man's nature, in the midst of his pride, is conscious of the fallibility and frailty of his own understanding. And thence it is that men are so fearful in great matters of being overreached. And wherever any conclusion dependeth upon a contexture of many proofs, or on any long, operous work of reason, men have a natural consciousness of the uncertainty of it. Yea, though our doctrines of the immortality of our own souls, and of the life of retribution after this, and the truth of the gospel, have so much certain evidence as they have, yet a lively, certain faith is the more rare and difficult, because men are so conscious of the fallibility of their own understandings, that about things unseen and unsensible, they are still apt to doubt whether they be not deceived in their apprehensions of the evidence.

By these twenty instances it is too plain that there is little solid wisdom in the world; that wise men are few, and those few are but a little wise. And should not this suffice to make all men, but especially the unlearned and half-learned, the young and unexperienced to abate their ungrounded confidence, and to have humble and suspicious thoughts of their own apprehensions?

CHAPTER XVII.

INFERENCE 5. THAT IT IS NOT THE DISHONOUR, BUT THE PRAISE OF CHRIST, HIS APOSTLES, AND THE GOSPEL, THAT THEY SPEAK IN A PLAIN MANNER OF THE CERTAIN NECESSARY THINGS, WITHOUT THE VANITY OF SCHOOL UNCERTAINTIES, AND FEIGNED, UNPROFITABLE NOTIONS.

I HAVE been myself oft scandalized at the fathers of the fourth Carthage council,[a] who forbad bishops the reading of the heathens' books; and at some good old unlearned christian bishops, who spake to the same purpose, and oft reproach Apollinaris, Ætius, and other heretics for their secular or gentile learning, logic, &c. And I wondered that Julian and they should prohibit the same thing. But one that is so far distant from the action, is not a competent judge of the reasons of it. Perhaps there were some christian authors then, who were sufficient for such literature as was best for the church: perhaps they saw that the danger of reading the heathens' philosophy was like to be greater than the benefit; both because it was them that they lived among, and were to gather the churches out of; and if they put an honour upon logic and philosophy, they might find it more difficult to draw men from that party which excelled in it, to the belief of the Scriptures which seemed to have so little of it: and they had seen also how a mixture of Platonic notions with christianity, had not only been the original of many heresies, but had sadly blemished many great doctors of the churches.

Whatever the cause was, it appeareth that in those days it was the deepest insight into the sacred Scrip-

[a] Concil. Carth. 4. Can. 16.

tures which was reckoned for the most solid learning; philosophy was so confounded by differences, sects, uncertainties, and falsehoods, that made it the more despicable, by how much the less pure. And logic had so many precarious rules and notions, as made it fitter to wrangle and play with, than to further grave men in their deep and serious inquiry in the great things of God, and mysteries of salvation.

But yet it cannot be denied but that true learning of the subservient arts and sciences is of so great use to the accomplishing of man's mind with wisdom, that it is one of the greatest offences that ever was taken against Christ and the holy Scriptures, that so little of this learning is found in them, in comparison of what is in Plato, Aristotle, Demosthenes, or Cicero. But to remove the danger of this offence, let these things following be well considered:

I. Every means is to be judged of by its aptitude to its proper use and end: morality is the subject and business of the Scriptures: it is not the work of it to teach men logic and philosophy, any more than to teach them languages. Who will be offended with Christ for not teaching men Latin, Greek, or Hebrew, architecture, navigation, or mechanic arts? And why should they be more offended with him for not teaching them astronomy, geometry, physics, metaphysics, logic, &c.? It was none of his work.

II. Nature is presupposed to grace; and God in nature had before given man sufficient helps to the attainment of so much of the knowledge of nature, as was convenient for him. Philosophy is the knowledge of God's works of creation. It was not this (at least chiefly) that man lost by his fall: it was from God, and not from the creature, that he turned; and it was to the knowledge of God, rather than of the creature, that he was to be restored. What need one be sent from heaven to teach men the order and rules of speaking? or to teach men those arts and sciences which they can otherwise learn themselves? As it is presupposed that men have reason, so that they have among them the common helps and crutches of reason.

III. The truth is, it is much to be suspected, lest as an inordinate desire of creature knowledge was a great part of our first parents' sin, so it hath accordingly corrupted our nature with an answerable vicious inclination thereunto: not that the thing in itself is evil to know God's works; but good and desirable in its place and measure; but it is such a good as by inordinacy may become a dangerous evil. Why should we not judge of this desire of knowing the creatures as we do of other creature affections? It is lawful and meet to love all God's creatures: his works are good, and therefore amiable. And yet I think no man is damned but by the inordinate loving of the creature, turning his heart from the love of God. And as our appetites are lawful and necessary in themselves, and yet nature's pravity consisteth much in the prevalency of them against reason, which is by reason's infirmity, and the inordinacy of the sensitive appetite; even so a desire to know God's works is natural and good, but its inordinateness is our pravity, and a sinful lust.

Doubtless the mind and fantasy may find a kind of pleasure in knowing, which is according to the nature and use of the thing known. When it is vain, or low, and base, the pleasure is vain, and low, and base: when the object is insnaring and diverting from higher things, it doth this principally by delight. Verily this inordinate desire of creature knowledge is a lust, a vicious lust. I have been guilty of it in some measure myself, since I had the use of reason: I have lived a life of constant pleasure, gratifying my intellect and fantasy with seeking to know as much as I could know: and if I could not say truly, that I referred it as a means to the knowledge and love of God, I should say that it was all sin: but because I have loved it too much for itself, and not referred it to God more purely and entirely, I must confess that it was never blameless.

And the corruption of the noblest faculty is the worst: the delights of eating, drinking, venery, are the matter of common sensuality, when they are inordinately desired; and is not the inordinate desire of creature knowledge (if it be desired from the like principle, and to the like ends) as bad or worse in some respects? Consider,

1. I am sure that it doth as much take up and prepossess the mind, which should be employed on God, and take up those thoughts and affections which should be holy. Tell me why one man should be accounted carnal and ungodly, for delighting to see his own houses, fields, woods, corn, rivers, cattle, &c. rather than another that hath as much delight to peruse a map of pleasant countries, setting aside the covetous desire of having much. Do we not justly account it as unfit a work for the Lord's day to be for pleasure perusing maps, as to be for pleasure viewing the woods and fields? Many a poor student is as long and perilously entangled in his thoughts and affections, and kept from God, and heaven, and holiness, by deep study of languages, customs, counties, chronology, logic, physics, mathematics, metaphysics, laws, &c. as worldlings are by overminding the world.

2. And it wasteth their precious time as much as other lusts do. One sensualist spendeth his hours in gaming, feasting, wantonness, idle courtship, hunting, hawking, bowling, and other excess of sports; another spends his precious time in hearing comedies; and another in reading play-books and romances; and another in reading true and useful history, and other parts of useful learning: and though the matter of the latter be better than the former, a man may make up the same sensuality in one as in the other; in reading mathematics or history, as in reading, or beholding, and hearing comedies.

3. And some turn this learning to as powerful a perversion of the mind, as others do their sensual delights. Many think so highly of their languages, and chronology, and philosophy, that secretly they are drawn by it to despise the gospel, and to think a holy life to be but an employment for women, and persons that live more by affection than by judgment: so perniciously doth learning make them mad.

4. And abundance make it the fuel of their pride, and think that they are excellent persons, because they have got some ornaments of the mind: as vain women are proud of fine clothes instead of real comeliness and worth. I will not dishonour some famous writers by naming them here, lest I seem to take down their due praise; but in general I may say, that it is more than one of our late famous philological and grammatical critics, who openly show so much pride of their kind of worldly knowledge, as may warn humble men to fear such temptations, and to see that this learning may be made a snare.

5. And the worst of all is, that while such learned men think highly of themselves for that, they are kept from the knowledge and sense of their sinful corruption and misery, and feel not the need of a Saviour and a Sanctifier: they cry not for grace; they seek not after God and everlasting happiness; they neglect a holy, heavenly life; they take up some easy formalities and words to make up an image of religion of; and then they think that (in their unhumbled, unsanctified state) they have as

good right to be esteemed godly, as any other; and if any question it, they are accounted proud, self-conceited fanatics, who appropriate the reputation of holiness to themselves: and to question a learned formalist's sincerity, (as Martin and Sulpitius Severus did Ithacius's and his fellow-bishops,) is to expose himself to the censure of proud hypocrisy. Yea, no man is so fit for church preferment and honour, and to be the governor of all the religious persons and affairs, as one of these unsanctified, learned men is in his own eyes: from whence it is that the state of the churches is so low in the East and West, (the Roman I mean,) because those that have truly no religion must dispose of religion, and the churches of Christ must be instructed and ruled by his real enemies; and those that hate godliness at the heart, must be the teachers of godliness, and the chief managers of the sacred work.

Lay all this together, and think whether our inordinate desire of common learning, which is the knowledge of the creature, be not the fruit of Adam's sin.

And if it prove so, consider how far it was the work of Christ to cure it. Sure he was sent to destroy the works of the devil (not learning, but this inordinate desire of it). And he was to mortify it in the same way as he mortified other sinful lusts. Therefore as he mortified venereous and all sensual lusts, by holy example, and by condemning them, and calling men off from them to spiritual delights; and as he mortified worldliness in men, by living himself a life of poverty and inferiority in the world, and calling men off from the love of the world to the love of God and glory: even so no wonder if he mortified in men the inordinate desire of greater knowledge, by calling them up to higher things, and showing them the vanity of this alone. And as he saith, "Love not the world, nor the things that are in the world: if any man love the world, the love of the Father is not in him," 1 John ii. 15; when yet the ordinate love of the world is lawful: and as he saith, John vi. 27, "Labour not for the meat that perisheth," when he meaneth, labour not for it inordinately: even so no wonder if Christ omit this common philosophy, and if Paul bid them take heed that none deceive them by vain philosophy, when it is the inordinacy only which they condemn.

If you ask me, when this desire of common learning is inordinate? I answer, 1. When it is desired most for the fantastical, sensual, or intellectual delight of knowing; or from the overvaluing of the thing known: not but a delight in knowledge as such is good and lawful, but not as our chief end. 2. When it is desired as a step to serve a proud, aspiring mind, that we may be magnified as learned men; or to serve any worldly, covetous design. 3. When it is not duly subordinate and subservient to the love of God, and to his service, and the common good: if God be not first intended, and all our studies and learning desired purely as a means to God, that is, as a means to know him, and to love him, and to please him, and praise him, and do him service in the world, and enjoy him for ever, but be desired for itself or carnal ends, it is a carnal lust. 4. When it hath a greater measure of our time, and affection, and industry, comparatively than its due; and the study of higher things is put behind it, or neglected by it, at least in a great degree. 5. When it cometh not in due order, but is taken first, and in the hours and place which higher things should have.

In a word; God, and our duty to him, and the common good, and our salvation, are the great and necessary things, in comparison of which all other things are vain: as riches and pleasure with its appetite may be used holily, as God's mercies, to raise us unto spiritual delights, and to serve him the better ourselves, and to be helpful to others: and for these ends they are given us, and may be sought and used; when yet, as they are the fuel of lust, they are the snares of Satan, the mammon, the god of this world, the damnation of souls: so is it with the knowledge of the creature; sanctified and made serviceable to God and holiness it is of great utility, but out of its place it is poison and perdition.

Yea, as appetite and sensual delight is necessary, while we are in a body in which the soul must operate and receive; even so is some knowledge of creatures and common things (called learning) of necessity, as a means to better. And while we see as in a glass, we must not cast away the glass, nor neglect it, though it be but a help to see the species.

I conclude then, 1. That it is hard to say that any man can know too much, except it be, 1. Matter of temptation. 2. And of penal knowledge, raising terrors, and tormenting the soul. In these two cases we may know too much; and I fear some men's knowledge is much of the first sort. But so far am I from dissuading any from true knowledge, or studies to attain it, that I think ignorance is the mother, as pride is the father of all heresies, and almost all sins: and that the lazy student shall never be wise, though one may take his years in the university, the greatness of his library, or the titles which he hath obtained, instead of wisdom; and another as slothful, may boast that the Spirit hath saved him the labour of long and hard studies: for my part I shall account both sorts as they are, and leave them to be admired by such as themselves; and verily they have their reward. He that will be wise, must spare no pains, and be diverted by no worldly things, but take wisdom for his welfare here, and the getting and using it for all his work. Never was slothful, or impatient, or presumptuous person wise.

2. God hath not made and set before us his works in vain: "Great and wonderful are all his works, sought out of them that have pleasure therein," Psalm cxi.; the image of his power, wisdom, and goodness is imprinted on them all. Who can look up to the sun, and moon, and stars; to the vast and numerous globes above us; to this earth, and all its furniture and inhabitants, and not see the footsteps of the great, and wise, and good Creator, and be edified and made more holy; that doth not use the eye of sense alone, while he winketh with the eye of reason? Our Redeemer came to recover us to the knowledge, love, and obedience of our Creator, and by faith to lead us up to the love of God, and to sanctify us to our Maker's praise and service. Far was it from his design to call us from studying the works of creation; which he prepareth us better to understand and use: nor would he deprive reason of its spectacles, but help us to better than we had before. Man's wit and tongue are apt to be so irregular, that we have need of the rules of true logic to keep them to order, and save them from deceit. Too little true logic and philosophy is much of their unhappiness who think they have enough to deserve veneration and applause.

3. But all this is dreaming, insignificant, incoherent nonsense, deliration, worse than children's chat, (as it troubleth the world more,) if God be not the beginning, guide, and end of it, and if we know not how to please him and be saved; and if all learning be not directly or indirectly a learning to know God and life eternal: when conscience is awakened all things are as dreams, and signify nothing in comparison of God and life eternal, to be obtained by

Christ. When men come to die, the most learned die in this mind; and further than it is divine and holy and felicitating, they cry out of all their fame and learning, "Vanity of vanities, all is vanity;" though learning be the most splendid of all vanities. Fear God and keep his commandments, is the end of true learning, and the whole learning of man. Of writing many books there is no end; and much reading is a weariness to the flesh; and he that increaseth knowledge contracteth envy and contradiction, and increaseth sorrow: but sanctified learning maketh a man indeed; so it be true, and not false pretended learning.

4. Therefore the industry of a man's study, the most of his time, the zeal of his soul, must be laid out on God, and the great and endless concernments of his own and others' souls; and learning must be desired, esteemed, sought, and used, according to its usefulness to these high and glorious ends: then it is the lower part of wisdom; which all that want it must esteem, and honour, and desire; else it is a dream and folly, which leaveth the awakened soul in shame. But I have been too long on this.

IV. Consider next, that as this lower sort of learning is presupposed by Christ as true, and the desire of it cured as it is a lust; so plainness and intelligibleness were altogether necessary to his ends; what came he on earth to do, but to reconcile us to God, and make known his kingdom and his love to sinners? to procure us pardon, and a spirit of vivification, illumination, and sanctification? And the word that must be the means of this must be fitted to its end, and be intelligible to the unlearned; or else he should have been the Saviour of a few learned men only, and not of the world. Kings and parliaments write their laws in a style suitable to the matter; and so do men draw up their covenants, and princes their pardons, and physicians their bills and directions: and none of these useth to write a grammar or logic instead of their proper work, nor to fill their writings with ludicrous, logical tricks and toys. He that is but to tell men how to be saved from sin and hell, and brought to heaven, and live so here that he may live with God and angels for ever, must speak in plainness and in good earnest.

V. And consider that the Scripture is not void of so much logic and philosophy as is suitable to its design. In a well-fleshed body the distinction and compagination of the parts are hid, which in an ugly skeleton are discerned. So the Scripture is a body of essentials, integrals, and accidentals of religion, and every unstudied fellow cannot anatomize it: but it hath its real and excellent method, for all that it is hid to the unskilful. There is a method of Scripture theology, which is the most accurate that ever the world knew in morality. I have drawn up the body of theology into schemes, in which I doubt not but I have shown, that the method of theology contained in the holy Scriptures, is more accurate than any logical author doth prescribe; and the Lord's prayer and decalogue especially will prove this, when truly opened: and the doctrine of the Trinity, and the baptismal covenant, is the foundation of all true method of physics and morality in the world. What if a novice cannot anatomize Cicero or Demosthenes, doth it follow that they are immethodical? Brandmiller and Flaccher upon the Scripture text, and Steph. Tzedegine, Sohnius, Gomarus, Dudley, Fenner, and many others upon the body of theology, have gone far in opening the Scripture method. But more may be yet done.

VI. Consider also that the Eternal Wisdom, Word, and Son of God our Redeemer, is the fountain and giver of all knowledge: nature to be restored, and grace to restore it, are in his hands. He is that true light that lighteneth every one that cometh into the world: the light of nature, and arts and sciences, are from his Spirit and teaching, as well as the gospel. Whether Clemens Alexandrinus and some other ancients were in the right or not, when they taught that philosophy is one way by which men come to salvation, it is certain that they are in the right, that say it is now the gift of Christ: and that as the light which goeth before sun-rising (yea, which in the night is reflected from the moon) is from the sun, as well as its more glorious beams; so the knowledge of Socrates, Plato, Zeno, Cicero, Antonine, Epictetus, Seneca, Plutarch, were from the Wisdom and Word of God, the Redeemer of the world, even by a lower gift of his Spirit, as well as the gospel and higher illumination: and shall Christ be thought void of what he giveth so many in the world?

VII. Lastly, let it be considered above all, that the grand difference between the teaching of Christ and other men, is that he teacheth effectively (as God spake when he created, and as he said to Lazarus, Arise). He giveth wisdom by giving the Holy Ghost: all other teachers speak but to the ears; but he only speaketh to the heart: were it not for this he would have no church.—I should never have else believed in him myself, nor would any other, seriously and savingly. Aristotle and Plato speak but words, but Christ speaketh LIFE and LIGHT and LOVE, in all countries, through all ages to this day. This above all is his witness in the world. He will not do his work on souls by ludicrous enticing words of the pedantic wisdom of the world; but by illuminating minds, and changing hearts and lives, by his effectual operations on the heart. God used not more rhetoric nor logic than a philosopher, when he said only, "Let there be light," but he used more power. Indeed the first chapter of Genesis (though abused by ignorants and cabalists) hath more true philosophy in it than the presumptuous will understand (as my worthy friend Mr. Samuel Gott, lately gone to God, hath manifested in his excellent Philosophy; excepting the style, and some few presumptions). But operations are the glorious oratory of God, and his wisdom shineth in his works, and in things beseeming the heavenly Majesty; and not in childish laces, and toys of wit.

Let us therefore cease quarrelling, and learn wisdom of God, instead of teaching and reprehending him. Let us magnify the mercy and wisdom of our Redeemer, who hath brought life and immortality to light, and certified us of the matters of the world above, as beseemed a messenger sent from God; and hath taught us according to the matter, and our capacity, and not with trifling, childish notions.

CHAPTER XVIII.

INFERENCE 6. THE TRUE AND FALSE WAYS OF RESTORING THE CHURCHES, AND HEALING OUR DIVISIONS, HENCE OPENED AND MADE PLAIN.

HAVING opened to you our disease, it is easy, were not the disease itself against it, to discern the cure. Pretended knowledge hath corrupted and divided the christian world. Therefore it must be CERTAIN VERITIES, which must restore us, and unite us. And these must be things PLAIN and NECESSARY, and such as God hath designed to this very use; or else they will never do the work. One would think that it should be enough to satisfy men of this, 1. To read Scripture. 2. To peruse the terms of concord in the primitive church. 3. To peruse the sad histories of the church's discord and divisions, and the causes. 4. To peruse the state of the world at this day, and make use of universal experience. 5. To know what a christian is, what baptism is, and what a church is. 6. To know what man is; and that they themselves, and the churches, are but men. But penal and sinful infatuation hath many ages been upon the minds of those in the christian world, who were most concerned in the cure; and our sin is our misery, as, I think, to the damned it will be the chief part of their hell.

But this subject is so great and needful, and that which the wounds and blood of the christian world do cry for a skilful cure of; that I will not thrust it into this corner, but design to write a treatise of it by itself, as a second part of this.[a]

CHAPTER XIX.

VIII. OF THE CAUSES OF THIS DISEASE OF PREFIDENCE, OR PROUD PRETENDED KNOWLEDGE, IN ORDER TO THE CURE.

THE cure of prefidence and pretended knowledge, could it be wrought, would be the cure of souls, families, churches, and kingdoms. But alas, how low are our hopes! Yet that may be done on some, which will not be done on all or most. And to know the causes, and oppugn them, is the chief part of the cure, so far as it may be hoped for.

I. The first and grand cause is the very nature of ignorance itself; which many ways disableth men from knowing that which should abate their groundless confidence. For, 1. An ignorant man knoweth but little parcels and scraps of things; and all the rest is unknown to him: therefore he fixeth upon that little which he knoweth; and having no knowledge of the rest, he cannot regulate his narrow apprehensions by any conceptions of them. And all things visible to us (not light itself excepted, which, as seen by us, is fire incorporated in air) being compounds, the very nature or being of them is not known, where any constitutive part is unknown. And in all compounds, each part hath such relation and usefulness to others, that one part which seemeth known, is itself but half known, for want of the knowledge of others. Such a kind of knowledge is theirs, that knowing only what they see, do take a clock or watch to be only the index moving by the hours, being ignorant of all the casual parts within; or that know no more of a tree, or other plant, than the magnitude, site, colour, odour, &c.; or that take a man to be only a body, without a soul, or the body to be only the skin and parts discerned by the eye in converse.

Now that which such persons do sensibly apprehend, they are confident of, because that nature teacheth them to trust their senses; but not knowing the rest, their little partial conceptions are lame, defective, and deceitful. For most will hence rashly conclude of the negative, that there is no more, because they know no more. But if any be more wise and modest, yet do they want the conception of the unknown parts, to make the rest to be true knowledge, or to tell them what is yet unknown; and such use to turn a judicial rule into a physical, that *non apparere et non esse* are to them all one.

2. And an ignorant man doth not know what conceptions other men have of the same things which he is ignorant of: so that he neither knoweth the thing intelligible, (what it is,) nor yet the act of knowing it, which he never had: but as a man born blind hath no formal conception, either of sight, or of light, or visible objects; so is it here.

3. Nor hath he usually a true knowledge of his own ignorance; how imperfect his understanding is, and how much to be suspected, as liable to mistake: though in some sensible matters it is easy to convince men of a total ignorance; yet when they know any thing, it is hard to convince them what more is to be known, and to keep them from false and hasty conclusions. A man that cannot read at all, is easily convinced that he cannot read; but he that can read a little, is apt to think that he readeth rightly, when he doth not. A man that never heard of physic, is easily convinced that he hath no skill in it; but if he have read, heard of, and tried a few medicines, he is apt to grow conceited, and venture men's lives upon his skill. A man that never saw building, navigation, or any art or manufacture, is easily convinced that he is ignorant of it; but if he have got some smattering knowledge, he is ready to think that it is more than it is, because he knoweth not what he wants.

And to err, and know that a man erreth, (at the same time, about the same thing,) is a contradiction; for he that erreth, judgeth a falsehood to be a truth: but to know that so to judge is to err, is certainly not so to judge; for *intellectus vult verum;* that is, truth is the object which it is naturally inclined to. The same light which discovereth error, cureth it; and that light which discovereth the thing itself, is it that must convince me that I before erred about it, by misapprehensions.

4. And an ignorant man doth not so much as know the difficulties of the case, and what may be said on the other side; what contrary evidence convinceth others, or what weight there is in the objections, which are or may be brought against him. So that all men being naturally ignorant, and little being known for much that is unknown, even to the wisest; alas, the temptation to error and false confidence is so strong, that few escape it.

II. Another cause of it is, the radical master sin of pride: an unhumbled mind, never well acquainted with its own dark and erroneous condition, and its great need of natural and supernatural helps. I find it hard to convince men of this; but the forementioned effects do certainly prove it. The vice is born with us at the very heart. It is the devil's image: he that is not naturally proud, is not a son of Adam. It liveth first, and dieth last: and there is nothing that man is apter to be proud of, than his reason, which is his humanity, and next to that of his goodness, and of his greatness. Men perceive not this in themselves, because they know not what pride is, while it ruleth in them. They think that it is only some womanish or childish extrinsical ostentation, (boasting,) or perking up above others in garb and place, or peacock-like looking upon their own train, or setting it up for others to look on. But pride is (as I said before) an overvaluing ourselves, and a desire that others should overvalue us: and how few be there that be not tickled when their wisdom is applauded, and nettled when it is accounted small! it is hard to bear to be accounted and reported a

[a] This book is since printed with some alteration, and called "The True and Only Way of the Concord of the Churches."

fool, or a person of little wit. Many a man spendeth all the studies of his life, more for a fame of learning than for learning itself. What is pride if this be not? What grosser pride, than for a woman, or unexperienced lad, to scorn and despise the oldest and hardest students in divinity, as dark souls in comparison of them? The quakers in their shops, when I go along London streets, say, Alas, poor man, thou art yet in darkness. They have oft come into the congregation, (when I had liberty to preach Christ's gospel,) and cried out against me as a deceiver of the people. They have followed me home, crying out in the streets, The day of the Lord is coming, when thou shalt perish as a deceiver. They have stood in the market-place, and under my window, year after year, crying out to the people, Take heed of your priests, they deceive your souls. And if they saw any one wear a lace or neat clothing, they cried to me, These are the fruit of thy ministry. If they spake to me with the greatest ignorance or nonsense, it was with as much fury and rage, as if a bloody heart had appeared in their faces; so that though I never hurt or occasioned the hurt of one of them, that I know of, their truculent countenances told me what they would have done had I been in their power: (this was in 1656, 57, 58, 59.) And yet they were poorly clothed, (some of them went through the streets stark naked,) and cried out over and over all the year, Woe to the proud! Wonderful! wonderful! Oh the blindness of a corrupted mind! that these poor souls did not perceive their superlative pride. How highly did these people think of their own wisdom and holiness, while they cried down laces, points, and cuffs!

And when did I ever know either a true church tyrant, or a true sectarian, separating humorist, which were not both notorious proud overvaluers of their own conceits; to which those that bowed not must be persecuted as unruly schismatics by the one sort, and excommunicated, separated from, and damned as ungodly, carnal, or antichristian by the other sort?

Several ways doth PRIDE cause pretended knowledge. 1. By thinking that our understandings are so good as that without great study we can know truth from falsehood; and so making us venture to judge of things at the first hearing or reading, which we cannot be capable of judging of under long and diligent studies; because *recipitur ad modum recipientis.* Therefore it is that when a man by great success in studies hath made things as plain as words can make them, so that you would think that all students should presently be wise at easy rates by the light which he hath set up to them, they are half as long in learning for all that, as if he had never given them such a help. And therefore it is, that we cannot leave our learning to posterity; because still the stop is in the receiver's incapacity; and he cannot be capable of the plainest precepts, but by much time and study.

2. Pride maketh men hasty in concluding, because they are not humbled to a just suspicion of their own apprehensions. And men stay not to prove and try things before they judge.

3. Pride maketh men insensible how much they are ignorant of, in all their knowledge.

4. And it causeth men to slight the reasons and judgments of other men, by which they might learn, or at least might be taught to judge considerately, and suspend their own.

If overvaluing a man's own apprehensions be pride, (as it is,) then certainly pride is one of the commonest sins in the world, and particularly among men professing godliness, who upon every poor surmise or report are condemning those that they do not thoroughly know; and in every petty controversy they are all still in the right, though of never so many minds.

III. Another cause of pretended knowledge is the want of a truly tender conscience: which should make men fear, lest they should err, lest they should deserve the curse for putting "light for darkness and darkness for light, evil for good and good for evil," Isa. v. 20; and should make them afraid lest they should defile their minds, resist the truth, blaspheme God or dishonour him, by fathering errors on him; and lest they should prove snares to men's souls, and a scandal and trouble to the church of God. A tender conscience would not have espoused such opinions under one or two or many years' deliberation, which an antinomian or other sectary will take up in a few days (if they were true). Oh, saith the tender conscience, what if I should err, and prove a snare to souls, and a scandal and dishonour to the church of God! &c.

IV. Another cause of pretended knowledge, is a blind zeal for knowledge and godliness in the general, while men know not what it is they are zealous of. They think that it is a necessary part of sincerity to receive the truth speedily without delay; and therefore they take a present concluding for a true receiving it. And he that soonest taketh up that which is offered him, probably as a part of godliness, is taken for the most resolved downright convert. Which is true in case of evident truths, where it is the will that by vice suspendeth the mind; but not in dark and doubtful cases.

V. Another cause is, an inordinate trust in man; when some admire the learned too much, and some the religious, and some this or that particular person, and therefore build too confidently on their words; some on great men, some on the multitude, but most on men of fame for great learning or great piety. A credit is to be given by every learner to his teacher: but the confounding this with our belief of God, and making it a part of our religion, and not trusting man as man only, that is, as a fallible wight, doth cause this vice of pretended knowledge to pass with millions for divine faith. Especially when men embody themselves into a sect, as the only orthodox or godly party, or as the only true church (as the papists do); then it imboldeneth them to believe any thing which their sect or church believeth. For they think that this is the church's faith, which cannot err, or is the safest; and that God would not let so many good men err. And thus they that should be made their teachers, and the helpers of their faith, become the lords of it, and almost their gods.

VI. And it much increaseth this sin, that men are not sufficiently acquainted with the original and additional corruption of man's nature, and know not how blind all mankind are. Alas, man is a dark creature: what error may he not hold! What villany may he not do; yea and maintain! Truly said David, "All men are liars." Pitifully do many expound this as an effect of his unbelief and passion, because he saith, "I said in my haste;" when it is no more than Paul saith, "Let God be true, and every man a liar," Rom. iii.; and than Solomon and Isaiah say, "All men are vanity;" and Jeremiah, "Cursed be he that trusteth in man!" All men are untrusty in a great degree; weak, false, and bad. And his *haste* was either, as Dr. Hammond translateth it, his *flight*, or else that his trial and distress made him more passionately sensible of the vanity or untrustiness of man than he was at other times. For *vanity* and a *lie* to the Hebrews were words of the same importance, signifying deceivableness and untrustiness. And indeed among mankind there is so great a degree of impotency, selfishness, timorousness, ignorance, error, and viciousness, as that few wicked men are to be believed, where there is any strong temptation to lying. And the devil is seldom unprovided of temptations: and abundance of hypocrites are as untrusty as open wicked men: and abundance of sincere godly persons, especially women, have loose tongues, and hasty passions, and a stretching conscience, but especially injudicious heads, so that frequently they know not truth from falsehood, nor have the tenderness of conscience to be silent till they know: so that if one say it, another will say it, till a hundred say it, and then it goeth for current truth.

Good men's over-much credulity of one another hath filled the church with lies and fables. Many of the papists' superstitions, purgatory, praying to saints and angels, praying for the dead, &c. were bred by this credulity. It is so visible in Venerable Bede, Gregory the first, yea before them in Sulpitius Severus of Martin's Life, and abundance more, that to help up christianity among the pagans, they laid hold of any old woman's or ignorant man's dreams, and visions, and stories of pretended miracles and revelations, that it made even Melchior Canus cry out of the shameful, ridiculous faith, that hence had filled their legends. Even Baronius, upon trial, retaineth no small number of them, and with his brethren the Oratorians, on their prophesying days, told them to the people. I am ashamed, that I recited one out of him, before my treatise of "Crucifying the World," though I did it not as persuading any that it was true: for I quickly saw, that Sophronius, on whom he fathered it, was none of the reporters of it, that book being spurious, and none of Sophronius's work.

Indeed I know of such impudent false history lately printed, of matters of public fact in these times, yea, divers concerning my own words and actions, by persons that are far from contemptible, that strangers and posterity will scarce believe that human nature could be guilty of it in the open light. And I know it to be so customary a thing, for the zealots professing the fear of God, on one side and the other, to receive and rashly tell about lies of one another, that I confess I am grown to take little heed of what such say, in such a case; unless the report continue a year uncontrolled: for it is common for them to tell those things as unquestionable, which a few months prove false; and yet never to manifest any repentance, but to go on with the like, one month disproving what the former hatched and vended.

And indeed the very wisest and best of men are guilty of so much ignorance, temerity, suspiciousness of others' partiality, &c. that we must believe them (though far sooner than others, yet) still with a reserve to change our minds, if we find them mistaken, and still on supposition that they are fallible persons, and that all men are liars.

VII. Another great cause of pretended false knowledge and confidence, is the unhappy prejudices which our minds contract even in our childhood, before we have time, and wit, and conscience to try things by true deliberation. Children and youth must receive much upon trust, or else they can learn nothing: but then they have not wit to proportion their apprehensions to the evidence, whether of credibility or certainty: and so fame, and tradition, and education, and the country's vote, do become the ordinary parents of many lies; and folly maketh us to fasten so fearlessly in our first apprehensions, that they keep open the door to abundance more falsehoods; and it must be clear teachers, or great, impartial studies, of a self-denying mind, with a great blessing of God, that must deliver us from prejudice, and undeceive us. And therefore all the world seeth, that almost all men are of the religion of their country or their parents, be it never so absurd; though with the Mahometans they believe the nonsense of a very sot (once reading a quarter of whose Alcoran one would think should cure a man of common reason of any inclination to his belief). And among the Japonians, even the eloquent Bonzii believe in Amida and Xaca; to mention the belief of the Chinese, the people of Pegu, Siam, and many other such; yea, the Americans, the Brazilians, Lappians, &c. that correspond with devils, would be a sad instance of the unhappiness of men's first apprehensions and education. And what doth the aforesaid instance of popery come short herein, which tells how prejudice, and education, and company can make men deny all men's common sense, and believe common, unseen miracles, pretended in the stead?

VIII. Another cause is the mistaking of the nature of the duty of submitting our judgment to our superiors and teachers, especially to the multitude, or the church, or antiquity. No doubt but much reverence, and a human belief, is due to the judgment of our teachers credibly made known. But this is another thing quite different, 1. From knowing by evidence. 2. And from believing God (of which, before and after).

IX. Another cause is base slothfulness, which makes men take up with the judgment of those in most reputation for power, wisdom, or number, to save them the labour of searching after the scientific evidence of things, or the certain evidence of divine revelations.

X. Another frequent cause is, an appearance of something in the truth, which frighteneth men from it; either for want of a clear, methodical, advantageous representation; or by some difficult objection, or some miscarriage in the utterance, carriage, or life of them that seem most zealous for it: such little things deceive dark man; and when he is turned from the truth, he thinks that the contrary error may be embraced without fear.

XI. Another great cause of confidence in false conceits, is the bias of some personal interest prevailing with a corrupted will, and the mixture of sense and passion in the judgment. For, as interested men hardly believe what seemeth against them, and easily believe that which they would have to be true; so sense and passion (or affections) usually so bear down reason, that they think it their right to possess the throne. Not but that sense is the only discerner of its own sensible object as such (and reason by sense as it is intelligible): but that is not the matter in hand. But the sensualist forceth his reason to call that best for him which his sense is most delighted with, and that worst which most offendeth sense. The drunkard will easily judge that his drinking is good for him, and the glutton that his pleasant meats are lawful, and the time-waster that his plays are lawful, and the fornicator the wrathful revenger, &c. that their lusts and passions are lawful, because they think that they have feeling on their side. It is hard to carry an upright judgment against sense and passion.

XII. Sometimes a strong, deluded imagination maketh men exceeding confident in error; some by melancholy, and some by a natural weakness of reason, and strength of fantasy; and some by misapprehensions in religion; grow to think that every strong conceit which doth but come in suddenly, at reading, or hearing, or thinking on such a text, or in time of earnest prayer, especially if it deeply affect themselves, is certainly some suggestion or inspiration of God's Spirit. And hence many errors have troubled poor souls and the church of God, which afterwards they have themselves retracted. Hence is the confidence of some ignorant christians in expounding difficult Scripture prophecies; and the boldness of others in expounding dark providences, and also in foretelling by their own surmises things to come.

XIII. And not a few run into this mischief in some extremes, by seeing others run into error on the other side. Some are so offended at the credulity of the weak, that they will grow confident against plain certainties themselves. As, because there are many feigned miracles, apparitions, possessions, and witchcrafts in the world, divulged by the credulity of the injudicious, therefore they will more foolishly be confident that there are no such things at all. And because they see some weak persons impute more of their opinions, performances, and affections to God's Spirit, than they ought; therefore they grow mad against the true operations of the Spirit, and confident that there is no such thing. Some deride praying by the Spirit, and preaching by the Spirit, and living by the Spirit; whenas they may as well deride understanding, willing, working, by a reasonable soul; no holy thing being holily done without God's Spirit, any more than any act of life and reason without the soul. And they may, on the same grounds, deride all that live not after the flesh, and that are christians, Rom. viii. 5—9, 13; or that love God, or that seek salvation. Yea, some run so far from spiritual fanaticisms, that they deny the very being of spirits; and many confidently set up a dead image of true religion, in bitter hatred and opposition of all that hath life and serious holiness: so mad are some made, by seeing some feverish persons dote.

XIV. Another cause is, conversing only with those of our own mind, and side, and interest; and not seeking familiar, loving acquaintance with those that differ from us: whereby men deprive themselves of hearing half that is to be heard, and of knowing much that is to be known. And their proud vice hardeneth them in this way, to say, I have read and I have heard enough of them; I know all that they can say. And if a man soberly speak to them, their vices of pride, presumption, and passion, will scarce patiently bear him to go on without interruption to the end; but the wizard saith, I know already what you will say, and you are tedious; and do you think that so wise a man as I hath nothing to do but hear such a fool as you talk? Thus proud men are ordinarily so full of themselves, that they can scarce endure to hear, or at least learn any thing from others, nor restrain their violent list to speak, so long as either just information or human civility requireth.

XV. Another cause is, malignity and want of christian love; whereby men are brought, if not to a hatred, yet to a proud contempt of others, who are not of their mind, and side, and way. O they are all—as foolish and bad as any one hath list to call them; and he that raileth at them most ingeniously and impudently, giveth them but their due. And will a man, full of himself and his own, be moved from his presumptions, by any thing that such a hated or scorned people can say? Nay, will he not be hardened in his self-conceit, because it is such as these that contradict him?

Many such causes of this vice there be; but pride and ignorance are the proper parents of it, whatever else be the nurse or friend.

CHAPTER XX.

OBJECTIONS ANSWERED.

I EASILY foresee, that besides the foresaid impediments, all these following objections will hinder the cure of false pretended knowledge, and self-conceitedness, and false belief, if they be not answered.

Object. I. You move men to an impossibility; to see without light; and for an erring man to believe that he erreth. He that hath not light to see the truth, hath not light to see his ignorance of it. This is no more, than to persuade all men to be wise, and not to err; which you may do long enough to little purpose.

Answ. It is impossible indeed for an erring man, while such, to know that he erreth: but it is not impossible, 1. For an ignorant man to know that he is ignorant (nor for a man without light or sight, to know that he seeth not; though he cannot see that he seeth not). For though nescience be nothing; and nothing is not properly and directly an object of our knowledge, no more than of our sight: yet as we see the limited quantity of substances, and so know little from big, by concluding that it hath no more quantity than we see; so we know our own knowledge, both as to object and act, and we know the degree of it, and to what it doth extend; and so can conclude, I know no more. And though nescience be nothing, yet this proposition, I know no more, is not nothing. And so nothing is usually said to be known reductively; but indeed it is not properly known at all; but this proposition, *de nihilo*, is known, which is something. (I will not here meddle with the question, whether God know nonentities.)

2. To think, and to know, are not all one: for I may think that I may know; that is, I study to know. Now I can know that I study, or think; and I can perceive, that my studies reach not what I desire to reach, but fall short of satisfaction: and so as in the body, though emptiness be nothing, and therefore not felt as nothing; yet a hungry man feeleth it in the consequents, by accident; that is, feeleth that by which he knoweth that he is empty: and so it is with a student as to knowledge.

3. And a man that hath so much experience, as we all have of the stated darkness of our understandings, and frequent errors, may well know, that this understanding is to be suspected, and so blind a guide not over-confidently and rashly to be trusted.

4. And a man that knoweth the danger of error, may know that it is a thing that he should fear: and fear should make him cautelous.

5. And though an erring man, while such, cannot know that he erreth; yet, by the aforesaid means, he may cease to err, and know that he hath erred.

6. And lastly, It is a shame for a man to be unacquainted with himself, and especially with his understanding, and not to know the measure of his knowledge itself.

Object. II. You talk like a Cartesian, that must have all that would know suppose first that they know nothing, no not that he feeleth and liveth.

Answ. No such matter. Some things we know necessarily, and cannot choose but know; for the intellect is not free of itself, but only as *quoad exercitium actus*, it is *sub imperio voluntatis*. And it is vain to bid men not to know what they cannot choose but know. And it is as vain to tell them that they must suppose (falsely) that they know not what they know, as a means to know: for ignorance is no means to knowledge, but knowledge is. One act of knowledge being necessary to more, and therefore not to be denied. I have told you before what the certainties are, which must be known, and never forsaken.

Object. III. But your discourse plainly tendeth to draw men to scepticism, and to doubt of all things.

Answ. 1. I tell you, I describe to you many certainties not to be doubted of. 2. And it is indeed your prefidence that tendeth to scepticism, as is showed; for men that believe hastily and falsely, find themselves so oft deceived, that at last they begin to doubt of all things: it is scepticism which I prevent. 3. But I confess to you, that I am less afraid of scepticism in the world, than ever I was; as finding corrupt nature so universally disposed the contrary way. As when I first saw the books of Jacob Behmen, and some such others, I adventured to prognosticate, that the church would never be much endangered by that sect, or any other which a man cannot understand and join in without great study and acuteness, because few men will be at so much labour; even so I say of scepticism; here and there a hard, impatient, half-knowing student, may turn sceptic; but never any great number. For pride and ignorance, and other causes of self-conceitedness, are born in all men; and every man that apprehendeth any thing, is naturally apt to be too confident of his apprehensions; and few will have the humility to suspect themselves, or the patience and diligence to find out difficulties. I must say in my experience, that except the congregation which I long instructed, and some few such, I meet with few women, boys, or unlearned men, when they are past eighteen or twenty years old, but they are in conceit wiser than I, and are still in the right, and I am in the wrong, in things natural, civil, religious, or almost any thing we talk of, if I say not as they say; and it is so hard to abate their confidence, or convince them, that I have half ceased to endeavour it, but let every one believe and say what he will, so it be not to the dishonour of God, the wrong of others, and the hazard of his salvation: for I take it for granted beforehand, that contradiction ofter causeth strife than instruction; and when they take not themselves for scholars, they seldom learn much of any but themselves: and their own thoughts and experience must teach them that in many years which from an experienced man they might have cheaplier learned in a few days.

Object. IV. You speak against taking things on trust, and so would keep children from believing and learning of their parents and masters, and from growing wise.

Answ. I oft tell you that human faith is a necessary help to divine faith; but it must not be mistaken for divine faith. Men are to be believed as fallible men; but in some things with diffidence, and in some things with confidence, and in some things (where it is not the speaker's credit that we rely on, but a concurrence of testimonies, which make up a natural certainty) belief and knowledge go together, and the thing is sure. But man is not God.

Object. V. May not a man more safely and confidently believe by the church's faith than his own? that is, take that for more certain which all men believe, than that which I think I see a divine word for myself?

Answ. This is a popish objection thus confusedly and fallaciously often made. 1. Properly, no man can believe by any faith but his own, any more than understand with any understanding but his own. But the meaning being, that we may better trust to the church's judgment that this or that is God's word, than to our own persuasion that it is God's word, from the evidence of the revelation; I further answer; 2. That the church's judgment is one part of our subordinate motive; and therefore not to be put in competition with that divine evidence which it is always put in conjunction with. And the church's teaching is the means of my coming to know the true evidences of divinity in the word. And the church's real holiness caused by that word, is one of the evidences themselves, and not the least. Now to put the question, whether I must know the Scripture to be God's word because I discern the evidences of its divinity, or rather because the church teacheth me that it is God's word, or because the church saith it is God's word, or because the church is sanctified by it, are all vain questions; setting things conjunct and co-ordinate as opposite. 1. By the church's judgment or belief, I am moved to a high reverence of God's word, by a very high human faith, supposing it credible that it may be God's word indeed. 2. Next, by the church's (or minister's) teaching, the evidences of its divinity are made known to me. 3. The effect of it, in the church's holiness, is one of these evidences. 4. And by that and all other evidences I know that it is God's word. 5. And therefore I believe it to be true. This is the true order and resolution of our faith.

3. But because the popish method is, barely to believe the Scripture to be God's word, because a pope and his council judgeth so, I add, 1. That we have even of that human sort of testimony far more than such. For theirs is the testimony of a self-exalting sect of christians, about the third part of the christian world: but we have also the testimony of them and of all other christians; and in most or much of the matter of fact, (that the Scriptures were delivered down from the apostles,) the testimony of some heathens and abundance of heretics. 2. And with these we have the evidences of its divinity themselves. 3. But if we had their church's (or pope and council's) decrees for it alone, we should take it but for a human, fallible testimony.

For, 1. They cannot plead God's word here as the proof of their infallibility: for it is the supposed question, what is God's word, which (they say) cannot be known but by their infallible judgment. 2. And they cannot plead number; for, 1. The Mahometans are more than the christians in the world: Brierwood reckoneth that they are six parts of thirty, and we but five. And yet not therefore infallible nor credible. 2. And the heathens are more than the Mahometans and christians, (being four-sixth parts of the world,) and yet not infallible. But of this I have the last week wrote a book of the "Certainty of Christianity without Popery;" and heretofore my "Safe Religion," and others.

Object. VI. At least this way of believing and knowing things by proper evidences of truth, will loosen the common sort of christians (even the godly) from their faith and religion: for whereas now they quietly go on without doubting, as receiving the Scriptures from the church or their teachers as the word of God, when they fall on searching after proofs, they will be in danger of being overcome by difficulties, and filled with doubts, if not apostatizing to infidelity, or turning papists.

Answ. Either these persons have already the knowledge of certain evidence of the divinity of the Scripture, or christianity, or they have none. If they have any, the way of studying it more will not take it from them, but increase it: else you dishonour christianity to think that he that knoweth it to be of God, will think otherwise if he do but better try it. Upon search he will not know less, but more,

But if he have no such certainty already, 2. I further answer, that I take away from him none of that human belief which he had before: if the belief of his parents, teachers, or the church only, did satisfy him before, which was but a strong probability, I leave with him the same help and probability, and only persuade him to add more and surer arguments. And therefore that should not weaken, but confirm, his faith.

Object. But you tell him that the church's or his teacher's judgment or word is uncertain, and that sets him on doubting.

Answ. 1. I tell him of all the strength and credibility that is in it, which I would have him make use of. 2. And it is not alone, but by his teacher's help, that I would have him seek for certainty. 3. But if he did take that testimony for certain which was not certain; if he took man for God, or took his teachers, or pope, for inspired prophets, and a human testimony for divine, do you think that this error should be cherished, or cured? I think that God nor man have no true need of a lie in this case; and that lies seldom further man's salvation; and that though they do some job of present service the next way, at the end we shall find that they did more harm than good. And that to say the contrary, and that men will cease to be christians unless they be kept to it by deceit, is the way to downright infidelity.

And yet that you may see how much more than ordinary I favour the weaknesses of such, I will here answer a great question.

Quest. Whether a man can have a true saving faith, who believeth the gospel or Scripture to be God's word, and Christ to be the Saviour of the world, upon reasons or grounds not sure nor cogent and concluding; yea, possibly not true, for the most part.

Answ. He that readeth Mr. Pink's excellent sermons, and many other such divines, will find them thus describing the faith of hypocrites, (that they conclude have no true saving faith,) that they believe in Christ, but on the same or like reasons as a Turk may believe in Mahomet; that is, because the most, the greatest, the learnedest and the best, and all the country, are of their minds, and in that way their parents did educate them in. For my part, I easily confess, 1. That such a belief which buildeth on unsound grounds, is wanting proportionably in its own soundness. 2. And that it should not be rested in. 3. Much less cherished against all counsels that would cure it. 4. And that though uncertain reasons are, 1. The first; 2. And the most prevailing with him afterwards; yet every true believer discerneth some intrinsic signs of divinity at least as probable in the word itself. But yet supposing that wrong motives be his chief, and that he discerneth not that in the word itself which most prevaileth with him, I am of opinion that, 1. If the end of such a believer be sound (the reducing of the soul to God, and attainment of glory, and the perfect love of God); 2. And if that man unfeignedly believe all that is God's word to be true; 3. And if he believe all the substance of the gospel to be God's word, though by an unsound and non-concluding medium as his chief; 4. And if he by this belief be brought himself to the actual love of God as God; this unsound believer is sound in the essentials of christianity, and shall be saved.

The *Objection* is, An uncertain, yea, deceived belief upon false suppositions, is no true belief, and therefore cannot save.

I answer, There is a double truth in such a belief: 1. That all God's word is true. 2. That this gospel is God's word, and Christ is the Messiah.

You will say, that there can be no more, no surer, no better in the conclusion, than is in the weaker of the premises.[a] I answer, I grant it. And all that will follow is, that the conclusion is not necessary from these premises; and that the believer was mistaken in the reason of his inference, and that he concluded a truth upon an unsound medium: I grant all this, and consequently that his faith hath some unsoundness or diseasedness in it. But for all this, I see not but such a believer may be saved: 1. Because Christ's promise is, that whoever "believeth in him shall not perish, but have everlasting life," without excepting such as are drawn to it by noncogent arguments. And he that will put in an exception against the covenant of grace, must prove it, or be injurious to Christ, to his gospel, and to men's souls.

2. Because by experience I find, that it is but a small part of serious, godly christians, who believe the Scriptures upon cogent evidence (or at least many do not): but abundance take it upon trust from godly preachers or parents, and go on without much examining of their grounds; and are not able to bring a cogent proof of the divinity of the Scriptures, when they are called to it. And I am not willing to conclude so great a part of humble, upright christians, to damnation, as know not such reasons for their faith as would hold good in strict disputation. Not that our charity must bend the Scripture to it. But that Scripture commandeth such charity; and it no where condemneth any man that believeth upon uncogent reasons. For he that doth so, may yet firmly trust on Jesus Christ, and firmly believe that the gospel is true, as being the very word of God, and may take heaven for his portion, and love God as God, and therefore may be saved. Though yet I think it impossible that any man should truly believe the Scriptures, and not perceive in them some characters of divinity, which as an intrinsical evidence much encourage and induce him to believe them: and though this secret gust and perception be not the medium that he useth in arguing, or be not the chief, yet it may have an effectual force with his soul to hold him close to Christ. But if you suppose the man to have no spiritual sight and taste of a difference between God's word and a common book, then he cannot be supposed to be a sound believer.

As a man that hath one ingredient in his medicine which is effectual, may be cured, though in the composition the main bulk be vanities; or as a debtor that hath many insufficient sureties, may do well if he have one sufficient one, though he more trust the rest; or as a man's cause may go for him in judgment that hath one or two good witnesses, and twenty bad ones which he put more trust in; and as he truly proveth his position, who bringeth one sound argument for it, and twenty bad ones: so I think that the common way of the illiterate in believing is, first to believe God's word *to be his word* by human faith, and after upon trial to find a spiritual light and goodness in the word itself, and by both together to believe that it is God's word. And the worse reasons may be the more powerful with him, and yet not destroy the sincerity of his faith.

Nor doth this make his faith merely human: for the question now is not, why he believeth God's word to be true, and trusteth on it; for that is, because it is God's word (discerned by him so to be); but he that by an insufficient medium (at least with a better, though less understood) doth take it to be God's, may yet by a divine faith believe it, because he judgeth it his word.

[a] Of which see Smiglecius' Logics, and Albertinus in his Philosoph. Disputat. at large.

If a man should counterfeit himself an angel from heaven, and come in some splendid, deceitful appearance in the night to a heathen, and tell him that he is sent from God to bring him this Bible as his certain word; and if the man receive it, and believe it on his credit to the death, and by that believing it be brought to see an excellency and credibility, and taste a spiritual sweetness in it, and be brought by it (as he may be) to holiness and the love of God, that man shall be saved; though I cannot say that the intrinsic evidence of the word alone would have prevailed with him without that false belief of a deceiver: when it is once become a sanctifying belief, then there is no doubt but the man hath better evidence than the uncertain word of man; he hath the witness in himself. And it is not a glorifying faith, till it be sanctifying faith. But the question is, what soundness of reason or proof that this is God's word, is necessary to make it a sanctifying faith; at least, as most prevalent and trusted in?

By this you may know what I judge of the faith of honest illiterate papists, and of illiterate protestants, for there are a great number of them, who live in love and obedience to God.

And yet to speak both more concisely and distinctly, I. I may believe by historical tradition all that matter of fact, which those that saw Christ's and the apostles' miracles, and heard their words, did know by sense; and those that saw not, believed on the credit of the reporters. II. And yet I may know by reason, through God's help, that these miracles, and this Scripture impress and efficacy, are God's attestation; and none but God could do it. And of this all believers have some perception in various degrees. III. And then we know it to be true, because it is sealed by those attestations, and is the word of God.

Object. VII. But would you have men take the matter of fact for uncertain, (that this is a true Bible and copy, and was given the church by the apostles, &c.) and so not pretend to be certain of them.

Answ. I have oft said, and elsewhere largely proved, that as, 1. A human faith of highest probability prepareth the way; so, 2. These things are known by an historical evidence, which hath a proper certainty above mere human faith: for human faith resteth on men's veracity or fidelity, which is uncertain: but there is a history (such as that there is such a city as Rome, Venice, &c.) which is evident by a surer ground than men's fidelity; even from such a concurrence of consenters and circumstances, as will prove a forgery impossible.

Object. VIII. You seem to favour the popish doctrine of ignorance, while you would have all our knowledge confined to a few plain and easy things, and persuade men to doubt of all the rest.

Answ. 1. I persuade no man to doubt of that which he is certain of, but not to lie, and say he is certain when he is not. 2. I am so far from encouraging ignorance, that it is ignorance of your ignorance which I reprove; I would have all men know as much as possibly they can of all that God hath revealed. And if the self-conceited knew more, they would doubt more; and as they grow wiser, will grow less confident in uncertainties. It is not knowing, but false pretending to know, that I am against. Do you think that a thousand self-conceited men and women do really know ever the more for saying they know, or crying down that ignorance, doubting, and uncertainty which they have themselves. How many a one (yea preachers) have cried down the popish doctrine of uncertainty of salvation, who had no certainty of their own; but their neighbours thought by their lives were certainly in the way to hell.

Object. IX. But you would have men resist the Spirit that convinceth them, and make so long a work in doubting, and questioning, and proving every thing, as that christians will come but to little knowledge in your way.

Answ. They will have the more knowledge, and not the less, for trying. Peremptory confidence is not knowledge, the next way here is farthest about. Receive all evidence from God and man, from the word and Spirit, with all the desire, and all the delight, and all the speed that you possibly can; study earnestly; learn willingly; resist no light; neglect no truth. But what is all this to the foolish conceit that you know what you do not? What is this to the hasty believing of falsehoods, or uncertainties, and troubling the church and world with self-conceit and dreams? I remember two or three of my old acquaintance, who suddenly received from a seducer the opinion of perfection, that we might be perfectly sinless in this life: and because I denied it, they carried it as if I had pleaded for sin against perfection; and they presently took themselves to be perfect and sinless, because they had got the opinion that some are such. I told them that I desired perfection as well as they, and that I was far from hindering or dissuading any from perfection; but wished them to let us see that they are so indeed, and never to sin more in thought, word, or deed; and ere long they forsook all religion, and by drunkenness, fornication, and licentiousness, showed us their perfection. So here, it is not a conceit that men have faith and knowledge, and quickly saying, I believe, or turning to the priest or party that persuadeth them, which maketh them ever the wiser men, or true believers.

Object. X. But that may seem certain to another which seemeth uncertain or false to you: therefore every man must go according to his own light.

Answ. 1. Nothing is certain which is not true: if that seem true to you which is false, this is your error: and is every man, or any man, bound to err, and believe a falsehood? Being is before knowing: if it be not true, you may think it to be so, (which is that which I would cure;) but you cannot know it to be so, much less be certain of it. 2. If it be certain to you, it is evidently true; and if so, hold it fast, and spare not: it is not any man's certainty, but error, which I oppose.

Object. XI. But if we must write or utter nothing but certainties, you would have but a small library.

Answ. 1. The world might well spare a great many uncertain writings. 2. But I say not that you must think, say, or write nothing but certainties: there is a lawful, and, in some cases, necessary exercise of our understandings about probabilities and possibilities. The husbandman when he plougheth and soweth is not certain of an increase. 1. But call not that certain which is not. 2. And be not as vehement and peremptory in it as if it were a certainty. 3. And separate your certainties and probabilities asunder, that confusion fill not your minds with error.

Object. XII. While you persuade us to be so diffident of men's reports, and to suspend our belief of what men say, you speak against the laws of converse.

Answ. I persuade you not to deny any man such a belief as is his due: but give him no more. If a man profess himself a christian, and say that he sincerely believeth in Christ, and consenteth to his covenant, though you may perceive no ascertaining evidence that he saith true, yet you must believe him, because he is the only opener of his own mind, and the laws of God and human converse require it.

But what is this believing him? Not taking it for a certain truth, but taking it for a thing probable, which may be true for aught you know, and which you must hope is true; and this in different degrees, according to the different degrees of the person's credibility.

If you hear men confidently report any news in these times, when half that we hear oft proveth false, you may believe the reporter as a fallible person, that is, believe that he doth not wilfully lie, and so not uncivilly contradict him; and yet suspend your belief of the thing itself, and whether he took it up rashly on uncertain rumours.

But if you hear a man speak evil of another behind his back, when the thing is not notorious and certain other ways, the law of justice and charity obligeth you not to believe him, but to suspend your belief till you hear both sides, or have surer proof; yea, and to suspend, not with an indifferency, but with a hope that it is not true which he speaketh.

Object. XIII. But then I shall be as uncharitable in judging the reporter (who perhaps is a godly man) to be a liar and slanderer, as I should be in believing that the other is guilty.

Answ. 1. I say not that you are to conclude that certainly he lieth, and that it is false, but to suspend your belief, and to hope that it is false. 2. He that maketh himself the accuser of another man behind his back in a way of talk, doth expose himself to that disadvantage, and maketh it our duty to begin our charitable opinion on the side of him that is accused, and rather to hope that he is innocent *(cæteris paribus)* than the accuser. For God forbiddeth backbiting and slandering, and biddeth us speak evil of no man. And he that in our hearing backbiteth and speaketh evil, how godly otherwise soever, without a clear necessary cause, doth forfeit our charity and belief, more than a man can do whom we do not see or hear. For if I was bound to judge him innocent before this backbiting, I am bound so to judge him still. Therefore I do but continue that good opinion of my neighbour which I was bound to: and that I must suspect the backbiter of a lie, is the consequent of his own act, and long of himself. For I cannot believe contraries; and it is not his backbiting that will disoblige me from my former duty, of judging the other innocent. So that it is the reporter that casteth away the reputation of his own veracity.

Object. XIV. When you have written all this against pretended knowledge, who is more guilty than yourself? Who so oppresseth his reader with distinctions? Are all your large writings evident certainties? even those controversies in which you have so many adversaries?

Answ. I put in this objection, because I have a book called "Methodus Theologiæ," which I know will occasion such thoughts in many readers. But, 1. It is one thing to assert uncertainties, and another thing to anatomize, and distinctly and methodically explain a certain truth. In all my large writings, if you find that I call any thing certain which is uncertain, that is, which I give not ascertaining evidence of, acquaint me with the particulars, and I shall retract them.

2. I never persuaded any man to write or say no more than all men certainly know already, no not all learned divines; for then how should we receive edification? Subjective certainty is as various as men's intellects, where no two are of a size. And objective certainty must be tried by the evidence, and not by other men's consenting to it. Nor must a major vote of dissenters go for a proof of objective uncertainty: for heathens are more than the rest of the world; and Mahometans more than christians; and papists more than protestants; and the ungodly more than the godly; and yet this is no proof of our own or the thing's uncertainty.

3. Part of my writings are against uncertainties; and to deliver the church from false opinions that go for certainties; and these are they that have most contradicters: and may I not write against false and uncertain opinions which religion is corrupted with, and defend the ancient simplicity, without being guilty of the introduction of uncertainties myself.

4. I deny not but I have many things that are uncertain; but then I acknowledge them uncertain, and treat of them but as they are.

5. Lastly, If really my writings are guilty of that which I here reprehend, false pretended knowledge, the sin is never the better for that, nor my accusation of it ever the less true, nor your duty to avoid it ever the less. Think what you will of me, so you will but think rightly of sin and duty. If I go contrary to my doctrine, and you can prove it, take warning by me, and do not you the like.

CHAPTER XXI.

IX. DIRECTIONS FOR THE CURE OF PRETENDED KNOWLEDGE, OR SELF-CONCEIT.

THE cure of this plague of prefidence or pretended knowledge is it which all the rest is written for; and must now be the last in execution as it was the first in my intention.[a] And could men be persuaded to this following course it might be done; but nature's vicious inclination to the vice, and the commonness and strength of temptations to it, do make me expect to prevail but with a few.

Direct. I. Labour to understand the true nature and principles of certainty before opened. False measures will make you judge certainties to be falsehoods or uncertain, and falsehoods to be certain truths. And when you know the conditions of certainty, try all things by them accurately; and if any would by art persuade you of the uncertainty of nature's just perceptions, by sense or intellect, remember that be they what they will you have no better or surer; they are such as our Creator hath given you to trust to for your use, even for the ends of life.

Direct. II. Discern the helps of knowledge from knowledge or certainty itself. Believing your teachers as men, and believing historians according to their credibility, and reverencing the judgment of seniors, and of the church, are all preparative helps to certainty: and human faith is such as to divine faith. But do not therefore think that it is the same; nor give men that prerogative of infallibility which belongeth to God, or to inspired prophets, who prove their word by God's attestation. The belief of logicians is needful to your understanding logic, and logic is a great help to your certain discerning of physical and metaphysical and moral verities. And yet many rules of your logic may be uncertain, and you must not take the helps of your knowledge for evidence itself.

Some think that nothing is known till we have second notions for it, or can define it; when things sensible are better known by sensing them, and

[a] Because I must not oft repeat the same things, I must refer the reader to what I have more fully said of this in twenty-seven directions for certainty of knowledge in my Christian Directory, part iii. chap. 7.

usually second notions deceive men, and make them doubt of what they better apprehended without them.

Be very suspicious of all words or terms; 1. As ambiguous, as almost all are: and therefore he that cannot distinguish them must needs err by confusion. 2. Lest you take the names for things, most disputes using to carry controversies *de nomine* as if they were *de re*, or slide from this into that.

Direct. III. Therefore also trust not too far to the artificial forms or argument, without, or instead of, the evidence of the truth of the thing itself. For there are many things supposed to the infallibility of your art, which may not themselves be infallibly true: and man's wit is conscious of its own fallibility; and therefore is doubtful lest it should be deceived in its collections and ratiocinations; especially when the engine hath many tacklings, and the chain many links, we are still in doubt lest some one should break: but the evidence of the thing in its own reality, which is not wholly laid on the form of an artificial argument, which is of great use, doth satisfy more.

Direct. IV. Take truths in order; the principles first, and the rest in their true exurgence and dependence upon them: and take nothing to be well known, which is not known, not only in a method, but in a method clearly suitable to the things. As words and notions, so rules and methods, must be fetched from the things, and fitted to the things, or they are vain. Sense and intellect must first perceive the things themselves, and be your first tutors in somatology and pneumatology; and then these must do much in making your logic. The foot must be the measure of the shoe. And remember that you have but a half, fallacious knowledge, till you know the true place, and order, and respects of the thing, as well as the nature and quality of it in itself; and till you can draw up a true scheme of the things which you know: it is dreams that are incoherent.

Direct. V. Let the great radical verities have your greatest confidence, and not only so, but the most of your thoughts, and estimation, and time; and proportionably let the lesser things have but that share of your esteem, and time, and studies which they deserve; which comparatively will be little. And make them the test of what is further offered to you: and believe nothing which is certainly contrary to them. Argue always *a notioribus*, and reduce not certainties to uncertainties, but contrarily.

Direct. VI. Keep all your perceptions distinct according to the distinction of their natures. Let both your books and your intellects be like an apothecary's shop, where there are different boxes with different titles for different things. Let sensible perceptions be by themselves: and the intellective perception of things sensate be by themselves: and the intellect's perception of its own and the will's acts be by themselves: and the collection of the nature of spirits and intellective agents thence, be by themselves: and the knowledge of principles, physical and moral, be by themselves: and the certainty of conclusions be ranked according to the variety of their degrees. The confusion of these different things causeth so confused a kind of knowledge, as is next to no knowledge, and fitter to trouble than to satisfy.

Direct. VII. Look to all things, or as many as is possible. When half is unknown, the other half is not half known. *Respicere ad omnia* is proper to God: *respicere ad plurima* is necessary to the competent wisdom of a man: to be of a narrow mind and prospect, is the property of the ignorant and erroneous. He that seeth only a hand or foot knoweth not what a man is by it: and he that seeth only a word knoweth not by that what a sentence is. God's works are all one. I know not what we shall see in Commenius's Pansophy, which they say is yet to see the light; how far he hath reduced all sciences to one. But I little doubt but they may and should be all reduced to two, which are as the soul and body that yet make up one man, though not one nature; viz. 1. The ontological or real part, distinguished into that of substances and of modes, where morality cometh in, &c. 2. The organical part, which fitteth words and notions to things. And I am sure that as the knowledge of one thing, or of many, much conduceth to further knowledge; so the ignorance of one thing conduceth to ignorance and error about others. It is here as in the knowledge of a clock or watch, or musical instrument. Know all or you know little, and next to none. No man is a fit judge of church affairs, who hath not the state of the world in some good measure in his eye; else he will be like most sectaries, who judge, and talk, and live, as if the world were no bigger than their synagogues or sects. He must have all the Scripture in his eye, and all the body of divinity, and all the world in his eye; and God himself, who is more than all, who will not, by a narrow mind, be cheated into a multitude of errors. There are abundance of truths unknown to you which, were they known, would rectify your other errors.

Direct. VIII. Conclude not hastily of negatives. You may easilier know, that you do know what you do know, than know what it is that you do not know. It doth not follow that there is no more because you know no more. St. John tells you, that if all that Christ did should be written, the world could not contain the books: you cannot therefore conclude from what is recorded, that he said and did no more than is recorded: though I am sure against popery, by my sense and intellect, that there is real bread and wine in the sacrament, I am not sure by sense that there is no spiritual body of Christ: the negative must be otherwise proved. I am sure by my five senses (as they are commonly distinguished and numbered) that there are existent all the sensible qualities, which are their objects: but whether the world may not have more sensible qualities, suited to many other sort of senses, which we have no conception, notion, or name of, is a thing that no mortal man can know.

You hear many things, and know many things by another man, which make his cause seem bad: but do you know how many more things may be existent unknown to you, which if you knew would change your judgment?

Allow still room and supposition for abundance of unknown things, which may come hereafter to your knowledge, and make things seem to you quite other than they do. How can you possibly know how much more may be unknown to you? If I have a servant that stayeth much longer than I expected, I may conjecture that he could have no business to stay him, but his negligence; but there may be many accidents to cause it, which I cannot judge of till I hear him speak.

Direct. IX. Be sure that you suspect your first apprehensions of things: and take few conceptions (conclusive) for certain, that are not digested. Fasten not over-tenaciously upon opinions, in the beginning, at the first hearing: take it for granted, that your first conceptions of things must alter, either as to the truth, or the evidence, or the order, or the degree. Few men are so happy in youth, as to receive at first such right impressions, which need not after to be much altered. When we are children, we know as children; but when we become men, childish things are done away. Where we change not our judgment of the matter, yet we come to have very different apprehensions of it. I would not have boys to be mere sceptics; for they must be godly, and christians. But I would have them leave room for increase of knowledge, and not be too peremptory with their juvenile conceptions, but suppose that a further light will give them another prospect of the same things.

Direct. X. Choose such teachers, if possible, as have themselves attained the things you seek; even that most substantial wisdom which leadeth to salvation. For how else shall they teach others what they have not learned themselves? Oh the difference between teachers and teachers! between a rash, flashy, unexperienced, proud wit; and clear-headed, well-studied, much-experienced, and godly men! Happy is he that hath such a teacher, that is long exercised in the ways of truth, and holiness, and peace; and hath a heart to value him.

Direct. XI. Value truth for goodness, and goodness above truth; and estimate all truths and knowledge by their usefulness to higher ends. That is good as a means, which doth good. There is nothing besides God that is simply good, in, of, and for itself; all else is only good derivatively from God the efficient, and as a means to God the final cause. As a pound of gold more enricheth than many loads of dirt; so a little knowledge of great and necessary matters, maketh one wiser than a great deal of pedantic, toyish learning. No man hath time and capacity for all things: he is but a proud fool, that would seem to know all, and deny his ignorance in many things. Even he that with Alstedius, &c. can write an Encyclopædia, is still unacquainted with abundance that is intelligible. For my own part, I humbly thank God, that by placing my dwelling still as in the church-yard, he hath led me to choose still the studies which I thought were fittest for a man that is posting to another world. He that must needs be ignorant of many things, should choose to omit those which he can best spare. Distinguish well between studying and knowing for use, and for lust; for the true ends of knowledge, and for the bare delight of knowing. One thing is necessary, (Luke x. 42,) and all others but as they are necessary to that one: mortify the lust of useless knowledge, as well as other lusts of flesh and fantasy. Dying men commonly call it vanity. Remember what a deal of precious time it wasteth; and from how many greater and more necessary things it doth divert the mind; and with what wind it puffs men up; as is aforesaid. How justly did the rude Tartarians think the great libraries, and multitudes of doctors and idle priests, among the Chinese to be a foolery; and call them away from their books to arms, as Palafox tells us; when all their learning was to so little purpose as it was, and led them to no more high and necessary things!

Direct. XII. Yet because many smaller parts of knowledge are necessary to kingdoms, academies, and churches, which are not necessary, nor greatly valuable, to individual persons; let some few particular persons be bred up to an eminency in those studies, and let not the generality of students waste their time therein. There is scarce any part of knowledge so small and useless, but it is necessary to great societies that some be masters of it, which yet the generality may well spare. And all are to be valued and honoured according to their several excellences. But yet I cannot have while to study as long as Politian how Virgil should be spelt; nor to decide the quarrels between Phil. Pareus and Gruter, nor to digest all his grammatical collections, nor to read all over abundance of books which I allow house-room to. Nor to learn all the languages and arts which I could wish to know, if I could know them without neglecting greater things. But yet the excellent professors of them all I honour.

Direct. XIII. Above all, value, digest, and seriously live upon the most great and necessary certain truths. Oh that we knew what work, inward and outward, the great truths of salvation call for from us all! If you do not faithfully value and improve these, you prepare for delusion: you forget your premises and principles: God may justly leave you in the dark, and give you up to believe a lie. Did you live according to the importance of your certain principles, your lives would be filled with fruit, and business, and delight, and all this great: so that you would have little mind or leisure for little and unnecessary things. It is the neglect of things necessary, which fills the world with the trouble of things unnecessary.

Direct. XIV. Study hard, and search diligently and deeply, and that with unwearied patience and delight. Unpleasant studies tire and seldom prosper. Slight running thoughts accomplish little. If any man think that the Spirit is given to save us the labour of hard and long studies, Solomon hath spent so many chapters in calling them to dig, search, cry, labour, wait for wisdom, that if that will not undeceive them, I cannot: they may as well say, that God's blessing is to save the husbandman the labour of ploughing and sowing; and that the Spirit is given to save men the labour of learning to read the Bible, or to hear it, or think of it, or to pray to God. Whereas the Spirit is given us to provoke and enable us to study hard, and read, and hear, and pray hard, and to prosper us herein.

And as vain are our idle lads, that think that their natural wits, or their abode and degrees in the universities, will serve the turn instead of hard studies! And so they come out almost as ignorant, and yet more proud than they went thither, to be plagues in all countries where they come, to teach others by example the idleness and sensuality which they learned themselves; and being ignorant, yet the honour of their functions must be maintained, and therefore their ignorance must be hid, which yet themselves do weekly make ostentation of in the pulpit, where they should be shining lights; and when their own tongues have proclaimed it, those of understanding that observe and loathe it, must be maligned and railed at for knowing how little their teachers know.

Nothing without long and hard studies furnisheth the mind with such a stock of truth, as may be called real wisdom. "That God is the rewarder of them that diligently seek him," (and not of the lazy neglecters of him,) is the second principle in religion, Heb. xi. 6. They that cannot be at this labour, must be content to know but little, and not take on them to know much. For they are not able to discern truth from falsehood: but while they sleep the tares are sowed: or while they open the door, all crowd in that can come first; and they cannot make a just separation. Ignorant persons will swarm with errors, and he that erreth will think that he is in the right: and if he think that it is a divine and necessary truth which he embraceth, how zealously may he pursue it!

Direct. XV. Take heed of a bias of carnal interest, and of the disturbing passions which selfish partiality will be apt to raise. Men may verily think, that they sincerely love the truth, when the secret power of a carnal interest, their honour, their profit or pleasure, is it that turneth about their judgment, and furnisheth them with arguments, and whets their wits, and maketh them passionately confident, and they are not aware of it. Is your worldly interest on that side that your opinion is for? Though that prove it not false, it proveth that you should be very suspicious of yourselves.

Direct. XVI. Keep up unfeigned fervent love to others, even as to yourselves. And then you will not contemn their persons and their arguments, beyond certain cause. You will not turn to passionate contentions, and reproaches of them when you differ; and the reverence of your elders, teachers, superiors, will make you more ready to suspect yourselves than them. Most of our self-conceited pretenders to knowledge, have lost their love and reverence of dissenters, and are bold despisers of the persons, reasons, and writings of all that contradict their error. And most that venture to cast the churches into flames, and their brethren into silence and sufferings, that they may plant their own opinions, are great despisers of those that they afflict, and either hate them, or would make them hateful, lest they should be thought to be unjust in using them like hateful persons. "Love that thinketh not evil of others, is not apt to vaunt itself," 1 Cor. xiii.

Direct. XVII. Reverence the church of God, but give not up your understandings absolutely to any men; but take heed of taking any church, sect, or party, instead of the infallible God. With the universal church you most embody and hold concord: it is certain, that it erreth not from the essentials of christianity: otherwise the church were no church, no christians, and could not be saved. If a papist say, And which is this church? I answer him, it is the universality of christians, or all that hold these essentials; and when I say, that this church cannot fall from these essentials, I do but say, it cannot cease to be a church: the church is constituted of, and known by, the essentials of faith; and not the essentials of faith constituted by the church, nor so known by it; though it be known by it as the teacher of it.

He that deserteth the christian universality, in deed though not in words, and cleaveth too close to any sect, whether papal or any other, will be carried down the stream by that sect, and will fill his understanding with all their errors and uncertainties, and confound them with the certain truths of God, to make up a mixed religion with; and the reverence of his party, church, or sect, will blind his mind, and make him think all this his duty.

Direct. XVIII. Fear error and ungrounded confidence. Consider all the mischiefs of it, which the world hath long felt, and the churches in the East and West are distracted by unto this day; and which I have opened to you before. He that feareth not a sin and mischief, is most unlikely to escape it. A tender conscience cannot be bold and rash, where the interest of God, the church, and his own and others' souls, is so much concerned. When you are invited to turn papist, or quaker, or anabaptist, or antinomian, or separatist, think, What if it should prove an error; and as great an error as many godly, learned men affirm it to be? Alas, what a gulf should I plunge my soul in! What injury should I do the truth! What wrong to souls! And shall I rashly venture on such a danger, any more than I would do on fornication, drunkenness, or other sin? And doth not the sad example of this age, as well as all former ages, warn you to be fearful of what you entertain? Oh what promising, what hopeful, what confident persons, have dreadfully miscarried, and when they once began to roll down the hill, have not stopped till some of them arrived at infidelity and profaneness, and others involved us in confusions! And yet shall we not fear, but rage and be confident?

And to see on the other side, what darkness and delusion hath fallen upon thousands of the papal clergy, and what their error hath cost the world, should make those that are that way inclined also fear.

Direct. XIX. Above all pray and labour for a truly humble mind, that is well acquainted with its own defects; and fear and fly from a proud overvaluing of your own understanding. Be thankful for any knowledge that you have, but take heed of thinking it greater than it is. The devil's sin, and the imitation of Adam, are not the way to have the illumination of God's Spirit. It is not more usual with God to bring low those that are proud of greatness, than to leave to folly, deceit, and error, those that are proud of wisdom, and to leave to sin and wickedness those that are proud of goodness. A proud understanding cannot be brought to suspect itself, but is confident of its first undigested apprehensions: it either feeleth no need of the Spirit's light, but despiseth it as a fancy; or else it groweth conceited, that all its conceptions are of the Spirit, and is proud of that Spirit which he hath not. Nothing maketh this peremptory confidence in false conceits so common, as pride of a knowledge which men have not. Would the Lord but humble these persons thoroughly, they would think, Alas! what a dark, deceitful mind have I! how unfit to despise the judgment of them that have laboured for knowledge far more than I have done, and how unfit to be confident against such as know much more than I!

But so deep and common is this pride, that they that go in rags, and they that think themselves unworthy to live, and are ready to despair in the sense of sin, do yet ordinarily so overvalue their own apprehensions, that even these will stiffly hold their vain and unpeaceful opinions, and stiffly reject the judgment and arguments of the wisest and best that will not be as envious as they.

Direct. XX. Lastly, Keep in a child-like, teachable, learning resolution, with a sober and suspended judgment, where you have not sure evidence to turn the scales. When Christ saith, "Except ye be converted and become as little children, ye shall in no wise enter into the kingdom of heaven," Matt. xviii. 3; as he hath respect to the humility of children in general, (and their inception of a new life,) so in special he seemeth to respect them as disciples. Set children to school, and their business is to hear and learn all day; they set not their wits against their master's, and do not wrangle and strive against him, and say, It is not so; we know better than you. But so abominably is human nature corrupted by this intellectual pride, that when once lads are big enough to be from under a tutor, commonly, instead of learning of others, they are of a teaching humour, and had rather speak two hours than hear one; and set their wits to contradict what they should learn, and to conquer those that would instruct them; and to show themselves wiser than to learn to be more wise; and we can scarce talk with man or woman, but is the wisest in the company, and hardliest convinced of an error.

But two things here I earnestly advise you: 1. That you spend more time in learning than in disputing: not but that disputing in its season is necessary to defend the truth; but usually it engageth men's wits in an eager opposition against others, and so against the truth which they should receive; and it goeth more according to the ability of the disputants, than the merits of the cause. And he that is worsted is so galled at the disgrace, that he hateth the truth the more for his sake that hath dishonoured him: and therefore Paul speaketh so oft against such disputing, and saith that the servant of the Lord must not strive, but be gentle, and apt to teach, and in meekness instruct opposers.

I would ordinarily, if any man have a mind to wrangle with me, tell him: If you know more of these things than I, if you will be my teacher, I shall thankfully hear and learn; and desire him to open his judgment to me in its fullest evidence: and I would weigh it as the time and case required; and if I were fully satisfied against it, I would crave leave to tell him the reasons of my dissent, and crave his patient audience to the end. And when we well understood each other's mind and reasons, I would crave leave then to end in peace; unless the safety of others required a dispute to defend the truth.

2. And my special repeated counsel is, that you suspend your judgment till you have cogent evidence to determine it. Be no further of either side than you know they are in the right; cast not yourself into other men's opinions hastily, upon slight reasons, at a blind adventure. If you see not a certainty, judge it not certain. If you see but a probability, judge it but probable. "Prove all things, and hold fast that which is good," 1 Thess. v. The Bereans are commended for searching the Scripture, and seeing whether the things were so which Paul had spoken, Acts xvii. Truth feareth not the light. It is like gold, that loseth nothing by the fire. Darkness is its greatest enemy and dishonour. Therefore look before you leap: you are bid, "Believe not every spirit, but try the spirits whether they be of God," 1 John ii. Stand still till you know that the ground is safe which you are to tread on. When poisoners are as common as physicians, you will take heed what you take. It is safer when once you have the essentials of christianity, to take too little than too much: for you are sure to be saved if you are mere true christians; but how far popery, antinomianism, &c. may corrupt your christianity is a controversy. Wish them that urge you, to forbear their haste in a matter of everlasting consequence: these are not matters to be rashly done. And as long as you are uncertain, profess yourselves uncertain; and if they will condemn you for your ignorance when you are willing to know the truth, so will not God. But when you are certain, resolve in the strength of God, and hold fast, whatever it cost you, even to the death, and never fear being losers by God, by his truth, or by fidelity in your duty.

PART II.

OF TRUE SAVING KNOWLEDGE: I. CAUSING OUR LOVE TO GOD. II. THEREBY QUALIFYING US FOR HIS LOVE.

1 CORINTHIANS viii. 3.

BUT IF ANY MAN LOVE GOD, THE SAME IS KNOWN OF HIM.

CHAPTER I.

KNOWLEDGE IS TO BE ESTIMATED MORE BY THE END IT TENDETH TO, THAN BY ITSELF.

HAVING done with that epidemical, mortal disease, SELF-CONCEITEDNESS, or PREFIDENCE, or over-hasty judging, and pretending to know that which we know not, which I more desire than hope to cure; I have left but little room for the nobler part of my subject, True saving Knowledge, because the handling of it was not my principal design.

The meaning of the text I gave you before. The true paraphrase of it is as followeth: as if Paul had said: You overvalue your barren notions, and think that by them you are wise; whereas knowledge is a means to a higher end; and that end is to make us lovers of God, that so we may be known with love by him; for to love God and be beloved by him is man's felicity and ultimate end; and therefore that which we must seek after and live for in the world: and he is to be accounted the wisest man that loveth God most; when unsanctified notions and speculations will prove but folly.

This being the true meaning of the text, I shall briefly speak of it by parts, as it containeth these several doctrines or propositions.

Doct. I. Knowledge is a means to a higher end, according to which it is to be estimated.

Doct. II. The end of knowledge is to make us lovers of God, and so to be known with love by him.

Doct. III. Therefore knowledge is to be valued, sought, and used, as it tendeth to this holy, blessed end.

Doct. IV. And therefore those are to be accounted the wisest or best-knowing men, that love God most; and not those that are stored with unholy knowledge.

For the first of these, that knowledge is a means to a higher end, I shall first open it, and then prove it.

I. Aquinas and some other schoolmen make the vision or knowledge of God, to be the highest part of man's felicity: and I deny not but that the three faculties of man's soul, *vital activity*, *intellect*, and *will*, as the image of the Divine Trinity, have a kind of inseparability and co-equality. And therefore each of their perfections and perfect receptions from God, and operations on God, is the ultimate end of man: but yet they are distinguishable, though not divisible; and there is such an order among them, as that one may in some respects be called the incepter and another the perfecter of human operations; and so the acts of one be called a means to the acts of the other. And thus though the vision or knowledge of God be one inadequate conception, if not a part of our ultimate end; yet the love of God, and living to God, are also other conceptions or parts of it: yea, and the more completive, perfect parts, which we call *finis ultimate ultimus.*

II. The proof shall be fetched, 1. From the order and use of the faculties of the soul. 2. From the objects. 3. From the constitution of the acts. 4. From express Scripture.

I. It is evident to our internal perception; 1. That the understanding is but the guide of the will, and its acts but mediate to determine the will: as the eye is to lead the appetitive and executive faculties, by presenting to them their proper objects. To know is but an initial, introductory act.

Yea, 2. It is evident that the soul is not satisfied with bare knowing, if no delight or complacency follow: for what is that which we call satisfaction, but the complacency of the will? Suppose a man to have no effect upon his will, no pleasure, no contentation in his knowledge, and what felicity or desirable good to him would there be, in all the knowledge in the world? Yea, when I name either *good* or *desirable,* every one knoweth that I name an object of the will. Therefore if you stop at bare intellection, it is not to be called good or desirable as to the intellect, these being not proper intellectual objects: though remotely I confess they are; that is, that which is called good, amiable, and desirable primarily as the proper object of the will, must be discerned to be such by the understanding: when yet the formal notion of the intellect's object, is but *quid intelligibile,* which materially is *ens, unum, verum, bonum:* but goodness is the formal notion of the object of the will, and not only the material.

If any say that I seem here to take part with Epicurus, and Cicero's Torquatus, who erred by placing the chief excellency of virtue in the pleasure of it; and consequently making any thing more excellent which is more pleasant, though it be sin itself; I answer, He that will decide that great controversy, must distinguish, 1. Between sensitive pleasure, and the complacency of the will. 2. Between that which is good only to me, and that which is good to others, and that which is good in relation to the supreme and final will of God. 3. Between the exterior and the interior acts of virtue, and then you shall see Cicero and Torquatus easily reconciled, thus:—

1. It is certain that GOODNESS and the WILL are so essentially related to each other, that they must each enter the other's definition. To be *bonum* is to be *volibile;* and to will is ever *velle bonum.*

2. It is certain that God's will is the original and end of all created good, which hath its essence in relation to his will. And therefore if it were possible for virtue to be unpleasant or pernicious to the possessor, it would be good as it is suited and related to the will of God.

3. Therefore it cannot be said, that virtue as virtue is better than virtue as it pleaseth God: but it is most certain that virtue as virtue is pleasing to God, (as to the objective aptitude,) and that virtue as pleasing to God, and consequently as virtue, is better than virtue as it is pleasant to the possessor.

4. And it is certain that virtue, as it is profitable, and justly pleasing to mankind, to the church, to kingdoms, to public societies or multitudes, is better than as it is pleasing unto one. Because the good of many is better than of one.

5. And it is certain that virtue, as it pleaseth the rational will, is better than as it pleaseth the mere sensitive appetite, which it seldom doth: and therefore sensuality hath no advantage hence.

6. And virtue as it profiteth, though at present it occasion sorrow or displicence in its consequents, is better than that which at the present only pleaseth, and quickly vanisheth. But that profit lieth in this, that it prepareth for everlasting or more durable pleasure. And a long pleasure attained by present sorrow, is better than a momentary pleasure; which is another difference between sensual sinful, and spiritual durable delights.

7. And to end all this controversy between us and Epicurus, it is notorious, that the internal vital acts of true virtue are nothing else radically but pleasure itself: for it is radically and summarily nothing but the love of God and goodness; and love in its properest notion is nothing but the complacency of the will. To say, I love it, is but to say, It pleaseth me; unless when you speak of either sensual appetite and delight, or love as conjunct with some other act or passion. And (though Occum here stretch it a little too far) it is certain that the external act of man hath no virtue in it that is moral, but secondary, and derived from the will, even as far as it is voluntary. So that the informing root of all virtue is will, love, or complacency; which Austin useth to call delectation, asserting what I now assert. So that the question now is, Whether virtue, which is nothing but complacency in good, be better as complacency or as virtue; that is, under one name or another? or whether it be better as virtue, or as virtue? as complacency, or as complacency?

If you think I make Cicero and the old philosophers fools, by feigning them to agitate such a question; I answer, 1. If they do so, it is not my doing, but their own. 2. But I think Cicero meant not so foolishly, but understood Epicurus only of sensual pleasure, and not of rational. 3. Or at least, of private pleasure of a single person, as opposite to the utility and pleasure of multitudes. 4. And whether he had so much theology as to remember that which is it that resolveth the whole doubt, I know not, viz. that virtue as virtue is objectively pleasing to the will of God: and as pleasing to God, it is better than as pleasing to me, and all the world.

So that notwithstanding this objection, thus fully answered, the acts of the intellect merely as such, without their respect to some will, either of God or man, are not so much as formally amiable, desirable, or good.

3. I further add, that the acts of the intellect may be forced, involuntary, displeasing, and both morally and penally evil. A man may by God be forbidden to search after and to know some things; and to know them (as voluntarily done) may be his sin. And all know that a man may be necessitated to know many things; and that knowledge may torment him: as to know dangers, losses, enmities, injuries, future evils; especially sins by an accusing conscience, and God's displeasure: and devils and damned souls have such knowledge.

Object. All this is true of some knowledge, but not of the knowledge of God or goodness.

Answ. 1. It is granted then that knowledge, as such, is not sufficient to be man's felicity, or final act. 2. And as to the object, I easily grant that the true knowledge of God is the initial part of man's felicity: but that is much, because it ever inferreth that love or complacency of the will, which is the more completive part. 3. But there is a knowledge even of God, which being separated from love, is sin and misery. As the devils and damned that believe, and tremble, and hate, and suffer, are not without all knowledge of God. So much for the first proof, fetched from the order of the faculties of the soul.

II. The second proof is fetched from the objects: it is not mere intelligibility that blesseth a man, but goodness, which as such is the formal object of the will, though the material object of the understanding. It is a pleasant thing for the eyes to behold the sun: and as pleasant, it is good; and also as useful to further pleasure of ourselves or others. Nothing maketh a man good or happy, but as it is good. Therefore the goodness of God (his transcendent perfection by which he is first essentially good in himself, and amiable to himself, and then good and amiable to us all) is the ultimately ultimate object of man's soul, to which his intelligibility is supposed.

III. The third proof is from the constitution of these several acts: knowledge being but an introductive act, supposeth not love, as to its essence, though it produce it as an effect: but love includeth knowledge in it; as the number of two includeth one, when one doth not include two. Therefore both together must needs be perfecter than one alone.

IV. The fourth proof is from express Scripture. I will only cite some plain ones which need no tedious comment. 1. For love it is said, "We have known and believed the love that God hath to us: God is love, and he that dwelleth in love dwelleth in God, and God in him. Herein is our love made perfect, (or in this the love with us is perfected,) that we have boldness in the day of judgment: because as he is, so are we, in this world. There is no fear in love, but perfect love casteth out fear. He that feareth is not made perfect in love," 1 John iv. 16—18. So that love is the perfection of man.

1 Cor. xii. 31; xiii. 2, &c. "Yet show I unto you a more excellent way: though I understand all mysteries, and all knowledge, and have not charity, I am nothing.—Charity never faileth." Ver. 13, "The greatest of these is charity."

Rom. viii. 35, "Who shall separate us from the love of God," &c.

Rom. xiii. 10, "Love is the fulfilling of the law."

Rom. v. 5, "The love of God is poured out on our hearts by the Holy Ghost which is given to us."

Gal. v. 6, "Faith which worketh by love."

Matt. xxii. 37, "The first and great commandment is, Thou shalt love the Lord thy God with all thy heart," &c.

Luke x. 27; Deut. x. 12; xi. 1, 13, 22; xix. 9; xiii. 3; xxx. 6, 16, 20; Josh. xxii. 5; xxiii. 11; Psal. v. 11; xxxi. 23; lxix. 36; cxix. 165; cxlv. 20. Jam. i. 12, "He shall receive the crown of life, which the Lord hath promised to them that love him." So chap. ii. 5.

Prov. viii. 17, "I love them that love me."

See John xiv. 21; xvi. 27; 1 John iv. 19; John xxi. 15—17; 1 John iii. 22; Heb. xi. 6, &c.

And of knowledge it is said, John xiii. 17, "If ye know these things, happy are ye if ye do them."

See James ii. 14, to the end. John xv. 24, "But now they have both seen and hated both me and my Father."

Luke xii. 47, knowing God's will, and not doing it, prepareth men for many stripes. See Rom. ii. And as barren knowledge is oft made the aggravation of sin, so true knowledge is usually made the cause or means of love and obedience. 1 John iv. 8, "He that loveth not, knoweth not God." 2 Pet. i. 2, "Grace and peace be multiplied to you, through the knowledge of God." 2 Pet. ii. 20, and many such like.

I conclude therefore that the knowledge of creatures is not desirable ultimately for itself, but as it leadeth up the soul to God. And the knowledge of God, though desirable ultimately for itself, yet not as the perfect, but the initial part of our ultimate act or end, and as the means or cause of that love of God, which is the more perfect part of that ultimate perfection.

CHAPTER II.

THE END OF KNOWLEDGE IS TO MAKE US LOVERS OF GOD, AND SO TO BE KNOWN WITH LOVE BY HIM.

THIS is the second doctrine contained in the meaning of the text: where is included, 1. That all knowledge of creatures, called learning, must be valued and used but as a means to the knowledge and love of God: which is most evident in that the whole creation is the work of God, bearing the image or impress of his perfections, to reveal him to the intellectual creature, and to be the means of provoking us to his love, and helping us in his service. To deny this therefore is to subvert the use of the whole creation, and to set up God's works as a useless shadow, or as an idol, in his place.

2. It is included, as was before proved, that all our knowledge of God himself, is given us to kindle in us the love of God. It is the bellows to blow up this holy fire. If it do not this, it is unsound and dead. If it do this, it hath attained its end; which is much of the meaning of James in that chap. ii. which prejudice hindereth many from understanding.

3. This love of God hath its degrees and effects. Knowledge first kindleth but some weak initial act of love; which through mixtures of fear, and of carnal affections, is hardly known to be sincere by him that hath it. But afterwards it produceth both stronger acts, and the Holy Ghost still working as the principal cause, infuseth or operateth a radicated habit. So that this holy love becometh like a nature in the soul, even a divine nature; and it becometh in a sort natural to us to love God and goodness, though not as the brutish nature, which is exercised by necessity, and without reason. And this new nature of holy love, is called the new creature and the Holy Ghost dwelling in us, and the Spirit of adoption; and is our *new name*, the *white stone*, the *witness* in ourselves that Christ is the Saviour, and that we are the regenerate children of God, the pledge, the earnest, the first-fruits, and the foretaste of life eternal.

And all the works of a christian are so far truly holy, as they are the effects of holy love: for, 1. Holy love is but a holy will; and the will is the man, in point of morality. 2. And the love of God is our final act upon the final object; and all other gracious acts are some way means subservient to this end: and the end is it that informeth all the means, they being such only as they are adapted to the end.

And in this sense it is true which is said in the schools, (though many protestants misunderstanding it, have contradicted it,) that love is the form of all other graces; that is, it is the heart of the new creature; or it is that by which the man is morally to be reputed and denominated: and it is the final grace which animateth or informeth the rest as means.

And thus it is true, that when you will prove any grace to be sincere and saving, or any evidence certain, you must prove it to participate of the love of God and goodness, or you have failed and said nothing. Yea, you must prove it to be conjunct with predominant love, which setteth God above all creatures. And if you will prove any good work to be acceptable to God, prayer, praise, alms, justice, &c.

you must prove that it cometh from this predominant love. For it is so far and no further acceptable to God.

And their ignorance is but to be pitied, who tell you that this is to make our love of God to be instead of Christ to us, or to set up an acceptable righteousness or merit in ourselves: for we dream not that our love of God was a sacrifice for our sins, and the expiatory atonement and satisfaction to justice, nor that merit which procured us love itself, or purchased us the Holy Ghost. Our meaning is, that goodness is the only proper object of love; and God loveth his essential goodness first, and created goodness next: and our moral goodness, which is his image, is holy love, produced by and joined with holy wisdom and vitality. And so though God love us in Christ, or as related to him, it is as holy members of him; and not that he loveth complacentially the haters of God for their relation to Christ, without respect to any goodness in themselves. And to say that Christ maketh us acceptable and amiable to God, is all one as to say that he procureth us the pardon of sin, and the gift of the Holy Ghost, and maketh us holy lovers of God; or that he is indeed our Saviour. He that commendeth health as wrought by his physician, doth not set health instead of the physician. Christ is the physician; the Holy Ghost or holy love in us, is our health: to procure and give us the Holy Ghost, is Christ's office. He pardoneth our sin when he pardoneth the punishment: the privation of the Holy Ghost and his operations is our principal punishment; and therefore not all, but the principal part, of our pardon lieth in the giving us the Holy Ghost.

But some will say, That if God love nothing but goodness, and love us no further than we are good, how then did he love us first, and while we were his enemies? Are not election, creation, redemption, and conversion acts of love? And is not our love the fruit of his love?

Answ. Thus names not opened by confounding heads, are made the matter of a thousand controversies. As our love is nothing but our will, so the word *love* is taken strictly and properly, or largely and less properly. A man's will is considered as efficient or as final; as it respecteth a future effect, or a present exigent good. And so God's will, as it is final, and respecteth things existent, either, 1. *In esse cognito*, 2. Or *in esse reali*, is called complacence, and only complacence is love in the strict and properest sense. But God's will as efficient of good, may in a laxer sense be called love. God's will is the fountain or efficient cause of all good, natural and moral, in the world. And so you may call God's causing or making good, by the name of love, if you please; remembering that it is but the name that is questioned: but his complacency in good foreseen, or existent, is strictly called his love. And so still God loveth nothing in either sense but good. For, 1. He causeth nothing but good. 2. And he is pleased in nothing but good as good.

Quest. But how then doth God love his enemies?

Answ. 1. He maketh us men, which may be called one act of efficient love: and he redeemeth them; and he giveth them all the good things which they possess; and he sanctifieth some, and maketh them lovers of him, that is, holy. And thus he willeth their good, while they are nothing or evil; which is called benevolence, and love efficient.

2. And he hath true love of complacency in them, 1. As they have the good of human nature. 2. And thereby are capable of grace, and all the love and service which after they may perform. 3. And as they are related to Christ as his redeemed ones. 4. And as by relation they are those that God foreknoweth will love and serve him here, and in the perfections of eternal glory. There is all this good in some enemies of God, to be the matter of his complacency. And beyond their goodness he hath no complacency in them.

3. And to clear up all this, still remember that though man's will is changed by or upon the various objects, yet so is not the will of God. And therefore all these words signify no variety or change in God; but only how his simple, immutable, essential will is variously related to and denominated from the connotation of effects and objects.

4. Also it must be noted, as included in the text, that God loveth all that truly love him; for to be known of him, here meaneth to be known with approbation and love as his peculiar people. As Psal. i. 6, it is said, "The Lord knoweth the way of the righteous;" and so oft: and of the wicked, (Matt. xxv. 12,) "Depart from me, I know you not." God owneth with love all those that love him. What parts, what quality, what degree soever men are of, whatever difference else there be among them, if they are true lovers of God, they are certainly approved and beloved by him. This being the very heart and essence of the new creature, and the Divine nature in us, must needs prove that man to be amiable to God that hath it. Other things are true marks of a child of God only so far as they participate of love: but love is the primary proper character, which proveth us adopted directly of itself.

And here you may resolve the question that seemeth so difficult to many: whether when the Scripture either by describing the godly, or by promising life, doth mention some one grace or duty, as the character of a saint, or the condition of salvation, it be to be understood with a *cæteris paribus*, if other graces and duties concur, as supposing them separable? or absolutely, as supposing that one mark infallible, because it is never separated from the rest?

Answ. The new man hath, 1. Its essential parts; and, 2. Its integrals; and, 3. Its accidents. The essentials are ever infallible marks, and are inseparable from each other: any one of them will prove us holy, and will prove the presence of the rest. These essentials are a united trinity of graces, holy life, light, and love, where each one hath the common essence of holiness, which is their objective termination upon God; and each is linked by participation to another. Holy vitality is vital activity towards God in mind, will, and practice. Holy light is that knowledge and belief which kindleth love, and causeth a holy life. Holy love is that complacency of will in God and goodness, which is kindled by holy life and light, and operateth in holy practice. Any one of these thus described, where love is the heart of all, is an infallible mark of holiness. But all other graces and duties which are but the integrals of holiness, are in all characters and promises to be understood with a *cæteris paribus;* that is, supposing them to be animated with holy love, and caused by holy life and light (knowledge and belief).

And that God doth most certainly love all that love him, besides the forementioned proofs from Scripture, is further evident.

1. The love of God and goodness is the divine nature; and God cannot but love his own nature in us: it is his image, which, as in its several degrees, he loveth for himself, and next to himself.

2. The love of God is the rectitude of man's soul, its soundness, health, and beauty: and God loveth the rectitude of his creatures.

3. The love of God is the final, perfect operation of the soul; even that end which it was created and redeemed for: and God loveth to have his works

attain their end, and to see them in their perfection.

4. The love of God is the goodness of the soul itself: and goodness is amiableness, and must needs be loved by him that is goodness and perfection himself.

5. The love of God is our uniting adhesion to him: and God that first draweth up the soul to this union, will not himself reject us, and avoid it.

6. Love is a pregnant, powerful, pleasing grace: it delivereth up ourselves, and all that we have, to God: it delighteth in duty: it conquereth difficulties: it contemneth competitors, and trampleth on temptations: it accounteth nothing too much nor too dear for God. Love is the soul's nature, appetite, and *pondus*, according to which it will ordinarily act. A man's love is his will, his heart, himself; and if God have our love, he hath ourselves, and our all: so that God cannot but love the soul that truly loveth him as God.

But here are some doubts to be resolved.

Quest. 1. What if the same soul have love and sin mixed; or sincere love in a degree that is sinfully defective, and so is consistent with something of its contrary: God must hate that sin; how then can he love that soul?

Answ. Remember still that diversity is only in us, and not in God: therefore God's will is related and denominated towards us, just as its object is. All that is good in us God loveth: all that is evil in us he hateth. Where goodness is predominant, there God's love is predominant, or greatest, from this relation and connotation. Where sin is predominant, God's aversation, displicency, or hatred is the chief: and we may well expect that the effects be answerable.

Object. But we are beloved as elect before conversion.

Answ. That was answered before. That is, God from eternity purposed to make us good, and amiable, and happy; if you will call that (as you may) his love.

Object. But we are beloved in Christ, for his righteousness and goodness, and not for our own.

Answ. The latter is false: the former is thus true: for the merits of Christ's righteousness, and goodness, God will pardon our sins, and make us good, holy, and happy; and will love us as the holy members of his Son; that is, both as related to him and as holy.

Object. But if God must needs love sincere imperfect lovers of him as such, with a predominant love, (which will not damn them,) then sin might have been pardoned without Christ's death, and the sinner be loved without his righteousness, if he had but sincerely loved God.

Answ. The supposition is false, that a sinner could have loved God without pardon and the Spirit, purchased by the death and righteousness of Christ. God perfectly loveth the perfected souls in glory, for their own holy perfection, but they never attained it, but by Christ. And God loveth us here, according to the measure of our love to him: but no man can thus love him, till his sin be pardoned; for which he was deprived of the Spirit, which must kindle love. And imperfect love is ever joined with imperfect pardon (whatever some falsely say to the contrary); I mean that love which is sinfully imperfect.

Quest. 2. Doth not God's loving us make us happy? And if so, it must make us holy. And then none that he loveth will fall away from him: whereas the fallen angels and Adam loved him, and yet fell from him: how then were they beloved by him?

Answ. I before told you that God's will (or love) is first efficient, causing good, and then final, being pleased in the good that is caused. God's efficient will or love, doth so far make men holy and happy as they are such, even efficiently; but God's will, or love, as it is our *causa finalis*, and the terminating object of our love, and is pleased in us, and approveth us, is not the efficient cause of our holiness and happiness; but the objective and perfect constitutive cause. Now you must further note, that God's benevolent efficient will, or love, doth give men various degrees of holiness. To Adam in innocency he gave but such a degree, and upon such terms, as he could lose and cast away; which he did. But to the blessed in glory, he giveth that which they shall never lose. These degrees are from God's efficient love, or will; which, therefore, causeth some to persevere, when it left Adam to himself, to stand or fall. But it is not God's final love of complacency, as such, that causeth our perseverance: for Adam had this love, as long as he loved God, and stood; and he after lost it: so that it is not that final complacency, which is the *terminus* of our holiness, and constitutive cause of our happiness, which alone will secure the perpetuity of either of them.

Object. Thus you make God mutable in his love, loving Adam more before his fall than after.

Answ. I told you, loving and not loving the creature, are no changes in God, but in the creature. It is man that is mutable, and not God. It is only the relation of God's will to the creature, as varying in itself, and the extrinsic denomination, by connotation of a changed object, which is changed as to God. As the sun is not changed when you wink and when you open your eyes; nor a pillar changed when your motion sets it sometimes on your right hand, and sometimes on your left.

5. Lastly, it must be noted, as included in the text, That our own loving God, is not the only or total notion of our end, perfection, or felicity; but to be known and loved by God, is the other part which must be taken in, to make up the total notion of our end.

In our love, God is considered as the object: but in God's complacential love to us, he is considered as active, and his love as an act, and man as the object: but yet not as an object of efficiency, but of approbation, and a pleased will or delight. Here then the great difficulty is, in resolving which of these is the highest perfective notion of man's felicity, perfection, or ultimate end; our love to God, or God's love to us.

Answ. It is mutual love and union which is the true and complete notion of our end; and to compare God's love and ours as the parts, and tell which is the final principal part or notion, is not easy, nor absolutely necessary. But I conceive,

1. That our love to God is objectively, or as to the object of it, infinitely more excellent than God's love to us, as to the object: which is but to say, that God is infinitely better than man. God loveth man who is a worm; but we love God who is perfect goodness.

2. God's love to us, as to the agent and the act *ex parte agentis*, is infinitely more excellent than our love to him: for it is God's essential will which loveth us; and it is the will of a worm that loveth God.

3. That man's felicity, as such, is not the chief notion of his ultimate end; but he must love God as God, better than his own felicity as such, or better than God as our felicity.

4. That man's true ultimate end containeth these five inadequate conceptions. 1. The lowest notion or part of it is, our own holiness and felicity 2.

The next notion of it is, the perfection of the church and universe, to which we contribute, and which we must value above our own; including the glory of Christ's humanity. 3. The third notion is, the glory or lustre of God's perfections, as they shine forth in us and all his perfected glorious works. 4. The fourth notion is, God's own essential goodness, as the object of our knowledge, love, and praise. 5. The fifth and highest notion is, the active love or complacency of God's fulfilled will, in us, and in the whole creation. So that the pleasing of God's will is the highest notion of man's ultimate end; though all these five are necessarily contained in it.

CHAPTER III.

DOCT. 3. THEREFORE KNOWLEDGE IS TO BE VALUED, SOUGHT, AND USED, AS IT TENDETH TO OUR LOVE OF GOD.

This third doctrine is much of the scope of the text: all means are for their end: so far as knowledge is a means of love, it must needs hence have the measure of its worth, and we the motives of our desires of it, and the direction for our using of it.

1. All knowledge that kindleth not the love of God in us, is so narrow and small that it deserveth not indeed the name of knowledge; for the necessary things that such a person is ignorant of, are a thousand times more or greater, than that little which he knoweth: for, (1.) What is it that he is ignorant of?

1. He hath no sound and real knowledge of God. For if he knew God truly, he could not but love him: goodness is so naturally the object of the will, that if men well knew the infinite Good, they must needs love him: however there is a partial knowledge that is separable from sincere love.

2. He that knoweth not and loveth not God, neither knoweth nor loveth any creature truly and effectually either as it is *of God*, or *through him*, or *to him;* either as it beareth the impress of the glorious efficient, or as it is ordered to its end by the most wise Director, or as it is a means to lead up souls to God, or to glorify and please him, no nor to make man truly happy. And can he be said indeed to know any creature that knoweth it not in any of these respects, that knoweth neither its original, order, or use? Doth a dog or a goose know a book of philosophy, because he looketh on it, and seeth the bulk? Doth he know a clock or watch, who knoweth no more of it, but that it hath such parts and shapes, made of iron and brass? It is most evident that an unholy person knoweth nothing; that is, no one being, though he may know *aliquid de re aliqua*, something of some being: for he that knoweth not the nature, order, or use and end of a being, cannot properly be said to know that being; but only *secundum quid*, or some accidents of it, or to have a general knowledge that it is a substance, or a something, he knoweth not what. As an Epicurean can call all things compacted atoms, or matter and motion. An ungodly man is just like one that studieth the art of a scrivener or printer, to make the letters, and place them by art, but never learned to read or know the signification of the letters which he maketh or composeth.

Or if any may be said to have a speculative knowledge of all this in the creature, (the nature, order, and use,) yet he is without the true practical knowledge, which is it that only is knowledge indeed, and of use and benefit to man; for to be able to speak or write a true proposition about God or the creature, is not properly to know God or the creature, but to know names and words concerning them: it is but a logical knowledge of notions, and not the knowledge of the thing itself, to be able to say and know that this or that concerning it is true or false. Nothing more deceiveth mankind, both in point of learning, and of religion, and salvation, than mistaking the organical or logical knowledge of second notions, words, propositions, inferences, and methods, for the real knowledge of the things themselves; and thinking that they know a thing, because they know what to say of it.

He knoweth not a country, who is only able by the map or hearsay to describe it. He knoweth not motion, light, heat, cold, sweet, bitter, that knoweth no more than to give a true definition of it. And as this is true of things sensible, which must themselves be perceived first by sense, so is it of things spiritual, which must themselves be perceived first by intellection, and not only the notions and definitions of them. He that doth not intuitively, or by internal immediate perception, know what it is to understand, to remember, to will and nill, to love and hate, and consequently to be able to do these acts, doth not know what a man is, or what a reasonable soul is, and what an intellectual spirit is, though he could (were it possible) without these learn the definition of a man, a soul, a spirit. A definition or word of art spoken by a parrot or a mad-man, proveth not that he knoweth the thing.

Practical objects are not truly known without a practical knowledge of them. He knoweth not what meat is, that knoweth not that it must be eaten, and how to eat it. He only knoweth his clothing that knoweth how to put it on. He only knoweth a pen, a gun, or other instrument, that knoweth how to use it. Now the ungodly, not knowing how any creature signifieth the divine perfections, nor how by it to ascend to the knowledge and love of God, do indeed know nothing with a proper, formal knowledge.

(2.) And what is it that such men know, or seem to know, which may be compared with their ignorance? To give them their due praise, they know how to eat as well as a dog, though not so subtlely as an ox or sheep, that can distinguish grass before he taste it. He can tell how to drink, though not by so constant a temperance as a beast. He can speak better than a parrot. He can build him a house as apt for his use, as a swallow or other birds can do for theirs. He can lay up for the time to come more subtlely than a fox, or ant, though nothing so orderly, and by wonderful self-conficiency, as the bees. He can look upwards, and see the birds that soar and fly in the air, though he cannot imitate them. He can look into the surface of the waters, and artificially pass over them in ships, though he cannot live in them, or glide through them as the fish. He can master those that are weaker than himself, as the great dogs do the little ones, and carry away the bone from them all. He can glory in his strength, though it be less than a horse's, on ox's, an elephant's, or a whale's. He can kill and eat his fellow animals, as well as a pike among the fishes, a kite among the birds, or a wolf or dog among the beasts. He can more craftily than the fox entrap and insnare them (the fishes, birds, and beasts); yea, as artificially as a spider does the flies, to make up what he wants of the hawk or dog for swift pursuit, or of the lion for rapacious strength. He can sing; and so can the linnet, the ousel, the lark, and nightingale. He can make his bed as soft as the birds their nests, or as other creatures that love their ease: he can generate and breed up his offspring, though not with that constancy of affection, and accurateness of skill and industry, as a hen her chickens, or most other animals do their young. Yea, he can live in societies, families, commonwealths, though much more disorderly, contentiously, and to the disturbance, if not destruction of each other, than pigeons in their dove-house, or the flight of stares, or larks, or lapwings, or the flocks of sheep, and less accurately than the bees do in their hive.

All this and more we can speak of the praises of the knowledge or wisdom of an ungodly man, that never learned to know or love his God, nor any thing truly worthy of a man: and is all this worthy the name of knowledge? Their character could not be fitlier given than here it is by the apostle: "They know nothing as they ought to know." But of this more next.

CHAPTER IV.

DOCT. 4. AND THEREFORE THOSE ARE TO BE ACCOUNTED THE WISEST AND BEST KNOWING MEN, THAT LOVE GOD MOST; AND NOT THOSE THAT ARE STORED WITH UNHOLY KNOWLEDGE.

THIS fourth doctrine is also a discernible part of the meaning of the apostle in the text. His purpose is to humble those that judge themselves wise for that which is no wisdom, but useless, ludicrous notions and self conceitedness; and to show men wherein true wisdom doth consist. Many thousands there are that heartily love God, and are devoted to him, and live to his service in the world, who never read logic, physics, metaphysics, or mathematics; nor laid in that stock of artificial notions, which are the glory and utensils of the learned world. And yet that these are truly and happily wise and knowing, the apostle judgeth, and I thus further prove.

1. Because they know the things themselves, and not only the names and definitions of them: as he that knoweth food by eating it, the military art, or navigation, by experience, or a country by travelling or dwelling in it. Others lick the outside of the glass, but taste not the sweet that is within.

2. Because they know the greatest and most excellent things: God is infinitely greater and better than the creatures; and heaven incomparably better than the riches and pleasures of this earth. To know how to build a city, or a navy, and how to govern an army or a kingdom, is more than to know how to pick sticks or straws, or to dress and undress us. Understanding is valuable by the dignity of its objects; therefore how much doth the wisdom of a holy soul excel all the craft and learning of the ungodly! Let not the rich man glory in his riches—But let him that glorieth glory in this, that he knoweth God; if he so know him as to love him.

3. Because they know the most necessary things, and the most profitable. They know how to be good, and how to do their duty, and how to attain their end, and how to please God, and how to escape damnation, and how to be happy in everlasting joy and glory. And I think he is wise, that is wise enough to be happy, and to attain all that the soul of man can well desire.

But who will desire the wisdom that maketh a man never the better; and that will not save his soul from hell? What soul in hell doth think that wisdom brought him thither? It were a thousand times better, not to know how to speak or go, to dress or undress us, than not to know how to be holy and happy, and to escape sin and everlasting misery.

4. A holy soul understandeth that which his understanding was made for; and for which he hath his life, and time, and teaching; which is but to be good, and love God and goodness, and to do good. And wisdom, as is before proved, as all other means, is to be estimated by its end.

But an ungodly man knoweth not that which he was made for. He is like a knife that cannot cut; a ship that will not endure the water; a house that is not fit to dwell in. What is a man's wit worth, but for its proper end? If man was made but to eat, and drink, and play, and sleep, and build, and plant, and stir awhile about the earth, and have his will over others, and his fleshly pleasure, and then die, then the ungodly may be called wise; but if he be made to prepare for another world, and to know, and love, and to live to God, they are then worse than Bedlams, and more dangerously beside themselves.

5. A holy soul knowing God the beginning and end, knoweth all things: because he knoweth them, 1. In the chiefest excellency of their natures, as they bear the impress of God; 2. And in their order, as governed by him; 3. And in their usefulness, as tending to him: though neither they, nor any others, be well acquainted with their material part, which the philosopher thinketh that he knoweth best. Who think you best knoweth what money is? He that knoweth the king's impress, and the value, and what it is good for, and how to get and use it? or he that can only tell you whether it be copper, or silver, or gold, (not knowing well what any of these are,) and knoweth nothing of the impress, or value, or use? I tell you, the humble, holy person, that seeth God in all, and knoweth all things to be *of him*, and *by him*, and *to him*, and loveth him in and for all, and serveth him by all, is the best philosopher, and hath the greatest, most excellent, and profitable knowledge. In comparison of which, the unholy learning of the world is well called foolishness with God. (For I believe not that paraphraser who would persuade us that it is but the fanatic conceits and pretensions of the Gnostics, that the apostle here and elsewhere speaketh of. But I rest satisfied, that it is primarily the unholy arts and sciences of the philosophical heathens; and secondarily, the Platonic heretics' pretensions to extraordinary wisdom, because of their speculations about angels, spirits, and other invisible and mysterious things, which they thought were peculiarly opened unto them.) Doting about questions that engender strife, and not edification, and to increase to more ungodliness, is the true description of unholy learning.

6. The lovers of God are wise for perpetuity: they see before them: they know what is to come; even as far as to eternity. They know what will be best at last, and what will be valued and serve our turn in the hour of our extremity; they judge of things as all will judge of them; and as they shall constantly judge of them for ever. But others are wise but for a few hours, or a present job: they see not before them: they are preparing for repentance. They are shamefully mutable in their judgments; magnifying those pleasures, wealth, and honours today, which they vilify and cry out against at death and to eternity! A pang of sickness, the sight of a grave, the sentence of death, the awakening of conscience, can change their judgments, and make them speak in other language, and confess a thousand times over that they were fools: and if they come to

any thing like wisdom, it is too late, when time is past, and hope is gone. But the godly know the day of their visitation, and are wise in time; as knowing the season of all duties, and the duties of every season. And as some schoolmen say, that all things are known to the glorified, *in speculo Trinitatis;* so I may say, that all things are morally and savingly known to him that knoweth and loveth God, as the efficient Governor and End of all.

Yet, to avoid mistakes and cavils, remember, that I take no true knowledge as contemptible. And when I truly say that he knoweth nothing as he ought to know, that doth not know and love his God, and is not wise to his duty and salvation; yet if this fundamental knowledge be presupposed, we should build all other useful knowledge on it, to the utmost of our capacity: and from this one stock may spring and spread a thousand branches, which may all bear fruit. I would put no limits to a christian's desires and endeavours to know, but that he desire only to know useful and revealed things. Every degree of knowledge tendeth to more: and every known truth befriendeth others; and like fire, tendeth to the spreading of our knowledge, to all neighbour truths that are intelligible. And the want of acquaintance with some one truth among a hundred, may hinder us from knowing rightly most of the rest; or may breed a hundred errors in us: as the absence of one wheel or particle in a watch, or the ignorance of it, may put all the rest into a useless disorder. What if I say that wisdom lieth more in knowing the things that belong to salvation, to public good, to life, health, and solid comfort, than in knowing how to sing, or play on the lute, or to speak or carry ourselves with commendable decency, &c.; it doth not follow that all these are of no worth at all; and that in their places these little matters may not be allowed and desired: for even hair and nails are appurtenances of a man, which a wise man would not be without; though they are small matters in comparison of the animal, vital, and nobler parts. And indeed he that can see God in all things, and hath all this sanctified by the love of God, should above all men value each particle of knowledge, of which so holy a use may be made; as we value every grain of gold.

CHAPTER V.

INFERENCE 1. BY WHAT MEASURES TO ESTIMATE MEN'S KNOWLEDGE.

FROM hence then we may learn how to value the understandings of ourselves and others: that is good which doth good. Would God but give me one beam more of the heavenly light, and a little clearer knowledge of himself, how joyfully could I exchange a thousand lower notions for it! I feel not myself at all miserable for want of knowing the number and order of the stars, the nature of the meteors, the causes of the ebbing and flowing of the sea, with many hundred other questions in physics, metaphysics, mathematics: nor do I feel it any great addition to my happiness, when I think I know somewhat of such things which others know not. But I feel it is my misery to be ignorant of God, and ignorant of my state and duty, and ignorant of the world where I must live for ever. This is the dungeon where my wretched soul doth lie in captivity night and day, groaning and crying out, Oh when shall I know more of God! and more of the celestial habitations, and more of that which I was made to know! Oh when shall I be delivered from this darkness and captivity! Had I not one beam that pierceth through this lantern of flesh, this dungeon were a hell, even the outer darkness. I find books that help me to names, and notions; but oh for that Spirit that must give me light to know the things, the spiritual, great, and excellent things, which these names import! Oh how ignorant am I of those same things, which I can truly and methodically speak and write of! Oh that God would have mercy on my dark understanding, that I be not as a clock, to tell others that which itself understandeth not! Oh how gladly would I consent to be a fool in all common arts and sciences, if I might but be ever the wiser in the knowledge of God! Did I know better him by whom I live, who upholdeth all things, before whom my soul must shortly appear; whose favour is my life; whom I hope to love and praise for ever; what were all other things to me? Oh for one beam more of his light! for one taste of his love! for one clear conception of the heavenly glory! I should then scarce have leisure to think of a thousand inferior speculations, which are now magnified and agitated in the world.

But much more miserable do I find myself, for want of more love to the blessed God who is love itself! O happy exchange! did I part with all the pleasures of the world, for one flame, one spark more of the love of God! I hate not myself for my ignorance in the common arts and sciences; but my God knoweth that I even abhor and loathe myself, because I love and delight in him no more! Oh what a hell is this dead and disaffected heart! Oh what a foretaste of heaven would it be, could I but feel the fervours of Divine love! Well may that be called the first-fruits of heaven, and the divine nature and life, which so uniteth souls to God, and causeth them to live in the pleasures of his goodness. I dare not beg hard for more common knowledge: but my soul melteth with grief for want of love; and forceth out tears, and sighs, and cries; Oh when will heaven take acquaintance with my heart, and shine into it, and warm and revive it, that I may truly experience the delightful life of holy love! I cannot think them loathsome and unlovely, that are unlearned, and want the ornaments of art. But I abhor and curse those hateful sins, which have raised the clouds, and shut the windows, and hindered me from the more lively knowledge and love of God. Would God but number me with his zealous lovers, I would presume to say, that he had made me wise, and initially happy. But, alas! such high and excellent things will not be gotten with a lazy wish, nor will holy love dwell with iniquity in unholy and defiled souls.

But if wisdom were justified of none but her children, how confidently durst I call myself a son of wisdom? For all my reason is fully satisfied, that the learned, ungodly doctors are mere fools, and the lovers of God are only wise: and oh that my lot may be with such, however I be esteemed by the dreaming world!

CHAPTER VI.

INFERENCE 2. TO ABATE OUR CENSURES AND CONTEMPT OF THE LESS LEARNED CHRISTIANS AND CHURCHES UPON EARTH.

I MUST confess that ignorance is the great enemy of holiness in the world; and the prince of darkness in his kingdom of darkness, oppugneth the light, and promoteth the works of darkness by it: and it is found that where vision ceaseth, the people perish, even for lack of knowledge; and the ignorantest countries are the most ungodly. But I must recant some former apprehensions: I have thought the Armenians, the Syrians, the Georgians, the Coptics, the Abassines, the Greeks, more miserable for want of polite literature, than now I judge them. Though I contemn it not as the Turks do, and the Muscovites; yet I perceive that had men but the knowledge of the holy Scriptures, yea, of the summaries of true religion, they might be good and happy men, without much more. If there be but some few among them skilled in all the learning of the world, and expert in using the adversaries' weapons against themselves as champions of the truth, the rest might do well with the bare knowledge of God, and a crucified Christ. It is the malice of assaulting enemies, that maketh all other learning needful in some for our defence. But the new creature liveth not on such food, but on the bread of life, and living waters, and the sincere milk of the sacred word.

The old Albigenses and Waldenses in Piedmont, and other countries, did many ages keep up the life and comfort of true religion, even through murders and unparalleled cruelties of the worldly learned church; when they had little of the arts and common sciences. But necessary knowledge was propagated by the industry of parents and pastors: their children could say over their catechisms, and could give account of the principles of religion, and recite many practical parts of Scripture: and they had much love and righteousness, and little division or contention among them; which made the moderate emperor Maximilian profess to Crato, that he thought the Picards of all men on earth were likest the apostolic, primitive churches.

And Brocardus, who dwelt among them in Judea, tells us that the christians there that by the papists are accounted heretics, (as Nestorians or Eutychians,) were indeed good, harmless, simple men, and lived in piety, and mortifying austerities, even beyond the very religious sort (the monks and friars) of the church of Rome, and shamed the wickedness of our learned part of the world.

And though there be sad mixtures of such superstitions and traditions, as ignorance useth to breed and cherish, yet the great devotion and strictness of many of the Abassines, Armenians, and other of those ruder sort of christians, is predicated by many historians and travellers. And who knoweth but there may be among their vulgar, more love to God, and heaven, and holiness, than among the contentious, learned nations, where the pastors strive who shall be the greatest, and preach up that doctrine and practice which is conformable to their own wills and worldly interests; and where the people, by the oppositions of their leaders, are drawn into several sides and factions, which, as armies, militate against each other. Is not the love of God like to be least, where contentions and controversies divert the people's minds from God and necessary saving truths? and where men least love one another? and where mutual hatred, cruelty, and persecution proclaim them much void of that love which is the christian badge?

I will not cease praying for the further illumination and reformation of those churches: but I will repent of my hard thoughts of the providence of God, as if he had cast them almost off, and had few holy souls among them. For aught I know they may be better than most of Europe.

And the like I say of many unlearned christians among ourselves. We know not what love to God and goodness doth dwell in many that we have a very mean esteem of. The breathings of poor souls towards God by Christ, and their desires after greater holiness, is known to God that kindleth it in them, but not to us.

CHAPTER VII.

INFERENCE 3. BY WHAT MEASURES TO JUDGE OF THE KNOWLEDGE NECESSARY TO CHURCH COMMUNION.

I KNOW that there are some that would make Christ two churches; one political and congregate, as they phrase it, and the other regenerate; or one visible and the other invisible: and accordingly they say, that professed faith is the qualification of a member of the church-congregate; and obedience to the pope, say the papists, and real love, is the qualification of the church regenerate.

But as there is but one catholic church of Christ, so is there but one faith, and one baptism, by which men are stated as members in that church. But as heart consent and tongue consent are two things, but the latter required only as the expression and profession of the former; so heart consenters and tongue consenters should be the same men; as body and soul make not two men, but one. But if the tongue speak that consent which is not in the heart, that person is a hypocrite; and is but analogically or equivocally called a christian or member of Christ: and such among the sincere are not a distinct church or society (if they were, they should be called the hypocritical church, and not the political or congregate church). But they are as traitors in an army, or as stricken ears in a corn-field. But the true church being one, is considered as consenting with the heart and with the tongue: as a corn-field hath straw, chaff, and grain; and as a man hath soul and body. So that it is the same church that is visible by baptism and profession, and invisible by heart consent or sincerity.

But it is the same thing, and not divers, that is in the hearts of the sincere, and that is to be professed by the tongue: even that voluntary practical faith which is described in baptism, and no other. The same faith which is accepted to salvation in the sincere and invisible members of the church, as they are called, must be professed by all that will, at age, be visible members.

And the knowledge and belief required in baptism is so much as prevaileth with the person to give up himself to God the Father, Son, and Holy Ghost, as his reconciled Creator, his Saviour and Sanctifier. And he that hath so much knowledge as will do this, hath as much as is necessary to his reception into the church.

Doubtless he that is capable of baptism, is capable of church membership; and he that is capable of church membership, is capable *de jure*, as to right, of so much church communion as he is capable of by real aptitude. An infant is not naturally capable of the actions of the adult; nor half-witted persons of the receptions and performances of the judicious: some cannot understand a sermon, or prayer, or praise, the twentieth part so well as others can do, and so cannot receive and do beyond their understanding. Some may not so well understand the nature of the Lord's supper, as to be really fit at present to receive it; and some may be unfit through some extraordinary doubts, opinions, or lapses; but still *de jure* a church member hath right to so much church communion as their real qualifications make them capable of. For that right is part of the definition of a church member; and to be made a church member is the work of baptism.

And here we must consider of the reason why God would have baptism to be the profession of that faith which maketh us christians. Sometimes we are called believers, and said to be justified by faith, as if it were faith alone that were our christianity; and yet when it cometh to church entrance, and to the solemn profession of our faith, and reception of a sealed and delivered pardon, we must do more than profess that we believe with the understanding; we must give up ourselves absolutely by a vow and covenant, to God the Father, Son, and Holy Ghost, renouncing the flesh, the world, and the devil; which is the act of a resolved will: and to will is rationally to love and choose. By which Christ telleth us, that (as words of knowledge in Scripture usually imply affection, so) the faith that he means and requireth to our justification, is not a mere assent or act of intellection; but it is also the will's consent, and a practical affiance: as a man believing the skill and fidelity of a physician, doth desire, will, or choose him for his physician, and practically trust him, or cast himself upon his fidelity and care for cure. Therefore Christ joineth both together, "He that believeth and is baptized, shall be saved," Mark xvi. 16; not principally intending the washing of the flesh, but the answer of a good conscience, as Peter expoundeth it: that is, he that so believeth as by hearty consent to devote and give up himself openly and absolutely, and presently, to God the Father, Son, and Holy Ghost, shall be saved.

And so the apostle saith, (Eph. iv. 4, 5,) there is one baptism, as part of the uniting bond of christians: that is, there is one solemn covenant between God and man, in which we profess our faith, and give up ourselves to God the Father, Son, and Holy Ghost, and are stated in a gracious relation to him and one another.

And thus it is that baptism is reckoned (Heb. vi.) among the principles; and that the ancient doctors unanimously conclude, that baptism washeth away all sin, and certainly puts us into a present state of life; that is, the delivering up ourselves sincerely to God in the baptismal covenant, is the condition of our right to the benefits of that covenant from God.

From all which it is plain, that the head is but the guide of the heart, and that God looketh more to the heart than to the head, and to the head for the heart: and that we are not christians indeed, till Christ have our hearts indeed; nor christians by profession, till by baptismal covenant and profession we deliver up the heart to Christ. Now so far as consent and will may be called love, so far even love is essential to our christianity, and to this faith, which is required to our baptism and justification; and no other faith is christianity, nor will justify us.

But to them that are here stalled with the great difficulty, how love is that grace of the Holy Ghost which is promised to believers in the covenant, as consequent, if it go before it in the covenanters; I answer at present, that they must distinguish between, 1. Love to Christ, as a Saviour of ourselves, proceeding principally from the just love of ourselves and our salvation; and love to God above ourselves, for his own infinite goodness, as our ultimate end: 2. Between the act of love, and a habit: 3. Between that spark of love which consisteth in the said consent, and is contained in true faith; and that flame of love which itself carrieth the name, as being the most eminent operation of the soul. And if hereupon they cannot answer this question themselves, I must refer them to the Appendix of the third chapter of my "Christian Directory," in which I have largely opened this case, with as much exactness as I could reach unto.

All that remaineth very difficult then as to our judging of the knowledge of men to be admitted to christian church communion, is but what knowledge is necessary in the adult unto their lawful baptism. And to that I say, so much as is necessary to an understanding consent to the baptismal covenant, or to a hearty giving up themselves to God the Father, Son, and Holy Ghost. And here we must know that the same covenanting words being comprehensive, are understood in different degrees, according to man's different capacities, even of true believers: insomuch that I do not think that any two men in the world have in all notions and degrees just the same understanding of them. And therefore it is not the same distinctness and clearness of understanding which we must expect in all, which is found in some, or which is desirable. When one man nameth GOD, he hath an orderly conception of his several attributes (in which yet all men are defective, and most divines themselves are culpably ignorant): when another man conceiveth but of fewer of them, and that disorderly: and yet these must not be accounted atheists, or denied to believe in the same God, or refused baptism; nor is it several gods that men so differently believe in.

I. He that knoweth God to be a most perfect Spirit, most powerful, wise, and good; the Father, Son, and Holy Ghost; the Creator of the world; our Owner, Governor, and most amiable Lover, Benefactor, and End: I think, knoweth as much of God, as is of necessity to baptism and church communion.

II. He that knoweth that Jesus Christ is God and man, the Redeemer of the sinful world, and the Mediator between God and man; who was conceived by the Holy Ghost in the Virgin Mary, fulfilled all righteousness, was crucified as a sacrifice for man's sin; and being dead and buried, rose again, and ascended into heaven; and is the Teacher, King, and Intercessor of his Church; and hath made the new covenant, and giveth the Holy Ghost to sanctify believers, and pardoneth their sins; and will raise our bodies at last, and judge the world in righteousness according to his gospel, and will give everlasting happiness to the sanctified: I think, knoweth as much of Christ, as is necessary to baptism and church communion.

III. He that knoweth, that the Holy Ghost is God, proceeding from the Father and the Son, the Sanctifier of souls, by holy life, and light, and love; by the holy gospel, of which he is the inditer, and the seal: I think, knoweth all that is necessary unto baptism, concerning the Holy Ghost.

IV. And as to the act of knowing this Trinity of objects, there is a great difference between, 1. Knowing the notions, or words, and the matter. 2. Between an orderly, clear, and a dark and more confused knowledge. 3. And between apt significant words, and such as any way notify a necessary true conception of the mind. 4. Between such a knowledge as maketh a man willing, and consent to give up himself to this Trinity in covenant, and that which prevaileth not for such consent. And so,

1. It is true, that we know not the heart immediately; and therefore must judge by words and deeds: but yet it is the knowledge of the things, as is aforesaid, that is necessary to salvation; because it is the love of the things that is chiefly necessary. But by what words to express that love or knowledge is not of equal necessity in itself.

2. There being no man, whose conceptions of God, Christ, the Holy Ghost, the covenant, &c. are not guilty of darkness and disorder; a great degree of darkness and disorder of conceptions may consist with true grace in those of the lowest rank of christians.

3. The second notions and conceptions of things, (and so of God our Redeemer and Sanctifier,) as they are *verba mentis* in the mind itself, are but logical, artificial organs; and are not of that necessity to salvation, as the conception of the matter or incomplex objects.

4. Many a man in his studies, findeth that he hath oft a general and true knowledge of things in themselves, before he can put names and notions on them, and set those in due order, and long before he can find fit words to express his mental notions by; which must cost him much study afterwards. And as children are long learning to speak, and by degrees come to speak orderly, and composedly, and aptly (mostly not till many years' use hath taught them); so the expressive ability is as much matter of art, and got by use, in men at age; and they must be taught yet as children to speak of any thing new and strange, and which they learned not before: as we see in learning arithmetic, geometry, and all the arts and sciences. Even so men, how holy, internally soever, must by study and use, by the help of God's Spirit, learn how to speak of holy things, in prayer, in conference, in answering such as ask an account of their faith and knowledge: and hypocrites, that are bred up in the use of such things, can speak excellently in prayer, conference, or preaching; when true christians at first, that never used them, nor were bred up where they heard them used, cannot tell you intelligibly what is in their minds; but are like men that are yet to learn the very language in which they are to talk. I know this by true experience of myself, and many others that I have examined.

5. Therefore, I say again, if men cannot aptly answer me, of the very essentials of religion, but speak that which in its proper sense is heresy, or unsound and false; yet if when I open the questions to them myself, and put the article of faith into the question, and ask them, e. g. Do you believe that there is but one God? or, are there many? Doth God know all things, or not? Is he our Owner, or not? Doth he rule us by a law, or not, &c.? If they, by yea or nay, do speak the truth, and profess to believe it; I will not reject them for lack of knowledge, if the rest concur. I meet with few censorious professors, (to say nothing of teachers,) that will not answer me with some nonsense or falseness, or ineptitude, or gross confusion, or defectiveness, if I examine them of the foregoing notions of the very baptismal covenant: as, What is a spirit? What doth the word God signify? What is power in God? What, knowledge? What, will? What, goodness? What holiness? What is a person in the Trinity? What is the difference between the three persons? How is God our end? Had Christ his human soul from the Virgin, or only his flesh? Had he his manhood from man, if not his soul, which is the chief essential part? What is the union of the divine and human nature? Wherein different from the union of God and saints, or every creature? with a hundred such; in which I must bear with ignorant false answers from eminent professors, that separate from others as too ignorant for their communion: and why then must I not bear with more in those that are new beginners, and have not had their time and helps?

6. But if a man can speak never so well, and profess never so confident a belief; if he consent not to the covenant and vow of baptism, to give up himself presently and absolutely to Christ; I must reject that man from the communion of the church. But if these two things do but concur in any, 1. The aforesaid signification of a tolerable knowledge and belief, by yea or nay (Dost thou believe in God? &c. as the ancient churches used to ask the baptized); 2. And a ready professed consent to be engaged by that holy vow and covenant to God the Father, Son, and Holy Ghost; I will not deny baptism to such, if adult, nor after church communion to them, if they are already in the covenant.

And all this is because that the will is the man; and if any man truly love Jesus Christ, he is a true believer in Christ; and if any man love God, the same is known and loved of him, and hath so much knowledge as will save his soul. I confess in private catechising and conference, I have met with some ancient women that have long lived as godly persons, in constant affectionate use of means, and an honest, godly life, and been of good repute in the church where they lived, who yet have spoken downright heresy to me, through ignorance, in answering some questions about Jesus Christ: but I durst not therefore suspend their communion, nor condemn their former communion; for as soon as I told them better; they have yielded, and I could not perceive whether it was from gross ignorance, or from unreadiness of notions, or from the want of memory, or what, that they spake amiss before. So that I shall be very loth to reject one from communion, that showeth a love of God, and Jesus Christ, and holiness, by diligent use of means, and an upright life.

7. And he that will impartially be ruled by the holy Scriptures, will be of the same mind. For no one was ever taken to be a church member at age, without so full a consent, as was willingly expressed by devotedness to God in the solemn covenant: the Jews by the sign of circumcision, and the christians by baptism, and both by covenanting with God, were initiated; and consent is love. But the articles and objective degrees of knowledge and belief have greatly varied. The Jews were to know and profess more than the gentiles; and the Jews since the Egyptian deliverance, more than before; and John baptized upon a shorter profession than the apostles did; and the apostles till Christ's resurrection, believed not many great articles of our faith, not knowing that Christ must die, and be an expiatory sacrifice for sin, and sin to be pardoned by his blood; nor that he was to rise again, and send the Holy Ghost for the work which he was sent for, &c. And Acts xix. there were disciples that had not heard that there was a Holy Ghost (I confidently think, twice baptized).

And if we mark how the apostles baptized, with what orders for it they received from Christ, it will confirm my conclusion. For Christ could have given a particular creed, and profession of faith, if he had pleased; but he taketh up with the general three articles, of believing the Father, Son, and Holy Ghost, (Matt. xxviii. 19, 20,) lest any should cast out his weak ones, for want of distinctness of knowledge and belief. And he maketh the covenant consent in baptism the necessary thing, as the end and measure of their knowledge. He that hath knowledge enough to cause him to thirst, may come and drink of the waters of life, Rev. xxii. 17. And he that hungereth and thirsteth after righteousness shall be satisfied; and he that cometh to Christ, he will in no wise cast out.

And the apostles baptized so many thousands in a short time, that they could not examine each person about a more particular knowledge and belief, (Acts ii. &c.;) nor do we read in Scripture of such particular large professions, as go much beyond the words of baptism. And though, no doubt, they did endeavour to make the ignorant understand what they professed and did, and so had some larger creed, yet was it not all so large as the short creed called the Apostles' now is; several of its articles having been long since added.

I have spoken all this, not only to ministers, who have the keys of admission, but especially for the religious persons' sakes, who are too much inclined to place godliness in words and ability to speak well, in prayer or conference, or answering questions, and that make a more distinct knowledge and profession necessary than God hath made: yea, if all the articles of the creed are professed, when the understanding of them is not clear and distinct, they deride it, and say, a parrot may be taught as much; and they separate from those pastors and churches that receive such to their communion. Many do this of a godly zeal, lest ignorance and formality be encouraged, and the godly and ungodly not sufficiently distinguished: but their zeal is not according to knowledge, nor to the holy rule; and they little know how much pride oft lurketh unobserved, in such desires to be publicly differenced from others, as below us, and unmeet for our communion: and less know they how much they injure and displease our gracious Lord, who took little children in his arms, and despiseth not the weak, and carrieth the lambs, and refuseth no one any further than they refuse him.

I tell you, if you see but true love and willingness in a diligent, reformed, pious, and righteous life, there is, certainly there is, saving knowledge and faith within; and if words do not satisfactorily express it, you are to think that it is not for want of the thing itself, but for want of use and exercise, and for want of well-studied notions, or for want of natural parts, education, or art to enable them to act that part aright. But if God know the meaning of Abba, Father, and of the groans of the Spirit, in his beloved infants, I will not be one that shall condemn and reject a lover of God and Christ and holiness, for want of distinct particular knowledge, or of words to utter it aright.

CHAPTER VIII.

INFERENCE 4. THE APTNESS OF THE TEACHING OF CHRIST, TO INGENERATE THE LOVE OF GOD AND HOLINESS.

If love be the end and perfection of our knowledge, then hence we may perceive, that no teacher that ever appeared in the world, was so fit for the ingenerating of true saving knowledge as Jesus Christ; for none ever so promoted the love of God.

1. It was he only that rendered God apparently lovely to sinful man, by reconciling us to God, and rendering him apparently propitious to his enemies, pardoning sin, and tendering salvation freely to them that were the sons of death. Self-love will not give men leave to love aright a God that will damn them, though deservedly for sin. But it is Christ that hath made atonement, and is the propitiation for our sins, and proclaimeth God's love, even to the rebellious: which is more effectually to kindle holy love in us, than all the precepts of naturalists without this could ever have been. His cross, and his wounds and blood, were the powerful sermons, to preach God's winning love to sinners.

2. And the benefits are so many and so great which he hath purchased and revealed to man, that they are abundant fuel for the flames of love. We are set by Christ in the way of mercy, in the household of God, under the eye and special influence of his love; all our sins pardoned, our everlasting punishment remitted, our souls renewed, our wounded consciences healed, our enemies conquered, our fears removed, our wants supplied, our bodies, and all that is ours, under the protection of Almighty Love; and we are secured by promise, that all our sufferings shall work together for our good. And what will cause love, if all this will not? When we perceive with what love the Father hath loved us, that of enemies we should be made the sons of God, and of condemned sinners we should be made the heirs of endless glory, and this so freely, and by so strange a means, we may conclude that this is the doctrine of love, which is taught us from heaven by love itself.

3. And especially this work of love is promoted, by opening the kingdom of heaven to the foresight of our faith; and showing us what we shall enjoy for ever; and assuring us of the fruition of our Creator's everlasting love; yea, by making us foreknow that heaven consisteth in perfect, mutual, endless love. This will both, of itself, draw up our hearts and engage all our reason and endeavours, in beginning that work which we must do for ever, and to learn on earth to love in heaven.

4. And besides all these objective helps, Christ giveth to believers the Spirit of love, and maketh it become as a nature in us; which no other teacher in the world could do. Others can speak reason to our ears, but it is Christ that sendeth the warming beams of holy love into our hearts.

If the love of God and holiness were no better than common philosophical speculations, then Aristotle, or Plato, or such other masters of names and notions, might compare with Christ and his apostles, and Athens with the primitive church; and the schoolmen might be thought the best improvers of theology. But if thousands of dreaming disputers wrangle the world into misery, and themselves into hell, and are ingenious artificers of their own damnation; if the love of God and goodness be the healthful constitution of the soul, its natural content and pleasure, the business and end of life, and all its helps and blessings, the solder of just societies, the union of man with God in Christ, and with all the blessed, and the foretaste and first-fruits of endless glory; then Christ the Messenger of love, the Teacher of love, the Giver of love, the Lord and commander of love, is the best promoter of knowledge in the world. And as Nicodemus knew that he was a teacher come from God, because no man could do such works unless God were with him; so may we conclude the same, because no man could so reveal, so cause, and communicate love, the holy love of God and goodness, unless the God of love had sent him. Love is the very end and work of Christ, and of his word and Spirit.

CHAPTER IX.

INFERENCE 5. WHAT GREAT CAUSE MEN HAVE TO BE THANKFUL TO GOD FOR THE CONSTITUTION OF THE CHRISTIAN RELIGION; AND HOW INEXCUSABLE THEY ARE THAT WILL NOT LEARN SO SHORT, AND SWEET, AND SAFE A LESSON.

So excellent and every way suitable to our case is the religion taught and instituted by Christ, as should render it very acceptable to mankind; and that on several accounts.

1. The brevity and plainness of christian precepts

greatly accommodateth the necessity of mankind. I say his necessity, lest you think it is but his sloth. *Ars longa, vita brevis,* is the true and sad complaint of students. Had our salvation been laid upon our learning a body of true philosophy, how desperate would our case have been! For, 1. Man's great intellectual weakness; 2. His want of leisure; would not have allowed him a knowledge that requireth a subtle wit and tedious studies.

1. Most men have wits of the duller sort: such quickness, subtlety, and solidity as is necessary to great and difficult studies, are very rare; so rare, as that few such are found even amongst the preachers of the gospel: of a multitude who by hard studies, and honest hearts, are fit to preach the doctrine of salvation, scarce one or two are found of so fine and exact a wit as to be fit judiciously to manage the curious controversies of the schools. What a case then had mankind been in, if none could have been wise and happy indeed, but these few of extraordinary capacity! The most public and common good is the best. God is more merciful than to confine salvation to subtlety of wit; nor indeed is it a thing itself so pleasing to him as a holy, heavenly heart and life.

2. And we have bodies that must have provision and employment: we have families and kindred that must be maintained: we live in neighbourhoods and public societies, which call for much duty, and take up much time. And our sufferings and crosses will take up some thoughts. Were it but poverty alone, how much of our time will it alienate from contemplation! Whilst great necessities call for great care, and continual labour; can our common, poor labourers (especially husbandmen) have leisure to inform their minds with philosophy or curious speculations?

Nay, we see by experience, that the more subtle and most vacant wits, that wholly addict themselves to philosophy, can bring it to no considerable certainty and consistency to this day, except in the few rudiments or common principles that all are agreed in. Insomuch that those do now take themselves to be the chief or only wits, who are pulling down that which through so many ages, from the begining of the world, hath with so great wit and study been concluded on before them; and are now themselves no higher than new experimenters, who are beginning all anew again, to try whether they can retrieve the errors of mankind, and make any thing of that which they think the world hath been so long unacquainted with: and they are yet but beginning at the skin or superficies of the world, and are got no further with all their wit, than matter and motion, with figure, site, contexture, &c. But if they could live as long as Methuselah, it is hoped they might come to know that besides matter and motion, there are essential virtues called substantial forms, or active natures, and that there is a *vis motiva,* which is the cause of motion, and a *virtus intellectiva,* and wisdom, which is the cause of the order of motion, and a vital will and love, which is the perfection and end of all: in a word, they may live to know that there is such a thing in the world as life, and such a thing as active nature, and such a thing as sense and soul, besides corporeal matter and motion, and consequently that man is indeed man. But, alas! they must die sooner, perhaps before they attain so far, and their successors must begin all anew again, as if none of all these great attempts had been made by their predecessors; and so, by their method, we shall never reach deeper than the skin, nor learn more than our A B C. And would we have such a task made necessary to the common salvation, even for all the poor and vulgar wits, which is so much too hard for our most subtle students?

2. And christianity is as suitable to us, in the benefit and sweetness of it. What a happy religion is it that employeth men in nothing but receiving good to themselves, and in doing good to themselves and others; whose work is only the receiving and improving of God's mercies, and loving and delighting in all that is good, rejoicing in the taste of God's love on earth, and in the hopes of perfect felicity, love, and joy for ever! Is not this a sweeter life than tiresome, unprofitable speculations?

Oh, then, how unexcusable are our contemners of religion, that live in wilful ignorance and ungodliness, and think this easy and sweet religion to be a tedious and intolerable thing! What impudent calumniators and blasphemers are they of Christ and holiness, who deride and revile this sweet and easy way to life, as if it were a slavery and an irksome toil, unnecessary to our salvation, and unfit for a free-man, or at least a gentleman, (or a servant of the flesh and world,) to practise. If Christ had set you such a task as Aristotle or Plato did to their disciples, so many notions, and so many curiosities to learn; if he had written for you as many books as Chrysippus did; if he had made necessary to your salvation, all the arbitrary notions of Lullius, and all the fanatic conceits of Campanella, and all the dreaming hypotheses of Cartesius, and all the astronomical and cosmographical difficulties of Ptolemy, Tycho-Brache, Copernicus, and Galilæus, and all the chronological difficulties handled by Eusebius, Scaliger, Functius, Capellus, Petavius, &c.; and all the curiosities in philosophy and theology of Cajetan, Scotus, Ockam, Gabriel, &c.; then you might have had some excuse for your aversation: but to accuse, and refuse, and reproach so compendious, so easy, so sweet, so necessary a doctrine and religion, as that which is brought and taught by Christ; this is an ingratitude that hath no excuse, unless sensuality and malignant enmity may pass for an excuse.

Doth Christ deliver you from the maze of imaginary curiosities, and from the burdens of worldly wisdom, called philosophy, and of Pharisaical traditions and Jewish ceremonies, and make you a light burden, an easy yoke, and commandments that are not grievous; and after all this, must he be requited with rejection and reproach, and your burdens and snares be taken for more tolerable than your deliverance? You make a double forfeiture of salvation, who are so unwilling to be saved.

Be thankful, O christians, to your heavenly Master, for tracing you out so plain and sweet a way. Be thankful that he hath cut short those tiresome studies, by which your taskmasters would confound you, under pretence of making you like gods, in some more subtle and sublime speculations than vulgar wits can reach. Now all that are willing may be religious, and be saved: it is not confined to men of learning. The way is so sweet, as showeth it suitable to the end. It is but, believe God's love and promises of salvation by Christ, till you are filled with love and its delights, and live in the pleasures of gratitude and holiness, and in the joyful hopes of endless glory! and is not this an easy yoke? Saith our heavenly poet Mr. G. Herbert, in his poem called "Divinity," p. 127.

"As men for fear the stars should sleep and nod,
  And trip at night, have spheres supply'd;
As if a star were duller than a clod,
  Which knows his way without a guide:
Just so the other heaven they also serve,
  Divinity's transcendent sky,
Which with the edge of wit they cut and carve,
  Reason triumphs, and faith lies by.
——But all his doctrine which he taught and gave,
  Was clear as heav'n from whence it came;

At least those beams of truth which only save,
  Surpass in brightness any flame:
Love God, and love your neighbours, watch and pray,
  Do as you would be done unto.
Oh dark instructions! even as dark as day!
  Who can these Gordian knots undo?"

CHAPTER X.

INFERENCE 6. HOW LITTLE REASON UNGODLY MEN HAVE TO BE PROUD OF THEIR LEARNING, OR OF ANY SORT OF KNOWLEDGE OR WISDOM WHATSOEVER.

As the ancient Gnostics, being puffed up with their corrupt Platonic speculations, looked down with contempt upon ordinary christians, as silly ignorants in comparison of them, and yet had not wisdom enough to preserve them from the lusts and pollutions of the world; even so is it with abundance of the worldly clergy and ungodly scholars in this age. They think their learning setteth them many degrees above the vulgar, and giveth them right to be reverenced as the oracles or rabbies of the world; when yet, poor souls! they have not learned, by all their reading, studies, and disputings, to love God and holiness better than the riches and preferments of the world; and some of them not better than a cup of strong drink, or than the brutish pleasures of sense and flesh. It is a pitiful thing to see the pulpit made a stage for the ostentation of this self-shaming, self-condemning pride and folly. For a man under pretence of serving God, and helping other men to heaven, to make it his errand to tell the hearers, that he is a very wise and learned man, who hath not wit enough to choose a holy, humble life, nor to make sure of heaven, or to save his soul; nor perhaps to keep out of the tavern or ale house the next week, nor the same day to forbear the venting of his worldly, carnal mind: what is such learning but a game of imagination, in which the fantasy sports itself with names and notions; or worse, the materials which are used in the service of sin, the fuel of pride, the blinder and deceiver of such as were too ignorant before, being a mere shadow and name of knowledge? What good will it do a man tormented with the gout, or stone, or by miserable poverty, to know the names of various herbs, or to read the titles of the apothecaries' boxes, or to read on a sign-post, Here is a good ordinary? And what good will it do a carnal, unsanctified soul, that must be in hell for ever, to know the Hebrew roots or points; or to discourse of Cartesius's Materia Subtilis, and Globuli Ætherei, &c. or of Epicurus' and Gassendus' Atoms; or to look on the planets in Galileus' glasses; while he casteth away all his hopes of heaven, by his unbelief, and his preferring the pleasures of the flesh? Will it comfort a man that is cast out of God's presence, and condemned to utter darkness, to remember that he was once a good mathematician, or logician, or musician, or that he had wit to get riches and preferments in the world, and to climb up to the height of honour and dominion? It is a pitiful thing to hear a man boast of his wit, while he is madly rejecting the only felicity, forsaking God, esteeming vanity, and damning his soul: the Lord deliver us from such wit and learning! Is it not enough to refuse heaven, and choose hell, (in the certain causes,) to lose the only day of their hopes, and in the midst of light, to be incomparably worse than mad, but they must needs be accounted wise and learned, in all this self-destroying folly? As if (like the physician who boasted that he killed men according to the rules of art) it were the height of their ambition to go learnedly to hell; and with reverend gravity and wit, to live here like brutes, and hereafter with devils for evermore.

CHAPTER XI.

INFERENCE 7. WHY THE UNGODLY WORLD HATETH HOLINESS, AND NOT LEARNING.

FROM my very childhood, when I was first sensible of the concernments of men's souls, I was possessed with some admiration, to find that every where the religious, godly sort of people, who did but exercise a serious care of their own and other men's salvation, were made the wonder and obloquy of the world; especially of the most vicious and flagitious men; so that they that professed the same articles of faith, the same commandments of God to be their law, and the same petitions of the Lord's prayer to be their desire, and so professed the same religion, did every where revile those that did endeavour to live according to that same profession, and to seem to be in good sadness in what they said. I thought that this was impudent hypocrisy in the ungodly, worldly sort of men; to take them for the most intolerable persons in the land, who are but serious in their own religion, and do but endeavour to perform what all their enemies also vowed and promised. If religion be bad, and our faith be not true, why do these men profess it? If it be true and good, why do they hate and revile them that would live in the serious practice of it, if they will not practise it themselves? But we must not expect reason, when sin and sensuality have made men unreasonable.

But I must profess that since I observed the course of the world, and the concord of the word and providences of God, I took it for a notable proof of man's fall, and of the verity of the Scripture, and the supernatural original of true sanctification, to find such a universal enmity between the holy and the serpentine seed, and to find Cain and Abel's case so ordinarily exemplified, and him that is born after the flesh to persecute him that is born after the Spirit. And methinks to this day it is a great and visible help for the confirmation of our christian faith.

But that which is much remarkable in it is, that nothing else in the world, except the crossing of men's carnal interest, doth meet with any such universal enmity. A man may be as learned as he can, and no man hate him for it. If he excel all others, all men will praise him and proclaim his excellency: he may be an excellent linguist, an excellent philosopher, an excellent physician, an excellent logician, an excellent orator, and all commend him. Among musicians, architects, soldiers, seamen, and all arts and sciences, men value, prefer, and praise the best; yea, even speculative theology, such wits as the schoolmen and those that are called great divines are honoured by all, and meet, as such, but with little enmity, persecution, or obloquy in the world. Though I know that even a Galilæus, or Campanella, and many such, have suffered by the Roman inquisitors, that was not so much in enmity to their speculations or opinions, as through a fear lest new philosophical notions should unsettle men's minds and open the way to new opinions in theology, and so prove injurious to the kingdom and interest of Rome. I know also that Demosthenes, Cicero, Seneca, Lucan, and many other learned men, have died by the hands or power of tyrants. But that was not for their learning, but for their opposition to those tyrants' wills and interests. And I know that some religious men have suffered for their sins and follies, and some for their meddling too much with secular affairs, as the counsellors of princes, as Functius, Justus Jonas, and many others. But yet no parts, no excellency, no skill or learning, is hated commonly, but honoured in the world, no not theological learning, save only this practical godliness and religion, and the principles of it, which only rendereth men amiable to God, through Christ, and saveth men's souls. To know and love God, and live as those that know and love him; to seek first his kingdom and the righteousness thereof; to walk circumspectly, in a holy and heavenly conversation, and studiously to obey the laws of God; this which must save us, this which God loveth and the devil hateth, is hated also by all his children; for the same malignity hath the same effect.

But methinks this should teach all considering men to perceive what knowledge it is that is best, and most desirable to all that love their happiness. Sure this sort of learning, wit, and art, which the devil and the malignant world do no more dispraise, oppose, and persecute, (though as it is sanctified to higher ends it be good, yet) of itself is comparatively no very excellent and amiable thing. I know Satan laboureth to keep out learning itself (that is truly such) from the world, because he is the prince and promoter of darkness, and the enemy of all useful light: and lower knowledge is some help to higher, and speculative theology may prepare for practical; and the most gross and brutish ignorance best serveth the devil's designs and turn. And even in heathen Rome the arts prepared men for the gospel; and learning in the church reformers hath ever been a great help and furtherance of reformation. But yet if you stop in learning and speculation, and take it as for itself alone, and not as a means to holiness of heart and life, it is as nothing. It is Paul's express resolution of the case, that if "we have all knowledge without this holy love we are nothing," but as "sounding brass, or a tinkling cymbal," 1 Cor. xiii.

But surely there is some special excellency in this holy knowledge, and love, and obedience, which the devil and the malignant world so hate, in high and low, in rich and poor, in kindred, neighbours, strangers, or any, where they meet with it. It is not for nothing. This is the image of God; this is it that is contrary to their carnal minds, and to their fleshly lusts and sinful pleasures. This tells them what they must be and do, or be undone for ever, which they cannot abide to be or do.

Let us therefore be somewhat the wiser for this discovery of the mind of the devil and all his instruments. I will love and honour all natural, artificial, acquired excellences in philology, philosophy, and the rest; as these expose not men to the world's obloquy, so neither unto mine or any sober man's. In their low places they are good, and may be used to a greater good. But let that holy knowledge and love be mine, which God most loveth, and the world most hateth, and costeth us dearest upon earth, but hath the blessed end of a heavenly reward.

CHAPTER XII.

INFERENCE 8. WHAT IS THE WORK OF A FAITHFUL PREACHER, AND HOW IT IS TO BE DONE.

If that knowledge which kindleth in us the love of God, be the only saving knowledge, then this is it that ministers must principally preach up and promote. Could we make all our hearers never so learned, that will not save their souls; but if we could make them holy, and kindle in them the love of God, and goodness, they should certainly be saved. The holy practica preacher therefore is the best preacher, because the holy practical christian is the best and only true christian. We work under Christ, and therefore must carry on the same work on souls which Christ came into the world to carry on. All our sermons must be fitted to change men's hearts, from carnal into spiritual, and to kindle in them the love of God. When this is well done, they have learned what we were sent to teach them; and when this is perfect, they are in heaven.

Those preachers that are enemies to the godliest of the people, and would make their hearers take them all for hypocrites, that go any further than obedience to their pastors, in church forms and orders, observances and ceremonies, and a civil life, are the great enemies of Christ, his Spirit, his gospel, and the people's souls; and the eminent servants of the devil, in his malignant war against them all. All that knowledge, and all those formalities, which are set up instead of divine love and holy living, are but so many cheats, to deceive poor souls till time be past, and their convictions come too late.

I confess that ignorance is the calamity of our times, and people perish for lack of knowledge: and that the heart be without knowledge it is not good: and lamentable ignorance is too visible in a great degree, among the religious sort themselves; as their manifold differences and errors too openly proclaim: and therefore to build up men in knowledge, is much of the ministerial work. But what knowledge must it be? Not dead opinions, or uneffectual notions, or such knowledge as tendeth but to teach men to talk, and make them pass for men of parts; but it is the knowledge of God and our Redeemer, the knowledge of Christ crucified, by which we crucify the flesh with all its affections and lusts; and by which the world is crucified to us, and we to it. If the gospel be hid, it is hid to them that are lost, in whom the god of this world hath blinded their eyes. When there is no truth and mercy, and knowledge of God, in the land, no wonder if such a land be clad in mourning. When men have not so much knowledge of the evil of sin, and their own sin and misery, and of the need and worth of Christ, of the truth of God's word, of the vanity of the world, of the greatness, wisdom, and goodness of God, and of the certain, most desirable glory of heaven, as shall humble their souls, and turn them from the world to God, and absolutely deliver them up to Christ, and mortify fleshly lusts, and overcome temptations, and renew them unto the love of God and goodness, and set their hearts and hopes on heaven: this is the ignorance that is men's damnation; and the contrary effectual knowledge it is which saveth souls.

CHAPTER XIII.

INFERENCE 9. THOSE THAT KNOW GOD SO FAR AS TO LOVE HIM ABOVE ALL, MAY HAVE COMFORT, NOTWITHSTANDING THEIR REMAINING IGNORANCE.

A great number of upright-hearted christians, who love God sincerely, and obey him faithfully, are yet under so great want of further knowledge, as is indeed a great dishonour to them, and a hinderance of them in their duty and comfort, and to many a great discouragement. And oh that we knew how to cure this imperfection, that ignorance might not feed so many errors, and cause so many factions and disturbances in the church, and so many sinful miscarriages in its members!

But yet we must conclude that the person that hath knowledge enough to renew his soul to the love of God, shall be loved by him, and shall never perish, and therefore may have just comfort under all the imperfections of his knowledge. More wisdom might make him a better and more useful christian; but while he is a christian indeed, he may rejoice in God. I blame not such for complaining of the dulness of their understandings, the badness of their memories, their little profiting by the means of grace: I should blame them if they did not complain of these: and I think their case far more dangerous to the church and to themselves, who have as much ignorance and know it not, but proudly glory in the wisdom which they have not. But many a thousand christians, that have little of the notional and organical part of knowledge, have powerful apprehensions of the power, wisdom, and love of God, and of the great mercy of redemption, and of the evil of sin, the worth of holiness, and the certainty and weight of the heavenly glory: and by how much these men love God and holiness more than the more learned that have less grace, by so much they are more beloved of God, and accounted wiser by the God of wisdom; and therefore may rejoice in the greatness of their felicity. I would have none so weak as to undervalue any real useful learning; but if Pharisees will cry out against unlearned, godly christians, "These people know not the law and are accursed;" remember the thanksgiving of your Lord, "I thank thee, Father, Lord of heaven and earth, that thou hast hid these things from the wise and prudent, and hast revealed them to babes." And as the (reputed) foolishness of God, that is, of God's evangelical mysteries, will shortly prove wiser than all the reputed wisdom of men; so he that hath wisdom enough to love God and be saved, shall quickly be in that world of light, where he shall know more than all the doctors and subtle disputers upon earth; and more, in a moment, than all the books of men can teach him, or all their authors did ever here know. "Thus saith the Lord, Let not the wise man glory in his wisdom, neither let the mighty man glory in his might, let not the rich man glory in his riches; but let him that glorieth glory in this, That he understandeth and knoweth me, that I am the Lord, which exercise loving-kindness and righteousness in the earth: for in these things do I delight, saith the Lord," Jer. ix. 23, 24.

CHAPTER XIV.

QUESTIONS AND OBJECTIONS ANSWERED.

Quest. I. IF so much knowledge will save a man, as helpeth him to love God as God, may not heathens or infidels at least be saved? For they know that there is one God who is infinitely good and perfect, and more amiable than all the world, and the great Benefactor of man, and of the whole creation: so that there is no goodness but what is in him, or from him, and through him, and finally to him: and man's will is made to love apprehended good, and followeth the last practical act of the intellect, at least where there is no competitor, but *omnimoda ratio boni.* And all men know that God is not only best in himself, but good, yea, best to them, because that all they have is from him; and they have daily experience of pardoning grace contrary to their demerit. It seemeth therefore that they may love God as God.

Answ. 1. To cause a man to love God as God, there is necessary both objective revelation of God's amiableness, and such subjective grace which consisteth in a right disposition of the soul. 2. Objective revelation is considered as sufficient either to a well-disposed, or to an ill-disposed soul. 3. This right disposition consisteth both in the abatement of men's inclinations to contrary, sensual objects, and in the inclining them to that which is divine and spiritual. And now I answer,

1. It cannot be denied, but that so much of God's amiableness or goodness is revealed to infidels that have not the gospel, by the means mentioned in the objection, as is sufficient to bring men under an obligation to love God as God, and to leave them inexcusable that do not.

2. Therefore, to such, the impossibility is not physical, but moral.

3. And there is in that objective revelation, so much sufficiency, as that if the soul itself were sanctified and well disposed, it might love God upon such revelation: which Amyraldus hath largely proved.

4. But to an unholy and undisposed soul, no objective revelation is sufficient without the Spirit's help and operations.

5. Only the Spirit of Christ the Mediator, as given by and from him, doth thus operate on souls, as savingly to renew them.

6. Whether ever the Spirit of Christ doth thus operate on any that hear not of Christ's incarnation, must be known either by the Scripture or by experience.[a] By the Scripture I am not able to prove the universal negative, though it is easy to prove sanctification incomparably more common in the church, than on those without, if any there have it. The case of infants, and of the churches and the world before Christ's incarnation, must here come into consideration. And by experience no man can prove the negative; because no man hath experience what is in the hearts of all the persons in the world.

Quest. 2. May a papist or a heretic by his knowledge be a lover of God as God?

Answ. What is said to the former question is here to be reviewed. And further, 1. A papist and such heretic as positively holdeth all the essentials of christianity, and seeth not the opposition of his false opinions thereto, and holdeth christianity more practically than those false opinions, may be saved in that state, for he is a lover of God: but no other papists or heretics can be saved but by a true conversion. 2. There is a sufficiency in the doctrine of christianity which they hold, to save them, as to objective sufficiency. And that God giveth not subjective grace of sanctification to any such, notwithstanding their errors, is a thing that no man can prove, nor any sober, charitable christian easily believe: and experience of the piety of many maketh it utterly improbable, though we know not certainly the heart of another.

There are many murmurings against me in this city, (behind my back; for never one man of them to my remembrance to this day, did ever use any charitable endeavour to my face, to convince me of my supposed error,) as one that holds that a papist may

[a] Of all this I have discoursed more largely in my "Catholic Theology," and the annexed Epitome.

be saved, yea, that we are not certain that none in the world are saved besides christians: and the sectaries whisper me to one another to be like Origen, a person, in these dangerous opinions, forsaken of God, in comparison of them. What really I assert about these questions, I have here briefly hinted; but more largely opened in my "Catholic Theology:" but I will confess that I find no inclination in my soul, to desire that their doctrine may prove true, who hide the glorified love of God, and would contract his mercy and man's salvation into so narrow a room, as to make it hardly discernible by man, and the church to be next to no church, and a Saviour to save so very few, as seem scarce considerable among the rest that are left remediless; and who would make us believe that the way appointed to bring men to the love of God, is, to believe that he hath elected that particular person, and left almost all the world (many scores or hundreds to one) unredeemed, and without any promise or possibility of salvation. I am sure that the covenant of innocency is ceased, and I am sure that all the world was brought under a law of grace, made after the fall to Adam and Noah: and that this law is still in force, to those that have not the more perfect edition in the gospel: and that Christ came not to bring the world that never hear of him, nor can do, into a worse condition than Jews and gentiles were in before: nor hath he repealed that law of grace, which he before made them; nor hath God changed that gracious name which he proclaimed even to Moses, Exod. xxxiv. 6, 7. And I am sure that Abraham, the father of the faithful, conjectured once, even when God told him that Sodom was ripe for destruction, that yet there might be fifty righteous persons in it; by which we may conjecture what he thought of all the world.[b] And I know "that in every nation he that feareth God, and worketh righteousness, is accepted of him;" and that "he that cometh to God, must believe that God is, and that he is the rewarder of them that diligently seek him;" and therefore without faith none can please God; and that men shall be judged by that same law, which they were under and obliged by, whatever it be: and they that have sinned under the law of Moses, shall be judged by it; and they that sinned without that law shall be judged without it. And know that God is love itself, and infinitely good; and will show us his goodness in such glorious effects to all eternity, as shall satisfy us, and fill us with joyful praise. And as for the papists, I know that they are seduced by a worldly clergy, and that by consequence many of the errors in that church do subvert the fundamentals; and so do many errors of the antinomians and others among us, that are taken for religious persons; yea, and as notoriously as any doctrines of the popish councils do. But I know that as a logical faith or orthodoxness, which consisteth in holding right notions and words, deceiveth thousands that have no sound belief of the things themselves expressed by these words; so also logical errors about words, notions, and sentences, may in unskilful men consist with a sound belief of the things which must necessarily be believed. And that Christ and grace may be thankfully received by many that have false names, and notions, and sayings about Christ and grace. And I know the great power of education and converse, and what advantage an opinion hath even with the upright, which is commonly extolled by learned, godly, religious men, especially if by almost all. Therefore I make no doubt but God hath many among the papists, and the antinomians, to name no others, who are truly godly, though they logically or notionally hold such errors, as if practically held would be their damnation, and if the consequents were known and held; much more when thousands of the common people hold not the errors of the church which they abide in. And it shall not be my way of persuading my own soul or others to love God, by first persuading them that he loveth but few besides themselves. And when such have narrowed God's love and mercy to all save their own party, and made themselves easily believe that he will damn the rest of the world, even such as are as desirous to please God as they are, they have but prepared a snare for their own conscience; which may perhaps, when it is awakened, as easily believe that he will damn themselves. Let us give "all diligence to make our own calling and election sure," and leave others to the righteous God, to whose judgment they and we must stand or fall. "Who art thou that judgest another's servant?"

As the covenant of peculiarity was made only with the Israelites, though the common law of grace, made to Adam and Noah, was in force to other nations of the world; so the more excellent covenant of peculiarity is, since Christ's incarnation, made only with the christian church, though the aforesaid common law of grace be not repealed to all others: nor can it be said that they sin not against a law of grace, or mercy leading to repentance.

And as the covenant of peculiarity was not repealed to the ten tribes, (though the benefits were much forfeited by their violation,) but God had still thousands among them in Elias's time, that bowed not the knee to Baal, and such as Obadiah to hide the prophets; though yet the Jews were the more orthodox: even so though the reformed churches, as the two tribes, stick closer to the truth, the kingdoms where popery prevaileth have yet many thousands that God will save; and, notwithstanding their errors and corrupt additions, they have the same articles of faith and baptismal covenant as we. And if any man think himself the wiser or the happier man than I, for holding the contrary, and thinking so many are hated of God more than I do, (and consequently rendering him less lovely to them,) I envy not such the honour nor comfort of their wisdom.

Object. III. You will thus confirm our ignorant people in their presumption, that tell professors of godliness, I love God above all, and my neighbour as myself; though I do not know, and talk, and pray so much as you do.

Answ. Either they do so love God and man, or they do not. If they do they are good and happy men, though you call them ignorant: yea, he is far from being an ignorant man, that knoweth God and Christ, and heaven and holiness, so well, as to be unfeignedly in love with them. But if he do not, what say I to his encouragement in presumption? But you must take another course to cure him, than by calling him to a barren sort of knowledge. You must show him, that the love of God is an operative principle; and where it is will have dominion, and be highest in the soul: and that telling God that we love him, while we love not his law, his service, or his children; yea, while we love our appetite, our wealth, our credit, and every beastly lust above him; and while we cannot abide much to think or hear talk of him; this is but odious hypocrisy, which deceiveth the sinner, and maketh him more abominable to God.

But if really you see a poor neighbour, whom you count ignorant, live as one that loveth God and goodness; take heed that you proudly despise not Christ's little ones, but love and cherish those sparks that are kindled and loved by Christ. The least are called by Christ his brethren, and their interest made

[b] Read Mal. i. 14, with all the old translations in the Polyglot Bible, and consider it.

as his own, Matt. xxv. And the least have their angels, which see the face of God in heaven.

Object. IV. How then are infants saved, that neither have knowledge nor love?

Answ. 1. While they have no wills of their own, which are capable of holy duties, they are as members of their parents, whose wills are theirs; or who know God, and love him, for themselves and their infants. As the hand and foot doth not know and love God in itself, and yet is holy, in that it is the hand or foot of one that doth know and love him.

2. Sanctified infants have that grace which is the seed of holy love, though they have not yet the act nor proper habit of love. I call it a seed, because it is a holy disposition of the soul; by which it is (not only physically, as all are, but) morally able to love God, when they come to the use of reason, or at least mediately to do that which shall conduce to holy love.

3. And in this state being loved of God, and known of him as the children of his grace and promise, they are happy in his love to them: for he will give their natures their due capacity, in his way, which we are not yet fit to be fully acquainted with; and he will fill up that capacity with his love and glory.

Object. V. If this hold, away with universities, and all our volumes and studies of physics, mathematics, and other sciences; for they must needs divert our thoughts from the love of God! And then Turks, Muscovites, and other contemners of learning, are in the right.

Answ. There is a right and a wrong use of all these, as there is of arts and business of the world. One man so followeth his trade and worldly business, as to divert, distract, or corrupt his mind, and drown all holy thoughts and love, and leave no due place for holy diligence. And another man so followeth his calling, as that heaven hath still his heart and hope, and his labour is made but part of his obedience to God, and his way to life eternal; and all is sanctified by holy principles, end, and manner. And so it is about common learning, sciences, or arts. And I have proved to you, that among too many called great scholars in the world, many books, and much reading and acquaintance with all the arts of speaking, with grammar, logic, oratory, metaphysics, physics, history, laws, &c. is but one of Satan's last and subtlest means of wasting precious time, deceiving souls, and keeping such persons from pursuing the ends of their excellent wit, and of life itself, that would not have been cheated, diverted, and undone, by the grosser way of brutish pleasures: but holy souls have a sanctified use of all their common knowledge, making it serve their high and holy ends. But oh that some learned men would in time, as well understand the difference between common learning, (which serveth fancy, pride, or worldly hopes,) and the love of God and a heavenly life, as they must know it when they come to die!

CHAPTER XV.

USE. EXHORT. 1. NOT TO DECEIVE OURSELVES BY OVERVALUING A DEAD OR AN UNHOLY KNOWLEDGE.

IT grieveth my soul to observe how powerfully and how commonly Satan still playeth his first deceiving game, of calling off man from love, trust, and obedience, to an insnaring and troublesome, or unprofitable, sort of knowledge. And how the lust of knowing carrieth away many unsuspected to misery, who escape the more dishonourable sort of lust! And especially, what abundance in several ways take notional knowledge, which is but an art of thinking and talking, for real knowledge, which is our acquaintance with God and grace; and which changeth the soul into the image of him that we seek and know; and filleth us with love, and trust, and joy.

Two sorts are especially here guilty.

I. The learned students before described.

II. The superficial sort of people accounted religious.

I. I have already showed how pitiful a thing it is, that so many academical wits, and so many preachers, (to say nothing of the grossly proud, tyrannical, and worldly clergy,) do spend so many years in studies, that are used but in the service of the flesh, to their own condemnation; and never bend their minds to kindle in themselves the love of God, nor a heavenly desire or hope, nor to live in the comfortable prospect of glory. How many preach up that love and holiness, (as the trade that they must live by,) which they never fervently preached to themselves, nor practised sincerely one hour in their lives! How many use to preach funeral sermons, and bury the dead, that are unprepared for death themselves, and hardened in their security and unholy state, by those sights, those studies, those words, which should awaken and convince them, and which they plead themselves for the conviction of their hearers! O miserable scholars! miserable preachers! miserable doctors and prelates! who study and preach to their own condemnation; and have not knowledge enough to teach them to love God, nor to set more by the heavenly glory than this world; but by spiritual words, do both hide and cherish a fleshly and a worldly mind! You will find at death, that all your learning was but a dream, and one of the vanities that entangle fools; and you will die as sadly as the unlearned, and be beaten with more stripes than they that knew not their Master's will.

1. Unholy knowledge is but a carcass, a shadow, the activity of a vain mind, or a means without the end, and unfit to attain it. A map is not a kingdom, nor doth it much enrich the owner. The names of meats and drinks will not nourish you; and to know names and notions, giveth you no title to the things so named. You may as well think to be saved for being good musicians, physicians, or astronomers, as for being learned divines, if your knowledge cause not holy love: it may help others to heaven, but it will be but vanity to you; and you will be as "sounding brass, or a tinkling cymbal," 1 Cor. xiii. 1. You glory in a lifeless picture of wisdom; and hell may shortly tell you, that you had better have chosen any thing to play the fool with, than with the notions and words of wisdom mortified.

2. Nay, such profanation of holy things is a heinous sin. Who is liker the devil than he that knoweth most, and loveth God least? To know that you should love and seek God most, and not to do it, is wilfully to despise him in the open light. As the privation of God's love is the chief part of hell, so the privation of our love to God is the chief part of ungodliness or sin; yea, and much of hell itself. Knowledge puffeth up, but charity edifieth. Unholy knowledge is a powerful instrument of Satan's service: in the service of pride, and ambition, and heresy, one learned and witty, ungodly man will merit more of the devil by mischieving mankind, than many of the common, unlearned sort; and none are so like impenitently to glory in this sin. They

will be proud of such adorned fetters; that they can sin philosophically, and metaphysically, in Greek and Hebrew, and with logical subtlety, or oratorical fluency, prove against unlearned men, that they do well in damning their own souls, and that God and heaven are not worthy of their chiefest love and diligence. Such men will offend God more judiciously than the ignorant, and will more discreetly and honourably fool away their hopes of heaven, and more successfully deceive the simple. Their wisdom, like Ahithophel's, will serve turn to bring them to destroy themselves: and is it any wonder if this be foolishness with God? 1 Cor. iii. 19.

The understanding of a man is a faculty unfit to be abused and prostituted to the slavery of the flesh. The abuse of the senses is bad, but of the understanding worse; because it is a nobler faculty. When they that "knew God, glorified him not as God, but became vain in their imagination, their foolish heart was darkened, and professing themselves wise (philosophers or Gnostics) they became fools," Rom. i. 21, 28; "and as they did not like to retain God in their knowledge, God gave them up to vile affections." And yet many are proud of this mortal tympanite, as if it were a sound and healthful constitution; and think they have the surest right to heaven for neglecting it knowingly, and going learnedly in the way to hell.

3. You lose the chiefest delight of knowledge. Oh that you knew what a holy quietness and peace, what solid pleasure, that knowledge bringeth, which kindleth and cherisheth holy love, and leadeth the soul to communion with God; and how much sweeter it is to have a powerful and experimental knowledge, than your trifling dreams! The learnedest of you all have but the husks or shells of knowledge; and what great sweetness is in shells, when the poorest holy, experienced christian hath the kernel, which is far more pleasant! Oh try a more serious, practical religion, and I dare assure you, it will afford you a more solid kind of nourishment and delight. The pleasure of the speculative divine in knowing, is but like the pleasure of a mathematician or other speculator of nature; yea, below that of the moral philosopher: it is but like my pleasure in reading a book of travels or geography, in comparison of the true, practical christian's, which is like their pleasure that live in those countries, and possess the lands and houses which I read of.

4. Nay, yet worse, this unholy knowledge doth often make men the devil's most powerful and mischievous instruments; for though Christ oft also so overrule the hearts of men, and the course of the world, as to make the knowledge and gifts of bad men serviceable to his church, (as wicked soldiers oft fight in a good cause, and save the lives of better men,) yet a worldly mind is likest to follow the way of worldly interest; and it is but seldom that worldly interest doth suit with and serve the interest of truth and holiness, but more commonly is its greatest adversary: therefore most usually it must be expected that such worldly men should be adversaries to the same truth and holiness which their worldly interest is averse to. And hence hath arisen that proud, worldly, and tyrannical clergy, which hath set up and maintained the Roman kingdom, under the name of the holy catholic church; and which hath by their pope and pretended general councils, usurped a legislative and executive power over the whole christian world, and made great numbers of laws without authority, and contrary to the laws of Christ; multiplying schisms on pretence of suppressing them, and making so many things necessary to the concord of christians, as hath made such concord become impossible; presumptuously voting other men to be heretics, while their own errors are of as odious a kind; yea, when holy truth is sometimes branded by them as heresy. And when they cannot carry the judgments, consciences, and wills of all men along in obedience to their tyrannical pride, lust, and interest, they stir up princes and states to serve them by the sword, and murder and persecute their own subjects, and raise bloody wars against their neighbours, to force them to obey these proud seducers. Yea, and if kings and states be wiser, than thus to be made their hangmen or bloody executioners, to the ruin of their best subjects, and their own everlasting infamy and damnation, they stir up the foolish part of the subjects against such rulers; and in a word, they will give the world no peace: so that I am past all doubt that the ten heathen persecutions so much cried out of, was but a small matter as against the christians' blood, in comparison of what hath been done by this tyrannical clergy: and the cruellest magistrates still seem to come short of them in cruelty, and seldom are very bloody or persecuting, but when a worldly or proud clergy stirs them up to it. And all the heresies that ever sprang up in the church, do seem to have done less harm on one side, than by pretences of unity, order, and government, they have done on the other. Oh how unspeakably great have been, and still are, the church's sufferings, by a proud and worldly clergy, and by men's abuse of pretended learning and authority!

5. I will add yet one more considerable mischief; that is, that your unholiness and carnal minds, for all your learning, corrupteth your judgments, and greatly hindereth you from receiving many excellent truths, and inclineth you to many mortal errors. To instance in some particulars:

1. About the attributes and government of God. A bad man is inclined to doubt of God's particular providence, his holy truth and justice, and to think God is such a one as he would have him to be. Whereas they that have the love of God and goodness, have his attributes, as it were, written on their hearts; that he is good, and wise, and holy, and just, and true, they know by an experimental, certain knowledge, which is to them like nature and life itself, John xvii. 3; Hos. ii. 20; Psal. xxxiv. 8, &c.

2. The very truth of the gospel and mystery of redemption is far hardlier believed by a man that never felt his need of Christ, nor ever had the operations of that Spirit on his soul, which are its seal, than by them that have the witness in themselves, and have found Christ actually save them from their sins: who are regenerated by this holy seed, and nourished by this milk, 1 John v. 10—12; 1 Pet. i. 22, 23; ii. 2.

3. Yea, the very truth of our soul's immortality, and the life and glory to come, is far hardlier believed by them, who feel no inclination to such a future glory, but only a propensity to this present life, and the interests and pleasures of it, (Rom. v. 2, 3; 2 Cor. iv. 16—18; v. 1—3, &c.) than by them that have a treasure, a home, a heart, and a conversation in heaven, and that long for nearer communion with God, and that have the earnest and first-fruits of heaven within them, Matt. vi. 20, 21; Phil. iii. 20, 21; Col. iv. 1—4; Rom. viii. 17—20.

4. The evil of sin in general, and consequently what is sin in particular, is hardlier known by a man that loveth it, and would not have it to be sin, than by one that hateth it, and loveth God and holiness above all: they that love the Lord, hate evil, 1 Cor. ii. 14; John ix. 40.

5. Most controversies about the nature of grace, are hardlier understood by them that have it not, than by them that have it as a new nature in them. And consequently what kind of persons are to be well thought of, as the children of God. The Pharisees were strict, and yet haters of Christ and christians. Many preach and write for godliness, that yet when it cometh to a particular judgment, deride the godly as hypocrites or superstitious.

6. In cases about the worship of God, a carnal mind, how learned soever, is apt to relish most an outside, carnal, ceremonious way, and to be all for a dead formality, or else for a proud ostentation of their own wits, opinions, and parts, or some odd singularity that sets them up to be admired as some extraordinary persons, or teacheth their own consciences so to flatter them: when a spiritual man is for worshipping God (though with all decent externals, yet) in spirit and in truth; and in the most understanding, sincere, and humble manner, and yet with the greatest joy and praise, Rom. viii. 16, 26, &c.

7. Especially in the work of self-judging, how hard a work have the most learned that are ungodly truly to know themselves; when learning doth but help their pride to blind them! And yet none so apt to say as the Pharisees, (John ix. 10,) "Are we blind also?" and to hate those that honour them not as erroneously as they do themselves: and therefore Augustine so lamenteth the misery of the clergy, and saith that the unlearned take heaven by violence, when the learned are thrust down to hell with all their learning! Who are prouder and more self-ignorant hypocrites in the world (expecting that all should bow to them and reverence them, and cry them up as wise and excellent men) than the unholy, worldly, fleshly clergy?

8. And in every case that themselves are much concerned in, their learning will not keep them from the most blind injustice. Let the case be but such as their honour, or profit, or relations and friends, are much concerned in, and they presently take all right to be on their side; and all these to be honest men that are for them, and all those to be wicked hypocrites, heretics, schismatics, factious, or liars, that are against them; and dare print to the world that most notorious truths in matters of fact are lies, and lies are truths, and corrupt all history where they are but concerned: so that experience hath taught me to give little credit to any history written by men, in whom I can perceive this double character: 1. That they are worldly and unconscionable: 2. And concerned by a personal interest; especially when they revile their adversaries. And money, friends, or honour will make any cause true and just with them, and confute all evidences of truth and innocency. Learned judges are too oft corrupt.

9. And in cases of great temptation, how insufficient is learning to repel the tempter, when it is easily done by the holy love of God and goodness! How easily is a man's judgment tempted to think well of that which he loveth, and ill of that which his heart is against!

Many such instances I might give you, but these fully show the misery and folly of ungodly scholars, that are but blinded by dead notions, and words of art, to think they know something, when they know nothing as they ought to know; and to hate truth and goodness, and speak evil of the things they know not; while for want of holy love, these tinkling cymbals do but deceive themselves, and ascertain their own damnation.

II. I should next have said as much of the vanity and snare of the knowledge of such Gnostics, as in an overvaluing of their own religious skill and gifts, cry out as the Pharisees, "This people that know not the law are cursed." But what is said is applicable to them.

CHAPTER XVI.

EXHORT. 2. LOVE BEST THE CHRISTIANS THAT HAVE MOST LOVE TO GOD AND MAN.

If God love those most that have most love, and not those that have most barren knowledge; then so must we, even all that take God's wisdom as infallible. Of whom can we know better, whom to love and value, than of him that is wisdom and love itself? There is more savoury worth in the experience, affections, and heavenly tendency of holy souls, than in all the subtleties of learned wits. When a man cometh to die, who savoureth not more wisdom in the sacred Scripture, and in holy treatises, than in all Aristotle's learned works? And who had not then rather hear the talk and prayers of a holy person, than the most accurate logic or mathematics? Alas! what are these but trifles to a dying man! And what they will be to a dying man, they should be much to us all our life; unless we would never be wise till it is too late.

And among men seeming religious, it is not the religious wrangler or disputer, nor the zealous reviler of his brethren, that can hotly cry down on one side, These men are heretical; or on the other, These are antichristian, that are the lovely persons: not they that on one side cry out, Away with these from the ministry and church as disobedient to us; or on the other, Away with these from our communion as not holy enough to join with us. It is not they that proudliest persecute to prove their zeal, nor they that proudliest separate from others to prove it; but it is they that live in the love of God and man, that are beloved of God and man. Nature teacheth all men to love those that love them. And the divine nature teacheth us to love those much more that love God and goodness. Though love be an act of obedience as commanded, yet hath it a nature also above mere obedience; and bare commanding will not cause it. No man loveth God or man, only because he is commanded so to do; but because he perceiveth them to be good and amiable. And the most loving are the most lovely, so be it their love be rightly guided. Doth it not kindle love in you to others, more, to hear their breathings after God, and grace, and glory, and to see them loving and kind to all, and delighting to do all the good they can, and covering tenderly the infirmities of others, and practising 1 Cor. xiii. and living at peace among themselves, and as much as is possible with all men, and loving their enemies, and blessing those that curse them, and patiently bearing and forgiving wrongs; than to come into one congregation and hear a priest teach the people to hate their brethren as schismatics or heretics; or in another, and hear a man teach his followers to hate others as antichristian or ceremonious? Or to hear silly men and women talk against things that are quite beyond their reach, and shaking the head to talk against dissenters, and say, Such a one is an erroneous or dangerous man, take heed of hearing him? Such a one is for or against reprobation, free-will, universal redemption, man's power, and such like, which they little understand. In a word, the proudly tyrannical and the proudly schismatical, with all their pretence of learning on one side, or of the Spirit, and holiness, and gifts on the other, are no whit so amiable as the single-hearted, honest, peaceable christian, who preacheth love, and prayeth love, and liveth, and breatheth, and practiseth love. Paul saith, that all the law is fulfilled in love; and fulfilling is more than knowing it. And Christ himself did not in vain sum up all the commandments in the love of God and man; nor in vain ask Peter thrice, "Lovest thou me?" nor in vain so often charge it on them, as his new, that is, his last commandment, that they love one another! Nor doth his beloved apostle John in vain so earnestly write for love.

CHAPTER XVII.

EXHORT. 3. PLEAD NOT AGAINST LOVE OR WORKS OF LOVE, UPON PRETENCE OF A CROSS INTEREST OF LEARNING, KNOWLEDGE, GIFTS, CHURCH ORDER, DISCIPLINE, &C. OR ANY OTHER THING.

IF love be that which is most amiable in us to the God of love, then as nothing in the world can excuse him that is without it, nor render him lovely indeed to God and man, so nothing must be made a pretence against it; and no pretence will excuse that man, or that society, that is against it. Even corrections and severities, when they must be used, must come from love, and be wholly ordered to the ends and interest of love. And when necessity calls for destructive executions, which tend not to the good of him that is executed, yet must they tend to the good of the community or of many, and come from a greater love than is due to one; or else that which otherwise would be laudable justice, is but cruelty; for the punishment of offenders is good and just, because tending to the common good, *debentur reipublicæ*, the community have *jus*, a right to them as a means to their good; so that it is love that is the amiableness of justice itself.

If any think that God's justice is a cross instance; let him consider, 1. That though the most public or common good be our end next the ultimate, yet the true ultimate end of all things, is God himself: and the love of God is the highest love: and God's justice is not without that love of himself, and tendeth to that good which he is capable of receiving; which is but the fulfilling or complacency of his own will, which is, but improperly, called his receiving. 2. And we little know how many in another world, or in the renewed earth, are to be profited by his justice on the damned, as angels and men are by his justice on the devils.

1. LOVE is the life of religion, and of the soul, and of the church: and what can be a just pretence for any to destroy or oppose the very life of religion, the life of souls, and the life of the church of Christ? Physic, blood-letting, and dismembering may be used for life; but to take away life, except necessarily for a good that is better that that life, is murder. And what is it that is better than the life of religion, in all matters of religion? or than the life of the church, in all church affairs? or than the life of men's souls, in all matters of soul-concernment?

2. LOVE is the great command and summary of all the law; and what can be a just pretence for breaking the greatest command, yea, and the whole law?

3. LOVE is God's image; and he that dwelleth in love, dwelleth in God, who is LOVE, and God in him: and what can be a pretence sufficient for destroying the image of God, which is called by his name?

4. There is nothing in man that God himself loveth better than our love: and therefore nothing that as better can be set against it.

And yet, alas, what enmity is used in the world against the *love* of God and man! and many things alleged as pretences to justify it! Let us consider of some few of them.

1. The great tyrants of the world, such as in several ages have been the plagues of their own and neighbour nations, care not what havoc they make of religion, and of men's lives, by bloody wars, and cruel persecutions! destroying many thousands, and undoing far more thousands of the country families where their armies come; and sacrificing the lives of the best of their subjects by butcheries or flames! And what is the pretence for all this? Perhaps they would be lords of more of the world, and would have larger kingdoms, or more honour. Perhaps some prince hath spoken a hard word of them, or done them some wrong. Perhaps some subjects believe not as they bid them believe; or forbear not to worship God in a manner which they forbid them. Perhaps Daniel will not give over praying for a time; or the apostles will not give over preaching; or the three confessors will not fall down to the golden image; and so Nebuchadnezzar or the other rulers seem despised: and their wills and honour are an interest that with them seemeth to warrant all this. But how long will it seem so? I had rather any friend of mine had the sins of a thief or drunkard, or the most infamous sinner among us, to answer for, than the sins of a bloody Alexander, Cæsar, or Tamerlane.

2. The Roman clergy set up inquisitions, force men by cruelties to submit to their church keys, whose very nature is to be used without force; and they silence, yea, torment the faithful ministers of Christ, and have murdered thousands of his faithful people, raised rebellions against princes, and wars in kingdoms; and taught men to hate God's servants, as heretics, schismatics, rebels, factious, and what not? And what pretence must justify all this? Why, the interest of the pope and clergy; called in ignorance, or craft, by the name of the *holy church, religion, unity*, and such other honourable names! But must their church live on blood, and holy blood; and be built or preserved by the destruction of Christ's church? Must their doctrine be kept up, by silencing faithful ministers; and their worship by destroying or undoing the true worshippers of Christ? Are all these precious things which die with love, no better than to be sacrificed to the clergy's pride and worldly lusts?

3. Among many schismatics and sectaries, that are not miscalled so, but are such indeed; their discipline consisteth in separating from most other christians, as too bad (and that is, too unlovely) to be of their communion; and their preaching is much to make those seem bad (that is, unlovely) that are not of their way. And their worship is much such as relisheth of the same envy and strife, to add affliction or reproaches to their brethren; or to draw the people from the love of others unto them: and their ordinary talk is backbiting others for things that they understand not; and reporting any lie that is brought them; and telling the hearers something of this minister, or that person, or the other, that is unlovely; as if Satan had hired them to preach down love, and prate and pray down love; and all this in the name of Christ. And the third chapter of James is harder than Hebrew to them; they do not under-

stand it; but though they tear it not out of the Bible, they leave it out of the law in their hearts, as much as the papists leave the second commandment out of their books. And it is one of the marks of a good man among them, to talk against other parties, and make others odious, to set up them. And what are the pretences for all this? Why, truth and holiness. 1. Others have not the truth which they have. And, 2. Others are not against the same doctrines, and ceremonies, and bishops, and church orders, and ways of worship, which they are against; and therefore are ungodly, antichristian, or men of no religion.

But truth seldom dwelleth with the enemies of love and peace. They that are strangers and enemies to it, indeed, do often cry it up, and cry down those as enemies to it that possess it. The wisdom that hath bitter envying and heart-strife, is from beneath, and is earthly, sensual, and devilish. I admonish all that care for their salvation, that they set up nothing upon love-killing terms. If you are Christ's disciples, you are taught of God to love each other; you are taught it as Christ's last and great commandment; you are taught it by the wonderful example of his life; and especially (John xiii. 14) by his washing his disciples' feet. You are taught it by the Holy Ghost's uniting the hearts of the disciples, and making them by charity to live as in community, Acts iii.; iv. You are taught it by the effective operation of the Spirit on your own hearts; the new nature that is in you, inclineth you to it. And will you now pretend the necessity of your own interest, reputation, your canons, and things indifferent, your little church orders of your own making, yea, or the positive institutions of Christ himself, as to the present exercise, against this love? Hath Christ commanded you any thing before it, except the love of God? You say, if such and such men be suffered, this and that disorder and inconvenience will follow: but is it a greater thing than love that you would maintain? Is it a greater evil than the destruction of love that you would avoid? Did not Christ prefer mercy before sabbath rest, and before the avoiding familiarity with sinners? Pretend nothing against love, that is not better than love!

Object. But what is this to the love of God, which the text speaketh of?

Answ. As God is here seen as in a glass, so is he loved. He that loveth not his brother whom he seeth daily, how shall he love God, whom he never saw? He that saith he loveth God, and hateth his brother, is a liar! What you do to his brethren you do as to Christ. If you can find as full a promise of salvation to those that observe your canons, ceremonies, orders, or are of your opinion and sect, as I can show you for them that love Christ and his servants, then prefer the former before love.

I know that the love and good of church and state and of many must be preferred before the love and good of few. But take heed of their hypocrisy that make these also inconsistent when they are not; and make public good and peace a mere pretence for their persecutions on one side, or their schisms on the other. Love is so amiable to nature itself, that few of its enemies oppose it but under pretence of its own interest and name: it is as in love to the church and to men's souls that the inquisition hath murdered so many, and the laws *de hereticis comburendis* have been made and executed. But this burning, hanging, tormenting, and undoing kind of love, needeth very clear proof to make good its name and pretences, before impartial men will take it for love indeed. Whatever good you seem to do, by the detriment of love to God and man, you will find it will not bear your charges.

CHAPTER XVIII.

EXHORT. 4. BEND ALL YOUR STUDIES AND LABOURS TO THE EXERCISE AND INCREASE OF LOVE, BOTH OF GOD AND MAN, AND ALL GOOD WORKS.

THE greatest, best, and sweetest work should have the greatest diligence. This great commandment must be obeyed with the greatest care. The work of love must be the work of our whole life: if you cannot learn to pray and preach, no nor to follow a worldly trade, without study and much exercise, how think you to be proficients in the love of God without them? Do this well, and all is done. O happy souls, that are habituated and daily exercised in this work; whose new nature, and life, and study, and business, is holy love!

1. How divine, how high and noble is this life; to live in a humble friendship with God and all his holy ones! All animals naturally love their like, and converse according to their love: and men as men have as much sociable love to men as the love of sin and inordinate self-love will allow them: and they that truly love God and holiness and saints, do show that they have some connatural suitableness to these excellent objects of their love. Nothing more aptly denominateth any man divine and holy, than divine and holy love. How else should souls have communion with God? His common influx all creatures receive; in him all live, and move, and have their being; but when his love kindleth in us a reflecting love, this is felicity itself. Yea, it is much nobler than our felicity; for though our felicity consist in loving God, and being beloved of him, yet it is a far more excellent thing, by reason that God is the object of our love, than by reason that it is our felicity: God's interest advanceth it more than ours; and though they are not separable, yet being distinguishable, we should love God far more as God, and perfect goodness in himself, than as he or this love is our own felicity.

2. This life of love is the true improvement of all God's doctrines, ordinances, mercies, afflictions, and other providences whatsoever; for the use of them all is to lead us up to holy love, and to help us in the daily exercise of it. What is the Bible else written for, but to teach us to love, and to exercise the fruits of love? What came Christ from heaven for, but to demonstrate and reveal God's love and loveliness to man; and by reconciling us to God, and freely pardoning all our sins, and promising us both grace and glory, to show us those motives which should kindle love, and to show that God is most suitable and worthy of our love, and to fill us with the Spirit of love, which may give us that which he commandeth us? What is it that we read books for, and hear sermons for, but to kindle and exercise holy love? What join we for in the sacred worship of the assemblies, but that in a united flame of holy love, we might all mount up in praise to Jehovah? What is the Lord's day separated to, but the tidings of love, the sufferings, victories, and triumphs of our Saviour's love, the tastes and prospects of God's love to us, and the lively and joyful exercise of ours to him, and to each other? What use are the sacraments of, but that being entertained at the most wonderful feast of love, we should taste its sweetness, and pour out the

grateful sense of it in holy thanksgiving and praise, and the exercise of uniting love to one another? What are church societies or combinations for, but the loving communion of saints? which the primitive christians expressed by selling all, and living in a community of love, and stedfastly continuing in the apostles' doctrine and fellowship, and breaking of bread and prayer. What are all God's mercies for, but that as by love-tokens we should taste that he is love and good, and should by that taste be inclined to returns of love? Nay, what are civil societies, but loving communions, if used according to their natures? Did they not love each other, so many bees would never hive and work together, nor so many pigeons dwell peaceably in one dove-house, nor fly together in so great flocks. What is the whole christian faith for, but the doctrine of holy love believed, for the kindling and exercise of our love? What is faith itself but the bellows of love? What is the excellency of all good works, and gifts, and endowments, but to be the exercises of love to God and man, and the incentives of our brethren's love? Without love all these are dead carcasses and as nothing, and without it we ourselves are as nothing; yea, though we give all that we have to the poor, or give our bodies like martyrs to be burnt, or could speak with the tongue (the orthodoxness and elegancy) of angels, we were but "as sounding brass, and as a tinkling cymbal." James knew what he said, when he said that "Faith without works is dead," because without love it is dead, which those works are but the body or the fruit of.

3. This life of love is the perfection of man's faculties as to their intended end and use. As all the operations of the lower faculties, vegetative and sensitive, are subordinate to the use and operations of the intellectual part, which is the higher, so all the acts of the intellect itself, are but subservient and dirigent to the will, or love and practice. The understanding is but the eye by which the soul seeth what to love and choose or refuse, and what to do or to avoid. Love is the highest act of our highest faculty; and complacency in the highest infinite good, is the highest of all the acts of love. This is the state of the soul in its ripeness and mellow sweetness, when it is delightful, embracing its most desired object, and is blessed in the fruition of its ultimate end. All other graces and duties are servants unto this. They are the parts indeed of the same new creature, but the hands and feet are not the heart.

4. For love is the very foretaste of heaven; the beginning of that felicity which shall there be perfect. In heaven all saints shall be as one; and all united to their glorious Head, as he is united to the Father, disparities allowed, John xvii. 24. And what more uniteth souls than love? Heaven is a state of joyful complacence; and what is that but perfect love? The heavenly work is perfect obedience and praise; and what are these but the actions and the breath of love?

5. Therefore they that live this life of love, are fitter to die, and readier for heaven, than any others. Belief is a foresight of it; but love is a foretaste; the first-fruits, and our earnest and pledge. He that loveth God, and Christ, and angels, and saints, and perfect holiness, and divine praise, is ready for heaven, as the infant in the womb is ready for birth, at the fulness of his time: but other christians, whose love is true, but little to their fears, and damped by darkness, and too much love of the body and this world, do go as it were by untimely birth to heaven; and those in whom the love of the body is predominant, come not thither, in that state, at all. The God of grace and glory will meet that soul with his felicitating embracements, who panteth and breatheth after him by love; and as love is a kind of union with the heavenly society, the angels, who love us better than we love them, will be ready to convey such souls to God. As the living dwell not in the graves among the dead, and the dead are buried from among the living, so holy souls, who have this life of love, cannot be among the miserable in hell, nor the dead in sin among the blessed.

6. Therefore this life of holy love doth strengthen our belief itself. Strong reasons that are brought for the immortality of souls, and the future glory, are usually lost upon unsanctified hearers, yea with the doctors themselves that use them: when they have persuaded others that there is a heaven for believers, and that by arguments in themselves unanswerable, they have not persuaded their own hearts; but the predominant love of flesh and earth doth bias their understandings, and maketh them think that they can confute themselves. Their gust and inclination prevaileth against belief: and therefore the greatest scholars are not always the strongest believers. But holy love, when it is the habit of the soul, as it naturally ascendeth, so it easily believeth that God, that glory to which it doth ascend. The gust and experience of such a soul assureth it that it was made for communion with God, and that even in this life such communion is obtained in some degree; and therefore it easily believeth that it is redeemed for it, and that it shall perfectly enjoy it in heaven for ever. Though glory be here but seminally in grace, and this world be but as the womb of that better world for which we hope, yet the life that is in the embryo and seed, is a confirming argument for the perfection which they tend to. Oh that men knew what holy love doth signify and foretell! As the seed or embryo of a man becometh not a beast or serpent; so he that hath the habitual love of God, and heaven, and holiness, is not capable of hell, no more than the lovers of worldliness and sensuality are capable of present communion with God, and of his glory. God doth not draw men's hearts to himself, nor kindle heavenly desires in them, in vain. He that hath the Spirit of Christ, hath the witness in himself, that Christ and his promises of life are true, 1 John v. 10—12. And what is this Spirit but the habit of divine and heavenly love, and its concomitants? May I but feel my soul inflamed with the fervent love of the heavenly perfection, surely it will do more to put me quite out of doubt of the certainty of that blessed state, than all arguments without that love can do.

7. And holy love will be the surest evidence of our sincerity; which many old writers meant, that called it, The form of faith and other graces: as means, as means, are informed by their aptitudinal respect unto the end; so love, as it is the final act upon God the final object, thus informeth all subordinate graces and duties as they are means. And as all morality is subjected in the will as the proper primary seat, and is in the intellect, executive power, and senses only by participation, so far as their acts are imperate by the will; so love and volition being really the same thing, it may accordingly be said, that nothing is any further acceptable to God than it is good; and nothing is morally good any further than it is voluntary or willed; and to be willed (as good, as end, or as means) and to be loved, are words that signify the same. No preaching, praying, fasting, &c. no fear of punishment, no belief of the truth, &c. will prove us sincere and justified, any further than we can prove, that all this either cometh from, or is accompanied with, love, that is, with a consenting will. "With the heart

man believeth unto righteousness," Rom. x. And, "If thou believe with all thy heart, thou mayest be baptized," saith Philip to the eunuch, Acts viii. "My son, give me thy heart," is Wisdom's invitation. All is nothing without the heart, that is, without willingness or love. They that love most are sureliest forgiven, and have most holiness or grace, how unskilful soever they may be in their expressions. The sealing Spirit of adoption is the Spirit of love; and the Abba, Father, and the unexpressed groans of filial love, are understood and acceptable to God. A loving desire after God and holiness, is a better evidence than the most taking tongue or largest knowledge.

8. This life of holy love will make all our religion and obedience easy to us; it will give us an alacrity to the performance, and a pleasure in the practice of it; and so our obedience will be hearty, willing, and universal. Who is averse to that which he loveth, unless for something in it which he hateth? All men go willingly and readily to that which they truly love. Therefore it is said that the law is not made for a righteous man; that is, a man that loveth piety, temperance, and justice, and their several works, so far hath no need of threatening laws and penalties to constrain him to it; and he that hateth sin, so far hath no need of legal penalties to restrain him from it. Thus is the law said to be "written in our hearts;" not as it is merely in our knowledge and memory, but as the matter commanded is truly loved by us, and the sin forbidden truly hated. Even our horses will carry us cheerfully that way which they love to go, and go heavily where they go against their wills. Win men's love, and the life, and lips, and all (according to power) will follow it.

9. And such persons therefore are likest to persevere: men go unweariedly, if they be but able, where they go with love. Especially such a love which groweth stronger as it draweth nearer the state of perfection which it loveth; and groweth by daily renewed experiences and mercies, as rivers grow bigger as they draw nearer to the sea. We easily hold on in that we love; but that which men loathe, and their hearts are against, they are quickly weary of: and the weary person will easily be persuaded to lie down. The root of apostasy is already in those persons, who love not the end which they pretend to seek, nor the work which they pretend to do.

10. Lastly, holy love is a pregnant, spreading, fruitful grace: it kindleth a desire to do good to others, and to draw men to love the same God, and heaven, and holiness which we love. It made God's word to be to Jeremiah as a "burning fire shut up in his bones, he was weary of forbearing," Jer. xx. 9. As a fire kindleth fire, and is the active principle of vegetation, as I suppose, so love kindleth love, and is a kind of generative principle of grace. God's love is the first cause; but man's love maketh them meet instruments of God's love: for love will be often praising the God and holiness which is loved; and earnestly desireth that all others may love and praise the same. The soul is not indeed converted, till its love is won to God and goodness: a man may be terrified into some austerities, superstitions, or reformations, but he is not further holy than his heart is won. And as every thing that generateth is apt to produce its like, so is love, and the words and works of love. And as love is the heart of holiness, so must it be of all fruitful preaching and conversation; whatever the words or actions are, they are like no further to win souls, than they demonstrate the love of God, and of holiness, and of the hearers or spectators. As among amorous and vain persons, strong love appearing, though by a look or word, doth kindle the like more than all compliments that are known to be but feigned and affected words; so usually souls are won to God, as by the preacher's words and works of love, the love and loveliness of God in Christ are fulliest made known.

Quest. But how should we reach this excellent life of holy love, which doth so far excel all knowledge?

Answ. I have said so much of this in the first part of my "Christian Directory," and other writings, that I must here say but little of it, lest I be overmuch guilty of repetitions. Briefly,

Direct. 1. Believe God's goodness to be equal to his greatness. God's three great primary attributes are coequal, viz. his power, his wisdom, and his goodness. And then look up to the heavens, and think how great and powerful is that God that made and continueth such a frame, as that sun, and those stars, and those glorious unmeasurable regions where they are: think what a world of creatures God maintaineth in life, on this little lower orb of earth, both in the seas and on the land. And then think, Oh what is the goodness which is equal to all this power!

Direct. 2. Consider how communicative this infinite goodness is: why else is he called LOVE itself? Why else made he all the world? and why did he make the sun so glorious? why else did he animate and beautify the universe, with the life and ornaments of created goodness? All his works shine by the splendour of that excellency which he hath put upon them: all are not equal, but all are good, and their inequality belongeth to the goodness of the universe. The communicative nature with which God hath endowed all active beings, (and the most noble most,) is an impress of the infinite communicative LOVE. Fire would communicate its light, heat, and motion, to all passive objects which are capable of receiving it: how pregnant and fertile is the very earth with plants, flowers, and fruits of wonderful variety, usefulness, and beauty! what plant is not natured to the propagation of its kind, yea, to a plenteous multiplication? How many seeds, which are virtual plants, doth each of them bring forth at once; and yet the same plant, with all its offspring, perhaps liveth many years for further multiplication; so that did not the far greatest part of seeds yearly perish, there must be very many such earths to receive and propagate them: this earth hath not room for the hundredth part: to show us that the active natures even of vegetatives, do quite exceed in their pregnant communicative activity the receptive capacity of all passive matter; which teacheth us to observe that all created patients are unconceivably too narrow to receive such communicative influences, as infinite pregnant LOVE can communicate, were their subjects to receive them.

It is wonderful to observe in all sorts of animals, the same multiplying communicative inclination; and what use the God of nature maketh even of sensual LOVE to all generation! Uniting and communicating LOVE is in all creatures the incentive principle of procreation. And what a multitude of young ones will some one creature procreate, especially fishes to admiration! so that if other fishes, with men and other creatures, did not devour them, all the waters on earth could not contain them.

Yea, our moral communicativeness also hath the same indication. He that knoweth much, would fain have others know the same; secret knowledge kept to ourselves only hath its excellent use; but it satisfieth not the mind, *nisi te scire hoc sciat alter*, unless others know that you have such knowledge, and unless you can make them know what you know. Holy souls therefore have a fervent, but a regular desire, and endeavour by communicative teaching to make others wise: but proud, heretical persons, that overvalue their conceits, have an irregular, fornicating lust of teaching, and adulterously invade the charge of others, presuming that none can do it so wisely and so well as they. Men "will compass sea and land to make a proselyte;" and tares and weeds are as much inclined to propagation as the wheat. There is a marvellous desire in the nature of man, to make others of their own opinion; and when it is governed by God's laws, it is greatly beneficial to the world.

And even in affections, as well as knowledge, it is so: we would have others love those that we love, and hate what we hate. Though where, by the insufficiency of the narrow creature, men must lose and want that themselves, which they communicate to others, selfishness forbiddeth such communication.

And doubtless all the creatures in their several ranks, have some such impresses from the Creator, by which his transcendent perfections may be somewhat observed. That God is now so communicative as to give to all creatures in the world whatever being, motion, life, order, beauty, harmony, reason, grace, glory, any of them possess, is past all question to considering, sober reason. Which tempted Aristotle to think that the world was eternal; and some christians to think that though this present heaven and earth were created, as in Genesis i. is said, yet that from eternity some intellectual world at least, if not also corporeal, did flow from the Creator, as an eternal effect of an eternal cause, or an eternal accident of the Deity; because they could not receive it, that a God so unspeakably communicative now, (who hath made the sun to be an emblem of his communicativeness,) should from all eternity be solitary and not communicative, when yet to all eternity he will be so. But these are questions which uncapable mortals were far better let alone than meddle with, unless we desire rather to be lost than to be blessed in the abyss of eternity, and the thoughts of infinite pregnant LOVE.

But it is so natural for man and every animal to love that love and goodness which is beneficent, (not only to us, but to all,) rather than a mere self-lover, that doth no good to others, that it must needs conduce much to our love of God, to consider that "he is good to all, and his mercy is over all his works;" and that as there is no light in the air but from the sun, so there is no goodness but from God in all the world, who is more to the creation than the sun is to this lower world. And a sun that lighteth all the earth, is much more precious than my candle: a Nile which watereth the land of Egypt, is more precious than a private well; it is the excellency of kings and public persons, that if they are good, they are good to many: and oh what innumerable animals in sea and land, besides the far greater worlds of nobler wights, do continually live by one God of love! Study this universal, infinite Love.

Direct. 3. Especially study divine love and goodness in the face of our Redeemer Jesus Christ, and all the grace which he hath purchased and conferreth. As we may see that magnitude of the stars in a telescope, which without it no eye can discern; so may we see that glory of the love of God by the gospel of Jesus, which all common natural helps are insufficient to discover to such minds as ours. Love is the great attribute which Christ came principally to manifest, as was aforesaid, John iii. 16; 1 John iii. 1, &c. And love is the great lesson which he came to teach us; and love is the new nature which by his Spirit he giveth us; and love is the great duty which, by law and gospel, he requireth of us. Love hath wrought its miracles in Christ to the posing of the understandings of men and angels. There we may see God in the nearest condescending unity with man; in Christ we may see the divine Wisdom and Word incorporate in such flesh as ours, conceived in a virgin by the power of the Spirit of love; by which Spirit this incorporate Word did live, preach, converse familiarly with man; work miracles, heal diseases, suffer reproachful calumnies and death; rising, triumphing, ascending, interceding, sending the embassies of love to the world, calling home the greatest sinners unto God, reconciling enemies, and making them the adopted sons of God, forgiving all sin to penitent believers, quickening dead souls, illuminating the blind, and sanctifying the wicked by the Spirit of life, and light, and love; and making it his office, his work, his delight, and glory, to rescue the miserable captives of the devil, and to make heirs of heaven of those that were condemned to hell, and had forsaken life in forsaking God. As this is shining, burning love, so it is approaching and self-applying love; which cometh so near us, in ways and benefits so necessary to us, and so exceeding congruous to our case, as that it is easier for us to perceive and feel it, than we can do things of greater distance. The clearer the eye of faith is, by which we look into this mysterious glass, the more the wonders of love will be perceived in it. He never knew Christ, nor understood the gospel, that wondered not at redeeming, saving love; nor did he ever learn of Christ indeed, that hath not learned the lesson, work, and life of love.

Direct. 4. Keep as full records as you can of the particular mercies of God to yourselves; and frequently peruse them, and plead them with your frozen hearts.

These are not the chiefest reasons of christian love; because we are such poor, inconsiderable worms, that to do good to one of us, is a far smaller matter, than many things else that we have to think of for that end. But yet when love doth choose a particular person for its object, and there bestow its obliging gifts, it helpeth that person far more than others to returns of thankfulness and love: it is that place, that glass, which the sun doth shine upon, doth reflect its beams, rather than those that are shut up in darkness. Self-love may and must be regulated and sanctified, to the furthering of higher love. It is not unmeet to say with David, (Psal. cxvi. 1,) "I love the Lord, because he hath heard the voice of my supplication." We should say as heartily, I love the Lord, because he hath prospered, recovered, comforted my neighbour: but this is not all out so easy as the other. And where God by personal application maketh our greatest duty easy, we should use his helps.

Object. But if it be selfishness, as some tell us, to love one that loveth us, better than another of equal worth, who doth not love us, is it not selfishness to love God on so low an account as loving us? God may say well, "I love those that love me," (Prov. viii. 17,) because to love him is the highest virtue, but to love us is as inconsiderable as we are.

Answ. 1. You may love another the more for loving you, on several accounts. 1. As it is a duty which God requireth him to perform (but so you must love him equally for loving others also). 2. As he rendereth himself more congruous and obliging to you, by choosing you for the special object of his love, by which he taketh the advantage of your natural self-love, to make your love to him both due and easy, as it is said of the reflection of the sunbeams before.

2. But two things you must take heed of: 1. That

you undervalue not your neighbours' good, but love another for loving your neighbours also, and doing them good; and he that arriveth at that impartial unity as to make the smallest difference between his neighbour and himself, doth seem to me to be arrived at the state that is likest to theirs that are one in heaven. 2. And you must not overlove any man by a fond partiality for his love to you; as if that made a bad man good, or fitter for your love: they that can love the worst that love them, and cannot love the best that set light by them, (deservedly, or upon mistake,) do show that self-love overcometh the love of God. But God cannot be loved too much, though he may be loved too selfishly and carnally. His greatest amiableness is his essential goodness and infinite perfection: the next is his glory shining in the universe, and so in the heavenly society, especially Christ and all his holy ones; and so in the public blessings of the world, and all societies. And next his goodness to yourselves, not only as parts of the said societies, but as persons whose natures are formed by God himself to a capacity of receiving and reflecting love.

Who findeth not by experience that God is most loved, when we are most sensible of his former love to us in the thankful review of all his mercies, and most assured or persuaded of his future love in our salvation? Therefore make the renewed commemoration of God's mercies the incentives of your love.

Direct. 5. But yet could you get a greater union and communion not only with saints as saints, but with mankind as men, it would greatly help you in your love to God: for when you love your neighbours as yourselves, you would love God for your neighbours' mercies, as well as for your own. And if you feel that God's love and special mercies to one person, even yourselves, can do so much in causing your love, what would your love amount to, if thousand thousands of persons to whom God showeth mercy, were every one to you as yourselves, and all their mercies as your own? Thus graces mutually help each other. We love man, because we love God; and we love God the more for our love to man.

Direct. 6. Especially dwell by faith in heaven where love is perfect, and there you will learn more of the work of love. To think believingly that mutual love is heaven itself, and that this is our union with God, and Christ, and all the holy ones, and that love will be an everlasting employment, pleasure, and felicity, this will breed in us a desire to begin that happy life on earth. And as he that heareth excellent music will long to draw near and join in the concert or the pleasure; so he that by faith doth dwell much in heaven, and hear how angels and blessed souls do there praise God in the highest fervours of rejoicing love, will be inclined to imitate them, and long to partake of their felicity.

Direct. 7. Exercise that measure of love which you have in the constant praises of the God of love. For exercise exciteth, and naturally tendeth to increase, and praise is the duty in which pure love to God above ourselves and all, even as good and perfect in himself, is exercised. As love is the highest grace, or inward duty; so praise is the highest outward duty, when God is praised both by tongue and life. And as soul and body make one man, of whose existence generation is the cause; so love and praise, of mouth and works, do make one saint, who is regenerated such by believing in the Redeemer, who hath power to give the Spirit of holiness to whom he pleaseth. But of this more afterwards.

Direct. 8. Exercise your love to man, especially to saints, in doing them all the good you can; and that for what of God is in them. For as this is the fruit of the love of God, and the evidence of it, so doth it tend to the increase of its cause; partly as it is an exercise of it, and partly as it is a duty which God hath promised to reward. As it is the Spirit of Christ, even of adoption, which worketh both the love of our Father and our brethren in us; so God will bless those that exercise love, especially at the dearest rates, and with the fullest devotedness of all to God, with the larger measures of the same Spirit.

CHAPTER XIX.

EXHORT. 5. PLACE YOUR COMFORTS IN HEALTH AND SICKNESS IN MUTUAL DIVINE LOVE. 2. SEE THAT YOU SINCERELY LOVE GOD. HOW KNOWN? DOUBTS ANSWERED.

It is of greatest importance to all mankind, to know what is best for them, and in what they should place and seek their comforts: to place them most with the proud, in the applauding thoughts or words of others, that magnify them for their wit, their beauty, their wealth, or their pomp and power in the world, is to choose somewhat less than a shadow for felicity, and to live on the air, even an unconstant air. And will such a life be long or happy? Should not a man in misery rather take it for a stinging, deriding mockery or abuse, to be honoured and praised for that which he hath not, or for that which is his snare, or consisteth with his calamity? Would not a malefactor at the gallows take it for his reproach, to hear an oration of his happiness? Will it comfort them in hell to be praised on earth? This common reason may easily call, an empty vanity.

To place our comforts in the delights of sensuality, had somewhat a fairer show of reason, if reason were made for nothing better; and if these were the noble sort of pleasures that advanced man above the brutes; and if they would continue for ever, and the end of such mirth were not heaviness and repentance, and they did not deprave and deceive men's souls, and leave behind them disappointment and a sting. But he is unworthy the honour and pleasures of humanity, who preferreth the pleasures of a beast, when he may have better.

To place our comforts in those riches which do but serve this sensuality with provisions, and leave posterity in as vain and dangerous a state as their progenitors were, is but the foresaid folly aggravated.

To place them in domination, and having our wills on others, and being able to do hurt, and exercise revenge, is but to account the devils happier than men, and to desire to be as the wolf among the sheep, or as the kite among the chickens, or as the great dogs among the little ones.

To place them in much knowledge of arts and sciences, as they concern only the interests of the body in this life, or as knowledge is but the delight of the natural fantasy or mind, doth seem a little finer, and sublime, and manly; but it is of the same nature and vanity as the rest. For all knowledge is for the guidance of the will and practice; and therefore mere knowing matters that tend to pride, sensuality, wealth, or domination, is less than the enjoyment of sensual pleasures in the things themselves. And the contemplation of superior creatures, which hath no other end than the delight of knowing, is but a more refined sort of vanity, and like the mind's activity in a dream.

But whether it be the knowledge or the love of

God, that man should place his highest felicity in, is become among the schoolmen and some other divines a controversy that seemeth somewhat hard. But indeed to a considering man, the seeming difficulty may be easily overcome; the understanding, and will, and executive activity, are not several souls, but several faculties of one soul; and their objects and order of operation easily tell us, which is the first, and which the last, which tendeth to the other as its end, and which object is the most delightful and most felicitating to the man; viz. That truth is for goodness, and that good as good is the amiable, delectable, and felicitating object; and therefore that the intellect is the guide of the will, and faith and knowledge are for love and its delight. And yet that man's felicity is in both, and not in one alone, as one faculty alone is not the whole soul, though it be the whole soul that acteth by that faculty. Therefore the latter schoolmen have many of them well confuted Aquinas in this point.

And it is of great in portance in our christian practice. As the desire of more knowledge first corrupted our nature, so corrupted nature is much more easily drawn to seek after knowledge than after love. Many men are bookish that cannot endure to be saints: many can spend their lives in the studies of nature and theology, and delight to find increase of knowledge, who are strangers to the sanctifying, uniting, delightful exercise of holy love. Appetite is the *pondus* or first spring of our moral actions, yea, and of our natural, though the sense and intellect intromit or illuminate the object. And the first act of natural appetite, sensitive and intellectual, is necessitated. And accordingly the appetite as pleased is as much the end of our acts and objects, as the appetite as desiring is the beginning: even as (*si parvis magna*, &c.) God's will as efficient is the absolutely first cause, and his will as done and pleased is the ultimate end of all things. It is love by which man cleaveth unto God as good, and as our ultimate end. Love ever supposeth knowledge; and is its end and perfection. Neither alone, but both together, are man's highest state; knowledge as discerning what is to be loved, and love as our uniting and delighting adherence to it.

1. Labour therefore, with all your industry, to know God that you may love him; it is that love that must be your comforting grace, both by signification, and by its proper effective exercise. 1. True love will prove that your knowledge and faith are true and saving, which you will never be sure of, without the evidence of this and the consequent effects. If your expressive art or gifts be never so low, so that you scarce know what to say to God or man, yet if you so far know God as sincerely to love him, it is certainly true saving knowledge, and that which is the beginning of eternal life. Knowledge, belief, repentance, humility, meekness, patience, zeal, diligence, &c. are so far and no further sure marks of salvation, as they cause or prove true love to God and man predominant. It is a hard thing any otherwise to know whether our knowledge, repentance, patience, zeal, or any of the rest, be any better than what an unjustified person may attain: but if you can find that they cause, or come from, or accompany, a sincere love of God, you may be sure that they all partake of sincerity, and are certain signs of a justified soul. It is hard to know what sins for number, or nature, or magnitude, are such as may or may not consist with a state of saving grace. He that considereth of the sins of Lot, David, Solomon, and Peter, will find the case exceeding difficult: but this much is sure, that so much sin may consist with a justified state, as may consist with a sincere love to God and goodness. While a man truly loveth God above all, his sin may cause correction, but not damnation; unless it could extinguish or overcome this love. Some question whether that the sin of Lot or David, for the present, stood with justification: if it excussed not predominant habitual love, it intercepteth not justification: if we could tell whether any or many heathens that hear not of Christ, have the true love of God and holiness, we might know whether they are saved.

The reason is, because that the will is the man in God's account; and as voluntariness is essential to sin, so a holy will doth prove a holy person. God hath the heart of him that loveth him. He that loveth him would fain please him, glorify him, and enjoy him: and he that loveth holiness would fain live a holy life.

Therefore it is that divines say here, that desire of grace is a certain sign of grace, because it is an act of will and love. And it is true, if that desire be greater or more powerful than our averseness, and than our desire after contrary things, that so it may put us on necessary duty, and overcome the lusts and temptations which oppose them: though cold wishes, which are conquered by greater unwillingness and prevailing lusts, will never save men.

2. And as love is our more comforting evidence, so it is our most comforting exercise. Those acts of religion which come short of this, come short of the proper life and sweetness of true religion. They are but either lightnings in the brain that have no heat; or a feverish zeal, which destroyeth or troubleth, but doth not perform the acts of life; or else, even where love is true, but little, and oppressed by fears, and grief, and trouble, it is like fire in green wood, or like young green fruits, which is not come to mellow ripeness. Love of vanity is disappointing, unsatisfactory, and tormenting: most of the calamities of this life proceed from creature love. The greatest tormentor in this world, is the inordinate love of life; and the next is the love of the pleasures and accommodations of life: which cause so much care to get and keep, and so much fear of losing, and grief for our losses, especially fear of dying; that were it not for this, our lives would be much easier to us (as they are to the fearless sort of brutes). And the next tormenting affection is the love of children, which prepareth men for all the calamity that followeth their miscarriages in soul and body: their unnatural ingratitude, their lewdness, and debauchery, and prodigality, their folly and impiety, would nothing so much torment us, were they no more loved than other men. And our dearest friends do usually cost us much dearer than our sharpest enemies. But the love of God and satisfying, everlasting good, is our very life, our pleasure, our heaven on earth. As it is purest and highest, above all other, because of the object; so is it yet more pleasant and contenting, because it includeth the hopes of more, even of those greater delights of heavenly, everlasting love, which, as a pledge and earnest, it doth presignify. As in nature, conception and the stirring of the child in the womb, do signify that same life is begun, which must shortly appear and be exercised in the open world; so the stirrings of holy love and desires towards God, do signify the beginning of the heavenly life.

Humility and patience, and diligent obedience, do comfort us by way of evidence, and as removing many hinderances of our comfort; and somewhat further they go. But faith, hope, and love, do comfort us by way of direct efficiency: faith seeth the matter of our joy; love first tasteth it, so far as to stir up desires after it; then hope giveth some pleasure to us in expecting it. And lastly, complacential love delightfully embraceth it, and is our very joy itself, and is that blessed union with God and holy souls, the amiable objects of true love, which is our felicity itself. To work out our comforts by the view of evidences and signs, is a necessary thing indeed: but it requireth a considerate search, by an understanding and composed mind; and it is often much hindered and interrupted by men's ignorance of themselves, and weakness of grace, and darkness or smallness of evidence, and divers passions, especially fear (which in some is so tyrannical, that it will not suffer them to believe or feel any thing that is comfortable). But love taketh in the sweetness of that good which is its object, by a nearer and effectual way, even by immediate taste: as we feel in the exercise of our love to a dear friend, or any thing that is amiable and enjoyed.

The readiest and surest way, therefore, to a contented and comfortable life, is (to keep clear indeed our evidence, especially sincere obedience, but) especially to bend all our studies and religious endeavours, to the kindling and exercise of holy love; and to avoid all (though it may come on religious pretence of humiliation or fear) which tendeth to quench or hinder it.

I. In health and prosperity, as you live upon God's love, be sure that you do not atheistically overlook it, but take all as from it, and savouring of it. The hand of divine love perfumeth each mercy with the pleasant odour of itself, which it reacheth to us: every bit that we eat is a love-token; and every hour or minute that we live: all our health, wealth, friends, and peace are the streams which still flow from the spring of unexhausted love. Love shineth upon us by the sun; love maketh our land fruitful, our cattle useful, our habitations convenient for us, our garments warm, our food pleasant and nourishing. Love keepeth us from a thousand unknown dangers night and day; it giveth us the comforts of our callings, our company, our books, our lawful recreations: it blesseth means of knowledge to our understandings, and means of holiness to our wills, and means of health and strength to our bodies. Mercies are sanctified to us, when we taste God's love in them, and love him for them, and are led up by them to himself; and so love him ultimately for himself, even for his infinite essential goodness. As God is the efficient life of our mercies, and all the world (without his love) could never give us what we have; so is God's love the objective life of all our mercies, and we have but the corpse or carcass of them, and love them but as such, if we love not in them the love that giveth them.

II. And even in adversity, and pain, and sickness, whilst God's love is unchanged, and is but changing the way of doing good, our thoughts of it should be unchanged also. We must not think that the sun is lost when it is set, or clouded: we live by its influence in the night, though we see not its light, unless as reflected from the moon. Our mothers brought us into the world in sorrow, and yet they justly accounted it a mercy that we were born; our lives are spent in the midst of sorrows, and yet it is a mercy that we live; and though we die by dolour, all is still mercy to believers, which faith perceiveth contrary to sense. All here is the greatest and final victory which faith obtaineth against the flesh, to believe even the ruin of it to be for our good. Even Antonine the emperor could say, that it was the same good God, who is the cause of our birth and of our death; one as well as the other is his work, and therefore good: it was not a tyrant that made us, and it is not a tyrant that dissolveth us. And that is the best man, and the best will, which is most pleased with the will of God, because it is his will. Yet just self-love is here a true coadjutor of our joy; for it is the will of God, that the justified be glorified: and Infinite Love is saving us, when it seemeth to destroy us.

To live upon the comforts of divine love in sickness, and when death approacheth, is a sign that it is not the welfare of the body that we most esteem; and that we rejoice not in God only as the preserver and prosperer of our flesh, but for himself and the blessings of immortality.

It is a mercy indeed, which a dying man must with thankfulness acknowledge, if God have given him a clear understanding of the excellent mysteries of salvation. Knowledge, as it kindleth and promoteth love, is a precious gift of grace, and is with pleasure exercised, and may with pleasure be acknowledged. But all other knowledge is like the vanities of the world, which approaching death doth take down our esteem of, and causeth us to number it with other forsaking and forsaken things. All the unsanctified learning and knowledge in the world, will afford no solid peace at death; but rather aggravate nature's sorrows, to think that this also must be left. But love and its comforts, if not hindered by ignorance or some strong temptation, do then show their immortal nature: and even here we feel the words of the apostle verified, of the vanishing nature of knowledge, and the perpetuity of holy love; whilst all our learning and knowledge will not give so much comfort to a dying man, as one act of true love to God, and holiness kindled in us by the communication of his love. Make it therefore the work of your religion, and the work of your whole lives, to possess your minds with the liveliest sense of the infinite goodness and amiableness of God, and hereby to live in the constant exercise of love.

III. And though some men hinder love, by an over-fearful questioning whether they have it, or not; and spend that time in doubting and complaining that they have it not, which they should spend in exciting and exercising it; yet reason requireth us to take heed lest a carnal mind deceive us with any counterfeits of holy love. Of which having written more in my "Christian Directory," I shall here give you but these brief instructions following.

It is here of grand importance, I. To have a true conception of God as he must be loved. II. And then to know practically how it is that love must be exercised towards him.

I. GOD must be conceived at once, both, 1. As in his essence. 2. And as in his relations to the world, and to ourselves. 3. And as in his works. And those that will separate these, and while they fix only on one of them, leave out the other, do not indeed love God as God, and as he must be loved.

1. To think in general, that there is an Infinite Eternal Spirit of life, light and love; and not to think of him as related to the world as its Creator, Preserver, and Governor; nor as related to us and to mankind as our Owner, Ruler, and Benefactor; is not to think of him as a God to us, or to any but himself: and a love thus exercised cannot be true saving love.

2. And because his relations to us result from his works, either which he hath done already, or which he will do hereafter; therefore without the knowledge of his works, and their goodness, we cannot truly know and love God in his relations to us.

3. And yet when we know his works, we know but the medium, or that in which he himself is made known to us: and if by them we come not to know him, and to love him in his perfect essence, it is not God that we know and love. And if we knew him

only as related to us and the world, (as that he is our Creator, Owner, Mover, Ruler, and Benefactor,) and yet know not what he is in his essence, that is thus related; (viz. that he is the perfect, First Being, Life, Wisdom, and Love;) this were not truly to know and love him as he is God. These conceptions therefore must be conjunct.

God is not here known to us, but by the revelation of his works and word; nor can we conceive of him, but by the similitude of some of his works. Not that we must think that he is just such as they, or picture him like a creature; for he is infinitely above them all: but yet it is certain that he hath made some impressions of his perfections upon his works; and on some of them so clear, as that they are called his image.

Nothing is known to us, but either, 1. By sense immediately perceiving things external, and representing them to the fantasy and intellect. Or, 2. By the intellect's own conceiving of other things by the similitude of things sensed. 3. Or by immediate internal intuition or sensation of the acts of the soul in itself. 4. Or by reason's collection of the nature of other things, from the similitude and effect of such perceived operations.

I. By the external senses we perceive all external sensed things, and we imagine and know them as so perceived.

II. By the intellection of these, we conceive of other things as like them; forming universal conceptions, and applying them to such individuals as are beyond the reach of our senses. (As we think of men, trees, beasts, fishes, &c. in the Indies, as like those which we have seen; and of sounds there, as like those which we have heard; and of the taste of fruits, by the similitude of such as we have tasted, &c.)

III. How sense itself, intellection itself, volition itself, and internal affections, are perceived, is no small controversy among philosophers. That we do perceive them, by the great wisdom and goodness of our Creator, we are sure; but how we do it we can scarcely describe; as knowing it better by the experience of that perception itself, than by a knowledge of the causes and nature of the acts. It is most commonly said, that the intellect knoweth its own acts by reflection, or, as Ockham, by intuition; and that it knoweth what sense is, and what volition, by some species or image of them in the fantasy which it beholdeth. But such words give no man a true knowledge of the thing inquired of, unless withal he read the solution experimentally in his own soul. I know not what the meaning of a reflect act is: is it the same act which is called direct and reflect? and doth the intellect know, that it knoweth by the very same act by which it knoweth other things? If so, why is it called reflect; and what is that reflection? But the contrary is commonly said, that divers objects make divers acts; and therefore to know e. g. that this is paper, and to know that I know this, are two acts, and the latter is a reflecting of the former. But the former act is gone, and nothing in the instant that it is done; and therefore is in itself no intelligible object of a reflecting act: but, as remembered, it may be known; or rather, that remembering is knowing what is past, by a marvellous retention of some impress of it, which no man can well comprehend, so as to give an account of it. And why may not the same memory, which retaineth the unexpressible record of an act past an hour or many years ago, be also the book where the intellect readeth its own act as past immediately in the foregoing instant? But surely this is not the first knowing that we know. Before the act of memory, the intellect immediately perceiveth its own particular acts; and so doth the sense. By one and the same act, we see, and perceive that we see; and by one and the same act, I think, we know, and know that we know, and this by a consciousness or internal sense, which is the immediate act of the essence of the faculty: and choose whether you will say that such two objects may constitute one act; or whether you will say, that the latter (the act itself) is not properly to be called an object. For the various senses of the word object must be considered in the decision of that. Man's soul is God's image: when God knoweth himself and his own knowledge, and when he willeth or loveth himself and his own will or love; here we must either say, that himself, his knowledge and will, is not properly to be called an object; or else that the object and the act are purely the same, without the least real difference; but we name them differently, as inadequate conceptions of one being; and why may it not be so in a lower sort in the soul that is God's image? that is, that the understanding's most internal act, viz. the knowing or perceiving when it knoweth any thing that it knoweth. It is not really compounded of an act and an object (as the knowledge of distinct objects is); but that either its act is not properly to be called its object, or that act and object are not two things, but two inadequate conceptions of one thing.

And how doth the soul perceive its own volitions? To say that volitions, which are acts of the intellectual soul, must be sensate, and so make a species on the fantasy, as sensate things do, and be known only in that species, is to bring down the higher faculty, and subordinate it to the lower, that it may be intelligible: while it is certain that we shall never here perfectly understand the solution of these difficulties, is it not pardonable, among other men's conjectures, to say, that the noble faculty of sense (because brutes have it) is usually too basely described by philosophers? And that intellection and volition in the rational soul are a superior, eminent sort of sensation, transcending that of brutes; and that *intelligere et velle* are *eminenter sentire;* and that the intellect doth by understanding other things eminently see or sense, and so understand that it understandeth; and that the will doth by willing feel that it willeth: when I consult my experience, I must either say thus, or else that intellection and volition so immediately ever move the internal sense, that they are known by us only as acts compounded with that sense.

But I am gone too far before I was aware.

IV. The soul thus knowing or feeling its own acts, doth in the next place rationally gather, 1. That it hath power to perform them, and is a substance so empowered. 2. That there are other such substances with the like acts. 3. And there is one prime transcendent substance, which is the cause of all the rest which hath infinitely nobler acts than ours.

And thus sense and reason concur to our knowledge of God, by showing us, and perceiving that image in which by similitude we must know him. The fiery, ethereal, or solar nature is (at least) the similitude of spirits: and by condescending similitude, God in Scripture is called Light, and the FATHER of LIGHTS, in whom is no darkness; allowing and inviting us to think of his glory by the similitude of the sun or light. But intellectual spirits are the highest nature known to us, and these we know intimately by most near perception; by the similitude of these therefore we must conceive of God.

A soul is a self-moving life or vital substance, actuating the body to which it is united. God is supereminently essential life, perfect in himself, as living infinitely and eternally, and giving being to all that is, and motion to all that moveth, and life to all that liveth.

A reasonable soul is essentially an understanding power: and God is super-eminently an infinite understanding, knowing himself and all things perfectly.

A reasonable soul is essentially a rational appetite or will, necessarily loving himself, and all that is apprehended every way, and congruously good. God is super-eminently an infinite will or love, necessarily loving himself; and his own image, which yet he freely made by communicative love.

All things that were made by this Infinite Goodness, were made good and very good. All his works of creation and providence (however misconceived of by sinners) are still very good. All the good of the whole creation is as the heat of this Infinite, Eternal Fire of Love. And having made the world good, in the good of nature, and the good of order, and the good of mutual love, he doth by his continual influx maintain and perfect it. His power moveth, his wisdom governeth, and his love felicitateth. And man he moveth as man, he ruleth him by moral laws as man; and he is his perfect lover, and perfect amiable object and end: as our Creator making us in this natural capacity and relation; as our Redeemer restoring and advancing us to blessed union with himself; and as our Sanctifier and Glorifier preparing us for, and bringing us to, celestial perfection. And thus must God be conceived of that we may love him: and false and defective conceptions of him are the great impediments of our love: and we love him so little, (much,) because we so little know him: and therefore it is not the true knowledge of God, which Paul here maketh a competitor with love.

II. And as we know God by ascending from his works and image, in the same order must our love ascend. The first acts of it will be towards God in his works, and the next will be towards God in his relation to us, and the highest towards God as essentially perfect and amiable in himself.

I will therefore now apply this to the soul that feareth lest he love not God, because he perceiveth not himself either to know or love him immediately in the perfection of his essence.

1. Do you truly love the image of God on the soul of man; that is, a heavenly life, and light, and love? Do you not only from bare conviction commend, but truly love a soul devoted to God, full of his love, and living in obedience to his laws, and doing good to others according to his power? This is to love God in his image? God is infinite power, wisdom, and goodness, or love: to love true wisdom and goodness as such, is to love God in his works.

Especially with these two qualifications: 1. Do you love to have wisdom, and goodness, and love as universal as is possible? Do you long to have families, cities, kingdoms, and all the world, made truly holy, wise, and united in love to one another? The most universal wisdom and goodness is most like to God; and to love this is to love God in his image.

2. Do you love wisdom and goodness in yourselves, and not in others only? Do you long to be liker to God in your capacity, and more near him and united to him? that is, do you long to know him and his will more clearly, and to enjoy a holy communion with him and his holy ones in the fullest mutual love, (loving and being beloved,) and to delight your souls in his joyful praises, in the communion of saints? This is certainly the love of God. Our union is by love: he that would be united to God and his saints in Jesus Christ, that would fain know him more, and love him better, and praise and obey him joyfully in perfection, doth undoubtedly love him.

And here I would earnestly caution you against two common deceits of men by counterfeit love. I. Some think that they love God safely, because they love him as the God of nature, and cause of all the natural being, order, and goodness which is in the whole frame of heaven and earth: this is to love somewhat of God, or to love him *secundum quid*, in one respect; but if they love him not also as he is the wise, and holy, and righteous Ruler of mankind, and as he requireth us to be holy, and would make us holy, and love not to please his governing will, they love him not as God with a saving love. I have elsewhere mentioned the saying of Adrian (after pope) in his Quodlib. that an unholy person may not only love God, as he is the glorious cause of the world and natural good, but may rather choose to be himself annihilated, and be no man, than that there should be no God, were it a thing that could be made the matter of his choice: and indeed I dare not say that every man is holy, who had rather be annihilated than one kingdom should be annihilated, when many heathens would die to save their country or their prince; much less dare I say that all shall be saved that had rather be annihilated than there should be no world, or be no God; but, saith the aforesaid schoolman, it is the love of God as our holy Governor, and a love of his holy will, and of our conformity thereto, that is saving love.

II. And I fear that no small number do deceive themselves in thinking that they love holiness, as the image of God in themselves and others, when they understand not truly what holiness is, but take something for it that is not it. Holiness is this uniting love to God and man, and a desire of more perfect union. To love holiness, is to love this love itself; to love all of God that is in the world, and to desire that all men may be united in holy love to God and one another, and live in his praise, and the obedience of his will. But I fear too many take up some opinions that are stricter than other men's, and call some things sin which others do not, and get a high esteem of some particular church order, and form or manner of worshipping God, which is not of the essence or holiness; and then they take themselves for a holy people, and other men for profane and loose, and so they love their own societies for this which they mistake for holiness; and instead of that uniting love which is holiness indeed, they grow into a factious enmity to others, reproaching them and rejoicing in their hurt, as taking them for the enemies of God.

2. And as God must be loved in his image on his servants, so must he in his image on his word. Do you love the holy laws of God, as they express that holy wisdom and love which is his perfection? Do you love them as they would rule the world in holiness, and bring mankind to true wisdom and mutual love? Do you love this word as it would make you wise and holy; and therefore love it most when you use it most, in reading, hearing, meditation, and practice? Surely to love the wisdom and holiness of God's laws and promises, is to love God in his image there imprinted, even in that glass where he hath purposely showed us that of himself which we must love.

3. But no where is God's image so refulgent to us, as in his Son, our Saviour Jesus Christ: in him therefore God must be loved. Though we never saw him, yet what he was, even the holy Son of God, separate from sinners, the gospel doth make known to us; as also what wondrous love he hath manifested to lost mankind. In him are all the treasures of wisdom and goodness: both an example, and a doctrine, and a law of wisdom, holiness, and peace

he hath given to the world: in this gospel faith seeth him, yea, seeth him as now glorified in heaven, and made Head over all things to the church; the King of love, the great High Priest of love, the Teacher of love, and the express image of the Father's person. Are the thoughts of this glorious image of God now pleasing to you, and is the wisdom, holiness, and love of Christ now amiable to you in believing? If so, you love God in his blessed Son. And as he that hath seen the Son hath seen the Father, so he that loveth the Son loveth the Father also.

4. Yet further, the glory of God will shine most clearly in the celestial glorified church, containing Christ and all the blessed angels and saints, who shall for ever see the glory of God, and love, obey, and praise him, in perfect unity, harmony, and fervency! You see not this heavenly society and glory, but the gospel revealeth it, and faith believeth it: doth not this blessed society, and their holy work, seem to you the most lovely in all the world? Is it not pleasing to you to think in what perfect joy and concord they love and magnify God, without all sinful ignorance, disaffection, dulness, discord, or any other culpable imperfection? I ask not only, whether your opinion will make you say that this society and state is best; but whether you do not so really esteem it as that it hath the pleasing desires of your souls? Would you not fain be one of them, and be united to them, and join in their perfect love and praise? If so, this is to love God in that most glorious appearance where he will show forth himself to man to be beloved.

But here true believers may be stopped with doubting, because they are unwilling to die, and till we die this glory is not seen. But it is one thing to love heaven, and God there manifested; and another thing to love death which standeth in the way. Nature teacheth us to loathe death as death, and to desire, if it might be, that this cup might pass by us; though faith make it less dreadful, because of the blessed state that followeth: but he that loveth not blood-letting, or physic, may love health. It is not death, but God and the heavenly perfection in glory, which we are called to love. What if you could come to this glory without dying, as Enoch and Elias did, would you not be willing to go thither?

5. And he that loveth God in all these his appearances to man, in his works and image on his saints, in the wisdom, holiness, and goodness of his word, in the wisdom, love, and holiness of his Son, and in the perfection of his glory in the heavenly society, doth certainly also love him in the highest respect, even as he is himself that blessed essence, that perfect greatness, wisdom, and goodness, or life, light, and love, which is the beginning and end of all things, and the most amiable object of all illuminated minds, and of every sanctified will, and of all our harmonious praise for ever. For whatever become of that dispute, whether we shall see God's essence in itself, as distinct from all created glory, (the word *seeing* being here ambiguous,) it is sure that we can even now have abstracting thoughts of the essence of God as distinct from all creatures, and our knowledge of him then will be far more perfect.

It should be most pleasant to every believer to think that God is; even that such a perfect glorious being is existent: as if we heard of one man in another land, whom we were never like to see, who in wisdom, love, and all perfections excelled all men that ever were in the world, the thoughts of that man would be pleasing to us; and we should love him because he is amiable in his excellency. And so doth the holy soul when it thinketh of the infinite amiableness of God.

6. But the highest love of the soul to God, is in taking in all his amiableness together; and when we think of him as related to ourselves, as our Creator, Redeemer, Sanctifier, and Glorifier, and as related to all his church, and to all the world, as the cause and end of all that is amiable; and when we think of all those amiable works which these relations do respect, his creation and conservation of the whole world, his redemption of mankind, his sanctifying and glorifying of all his chosen ones, his wonderful mercies to ourselves for soul and body, his mercies to his church on earth, his inconceivable mercies to the glorified church in heaven, the glory of Christ, angels, and men, and their perfect knowledge, love, and joyful praises, and then think what that God is in himself that doth all this: this complexion of considerations causeth the fullest love to God. And though unlearned persons cannot speak or think of all these distinctly and clearly, as the Scripture doth express them, yet all this is truly the object of their love, though with confusion of their apprehensions of it.

But I have not yet done, nor indeed come up to the point of trial. It is not every kind or degree of love to God in these respects that will prove to be saving. He is mad that thinks there is no God: and he that believeth that there is a God, doth believe that he is most powerful, wise, and good, and therefore must needs have some kind of love to him. And I find that there are a sort of deists or infidels now springing up among us, who are confident, that all, or almost all men shall be saved, because, say they, all men do love God. It is not possible, say they, that a man can believe God to be God, that is, to be the best, and to be love itself, and the cause of all that is good and amiable in heaven and earth, and yet not love him: the will is not so contrary to the understanding, nor can be. And say the same men, he that loveth his neighbour, loveth God; for it is for his goodness that he loveth his neighbour, and that goodness is God's goodness appearing in man: he that loveth sun, and moon, and stars, meat, and drink, and pleasure, loveth God, for all this is God's goodness in his works; and out of his works he is unknown to us: and therefore, they say, that all men love God, and all men shall be saved; or at least, all that love their neighbours; for God by us is no otherwise to be loved.

For answer to these men, 1. It is false that God is no otherwise to be loved than as in our neighbour: I have told you before, undeniably, of several other respects or appearances of God, in which he is to be loved: and he that is not known to us as separate from all creatures, is yet known to us as distinct from all creatures, and is and must be so loved by us: else we are idolaters if we suppose the creatures to be God themselves, and love and honour them as God: even those philosophers that took God for the inseparable soul of the world, yet distinguished him from the world, which they thought he animated, and indeed doth more than animate.

2. And it is false that every one loveth God who loveth his neighbour, or his meat, drink, and fleshly pleasure, or any of the accommodations of his sense. For nature causeth all men to love life, and self, and pleasure for themselves: and these are beloved even by atheists that believe not that there is a God; and consequently such men love their neighbours not for God, but for themselves, either because they are like them, or because they please them, or serve their interest, or delight them by society and converse; as birds and beasts do love each other that think not of a God. And if all should be saved that so love one another, or that love their own pleasure, and that

which serveth it, not only all wicked men, but most brute creatures should be saved. If you say, they shall not be damned, it is true, because they are not moral agents, capable of salvation or damnation, nor capable of moral government and obedience; and therefore even the creatures that kill one another are not damned for it: but certainly as man is capable of salvation or damnation, so is he of somewhat more as the means or way, than brutes are capable of, and he is saved or damned for somewhat which brutes never do. Many a thousand love the pleasure of their sense, and all things and persons which promote it, that never think of God, or love him. And it is not enough to say that even this natural good is of God, and therefore it is God in it which they love; for it will only follow that it is something made and given by God which they love, while they leave out God himself. That God is essentially in all things good and pleasant which they love, doth not prove that it is God which they love, while their thoughts and affections do not include him.

3. But suppose it were so, that to love the creature were to love God, is not then the hating of the creature the hating of God? If those same men that love meat and drink, and sensual delight, and love their neighbours for the sake of these, or for themselves, as a dog doth love his master, do also hate the holiness of God's servants, and the holiness and justice of his word and government, and that holiness and order of heart and life which he commandeth them, do not these men hate God in hating these? And that they hate them, their obstinate aversation showeth, when no reason, no mercy, no means, can reconcile their hearts and lives thereto.

4. I therefore ask the infidel objector, whether he shall be saved that loveth God in one respect, and hateth him in another? that loveth him as he causeth the sun to shine, the rain to fall, the grass to grow, and giveth life and prosperity to the world; but hateth him as he is the author of those laws, and duties, and that holy government, by which he would bring them to a voluntary right order, and make them holy, and fit for glory, and would use them in his holy service, and restrain them from their inordinate lusts and wills? How can love prepare or fit any man for that which he hateth or doth not love? if the love of fleshly interest and pleasure prepare or fit them to seek that, and to enjoy it, (the little time that it will endure,) how should this love make them fit for heaven, for a life of holiness with God and saints? It is this that they love not, and will not love (for if they truly loved it they should have it); yea, it is this that they hate, and will not accept or be persuaded to. And what a fond conceit then is it to think that they shall have heaven that never loved it, no nor the small beginnings here of the heavenly nature and life, and all because they loved the pleasures of the flesh on earth, and loved God and their neighbours for promoting it?

5. Yea, I would ask the infidel, whether God will save men for rebelling against him? Their love to their flesh and to the creature, as it is inordinate, and taketh God's place, and shutteth out the love of holiness and heaven, is their great sin and idolatry; and shall this be called a saving love of God? What gross self-deceit hath sensuality taught these men!

6. I grant them therefore that all men that believe that there is a God, do love somewhat of God, or *secundum quid*, or in some partial respect, have some kind of love to God. But it is not a love to that of God, which must save, felicitate, and glorify souls: meat and drink, and fleshly sports, do not this; but heavenly glory, wisdom, holiness, and love to God, and man for God; and this they love not, and therefore never shall enjoy: nay, that of God which should save and felicitate them they hate; and hated holiness is none of theirs, nor ever can be, till they are changed. And so much to the infidel's objection.

7. I add therefore in the last place, to help men in the trial of their love to God, that their love must have these two qualifications.

1. They must love that of God which maketh man happy, and is indeed the end of his nature, and sanctification; and that is, not only the comforts of this transitory natural life and flesh, but the fore-described union and communion with God, in perfect knowledge, love, and praise. 2. This love to God must be predominant, and prevail against the power of alluring objects, which Satan would use to turn our hearts from him, and to keep out holy, heavenly love. Damning sin consisteth in loving somewhat that is good and lovely, and that is of God; but it is not simply in loving it, but in loving it inordinately, instead of God or greater things, and out of its due time, and rank, and measure, and so as to hinder that love which is our holiness and happiness. Moral good consisteth not in mere entity, but in order; and disorderly love even of real good is sinful love.

Therefore when all is said, the old mark which I have many and many times repeated, is it that must try the sincerity of your love; viz. If, 1. in the esteem of a believing mind; 2. And in the choice and adherence of a resolved will; 3. And in the careful, serious endeavours of your lives; you prefer the knowing, loving, obeying, and joyful praising of God, begun here and perfected in glory, as the benefit of our redemption by Christ, before all the interests of this fleshly life, the pleasures, profits, and honours of this world; that is, before the pleasures of sin and sensuality for this transitory season. Or, in Christ's words, (Matt. vi. 33,) if you SEEK FIRST THE KINGDOM OF GOD, AND HIS RIGHTEOUSNESS, and trust him to superadd all other things. This is that love of God and goodness which must save us: and he that loveth God, even in these high respects, a little, and loveth his fleshly pleasure so much more, as that he will not consent to the regulating of his lusts, but will rather venture or let go his salvation than his sins, hath no true saving love to God.

Object. There is scarce any fornicator, drunkard, glutton, swearer, or other rash and sensual sinner, but believeth that God is better than the creature, and that it were better for him to live to God in love and holiness, than to live in sinful pleasures: and therefore though he live in sin against this knowledge, it seemeth that with the rational will he loveth God and goodness best, because he judgeth them best.

Answ. 1. It is one thing, what the judgment saith, and another thing how it saith it. A speculative judgment may drowsily say, that God and holiness are best, when yet it saith it but as a dreaming opinion, which prevaileth not with the will to choose them, having at the same time so strong an apprehension of the pleasures of sin as carrieth away the will and practice.

2. It is one thing therefore to love God under the notion of being best, and another thing to love him best. For the will can cross such a notion of the understanding; at least by an omission, as appeareth by the sin of Adam, which began in the will (or else had been necessitated). The same understanding which sluggishly saith God or holiness is better, yet may more clearly and vehemently say, lust is pleasant, or pleasure of the flesh is good; and being herein seconded with the strong apprehensions of sense

and fantasy, the will may follow this simple judgment, and neglect the comparate.

3. It is one thing for the understanding to say, that God is more amiable to one that hath a heart to love him, and a suitable disposition; and another thing to say, he is now more amiable to me: those can say the first that cannot truly say the latter, and therefore love not God as best, and above all.

4. It is one thing for the understanding sometimes under conviction to say, God and holiness are best for me, and I ought to love them best, and then to lay by the exercise of this judgment in the ordinary course of life, (though it be not contradicted,) and to live in the continual apprehension of the goodness of sensual pleasure; and another thing to keep the judgment that God and holiness are best, in ordinary exercise. For the will doth not always follow the judgment that we had before, but that which we have at present; and that which we exercise not, we have not at that time in act: and it is not a mere power or habit of knowledge which ruleth the will, but the present act. Many a man is said to know that which he doth not think of, when indeed he doth not know it at that time, but only would know it if he thought of it; as a man in his sleep is said to know what he knew awake, when indeed he knoweth it not actually till he be awake.

Object. But true grace is rather to be judged by the habit, than by the present acts.

Answ. By the habit of the will it is, that is, by habitual love, for that will command the most frequent acts: but I propose it to the consideration of the judicious, whether an ordinary habit of drowsy knowledge, or belief that God and holiness are best, may not be ordinarily kept out of act, and consist with a prevailing habit of sensuality or love of forbidden pleasure in the will, and with a privation of prevalent habitual love to God and holiness. I suppose with most such sinners this is the true case: the understanding said lately, It is best for thee to love God, and live to him, and deny thy lust; and it oft forgetteth this, while it still saith with sense, that fleshly pleasure is desirable: and at other times it saith, Though God be best, thou mayst venture at the present on this pleasure; and so lets loose the corrupted will, reserving a purpose to repent hereafter, as apprehending most strongly at the present, that just now sensual delight may be chosen, though holiness will be best hereafter.

Object. But if a habit will not prove that we sincerely love and prefer God, how shall any man know that he loveth and preferreth him, when the best oft sin; and in the act of sin God is not actually preferred.

Answ. 1. I told you that a habit of true love will prove sincerity, though not a habit of true opinion or belief, which is not brought into lively and ordinary act: uneffectual faith may be habitual. Yea, such an uneffectual counterfeit half love, which I before described to you, may be habitual, and yet neither act nor habit saving.

2. The sins of godly men are not prevalent absolutely against the being, operation, or effects of the love of God and holiness; for even when they sin, these live and are predominant in all other things, and in the main bent and course of life; but only they prevail against some degree of holy love, perhaps both in the act and habit, for such sins are not ungodliness, but imperfection of godliness, and the effects of that imperfection.

3. When godly men fall into a great extraordinary sin, it is not to be expected that they should comfortably discern the sincerity of their love to God either by that sin, or in that sin; but they may discern it, 1. By the course of a godly life, where the prevalence of the habit appeareth in the power and stream of acts; and, 2. By their repentance for, and abhorring and forsaking of, that sin, which stopped and darkened their love to God. And these two together, viz. a resolved course of living unto God, and repentance and hatred of every sin which is against it, and especially of greater sins, will show the sincerity and power of holy love.

Object. But then one that sinneth daily, e. g. by passion, or too much love to the world, or creatures, and by omissions, &c. shall never be sure that he sincerely loveth God, because this is a course of sin, and he cannot have such assurance till he forsake it.

Answ. One that ordinarily committeth gross and wilful sin, that is, such sin as he had rather keep than leave, and as he would leave if he were but sincerely willing, hath no predominant love of God; at least in act; and therefore can have no assurance of it: but one that is ordinarily guilty of mere infirmities may at the same time know that the love of God doth rule both in his heart and life. The passion of fear, or of anger, or of sorrow may be inordinate, and yet God loved best, because the will hath so weak a power over them, that a man that is guilty of them may truly say, I would fain be delivered from them. And some inordinate love of life, health, wealth, friends, honour, may stand with a more prevailing love of God, and the prevalency be well perceived. But what greater actual sins (as Noah's or Lot's drunkenness, David's adultery and murder, Peter's denial of Christ) are or are not consistent with true love to God, is a case that I have elsewhere largely handled, and is unmeet for a short decision here.

Object. But when I feel my heart, desires, and delights all cold to God and holiness, and too hot after fleshly, worldly things, may I not conclude that I love these better?

Answ. Sensible near things may have much more of the passionate part of our love, our desires, and delights, and yet not be best loved by us. For God and things spiritual being out of the reach of sense, are not so apt or like to move our sense and passion immediately to and by themselves. As I said before, that is best loved, which hath, 1. The highest esteem of the understanding. 2. The most resolved prevalent choice of the will. 3. And the most faithful endeavours of our life.

And many a christian mistaketh his affection to the thing itself, because of his strangeness to the place and to the change that death will make. If the weakest christian could have, without dying, the clear knowledge of God, the communion of faith and love by his Spirit; could he love God but as much as he would love him, and answerably taste his love, in every prayer, in every promise, in every sacrament, in every mercy; could his soul keep a continual sabbath of delight in God, and in his saints and holy worship, this seemeth to him more desirable and pleasing than all the treasures of the world. And he that desireth this communion with God, desireth heaven in reality, though he fear the change that death will make, because of the weakness of faith, and our strangeness to the state of separate souls.

CHAPTER XX.

THE SECOND PART OF THE EXHORTATION; REST IN THIS, THAT YOU ARE KNOWN WITH LOVE TO GOD.

2. To be KNOWN OF GOD here signifieth to be approved and loved of him, and consequently that all our concerns are perfectly known to him and regarded by him.

This is the full and final comfort of a believer. Our knowledge and love of God, in which we are agents, are, 1. The evidence that we are known with love to God, and so our comfort (as is said) by way of evidence. 2. And they are our comfort in their very exercise. But the chief part of our comfort is from God, not only as the object of our love, but as the lover of us and all his saints, even in our passive receiving of the blessed effects of his love for ever: when a christian therefore hath any discerning of his interest in this love of God, by finding that he loveth God and goodness, here he must finally anchor his soul, and quietly rest in all temptations, difficulties, and tribulations.

1. Our enemies know us not, but judge of us by blinding interest, and the bias of their false opinions, and by an easy belief of false reports, or by their own ungrounded suspicions: and therefore we are odious to them, and abused, slandered, and persecuted by them. But God knoweth us, and will justify our righteousness, and bring all our innocency into light, and stop the mouth of all iniquity.

2. Strangers know us not, but receive such characters of us as are brought to them with the greatest advantage: and even good men may think and speak evil of us (as Bernard and other of the Waldenses, and many fathers of many godly men that were called heretics, and many called heretics of such fathers). But to us it is a small thing to be judged of man, that is not our final judge and knoweth not our cause, and is ready to be judged with us; we have one that judgeth us and them, even the omniscient God, who knoweth every circumstance of our cause.

3. Our very friends know us not; no, not they that dwell with us: in some things they judge us better than we are, and in some things worse: for they know not our hearts; and interest and cross dispositions may deceive them; and even our bosom friends may slander us and think they speak the truth.

And when they entirely love us, their love may hurt us, while they know not what is for our good: but God knoweth us perfectly, and knoweth how to counsel us, conduct us, and dispose of us: he seeth the inwards and the outwards, the onwards and the upwards of our case, which our dearest friends are utter strangers to.

4. We know not ourselves thoroughly, nor our own concerns: we oft take ourselves to be better or worse than indeed we are: we are oft mistaken in our own hearts, and our own actions, and in our interest: we oft take that to be good for us that is bad, and that to be bad which is good and necessary. We long for that which would undo us, and fear and fly from that which would save us: we oft rejoice when we are going to the slaughter, or are at least in greatest danger; and we lament and cry when God is saving us, because we know not what he is doing. Paul saith, " I know nothing by myself, yet I judge not my own self;" that is, though I have a good conscience, yet that is not my final judge: it must go with me as God judgeth of me, and not as others or myself.

Is it not then an unspeakable comfort in all these cases, that we are known of God?

Desiring to know inordinately for ourselves, was our first sin; and this sin is our danger, and our constant trouble: but to be to God as a child to his father, who taketh care to love him and obey him, and in all things trusteth his father's love, as knowing that he careth for him, this is our duty, our interest, and our only peace.

Remember then with comfort, O my soul, 1. Thy Father knoweth what it is fittest for thee to do. His precepts are wise, and just, and good: thou knowest not but by his word. Love, therefore, and submit to all his laws: the strictest of them are for thy good. Thy Guide, and not thou, must lead the way: go not before him, nor without him; nor stay behind him: in this night and wilderness, if thou have not his light and presence, how forlorn, erroneous, and comfortless wilt thou be! He knoweth thy heart, and knoweth thy enemies, temptations, and dangers, and therefore best knoweth how to guide thee, and what to put into his laws and into thy duty.

2. He knoweth what place, what state of life, of health, of wealth, of friends is best for thee. None of these are known to thee. He knoweth whether ease or pain be best: the flesh is no fit judge, nor an ignorant mind. That is best which will prove best at last; which he that foreknoweth all events knoweth. That therefore is best which Infinite wisdom and love doth choose. Ease and pain will have their end: it is the end that must teach us how to estimate them: and who but God can foretel thee the end?

He knoweth whether liberty or imprisonment be best. Liberty is a prison, if sin prevail, and God be not there. A prison is a palace, if God by his love will dwell there with us. There is no thraldom but sin and God's displeasure; and no true liberty but his love.

3. He knoweth whether honour or dishonour be best for thee. If the esteem of men may facilitate their reception of the saving truth of God which is preached to them, God will procure it, if he have work to do by it; if not, how little is it to be regarded! What doth it add to me to be highly esteemed or applauded by men, who are hasting to the dust, where their thoughts of me and all the world are at an end? When I see the skulls of the dead, who perhaps once knew me, how little doth it now concern me what thoughts of me were once within that skull? And as for the immortal soul, if it be in the world of light, it judgeth as God judgeth by his light: if in hell, I have no more cause to be troubled at their malice than at the devil's; and I have little cause to rejoice that those damned souls did once applaud me.

Oh miserable men, that have no better than the hypocrites' reward, to be seen and honoured of men! God's approbation is the felicitating honour! He will own all in me that is his own, and all that he owneth is everlastingly honoured. "The Lord knoweth the way of the righteous," Psal. i. 6; for it is his way; the way which he prescribeth them, and in which he did conduct them. Good and evil are now so mixed in me, that it is hard for me fully to discern them; but the all-seeing God doth discern them, and will separate them.

4. Thy heavenly Father knoweth whether it be best for thee to abound or want; and with what measure of worldly things it is fittest for thee to be intrusted. Abundance hath abundant snares, and cares, and troubling employments, which divert our thoughts from things of real and perpetual worth:

provision is desirable according to its usefulness to our work and end. It is far better to need little and have little, than to have much, and need it all; for it cannot be got, or kept, or used, without some troublesome and hurtful effects of its vanity and vexation. Let the foolish desire to be tired and burdened with provision, and lose the prize by turning their helps into a snare, and miss of the end by overloving the way: my Father knoweth what I want, and he is always able to supply me with a word. It doth not impoverish him to maintain all the world. His store is not diminished by communication. "The Lord is my Shepherd, what then can I need?" Psal. xxiii. 1. How oft have I found that he careth for me, and that it is better to be at his finding and provision, than to have been my own carver, and to have cared for myself! Blessed be my bounteous Father, who hath brought me so near to the end of my race, with very little care for provision in my way, and with lesser want: necessaries I never wanted, and superfluities are not wanted. Blessed be that wise and gracious Lord, that hath not given me up to greedy desires, nor insnared and burdened me with needless plenty. How safe, how easy and comfortable a life is it, to live in the family of such a Father, and with a thankful carelessness to trust his will, and take that portion as best which he provideth for us! and into what misery do foolish prodigals run, who had rather have their portion in their own hand than in their Father's!

5. Thy heavenly Father knoweth with what kind and measure of trials and temptations it is fit that thou shouldst be exercised: it is his work to permit, and bound, and order them; it is thy work to beg his grace to overcome them, and watchfully and constantly to make resistance, and in trial to approve thy faithfulness to God: "Blessed are they that endure temptations; for when they are tried they shall receive the crown of life," James i. If he will try thee by bodily pain and sickness, he can make it turn to the health of thy soul: perhaps thy diseases have prevented some mortal soul diseases which thou didst not fear. If he will try thee by men's malice, injury, or persecution, he knoweth how to turn it to thy good; and in season to bring thee out of trouble: he will teach thee by other men's wickedness to know what grace hath cured or prevented in thyself; and to know the need of trusting in God alone, and appealing to his desirable judgment: he that biddeth thee, when thou art reviled and persecuted, and loaded with false reports for righteousness' sake, to rejoice and be exceeding glad, because of the great reward in heaven, can easily give thee what he doth command, and make thy sufferings a help to this exceeding joy.

If he will try thee by Satan's molesting temptations, and suffer him to buffet thee, or break thy peace, by melancholy disquietments and vexatious thoughts, from which he hath hitherto kept thee free, he doth but tell thee from how much greater evil he hath delivered thee, and make thy fears of hell a means to prevent it, and call thee to thy Saviour to seek for safety and peace in him.

If it please him to permit the malicious tempter to urge thy thoughts to blasphemy, or other dreadful sin, (as it ordinarily falleth out with the melancholy,) it telleth thee from what malice grace preserveth thee, and what Satan would do were he let loose: it calleth thee to remember that thy Saviour himself was tempted by Satan to as great sin as ever thou wast, even to worship the devil himself; and that he suffered him to carry about his body from place to place, which he never did by thee: it tells thee therefore that it is not sin to be tempted to sin, but to consent; and that Satan's sin is not laid to our charge: and though our corruption is such, as that we seldom are tempted, but some culpable blot is left behind in us, for we cannot say, as Christ, that Satan hath nothing in us; yet no sin is less dangerous to man's damnation, than the melancholy thoughts which such horrid vexatious temptations cause; both because the person being distempered by a disease, is not a volunteer in what he doth; and also because he is so far from loving and desiring such kind of sin, that it is the very burden of his life; they make him weary of himself, and he daily groaneth to be delivered from them. And it is certain that love is the damning malignity of sin; and that there is no more sin than there is will; and that no sin shall damn men which they had rather leave than keep; and therefore forgiveness is joined to repentance: drunkards, fornicators, worldlings, ambitious men, love their sin; but a poor, melancholy soul that is tempted to ill thoughts, or to despair, or terror, or to excessive griefs, is far from loving such a state. The case of such is sad at present; but oh how much sadder is the case of them that are lovers of pleasure more than of God, and prosper and delight in sin!

6. God knoweth how long it is best for me to live. Leave then the determination of the time to him. All men come into the world on the condition of going out again: die we must, and is it not fitter that God choose the time than we? Were it left to our wills how long we should live on earth, alas, how long should many of us be kept out of heaven, by our own desires! And too many would stay here till misery made them impatient of living. But our lives are his gift, and in his hand, who knoweth the use of them, and knoweth how to proportion them to that use, which is the justest measure of them. He chose the time and place of my birth, and he chooseth best: why should I not willingly leave to his choice, also, the time, and place, and manner of my departure? I am known of him; and my concerns are not despised by him. He knoweth me as his own, and as his own he hath used me, and as his own he will receive me. "The Lord knoweth the days of the upright, and their inheritance shall be for ever," Psal. xxxvii. 18. And if he bring me to death through long and painful sickness, he knoweth why, and all shall end in my salvation. "He knoweth the way that is with me, and when he hath tried me, I shall come forth as gold," Job xxiii. 10. He forsaketh us not in sickness or in death. "Like as a father pitieth his children, the Lord pitieth them that fear him; for he knoweth our frame, he remembereth that we are dust. As for man, his days are as grass; as a flower of the field, so he flourisheth; for the wind passeth over it, and it is not, and the place thereof shall know it no more: but the mercy of the Lord is from everlasting to everlasting to them that fear him." If the ox should not know his owner, nor the ass his master's crib, the owner will know his own and seek them. That we understand and know the Lord, is matter of greater joy and glorying, than all other wisdom or riches in the world, Jer. ix. 24. But that he knoweth us in life and death, on earth and in heaven, is the top of our rejoicing. "The Lord is good, and strength in the day of trouble; and he knoweth them that trust in him," Nah. i. 7. Sickness may so change my flesh that even my neighbours shall not KNOW ME; and death will make the change so great, that even my friends will be unwilling to see such an unpleasing, loathsome spectacle: but while I am carried by them to the place of darkness, that I may not be an annoyance to the living, I shall be there in the sight

of God, and my bones and dust shall be owned by him, and none of them forgotten or lost.

7. It may be that under the temptations of Satan, or in the languishing weakness or distempers of my flesh, I may doubt of the love of God, and think that he hath withdrawn his mercy from me; or at least may be unmeet to taste the sweetness of his love, or to meditate on his truth and mercies: but God will not lose his knowledge of me, nor turn away his mercy from me. "The foundation of God standeth sure, having this seal, The Lord knoweth them that are his; and, Let him that nameth the name of Christ depart from iniquity," 2 Tim. ii. 19. He can call me his child, when I doubt whether I may call him Father: he doubteth not of his right to me, nor of his graces in me, when I doubt of my sincerity and part in him. "Known unto God are all his works," Acts xv. 18. What meaneth Paul thus to describe a state of grace, (Gal. iv. 9,) "Now after ye have known God, or rather are known of God;" but to notify to us, that though our knowledge of God be his grace in us, and our evidence of his love, and the beginning of life eternal, (John xvii. 3,) yet that we are loved and known of him is the first and last, the foundation and the perfection of our security and felicity? He knoweth his sheep, and none shall take them out of his hand. When I cannot through pain or distemper remember him, or not with renewed joy or pleasure, he will remember me, and delight to do me good, and to be my salvation.

8. And though the belief of the unseen world be the principle by which I conquer this, yet are my conceptions of it lamentably dark: a soul in flesh, which acteth as the form of a body, is not furnished with such images, helps, or light, by which it can have clear conceptions of the state and operations of separated souls: but I am known of God, when my knowledge of him is dark and small: and he knoweth whither it is that he will take me, and what my state and work shall be! He that is preparing a place for me with himself, is well acquainted with it and me. All souls are his; and therefore all are known to him: he that is now the God of Abraham, Isaac, and Jacob, as being living with him while they are dead to us, will receive my departing soul to them, and to himself, to be with Christ, which he hath instructed me to commend into his hands, and to desire him to receive. He that is now making us living stones for the new Jerusalem, and his heavenly temple, doth know where every one of us shall be placed. And his knowledge must now be my satisfaction and my peace. Let unbelievers say, "How doth God know?" Psal. lxxiii. 11. But shall I doubt whether he that made the sun, be Father of lights, and whether he know his dwelling, and his continued works? Be still, O my soul, and know that he is God, Psal. xl. 10; and when he hath guided thee by his counsel, he will take thee to glory; and in his light thou shalt have light: and though now it appear not, to sight, but to faith only, what we shall be, yet we know that we shall see him as he is, and we shall appear with him in glory.

And to be KNOWN of God, undoubtedly includeth his PRACTICAL LOVE, which secureth our salvation and all that tendeth thereunto. It is not meant of such a knowledge only as he hath of all things, or of such as he hath of the ungodly. And why should it be hard to thee, O my soul, to be persuaded of the love of God.

Is it strange that he should love thee, who is Essential, Infinite Love; any more than that the sun should shine upon thee, which shineth upon all capable, recipient objects, though not upon the uncapable, which through interposing things cannot receive it? To believe that Satan, or wicked men, or deadly enemies should love me, is hard: but to believe that the God of love doth love me, should in reason be much easier than to believe that my father or mother, or dearest friend in the world, doth love me: if I do not make and continue myself incapable of his complacence by my wilful continued refusing of his grace, it is not possible that I should be deprived of it. Prov. viii. 17, "I love them that love me." Psal. cxlvi. 8, "The Lord loveth the righteous;" John xvi. 27.

2. Why should it be hard to thee to believe that He loveth thee, who doth good so universally to the world, and by his love doth preserve the whole creation, and give all creatures all the good which they possess? When his mercy is over all his works, and his goodness is equal to his wisdom and his power, and all the world is beautified by it, shall I not easily believe that it will extend to me? "The Lord is good to all," Psal. cxlv. 9; Luke xviii. 19. None is good (essentially, absolutely, and transcendently) but he alone. "The earth is full of the goodness of the Lord," Psal. xxxiii. 5. "The goodness of God endureth continually," Psal. lii. 1. "He is good and doth good," Psal. cxix. 68. And shall I not expect good from so good a God, the cause of all the good that is in the world?

3. Why should I not believe that He will love me, who so far loved the world, yea, his enemies, as to give his only begotten Son, "that whosoever believeth in him, should not perish, but have everlasting life?" John iii. 16. Having given me so precious a gift as his Son, will he think any thing too good to give me? Rom. viii. 32. Yea, still he followeth his enemies with his mercies, not leaving himself without witness to them; but filling their hearts with food and gladness, and causing his sun to shine on them, and his rain to fall on them, and by his goodness leading them to repentance.

4. Why should I not easily believe His love, which he hath sealed by that certain gift of love, the Spirit of Christ, which he hath given? "The giving of the Holy Ghost, is the shedding abroad of his love upon the heart," Rom. v. I had never known, desired, loved, or served him sincerely, but by that Spirit: and will he deny his name, his mark, his seal, his pledge, and earnest of eternal life? Could I ever have truly loved him, his word, his ways, and servants, but by the reflection of his love? Shall I question whether he love those whom he hath caused to love him? When our love is the surest gift and token of his love, shall I think that I can love him more than he loveth me, or be more willing to serve him than he is willing and ready to reward his servants? Heb. xi. 6; 1 John iii. 24; iv. 13.

5. Shall I not easily hope for good from Him, who hath made such a covenant of grace with me in Christ? who giveth me what his Son hath purchased, who accepteth me in his most Beloved, as a member of his Son? who hath bid me ask, and I shall have? and hath made to godliness the promise of this life, and that to come; and will withhold no good thing from them that walk uprightly? Will not such a gospel, such a covenant, such promises of love, secure me that he loveth me, while I consent unto his covenant terms?

6. Shall I not easily believe that he will love me, who hath loved me while I was his enemy, and called me home when I went astray, and mercifully received me when I returned? who hath given me a life full of precious mercies, and so many experiences of his love as I have had? who hath so often signified his love to my conscience; so often heard my prayers in distress, and hath made all my life,

notwithstanding my sins, a continual wonder of his mercies? Oh unthankful soul, if all this will not persuade thee of the love of him that gave it! I that can do little good to any one, yet have abundance of friends and hearers, who very easily believe that I would do them good, were it in my power; and never fear that I should do them harm. And shall it be harder to me to think well of Infinite love and goodness, than for my neighbours to trust me, and think well of such a wretch as I? What abundance of love-tokens have I yet to show, which were sent me from heaven, to persuade me of my Father's love and care!

7. Shall I not easily believe and trust His love, who hath promised me eternal glory with his Son, and with all his holy ones in heaven? who hath given me there a great Intercessor, to prepare heaven for me, and me for it; and there appeareth for me before God? who hath already brought many millions of blessed souls to that glory, who were once as bad and low as I am? and who hath given me already the seal, the pledge, the earnest, and the first-fruits of that felicity?

Therefore, O my soul, if men will not know thee, if thou were hated of all men for the cause of Christ and righteousness; if thine uprightness be imputed to thee as an odious crime; if thou be judged by the blind, malignant world, according to its gall and interest; if friends misunderstand thee; if faction, and every evil cause which thou disownest, do revile thee, and rise up against thee; it is enough, it is absolutely enough, that thou art known of God. God is all; and all is nothing that is against him, or without him. If God be for thee, who shall be against thee? How long hath he kept thee safe in the midst of dangers; and given thee peace in the midst of furious rage and wars! He hath known how to bring thee out of trouble, and to give thee tolerable ease, while thou hast carried about thee night and day the usual causes of continual torment! "His loving-kindness is better than life," Psal. lxiii. 3; but thou hast had a long unexpected life, through his loving-kindness. "In his favour is life," Psal. xxx.; and life thou hast had by and with his favour. Notwithstanding thy sin, while thou canst truly say thou lovest him, he hath promised, "that all shall work together for thy good," (Rom. viii. 28,) and he hath long made good that promise. Only ask thyself again and again, as Christ did Peter, whether indeed thou love him? And then take his love as thy full, and sure, and everlasting portion, which will never fail thee, though flesh and heart do fail: for thou shalt dwell in God, and God in thee, for evermore. Amen. 1 John iv. 12, 15, 16.

CATHOLIC UNITY:

OR

THE ONLY WAY TO BRING US ALL TO BE OF ONE RELIGION.

TO BE READ BY SUCH AS ARE OFFENDED AT THE DIFFERENCES IN RELIGION, AND ARE WILLING TO DO THEIR PART TO HEAL THEM.

TO ALL THOSE IN THE SEVERAL PARISHES OF THESE NATIONS, THAT COMPLAIN OF THE DISAGREEMENTS IN MATTERS OF RELIGION.

MEN AND BRETHREN,

As in the midst of all the impiety and dishonesty of the world, it is some comfort to us, that yet the names of piety and honesty are still in credit, and ungodliness and dishonesty are terms of disgrace; so that those that will be ungodly and dishonest, are fain to use the mask and veil of better names, to hide their wickedness; so also it is some comfort to us, in the midst of the uncharitableness and discords of this age, that yet the names of love and concord sound so well, and are honoured by those that are farthest from the things: for thus we seem agreed in the main cause, and have this advantage in our debates, that whatever shall be proved to be against love, and unity, and peace, we are all of us obliged by our professions to disown. I may suppose that all that read these words, will speak against the uncharitableness, and contentions, and divisions of the present times, as well as I. Doth it grieve my soul to hear professed christians so censoriously condemning and passionately reviling one another, while they are proudly justifying themselves? I suppose you will say, it grieves you also. Do I mourn in secret, to see so many divisions and subdivisions, and church set up against church, and pastors against pastors, in the same parishes; and each party labouring to disgrace the other and their way, that they may promote their own? I suppose you will say, you do so too. Do I lament it as the nation's shame, that in religion men are of so many minds, and manage their differences so unpeaceably, that it is become the stumbling block to the ungodly, the grief of our friends, and the derision of our enemies? I know you will say, that this also is your lamentation. And is it not a wonder indeed, that such a misery should be continued, which all men are against; and which cannot be continued but by our wilful choice? Is it not strange that we are so long without so great a blessing as unity and peace, while all men say they love it and desire it; and while we may have it if we will? But the cause is evident; while men love unity, they hate the holiness in which we must unite: while they love peace, they hate the necessary means by which it must be obtained and maintained: the way of peace they have not known; or knowing it, they do abhor it. As well as they love unity and peace, they love the causes of discord and division much better. The drunkard, and whoremonger, and worldling say they love the salvation of their souls: but yet while they love and keep their sins, they will miss of the salvation which they say they love. And so while men love their ungodliness and dividing ways, we are little the better for their love of peace. If men love health, and yet love poison, and hate both medicine and wholesome food, they may miss of health, notwithstanding they love it.

Where know you a parish in England, that hath no disagreements in matters of religion? In this parish where I live, we have not several congregations, nor are we divided into such parties as in many other places; but we have here the great division: some are for heaven, and some for earth; some love a holy, diligent life, and others hate it; some pray in their families, and teach them the word and fear of God, and others do not; some spend the Lord's day in holy exercises, and others spend much of it in idleness and vanity; some take the service of God for their delight, and others are weary of it, and live in ignorance, because they will not be at the pains to learn: some make it the principal care and business of their lives to prepare for death, and make sure of everlasting life; and others will venture their souls on the wrath of God, and cheat themselves by their own presumption, rather than be at this sweet and necessary labour to be saved. Some hate sin, and make it their daily work to root out the relics of it from their hearts and lives; and others love it and will not leave it, but hate those that reprove them, and endeavour their salvation.

And as long as this great division is unhealed, what other means can bring us to any happy unity? It would make a man's heart bleed to consider of the folly of the ungodly rout, that think it would be a happy union, if we could all agree to read one form of prayer, while some love, and others hate, the holiness which they pray for: and if we could all agree to use the sign of the cross in baptism, while one half either understand not the baptismal covenant, or wilfully violate it, and neglect, or hate and scorn that mortified, holy life, which by that solemn vow and covenant they are engaged to. They are solicitous to bring us all to unity in the gesture of receiving the sacrament of the Lord's supper, while some take Christ and life, and others take their own damnation. When they should first agree in being all the faithful servants of one Master, they make a great matter of it, that the servants of Christ and of the devil may use the same bodily posture in that worship where their hearts are as different as spirit and flesh. Poor people think that it is the want of uniformity in certain ceremonies of man's invention, that is the cause of our great divisions and distractions; when, alas! it is the want of unity in matters of greater consequence, even of faith, and love, and holiness, as I have here showed. If once we were all children of one Father, and living members of one Christ, and all renewed by one sanctifying Spirit, and aimed at one end, and walked by one rule, (the word of God,) and had that special love to one another which Christ hath made the mark of his disciples, this were an agreement to be rejoiced in indeed, which would hold us together in the most comfortable relations, and assure us that we shall live together with Christ in everlasting blessedness. But, alas! if our agreement be no better, than to sit together in the same seats, and say the same words, and use the same gestures and ceremonies, our hearts will be still distant from each other, our natures will be contrary, and the malignity of ungodly hearts will be breaking out on all occasions. And as now you hear men scorning at the practice of that religion which themselves profess, so, if God prevent it not, you may shortly see another war take off their restraint and let them loose, and then they will seek the blood of those that now they seem to be agreed with. At furthest we are sure, that very shortly we shall be separated as far as heaven and hell, if there be not now a nearer agreement than in words and outward shows and ceremonies.

It being then past doubt, that there is no happy, lasting unity, but in the Spirit and a holy life, what hindereth us from so safe, so sweet, so sure a peace? Why might not all our parishes agree on such necessary, honourable, and reasonable terms? Why is there in most places but here and there a person, or a family, that will yield to the terms of an everlasting peace, and live as men that believe they have a God to serve and please, and immortal souls to save or lose? Is not God willing that "all should be saved, and come to the knowledge of the truth," 1 Tim. ii. 4; and that all should agree in so safe a path? Why then doth he invite all, and tender them his saving mercy, and send his messengers to command and importune them to this holy concord? He would take them all into the bond of his covenant: how oft would Christ have gathered all the children of Jerusalem to him, as the hen gathereth her chickens under her wings; but it was they that would not, Matt. xxiii. 37. He would have the gospel preached to every creature, Matt. xvi. 15, 16; and would have the kingdoms of the world become the kingdoms of the Lord and of his Christ.

What then is the cause of this sad division in our parishes? Are ministers unwilling that their people should all agree in holiness? No, it would be the greatest favour you could do them, and the greatest joy that you could bring to their hearts: they would be gladder to see such a blessed unity, than if you gave them all that you have in the world. Oh how a poor minister would boast and glory of such a parish! He would bless the day that ever he came among them; and that ever he was called to the ministry; and that ever he was born into the world for their sakes. How easy would all his studies and labours be, if they were but sweetened with such success! How easily could he bear his scorns, and threatenings, and abuses, and persecution from others, if he saw but such a holy unity among his people to encourage him! So far are your teachers from excluding you from this happiness, that it is the end of their studies, and preaching, and prayers, yea, and of their lives, to bring you to partake of it. And glad would they be to preach to you, and exhort you, in hunger and thirst, in cold and nakedness, in all the contempt and derision of the world, if thereby they could but bring their parishes to agree in a life of faith and holiness.

And sure our difference is not because the godly will not admit you to join with them in the ways of God; for they cannot hinder you if they would; and they would not if they could. It is their joy to see the house of God filled with guests that have on the wedding garment.

We must conclude therefore, that it is the ungodly that are the wilful and obstinate dividers. They might be united to Christ, and reconciled to God, and they will not. They might be admitted into the communion of saints, and into the household of God, and partake of the privileges of his children; and they will not. They have leave to read, and pray, and meditate, and walk with God in a heavenly conversation, as well as any of their neighbours; but they will not. It is themselves that are the refusers, and continue the division, to the displeasing of God, and the grief of their friends, and the gratifying of Satan, and the perdition of their own immortal souls. We might all be united, and our divisions be healed, and God much honoured, and ministers and good christians be exceedingly comforted, and the church and common wealth be delivered and highly honoured, and themselves be saved from everlasting misery, if we could but get the hearty consent of these foolish, obstinate, ungodly men.

What say you, wretched souls, can you deny it? How long have your teachers been labouring in vain, to bring you to the hearty love of God, and heaven, and serious holiness! How long have they been persuading you to set up reading, and catechising, and constant fervent prayer in your families, and yet it is undone! How long have they in vain been persuading the worldling from his worldliness, and the proud person to humility, and the sensual beast from his tippling, and gluttony, and other fleshly pleasures!

And besides this, most of the disorders and divisions in the churches are caused by ungodly men. I will instance in a few particulars.

1. When we ask any godly, diligent ministers, either in London, or the country, why they do not unanimously catechise, instruct, and confer with all the inhabitants of their parishes, man by man, to help them to try their spiritual state, and to prepare in health for death and judgment? they usually answer us, that, alas! their people will not consent, but many would revile them if they should attempt it.

2. When we ask them why they do not set up the practice of discipline, which they so unanimously plead for; and why they do not call their people to confirmation, or open profession of faith and holiness, in order thereto? they tell us, that their people will not endure it; but many will rather set themselves against the ministry, and strengthen the enemy that now endangereth the church's safety, or turn to any licentious sect, than they will thus submit to the undoubted ordinances of Christ, which the churches are so commonly agreed in as a duty.

3. We have an ancient, too-imperfect version of the Psalms, which we sing in the congregations; and in the judgment of all divines that ever I spoke with about it, (of what side soever,) it is our duty to use a better version, and not to perform so excellent a part of the public worship, so lamely, and with so many blemishes. And if you ask the ministers why they do not unanimously agree on a reformed, corrected version, most of them will tell you, that their people will not bear it, but proudly and turbulently reproach them, as if they were changing the word of God.

4. In many places the sacrament of baptism is ofter used in private houses, than in the public assemblies; and if we ask the reason of so great a disorder, the ministers will tell us that it is the unruliness and wilfulness of the people, that proudly set themselves above their guides, and instead of obeying them, must rule them, and have their humours and conceits fulfilled, even in the holy things of God, or else they will revile the pastors, and make divisions in the church: and this is done by them that in other cases do seem sufficiently to reverence the place of public assembly as the house of God; and that speak against private meetings, though but for prayer, repeating sermons, or singing to the praise of God, while yet themselves are wilfully bent for such private meetings as are set up in opposition to the public, and that for the administration of so great an ordinance as the sacrament of baptism, and in cases where there is no necessity of privacy: and who knows not that our sacramental covenant with God, and engagement to a christian life, and reception into a christian state and privileges, is fitter to be done with the most honourable solemnity, than in a conventicle, in a private house?

Too many more such instances I could give you, which show who they be that are the enemies of our unity; even those that cry out against divisions while they cause them, and cry up unity, concord, and obedience, while they destroy them.

And shall we thus continue a division that doth prognosticate our everlasting division? Is there no remedy for so great a misery, when yet our poor ungodly neighbours may heal it if they will? What if the ministers of the several parishes should appoint one day of public conference with all the people of their parishes together, and desire all that are fit to speak, to debate the case, and give their reasons, why they concur not in their hearts and lives with the holy, diligent servants of the Lord? And let them hear the reasons why the godly dare not and cannot come over to their negligent, ungodly course? And so try who it is long of among them, that they are not of one mind and way? What if the ministers then urged it on them, to agree all before they parted, to unite on the terms which God will own, and all unanimously to take that course that shall be found most agreeable to his word; and whoever doth bring the fullest proof that his course is best, in reason, the rest should promise to join with him? What if we call the people together, and bespeak them as Elijah did, (1 Kings xviii. 21,) " How long halt ye between two opinions? If the Lord be God, follow him: but if Baal, then follow him." If a careless, ungodly, worldly, fleshly life be best, and most please God, and will comfort you most at death and judgment, then hold on in the way that you are in, and never purpose hereafter to repent of it, but let us all become as sensual as you. But if it be only the life of faith and holiness, and seeking first the kingdom and righteousness of God, that God, and Scripture, and reason will justify, and that will comfort the soul in the hour of extremity, and that you shall wish a thousand times you had followed, in everlasting misery, when wishing is too late, if now you continue to neglect it; doth not common reason then require, that we all now agree to go that way which all will desire to be found in at the last?

One would think, if a minister should treat thus with his parishioners, and urge such a motion as this upon them, they should not have the hearts or faces to deny, or delay, such a necessary agreement and engagement that would make their parish and their souls so happy, and which nothing but the devil and the befooled, corrupted minds of sinners hath any thing to say against! And yet it is likely we should either have such an answer as Elijah had, even silence, (" The people answered him not a word," ver. 21,) or else some plausible promise, while we have them in a good mood, which would quickly be broken and come to nothing. For indeed they are all engaged already by their baptismal covenant and profession of christianity, to the very same thing; and yet we see how little they regard it.

But yet because it is our duty to use the means for the salvation and concord of our people, and wait on God by prayer for the success, I have here showed you the only way to both. Read it impartially, and then be yourselves the judges, on whom the blame of our greatest and most dangerous divisions will be laid; and for shame, either give over complaining that men are of so many minds, and profess yourselves the enemies of unity and peace; or else give over your damning and dividing course, and yield to the Spirit of Christ, that would unite you to his body, and walk in communion with his saints: and let not these warnings be hereafter a witness against you to your confusion, which are intended for your salvation, and the healing of our discords, by

An unworthy servant of Jesus Christ, for the calling and edifying of his members,

December 10, 1659. RICHARD BAXTER.

EPHESIANS iv. 3.

ENDEAVOURING TO KEEP THE UNITY OF THE SPIRIT IN THE BOND OF PEACE.

It seems that unity and felicity are near kin, in that the world is so like affected to them both. As our felicity is in God, and we lost it by falling from God, so our unity is in God, and we lost it by departing from this Centre of unity. And as all men have still a natural desire after felicity in general; but God, who is their felicity, they neither know nor desire: so have we still a natural desire after unity in itself considered; but God, who is our unity, is little known or desired by the most. And as nature can perceive the evil of misery which is contrary to felicity, and cry out against it, and yet doth cherish the certain causes of it, and will not be persuaded to let them go; so nature can perceive the evil of division, which is contrary to unity, and cry out against it, and yet will not forbear the causes of division. And therefore as we say of felicity, Nature by philosophy seeks it, Divinity findeth it, and Religion possesseth it; so may we say of true unity, Philosophy or nature seeks it, Divinity findeth it, and Religion or holiness possesseth it. And as most of the world do miss of felicity, for all their high esteem of it, and fall into misery, for all their hatred of it, because they love not the object and way of felicity, and hate not the matter and way of misery; even so most of the world do miss of unity, for all their high esteem of unity, and fall into miserable distractions and divisions, for all their hatred of divisions, because they love not the centre and way of unity, and hate not the occasion and causes of division. And as the very reason why the most are shut out of happiness, is their own wilful refusing of the true matter and means of happiness, and no one could undo them but themselves, for all that they are loth to be undone: even so the very reason why the world attaineth not to unity, is their own wilful refusing of the true centre and means of unity; and it is themselves that are the wilful causes of their own divisions, even when they cry out against divisions. And as there is no way to happiness, but by turning to God from whom we fell, that in him we may be happy; and no way to God but by Jesus Christ as the Saviour, and the Holy Ghost as the Sanctifier; so there is no way to true unity, but by turning to God that we may be one in him; and no way to him, but being united to Christ, and being quickened by that one most Holy Spirit that animateth his members. And yet as poor souls do weary themselves in vain, in seeking felicity in their own ways and devices; so do they deceive themselves in seeking unity in ways that are quite destructive to unity. One thinks we must be united in the pope, and another in a general council; another saith, we shall never have unity till the magistrate force us all one way; and yet they would not be forced from their own way. Another turns the atheist, or infidel, or impious, by observing the divisions that be among christians; and saith, It is the Scripture, and religion, and Christ, that hath set the world together by the ears; and we shall never have unity till we all live according to nature, and cast off the needless cares and fears of another life. And thus the miserable, deluded world are groping in the dark after unity and felicity, while both are at hand, and they wickedly reject them; and many of them become so mad, as to run away from God, from Christ, from the Spirit, as if He were the cause of misery and division, who is the only Centre of felicity and unity. And thus as it is but few that arrive at happiness for all their desire of it, so it is but few that attain to unity, to such a unity as is worth the attaining to.

I dare presume to take it for granted, that all you that hear me this day, would fain have divisions taken away, and have unity, and concord, and peace through the world. What say you? would you not have us all of one mind, and of one religion? And would you not fain have an agreement, if it might be, through all the world? I am confident you would. But you little think that it is you, and such as you, that are the hinderers of it. All the question is, What mind that is that all should be one in? and what religion that is that all men should agree in? Every man would have all men of one mind, and one religion; but then it must be of his mind, and of his religion; and so we are never the nearer an agreement.

Well! what would you give now to be certainly told the only way to unity and agreement? There is but one way; when you have sought about as long as you will, you must come to that one way, or you will be never the nearer it. What would you give to know undoubtedly, which is that one way? Oh that the world were but willing to know it, and to follow it when they know it. Well! I dare promise you from the information of the Holy Ghost, here given us in this text, that now I have read to you, to tell you the only way to true unity; and blessed is he that learneth it, and walketh in it.

This text is a precept containing the work required of us, with its double object; the one the means to the other. The next verse is an exposition of this. As the natural man hath one body, and one soul, which constitute it a man, so the church which is the mystical body of Christ, is one body, consisting of many members united by one Spirit. Every commonwealth or political body hath, 1. Its constituent causes that give it its being and its unity; and, 2. Its administration and preserving causes, as laws, execution, obedience, &c. that exercise, and preserve, and perfect its being. The constitutive cause is the sovereign and the subject conjoined in their relation. So is it with the church, which is a political body, but of a transcendent kind of policy. The constitutive causes of the church, are Christ and the members united in one Spirit: and this is the final part of the duty here required, "to keep the unity of the Spirit." The preserving cause is the peaceable behaviour of the members; and this is the mediate duty here required "in the bond of peace." Our own endeavours are hereto required; because as every natural body must be eating and drinking, and fit exercise and usage be a cause of its own preservation, and not forbear these under pretence of trusting the all-sufficiency of God; and as every political body must, by government and arms, in case of need, preserve themselves under God; so must the body of Christ, the church, be diligent in using their best endeavours to preserve the being and well-being of the whole. So that you see here are two causes of the church's unity expressed: 1. The principal constitutive cause, in which our unity consisteth; and that is, "the Spirit." 2. The preserving cause, by which our unity is cherished, and that is "peace," which therefore is called "the bond" of it. The fifth and sixth verses do open this unity of Spirit in its parts, effects, and ends. "There is one hope of our calling," that is, one heaven or life eternal, which is the end of our christianity and church constitution. "There is one Lord," Jesus Christ; one Head, one Saviour, one sovereign Redeemer, to whom by this Spirit the members are all united. "There is one faith," both one sum of holy doctrine, which all that will be saved must believe, which was used to be professed by the adult at baptism, and one internal saving faith, which this Spirit causeth in our spirits, and useth it as a means of our union with Christ, in whom we do believe. "There is one baptism," or solemn covenanting with God the Father, Son, and Holy Ghost; and the same promise there to be made by all. And "there is one God the Father of all," from whom we fell, and to whom we must be recovered, and who is the end of all, and to whom Christ and all these means are the way. So that all these are implied in, and conjunct with, the "unity of the Spirit."

The sense of the text then briefly is this: as all the living true members of Christ and the church have one Spirit, and so one faith, by which they are all united to Christ the Head, and so to the Father in and by him; which union in one Spirit is your very life, and is it that constituteth you true members of Christ and his church; so it must be your care and great endeavour to preserve this Spirit in you, and this vital unity, which by this Spirit you have with Christ and one another: and the way to preserve it, is by the bond of peace among yourselves. It is here evident then, that all the members of Christ and his body have one Spirit, and in that is their union. All the question is, what Spirit this is? And that is left past all doubt in the chapter; for though the common gifts of the Spirit are sometimes called by that name, yet these are no further meant in the text than as appurtenances or additions to greater gifts. As godliness hath the promise of the common mercies of this life, as well as of the special mercies of the life to come; but yet with great difference, the latter being absolutely promised, and the former but limited, so far as God sees best for us: even so the Spirit gave to the members of the church both sanctifying grace, and common gifts; but with great difference; giving sanctification to all, and only, the members of Christ; but giving common gifts also to some others, and to them but with limitation, for sort, and season, and measure, and continuance, as God shall see good. It is then the same Holy Ghost as our Sanctifier, into whose name we are baptized, as well as into the name of the Father and the Son, and in whom we all profess to believe, that is here meant in my text. And it is only the sanctified that are the people united to Christ, and to one another. This is proved expressly by that which followeth. It is those that have the "one hope, one Lord, one faith, one baptism, one God the Father," ver. 6, 7. It is the saints and body of Christ that are to be perfected by the ministry, ver. 12. It is those that must come in the unity of faith, and knowledge of the Son of God, to a perfect man, to the measure of the stature of the fulness of Christ; and that grow up in all things in Christ the Head: it is the body that is united to him, and compacted in love, and edifieth itself in love, ver. 13, 15, 16. It is those that have so learned Christ, as to put off the old man that is corrupt, and are renewed in the spirit of their minds, and put on the new man, which after God is created in righteousness and true holiness," ver. 20—24. If therefore any words be plain, it is plain that it is true saints only that are here spoken of, that have the "unity of Spirit," which they must preserve in the "bond of peace." And therefore I shall make this observation the ground of my discourse.

Doct. The true unity of the catholic church of Christ consisteth in this, that they have all one sanctifying Spirit within them.

By the Holy Ghost within them they are all united to Christ and to one another: by this one Spirit they are all made saints, or a holy people, having one heaven for the matter of their hopes, one Christ their head, one sum of christian doctrine, which they believe, containing all the essentials of christian faith; and one living principle of faith to believe it; one solemn covenant with Christ; and one God the Father, their end and all.

It is only the sanctified that have true christian unity; and it is unholiness or ungodliness that is the cause of the miserable divisions of the world. Now, sirs, you see the only way to unity; even to have one sanctifying Spirit within us, and be all a holy people; and there is no way but this. Now you see the principal cause of division; even unholiness, and refusing the Spirit of grace.

In handling this point, I. I shall give you some propositions that are necessary for the fuller understanding of it. II. I shall demonstrate the point to you by fuller evidence of reason. III. I shall make application of it.

I. *Prop.* 1. Though it be only the sanctified that have the true union of members with Christ and the body; yet all that make profession of sanctification, and null not that profession, have an extrinsic, analogical union in profession: as the wooden or dead leg is united to the body, and the dead branch to the vine. And so even hypocrites must not only dwell among us, but be of the same visible church with us, as the chaff and tares are in the same corn-field. And as long as they seem saints we must value them and use them as saints, and love them, and have communion with them as saints: not as conceiving them certainly to be such, but probably, and by that human faith, by which we are bound to believe their profession; not as we believe God, who is infallible, but as men that are fallible; and this in several degrees, according to the several degrees of their credibility, and the probability of their profession. So that you must not after this mistake me, as if I tied our external church communion only to true saints; for then we must have communion with none; because being not able to search the hearts, we know not what professors are sincere. But yet even this external church communion belongs only to them that make profession of love and holiness, as well as of belief; and no lower profession must serve the turn.

Prop. 2. There is a common unity of human nature that we have with all men, and a common peace, that as much as in us lieth we must hold with all, Rom. xii. 18. But this is nothing to the unity in question, which belongeth to our happiness. The devils have a unity of nature, and some order and accord in evil; for if "Satan be divided, how can his kingdom stand?" Matt. xii. 26.

Prop. 3. The unity of the saints in the Spirit of holiness, consisteth in this life with much imperfection and discord, according to the imperfection of their holiness. But as grace is the seed of glory, and the beginning of eternal life, for all its weakness, and the sins that accompany it, John xvii. 3; so the unity of the Spirit of holiness is the seed and beginning of the perfect unity in heaven, for all the differences and discord that here accompany it.

II. Having showed you the only bond of unity, I come, now by fuller evidence, to convince you of the truth of what is said, and even to force it into your understandings, if you will but use your reason, and believe the word of God. It is unholiness and ungodliness that causeth our discord; and it is the spirit of holiness that is the uniting principle; and there is no true christian unity to be had with ungodly men: never think of unity by any other way than sanctification. You are as on the other side of the river, and cannot be united to the servants of Christ, till the Spirit convert you, and pass you over. You are dead men, and unfit to be united to the living; and it is the "Spirit that quickeneth," and this life must be our union. You madly rail against division, and yet stand at a distance from Christ and his church, and maintain the greatest division in the world. Believe it, you do but dote and dream, if you think to have true christian unity on any other terms, than by the sanctifying Spirit of Christ. And this I shall now evince as followeth.

1. You know sure that there can be no christian unity, but in God as your Father, and the centre of unity: all the true members of the catholic church must say, "Our Father," and be as his children united in him. If you will have unity without the favour of God, it must be the unity of rebels, and such a concord as is in hell: the family of God do all unite in him. As all the kingdom is united in one king, so is all the church in God. Can you think it possible to have unity as long as you will not unite in God? Well then, there is nothing plainer in the Scripture, than that all men by nature are departed from God, and none are united to him but those that are regenerate and made new creatures; not a man is his child by grace, and in his favour, but only those that are sanctified by his Spirit, John iii. 3—5; Matt. xviii. 3; 2 Cor. v. 17; Heb. xii. 14. So that there is no true unity without sanctification, because there is no reconciliation with God, nor unity with him, without it.

2. There can be no true christian unity but in Christ the Redeemer and Head of the church: for how can the members be united but in the head? or the scholars but in their teacher? or the subjects but in their sovereign? You know there is no christian unity but in Christ. Well then, what unity can we have with those that are not in Christ? The unsanctified have indeed the name of christians; but what is that to the nature? Some branches not bearing fruit are said to be in him the Vine, by outward profession; but they are dead and withered, and must be cut off and cast away for the fire; and so are unfit for communion with the Vine, John xv. "He that is in Christ is a new creature: old things are passed away; behold, all things are become new," 2 Cor. v. 17. "If any man have not the Spirit of Christ, (which is this sanctifying Spirit,) the same is none of his." I pray you mark the plainness of these passages. All you that are unconverted and unsanctified are out of Christ, and none of his, though you may talk and boast of him as long as you will. And therefore you cannot have unity with christians till you first have unity with Christ himself. Till you are ingrafted into him, you are not ingrafted into the catholic church, but only seem to be what you are not.

3. The dead cannot be united to the living: who will be married to a dead corpse? or would be tied to it, and carry it about? It is life that must unite us. The unsanctified are dead in sin, (Eph. ii. 5,) and the Spirit is given to quicken the dead, that they may be fit for converse. What union can there be between a block and a man; or a beast that hath but a sensitive life, and a man that hath a rational soul? So what union between the sensual world and the sanctified believer? If you could have unity without the sanctifying Spirit, why are you then baptized into the name of the Holy Ghost as your Sanctifier? To have a unity of being is common to us with the devils; for they are God's creatures, and so are we. To have a union of specific being is common to us with all the damned, for they are men as well as we; and common to the devils among themselves. But it must be a unity in the Spirit of holiness that must prove us happy, and afford us comfort.

4. There is no possibility of having unity with those that have not the same ultimate principal end. But the sanctified and the unsanctified have not the same end, nay, have contrary ends. If one of you will go to York, and the other to London, how can you possibly go one way? This is the great difference that sets the world and the sanctified by the ears: you serve mammon, and they serve God: you have one portion, and they another. Your portion is in this life, Psal. xviii. 14; here you have your good things, (Luke xvi. 25,) and here you lay up your treasure, Matt. vi. 19, 21. Your belly is your god, and you mind earthly things, Phil. iii. 18. But it is the Lord that is the portion of the saints, Psal. xvi. 5. They lay up a treasure in heaven, (Matt. vi. 20,) and there they have their conversations, Phil. iii. 20. Being risen with Christ, they seek the things that are above, where Christ sitteth at the right hand of God: for they are dead, and their life is hid with Christ in God, Col. iii. 1, 3, 4. The business that the saints and that the ungodly have in the world, is clean contrary. Their business is for heaven, and yours is for earth; they are sowing to the Spirit, in hope of everlasting life, and you are sowing to the flesh, and shall reap corruption, Gal. vi. 6, 7. They are making provision for another life, that never shall have end; and you are making provision for the flesh, to satisfy its desires, Rom. xiii. 14. And how is it possible for these to be united? What concord between light and darkness? or Christ and Belial? or righteousness with unrighteousness? 2 Cor. vi. 14, 15. "Can two walk together, except they be agreed?" Amos iii. 3. We must better agree of our business in the world, and of our journey's end, before we can keep company with you. While you are for earth and we for heaven, it is not possible that we should go one way. While one is for the world, and another for God, they must needs differ: for God and the world are masters that are irreconcilable. If you will cleave to one, you must despise the other.

The work of the butcher and the soldier is to kill; and the work of the surgeon and physician is to cure. And do you think these will ever take one course? The soldier studies how to wound and kill; the surgeon studies how to close these wounds and heal them: and surely these must go contrary ways. Sirs, as long as your business is principally for the flesh and the world, and the business of the sanctified is against the flesh and world, and for the Spirit and the world to come, how is it possible that you should be agreed? You must bring heaven and earth together first, yea, heaven and hell together first, before you can have a christian unity and agreement between the sanctified and the unsanctified.

5. There is no unity to be had but in the gospel. The apostle tells us, "there is one faith," Eph. iv. 5. If an angel from heaven would preach another gospel, he must be accursed, Gal. i. 10, 11. But the unsanctified do not truly and heartily entertain this gospel. You think and say you truly believe it,

when you do not. If you truly believed it, your lives would show it. He that indeed believes an everlasting glory, will sure look after it, more than after the world or the flesh.

6. There is no christian unity, but in the christian nature. Contrary natures cannot close. Fire and water, the wolf and the lamb, the bear and the dog, will not well unite. The sanctified have a new, divine, and heavenly nature, John iii. 6; 2 Pet. i. 4; 2 Cor. v. 17. Their disposition is another way than it was before. But the unsanctified have the old corrupt, fleshly nature still: one is as the fire, still bending upward; the other as the earth or stone, still bending downward to the earth: and how can these agree together?

7. There is no christian unity to be had, where the affections run quite contrary ways. But so it is with the sanctified and the unsanctified. One loves God above all, and cannot live without holy communion with him, and retireth into him from the distractions of the world, and maketh him his rest, content, and solace: the other mentions the goodness of God, but findeth no such sweetness in him, nor desires after him. One treads a world under-foot as dirt, or valueth and useth it but as a help to heaven; and the other makes it his happiness, and sets his heart on it. One delighteth in holiness, and the other hateth it, or regardeth it not. One hateth sin as a serpent, or as death; and the other makes it his meat, and drink, and business. And how is it possible for men of such contrary affections to be agreed, and nature at such enmity to unite?

8. The sanctified and unsanctified are moved by contrary objects: one lives by faith on things that are out of sight, and strives for heaven as if he saw it, and strives against hell as if he saw it; for his "faith is the evidence of things not seen," Heb. xi. 1, 7. We live by faith, and not by sight, 2 Cor. v. 7; iv. 18. But the unsanctified live upon things that are seen, and things believed little move them, because they are not heartily believed.

9. The holy and the unholy do live by contrary laws. One liveth by the law of God, and there asketh counsel what he must think, or say, or do, resolving to obey God, before his flesh, and all the world. The other will say, he will be ruled by God's laws, till his flesh and carnal interest contradict it, and then he will take his lusts for his law: his pride is a law to him, and the pleasures and profits of the world are a law to him; and the will of great ones, and the customs of men, are his law. And how is it possible for men to agree that walk by such contrary rules as these?

10. There is no true unity but in the covenant with Christ. As marriage uniteth man and wife, so every truly sanctified man hath delivered up himself to Christ in a peremptory absolute covenant, and hath quit all claim of interest in himself, and is wholly God's. But the unsanctified will not be brought to this, any further than the lips, and therefore they cannot be well united.

11. The true members of the church are "built on the foundation of the apostles and prophets," Eph. ii. 20, 21. But the unsanctified regard them not, if they cross their minds.

12. There is no true christian unity, but with the holy catholic church. The body is but one, 1 Cor. xii. 12, 13; Eph. iv. 4. But the unsanctified are not of the holy catholic church, but only in the visible external communion of it.

13. There can be no true christian unity with the saints, without a special love to the saints. For by this "we know that we are passed from death to life, because we love the brethren; he that loveth not his brother abideth in death," 1 John iii. 14. "By this must all men know that we are Christ's disciples," John xiii. 35. Love is the bond and cement of the church. He that doth not heartily love a godly, sanctified man, because he is such, hath no true unity with the church. But the ungodly love them not as such: they see no such beauty and loveliness in holiness. Though Scripture calls it God's image, they be not in love with God's image, but think it a conceit, or hypocritical pretence, or a wearisome thing. Why, poor carnal wretches, do you hate the godly, and yet would you have unity with them? Do you hate them, and yet cry out against divisions, when your hearts are thus divided from God and his servants? You must learn to love them with a special love, and Christ in them, before you can be united with them.

14. There is no unity to be had without a love to the body that you are united to. You must love the church, and long for its prosperity, and the success of the gospel, and the downfal of wickedness. Thus do the saints; but thus do not the ungodly. Nay, many of them are glad when they hear of any evil befall the godly.

15. There is no true unity without a singular respect to the special members that are ligaments and chief instruments of unity; even the officers of the church and most useful members. The overseers of the church must "be highly esteemed in love for their work's sake," 1 Thess. v. 12. Thus do the godly, but not the ungodly.

16. There must be an inward inclination to the communion of saints, before there can be any agreement and unity. All that are of the holy catholic church, must desire the communion of saints. Their "delight must be in them," Psalm xvi. 3. But the ungodly have no such delight in their communion.

17. If you will have unity and communion with the church, you must have a love to the holy ordinances, which are the means of communion; as to the word of God, heard and read, to prayer, sacraments, confession, &c.; but the ungodly have either a distaste of these, or but a common delight in the outside, and not in the spirit of the ordinance; and therefore they cannot agree with the church. When you loathe that which is our meat and drink, and we cannot feed at one table together, what agreement can there be?

18. If you will agree, you must work in the same vineyard, and labour in the same employment, and walk the same way as the sanctified do: and that is in a way of holiness and righteousness, "giving all diligence to make your calling and election sure," 2 Pet. i. 10. If you live to the flesh, and they live to the Spirit, (Rom. viii. 5, 13,) what unity and agreement can there be?

19. There is no unity to be had, unless you will join in a defensive and offensive league, and in opposition to that which would tend to our destruction. What commonwealth will unite with them that defend their enemies and rebels? There is an enmity put in the beginning between the seed of the woman and of the serpent, Gen. iii. 15. "Because we are not of the world, the world will hate us," John. xv. 19. If you will be united to the church and people of Christ, you must be at enmity with sin, and hate it, and join for the destroying of it; and you must be soldiers in Christ's army, which the devil and his army fight against; and you must fight against the flesh, the world, and the devil, and not live in friendship with them. But this the unsanctified will not do.

20. And therefore because you will not be united to them in the state and kingdom of grace, you shall

not be united with them in the state and kingdom of glory.

And thus I have made it plain to you, that none can have true union with the church of Christ, but only they that are sanctified by the Spirit.

Use 1. By this time you may see, if you are willing to see, who it is long of that the world is all in pieces by divisions, and who are the greatest hinderers of unity: even unsanctified, ungodly men. And you may see how fit these men are to cry out against divisions, that are the principal causes of them; and how wisely they deal to cry up unity, and in the mean time resist the only ground and way of unity. As Joshua said to Achan, "Why hast thou troubled us? the Lord shall trouble thee this day," Josh. vii. 25; so I may say to all the ungodly, Why trouble you the church, and hinder unity? you shall one day have trouble yourselves for this. They cry out against the ministry and others that fear God, as Ahab did to Elijah, "Art thou he that troubleth Israel?" But saith Elijah, "It is thou and thy father's house that trouble Israel, in that ye have forsaken the commandments of the Lord," 1 Kings xviii. 17, 18. Sirs, I tell you, (and I may confidently tell you when I have proved it so fully,) that it is the ungodly that are the great dividers of the world. It is you that make the breach, and keep it open. We are willing to agree to any thing that is reasonable or possible; but there is no possibility of agreeing with the ungodly, unless they will turn. It would make any honest heart to ache, to see these wretches set all on fire, and then cry out against others as the authors of it. As Nero set Rome on fire, and then persecuted the christians for it, as if it had been done by them. They pluck up the foundations, and hold most damnable, practical errors; and when they have done, they go about reviling other men as erroneous. I speak not in the excuse or extenuation of other men's errors; I have spoke my part against them also: but I tell you, it is the profane and ignorant rabble, and all the ungodly, whether gentlemen, scholars, or of what rank soever, that are the great dividers, and stand at the greatest distance from christian unity. Oh what a happy church should we have, for all the sects that trouble us so much, if it were not for ungodliness that animateth some of those sects, and virtually containeth many more! Had we none but men fearing God to deal with, we should have no opposition to the essentials of religion; and we should still have the comfort of agreeing with them in all things necessary to salvation. They would carry on their differences in christian meekness, charity, and moderation; and at the worst our agreement would be greater than our disagreement. But when we have to deal with haters of holiness, or at least with men that are strangers to the sanctifying work of the Spirit, we have predominant pride, and selfishness, and covetousness to strive against: we have radicated infidelity, and enmity to God and holiness, giving life and strength to all their errors, and making them stubborn, and wilful, and scornful, against the clearest truths that can be showed them. There is no dealing effectually with a carnal heart, for any but God himself. Unless we can create light in them, as well as reveal the truth to them, what good can we do them? What good doth the sun to a man that is blind? They have understandings left, and therefore they can err; but they have no heavenly light in them, and therefore they cannot choose but err. They have wills, and therefore are capable of sin; but they have no holy rectitude of them, and therefore sin they will with obstinacy. When we dispute with the godly, that err through weakness, we deal with men that have eyes in their heads, and life in their souls, and some savour and experience of the matters of God. But when we dispute with the ungodly, we deal with the blind, we talk to the dead, we offer the bread of life to men that have no appetite or savour of it; yea, we speak for God, to enemies of God; and for truth, to the natural enemies of such truths; and the more obstinate enemies, because they know it not. Had we nothing but mistakes to argue against, and had we but to do with men that have the free use of their reason, we should do well enough with them. But when we must persuade the deaf, the distracted, and the dead; when we must dispute with pride, and passion, and enmity, and persuade a lion to become a lamb, and a serpent to lay by his venom, no wonder if we find a difficult task of it. Had we none but the godly to deal with, we should have abundant advantage for success; we should deal with men that love the truth, and are willing to use right means to discover it: they would pray with us for truth, as well as dispute; they would with meekness search the Scripture, and see whether these things be so or not: they would yield to light when it appeareth to them, and not imprison it in unrighteousness. And it would move us to more tender dealing with them, while we see and love Christ in them, and when we remember that the men that we now dispute with, we must live with in heaven, and join with in the everlasting praises of the Lord. I profess, sirs, I speak to you from sad experience, I have been troubled with antinomians, and anabaptists, and other errors in well-meaning men, as much as most; and many a day's work they have made me in writing and disputing against them. But, alas! this is nothing to the trouble that the profane, ungodly do put me to. I thank God I have dealt with all these errors with so good success, that I live in peace by them; and I know not of an anabaptist, or Socinian, or Arminian, or quaker, or separatist, or any such sect in the town where I live; except half a dozen papists that never heard me. But infidels, atheists, ungodly wretches, I am pestered with still: one heresy called drunkenness, that denieth the use of reason itself, doth still walk the streets in despite of all that I can say, or all that the magistrates will do, and none of us all are able to confute them. In one hour's time they will fetch more arguments from the ale-house, than all the reason in the town can effectually answer.

And as the ungodly are most desperately principled of any heretics in the world, both for the quality and the radication of their errors: so there are far greater numbers of them, than of all other heresies set together. It may be we have one or two anabaptists in a parish, and in some parishes none; in some few it may be twenty: but oh that I could say, I had not twenty, and twenty, and twenty, and twice twenty more, unsanctified, ungodly persons in my parish, though I hope there are as many better, as in any parish I know. Alas, sirs, into how many parishes may you go, and find gross ignorance, profaneness, worldliness, contempt of God and heavenly things, to be their common air which they breathe in, and the natural complexion of the inhabitants, as blackness is to the Æthiopians. It is a blessed parish, that of three thousand inhabitants, hath not above two thousand natural heretics, even ungodly persons that are strangers to sanctification. And who then do you think is likest to be the cause of our distractions and divisions?

Moreover, let me tell you, profaneness and ungodliness is not a single error or heresy; but it is the sum of all the heresies in the world. You will think this strange, when you see so many that join with us in a sound profession, and some of them zealous defenders of the truth; and many of them cry out against errors: but, alas! they believe not that which they think they do believe. They hold not that which they say they hold. There is much in their creed, that was never in their belief. Doubtless ungodliness is the nest of all the heresies in the world.

Will you give me leave to instance in some particulars. The greatest error in the world is atheism, when men deny the. Godhead itself. And do not the most of the ungodly deny him in their hearts? If he be not just, he is not God; and they deny and hate his justice: if he be not holy, he is not God; and they deny in their hearts, and hate his holiness: if he be not true, he is not God; and they commonly believe that he is not true. Show them where he hath said, that none but the converted, the sanctified, the regenerate, the heavenly, the self-denying shall be saved; and they will not believe that this will be made good, but hope it is false. If he be not wise, and be not the Governor of the world, he is not God. And these wretches quarrel with his holy laws, as if they could tell how to mend them themselves, and were wiser to make a law than God is; and by flat rebellion deny his government. So that we may truly say with David, (Psal. xiv.) that these fools say in their hearts, that "There is no God;" or else they durst not say and do in his presence as they do.

Moreover, idolatry, which is the setting up of false gods, is a most abominable, damning sin. And every ungodly man is guilty of it. Covetousness is idolatry, (Eph. v. 5,) and the sensual make their belly their God, Phil. iii. 19. And pride and selfishness, which are the heart of the old man, are nothing else but making ourselves our idols. Every unsanctified man is his own idol; giving to himself the honour, and pleasure, and love that is due to God alone; and setting up his own will instead of God's.

Polytheism, which is the feigning of many gods, is a most damnable error. And how many gods have all that are ungodly! No man departeth from the one true God, but he makes to himself many false gods in his stead. His wealth, and his credit, and his throat, and his recreations, and the rulers that are capable of hurting him, are all as his gods, and to them he gives that which is due to God only.

Infidelity is one of the most damning errors in the world, when men believe not in Christ that bought them: but this is the case of all the unsanctified. An opinion they have that the gospel is true; and Christ is the only Lord and Saviour; but infidelity is predominant in them, and therefore should denominate them; or else they should be saved, if they were true believers. Never did they give an hour's true entertainment to Christ in their hearts.

To set up a false Christ, is one of the most damning sins in the world. And what else do all the ungodly, that place their hopes for pardon and salvation, either in their own good works or carnal shifts, or at least, by false conceptions do make Christ not indeed to be Christ?

To have many saviours, is a damnable error. And how many do the ungodly make to themselves, while they depart from the Lord Christ?

To deny the Holy Ghost, is a damnable error. And what else do all the ungodly in the world, that will not be sanctified by him? This is the most palpable error that they are guilty of. They are baptized into the name of the Holy Ghost as their Sanctifier, and yet they will not be sanctified by him: nay, some of them make a mock of the Spirit, and of sanctification. And some of them will hearken to false, deceiving spirits, instead of the Holy Spirit of God.

Some heretics have denied some parts of the Scripture, and infidels deny it all. And what less do all ungodly men, that believe it not heartily, and will not obey it, but deny it in parts, and refuse subjection to it? They will not be so holy, not they, let Scripture say what it will. Are not all the ungodly against the Scripture? Many a time have I heard them, when the times more encouraged them, deriding the Bible, and those that did but carry a Bible, or speak of the Scripture, or read it in their houses. Certainly, he that fights against Scripture in his life, is more against it than he that only denies it with his tongue.

Moreover, the Pelagian heretics denied original sin, and justified man's nature: and so doth profaneness in a very great measure. Never were the ungodly truly humbled for their original sin, nor saw any such matter in themselves, as to make them abhor themselves: and what is this but actually to deny it?

The same Pelagians made light of grace, which is God's image upon the soul. But in this the ungodly go quite beyond them: they make a matter of nothing of holiness, but account it a fancy, or a needless thing; and many of them hate it, and if the times did but favour their malice, there were no living near them for any that fear God. In this they are devils in flesh; I cannot liken them to any heresy but devilism, they go so far beyond the professors of them all.

One sect is against those that are their opposers, and another sect against their opposers; but ungodliness is against all that are godly of every party whatsoever; and is in open arms or secret enmity against the army of Christ, and against himself.

The Simonians, and Nicolaitans, and Gnostics of old, did hold that men might do any outward action, when there is no other way to escape suffering, as long as they keep their hearts to God. So think the ungodly, as appeareth by their practice. Before they will lose their estates and be brought to poverty, or before they will lie in prison, or be burnt at a stake, they will say any thing, or do any thing: they would worship a piece of bread as if it were God; they would turn to papists or any that can do them a mischief, if it were the Turks.

Alas! the particular sects among us do play a small game in comparison of the ungodly; and hold but petty errors to theirs. One sect is against one ordinance, and another sect is against another ordinance; but the ungodly are against all. The sectaries are against something in the manner or outside of the work, but the ungodly are against the spirit, and life, and substance of the duty itself. One sect depraveth the doctrine of faith, and another the doctrine of repentance, and another the doctrine obedience; but the ungodly deprave all the doctrine of godliness; yea, deny it, and not only deprave it: they sweep away all before them, and go by wholesale: they stand not to speak as other heretics, against this grace or that grace, but against all: it is godliness itself that the ungodly are against.

The sectaries oppose all parts of the catholic church, saving their own; but the ungodly are against the holy catholic church itself; as it is a church, and as it is holy, they are against it. The church is a society combined for holy obedience to Christ; and the ungodly are against that holy obedience.

The sectaries would have no communion of saints, but in their own way. But the ungodly are against the communion of saints in itself; for they are against the saints that hold this communion.

The papists and quakers are against our ministry, and rail at them, and labour to bring them into hatred. So do the worser sort of the ungodly, even of them that say they are protestants, of our own religion. In their houses, and in the ale-houses, in their ordinary discourse, they are cavilling against the ministers, or reproaching them: and some of them are more bitter haters and revilers of them than almost any heretics that we meet with; yea, some of them are glad to hear the quakers and anabaptists reproach them, and secretly set them on; only they are ashamed to own these revilers, because they see them come off in the end with so much disgrace. But if they were but sure that papists, or quakers, or any sect that is against a godly ministry, had power in their hands to go through with their work, the multitude of the ungodly among us would soon join with them. How plainly did this appear in our late wars! When few ministers of noted diligence and piety, that desired to have lived at home in quietness, could be suffered to live among them; but the ungodly rise up against them as if they had been Turks or Jews, and drove them into garrisons to save their lives. The separatists and quakers, and other sects, dispute against the ministry with cavils and railings; but the ungodly would dispute them down with halters and hatchets, with fire and sword, if the merciful Governor of the world did not tie their hands.

The quakers, and many anabaptists and separatists, are against tithes, and all settled maintenance of the ministry. And do I need to tell you, that the ungodly, covetous worldlings are of the same mind? What need had ministers else to sue for their tithes? Were it not for fear of treble damages, the ministers in many parishes of England should not have bread to their mouths, nor clothes to their backs, before they got it by suit at law. How commonly do they think that all is won, and is currently their own, that they can but defraud the minister of! If it were not that they are under disgrace, the quakers would soon have disciples enough upon this very account, because they are against tithes. And gladly do the ungodly covetous people hearken to that doctrine, and get their books, and would fain have that opinion take as orthodox. If the prince and parliament would but turn quakers, and cry down tithes, yea, and ministry too, the miserable ungodly multitude would quickly be of that religion, and entertain their laws with ringing of bells, and shouts, and bonfires.

Another heresy there is, even the old sect of anabaptists, that are against christian magistracy; and another heresy, the libertines, that would have the magistrates give men leave to sin. And are not all the profane of the same opinion? They dare not speak so freely indeed against the magistrate as against the ministry, unless when they are up in arms against him; but their very hearts detest that magistrate that takes part with godliness, and promotes religion, and puts down ale-houses, and punisheth swearers, and drunkards, and profaners of the Lord's day. They are commonly for the doctrine that Dell preached to the parliament, that They should let Christ alone with reformation, and let him do his work himself: or as another hath written, that He will never serve such a God that is not able to defend his own cause without the magistrate's sword. The wretches might as well have said, We will have no such God as cannot govern us himself without a magistrate; or cannot defend us against enemies without wars; or cannot preserve our estates without the charge and trouble of law-suits; or save our goods or lives without punishing thieves or murderers; or that cannot teach the world without ministers, or give us corn without ploughing and sowing: we will never serve such a God as cannot preserve our lives without meat and drink, and clothes; and lighten the world himself without a sun. God can do all this! But must these dunghill worms impose it on him, and give him a law, and take down his creatures, and institutions, and means, and bid him do all without them himself, or else he is no God? Oh wretched blasphemers! Why how much of this blasphemy are the ungodly guilty of, that hate the magistrate, or any other that executes God's laws, and would hinder them from sin, and drive them to the means that should make them better!

The antinomians corrupt the doctrine of faith, and take it to be a believing that their sins are pardoned, that Christ hath even repented and believed in their stead; and he that hath this belief they think is safe, and that a man cannot thus believe too much or too soon. And this is just the common faith of the ungodly: they trust in Christ to save and pardon them, even without sanctification or conversion; and trust they will, let ministers say what they can: presumption is taken to be true believing, and by it they think to be saved. They believe that God will save them, and therefore they think they are true believers.

The antinomians say, that no man should be discouraged from such a belief by any sin whatsoever. And this the ungodly hold and practise. The antinomians hold that no man should stay for any evidences of grace in himself, before he thus believe that he is a child of God, and justified. And this the ungodly hold and practise. They believe and hope that they are justified and shall be saved, when they have not a word of proof for their hopes, nor any reason why they should be saved more than the rest of the world that will be condemned: only they believe it and hope it, and that they think shall serve the turn.

The antinomians are against repenting and grieving for sin, and confessing it, as a means of pardon. And I am sure the ungodly are practically against it. Repent, and mourn, and turn from sin, they will not; nor confess any more but what they know not how to deny; but as much as they can they will hide it, excuse it, and defend it.

The antinomians would not have one of their believers, if he fall into the grossest sins, to make the least question of his pardon and justified state for that. And so it is with the ungodly: they will confess, when they swear or are drunk, that they sin, (because they cannot deny it,) but they will not believe that they are graceless and unpardoned; but all are sinners; and the best have their faults, and so have they; and this is the worst they make of their sin.

The Pelagians say, that the will of man is so free, that he can turn and become a new creature at any time. And if this were not the opinion of the ungodly, how could they put off conversion, and say, It is time enough hereafter: but that it seems they think they can turn at any time, as if they had the Spirit and grace of God at their command.

And yet they hold the contrary to this. (And this is no wonder; for there is the very Babel of confusion in the soul of the unsanctified.) The antinomians say, that man can do nothing to his own conversion, but is merely passive: if God have justified him before he was born, he shall be a justified person; and if God will give him grace, well and good; if not, he cannot help it. Just so say many of the ungodly: If we are elected we shall be saved; if not, let us do what we can, we cannot be saved: if God will not give us grace, we cannot have it; and if we perish, what remedy? As if God did deny his grace to any of you, but those that forfeit it by wilful sin; or as if your wilful resisting of it were no fault or forfeiture; or as if God did predestinate any besides the sanctified to salvation.

Abundance more such heresies I might reckon up, that are all comprised in ungodliness. Some infidels question the immortality of the soul: and so do many of the ungodly: I have heard some of them flatly deny it, and others of them do not well believe it.

Some infidels question whether there be any hell. And so do the ungodly in their hearts, or else they durst never so boldly venture on it, and so merrily live in the sudden danger of it.

Some infidels question the joys of heaven. And if the ungodly did not so in their heart, they would not think a holy life too much ado to get it, nor would they part with it for the pleasure of a filthy sin.

There is never an article of the creed but some heretic or other doth oppose it. And the ungodly are against them altogether, even while they profess to believe them all.

There is never a one of the ten commandments, but ungodliness is against it. There is never a petition in the Lord's prayer, but ungodliness is against it; for all that they are content to use the words. Instead of hallowing the name of God, they dishonour it; and instead of living to the glory of God, they seek themselves and their own honour. The kingdom of Christ they are enemies to: in the church without them, they love not his government; in their hearts within, they will not endure it; and the coming of his glorious kingdom they are afraid of. Instead of doing his will, they will quarrel with it, and murmur at it, and disobey it, and do their own wills, and would have God do their wills too, and have all others do them. Instead of being content with daily bread to fit them for God's service, they drown themselves in pleasure, or in worldly cares, to make provision to satisfy their flesh. Instead of valuing and accepting the forgiveness of sin, as purchased by Christ, and offered in the gospel, they have slight apprehensions of so great a mercy, and refuse the conditions of it as too hard, and run deeper into debt, and wilfully sin more. Instead of avoiding temptations, and flying to Christ for deliverance from evil, they tempt themselves, and run into temptations, and seek after them, and love the evil of sin, and are loth to leave it and be delivered from it. So that they are against every petition in the Lord's prayer, though they use the words.

They are also against every ordinance of God, and lick up the vomit of all sects that do oppose them. One sect is against the Lord's day; and so are the ungodly against the sanctifying of it, and spending it in holy worship, and delighting themselves thereon in God. Else what need so many acts to restrain them from sports and other profanation of it? and all will not do.

Another sect is against praying but by the book, and would have a minister restrained from praying in any other words than are commanded him. And the ungodly easily receive this opinion, and reproach all other prayers as extemporate and disorderly.

Another sect is against church government by any but magistrates; these are called Erastians. And the ungodly are not only against it, but detest it, and reproach it. Let them be called to public repentance and confession for any public sin, and try whether they be not against this discipline. I know no outward duty that they are more against. They will hear us preach with some patience and quietness; but when we come to reprove them personally, and recover them from scandalous sins by necessary discipline, they storm and rage against us, and will not endure it.

Some separatists are for the people's governing of the church by a major vote, and consequently ruling those that God doth call their rulers, and commandeth them to obey, Heb. xiii. 17. And so are the ungodly; they would rule their rulers, the ministers, and have them administer the ordinances of God according to their fancies, but they will not be ruled by them. Let the minister but require them to come to him to be instructed or catechised, and they will not be ruled by him, they are too old to be catechised: let him call them to any necessary profession or other duty, and they will do what they list: let him but cross any of their conceits and customs, and they will sooner revile him than be ruled by him.

The separatists will withdraw themselves from our churches and God's ordinances, if things be not suited to their mind. And so will many of the ungodly. Most parishes in England, that I hear of, where any kind of discipline is exercised, have more separatists than communicants. The far greater part of many parishes forbear the communion of the church in the Lord's supper, and have done many years together; even because they cannot be admitted without examination, or without some necessary or lawful profession, or because they cannot have the sacrament kneeling, or put into their hands, or the like. They will separate and be without the sacrament, or take it in a separate society, rather than they will be ruled by the pastors of the church in a gesture or undoubtedly lawful thing.

Another sect of late will not sing David's Psalms; and the ungodly will not do it heartily and reverently, but only with the voice.

Another sect, the anabaptists, are against baptizing infants. And the ungodly do not holily and heartily devote themselves and their infants to God; they do not themselves renounce the world, the flesh, and the devil, and take God for their God, and Christ for their Saviour, to heal and rule them, and the Holy Ghost for their Sanctifier to make them holy: and how then can they do this for their children, which they refuse themselves? When they have offered their children to God in baptism, they bring them up to the flesh, and the world, and the devil, in their lives, and teach them to break the covenant which they made. So that they are far worse than anabaptists.

Another late sect will not pray morning and evening in their families, nor crave God's blessing on their meat, nor teach their children and servants the duties of religion: and so it is with the ungodly. How many of you that hear me to-day, have prayerless families; that let your people go about their labour as an ox to the yoke, without calling upon God! How few use to instruct and admonish their families, and help to prepare them for death and judgment! All that are about you may see that you are guilty of this heresy.

Another sect of late is risen up, that will not keep any constant times of prayer neither in family or in private, but only when they find themselves in a good mood, then they will pray. And so is it with many of the profane.

I am weary of mentioning these desperate errors: more of them might be mentioned, and the case made plain, that almost all the heresies in the world are met together in the ungodly and unsanctified.

Would you see the sum of all my charge, in order? It is this: 1. Many sects that trouble us much, do yet hold no errors but what may stand with christianity and salvation. But the ungodly err in the essentials, and overthrow the very foundation of religion. Their errors will not consist with grace or salvation. They are damnable heresies. Yea, beside all that the sects aforesaid hold, they have many damning heresies of their own. These deadly heretics hold, that the world is rather to be sought than everlasting glory; that the pleasure of sin is to be chosen before the holiness of the saints; that their flesh is to be pleased before God; that it is better venture on their beloved sins, and keep them yet a little longer, than presently forsake them; that the way to heaven which God commandeth, and Christ and all his apostles went in, is puritanism and preciseness, and godliness is more ado than needs; and that the body must have more care and diligence than the soul; and the trifles of this world be more looked after than the one thing necessary!

These, and abundance such damnable heresies, do dwell in our cities and countries, in the minds of those that cry out against heresies. Ungodliness is the greatest heresy in all the world.

2. Other heretics have some of them but one or two errors, but the ungodly have all these together: they are the sink of all errors. As all God's graces make up the new creature in the sanctified; so all deadly errors and vices go to make up the body of ungodliness, when it is complete. Its name is Legion, for there are many of these evil spirits in it. The anabaptist hath a scab, and the separatist hath a wound; but the common ungodly multitude have the leprosy and plague sores from top to toe.

Profaneness is a hodgepodge and gallimaufry of all the heresies of the world in one.

3. Many other heretics do err but in speculation, and only the brain is infected, and they do not at the heart digest their own mistakes. But the heresies of the profane ungodly people are practical, and have mastered the will: the poison is working in the heart and vital parts, so that it is far the more mortal for this.

4. Many sects at least do not practise their errors; but the ungodly live upon them: yea, their lives are worse than their opinions; they say bad, and do worse. You may see more heresy than you can hear from them.

5. Some erring persons have the substance of christian truth mixed with their error, by which the power of the venom is abated, and they do good in the church as well as hurt. But the ungodly do not savingly, heartily, and practically hold fast any the most fundamental truth.

6. Some sects are meek and temperate in their way; but the ungodly are carried on with fury and malice, against the whole body of the holy catholic church.

7. And some heretics are so thin and few, that where we have one of them to do hurt, we have a hundred or a thousand to contradict them. But the unsanctified and ungodly are the greater number, and think they should rule because they are the most; and the flock of Christ is a little flock. And so many thousands swarming all over the world, and making up the far greatest part of the world, is like to do more against the truth and peace, than here and there a poor sectary in a corner.

8. And lastly, the errors of some others are easier cured; but the whole nature of the ungodly is turned as it were into error; it is rooted so at the heart, that no power on earth is able to cure it, till God Almighty, by insuperable light and life of grace, will do the cure.

And now I beseech you judge impartially, who they be that are the deadly and dangerous heretics, and who are the hinderers of unity in the church; and how unfit these miserable people are to call for unity, and cry out against our many religions, who are heartily of no religion themselves, but against the life and practice of all. To hear an ungodly man go crying out of sects, of separatists, of anabaptists, and this and that, is as if we should hear a blackamoor scorn one for a spot on his face; or a murderer rebuke a man for an angry word; or a soldier that kills as many as he can, cry out of the surgeons for curing no more, or blame others for a foul word; or a common whore reproach another for a wanton word, or uncomely garments: or as if a mad-man should revile men for every slip he findeth in their speeches, and call them fools. Oh that we knew how to cast out this master-devil of ungodliness! this Beelzebub the prince of devils! and then I should not fear the rest; no, not all the sects and errors in the world, that are found with true godliness.

Yet still remember these two cautions. 1. I do not excuse the errors of the best; and I lament that they have lamentably wronged the church, and in some respects they have the greatest aggravations. 2. And I still confess that some of the unsanctified are so civil and orthodox, as to be very useful in the church, and helpful against sects and heresies, because they are right in the brain as to speculation, and right in the tongue; and their error is kept buried deep in the heart, and therefore they err more to themselves than to others. I doubt not but many such are profitable preachers and defenders of the truth; and the church must be thankful to God for their gifts. And yet all that I have affirmed standeth good, that ungodliness is the transcendent heresy and schism.

Use 2. By what hath been said, you may easily perceive how little cause the papists, or ceremonious, or any others, have to glory in such members of their churches as I have described. Can they expect a unity of the Spirit with these? If they glory that they have men and multitudes on their side, so may the Turks that have more than they, and so may the heathens that have more than either. And yet when a papist hath deceived a poor licentious or ignorant man, or a proud or vicious silly woman, they glory in their convert. Never yet did I know any protestant turn papist, that was not an ungodly wretch before, and without the power of the religion which he professed. Do not say I speak censoriously or uncharitably in this; for I think, upon consideration, all papists will confess it: for they teach, that all that be not of their church are void of charity, and cannot so be saved; and that all must therefore come in to their church, because there is no charity or salvation without it. Though this be false, yet you see by it, that they confess that never any but graceless, unsanctified protestants did turn to them; nor can they invite any to them but ungodly people. And whoever turneth papist, doth thereby confess that he was ungodly before, and that he was not an honest, godly man; for in turning papist, he professeth to go into that church out of which there is no salvation, and consequently no charity or saving grace. And if indeed you desire none but the ungodly to turn to you, take them if they will needs go, and try whether you can do any more good on them than we have done. I think we have little cause (but for their own sakes) to lament our loss of such as these; and that you have little cause to glory in your proselytes. And I have yet seen none that show us any more holiness since their change than they had before. A fair church you have, that is the common sty for all that will come to you; and that is glad of any to make up the number, that you may have that in quantity that is wanting in quality.

Use. 3. From hence also let quakers and papists, and all reproachers of our churches, take notice how groundlessly they hit us in the teeth with the ungodly that live among us. These are your protestants, say they; these are your churches! these are the fruit of your ministry! say the quakers. No, these are the enemies of our ministry and doctrine; these are they that join with you, and such as you, to reproach us and revile us! These are the obstinate despisers of our ministry, that instead of learning of us do revile us, and instead of obeying our doctrine do make a mock at it. If they are any of them brought to a sound confession, and restrained from any vice, they may thank the doctrine which we preach for that (unless they do it only for fear of the laws). But their profaneness is it that we have endeavoured to cure them of, and cannot; for they are obstinate.

If papists or quakers accuse our doctrine as dead and weak, because it cannot cure all our hearers; what forgetful dotards are they, that observe not how they condemn themselves! Do the quakers or papists change us all to their opinions, by their books or preaching? Beyond sea they are fain to keep men in their church by fire and sword, for fear of losing them; and here it is but here and there an ignorant, ungodly wretch, or a proud, raw novice, that turns to them.

You may therefore as well hit us in the teeth with yourselves, that revile us, and say, We are the fruit of your ministry, as with the ungodly, and tell us that they are the fruit of our ministry. For though they live among us, they are not of us. And we teach men no more to be ungodly than to be quakers or papists. If you say, that they are in our churches; I answer, Where discipline is exercised, the most of them are out, and the rest we weed up as fast as they so discover themselves, that we may do it without danger of pulling up the wheat with them. Many of us reject them by discipline; and all of us rebuke and disown them by doctrine. If Jews and heathens were among us, we could not preach more against them, than we do against the ungodly; nor could we labour harder to cure them. Tell us not therefore of them; they are none of ours, they disown us, and we disown them: they are our persecutors, as you are, that hate us when we have done our best for them, and love us least when we love them most; and cast back all our instruction in our faces, or cast it behind their backs and tread it under feet. They are those against whom we shake off the dust of our feet: they are not our disciples, but such as refuse to be Christ's own disciples.

Nay, I wonder that papists and quakers do not to their shame observe, that it is like to be some evil spirit that sets them a-work to rail against us, seeing all the drunkards, and whoremongers, and covetous wretches, and ungodly, malicious people in our parishes, be of their mind, and rail against us as they do: it is like to be the same cause that hath the same effect. If it be the devil that sets the profane to revile us, judge who it is that sets these sects to speak the same or like words against the same persons.

And you that are profane and ungodly, I pray you here take notice what a case you are in! You are so vile, that few besides yourselves will own you. We disown you: you are none of ours, because you will be none of Christ's. And the very quakers, and other sects, disown you, and hit us in the teeth with you, as if you were our shame: all these bear witness against your ungodliness: and therefore if yet you will be ungodly, when quakers are against you, and all are against you almost as well as we; if you will hear neither ministers nor sectaries, neither teachers nor railers, how many witnesses will rise up against you, and how speechless will you be!

Use 4. I have been all this while but about preparatives; and now I come to the work that I intended. Do not think that I have spoken all this of the ungodly, to hinder a union and christian concord, but to prepare for it, by telling you the reason of our distance, and division, and what must be removed before we can be one. Truly, sirs, I come to you with peaceable intentions. I come upon a treaty with you, to see whether you will become one with us, and be reconciled, or not. For the Lord's sake attend me considerately and impartially, for it is a weighty business that I have to propound to you, and a most excellent motion that I have to make. As you regard the God of unity that sends to you, and Christ the Prince of peace, and the Spirit who is the principle of unity, and the church that is the seat of unity, and yourselves that may have the blessing of unity, hearken to the motion of peace and unity that I have to make to you from the Lord. Sirs, what think you? hath the world been long enough divided or not? Are we cut into shreds enough, and broken into pieces enough, or not? Are our distances from one another great enough, and our spirits bitter enough, or not? Is it not time, think you, to sound a retreat to our foolish wars? You call for unity; you talk for unity, and against sects and divisions: do you mean as you speak; and are you in good sadness, or are you not? Would you have us to be all of one mind and way, or not? You talk against being of so many religions: is it the true desire of your hearts, that we should be all of one religion? If it be, hold fast to this. So far we are agreed. Let us lay this as a groundwork; We must be all of one church, one faith, one religion, if we will be saved.

Well then, it lies next before us, in order, to inquire, What one religion and way we must be of; and what is our distance, and what course must be taken to make us one? Are you willing to lay by passion, and scorn, and hatred, and bitterness, and come to a treaty about the matter? O sirs, if you were but all truly willing to search out the business, and to be ruled by God and reason, we should soon be agreed for all our differences. And how happy would this be for the troubled church; how happy for the offended, distracted world; how happy for your own souls! Well; what terms shall we agree upon? Somebody must begin the motion; sitting still will not heal us. I will make a motion that never a man of you, that hath the face of a christian, can tell what justly to except against. Let us set the word of God before us, and take the best helps on both sides to understand it, and let this decide the case with us. What say you; will you stand to the word of God? Shall we appeal all to Christ, and try our differences by his revealed word? If this may carry it, we shall soon be agreed.

But if any of you have catched the popish perverseness, and say, The Scripture is dark, and a dead letter; every sect pleads Scripture for their way: this will not serve our turn; we must have a living judge: I answer such a one as followeth: 1. Is the Scripture the law of God or not? If you say, not, you may as well say you are infidels. If you confess it is, then it must have the use of a law. And, 2. Must not subjects understand a law to live by it, though they be not judges? And when estate and life depend on our obedience to the law, if this law now be so dark that the subjects cannot understand it, then it is no law, as not being capable of the use and ends of a law. And so if our salvation or damnation lie on our obedience to God's word and law, it is an intolerable reproach to God and it, to say it is such as we cannot understand. 3. Must we not be judged by this law? Undoubtedly we must. And then should we not measure our causes by it now? 4. May not abitrators make use of a law to decide a controversy, before it come to the judge? Doubtless they may. 5. What judge would you have? There are but two in the world, that pretend to be the universal, infallible judge of controversies; and that is a pope and a general council. For a general council, there is none now in the world, nor like to be to the end of the world. God forbid we should defer our peace till then! And its decrees are as dark, and much more uncertain than the word of God. And for the pope, he is the head of a sect or party, and therefore not fit to be judge: you may well know he will judge on his own side. He must be judged by this word of God himself. He is too far off, of all conscience, for us to go or send to. Where Rome is, the most of you know not: a shorter journey may better despatch our work. The papists themselves tell us, that many popes have been murderers, adulterers, simonists, perjured persons, and some heretics and infidels. And must such as these be our only judges? They have erred oft already, and therefore they may deceive us: and if you send for the pope's sentence, you must take the messenger's word that he was there, and that it is true.

But yet if all this will not serve turn, I will make a motion, that none can gainsay that hath the face of a christian. Let us first agree in all those points that papists and protestants, Calvinists and Lutherans, Arminians, and anabaptists, and separatists, and all parties that desire to be called christians, are agreed in. What? say you is not this a reasonable motion? O happy you, and happy the places where you live, if you would but stand to it!

And let us consider of this motion, first in the general state of our difference, and then in the particular parts of it.

Truly, sirs, the main difference in this world is between the godly and the ungodly; and all other differences that are not parts of this, are nothing to this, being of lesser danger and easier toleration or cure. The whole world is divided into two armies: Christ is the Captain-general of one, and the saints only his true soldiers, and the seeming saints his seeming soldiers. The devil is the general of the other, and all the unregenerate or ungodly are his soldiers. An enmity is put, since the beginning, between the seed of the woman and of the serpent, Gen. iii. 15. And there is no middle state, nor one man on earth that is not in one of these armies. I come not to reconcile the commanders, Christ and Satan, for they are irreconcilable; but to reconcile you to Christ, and draw you from a deceiver. I tell you, sirs, this great difference between the holy and the unholy is the first that must be healed. We can go no farther with you, if you will not begin here at the heart of the difference. When this is done, you shall see, before I have done with you, that I will quickly tell you how we may do well, for all our other differences. You know if one of us believe that there is a God, and another that there is none, it were foolery for us to dispute how God must be worshipped, before we are agreed that there is a God. So here, when it is the nature of ungodliness to make men false to the very truths that they do profess, and heartily to be of no religion at all, it is in vain to dispute about circumstances and modes with such kind of men. Who would dispute whether infants should be baptized with a man that knows not what baptism is? even an accepting of God for our God, and Christ for our Lord and Saviour, and the Holy Ghost for our Sanctifier; and an absolute delivering up ourselves to the blessed Trinity in these relations, by a solemn covenant professed and sealed by water, renouncing the flesh, the world, and the devil. Oh were but this much practically known, we should be all united in this one baptism. Still I say, unholiness is the great point of difference, and the dungeon of confusion, and puddle, where all the heresies of the world are blended and made into a body that is something worse than heresy. When you cry up unity, and cry down holiness, you are distracted, and know not what you say. You talk of joining us together, and you cast away the glue and solder. You talk of building the church in unity, and you cast away the lime and mortar, the pins and nails, and all that should fasten them. You complain that the garment of Christ is rent, and you throw away the needle and thread that should sew it up. You see our wounds and blood, and take on you to have pity on the church, and call for healing; but you hate and cast away the only salve. Do you not yet know that the church's unity is a unity of the Spirit, and of holiness? and that there is no way in the world for us and you to be united, unless you will be sanctified, and live in the Spirit, as you have done in the flesh?

Sirs, let us come nearer the matter: I know our towns and countries have two sorts of persons in them: some are converted, and some unconverted; some holy, and some unholy; some live for heaven, and some are all for earth; some are ruled by the word of God, and some by their own flesh or wills. If ever these agree and be united, one party must come over to the other. Either the godly must become ungodly, or the ungodly must become saints and godly: which must it be? Which do you think in your consciences is the way? Must we yield to you, or should you come away to us? (Pardon that I number myself with the sanctified; for I dare not deny the mercies of God, and the privileges of his house.) Let us come fairly to debate the case, and lay our reasons together, and I will here protest to you, if you can give us better reasons why we should forsake a godly life, I will turn to you; and if we can give you better reasons why you should embrace a holy life, will you here promise to turn to us? And let them carry it that have the better cause, and let us be resolved to go away united, and fall all together into that one way that shall be proved to be the best.

Well, let us come to a debate, and see whether we must come to you, or you to us.

1. If we ever agree and unite, you know it must be on terms that are possible. He that propoundeth impossibilities to be agreed on, is the enemy of agreement. But it is impossible for us to come to you, and so to unite with you. This I now prove. (1.) It is impossible to have any universal unity but in a universal head and centre, and that is only God, the Father, Son, and Holy Ghost. As I told you, the army must unite in the general, the kingdom in the sovereign, the family in the master, the school in the schoolmaster. In order of nature, you must unite with God in the Redeemer by the sanctifying Spirit, before you can unite with us. But while you are unsanctified you are divided from God. Do you not feel your minds strange to him, your hearts draw back from him, and find by his strangeness to you that there is a division? Is it impossible for us to be united to you, till Christ be united to you. For

it is against nature, seeing he is the centre, and the head and fountain of life: and what good would it do you to be one with us, and not with him? God is against any unity without him: if you will not begin with him, he will take it but as a treasonable conspiracy, and will break it. We dare not go without him, lest he be angry and destroy us: soldiers must not make either peace or war, nor so much as treat, without the general. Do you not remember how Jehoshaphat had like to have sped by a friendship and confederacy with Ahab?

(2.) Moreover the godly and ungodly are of contrary natures: I told you God hath put an enmity between them. You must change your nature or we ours, before we can unite. You may as well think else to unite fire and water, or to build in the air, or to incorporate fire and gunpowder; or to reconcile men and serpents; and marry the dog and the bear together. Sirs, these things are mere impossibilities. There is no agreement between Christ and Belial, righteousness and unrighteousness, light and darkness, death and life, the members of Christ and the members of a harlot, or a drunkard, or such like, 2 Cor. vi. 14. We have contrary spirits; how then can we be one? One hath the Spirit of holiness, and the other the spirit of profaneness; one is led by the Spirit of God, and the other by the flesh. We live not by one law: God's will revealed in his word is our law; and the will of the flesh, and the course of the world, is your law. We live not on one sort of food; how then can we accord together? Christ, and his heavenly truth, and Holy Spirit, and ordinances, is the meat and drink of the saints; they cannot live without them. And the world and fleshly delights are your food; you cannot be without it. Your food would be our poison; your worldly cares, your drunkenness, and profaneness, would be a torment to an honest heart. They cannot live without some communion with God in faith and love, by prayer and meditation; and your heart is against it. They have not the same end as you have. Their work is all for heaven, and yours is all principally for earth. Their work and yours are contrary: they go one way, and you another: so that it is impossible to be united and agree, till one side change. And we cannot possibly turn to you; God holds us fast by his love and Spirit, and will not let us go, nor suffer us ever to be willing to go. Do you not read Christ telling you, that it is impossible to deceive the elect? that is, so far as to turn them away from Christ. We are kept by the mighty power of God, through faith, to salvation, 1 Pet. i. 5; and who can break away from the upholding arms of Almighty power? Christ hath such hold of us, that he is resolved none shall take us out of his hands, John x. 28; so that we cannot come over again to you.

But you may come over to us if you will. God calls you, and Christ would welcome you, and the Holy Ghost would help you: the door is set open by the blood of Christ: the promise is to you and to your children, that you may and shall have Christ and life if you will come in, and accept the offer. The devil cannot hinder you against your wills, he holds you but in the fetters of your own wilfulness, by his mere deceits. Seeing, therefore, that you may come over to the sanctified, and they cannot possibly come to you, let any reasonable man be judge on what terms we should unite and agree.

2. Moreover, if we agree, it must be on terms of wisdom and honesty. A dishonest agreement is not to be desired, but abhorred. For you to leave your ungodliness, and turn to the love and fear of God, is an honest course of agreement; for it is but to leave dishonesty itself and become honest. I hope none of you dare charge the way of God and godliness with any dishonesty: God calls you to nothing but what is holy, and just, and good; and, therefore, honesty requireth you to yield.

But for the sanctified to become unsanctified, for the godly to become ungodly, to be one with you, this were the basest dishonesty in the world. We know your way to be of the devil and the flesh: and is it honest then to join with you in it? We have tried too long already in the days of our ignorance, and have found it dishonest and deceitful; and would you have us go against our own experience? We were once in the way that you are in, and were forced to renounce it, or else we had been undone body and soul for ever; and should we lick up the vomit which we were forced to cast out? We were once agreed with you, and God constrained us to break that agreement; and shall we renew it again? Alas, your way hath cost us dear; many a bitter repenting day, and many a sad thought, to the breaking of our hearts, and the very sense of God's displeasure; a taste of hell was cast into our consciences; many a groan, and tear, and prayer it cost us, before we could recover the hurt that we caught in the way of ungodliness; and yet we have not fully recovered it to this day. And would you have us stark mad, to forget so soon our former sorrows, and turn to a life that hath cost us so dear already? No, we have paid too dear for it, and smarted too much for it, to go that way any more: it brought us to the very brink of hell; and if we had but died in that condition, we had been damned at this hour; and would you be so unreasonable as to wish us to go back again? No, by that time you know as much of an unsanctified state as we do, you will run from it yourselves as fast as you can run; as the Israelites did from the cry of the company of Dathan and Abiram, "lest the earth should swallow them up also," Numb. xvi. 34.

We are certain that the Lord, whom we serve, is the only God, and that he, and none but he, should rule us; and that we have grievously wronged him, by disobeying him so long. And yet would you have us again forsake him? If we should lie in tears till we die, it were too little to satisfy his justice for one of the sins we have already committed; and if it had not been for the wonderful love and suffering of the Son of God, we had been lost for ever. And yet must we turn to this course again? God forbid. It was not so wise nor honest a course. "We ourselves," saith Paul, "were sometime foolish, disobedient, deceived, serving divers lusts and pleasures, living in malice and envy, hateful and hating one another." (You hear how he calls his former life.) "But after that the kindness and love of God our Saviour toward man appeared; not by works of righteousness which we have done, but according to his mercy he saved us, by the washing of regeneration and renewing of the Holy Ghost," Tit. iii. 3—5. And should Paul have turned a fool again, and be deceived and disobedient again, to agree with the rest of the deceived world? O sirs, we have seen that which you have not seen, and tasted that which you never tasted. Had you seen and tasted the love of God in Christ, and the delightful hopes of eternal life, and felt the comfort of his service, and the joys of the Holy Ghost, you would never wish us to come back again to agree with you in sin; but you would abhor yourselves the very thoughts of your former folly. Why, you may better persuade a man to repent that he was born, and to go into the womb again, than to persuade us to repent that we are new-born, and return to our former state of death. Death is not so sweet to us, nor hell, nor the wrath of God so lovely, nor sin, with all its pleasures, so desirable, that we should turn to them again for peace with you. If we have escaped them once, and will not take that for a warning to come there no more, we deserve to pay for it.

Why, sirs, we have made a solemn covenant with God, in the face of the congregation, in our baptism, and oft renewed it in the Lord's supper, and vowed that we would be his, and absolutely and unreservedly his. And would you wish us to break so solemn a covenant? What honesty is in such perfidiousness? We have renounced the flesh, the world, and the devil; and should we turn to them again for peace with you? Oh what a cursed peace were that! Let me tell you, that we have not found God so bad a master, as to forsake him for the sake of you or any creature. We have tried him, and found him better to us than all the world. He hath never given us cause to forsake him. And if we should now, after all the trials of his love, turn back to the way of sin and ungodliness, the devil himself would charge us with dishonesty. What! must the godly turn drunkards, and worldlings, and haters of godliness to have peace with you? Why, you may next persuade us even to turn devils, that we may be reconciled to you. The God that made us, hath forbid us, upon pain of his hot displeasure, to walk in your ways. He saith to every one of us, as to Jeremiah, "Let them return unto thee, but return not thou unto them," Jer. xv. 19. And should we obey God or men? Judge you whether. Why, sirs, are you so utterly unreasonable as to wish us, or any man living, to love you better than God, or to regard you more than God, or obey you before God? Or should we be so much worse than mad, as to yield to you if you did desire it? Why, what are you in comparison with the Almighty! O poor worms, that are even dying while you are speaking! that are but as bubbles ready to burst, when you are swelled to the highest in ungodly pride! that even while you are eating and drinking, and making merry, are passing on apace to weeping and gnashing of teeth, and everlasting woes and lamentations! what, should we regard such dust and dirt as you are, before the glorious God? It were far greater wisdom and honesty, for your children to set up a dog or a toad, and say, This is more to be loved and honoured than my father. If a traitor against an earthly prince deserve to be hanged, drawn, and quartered; certainly that man that would forsake God and his laws, to please such silly worms as you, did deserve to be hanged in the flames of hell, and to be tormented by infernal fiends, and ground to powder by the wrath of the Almighty! Well, if you have eyes that can see, you may see now past doubt, that we cannot turn to you that are ungodly, with any wisdom or honesty in the world, nor without the highest madness and dishonesty. But can you say so of your turning in to us? Is it contrary either to wisdom, or honesty, for you to turn unfeignedly to God, and to become a sanctified, godly people? Methinks you should not have such a thought in your hearts; and, therefore, if we be not all of a mind, and go not all one way, it is most apparent that it is not long of us, but of you.

3. If we do unite and agree, it must be upon terms of safety. This much I hope you cannot deny us. You would not sure wish us to agree to our own destruction, and to make a bargain with you, that we may all join together in cutting our own throats! Do you think that this were a wise combination? How much less should we make an agreement to go the certain way to hell, and to join together in damning our own souls for ever! Sirs, if you dislike the way of holiness, do but find out any other way that will safely bring a man to heaven, and we will promise you to join in it. But unholiness will never do it. God hath told us as plain as can be spoken, "That except a man be born again, and be converted, he cannot enter into the kingdom of heaven," John iii. 3, 5; Matt. xviii. 3; and that "without holiness no man shall see the Lord," Heb. xii. 14: and that "the righteous themselves are scarcely saved," 1 Pet. iv. 18: and that "if any man be in Christ, he is a new creature; old things are passed away, and all things become new," 2 Cor. v. 17: and that "if any man have not the Spirit of Christ, he is none of his," Rom. viii. 9. So that if God know who shall be saved, it is as certain as any thing in the world, that no unsanctified man can be saved. If leaping into the water be the way to drowning, or leaping into the fire be the way to burning, or leaping down from the top of a steeple be the way to break your necks, as sure is an unholy life the way to everlasting torment. And would you wish us to undo ourselves everlastingly for your friendship? What can you say to this now? If you say that your way is not so dangerous, it is but our precise, uncharitable conceit. We have showed you the word of God for it; and forty times more we could easily show you. And shall we believe you, or such as you, before God? You are liars, but God cannot lie. You see not what is done in another world; but God seeth it. You know not what is in heaven or hell; but God knoweth. And shall we not believe God that knoweth and disposeth of all, better than moles that never saw it, and ignorant souls that never knew it? God saith, that "fornicators, adulterers, drunkards, covetous persons, revilers, or the like, shall not inherit the kingdom of God," 1 Cor. vi. 10, 11. And that "they that are in the flesh cannot please God;" and that "if you live after the flesh ye shall die," Rom. viii. 5—7, 13. And would you have us believe you, that there is no danger in a fleshly life? Sirs, we desire heartily to be united and agreed with you, but we are loth to buy it so dear, as the loss of God and heaven comes to. We are willing of concord with you, but we are loth to be damned with you: and do you blame us for this? And, alas, if you should tell us a thousand times, that you hope there is no such danger, or that you hope to escape as well as the godly, this is but poor security to us. Shall we be so mad, as to venture ourselves on such words as these, against the word of the Ruler of the world? What security can you give us, that we shall escape damnation if we turn ungodly? Are you able to save us from the wrath of God? Will you undertake to stand between us and his displeasure? What say you? If we will forsake a holy life, and live as careless worldlings do, and neglect God and our souls, and please the world and our flesh, will you undertake to answer for us in judgment? And will you venture to bear the punishment that we should bear? If you dare not undertake to save us harmless, why will you persuade us to do as you do? Nay, if you would undertake it, he were a mad-man that would trust you, and venture his salvation upon such undertakings; for we know you are not able to make them good. Alas! poor souls, how unable will you be to save yourselves, or to stay out of hell an hour longer, when devils have commission to carry you away! And shall we trust our souls upon your boasting words, when we know you are unable to help yourselves? Let us see first what you can do for yourselves or us, against the present hand of God. Can you keep off death, and rebuke diseases, and live here in health and wealth for ever, whether God will or no? How comes it to pass then that here is never a one of you near two

hundred years of age? Let us see you chide back approaching death, and raise the dead bodies from their graves, and heal all the diseases that cut off mankind: if you cannot do these smaller matters, would you have us believe that you can save us from damnation? Why, sirs, must your neighbours lie some of them in poverty, and some in pain, some sick of one disease, and some of another, and you look on them and cannot cure them, or relieve them, and yet must we venture our souls upon your words? You cannot make an old man young again; and can you make the word of God prove false, or save those that God hath said shall perish, and bring unsanctified men to heaven whether God will or no? Well, sirs, let them that hate their souls, or care not whether they are saved or damned, forsake the Lord and a holy life, and join with you, and see whether you can save them: but for my part, I believe the word of God, and upon this word only I am resolved to build my hopes, and venture my soul, and all that little that I have in this world: trust you on what you please, this shall be my trust; and they that can find a surer ground to build upon, let them take their course.

But I must tell you, that if you would wish us all to cast away God, and Christ, and heaven, to agree with you, you are monsters and not men; and if you are so cruel as to desire us to damn our souls for company, we must be so careful of ourselves as to abhor your motion, and rather to hate the dearest thing or person in the world, as they would draw us from Christ and everlasting life, Luke xiv. 26.

You see then what it is that standeth in our way, to hinder us from turning back to you. But what danger would you be in if you should turn to us? Would it hurt or hazard you to forsake your sensual, ungodly lives? Is there any danger in turning to God, and living a holy, heavenly life? What is the danger? Forsooth you may lose your estates or lives! A great matter indeed in comparison of eternal life: and must you not lose them shortly whether you will or not? And are they not in the power of God? And cannot he preserve them if he please? And if it be good for them, he is liker to do it for his own, than for his enemies. But indeed he hath told you himself, that "he that will save his life shall lose it, and he that loseth his life for his sake, shall find it; even in life everlasting," Matt. xvi. 25; x. 39. And yet as the world now goeth in England, through the mercy of God, your lives are in no danger. It is but the scorn of ignorant, miserable men that you must endure. And will you stick at this, in the cause of God and your salvation? Nay, indeed you are in most dreadful danger every day, and night, and hour, till you forsake your former fleshly lives, and turn to Christ! You are all the while even within a step of death and hell, till you are converted and made a holy people; it is but one stroke of death to put an end to your lives and hopes, and you are gone for ever. So that you have nothing to lose, but a heaven to gain, if you join with the godly. There is no danger can come to you by turning, unless it be the loss of your sins; and that is a loss no more to be feared, than a man should fear to lose the plague, or pox, or leprosy, that hath it.

Now I beseech you, sirs, as men of conscience or of reason, set both together, and equally consider how the case stands between us. If we join with the unholy, we run into hell, and lose God, and Christ, and grace, and salvation for evermore; but if you turn to the godly, you get out of danger, and make the gainfullest match that ever was made by mortal men; and you can lose nothing but the sensual pleasures of sin, which are but exchanged for the joys of saints, as sickness is exchanged for health. And which now do you think in reason is the fitter, that you turn to the godly, or they to you? Truly, if you make so great a matter of leaving your sins, which are viler than your dung, that you will rather break with God and us, you must give us leave to make so great a matter of leaving Christ and his holy ways and people, that we will much rather break with you and all the wicked in the world, and with our carnal selves, and that which is most dear to them: and I think we have good reason for it.

4. Moreover, this must be considered in our treaty, that if we agree, it is fit that our dearest friends be taken into the agreement: should we cast off them to agree with adversaries, and leave our old friends in hope of new? But if we come over to you, and turn unholy, we shall never have God's consent to the agreement; we must leave him out, and utterly lose him: when, alas, we cannot live, nor move, nor breathe, without him; we cannot have our daily bread, or one night's rest, but by his gift. And such a friend is not to be lost for you. And we shall lose the Lord Jesus, and the Holy Ghost, and the communion of saints, and the peace of our own consciences. Oh what a peal would conscience ring us night and day! It would open hell to us: it would kindle the fire of God's wrath in our bosoms; and be scorching us as we lie down and as we rise up: and who would endure such a life as this for all the world? It is like it is not thus with you; but that is because you know not what a case you are in, nor what a dreadful thing ungodliness is; but we know it: and therefore what shift soever you make to keep your consciences asleep, I know not how I should quiet mine, if I were in your case, and knew but what I know of it.

But now if you will join with Christ and us, your true friends will be glad of it; you should not lose one friend in the world by it, unless you take the devil and his servants for your friends, that would destroy you. Judge then, whether you should come to us, or we to you.

5. Moreover, this must be considered in our treaty, that if we agree with you, we have some regard to our honour. And what honour is it to us to become the servants of sin and the devil, and be forsaken of God, and return to the slavery that lately we were delivered from? A hangman is ten thousand times more honourable than this.

But on the other side, if you will turn to Christ, you will come out of the greatest shame, and obtain the greatest honours, that you are capable of: you will be the sons of God, and heirs of heaven, coheirs with Christ, fellow-citizens of the saints, and of the household of God, John i. 12; Rom. viii. 17; Eph. ii. 19; and be built up an habitation of God through the Spirit, Eph. ii. 22.

6. Moreover, this is most considerable in our treaty, that if we agree, it must be upon universal terms that all will agree upon; or else it can be no universal agreement. If a few should agree with you, this would not make a unity in the world. We must have terms that are fit for all to agree upon. And in good sadness, would you have all the world be such as you? Tell me, you that are covetous and proud, would you have all the world become proud and covetous to agree with you? Nay, if they should, when they are likest you, they would not agree with you: for the proud will envy the proud, and their pride will set them together by the ears: and the covetous would be greedily snatching the prey out of one another's jaws, and their mam-

mon would be the matter of their strife. Tell me, also, you that are drunkards or unclean, would you have all the world become drunkards and unclean for unity with you? You that are careless about your souls, and prayerless in your families, and forget the matters of everlasting life, would you have all the world set as light by God, and Christ, and heaven as you? Could the worst of you all have the face to make such a motion as this? What! would you have all holiness and heavenly-mindedness banished out of the world, because you have banished it from yourselves? Would you have all men shut their Bibles as much as you, and instruct their children and servants no more than you, and love God and serve him no more than you? Is it possible that such a heart as this can be in the breast of the worst on earth? What! would you have all the world be drunkards, or fornicators, or haters of godliness, or at least unsanctified, because you are so? How quickly then would earth turn hell, and the flames of the wrath of God consume it! How certainly then would God forsake the world, as a man would be gone from toads and serpents! Can there be such cruelty in any but the devils, as to wish all the world to be damned with you for company, or to agree with you on such terms, that you may go hand in hand together to damnation? Or if you had such devilish hearts within you, as to desire such an agreement as this, can you think that all the godly would yield to it? No, let me tell you, not one of them in all the world will yield to it. If you set no more by the love of God, the blood of Christ, the presence and comforts of the Holy Ghost, and the hopes of glory, yet they do, and will do. If you will run into hell, you shall never get them thither with you for company.

But on the other side, there is nothing in the way of holiness, but what is fit for all men to agree upon. I know all will not; and therefore we expect not an agreement with all. But that is their unhappiness. There is no fit means of agreement but this.

7. Lastly, this also must be considered in our treaty; that we agree upon terms that are like to hold, and not to be repented of hereafter. For what good will it do to agree to-day, and to break it or bewail it to-morrow? Why, alas, sirs, we know as sure as we breathe, that if we should agree with you in unholiness, we should quickly repent it, either by grace, or in hell-fire. Nay, we know that you will repent of these unholy ways and hearts yourselves, either by grace or judgment. Nay, there are even now some kind of purposes in many of you to repent. I have heard abundance of ungodly men profess that they hope to repent hereafter, and mend their lives, and leave their sins. And would you wish us to come and join with you in a way that you hope to forsake yourselves, and in a way that you propose hereafter to repent of? I know as sure as that the sun will set, that every ungodly soul among you will shortly change their false opinions; and they that derided the servants of Christ, would wish then that they might be but door-keepers among them: you will wish and wish a thousand times that you had done as they did, and lived as holily as the best on earth: you will then wish, Oh that it were to do again! and that my life were again to be lived; and God would but try me on earth once more! Those tongues that railed against religion, will a thousand times more reproach yourselves for those reproaches, and the neglect of this religion. You will then cry out, Where was my wit and reason, when I made so mad a change, as of God for the creature, Christ for sin, and heaven for hell! Do you think, sirs, that it were any wisdom for us to agree with you now in that, for which you will fall out with yourselves for ever? and to go with you in that loose ungodly way, which you will wish yourselves that you had never known?

Besides, we know that it is only the saints that we must live with for ever; and therefore you must become saints, if you would be united to us here. What! should we be so careful to agree with you awhile and be separated from you eternally, or do worse by suffering with you? But if you will unite with us in Christ and holiness, this will be a lasting unity; which you will never have occasion to repent of. The union between the Lord Jesus and his members, shall never be dissolved. Heartily join with his servants now in the ways of holiness, and you shall certainly join with them in the state of happiness, and in the joyful fruition and praises of the Lord.

Well, sirs, in this much of our treaty, I have laid the case plain and open before you, and showed you that we cannot come over to you: it is not possible, nor honest, nor safe; we cannot forsake a holy life without forsaking God, and our Redeemer, and our salvation, which no man, that is a man indeed, should desire us to do; nor can we do it till we first forsake our understandings. But on your side the case is otherwise: you may turn to God and a holy life without any hurt or wrong to you at all; nay, it is the only way to your felicity, and if you do it not, you are undone for ever: so that the case is past all controversy before you, that there is no way in the world to unity, but by consent in piety. If half the commonwealth turn rebels, and so shall make a division in the body, the way to unite them is by the returning of the rebels to their allegiance, and not for the true and lawful subjects to turn all rebels and join with them. For without the head there cannot be a union. So that if the world be still divided and disagreed, it is not long of the godly, but of the ungodly; and if you would have an agreement, it is you that must yield, who cause the disagreement. You may do it, and must do it, or do worse; but the godly may not yield to you.

What say you now, would you have unity or division? Would you have peace or no peace? You complain that the world is of so many minds: would you have them all reconciled and of one mind? If you would, let us see it. The work sticks with you; on your hands it lieth, and it is you that must do it, if ever it be done. If you would have all ungodly, you deserve not to live on the earth. Shall we then without any more ado agree all upon a life of holiness? Oh that our towns and parishes would all join together in this agreement! And it must be this or none.

But perhaps some of you will say, What need you make so many words about a matter that nobody doth deny? We all know we should be holy and godly, and none should be ungodly; who doubts of this? But the question is, What holiness and godliness is? Tell us therefore what you mean by it, and who those be that you take to be the godly, sanctified people?

Answ. If we are all agreed of the necessity of holiness, then those that are not yet agreed to be holy themselves, do sin against their own consciences, and condemn themselves in the things which they allow, and wilfully divide themselves from Christ and from his church. And if any of you have been so long baptized into the name of the Holy Ghost as your Sanctifier, and yet know not what sanctification is, and who are to be accounted sanctified and godly, you show that you have perfidiously cast away and broke your covenant with God; and made but an ill use of your baptism, or any means and ordinances since. But if you know not who are godly or ungodly, I shall quickly tell you.

A godly man is one that being formally in a state of sin and misery, both strange and backward to God and heaven, and a holy life, and prone to earthly, fleshly pleasures, is now, by the powerful work of the word and Spirit of God, converted to unfeigned faith and repentance, broken-hearted for his former sin and misery, flying to Christ as the only hope and physician of his soul; and so is made a new creature, having his heart set upon God and everlasting life, and contemning all the pleasures of the flesh, and the things of this world, in comparison of his hopes and glory; hating all known sin, and not wilfully living in any; and loving the highest degree of holiness, and willing to use the means that God hath appointed to destroy the remnants of sin, and bring him nearer to perfection: this is a truly godly man. And he that is not such, is ungodly. He that yet remaineth in his natural depraved state, and is unacquainted with this great and holy change, that hath any sin that he had rather keep than leave, and any that he wilfully liveth in; and wilfully neglecteth known duties, as one that had rather be free from them than perform them, and had rather live a fleshly life than a spiritual and a holy life, and is more in love with the creature than with God; with his life on earth in flesh and sin, than a life in heaven with God and his saints in perfect holiness; this man is undoubtedly a wicked and ungodly man, how civilly or religiously soever he may seem to live in the world. And so I have in a few words told you, who they be that are godly, and who are the ungodly. The question now that we are treating about is, whether we shall all agree together to be godly? Do you not believe it to be best and necessary? If not, you are blind: if you do, let us agree on it without delay. You tell us with many great complaints of the many differences and divisions that are among us; but shall we agree so far as we are agreed? That is, shall we agree in heart and practice, so far as we are agreed in opinion and profession? Oh that you would make a solemn covenant, that you will but consent and go along with the godly so far as you confess you ought to do; and would but unite with us in faithfulness to the truths which you cannot deny. I think it will be best to call you to the trial in some particulars.

1. I hope we are all agreed that there is one only God that made us, and preserveth us, and redeemed us; and therefore that we are wholly his, and should resign ourselves, and all that we have, absolutely to him for his service. He is not worthy the name of a man that denieth this. And shall we all agree now in the practice of this much? Shall we wholly resign ourselves and all that we have to God, and labour to know what God would have us be and do, and that let us resolve upon, whatever the flesh or the world say to the contrary? Were but this much well resolved on, we were in a fair way to a full agreement.

2. We are all agreed in opinion or profession, that this God is our only happiness, and his favour is better than all the world, and that he is infinitely wise, and good, and powerful; and therefore that he must be loved above all things whatsoever, and must be most feared, and served, and trusted, and depended on.

And shall we but agree all in the practice of this much? Oh that you would but heartily consent and do it! Did we but join together in loving God above all, and fearing, and trusting, and serving him before all, we should quickly be of one heart and soul, and in a very fair way to a perfect agreement.

3. We are all agreed (that profess christianity) that sin hath made us miserable, and brought us under the wrath and curse of God; and that the Lord Jesus Christ having redeemed us by his blood, is the only physician and remedy of our souls; and having manifested such infinite love in our redemption, and also purchased dominion over us, we are strongly bound to rejoice in his salvation, and fly to him for safety, and rest upon him, and live in the thankful admirations of his love, and in careful obedience to his gracious laws.

And shall we all agree in the practice of this much? Will you fly to Christ with broken, bleeding hearts, for safety from sin, and wrath, and hell, and set more by him than by all the world? Will you study with all saints to comprehend his love, Ephes. iii. 18, 19; and admire him and his mercies, and devote yourselves to him, and be ruled by him? Oh that we were but all agreed in this much.

4. We are all agreed in opinion or profession, that the Holy Ghost is the Sanctifier of God's elect, or of all that shall be saved; and that except a man be born again by the Spirit, he cannot enter into the kingdom of heaven; and that without holiness none shall see God; and that no man is the son of God that hath not in him the Spirit of his Son, 1 Cor. xii. 12, 13; Eph. iv. 5; John iii. 5, 6; Heb. xii. 14; Rom. viii. 9; Gal. iv. 4.

Were we but all such now as we are agreed we must be, and would you but all consent to this sanctification and newness of life, the great difference were healed, and the work were done.

5. Moreover we are all agreed, or seem to be so, that the holy Scripture is the word of God, and of infallible truth, and therefore must be believed and made the rule of our judgments and our lives.

Shall we all agree now in the practice of this? Will you appeal to the Scripture, and shall it be our rule? If the flesh persuade you to another course, and murmur at the strictness of God's word; if custom be against it, and the greater number be against it; if your profits, or pleasures, or worldly honours be against it, and your former opinions and practice have been against it; will you yet believe the Scripture before all, and be ruled by it above all the world? You are agreed I hope that God is to be obeyed rather than men, or than the flesh and the devil? Will you resolve that it shall be so? Oh if the word of God might be the rule, how quickly should we be agreed! for all the popish cavils at its difficulty, and men's divers expositions, yet how soon should we be agreed!

6. We are all agreed in opinion or profession, that there is a heaven for the sanctified, even an endless unconceivable glory with God, in the seeing of his face, and enjoying him in perfect love and joys; and that the seeking of this everlasting glory should be the main and principal business of our lives, which all things must give place to. He that will deny this can have no pretence to call himself a christian.

Oh that we might but all agree in the practising of this! and that the principal love and desire of our souls were set upon the heavenly blessedness, and the chiefest of our care and labour might be laid out for the obtaining of it! Agree in this, and all will be agreed at last.

7. We are all agreed in our profession, that there is a hell, or state of endless torments, where all the finally unsanctified and ungodly must be for ever.

But why do we not agree in the diligent avoiding of such a dreadful misery, and using our best endeavours to escape it?

8. We are all agreed in profession, that the flesh is our enemy, and must be mortified. But will you

agree in the practice of this mortification? We are agreed in profession, that the world is our enemy, and must be contemned, and that it is a vain and worthless thing compared with the glory that is to come: but yet men will not agree to renounce the world unfeignedly, and to be strangers to it, and part with all rather than with God and a good conscience; but while men speak contemptuously of the world, they seek it far more eagerly than heaven. We are agreed that the devil is our enemy, and yet men will not forsake his service.

9. We are all agreed in profession, that sin is a most hateful thing, hated of God, condemned by his word, and the only cause of the damnation of souls: and yet men love it, and live in it with delight. Shall we agree all to deal with sin as we speak of it? Will magistrates, and ministers, and people join together, to banish it out of town and country? Particularly we are agreed, I hope, that whoredom, and wantonness, and gluttony, and drunkenness, and strife, and envying, and lying, and deceit, and cursing, and swearing, and railing, and backbiting, and speaking against a holy life, are all gross, hateful, damning sins, which every christian must abhor. But why do you not agree in the hating, and forsaking, and beating down these sins? But town and country swarmeth with them as a carcass doth with maggots, or a stinking pond with frogs and toads: so that magistrates and ministers, punishments and persuasion, the laws of the land, and the laws of God, can do but little to rid the country of them; but the same men that confess all these to be great and grievous sins, will keep them and delight in them, as if it were in despite of God and man, or as if they bore a deadly grudge to their own immortal souls.

10. There is none of you that bears the face of a christian, but must agree with us in profession, that "one thing is needful, and that we must seek first the kingdom of God and his righteousness, and labour most for the food that will not perish," Luke x. 41, 42; Matt. vi. 33; John vi. 27; and that "God should be loved with all our heart, and soul, and might," and that no man can love him too much, nor serve him too carefully, nor be too diligent in the seeking of his salvation. Why then will you not all agree to do thus? But the very same tongues that confess all this, will yet speak against the service of God, and call it puritanism and preciseness, and say it is more ado than needs. Why, sirs, if you will say and unsay, there is no hold to be taken of your words, and therefore what agreement can be with you? Will you confess that all should take more care for their souls than for their bodies; and take more care for heaven than earth, and yet will you not agree to do it, but rather speak against them that do it, when you confess that it is best? Why, if you can agree no better with yourselves, how can you agree with us? If your own opinions and profession be at such odds with your wills and practices, no wonder if you be at odds with others.

More particularly, I hope you will all confess, that it is the duty of all that can, to hear the word of God, and frequently to read it, and labour to understand it, and to meditate in it day and night; and for parents daily to teach it their children at home and abroad, lying down and rising up, Deut. vi. 6—8; xi. 18, 19; Psal. i. 2, 3; and to pray in their families, and in private, even always or frequently to pray, and not to wax faint, but in all things to make known their requests to God, that all things might be sanctified to them by the word and prayer. All this is plain in the word of God, Dan. vi. 10, 11; Luke xviii. 1; 1 Thess. v. 17; Psal. lv. 17; 1 Tim. iv. 5; Phil. iv. 6.

But will you all agree with us in the practice of these things? Will all the families in town and country agree together, to pray morning and evening reverently to God, and to banish profaneness out of their doors, and to instruct their children and servants in the fear of God, and spend the Lord's day in holy exercises, and help one another to prepare for death and judgment, and exhort one another daily, while it is called to-day, lest any be hardened by the deceitfulness of sin? Heb. iii. 13.

To what purpose should I mention any more particulars, till we see whether you will unite and agree in these? All these are your own professions. I know you cannot deny any one of them, and yet we cannot persuade you to consent with us in the practice of what yourselves profess; no, nor scarce to forbear the open opposing of it: either resolve now that you will all agree with us in these things, which you confess the Lord hath made your duty, or else tell us plainly that you are the deadly enemies of unity and peace, that we may take you to be as you are, and trouble ourselves no more about you. If you are resolved against agreement and unity, tell us so, and save us the labour of any further treaties with you. Talk no more childishly about our petty differences in ceremonies and forms of worship, about bishops and common prayer books, and holydays, and such like, as long as you refuse agreement in the main. There is a difference between you that is a hundred times greater than these: some of you are for heaven, and some for earth; some of you live to the Spirit, and some to the flesh; some of you are hearing, reading, or meditating on the word of God, when others think it needless, and had rather have a pair of cards or dice in their hands: some of you make God's law your rule, and some are ruled by the world and the flesh; some are drunkards, gluttons, wantons, worldlings, and some are sober, temperate, chaste, and heavenly; some think almost any thing enough in the worship of God, and for the saving of their souls, and others think the best they can do too little; and when they have done most, lament that they do no more: some families use daily prayer, reading, and holy instructions; and others use daily swearing, railing, ribaldry, and perhaps deriding of holiness itself. In a word, some give up themselves to God and heaven, and others to the world, the flesh, and the devil; some are converted and become new creatures by the sanctifying work of the Holy Ghost, and others are yet in the state of nature, and never knew a true conversion.

This is the great difference of the world, sirs: till this be healed, it is in vain to talk of the healing of our petty differences. And therefore once more I tell you, if you will not be converted to a holy life, and unite with us on these terms, you are the enemies of peace and unity, and the great incendiaries of the world.

And now having proceeded thus far in the treaty with you, because I will either bring you to agreement, or leave you at least without excuse, I will here annex some further reasons to move you, if it may be, to so happy a work.

1. Consider, I pray you, that if you will not agree with us in the things that you make profession of, and confess to be your duty, you are then treacherous and false to God, and to yourselves, and therefore not fit for any to make agreement with, till you change your minds. Do you know that God is best, and yet will you not love him better than the world? Do you know that heaven is the only happiness,

and yet will you not seek it more than earth? Do you know that a holy life is best, and yet will you be unholy? Do you know sin is the worst and most dangerous thing in the world, and yet will you not let it go? Who will trust such men as you, that will go against their own knowledge and confessions? If you will be false to God, and false to your own souls, no wonder if you be false to us.

2. Moreover, all your pretended desires of unity and concord are base hypocrisy, as long as you refuse to unite with us in the way and state of holiness. To take on you that you are troubled at the divisions of the world, and to wish that we were all of one religion, and to talk against sects and opinions as you do, is mere self-condemning, and such gross dissembling as exposeth you to shame. What! would you have us think you are against divisions when you divide from God, and Christ, and the Holy Ghost; from the Scripture, from the holy catholic church, and from the communion of saints? Can you for shame say, that you are for unity and agreement, when you are dividing from us, and will not agree with us, unless we will be as mad as you, and damn our souls for company with you? To hear these ungodly men talk against sects and divisions in the church, is as if we heard a man that hath the leprosy cry out against those that have the itch, or a murderer chide another for foul words.

3. And I must tell you, while you remain ungodly, you are the great heretics and separatists that trouble the church of God, more than abundance of those that you reproach. I excuse not the least; but none of them are like you. As death is worse than sickness, as being that which all sickness tends to, and the worst that it can do; so ungodliness is worse than sects, and particular errors or heresies, it being the worst that any error can do, to make a man ungodly. There are no such separatists in the world as you. It is not only from a particular church or ordinance that you separate; but, as I said even now, you separate from God that made you, from Christ that bought you, from the Spirit that should sanctify you, from the word of God that must rule you or condemn you, from the body of Christ, and the holy communion of his people. The church would have you join with them in holy worship; and your godly neighbours would have you join with them in prayer and holy lives, and you will not, but separate from them all. They cannot have your help against the sins of the time and place you live in: they cannot have your company in the way to heaven; but when they go one way, you go another way. You are the great troublers of the world, and break the peace of church and state, and of all that you have to do with. You trouble magistrates, and make work for lawyers; you trouble ministers, and frustrate their labours, and make their lives grievous to them, when it is much in your hands to make them joyous. You trouble all the godly that are about you, and you will find at last that you have most of all troubled your own souls. For shame therefore, before you speak any more against sects and separatists, or any other troublers of the church, give over the ungodly separation which you continue in, and come in to the unity of the church yourselves, and live in that communion of saints which you say you do believe, and do not go on to trouble the church abundance more than those that you speak against.

4. Consider, also, whether you have not as much reason to live a diligent, holy life, and seek God and your salvation with all your might, as any of your neighbours have; and, therefore, whether your own necessity doth not call aloud to you, to unite with them, and to do as they do. Your godly neighbours are meditating on the word of God, when you are thinking of the world, or on vanity: they are discoursing of the life to come, when you are talking of your worldly business, or pouring out a company of idle words. Ask your consciences now, whether you have not as much need to study the Scripture, and prepare for the life to come, as they? Your godly neighbours are at prayer, when you are sinning and drowned in the inordinate cares of the world, and have no heart to their employment. Let conscience speak, whether you have not as much need to pray as they. They abhor sin and are afraid of it, when you boldly venture on it. Let conscience tell you, whether you have not as much cause to be afraid of sin as they: yea, and a hundred times more; for you are under the guilt and power of it. Oh wonderful madness of the ungodly world, that the example of the godly should not bring them to some consideration! A man that is converted and reconciled to God, and hath a pardon of all his sins, and is in a state of salvation, and walketh humbly and uprightly with God, doth yet think all too little that he can do; but fasteth, and prayeth, and watcheth against temptations, and humbleth his flesh, and followeth after God continually, and lamenteth after all that he is so bad, and can do no more. And his neighbour that liveth by him is an ignorant, stupid sinner, unconverted, and under the guilt of his sin, and under the curse and wrath of God, having no assurance of salvation; nay, it is certain that he would be cast into hell the next hour if he die in that condition; and yet this man feels not any such need of prayer, and holy meditation, and conference, and so religious and strict a life. He that hath lost almost all the time of his life, and is not only quite behindhand in knowledge and abilities, but is an unsanctified miserable wretch, not sure to be out of hell an hour; this man perceiveth no such necessity of a holy life, nor why he should make so much ado. As if a rich man should be put to daily labour, and a man that hath nothing should think it needless: or as if a man that hath the tooth-ache, or a slight disease, should send to the physician; and he that hath the plague should sit still and say, "What needs this trouble?" Sirs, I beseech you look upon the holiest and most heavenly neighbours you have, and bethink you whether you have not much more need to be diligent than they. Have not you immortal souls to lose as well as they? Are not you in danger of damnation as much, and a hundred times more than they? Should not God be your master as well as theirs? and his law your ruler as well as theirs? and heaven be as dear to you as to them? Bethink yourselves when you hear them praying, or reading, or repeating sermons, and sanctifying the Lord's day, and fearing to offend, Have not I as much need to do all this as any of them? If then you have as much cause and need to live a godly life as others, join with them in it, and let all the town agree together, and none withdraw but he that can say, I have no need of it.

5. And I pray you consider also, how easy it would make the way to heaven, if we would but all unite and agree to go together in it. This is it that discourageth the weak, and makes it so hard a matter to be saved, because there are so few that are godly: but if one or two poor people be resolved to seek first the kingdom of God and his righteousness, and to please God and save their souls, the rest do either look on and refuse to join with them, or else speak against them, and make them their ordinary scorn. And thus he that will be saved, must not only go to

heaven without the company of the most of his neighbours, but must go through their opposition, and reproaches, and discouragements : and (the Lord be merciful to the miserable world !) most places that one shall come into, are more agreed against holiness and salvation than for it, and had rather that all the parish would agree together against a godly life (which is indeed against Christ, and heaven, and their own souls) than for it. And some places are so miserable, that you may hear them thank God that they have not one puritan in their parish, or but few at most; meaning by puritans, men that seek heaven above earth, and had rather leave their sins than be damned. And this disheartencth many that have some mind to godliness, to see almost all the town and parish against it.

But now if you had all but so much wit and grace, as to meet together and make an agreement, that you will all be a holy people to the Lord, and you will all join together in a godly life, and you will all be the sworn professed enemies of the way to hell, and join together against your ignorance, and pride, and covetousness, and drunkenness, and swearing, and railing, and all profaneness and iniquity ; and if you would all agree together to set up prayer, and reading, and holy exercises, in every house in town and parish ; and that you will all redeem the time for your souls, especially that you will wholly spend the Lord's day in the necessary delightful work of God ; then what abundance of your difficulties would be removed! and how easy and pleasant would the way to heaven be ! Then there would be none to discourage poor ignorant souls, by deriding at a godly life; nor any to entice them to wicked courses; nor any to tempt them by their ill examples ; and the number of the godly would encourage men, as the fewness of them now discourageth. This troubleth men in their passage to heaven, when we are ill-yoked together, and one draws backward as the other draws forward: and if the husband be for God, the wife is for the world; or if the wife be for heaven, the husband will needs go the way to hell: and if one neighbour be godly, the two, if not ten or twenty, next him will be ungodly : and, as the Israelites' spies, they raise up false reports of the land, of the state of godliness, and of the persons themselves, to discourage others ; whereas if you would all agree together, you might march on comfortably without all this ado.

Oh how sweet and pleasant a life is it, to see brethren dwell together in such a holy unity as this, Psal. cxxxiii. 1. Happy are they that dwell in such towns and parishes as these, if there be any such in the world! Where neighbours go all hand in hand together towards heaven, and take sweet counsel together; and go to the house of God in company: and when others meet in ale-houses, and about fooleries and profaneness, they will meet together to talk of their meeting in the presence of God, and the joy and praises of the living God, and the communion with Christ, and with angels, and with one another, which we shall then possess: when they will pray together, and comfort one another with such words, 1 Thess. iv. 18. And when others are talking idly, or of the world, they will be admonishing and exhorting one another, and speaking words that are edifying to the hearers, Col. iii. 16; Ephes. iv. 29; and opening their cases and experiences to each other, and faithfully watching over one another, agreeing to tell one another plainly and lovingly of their sins, and to take it thankfully of those that do so, and endeavour presently to amend. What a sweet and blessed life were this, if all our towns and parishes would agree in it! Who would not rather live with bread and water in such a town as this, than be a lord or prince among the ungodly! Well, sirs, it is much in your hands now to make your own and your neighbours' lives thus sweet and comfortable, and to make the way to heaven thus easy: why then will you not agree and do it?

6. Moreover, such a holy unity and concord would be the highest honour to your towns and countries that in this world they can possibly receive. It is the highest glory of the kingdoms of thé world, to become the kingdoms of the Lord and of his Christ, Rev. xi. 15. You think it a great honour for your towns to be rich, and have fair buildings, and to have worldly privileges : but, alas, these are baubles in comparison of the other! Oh if it were but the happiness of this town and parish to be brought to such a holy agreement as I mentioned, that you would all join together in a godly life, and every family agree to worship God with holy reverence, and all set together against profaneness and all known sin, what an honour would it be to you of this place! How would your fame go through all the land ! All countries would ring of Kidderminster, what a victory Christ had gotten there, and what an overthrow the devil and sin had there received! and what a blessed place and people it is, where they are all agreed to be holy and to be saved, and are all like the ancient primitive believers, that were of one heart and one soul! Acts iv. 32. Oh how the world would ring of such a town, where there is not one family that is ungodly, that serveth the devil by worldliness, swearing, drunkenness, or any ungodly course ; but all are united in Christ and holiness, and are like to live together in heaven! Truly, neighbours, this would be a greater honour to you, and to the town, than if you were every man a lord or prince! In the eyes of God and all wise men, it would be the greatest honour in the world. And oh what an excellent example would it be to all the towns and parishes in the land! When they see your holy unity and peace, or hear of a place that is so happily agreed, it may shame them out of their ungodliness, and kindle in them a strong desire to be like you, and agree together as you have done. Oh that you would but give them such an example, and try the issue!

7. And I desire every one singly to consider, that it is the unspeakable mercy of God, that he calleth you to this holy union with Christ, and communion of saints; and that he doth not thrust you away, and forbid you coming near, but will give you leave to be of the holy society, fellow-citizens with the saints, and of the household of God. God hath made his promise and offer so large, that you may have part in it as well as others, if you will not wilfully shut out yourselves. The feast is prepared; all things are ready, and you are every man and woman invited. Christ hath opened to you a door of admittance and access to God. And will you now refuse and undo yourselves? The sanctified are God's jewels, Mal. iii. 17; his treasure and peculiar people; the beloved of his soul, and his delight; and the only people in the world that shall be saved. This is true; for God hath spoken it: and you may be of this blessed number if you will. God hath not separated you from them, or shut you out by forbidding you to come among them. O do not you separate and shut out yourselves. You see your godly neighbours in possession of this privilege; and may not you have it if you will? May not you study the word of God, and call upon him in prayer, and set yourselves for heaven. as well as they? Where doth the Scripture command them to it, any more than

you? or forbid you any more than them? The door is open, you may come in if you will. You have the same means, and call, and offer, and time, and leave, to lead a holy life as they. And will you make so much of the difference yourselves as to be the only refusers? God hath done so much for you by the death of Christ, and so ordered the matter in the promises and offers of the gospel, that none of you shall be able to say at last, I would fain have been one of the blessed society, and fain have lived in the union and communion of saints, but I could not; God would not give me leave, and Christ and his church would not receive me and entertain me. Not a man or a woman of you shall have this excuse; and therefore come in and join with the saints, and thank God that you may.

8. And consider, also, that if you will not agree with us in matters of holiness, we can never well make up the rest of our differences: our smaller controversies will never be well agreed, if you will not agree in the main. But if this were agreed, we should in season certainly heal the rest. It would make a man's heart ache to hear wretched sinners talk of our differences about bishops, and ceremonies, and common prayer, and holy days, and infant baptism, and the like, that are dead in their sins, and are yet disagreed from us in the very bent of heart and life. Alas, sirs, you have other matters than these first to talk of, and trouble yourselves with. A man that is ready to die of a consumption, should not be taking care to cure the warts or freckles in his face. We have greater matters wherein we differ from you, than kneeling at the sacrament, or observation of days or other ceremonies, or doubtful opinions in matters of doctrine. Let us first be agreed all to serve one Master, and seek one end, and be ruled by one law, and hate known sin, and live a holy life, and then we shall be ready to treat with you about a further agreement. But to talk of small matters, when we differ in the greatest matters in the world, as much as your souls are worth, and in matters which heaven or hell lieth on, this is but childish trifling; and whatever we may do for the peace of the church with such, yet to yourselves that will be small advantage.

Nay, I must tell you, that it is usually but the cunning of the devil, and the hypocrisy of your own hearts, that makes you turn your talk to these controversies, when the great breach is unhealed between Christ and you. It is commonly made a shift to delude and quiet a debauched conscience. Our poor people will not by any persuasion be drawn to a holy, heavenly life, but live in worldliness and fleshliness, in swearing and drunkenness, and lying and deceit, and filthiness and profaneness, and hate the minister or christian that doth reprove them; and then forsooth they talk of Common Prayer book, and holy days, and bishops, and kneeling at the sacrament, to make others, and perhaps their deluded hearts, believe, that this is the controversy and difference. And so a wretched drunkard, or worldling, persuades himself that he is a religious man; as if the difference between him and the godly were but about these ceremonies or church orders: when, alas, we differ in greater matters, as light and darkness, life and death, yea, next to the difference between heaven and hell.

And I must tell you, that you do but wrong the party or cause that you pretend to, when you will needs engage yourselves among them. What hath done more to the dishonour of the bishops, and Common Prayer book, and other late orders and ceremonies of the church, than to see and hear the rabble of drunkards, swearers, scorners at holiness, and such like, to plead for them, and be violent defenders of them? If you would devise how to shame these things, and bring them down, you can scarce contrive a more effectual way, than to set all the ungodly scandalous wretches to cry them up, and become their patrons; for it will make abundance of soberer people begin to question, whether it be likely to be good, that hath such defenders on one side, and adversaries on the other side.

And therefore, sirs, let us begin our closure and agreement in the main, if you would be ever the better for it, and have unity indeed. And if you say, What the nearer shall we be for agreement in the other things? Do not the godly still differ about church government, and orders, and ceremonies? I answer, 1. If we never should be agreed in these on earth, we might bear it the more quietly, because our very hearts and souls are united in the main, even in matters abundance greater, and in all that salvation is laid upon; and, therefore, we have this comfort in the midst of our differences, that we shall all shortly come to heaven, and that perfection and the blessed face of God will unite and perfectly agree us in all things.

2. In the mean time we could hold a holy communion with them in the substance of God's worship; and we have a daily communion with them in the Spirit, and an endeared love to one another.

3. And the holiness of their natures will incline them to manage our remaining differences with meekness, humility, self-denial, moderation, and with great respect to the safety of the whole church, and the honour of God and of the gospel.

4. And yet I must add, that with such there is a far greater advantage to heal the smallest difference that remains, than with any other. When we have one God to awe us, and one heaven to draw us, and one Christ for our Head, and one Spirit and new nature to principle us and dispose us, and one law to rule us, and have all one ultimate end and interest, here is a great advantage for healing of any particular differences that may arise. If the liver, or spleen, or stomach, or brain, or lungs be unsound, the sores that are without will hardly be cured; yea, if there were none, these inward diseases may breed them; but when all is well within, the strength of nature, without a medicine, will do much to cure such small distempers that arise without. The life of faith, the love of God, the love of the brethren, and the church's peace and welfare, with the humility and self-denial that is in every christian, will do a great deal to the healing of divisions among the godly. They will be content to meet together in love, and pray it out, and refer the matter to the holy Scripture, and they have all some special illumination of the Spirit.

But perhaps you will say, Why are they not more fully agreed? I answer, 1. Because there are such a multitude of ungodly persons among them, that hinder them from opportunities and advantages for agreement. And many of these ungodly ones are hypocrites, that take on them to be godly, and so are traitors in our bosoms, and hinder peace the more by seeming to be godly, when they are not. 2. Because of the remnant of sin that is yet in the sanctified, and because they are not yet perfect and in heaven. If they had no sin, they would have no divisions: and as their sin is healed as to the dominion of it, but not perfectly till they come to heaven; so their divisions are healed in the main, but not perfectly, till they are perfectly united to God in glory.

9. Consider, also, I beseech you, what a joy it would be to Christ, and to the angels of heaven, and

to all good men, if you would but all make such an agreement, and heartily join together in holiness! The whole fifteenth chapter of Luke is by divers parables to tell you this, what joy there is in heaven itself for the conversion of one sinner. Oh what would there be then, if towns and countries would agree in holiness! And I am certain it should be a joy to the princes and rulers of the earth; for such a unity only will hold, and be a blessing to their dominions. Plutarch makes it Agesilaus' reason, why the Spartans had no walls, because the people being all of one mind, had no need of walls. And Pliny tells us of a stone that will swim if it be whole, and sink if it be broken. And so will commonwealths that are broken from Christ, and void of the cement of the Spirit that should unite them.

And to the ministers of the gospel, and all good christians, such a unity as this would be an unspeakable joy. Somewhat I know of other men's hearts by mine own. Could I but prevail with this nation, yea with this one town and parish, to meet all together, and heartily consent, agree, and resolve to join all together in a heavenly life, I should more rejoice in it than if I had the house full of gold and silver, yea, (as to mine own interest,) than if I were lord of all the world. Oh what a joyful day were this, if I could this day bring you to this holy unity and agreement! How comfortably should I spend the remaining days of my pilgrimage among you, if you would but all be brought to this! Whereas I may now say as David, Psal. cxx. 5, for all the godly that are among you, "Woe is me, that I sojourn in Mesech, that I dwell in the tents of Kedar! My soul hath too long dwelt with him that hateth this holy peace. I am for peace; but when I speak, and persuade men to it, they are for war," and continuance in the dividing course of ungodliness. Alas, it grieveth us to see such divisions in all the churches and nations of the christian world: and oh that we did know how to heal them! But when we cannot heal the most ungodly separations and divisions of one town and parish, it discourageth us from hoping for any great matters of such large extent. Some attempts I have made, and more I would fain make, to further a union and peace among the churches through the land: but when I cannot procure the unity of this one town and parish, what hope can I have to look any further? Alas, what a shame is this to you, and what a grief to us, that we cannot bring one parish, one village that ever I knew of, in all England, to be all of a mind in those great, those weighty, needful things, where it is worse than a madness for men to be unresolved or disagreed! As Melanthus made a jest of a great man that went about to reconcile all Greece, and bring all the princes and states to peace, when he could not bring his wife and her servant maid to agreement in his own house; so with what hopes can we attempt any public peace, when we cannot bring one parish, one village, yea but very few families, to agree in that which they must agree in, or else the refusers will be certainly condemned! I beseech you, sirs, make glad the hearts of your teachers, and of all good men, by your agreement. You owe us this comfort; and you owe it to Christ, and the angels of heaven: deny us not our due, but without any more delay agree together to live as saints. What a joy it would be to your pastors, you are not easily able to believe. When Gregory Thaumaturgus came first to be bishop of Neocæsarea, he found but seventeen christians in the city: and when he lay on his deathbed, he desired them to make inquiry how many infidels were unconverted; and they found but just seventeen infidels left, and all the rest were converted to christianity. And though he rejoiced that he left but just as many unconverted infidels as he found converted christians; yet he grieved withal, that he should leave those seventeen in the power of the devil. When I came to you, I found you all professed christians; but oh that I could say that I shall leave but seventeen unconverted when I am called from you, for all that! Oh that there were no more that are infidels or impious, under the name of christians! But I and you are unworthy of so great a mercy.

10. And I pray you consider this in time, that all of you that now refuse this agreement in holiness, will wish, ere long, that you had heartily embraced it, and joined with the godly, and done as they. And why will you not be of the mind that you will be shortly of? And why will you be of that way and company that you will wish at last you had not been of? The prodigal in Luke xv. did think it a slavery to be kept up so strictly by his father's eye; he must have his portion in his own possession, and abroad he must be gone: but when smart had taught him another lesson, and misery had brought him to himself, then he is glad to be a hired servant, and casteth himself at his father's feet, in the confession of his unworthiness to be called a son. God grant that this may prove your case. But let me tell it you for a certain truth, there is not one of you that now is loth to become so holy, and join yourselves in the ways of God, but the time is at hand, when either grace or hell shall make you wish and wish again, that you might have but the poorest, lowest place in the society which you so despised. Mark what I say to you, sirs, in the name of God. If the Lord of heaven do not shortly make the dullest heart, the greatest derider of godliness among you, that heareth these words, to wish, and wish a hundred times, that he had lived as holy and heavenly a life as the strictest of those that he had formerly derided, then call me a false prophet for ever, and spare not. When you feel the misery of unholy souls, and see the happiness of the saints above you, then oh that you had been but such as they, and lived as they, whatever it cost you! And as Balaam you will shortly say, "Oh that I might die the death of the righteous, and that my last end may be as his!" Numb. xxiii. 10. There is never a one of you all but would fain be among the saints at judgment, and receive their sentence and reward; and therefore it is best for you to join with them now; or it will be too late to wish it then.

11. If all this will not serve the turn, but you will needs stand off, and separate yourselves from the servants of Christ, be it known to you, you shall ere long have separation enough, and be further from them than your hearts can wish. As you would not be united to them, and join with them in holiness, so you shall not be partakers with them of their happiness. One heaven will not hold you both; and there is but one to hold you; and therefore an everlasting separation shall be made: between them and you will a great gulf be set, so that they that would pass from you to them shall never be able, Luke xvi. 26. When they stand on the right hand, you shall be set upon the left; and when they hear "Come ye blessed," you shall hear "Go ye cursed;" and when they "go away into life eternal," you shall "go away into everlasting punishment," Matt. xxv. 31, 32, 41, 46. Then you shall see that "the man is blessed that walketh not in the counsel of the ungodly, nor standeth in the way of sinners, nor sitteth in the seat of the scornful; but his delight is in the law of the Lord, and in his law doth he meditate day and night.—The ungodly are not so, but

are like the chaff which the wind driveth away: therefore the ungodly shall not stand in the judgment, nor sinners in the congregation of the righteous: for the Lord knoweth the way of the righteous, but the way of the ungodly shall perish," Psal. i. Then you will say to them that now you differ from, "Give us of your oil, for our lamps are gone out." Oh that we had part in your holiness and your hopes! But they will answer you, "Not so, lest there be not enough for us and you." We have little enough for ourselves, you should have done as we did; but then it will be too late, Matt. xxv. 8—10. It will then make the proudest heart to shake, to hear, "Depart from me, all ye that are workers of iniquity, I never knew you," Matt. vii. 23. You departed from me, and would not live in the communion of saints; and now Christ himself, of whom you boasted, and in whom you trusted, will not know you, but cause you to depart much farther than you desired, both from his saints and him. These are the true revelations of God, which may be laughed at and slighted now, but will certainly be made good on all that are not in time united to Christ and his church.

12. And let me tell you, to consummate your misery, when that day of everlasting separation comes, those servants of Christ whom you refused to join with in a holy life, will be so many witnesses against you to your condemnation: as Christ tells you, Matt. xxv. he will say, "Inasmuch as you did it not to one of these, you did it not to me." So, inasmuch as you refused the communion of saints, and perhaps derided them, you refused communion with Christ himself, and derided him. Then they must testify against you, We were willing to have had his company in the way of holiness, but he refused it. And when you see them set so far above you, then your own consciences will say, We might have been of this blessed society, and would not; we might have done as they, and now sped as they; we were often entreated to it by our teachers; and full glad would the godly have been of our company in a holy life; but we obstinately refused all! Wretches that we are, we refused all! we thought it needless, our hearts were against it; we preferred our pleasures, and profits, and credit, and the customs of the world before it, and now how justly do we perish in our wilfulness, and must lie in yonder burning flames, and be separated as far as hell is from heaven, from those that we wilfully separated from on earth!

Beloved hearers, I were not a believer, if I did not foresee this dreadful day; and I were not a man, if I did not desire that you might escape this misery; and therefore I could do no less than warn you, as you love yourselves, and would not be separated from them for ever, that you would presently be united to the godly, and live in the true communion of the saints, and withdraw yourselves from the ways of the ungodly, lest you be found among them, and perish with them. I have done my part in telling you the truth, and now must leave the success to God.

Use ult. But I must conclude with a word of advice to the godly. I have made a very large, ambitious motion, for the conversion of all at once; but alas, it is far from my expectation that it should prevail. I am not so unacquainted with the power of sin, and the subtlety of the devil, and the wilfulness of blind, unsanctified men, and the ordinary course of providence in this work, as to cherish any hopes that all the town and parish should consent. If many or any more do, I shall be glad. But *plurima quæras, ut pauca feras:* a high motion, when reasonable, may be serviceable to lower hopes. By what I have here said, you may see how little hope there is that ever the church should have any such peace on earth as we desire. If unholiness be the hinderance, and the greatest part of the world are so unholy, and so our unity is like to rise no higher than our piety, you may see then how much unity to look for.

But for your own parts, be sure among yourselves to maintain the "unity of the Spirit in the bond of peace." "Love the brotherhood, even saints as saints." And because you are not the searchers of the heart, proceed according to the word of God. Let all that profess themselves a sanctified people, and live so as that you cannot certainly disprove their profession, be used as saints by you, and leave the infallible judgment to God. It is only real saints that have the internal special "unity of the Spirit," and saving communion; but it is professors of faith and holiness that must have external communion with us in ordinances, as they have a visible union of profession with the church. But if they profess not holiness, they ought not to have any christian communion at all.

O christians, keep close to Christ the centre of your unity, and the Scripture which is the rule of it, and cherish the Spirit which is the vital cause; walk evenly and uprightly in a dark generation, and give no offence to those without, nor to the church of God. Know them that are over you in the Lord, and be at peace among yourselves, "and the God of peace shall be with you," 1 Thess. v. 12; Phil. iv. 8, 9.

Object. But may not a profession of the same faith procure a sufficient unity among us, though all be not saints, and savingly regenerate? Let us first be of one religion, and then we may come to be sincere in the practice of that religion by degrees.

Answ. 1. For the church's sake, we are thankful to God, when we see a common concord in profession, though most are false in and to the religion which they profess. Many ways God doth good to his church by unsound professors.

1. Their professing the same faith doth somewhat tie their hands from persecuting it. And of the two, we can better bear hypocrites than persecutors.

2. And it somewhat tieth their tongues from reproaching the faith, and arguing against it, and seducing others from it. And of the two, it would be more hurtful to the church to have these men open enemies to the truth, and bend their wits and tongues against it, and to have the multitude assaulting their neighbours with invectives and cavils against religion, than to have them falsely pretend to be religious.

3. And it is a great mercy to the church, hereby to have the benefit of these men's common parts and interests. When they profess the same religion with us, though unsoundly, yet it engageth them to stand for the religion which they profess; and their illumination and conviction may lead them to do much service for the truth. By this means many hands are at work to build up the church of Christ. And by this means the lives of many faithful christians are preserved, and their estates much spared. Many have skill in building, that are not true heirs of the house which they build. Many have excellent gifts for preaching and expounding Scripture, by which the church may be edified, and the truth defended against the adversaries, when yet the same men may themselves be destitute of the power of this truth. The church hath great cause to be thankful to God for the gifts of many an unsanctified man: had the church denied the ministry and gifts of all men except saints, it would have been confined to a narrower

room, and many a soul might have been unconverted that have been by the ministry called of unsanctified men. By some such did God work miracles themselves for the confirmation of the christian faith. And in times of war, if the church had none but saints to fight for them, it could not stand without a continued miracle. And if we had not the daily help of others in civil and secular affairs, we should find by the miss of it, what a mercy we undervalued. Were every unregenerate man an open enemy to the church, we should live as partridges, and such other birds, that must hide themselves from every passenger.

4. Moreover, this profession of hypocrites doth much restrain them from many a sin, by which God would be much dishonoured, and the church more wronged, and the godly more grieved, and the open enemies more encouraged.

5. And also it is some honour to the gospel in the eyes of men, to have a multitude of professors. Should Christ's visible church be as narrow as the mystical, and should none be professors of the faith, but those few that are sanctified believers, the paucity of christians, and narrowness of the church, would be a dishonour to Christ in the eyes of the world, and would hinder the conversion of many a soul.

All this I have said, that you may see that we do not despise a unity in profession, and that we are not of those that would have all hypocrites and common professors shut out: yea, that we take ourselves bound to be very thankful to God for the mercy which he vouchsafeth us, by the gifts, and favour, and help, and interest of many such professors. And such a unity of profession we shall endeavour to our power heartily to promote, as knowing that the church, as visible, consisteth of such professors.

2. But yet for all this, I must come closer to your objection, and tell you, that this unity of mere profession is comparatively so poor a kind of unity, that this will not, this must not satisfy us, and serve the turn, which I desire you to observe in these discoveries.

1. This unity in mere profession is properly no christian unity, because you are not properly christians. If this be all, it is but in the bark and shell that we are agreed; it is but a seeming agreement, from the teeth outward; but not a hearty agreement to be christians. What! shall we all agree to say we are christians, when with most it is not so? For all this agreement, you will still have one father, and we another. You will not be united with us in Christ the Head; you will not have the same Holy Spirit, who is the life of the new creature: you will be contrary to us in nature or disposition. You will not have the same intention and ultimate end with us, but you will aim at one thing, and we at another: you will not go the same way, nor walk by the same rule and law as we: it will be but a tying together the living and the dead. Bellarmine himself confesseth that the ungodly are but dead members. It is not life that uniteth a dead member to the living. You will be still either openly or secretly betraying the body to which you profess yourselves united, and taking part with its deadly enemies, the flesh, the world, and the devil! Your very hearts and ours will still be contrary: you will love the sin that we hate and set ourselves against; and you will disrelish that holy, heavenly life, which must be our business and delight. Your affections will go one way, and ours another. You will live by sense, when we must live by faith; and you will be laying up a treasure on earth, when we are laying up a treasure in heaven: you will be asking counsel of flesh and blood, when we must advise with God and his holy word. You will look first to your bodies, when we must look first and principally to our souls. It will be your business to feed those sins, which it is our daily work to kill. You will make and apprehend it to be your interest to go contrary to us: and what agreement can there be, where there are contrary interests? Under all your outward profession, you will still retain a secret enmity and hatred to the life of holiness; and will not have that hearty love to the saints, as beseems all those that are members of Christ, and of the holy catholic church. So that when you have communion with the saints, it will be but an external and superficial communion in some common things; but you will have no communion with them in the same Head, and Spirit, and promise, and holy nature, and saving benefits of the gospel. And shall this be called unity, that leaveth you at so sad a distance as this? This is but such a union as a wooden leg hath to the body; or as the vessels of honour and dishonour have by being in the same house together. In their higdest professions, the Lord himself saith of unsanctified professors, that they "are none of Christ's," (Rom. viii. 9,) and that "they cannot be his disciples," (Luke xiv. 33,) that they "are not Israel, though of Israel, nor are they children of God, nor the seed of promise," Rom. ix. 6—8; and when they plead their highest privileges, at last, Christ will tell them that he "knoweth them not," Matt. vii. 23; xxv. 12; Psal. i. 5, 6. And if in mercy to the church, God cause the lion and the lamb to lie down together, yet will he not therefore mistake a lion for a lamb. So that you see what a poor kind of unity, and next to none, it is that mere profession maketh. And therefore this will not serve our turn.

2. Moreover, if we have no other unity, we are unlike to live in peace together. Though it be our duty to endeavour to have peace with all men, yet we can have but little hope of it. As long as there is so much difference and contrariety as I have mentioned, and as long as there is a secret enmity at the heart, it will be working into dissension, if God, for the sake of his church, restrain it not. The godly will be crossing your carnal interest, and hindering you in the sinful ways of your commodity, pleasure, or vain-glory! They will be calling you to self-denial, which you cannot endure; and putting you upon duties of holiness, righteousness, and mercy, which your sinful flesh will utterly refuse. If you are scandalous, you will be called to confession, repentance, and reformation, or by church censures be cut off from them to your shame: and the magistrate also must trouble you by the penalties of the law. The very examples of a strict and holy living, which are given you by the godly, will displease you, because they are so unlike to your lives, and therefore witness against your negligence and ungodliness. So that it is not possible that we should avoid offending you; for our very obedience to God will offend you, and our studying and following the holy Scripture will offend you, and our diligent labour to save our souls will offend you, and our hating and avoiding the poison of sin will offend you. And how then shall we live in peace with such? If you yoke a swine and a sheep together, one will be drawing to the wash-tub, when the other would be at grass; and one would be drawing to lie down in the mire, when the other would lie clean; one will be routing in the earth, and eating dung, which the other's nature is against. It is Christ, before me, that calleth the wicked by the name of *swine*, and the godly *sheep:* and if you will come no nearer us than this, we are like to have but poor agreement.

And as our ways will displease you, so your galled,

malicious hearts will manifest the offence, and will be girding, and maligning, if not slandering, deriding, or openly persecuting, as far as you have power, those that thus offend you. And what unity is this?

3. If reason persuade you not, do but ask experience itself, whether, in all ages, men that profess the same religion with zealous godly men, have not been their persecutors, and ofttimes more cruel than infidels themselves? The Arians, that call themselves christians, were as cruel to the true believers as the heathens. The papists profess the same christianity as we, and take the whole Scripture as the word of God: and yet none of the heathenish persecutions do match or come near to the French massacres, and Spanish Inquisition, and the cruelty that in Ireland, England, and their part of the christian world, they have exercised upon the sheep of Christ. The many ministers that were silenced in Germany, and some imprisoned, and many families undone, was by the Lutherans, against men that were protestants as well as they. And they that cast out so many learned, holy ministers in England, and occasioned the expulsion of so many thousand persons fearing God, were professed protestants as well as we. And that there may not be the appearance so much as of a difference in ceremonies to cover their proceedings, abundance of conformable men are troubled and undone as well as others, and they gave out that none were worse than the conformable puritans. It was a holy observation of the Lord's day, and opposition to the abuse of it by dancings; and it was hearing sermons, and instructing men's families, and praying together, that were the things inquired after, that occasioned our troubles. And (whoever was in the right or wrong) you all know that the late miserable wars among us, was between men that professed themselves to be of the same religion, not only as christians, but as protestant and reformed (in the main). To this day you see among ourselves in towns and countries, that those that do not only dwell with us, and come to the same assemblies with us, and profess themselves of the same protestant, reformed religion, have yet many of them a secret malignity against the godly, that will not be as loose and negligent as they, and will not as madly cast away their souls: and also even many greater hypocrites, that rank themselves with us in the same church order, and seem to own all ordinances of God, and government of the church, yet when this government crosseth them in their carnal ways, and these ordinances open the nakedness of their miscarriages, they prove stark enemies to the government, officers, and ordinances themselves.

Indeed however we may abide together, (as the clean and unclean creatures in Noah's ark,) yet still at the heart there is so much enmity or distance, and in our ends and interests there are so much contrariety, that if the ministers and other followers of Christ will faithfully discharge the duty that is required of them, they will certainly be persecuted by men of the same profession in religion; especially by the prouder and loftier sort of wicked men: because some will receive the same truth better from one than from another. I will give you my assertion in the words of a man, that you shall confess did speak impartially, and not out of any intemperance or singularity; who in a prosperous university, in peaceable times, being himself in favour, and of that judgment and of such learning as was likely to continue him in favour, did yet write thus concerning persecution: I mean Doctor Jackson, in his book of "Saving Faith," sect. 2, chap. iv. page 185. "The ministers of Christ may deny Christ, or manifest their ashamedness of his gospel, as directly by not laying his law as closely to the great Herods of the world, as John Baptist did, (suppose the case be as notorious, and as well known to them,) as if they had been afraid to confess him, for fear of being put out of the synagogues; or said with those other Jews, We know that God spake with Moses, and gave authority to magistrates; but this man we know not whence he is, nor do we care for his counsels. Yet were John Baptist's kind of preaching used in many kingdoms, though by such as profess the same religion with the potentates they should offend with their boldness, I think it would prove matter of martyrdom in the end. That any age, since the christian religion was first propagated, hath wanted store of martyrs, is more to be attributed to the negligence, ignorance, and hypocrisy, or want of courage in Christ's ambassadors, or appointed pastors, than unto the sincerity, mildness, or fidelity of the flock; especially of the belwethers or chief ringleaders. Or, if Satan had not abated the edge of primitive zeal and resolution, by that dishonourable peace concluded between christianity and gentilism, after the settling of the Goths and Vandals in these parts of Christendom; had he not utterly benumbed mankind by locking up their spiritual senses in midnight darkness, and fettering their souls in superstition, since the time he himself was let loose; Rome *christian* had seen more martyrs, even of such as did not much dissent from her in most opinions held within six hundred years of Christ, in one year, than Rome *heathen* at any time had known in ten. Even in churches best reformed, it would be much easier, I think, to find store of just matter of martyrdom, than of men fit to make martyrs. And he that hath lived any long time in these quiet mansions, and seats of muses, secure from Mars his broils, or external violence, hath great cause either to magnify the tender mercies of his gracious God, or suspect himself for a hypocrite, if he have not suffered some degrees of martyrdom: but unto such as have been exercised therein, it bringeth forth the quiet fruit of righteousness."

Thus you see this learned doctor, though in favour with the rulers of the age he lived in, did think that a man that would not be a hypocrite, but faithfully discharge his duty, was likely to suffer martyrdom from those of the same profession with himself; and that it must be by very great mercy from God, or by hypocrisy and unfaithfulness in us, if any minister do escape the hands of the wicked that are of his own profession. So that you may see that mere profession will make but a poor agreement or union among us: sin will be sin still, and the flesh will rage still after its prey in unmortified professors; and the word of God will still disgrace them and condemn them, and consequently trouble them and exasperate them; so that if you come no nearer to us than a profession of the christian protestant religion, you will still be soldiers in the army of the devil, and be still flying in the faces of true believers, whenever they do but cross you in your sins.

3. Consider, also, what a poor benefit comparatively it is to yourselves, to be joined with the saints by a bare profession, and no more. Will it make you happy to see their faces, or to live among them? So do the brute beasts, and so do their persecutors. Will it make you happy to be called by the name of christians? No more than it maketh a picture rational to be called by the name of a man. And what if, by your parts and moral virtues, you are some way helpful to the church? So is the wooden leg to the body, which yet is not a member, but a crutch.

4. Yea, methinks it should rather double your

sorrows, that you are so miserable among the happy. You live with them that have part in Christ, when you have none in him. You join with those that have the Spirit of God, and a holy disposition and conversation, when you have none: you kneel by them whose spirits are importunate with God in prayer, when your hearts are dead: you sit by them that are quickened and sanctified by the word, which to you is but a dead and empty sound. You are famished among them that are feasting upon Christ, and upon the precious promises of eternal life. You are but as carcasses among the living: their company maketh not you alive; but your noisome conversation is grievous unto them, unless it be some of you that are embalmed and beflowered with some common graces, for the sakes of those that else would be more troubled with you. And is this so great a comfort to you, to be dead among the living, and to be heirs of hell in the midst of them that are heirs of heaven? Methinks (till you are sanctified) it should be a daily honour to you, to look them in the faces, and think that they have Christ and grace, and you have none; and to hear in the holy assemblies the mention of their happiness, and the name of that God, that Christ, that heaven, where they must live for ever, and in which their blessedness consisteth, when you must be turned out into everlasting misery.

That you may not think I am singular in all this, I will add here some human testimony for confirmation of it. Zonoras, Comment. in Epist. Canon. Can. 45, ex Basil. M. Epist. 2, ad Amphiloch. gives us this as one of the canons of the Greek church received from Basil, "If any one receiving the name of christianity shall be a reproach to Christ, (that is, saith Zonoras, by a wicked life,) his name or appellation is no profit at all to him." And even in the Roman canon law, this is one canon taken out of Augustine, *Parvulus qui baptizatur, si ad annos rationales veniens, non crediderit, nec ab illicitis abstinuerit, nihil ei prodest quod parvulus accepit.* Decret. part 3, disl. 3, p. 1241, That is, A baptized infant, if when he comes to years of discretion doth not believe, nor abstain from things unlawful, it profiteth him nothing which he received in his infancy. If it were needful after the canons both of the Greek and Latin church, to give you the like words from particular fathers, I could soon perform it.

5. You are so far from being happy by your visible church state, and outward profession, and communion with the church, that you have the greater sin, and will have the sorer punishment, because among such examples, such means, and calls, and mercies, you yet resist the grace of Christ, and are void of that holiness which your tongues profess. The poor Indians hear not that which you daily or weekly hear; nor have the opportunities in public and private that you have had. If they lie in ignorance and unbelief, they can say, it is because they never read or heard the Scripture, nor ever had a man to tell them of the blessed tidings of redemption, or open to them the way to life: but so cannot you say for yourselves. They were the less excusable, if they had seen but one of your days, or joined but once in those holy assemblies which you profane. The mouth of Christ himself hath told us concerning the rejecters of his ministers and his gospel, that it shall be easier for Sodom in the day of judgment than for them, Matt. x. 15. You will find a hotter place in hell, that pass thither from those seats, from this assembly, from such a neighbourhood, and such a nation, than if you had passed thither from among the Turks or Indians.

6. Moreover, there is in some respects less hope of your salvation, that have long lived unconverted in the outward communion of the church, than of other men: as a sick man is in a more desperate case that hath long used the best and only means, and all in vain, than he that never used any. I confess you have the advantage of being still under the means; and that is your hope (as long as it lasteth): but then you have the dreadful symptom of frustrating these means; and that is your terror, above those that yet remain without.

7. Moreover, if you agree with us but in profession and outward communion, you will be thereby more capable of doing us the greater mischief. I know God doth benefit his church by many of the unsanctified, as I said before. But many others of them are the greatest plagues to it. One enemy in our own armies, or in our councils, may do more against us, then ten thousand open enemies abroad. False-hearted bishops, pastors, yea, and magistrates, that have the name and not the nature of christians, are they that have betrayed the church, and broken it in pieces, and made the cause of Christ a stepping-stone to their worldly ends. It was a Doeg that betrayed David and Abimelech. It was a Judas that betrayed Christ himself. You are now our daily hearers, and live some of you civilly among us, and take yourselves confidently for christians and saints as well as others, and secretly scorn those that would rob you of that honour, as appropriating it unto themselves, and say as Zedekiah to Micaiah when he struck him, "Which way went the Spirit of the Lord from me to speak unto thee?" 1 Kings xxii. 24. But if the times should turn, and you had but your will, at least if you were but forced or driven by authority, we should soon find many of you to be blood-thirsty enemies, that now are so confident that you are christians and true servants of God. A little money would hire those Judases to betray Christ, and his cause and church, that now are our familiars, and put their hands into the same dish with the true disciples. While they are among us, they are not of us; and therefore when temptations come, they will be gone from us. It is well if half this assembly that are now hearing me, would stick to godliness, if godliness were but the persecuted, scorned way of the times: yea, if they would not forsake even the name itself of christian, and forsake these assemblies and outward worship, if the rulers were against it, and did but persecute it, so that it must cost them any thing dear to hold it.

8. Moreover, these hollow-hearted christians, that agree with us but in the outside and the name, are capable of dishonouring Christ and the gospel, much more than if they were open enemies. If a professed heathen or infidel live wickedly, this cannot be cast upon the gospel or the christian name, nor can Christ and his servants be hit in the teeth with it, or reproached by it: but when those that take on them to be christians, and join with christians in their public worship, shall live like heathens, or worse than some of them, what greater wrong can be done to Christ? Will he not one day take such wretches by the throat, and say, "If thou must have thy pride, and drunkenness, and covetousness; if thou must needs swear, and curse, and rail, or live an ungodly, fleshly life, thou shouldst have kept thee out of my church, and not have called thyself a christian, and taken an easier place in hell. Must thou bring thy wickedness into my house, and among my servants, to dishonour me? Must I and my servants be reproached with thy crimes?"

And this is one great cause why Christ hath appointed discipline in his church to admonish and reform, or reject, the scandalous. And this is the reason, among many others, why faithful christians (though they would make no unjust divisions and separations) would yet have the church of Christ kept clean, by use of holy discipline, as he hath appointed; because it is from such false-hearted professors, usually, that the name of Christ is reproached in the world. These are they for the most part that make Turks and Jews, and all other enemies, say, that christians are as bad as others, because those that are as bad as others do take on them to be christians. When drunkards, and fornicators, and covetous persons, and profane, do come to the congregation, and say they are christians, when in heart and deed they are not, what wonder then if infidels and enemies of the church reproach us and say, You see what christians are? How could a papist do the protestants a cunninger and surer mischief, than to take on him a protestant, and then commit fornication or other horrid lewdness, or join with some abominable sect, to make men think that the protestants are such as these? And how can you do Christ a greater wrong than to carry the dung of the world into his church; and to cover all the crimes of infidels with the name and garb of christianity, that it may be said, All these are the crimes of christians? And therefore it is that Christ and his faithful ministers, though they would have as many as is possible to be saved, yet are not so forward to take in all, as others be: for Christ needeth not servants, but it is they that need him; and he had rather have a few that will honour him by mortified holy lives, than a multitude that will but cause his name and gospel to be reproached. It is certain from church history, that the holy life of some one or few persons (as Gregory Thaumaturgus, Macarius, and many the like) hath drawn in multitudes, and converted countries to the faith: when the wickedness of whole towns and countries of professed christians, hath caused many to fall off, and caused the enemy to insult.

We will not for all this break our rule, nor presume to search the hearts of men any further than they appear in outward evidence. We will still take all professors of christianity as christians, that null not their own profession. Basil was advised by Athanasius himself, to receive the Arians themselves into communion, if they did but disown their former errors, and subscribe to the Nicene creed, and seek the communion of the churches. And he practised this, though many were offended at it. But yet we must needs say, that it is better for the church to have a few that are holy, and answer the nature of their holy calling, than to have multitudes that will but prove our shame, and make the infidel world believe that christianity is not what it is. Yea, and these are they most commonly too (though they may proceed to a higher profession) that are carried about with every wind of doctrine, and that turn to heresies, and cause and continue the divisions of the church: for they that are such, serve not the Lord Jesus, when they profess to serve him, Rom. xvi. 17. When heresies do arise, it is such chaff as this that is carried away, that the approved christians indeed may be made manifest, 1 Cor. xi. 19. Abundance of proud, unsanctified persons do us as much good in the church as fire in our thatch, or as mutinous soldiers that are but the enemy's agents in the army, to set all the soldiers together by the ears, or discover their councils, or blow up their magazines. And would you have us contented with such a kind of agreement and communion with you as this, which you and we are like to be so little the better for, if not the worse?

9. Furthermore, it is not this mere agreement in profession that will satisfy Christ himself, and, therefore, it must not satisfy us. It is not in this that he attaineth the principal ends of his redemption, nor seeth the travail of his soul. Alas, the blood of Christ is lost to you, and all the ordinances and means are lost, and all the labour of ministers is but lost to you, as to any pardon of sin, or life, or heaven, that ever you shall have by them, if you go no further. And would you have us be contented with such an agreement as this?

10. Lastly, Consider that if we agree no further than in an outward profession of the christian faith, alas, it will be but a short agreement. We may be together here awhile in the church, as fishes good and bad in one net; but when it is drawn to the shore, a separation will be made. Here you may sit and kneel among us awhile, and go away with the name of christians: but, alas, it is but a little while till this agreement will be broken, and a dreadful everlasting separation must be made. Dreadful to the unsanctified, but joyful to the saints. And what great good will it do to you or us, to be tied together a little while, by words and shows, and then to be everlastingly separated, as far as light from darkness, heaven from hell, and the greatest joys from the greatest sorrows. O blame us not if we motion to you, and beg of you a far nearer union and agreement than this!

I think I have now sufficiently proved, that if we will be indeed of one religion, and ever come to a right agreement, it is the unity of the sanctifying Spirit that must do it. It must be a union and agreement in true conversion and holiness of life, and nothing lower will serve the turn. If God do us any good by the profession, gifts, or interest of hypocrites and unsanctified professors, we will thank him for it, and take it as a mercy; but it is a higher design that must be in our hearts; and woe be to them that come no nearer the holy catholic church, and the unity of the Spirit, and the communion of saints, than by an outward profession and participation of sacraments, and such like outward ordinances of communion!

Quest. But suppose we should be united in the Spirit, and agree in holiness, do you think this would heal the divisions of the church? Do you not see that the most godly are all in pieces, as well as others? Is it not such that have been the principal causers of our late divisions? You promised to show us how we might do well, for all our other differences, if we were but agreed in holiness; will you now show us what advantage that would be?

Answ. To be agreed in holiness, and to be heartily one in the essentials of christianity, is an exceeding advantage to us in all our disagreements about lesser things: as,

1. Were we but once united in the main, and sanctified by the uniting Spirit of Christ, our principal differences were healed already. We should no longer be of different minds, whether sin or holiness be best; or whether earth or heaven should be chosen for our portion; nor whether God, or the flesh, or the world, should be obeyed. You little think what abundance of differences are at once reconciled in the very hour of a sinner's conversion. Before that hour, we differed in judgment from all wise men, from all the saints of God, from all the holy prophets, apostles, and martyrs, as well as from all the godly about us; and from all men of right reason, and faith, and experience; yea, we differed from the Holy Ghost, from Christ, from God himself; yea, from none so much as him. Wicked wretches! you differ from the godly because they agree with God; but you differ more from God than

from them. When you despise a holy life, are his thoughts like your thoughts? When you revile his servants, and scorn his yoke and burden as too heavy, are you then of the mind of Christ? O no; your darkness and his light are far more distant than you are able to conceive. Were you but once reconciled to God, by converting, sanctifying light, you would at once be reconciled to his servants; for in the matters of chief concernment to the soul, they are all of his mind; for he is their instructor. And then what a day of healing would that be! Oh what abundance of differences are ended upon the day of true conversion! And withal, what abundance of differences would be new made! For now you agree with the devil, and with your fleshly desires, and with distracted, wicked men, and all this agreement would then be broke: for this friendship with the world is enmity to God, James iv. 4; and such divisions as these Christ tells us that he came to send, Luke xii. 51. But you would presently be agreed with God, with the holy Scriptures, with all the apostles and servants of the Lord, and with all men of spiritual wisdom and experience in the world, in the great and principal matters of your lives. And it is a multitude of particulars that is contained in this agreement that is made when a sinner is truly sanctified.

2. If once you were united in the Spirit, and agreed in a holy life, you would differ in nothing that could keep you out of heaven. And if we have some small differences on earth, as long as they are such as cannot hinder our salvation, they may be the more easily borne. Paul and Barnabas had a little falling out; but oh how sweetly are they now reconciled! Jerom and Chrysostom, Epiphanius and John of Jerusalem, Theophilus and Chrysostom, were at odds; Luther and Zuinglius had their disagreements: but oh how happily are they now agreed! Our imperfection of knowledge causeth us here to err and differ in part: but if we are all united in Christ, and agreed in the main, how quickly shall we see that blessed light that will reconcile all our controversies! Marvel not to find some contests among the most learned and most godly, unless you will marvel that earth is not heaven; or that in that body we see not the face of God, which is the all-disclosing, reconciling light. If we were all here together in the dark, and were of many opinions about the things before us; if one did but come in among us with a candle, it might end all our differences in a moment. When we are newly out of this obscuring flesh, and this dark, deceitful, earthly world, oh what an unconceivable reconciliation will be made by that blessed light! There is no contending or quarrelling; for there are none of those errors or passions that should occasion it. As imperfect holiness produceth an answerable imperfect unity, so perfect holiness will perfectly unite. And is not this then the only way to unity, which will help us here to what is here attainable, and secure us of eternal perfect concord in the world that we are passing to? O see that you be once agreed in the things that are necessary to salvation, and then the hour is near at hand that will end all your differences, and agree you in the rest.

3. If once you be but agreed in holiness, you will have no difference left that shall destroy any grace in you that is necessary to salvation. The power of divine faith, and love, and hope, and fear, and zeal, will still be safe. Your diseases will not destroy your vital faculties. And if the head, the heart, and principal parts be sound, you may the better bear a small distemper. The disagreements of the ungodly from God, from Scripture, and the saints, are mortal to them, and prove them under the power of darkness and of Satan, that leads them captive at his will, 2 Tim. ii. 26; Ephes. ii. 23; Acts xxvi. 18. But the differences of the sanctified are but as the different complexions or statures of children, or at worst but as their falling out, which will not cause the father to turn them out of his family; so that as long as faith, and love, and hope, and other graces are kept sound, we shall certainly do well for all our differences. And this is the benefit of agreeing in holiness.

4. Moreover, if once we were all agreed in the Spirit, and in holiness of heart and life, we should escape all heresies or errors that effectually subvert the essentials of the christian faith. Mistaken we might be, but heretics we could not be. I stick not upon the bare word, whether small errors may be called heresy; but taking heresy as commonly it is taken, a sanctified person cannot (at least habitually) be a heretic. For should a man so hold a point inconsistent with any one essential point of the christian faith, (at least habitually and practically hold it,) it is as impossible that this man should be then a christian, as that contradictories should be true. And therefore, certainly, whosoever is a true christian, is free from such heresies. And therefore, as if you are sure a man so holds a heresy, you have no reason to believe his shows of holiness; so where you see a great appearance of real holiness, you must long deliberate and have good evidence, before you judge that man a heretic: for this is the certain privilege of the sanctified, that they cannot be heretics, though they may have many errors, (as *in sensu composito* all confess.)

5. Moreover, if we were but all agreed in true holiness, we should be freed from most of those scandalous sins which are the common occasion of our reproaches and divisions. It is sin that is the great trouble of the church, and of the world, John vii. 25. This breeds our quarrels. This setteth all into a flame. When a drunkard, or an unclean person, or a slanderer, or a railer, or any scandalous person, is reproved, or openly admonished, or for impenitency rejected, then the devil and sin bestir themselves, and rage against the church, and officers, and ordinances of God. It is sin within that animateth the malignant to be contentious: and it is to defend and take part with sin, that they fall out with God, and his word and servants. Now holiness is contrary to this sin that troubleth us. Mortification of sin is part of sanctification. If therefore we were agreed in holiness, it were as ready a way to procure our peace, as quenching the fire in your thatch is the ready way to save your house. I know there are too many scandals given by the best. But it is commonly but by the weaker, worser sort of the best. And it is not a common thing with them neither. And none of them make a trade of sinning, nor have any unmortified reigning sin. If a Noah, a Lot, a David, be once scandalous in all his life, this is not the case of all the godly; and it is not like the case of the ungodly that are either often or impenitent in it. And therefore though it may disturb the church, yet not so much as the frequent and impenitent scandals of the ungodly. Oh could we but all agree against this make-bate, this great disturber and troubler of the world, what peace might we enjoy!

6. And also, if once we could agree in holiness, the matter and occasion of offences, separations, and contentions would cease. What caused the Donatists' separation of old, but the scandals in the church; and the receiving of such, upon repentance, into communion or ministry? And so the Novatian schism also was occasioned. And though the Donatists and Novatians were to blame to be against the ordination or reception of such penitents; yet the

prevention of the sin would have been the prevention of the breach. What hath caused so many to turn separatists in England, but seeing so many ungodly persons in our churches and communion? You that are most offended at schisms and private churches, are the common occasions of it yourselves. If such ungodly persons were not in our assemblies, few godly persons would separate from them. Though I do not justify them, yet I must needs condemn you as the cause. Were it not for you, we should be more of a mind among ourselves. But when your rotten ulcers and corrupted lives have raised a stink in our assemblies, this causeth our division: the separatists stop their noses and are gone, and will come here no more: and the rest of us think that for your sakes, and the peace of the church, we should stay as long as we well can; like patient surgeons, that will not forsake their patient because of a rotten, stinking sore, as long as there is any hope of cure, or of saving the body, by cutting off the rotten member. And thus while some are more patient and charitable towards you, and some are more impatient of your sin, or else afraid of God's displeasure for having communion with you, here comes our divisions among ourselves, for your sakes. And therefore if we were but agreed in holiness, all this were ended. There would then be no habituated drunkard, or worldling, or railer, or swearer, or other ungodly persons in our churches; and then who could scruple communion with them? And so what should hinder but we might all be one? And yet will you not agree in this?

7. Yea, if we were united in the Spirit of holiness, the very dividing, unpeaceable disposition of men would itself be healed, and so we should have peace. For an uncharitable, dividing disposition is part of the old man, and of that unholiness which we must forsake. And charity and meekness, and a peaceable, healing temper, is holiness itself. And therefore this must needs do much to heal and reconcile us. Read but James iii. throughout, and it will satisfy you of this, if you will be satisfied. Those that pretend to be wiser than the rest of the godly, and to have more illumination, "if yet they have bitter envying and strife in their hearts, they glory in vain, and lie against the truth: for this wisdom descendeth not from above, but is earthly, sensual, and devilish. He that is truly wise and endued with knowledge in the church, must show out of a good conversation his works with meekness of wisdom. For the wisdom that is from above, is first pure, then peaceable, gentle, easy to be entreated, full of mercy and good fruits, without partiality, and without hypocrisy. But where envying and strife is, there is confusion and every evil work," James iii. 13—17. See here what a spirit sanctification doth contain, and whether this be not the only healing way. It is first indeed pure; but next it is "peaceable, gentle, and easy to be entreated." They that cause divisions and offences contrary to the doctrine which is taught, do not serve the Lord Jesus, whatever they may pretend or think. Peace and holiness must be followed together, Heb. xii. 14. Yea, "peace with all men," if it be possible, and in our power, (Rom. xii. 18,) so that by changing the unpeaceable disposition, and drying up the fountain of our strifes, an agreement in the Spirit would reconcile us.

8. Moreover, if we would all agree in the Spirit of holiness, it would destroy that carnal, selfish disposition, and that end which is the dividing interest, and take away the bone of our contentions. It is selfishness that causeth the great divisions in church and state, and sets the world together in wars and quarrels: every unsanctified man is selfish; his self and selfish interest is more to him than God and his interest. And such men as these will never live with any man in peace, any longer than they may have their will and way. They will not agree with neighbours if self be but touched by any. They will hate the magistrate whenever he would punish them. They will hate the pastors of the church if they faithfully discharge their offices in reproving them, and calling them to repentance, and such confession as is necessary to their cure. If it were father or mother, a selfish person cannot bear it, if they go against his selfish interest. There is no living at peace with selfish men, if you do but cross them in their credit, or profit, or sensual delights; and this we must do, unless we will incur the displeasure of our Lord. We are cast upon an impossibility of living in peace with wicked men. For God hath commanded us to "rebuke them plainly, and not to suffer sin upon them." And if we disobey God to please men, it will cost us dearer than their favour can repay. But if we obey God and do our duty, we are as sure to be hated and reproached with the most, as that the earth is under our feet. Give a wicked, selfish sinner as plain Scripture and reason as can be given, and you shall not stir him from his selfish interest: if you punish him, or reprove him openly, or exercise church censures on him, or any way touch his carnal, selfish interest, and when you have done, go about to satisfy him with reason, you may as well almost go reason a hungry dog from his carrion, or reason a wolf into the nature of a lamb, or reason a mastiff to be friends with a bear. Many a trial I have made; and many a time I have stopped their mouths, and satisfied them in reason, that they ought to deny themselves, and confess and forsake their sins, and yield to God (or made them confess so much at least); but their selfish minds were no more satisfied, for all that, than if I had never spoken to them. Scripture is no Scripture, and reason is no reason to them; and God shall be no God to them, if self do but contradict it; and that is, whenever he contradicteth self. They can no more believe, and like, and love that doctrine, or duty, or counsel, or course of life, that crosseth self, and calls them to any great self-denial, than a child can love to be corrected. So that self being so certain a peace-breaker and disturber of the world, and yet being the reigning principle in all that are unsanctified, you may easily see that this is the hinderance of our unity and concord; and that sanctification must needs be the principal remedy. For sanctification is the destruction of selfishness, and teacheth men self-denial, and centreth all men in one interest, which is God. Among the unsanctified, there are as many ends and interests as men; for every one of them hath a self to please: and then what unity can there be? But the sanctified are all united in God, as their common principle, end, and all; and therefore must needs be reconciled.

9. Moreover, if we could but all agree in the Spirit of holiness, we should then overcome that pride and self-conceitedness, that breaks our peace, and raiseth errors, and puts us into dissensions. What makes us all so hardly to agree, and to be of so many minds and ways, but that every man naturally is proud and self-conceited, and wise in his own eyes, and confident of every fancy of his own? All his own reasons seem strong to him; and God's own reasons do seem unreasonable to him: and can we ever agree with such men as these, that think themselves wiser than God and Scripture, and dare prefer the very folly of their own muddy brains before the word and wisdom of their Maker? Give these men as plain Scripture and reason as you will,

they have more wit (as they think) than to believe you; and what they want in reason, they have in pride and self-conceit; and therefore your wisdom is folly to them. But now when the Spirit of holiness comes, it takes them down, and abaseth and humbleth the proud and self-conceited, and makes them ashamed of the folly and weakness of their own understandings, so that a man may speak to them now as to men of reason, and have a hearing and consideration of his words. A humble godly man is low in his own eyes; and therefore suspicious of his own understanding in doubtful things; and therefore is more flexible and yielding to the truth; when others are so stiffened by pride that they are readier to deride the wisest that shall contradict them: if therefore we could but all agree in holy meekness and humility, what readier way could there be in the world to draw to an end of our differences and divisions?

10. Moreover, if we could but agree in holiness, it would free us from that uncharitableness that causeth our disagreement in other things; and it would possess us with a special endeared love one to another: and who knoweth not that love is a uniting, healing thing? Sanctification principally consisteth in love to God and man, and this the unsanctified principally want. It is want of love that makes men surmise the worst of one another, and make the worst of all that they say and do, and draw matter of contention from that which never gave them cause. Love would put a better sense upon men's words and deeds, or at least would bear them far more easily. But instead of love, there is a natural enmity in all that are unsanctified to all the servants and the ways of God. And can we ever be agreed with our natural enemies? Why, malice will so pervert their understandings, that all that we say or do will be misconstrued: and as a man that looks through a red glass thinks all things to be red that he looks upon; so these men, through the distemper of their malicious minds, will find matter of quarrelling with all that we can say or do. Ill-will never saith well. Our very obedience to the law of God, and seeking to save our own souls, will be matter of quarrel, and taken to be our crime. If we will not run into hell-fire with them, and think there is no danger, when we know the contrary, it will be a fault sufficient for their malice to reproach us with: so that if we should agree with ungodly men, in all our opinions of religion; yet if we will not damn our souls, and make no bones of displeasing the great and dreadful God, there is no peace to be had with them. They have no peace with God, and they have no solid peace with themselves; (for God hath professed "that there is no peace to the wicked," Isa. xlviii. 22;) and how then can we expect that they should have peace with us? But sanctification doth beget that effectual love, that is as healing to a divided church, or to disagreeing persons, as the most precious balsam or wound-salve is to bodily wounds. Love will not let you rest in wrath, but will keep you under smart and disquietness, till you are either at peace, or have done your part to have procured it. Husband and wife, parents and children, brethren and sisters, do seldom fall into greater dissensions than strangers do: and when they do fall out they are easilier reconciled. The Spirit of grace doth possess unfeigned christians with as dear a love to one another, as is between the nearest relations. For by our new birth the saints are brethren in Christ. If you saw an army fighting, or a company of people quarrelling and scolding at one another, do you think there could be a readier way to make them all friends, and end their quarrels, than to possess them all with a dear and tender love to one another? If it were in my power to cause all contenders to love those that they contend with as themselves, do you think I should not soon agree them? Why, you know, if you know any thing in christianity, that sanctification causeth men to love their neighbours as themselves, and to "love one another with a pure heart fervently," 1 Pet. i. 22. "For by this we know that we are passed from death to life, because we love the brethren: he that loveth not his brother abideth in death," John iii. 14. And therefore it is a case exceeding plain, that the readiest way in the world to reconcile our lesser differences is, to be united in the Spirit, and to agree upon a holy life.

11. Moreover, were we all united in the Spirit, we should have all one God, one Master of our faith, and one Lawgiver and Judge of all our controversies: and this would be an exceeding help to unity. The principal cause of divisions in the world, are the multitude of rulers, and masters, and judges. For with unsanctified men, their own conceits and carnal interest are their counsellor and judge. The rulers of the world, that have the power of the sword, and can do them good or hurt in their estates, are the masters of their religion more than God. They will follow this man or that man, that best pleaseth their fancies and fleshly desires; and so will never be of one mind. But sanctification takes down all other masters of our faith, save Christ and those that declare his will. Let flesh and blood say what it will, let all the world say what they will, if God say the contrary, his word shall stand and be a law to them. And can there be a readier way to unity, than to bring us all into one school, and subject us all to one Lord and Master, and to bring us all to refer our differences to one most wise infallible Judge? Though we do not yet understand his will in all things, yet when we understand it in the main, and are resolved to search after the knowledge of the rest, it is a great preparative to our agreement, when we all look but to one for the deciding of our controversies. Whereas the unsanctified have as many judges and guides as persons; for every man is a guide and judge to himself.

12. Moreover, were we but once agreed in holiness, we should all have one light for the ending of our differences; and that light would be the true infallible light. For we should all have the same holy word of God, as the extrinsic light, which is most true, as coming from the Lord of truth: and we should all have the Spirit of truth within, to teach us the meaning of that word without, and to help our understandings, and assist us in the application, and destroy the corruptions that blind us and hinder us from perceiving the truth: whereas the unsanctified are all in the dark; and what wonder, if there they disagree, and are of many minds! They be not guided by the word and Spirit, and they are strangers to the light that must reconcile us, if ever we be reconciled. It is true, too true, that the godly are illuminated but in part, and therefore as yet they differ in part. But yet this imperfect illumination doth more to a true and safe agreement, than all the world can do besides. If you would stop your ears against the flesh, and yield all to the teachings of the word and Spirit, we should be sooner agreed.

13. And if we were once united in the Spirit and holiness, we should all have the use and benefit of all the reconciling, healing means and ordinances of God; which would be an exceeding great advantage to us. The unsanctified have but the outside, the sound, and shell of ordinances; but it is the sanctified that have the light, and life, and fruit of them.

Every chapter that you read, and every sermon that you hear, will do somewhat towards the healing of our breaches; it will further our knowledge and our love. The communion of the saints in all holy duties, especially at the Lord's supper, when they partake of one Christ, will inflame their love, and humble them for their divisions, and solder and glue their hearts together, as being all one bread and one body: and so they will be all as of one heart and soul, Acts iv. 32; 1 Cor. x. 16, 17; Acts ii. 42—44, 46. When we hear of the tender love of Christ to his weakest members, how can we choose but love them if we be his disciples? When we hear how much and how freely he hath forgiven us, how can we choose but forgive them? Matt. xviii. 35. When we have communion with them in holy worship, as servants of the same Lord, as members of the same body, how can we choose but have the affections of fellow-members? 1 Cor. xii. 26. When we join with them in prayer, or holy conference, and perceive the fragrant odour of their graces, and the holy breathings of their souls after God, we cannot choose but love Christ in them. As the new commandment so frequently pressed in the gospel, is the law of love, (John xv. 12, 17,) and the new nature of the saints is a disposition of love, for this they are taught of God effectually, 1 Thess. iv. 9; so the ordinances do all of them exercise that love, and engage us to it. We must leave our gift at the altar, and go first and be reconciled to our brother if we remember that he hath any thing against us, Matt. v. 23, 24. We must pray for forgiveness, but on condition that we do forgive. Differences and divisions that make a breach in christian charity, are so insufferable among the saints, that they long for healing, and smart as the wounded body doth, till the time of healing; and are pained as a bone out of joint, till it be set again. And as they cannot bear it themselves, (when they are themselves,) so the church cannot bear it, but is engaged to watch over them, and set them in joint again; so that God hath hedged in his servants into one holy society, that they should not straggle from him, or from each other, and hath set pastors over them for this very end, to guide them and keep them in holy unity, Eph. iv. 11—14. Now all these uniting, healing ordinances are effectual upon the sanctified; for their hearts are open to them, and their new nature is suited to the new commandment and work: but to others they are in a manner as food or physic to the dead: they hate the power of them: they break the holy enclosure of discipline, and proudly rebel against their guides; and say, "Let us break their bands, and cast away their cords from us," Psal. ii. 3. What! must we be ruled by such and such? It is but the outside of sacraments, praises, and prayers that they are acquainted with; and these have no such healing force: so that in this you see the great advantage that we should have for full agreement, if we were but once agreed in the main, and united by the sanctifying Spirit.

14. Moreover, if once we were united in the Spirit, and in holiness, we should manage all our differences in a holy manner, and be awakened and disposed to seek after healing in a healing way. It would put us upon inquiring after peace, and studying the meetest terms of peace, till we had found out the way in which we should accord. The Spirit of love and holiness would provoke us to begin and seek for peace with those that will not seek to us, and that seem averse to it; and to follow after peace when it flieth from us, Heb. xii. 14; and even to lie down at the feet of men, and deny our honour and worldly interest, if it might procure brotherly love and peace. Whereas a proud, unsanctified heart will scorn to stoop, especially to those that are below them, or have wronged them, and will scorn to ask forgiveness of those that they have wronged! When you have showed them the plainest word of God for it, and persuaded them to it with undeniable reasons, you lose your labour, and may almost as well persuade the fire to be cold. If you will stoop and humble yourself to him, and ask him forgiveness, and give him the honour, or change your mind, and be of his opinion, and say as he saith, and do as he would have you, perhaps you may have some peace with the most ungodly man. But the servants of Christ have a spirit of meekness, and humility, and self-denial; and therefore if there be fallings-out among them, they can humble themselves and seek for reconciliation. If there be difference in judgment about any weighty matters, they will go or send to one another as brethren, and confer about it in love and meekness, and search the Scripture, and seek after truth, and compare their evidences, and pray together for that light and love that must reconcile them. If they fall out they can say to one another, We are brethren, and must not live at a distance, nor suffer any wounds in our affections, or any breach of charity to remain. The sun must not go down upon our wrath. Come, let us go together in private, and beg of God that he would repair our love, and reconcile us, and prevent such breaches for the time to come. And thus they can pray themselves friends again. I am persuaded that one quarter of an hour's fervent prayer would do more to quiet our distempered minds, and reconcile us, if thus we would get together in private, than many hours' debates without it. Now the Spirit of holiness is a Spirit of prayer; and therefore disposeth the servants of Christ, as meekly and lovingly to search for truth, so earnestly to pray themselves into agreement.

15. Moreover, were we once united in the Spirit, we should be under the promise of divine assistance, which the unsanctified have no part in. When we pray for light, and peace, and concord, we have a promise to be heard and helped, at least, in the time and measure as shall be fittest; we have a promise of the Spirit to be our teacher, and to lead us into truth: we have promises for the maintaining and repairing of our healing graces, and our communion graces; our love to Christ and one another; our patience and meekness, and the rest. And this must needs be a great advantage to unity and agreement. For God is partly engaged for it.

16. And if we were united in the Spirit, and agreed in the main, the great truths which we are agreed in would very much direct us to find out the rest which yet we differ in. For these have an influence into all the rest, and the rest are all connected to these, and also linked and knit together, that we may find out many by the help of one. All holy truths do befriend each other, but especially the great and master points which the rest depend upon, and flow from. There is no way to a right agreement in other points, but by agreeing first in these fundamental rudiments.

17. Also if we were once agreed in holiness, we should have that continually within us and before us, that would much take us off from vain contendings, and from an over-zealous minding of smaller things. We should have so much to do with God in holy duties, and so much to do with our own hearts in searching them, and watching them, and exciting them, and mending them, reproving and correcting them, supporting and comforting them by the application of the promises, that we should have less time for quarrelling, and less mind of it, than the unsanctified have. We should have so many great and prac-

tical truths to digest and live upon, that lesser and unnecessary matters, which are the common causes of contention, would find less room: or at least, we should allow each truth its due proportion of our study, and talk, and zeal; and so the lesser would have comparatively so small a share, and be so exceeding seldom and remissly meddled with, that there would be the less danger of contentions.

18. Yea, if once we were united in the Spirit, the very forethought of an everlasting union in heaven would have a continual influence upon our hearts, for the healing of our breaches. We should be thinking with ourselves, Shall we not shortly be all of one mind and heart? and all be perfected with the blessed vision, and reconciling light of the face of God? There will then be no dissension or division, or unbrotherly censures, or separations. And should we now live so unlike our future life? Shall we now be so unlike to what we must be for ever? Shall we now cherish those heart-burnings and dissensions, that must not enter with us into heaven, but be cast off among the rest of our miseries, and shut out with the rest of our enemies, and hated for ever by God and us? Must we there be closed in perfect love, and be all employed in the same holy praise of God and our Redeemer; and does it beseem us now to be censuring, contending, and separating from each other? Thus the belief of the life to come will be a more effectual means with the godly for agreement, than any that unsanctified men can use.

19. Moreover, they that have the Spirit of holiness, have a dear and special love to truth as well as unto peace. And therefore they have a great advantage for the receiving of it in all debates; and consequently they are fairer for a just agreement. They are friends with the most searching, spiritual truths; but the ungodly have an enmity to all that truth that would show them their sin, and misery, and duty, and make them holy, and lead them up from the creature unto God. And as the proverb is, He that would not know, cannot understand. When you deal with a wicked, graceless heart, you do not set reason against reason, (for if that were all, we should soon have done,) but you set reason against will, and passion, and appetite, and fleshly interest; and when you have convinced them, you are little the nearer prevailing with them. You may as well think to satisfy a hungry belly with reasons, or to tame a wild beast with reasons, as to humble the proud, and bring the sensual person to self-denial, by all your reasons. For they love not the truth, because they love not the duty that it would persuade them to, and because they love the sin that it would take from them. There are two forts of Satan in a wicked man, that none but God can batter, so as to win them: that is, a proud and ignorant mind, and a hard and sensual heart. Many a year have I been battering them by the word of God, from this place, and yet with many can do no good. But the sanctified heart that loveth the truth will meet it, and welcome it, and thankfully entertain it. Love maketh a diligent hearer and a good scholar, and giveth us hope that informations and debates may be successful. A godly man is so far from hating truth, and flying from it, that he would give all the riches of the world to purchase it; he prays, and reads, and studieth for it; and therefore hath great advantage to attain it.

20. Moreover, if we were all agreed in holiness, and united in the Spirit of Christ, we should love the truth in a practical manner, and we should know that every truth of God hath its proper work to do upon the soul; and therefore we should love the end of each truth better than the truth itself. And therefore we could not pretend the truth against the ends of truth. And therefore we should see to the security of those ends in all our debates and controversies. We should not make havoc of the church of Christ, nor easily be guilty of divisions, nor quench our love of God and of our brethren, under pretence of standing for the truth; which unsanctified men will easily do. Truth is for holiness and love as its proper end. Ungodly men will tread down love and holiness, or at least disadvantage it, and hinder it in the world, for the exalting of their own conceits, under the name of truth. They will cure the church by cutting it in pieces, or by cutting the throat of it, and are presently dismembering for every sore: but with the godly it is not so.

21. Moreover, the sanctified have a great advantage for agreement, in that they have hearts that are subject to the truth, and will be true to it when they understand it. Did they but know the right way, they would presently walk in it. Nothing is so dear to them that should not be forsaken for it, or sacrificed to it. But the wicked are false to the truths which they are acquainted with. They hold it or imprison it in unrighteousness, (Rom. i. 18,) and therefore is wrath revealed against them. "They like not to retain God in their knowledge;" and therefore God doth often give them up to a reprobate mind, Rom. i. 28. "They receive not the truth in the love of it, that they might be saved:" no wonder therefore if "God give them up to strong delusions to believe a lie, that all they might be damned that believed not the truth, but had pleasure in unrighteousness," 2 Thess. ii. 10—12. "When they know the judgment of God, that they that do such things are worthy of death; yet they do them, and have pleasure in them that do them," Rom. i. 32. We may well think that God will sooner reveal his truth to them that will obey it, than to them that will but bury it in the dunghill of a corrupted heart. And that he will rather hold the candle to his servants that will work by it, than to loiterers that will but play by it; or thieves or fornicators, that had rather it were put out; or to enemies, that would do mischief by it, and will throw away the candlesticks, (the ministers,) and put the candle into the thatch. Is there not many an ungodly person that hears me this day, that is convinced in his conscience that a holy life is best, and yet will not follow it and obey his conscience? Are there not convictions at the bottom, that the diligent, heavenly christian, whom thou reproachest, is in a safer condition than thyself; and yet thou wilt not imitate such. Can you expect that God should acquaint such with his truth, that are so false to it?

22. If we were but all agreed in true holiness, we should have the great advantage of a tender conscience, together with an illuminated mind. For spiritual wisdom, with tenderness of conscience, is a great part of sanctification. And it is a great advantage in controversies and debates, to be wise and tender-conscienced: for wisdom makes men able to discern, and a tender conscience will make them afraid of mistaking and contradicting the truth; and will keep them from rashness, and unadvisedness, and levity; so that such a one dare not venture so easily upon new conceits, and will be more suspicious of himself, and of any thing wherein himself is much concerned: especially if he see great probabilities against it, or the judgment of the universal church, or of many wise and godly men, against it, and see that it is like to have ill effects; in all such cases a godly man will be tender-conscienced, and therefore cautelous. But is it so with the ungodly? No; but clean contrary. None so bold as the blind. Solomon's words describe them exactly; "The fool rageth

and is confident," Prov. xiv. 16. If he be in an error, or entangled in any evil cause or way, you know not what to say to him for his recovery. The less he knows, the more he despiseth knowledge, and sets his face against his teachers, as if they were but fools to him, and scorns to be ruled by such as they, whom God hath made his rulers. Will you go to dispute or debate the case with one of these? Why be sure of it, they will put you down and have the day. It would do a man good to dispute with a wise, and learned, or sober, rational man, and to be overcome by reason and by truth: but no man will have so sure a conquest against you, as he that hath the least of sense or reason. He will go away and boast that you could not convince him: as if a mad-man should boast that the physicians could not all of them cure him. An obstreperous, proud, self-conceited fellow, will never yield to the clearest reason, nor ever be put down. We have a proverb, that There's no gaping against an oven, especially if it be hot. If he have passion as well as ignorance, and a tongue, he will have the best. He that speaks nonsense saith nothing while he seems to speak. These men have the faculty of saying nothing, an hour or two together, in abundance of words. And there is no confuting a man that saith nothing. Nonsense is unanswerable, if there be but enough of it. Who would dispute against a pair of bagpipes, or against a company of boys that hoot at him? If you will make a match at barking or biting, a cur will be too hard for you: and if you will try your skill or strength at kicking, a horse will be too hard for you: and if you will contend with multitude of words, or by rage and confidence, a fool will be too hard for you (as you may see by Solomon's descriptions, and by daily experience). But if you will dispute by equal, sober reasoning, it is only a wiser man by evidence of truth that can overcome you: and to be thus overcome is better than to conquer: for you have the better if truth overcome you; and you have the worse if you overcome the truth.

So that you may easily perceive what an exceeding hinderance to unity and peace it is to have to do with ungodly persons, that are blind, and proud, and brazen-faced, and of seared consciences, that fear not God, and therefore dare say any thing, as if they could out-face the truth, and the God of truth. But the sanctified have illuminated minds, and therefore are the more capable of further information; and they have tender consciences, and therefore dare not be unadvised and contentious, and strive against the light; and therefore have great advantage for agreement.

23. And if all these advantages should not yet so far prevail, as to bring us up to a full agreement, yet if we be but united in the Spirit and a holy life, we should be the more easily able to bear with one another under all our lesser differences, until the time of full agreement come. We should hold our differences (as brethren their diversity of statures and complexions, or at least as common human frailties) with love and compassion, and not with hatred and divisions. We should lovingly consult together upon rules or terms on which we might manage our unavoidable differences, to the least disadvantage to the cause of Christ, and to the common truths that we all maintain, and to the work of God for other men's conversion, and to the least advantage to sin and Satan, and the malice of ungodly men. And I think this is a fair agreement for imperfect persons, short of heaven; to have unity in the Spirit, and agreement in things of greatest weight, and to bear with one another in smaller matters, and manage our differences with meekness and with peace.

24. Lastly, If all this be not enough, there is yet more for our encouragement. 1. If we are but once united in the Spirit, and agree in a holy heart and life, we have the infallible promise of God, that we shall shortly all arrive in heaven, at the place and state of full perfection, where all our differences will be ended, and we shall be perfectly agreed in mind and will, being one in him that is the only centre of universal peace and concord. And it is a great comfort to us in our darkness and differences, that we are in the sure and ready way to perfect light and harmony of mind. 2. Yea, and till we do come thither, we are still on the mending hand; and if we do but thrive in holiness, we shall certainly thrive in concord and in peace. And it is a comfort to a sick man, not only to be certain of a full recovery, but to feel himself daily on the mending hand. 3. And in the mean time God himself will bear with all our differences, though not so far as to approve or cherish them, yet so far as to own us for his children, though we are too often falling out with one another; and so far as to pity our frailty and infirmity, and to pardon us, and deal as a father with us. And if our quarrels cause him to use the rod, it is but to keep us in quietness afterwards; that as we had the taste of the sour fruits of our contentions, so we may after have the quiet fruits of righteousness.

And thus I have given you in four and twenty particular discoveries, a sufficient proof, that a unity in the Spirit, and an agreement in holiness, hath abundant advantages for our further agreement in lower things; and such as all other men are destitute of; and therefore that there is no way possible for a just, a safe, a durable agreement, but that we all agree in a holy life, and be united in the sanctifying Spirit of Christ.

But perhaps you will object, If all this be so, whence comes it to pass that there are so many differences still among those that you call the sanctified? Do we not see that they are more contentious and divided into parties, and make more stir about religion, than any others?

Answ. 1. The differences among the godly are nothing for number, or greatness, or weight, in comparison of yours. I have showed you in my discourse of "The Catholic Church," twenty great and weighty points, in which they all agree together, and in which the ungodly agree not with them. What if they agree not, whether church government should be exercised by the elders only, the flock consenting; or by all the flock, the pastors guiding? Or whether one among the pastors should be of a superior degree, or of a superior order, or whether they should only be of the same degree and order, though chosen to preside and moderate for the time? What if one think that it is necessary to read the public prayers out of a book; and another think it is necessary to pray without book; and a third more truly thinks it is in itself indifferent, whether it be within book or without? With other such like differences as these, which will keep no man out of heaven? Are these like our differences with ungodly men? Our differences with you are, Whether heaven or earth is chiefly to be loved and sought after? Whether grace and holiness, or sin and carelessness, be the better; whether it be the more sweet and desirable life, to be heavenly-minded, and live in the love and service of God, and to be much in holy communion with him, and meditating upon his law, and upon the life to come; or on the contrary, to live to the world and to the flesh? Whether it be better to obey the word of God, and his ministers that speak it in his name; or to obey our fleshly desires, and the proud conceits of ignorant minds? In a word, our difference with the ungodly, though they will not confess it and speak out, is plainly this, Whether heaven or earth be better? And whether God be God, and shall be our God? And whether Christ be Christ, and shall be our Christ? And whether the Holy Ghost shall be our Sanctifier? Or whether we shall live after the flesh and rule ourselves, against the will and word of God, and so in effect, whether God be God, and man be man? And whether we should live as men or as beasts? And so whether we should choose salvation or damnation? If you could but understand yourselves, and the depth of your deceitful hearts, you would see that here lieth the difference. For though some of the unsanctified have a fair and plausible deportment, and will speak handsomely of the christian religion, because they have had an ingenuous christian education; yet all this is indeed but little more than formal compliment, so far are they from a heavenly mind and a heart that is truly set on God, as their careless lives, and carnal, unsavoury confidence showeth, if not their scorns at a state of holiness. So that our differences are nothing in comparison of the difference with you.

2. Moreover, the servants of God do mind the matters of religion more seriously than others do; and therefore their differences are brought to light, and made more observable to the world. Their very heart is set upon these heavenly things, and therefore they cannot make light of the smallest truth of God; and this may be some occasion of their difference: whereas the ungodly differ not about religion, because they have heartily no religion to differ about; they trouble not themselves about these matters, because they do not much regard them. And is this a unity and peace to be desired? I had rather have the discord of the saints, than such a concord of the wicked. They are so careful about their duty that they are afraid of missing it in the least particular; and this (with their imperfect light) is the reason of their disputings about these matters. But you that are careless of your duty, can easily agree upon a way of sin, or take any thing that comes next to hand. They honour the worship of God so much, that they would not have any thing out of order; but you set so little by it, that you will be of the religion that the king is of, let it be what it will be: and it is easy to agree in such an ungodly, careless course. Astronomers have many controversies about the positions and motions of the heavens; and all philosophers have many controversies about the matter of their sciences: when ignorant men have none of their controversies, because they understand not, and therefore regard not, the things that the learned differ about. And will you think ever the better of ignorance, or ever the worse of learning, for this? The controversies of lawyers, of historians, chronologers, geographers, physicians, and such like, do never trouble the brains of the ignorant; but for all that, I had rather be in controversy with the learned, than without such controversy with you. If you scatter a handful of gold or diamonds in the street, perhaps men will scramble for them, and fall out about them, when swine will trample on them and quietly despise them, because they do not know their worth: will you therefore think that swine are happier than men? The living are vexed with strifes and controversies, about almost all the matters in the world, when the dead carcasses in the grave lie still in peace, and are not troubled with any of these differences. And will you say therefore that the dead corpse is happier than the living? Sirs, the case is very plain, if you will see, that thus it is as to the matter in hand. It is a death in sin, and compliance with the times and carnal interest, and a disesteem of spiritual, holy things, that is the cause of the agreement of the wicked. But the godly know the worth of the things that you set light by, and therefore make a greater matter of them than you; and therefore no wonder if they have more debates and controversies about them.

3. And this also is another reason of the difference. It is the interest of Satan to divide the servants of Christ, but to keep his own in unity and peace: and therefore he will do what he can to accomplish it. He knows that a kingdom divided cannot stand: and therefore he will do his worst to divide Christ's kindom, and to keep his own from being divided. By a deceitful peace it is that he keeps his servants to him. And by casting among them the matter of contentions and divisions, he hopeth to get Christ's followers from him. So that the devil himself is the promoter of your unity and concord, but the destroyer of ours; and therefore no wonder if you have fewer differences.

4. Besides, the way that ungodly men go in is so suited to the common corruption of nature, that it is no wonder if they be all agreed. All the world can agree to eat, and drink, and sleep; and therefore all the sensual sinners in the world may easily agree upon an overloving of meat, and drink, and sleep; and so of riches, and honours, and pleasures. And as it is easy, so it is not much desirable, no more than if you should all agree to cast yourselves headlong into the sea. When every house is infected with the plague, there is an agreement among them: but had you not rather be one of those that disagree from them? But to agree in a holy, heavenly life, is contrary to corrupted nature; and therefore no marvel if it be more difficult. When a physician hath a hundred patients in hand, he may easily get them all to agree to eat and drink that which they desire; but if he require them to forbear the things that they most love, because they will hurt them, the understanding sort will agree to him, but so will not the rest. In a rotten house, the fall of one bearer may occasion the fall of all the house, because their weight inclines them downward: but if you take up one stone and cast it upward, all the rest of the stones in the heap will not fly upward with it. It is easier to draw others with us down-hill, than up the hill.

5. And it is considerable that the differences among the servants of Christ are not always from themselves, but from the ungodly enemies that contrive their dissensions, and set them together by the ears, that they may fish in troubled waters, and the better attain their wicked ends. It is the envious man that soweth these tares while we are asleep, and casteth in this wildfire among us.

6. Moreover, one of the greatest causes of the troublesome breaches and divisions in the church, is because there are so many unsanctified persons among us, that seem to be of us, and to be truly godly, when it is not so. You think it is the godly that have these divisions, when the most and worst of all our divisions proceed from the ungodly, that have an unsound and unrenewed heart, under the cloak of piety and zeal: for if they were truly gracious persons, they durst not do as many of them do. 1. They durst not so rashly and easily venture on novelties as they do, without deliberation, and reading, and hearing what can be said on the other side. 2. They durst not so easily make a division in the church of Christ. 3. Nor so easily cast a stumblingblock before the weak; and matter of reproach to our christian profession before the wicked. 4. Nor durst

they so easily reproach, and condemn, and cast off the unanimous faithful ministers of Christ. 5. Nor durst they so easily censure the universal church in former ages, as many of them do. 6. Nor durst they sacrifice the success and honour of the gospel, and the common acknowledged truths, and the saving of men's souls thereby, to their private opinions and ends. 7. Nor durst they make so great a breach in charity, nor so arrogantly condemn or slight their brethren, whose piety and soberness they cannot deny. These, with many other evidences, do let us know, that ungodly men, crept in among us, are the causes of most of our most dangerous divisions. And will you lay the blame of this upon religion, which the devil and the secret enemies of religion do perform? It is your dishonour, and not ours; for these men are of your party, though they seem to be of us. Satan knows well enough, that if he have not some of his followers to be spies in Christ's army, and to raise mutinies there and betray the rest, he is like to be the more unsuccessful in his attempts. Was Judas more a dishonour to Christ, or to the devil? He was among the followers of Christ indeed; but he told them beforehand of him, that he was a devil; and he never betrayed Christ till Satan had entered into him.

7. Lastly, The saints themselves are sanctified but in part, and many in a low degree; and being imperfect in holiness, must needs be as imperfect in holy unity and peace. It is not their holiness that causeth their contentions, but the remnants of their sin. And therefore it is but small credit to the way of sinners. Were we but perfectly rid of the vices that you cherish, and perfectly separated from the ways that you so much delight in, and had we no remnants of your disease and sinful nature in us, we should then have perfect unity and peace. Do you think that it is long of our religion that we disagree: no; if we were but perfectly religious we should be perfectly agreed. It is because we are holy in no greater a measure, and not because we are holy at all. It is not because of the way of godliness that we have chosen; but because we walk no faster, and no more carefully, in that way. It is our too oft stepping out of it, and not our walking in it, that breaketh our peace with God and man, and our own consciences. Search all the Scripture, and see where you can find, that ever God encouraged his servants to divisions. No: but on the contrary, he oft and earnestly cries them down, and warneth all his followers to avoid them, and the causers and fomenters of them. There was never master so much for unity as Christ, and never was there a law, or a religion, that did so much condemn divisions, and command brotherly love, and peace, and concord, and forbearing and forgiving one another, as the christian law and religion doth. And will you yet say that our divisions are long of our religion, or of Christ the author of it? You may as wisely say, that eating is the cause of weakness, because that some are weak for all their meat. But you will find that none can live without it. Or you may say as wisely, that physicians are the causes of the diseases of the world, because they do not cure them all. I tell you, there is none in all the world that have done so much for unity and peace, as Christ hath done. No; all the world set together have not done half so much for it as he. He hath preached peace and unity, forgiving and forbearing, and loving one another, yea, loving our enemies; and he hath gone before us in the perfect practice of what he taught. He hath offered himself a sacrifice to the justice of his Father, that by his blood he might reconcile us unto God. He is the great Peace-maker between God and man, between Jews and gentiles, taking away the enmity, and becoming himself the Head of our unity; and giving us one Spirit, one faith, one baptism, that we might be one in him who is one with the Father. So that to charge the Centre of unity with our divisions, and the Prince of peace himself with our discords, or his holy word or ways with our disagreements, is all one as to charge the sun with darkness, and to say that our lawgivers and laws are the causes of theft, and murder, and adultery, which condemn them to death that are approved guilty of them. The cause of all our disagreements and divisions is, because we are no more holy than we are, and because we are no more religious. So that I may leave it now as a proved truth, that we must unite in the Spirit, and agree in holiness of heart and life, if ever we will have true unity and agreement.

And now, sirs, you have seen the only way of unity opened to you: it is plain and past all doubt before you. If yet you will divide from God and his servants, and if yet you will be numbered with the stragglers or quarrellers, do not say but peace was opened and offered to you. Do not say, you could have peace, but that you would not. Do not say any more hereafter, that there were so many religions and so many ways that you could not tell which to join with! never more pretend the differences of the godly as a cloak for your ungodliness. I have opened the nakedness of such pretences. You shall not be able, when your lives are scanned, to look God in the face with such an unreasonable impudent pretence. Your consciences and the world shall then be witnesses of your shame; that while you cried out of sects and heresies, and were offended at the divisions of the church, it was yourselves that were the cause of it. It was you, and such as you, that were the great dividers; and that obstinately proceeded in your divisions, when the way of peace was opened to you; and would not be united in the Spirit to Christ, and would not agree in holiness with his church, when you were acquainted that there was no other way to peace. Would you but have joined in a firm and everlasting covenant to God the Father, Son, and Holy Ghost, as your only Creator, Redeemer, and Sanctifier, as members of the holy catholic church, and have lived in the communion of the saints, you should have received the forgiveness of sins, the resurrection of the just, and everlasting life: but in refusing, and obstinately refusing these, you refused all your hopes of blessedness, and wilfully cast yourselves on the wrath of God; and therefore must endure it for ever.

The last advice that I have to give, upon the ground of this doctrine, is, To all that are united in the Spirit, and agreed upon a holy life. I mean to say but little to you now; but briefly to tender you these two requests.

1. I beseech you, christians, but to live as christians, in that holy unity as your principles and profession do engage you to. Hath true christianity and holiness such abundance of advantages against division, and yet will you be guilty of it? Against all these bonds and healing principles and helps, will you be dividers? Doth it not grieve you, and even break your hearts, to hear ungodly persons say that professors are of so many minds and parties, that they know not which of them to follow; and that we had never concord since you bore sway? O do not seek by your contentious ways, to persuade people that holiness is a dividing thing, and that religion doth but tend to set the world together by the ears. Is it not a precious mercy to us of this place, that we have among us but one church, and one

religion, and have not church against church, and christian against christian? I charge you from the Lord, that you be thankful for this benefit; and that you look upon divided places, and compare their case with yours, that if ever dividers come amongst you, the sense of your felicity in this blessed unity may cause you to reject them; and that you do not suffer any Delilah to rob you of your strength and glory. Were you but once here in pieces among yourselves, what a scorn would you be to all the ungodly! What sport would it be to them, to hear you disputing against one another, and reproaching and condemning one another, as bitterly as the wicked do reproach you all! Do you not pity those places where divisions have made religion to be a scorn, and the tender love and unity of the saints is turned into uncharitable censures and separations? Take warning then that you come not to the like. If you should, you would be as unexcusable as any people in the world, because you have tried and tasted so much of the sweetness and benefits of unity as you have done; show men by your lives, that holiness is the most certain way to unity, as ever you desire either to propagate holiness, or to have any evidence of it in yourselves.

2. Judge by this undoubted truth, of any doctrine that shall be offered you, and of the ways of men and of yourselves.

1. Suspect that doctrine that tendeth to divisions in the church. If it be not for unity, it is not of God, Rom. xvi. 17. Christ came to heal and reconcile, and is the Prince of peace; and, therefore, sendeth not his servants on a contrary errand. He will justify your dividing from the unbelieving world; but he hateth dividing among his servants. He that is for church division, is not (in that) for Christ or you.

2. Whatever holiness they may pretend to, adhere not to those men, and think not too highly of them that are for divisions among the churches or servants of the Lord. You will see them repent, or come to shame and confusion at the last. You fly from Christ, if you fly from unity.

3. Think not that you have any more of the Spirit, or of holiness, than you have of love to the unity of the saints. It is the spirit of Satan, and not of Christ, that leadeth you to church divisions: it is a counterfeit holiness that maketh you not desirous of unity with all the saints. If you be not first pure and then peaceable, your wisdom is not from above. As you would all take that man to be an enemy to holiness, that is an enemy to chastity, temperance, or common honesty; so have you reason to think of him that is an enemy to the church's unity and peace. Show that you have the Spirit by the unity of the Spirit; and show that you are holy by loving the union and communion of the saints.

ROMANS XIV. 1.

HIM THAT IS WEAK IN THE FAITH RECEIVE YE, BUT NOT TO DOUBTFUL DISPUTATIONS.

I HAVE already proved to you in the foregoing discourse, 1. That the true unity of the church of Christ is a unity of the Spirit, and that the unsanctified are the causes of our divisions. 2. That a unity in mere profession, is but a low and miserable unity, which will not satisfy nor serve the turn. That a unity in the Spirit of holiness, is a great advantage for the healing of all our lesser differences, or that we may do well for all those differences, if we are truly sanctified. I come now to the fourth and last part of my discourse, which is to show you, that it is not the will of God that the unity of his church should consist in things indifferent, or in the smaller matters, or in points of doubtful disputation. To which end I have chosen this text, in which Paul doth purposely and plainly lay down this point, in order to the reconciling of a difference that was then among the Romans. I shall not now stand to discuss whether the weak that Paul here speaks of, were some christians tainted with a Pythagorean conceit, and guilty of some excessive austerities (which some have thought, 1. because here is no mention of circumcision; 2. and because they are said to eat herbs only); or whether it were some converts of the Jews, that scrupled the forsaking of their ancient ceremonies, which is the common and likelier exposition. 1. The person here spoken of is "him that is weak in the faith," that is, who is yet so ignorant in the doctrine of faith, as not to know that these ceremonies are abolished, or these matters are no part of duty, which he placeth duty in; and, consequently, who is so weak in conscience as that he dare not omit the observation of these days and ceremonies. The points in which the weakness of these persons are said to be manifested, are, 1. In their abstaining from flesh, and eating herbs. 2. In their observation of certain days as holy.

2. The thing commanded is, that these persons, for all their weakness, be received; that is, 1. Into brotherly internal charity. 2. Into christian external communion. For it seems, that by reason of this their weakness, there grew divisions in the church. The weak were so self-conceited, as to censure the strong, because they did not observe their ceremonies. And the strong were too contemptuous of the weak, and made light of them as a superstitious people, unfit for their communion. Paul chides them both; the weak for censuring the strong, and the strong for contemning the weak; and commandeth that for the future, the weak forbear his judging, and the strong receive the weak whom they contemned, and so that they join in inward love and external communion.

3. And he addeth this caution, for the manner of their reception and behaviour, that it must not be "to doubtful disputations," either to the censuring of one another, or to unseasonable, uncharitable contendings and disputes about these smaller things. Three things Paul seemeth to suppose in the matter of their controversy. 1. That they were matter of some indifferency. 2. That they were small, and of lowest consideration in religion. 3. That to the weak they were so dark and doubtful, as to be the matter of disputes. But for all these, he would have no breach in their charity or communion.

One doubt we must not overpass; and that is, how this will stand with what he saith in the epistle to the Galatians. Here he saith, "Let not him that eateth despise him that eateth not. One man esteemeth one day above another; another esteemeth every day alike. Let every man be fully persuaded in his own mind." But there he saith, "Ye observe days, and months, and times, and years: I am afraid of you, lest I have bestowed upon you labour in vain," Gal. iv. 10, 11. And of circumcision, "Behold, I Paul say unto you, if ye be circumcised, Christ shall profit you nothing; for I testify again to every man that is circumcised, that he is a debtor to do the whole law," Gal. v. 2, 3. For the understanding of this you must observe, 1. That there is a great difference between circumcision and the ceremonies here spoken of. 2. And between the outward act of circumcision, and the sacrament of circumcision as appointed by God. 3. And there is a great difference between the using it as necessary to justification, and the using the outward part only for some lawful end. 4. And between the time when the gospel was but newly revealed, and the time when it was oft and fully declared to the world. 5. And between those that are ignorant for want of full information, and those that are obstinate after long instruction. 6. And between those that scruple the omission of such ceremonies themselves; and those that would obtrude them as necessary upon others. Observing these distinctions, you may see the difficulty plainly resolved, as followeth. 1. In this text, Rom. xiv. Paul speaketh not of circumcision, but of meats and days only. For circumcision engaged men further to Moses's law, than these single ceremonies. 2. When Paul saith he was afraid of the Galatians, because of their observation of days, and weeks, and months, he means because they still adhered to the abrogated law, after so long and plain instruction. 3. And though he circumcised Timothy, (Acts xvi. 3,) and yet speaks against it, (Gal. v. 2, 3,) the difference of the cases is exceeding great. For, 1. It was but the outward circumcision of the flesh that he used with Timothy (as with one that did not intend by it any engagement to Moses, or necessity of it to justification); but it was the entire sacrament of circumcision which was pretended to continue necessary, by the false teachers, and which he exhorted the Galatians to refuse. And circumcision as a sacrament doth signify two principal things. 1. An engagement to and profession of faith in the promised Seed, as promised and future. 2. An engagement to Moses's law (for this use it had after the law was given). Now when Christ was come, that man that would still be circumcised into, and profess to expect, a Messiah yet to come, and that would engage himself to that law which contained the types of a future Messiah, and was but a schoolmaster to lead to Christ, I say that person that was thus circumcised (as all were that received it according to the institution) did plainly deny that Christ was come, and therefore Christ could profit them nothing. But yet a man that used but the outward sign to avoid an impediment to the gospel, (as Paul did in the case of Timothy,) or if it were erroneously, as a mere custom, as the Abassines now do, might yet be saved by Christ nevertheless. 2. And when Paul used it, it was as an indifferent thing: but he condemned it as supposed necessary. 3. When he used it, it was in the beginning of the publication of the gospel, that (as Austin speaks) he might give the ceremonies an honourable burial: but when he condemned it, it was after the full publication of the abolition of the law, against those that would have raked it out of the grave again. 4. He bore with it in the weak; but he condemned it in the wilful. 5. He bore with it in those that scrupled the forsaking it as they were Jews; but he condemned it in those that would have laid this yoke as necessary on the gentiles.

Object. But it seems here that Paul is against the necessary observation of the Lord's day, when he is for esteeming all days alike.

Answ. If you understand the subject of the debate, you will understand his speech. It is only Jewish holy-days that was the matter in question, and therefore of these only is he to be understood. As for the Lord's day, it is plain in the New Testament, that Christ did not only rise upon it, and appear to his disciples on it, and send down the Holy Ghost upon it; but that the disciples presently after Christ's resurrection, began their religious assemblies on it, and so continued them, by the guidance of the Holy Ghost; and so settled that day for the use of the holy assemblies of the church, calling it the Lord's day, John xxi. 19, 26; Acts ii. 1; xx. 7; 1 Cor. xvi. 2; Rev. i. 10. And it is past all doubt in the history of the church, that since the apostles' days till now, the church hath constantly kept this day as thus established, by the name of the Lord's day; which the fathers called the christian sabbath, as they applied the name of an altar to the table, and of a sacrifice to the supper of the Lord: so that he that will reject the observation of the Lord's-day, must take on him to be wiser than the Holy Ghost in the apostles, and than all the catholic church of Christ, from the beginning, till these contentious persons did arise.

The text being thus explained, the doctrine before-mentioned is plain in it before us, viz.

Doctrine. It is the will of God that the unity of the church should not be laid upon indifferent, small, and doubtful points; but that true believers, who differ in such things, should notwithstanding have inward charity and outward communion with one another, not censuring, nor despising, nor dividing from each other upon this account.

In handling this point, I shall briefly show you, 1. What I mean by things indifferent. 2. What I mean by smaller matters. 3. What by doubtful things or disputations: and then I shall give you the reasons of it, and then apply it.

I. For the explication. 1. By things indifferent I do not mean things, *hic et nunc*, indifferent in the use; but things that are not ordinarily in themselves either commanded as duties or forbidden as sins, but left as lawful or indifferent by the Scriptures, unless as some accident or circumstance may make them to be good or evil.

2. By smaller matters, it is none of my intent to persuade you, that any thing that is but an appurtenance to faith or piety is absolutely small: but they are small in comparison of the far greater things, and so small that many are saved without them, and they are not of flat necessity to salvation; and the greater matters must be preferred before them.

3. By things doubtful, I do not mean such as are not certainly revealed in the Scripture, nor yet such as perverse heretical men do raise doubts about when they are plain in themselves: but I mean such points as are revealed certainly, but more darkly than the greater points, and therefore cannot be so clearly known; so that the sum is this, 1. Indifferent things must not be taken to be necessary, or sinful, but to be indifferent. 2. Lower and lesser points must not be taken to be greater or weightier than they are. 3. Points of less certainty that are more darkly revealed, must not be taken to be more clear and certain to us than they are. 4. And it is not on such darker, smaller matters that God hath laid our salvation; or that the church's unity and peace dependeth.

II. For the fuller demonstration of this, let these reasons be observed: 1. If our unity were laid on these smaller matters, the multitude of them is such, that we should never agree in all. The essentials of christianity are so few, that all men may well be expected to learn, and know, and entertain them. But the smaller points are so many, that there is no hope of a universal agreement in them all. You know in the body of man or beast, the great master veins that are the stock of all the rest, are but a few; but follow them farther, and you shall have so many divisions, and sub-divisions, till you find them to be many hundreds or thousands. So is it with the arteries, and with the nerves. The body of a tree is but one, and the first division perhaps is but in two or three parts; but follow it to the very ends of the branches, and you may find many thousands. So is it in divinity: and therefore if none should be in unity with the church, but those that understand every branch of christian verity, what hope of union could there be.

2. Moreover, the smaller points are far less discernible than the greater be; and therefore there is the less hope that ever the church should have unity in these. The great arms of a tree are easily discerned, when the extremities of the branches are very small. The trunks of the master veins are great and easily seen, but the points and capillary veins are so small, as hardly to be perceived. So God in mercy hath made very plain those few essential points of faith that salvation lieth on; but if you follow on these generals to all the particulars and appurtenances, you shall find them run so small, as well as so many, as that it is impossible that unity should consist in these.

3. Furthermore, if our unity were laid on these, religion would be for none but the learned, and (as the ancients ordinarily argue against the heathens that cavilled at the plainness of the Scripture) God should be then partial, and should make a way to heaven that poor men cannot go. For the poor cannot possibly attain to so much learning, and spend so much of their lives in study, as may bring them to the knowledge of all these lower, difficult points.

4. Yea, if our unity or salvation lay on these, it is certain it would shut us all out, both from unity and salvation; so that there would no two be at unity in all the world, and no one be saved. For all men on earth are ignorant in many lesser truths, even such as are revealed to us in the Scripture, and we should endeavour to understand. What man dare affirm that he understandeth every word of the holy Scripture? Did the pope himself think that he had attained to this infallibility, he would ere this have written us an infallible commentary. If the best must say with Paul himself, "We know but in part," then sure those smaller, doubtful things, which all the truly sanctified know not, are not the matter of the unity of the church.

5. I have showed in my discourse of "The Catholic Church," that to shut out all from the church and our communion, that differ from us in such lower things, is utterly against the design of Christ, and the tenor of the gospel, and very dishonourable to him and to his church: God hath more mercy than to shut out the weak; and will you dishonour him so far as to persuade the world that he hath no such mercy? The design of the gospel is grace and love! How tender was Christ, even of his little ones that believe in him! how compassionate is he to them in their infirmities! And would you go about to persuade the world that he hath so little of this compassion, as that he will admit none to heaven, or to the communion of his church, but those that attain to knowledge and agreement in all these lesser, doubtful controversies, and indifferent things? The church is small enough already; but if you would cut off all that do not agree in every circumstance, you would make it small indeed. This is no better than, under pretence of faith and unity, to unchurch the church, and damn yourselves and all the world.

6. The arguments in the text are very forcible: "For God hath received him," ver. 3. As if he should say, Dare you despise or cast out him that God receiveth? "Who art thou that judgest another man's servant?" ver. 4. "Why dost thou judge thy brother? or why dost thou set at nought thy brother? We shall all stand before the judgment-seat of Christ," ver. 10. The church doth not censure men for small or doubtful things; nor must we condemn those that God doth not condemn.

7. The laying such stress on smaller things, doth multiply controversies, and fill the minds of men with scruples, and insnare their consciences, and engage men in parties against each other to the certain breach of charity, and ruin of the peace of the church, and of their souls. The fire of contention will never go out for want of fuel, if unnecessary things be made necessary, and small things pretended be great, and uncertain things pretended to be certain. Abundance of vice will be daily set and kept at work, upon this borrowed stock.

8. And what a world of precious time will be wasted by this means, while men are studying and reading to maintain their own opinions; and when they must waste their hours when they are together, in conferences and wrangling disputations, to the discomposing of their own and others' minds, and certain troubling the church of God! Oh what use have we for those precious hours, for surer, greater, and more needful things!

9. The things that our salvation, and the church's peace, are indeed laid upon, are so great, so necessary, so pleasant, and so profitable, that it leaveth us the more without excuse, to waste our time in things unnecessary. We have our great Creator to know and honour; we have the mystery of redemption to search into and admire; we have the nature, and life, and death, and resurrection, and ascension, and glorification, and intercession of Christ, to study and believe; and all the love and wisdom of God, the mercy, and the holiness and justice, that was revealed in him; we have judgment to prepare for; and all the graces of the Spirit of Christ to be received, or cherished, increased, and exercised in our souls. We have a hell to escape, and a heaven to obtain, and the foreseen glory of it to feed upon, for the strengthening and delighting of our souls; we have many particular duties of holiness and righteousness to attend: and in the midst of all this great employment, should we make more work and trouble to ourselves, and that about unnecessary things?

10. These unnecessary or lower things, when once they are advanced above their rank, do undermine and wrong the greater matters, which they pretended to befriend. They divert the thoughts and speeches from them, and take up the affections, and will not be contented with their due proportion; but are, as the proverb is, Like a beggar on horse-back, that will never light. If men be set upon ceremonies, or private opinions of their own, they are upon it in all companies; and you shall sometimes have almost nothing else from them. And that is not all; but the interest of their unnecessary or lower points, is ordinarily set up against the interest of that body of christian verities which we are all agreed in; so that they can be contented that christianity lose much advantage in the greater points, that their cause may be advantaged. If this were not so, we should not have had ceremonies and formalities cast out such abundance of excellent preachers heretofore; nor private opinions have set so many against the labours of faithful ministers, as, to our grief and shame, we have lately seen: and the mischief is, that unnecessary things made necessary, do so involve the imposers' interest with their own, that they think they are necessitated to drive them on, and see their impositions obeyed, or else their wisdom or authority is despised.

11. And thus they directly lead men to persecution, and occasion those that must needs have their wills, to lord it over God's heritage, 1 Pet. v. 3. When the desire of being the church's god, hath prevailed

so far with any of its members, as to set them upon a course of law-giving and domineering, and bringing others into a conformity to their wills; they look upon all men as sinners that disobey them, and think that their power will warrant them to force obedience to their commands, or else to deprive the church of her pastors. Many a congregation have I known change preachers for ceremonies; whenas if God's will and word in necessary things to men's salvation, had but been preferred to the will and word of the bishops, about things called indifferent by themselves, the case had been altered; and they would rather have let the ignorant have been without a ceremony than a sermon. It is the unhappy fate of almost all that are set upon unnecessary things, that they cannot endure that others should have the liberty of differing from them. It is not enough to them to enjoy the freedom of their own consciences, about meats, or holy-days, or gestures, or vestures, or other formalities, unless all others be compelled to do as they do. When they are but moved to comply with others, though plain Scripture and the practice of the primitive catholic church be justly alleged for it, yet it moveth them little or nothing. But if others will not comply with them, they cry out against them as enemies to unity and peace; and say, It is not fit to suffer men to be of so many minds and ways; that is, it is fit all should be compelled to do as they would have them.

12. And another mischief that followeth the making unnecessary things to be nĕcessary, is, that it openeth a gap to so many more of the same kind, that no man knows how to stop it, nor when we have ceremonies and inventions enough: but upon the same ground that these are brought in to-day, the next pope or bishop thinks he may bring another to-morrow; and so we can never tell when we have all, nor when will be an end.

13. And then in the multitude of things unnecessary, we shall be in danger of losing the things that are necessary, they will be so buried or obscured in the crowd; the substance will scarcely be perceived for the ceremony.

14. And methinks it is such height of pride for mortal men to arrogate such a power, and to desire and endeavour such a thing, that I wonder how they dare attempt it; I mean, to make universal or unnecessary laws for the church, in the matters of faith or worship. Can a man that hath one spark of humility left in him, desire that his will may be a law to all others, in doubtful or indifferent things? and proceed so far as to desire, that none may have liberty in the church that are not of his opinion, or will not be ruled by him, in things indifferent, or of no necessity? Surely a man of any humility would think with himself, Am not I also imperfect in knowledge? And may I not be mistaken? What is my judgment that it should be a law to the church, and that I should be so highly conceited and confident of it, as to turn out godly ministers or people from the church or worship of God, for not conforming themselves to my opinion in things of such a low and indifferent nature! He that would be the lawgiver to the church, and suffer none but those of his own opinion in such points, would be the lord of the church, which can know the voice of none but Christ, and owneth no other lord but him.

15. And the sin is the greater, because they have so little interest or pretence to lead them to these usurpations: they must have their will, though it get them nothing. Who made them lawgivers to the church of Christ? Cannot they allow Christ this part of the sovereignty, to make laws for his church? And cannot they be content with a ministerial power, to proclaim and promote the laws of Christ, and according to these to guide his church?

16. And hereby men are drawn to a human kind of religion; and they do more properly believe, obey, and worship these imposers than Jesus Christ: when they must fetch the very matter of their religion, not from the Bible, but the canons or decrees of men, their conscience, obedience, and reward will be according thereunto.

17. And hereby the adversaries of the church have occasion to insult over us, and think our differences to be more than indeed they are. When the unity of the church is laid upon things indifferent or of smallest moment, there will presently be disagreements, and these will be the enemy's matter of reproach. It is this that makes the papists tell us of our differences among ourselves, because we have made them seem something to them, when they are next to nothing. Oh, say they, where is your church of England now? Why! what is the matter? Is the church of England dead? Or is any thing taken down that was essential to the church of England? Was a prelacy ruling by a lay-chancellor over many hundred parishes, chosen and governing without the body of the clergy, essential to the church of England? I am confident the most of the sober, godly ministers in England, are for the apostolical, primitive episcopacy still. Was the book of canons, or the book of Common Prayer, or the ceremonies essential to the church of England? Sure they were not; and if so, it is living still. But if any say, that these were essential to it, we may thank them for the death of it, that made it of such a human mortal frame, which any prince might spurn down at his pleasure. Surely the church or churches of Christ in England, are of a more heavenly, durable frame, that may be persecuted, but hardly destroyed, while the men are living of whom it doth consist.

Hence also it is, that the papists tell us that we have changed all our worship. And wherein? Why we have not the same baptism that we had; nor the same administration of the Lord's supper, nor the same public prayer, nor the same way of marrying, churching, burying, &c. And what is the difference? Is it that we say not at every time the very same words? Why so you may as well say, that Paul was mutable, because he wrote not the same words in every one of his epistles, nor spoke not the same words in all his prayers, no not in public. And so both you and we are mutable, because we preach not the same words every day in our sermons. God hath bid us pray; but he hath prescribed us no necessary form of words, but the Lord's prayer. If the difference be, that we use not the Common Prayer book; doth that make a different sort of worship? Is it not the same sort of worship if we say the same words, or words to the same sense, either on the book or off it? If once men lay the nature of worship, and the unity of the church, upon things unnecessary, then what changes will seem to be in our worship, when indeed there are none! Then the papists may tell us of our divisions in worship, because one man sitteth at the singing of psalms and another stands; and one readeth with spectacles and another without; and one weareth a cap, and another weareth none; and one preacheth on one text, and another upon another. But be it known to all the papists in the world, that our religion is not changed at all; our worship is the same whether within book or without. Our prayers are the same for matter with those in the Common Prayer book. And if I should one day use the Common Prayer book, and another day forbear it, I should not change the worship of God. To pray is part of his worship: but whether it be on a book or off it, is no part at all, but only a mode or circumstance, which may be altered as occasion serveth. I doubt not but a book is fittest for some; but not for all. And do they think, that we know not what adding, and chopping, and changing they have made with their mass-book? Who is it then that hath changed their worship? Is it like the same book that it was before the changes made by Gregory the Great? It was so ordinary a thing to change the manner and forms of worship, that private bishops did it without any synods: whence else had the world the forms that are now in use? Tell us how many of those in the Biblioth. Patrum were made by apostles, or general council, if you can. When Basil the Great had set up a new way of singing to God, and made some other changes in worship, the clergy of Neocæsarea were offended with him for the novelty, and told him, that none of that was used in Gregory's days. To whom he answers, that neither was their own litany known in Gregory's days, (who yet had lived not one hundred and forty years before, and was the famous founder of their church by miracles,) Basil, Epist. 63. And Basil added to the clergy of Neocæsarea, But how can you tell that these things were not in use in Gregory's days, when you have kept nothing unchanged which he was used to? And that you may see his mind in this, he adds, But I pardon all these things (though God will examine all): only let the principal things be kept safe. If we had changed the sacraments, as the papists have done, viz. a commemorative sacrifice into a real sacrifice of Christ himself; the sacramental body and blood of Christ into the real body and blood; the administration of it in both kinds into one kind alone, defrauding the people of the cup; the communion into a private mass, the people only looking on the priest, when he receiveth alone himself, &c.: I say, had we made such changes as these, they might have called us changelings indeed, and have told us of novelties in the worship of God.

18. Moreover, this laying so much upon lower and unnecessary things, doth impoverish the soul, and make it low, and empty, and formal, according to the matter that it hath to work upon. As the great unquestionable truths of God are they that sanctify and elevate the soul, and leave their image on it; so will contending about private opinions, or laying out our zeal in ceremonies and shadows, depress the soul and famish it, and turn our religion into a shadow. We find, by sad experience, that people are so prone to turn all religion into mere words, and shows, and customary formalities, that when we have done our best, we cannot cure them of this mortal sin: "God is a Spirit, and will have such worshippers as worship him in Spirit and in truth," John iv. 25. We have little need to cherish this disease of hypocrisy and seeming histrionical outside religiousness, when we see so many perish by it, after all that we can do for their deliverance.

19. And this making a religion of unnecessary things, or laying the church's unity thereon, is a dangerous snare to delude the ignorant and ungodly, and make them believe that they are godly people, and in the way to heaven, as well as others. I use not this, or any argument, against the profitable use of any forms, in order to the understanding of the matter; nor against the due circumstantiating of the worship of God. But if profitable forms, and God's own ordinances, are somewhat liable to this abuse, we cannot devise how to increase the danger, and quite enthral these miserable souls, more certainly, than by multiplying unnecessary formalities, and placing religion and unity in them. For they that are most ignorant, and empty of the love and fear of God, and the bitterest enemies to a heavenly life, will presently set in with these formalities, and make themselves a religion of these; and then they will take themselves to be as godly as the best. You shall never make them believe that they are ungodly. They think the difference lieth but in the way and manner of serving God: you serve him one way and they another; but yet they serve him as well as you: yea, they will overdo in these indifferent things, that they may make up that which is wanting in true godliness; and then they will think that they are better and righter than you. Thus did the heathens cry out against the ancient christians, with a *Tollete impios*, Away with the ungodly; and killed them, and cast them to wild beasts to be torn by them, because they would not worship their idols. And so many ungodly wretches now, that will not be persuaded to a holy life, will yet cry down others as impious, because they observe not all the ceremonies which they observe. When we have used all the means we can to bring them to the study of the Scripture, and to meditate in the law of the Lord, and to holy conference, and fervent prayer; to hatred of sin, the contempt of the world, the mortifying of the flesh, to the love of God above all, to a thankful admiration of the love of Christ and the great mystery of redemption, to the believing, delightful forethoughts of everlasting life, and preparation for it, &c.; I say, when we have done all to bring them to this which is godliness indeed, we lose our labour, and leave them as we find them. They cannot away with so precise a life: but yet a religion they will have instead of it, to deceive their souls, and quiet them in the way to hell. For instance, I must speak it with grief of heart, that I meet with no small number among us that know not who Christ is. Some say he is God and not man; some say he is man and not God; some say he was made both God and man at once; some say he is neither God nor man, but a spirit; some say he is not God, but the Son of God, and hath the power of God given him; abundance say, that he is God only and not man, now he is in heaven, though he was both on earth. And very many know not what christianity is, nor wherein the christian religion doth consist. And yet all these persons, that are heathens rather than christians, are the most zealous keepers of Christmas, (as it is called,) and the bitterest condemners of those that do not; and so do make themselves believe that they are christians as well as others. The same persons that know not who Christ is, nor what it is to be a christian, are so much for kneeling at the taking of the Lord's supper, that they dare not be so irreverent as to sit or stand; but will rather never receive at all: (nor are they fit till they change in a greater matter than the gesture:) and yet, poor souls, they think themselves to be very religious, and more reverent than others, and that here lieth the difference between them. It would grieve the heart of a considerate man, to see a multitude of miserable sinners to live in wickedness, in cursing, swearing, drunkenness, filthiness, neglect of God and a holy life, drowned in worldly-mindedness, and as regardless of the life to come as if they thought they should die like the beasts; and even hating those that will not be ungodly as well as they; and yet as hot for ceremonies, and holy-days, and kneeling at the sacrament, and the Common Prayer book, as if they were more devout than others; and it seems they have made themselves believe in good earnest, that they are true christians and godly men, because in the depth of their ungodliness they can make a stir against

those that will not be of their mind, and use these ceremonies as well as they.

If any of you say, that I am now speaking against your opinions or ceremonies themselves, as if I could not give you leave to use them, you will but show yourselves mistaken hearers, and false reporters. No, it is the laying too much stress on these matters, and making indifferent things seem necessary, as if God's worship, or the unity of the church, lay on them, which I speak against. And therefore I must needs say, that both sides may be guilty of this sin: principally the imposers of them, that would have all men forced to do as they do; and next them there may be too much guilt in those that make indifferent things seem evil, or lesser evils to be much greater than they are, and so would make a religion of avoiding what others make it their religion to observe. And whether your religion lie in being for or against these points (in such as the apostle speaks of in my text) is no great difference: for the religion of both will prove but a mere shadow; yea, an over-hot opposing of such middle things, doth teach those that are for them to believe that they are matters of very great moment, or else they think you would not make so great matter of them. And then when you have taught them by your fierce opposition to make a great matter of them; and custom and their party hath taught them to think their way is best; both these set together do delude their souls, and make them think that because of their formalities, they are godly men, in the depths of their ignorance, ungodliness, and misery.

20. Lastly, observe how we sin against the sad experience of the church in all ages, by laying our religion or unity upon these smaller or unnecessary things. What hath distracted the church so much as contendings about their ceremonies and orders, and precedency and superiority? Heresies I know have done their part (especially the Arians); but smaller matters have had too great a hand in it. What plentiful evidence could I give you of this! The lamentable divisions of the christian world about Easter-day, which the first general council was fain to meet about and decide, is too sad an instance. But alas, the present age itself hath given us too sad and plenteous proofs of it. By a heap of ceremonies, and unnecessary things, the Roman church hath almost drowned both the doctrine, worship, and discipline of Christ, and miserably torn the church in pieces, and so continues to do. And what work this mistake hath made in England, I have no mind to tell you, while our smart and sufferings tell you of it more plainly than is fit for me to do. Indifferent things have shut out that which was better than indifferent. Consider well these twenty reasons, and then judge whether the religion or unity of the church should be placed in unnecessary things. The imposing of them I shall speak of by itself.

Use. From the text and doctrine explained and confirmed, we may see these following consectaries arise.

1. Hence we see the tender mercy of God to them that are sincere in the faith, though weak. If their understandings be dark, and their judgments in lesser things mistaken, and their consciences therein erroneous; yet if they be but true believers, and right in the main, and willing to know the mind of God, and to obey it, God would not have them excluded from the communion of the saints, but rather received with charity and compassion; and would have the stronger bear with their infirmities, Rom. xv. 1. He will not himself reject them; and therefore he would not have them rejected or despised by his servants.

Use 2. Hence also we may see, that God will bear more, and so must his church, with smaller errors, than with the uncharitable or dividing management of those errors. Though men should err about meats, or days, or such-like matters, we must yet receive them and love them as believers: but yet if they will hereupon despise or censure one another to the breach of charity, and trouble of the church, for this must be sharply rebuked, as Paul here doth.

Use 3. Hence also you may learn, how far men should desire and enjoy a liberty in matters of religion, and how far the magistrate should interpose with force, and how far not. A liberty to live in sin, or to subvert the gospel, and the souls of others, the magistrate should give to none; but a toleration in things of a lower nature, that hazardeth not mens' souls, nor the unity of the church, should be granted to the weak. Can we be bound with charity to receive them, and yet to provoke the magistrate to punish them, and deal severelier with them than we? This may not be desired.

Use 4. Hence also you may see what an enemy popery is to the unity of the church, and how impossible it is that the church should have unity upon their terms; when they have composed a religion of so many ceremonies, and unnecessary things, and new-devised articles, and sacraments; and none must be a catholic christian with them that will not be of this religion, and vow or practise all their novelties. So far are they from practising the doctrine of my text, that they set themselves in opposition to it, and place their religion and the unity of their church in such things as Paul here requireth us not so much as to judge one another in; or in worse than these. A catholic unity is impossible on their terms.

Use 5. To conclude, I advise all that are unfeigned friends to the unity of the church, to practise the wholesome doctrine of this text. If you have zeal, there is sin enough in yourselves and others to lay it out upon: bear not with infidelity, sensuality, impenitency, or any ungodly course. If men be not so much as weak believers, and seem not saints at least of the lower form, receive not these into your communion; but leave them under your common, compassionate charity. If you can prove that God receiveth them not, then do not you receive them. But as you are christians, take heed of cutting off or despising the members of Christ; and of giving a bill of divorce to any soul that is truly espoused to him: you have drunkards, and railers, and notorious ungodly ones enough to exercise all your zeal, if you join both head and heart and hand against them: and can you find in your hearts to fall upon one another for indifferent things, or smaller matters, which the unity of the church doth not consist in? I speak to both sides impartially; and I beseech you so understand me. What if thy weak brother pray upon a book, darest thou therefore despise him? And what if thy brother pray without book, darest thou therefore judge him? Nay, darest thou desire that none but such should have liberty to preach or worship in the church? What if thy weak brother dare not receive the sacrament, unless he kneel in the act of receiving it? Darest thou therefore despise him? And what if thy brother on the other side, do rather take it in another gesture, because he is sure that Christ and his apostles sinned not in so doing, and because he finds that our kneeling is contrary to the practice of the ancient church, (yea, *ad hominem*, I may say,) contrary to general councils, yea, to the last canon of the first general council itself, which even the canonists say that no provincial council or bishops can repeal (with many other reasons); dare you therefore judge him, because he dare not imitate you rather than Christ and his apostles, and the primitive church for many hundred years? If any imagine that I go against this necessary toleration myself, because all here receive the sacrament sitting; I answer, let them prove that ever I refused one person merely because they would take it kneeling, if they can. If you say, Why then are not all admitted to take it kneeling? I answer, soft and fair; there are greater matters than kneeling in the way. Do but first let go your vicious courses, and agree with us in a holy life, and turn unfeignedly to God, and live in the church order that he hath plainly commanded; and then, if I cannot give you satisfaction, you shall have liberty to take it in the gesture that you desire, so be it you will grant me my liberty as I grant you yours.

One instance more: To-morrow is the day called Christmas day, and many days called holy-days do follow it; if you will but read and mark this chapter, Rom. xiv. I am persuaded it may prevent a great deal of sin, that many of you on both sides may be guilty of. Is it not a wonder that after so large and plain a decision by the Holy Ghost, as here you find, there should yet be any controversy among us about this case? Do you take the word of God for your rule or not? If you do, why then doth it not rule you, and end the difference? Do you not read the apostle's words, "One man esteemeth one day above another; another esteemeth every day alike: let every man be fully persuaded in his own mind," verse 14. If you were papists that would say the Scripture is obscure, and therefore you must have a general council, you could scarce devise how a council should speak more plain than this. But nothing will serve some men, but their own wills. Dare you, on the one side, despise your weak brother now for esteeming these days above the rest? Why, perhaps it is to God that he esteemeth them, and the ancient custom of the church, and practice of many godly persons, do persuade him that is right. And dare you, on the other side, condemn or reproach them that make not this difference of days as you do? If we are contented that you have your liberty, (which truly I would not deprive you of, if it were in my power,) cannot you be contented that we have ours? There are three opinions about these holy-days. 1. Some think the observance of them a necessary religious duty. 2. Some think the very outward observance to be an intolerable sin. 3. Some know that both these extremes are erroneous, and therefore they take the thing in itself to be indifferent, but as circumstances or accidents may make it good or evil: and these are in the right. They that are in the middle can bear with others, but the other cannot bear with them, nor with each other. There is no proof that ever I saw, that the church observed any of these days, of many hundred years after Christ. For the Clement, the Dionysius, the Cyprian, that are cited for it, are known to be spurious. And it is unlikely that none of these would have been mentioned as well as the Lord's day, if they had been then observed, when there was so much ado about the time of Easter-day. Yea, it is certain that of divers hundred years after Christ, it was not agreed on, which was the day of Christ's nativity; some thought it was on January 6, and therefore called it the Epiphany, or appearance: and of old, both the birth-day and circumcision of Christ were supposed to be on that same day; that is, on the sixth of January. Cassianus witnesseth that the Egyptians were of that mind, Collat. l. 10, c. 11. And Epiphanius witnesseth the same of the Greek, and Asian, and Syrian churches. Epiphanius himself, and Nazianzen, and many others, were of this mind, that it was on January 6, and that thence it was called the Epiphany. And Chrysostom in Hom. in Natal. Dom. tells us, that it was but ten years before he wrote it, that the Romans had persuaded the church of Constantinople to change the day to December 25. And yet the countries about Jerusalem held to the sixth of January, as Casaubon hath showed, Exercit. 2, cap. 4, p. 170, 171, and cap. 11, p. 186, 187. Yea, indeed, the day of Christ's nativity is yet unknown, as if God had kept us ignorant of purpose. Many very learned men, as Broughton, Helvicus, Scaliger, Beroaldus, think that the day was about autumn, in the beginning of October. Calvisius, Paræus, and many more are for other times than December 25, and Jac. Cappellus, and many others, still go the old way for January 6. And Th. Lydias, out of Clem. Alexandr. is for May 20. Scultetus, Clopenburgius, and many others, do show, that indeed the time is utterly uncertain. And no wonder if the day be uncertain when the very year is so uncertain, that there is no probability of ever coming to a full agreement about it among the learned in chronology, till the last coming of Christ agree them! Our late most learned chronologer, Bishop Usher, was confident that we were about four years too late in our common account, as in his "Annals" may be seen. And what man can reveal the things that God hath purposely concealed? For my part, I dare not judge men for keeping or not keeping such days as these. But if any will make it a necessary thing to the universal church, I must resist that usurpation; as Paul, that had circumcised Timothy, did cry down circumcision when some would have obtruded it as a necessary thing. And for this I have an argument that sustaineth my religion itself; even the sufficiency of the holy Scripture. If this be not the law of God, then farewell christianity. If it be his law, it is sufficient in its kind, and to its ends; which is, 1. To determine of all things that were then fit to be determined of: 2. And to determine of all that the universal church in all times after must be bound to. There is no universal lawgiver but Christ. If this day be of necessity, it was so then as well as now, and it is so to one country as well as another; for there is the same reason for it in one age and place as in another. And, therefore, if Scripture be not a sufficient rule for universal duties of religion, then we are utterly at a loss; and as popery will come first in, so infidelity is likely to come next. I doubt not but *pro re nata*, upon emergent occasions, church governors may appoint religious anniversary solemnities. For the occasion of these being, 1. To some one place or province only; 2. And not existent in Scripture times; it did not belong to the universal law to determine of them. But in cases that equally belong to the universal church, and where the reason and occasion was existent in the apostles' days as well as now, if there we have not their determination, no others can come after them and make it universally necessary. And indeed neither general councils nor apostolic tradition can be pleaded for the necessity. And sure I am, that the one day in seven, even the Lord's day, of his own appointment, which the universal church hath constantly observed, is a festival for the commemoration of the whole work of redemption, and therefore of the birth of Christ, though especially of the resurrection: and therefore we are not without a day for this use.

I speak not all this to condemn any that use these days, but to excuse those that use them not; and by telling you a few of those many reasons which they have to give for themselves, to persuade you both to lay by the opinion of necessity, and to forbear condemning those that differ from you, and be content that they have their liberty, as we are freely content that you have yours; and lay not the unity and peace of the church upon such things as these, when the Holy Ghost hath so plainly decided the case. And I could heartily wish that the Lord's own day were not most wilfully neglected by many that are most forward for other holy-days. It is a fearful self-delusion of ungodly people, that no means can bring them to a new, a holy, and heavenly life; and yet they will make themselves believe that they are religious, by pleading for forms, and days, and ceremonies. Alas! poor soul, if thy eyes were but opened, thou wouldst see that thou hast other kind of matters first to look after! It would grieve one to hear a man contending for kneeling, and holy days, and prayer books, that is in a state of unregeneracy, and a stranger to sanctification, and under the dominion of his sins, and under the curse and wrath of God. Get first a new and holy nature; make sure of the pardon of sin, and of peace with God, and then the discourse of lower matters will be more seasonable and more savoury.

Is it not a shameful self-condemning, to keep holy-days for the dead saints, and to hate and rail against the living? Do you know what kind of men those were that are called *saints*, and holy-days were kept in remembrance of them? They were such as those that now are hated by the world, and took the course in a holy and diligent care of their salvation, as these do, and therefore were hated by the world, as the godly now are; and when wicked men had put them to death, the godly that survived would keep a day in remembrance of their martyrdom, to encourage others to constancy for Christ. And also because the unruly multitude were so set upon their pleasure, that they kept the idols' festivals for their sport sake; therefore some pastors of the church did think it better to let them have festivals for the saints to take their pleasure in, to turn them off from the idols' festivals. So Gregory Nyssen tells us of Gregory Thaumaturgus in his Oration of his Life, that he made holy days for his neighbours of Neocæsarea, when the Roman fury had martyred many; and he used this as a pious wile, to draw the licentious vulgar from the idols' festivals, by letting them play on the martyrs' days, till they could be drawn up to a holy observation of them. Whether the course were right or wrong, by this you may see the original of such days. And Gregory the Great of Rome would, for this very end, have all the heathens' festivals turned into christian festivals. But if any of you will hate a saint, and refuse the communion of saints, and will not imitate them in holiness, and yet will keep holy days for them that are dead, Christ himself hath given you your doom, Matt. xxiii. 29—33, which I desire you to read.

Well, sirs, I have said enough, if enough will serve, to prove that the unity of the church must not be laid on things indifferent, nor upon low and doubtful points; but it must be a unity in the spirit of sanctification. It is the few, the great, the certain, and the necessary points, that we must all agree in if ever we will agree, and compassionately tolerate the differences that are tolerable.

If, after all this, there be any so proud, and selfish, and ungodly, and unmerciful, that they will set up their own conceits and wills against the plain commands of God, the long and sad experience of the world, and against the peace of their brethren, and the unity of the church, and will have no agreement unless all others will be conformed to their wills, I shall say no more to such, but that these are not the sons of peace, nor the living compassionate members of the church, but self-idolizers, that God is engaged to pull down: and it is not by such as these that the church must be healed and repaired; but it is by them that are sensible of their own infirmities, and compassionate to others, that are of a christian, catholic spirit, and have catholic principles and affections, and see such a beauty in the image of Christ, that they can heartily love a gracious person, notwithstanding his many tolerable infirmities, and think themselves more unworthy to be tolerated by others, than such as I have described to be tolerated by them.

Preached December 24, 1657.

THE

TRUE AND ONLY WAY OF CONCORD

OF ALL

THE CHRISTIAN CHURCHES.

Acts xv. 28, "It seemed good to the Holy Ghost, and to us, to lay upon you no greater burden than these necessary things."
Rom. xiv. 17, 18, "The kingdom of God is not meat and drink; but righteousness, and peace, and joy in the Holy Ghost. For he that in these things serveth Christ is acceptable to God, and approved of men."
2 Tim. iv. 1, 2, "I charge thee therefore before God, and the Lord Jesus Christ, who shall judge the quick and the dead at his appearing and his kingdom; preach the word; be instant in season, out of season."
Acts iv. 19, "Whether it be right in the sight of God to hearken unto you more than unto God, judge ye."
1 Thess. ii. 15, 16, "They please not God, and are contrary to all men: forbidding us to speak to the gentiles that they might be saved, to fill up their sins alway: for the wrath is come upon them to the uttermost."
Mr. Jones of The Heart and its Sovereign, p. 344, "*Id fit quod jure fit:* Tyrants are but great lords of nullities, by the exemption of the will and soul from, and the frown of Heaven upon, all brutish injustice and force." Read him also, p. 23.

THE PREFACE.

TO THE HONOURABLE AND REVEREND DR. GEORGE MORLEY,

LATE LORD BISHOP OF WORCESTER, AND NOW OF WINCHESTER;

AND DR. PETER GUNNING, LORD BISHOP OF ELY.

It is now about eighteen years since you and many others were appointed by his Majesty's commission, with divers of us, who desired some reformation of the church discipline and worship, to consider what alterations of the liturgy were necessary and expedient for the satisfaction of tender consciences, and the restoring and continuance of peace and unity to the churches under his Majesty's protection and government. His Majesty's gracious declaration about ecclesiastical affairs had before showed so much of his wisdom and care to attain this unity, as we thought had almost done the cure; the differences about church government, and most of the rest being thereby, as we hoped, fairly ended: as (with the help of the Reverend Dr. Sparrow, now Bishop of Norwich, and Dr. Pierson, now Bishop of Chester) you maintained that no alteration was necessary to these ends, so I with others endeavoured to prove the contrary: but since the said declaration being dead, such alterations were made as greatly increased our impossibility of conforming. We never treated with you for presbyterian government, or independent, but for unity and peace; nor did we herein offer you any worse than Archbishop Usher's form of the primitive episcopal government, (which I had declared my judgment of before in print); and I never heard of the name of episcopal presbyterians, or presbyterian archbishops, till of late. And we thankfully accepted much less than that form, as granted in his Majesty's foresaid declaration. As I doubt not but you still think that your way was best for the healing of the church and land; so I know that I have greatly incurred both your displeasures for what I have said and done against your way. One of you showed it in a printed letter long ago, which when I had answered, I cast that aside for peace, believing that the opening of so many mistakes in matter of fact would not be easily borne. The other of you since told me, that he would petition authority that we might be compelled to give our reasons; as if we kept up a schism, and would not tell why! I rejoiced at the motion, and offered to beg leave on my knees to do it. Since then your Mr. Walton, in his "Life of Bishop Sanderson," hath called me by name to remember our debate aforesaid. I know not of any two men living that I am now more obliged to give an account to of my continued dissent than unto you. My judgment is not in my own power, nor in yours. Many are dead who were in that consultation: you and I by God's great mercy are yet alive, and may review our actions before we come to the bar of God, which is like to be speedily to me, and to you it cannot be far off, especially to the elder of you; so that I suppose that all three of us are really beyond the motives of any personal worldly interest. What is this world to us who are taking our farewell of it for ever? All the doubt then remaining is, whether your terms, or those desired by us, are the true way of love and concord? And which are the true causes of schisms, and the attendant evils?

I doubt not but you still think that the good which you have done, doth far weigh down all the direct and accidental hurt. What that good is you know better than I. Dr. Heylin, in the "Life of Archbishop Laud," tells us what some accounted then most desirable; and how much more desirable it is to open the church doors so wide as that moderate loyal Romanists may come in, as they did in Queen Elizabeth's first years, and to reconcile them by nearer approaches or concessions, rather than to go further from them, to unite with a few inconsiderable puritans, whose principles are against the power and wealth of the church, we have often heard from others: as also that the ejection of the near two thousand nonconforming ministers, was the church's deliverance from them that would have done more hurt within than they can do without. The converted priest, Mr. Smith, in his narrative of the popish plot, dedicated to the king, nameth more reasons, which I will not name, which some were moved by.

For my part, as with fear I foresaw, so with grief I see, so many hundred ministers under the restraints and penalties which you know of, of whom I have better thoughts than you have; believing from my heart, by the acquaintance which I have had with very many, that notwithstanding the faulty former actions of some few of them, and the unjustifiable scruples of others, you cannot name that nation under heaven, out of our king's dominions, which hath this day so many ministers, more sound in doctrine, heart, and life, and liker to further men's salvation, than those that in England have been silenced and cast out. Name that country if you can! And I believe that Christ hath given us no supernumeraries of such useful men; but if all faithful ministers, conformists and nonconformists, were employed and encouraged, they would be still too few to do the work upon the ignorant, ungodly, and vicious, which is to be done. And considering, how many souls a faithful minister may hope to edify and save, I consider then how many thousands are like to be losers where such are lost and wanting. It grieveth my soul to see what advantage Satan hath got in England against that christian love which is the life and character of Christ's disciples, and to cause wrath, envy, hatred, and strife, when God saith, "He that hateth his brother is a murderer, and no murderer hath eternal life in him," 1 John iii. 15. It grieveth me to see preachers against preachers, and churches against churches, and in press and pulpit learning and oratory employed to render brethren odious, and keep up a heart war against each other, and all this (oh fearful!) as in the name of Christ, and as for the safety of the church and kingdom. To see families against families, and father against son, and as Guelphs and Gibelines, cities and countries in their ordinary discourses (at the least) accusing, contemning, and reproaching one another! It grieveth me to think how much, first the honour, and then the success, of the ministry on both sides, is hereby hindered, and what temptations some have to further injuries, which I am loth to name; and how by all this the wicked and infidels are hardened, the weak are scandalized, the papists are encouraged to despise us all, and many turn to them, scandalized by our discord; sects are advantaged, the church and kingdom by divisions weakened, and the king denied the comfort which he might have in a loving, united, and concordant people.

I believe that you dislike all this as well as I. All the question hath been and still is, Which is the true way of cure? And one would think that, first, The nature of the thing, and, secondly, The experience of all the christian world, thirdly, And our new experience these seventeen or eighteen years, might resolve men of lower parts than ours! Is there no better way to the church's concord, than that which must cast out either such men as you or I, and that so many? Can a wise physician (a true peace-maker) find out no remedy which may better avoid the aforesaid evils? Oh what a loss had England in the removal of such healing men as Bishop Usher, Hall, Davenant, Brownrig, &c.! Far was I, and am I, from liking any former injury to such men by covenant or abuse. But it hath been ever the just misery of the persecutors of worthy men, to have the stone fly back on their own heads, and to be themselves undone by striving to undo others, while they first make, and then stir up, a multitude of enemies for their own defence, who else would be friends, and live in peace.

I am fully persuaded that in this book I have told you a righter way of christian church concord; more divine, sure, harmless, and comprehensive; fitted by Christ himself to the interest of all good men, yea, of the church, and all the world. I offer it first to you, that you and posterity may see what it was that I desired; and that if I here err you will faithfully detect my error, that I may repent before I die, and may leave behind me the recantation of this and all my other mistakes and miscarriages, as I intend to do upon just conviction. But do it quickly, or else I am not like to see it; and I purpose not to provoke you by any confutation, but to improve your evidence for myself.

And to answer the earnest demand of our reasons by you the Lord Bishop of Ely, I have also published an historical narrative of our case and judgment in another book, called "The Nonconformist's Plea for Peace."

If (much contrary to my expectation) you should be convinced that these terms of unity and concord are righter than those which you (above all men that I know) have effectually helped to bring us under, I humbly crave that you will use as much earnestness and diligence to procure the church's concord, by promoting them, as you did for that which you then thought righter. I have here opened those reasons which made me believe that the fourteenth and fifteenth chapter to the Romans decideth our controversy, and is to be understood as I then maintained.

If it prove the necessary truth which is here offered you, I beseech you see that prejudice resist it not. It would be a happy work, could we procure the reviving of christian love, unity, and concord, that all Christ's servants might strive together for the hallowing of God's name, the promoting of his kingdom, and the doing of his will with love and concord, as it is done in heaven. And when instead of worldly wealth and grandeur, we are contented with our daily bread; and instead of cruelty to the innocent or weak, we bewail our own sins, and forbear and forgive one another; and instead of tempting men to the evil of wrath, and making battering cannons and tearing engines of schism, we cease to be over-wise in our own conceits, and to judge, despise, and ruin others, then we shall be in a hopeful way to this: we shall then receive him that is weak even in the faith, (much more about our lesser matters,) even as Christ received us, and not to doubtful disputations; and he that pleaseth God by that in which his kingdom doth consist, will be also approved by us; and we shall better learn what that meaneth, I will have mercy, and not sacrifice; and that none of our church power is given for destruction, but for edification; and so we shall not condemn the guiltless, nor smite the shepherds, and scatter the flocks, and then hunt them about as schismatics, and see the mote of dissent from a formality, ceremony, or word, in their eye, while we see not this great beam in our own. How joyfully should we die, might we leave behind us by our endeavours a healed church and nation, and see first this desired unity, which would be the strength, ease, and joy of ministers and people, king and subjects, and a hopeful pattern to the divided churches abroad to imitate! If you will not contribute your help hereto, those will who shall have the honour and comfort of being the blessed instruments of our concord, if God have so much mercy for us.

I once more repeat to you the pacificator's old despised words.

Si in necessariis sit unitas non necessariis libertas,
In utrisque charitas, optimo certe loco essent res nostræ.

Pardon this freedom, and accept this account of the reasons of all his former and latter dissent from your judgment, words, and way, to

Your unfeigned well-willer,

November 15, 1679. RICHARD BAXTER.

A PREMONITION.

READER,

UPON the review of this book I find some things which may be to some an occasion of offence, if this premonition prevent it not.

First, Some may think when I say "diocesan prelacy, archbishops, and patriarchs are not to be made necessary to universal, or subordinate church concord, as being uncapable terms or means thereof," that I speak against the lawfulness of all episcopacy, when I speak but against such necessity of that sort. Know therefore, 1. That I meddle not with the question, Whether every particular church (of pastor and people associate for personal church communion, such as Ignatius describeth) should have a bishop with his presbyters and deacons?

2. Nor with the question, Whether these should have archbishops over them, as successors to the apostolical and other general overseers of the first age, in the ordinary continued parts of their office?

3. Nor, whether patriarchs, diocesans, and lay chancellors, as officers of the king, exercising under him such government of the church as belongeth to kings, (according to our oath of supremacy,) be lawful, to which in such exercise all subjects must for conscience sake submit?

4. Nor, whether it was well done, (or of divine appointment,) that about temporal matters, as well as church controversies, the bishops were chosen arbitrators by the ancient christians, and so did that which christian magistrates now must do, till upon the conversion of princes and states the said power of externals *circa sacra* fell into their hands?

5. Nor yet if diocesans become the sole bishops *(infimi ordinis)* over many hundred parishes, all the bishops and parish churches under them being put down, and turned into curates and chapels, *(partes ecclesiæ infimæ speciei,)* whether a minister and every subject ought yet to live quietly and peaceably under them? It is none of these that are the questions which I decide.

Secondly, In my confutation of Mr. Dodwell some may mistake me, as if I denied that our religion had come down to us by a continued succession from the apostles, or that the ministerial office *in specie*, or that the universal church, had ever been without a true ministry or religion. I have proved where our church was in all ages before Luther in my second book against Johnson, alias Terret: nor do I say what I do to avoid deriving our ministerial succession from Rome; for history puts me out of doubt, that the multitude of uncapable popes and schisms will prove a far greater interruption of canonical and legitimate succession at Rome, than can be proved of England, and perhaps than hath happened to almost any other church in the world. And I am fully satisfied that the present church of England, as national, deriveth its succession from the ancient British and Scottish church, and not from Rome; and that christianity was the religion of England long before Gregory or Augustine the monk's days; and that notwithstanding Gildas's smart reproofs, when the British and Scottish clergy and people disclaimed all obedience to the pope, and would not so much as eat or lodge in the same house with Gregory's clergy, the persons were better, or at least their doctrine and religion more sound, than that which Rome did afterwards obtrude. And as the blood of this nation, though called English, will upon just consideration be found to be twenty, if not a hundredfold, more British than either Roman, Saxon, or Norman, so the ordination of the bishops is derived so much more from the Britains and Scots than from Rome, as that Augustine the monk's successors were afterward almost quite extinct, only one Wini a simonist being left in anno 668, the rest of the bishops being all of British ordination: all which, with much more of great importance, is so fully proved (after Usher) by M. T. Jones of Oswestry, late chaplain to the duke of York, in an excellent historical treatise hereof, called "Of the Heart, and its right Sovereign," that I am sorry that book is no more commonly bought and read.

But withal, I must say that this our certain succession disproveth the papists' and Mr. Dodwell's plea for the necessity of their sort of episcopal canonical uninterrupted succession: for (as the bishops of Denmark have their succession but from Bugenhagius Pomeranus, a presbyter, his ordination, so) Aidan and Finan that came from Scotland out of Columbanus' monastery were no bishops, as Beda and others fully testify: and after Beda and others, Mr. Jones hath cleared it, that it was not only the northern bishops that were ordained by Aidan, and Finan, and Dhuma, but that the bishops of the whole land had their ordination derived from them, and such as they, and those whom they ordained; so that the denying of the validity of the ordination by presbyters, shaketh the succession of the episcopal church of England; and proveth it on that supposition interrupted: and if they derive it from Rome it will be as much shaken.

Thirdly, In perusal I find that I have more than once mentioned some things in this treatise, and the repetition may be an offence to some. To which I say, 1. That this is usual in controversies, where several objections and occasions call for the same material answer. 2. But I confess it is the effect of my haste and weakness: and it is my judgment, while I think that I write no needless books, that I should rather write any one that is truly useful with such imperfections of manner and style, as only so far disgrace the author, than for want of time to leave it undone, to the loss of others: but if it be needless, it is a greater fault to write it, than to write it no more accurately.

My dear friend, and judicious brother, Mr. John Corbett, hath newly published a small book to the same purpose with this, of the "True State of Religion," and "Interest of the Church," with a "Discourse of Schism," which I commend to the reader as much worthy of his perusal, and which if written on the hearts of rulers, and teachers, and people, according to its certain truth and weight, would heal us all. The Lord forgive our heinous sins, which deserve that he should excommunicate and forsake us; and save England from Englishmen; and save us all from ourselves, our most dangerous enemies; and christians, and pastors, and friends, from one another. For as Mr. Jones's Welsh proverb saith, "Though thy dog be thy own, trust him not when he is mad."

Fourthly, I hear some say of my book that cometh out with this, (of the case of the Nonconformists,) and may say of this, that, 1. It is unseasonable to mention our own differences when we are called to unite against the papists. 2. And that too hard accusations of conformity are intimated.

I answer to the first, 1. That it is never more seasonable to write for unity than when we are most obliged to unite; though indeed it can never be unseasonable. And to take nonconformists for heinous schismatics, and call on magistrates to silence, and imprison, and ruin them, is not the way to unity, nor consistent with it; and therefore to deprecate such unpeaceable ways, is the necessary work of a peace-maker. 2. I have waited in vain these seventeen years for a fit season; and with me in likelihood it must be now or never; for there is no doing it in the grave; and I dare not die, and leave it undone, on pretence that it was not seasonable.

To the second I say, 1. I have professed that I write not to accuse conformists; but if men accuse us as enemies to order, obedience, and peace, and as fit for silencing and utter ruin, and tell the world falsely that it is but things indifferent that we deny obedience to, and call on us to tell them what it is that we fear if we conform; and when we tell them, they make this also our crime because they think themselves accused, what remedy have we against such men? 2. I love and honour all good and pious men that conform; for I consider how variously the same thing is represented to and apprehended by men of various educations, converse, and advantages; so that the same sin materially heinous, may formally be much less in some than in others; as was Paul's ignorant unbelief and persecution. Or else, saith the papist answerer of the "Three Books for the Jesuits' Loyalty," Most princes must be most heinous sinners that make wars against each other, in which multitudes are killed, when both sides cannot have a just cause, unless the supposition that their cause was good by mistake excuse them.

THE REASONS FOR CHRISTIAN UNITY AND CONCORD: WHAT IT IS: AND HOW MUCH MAY BE HOPED FOR ON EARTH.

EPHESIANS IV. 3.

Σπουδάζοντες τηρεῖν τὴν ἑνότητα τοῦ Πνεύματος ἐν τῷ συνδεσμῷ τῆς εἰρήνης.

ENDEAVOURING (OR CAREFULLY OR DILIGENTLY STUDYING) TO KEEP THE UNITY OF THE SPIRIT IN THE BOND OF PEACE.

CHAPTER I.

THE TEXT OPENED, AND THE DOCTRINES AND METHOD PROPOSED.

HAD not the distempers of the minds even of religious persons, and the long and sad divisions and distractions of christians, assured me that this text is not commonly understood and regarded, as the apostle's vehement exhortation, and the importance and reason of the matter, do bespeak; yea, had not the long bleeding wounds of the church, made by its pastors and most zealous members, still cried out aloud for pity and help; I had not chosen this subject at this time. But after the complaints, and exhortations, and tears of the wisest and best men since the days of Christ, after the long miseries of the church, and the long and costly experience of all ages, the destroying spirit of division still possesseth the most, and maketh some of the possessed to rage, and foam, and tear themselves, and all that are in their power; it haunteth the holy assemblies, and disquieteth the lovers of unity and peace, and by the scandals which it raiseth it frighteneth children and unstable persons out of their religion, and their wits. And therefore after the many books which I have written for unity, love, and peace, and the many years preaching and praying to that end, I find it yet as necessary as ever to preach on the same subject, and to recite the same things; and while I am in this tabernacle, which I must shortly put off, to stir you up, that after my decease you may have it in remembrance, 2 Pet. i. 12—14. And could I persuade the churches of Christ to seek by fasting and fervent prayer the dispossessing of this distracting spirit, (by which only this evil kind goeth out,) our languishing hopes might yet revive.

If Paul found it necessary to cry down division, and plead for unity so frequently and so vehemently as he doth to those new-planted churches of Rome, Corinth, Ephesus, Galatia, Philippi, Thessalonica, &c. which had been founded by the means of miracles, and had so much of the spirit of unity and community, and had apostles among them to preserve their peace; what wonder if we that are much ignorant of the apostles' minds, and of the primitive pattern, and have less of the Spirit, have need to be still called upon to study to keep the unity of the Spirit in the bond of peace? They that preach twenty, or a hundred sermons for purity, and scarce one with equal zeal for unity and peace, do not sufficiently discern that purity and peace are the inseparable fruits of the wisdom from above, (James iii. 17,) which live and die together, and with them the souls and societies of believers.

This famous church of Ephesus is it which Paul had so long laid out his labours in; even publicly and from house to house, night and day, with tears, Acts xx. 28—30: which was famous for its greatness, and the open profession of Christ; where even the price of the vain unlawful books which they openly burnt came to fifty thousand pieces of silver, Acts xix. 19.[a] This is the church that first of the seven is written to by Christ, (Rev. ii.) whose works, labour, and patience, even without fainting, were known and praised by the Lord, Rev. ii. 2—6; which proved and disproved the false apostles, which hated the deeds of the Nicolaitans. And yet Paul saw cause, (Acts xx. 30,) to foretell them prophetically of their temptations to division; that they should be tried by both extremes, as other churches were and are: that on one side grievous wolves, or church tyrants, should enter, not sparing the flock; and on the other side, of themselves should men arise, speaking perverse things, to draw away disciples (by schism and separation) after them. And to this excellent church he seeth cause here to urge the persuasives to the vigilant preservation of unity in this chapter.

Having in the three first chapters instructed them in the high mysteries of election, redemption, and the fruits thereof, and magnified the riches of grace in Christ, and the spiritual knowledge thereof, that we may know what use he principally intended, he here beginneth his application, 1. With a moving reason from his person and condition, ver. 1, "I the prisoner of the Lord." As if he should say, As ever you will regard the doctrine and counsel of your teacher, and Christ's apostle, now I am in bonds for the doctrine which I preach. 2. With words of earnest request, "I beseech you." 3. With the matter of his request, 1. In general, that "they walk worthy the calling wherewith they were called." Beza need not have avoided the vulgar and proper translation of ἀξίως, and put *quod convenit* for worthy; for worthiness can signify nothing but moral congruity. 2. Specially this worthiness consisteth in the holy and healthful constitution of their souls, and the exercise thereof; in their inward disposition, and their answerable practice.

First, The inward qualifications are, 1. All lowliness. 2. Meekness. 3. Love.

Secondly, The fruits of these are, 1. Long-suffering; 2. Forbearing one another; 3. And studying to keep the unity of the Spirit in the bond of peace. Which unity is particularly described in the terms and reasons of it, which are seven. 1. One body. 2. One Spirit. 3. One hope. 4. One Lord. 5. One faith. 6. One baptism. 7. One God and Father, who is above all, and through all, and in them all. But negatively, not in an equality of grace in all the members, for that is various, according to the measure of the gift of Christ, the free Benefactor.

I must pass by all unnecessary explication, and the handling of the many useful lessons which offer themselves to us in the way; such as these following.

Doct. I. It should not depreciate the counsels of Christ's ministers, that they are sent or written from a prison or bonds, but rather procure their greater acceptance; when they are not imprisoned for evil doing, but for preaching or obeying the gospel and law of Christ, it is their honour, and the honour of that doctrine which they suffer for: why else keep you days of thanksgiving and commemoration of the martyrs? On the persecutors' part Christ is evil spoken of, or blasphemed, but by the sufferers he is glorified, (1 Pet. iv.) and therefore he will glorify them. I was once blamed for dating a book (out of the common gaol or prison in London) as if it reflected on the magistrate: but I imitated Paul, and mentioned nothing which the rulers took for a dishonour, as their actions showed.

Doct. II. Beseeching is the mode and language of wise and faithful pastors, in pleading for unity and against schism in the church. For they are not lords over the flocks, but helpers of their faith: they have no power of the sword, but of the word. They rule not by constraint, but willingly; nor such as are constrained by them, but volunteers. It is not the way to win love to God, to pastors, or to one another, to say, Love me, or I will lay thee in a gaol. Stripes are useful to cause fear, and timorous obedience, but not directly to cause love; and hated preachers seldom prosper in converting or edifying souls, or healing disordered, divided churches.

Doct. III. Though grace find us unworthy, it maketh men such as walk worthy of their high and heavenly calling; that is, in a suitable conversation, answerable to the principles of their faith and hope. Christianity were little better than the false religions of the world, if it made men no better. If Christ made not his disciples greatly to differ from the disciples of a mere philosopher, he would not be thought greatly to differ from them himself; the fruits of his doctrine and Spirit on our hearts and lives are the proofs and witness of his truth: we wrong him heinously when we live but like other men; and we weaken our own and other men's faith by obscuring a great evidence of the christian verity. And those that are of eminent holiness and righteousness of life, are the great and powerful preachers of faith, and show men by proofs, and not only by words, that Christ is true.

Doct. IV. Lowliness is a great part of christian worthiness, and a necessary cause of christian unity and peace. This μετὰ πάσης ταπεινοφροσύνης is but the same thing which Paul elsewhere (Acts xx. 19) tells this same church, that he practised towards them exemplarily himself. Lowliness of mind containeth both low and humble thoughts of ourselves, and low expectations as to honour and respect from

[a] See Beza's conjecture of the sum, in loc

others; with a submissive temper, that can stoop and yield, and a deportment liker to the lower sort of people, than to the stout and great ones of the world. As (Matt. v.) to be poor in spirit, is to have a spirit fit for a share of poverty; not in love with riches, but content with little, and patient with all that poor men must endure; so lowliness of mind is a disposition and deportment, not like the grandees of the world, but suited to low persons and low things, condescending to the lowest persons, employments, and indignities, or contempt that shall be cast upon us. A proud, high-minded person, that is looking for preferment, and must be somebody in the world, is of a spirit contrary to that of christianity, and will never lie even in the sacred edifice, nor be a healer, but a troubler of the church of Christ, and must be converted and become as a little child, before he can enter into the kingdom of heaven, Matt. xviii. 3. And indeed only by selfishness and pride have become the divisions and contentions in the church, even by those that have made it the means of their domination to cry down division, because they must have all to unite in them, in conformity to their opinions, interests, and wills. A humble soul, that can be content to follow a crucified Christ, and to be made of no reputation, (Phil. ii. 7; Heb. xii. 1—3,) and to be a servant to all, and a lord of none, and can yield, and stoop, and be despised, whenever the ends of his office do require it, is a christian indeed, and fit to be a healer.

Doct. V. Meekness or lenity is another part of christian worthiness, and a necessary cause of unity and peace.

Though in some this hath extraordinary advantage or disadvantage in the temperature of the body, yet it is that which persons of all tempers may be brought to by grace. A boisterous, furious, or wild kind of disposition, is not the christian healing spirit. If passion be apt to stir, wisdom and grace must repress it, and lenity must be our ordinary temper: we must be like tame creatures, that familiarly come to a man's hand, and not like wild things that fly from us as untractable; otherwise how will such in love, and peace, and sociable concord, ever carry on the work of Christ?

Doct. VI. Love to each other is a great part of christian worthiness, and a most necessary cause of unity and peace. Of which I hope to say so much by itself (if God will) as that I shall here pass it by, it being the very heart and life of unity.

Doct. VII. Long-suffering, or a patient mind, not rash or hasty, is another part of christian worthiness, and a necessary cause of unity and peace.

Μακροθυμία hath more in it than many well consider of. I know it is commonly taken for restraint of anger by patient long-suffering; but I think that it chiefly signifieth here, and elsewhere in Paul's epistles, that deliberate slowness and calmness of mind, which is contrary to passionate haste and rashness. When a passionate man is hasty and rash, and cannot stay to hear another speak for himself, nor to deliberate of the matter, and search out the truth, nor forbear revenge while he thinketh whether it will do good or harm, or what the case will appear in the review, this longanimity will stay men, and compose their minds, and cause them to take time before they judge of opinions, practices, or persons, and before they venture to speak or do, lest what they do in haste they repent at leisure. It appeaseth those passions which blind the judgment, when wrath doth precipitate men into those conceptions, words, and deeds, which they must after wish that they had never known. Hasty rashness in judging and doing, for want of the patience and lenity of a slow, deliberating mind, is the cause of most errors, heresies, and divisions, and of abundance of sin and misery in the world.

Doct. VIII. Bearing, supporting, and forbearing one another in love, is another part of gospel worthiness, and needful means of unity and peace.

Doubtless to forbear each other patiently under injuries and provocations is a great part of the duty here meant; but both Beza, who translated it *sustinentes*, and the vulgar Latin, which translateth it *supportantes*, seemed to think that *ἀνεχόμενοι* signifieth something more. While we are imperfect sinful men we shall have need of mutual support and help, yea, we shall be injurious, provoking and troublesome to each other: and when christians (yea church pastors) are so far from supporting and sustaining the weak, that they cannot so much as patiently bear their censures, neglects, or other effects of weakness, unity and peace will hardly prosper, much less if their spiritual nurses become their chief afflicters.

Doct. IX. Unity of the Spirit is most necessary to the church of Christ, and to its several members, though their measures of grace be divers.

Doct. X. The bond of peace must preserve this unity.

Doct. XI. This unity consisteth in these seven things: 1. One body. 2. One Spirit. 3. One hope. 4. One Lord. 5. One faith. 6. One baptism. 7. One God.

Doct. XII. This unity must be studied carefully, and diligently endeavoured and preserved, by all the faithful members of the church.

These last doctrines being the subject which I design to handle, I shall speak of them together in the following order.

I. I shall tell you, what the unity of the Spirit is which is so necessary.

II. I shall tell you, what necessity there is of this unity, and what are its happy fruits.

III. I shall open the seven particulars in which it doth consist; and defend the sufficiency of them to the use here intended in the text.

IV. I shall open the nature and terms of counterfeit unity.

V. I shall open the nature and mischiefs of the contrary division.

VI. I shall show you what are the enemies and impediments of this unity.

VII. I shall show you, what are the study and endeavour, and the bond of peace, by which this unity must be kept.

VIII. I shall conclude with some directions for application, or use of all.

CHAPTER II.

THE NATURE OF UNITY, AND THIS UNITY OF THE SPIRIT, OPENED.

I. What unity in general is, and what this unity of the Spirit in special, I shall open in these following connexed propositions.

1. I must neither here confound the ordinary reader by the many metaphysical difficulties about unity, nor yet wholly pass them by, lest I confound him for want of necessary distinction.

2. Unity is sometimes the attribute of a universal, which is but *ens rationis*, or a general inadequate partial conception of an existent singular Being: and so all men are one as to the species of humanity;

and all living things are one in the genus of vitality: and so of bodies, substances, creatures, &c. It is much more than this that we have before us.

3. Some think that the word ONE, or UNITY, signifieth only negatively an undividedness in the thing itself. But this conception is more than negative, and taketh in first in compounds, that peculiar connexion of parts by one form, and in simple, spiritual beings, that more excellent indivisible essentiality and existence, whence the being is intelligible, as such a subsistence as is not only undivided in itself, but divisible or differenceable from all other existent or possible beings, so far as it is one.

4. Passing by the distinction of *unum per se et per accidens*, and some such other, I shall only further distinguish of unity according to the differences of the entities that are called one: where indeed the difference of things maketh the word ONE of very different significations.

5. GOD is supereminently and most perfectly ONE, as he is ENS, BEING; no creature hath unity in the same perfect sort and sense as God is one. He is so ONE as that he is perfectly simple and indivisible, and so as that he cannot be properly a part in any composition.

6. Therefore God and the world, or any creature, are not compounding parts; for a part is less than the whole; and that which is less is not infinite.

7. Yet God is more intimate to every creature than any of its own parts are: no form is more intimate to the matter, no soul to the body, no formal virtue to a spirit, than God is to all and every being. But his perfection and the creatures' imperfection is such, as that creatures can be no addition to God, nor compounding parts, but like to accidents.

8. The same must be said therefore of Christ's divine and human natures. The schoolmen therefore say that Christ's soul and body are parts of his human nature; but his Godhead and manhood are not to be called parts of Christ, because the Godhead can be no part of any thing.

9. When Paul saith that God is πάντα ἐν πᾶσι, All in all things, he meaneth not that he is formally all things themselves; but yet not that he is less, or is more distant from them, than the form; but is eminently so much more, as that the title is below him: so he is said here, (Eph. iv. 6,) to be Πατὴρ πάντων, ὁ ἐπὶ πάντων, καὶ διὰ πάντων, καὶ ἐν πᾶσιν ἡμῖν, the Father of all, above all, and through all, and in us all. And 1 Cor. xii. 16, it is said that the same God worketh all in all, as to the diversity of operations. He is the most intimate prime Agent in all that acteth (though he hath enabled free agents to determine their own acts morally to this or that, *hic et nunc*, &c.); "for in him we live, and move, and have our being; for we are his offspring," Acts xvii.

10. Somewhat like this must be said of the special union of Christ and all true believers. As to his divine nature, (and so the Holy Ghost,) he is as the Father, intimately in all, but more than the form of all, or any. But he is specially by relation and inoperation in his members, as he is not in any others. So, Col. iii. 11, Christ is said to be πάντα ἐν πᾶσι, All in all, that is, to the church. And so I conceive that it is in a passive or receptive sense that the church is said to be the "fulness of him that filleth all in all," Eph. i. 23. Whether it be spoken of Christ's Godhead only, or of his human soul also, as being to the redeemed world what the sun is to the natural illuminated world, I determine not; but whichever it is, Christ filling all in all, the church is called his fulness, as being eminently possessed and filled by him, as the head is by the human soul, more than the hand, or other lower parts.

11. The trinity of persons is such as is no way contrary to the perfect unity of the divine essence; as the faculties of motion, light, and heat in the sun, and of vital activity, intellection, and volition in man, is not contrary to the unity of the essence of the soul; yet man is not so perfectly one as God is.

12. The unity of a spirit in itself is a great image or likeness of the divine unity, as having no separable parts, as passive matter hath, but being one without divisibility, even one essential virtue, or virtuous substance.

13. The most large extensive unity (as far as spirits may be said to have extension or degrees of essence) is likest to God; and the unity of a material atom is not more excellent than the unity of the material part of the world, made up of such atoms. (Whether there are such atoms physically indivisible I here meddle not, but the shaping of an atom into cornered, hollow, and such other shapes, is to common reason a palpable contradiction.)

14. Whether there be any one passive element (earth, water, or air) any where existent in a union of its proper atoms, without a mixture of any other element, is a thing unknown to mortals.

15. So is it whether there be any where existent a body of the united atoms of the several passive elements, without the active.

16. The mixed beings known to us do all consist of a union of the passive and active elements (or of these united).

17. We perceive by sense what union and division of passive matter is, which hath separable parts; but how far spirits are passive, (as all under God are in some degree,) and whether that passivity signify any kind of materiality as well as substantiality; and how far they are extensive, or partible, or have any degrees analogous to parts, and so what their unity is in a positive conception; and how spirits are many, and how one, and whether there be existent one universal spirit of each kind, vegetative, sensitive, and intellective; and whether they are both one and many in several respects, with many such like questions, these are all past human certain knowledge in this life: many it is certain that there be; but whether that number here be *quantitas discreta*, and how they are individuate and distinguishable, and how it is that many come from one or two in generation, are questions too hard for such as I.

18. But we see in passive matter, that the parts have a natural propensity to union, and the aggregative inclination is so strong, as that thence the learned Dr. Glisson (Lib. de Vita Naturæ) copiously maintaineth that all matter hath life, or a natural, vital, self-moving virtue, not as a compounding part, but as a formal inadequate conception: in which, though I consent not, yet the aggregative inclination is not to be denied. All heavy terrene bodies hasten to the earth by descent, and all the parts of water would unite; and air much more.

19. The grosser and more terrene any body is, the easilier the parts of it continue in a local separation; you may keep them easily divided from one another, though they incline to the whole: but liquids more hasten to a closure; and air yet much more.

20. Whether this their strong inclination to unity, be a natural principle in the passive elements themselves, or be caused by the igneous active part which is ever mixed with them, and whose unity in itself is more perfect; or whether it principally proceed from any spiritual substance which animateth all things, and is above the igneous substance, I think is too hard for man to determine.

21. But so great is the union of the whole igneous substance that is within our knowledge, that we can hardly tell whether it have divisible, separable parts, and more hardly prove that there are any parts of it actually separated from the rest, even where by termination and reception in the passive matter there is the most notable distinction. The light of the sun in the air is one, and that light seemeth to be the effect of the present substance of the solar fire, and not a quality or motion locally distant from it: a burning-glass may by its receptive aptitude occasion a combustion by the sun-beams in one place which is not in another; but those beams that terminate on that glass are not separated from the rest. As there are in animals fixed spirits which are constitutive parts of the solid members, and moved spirits which carry about the humours, and yet these are not separated from each other; so the earth itself, and its grosser parts, have an igneous principle still resident in them, as fire is in a flint or steel, and indeed in every thing: and this seemeth to be it which many call *forma telluris*. But that all these are not contiguous or united also to the common solar fire, or igneous element, is not to be proved. The same sun-beams may kindle many things combustible, and light many candles, which yet are all one undivided fiery substance, though by the various receptivity of matter, so variously operating, as if there were various separate substances. And as all these candles or fires are one with the solar fire in the air, so are they therefore one among themselves, and yet not one candle; because that word signifieth not only the common fire, but that fire as terminated and operative on that particular matter. The stars are many; but whether they be not also one fiery substance, diversified only by contraction and operation of its parts upon some suitable receptive matter, (or contracted simply in itself,) without separation from all other parts, is more than we are able to determine.

22. They that hold that *non datur vacuum*, must hold that all things in the world are one, by most intimate conjunction or union of all the parts of being, and yet distinguishable several ways.

23. We constantly see a numerical difference of substances made by partible receptive matter, when yet the informing substance in them all is one in itself thus variously terminated and operating: so one vine or pear tree hath many grapes or pears numerically different; and many leaves, and branches, and roots; and yet it is one vegetative substance which animateth or actuateth them all, which consisteth not of separated parts: and that tree which is thus principled, is itself united to the earth, and radicated in it, is a real part of it, as a man's hair is an accident (or as some will call it, an accidental part) of the man, or the feathers of a bird. And consequently the *forma arboris*, or its vegetative spirit, and the *forma telluris*, are not separated, but one. And we have no reason to think that there is not as true a union between that *forma telluris*, and the forms or spirits of the sun, stars, or other globes of the same kind, as there is between the spirits of the earth and plants. So that while vegetative spirits are many by the diversity of receptive or terminative matter, (and perhaps other ways to us unknown,) yet seem they to be all but one thus diversified, as one soul is in many members.

24. Seeing the noblest natures are most perfect in unity, (and the basest more divisible,) we have no reason to think that the vital principles of the divers sensitive animals (merely such) are not as much one as the divers principles of plants or vegetables are.

25. And as little reason have we to think that there is no sort of unity among the divers intellectual substances, seeing their nature is yet more perfect, and liker to God, who is perfectly one.

26. It is not to be doubted but the universe of created being is one, consisting of parts compaginated and united, though the bond of its union be not well known to us.

27. But it is certain that they are all united in God (though we know not the chief created cause of unity;) and that though it be below him to be the informing soul of the world, yet is he more than such a soul to it; and of him, and through him, and to him are all things, who is all things in all things, above all, and through all, and in us all (as is aforesaid); and being as intimate to all things as their proper form, is the first united principle of all being, as he is the first cause and the end of all. And yet it is above the creatures to be accounted parts of God, for they are not his constitutive parts, (who is most simple), but flow from him by his causal efflux, and so are by many not falsely called, *una emanatio divina*, or a continued effect of one *divine creative* or efficient volition; all one, as in, and of, and to one God, and as compaginated among themselves, and yet many by wonderful incomprehensible diversities; *ab uno omnia.*

28. God is said to be more one with some creatures than with others, as he operateth more excellent effects in one than in others, and as he is related to those effects; but not as his essence is nearer to one than to another.

29. Accordingly his union with the intellectual spirits, and souls of men, is said to be nearer than with bodies, and his communion answerably; but that is because they are the nobler product of his creating or efficient power and will.

30. And so he is said to be more united to holy souls than to the unholy, to the glorified than to the damned; because he maketh them better, and communicateth to them more of his glory, and the effects of his power, wisdom, and love: as the sun is more united to a burning-glass, or to a place where it shineth brightly, or to some excellent plant which it quickeneth, than to others.

31. Accordingly we must conceive of that union (before mentioned Thes. 10.) of Christ with believers here, and with the glorified hereafter, as to his divine nature; which may well be called mystical, and is of late become the subject of some men's contentious opposition, and is matter of difficult inquiry to the wisest. And yet it is hard to say that in all their hot opposition any sober men are in this disagreed: for, first, It is by such commonly confessed, that the Spirit of Christ doth operate more excellent effects on believers than on others, and on the blessed than on the damned; even making them liker unto God. Secondly, And that this Holy Spirit is by covenant related to them, to operate for the future more constantly and eminently in them than in others. Thirdly, And that this Spirit proceedeth and is sent from the Father and the Son to do these works. Fourthly, And that Christ is related to each believing and each glorified soul, as one in covenant, self-obliged (or a promiser) thus by his Spirit to operate on them. Fifthly, And that he is thus related to the whole church or society of such persons, whereof each individual is a part.

So that all this set together telleth us, That every believing, and every glorified soul, is said to be united to Christ in all these several conjunct respects (as to his Godhead.) First, In that he eminently operateth grace and glory in them, that is, holy life, light, and love, by the Holy Ghost: and this he doth (as God doth all things) *per essentiam*, and not as distant by an intermediate virtue, which is neither Creator nor creature: as the very sun-beams touch the illuminated and heated object. Secondly, By a moral relative union by covenant to that individual person, to do such things upon him. (As husband and wife are united by covenant for certain uses.) Thirdly, By a political relative union, as that person is a member of the church or political body, to which Christ is united by promise, as aforesaid. Who denieth any of this? and who asserteth more?

32. And then our union with Christ's human nature (besides the general and special logical union, as he is a creature, a man, of the same nature with us) can be of no higher or nearer a sort; but differeth from the former so far as the operations and relations of a created medium differ from those of the Creator: that is, first, The human nature is honoured and used by the divine, as a second cause of the foresaid effects of grace and glory on us. Secondly, The human nature (being of the same species with ours) is by a law, obligation, and consent, related to each believer, and to all the church, as the root, and chief medium, administrator, and communicator of this grace and glory; and so as our relative head in the foresaid moral and political sense, communicating those real benefits. Thirdly, And Christ in his humanity is the authorized Lord and Governor of all inferior means and causes, by which any grace and glory is conveyed to us (as of angels, ministers, word, sacraments, changing providences, &c.) Fourthly, But whether his own human soul *per essentiam et immediatam attingentiam*, do operate on all holy souls, and so be physically also united to them, as the sun is to the quickened plants or animals, I told you before I know not yet, but hope ere long to know.

33. Christ's divine nature is united to his human in a peculiar sort, as it is not to any other creature. But it is not by any change of the divine; but by that peculiar possessing operation and relation, which no other created being doth partake of, and which no mortal can comprehend, of which I have said more elsewhere.[b]

34. All creatures as such are united in God as the root, or first cause of nature: all believers and saints are united in Christ, as the head of the church, as aforesaid; and in the Holy Spirit as the principle of their sanctification.

35. The political, relative union of such saints among themselves, is intelligible and sure, as having one God, one Head, one Holy Spirit: but (as I said before) how and how far their very substance is one, by a unity analogous to physical continuity, (like the solar light, &c.) and how far and how they are substantially divers; and how and how far the Spirit of holiness doth in a peculiar manner unite the substances of holy souls among themselves, (by analogy to the illuminated air, &c.) and how all souls and angels are individuate and distinguished, I say again is past our reach.

36. Seeing union is so naturally desired as perfection by all creatures known to us, it is great inordinateness and folly to fear lest death will by too near a union end our individuation.

37. And as things sensible are the first known by man in flesh, and we see that among them union destroyeth no part of their substance; but a sand or atom is the same thing in union with others, as it would be if separate or solitary, and a drop of water hath as true and much existing substance in the ocean, as in its separate state, and so of a particle of air; we have reason to conclude no worse of the igneous element, nor yet of sensitive or intellectual spirits. For, 1. How far they are passive and partible (being many) we know not. Most of the old fathers, especially the Greeks, (as Faustus Regiensis cited them in the book which Mammertus answered,) thought that God only was totally immaterial or incorporeal; and it must not be denied that every creature doth *pati a Deo*, is passive, as from God the first cause; and many philosophers think that all passivity is a consequent or proof of answerable materiality; and many think that we have no true notion of *substantia*, besides relative, (as it doth subsist of itself, and *substare accidentibus,)* but what is the same with *materia purissima*. 2. But, supposing all this to be otherwise, spirits being true substances, of a more perfect nature than gross bodies, as they are more inclined to union *inter se*, so there is as little, if not less, danger that they should be losers by that union, than that a drop of water should be so: for the perfection of the highest nature must needs be more the perfection of all the parts, (physical or intelligible,) than the perfection of the lowest; and the noblest inclineth not to its own loss, by desiring union, which to the lowest is no loss.

38. It is called in the text "the union of the Spirit," first, As it is one species of spiritual grace, which all the members are endowed with, which is their holiness, or God's image on them, which is called, the Spirit in us, because it is the immediate and excellent work of God's Spirit; as the sun is said to be in the room, because it shineth there. Secondly, As the Spirit is the efficient cause hereof. Thirdly, And because this one Spirit in all the members inclineth them to unity; even as the soul of every animal inclineth it to preserve the unity of all its parts, and to abhor wounding and separation, as that which will be its pain, and tendeth to its destruction by dissolution.

39. The holiness, or spiritual qualification, of souls, which is called the Spirit, is holy, or divine, life, light, and love, or the holy disposition of the soul's three natural faculties, vital power, (or activity,) understanding, and will. As all men have one species of humanity, so all saints have this one Spirit.

40. Though quickening (by holy life) and illumination be parts of sanctification, (or this Spirit,) yet the last part, "love," is the completing perfective part, and therefore is oft called sanctification specially; and by the word "Spirit" and "love" is oft meant the same thing. And when the Spirit is said to be given to believers, the meaning is, that upon and by believing the wonderful demonstrations of God's love in Christ, the habit of holy love is kindled in us.

41. This holy love, which is God's image, (for God is love,) usually beginneth at things visible, as being the nearest objects to man in flesh; and as we see God here as in a glass, so we first see the glass before we see God in it; and accordingly we first see the goodness and loveliness of God's blessings to us, and of good people, and of good words and actions; but yet when we come up to the love of God, it is he that is the chiefest object, in whom all the church by love is centred: so that we thenceforth love God for himself, and all his servants and word as for his sake, and impress on them. And our union by love would not be perfect, if it united us together only among ourselves, and did not unite us all in God and our Redeemer. So that the unity of the Spirit is the love of God in Christ, and of all the faithful, (yea, and of all men, so far as God appeareth in them,) to which God's Spirit strongly inclineth all true believers; including holy life and light as tending to this unity of spiritual love.

[b] In Methodo Theologiæ, part 2.

42. Therefore love is not distinctly named after, among the particular terms of unity, as faith and hope are, because it is meant by that word, "There is one Spirit."

43. The love and unity of christians as in one church, supposeth in nature a love to man as man, and a desire of the unity and concord of mankind, as christianity supposeth humanity.

44. But experience and faith assure us that this human love and unity is woefully corrupted and much lost; and that though man's soul be convinced by natural light that it is good, and have a general languid inclination to it, yet this is so weak and uneffectual, as that the principles of wrath and division prevail against it, and keep the world in miserable confusion.

45. It is the predominancy of the corrupt selfish inclination which is the great enemy and destroyer of love and unity.

46. Christianity is so far from confining all our love to christians, that it is not the least use of it to revive and recover our love to men as men; so that no men have a full and healing love to mankind, and desire of universal unity, but believers.

47. The purest and strongest love and unity is universal. And it is not genuine christianity if it do not incline us to love all men as men, and all professed christians as such, and all saints as saints, according to their various degrees of amiableness.

48. Love and unity which is not thus universal partaketh of wrath and schism. For he that loveth but a part of men, doth not love the rest; and he that is united but to a part (whether great or small) is schismatically divided from all the rest.

49. But love to all must not be equal to all, nor our unity with all equal, as on the same terms, or in the same degree. As the goodness of mere humanity, and the mere profession of christianity, is less, and so less amiable, than is the goodness of true sanctification, so our love and unity must be diversified. All the members of the body must be loved, and their unity carefully preserved: but yet not equally; but the head as a head, and the heart as a heart, and the stomach as a stomach, and all the essential parts as essential, without which it is not a human body; and all the integral parts as such, but diversely according to their worth and use; the eye as an eye, and a tooth but as a tooth. Goodness being the object of love, and love being the life of our unity, it varieth in degrees as goodness varieth.

50. That love and unity which is sincere in kind, may be mixed with lamentable wrath and schism (as all our graces are with the contrary sin in our imperfect state): not but that all christians have an habitual inclination to universal love and unity; but the act may be hindered by the want of due information, and by false reports and misrepresentations of our brethren, which hide their amiableness, and render them to such more odious than they are.

51. Sincere and genuine love and unity hath a universal care of all mankind, and is very apt to inquire and take knowledge how it goeth with all the world, and specially with all the churches: for none can much love and desire that which they mind not, or take no thought of. And this is the chief news which a true christian inquireth after, whether God's name be hallowed, his kingdom come, and his will be done on earth, as it is done in heaven: and of this he is solicitous even on his death-bed.

52. The unity of the Spirit inclineth men to mourn much for the sects, schisms, divisions, and discords of believers; and to smart in the sense of them, as the body does by its wounds. And they that bewail them not, are so far void of the unity of the Spirit.

53. The unity of the Spirit helpeth a man greatly to distinguish between wounding and healing doctrines, wounding and healing courses of practice, and between wounding and healing persons; even as nature teacheth us to discern and abhor that which would dismember or divide the body as painful and destructive.

54. Therefore holy experienced christians, who have most of the unity of the Spirit, are most against the dividing impositions of church tyrants, and also against the quarrelsome humour and causeless separations of self-conceited singularists, whether dogmatical or superstitious; who proudly overvalue their own conceptions, forms, and modes of worship and doctrine, and thence aggravate all that they dislike into the shape of idolatry, antichristianism, false worship, or some such heinous sin, when the beam of self-conceit and pride in their own eye is worse than the mote of a modal imperfection of words, method, or matter, in another's eye.

55. The unity of the Spirit inclineth men to hope the best of others, till we know it to be untrue, and to take more notice of men's virtues than of their faults; and love covereth such infirmities as may be covered; and beareth one another's burdens, while we consider that we also may be tempted, Rom. xiv. 17; xv.; 1 Cor. xii.; xiii.; Gal. vi. 1—3.

56. The unity of the Spirit teacheth and inclineth men to yield for peace and concord to such lawful things, (whose practice doth truly conduce to unity,) yea, and to give up much of our own right for unity and peace.

57. This love and unity of the Spirit inclineth men to vigorous endeavours for concord with all others; so that such will not slothfully wish it, but diligently seek it; they will pursue and follow peace with all men, Heb. xii. 14; as far as is possible, and as in them lieth, Rom. xii. 18; they that are true peace-lovers, are diligent peace-makers, if it be in their power and way.

58. This love and unity of the Spirit will prevail with the sincere to prosecute it through difficulties and oppositions, and to conquer all: and it teacheth them at the first hearing to abhor backbiters, and slanderous censurers, who on pretence of a (blind) zeal for orthodoxness, or piety, or purity of worship, are ready to reproach those that are not of their mind and way in points where difference is tolerable: and when children that are tossed up and down, and carried too and fro with every wind of doctrine, (Eph. iv. 14.) are presently filled with distaste and prejudice, when they hear other men's tolerable opinions, forms, and orders aggravated, the right christian is more affected with displeasure against the self-conceited reproacher, who is employed by Satan (though perhaps he be a child of God) against the love and unity of believers.

59. The more any man hath of love, and the unity of the Spirit, the greater matter he maketh of universal unity, and the more zealous he is for it. A small fire or candle giveth but a faint and little light and heat, and that but a little way: but the sun-light and heat extendeth to all the surface of the earth, and much farther; and that so vigorously as to be the life of the things that live on earth: so strong love is extensive.

60. The more any man hath of love, and the unity of the Spirit, the more resolved and patient he is in bearing any thing for the furthering of unity. If he must be hated for it, or undone for it; if his friends censure and forsake him for it; if church tyrants will ruin him, he can joyfully be a martyr for love and unity: if dogmatists condemn him as a heretic, he can joyfully bear the censure and reproach: if

blind, superstitious persons charge him with lukewarmness, or sinful confederacies, or compliance, or corrupting God's worship, or such like, as their error leadeth them, he can bear evil report, and to be made of no reputation, and to be slandered and vilified by the learned, by the zealous, by his ancient friends, rather than forsake the principles, affections, and practice of universal charity, unity, and peace.

61. Though perfection must be desired, it is but a very imperfect unity which can be reasonably hoped for on earth.

62. There must go very much wisdom, goodness, and careful diligence, to get and keep unity and peace in our own souls, (it being that healthful, equal temperature and harmony of all within us which few obtain,) and most have a discord, and war, or disquiet in themselves; but to have a family of such is harder, and to have a church of such yet harder; and much more to have a kingdom of such, and a conjunction of such churches; and most of all, to bring all the world to such a state. And they that have a war in themselves, are not fit to be the peace-making healers of the church (in that degree).

63. Yet as every christian hath so much concord and peace at home as is necessary to his salvation, so we may well hope that by just endeavours the churches may have so much as may preserve the essentials of christianity and communion, and also may fortify the integrals, and may much increase the greatness and glory of the church, and much further holiness and righteousness in its members, and remove many of the scandals and sinful contentions, which are the great hinderers of piety, and are Satan's advantages against man's recovery and salvation: this much we may seek in hope.

64. Despair of success is an enemy to all pacificatory endeavours; and low and narrow designs show a low spirit, and a little degree of holy love, and all other uniting grace.

65. An earnest desire[c] of the world's conversion, and of the bringing in the barbarous, ignorant, infidels, and impious, to the knowledge of Christ, and a holy life, doth show a large degree of charity, and of the unity of the Spirit, which would fain bring in all men to the bond of the same unity, and participation of the same Spirit.

66. The most public endeavours therefore of the good of many, of churches, of kingdoms, of mankind, are the most noble, and most beseeming christianity; though it is possible that a hypocrite may attempt the like to get a name, or for other carnal ends.

67. And it is very savoury and suitable to the unity of the Spirit to hear men, in prayer and thanksgiving, to be much and fervent for the church, and for all the world; and to make it the first and heartiest of their requests, that God's name may be hallowed, his kingdom come, and his will be done on earth as it is in heaven; and not to be almost all for themselves, or for a sect, or a few friends about them, as selfish persons use to be.

68. A very fervent desire of union confined to some few that are mistaken, for all or the chief part of the church, with a censorious undervaluing of others, and a secret desire that God would weaken and dishonour them, because they are against the opinions and the interest of that sect or party, is not only consistent with schism, (as I said before,) but is the very state of schism (called heresy of old): and the stronger the desire of that inordinate separating unity is, as opposite to the common unity of all christians, the greater is the schism. Even as a bile, or other aposteme or inflammation, containeth an inordinate burning collection or confluence of the blood to the diseased place, instead of an equal distribution.

CHAPTER III.

THE NECESSITY AND BENEFITS OF THIS UNITY AND PEACE.

II. THE necessity and excellency of the unity of the Spirit and peace will appear in these respects: 1. For the good of the particular persons that possess it. 2. For the good of christian societies. 3. For the good of the uncalled world. 4. For the glory and well-pleasing of Jesus Christ, and of the Father: of these in order.

1. For the good of each particular person that possesseth it.

1. It is the very health and holiness of the soul, and the contrary is the very state of sin and death. What is holiness but that uniting love by which the will adhereth to God, and delighteth in his goodness, as it shineth to us in his works, and specially in Christ, and in all his members, (and in a common sort in all mankind)? And what is the unholy state of sin and death, but that contractedness and retiring to ourselves, by which the selfish person departeth from the due love of God and others, and of that holiness which is contrary to this his selfishness? So far as any man's love is contracted, narrowed, confined to himself, and to a few, so far his soul is indeed unsanctified, and void of the unity of the Spirit, or the Spirit of unity. If a man lived in banishment, or a prison, uncapable of doing others any good, yet if he have that love and Spirit of unity which inclineth him to do it if he could, this is his own health and rectitude, and acceptable unto God. Little do many religious people think how much they do mistake unholiness and sin itself, for a degree of holiness above their neighbours, when they contract and narrow their christian love and communion to a party, and talk against the churches of Christ, by disgraceful and love-killing censures and reproaches, as being not holy enough for their communion; this want of the Spirit of love and unity is their own want of holiness itself. It was the old deceit of the Pharisees which Christ the messenger and mediator of love condemned, to think that holiness lay more in sacrifices and ritual observances, and in a strict keeping of the sabbath's rest, and such like, than in the love of God and all men: and the lesson that Christ twice set them to learn was, "I will have mercy, and not sacrifice." He hath most grace and holiness who hath most of the Spirit of love and unity.

2. It is the soul's necessary qualification for that life of true christianity which God hath commanded us in the world. It is this inward health which must enable us to all our duty.

1. Without the Spirit of unity we cannot perform the duties of the first table unto God: our sacrifices will be as loathsome as theirs described, Isa. i.; lviii. If we lift not up pure hands without wrath, and

[c] Such as now worketh in Mr. Eliot in New England, and Mr. Thomas Gouge in England, towards the Welsh; and in many worthy ministers, who suffer the reproach and persecutions of men, because they will not consent to be as lights put under a bushel.

wrangling, (or disputing,) (for so I would rather translate διαλογισμοῦ, 1 Tim. ii. 8, than doubting,) our prayers will not be acceptable to God. Though it be Christ's worthiness for which our prayers and services are accepted, yet there must be the subordinate worthiness of necessary qualification in ourselves. For Christ himself hath annexed specially the express mention of this one qualification in the Lord's prayer itself, "forgive us our trespasses, as we forgive them that trespass against us;" and he repeateth it after, "for if ye forgive men their trespasses, your heavenly Father will forgive you your trespasses; but if ye forgive not men their trespasses, neither will your heavenly Father forgive you," Matt. vi. 13, 14. Love is here included in forgiving as a cause in its effect; and Christ rather nameth forgiving than love, because men may pretend to that act which is secret in the heart; but if it should not work in the necessary fruits (of which forgiving others is one) it would be but a vain pretence.

And here I entreat the reader to consider a while the singularities of this passage of Christ. 1. That men that must trust in Christ's merits and mediation must yet be told of such an absolute necessity of a condition or qualification in themselves. 2. That forgiving others as an act of love is singled out as this qualification. 3. That this condition must be put into the very prayer itself, that our own mouths may utter it to God. 4. That it must be annexed to this one petition of forgiveness rather than any of the rest, where men are apt to confess their own necessity, and where many are readiest to think that God's mercy, and Christ's merits and mediation, must do all, without any condition on their part. They that know that their daily bread, and deliverance from temptation and evil, must have some care and endeavours of their own, are yet apt to think that the forgiveness of sin needeth nothing on their part but asking and receiving. 5. That Christ should after single out this one clause to repeat to them, by urgent application; and yet how little is this laid to heart!

And indeed the first word in the Lord's prayer, "Our Father," teacheth us the same lesson, how needful a qualification love and unity are to all that will come to God in prayer. He that teacheth us that to love our neighbour as ourselves is the second summary commandment, and even like to the first, which is love to God, (for it is loving God in his likeness on his works,) doth here call us in all our prayers to express it, by praying for our brethren as for ourselves. Oh that men of wrath and wrangling were truly sensible what affections should be expressed by that word "our Father," and with what a heart men should say "give us" and "forgive us;" and how far us must extend beyond me, and beyond our party, or our side, or our church, in the divider's sense. I tell you, if you will be welcome to God in your prayers, or any other religious services, you must come as in union with Christ and with his universal church. God will receive no one that cometh to him as alone, and divided from the rest. As you must have union with Christ the Head, so must you have with his body: a divided member is no member, but a dead thing. Little think many ignorant persons of this, who think that the singularity and smallness of their sect or party is the necessary sign of their acceptance with God. Because they read "Fear not little flock," as if a little flock must separate from Christ's little flock, for fear of being too great; and as if his flock, which then was but a few hundreds, must be no greater, when the kingdoms of the world are become his kingdoms. Yet such have there been of late among us, who first became (as they were called) puritans, or presbyterians, when they saw them a small and suffering party; but when they prospered and multiplied they turned independents, or separatists, thinking that the former were too many to be the true church. And on the same reason, when the independents prospered, they turned anabaptists; and when they prospered they turned quakers; thinking that unless it were a small and suffering party it could not be the little flock of Christ. As if he that is called the Saviour of the world, would take it for his honour to be the Saviour only of a few families or villages, and his kingdom must be as little as Bethlehem, where he was born.

Should they take the same course about their language, and say that it is not the language of Canaan, but of the beast, if it grow common, and so take up with a new one, that it might be a narrow one, the folly of it would discover itself. And what is the excellency of a language but significancy and extensive community? And what greater plague since Adam's sin hath befallen mankind than the division of tongues, as hindering communication and propagation of the gospel? And what greater blessing as a means to universal reformation could be given men, than an universal, common lauguage? And what is the property of Babel but division and confusion of tongues? And doth not all this intimate the necessity of a union of minds?

While we keep in the unity of the body and Spirit, we may, we must strive for such a singularity as consisteth in an excellency of degree, and endeavour to be the best and holiest persons, and the usefullest members in the body of Christ. But if once you must separate from the body as too good to be members of so great or so bad a society, you perish.

God will own no church which is so independent, as not to be a member of the universal; nor any person who is so independent, as not to come to him as in communion with all the christians in the world. We must not approve of the faults of any church or christian, and so communicate with their sin by voluntary consent: but disowning their sin, we must own them as Christ's members, and have communion with them in faith and love, and holy profession of both; and while we are absent in body, must be as present in spirit with them, and still come to God as in communion with all his church on earth, and offer up our prayers as in conjunction with them, and not as a separated independent thing.

2. And as our unity is part of our necessary fitness for duties of holy worship, so is it also for duties of the second table; that is, of justice and charity to men: and this is evident in the nature of the thing. No man will be exact in justice, till he do as he would be done by: and who can do that who loveth not his neighbour as himself? What is our unity, but our love to others as ourselves? and how can we do the works of love without love? It is divided self that is the cause of all the unmercifulness and injustice in the world. Unity maketh my neighbour to be to me as myself, and his interest and welfare to be to me as my own, and his loss and hurt to be as mine: and were he indeed myself, and his welfare and his hurt mine own, you may judge without many words how I should use him; whether I should show him mercy in his wants and misery; whether I should rejoice with him in his joy, and mourn with him in his sorrows; whether I should speak well or ill of him behind his back; and whether I should persecute him, and undo him: whether I should defame him, and write books to render him odious, and to persuade the rulers that he is unworthy to have the liberty of a christian or of a man to preach,

to pray, to be conversed with, or to live! Would not uniting love make a wonderful change in some men's judgments, speeches, and behaviour, and make those men good christians, or good moralists at least, who now when they have cried up morality, and charity, and good works, would persuade men by the commentary of their practice, that they mean malignity, cruelty, and the propagating of hatred, and all iniquity? Where there is not a dominion of love and unity, there is a dominion of selfishness and enmity; and how well these will keep the commandments, which are all fulfilled in love, how well they will do good to all men, especially to them of the household of faith, and provoke one another to love and to good works, (Rom. xiii. 12, 13; Gal. vi. 6—8,) it is easy for any man to judge. Once alienate men's hearts from one another, and the life will show the alienation.

3. This unity of Spirit (and Spirit of unity) is our necessary preservation against sins of commission, (as well as of omission, as aforesaid,) even against the common iniquities of the world. Love and unity tyrannize not over inferiors, contrive not to tread down others that we may rise, and to keep them down to secure our domination. They oppress not the poor, the weak, or innocent: they make not snares for other men's consciences, nor lay stumbling-blocks before them to occasion them to sin, nor drive men on to sin against conscience, and so to hell, to show men's authority in a thing of nought. Had this ruled in Ahab and his prophets, Micaiah had not been smitten on the mouth, nor fed in a prison with the bread and water of affliction; nor had Elijah been hunted after as the troubler of Israel. Had this unity of Spirit ruled in Jeroboam and in Rehoboam, one had not stretched out his hand against the prophet, nor the other despised experienced counsellors, to make heavier the burdens of the complaining people. Had it overcome the selfishness of the kings of Israel, their calves and high places had not engaged them against the prophets, and been their ruin. Had it prevailed in the kings of Judah and their people, Jeremiah had not been laid in the dungeon, nor had they forbid Amos to prophesy at the king's chapel or his court; nor had they mocked the messengers of God, and despised his prophets, till the wrath of the Lord arose, and there was no remedy, 2 Chron. xxvi. 16.

Had this Spirit of unity been in the persecuting Jews, they would not have counted Paul a pestilent fellow, and a mover of sedition among the people, nor have hunted the apostles with implacable fury, nor have forbidden them to preach to the gentiles that they might be saved, and have brought God's wrath upon themselves to the uttermost, 1 Thess. ii. 15, 16.

Had this unity of Spirit prevailed in the Nicolaitans, and other heretics of old, they had not so early grieved the apostles, and divided and dishonoured the primitive church, nor raised so many sects and parties among christians, nor put the apostles to so many vehement obtestations against them, and so many sharp objurgations and reproofs: nor had there been down to this day a continuation for so many hundred years of the church's woeful distractions and calamities by the two sorts of afflicters, viz. the clergy tyrants on one side, and the swarms of restless sectaries on the other.

And if the Spirit of unity ruled in the people, there would be less rebelling, repining, and murmuring against governors, but subjects would render to all their dues; "tribute to whom tribute, custom to whom custom, fear to whom fear" is due, and "honour to whom honour," Rom. xiii. 7. They would owe nothing to any man, but to love one another, ver. 8. "For he that loveth another hath fulfilled the law. For this, Thou shalt not commit adultery, Thou shalt not kill, Thou shalt not steal, Thou shalt not bear false witness, Thou shalt not covet; and if there be any other commandment, it is briefly comprehended in this saying, namely, Thou shalt love thy neighbour as thyself. Love worketh no ill to his neighbour: therefore love is the fulfilling of the law," ver. 9, 10. "Love is long-suffering and kind: love envieth not: love vaunteth not itself, (or is not rash,) nor is puffed up; doth not behave itself unseemly; seeketh not her own; is not easily provoked (or fiercely angry); thinketh no evil; rejoiceth not in iniquity, but rejoiceth in (or with) the truth. Love beareth (or concealeth) all things, believeth all things, hopeth all things, endureth all things," 1 Cor. xiii. 4, &c.

Did the unity of the Spirit and love prevail, it would undo most of the lawyers, attorneys, solicitors, proctors: it would give the judges a great deal of ease: it would be a most effectual corrector of the press, of the pulpit, of the table-talk of calumniators and backbiters: it would heal factious preachers and people, and many a thousand sins it would prevent. In a word, love and unity are the most excellent law, they are a law *eminenter*. For it is to such that the apostle saith there needeth no law; that is, no forcing, constraining law, which supposeth an unwilling subject: for what a man loveth, he need not be constrained to by penalties; and men need not many threats to keep them from beating, or robbing, or slandering themselves. And did they but love God, and the church, and their neighbours, and their own souls, as they do their bodies, piety, and justice, and concord, and felicity, would be as common as humanity is.

As the best physicians are most for strengthening nature, which is the true curer of diseases, so he that could strengthen unity and love would soon cure most of the persecutions, schisms, reproaches, contentions, deceivings, overreaching, rash censuring, envy, malice, revenge, and all the injuries which selfishness causeth in the world.

4. The unity of the Spirit is necessary to the fulness of our joy, and the true consolation of our lives. A private, selfish spirit hath very little matter to feed his joy, even his own poor, narrow, and interrupted pleasures: and what are these to the treasures which feast the joy and pleasure of a public mind? If love unite me as a christian to all christians, and as a man to all the world, the blessings of christians and the mercies of all the world are mine. When I am poor in my own body I am rich in millions of others, and therefore rich in mind. When I am sick and pained in this narrow piece of flesh, I am well in millions whose health is mine, and therefore I am well in mind. When I am neglected, abused, slandered, persecuted in this vile and perishing body, I am honoured in the honour of all my brethren, and I prosper in their prosperity, I abound in their plenty, I am delivered in their deliverances, I possess the comfort of all the good which they possess.

Object. By the same reason you may say, that you are holy in their holiness, and righteous in their righteousness, which will be a fanatical kind of comfort to ungodly persons.

Answ. He that is himself unholy and unrighteous, hath not this unity with holy, righteous persons; he that hath not the Spirit, hath not the unity of the Spirit. This frivolous objection therefore goeth upon a mistake, as if this unity were common to the ungodly. But to those that have the Spirit of unity indeed, the comfort of all other men's holiness is theirs, and that in more than one respect. 1. By some degree of causal participation; as the common health of the body is extended to the benefit of each particular member, and the common prosperity of the kingdom doth good to the particular subjects. Goodness in all men is of a communicative nature, as light and heat are; and therefore as a greater fire, much more the sun, doth send forth a more extensive light and heat than a spark or candle, so the grace of life in the united body of Christ doth operate more powerfully for every member, than it would do were it confined to that member separatedly; as in the holy assemblies we find by sweet experience, that a conjunction of many holy souls doth add alacrity to every one in particular. And it is a more lively, joyful work, and liker to heaven, to pray and praise God with many hundreds or thousands of faithful christians than with a few. I know not how the conceit of singularity may work on some, but for my part God's praises sung or said in a full assembly of zealous, sincere, and serious persons, is so much sweeter to me than a narrower communion, (yea, though many bad and ignorant persons should be present,) that I must say that it is much against my will whenever I am deprived of so excellent a help.

2. And as efficiently, so objectively, a holy soul by this unity of Spirit hath a part in the blessings and graces of all the world. He can know them, and think of them, (so far as he is one with them,) with such pleasure as he thinketh of his own. For what should hinder him? Do we not see that husband and wife are pleased by the riches and honour of each other, because their union maketh all to be common to them? Are not parents pleased to see their children prosper, and every one delighted in the welfare of his friend? What then if all the world were as near and dear to us as a husband, a child, or a bosom friend? Would it not be our constant pleasure to think of God's blessings to them as if they were our own? A narrow spot of ground doth yield but little fruit in comparison of a whole kingdom, or all the earth: and he that fetcheth his content and pleasure from so little a clod of earth as his own body, must have but a poor and pitiful pleasure in comparison of him that can rejoice in the good of all the world. It is uniting love which is the great enriching, contenting, and felicitating art. (An art I call it, as it is a thing learned and practised by rule; but more than an art, even a nature, as to its fixed inclination.)

3. And union maketh other men's good to be all ours (as efficiently and objectively, so also) finally; as all is but a means to one and the same end in which we meet: it is my ends that are attained by all the good that is done and possessed in the world. They that have one Holy Spirit, have one end. The glorifying of God in the felicity of his church, and the perfection of his works, and the fulfilling and pleasing of his blessed will in this his glory, is the end that every true believer doth intend and live for in the world. And this one end, all saints, all angels, all creatures, are carrying on as means. If I be a christian indeed, I have nothing so dear to me, or so much desired, as this pleasing and glorifying of God in the good and perfection of his works. This is my interest; in this he must gratify me that will be my friend. All things are as nothing to me, but for this; and in this all the world, but specially all saints, are continually serving me. In serving God they are serving me, while they serve my chiefest end and interest. If I have a house to build, or a field to till, or a garden to dress, do not the labours of all the builders and workmen serve me, and please me, while it is my work that they do. This is no fancy, but the real case of every wise and holy person: he hath set his heart and hope upon that end, which all the world are jointly carrying on, and which shall certainly be accomplished. Oh blessed be that infinite wisdom and love, which teacheth this wisdom, and giveth this uniting love to every holy soul! All other ways are dividing, narrow, poor, and base: this is the true and certain way for every man to be a possessor of all men's blessings, and to be owner of the good of all the world. They are all doing our heavenly Father's will, and all are bringing about the common end, which every true believer seeketh. It is this base and narrow selfishness, and inordinate contractedness of spirit, and adhering to individual interest, which contradicteth all this, and hindereth us from the present joyful taste of the fruits of unity which we now hear and read of.

Yea, I can die with much the greater willingness, because (besides my hopes of heaven) I live even on earth when I am dead: I live in all that live, and shall live till the end of all. I am not of the mind of the selfish person, that saith, When I am dead, all the world is dead or at an end to me: but rather, God is my highest object; his glory and complacency is my end; these shine and are attained more in and by the whole creation than by me: while these go on, the end is attained which I was made for; and I shall never be separated living or dead from the universal church, or universal world: so that when I am dead, my end, my interest, my united fellow-christians and creatures, will still live. If I loved my friend better than myself, it would be less grief to me to be banished than for him to be banished; and so it would be less grief to me to die than for him to die. And if I loved the church and the world but half as much more than myself, as my reason is fully convinced there is cause, it would seem to me incomparably a smaller evil to die myself, than that the church or world should die. As long as my garden flourisheth, I can bear the death of the several flowers, whose place will the next spring be succeeded by the like. And as long as my orchard liveth, I can bear the falling of a leaf or an apple; yea, of all the leaves and fruit in autumn, which the next spring will repair and restore in kind, though not those individuals. What am I, that the world should miss me, or that my death should be taken by others, or by me, for a matter of any great regard? I can think so of another, and another can think so of me. But unhappy selfishness maketh it hard for every man or any man to think so of himself. Did unity more prevail in men, and selfishness less, it would more rejoice a dying man, that the power, wisdom, and goodness of God will continue to shine forth in the church and world, and that others should succeed him in serving God and his church when he is dead, than it would grieve him that he must die himself.

Yea, more than all this, this holy unity will make all the joys of heaven to be partly ours. Even while we are here in pain and sorrows, we are members of the body, whose best part is above with Christ; and therefore their joys are by participation ours, as the pleasure of the head and heart extendeth to the smallest members. Would it be nothing to a mother if all her children, or to a friend if all his friends, had all the prosperity and joy that he could wish them?

The nearer and stronger this holy unity is, the more joyfully will a believer here look up, and say, Though I am poor, or sick, or suffer, it is not so with any of the blessed ones above; my fellow-christians now rejoice in glory; the angels with whom I shall live for ever are full of joy in the vision of Jehovah. My blessed Head hath kingdom, and power, and glory, and perfection. Though I am yet weak, and must pass through the gates of death, the glorified world are triumphing in perpetual joys; their knowledge, their love, their praises of God, are perfect and everlasting, beyond all fears of death, or any decay or interruption. Unity giveth us a part in all the joys of earth and heaven; and what then is more desirable to a believer?

5. And in all that is said it appeareth that unity is a great and necessary part of our preparation for sufferings and death. Without this men want the principal comforts that should support them. They that can fetch comfort neither from earth, nor from heaven, but only from the narrow interest of themselves, are like a withering branch that is broken from the tree, or like a lake of water separated from the stream, that will soon dry up: a selfish person hath neither the motives to right suffering, nor the truest cordials for a dying man. Something or other in this sinful self will be still amiss; and a selfish person will be still caring, fearing, or complaining; because he can take but little pleasure in remembering that all is well in heaven, and that if he were nothing, God would be still glorified in the world. Therefore the more selfish true christians are, the less is their peace, and the more their hearts do sink in suffering. Their religion reacheth little higher than to be still poring on a sinful, confused heart, and asking, How should I be assured of my own salvation? When a christian that hath more of the Spirit of unity, is more taken up with sweeter things, studying how to glorify God in the world, and rejoicing in the assurance that his name shall be hallowed, his kingdom shall come, and his will shall be done, yea, and is perfectly done in heaven: that which is first in his desires and prayers, is ever the chiefest in his thanksgivings and his joys.

CHAPTER IV.

THE UNITY OF THE SPIRIT IN THE WELFARE OF THE CHURCH.

II. As the unity of the Spirit is the personal welfare of every christian, so is it the common interest of the church, and of all christian societies, kingdoms, cities, schools, and families; and that in all these respects.

I. Unity is the very life of the church (and of all societies as such). The word life is sometimes taken for the living principle or form, and so the soul is the life of a man, and the Spirit, as dwelling and working in us, is the moral or holy spiritual life of the soul, and of the church as mystical. And sometimes life is taken for the union of the said vital principle with the organical body, or matter duly united in itself; and so the union of soul and body is the life of a man; and the union of the political head and body is the life of political societies: and so the union of Christ and the church is the life of the church; and the union of the members among themselves, is (as the union of the parts of the organical body) the necessary *dispositio materiæ*, without which it cannot have union with the Head; or the effect of union with the vital principle, and so the union which is essential to the church. As that is no body whose parts are not united among themselves, nor no living body which is not united to the soul (and in itself); so that is no church or no society which is not united in itself, and no christian society or church which is not united unto Christ.

It is a gross oversight of them that look at nothing but the regeneration of the members as essential to the church, and take unity to be but a separable accident. Yea, indeed regeneration itself consisteth in the uniting of persons by faith and love to God and the Redeemer, and to the body of the church; and if union be life, then division is no less than death. Not every degree of division; for some breaches among christians are but wounds. (But to be divided or separated from Christ, or from the universal church, which is his body, is death itself: and even wounds must have a timely cure, or else they threaten at least the perishing of the wounded part.)

II. Unity is the health, ease, and quiet of the church and all societies, as well as of each person; and division is its smart and pain; and a divided, disagreeing society is a wounded or sick society, in continual suffering and disease. But how easy, sweet, and pleasant is it when brethren dwell together in unity! when they are not of many minds, and wills, and ways; when they strive not against each other, and live not in wrangling and contention; when they have not their cross interests, wills, and parties, and envy not or grudge not against each other, but every one taketh the common interest to be his own, and smarteth in all his brethren's sufferings and hurts; when they speak the same things, and mind the same interest, and carry on the same ends and work!

> "O felix hominum genus
> Si vestros animos amor
> Quo cœlum regitur, regat," saith Boetius.

Many contrivances good men have had for the recovering of the peace and felicity of societies; and they that despaired of accomplishing it, have pleased themselves with feigning such societies as they thought most happy: whence we have Plato's Commonwealth, Moor's Utopia, Campanella's Civitas Solis, &c. But when all is done, he is the wisest and happiest politician, and the best friend and benefactor to societies and to mankind, who is the skilfullest contriver and best promoter of uniting love. I know that this is (like life in man) a work that requireth more than art; but yet I will not say *hoc non est artis, sed pietatis opus*, as if art did nothing in it; it is God's work blessing man's endeavours. Even in the propagation of natural life, though *Deus et sol vivificant*, God is the quickener and fountain of all life; yet man is the generator, (even if it prove true that the soul is created,) and God will not do it without the act of man. So God will not bless churches, and kingdoms, and families, with uniting love, without the subordinate endeavours of men; and the skill and honesty of the endeavours greatly conduceth to the success of the work. Men that stand in a significant capacity, (as rulers and public teachers do,) may do much by holy art to promote uniting love in all societies; by contriving and uniting of interests, (and not by cudgelling them all into the same temples or synagogues, as prisoners into a gaol,) and by diligent clear teaching them the excellency and necessity of unity and love, and mischiefs of dividing selfishness. But of this more after in due place. All the devices in the world for the felicity of societies which tend not unto unity, and all ways of unity which promote not love, are erroneous, and merely frivolous; and all that are contrary to love are pernicious, whatever the contrivers pretend to dream.

III. Unity is the strength and preservation of societies, and selfishness and division is their weakness, their dissolution, and their ruin. As in natural, so in political bodies, the closest and perfectest union of parts maketh the firmest and most durable composition. What is the strength of an army but their unity? When they obey one general commander, and cleave inseparably together, and forsake not one another in fight, such an army would conquer far greater multitudes of incoherent separable men: when every soldier thinketh how to shift for himself, and to save his own life whatever become of others, a few run away first, and show the rest the way, and they are quickly all made conquered fugitives: when they that resolve, We must all stand or fall together, and we will not live or escape alone; it is more the army than my life that I would preserve; these are seldom overcome by any policy or power. What is the conquest of an army but the routing and scattering of them? The strength of composed bodies lieth in the great number of parts most inseparably conjoined. Small cities and republics are made a prey to potent princes, because they are insufficient for their own defence, and are hardly united with their neighbours for mutual preservation. A united flame of many combustibles consumeth all without resistance, when divided sparks and candles have no such power. Divided drops of rain are easily borne, when united streams and floods bear down all before them. He can break a single thread, that cannot break a cord that is made of multitudes. And though the chief strength of the church of Christ be not in themselves, but in their God and Head, yet God fitteth every thing to the use that he designeth it to, and maketh that creature, that person, that society strong, which he will have to be most safe and durable, and to do the works and bear the burdens that require strength. Though we have all one God, and Christ, and Spirit, yet are there great variety of gifts and graces; and as there are strong and weak christians, so there are strong and weak churches and commonwealths.

Oh what great things can that church or kingdom do which is fully united in itself! what great assaults can they withstand and overcome! But the devil himself knoweth that a kingdom or a house divided cannot stand, Matt. xii. 25, 26. And therefore by some kind of concord (whatever it is) even Satan's kingdom is upheld, Mark iii. 24, 25; Luke xi. 17, 18. And by discord it is that he hoped and laboureth to destroy Christ's kingdom. And he that would have Christ's kingdom to be stronger than the devil's, must do his part that it be more united, and less divided. All living creatures perish by the dissolution of parts: what concord and discord do in kingdoms and all societies, he must be stupidly ignorant that knoweth not after so long experience of the world. Therefore they who agree in error, are hardliest convinced, (which is the Roman strength,) and they take their own concord for an evidence of truth: and those that disagree, and divide, and wrangle, are apt to be drawn at last to suspect, if not forsake, that truth in which they are agreed. Concord corroborateth even rebels and thieves in evil, much more the servants of God in good.[a]

O unhappy people of God (saith Jerom in Psal. lxxxii.) that cannot so well agree in good as wicked men do in evil! But, by his leave, there is more unity and concord among all Christ's true servants, than among any wicked men: else the devil's kingdom would be stronger and perfecter than Christ's.

Object. But this of Jerom's is a common saying, and common experience seemeth to confirm it. How unanimous were the Sodomites in assaulting the house of Lot! And what multitudes every where agree in ignorance and enmity to the godly! And how divided and quarrelsome are the religious sort!

Answ. The question whether Christ's kingdom or Satan's hath more unity and concord, requireth a distincter kind of answer; which is, 1. Unity is one thing, and similitude is another. 2. Active concord, or union of excellent, coherent, and co-operative natures, is one thing, and negative non-repugnancy of dead or baser creatures is another.

1. As there is a great similitude between incoherent sands or drops of rain, so is there between ungodly men; they are very like in their privations and ungodliness, but this is no unity at all. But the faithful are not only like, but united, as many drops in one ocean, or as many candles united in one flame, or many sun-beams in one sun and air. 2. All these sands, or dust, or dead bodies, quarrel not among themselves, because they are unactive beings, whose nature is to lie still; while parents, and children, and brethren, may have many fallings-out: and yet there is that unity in parents and children, inclining them to the loving communion of each other, which is not in the sand, or dust, or dead.

And so wicked men in some cases have not those vital principles which are necessary to an active quarrel, and yet may have far less union than the godly in their scandalous discord. Swine and dogs will not strive or fight for gold, or lands, or lordships, as men do; nor asses for the food or delicates of men; nor yet for our ornaments or gay clothes: brutes never contend for pre-eminence in learning, nor fall out in argumentation as men do, because their faculties are as dead to all these things; and that which moveth not, doth not strive: so wicked men strive not who shall please God best, or who shall be soundest in the faith, or the greatest enemy to sin, which is the commonest contention of good men (while some of them mistake some sin for no sins, and some take those to be sins that are none).[b] But brethren that oft fall out have yet more unity than strangers that never think of one another, or than fellow-travellers that quietly travel in the way. Godly persons are all closely united in one God, one Christ, one faith, one hope, one bond of love to one another, one mind, and one design and work, as to the main. There is no such union as this among the ungodly. It is true, that they all agree by way of similitude, in being all blind, all bad, all worldly and fleshly, all void of God's Spirit, and all enemies to the godly: but so all dead carcasses agree in being dead, and all toads agree in being toads and poisonous: and yet when the fable feigneth the belly, and the hands, and feet, to fall out because the hands and feet must labour for the belly, they had then more unity than several carcasses, toads, or serpents, that never fall out; yea, if a gouty foot be a torment to all the body, it hath yet more unity with the body than another man's foot hath that putteth it to no pain.

But yet the perfectest unity hath also ease, and strength, and safety. Things united are durable. Death, when it creepeth upon decaying age, doth it by gradual separations and dissolution. The fruit and the leaves first fall from the tree, and then one

[a] Sicut noxium est si unitas desit bonis, ita perniciosum est si sit in malis: perversos quippe unitas corroborat dum concordant, et tanto magis incorrigibiles quanto unanimes facit. Greg. Moral. l. 33.

[b] See Whateley's notable discourse of this in his Cerecloth, Doct. 1.

branch dieth, and then another. The combined parts of our nutritious juices are first loosened, and then separated, in our decaying bodies, and then the pained parts feel the ill effects: the hair falleth off, the teeth rot and fall out, and we die by degrees, as by a coalition of parts we lived by degrees in our generation and augmentation; saith Boetius, de Consol. Philos. l. 4, *Omne quod est, tam diu manet et subsistit, quam diu sit unum; sed interit et dissolvitur quando unum esse desierit.* We live while we are one; we die when we cease to be one; and we decay when by separation we hasten towards it; and we grow weak when by looseness we grow more separable. Therefore all loosening opinions or principles, which tend to abate the love and unity of christians, are weakening principles, and tend to death. Schisms in the church, and feuds or wars in the commonwealth, and mutinies in armies, are the approaches or threatenings of death: or if such fevers and bloody fluxes prove not mortal, the cure must be by some excellent remedy, and divine clemency and skill. *Discordia ordinum est reipublicæ venenum,* saith Livy. For (as Sallust saith) war is easily begun, (as fire in the city easily kindled,) but to end it requireth more ado. And the end is seldom in the power of the same persons that began it, much less will it end as easily as it might have been prevented. It is like the eruption of waters, that begin at a small branch in the dam or banks, but quickly make themselves a wider passage. Prov. xxvi. 17, "He that passeth by and meddleth with strife which is not to him, is like one that taketh a dog by the ears." Prov. xvii. 14, "The beginning of strife is as when one letteth out water; therefore leave off contention before it be meddled with" (or exasperated, or stirred up to rage). As passion inclineth men to strive, rail of some way hurt, so all discord and division inclineth men to a warring, depressing way against others. As Gregory saith, Moral. l. 9, When perverse minds are once engaged *ad studium contrarietatis,* to a study of contrariety, they arm themselves to oppugn all that is said by another, be it wrong or right; for when the person through contrariety is displeasing to them, even that which is a right, when spoken by him, is displeasing. And when this is the study of each member, to prove all false or bad that another saith or doth, and to disgrace and weaken one another, what strength, what safety, what peace, what duration can be to that society?

IV. Unity is also the beauty and comeliness of the church and all societies. Perfect unity without diversity is proper to God. But *ab uno omnia:* that all the innumerable parts of his creation should by order and unity make one universe or world; that all the members of the church of Christ, of how great variety of gifts, degrees, and place soever, should make one body; this is the divine skill, and this order and unity is the beauty of his works. If the order and unity of many letters made not words, and of many words made not sentences, and of many sentences made not books, what were their excellency or use? If many notes ordered and united made not harmony, what were the pleasure of music or melody? And how doth this concord make it differ from a discordant, odious noise? The united of well-ordered materials is the beauty of an edifice: and the unity of well-ordered and proportioned members is the symmetry and beauty of the body. It delighteth man's nature more to read the history of loves, and amiable concord, (which is the charming snare in tempting lust books,) than to read of odious and ruinating discords: and no doubt but the many histories of sinful discord, and their effects, are purposely recorded in Scripture, to make it the more hateful to all believers. This is the use of the recorded malice of Cain to Abel; of the effect of the Babel division of tongues; of the disagreement of the servants of Abraham and Lot; of the envy of Joseph's brethren; and of Esau's thoughts of revenge against Jacob, and of Jacob's fear of him; of the discord of Laban and Jacob; of the bloody fact of Simeon and Levi, and Jacob's dying detestation of it, and his curse; of the two Hebrews that strove with each other, and one of them with Moses; of the Israelites' murmurings and mutinies against Moses; Abimelech's cruelty against his brethren; of the tribe of Ephraim's quarrel with Jephthah; and the Israelites with the Benjamites, and their war; of the envy of Saul against David, and his pursuit; of his and Doeg's cruelty against the priests; of Absalom's rebellion against David; of Joab's murders, and his death; of Solomon's jealousy, and execution of Adonijah; of Rehoboam's foolish differences with his subjects, and the loss of the ten tribes, and Jeroboam's reign; of the continual wars of Judah and Israel; of the many malicious actions of priests and people against Jeremiah, Amos, and other prophets and messengers of God; of the persecuting cruelty of Herod against Christ and the infants; of his jealousies about his crown; of the Jews' malicious and foolish opposition to Christ; of Christ's disciples striving which should be the greatest; and the aspiring request of James and John; of the short dissension of Paul and Barnabas, &c.:[c] are not all these unpleasant histories to us, and written to make dissensions odious? To this end it is that we have the sad history of the early contentions between the Jewish and the gentile christians about circumcision, and the law, and the reconciling assembly, Acts xv. To this end we have the sad history and sharp reproofs of the factions and sidings among the Corinthians; of the false apostles' envy raised against Paul among the Corinthians and Galatians, 1 Cor. i. and iii. &c.; and of those that preached Christ out of envy, and in strife, to add affliction to his bonds, Phil. i.; of the many heresies that rose up even in those first churches to trouble, defile them, and disgrace them. To this end we have the abundance of sharp rebukes of contentious persons, and such as strove about words, and genealogies, and the law; and the reproofs of many of the Asian churches, (Rev. ii. and iii.) and the odious description of the heretics, (2 Pet. ii. and Jude, &c.) not only as corrupters of doctrine, but in a special manner as separatists and dividers of and from the christian churches. To this end we have the sad predictions that two sorts should arise and tear the churches, (Acts xx.) grievous wolves that should not spare the flocks, and some of themselves that should speak perverse things to draw away disciples after them. To this use we have so many vehement obtestations and exhortations against discord and divisions, even in those times of vigorous love and concord; such as 1 Cor. i. 10, &c. and iii. &c. Phil. ii. 1, 2, &c. iii. 14—16, and abundance such of which hereafter. And even those that by their Master are taught not to be too forward in seeing the mote in another's eye, must yet be entreated to mark them that cause divisions and offences, and avoid them; and whereas they that were such pretended to be the most excellent servants of Christ, and to speak more sublimely and spiritually, for

[c] Gen. iv. 8, 9; xiii. 7, &c.; xix. 4; xxvi. 20; xxvii. 41; xxxi. 36; xxxiv. 35, &c.; xlix. 1; Exod. ii. 13; xvi. 2; xvii 3; Numb. xxi. 4—6; Judg. ix.; xii.; xx.; 1 Sam. xviii.; 2 Sam. iii.; xv.; xix.; 1 Kings xii. &c.; 2 Chron. xxxvi. 16; Matt. ii.; iii.; Luke xxii.; Acts xv. 39, 40.

greater edification and advancement of knowledge than the apostles did, it was no ill censoriousness to judge, that being the causes of divisions and offences, contrary to Christ's doctrine of love, unity, and peace, they did not serve the Lord Jesus, (whose great and last command was love, which he made the nature, and character, and badge of his true disciples,) but by those good words and fair speeches, deceived the hearts of the simple and deceivable. Here there are four words especially to be noted. 1. Χρηστολογία, which we translate good words, is commonly translated flattery; but as Beza well noteth, it signifieth a speaking of things that are plausible in themselves, for some good that is in them, and that are pretended to be all spoken for the hearers' good, as Satan pretended when he tempted Eve; yea, perhaps to be necessary to their salvation, or to make them the most knowing and excellent sort of christians. 2. 'Ελογία, which signifieth both to bless them, as ministers do that desire their happiness, and to praise them, and speak well or highly of them. And so almost all sects and divided bodies are gathered by flattering the hearers into a conceit that thus they shall become the surest and most excellent christians, and all others are far inferior to them. 3. Καρδίας, it is the hearts of such hearers that are deceived, and not their heads, or reason, only or chiefly; for the good words first take with them, by moving their passions or affections, and then the praise, fair promises, and speeches kindle a kind of secret spiritual pride and ambition in the heart, as Satan's words did in Eve, to be as gods in knowledge. And the heart thus infected and puffed up promoteth the deceit of the understanding. 4. And this is *των ἀκάκων, hominum minime malorum*, as Beza translates. It is not simple fools, but such simple persons as we call harmless, or innocents, (as the vulgar Latin translates it,) well-meaning men, or not ill men: people that fear God, and have good desires and meanings, are for want of judgment and watchfulness overcome by dividers.

And on the contrary, the amiable examples of unity and concord, and their happy effects, are recorded in Scripture, to make us in love with them. But none so eminent as that of the first christians. It is very remarkable, that when Christ would show the world the work of his mediation in its notable effects, and when he should show them the excellency of his disciples above the common world, and of his church under the gospel above that under Moses' law, he doth it by showing them in the power and exercise of uniting love. Love was it which he came to exercise and demonstrate (his Father's and his own): love was that which he came to kindle in their souls, and bring them to possess and practise. Perfect love is the perfect felicity which he hath promised them: love and unity are the matter of his last and great command. These are the characters of his genuine disciples, and of the renewed divine nature in them. It was love and unity which must in them be the witness of Christ's Spirit and power, to convince the unbelieving world; and therefore it is love and unity which is the matter of his last excellent prayer for them, John xvii. 22—25; xv. 12, 17; xiii. 34; 1 John iii. 14, 23; iv. 21. And all these his preparations, precepts, examples, and prayers, were accordingly exemplified in the wonderful love and concord of his followers. When the day of Pentecost was come, in which the Holy Ghost must be most eminently communicated to them, they "were all with one accord in one place," Acts ii. 1. The apostles had a unanimity and concord before proportionable to the measure of their grace, which was preparatory to their reception of the eminent gift of the Spirit, which increased their unanimity. And, ver. 41—46, "The three thousand that were suddenly added to the church, continued stedfastly in the apostles' doctrine and fellowship, and in breaking of bread, and in prayers: and all that believed were together, and had all things common, and sold their possessions and goods, and parted them to all men as every man had need. And they continued daily with one accord in the temple; and breaking bread from house to house, did eat their meat with gladness, and singleness of heart, praising God and having favour with all the people." What greater demonstration could be given that Christ is the great Reconciler, the Messenger, Gift, and Teacher of love, the Prince of peace, and the great Uniter of the divided world, both with his Father and himself, and with one another?

In this text, Acts ii. and marvellous example, you see the design and work of the great Reconciler: when men fall out with God, they fall out with one another; when they depart from the only centre of unity, they can have no true unity among themselves; when they lose the love of God, they love the love of man as for God's sake and interest. And he that cannot see and love God in man, can see nothing in man that is worthy of much love. As he that loveth not a man for his soul and its operations, more than for his body, loveth him not as a man; and few have any great love to a dead corpse. Cicero could say, It is your soul that we speak to, and converse with: were that departed we should speak to you no more. God is more to every man than his soul: if God were not their life and amiableness, all men would be unlovely, loathsome carcasses. Therefore wicked men that cannot love God and goodness, can love none thoroughly but themselves, and for themselves, or as brutes, by a low or sensitive kind of love; for it is self that they are fallen to from God and man: and yet while self is carnally and inordinately loved instead of God and man, it is but destroyed and undone by that inordinate, idolatrous love; and he that loveth himself to his own destruction, (with a love more pernicious than another's hatred,) doth love his friends but with such a kind of killing love (as I have seen some brutes kill their young ones with the violence of their love, that would not suffer them to let them alone). Thus all love to man, saving a pernicious love, doth die, where the love of God and goodness dieth. And Cain giveth the world the first specimen or instance of depraved nature in envy and wrath, and finally in the murder of his brother, and undoing himself, by setting up and adhering inordinately to himself.

But when Christ reconcileth God and man, he reconcileth men to one another: for he teacheth men to love God in man, and man for God, with a holy, noble, reasonable kind of love: and so to love all men, as far as God hath an interest in all; and to love all christians with an eminent love, as God is eminently interested in them. And this is Christ's work on the souls of men; and much of his business which he came for into the world; and therefore he would have his first disciples to give the world such a specimen of love in this extraordinary way of community: for as extraordinary works of power (that is, miracles) must be wrought by the first preachers of the gospel, to show Christ's power, and convince the unbelieving world; so it was as needful that then there should be extraordinary works of love, to show Christ's love, and teach them the great work of love which he came to call and bring men to; for the first book that Christ wrote was on the hearts of men (which no philosopher could do); in fleshly tables he wrote love to God and man by the finger of his Spirit (many a year before any book of the New Testament was written). And as his doctrine was, "Love one another," and "Love your enemies, forbear and forgive," &c.; so his first churches must extraordinarily exemplify and express this doctrine, by living in this extraordinary community, and selling all, and distributing as each had need; and afterwards their love-feasts did long keep up some memorial of it. For they were the first sheet, as it were, of the new book which Christ was publishing; and love was the sum of all that was imprinted on them: and their practice was to be much of the preaching that must convert the world. Christ was not a mere orator or teacher of words: and *non magna loquimur, sed vivimus*, was the profession of his disciples. He came not merely to talk, and teach men to talk; but to do, to teach men to do; even to do that himself which none else ever did, and to teach his followers to do that which no other sort of men did in this world. But this leadeth me up to the next use of unity.

V. The Spirit of unity and love is the great means of the church's increase. There is a twofold augmentation of the church: 1. Intrinsic and intensive; when it increaseth in all goodness, and hasteth to perfection: and it is this vital principle of uniting love, or the Spirit of unity, which is the immediate cause of this. 2. Extensive, when the church is enlarged, and more are added to it: and it is a life of uniting love among christians that must do this, as much or more than preaching: or at least, if that preaching which is but the effect of knowledge produce evangelical knowledge in the hearers, yet a life of love and unity is the adapted means of breeding love and unity, the life of religion in the world. Light may cause light, but heat must cause heat; and it must be a living thing that must generate life by ordinary causation. That which cometh from the head may reach the head, and perhaps the heart, but is not so fit to operate on hearts as that which cometh from the heart. Undoubtedly if christians did commonly live in such love and unity among themselves, and show the fruits of common love to all about them, as their great Master and his religion teacheth them, they would do wonders in converting sinners, and enlarging the church of Jesus Christ. Who could stand out against the convincing and attractive power of uniting love? Who could much hate and persecute those that love them, and show that love? This would heap melting coals of fire on their heads. Our Saviour knew this when he made this his great lesson to his disciples, and when he prayed (John xvii. 21—24) over and over "for them which should believe on him, through" the apostles' "word, that they all may be one, as thou Father art in me, and I in thee; that they also may be one in us, that the world may believe that thou hast sent me. And the glory which thou gavest me I have given them, that they may be one, even as we are one: I in them, and thou in me, that they may be made perfect in one, and that the world may know that thou hast sent me, and hast loved them as thou hast loved me." Oh when will Christ revive this blessed principle in his followers, and set them again on this effectual way of preaching, that love may draw the world into the church's unity! Some look for new miracles for the converting of the now forsaken nations: what God will do of that kind we know not, for he hath not told us; but holy, uniting, universal love is a thing which he hath still made our certain duty, and therefore we are all bound to seek and do it, and therefore we may both pray and labour for it in hope. And could we but come up to this known duty, we should have a means for the world's conversion as effectual as miracles, and more sweet and pleasant to them and us.

Object. But why then is the world still unconverted when all true christians have this love?

Answ. 1. Alas, those true christians are so few, and the hypocrites that are selfish worldlings are so many, that the poor people that live among professed christians do judge of christianity by those false professors, who are indeed no christians: men see not the hearts of one another. Thousands of ungodly persons, for interest, education, and custom, take on them the name of christians, who never were such indeed by heart consent. When these counterfeit christians live like infidels, men think that christians are no better than infidels; for they think they must judge by the greater number of such as go under the christian name. But if the world could tell who they be that are truly christians at the heart, they would see that they have that Spirit of love which is not in unbelievers. 2. And alas, the love and unity even of true christians is yet too imperfect, and is darkened and blemished with too much of the contrary vice. Were christians perfect christians, they would indeed be the honour of their profession. Then love would be the powerful principle of all their works, which would taste of its nature; and as it is said of wine, (Judg. ix. 13,) it cheereth God and man, so I may say, God and man would be delighted in the sweetness of these fruits; for with such sacrifice God is well pleased, Heb. xiii. 16. But alas, what crabbed and contrary fruits, how sour, how bitter, do many distempered christians bring forth! If it will increase the church, and win men to the love of christianity, to be reviled or persecuted, to be contemned and neglected, to be separated from as persons unworthy of our love and kindness, then christianity will not want propagators: the pouring out of the Spirit was the first planting of the christian church; and where there is most of love, there is most of the Spirit. As there needeth no forcing penal laws to compel men to obey God so far as love prevaileth in them; so if love were more eminent in the church pastors and professors, that they preached, and ruled, and lived towards all men in the power of sincere and fervent love, there would be less pretence for all that violence, oppression, and cruelty, which hath been long exercised by the worldly clergy, and so much the more odiously by how much the more the sacred name of religion hath been used for its justification or excuse.

VI. Uniting love is the glory and perfection of the church; and therefore there will be in heaven much greater love, and much nearer unity, than there is of the dearest friends on earth, yea, greater and nearer than we can now distinctly understand.

And again I say, That they that in thinking of the state of separated souls, do fear lest all souls do lose their individuation, and fall into one common soul, do foolishly fear a greater unity than is to be expected. (And yet nothing else about the soul's immortality is liable to a rational doubt. For, 1. Its substance certainly is not annihilated. 2. Nor its formal essential virtues lost, by mutation into some other species. 3. Nor doth the activity of such an active nature cease. 4. Nor will there want objects for it to act upon.) Were it well considered that love is as natural to a soul as heat is to the sun, that is, an effect of that act which its very essence doth perform. 2. And that our unity is a unity of love, (voluntarily performed,) it would much abate such selfish fears of too much unity: for who ever feared too much love? too extensive, or too intensive? too large, or too near a union of minds? And as the beloved apostle saith, that God is love, as a name which signifieth his essence, why may not the same be said of souls, which are his image? that a soul is love?

Not that this is an adequate conception of a soul (much less of God); but of the partial or inadequate conceptions, it seemeth to be the chiefest. The soul of man is a pure (or spiritual) substance, informed by a virtue of vital activity, intellection, and volition, (which is love,) informing (or animating) an organical body for a time, and separable at the body's dissolution. And as the calefactive virtue is the essence of the fire, (though not an adequate conception of its essence; for it is a pure substance formally endued with the virtue, motive, illuminative and calefactive,) and the act of calefaction is its essence as operative on a due recipient); so love is the soul's essence in the faculty or virtue, and its essence as operative on a due object in the act; which act, though the soul exercise it not *ad ultimum posse*, by such a natural necessity as the fire heateth, yet its nature or essence immediately exerciseth it, though in a freer manner; yea, some acts of love, *quoad specificationem*, though not *quoad exercitium*, are exercised as necessarily as calefaction by the fire; yea, more, though now in the body the exercise by cogitation and sense be not so necessary, we cannot say that in its separated state it will not be so; yea, yet more, even in the body the love of a man's self, and of felicity, or pleasure, seemeth to be a deep, constant, or uncessant act of the soul, though not sensibly observed. And if love be so far essential to it, the perfection of love is the soul's perfection, and the exercises of love are the chief operations of the soul: and consequently the perfection and glory of the church (which is but a conjunction of holy persons) consisteth in the same uniting love which perfecteth souls.

And indeed uniformity in circumstantials and in external polity, were but a carcass or image of unity, without uniting love, which is its soul. As much external union in good as we are capable of, doth advantage unity of Spirit: but all union in evil, and all in unnecessary circumstantials, which is managed to the diminution of christian love, are to the church but as the glory of adorned clothing, or monuments, or pictures, to a carcass: and the church tyrants that would thus unite us, and sacrifice love and the means of it to their sort of unity, are but like the physician that prescribeth a sick man a draught of his own heart-blood to cure him. The inquisitors that torture men's bodies to save their souls, are not more unskilful in their pretended charity to save men, than is he that hindereth or destroyeth love, while he seeketh the church's unity in human ordinances by fraud or fear. When they have killed any church by love-killing snares and practices, and glory that it is united in papal power, splendour, and decrees, it is but as if they cut all a man's nerves, or cast him into a palsy, or killed him, and gloried that they have tied their limbs together with strings, or bound them all up in the same winding-sheet and coffin. That edifieth not the church which tendeth not to save, but to destroy, men's souls.

CHAPTER V.

THIS UNITY CONDUCETH TO THE GOOD OF THE WORLD WITHOUT THE CHURCH.

THE chief hopes of the heathen and infidel world, consist in their hopes of being brought into the faith and church of christians; and as God addeth to the church such as shall be saved, so the means that our charity must use to save them is to get them into this ark. The measure of their other hopes, or what possibility there is of their salvation, I have elsewhere plainly opened: it sufficeth us here to remember, that no man cometh to the Father but by the Son; and that he is the Saviour of his body, however he be called also the Saviour of the world.

And as in nature it is the principle of life in the seed and womb, which is the generating cause of formation and augmentation of the fœtus; and it is the vital powers in man, which maketh his daily nourishment become a living part of himself, and causeth his growth; so is it the Spirit in the church that is God's appointed means to quicken and convert the infidel world. And it is those christian countries which are adjoining to Mahometans and heathens, that should do most to their conversion; who have far easier means than others by proximity and converse to do it, and therefore are under the greatest obligations to attempt it; as also those remoter countries that are most in amity and traffic with them.

And as instruction by evidence must do much, so this uniting Spirit of love must do a great part of this work; and that both as it worketh inwardly on ourselves in the communion of saints, and as it worketh outwardly by attraction and communication, to draw in and assimilate others.

I. The church's unity of Spirit doth fortify and fit it for all its own offices in order to the conversion of the world: all parts are better qualified for the work by that wisdom, goodness, and life which they must work by; and each member partaketh of the common strength which their unity causeth. A united army is likest to be victorious; their routing is their flight and overthrow; and the army or kingdom that is mutinous, or in civil wars, or not unanimous, is unfit to enlarge dominion, and conquer others; they will have work enough at home.

Were but christian princes and people united, as they would be a terror to Turkish and other infidel oppressors, (and in likelihood easily able to vanquish them,) so they might easily contribute their endeavours to instruct and convince these infidels, with probability of greater success than any attempts have yet had upon them. They might with greater advantage send out and maintain men of learning, and other fitness to perform it. The Eastern christians by divisions were broken off from the Greeks. The Greeks by division and wickedness fell into the hands of the Turks. The divisions of the Western nations furthered their conquest, and hindered the Greeks' recovery. The divisions of the military forces lost Palestine, and frustrated their vast labours and expenses; lost also Armenian aids, and destroyed the hopeful beginnings of the conversion of the Tartarians. The division of christian princes hath set up the papal kingdom as the umpire of their feuds. That which hath done so much to destroy churches and kingdoms, and hath murdered many hundred thousand christians, and gone far towards the extirpating of true christianity out of much of the (formerly christian) world, must needs unfit us all to recover the world, and convert unbelievers.

6. And were but christian preachers and pastors united, instead of their pernicious, church-destroying contentions, how great things might their united diligence have done! If all the mischievous, unskilful, proud, wrangling, and worldly, ambitious strife, by which the christians are divided into Nestorians, Eutychians, Monothelites, Phantasiasts, Donatists, Novatians, and their anathematizers, &c. had been turned into a united force and diligence, by light

and love to have converted infidels, what a happy case had the world been in! And what blessings had that part of the clergy been, that now have left their names and history to reproach and shame!

II. And as efficiently, so objectively, and morally, the union of christians tendeth to convert the world, as it is notorious that their divisions have hindered their conversion. Men commonly suspect them to be deceived, or deceivers, that do not agree among themselves. They that reverence united christians, despise them when they see them fall into divisions, and learn of themselves to condemn them all, by hearing them revile and condemn each other. Christ had never made it so great a part of his prayer to his Father, that his disciples might be one, even as the Father and he were one, to this end, "that the world may know that the Father sent him," if this their union had not been a special means of convincing unbelievers. And this was not by a political union of the rest of his disciples under some one of them, as the governing head of all the rest; for no such head was set over them by Christ, nor ever claimed or exercised any such authority. But it was a holy union of mind in knowledge and faith, and of hearts in love, and of life in their published doctrine and their communion and conversation. The common sun-light maketh all men's sight (whose organs and visive faculty are sound) to agree; and though a man hath two eyes, they see unitedly as if they were one. The more united fuel make one fire, the more powerful it is to kindle on all other combustible matter near it. When many ministers of the same or several churches agree, it much availeth to procure the belief and obedience of their flocks; and when pastors and people agree, it strongly inviteth the reverence and consent of those without. By wilful dissensions we are scandals and snares to unbelievers; and if christians live not in unity, love, and peace, they rob the world of a great appointed means of their conversion: and they who for so doing do justly exclaim against persecutors and hinderers of the gospel, should also remember how much they participate in that guilt, while the love of christians to one another is made almost as needful as preaching to the winning of men's love to faith and holiness.

As in the solemn singing of psalms, the harmony of consenting, well-tuned voices, inviteth the hearers to join with them by delight, when bawling confusion and discord (one singing one tune, and another another) is loathsome and tiresome, and driveth men away; so would the sweet consent of christians have won unbelievers to the love of christian faith and piety, when their divisions and wicked lives have had contrary lamentable effects. Woe to the world because of offences! and woe to them by whom offences come!

CHAPTER VI.

THE UNITY OF CHRISTIANS IS DUE TO THE HONOUR OF CHRIST, AND IS PLEASING AND AMIABLE TO GOD.

IT is not only miracles that are Christ's witness in the world, the Spirit of prophecy also is called his witness, Rev. xix. 10. And if many prophets should all say that they speak from Christ, and speak contrary things, and charge each other with falsehood and deceit, would this be to his honour, or to the credit of their testimony? It is the great concord of the prophecies, promises, and types of the Old Testament, with the history and doctrine of the New, and the great concord of all the writers of the New Testament among themselves, which greatly facilitateth our belief, both of the Old and New. And all infidels who accuse the Scripture of untruth, do accuse it also of contradictions: and if they could prove the latter, they would prove the former.

And the Spirit of holiness, as it regenerateth and sanctifieth sinners from generation to generation, is no less a witness of the truth, and love, and glory of Christ, than prophecies and miracles. The same Spirit that is the author of prophecy and sacred doctrine, is also the author of believers' renovation to the image of God. And illumination is not the least or last part of this sanctifying work. Christ is the Light of the world, and his word and Spirit are given to enlighten blinded minds, and to bring them out of darkness into his marvellous light; and from the power of the prince of darkness, and from doing the works of darkness, to the Father of lights, who giveth wisdom liberally to them that ask it, that they may walk as children of the light. Light is usually called glory; heaven is the place of the greatest light, and greatest glory; and heavenly wisdom in believers is much of their glory here begun, in which their Father, their Saviour, and their Sanctifier is glorified. Whatever therefore obscureth or diminisheth this sacred Light in saints, opposeth that glory of God and our Redeemer which must appear and shine forth in them. The holy learning of his disciples is the honour of the heavenly Teacher of the church. All true believers are taught of God: were they no wiser, nor no better than other men, where were the testimony and the honour of their Teacher? and who would believe that he were a happier teacher than philosophers? or that he were the true Saviour of the world, that doth not save his own disciples from sin and folly? No wonder that God hath no pleasure in fools, and that the foolish shall not stand in his sight, when they are such a dishonour to Christ and him: what fellowship hath light with darkness?

And who knoweth not that disagreement proveth ignorance and error in one party at least? When they hold and plead for contrary opinions, both cannot be in the right. And when this is but in dark and difficult matters, of no great influence on our hearts, and lives, and future hopes, it is tolerable; and no more to be wondered at, than that we are yet but imperfect men in flesh, and in this low and darksome world; but when it amounteth to that which maketh christians judge it necessary to anathematize one another, and to cast out each other from their communion as intolerable, and perhaps to seek one another's destruction, do they not loudly proclaim their shameful ignorance to the world?

I know that discipline must be exercised, and the precious separated from the vile; and this especially for the honour of christianity. For if the church be as a swine sty, and the clean and unclean, the sober and the drunken, the chaste and the fornicators, equally members of it, such a society and their religion will be contemned. For "sin is a reproach to any people," Prov. xiv. 34; and vi. 33; xix. 26; Jer. xxiii. 40; xxix. 18; xlii. 18; xliv. 8; Ezek. v. 14, 15; xxii. 4.

But casting a felon or murderer into gaol, doth much differ from a civil war. For the church to cast out the impure that repent not is necessary to their honour; but to divide and subdivide among themselves, is their reproach, though the dividers have never so fair pretences.

I know also what pretences against heresy, &c. the dividing sects have had in all ages. They have pretended that they only being the true church, the condemning and rejecting of all others was necessary to the church's honour: but is it indeed to the honour of the christian name, that so great bodies for so many ages have continued to condemn and anathematize each other? that the Greek church condemneth the Western, and the Western them? That the Eastern and Southern are separated from both? and the Western christians so divided among themselves? Who that is not a stranger to man and history, knoweth not that it hath been to exercise a dominion over others, and also to extol the skill of their understandings, as speaking rightlier than others, when they strove about ambiguous words, that very much of their anathematizing hath been used? And when the pope hath anathematized the patriarch of Constantinople, he hath anathematized him again; yea, so hath the patriarch of Alexandria also. And when the three parties (the orthodox, the Nestorians, and the Eutychians) for so many ages have continued anathematizing each other, the dishonour falleth on them all in the eyes of beholders, and no party recovereth their honour with the rest.

Undoubtedly it is they that God shall make the blessed instruments of restoring the necessary means of concord, and thereby of reviving christian love and peace, that will be the chief and honourable agents for the repairing of the honour of the christian church, if ever it be repaired in this world. All parties seem agreed in this, even they that most foolishly and cruelly tear and distract the church, that it must be love and concord that at last must heal it, and recover its glory, if ever it be healed. And how much Christ is pleased to see his servants live in love and peace, his office, his nature, his many and vehement commands, do tell us.

CHAPTER VII.

III. WHAT OBLIGATIONS ARE ON ALL CHRISTIANS TO AVOID SINFUL DIVISIONS AND DISCORD, AND TO PROMOTE THIS UNITY AND PEACE.

FROM what is already said, it is easy to gather, that many and great obligations are on all christians to be promoters of concord, and enemies of discord and divisions. I. The many and express commands of Christ in Scripture do oblige them. This is no dark or controverted point, written in words which are hard to be understood, but plainly uttered, and often urged; yea, when several of God's commands are mentioned, this is still preferred before most others that can be imagined to stand in competition against it: as the uniting love of God is called the first and great command, so the uniting love of man is called the second like to that, and the sum of the second table, and the fulfilling of the law. It is not mentioned as an accident of the new creature, but as an essential part; not as the high qualification of some rare christian, but as that which is necessary and common to all that are the living members of Christ: not only as needful to some inferior uses, but as necessary to all the great ends of our religion, preferred before sacrifice, and all the rituals, and not to be dispensed with on any pretence.

II. No man therefore can be an obedient servant of Christ, that seeketh not to keep the unity of the Spirit in the bond of peace: if he that breaketh one of the least commands, and teacheth men so to do, shall be called least in the kingdom of God; what shall he be called, and where shall be his lot, that breaketh the greatest?

III. The love of God our Father, and of Christ our Redeemer, doth oblige us: for if he that loveth not his brother whom he seeth daily, cannot love God whom he never saw; how much less he that loveth not the multitude of believers, and so great an interest of God in the world, as is that unity and concord of the body of Christ! And if he that doth or doth not good to one of the least of the servants of Christ, is supposed to have done it or not done it to himself, how much more he that doth or omitteth that which Christ and his whole church is so much concerned in!

IV. The love of our own souls obligeth us, considering how many and great impediments discord doth raise against all grace and duty, and against our holiness, comfort, and salvation; and how much christian love and concord do conduce to the preservation of all grace, and to the attainment of glory. All men in true concord are our helpers, and all men in discord are our hinderers and tempters. How fair and easy is the way to heaven among true loving and agreeing christians, and how hard is it where divisions and contentions take place!

V. The love of our neighbours' souls obligeth us to this: that which is best for us is best for them. Alas, carnal minds deceived by sin need not to have the way to heaven made harder, nor to be tempted by the discords of christians to despise them: their own malignity, and the devil's temptations, when we have done our best, may suffice to deceive them, and undo them. Every christian should be a helper to the salvation of all about him, and a soldier under Christ to fight against Satan, as he is the great divider and destroyer. As ever therefore we pity the souls of sinners, and would not be guilty of their damnation, we should keep the unity of the Spirit in the bond of peace.

VI. Our love to the church and sacred ministry doth oblige us. Our discords unsay too powerfully what Christ's ministers say, when they set forth the power of grace, and the excellency of christianity. All the opposition of the arguments and reproaches of quakers, or malignant profane enemies, is of far less force against the gospel than the discords of professed christians. The labours of many worthy ministers have been hindered, and their hearts even broken, with such sinful and scandalous divisions. When the enemies hit us in the teeth with these we are ashamed, and cannot deny the fact, though we can deny their false conclusions. How much of the designs of Satan and his agents have lain in dividing the servants of Christ! Some of the moderate and peaceable emperors in the more flourishing state of the church and empire, by the discords and mutinies of factious christians were made weary of their crowns: yea, some of those that the hasty hereticating orthodox party too hastily pronounced heretics and heretical, (such as Theodosius junior, Zeno, Anastasius, Justinian, &c.) were tired out with labouring in vain to keep the christian bishops in peace, and by historians are recorded to be men of better qualities than the bishops; and one of them (Anastasius) laid down his crown, and told them he would not be the ruler of such contentious and unruly men, till the necessities of the people brought them to remorse, and to entreat him to continue emperor, and promised to cease their mutinous contentions.

And what the divisions in the church of Rome did to shame, and thus far abase, the papacy, is past all doubt: when there have been in many generations sometimes two, and sometimes three, called popes at once; when some kingdoms owned one, and some another; and when they often fought it out, and (as Victor the Third, and many another) got their pretended right by victory, not by the word, but by the sword: when one pope for forty years together lived in France at Avignon, and the other at Rome; when they fought it out with many emperors and kings: when Italy was kept by them many ages in divisions and bloody wars; and when the very citizens of Rome and their popes were put to fight it out at home in their streets; and when the popes have excommunicated the people of Rome itself, (where then was the church of Rome?) All this church history recordeth to their perpetual shame.

And have not the dissensions between Luther, and Carolostadius, and Zuinglius, Lutherans and Calvinists, to name no more, been a reproach to the Reformation (as I said before)? As we love the church then, and as we regard the honour and success of the ministry, and would not have Christ's house and kingdom fall, or be shaken, or disgraced by our sinful discords, let us keep this spiritual unity and peace.

VII. And indeed experience is not the least of our obligations. A danger never tried, is seldom so cautelously avoided as those into which we have formerly fallen, and out of which we have narrowly escaped. They that have read church history, what the factions and heresies of the bishops and people have done from the days even of the apostles to this day; yea, they that have but seen and felt what religious discords have done in this generation, even at home in England, Scotland, and Ireland, and yet do not hate such discord as death, and love peace and spiritual unity as life, and health, and safety, they are hardened past all excuse.

CHAPTER VIII.

WHAT SORT AND MEASURE OF UNITY MAY NOT OR MAY BE GROUNDEDLY HOPED FOR ON EARTH.

THE prognostics in diseases are needful to direct physicians in their attempts: he that either pretendeth to cure incurable diseases, and thereby doth but torment the patient, and hasten death; or else will hastily prevent the crisis, or will open inflammations before the time; may be called a physician or surgeon, but will prove a hurtful or pernicious enemy. Some diseases will admit of no better than palliating and delay: some that are curable are made mortal by temerarious haste. Who will break the egg to get the chicken before it is ripened by nature for exclusion? Yet hath the church had too many such midwives that will hasten abortion and untimely birth, and cannot stay till nature's time; such mischievous surgeons as are presently lancing unripe apostemes. It is of mischievous consequence to expect such concord, and accordingly set upon the hastening of it, which certainly will never be: and it is of great and necessary use to know how much and what unity may be expected in the church militant, and what not.

I. Negatively: 1. It is certain that christians will never be all of one stature or degree of grace. The apostle hath fully opened this, 1 Cor. xii. and here, Eph. iv. and Rom. xiv. and xv. and elsewhere. Some will be of more blameless lives, and some more offensive; some will be more fruitful and useful in the church than others; some will have greater gifts than others for that end; some will be more patient and meek, and others more passionate and hot; some will be more considerate and prudent, and some more rash and of indecent carriage; some will be more humble and condescending, and abhor pride much more than others will do; some will be more zealous, and some more frigid and lukewarm; some will be much more heavenly, and make less of earthly things than others; some will be more self-denying and patient under sufferings, and some will too much seek their own transitory things, and with greater impatience bear both crosses from God and injuries from man; some will be more cheerful, and rejoice in God, and the hope of glory, and others will be more sad, and timorous, and heavy; some will have a strong faith, and some a weak; some will have assured, sealed hopes, and others will be doubting of their salvation. But in nothing will there be more certain and notable difference, than in men's knowledge and conceptions of spiritual things. Undoubtedly there is scarce a greater difference of visages, than there is of intellectual apprehensions; nay, perhaps the likeness of all men's faces is greater than of their understandings. Some will still know little, (and none very much, but) others comparatively much more; some that know much in one kind, will be ignorant in others; and as all men are not of the same trade, nor all scholars prosecute the same studies, but some excel in one thing, and some in another, and some in nothing; so in religion such proportions and differences of understanding there will be.

No observing man that converseth with mankind one would think could be ignorant of this; and yet the talk and actions of too many church leeches, in most parts and ages of the christian world, hath showed that they did not well understand it. If universal, constant, undeniable experience be not enough to prove that it is so, and hath been so, and therefore will be so, let the certain causes of it be considered.

1. Men are born of much different intellectual complexions and degrees of capacity: some are idiots, or natural fools, some are half such; some are very phlegmatic and dull of wit, and must have long time and teaching to learn a little, and of memories as weak to retain what they learn; some have naturally strong wits, and as strong memories. If these be bred up in the same house, will they therefore have the same knowledge and conceptions?

2. And as men naturally differ in quickness and dulness of wit, so they do in the temperature of all their humours and bodies, which accidentally will cause great difference in their minds. A sanguine man hath usually other thoughts and perceptions than a phlegmatic man, and a phlegmatic man hath other thoughts and sense of things than the choleric have; and the melancholy man differeth from them all, and often from himself. As these tempers variously affect the phantasy and the passions, so consequently they do usually the intellect and the will.

3. The countries that men are born in, if not by the air and soil, at least by the great diversity of languages, laws, governments, and customs, do make much difference in men's conceptions; as we see by experience in the difference of many nations.

4. The very sins or merits of parents may do much to the hurt or benefit of children; partly by corrupting or bettering their bodily temperature, and partly by God's curse or blessing on their souls, as I have fully proved in my second disputation of original sin.

5. And were there no other cause of different conceptions than the different education of children

by their parents, it would make a very great difference in the world. When one is brought up in learning, and another in barbarism; one in reading and hearing God's word, and another in contemning and deriding it: one is taught to reverence God's name and truth, and another to blaspheme them, or despise them: one is taught one religion, and another another; one is taught to lay all his salvation on that which another is taught to abhor. And it is not only in divers lands, but in the same cities, towns, and streets, yea, among men that publicly profess the same religion in name and generals, that this difference is found.

6. And if parents make no difference, yet schoolmasters often will. With their grammar learning, one teacheth his scholars to deride such or such a party of christians as heretics, heteroclites, or anomalous; and others say the same of others, as they themselves do like or dislike; and boys usually take deeply their masters' dictates, especially if they be cunning and malignant, and such as the devil and flesh befriend.

7. And it is no small difference that company and converse cause, even among children and servants in families, and boys at school; from whom they are as apt to receive ill impressions, as from evil teachers; and therefore variety of company in youth is like to breed variety of sentiments.

8. And the different books which they read will make the like difference; while one writeth against that which another proclaimeth to be excellent and necessary, and all set off the matter with such plausibility and confidence, as young and unexercised persons are unable to see through, and perceive the error.

9. And when they go abroad in the world, the difference among those that they converse with all their lives, may well be expected to cause much difference in their thoughts. If they be set apprentices, one falls into a family of one mind, and another of another; and so if they be servants: and their friends and companions will occasion as much: and if they marry, the different judgments of husbands and wives may do the same.

10. And especially when differences in religion have already got possession of all mankind, (in some degree,) and they set themselves to inquire after the nature of these differences, and being at first unskilful are unable to try and judge aright, they must needs fall into great variety of judgments.

11. And the great difference among preachers and pastors of the church will be as powerful a cause of discord to youth and learners, as almost any of the rest; while one preacher condemneth that as a dangerous error, and frighteneth them from it as a heinous sin, which another extolleth as necessary truth or duty. And yet thus it is in many particulars, even where men profess the same religion; witness the many loads of books that are written by the papists against each other, as the Dominicans against the Jesuits, and the Jesuits against them; the Jansenists against both, and their odious charges of highest false doctrines and crimes in their provincial letters, and the Jesuits' morals; Gulielmus de Sancto Amore and his partners against the friars; the secular priests against the regulars, such as Watson in his Quodlibets, and abundance more such like. And in what country almost, or city, do not preachers in some measure differ, and breed diversity of senses in the people? Which Paul foretold even in the purest times and church, that of their ownselves should men arise, speaking perverse things to draw away disciples after them: besides the grievous wolves that should enter and devour the flock, Acts xx. 30. It must be that heresies must arise, that they that are approved may be made manifest. In Corinth some were of Paul, and some of Apollos, and some of Cephas; and they had such divisions as showed them to be much carnal. At Rome they judged and despised one another about meats, and drinks, and days, Rom. xiv. and xv. And some caused divisions and offences contrary to the doctrine which they had learned, Rom. xvi. 16, 17. In Galatia they had judaizing teachers that troubled them: and at Antioch some taught them that except they were circumcised, and kept the law of Moses, they could not be saved, Acts xv. 1, &c. In Asia some churches had Nicolaitans, and such as taught them to eat things offered to idols, and to commit fornication, and the woman Jezebel that seduced them: and some had such as Diotrephes, that received not the brethren, and cast out those that did, and prated even against the beloved apostle with malicious words. Divers churches had perverse disputers about the law and genealogies, and such as strove about words that profited not, but to the subverting of the hearers; and some whose doctrine fretted like a cancer, who subverted whole houses, whose mouths were to be stopped: and the Colossians had such as were for human ordinances, Touch not, taste not, handle not, and for worshipping angels, and prying into unknown things, Col. ii. And Paul telleth the Philippians, that some preached Christ not sincerely, but in envy and strife, to add afflictions to his bonds; whom yet he silenced not, but rejoiced that Christ was preached even by such: and he foretelleth Timothy, that in the latter days much false doctrine should be vented; and even then he had none like-minded to Timothy, that naturally sought the church's good; but all sought their own, (too much,) and the things of Jesus Christ too little. And the apostle John met with such as he would not have christians bid good speed to, nor receive them into their houses. And James was put sharply and largely to reprove such as in conceited wisdom would needs be masters, and had the envious wisdom which is from beneath, and is earthly, sensual, and devilish, producing strife, confusion, and every evil work, James iii. And could it then be expected that all christians be of the same opinions in all things?

12. But now this temptation to differences of judgment is grown much greater, in that the christian world is so publicly and notoriously divided into different parties. The Greeks are one party; the Armenians and Georgians somewhat differ; the Syrians, and the Abassines, and Coptics, in Egypt, and other Eastern and Southern countries, are of divers sentiments in many things; the papists differ from all, and the protestants from them; and too many divisions are among themselves, which I need not name. And can it be expected, that in such a world particular christians should be found without their personal differences?

13. And the variety of governments and laws will also produce the like disagreements; while one prince or state is of one mind, and another of another; one is a papist, another a protestant; one a Lutheran, and another Reformed; one a Greek, and another against all sorts of christians; and in the same kingdom in one age the prince is of one mind, and in the next his successor of another; and this must needs cause disagreement in the subjects.

14. And even the variety of God's providences will occasion diversity of thoughts; when some are in health, and some in sickness; some in wealth, and some in poverty; some high, and some low; some favoured and preferred, and some persecuted, imprisoned, slandered, and distressed, whence different impressions will arise.

15. Yea, men's different trades and callings will occasion different impressions; whilst their business leadeth them several ways, and into several companies and altering employments.

16. And almost all men have some different interests; the teacher and the hearer, the landlord and the tenant, the soldier and the countryman, the buyer and the seller, the master and the servant, the ruler and the subject, which will occasion different inclinations.

17. And men have great difference of temptations and provocations, from Satan and from men. Some Satan tempteth one way, and some another; some are abused and provoked by one sort of men, and some by another; some are called out to dispute with one sex, and some with another: and when they are engaged they usually bend all their studies one way, and little consider what may be said on the other side, or of other matters.

18. And when once a man hath received some one great opinion, true or false, it draweth on abundance of consequences, which those that received not that point did never think of.

19. And some have much more time and leisure to study, and happy counsellors to help them. And some follow hard labour, and have little leisure to read, hear, or think; or else live retiredly, where they have little notice of affairs, and miss the help of sound and faithful counsellors and helpers.

20. Lastly, God's own grace is free, and given to men in great diversity; some that have the same Spirit have more illumination, and some less, as the apostle at large declareth, 1 Cor. xii. and elsewhere. "There is one glory of the sun, and another of the moon," saith Paul; and as one star differs in glory from another, so doth one man in gifts and understanding; and the face of the whole creation showeth that God delighteth to make a wonderful diversity in his works: scarce two stones in the street, two sheep, two beasts, two birds, two fishes, two trees, &c. so like, but we may know one from another by their differences: no, nor two sons of the same parents, or two of the offspring of any animals.

And is not all this, joined to the constant experience of all ages, enough to prove, that even among christians, and good and tolerable christians, yea, among all, there will still be differences in degrees of knowledge and virtue, and consequently discords in some matters of religion, higher or lower, more or less?

2. It is therefore certain, that while there will be discord in judgment, there will be also discord in professions, and in practice. For honest men's professions and practices will agree with their judgments in the main. Even Paul and Barnabas will part when their judgments lead them so to do. When men have not the same measure of skill and accurateness in expressing their own minds, and in speaking properly, grammatically, logically, significantly, agreeably to the thing spoken; nor the same skill in defining, or distinguishing, or sifting the true sense of words, they will really differ; and they will verbally differ, and seem to most unskilful judges to differ really, when they do not.

It is not therefore to be expected, that if some men think long doctrinal confessions, formed in men's private words or liturgies, or other human forms, have nothing in them untrue, or evil, or which all men may not consent to, therefore all others must think so too, and say as they: who can think that in many thousand uncertain words all men can and must be of the same mind, and approve them all alike? or that honest men can lie, and say that they assent to what they do not?

And if men's judgments differ about matters of practice in essentials, integrals, or accidents, their practice will accordingly differ. He that judgeth a thing unlawful will not do it, if he fear God, and be truly conscionable. Had these been lawfully used in places or exercises of God's worship, yet it was inhuman and unchristian in those bishops and councils who cursed from Christ all that were of the contrary mind, and pronounced it an intolerable heresy, and ejected and silenced dissenters, and raised wars and bloodshed for such a difference. Much more unchristian was it for the Roman pope to rebel against his proper prince, the Greek emperor, and alienate the Western empire from him to the French on that account, and to excommunicate and depose emperors as heretics, called iconoclasts, as if imagery had been an article of faith, or a necessary universal command of God. For how can that be a heresy that is not a plain denial or subversion of any necessary article of faith or practice? And sure no such for images is in the creed or decalogue.

The same I may say of ma y other religious practices: as St. Paul speaketh of meats, and drinks, and days, (Rom. xiv. xv.) so must we say of all things that are of no greater necessity. If men in all these must be brought to uniformity and practising in the same mode, it must be either by argument and persuasion, or by force: the first we are sure will never do it in all things, though it may in many. All the twenty reasons before mentioned prove it, and many hundred years' experience much more. It is certain to all, save blinded persons, that all christians will never be in all things of a mind about lawful and unlawful, duty and sin. And it is as certain that force will never do it. St. Paul saith of things indifferent, that he that doubteth is damned if he eat, because he eateth not of faith; for whatsoever is not of faith is sin. Ungodly persons that have no true conscience, may go against their false consciences for worldly ends, and wilfully sin for fear of men. But so will no true christian, unless in the hour of such a temptation as Peter's, by a fall from which he will rise again to a stronger resolution than he had before. No sound believer will sell his soul to save his flesh, nor hazard heaven by wilful sin to save his interest on earth. So that this way of forcing men to practise contrary to their consciences in points in which good and tolerable christians differ, will but make up churches of wicked men that have no conscience, joined with one party that is therein agreed. And I shall show you in due place that they will never devise what to do with the conscionable dissenters, that shall not be far worse than a charitable and peaceable forbearance.

3. It is certain that there will never be so great concord, as that all disputings, opposition, and passionate and injurious words and writings, will cease among all sorts of christians; no, nor among all that are honest and upright in the main. For as long as one taketh that for a dangerous error or sin which another taketh for a necessary truth or duty, men will (even on God's account) think ill of one another, and in some measure speak ill as they think. They that know that they must not call evil good, and good evil, nor put darkness for light, and light for darkness, will abuse and injure one another in things where they confidently err. A Lutheran, though pious, will speak and dispute against a Calvinist, and a Calvinist against a Lutheran, and so of many other parties. And though it is greatly to be wished that all christians had humble thoughts of their own understandings, and would stay till they know well what they say, before they talk much against things or persons; and though it be so with wise, and eminently

sober, humble men, yet with too many it is far otherwise, and like so to continue. Perverse disputings, and shameful backbitings, and speaking evil of things and persons not understood, have such unhappy causes in the remnants of dark corrupted nature, that they seem to be like to live till a golden age or heaven do cure them. Talking and writing against one another, even of the same religion, yea, praying and preaching against one another, must be expected in some degree. I would I need not say silencing and persecuting one another; yea, excommunicating and anathematizing among the worser sort of men: such usage as Nazianzen had from one of the famous general councils; and such usage as Chrysostom had from such bishops, as Theophilus Alexand. and Epiphanius, and a council of other bishops, and such as abundance of excellent men in most ages have met with in the like kind and way, may be expected again till bishops and christians become more wise and refined persons.

II. But, affirmatively, there is yet an excellent sort and degree of unity and concord to be sought with hope among christians, worthy of all our utmost labour; yea, there is a true and excellent unity and concord, which all true christians do already enjoy, consisting in the following things.

1. All christians (truly such) believe in one God, and believe the incomprehensible Trinity, and believe God's essential attributes and grand relations to man. They believe that he is infinite in immensity, and eternity, and perfection, even a most perfect Spirit, life, understanding, and will, most powerful, wise, and good, the Creator and Preserver, the Governor and the End of all; of whom, and through whom, and to whom are all things; in whom we live, and move, and have our being; most holy, and true, and merciful, and just; whom we are bound to believe, and trust, and love, and serve, and obey, and praise with all our heart, and mind, and strength: and perfectly and everlastingly to see, love, and praise him, (to please him and be pleased in him) in glory, is the end and happiness of saints.

2. All true christians believe in one Mediator between God and man, Jesus Christ, the eternal Word, God, and one in essence with the Father, incarnate, assuming the whole nature of man, conceived by the Holy Ghost, born of the Virgin Mary; and was holy, harmless, undefiled, separate from sinners, fulfilling all righteousness, and overcame the devil and the world, and gave himself a sacrifice for man's sin, by suffering a cursed death on the cross to ransom us, and reconcile us unto God; was buried, and went to the departed souls in hades, and the third day rose again from the dead, having conquered death. And having declared the new covenant, or law of grace, and commanded his apostles to preach the gospel to all the world, and promised them to send the Holy Spirit, he ascended into heaven before their faces. The said covenant of grace is summarily this, That whereas all have sinned, and come short of the glory of God, sin by one man entering into the world, and death by sin, and so death and condemnation passed upon all, in that all have sinned; God so loved the world that he gave his only begotten Son, that whosoever believeth in him should not perish, but have everlasting life: that is, God freely giveth to lost, undone sinners himself to be their reconciled God and Father, Jesus Christ to be their Saviour, and the Holy Ghost to be their Sanctifier, if they will believe and trust him, and accept the gift, and will in serious covenant (which baptism celebrateth accordingly) give up themselves to him, repenting of their sins, and consenting to forsake the devil, the world, and the flesh, as opposite to God, and sincerely (though not perfectly) obey Christ and his Spirit to the end, according to the law of nature and his gospel institutions, that so they may overcome and be glorified for ever.

And they believe that Christ will come at last in glory, and judge all men according to his laws, and to their works.

3. And they all believe that the Holy Spirit being God, and one in essence with the Father and the Son, proceeding from the Father and (or by) the Son, is the great Witness, Agent, and Advocate of Christ, before, at, and after his coming into the world incarnate; by his gifts of prophecy, miracles, and sanctification, convincing sinners, and drawing them to repent and believe, and dwelling in believers as an operating cause of divine life, and light, and love; thus uniting them to God in Christ their Head, and to each other in faith and love, by which they are gathered to him as his church or body, having the forgiveness of their sins, and the adoption of sons, and right to the heavenly inheritance; and living in holy communion on earth, their souls at death are received to happiness with Christ, and their bodies shall be raised, and soul and body glorified at the last with Jesus Christ, and all the blessed, in the perfect vision, love, and joyful praise of the most glorious Jehovah.

And as, 1. All christians agree in this belief, so also, 2. They all solemnly in and by the baptismal covenant, and their holy eucharistical communion and other duties, profess the consent of their wills to these relations to God their Creator, Redeemer, and Sanctifier, and to his church or body, and their thankful acceptance of the foresaid gifts: and they profess and express their seeking desires hereof, according to the contents of the Lord's prayer.

3. And as to practice, they all agree in professing and promising obedience to Christ, according to the law of nature, the decalogue, and all his written laws, so far as they understand them, and their desire to learn them to that end.

All sincere christians agree in the true and hearty consent to all this; and these are the true saved church of Christ called invisible, because their heart's consent is invisible. All other baptized and professing christians with them agree in the profession of all this, and are called the church visible, their profession being visible. And all this being truly included in baptism, which is our entrance into the catholic (or universal) church, in this before described consisteth our catholic communion in Christ's body, as spiritual or invisible, and as visible.

II. But besides this universal church union and communion, for order and advantage to our great end, God hath instituted the order of christian assemblies or particular churches, which are to the universal church as cities and corporations to a kingdom; which are the noblest and most privileged parts of the kingdom; but yet not essential parts, but eminently integral: for it may be a kingdom without them, and would be if they were all disfranchised, and laid common. And if apostles and evangelists as itinerant preachers convert and baptize men, they are part of the church universal before they are gathered into distinct societies under proper pastors of their own. The eunuch (Acts viii.) was baptized into no particular church, but into the universal only; and so were many others: and mere baptism, as such, without any additional contract, doth no more. If thousands were converted in America, or cast there without pastors, they were parts of the universal church, if baptized professing christians. And before the apostles ordained any fixed bishops or pastors of particular churches, the church universal was in being, though small.

But these particular churches being a great part of Christ's institutions, and necessary, not only by precept, but as a means to the well-being of the universal, and the edification of it, and the particular members, it must be endeavoured, and that with good hope of success, that there may so much particular church union be obtained and maintained as shall much conduce to its great and excellent ends: that is, 1. So much as that in them, God the Father, Son, and Holy Ghost, may be publicly, solemnly, and constantly confessed, by sound doctrine, holy worship, and holy discipline and conversation.

2. So much as that hearty christian love may be exercised and maintained, and christians edified in communion of saints.

3. So much as that God shall accept them, delight in them, and bless them, to their converting, edifying, and comforting souls, hearing their prayers and praises, and owning them by his ministry, covenants, and grace, and differencing them from the people that do not thus confess and worship him, and promoting hereby their salvation.

And if this much be attained, it is not to be vilified for want of more, nor blotted with reproachful names, but acknowledged with thankfulness and praise.

III. And yet there is a further degree of concord to be hoped for and endeavoured, and that is the concord of these particular churches with one another: that they may all profess, 1. The same faith, and necessary doctrine. 2. And the same love to God and one another. 3. And the same hope of life eternal. 4. And may offer to God the same necessary and acceptable sort of worship; viz. by preaching and applying his holy word, recorded in the holy Scriptures, preserving and reading them, calling upon his holy name by confession, prayer, thanksgiving, and praises, and holding respective communion in the use also of the sacraments of his covenant: and exercising in some measure such holy government and discipline, by pastors overseeing their several flocks, as he himself by his institution hath made universally necessary. And all this, though not in perfection, nor every where with the same degree of purity and care, yet so far, 1. As that God's word and ordinances be kept up in soundness in all parts and respects necessary to salvation. 2. And as may tend to the edifying of the churches by love and concord in necessary things, and their mutual help by counsel, and strength by that concord. 3. And the avoiding of pernicious feuds and divisions.

The means by which this is to be done, 1. By communicatory letters, 2. By synods, 3. And by civil governors, is after in due place to be explained.

Thus much of christian unity and concord may be well hoped for upon just endeavours here on earth; but neither perfection in these, nor those unnecessary terms of concord which some have long taken to be necessary.

And indeed so much as may be hoped for, is so very hardly to be obtained, that if we trusted not to God's extraordinary grace, more than to any natural probability that appeareth to us in man, we should be ready to despair that ever christians should live long in so much peace and concord: and though the great difficulty must not kill our hopes, it must much quicken us to strenuous endeavours: of which more anon. Satan is so great an enemy to it, and every sin in man is so much against it, (as every disease in the body is against its ease and peace,) and the multitude and malignity of sins and sinners is so great, and the very healers so few, and faulty, and unskilful, and do so much against their own desired ends, that instead of accusing the providence of God, we should thankfully wonder that there is so much peace and concord as there is; and that all men live not as enemies to each other, in continual war; or that the devouring pikes leave so many of the lesser fish alive, and the weak and innocent are not wholly a prey to the oppressors.

CHAPTER IX.

THAT CHRIST HIMSELF, WHO COMMANDED THE UNITY, LOVE, AND CONCORD OF CHRISTIANS, DID PRESCRIBE THE NECESSARY TERMS.

If it be once proved that Christ himself hath prescribed the conditions or terms of christian union and communion, what remaineth to christians but to inquire what are those terms? Whereas for want of that necessary supposition, while men think it is left to them, no man knoweth who should do it, and the pope prescribeth his terms, and others prescribe their terms, and almost each sect hath different terms.

That Christ did prescribe them I shall prove, I. Antecedently, *a causis*. II. Consequently, *ab effectis*. III. By proving the necessary exclusion of any other competent prescribers.

I. Antecedently it is proved from, 1. The universal necessity of the thing. 2. And from the office of Christ to do things of such universal necessity, and his faithfulness therein.

1. There are few christians so ignorant or inconsiderate but will confess that the union of christians is necessary, not only to the edification and well-being, but to the very being of the church (both universal and particular). For what is a church, but many christians united and associated for church ends? Pull all the bricks or timber of the house asunder, and it is no house: pull all the planks and parts of a ship asunder, and it is no ship: pull all the leaves and sentences of a book asunder, and it is no book: pull all the parts of a man's body asunder, and there remaineth no body of a man, considered formally, but only materially, and in their aptitude to re-union at the resurrection. An army disbanded and dissipated, is no army. And certainly it is no church that hath not church unity of parts.

2. And all that believe in Christ, believe that he came into the world to call and gather his church, and to save them; and that he sent his word, his ministers, and Spirit to this end. He is the principle of life to the church his body; who first by aggregation uniteth them to himself, and one another, and then is their constitutive, and governing, and quickening Head. It is his undertaken office first to make all his own members, and then to govern, preserve, edify, and save them. And how can Christ make his church without uniting the members? Can he build his house, and never set the bricks, stones, or timber together? Can you make a clock or watch, without adapting and uniting the parts? And can Christ gather, build, compaginate, and unite his church, and not so much as tell men (either pastors or people) what are the conditions and terms of union, and the cement or solder that must unite them?

And all christians confess Christ's sufficiency for his office, and his perfect faithfulness in performing it. He wanted neither power, wisdom, nor love (or will) to gather his own church or body. He was faithful as Moses in all God's house. And he that fulfilled all the righteousness of the law, and whatever was imposed on him as a humbled satisfier of justice, surely no less fulfilled all that belonged to him as the grand Administrator, and Benefactor, and Executor of God's mercy and his own will, and as Head over all things to his church, Eph. i. 22, 23.

Nay, as he was the King and Lawgiver of the church, who was to give them all their universal laws, (binding all men,) could he be supposed to have done this faithfully, if he had left out the very terms of church unity and concord, when such unity is essential to the church? Did he send the apostles to disciple and baptize all nations, and be in God's house, (the church,) as Paul calleth Timothy, "pillars and bases of truth," yea, foundations, and master-builders, that must gather his church out of all the world, and yet never tell them what a church is? that is, how the parts must be united?

As he is the Teacher of the church, did he never teach them so necessary a thing, as what essential church unity is? These are such imputations against Christ, as seem to deny him to be Christ; as he would deny God to be God, that would deny his providence and government of the world.

Christ's law is to be both the rule of our actions and his judgment. And if he have left out so great a point as the essentiating terms of church union, what momentous acts of our lives are left to be ungoverned and unjudged by the laws of Christ!

Above all men those are bound to consent to what I say, who hold that Christ's laws have not left so much as a ceremony undetermined, and that nothing may be added or diminished in his worship. How much less then hath he left the essentiating terms of church unity unprescribed!

II. And consequently *ab effectis* we find that Christ did it.

1. He plainly declared what maketh a christian. 2. He declared how all christians should live in love and concord. 3. And how the coalition of these christians maketh his church.

1. It had been strange, if he that came into the world to make men christians, had never told men what a christian is. And if he that sent his apostles to make christians, had set them to do they knew not what, and never told them what a christian is, and consequently what they must persuade men to. And if he that promised justification, pardon, adoption, and glory to all true believers, (that is, to true christians,) had yet never told them how they may know that they are such. And that he that commanded so much christian duty, public and private, and required christians to suffer so much for his sake, and to look for a reward in heaven, should yet never tell them what christianity is. If Christ made christianity, (that is, the laws and description, objects and principle,) then he made a determinate thing: if not, hath he left it to man to make christianity (objectively)? Then how shall we know to whom he gave this power? and how many several species of christianity (or faith) may be made in the world?

It is evident in Scripture, that Christ sent his apostles, and that he taught them what to preach, and particularly that he said, Matt. xxviii. 19, 20, "Go and disciple me all nations, baptizing them in the name of the Father, the Son, and the Holy Ghost, teaching them to observe all things whatever I command you." And it is certain, that a baptized person was then accounted a christian, and baptism was their christening, and that this was the church entrance, and visible symbol of a christian and church member: and that all Christ's church hath so accounted of baptism, to this day; and true tradition is in no one point so full and constant as in this. And moreover, the very nature of the thing itself declareth it. Is not he a christian that believeth according to the sense of the institution, in God the Father, Son, and Holy Ghost, and by a solemn vow and covenant, devoteth himself to him as his God and Father, his Redeemer and Saviour, and his Sanctifier and Comforter, and the Witness of Christ; and that hereupon hath right to justification, adoption, and the heavenly inheritance? Who is a christian, if this be not?

The sense of the catholic church is so notorious in this, that I think there is little disagreement about it. The papists confess it; the protestants confess it. See but Vossii Theses de Baptismo, and Davenant de Bapt. and especially Gataker's Animadversions on that of Davenant. All confess, that all the ancient churches held, that to the duly qualified receiver all sin was pardoned in baptism, and the person put into a state of life; and therefore was a member of the church.

2. And that Christ commanded all christians to take each other as brethren, and to live in love; and that all men by this were to know them to be his disciples, is so fully revealed in Scripture, that it is needless among christians to prove it.

3. As also that such christians united to him their Head are *eo nomine* his church; and living in this love, live as the members of his church must do.

And here three things are to be noted. 1. That what was done by the Holy Spirit, as given extraordinarily to the apostles as founders or architects of the church, to lead them into all truth, was truly done by Christ himself; the Holy Ghost so extraordinarily given, being his promised Agent.

2. That yet this work of instituting baptism as the terms of church union, he would not leave to the Spirit in the apostles, but was the immediate author of it himself.

3. But yet two things hereabout he left to the apostles: 1. To explain to the baptized the true sense of the general words in the baptismal covenant. 2. And to institute part of the terms of particular church order and unity, who accordingly settled (or ordained) elders, bishops, or pastors, in every particular church, which at first was for the most part in every city (or great town) where the gospel was received by any competent number; and after they added deacons and deaconesses, or widows *ad melius esse* only, and they taught them by word and writing to observe all that Christ commanded.

III. And as I have proved, 1. That it must be done; 2. And that Christ did it; so, 3. It is part of our proof that no other did it, or could do it.

1. No other had authority to institute church essentials, and to give such necessary universal laws. 2. No other came early enough to do it, but as his ministers after Christ had done it. 3. No other had wisdom and fitness enough for it, nor were fit to agree to make church essentials. 4. *De facto* history proves they did it not. 5. To undertake it is to invade Christ's office. The apostles themselves found it done to their hands. Much less can any ordinary pastors since prove any authority from God, or any true capacity in themselves, for such a work.

And if any pretend to it, they must be such as lived before Christ had any evangelical church, (that is, of the same species as hath been since the institution of christian baptism,) or such as have lived only since. The former came not in as competitors; the latter were too late to be the doers of that which was done before. Union is essential to the church in general: the necessary terms of union are essential to it *in specie* as the christian church: for *necessarium est sine quo res esse non potest.* It is no christian church without the necessary terms of church union. And therefore before those terms were first made or instituted there was no church of that species; and after there was such a church, and consequently such terms of its union, none could make them, they being made before.

If any that came after did or shall hereafter attempt to make such terms, it must be new ones, and not the same that constituted the first church: and then their church will be new, and not of the same species as the first. Indeed God did make new laws of administration, and so may a kingdom, without changing the constitution; but not new constituting terms. Governing laws which follow the constitution, are not to make the kingdom a kingdom, or the church a church; but to preserve the church and its order, and promote its welfare: and the oath of allegiance maketh a man a subject, without subscribing to the governing laws; but as a subject he consenteth to live under those laws; and if he break them, he is punishable according to them, and for breaking some of them may be cut off; and for some crimes a man may be excommunicate.

But yet excommunication must be distinguished: that which totally cuts a man off from the church, must be but a sentence upon proof that he hath first morally cut off himself. Lesser crimes must be punished with the lesser excommunication, which is but a suspension, and that which Paul speaketh of, 2 Thess. iii. 15, "Yet take him not for an enemy, but admonish him as a brother."

By all this it is most evident, that Christ himself, the Institutor and Maker of his church, hath made the terms of essential catholic union; and that we have nothing to do herein, but to find out what are the terms that he hath made, and not to inquire what any men since have made or added, as being not authorized thereto.

CHAPTER X.

NO HUMAN TERMS, NOT MADE BY CHRIST, OR HIS SPIRIT EXTRAORDINARILY GIVEN TO THE APOSTLES, ARE NECESSARY TO THE BEING OF PARTICULAR CHURCHES: BUT DIVERS HUMAN ACTS ARE NECESSARY TO THEIR EXISTENCE AND ADMINISTRATION.

Divers men speak diversely of this matter: 1. Some say that no form of the polity of particular churches is of divine institution, but that God hath left all the forming of them to the will of man.

2. Others say, that no form of them is lawful but what is of divine institution.

And of the first, some say that Christ instituted the papal form, and some say general councils, the *summam potestatem* to the universal church, and left it to them to form particular churches. Others say that magistrates are to do it; and others that the diocesan bishops of every nation in national or provincial synods may do it. But all agree that the form of particular churches must be made by some that had authority from Christ to do it.

Of the second sort, (who hold no form of a particular church lawful, but what is of divine institution,) some hold that only a diocesan church (that hath many congregations and altars) is of divine institution, and that the parochial are not churches, but oratories, or chapels, or parts of a church. Others hold that only parochial churches (of one altar, or associated for personal communion in presence) are of divine institution: some that both diocesan and parochial churches are of divine institution; and some that these and provincial, national, patriarchal, (and the papal,) are of divine institution: thus do men's judgments vary.

A third sort hold that God hath instituted some church forms besides the universal, and left men to make others: and here some think that God instituted patriarchal, and left them to make the diocesans and parochial; some hold that God instituted only the diocesan, and left them power to make the patriarchal and the parochial; some hold that he made only the parochial, (I mean single societies associated for present personal communion,) and left them by voluntary associations to make the greater over them.

Among these opinions let us first try whether Christ hath instituted any church form besides the universal. And, 2. What that is.

I. And, 1. If Christ hath instituted a holy christian society for ordinary holy communion and mutual help in God's public worship and holy living, consisting of pastors authorized and obliged to teach, and guide, and speak for the flock in God's public worship, and administer his sacraments according to Christ's word, and of a flock obliged to hear them, learn, obey, and follow such their conduct to the foresaid ends, then Christ hath instituted a form of a particular church, and its policy. But the antecedent is true, as shall be proved; and the consequent or major is proved, *a definito ad denominatum;* this definition containeth the essentials of a church. No man can deny that to be a christian church which hath this definition.

Here still it is supposed that the Spirit in the apostles, who were designed to be founders and master-builders, and to gather and order churches, and teach them to observe all Christ's commands, was Christ's promised Agent (as Tertullian calls him); and that Christ did what the Spirit did by the apostles in their proper work, to which he was promised them as their Guide; as it is aforesaid.

And that Christ and his apostles instituted sacred ordinary assemblies of christians for holy worship and communion, is so clear in the New Testament that it were vain to prove it.

And, 2. As notorious and past doubt it is that the end of these assemblies was such as is here mentioned. 3. And as plain that such pastors as are here described were set over all these congregations, and authorized and obliged to the foresaid work, that is under Christ the great Teacher, Priest, and Ruler of the church, to teach them God's word, to intercede under Christ for them to God, and from Christ to them in prayer and sacraments, &c. and to guide them by that called the keys of the church, discerning whom to receive by baptism, whom to reprove, exhort, comfort, or absolve. Acts xiv. 23; xx.; 1 Tim. iii.; Tit. i. and many other places show this.

And it is no less plain that the people were bound to continue in their doctrine, communion, and prayer, and to obey them in that which they were commissioned to do, Heb. xiii. 7, 13, 24; x. 25, 26; 1 Thess. v. 12, 13; 1 Tim. v. 17; xx.; and many other places; so that the form of such churches, as consist of such congregations and their pastors, is past all denial and just doubt.

And as to all other church forms, classical, diocesan, metropolitical, provincial, national, patriarchal, and papal, it is these only that fall under reasonable doubt and controversy. And, 1. For classical churches, I can say but this, 1. That the general commands of holding christian love and concord, and doing all to edification, require such churches as live near together to be helpers to each other, and that counsel and correspondency is necessary hereto, which the churches have still laudably exercised by synods; and if these associations for order sake be agreed on, as to stated times, and numbers, and bounds, it is but the circumstantiating of a known duty: and if any will call this a distinct policy or church form, I contend not against their liberty of speech, while we agree *de re;* but I judge it perilous to give the same name to such an assembly or association as to a church of Christ's institution, lest it seduce men to think that the word is not equivocally used. If the agents of several kingdoms met at a common diet, I had rather not call them a superior kingdom, were their meeting never so necessary. An assembly, that is the *pars imperans* of one body politic, having legislative power, is one thing; and an assembly of agents or princes for mere concord and strength, and help of distinct kingdoms, schools, armies, &c. is another thing. And I know no proof that such councils must be ordinary, or at stated times and places, but sometimes that is best, and sometimes not, as the case standeth, as even the papists confess. And when they begin to degenerate from a council for concord to a majesty or highest governing power, it is time to cross their claim, and interrupt the occasions of it.

And if men at such classes and councils choose one to keep order as a moderator, yea, if they fix him, it is but the circumstantiating of the assemblies' work: but if it will claim hereupon a distinct order, office, and proper political church relation, so as hence to make himself the regent part of a species of a church, yea, and claim this as of God and unalterable, I cannot justify such a church form.

This holds as to the presidents of all ranks of synods, classical, diocesan, metropolitical, provincial, national, or patriarchal. To use them as presidents of councils for concord is one thing; and to use them as the *pars imperans,* or the constitutive heads of a distinct church species, is another. Archbishop Usher told me himself his judgment, that councils were but for counsel and concord, and not for the government of each other, or any of the members; and that they had no proper governing power, either over their minor part, or over any absent bishops: though each bishop was still the governor of his own flock, and their power over their flocks was exercised with the greater advantage by their concord in councils. Diets and councils of distinct independent bishops are not distinct forms of policy or churches.

And if this hold true, that the councils themselves are not thereby rectors of a distinct political society, but for concord of many, then it will follow that a president of such a council, whether diocesan, provincial, national, or more general, is not as such a rector of the bishops under him and their people, but only the orderer or guide of the modes and circumstances of the council as such. And therefore could the pope prove a right to preside in general councils, *(orbis Romani, vel orbis terrarum,)* which he cannot, it were no proof that he is regent head of the church universal. The same I may say of the other presidents.

If it hold that God instituted only congregational or parochial churches, (as for present communion,) then it must needs follow that none of the rest instituted by man have power to deprive such single churches of any of the privileges granted them by Christ: and therefore whereas Christ hath made the terms of catholic communion himself, and hath commanded all such to worship him publicly in holy communion under faithful pastors, chosen, or at least consented to, by themselves, (which many hundred years was the judgment of the churches,) no human order or power can deprive them of any of this benefit, nor disoblige them from any of this duty, by just authority.

Nay, seeing that the universal church is certainly the highest species, none hath authority on pretence of narrower communion in lower churches, to change Christ's terms of catholic communion, nor to deprive christians of the right of being loved and received by each other, or disoblige them from the duty of loving and receiving each other. Human power made by their own contracts cannot change Christ's laws, nor the privileges or forms of Christ's own churches.

They that say that these several church species are of God, must prove that God instituted them; and that can be only by Scripture: or else that he gave some power to institute them since Scripture times: which till they prove, none are bound to obey them, at least when they overrule Christ's own institutions.

To devise new species of churches, without God's authority, and impose them on the world, (yea, in his name,) and call all dissenters schismatics, is a far worse usurpation than to make and impose new ceremonies or liturgies.

Dr. Hammond (Dissert. cont. Blond. et Annot. in Act. xi. et pass.) affirmeth that it cannot be proved that the order of subject-presbyters was existent in Scripture times; and consequently holdeth that bishops had but single congregations (as Ignatius speaketh, with one altar). Now if diocesans, metropolitans, provincials, patriarchs, or pope, as constitutive of church species, were made after, either these new churches were made by the bishops of parochial churches, or by those that were no bishops or pastors of any churches at all. (For the apostles were dead, and no institution of these but Scriptural can be truly proved. And other churches besides the catholic and parochial, or single, (distinct from a compound of churches) there were then none.) For the lower to make the higher churches is that which they will not grant, who grant not that presbyters may propagate their own species; and deny that power ascendeth *ab inferioribus.* And that men of no church made all these new church species is no honour to them.

Two contrary opinions herein now reign: one of the papists, that think Christ instituted the pope with power to make inferior church species; the other is, that Christ or his apostles instituted diocesans, giving them power, both as rulers to make parish churches (or chapels) under them, and by contract or consent to make the highest species over them (provincial, national, patriarchal, and, say some, papal). But as to the papists so much is said against their supposition, that it is not here to be confuted: and it is certain that single church order was constituted by no pope, and that all the apostles had power thereto. And as for the latter, which affirmeth the lower degrees to make their higher, we still want the proofs of their authority so to do; of which more afterwards.

As for them that say, that it is magistrates that have power to make new species of churches, I grant them that whatever alterations of church orders may be made, magistrates may do much in them. The power of princes, and the guidance of pastors, and the consent of the people, have each herein their special place. But what these alterations or additions are which they may make is the chief question: both the catholic church, and single church assemblies, being instituted by Christ, are not left to them. The circumstantiating of other assemblies and associations are left to them, to be done according to God's general law: but that making new political societies that are properly called churches, or religious bodies, consisting of the *pars regens*, and *pars subdita*, is left to them by Christ, I never saw proved, any more than the making of new sacraments. But if that could be proved, yet that these human churches or their makers may change those that are of divine institution, or deprive them of their privileges, or forbid them commanded duty, cannot be proved.

And it is certain, 1. That if princes, or bishops, or the people, did institute diocesan or metropolitan, provincial or patriarchal churches, they may yet make more and other species: and who knoweth how many new forms of churches we may yet expect? 2. And they that made them, upon good reason, may unmake them, or alter them when they please.

But though the legislator, and not the subjects, be the institutor of the universal and particular church policies, yet men are the constitutive matter, and man's consent and faith is the *dispositio materiæ*, without which the form is not received: and man's welfare is part of the final cause; and ministers are the instruments (and God's word written and preached) for the gathering of churches by such qualification of the persons, and also of revealing the institution of Christ, and investing of particular persons in their church relations.

By all this it appeareth, that as it belongeth to Christ to institute the political species of churches, (though circumstantiating may be left to man,) at least, undoubtedly of the universal and of the single species; so it belongeth to Christ, and not to man, to institute and describe their terms of union; for this is the very institution of the species: and we are not to receive human church policies without good proof of men's authority, to make them, and impose them.

CHAPTER XI.

THE DANGER OF THE TWO EXTREMES: AND FIRST OF DESPAIRING OF ANY CONCORD, AND OF UNJUST TOLERATIONS.

SOME men having seen the christian world so long in sects and contending parties, do think that there is no hope of unity and concord, and therefore that all should be left at liberty; and others think that there is no hope but on terms so wide as shall take such as Christ receiveth not, nor would have us receive. And on such accounts there were very early great contentions about the qualifications of the baptizers and baptized, and the validity of baptism, and about re-baptizing.

As to the baptizers, some thought that only priests should baptize (none appropriated it to bishops): some thought lay-men might baptize in case of necessity, and some thought that women also might do it: and some thought that though women or lay-men might not do it lawfully, yet *factum valet*, being done, such should not be re-baptized. And some thought that those that were baptized, even by priests that were schismatics, (or as they called them, heretics, when they separated from common concord and communion,) must be re-baptized. And they thought that if they were baptized in such a schismatical (or heretical) society, by whomsoever, it was not into the true church. In this case Cyprian and the African bishops, with Firmilian and his colleagues, were in the wrong, when the bishop of Rome was in the right. And the Donatists thought they were but of Cyprian's mind; for it seems they had there the greater number of bishops; and the greater number went for the church, and the less for heretics; and so they called themselves the church (though out of Africa the number against them, or that meddled not in the quarrel, was far greater). And all this arose but by the contests of two men for the bishopric of Carthage, some following one, and some the other.

This error of Cyprian and the Donatists arose, 1. From their not sufficiently distinguishing the church universal, from the associated churches of their country; nor well considering that baptism as such is but our entrance into the universal church, and not into this or that particular church. 2. By an abusive or equivocal use of the name heretic, their doctrine being true of heretics strictly so called, who deny in baptizing any essential part of christianity, but false of heretics laxly so called, that are only schismatics, or deny only or corrupt some lower doctrines, precepts, or practices of religion.

Therefore the council of Nice truly decided the case by distinction, decreeing the re-baptizing of some, (as such as the Paulinists baptized,) and not of others. That is, all that had not true christian baptism, consisting of all the true essentials, were to be re-baptized, and not others, whatever particular church they were of.

Hereupon also among the Roman doctors it hath been a great debate, whether the priest's intention was necessary to the validity of baptism: the true answer to which is this.

It is one question, what is necessary to the justifying of the priest before the church? and another, before God? and another question, What is necessary to the validity of baptism to the receiver before the church? and another, before God? And so I answer:

Supposing that no man shall suffer for another's fault, but for his own: 1. If the priest profess an intention to baptize in general, and express it in the true words of baptism, his act *ex parte sui* is valid *coram ecclesia*, though he dissemble.

2. If the priest dissemble, his act is a crime, and shall be punished by God.

3. If he profess not to intend to baptize the person, or to intend it in general, but to corrupt it in the essentials, it is as a ministration invalid *coram ecclesia*, and should be done again.

4. If the adult person baptized profess baptismal consent dissemblingly, it is valid baptism *coram ecclesia*, as to what the church must do upon it, but invalid as to what God is to do as the performer of the covenant.

5. If the person baptized do not so much as profess consent, or profess not to consent, nor to intend to be then baptized, it is no baptism before God or the church.

6. If he profess to be baptized in general, but deny any essential in particular, it is not the true christian baptism, but must be better done.

When any came in so great error, as that the church scarce knew whether it was an essential part of faith and baptism that was denied, it made the controversy hard about their re-baptizing. Many thought that the Photinians and Arians, denying Christ's Godhead as of the same substance with the

Father, denied an essential article, and were to be re-baptized if they so entered at first: our Socinians are much worse, that deny Christ's Godhead in a fuller sense. And how doth he believe in Christ that believeth him not to be God, which is most eminently essential to him?

They that are over-bold in altering Christ's terms of church union and communion, making them less, or more, or other, if they knew what they do, would find themselves more concerned in these controversies of baptizing and re-baptizing, and consequently greater corrupters than they have thought.

To think that church union is impossible, is to deny that there is any church, and consequently any Christ. To think that necessary concord in communion is impossible, is so great a disparagement to the church, as tempteth men by vilifying it to doubt of christianity: for if christians cannot live in unity of faith, and love, and converse, what is their christianity? And such despair of concord will make men suspend all endeavours to attain it: for despair useth no means.

And to take into the church of Christ such as want the essentials, and Christ would not have received, is to corrupt his church, and bring in confusion, and such as will dishonour him, and will be more hurtful in the church than they would be without: like rebels in a kingdom, or mutineers in an army, or enemies in a family: the nearer the worse.

It is for this use especially that Christ hath committed the church keys to the pastors. And the key of entrance is the chief. Therefore he that judgeth who is to be baptized, exerciseth the chief act of the church keys; and he that baptized was held to have the power of judging whom to baptize: which was never denied to the presbyters, till after for order some restrained them.

It is a strange contrariety of some pastors to themselves, who judge that all infants of heathens, Jews, Turks, or wicked men, are without exception to be taken into the church, if any ignorant christian will but offer them, and say over a few words; and the adult also if they can but say over the creed by rote, and a few words more; and thus fill the church with enemies of Christ: and yet when they are in, deny them communion, unless they will strictly come up to many human unnecessary impositions; as if far stricter obedience to men (perhaps in usurpations) were necessary, than to Jesus Christ.

How far infidels, catechumens, or heretical or schismatical assemblies, may be tolerated in the world about us by magistrates, is not here to be inquired, but hereafter; but that the churches themselves should not corrupt their own communion, by taking and keeping in uncapable persons, the nature of the church and discipline, and its ends, and the reproof of the churches, Rev. ii. and iii. and the judgment of the universal church, do tell us.

CHAPTER XII.

THE SIN AND DANGER OF MAKING TOO MUCH NECESSARY TO CHURCH UNION AND COMMUNION.

Addition to Christ's terms are very perilous as well as diminution: when men will deny either church entrance or communion to any that Christ would have received, because they come not up to certain terms which they or such as they devise. And though they think that Christ giveth them power to do thus, or that reason or necessity justifieth them, their error will not make them guiltless: imputing their error to Christ untruly, is no small aggravation of the sin.

Nor is it a small fault to usurp a power proper to Christ; to make themselves lawgivers to his church without any authority given them by him: their ministry is another work.

And it is dangerous pride to think themselves great enough, wise enough, and good enough, to come after Christ, and to amend his work, and do it better than he hath done.

Much less when they hereby imply an accusation against him and his institutions, as if he had not done it well, but they must amend it, or all will be intolerable.

And indeed man's work will be like man, weak, and faulty, and full of flaws; when God's work will be like God, the effect of all-sufficience, power, wisdom, and love.

And the merciful Lord and Saviour of the church, that came to take off heavy burdens and intolerable yokes, will not take it well to have men come after him, and as by his authority, to make his easy yoke more strait, and his light burden heavy, and to cast or keep out those that he hath redeemed, and doth receive, and to deal cruelly with those that he hath so dearly bought, and tenderly loveth.

And indeed it is ofter for men's own interest and dominion, to keep up their power and honour of superiority, that men thus use the servants of Christ, than truly to keep clear the church, and to keep out the polluters.

But when it is done by too much strictness, and as for church purity, yet this also hath its aggravations: for men so far to forget themselves, that they are servants and not lords, sinners that have need themselves of mercy, unfit to be too forward to cast the first stone, to seem more wise and holy than Christ, is but specious offending him.

And as spiritual privileges excel temporal, so is it an aggravated tyranny to deprive Christ's servants of benefits so precious, and so dearly bought. As it was not with silver and gold that we were redeemed, so neither for the enjoying of silver and gold. Communion with Christ, his body and blood, and his saints in his ordinances, is a blessing so great, that he that robs such of it that have right to it, may answer it dearlier than if he had robbed them of their purses. Oh what then hath the Roman usurper done that hath oft interdicted whole kingdoms of christians the use of holy privileges and duties!

Little do many men, that cry up faith, and orthodoxness, and catholicism, and obedience, and cry down heresy, schism, error, and disobedience, believe how much guilt lieth on their souls, and without repentance how terrible it will prove, to be charged with the cruelties which they have used to good christians, in reproaching them, and casting them out of the church, and destroying them as heretics and schismatics, that should have been loved and honoured as saints. But some men cannot see by the light of the fire, till they come so near it as to be burned.

These self-made or overdoing terms of church union and concord will prove the certainest engines of schism; and none are so heinous schismatics, as they that make unnecessary terms of union, and then call all schismatics that consent not to them. For, 1. These are the leaders of the disorder, when other sort of schismatics usually are but followers. 2. These do it by law, which is of most extensive mischief, even to all that are subject to them, when others do it but by local practice, extending but to those that are about them, or the particular assemblies which they gather. 3. These make the schism unavoidable, when private seducers may be resisted: for it is not in the power of good men to bring their judgments to the sentiments of every or any dictator, or yet to go contrary to their judgments. *Illicitum stat pro impossibili.* 4. These aggravate the crime by pretending power from God, and fathering schism on so good a thing as government, and causing it as for unity itself. 5. They condemn themselves by crying down schism, while they unavoidably cause it.

And this over-doing and making unnecessary terms, unavoidably involveth them in the guilt of persecution; and when they have begun it, they know not where to stop. Suppose they decree that none shall preach the gospel, or assemble for holy communion in public worship, but those that subscribe, or swear, or promise, or profess, or do, somewhat accounted sinful by the persons commanded, and not necessary indeed, however esteemed by the imposer (who yet perhaps calls it but indifferent). It is certain that no honest christian will do that which he judgeth to be sin: it is certain that other men's confident talk will not make all men of their minds, to take all for lawful which they take for such. What then will the imposers do? They will make strict laws to punish severely all that disobey; for say they, our commands must not be contemned, nor disobedience tolerated: so do the papists as to the Trent oath, &c. so did Charles the Fifth awhile about the Interim, and so many others. These laws then must be executed; the pastors must be cast out, the preachers silenced: they still believe as Daniel did about praying, and the apostles about preaching, that God commandeth what men forbid, and it is a damnable sin to forsake their calling and duty, no less than sacrilege, and cruelty to souls, and deserting the church, and worship, and cause of Christ; and the people will still believe that no man's prohibition can excuse them if they forsake God's public worship, and comply with sin. The prelates will say that all this is but error, wilfulness, and rebellion, and they can prove the contrary. Their words will not change the judgments of dissenters. The pastors and preachers then must be fined, imprisoned, or banished for preaching, and the people for public worshipping God. When they are fined they will go on; when they are out of prison they will return to their work: nothing is left then to remedy it, but either perpetual imprisonment, banishment, or death. When that is done, more will still rise of the same mind, and continue the work that others were disabled to perform: and the prelates that cause this will be taken by the suffering people for thorns and thistles, and grievous wolves that devour the flocks, and the military ministers of the devil. The indifferent common people, knowing their neighbours to be conscionable men of upright lives, will become of the same minds, and look on the persecutors as the enemies of good men and of public peace, that do all this by pride and domination: the ungodly rabble of drunkards, profane swearers, adulterers, and such like, for the part hating godliness and strict living, will cry up the prelates, and triumph over the sufferers. And thus the land will be divided; the prelates and other persecutors, with the dirty, malignant rabble of the licentious, will make one party, and these will call themselves orthodox and the church; the sufferers, and all that pity them, and like them better than the persecutors, will be the other party. The conjunction of the debauched and malignant rabble, with the prelates and their party, will increase sober men's disaffection to them, and make men take them for the patrons of impiety: and how sad a condition must such churches be in! to say nothing of the state concussions and diseases that usually follow. Whatever ignorant men may dream, these prognostics are most certain, as any man that can discern effects in moral causes may see, and as history and sad experience prove to all men of reading, observation, and understanding.

And in pastors of the church this will be a double crime and shame: because, 1. It is their office to gather and edify Christ's flock, and not to scatter and afflict them. 2. Because they should most imitate Christ in tender bowels, gentleness, and long-suffering, bearing the lambs in their arms, and not breaking the bruised reed, nor quenching the smoking flax: nurses or mothers use not to kill their children for crying, nor to turn them out of doors because they are unclean, nor to cut their throats to make them swallow bigger morsels, instead of cutting their meat; much less to cast them off for obeying their father. 3. Because it is supposed that they best know the will of Christ, and should be best acquainted with the ways of peace. And therefore should understand Rom. xiv. and xv. "Him that is weak in the faith receive ye; but not to doubtful disputations. The kingdom of God is not meats and drinks, but righteousness, peace, and joy in the Holy Ghost. And he that in these things serveth Christ, is acceptable to God, and approved of men;" that is, of wise and good men, but not of proud persecutors, Rom. xiv. 17, 18. "Wherefore receive ye one another, as Christ also received us to the glory of God," Rom. xv. 7. If the people were schismatical, and inclined to fall in pieces, the guides and builders should solder and cement them, and as pillars and bases in the church, which is the house of the living God, (as Timothy is called,) should bear them up that they fall not by division.

In a word, whoever will impartially read church history, especially of the councils and popes, shall find that the self-conceited usurpation of proud prelates, imposing unnecessary devices of their own (professions or practices) on the churches, and this with proud and fierce impatience toward dissenters, and usurping a legislation which Christ never gave them, hath been the great cause of much of the hatred, schisms, persecutions, wars, rebellions, against emperors and kings, false excommunications, interdicts, and the disgrace of christianity, weakening of the church, and hindering the conversion of Jews and infidels, and been a chief grenado, thunderbolt, or wild-fire, by which Satan much prospered in storming of the church.

CHAPTER XIII.

TO CRY OUT OF THE INTOLERABLE MISCHIEFS OF TOLERATION, AND CALL FOR SHARPER EXECUTION, WHILE DIVIDING SNARES ARE MADE THE TERMS OF UNION, IS THE WORK OF IGNORANT, PROUD, AND MALIGNANT CHURCH DESTROYERS.

To tolerate all evil that pretendeth religion, is to be no friend to religion, government, or peace. To tolerate no error in religion, is for no prince to tolerate himself, his wife, his child, or any one subject; and to pretend to this, is to crave self-destruction, *(neque enim lex justior ulla est, &c.)* and to proclaim himself ignorant, yea, grossly ignorant, what is a church, a pastor, a government, a christian, or a man.

Multitudes of books are written for and against toleration. They that are lowest usually write for it. (Even Jer. Taylor's "Liberty of Prophesying," before he was a bishop, was thought a commendable or tolerable book.) But most are against it that are in power, and think they can force others to their wills. But it is wise, and just, and impartial men, that are here the discerners of the truth, whose judgments are not biassed by interest or passion, nor blinded by unacquaintedness with their adversaries or their cause, or perverted by using only one ear and one eye. He knoweth not mankind, who knoweth not how greatly (not only the common gang, but) even learned men, yea, and zealous religious men, are to be suspected in their evil characters and reports of those that are speaking against as adversaries. It grieveth me to know and think how little most adversaries in this case are to be believed.

To describe the due bounds of toleration is far from being impossible or very difficult to an understanding and impartial man; but to stop the mouth or rage of contradicters, and to reconcile the multitude of ignorant, proud, tyrannical, uncharitable, interested, factious, partial men to such certain measures, is next impossible, and never yet even among the clergy was attained, since the spirit of infallibility, simplicity, and love departed, and the spirit of darkness, pride, and malignity in most places got the upper hand.

Many and many books of this nature I have lately read, that cry down liberty and toleration, and call for greater severities, and describe those whose ruin or sufferings they plead for, as ignorantly and falsely, as if they talked of men at the antipodes, whom they had never seen, and as if they had never heard their cause; and as cruelly, as if they had been preaching to soldiers, and confuting John Baptist, or preaching a visitation sermon to Bonner or Gardiner; and yet the falsehoods or injuries set off with so great confidence, and well composed words and zeal against schism and error, and especially for the church and government, that it grieveth my soul to think how difficult such men do make it to strangers that must know all on trust from others, and men of other business, that cannot have while to search into the truth, to escape deceit and the consequent mischiefs. Zeal for piety is not more abused by sectaries, than zeal for themselves and their power and wealth, called zeal for the church, and truth, and order, is abused by bad, domineering men; or else the world had not been embroiled by the clergy these twelve hundred years at least, nor Rome arrived at its pernicious greatness and power to destroy.

And let men's different religions or opinions be never so many and notable, yet every where the same plea against toleration is used, and the same arguments seem good for every party that is in power. In Japan, and China, and heathen lands, they can copiously declaim against the mischiefs of tolerating christianity. The papists think tormenting inquisitions, and burning christians, and murdering thousands and hundreds of thousands, better than to tolerate protestants. The Lutherans cry down the toleration of Calvinists. What need I name more? As the papists say, that every sect pleadeth the Scripture, so we may say, that every powerful party, be their cause never so false, cry out against tolerating others, though in the truth.

And doubtless concord even in perfection is so desirable, that it is easy for a man to set forth the beauty and excellency of it; and discord is so bad, that it is easy to declaim against it: but for him that causeth it, to do it, is self-condemnation; and for him that falsely describeth the cause, and justifieth the schismatic, and accuseth the innocent, to write books and preach sermons against schism and toleration, is but delusion, tending to their own shame, and others' deceit and ruin.

And he never was a good musician, builder, watchmaker, nor good at any art or science, that thought all diversity was discord. He that would with zeal and learning write a book to prove that a lute or organs must not be tolerated, if each string and key be not of the same sound; or that all the parts in a clock, watch, building, &c. must be of the same shape and magnitude; or all men of one language or complexion, &c.; would scarce get so much credit as most of our hereticaters do, when they call for fire, and faggot, and jailers, as more meet and able confuters of error than themselves.

The men on whom they cry for vengeance, either are really religious, or not; if not, it is a marvel that they are not of the accusers' mind, being supposed to follow the upper side. It is possible that some advantage may turn a man that hath no religion out of the king's highway, into some sectarian cottage, especially in some storms; but it is very rarely that gain goeth not for godliness, and the way of reputation, ease, and profit, for religion, with such as indeed have none at all. But if they are seriously religious, they take it as from the law of the Almighty, the King of kings, and Lord of lords, to whom all men are less than the vilest worms to us; and they take it to be that which they lay their salvation and everlasting hopes on; believing that God will bear them out; and if they die for it, will reward them with the crown of glory: they believe that they shall be damned in hell for ever if they break God's law, and obey man against him; and in this case it should not be hard to reasonable men, especially bishops and teachers, to know what means and measures are meetest to be used with such men; and when he that must suffer, hath flesh that is as unwilling to suffer as other men's, it should be considered how far Satan be flesh for his interest, and how far the pastors of the church should take part with it; whenas St. Paul saith, He that doubteth is damned if he eat, because he eateth not of faith.

There is no heed to be taken by men's crying out against error or schism, to discern who is the erroneous or schismatic. None more cry out against them than the guilty. Who condemneth error and schism more than the papists? And who are greater causes and authors of them than the pope? As our common profane rabble are so great hypocrites, that they live quite contrary to their baptismal vow, and the religion which they nominally profess, and yet commonly cry out against hypocrisy, and call all men hypocrites that seem to be serious in living as they vowed and profess; even so the greatest schismatics and heretics, partly in blindness, and partly to avert both men and conscience from accusing themselves, do usually first cry down schismatics and heretics, and perhaps preach and write most vehemently against them. I take a man to be never the more orthodox, catholic, or of the true church, for crying up the true church catholicism and orthodoxness, and crying down the contrary, and accusing others.

I have long observed with the best judgment I have, that usually those divines that write most for peace and reconciliation of hot contenders, are men of clearer judgment than others, and usually see further into the cause, than either of the fierce contending parties. Though the Turks in policy give some liberty to christians, as a necessary preservation of their empire; and the Socinians have much pleaded for peace and concord, partly by necessity for themselves, and partly from common light of reason; yet among real reformed christians, the greatest judgment is found in the greatest pacificators; such as Le Blank, Amyrald, Placeus, Camero, Lud. Crocius, Bergius, Martinius, Calixtus, Dallæus, Blondel, Usher, Davenant, Hall, Morton, Chillingworth, and such others: darkness doth best fit the spirit of contention.

There is nothing in human actions that is free from inconveniences; especially actions of public consequence. And the collecting and aggravating of such inconveniences, and making tragical exclamations thereupon, without looking to the mischiefs that men imagine must be the remedy, or seeing the evils on the other side, is the common practice of these church mountebanks. How easy is it to say, If we be not all of one religion, it will cherish contention, bring ministers into contempt, scandalize the weak, harden the enemies, raise factions, shake the peace of kingdoms; and more such like! How easy is it to say, If men be tolerated to break the laws, and gather conventicles, souls will be poisoned, error propagated, christianity disgraced, &c.! When in the mean time, 1. Their course tendeth not at all to make men of one religion. 2. Nay, they plead for that which is the great divider: where do fire, and banishment, or prisons, cause true faith, or make men think that their persecutors are in the right? Is there any thing in the nature of the thing so to persuade men? Nay, what more inclineth men to think that other men's opinions are false, than to feel that their practice is hurtful? All will say, Do men gather grapes of thorns, or figs of thistles? By their fruit they may be known. If it be forcing some to dissemble, and destroying the rest, that they mean by making men of one religion; thus saith Tertullian did the heathen persecutors. *Solitudinem faciunt et pacem vocant*. But, 1. This will not do: France, Ireland, Belgia, and Queen Mary in England, tried it in vain. God will still have some that shall be seriously religious, and shall fear him more than man, and not sell their souls to save their bodies. If you have no hope of making men to be of one religion, but by making them to be of no religion, (as all are that fear not God more than man,) your hopes are vain as well as wicked. There is so full testimony given to the world, that there is a God, and a life to come, that still some men will believe it, and will think whither they must go next, and therefore will not forsake their religion through fear, seeing that is to forsake their God and their salvation.

2. And if you could accomplish it, it were not worth your labour. If all the princes on earth should force their subjects to be of one religion, it would be their own: and then five parts of six would be heathens and Mahometans, and of the sixth part a third or fourth would be papists, and above two parts of the other three would have foul corruptions, for which they would be sharply censured by the rest. Is it not better that in Congo, China, &c. christianity is tolerated, than that they had all continued of their one religion? And so is it that the Turks do tolerate the Greeks and other christians. And I think if Spain had both papists and protestants, it were better than to have but papists only; and if the Swedes, Danes, and Saxons, did tolerate the more reformed, it would do more good than harm. If prelacy were banished out of Scotland and England, many would think it better to tolerate it.

It is certain that unity and concord is most desirable; and as certain that these over-doers do destroy it, while they lay it upon impossible terms. 1. The most desirable concord is in common perfection of wisdom and holiness: but it is certain it will not be, nor are any perfect.

2. The next desirable concord is in such high degrees of wisdom and goodness, as that all christians be strong and excellent, and err not notably in a word, ceremony, or mode: but it is certain this is not to be expected.

3. The next degree desirable is, that all should be so far teachable and persuadable, as to yield to every truth and lawful imposition, when reason is set before them: but it is certain this is not to be expected; and he that denieth it, knoweth not man.

A peace-maker therefore must understand, 1. What concord is already among all christians, and what is of necessity to communion with the church universal. 2. And what more is necessary to communion in a particular church. 3. And what more is necessary to the association and concord of such particular churches. 4. And what is necessary only to eminency, praise, and special encouragement. 5. And what is necessary to mere human neighbourhood and converse.

And accordingly he should study, 1. How all men may be used like men, and all peaceable men as peaceable. 2. How all christians may be used as christians. 3. How all the members of particular churches may hold such concord as the ends of their society require. 4. How all such churches may keep such love and correspondency as tendeth to the good of all. 5. And how eminent christians may be used according to their worth. 6. And how heresy and sin may be suppressed without contradicting any of these ends.

If once unnecessary terms of unity and concord be taken for necessary, even multitudes of honest, well-meaning men, will hence bend all their strength to do mischief: they will think that all peacemakers must promote these terms; and all must be used as schismatics that are against them. And so all the forementioned accusations, cruelties, and persecutions will (alas) go for the work even of peacemakers: and so the common engine of church division, and persecution, and discord, will be preaching and writing against schism, and crying up peace, and aggravating dissent as a heinous crime, even when it is a duty, and making all odious as far as they can, that are not of their mind.

THE TRUE CATHOLIC,

AND

CATHOLIC CHURCH DESCRIBED;

AND THE VANITY OF THE PAPISTS, AND ALL OTHER SCHISMATICS, THAT CONFINE THE CATHOLIC CHURCH TO THEIR SECT, DISCOVERED AND SHAMED.

THE PREFACE.

READER,

THE tumultuary contentions and distractions about the *catholic church*, which have been raised by many heretical and schismatical firebrands, have moved me to publish these popular sermons, in order to the satisfaction and settlement of such minds as have been insnared to a misunderstanding of this article of the creed. It grieved me to hear so many christians, that were all baptized into the catholic church, and there received the badge of christianity and catholicism, to be doubtfully inquiring which is the true catholic church, and many dividers confining it to their sects; and lastly, the seekers (instructed by the papists) with seeming seriousness questioning whether there be any church and ministry at all. But never any sect did cause my admiration so much as the papist; that ever so many princes and learned men should so odiously vilify the catholic church, and that under pretence of magnifying it, and appealing to it. They are not contented in their doctrine of transubstantiation, to deny sense and reason, *(et contra rationem nemo sobrius,)* and in many writings to speak diminutively and dishonourably of the holy Scriptures, (too like to infidels: *et contra Scripturas nemo christianus);* but they also cut off themselves (as sectaries) from the universal church, as far as an uncharitable, odious condemning of the far greatest part of the church can do it, and call the church (even that greatest part) by the name of heretics and schismatics *(et contra ecclesiam nemo pacificus).* And as confidently and contentiously do they labour to cut off the main body of believers, and to appropriate the catholic church to themselves, and to make their corrupted sect to be the whole, as if the catholic church had been limited to the *Roman* in the Scripture, or the creed; or as if they had the consent of Christ himself for the divorcing of his spouse. And the men that call charity the form, and soul, and life of the new creature, do seem to be insensible of the brand of their unhappiness; and that there is no greater uncharitableness to be found on this side hell, than the malicious reproaching, condemning, and unchurching of the far greatest part of the church of Christ; except that of infidels, who condemn the whole. When you hear them glorifying of their charity, come hither and rub your eyes, and see what popish charity is.

For the right understanding of this following discourse, I shall only desire the reader to observe, 1. That it is not a particular church, but the universal, that I am here inquiring after. 2. That I do not intend hereby to equalize the several parts of the catholic church, as to purity of doctrine, discipline, or worship. 3. That yet I would have all christians join themselves in actual particular communion with the purest churches, if they can obtain it, without greater hurt to themselves or others, than the benefits will countervail. And that I do not intend that we must hold local communion with every congregation, which must be owned as a part of the catholic church. It is possible they may require a participation in some sin of all those that they will admit to their communion; and in such cases (when they exclude us) we can hold but such a general distant communion, which they cannot prohibit. 4. That when I condemn the schism and uncharitableness of the papists, or any others, I yet condemn not, but commend, our exercise of charity to them; and shall own all that is of Christ in them, as far as I can discern it.

Lastly, be advertised, that whereas in another book, that comes out with this, (called "Catholic Unity,") I have again taken up many of the particulars wherein the godly are united; I think it need not offend the reader, as an unnecessary repetition, that being but the application of the truth which is here asserted. There I labour to convince the ungodly, that concord can be obtained by no other means, and no other terms, than those which I have here showed the godly are all agreed in.

Reader, if indeed thou love the church of Christ, join with me in thy heartiest daily prayers, and in thy faithful, diligent endeavours, for the destroying of divisions, and the repairing of decayed charity, and restoring of catholic principles and affections to all the members of the church.

RICHARD BAXTER.

December 12, 1659.

1 CORINTHIANS XII. 12.

FOR AS THE BODY IS ONE, AND HATH MANY MEMBERS, AND ALL THE MEMBERS OF THAT ONE BODY, BEING MANY, ARE ONE BODY: SO ALSO IS CHRIST.

It is a pitiful case with the poor afflicted church of Christ, that almost all her members cry out against division, and yet cause and increase it while they speak against it. And that all cry up unity, and yet very few do any thing that is very considerable to promote it; but multitudes are destroying unity, while they commend it: and those few that would heal and close the wounds, are not able by the clearest reasons, and most importunate requests, to hold the hands of others from opposing it; and to get leave of the rest to do that work, which they will not do themselves while they extol it. You would think this were rather the description of a Bedlam, than of a christian; to set all on fire, and furiously to rail at all that would quench it, and at the same time to rail as much at incendiaries, and cry out for concord, and against division, and call other men all that is naught, for doing that which they do themselves, and will not be persuaded from! But to the injurious dishonour of christianity itself, it is thus with millions of professed christians! thus is the church used: the sin and shame is made so public, that no charity can much excuse it, and no shift can cover it from the reproachful observation of those that are without. Alas, our flames do rise so high, that Turks, and Jews, and heathens stand looking on them, and ask, What is the matter that these christians thus irreconcilably worry one another? Do we need any proof, when we feel the smart? when we see the blood? when we hear the noise of revilers at home, and see the scornful laughters of those abroad? when almost all christendom is up in arms? when the churches are of so many by-names, and broken into so many odious fractions; and so many volumes fly abroad, containing the reproaches and condemnations of each other? and (which is enough to break an honest heart to think or speak of) that all this hath continued so long a time? And they be not so wise as the passionate, or the drunken, that in time will come to themselves again; and that it hath continued notwithstanding the greatest means that are used for the cure: mediation prevaileth not; pacificatory endeavours have done almost nothing; nay, sin gets advantage in point of reputation, and dividing is counted a work of zeal, and ministers themselves are the principal leaders of it, yea, and ministers of eminent parts and piety; and piety itself is pretended for this, which is the poison of piety; and pacification is become a suspected or derided work; and the peace-makers are presently suspected of some heresy, and perhaps called dividers for seeking reconciliation. It made my heart ache with grief, the other day, to read over the narrative of the endeavours of one man (Mr. John Dury) to heal the protestant churches themselves, and to think that so much ado should be necessary to make even the leaders of the christian flocks to be willing to cease so odious a sin, and come out of so long and doleful a misery; yea, and that all should do so little good, and get from men but a few good words, while they sit still and suffer the flames to consume the deplorable remnant: yea, such havoc hath division made, and cut the church into so many pieces, that it is become one of the commonest questions among us, which of these pieces it is that is the church: one saith, We are the catholic church; and another saith, No, but it is we; and a third contendeth that it is only they: and thus men seem to be at a loss; and when they believe the holy catholic church, they know not what it is which they say they believe. Though I dare not presume to hope of much success in any attempts against this distraction, after the frustration of the far greater endeavours of multitudes that have attempted it with far greater advantage, yet I have resolved by the help of Christ to bear witness against the sin of the dividers, and leave my testimony on record to posterity, that if it may not excite some others to the work, yet at least it may let them know, that all were not void of desires for peace in this contentious age.

To which purpose I intend, 1. To speak of the unity and concord of the catholic church. 2. Of the unity and concord of christians in their particular churches, and in their individual state. And the first discourse I shall ground upon this text, which from the similitude of a natural body doth assert, 1. The multiplicity of members; and, 2. The unity of the body or church of Christ, notwithstanding the multiplicity of the members. The members are here said to be many for number, and it is intimated (which after is more fully expressed) that they are divers for office, and use, and gifts. The church here spoken of is the universal church, as it is both in its visible and mystical state. It is only a particular church that is here meant; nor is it the catholic church only as a mystical, or only as visible, but as it containeth professors and believers, the body and soul, which make up the man, having both ordinances and spirit in their possession. That it is the catholic church is apparent, 1. In that it is denominated in the text from Christ himself, "So also is Christ." And the universal church is more fitly denominated from Christ as the Head, than a particular church. It is not easy to find any text of Scripture that calleth Christ the Head of a particular congregation, (as we use not to call the king the head of this or that corporation, but of the commonwealth,) though he may be so called, as a head hath respect to the several members: but he is oft called the Head of the catholic church, Eph. i. 22; iv. 15; Col. i. 18; ii. 19; Eph. v. 23. The head of such a body is a commoner phrase than the head of the hand or foot. 2. Because it is expressly called "the body of Christ," which title is not given to any particular church, it being but part of the body, ver. 27. 3. It is such a church that is here spoken of, to which was given apostles, prophets, teachers, miracles, healings, helps, governments, tongues, &c. ver. 28, 8—10. But all particular churches had not all these; and it is doubtful whether Corinth had all that is here mentioned. 4. It is that church which all are baptized into, Jews and gentiles, bond and free: but that is only into the universal church. The Spirit doth not baptize, or enter men first or directly into a particular church; no, nor the baptism of water neither always, nor primarily. The scope of the chapter, and of the like discourse of the same apostle, (Eph. iv.) do show that it is the catholic church that is here spoken of.

The sense of the text then lieth in this doctrine:

Doct. The universal church being the body of Christ is but one, and all true christians are the members of which it doth consist.

Here are two propositions: first, that the catholic church is but one. Secondly, that all christians are members of it, even all that by the one Spirit are baptized into it. These are both so plain in the text, that were not men perverse or very blind, it were superfluous to say any more to prove them. And for the former proposition, that the catholic church is but one, we are all agreed in it. And therefore I will not needlessly trouble you with answering such objections as trouble not the church, which are fetched from the difference of the Jewish church and the gentile church, (or strictly catholic,) or between the called (the true members) and the elect uncalled; or between the church militant and triumphant.

And as for the second proposition, that the catholic church consisteth of all christians, as its members, it is plain in this text, and many more. It is all that (heartily) say "Jesus is the Lord," (verse 3,) and all that "are baptized by one Spirit into the body," (verse 13,) and all that Paul wrote to, and such as they: and yet some of them were guilty of division, or schism itself, and many errors and crimes, which Paul at large reprehendeth them for. The Galatians were members of this church, Gal. iii. 26—29; for all their legal conceits and errors, and for all that they dealt with Paul as an enemy for telling them the truth. This church consisteth of all that have the "one Spirit, one faith, one baptism, one God and Father of all," &c.; and of all that "have so learned Christ, as to put off the old man, and to be renewed in the spirit of their minds, and put on the new man, which after God is created in righteousness and true holiness," Eph. iv. 4—6, 20—24. This church consisteth of all that "Christ is a Saviour of," and that are "subject" unto Christ, and for "whom he gave himself, that he might sanctify and cleanse them by the washing of water by the word," Eph. v. 23—26. It containeth all such as the Romans then were to whom Paul wrote, (Rom. xii. 4, 5,) however differing among themselves to the censuring of each other. It containeth in it all "such as shall be saved," Acts ii. 47. These things are beyond all just dispute.

When I say, that all christians are members of the catholic church, I must further tell you that men are called christians, either because they are truly and heartily the disciples of Christ, or else because they seem so to be by their profession. The first are such christians as are justified and sanctified, and these constitute the mystical body of Christ, or the church as invisible. Professors of this inward true christianity do constitute the church as visible to men. Professors of some pieces only of christianity, leaving out or denying any essential part of it, are not professors of christianity truly, and therefore are no members of the visible church: and therefore we justly exclude the Mahometans.

And whereas it is a great question, Whether heretics are members of the catholic church? the answer is easy: Contend not about a word. If by a heretic you mean a man that denieth or leaves out any essential part of christianity, he is no member of the church: but if you extend the word so far as to apply it to those that deny not, or leave not out, any essential part of christianity, then such heretics are members of the church. It is but the perverseness of men's spirits, exasperated by disputation, that makes the papists so much oppose our distinction of the fundamentals of religion from the rest; when at other times they confess the thing in other words themselves. By the fundamentals we mean the essentials of the christian faith, or religion. And do they think indeed that christianity hath not its essential parts? Sure they dare not deny it, till they say, it hath no essence, and so is nothing, which an infidel will not say. Or do they think that every revealed truth, which we are bound to believe, is essential to our christianity? Sure they dare not say so, till they either think that no christian is bound to believe any more than he doth believe, or that he is a christian that wants an essential part of christianity, or that christianity is as many several things, as there be persons that have several degrees of faith or knowledge in all the world. For shame, therefore, lay by this senseless cavil, and quarrel not with the light by partial zeal, lest you prove your cause thereby to be darkness. But if you perceive a difficulty (as who doth not, though it be not so great as some would make it) in discerning the essential parts from the integrals, do not therefore deny the unquestionable distinction, but join with us for a fuller discovery of the difference.

In a few words, every man that doth heartily believe in God the Father, Son, and Holy Ghost, by a faith that worketh by love, is a true christian. Or every one that taketh God for his only God, that is, his Creator, Lord, Ruler, and felicity, or end; and Jesus Christ for his only Redeemer, that is, God and man, that hath fulfilled all righteousness, and given up himself to death on the cross in sacrifice for our sins, and hath purchased and promised us pardon, and grace, and everlasting life; and hath risen from the dead, ascended into heaven, where he is Lord of the church, and intercessor with the Father, whose laws we must obey, and who will come again at last to raise and judge the world, the righteous to everlasting life, and the rest to everlasting punishment: and that taketh the Holy Ghost for his Sanctifier, and believeth the Scriptures given by his inspiration, and sealed by his work, to be the certain word of God. This man is a true christian, and a member of the catholic church; which will be manifested when he adjoineth a holy, sober, and righteous life, using all known means and duties, especially baptism at first, the Lord's supper afterward, prayer, confession, praise, meditation, and hearing the word of God, with a desire to know more, that his obedience may be full; living under Christ's ministers, and in communion of saints, denying himself, mortifying the flesh and world, living in charity and justice to man: he that doth this is a true christian, and shall be saved, and therefore a member of the catholic church as invisible; and he that professeth all this, doth profess himself a true christian, and if he null not that profession, is a member of the catholic church as invisible. These things are plain, and in better days were thought sufficient.

He that hath all that is contained but in the ancient creed, the Lord's prayer, and ten commandments, with baptism and the Lord's supper, in his head, and heart, and life, is certainly a member of the catholic church. In a word, it is no harder to know who is a member of this church, than it is to know who is a christian. Tell me but what christianity is, and I will soon tell you how a church member may be known.

But because it will tend both to the further clearing of this, and the text itself, I shall next show you in what respects the members of the church are divers, and then in what respects they are all one, or in what they are united.

And as the text tells you, that the members are many numerically, so they are divers in their respects.

1. They are not of the same age or standing in Christ. Some are babes, and some are young men, and some are fathers, 1 John ii. 12—14. Some are novices, or late converts, and raw christians, (1 Tim.

iii. 6,) and some are of longer standing, that have "borne the burden and heat of the day," Matt. xx. 12.

2. The members are not all of the same degree of strength. Some are of small understanding, that reach little further than the principles of holy doctrine, and have need to be fed with milk, being unskilful in the word of righteousness: yea, they have need to be taught the very principles again, not as being without a saving knowledge of them (for they are all taught of God, and these laws and principles are written in their hearts); but that they may have a clearer, more distinct and practical knowledge of them, who have but a darker, general, less effectual apprehension, Heb. v. 11—13; vi. 1. And some being at full age, are fit for "stronger meat," that is harder of digestion; Heb. v. 14, "Who by reason of use have their senses exercised to discern both good and evil." Some have faith and other graces but as a "grain of mustard seed," and some are thriven to a greater strength, Matt. xvii. 20; xiii. 31. Some grow in grace, and are able to resist a temptation, and do or suffer what they are called to, (2 Pet. iii. 18,) being "strengthened with might by the Spirit in the inner man, according to the glorious power of grace," (Ephes. iii. 17; Col. i. 11,) being "strong in faith, giving glory to God," Rom. iv. 20; having accordingly "strong consolation," Heb. vi. 18. And some are "weak in the faith," apt to be offended, and their consciences to be wounded, and themselves in greater danger by temptations; whom the stronger must receive, and take heed of offending, and must support them, and bear their infirmities, Rom. xiv. 1, 2, 21; xv. 1; 1 Cor. viii. 7, 10—12; ix. 22; 1 Thess. v. 14; Acts xx. 35.

3. Moreover the members have not all the same stature or degree of gifts; nor in all things the same sort of gifts: some excel in knowledge, and some in utterance; some in one sort of knowledge, and some in another; and some are weak in all. But of this the chapter speaks so fully, that I need say no more but refer you thither.

4. The members are not altogether of the same complexion. Though all God's children be like the Father, being holy as he is holy, yet they may be known from one another. Some are naturally more mild, and some more passionate: some of colder and calmer temper, and some so hot that they seem more zealous in all that they say or do: some of more orderly, exact apprehensions, and some of more confused: some quick of understanding, and some dull, Heb. v. 11.

5. The members are not all of the same degree of spiritual health. Some have much quicker and sharper appetites to the bread of life than others have: some are fain to strive with their backward hearts before they can go to secret duties, or hold on in them, and before they can get down the food of their souls; and some go with cheerfulness, and find much sweetness in all that they receive: some are of sounder understandings, and others tainted with many errors and corrupt opinions: as appears in Paul's writings to the Romans, Corinthians, Galatians, and others. Some relish only the food that is wholesome, and some have a mind of novelties, and vain janglings, and contentious, needless disputes, like stomachs that desire coals and ashes, or hurtful things. Some in their conversations maintain their integrity, and walk blamelessly, and without offence, Luke i. 6; Phil. ii. 15. And some are overcome by temptations, and give offence to others and grievously wound themselves; as David, Lot, Noah, Peter, &c. And being overcome with creature respects many good men walk not uprightly in some things, nor according to the truth of the gospel; and others that are good also are led away in a party by the example of their miscarriages, and the high estimation of their parts and persons, Gal. ii. 11—14. Some are firm and stedfast in the truth, and some hold it with shaking, and are oft looking behind them, and sometimes are declining and going backward, and have need to be called upon to return to their first love, and to strengthen the things that remain: yea, some grow to forsake many excellent truths, and neglect many weighty duties, yea, to oppose these truths and duties, and speak against them, as thinking them to be none. Hence it follows that some live in a holy peace and joy, as health is mostly accompanied with ease; when others live in continual lamentations and complaints; and some in too much stupidity and carelessness; and some with dangerous mixtures of an ungrounded, misguided, deluding peace.

6. Hence also it follows, that the members are not all of the same usefulness and serviceableness to the church and cause of Christ. Some are as pillars to support the rest, (Gal. ii. 9; 1 Thess. v. 14,) and some are a trouble to others, and can scarce go any further than they are guided and supported by others. Some lay out themselves in the helping of others; and some are as the sick, that cannot help themselves, but trouble the house with their complaints and necessities, which call for great and continual attendance. Some are fit to be teachers of others, and to be pastors of the flock, and guide the Lord's people in the way of life, and give the children their meat in season, rightly dividing the word of truth. And some are still learning, and never come to much knowledge of the truth, and do no great service to God in their generations: yea, too many weary their teachers and brethren by their frowardness and unfruitfulness; and too many do abundance of wrong to the church, and gospel, and the world by their offensive miscarriages: yea, too many prove as thorns in our sides, and by some error in their understandings, cherished and used by the too great remnant of pride, self-conceitedness, passion, and carnality, are grievous afflicters of the church of Christ, and causes of dissension; one saying, I am of Paul, and another, I am of Apollos, and another, I am of Christ, as if Christ were divided, or else appropriated to them, and Paul or Apollos had been their saviours, 1 Cor. iii. 1—5. Some live so as that the church hath much benefit by their lives, and much loss by their death: and some are such troublers of it, by their weakness and corrupt distempers, that their death is some ease to the places where they lived. And yet all these may be truly godly, and living members of the catholic church.

7. Moreover, the members are not all the same in regard of office. Some are appointed to be pastors, teachers, elders, overseers, to be stewards of God's mysteries, and to feed the flock, taking heed to them all, as being over them in the Lord, as their rulers in spiritual things, Ephes. iv. 11; Acts xiv. 23; Tit. i. 5; 1 Cor. iv. 1; Acts xx. 17, 28; 1 Thess. v. 12; Heb. xiii. 7, 17. And some are the flock, commanded to learn of them, to have them in "honour, and highly esteem them for their work's sake, and to obey them," 1 Thess. v. 12; Heb. xiii. 17; 1 Tim. v. 17. In this chapter saith Paul, "If the whole body were an eye, where were the hearing? If the whole were hearing, where were the smelling? Are all apostles? are all prophets? are all teachers?" 1 Cor. xii. 17, 29. As there are diversity of gifts, so also of offices; for God hath designed men to use the gifts they have in such order and manner as may edify the church. All the body is not the bonds, or nerves, and ligaments, by which the parts are joined together, Eph. iv. 16. All are not "pastors and teachers, given for perfecting of the saints, the work of the ministry,

and edifying of the body of Christ," Ephes. iv. 11—13.

8. Consequently the members have not all the same employment. Magistrates must rule by force, and ministers must guide or rule by the light and force of the word of God: all must not administer sacraments; all must not be the overseers of the flock. Masters and parents have their own work, and servants and children have theirs. Nay, difference of understanding may cause a great deal of difference among ministers and people in the manner of God's worship, when yet all worship him acceptably and in sincerity. Some may be too much ceremonious in meats, and drinks, and observation of days, (Rom. xiv. and xv.) in gestures, vestures, and other circumstances, sinfully laying much more in these than God would have them; and others may be as rigorous against them; and others more temperate between both. Some may pray and praise God in forms composed by themselves or others, or read them in a book; and some may abhor all this as unlawful; and some may be so wise as to know that it is a matter that God hath left in itself indifferent, and is to be determined according to the suitableness of times and persons. And thus many modal, circumstantial differences there may be in the true worshipping of God, by the members of this one universal church.

9. And from what is said already, it follows, that all the members of the church are not all equally to be honoured and loved. Even among the elders, there are some that are worthy of double honour, and some of more than they, 1 Tim. v. 17. Some are of high and excellent gifts and graces; and as more of God doth shine forth in them, so a greater love and honour is due to them. Some are so eminently self-denying, and of public spirits, and wholly carried to the service of God, and the good of the church, that few others are "like-minded, naturally caring for the people's state, but all do too much seek their own, and too little the things that are Jesus Christ's," Phil. ii. 20, 21. The body hath some parts that are less honourable, and less comely, 1 Cor. xii. 22—24; though these also have their honour and comeliness: those that most honour God shall be most honoured, 1 Sam. ii. 30; Job xii. 26; and they that will be the "servants of all, shall be the greatest," Luke xxii. 26; Matt. xxiii. 11.

10. To conclude, from all this imparity it will follow, that the members will not have an equal degree of glory, as not having an equal preparation and capacity. All are not in Abraham's bosom, as Lazarus was. "To sit on Christ's right hand and left in his kingdom will not be the lot of all, but of those to whom the Father will give it," Matt. xx. 23. All are not to sit on thrones, in full equality with the apostles, Luke xx. 30. There are of the first for time of coming in, that shall be last in dignity, and of the last that shall be first, Matt. xix. 30; xx. 16. All shall not be rulers of five cities, but only they that have double five talents, Matt. xxv. And thus I have showed you the disparity of the members, wherein they differ.

Secondly, I am now to show you the unity of them, and of the body which they constitute. The members of the catholic church are united in all these following respects:

1. They have all but one God, the fountain of their being and felicity, and are all related to him as children to one Father, reconciled to them, and adopting them in Jesus Christ, John i. 12. "Ye are all the children of God by faith in Christ Jesus," Gal. iii. 26. "There is one God and Father of all," &c. Gal. iv. 5, 6; Eph. iv. 6.

2. The members of the church have all one Head, the Redeemer, Saviour, Mediator, Jesus Christ, Eph. iv. 5. As the commonwealth is denominated from the unity of the sovereign power that heads it; so the church is hence principally denominated one from Christ, who is the Head, the Sovereign, and the Centre of it. And therefore it is called frequently his body, and he the Head of it, Eph. iv. 15; i. 22; Col. i. 18; ii. 19; Eph. v. 23; Col. iii. 15; Rom. xii. 4, 5; 1 Cor. x. 17; Eph. ii. 16. He is the foundation, and the church is the building that is erected upon him, "and other foundation can no man lay," 1 Cor. iii. 11, 12. "From this Head the whole body fitly joined together, and compacted by that which every joint supplieth, according to the effectual working of the measure of every part, maketh increase of the body to the edifying of itself in love," Eph. iv. 16. All therefore are members of the catholic church that are members of Christ. He is "the chief Corner-stone that is laid in Zion, elect and precious, and he that believeth on him shall not be confounded; to whom coming as to a living stone, we also as lively stones are built up a spiritual house," 1 Pet. ii. 4—6. As this "One died for all," (2 Cor. v. 14,) "because all were dead; so by the righteousness of this One, the free gift cometh on all to justification of life, and by the obedience of this One shall many be made righteous," Rom. v. 18, 19. "And by one Jesus Christ we shall reign in life," Rom. v. 17. "In him the church of Jews and gentiles are made one," Eph. ii. 14, 15. "To this one Husband we are all espoused," 2 Cor. xi. 2. So that we "are all one in Christ Jesus," Gal. iii. 28. And "to us there is but one God the Father, of whom are all things, and we in him; and one Lord Jesus Christ, by whom are all things, and we in him," 1 Cor. viii. 6.

3. The whole catholic church (strictly taken, as comprehending only the living members) have only one Holy Ghost dwelling in them, illuminating, sanctifying, and guiding them, and are animated as it were by this one Spirit. "By this one Spirit we are all baptized into one body, and have been all made to drink into one Spirit," 1 Cor. xii. 13. And "whoever hath not this Spirit of Christ, the same is none of his," Rom. viii. 9. "By this one Spirit we have all access to the Father," Eph. ii. 18. And through this Spirit we are "one habitation of God," Eph. ii. 22. And therefore "he that is joined to the Lord is called one Spirit," 1 Cor. vi. 17. And as it is said of Christ, so may it be of the Spirit in a sort, "He that sanctifieth and they that are sanctified are all of one," Heb. ii. 11. This is the scope of the chapter that my text is in.

4. The church is *one* as to their principal, ultimate end. The same God is their end who is their beginning. The same eternal glory with him, is purchased and prepared for them, and intended by them through their christian course. The wicked have a lower end, even flesh and self: but all the members of Christ are united in the true intention of this end. They are all the "heirs of life, and partakers of the inheritance of the saints in light, and have all lain up their treasure in heaven," Matt. vi. 20, 21; Col. i. 12; Gal. iv. 7; Rom. viii. 17; 1 Pet. iii. 7; Tit. iii. 7; Gal. iii. 29; Heb. i. 14; Eph. iii. 6. "All that are risen with Christ, do seek the things that are above," Col. iii. 1; "and have their conversation with him in heaven," Phil. iii. 20, 21.

5. All the members of the catholic gospel church have one gospel to teach them the knowledge of Christ, Gal. i. 10, 11; and one word of promise to be the charter of their inheritance, 1 Tim. iv. 8; Heb. ix. 15; Gal. iii. 22, 29; and one holy doctrine

to be the instrument of their regeneration, and the "seed of God abiding in them," 1 Pet. i. 23, 25; Luke viii. 11. It is but one that God hath appointed for them; and it is one in the substance that is the instrument of their change.

6. It is one kind of faith, that by this one holy doctrine is wrought upon their souls. Though the degrees be various, yet all believe the same essential points of faith, with a belief of the same nature. There is "one faith," Eph. iv. 5; and in all these essentials the church is of "one mind," (John xvii. 21; Acts iv. 32; 1 Pet. iii. 8; 1 Cor. xv. 2—4,) though in lesser things there be exceeding great diversity.

7. There is one new disposition, or holy nature, wrought by the Spirit of God in every member of the catholic church. This is called their holiness, and the new creature, and the divine nature, and the image of God, 1 Pet. i. 16; 2 Pet. i. 4; John iii. 6. "That which is born of the Spirit, is spirit," Col. iii. 10; 2 Cor. v. 17.

8. The affections which are predominant in all the members of the church, have one and the same object. Sin is the chiefest thing that all of them hate, and the displeasure of God the chief thing they fear, and God in Christ is the prime object of their love; and they have all the same object of their desires and hopes, even the favour of God, and everlasting life: and they all chiefly rejoice in the same hopes and felicity; as were easy to manifest and prove in the particulars, as to all the essentials of christianity that are the objects of the will, Phil. i. 27; ii. 3; Eph. iv. 4; Matt. xxii. 37, 38; Rom. viii. 28; 1 Cor. ii. 9. And thus they are all of one heart and soul, as uniting in the same objects.

9. They have also all one rule or law to live by, which is the law of faith, of grace, of liberty, of Christ, Rom. iii. 27; viii. 2; Jam. i. 25; Gal. vi. 2. And as one law is appointed for them all, so one law in the points of absolute necessity is received by them all; for "it is written in their hearts," and put into "their inward parts," Jer. xxxi. 32; Heb. viii. 10, 16; though in the other points of the law of Christ there be much diversity in their reception and obedience. All of them are sincerely obedient to what they know, and all of them know that which God hath made of necessity to life.

10. Every member of the church is devoted to God in one and the same covenant. As the covenant on Christ's part is one to them all; so is it one on their part. They all renounce the world, the flesh, and the devil, and give up themselves to God the Father, Son, and Holy Ghost. And this being used by God's appointment, to be solemnly done in baptism, therefore baptism is called the principle or foundation, Heb. vi. 1. And there is said to be but one baptism, (Eph. iv. 5,) and baptism is said to save us; "Not the putting away the filth of the flesh, (that is, not the outward washing,) but the answer of a good conscience to God," (1 Pet. iii. 21,) that is, the sincere, internal covenant of the heart, and delivering up ourselves to Christ. So also the fathers, when they (usually) speak of the necessity of baptism, they mean principally our becoming christians, and entering into the holy covenant, which was done by baptism. Though if any be so weak as to think that this outward baptism is to be delayed, (as Constantine and many of the fathers did,) if in the mean time he make and profess his covenant with Christ, he is to be taken as a christian and church member: but as a soldier without colours, or a king not crowned; he is a christian not orderly admitted, which is his sin.

11. Every member of the catholic church hath the same instrumental founders of his faith under Christ, that is, the prophets and apostles, infallibly inspired by the Holy Ghost. "We are built upon the foundation of the apostles and prophets, Jesus Christ himself being the chief Corner-stone; in whom all the building fitly framed together groweth unto an holy temple in the Lord," Eph. ii. 20, 21. These were the eye-witnesses of the resurrection of Christ, and the ear-witnesses of his holy doctrine, who have delivered it to us as confirmed by the miracles of the Holy Ghost by Christ and by themselves. And though possibly some ignorant christian may not well understand his relation to these founders of his faith, yet from them he had it, and is thus related to them: and commonly this is understood and acknowledged by them.

12. Every member of the church is related to all the body, as a member of it; and are "no more strangers and sojourners, but fellow-citizens of the saints, and of the household of God," Eph. ii. 19. But this the very term itself doth sufficiently import to you.

13. Every member of the church hath an habitual love to each particular member of the same church. Though mistakes and infirmities may occasion fallings-out, even as Paul and Barnabas, to a parting; and there may be dislikes and bitterness against one another upon misunderstandings, and not discerning God's graces in each other; yet still, as christians, they are heartily loved by each other; and did they know more of the truth of each other's christianity, they would love each other more. Every member is united by love to the rest; for this is a lesson that is taught us inwardly of God: "And by this we know that we are translated from death to life," 1 Pet. i. 22; 1 John iii. 11, 14, 23; iv. 12, 20, 21, 8; 1 Thess. iv. 9; John xiii. 34, 35.

14. Every member of the church hath a special love to the whole, and desire after the church's welfare and prosperity. Yea, their love to the body exceedeth their love to the particular members, (Psal. cxxii. 2,) and therefore they desire and pray for its safety and increase.

15. Every member of the church hath a special love to the more noble sort of members. As every man is more careful of the heart, the stomach, the lungs, the liver, than of his finger; so are christians as christians, in greatest love to those that have most of Christ in them, and on whom the church's welfare doth most depend; of them are they most solicitous, so far as they understand it. This is true both of men's graces, gifts, and offices. He that loveth grace, loveth those most that have most grace. And he that loveth the church, honoureth those in a special manner whom he discerneth best gifted for the benefit of the church, and to employ his gifts most faithfully thereto. And though I will not say but it is possible for some christians to be converted by a private man, and die before they know a church officer, and for some weak ones in a temptation to deny and disclaim, or quarrel with their officers; yet so far as any true christian is acquainted with the necessity or usefulness of the ministry to the church's good, and God's honour, (as ordinarily all know it in some measure, and they that know it not are in some fit of a frenzy,) so far they cannot choose but love and honour them. And thus far all christians join for the ministry: as God's intention was for all their good in giving pastors, teachers, and gifts of special service for the church, Eph. iv. 11—14.

16. All members have an inward inclination to hold communion with fellow-members, so far as they discern them to be members indeed. As fire would to fire, and water would to water, and earth to earth,

and every thing to its like; so christians would have actual communion with christians, as delighting in each other, and loving Christ in each other, and finding benefit by each other's communion. Though I know that this inclination may be much kept from execution, and communion much hindered, by mistakes about the nature, and manner, and requisites of it, and by infirmities and passions of our own. Brethren may fall out, but there is naturally in them a brotherly love, and when the mistake or passion is over, they will get together again, Acts iv. 32, 33; ii. 42, 44; Heb. x. 25; Psal. xvi. 3.

17. There is in every true member of the church an inward inclination and propensity to all the instituted means of grace, and a suitableness of spirit to them, which fitteth them to relish them, and highly to value them: and ordinarily this disposition is brought forth into act. The word of God is ingrafted or innaturalized to them, James i. 21. It is to them as milk to the new-born babe, 1 Pet. ii. 1, 2. The Lord's supper is sweet to him, as representing Christ sacrificed, and offering him Christ the food of the soul, and affording him special communion with the saints. "For the cup of blessing which we bless is the communion of the blood of Christ; and the bread which we break is the communion of the body of Christ: for we being many are one bread, and one body; for we are all partakers of that one bread," 1 Cor. x. 16, 17. The same holy disposition have they to prayer, confession, the praises of God, and all other parts of his service. Though it is too true, that as diseases may put our mouths out of relish to our meat; so temptations may bring some christians to mistakes about some ordinances, especially as to the manner, and so may make them guilty of too long forbearance of them.

18. So also every member of the church hath in the main the same holy employment and conversation; that is, the service of God, so far as they know his will, is the business of their lives, Rom. xii. 1. "We are his workmanship, created to good works in Christ Jesus," Eph. ii. 10, 11.

19. And every member hath an inward enmity to that which is destructive to itself, or to the body, so far as he knoweth it; that is, 1. To sin in general. 2. To all known sin in particular. And, 3. Specially to divisions, distractions, and diminution of the church. These things their inward disposition is against; and when they are led to them, it is by temptation producing mistakes and passions against the bent of their hearts and lives. They abhor that which is destructive to the body, as such.

20. Lastly, They shall all at the end of their course obtain the same crown of glory, and see and enjoy the same blessed God and glorified Redeemer, and be members of the same celestial Jerusalem, and employed everlastingly in the same holy love, and joy, and praise, and glorify and please the Lord in all, and centre and be united perfectly in him, John xvii. 21, 23, 24. "For of him, and through him, and to him are all things, to whom be glory for ever, Amen," Rom. xi. 36.

And thus I have showed you in twenty particulars the unity of the saints; though it is not from every one of these that they are called one church, yet all these are inseparable as to possession from the true members, and as to profession from the seeming members that are adult.

Use 1. The truth being thus plain and certain as it is, that the catholic church is one, and consisteth of true christians, as its real living members, and of all professors of true christianity, as its visible members, we have here too great occasion of sad lamentation, for the common ignorance of the contenders of the world about this matter, and the great inconsiderateness and abuse of this unquestionable verity. To four sorts of people I shall direct my expostulations. 1. To the seekers, or whoever else deny the very being of the catholic church. 2. To the blind contending parties of these times, and the offended ignorant people, that are much perplexed among so many pretenders, to know which is the church. 3. To the several sects that would appropriate the church to themselves only. 4. To the papists, that ask us for a proof of the continued visibility of our church, and where it was before Luther. To these in order: and,

I. For the seekers; because it is not their persons that I have to speak against, but the errors which they are said to hold, and because they purposely hide their opinions, and because I meet with them of so many minds, I shall therefore deal only with the opinions commonly supposed to be theirs, not determining whether indeed they are theirs, or no; for I care not who maintains them, so I do but effectually confute them. And here are four degrees of this error supposed to be held by the seekers. 1. Some of them are said to deny the universal mystical church itself. 2. Some are said to deny only the universal visible church, as such. 3. Some yielding both these, deny the universal church as political only. 4. Some only deny the truth of particular churches, as political, that is, the truth of the ministry. Of these in order.

1. Let that man that questioneth the being of the catholic mystical church, and yet pretends to believe in Christ, read but these three or four arguments, and blush.

Argum. 1. If there be no such universal church, then there are no christians: for what is the church but all the christians of the world? And I pray inquire better, whether there be any christians in the world or not? Read the church history, and the books of the infidels, and see whether there have been christians in the world since the apostles. He that believeth not that there are christians in the world, when he dwells among them, and daily converseth with them, deserveth to be otherwise disputed with than by argument. He hath only cause to doubt whether there be any christian magistrate in this part of the world, that such as he are suffered to rave against christianity.

And certainly he that thinks there are no christians in the world, is none himself, nor would be thought one.

Argum. 2. If there be no church, there is no Christ: no body, no head: no kingdom, no king: no wife, no husband: no redeemed ones, no Redeemer or Mediator. Though the person of Christ should be the same, yet the office and relation must cease, if the church cease. This is beyond all dispute. And if this be your meaning, that there is no Christ, no Mediator, no Head, or Teacher, or King of the church, speak out, and call yourselves infidels as you are.

Argum. 3. If there be no church or christians, then there is no salvation; for salvation is promised to none but christians, or members of Christ. He is the "Saviour of his body," Eph. v. 23. And he that thinks there is none on earth that shall be saved, it seems expecteth no salvation himself: and how much the world is beholden to him for his doctrine, and how ready they will be to receive it, if they be in their wits, is easy to be conjectured.

Argum. 4. If there be no church, there is no pardon of sin, or adoption, nor any fruit of the promise. For the church only are the heirs of promise, pardoned, adopted. (I would heap up plain Scriptures for these things, if I thought it to any purpose.) And he that thinks the promises are ceased, and the pardon of sin and adoption ceased, doth sure think the gospel and christianity are ceased, or never were.

2. As to the second opinion, let them that deny the church as visible, consider of the same arguments again, with the necessary addition, and be ashamed.

Argum. 1. If there be no visible church, there are no visible christians; for christians are the church: and if there are no visible christians, then no man can say, that there are any christians at all; for how do you know it if they are not visible?

Argum. 2. And consequently no man can tell that there is a Christ, the Head and King of the church; for who can judge of that which is inevident? And if you know not that there is a church, you cannot know that there is a Christ.

Argum. 3. And thus you must be uncertain of any to be saved, because they are not visible.

Argum. 4. And you must be uncertain of the continuance of the force of the promise, and of pardon, and sanctification.

Argum. 5. Experience and sense itself confutes you. Open your eyes and ears: do you not see christians in holy exercises? Do you not hear them make profession of their faith? It is a fine world, when we must be fain to dispute whether there be such a people whom we every day converse and talk with! You may better question, whether there be any Turks or Jews in the world! and as well question, whether there be any men in the world! And how should such be disputed with?

3. For the third opinion, which yields a universal visible church, but not a political, it is a gross contradiction.

Argum. Where there is a sovereign, and subjects, and ruler, and such as are under his rule, there is a political body or society. For the *pars imperans*, and *pars subdita*, do constitute every commonwealth: and the relations of these two parties, the ruling part and the ruled part, is the form of the republic. This is undeniable. But here are these two parts: for Christ is the ruling part, and the church or christians are the ruled part: and therefore you must either deny that there is a Christ to be King, or that there are christians his subjects; or else you must confess a political church.

But some of this opinion say, We confess there is a visible body headed by Christ, who is to us invisible, though visible in the heavens; but this makes not the church to be visibly political, unless *secundum quod;* but here is no visible universal head.

Answ. 1. We perceive now whereabout you are, and from whom and for whom you fetch your arguments. You must have a pope, it seems, or else no visible political church. We deny that either pope or general council are the visible heads of the church. We maintain that the church is no otherwise visible in its policy, than in these respects. 1. As the body is visible, and their obedience. As, 2. The laws are visible by which they are governed. 3. As the inferior officers or ministers are visible. And, 4. As Christ the Head is visible in heaven. There is no other visibility of polity to be here expected.

4. The next opinion denieth only that there are any true particular political churches. Against this I argue thus:

Argum. 1. If there be no particular churches, there is no universal church: for there can be no whole, if there be no parts; and political particular churches are those principal constitutive parts of the universal, which the Scripture mentioneth. But I have proved that there is a universal church, which is the whole: therefore there are particular political churches, which are the parts.

Argum. 2. If there be particular christian societies with overseers, then there are particular political churches: for a church hath but two essential parts; the guiding or ruling part, which is the elders or overseers, and the guided and ruled part, which are the people. Now here are both these: therefore there are particular political churches. That here are christian assemblies methinks I should not need to prove, to men that see them day by day, and plead against them. The only question, therefore, remaining is, Whether the elders or teachers be true officers or elders, or not? And in the upshot this is all the question, and you can stick on no other (nor well on this) without declaring yourselves to be infidels: and this is a question that belongs not to this place, but I purposely refer you to what I have already published hereupon.

II. My next address is, to them that are so solicitous to know which is the true church among all the parties in the world that pretend to it. Silly souls! they are hearkening to that party, and to that party, and turn it may be to one, and to another, to find the true universal church: I speak not in contempt, but in compassion; but I must say, you deal much liker Bedlams than christians, or reasonable men. You run up and down from room to room to find the house, and you ask, is the parlour it? or is the hall it? or is the kitchen or the coal-house it? Why, every one is a part of it; and all the rooms make up the house. You are in the wood, and cannot find it for trees: but you ask, which of these sort of trees is the wood? Is it the oak, or the ash, or the elm, or poplar? or is it the hawthorn, or the bramble? Why, it is all together. You are studying which of the members is the man: is the hand the man? or is it the foot? or is it the eye? or the heart? or which is it? Why, it is the whole body and soul, in which all parts and faculties are comprised. You wisely ask, Which part is the whole? Why, no part is the whole. Which is the catholic church? Is it the protestants, the Calvinists, or Lutherans, the papists, the Greeks, the Ethiopians? or which is it? Why, it is never an one of them, but all together, that are truly christians. Good Lord! what a pitiful state is the poor church in, when we must look abroad and see such abundance running up and down the world, and asking which is the world? whether this country be the world, or that country be the world? They are, as it were, running up and down England to look for England, and ask, whether this town be England, or whether it be the other? They are as men running up and down London to inquire for London, and ask, whether this house be London, or that street be London? or some other? Thus are they in the midst of the church of Christ inquiring after the church, and asking, Whether it be this party of christians, or whether it be the other? Why, you doting wretches, it is all christians in the world, of what sort soever, that are truly so, that constitute the catholic church.

Indeed if your question were only, Which is the purest, or soundest, or safest part of the church, then there were some sense in it, and I could quickly give you advice for your resolution; but that is reserved for a following part of the discourse. If you only ask, whether the parlour or the coal-house be the better part or room of the house? or whether the oak or the bramble be the better part of the wood? I should soon give you an answer. So if you ask, whether the protestants, or papists, or Greeks, be the sounder part of the church? I should soon answer you. The same family may have in it both infants and men at age, sound men and sick men; some that have but small distempers, and some that have the plague or leprosy: and yet all are men and members of the family: and so hath the church of God such members.

Object. But will you make all sects and heretics in the world to be members of the catholic church?

Answ. No: there are none members of the church but christians. If you call any christians heretics, those are members of the church: but those heretics that are no christians, are no church members. If they deny any essential point of christianity, they are not christians, but analogically, equivocally, or *secundum quid.* I tell you, all that are true believers, justified and sanctified, are true living members of the church: and all that profess true faith and holiness, are true members, and no others, at age and use of reason. Your inquiry, therefore, should be, which are true christians? And what is true christianity? And what heresies deny the essentials of christianity? And then you may soon know who are of the church.

Object. Abundance of the errors now common in the world, do subvert the foundation, or destroy the essentials of christianity.

Answ. It is not every consequential destroying of the essentials that will prove a man no christian. For almost every error in the matters of faith and morality doth consequentially subvert the foundation, because of the concatenation of truths together, and their dependence on each other. And so every man on earth should perish if this were inconsistent with christianity: for all men err in matters revealed and propounded by God in Scripture to their knowledge and belief. He that holdeth fast the essentials of religion by a practical belief, shall be saved by it, though he hold any opinions which consequently subvert the truth, and doth not understand that they do subvert it: for this is the best men's case. But if he so hold the error, as seeing that it overthrows an essential point, and so holdeth not that point which it is against, this man is not a christian. Every drop of water is contrary to fire, and yet a great fire is not put out by a single drop. Every degree of sickness, or natural decay, hath a contrariety to health and life; and yet every man is not dead that is sick; nor any man, I think: nor is it every sickness that procureth death. The promise is, "He that believeth shall be saved:" and, therefore, as long as he believeth all the essential verities, it is no contrary opinion that can unchristen him, or unchurch him.

Object. But how shall we know a visible christian by this, when we know not whether he hold the truth, or not?

Answ. By men's profession the visibility of their faith is easily discerned. If they say they believe that Christ rose from the dead, I am to take them as believers of it, notwithstanding they should hold some error, that hath a remote opposition to it. But if they directly deny it, I have no reason to think they believe it; and if they will hold two directly contradictory propositions, they are mad-men, and to be believed in neither. The Lutherans maintain, that Christ hath a true human nature; and yet some of them say, that it is every where. Though this be contrary to the former by consequence; yet I am bound to judge that they take Christ to be true man still, because indeed they do so, not seeing the contradiction.

But if a man by his contradiction in other terms, do manifest that he doth not believe the truth which he professeth to believe, but speaks the words while he denies the sense, this is to deny the matter itself; for it is the sense that is the doctrine: and so he denies himself to be a christian. For example: If he say, that Christ is risen, and by Christ tell you he meaneth his own spirit; and by rising he meaneth his rising from sin, as the familists do, and no more; this is to deny the resurrection of Christ.

Object. But you will dishonour Christ and his church by taking in all sects and erroneous persons, that held the essentials. What a linsey-woolsey garment will this be! What a large and mingled church will you make!

Answ. The largeness is no dishonour to it: but by overnarrowing it many sects do dishonour it. The corruptions and infirmities are indeed a dishonour to it: but that reflects not at all on Christ, yea, it maketh for his honour, both that he is so exceeding compassionate as to extend his love and mercy so far, and to bear with such distempers, and pardon such miscarriages of his servants. And should your eye be evil because he is good? Oh how ill doth it beseem that man that needeth exceeding mercy himself, even to save him from damnation, to be opening his mouth against the mercy of Christ to others! yea, to repine at, and even reproach the mercy that he liveth by, and must save him, if ever he be saved! Why, man, hast not thou as much need of tender indulgence and mercy thyself, to keep thee in the church, and in the favour of God, and bring thee to heaven, as anabaptists, separatists, Arminians, Lutherans, and many such sects have, to continue them in the number of catholic christians? If thou have not their errors, thou hast others, and perhaps as bad, which thou little thinkest of: and if thou have not their errors, hast thou not sins that are as provoking to God as they? Really, speak thy heart, man, be thou papist or protestant, or what thou wilt: wouldst thou have God less merciful than he is? Or wouldst thou wish him to be so little merciful, as to damn all that be not of thy opinion, or to unchristen and unchurch all these that thou speakest against? Or wouldst thou have him to condemn and cast away all men that have as great faults as the errors of these christians are? and consequently to condemn thyself? Moreover, it is Christ's honour to be the healer of such great distempers, and the cure at last shall magnify his skill. In the mean time the church, though black, is yet comely in the eyes of Christ, and of all that see by the light of his Spirit. And our tender-hearted Saviour disdaineth not to be the Physician of such an hospital as hath many sorts of diseases in it, and many of them very great. And when Pharisees make it his reproach that he thus converseth with publicans and sinners, he takes it as his glory to be the compassionate Physician of those that are sick.

I beseech you therefore, poor, peevish, quarrelsome souls, give others leave to live in the same house with you. Do not disown your brethren, and say, they are bastards, because they somewhat differ from you in complexion, in age, in strength, in health, in stature, or any of the points wherein I told you a little before that the members of the church do usually differ in. Show not yourselves so ignorant or froward as to make a wonder of it, that God should be the Father both of infants and men at age, of weak and strong, and that the sick and the sound should both be in his family. Doth such cruelty beseem the breast of a christian, as to wish God to cast out all his children from his family that are weak and sick? Do not make it such a matter of wonder, that God's house should have many rooms in it; and think it not a reproach to it, that the kitchen or the coal-house is part of the house. Wonder not at it as a strange thing, that all the body is not a hand or eye; and that some parts have less honour and comeliness than the rest. Hath God told you so plainly and fully of these matters, and yet will you not understand, but remain so perverse? I pray hereafter remember better that the catholic church is one, consisting of all true christians as the members.

III. My next address is to those several sects (I call them not so in reproach, but because they make themselves so) that sinfully appropriate the catholic church to themselves. Thus did the Donatists in Augustine's time, to whom he gives a confutation of very great use to all that are guilty of that sin in our days. But I shall only speak particularly now to these three sects that are most notoriously guilty: 1. The quakers. 2. Some anabaptists. And, 3. The papists.

1. The quakers are but a few distempered people, risen up within a few years in this corner of the world: and yet they are not ashamed to condemn the most godly christians, ministers, and churches of the world, that are not of their way; as if the church were confined to these few poor, distracted, erroneous persons. Do not think that they are all of a mind among themselves; some of them plainly deny the very essentials of christianity. And for these to reproach the church is no wonder: but to appropriate it to themselves that are themselves no members of it, is as if Turks or heathens should have persuaded the world that they are the only christians. In the mean time I thank God that christianity is in so much esteem, that even the enemies of it do pretend to it: but for those that go under that name, and deny not the fundamentals, let them consider what I said before to the seekers: if there be no church, there is no Christ; no body, no head; and no church, no christians, and no justification or salvation. And therefore I would know of them, where was the true church before the other day that the quakers rose? If there were any, where was it? If there were none, then there was no Christ, no Head! I remember what a boy told them lately near us, Your church and religion (saith he) cannot be the right, for I can remember since it first begun. Sure Christ had a church before the quakers.

2. The rigid anabaptists do run the same strain, and appropriate the church to their sect alone; and this upon the popish conceit, that baptism is either necessary to salvation, or else to the being of a member of the church. None but the re-baptized, or those that are baptized at age, are taken by them to be members of the church (though I know that many of the anabaptists are more moderate, and make re-baptizing necessary only in point of duty, and *ad bene esse.)* Of these men also I would know, 1. Where was a church that was against infant baptism, since the days of the apostles, (much less among them,) till within these five hundred or six hundred years at most (perhaps these two hundred or three hundred)? Had Christ a visible church of such in all ages? If so, tell us where it was, and prove it. If not, tell us how Christ could be a King without a kingdom, a Head without a body. 2. And can your hearts endure so cruel a doctrine, as to unchurch all the churches of the world, except so few, and such as you? 3. And would you have men in their wits believe that Christ hath been so many hundred years without a visible church? Or that his church hath had a false constitution, and that now he is constituting his church aright in the end of the world? 4. Your error is so much the greater and more cruel, as your party is the smaller, and more lately sprung up; that ever it can enter into your hearts to imagine that God hath no church in all the world but you. But I shall say no more to you particularly, partly because you are an impatient generation, that take a confutation for a persecution; and partly because I shall offend the more sober, by such needless words, to so gross an error; and chiefly because that which I shall speak to the next party, will be also useful to your information.

3. The principal sect that appropriate the church to themselves, is the papists. And to them I shall more largely open my mind. They make a great noise against all other parties with the name of the Roman catholic church, and the confident ostentation that it is only they. They make the pope the visible head of it, and exclude all from the church besides his subjects; and all that are not of that church they exclude also from salvation, with an *extra ecclesiam nulla salus.* What shall we say to these things?

1. Sure it must needs be some admirable qualification that must thus advance the church of Rome to be the whole and only catholic church! And what should this be? Is it their extraordinary holiness? I know they talk much of the holiness of their church: but they dare not put it upon that issue, and let us take that for the church which we find to be most holy. On those terms I think we should soon be resolved, by a little observation and experience. However, it would not serve their turn, unless they could prove that none are holy at all but they. What then is the ground of this pretended privilege? Why, because they take the bishop of Rome for the universal bishop, and are under his government. And is this it that salvation is confined to?

2. And sure it must be some very heinous matter, that all the rest of the christian world must be unchurched and damned for! And what is that? Is it for denying any article of the faith? Which is it that we deny? When they would set them against protestants, they boast that the Greeks are in all things of their mind, except the pope's supremacy; and therefore this is the only heresy that might unchurch and damn them. And it is not for ungodliness; for we are ready to join with them in severer censures of ungodliness than we know how to bring them to. The damning crime is, that we believe not the church of Rome to be the mistress of all the churches, and the pope to be their head. And indeed is this a damning sin, and inconsistent with christianity, or church membership? I prove the contrary, that the catholic church is not confined to the Roman, but containeth in it all that I have mentioned before.

Argum. 1. If many are true christians that believe not in the pope, or Roman church, as the ruler of the rest, then many may be church members and saved that believe not in them: but the antecedent is certain. For,

1. He that truly believes in God the Father, Son, and Holy Ghost, renouncing the flesh, the world, and the devil, is a christian: but so do many millions that believe not in the pope or Roman sovereignty.

2. He that hath the sanctifying Spirit of Christ is a christian; for Christ giveth it to no other: but so have millions that believe not the Roman sovereignty, as I shall further show anon.

3. Those that have all that is essential to a christian, are true christians: but so have millions that believe not the Roman sovereignty. For they have

faith, hope, charity, repentance, and sincere obedience, and therefore are true christians. If you say, that the belief of the Roman sovereignty is essential to christianity, you must well prove it, which yet was never done.

I prove the contrary by many arguments.

1. No Scripture tells us that your sovereignty is a truth, much less of the essence of christianity. Therefore it is not so to be believed. What Bellarmine brings but to prove the truth of it, I have manifested to be utterly impertinent in my book against popery.

2. If it had been essential to christianity, and necessary to salvation, to believe the sovereignty of the church of Rome, the apostles would have preached it to all the people, whose conversion they endeavoured, and have established the churches in it: but there is not a word in Scripture, or any church history, that ever the apostles, or any preachers of those times, did teach the people any such doctrine: much less that they taught it all the people. And sure they would not have omitted a point of necessity to salvation.

3. If the sovereignty of the pope, or of Rome, is of necessity to christianity and salvation, then the apostles and pastors of the primitive church would either have baptized men into the pope and Roman church, or at least have instructed their catechumens in it, and required them to profess their belief in the pope and Roman church. But there is not a word in Scripture, or any church records, intimating that ever such a thing was once done either by orthodox or heretics; that ever any did baptize men into the name of the pope or Roman church, or did require of them a confession of the Roman sovereignty; no, nor ever taught any church or christian to obey the church of Rome, as the ruler of other churches. Paul was more certainly an apostle at Rome (a bishop they call him) than Peter, and you may know his practice by 1 Cor. i. 14, 15, "I thank God that I baptized none of you, but Crispus and Gaius, lest any should say that I baptized in my own name." The ancient forms of baptism are recorded in Scripture and church history; but this is never in. He that believed in God the Father, Son, and Holy Ghost, for remission, justification, sanctification, and everlasting life, was baptized as a christian.

4. If the sovereignty of the Roman church were necessary to christianity and salvation, we should have had it in some of the creeds of the primitive church, or at least in the exposition of those creeds. But there we have no such thing. For their affirmation, that the word "catholic church" in the creed signifieth as much as the Roman catholic church, doth signify no more to us, but the dreaming ungrounded confidence of the affirmers.

5. Thousands and millions were saved in the primitive church, without ever believing or confessing the Roman sovereignty; therefore it is not essential to christianity. No man can prove that one christian believed Rome to be the mistress of other churches for many hundred years after Christ, much less that all believed it.

6. If it be an article of faith, and so essential to christianity, that Rome is the mistress of other churches, then either it was so before there was a church at Rome, or else it begun after. Not before: for when there was no church, it could not be the mistress of all churches. Not after: for then christianity should have altered its specific nature, and become another thing, by the adding of a new essential part. But christianity is the same thing since there was a church at Rome, as it was for many years before. And the catholic church is the same thing. It was many years a catholic church before there was any church at Rome at all.

7. If it be necessary to christianity or salvation to believe that Rome is the mistress and head of the catholic church, then it is as necessary to know who it is that is this head and mistress; whether it be the pope, or the particular church of Rome, or the general council. For else the bare name of Rome should be the thing of necessity. But if we know not what that name doth signify, it is no more to us than a nonsense word, which a parrot may utter. But what it is that is this head or sovereignty the papists themselves are utterly disagreed in. The council of Constance and Basil defined, That the general council is the head, above the pope, and may judge and depose him, as they did divers. The Lateran council thought otherwise; and Bellarmine saith the aforesaid council judged the judge of the whole world, and maintains the pope to be the head and seat of sovereignty. The Italians go one way, and the French another. But if these be true general councils, then the matter is determined against the pope; and therefore is an article of faith to be believed on pain of damnation, that the council is above the pope: and yet it is also an article of faith to be believed on the same penalty, that the pope is above the general council: for the council at the Lateran under Leo X. hath determined it, sess. 11. So that councils are contrary, and articles of faith are contrary, and he that will be a papist must believe contradictions. If to evade this any say, that either the council of Constance, or that at the Lateran, were not true general councils, or not approved by the pope; for that of Constance Bellarmine answers after Turrecremata, Campegius, Sanders, &c. that it was a true and approved council, lib. 2. de Concil. cap. 19. But they say, that it determined only that the council is above the pope in case of a schism, when the true pope is not known. But Bellarmine durst not stand to this answer; for the express words of the council are, that a general council hath immediate authority from Christ, which all are bound to obey, though of papal dignity. Can plainer words be spoke? But Bellarmine's other shift is worse, that P. Martin V. confirmed all that was done in his council, *conciliariter;* but this (saith he) was not *conciliariter*. See what juggling the articles of the Romish faith are liable to, and how clear an interpreter of the Scriptures and decider of controversies we have, that speaks so enigmatically when he seems to speak most plainly, even in confirming a general council, that his own cardinals, nor the council itself, are able to understand him. But perhaps the council at the Lateran was false, that determineth of the contrary, that the pope is above councils: no, not in the judgment of Bellarmine and his party. For (lib. 2 de Concil. cap. 17) he saith, that *vix dici potest*, it can scarce be said that the council was not general. And the pope was in it, and confirmed it, and the non-reception of it by others he saith is nothing, because degrees of faith are immutable, and the not receiving cannot change them. What a case then are they in, that must needs be damned, whether they believe the pope to be the supreme, or the council to be the supreme! One council is against one way, and the other against the other way, and both councils confirmed by undoubted popes. But yet they have a remedy, and that is, that yet the matter is doubtful: and where is the doubt? Why it is, whether the council defined this as an article of faith, or no? And therefore saith Bellarmine, they are not properly heretics that hold the contrary, but cannot be excused from great temerity. So that you see what

certainty the papists are at in their faith. It cannot be known, nor will any succeeding popes determine it, when a council hath decided a point, whether or no they intended it as an article of faith. (And yet in the Trent oath they are to swear obedience to all things defined and declared by the sacred canons and œcumenical councils.) One council decrees, that the pope is highest, another or two decree, that the council is highest; and the pope must obey them: yea, both these are confirmed by the pope. The subjects are sworn to obey both contradictories: and yet after this contrary decision, the case is still undecided with them, and for fear of losing half their party, they dare not say that either are properly heretics. (Mark, *properly*.) Yea, (saith Bellarmine, de Concil. lib. 2. c, 13,) though afterwards in the Florentine and Lateran council the question seems to be defined, (having before been contrarily defined at Constance and Basil,) yet to this day it remaineth a question among catholics; because the council of Florence seems not to define it so expressly; and of the council of Lateran, which most expressly defined it, some doubt. So that as there is no understanding their councils in their highest decrees, so we have the confession of the papists themselves, that it is yet undetermined, and no point of faith, which is the sovereign power in the church: and if it be not so much as determined, then much less is it essential to christianity. And if it be not necessary to know who hath the sovereignty, then it cannot be necessary to know that it is in the church of Rome: for the name of the church of Rome is nothing but a sound, without the thing that is signified by it: moreover, the pope is not the church of Rome; for it was never heard that one man was called a church; and a general council is not the churches of Rome; for if there be such a thing, it representeth all churches as much as Rome. And therefore whichever be the sovereign, it cannot be the church of Rome. And as for the particular Roman clergy or people, no man that ever I heard of did yet affirm that it was the sovereign ruler of the churches. It is only the pope and council that are competitors.

If any say, that it is the pope and council only conjunct. I answer, 1. That two that are both fallible, set together, will not make one infallible power. 2. Then the far greatest part of the papists are erroneous in holding the contrary: for almost all make either the pope or the council to be the seat of supremacy and infallibility. 3. Then what is become of the church when these two disagree, as frequently they have done? 4. The pope and council agreeing do oft contradict a former pope and council agreeing. 5. Then the church is without a head, all this while that there is no council in being. See Bellarmine's arguments against this opinion.

8. Another argument to prove that it is not essential to christianity, to believe the sovereignty of the pope or church of Rome, is this, it is not necessary to salvation to know that there is such a place as Rome in the world, or whether there be one, or two, or ten places of that name, or which of them it is that hath the sovereignty; and therefore it cannot be necessary to believe that it is the catholic or mistress church: would God lay men's salvation upon the title of a city many thousand miles from some parts of his church, which they have no knowledge of? Many papists say, that heathens have sufficient means of salvation that never heard of Christ; and yet will they damn christians that never heard of the city or pope of Rome? For about three hundred years after Christ it was the seat of the greatest idolatry, impiety, and persecuting cruelty in the world. And would God all that while so advance that wicked place as to make it essential to christianity to believe Rome to be the seat of the sovereignty of the church.

9. We have no certainty of faith that Rome shall not be burned, or be possessed by Mahometans, or turn to infidelity: therefore we have no certainty that it shall be any church at all, much less the true ruling or catholic church.

10. If it were necessary to salvation to believe Rome's sovereignty, God would afford the world sufficient evidence of it, and commission preachers to preach it to the world: "For how should they believe without a preacher; and how shall he preach except he be sent?" But no such commissions are proved to be given to any from the Lord.

Having thus backed my first argument, and proved others besides papists to be christians, and consequently members of the catholic church, I may proceed to the rest.

Argum. 2. If millions besides papists have the Spirit of God, and true faith, and charity, and holiness, then are they members of the catholic church. For out of the church is no salvation; but all that have the Holy Ghost and charity shall be saved, as the papists confess, if they continue in it. But that many besides papists have charity and sanctification, we have large experience to persuade us to conclude: for though no man can know the certain truth of another man's profession, or heart; yet as far as men can know by one another, we have ground to be exceeding confident of the sanctity and charity of multitudes among us. I profess if it were but this one thing that hindered me, I could not be a papist upon any terms. I live among humble, holy, and heavenly people, that live in continual breathings after God, hating a sinful thought, in great mortification, and willingness to know God's will, that they may obey it; and accordingly abundance have ended their lives in peace and joy in the Holy Ghost: none of these were papists: and now it is impossible for a man to be a papist, that will not conclude all these to be out of the catholic church, and consequently to be unsanctified and condemned. And if so, I am resolved never to be a papist. If I cannot be a papist without condemning a multitude of the holiest persons that ever I could meet with, and shutting my eyes against the admirable lustre of their graces, let them be papists that will for me.

Argum. 3. The Lord Jesus shed his blood for all christians as well as papists, with a special intent to sanctify and save all that are such indeed: therefore they are members of the catholic church, Eph. v. 25—27.

Argum. 4. All christians are subject to Christ, though they be not subject to the pope: therefore they are the church of Christ, Eph. v. 24.

Argum. 5. Those that are loved of the Father, and reconciled to him, are to be taken for members of the church. But all that believe in the Son, and love him, are loved by the Father, and reconciled to him, John xvi. 27; Rom. v. 1, 2.

Argum. 6. All that are justly baptized are visible members of the church; but many are justly baptized that believe not the sovereignty of Rome: therefore, &c. the minor is evident by the Scripture direction for baptizing, and examples of it; and millions at this day in the church of God confirm it to us.

Argum. 7. They that have a promise of pardon, and are the adopted sons of God, and heirs of glory, are members of the church (beyond all question): but so are all that believe in Christ, and love God, whether they believe in the pope or not; as you may see expressly, John i. 12; iii. 15, 16, 18; xvii. 20—22, 24; Mark xvi. 16; John iii. 36; v. 24; vi. 35, 40, 47; vii. 38; xi. 25, 26; xii. 46; Rom. iii. 22, 26; iv. 11, 24; ix. 33; x. 9; Gal. iii. 22; 2 Thess. i. 10; Heb. iv. 3; Acts v. 14; 1 Pet. ii. 6; 1 John v. 1, 5, 10; Acts xiii. 39.

Argum. 8. If they must live in heaven with us, we have reason to take them for members of the church on earth: but all that truly love God, and believe in Christ, shall live in heaven with us though they never believed in the pope. Therefore, &c.

Argum. 9. They that are united in all the twenty particulars in the beginning expressed, are certainly members of the catholic church: but so are many that believe not in the pope. Therefore,

Argum. 10. The papists' doctrine goes against the certain experience of the sanctified. Some measure of assurance I have myself of the love of God in me; and much more many others have, as I see great reason to believe. Now popery binds me to conclude that I am void of charity, and all saving, special grace, because I believe not in the pope; that is, to renounce the experience of God's grace in my soul, and unthankfully to deny all these mercies of God. So that as sure as any protestant can be of charity or saving grace in himself, so sure may he be that popery is false doctrine; and that is enough.

Having spoken thus much to these several sects that would appropriate the catholic church to themselves, I shall once more speak to them altogether. Whether you are papists, or what sect soever, that are guilty of this grievous crime, I beseech you think of these following aggravations of your sin:

1. How evidently is your doctrine against the merciful nature of God, and contrary to that abundant grace which he hath manifested to mankind! Is he love itself; and his mercy over all his works reaching unto the heavens, and unconceivable by sinners? Hath he not thought the blood of his Son too dear for us? And yet can you believe those men that would persuade you that the far greatest part of the christians of the world are out of the church, and shall be damned, because they believe not in the pope of Rome, or because they are not rebaptized, or the like, how holy soever they are in other repects? Is this like God? or hath he thus described himself in his word? We are as willing as you to know the truth; and study, and pray, and seek as much after it, and would most gladly find it at any rates; and the more we search, and study, and pray, the more confident we are that your way is wrong: and must we yet be all unchristened that are not of your opinion?

2. How much do you wrong and dishonour the Lord Jesus in many respects! 1. Hath he purchased his church with his own blood; and now dare you presume to rob him of the far greater part of his purchase, because they be not of your opinion? I would not stand before him with the guilt of such a sin for all the world. 2. Dare you charge so great unmercifulness on Christ, that hath so wonderfully showed his mercy, and at so dear a rate? After all his blood and sufferings, dare you feign him to say to the world, Believe in me, and love me never so much: if you obey not the church of Rome, you cannot be my disciples, or be saved? Yea, and would he lay our salvation on this, and yet not reveal it to us, but say so much against it? Let him be of these men's minds that can, for I cannot. 3. Moreover, the weaknesses and diseases of the saints do honour the skill of Christ their Physician, that hath undertaken the cure, and in due time will accomplish it. And will you go and turn them all out of his hospital, and say they are none of his patients?

3. Your design is against the very nature of the catholic church, and the communion of saints. The design of Christ in the work of redemption was to gather all into one body, and bring them to God; to break down the partition wall between Jew and gentile, and take away the ordinances and ceremonies that occasioned the division, and to unite them all in himself the universal Head, Ephes. ii. 13—15; "that he might reconcile both to God in one body by the cross, having slain the enmity thereby," ver. 16. To this end, when he ascended, "he gave pastors and teachers, as well as apostles, prophets, and evangelists, for the perfecting of the saints, for the work of the ministry, for the edifying of the body of Chrst, till we all come in the unity of the faith, and of the knowledge of the Son of God, unto a perfect man, to the measure of the stature of the fulness of Christ,—that we may grow up into him in all things, which is the Head, even Christ; from whom the whole body fitly joined together, and compacted by that which every joint supplieth, according to the effectual working in the measure of every part, maketh increase of the body unto the edifying of itself in love," Ephes. iv. 11—13, 15, 16. In these several particulars you directly strike at the very nature of the catholic church. 1. The church is but one, and you tear off a member, and call it the whole, and so would make it many, or divide it. It was the design of Christ to unite all the differing parts; and you cross his design, and go about to separate that which he hath conjoined and cemented, even by his precious blood. 2. The church is united and centred in Christ, and knows no other head: the papists would set up a mortal and incapable man, and have all unite in him as a vicar head: and having not a word for this from Christ, they pervert one text, "The eye cannot say to the hand, &c. or the head to the feet, I have no need of you," 1 Cor. xii. 21. See here, say they, is a visible head: but, 1. It is visible to any man that will understand, that the term *head* is used of the natural body's head, by way of similitude; but when the thing assimilate (the mystical body) is mentioned, there is not a word of a head; but the application is of the more honourable or comely parts in general: many such heads there be, that is, more honourable parts, but no universal governor, that is it they should prove; they may else as well pretend, that beside the pope who is the head, there must be one or two universal eyes, and two universal hands, or feet, for the whole church. Thus men abuse themselves, when they will dare to wrest the Scripture to their interests. 2. But if it had spoke of one universal head, must it needs be the pope, or an earthly man? I must profess that very chapter is so full and plain against popery, that were there no more I could hardly be a papist. For mark, I pray you, 1. The Lord Jesus himself is expressly named in verse 12. And yet must we seek for another exposition of the word head? "All the members of that body being many, are one body; even so is Christ." It is Christ that the church is united in.

Object. But Christ may say to the feet, I have no need of you.

Answ. For himself he hath no need of any creature: but, 1. For the completing of the body he hath need of the members, which is the thing here mentioned. 2. And to his own glory he hath use for them. He that said of a colt, when he was to ride into Jerusalem, "The Lord hath need of him," may as well be said to have need of his members. 3. If neither prophet, apostle, or teacher, were head of the church, then the pope is not: for he pretends not to be greater than Peter the apostle. But none of these were the head, as is most plain; "Now ye are the body of Christ, and members in particular; and God hath set some in the church, first apostles, secondarily prophets, thirdly teachers," verses 27, 28. So that Christ only is made the Head, and apostles are altogether numbered with the prime or most honourable members, and no more.

So Colos. i. 18—20, "And he is the head of the body, the church.—For it pleased the Father, that in him should all fulness dwell; and, having made peace by the blood of his cross, by him to reconcile all things to himself." What a daring, vile attempt is it of that man, that would tear the greater half of the members from his body, when it hath cost him so dear to unite them in himself!

4. Moreover, your course is dishonourable to the church and cause of Christ. I know his flock is small; but to narrow it, as you would do, is exceedingly to dishonour it. To make men believe that God hath no more in all the world but your party, is to raise temptations and hard thoughts of God in the minds of men without any cause.

5. And if such a dividing censure must needs be passed, there is none less fit to do it than you, that are commonly forwardest to divide. If most of the christian world must needs be unchurched, to whose share were it liker to fall to you? Quakers I will say nothing to, their folly being so gross. Anabaptists are setting up a new church entrance in the end of the world: and if they know any thing of church history, they must needs know that, comparatively, there are few in heaven that were of their mind on earth. And for the papists, we have much ado to maintain our charity, in proving them to be a church at all. And the truth is, the question hath some difficulty, whether the church of Rome be a true church or no: to which I give this true and plain answer in brief.

The word *church* signifieth four things (pertinent to our present purpose). 1. The universal or catholic church as visible: so the church of Rome is not the church at all. 2. The universal church as invisible: so the church of Rome is not the church. 3. A particular political church of Christ's institution. And, 4. A community or mere country or company of christians, as part of the catholic church. Now as to these two last, the church of Rome signifieth, 1. Either all the papists formally as such, that is, as united to a pretended universal bishop. And in this formal respect the church of Rome is a false church, and no true church at all of Christ's appointing. 2. By the church of Rome may be meant, the persons that live under the papal captivity and subjection; not as his subjects formally, but as christians, and the subjects of Christ: and thus all christians in the church of Rome are a part of the universal church of Christ: a part, and but a part, as christians: no part, but the plague of the church, as papists. This is the plain truth. Your errors are great and numerous; yet we are willing to extend our charity as far as is possible, to take you for brethren: and will you be so froward as to unchurch others, even all the rest of the christian world, that have need of so much charity to yourselves? You cry out of the heresy of the Jacobites, Georgians, Syrians, Armenians, &c. Some are Nestorians, some are Eutychians, and I know not what: but woe to Rome, if worse men and more erroneous than they, may not be of the church, and saved! Shall I set down the words of the one of your own monks that dwelt among them in Judea? It is Bochardus Descript. Terra Sanct. 323—326. *Sunt in Terra promissionis*, &c. "There are in the Holy Land (saith he) men of every nation under heaven; and every nation liveth after their own rites: and to speak the truth, to our great confusion, there are none found in it that are worse, and of more corrupt manners, than the christians." (He means the papists.) Page 235, he saith, "Moreover those that we judge to be damned heretics, Nestorians, Jacobites, Maronites, Georgians, and the like, I found to be for the most part good and simple men, and living sincerely towards God and men, and of great abstinence," &c. ——And page 324, he tells you, "That the Syrians, Nestorians, Nubians, Jabeans, Chaldeans, Maronites, Ethiopians, Egyptians, and many other nations of christians there inhabit, and some are schismatics, not subject to the pope; and others called heretics, as the Nestorians, Jacobites," &c. "But (saith he) there are many in these sects exceeding simple, (or plain,) knowing nothing of heresies, devoted to Christ, macerating the flesh with fastings, and wearing the most simple garments, so that they even far exceed the very religious of the Roman church."

Thus by the testimony of your own eye-witnesses, even these that you cast out for heretics and schismatics, are far beyond even the religious of your church: what then are the reformed churches? Truly sirs, it is intolerable for the parlour to say, I am all the house; but for the chimney, kitchen, or coal-house, it is more intolerable. If your chief servant shall say, the rest are no servants, it is not well; but for the scullion or groom to say so, is worse. If the oak say, I am the whole wood, it is ill; but if the bramble say so, it is worse. If the best of your children should say, that all the rest are bastards, it is not well; but if the most vicious and deformed say so, it is worse.

And as you are unfit for quality to exclude all others, so also for number you are very unfit. As for the anabaptists, and such inconsiderable parties, that are not past the thousandth part of the church, or perhaps the many thousandth part of it (when yet the whole visible church is supposed to be but the sixth part of the world); I do admire how any christian can make himself believe that the love and grace of Christ is confined to so narrow a room, and his church so small. I think he that believeth once that Christ hath not one of so many thousands, is next to believing that he hath no church at all, and consequently that there is no Christ at all.

And for the papists, how deeply also are they guilty in this! As I said, in their greatest height now they are not near one half the christians in the world: a great part of their church are the poor Americans, whom they drive to baptism as cattle to water (yet not leaving it to their choice so much as to drink when they come thither): so that their own writers tell us, that multitudes of them know nothing of christianity but the name, and many forget that too. Awhile ago the papists were but a small part of the church, before Tenduc, Nubia, and other kingdoms fell away. One of their own bishops, and legate there resident, speaks upon his own knowledge of the state of the church in the eastern parts, "That in the easterly parts of Asia alone, the christians exceeded in multitudes both the Greek and Latin churches." (Jacob a Vitriaco Histor. Oriental. cap. 77.) And a most learned writer of their own, (Melch. Canus Loc. Theol. lib. 6, cap. 7, fol. 201,) saith, *Pugnatum est*, &c.——"Both the Greeks, and almost all the rest of the bishops of the whole world, did vehemently fight to destroy the privilege of the Roman church: and they had on their side both the arms of emperors, and the greater number of churches, and yet they could never bring it to pass, that the power of this one Roman pope should be abrogated." You see here by their own most express confession which way the most of the churches went, and that almost all or most of all the bishops of the world were against them (and so where our church was before Luther): and yet are these men a competent number to condemn all the rest of the churches of Christ, and appropriate all the catholic church to themselves? Oh what a world of faction do we live in! I am bitterly censured on one side for believing that any papists are parts of the catholic church: and, on the other side, we cannot persuade the papists, that any other are parts of it: and so they will needs be either the whole church, or none of it.

6. This factious course of unchurching all christians, saving yourselves, is contrary to the very internal nature of christianity. Every christian as a christian is taught of God to love the brethren, and by this all must know that we are Christ's disciples; and "he that loveth not his brother abideth in death." There is a holy disposition to unity and closure in all christians. And if you have not this disposition yourselves, you are but hypocrites: if you have it, how dare you sin against it? Though you must not unite with any in their sin, you must unite with all that are christians in their christianity.

7. Moreover, your course is contrary to christian humility, and proclaimeth the most abominable pride of the dividers. That you should call all the rest of the christian world schismatics and heretics, and say, that none are christians but you: why, what are you above other men, that you should say, Come not near me, I am holier than thou? Have none in the world, think you, faith, hope, and charity, but you? Can you indeed believe that none shall be saved but you? Alas, that you should not only so much overlook God's graces in your brethren, but also be so insensible of your own infirmities! Have you so many errors and sins among you, and yet are none of the church but you? Methinks a humble soul should say, Alas, I am so bad, that I am liker to be cast out than they; I am unworthy of the communion of the saints!

8. Yea, you trespass against common reason itself. Do you think it reasonable for us to believe, that all those that we see walk uprightly with God and men, earnest in prayer and study to know the truth, holy, and humble, and heavenly christians, are yet out of the church, and state of life, because they be not re-baptized with the anabaptists, or because they believe not in the pope of Rome with the papists? It is hard to imagine that he that pretends to believe such unreasonable things as these, doth well believe christianity itself.

9. And how could you honour and gratify the devil more, and magnify his kingdom, than by teaching men that most of the churches are his? Will you not be content to let him go away with all the unbelieving world, and all the hypocrites also in the church, but you will proclaim him the king of Christ's inheritance, even of the best and greatest part of his disciples, because they are not of your opinion, or your sect? What dealing is this for a christian to be guilty of?

10. Lastly, consider what uncomfortable doctrine it is that you deliver, especially to yourselves. You will not believe that all these sects and differing parties that hold the essentials are members of the catholic church: you scorn at such a church, and say, What a medley church is this! Will Christ entertain men of so many opinions, and of so much corruption? Yea, or else woe to you, and such as you are! Methinks you should rather say, Alas, what will become of me, if sinners and erring persons may not be christians, but must all perish? Oh what sins have I that are greater than many of their errors! And who is liker to err than such an ignorant wretch as I? Take heed lest you cut a shoe too little for your own foot; and lest you shut out so many that you must yourselves go out with the first. I must profess, after long, impartial studies, if I were of the opinion that most of the christian world are, out of the catholic church, I could not believe that the papists are in it.

Consider now of these aggravations of your sin: to think and say, 1. That one piece of the church is the whole church: 2. Yea, and a piece that is no greater: 3. That none of the best, nor far from the worst: 4. Nor any of the ancientest, whatever is pretended. 5. And to exclude the greatest part of christians for such a matter, as not believing in the pope of Rome. And, 6. Lastly, to do all this in pretence of unity, even to cast away the most of the church to unite it. What an unreasonable, unchristian course is this! Dividing spirits may plead what they will, but God will one day show them their sin in a fouler shape than here I have opened it, though it seem to them but pious zeal.

IV. My next address is to the papists, for answer to their great question, Where was your church before Luther? Give us a catalogue of the persons of all ages that were of your church?

Answ. Of OUR CHURCH! Why, sirs, do you think we have a catholic church by ourselves? Is there any more universal churches than one? Do you not know where the catholic church was before Luther, and in all ages? Why, *there* was *our* church; for we have no other, we know but one. Do you not know where there were any christians before Luther, or in all ages? Or would you have us give you a catalogue of christians? Wherever there were true christians, there was our church. Would you have the world believe that there were no christians but the subjects of the pope? Can you believe it yourselves? Doth not your Canus confess, as before cited, that most of the churches and bishops of the whole world were against the privileges of the church of Rome, and had the arms of emperors on their sides? Doth not your Reinerius long ago say, or whoever was the author of that conclusion, "The churches of the Armenians, Ethiopians, and Indians, and the rest which the apostles converted, are not under the church of Rome," Contr. Waldens. Catal. in Biblioth. Patr. T. 4, page 773. What fuller confessions can we desire? Nay, do we not know how small a part of the world did believe your universal sovereignty till almost a thousand years after Christ; and none at all for many hundred years after him, that any credible history tells us of? and yet do you ask us, where was our church?

But you must have us tell you where was a church that had all our opinions? To which I answer, 1. When you have showed us a catholic church that held all your opinions, we shall quickly tell you of one that held ours. 2. It is not all our opinions that are essential to a christian, and the catholic church. It is christianity that makes us christians and members of the church: it is not inferior truth. That which makes us christians and catholics, all true christians in the world have as well as we: and, therefore, we are of the same catholic church. Æthiopians, Syrians, Armenians, Egyptians, Jacobites, the many nations of Greeks, Muscovites, and Russians, and all other that are against the Roman sovereignty, are of the same religion and catholic church as we; and so are all among yourselves too that are christians indeed. The points which we agree in make us all christians, and church members; but the points in which we differ from the papists do make us so much sounder and safer christians than these, that I would not be one of them for all the world. A sound man is but a man; and so is a man that hath the plague: but yet there is some difference, though not in their manhood.

If, therefore, you will at any time try whether your doctrines or ours be the sounder, we are heartily willing to appeal to antiquity! Spit in his face, and spare not, that will not stand to this motion: That the oldest way of religion shall carry it; and they that are of latest beginning shall be judged to be in the wrong. I abhor that religion that is less than sixteen hundred years of age, and therefore I cannot be a papist. I confess in the streams of after-ages there have been divisions in the integrals of christianity, or the points that tend to the soundness of the churches. And in this, I say, let the oldest be held the best. But for the essentials of christianity, and the church, there never was division among true christians; for they could not be christians that wanted any essential part. And, therefore, that one church which contained all the christians in the world was our church before Luther; and the catalogues of the professors are our church rolls: but we count by thousands, and by countries, and not by names.

But perhaps you will say, You cannot be of the same church with the Greeks, or us, or the other parties that you name; for we and they do all renounce you. I answer, As if it were in your power who shall be no member of Christ and his church by your renouncing him! Your renouncing may prove you no christians yourselves perhaps, by proving you, in some cases, uncharitable; but it can do nothing to unchurch or unchristen others. If I should say myself, I am no member of the church, that doth not make me none, as long as I am a christian: much less can your saying so. Saith Paul, "If the foot shall say, Because I am not the hand, I am not of the body; is it therefore not of the body? and if the ear shall say, Because I am not the eye, I am not of the body: it is therefore not of the body?" 1 Cor. xii. 15, 16. The words of a man's mouth make not another to be what he is not, or cease to be what he is. Every one is not a bastard, or a whore, that another in railing passion calleth so. If Christ do but consent, we will be members of his body, whether the pope will or not.

And now, beloved hearers, you have been acquainted from the word of God, of the nature and unity of the catholic church, I beseech you resolve to retain this doctrine, and make use of it for yourselves and others. If any man ask you what church you are of, tell him that you are of that particular church where you dwell; but for the catholic church you know but one, and that you are of. Thrust not yourselves into a corner of the church, and there stand quarrelling against the rest: make not sectaries of yourselves, by appropriating Christ, and the church, and salvation to your party: abhor the very thoughts and name of any universal church of Christ, which is of narrower extent than christianity, and containeth fewer than all true christians, and is pretended to be confined to a sect. It is not the papists that are the catholic church, nor is it the Greeks, no, nor the protestants, much less the new prelates alone; but it is all christians through the world, of whom the protestants are the soundest part, but not the whole. Again, consider what a lamentable case it is, that so great a part of the church do seem to be at a loss about the church, as if they knew not where it is! That they run up and down the house of God, complaining that they cannot find the house, and know not which room it is that is the house. But in the house of God are many rooms and mansions: one for Greeks, and one for Æthiopians; one for Armenians, Georgians, and Syrians; one for many that are called papists; one for Lutherans and Arminians; one for anabaptists, and one for many that are truly guilty of schism and separation from particular churches: there is room for episcopal, presbyterians, independents, and Erastians; there is room for Augustinians, called Jansenists, and room for Calvinists; but yet no room for any but christians and catholics. Alas, that after so many warnings in plainest words of Scripture, and the history of so many ages, so many christians should yet be so carnal, as to be saying, I am of Paul, and I am of Apollos, and I of Cephas, that is, Peter; yea, that after Cephas is here named as a party, the papists should be so wilfully blind as still to make him the head of a party! That one is for Rome, and another for Constantinople, and another for Alexandria! When that Augustine hath so long ago decided this point against the Donatists, and told them which is the catholic church, even that which begun at Jerusalem, and is extended over the world wherever there be christians: alas, that still men are so stupid in their divisions, as to be crying out, Here is Christ, and there is Christ: here is the church, and there is the church: we are the church, and you are none of it: when the body of Christ and its unity is so frequently and plainly described in the Scripture. I know that none are members of the church that deny any essential point of christianity; but I know that many other mistaken parties are. Consider what an uncharitable, dangerous thing it is to give Christ's spouse a bill of divorce, or cast his children out of his family. And in the name of God take heed whilst you live, 1. That you never confine the church to a sect or party. 2. Nor ever cast out the least true christians, seeing Christ will never cast them out.

But because this disease hath miserably tormented us for so many ages, and because we see so many sick of it at this day, distractedly looking for the catholic church in this or that party, and thinking that all others are shut out, I shall here tell you what are the causes of this distraction, and in the discovery of the causes you may see the remedies. And withal I shall show you the hinderances of the concord and peace of the church, while so many seem to be all for peace! For it may seem a wonderful thing to hear almost all men cry up the church's peace and concord, and yet that it flieth further from us, when it is in our power to be possessors of it, if we were but truly and generally willing, as we pretend to be, and think that we are.

1. Some men understand not the nature of the union and concord of the church, nor how much is to be expected in this life, and therefore looking for more than is to be looked for, they think we have no unity, because we have not that which they ignorantly expect: and thereupon finding greater unity in this or that sect among themselves than they find in the whole body, they presently conclude that that sect is the church: they see a great many differing parties, and hear them condemning one another, and therefore they foolishly think that all these cannot possibly be of the true church: and then they hear the papists boast of their unity, as having one head, and one judge of controversies, and one expounder of Scripture, and being all of one belief, and therefore they think that the papists are the true church.

But consider before you run past your understandings of these two things: First, There is no perfect concord to be expected upon earth: this is the glory that is proper to the life to come. You might easily see this if you were but considerate. For, 1. There can be no perfect concord but where there is perfect light and knowledge; for while we are ignorant, we shall unavoidably err and differ. What do we quarrel about but matter of opinion? One thinks this is the right, and another thinks that is the right: and if we had all so much knowledge as to resolve all these doubts, do you think we should not be sooner agreed? Doubtless our disagreements are much for want of knowledge; we quarrel in the dark: if such a light would come in among us, as would show us all the truth, it would soon make us friends. But this is not to be expected in this life: even Paul saith, that here we know but in part: we understand as children; and think and speak as children; and is it any wonder to have children fall out? "But when that which is perfect is come, then that which is in part shall be done away: now we see through a glass darkly; but then face to face: now we know in part; but then we shall know even as we are known," 1 Cor. xiii. 9—12. And therefore we find even Paul and Barnabas so far disagreed as to part asunder, because they had not both so much knowledge as to know whether Mark should be taken with them or not. In heaven only we shall know perfectly; and therefore in heaven only we shall be united, and agree perfectly.

2. And we can never be perfect in union and agreement among ourselves till we are perfect in union and agreement with Christ. For we cannot regularly be nearer to each other than we are to our Centre; for it is the Centre only in which we must unite. It is not possible to be nearlier united among ourselves by a christian union than we are to Christ: and therefore seeing it is only in heaven that we are perfectly united to Christ, and at agreement with him, it is only in heaven that we must be perfectly united among ourselves. You marvel that we so much differ from one another, but you forget how much we all differ yet from Jesus Christ; and that this is the difference that must be first made up before we do any good of the rest.

3. Moreover, we can never be perfectly united and agreed till we are perfectly holy, and every grace be perfect in us: for holiness is that new nature in which we must be one; and every grace hath a hand in our accord. When we are perfect in love, and perfect in humility, and meekness, and patience, and perfect in self-denial, and all other graces, then, and never till then, shall we be perfect in our union and agreement among ourselves: while there is the least sin in the soul it will hinder our full agreement with God and men. It is sin that woundeth both the soul and the church, and makes all the debate and divisions among us; and when all sin is gone, then all differences will be done, and never till then. What an ignorant thing then is it of you to wonder so much at our many differences, and yet not to wonder at our sinfulness, and unholiness, and difference with Christ, in whom we must agree. Well, remember hereafter, that unity and concord is here to be expected but according to the proportion of our holiness, and therefore so much sin and ignorance as remain, no wonder if so much division remain.

The second thing which I desire you to remember is this, That in all the essential matters of christianity there is as true a unity among all the differing sorts of christians, as there is among the papists, or any one sect; even in all the twenty points of union, which I named in the beginning. And this is the union that is most to be esteemed; or at least this is enough to make us of one Christ. As the great essential points of faith are of far greater moment and excellency than our several controverted by-opinions, so is a union in these great essential points more excellent than a union in smaller matters; though both together is best of all, if joined with the truth.

To these let me add also a third consideration; That it is no wonder to find the papists as a sect agreed among themselves; for so are other sects as well as they: yea, let me add more, that I know not of any one sect in the world that differ so much among themselves as the papists do. The Greeks are kept from so much difference by their want of learning, which keeps them from meddling so much with niceties, and running into so many controversies as the papists do. The like may be said of the Ethiopians, Armenians, and many more. The protestants differ not in half nor a quarter so many points as the papists do. Nay, the very anabaptists themselves do not differ among themselves in the tenth part so many points as the papists. If the many hundred differences among their commentators, schoolmen, casuists, and other writers, were collected and presented to your view, I much doubt whether there be any one sect on the face of the earth that hath the twentieth part so many differences among themselves as the papists have. Though they think they salve all by saying that they differ not in articles of faith, yet their differences are never the fewer for that. And others may say more in that than they can do.

Well! remember this advice: expect not a heavenly perfection of unity and concord till you come to heaven.

2. Another cause of our distractions and hinderance of concord is, that very few men have peaceable spirits, even when they are extolling peace. A peaceable spirit must have these qualifications, which most men want. 1. He must be united to Christ, the Head and Centre of union, and have a sanctified nature, and value God's honour above all things else; that so his desires of peace may flow from a right principle, and may proceed upon right grounds, and to right ends; and he may seek a holy peace: and, alas, how few such spirits have we!

2. A peaceable spirit must be a public spirit, highly esteeming the welfare of the whole body, above any interest of his own, or of any sect or party. The great grace of self-denial is of necessity herein. No man hath a christian, peaceable spirit, that doth not most highly value the peace and prosperity of the universal church, so far as to submit to losses or sufferings himself for the obtaining of it; and that had not rather his party suffered than the whole. But, alas, how rare is a public spirit in any eminency! how private and selfish are the most! The good of the church can no further be endeavoured, with too many, than self will give leave, and than their party will give leave: these must be made the masters of the consultation.

3. A peaceable spirit must be a charitable spirit; loving all the saints as saints; and that with a pure heart, and fervently: this would put by the matter of contentions: this would provoke men to healing endeavours; and it would put the best construction on men's opinions, words, and actions, that they can bear. "Charity suffereth long, and is kind; charity envieth not; charity vaunteth not itself, is not puffed up, doth not behave itself unseemly, seeking not her own, is not easily provoked, thinketh no evil; rejoiceth not in iniquity, but rejoiceth in the truth; beareth all things, believeth all things, hopeth all things, endureth all things," 1 Cor. xiii. 4—7. Oh what an effectual healer is charity! what a tender hand will it bear to any distressed member! much more to the whole church. What causeth our dis-

tractions more than want of charity; what else makes men look so scornfully, and speak so disgracefully of every sort of christians but themselves? And to endeavour to make others as odious as they can; and to make mere verbal differences seem real, and small ones seem exceeding great; and to find out a heresy or a blasphemy in the smallest error, and perhaps in a harmless word: all is blasphemy with some men, or error at least, which they do not understand. Alas, we have real heresies and blasphemies enough among Arians, Socinians, ranters, quakers, seekers, libertines, familists, and many others; let us reject these that are to be rejected, and spare not; but we need not feign heresies and blasphemies where they are not, as if we wanted matter for our indignation.

4. A peaceable spirit must be in some measure meek and patient, with a humble consciousness of its own frailties and offences: but, alas, what passionate, rash, and turbulent spirits do abound in the poor divided church! Such as are made of gunpowder, and speak fire and sword; that will do no right, nor bear any wrong; that will speak well of few but their own party, and yet cannot endure to be ill spoken of themselves; that are possessed with the "wisdom which is from beneath, which is earthly, sensual, and devilish," and are strangers to the heavenly "wisdom, which is first pure, and then peaceable, gentle, and easy to be entreated," James iii. 15, 17. Even preachers of peace are some of them become the fervent agents of the divider, and go up and down with destroying rage, and make their tongues the bellows of hell, resisting the peaceable endeavours of their brethren.

5. A peaceable spirit must have a high esteem of peace, and be zealous for it, and industrious to obtain it. Only against ungodliness and unpeaceableness must he be unpeaceable. Many have a good wish and a good word for peace, as hypocrites have for godliness, but this will not serve the turn. He that is not for us is against us, and he that gathereth not with us scattereth abroad. The wicked and unpeaceable are zealous and industrious against peace; and those that are for peace are cold and indifferent for the greater part; and the zealous and industrious are so few, that their voices cannot be heard in the contentious crowd. The unpeaceable are commonly the loudest, and are actuated by a fervent zeal, which nature agreeth with, and Satan cherisheth and excites: such will, even as the quakers, go up and down from one assembly to another, and in the market-places, and other places of concourse, revile, and rail, and reproach the ministry, and speak as earnestly as if they were the agents of Christ. And others are busy in secret, that will not incur the disgrace of such visible impiety. And when the enemies of unity and peace are many, and hot, and loud, and the friends of unity and peace are either few, or cold, and dull, and silent, what is like to be the issue but even the mischiefs which we feel? Forsooth, some dare not be fervent for peace, lest they be censured for their fervour to be unpeaceable: these show how much they love the praise of men, and stick yet in the power of self. There is need of zeal for peace, as well as for other parts of holiness. All the resistance that the enemies of hell and earth can make will be made against it: and will it be carried on against all by sleepy wishes, and sitting still? I am sure this agrees not with the precepts of the Spirit: "Follow peace with all men," Heb. xii. 14. "If it be possible, as much as in you lieth live peaceably with all men," Rom. xii. 18. It is a sorry surgeon, or a physician, that will think it enough to wish well to their patient. The house of God will be neither built nor repaired without zeal, and industry, and patience in the work. If men's hearts were set upon the church's peace, and they did but feel the disjointing of her members, the breaking of her bones, and the smart of her wounds, as sensibly as they feel the like in their own bodies; and if ministers, and other christians, were as sensible of the evil of divisions as they are of drunkenness and whoredom, and such other sins; and if we were all awakened to quench the flames of the church, as earnestly as we would do the fire in our houses, and would preach for peace, and pray for peace, and plead, and labour, and suffer for peace, then some good might be done on it against the rage and multitude of dividers.

3. One of the greatest hinderances of concord and peace, is the setting up of a false centre, and building peace on grounds that will never bear it. Christian unity is no where centred but in Christ the Head, and no way maintained but by the means which he hath ordained to that end. But the miserable world will not discern or take up with this. The papists are of two churches; for they have two heads, or sovereigns, which specify the society. One of the popish churches make the pope the head and centre, and all the church must unite in him, or it can be no church. The other popish church do make a general council the head, and the pope only the subordinate sovereign in the vacancy. And these think to have the whole church to unite upon these terms. But it will never be. As divine faith will have no formal object but divine veracity, so neither can christian unity have any universal proper centre but Christ. As at the building of Babel, when men would unite for their future security in their own devices, it brought them to utter confusion, which the world groaneth under to this day; so when men will build a Babel of their own invention, for the preventing of the inundation of heresies, they are upon the most dreadful work of confusion. The church is taught by the Scripture, and the Holy Ghost within them, to take up no where short of God; to call no man on earth the father or master of our faith, nor to trust in man, and make flesh our arm. Man is too dark and too weak a creature to be the head or centre of the church-deluded papists! You think you befriend the church's unity, when you hang it by a hair, and build it on the sand, and found it on mere weakness; could you prove that ever God had promised abilities and gifts to the pope of Rome, proportionable to such a work, we should most gladly look out to him for the exercise of those abilities. God setteth none on work but he furnisheth them with a suitableness for it. Have all popes or councils prophetical and apostolical inspirations and directions? What! those that have been censured, and some of them deposed, for blasphemy, heresy, sodomy, adultery, murder, simony, and such works of darkness? The Spirit useth not to dwell in such persons, nor light to have communion with such darkness. Nay, if all popes were holy, yea, as holy as Peter, they were too weak to bear up the unity of the church. It is Christ, and not Peter, that is called the Rock, on which the church is built, against which the gates of hell shall not prevail. This Rock is Christ, 1 Cor. x. 4. The church is the spouse of Christ, and must not be made a harlot, by being wedded to the pope, or any other. Nothing hath more hindered the fuller union of the church than this idol, self-exalting head, and false centre of union.

And if any would unite the church in kings, in councils, in any human devices, they will but divide it.

4. And the same course take they that must needs build our union on insufficient subordinate means.

Some must have confessions in words of their own, to which all that will be accounted christians must subscribe; or at least, all that would have communion with them. Though we would subscribe to the whole Scripture, or any confession drawn up in its phrase and matter, yet this will not serve for union and communion. They tell us, heretics will subscribe to the Scripture: and I tell them, that heretics may subscribe also to their confessions, and force a sense of their own upon them; and that God never left them to make better confessions, and fitter to discover heresies, than Scripture doth afford. But if heretics will subscribe to the Scriptures, or confessions taken wholly out of them, they should be no heretics in our account till they discover that they maintain some heresy against the sense of the Scripture, or confession which they subscribed to: and then they are to be censured by the churches accordingly; not for want of subscribing to a sufficient confession, but for abusing and contradicting the confession which they did subscribe; and so to be corrected for it as a crime against a sufficient law and rule; and we must not think to prevent it by making a better law or rule, which shall tie them stricter, and which they cannot break. It is a strange rule, which can necessitate the subject to observe it, and which cannot be violated. And it is a wild head that must have new laws and rules made, because he sees that malefactors can break these! The law is sufficient to its own part, which is to be the rule of duty, and of judgment. It tells men sufficiently what they must believe and do; but if they will not do it, it judgeth them as offenders. You will never form a confession, or make a law that cannot be misinterpreted and broken. The papists have set up whole volumes of councils and decrees for the *rule* forsooth, because the Scripture is dark, and all heretics plead Scripture. And what have they done by it, but cause more darkness, and set the world and their own doctors too in greater contentions; so that now councils cross councils, and they can neither agree which be true approved councils, and which not; nor when they intend a decree to be an article of faith, and when not; no, nor what sense to take their words in, and how to reconcile them. And thus men lose themselves, and abuse the church, because God's word will not serve their turn as a rule for us to unite upon. This is the one rule that God hath left, and men will needs blame this as insufficient, and mend God's works by the devices of their addle brains, and then complain of divisions, when they have made them! One company of bishops must needs make a company of canon laws for the church, and all must be schismatics that will not be ruled by them: another company that are of another mind make contrary canons, and those must be obeyed, or else we are schismatics. They must make us our sermons, and call them homilies, and make us our prayers, and call them a liturgy; and the fruit of their brains must be the rule of all others, or else they are schismatics. So wise and holy are they above all their brethren, that none must publicly speak to God in any words but what they put into their mouths. (Read Dr. Heylin's Discourse of Cant. v. 5, against ministers praying in the church in any other words but what is in the Common Prayer book.) So they do also by their vestures, and gestures, and other ceremonies: nothing hath more divided the church than the proud impositions of men, that think so highly of their own words and forms, and ceremonious devices, that no man shall have communion with Christ and the church in any other way. Never will the church unite on such terms. The rule that all must agree in must be made by one that is above all, and whose authority is acknowledged by all. Experience might tell these men, that they are building but a Babel, and dividing the church. In the Lord's supper, where they have limited us to a gesture, we are all in pieces. In singing psalms, where they left us free, we have no dissension. In the places where garments and other ceremonies are not imposed, God's worship is performed without contention, and with as little uncomeliness as with them. Proud, quarrelsome men, that must needs be lording it over the church, and turning legislators, may set all on fire for the promoting of their ways, and rail at all that will not be under their yoke: but when they have all done, they will find they are but busily dividing the church, and their canons are but fiery engines to batter its unity and peace. A thousand years' experience and more, might have taught us this to our cost. Never will the church have full unity, till the Scripture sufficiency be more generally acknowledged. You complain of many opinions and ways, and many you will still have, till the one rule, the Scripture, be the standard of our religion. As men that divide and separate from us, do use to accuse the ministers, and then be every man a teacher to himself; so they use to accuse the Scriptures, and, as the papists, call them dark, and dangerous, and insufficient; and then every sect must make us a new rule, when they have disparaged that which Christ hath given us. Then one makes the pope a rule by his decretals, and another a council, and another the bishops, canons, or articles, and another his own suggestions and impulses. Stick close to this one Bible, and let nothing come into your faith or religion but what comes thence; and when controversies arise, try them by this; and if you cannot do it yourselves, then take the help of ministers or synods, and use them not as masters, but as helpers of your faith; not to make you another rule, but to help you to understand this only rule; and thus you may come to be of one religion, but never otherwise.

5. To these I may add the damnable sin of pride and selfishness, touched at before. All men would have peace; but most would have it on their own terms; yea, and most parties would be the very centre of the churches. If all the world will come over to them, they will be at peace with them, otherwise not. If we will all swear allegiance to the pope, and turn to them, we shall have concord with the papists. If we will all renounce presbyterian ordination, and submit to episcopacy, with all their canons, forms, and ceremonies, we shall have concord with the rigid of that party. If we will all be for an office of unordained elders, that have no power to meddle with preaching or sacraments, we shall have peace with the rigider sort of that way. If we will causelessly separate, and make the major vote of the people to be church governors, we may have peace with men of that way. And if we will be re-baptized, we may have peace with the anabaptists. But can all the catholic church unite upon these private, narrow terms? Every man would be the pope or the general council himself: or rather every one would be the god of the world; that all men may receive the law at his mouth, and his name may be honoured, and his kingdom may be set up, and his will may be done throughout the world: this is the nature of self-idolizing pride. And hence it is that the church hath as many dividers as unsanctified men; because every unsanctified man is thus made an idol by his pride, and knows no further end but self. Is there never a man of you that hears me this day, that would not have all the town, and country, and world to be of one mind? I think there is not one but

wisheth it. But what mind must it be? It must be of your mind; or else it will not satisfy you! And alas, you are so many, and of so many minds among yourselves, that this way will never unite the world! One must have all of his mind, and another must have all of his mind, when no man well agrees with another, and yet none will be brought to another's mind. But God is one, and his mind is certainly right and good: and the Spirit is one, and the Scripture indited by it is one; and if you would come to that as the only rule, you might be of one religion, and mind, and way; but till then you do but labour in vain. But you will say still, that every sect pretendeth to the Scripture, and there is so many expositions of it, that we see no hopes that this way should unite us: to this I next answer.

6. It is the bane of unity when men must make every inferior opinion the seat of unity, and will not unite in the essentials of christianity, endeavouring in love to accord as well as they can in the rest. Though the truth of the whole Scripture, that is known to be holy Scripture, must be acknowledged; yet the understanding of the meaning of the whole Scripture is not of necessity to salvation, or church unity: otherwise woe to every one of us! For there is no man on earth that hath the perfect understanding of all the holy Scriptures. And yet all that is in it propounded to be believed is *de fide*, matter of faith, and it is our duty to believe it, and understand it, and our sin that we do not; but not a sin that proves us graceless, or unjustified. I wonder the papists have not venial errors in matters of faith, as well as venial sins against moral precepts! But all that is *de fide*, must with some of them be fundamental or essential to christianity. The Scripture is a full and beautiful body, which hath its flesh, and skin, and a multitude of nerves, and veins, and arteries, as well as the head, the heart, and stomach, and other natural parts; without which parts, that are the seat or chief instruments of the animal, vital, and natural spirits, the body were no body. All in the Scripture is true and useful, but all is not essential to christianity. And in the essentials all christians do agree; and if you would know how such should behave themselves to one another, hear the Holy Ghost himself, (Phil. iii. 12—16,) "Not as though I had already attained, or were already perfect; but I follow after, if that I may apprehend that for which also I am apprehended of Christ Jesus. Brethren, I count not myself to have apprehended; but this one thing I do, forgetting those things which are behind, and reaching forth to those things that are before, I press towards the mark for the prize of the high calling of God in Christ Jesus. Let us therefore, as many as be perfect, be thus minded; and if in any thing ye be otherwise minded, God shall reveal even this unto you: nevertheless, whereto we have already attained, let us walk by the same rule, let us mind the same thing." So 1 Cor. iii. 11—15, "Other foundation can no man lay, than that is laid, which is Jesus Christ. Now if any man build on this foundation gold, silver, precious stones, wood, hay, stubble, every man's work shall be made manifest: for the day shall declare it, because it shall be revealed by fire, and the fire shall try every man's work of what sort it is. If any man's work abide which he hath built thereupon, he shall receive a reward: if any man's work shall be burnt, he shall suffer loss; but he himself shall be saved, yet so as by fire." Errors may bring heavy judgments in this life, and out of this fire the erroneous may escape, and not fall into the eternal fire; for thus will God "sit as a refiner, and purifier of silver, and will purify the sons of Levi, and purge them as gold and silver, that they may offer to the Lord an offering in righteousness," Mal. iii. 2, 3. Dislike every error, and escape as many as you can; but think not that every error must dissolve our unity, or that every truth is necessary to our unity.

And where you say that all sorts do plead the Scriptures, I answer, 1. That all sorts of christians in the essentials do rightly understand the Scripture. 2. And for the rest, their very pleading that, shows that all sorts are convinced that it is the rule of truth, even where they do not understand it. 3. And this is no proof of the insufficiency of Scripture, but of the imperfection of men's understandings; and instead of seeking for another rule, you should labour for a better understanding of this, and use the help of ministers thereto. The law of the land is the rule of the subjects' actions, and tenures; and yet what controversies are about it, even among the wisest lawyers! and one pleadeth it for one cause, and another saith that the law is for the contrary cause! Yea, one judge differs from another. What then? must we cast away the law? Let us know where to have a better first! But rather, men should labour to know it better, and live quietly in obedience of what they know, and meddle not contentiously with the niceties of it without need. And thus we must do about the law of God; agree in the essentials, and learn the rest as well as we can.

7. Another great impediment to our concord is, abundance of dividing, unpeaceable principles, that be grown into credit, or entertained in the world: and if such principles meet with the most peaceable disposition, they will make the man become unpeaceable. For the best men that are will think they must obey God; and therefore when they mistake his will, they will think they do well when they are sinning against him. There are too few in the world of a peaceable principle: some lay all peace, as is said, on the opinions of their own parties; and some lay it on a multitude of such low opinions, and such doubtful things, that they might know can never be the matter of universal consent. Some think they must not silence any thing which they conceive to be a truth, for the peace of the church, or the promoting of greater undoubted truths. Some think they ought to reproach and disgrace all that are not of their mind; and some think they ought to destroy them, or cast them out, and think this a part of their faithfulness to the truth of Christ, and that this is but to help him against his enemies. And there is no more desperate principle of division and persecution than this uncharitableness, which makes the children of God, and the members of Christ, to *seem* his enemies, and then use them as his enemies: to dress them in a false attire, as they did Christ, and then smite him: to put them in the shape of schismatics, or heretics, or devils, as the papists do when they burn them, and then use them accordingly. Many more unpeaceable principles I might recite; and if it were not too tedious, I think it would be useful.

8. Another hinderance of unity and peace is, a carnal zeal in matters of religion, which is frequently mistaken for the true zeal of the saints. When men are confident that their opinions are the truth, and overvalue them as to the necessity, because they are their own, though they observe not the reason, they presently think they must be hot against all the gainsayers of their opinions; and herein they place the most, or at least too much of their religion.

There is not one of many that hath this zeal, but thinks it is of God, and is part of their holiness. Whenas it is often from the devil and the flesh, even when the doctrine is true which they contend for. You may know it from true zeal by these following marks. 1. It is more for controversies and speculations than for practical holiness. 2. It is selfish, and kindled by an overvaluing their own conceits or ways. 3. It is private, and would promote a lower truth to the loss of a greater, or a doubtful point to the loss of undoubted truth; or a single truth to the loss or hinderance of the body of common truth; and it is hotter for a party than for the catholic church, and will promote the interest of an opinion or party, to the wrong of the common interest of the church. 4. It is blind, and carries men to sinful means; as resisting authority, order, or ordinances, or the like. 5. It is unmerciful and unpeaceable, and little sensible of the case of others, or smart of the divided church. Many are calling for fire from heaven for the cause of Christ, that little "know what spirit they are of;" Luke ix. 55. Oh how true is this of many, that think they excel in knowledge or zeal, and are but defending the truth against erroneous adversaries! But "who is the wise man, and endued with knowledge among you? let him show out of a good conversation his works with meekness of wisdom. But if ye have bitter envying and strife in your hearts, glory not, and lie not against the truth. This wisdom descendeth not from above, but is earthly, sensual, devilish. For where envying and strife is, there is confusion and every evil work. But the wisdom that is from above is first pure, then peaceable, gentle, and easy to be entreated, full of mercy and good fruits, without partiality, and without hypocrisy. And the fruit of righteousness is sown in peace of them that make peace," James iii. 13, to the end. But of this I have formerly spoken at large in many sermons on these words of James. Dividing zeal is a grievous distracter of the church's peace.

9. Another hinderance is, that of the many that are for peace and unity, there are few that have any great skill to promote it; and those few that have skill, want opportunity or interest, and are cried down by the opposers. There is a great deal of skill necessary to discern and manifest the true state of controversies, and to prove verbal quarrels to be but verbal, and to take off the false visors which ignorance and passion puts on them, to aggravate the differences that are debated. There is much wisdom necessary for the securing of truth, while we treat for peace, and the maintaining peace, while we defend the truth. Alas, how few escape one of the extremes in most differences themselves! and, therefore, are unfit reconcilers of others. Few are possessors of that blessed light that doth show the error of both extremes, and must be the means of our concord, if ever we agree. Few know that truth between contrary errors in which both must meet. How much skill also is necessary to deal with touchy, froward spirits, and to handle both nettles and thorns that must be dealt with! And how few men of wisdom and peace are much regarded by the firebrands of the churches! and how few of them have language, and health, and maintenance, and authority, and a skilful activity to set others on work, which are almost needful for this healing design! And what abundance of private wishes have been buried by the skilfullest men for want of opportunities! And how many private writings cast by, that have that in them that deserved public entertainment, and might have been very fit instruments for this healing work!

10. And the various carnal interests of the world, are an exceeding hinderance to the church's peace. The interest of one prince lieth for one party; and another is for another party: one prince thinks it for his interest to unite, and another thinks it for his interest to divide, or secretly to cherish and continue divisions. The ministry also have too oft a carnal interest, which lieth usually in siding with the prince; and the great carnal interest of the Roman clergy lieth in sticking close to the pope. The people hereupon are commonly in such distractions and disturbances, by wars or secular cares and wants, that motions of peace can scarce be heard, or attended to; but the noise of guns, drums, and lamentations, and reproaching of enemies, drowneth all. And when the crossing of secular interests hath made them one another's enemies, they will hardly treat as friends for unity in religion, or the healing of the church.

11. And it is no small hinderance that the princes of the earth are commonly so bad, as either to be strangers to the true interest of Christ and his church, or else to prefer their own before it. It is they that have the greatest interests and opportunities, and might do most for unity if they would. And withal they think that nobody should meddle without their leave; and commonly when they do nothing themselves, they will not suffer the ministers to do it that are their subjects. How easy were it with the christian princes and states, if they had so much wit and grace to agree together, to bring the churches in their dominions to much agreement! But alas, highest places have greatest temptations, and therefore too oft the worst men: so that they that should do it, and might do it, have no heart to it. And the princes are very rare that prefer Christ's interest before their own; and have truly learned the lesson of denying themselves, and forsaking all they have for him. The great work of converting the heathen world should be promoted by them; but how little is there done in it by any princes!

12. Moreover, the multitude are every where almost averse to holy unity and peace: their dispositions are against it; their principles are against it: their parts unfit for it: and yet how to do it without them will be hard. For, 1. They have all of them almost conceits of their own fitness; and think all matters in religion should be regulated by them. They detest that a few should overtop them, and do the work while they stand by; and they grow to a hatred of those few, because they are counted wiser and better than they; yea, they naturally hate the godly, and the practical truths of God: and yet the greater vote must carry it, or else the swarm will be about your ears: when it is a hundred to one, but a hundred for one in most places of the world are in the wrong, if not bitter enemies to the right. And in the best parts of the world, it is a wonder if the greater part be not the worse. Or if in a corner or two it should be better, what is that to all the christian world? 2. At least if they will not be passively peaceable, how little can we do, when it is they that must, in part, consent, and it is they that have the strength to resist.

13. And even among the godly the peace-makers are far the smaller number, I mean as to the healing of our common divisions. For the younger sort of christians, in age, or grace, or gifts, are the greatest number: and these also are of the most active, hot dispositions, and will be forwardest in all agitations, and will not stand by. And alas, how few of them have meekness, prudence, and charity, answerable to their heat and activity! They will lead their leaders; and their way must carry it, or else all are censured and trod down by them: and how ordinarily is their way unpeaceable and confusive! And how seldom doth it end according to their expectations, for the churches' good! But for the wise and judicious, experienced, sober, peaceable men, alas, how few are they! till they grow aged few attain to this. And yet nothing will be done for the peace

and welfare of the church but by the conduct and direction of these few experienced, judicious, moderate men. None else can do it; and yet few other will suffer them to do it. And thus we see here in these nations, that even religious men have been the hinderers of our peace.

14. And withal, the devil, who is the great enemy of peace and unity, is still watching to cast in some bone of contention, and to make use of the opinions and passions of all, both good and bad, for the accomplishing of his ends. And alas, his subtlety overreacheth not only the ignorant people, but the most learned divines, and prudent princes. They shall not manage their affairs of state so carefully, but he will engage them against Christ and the peace of the church, before they are aware. He will do his utmost to make the interest of Christ and the prince, of the church and the commonwealth, to seem to stand at an enmity to each other, and make princes walk in a jealousy of Christ, and his gospel, and ministers, lest they should encroach upon their honour and greatness: and too oft he engageth them in flat opposition, till this stone fall upon them, and grind them to powder.

And the ministers of the gospel shall scarcely manage their work so wisely, but he will cast in some wildfire, and find some occasion to make a dissension by. Either the subtlety of men too wise and learned, in their own eyes, shall start some dividing, fruitless controversies; or the zeal of men that are orthodox over-much, shall rise up unpeaceably against all dissenters: or he will entangle the godly in some dangerous errors; or he will seek to make men lay snares for their brethren, by needless impositions, under pretence of order, and decency, and unity, and authority; or some passionate words shall kindle the fire. There are many unsound hypocrites among godly ministers; and there is too much pride and passion in the best, and Satan knows how to make use of all. What! saith he to the proud, shall such a one be preferred before thee? shall he bear away the applause? shall he eclipse and stand in the way of thy reputation? Did he not speak dishonourably of thee; or carry himself disregardfully towards thee? Did he not disgrace thee by such an opposition or dispute? A hundred temptations hath Satan at hand to kindle dissension, even among the ministers of Christ: and where he meets with proud hearts he seldom misseth of his purpose. If the disciples were striving which should be the greatest, and if Paul and Barnabas fall out to a parting, no wonder if pride and dissension be yet found among the most renowned men. Though it is a sad case that it should be so, when we daily preach humility to our people, and know, that except conversion make us little children, we can in no wise enter into the kingdom of God, Matt. xviii. 3.

How hard a task hath a peaceable minister to keep one congregation of christians in peace! But differences will be rising, and one will be provoking another by injuries, or hard words, and few can bear, and forbear, and forgive. Yea, a master of a family finds it hard to keep one small family in peace. Yea, two persons find somewhat to do to keep peace, especially if they have much trading, or dealing with each other, or any crossing in matters of commodity. Yea, husband and wife, that are as one flesh, have much ado to avoid dissensions. No wonder then if the enemy of peace can disturb the church of Christ.

15. Another cause of divisions is, living among and hearkening to schismatical persons that are still blowing the coals. It is a dangerous case, especially to young, unexperienced christians, to fall among those that make it their religion to vilify others as enemies of Christ. When they hear one sect only extolled, and all others spoken of as ignorant, or carnal, or enemies to the church, it is two to one but this imprinteth a schismatical disposition in the hearers' minds. Conversing only with one party doth usually occasion great uncharitableness towards all others, and sear the conscience, so that it grows insensible of revilings, and opprobrious speeches, against those that differ from them.

16. And the unity of the church is exceedingly hindered by an unworthy privacy and retiredness of most christians, that live like the snail in a shell, and look but little abroad into the world. Some know not the state of the world, or of the church, nor much care to know it; but think it is with all the world as it is with us in England: whenas if they knew the fewness of christians, the huge numbers of infidels, the corruptions of other churches, in comparison of ours, it would surely set them a-lamenting, and praying that the kingdom of Christ might come. Yea, many ministers are of so base a privacy of spirit, that they look little further than their own parishes, and think if all be well there, all is well every where; and seldom inquire how it goes with the church in the rest of the world: nor will scarce be brought to associate and keep correspondence with their brethren, for the union and communion of the several churches and the common good: far unlike the temper of Paul, and the other apostles and servants of Christ in those days. They have not a care of all the churches. They long not to hear of their welfare. They would think it much to travail and labour for it the thousandth part so much as they. They cannot say, "Who is weak, and I am not weak," &c.

17. Yea, some are drawn from the church's unity and peace by misunderstanding those texts of Scripture that call for separation from the world, and that speak of the fewness of those that shall be saved. I have heard of one that turned separatist upon this conceit, because he thought that, seeing the flock of Christ is little, the protestants were too many to be it: at last the separated church grew so big, that he thought, Sure this is not the flock, and so turned to the anabaptists: at last the anabaptists' church so increased, that he thought, Sure this is too big to be the little flock: and so went seeking about for the least, as thinking that must needs be in the right. Alas, what low thoughts have such of the church of God! yea, and of the love and gracious nature of God, and of the great design of Christ in the work of redemption! But the main cause of the delusion of these poor souls is, because they know not the state of the world abroad. If they did but know that it is the sixth part of the world that are baptized common christians, and not past a sixth or seventh part of that sixth part that are common protestants, but all the rest are papists, and Greeks, and many sorts of more ignorant, unreformed christians; and among the protestants, no country for godliness is like to England; they would not go about to pen up the church into a narrower room. To believe that Christ died, and made so much ado, for so small a part of the world, as comes not to one of forty, or fifty, or a hundred thousand, is next to flat infidelity itself, which thinks died for none at all.

And for the command, "Come out from among them, and be ye separate," it is pity that any christian should need be told, that it speaks only to the church to come out of the heathen, infidel world (such as are Jews, and Mahometans, and heathens); but there is never a word in all the Bible that bids you, Come out of the church, and be ye separate! Wonderful! that God should be so abused by misunderstanding christians! Because he commands men to come out of the infidel world into the church, they plead it as if he commanded them to come out of the church into a separated sect. The church is the house of Christ; forsake it not, while *he* stays in it: forsake it not, for he hath promised never to forsake it. Particular churches indeed he may cast off, but never the universal. Dwell therefore where he dwells.

18. Another hinderance of peace is, that so many christians, as they have carnal dispositions, so they are still looking at carnal means. The endeavours of the ministry they account as nothing; but they are still looking what the magistrate will do; and till he force them they will not stir, and till he do it they think there is nothing done: such base thoughts have some, even ministers, of their own callings. And hence it is that such men are always on the stronger side, and of the king's religion; or else are seeking carnal advantages to carry on their cause. So the Jesuits are more busy to get the princes of the world engaged for them, and the arms of the nations employed for their ends, than we are to treat of unity and peace: and every party, instead of seeking peace, is seeking to get highest, that they may be able to force all others to their will: and we can never get any peaceable debates upon equal terms, because the several parties do seldom stand on equal terms; but still one is up, and another is down: and he that is in the saddle will not light to treat of peace, nor hearken to any equal motions, but must have his will, and nothing less will serve the turn; and when he is down, and the other party is up, the case is the same. Still he that is lowest is most reasonable and peaceable (except some impious, implacable spirits); but the party that is highest will not be brought to reason. And thus the peace of the church is hindered, to our grief and shame.

19. Another great hinderance of unity and concord is, the great weaknesses and miscarriages of the professors of godliness, partly because of hypocrites among them, and partly because they are sanctified but in part. Among others, by these several ways, they do disturb our peace.

1. By an ignorant quarrelling with their teachers, thinking themselves fit to correct their guides before they are considerably grounded in the catechism.

2. By entertaining false opinions, and making a disturbance for them.

3. By the great diversity of opinions among themselves, by which they become a scorn or stumbling-block to many about them.

4. By the uncharitable bitterness of their spirits, in rash censures and contendings.

5. By their scandalous lives, and falls, disgracing their profession, and hardening and alienating the minds of others.

And, 6. By their imprudent and intemperate dealing with others; using proud or provoking language, or carriage that more savoureth of contempt than of compassion. And thus the children of the church do divide it. Especially by their childish fallings-out with one another, and hearkening to malicious, contentious hypocrites, that would lead them to despise their guides, and break them into shreds among themselves, Rom. xvi. 17.

20. Lastly, The greatest hinderance of our unity is, the ungodliness of the most that profess themselves christians, whereby they become uncapable matter for our truest, nearest union, and yet think that we must be united to them all: when they will not join with us in the vitals of christianity, but stick in the bark, and take up with the name, yet do they think that we must join with them, and be of their communion and opinions in all external things, and if we differ from them they think we are schismatics. Men lay the church's unity too much in mere speculations, which they call the articles of faith, and too little in practicals, and holiness of life; whereas there is no article of faith, but is for practice; and as truly as the understanding and will are both essential to the soul, so truly the sanctity of understanding and will are both essential to a christian: and as the holiness of the heart is as essential as faith to a real christian, or member of the church regenerate; so the profession of holiness is as essential as the profession of faith to make a man a member of the church visible or congregate. And therefore as we can have no inward union and communion with any but the truly sanctified, so can we have no visible church union or communion but with those that profess to be truly sanctified. It is a shameful thing to hear every drunkard and scorner at godliness to rail at the many divisions in the church, and to call for unity and concord, when it is he, and such as he, that hinder it, that will not be united to Christ himself, nor join with us in the only centre of union, nor in the greatest and most necessary things, without which all christian union is impossible. But because I take this to be a necessary point, I shall handle it, God willing, more fully by itself.

To conclude all, let me exhort all christians to drink in this truth into their judgments and affections. If you are christians indeed, you are catholics. And if so, you must have, 1. Catholic principles; and, 2. Affections. I beseech you look to both these well.

And as you must keep the great catholic principle, which is the subject of our discourse, viz. to know what a true catholic is, and which is the catholic church, that so you may not do as the papists, that take up a sect under the abused name of catholicism, and plead against the catholic church for that sect under the name of the catholic church; so also you must know and keep close to the true catholic rule; and not do as the papists, that have honoured a private and crooked rule by that name, to the church's trouble, and their own delusion: and also you must keep close to the true catholic Governor of the church, and judge of controversies, and turn not aside with papists and others, to a usurper, or a private judge. In these three your catholicism must much consist. The first, what the catholic church is, and what a true catholic, I have said as much to as I conceive necessary. The other two I shall say a little more to, viz. the catholic rule, and the catholic Judge, and then of the fourth and last, which is, the catholic spirit or affections.

1. We are all agreed that the will of God revealed, must be, and is, the catholic rule of faith and life. But we are not all agreed which is this revelation of the will of God. That the book of the creatures and the principles of nature do reveal much natural moral verity and duty we are agreed: but the doubt is of supernatural revelation. And of this we are agreed, that whatsoever is certainly delivered to the church by prophet or apostle, or any person infallibly proving a divine inspiration or command to deliver what he speaks, must be received as from God. And whatever is so revealed concerning faith or duty, by way of imposition, is our rule: and if revealed to all, it is the rule to all. We are agreed also, that the holy Scriptures containing those books which the Reformed churches take for the canon are a divine, infallible revelation concerning faith and duty. And therefore we are all agreed that the holy Scriptures are the rule. But whether they be the whole rule we are not agreed. The Reformed churches say, that the sign is but to make known the doctrine

signified; and that while the inspired apostles were themselves alive, their own voices were the sign, and instead of a written word to all that heard them, and more. But knowing that they must die, and that the word of persons not infallibly inspired, is no rule of faith, and how hardly things not written are preserved from alteration and deprivation, therefore they left their doctrine in writing, for the easier, and surer, and more universal communication and preservation. And that universal, infallible tradition hath delivered us down both this Scripture, and also (by itself) the sum of christianity, in the creed and baptismal covenant, and in the hearts of the faithful from age to age. So that we make very high account of tradition, as bringing us in one hand the essentials of christianity, and in the other the whole body of sacred doctrine in the Scriptures, containing all these essentials, and more. And this is the rule of our faith and life: yet we confess, that if any could prove a certain delivery of any more from the apostles to the church, we are ready to receive it, which way ever it be delivered. But the papists add, that partly tradition, and partly the canons and decrees of the church, are to be received as the rule as well as Scripture, and that much is revealed by verbal tradition to that end, which is not in Scripture, which is with equal pious affection and reverence to be received; and that the church, which is the keeper of this tradition, is only the Roman church, or all that believe in the pope of Rome, as the universal head or sovereign of the church.

Now the question is, Whether theirs or ours be the catholic rule?

And here the wickedness of factious disputers hath done the church a world of wrong on both sides. Some are so mad in their contentions, that they care not what they say scarce, so they do but cry down one another. The papists cannot cry up their tradition, but they must speak so reproachfully, impiously, foolishly of the Scriptures, as if they were stark infidels. To omit others, the reading of Rushworth's Dialogues, and White's Additions and Defence, is a notable bait to tice men to infidelity, and those Dialogues contain the very same arguments which the new apostate infidels use. And on the other side, many, to say as much as they can against the papists, do so cry down traditions, that they *(tantum non)* disable themselves to make good the Scripture itself. Oh perverseness! Oh doleful fruits of contentions! Whereas a true catholic should be glad of any light from heaven whatsoever: and must know, that God in great mercy to his church hath by these two hands delivered us his will: not some part in Scripture, and the rest by unwritten traditions, as say the papists; but some part by such tradition, and all by Scripture, and that Scripture by tradition. So that God hath given us two strings to one bow: and the papists will have two bows also; and others will have but one string.

Well; 1. I prove that the Scripture is the catholic rule.

That is the catholic rule of faith, which the whole church in all ages and places hath received as the rule: but such is the Scripture. Papists and protestants, Greeks and Armenians, Abassines and all christians, confess that the canonical Scriptures are the revelation of the will of God: so that this must be catholic, which the catholic church receiveth.

2. And I prove that the papists' rule is a sectarian, crooked rule, and not catholic. 1. That is not the catholic rule of faith which the catholic church did never receive; but such is the popish rule of Roman tradition: therefore if you take it in the general, viz. the tradition of the Roman church to be received by her particular authority. (1.) The Reformed churches now disown it. (2.) The Greeks and other Eastern and Southern churches now disown it. (3.) The primitive church did never own it. So that all the church was once a stranger to their rule, and the most of it is an adversary to it at this day. And can that be the catholic rule which most of the catholic church disclaims? The Eastern and Southern churches think that the Roman traditions are of no more authority than their own; nay, of far less, and much of them false. 2. If you look to their additions of the apocryphal books, to the canon of the Scriptures, the ancient catholic church was against them; as Dr. Reignolds, the newly Dr. Cosin at large, and through every age, hath showed it. 3. If you come to particulars: the very essence of the Roman catholicism and church, and the universal headship still of their pope, which are the master-points of their tradition, are denied and detested by the far greater part of the catholic church on earth to this day. And is this a catholic rule which the catholic church denieth? A great stir the papists make about catholic tradition, and the judgment of the catholic church. But what good would this do them, if we were as much for tradition as they? when the most of the catholic church condemneth them and their traditions, or own them not, even in the principal points essential to their religion?

And what have they to say to this? Nothing but what any thief may say of a true man when he hath cut his purse, even to call him thief first! Forsooth, most that are called christians, by far, are all heretics, and therefore none of the catholic church; and therefore their votes are no impeachment to the papal claim. And how prove you that? Why the pope saith so, and so do this faction. Why, but he is a party! How know we that he saith true? Why, here you must leave them: he saith that he saith true; therefore he saith true: he saith that the most of the church are not of the church, but heretics, and that none but his subjects are of the church, therefore it is true. And so he must be the judge in his own cause, and be believed by the catholic church on his own authority. Read but the third section of Rushworth's Second Heathenish Dialogues, and see what a silly shift the self-conceited disputant is at in answering this objection, All christians agree in the acceptation of the Scripture, and far fewer in divers points of doctrine: for the churches of the Roman communion are no such extraordinary part of christendom, compared to all the rest. *Answ.* For the extent of the churches I cannot certainly tell you the truth, because I fear many are called christians, who have little either in their belief or lives to verify that name: but you know in witnesses the quality is to be respected, as well and more than the quantity; so that those countries in which christianity is vigorous, are to be preferred before a greater extent of such where little remains more than the name. Suppose, in a suit of law, one party had seven legitimate witnesses, the other as many, and besides them twenty knights of the post, (known perjured knaves,) would you cast the cause for this wicked rabble? Thus Rushworth.

And is this all? And is this a catholic cause or rule? You see now from their most violent, subtle disputers, that they dare not stand to the major vote. They cannot deny but the papists are the far smaller number: and most must not carry it! How then? Why we must be judged by the best, and not by the most. Content: and I must solemnly profess, that if my salvation lay upon it, and I were to go to-morrow, either to heaven or hell, according to my choice of the holier party to trust my faith upon, I should make as little doubt whether the Reformed or the Roman professors be more holy, (as far as ever I was able to discern,) as I should do whether the Latin or the Greek church be the more learned. If godliness and honesty of witnesses must carry it, I must live and die where I am. But especially when the papists are worsted at both, and have neither the greater part, nor the honester, (of which I am quite past doubt, as I am whether England be better and greater than the Orcades,) where then is their catholic faith and rule?

As for all the heathenish cavils of Rushworth against the certainty of Scripture, because of the language, the translations, and such like blind, malignant exceptions, I shall answer them, if God will, in a fitter place.

2. Having spoken of the catholic rule, let me next advise you to keep close to the catholic Governor and Judge. And who is that? Even Jesus Christ himself, and none but he. Why, but is there not a visible head and catholic judge of controversies on earth? To deny this seems an intolerable absurdity to a papist: then every man may believe what he list, or what his own fancy leads him to! *Answ.* 1. And if the pope can cure heresy or infidelity, why doth he suffer most of the world to be infidels, and most of professed christians to be, in his judgment, heretics? And if he can decide all controversies, why suffers he so many hundreds to be undecided among his followers. And it seems by the late determination of the Five Jansenian Articles, that neither he nor his subjects know when he hath decided a controversy, and when not. He said he condemned five points of the doctrine of Jansenius: the Jesuits say so too: the Jansenists say, It is not so, they are none of his doctrines, nor to be found in him in word or sense. 2. The catholic judge doth not contradict the catholic rule; but the pope and his council doth. 3. The catholic judge contradicteth not himself, but so do popes and councils. 4. That is not the catholic judge whom most of the catholic church disowneth, and never did own: but most of them never owned the pope. But of all this I entreat the unsatisfied reader to peruse but what I have written in the Second and Third Disputation against Popery.

Object. But what! will you have no visible judge of controversies? *Answ.* Yes: but not over all the catholic church. *Quest.* But who then shall be judge? *Answ.* The case is plain, if men were but impartial. Discerning is one thing, teaching is another, and deciding or determining is another. A discerning judgment, as far as they are able, belongs to all: a directing or teaching judgment occasionally and *ex charitate* belongs to all that are able; and publicly and ordinarily, *ex officio*, it belongs to all pastors and teachers. Neither of these is the judgment now inquired after, but the third. If a man know not the articles of faith, the teachers of the church are to instruct him. But if a man deny the articles of faith, the same teachers of the church are to endeavour to convince him of his error, and better inform him: and thus far judicial decisive power is unnecessary. But if he will not be convinced, but still deny the articles of the faith, then comes in the judicial decisive power in order to his punishment. The articles of faith are to be discerned, and judged by, but not judged themselves any otherwise than to be taught: but it is the heretic or offender that is to be judged. And the judgment being in order to execution, there is a twofold judgment, as there is a twofold execution. 1. If the question be, Who shall be taken for a heretic, in order to the corporal punishment or forcible coercion of him by the sword, here the magistrate only is the judge: and it is, 1. A vile usurpation in the pope to take this power out of his hands. And it is an intolerable abuse of magistrates: it makes them but like hangmen, or mere executioners, when the pope and his clergy must be the judges of heresies, and the magistrate must but execute their judgment: what if the church or pope judge a catholic to be a heretic, must the magistrate therefore burn an innocent member of Christ? They confess themselves that the pope may err in matter of fact, and judge a man to be a heretic that is none: and if he could not err, yet sure his clergy may: yea, they confess a general council may, and say, they did err in condemning Pope Honorius of heresy. And must kings, and judges, and all magistrates, hang and burn all innocent people that the popish clergy shall falsely judge heretics? Will it justify them before God to say, The pope or bishops bid us burn them? No, I had rather be a dog, than be a king upon these conditions. 3. And indeed it is impossible for the pope himself to be judge of all men through the world that are guilty of heresy. For he is many hundred or thousand miles off; and there must be a present judge that shall hear the cause and witnesses; and there must be many thousand of these judges to the whole world: and can the pope or council then serve alone? If every heretic in England escape till a pope or council have the hearing or judging of him, he will not fear.

Object. But the pope and council are to judge what is heresy, and what not, though not to judge all particular causes; and then the bishops must judge the causes.

Answ. God hath told us already in his word, which are the articles of our faith, and the universal church hath delivered us all the essential articles in creeds, professions, and the baptismal covenant! And therefore here is no work for a judge, but for a teacher. The pastors of the church must teach us *ex officio*, with authority, which are the articles of faith; but they have no power to judge an article to be no article, nor to make any new article: and to judge an article to be an article, any man may do by judgment of discerning, and any teachers by a judgment of direction. If moreover you would have no article of faith be believed to be such, but on the word or credit of the pope or council, and so resolve our faith into them, I have fully confuted this in my Third Dispute against Popery. The word of God must be believed, whether men know the mind of the pope and council, or not: but this is the highest arrogancy of the papal sect, that they must not have God's own laws believed, or received by any, but upon their word and credit; and so we must know that they are authorized hereto, and infallible, before we know the articles of our faith; and so we must believe in Christ's vicar before we can believe in Christ. This is the ground of the papal cause. Well, I think I may take it for granted by this time, that with reasonable, impartial, considerate men the case is plain, that it is magistrates, and not the pope, that are judges who is to be corporally punished for heresy! And if every bishop must do it, then, 1. They must prove every bishop infallible; and, 2. Then they have not one catholic judge of faith, but many.

And what if we had granted them a power in the pope or council to judge of God's law, and what is an article of faith, and what is heresy? Yet this will be far from restraining heresies, as long as there is no judge of the particular case: and if we have as many judges of the cause and person as there be bishops, then we have not one catholic judge of persons and causes; and if we must have fallible bishops, yea, and popes, to judge of the person and fact, then we have but fallible restrainers of heresy.

2. The second sort of judgment is in order to church punishments. When the question is not, Who shall be punished by the sword? But, Who shall be avoided by the church as a heretic? Here it is the church that is to judge; even that church that must avoid or reject them from communion. And therefore as communion is of narrower or wider extension, so must excommunication and judging of heretics be. If the question be only, whether this man be to be avoided as a heretic by this particular church where he liveth? that church must judge. If the question be, whether he be to be avoided as a heretic by all the churches of the country or nation? it is all these churches that must judge. For who should judge but those that must practise, and answer for their practice? And how can the pope or council be able to judge persons and causes that they know not; and to judge so many millions throughout the world? If you could prove that the whole catholic church were bound to take notice of this individual heretic, and were capable of actual communion, and avoiding communion with him, and of congregating to judge him, then I should consent that all christendom should meet to excommunicate a heretic, if they had no better work the while to do. But the case is plain, that the church that must execute, must judge: the church that must avoid the communion of the heretic, must judge him to be avoided: and I think the pope and general councils will not undertake all this work.

You have nothing therefore to say, but to recur to the former way in your objection, viz. That it is the work of pope and general councils to judge what is faith and heresies, and the work of provincial synods or bishops to judge the offenders by their canons.

Answ. That is plainly, the pope and council must make the law, and the bishops judge by it. But, 1. God hath made the church's law already: we know but this one Lawgiver to the church, to constitute articles of faith and spiritual duty. And is this all that you make such a noise about, when you say, Who shall be judge of faith, and heresy, and controversy? That is, Who shall make laws against them, to tell us which is faith, and which is heresy? Why God hath done this already in the Scripture. 2. And this will not answer your own expectations in resolving your doubt: for if the pope's legislation be all his judging of controversies, there will be never the fewer controversies or heresies in the world: for there is no law that hath a virtue sufficient to compel all the subjects to obey it. If God's law cannot do it, neither can the pope's.

Object. But every heretic pleadeth Scripture, and saith, it is for him; and shall there be no judge to put an end to all these controversies about the sense of Scripture?

Answ. 1. If there be any absolute judge of the sense of Scripture, his work is to give the world a decisive commentary upon it; which no pope or council hath done. 2. And he should actually decide all the controversies afoot, which the pope dare not attempt; but leaves hundreds undecided among themselves, and more than ever were among the protestants. 3. It is the work of a teacher, and not a catholic judge, to acquaint men with the meaning of the law. 4. For all their malignant accusation of the Scriptures, they do as plainly deliver us the articles of christian faith, and the necessary christian duties, as any pope or council hath done. And if all the work for a pope or council be to teach God how to speak or mend his word, and make sense of it, when God hath made it but nonsense, in their presumptuous judgments, then we can well spare such a judge as this. 5. There is as much contention among yourselves about the meaning of the canons of councils, and the pope's decretals: and who must be judge of all these controversies? Even the late council of Trent is pleaded by one party for one side, and by another for the contrary; yea, even by the particular divines that were members of the council: and yet no deciding judge steps up, but let the contenders worry one another, and there is no end of their disputes.

So that the case is as plain as can be desired, 1. That constituting by a law or universal rule, to determine what shall be taken for faith, and what for heresy, this God hath done, who is the only universal Lawgiver, and we need no pope for it. 2. To judge who is to be corporally punished as a heretic belongs to the magistrate in his own jurisdiction, and not to pope or bishops (as hath been made good in ages against them, since they claimed it, as the many tractates of Goldastus' collection manifest.) 3. To judge who shall be cast out of the communion of the church as a heretic, and avoided, belongs to the church that hath communion with him, and that is to avoid him; and to all other churches, so far as they are naturally capable of communion and non-communion with him, and of the cognizance of the case, and bound to take notice of it. So that all human judgment is but limited, and *ad hoc*, the judgment being but in order to the execution. 4. And therefore the absolute final judgment is only that of Christ himself, to whom we must make our appeals, and from whom there is no appeal. And this is the true decision of this question, that makes so loud a noise, Who shall be judge of controversies in faith, and of heresies? And thus you see that Scripture is the catholic rule, and Christ the catholic Judge, and the magistrate the judge *ad hoc*, who shall be corporally punished, and the pastors and church where communion or avoiding the party is a duty, are judges *ad hoc*, whether he be to be avoided. And this is the next catholic principle.

Before I come to speak of the last, (which is, catholic affections,) I shall briefly name some principles contrary to the catholic principles, which I would warn you to avoid: and I shall not stand upon them, but touch them.

1. It is a private and not-catholic principle, to hold that we are not baptized into the catholic church, but into a particular church only. As the case of the eunuch, (Acts viii.) and the baptismal institution, show.

2. It is a private principle, contrary to catholicism, to hold that an authorized minister of Christ is only a minister in that church which is his special charge, and where we confess he is bound to exercise his ordinary labours; and that he may not preach, baptize, administer the Lord's supper, yea, and rule *pro tempore*, as a minister in another church to which he is called. As physicians must first have a general licence, upon exploration and approbation, to practise physic when they are called, and afterward may have a special call and engagement to a particular hospital or city as their charge, and so do practise occasionally upon a particular call abroad, but ordinarily at home, as to their special charge, but to both as physicians; so is it with a pastor in the church of Christ.

3. It is a private and uncatholic principle, that a minister is so bound to that one congregation which is his special charge, as that he must prefer them

and their service before the more public service of the churches, and must neglect opportunities of doing apparently much greater good, for fear of neglecting them. All our obligations are strongest to our ultimate end, and next to that which is next that end, and so more to the public than to any particulars as such.

4. And it is a private, uncatholic principle, that a minister should more fear or avoid the offending or hurting of his own particular flock, than the offending and hurt of the catholic church, or of many particular churches: where the interest of Christ and the gospel is greater, we are more obliged to God, and the catholic church, than we can be to any man or particular church. A physician of an hospital, *cæteris paribus*, must prefer his own charge before any others, and rather neglect a stranger's life than theirs: but he should rather neglect one of his own charge, than a prince, or many considerable persons abroad; or all his own charge, than persons, or cities, or countries of far more public use and interest.

5. It is a private, uncatholic principle, that ministers may satisfy their consciences if they stay at home, and only look after their own congregations, and never go to the assemblies of the ministers, where more public affairs of the churches are transacted, nor by preaching abroad where necessity requireth it, be helpful to other places.

6. And it is an uncatholic principle, to hold that the assemblies and associations of pastors, and concatenation of churches by them, is a needless thing; or that they are not to be ordinary, and fixed, for a certain settled way of the communion of churches and brethren, but only occasional and seldom; and that it is indifferent whether we be there.

7. And it is an uncatholic, dividing principle to hold, that when the churches agree upon a circumstance of worship as convenient, any particular persons shall walk singularly, and refuse to consent to that agreement, unless it be against the word of God.

8. It is not according to catholic principles, for any man of another church to make light of the reproofs, advice, or teaching, of any faithful minister of Christ, because they are not members of his charge.

9. Nor is it a catholic principle for a minister to hold, that a fit person of another church may not have communion with him and his charge, and partake of the ordinances among them, when they are for a time cast into their neighbourhood, and give sufficient testimony of their fitness.

10. It is a dividing, uncatholic principle, to think that for every disorder, or gross sin, that (against our wills) is connived at in the church, we must therefore withdraw from the communion of that church, before sufficient means and patience have been used with them, and before the church do own the sin.

11. It is a dividing, uncatholic principle, to hold that we must necessarily require the profession of more than the essentials of christianity in order to the baptizing of any into the church, or that profession is no satisfactory evidence, (though there be no proof on the contrary to invalidate it,) unless there be some other discovery of the truth of grace. To deny the catholic qualification of visible members is not catholic.

12. It is a dividing, and not a catholic principle, that we must needs preach, profess, or declare every thing that we take to be a truth, though to the apparent hazard of the church, and hinderance of the great essential truths; and that no truth must be silenced for the church's peace, and the advantage of the more necessary truths: and that we may not hold communion with those that agree not with us in some integrals of the christian faith, though they agree in the essentials, and forfeit not the communion of the church by wicked lives.

Too many more such principles might be named, but I only warn you briefly of these few.

3. The last part of my advice is, that you labour to preserve a catholic spirit and affections. And a catholic spirit consisteth, 1. In a catholic love. 2. A catholic compassion. 3. A catholic care. And 4. A catholic endeavour to be serviceable to all.

I. A catholic love consisteth in these particulars: 1. That you love a christian as a christian, for the sake of Christ, and not for by-respects only: not chiefly because he is rich, or honourable, or of eminent place, or parts, or personage, or because he loveth you, or any such lower respects; though these may have their parts in subserviency to the main; but the chief reason of your love must be, because he is a member of Christ, and beareth his image, and is serviceable to the glory of God, and one that is like to join with you in his everlasting praises.

2. That your love may be catholic, it must be a love to all that are christians, as far as you can discern them, and have opportunity to observe them. Though he should differ from you in many points of religion, yet if he hold the essentials, and manifest the grace of God in his life, you must love him with the special love of a christian. Though he have fallen out with you, or wronged you by word or deed, or have a low esteem of you, and slight you, whether deservedly or in a mistake, yet if he manifest the image of God, by his holy profession and conversation, you must afford him this special christian love. Though he be a very weak christian of parts, or graces, and subject to passions and infirmities, (consistent with grace,) and his profession reach not to that height as may make him eminent, nor his life to that degree of diligence as may make you confident of his sincerity, yet if he have a profession of true faith, and repentance, and holiness, seemingly serious, and not invalidated or disproved by a contrary profession or practice, you must allow him the special love of a christian. He that loveth a christian as a christian, must needs love all christians that he discerneth to be such; and he must not by uncharitableness hinder that discerning.

3. And catholic love will be somewhat suitable to the excellency of the object, which is a member of Christ. He that loveth a christian truly, doth love him above gold, and silver, and worldly things; and therefore can part with his substance to relieve him, and venture his life for him, when God and his honour do require it. And therefore it is that Christ will not at the last day barely ask, whether we have loved him in his members? but whether our love were such as could carry us to clothe, and feed, and visit, and relieve them to our power?

4. Lastly, Catholic love must be diversified in the degree according to the apparent degree of men's graces and serviceableness to God. He that loveth men as christians and godly, will love those best where he seeth most christianity and godliness, and those least where he seeth least of it.

There is, 1. A common love of men as men; and this you owe to all, even to an enemy; and this may consist with a dislike or hatred of them as wicked, and God's enemies. 2. There is a love to men for some lovely, natural, or acquired parts; as wit, learning, eloquence, gentleness, a loving nature, and the like; and this is proper to them that are the qualified objects of it; you owe it not to all, and yet you may allow it to those that are no saints. But this is not the catholic love which I speak of. 3. There is the fore-described love to a christian, as a christian;

and this is the catholic love which is due to all that seem christians. 4. There is a special degree of this love, which you owe to stronger and more excellent christians, and to those whose profession and conversation doth put you into a more confident persuasion of their sincerity, than you have of many or most common professors. And this special degree is not due to all christians. As we have but very small and doubtful persuasions of some men's sincerity, and more confident persuasions of others; so our love must be greater to one than to another, even where a special christian love is due to them all. 5. There is a special suitableness in the spirits of but few, even of those that are stronger christians, whereby they are fitted to be your bosom friends. And this extraordinary love of a bosom friend, such as was between David and Jonathan, and should be between husbands and wives, is not due to all, no, not all that are strong christians.

For natural love to parents, and children, and other natural relations, and for grateful love to benefactors, I shall say nothing to them, as not pertaining to our business; nor yet of the heavenly degree of love which is proper to glory. But I have showed you what that special christian love is which is truly catholic; and that it must be to all, and to all with a high degree; but not to all with an equal degree, but must be much diversified by their degrees of grace.

The love which is called, "The fulfilling of the law," containeth all these sorts before mentioned; but the love which is the new commandment of the gospel, is this special endearedness of christians to one another in their new relation; even, 1. As they believe in the Messiah as come, in whom they are all fellow-members and brethren. And, 2. As they are disposed and elevated to this love, by a special measure of sanctification by the Spirit, proper to gospel times.

This is the love to the brethren, by which we may know that we are translated from death to life, and so that we are true catholic christians, 1 John iii. 14. He that hath not this love abideth in death. By this it is that all men must know us to be Christ's disciples, that is, catholic christians, John xiii. 35. If Christ have more skill in knowing his own sheep and sheep-mark than the papists have, then this is a better mark of a catholic than believing in the pope, as the universal sovereign of the church: even loving one another as christians, for Christ's sake, and that "with a pure heart fervently," 1 Pet. i. 22. "Not in word and tongue, but in deed and in truth," so as to part with worldly goods for our brethren's relief, 1 John iii. 17, 18; Matt. xxv. 34, 40.

Reader, thou art a blessed man if thou hast this charitable, catholic spirit, that thou canst love all christians, as far as thou canst discern them, with a special christian love. When others hate and reproach all those that are not of their sect, or at least have no special christian love for them, let them be dear to thy heart, and amiable, because of the image and interest of thy Lord, even when thou art called to disown and rebuke (yea, or chasten, if a governor) their errors and imperfections. This lesson is written in the very heart of a true catholic; for "they are all taught of God to love one another," 1 Thess. iv. 9. Those, therefore, that malign all dissenters, and malice those that are not of their party, do carry about with them the brand of sectaries, how much soever they may seem to detest them. Those that deny the essentials of christianity are not the objects of christian love, but of common love only; but whatever infirmities are consistent with christianity are insufficient to excuse us from this special love.

And here let me mind you of one other principle, which is notoriously uncatholic, while it pretendeth to be most catholic, and is here most fitly to be mentioned, as being the bane of catholic, christian love; and that is the doctrine of many papists, and some few protestants, that make the necessary qualification of a church member to be (the reality, *coram Deo,* and the profession, *coram ecclesia,* of) a kind of dogmatical faith, which is short of justifying faith. From whence it followeth, that visible church members, as such, are not to be taken by us for true living members of the body of Christ; but that esteem is due only to some few that manifest their holiness by an extraordinary profession, or fuller discovery: and consequently, that we are not bound to love any as living members of Christ, but such eminent professors: and so the special catholic love, which is the new commandment, and the badge of a disciple, is turned into a common love specifically different from it, and answerable to the common not-justifying faith; and the special catholic love is reserved as another thing for some few of the visible church: whereas indeed we may say of all that are duly visible members, by profession of a saving faith, not nulled, that as it is the same faith with that of the holiest saints which they profess, so is it the same specific love that is due to the holiest saint, that they must be loved with: a great difference there must be in degree, but none in kind. We love none of them as infallibly known to be true living christians, but all of them as probably such by profession; but with very different degrees, because of the different degrees of probability.

And let me add another corrupt principle, that tendeth to corrupt this catholic love, and that is theirs that would have the church lie common; and men that profess not saving faith, or that null that profession by a wicked, impenitent course of life, to be permitted in the church, and discipline laid aside, and so the common and unclean to be numbered with the visible saints. And so when the permitted members are such as by right are no members, nor so much as seeming saints, they cannot be the objects of catholic love. Destroy the object and you destroy the art.

II. The second catholic affection is, compassion towards a christian as a christian in his sufferings. A sensibleness of their sufferings, as if we suffered with them: "And whether one member suffer, all the members suffer with it, or one member be honoured, all the members rejoice with it," Heb. xiii. 3; 1 Cor. xii. 26. "Rejoice with them that do rejoice, and weep with them that weep: be of the same mind one towards another," Rom. xii. 15, 16. "Who is weak, and I am not weak? Who is offended, and I burn not?" 2 Cor. xi. 29. A true catholic is grieved to see his brother's calamity, and especially to hear of the dangers, and losses, and sufferings of the churches: be they never so distant from him, it is near to his heart, for their interest is his own.

He that feels nothing but his own afflictions, and can make a small matter of the losses and sufferings of the church, perhaps under pretence of trusting God, so that if all be but well with himself, is certainly no catholic or christian. And he that little feels the losses of the church, if his own sect or party do but gain or increase by it, doth show that he hath more of a sectary than of a christian. Catholic compassion (to which I adjoin also catholic rejoicing) do prove a true catholic.

III. Another catholic affection is, a special care of the common christian state and cause, and of the case of all our brethren that are known to us. I mean not that care which belongs to God only, and which we are forbidden to use, even for ourselves; but, 1. An estimation of the interest of the church and brethren as our own; and, 2. An ordinate solicitousness about their welfare, containing an earnest desire of it, and a care to use the means that should obtain it. A catholic spirit is busily careful about the church's and brethren's welfare as well as his own. "That there should be no schism in the body, but that the members should have the same care one for another," 1 Cor. xii. 25. Timothy naturally cared for the state of the churches: such a care by grace he had of the churches, as he had by nature of himself; proceeding from so deep a love, as was a kind of new nature to him, Phil. ii. 20. "That our care for you in the sight of God might appear to you," 2 Cor. vii. 12. Titus had an earnest care for the Corinthians, 2 Cor. viii. 16. Every pastor must have a care of his church, (1 Tim. iii. 5,) but not stop there; but with Paul, "have a care of all the churches," (2 Cor. xi. 28,) though not an apostolical charge of them like his. Carelessness of the church and brethren is not catholic.

IV. Lastly, A true catholic spirit must appear in catholic endeavours for the good of all the members of the church. 1. It is contrary to a base, covetous, selfish spirit, which causeth men to mind and seek only their own, and not the things of Jesus Christ, and of their brethren; and will not allow men to part with any more than some inconsiderable pittance out of their superfluity, for their brethren's relief, or the church's service. "But whoso hath this world's goods, and seeth his brother have need, and shutteth up his bowels of compassion from him, how dwelleth the love of God in him?" 1 John iii. 17. He that cannot pinch himself, and deny himself even in his daily bread for the church and brethren, when God requireth it, is not a true catholic christian.

2. And it is contrary much more to a spirit of malignity, by which men envy the good of others, or of those that are not of their party; and yet more to persecution, when men would tread down and destroy their brethren, and the inheritance of the Lord, in a selfish, devilish zeal.

3. But yet it is not contrary to a charitable, moderate correction of offenders, which tendeth either to their own or the church's good, and is necessary to the restraint of iniquity, and the preserving of others from the infection of error; and therefore the sword of the magistrate and the discipline of the church must both be employed in the cause of God; and this is so far from being contrary to the endeavours of a catholic spirit, that it is a necessary part of it. Correction first proceedeth from love; and secondly, tendeth to good; and thirdly, is not used but in necessity: and this differeth from persecution, as the whipping of a child from the malignant hurting of the innocent.

Quest. But how can the endeavours of a private christian be extended to the catholic church?

Answ. 1. His daily and earnest prayers to God may be extended to the whole; and must be. He is not of a catholic spirit that is not disposed to fervent prayers for the universal church of Christ. 2. And his actual assistance must reach as far as he can extend it; and then he that doth good to a part of the church, may well be said to do good to the catholic church in that part.

Quest. But what good is it that we should do?

Answ. Besides that of prayer before mentioned, 1. Maintain catholic truths and principles; earnestly contend for the catholic faith; and resist dividing, uncatholic principles and errors. 2. Maintain catholic affections in others to your power, and labour to draw them from privateness of spirit, and selfish or dividing affections. 3. Endeavour the actual healing of breaches among all catholics as soon as you perceive them. To that end, 1. Acquaint yourselves with healing truths; and labour to be as skilful in the work of pacifying and agreeing men, as most are in the work of dividing and disagreeing. Know it to be a part of your catholic work to be peace-makers; and therefore study how to do it as a workman that needeth not be ashamed. I think most divines themselves in the world do study differences a hundred hours, for one hour that ever they study the healing of differences; and that is a shameful disproportion. 2. Do not bend all your wits to find what more may be said against others, and to make the differences as wide as you can; but study as hard to find out men's agreements, and to reduce the differences to as narrow a compass as is possible. 3. And to that end, be sure that you see the true state of the controversy, and distinguish all that is merely verbal from that which is material; and that which is but about methods, and modes, and circumstances, from that which is about substantial truths; and that which is about inferior truths, though weighty, from that which is about the essentials of christianity. 4. Be as industrious for peace among others as if you smarted by it yourself; seek it, and beg it, and follow it, and take no nay. Make it the work of your lives. When once God hath so awakened the hearts of his servants to see the beauty, and feel so much of the necessity, of unity and peace in the church, as shall make them generally more zealous, and diligent, and unwearied in seeking them, than dividers are in seeking to destroy them, then may we expect a healing, and strength, and glory to the catholic church: but wishing will not serve the turn, nor will we much thank wishers for it if we be healed.

Lastly, Lay the unity of the church upon nothing but what is essential to the church. Seek after as much truth, and purity, and perfection as you can: but not as necessary to the essence of the church, or any member of it; nor to denominate and specify your faith and religion by. Tolerate no error or sin, so far as not to seek the healing of it: but tolerate all error and sin, consisting with christian faith and charity, so far as not to unchristian and unchurch men for them. Own no man's errors, or sins, but own every man that owneth Christ, and whom Christ will own, notwithstanding those errors and infirmities that he is guilty of. Bear with those that Christ will bear with; especially learn the master-duty of self-denial: for it is self that is the greatest enemy to catholicism. Self-conceitedness, and self-love, and self-willedness, and selfish interests, are the things that divide, and would make as many religions in the world as selfs. Even among many accounted orthodox, pride and selfishness causeth them so far to overvalue their own judgments, as to expect that all should be conformable to them, and bow to their arguments which have no strength, if not to their sayings and wills without their arguments; and to disdain, and passionately censure and reproach, all that dissent and gainsay them. And thus every man, so far as he is proud and selfish, would be the pope or centre of the catholic church. And therefore it is observable that Christ hath told us, "That except we be converted, and become as little children, we cannot enter into his kingdom," Matt. xviii. 3. "And if we deny not ourselves, we cannot be his disciples," Luke ix. 23. But of this I have spoken in another treatise.

And thus I have plainly from the word of God declared to you the true nature of catholicism, and which is the catholic church, and who a catholic.

I hope it may do somewhat to cure the frenzy of the world, that makes men cry, Here is the church, and there is the church; that makes one sect say, We are the church, and another say, We are the church. I hope it may do somewhat to the confounding of the arrogancy and presumption of all sects, especially the sect of papists, that being but a piece of the church, and that none of the best, dare pretend to be the whole, and restrain the name of catholics or christians to themselves! And I hope it may do somewhat to awake the servants of Christ to more catholic considerations, and principles, and affections, and endeavours, that those that have lived too much to themselves, and too much to their own parties, as if the church had been confined to their narrow provinces, may hereafter look more abroad into the world, and remember the extent of the kingdom of Christ, and not think so dishonourably of it as they have done. I hope also it may help to abate the censoriousness and presumption of those that would rob Christ of the greatest part of his inheritance, and deliver it up to Satan, his enemy. And I hope it may somewhat disgrace the dividing principles and practices of these times, and turn soldiers into surgeons, wounding into healing, and excite in some a stronger desire for unity and peace, and cause them to extend their care and charity further than they have done. However, this here described is the catholic church which God will own. This is it that is built on Christ the Rock, which the gates of hell shall not prevail against. Here is the safe standing, from whence you may look with boldness, thankfulness, and compassion, upon the many sects and furious contentions of the world; and lament their giddiness, without being brought yourselves to a loss about the truth of your church or faith; and may see the folly of them that are puzzled to find out the true catholic church and religion. And here you may see the admirable privilege of a truly regenerate, sanctified person, that is most certainly a member of the true catholic church, whoever deny it. To conclude, you may hence see that it is not as Romanists, Greeks, Armenians, Abassines, Jacobines, Lutherans, Calvinists, Arminians, &c. that men are saved, but as catholic christians, aspiring to the highest perfection.

THE

ONE THING NECESSARY:

OR

CHRIST'S JUSTIFICATION OF MARY'S CHOICE;

AND

OF HIS SERVANTS WRONGFULLY ACCUSED.

THE PREFACE.

It is not a needless subject which I here offer about needless or less needful things. Little do most men think how much of their wisdom or folly lieth in their right or wrong valuing and using things lawful, and that have an inferior sort of goodness; and how much their salvation or damnation is herein concerned. Men are condemned for an evil love, but not for the love of evil as evil. Nature is against that. To love a lesser good too much, and a greater too little; to love the end but as the means, and the means as the end, is an evil love; *Non malum volumus, sed male.* It is the act that is evil when the object is good, either in deed, or in the apprehension of the lover. He may will hurt as hurt to another, but it is as conceited to be some good to himself. Apprehension of good or evil, that is, practical judgment, ruleth the wills and actions of the world. Of how great moment then is it to have a truly informed judgment, and to have teachers that will thus truly inform us! Not about matter of mere talk and dispute, that little concerneth us, but about that which is good or evil to ourselves, and to know indifferent things to be indifferent. It is the pernicious enmity of the fleshly appetite to the soul, that it biasseth the practical judgment and will to take things indifferent to be good and desirable, and almost necessary; and a small sensible good to be a great one, and a great good, which displeaseth sense and appetite, to be small, if not a hurtful evil.

And indeed the Holy Ghost hath told us, (Rom. viii. 5—8,) that this is the difference between the truly godly and ungodly, that one is spiritually-minded, and the other carnally; that is, one savoureth things spiritual, and judgeth of things according to spiritual reason and interest, and loveth and chooseth them for spiritual goodness; but the carnal have no such gust, judgment, or love, but value things as the appetite and interest of the flesh inclineth them. Be they both of the same calling, education, and profession, if both were pastors of the same churches, and preachers of the same doctrine, yet this difference is at the hearts of spiritual and carnal men; and it usually appeareth to others in their lives. If they be public persons, they will show men what things they value, and what gain it is that they pursue. The flesh loveth not mortification, nor the cross; it is always against spiritual laws and life, and spiritual worship and persons, so far as they cross their carnal interest. He that will worship God, that is a Spirit, in spirit and truth, must have a judgment that most valueth spiritual things, and place his love and hope on spiritual delights and happiness. A carnal mind that savoureth only carnal things, and neither is nor can be subject to God's spiritual law, will hardly relish spiritual worship or a spiritual kind of life.

One of the greatest signs of a hypocrite is, making a great matter of little (worldly and fleshly) things, and making a little matter of great things. All the things of the flesh and world are things indifferent in themselves, or almost indifferent, further than their relation to spiritual good doth make them become good or evil; good if they further it, and evil if they hinder it. But the hypocrite is never indifferent toward them; he feeleth no great need of spiritual thoughts, spiritual counsel, or discourse, or preaching, or books, or company. Perhaps he can bear them, but he can be without them; and doth neither much desire them, or delight in them. A history, or romance, or merry jest, or game, is pleasanter to him. But his thoughts are serious for his carnal commodity, pleasure, and reputation; what he shall eat and drink, and wherewith he shall be clothed. If his house, his maintenance, his meat and drink be not such as the flesh desireth, especially if it be put to straits and sufferings, his sense of it is as quick, and his complaint as serious, as if he were half undone, or it were some great matter at least that he complaineth of. The complaints and tears of many that are in some straits or sufferings should cause wiser tears from serious believers, to see men so miserably carnal, like children that cry for a pin or a feather, as if they had lost their greatest good.

Seriousness is it that showeth what is next to a man's heart. It is seriousness and earnestness about fleshly vanity, and want of seriousness about things spiritual and eternal, which is the temperament and character of the hypocrite.

And here I would entreat some that I hope are godly, to forbear so suspicious and disgraceful a course as they are openly guilty of; I mean when they talk so concernedly and eagerly about their meat, and drink, and clothes, and every fleshly thing, as if their hearts were set upon them. Passion and chiding if all be not as their fancies or appetite would have it, doth show that they are dangerously diseased at least. This meat is not well drest, and the other is too little, or too much; and that sauce is not rightly made, and something or other is still amiss. And all these are talked of as seriously as if the fleshly appetite were the man. In a word, the more serious any man is about great things, the more indifferent he will be about things indifferent. And the more indifferent a man is about the greatest things, the more earnest and serious will he be about things indifferent; and *vice versa*, the more serious he is about things indifferent, the more indifferent he will be about the one thing necessary. Taking great things for small, and small things for great; necessary things for indifferent, and indifferent or smaller things for necessary, is the folly, and the sin, and the damnation of the ungodly. And because all men will do as they are, it is also the corrupter, troubler, and divider of the christian societies, in doctrine, worship, discipline, and conversation, and the confounder of the world. Of which faith and serious godliness is the remedy, which valueth and useth all things as they are.

September 29, 1684.

LUKE X. 41, 42.

JESUS ANSWERED AND SAID UNTO HER, MARTHA, MARTHA, THOU ART CAREFUL AND TROUBLED ABOUT MANY THINGS: BUT ONE THING IS NEEDFUL.

HAVING long ago published some sermons on the One Thing Needful, in a Treatise called, "A Saint or a Brute," I find by more experience than I had then, that it is more necessary to say something on the former part of the text than I thought it was. I then lived among poor, labouring, honest people, who had indeed some temptations from outward wants, but little from wealth and superfluities, nor had leisure to waste time upon so many trifles as I see rich and idle persons think they have.

It is here very considerable, 1. That the Author of this reproof was one who was not to be suspected to mistake through ignorance, or want of love to Martha. And though he lived in a low manner, and not as the rich, yet it was not because he wanted such things that he blameth the minding of unnecessary things, for he was Lord of all; and for our sakes he became poor, yet suffered as rich men, that are supposed to be usually the greatest sinners. "He made his grave with the wicked, and with the rich in his death," Isa. liii. 9.

2. And that his reproof was very serious and compassionate, repeating her name, "Martha, Martha."

3. The person reproved was not a wicked, fleshly, worldly person; but one that was beloved by him, and a religious believer.

4. The matter which she is reproved for is partly positive expressed, (being "careful and troubled about many things,") and partly implied as privative; not preferring the one thing needful at that time so much as she should have done. Which implieth, 1. That the many things were needless, or less needful things. 2. That they took up both her unseasonable time, and the cares of her mind, unto her trouble.

I need no more words to convince you that Christ here teacheth us this lesson, viz.

That care and trouble about many needless or less needful things, hindering them from the due minding of the one thing needful, is a sin which Christ reproved in Martha, and therefore blameth in all others who are guilty of it.

Here, I. Let us consider what Martha's sin in particular was. II. Whether we are not like to be more guilty of the like. III. In what kind this sin is usually committed. IV. What are the excuses for it. V. What is the evil of it which deserveth such reproof. VI. What use we should make of Christ's reproof.

I. Martha's sin (already mentioned) was overmuch care and trouble about her table for Christ's entertainment, while Mary sat hearing his holy discourse; which showed that she had less appetite than Mary to the holy doctrine of Christ, that could easilier be without it. 2. And that she overvalued the lower part, his bodily entertainment.

Yet there were these extenuations of it. 1. It was not doing any sinful work in itself.

2. It was not needless in its time and measure. We are allowed to pray for our daily bread; and here is no mention of any superfluities or excess: and so worthy a guest deserved the best provisions; and it is probable that Martha was the chief housekeeper, to whom it most belonged. And no doubt it was a work of love and honour to Christ. Yet though it was for his own person, and had such excuses, Christ would not take part with it, or forbear to blame it.

And indeed one half of her fault lay in blaming her sister that was wiser, and chose better than herself; and Christ spake this as much to justify Mary, as to blame Martha, as the following words show.

II. And if we judge but by her quality and case, and ours, we are far liker to be thus culpable than Martha was. For, 1. That country was poor in comparison of ours, and had not half the temptations to many needless things, as we have by our riches and their effects.

2. Christ would not have endured such vanities and excesses as we are usually guilty of.

3. It is like Martha, that was so familiar with Christ, was less addicted to vanities than we now are.

4. Our common vanities, for which few of the better sort blame themselves, have no such extenuations or excuses as the case of Martha had.

III. But we need no more to convince us, than to name some of the many instances in which our sin is far, yea, very far worse than Martha's.

1. How much of most men's thoughts and time is taken up with the needless cares to grow richer, and be better provided in the world! From one end of the year to the other, how great a proportion is thus laid out! Cannot we serve God's providence, and labour in our callings, and do our duty, without such a measure of care and trouble? Into how narrow a compass do worldly cares and troubles cast God's service, and men's cares and thoughts of their endless state, in the hearts and houses of most men! These thorns and briers are so rank and plentiful, that they choke much of the seed of the gospel, and make true godliness and heavenly delight to wither away, and come to little.

2. How many needless cares and troubles have most about God's part and providence, which belong not to them; fearing what may befall them, lest they should be poor or oppressed, or suffer by others; when they should spend those thoughts in caring for their duty, and trusting the love and faithfulness of God! And no other care will avoid their suffering.

3. How much needless, yea, and brutish thoughts and works have many to please and gratify their appetites! What a base and yet costly service have they that serve a greedy throat and a beastly fancy!

Had God taken away many men's health, and appetite, that meat and drink had been loathsome to them, it had been a mercy to many such, who by the pleasure that they have in these, are made slaves to the flesh, and sinks of shameful sin, and the football of temptations, and live under continual wounds of conscience; and when the cup is absent, they are sinning in their imaginations and desires, and are contriving how the next meal or day to gratify their appetites again. I speak not of the reeling, befooled drunkard, or the spewing glutton, but of them whose care is for throat and belly, that make a great matter of the pleasing or displeasing of their appetites, and think and talk of it so seriously, as if it were some needful or important thing; that are displeased in mind if their throats be not pleased, and they fare not sumptuously or deliciously every day. When the poor Israelites had not tasted bread or flesh for many years in a wilderness, nor so much as the Egyptian onions, but only manna, they are killed by God's justice because they murmured; and when they asked flesh, it is said, "They asked meat for the lusts," (Psa. lxxviii.) that is, for their mere appetites, without necessity for life or health. But how much further do most go now, exceeding even the princes or great men in Israel in the matter and manner of their diet, (as I believe the most in England do,) and yet never blame or suspect themselves! Turks can forbear wine at Mahomet's command, and the Rechabites, because their father bid them; and if the physician forbid strong drink or wine to the sick they can forbear; but sensual sinners will rebel against God for their desired bait, and their heart and thoughts are set upon it.

4. How much also of many vain people's thoughts and care is spent about needless ornaments of apparel! Do we need any other proof than the opening of our eyes in the streets, yea, in the holy assemblies, as well as in places of evil fame? Dives is noted by Christ to wear purple and silk, or as we translate it, fine linen; and then those that were gorgeously apparelled were in king's houses; but how few here of the vulgar, yea, of servants, affect it not now that can but procure it! If the highest do but take it up, inferiors quickly strive to imitate them. In my short time the garb of England is so changed, that but fifty years ago men would have gazed at such as painted Indians, or outlandish strangers, or ugly ruffians, that had gone as most civil and religious people do in this city now. Paul would have forborne wine and flesh while he had lived, rather than this liberty should hurt his weak brother's soul. But if the scandal of our pride or gaudery do make many weak persons turn quakers to fly from it, how few for to avoid this would avoid the most gaudy, and effeminate, or ruffianly fashion of clothes or hair! And instead of receiving reproof from such quakers, they are hardened the more because of the weakness of their reprovers. I am loth to name those gauds with which especially the female sex do openly show their vanity, which tell all beholders what needless trifles take up much of their time, and cost, and care. And alas, for men's stupid folly all this is, while thousands want food and raiment, while whole countries are impoverished by cruel wars, when dreadful flames have consumed our wealth and rebuked our pride, and humbling diseases have showed us what flesh is; and when our daily feeling tells us it is perishing; and while we are going to a loathsome grave, and see the dust and bones of those whom we are following; and the plain warnings of Peter, (1 Pet. iii. 3—6,) and many such, stand in the Bible as ciphers to them.

5. How many needless things take up the rich, about their houses, furniture, retinue, and entertainments! Especially those that are most proud, and most curious and vain. Conveniency must be a pretence for sinful cost and labour; handsomeness or decency must be a pretence for needless charge in furniture, while the poor go almost naked. Cleanliness must be a pretence for their servants spending much of the day and year in needless vanities, which might be much better spent. Not to be accounted careless or uncleanly by others of the like vanity, seemeth excuse enough for a multitude of needless curiosities. To find poor people work, doth pass for an excuse for employing servants and tradesmen in making and providing all these need-nots, as if they might not have been better employed for the common good, and encouraged to learn some better trades; as if they knew not how narrow a coffin and little furniture must shortly serve them. The report of good housekeeping and entertainments must justify the excesses, and chargeable, needless superfluities of the rich.

6. What needless cares and business have many to avoid the contempt or hard thoughts of others! How near goeth it to a proud heart what is thought and spoken of them! And their avoiding of contempt must be the reason of most of the forementioned vanities, in their dress, their houses, their retinue, and the rest; when alas, they have another kind of judgment to prepare for, and they, and those whose thoughts they so much regard, are almost dead and dust already.

7. What a deal of some men's care and thoughts are spent in needless contrivances for power and greatness in the world! What works find some Ahithophels and Hamans for their minds! As if it were needful for a man to fall at last from a higher place than the rest about him; or to have his will fulfilled by all others; or to have the souls or lives of many to answer for; or to be stronglier allured to the damning love of this world than other men; or to be envied by many; or to be a ruler of others, before one knoweth how to be obedient to God, and to rule himself. And oh what worse than needless troubles, even horrible wickedness, doth this

ambition lead many to! Even to be the plagues of the earth, and incarnate devils, by bloody wars, and cruel oppressions, desolations, and persecutions.

8. Yea, some of lower rank have such imperious idol wills that nothing must cross them, or be said or done by any about them, but as they would have it. And yet it is two to one but so many persons and things will cross them, and go quite contrary to their wills, as that their disease will be their continual torment. And they will be like one in winter that cannot bear the cold, and yet must bear it; or like a poor man that is a servant to his appetite, and hath not wherewith to please it; or like one that dwelleth by the sea, and cannot bear the sight of the water; or in a wood, and cannot bear the shaking of a leaf. Such worse than needless troubles doth an idol will produce.

9. And how much time is lost in vain and needless talk about things not justly pleasing, and no way profiting ourselves and others! A vain tongue being the index of a vain mind, as if mind and tongue had no higher or better subjects or employment.

10. And in this city it is not a little time that is taken up with needless sports and recreations. I will not honour the gamester's trade with so soft a name as needless work; nor the play-houses, nor the houses of excess and lust. But if cards, dice, and stage-plays had never been branded and condemned by the ancient canons of the christian churches, and did not notoriously bear the marks of temptation, and much gross folly and sin, yet vanity and needlessness should be enough to make men that believe in another world, and the shortness of this life, to abhor them, and better spend their time. There is a sort of pleasure and recreation that is needful. That which fits us best for our necessary works and duties, preserving by motion the health of the body, or refreshing the weary spirits of hardy students. But God hath left no man in such a penury of recreation but that he may find more useful, profitable, manly, time-saving, and safe ones, than gaming, or stage-plays, or romances, and such insnaring, befooling, unprofitable time-wasters are.

11. And among all the needless, deceitful vanities, unprofitable studies and arts are not the least. When Cornelius Agrippa had strained his brain to such curiosities that he passed for a conjurer, and had written a commentary upon Lullius' arts after many others; he concludeth all with an honest and christian-like treatise, De Vanitate Scientiarum, commending the study and practice of God's word as the only true wisdom. And though I have marvelled at the Carthage council, which forbade the reading of heathens' books, I never wondered that men's excess herein should be rebuked, nor that Paul called men to beware lest they were deceived by vain philosophy, and to avoid opposition of sciences falsely so called. Languages, logic, metaphysics, physics, mathematics, &c. have their use; but he is a learned man indeed who rightly applieth them to that use, and separateth the needful from the needless part, the certain from the uncertain, truth from falsehood, and presumptuous conceits: the plausibleness of the thing inviteth many to waste their time in unprofitable studies, who durst not have spent it in play-houses and gaming; and yet I doubt to many it will prove no better.

Query. But the doubt is, What are these needless, sinful things, that seemeth needless to one that is not so indeed, or to another? Cynics call decencies, and ornaments, and conveniences, and pleasure needless.

Answ. 1. That is needless which doth no good.

2. Those things that do more hurt than good.

3. Those things which answer not the cost and labour which is bestowed for them.

4. Those things that are good, but hinder and deprive us of a greater good, which we may well spare, but are hinderances to the one thing necessary, which we cannot spare; all these are certainly needless, if not worse.

But because vain persons are hardly convinced, till God by light or fire do convince them, I will help them by these few questions following.

Quest. 1. Is that act which you plead for a thing which God doth any way command you directly or indirectly? If not, how can it be needful to you? You will say, Are there not some things indifferent and lawful which are no duties? *Answ.* 1. There are natural things which are not moral (either virtue or vice); as your health or sickness, and such things as are God's works, and not yours; of these I speak not. 2. There are actions of your own which are merely natural, neither commanded nor forbidden, and that is all those which are no matter for rational choosing or refusing, such as have no moral use; as winking with the eye, which foot I shall first put forward; which of two equal things, in meat, drink, apparel, &c. I shall take, (not choose,) when it is needful that I do one, but it is perfectly indifferent which. But the things which I am speaking of are of no such nature, but such as belong to rational choice, and are accordingly chosen by you.

Quest. 2. Would your consciences trouble you for it as any sin, if you omitted the thing which I call needless? I suppose not.

Quest. 3. Is it to please God as an act of obedience that you do them? Is your curiosity, and your vain attire, and the rest forementioned, chosen to please God, or to please your fleshly sense and fancy, or the world?

Quest. 4. Will it be any hurt to you, or real loss, if they be omitted, or be denied you?

Quest. 5. Have you got any thing by them already, or not lost more than you have gotten?

Quest. 6. Are they things that the better or the worser sort of persons more mind and plead for? Whose delights are cards, and dice, and plays, and vain fashions? Is it the most heavenly, or the most fleshly persons that are most eager of them, and most use them?

Quest. 7. Do you find that they more help or hinder you in prayer and other holy exercises; especially your heavenly delights?

Quest. 8. How do they relish with you when you think of death and judgment? Are they a comfortable part of your preparation? Had you rather then review and answer for your time spent in these than in greater things?

If you will but set conscience to answer these questions, methinks you should soon perceive yourselves what things they be that are needless, and therefore not to be chosen, and consequently unlawful.

But that you may see that I drive you not to any tremes, I shall negatively add,

1. I do not number all our thoughts, care, and labour for our bodies, children, or others, about things needful and convenient, to be these needless things.

2. Nor is our diligent labour in a constant calling needless; he that will not labour, St. Paul saith, should not eat: this is a part of our obedience to God, " Six days shalt thou labour."

3. Nor is it needless to labour for more than we need ourselves, that we may have to give to him that needeth, and to do good to others.

4. Nor is it needless to do our best for our bodily health to fit our bodies to be able and cheerful ser-

vants to our souls. That food, that recreation and pleasure, which is necessary to fit body or mind for service, and the work of a christian life, is not vain.

5. All men are not called to the same kind of labour and employment. That is needful to one, which is not to another.

6. The lowest things which we do in obedience to God, if it were but sweeping the streets or chimneys, is not to be numbered with the needless things, but rather a comfortable exercise of humility and obedience.

But every man must prefer the greatest thing.

IV. What are the common excuses of this sin?

Object. 1. Some say, that it is but few persons, at least not all, that are fitted for and called to great employments. They that cannot do greater matters must do lesser.

Answ. All are not called to govern kingdoms, nor to be teachers and pastors of the church; but all have some talent, which they must use and answer for; and all may do somewhat which tendeth to the common good: the servant or labourer that plougheth, soweth, and reapeth, doth serve the commonwealth; and if his master live idly, and spend his time in gaming, plays, or other vanity, can he excuse it by pleading a greater incapacity than his servant had? A mason, a carpenter, a tailor, a chimney-sweep, do that which is needful to be done; and shall rich men live idly, and do no good, because they are rich?

Object. 2. I was not bred up to labour; they that were bred up to it must use it.

Answ. If you were not bred up to some calling or employment, profitable to yourself and others, you were bred in sin, and then it is time to break it off. Idleness, with pride, and fulness, are noted to have been Sodom's sins; and will you not amend because you were bred in sin? Can you bear the doom of the unprofitable, slothful servant? Matt. xxv. Or will it excuse you because you have been slothful from your youth?

Object. 3. God doth not require toil and labour from those that are rich, and need it not.

Answ. God doth not require the same kind of labour from all; but if he give you more than the poor, he requireth not less, but more from you; that is, your constant diligence in more profitable work; else you may as well say, that God is the Governor of none but the poor; or that he looketh for least service where he giveth most wages.

Your labour is not only to supply your own needs, but to profit others, and for the common good.

And the more you do in way of duty, the more you receive and profit yourselves. Idleness is your own loss to soul and body.

Object. 4. Men need recreation and relaxation.

Answ. What do you need it for? Is it not for your work, and your health, to enable you to work? Use no more than furthereth your health and work, and that shall not be called needless.

Object. 5. Little things are useful in their places: Christ saith of some such, "These ought ye to have done, and not to leave the other undone."

Answ. No doubt but there are things good and needful of several degrees; all are not of the most needful kind. But what is this to that which is not needful? or that hindereth more needful things, as afore described?

Object. 6. Old men are incompetent judges of the case of youth, as not having their inclinations to sports and pleasures; and all men, especially divines and lawyers, and such-like grave men, who are themselves taken up with greater matters, are incompetent judges of the affairs of women, their clothes, their furniture, their expenses, and their employments, and are apt to call all needless which is below their work.

Answ. Yet Christ thought himself meet to judge of the choice of Martha and Mary, and Solomon to give directions to women, and so did St. Peter and St. Paul. Old men were once young, and know what youthful inclinations are; and grave men that live among women, see their business, and know their reasons. And if all sorts of persons shall judge ministers, lawyers, and judges incompetent to judge of their tradings, actions, and affairs, and so appropriate the judgment of them to themselves alone, then all persons will by their own judgments be always in the right, and none will be capable of amendment; the proverb is, A stander-by may see more than a player; but it is confessed that a just judge must hear and consider the whole case.

Object. 7. We shall be derided if we are singular.

Answ. Will God deride you for obeying him? Hath not he said, "Be not conformed to this world?" You will be derided and persecuted too by wicked men, if you will be true to Christ, to godliness, sobriety, and honesty: and is that a good reason why you should be sensual, worldly, and ungodly?

V. But what is the sin here reproved, &c.? What harm is it to be thus careful and troubled about many things that are not comparatively needful?

Answ. 1. To prefer little things before greater, and thus to employ ourselves, is a wilful debasing of our souls, which should be exercised about that which is answerable to the dignity of their natures: as it is a debasing of a prince to use him as beggars, or in sordid work; and as it were below a wise man to talk at the rate of fools and children; so is it a debasing of a soul that is made for things of endless consequence to employ it upon needless trifles. Pride maketh men think well of themselves, and look high in the world, and disdain to be set low in men's thoughts, words, or employments; and yet when God commandeth them to look higher, they choose a low and sordid life.

2. It is a wilful contempt of the most excellent things: God and our Redeemer, grace and glory, are before us, and should be remembered and sought in the first place; and it is a contempt of them needlessly to turn from them our minds and time to vanity. The mind of man is not infinite, but narrow, and cannot be employed on many things at once; if it be taken up with trifles, it cannot choose but neglect greater things. And for God, and Christ, and heaven, to be set by, while we play with toys, is profane contempt.

Object. We cannot be always thinking of God and heaven.

Answ. But you must always be serving God in one kind or other, and always doing that which tends to heaven; as you are not all day meditating of the light, but you are all day using it.

3. This taking up our minds and time with needless things, is a great injury to ourselves by neglect of our own greatest benefit and necessities. Did but men know what they have to mind and seek, it would be their speedy cure. Alas! we are all behindhand in our great and necessary business; and these triflers usually are more behindhand than others. They have more to do of unspeakable consequence than all their time and diligence will serve for, as it deserveth, (having lost so much already,) and yet have they so much to spare for trifles.

Oh that these loiterers knew their necessity and their work! 1. You have a God to know, of whom you are too ignorant; you have his word and will to know, which you are yet much unacquainted with.

2. Do you know what it is to get, keep, use, and strengthen a lively belief of the word of God, and the unseen world? 3. Do you know what it is to get assurance that God is your reconciled Father, that Christ and salvation are yours; that you are truly sanctified, and shall live in heaven for ever? 4. Do you know what it is to get the heart in love with God, and to long after communion with him in glory? 5. Do you know what it is to get down all the lusts of the flesh, and watch against all the snares of sense and vain imagination, and to escape the love of these alluring pleasures, and the danger of particular sins of sensuality? 6. Do you know what it is to subdue all your carnal affections and passions, and to get in their stead a zeal for God, and to be fervent in his service? 7. Do you know what it is to get above the love of riches, and to escape all the snares of covetous desires? 8. Do you know what it is to keep a holy government of your thoughts, and to employ them in their proper work? 9. Do you know what it is to rule your tongues, in forbearing evil, and using them for that which they are made for? 10. And do you know what the spiritual, sincere, and constant use of all God's worship is, word, prayer, sacraments, &c. 11. Do you know what it is to renew repentance for our renewed sins? 12. And to keep down all pride, and to walk humbly before God and man? 13. Do you know what it is to love others as yourselves; to do as much good to all men's souls and bodies as you can? 14. And what it is to discharge all the duties of your several relations, to all your superiors, inferiors, and equals? 15. And what it is to find out the corruptions and deceitfulness of your own hearts, and well to understand yourselves? 16. And what it is to understand the nature and danger of all Satan's temptations, and to escape or overcome them? 17. And what it is to obey all the motions of God's Spirit? 18. And to use all our daily mercies well? 19. And to bear afflictions patiently, and profitably? 20. And to be above the love of this body and life, and ready to die? 21. And to live in the joy and comfort which beseemeth the children of God, the members of Christ that wait in hope of endless glory? Do but understand what all, or half this is, and conscionably do it, and then spend the rest of your time in cards, dice, plays, vain adornings, curiosities, and other trifles.

4. Consider also that time and life are very short, and very uncertain, and therefore not to be spent on needless things by one that standeth at the door of eternity.

5. The experience of other men should move us: all right repenting men, and most dying men, wish that their time had not been so wasted, but spent on that which was necessary to the great ends of life.

6. Conscience telleth most that have not seared it, that at death and judgment we are like to wish that needful things had taken up all our time.

7. It is a wrong to our great Creator and Preserver, that we should thus waste our time while he maintaineth us, as if he gave us life and mercy for such vanity.

8. The example of Christ and his saints is a reproof of all such vanity; we find not that they thus spent their thoughts and time.

VI. The uses we should make of this are these.

1. Parents may hence learn for what employment they should educate their children in the world, what they should teach them, and to what trades and callings they should set them; not to such as will spend their lives in vanities; but such in which they may be most useful to themselves and others in the world. Not that all can be of the best or highest callings, but all should be educated for the most use and service, and all employed in the best which they are fit for. It is a debasing of your children to intend them for no better than to live at ease to get money; a heathen would tell you, that usefulness to the commonwealth is more to be regarded; and a christian knoweth that the serving of God in the greatest profiting of ourselves and others, must be preferred.

2. Let us all review our lives, and see here how much we have to repent of; and let us see also what cause of lamentation we have for the common guilt of all sorts, against these and such-like words of Christ.

But to prevent your misunderstanding of me, I first profess that I intend not to make you cynics, or superstitious, nor to persuade you that it is necessary to your salvation to live nastily and undecently; nor that it is any part of your holiness or perfection to be singularly sordid, and to avoid things comely and convenient, as some old hermits and anchorites, and divers popish saints seemed to think. I am not drawing you to imitate that present sect among us, that set up at first with a holiness which consisted much in forbearing cuffs, and bands, and hatbands, and ribands, and saying thou instead of you, and withal in open reviling the most faithful ministers. It is not a superstitious "Touch not, taste not, handle not," (Col. ii. 20, 21,) I am commending to you; but I fear lest the contrary common extreme be much more dangerous. I would not speak against your smallest convenience, so far as it become not a time-wasting snare, and hindered not your heads, hearts, and lives from greater necessary things. I know that when St. Paul speaketh often for providing things honest, and living honestly, he meaneth things decent, and of good report; to expose oneself purposely to be laughed at, as St. Francis and such others are said to have done, is no just exercise of piety or humility.

But alas, what a doleful spectacle is it, to one that believeth whither we are going, to see what it is that most men are doing, and what it is that they leave undone! I am not now speaking of the time that is spent in direct evil; but little do men know how dangerously they sin in spending too much in things that have some good, and in preferring conveniences, and small bodily pleasures and commodities, before the great and needful things. Who can doubt but it was a decent and good thing for Martha to make provision for Christ, and to attend and serve him? Are not most of your unseasonable cares and troubles about much smaller matters than this? But at the time when greater things should be done, even these are culpable cares and troubles; much more those many little trifles, which only pride and folly calleth needful. And verily we have all so much of this necessary work to do, that leaveth us little room or time to spare for things which most men spend much of their lives in; so great and urgent are our main concerns, as should make every wise man study diligently to put by as many of the less diverting matters as he can. He that had money to lay out for his ransom, or for his life, or necessary livelihood, would spend little on small matters, till he were sure he had enough to spare. Hearken but wisely to God and conscience; foresee whither you are going, and what you have to do, and of what inconceivable importance, and then consider whether you have room and time for all or any of those diverting trifles which are the chiefest care and business of the unbelieving carnal world.

This needless business plainly showeth that you have low and little souls. As children playing in the sand show their difference from men that apply themselves to manly business, so your over-business about your ornaments, dresses, compliments, rooms, and many such trifles, doth tell others, (whether you will know it yourselves or not,) that you have both childish understandings, (and worse, because you are at age,) that set too much by little things; and that you have too much carnality of affection, when you have so much mind of trifling need-nots. And worst of all, it plainly showeth that you greatly want a sounder belief and deeper sense of your great business and interest in the world, and live not in the sense of the nearness of death, and things eternal, as wise believers should still do.

I am not saying that you should always have the sinful fears and sadness, which the sentence of death doth bring on most; I had rather you were quite above these to the last. Nor do I say that you should always have just the same kind of passions, or do all things just in the same manner, as you ought to have and do if you were sure to die to-morrow. But I must say, that you should have the same wisdom, and the same esteem of God, and of the world, of soul and body, of heaven and earth, of eternity and time, of duty and sin, of necessaries and trifles, as you will then have; and the same holy affections, and diligence, and practice of life, which this wisdom will then teach you to wish that you had sooner had. O let there not be too great and shameful a difference between your living and your dying thoughts. If your father, or child, or husband, or wife, were on their death-bed, or going to execution, would not all be ashamed of you, that should hear you talk to them about cards, or plays, or fine clothes, or laces, or greater worldly toys than these? Yea, if you were taken up yourselves about your own ornaments, dressings, curiosities, and troublesome triflings, who would not say that you were disgracefully senseless of your own and your dying friend's condition? O promise not yourselves more time than God hath promised you! Dream not that you dwell further from the grave than you do: you know not what it is to live as christians, or as men, if you know not that all our life should be spent in our best preparation for death. Though you must do much which you would not be just found doing, you must do nothing but what you can then comfortably review, nor spend a moment in that which then you must wish that you had not spent it in. And whether time-wasting trifles and need-nots will be comfortably remembered then, by one that hath reason and faith, and had so little time, and so much to do with it, methinks it might be easy to foresee.

Verily if you spent your time in no greater matters, than in getting gold and worldly glory, crowns and kingdoms, merely for your flesh, and the greatest pleasures of a carnal, transitory life, you will in the everlasting review be confounded and tormented in remembering your self-abasing folly. And are your many little trifles then of more worth to make you a just excuse? Gentlemen, ladies and gentlewomen, do not only bear with me, but be willing and thankful that I deal plainly with you, when it is not for me, but for yourselves: it is such as you that are most ordinarily and unexcusably guilty of this sin and folly. The poor labouring countryman and tradesman indeed is unexcusable that will be diverted from the care of his everlasting state, even by his most lawful and necessary labours; but usually their guilt is less far than yours in all these following respects.

1. That which they do is profitable to the commonwealth, and so is good, and part of their duty in itself considered; to plough, and sow, and reap, and make you bread, and drink, and clothes, &c. But what good cometh to the commonwealth by your curiosities, and vanities, and plays, and compliments, though decency, and cleanliness, and handsomeness, and avoiding contempt and reproach, be vainly pretended for them. They gather, and you waste. They are the bees, and you are the drones. They labour, and you consume it on your lusts and fancies. God bid them labour six days, but he never bade you make such a stir for mere unnecessary vanities.

2. Necessity is some reason for what they do, though it be no good excuse for leaving undone greater things. They must maintain themselves and families, and pay you your rents. But what necessity have you to waste thoughts and times about your many unprofitable toys? Martha had some excuse, but you have none.

3. God giveth you more wages, and therefore doth expect more work; you are stewards of more trust, and therefore have more to give up an account of.

4. They can say, Christ and his apostles, and all good men, have laboured and done such things as we do; and it is part of his law, that if we will not work we shall not eat; and Solomon's mother, a queen, and he the wisest king by her teaching, describeth the virtuous woman to be one that worketh willingly with her hands on wool and flax, that riseth before day to look to her household, and her candle goeth not out by night; and eateth not the bread of idleness (when too many of the rich do eat no other). The labours of your tenants have such precedents as these. But have you any such for your needless formalities and toys? Did Christ or his apostles spend their time in prating of unprofitable things, or in idleness, or plays, or gaming, or in childish neatifying their bodies, or such like? Was St. Peter of your mind when he wrote to christian women, that "their adorning be not outward, of plaiting the hair, and of wearing gold, or of putting on of apparel, but the hidden man of the heart; in that which is not corruptible, even of a meek and quiet spirit, which is in God's sight of great price?" 1 Pet. iii. 3. That is, regard that which is precious, and adorneth you in the sight of God, and affect not neatness or costliness, to make you seem either rich or comely in the sight of man, but clothe your corruptible flesh with cheap and easy plainness, as beseemeth those that are going to the grave. It is not apparel, but ornaments, that he forbids, and a vain desire by our apparel to seem somewhat higher or handsomer than we are to men.

Perhaps you will say, that Christ and his apostles were poor men, and therefore neither patterns nor fit judges for you. *Answ.* But yet they shall judge you whether you will or not; and they who tell men by their lives, that they take not their doctrine or example for their rule, or Christ for their Governor, shall find that unbelief and rebellion are not the way to their justification. But though they that are gorgeously clothed then dwelt in kings' houses, do you but read the thirty-first chapter of the Proverbs, and take there the counsel and pattern of a queen and king, and I will reprove you no more.

And you that are so regardful of the thoughts and eyes of men, and whose pride maketh so great a matter of your reputation, that all about you be sightly, and liable to no contempt, why do you not most regard your reputation with the wisest and the best? St. Peter before told you what are the precious ornaments in the sight of God: and wise men and good men come nearest to God in all their estimations. Who will bestow much cost or time, or hire servants, to trim themselves, or their houses, for children or Bedlams to look on and admire? None but such as yourselves do think ever the better of you for all your costly or troublesome curiosities: wise men look at you as at players, or morrice dancers, some with laughter, and all with pity; and think what empty souls are these that mind such little, childish things.

And seeing common reason tells you, that a man's dignity or baseness lieth in the dignity or baseness of the things which he mindeth, hopeth for, and seeketh, and of the work in which his life is spent, why will you set yourselves so far below your poor tenants and labouring servants, as to choose employments so far baser than theirs? That is basest which is most vain, and of little benefit to yourselves or others. Your ploughman, your baker, your brewer, your cook, yea, your chimney-sweeper, live upon more useful employments, than some rich, vain, curious, idle persons.

And as all sin blindeth and befooleth sinners, it is two to one but these self-abasing persons will distaste what I say, as thinking that it is against them; when common reason might tell them that all this that I speak is for them, even for their honour, their commodity, their conscience, and their salvation. Should I persuade one that selleth pins and points, or the scavengers that carry out dust and dung, to become merchants that trade for gold and enriching merchandise, few of them would be so sottish, as to think I speak against them, to their dishonour or their loss.

And still I confess that many little things are needful in their place and season. We should miss pins and points if we were without them. Dirt and uncleanness must be swept and washed away. Garments should be warm and comely. Rooms that are convenient are desirable. Comely and stately buildings and furniture for princes and rulers are a due ornament to magistracy, and splendid cities and temples are an honest imitation of the great and glorious works of God. Sweet harmony and melody exhilarate the spirits for and in God's holy praise. All his mercies should be used to fit us to serve him with gladness and joyfulness of heart. It is not a cynical life that I plead for, but a base and childish life that I am dispraising; when comeliness, and decency, and cleanliness, and reputation is made a pretence for such trifling away your own and your servants' time, and setting up such toyish trades and employments, as nothing but your own sinful disease and folly could keep you from being ashamed of, and your consciences from accusing you for. I am ashamed to name over the trifles within doors and without which I mean.

But Satan is subtle as well as malicious, and knoweth that all fish bite not at the same bait. Crowns and enlarged dominions are the diversions of some who think their designs are high and honourable, while they go to damnation with more applause than worldly peasants. Brave speculations and pleasing knowledge of things unnecessary, are the bait of others, that scorn to neglect God, and cast away their salvation for such low and little things as the wanton and the glutton or drunkard do. Yet these that are pleased in satisfying their appetites, think that they make a wiser bargain, and have somewhat more instead of heaven than sick-brained childish women, that have no better in exchange than things and businesses which I am ashamed to name.

Oh that God would awaken all our reason by a lively faith, to see where we stand, and what is before us, and with whom we have to do, and how little transitory things of the flesh do signify to a sound understanding! We should then see that time and life are of greater use than to be played and fooled away. Every moment of it would then appear to be very precious, and of great use. Whereas that is vile which is good for nothing but vile employments. That hour which is useful for no greater work than your trifling need-nots, is of no greater worth than the work which it is for. Had you no more to do with it, how undesirable were life! Surely the gain or pleasure of an idle or a trifling life will never compensate the cares, and troubles, and sufferings which we must all undergo. Were a prince, judge, or doctor, set up as a picture only to adorn a room, or as a mawkin to frighten away crows from the corn or garden, this were not useless, yea, it were better than many of your time-wasting vanities; but sure it would be a great debasing of such persons, as scarce worth the cost and trouble of living.

The Scripture tells us, indeed, that man walketh in a vain show, and that "verily every man at his best estate is vanity;" yea, all under the sun is "vanity and vexation of spirit." But all this is said only of man as seeking a felicity in this world, and of all that he is and doth with no higher respect than to the present prosperity and pleasure of the flesh. But there are greater things offered us which are not vanity, even the pleasing of God, and the fruition of his love and glory for ever; and were our life and time devoted to these high and noble ends, were our waking and sleeping, our eating and drinking, our health and sickness, our labours, yea, and our needful recreations, employed for these, and measured accordingly as means hereto, they would be holy and comfortable, and the lowest things would be thus honoured and precious. They that are "stedfast, unmovable, always abounding in the work of the Lord," do find their "labour not in vain," 1 Cor. xv. 58. The same house, goods, money, food, raiment, time, as used by holy believers, and by carnal worldlings, &c. differ more than we can now conceive. HOLINESS TO THE LORD is the name of the one, and VANITY, VEXATION, and SIN, of the other.

But alas, man who as a shadow passeth away, doth set his heart on transitory shadows, and dreaming, and seeming, and stage-employments and enjoyments, make up his hypocritical life and comforts. His religion is naturally (till grace amend him) but show and ceremony; his heart-work, and house-work, and public-work, is little but shadow and ceremony. Time is spent, and money spent, and talk spent, and thoughts spent, upon shadow and ceremony. Servants are employed too often also in wasting their time to serve their master's fancies in mere shadow and ceremony. You can see and hear but little that is better, or of greater use, in many rich persons' daily conversations, in their retinue, in their splendid houses, and curious adorned rooms, or any thing even of that which commandeth their hearts and time, and in which they place their dignity and pleasure; until either grace happily, or death miserably, awake their wit, and then they cry out, All is vanity and vexation; oh that we had better spent our time! "This their way is their folly, and yet their posterity approve their sayings," Psal. xlix. 11—13. And still others rise up that tread in their unhallowed steps; and Satan's kingdom can truly boast of an uninterrupted succession, even from the days of Cain until now.

I shall end with some directions how to judge, 1. Of needless things. 2. And an answer to some cases of conscience.

I. 1. All things are culpably needless which answer not the cost, and labour, and time, which is laid out upon them. You may judge by the good which they are like to do.

2. Those things are culpably needless which are but to serve a desire or humour, which we have no need to please. If the lust or fancy be vain, the means that serve it can be no better; whether it be the lust of the flesh, the lust of the eyes, or pride of life, which are not of the Father, but of the world. Men say, We delight in this or that, in curiosity, in costly or time-wasting sports, or such as profit not their bodily health, in gaudy dresses, or such like; and why may we not gratify our delight? Why, it is supposed to be a needless, unprofitable delight, proceeding from a vain fancy, which should rather be cured than pleased.

3. All things are much more culpably needless which proceed from a vicious, sinful humour, desire, or lust. "Make no provision for the flesh, to satisfy the lust thereof," Rom. xiii. 13, 14. To mind the things of the flesh is enmity to God, and to the minding of spiritual things, Rom. viii. 6, 7. Unnecessary, sensual delights corrupt the soul, and strongly turn down the mind from God and holy pleasures; and the mortifying of such fleshly lusts or pleasures is no small part of our religion.

4. All those are culpably needless and worse which are preferred before truly needful things; and which are against them, and shut them out, or take up that same time and room which they should have; if you have any thing of greater moment, which should be done at that same time, whatever hindereth it is vanity, and worse: and therefore there is no cure for vanity of mind and life, till men come to know their great necessities, and important business, which they have for all their thoughts and time, even the regard of their end and all the means, the duties of their spiritual and temporal callings, and see that they have no time to spare.

II. *Quest.* It is lawful to be of a trade which serveth the humours of vain persons; as to make cards, or dice, or stage-plays; or vain attire, as ribands, periwigs, and such like?

Answ. 1. These things are of very different natures. Some of them, as stage-plays, cards, and dice, (though instances may be devised in which it is possible to use them lawfully,) are so ordinarily used sinfully and so seldom well, that the trade that maintaineth them may well be supposed to be a trade of maintaining sin. And had I a son, I had rather he begged his bread than have such a trade. But laces, and ribands, and fine clothes, and feathers, and divers such things, have (among some that they are fit for) a more ordinary lawful use; and therefore I cannot say such trades are sinful. 2. But yet because they are of so little benefit to the commonwealth, and so very frequently used to serve a vain and sinful lust and fancy, I take it to be a sin for any one to prefer such a trade before one that is more blameless and profitable, though the person might get more money by it. 3. And they that will use such a trade without sin, must necessarily be so careful in distinguishing of customers, and not promiscuously sell to all who they perceive will serve their sin by it, that it will much diminish their gain. The case is much like an ale-seller's or vintner's, which is lawful in itself, but must be used with so much distinguishing care as I doubt few practise, lest their gain be hindered. And therefore a safer trade is much to be preferred, which is not a continual temptation.

Quest. 2. May a servant dwell with and obey such a master, or lady, or mistress, as will command them to spend much of their time in trifles and vanities, that are but to please a proud or curious fancy?

Answ. 1. It must be supposed that many times servants, through sloth or education, misjudge those things to be needless or evil which are not such; and think that their superiors should command them no other labour than what they like themselves. In this case their error will not justify their neglect. Persons of honour and dignity may lawfully go much further in employing their servants in dressing, and adornings, and attendance, and in washing and rubbing rooms, and such smaller things, than lower persons, from whom it is not expected, and to whom the marks of wealth agree not; though none must be inordinate.

2. In mere doubtful cases servants are not the judges of their governor's commands and business; and where they are no judges, and know no sin, they must submit.

3. Sometimes that which is sinfully commanded may be lawfully and dutifully obeyed. As it is a sin in a sick man to be peevish, and hardly pleased, and to command many needless things to a servant in that peevish humour; when yet (they being lawful things to be done) the servant may be bound to obey them. A patient may sinfully be humorous in his expectations, when a physician may yet lawfully please his humours for his health. A child may faultily cry for something, when the nurse may without fault give him that which he crieth for to quiet him. All is not forbidden the servant to do, which is forbidden the government to command.

4. But all that is sin in the doer must be forborne; and to serve and cherish the sin of others when we may choose, is sinful.

5. Therefore in such cases, though it be lawful for a servant to do many needless things (not forbidden him by God) when commanded, it is unlawful to choose such a service, in which he shall be so employed, to spend his time in vanity, to satisfy a ruler's pride and humour, unless it be in case of true necessity, or probably to attain a greater good, which will compensate all the inconvenience. As if a pirate or tyrant command me to say some idle words, or do some needless action, or else my friend or I should be murdered; in this case they are not idle, or needless, or unlawful, but a duty, which voluntarily chosen would be a sin.

Object. By this you will make it a duty to obey papal commands of idle ceremonies if we doubt, or if they be not things forbidden us.

Answ. 1. God hath not left us to so much liberty how to worship him, as he hath left us about our houses and dresses, and common things.

2. The pope and his ministers are unlawful governors, as setting up an unlawful church policy, even a universal, human, ecclesiastical monarchy, (or aristocracy, as the conciliar party hold,) and therefore we owe them no obedience even in lawful things, and it is a sin to become their subjects.

3. Doubting whether real sin be sin, will not make it no sin, nor change the law of God. Should men be uncertain whether rebellion, schism, fornication, perjury, or lying be sin, they may not therefore do it though it were commanded them; for no one hath true authority to command them.

4. But if really the thing be lawful to be done, we must do it, if commanded by such as have true authority to do it, though they mistake and sin in the reasons, ends, and manner of their command.

5. If a lawful magistrate or ruler sinfully command, [say such or such a needless word, or do such a vain action, or wear such a vain habit, (not forbidden us by God,) or else you shall be silenced, banished, imprisoned,] it ceaseth to be vain in the user, when it is made necessary to such ends, though it be sinfully commanded. But what God forbiddeth must never be done.

Quest. May the husband and master bear with sinful vanities in his wife and servants in his house? Seeing he is the ruler, is it not his sin to tolerate them?

Answ. 1. It is undoubtedly his sin to consent, or not to remedy it, if he can do it by lawful means. 2. It oft falls out that not only needless toys and vanities, but some downright great sins, cannot be hindered effectually without so great inconveniences and mischiefs, as that such hindering becometh an unlawful means. If a man have a wife so passionate or unquiet, as that no means would restrain her tongue or hands but turning her away, or using such violence as is unsuitable to a conjugal relation, he must patiently endure her sin.

If he have a wife that will fall into some dangerous disease or grow distracted, if she may not please her pride in apparel, or sinfully waste much in vain expenses, or may not use an unruly tongue to sin; or at least, if the restraint would cost the husband so dear as would by unquietness unfit him to serve God in his place; in this case it is no sinful toleration to endure it. He is far from consenting to it; he only restraineth not that which he cannot restrain. For what a man cannot do by lawful means, and without doing more hurt than good, it must be said that he cannot do it at all. And so much as a man may lawfully give to purchase his own peace and quietness, or to cure his wife of such a disease or distraction, so much he may lawfully suffer her to spend (though sinfully) to prevent it, as long as he disowneth the sin, and would remedy it, if he could by lawful means.

Object. If you tell women this, some will give their husbands no quietness, and some will waste their estates in sin, or vain expenses, to satisfy their lusts.

Answ. 1. We must use no false doctrine for the preventing of such persons' sin. If it be true, some men have need to know it. 2. It is possible that some rates of expense or suffering may be greater than the preventing of the wives' calamity and its consequences are worth; and in such cases it cannot be so prevented. 3. And I hope the case is so rare, that most women's pride, exorbitancy, and passion, and the sins thence proceeding, may be restrained by other means at easier rates.

Object. 2. But by this you would infer, that evils may also be tolerated in the church, if so far in the family.

Answ. Consenting to any sin is sin, and so is doing that by promoting or tolerating, which signifieth consent; but not to hinder that which we cannot hinder by lawful means, and without doing greater hurt than good, is no consenting or sinful toleration. Papists that are for burning and banishing dissenters, yet confess this, that they must tolerate them, when else they should more hurt the church by what is done against them.

It is no sin to bear with the greatest sin in the world which we cannot remedy, much less with human, common frailties, in which all mortal men must bear with one another, or else forsake all love and peace.

And this objection mindeth me humbly but earnestly (though almost hopelessly) to desire all governors to take notice, that the pastoral government of Christ's church (being exercised under him, who calleth it his spouse and body) is very like the government of a husband over his wife, which must be done by no means inconsistent with love, and conjugal offices, and communion to the last. And therefore if men must bear with so many and great offences and inconveniences, yea, and sufferings, in and from a wife, for their household peace and quietness, let them consider whether for church peace, much evil is not to be endured when it cannot be lawfully hindered.

And if human frailty and darkness be such as that few persons living have the same apprehensions of many or most things, and husband and wife about their ordinary affairs will daily manifest such difference of opinions and humours, as must be borne, (or they must bear much worse,) let pastors consider, while we agree in all things necessary to salvation and the common peace, how much diversity of sense, and consequently of practice, must be endured in the numerous difficulties of religion by them that know the way of peace. And whether they that will not bear a little are not preparing to bear much. And perhaps if the Roman clergy had not been so much against priests' marriage, the experience of their families, and what differing apprehensions and actions must there be borne by conjugal love, might have better taught them how far to bear with differing opinions and practices in religion, instead of their unchristian, inhuman laws and practices of burning, exterminating, and ruining all such as their judgments shall stigmatize as heretics.

Quest. 4. What are to be taken for sinful, needless studies, which scholars should avoid?

Answ. 1. There is great cause to put this question, considering how many years are this way lost, and how little it is repented of, and how much is still owned and applauded by men of greatest reputation.

The case may be resolved by the same rules before given. 1. All learning and studies which are not worth the cost and labour. 2. All that do but serve that vain desire of knowledge which first tempted Eve to sin. 3. Much more all that which is but to serve men's sinful pride and worldly designs: and it were well with many students if their learning (or science, falsely so called, saith Paul) became not more plentiful and dangerous matter of pride and self-deceit than fine clothes and trifles do to women.

4. All that is worse than vain, which keepeth out greater and necessary things, and turneth the mind from holiness and heaven.

But the same knowledge in its proper place, and used in due subordination to the greatest things, and as a true means to the true end, is good and holy, which otherwise placed and used is doting vanity and delusory dreaming; as too many ungodly students will find to their cost when it is too late. Therefore a sound judgment and holy will, by right intention of the end, and true discerning the aptitude of means, must resolve this case, and most of such cases through all our lives. Happy is he that is wise in things spiritual, and of everlasting consequence to God, and to salvation, though the world should deride him as unlearned, or a fool. And woe to him that is honoured for wit and policy, for many languages, and a rolling tongue, for the prudence of Ahithophel, or the learning of Aristotle, and hath not wisdom to live to God, to resist temptation, to escape damning sin, and to save his soul. It will do him no more good in hell that he was cried up for a learned, or wise, or reverend man on earth, than it will do to Dives, (Luke xvi.) that he was clothed in purple and silk, and fared sumptuously every day, and had his portion and good things where Lazarus had sorrow and contempt. More than one of the most famous scholars have at last cried out that all learning is vanity, save the knowledge of God in Christ, our duties, and our spiritual and endless benefits and hopes.

I have told you of many evils that come by the

preference of unnecessary or less necessary things, but one remaineth to be noted, which the text expresseth in Martha's instance. While she is over-careful, and troubled about many things, which were then less necessary, she thinks her sister should have been of the same mind, and done as she did, and grudgeth at her, and accuseth her to Christ, as if Mary's work had been less necessary than hers; which showeth us,

Obs. That they that choose unnecessary or less necessary employments, are apt to account religious exercises less necessary, and to censure those that choose them.

The wrong censuring of Mary's choice and work was as much of Martha's fault as her own worst choice and needless trouble. Those that sin against knowledge, and confess that they do ill, are often desirous that their children and friends should do better. But they that think their sin is their duty, will censure those that sin not with them, as if it were sin to fear sin, and avoid it. And no wonder. For, 1. That which is true to one, is true to another; and that which is best to one, as a common duty, is best to another. And it is natural to us to desire that our friends should know what we know, and choose that common good which we choose, and avoid the error, sin, and misery which we avoid. Our love to truth and goodness will make us desire that they may be common. And our love to our friends will make us desire that they may be happy by choosing what is best. And the love of ourselves maketh men desire that others may be of their mind and way. As God first loveth himself, and next that which is most like himself, so naturally doth a selfish man. Though a holy man as such first loveth God, and then that which is likest God; yet when he erreth, he thinketh that to be like God which is not. And then even the love of God also will be abused to the promoting of error, and the angry censuring of truth and duty. No doubt but Martha's love to Christ himself, was abused by her error, to censure her sister that did not serve him in the way that she thought then most necessary.

2. And when several things are contrary or inconsistent, the overvaluing of the one must needs cause the undervaluing and rejecting of the other; the weighing down of one end of the balance will lift up the other. As all men that are earthly-minded are so much the less spiritual and heavenly, and he that loveth the world hath the less love to God; so they that overvalue unnecessary things, will naturally grow into a greater disesteem of things truly necessary: contrary things cannot be both at once preferred (in the same respect); when unnecessary things seem necessary, inconsistent necessary things will seem unnecessary.

All this we see verified constantly in our experience, in men's judging both for themselves and others.

1. Mark any that grow more in loving and caring for unnecessary worldly, fleshly things, and you shall find that they grow more indifferent to prayer, and to all holy exercises that employ the mind; a little of this will serve their turn. Mark them that overmind their ornaments, their conveniences, their appetites, or their worldly gain, and you shall see how heartless and dead they grow towards God, and holiness, and heaven; when shadows seem substances, the substance goeth but for a shadow. A little of God will serve them, when a little of the world will not serve them; and spiritual things lose all their sweetness, when fleshly pleasures and hopes grow too sweet.

2. And you shall see that such persons do judge accordingly of others. Their love of vanity maketh serious religion seem a vanity to them. When they are over-eager for the flesh or the world, they judge God's servants to be over-earnest in religion. When we wonder what they can find in an empty world to take up all their thoughts and hearts, their talk, labour, and time, they wonder what we find in religion to take up ours. As we say to them, What needs all this ado for vanity? cannot you have food and a grave without this over-much care and trouble? so they say to us, What needs all this ado in religion? Cannot a man be saved without so much violence and stir? is God so ill-natured that no less will please him?' Thus God must be thought to be like them, (Psal. l.) and to leave his holiness when they leave theirs, (or never had it,) and to grow indifferent and reconcilable to sin when once they love it.

And when serious godliness is thus rejected by themselves, it first seemeth in others to be but a needless, honest superstition, the effect of a weak judgment, and a timorous and trembling heart; and afterward they grow on to call it foolishness, and entitle it as Christ did Martha's case, a care and trouble about many unnecessary things. And from thence many grow to think it evil; and from thence to think it the most insufferable evil, and to take serious conscience of our duty to God to be the greatest rebel against kings, and the greatest troubler of the land, the greatest schismatic, and the most dangerous enemy, and most intolerable plague: and so they proceed to hellish malignity and cruel persecution. This is the natural progress of overvaluing and overminding needless things.

3. And alas, not only the history of thirteen hundred years, but the notice of our own age hath told us, that even in the churches the same cause hath produced the same effect, when many needless and troublesome things are overvalued and thought necessary. Mary is accused, and her hearing so much preaching is taken for the effect of idleness, or itching ears. In the church of Rome, where things first called indifferent have been preferred, true knowledge, explicit faith, spiritual worship, and a holy life, are taken to be necessary only to some few votaries, or saints that are to be canonized as wonders, and not to all that will be saved; and a mass of ceremonies hath shut out mostly serious preaching, praying, and holy living; their tree beareth sometimes only leaves, and at other times the pricks of thorns and thistles. Images pretended to be for the honour of departed saints are cherished, where saints and sanctity are hated; as their forefathers the Pharisees, (Matt. xxiii.) " they build the sepulchres of the prophets and righteous men," and condemn those that murdered them, and keep holy days in honour of them, and go on implacably to kill those that imitate them, and to do as their forefathers did that persecuted them. Ceremony is become the substance of too many men's religion, and an image and shadow of faith and godliness. Justice and charity hath taken place of life and substance. Too many churches are filled with statues and carcasses instead of real saints. The shell, which is but to keep the kernel, is valued in its stead, and the kernel cast away instead of the shell. The letter, which is for the signification of the sense, is first taken up as enough without it, and then turned as an enemy against it; and the oft-repeated names of Jesus, and Mary, and saints, are used first instead of holy love to Jesus and saints, and then to cherish a malignant, murderous hatred of them that are saints indeed within their reach. It was

St. Dominic, and such other of their holy men, that promoted the murder of real saints, even of many thousands, if not hundred thousands: do but call them heretics, Waldenses, Albigenses, Lutherans, Zuinglians, Calvinists, hugonots, bigots, lollards, whigs, puritans, and then conscience is as loose and free to hate, revile, imprison, silence, or murder them, as if they were so many robbers or rebels, or as bad as their accusers and persecutors feign them. Paul doth foretell that in the last days some shall be haters of those that are good, and διάβολοι, devils, which we translate false accusers, and yet have a form of godliness, while they deny the power. Diabolism begins in false accusation, and proceedeth to the cruellest persecution. What on earth can be liker a devil, than first to print such horrid lies of the servants of Christ, as they have done of Luther, Zuinglius, Bucer, Calvin, Beza, and the Reformed churches, and then to torture and burn such as heretics, and to make it a law and part of their religion to compel princes to do the like in all generations to come; and even to burn the bones of the dead, as they did by Bucer, Phagius, and Wickliff; yea, to murder them by thousands, as in France, and by hundred thousands, as in Ireland: and all this began with the overvaluing unnecessary things, worldly pomp, and power, and wealth, and pleasure, and images, ceremonies, and formalities! What dreadful work was made about images against the Eastern emperors! How many councils of bishops were the authors of schism and rebellion for them! And at last for them did the pope rebelliously cast off his sovereign, and cut off the Western empire from him, and give it (as if it had been his own) to the French. To this day, do but speak against their deified wafer, or their mass, of ceremonies, or their adoring images, or their false doctrine, or their papal or prelatical tyranny and usurpation, and you presently deserve to be painted with the picture of devils, and after the torment of the inquisition, to be cursed from Christ, and burned to ashes; and all this as for Christ, the church, and faith.

And the German Interim told the world whither the overvaluing of things, called indifferent, doth tend, when the churches were deserted, the ministers silenced and persecuted, and sadly divided among themselves, and the Reformation almost overthrown; and all because the pastors refused to conform to a book compiled by the emperor's command, by a few self-conceited bishops, pretending to be moderate reconcilers, obtruding divers of the Romish formalities as the means of the peace and concord of the churches. It would grieve one's heart to read what confusions this imposed book, called "The Interim," did cause.

But alas, they are not the only instances of the calamitous effects of the overvaluing and obtruding unnecessary things. As the ruins of Troy long told spectators what a war for one Helena, a beautiful whore, did cost that part of the world (which became the subjects of the famous poems of divers ages); even so the ruins of the Eastern churches, sometime the most great and famous in the world, and now the habitations of owls and serpents, deluded Mahometans, with some ignorant, sad, oppressed christians, proclaim to all that read, hear, or see them, what are the fruits of striving about unnecessary things, even about worldly pre-eminence and wealth; which patriarch should be greatest, and which bishop should sit highest, and go first, and have his will, and pass for the most orthodox, or have most followers; and about ambiguous words, who it was that spake wiseliest, and who should make the words of other men's creeds and professions (for the trade of making liturgies, which whole nations or provinces must be confined to, was not set up till after that of making creeds). In a word, church wars, 1. About the jurisdiction of prelates; especially whether Rome or Constantinople should be the chief; 2. And about hard and doubtful words; 3. And about images and ceremonies; have laid East and West in the condition of apostasy, desolation, shame, and slavery, in which with amazement we see them at this day.

And what are all the religious wars, murders, and cruelties exercised for by the papal party, but that one prelate and his confederates may be the masters of all the christian world, and may have their wills in all religious matters directly, and in all civil matters in order to the religious; and that all their laws may be obeyed, their formalities used, and their words believed? Killing, burning, tormenting, and confounding, seem not too dear to accomplish this. "Behold how great a matter a little fire kindleth!" Who would think, that never before saw it, that a little gunpowder should blow up houses as it doth? And who would have thought that so many churches, kingdoms, lives, and souls should have been blown up, or ruined, as they have been, for the unnecessary domination, wealth, formalities, and ceremonies of the clergy?

I have often, too often, heard preachers themselves, instead of a sermon, pour out scorns against those that preached and lived more seriously, strictly, and holily than themselves. And I have too oft heard the common rabble revile them that were most careful and diligent for salvation, as a company of precisians, puritans, and hypocrites. And I have thought with myself, Have these men found better and greater things to lay out their own care, time, and labour for? And alas, I perceived that instead of God, and Christ, and holiness, and heaven, they had nothing to take them up but vanity and vexation; their bellies, and their purses, and their walls, and titles, and their pride, and lust, and selfish wills; and are these more necessary than Mary's choice? Mark what those persons are saying and doing every day, who think serious godliness to be overdoing; and you shall see, that instead of it, some are doing nothing, and some worse than nothing; wasting their short time, deceiving and destroying themselves and others.

And indeed it is not possible that any one that is a serious christian himself, and hath tried truly a holy life, should think it needless, or make it a matter of reproach to others. But we grant that particular duties may be misplaced, and prudence is necessary to know their time, and length, and manner; and it is possible, both that a Mary may sometimes here imprudently overdo, and that a Martha may by mistake be quarrelsome, and accuse the innocent, that yet is not against serious piety itself. Therefore I think meet to annex these two cautions to the hearers in this case.

I. Do not presently take yourselves to be truly godly, because some others accuse you of overdoing, or of being religious over-much. Every one is not a saint that is derided for sanctity; every one doth not sincerely preach, hear, pray, or practise, that is derided for these things. If you have no better evidence of grace, than that some call you puritans, precisians, or such like, it will be an insufficient evidence. 1. Bad men will deride those that seem holy, though they are not so. 2. And good men in their faulty weakness, may misjudge of the circumstances of your duty, and unjustly blame you, and yet you may not be sincere in the main. 3. And you may actually mistake in circumstances yourselves, and deserve the blame that is cast upon you. The

Pharisees were over-strict for the sabbath, and in avoiding publicans and sinners, and thought Christ too loose. Judas pretendeth more charity to the poor than Christ had. That is not rightest which seemeth strictest, but that which is most agreeable to the law of God. Though some misapply Solomon's words, Eccles. vii. 16, "Be not righteous over-much, neither make thyself over-wise;" as if it had been written against serious, diligent obedience to God, and true, proper righteousness and wisdom; yet we must know that it was written by the Holy Ghost, and not in vain. A pharisaical, superstitious sort of religion, and observation of vain traditions, and a zealous strictness which God never commanded, is a righteousness equivocally so called, and it is over-much. Such is much of the popish righteousness, and such is the affected austerity of several sects, old and new. "Touch not, taste not, handle not," are oft a human, counterfeit righteousness, which God doth neither require nor accept. As God liketh not a popish charity, that killeth or tormenteth men in love to God and religion; so neither doth he like those superstitious austerities which destroy our own bodies, and disable us from cheerful thankfulness and obedience; which maketh Solomon say, "Why should thou be desolate" (or destroy thyself)? That is good which is fitted to do good. All grace and duty is for edification.

II. And as every one is not truly godly who is derided as godly by the profane, or blamed for some superstitious strictness, so you must not take every one for malignant or ungodly who speaketh against such strictness, as either is real superstition, or seemeth so or worse to him.

For, 1. If you are guilty of superstition, it is a friendly office to show you your mistake. 2. And if you are in the right, and another that is in the wrong misaccuseth you, in many cases his error may stand with love to truth and holiness in the main. Every one is not ungodly who misreproach us with the anabaptists for baptizing infants; or with the antinomians as setting up the abrogated law; and so of many others. As men differ in judgment about God's law, they will accuse each other's differing practice. But opposing serious godliness as such is another thing.

And indeed it is usual with malignant enemies of a holy life, to make themselves a religion of formalities, and imagery, and shadows, to quiet their consciences while they resist the truth, that it may not seem to be an act of impiety and malignity which they do, but an opposition to the faults of others.

But the use which you should make of this lesson is this: Take heed lest you be tempted to an overvaluing of any unnecessary or less needful things, whether it be wealth, and honour, and fleshly interest; or else any formalities, or things indifferent about religion; lest before you are aware (as imagery stole away the hearts of the old idolaters from God, so) these should secretly consume your holy zeal, and turn your hearts from the life and serious exercise of religion, and worshipping God in Spirit and truth, and afterwards draw you to condemn that zeal and diligence in others which you want yourselves. We have bodies as well as souls, and must have a just regard to bodily necessaries, and a care that our bodies do their duty. But let the body and its interest keep their place. Remember how far it is below the soul, and use it and all its interests accordingly. The least things that are good are not to be despised. But alas, what work is made by preferring little things! The traditions of their fathers, their tithing mint and anise, their washings, their building the sepulchres of the prophets, their domination, pomp, and ceremonies, did pass with the Pharisees instead of the great things of the law, and sacrifice went before mercy, truth, and judgment; yea, and became a cloak for devouring widows' houses, and for persecuting and silencing the preachers of the gospel, and for slandering and murdering Christ himself.

What ruins this hath made in souls, churches, and kingdoms, I have already told you. Know therefore wherein God's kingdom doth consist, Rom. xiv. 17, 18; and what and whom God bindeth you to approve; and learn what this meaneth, "I will have mercy, and not sacrifice," that you may not deceive yourselves, or condemn the guiltless. Even Martha will murmur at her dear sister, and accuse her, if she be herself but tainted with this ill disease.

But whose part doth Christ take? and which of them doth he justify? The defendant Mary; and that, 1. With a compassionate reproof of Martha. 2. With the reason of Mary's justification. 3. And with a sentence of blessing added to her defence. Whence we learn,

Doct. 2. That when wiser christians, and their better choice and work, are accused by them that preferred less needful things, Christ will be the Advocate and Judge, and will defend and justify the wrongfully accused. He will in this case take the accused's part.

Martha accuseth her sister to Christ, she expecteth that he should blame her as neglecting her duty, and leaving all the trouble and care on Martha. But Christ doth not answer her expectation, but justifieth the wise and innocent.

Reason 1. For it is his office to be both the Advocate and the Judge. And he will do it in perfection, without error or injustice. He well knoweth who is in the right, and none can deceive him by false accusations or false witnesses.

2. He is so nearly related and deeply obliged to defend the innocent or just, that he will never fail them. They are his members, and his love engageth him. He spared not his life and blood for them, and will he not speak for them? They are his purchase and interest, his peculiar redeemed ones, and will he forsake his interest, and his own?

3. Indeed in plain justice he is bound to justify them against such injurious accusations. For it is he that commandeth them to do what they are accused of. It is for obeying him. If it were a fault, it would be his that bid them do it. Nay, how much hath he done to bring his servants to that holy choice, and faithful duty, which in the world they are commonly accused for! Alas, we were not forward to it of ourselves. It was not we that made the law, which so strictly forbiddeth sin, and commandeth duty. The Bible is not of our making. It is not we that made the law to "love God with all our heart, and soul, and might; and our neighbour as ourselves; not to take his name in vain, to worship God in spirit and in truth," &c. And it was a higher cause than our own power which taught us, and inclined our hearts to obey these. Many a message did Christ send us, by his Bible, ministers, and Spirit, before we were heartily drawn to yield. Many a day's patience did he use, and many a threatening to drive us to it, and many a mercy and promise to draw us, and many a book and teacher to instruct us, yea, and many an affliction to correct us; and will he not justify us for that which he so earnestly commandeth us, and with so much ado doth bring us to obey? Did he come into the world, and live, and die, to save his people from their sins, and purify to himself "a peculiar people, zealous of good works," (Tit. ii. 14,) and will he forsake them when they are accused for

obeying him? Where shall we meet with a man of any common honesty that would do thus by his poorest servant? And shall not the Judge of all the earth do righteously? For our parts, if we are accused for serious piety, or any duty which Christ commandeth us, it is his command that was our reason and obligation, and which we have to allege for our defence. If that have not authority and truth enough to justify us, we have no other justification. Indeed Christ should forsake himself if he thus deserted us. He should take the blame upon his own laws, yea, and on all the works of his grace and Spirit, and all that he hath done to bring us to that which the world and our flesh was so much against.

4. He defendeth his disciples against the Pharisees' accusations on earth; and will he afterwards forsake them?

5. He hath appointed the great day to judge the world in righteousness, even the secrets of men, and to bring all things open into the manifesting light, even all truth and falsehood, and all the hidden works of darkness. Therefore undoubtedly all truth, all righteousness, and all that is of God, shall be fully justified, and God's truth in all, when false accusers shall be all found liars.

Use. This being then so plain and sure, I would commend the consideration of it to several sorts, and in several instances. I. To the accusers of the godly for their duty to God. II. To the accused. III. To those that are yet in doubt what cause to choose.

I. The unjust accusers of just men are of divers degrees or sorts.

1. Some there be that only accuse them in their thoughts, and take them to be guilty when they are not.

2. Others go further, and too easily believe false reports from others; and then think that they are allowed to tell what they have heard, and so to vend such false reports. And if they can but say, either that it was a great man, or a learned man, or a minister, or a religious man, that said it, they think that their calumny or backbiting is no sin. But much more, if many such report it; and yet more, if they heard none contradict it.

3. Others there be, that because it serveth their interest or design, or pleaseth their malignant minds, do make it part of their business purposely to carry about such reports, and persuade as many as they can to believe them, and plead down those that contradict them.

4. Others go further, and are the first devisers, or the malicious increasers, of the slanderous reports themselves; not only the spreaders or carriers, but the fathers of the lies which they send about by others.

5. Yet some go further, and studiously and maliciously publish them in pulpits, or in print, to draw the world and posterity to believe them; yea, and this as for God, and as for the church and truth; as if it were but the detecting of heresies or lies, or dangerous faults or practices of others.

6. And yet further, some in most ages and countries, in offices and places of judicature, who should be the pillars of justice, do pass false sentences against the just, and pronounce them guilty, and persecute and oppress them by their unrighteous punishments.

7. And yet worse; some slander not only the persons, but the cause of truth, piety, and righteousness itself, and make false laws and canons, calling good evil, and decreeing the common slandering of the truth, and the punishing of the innocent, because they will not break the laws of God, and please proud, mistaken men before him.

To all these sorts of accusers of the just, I would give (would they hear me) this following advice.

1. I advise you to stay, and think well of the matter, and be sure that you have thoroughly tried it before you venture to pass your judgment. It is not so small a matter as you think, to wrong the just, and say, I was mistaken. And especially will you be first sure what side Christ will take? and whether he will be of the accuser's mind?

And Christ hath so fully told us his mind already in his word, that we may certainly foreknow what judgment he will pass.

(1.) Do you accuse men for pretending to the Spirit, and to be holy? Why, Christ hath said, that "Except a man be born of water, and the Spirit, he cannot enter into the kingdom of heaven," John iii. 6. And, "Without holiness none shall see God," Heb. xii. 14. And, "If any man have not the Spirit of Christ, the same is none of his," Rom. viii. 9.

(2.) Do you accuse godly men for singularity, and for differing from others in their religious diligence and zeal? If they differ from the common faith of christians, or single themselves from the communion of saints, or from the love and concord of believers, Christ will not justify them in this. For he hath said, "A man that is an heretic, after the first and second admonition avoid," Tit. iii. 10. And, "By this shall all men know that you are my disciples, if ye have love one to another," John xiii. 34, 35. And, "Mark those that cause divisions and offences, contrary to the doctrine which ye have learned, and avoid them," Rom. xvi. 17.

But if it be differing from unbelievers, or ungodly men, or formal hypocrites, by a holy resolution to live wholly to God, and obey his laws, whoever be against it; if this be the singularity you mean, Christ is engaged to bear them out. For it is he that hath commanded this, and said, "Ye are my friends if ye do whatsoever I command you," John xv. 14. "If ye keep my commandments ye shall abide in my love," ver. 10. "Except your righteousness exceed the righteousness of the scribes and Pharisees, ye shall in no case enter into the kingdom of heaven," Matt. v. 20. "What do you more than others?" ver. 47. "He purifieth to himself a peculiar people, zealous of good works," Tit. ii. 14. Lot differed from Sodom, and Noah differed from all the old world. The wise differ from the foolish, and the righteous from the wicked; or else there would not be hereafter so great a difference as of heaven and hell. What is a physician good for if he make not his patients to differ from the sick? And what came Christ to do, or how is he a Saviour, if he make not his disciples differ from the ungodly world? Even a philosopher would not set up a school, but to make his scholars to differ from the unlearned.

(3.) Is it for so much preaching and hearing that you accuse men? It is possible indeed to do a duty unreasonably, and to overdo in one thing, when it causeth the omission of other duties. But certainly Christ, that so strictly commandeth his ministers to preach, and as they love him to feed his flock, will justify them for so doing. "How shall they believe without a preacher? And how shall they preach unless they are sent?" Rom. x. And he that said, "He that heareth you, heareth me," and that here justifieth Mary's hearing, will justify all others in the like case: for he hath bid us (by Solomon) to "get wisdom as the principal thing," Prov. iv. 5, 7. "To incline the ear, and apply the heart to it; to cry after knowledge, and lift up the voice for understanding; to seek her as silver, and search for her as for hidden treasure," Prov. xxii. 3, 4. "Hear instruction, and be wise, and refuse it not. Blessed is the man that heareth me, watching daily at my gates, waiting at the posts of my doors. For whoso findeth me, findeth life, and shall obtain favour of the Lord," Prov. viii. 33—36.

(4.) Is it for much praying that you accuse men? Why, Christ bid his disciples "pray always, and not faint," Luke xviii. 1, 2; and pray continually, 1 Thess. v. 17.

(5.) Is it for so much ado in their families, in the religious education of their children, and reading the Scriptures, that you accuse men? Why, it is God that hath said, "These words which I command thee this day shall be in thy heart, and thou shalt teach them diligently to thy children, and shalt talk of them when thou sittest in thy house, and when thou walkest by the way, and when thou liest down, and when thou risest up," &c. Deut. vi. 7—10; xi. 18—20. An angel was sent from heaven unto Cornelius when he was fasting and praying in his house, to signify God's acceptance, and tell him further how to be saved. Daniel would rather be cast to lions, than forbear praying in his house for certain days, when the king and laws forbad him. You may easily know then which side Christ will take.

(6.) Is it for scrupling things which others scruple not; and taking that for sin which others say is none, and so not doing as others do, that you accuse men?

If they mistake, and think that to be sin which is not, Christ will justify their desire to please him, and their fear of sinning, but he will not justify their mistake. But if it be sin indeed, whatever men call it, he will justify our avoiding and abhorring it. He that died for sin, would not have us love it, nor run into the consuming fire, from which he came to save us. "It is a fearful thing to fall into the hands of the living God." The accuser may call it folly, and precise scrupulosity, but God saith to man, "Behold, the fear of the Lord, that is wisdom, and to depart from evil is understanding," Job xxviii. 28. If we sin with others, we must suffer with them.

(7.) But perhaps it is for not keeping their faith and religion to themselves, but making so much ado to propagate them, that you accuse men.

Indeed Paul, speaking of the knowledge and belief of the lawfulness of lawful, necessary things, saith, "Hast thou faith? Have it to thyself before God," Rom. xiv. 21. That is, enjoy thy own knowledge and liberty, but use it not so as to tempt and ruin others. But surely it is Christ that hath said, "Ye are the lights of the world, that must not be put under a bushel," Matt. v. And, "He that gathereth not with us, scattereth abroad," Matt. xii. 30. And, "Whoever shall confess me before men, him will I confess before my Father," &c. Matt. x. 32. And, "With the heart man believeth unto righteousness, and with the mouth confession is made unto salvation," Rom. x. 10. We must love our neighbours as ourselves, and therefore desire and seek their salvation: "He that seeth his brother have need, (for his body,) and shutteth up the bowels of his compassion from him, how dwelleth the love of God in him?" much less if he have no pity for souls. While we have opportunity we must do good to all men, Gal. vi. 10. The slothful servant that hid his talent is condemned to utter darkness, Matt. xxv. What do we in the world but to receive good, and do good? And how little goodness is in that which tendeth not to men's salvation? What are we made, redeemed, and preserved for, but to serve God, and seek the good of ourselves and others? You accuse not men for giving money to the poor and needy; and is not holiness much better? If money be better than grace, not only Simon Magus was excusable, but Cæsar might be a greater benefactor than Christ. Do you believe a heaven, and do you accuse men for seeking to help men to attain it? Unthankful, miserable sinners, that accuse men for endeavouring to save them from sin and endless misery! Were they drowning, they would not accuse men for labouring to save their lives. None but mad-men strive against those that would heal or help them; but it is here no wonder, when the Saviour of the world was as madly and unthankfully used by such sinners: how can we expect that he will accept our help, who despiseth or refuseth God's?

(8.) But perhaps it is their zeal and earnestness in religion that you accuse; and think that they should be, as you call it, more moderate; that is, indifferent and cold.

Indeed, imprudent, passionate rashness, and erroneous zeal and factious violence, which is more for self-interest and self-conceit, than for the truth and cause of Christ, is a thing which he will never justify. If James and John have such a feverish zeal, he will tell them, "You know not what manner of spirit ye are of." Where an envious, striving, masterly zeal is, he tells them it is not from above, but the wisdom which it pretendeth to is earthly, sensual, and devilish, tending to confusion, and every evil work. Christ is no patron of popish, tyrannical, persecuting, destroying, hurtful zeal; but surely he will justify the zeal of love, and of good works: not zealous slandering, railing, and false censuring; but zealous preaching, praying, and praising God, and a zealous diligence in all that he commandeth, and a zealous care to mortify fleshly lusts, and avoid sin, and escape damnation, and to glorify God. It is a base contempt and dishonouring of God, and Christ, and holiness, and heaven, to think or speak of them, or seek them, with a cold indifferency, as if they were but common needless things.

How eagerly do worldlings seek the world, and proud men strive to climb into some honour, before they fall into the grave and hell! How violent do many earthly rulers strive to enlarge their dominions, and have their wills, though by the ruin of countries, and the blood of many thousand innocents! How hot are all these worldly men (even popes and prelates, that say they believe a better world) against all, how wise and holy soever, that are against their worldly interest! How fervently did they cry against Christ himself, "Away with him, crucify him!" How furiously did they gnash their teeth at Stephen, and stone him! And cried out against Paul, "Away with such a fellow from the earth, it is not fit that he should live!" The devil is earnest to destroy us. The zeal of infidels, papists, and church tyrants is burning hot, and no reason, no worth or innocency of the just, will serve to quench it. And is it only God's service and our salvation that must be coldly managed and sought? Is it only that which we are born for, and live for, that must be thrust behind the door, or done as if we did it not? Is it heaven and hell that must be jested with? and souls that must be ventured for a little wealth, or lust, or our endless hope cast away for nothing? Idols that have eyes and see not, deserve no better service than the hypocrite's imagery, and stage religion; but do you think the God of love and glory can be loved, honoured, or obeyed too much? None but the atheistical fool can think so. How quickly, how certainly will you all wish that God and your salvation had been loved, and sought with all your hearts, and strength, and time, and that he that is All had had your all, and that you had been as holy as the holiest men! O hypocrites, that daily pray that "God's name may be hallowed, his kingdom come, and his will done on earth as it is done in heaven;" and yet accuse those as doing too much, that, alas! fall far short of the lowest of all the heavenly inhabitants!

(9.) But perhaps they are accused for not serving God just as men command them, and not being of the religion of those that are uppermost.

This hath indeed been the common accusation. But, 1. God is uppermost, and will be; therefore they are resolved to be as near as they can of his mind that is uppermost, and will prevail.

2. Christ went against the rulers of his time, and commanded his apostles so to do; and so did they, and so did the church for three hundred years, and in much of the world ever since.

3. Must we have as many religions as princes have? And must we change our religion as oft as we change our country? Must a man be a heathen under heathens, and a Mahometan under Turks and Persians? and a papist under papists, and a Socinian under Socinians, and so on? If not, how shall we know which prince's religion it is that we must be of, and which we must refuse, but by the word of God, which we must ourselves discern (using the best helps of teachers that we can get)? We thank God that we have rulers that so far own truth and righteousness as they do; but even the apostle saith, they were not lords, nor had dominion over their faith, but were their helpers, 2 Cor. i. 24, "as stewards of the mysteries of God," 1 Pet. v. 1, 3.

4. Why do you honour the martyrs, and keep holidays in remembrance of their sufferings, who died rather than they would obey man against God, if you think we must always be of the ruler's religion? Did the three witnesses so? Dan. iii. or Daniel himself? Dan. vi. The common case is much like Daniel's; "We shall not find any occasion against this Daniel, except we find it against him concerning the law of his God," Dan. vi. 5; which they did for praying when the law forbad him. They could find no fault with Christ and his apostles, but for not observing their traditions, and for worshipping God contrary to the law, and doing contrary to the decrees of Cæsar, Acts xviii. 13; xvii. 5; Matt. xv. God's law is perfect, man's is not so; though we cannot ourselves attain perfection in understanding our practice, yet we will choose and set before us a perfect rule, even the perfect law of the perfect Ruler of the world. If we must be all of the prince's or state's religion, where one country hath the true religion, many will have a false one; and when we are right in one point, we may be wrong in another, our copy being so.

(10.) But perhaps it is error, sin, sedition, sects, schism, scandal, that you accuse men of: if that be it, if you do it truly, and do not slander them, certainly Christ will not justify them in these.

1. If you accuse them falsely he will justify them.

2. If they have sinned, and truly believe, and repent, and amend, he will pardon them through his meritorious righteousness and sacrifice, and will make them and pronounce them just.

3. And he will justify in them all that is his own and good, notwithstanding their pardonable infirmities, and will not make their faults greater than they are, but will see the willingness of the spirit when the flesh is weak. If malignant men will see the mote of a ceremonious error or frailty in their brother's eye, and call it a beam because a beam is in their own, Christ will not join with them in their malignity and injustice, but will bid him cast the first stone that is without sin, John viii. 7.

4. And yet he will not justify the least sinful thought, or word, or deed, nor the least faulty imperfection in their faith, love, or obedience: for no man hateth any of these so much as Christ doth, in whomsoever they are found. Do you cry out against error, sedition, rebellion, disobedience, schism, divisions? So doth Christ, and so do all his true disciples; we all agree with you in this. But if the question be either, Who they are that are herein guilty? or, in whom any sin is reigning, wilful, and unpardoned? here see that you go not beyond proof; for Christ will not own the condemners of the just, nor confirm any man's unrighteous and malicious censure.

2. And as I advise you before you accuse any, to know whether Christ be of your mind, and will be against them, or will take their parts; so next I advise you, as you love yourselves, to think well how great a sin malignant and false accusing is.

1. It showeth much of the devil in your hearts; whether you see it or not, it is no better: he is malicious, a murderer, a liar, and the accuser of the just, and slanders are called by his name, διάβολοι, as aforesaid.

2. If it be for Christ's cause, for truth or righteousness, or done in malice, against godliness or faith, Christ taketh it all as done against himself, Matt. xxv. For it is not only against his servants, but also for their obeying and serving him: it is he that commanded them, as is aforesaid.

3. You set yourself against the office also of Christ: he is the Advocate of his servants, he hath undertaken their defence, and do you think to overcome him? It is he that justifieth us, (for all that faith, and zeal, and holiness, for which we are accused and persecuted by the world,) who then shall condemn us? It is he that is for us, who then is he that will be against us? Shall we not be more than conquerors through him whose power hath conquered for us, and whose victorious love will not forsake us? Rom. viii. 34, &c. Remember in what a manner he said, "Saul, Saul, why persecutest thou me? It is hard for thee to kick against the pricks," Acts ii. And to him that offendeth one of those little despised ones that believe in him, that "it were better for him that a millstone were hanged about his neck, and he were cast into the sea."

And it is not only to the gross persecuting accusers of the just, that I give this advice, but I beseech you all to take heed of any rash accusing of the just; for the wrong is most to God himself, and the hurt to you, and Christ will be against you.

1. Some there are, that when they have by ignorance, or a stretching conscience, for worldly interest consented to some sinful practices, are led by that same unhappy interest, to justify first what they do themselves, and then to accuse all those as erroneous, precise, or schismatical, that are against their choice and practice. Most men that live in sin for interest, do think that they must be secured from the accusations of conscience, and the disgrace of sinning, by justifying their sin, and accusing those as the sinners that are against it, and dare not sin as much as they; but how sad a defence will this prove at last, which so much addeth to their crime!

2. There are some on the contrary, that in ignorance having taken a duty or lawful practice for a sin, (as baptizing infants, singing David's psalms, praying constantly in families, observing the Lord's day, praying oft in the same words, communicating with some faulty churches, or such as these men condemn, and such like,) they hereupon become the rash and false accusers of those that be not as erroneous as themselves: thus did the Pharisees by Christ and his apostles; thus did the Jewish teachers, that said, "Except ye be circumcised, and keep the law of

Moses, ye cannot be saved," Acts xv. Thus did the Jewish christians against Peter, "They contended with him, saying, Thou wentest in to men uncircumcised, and didst eat with them," Acts xi. 23. And after his miraculous conviction by this censoriousness, they drew him to that separation which Paul doth blame him for, Gal. ii. 12—14; and Barnabas and others dissembled with him, for fear of the censures of these erroneous men: for it is not the least mischievous effect of these false accusations and censures, that they frighten many weak christians from duty and into sin, while they hear that this or that is no duty, or is some heinous sin, and have not the understanding to try and judge, they are carried away with the name and noise; and some such as Peter and Barnabas walk not uprightly, but step out of the way for fear of displeasing them, or being accused by them, as others are; and it is not a little shame, guilt, and suffering, that this course hath brought upon the ministers themselves.

3. And there are some that here more heinously offend, familists, ranters, seekers, quakers, and too many more; that while they are guilty themselves of lamentable errors, fear not to accuse almost all the churches of Christ on earth, as if they were not his church at all, and had no true religion, ministry, ordinances, and were not to be communicated with. The papists that burn men as heretics for the truth, I think, accuse not so many of Christ's ministers and churches, nor so deeply, as some of these sects do; yea, and father this malignity on the Spirit of God: but Christ will defend and justify his churches against all these false accusers.

Oh, little do either papists or any other sectaries know how heinous a crime Christ will take it, to accuse the greatest part of christians on earth as being heretics, schismatics, or no true churches, or having no true religion or part in Christ, or in his Spirit; and for a worldly faction on one side, or a sick-brained, self-conceited sect on the other side, to appropriate the title of the church or saints to themselves alone, and say to most of the members of Christ, "You are none of his!" If to accuse falsely one man when his estate only is concerned in it, and that before a single judicature, be so great a crime as Scripture maketh it, what is it openly before God and the world, rashly or falsely to accuse whole churches and countries of christians, yea, the faithfullest of Christ's ministers, with bitter scorns, as many of the aforesaid sectaries do; yea, almost all the church of Christ, in this and almost all former ages! For my part, (though some censure me for it,) I am afraid of too bold censuring even of papists, or of honest heathens, such as were Antonine, Cicero, and such others that never heard the gospel of Christ.

II. My next advice is to those that are thus accused by others about religion, or of sin.

1. Do not presently justify yourselves, because you love not to be blamed; rash self-justifying may be more hurtful to you than other men's rash accusing you. Error and sin are not so rare things, even among good men, that it should be taken for hard measure to be judged erroneous and sinners: who knoweth his secret faults? Psal. xix. We must daily pray, "Forgive us our trespasses." Little do most know how great a number of falsehoods are received into the minds of most good christians in the world, yea of the best, much more of the more ignorant sort; and therefore we have great cause to be still cautiously suspicious of ourselves: and it is a mercy to have notice of our sins and errors from whomsoever, friends or foes.

Try, therefore, lest it should prove an error or sin that you are accused of; confess it not to be such because another calleth it such; but yet let him know that you are willing of his help for your information and conviction.

It is supposed that none of us love error as error, or sin as sin, or any evil as such; it is no evil that is the object of a sinner's will and choice, but a misplaced good, even a lesser good set against or instead of a greater: (as the creature instead of the Creator, and corporal instead of spiritual, &c.) We do not love and will *malum, sed male,* not evil, but evilly: it is not the thing loved that is evil itself, but the act of loving it (or doing it). The fruit that Adam did eat was not evil, but eating it was; meat, drink, pleasurable objects, beauty, money, lands, honours, are all good, but the inordinate love and use of them is the evil.

Our nature therefore giveth this advantage to our monitors; we would all be delivered from evil as evil, and therefore thankfully accept their help.

Humanum est errare; how little doth that man know himself, or what man is, who taketh it for an injury to be supposed to have errors! But to deny necessary saving verities, or to be unwilling to see our errors by finding out the truth, or proudly to defend them, because we have once owned them, and to be rash and confident propagators of such errors, and to rage against wiser men that are against our folly, and ignorantly to cry them down as ignorant, and to charge all this on the Spirit of God, this is an unchristian and inhuman sort of erring. Try therefore with a due suspicion of yourselves, lest your accusation should be true, and you be found in the mistake.

The same I say when you are accused of any sin: alas, sin is not so rare a thing with any of us, but that we may well fear and try the case, lest we should be guilty.

2. My next advice is, Take heed lest you go about to interest Christ in any of your sins or errors, or lest you expect that he should justify them. It is a greater sin which many erring men are guilty of in this kind, than is commonly perceived. It is well that men would do that which God owneth if they knew it; but it is dangerous so say that he owneth what he abhorreth: to father falsehood on the God of truth, and sin on the God of holiness, is a fearful crime. God that would not endure false fire, (Lev. x.) or to be worshipped like an idol, no, nor to have holy things profaned, will much less endure to be made the father of lies and wickedness.

(1.) Consider that this is to set him against himself, who is the God of truth and holiness.

(2.) This is to use his name against his word, which is the word of truth and holiness.

(3.) This is to put him in the place of Satan, and to father on him the devil's works, who is a liar and the father of it.

(4.) This is it which the false prophets are so heavily threatened for in Scripture.

(5.) This is to fight against God's kingdom, and the grace of Christ, and the work of the Spirit in his own name.

(6.) This is the direct breach of the third commandment, "Thou shalt not take the name of the Lord thy God in vain:" a lie and vanity oft signify the same thing in Scripture. This sin is of the nature of perjury, which is appealing to God, as owning and approving a falsehood; and do not they so that falsely say, God saith this, and that, and the other thing in the Scripture, and by his Spirit in me, which he never said, yea, which no one so much abhorreth as he; and will you father on God that one thing which he hateth? God tells you that he will not hold him guiltless, that is, he will notably condemn and punish, such as thus profanely and audaciously take his name in vain, or use it to patronize a lie.

I am often near trembling, to hear some of our tremblers, yea, and some others, abuse abundance of plain texts of Scripture, and expound them with palpable falsehood, and deny the articles of the christian faith, about Christ's person, his intercession, his coming again, his laws, his kingdom, his judgment, and pouring out many heathenish and gross errors, and fathering all this with raging confidence on God himself, and saying, I am sure this is true; the Spirit infallibly tells me so; God speaketh it in me; I no more doubt of it than whether I live; he that doubteth is damned; the light within me assureth me that this is true, and the meaning of the Scripture. O patient God! O sinful man! O subtle serpent! O dark, unhappy world! O pitiful professors of faith, that will be changed or shaken by such heinous sin, as if they heard an oracle of God! Our God is love, and yet he is a consuming fire: take heed what you say of him, and what you father on him: if pride, blindness, and deceit do carry you to blaspheme him, your confidence will not make Christ justify it.

3. But I further advise you, If indeed it be truth and duty which men accuse you for, even such as Christ in the sacred Scriptures did prescribe, doubt not but he will justify you against all accusers; and let this satisfy you, however you are slandered, against all. As, if your sins were few and small, there would be less use of a Saviour to forgive them; so, if your slanders by malignant liars be few and small, you will have the less use for Christ to justify you. If it be "all men that revile you, and persecute you, and shall say all manner of evil against you falsely (or lying) for Christ's sake, blessed are ye," saith Christ, Matt. v. 11. And if you believe him, you may "rejoice, and be exceeding glad, for great is your reward in heaven; and so persecuted they the prophets before you." How many things are here to be observed! It is supposed to be lies that are reported of you; and this not of one sort only, but "all manner of evil;" as if you were impious against God, uncharitable and unjust towards men, heretics against truth, schismatics against unity, rebels and disobedient against authority, and all the rest: and of all these have the just been ordinarily accused; and this is not by some one exasperated person in a corner, whom few believe, but by all men, that is, the common voice of deluded adversaries; and it is not only belying, but reviling, yea, and persecuting; yet must you not only be patient, but joyful and exceeding glad, because it is for Christ, and he will justify you and give you a great reward in heaven. Here is a noble work for faith, to learn and practise this lesson of cross-bearing, hope and joy. The judge is at the door, who seeth us and all our case, and is more concerned in it than we are: be not too hasty for a full vindication; cannot you stay till the assizes? Were it not that slanderers hurt others and themselves, how small a matter were their thoughts and words to you! Will a malignant thought of a dying worm deject you from any real honour or felicity? Is it in the power of a lying tongue, or of many, how high or how credible soever esteemed, to deprive you of your innocency, or the approbation of God, or your adoption, or Christ's justification, or your everlasting glory and reward? Do you trust Christ for your souls, and cannot you trust him with your names? Is God your God, and is not his approbation enough for you? Is man nothing to you, who is posting to dust and judgment, and yet cannot you bear his lying words or thoughts? How will you bear the cross of martyrdom, which is to die for well-doing, under the reputation of malefactors, if you cannot bear false words or thoughts? If you say, It is the truth that is dishonoured through my dishonour, I answer,

(1.) God is sufficient to vindicate his truth: every slanderous mouth shall soon be stopped, and God will be proved true, and all men liars, Rom. iii.

(2.) And he hath promised to bring forth your righteousness as the light; your name shall rise as the morning sun, when the most malignant darkness seemed to bury them. Christ is not in heaven reputed a blasphemer, nor a rebel against Cæsar; nor is Paul there taken for a pestilent fellow, or a mover of sedition amongst the people; nor the cross of Christ for foolishness or a stumbling block; nor are true christians there reproached or excommunicated, as heretics or evil-doers. Of how small regard is the judgment of man to him that fully trusteth to Christ's justification! which you may be sure of so far as the Scriptures truly understood do justify you.

III. My next counsel is to those that are unresolved which cause or side is right, and to be chosen, whilst most men are accusers of each other: one talketh against this thing, and another against that, one against this doctrine and practice, and another against that, and so many parties accuse all the rest that it distracteth ignorant persons.

Either the things which they differ about are such as Christ hath told us his mind of in the Scripture, or not; if not, then pity and bear with the contenders on both sides; interpose not your judgment rashly, but let every one enjoy his own. Paul and Barnabas, as well as Martha and Mary, may differ about persons and circumstances of duty; but if Christ have already decided the case, let that determine you: what need you more? Is the controversy whether God or man should be first obeyed? Whether heaven or earth, Christ or the pleasures of sin, should be preferred? Whether we should live after the flesh or the Spirit? In all such cases it is easy to know what Christ doth judge. I hope you do not think that he will take part with the sensual, or the covetous, or the malignant enemies of a godly life; nor that he will turn to the oppressors or persecutors of the just; nor that he will renounce his own word, because any men, how great or reverend soever, misapply it, or contradict it; nor that he will call drunkenness, gluttony, worldliness, idleness, filthiness, or pride, by gentle, extenuating, deceitful names, though the guilty and impenitent do so.

Some would persuade you that Christ and his Spirit could not speak so much sense as to become intelligible; and though every friend can intelligibly write you his mind, yet Christ could not, or would not: and that you may understand poets and orators, Virgil, Horace, Cicero, Seneca, and philosophers, lawyers, physicians, historians, yea, the voluminous statutes of law-givers, and canons of the church; but the holy Scriptures you cannot understand. But it is not reproaching Christ that is the way to have him justify your cause or you. Though ambiguity of words make Scripture, as all other writings, so far difficult as to need some skill in those words to him that will understand them; and though a carnal, blinded mind cannot (savingly in love and lively sense) receive the spiritual things of God; yet men shall shortly be convinced, that the Light of the world was not invisible, though the darkness comprehend it not, and that the wisdom of God hath spoken intelligibly, and in all necessary things you may certainly know which part Christ taketh.

But alas, Christ is unseen, and therefore little regarded by multitudes who customarily honour his name. As among the Turks, we blame not him that rather asketh what the emperor or bashaw commandeth, than what Mahomet commandeth; so these that honour Christ but as the Turks honour Mahomet, do far more regard which side their landlord takes, or which side such a lord, or bishop, or prince is for, than which part Christ is for. O sirs! you would all fain have Christ to be your advocate at last: as ever you would have him be for you then, be now for that which he is for, and hath foretold you he will justify.

Oh that you were all but truly willing to know what it is that Christ is for (whether for a holy, or a worldly or fleshly mind and life); and that you were but resolved to be for that which Christ is for, as far as by diligent search you can know it! I should hope then that he would not leave you to damnable mistake, but help you to understand his will for your salvation.

Use. And here you may see, that it is false doctrine which some men confidently preach, that there is no such thing as Christ justifying his people against false accusations; as when we tell them, that against the accusation of being finally impenitent, unbelievers, unconverted, unholy, they must be justified by their own personal repentance, faith, conversion, and holiness, or not at all; they have no shift against the plain truth, but to tell us, that we have need of no such justification; the devil will have something else to do than falsely to accuse us. But on the contrary,

1. Is not the devil the accuser of the brethren? And is he not the father of lies? Is not his name Diabolus, a false accuser?

2. Doth he not set the wicked on his work in this life falsely to accuse the faithful, and their faith and duty, that it may reflect on God himself? Yea, through the remnant of ignorance and sin Christ's servants too oft falsely accuse one another, as unsound, erroneous, heretical, &c. Yea, darkness causeth good men's consciences too often falsely to accuse themselves. And is it not Christ's office to be the Advocate of the just? and in justifying them to justify himself, and his cause and truth? Rom. iii. 4, 26. And is it not much of the work of that glorious day, to bring all hidden things to light, and to justify his cause and servants against all the false accusations that ever were brought against them, and thus to shame all falsehood and unrighteousness, and to judge the world in truth?

3. Was it not a false accusation that Satan brought against Job; and did not God solemnly justify him against it? Is not Satan's kingdom upheld in the world, by making men in all nations believe that believers are deceived, false believers, and that Christ's servants are wicked hypocrites, the plagues and troubles of the earth? And is there not a day to justify them against all this?

4. If we are not justified against false accusation, we are justified against none at all; for Christ will not justify us against the truth. It is justification by plea and sentence that we are now speaking of: justification sometimes signifieth making us just, and sometimes judging and maintaining us to be just. The first doth make an unrighteous and ungodly man just by converting him, and giving him repentance toward God, and faith towards our Lord Jesus Christ; and pardoning his sins, and giving him right to the heavenly inheritance: this is our first constitutive justification. But when God hath thus made us just by the merits of Christ's righteousness,

1. He virtually by the law of grace doth pronounce us just, and this against the curse of the condemning law of innocency.

2. And in judgment Christ as our Advocate will maintain us just.

3. And Christ our Judge will judge us just, against all that can be brought against us. But how far just? Not such as never sinned; nor such as by imputation of his righteousness are by God accounted never to have sinned, nor such as never deserved death: but such as are not to be condemned to pain of sense or loss, but have right to the free gift of life eternal, because Christ for them satisfied justice, and fulfilled all righteousness, and merited all this for them, even forgiveness, grace, and glory, and they being penitent believers have part in him, and sincerely obeyed him to the death.

And if it were never so true, that no actual false accusation would be urged against believers, yet is it true that we shall be justified against even a virtual and possible accusation: and where there is not so much as this, there needeth no justification by plea, by witness, or by sentence.

And if we are accused to have been sinners, it is not to be denied: if it be said that our sin deserved death, it must be granted; but if it be said,

1. That we were finally impenitent unbelievers.
2. Or have no part in Christ.
3. Or had no pardon of sin.
4. Or had no right to life eternal.
5. And therefore are to be condemned; all this being false, Christ will justify us against it, and against all other false accusation of men or devils.

Doct. Last. Christ doth not only plead his own righteousness for Mary's justification, but justify her choice of the better part, and decree that it shall not be taken from her.

I. Indeed all the good that we have is his own as the Giver, though some be also ours as the actors and possessors: and Christ will justify all that is of himself. Nothing but good cometh from infinite good, or him that came to destroy the works of the devil. They that accuse our grace or duty, accuse Christ, his Spirit, and his law. And will he not justify himself? (But of this before.)

II. He that praiseth his servants' holiness and duty, and will praise them in judgment, doth so far justify them. "Well done, good and faithful servant!" Matt. xxv. Yea, he that calleth eternal glory their reward, and the crown of righteousness given by God the righteous Judge, to such as have fought a good fight, and finished their course, and love the appearing of Christ; and he that is the Author of eternal salvation to all them that obey him; and will judge all men according to their works, and pronounceth them blessed that do his commandments, that they may have right to the tree of life, (2 Tim. iv. 8, 9; Heb. v. 9; Rev. xxii. 14, &c.) doth surely so far justify this personal obedience and righteousness of theirs.

But he justifieth only against false accusations, and not against the charge of culpable imperfection. And do they therefore talk wisely that say, it is no righteousness, and no justification, because it is imperfect? Doth any wise man pretend to personal perfect righteousness? And doth not God many hundred times in Scripture call that righteousness and equivalent which is imperfect? And will he justify or save any that hath no such righteousness? Christ was perfectly righteous for us to merit the pardon and salvation of believers, and the acceptance of their imperfect righteousness; and not to bring any to heaven that hath no inherent personal righteousness.

There are some that seem by their arguing to think that so much honour as we give to our holiness and duty, so much we take from Christ, and to praise his saints is to dishonour him. (And yet these men love and look for praise.) But wise men will not believe that the greatness of the gift is a dishonour to the giver, or the excellency of the house or work a dishonour to the builder or workman, or the recovered health of the patient a dishonour to the physician; else what a dishonour will our salvation be to Christ, when we are perfectly holy, without spot or wrinkle, and have no sin! It will be then by the communication of his holiness, as motion, light, and heat is from the sun; and so it is now, though we are imperfect: God accepteth, praiseth, and *in tantum* proportionably justifieth our imperfect righteousness for the sake and merits of his that was perfect.

I never met with any of this mind, but if one accuse them of less than infidelity, impenitence, impiety, and hypocrisy, they will seek to justify themselves. And why will they justify themselves in that which God will not justify the generation of the just, when malignants call them all deluded hypocrites? And I know no sober man but expecteth that every judge should justify the wrongfully accused and their cause.

Object. To justify a good cause is not to justify the person.

Answ. Untrue. It is not to justify him in all respects, but it is to justify him as to that cause.

Object. This is but before men.

Answ. God doth more hate the condemning of the just than any man doth.

Object. This is but as to a particular cause, and not a universal justification.

Answ. And the justifying of a believer and penitent obedient saint by his faith, and repentance, and obedience, is but the justifying him in that particular cause, which is the medium of his part in Christ; the merit of whose righteousness and sacrifice procureth the pardon of all his sins, and his right to the free gift of life eternally, and so far justifieth him against the guilt of his sin, and the condemnation of the law.

He that is not first made a penitent believer, and justified against chargeable infidelity, impenitence, and hypocrisy, shall never be justified by Christ's merits and sentence against the curse and penalty of the law.

II. But Christ doth not only justify Mary and her choice, but decree that it shall not be taken from her. For,

1. He hath by his covenant given the best and greatest things, and that for ever, to every one that will but thankfully accept and choose them.

2. And what he offereth and promiseth he decreeth.

3. And what he decreeth and promiseth he performeth.

For who is it that should take it from her, or from any believer? Or "who shall separate us from the love of God?"

1. Not the malice of Satan; else no believer should be saved. If the devil could deprive us of the gospel, or of grace, it should be surely done; if he could have kept the world from being redeemed by Christ, it had never been redeemed; if he could keep men unconvinced, unconverted, and unpardoned, he would surely do it.

2. Not any of his malignant instruments; for God will not give them power to make a godly man ungodly, and the devil hath no such power to give them.

3. Not the envy of erroneous zealots, or uncharitable hypocrites. The prodigal shall not be turned out of doors because his elder brother envieth his entertainment. The envy of the Jews shall not hinder the blessing of the gentiles. Resolvedly choose the best, and you shall have it.

Use 1. Oh that all men would take this sure and necessary direction of Christ for the choice of their comforts, hopes, and happiness. All men had rather be happy for ever, than for a little while; and what else but holiness and heaven, Christ, grace, and glory, will be such a durable felicity? Will you choose the favour of great men, and hopes of preferment and worldly honours; and can you say that this shall not be taken from you? Will you choose lands and money, and the prospering of your endeavours in growing rich; and can you say that these shall not be taken from you? Will you choose mirth and sport, and fleshly lust, and the pleasing of your appetites and fancies; and can you say that these shall not be taken from you? Must not life itself be shortly taken from you, and therefore all the pleasures of this life? If these things be your choice, Christ hath already foretold you what you may expect; "Thou fool, this night shall thy soul be required of thee; and then whose shall all these things be which thou hast provided? So is he that layeth up treasure for himself, and is not rich towards God," Luke xii. 19, 20. And Luke xvi. 25, "Son, remember that thou in thy lifetime receivedst thy good things, and Lazarus evil things, but now he is comforted, and thou art tormented." "Wherefore then do you spend money for that which is not bread, and your labour for that which satisfieth not? Hearken diligently to Christ, and eat that which is good, and let your soul delight itself in fatness. Incline your ear, and come unto him; hear, and your soul shall live; and he will make an everlasting covenant of sure mercies with you," Isa. lv. 2, 3. "Labour not for the food which perisheth, but for that which endureth to everlasting life," which Christ will give you, John vi. 27. "Lay not up for yourselves treasures on earth, where moth and rust doth corrupt, and where thieves break through and steal; but lay up for yourselves treasure in heaven, where neither moth nor rust do corrupt, nor thieves break through and steal," Matt. vi. 19, 20. "The time is short, therefore weep and rejoice, buy and possess, and use the world, as though you did it not; for the fashion of this world passeth away," 1 Cor. vii. 29—31. O be not as the wicked, who have their portion in this life, in the treasure of their bellies; "for their hopes soon perish, as the rush that groweth but in the mire, and as the spider's web, and as the giving up of the ghost," Psal. xvii. 14. Flesh will fail you, and the world will fail you; but God will be a never-failing portion to all that do but sincerely choose him, Psal. lxxiii. 25, 26. If you drink here you shall thirst again, and if you eat here, you shall hunger again; but if Christ and his Spirit be your meat and drink, "you shall hunger and thirst no more for ever." "Blessed are they that hunger and thirst after righteousness, for they shall be satisfied." O do not profanely sell such a birthright for a morsel; you shall have no better than you choose: show not yourselves unworthy of eternal life, by preferring known vanity before it. If you lost heaven because you could not have it, and would have a Christ and holiness, but could not, your case would not be all so bad, as to be the wilful refusers of your own salvation, and lose it because you would not have it. Do not say, We would be saved, if you would not be saved from your sin, and have that holiness and communion with God which is your salvation; and do not say, We would have God, and Christ, and holiness, if the pleasures of sin seem better to you, and you choose them first! You may as well say plainly, We will have no God no Christ, no heaven, as say, We had rather have the pleasures of sin; and you may as well say so, as choose so, and do so. There are some deceived libertines that think that every good desire is the mark of a justified soul, especially if it be accompanied with a willingness that Christ's righteousness should justify them, and a belief that it will do so, though they love sinful pleasure, profit, and honour, better than God, and holiness, and heaven; and had rather have the felicity of an epicure, than of a saint.

But Christ himself hath judged contrarily. He saith, he cannot be his disciple that loveth any thing more than him, Matt. x.; Luke xiv. 23, 26. And he that will have this pearl of greatest price, must think nothing too dear, but sell all that he hath to buy it, Matt. xiii. 46. To be "lovers of pleasure more than lovers of God," is the brand of the worst times and persons, 2 Tim. iii. 4. Let any man that can show us one promise of God for the saving of any that seek not first God's kingdom and its righteousness, Matt. vi. 33; and labour not chiefly for the food that perisheth not; and loveth not God above the world, and holiness more than the pleasures of sin.

If this be not so, where can you fix the difference between the justified and them that perish? Would God make such a difference in the world to come, if there were none here? Doth Christ and his Spirit do no more noble a work in sanctifying souls than so? If one may be justified that loveth one sinful pleasure better than God, and grace, and glory, why not he that loveth another, and another, and all? if fornication, why not gluttony? if gluttony, why not drunkenness? if drunkenness, why not covetousness, and ambition, and all evil? But Paul saith, "Let no man deceive you with vain words, for because of these things cometh the wrath of God on the children of disobedience," Eph. v. 6. And "without holiness no man shall see the Lord," Heb. xii. 14. "Not every one that saith, Lord, Lord, shall enter into heaven;" no, not those believers that prophesied, and did wonders, and cast out devils in Christ's name, but only they that do the will of God. To the rest he will say, "Depart from me, ye workers of iniquity, I know you not."

How oft is it said that all shall be judged according to their works! And Christ so describeth his own judgment, Matt. xxv. Can any man believe James ii.; 1 John iii. iv.; Rom. viii. 1—14; Rom. ii. and a multitude of such texts, and yet believe that a bare belief that Christ's righteousness is imputed to us, will prove any one justified who loveth his sin better than God, grace, and glory; and consequently that Christ's members differ but imputatively from the children of the devil? For wherein is a wicked man worse than the godly, but in this? "He that loveth the world, (more than God,) the love of the Father is not in him." Why may not life or pleasure separate us from the love of God if we love them better? Rom. viii. 38, 39. Nay, he loveth not God at all in a proper sense, who loveth him not as God; and he loveth him not at all as God, who loveth him not as better than the pleasure of sin, but only as a lesser good.

Object. To love God above all sinful pleasure is the fruit and ripeness of grace, but the seed doth not reach so high.

Answ. It is true, if you call preparatory grace that seed; but such are in no justified state; but it is not true if you mean by the seed any thing proper to a justified man, as all the texts forecited show.

Object. What can the strongest christian do more than love God above all?

Answ. Among those that love God above all, and holiness more than sin, there may be a hundred different degrees; one may love him so much as to long after him, and delight in him, and contemn all vanities, and overcome temptations, much more easily and effectually than others; and another may do these more faintly, hardly, and with less delight.

Object. Did David, Peter, and the disciples that all forsook Christ and fled, love him better than life at such a time?

Answ. 1. We must distinguish between the rational will, or love, and sensitive passion. 2. Between the habit and the act. 3. Between the ordinary course of action, and a particular extraordinary action.

The weakest true justified christian loveth God above the creature, and perfect holiness above sinful pleasure;

1. As to the fixed inclination and habit of the soul, (which is the divine nature).

2. And in the ordinary act or exercise of his rational love, and deliberate choice, and the seeking endeavour of his life.

3. But not always with the most passionate sensitive love.

4. And passion (of fear or creature love) may in an extraordinary act both weaken the activity of rational, spiritual love, and bear down the executive power into outward contrary sinful acts. But the predominancy of the holy nature will show itself, in raising the soul from such a fall, and causing it the more to hate and fear the sin. There is difference between a swoon and death, and between an infant and an image: and so there was between the falls of David, Lot, Peter, and a wicked man, that had rather keep his sin than leave it, and loveth such pleasure more than God.

Use 2. Be thankful then, christians, for that grace of Christ which caused you to make the wisest choice; even of that which is the real durable felicity, and shall never be taken from you.

Had you chosen houses, they might have been burnt; had you chosen wealth or worldly honours, they might all have been taken from you; yea, all would certainly have left you in distress. Men might have taken away your estates, your liberties, your lives, but not your God, your Christ, your heaven. They may take away your Bibles, and other books, but they cannot take away your grace. They may shut you out of the synagogues, but not out of the love of God. They may imprison you, banish you, cut out your tongues, that you can neither preach nor speak, but still your souls may have communion with God. A Tertullus may call us pestilent fellows and seditious; schismatics may call us the schismatics, and heretics may call us the heretics, and hypocrites may call us hypocrites; but none of them can make us what they call us. They may with some (by God's permission) take away the reputation of your innocency, but not your innocency itself. When a man's food is but on his table, it may be taken from him; if it be but in his stomach, he may cast it up; but it is safer when it is digested and turned into his substance. So may your teachers, and Bibles, and churches, be taken from you, but not the law and gospel which is written in your hearts, and become a spiritual nature in you. What triumphant challenges doth St. Paul make? "Who shall be against us? who shall condemn us? what shall separate us from the love of God?" Rom. viii. 37, 38, &c. The power of men and devils cannot do it. Death itself, the last enemy, shall not do it. He will dissolve this frame, and lay our flesh in dust and darkness, and take away from us all the pleasure and possession of this world, but none of our chief good. Tyrants may deprive us of such things as they choose themselves, but not of that which we have chosen! If the devil had said truly, (Matt. iv.; Luke iii. 6, 7,) "All this power will I give thee, and the glory of them, for that is delivered to me, and to whom I will I give it;" he might have said also, From whom I will I take it away. But sure he is no giver of grace or glory, and therefore cannot forcibly take them from us. Nay, by taking life and all from us, men shall but hasten our perfect fruition of what we choose. Malice may snarl, and rail, and slander, but cannot abate the love of the Father, the grace of the Son, the communion of the Spirit, or deprive us of expected glory.

Let not then worldly fury think that it hath undone us by taking away worldly things. They were none of our choice, nor our trust, nor treasure. If we are true believers, our treasure, heart, and conversation are in heaven: let thieves get in and steal it thence if they can. Papal usurpers may pretend Peter's keys to shut out all that obey not their domination; but while God is our choice, and we shut not out ourselves from heaven, they talk more to their own hurt than ours, and can never take our chosen treasure from us.

Use 3. But if none can take it from us, let us not cast it away ourselves. All that men and devils can do against us is but by allurements, or fear, or other temptations, to deceive us into self-destruction, and to cast away that ourselves which none can take from us. Great disputes we have about free-will and perseverance; whether it be possible to fall away. But it is past dispute with men that believe the word of God, that we have such freedom, as that Christ, and grace, and glory, are freely offered to our accepting choice; and that he that truly chooseth them shall have them; and that all that choose them not before that pleasure of sin which is set in competition against them, shall never have them; and that it is just so far possible or impossible to fall from grace, as it is possible or impossible for the will of one that hath grace to change: so far as your serious choice continueth, you persevere; and so far as you change it, you lose your grace. While you plead for the impossibility of the ill changing of your own wills, confute not yourselves by your actual change; but when you feel them again pleased with the forbidden things of the flesh and world, and your appetite to holy pleasure groweth dull and cold, methinks you should perceive that in yourselves there is no impossibility of a change: if there be any, it is out of you, in God; and no doubt but a change of his decree and will is impossible. All the doubt is, whether he have decreed that no gracious will shall change. It is certain that being so very mutable in ourselves, that we could not persevere were we left to ourselves. We are all under many and great obligations to "keep ourselves in the love of God," Jude 21, and to "continue in the love of Christ," John xv. 9. And we have need of commands to "abide in Christ, and he in us," John xv. 4; and need of threatenings of destruction if we fall away. "If a man abide not in me, he is cast forth as a branch, and is withered, and men gather them, and cast them into the fire, and they are burned," John xv. 6. "Let him that thinketh he standeth, take heed lest he fall," 1 Cor. x. 12. "Let us fear lest a promise being left of entering into his rest, any of you should seem to come short of it," Heb. iv. 1. And all God's threatenings are the objects of our belief and fear. "If we sin wilfully after the knowledge of the truth, there remaineth no more sacrifice for sins, but a certain fearful expectation of judgment and fiery indignation, which devoureth the adversaries. Of how much sorer punishment suppose ye shall he be thought worthy, who hath trodden under-foot the Son of God, and hath counted the blood of the covenant wherewith he was sanctified an unholy thing, and done despite to the Spirit of grace.——If any draw back, my soul shall have no pleasure in him," Heb. x. 26, 27, 29, 38. Which is the same with Ezek. xxxiii. 18, "When the righteous turneth from his righteousness he shall die."

Yea, God seeth it meet to give us the comforts of the faithful still conditionally: Rev. ii. iii. "To him that overcometh," &c. "He that endureth to the end shall be saved." Col. i. 21—23, "If ye continue in the faith, and be not moved away from the hope of the gospel."

All this tells us, that notwithstanding God's unchangeable decree, the care and diligent labour to persevere is our duty, and that falling away must be our fear, and that there is no such impossibility as excludeth this care and fear: and that so far as it is impossible to fall away, so far it is impossible not to fear falling away, with a preserving, watchful fear: and how far a known impossibility is the object of due fear I leave to further consideration.

God hath put us into the hands of Christ, in whose care and trust is our chief security; but he hath also trusted us, or put our perseverance and salvation more in our own hands, than in any others; and so far that if we do not undo ourselves by wilful and final neglect, or refusal of offered grace and mercy, we are safe. Choose Christ as Christ, and God as God; choose grace and glory before all the vanities of the world, and before all the pleasures of sin for a season, and stand to this choice unto the end, expressing it in faithful victorious endeavours, and then neither men nor devils, life or death, shall take your chosen treasure from you.

Object. I can easily keep up a resolved choice of God, and holiness, and heaven, but I cannot so constantly keep up the rejection of fleshly pleasures, and profit, and honour, which would be for the time preferred.

Answ. The worst man would have God and heaven so far as to give him the desires of his flesh, and keep him from all pain and misery; but is it not a plain contradiction to say in proper speech, I would have God as God, that is, as best, but I would have pleasant vanity as better? I can easily love my wife as a wife, but I cannot forbear loving harlots better. I can resolve for temperance, but I cannot resolve against gluttony and drunkenness. I am resolved for truth, but not against lying? Just such is that, to resolve for God and holiness, but not against the pleasures of sin, which alienate the heart from God.

Object. But how doth a man choose God and holiness in the hour of sin, when he is choosing forbidden pleasure?

Answ. The act of sin is not a choosing God and holiness, but somewhat that is contrary; but every act of the will which is against God and holiness is not a rejecting of them, or a retracting of our choice, nor inconsistent with it; but perhaps only an interruption of the exercise, and an abatement of the degree. Play-fellows may draw a child to disobey a father for love of play and them, when yet he doth not forsake his father, nor love them better; but only forgets him, or abateth desire through the diversion of the sport.

Quest. What is it that is our duty in order to the unchangeableness of our own wills and choice?

Answ. 1. Trust not yourselves too far: the will goeth not against the mind's apprehensions; and a man's mind is a very dark, weak, mutable thing: what a temptation, or a subtle wrangler or argument, or a new thought, may do upon us, we do not well know. Presumption seldom escapeth danger. A wise man feareth, and departeth from evil: confidence in your own understanding, goodness, and stability, is the prognostic of backsliding.

2. Away from the temptations which do most strongly allure the flesh: to be over-pleased with things temporal and sensible, turneth the heart from things spiritual and eternal. To desire a more pleasing condition to the flesh, is to desire stronger temptations, and greater danger to the soul.

3. Think much and seriously on the great and certain things which first converted and resolved your wills: they are the same, and as good now as they were then, and you should know them better. A man that loveth and chooseth rationally, knoweth why he doth it: and the fixing and renewing of your knowledge and belief, is it that must fix your love and choice. The greatest things forgotten do not affect us.

4. Flatter not yourselves with the hope of living long on earth, and look not at death and the following life as a great way off. The power of tempting vanities lieth in men's hopes of long enjoying them: to a man under the sentence of present death they have little power. And the best things that seem far off, do not much and powerfully affect us. Live therefore as dying men, and you will have the mind and choice of dying men.

5. See that your meditations and belief be practical, and brought close to the heart: and take not bare thinking of God and heaven as enough, but know that holy thoughts fall short of their use and end, if they come not to the heart and life. It is not the speculative, disputing christian that hath the fixed will and choice, unless he be also a hearty practising, experienced christian. He that hath a heavenly heart and conversation, and hath felt the power and sweetness of things spiritual, will hold them fast, when bare hearsay and opinion will let them go.

6. Depend in the constant exercise of faith and prayer upon the love of the Father, the grace of the Son, and the communion of the Holy Spirit, and seek to please God as your greatest pleasure, and so live by the faith of the Son of God, that you may say, "it is Christ that liveth in you," Gal. ii. 19, 20. And then none can take you out of his hands, nor separate you from the love of God, (Rom. viii. 38, 39,) nor take your chosen portion from you.

In a word, that your choice may be unchangeable, you must firmly trust to the unchangeable promise of the unchangeable God, for the unchangeable kingdom, as purchased by Christ, and our title sealed by his Spirit. The world and the flesh must be crucified, dead, and buried to you by the virtue of his cross believed, and you must be risen with him to a heavenly mind, and hope, and conversation: every weight must be laid by, and the sin which doth so easily beset us, Heb. xii. 1; and we must not look back to the forsaken world behind us, but press forward for the prize unto the mark, Phil. iii.; looking still to Jesus, the author and finisher of our faith, who for the joy that was set before him, endured the cross, and despised the shame, and is set down at the right hand of the throne of God. We must consider him that endured such contradiction of sinners, lest we be weary and faint. We must count nothing dear to us that we may finish our course with joy; and must know by faith that "our labour is not in vain in the Lord," if we would be "stedfast and unmovable, always abounding in the work of the Lord," 1 Cor. xv. 58. We must serve God acceptably, with reverence and godly fear, as for a kingdom which cannot be moved; and all this in dependence on the grace of Christ, Heb. xii. 28. Considerate men know by sense and experience that this world is vanity and vexation: if we know also by a living constant faith, that a better world of holy joy is the near and certain portion of the faithful, it will fix the will in a resolved choice, and we shall not be like profane Esau, that sold his birthright for one morsel; and the living eternal God will be eternally our Life and Joy, to whom all the blessed with Christ shall give glory and praise for ever. Amen.

TRUE CHRISTIANITY;

OR,

CHRIST'S ABSOLUTE DOMINION,

AND

MAN'S NECESSARY SELF-RESIGNATION AND SUBJECTION.

IN TWO ASSIZE SERMONS,

PREACHED BEFORE THE HONOURABLE JUDGE OF ASSIZE, AT WORCESTER, AUGUST 2, 1654.

"For to this end Christ both died, and rose, and revived, that he might be Lord both of the dead and living."—Rom. xiv. 9.

TO THE RIGHT HONOURABLE SERJEANT GLYN,

NOW JUDGE OF ASSIZE IN THIS CIRCUIT.

My Lord,

Could my excuse have satisfied you, this sermon had been confined to the auditory it was prepared for. I cannot expect that it should find that candour and favour with every reader, as it did with the hearers. When it must speak to all, the guilty will hear, and then it will gall. Innocency is patient in hearing a reproof, and charitable in the interpretation, but guilt will smart and quarrel, and usually make a fault in him that findeth one in them. Yet I confess this is but a poor justification of his silence that hath a call to speak. Both my calling and this sermon would condemn me, if, on such grounds, I should draw back; but my backwardness was caused by the reason which I then tendered your Lordship as my excuse, viz. because here is nothing but what is common, and that it is in as common and homely a dress. And I hope we need not fear that our labours are dead, unless the press shall give them life. We bring not sermons to church, as we do a corpse for a burial. If there be life in them, and life in the hearers, the connaturality will cause such an amicable closure, that through the reception, retention, and operation of the soul, they will be the immortal seed of a life everlasting. But yet seeing the press hath a louder voice than mine, and the matter in hand is of such exceeding necessity, I shall not refuse, upon such an invitation, to be a remembrancer to the world of a doctrine and duty of such high concernment, though they have heard it never so oft before. Seeing, therefore, I must present that now to your eyes, which I lately presented to your ears, I shall take the boldness to add one word of application in this epistle, which I thought not seasonable to mention in the first delivery; and that shall be to your Lordship, and all others in your present case, that are elected members of this expected parliament. Be sure to remember the interest of your Sovereign, the great Lord-protector of heaven and earth. And as ever you will make him a comfortable account of your power, abilities, and opportunities of serving him, see that you prefer his interest before your own, or any man's on earth. If you go not thither as sent by Him, with a firm resolution to serve him first, you were better sit at home. Forget not that he hath laid claim to you, and to all that you have, and all that you can do. I am bold with all possible earnestness to entreat you, yea, as Christ's minister to require you, in his name, to study and remember his business and interest, and see that it have the chief place in all your consultations. Watch against the encroachments of your own carnal interests, consult not with flesh and blood, nor give it the hearing when it shall offer you its advice. How subtilly will it insinuate! How importunately will it urge you! How certainly will it mar all, if you do not constantly and resolvedly watch! Oh how hard, but how happy is it to conquer this carnal self! Remember still that you are not your own; that you have an unseen Master that must be pleased, whoever be displeased, and an unseen kingdom to be obtained, and an invisible soul that must be saved, though all the world be lost. Fix your eyes still on him that made and redeemed you, and upon the ultimate end of your christian race, and do nothing wilfully unworthy snch a Master and such an end. Often renew your self-resignation, and devote yourself to him; sit close at his work, and be sure that it be his, both in the matter, and in your intent. If conscience should at any time ask, Whose work are you now doing? or a man should pluck you by the sleeve, and say, Sir, whose cause are you now pleading? see that you have the answer of a christian at hand; delay not God's work till you have done your own, or any one's else. You will best secure the commonwealth, and your own interest, by looking first to his. By neglecting this, and being carnally wise, we have wheeled about so long in the wilderness, and lost those advantages against the powers of darkness, which we know not whether we shall ever recover again. It is the great astonishment of sober men, and not the least reproach that ever was cast on our holy profession, to think with what a zeal for the work of Christ men seemed to be animated in the beginning of our disagreements, and how deeply they did engage themselves to him in solemn vows, protestations, and covenants, and what advantages carnal self hath since got, and turned the stream another way! So that the same men have since been the instruments of our calamity, in breaking in pieces and dishonouring the churches of Christ, yea, and gone so near to the taking down, as much as in them lay, the whole ministry that stand approved in the land. O do not, by trifling, give advantage to the tempter to destroy your work and you together! Take warning by the sad experiences of what is past; bestir you speedily and vigorously for Christ, as knowing your opposition, and the shortness of your time. Blessed is that servant whom his Lord, when he cometh, shall find so doing. If you ask me wherein this interest of Christ doth consist, I shall tell you, but in a few unquestionable particulars. 1. In the main, that truth, godliness, and honesty be countenanced and encouraged, and their contraries by all fit means suppressed. 2. In order to this, that unworthy men be removed from magistracy and ministry, and the places supplied with the fittest that can be had. 3. That a competent maintenance may be procured where it is wanting, especially for cities and great towns, where more teachers are so necessary in some proportion to the number of souls, and on which the country doth so much depend. Shall an age of such high pretences to reformation and zeal for the churches, alienate so much, and then leave them destitute, and say it cannot be had? 4. That right means be used, with speed and diligence, for the healing of our divisions and the uniting of all the true churches of Christ at last, in these nations; and oh that your endeavours might be extended much further! To which end I shall mention but these two means of most evident necessity. 1. That there be one Scripture creed, or confession of faith, agreed on by a general assembly of able ministers, duly and freely chosen hereunto, which shall contain nothing but matter of evident necessity and verity. This will serve, 1. For a test to the churches to discern the sound professors from the unsound, (as to their doctrine,) and to know them with whom they may close as brethren, and whom they must reject. 2. For a test to the magistrate of the orthodox to be encouraged, and of the intolerably heterodox, which it seems is intended in the 37th article of the late formed government, where all that will have liberty must profess faith in God by Jesus Christ, which, in a christian sense, must comprehend every true fundamental or article of our faith: and, no doubt, it is not the bare speaking of those words in an unchristian sense that is intended; as if a ranter should say, that himself is God and his mate is Jesus Christ.

2. That there be a public establishment of the necessary liberty of the churches, to meet by their officers and delegates on all just occasions, in assemblies smaller or greater, (even national, when it is necessary,) seeing, without such associations and communion in assemblies, the unity and concord of the churches is not like to be maintained. I exclude not the magistrates' interest, or oversight, to see that they do not transgress their bounds. As you love Christ, and his church, and gospel, and men's souls, neglect not these unquestionable points of his interest, and make them your first and chiefest business, and let none be preferred before him until you know them to be of more authority over you, and better friends to you, than Christ is. Should there be any among you that cherish a secret root of infidelity, after such pretences to the purest christianity, and are zealous of Christ lest he should over-top them, and do set up an interest inconsistent with his sovereignty, and thereupon grow jealous of the liberties and power of his ministers, and of the unity and strength of his church, and think it their best policy to keep under his ministers, by hindering them from the exercise of their office, and to foment divisions, and hinder our union, that they may have parties ready to serve their ends; I would not be in the case of such men, when God ariseth to judge them, for all the crowns and kingdoms on earth! If they stumble on this stone, it will break them in pieces, but if it fall upon them, it will grind them to powder. They may seem to prevail against him awhile, when their supposed success is but a prosperous self-destroying; but mark the end, when his wrath is kindled, yea, but a little; and when these, his enemies that would not he should reign over them, are brought forth and destroyed before him, then they will be convinced of the folly of their rebellion. In the mean time, let wisdom be justified of her children.

My Lord, I had not troubled you with so many words, had I not judged it probable that many more whom they concern may peruse them.

I remain,

Your Lordship's servant in the work of Christ,

RICHARD BAXTER.

August 5, 1654.

A SERMON

OF THE

ABSOLUTE DOMINION OF GOD-REDEEMER; AND THE NECESSITY OF BEING DEVOTED AND LIVING TO HIM.

I CORINTHIANS VI. 19, 20.

AND YE ARE NOT YOUR OWN, FOR YE ARE BOUGHT WITH A PRICE; THEREFORE GLORIFY GOD IN YOUR BODY, AND IN YOUR SPIRIT, WHICH ARE GOD'S.

FUNDAMENTALS in religion are the life of the superstructure. Like the vitals and naturals in the body, which are first necessary for themselves and you also, for the quickening and nourishing of the rest; there being no life or growth of the inferior parts, but what they do receive from the powers of these: it is but a dead discourse which is not animated by these greater truths, whatever the bulk of its materials may consist of. The frequent repetition, therefore, of these is as excusable as frequent preaching: and they that nauseate it as loathsome battology, do love novelty better than verity, and playing with words to please the fancy, rather than closing with Christ to save the soul. And as it is the chief part of the cure, in most external maladies, to corroborate the vital and natural powers, which then will do the work themselves, so is it the most effectual course for the cure of particular miscarriages in men's lives, to further the main work of grace upon their hearts. Could we make men better christians, it would do much to make them better magistrates, counsellors, jurors, witnesses, subjects, neighbours, &c. And this must be done by the deeper impress of those vital truths and the good in them exhibited, which are adequate objects of our vital graces. Could we help you to wind up the spring of faith, and so move the first wheel of christian love, we should find it the readiest and surest means to move the inferior wheels of duty. The flaws and irregular motions without, do show that something is amiss within, which, if we could rectify, we might the easier mend the rest. I shall suppose, therefore, that I need no more apology for choosing such a subject at such a season as this, than for bringing bread to a feast. And if I medicate the brain and heart, for the curing of senseless paralytic members, or the inordinate convulsive motions of any hearers, I have the warrant of the apostle's example in my text. Among other great enormities in the church of Corinth, he had these three to reprehend and heal: first, their sidings and divisions, occasioned by some factious, self-seeking teachers. Secondly, their personal contentions by law-suits, and that before unbelieving judges. Thirdly, the foul sin of fornication, which some among them had fallen into. The great cure which he useth to all these, and more especially to the last, is the urging of these great foundation truths, whereof one is in the words before my text, viz. the right of the Holy Ghost; the other in the words of my text, which contains, first, a denial of any right of propriety in themselves. Secondly, an asserting of Christ's propriety in them. Thirdly, the proof of this from his purchase, which is his title. Fourthly, their duty concluded from the former premises, which is to glorify God, and that with the whole man; with the spirit, because God is a Spirit, and loathes hypocrisy; with the body, which is particularly mentioned, because it seems they were encouraged to fornication by such conceits, that it was but an act of the flesh, and not of the mind, and therefore, as they thought, the smaller sin. The apostle's words, from last to first, according to the order of intention, do express, first, man's duty to glorify God with soul and body, and not to serve our lusts. Secondly, the great fundamental obligation to this duty, God's dominion or propriety. Thirdly, the foundation of that dominion, Christ's purchase. According to the order of execution, from first to last, these three great fundamentals of our religion lie thus: first, Christ's purchase. Secondly, God's propriety thence arising. Thirdly, man's duty — wholly to glorify God, arising from both. The argument lies thus: They that are not their own, but wholly God's, should wholly glorify God, and not serve their lusts: but you are not your own, but wholly God's; therefore you should wholly glorify God, and not serve your lusts. The major is clear by the common light of nature. Every one should have the use of their own. The minor is proved thus: They that are bought with a price, are not their own, but his that bought them: but you are bought with a price; therefore, &c. For the meaning of the terms briefly; ἑαυτῶν, *vestri*, as the Vulgar; *vestri juris*, as Beza, and others; is most fitly expressed by our English, "your own;" "ye are bought:" a *synecdoche generis*, saith Piscator, for "ye are redeemed with a price." There is no buying without a price." This, therefore, is an emphatical *pleonasmus*, as Beza, Piscator, and others; as to see with the eyes, to hear with the ears. Or else, "a price," is put for "a great price," as Calvin, Peter Martyr, and Piscator, rather think: and therefore the Vulgate adds the epithet *magno*, and the Arabic *pretioso*, as Beza notes, as agreeing to that of 1 Pet. i. 18. I see not but we may suppose the apostle to respect both the purchase and the greatness of the price, as Grotius and some others do. "Glorify God," that is, by using your bodies and souls wholly for him, and abstaining from those lusts which do dishonour him. The Vulgate adds *et portate*, *q. d.* bear God about in your hearts, and let his Spirit dwell with you instead of lust. But this addition is contrary to all our Greek copies. Grotius thinks that some copies had ἀρατὸν θεὸν, and thence some unskilful scribe did put ἄρα τε: however, it seems that reading was very ancient, when not only Austin, but Cyprian and Tertullian followed it, as Beza noteth. The last words, "and in your spirit, which are God's," are out of all the old Latin translations, and therefore it is like out of the Greek, which they used: but they are in all the present Greek copies, except our manuscript, as also in the Syriac and Arabic version.

The rest of the explication shall follow the doctrines, which are these.

Doct. 2. Because we are so bought we are not our own, but his that bought us.

Doct. 3. Because we are not our own, but wholly God's, therefore we must not serve our lusts, but glorify him in the body and spirit. In these three conclusions is the substance of the text; which I shall first explain, and then make application of them in that order as the apostle here doth.

The points that need explication are these.

First, In what sense we are said to be bought with a price. Who bought us? And of whom? And from what? And with what price?

Secondly, How we are God's own upon the title of this purchase.

Thirdly, How we are not our own.

Fourthly, What it is to glorify God in body and in spirit on this account.

Fifthly, Who they be that, on this ground, are or may be urged to this duty.

1. For the first of these, whether buying here be taken properly or metaphorically, I will not now inquire.

First, Mankind by sin became guilty of death, liable to God's wrath, and a slave to Satan, and his own lusts. The sentence in part was past, and execution begun: the rest would have followed, if not prevented. This is the bondage from which we were redeemed.

Secondly, He that redeemed us is the Son of God—himself God and man, and the Father by the Son. "He purchased us with his own blood," Acts xx. 28.

Thirdly, The price was the whole humiliation of Christ; in the first act whereof, his incarnation, the Godhead was alone, which, by humbling itself, did suffer reputatively, which could not really. In the rest, the whole person was the sufferer, but still the human nature really, and the divine but reputatively. And why we may not add, as part of the price, the merit of that obedience, wherein his suffering did not consist, I yet see not. But from whom were we redeemed?

Answ. From Satan, by rescue against his will; from God's wrath or vindictive justice, by his own procurement and consent. He substituted for us such a sacrifice, by which he could as fully attain the ends of his righteous government, in the demonstration of his justice and hatred of sin, as if the sinner had suffered himself: and in this sound sense it is far from being an absurdity, as the Socinian dreameth, for God to satisfy his own justice, or to buy us of himself, or redeem us from himself.

2. Next let us consider how we are God's, upon the title of this purchase. By "God," here, is meant both the Son, who being God, hath procured a right in us by his redemption, and also the Father, who sent his Son, and redeemed us by him, and to whom it was that the Son redeemed us. "Thou hast redeemed us to God by thy blood," Rev. v. 9. In one word, it is God as Redeemer, the manhood also of the Second Person included, that hath purchased this right. Here you must observe that God, as Creator, had a plenary right of propriety and government, on which he founded the law of works that then was. This right he hath not lost. Our fall did lose our right in him, but could not destroy his right in us. Because it destroyed our right, therefore the promissory part of that law was immediately thereupon dissolved, or ceased through our incapacity, and therefore divines say that, as a covenant, it ceased; but because it destroyed not God's right, therefore the preceptive and penal parts of that law do still remain. But how remain? In their being; but not alone, or without remedy: for the Son of God became a sacrifice in our stead; not that we might absolutely, immediately, or, *ipso facto*, be fully delivered, or that any man should, *ab ipsa hostia*, from the very sacrifice as made, have a right to the great benefits of personal, plenary reconciliation, and remission, and everlasting life; but that the necessity of perishing through the unsatisfiedness of justice for the alone offences against the law of works being removed from mankind, they might all be delivered up to him as Proprietary and Rector, that he might rule them as his redeemed ones, and make for them such new laws of grace, for the conveyances of his benefits, as might demonstrate the wisdom and mercy of our Redeemer, and be most suitable to his ends. The world is now morally dead in sin, though naturally alive. Christ hath redeemed them, but will cure them by the actual conveyance of the benefits of redemption, or not at all. He hath undertaken to this end himself to be their Physician, to cure all that will come to him and take him so to be, and trust him, and obey him in the application of his medicines. He hath erected an hospital, his church, to this end, and commanded all to come into this ark. Those that are far distant he first commandeth to come nearer, and those that are near he inviteth to come in. Too many do refuse, and perish in their refusal. He will not suffer all to do so, but mercifully boweth the wills of his elect, and, by an insuperable powerful drawing, compels them to come in. You may see, then, that here is a *novum jus, et dominii, et imperii*, a new right of propriety and rule, founded on the new bottom of redemption: but that this doth not destroy the old, which was founded on creation; but is in the very nature and use of it an emendative addition. Redemption is to mend the creature, not of any defect that was left in the creation, but from the ruin which came by our defacing transgression. The law of grace upon this redemption is superadded to the law of nature given on the creation; not to amend any imperfections in that law, but to save the sinner from its insufferable penalty by dissolving its obligation of him thereto: and thus, in its nature and use, it is a remedying law. And so you may see that Christ is now the Owner, and, by right, the Governor of the whole world, on the title of redemption, as God before was, and still is, on the title of creation.

3. By this you may also perceive in what sense we are not our own. In the strictest sense, there is no proprietary, or absolute lord, in the world, but God. No man can say this is fully and strictly mine. God gives us, indeed, whatever we enjoy; but his giving is not as man's. We part with our propriety in that which we give, but God gives nothing so. His giving to us makes it not the less his own. As a man giveth his goods to his steward to dispose of for his use, or instruments to his servant to do his work with, so God giveth his benefits to us; or, at the utmost, as you give clothes to your child, which are more yours still than his, and you may take them away at your pleasure. I confess, when God hath told us that he will not take them away, he is, as it were, obliged, in fidelity, to continue them, but yet doth not, hereby, let go his propriety: and so Christ bids us call no man on earth Father, that is, our absolute lord or ruler, because we have but one such Master, who is in heaven, Matt. xxiii.

7—10. So that you may see by this what propriety is left us, and what right we have to ourselves and our possessions. Even such, as a steward in his master's goods, or a servant in his tools, or a child in his coat, which is a propriety in proper subordinate and *secundum quid*, and will secure us against the usurpation of another. One servant may not take his fellow's instrument from him, nor one child his brother's coat from him, without the parent's or master's consent. They have them for their use, though not the full propriety. It may be called a propriety, in respect to our fellow-servant, though it be not properly so as we stand in respect to God. We have right enough to confute the leveller, but not exempt either us or ours from the claim and use of our absolute Lord.

4. What is it to glorify God in body and spirit? I answer, in a word, it is when, upon true believing apprehensions of his right to us, and of our great obligations to him as our Redeemer, we heartily and unfeignedly devote ourselves to him, and live as a people so devoted; so bending the chiefest of our care and study how to please him in exactest obedience, that the glory of his mercy and holiness, and of his wise and righteous laws, may be seen in our conversations; and that the holy conformity of our lives to these laws may show that there is the like conformity in our minds, and that they are written in our hearts; when the excellency of the christian religion is so apparent in the excellency of our lives, causing us to do that which no others can imitate, that the lustre of our good works may shine before men, and cause them to glorify our Father in heaven. To conclude; when we still respect God as our only absolute Sovereign, and Christ as our Redeemer, and his Spirit as our Sanctifier, and his law as our rule; that the doing of his will, and the denying of our own, is the daily work of our lives, and the promoting of his blessed ends is our end: this is the glorifying of God who hath redeemed us.

5. The last question is, Who they be that are and may be urged to glorify God, on this ground, that he hath bought them? Doubtless only those whom he hath bought; but who are those? It discourageth me to tell you, because among the godly it is a controversy; but if they will controvert points of such great moment, they cannot disoblige or excuse us from preaching them. Among the variety of men's opinions it is safe to speak in the language of the Holy Ghost, and accordingly to believe: viz. that, "As by the offence of one, judgment came upon all men to condemnation; even so by the righteousness of one the free gift came upon all men, to justification of life," Rom. v. 18; and, "That he gave himself a ransom for all, and is the only mediator between God and man," 1 Tim. ii. 5, 6. "That he is the propitiation for our sins; and not for ours only, but also for the sins of the whole world," 1 John ii. 2. "That God is the Saviour of all men, especially of those that believe," 1 Tim. iv. 10. "That he is the Saviour of the world," John iv. 42; 1 John iv. 14, 15. "That he tasteth death for every man," Heb. ii. 9; with many the like. It is sad to consider how men's unskilfulness to reconcile God's general grace with his special, and to assign to each its proper part, hath made the Pelagians, and their successors, to deny the special grace; and too many of late no less dangerously to deny the general grace; and what contentions these two erroneous parties have maintained, and still maintain, in the church, and how few observe or follow that true and sober mean which Austin, the maul of the Pelagians, and his scholars, Prosper and Fulgentius, walked in! If when our dark confused heads are unable to assign each truth its place, and rightly to order each wheel and pin in the admirable fabric of God's revelations, we shall, therefore, fall a wrangling against them, and reject them, we may then be drawn to blaspheme the Trinity, to reject either Christ's human nature or his divine; and what truth shall we not be in danger to lose? To think this general grace to be inconsistent with the special, is no wiser than to think the foundation inconsistent with the fabric that is built thereupon; and that the builders themselves should have such thoughts is a matter of compassionate consideration to the friends of the church. Doubtless Christ died not for all alike, nor with equal intentions of saving them; and yet he hath borne the sins of all men on the cross, and was a sacrifice, propitiation, and ransom for all; even they that bring in damnable heresies, deny the Lord that bought them, and bring on themselves swift destruction, 2 Pet. ii. 1. "God sent not his Son into the world to condemn the world, but that the world through him might be saved. He that believeth on him is not condemned; but he that believeth not is condemned already, because he hath not believed in the name of the only begotten Son of God. And this is the condemnation, that light is come into the world, and men loved darkness rather than light, because their deeds were evil," John iii. 17—19. I doubt not but my text doth warrant me to tell you all that you are not your own, but are bought with a price, and, therefore, must glorify him that bought you; and I am very confident, that if any one at judgment will be the advocate of an unbeliever, and say, he deserves not a sorer punishment for sinning against the Lord that bought him, his plea will not be taken; or if any such would comfort the consciences in hell, or go about to cure them of so much of their torment, by telling them that they never sinned against one that redeemed them, nor ever rejected the blood of Christ shed for them, and, therefore, need not accuse themselves of any such sin, those poor sinners would not be able to believe them. If it be only the elect with whom we must thus argue, You are not your own, you are bought with a price, therefore glorify God, then can we truly plead thus with none till we know them to be elect, which will not be in this world. I do not think Paul knew them all to be elect that he wrote to, I mean, absolutely chosen to salvation; nor do I think he would so peremptorily affirm them to be bought with a price, who were fornicators, defrauders, contentious, drunk at the Lord's supper, &c. and from hence have argued against their sins, if he had taken this for a privilege proper to the elect. I had rather say to scandalous sinners, You are bought with a price, therefore, glorify God, than, You are absolutely elect to salvation, therefore, glorify God. And I believe, that as it is the sin of apostates to "Crucify to themselves the Son of God afresh," Heb. vi. 5, 6; so is it their misery, that "There remaineth no more sacrifice for sins, but a certain fearful looking for of judgment, and fiery indignation, which shall devour the adversaries, because they have trodden under-foot the Son of God, and counted the blood of the covenant wherewith they were sanctified an unholy thing," Heb. x. 26—28. Lastly, I judge it also a good argument to draw us from offending others, and occasioning their sin, that "Through us our weak brother shall perish, for whom Christ died," 1 Cor. viii. 11. So much for explication.

I would next proceed to the confirmation of the doctrines here contained, but that they are so clear in the text, and in many others, that I think it next to needless, and we have now no time for needless work, and, therefore, shall only cite these two or three texts, which confirm almost all that I have said together: Rom. xiv. 9, "For to this end Christ both died, and rose, and revived, that he might be Lord both of the dead and living." 2 Cor. v. 14, 15, "We thus judge, that if one died for all, then were all dead; and that he died for all, that they which live should not henceforth live unto themselves, but unto him which died for them and rose again." Matt. xxviii. 18—20, "All power is given me in heaven and in earth. Go ye, therefore, disciple all nations, baptizing them, &c. teaching them to observe all things whatsoever I have commanded you," 1 Pet. i. 17, 18, "If ye call on the Father, who without respect of persons judgeth every man according to his works, pass the time of your sojourning here in fear; forasmuch as ye know that ye were not redeemed with corruptible things, as silver and gold, from your vain conversation, but with the precious blood of Christ, as of a lamb without blemish and without spot." These texts speak to the same purpose with that which I have in hand.

Use. In applying these very useful truths, would time permit, I should begin at the intellect, with a confutation of divers contrary errors, and a collection of many observable consectaries. It would go better with all the commonwealths and princes on earth, if they well considered that the absolute propriety and sovereignty of God-redeemer is the basis of all lawful societies and governments; and that no man hath any absolute propriety, but only the use of the talents that God doth intrust him with: that the sovereignty of the creature is but analogical, *secundum quid;* improper and subordinate to God, the proper Sovereign: that it belongs to him to appoint his inferior officers: that there is no power but from God, and that he giveth none against himself: that a theocracy is the government that must be desired and submitted to, whether the subordinate part be monarchical, aristocratical, or democratical; and the rejecting of this was the Israelites' sin in choosing them a king: that it is still possible and necessary to live under this theocracy, though the administration be not by such extraordinary means as among the Israelites: that all human laws are but by-laws, subordinate to God's. How far his laws must take place in all governments: how far those laws of men are *ipso facto* null, that are unquestionably destructive of the laws of God: how far they that are not their own, may give authority to others: and what aspect these principles have upon liberty in that latitude as it is taken by some; and upon the authority of the multitude, especially in church government. Should I stand on these and other the like consequents, which these fundamentals in hand might lead us to discuss, I should prevent that more seasonable application which I intend, and perhaps be thought, in some of them, to meddle beyond my bounds. I will only say, that God is the first and the last in our ethics and politics, as well as in our physics; that as there is no creature which he made not, so it is no good right of property or government which he some way gives not; that all commonwealths not built on this foundation, are as castles in the air, or as children's tottering structures, which in the very framing are prepared for their ruin, and strictly are no commonwealths at all; and those governors that rule not more for God, than for themselves, shall be dealt with as traitors to the universal Sovereign. Thus far, at least, must our politics be divine, unless we will be mere confederate rebels.

But it is yet a closer application which I intend. Though we are not our own, yet every man's welfare should be so dear to himself, that methinks every man of you should presently inquire how far you are concerned in the business which we have in hand. I will tell you how far. The case here described is all our own. We are bought with a price, and, therefore, not our own, and, therefore, must live to him that bought us. We must do it, or else we violate our allegiance, and are traitors to our Redeemer. We must do it, or else we shall perish as despisers of his blood. It is no matter of indifferency, nor a duty which may be dispensed with. That God who is our Owner by creation and redemption, and who doth hitherto keep our souls in these bodies, by whose mere will and power you are all here alive before him this day, will shortly call you before his bar, where these matters will be more seriously and searchingly inquired after. The great question of the day will then be this, Whether you have been heartily devoted to your Redeemer, and lived to him; or to your carnal selves. Upon the resolution of this question your everlasting salvation or damnation will depend. What think you then? Should not this question be now put home by every rational hearer to his own heart? But I suppose some will say, There is no man that wholly lives to God, for all are sinners; how then can our salvation depend so much on this? I answer in a word: Though no man pay God all that he oweth him, yet no man shall be saved that giveth him not the pre-eminence: he will own none as true subjects that do not cordially own him in his sovereignty. Be it known to you all, there shall not a man of you enter into his kingdom, nor ever see his face in peace, that giveth him not the chiefest room in your hearts, and maketh not his work your chiefest business. He will be no underling, or servant, to your flesh; he will be served with the best, if he cannot have all. And in this sense it is that I say the question will be put, in that great day, by the Judge of all, whether God or our carnal selves were preferred? and whether we lived to him that bought us, or to our flesh? Beloved hearers, I will not ask you whether you, indeed, believe that there will be such a day. I will take it for granted, while you call yourselves christians. Much less will I question whether you would be saved or condemned. Nature will not suffer you to be willing of such a misery, though corruption make you too willing of the cause. But the common stupidity of the world doth persuade me to ask you this, whether you think it meet that men who must be so solemnly examined upon this point, and whose life or death depends on the decision, should not examine themselves on it beforehand, and well consider what answer they must then make? And whether any pains can be too great in so needful a work? And whether he that miscarrieth to save a labour, do not madly betray his soul unto perdition? As if such rational diligence were worse than hell, or his present carnal ease were more desirable than his salvation? Let us then rouse up ourselves, brethren, in the fear of God, and make this a day of judgment to ourselves. Let us know whether we are children of life or death. Oh, how can a man that is well in his wits enjoy with any comfort the things of this world, before he know, at least in probability, what he shall enjoy in the next! How can men go cheerfully up and down about the business of this life, before they have faithfully laboured to make sure that it shall go well with them in the life to come! That we may now know this without deceit, let us all, as in the presence of the living God, lay bare our hearts, examine them, and judge them, by this portion of his word, according to the evidence.

1. Whoever he be that takes not himself for his own, but lives to his Redeemer, he is one that hath

found himself really undone, and hath unfeignedly confessed the forfeiture of his salvation; and finding that redemption hath been made by Christ, and that there is hope and life to be had in him, and none but him, as he gladly receives the tidings, so he cheerfully acknowledgeth the right of his Redeemer, and in a sober, deliberate, and voluntary covenant, renounceth the world, the flesh, and the devil, and resigneth up himself to Christ as his due. He saith, Lord, I have too long served thine enemies and mine own; by cleaving to myself, and forsaking God, I have lost both myself and God: wilt thou be my Saviour, and the Physician of my soul, and wash me with thy blood, and repair the ruins of my soul by thy Spirit, and I am willing to be thine; I yield up myself to the conduct of thy grace, to be saved in thy way, and fitted for thy service, and live to God, from whom I have revolted. This is the case of all that are sincere.

By many Scriptures we might quickly confirm this, if it were liable to question. "If any man come to me, and hate not his father, and mother, and wife, and children, and brethren, and sisters, yea, and his own life also, he cannot be my disciple: and whosoever doth not bear his cross, and come after me, cannot be my disciple," Luke xiv. 26, 27. So verse 33, "Whosoever he be of you that forsaketh not all that he hath, he cannot be my disciple." Which is expounded, Matt. x. 37, "He that loveth father or mother more than me, is not worthy of me." "If any man will come after me, let him deny himself, and take up his cross, and follow me. For whosoever will save his life, shall lose it: and whosoever will lose his life for my sake, shall find it," Matt. xvi. 24. "Whom have I in heaven but thee, and there is none upon earth that I desire besides thee," Psal. lxxiii. 25—27. "The Lord is the portion of mine inheritance," &c. Psal. xvi. 5. Moses refused honour, and chose "rather to suffer affliction with the people of God, than to enjoy the pleasures of sin for a season, esteeming the reproach of Christ greater riches than the treasures of Egypt, for he had respect to the recompence of the reward," Heb. xi. 24—26. I forbear citing more, the case being so evident, that God is set highest in the heart of every sound believer, they being in covenant resigned to him as his own. On the contrary, most of the unsanctified are christians but in name, because they were educated to this profession, and it is the common religion of the country where they live, and they hear none make question of it, or if they do, it is to their own disgrace; the name of Christ having got this advantage, to be every where among us well spoken of, even by those that shall perish for neglecting him and his laws. These men have resigned their names to Christ, but reserved their hearts to flesh-pleasing vanities. Or if under conviction and terror of conscience, they do make any resignation of their souls to Christ, it comes short of the true resignation of the sanctified in these particulars.

1. It is a firm and rooted belief of the gospel, which is the cause of sincere resignation to Christ. They are so fully persuaded of the truth of those things which Christ hath done, and promised to do hereafter, that they will venture all that they have in this world, and their souls, and their everlasting state, upon it. Whereas the belief of self-deceivers is only superficial, staggering, not rooted, and will not carry them to such adventures, Matt. xiii. 21—23.

2. Sincere self-resignation is accompanied with such a love to him that we are devoted to, which overtoppeth (as to the rational part) all other love. The soul hath a prevailing complacency in God, and closeth with him as its chiefest good, Psalm lxxiii. 25; lxiii. 3. But the unsanctified have no such complacency in him; they would fain please him by their flatteries, lest he should do them any hurt, but might they enjoy but the pleasures of this world, they could be well content to live without him.

3. Sincere self-resignation is a departing from our carnal selves, and all creatures as they stand in competition with Christ for our hearts; and so it containeth a crucifying of the flesh, and mortification of all its lusts, Gal. v. 24; Rom. viii. 1—14. There is a hearty renouncing of former contradictory interest and delights, that Christ may be set highest, and chiefly delighted in. But self-deceivers are never truly mortified when they seem to devote themselves most seriously to Christ; there is a contrary prevailing interest in their minds, their fleshly felicity is nearer to their hearts, and this world is never unfeignedly renounced.

4. Sincere self-resignation is resolved upon deliberation, and not a rash, inconsiderate promise, which is afterwards reversed. The illuminated see that perfection in God, that vanity in the creature, that desirable sufficiency in Christ, and emptiness in themselves, that they firmly resolve to cast themselves on him, and be his alone, and though they cannot please him as they would, they will die before they will change their Master; but with self-deceivers it is not thus.

5. Sincere resignation is absolute and unreserved: such do not capitulate and condition with Christ, I will be thine so far, and no farther, so thou wilt but save my estate, or credit, or life. But self-deceivers have ever such reserves in their hearts, though they do not express them, nor, perhaps, themselves discern them. They have secret limitations, expressions, and conditions; they have ever a salve for their worldly safety or felicity, and will rather venture upon a threatened misery which they see not, though everlastingly, than upon a certain temporary misery which they see. These deep reserves are the soul of hypocrisy.

6. Sincere self-resignation is fixed and habituate; it is not forced by a moving sermon, or a dangerous sickness, and then forgotten and laid aside, but it is become a fixed habit in the soul. It is otherwise with self-deceivers; though they will oblige themselves to Christ with vows, in a time of fear and danger, yet so loose is the knot, that when the danger seems over, their bonds fall off. It is one thing to be affrighted, and another to have the heart quite changed and renewed. It is one thing to hire ourselves with a master in our necessities, and yet serve ourselves, or run away; and another thing to nail our ears to his door, and say, I love thee, and therefore will not depart.

So much for the first mark of one that lives not as his own, but as God's, to wit, sincere self-resignation. The second is this.

2. As the heart is thus devoted to God, so also is the life, where men do truly take themselves for his. And that will appear in these three particulars.

1. The principal study and care of such men is how to please God, and promote his interest, and do his work. This is it that they most seriously mind and contrive. Their own felicity they seek in this way, 1 Cor. vii. 32, 33; Rom. vi. 11, 13, 16; Col. i. 10; iii. 1—3; Phil. i. 20, 21, 24. It is not so with the unsanctified, they drive on another design. Their own work is principally minded, and their carnal interest preferred to Christ's. They live to the flesh, and make provision for it, to satisfy its desires, Rom. xiii. 14.

2. It is the chiefest delight of a man devoted to God to see Christ's interest prosper and prevail. It doth him more good to see the church flourish, the gospel succeed, the souls of men brought in to God, and all things fitted to his blessed pleasure, than it would do him to prosper himself in the world; to do good to men's bodies, much more to their souls, is more pleasing to him than to be honourable or rich. To give is sweeter to him than to receive. His own matters he respects as lower things, that come not so near his heart as God's. But with the unsanctified it is not so, their prosperity and honours are most of their delight, and the absence of them their greatest trouble.

3. With a man that is truly devoted to God, the interest of Christ doth bear down all contradicting interest in the ordinary course of his life. As his own unrighteous righteousness, so his own renounced carnal interest, is loss and dung to him in comparison of Christ's, Phil. iii. 8, 9. He cannot take himself to be a loser by that which is gain to the souls of men, and tendeth to promote the interest of his Lord. He serveth God with the first and best, and lets his own work stand by till Christ's be done, or rather owneth none but Christ's, his own dishonour being lighter to him than Christ's, and a ruined estate less grievous than a ruined church; therefore doth he first seek God's kingdom and its righteousness, Matt. vi. 33; and chooseth rather to neglect his flesh, his gain, his friends, his life, than the cause and work of Christ. It is far otherwise with the unsanctified; they will contentedly give Christ the most glorious titles, and full-mouthed commendations, Luke vi. 46; but they have one that is nearer their hearts than he, their carnal self must sway the sceptre. God shall have all that the flesh can spare; if he will be content to be served with its leavings, they will serve him; if not, they must be excused, they can allow him no more. The trying time is the parting time, when God or the world must needs be neglected. In such a strait, the righteous are still righteous, Rev. xxii. 11. But the unstedfast in the covenant do manifest their unstedfastness, and though they will not part with Christ professedly, nor without some witty distinctions and evasions, nor without great sorrow, and pretence of continued fidelity, yet part they will, and shift for themselves, and hold that they have as long as they can, Luke xviii. 23. In a word, the sanctified are heartily devoted to God, and live to him, and were they uncapable of serving or enjoying him, their lives would afford them little content, whatever else they did possess. But the unsanctified are more strongly addicted to their flesh, and live to their carnal selves, and might they securely enjoy the pleasures of this world, they could easily spare the fruition of God, and could be as willing to be dispensed with for his spiritual service, as to perform it. And thus I have given you the true description of those that live to their Redeemer, as being not their own, and those that live to themselves, as if they were not his that bought them.

Having thus told you what the world saith, it followeth that we next inquire what your hearts say: you hear what you must be, will you now consider what you are? Are all the people that hear me this day devoted in heart and life to their Redeemer? Do you all live as Christ's, and not your own? If so, I must needs say it is an extraordinary assembly, and such as I had never the happiness to know. Oh that it were so indeed! that we might rejoice together, and magnify our Deliverer, instead of reprehending you, or lamenting your unhappiness. But, alas! we are not such strangers in the world, as to be guilty of such a groundless judgment. Let us inquire more particularly into the case.

1. Are those so sincerely devoted to Christ, and do they so deny themselves, whose daily thoughts, and care, and labour, is, how they may live in more reputation and content, and may be better provided for the satisfying of their flesh? If they be low and poor, and their condition is displeasing to them, their greatest care is to repair it to their minds; if they be higher, and more wealthy, their business is to keep it, or increase it: that hunt after honour, and thirst after a thriving and more plenteous state; that can stretch their consciences to the size of all times, and humour those that they think may advance them, and be most humble servants to those above them, and contemptuously neglect whosoever is below them; that will put their hands to the feet of those that they hope to rise by, and put their feet on the necks of their subdued adversaries, and trample upon all that stand in their way; that applaud not men for their honesty but their worldly honours; and will magnify that man while he is capable of advancing them, whom they would have scorned if Providence had laid him in the dust; that are friends to all that befriend their interests and designs, and enemies to the most upright that cross them in their course; that love not men so much because they love God, as because they love them. Are these devoted to God, or to themselves? Is it for God, or themselves, that men so industriously scramble for honours, and places of government, or of gain? Will they use their offices or honours for God, that hunt after them as a prey, as if they had not burden enough already, nor talents enough to answer for neglecting? Are those men devoted to God, that can tread down his most unquestionable interest on earth, when it seems to be inconsistent with their own? Let the gospel go down, let the church be broken in pieces, let sound doctrine be despised, let ministers be hindered or tired with vexations, let the souls of people sink or swim, rather than they should be hindered in the way of ambition! I shall leave it to the trial of another day, whether all the public actions of this age, with their effects, have been for God or for self. This doth not belong to my examination, but to his that will thoroughly perform it ere long, and search these matters to the quick, and open them to the world. There were never higher pretences for God in an age, than have been in this; had there been but answerable intentions and performances, his affairs and our own had been in much better case than they are; but enough of this. Should we descend into men's particular families and conversations, we should find the matter little better with the most. Are they all for God that follow the world so eagerly, that they cannot spare him a serious thought? an hour's time for his worship in their families, or in secret? that will see that their own work be done; but for the souls of those that are committed to their charge they regard them not? Let them be ever so ignorant they will not instruct them, nor cause them to read the word, or learn a catechism; nor will spend the Lord's peculiar day in such exercises; and it is much if they hinder not those that would. Is it for God that men give up their hearts to this world, so that they cannot have once a day or week, to think soberly what they must do in the next; or how they may be ready for their great approaching change? Is it for God that men despise his ministers, reject his word, abhor reformation, scorn a church government, and deride the persons that are addicted to his fear, and the families that call upon his name? These men will shortly understand a little better than now they

will do, whether indeed they live to God or to themselves.

2. If you are devoted to God what do you for him? Is it his business that you mind? How much of your time do you spend for him? How much of your speech is for him? How much of your estates yearly is serviceable to his interest? Let conscience speak, whether he have your studies and affections; let your families be witnesses whether he have your speeches and best endeavours; let the church witness what you have done for it; and the poor witness what you have done for them; and the souls of ignorant and ungodly men, what you have done for them. Show by the work you have done who you have lived to, God or your carnal selves. If, indeed, you have lived to God, something will be seen that you have done for him; nay, it is not a something that will serve the turn, it must be the best. Remember that it is by your works, that you shall be judged, and not by your pretences, professions, or compliments; your Judge already knows your case, he needs no witnesses, he will not be mocked with saying you are for him; show it, or saying it will not serve.

Methinks now the consciences of some of you should prevent me, and preach over the sharper part of the sermon to yourselves, and say, I am the man that have lived to myself, and so consider of the consequence of such a life; but I will leave this to your meditation when you go home, and next proceed to the exhortative part of application.

Men, brethren, and fathers, the business that I come hither upon is to proclaim God's right to you and all that is yours, even his new right of redemption, supposing that of creation; and to let you know, that you are all bought with a price, and therefore are not your own, but his that bought you, and must accordingly be dedicated and live to him. Honourable and worshipful, and all men, of what degree soever, I do here, on the behalf and in the name of Christ, lay claim to you all, to your souls and bodies, to all your faculties, abilities, and interests, on the title of redemption; all is God's. Do you acknowledge his title, and consent unto his claim? What say you? Are you his; or, are you not? Dare you deny it? If any man dare be so bold I am here ready to make good the claim of Christ. If you dare not deny it, we must take it as confessed. Bear witness all, that God laid claim to you and yours, and no man durst deny his title. I do next, therefore, require you, and command you, in his name, give him his own; render to God the things that are God's. Will you this day renounce your carnal selves, and freely confess you are not your own; and cheerfully and unreservedly resign yourselves to God, and say, as Josh. xxiv. 15, "As for me and my household, we will serve the Lord?" Do not ask what God will do with you; or how he will use you, or dispose of you. Trust him for that, and obey his will. Fear not evil from the chiefest good, unless it be in neglecting or resisting him. Be sure of it, God would use you better than Satan would, or than this world would, or better than you have used or would use yourselves. He will not employ you in dishonourable drudgeries, and then dash you in pieces. He will not seduce you with swinish sensualities, and keep you in play with childish vanities, till you drop into damnation before you are aware: nor will he lull you asleep in presumptuous security, till you unexpectedly awake in unquenchable fire. You need not fear such dealing as this from him: "His commandments are not grievous," 1 John v. 3. "His yoke is easy, his burden is light," and tendeth to the perfect rest of the soul, Matt. xi. 28—30. What say you? Will you hereafter be his, unfeignedly his? resolvedly, unreservedly, and constantly his? or will you not? Take heed "that you refuse not him that speaketh," Heb. xii. 25. Reject not, neglect not, this offer, lest you never have another on the like terms again. He is willing to pardon all that is past, and put up all the wrongs that you have done him, so you will but repent of them; and now at last be heartily and entirely his; not only in tongue, but in deed and life. Well, I have proclaimed God's right to you, I have offered you his gracious acceptance; if yet you demur, or sleepily neglect it, or obstinately resist him, take that you get by it; remember you perish not without warning. The confession of Christ's right, which this day you have been forced to, shall remain as on record, to the confusion of your faces; and you shall be then forced to remember, though you had rather forget it, what now you are forced to confess, though you had rather you could deny it. But I am loth to leave you to this prognostic, or to part on terms so sad to your souls, and sad to me: I will add, therefore, some reasons to persuade you to submit; and though it be not in my power to follow them so to your hearts as to make them effectual, yet I shall do my part in propounding them, and leave them to God to set them home, beseeching him that maketh, new maketh, openeth, and softeneth hearts at his pleasure, to do these blessed works on yours, and to persuade you within, while I am persuading you without, that I may not lose my labour and my hopes, nor your souls, nor God his due.

1. Consider the fulness of God's right to you. No creature is capable of the like. He made you of nothing, and, therefore, you have nothing which is not his. He redeemed you when you were fallen to worse than nothing. Had not Christ ransomed you by being a sacrifice for your sin, you had been hopelessly left to everlasting perdition; give him, therefore, his own which he hath so dearly bought, 1 Pet. i. 18.

2. Consider that you have no right of propriety to yourselves. If you have, how came you by it? Did you make yourselves? Did you redeem yourselves? Do you maintain and preserve yourselves? If you are your own, tell God you will not be beholden to him for his preservation. Why cannot you preserve yourselves in health if you are your own? Why cannot you recover yourselves from sickness? Is it yourselves that gives power to your food to nourish you? to the earth to bear you, and furnish you with necessaries? to the air to cool and recreate your spirits? If you are your own, save yourselves from sickness and death; keep back your age; deliver your souls from the wrath of God; answer his pure justice for your own sins; never plead the blood of a Redeemer, if you are your own. If you can do these things I will yield that you are your own. But no man can ransom his soul from death, it cost a dearer price than so, Acts xx. 28. You are not debtors, therefore, to the flesh, to live after it, (Rom. viii. 12,) but to him that died to subdue the flesh, Rom. vi. 11.

3. None else can claim any title to you, further than under God upon his gift. Men did not create you or redeem you; "Be not, therefore, the servants of men," (1 Cor. vii. 23,) unless it be under Christ, and for him. Certainly Satan did not create you, or redeem you; what right then hath he to you, that he should be served?

4. Seeing then that you are God's, and his alone, is it not the most heinous thievery to rob him of his right? If they must be hanged that rob men of so small a thing as earthly necessaries, wherein they

have but an improper derived propriety, what torments do those deserve that rob God of so precious a creature, that cost him so dear, and might be so useful, and wherein he hath so full and unquestionable propriety! The greatest, the richest, and wisest men that are trusted with most, are the greatest robbers on earth, if they live not to God, and shall have the greatest punishment.

5. Is it not incomparably more honourable to be God's, than to be your own; and to live to him, than to yourselves? The object and end doth nobilitate the act, and thereby the agent. It is more honourable to serve a prince than a ploughman. That man that least seeks his own honour or carnal interests, but most freely denieth it, and most entirely seeks the honour of God, is the most highly honoured with God and good men, when self-seekers defraud themselves of their hopes. Most men think vilely, or at least suspiciously, of that man that seeks for honour to himself; they think if the matter were combustible he need not to blow the fire so hard; if he were worthy of honour, his worth would attract it by a sweet, magnetic power; so much industry they think is the most probable mark of indignity, and of some consciousness of it in the seeker's breast. If he attain some of his ends, men are ready to look on his honour but as alms, which he was fain to beg for before he got it. And could he make shift to ascend the throne, so much in the eyes of the wisest men would be detracted from his honour, as they did believe himself to have a hand in contriving it, *quod sequitur fugio*, &c. They honour him more that refuseth a crown when it is offered, than him that ambitiously aspireth after it, or rapaciously apprehendeth it. If they see a man much desire their applause, they think he needeth it rather than deserveth it. Solomon saith, "To search their own glory is not glory," Prov. xxv. 27.

6. You can never have a better master than God, nor yet a sweeter employment than his service. There is nothing in him that may be the least discouragement to you, nor in his works that should be distasteful. The reason why the world thinks otherwise, is because of the distempered averseness of their souls. A sick stomach is no fit judge of the pleasantness of meat. To live to God is to live to the truest and highest delights. His kingdom is not in meats and drinks, but in righteousness, peace, and joy in the Holy Ghost. His servants, indeed, are often troubled; but ask them the reason, and they will quickly tell you that it is not for being his servants, or for serving him too much; but for fear lest they are not his servants, or for serving him no better. It is not in his ways, or at least not for them, that they meet with their perplexities, but in stepping out of them, and wandering in their own. Many, besides the servants of God, do seek felicity and satisfaction to their minds, and some discover where it lieth; but only they attain it, and enjoy it.

But, on the contrary, he hath an ill master that is ruled by himself. A master that is blind, and proud, and passionate, that will lead you unto precipices, and thence deject you; that will most effectually ruin you when he thinks he is doing you the greatest good; whose work is bad, and his wages no better; that feedeth his servants in plenty but as swine, and in the day of famine denieth them the husks. Whatever you may now imagine, while you are distracted with sensuality, I dare say, if ever God bring you to yourselves, you will consider that it is better be in your Father's house, where the poorest servant hath bread enough, than to be fed with dreams and pictures, and to perish with hunger. Reject not God till you have found a better master.

7. If you will needs be your own, and seek yourselves, you disengage God from dealing with you as his in a gracious sense. If you will not trust him, nor venture yourselves upon his promise and conduct, but will shift for yourselves, then look to yourselves as well as you can; save yourselves in danger, cure your own diseases, quiet your own consciences, grapple with death in your own strength, plead your own cause in judgment, and save yourselves from hell if you can; and when you have done, go and boast of your own sufficiency and achievements, and tell men how little you were beholden to Christ. Woe to you, if, upon these provocations, God should give you over to provide for yourselves, and leave you without any other salvation than your own power is able to effect! Mark the connexion of this sin and punishment in Deut. xxxii. 18—20. Of the Rock that begat thee thou art unmindful, and hast forgotten God that formed thee. And when the Lord saw it, he abhorred them, because of the provoking of his sons, and of his daughters: and he said, "I will hide my face from them, I will see what their end shall be." As if he should say, I will see how well they can save themselves, and make them know by experience their own insufficiency.

8. Those men that seek themselves, and live to themselves, and not to God, are unfaithful and treacherous both to God and man. As they neglect God in prosperity, so they do but flatter him in adversity, Psal. lxxviii. 34—37. And he that will be false to God, whose interest in him is so absolute, is unlikely to be true to men, whose interest in him is infinitely less: he that can shake off the great obligations of creation, redemption, preservation, and provision, which God layeth on him, is unlikely to be held by such slender obligations as he receives from men. I will never trust that man far, if I know him, that is false to his Redeemer. He that will sell his God, his Saviour, his soul, and heaven for a little sensuality, vain-glory, or worldly wealth, I shall not wonder if he sell his best friend for a groat. Self-seeking men will take you for their friend no longer than you can serve their turns; but if once you need them, or stand in their way, you shall find what they esteemed you for. He that is in haste to be rich, and thereupon respecteth persons for a piece of bread, that man will transgress, saith Solomon, Prov. xxviii. 20, 21.

9. Sanctification consisteth in your hearty resignation and living to God; and therefore you are unsanctified if you are destitute of this. "Without holiness none shall see God," Heb. xii. 14. And what is holiness, but our sincere dedication and devotedness to God? Being no longer common and unclean, but separated in resolution, affection, and conversation, from the world and our carnal selves to him. It is the office of the Holy Ghost to work you to this; and if you resist and refuse it, you do not soundly believe in the Holy Ghost, but instead of believing in him you fight against him.

10. You are verbally devoted to Christ in solemn covenant, entered into in baptism, and frequently renewed in the Lord's supper, and at other seasons. Did you not there solemnly, by your parents, resign yourself to Christ as his? and renounce the flesh, the world, and the devil, and promise to fight under Christ's banner against them to your lives' end? O happy person that performeth this covenant, and everlastingly miserable are they that do not. *Fides non recepta, sed custodita vivificat*, saith Cyprian. It is not covenant-making, without covenant-keeping, that is like to save you. Do you stand to the covenant that you made by your parents? or do you

disclaim it? If you disclaim it, you renounce your part in Christ, and his benefits in that covenant made over to you. If you stand to it, you must perform your promise, and live to God, to whom you were resigned. To take God's oath of allegiance so solemnly, and afterward to turn to his enemies which we renounced, is a rebellion that shall not be always unrevenged.

11. God's absolute dominion and sovereignty over us is the very foundation of all religion, even of that little that is found left among infidels and pagans, much more evidently of the saving religion of christians. He that dare say he believeth not this, will never, sure, have the face to call himself a christian. Is it not a matter of most sad consideration, that ever so many millions should think to be saved by a doctrine which they believe not, or by a religion that never went deeper than the brain, and is openly contradicted by the tenour of their lives? Is a true religion enough to save you, if you be not true to that religion? How do men make shift to quiet their consciences in such gross hypocrisy? Is there a man to be found in this congregation that will not confess that he is rightfully his Redeemer's? But hath he indeed their hearts, their time, their strength, and their interest? Follow some of them from morning to night, and you shall not hear one serious word for Christ, nor see any serious endeavours for his interest, and yet men will profess that they are his. How sad a case is it, that men's own confessions should condemn them, and that which they called their religion should judge them to that everlasting misery which they thought it would have saved them from! And how glorious would the christian religion appear if men were true to it; if Christ's doctrine had its full impression on their hearts, and were expressed in their lives! Is he not an excellent person that denieth himself, and doth all for God: that goeth on no business but God's: that searcheth out God's interest in every part of his calling and employment; and intendeth that, "whether he eat or drink, or whatever he doth, doth all to the glory of God," 1 Cor. x. 31; that can say, as Paul, "I am crucified with Christ, nevertheless I live, yet not I, but Christ liveth in me," Gal. ii. 20; and, "What things were gain to me, those I counted loss for Christ: yea, doubtless, and I count all things but loss for the excellency of the knowledge of Christ Jesus my Lord; for whom I have suffered the loss of all things, and do count them but dung, that I may win Christ, Phil. iii. 7, 8; and, "For me to live is Christ, and to die is gain," Phil. i. 21. Perhaps you think that the degree of these examples is inimitable by us; but I am sure all that will be saved must imitate them in the truth.

12. Self-seeking is self-losing, and delivering up yourself and all you have to God, is the only way to save yourselves, and to secure all. The more you are his, the more you are your own indeed; and the more you deliver to him, and expend for him, the greater is your gain. These paradoxes are familiar, tried truths to the true believer: these are his daily food and exercise, which seem to others such scorpions as they dare not touch, or such stones as they are not able to digest. He knoweth that self-humbling is the true self-exalting, and self-exalting is the infallible way to be brought low, Luke xiv. 11; xviii. 14; Matt. xxiii. 12. He believeth that there is a losing of life which saves it, and a saving of it which certainly loseth it, Matt. x. 39; xvi. 25. Oh that I could reach the hearts of self-seekers, that spend their care and time for their bodies, and live not unto God! that I were but able to make them see the issue of their course, and what it will profit them to "win all the world, and lose their souls!" O all you busy men of this world, hearken to the proclamation of him that bought you: "Ho, every one that thirsteth, come ye to the waters! Buy wine and milk without money and without price. Wherefore do you spend money for that which is not bread, and your labour for that which satisfieth not? Hearken diligently to me, and eat ye that which is good, and let your soul delight itself in fatness. Incline your ear, and come unto me: hear, and your soul shall live, and I will make an everlasting covenant with you," Isa. lv. 1—3. O sirs, what a deal of care and labour do you lose! How much more gainfully might your lives be improved? "Godliness with contentment is the great gain," 1 Tim. vi. 6. That which you now think you make your own, will shortly prove to be least your own; and that is most lost which you so carefully labour for. You that are now so idly busy in gathering together the treasure of an ant-hillock, and building children's tottering piles, do you forget that the foot of death is coming to spurn it all abroad, and tread down you and it together? You spend the day of life and visitation in painting your phantasies with the images of felicity, and in dressing yourselves, and feathering your nest with that which you impiously steal from God: and do you forget that the night of blackness is at hand, when God will undress you of your temporary contents, and deplume you of all your borrowed bravery. How easily, how speedily, how certainly will he do it! Read over your case in Luke xii. 16—22. How can you make shift to read such texts, and not perceive that they speak to you? When you are pulling down and building up, and contriving what to do with your fruits, and saying to yourselves, I have so much now as may serve me so many years, I will take mine ease, eat, drink, and be merry; remember, then, the conclusion: but God said unto him, "Thou fool, this night thy soul shall be required of thee. Then whose shall these things be which thou hast provided? So is he that layeth up treasure for himself, and is not rich towards God." Are these things yours or mine? (saith God.) Whose are they? If they are yours, keep them now if you can: either stay with them, or take them with you. But God will make you know that they are his, and disrobe such men as thieves, who are adorned with that which is none of their own. This honour, (saith God,) is mine; thou stolest it from me: this wealth is mine; this life and all is mine; only thyself he will not own. They shall require thy soul that have conquered and ruled it. Though it was his by the right of creation and redemption, yet seeing it was not his by a free dedication, he will not own it as to everlasting salvation, but say, "Depart from me, I know you not, ye workers of iniquity," Matt. vii. 23. Oh with what hearts then will self-seeking gentlemen part with their honours and estates, and the earthly-minded with their beloved possessions! When he that resigned all to God, and devoted himself and all to his service, shall find his consumed estate to be increased, his neglected honour abundantly repaired, and in this life he shall receive a hundred-fold, and in the world to come eternal life, Matt. x. 30; John iv. 56; 1 Tim. vi. 12, 19.

13. Lastly, Consider, when judgment comes, inquiry will be made whether you have lived as your own, or as his that bought you. Then he will require his own with the improvement, Luke xix. 23. The great business of that day will be, not so much to search after particular sins, or duties, which were contrary to the scope of heart and life; but to know whether you lived to God, or to your flesh; whe-

ther your time, and care, and wealth, were expended for Christ in his members and interest, or for your carnal selves, Matt. xxv. Inasmuch as you did it not to these, you did it not to him. You that Christ hath given authority to shall then be accountable whether you improved it to his advantage. You that he hath given honour to must then give account whether you improved it to his honour. In the fear of God, sirs, cast up your accounts in time, and bethink you what answer will then stand good. It will be a doleful hearing to a guilty soul, when Christ shall say, I gave thee thirty or forty years' time: thy flesh had so much in eating and drinking, and sleeping, and labouring, in idleness, and vain talking, and recreations, and other vanities; but where was my part? how much was laid out for the promoting of my glory? I lent you so much of the wealth of the world; so much was spent on your backs, and so much on your bellies, so much on costly toys or superfluities, so much in revengeful suits and contentions, and so much was left behind for your posterity; but where was my part? how much was laid out to further the gospel, and to relieve the souls or the bodies of your brethren? I gave thee a family, and committed them to thy care to govern them for me, and fit them for my service; but how didst thou perform it? O brethren, bethink you in time what answer to make to such interrogatories: your Judge hath told you that your doom must then pass according as you have improved your talents for him; and that he that hideth his talent, though he give God his own, "shall be cast into utter darkness, where is weeping and gnashing of teeth," Matt. xxv. 30. How easily will Christ then evince his right in you, and convince you that it was your duty to have lived unto him! Do you think, sirs, that you shall then have the face to say, I thought, Lord, that I had been made and redeemed for myself? I thought I had nothing to do on earth, but live in as much plenty as I could, and pleasure to my flesh, and serve thee on the by, that thou mightest continue my prosperity, and save me when I could keep the world no longer. I knew not that I was thine, and should have lived to thy glory. If any of you plead thus, what store of arguments hath Christ to silence you! He will then convince you that his title to you was not questionable. He will prove that thou wast his by thy very being, and fetch unanswerable arguments from every part and faculty: he will prove it from his incarnation, his life of humiliation, his bloody sweat, his crown of thorns, his cross, his grave. He that had wounds to show after his resurrection, for the convincing of a doubting disciple, will have such scars to show then as shall suffice to convince a self-excusing rebel. All these shall witness that he was thy rightful Lord. He will prove it also from the discoveries of his word, from the warnings of his ministers, from the mercies which thou receivedst from him, that thou wast not ignorant of his right, and of thy duty; or at least not ignorant for want of means. He will prove it from thy baptismal covenant and renewed engagements. The congregation can witness that you did promise to be his, and seal to it by the reception of both his sacraments. And as he will easily prove his right, so will he as easily prove that you denied it to him. He will prove it from your works, from the course of your life, from the stream of your thoughts, from your love, your desires, and the rest of the affections of your disclosed hearts.

O brethren, what a day will that be, when Christ shall come in person, with thousands of his angels, to sit in judgment on the rebellious world, and claim his due, which is now denied him! when plaintiff and defendant, witnesses and jurors, counsellors and justices, judges and all the princes on earth, shall stand equal before the impartial Judge, expecting to be sentenced to their unchangeable state! Then, if a man should ask you, What think you now, sir, of living to God? Is it better to be devoted to him, or to the flesh? Which now do you take for the better matter? What would you do now if it were all to do again? What would you then say to such a question? How would you answer it? Would you make as light of it as now you do? O sirs, you may hear these things now from your poor fellow-creature, as proud-hearted gallants, or as self-conceited deriders, or as besotted worldlings, or senseless blocks, or secret infidels, that as those, Deut. xxix. 19, do bless themselves in their hearts, and say, We shall have peace, though we walk in the imagination of our hearts. But then you will hear them as trembling prisoners. Read the 20th verse at leisure. Such a sight will work when words will not, especially words not believed, nor considered of. When you shall see the God that you disowned, the Redeemer whom you neglected, the glory which you forfeited, by preferring the pleasures of the flesh before it, the saints triumphing whom you refused to imitate, and a doleful eternity of misery to be remedilessly endured, then saints will seem wiser men in your eyes, and how gladly would you then be such! But oh, too late! What a thing is it, that men who say they believe such a judgment, and everlasting life and death, as all christians profess to do, can yet read, and hear, and talk of such things as insensibly as if they were dreams or fables! I know it is the nature of sin to deceive, and of a sinful heart to be too willing of such deceiving; and it is the business of Satan by deceiving to destroy, and with the most specious baits to angle for souls; and therefore I must expect that those of you that are taken and are the nearest to the pit, should be least fearful of the danger, and most confident to escape, though you are conscious that you live not to God, but to yourselves. But for my part, I have read and considered what God saith in his word, and I have found such evidence of its certain truth, that I heartily wish that I might rather live on a dunghill, and be the scorn of the world, and spend my few days in beggary and calamity, than that I should stand before the Lord, my Judge, in the case of that man, whatever he be, that is not in heart and life devoted unto God, but liveth to his flesh. For I know that if we live after the flesh, we shall die, Rom. viii. 13. I had rather lie here in Lazarus's poverty, and want the compassion and relief of man, than to be clothed with the best, and fare deliciously, and hereafter be denied a drop of water to cool the flames of the wrath of God.

I confess this is likely to seem but harsh and ungrateful preaching to many of you. Some pleasant jingles, or witty sayings, or shreds of reading, and pretty cadency of neat expressions, were liker to be accepted, and procure applause with them who had rather have their ears and fantasy tickled than rubbed so roughly, and be roused from their ease and pleasing dreams. But shall I preach for myself, while I pretend to be preaching you from yourselves to God? Shall I seek myself, while I am preaching of the everlasting misery of self-seekers? God forbid. Sirs, I know the terrors of the Lord, 2 Cor. v. 11. I believe, and therefore speak. Were I a christian no deeper than the throat, I would fish for myself, and study more to please you than to save you. I love not to make a needless stir in men's consciences, nor to trouble their peace by a doctrine which I do not believe myself. But I believe that our Judge is even at the door, and that we shall shortly see him coming in his glory, and the host of heaven attending him with acclamations. In the mean time, your particular doom draws on; the fashion of all these things passeth away; as those seats will anon be empty when you are departed, so it is but a moment till all your habitations shall change their possessors, and the places of your abode, and too great delight, shall know you no more. I must needs speak to you as to transient, itinerant mortals, who must, ere long, be carried on men's shoulders to the dust, and there be left by those that must shortly follow you: then farewell honours and fleshly delights; farewell all the accommodations and contents of this world. Oh that you had sooner bid them farewell! Had you lived to Christ as you did to them, he would not so have turned you off, nor have left your dislodged souls to utter desolation.

In a word, as sure as the word of God is true, if you own him not now as your Lord and Sovereign, he will not own you then as his chosen to salvation. And if now you live not to him, you shall not then live with him. "Be not deceived; God is not mocked: for whatsoever a man soweth, that shall he also reap. For he that soweth to his flesh shall of the flesh reap corruption; but he that soweth to the Spirit shall of the Spirit reap everlasting life," Gal. vi. 7, 8. "Consider this, ye that forget God, lest he tear you in pieces, and there be none to deliver you," Psalm l. 22.

Beloved hearers, believe as you pretend to believe, and then live as you do believe. If you believe that you are not your own, but his that made you, and bought you with a price, and that he will thus try you for your lives and everlasting comforts on this question, whether you have lived to him, or to yourselves; then live as men that do indeed believe it. Let your religion be visible, as well as audible, and let those that see your lives, and observe the scope of your endeavours, see that you believe it. But if you believe not these things, but are infidels in your hearts, and think you shall feel neither pain nor pleasure when this life is ended, but that man dieth as the beast, then I cannot wonder if you live as you believe. He that thinks he shall die like a dog, is like enough to live like a dog, even in his filthiness, and in snarling for the bone of worldly vanities, which the children do contemn.

Having spoken thus much by way of exhortation, I shall add a few words for your more particular direction, that you may see to what my exhortation doth tend, and it may not be lost.

1. Be sure that you look to the uprightness of your heart, in this great business of devoting yourselves to God; especially see,

1. That you discern, and soundly believe, that excellency in God which is not in the creature, and that perfect felicity in his love, and in the promised glory, which will easily pay for all your losses.

2. And that upon a deliberate comparing him with the pleasures of this world, you do resolvedly renounce them, and dedicate yourselves to him.

3. And especially that you search carefully lest any reserve should lurk in your hearts, and you should not deliver up yourselves to him absolutely, for life and death, for better and worse, but should still retain some hopes of an earthly felicity, and not take the unseen felicity for your portion. "It is the lot of the wicked to have their portion in this life," Psal. xvii. 14. And let me here warn you of one delusion, by which many thousands have perished, and cheated themselves out of their everlasting hopes. They think that it is only some grosser disgraceful sins, as swearing, drunkenness, whoredom, injustice, &c. that will prove men's perdition, and because they are not guilty of these, they are secure; whenas it is the predominancy of the interest of the flesh against the interest of God in their hearts and lives, that is the certain evidence of a state of damnation, which way soever it be that this is expressed. Many a civil gentleman hath his heart more addicted to his worldly interest, and less to God, than some whoremongers and drunkards. If you live with good reputation for civility, yea, for extraordinary ingenuity, yea, for religious zeal, and no disgraceful vice is perceived in your lives, yet if your hearts be on these things which you possess, and you love your present enjoyments better than God, and the glory that he hath promised, your case is as dangerous as the publicans and harlots. You may spend your days in better reputation, but you will end them in as certain desolation as they. The question is only whether God have your hearts and lives, and not whether you denied them to him with a plausible civility. Nay, it is merely for their carnal selves to preserve their reputation, that some men do forbear those grosser crimes, when yet God hath as little of them as of the more visibly profane. "Love not the world, nor the things that are in the world. If any man love the world, the love of the Father is not in him," 1 John ii. 15.

2. If you are wholly God's, live wholly to him, at least do not stint him, and grudge him your service. It is grown the common conceit of the world, that a life of absolute dedication to God is more ado than needs. What needs all this ado? say they. Cannot you be saved with less ado than this? I will now demand of these men but an answer to these few sober questions.

1. Do you fear giving more to God than his due? Is not all his own? And how can you give him more than all?

2. He is not so backward in giving to you, that owes you nothing, but gives you plenty, variety, and continuance of all the good you enjoy; and do you think you well requite him?

3. Christ said not of his life and precious blood, it is too much; and will you say of your poor unprofitable service, it is too much?

4. Who will you give that to which you spare from God? that time, and study, and love, and labour? To any that hath more right to it, or better deserves it, or will better reward you than he will do?

5. Are you afraid of being losers by him? Have you cause for such fears? Is he unfaithful, or unable to perform his promises? Will you repent when you come to heaven that you did too much to get it? Will not that blessedness pay you to the full?

6. What if you had no wages but your work? Is it not better to live to God than to man? Is not purity better than impurity? If feasting be grievous, it is because you are sick. If the mire be your pleasure, it is because you are swine, and not because the condition is desirable.

7. Will it comfort you more in the reckoning and review to have laid out yourselves for God, or for the world? Will you then wish that you had done less for heaven, or for earth? Sirs, these questions are easily answered if you are but willing to consider them.

8. Doth it beseem those to be afraid of giving God too much, that are such bankrupts as we are, and are sure that we shall not give him the twentieth part of his due, if we do the best we can? and when the best, that are scorned by the world for

their forwardness, do abhor themselves for their backwardness? Yea, could we do all, we are but unprofitable servants, and should do but our duty, Luke xvii. 10. Alas! how little cause have we to fear lest we should give God too much of our hearts, or of our lives!

3. If you are not your own, remember that nothing else is your own. What can be more your own than yourselves?

1. Your parts and abilities of mind or body are not your own; use them, therefore, for him that owneth them.

2. Your authority and dignities are not your own; see, therefore, that you make the best of them for him that lent them you.

3. Your children themselves are not your own; design them for the utmost of his service that trusts you with them, educate them in that way as they may be most serviceable to God. It is the great wickedness of too many of our gentry, that they prepare their posterity only to live plenteously, and in credit in the world, but not to be serviceable to God or the commonwealth. Design them, all that are capable, to magistracy or ministry, or some useful way of life. And whatever be their employment, endeavour to possess them with the fear of the Lord, that they may devote themselves to him. Think not the preaching of the gospel a work too low for the sons of the noblest person in the land. It would be an excellent furtherance to the work of the gospel, if noblemen and gentlemen would addict those sons to the ministry that are fit for it, and can be spared from the magistracy. They might have more respect from their people, and easier rule them, and might better win them with bounty than poor men can do. They need not to contend with them for tithes or maintenance.

4. If you are not your own, your whole families are not your own. Use them, therefore, as families that are dedicated to God.

5. If you are not your own, then your wealth is not your own. Honour God, therefore, with your substance, and with the first-fruits of your increase, Prov. iii. 9. Do you ask how? Are there no poor people that want the faithful preaching of the gospel for want of means, or other furtherance? Are there no godly scholars that want means to maintain them at the universities, to fit them for this work? Are there no poor neighbours about you that are ignorant, that if you buy them Bibles and catechisms, and hire them to learn them, might come to knowledge and to life? Are there no poor children that you might set apprentices to godly masters, where soul and body might both have helps? The poor you have always with you. It is not for want of objects for your charity; if you hide your talents, or consume them on yourselves, the time is coming when it would do you more good to have laid them out to your Master's use, than in pampering your flesh.

Some grudge that God should have the tenths, that is, that they should be consecrated to the maintenance of his service. But little do these consider that all is his, and must all be accounted for. Some question whether now there be such a sin as sacrilege in being, but little do they consider that every sin is a kind of sacrilege. When you dedicated yourself to God, you dedicated all you had, and it was God's before; do not take it from him again. Remember the halving of Ananias, and give God all.

Object. But must we not provide for our families?

Answ. Yea, because God requires it, and in so doing you render it to him. That is given to him which is expended in obedience to him, so be it you still prefer his most eminent interest.

Lastly, if you are not your own, then must not your works be principally for yourselves, but for him that oweth you. As the scope of your lives must be to the honour of your Lord, so be sure that you hourly renew these intentions. When you set your foot out of your doors, ask whether your business you go upon be for God. When you go to your rest, examine yourselves what you have done that day for God; especially let no opportunity overslip you wherein you may do him extraordinary service. You must so perform the very labours of your callings, that they may be ultimately for God; so love your dearest friends and enjoyments, that it be God that is principally loved in them.

More particularly as to the business of the day, what need I say more than in a word to apply this general doctrine to your special works?

1. If the honourable judges and the justices will remember that they are God's, and not their own, what a rule and stay will it be to them for their work! What an answer will it afford them against all solicitations from carnal self, or importunate friends! viz. I am not mine own, nor come I hither to do mine own work; I cannot therefore dispose of myself or it, but must do as he that owes me doth command me. How would this also incite them to promote Christ's interest with their utmost power, and faithfully to own the causes which he owneth!

2. If all counsellors, and solicitors of causes, did truly take themselves for God's, and not their own, they durst not plead for nor solicit a cause they knew which God disowneth. They would remember that what they do against the innocent, or speak against a righteous cause, is done and said against their Lord, from whom they may expect, ere long, to hear, Inasmuch as you said or did this against the least of these, you said or did it against me. God is the great patron of innocency, and the pleader of every righteous cause; and he that will be so bold as to plead against him, had need of a large fee to save him harmless. Say not it is your calling which you must live by, unless you that once listed yourselves in your baptism under Christ, will now take pay, and make it your profession to fight against him. The emptier your purses are of gain so gotten, the richer you are; or at least, the fuller they are, you are so much the poorer. As we that are ministers do find by experience, that it was not without provocation from us that God of late hath let loose so many hands, and pens, and tongues against us, though our calling is more evidently owned by God than any one in the world besides, so I doubt not but you may find, upon due examination, that the late contempt which hath been cast upon your profession, is a reproof of your guilt from God who did permit it. Had lawyers and divines less lived to themselves, and more to God, we might have escaped, if not the scourge of reproachful tongues, yet at least the lashes of conscience. To deal freely with you, gentlemen, it is a matter that they who are strangers to your profession can scarce put any fair construction upon, that the worst cause, for a little money, should find an advocate among you. This driveth the standers-by upon this harsh dilemma, to think that either your understandings or your consciences are very bad. If, indeed, you so little know a good cause from a bad, then it must needs tempt men to think you very unskilful in your profession. The seldom and smaller differences of divines, in a more sublime and mysterious profession, is yet a discovery so far of their ignorance, and is imputed to their disgrace. But when almost every cause, even the worst that comes to the bar, shall have some of you for it, and some against it,

and in the palpablest cases you are some on one side and some on the other, the strange difference of your judgments doth seem to bewray their weakness. But if you know the causes to be bad which you defend, and to be good which you oppose, it more evidently bewrays a deplorate conscience. I speak not of your innocent or excusable mistakes in cases of great difficulty; nor yet of excusing a cause bad in the main from unjust aggravations: but when money will hire you to plead for injustice against your own knowledge, and to use your wits to defraud the righteous, and spoil his cause, or vex him with delays, for the advantage of your unrighteous client, I would not have your conscience for all your gains, nor your account to make for all the world. It is sad, that any known unrighteous cause should have a professed christian, in the face of a christian judicature, to defend it, and Satan should plead by the tongues of men so deeply engaged to Christ: but it is incomparably more sad, that almost every unjust cause should find a patron; and no contentious, malicious person should be more ready to do wrong, than some lawyers to defend him, for a (dear-bought) fee! Did you honestly obey God, and speak not a word against your judgment, but leave every unjust man to defend his own cause, what peace would it bring to your consciences; what honour to your now reproached profession; what relief to the oppressed; and what an excellent cure to the troublesome contentions of proud or malicious men!

3. To you, juries and witnesses, I shall say but this, You also are not your own; and he that owneth you hath told you, that he "will not hold him guiltless that taketh his name in vain." It is much into your hands that the law hath committed the cause of the just; should you betray it by perjury and false witness, while their is a conscience in your guilty breast, and a God in heaven, you shall not want a witness of your sin, or a revenger of the oppressed, if the blood of Christ on your sound repentance do not rescue you.

4. If plaintiff and defendant did well consider that they are not their own, they would not be too prone to quarrels, but would lose their right, when God, the chief Proprietor, did require it. Why do you not rather take wrong, and suffer yourselves to be defrauded, than do wrong and defraud, and that your brethren? 1 Cor. vi. 7—9.

To conclude: I earnestly entreat you all, that have heard me this day, that when you go home, you will betake yourselves to a sober consideration of the claim that God hath laid to you, and the right he hath in you, and all that you have: and resolve, without any further delay, to give him his own; and give it not to his enemies, and yours. When you see the judgment seat, and the prisoners waiting to receive their sentence, remember with what inconceivable glory and terror your Judge will shortly come to demand his due; and what an inquiry must be made into the tenour of your lives. As you see the eclipsed sun withdraw its light,[a] so remember how before this dreadful final judgment, the sun and moon, and the whole frame of nature, shall be dissolved! and how God will withdraw the light of his countenance from those that have neglected him in the day of their visitation. As ever you would be his, then see that you be his now; own him as your absolute Lord, if you expect he should own you then as his people. Woe to you that ever you were born, if you put God then to distrain for his due, and to take that up in your punishment, which you denied to give him in voluntary obedience. You would all be his in the time of your extremity; then you cry to him as your God for deliverance. Hear him now, if you would then be heard: live to him now, and live with him for ever. A popish priest can persuade multitudes of men and women to renounce the very possession of worldly goods, and the exercise of their outward callings in a mistaken devotedness to God. May not I, then, hope to prevail with you to devote yourselves, with the fruit of your callings and possessions, to his unquestionable service? Will the Lord of mercy but fasten these persuasions upon your hearts, and cause them to prevail, what a happy day will this prove to us all! God will have his own, the church will have your utmost help, the souls of those about you will have the fruit of your diligence and good examples, the commonwealth will have the fruit of your fidelity, the poor will have the benefit of your charity, I shall have the desired end of my labour, and yourselves will have the great and everlasting gain.

A SERMON

OF THE

ABSOLUTE SOVEREIGNTY OF CHRIST; AND THE NECESSITY OF MAN'S SUBJECTION, DEPENDENCE, AND CHIEFEST LOVE TO HIM.

PREACHED BEFORE THE JUDGES OF ASSIZE, AT WORCESTER.

"But those mine enemies, which would not that I should reign over them, bring hither, and slay them before me."
Luke xix. 27.

CHRISTIAN READER,

WHEN I had resolved, at the desire of the Honourable Judge of Assize, to publish the foregoing sermon, I remembered that, about six years before, I had preached another on the like occasion, on a subject so like, and to so like a purpose, that I conceived it not unfit to be annexed to the former. I have endeavoured to

[a] This sermon was preached in the time of the eclipse.

show you, in both these sermons, that Christ may be preached without antinomianism; that terror may be preached without unwarrantable preaching the law; that the gospel is not a mere promise, and that the law itself is not so terrible as it is to the rebellious: as also what that superstructure is, which is built on the foundation of general redemption rightly understood; and how ill we can preach Christ's dominion in his universal propriety and sovereignty, or yet persuade men to sanctification and subjection, without this foundation. I have laboured to fit all, or almost all, for matter and manner, to the capacity of the vulgar. And though, for the matter, it is as necessary to the greatest, yet is it for the vulgar, principally, that I publish it; and had rather it might be numbered with those books which are carried up and down the country from door to door in pedlars' packs, than with those that lie on booksellers' stalls, or are set up in the libraries of learned divines. And to the same use would I design the most of my published labours, should God afford me time and ability, and contentious brethren would give me leave.

RICHARD BAXTER.

August 7, 1654.

PSALM II. 10—12.

BE WISE NOW THEREFORE, O YE KINGS: BE INSTRUCTED, YE JUDGES OF THE EARTH. SERVE THE LORD WITH FEAR, AND REJOICE WITH TREMBLING, &c.

To waste this precious hour in an invective against injustice and its associates, is none of my purpose; they are sins so directly against the principles in nature, so well known, I believe, to you all, and so commonly preached against upon these occasions, that upon the penalty of forfeiting the credit of my discretion, I am bound to make choice of a more necessary subject. What! have we need to spend our time and studies to persuade christians from bribery, perjury, and oppression; and from licking up the vomit which pagans have cast out? and that in an age of blood and desolation, when God is taking the proudest oppressors by the throat, and raising monuments of justice upon the ruins of the unjust? And I would fain believe that no corrupt lawyers do attend your judicatures, and that Jezebel's witnesses dwell not in our country, nor yet a jury that fear not an oath. I have therefore chosen another subject, which being of the greatest moment, can never be unseasonable; even to proclaim him who is constituted the King and Judge of all, to acquaint you with his pleasure, and to demand your subjection.

The chief scope of the Psalm is, to foretell the extent and prevalency of the kingdom of Christ, admonishing his enemies to submit to his government, deriding the vanity of their opposing projects and fury, and forewarning them of their ruin if they come not in.

The verses which I have read are the application of the foregoing prediction, by a serious admonition to the proudest offenders: they contain, 1. The persons admonished, "kings and judges." 2. Their duty: 1. In general to God, "serve him;" with the adjuncts annexed: 1. Rejoicing. 2. Fear and trembling. 2. More especially their duty to the Son, "kiss him." 3. The motives to this duty. 1. Principally and directly expressed, "lest he be angry;" which anger is set forth by the effect, "and ye perish:" which perishing is aggravated, 1. From the suddenness and unexpectedness, "in the way." 2. From the dreadfulness, "kindled." 1. It is fire, and will kindle and burn. 2. A little of it will produce this sad effect. 3. It will be woe to those that do not escape it; which woe is set forth by the contrary happiness of those that by submission do escape. 2. The motives subservient and implied are in the monitory words, "be wise, be learned," *q. d.* else you will show and prove yourselves men of ignorance and madness, unlearned and unwise.

Some questions here we should answer for explication of the terms: as,

1. Whether the Lord in verse 11, and the Son in verse 12, be both meant of Christ the Second Person?

2. Whether the anger here mentioned be the anger of the Father or the Son, "lest he be angry?" I might spend much time here to little purpose, in showing you the different judgment of divines of these, when in the issue there is no great difference, whichever way we take them.

3. What is meant by "kissing the Son?" I answer, according to its threefold object, it hath a threefold duty contained in it.

1. We kiss the feet in token of subjection; so must we kiss the Son.

2. We kiss the hand in token of dependence; so must we kiss the hand of Christ; that is, resign ourselves to him, and expect all our happiness and receivings from him.

3. We kiss the mouth in token of love and friendship; and so also must we kiss the Son.

4. What is meant by "perishing in the way?" I answer, (omitting the variety of interpretations,) it is their sudden, unexpected perishing in the heat of their rage, and in pursuit of their designs against the kingdom of Christ.

I know no other terms of any great difficulty here.

Many observations might be hence raised: as,

1. Serving the Lord is the great work and business that the world hath to do.

2. This service should be accompanied with rejoicing.

3. So should it also with fear and trembling.

4. There is no such opposition between spiritual joy and fear, but that they may and must consist together.

5. Scripture useth familiar expressions concerning man's communion with Christ, such as this, "kiss the Son."

6. There is anger in God, or that which we cannot conceive better of than under the notion of anger.

7. There is a way to kindle this anger; it is man that kindleth it.

8. The way to kindle it chiefly is not kissing the Son.

9. The kindling of it will be the perishing of the sinner.

10. The enemies of Christ shall perish suddenly and unexpectedly.

11. A little of God's anger will utterly undo them.

12. They are blessed men that escape it, and miserable that must feel it.

13. It is therefore notorious folly to neglect Christ, and stand out.

14. Kings, judges, and rulers of the earth, are the first men that Christ summons in, and the chief in the calamity if they stand out.

But I will draw the scope of the text into this one doctrine; in the handling whereof I shall spend the time allotted me.

Doct. No power or privilege can save that man from the fearful, sudden, consuming wrath of God, that doth not unfeignedly love, depend upon, and subject himself unto the Lord Jesus Christ.

If they be the greatest kings and judges, yet if they do not kiss the mouth, the hand, the feet of Christ, his wrath will be kindled, and they will perish in the way of their rebellion and neglect.

In handling this point I shall observe this order.

1. I will show you what this love, dependence, and subjection are.

2. What wrath it is that will thus kindle and consume them.

3. Why this kissing the Son is the only way to escape it.

4. Why no power or privilege else can procure their escape.

5. The application.

For the first, I shall only give you a naked description, wishing that I had time for a fuller explication.

1. Subjection to Christ is, the acknowledging of his absolute sovereignty, both as he is God, Creator, and as Redeemer over all the world, and particularly ourselves; and a hearty consent to this his sovereignty, especially that he be our Lord, and his laws our rule; and a delivering up ourselves to him to be governed accordingly.

2. This dependence on Christ is, when, acknowledging the sufficiency of his satisfaction, and his power and willingness to save all that receive him, manifested in his free universal offer in the gospel, we do heartily accept him for our only Saviour, and accordingly, renouncing all other, do wait upon him believingly for the benefits of his sufferings and office, and the performance of his faithful covenant to us, in restoring us to all the blessings which we lost, and advancing us to a far greater everlasting glory.

3. This affection to Christ is, when, in the knowledge and sense of his love to us, both common and especial, and of his own excellency, and the blessedness of enjoying him, and the Father and life by him, our hearts do choose him, and the Father by him, as our only happiness, and accordingly love him above all things in the world.

As this threefold description containeth the sum of the gospel, so hath it nothing but what is of necessity to sound christianity. If any one of these three be not found in thy heart, either I have little skill in divinity, or thou hast no true christianity, nor canst be saved in that condition.

Object. But do not the Scriptures make believing the condition of the covenant? But here is a great deal more than believing.

Answ. Sometimes faith is taken in a narrower sense, and then it is not made the sole condition of the new covenant; but repentance, and forgiving others, are joined with it as conditions of our forgiveness; and obedience and perseverance, as conditions of our continued justification and salvation. But when faith is made the sole condition of the covenant, then it comprehendeth essentially, (not only supposeth as precedent or concomitant,) if not all three, yet at least the two first of the fore-described qualifications; viz. dependence and subjection, which, if it were well understood, would much free the common sort of christians from their soul-destroying mistakes, and the body of divinity from a multitude of common errors, and our religion from much of that reproach of solifidianism which is cast upon it by the papists.

2. I must be as brief in opening the second thing, viz. What wrath it is that will thus kindle and consume them. What wrath is in God we need not here trouble ourselves to inquire, but only what is intimated in the threats or curses of the covenants. As there are two covenants, so each hath his proper penalty for its violation.

1. Then till men do come in and submit to Christ they lie under the wrath of God for all their sins, as they are against the covenant of works, or they are liable to the curse of that covenant. Christ's death hath taken away the curse of that covenant; not absolutely from any man, but conditionally, which becomes absolute when the condition is performed. The elect themselves are not by nature under the covenant of grace, but remain under the curse of the first covenant till they come in to Christ.

2. Whosoever rejecteth or neglecteth his grace, and so finally breaketh the new covenant, must also bear the curse or penalty thereof, besides all the former, which will be a far greater curse, even as the blessings of this covenant are far greater than those of the first. It was a heavy punishment to be cast out of Paradise, and from the presence and favour of God, and to be cursed by him, and subjected to eternal death, and all creatures below cursed for our sakes; to bear all those curses and plagues threatened in Deut. xxvii. and xxviii. and to have the wrath of God smoke against us, &c. as Deut. xxix. 20. "But of how much sorer punishment shall he be thought worthy, that doth tread under-foot the blood of this covenant, and do despite to the Spirit of grace?" Heb. x. 28, 29. It is true, that for all other sins the wrath of God cometh upon the children of disobedience, (or unpersuadableness,) that is, on them that will not be persuaded to obey the Lord Christ, Eph. v. 6. But it is on no other with us; for this is the condemnation, "that light has come into the world, and men love darkness rather than light," John i. 19.

3. Why is this kissing the Son, that is, loving, depending on, and submitting to him, the only way to escape these curses?

Answ. 1. The most proper and primary reason which can be given, is, the will of the great Lawgiver, who, having absolute sovereignty over us, might dispose of us as he please, and make us such laws and conditions as seem best to his wisdom, upon which our justification and salvation should depend: he hath resolved that this shall be the only condition and way; and that, as no man shall be justified by a mere Christ, or his death, abstracted from faith, (that is of age and use of reason,) so this faith shall be the condition upon which they shall be justified: or, as a Christ neglected shall save no man, so the accepting or receiving of him shall justify and save them, as the condition of the covenant performed, under which notion it is that faith justifieth.

2. Yet other improper or subordinate reasons (which receive their life from the former, and without it would be no reasons) may be given: as, 1. from the equity; and, 2. from the suitableness and conveniency.

1. It is but equal that he who hath bought us, and that so dearly, and from a state so deplorable and desperate as we were in, should be acknowledged and accepted for our Saviour and our Lord; and that we who are not our own, "but are bought with a price, should glorify him with our bodies and souls.

which are his," 1 Cor. vi. 20; vii. 23; especially when for that end he both died and rose again, that he might rule, or be Lord over, both quick and dead, Rom. xiv. 9. If one of you should buy a man from the galleys or gallows, with the price of your whole estate, or the life of your only son, would you not expect that he should be at your disposal? that he should love you, depend on you, and be subject to you?

2. And as salvation by free grace through Christ is a way most suitable to God's honour, and to our own necessitous and low condition, so, in subordination thereto, the way of believing is most rationally conducible to the same ends. As we could not have had a fitter way to the Father than by Christ, so neither could there be a fitter way to Christ, or means to partake of him, than by faith: for though I cannot call it the instrumental cause of our justification, either active or passive, yet is this faith, or acceptation of Christ for our Saviour and King, which is here called "kissing the Son," the fairest condition that we could reasonably expect, and the most apparently tending to the honour of our Redeemer; applying and appropriating to ourselves the person, righteousness, and benefits procured and offered, but not the least of the honour of the work. All we do is but to accept what Christ hath procured, and that must be by the special assistance of his Spirit too.

4. The fourth thing I promised, is to show you why no other privilege or power in the world can save him that doth not kiss the Son. It may here suffice that I have showed you God's determination to the contrary. But further consider, (if any should hope to escape by their dignities, titles, friends, strength, or any other endowments or virtuous qualifications,) 1. What is their task. 2. What is their power to perform it.

1. They must resist the irresistible will of God. They must do that which heaven or earth, men or devils, were never able yet to do. They have resisted his laws and his love, but they could never resist his purpose or his power. The power that undertaketh to save an enemy, or neglecter of Christ, must first overcome the power of the Almighty, and conquer him that doth command the world. And who hath the strength that is sufficient for this? Sinner, before thou venture thy soul upon such a mad conceit, or think to be saved whether God will or not, try first thy skill and strength in some inferior attempt; bid the sun or moon stand still in the firmament, invert the several seasons of the year, bid the snow and frost to come in summer, and the flowers and fruits to spring in winter; command the streams to turn their course, or the tide its times, or the winds their motion. If these will obey thee, and thy word can prevail with them against the law of their Creator, then mayst thou proceed with the greater confidence and courage, and have some hope to save the neglecters of Christ. Or try first whether thou canst save thy present life against the course of nature and will of God: call back thine age and years that are past; command thy pains and sickness to be gone; chide back this bold approaching death? Will they not obey thee? Canst thou do none of these? How then canst thou expect the saving of thy soul against the determinate will and way of God? Where dwelleth that man, or what was his name, that did neglect Christ, and yet escape damnation? Who hath hardened himself against him and hath prospered? Job ix. 4. And dost thou think, then, to be first? Thou mayst, perhaps, knock boldly at the gate of heaven, and plead thy greatness, thy virtues, thy alms deeds, and formal devotion, but thou shalt receive a sadder answer than thou dost expect. Jesus we know, and obediential faith in him we know, but who are ye?

2. He that will save the soul, that loveth not, dependeth not on, and subjecteth not himself to Christ, must first make false the word of God, and make the true and faithful God a liar? This is another part of his task: God hath given it under his hand for truth, that "he that believeth not is condemned already," John iii. 18; that "he shall not see life, but the wrath of God abideth on him," John iii. 36; that they who are invited to Christ, and make light of it, or make excuses, "shall never taste of his supper," Luke xiv. 24; Matt. xxii. 5. 8; that "it shall be easier for Sodom in the day of judgment, than for that city which refuseth the offers of the gospel," Matt. x. 15; that whosoever would not have Christ to reign over them "shall be brought forth at last and destroyed before him as his enemies," Luke xix. 27; that "they shall all be damned that believe not the truth, but have pleasure in unrighteousness," 2 Thess. ii. 12, &c. And hath the Almighty said that thus it shall be? Who, then, is he that dare say it shall not be? Is this the concluded decree of Heaven? What power or policy is able to reverse it? Hath God said it, and will he not do it?

Thus you see his task that will undertake to save one neglecter of Christ.

2. Let us now consider what power that is which must perform it. If it be done it must be either, 1. By wisdom; or, 2. By strength; whereas, the chiefest of men, even the kings and judges of the earth, are both ignorant and impotent.

1. Ignorant. Though judges are learned in the repute of the world, alas! poor crawling, breathing dust! do you know the secrets of your Maker's counsel? And are you able to overreach them, and frustrate his designs? Doth this book know what is written in it? Can the seat you sit on overtop your counsels? More likely than for you to overtop the Lord. Silly worms! you know not what God is, nor know you any one of his unrevealed thoughts, no more than that pillar doth know your thoughts. You know not what you are yourselves, nor see any further than the superficies of your skin. What is thy soul; and when didst thou receive it? Dost thou know its form; or didst thou feel it enter? Which part didst thou feel it first possess? Thou canst call it a spirit, but knowest thou what a spirit is; or rather only what it is not? Thou knowest not that whereby thou knowest. And how was thy body formed in the womb? What was it a hundred years ago? what is that vital heat and moisture? what causeth that order and diversity of its parts? when will the most expert anatomists and physicians be agreed? Why, there are mysteries in the smallest worm, which thou canst not reach; nor couldst thou resolve the doubts arising about an ant or atom, much less about the sun, or fire, or air, or wind, &c. and canst thou not know thyself, nor the smallest part of thyself, nor the smallest creature; and yet canst thou overreach the everlasting counsels.

2. And is thy might and power any greater than thy policy? Why, what are the kings and rulers of the earth but lumps of clay, that can speak and go; moving shadows, the flowers of a day, a corruptible seed, blown up to that swelled consistence in which it appears, as children blow their bubbles of soap, somewhat invisible condensate; which, that it may become visible, is become more gross, and so more vile, and will shortly be almost all turned into invisible again; and that little dust which corruption

leaves by the force of fire, may be dissipated yet more, and then where is this specious part of the man? Surely now that body, which is so much esteemed, is but a loathsome lump of corruptible flesh, covered with a smooth skin, and kept a little while from stinking by the presence of the soul, and must shortly be cast out of sight into a grave, as unfit for the sight or smell of the living, and there be consumed with rottenness and worms. These are the kings and rulers of the earth; this is the power that must conquer heaven, and save them that rebel against Christ the Lord. They that cannot live a month without repairing their consuming bodies by food, one part whereof doth turn to their vital blood and spirits, and the other to most loathsome, unsufferable excrements, so near is the kin between their best and worst; judge all you that have common reason, whether he that cannot keep himself alive an hour, and shortly will not be able to stir a finger to remove the worms that feed upon his heart, be able to resist the strength of Christ, and save the soul, that God hath said and sworn shall not be saved. Ah! poor souls, that have no better saviours. And well may Christ, his truth, and cause, prevail, that have no stronger enemies.

Use 1. You have here a text that will fully inform you how you are like to speed at the bar of Christ; who shall die and who shall live. The great assize is near at hand, the feet of our Judge are even at the door. Go thy way, unbelieving sinner; when thou hast had all the pleasure that sin will afford thee, lie down in the dust and sleep awhile, the rousing voice shall quickly awake thee, and thine eyes shall see that dreadful day. Oh blessed day! Oh doleful day! Blessed to the saints, doleful to the wicked. Oh the rejoicing! oh the lamenting that there will be! The triumphant shoutings of joyful saints; the hideous roaring cries of the ungodly, when each man hath newly received his doom, and there is nothing but eternal glory and eternal fire. Beloved hearers, every man of you shall shortly there appear, and wait as the trembling prisoner at the bar, to hear what doom must pass upon you. Do you not believe this? I hope you do believe it. Why what would you give now to know, for certain, how it shall then go with you? Why here is the book by which you must be judged, and here is the sum of it in my text, and the grounds upon which the Judge will then proceed. Will you but go along with me, and answer the questions which hence I shall put to you, and search and judge yourselves by them as you go, you may know what doom you may then expect: only deal faithfully, and search thoroughly, for self-flattery will not prevent your sorrow.

And here you must know that it is the kiss of the heart, and not of the lips, which we must here inquire after. The question will not be at the great day, who hath spoken Christ fair; or who hath called themselves by the name of christians; or who hath said the creed or the Lord's prayer oftenest; or cried, Lord, Lord; or come to church; or carried a Bible; or who hath held this opinion, or who that. It would make a man's heart ache to think how zealously men will honour the shadow of Christ, and bow at his name, and reverence the image of the cross which he died on, and the names and relics of the saints that died for him, and yet do utterly neglect the Lord himself, and cannot endure to be governed by him, and resist his Spirit, and scorn his strict and holy ways, and despitefully hate them that most love and obey him, and yet believe themselves to be real christians. For God's sake, sirs, do not so delude your immortal souls, as to think your baptism, and your outward devotion, and your good meanings as you call them, and your righteous dealing with men, will serve the turn to prove you christians. Alas! this is but, with Judas, to kiss the mouth of Christ, and indeed to fetch your death from those blessed lips, from whence the saints do fetch their life. I will show you some surer signs than these.

1. And, first, let me a little inquire into your subjection to Christ. Do you remember the time when you were the servants of sin, and when Satan led you captive at his will, and the prince of darkness ruled in your souls, and all within you was in a carnal peace? Do you remember when the Spirit in the word came powerfully upon your hearts, and bound Satan and cast him out, and answered all your reasonings, and conquered all your carnal wisdom, and brought you from darkness to light, and from the power of Satan to God? Acts xxvi. 18. Or, at least, are you sure that now you live not under the same lord and laws as the ungodly do? Hath Christ now the only sovereignty in your souls? Is his word thy law, which thou darest not pass? Doth it bound thy thoughts, and rule thy tongue, and command thyself, and all thou hast? Hast thou laid all down at the feet of Christ, and resigned thyself and all to his will, and devoted all to his disposal and service? If custom bid thee curse and swear, and Christ forbid thee, which dost thou obey? If thy appetite bid thee take thy cups, or fare deliciously every day; if thy company bid thee play the good fellow, or scorn the godly; if thy covetousness bid thee love the world, and Christ forbid thee, which dost thou obey? If Christ bid thee be holy, and walk precisely, and be violent for heaven, and strive to enter in, and the world and the flesh be enemies to all this, and cry it down as tedious folly, which dost thou obey? Dost thou daily and spiritually worship him in private, and in thy family, and teach thy children and servants to fear the Lord? I entreat you, sirs, deal truly in answering these questions: never man was saved by the bare title of a christian. If you are not subject to Christ, you are not christians, no more than a picture or a carcass is a man, and your salvation will be such as your christianity is. Subjection is an essential part of thy faith, and obedience is its fruit. In short, then, dost thou make him thy fear, and tremble at his word? Darest thou run upon fire or water, sword or cannon, rather than wilfully run upon his displeasure? Wouldst thou rather displease thy dearest friend, the greatest prince, or thine own flesh, than wittingly provoke him? When Christ speaks against thy sweetest sin, thy nature, or custom, or credit, or life, against thy rooted opinions, or thy corrupt traditions, art thou willing to submit to all that he revealeth? Dost thou say, "Speak, Lord, for thy servant heareth? Lord, what wouldst thou have me to do? I am ready to do thy will, O God."

Beloved hearers, this is the frame of every servant of Christ, and this is the acknowledging and accepting him for your Lord. I beseech you cozen not your souls with shows and formalities. If ever you be saved without this subjection, it must be without Christ's merits or mercy. It must be in a way that Scripture revealeth not, nay, it must be in despite of God, his truth must be falsified, and his power must be mastered, before the disobedient can be saved from his wrath.

2. Examine, also, your dependence on Christ, whether you kiss his hand as well as his feet. Do you understand that you are all by nature condemned men, and liable to the everlasting wrath of God; that Christ hath interposed and paid this debt, and bought us as his own by the satisfaction of that

justice; that all things are now delivered into his hands, (John xiii. 3,) and he is made Head over all things to his church? Eph. i. 21, 22. Dost thou take him for thy only Saviour, and believe the history of his life and passion, the truth of his divine and human nature, his resurrection, his office, and his approaching judgment? Dost thou see that all thy supposed righteousness is but vanity and sin, and that thyself art unable to make the least satisfaction to the law by thy works or sufferings, and if his blood do not wash thee, and his righteousness justify thee, thou must certainly be damned yet, and perish for ever? Dost thou, therefore, cast thyself into his arms, and venture thy everlasting state upon him, and trust him with thy soul, and fetch all thy help and healing from him? When sin is remembered, and thy conscience troubled, and the forethoughts of judgment do amaze thy soul, dost thou then fetch thy comfort from the views of his blood, and the thoughts of the freeness and fulness of his satisfaction, his love, and gospel offers and promises? Dost thou so build upon his promise of a happiness hereafter, that thou canst let go all thy happiness here, and drink of his cup, and be baptized with his baptism, and lose thy life upon his promise that thou shalt save it? Canst thou part with goods and friends, and all that thou hast, in hope of a promised glory which thou never sawest? If thou canst thus drink with him of the brook in the way, thou shalt also with him lift up the head, Psalm cx. 7. Dost thou perceive a Mediator as well as a God in all thy mercies, both special and common, and taste his blood in all that thou receivest, and wait upon his hand for thy future supplies? Why, this is kissing the hand of Christ, and depending upon him. Oh how contrary is the case of the world, whose confidence is like the Samaritan's worship! they trust God and their wits and labours, Christ and their supposed merits; I would I might not say Christ and deceit, and wicked contrivances. Oh blasphemous! joining of heaven and hell to make up one foundation of their trust!

3. Examine a little also your love to Christ. Do you thus kiss the Son? Do your souls cleave to him, and embrace him with the strongest of your affections? Sirs, though there is nothing that the blind world is more confident in than this, that they love Christ with all their hearts, yet there is nothing wherein they are more false and faulty. I beseech you, therefore, deal truly in answering here. Are your hearts set upon the Lord Jesus? Do you love him above all things in this world? Do you stick at your answer? Do you not know? Sure, then, at best you love him but little, or else you could not choose but know it. Love is a stirring and sensible affection; you know what it is to love a friend. Feel by this pulse whether you live or die. Doth it beat more strongly toward Christ than to any thing else? Never question, man, the necessity of this; he hath concluded, If thou love any thing more than him, thou art not worthy of him, nor canst be his disciple. Are thy thoughts of Christ thy freest and thy sweetest thoughts? Are thy speeches of him thy sweetest speeches? When thou awakest art thou still with him; and is he next thy heart? When thou walkest abroad, dost thou take him in thy thoughts? Canst thou say, and lie not, that thou wast ever deeply in love with him, that thou dost love him but as heartily as thou dost thy friend, and art as loth to displease him, and as glad of his presence, and as much troubled at his strangeness or absence? Hath thy minister, or godly acquaintance, ever heard thee bemoaning thy soul for want of Christ, or inquiring what thou shouldst do to attain him? or thy family heard thee commending his excellency, and labouring to kindle their affections towards him? Why, love will not be hid; when it hath its desire, it will be rejoicing, and when it wants it, it will be complaining. Or, at least, can thy conscience witness thy longings, thy groans, thy prayers for a Christ? Wilt thou stand to the testimony of these witnesses? Do you love his weak, his poor, despised members? Do you visit them, clothe them, feed them, to your power? Not only in a common natural compassion to them as they are your neighbours, but do you love or relieve a prophet in the name of a prophet, or a disciple in the name of a disciple? Matt. x. 40, 42. Shall all these decide the question?

Beloved hearers, I profess to you all, in the name of our Lord, that it is not your bold and confident affirming that you love Christ, which will serve your turn when Christ shall judge; he will search deep, and judge according to the truth in the inward parts. How many thousands will then perish as his utter enemies, that verily thought themselves his friends! How easily now might they find their mistake if they would but be at the pains to examine themselves! O try, try, sirs, before God try you; judge yourselves before Christ try you. It would grieve a man's heart that knows what it is to love Christ, to believe, to be subject to him, to see how rare these are in the world, and yet how confident and careless most men are. It may be you may think much that I so question your love, yet Christ that knew all things, questioned Peter's love to him, and that three times, till it grieved Peter. I am a stranger to the most of you, and therefore know not your conditions or inclinations. Yet judge me not censorious if I fear the worst, and if I measure you by the rest of the world; and then I may confidently and sadly conclude that Christ hath few loving subjects among you. If we could hear your oaths and vain speeches turned to heavenly, soul-edifying discourse, and your covetousness to conscionableness, and see that the word of Christ were your law, and that you laid out your endeavours for heaven in good earnest, then we should say, These people are the loving subjects of Christ. But when men are enemies to Christ's doctrine, and ways, and worship, and had rather live after the flesh, and the world, and the traditions of their fathers, and are notorious for profaneness, superstition, and enmity to reformation, who can choose but condole your case? And if your obstinacy will not endure us to help you, yet you shall give us leave, whether you will or no, to lament you.

Use 2. But it is time that I turn my speech to exhortation, and oh that you would encourage me with your resolutions to obey! My business here to-day is, as his herald and ambassador, to proclaim the Lord Jesus your King and Saviour, and to know whether you will heartily acknowledge and take him so to be or not. And to persuade you to take so fair an offer while you may have it, and to kiss the Son lest his wrath be kindled. This is my business here, in which if I had not some hope to speed, the Lord knows I would not have been here to-day. You will say, This is a common errand; do you think we never heard of Christ before? I confess it is common, blessed be God for it, (and long may it so continue and increase, and let it be as constant and durable to us as the sun in the firmament: and the Lord grant that England's sins or enemies may never bereave them of the blessing of the gospel, and then it will be a happier land than yet ever was any on the face of the earth,) but is it as common to receive Christ in love and obedience? I would it were. I know the name of Christ is common. The swearer doth swear by it, the beggar begs by it, the charmer puts it into his charms, and the jester into his jests, and every papist and ignorant protestant doth mutter it ofttimes over in his prayers. But who trembleth at it? or triumpheth in it? Who maketh it his fear and his joy? and give up their souls and lives to be governed by Christ? I do here solemnly proclaim to you that the Lord Jesus will not be put off with your compliments; he cares not for your mere name of christianity, nor your cap, nor your knee. If thy heart be not set upon him, thou art none of his. His word must be your law, and you must depend on him alone for soul and body, or never look for mercy at his hands. He is the author of eternal salvation to them only that obey him, Heb. v. 9.

What say you then, sirs, in answer to my message? And what course do you resolve upon? Shall Christ be your love, and your Lord, or not? Will you kiss the Son, or will you slight him still? Methinks you should easily be resolved, and say, Away with pleasure, and credit, and worldly gain; away with these bewitching delights and companions: Christ hath bought my heart, and he shall have it; he is my Lord, and I will be ruled by him. Hearers, I hope God hath kept you alive till now to show you mercy, and brought some sinners hither to-day to prevail with their hearts; and my hope is somewhat strengthened by God's disposal of my own spirit: I was strongly tempted to have preached this sermon in the enticing words of human wisdom, tending to a proud ostentation of parts; but Christ hath assisted me to conquer the temptation, and commanded me to preach him in plainness, and evidence of the Spirit. I come not to persuade you to opinions or factions, to be for this side, or for that, but to be with all your hearts for Christ, as ever you look that Christ should be for you: to love him as he that hath bought you from eternal wrath, and died to save you from the everlasting burnings; to lay hold on him with most earnest affectionate apprehension, as a man that is ready to drown would do upon a bough, or upon the hand of his friend that would pull him to the shore; to wait for the law of thy direction from him, and do nothing till thou hast asked counsel at his word, and know his mind, whether thou shouldst do it or no, till thou feel thy conscience bound by his law, that thou canst not stir till he give thee leave; that the commands of parents and princes may stoop to his, much more the commands of custom and company, of credit or pleasure, of the world or flesh: these are the things that I exhort you to; and I must tell you that Christ doth flatly expect them at your hands.

I will here back these exhortations with some persuading considerations. Think of what I say, and weigh it as we go. If I speak not truth and reason, then reject it with disdain, and spare not; but if it be, and thy conscience tell thee so, take heed then how thou dost neglect or reject it, lest thou be found a fighter against the Spirit, and lest the curse of God do seize upon that heart that would not yield to truth and reason.

And I will draw these considerations only from my text:

1. Thou art else a rebel against thy sovereign Lord. This I gather from the command in my text; and, indeed, the scope of the whole Psalm. God hath given thee into the hands of his Son, and made him Lord and King of all, and commanded all men to accept him, and submit unto him. Who can show such title to the sovereignty, such right to rule thee, as Christ can do? He is thy Maker, and so is not Satan; he dearly bought thee, and so did not the world; "Thou wast not redeemed with silver, and gold, and corruptible things," 1 Pet. i. 18. I make this challenge here in the behalf of Christ; let any thing in the world step forth and show a better title to thee, to thy heart, and to thy life, than Christ doth show, and let them take thy heart, and take the rule. But why do I speak thus? I know thou wilt confess it; and yet wilt thou not yield him thy chiefest love and obedience: out of thy own mouth then art thou condemned, and thou proclaimest thyself a knowing and wilful rebel.

2. To deny thy affections and subjection to Christ is the most barbarous unkindness that a sinner can be guilty of. Did he pity thee in thy lost estate, and take thee up when thou layest wounded in the way, and make thee a plaster of the blood of his heart? And is this thy requital? Did he come down from heaven to earth, to seek thee when thou wast lost, and take upon him all thy debt, and put himself into the prison of the world and flesh? Hath he paid for thy folly, and borne that wrath of God which thou must have suffered for ever? And doth he not now deserve to be entertained with most affectionate respect? But with a few cold thoughts instead of hearty love; and with a few formal words instead of worship? What hurt had it been to him if thou hadst perished? What would he have lost by it if thou hadst lain in hell? Would not justice have been glorified upon a disobedient wretch? Might not he have said to his Father, What are these worms and sinners to me? must I smart for their folly? must I suffer when they have sinned? must I debase myself to become man because they would have exalted themselves to become as God? If they will needs undo themselves, what is it to me? If they will cast themselves into the flames of hell, must I go thither to fetch them out? Thus Christ might have put off the suffering and the shame, and let it fall and lie where it was due: but he did not; his compassion would not suffer him to see us suffer; justice must be satisfied, the threat must be fulfilled; Christ seeth that we cannot overcome it, but he can; therefore, he comes down into flesh, he lives on earth, he fasteth, he weepeth, he is weary, he is tempted, he hath not a place to put his head, he is hated, he is spit upon, he is clothed as a fool and made a scorn, he sweateth blood, he is crucified with thieves, he bears the burden that would have sunk us all to hell; and must he after all this be neglected and forgotten, and his laws that should rule us be laid aside, and be accounted too strict and precise for us to live by? O let the heavens blush, and the earth be ashamed, at this barbarous ingratitude! How can such a people show their faces at his coming, or look him in the face when he shall judge them for this? Would you use a friend thus? No, nor an enemy. Methinks you should rather wonder with yourselves that ever Christ should give you leave to love him, and say, Will the Lord endure such a wretch to kiss him? Will he suffer himself to be embraced by those arms, which have been defiled so oft by the embracements of sin? Will he so highly honour me as to be his subject and his servant, and to be guided by such a blessed and perfect law? And doth he require no harder conditions than these for my salvation? Take, then, my heart, Lord, it is only thine; and oh that it were better worth the having, or take it and make it better: the spear hath opened me a passage to thy heart, let the Spirit open thee a passage into mine: deservedly may those gates be fuel for hell, that would not open to let in the King of glory.

3. To deny thy affection and subjection to the Son is the greatest folly and madness in the world.

Why doth he require this so earnestly at thy hands? Is it for thy hurt, or for thy good? Would he make a prey of thee for his own advantage? Is it any need that he hath of thee or of thy service, or because thou hast need of him for thy direction and salvation? Would he steal away thy heart, as the world doth, to delude it? Would he draw thee as Satan doth, to serve him, that he may torment thee? If so, it were no wonder that thou art so hardly drawn to him. But thou knowest sure that Christ hath none of these ends.

The truth is this: his dying on the cross is but part of the work that is necessary to thy salvation; this was but the paying of the debt; he must give thee moreover a peculiar interest, and make that to be absolutely thine, which was thine but conditionally; he must take off thy rags, and wash thy sores, and qualify thy soul for thy prepared glory, and bring thee out of the prison of sin and death, and present thee to his Father blameless and undefiled, and estate thee in greater dignity than thou fellest from: and all this must he do by drawing thee to himself, and laying himself upon thee as the prophet upon the child, and closing thy heart with his heart, and thy will with his will, and thy thoughts and ways with the rule of his word: and is this against thee, or for thee? Is there any hurt to thee in all this? I dare challenge earth and hell, and all the enemies of Christ in both, to show the least hurt that ever he caused to the soul of a believer, or the least wrong to the soul of any.

And must he then have such a stir to do thee good? Must he so beseech thee to be happy, and follow thee with entreaties? And yet art thou like a stock that neither hears nor feels? Nay, dost thou not murmur and strive against him, as if he were about to do thee a mischief, and would rather cut thy throat than cure thee, and were going to destroy thee, and not to save thee? I appeal to any that hath not renounced his reason, whether this be not notorious brutish unreasonableness; and whether thou be not like a beast, that must be cast or held while you dress his sores, than to a man that should help on his own recovery. Foolish sinner! it is thy sin that hurts thee, and not thy Saviour; why dost thou not rather strive against that? It is the devil that would destroy thee, and yet thou dost not grudge at thy obedience to him. Be judge thyself, whether this be wise or equal dealing.

Sinner, I beseech thee in the behalf of thy poor soul, if thou have such a mind to renounce thy Saviour, do it not till thou hast found a better master: say as Peter, "Whither shall we go, Lord? thou hast the words of eternal life:" and when thou knowest once where to be better, then go thy way, part with Christ, and spare not. If thy merry company, or thy honour, or thy wealth, or all the friends and delights in the world, will do that for thee which Christ hath done, and which at last he will do if thou stick to him, then take them for thy gods, and let Christ go. In the mean time let me prevail with thee, as thou art a man of reason, sell not thy Saviour till thou know for what; sell not thy soul till thou know why; sell not thy hopes of heaven for nothing. God forbid that thy wilful folly should bring thee to hell, and there thou shouldst lie roaring and crying out for ever, This is the reward of my neglecting Christ; he would have led me to glory, and I would not follow him; I sold heaven for a few merry hours, for a little honour, and ease, and delight to my flesh; here I lie in torment, because I would not be ruled by Christ, but chose my lusts and pleasures before him. Sinner, do not think I speak harshly or uncharitably to call this neglect of Christ thy folly: as true as thou livest and hearest me this day, except thy timely submission do prevent it, which God grant it may, thou wilt one of these days befool thyself a thousand times more than I now befool thee, and call thyself mad, and a thousand times mad, when thou thinkest how fair thou wast for heaven, and how ready Christ was to have been thy Saviour and thy Lord, and how light thou madest of all his offers; either this will prove true to thy cost, or else am I a false prophet, and a cursed deceiver. Be wise, therefore, be learned, and kiss the Son.

The former considerations were drawn from the aggravations of the sin; the following are drawn from the aggravations of the punishment, and from the words of the text too.

1. God will be angry if you kiss not the Son. His wrath is as fire, and this neglect of Christ is the way to kindle it. If thou art not a believer thou art condemned already; but this will bring upon thee a double condemnation. Believe it for a truth, all thy sins, as they are against the covenant of works, even the most heinous of them, are not so provoking and destroying as thy slighting of Christ. Oh! what will the Father say to such an unworthy wretch! Must I send my Son from my bosom to suffer for thee? Must he groan when thou shouldst groan, and bleed when thou shouldst bleed, and die when thou shouldst die? and canst thou not now be persuaded to embrace him, and obey him? Must the world be courted whilst he stands by? Must he have the naked title of thy Lord and Saviour while thy fleshly pleasures and profits have thy heart? What wrath can be too great, what hell too hot, for such an ungrateful, unworthy wretch! Must I prepare thee a portion of the blood of my Son, and wilt thou not be persuaded now to drink it? Must I be at so much cost to save thee, and wilt thou not obey that thou mayst be saved? Go seize upon him, justice, let my wrath consume thee, let hell devour thee, let thy own conscience for ever torment thee; seeing thou hast chosen death, thou shalt have it, and as thou hast rejected heaven, thou shalt never see it, "but my wrath shall abide upon thee for ever," John iii. 36. Woe to thee, sinner, if this be once thy sentence! Thou wert better have all the world angry with thee, and bound in an oath against thee, as the Jews against Paul, than that one drop of his anger should light upon thee; thou wert better have heaven and earth to fall upon thee, than one degree of God's displeasure.

2. As this wrath is of fire, so is it a consuming fire, and causeth the sinner utterly to perish. All this is plain in the text: not that the being of the soul will cease, such a perishing the sinner would be glad of; a happy man would he think himself, if he might die as the brutes, and be no more: but such wishes are vain. It is but a glimpse of his own condition, which he shall see in the great combustion of the world; when he seeth the heaven and earth on fire, he seeth but the picture of his approaching woe; but alas! it is he that must feel the devouring fire. The world will be but refined or consumed by its fire; but there must he burn, and burn for ever, and yet be neither consumed nor refined. The earth will not feel the flames that burn it, but his soul and body must feel it with a witness. Little know his friends that are honourably interring his corpse what his miserable soul is seeing and feeling. Here endeth the story of his prosperity and delights, and now begins the tragedy that will never end. Oh! how his merry days are vanished as a dream, and his jovial life as a tale that is told; his witty jests, his pleasant sports, his cards and dice, his merry company and wanton dal-

liance, his cups and queans, yea, his hopes of heaven and confident conceits of escaping this wrath, are all perished with him in the way: as the wax melteth before the fire, as the chaff is scattered before the wind, as the stubble consumeth before the flames, as the flowers do wither before the scorching sun; so are all his sinful pleasures withered, consumed, scattered, and melted. And is not the hearty embracing of Christ, and subjection to him, a cheap prevention of all this? Oh! who among you can dwell with the devouring fire? who can dwell with the everlasting burnings? Isa. xxxiii. 14. This God hath said he will surely do if you are able to gainsay and resist him: try your strength, read his challenge, "Who would set the briers and thorns against me in battle? I would go through them, I would burn them together," Isa. xxvii. 4.

3. This perishing will be sudden and unexpected, in the way of their sin and resistance of Christ, in the way of their fleshly delights and hopes; "They shall perish in the way," 1 Thess. v. 3; Matt. xxiv. 37. As fire doth terribly break out in the night when men are sleeping, and consumeth the fruit of their long labours; so will this fire break forth upon their souls: and how near may it be when you little think on it! A hundred to one but some of us present shall within a few months be in another world; and what world it will be you may easily conceive if you do not embrace and obey the Son. How many have been smitten, with Herod, in the midst of their vain glory! How many, like Ahab, have been wounded in fight, and dunged the earth with their flesh and blood, who left the Lord's people to be fed with bread and water of affliction, in confidence of their own return in peace! How many have been swallowed up like Pharaoh and his host, in their rash and malicious pursuit of the godly! Little thinks many an ignorant, careless soul what a change of his condition he shall shortly find: those thousands of souls that are now in misery did as little think of that doleful state while they were merrily pleasing the flesh on earth, and forgetting Christ and their eternal state, as you do now; they could as contemptuously jeer the preacher as you, and verily believed that all this talk was but words, and wind, and empty threats, and ventured their souls as boldly upon their carnal hopes. Little thought Sodom of the devouring fire when they were furiously assaulting the door of their righteous reprover! as little do the raging enemies of godliness among us think of the deplorable state which they are hastening to! They will cry out themselves then, Little did I think to see this day, or feel these torments! Why, thou wouldst not think of it, or else thou mightest; God told thee in Scripture, and ministers in their preaching, but thou wouldst not believe till it was too late.

4. A little of God's wrath will bring down all this upon those that embrace not and obey not the Son. If his wrath be kindled, yea, but a little, &c. As his mercy being the mercy of an infinite God, a little of it will sweeten a world of crosses; so therefore will a little of his wrath consume a world of pleasures: one spark fell among the Bethshemites, and consumed fifty thousand and seventy men, but for looking into the ark, till the people cry out, "Who can stand before this holy Lord God?" 1 Sam. vi. 19, 20. How then will the neglecters of Christ stand before him? Sirs, methinks we should not hear of this as strangers, or unbelievers! There did but one spark fall upon England, and what a combustion hath it cast this kingdom into! How many houses and towns hath it consumed! How many thousands of people hath it impoverished! How many children hath it left fatherless! and how many thousand bodies hath it bereaved of their souls! And though there are as many hearty prayers and tears poured forth to quench it as most kingdoms on earth have had, yet is the fire kindled afresh, and threateneth a more terrible desolation than before, as if it would turn us all to ashes. One spark fell upon Germany, another upon Ireland, and what it hath done there I need not tell you. If a little of this wrath do but seize upon thy body, what cries, and groans, and lamentations doth it raise! If it be on one member, yea, but a tooth, how dost thou roar with intolerable pain, and wouldst not take the world to live for ever in that condition! If it seize upon the conscience, what torments doth it cause, as if the man were already in the suburbs of hell! he thinketh every thing he seeth is against him; he feareth every bit he eateth should be his bane. If he sleep, he dreams of death and judgment; when he awketh, his conscience and horror awake with him: he is weary of living, and fearful of dying; even the thoughts of heaven are terrible to him, because he thinks it is not for him. Oh! what a pitiful sight is it to see a man under the wrath of God! And are these little sparks so intolerably hot? What then do you think are the everlasting flames? Beloved hearers, if God had not spoke this I durst not have spoke it: the desire of my soul is, that you may never feel it, or else I should never have chosen so unpleasing a subject, but that I hope the foreknowing may help you to prevent it: but let me tell you from God, that as sure as the heaven is over your head, and the earth under your feet, except the Son of God be nearer thy heart, and dearer to thy heart, than friends, or goods, or pleasures, or life, or any thing in this world, this burning wrath will never be prevented, Matt. x. 37; Luke xiv. 26.

5. When this wrath of God is thoroughly kindled, the world will discern the blessed from the wretched. "Then blessed are they that trust in him." It is the property of the wicked to be wise too late. Those that now they esteem but precise fools, will then be acknowledged blessed men. Bear with their scorns, christians, in the mean time; they will very shortly wish themselves in your stead, and would give all that ever they were masters of, that they had sought and loved Christ as earnestly as you, and had a little of your oil when they find their lamps are out, Matt. xxv. 8.

And now, hearers, what is your resolution? Perhaps you have been enemies to Christ, under the name of christians; will you be so still? Have you not loathed this busy, diligent serving of him; and hated them that most carefully seek him, more than the vilest drunkard or blasphemer? Have not his word, and service, and sabbaths, been a burden to you? Have not multitudes ventured their lives against his ordinances and government? Nay, is it not almost the common voice of the nation in effect: Give us our sports, and liberty of sinning; give us our readers, and singing men, and drunken preachers; give us our holidays and ceremonies, and the customs of our forefathers; away with these precise fellows, they are an eyesore to us; these precise preachers shall not control us, this precise Scripture shall be no law to us: and consequently, this Christ shall not rule over us?

How long hath England rebelled against his government! Mr. Udal told them, in the days of Queen Elizabeth, that if they would not set up the discipline of Christ in the church, Christ would set it up himself in a way that would make their hearts to ache. I think their hearts have ached by this time; and as they judged him to the gallows for his prediction, so hath Christ executed them by thousands for their rebellion against him; and yet they are as unwilling of his government as ever. The kings of the earth are afraid lest Christ's government should unking them; the rulers are jealous lest it will depose them from their dignities; even the reformers that have ventured all to set it up, are jealous lest it will encroach upon their power and privileges; kings are afraid of it, and think themselves but half kings, where Christ doth set up his word and discipline; parliaments are afraid of it, lest it should usurp their authority; lawyers are afraid of it, lest it should take away their gains, and the laws of Christ should overtop the laws of the land; the people are afraid of it, lest it will compel them to subjection to that law and way which their souls abhor: indeed, if men may be their own judges, then Christ hath no enemies in England at all, we are his friends, and all good christians. It is precisians and rebels that men hate, and not Christ: it is not the government of Christ that we are afraid of, but the domineering of aspiring, ambitious presbyters (viz. that generation of godly, learned, humble ministers, who have done more than ever did any before them, to make themselves uncapable of preferment or domineering); and when men disobey and disregard our doctrine, it is not Christ, but the preacher, that they despise and disobey. And if the Jews might so have been their own judges, it was not the Son of God whom they crucified, but an enemy to Cæsar, and a blasphemer that works by the devil. It was not Paul, a saint, that they persecuted, but one that they found to be a pestilent fellow, and a mover of sedition amongst the people. But were there no seditious persons but apostles and christians; nor no troublers of Israel but Elias; nor no enemies to Cæsar but Christ and his friends? Oh! God will shortly take off the veil of hypocrisy from the actions of the world, and make them confess that it was Christ they resisted, and that it was his holy ways and word that did kindle their fury; else would they as soon have fallen upon the ungodly rabble, as they did upon the most zealous and conscionable christians: and, however you mangle and deform them with your false accusations and reproach, he will then know and own his people and his cause, and will say to the world, In despising them you despised me; and, Inasmuch as you did it to one of these little ones, you did it unto me. As Dr. Stoughton saith, If you strike a schismatic, and God find a saint lie a-bleeding, and you to answer it, I would not be in your coat for more than you got by it. Hath the world ever gained by resisting Christ? Doth it make the crown sit faster on the heads of kings? Or, must they not rather do to Christ as King John to his supposed vicar, resign their crowns to him, and take them from him again as his tributaries, before they can hold them by a certain tenure? Read over but this Psalm and judge. Herod must kill the child Jesus to secure his crown: the Jews must kill him lest the Romans should come and take away their place and nation, John xi. 41. And did this means secure them; or did it bring upon them the destruction which they thought to avoid?

Or have the people been greater gainers by this than by their kings? What hath England got by resisting his gospel and government, by hating his servants, and by scorning his holy ways? What have you got by it in this city? What say you? Have you yet done with your enmity and resistance? Have you enough; or would you yet have more? If you have not done with Christ, he hath not done with you; you may try again, and follow on as far as Pharaoh if you will; but if you be not losers in the latter end, I have lost my judgment; and if you return in peace, God hath not spoken by me, 1 Kings xxii. 28.

Sirs, I am loth to leave you till the bargain be made. What say you? Do you heartily consent that Christ shall be your Sovereign, his word your law, his people your companions, his worship your recreation, his merits your refuge, his glory your end, and himself the desire and delight of your souls? The Lord Jesus Christ now waiteth upon you for your resolution and answer; thou wilt very shortly wait upon him for thy doom: as ever thou wouldst then have him speak life to thy soul, do thou now resolve upon the way of life. Remember thou art almost at death and judgment. What wouldst thou resolve if thou knewest that it were to-morrow? If thou didst but see what others do now suffer for neglecting him, that doth now offer thee his grace, what wouldst thou then resolve to do? Sirs, it stirreth my heart to look upon you, (as Xerxes upon his army,) and to think that it is not a hundred years till every soul of you shall be in heaven or in hell! and it may be, not a hundred hours till some of your souls must take their leave of your bodies! When it comes to that, then you will cry, Away with the world, away with my pleasures; nothing can comfort me now but Christ! Why, then, will you not be of the same mind now? When the world cries, Away with this holiness, and praying, and talking of heaven! give us our sports, and our profits, and the customs of our forefathers, that is; "Away with Christ, and give us Barabbas;" then do you cry, Away with all these, and give us Christ.

Oh! if it might stand with the will of God that I might choose what effect this sermon should have upon your hearts, verily, it should be nothing that should hurt you in the least; but this it should be, it should now be to fasten upon your souls, and pierce into your consciences, as an arrow that is drawn out of the quiver of God; it should follow thee home to thy house, and bring thee down on thy knees in secret, and make thee there lament thy case, and cry out in the bitterness of thy spirit, Lord, I am the sinner that have neglected thee; I have tasted more sweetness in the world than in thy blood, and taken more pleasure in my earthly labours and delights than I have done in praying to thee, or meditating on thee; I have complimented with thee by a cold profession, but my heart was never set upon thee. And here should it make thee lie in tears and prayers, and follow Christ with thy cries and complaints, till he should take thee up from the dust, and assure thee of his pardon, and change thy heart, and close it with his own. If thou were the dearest friend that I have in the world, this is the success that I would wish this sermon with thy soul, that it might be as a voice still sounding in thine ears, that when thou art next in thy sinful company or delight, thou mightest, as it were, hear this voice in thy conscience, Is this thine obedience to him that bought thee? That when thou art next forgetting Christ, and neglecting his worship in secret, or in thy family, or public, thou mightest see this sentence, as it were, written upon thy wall, "Kiss the Son, lest he be angry, and thou perish." That thou mightest see it, as it were, written upon the tester of thy bed, as oft as thou liest down in an unregenerate state; and that it may keep thine eyes waking, and thy soul disquieted, and give thee no rest, till thou hadst rest in Christ. In a word; if it were but as much in my hands as it is in yours, what should become of this sermon, I hope it would be the best sermon to thee that ever thou heardest; it should lay thee at the feet of Christ, and leave thee in his arms. Oh! that I did but know what arguments would persuade you, and what words would work thy heart hereto! If I were sure it would prevail, I would come down from the pulpit, and go from man to man, upon my knees, with this request and advice in my text: Oh! "kiss the Son, lest he be angry, and you perish."

But if thy hardened heart make light of all, and thou go on still in thy careless neglect of Christ, and yet wilt not believe but thou art his friend and servant, I do here from the word and in the name of Christ, pass this sentence upon thy soul: Thou shalt go hence, and perhaps linger out in thy security a few days more, and then be called by death to judgment, where thou shalt be doomed to this everlasting fiery wrath. Make as light of it as thou wilt, feel it thou shalt: put it off and escape if thou canst; and when thou hast done, go boast that thou hast conquered Christ. In the mean time I require this congregation to bear witness that thou hadst warning.

This to all in general: my text yet directeth me to speak more particularly to the rulers and judges of the earth.

Honourable and reverend judges, worshipful magistrates, if you were all kings and emperors, all is one to Christ, you were but high and mighty dust and ashes: Christ sendeth his summons first to you, he knows the leaders' interest in the vulgar; you are the commanders in the host of God, and must do him more service than the common soldiers: if one of you should neglect him, and stand out against him, he will begin with you in the sight of the rest, and make your greatness a stepping-stone to the honour of his justice, that the lowest may understand what they have to do when they see the greatest cannot save themselves.

Shall I say you are wiser than the people, and therefore that this admonition is needless to you? No, then I should accuse the Spirit in my text: the cedars of the earth have always hardly stooped to Christ, which hath made so many of them rooted up. Your honours are an impediment to that self-abasing which he expecteth: your dignities will more tend to blind you than to illuminate. There are few of any sort, but fewest of the great, and wise, and mighty, that are called: yet a man would think that among those that have held out, in these trying times, there should be no need of these suspicions: but hath there not been always a succession of sinners, even of those that have beheld the ruin of their predecessors? Who would have thought that a generation that had seen the wonders in Egypt, and had passed through the sea, and been maintained in a wilderness with constant miracles, should yet be so vile idolaters, or murmuring unbelievers, that only two of them should enter into rest? The best of saints have need of self-suspicion and vigilancy. My advice to you, therefore, is this, learn wisdom by the examples that your eyes have seen: "Them that honour God, he will honour; and they that despise him, shall be lightly esteemed," 1 Sam. ii. 30.

More particularly, let me advise you as your duty to the Son, 1. That you take your commission and office as from him. I think it a doctrine more common than true, that ministers only are under Christ the Mediator, and magistrates are only under God as Creator. Christ is now Lord of all, and you are his servants; as there is no power but from God, so none from God but by Christ. Look upon yourselves as his vicegerents, therefore do not that which beseemeth not a vicegerent of Christ. Remember that as you see to the execution of the laws of the land, so will Christ see that his laws be obeyed by you, or executed on you. Remember when you sit and judge offenders, that you represent him that will judge you and all the world. And oh how lively a resemblance have you to raise your apprehension! Think with yourselves, Thus shall men tremble before his bar; thus shall they wait to hear their doom: and be sure that your judgment be such as may most lively represent the judgment of Christ, that the just may depart from your bar with joy, and the unjust with sadness. Let your justice be most severe where Christ is most severe; and so far as you can exercise your clemency, let it be about those offences which our laws are more rigorous against than the laws of God. Be sure yet that you understand the extent of your commission, that you are not the sole officers of Jesus Christ: you are under him as he is Head over all; ministers are under him as he is Head to his church, Eph. i. 22. Ministers are as truly the magistrates' teachers, as magistrates are their governors; yea, by as high and undoubted authority must they oversee, govern, and command ministerially, as their Lord's ambassadors, both kings and parliaments, to do whatsoever is written in this Bible, as you may command them to obey the laws of the land; yea, and as strict a bond lieth on you to obey them so far as they speak according to this word, and keep within the bounds of their calling, as doth on them to obey you in yours, Heb. xiii. 7, 17. Deal not with them so dissemblingly as to call them your pastors, teachers, overseers, and rulers, (as Scripture bids you,) and yet to learn of them but what you list, or to deny them leave to teach or advise you, further than they receive particular warrant and direction from yourselves. Should our assembly limit all their ministerial advice to the warrant and direction of parliament, and not extend it to the warrant and directions of Christ, would they not become the servants and pleasers of men? If you do not your best to set up all the government of Christ, even that in and proper to his church, as well as that which is over them, and for them, men may well think it is your own seats, and not Christ's, that you would advance. I would all the magistrates in England did well consider that Christ hath been teaching them this seven years, that their own peace or honours shall not be set up before his gospel and government; and that they do but tire themselves in vain in such attempts; then they would learn to read my text with the vulgar, *apprehendite disciplinam.* And if the decisive power of the ministry be doubtful, yet at least they would set up their nunciative in its vigour. Christ will rule England either as subjects or as rebels, and all that kings and states do gain by opposing his rule, will not add one cubit to the stature of their greatness. Yet do I not understand by the government of Christ, a rigid conformity to the model of this or that party, or faction, with a violent extirpation of every dissenter. It is the ignorant part of divines, (alas! such there are,) who, with the simple fellow in Erasmus, do expound Paul's *hæreticum hominem devita*, i. e. *de vita tolle.* It is the essentials, and not the accidentals, of discipline that I speak of: and if some disengaged standers-by be not mistaken who have the advantage by standing out of the dust of contention, each party hath some of these essentials, and the worst is nearer the truth than his adversary is aware of: and were not the crowd and noise so great that there is no hope of being heard, one would think it should be possible to reconcile them all. However, shall the work be undone while each party striveth to have the doing of it? I was afraid when I read the beginning and end of this controversy in France. The learned Ramus pleadeth for popular church government in the synods; they reject it as an unwarrantable novelty; the contention grew sharp, till the Parisian massacre silenced the difference. And must our differences have so sharp a cure? Will nothing unite disjoined christians but their own blood? God forbid. But in the mean time, while we quarrel, the work standeth still. Some would have all the workers of iniquity now taken out of the kingdom of Christ, forgetting that the angels must take them out at last, Matt. xiii. Some ministers think as Myconius did, when he was called to the ministry; by a vision leading him into a corn-field, and bidding him reap, he thought he must put in his sickle at the bottom, till he was told *Domino meo non opus est stramine, modo aristæ in horrea colligantur.* My Master needeth not straw; gather but the ears, and it shall suffice.

Once more: I know I speak not to the parliament that should remedy it, but yet that you may be helpful in your places to advance this work of Christ, let me tell you what is the thing in England that cries for reformation next our sins; even the fewness of overseers in great congregations, which maketh the greatest part of pastoral work to lie undone, and none to watch over the people in private, because they are scarce sufficient for the public work. It is pity that Musculus, that may be head of a society of students if he will continue a papist, must weave and dig for his living if he will be a protestant. It is pity that even Luther's wife and children must wander destitute of maintenance when he is dead, when Æsop, the stage-player, can leave his son one hundred and fifty thousand pounds; and Roscius have thirty pounds a-day for the same trade; and Aristotle be allowed eight hundred talents to further his search into the secrets of nature. But am I pleading that ministers may have more maintenance? No, be it just or unjust, it is none of my errand. But oh that the church had more ministers, which, though at the present they cannot have for want of men, yet hereafter they might have if it were not for want of maintenance. Alas! then, what pity is it that every reformation should diminish the church's patrimony! If the men have offended, or if the office of bishops or deans be unwarrantable, yet what have the revenues done? Is it not pity that one troop of a hundred men shall have seven commanding officers allowed them, besides others, and ten thousand, or forty thousand, shall have but one or two overseers allowed them for their souls, when the ministerial work is more laborious, and of greater concernment, than the work of those commanders? I tell you again, the great thing that cries for reformation in England, next to sin, is the paucity of ministers in great congregations. I tell you this, that you may know which way to improve your several interests for the advancement of the kingdom of Christ in England.

To you, lawyers and jurors, my advice is this, "Kiss the Son." Remember the judgment is Christ's, every cause of truth and innocency doth he own, and will call it his cause. Woe, therefore, to him that shall oppose it! Remember every time you take a fee to plead against a cause that you know to be just, you take a fee against a cause of Christ. Will you be of counsel against him that is your Counsellor and King? Dare you plead against him that you expect should plead for you? or desire judgment, as the Jews, against your Lord and Judge? Hath he not told you that he will say, "Inasmuch as ye did it to one of these little ones, ye did it unto me?" Remember, therefore, when a fee is offered you against the innocent, that it is a fee against Christ; and Judas's gain will be loss in the end, and will be too hot to hold long; you will be glad to bring it back, and glad if you could be well shut of it, and cry, I have sinned in betraying the cause of the innocent. Say not, It is our calling that we must live upon. If any man of you dare upon such grounds plead a cause against his conscience, if his conscience do not plead it again more sharply against him, say I am a false prophet. If any, therefore, shall say of you, as the cardinals of Luther, *Cur homini os non obstruitis auro, et argento,* let the same answer serve turn, *Hem pecuniam, non curat,* &c. If any honourable or worshipful friend must be pleasured, inquire first whether he be a better friend than Christ. Tell him the cause is Christ's, and you cannot befriend him, except he procure you a dispensation from him. When Pompey saw his soldiers ready to fly, he lay down in the passage, and told them they should tread upon him then; which stopped their flight. So suppose every time you are drawn in to oppose a just cause, that you saw Christ saying, Thou must trample upon me, if thou do this. As Luther to Melancthon, *Ne causa fidei sit sine fide,* so say I to you all, *Ne causa justitiæ sit sine justitia.* When you begin to be cold in a good cause, suppose you saw Christ showing you his scars, as the soldier did to Cæsar when he desired him to plead his cause, See here, I have done more than plead for you. We have had those that have had a tongue for a fee or a friend, but none for Christ; but God hath now, therefore, shut their mouths, and we may say of them, as Granius by his bad lawyer, when he heard him grown hoarse, If they had not lost their voices, we had lost our cause. To conclude; remember, all of you, that there is an appeal from these earthly judgments; these causes must all be heard again, your witnesses re-examined, your oaths, pleadings, and sentences reviewed; and then, as Lampridius saith of Alexander Severus, that he would vomit choler if he saw a corrupt judge, so will Christ vomit wrath, and vomit you out in wrath from his presence, if corrupt. Therefore, "kiss the Son, lest he be angry, and you perish," &c. I am sensible how I have encroached on your great affairs. Melancthon was wont to tell of a priest that begun his sermon thus, *Scio quod vos non libenter auditis, et ego non libenter concionor, non diu igitur vos teneam.* But I may say contrary: I am persuaded that you hear with a good will, and I am certain that I preach willingly, and therefore I was bold to hold you the longer.

MAKING LIGHT OF CHRIST

AND SALVATION,

TOO OFT

THE ISSUE OF GOSPEL INVITATIONS.

MANIFESTED IN A SERMON PREACHED AT LAURENCE JURY, IN LONDON.

"How shall we escape if we neglect so great salvation?"—Heb. ii. 34.

TO THE READER.

Reader,

Being called on in London to preach, when I had no time to study, I was fain to preach some sermons that I had preached in the country a little before. This was one, which I preached at St. Laurence, in the church where my reverend and faithful brother in Christ, Mr. Richard Vines, is pastor: when I came home I was followed by such importunities by letters to print the sermon, that I have yielded thereunto, though I know not fully the ground of their desires. Seeing it must abroad, will the Lord but bless it to the cure of thy contempt of Christ and grace, how comfortable may the occasion prove to thee and me! It is the slighting of Christ and salvation, that undoes the world. O happy man if thou escape but this sin! Thousands do split their souls on this rock which they should build them on. Look into the world, among rich and poor, high and low, young and old, and see whether it appear not by the whole scope of their conversations that they set more by something else than Christ? And for all the proclamations of his grace in the gospel, and our common professing ourselves to be his disciples, and to believe the glorious things that he hath promised us in another world, whether it yet appear not by the deceitfulness of our service, by our heartless endeavours to obtain his kingdom, and by our busy and delightful following of the world, that the most who are called christians do yet in their hearts make light of Christ; and if so, what wonder if they perish by their contempt? Wilt thou but soberly peruse this short discourse, and consider well as thou readest of its truth and weight, till thy heart be sensible what a sin it is to make light of Christ and thy own salvation, and till the Lord that bought thee be advanced in the estimation and affections of thy soul, thou shalt hereby rejoice, and fulfil the desires of

Thy servant in the faith,

RICHARD BAXTER.

MATT. XXII. 5.

BUT THEY MADE LIGHT OF IT.

The blessed Son of God, that thought it not enough to die for the world, but would himself also be the preacher of grace and salvation, doth comprise in this parable the sum of his gospel. By the king that is here said to make the marriage, is meant God the Father, that sent his Son into the world to cleanse them from their sins, and espouse them to himself. By his Son, for whom the marriage is made, is meant the Lord Jesus Christ, the eternal Son of God, who took to his Godhead the nature of man, that he might be capable of being their Redeemer when they had lost themselves in sin. By the marriage is meant the conjunction of Christ to the soul of sinners, when he giveth up himself to them to be their Saviour, and they give up themselves to him as his redeemed ones, to be saved and ruled by him; the perfection of which marriage will be at the day of judgment, when the conjunction between the whole church and Christ shall be solemnized. The word here translated *marriage*, rather signifieth the marriage-feast; and the meaning is, that the world is invited by the gospel to come in and partake of Christ and salvation, which comprehendeth both pardon, justification, and right to salvation, and all other privileges of the members of Christ. The invitation is God's offer of Christ and salvation in the gospel; the servants that invite them are the preachers of the gospel, who are sent forth by God to that end; the preparation for the feast there mentioned, is the sacrifice of Jesus Christ, and the enacting of a law of grace, and opening a way for revolting sinners to return to God. There is a mention of sending second messengers, because God useth not to take the first denial, but to exercise his patience till sinners are obstinate. The first persons invited are the Jews; upon their obstinate refusal they are sentenced to punishment: and the gentiles are invited, and not only invited, but by powerful preaching, and miracles, and effectual grace, compelled; that is, infallibly prevailed with to come in. The number of them is so great that the house is filled with guests: many come sincerely, not only looking at the pleasure of the feast, that is, at the pardon of sin, and deliverance from the wrath of God, but also at the honour of the marriage, that is, of the Redeemer, and their profession by giving up themselves to a holy conversation: but some come in only for the feast, that is, justification by Christ, having not the wedding-garment of sound resolution for obedience in their life, and looking only at themselves in believing, and not to the glory of their Redeemer; and these are sentenced to everlasting misery, and speed as ill as those that came not in at all; seeing a faith that will not work is but like that of the devil; and they that look to be pardoned and saved by it are mistaken, as James showeth, chap. ii. 24.

The words of my text contain a narration of the ill entertainment that the gospel findeth with many to whom it is sent, even after a first and second invitation. They made light of it, and are taken up with other things. Though it be the Jews that were first guilty, they have too many followers among us gentiles to this day.

Doct. For all the wonderful love and mercy that God hath manifested in giving his Son to be the Redeemer of the world, and which the Son hath manifested in redeeming them by his blood; for all his full preparation by being a sufficient sacrifice for the sins of all; for all his personal excellences, and that full and glorious salvation that he hath procured; and for all his free offers of these, and frequent and earnest invitation of sinners; yet many do make light of all this, and prefer their worldly enjoyments before it. The ordinary entertainment of all is by contempt.

Not that all do so, or that all continue to do so, who were once guilty of it; for God hath his chosen whom he will compel to come in. But till the Spirit of grace overpower the dead and obstinate hearts of men, they hear the gospel as a common story, and the great matters contained in it go not to the heart.

The method in which I shall handle this doctrine is this.

I. I shall show you what it is that men make light of.

II. What this sin of making light of it is.

III. The cause of the sin.

IV. The use of the doctrine.

I. The thing that carnal hearers make light of is, 1. The doctrine of the gospel itself, which they hear regardlessly. 2. The benefits offered them therein: which are, 1. Christ himself. 2. The benefits which he giveth.

Concerning Christ himself, the gospel, 1. Declareth his person and nature, and the great things that he hath done and suffered for man; his redeeming him from the wrath of God by his blood, and procuring a grant of salvation with himself. Furthermore, the same gospel maketh an offer of Christ to sinners, that if they will accept him on his easy and reasonable terms, he will be their Saviour, the Physician of their souls, their Husband, and their Head.

2. The benefits that he offereth them are these. 1. That with these blessed relations to him, himself and interest in him, they shall have the pardon of all their sins past, and be saved from God's wrath, and be set in a sure way of obtaining a pardon for all the sins that they shall commit hereafter, so they do but obey sincerely, and turn not again to the rebellion of their unregeneracy. 2. They shall have the Spirit to become their Guide and Sanctifier, and to dwell in their souls, and help them against their enemies, and conform them more and more to his image, and heal their diseases, and bring them back to God. 3. They shall have right to everlasting glory when this life is ended, and shall be raised up thereto at the last; besides many excellent privileges in the way, in means, preservation, and provision, and the foretaste of what they shall enjoy hereafter: all these benefits the gospel offereth to them that will have Christ on his reasonable terms. The sum of all is in 1 John v. 11, 12, "This is the record, that God hath given us eternal life, and this life is in his Son: he that hath the Son hath life, and he that hath not the Son hath not life."

II. What this sin of the making light of the gospel is. 1. To make light of the gospel is to take no great heed to what is spoken, as if it were not a certain truth, or else were a matter that little concerned them; or as if God had not written these things for them. 2. When the gospel doth not affect men, or go to their hearts; but though they seem to attend to what is said, yet men are not awakened by it from their security, nor doth it work in any measure such holy passion in their souls, as matters of such everlasting consequence should do: this is making light of the gospel of salvation. When we tell men what Christ hath done and suffered for their souls, and it scarce moveth them: we tell them of keen and cutting truths, but nothing will pierce them: we can make them hear, but we cannot make them feel; our words take up in the porch of their ears and fancies, but will not enter into the inward parts; as if we spake to men that had no hearts or feeling: this is a making light of Christ and salvation. Acts xxviii. 26, 27, "Hearing ye shall hear, and shall not understand; seeing ye shall see, and shall not perceive. For the heart of this people is waxed gross, and their ears are dull of hearing, their eyes are closed," &c.

3. When men have no high estimation of Christ and salvation, but whatsoever they may say with their tongues, or dreamingly and speculatively believe, yet in their serious and practical thoughts they have a higher estimation of the matters of this world, than they have of Christ, and the salvation that he hath purchased; this is a making light of him. When men account the doctrine of Christ to be but a matter of words and names, as Gallio, (Acts xviii. 4,) or as Festus, (Acts xxv. 19,) a superstitious matter about one Jesus who was dead, and Paul saith is alive; or ask the preachers of the gospel, as the Athenians, "What will this babbler say?" Acts xvii. 18: this is contempt of Christ.

4. When men are informed of the truths of the gospel, and on what terms Christ and his benefits may be had, and how it is the will of God that they should believe and accept the offer; and that he commandeth to do it upon pain of damnation; and yet men will not consent, unless they could have Christ on terms of their own: they will not part with their worldly contents, nor lay down their pleasures, and profits, and honour at his feet, as being content to take so much of them only as he will give them back, and as is consistent with his will and interest, but think it is a hard saying, that they must forsake all in resolution for Christ: this is a making light of him and their salvation. When men might have part in him and all his benefits if they would, and they will not unless they may keep the world too; and are resolved to please their flesh, whatever comes of it; this is a high contempt of Christ and everlasting life, Matt. xiii. 21, 22; Luke xviii. 23. You may find examples of such as I here describe.

5. When men will promise fair, and profess their willingness to have Christ on his terms, and to forsake all for him, but yet do stick to the world and their sinful courses; and when it comes to practice, will not be removed by all that Christ hath done and said; this is making light of Christ and salvation, Jer. xlii. 5, compared with xliii. 2.

III. The causes of this sin are the next thing to be inquired after. It may seem a wonder that ever men, that have the use of their reason, should be so sottish as to make light of matters of such consequence. But the cause is,

1. Some men understand not the very sense of the words of the gospel when they hear it; and how can they be taken with that which they understand not? Though we speak to them in plain English, and study to speak it as plain as we can, yet people have so estranged themselves from God, and the matters of their own happiness, that they know not what we say; as if we spoke in another language, and as if they were under that judgment, Isa. xxviii. 11, "With stammering lips, and with another tongue, will he speak to this people."

2. Some that do understand the words that we speak, yet because they are carnal, understand not the matter. "For the natural man receiveth not the things of the Spirit of God, neither can he know them, because they are spiritually discerned," 1 Cor. ii. 14. They are earthly, and these things are heavenly, John iii. 12. These things of the Spirit are not well known by bare hearsay, but by spiritual taste, which none have but those that are taught by the Holy Ghost, (1 Cor. ii. 12,) that we may know the things that are given us of God.

3. A carnal mind apprehendeth not a suitableness in these spiritual and heavenly things to his mind, and therefore he sets light by them, and hath no mind of them. When you tell him of everlasting glory, he heareth you as if you were persuading him to go play with the sun: they are matters of another world, and out of his element; and therefore he hath no more delight in them than a fish would have to be in the fairest meadow, or than a swine hath in a jewel, or a dog in a piece of gold: they may be good to others, but he cannot apprehend them as suitable to him, because he hath a nature that is otherwise inclined: he savoureth not the things of the Spirit, Rom. viii. 5.

4. The main cause of the slighting of Christ and salvation is, a secret root of unbelief in men's hearts. Whatsoever they may pretend, they do not soundly and thoroughly believe the word of God: they are taught in general to say the gospel is true; but they never saw the evidence of its truth so far, as thoroughly to persuade them of it; nor have they got their souls settled on the infallibility of God's testimony, nor considered of the truth of the particular doctrines revealed in the Scripture, so far as soundly to believe them. Oh did you all but soundly believe the words of this gospel, of the evil of sin, of the need of Christ, and what he hath done for you, and what you must be and do if ever you will be saved by him; and what will become of you for ever if you do it not; I dare say it would cure the contempt of Christ, and you would not make so light of the matters of your salvation. But men do not believe while they say they do, and would face us down that they do, and verily think that they do themselves. There is a root of bitterness, and an evil heart of unbelief, that makes them depart from the living God, Heb. ii. 12; iv. 1, 2, 6. Tell any man in this congregation that he shall have a gift of ten thousand pounds, if he will but go to London for it; if he believe you, he will go; but if he believe not, he will not; and if he will not go, you may be sure he believeth not, supposing that he is able. I know a slight belief may stand with a wicked life; such as men have of the truth of a prognostication, it may be true, and it may be false; but a true and sound belief is not consistent with so great neglect of the things that are believed.

5. Christ and salvation are made light of by the world, because of their desperate hardness of heart. The heart is hard naturally, and by custom in sinning made more hard, especially by long abuse of mercy, and neglect of the means of grace, and resisting the Spirit of God. Hence it is that men are turned into such stones: and till God cure them of the stone of the heart, no wonder if they feel not what they know, or regard not what we say, but make light of all: it is hard preaching a stone into tears, or making a rock to tremble. You may stand over a dead body long enough, and say to it, O thou carcass, when thou hast lain rotting and mouldered to dust till the resurrection, God will then call thee to account for thy sin, and cast thee into everlasting fire, before you can make it feel what we say, or fear the misery that is never so truly threatened: when men's hearts are like the highway that is trodden to hardness by long custom in sinning, or like the clay that is hardened to a stone by the heat of those mercies that should have melted them into repentance; when they have consciences seared with a hot iron, as the apostle speaks, (1 Tim. iv. 2,) no wonder then if they be past feeling, and working all uncleanness with greediness do make light of Christ and everlasting glory. Oh that this were not the case of too many of our hearers! Had we but *living souls* to speak to, they would hear, and feel, and not make light of what we say. I know they are naturally alive, but they are spiritually dead, as Scripture witnesseth, Eph. ii. 3. Oh if there were but one spark of the life of grace in them, the doctrine of salvation by Jesus Christ would appear to them to be the weightiest business in the world! Oh how confident should I be, methinks, to prevail with men, and to take them off this world, and bring them to mind the matters of another world, if I spake but to men that had life, and sense, and reason! But when we speak to blocks and dead men, how should we be regarded? Oh how sad a case are these souls in, that are fallen under this fearful judgment of spiritual madness and deadness! to have a blind mind, and a hard heart, to be sottish and senseless, (Mark iv. 12; John xii. 40,) lest they should be converted, and their sin should be forgiven them.

6. Christ and salvation are made light of by the world, because they are wholly enslaved to their

sense, and taken up with lower things: the matters of another world are out of sight, and so far from their senses, that they cannot regard them; but present things are nearer them, in their eyes, and in their hands. There must be a living faith to prevail over sense, before men can be so taken with things that are not seen, though they have the word of God for their security, as to neglect and let go things that are still before their eyes. Sense works with great advantage, and therefore doth much in resisting faith where it is; no wonder then if it carry all before it, where there is no true and lively faith to resist, and to lead the soul to higher things. This cause of making light of Christ and salvation is expressed here in my text: one went to his farm, and another to his merchandise: men have houses and lands to look after; they have wife and children to mind; they have their body and outward estate to regard; therefore they forget that they have a God, a Redeemer, a soul to mind: these matters of the world are still with them. They see these, but they see not God, nor Christ, nor their souls, nor everlasting glory. These things are near at hand, and therefore work naturally, and so work forcibly; but the other are thought on as a great way off, and therefore too distant to work on their affections, or be at the present so much regarded by them. Their body hath life and sense, therefore if they want meat, or drink, or clothes, will feel their want, and tell them of it, and give them no rest till their wants be supplied, and therefore they cannot make light of their bodily necessities; but their souls in spiritual respects are dead, and therefore feel not their wants, but will let them alone in their greatest necessities; and be as quiet when they are starved and languishing to destruction, as if all were well, and nothing ailed them. And hereupon poor people are wholly taken up in providing for the body, as if they had nothing else to mind. They have their trades and callings to follow, and so much to do from morning to night, that they can find no time for matters of salvation: Christ would teach them, but they have no leisure to hear him: the Bible is before them, but they cannot have while to read it: a minister is in the town with him, but they cannot have while to go to inquire of him what they should do to be saved: and when they do hear, their hearts are so full of the world, and carried away with these lower matters, that they cannot mind the things which they hear. They are so full of the thoughts, and desires, and cares of this world, that there is no room to pour into them the water of life. The cares of the world do choke the word, and make it become unfruitful, Matt. xiii. 32. Men cannot serve two masters, God and mammon; but they will lean to the one, and despise the other, Matt. vi. 24. He that loveth the world, the love of the Father is not in him, 1 John ii. 15, 16. Men cannot choose but set light by Christ and salvation, while they set so much by any thing on earth. It is that which is highly esteemed among men that is abominable in the sight of God, Luke xvi. 15. Oh this is the ruin of many thousand souls! It would grieve the heart of any honest christian to see how eagerly this vain world is followed every where, and how little men set by Christ and the world to come; to compare the care that men have for the world, with the care of their souls; and the time that they lay out on the world, with that time they lay out for their salvation: to see how the world fills their mouths, their hands, their houses, their hearts, and Christ hath little more than a bare title: to come into their company, and hear no discourse but of the world; to come into their houses, and hear and see nothing but for the world, as if this world would last for ever, or would purchase them another. When I ask sometimes the ministers of the gospel how their labours succeed, they tell me, People continue still the same, and give up themselves wholly to the world; so that they mind not what ministers say to them, nor will give any full entertainment to the word, and all because of the deluding world: and oh that too many ministers themselves did not make light of that Christ whom they preach, being drawn away with the love of this world! In a word, men of a worldly disposition do judge of things according to worldly advantages, therefore Christ is slighted; "He is despised and rejected of men, they hide their faces from him, and esteem him not, as seeing no beauty or comeliness in him, that they should desire him," Isa. liii. 3.

7. Christ and salvation are made light of, because men do not soberly consider of the truth and weight of these necessary things. They suffer not their minds so long to dwell upon them, till they procure a due esteem, and deeply affect their heart; did they believe them and not consider of them, how should they work! Oh when men have reason given them to think and consider of the things that most concern them, and yet they will not use it, this causeth their contempt.

8. Christ and salvation are made light of, because men were never sensible of their sin and misery, and extreme necessity of Christ and his salvation; their eyes were never opened to see themselves as they are; nor their hearts soundly humbled in the sense of their condition: if this were done, they would soon be brought to value a Saviour: a truly broken heart can no more make light of Christ and salvation, than a hungry man of his food, or a sick man of the means that would give him ease; but till then our words cannot have access to their hearts: while sin and misery are made light of, Christ and salvation will be made light of; but when these are perceived an intolerable burden, then nothing will serve the turn but Christ. Till men be truly humbled, they can venture Christ and salvation for a lust, for a little worldly gain, even for less than nothing: but when God hath illuminated them, and broken their hearts, then they would give a world for a Christ; then they must have Christ or they die; all things then are loss and dung to them in regard of the excellent knowledge of Christ, Phil. iii. 8. When they are once pricked in their hearts for sin and misery, then they cry out, "Men and brethren, what shall we do?" Acts ii. 37. When they are awakened by God's judgments, as the poor jailer, then they cry out, "Sirs, what shall I do to be saved?" Acts xvi. 30. This is the reason why God will bring men so low by humiliation, before he brings them to salvation.

9. Men take occasion to make light of Christ by the commonness of the gospel; because they do hear of it every day, the frequency is an occasion to dull their affections; I say, an occasion, for it is no just cause. Were it a rarity it might take more with them; but now, if they hear a minister preach nothing but these saving truths, they say, We have these every day: they make not light of their bread or drink, their health or life, because they possess them every day; they make not light of the sun because it shineth every day; at least they should not, for the mercy is the greater; but Christ and salvation are made light of because they hear of them often; This is, say they, a good, plain, dry sermon. Pearls are trod into the dirt where they are common: they loathe this dry manna: "The full soul loathes the honey-comb; but to the hungry every bitter thing is sweet," Prov. xxvii. 7.

10. Christ and salvation are made light of, because of this disjunctive presumption; either that he is

sure enough theirs already, and God that is so merciful, and Christ that hath suffered so much for them, is surely resolved to save them, or else it may easily be obtained at any time, if it be not yet so. A conceited facility to have a part in Christ and salvation at any time doth occasion men to make light of them. It is true, that grace is free and the offer is universal, according to the extent of the preaching of the gospel; and it is true, that men may have Christ when they will; that is, when they are willing to have him on his terms; but he that hath promised thee Christ if thou be willing, hath not promised to make thee willing: and if thou art not willing now, how canst thou think thou shalt be willing hereafter? If thou canst make thine own heart willing, why is it not done now? Can you do it better when sin hath more hardened it, and God may have given thee over to thyself? O sinners! you might do much, though you are not able of yourselves to come in, if you would now subject yourselves to the working of the Spirit, and set in while the gales of grace continue. But did you know what a hard and impossible thing it is to be so much as willing to have Christ and grace, when the heart is given over to itself, and the Spirit hath withdrawn its former invitations, you would not be so confident of your own strength to believe and repent; nor would you make light of Christ upon such foolish confidence. If indeed it be so easy a matter as you imagine, for a sinner to believe and repent at any time, how comes it to pass that it is done by so few; but most of the world do perish in their impenitency, when they have all the helps and means that we can afford them? It is true, the thing is very reasonable and easy in itself to a pure nature; but while man is blind and dead, these things are in a sort impossible to him, which are never so easy to others. It is the easiest and sweetest life in the world to a gracious soul to live in the love of God, and the delightful thoughts of the life to come, where all their hope and happiness lieth: but to a worldly, carnal heart, it is as easy to remove a mountain as to bring them to this. However, these men are their own condemners; for if they think it so easy a matter to repent and believe, and so to have Christ, and right to salvation, then have they no excuse for neglecting this which they thought so easy. O wretched, impenitent soul! what mean you to say when God shall ask you, Why did you not repent and love your Redeemer above the world, when you thought it so easy that you could do it at any time?

IV. *Use* 1. We come now to the application: and hence you may be informed of the blindness and folly of all carnal men. How contemptible are their judgments that think Christ and salvation contemptible! And how little reason there is why any should be moved by them, or discouraged by any of their scorns or contradictions!

How shall we sooner know a man to be a fool, than if he know no difference between dung and gold? Is there such a thing as madness in the world, if that man be not mad that sets light by Christ, and his own salvation, while he daily toils for the dung of the earth? And yet what pity is it to see that a company of poor, ignorant souls will be ashamed of godliness, if such men as these do but deride them! or will think hardly of a holy life, if such as these do speak against it! Hearers, if you see any set light by Christ and salvation, do you set light by that man's wit, and by his words, and hear the reproaches of a holy life as you would hear the words of a mad-man, not with regard, but with a compassion of his misery.

Use 2. What wonder if we and our preaching be despised, and the best ministers complain of ill success, when the ministry of the apostles themselves did succeed no better? What wonder if for all that we can say or do, our hearers still set light by Christ and their own salvation, when the apostles' hearers did the same? They that did second their doctrine by miracles, if any men could have shaken and torn in pieces the hearts of sinners, they could have done it; if any could have laid them at their feet, and made them all cry out as some, "What shall we do?" it would have been they. You may see then that it is not merely for want of good preachers that men make light of Christ and salvation. The first news of such a thing as the pardon of sin, and the hopes of glory, and the danger of everlasting misery, would turn the hearts of men within them, if they were as tractable in spiritual matters as in temporal: but alas, it is far otherwise. It must not seem any strange thing, nor must it too much discourage the preachers of the gospel, if when they have said all that they can devise to say, to win the hearts of men to Christ, the most do still slight him; and while they bow the knee to him, and honour him with their lips, do yet set so light by him in their hearts, as to prefer every fleshly pleasure or commodity before him. It will be thus with many: let us be glad that it is not thus with all.

Use 3. But for closer application, seeing this is the great condemning sin, before we inquire after it into the hearts of our hearers, it beseems us to begin at home, and see that we who are preachers of the gospel be not guilty of it ourselves. The Lord forbid that they that have undertaken the sacred office of revealing the excellences of Christ to the world, should make light of him themselves, and slight that salvation which they do daily preach. The Lord knows we are all of us so low in our estimation of Christ, and do this great work so negligently, that we have cause to be ashamed of our best sermons; but should this sin prevail in us, we were the most miserable of all men. Brethren, I love not censoriousness; yet dare not befriend so vile a sin in myself or others, under pretence of avoiding it: especially when there is so great necessity that it should be healed first in them that make it their work to heal it in others. Oh that there were no cause to complain that Christ and salvation are made light of by the preachers of it! But, 1. Do not the negligent studies of some speak it out? 2. Doth not their dead and drowsy preaching declare it? Do not they make light of the doctrine they preach, that do it as if they were half asleep, and feel not what they speak themselves?

3. Doth not the carelessness of some men's private endeavours discover it? What do they for souls? How slightly do they reprove sin! How little do they when they are out of the pulpit for the saving of men's souls!

4. Doth not the continued neglect of those things wherein the interest of Christ consisteth discover it? 1. The church's purity and reformation. 2. Its unity.

5. Do not the covetous and worldly lives of too many discover it, losing advantages for men's souls for a little gain to themselves? And most of this is because men are preachers before they are christians, and tell men of that which they never felt themselves. Of all men on earth there are few that are in so sad a condition as such ministers: and if indeed they do believe that Scripture which they preach, methinks it should be terrible to them in their studying and preaching it.

Use 4. Beloved hearers, the office that God hath called us to, is by declaring the glory of his grace, to help under Christ to the saving of men's souls.

I hope you think not that I come hither to-day on any other errand. The Lord knows I had not set a foot out of doors but in hope to succeed in this work for your souls. I have considered, and often considered, what is the matter that so many thousands should perish when God hath done so much for their salvation; and I find this that is mentioned in my text is the cause. It is one of the wonders of the world, that when God hath so loved the world as to send his Son, and Christ hath made a satisfaction by his death sufficient for them all, and offereth the benefits of it so freely to them, even without money or price, that yet the most of the world should perish; yea, the most of those that are thus called by his word! Why, here is the reason, when Christ hath done all this, men make light of it. God hath showed that he is not unwilling; and Christ hath showed that he is not unwilling that men should be restored to God's favour and be saved; but men are actually unwilling themselves. God takes not pleasure in the death of sinners, but rather that they return and live, Ezek. xxxiii. 11. But men take such pleasure in sin, that they will die before they will return. The Lord Jesus was content to be their Physician, and hath provided them a sufficient plaster of his own blood: but if men make light of it, and will not apply it, what wonder if they perish after all? This Scripture giveth us the reason of their perdition. This sad experience tells us the most of the world is guilty of. It is a most lamentable thing to see how most men do spend their care, their time, their pains, for known vanities, while God and glory are cast aside; that he who is all should seem to them as nothing, and that which is nothing should seem to them as good as all; that God should set mankind in such a race where heaven or hell is their certain end, and that they should sit down, and loiter, or run after the childish toys of the world, and so much forget the prize that they should run for. Were it but possible for one of us to see the whole of this business, as the all-seeing God doth; to see at one view both heaven and hell, which men are so near; and see what most men in the world are minding, and what they are doing every day, it would be the saddest sight that could be imagined. Oh how should we marvel at their madness, and lament their self-delusion! O poor distracted world! what is it you run after? and what is it that you neglect? If God had never told them what they were sent into the world to do, or whither they were going, or what was before them in another world, then they had been excusable; but he hath told them over and over, till they were weary of it. Had he left it doubtful, there had been some excuse; but it is his sealed word, and they profess to believe it, and would take it ill of us if we should question whether they do believe it or not.

Beloved, I come not to accuse any of you particularly of this crime; but seeing it is the commonest cause of men's destruction, I suppose you will judge it the fittest matter for our inquiry, and deserving our greatest care for the cure. To which end I shall, 1. Endeavour the conviction of the guilty. 2. Shall give them such considerations as may tend to humble and reform them. 3. I shall conclude with such direction as may help them that are willing to escape the destroying power of this sin. And for the first, consider,

1. It is the case of most sinners to think themselves freest from those sins that they are most enslaved to; and one reason why we cannot reform them, is because we cannot convince them of their guilt. It is the nature of sin so far to blind and befool the sinner, that he knoweth not what he doth, but thinketh he is free from it when it reigneth in him, or when he is committing it: it bringeth men to be so much unacquainted with themselves, that they know not what they think, or what they mean and intend, nor what they love or hate, much less what they are habituated and disposed to. They are alive to sin, and dead to all the reason, consideration, and resolution that should recover them, as if it were only by their sinning that we must know they are alive. May I hope that you that hear me to-day are but willing to know the truth of your case, and then I shall be encouraged to proceed to an inquiry. God will judge impartially; why should not we do so? Let me, therefore, by these following questions, try whether none of you are slighters of Christ and your own salvation. And follow me, I beseech you, by putting them close to your own hearts, and faithfully answering them.

1. Things that men highly value will be remembered, they will be matter of their freest and sweetest thoughts. This is a known case.

Do not those then make light of Christ and salvation that think of them so seldom and coldly in comparison of other things? Follow thy own heart, man, and observe what it daily runneth after; and then judge whether it make not light of Christ.

We cannot persuade men to one hour's sober consideration what they should do for an interest in Christ, or in thankfulness for his love, and yet they will not believe that they make light of him.

2. Things that we highly value will be matter of our discourse; the judgment and heart will command the tongue. Freely and delightfully will our speech run after them. This also is a known case.

Do not those then make light of Christ and salvation, that shun the mention of his name, unless it be in a vain or sinful use? Those that love not the company where Christ and salvation is much talked of, but think it troublesome, precise discourse: that had rather hear some merry jests, or idle tales, or talk of their riches or business in the world. When you may follow them from morning to night, and scarce have a savoury word of Christ; but perhaps some slight and weary mention of him sometimes; judge whether these make not light of Christ and salvation. How seriously do they talk of the world, (Psal. cxliv. 8, 11,) and speak vanity! but how heartlessly do they make mention of Christ and salvation!

3. The things that we highly value we would secure the possession of, and therefore would take any convenient course to have all doubts and fears about them well resolved. Do not those men then make light of Christ and salvation that have lived twenty or thirty years in uncertainty whether they have any part in these or not, and yet never seek out for the right resolution of their doubts? Are all that hear me this day certain they shall be saved? Oh that they were! Oh, had you not made light of salvation, you could not so easily bear such doubtings of it; you could not rest till you had made it sure, or done your best to make it sure. Have you nobody to inquire of that might help you in such a work? Why, you have ministers that are purposely appointed to that office. Have you gone to them, and told them the doubtfulness of your case, and asked their help in the judging of your condition? Alas, ministers may sit in their studies from one year to another, before ten persons among a thousand will come to them on such an errand! Do not these make light of Christ and salvation? When the gospel pierceth the heart indeed, they cry out, "Men and brethren, what shall we do to be saved?" Acts xvi. 30. Trembling and astonished, Paul cries out, "Lord, what wilt thou have me to do?" Acts ix. 6. And so did the

convinced Jews to Peter, Acts ii. 37. But when hear we such questions?

4. The things that we value do deeply affect us, and some motions will be in the heart according to our estimation of them. O sirs, if men made not light of these things, what working would there be in the hearts of all our hearers! What strange affections would it raise in them to hear of the matters of the world to come! How would their hearts melt before the power of the gospel! What sorrow would be wrought in the discovery of their sins! What astonishment at the consideration of their misery! What unspeakable joy at the glad tidings of salvation by the blood of Christ! What resolution would be raised in them upon the discovery of their duty! Oh what hearers should we have, if it were not for this sin! Whereas now we are liker to weary them, or preach them asleep with matters of this unspeakable moment. We talk to them of Christ and salvation till we make their heads ache: little would one think by their careless carriage that they heard and regarded what we said, or thought we spoke at all to them.

5. Our estimation of things will be seen in the diligence of our endeavours. That which we highliest value, we shall think no pains too great to obtain. Do not those men then make light of Christ and salvation, that think all too much that they do for them; that murmur at his service, and think it too grievous for them to endure? that ask of his service as Judas of the ointment, What need this waste? Cannot men be saved without so much ado? This is more ado than needs. For the world they will labour all the day, and all their lives; but for Christ and salvation they are afraid of doing too much. Let us preach to them as long as we will, we cannot bring them to relish or resolve upon a life of holiness. Follow them to their houses, and you shall not hear them read a chapter, nor call upon God with their families once a day: nor will they allow him that one day in seven which he hath separated to his service. But pleasure, or worldly business, or idleness must have a part. And many of them are so far hardened as to reproach them that will not be as mad as themselves. And is not Christ worth the seeking? Is not everlasting salvation worth more than all this? Doth not that soul make light of all these, that thinks his ease more worth than they? Let but common sense judge.

6. That which we most highly value, we think we cannot buy too dear: Christ and salvation are freely given, and yet the most of men go without them, because they cannot enjoy the world and them together. They are called but to part with that which would hinder them from Christ, and they will not do it. They are called but to give God his own, and to resign all to his will, and let go the profits and pleasures of this world, when they must let go either Christ or them, and they will not. They think this too dear a bargain, and say they cannot spare these things: they must hold their credit with men; they must look to their estates: how shall they live else? They must have their pleasure, whatsoever becomes of Christ and salvation: as if they could live without Christ better than without these: as if they were afraid of being losers by Christ, or could make a saving match by losing their souls to gain the world. Christ hath told us over and over, that if we will not forsake all for him we cannot be his disciples, Matt. x. Far are these men from forsaking all, and yet will needs think that they are his disciples indeed.

7. That which men highly esteem, they would help their friends to as well as themselves. Do not those men make light of Christ and salvation, that can take so much care to leave their children portions in the world, and do so little to help them to heaven? that provide outward necessaries so carefully for their families, but do so little to the saving of their souls? Their neglected children and friends will witness, that either Christ, or their children's souls, or both, were made light of.

8. That which men highly esteem, they will so diligently seek after, that you may see it in the success, if it be a matter within their reach. You may see how many make light of Christ, by the little knowledge they have of him, and the little communion with him, and communication from him; and the little, yea, none of his special grace in them. Alas! how many ministers can speak it to the sorrow of their hearts, that many of their people know almost nothing of Christ, though they hear of him daily! Nor know they what they must do to be saved: if we ask them an account of these things, they answer as if they understood not what we say to them, and tell us they are no scholars, and therefore think they are excusable for their ignorance. Oh if these men had not made light of Christ, and their salvation, but had bestowed but half so much pains to know and enjoy him, as they have done to understand the matters of their trades and callings in the world, they would not have been so ignorant as they are: they make light of these things, and therefore will not be at the pains to study or learn them. When men that can learn the hardest trade in a few years, have not learned a catechism, nor how to understand their creed, under twenty or thirty years' preaching, nor cannot abide to be questioned about such things; doth not this show that they have slighted them in their hearts? How will these despisers of Christ and salvation be able one day to look him in the face, and to give an account of these neglects?

Thus much I have spoken in order to your conviction. Do not some of your consciences by this time smite you, and say, I am the man that have made light of my salvation? If they do not, it is because you make light of it still, for all that is said to you. But because, if it be the will of the Lord, I would fain have this damning distemper cured, and am loth to leave you in such a desperate condition, if I knew how to remedy it, I will give you some considerations, which may move you, if you be men of reason and understanding, to look better about you; and I beseech you to weigh them, and make use of them as we go, and lay open your hearts to the work of grace, and sadly bethink you what a case you are in, if you prove such as make light of Christ.

Consider, 1. Thou makest light of him that made not light of thee who didst deserve it. Thou wast worthy of nothing but contempt. As a man, what art thou but a worm to God? As a sinner, thou art far viler than a toad: yet Christ was so far from making light of thee and thy happiness, that he came down into the flesh, and lived a life of suffering, and offered himself a sacrifice to the justice which thou hadst provoked, that thy miserable soul might have a remedy. It is no less than miracles of love and mercy, that he hath showed to us: and yet shall we slight them after all?

Angels admire them, whom they less concern, (1 Pet. i. 12,) and shall redeemed sinners make light of them? What barbarous, yea, devilish, yea, worse than devilish ingratitude is this! The devils never had a Saviour offered them, but thou hast, and dost thou yet make light of him?

2. Consider, the work of man's salvation by Jesus

Christ, is the master-piece of all the works of God, wherein he would have his love and mercy to be magnified. As the creation declareth his goodness and power, so doth redemption his goodness and mercy; he hath contrived the very frame of his worship so, that it shall much consist in the magnifying of this work; and after all this, will you make light of it? "His name is Wonderful," Isa. ix. 6. "He did the work that none could do," John xv. 24. "Greater love could none show than his," John xv. 13. How great was the evil and misery that he delivered us from! the good procured for us! All are wonders, from his birth to his ascension, from our new birth to our glorification, all are wonders of matchless mercy; and yet do you make light of them?

3. You make light of matters of greatest excellency and moment in the world: you know not what it is that you slight: had you well known, you could not have done it. As Christ said to the woman of Samaria, John iv. 10, Hadst thou known who it is that speakest to thee, thou wouldst have asked of him the waters of life: had they known they would not have crucified the Lord of glory, 1 Cor. ii. 8. So had you known what Christ is, you would not have made light of him; had you been one day in heaven, and but seen what they possess, and seen also what miserable souls must endure that are shut out, you would never sure have made so light of Christ again.

O sirs, it is no trifles or jesting matters that the gospel speaks of. I must needs profess to you, that when I have the most serious thoughts of these things myself, I am ready to marvel that such amazing matters do not overwhelm the souls of men; that the greatness of the subject doth not so overmatch our understandings and affections, as even to drive men beside themselves, but that God hath always somewhat allayed it by the distance: much more that men should be so blockish as to make light of them. O Lord, that men did but know what everlasting glory and everlasting torments are; would they then hear us as they do? would they read and think of these things as they do? I profess I have been ready to wonder, when I have heard such weighty things delivered, how people can forbear crying out in the congregation; much more how they can rest till they have gone to their ministers, and learned what they should do to be saved, that this great business might be put out of doubt. Oh that heaven and hell should work no more on men! Oh that everlastingness should work no more! Oh how can you forbear when you are alone to think with yourselves what it is to be everlastingly in joy or in torment! I wonder that such thoughts do not break your sleep; and that they come not in your mind when you are about your labour! I wonder how you can almost do any thing else! how you can have any quietness in your minds! how you can eat, or drink, or rest, till you have got some ground of everlasting consolations! Is that a man or a corpse that is not affected with matters of this moment? that can be readier to sleep than to tremble when he heareth how he must stand at the bar of God? Is that a man or a clod of clay that can rise and lie down without being deeply affected with his everlasting estate? that can follow his worldly business, and make nothing of the great business of salvation or damnation; and that when they know it is hard at hand! Truly, sirs, when I think of the weight of the matter, I wonder at the very best of God's saints upon earth that they are no better, and do no more in so weighty a case. I wonder at those whom the world accounteth more holy than needs, and scorns for making too much ado, that they can put off Christ and their souls with so little; that they pour not out their souls in every supplication; that they are not more taken up with God; that their thoughts be not more serious in preparation for their account. I wonder that they be not a hundred times more strict in their lives, and more laborious and unwearied in striving for the crown, than they are. And for myself, as I am ashamed of my dull and careless heart, and of my slow and unprofitable course of life; so the Lord knows I am ashamed of every sermon that I preach: when I think what I have been speaking of, and who sent me, and what men's salvation or damnation is so much concerned in it, I am ready to tremble, lest God should judge me as a slighter of his truth, and the souls of men, and lest in the best sermon I should be guilty of their blood. Methinks we should not speak a word to men in matters of such consequence without tears, or the greatest earnestness that possibly we can: were not we too much guilty of the sin which we reprove, it would be so. Whether we are alone, or in company, methinks our end, and such an end, should still be in our mind, and as before our eyes; and we should sooner forget any thing, and set light by any thing, or by all things, than by this.

Consider, 4. Who is it that sends this weighty message to you. Is it not God himself? Shall the God of heaven speak, and men make light of it? You would not slight the voice of an angel, or a prince.

5. Whose salvation is it that you make light of? Is it not your own? Are you no more near or dear to yourselves than to make light of your own happiness or misery? Why, sirs, do you not care whether you be saved or damned? is self-love lost? are you turned your own enemies? As he that slighteth his meat doth slight his life; so if you slight Christ, whatsoever you may think, you will find it was your own salvation that you slighted. Hear what he saith, "All they that hate me love death," Prov. viii. 36.

6. Your sin is greater, in that you profess to believe the gospel which you make so light of. For a professed infidel to do it that believes not that ever Christ died, or rose again; or doth not believe that there is a heaven or hell; this were no such marvel: but for you that make it your creed, and your very religion, and call yourselves christians, and have been baptized into this faith, and seemed to stand to it, this is the wonder, and hath no excuse. What! believe that you shall live in endless joy or torment, and yet make no more of it to escape torment, and obtain that joy! What! believe that God will shortly judge you, and yet make no more preparation for it! Either say plainly, I am no christian, I do not believe these wonderful things, I will believe nothing but what I see; or else let your hearts be affected with your belief, and live as you say you do believe. What do you think when you repeat the creed, and mention Christ's judgment and everlasting life?

7. What are these things you set so much by, as to prefer them before Christ and the saving of your souls? Have you found a better friend, a greater and surer happiness than this? Good Lord! what dung is it that men make so much of, while they set so light by everlasting glory! What toys are they that they are daily taken up with, while matters of life and death are negected! Why, sirs, if you had every one a kingdom in your hopes, what were it in comparison of the everlasting kingdom? I cannot but look upon all the glory and dignity of this world, lands and lordships, crowns and kingdoms, even as

on some brain-sick, beggarly fellow, that borroweth fine clothes, and plays the part of a king or a lord for an hour on a stage, and then comes down, and the sport is ended, and they are beggars again. Were it not for God's interest in the authority of magistrates, or for the service they might do him, I should judge no better of them. For as to their own glory, it is but a smoke: what matter is it whether you live poor or rich, unless it were a greater matter to die rich than it is? You know well enough that death levels all. What matter is it at judgment, whether you be to answer for the life of a rich man or a poor man? Is Dives then any better than Lazarus? Oh that men knew what a poor deceiving shadow they grasp at, while they let go the everlasting substance! The strongest, and richest, and most voluptuous sinners, do but lay in fuel for their sorrows, while they think they are gathering together a treasure. Alas! they are asleep, and dream that they are happy; but when they awake what a change will they find! Their crown is made of thorns: their pleasure hath such a sting as will stick in the heart through all eternity, except unfeigned repentance do prevent it. Oh how sadly will these wretches be convinced ere long, what a foolish bargain they made in selling Christ and their salvation for these trifles! Let your farms and merchandise then save you if they can; and do that for you that Christ would have done. Cry then to thy Baal to save thee! Oh what thoughts have drunkards and adulterers, &c. of Christ, that will not part with the basest lust for him! "For a piece of bread," saith Solomon, "such men do transgress," Prov. xxviii. 11.

8. To set so light by Christ and salvation, is a certain mark that thou hast no part in them, and if thou so continue, that Christ will set as light by thee: "Those that honour him he will honour, and those that despise him shall be lightly esteemed," 1 Sam. ii. 30. Thou wilt feel one day that thou canst not live without him; thou wilt confess then thy need of him; and then thou mayst go look for a Saviour where thou wilt; for he will be no Saviour for thee hereafter, that wouldst not value him, and submit to him here. Then who will prove the loser by thy contempt? Oh what a thing will it be for a poor miserable soul to cry to Christ for help in the day of extremity, and to hear so sad an answer as this! Thou didst set light by me and my law in the day of thy prosperity, and I will now set as light by thee in thy adversity. Read Prov. i. 24, to the end. Thou that as Esau didst sell thy birthright for a mess of pottage, shalt then find no place for repentance, though thou seek it with tears, Heb. xii. 17. Do you think that Christ shed his blood to save them that continue to make light of it? and to save them that value a cup of drink or a lust before his salvation? I tell you, sirs, though you set so light by Christ and salvation, God doth not so: he will not give them on such terms as these: he valueth the blood of his Son, and the everlasting glory; and he will make you value them if ever you have them. Nay, this will be thy condemnation, and leaveth no remedy. All the world cannot save him that sets light by Christ, Heb. ii. 3; Luke xiv. 24. None of them shall taste of his supper, Matt. x. 37. Nor can you blame him to deny you what you made light of yourselves. Can you find fault if you miss of the salvation which you slighted?

9. The time is near when Christ and salvation will not be made light of as now they are. When God hath shaken those careless souls out of their bodies, and you must answer for all your sins in your own name; oh then what would you give for a Saviour! When a thousand bills shall be brought in against you, and none to relieve you; then you will consider, Oh! Christ would now have stood between me and the wrath of God: had I not despised him, he would have answered all. When you see the world hath left you, and your companions in sin have deceived themselves and you, and all your merry days are gone; then what would you give for that Christ and salvation that now you account not worth your labour! Do you think when you see the judgment set, and you are doomed to everlasting perdition for your wickedness, that you should then make as light of Christ as now? Why will you not judge now as you know you shall judge then? Will he then be worth ten thousand worlds, and is he not now worth your highest estimation, and dearest affection?

10. God will not only deny thee that salvation thou madest light of, but he will take from thee all that which thou didst value before it: he that most highly esteems Christ shall have him, and the creatures so far as they are good here, and him without the creature hereafter, because the creature is not useful; and he that sets more by the creature than by Christ, shall have some of the creature without Christ here, and neither Christ nor it hereafter.

So much of these considerations, which may show the true face of this heinous sin.

What think you now, friends, of this business? Do you not see by this time what a case that soul is in that maketh light of Christ and salvation? What need then is there that you should take heed lest this should prove your own case! The Lord knows it is too common a case. Whoever is found guilty at the last of this sin, it were better for that man he had never been born. It were better for him he had been a Turk or Indian, that never had heard the name of a Saviour, and that never had salvation offered to him: for such men "have no cloak for their sin," John xv. 22. Besides all the rest of their sins, they have this killing sin to answer for, which will undo them. And this will aggravate their misery, that Christ whom they set light by must be their Judge, and for this sin will he judge them. Oh that such would now consider how they will answer that question that Christ put to their predecessors, "How will ye escape the damnation of hell?" Matt. xxiii. 33; or, "How shall we escape if we neglect so great salvation?" Heb. ii. 3. Can you escape without a Christ? or will a despised Christ save you then? If he be accursed that sets light by father or mother, (Deut. xxvii. 16,) what then is he that sets light by Christ? It was the heinous sin of the Jews, that among them were found such as set light by father and mother, Ezek. xxii. 7. But among us, men slight the Father of spirits! In the name of God, brethren, I beseech you to consider how you will then bear his anger which you now make light of! You that cannot make light of a little sickness or want, or of natural death, no, not of a tooth-ache, but groan as if you were undone; how will you then make light of the fury of the Lord, which will burn against the contemners of his grace! Doth it not behove you beforehand to think of these things?

Hitherto I have been convincing you of the evil of the sin, and the danger that followeth: I come now to know your resolution for the time to come. What say you? Do you mean to set as light by Christ and salvation as hitherto you have done; and to be the same men after all this? I hope not. Oh let not your ministers that would fain save you, be brought in as witnesses against you to condemn you; at least, I beseech you, put not this upon me. Why, sirs, if the Lord shall say to us at judgment, Did you never tell these men what Christ did for their souls, and what need they had of him, and how nearly it did concern them to look to their salvation, that they made light of it? We must needs say the truth; Yea, Lord, we told them of it as plainly as we could; we would have gone on our knees to them if we had thought it would have prevailed; we did entreat them as earnestly as we could to consider these things: they heard of these things every day; but, alas, we could never get them to their hearts: they gave us the hearing, but they made light of all that we could say to them. Oh! sad will it prove on your side, if you force us to such an answer as this.

But if the Lord do move the hearts of any of you, and you resolve to make light of Christ no more; or if any of you say, We do not make light of him; let me tell you here in the conclusion what you must do, or else you shall be judged as slighters of Christ and salvation.

And first I will tell you what will not serve the turn.

1. You may have a notional knowledge of Christ, and the necessity of his blood, and of the excellency of salvation, and yet perish as neglecters of him. This is too common among professed christians. You may say all that other men do of him: what gospel passages had Balaam! Jesus I know, and Paul I know, the very devils could say, who believe and tremble, James ii.

2. You may weep at the history of his passion, when you read how he was used by the Jews, and yet make light of him, and perish for so doing.

3. You may come desirously to his word and ordinances. Herod heard gladly; so do many that yet must perish as neglecters of salvation.

4. You may in a fit of fear have strong desires after a Christ, to ease you, and to save you from God's wrath, as Saul had of David to play before him; and yet you may perish for making light of Christ.

5. You may obey him in many things so far as will not ruin you in the world, and escape much of the pollutions of the world by his knowledge, and yet neglect him.

6. You may suffer and lose much for him, so far as leaveth you an earthly felicity; as Ananias; the young man. Some parcels of their pleasures and profits many will part with in hope of salvation, that shall perish everlastingly for valuing it no more.

7. You may be esteemed by others a man zealous for Christ, and loved and admired upon that account, and yet be one that shall perish for making light of him.

8. You may verily think yourselves, that you set more by Christ and salvation than any thing, and yet be mistaken, and be judged as contemners of him: Christ justifieth not all that justify themselves.

9. You may be zealous preachers of Christ and salvation, and reprove others for this neglect, and lament the sin of the world in the like expression as I have done this day; and yet if you or I have no better evidence to prove our hearty esteem of Christ and salvation, we are undone for all this.

You hear, brethren, what will not serve the turn; will you now hear what persons you must be if you would not be condemned as slighters of Christ? Oh search whether it be thus with your souls, or no.

1. Your esteem of Christ and salvation must be greater than your esteem of all the honours, profits, or pleasures of this world, or else you slight him: no less will be accounted sincere, nor accepted to your salvation. Think not this hard, when there is no comparison in the matters esteemed. To esteem the greatest glory on earth before Christ and everlasting glory, is a greater folly and wrong to Christ, than to esteem a dog before your prince, would be folly in you, and a wrong to him. Scripture is plain in this; "He that loveth father or mother, wife, children, house, land, or his own life, more than me, is not worthy of me, and cannot be my disciple," Matt. x. 37; Luke xiv. 26.

2. You must manifest this esteem of Christ and salvation in your daily endeavours and seeking after him, and in parting with any thing that he shall require of you. God is a Spirit, and will not take a hypocritical profession instead of the heart and spiritual service which he commandeth. He will have the heart or nothing; and the chief room in the heart too: these must be had.

If you say that you do not make light of Christ, or will not hereafter; let me try you in these few particulars, whether indeed you mean as you say, and do not dissemble.

1. Will you for the time to come make Christ and salvation the chiefest matter of your care and study? Thrust them not out of your thoughts as a needless or unprofitable subject; nor allow it only some running, slight thoughts, which will not affect you. But will you make it your business once a day to bethink you soberly, when you are alone, what Christ hath done for you, and what he will do, if you do not make light of it; and what it is to be everlastingly happy or miserable? And what all things in this world are in comparison of your salvation; and how they will shortly leave you; and what mind you will be then of, and how you will esteem them? Will you promise me now and then to make it your business to withdraw yourselves from the world, and set yourselves to such considerations as these? If you will not, are not you slighters of Christ and salvation, that will not be persuaded soberly to think on them? This is my first question to put you to the trial, whether you will value Christ, or not.

2. Will you for the time to come set more by the word of God, which contains the discovery of these excellent things, and is your charter for salvation, and your guide thereunto? You cannot set by Christ, but you must set by his word: therefore the despisers of it are threatened with destruction, Prov. xiii. 13. Will you therefore attend to the public preaching of this word; will you read it daily; will you resolve to obey it whatever it may cost you? If you will not do this, but make light of the word of God, you shall be judged as such as make light of Christ and salvation, whatever you may fondly promise to yourselves.

3. Will you for the time to come esteem more of the officers of Christ, whom he hath purposely appointed to guide you to salvation; and will you make use of them for that end? Alas, it is not to give the minister a good word, and speak well of him, and pay him his tithes duly, that will serve the turn: it is for the necessity of your souls that God hath set them in his church; that they may be as physicians under Christ, or his apothecaries to apply his remedies to your spiritual diseases, not only in public, but also in private: that you may have some to go to for the resolving of your doubts, and for your instruction where you are ignorant, and for the help of their exhortations and prayers. Will you use hereafter to go to your ministers privately, and solicit them for advice? And if you have not such of your own as are fit, get advice from others; and ask them, What you shall do to be saved? how to prepare for death and judgment? And will you obey the word of God in their mouths? If you will not do this much, nor so much as inquire of those that should teach you, nor use the means which Christ hath established in his church for your help,

your own consciences shall one day witness that you were such as made light of Christ and salvation. If any of you doubt whether it be your duty thus to ask counsel of your teachers, as sick men do of their physicians, let your own necessities resolve you, let God's express word resolve you; see what is said of the priests of the Lord, even before Christ's coming, when much of their work did lie in ceremonials: "My covenant was with him of life and peace: and I gave them to him (to Levi) for the fear wherewith he feared me, and was afraid before my name. The law of truth was in his mouth, and iniquity was not found in his lips; he walked with me in peace and equity, and did turn many away from iniquity. For the priest's lips should keep knowledge, and they should seek the law at his mouth: for he is the messenger of the Lord of hosts," Mal. ii. 5, 6.

Nay, you must not only inquire, and submit to their advice, but also to their just reprehensions, and church censures; and without proud repining submit to the discipline of Christ in their hands, if it shall be used in the congregations whereof you are members.

4. Will you for the time to come make conscience of daily and earnest prayer to God, that you may have a part in Christ and salvation? Do not go out of doors till you have breathed out these desires to God; do not lie down to rest till you have breathed out these desires: say not, God knoweth my necessity without so often praying; for though he do, yet he will have you to know them, and feel them, and exercise your desires and all the graces of his Spirit in these duties: it is he that hath commanded to pray continually, though he know your needs without, 1 Thess. v. 17. Christ himself spent whole nights in prayer, and encourageth us to this course, Luke xviii. 1. If you will not be persuaded to this much, how can you say that you make not light of Christ and salvation?

5. Will you for the time to come resolvedly cast away your known sins at the command of Christ? If you have been proud, or contentious, or malicious, and revengeful, be so no more. If you have been adulterers, or swearers, or cursers, be so no more. You cannot hold these, and yet set by Christ and salvation.

What say you? Are you resolved to let them go? If not, when you know it is the will of Christ, and he hath told you such shall not enter into his kingdom, do not you make light of him?

6. Will you for the time to come serve God in the dearest as well as in the cheapest part of his service? not only with your tongues, but with your purses and your deeds? Shall the poor find that you set more by Christ than this world? Shall it appear in any good uses that God calls you to be liberal in, according to your abilities? "Pure religion and undefiled before God is this, To visit the fatherless and the widows in their affliction," James i. 27. Will you resolve to stick to Christ, and make sure this work of salvation, though it cost you all that you have in the world? If you think these terms too dear, you make light of Christ, and will be judged accordingly.

7. Will you for the time to come make much of all things that tend to your salvation; and take every help that God offereth you, and gladly make use of all his ordinances? Attend upon his strengthening sacraments, spend the Lord's own day in these holy employments; instruct your children and servants in these things, Deut. vi. 6, 7; get into good company that set their faces heavenward, and will teach you the way, and help you thither; and take heed of the company of wicked scorners, or foolish, voluptuous, fleshly men, or any that would hinder you in this work. Will you do these things? Or will you show that you are slighters of Christ by neglecting them.

8. Will you do all this with delight; not as your toil, but as your pleasure? And take it for your highest honour that you may be Christ's disciples, and may be admitted to serve and worship him; and rejoice with holy confidence in the sufficiency of that sacrifice by which you may have pardon of all your failings, and right to the inheritance of the saints in light? If you will do these things sincerely, you will show that you set by Christ and salvation; else not.

Dearly beloved in the Lord, I have now done that work which I came upon; what effect it hath, or will have, upon your hearts, I know not, nor is it any further in my power to accomplish that which my soul desireth for you. Were it the Lord's will that I might have my wish herein, the words that you have this day heard should so stick by you, that the secure should be awakened by them, and none of you should perish by the slighting of your salvation. I cannot now follow you to your several habitations to apply this word to your particular necessities; but oh that I could make every man's conscience a preacher to himself, that it might do it, which is ever with you: that the next time you go prayerless to bed, or about your business, conscience might cry out, Dost thou set no more by Christ and thy salvation? That the next time you are tempted to think hardly of a holy and diligent life, (I will not say to deride it as more ado than needs,) conscience might cry out to thee, Dost thou set so light by Christ and thy salvation? That the next time you are ready to rush upon known sin, and to please your fleshly desires against the command of God, conscience might cry out, Is Christ and salvation no more worth, than to cast them away, or venture them for thy lusts? That when you are following the world with your most eager desires, forgetting the world to come, and the change that is a little before you, conscience might cry out to you, Is Christ and salvation no more worth than so? That when you are next spending the Lord's day in idleness or vain sports, conscience might tell you what you are doing. In a word, that in all your neglects of duty, your sticking at the supposed labour or cost of a godly life, yea, in all your cold and lazy prayers and performances, conscience might tell you how unsuitable such endeavours are to the reward; and that Christ and salvation should not be so slighted. I will say no more but this at this time, It is a thousand pities that when God hath provided a Saviour for the world, and when Christ hath suffered so much for their sins, and made so full a satisfaction to justice, and purchased so glorious a kingdom for his saints, and all this is offered so freely to sinners, to lost, unworthy sinners, even for nothing, that yet so many millions should everlastingly perish because they make light of their Saviour and salvation, and prefer the vain world and their lusts before them. I have delivered my message, the Lord open your hearts to receive it: I have persuaded you with the word of truth and soberness, the Lord persuade you more effectually, or else all this is lost.

A TREATISE OF DEATH,

THE LAST ENEMY TO BE DESTROYED.

SHOWING WHEREIN ITS ENMITY CONSISTETH, AND HOW IT IS DESTROYED.

PART OF IT WAS PREACHED AT THE FUNERAL OF ELIZABETH, THE LATE WIFE OF MR. JOSEPH BAKER, PASTOR OF THE CHURCH AT ST. ANDREW'S IN WORCESTER;

WITH SOME FEW PASSAGES OF THE LIFE OF THE SAID MRS. BAKER OBSERVED.

"In whose eyes a vile person is contemned: but he honoureth them that fear the Lord."—Psal. xv. 4.

"O death, where is thy sting? O grave, where is thy victory? The sting of death is sin, and the strength of sin is the law. But thanks be to God, who giveth us the victory through our Lord Jesus Christ."—1 Cor. xv. 55—57.

TO THE WORSHIPFUL THE MAYOR, ALDERMEN, AND SHERIFF OF THE CITY OF WORCESTER, WITH THE REST OF THE INHABITANTS; ESPECIALLY THOSE OF THE PARISHES OF ANDREW'S AND HELEN'S.

WORSHIPFUL, AND THE REST BELOVED,

THE chief part of this following discourse being preached among you, and that upon an occasion which you are obliged to consider, (Isa. lvii. 1,) being called to publish it, I thought it meet to direct it first to your hands, and to take this opportunity plainly and seriously to exhort you in some matters that your present and everlasting peace is much concerned in.

Credible fame reporteth you to be a people not all of one mind or temper in the matters of God; but that, 1. Some of you are godly, sober, and peaceable; 2. Some well-meaning and zealous, but addicted to divisions; 3. Some papists; 4. Some hiders, seduced by your late deceased neighbour Clement Writer (to whom the quakers do approach in many opinions); 5. And too many profane and obstinate persons, that are heartily and seriously of no religion, but take occasion, from the divisions of the rest, to despise or neglect the ordinances of God, and join themselves to no assemblies.

1. To the first sort (having least need of my exhortation) I say no more, but "as you have received Christ Jesus the Lord, so walk ye in him, rooted and built up in him, and established in the faith, as ye have been taught, abounding therein with thanksgiving. And beware lest any man spoil you by deceit," &c. Col. ii. 6—8. Walk as "a chosen generation, a royal priesthood, a holy nation, a peculiar people; to show forth the praises of him that hath called you out of darkness into his marvellous light: having your conversation honest among the ungodly; that, whereas they are apt to speak against you as evil-doers, they may by your good works, which they shall behold, glorify God in the day of visitation; for so is the will of God, that with well-doing ye may put to silence the ignorance of foolish men," 1 Pet. ii. 9, 11, 12, 15. Your labour and patience is known to the Lord, and how ye cannot bear them which are evil, but have tried them which say they speak from the Lord, and are apostles, and are not, and have found them liars; even the woman Jezebel, that is suffered to teach and seduce the people, calling herself a prophetess, who shall be cast into a bed of tribulation, and all that commit adultery with her, except they repent; and her children shall be killed with death; and all the churches shall know that Christ is he who searcheth the reins and hearts, and will give to every one according to their work. As for yourselves, we put upon you no other burden but that which you have already; hold fast till the Lord come, Rev. ii. Be watchful that ye fall not from your first love. And if any have declined, and grown remiss, remember how you have received, and heard; and hold fast, and repent, and strengthen the things that remain, which are ready to die, lest your candlestick should be removed, Rev. iii. 2, 3, &c. And "beware, lest ye also, being led away with the error of the wicked, fall from your own stedfastness. But grow in grace, and in the knowledge of our Lord and Saviour Jesus Christ," 2 Pet. iii. 17, 18. And I beseech you, brethren, "do all things without murmurings and disputings: that ye may be blameless and harmless, the sons of God, without rebuke, in the midst of a crooked and perverse nation, amongst whom you, and your brethren, shine as lights in the world," Phil. ii. 14, 15. And if in well-doing you suffer, think it not strange, but rejoice that ye are partakers of the suffer-

ings of Christ, that when his glory shall be revealed, ye may be glad also with exceeding joy. If ye be reproached for the name of Christ, happy are ye, for the Spirit of glory and of God resteth upon you, being glorified on your part, while he is evil spoken of on theirs," 1 Pet. iv. 12—14.

2. To the second sort, inclinable to divisions, let me tender the counsel of the Holy Ghost. "My brethren, be not many masters, (or teachers,) knowing that ye shall receive the greater condemnation. The wisdom that is from above, is first pure, and then peaceable, gentle, and easy to be entreated, full of mercy and good fruits, without partiality, and without hypocrisy; and the fruit of righteousness is sown in peace of them that make peace," Jam. iii. 1, 17, 18. "Who is a wise man and endued with knowledge among you? let him show out of a good conversation his works with meekness of wisdom. But if ye have bitter envying and strife in your hearts, glory not, and lie not against the truth. This wisdom descendeth not from above, but is earthly, sensual, devilish,—for where envying and strife is, there is confusion, and every evil work," Jam. iii. 13—16. Look on those assemblies where the people, possessing the fear of God, are of one heart and mind, and walk together in love and holy order, and people give due honour and obedience to their faithful guides; and compare them with the congregations where professors are self-conceited, unruly, proud, and addicted to ostentation of themselves, and to divisions; and see which is likest to the primitive pattern, and in which it is that the power of godliness prospereth best, and the beauty of religion most appears, and christians walk as christians indeed. If pride had not brought the heavy judgment of infatuation or insensibility on many, the too clear discoveries of the fruits of divisions, in the numerous and sad experiences of this age, would have caused them to be abhorred as odious and destructive, by those that now think they do but transcend their lower brethren in holiness and zeal. "Now I beseech you, brethren, in the name of our Lord Jesus Christ, that ye all speak the same thing, and that there be no divisions among you; but that ye be perfectly joined together, in the same mind, and in the same judgment," 1 Cor. i. 10. "The God of patience and consolation grant you to be like-minded one toward another, according to Christ Jesus; that ye may with one mind and one mouth glorify God," Rom. xv. 5, 6. "And I beseech you, brethren, to know them which labour among you, and are over you in the Lord, and admonish you; and esteem them very highly in love for their work's sake; and be at peace among yourselves," 1 Thess. v. 12, 13. And "mark them that cause divisions and offences, contrary to the doctrine which ye have learned, and avoid them," Rom. xvi. 17. And "if there be any consolation in Christ, if any comfort of love, if any fellowship of the Spirit, if any bowels and mercies, fulfil ye our joy, that ye be like-minded, having the same love, being of one accord, of one mind. Let nothing be done through strife or vain-glory; but in lowliness of mind let each esteem other better than themselves. Look not every man on his own things, (his own gifts and graces,) but every man also on the things (the graces and gifts) of others. Let this mind be in you which was also in Christ Jesus; who being in the form of God, thought it not robbery to be equal with God; but made himself of no reputation, (or emptied himself of all worldly glory,)" Phil. ii. 1—7; as if he had had no form or comeliness, and no beauty to the eye, for which we should desire him; but was despised and rejected of men, and not esteemed, Isa. liii. 2—4. It is not (as you imagine) your extraordinary knowledge, zeal, and holiness, that inclineth you to divisions, and to censuring of your brethren; but it is pride and ignorance, and want of love. And if you grow to any ripeness in knowledge, humility, self-denial, and charity, you will bewail your dividing inclinations and courses, and reckon them among the greater and grievous of your sins, and cry out against them as much as your more charitable and experienced brethren do.

3. To the third sort (the papists) I shall say nothing here, because I cannot expect they should read it and consider it; and because we are so far disagreed in our principles, that we cannot treat with them on those rational terms as we may do with the rest of the inhabitants of the world, whether christians, infidels, or heathens. As long as they build their faith and salvation on this supposition, that the eyes, and taste, and feeling of all the sound men in the world are deceived, in judging of bread and wine; and as long as they deny the certain experience of true believers (telling us that we are void of charity and unjustified, because we are not of their church); and as long as they fly from the judgment and tradition of the ancient and present church (unless their small part may be taken for the whole, or the major vote); and as long as they reject our appeal to the holy Scriptures; I know not well what we can say to them, which we can expect they should regard, any more than music is regarded by the deaf, or light by the blind, or argument by the distracted. If they had the moderation and charity impartially to peruse our writings, I durst confidently promise the recovery of multitudes of them, by the three writings which I have already published, and the more that others have said against them.

4. And for the fourth sort, (the hiders and the quakers,) I have said enough to them already in my book against infidelity, and those against popery and quakers; but in vain to those that have sinned unto death.

5. It is the fifth sort, therefore, that I shall chiefly address my speech to, who, I fear, are not the smallest part. It is an astonishing consideration to men that are awake, to observe the unreasonableness and stupidity of the ignorant, careless, sensual part of men, how little they love or fear the God whom their tongues confess; how little they value, or mind, or seek the everlasting glory which they take on them to believe; how little they fear and shun those flames which must feed for ever on the impenitent and unholy; how little they care or labour for their immortal souls, as if they were of the religion of their beasts; how bitterly many of them hate the holy ways commanded by the Lord, while yet they pretend to be themselves his servants, and to take the Scriptures to be his word; how sottishly and contemptuously they neglect and slight the holiness, without which there is no salvation, Heb. xii. 14; how eagerly they desire and seek the pleasing of their flesh, and the matters of this transitory life, while they call them vanity and vexation; how madly they will fall out with their own salvation, and, from the errors and sins of hypocrites or others, will pick quarrels against the doctrine, and ordinances, and ways of God; as if other men's faults should be exceeded by you, while you pretend to loathe them. If it be a sin to crack our faith by some particular error, what is it to dash it all to pieces? If it be odious in your eyes to deny some particular ordinance of God, what is it to neglect or profane them all? If it be their sin that quarrel in the way to heaven, and walk not in company, as love requireth them, what is it in you to run towards hell, and turn your backs on the holy laws and ways of God? If it be so lamentable to the nation and themselves, that so many have fallen into schism and disorder, what is

it, then, that so many are ungodly, sensual, and worldly, and have no true religion at all in sincerity, and life, and power? Ungodliness is all heresy transcendently in the lump, and that in practice. A man that is so foolish as to plead that arsenic is better than bread, may yet live himself, if he do not take it; but so cannot he, that eateth it instead of bread. Heretics only in speculation may be saved, but practical heretics cannot. You think it heinous to deny with the mouth, that there is a God, who made us, and is our only Lord and happiness (and so it is); and is it not heinous, then, to deny him with the heart and life, and to deny him the love and obedience that is properly due to God? It is odious idolatry to bow to a creature as to God; and is it not odious to love, and honour, and obey a creature before him, and to seek it more eagerly, and mind it more seriously, than God? If it be damnable infidelity to deny Christ to be the Redeemer, is it much less to turn away from him, and make light of him, and refuse his grace, while you seem to honour him? If it be damnable blasphemy to deny the Holy Ghost, what is it to resist and refuse him when he would sanctify you, and, perhaps, to make a scorn of holiness? If it be heresy to deny the holy catholic church, and the communion of saints, what is it to hate the holy members of the church, and to avoid, if not deride, the communion of saints? Be not deceived; God is not mocked; a mock religion and the name of christianity will never save you. Do you know how near you are to judgment? and will you fearlessly thus heap up wrath, and lay in fuel for the everlasting flames? Do you know how speedily you shall wish, in the bitterness of your souls, that you had heard, and prayed, and laboured as for your lives, and redeemed your time, and obeyed your teachers? and yet will you now stand loitering, and quarrelling, and jesting, and dallying in the matters of salvation? and will you live as if you had nothing but the world to mind, when you are even ready to step into the endless world? O sirs, do you know what you are doing? You are abusing the living God, and wronging the Lord Jesus, and trampling upon that mercy which would comfort you in your extremity, a drop of which you would then be glad of: you are grieving your poor friends and teachers, and preparing for your endless grief. Alas! what should a faithful minister do for the saving of your souls? He seeth you befooled in your security, and carelessly passing on towards hell, and cannot help it: he sees you posting to your misery, where you will be out of the reach of all our exhortations, and where mercy will not follow you to be accepted or rejected: and though he see you almost past remedy, he cannot help you. He knoweth not, when he speaks to you, whether ever he shall speak unto you more, and whether ever you shall have another call and offer; and, therefore, he would fain speak effectually if he could; but it is not in his power. He knows that the matter sticks all at your own wills; and that if he could but procure your own consent to the most reasonable and necessary business in the world, the work were done, and you might escape the everlasting flames; and yet this is it that he cannot procure. Oh! wonderful, that any man should be damned; yea, that many men, and most men, should be damned, when they might be saved if they would, and will not. Yea, that no saying will serve to procure their consent, and make them willing. That we must look on our poor miserable neighbours in hell, and say, They might have been saved once, but would not: they had time and leave to turn to God, and to be holy and happy as well as others; but we could never prevail with them to consent, and know the day of their visitation. Oh! what should we do for the saving of careless, senseless souls? Must we let them go? Is there no remedy? Shall ministers study to meet with their necessities, and tell them, with all possible plainness and compassion, of the evil that is a little before them, and teach them how they may escape it? Why this they do from day to day, and some will not hear them, but are tippling or idling, or making a jest of the preacher at home; and others are hearing with prejudice and contempt; and most are hardened into a senseless deadness; and all seems to them but an empty sound: and they are so used to hear of heaven and hell, that they make as light of them, as if there were no such states. Alas! that while millions are weeping and wailing in utter desperation for the neglecting of their day of grace, and turning away from him that called them, our poor hearers at the same time should wilfully follow them, when they are told from God what others suffer. Alas! that you should be sleepy and dead under those means that should waken you to prevent eternal death; and that ever you should make merry so near damnation, and be sporting yourselves with the same kind of sins, that others at the same hour are tormented for. And is such madness as this remediless in people that seem as wise as others for worldly things? Alas! for any thing that we can do, experience tells us, that with the most it is remediless. Could we remedy it, our poor people should not wilfully run from Christ, and lie in the flames of hell for ever: could our persuasions and entreaties help it, they should not for ever be shut out of heaven, when it is offered to them as well as others. We bewail it from our hearts before the Lord, that we can entreat them no more earnestly, and beg not of them, as for our lives, to look before them, and hearken to the voice of grace, that they may be saved; and a thousand times, in secret, we call ourselves hard-hearted, unmerciful, and unfaithful, (in too great a measure,) that speak no more importunately for the saving of men's souls, when we know not whether we shall ever speak to them any more. Is this all that we can say or do in so terrible a case, and in a matter of such weight as men's salvation? The Lord forgive our great insensibility, and awaken us, that we may be fit to awaken others. But yet for all this, with grief we most complain, that our people feel not when we feel, and that they are senseless or asleep when we speak to them as seriously as we can; and that tears and moans do not prevail; but they go home and live as stupidly, in an unconverted state, as if all were well with them, and they were not the men we speak to.

Oh! that you knew what a fearful judgment it is to be forsaken of God, because you would have none of him; and to be given up to your hearts' lust, to walk in your own counsels, because you would not hearken to his voice, Psalm lxxxi. 11—13; and to have God say, Let those wretches be ignorant, and careless, and fleshly, and worldly, and filthy still, Rev. xxii. 11. Oh! that you knew (but not by experience) what a heavy plague it is to be so forsaken, as to have eyes that see not, or seeing, do not perceive; and to have ears that hear not, or to hear, and not understand; and so to be unconverted and unhealed, Mark iv. 12; and to be hardened and condemned by the word, and patience, and mercies, that do soften and save others, and should have saved you. Take heed lest Christ say, I have sent them my messenger long enough in vain; from henceforth never fruit grow on them; because they would not be converted, they shall not. Take heed, lest he take you away from means, and quickly put an end to your opportunities. You see how fast men pass away, but little do you know how many are lamenting that they made no better use of time, and helps, and mercies, while they had them. Oh! hear while you may hear, for it will not be long; read while you may read, and pray while you may pray, and turn while you may turn, and go to your christian friends and teachers, and inquire of them, what you must do to be saved, before inquiring be too late. Spend the Lord's day, and what other time you can redeem, in holy preparations for your endless rest, while you have such a happy day to spend. Oh! sleep no longer in your sins, while God stands over you, lest, before you are aware, you awake in hell. Patience and mercy have their appointed time, and will not always wait and be despised. Oh! let not your teachers be forced to say, We would have taught them publicly and privately, but they would not. We would have catechised the ignorant, and exhorted the negligent, but some of them would not come near us, and others of them gave us but the hearing, and went away such as they came. If once, by forfeiting the gospel, the teachers whom you slight be taken from you, you may then sin on and take your course, till time, and help, and hope, are past.

The providence that called me to this work was some warning to you. Though it was a removing of his helper, a pattern of meekness, and godliness, and charity, and he is left the more disconsolate in the prosecution of his work. God hath made him faithful to your souls, and careful for your happiness: he walks before you in humility, and self-denial, and patience, and peaceableness, and inoffensive life; he is willing to teach you publicly and privately in season; he manageth the work of God with prudence and moderation, and yet with zeal; carefully avoiding both ungodliness and schism, or the countenancing of either of them. Were he not of eminent wisdom and integrity, his name would not be so unspotted in a place where dividers and disputers, papists and quakers, and so many bitter enemies of godliness, do watch for matter of accusation and reproach against the faithful ministers of Christ. As you love the safety and happiness of your city, and of your souls, undervalue not such mercies, nor think it enough to put them off with your commendations and good word: it is not that which they live, and preach, and labour for; but for the conversion, edification, and salvation of your souls. Let them have this, or they have nothing, if you should give them all you have. The enemies of the gospel have no wiser cavil against the painful labourers of the Lord, than to call them hirelings, and blame them for looking after tithes, and great matters in the world. But as among all the faithful ministers of this country, through the great mercy of God, these adversaries are now almost ashamed to open their mouths with an accusation of covetousness, so this your reverend, faithful teacher hath stopped the mouth of all such calumny, as to him. When I invited him from a place of less work, and a competent maintenance, to accept of less than half that maintenance, with a far greater burden of work among you, he never stuck at it, as thinking he might be more serviceable to God, and win that which is better than the riches of this world. And if now you will frustrate his expectations, and disappoint his labours and hopes of your salvation, it will be easier for Sodom in the day of judgment than for you. Alas! how sad is it to see a faithful minister longing and labouring for men's salvation, and many of them neglecting him, and others picking groundless quarrels; and the proud, unruly, selfish part rebelling, and turning their backs upon their teachers, whenever they will not humour them in their own ways, or when they deal but faithfully with their souls! Some, even of those that speak against disobedience, conventicles, and schism, turn away in disdain, if their children may not be needlessly baptized in private houses, and if that solemn ordinance may not be celebrated in a parlour conventicle. How many refuse to come to the minister in private to be instructed or catechised, or to confer with him about their necessary preparation for death and judgment! Is not this the case of many among you? Must not your teacher say he sent to you, and was willing to have done his part, and you refused? Little will ye now believe how heavy this will lie upon you one day, and how dear you shall pay for the causeless grieving and disappointment of your guides. It is not your surliness and passions that will then serve turn to answer God. Nor shall it save you to say, that ministers were of so many minds and ways that you knew not which of them to regard; for it was but one way that God in the holy Scripture did prescribe you; and all faithful ministers were agreed in the things which you reject, and in which you practically differ from them all. What! are we not all agreed that God is to be preferred before the world? and that you must first seek the kingdom of God, and his righteousness? and that no man can be saved except he be converted and born again? and that he that hath not the Spirit of Christ is none of his? Matt. vi. 33; John iii. 3, 5; Matt. xviii. 3; Rom. viii. 9; and that you and your households should serve the Lord? Josh. xxiv. 15. Are we not all agreed that the law of the Lord must be your delight, and that you must meditate in it day and night? Psalm i. 2, 3; and that you must be constant and fervent in prayer? 1 Thess. v. 17; Luke xviii. 1, &c.; and that all that name the name of Christ must depart from iniquity? and that if ye live after the flesh ye shall die? 2 Tim. ii. 19; Rom. viii. 13. You shall find one day that it was you only, and such as you, that practically differed from us in these points; but we differed not in these, or such as these, among ourselves. I never read that a man shall not see God because he is episcopal, presbyterian, independent, no, nor anabaptist; or because he readeth not his prayers, or such like; but I read that no man shall see God without holiness, Heb. xii. 14.

It will not serve your turn in judgment to say that you were for this side, or that side, and, therefore, you hearkened not to the other side, as long as all those sides agree in the necessity of holiness, which you neglect. Why did you not learn of your own side, at least to forsake your tippling, and swearing, and worldly-mindedness, and to make it the daily trade of your lives to provide for life everlasting, and make sure work in the matter of your salvation? If you had learnt but this much of any side, you would cast away your siding more, and have loved and honoured them that feared the Lord, of what side soever, (Psal. xv. 4,) and have contemned the ungodly as vile persons, though they had been of your side. The catholic church is one, and containeth all that heartily and practically believe in God the Father, Son, and Holy Ghost, the Creator, Redeemer, and Sanctifier, and live a holy, heavenly life. Leave off your siding, and keep this blessed, simple unity, and you will then be wiser than in a passion to cast yourselves into hell, because some fall out in the way to heaven.

Nor will it serve your turn at the bar of God to talk of the miscarriages or scandals of some that took on them to be godly, no more than to run out of the ark for the sake of Ham, or out of Christ's family for the sake of Judas. Whatever men are, God is just, and will do you no wrong; and you are called to believe in God, and to serve him, and not to believe in men. Nothing but wickedness could so far blind men as to make them think they may cast off their love and service to the Lord, because some others have dishonoured him; or that they may cast away their souls by carelessness, because some others have wounded their souls by particular sins. Do you dislike the sins of professors of godliness? So much the better. We desire you not to agree with them in sinning. Join with them in a holy life, and imitate them so far as they obey the Lord; and go as far beyond them in avoiding the sins that you are offended at as you can: and this it is that we desire. Suppose they were covetous, or liars, or schismatical, imitate them in holy duties, and fly as far from covetousness, lying, and schism, as you will.

You have had learned and godly bishops of this city; search the writings of those of them that have left any of their labours to posterity, and see whether they speak for the same substantials of faith and godliness, which are now preached to you by those that you set so light by. Bishops Latimer, Parrey, Babington, &c. while they were bishops; and Robert Abbot, Hall, &c. before they were bishops; all excellent, learned, godly men, have here been preachers to your ancestors. Read their books, and you will find that they call men to that strictness and holiness of life which you cannot abide. Read your Bishop Babington on the Commandments, and see there how zealously he condemneth the profaners of the Lord's day, and those that make it a day of idleness or sports. And what if one man think that one bishop should have hundreds of churches under his sole jurisdiction, and another man think that every full parish church should have a bishop of their own, and that one parish will find him work enough, be he what he will, (which is the difference now amongst us,) is this so heinous a disagreement as should frighten you from a holy life, which all agree for?

To conclude, remember, this is the day of your salvation. Ministers are your helpers; Christ and holiness are your way; Scripture is your rule; the godly must be your company; and the communion of saints must be your desire. If now any scandals, divisions, displeasures, or any seducements of secret or open adversaries of the truth, or temptations of Satan, the world, or flesh, whatsoever, shall prevail with you to lose your day, to refuse your mercies, and to neglect Christ and your immortal souls, you are conquered and undone, and your enemy hath his will; and the more confidently and fearlessly you brave it out, the more is your misery, for the harder are your hearts, and the harder is your cure, and the surer and sorer will be your damnation. I have purposely avoided the enticing words of worldly wisdom, and a style that tends to claw your ears, and gain applause with airy wits; and have chosen these familiar words, and dealt thus plainly and freely with you, because the greatness of the cause persuaded me I could not be too serious. Whether many of you will read it, and what success it shall have upon them, or how those that read it will take it, I cannot tell; but I know that I intended it for your good; and that whether you will hear, or whether you will forbear, the ministers of Christ must not forbear to do their duty, nor be rebellious themselves; but our labours shall be acceptable with our Lord, and you shall know that his ministers were among you, Ezek. ii. 3—8. "Yet a little while is the light with you: walk while ye have the light, lest darkness come upon you; for he that walketh in darkness knoweth not whither he goeth," John xii. 35. Oh, take this warning from Christ, and from

An earnest desirer of your everlasting peace,

RICHARD BAXTER.

---

1 CORINTHIANS XV. 26.

THE LAST ENEMY THAT SHALL BE DESTROYED IS DEATH.

DEATH is the occasion of this day's meeting; and death must be the subject of our present meditations. I must speak of that which will shortly silence me, and you must hear of that which will speedily stop your ears: and we must spend this hour on that which waits to cut our thread, and take down our glass, and end our time, and tell us we have spent our last. But as it hath now done good by doing hurt, so are we to consider of the accidental benefits, as well as of the natural evil, from which the heavenly wisdom doth extract them. Death hath now bereaved a body of its soul, but thereby it hath sent that soul to Christ, where it hath now experience how good it is to be absent from the body and present with the Lord, 2 Cor. v. 8. It hath separated a faithful wife from a beloved husband; but it hath sent her to a Husband dearlier beloved, and taught her now, by experience, to say, that to be with Christ is best of all, Phil. i. 23. It hath deprived a sorrowful husband of a wife, and deprived us all of a faithful friend: but it hath thereby brought us to the house of mourning, which is better for us than the house of feasting; (a paradox to the flesh, but an undoubted truth;) for here we may see the end of all men, and we who are yet living may lay it to our hearts, Eccl. vii. 2, 3. Yea, it hath brought us to the house of God, and occasioned this serious address to his holiness, that we may be instructed by his word, as we are warned by his works; and that we may be wise to understand, and to consider our latter end, Deut. xxxii. 29.

It is like you will think, to tell men of the evil or enmity of death is as needless a discourse as any could be chosen; for who is there that is not naturally too sensible of this, and who doth not dread the name, or, at least, the face of death? But there is accidentally a greater evil in it than that which nature teacheth men to fear: and while it is the king of terrors to the world, the most are ignorant of the greatest hurt that it doth them, or can do them; or, at least, it is but little thought on; which hath made me think it a needful work to tell you yet of much more evil in that which you abhor as the greatest evil: but so as withal to magnify our Redeemer, who overshooteth death in its own bow; and causeth it, when it hits the mark, to miss it; and which causeth health by loathsome medicines; and, by the dung of our bodily corruption, manureth his church to the greater felicity.

Such excellent skill of our wise Physician we find expressed and exercised in this chapter, where an unhappy error against the resurrection hath happily occasioned an excellent discourse on that weighty subject, which may establish many a thousand souls, and serve to shame and destroy such heresies, till the resurrection come and prove itself. The great argument which the apostle most insisteth on to prove the resurrection, is Christ's own resurrection, where he entereth into a comparison between Christ and Adam; showing that, as Adam first brought death upon himself, and then upon his posterity, so Christ, who was "made a quickening Spirit," did first rise himself as the first-fruits, and then at his coming will raise his own; and "as in Adam all die, so in Christ shall all be made alive." And this Christ will do as our victorious King, and the Captain of our salvation, who, when he hath subdued every enemy, will then deliver up the kingdom to the Father; and the last enemy which he will subdue is death, and therefore our resurrection is his final conquest.

The terms of the text have no difficulty in them. The doctrine which they express must be thus unfolded:

I. I must show you that death is an enemy, and what is meant by this expression, and wherein its enmity doth consist.

II. I shall show you that it is an enemy to be destroyed, though last; and how, and by what degrees, it is destroyed. And then we shall make application of it to your further instruction and edification.

I. That you may know what is meant by an enemy here, you must observe that man, being fallen into sin and misery, and Christ having undertaken the work of our redemption, the Scripture oft speaketh of our misery and recovery metaphorically in military terms: and so Satan is said to take us captive, and we to be his slaves, and Christ to be the Captain of our salvation, and to redeem us from our bondage; and thus our sin and misery, and all that hindereth the blessed ends of his undertaking, are called enemies. Death, therefore, is called an enemy to be destroyed, that is, a penal evil to be removed by the Redeemer, in order to our recovery, and the glory of his grace. 1. It is an evil. 2. A punishment procured by our sin, and executed by God's justice. 3. It is an evil that hindereth our felicity. These three things are included in the enmity.

That death is an enemy to nature is a thing that all understand; but all consider not how it is an enemy to our souls, to the exercise of grace, and, consequently, to the attainment of glory. I shall, therefore, having first spoken briefly of the former, insist a little longer upon the latter.

1. How great an enemy death is unto nature doth easily appear, in that, 1. It is the dissolution of the man. It maketh a man to become no man, by separating the soul from the body, and dissolving the body into its principles. It pulls down in a moment a curious frame, that nature was long building, and tenderly cherishing and preserving. The mother long nourisheth it in her bowels, and painfully brings it forth, and carefully brings it up. What labour doth it cost our parents and ourselves to make provision for this life! and death in a moment cuts it off. How careful are we to keep in these lamps, and to maintain the oil! and death extinguisheth them at a blast. How noble a creature doth it destroy! To-day our parts are all in order, and busy about their several tasks; our hearts are moving, our lungs are breathing, our stomachs are digesting, our blood and spirits by assimilation making more; and to-morrow death takes off the poise, and all stands still, or draws the pins, and all the frame doth fall to pieces. We shall breathe no more, nor speak, nor think, nor walk no more; our pulse will beat no more; our eyes shall see the light no more; our ears shall hear the voice of man, delightful sounds, and melody, no more; we shall taste no more our meat or drink; our appetite is gone; our strength is gone; our natural warmth is turned into an earthy cold; our comeliness and beauty is turned into a ghastly, loathsome deformity; our white and red doth soon turn into horrid blackness; our tender flesh hath lost its feeling, and is become a senseless lump, which feeleth not whither it is carried, nor how it is used; that must be hidden in the earth, lest it annoy the living; that quickly turns to loathsome putrefaction, and after that to common earth. Were all the once comely bodies which are now rotting in one churchyard uncovered, and here presented to your view, the sight would tell you, more effectually than my words do, what an enemy death is to our nature. When corruption hath finished its work, you see the earth which once was flesh; you see the bones; you see the skulls; you see the holes where once were brains, and eyes, and mouth. This change death makes, and that universally and unavoidably. The prince cannot resist it by his majesty, for he hath sinned against the highest Majesty; the strong cannot resist it by their strength, for it is the messenger of the Almighty. The commanders must obey it; the conquerors must be conquered by it. The rich cannot bribe it; the learned orator cannot persuade it to pass him by; the skilful physician cannot save himself from the mortal stroke. Neither fields nor gardens, earth or sea, affordeth any medicine to prevent it. All have sinned, and all must die; "Dust we are, and to dust we must return," Gen. iii. 19: and thus should we remain if the Lord of life should not revive us.

2. And it is not only to the body, but to the soul also, that death is naturally an enemy. The soul hath naturally a love and inclination to its body, and therefore it feareth a separation before, and desireth a restoration afterward. Abstracting joy and torment, heaven and hell, in our consideration, the state of separation as such is a natural evil: even to the human soul of Christ it was so, while his body remained in the grave. Which separated state is the *hades*, which our English calleth hell, that Christ is said to have gone into. And though (the soul of Christ, and) the souls of those that die in him, do pass into a far more happy state than they had in flesh, yet that is accidentally, from rewarding justice and the bounty of the Lord, and not at all from death as death. The separation as such is still an evil; and therefore the soul is still desirous of the body's resurrection, and knoweth that its felicity will then be greater, when the re-union and glorification hath perfected the whole man: so that death, as death, is unwelcome to the soul itself, though death, as accidentally gainful, may be desired.

3. And to the unpardoned, unrenewed soul, death is the passage to everlasting misery, and in this regard is far more terrible than in all that hitherto hath been spoken. Oh! could the guilty soul be sure that there is no justice to take hold on it after death, and no more pain and sorrow to be felt, but that man dieth as a beast which hath no more to feel, or lose, then death would seem a tolerable evil; but it is the living death, the dying life, the endless woe, to which death leads the guilty soul, which makes it to be unspeakably terrible. The utter darkness, the unquenchable fire, the worm that dieth not, the everlasting flames of the wrath of God; these are the chief horror and sting of death to the ungodly. Oh! were it but to be turned into trees, or stones, or earth, or nothing, it were nothing, in comparison of this. But I pass by this, because it is not directly intended in my text.

4. The saints themselves being sanctified but in part, are but imperfectly assured of their salvation; and therefore, in that measure, as they remain in doubt, or unassured, death may be a double terror to them. They believe the threatenings, and know more than unbelievers do, what an unsufferable loss it is to be deprived of the celestial glory; and what an unspeakable misery it is to bear the endless wrath of God: and therefore, so far as they have such fears, it must needs make death a terror to them.

5. But if there were nothing but death itself to be our enemy, the foreknowledge of it would increase the misery. A beast that knoweth not that he must die, is not tormented with the fears of death, though nature hath possessed them with a self-preserving fear, for the avoiding of an invading evil: but man foreknoweth that he must die; he hath still occasion to anticipate his terrors. That which will be, and certainly and shortly will be, is, in a manner, as if it were already: and, therefore, foreknowledge makes us as if we were always dying. We see our graves, our weeping friends, our fore-described corruption and dismal state, and so our life is a continual death. And thus death is an enemy to nature.

2. But this is not all, nor the greatest enmity that death hath to the godly. It is a lamentable hinderance to the work of grace, as I shall show you next in ten particulars.

1. The fears of death do much abate our desires after God, as he is to be enjoyed by the separated soul. Though every believing, holy soul do love God above all, and take heaven for his home, and therefore sincerely longeth after it, yet when we know that death stands in the way, and that there is no coming thither but through this dreadful, narrow passage, this stoppeth, and lamentably dulleth our desires; and so the natural enmity turneth to a spiritual sorer enmity. For let a man be never so much a saint, he will be still a man, and therefore, as death will still be death, so nature will still be nature, and therefore, death, as death, will be abhorred. And we are such timorous sluggards, that we are easily discouraged by this lion in the way. The ugly porter affrighteth us from those grateful thoughts of the new Jerusalem, the city of God, the heavenly inheritance, which otherwise the blessed object would produce. Our sanctified affections would be mounting upwards, and holy love would be working towards its blessed object, but death, standing in the way, suppresseth our desires, and turns us back, and frighteneth us from our Father's presence. We look up to Christ and the holy city as to a precious pearl in the bottom of the sea, or as to a dear and faithful friend, that is beyond some dreadful gulf. Fain we would enjoy him, but we dare not venture; we fear this dismal enemy in the way. He that can recover his health by a pleasant medicine, doth take it without any great reluctancy; but if a leg or an arm must be cut off, or a stone cut out by a painful, dangerous incision, what a striving doth it cause between the contrary passions; the love of life, and the love of ease, the fear of death, and the fear of suffering!

Could we but come to heaven as easily as innocent Adam might have done if he had conquered, what wings would it add to our desires! Might we be translated as Enoch, or conveyed thither in the chariot of Elias, what saint is there that would not long to see the face and glory of the Lord? Were it but to go to the top of a mountain, and there see Christ with Moses and Elias, in a glimpse of glory, as did the three disciples, who would not make haste, and say, "It is good for us to be here?" Matt. xvii. 1—4. But to travel so cheerfully with Abraham to the mount of Moriah, to sacrifice an only son, or with a martyr to the flames, is a harder task. This is the principal enmity of death; it deterreth our desires and thoughts from heaven, and maketh it a far harder matter to us to long after God than otherwise it would be. Yea, it causeth us to fly from him, even when we truly love him; and where faith and love do work so strongly as to overcome these fears, yet do they meet with them as an enemy, and must fight before they overcome.

2. And as this enemy dulleth our desires, so doth it consequently cool our love, as to the exercise, and it hindereth our hope, and much abateth the complacency and joy that we should have in the believing thoughts of heaven, when we should be rejoicing in hope of the glory of God, Rom. v. 2; the face of death appearing to our thoughts, is naturally an enemy to our joy. When we think of the grave, and of dissolution, and corruption, and of our long abode in the places of darkness, of our contemned dust, and scattered bones, this damps our joyful thoughts of heaven, if supernatural grace do not make us conquerors.

But if we might pass from earth to heaven, as from one room to another, what haste should we make in our desires! How joyfully should we think and speak of heaven! Then we might live in the joy of the Holy Ghost, and easily delight ourselves in God, and comfort would be our daily food.

3. Moreover, as our natural enemy doth thus occasion the abatement of desire, and love, and joy, so also of our thankfulness for the glory that is promised us. God would have more praise from us, if we had more pleasing, joyful thoughts of our inheritance. We should magnify him from day to day, when we remember how we shall magnify him for ever. Our hearts would be turned into thankfulness, and our tongues would be extolling our dear Redeemer, and sounding forth his praise whom we must praise for ever, if dreadful death did not draw a veil to hide the heavenly glory from us.

4. And thus the dismal face of death doth hinder the heavenliness of our conversation. Our thoughts will be diverted when our complacency and desire is abated; our minds be willinger to grow strange to heaven, when death still mingleth terror in our meditations. Whereas if we could have come to God in the way that was first appointed us, and could be clothed with glory, without being stripped of our present clothing by this terrible hand, how familiarly should we then converse above! How readily would our thoughts run out to Christ! Meditation of that glory would not be then so hard a work; our hearts would not be so backward to it as now they are.

5. Faith is much hindered, and infidelity much advantaged, by death. Look either to the state of soul or body, and you will easily perceive the truth of this. The state of a soul incorporated we know by long experience. What kind of apprehensions, volitions, and affections belong to a soul while it acteth in the body, we feel or understand, but what manner of knowledge, will, or love, what joy, what sorrow, belong to souls that are separated from the bodies, it is not possible for us now distinctly and formally to conceive. And when men find themselves at a loss about the manner, they are tempted to doubt of the thing itself. The swarms of irreligious infidels that have denied the immortality and separated existence of the soul, are too full a proof of this, and good men have been haunted with this horrible temptation. Had there been no death, we had not been liable to this dangerous assault. The opinion of the sleeping of the soul till the resurrec-

tion is but a step to flat infidelity, and both of them hence receive their life, because a soul in flesh, when it cannot conceive to its satisfaction of the being, state, or action of a separated soul, is the easier drawn to question or deny it.

And in regard of the body, the difficulty and trial is as great. That a corpse resolved into dust, and perhaps first devoured by some other body, and turned into its substance, should be re-united to its soul, and so become a glorified body, is a point not easy for unsanctified nature to believe. When Paul preached of the resurrection to the learned Athenians, some mocked, and others turned off that discourse, Acts xvii. 32. It is no easier to believe the resurrection of the body, than the immortality or separated existence of the soul. Most of the world, even heathens and infidels, do confess the latter, but few of them comparatively believe the former. And if sin had not let in death upon our nature, this perilous difficulty had been prevented. Then we should not have been puzzled with the thoughts of either a corrupted body or a separated soul.

6. And consequently, by all this already mentioned, our endeavours meet with a great impediment. If death weaken faith, desire, and hope, it must needs dull our endeavours. The deterred, discouraged soul moves slowly in the way of life; whereas, if death were not in our way, how cheerfully should we run towards heaven! Our thoughts of it would be still sweet, and these would be a powerful spring to action. When the will goes with full sails, the commanded faculty will the more easily follow. We should long so earnestly to be in heaven, if death were not in the way, that nothing could easily stop us in our course. How earnestly we should pray! How seriously should we meditate and confer of heaven, and part with any thing to attain it! But that which dulls our desires of the end, must needs be an enemy to holy diligence, and dull us in the use of means.

7. This enemy also doth dangerously tempt us to fall in love with present things, and to take up the miserable portion of the worldling. When it hath weakened faith, and cooled our desires to the life to come, we shall be tempted to think that it is best to take such pleasure as may here be had, and feed on that where a sensual mind hath less discouragement. Whereas, if death did not stand in the way, and darken heaven to us, and turn back our desires, how easily should we get above these trifles, and perceive the vanity of all below, and how unworthy they are to be once regarded.

8. Moreover, it is much long of this last enemy that God is so dishonoured by the fears and droopings of believers. They are but imperfectly yet freed from this bondage, and accordingly they walk. Whereas, if the king of terrors were removed, we should have less of fear, and more of love, as living more in the sight and sense of love. And then we should glorify the God of love, and appear to the world as men of another world, and show them the faith and hope of saints in the heavenly cheerfulness of our lives, and no more dishonour the Lord and our profession by our uncomfortable despondencies, as we do.

9. Moreover, it is much long of this last enemy that many true christians cannot perceive their own sincerity, but are overwhelmed with doubts and troublesome fears, lest they have not the faith and hope of saints, and lest the love of God abide not in them, and lest their hearts are more on earth than heaven. When they find themselves afraid of dying, and to have dark, amazing thoughts about eternity, and to think with less trouble and fear of earth than of the life to come, this makes them think that they are yet but worldlings, and have not placed their happiness with God, when perhaps it is but the fear of death that causeth these unjust conclusions. Christian, I shall tell thee more anon, that God may be truly loved and desired by thee, and heaven may be much more valued than earth, and yet the natural fears of death that standeth in thy way may much perplex thee, and make thee think that thou art averse from God, when indeed thou art but averse from death, because yet this enemy is not overcome.

10. Lastly, this enemy is not the smallest cause of many of our particular sins, and of the apostasy of many hypocrites. Indeed it is one of the strongest of our temptations. Before man sinned, none could take away his life but God, and God would not have done it for any thing but sin. So that man had no temptations from the malice of enemies, or the pride of conquerors, or the fury of the passionate, or the power of tyrants, to be afraid of death, and to use any unlawful means to escape it. An avoidable death from the hand of God he was obliged moderately to fear, that is, to be afraid of sinning lest he die, else God would not have threatened him, if he would not have had him make use of a preventing fear. But now we have an unavoidable death to fear, and also an untimely death from the hand of man by God's permission. And the fear of these is a powerful temptation, otherwise Abraham would not have distrustively equivocated as he did to save his life, (Gen. xx. 11,) and Isaac after him do the same, when he sojourned in the same place, Gen. xxvi. 7. If the fear of death were not a strong temptation, Peter would not have thrice denied Christ, and that after so late a warning and engagement. Nor would all his disciples have forsaken him and fled, Matt. xxvi. 56. Nor would martyrs have a special reward; nor would Christ have been put to call upon his disciples, that they fear not them that can kill the body, (Luke xii. 4,) and to declare to men the necessity of self-denial in this point of life, and that none can be his disciple that loves his life before him, Matt. xvi. 25; Luke xiv. 26. He is a christian indeed that so loveth God that he will not sin to save his life. But what is it that a hypocrite will not do to escape death? He will equivocate and forswear himself with the Jesuit and familist; he will forsake not only his dearest friend, but Christ also and his conscience. What a multitude of the most heinous sins are daily committed through the fears of death. Thousands where the inquisition ruleth are kept in popery by it, and thousands are kept in Mahometanism by it. Thousands are drawn by it to betray their countries; to deny the truth; to betray the church and cause of Christ; and, finally, to betray their souls unto perdition. Some of them presume to deny Christ wilfully, because that Peter had pardon that denied him through surprise, and through infirmity, but they will not repent with Peter, and die for him after their repentance. He that hath the power of a hypocrite's life, may prescribe him what he shall believe and do; may write him down the rule of his religion, and tell him what changes he shall make, what oaths he shall take, what party he shall side with, and command him so many sins a day, as you make your horse go so many miles. Satan, no doubt, had much experience of the power of this temptation, when he boasted so confidently of it against Job, (ii. 4,) "Skin for skin, yea, all that a man hath will he give for his life." And it is true, no doubt, of those that love nothing better than their lives. Satan thought that the fear of death would make a man do any thing, and of too many he may boldly make this boast, Let me but have power of their lives,

and I will make them say any thing, and swear any thing, and be for any cause or party, and do any thing against God or man. When lesser matters can do so much, as common, sad experience showeth us, no wonder if the fear of death can do it.

3. In brief, you may see by what is said that death is become an enemy to our souls, by being first the enemy of our natures. The interest of our bodies works much on our souls, much more the interest of the whole man. The principle of self-love was planted in nature in order to self-preservation, and the government of the world. Nature doth necessarily abhor its own destruction. And therefore this destruction standing in the way, is become an exceeding great hinderance to our affections, which takes them off from the life to come.

1. It is a very great hinderance to the conversion of those that are yet carnal, imprisoned in their unbelief. It is hard to win their hearts to such a state of happiness that cannot be obtained but by yielding unto death.

2. And to the truly godly it is naturally an impediment, and a great temptation in the points before expressed. And though it prevail not against them, it exceedingly hindereth them. And thus I have showed you that death is an enemy, further than, I doubt, the most consider of.

If the unbeliever shall here tell me that death is not the fruit of sin, but natural to man, though he had never sinned, and therefore that I lay all this on God; I answer him, that mortality, as it signifieth a *posse mori*, a natural capacity of dying, was natural to us in our innocency, or else death could not be threatened as a penalty. And if I grant as much of a natural disposition in the body to a dissolution, if not prevented by a glorifying change, it will no whit advantage their impious cause. But withal, man was then so far immortal, as that he had a *posse non mori*, a natural capacity of not dying, and the *morietur vel non morietur*, the actual event of life or death, was laid by the Lord of life and death upon his obedience or disobedience. And man having sinned, justice must be done, and so we came under a *non posse non mori*, an impossibility of escaping death, (ordinarily,) because of the peremptory sentence of our Judge. But the day of our deliverance is at hand, when we shall attain a *non posse mori*, a certain consummate immortality, when the last enemy, death, shall be destroyed; and how that is done, I shall next inquire.

You have seen the ugly face of death; you are next to see a little of the love of our great Redeemer. You have heard what sin hath done; you are next to hear what grace hath done, and what it will do. You have seen the strength of the enemy; you are now to take notice of the victory of the Redeemer, and see how he conquereth all this strength.

1. The beginning of the conquest is in this world. 2. The perfection will not be till the day of resurrection, when this last enemy shall be destroyed.

1. Meritoriously death is conquered by death; the death of sinners by the Mediator's death. Not that he intended in his meritorious work to save us from the stroke of death by a prevention, but to deliver us from it after by a resurrection. "For since by man came death, by man came also the resurrection from the dead," 1 Cor. xv. 21. "Forasmuch as the children are partakers of flesh and blood, he also himself likewise took part of the same, that through death he might destroy him that had the power of death, that is, the devil; and deliver them who, through fear of death, were all their lifetime subject to bondage," Heb. ii. 14, 15. Satan, as God's executioner, and as the prosperous tempter, is said to have had the power of death. The fears of this dreadful executioner are a continual bondage, which we are liable to, through all our lives, till we perceive the deliverance which the death of the Lord of life hath purchased us. 1st. By death, Christ hath satisfied the justice that was armed by sin against us. 2nd. By death he hath showed us, that death is a tolerable evil, and to be yielded to in hope of following life.

2. Actually he conquered death by his resurrection. This was the day of grace's triumph: this day he showed to heaven, to hell, and to earth, that death was conquerable; yea, that his personal death was actually overcome. The blessed souls beheld it to their joy, beholding in the resurrection of their Head a virtual resurrection of their own bodies. The devils saw it, and therefore saw that they had no hopes of holding the bodies of the saints in the power of the grave. The damned souls were acquainted with it, and therefore knew that their sinful bodies must be restored to bear their part in suffering. The believing saints on earth perceive it, and therefore see that their bonds are broken, and that to the righteous there is hope in death; and that our Head being actually risen, assureth us that we shall also rise. "For if we believe that Jesus died and rose again, even so them also which sleep in Jesus will God bring with him," 1 Thess. iv. 14: and as "Christ being raised from the dead, dieth no more, death hath no more dominion over him," Rom. vi. 9; so shall we rise and die no more. This was the beginning of the church's triumph. "This is the day that the Lord hath made (even the day which the church on earth must celebrate with joy and praise, till the day of our resurrection); we will rejoice and be glad in it," Psal. cxviii. 24. The resurrection of our Lord, hath, 1st, assured us of the consummation of his satisfaction; 2nd, of the truth of all his word, and so of his promises of our resurrection; 3rd, that death is actually conquered, and a resurrection possible; 4th, that believers shall certainly rise when their Head and Saviour is risen to prepare them an everlasting kingdom, and to assure them that thus he will raise them at the last. A bare promise would not have been so strong a help to faith, as to the actual rising of Christ, as a pledge of the performance. "But now Christ is risen from the dead, and become the first-fruits of them that slept," 1 Cor. xv. 20: "for because he liveth, we shall live also," John xiv. 19.

3. The next degree of destruction to this enemy was by the gift of his justifying and sanctifying grace. Four special benefits were then bestowed on us, which are antidotes against the enmity of death. 1. One is the gift of saving faith, by which we look beyond the grave, as far as to eternity. And this doth most powerfully disable death to terrify and discourage us, and raiseth us above our natural fears, and showeth us (though but in a glass) the exceeding eternal weight of glory which churlish death shall help us to. So that when the eye of the unbeliever looketh no further than the grave, believing souls can enter into heaven and see their glorified Lord, and thence fetch love, and hope, and joy, notwithstanding the terrors of interposing death. The eye of faith foreseeth the salvation ready to be revealed in the last time, and causeth us therein greatly to rejoice, though now for a season, (if need be,) we are in heaviness through manifold temptations," 1 Pet. i. 5, 6. And so victorious is this faith against all the storms that do assault us, "that the trial of it, though with fire, doth but discover that it is much more precious than gold that perisheth, and it shall be found unto praise, and honour, and glory, at the appearing of Jesus Christ, whom having never

seen in the flesh, we love: and though now we see him not, yet believing we rejoice with unspeakable, glorious joy; and shall shortly receive the end of our faith, the salvation of our souls," 1 Pet. i. 7—9. Thus faith, though it destroy not death itself, destroyeth the malignity and enmity of death; while it seeth the things that are beyond it, and the time when death shall be destroyed, and the life where death shall be no more. Faith is like David's three mighty men that brake through the host of the Philistines to fetch him the waters of Bethlehem, for which he longed, 2 Sam. xxiii. 15, 16. When the thirsty soul saith, Oh that one would give me drink of the waters of salvation! faith breaks through death which standeth in the way, and fetcheth these living waters to the soul. We may say of death as it is said of the world; "Whatsoever is born of God overcometh the world: and this is the victory that overcometh the world, even our faith: who is he that overcometh the world, but he that believeth?" &c. 1 John v. 4, 5. "For greater is he that is in you, than he that is in the world," 1 John iv. 4. The believing soul, foreseeing the day when death shall be swallowed up in victory, may sing beforehand the triumphing song, "O death, where is thy sting? O grave, where is thy victory?" 1 Cor. xv. 54, 55. "For which cause we faint not; but though our outward man perish, yet the inward man is renewed day by day. For our light affliction (though it reach to death) which is but for a moment, worketh for us a far more exceeding and eternal weight of glory; while we look not at the things which are seen, but at the things which are not seen: for the things which are seen are temporal, (and therefore not worthy to be looked at,) but the things which are not seen are eternal," and therefore more prevalent with a believing soul, than either the enticing pleasures of sin for a season, or the light and short afflictions, or the death that standeth in our way, 2 Cor. iv. 16—18; Heb. xi. 24—26.

2. A second antidote against the enmity of death, that is given us at the time of our conversion, is, the pardon of our sins, and justification of our persons by the blood and merits of Jesus Christ. When once we are forgiven, we are out of the reach of the greatest terror, being saved from the second death. Though we must feel the killing stroke, we are delivered from the damning stroke. Yea, more than so, it shall save us by destroying us; it shall let us into the glorious presence of our Lord, by taking us from the presence of our mortal friends; it shall help us into eternity, by cutting off our time. For in the hour that we were justified and made the adopted sons of God, we were also made the heirs of heaven, even co-heirs with Christ, and shall be glorified with him, when we have suffered with him, Rom. viii. 17. As death was promoting the life of the world when it was killing the Lord of life himself, so is it hastening the deliverance of believers, when it seems to be undoing them. No wonder if death be that man's terror that must be conveyed by it into hell, or that imagineth that he shall perish as the beast. But to him that knows it will be his passage into rest, and that angels shall convey his soul to Christ, what an antidote is there ready for his faith to use against the enmity and excess of fears! Hence faith proceedeth in its triumph; "The sting of death is sin; and the strength of sin is the law. But thanks be to God, which giveth us the victory through our Lord Jesus Christ," 1 Cor. xv. 56, 57. Let him inordinately fear death that is loth to be with Christ, or that is yet the heir of death eternal. Let him fear that is yet in the bondage of his sin, and in the power of the prince of darkness, and is not by justification delivered from the curse. But joy and holy triumph are more seemly for the justified.

3. A third antidote against the enmity of death is, the holiness of the soul. By this the power of sin is mortified; and, therefore, the fears of death cannot actuate and use it, as in others they may do. By this the interest of the flesh is cast aside as nothing, and the flesh itself is crucified with Christ: and, therefore, the destruction of the flesh will seem the more tolerable, and the fears of it will be a less temptation to the soul. By this we are already crucified to the world, and the world to us; and therefore we can more easily leave the world. We now live by another life than we did before; being dead in ourselves, our life is hid with Christ in God; and being crucified with Christ, we now so live, as that it is not we, but Christ liveth in us: the life which we live in the flesh, is by the faith of the Son of God that hath loved us, Gal. ii. 20. The things that made this life too dear to us are now, as it were, annihilated to us; and when we see they are nothing, they can do nothing with us. Sanctification also maketh us so weary of sin, as being our hated enemy, that we are the more willing to die, that it may die that causeth us to die: and especially the Holy Ghost, which we then receive, is in us a divine and heavenly nature, and so inclineth us to God and heaven. This nature principally consisteth in the superlative love of God. And love carrieth out the soul to the beloved. As the nature of a prisoner in a dungeon carrieth him to desire liberty and light; so the nature of a holy soul in flesh inclineth it to desire to be with Christ. As love maketh husband, and wife, and dearest friends to think the time long while they are asunder; so doth the love of the soul to God. How fain would the holy, loving soul behold the pleased face of God, and be glorified in the beholding of his glory, and live under the fullest influences of his love. This is our conquest over the enmity of death. As strong as death is, love is stronger. "Love is strong as death,—the coals thereof are coals of fire, which hath a most vehement flame (which will not by the terrible face of death, be hindered from ascending up to God). Many waters cannot quench love, neither can the floods drown it: if a man would give all the substance of his house for love, (that is, to bribe it, and divert it from its object,) it would utterly be contemned," Sol. Song viii. 6, 7. If the love of David could carry Jonathan to hazard his life, and deny a kingdom for him, and the love of David to Absalom made him wish that he had died for him, and the love of friends (yea, lustful love) hath carried many to cast away their lives; no wonder if the love of God in his saints prevail against the fear of death. The power of holy love made Moses say, "Else let my name be blotted out of the book of life." And it made Paul say, that he could wish that he were accursed from Christ for his brethren and kindred according to the flesh, Rom. ix. 3. And doubtless, he felt the fire burning in his breast when he broke out into that triumphant challenge, "Who shall separate us from the love of Christ? shall tribulation, or distress, or persecution, or famine, or nakedness, or peril, or sword? As it is written, For thy sake we are killed all the day long; we are accounted as sheep for the slaughter. Nay, in all these things we are more than conquerors through him that loved us. For I am persuaded, that neither death, nor life, nor angels, nor principalities, nor powers, nor things present, nor things to come, nor height, nor depth, nor any other creature, shall be able to separate us from the love of God, which is in Christ Jesus our Lord," Rom. viii. 35—39. You see here what it is

that conquereth the enmity of death in our sanctification; even that powerful love of God that is then given us, which will go to him through the most cruel death.

4. A fourth antidote that is given us by Christ against the enmity of death, is the Holy Ghost, as he is the Comforter of the saints. He makes it his work to corroborate and confirm them. As sin hath woven calamities into our lives, and filled us with troubles, and griefs, and fears; so Christ doth send his Spirit to undo these works of Satan, and to be a Comforter, as well as a Sanctifier to his members. As the sanctifying Spirit striveth against the enticing, sinful flesh, so the comforting Spirit striveth against the troubling flesh; as also against the persecuting, as well as the tempting world, and the vexing, as well as the tempting devil. "And greater is he that is in you, than he that is in the world," 1 John iv. 4. The Spirit of Christ overcomes the disquieting, as well as the tempting spirit; but with some difference, because our comforts are not in this life so necessary to us as our holiness. Joy being part of our reward, is not to be expected certainly or constantly, in any high degree, till we come to the state of our reward: and, therefore, though the Holy Ghost will carry on the work of sanctification, universally, constantly, and certainly in the elect; yet, in many of them, his comforting work is more obscure and interrupted. And yet he is a conqueror here; for his works must be judged of in reference to their ends: and our comfort on earth is given us for our encouragement in holy ways, that we be not stopped or diverted by the fear of enemies; and also to help on our love to God, and to quicken us in thanks and praise, and draw up our hearts to the life to come, and make us more serviceable to others. And such a measure of comfort we shall have as conduceth to these ends, and is suitable to our present state, and the employment God hath for us in the world, if we do not wilfully grieve our Comforter, and quench our joys.

So that when death and the grave appear before, and our flesh is terrified with the sight of these Anakims, and say, We are not able to overcome them, and so brings up an evil report upon the promised land, and casts us sometimes into murmuring, lamentation, and weakening discouragements, yet does the Holy Ghost cause faith and hope (as Caleb and Joshua) to still the soul, (Numb. xiii.) and causeth us to contemn these giants, and say, "Let us go up at once and possess it, for we are well able to overcome it," ver. 30. The comforting Spirit showeth us his death that conquered death, (Heb. ii. 14, 15,) even the cross on which he triumphed openly when he seemed to be conquered, Col. ii. 15. He showeth us the glorious resurrection of our Head, and his promise of our own resurrection. He showeth us our glorified Lord, to whom we may boldly and confidently commend our departing souls, Acts vii. 59. And he showeth us the angels that are ready to be their convoy. And he maketh all these considerations effectual, and inwardly exciteth our love and heavenly desires, and giveth us a triumphing courage and consolation. So that death doth not encounter us alone, and in our own strength, but finds us armed and led on by the Lord of life, who helps us by a sling and stone to conquer this Goliath. If a draught of wine, or some spiritful reviving liquor, can take off fears and make men bold, what then may the Spirit of Christ do by his powerful encouragements and comforts on the soul. Did we but see Christ or an angel standing by our sick-beds, and saying, Fear not, I will convoy thy soul to God; this day shalt thou be with me in paradise; what an unspeakable comfort would this be to a dying man! Why, the Spirit is Christ's agent here on earth; and what the Spirit speaks, Christ speaks; and, therefore, we may take its comforting words as spoken to us by Christ himself; who spoke the like to the penitent thief, to show believers the virtue of his cross, and what they also may expect from him in their extremity. And our Physician is most wise, and keeps his cordials for a fainting time. The Spirit useth to sustain and comfort us most in our greatest necessities. We need not comforts against death so much in the time of prosperity and health as when death draws near. In health we have ordinarily more need of quickening than of comforting; and more need to be awakened from security to a due preparation for death, than to be freed from the terrible forethoughts of it: though inordinate fears of death be hurtful to us, security and deadness hurts us more; and therefore the Spirit worketh according to our necessities. And when death is nearest, and like to be most dreadful, he usually giveth the liveliest sense of the joys beyond it, to abate the enmity, and encourage the departing soul. And if the comfort be but small, it is precious, because it is most pure, as being then mixed with no carnal joys; and because it is most seasonable in so great a strait. If we have no more but mere support, it will be yet a precious mercy. And thus I have done with the third degree of the destruction of death's enmity, by these four antidotes, which we receive at our conversion, and the consequents thereof.

4. The fourth degree of this enemy's destruction is by itself, or rather by Christ, at the time, and by the means of death, which, contrary to its nature, shall advantage our felicity. When death hath done its worst, it hath half killed itself in killing us. It hath then dismissed our imprisoned souls, and ended even our fears of death, and our fears of all the evils of this life. It hath ended our cares, and griefs, and groans. It hath finished our work, and ended all our weariness and trouble. And more than this, it ends our sinning, and so destroyeth that which caused it, and that which the inordinate fears of itself had caused in us. It is the time when sin shall gasp its last, and so far our Physician will perfect the cure; and our greatest enemy shall follow us no further. It is the door by which the soul must pass to Christ in paradise.

If any papist shall hence plead that therefore all men must be perfect without sin before death, or else go to purgatory to be cleansed, because as we die, so Christ will find us; or if they ask how death can perfect us? I answer them, It is Christ our Physician that finisheth the cure, and death is the time in which he doth it. And if he undertake then to do it, it concerns not us to be too inquisitive how he doth it. What if the patient understand not how blood-letting cureth the infected blood that is left behind? Must he therefore plead against his physician? and say, It will not be done, because he knoweth not how it is done? We feel that here we have our sinful imperfections. We have for all that a promise that we shall be with Christ when death hath made its separation; and we are assured that no sin doth enter there. And is not this enough for us to know?

But yet I see not why the difficulty of the objection should trouble us at all. Death doth remove us from this sinful flesh, and admits the soul into the sight of God. And in the very instant of its remove it must needs be perfected, even by that remove, and by the first appearance of his blessed face. If you bring a candle into a dark room, the access of the light expelleth the darkness at the same instant; and you cannot say that they consist together one moment of time. So cold is expelled by the approach of heat. And thus when death hath opened the door, and let us into the immortal light, neither before nor after, but in that instant, all the darkness and sinful imperfections of our souls are dissipated. Throw an empty bottle into the sea, and the emptiness ceaseth by the filling of the water, neither before nor after, but in that instant.

If this should not satisfy any, let it satisfy them, that the Holy Ghost in the instant of death can perfect his work.

So that we need not assert a perfection on earth, (which on their grounds must be the case of all that will escape hell and purgatory,) nor yet any purgatory torments after death, for the deliverance of the soul from the relics of sin; seeing at the instant of death, by the Spirit, or by the deposition of the flesh, or by the sight of God, or by the sight of our glorified Redeemer, or by all, this work will be easily and infallibly accomplished.

5. The last degree and perfect conquest will be at the resurrection. And this is the victory that is mentioned in my text. All that is fore-mentioned doth abate the enmity, and conquer death in some degree; but the enmity, and the enemy itself, is conquered at the resurrection, and not till then. And therefore death is the last enemy to be destroyed. The body lieth under the penal effects of sin until the resurrection. And it is penal to the soul to be in a state of separation from the body, though it be a state of glory that it is in with Christ: for it is deprived of the fulness of glory, which it shall attain at the resurrection, when the whole man shall be perfected and glorified together. Then it is that the Mediator's work will be accomplished; and all things shall be restored; and all that are in the graves shall hear the voice of the Son of God, and shall come forth, John v. 28. "For this is the Father's will that sent him, that of all that he hath given him, he should lose nothing, but should raise it up again at the last day," John vi. 39, 40. We "have hope towards God, that there shall be a resurrection of the dead, both of the just and unjust," Acts xxiv. 15. "As by man came death, so by man came also the resurrection from the dead," 1 Cor. xv. 21. "And there shall be no more death, nor sorrow, nor crying, neither shall there be any more pain," Rev. xxi. 4. No more diseases, or fears of death, or grave, or of corruption. No terrible enemy shall stand betwixt us and our Lord, to frighten our hearts from looking towards him. Oh what a birthday will that be, when graves shall bring forth so many millions of sons for glory! How joyful will the soul and body meet that were separated so long! Then sin hath done its worst, and can do no more. Then Christ hath done all, and hath no more to do as our Redeemer, but to justify us in judgment, and give us possession of the joy that he is preparing. And then he will deliver up the kingdom to the Father.

If you expect now that I should give you reasons why death is the last enemy to be destroyed, though much might be said from the nature of the matter, the wisdom and will of God shall be to me instead of all other reasons, being the fountain and the sum of all. He knows best the order that is agreeable to his works and ends, to his honour, and to our good. And therefore to his wisdom we submit, in the patient expectance of the accomplishment of his promises.

Use 1. I now come to show you the usefulness of this doctrine, for the further information of our understandings, the well-ordering of our hearts, and the reforming of our lives. And first, you may hence be easily resolved, whether death be truly penal to the godly? which some have been pleased to make a controversy of late; though I am past doubt but the hearts of those men do apprehend it as a punishment whose tongues and pens do plead for the contrary. "Dust thou art, and to dust shalt thou return," was part of the sentence passed on Adam and all his posterity; which then proved it a punishment; and it was not remitted to Adam, that at the same time had the promise of a Redeemer, not is it remitted to any of us all. Were it not for sin, God would not inflict it; who hath sworn that he takes "no pleasure in the death of sinners;" and that he "afflicts not willingly, nor grieves the sons of men." But my text itself decides the controversy: sin and punishment are the evils that Christ removeth; and if death were no punishment, (as it is no sin,) how could it be an enemy, and the last enemy to be destroyed by the Redeemer? When we feel the enmity before described against our souls, and also know its enmity to our bodies, we cannot think that God would do all this, were it not for sin. Especially when we read that "death passeth upon all men, for that all have sinned," Rom. v. 12. And that "the wages of sin is death," Rom. vi. 23. Though Christ do us good by it, that proveth it not to be no punishment; for castigatory punishments are purposely to do good to the chastised. Indeed we may say, "O death, where is thy sting?" because that the mortal evil to the soul is taken out; and because we foresee the resurrection by faith, when we shall have the victory by Christ. But thence to conclude that death hath no sting now to a believer, is not only besides, but against the text; which, telling us that the sting of death is sin, and that the strength of sin is the law, doth inform us, that death could not kill us, and be death to us, if sin gave it not a sting to do it with; as sin could not oblige us to this punishment, if the threatening of the law were not its strength. But Christ hath begun the conquest, and will finish it.

Use 2. From all this enmity in death, we may see what it is that sin hath done; and, consequently, how vile and odious it is, and how we should esteem and use it. Sin hath not only forfeited our happiness, but laid those impediments in the way of our recovery, which will find us work, and cause our danger and sorrow while we live. And death is not the least of these impediments. O foolish man, that still will love such a mortal enemy! If another would rob them but of a groat, or defame them, or deprive them of any accommodation, how easily can they hate them, and how hardly are they reconciled to them! But sin depriveth them of their lives, and separates the soul and body asunder, and forfeiteth their everlasting happiness, and sets death betwixt them and the glory that is purchased by Christ, and yet they love it, and will not leave it. Though God has made them, and sustains them, and provides for them, and all their hope and help is in him, they are not so easily drawn to love him; and yet they can love the sin that would undo them. Though Christ would deliver them, and bring them to everlasting blessedness, and hath assumed flesh, and laid down his life to testify his love to them, yet are they not easily brought to love him; but the sin that made them enemies to God, and hath brought them so near to everlasting misery, this they can love, that deserves no love. A minister, or other friend, that would draw them from their sin to God, and help to save them, they quarrel against, as if he were their enemy; but their foolish companions, that can laugh and jest with them at the door of hell, and clap them on the back, and drive away the care of their salvation, and harden them against the fear of God, these are the only acceptable men to them. O christians! leave this folly to the world, and do you judge of sin by its sad effects. You feel, (if you have any feeling in you,) in some measure, what it hath done against your souls. The weakness of your faith and love, the distance of your hearts from God, your doubts and troubles, tell you that it is not your friend. You must shortly know what it will do to your bodies. As it keeps them in pain, and weariness, and weakness, so it will, ere long, deliver them up to the jaws of death, which will spare them no more than the beasts that perish. Had it not been for sin we should have had no cause to fear a dissolution; nor have had any use for a coffin or a winding-sheet; nor have been beholden to a grave, to hide our carcasses from the sight and smell of the living. But as Enoch and Elias were translated when they had walked with God, even so should we: as those that are alive, and remain at the coming of Christ, shall be caught up together in the clouds to meet the Lord in the air: and so shall they ever be with the Lord, 1 Thess. iv. 17.

Use sin, therefore, as it will use you. Spare it not, for it will not spare you. It is your murderer, and the murderer of the world. Use it therefore as a murderer should be used. Kill it before it kills you; and then, though it kill your bodies, it shall not be able to kill your souls; and though it bring you to the grave, as it did your Head, it shall not be able to keep you there. If the thoughts of death, and the grave, and rottenness, be not pleasant to you, let not the thoughts of sin be pleasant. Hearken to every temptation to sin, as you would hearken to a temptation to self-murder; and as you would do if the devil brought you a knife, and tempted you to cut your throat with it, so do when he offereth you the bait of sin. You love not death, love not the cause of death. Be ashamed to stand weeping over a buried friend, and never to weep over a sinning or ungodly friend, nor once to give them a compassionate, earnest exhortation to save their souls. Is it nothing to be "dead in trespasses and sins?" Eph. ii. 1, 5; Col. ii. 13. Yea, it is a worse death than this, that is the wages of sin, and the fruit which it brings forth, Rom. vi. 21, 23; vii. 5. Surely God would never thus use men's bodies, and forsake them soul and body for ever, if sin were not a most odious thing. What a poison is this that kills so many millions, and damneth so many millions, and cannot be cured but by the blood of Christ! that killed our Physician that never tasted it, because he came so near to us! O unbelieving, stupid souls! that smart and sin, and groan and sin, and weep and lament our bodily sufferings, and yet sin still! that fear a grave, and fear not sin! that have heard, and seen, and felt so much of the sad effects, and yet sin still! Psal. lxxviii. 32. Alas! that murderers should be so common, and that we should be no wiser, when we have paid so dear a price for wisdom!

Use 3. From the enmity of death we may further learn, that man hath now a need of grace for such exceeding difficulties which were not before him in his state of innocency. Though Adam was able to have obeyed perfectly without sin, and had grace sufficient to have upheld him, and conquered temptations, if he had done his part, which by that grace he might have done; yet whether that grace was sufficient to the works that we are called to, is a doubt that many have been much troubled with. It is certain that he was able to have done any thing that was suitable to his present state, if it were commanded him; and it is certain that much that is now our duty, would have been unsuitable to his state. But whether it belonged to his perfection, to be able and fit for such duties, (that were then unsuitable to him,) on supposition they had been suitable and duties, this is the difficulty which some make to prove that such works cannot now be required of us without suitable help, because we lost no such grace in Adam. But this need not trouble us; for, first, though Adam was put on no such difficulty in particular as to encounter death, yet the perfect obedience to the whole law required a great degree of internal, habitual holiness; and, to determine the case, whether our particular difficulties, or his sinless, perfect obedience, required greater strength and help, is a matter of more difficulty than use. For, secondly, it is but about the degrees of holiness in him and us, and not about the kind, that the difficulty lieth. For it is the same end that he was created for, and disposed to by nature, and that we are redeemed for, and disposed to supernaturally.

But yet it is worthy our observation what a difficulty sin hath cast before us in the way of life, which Adam was unacquainted with; that so we may see the nature of our works, and the excellency of the Redeemer's grace. Adam was but to seek the continuance of his life, and a translation to glory, without the terrors of interposing death; he was never called to prepare to die, nor to think of the state of a separated soul; nor to mind, and love, and seek a glory to which there is no (ordinary) passage but by death. This is the difficulty that sin hath caused, against which we have need of the special assistance of the example, and doctrine, and promise, and Spirit of the Redeemer. Adam was never put to study how to get over this dreadful gulf. The threatening of death was to raise such a fear in him as was necessary to prevent it; but those fears did rather hold him closer to the way of life, than stand between him and life, to his discouragement. But we have a death to fear which must be suffered, that cannot be avoided. The strange condition of a separated soul (so unlike to its state while resident in the body) doth require in us a special faith to apprehend it, and a special revelation to discover it. To desire, and love, and long for, and labour after such a time as this, when one part of us must lie rotting in the grave, and the separated soul must be with Christ alone till the resurrection, and to believe and hope for that resurrection, and to deny ourselves, and forsake all the world, and lay down our lives when Christ requireth it, by the power of this faith and hope, this is a work that innocent Adam never knew; this is the high employment of a christian. To have our hearts and conversations in heaven, (Matt. vi. 21; Phil. iii. 20,) when death must first dissolve us before we can possess it, here is the noble work of faith.

Use 4. Moreover, this enmity of death may help us to understand the reason of the sufferings and death of Christ. That he gave his life a ransom for us, and a sacrifice for sin, and so to make satisfaction to the offended Majesty, is a truth that every christian doth believe. But there was another reason of his death that all of us do not duly consider of, and improve, to the promoting of our sanctification as we ought. Death is so great an enemy, as you have heard, and so powerful to deter our hearts from God, and dull our desires to the heavenly felicity, that Christ was fain to go before us, to imbolden the hearts of believers to follow him. He suffered death (with the rest of his afflictions) to show us that it is a tolerable evil. Had he not gone before and overcome it, it would have detained us its captives. Had he not merited and purchased us a blessed resurrection, and opened heaven to all believers, and by death overcome him that had the power of death, (as God's executioner,) that is, the devil, we should, all our life-time, have been still subjected unto bondage, by the fears of death, Heb. ii. 14. But when we see that Christ hath led the way, as the victorious Captain of our salvation, and that he is made perfect by sufferings, (in his advancement unto glory,) and that for the sufferings of death (which by the grace of God he tasted for every man) he is crowned with glory and honour, Heb. ii. 9, 10: this puts a holy valour into the soul, and causeth us cheerfully to follow him. Had we gone first, and the task of conquering death been ours, we had been overcome. But he that hath led us on, hath hewed down the enemy before him, and first prepared us the way, and then called us to follow him, and to pass the way that he hath first made safe, and also showed us, by his example, that it is now made passable. For it was one in our nature, that calleth us his brethren, that took not the nature of angels, but of the seed of Abraham, that is one with us, as the Sanctifier and the sanctified are, and to whom as children we are given, who hath passed through death and the grave before us, and therefore we may the boldlier follow him, Heb. ii. 11—13, 16. "Being found in fashion as a man, he humbled himself, and became obedient unto death, even the death of the cross; wherefore God also hath highly exalted him, and given him a name which is above every name," Phil. ii. 8, 9. Hereby he hath showed us that death is not so dreadful a thing, but that voluntary obedience may and must submit unto it. As Abraham's faith and obedience were tried in the offering up his son to death at God's command, so the children of Abraham, and the heirs of the promise, must follow him in offering up themselves, if God require it, and in submitting to our natural death (for that he doth require of all). Examples work more than bare precepts; and the experiments of others do take more with us than mere directions. It satisfieth a sick man more to read a book of medicinal observations, where he meets with many that were in his own case, and finds what cured them, than to read the praxis or medicinal recipes alone. It encourageth the patient much, when the physician tells him, I have cured many of your disease by such a medicine; nay, I was cured thus of the same myself. So doth it imbolden a believer to lay down his life, when he hath not only a promise of a better life, but seeth that the promiser went that way to heaven before him. Oh, therefore, let us learn and use this choice remedy, against the immoderate fear of death. Let faith take a view of him that was dead and is alive, that was buried and is risen, and was humbled and is now exalted. Think with yourselves, when you must think of dying, that you are but following your conquering Lord, and going the way that he hath gone before you, and suffering what he underwent and conquered. And, therefore, though you walk through the valley of the shadow of death, resolve that you will fear no evil, Psal. xxiii. 4. And if he call you after him, follow him with a christian boldness. As Peter cast himself into the sea, and walked on the waters, when he saw Christ walk there, and had his command; so let us venture on the jaws of death, while we trace his steps, and hear his encouraging commands and promises, John xxi. 7; Matt. xiv. 28, 29.

Use 5. Moreover, from this doctrine we may be informed of the mistakes of many christians, that think they have no saving grace because they are afraid of dying, and because these fears deter their souls from desiring to be with Christ. And hence they may perceive that there is another cause of these distempers, even the enmity of death that standeth in the way. You think that if you had any love to Christ you should more desire to be with him, and that if your treasure were in heaven, your hearts would be more there, and that if you truly took it for your felicity, you could not be so unwilling to be removed to it, for no man is unwilling to be happy, or to attain his end. But stay a little, and better consider of your case. Is it Christ that your heart is thus averse to? or is it only death that standeth in the way? You are not, I hope, unwilling to see the face of God, nor unwilling to be translated from earth to heaven, but unwilling to die. It is not because you love the creature better than the Creator, but because you are afraid of death. You may love God, and long to be perfected in holiness, and to see his glory, and to have the most near communion with him, and yet at the same time you may fear this enemy that standeth in your way; I mean, not only the pain of death, but principally the dissolution of our natures, and the separation of the soul from the body, and its abode in a separated state, and the body's abode in dust and darkness. Grace itself is not given us to reconcile us to corruption, and make death, as death, to seem desirable, but to cause us patiently to bear the evil, because of the good that is beyond it. It is not our duty to love death as death. Had it not been naturally an evil to be dreaded and avoided, God would not have made it the matter of his threatening, nor would it have been a fit means to restrain men from transgression. To threaten a man with a benefit, as such, is a contradiction. Inquire, therefore, into your hearts, whether there be not a belief of heaven, a love to God, a desire to enjoy and please him, even while you draw back, and seem to be averse; and whether it be not only a lothness to die, and not a lothness to be with Christ.

For the fuller discovery of this, (because I find that our comfort much dependeth on it,) I shall try you by these following questions.

Quest. 1. What is it that is ungrateful to you in your meditations of your change? Is it God and heaven, or is it death? If it be only death, it seems it is not the want of love to God and heaven that causeth your averseness. If it be God himself that is ungrateful to your thoughts, it is because you desire not his nearer presence, or communion with him in the state of glory. Or is it only because you fear lest you have no interest in his love, and shall not attain the blessedness which you desire? If it be the first, I must confess it proves a graceless soul, and signifieth the want of love to God. But if it be the latter only, it may stand with grace, for desire is a true signification of love, though there be doubts and fears lest we shall miss the attainment of those desires.

Quest. 2. Would you not gladly hear the news of your removal, if you might be changed without death, and translated to heaven as Enoch and Elias were, and as Christ at his ascension? Had you not far rather be thus changed than abide on earth? If so, then it seems it is not God and heaven that you are against, but death. Nay, if you could reach heaven by travelling a thousand miles, would you not gladly take the journey as soon as you had got assurance of your title to it, and done the work of God on earth? If it were but as Peter, James, and John, to go with Christ into an exceeding high mountain, and there to see him in glory, (Matt. xvii. 1,) would you not gladly do it? It seems that thou desirest to see the Lord, and thy love is to him, though thou be afraid of death.

Quest. 3. Consider of the nature of the heavenly

felicity, and try whether you love it in the several parts. One part is our personal perfection, that our souls shall be free from ignorance, and error, and sin, and sorrow, and enlarged for the perfect love of God, and our bodies at the resurrection made like the glorious body of our Lord, Phil. iii. 21. And wouldst thou not be thus perfected in soul and body? Another part is, that we should live with the society of angels and glorified saints. And wouldst thou not rather have such society than the company of sinners, and enemies, and imperfect saints on earth? Another part is, we shall see our glorified Head, and be with him where he is, that we may behold his glory. And doth not thy heart desire this? But the perfection of our happiness is, that we shall see the face of the glory of God, which is the light of that world, as truly as the sun is the light of this; and that we shall be filled up with the feeling of his love, and abound with love to him again, and perfectly delighted in this communion of love, and express in the praises of the Lord, and thus make up the new Jerusalem, where God will place his glorious presence, and in which he will for evermore take pleasure. And is there any thing in this that thy soul is against, and which thou dost not value above this world? If thou find that all the parts are sweet, and the description of heaven is most grateful to thee, and that this is the state that thou wouldst be in, it seems then it is not heaven, but death, that thou art averse from, and that maketh thee so loth to hear the tidings of thy change.

Quest. 4. Couldst thou not joyfully see the coming of Christ, if it were this day, if thou have done thy work, and art assured of his love? The apostle hath told us by the word of the Lord, that "the Lord himself shall descend from heaven with a shout, with the voice of the archangel, and with the trump of God. And the dead in Christ shall rise first; and then we which are alive, and remain, shall be caught up together with them in the clouds, to meet the Lord in the air: and so shall we ever be with the Lord," 1 Thess. iv. 16, 17. And this is the doctrine that comforteth believers, verse 18. Would it not rejoice your hearts if you were sure to live to see the coming of the Lord, and to see his glorious appearing and retinue? If you were not to die, but to be caught up thus to meet the Lord, and to be changed immediately into an immortal, incorruptible, glorious state, would you be averse to this? Would it not be the greatest joy that you could desire? For my own part, I must confess to you, that death, as death, appeareth to me as an enemy, and my nature doth abhor and fear it. But the thoughts of the coming of the Lord are most sweet and joyful to me; so that if I were but sure that I should live to see it, and that the trumpet should sound, and the dead should arise, and the Lord appear before the period of my age, it would be the joyfullest tidings to me in the world. Oh that I might see his kingdom come! It is the character of his saints to love his appearing, (2 Tim. iv. 8,) and to look "for that blessed hope, and the glorious appearing of the great God, and our Saviour Jesus Christ," Tit. ii. 13. "The Spirit and the bride say, Come: even so, come, Lord Jesus," (Rev. xxii. 17, 20,) come quickly, is the voice of faith, and hope, and love. But I find not that his servants are thus characterized by their desires to die. It is, therefore, the presence of their Lord that they desire; but it is death that they abhor. And, therefore, though they can submit to death, it is the coming of Christ that they love and long for; and it is interposing death that causeth them to draw back. Let not christians be discouraged by mistakes, and think that they love not God and glory, because they love not this enemy in the way; nor think that they are graceless or unbelieving worldlings, because they are afraid of death, as death.

But perhaps you will say, that if grace prevail not against the fears of death, then fear is predominant, and we are not sincere. To which I answer, that you must distinguish between such a prevailing as maintaineth our sincerity, and such a prevailing as also procureth our fortitude and joy. If grace prevail not to keep us upright in a holy life, renouncing the world, and crucifying the flesh, and devoting ourselves entirely to God, though the fear of death would draw us from it, then it is a sign that we are not sincere. But if grace do this much, and yet prevail not against all fears and unwillingness to die, but leave us under uncomfortable, hideous thoughts of death, this proves us not to be unsound. For the soul may savingly love God that is afraid of death, and he may truly love the end, that fears this dark and dismal way. Yet must there be so much to prove our uprightness, as that in our deliberate choice we will rather voluntarily pass through death, either natural or violent, than lose the happiness beyond it. Though we love not death, yet we love God and heaven so well that we will submit to it. And though we fear it and abhor it, yet not so much as we fear and abhor the loss of heaven. Let not poor christians therefore wrong themselves, and deny the graces of the Spirit, as if they had more mind of earth than heaven, and of things temporal than of things eternal, because they are afraid to die. All suffering is grievous, and not joyous to our nature. Paul himself desired not to be unclothed, but "clothed upon with our house which is from heaven, that mortality might be swallowed up of life," (2 Cor. v. 2, 4,) it being better to be absent from the body, and present with the Lord. Even Christ himself had a will that desired that the cup might have passed from him, if it had been agreeable to his Father's will, and the ends of his undertaken office, Matt. xxvi. 41, 42. Raise therefore no unjust conclusions from these natural fears, nor from the imperfection of our conquest; but praise him that relieveth us, and abateth the enmity of death, and furnisheth us with his antidotes, and will destroy his enemy at last.

Use 6. From the enmity of death we may further learn to study and magnify the victorious grace of our Redeemer, which overcometh the enemy, and turneth our hurt into our benefit, and maketh death a door of life. Though death be the enemy that seemeth to conquer us, and to destroy and utterly undo us, yet being conquered itself by Christ, it is used by him to our great advantage, and sanctified to be a very great help to our salvation. The suffering of Christ himself was in the hour of his enemies, and the power of darkness, (Luke xxii. 53,) which seemed to have prevailed against him: when yet it was but a destroying of death by death, and the purchasing of life and salvation for the world. So also in our death, though sin and Satan seem to conquer, it is they that are conquered, and not we, who are supervictors through him that hath loved us, Rom. viii. 37. They destroy themselves when they seem to have destroyed us. As the serpent bruised but the heel of Christ, who bruised his head; so doth he bruise but our heel, who, in that conflict, and by the means of his own execution through the strength of Christ, do bruise his head, Gen. iii. 15. And this is the upshot of all his enmity against the woman's holy seed. Though death was unsuitable to innocent man, and is still a natural enemy to us all; yet unto sinners it is an evil that is suitable and fit to destroy the greater evil that did cause it, and to prevent the everlasting evil. The foreknowledge of our certain death is a very great help to keep us humble, and disgrace all the seducing pleasures of the flesh, and all the profits and honours of the world, and so to enervate all temptations. It is a singular help to quicken a stupid, careless sinner, and to awaken men to prepare for the life to come, and to excite them to seek first the kingdom of God, and to give all diligence to make their calling and election sure; and to consider, seeing all these things must be dissolved, what manner of persons they ought to be, in all holy conversation and godliness, looking for and hastening to the coming of the day of God, 2 Pet. iii. 11, 12. When we drop asleep, the remembrance of death may quickly awake us; when we grow slack, it is our spur to put us on to mend our pace. Who is so mad as wilfully to sin with death in his eye? Or who so dead as, with death in his eye, to refuse to live a godly life, if he have any spiritual light and feeling? Experience telleth us, that when health and folly cause us to promise ourselves long life, and think that death is a great way off, it lamentably cools our zeal, and strengthens our temptations, and dulls our souls to holy operations. And the approach of death puts life into all our apprehensions and affections. It is a wonderful hard thing to maintain our lively apprehensions, and strong affections, and tenderness of conscience, and self-denial, and easy contempt of earthly things, when we put far from us the day of death. We see what a stir men make for the profits and honours of this world, and how fast they hold their fleshly pleasures while they are in health, and how contemptuously they speak of all, and bitterly complain of the vanity and vexation when they come to die. And if our lives and the world be brought hereby into such disorders, when men live so short a time on earth, what monsters of ambition, and covetousness, and luxury would men be, if they lived as long as before the flood, even to eight hundred or nine hundred years of age! Doubtless long life was so great a temptation then to man, (in his corrupted state,) that it is no wonder if his wickedness was great upon the earth; and if it prepared for that great destruction of the universal deluge. Should men live now but to the age of three hundred or four hundred years, I fear it would so tempt them to overvalue the world, and so imbolden them to delay repentance, that one would be as a wolf to another, and the weak but be a prey to the strong, and wickedness would overwhelm the world, despising the reins, and bearing down religious and civil opposition. But when we stand over the grave, and see our friends laid in the dust, how mortified do we seem! How do we even shake the head at the folly of ambitious and covetous worldlings, and are ashamed to think of fleshly lusts! So far are men from owning their vanities, when that silent teacher standeth by. It is death that helps to humble the proud, and abate the arrogancy and obstinacy of the wicked, and make them regard the messengers of Christ, that before despised them and their message. It is death that allayeth the ebullition of distracting thoughts and passions, and helpeth to bring men to themselves, and fixeth giddy, discomposed minds, and helps to settle the light and the unsettled, and to restrain the worst. As we are beholden to the gallows for our purposes and our lives, so are we to the grave and hell for much of the order that is in the world, and our peace and freedom procured thereby. But it is a greater good that it procureth to believers.

If you ask, how is all this to be ascribed to Christ? I answer, many ways. 1. It is he that hath now the keys or power of death and hell, even he that liveth and was dead, and that liveth for evermore, (Rev. i. 18,) and therefore is to be feared by the world. 2. It is he that hath by his blood and covenant brought us the hope of everlasting life, which is it that giveth the efficacy to death. Without this, men would be but desperate, and think that it is better have a little pleasure than none at all; and so would give up themselves to sin, and desperately gratify their flesh by all the wickedness they could devise. 3. And it is Christ that teacheth men the right use of death, by his holy doctrine, having brought life and immortality to light by his gospel. 4. And it is Christ that sendeth forth the Holy Spirit, which only doth so illuminate the mind, and quicken and dispose the heart, that death may be savingly improved. The poison is our own, but it is his skill and love that hath made a sovereign antidote of it. And let our bodies die, so our sin may die. If the foresight of death destroy our sin, and further our sanctification, and the hour of death doth end our fears, and enter us into the state of glory; though we will love death as death never the better for this, much less the sin that caused it, yet must we admire the love of our Redeemer.

And it is not only the peril but also the terror of death that we are in part delivered from. Though Christ himself was in a bloody sweat in his agony before his death, and cried out on the cross, "My God, why hast thou forsaken me?" because he bore the sins of the world; yet death is welcome to many of his followers, that drink of his cup, and are baptized with his baptism: for they taste not of these dregs which he drank up, and they are strengthened by his supporting grace. He that doth comfort them against sin and hell, doth also comfort them against death. So great is the glory that he hath promised them, and so great is his comforting, confirming grace, that dreadful death is not great enough to prevail against them. As it was too weak to conquer Christ; so is it too weak to conquer his Spirit in his people's souls. Without Christ we could not live, and we durst not die; but through him we can do and suffer all things, and can boldly pass through this dark and shady vale of death; yea, we can desire to depart and to be with Christ as best for us: for to live is Christ, and to die is gain, Phil. i. 21, 23. For we know that if our earthly house of this tabernacle were dissolved, we have a building of God, a house not made with hands, eternal in the heavens. And therefore sometimes we can groan, earnestly desiring to be clothed upon with our house which is from heaven. And we are always confident, knowing that whilst we are at home in the body, we are absent from the Lord; we are confident, I say, and willing rather to be absent from the body and present with the Lord; and therefore labour, that whether present or absent, we may be accepted of him: for we walk by faith, and not by sight: and it is God that hath wrought us for the self-same thing, who also hath given us the earnest of the Spirit, 2 Cor. v. 1—10. Though we long not to die, yet we long to see the face of God. And though we lay down our bodies with natural unwillingness, yet we lay down our sin and sorrows with gladness and spiritual delight. And though our hearts are ready to faint, as Peter's when he walked to Christ upon the waters, yet Christ puts forth his hand of love, and soon recovereth us from our fear and danger.

Melancholy and impatience may make men weary of their lives, and rush upon death with a false conceit that it will end their sorrows; but this is not to conquer death, but to be conquered by a lesser evil; and it is not an effect of fortitude, but of an imbecility and impotency of mind. And if a Brutus, a Cato, or a Seneca, be his own executioner, they do but choose a lesser evil, (in their conceits,) even a death which they accounted honourable, before a more ignominious death, or a life of shame, and scorn, and misery. But the true believer is raised above the fears of death by the love of God, and the hopes of glory; and death (though ungrateful in itself) is welcome to him, as the way to his felicity.

Let tyrants and soldiers take it for their glory, that they can take away men's lives, (that is, they have the power of a serpent, or of ratsbane,) as if it were their honour to be their country's pestilence, and a ruler and a dose of poison were things of equal strength and use. But it is the glory of Christ to enable his disciples to conquer death, and bear the fury of the most cruel persecutors. The martyrs have been more joyful in their sufferings, than the judges that condemned them in their pomp and glory. When we are pressed above strength, and despair of life, and have the sentence of death in ourselves, we are then taught to trust in the living God that raiseth the dead, 2 Cor. i. 8—10. The saints by faith have been "tortured, not accepting deliverance; that they might obtain a better resurrection:" they have "had trial of cruel mockings and scourgings; yea, moreover of bonds, and imprisonment; they were stoned, they were sawn asunder, were tempted, were slain with the sword," Heb. xi. 35—37. "Thanks be to God, which giveth us the victory through our Lord Jesus Christ," 1 Cor. xv. 57. "They overcome by the blood of the Lamb, and love not their lives unto the death," Rev. xii. 11. They "fear not them that kill the body, and after that have no more that they can do," Luke xii. 4. They trust upon his promise that hath said, "I will ransom them from the power of the grave; I will redeem them from death. O death, I will be thy plagues: O grave, I will be thy destruction," Hos. xiii. 14. "Precious in the sight of the Lord is the death of his saints," Psal. cxvi. 15. "Blessed are the dead which die in the Lord, from henceforth; yea, saith the Spirit, that they may rest from their labours; and their works do follow them," Rev. xiv. 13.

Use 7. Moreover, from the enmity of death we may be directed which way to bend our cares; and seeing where our difficulty most lieth, we may see which way our most diligent preparations must be turned. Death cannot be prevented, but the malignant influence of it on our souls may be much abated. If you let it work without an antidote, it will make you live like unbelieving worldlings; it will deter your hearts from heaven, and dull your love to God himself, and make your meditations of him, and of your everlasting rest, to be seldom, and ungrateful to you; and it will make you say, "It is good to be here;" and have sweeter thoughts of this present life, than of your inheritance: it will rob you of much of your heavenly delights, and fill you with slavish fears of death, and subject you unto bondage all your lives, and make you die with agony and horror, so that your lives and deaths will be dishonourable to your holy faith, and to your Lord. If it were merely our own suffering by fears and horrors, or merely our loss of spiritual delights, the matter were great, but not so great. But it is more than this. For when our joys are overwhelmed with the fears of death, and turned into sorrows, our love to God will be abated, and we shall deny him the thanks and cheerful praises, which should be much of the employment of our lives. And we shall be much discomposed and unfitted for his service, and shall much dishonour him in the world; and shall strengthen our temptations to the overvaluing of earthly things. Think it not therefore a small or an indifferent matter, to fortify your souls against these malignant fears of death. Make this your daily care and work; your peace, your safety, your innocency, and usefulness, and the honour of God, do much lie on it. And it is a work of such exceeding difficulty that it requireth the best of your skill and diligence; and when all is done, it must be the illuminating, quickening beams of grace, and the shining face of the eternal love, that must do the work; though yet your diligence is necessary to attend the Spirit, and use the means in subservience to grace, and in expectation of these celestial rays.

And above all, take heed lest you should think that carnal mirth, or mere security, and casting away the thoughts of death, will serve to overcome these fears; or that it is enough that you resolve against them. For it is your safety that must be looked to, as well as your present ease and peace; and fear must be so overcome, as that a greater misery may not follow: presumption and security will be of very short continuance. To die without fear, and pass into endless desperation, which fear should have wakened you to prevent, is no desirable kind of dying. And besides, resolving against the terrors of death will not prevent them. When death draws near, it will amaze you in despite of all your resolutions, if you are not furnished with a better antidote. The more jocund you have been in carnal mirth, and the more you have presumptuously slighted death, it is likely your horror will be the greater when it comes. And therefore see that you make a wise and safe preparation, and that you groundedly and methodically cure these fears, and not securely cast them away. Though I have given you, to this end, some directions in other writings, (in the Saints' Rest, and in the Treatise of Self-denial, and that of Crucifying the World,) yet I shall add here these following helps, which, faithfully observed and practised, will much promote your victory over death, which conquereth all the strength of flesh, and glory of this world.

Direct. 1. If you would overcome the danger and the fears of death, make sure of your conversion that it is sound; and see that you be absolutely devoted unto God without reserves. Should you be deceived in your foundations, your life, and hopes, and joys would all be delusory things. Till sin be mortified and your souls reconciled to God in Christ, you are still in danger of worse than death, and it is but the senselessness of your dead condition that keepeth you from the terrors of damnation. But if you are sure that you are quickened by renewing grace, and possessed by the sanctifying Spirit, and made partakers of the divine nature, you have then the earnest of your inheritance, (Eph. i. 14; 2 Cor. i. 22, and v. 5,) and the fire is kindled in your breast, that in despite of death will mount you up to God.

Direct. 2. To conquer the enmity of death you must live by faith in Jesus Christ; as men that are emptied of themselves, and ransomed from his hands that had the power of death, and as men that are redeemed from the curse, and are now made heirs of the grace of life, being made his members, who is the Lord of life, even the second Adam, who is a quickening Spirit. The serious, believing study of his design and office, (to destroy sin and death, and to bring many sons to glory,) and also of his voluntary suffering, and his obedience to the death of the cross, may raise us above the fears of death. When we live by faith as branches of this blessed vine, and are righteous with his righteousness, justified by his blood and merits, and sanctified by his word and Spirit, and find that we are united to him, we may then be sure that death cannot conquer us, and nothing can take us out of his hands; for our life being hid with Christ in God, we know that we shall live, because he liveth, Col. iii. 3; John xiv. 19; and that when Christ, who is our life, appeareth, we shall also appear with him in glory, Col. iii. 4; and that he will "change our vile bodies, and make them like unto his glorious body, by his mighty power, by which he is able even to subdue all things unto himself," Phil. iii. 21. In our strength we dare not stand the charge of death, and with it the charge of the law, and of our consciences. How dreadfully should we then be foiled and nonplussed if we must be found in no other righteousness but what we have received from the first Adam, and have wrought by the strength received from him. But being gathered under the wings of Christ, as the chickens under the wings of the hen, (Matt. xxiii. 37,) and being found then in him, having the righteousness which is through the faith of Christ, the righteousness which is of God by faith, we may boldly answer to all that can be charged on us to our terror. If we "know him, and the power of his resurrection, and the fellowship of his sufferings, and are made conformable unto his death," Phil. iii. 10; if we are dead with him to the world, and risen with him to a holy life; if we have believingly traced him in his sufferings and conquest, and perceive by faith how we participate in his victories, we shall then be able to grapple with the hands of death; and though we know the grave must be for awhile the prison of our flesh, we can by faith foresee the opening of our prison doors, and the loosing of our bonds, and the day of our last and full redemption. It strengtheneth us exceedingly to look "unto Jesus, the author and finisher of our faith, who, for the joy that was set before him, endured the cross, despising the shame, and is set down at the right hand of the throne of God." When we consider what he endured against himself, we shall not be weary, nor faint in our minds, Heb. xii. 2, 3.

Direct. 3. Live also by faith on the heavenly glory. As one eye of faith must be on a humbled, crucified Christ, so must the other be on heaven, on a glorified Christ, and on the glory and everlasting love of God, which we shall there enjoy. This is it that conquereth the fears of death, when we believe that we shall pass through it into everlasting life. If a man for health will take the most ungrateful potion, (the bitterness being short, and the benefit long,) and if he will suffer the surgeon to let out his blood, and in case of necessity to cut off a member, how light should we make of death, that have the assured hopes of glory to encourage us? What door so strait that we would not pass through if we could to our dearest friend? What way so foul that we would not travel to our beloved home? And shall death seem intolerable to us, that letteth in our souls to Christ? Well might Paul say, "To die is gain," Phil. i. 21. When we gain deliverance from all those sins that did here beset us, and all those sorrows that sin had bred, we gain the accomplishment of our desires, and the end of our faith, the salvation of our souls. We gain the crown that fadeth not away; a place before the throne of Christ, in the temple of God, in the city of God, the new Jerusalem; to eat of the hidden manna, and of the tree of life which is in the midst of the paradise of God, Rev. ii. 3. We gain the place prepared for us by Christ in his Father's house, John xiv. 1, 2. For we shall be with him where he is, that we may behold his glory, John xvii. 24. We shall gain the sight of the glory of God, and the feeling of his most precious love, and the fulness of joy that is in his presence, and the everlasting pleasures at his right hand, Psal. xvi. 11. And shall we think much to die for such a gain? We will put off our clothes, and welcome sleep, which is the image of death, that our bodies may have rest, and refuse not thus to die every night, that we may rise more refreshed for our employments in the morning. And shall we stick at the unclothing of our souls in order to their everlasting rest? Set but the eye of faith to the prospective of the promise, and take a serious, frequent view of the promised land, and this, if any thing, will make death more welcome than physic to the sick, than unclothing to a beggar that puts on new or better clothes. Shall a poor man cheerfully ply his labour all day in hope of a little wages at night, and shall not a believer cheerfully yield to death in hope of everlasting glory? So far as heaven is soundly believed, and our conversations and hearts are there, the fears of death will be assuaged, and nothing else will well assuage them.

Direct. 4. Moreover if you will conquer the enmity of death, do all that you can to increase and exercise the love of God in you. For love will so incline you to the blessed object of it, that death will not be able to keep down the flame. Were God set as a seal upon our hearts, we should find that "Love is as strong as death, and the coals thereof are coals of fire, which hath a most vehement flame; many waters cannot quench it, neither can the floods drown it," Sol. Song viii. 6, 7. If carnal love have made the amorous to choose death that they might passionately express it, especially when they have heard of the death of their beloved; and if natural fortitude and love to their country have made many valiant men, though heathens, to contemn death, and readily lay down their lives; and if the love of fame and vain-glory in a surviving name have caused many to die through pride; how much more will the powerful love of God put on the soul to leave this flesh and pass through death, that we may see his face, and fully enjoy the object of our love. So much as you love God, so much will you be above the terrors of the grave, and passed through death for the enjoyment of your beloved. "Perfect love casteth out fear," and "he that feareth is not made perfect in love." In death and judgment we shall have boldness if our love be perfect, 1 John iv. 17, 18. This maketh the martyrs cheerfully lay down their lives for Christ; and love is glad of so precious an opportunity for its exercise and manifestation. Love is a restless, working thing, that will give you no rest till your desires are attained, and you be with God. Nothing is so valiant as love. It rejoiceth when it meeteth with difficulties, which it may encounter for the sake of our beloved: it contemneth dangers; it glorieth in sufferings; though it be humble, and layeth by all thoughts of merit, yet it rejoiceth in sufferings for Christ, and glorieth in the cross, and in the participation of his sufferings, and in the honourable wounds and scars which we received for him that died for us.

Direct. 5. To overcome the terrors and enmity of death, it is necessary that we keep the conscience clear from the guilt of wilful sin, and of impenitency. If it may be, see that you wound it not; if you have wounded it, presently seek a cure, and live not in a wounded state. The face of death will waken conscience, and cause it to speak much louder than it did in health and in prosperity; and then sin will seem another thing, and wrath more terrible than it did in your security. Conscience will do much to make your burden light or heavy. If conscience groundedly speak peace, and all be sound and well at home, death will be less terrible, the heart being fortified against its enmity. But to have a pained body and a pained soul; a dying body and a scorched conscience, that is afraid of everlasting death, this is a terrible case indeed. Speedily, therefore, get rid of sin, and get your consciences thoroughly cleansed by sound repentance and the blood of Christ. For so much sin as you bring to your death-bed, so much bitterness will there be in death. Away then with that sin that conscience tells you of, and touch the forbidden fruit no more, and kindle not the sparks of hell in your souls to make the sting of death more venomous. As it will quiet a believing soul through Christ, when he can say with Hezekiah, "Remember now, O Lord, I beseech thee, how I have walked before thee in truth and with a perfect heart, and have done that which is good in thy sight," Isa. xxxviii. 3. And it will be our rejoicing if we have "the testimony of our conscience, that in simplicity and godly sincerity we have had our conversation in the world," 2 Cor. i. 12. So will it be most terrible to die in the fears of unpardoned sin, and to have conscience scourging us with the remembrance of our folly, when God is afflicting us, and we have need of a well-composed mind to bear the troubles of our flesh. A little from without is grievous, when any thing is amiss within. Get home, therefore, to Christ without delay; and cease not till you have peace in him, that death may find your consciences whole.

Direct. 6. Redeeming time is another means to prevent the hurtful fears of death. When we foreknow that it will shortly end our time, let us make the best of time while we have it. And then when we find that our work is done, and that we did not loiter nor lose the time that God vouchsafed us, the end of it will be less grievous to us. A man that studieth his duty, and spareth for no cost or pains, and is as loth to lose an hour's time, as a covetous man is to lose a hundred pounds, will look back on his life, and look before him to his death, with greater peace, and less perplexity, than another man; but the thoughts of death must needs be terrible to a man that hath trifled away his life, and been an unthrift of his time. To think when you must die, that now you are at your last day or hour; and withal, to think how many hours you vainly lost, and that you knew not the worth of time till it was gone, will make death more bitter than now you can imagine. What else is death but the ending of our time? And what can be more necessary to a comfortable end, than faithfully to use it while we have it?

Direct. 7. Another help against the enmity of death is, the crucifying of the flesh, with its affections and lusts; and the conquest of the world by the life of faith, and crucifying it by the cross of Christ, and dying daily by the patient suffering of the cross ourselves. When we are loose from all things under the sun, and there is nothing that entangleth our affections on earth, a great part of the difficulty is then removed; but death will tear the heart that is glued to any thing in this world. Possess, therefore, as if you possessed not, and rejoice as if you rejoiced not, and use the world as not abusing it: for the fashion of this world doth pass away, 1 Cor. vii. 29—31. It is much for the sake of our flesh that must perish, that death doth seem so bitter to us. If, therefore, we can thoroughly subdue the flesh, and live above its pleasures and desires, we shall the more easily bear its dissolution. Set up your senses then a little more, and let your hearts grow stranger to this world; and if you have known any persons, relations, accommodations after the flesh, from henceforth know them so no more. How terrible is death to an earthly-minded man, that had neglected his soul for a treasure here, which must then be dissipated in a moment! How easy is death to a heavenly mind, that is thoroughly weaned from this world, and taketh it but for his pilgrimage or passage unto life; and hath made it the business of his days to lay up for himself a treasure in heaven! He that hath unfeignedly made heaven his end in the course of his life, will most readily pass to it on the hardest terms, for every man is willing to attain his end.

Direct. 8. It will much help us against the enmity of death, to be duly conformed to the image of God in the hatred of sin and love of holiness; and especially in the point of justice. When we hate sin thoroughly, and find it so incorporated into our flesh, that they must live and die together, it will make death the more easy to us, because it will be the death of sin; even of that sin which we most hate, and that God hateth, and that hath cost us so dear as it hath done. When we are in love with holiness, and know that we shall never be perfect in it till after death, it will make death the more welcome as the passage to our desired life. When the justice, even the castigatory and vindictive justice of God, is more amiable in our eyes, and we are not blinded by self-love, to judge of God and of his ways according to the interest of our flesh, we shall then consent to his dissolving stroke, and then see the bitterness of death proceedeth from that which is good in God, though from that which is evil in ourselves. Doubtless, as justice is one of the blessed attributes of God, so should it be amiable to man, there being nothing in God but what is lovely. It is the prevalency of self-love that makes men so insensible of the excellency of divine justice, while they speak so respectfully of his mercy. So far as men are carnal and selfish, they cannot love that by which they smart, or of which they are in danger; but the soul that is got above itself, and is united unto God in Christ, and hath that image of God which containeth the impress and effect of all his attributes, hath such a habit of impartial justice in himself, and such a hatred of sin, and such a desire that the honour of God should be vindicated and maintained, and such an approbation of the justice of God, that he can the more easily consent or submit to the dissolving stroke of death; he hateth his own sin, and loatheth himself for all his abominations, and is possessed with that justice that provoketh him to self-revenge in an ordinate sort, and therefore doth love and honour that justice that inflicteth on him the penalty of death; (especially since mercy hath made it a useful castigation); as some penitent malefactors have been so sensible of their crimes, that they have not deprecated death, but consented to it as a needful work of justice (as it is written of the penitent murderer lately hanged at London). So holiness doth contain such a hatred of our own sins, and such impartial justice on God's behalf, that it will cause us to subscribe to the righteousness of his sentence, and the more quietly to yield to the stroke of death.

Direct. 9. It will somewhat abate the fears of death, to consider the restlessness and troubles of this life, and the manifold evils that end at death. And because this consideration is little available with men in prosperity, it pleaseth God to exercise us with adversity, that when we find there is no hope of rest on earth, we may look after it where it is, and venture on death by the impulse of necessity. Here we are continually burdened with ourselves, annoyed by our corruptions, and pained by the diseases of our souls; or endangered most when pained least. And would we be thus still? We live in the continual smart of the fruit of our own folly, and the hurts that we catch by our careless or inconsiderate walking, like children that often fall and cry; and would we still live such a life as this? The weakness of our faith, the darkness of our minds, the distance and strangeness of our souls to God, are a continual languishing and trouble to our hearts. How grievous is it to us that we can love him no more, nor be more assured of his love to us; that we find continually so much of the creature, and so little of God upon our hearts; that carnal affections are so easily kindled in us, and the love of God will scarce be kept in any life by the richest mercies, the most powerful means, and by our greatest diligence! Oh! what a death is it to our hearts that so many odious temptations should have such free access, such ready entertainment, such small resistance, and so great success! that such horrid thoughts of unbelief should look into our minds, and stay so long, and be so familiar with us! that the blessed mysteries of the gospel, and the state of separated souls, and the happiness of the life to come, are known so slightly, and believed so weakly and imperfectly, and meet with so many carnal questionings and doubts! that when we should be solacing our souls in the forethoughts of heaven, we look toward it with such strangeness and amazement, as if we staggered at the promise of God through unbelief; and there is so much atheism in our affections, God being almost as no God to them sometimes, and heaven almost as no heaven to them, that it shows there is too much in our understandings! Oh! what a death is it to our minds, that when we should live in the love of infinite goodness, we find such a remnant of carnal enmity, and God hath such resistance, and so narrow, so short, so cold, so unkind entertainment in those hearts that were made to love him, and that should know and own no love but his! What a bondage is it that our souls are so entangled with the creatures, and so detained from the love of God; and that we draggle on this earth, and can reach no higher; and the delightful communion with God, and a conversation in heaven, are things that we have so small experience of! Alas! that we that are made for God, and should live to him, and be still upon his work, and know no other, should be so biassed by the flesh, and captivated by self-love, and lost at home, that our affections and intentions do hardly get above ourselves; but there we are too prone to terminate them all, and lose our God, even in a seeming religiousness, while we will be gods to ourselves. How grievous is it that such wondrous and glorious appearances of God, as are contained in the incarnation, life, and death of Christ, and in all the parts of the work of our redemption, should no more affect us than they do, nor take up our souls in more thankful admiration, nor ravish us into higher joys. Alas! that heaven commands our souls no more from earth. That such an infinite glory is so near us, and we enjoy so little of it, and have no more savour of it upon our souls. That in the hands of God, and before his face, we do no more regard him. That the great and wonderful matters of our faith do so little affect us, that we are tempted thereby to question the sincerity of our faith, if not the reality of the things believed; and that so little of these great and wondrous things appeareth in our lives, that we tempt the world to think our faith is but a fancy. Is not all this grievous to an honest heart? And should we not be so far weary of such a life as this, as to be willing to depart and be with Christ.

If it would so much rejoice a gracious soul to have a stronger faith, a more lively hope, a more tender conscience, a more humble, self-abhorring heart, to be more fervent in prayer, more resolute against temptations, and more successfully to fight against them; with what desire and joy then should we look towards heaven, where we shall be above our strongest faith and hope, and have no more need of the healing graces or the healing ordinances, nor be put upon self-afflicting work, nor troubled with the temptations, nor terrified by the face of any enemy!

Now, if we will vigorously appear for God against a sinful generation, how many will appear against us! How bitterly will they reproach us; how falsely will they slander us; and say all manner of evil against us! and it is well if we escape the violence of their hands. And what should be our joy in all these sufferings, but that "great is our reward in heaven?" Matt. v. 11, 12.

Alas! how are we continually here annoyed by the presence, and the motions, and the success of sin in ourselves and others. It dwelleth in us night and day; we cannot get it to stay behind; no, not when we address ourselves to God: not in our public worship, or our secret prayers; not for the space of one Lord's day, or one sermon, or one sacrament, in ordinary or extraordinary duty. Oh, what a blessed day and duty would it be, in which we could leave our sin behind us, and converse with God in spotless innocency, and worship and adore him without that darkness, and strangeness, and unbelief, and dulness, and doubtings, and distractions, that are now our daily miseries! Can we have grace, and not be weary of these corruptions? Can we have life, and not be pained with these diseases? And can we live in daily pain and weariness, and not be willing of release? Is there a gracious soul that groaneth not under the burden of these miseries? Yea, in every prayer, what do we else but confess them, and lament them, and groan for help and for deliverance? And yet shall we fear our day of freedom, and be loth that death should bring us news that our prayers are heard, and our groans have reached up to heaven; and that the bonds of flesh and sin shall be dissolved, and we shall have need to watch, and strive, and fear, and complain, and sigh, and weep no more? Shall the face of death discourage us from desiring such a blessed day, when we have so full assurance that, at last, this enemy also shall be destroyed? The Lord heal and pardon the hypocrisy of our complaints, together with the unbelief and cowardliness of our souls. Do we speak so much, and hear so much, and seem to do so much against sin, and yet had we rather keep it still than be stripped of it, together with the rags of our mortality? And yet had we rather dwell with sin, in tempting, troubling, corruptible flesh, than lay them by, and dwell with Christ? O Lord, how lamentably have we lost our wisdom, and drowned our minds in flesh and folly, by forsaking thee our light and life! How come our unreasonable souls to be so bewitched, as, after all our convictions, complaints, and prayers, to be still more willing of our sickness than of the remedy, and more afraid of this bitter cup than of the poison that lodgeth in our bowels, which it would expel? and that after all the labour we have used, we had yet rather dwell with our greatest enemy, than, by a less, to be transmitted to our dearest Friend? and had rather continue in a troublesome, weary, restless life, than by the sleep of death to pass to rest?

And this sin in others, also, is our trouble, though not so much as in ourselves. It maketh those our bitter enemies, whose good we most desire and endeavour, and causeth the unthankful world to requite us with malicious usage, for telling them the ungrateful truth, and seeking their salvation. It makes our friends to be but half friends, and some of them too like our enemies. It puts a sting into the sweetest friendship, and mixeth smart with all our pleasures; it worketh us grief from precious mercies, and abateth the comfort of our near relations; so that our smart by the pricks is often greater than our pleasure in the sweetness of the rose. No friend is so smoothed and squared to the temper and interest of another, but that some inequality and unevenness doth remain, which makes the closure to be less near and stedfast. Even family relations are usually so imperfectly jointed and cemented, that when the winds of trial are any thing high, they shake the frame; and though they are but low, they find an entrance, and cause such a coldness of affections as is contrary to the nature and duty of the relations. Either a contrariety of opinions, or of natural temperature and humours, or else of the dispositions of the mind; sometimes cross interests, and sometimes passions and cross words, do cause such discontents and sourness, such frowns, or jealousies, or distances; that our nearest friends are but as sackcloth on our skins, and as a shoe too strait for us, or as a garment that is unmeet, which pinch and trouble us in their use: and those that should be to us as the apple of our eyes, are as the dust or smoke to them that vex or blind them; and the more we love them, the more it grieveth us to be crossed in our love. There is scarce any friend so wise, so good, so suitable to us, or so near, that we can always please. And the displeasure of a friend is as gravel in our shoes, or as nettles in our bed, ofttimes more grievous than the malice of an enemy. There is no such doing as this in heaven, because there is no such guest as sin. We shall love each other far more than we do here, and yet that love shall never be inordinate, nor in the least divert our love from God, but every saint and angel in the society shall be loved with the most chaste and pure affections, in a perfect subordination to the love of God, and so as that God himself in them shall be the chiefest object of that love. It is there that our friends, being freed from all their imperfections, do neither tempt us to a carnal love, nor have any thing in them to discourage the love that is spiritual and pure. We have here our passionate friends, our self-conceited friends, our unkind, unthankful, selfish friends, our mutable and unfaithful friends, our contentious friends, that are like to enemies. And who have used us more hardly than our friends? But when we come to God, we shall have friends that are like God, that are wholly good, and are participatively turned into love; and having left behind them all that was unclean, and noisome, and troublesome to themselves, they have also cast off all that could be troublesome to us. Our love will be there without suspicions, without interruptions, unkindnesses, and discontents, without disappointments, frustrations, and dissatisfactions: for God himself will fully satisfy us; and we shall love his goodness and glory in his saints, as well as immediately in himself. Our friends are now lost at the turning of a straw. The change of their interest, their company, their opinions, the slanders of backbiters, and misrepresentations of malicious men, can cool their love, and kill their friendship. But heaven is a place of constant love; the love of saints, as all things else, is there eternal, and yet it declineth not with age. It is a world of love that we are hastening to; it is a life of love that we must there live; and a work of love, and perfect love, that we must be there employed in for ever. If here we have a pure, a dear, a faithful friend, that is without false-heartedness and deceit, that loveth us as his own soul, how quickly is he snatched away by death, and leaves us melted into tears, and mourning over his earthly relics, and looking upward with grieved hearts, as the disciples did after their ascending Lord, Acts i. 9—11. We are left almost as lifeless by such friends, as the body is left by the departed soul. We have nothing but grief to tell us that we live, and that our souls are not departed with them. We are left in greater lamentation than if we had never known faithful friends. And, alas! how quickly are they gone when once God sees them ripe for heaven, when drones and dullards live much longer. If we see a saint that is clear of judgment, and low in humility, and naked-hearted in sincerity, and that abounds in love to God and man, that is faithful and constant to his friend, and is above the pride and vanities of this world, and doth converse by a life of faith above, and is useful and exemplary in his generation; alas! how soon is he snatched away; and we are left in our temptations, repining and murmuring at God, as Jonah, when his gourd was withered, as if the Lord had destinated this world to be the dwelling of unfaithful, worthless men, and envied us the presence of one eminent saint, one faithful friend, and one that (as Moses when he had talked with God) hath a face that shineth with the reflected rays of the heavenly glory; when, indeed, it is because this world is unworthy of them, (Heb. xi. 38,) not knowing their worth, nor how to use them, nor how to make use of them for their good; and because, when they are ripe and mellow for eternity, it is fit that God be served before us, and that heaven have the best, and that be left on earth that is earthly. Must heaven be deprived of its inhabitants? Must a saint that is ripe be kept from Christ, and so long kept from his inheritance, from the company of angels and the face of God, and all lest we should be displeased, and grudge at God for glorifying those whom he destined to glory before the foundations of the world, and whom he purchased and prepared for glory? Must there be a place empty, and a voice be wanting in the heavenly choir, lest we should miss our friends on earth? Are we not hastening after them at the heels; and do we not hope to live with them for ever; and shall we grudge that they are gone a day, or week, or year, before us? Oh foolish, unbelieving souls! We mourn for them who are past mourning, and lament for our friends that are gone to rest, when we are left ourselves in a vexatious, restless, howling wilderness, as if it were better to be here. We mourn and weep for the souls that are triumphing in their Master's joy; and yet we say we believe, and hope, and labour, and wait for the same felicity. Shall the happiness of our friends be our sorrow and lamentation? Oh, did we but see these blessed souls, and where they are, and what they are enjoying, and what they are doing, we should be ashamed to mourn thus for their change! Do you think they would wish themselves again on earth? Or would they take it kindly of you if you could bring them down again into this world, though it were to reign in wealth and honour? Oh! how would they disdain or abhor the motion, unless the commanding will of God did make it a part of their obedience! And shall we grieve that they are not here, when to be here would be their grief?

But thus our lives are filled with griefs. Thus smiles and frowns, desires and denials, hopes and frustrations, endeavours and disappointments, do make a quotidian ague of our lives. The persons and the things we love do contribute to our sorrows, as well as those we hate. If our friends are bad, or prove unkind, they gall and grieve us while they live: if they excel in holiness, fidelity, and suitableness, the dart that kills them deeply woundeth us; and the sweeter they were to us in their lives, the bitterer to us is their death. We cannot keep mercy, but sin is ready to take it from us, or else to mar it, and turn it into vinegar and gall. And doth not death (accidentally) befriend us, that puts an end to all these troubles, and lands us safe on the celestial shore, and puts us into the bosom of perpetual rest, where all is calm, and the storms and billows that tossed us here shall fear or trouble us no more? And thus death shall make us some recompence at last for the wrong it did us; and the mortal blow shall hurt us less than did the dreadful apparition of it in our forethoughts. Let not our fears, then, exceed the cause: though we fear the pangs and throes of travail, let us withal remember that we shall presently rejoice, and all the holy angels with us, that a soul is born into the world of glory, and death shall gain us much more than it deprived us of.

Direct. 10. The last direction that I shall give you to conquer the enmity of death is this: Give up your wills entirely to the will of God, as knowing that his will is your beginning and your end, your safety, your felicity, and rest, in which you should gladly acquiesce. When you think of death, remember who it is that sends it; it is our Father's messenger, and is sent but to execute his will. And can there be any thing in the will of God that his servants should inordinately fear? Doubtless, his will is much safer and better for us than our own: and if, in general, it were offered to our choice, whether all particulars of our lives should be disposed of by God's will, or by ours, common reason might teach us to desire to be rather in God's hands than our own. The fulfilling of his will is the care and business of our lives; and therefore it should be a support and satisfaction to us at our death that it is but the fulfilling of his will. His justice and punishing will is good, though selfishness maketh it ungrateful to the offender. But his children that are dear to him, and taste no evil but that which worketh for their good, have no cause to quarrel at his will. Whatsoever our surest, dearest friends would have us take, or do, or suffer, we are ready to submit to, as being confident they will do nothing for our hurt (if they do but know what is for our good). And shall we not more boldly trust the will of God than of our dearest friend? He knows what he hath to do with us, and how he will dispose of us, and whither he will bring us, and his interest in us is more than ours in ourselves; and shall we then disturb him, as if we had to do with an enemy, or one that were evil, and not with love and infinite goodness? It is the will of God that must be the everlasting rest, the heaven, the pleasure of our souls: and shall we now so fear it, and fly from it, as if it were our ruin? Look which way you will through all the world, your souls will never find repose, nor satisfying quietness and content, but in the will of God. Let us, therefore, commit our souls to him, as to a faithful Creator, and desire unfeignedly the fulfilling of his will, and believe that there is no ground of confidence more firm. Abraham may boldly trust his son, his only son, on the will of God; and Christ himself, when he was to drink the bitter cup, submitted his own natural love of life to his Father's will, saying, "Not my will, but thine be done." It is a most unworthy abuse of God, that we could be quiet, and rejoice, if our own wills, or our dearest friends, might dispose of our lives, and yet are distressed when they are at the dispose of the will of God.

But perhaps you will say, It is the error of my own will that hath procured my death: if it had been merely the fruit of the will of God, I could be easily satisfied. *Answ.* Woe to us if we had not ground of comfort against the errors of our own wills! When our destruction is of ourselves, our help is of God. So much as is of ourselves in it is evil, but so much as is of God is good. I do not say that you should rest in your own wills, nor in your own ways, but in the will and ways of God. The rod is good, though the fault that makes it necessary be bad. The chastising will is good, though the sinning will be evil; and it is good that is intended to us, and shall be performed in the event.

Object. But how can we rest in the angry, afflicting will of God, when it is this that we must be humbled under; and it is the will of God that is the condemnation of the wicked? *Answ.* The effect being from a twofold cause, (the sinning will of man, and the punishing will of God,) is accordingly good as from the latter, and so far should be loved and consented to by all; and evil as from the former, and so may be abhorred. But to the saints there is yet greater consolation. Though affliction is their grief as it signifieth God's displeasure, and causeth the smart or destruction of the flesh; yet it is their mercy, as it proceedeth from the love of God, and prepareth them for the greatest mercies. And therefore, seeing God never bringeth evil on them that love him, but what is preparatory to a far greater good, we may well take comfort in our death, that it is our Father's will it should be so.

Use 8. If death shall be conquered as the last enemy, from hence christians may receive exceeding consolation, as knowing that they have no enemy to their happiness, but such as shall be conquered by Christ; sooner or later he will overcome them all. Let faith, therefore, foresee the conquest in the conflict; and let us not, with too much despondency, hang down our heads before any enemy that we know shall be trodden down at last. We have burdensome corruptions, that exercise our graces, and grieve the Spirit, and wrong our Lord; but all these shall be overcome. Though we have heard, and read, and prayed, and meditated, and yet our sins remain alive, they shall be conquered at last. Our love, and joy, and praise, shall be everlasting; but our ignorance, and unbelief, and pride, and passion, shall not be everlasting. Our holiness shall be perfected, and have no end; but our sin shall be abolished, and have an end. Our friends shall abide with us for ever, and the holy love and communion of saints shall be perfected in heaven; but our enemies shall not abide with us for ever, nor malice follow us to our rest. The wicked have no comforts but what will have an end; and the forethought of that is sufficient to imbitter even the present sweetness. And the godly have no sorrows but such as are of short continuance; and methinks the foresight of their end should sweeten the present bitter cup, and make our sorrows next to none. We sit weeping now in the midst of manifold afflictions; but we foresee the day when we shall weep no more, but all tears shall be wiped from our eyes by the tender hand of our merciful Redeemer. We are now afraid of love itself, even of our dear and blessed Father, lest he should hate us, or be angry with us for ever; but heaven will banish all these fears, when the perfect fruition of the eternal love hath perfected our love. Our doubtings and perplexities of mind are many and grievous, but they will be but short. When we have full possession we shall be past our doubts. Our work is now to pour out our grieved souls into the bosom of some faithful friend, or ease our troubled minds by complaining of our miseries to our faithful pastors, that from them we may have some words of direction and consolation; but, oh! how different a work is it that we shall have in heaven, where no more complainings shall be heard from our mouths, nor no more sorrow shall possess our hearts! And we shall have no need of men to comfort us; but shall have comfort as naturally from the face of God, as we have light and heat, in the summer, from the sun. When we all make one celestial choir, to sing the praises of the King of saints, how unlike will that melody be to the broken music of sighs, and groans, and lamentations, which we now take to be almost our best! We are now glad when we can find but words, and groans, and tears, to lament our sin and misery; but then our joy shall know no sorrow, nor our voice any sad and mournful tune. And may we not bear a while the sorrows that shall have so good an end? We shall shortly have laid by the hard, unprofitable, barren hearts, that are now our continual burden and disease. Love not your corruptions, christians; but yet be patient under the unavoidable relics that offend you; remembering that your conflict will end in conquest, and your faith, and watchfulness, and patience will be put to it but a little while. Who would not enter willingly into the fight, when he may, beforehand, be assured that the field shall be cleared of every enemy? All this must be ascribed to our dear Redeemer. Had not he wrought the conquest, the enemies that vex us would have destroyed us, and the serpent that now doth but bruise our heel, would have bruised our head; and the sorrows that are wholesome, sanctified, and short, would have been mortal, venomous, and endless.

What suffering, then, can be so great in which a believer should not rejoice, when he is, beforehand, promised a gracious end? What though at the present it be not joyous, but grievous (in itself)? We should bear it with patience, when we know that at last it shall bring forth the peaceable fruit of righteousness to all them that are exercised thereby, Heb. xii. 11. If we should be always abused, and always unthankfully and unkindly dealt with, or always under the scorns, or slanders, or persecutions of unreasonable men, or always under our poverty and toilsome labours, or always under our pains and pining sicknesses, we might then, indeed, dismiss our comforts. But when we know that it will be but a little while, and that all will end in rest and joy, and that our sorrows are but preparing for those joys; even reason itself is taught by faith to bid us rejoice in all our tribulations, and to lift up the hands that hang down, and the feeble knees, Heb. xii. 12. We make nothing to endure a sudden prick, that by blood-letting we may prevent a long disease. The short pain of pulling out a tooth is ordinarily endured to prevent a longer. A woman doth bear the pains of her travail because it is short, and tends to the bringing of a child into the world. Who would not submit to any labour or toil for a day, that he might win a life of plenty and delight by it? Who would not be spit upon, and made the scorn of the world for a day, if he might have his will for it as long as he liveth on earth? And should we not then cheerfully submit to our momentary afflictions, and the troubles of a few days, (which are light, and mixed with a world of mercies,) when we know that they are working for us a far more exceeding, eternal weight of glory? 2 Cor. iv. 17. Our clamorous and malicious enemies, our quarrelsome brethren, our peevish friends, our burdensome corruptions and imperfections, will shortly trouble us no more. As our life is short, and but a dream and shadow, and therefore the pleasures of this world are no better; so our troubles also will be no longer, and are but sad dreams, and dark shadows, that quickly pass away. Our Lord that hath begun, and gone on so far, will finish his victories, and the last enemy shall shortly be destroyed.

And if the fearful, doubting soul shall say, I know this is comfort to them that are in Christ, but what is it to me, that know not whether I have any part in him? I answer, 1. The foundation of God still standeth sure; the Lord knoweth his own, even when some of them know not that they are his own. He knoweth his mark upon his sheep, when they know it not themselves. God doubteth not of his interest in thee, though thou doubt of thy interest in him. And thou art faster in the arms of his love, than by the arms of thy own faith; as the child is surer in the mother's, than by its holding of the mother. And, moreover, your doubts and fears are part of the evil that shall be removed, and your bitterest sorrows that hence proceed shall with the rest of the enemies be destroyed.

2. But yet take heed that you unthankfully plead not against the mercies which you have received, and be not friends to those doubts and fears which are your enemies, and that you take not part with the enemy of your comforts. Why dost thou doubt, poor humbled soul, of thy interest in Christ, that must make the conquest? Answer me but these few questions from thy heart.

Quest. 1. Did Christ ever show himself unkind to thee? or unwilling to receive thee, and have mercy on thee? Did he ever give thee cause to think so poorly of his love and grace as thy doubts do intimate thou dost? Hast thou not found him kind when thou wast unkind; and that he thought on thee when thou didst not think on him? And will he now forget thee, and end in wrath that begun in love? He desired thee when thou didst not desire him, and gave thee all thy desires after him: and will he now cross and deny the desires which he hath caused? He was found of thee, (or rather found thee,) when thou soughtest not after him; and can he reject thee now thou criest and callest for his grace? O think not hardly of his wondrous grace till he give thee cause. Let thy sweet experiences be remembered, to the shame of thy causeless doubts and fears; and let him that hath loved thee to the death be thought on as he is, and not as the unbelieving flesh would misrepresent him.

Quest. 2. If thou say that it is not his unkindness, but thy own, that feeds thy doubts, I further ask thee, is he not kind to the unkind, especially when they lament their own unkindness? Thou art not so unkind to him as thou wast in thy unconverted state, and yet he then expressed his love in thy conversion. He then sought thee when thou wentest astray, and brought thee carefully home into his fold, and there he hath kept thee ever since; and is he less kind now when thou art returned home? Dost thou not know that all his children have their frowardness, and are guilty of their unkindnesses to him? And yet he doth not therefore disown them, and turn them out of his family; but is tender of them in their froward weakness, because they are his own. How dealt he with the peevish prophet Jonah, that was "exceedingly displeased, and very angry," that God spared Nineveh, lest it should be a dishonour to his prophecy, insomuch, that he wished that he might die, and not live; and after repined at the withering of his gourd, and the scorching of the sun that beat upon him? The Lord doth gently question with him, "Dost thou well to be angry?" and after hence convinces him that the mercy which he valued to himself he should not envy to so many, Jonah iv. How dealt he with his disciples that fell asleep, when they should have watched with Christ in the night of his great agony? He doth not tell them, You are none of mine, because you could not watch with me one hour, but tenderly excuseth that which they durst not excuse themselves: "The spirit is willing, but the flesh is weak." When he was on the cross, though "they all forsook him and fled," he was then so far from forsaking them, that he was manifesting to admiration that exceeding love that never would forsake them. And knowest thou not, poor, complaining soul, that the kindness of Christ overcometh all the unkindness of his children? and that his blood and grace is sufficient to save thee from greater sins than those that trouble thee? If thou hadst no sin, what use hadst thou for a Saviour? Will thy physician, therefore, cast thee off because thou art sick?

Quest. 3. Yea, hath not Christ already subdued so many of thy enemies as may assure thee he will subdue the rest? and begun that life in thee which may assure thee of eternal life? Once thou wast a despiser of God and his holy ways; but now it is far otherwise with thee. Hath he not broken the heart of thy pride, and worldliness, and sensuality, and made thee a new creature? And is not this a pledge that he will do the rest? Tell me plainly, hadst thou rather keep thy sin or leave it? Hadst thou rather have liberty to commit it, or be delivered from it? Dost thou not hate it, and set thyself against it as thy enemy? Art thou not delivered from the reign and tyranny of it, which thou wast once under? And will he not perfect the conquest which he hath begun? He that hath thus far delivered thee from sin, thy greatest enemy, will deliver thee from all the sad effects of it. The blessed work of the Spirit in thy conversion did deliver thee from the bondage of the devil, from the power of darkness, and translated thee into the kingdom of Jesus Christ; then didst thou enter the holy warfare under his banners that was never overcome, in the victorious army that shall shortly begin their everlasting triumph. The sin which thou hatest, and longest to be delivered from, and art willing to use God's means against it, is the conquered enemy, which may assure thee of a full and final conquest, supposing that thy hatred is against all known sin, and that there is none so sweet or profitable in thy account which thou hadst not far rather leave than keep.

Quest. 4. Moreover, art thou not truly willing to yield to all the terms of grace? Thou hast heard of the yoke and burden of Christ, and of the conditions of the gospel, on which peace is offered to the sinful world, and what Christ requireth of such as will be his disciples. What saith thy heart now to those terms? Do they seem so hard and grievous to thee, that thou wilt venture thy soul in thy state of sin, rather than accept of them? If this were so, thou hadst yet no part in Christ indeed. But if there be nothing that Christ requireth of thee that is not desirable in thy eyes, or which thou dost not stick at, so far as to turn away from him, and forsake him, and refuse his covenant and grace, rather than submit to such conditions, thou art then in covenant with him, and the blessings of the covenant belong to thee. Canst thou think that Christ hath purchased, and offered, and promised that which he will not give? Hath he sent forth his ministers, and commanded them to make the motion in his name, and to invite and compel men to come in, and to beseech them to be reconciled to God, and that yet he is unwilling to accept thee when thou dost consent? If Christ had been unwilling, he had not so dearly made the way, nor begun as a suitor to thy soul, nor so diligently sought thee as he hath done. If the blessings of the covenant are thine, then heaven is thine, which is the chiefest blessing? And if they be not thine, it is not because Christ is unwilling, but because thou art unwilling of his blessings on his terms. Nothing can deprive thee of them but thy refusal. Know, therefore, assuredly whether thou dost consent thyself to the terms of Christ, and whether thou art truly willing that he be thy Saviour; and if thy conscience bear thee faithful witness that it is so, dishonour not Christ, then, so far as to question whether he be willing, who hath done so much to put it out of doubt. The stop is at thy will, and not at his. If thou know that thou art willing, thou mayst know that Christ and his benefits are thine; and if thou be not willing, what makes thee wish, and groan, and pray, and labour in the use of means? Is it not for Christ and his benefits that thy heart thus worketh, and thou dost all this? Fear not, then; if thy own hand be to the covenant, it is most certain that the hand of Christ is at it.

Quest. 5. Moreover, I would ask thee, whether thou see not a beauty in holiness, which is the image of Christ, and whether thy soul do not desire it even in perfection; so that thou hadst rather, if thou hadst thy choice, be more holy than more rich or honourable in the world? If so, be assured that it is not without holiness that thou choosest and preferrest holiness. Hadst thou not rather have more faith, and hope, and love to God, and patience, and contentment, and communion with Christ, than have more of the favour and applause of man, or of the riches or pleasures of this world? If so, I would know of thee whether this be not from the Spirit of Christ within thee; and be not his image itself upon thee; and the motions of the new and heavenly nature, which is begotten in thee by the Holy Ghost? Undoubtedly it is. And the Spirit of Christ thus dwelling in thee is the earnest of thy inheritance. Dost thou find the Spirit of Christ thus working in thee, causing thee to love holiness, and hate all sin, and yet canst thou doubt of thy part in Christ?

Quest 6. Moreover, canst thou not truly say, that Christ's friends, so far as thou knowest them, are thy friends, and that which is against him thou takest as against thyself? If so, undoubtedly thy enemies also are to him as his enemies, and he will lay them at thy feet. Thy troubles are his troubles; and in all thy afflictions he is as careful of thy good as if he himself were thereby afflicted. Fear not those enemies that Christ takes as his own. It is he that is engaged to overcome them.

And now when conscience itself beareth witness that thus it is with thy soul, and thou wouldst fain be what God would have thee be, and desirest nothing more than to be more like him, and nearer to him, and desirest no kind of life so much as that in which thou mayst be most serviceable to him; consider what a wrong it is, then, to Christ, and to the honour of his covenant and grace, and to thy poor, dejected soul, that thou shouldst lie questioning his love, and thy part in him, and looking about for matter of accusation, or causeless suspicion, against his Spirit working in thee; and that thou shouldst cast away the joy of the Lord, which is thy strength, and gratify the enemy of thy peace. When sickness is upon thee, and death draws nigh, thou shouldst then, with joy, lift up thy head, because thy warfare is almost accomplished, and thy Saviour ready to deliver thee the crown. Is this a time to fear and mourn, when thou art entering into endless joy? Is it a time of lamentation, when thou art almost at thy journey's end, ready to see thy Saviour's face, and to take thy place in the heavenly Jerusalem, amongst those millions of holy souls that are gone before thee? Is it seemly for thee to lament thus at the door when they are feasted with such unconceivable joys within? Dost thou know what thy brethren are now enjoying, and what the heavenly host are doing? how full they are of God, and how they are ravished with his light and love? And canst thou think it seemly to be so unlike them that are passing to them? I know there is such difference between imperfection and perfection, and between earth and heaven, that it justifieth our moderate sorrows, and commandeth us to take up infinitely short of their delights, till we are with them. But yet let there not be too great a disproportion between the members of Jesus Christ. We have the same Lord, and the same Spirit; and all that is theirs in possession is, in right and title, ours. They are our elder brethren, and, being at age, have possession of the inheritance; but we that are yet in the lap of the church on earth, our mother, and in the arms of our Father's grace, are of the same family, and have the same nature in our low degree. They were once on earth as low as we, and we shall be shortly in heaven as high as they. Am I now in flesh, in fears, in griefs? So was David, and Paul, and all the saints, a while ago; yea, and Christ himself. Am I beset with sin, and compassed with infirmities, and racked by my own distempered passion? So were the many saints now glorified; but the other day, "Elias was a man subject to like passions as we are," James v. 17. Am I maliced by dissenting adversaries? Do they privily lay snares for me, and watch my halting, and seek advantage against my name, and liberty, and life? So did they by David, and many others, now with Christ. But now these enemies are overcome. Art thou under pains, and consuming sicknesses? Are thine eyes held waking; and doth trouble and sorrow waste thy spirits? Doth thy flesh and thy heart fail thee, and thy friends prove silly comforters to thee? So was it with those thousands that are now in heaven, where the night of calamities is past, and the just have dominion in the morning; and glory hath banished all their griefs, and joys have made them forget their sorrows; unless as the remembrance of them doth promote these joys. Are thy friends lamenting thee, and grieved to see the signs of thy approaching death? Do they weep when they see thy pale face, and consumed body, and when they hear thy sighs and groans? Why, thus it was once with the millions that are now triumphing with their Lord? They lay in sickness, and underwent the pains, and were lamented by their friends, as thou art now. Even Christ himself was once in his agony, and some shook the head at him, and others pitied him, who should rather have wept for themselves than for him. This is but the passage from the womb of mortality into the life of immortality, which all the saints have passed before thee that are now with Christ. Dost thou fear the dreadful face of death? Must thy tender flesh be turned to rottenness and dust? And must thou lie in darkness till the resurrection, and thy body remain as the common earth? And is not this the case of all those millions, whose souls now see the face of Christ? Did they not lie as thou dost, and die as thou must, and pass by death to the life which they have now attained? Oh! then commit thy soul to Christ, and be quiet and comforted in his care and love. Trust him as the midwife of thy departing soul, who will bring it safe into the light and life which thou art yet such a stranger to. But it is not strange to him, though it be strange to thee.

What was it that rejoiced thee all thy life, in thy prayers, and sufferings, and labours? Was it not the hopes of heaven? And was heaven the spring and motive of thy obedience, and the comfort of thy life? and yet wilt thou pass into it with heaviness? and shall thy approaches to it be thy sorrows? Didst thou pray for that which thou wouldst not have? Hast thou laboured for it, and denied thyself the pleasures of the world for it, and now art thou afraid to enter in? Fear not, poor soul! thy Lord is there; thy Husband, and thy Head, and life is there; thou hast more there, a thousand-fold more, than thou hast here. Here thou must leave poor mourning friends, that languish in their own infirmities, and troubled thee as well as comforted thee while thou wast with them, and that are hastening after thee, and will shortly overtake thee. But there thou shalt find the souls of all the blessed saints that have lived since the creation till this age; that are all unclothed of the rags of their mortality, and have laid by their frailties with their flesh, and are made up of holiness, and prepared for joy, and will be suitable companions for thee in thy joys. Why shouldst thou be afraid to go the way that all the saints have gone before thee? Where there is one on earth, how many are there in heaven! And one of them is worth many of us. Art thou better than Noah, and Abraham, and David? than Peter, and Paul, and all the saints? Or dost thou not love their names, and wouldst thou not be with them? Art thou loth to leave thy friends on earth? and hast thou not far better and more in heaven? Why then art thou not as loth to stay from them? Suppose that I, and such as I, were the friends that thou art loth to leave; what if we had died long before thee? If it be our company that thou lovest, thou shouldst then be willing to die, that thou mayst be with us. And if so, why then shouldst thou not be more willing to die, and be with Christ, and all his holy ones, that are so much more excellent than we? Wouldst thou have our company? Remove, then, willingly to that place where thou shalt have it to everlasting; and be not so loth to go from hence, where neither thou nor we can stay. Hadst thou rather travel with us, than dwell with us? and rather here suffer with us, than reign in heaven with Christ and us?

Oh! what a brutish thing is flesh! What an unreasonable thing is unbelief! Shall we believe, and fly from the end of our belief? Shall we hope, and be loth to enjoy our hopes? Shall we desire and pray, and be afraid of attaining our desires, and lest our prayers should be heard? Shall we spend our lives in labour and travel, and be afraid of coming to our journey's end? Do you love life, or do you not? If not, why are you afraid of death? If you do, why then are you loth to pass into everlasting life? You know there is no hope of immortality on earth. Hence you must pass whether you will or not, as all your fathers have done before you; it is therefore in heaven, or no where, that endless life is to be had. If you can live here for ever, do. Hope for it, if any have done so before you. Go to some man of a thousand years old, and ask him how he made shift to draw out his life so long. But if you know that man walketh in a vain show, and that his life is a shadow, a dream, a post; and that all these things shall be dissolved, and the fashion of them passeth away; is it not more reasonable that we should set our hearts on the place where there is hopes of our continuance, than where there is none? and where we must live for ever, than where we must be but for so short a time?

Alas! poor darkened, troubled soul! Is the presence of Christ less desirable in thy eyes than the presence of such sinful worms as we, whom thou art loth to part with? Is it more grievous to thee to be absent from us, than from thy Lord? from earth, than from heaven; from sinners, than from blessed saints; from trouble and frailty, than from glory? Hast thou any thing here that thou shalt want in heaven? Alas, that we should thus draw back from happiness, and follow Christ so heavily and sadly into life! But all this is long of the enemies that now molest our peace. Indwelling sin, and a flattering world, and a brutish flesh, and interposing death, are our discouragements that drive us back. But all these enemies shall shortly be overcome.

Fear not death, then, let it do its worst. It can give thee but one deadly gripe that shall kill itself, and prove thy life; as the wasp that leaves its sting behind, and can sting no more. It shall but snuff the candle of thy life, and make it shine brighter when it seems to be put out; it is but an undressing, and a gentle sleep. That which thou couldst not here attain by all our preaching, and all thy prayers, and cares, and pains, thou shalt speedily attain by the help of death. It is but the messenger of thy gracious Lord, and calleth thee to him, to the place that he hath prepared.

Hearken not now to the great deceiver that would draw thee to unbelief, and cause thee to stagger at the promises of God, when thou hast followed him so far, and they are near to the full performance. Believe it as sure as thou believest that the sun doth shine upon thee, that God cannot lie: he is no deceiver. It was his mere love and bounty that caused him to make the promises, when he had no need for himself to make them. And shall he be then unfaithful, and not fulfil the promises which he hath freely made? Believe it, faith is no delusion: it may be folly to trust man; but it is worse than folly not to trust God. Believe it, heaven is not a shadow, nor the life of faith and holiness a dream. These sensible things have least reality; these grosser substances are most drossy, delusory, and base. God is a Spirit, who is the prime Being, and the cause of all created beings: and the angels, and other celestial inhabitants that are nearest to him, are furthest from corporeity, and are spirits likest unto God. The further any thing is from spirituality, the further from that excellency and perfection which the creatures nearest God partake of: the earth is baser than the air and fire; the drossy flesh is baser than the soul; and this lumpish, dirty, visible world, is incomparably below that spiritual world which we believe and wait for. And though thy conceptions of spirits, and the spiritual world, are low and dark, and much unsatisfying, remember still that thy Head is there; and it belongeth to him to know what thou shalt be, till thou art fit to know it, which will not be till thou art fit to enjoy it. Be satisfied that thy Father is in heaven, and that thy Lord is there; and that the Spirit that hath been so long at work within thee, preparing thee for it, dwelleth there. And let it suffice thee, that Christ knoweth what he will do with thee, and how he will employ thee to all eternity. And thou shalt very shortly see his face, and in his light thou shalt behold that light that shall fully satisfy thee, and shame all thy present doubts and fears; and if there were shame in heaven, would shame thee for them.

Use 9. From the enmity of death, and the necessity of a conquest, we may see what a wonderful mercy the resurrection of Christ himself was to the church, and what use we should make of it for the strengthening of our faith. It was not only impossible to man to conquer death by his own strength, and therefore it must be conquered by Christ; but it was also beyond our power to believe it, that ever the dead should rise to life, if Christ had not risen as the first-fruits, and convinced men, by eyesight, or certain testimony, that the thing is possible, and already done. But now what a pillar is here for faith! what a word of hope and joy is this, that Christ is risen! With this we will answer a thousand cavils of the tempter, and stop the mouth of the enemies of our faith, and profligate our infidelity. As unlikely as it seems to flesh and blood, shall we ever doubt whether we shall rise again, when the Lord came down in flesh among us, that he might die and rise again himself, to show us as to our faces that we shall rise? This is the very gospel which we preach, and by which we must be saved; "That Christ died for our sins according to the Scriptures, and that he was buried, and that he rose again the third day according to the Scriptures; and that he was seen of Cephas, then of the twelve; after that he was seen of above five hundred brethren at once, of whom the greater part remained alive" when Paul wrote this, who was the last that saw him, 1 Cor. xv. 1—6. Read over this chapter again and again, where our resurrection is proved by the resurrection of Christ.

No wonder, therefore, that the church, in all ages, ever since the very day of Christ's resurrection, hath kept the first day of the week as a holy festival in remembrance of it. Wherein, though they commemorated the whole work of our redemption, yet was it from the resurrection as the most glorious part that the Spirit of Christ did choose the day. This hath been the joyful day to the church this 1625 years, or thereabouts; in which the ancient christians would assemble themselves together, saluting one another with this joyful word, "The Lord is risen." And this is the day that the Lord hath blessed with the new birth and resurrection of millions of souls; so that it is most probable that all the six days of the week have not begot half so many souls for heaven, as this blessed day of the Lord's resurrection hath done. Let infidels, then, despise it, that believe not Christ's resurrection; but let it still be the church's joyful day. "This is the Lord's doing; it is marvellous in our eyes. This is the day which the Lord hath made; we will rejoice and be glad in it," Psal. cxviii. 23, 24. In it "Let us sing unto the Lord; let us make a joyful noise to the Rock of our salvation. Let us come before his presence with thanksgiving, and make a joyful noise unto him with psalms," Psal. xcv. 1, 2. Every day let us remember the Lord's resurrection; but on this day let the joyful commemoration of it be our work.

We may see by the witness of the apostles, and their frequent preaching the resurrection of Christ, as if it were the sum of all the gospel, that this is a point that faith must especially build and feed upon, and that we must make the matter of our most frequent meditations. Oh, what vigour it addeth to our faith, when we are encountered by the sight of death, and of a grave, to remember seriously that "Christ is risen." Did he take flesh purposely that he might die and rise, and show us how he will raise his members? And will he, after all this, break his promise, and leave us in the dust for ever? It cannot be. Hath he conquered death for himself alone, and not for us? Hath he taken our nature into heaven, to be there alone, and will he not have all his members with him? Remember, then, christian, when thou lookest on thy grave, that Christ was buried, and hath made the grave a bed of rest, that shall give up her trust when his trumpet sounds; and that his resurrection is the pledge of ours. Keep, therefore, thy rising and glorified Lord continually in thy eye. If Christ were not risen, our preaching were vain and your faith were vain, and all men were miserable, but we most miserable that suffer so much for a life which we had no ground to hope for, 1 Cor. xv. 14, 17, 19. But now we have an argument that infidelity itself is ashamed to encounter with; that hath been the means of the conversion of the nations unto Christ; by which we may put even death itself to a defiance, as knowing it is now a conquered thing. If it could have held Christ captive, it might also have held us. But he being risen, we shall surely rise. Write it, therefore, christians, upon your hearts; mention it more in your conference for the encouragement of your faith; write it on the grave-stones of your friends, that "CHRIST IS RISEN," and that "BECAUSE HE LIVETH, WE SHALL LIVE ALSO," and that "OUR LIFE IS HID WITH CHRIST IN GOD," though we are dead, and when he shall appear who is our life, we shall also appear with him in glory, John xiv. 19; Col. iii. 3, 4. Though we must be sown in corruption, in weakness, and dishonour, we shall be raised in incorruption, strength, and honour, 1 Cor. xv. 42, 23. While our souls behold the Lord in glory, we may bear with the winter that befalls our flesh till the spring of resurrection come. "Knowing that he that raised up the Lord Jesus, shall raise up us also by Jesus—for which cause we faint not; but though our outward man perish, yet the inward man is renewed day by day—while we look not at the things which are seen, but at the things which are not seen, for the things which are seen are temporal, but the things which are not seen are eternal," 2 Cor. iv. 14, 16, 18. As we are risen with Christ to newness of life, so we shall rise with him to glory.

Use 10. Lastly, if death be the last enemy to be destroyed at the resurrection, we may learn hence how earnestly believers should long and pray for the second coming of Christ, when this full and final conquest shall be made. Death shall do much for us, but the resurrection shall do more. Death sends the separated soul to Christ, but at his coming both soul and body shall be glorified. There is somewhat in death that is penal, even to believers, but in the coming of Christ, and their resurrection, there is nothing but glorifying grace. Death is the effect of sin, and of the first sentence passed upon sinners, but the resurrection of the just is the final destruction of the effects of sin. And, therefore, though the fears of death may perplex us, methinks we should long for the coming of Christ, there being nothing in that but what tends to the deliverance and glory of the saints. Whether he will come before the general resurrection, and reign on earth a thousand years, which some expect, I shall not presume to pass my determination. But sure I am, it is the work of faith, and character of his people, to "love his appearing," (2 Tim. iv. 8,) "and to wait for the Son of God from heaven, whom he raised from the dead, even Jesus who delivered us from the wrath to come," 1 Thess. i. 10. And to wait "for the coming of our Lord Jesus Christ," 1 Cor. i. 7. And to wait "for the adoption, the redemption of our bodies," with inward groanings, Rom. viii. 23. Oh! therefore, let us pray more earnestly for the coming of our Lord! And that "the Lord would direct our hearts into the love of God, and into the patient waiting for Christ," 2 Thess. iii. 5. O blessed day, when the glorious appearing of our Lord shall put away all his servants' shame, and shall communicate glory to his members, even to the bodies that had lain so long in dust, that to the eye of flesh there seemed to be no hope. Though the majesty and glory will cause our reverence, yet it will not be our terror, to the diminution of our joy. It is his enemies that would not have him rule over them, whom he cometh to destroy, Luke xix. 27. "Behold, the Lord cometh with ten thousand of his saints, to execute judgment upon all, and to convince all that are ungodly among them of all their ungodly deeds which they have ungodly committed, and of all their hard speeches which ungodly sinners have spoken against him;" as Enoch, the seventh from Adam, prophesied, Jude, verses 14, 15. But the precious faith of the saints shall "be found to praise, and honour, and glory, at the appearing of Jesus Christ," 1 Pet. i. 7. "When the chief Shepherd shall appear, we shall receive a crown of glory that fadeth not away," 1 Pet. v. 4. He that was once offered to bear the sins of many, and now appeareth for us in the presence of God, shall, unto them that look for him, appear the second time, without sin, to salvation, Heb. ix. 24, 28. And "when Christ, who is our life, shall appear, then shall we also appear with him in glory," Col. iii. 4. The Lord shall then "come to be glorified in his saints, and to be admired in all them that believe in that day," 2 Thess. i. 10. This is the day that all believers should long, and hope, and wait for, as being the accomplishment of all the work of their redemption, and all the desires and endeavours of their souls. It is the hope of this day that animateth the holy diligence of our lives, and makes us turn from the carelessness and sensuality of the world. "For the grace of God that bringeth salvation hath appeared to all men; teaching us, that denying ungodliness and worldly lusts, we should live soberly, righteously, and godly in this present world: looking for that blessed hope, and the glorious appearing of our great God, and our Saviour Jesus Christ," Tit. ii. 11—13. "The heavens and the earth, which are now, by the same word, are reserved unto fire against the day of judgment and perdition of ungodly men." And though the Lord seem to delay, he is not slack concerning his promise, as some men count slackness: for a day is with the Lord as a thousand years, and a thousand years as one day. "But the day of the Lord will come as a thief in the night; in the which the heavens shall pass away with a great noise, and the elements shall melt with fervent heat, the earth also and the works that are therein shall be burned up. Seeing then that all these things shall be dissolved, what manner of persons ought ye to be in all holy conversation and godliness, looking for and hasting unto the coming of the day of God, wherein the heavens being on fire shall be dissolved, and the elements shall melt with fervent heat? Nevertheless we, according to his promise, look for new heavens and a new earth, wherein dwelleth righteousness," 2 Pet. iii. 7—13.

Beza marvelleth at Tertullian for saying that the christians in their holy assemblies prayed *pro mora finis*, Apologet. c. 39; and so he might well enough, if it were not that to christians the glory of God is dearer than their own felicity, and the salvation of millions more precious than the mere hastening of their own; and the glory of the church more desirable than our personal glory, and the hallowing of God's name were not to be prayed for before the coming of his kingdom, and the kingdom of grace must not necessarily go before the kingdom of glory. But as much as we long for the coming of our Lord, we are content to wait till the elect be gathered; and can pray that he will delay it, till the universal body be made up, and all are called that shall be glorified. But to ourselves that are brought out of Egypt into the wilderness, how desirable is the promised land! When we think on our own interest, we cry, "Come, Lord Jesus, come quickly." The sooner the better. Then shall our eyes behold him, in whom we have believed: not as he was beheld on earth in his despised state; but as the glorious King of saints, accompanied with the celestial host, coming in flaming fire to render vengeance to the rebellious, and rest and joy to believing souls, that waited for this day of his appearance. Then faith and patience shall give up their work; and sight, and fruition, and perfect love, shall everlastingly succeed them. The rage of persecutors shall no more affright us; the folly of the multitude shall no more annoy us; the falseness of our seeming, selfish friends shall no more betray us; the pride of self-conceited men shall no more disturb us; the turbulency of men distracted by ambition shall cast us no more into confusions; the kingdom that we shall possess shall not be liable to mutations, nor be tossed with pride and faction, as are these below; there is no monthly (or annual) change of governors and laws, as is in lunatic commonwealths: but there will be the same Lord and King, and the same laws and government, and the same subjects and obedience, without any mutinies, rebellions, or discontents, to all eternity. The church of which we shall then be members, shall not be divided into parties and factions, nor the members look strangely at each other, because of difference of opinions, or distance of affections, as now we find it, to our daily grief, in the militant church. We shall then need no tedious debates to reconcile us. Unity will be then quickly and easily procured. There will be no falling-out in the presence of our Lord. There will be none of that darkness, uncharitableness, selfishness, or passion left, that now causeth our dissensions. When we have perfect light, and perfect love, the perfect peace will be easily attained, which here we labour for in vain. Now there is no peace in church or state, in cities or countries, in families, or scarce in our own souls. But when the glorious King of peace hath put all his enemies under his feet, what then is left to make disturbance? Our enemies can injure us no more, for it is then their portion to suffer for all their former injuries to Christ and us: our friends will not injure us, (as here they do,) because their corruption and weakness is put off, and the relics of sin that caused the trouble are left behind. Oh, that is the sight that faith prepareth for; that is the day, the blessed day, that all our days are spent in seeking, and waiting, and praying for; then shall the glory of holiness appear, and the wisdom of the saints be justified by all, that now is justified by her children. Then it shall be known, whether faith or unbelief, whether a heavenly or earthly mind and life, was the wiser and more justifiable course. Then shall all the world "discern between the righteous and the wicked, between him that serveth God and him that serveth him not," Mal. iii. 18. Then sin (that is now so obstinately defended and justified by such foolish cunning) shall never more find a tongue to plead for it, or a patron to defend it more. Then where is the man that will stand forth and break a jest at godliness, or make a scorn of the holy diligence of believers? How pale then will those faces look that here were wont to jeer at piety! What terror will seize upon those hearts that here were wont to make themselves sport at the weaknesses of the upright servants of the Lord! That is the day that shall rectify all judgments, and cure the errors and contemptuous thoughts of a holy life, which no persuasions now can cure: that is the day that shall set all straight that now seems crooked; and shall satisfy us to the full that God was just, even when he prospered his enemies, and afflicted the souls that loved him, and walked in their integrity before him. We shall then see that which shall fully satisfy us of the reason and equity of all our sufferings which here we underwent; we shall marvel no more that God lets us weep, and groan, and pray, and turns away his face, and seems not to regard us. We shall then find that all our groans were heard, and all our tears and prayers did succeed, which we suspected had been lost. We shall then find that a duty performed in sincerity, through all our lives, was never lost; no, nor a holy thought, nor a "cup of cold water," that, from holy love, we gave to a disciple. We shall then see that our murmurings, and discontents, and jealous, unbelieving thoughts of God, which sickness, or poverty, or crosses did occasion, were all injurious to the Lord, and the fruit of infirmity; and that when we questioned his love on such accounts we knew not what we said. We shall then see that death, and grave, and devils, were all but matter for the glorifying of grace, and for the triumph of our Lord and us.

Up, then, my soul, and shake off thy unbelief and dulness. Look up, and long, and meet thy Lord. The more thou art afraid of death, the more desire that blessed day, when mortality shall be swallowed up of life, and the name of death shall be terrible no more. Though death be thy enemy, there is nothing but friendly in the coming of thy Lord. Though death dissolve thy nature, the resurrection shall restore it, and make thee full reparation, with advantage.

How glad would I have been to have seen Christ but with the wise men in the manger, or to have seen him disputing with the doctors in his childhood in the temple, or to have seen him do his miracles, or heard him preach! much more to have seen him as the three disciples, in his transfiguration, or to have seen him after his resurrection, and when he ascended up to heaven. But how far is all this below the sight that we shall have of him when he comes in glory; when the brightness of his shining face shall make us think the sun was darkness, and the glory of his attendants shall make us think what a sordid thing, and childish foolery, was all the glory of this world! The face of love shall be then unveiled, and ravish us into the highest love and joy that our natures are capable of. Then doubt, and fear, and grieve, if thou canst! What, then, wilt thou think of all these disquieting, distrustful thoughts that now so wrong thy Lord and thee? If going into the sanctuary, and foreseeing the end, can cure our brutish misapprehensions of God's providences, (Psal. lxxiii. 17,) how perfectly will they be cured when we see the glorious face of Christ, and behold the new Jerusalem in its glory, and when we are numbered with the saints that judge the world! We shall never more be tempted, then, to condemn the generation of the just, nor to think it vain to serve the Lord, nor to envy the prosperity of the wicked, nor to stagger at the promise through unbelief, nor to think that our sickness, death, and grave, were any signs of unkindness or unmercifulness in God. We shall then be convinced that sight and flesh were unfit to censure the ways of God, or to be our guides.

Hasten, O Lord, this blessed day! Stay not till faith have left the earth, and infidelity, and impiety, and tyranny have conquered the rest of thine inheritance! Stay not till selfish, uncharitable pride hath vanquished love and self-denial, and planted its colonies of heresy, confusion, and cruelty in thy dominions, and earth and hell be turned into one. Stay not till the eyes of thy servants fail, and their hearts and hopes do faint and languish with looking and waiting for thy salvation. But if yet the day be not at hand, O, keep up faith, and hope, and love, till the sun of perfect love arise, and time hath prepared us for eternity, and grace for glory.

SOME IMITABLE PASSAGES OF THE LIFE OF ELIZABETH, LATE WIFE OF MR. JOSEPH BAKER.

THOUGH I spoke so little as was next to nothing of our dear deceased friend, it was not because I wanted matter, or thought it unmeet; but I use it but seldom, lest I raise expectation of the like where I cannot conscionably perform it. But he that hath promised to honour those that serve and honour him, John xii. 26; 1 Sam. ii. 30; and will come at last "to be glorified in his saints, and to be admired in all them that believe," 2 Thess. i. 10; I know will take it as a great and acceptable act of service, to proclaim the honour of his grace, and to give his servants their due on earth, whose souls are glorified with Christ in heaven, though serpentine enmity will repine, and play the envious accuser.

It is not the history of the life of this precious servant of the Lord which I intend to give you, (for I was not many years acquainted with her,) but only some passages, which, either upon my certain knowledge, or her own diurnal of her course, or the most credible testimony of her most intimate, judicious, godly friends, I may boldly publish as true and imitable in this untoward, distempered generation.

She was born November, 1634, in Southwark, near London, the only child of Mr. John Godeschalk, *alias* Godscall. Her father dying in her childhood, she was left an orphan to the Chamber of London. Her mother after married Mr. Isaac Barton, with whom she had the benefit of religious education: but between sixteen and seventeen years of age, by the serious reading of the book called "The Saints' Everlasting Rest," she was more thoroughly awakened, and brought to set her heart on God, and to seek salvation with her chiefest care. From that time forward she was a more constant, diligent, serious hearer of the ablest ministers in London, rising early, and going far to hear them on the week days; waiting on God for his confirming grace in the use of those ordinances, which empty, unexperienced hypocrites are easily tempted to despise. The sermons, which she constantly wrote, she diligently repeated at home, for the benefit of others; and every week read over some of those that she had heard long before, that the fruit of them might be retained and renewed; it being not novelty that she minded.

In the year 1654, being near one-and-twenty years of age, after seeking God, and waiting for his resolving, satisfying directions, she consented to be joined in marriage to Mr. Joseph Baker, by the approbation of her nearest friends, God having taken away her mother the year before. With him she approved herself, indeed, such a wife as Paul (no papist) describeth as meet for a bishop or pastor of the church; "Even so must their wives be grave, not slanderers, sober, faithful in all things," 1 Tim. iii. 11. Some instances I shall give for the imitation of others.

I. She was very exemplary in self-denial and humility: and having said thus much, what abundance have I comprehended! Oh, what a beauty doth self-denial and humility put on souls! Nay, what a treasure of everlasting consequence do these two words express! I shall give you a few of the discoveries.

1. It appeared in her accompanying in London with the holiest, how mean soever, avoiding them that were proud, and vain, and carnal. She desired most to be acquainted with those that she perceived were best acquainted with God, neglecting the pomp and vain-glory of the world.

2. When she was called to a married state, though her portion, and other advantages, invited persons of greater estates in the world, she chose rather to marry a minister of known integrity, that might be a near and constant guide, stay, and comfort to her in the matters which she valued more than riches. And she missed not of her expectations for the few years that she lived with him. Even in this age, when the serpent is hissing in every corner at faithful ministers, and they are contemned both by profane and heretical malignants, she preferred a mean life with such a one, for her spiritual safety and solace, before the grandeur of the world.

3. When some inhabitants of the city of Worcester were earnest with me to help them to an able minister, Mr. Baker, then living in Kent, had about a hundred pounds per annum: and when, at my motion, he was readily willing to take a great charge in Worcester, upon a promise from two men to make the maintenance fifty pounds a year, by a voluntary contribution, of the continuance of which he had no security, his wife was a promoter, and no discourager, of his self-denial, and never tempted him to look after greater things. And afterward, when I was afraid lest the smallness and uncertainty of the means, together with his discouragements from some of his people, might have occasioned his remove, and have heard of richer places mentioned to him, as he still answered that he had enough, and minded not removing without necessity, so was she ever of the same mind, and still seconded and confirmed him in such resolutions, even to follow God's work while they had a competency of their own, and to mind no more.

4. Her very speech and behaviour did so manifest meekness and humility, that, in a little converse with her, it might easily be discerned.

5. She thought nothing too mean for her that belonged to her in her family and relation, no employment, food, &c.; saying often, that what God had made her duty was not too low a work for her. And, indeed, when we know once that it is a work that God sets us upon, it signifieth much forgetfulness of him and ourselves, if we think it too base, or think ourselves too good to stoop to it.

6. No neighbour did seem too mean or poor for her familiar converse, if they were but willing.

7. She had a true esteem and cheerful love for the meanest of her husband's relations, and much rejoiced in her comfort in his kindred, recording it among her experienced mercies.

II. She was very constant and diligent in doing her part of family duties; teaching all the inferiors of her family, and labouring to season them with principles of holiness, and admonishing them of their sin and danger: never failing, on the Lord's day at night, to hear them read the Scriptures and recite their catechisms, when public duty, and all other family duty, was ended, and, in her husband's absence, praying with them. How much the imitation of such examples would conduce to the sanctifying of families is easy to be apprehended.

III. In secret duty she was very constant, and lived much in those two great soul-advancing works, meditation and prayer, in which she would not admit of interruptions. This inward, holy diligence was it that maintained spiritual life within, which is the spring of outward acceptable works. When communion with God, and daily labour upon our own hearts, is laid aside, or negligently and remissly followed, grace languisheth first within, and then unfruitfulness, if not disorders and scandals, appear without.

IV. Her love to the Lord Jesus was evidenced by her great affection to his ordinances, and ways, and servants. A very hearty love she manifested to those on whom the image of God did appear, even the poorest and meanest, as well as the rich or eminent in the world. Nor did a difference in lesser matters, or any tolerable mistakes, alienate her affections from them.

V. She was a christian of much plainness, simplicity, and singleness of heart. Far from a subtle, crafty, dissembling frame, and also from loquacity or ostentation. And the world was very low in her eyes, to which she was long crucified, and on which she looked as a lifeless thing. Sensuality, and pampering the flesh, she much loathed. When she was invited to feasts she would oft complain that they occasioned a difficulty in maintaining a sense of the presence of God, whose company in all her company she preferred.

VI. She was a very careful esteemer and redeemer of her time. At home in her family the works of her general and particular calling took her up. When necessary business, and greater duties, gave way, she was seldom without a book in her hand, or some edifying discourse in her mouth, if there were opportunity. And abroad she was very weary of barren company, that spent the time in common chat, and dry discourses.

VII. She used good company practically and profitably, making use of what she heard for her own spiritual advantage. When I understood, out of her diary, that she wrote down some of my familiar discourses, with serious application to herself, it struck exceeding deep into my heart, how much I have sinned all my days, since I undertook the person of a minister of Christ, by the slightness and unprofitableness of my discourse; and how exceeding careful ministers should be of their words, and how deliberately, wisely, and seriously they should speak about the things of God, and how diligently they should take all fit opportunities to that end, when we know not how silent hearers are affected with what we say. For aught we know, there may be some that will write down what we say in their books, or hearts, or both. And God and conscience write down all.

VIII. In her course of reading she was still laying in for use and practice. Her course was, when she read the Scriptures, to gather out passages, and sort and refer them to their several uses; as, some that were fit subjects for her meditations; some for encouragement to prayer, and other duties; promises suited to various conditions and wants: as her papers show.

And for other books, she would meddle with none but the sound and practical, and had no itch after the empty books, which make ostentation of novelty, and which opinionists are now so taken with; nor did she like writing or preaching in envy and strife. And of good books she chose to read but few, and those very often over, that all might be well digested. Which is a course (for private christians) that tends to avoid luxuriancy, and make them sincere, and solid, and established.

IX. She had the great blessing of a tender conscience. She did not slightly pass over small sins without penitent observation. Her diary records her trouble when causelessly she had neglected any ordinance; or was hindered by rain, or small occasions; or if she had overslept herself, and lost a morning exercise in London, or came too late; or if she were distracted in secret duty. And if she missed of a fast, through misinformation and disappointments, and found not her heart duly sensible of the loss, that also she recorded. So did she her stirrings of anger, and her very angry looks, resolving to take more heed against them. Though all ought not to spend so much time in writing down their failings, yet all should watch and renew repentance.

X. She was very solicitous for the souls of her friends. As, for instance, her brothers-in-law, over whom she exercised a motherly care, instructing them, and watching over them, and telling them of miscarriages, and counselling them. Causing them to keep a constant course of reading the holy Scriptures, and meditating on it (as far as she could): causing them to learn many chapters without book, and to read other good books in season; earnestly praying for them in particular; much desiring one or both should be ministers: and when her father-in-law appointed the eldest to go to France, she was much troubled for fear of his miscarriage among strangers, especially those of the Romish way.

XI. She was a serious mourner for the sins of the time and place she lived in.

XII. In sum, for strict, close, watchful, holy walking with God, even her husband professeth that she was a pattern to him. As I hinted before, she kept a daily account in writing, (which is now to be seen, from the beginning of the year 1654,) especially of these particulars:

1. Of the frame of her heart in every day's duty; in meditation, prayer, hearing, reading, &c. whether lively or dull, &c.

2. Of those sins which she had especially to repent of, and watch against.

3. Of her resolutions and promises, and how she kept them.

4. Of all special providences to herself, husband, brothers, and others, and the improvement of them. As at the death of her son, who died with great sighs and groans, she recorded her sense of the special necessity of holy armour, and great preparation, for that encounter, when her turn should come to be so removed to the everlasting habitation.

5. Of her returns of prayer, what answers and grant of them she found.

6. Of the state of her soul upon examination; how she found it, and what was the issue of each examination: and in this it seems she was very exact and punctual. In which, though many times fears and doubtings did arise, yet hath she frequent records of the discovery of evidences, and comfortable assurance of sincerity. Sometimes when she hath heard sermons in London, that helped her in her search, and sometimes when she had been reading writings that tended that way, she recorded what evidences she found, and in what degree the discovery was; if imperfect, resolving to take it up, and follow the search further. And if she had much joy, she received it with jealousy, and expectation of some humbling consequent. When any grace languished, she presently turned to some apt remedy. As, for instance, it is one of her notes, "November, 1658, I found thoughts of eternity slight and strange, and ordinary employments very desirable; at which I read Mr. B.'s Crucifixion, and was awakened to mortification and humiliation," &c.

The last time that she had opportunity for this work, was two or three days before her delivery in child-bearing, where she finally recorded the apprehensions she had, both of her bodily and spiritual state, in these words, "Drawing near the time of my delivery, I am fallen into such weakness that my life is in hazard. I find some fears of death, but not very great, hoping, through grace, I die in the Lord." I only mention these hints to show the method she used in her daily accounts. To those christians that have full leisure, this course is good; but I urge it not upon all. Those that have so great duties to take up that time, that they cannot spare so much to record their ordinary passages, such must remember what others record, and daily renew repentance for their daily failings, and record only the extraordinary, observable, and more remarkable and memorable passages of their lives, lest they lose time from works of greater moment. But this excellent work of watchfulness must be performed by all.

And I think it was a considerable expression of her true wisdom, and care of her immortal soul, that when any extraordinary necessity required it, and she found such doubts, as of herself she was not able to deal with, she would go to some able experienced minister to open her case, and seek assistance, (as she did, more than once, to my dear and ancient friend Mr. Cross, who, in full age, is since gone after her to Christ,) and, therefore, chose a minister in marriage, that he might be a ready assistant in such cases of necessity, as well as a continual help.

At last came that death to summon her soul away to Christ, for which she had so seriously been preparing, and which she oft called a dark entry to her Father's palace. After the death of her children, when she seemed to be somewhat repaired, after her last delivery, a violent convulsion suddenly surprised her, which, in a few days, brought her to her end. Her understanding, by the fits, being at last debilitated, she finding it somewhat hard to speak sensibly, excused it, and said, "I shall ere long speak another language," which were the last words which she spake with a tongue of flesh, and laying speechless eighteen hours after, she departed, Aug. 17, 1659. "Blessed are the dead which die in the Lord, from henceforth: Yea, saith the Spirit, that they may rest from their labours; and their works do follow them," Rev. xiv. 13.

Our turn is coming. Shortly we shall also lay by flesh. This is our day of preparation; there is no preparing time but this. Did men but know the difference between the death of the holy and the unholy, which doth not appear to fleshly eyes, how speedily would they turn! how seriously would they meditate! how fervently would they pray! how carefully would they live! how constantly, painfully, and resolvedly would they labour! Did they well consider the difference between dying prepared and unprepared, and of what difficulty, and yet everlasting consequence, it is to die well; oh, then, what manner of persons would men be, in all manner of holy conversation and godliness! and all their lives would then be a continued preparation for death, as all their lives are a hastening towards it.

And now I shall only desire you, for the right understanding of all that I have here said, and to prevent the cavils of blinded malice, to observe these three or four particulars.

1. That though I knew so much of her as easily maketh me believe the rest, upon so sure a testimony, and saw her diary, yet the most of this history of her life is the collection and observation of such faithful witnesses as had much better opportunity than I to know the secrets of her soul and life.

2. That it is no wonder if many, that knew her, perceived not all this by her that is here expressed; for that knowledge of our outward carriage at a distance will not tell our neighbours what we do in our closets, where God hath commanded us to shut our door upon us, that our Father which seeth in secret, may reward us openly. And many of the most humble and sincere servants of the Lord are so afraid of hypocrisy, and hate ostentation, that their justification and glory is only to be expected from the Searcher of hearts, and a few of their more intimate acquaintance; though this was not the case before us, the example described being more conspicuous.

3. That I over-passed the large expressions of her charity, which you may hear from the poor, and her intimate acquaintance, as I have done; that I may not grate upon the modesty of her surviving friends, who must participate in the commendations.

4. That it is the benefit of the living that is my principal end. Scripture itself is written much in history, that we may have matter of imitation before our eyes.

5. If any say that here is no mention of her faults, I answer, Though I had acquaintance with her, I knew them not, nor ever heard from any other so much as might enable me to accuse her, if I were her enemy. Yet I doubt not but she was imperfect, and had faults, though unknown to me. The example of holiness I have briefly proposed. They that would see examples of iniquity, may look abroad in the world, and find enough; I need not be the accuser of the saints to furnish them. And I think if they inquire here of any thing notable, they will be hard put to it to find enough to cover the accuser's shame.

6. It is the honour of Christ, and grace in his members, more than the honour of his servants, that I seek.

7. And I would not speak that in commendation of the living which I do of the dead, who are out of the reach of all temptations of being lifted up with pride thereby; unless it be such whose reputation the interest of Christ and the gospel commandeth me to vindicate.

8. Lastly, I am so far from lifting up one above the rest of the members of Christ by these commendations, and from abasing others, whose names I mention not, that I intend the honour of all in one, and think that in the substance I describe all saints in describing one. I am not about a popish work, of making a wonder of a saint, as of a phœnix, or some rare, unusual thing. Saints with them must be canonized, and their names put in the calendar; and yet their blind malice tells the world that there are no such things as saints among us. But I rejoice in the many that I have communion with, and the many that have lately stepped before me into heaven, and are safe there, out of the reach of malice, and of sin, and all the enemies of their peace; and have left me mourning, and yet rejoicing; fearing, and yet hoping; and, with some desires, looking after them here behind: and the faster Christ calls away his chosen ones, whose graces were amiable in mine eyes, the more willing he maketh me to follow them, and to leave this world of darkness, confusion, wickedness, danger, vanity, and vexation, and to meet these precious souls in life, where we shall rejoice that we are past this howling wilderness, and shall for ever be with the Lord.

A SERMON OF JUDGMENT,

PREACHED AT PAUL'S,

BEFORE

THE HON. LORD MAYOR AND ALDERMEN OF THE CITY OF LONDON,

Dec. 17th, 1654,

AND NOW ENLARGED.

"Every one of us shall give account of himself to God."—Rom. xiv. 12.
"The hour is coming, in the which all that are in the graves shall hear his voice, and shall come forth; they that have done good, unto the resurrection of life; and they that have done evil, unto the resurrection of damnation."—John v. 28, 29.

TO THE RIGHT HON. CHRISTOPHER PACK,

LORD MAYOR OF LONDON;

WITH THE RIGHT WORSHIPFUL ALDERMEN.

RIGHT HONOURABLE,

BEING desired to preach before you at Paul's, I was fain to preach a sermon which I had preached once before to a poor ignorant congregation in the country, having little leisure for study in London. I was glad to see that the more curious stomachs of the citizens did not nauseate our plain country doctrine, which I seemed to discern in the diligent attention of the greatest congregation that ever I saw met for such a work. But I little expected that you should have so far esteemed that discourse, as to have thought it meet for the view of the world, as I understood by a message from you, desiring it may be printed. I readily obey your will, when it gives me the least intimation of the will of God. It is possible some others may afford it the like favourable acceptance and entertainment. I am sure the subject is as necessary as common, and the plainness makes it the fitter for the ignorant, who are the far greater number, and have the greatest need. I have added the ninth, tenth, eleventh, and twelfth heads, or common-places, which I did not deliver to you for want of time, and because the rest are too briefly touched (as contrived for an hour's work). I have enlarged these, though making them somewhat unsuitable to the rest, yet suitable to the use of those they are now intended for: the directions also in the end are added.

Blessed be the Father of lights! who hath set so many burning and shining lights in your city, and hath watered you so plenteously with the rivers of his sanctuary, that you have frequent opportunities for the refreshment of your souls, to the joy of your friends, the grief of your enemies, and the glory of that providence which hath hitherto maintained them, in despite of persecution, heresies, and hell! It was not always so in London: it is not so in all other places, or famous cities in the world; nor are you sure that it will be always so with you. It doth me good to remember what blessed lights have shined among you, that now are more gloriously shining in a higher sphere—Preston, Sibbes, Stoughton, Taylor, Stock, Randal, Gouge, Gataker, with multitudes more that are now with Christ. It did me good to read in the preface to Mr. Gataker's funeral sermon, by one of your reverend and faithful guides, what a number of sound and unanimous labourers are yet close at work in that part of Christ's vineyard: and it did me good in that short experience and observation, while I was there, to hear and see so much of their prudence, unity, and fidelity.

Believe it, it is the gospel of Christ that is your glory; and if London be more honourable than other great and famous cities of the earth, it is the light of God's face, and the plenty and power of his ordinances and Spirit, that doth advance and honour it. O know, then, the day of your visitation!

Three things I shall take leave to propound to your consideration, which, I am certain, God requireth at your hand. The first is, that you grow in knowledge, humility, heavenliness, and unity, according to the blessed means that you enjoy. In my eyes, it is the greatest shame to a people in the world, and a sign of barbarism or blockishness, when we can hear and read what a famous, learned, powerful minister such a place, or such a place, had, and yet see as much ignorance, ungodliness, unruliness, and sensuality, as if the gospel had scarce ever been there. I hope it is not thus with you, but I have found it so in too many places of England. We who never saw the faces of their ministers, but have only read their holy labours, have been ready to think, Sure there are few ignorant or ungodly ones in such a congregation! Sure they are a people rich in grace, and eminently qualified above their brethren, who have lived under such teaching as this! At least, sure there can be none left who have an enmity to the fear of God! But when we have come to the towns where such men spent their lives, and laid out their labours, we have found ignorant, sottish worldlings, unprofitable, or giddy, unstable professors, and some haters of godliness among them. Oh what a shame is this to them in the eyes of wise men! And what a confounding aggravation of their sin before God! Thrive, therefore, and be fruitful in the vineyard of the Lord, that it may not repent him that he hath planted and watered you.

The second is this; improve your interest to the utmost, for the continuance of a faithful ministry among you, and when any places are void, do what you can to get a supply of the most able men. Your city is the heart of the nation; you cannot be sick but we shall all feel it. If you be infected with false doctrines, the countries will, ere long, receive the contagion. You have a very great influence on all the land, for good or evil. And do you think the undermining enemies of the church have not a special design upon you in this point, and will not promote it as far as is in their power? Could they but get in popish or dividing teachers among you, they know how many advantages they should gain at once. They would have some to grieve and trouble your faithful guides, and hinder them in the work, and lessen that estimation which, by their unity, they would obtain: and every deceiver will hope to catch some fish that casteth his net among such store. We beseech you, if there be learned, holy, judicious men in England, that can be had for supply of such occasions, let them be yours, that you may be fed with the best, and guided by the wisest, and we may have all recourse to you for advice; and where there are most opposers and seducers, there may be the most-powerful, convincing helps at hand. Let us, in the country, have the honest, raw, young preachers, and see that you have the chief fathers and pillars in the church. I speak it not for your sakes alone, but because we have all dependence on you.

The third thing which I humbly crave is, that you will "know them which labour among you, and are over you in the Lord, and admonish you, and to esteem them very highly in love for their work's sake, and be at peace among yourselves," 1 Thess. v. 12, 13. And that you will, instead of grieving or rejecting your guides, "obey them that have the rule over you, and submit yourselves; for they watch for your souls as they that must give account, that they may do it with joy, and not with grief, for that is unprofitable for you," Heb. xiii. 17. Encourage your teachers, for their work is great, their spirits are weak, they are but frail men; the enemy is more industrious against them than any men, and their discouragements are very many, and the difficulties which they must encounter are very great. Especially obey, submit, and encourage them in the work of government and exercise of Christ's discipline, and managing the keys of the kingdom which he hath put into their hands. Do you not perceive what a strait your teachers are in. The Lord Jesus requireth them to exercise his discipline faithfully and impartially. He giveth them not empty titles of rule, but lays upon them the burden of ruling. It is his work more than their honour that he intends; and if they will have the honour, it must be by the work. The work is, as to teach the ignorant, and convince the unbelieving and gainsaying, so to admonish the disorderly and scandalous, and to reject and cast out of the communion of the church the obstinate and impenitent, and to set by the leprous that they infect not the rest, and to separate thus the precious from the vile by Christ's discipline, that dividing separation and soul-destroying transgressions may be prevented or cured. This work Christ hath charged upon them, and will have it done whoever is against it. If they obey him, and do it, what a tumult, what clamours and discontents, will they raise! How many will be ready to rise up against them with hatred and scorn! Though it be the undoubted work of Christ, which, even under persecution, was performed by the church guides. When they do but keep a scandalous, untractable sinner from the communion of the church in the Lord's supper, what repinings doth it raise! But, alas! this is a small part of the discipline. If all the apparently obstinate and impenitent were cast out, what a stir would they make; and if Christ be not obeyed, what a stir will conscience make: and it is not only between Christ and men, but between men and men that your guides are put upon straits. The separatists reproach them for suffering the impenitent to continue members of their churches, and make it the pretence of their separation from them, having little to say of any moment against the authorized way of government, but only against the slackness in the execution; and if we should set to the close exercise of it, as is meet, how would city and country ring of it; and what indignation should we raise in the multitude against us. Oh what need have your guides of your encouragement and best assistance in this strait! God hath set them on a work so ungrateful and displeasing to flesh and blood that they cannot be faithful in it, but twenty to one they will draw a world of hatred upon themselves, if not men's fists about their ears. Festered sores will not be lanced and searched with ease. Corrupted members are unwilling to be cut off and cast aside, especially if any of the great ones fall under the censure, who are big in the eyes of the world, and in their own; and yet our sovereign Lord must be obeyed, and his house must be swept, and the filth cast out, by what names or titles soever it be dignified with men. He must be pleased, if all be displeased by it. Withdraw not your help, then, from this needful work. It is by the word, Spirit, and ministry, that Christ, the King of his church, doth govern it; not separately, but jointly by all three. To disobey these is to disobey Christ; and subjection to Christ is essential to our christianity. This, well thought on, might do much to recover the unruly that are recoverable. You may conjecture by the strange opposition that church government meets with from all sorts of carnal and corrupted minds, that there is somewhat in it that is eminently of God. I shall say no more but this, that it is an able, judicious, godly, faithful ministry; not barely heard and applauded, but humbly and piously submitted to, and obeyed in the Lord, that must be your truest present glory, and the means of your everlasting peace and joy.

So testifieth from the Lord your servant in the faith of Christ,

RICHARD BAXTER.

TO THE IGNORANT OR CARELESS READER.

Seeing the providence of God hath commanded forth this plain discourse, I shall hope, upon experience of his dealing in the like cases with me, that he hath some work for it to do in the world. Who knows but it was intended for the saving of thy soul, by opening thine eyes, and awaking thee from thy sin, who art now in reading of it? Be it known to thee, it is the certain truth of God, and of high concernment to thy soul, that it treateth of, and therefore requireth thy most sober consideration. Thou hast in it, (how weakly soever it is managed by me,) an advantage put into thy hand from God, to help thee in the greatest work in the world, even to prepare for the great approaching judgment. In the name of God, I require thee, cast not away this advantage; turn not away thine ears or heart from this warning that is sent to thee from the living God! Seeing all the world cannot keep thee from judgment, nor save thee in judgment, let not all the world be able to keep thee from a speedy and serious preparation for it. Do it presently, lest God come before thou art ready! Do it seriously, lest the tempter overreach thee, and thou shouldst be found among the foolish self-deceivers when it is too late to do it better. I entreat this of thee on the behalf of thy soul, and as thou tenderest thy everlasting peace with God, that thou wouldst afford these matters thy deepest consideration. Think on them, whether they are not true and weighty: think of them lying down and rising up: and, seeing this small book is fallen into thy hands, all that I would beg of thee concerning it is, that thou wouldst bestow now and then an hour to read it, and read it to thy family or friends, as well as to thyself: and as you go, consider what you read, and pray the Lord to help it to thy heart, and to assist thee in the practice, that it may not rise up in judgment against thee. If thou have not leisure on other, take now and then an hour on the Lord's day, or at night, to that purpose: and if any passage, through brevity, especially near the beginning, seem dark to thee, read it again and again, and ask the help of an instructer, that thou mayst understand it. May it but help thee out of the snares of sin, and promote the saving of thy immortal soul, and thy comfortable appearance at the great day of Christ, I have the thing which I intended and desired. The Lord open thy heart, and accompany his truth with the blessing of his Spirit! Amen.

---

2 CORINTHIANS V. 10, 11.

FOR WE MUST ALL APPEAR BEFORE THE JUDGMENT SEAT OF CHRIST; THAT EVERY ONE MAY RECEIVE THE THINGS DONE IN HIS BODY, ACCORDING TO THAT HE HATH DONE, WHETHER IT BE GOOD OR BAD. KNOWING THEREFORE THE TERROR OF THE LORD, WE PERSUADE MEN.

It is not unlikely that some of those wits that are taken more with things new than with things necessary, will marvel that I chose so common a subject, and tell me that they all know this already; but I do it purposely upon these considerations. 1. Because I well know, that it is these common truths that are the great and necessary things which men's everlasting happiness or misery doth most depend upon. You may be ignorant of many controversies and inferior points, without the danger of your souls, but so you cannot be of these fundamentals. 2. Because it is apparent by the lives of men that few know these common truths savingly, that think they know them. 3. Because there are several degrees of knowing the same truths, and the best are imperfect in degree, the principal growth in knowledge, that we should look after, is, not to know more matters than we knew before, but to know that better, and with a clearer light and firmer apprehension, which we darkly and slightly knew before. You may more safely be without any knowledge at all of many lower truths, than without some further degree of the knowledge of those which you already know. 4. Besides, it is known, by sad experience, that many perish who know the truth, for want of the consideration of it, and making use of what they know, and so their knowledge doth but condemn them. We have as much need, therefore, to teach and help you to get these truths, which you know, into your hearts and lives, as to tell you more. 5. And, indeed, it is the impression of these great and master truths, wherein the vitals and essentials of God's image upon the soul of man doth consist; and it is these truths that are the very instruments of the great works that are to be done upon the heart by the Spirit and ourselves. In the right use of these it is that the principal part of the skill and holy wisdom of a christian doth consist; and in the diligent and constant use of these, lieth the life and trade of christianity. There is nothing amiss in men's hearts or lives, but it is for want of sound knowing and believing, or well using these fundamentals. 6. And moreover, methinks, in this choice of my subject, I may expect this advantage with the hearers, that I may spare that labour that else would be necessary for the proof of my doctrine; and that I may also have easier access to your hearts, and have a fuller stroke at them, and with less resistance. If I came to tell you of any thing not common, I know not how far I might expect belief from you. You might say, These things are uncertain to us; or all men are not of this mind. But when every hearer confesseth the truth of my doctrine, and no man can deny it without denying christianity itself, I hope I may expect that your hearts should the sooner receive the impression of this doctrine, and the sooner yield to the duties which it directs you to, and the easier let go the sins, which, from so certain a truth, shall be discovered.

The words of my text are the reason which the

apostle giveth, both of his persuading other men to the fear of God, and his care to approve to God his own heart and life. They contain the assertion and description of the great judgment, and one use which he makes of it. It assureth us, that judged we must be, and who must be so judged, and by whom, and about what, and on what terms, and to what end.

The meaning of the words, so far as is necessary, I shall give you briefly. "We all," both we apostles that preach the gospel, and you that hear it, "must," willing or unwilling, there is no avoiding it, "appear," stand forth, or make your appearance, and there have your hearts and ways laid open, and appear as well as we, "before the judgment-seat of Christ," that is, before th Redeemer of the world, to be judged by him as our rightful Lord. "That every one," even of all mankind, which are, were, or shall be, without exception, "may receive," that is, may receive his sentence, adjudging him to his due; and then may receive the execution of the sentence, and may go away from the bar with that reward or punishment that is his due, according to the law by which he is judged. "The things done in his body," that is, the due reward of the works done in his body; or, as some copies read it, "the things proper to the body," that is, due to man, even body as well as soul. "According to what he hath done, whether it be good or bad;" that is, this is the cause to be tried and judged, whether men have done well or ill, whilst they were in the flesh, and what is due to them according to their deeds. "Knowing, therefore," &c. that is, being certain therefore that these things are so, and that such a terrible judgment of Christ will come, we persuade men to become christians, and live as such, that they may then speed well, when others shall be destroyed; or, as others, "Knowing the fear of the Lord," that is, the true religion, "we persuade men."

Doct. 1. There will be a judgment. *Doct.* 2. Christ will be the judge. *Doct.* 3. All men shall there appear. *Doct.* 4. Men shall be then judged according to the works that they did in the flesh, whether good or evil. *Doct.* 5. The end of judgment is, that men may receive their final due by sentence and execution. *Doct.* 6. The knowledge and consideration of the terrible judgment of God, should move us to persuade, and men to be persuaded, to careful preparation.

The ordinary method for the handling of this subject of judgment should be this. 1. To show you what judgment is in the general, and what it doth contain: and that is, 1. The persons. 2. The cause. 3. The actions. 1. The parties are, 1. The accuser. 2. The defendant. 3. Sometimes assistants. 4. The judge. 2. The cause contains, 1. The accusation. 2. The defence. 3. With the evidence of both. 4. And the merit. The merit of the cause is as it agreeth with the law and equity. 3. The judicial actions are, I. Introductory, 1. Citation. 2. Compulsion, if need be. 3. Appearance of the accused. II. Of the essence of judgment. 1. Debate by, 1. The accuser. 2. Defendant, called the disceptation of the cause. 2. By the judge. 1. Exploration. 2. Sentence. 3. To see to the execution. But because this method is less suitable to your capacities, and hath something human, I will reduce all to these following heads:—

1. I will show you what judgment is.
2. Who is the judge; and why.
3. Who must be judged.
4. Who is the accuser.
5. How the citation, constraint, and appearance will be.
6. What is the law by which men shall be judged.
7. What will be the cause of the day; what the accusation, and what must be the just defence.
8. What will be the evidence.
9. What are those frivolous, insufficient excuses, by which the unrighteous may think to escape.
10. What will be the sentence: who shall die, and who shall live; and what the reward and punishment is.
11. What are the properties of the sentence.
12. What and by whom the execution will be. In these particular heads we contain the whole doctrine of this judgment, and in this more familiar method shall handle it.

I. For the first, judgment, as taken largely, comprehendeth all the forementioned particulars; as taken more strictly for the act of the judge, it is the trial of a controverted case. In our case, note these things following.

1. God's judgment is not intended for any discovery to himself of what he knows not already; he knows already what all men are, and what they have done, and what is their due: but it is to discover to others, and to men themselves, the ground of his sentence, that so its judgment may attain its end: for the glorifying his grace on the righteous, and for the convincing the wicked of their sin and desert, and to show to all the world the righteousness of the judge, and of his sentence and execution, Rom. iii. 4, 26; Rom. ii. 2.

2. It is not a controversy, therefore, undecided in the mind of God, that is there to be decided; but only one that is undecided as to the knowledge and mind of creatures.

3. Yet is not this judgment a bare declaration, but a decision, and so a declaration thereupon: the cause will be then put out of controversy, and all further expectation of decision be at an end; and with the justified there will be no more accusation, and with the condemned no more for ever.

II. For the second thing, who shall be the judge, I answer, the judge is God himself, by Jesus Christ.

1. Principally, God as Creator.

2. As also, God as Redeemer, the human nature of Jesus Christ having a derived subordinate power. God lost not his right to his creature, either by man's fall, or the redemption by Christ, but by the latter hath a new further right: but it is in and by Christ that God judgeth; for, as mere Creator of innocent man, God judgeth none, but hath committed all judgment to the Son, who hath procured his right by the redeeming of fallen man, John v. 22. But as the Son only doth it in the nearest sense, so the Father, as Creator, doth it remotely and principally.

1. In that the power of the Son is derived from the Father, and so standeth in subordination to him as fountain or efficient.

2. In that the judgment of the Son, (as also his whole mediatorship,) is to bring men to God their Maker, as their ultimate end, and to recover them to him from whom they are fallen; and so as a means to that end, the judgment of the Son is subordinate to the Father.

From hence you may see these following truths worthy your consideration.

1. That all men are God's creatures, and none are the workmanship of themselves, or any other; or else the Creator should not judge them on that right.

2. That Christ died for all, and is the Redeemer of the world, and a sacrifice for all, or else he should not judge them on that right. For he will not judge wicked men as he will do the devils, as the mere enemies of his redeemed ones, but as being themselves his subjects in the world, and being bought

by him, and therefore become his own, who ought to have glorified him that bought them, 2 Cor. v. 14, 15; 2 Pet. ii. 1; 1 Cor. vi. 9, 20; 1 John ii. 2; Heb. ii. 9; 1 Tim. ii. 6, 7.

3. Hence, it appeareth that all men were under some law of grace, and did partake of some of the Redeemer's mercy. Though the gospel came not to all, yet all had that mercy which could come from no other fountain but his blood, and which should have brought them nearer to Christ than they were, (though it were not sufficient to bring them to believe,) and which should have led them to repentance, Rom. ii. 4. For the neglecting of which they justly perish, and not merely for sinning against the law that was given man in innocency: were that so, Christ would not judge them as Redeemer, and that for the abuse or non-improvement of his talents, as he tells us he will do, Matt. xxv. *per totum.*

4. If God will be the judge, then none can expect, by any shifts or indirect means, to escape at that day. For how should it be?

1. It is not possible that any should keep out of sight, or hide their sin, and the evil of their actions, and so delude the judge. "God will not be mocked" now, nor deceived then, Gal. vi. 7. They grossly deceive themselves that imagine any such thing. God must be omniscient and all-seeing, or he cannot be God. Should you hide your case from men, and from devils, and be ignorant of it yourselves, yet you cannot hide it from God. Never did there a thought pass thy heart, or a word pass thy mouth, which God was not acquainted with; and as he knows them, so doth he observe them. He is not as imperfect man, taken up with other business, so that he cannot mind all; as easy is it with him to mind every thought, or word, or action of thine, as if he had but that one in the world to observe, and as easy to observe each particular sinner, as if he had not another creature to look after in the world. He is a fool indeed that thinks now that God takes no notice of him, (Ezek. viii. 12; ix. 9,) or that thinketh then to escape in the crowd: he that found out one guest that had not on a wedding garment, (Matt. xxii. 12,) will then find out every unholy soul, and give him so sad a salutation as shall make him speechless. "For he knoweth vain man; he seeth wickedness also; and will he not consider it?" Job xi. 11.

2. It is not possible that any should escape at that day by any tricks of wit, any false reasoning in their own defence. God knoweth a sound answer from an unsound, and a truth from a lie. Righteousness may be perverted here on earth, by outwitting the judge; but so will it not be then: to hope any of this, is to hope that God will not be God. It is in vain, then, for the unholy man to say he is holy; or a sinner to deny, or excuse, or extenuate his sin: to bring forth the counterfeit of any grace, and plead with God any shells of hypocritical performances, and to think to prove a title to heaven by any thing short of God's condition, all these will be vain attempts.

3. And as impossible will it prove by fraud or flattery, by persuasion or bribery, or by any other means, to pervert justice, by turning the mind of God, who is the judge. Fraud and flattery, bribery and importunity, may do much with weak men; but with God they will do nothing. Were he changeable and partial he were not God.

4. If God be judge, you may see the cavils of infidels are foolish, when they ask, How long will God be in trying and judging so many persons, and taking an account of so many words, and thoughts, and deeds? Sure it will be a long time, and a difficult work. As if God were as man, that knoweth not things till he seek out their evidence by particular signs. Let these fools understand, if they have any understanding, that the infinite God can show to every man at once all the thoughts, and words, and actions, that ever he hath been guilty of. And in the twinkling of an eye, even at one view, can make all the world to see their ways, and their deservings, causing their consciences and memories to present them all before them, in such a sort, as shall be equivalent to a verbal debate: Psal. l. 21, 22, he will set them in order before them.

5. If Jesus Christ be the judge, then what a comfort must it needs be to his members, that he shall be judge that loved them to the death, and whom they loved above their lives; and he who was their rock of hope and strength, and the desire and delight of their souls!

6. And if Jesus Christ must be the judge, what confusion will it bring to the faces of his enemies, and of all that set light by him in the day of their visitation, to see mercy turned against them; and he that died for them, now ready to condemn them; and that blood and grace, which did aggravate their sin, to be pleaded against them, to the increase of their misery; how sad will this be!

7. If the God of love, and grace, and truth, be judge, then no man need to fear any wrong. No subtlety of the accuser, nor darkness of evidence, no prejudice or partiality, or whatsoever else may be imagined, can there appear to the wrong of your cause. Get a good cause, and fear nothing: and if your cause be bad, nothing can deliver you.

III. For the third point, Who are they that must be judged?

Answ. All the rational creatures in this lower world, and it seems angels also, either all, or some. But because their case is more darkly made known to us, and less concern us, we will pass it by. Every man that hath been made or born on earth, except Christ, who is God and man, and is the judge, must be judged. If any foolish infidels shall say, Where shall so great a number stand? I answer him, that he knoweth not the things invisible, either the nature of spirits and spiritual bodies, nor what place containeth them, or how; but easily he may know that he that gave them all a being, can sustain them all, and have room for them all, and can at once disclose the thoughts of all, as I said before.

The first in order to be judged are the saints, Matt. xxv.; and then with Christ they shall judge the rest of the world, (1 Cor. vi. 2, 3,) not in an equal authority and commission with Christ, but as the present approvers of his righteous judgment. The princes of the earth shall stand then before Christ even as the peasants, and the honourable as the base; the rich and the poor shall meet together, and the Lord shall judge them all, Prov. xxii. 2. No men shall be excused from standing at that bar, and giving up their account, and receiving their doom. Learned and unlearned, young and old, godly and ungodly, all must stand there. I know some have vainly imagined that the righteous shall not have any of their sins mentioned, but their graces and duties only; but they consider not that things will not then be transacted by words as we do now, but by clear discoveries, by the infinite light; and that if God should not discover to them their sins, he would not discover the riches of his grace in the pardon of all these sins. Even then they must be humbled in themselves, that they may be glorified, and for ever cry, "Not unto us, Lord, but unto thy name, be the glory."

IV. For the fourth particular, Who will be the accuser?

Answ. 1. Satan is called in Scripture the accuser of the brethren, (Rev. xii. 10,) and we find in Job i. and other places, that now he doth practise even before God, and therefore we judge it probable that he will do so then. But we would determine of nothing that Scripture hath not clearly determined.

2. Conscience will be an accuser, though especially of the wicked, yet in some sense, of the righteous, for it will tell the truth to all. And, therefore, so far as men are faulty, it will tell them of their faults. The wicked it will accuse of unpardoned sin, and of sin unrepented of; the godly only of sin repented of, and pardoned. It will be a glass wherein every man may see the face of his heart and former life, Rom. i. 15.

3. The Judge himself will be the principal accuser, for it is he that prosecutes the cause, and will do justice on the wicked. God judgeth even the righteous themselves to be sinners, or else they could not be pardoned sinners. But he judgeth the wicked to be impenitent, unbelieving, unconverted sinners. Remember what I said before, that it is not a verbal accusation, but an opening of the truth of the cause to the view of ourselves and others, that God will then perform.

Nor can any think it unworthy of God to be men's accuser by such a disclosure, it being no dishonour to the purest light to reveal a dunghill, or to the greatest prince to accuse a traitor. Nor is it unmeet that God should be both accuser and judge, seeing he is both absolute Lord and perfectly just, and so far beyond all suspicion of injustice. His law, also, doth virtually accuse, John v. 45. But of this by itself.

V. For the fifth particular, How will the sinners be called to the bar?

Answ. God will not stand to send them a citation, nor require him to make his voluntary appearance, but willing or unwilling, he will bring them in.

1. Before each man's particular judgment, he sendeth death, to call away his soul, a surly serjeant, that will have no nay. How dear soever this world may be to men, and how loth soever they are to depart, away they must, and come before the Lord that made them. Death will not be bribed. Every man that was set in the vineyard in the morning of their lives, must be called out at evening to receive according to what he hath done. Then must the naked soul alone appear before its Judge, and be accountable for all that was done in the body, and be sent before till the final judgment, to remain in happiness or misery, till the body be raised again, and joined to it.

In this appearance of the soul before God, it seemeth by Scripture that there is some ministry of angels, for in Luke xvi. 22, it is said that the angels carried Lazarus, that is, his soul, into Abraham's bosom. What local motion there is, or situation of souls, is no fit matter for the inquiry of mortals. And what it is in this that the angels will do, we cannot clearly understand as yet, but most certain it is, that as soon as ever the soul is out of the body, it comes to its account before the God of spirits.

2. At the end of the world, the bodies of all men shall be raised from the earth, and joined again to their souls, and the soul and body shall be judged to their endless state, and this is the great and general judgment where all men shall at once appear. The same power of God that made men of nothing, will as easily then new-make them by a resurrection, by which he will add much more perfection even to the wicked in their naturals, which will make them capable of the greater misery; even they shall have immortal and incorruptible bodies, which may be the subjects of immortal woe, 1 Cor. xv. 53; John v. 28, 29.

Of this resurrection, and our appearance at judgment, the angels will be some way the ministers. As they shall come with Christ to judgment, so they shall sound his trumpet, (1 Thess. iv. 16,) and they shall gather the wicked out of God's kingdom, and they shall gather the tares to burn them, Matt. xiii. 39—41. In the end of the world, the angels shall come forth and sever the wicked from among the just, and shall cast them into the furnace of fire, Matt. xvii. 49, 50.

VI. For the sixth particular, What law is it that men shall be judged by?

Answ. That which was given them to live by. God's law is but the sign of his will, to teach us what shall be due from us and to us; before we fell, he gave us such a law as was suitable to our perfection; when we had sinned, and turned from him, as we ceased not to be his creatures, nor he to be our Lord, so he destroyed not his law, nor discharged or absolved us from the duty of our obedience. But because we stood condemned by the law, and could not be justified by it, having once transgressed it, he was pleased to make a law of grace, even a new, a remedying law, by which we might be saved from the deserved punishment of the old. So we shall be tried at judgment upon both these laws, but ultimately upon the last. The first law commanded perfect obedience, and threatened death to us if ever we disobeyed. The second law, finding us under the guilt of sin against the first, doth command us to repent, and believe in Christ, and so return to God by him, and promiseth us pardon of all our sins upon that condition, and also, if we persevere, everlasting glory. So that in judgment, though it must be first evinced that we are sinners, and have deserved death according to the law of purè nature, yet that is not the upshot of the judgment. For the inquiry will be next, whether they have accepted the remedy, and so obeyed the law of grace, and performed its condition for pardon and salvation; and upon this our life or death will depend. It is both these laws that condemn the wicked, but it is only the law of grace that justifieth the righteous.

Obj. But how shall heathens be judged by the law of grace, that never did receive it?

Answ. The express gospel some of them had not, and therefore shall not directly be judged by it, but much of the Redeemer's mercy they did enjoy, which should have led them to repent, and seek out after recovery from their misery, and to come nearer Christ, and for the neglect and abuse of this they shall be judged, and not merely for sinning against the law that was given us in pure innocency; so that Christ, as Redeemer, shall judge them as well as others. Though they had but one talent, yet must they give an account of that to the Redeemer, from whom they received it. But if any be unsatisfied in this, let them remember, that as God hath left the state of such more dark to us, and the terms on which he will judge them, so doth it much more concern us to look to the terms of our judgment.

Obj. But how shall infants be judged by the gospel that were uncapable of it?

Answ. For aught I find in Scripture, they stand or fall with their parents, and on the same terms, but I leave each to their own thoughts.

VII. For the seventh head, What will be the cause of the day to be inquired after? What the accusation? And what the defence?

Answ. This may be gathered from what was last said. The great cause of the day will be to inquire and to determine who shall die, and who shall live; who ought to go to heaven, and who to hell for ever, according to the law by which they must then be judged.

1. As there is a twofold law by which they must be judged, so will there then be a twofold accusation. The first will be that they were sinners, and so having violated the law of God, they deserve everlasting death, according to that law. If no defence could be made, this one accusation would condemn all the world, for it is most certain that all are sinners, and as certain that all sin deserveth death. The only defence against this accusation lieth in this plea; confessing the charge, we must plead that Christ hath satisfied for sins, and upon that consideration, God hath forgiven us, and therefore, being forgiven, we ought not to be punished: to prove this, we must show the pardon under God's hand in the gospel. But because this pardoning act of the gospel doth forgive none but those that repent and believe, and so return to God, and to sincere obedience for the time to come, therefore the next accusation will be, that we did not perform these conditions of forgiveness, and therefore, being unbelievers, impenitent, and rebels against the Redeemer, we have no right to pardon, but, by the sentence of the gospel, are liable to a greater punishment for the contempt of Christ and grace. This accusation is either true or false: where it is true, God and conscience, who speak the truth, may well be said to be the accusers. Where it is false, it can be only the work of Satan, the malicious adversary, who, as we may see in Job's case, will not stick to bring a false accusation.

If any think that the accuser will not do so vain a work, at least they may see that potentially this is the accusation that lieth against us, and which we must be justified against. For all justification implieth an actual or potential accusation.

He that is truly accused of final impenitency, or unbelief, or rebellion, hath no other defence to make, but must needs be condemned.

He that is falsely accused of such non-performance of the condition of grace, must deny the accusation, and plead his own personal righteousness as against that accusation, and produce that faith, repentance, and sincere obedience and perseverance by which he fulfilled that condition, and so is evangelically righteous in himself, and therefore hath part in the blood of Christ, which is instead of a legal righteousness to him in all things else, as having procured him a pardon of all his sin, and a right to everlasting glory.

And thus we must then be justified by Christ's satisfaction only, against the accusation of being sinners in general, and of deserving God's wrath for the breach of the law of works. But we must be justified by our faith, repentance, and sincere obedience itself, against the accusation of being impenitent unbelievers, and rebels against Christ, and having not performed the condition of the promise, and so having no part in Christ and his benefits.

So that in sum you see, that the cause of the day will be to inquire, whether, being all known sinners, we have accepted of Christ upon his terms, and so have a right in him and his benefits, or not? Whether they have forsaken this vain world for him, and loved him so faithfully that they have manifested it in parting with these things at his command? And this is the meaning of Matt. xxv. where the inquiry is made to be whether they have fed and visited him in his members, or not? That is, whether they so far loved him as their Redeemer, and God by him, as that they have manifested this to his members according to opportunity, though it cost them the hazard or loss of all, seeing danger, and labour, and cost are fitter to express love by, than empty compliments, and bare professions.

Whether it be particularly inquired after, or only taken for granted, that men are sinners, and have deserved death according to the law of works, and that Christ hath satisfied by his death, is all one as to the matter in hand, seeing God's inquiry is but the discovery and conviction of us. But the last question which must decide the controversy, will be, whether we have performed the condition of the gospel.

I have the rather also said all this, to show you in what sense these words are taken in the text, that "every man shall be judged according to what he hath done in the flesh, whether it be good or bad." Though every man be judged worthy of death for sinning, yet every man shall not be judged to die for it, and no man shall be judged worthy of life for his good works. It is, therefore, according to the gospel, as the rule of judgment, that this is meant. They that have repented and believed, and returned to true though imperfect obedience, shall be judged to everlasting life, according to these works; not because these works deserve it, but because the free gift in the gospel, through the blood of Christ, doth make these things the condition of our possessing it. They that have lived and died impenitent unbelievers, and rebels against Christ, shall be judged to everlasting punishment, because they have deserved it, both by their sin in general against the law, and by these sins in special against the gospel. This is called the merit of the cause, that is, what is a man's due according to the true meaning of the law, though the due may be by free gift. And thus you see what will be the cause of the day, and the matter to be inquired after and decided, as to our life or death.

VIII. The next point in our method is to show you what shall be the evidence of the cause.

Answ. There is a five-fold evidence among men. 1. When the fact is notorious. 2. The knowledge of an unsuspected competent judge. 3. The party's confession. 4. Witness. 5. Instruments and visible effects of the action. All these evidences will be at hand, and any one of them sufficient for the conviction of the guilty person at that day.

1. As the sins of all men, so the impenitency and rebellion of the wicked was notorious, or at least will be then: for though some play the hypocrites, and hide the matter from the world and themselves, yet God shall open their hearts and former lives to themselves, and to the view of all the world. He shall set their sins in order before them, so that it shall be utterly in vain to deny or excuse them. If any men will then think to make their cause as good to God as they can now do to us, who are not able to see their hearts, they will be foully mistaken. Now they can say they have as good hearts as the best; then God will bring them out in the light, and show them to themselves, and all the world, whether they were good or bad. Now they will face us down that they do truly repent, and they obey God as they can; but God, who knoweth the deceivers, will then undeceive them. We cannot now make men acquainted with their own unsanctified hearts, nor convince them that have not true faith, repentance, or obedience; but God will convince them of it: they can find shifts and false answers to put off a minister with, but God will not be so shifted off. Let us preach as plainly to them as we can, and do all that ever we are able, to acquaint them with the impenitence and unholiness of their own heart, and the necessity of a new heart and life; yet we cannot do it, but they will believe, whether we will or not, that the old heart will serve the turn. But how easily will God make them know the contrary! We plead with them in the dark; for though we have the candle of the gospel in our hands when we come to

show them their corruption, yet they shut their eyes, and are wilfully blind; but God will open their eyes whether they will or not; not by holy illumination, but by forced conviction, and then he will plead with them as in the open light. See here thy own unholy soul; canst thou now say thou didst love me above all? Canst thou deny but thou didst love this world before me, and serve thy flesh and lusts, though I told thee if thou didst so thou shouldst die? Look upon thy own heart now, and see whether it be a holy or an unholy heart; a spiritual or a fleshly heart; a heavenly or an earthly heart. Look now upon all the course of thy life, and see whether thou didst live to me, or to the world and thy flesh. Oh! how easily will God convince men then, of the very sins of their thoughts, and in their secret closets, when they thought that no witness could have disclosed them. Therefore, it is said that the books shall be opened, and the dead judged out of the books, Rev. xx. 12; Dan. vii. 10.

2. The second evidence will be the knowledge of the Judge. If the sinner would not be convinced, yet it is sufficient that the Judge knoweth the cause: God needeth no further witness: he saw thee committing adultery in secret, lying, stealing, forswearing in secret. If thou do not know thy own heart to be unholy, it is enough that God knoweth it. If you have the face to say, "Lord, when did we see thee an hungred?" &c. Matt. xxv. 44; yet God will make good the charge against thee, and there needeth no more testimony than his own. Can foolish sinners think to lie hid, or escape at that day, who will now sin wilfully before their Judge; who know every day their Judge is looking on them, while they forget him and give up themselves to the world, and yet go on, even under his eye, as if to his face they dared him to punish them?

3. The third evidence will be the sinner's confession. God will force their own consciences to witness against them, and their own tongues to confess the accusation. If they do at first excuse it, he will leave them speechless, yea, and condemning themselves before they have done.

Oh! what a difference between their language now and then! Now we cannot tell them of their sin and misery, but they either tell us of our own faults, or bid us look to ourselves, or deny or excuse their fault, or make light of it; but then their own tongues shall confess them, and cry out of the wilful folly which they committed, and lay a heavier charge upon them than we can now do. Now, if we tell them that we are afraid they are unregenerate, and lest their hearts are not truly set upon God, they will tell us they hope to be saved with such hearts as they have. But then, oh! how they will confess the folly and falseness of their own hearts. You may see a little of their case even in despairing sinners on earth, how far they are from denying or excusing their sins. Judas cries out, "I sinned in betraying the innocent blood," Matt. xxvii. 4. Out of their own mouth shall they be judged. That very tongue that now excuseth their sin, will, in their torments, be their great accuser; for God will have it so to be.

4. The fourth evidence will be the witness of others. Oh! how many thousand witnesses might there be produced, were there need to convince the guilty soul at that day!

1. All the ministers of Christ that ever preached to them, or warned them, will be sufficient witnesses against them. We must needs testify that we preached to them the truth of the gospel, and they would not believe it. We preached to them the goodness of God, yet they set not their hearts upon him. We showed them their sin, and they were not humbled. We told them of the danger of an unregenerate state, and they did not regard us. We acquainted them with the absolute necessity of holiness, but they made light of all. We let them know the deceitfulness of their hearts, and the need of a close and faithful examination, but they would not bestow an hour in such a work, nor scarce once be afraid of being mistaken and miscarrying. We let them know the vanity of this world, and yet they would not forsake it, no, not for Christ, and the hopes of glory. We told them of the everlasting felicity they might attain, but they would not set themselves to seek it.

What we shall think of it then the Lord knows; but surely it seemeth now to us a matter of very sad consideration, that we must be brought in as witnesses against the souls of our neighbours and friends in the flesh. Those whom we now unfeignedly love, and would do any thing that we were able to do for their good; whose welfare is dearer to us than all worldly enjoyments; alas! that we must be forced to testify to their faces for their condemnation. Ah! Lord, with what a heart must a poor minister study when he considereth this, that all the words that he is studying must be brought in for a witness against many of his hearers. With what a heart must a minister preach, when he remembereth that all the words that he is speaking must condemn many, if not most of his hearers? Do we desire this sad fruit of our labours? No; we may say with the prophet, "I have not desired the woeful day, thou knowest," Jer. xvii. 16. No; if we desired it, we would not do so much to prevent it: we would not study, and preach, and pray, and entreat men, that if it were possible we might not be put on such a task: and, doubtless, it should make every honest minister study hard, and pray hard, and entreat hard, and stoop low to men, and be earnest with men in season and out of season, that if it may be they may not be the condemners of their people's souls. But if men will not hear, and there be no remedy, who can help it? Christ himself came not into the world to condemn men, but to save them, and yet he will condemn those who will not yield to his saving work. God takes no pleasure in the death of a sinner, but rather that he repent and live, Ezek. xviii. 23, 32; and yet he will rejoice over those to do them hurt, and destroy them who will not return, Deut. xxviii. 63: and if we must be put on such a work, he will make us like-minded. The Holy Ghost tells us that the saints shall judge the world, 1 Cor. vi. 2, 3; and if they must judge, they will judge as God judgeth. You cannot blame us for it, sinners. We now warn you of it beforehand, and if you will not prevent it, blame not us, but yourselves. Alas! we are not our own masters. As we now speak not to you in our own names, so then we may not do what we list ourselves; or if we might, our will will be as God's will. God will make us judge you, and witness against you: can we absolve you when the righteous God will condemn you? When God is against you, whose side would you have us be of? We must be either against God or you; and can you think that we should be for any one against our Maker and Redeemer? We must either condemn the sentence of Jesus Christ, or condemn you; and is not there more reason to condemn you than him? Can we have any mercy on you, when he that made you will not save you, and he that formed you will show you no mercy? Isaiah xxvii. 11; yea, when he that died for you will condemn you, shall we be more merciful than God? But, alas! if we should be so foolish and unjust, what good would it do you? If we would be false witnesses and partial judges, it would not save you; we are not justified if we absolve ourselves,

1 Cor. iv. 5; how unable, then, shall we be, against God's sentence, to justify you! If all the world should say you were holy and penitent, when God knows you were unholy and impenitent, it will do you no good. You pray every day that his will may be done, and it will be done. It will be done upon you, because it was not done by you. What would you have us say if God ask us, Did you tell this sinner of the need of Christ, of the glory of the world to come, and the vanity of this? Should we lie, and say we did not? What should we say if he ask us, Did not you tell them the misery of their natural state, and what would become of them if they were not made new? Would you have us lie to God, and say we did not? Why, if we did not, your blood will be required at our hands; Ezek. xxxiii. 6; iii. 18; and would you have us bring your blood upon our own heads by a lie? yea, and to do you no good, when we know that lies will not prevail with God? No, no, sinners; we must unavoidably testify to the confusion of your faces: if God ask us, we must bear witness against you, and say, Lord, we did what we could, according to our weak abilities, to reclaim them: indeed, our own thoughts of everlasting things were so low, and our hearts so dull, that we must confess we did not follow them so close, nor speak so earnestly, as we should have done. We did not cry so loud, or lift up our voice as a trumpet to awaken them, Isaiah lviii. 1. We confess we did not speak to them with such melting compassion, and with such streams of tears beseech them to regard, as a matter of such great concernment should have been spoken with: we did not fall on our knees to them, and so earnestly beg of them, for the Lord's sake, to have mercy upon their own souls, as we should have done. But yet we told them the message of God, and we studied to speak it to them as plainly and as piercingly as we could. Fain we would have convinced them of their sin and misery, but we could not: fain we would have drawn them to the admiration of Christ, but they made light of it, Matt. xxii. 5. We would fain have brought them to the contempt of this vain world, and to set their mind on the world to come, but we could not. Some compassion thou knowest, Lord, we had to their souls: many a weeping or groaning hour we have had in secret, because they would not hear and obey, and some sad complaints we have made over them in public. We told them that they must shortly die, and come to judgment, and that this world would deceive them, and leave them in the dust. We told them that the time was at hand when nothing but Christ would do them good, and nothing but the favour of God would be sufficient for their happiness, but we could never get them to lay it to heart. Many a time did we entreat them to think soberly of this life, and the life to come, and to compare them together with the faith of christians and the reason of men, but they would not do it. Many a time did we entreat them but to take now and then an hour in secret to consider who made them, and for what he had made them, and why they were sent into this world, and what their business here is, and whither they are going, and how it will go with them at their latter end; but we could never get most of them to spend one hour in serious thoughts of these weighty matters. Many a time did we entreat them to try whether they were regenerate or not, whether Christ and his Spirit were in them or not, whether their souls were brought back to God by sanctification, but they would not try. We did beseech them to make sure work, and not leave such a matter as everlasting joy or torment to a bold and mad adventure, but we could not prevail. We entreated them to lay all other business aside a little while in the world, and to inquire, by the direction of the word of God, what would become of them in the world to come; and to judge themselves before God came to judge them, seeing they had the law and rule of judgment before them; but their minds were blinded, and their hearts were hardened, and the profit, and pleasure, and honour of this world did either stop their ears, or quickly steal away their hearts, so that we could never get them to a sober consideration, nor ever win their hearts to God.

This will be the witness that many a hundred ministers of the gospel must give in against the souls of their people at that day. Alas! that ever you should cast this upon us! For the Lord's sake, sirs, pity your poor teachers, if you pity not yourselves! We had rather go a thousand miles for you; we had rather be scorned and abused for your sakes; we had rather lay our hands under your feet, and beseech you on our knees with tears, were we able, than be put on such a work as this. It is you that will do it if it be done. We had rather follow you from house to house, and teach and exhort you, if you will but hear us, and accept of our exhortation. Your souls are precious in our eyes, for we know they were so in the eyes of Christ, and therefore we are loth to see this day; we were once in your case, and therefore know what it is to be blind, and careless, and carnal, as you are, and therefore would fain obtain your deliverance. But if you will not hear, but we must accuse you, and we must condemn you, the Lord judge between you and us, for we can witness that it was full sore against our wills. We have been faulty, indeed, in doing no more for you, and not following you with restless importunity; (the good Lord forgive us!) but yet we have not betrayed you by silence.

2. All those that fear God, that have lived among ungodly men, will also be sufficient witnesses against them. Alas! they must be put upon the same work, which is very unpleasant to their thoughts, as ministers are: they must witness before the Lord that they did, as friends and neighbours, admonish them; that they gave them a good example, and endeavoured to walk in holiness before them; but, alas! the most did but mock them, and call them puritans, and precise fools, and they made more ado than needs for their salvation: they must be forced to testify, Lord, we would fain have drawn them with us to hear the word, and to read it, and to pray in their families, and to sanctify the holy day, and take such happy opportunities for their souls; but we could not get them to it: we did in our places what we were able to give them the example of a godly conversation, and they did but deride us; they were readier to mark every slip of our lives, and to observe all our infirmities, and to catch at any accusation that was against us, than to follow us in any work of holy obedience, or care for our everlasting peace. The Lord knows it is a most heavy thing to consider now, that poor neighbours must be fain to come in against those they love so dearly, and by their testimony to judge them to perdition. Oh! heavy case to think of, that a master must witness against his own servant! yea, a husband against his own wife, and a wife against her husband; yea, parents against their own children; and say, Lord, I taught them by word, but they would not learn; I told them what would come on it if they returned not to thee; I brought them to sermons, and I prayed with them and for them. I frequently minded them of these everlasting things, and of this dreadful day which they now see. But youthful lusts, and the temptations of the flesh and the devil, led them away, and

I could never get them thoroughly and soundly to lay it to their hearts. Oh! you that are parents, and friends, and neighbours, in the fear of God, bestir you now, that you may not be put to this at that day of judgment. Oh, give them no rest, take no nay of them till you have persuaded their hearts from this world to God, lest you be put to be their condemners. It must be now that you must prevent it, or else never; now while you are with them, while you and they are in the flesh together, which will be but a little while. Can you but now prevail with them all will be well, and you may meet them joyfully before the Lord.

3. Another witness that will testify against the ungodly at that day, will be their sinful companions. Those that drew them into sin, or were drawn by them, or joined with them in it. Oh! little do poor drunkards think, when they sit merrily in an ale-house, that one of them must bear witness against another, and condemn one another. If they thought of this, methinks it should make them have less delight in that company. Those that now join with you in wickedness, shall then be forced to witness, I confess, Lord, I did hear him swear and curse; I heard him deride those that feared the Lord, and make a jest of a holy life; I saw him in the ale-house when he should be hearing the word of God, or reading, or calling upon God, and preparing for this day; I joined with him in fleshly delights, in abusing thy creature, and our own bodies. Sinners, look your companions in the face the next time you are with them, and remember this that I now say, that those men shall give in evidence against you that now are your associates in all your mirth. Little think the fornicator and lustful wanton, that their sinful mates must then bear witness of that which they thought the dark had concealed, and tell their shame before all the world. But this must be the fruit of sin. It is meet that they who encouraged one another in sin, should condemn one another for it. And marvel not at it, for they shall be forced to it, whether they will or no. Light will not then be hid; they may think to have some ease to their consciences by accusing and condemning others. When Adam is questioned for his sins, he presently accuseth the woman, Gen. iii. 12. When Judas's conscience was awakened, he runs to the Pharisees with the money that drew him to it, and they cast it back in his own face, "See thou to it, what is that to us?" Matt. xxvii. 4—6. Oh! the cold comfort that sinners will have at that day, and the little pleasure that they will find in remembering their evil ways! Now, when a fornicator, or a worldling, or a merry voluptuous man, is grown old, and cannot act all his sin again, he takes pleasure in remembering and telling others of his former folly, what he once was, and what he did, and the merry hours that he had; but then when sinners are come to themselves a little more, they will remember and tell one another of these things with another heart. Oh! that they did but know how these things will then affect them!

4. Another witness that will then rise up against them will be the very devils that tempted them; they that did purposely draw them to sin, that they might draw them to torment for sin. They can witness that you hearkened to their temptations when you would not hearken to God's exhortations. They can witness that you obeyed them in working iniquity. But because you may think the accuser's testimony is not to be taken, I will not stand on this, though it is not nothing where God knoweth it to be true.

5. The very angels of God also may be witnesses against the wicked, therefore are we advised in Scripture not to sin before them, Eccl. v. 6; 1 Cor. xi. 10; 1 Tim. v. 21, "I charge thee before the elect angels," &c. They can testify that they would have been ministering spirits for their good, when the wicked rather chose to be slaves to the spirit of maliciousness. The holy angels of God do many a time stand by when you are sinning. They see you when you see not them; they are employed by God in some sort for your good as well as we. And as it is the grief of ministers that their labours succeed not, so may we suppose that according to their state and nature it is theirs. For they that rejoice in heaven at the conversion of one sinner, may be said to sorrow, or to lose those joys, when you refuse to be converted. These noble spirits, these holy and glorious attendants of Christ, that shall wait upon him to judgment, will be witnesses against rebellious sinners, to their confusion. Sirs, you have all in you naturally a fear of spirits and invisible powers; fear them aright, lest hearkening to the deceiving spirits, and refusing the help of the angels of God, and wilfully sinning before their faces, you should cause them, at that day, to the terror of your souls, to stand forth as witnesses against you, to your condemnation.

6. Conscience itself will be a most effectual witness against the wicked at that day. I before told you it will be a discerner, and force them to a confession, but a further office it hath, even to witness against them. If none else in the world had known of their secret sins, conscience will say, I was acquainted with them.

7. The Spirit of Christ can witness against the ungodly that he oft moved them to repent and return, and they rejected his motions; that he spoke to their hearts in secret, and oft set in with the minister, and often minded them of their case, and persuaded them to God, but they resisted, quenched, and grieved the Spirit, Acts vii. 51. As the Spirit witnesseth with the spirits of the righteous that they are the children of God, (Rom. viii. 16,) so doth he witness with the conscience of the wicked, that they were children of rebellion, and therefore are justly children of wrath. This Spirit will not always strive with men; at last, being vexed, it will prove their enemy, and rise up against them, Gen. vi. 3; Isa. lxiii. 10. If you will needs grieve it now, it will grieve you then. Were it not a Spirit of grace, and were it not free mercy that it came to offer you, the repulse would not have been so condemning, nor the witness of this Spirit so heavy at the last. But it was the Spirit of Jesus that came with recovering grace, which you resisted, and though the wages of every sin is death, yet you will find that it will cost you somewhat more to reject this salvation, than to break the Creator's law of works. Kindness, such kindness, will not be rejected at easy rates.

Many a good motion is now made by the Spirit to the heart of a sinner, which he doth not so much as once observe, and therefore doth not now remember them. But then they shall be brought to his remembrance with a witness. Many a thousand secret motions to repentance, to faith, to a holy life, will be then set before the eyes of the poor, unpardoned, trembling sinner, which he had quite forgotten; and the Spirit of God shall testify to his confusion, At such a sermon I persuaded thy heart to repent, and thou wouldst not; at such a time I showed thee the evil of thy sin, and persuaded thee to have forsaken it, but thou wouldst not. I minded thee in thy secret thoughts of the nearness of judgment, and the certainty and weight of everlasting things, the need of Christ, and faith, and holiness, and of the danger of sinning, but thou didst drown all my motions in the cares and pleasures of the world. Thou hearkenedst rather to the devil than to me. The sensual inclinations of thy flesh did prevail against the strongest arguments that I used. Though I showed reasons, undeniable reasons, from thy Creator, from thy Redeemer, from nature, from grace, from heaven, and from hell, yet all would not so much as stop thee, much less turn thee, but thou wouldst go on; thou wouldst follow thy flesh, and now let it pay thee the wages of thy folly; thou wouldst be thy own guide, and take thine own course, and now take what thou gettest by it,

Poor sinners! I beseech you, in the fear of God, the next time you have any such motions from the Spirit of God, to repent, and believe, and break off your sins, and the occasions of them; consider then, what a mercy is set before you, and how it will confound you, at the day of judgment, to have all these motions brought in against you, and that the Spirit of grace itself should be your condemner. Alas! that men should choose their own destruction, and wilfully choose it, and that the foreknowledge of these things should not move them to relent!

So much concerning the witness that will be brought in against the sinner.

5. The fifth evidence that will be given against the sinner will be the instruments and effects. You know, among men, if a man be found murdered by the highway, and you are found standing by, with a bloody sword in your hand, especially if there were a former dissension between you, it will be an evidence that will prove a strong presumption that you were the murderer; but if the fact be certain by other evidence, then many such things may be brought for aggravation of the fault.

So a twofold evidence will be brought against the sinner from these things; one to prove him guilty of the fact, the other to aggravate the fault, and prove that his sin was very great.

For the former, 1. The very creatures which sinners abused to sin, may be brought in against them to their conviction and condemnation. For though these creatures shall be consumed with the last destroying fire, which shall consume all the world, yet shall they have a being in the memory of the sinner, an *esse cognitum.* The very wine or ale, or other liquor, which was abused to drunkenness, may witness against the drunkard. The sweet morsels by which the glutton did please his appetite, and all the good creatures of God which he luxuriously devoured, may witness against him, Luke xvi. 19, 25. He that fared deliciously every day in this life, was told by Abraham when he was dead, and his soul in hell, "Remember that thou in thy life-time receivedst thy good things, and likewise Lazarus evil things, but now he is comforted, and thou art tormented:" though their sweet morsels and cups are past and gone, yet must they be remembered at judgment and in hell. "Remember, son," saith Abraham; yea, and remember he must, whether he will or no. Long was the glutton in sinning, and many a pleasant bit did he taste, and so many evidences of his sin will lie against him, and the sweetness will then be turned into gall.

The very clothing and ornaments by which proud persons did manifest their pride, will be sufficient evidence against them, as his being clothed with purple and fine linen is mentioned, Luke xvi. 19.

The very lands, and goods, and houses of worldlings will be an evidence against them. Their gold and silver, which the covetous do now prefer before the everlasting riches with Christ, will be an evidence against them. "Go to now, ye rich men, weep and howl for your miseries that shall come upon you. Your riches are corrupted, and your garments are moth-eaten; your gold and silver is cankered, and the rust of them will be a witness against you, and shall eat your flesh as it were fire. Ye have heaped treasure together for the last days. Behold, the hire of the labourers, who have reaped down your fields, which is of you kept back by fraud, crieth; and the cries of them which have reaped are entered into the ears of the Lord of sabaoth. Ye have lived in pleasure on the earth, and been wanton; ye have nourished your hearts, as in a day of slaughter," James v. 1—5. Oh! that worldlings would well consider this one text, and therein observe whether a life of earthly pleasure, and fulness of worldly glory and gallantry, be as desirable as they imagine, and to what time and purpose they now lay up their treasures, and how they must hear of these things hereafter, and what effect the review of their jovial days will have upon their miserable, condemned souls.

2. The very circumstances of time, place, and the like, may evidence against his condemnation. The drunkard shall remember, in such an ale-house I was so oft drunk, and in such a tavern I wasted my time. The adulterer and fornicator shall remember the very time, the place, the room, the bed where they committed wickedness. The thief and deceiver will remember the time, place, and the persons they wronged, and the things which they robbed or deceived them of. The worldling will remember the business which he preferred before the service of God, the worldly matters which had more of his heart than his Maker and Redeemer had, the work which he was doing when he should have been praying, or reading, or catechising his family, or thinking soberly of his latter end. A thousand of these will then come into his mind, and be as so many evidences against him to his condemnation.

3. The very effects, also, of men's sins will be an evidence against them. The wife and children of a drunkard are impoverished by his sin; his family and the neighbourhood are disquieted by him. These will be so many evidences against him. So will the abuse of his own reason, the enticing of others to the same sin, and hardening them by his example.

One covetous, unmerciful landlord doth keep a hundred, or many hundred, persons or families in so great necessities, and care, and labour, that they are tempted by it to overpass the service of God, as having scarce time for it, or any room for it in their troubled thoughts; all these miserable families and persons, and all the souls that are undone by this temptation, will be so many evidences against such oppressors.

Yea, the poor whom they have neglected to relieve when they might, the sick whom they have neglected to visit when they might, will all witness then against the unmerciful, Matt. xxv.

The many ignorant, worldly, careless sinners, that have perished under an idle and unfaithful minister, will be so many witnesses against him to his condemnation. They may then cry out against him to his face, I was ignorant, Lord, and he never did so much as teach me, catechise me, nor tell me of these things. I was careless, and minded the world, and he let me go on quietly, and was as careless as I, and had never plainly and faithfully warned me, to waken me from my security. And so their blood will be required at his hands, though themselves also shall perish in their sins, Ezek. xxxiii. 7, 8.

And as these evidences will convince men of sin, so there are many more which will convince them of the greatness of their sin. And these are so many that it would too much lengthen my discourse to stand on them. A few I shall briefly touch.

1. The very mercy of God in creating men, in giving and continuing their being to them, will be an evidence for the aggravation of their sin against him. What! will you abuse Him by whom it is that you are men? Will you speak to his dishonour that giveth you your speech? Will you live to his dishonour who giveth you your lives? Will you wrong him by his own creatures, and neglect Him without whom you cannot subsist?

2. The redemption of men by the Lord Jesus Christ will be an evidence to the exceeding aggravation of their sins. You sinned against the Lord that bought you, 2 Pet. ii. 1. When the feast was prepared, and all things were ready, you made light of it, and found excuses, and would not come, Matt. xxii. 4—6; Luke xiv. 17, 18. Must Christ redeem you, by so dear a price, from sin and misery, and yet will you continue the servants of sin, and prefer your slavery before your freedom, and choose to be Satan's drudges, rather than to be the servants of God? The sorrows and sufferings that Christ underwent for you will then prove the increase of your own sorrows. As a neglected Redeemer it is that he will condemn you; and then you would be glad that it were but true doctrine that Christ never died for you, that you might not be condemned for refusing a Redeemer, and sinning against him that shed his blood for you. How deeply will his wounds then wound your consciences! You will then remember, that to this end he both died, rose, and revived, that he might be Lord both of the dead and the living, and that he therefore died for all, that they which live should not henceforth live to themselves, but to him that died for them, and rose again, Rom. xiv. 9; 2 Cor. v. 14, 15; Matt. xxviii. 18—20; 1 Peter i. 17, 18. You will then understand that you were not your own, but were bought with a price, and therefore should have glorified him that bought you, with your bodies and spirits, because they were his, 1 Cor. vi. 19, 20. This one aggravation of your sin will make you doubly and remedilessly miserable, that you trod under-foot the Son of God, and counted the blood of the covenant, wherewith you were sanctified, an unholy thing, Heb. x. 26—29; and crucified to yourselves the Son of God afresh, and put him to open shame, Heb. vi. 5, 6.

3. Moreover, all the personal mercies which they received will be so many evidences for the condemnation of the ungodly. The very earth that bore them, and yielded them its fruits, while they themselves are unfruitful to God, the air which they breathed in, the food which nourished them, the clothes which covered them, the houses which they dwelt in, the beasts that laboured for them, and all the creatures that died for their use, all these may rise up against them to their condemnation. And the Judge may thus expostulate with them, Did all these mercies deserve no more thanks? Should you not have served Him that so liberally maintained you? God thought not all these too good for you, and did you think your hearts and services too good for him? He served you with the weary labours of your fellow-creatures, and should you have grudged to bear his easy yoke? They were your slaves and drudges, and you refused to be his free servants and his sons. They suffered death to feed your bodies, and you would not suffer the short forbearance of a little forbidden fleshly pleasure for the sake of him that made you and redeemed you.

Oh! how many thousand mercies of God will then be reviewed by those that neglected them to the horror of their souls, when they shall be upbraided by the Judge with their base requital! All the deliverances from sickness and from danger, all the honours and privileges, and other commodities, which so much contented them, will then be God's evidence to shame them and confound them. On this supposition doth the apostle reprove such, "Despisest thou the riches of his goodness, and forbearance, and long-suffering, not knowing that the goodness of God leadeth thee to repentance? But after thy hardness and impenitent heart treasurest up unto thyself wrath against the day of wrath, and revelation of the righteous judgment of God, who will render to every man according to his deeds," Rom. ii. 4—6.

4. Moreover, all the means which God used for the recovery of sinners in the day of their visitation will rise up against impenitent souls in judgment to their condemnation. You can hear sermons carelessly and sleepily now; but, oh that you would consider how the review of them will then awake you! You now make light of the warnings of God and man, and of all the wholesome advice that is given you, but God will not then make light of your contempt. Oh! what cutting questions will they be to the hearts of the ungodly, when all the means that were used for their good are brought to their remembrance on one side, and the temptations that drew them to sin on the other side; and the Lord shall plead his cause with their consciences, and say, Was I so hard a master, or was my work so unreasonable, or were my wages so contemptible, that no persuasions could draw you into my service? Was Satan so good a master, or was his work so honest and profitable, or were his wages so desirable, that you would be so easily persuaded to do as he would have you? Was there more persuading reason in his allurements and deceits than in all my holy words, and all the powerful sermons that you heard, or all the faithful admonitions you received, or all the good examples of the righteous, or in all the works of God which you beheld? Was not a reason fetched from the love of God, from the evil of sin, the blood of Christ, the judgment to come, the glory promised, the torments threatened, as forcible with you, and as good in your eyes to draw you to holiness, as a reason from a little fleshly delight or worldly gain, to draw you to be unholy?

In the name of God, sinners, I entreat you to bethink yourselves in time, how you will sufficiently answer such questions as these. You should have seen God in every creature you beheld, and have read your duty in all his works: what can you look upon above you, or below you, or round about you, which might not have showed you so much of the wisdom, and goodness, and greatness of your Maker, as should have convinced you that it was your duty to be devoted to his will? and yet you have his written word which speaks plainer than all these; and will you despise them all? Will you not see so great a light? Will you not hear so loud and constant calls? Shall God and his ministers speak in vain? And can you think that you shall not hear of this again, and pay for it one day? You have the Bible and other good books by you, why do you not read them? You have ministers at hand, why do you not go to them, and earnestly ask them, Sir, "what must I do to be saved," and entreat them to teach you the way to life? You have some neighbours that fear God, why do you not go to them, and take their good advice, and imitate them in the fear of God, and in a holy diligence for your souls? Now is the time for you to bestir yourselves; life and death are before you. You have gales of grace to further your voyage. There are more for you than against you. God will help you, his Spirit will help you, his ministers will help you, every good christian will help you, the angels themselves will help you, if you will resolvedly set yourselves to the work; and yet will you not stir? Patience is waiting on you, mercies are enticing you, scourges are driving you, judgment stayeth for you, the lights of God stand burning by you to direct you, and yet will you not stir, but lie in darkness? And do you think you shall not hear of this; do you think this will not one day cost you dear?

IX. The ninth part of our work is to show you what are those frivolous excuses by which the unrighteous may then endeavour their defence.

Having already showed you what the defence must be that must be sufficient to our justification:

If any first demand whether the evidence of their sin will not so overwhelm the sinner, that he will be speechless, and past excuse, I answer, before God hath done with him he will be so. But it seems, at first, his dark understanding and partial corrupted conscience, will set him upon a vain defence; for Christ telleth us that "Many will say to me in that day, Lord, Lord, have we not prophesied in thy name? and in thy name have cast out devils? and in thy name done many wonderful works? And then will I profess unto them, I never knew you: depart from me, ye that work iniquity," Matt. vii. 22, 23. And in Matt. xxv. 11, the foolish virgins cry, "Lord, Lord, open to us:" and ver. 44, "Then shall they also answer him, saying, Lord, when saw we thee an hungred, or athirst, or a stranger, or naked, or sick, or in prison, and did not minister unto thee?" And ver. 24, 25, they fear not to cast some of the cause of their neglect on God himself: "Then he which had received the one talent came and said, Lord, I knew that thou art an hard man, reaping where thou hast not sown, and gathering where thou hast not strawed, and I was afraid, and went and hid thy talent in the earth; lo! there thou hast that is thine."

It is clear, then, that excuses they will be ready to make, and their full conviction will be in order after these excuses (at least, as in their minds, if not in words). But what the particular excuses will be, we may partly know by these scriptures which recite them, and partly by what the ungodly do now say for themselves: and because it is for their present benefit that I now make mention of them, that they may see the vanity of all such excuses, I will mention them as I now meet with them in the mouths of sinners in our ordinary discourse: and these excuses are of several sorts—some by which they would justify their estate; some excuses of particular actions, and that either in whole or in part; some by which they would put by the penalty, though they confess the sin; some by which they lay the blame on other men, and in some they would cast it upon God himself. I must touch but some of them very briefly.

The first excuse: I am not guilty of these things which I am accused of; I did love God above all, and my neighbour as myself; I did use the world but for necessity, but God had my heart.

Answ. The all-seeing Judge doth know the contrary; and he will make thy conscience know it. Look back, man, upon thy heart and life! How seldom and how neglectfully didst thou think of God! How coldly didst thou worship him, or make any mention of him! How carelessly didst thou serve him! And think much of all that thou didst therein. Thou rather thoughtest that his service was making more ado than needs, and didst grudge at those who were more diligent than thyself; but for the world, how heartily and how constantly didst thou seek and serve it! And yet wouldst thou now persuade the Judge that thou didst love God above all? He will show thee thy naked heart, and the course of thy former life, which shall convince thee of the contrary.

The second excuse: I lived not in any gross sin, but only in small infirmities: I was no murderer, or adulterer, or fornicator, or thief; nor did I deceive or wrong any, or take any thing by violence.

Answ. Was it not a gross sin to love the world above God, and to neglect Christ that died for thee, and never to do him one hour's hearty service, but merely to seek thy carnal self, and to live to thy flesh? God will open thine eyes then, and show thee a thousand gross sins, which thou now forgettest, or makest light of; and it is not only gross sin, but all sin, great or small, that deserveth the wrath of God, and will certainly bring thee under it for ever, if thou have not part in Christ to relieve thee. Woe to the man that ever he was born, that must answer in his own name for his smallest offences!

The third excuse: I did it ignorantly; I knew not that there was so much required to my salvation. I thought less ado might have served the turn; and that if I looked to my body, God would take care of my soul, and that it was better to trust him what would become of me hereafter, than to trouble my mind so much about it. Had I known better, I would have done better.

Answ. 1. If you knew not better, who was it long of but yourself? Did God hide these things from you? Did he not tell them you in his word as plainly as the tongue of man can speak, that except you were regenerate and born again, you should not enter into the kingdom of God, John iii. 3, 5; that without holiness none should see God, Heb. xii. 14; that you must strive to enter in at the strait gate; for many shall seek to enter, and shall not be able, Luke xiii. 24: that if you lived after the flesh you should die; and if by the Spirit you mortified the deeds of the body you should live, Rom. viii. 13: that if any man have not the Spirit of Christ, the same is none of his, Rom. viii. 9; and to be carnally-minded is death, but to be spiritually-minded is life and peace, Rom. viii. 9: that you must not lay up for yourselves a treasure on earth, where rust and moth do corrupt, and thieves break through and steal; but must lay up for yourselves a treasure in heaven, where rust and moth do not corrupt, and thieves do not break through and steal, Matt. vi. 19, 20: that you must seek first the kingdom of God, and the righteousness thereof, Matt. vi. 23; and not labour for the food that perisheth, but for the food that endureth to everlasting life, which Christ would have given you, John vi. 27; that if you be risen with Christ, you must seek those things which are above, where Christ sitteth at the right hand of God, and not the things that are on earth, Col. iii. 1—3; yea, your very conversation should be in heaven, Phil. iii. 19—21.

What say you? Did not God tell you all this and much more, and plainly tell it you? Turn to your Bibles and see the words, and let them witness against you.

2. And could you think with any reason that your souls being so much more precious than your bodies, you should yet do so much more for your bodies than your souls? Could you think all the labours of your lives little enough for a frail body that must lie shortly in the dirt, and that your immortal souls should be no more regarded? Could you think, with any reason, that your souls should do so much for a life of a few

year's continuance, and do no more for a life that shall have no end?

3. And whereas you talk of trusting God with your souls, you did not trust him: you did but on that pretence carelessly disregard them. If you trust God, show any word of promise that ever he gave you to trust upon, that ever an impenitent, carnal, careless person shall be saved? No, he hath told you enough to the contrary: and could you think that it was the will of God that you should mind your bodies more than your souls, and this life more than that to come? Why, he hath bid you strive, and run, and fight, and labour, and care, and seek, and use violence, and all diligence, for the safety of your souls, and for the life to come; but where hath he bid you do so for your bodies? No; he knew that you were prone to do too much for them, and therefore he hath bid you "care not, and labour not," that is, do it as if you did it not; and let your care and labour for earthly things be none, in comparison of that for heavenly things. You know God can as well maintain your lives without your care and labour, as save your souls without it; and yet you see he will not, he doth not. You must plough, and sow, and reap, and thrash, for all God's love and care of you, and not say, I will let all alone and trust God. And must you not much more use diligence in much greater things? If you will trust God, you must trust him in his own way, and in the use of his own means.

The fourth excuse: I was never brought up to learning, I cannot so much as read; nor did my parents ever teach me any of these things, but only set me about my worldly business, and provide food and raiment for me, but never once told me that I had a soul to save or lose, and an everlasting life to provide and prepare for, and therefore I could not come to the knowledge of them.

Answ. The greater is their sin who thus neglected you: but this is no sufficient excuse for you. Heaven is not prepared for the learned only; nor will Christ ask you at judgment whether you are good scholars, or not; no, nor so much as whether you could write or read. But, consider well, was not God's word so plainly written that the unlearned might understand it? Did he not put it into the most familiar style, though he knew it would be offensive to the proud scholars of the world, on purpose that he might fit it to the capacities of the ignorant? And if you could not read, yet tell me, could not you have learned to read at twenty or thirty years of age, if you had been but willing to bestow now and then an hour to that end; or, at least, did you not live near some that could read; and could you not have procured them to read to you, or to help you; and did you not hear these things read to you in the congregation by the minister, or might have done if you would; and if your parents did neglect you in your youth, yet when you came to a fuller use of reason, and heard of the matters of salvation from God's word, did it not concern you to have looked to yourselves, and to have redeemed that time which you lost in your youth, by doubling your diligence when you came to riper years? The apostles gathered churches among heathens who never heard of Christ before, and converted many thousand souls who were never once told of a Saviour, or the way to salvation, till they had passed a great part of their lives. If you loitered till the latter part of the day, it behoved you then to have bestirred yourselves the more; and not to say, Through the fault of my parents I lost the beginning of my life, and therefore I will lose all; they taught me not then, and therefore I will not learn now. Have you not seen some of your neighbours who were as ill educated as yourselves attain to much knowledge afterwards by their industry; and why might not you have done so if you had been as industrious as they? may not God and conscience witness that it was because you cared not for knowledge, and would not be at pains to get it, that you knew no more? Speak truth, man, in the presence of thy Judge! Was thy heart and mind set upon it? Didst thou pray daily for it to God? Didst thou use all the means thou couldst to get it? Didst thou attend diligently on the word in public, and think of what thou heardest, when thou camest home? Didst thou go to the minister, or to others that could teach thee, and entreat them to tell thee the way to salvation? Or didst thou not rather carelessly neglect these matters, and hear a sermon as a common tale, even when the minister was speaking of heaven or of hell? It was not, then, thine unavoidable ignorance, but thy negligence.

Yea, further, answer as in the presence of God: didst thou obey so far as thou didst know? or, didst thou not rather sin against that knowledge which thou hadst? Thou knewest that the soul was better than the body, and everlasting life more to be regarded than this transitory life, but didst thou regard it accordingly? Thou, sure, knewest that God was better than the world, and heaven than earth: at least, thou wast told of it; but didst thou accordingly value him, and love him more? Thou knewest, sure, that there was no salvation without faith, and repentance, and newness of life, and yet they were neglected. In a word, many a thousand sins which were committed, and duties that were omitted against thy own knowledge and conscience, will mar this excuse.

The fifth excuse: I lived not under a powerful minister to tell me of these things, but where there was no preaching at all.

Answ. And might you not have gone where a powerful minister was, with a little pains? Yea, did not the very plain word that you heard read tell you of these things; and might you not have had a Bible yourselves, and found them there?

The sixth excuse: I was a servant, and had no time from my labour to mind these matters: I lived with a hard master, that required all his own work of me, but would allow me no time for the service of God. Or else, I was a poor man, and had a great charge to look after, and with my hard labour had much ado to live, so that I had no time for heavenly things.

Answ. 1. Who should be first served, God or man? What should be first sought after, heaven or earth? Did not Christ tell thee, "One thing is necessary?" Luke x. 41, 42. Was it not as needful to see that you escape damnation, and get safe to heaven when this life is ended, as to see that you had food and raiment for yourselves and yours?

2. Did you spend no time in recreation, nor idleness, nor vain talking? Why might not that at least have been spent about heavenly things?

3. Could you have taken no time from your rest or eating, or at other intermissions? Man's body will not endure so great labours as have no intermission: and why then might not godliness have been your ease and recreation?

4. Or might you not have minded these things, even when you were about your labour, if you had but a heart to them?

5. At least you might have spent the Lord's own day in hearing, reading, and pondering of these matters, when you were forced to forbear your worldly labours, even by the wholesome law of the land. These, therefore, are all but vain excuses;

and God will shortly make thee speak out, and plainly confess, it was not so much for want of time, or helps, or warning, as for want of a heart to use them well. I should have found some time, though it had been when I should have slept, if my heart had been but set upon it.

The seventh excuse: Little did I think to have seen this day. I did not believe that ever God would be so severe. I thought his threatenings had been but to keep men in awe; and I suspected either that the Scripture was not his word, or else I thought he would be better than his word. I thought all that I heard of another life had been uncertain, and therefore was loth to let go a certainty for an uncertainty, and lose my present pleasures which I had in hand for the hopes of that which I never did see.

Answ. He that will not know his misery by believing to prevent it, shall know it by feeling to endure it. You were told, and told again, what your unbelief would bring you to. Did God's word make heaven and earth? Doth it support and secure them? And is not his word sufficient security for you to have trusted your souls upon? Did you know where was any better security to be had, and where was any surer ground for your confidence? And did you think so basely and blasphemously of God, that he would falsify his word, lest such as you should suffer, and that he was fain to rule the world by a lie? Did God make the world so easily? And can he not govern it by true and righteous means? What need God to say that which he will not do to awe sinners? Can he not awe them by truth? Is it not just that those should eternally perish who will entertain such desperate thoughts of God, and then, by such wicked imaginations, encourage themselves in sin against him?

And for the truth of Scripture, God did not bid you believe it without evidence. He stamped on it the image of his own purity and perfection, that you might know it by that image and superscription, if you had eyes to see them. He sealed it by uncontrolled multitudes of miracles. He delivered it down to your hands by infallible witnesses, so that he left you no room for rational doubting.

And you knew that the matters of this world were not only uncertain, but certainly vain and transitory, and would shortly come to nothing, and leave you in distress. If it had been uncertain whether there were a glory and misery hereafter, (as it was not,) should not reason have taught you to prefer the least probabilities of an everlasting, unspeakable happiness, before that which is certainly perishing and vain? These vain excuses will but condemn you.

The eighth excuse: I was so enticed and persuaded by sinners to do as they did, that I could not deny them: they would never let me rest.

Answ. And were you not as earnestly persuaded by God to forsake sin, and serve him, and yet that would not prevail with you? You could not deny the devils and fools, but you could deny God and all his messengers. Were not ministers as earnest with you every week to repent and amend? What did men entice you with? With a little deluding fleshly pleasure for a few days? And what did God entice you with? With the promise of endless, inconceivable felicity! And if this were a smaller matter in your eyes than the other, then you have had your choice, be content with it, and thank yourselves. In your life-time you had the good things which you chose, and preferred before heaven, and therefore cannot expect to have heaven besides.

The ninth excuse: I lived among ungodly persons, who derided all that feared God; so that if I had not done as they did, but had made any more ado to be saved, I should have been the very scorn of the place where I lived.

Answ. And was not heaven worth the enduring of a scorn? Is not he worthy to go without it who thinks so basely of it? Did not Christ tell you that if you were ashamed of him before men, he would be ashamed of you before his Father and the angels of heaven? Mark viii. 38. He suffered more than scorns for you; and could not you suffer a scorn for him and yourselves? Seeing you chose rather to endure everlasting torment, than a little derision from ignorant men, take that which you made choice of: and seeing so small a matter would drive you from heaven, and part God and you as a mock, as the wind of a man's mouth, no wonder if you be commanded to depart from him into everlasting fire.

The tenth excuse: I had ungodly persons for my parents, or masters, or landlord, or governors, who threatened to undo me if I had addicted myself to so strict a life, and if I would not believe and do as they did.

Answ. What if they threatened you with present death? Did not God also threaten you with everlasting death if you were not ruled by him? And whose threatening should you have chiefly feared? Is man more dreadful than God? Is death more terrible than hell? Did not Christ bid you "fear not them that can kill the body, and after that can do no more; but fear him that is able to destroy both body and soul in hell-fire? yea, I say unto you, fear him," Matt. x. 28; Luke xii. 4, 5. "Fear ye not the reproach of men, neither be afraid of their revilings: for the moth shall eat them up like a garment, and the worm shall eat them like wool; but my righteousness shall be for ever, and my salvation from generation to generation," Isaiah li. 7. Seeing, therefore, you have chosen rather to suffer from God for ever for your sin, than to suffer small matters for well-doing for a moment, you must ever bear your own choice. Christ told you beforehand, that if you could not forsake all the world, and your own lives, for him, you could not be his disciples, Matt. x. 37—39. And seeing you thought his terms too hard, and would needs seek you out a better service, even take what you have chosen and found.

The eleventh excuse: I saw so many follow their pleasure and their worldly business, and never look after these higher things, and so few go the other way, that I thought sure God would not damn so great a part of the world, and therefore I ventured to do as the most did.

Answ. God will make good his word upon many or few. Did you doubt of his will, or of his power? For his will—he hath told it you in his word; for his power—he is as able to punish many as one man. What is all the world to him, but as a drop of a bucket, as the dust of the balance? He told you beforehand that the gate was strait, and the way to heaven was narrow, and few did find it; and the gate to destruction was wide, and the way was broad, and many did enter in at it, Matt. vii. 13, 14. And if you would not believe him, you must bear what your unbelief hath brought you to. What if you had twenty children, or servants, or friends, and the greater part of them should prove false to you, and seek your destruction, or prove disobedient, and turn to your enemy, would you think it a good excuse if the rest should do the like because of their example? Will you therefore wrong God because you see others wrong him? Would you spit in the face of your own father, if you saw others do so? God warned you that you should not follow a multitude to do evil, Exod. xxiii. 2. And if yet you will do as most do, you must even speed as most speed.

You should not so much consider who they be, as what they do, and whither they go, and who they forsake, and what they lose, and what strength is in the reasons that move them to do this: and then you would find it is God they forsake, it is sin they choose; it is heaven they lose, it is hell they run into; and it is no true reason, but Satan's delusion, and sensual inclinations, that lead them to it: and should they be imitated, be they many, or be they few, in such a course as this?

The twelfth excuse: I saw so many faults in those that were accounted godly, and saw so much division among them, that I thought they were as bad as others; and among so many opinions I knew not what religion to be of.

Answ. 1. A spot is soonest seen in the fairest cloth; and the malicious world useth to make such far worse than they are.

2. But suppose all were true that malice saith of some, you could not say the like by others.

3. Or, if you could, yet it was God's law, and not men's faults, that was made the rule for you to live by: will it excuse you that others are bad?

4. And from their diverse opinions you should have taken counsel at God's word, which was right. Did you first search the Scripture impartially, as willing to know the truth, that you might obey it? And did you pray daily that God would lead you into the truth? And did you obey as much as you knew? Did you join with the godly so far as they are all agreed in the fundamental articles of christianity, and in all things absolutely necessary to a holy life, and to salvation; that all known sin is to be forsaken, and all known duty to be done. Why did you not so far, then, agree with them? Alas! the imperfections of the godly, and the false accusations of the malicious world, will prove but a poor cover for your wilful ungodliness, and Christ will convince you of the vanity of these excuses.

The thirteenth excuse: The Scriptures were so dark that I could not understand them. And I saw the wisest men differ so much in the exposition of them, that I thought it was in vain for me to trouble myself about them. If God would have had us live according to the Scriptures, he would sure have written them plainly, that men might understand them.

Answ. 1. It is all plainly written according to the nature of the subject, but a prejudiced, disaffected, yea, or but untaught, disused soul, cannot at first understand the plainest teaching. The plainest Greek or Hebrew grammar that can be written, will be utterly obscure to him that is but newly entered the English school, yea, after many years' time that he spends in learning. Did you study hard, and pray for God's teaching, and inquire of others, and wait patiently in Christ's school, that you might come to further knowledge by degrees? And were you willing to know even those truths that called you out to self-denial, and that did put you on the hardest flesh-displeasing duties? Had you done thus, you would have admired the light of the holy Scripture, and now have rejoiced that ever you saw them, and not have quarrelled at its seeming darkness. This word might have made you wise to salvation, as it hath done others, Acts xx. 32; 2 Tim. iii. 15—17. "The law of the Lord is perfect, converting the soul; the testimony of the Lord is sure, making wise the simple; the statutes of the Lord are right, rejoicing the heart; the commandment of the Lord is pure, enlightening the eyes," Psal. xix. 7, 8.

2. So much as is of necessity to salvation, is as plain as you could desire. Yet if you be judged by these, you will be condemned, for you did not obey that which was most plain. What darkness is in such words as these, "Except ye repent, ye shall all perish," Luke xiii. 3, 5. "Love not the world, nor the things in the world. If any man love the world, the love of the Father is not in him," 1 John ii. 15. "He that will come after me, let him deny himself," &c. Matt. xvi. 24.

3. If there had been nothing that seemed difficult to you, would you not have despised its simplicity, and have thought yourselves wise enough at the first reading, and needed no more?

The fourteenth excuse: There were so many seeming contradictions in the Scripture, and so many strange, improbable things, that I could not believe it.

Answ. 1. The contradictions were in your fancy, that did not understand the word which you read. Must the raw, unexperienced learner despise his book or teacher as oft as in his ignorance he thinks he meets with contradictions? Did you think God was no wiser than you, and understood not himself, because you understood him not? nor could reconcile his own words, because you could not reconcile them? You would needs be a judge of the law, instead of obeying it, and speak evil of it, rather than do it, James iv. 11.

2. And those things which you called improbable in the word, were the wonders of God, of purpose to confirm it. If it had not been confirmed by wonders, you would have thought it unproved, and yet now it is so confirmed, you will not believe the doctrine, because the witness seems incredible. And that is, because they are matters above the power of man, as if they were therefore above the power of God. You shall at last have your eyes so far opened, as to see those seeming contradictions reconciled, and the certainty of those things which you accounted improbable; that you may be forced to confess the folly of your arrogancy and unbelief; and then God will judge you in righteousness, who presumed unrighteously to judge him and his word.

The fifteenth excuse: It seemed so unlikely a thing to me, that the merciful God should damn most of the world to everlasting fire, that I could not believe it.

Answ. 1. And did it not seem as unlikely to you that his word should be false?

2. Should it not have seemed as unlikely that the Governor of the world should be unjust, and suffer his law to be unexecuted, and the worst to speed as well as the best; and to suffer vile, sinful dust to despise his mercy, and abuse his patience, and turn all his creatures against him without due punishment?

3. Did you not feel pain and misery begin in this life?

4. You saw toads and serpents, which had never sinned, and you would rather live in any tolerable suffering than to be a toad. And is it not reason that it should go worse with contemptuous sinners, than with those creatures that never sinned.

5. Could you expect that those should come to heaven that would not believe there was such a state, but refused it, and preferred the world before it? And to be out of heaven is to be out of all happiness; and he that is so out of all happiness, and knows that he lost it by his own folly, must needs torment himself with such considerations, were there no other torments: and as man is capable of greater felicity than brutes, so must he needs be capable of more misery.

The sixteenth excuse: The things which God promised in heaven, and threatened in hell, were all out of my sight, and therefore I could not heartily believe them. Had I but once seen them, or spoke with one that had seen them, I should have been satisfied, and have contemned the things of the world.

Answ. Will you not believe till you see or feel? Was not God's word sufficient evidence? Would you have believed one from the dead that had told you he had seen such things? And would you not believe Stephen that saw them? Acts vii. 56; or Paul, that heard and saw them? 2 Cor. xii. 3, 4. nor Christ, that came purposely from heaven to reveal them? Why, flesh and blood cannot see them. You see not God, will you not therefore believe that there is a God? Indeed, whatever you imagine, if you would not believe Moses and the prophets, Christ and his apostles, neither would you have believed though one had risen from the dead, for God's word is more credible than a dead man's, and Christ did rise from the dead to attest it. Blessed are they that have not seen, and yet believed. Noah saw no rain when he was preparing the ark, but because he believed, he made ready and escaped, (Heb. xi. 7,) when the world, that would not believe, did perish. But seeing God's word was of no more weight with you, and no knowledge would serve your turn but by seeing and feeling, you shall see and feel everlastingly to your sorrow.

The seventeenth excuse: It was so strict a law that God would have ruled me by, and the way to heaven was so strait and difficult, that I could not endure it. I was not able to deny my flesh, and live such a life.

Answ. 1. You are not able because you are not willing. What was there but your own wicked hearts that should make such a life seem grievous to you? Every thing is hard and grievous to him who loathes it, and whose heart is against it. The chief thing that God called you to was to love him, and make him your delight, and are love and delight such grievous things? It was not grievous to you to love your meat, or drink, or money. It was no hard matter to you to love a friend that loved you, no, nor to love your sin which was your enemy; and what should make it seem hard to love God but a wicked heart? Is not he better and more lovely than all these? And had you but loved him, all the rest of his service would have seemed easy to you. To think of him, to speak of him, to pray to him, to praise him, yea, to deny all and suffer for him, would have been sweet and pleasant to you, so far as you had loved him. It was not God, therefore, but your own naughty hearts, that made his work seem grievous to you, and the way to heaven seem hard. He told you truly that his yoke was easy, and his burden light, and his commandments were not grievous, Matt. xi. 29; 1 John v. 3. They that tried them found them the very joy and delight of their souls, and why could not you do so?

2. But what if the way to heaven had been harder than it was? Was not heaven worth your labour? Were you afraid of being a loser by it? Could not God requite your labour or sufferings? Doth any repent when they come to heaven that it cost them so dear to come thither? And is not hell worse than the hardest way to heaven? Seeing you have chosen hell to save you labour and suffering in this life, you must have your choice. And seeing you thought not everlasting life to be worth so much as God required, that is, the accepting thankfully, and minding, and seeking, and preferring it before this life, you have none to blame for the loss of it but yourselves.

The eighteenth excuse: It was God that made me of a sensual nature. He gave me an appetite to meat, and drink, and ease, and lust. He gave me that flesh which ruled me, how then can he condemn me for living according to the nature which he gave me?

Answ. He gave that appetite to be exercised moderately under the rule of reason, for the preservation and propagation of mankind. But did he not also give you reason to govern that appetite? and the revelation of his will to guide that reason? He gave you your flesh to be a servant, and not a master. Your beast hath fleshly appetite without reason, and therefore God hath put him under you who have reason, that you should rule him. Will you let your beast do what he list, and madly run upon whom you list, and say, you do but let him live according to his nature, which God hath given him? Why, God that gave him such nature, did intend him to be ruled by a higher nature, even by the reason which he gave to you; and so he did also by your flesh and sensual appetite.

The nineteenth excuse: But I lived among so many baits which enticed this flesh, that I could not resist them. My meat was a snare to me, my drink a snare, my clothes, my house, my land a snare, every beauty that I saw was a snare. And the better all these were, the stronger was my snare. If God would not have had my heart insnared and drawn from him, he should not have put so many baits in my way. Yea, and they were so near to me, and daily with me, that though I was resolved to forbear them before, yet when they were brought to my hand, I could not forbear.

Answ. 1. Is this the thanks that God hath for his mercies? He sent you all these as favours from his own hand. He wrote his own name upon them, that in them you might see his power, and wisdom, and goodness, and so be led up to the consideration of him, that you might fall in love with himself, who was the fountain, the life, the end of all. And do you overlook God in the creature, and live as without him in the world, and dote upon that which should have drawn you to himself, and then lay the blame on God? If he send a suitor to speak to you in his name, and write you a love-letter with his own hand, will you fall in love with the messenger or the letter, and neglect the sender, and then blame him that wrote his letter on so fair a paper, or in so neat a hand, or that sent it by such a comely messenger? Certainly these excuses are too gross to take with the wise and righteous God, or to seem sufficient to a well-informed conscience.

2. And whereas you speak of the power of these objects, was there not much more in God, in Christ, in the promised glory, to have drawn your heart another way? Why, then, did not these take as much with you as the other? You could not choose, forsooth, but be enticed with such baits as were fitted to your sensual appetite, and such things as a dog or a swine may enjoy as well as a man, but you could choose when Christ and glory were offered you. Yea, you did choose to refuse the offer, and tread them under-feet by your neglect. When Satan set your cups, and your harlots, and your profits before you, on one side, did not God set his favour and everlasting happiness on the other side? And was it wise or equal dealing to prefer your lusts before that glory?

3. Moreover, it was not in the power of any of those baits to force your will, or to necessitate you to choose them. They could be but baits to entice you, and it was still in your own choice whether you would yield to the enticement, and choose them or not. Shall every man be false to God that hath any bait to entice him from him? Will you excuse your child or friend if he would be false to you upon as

great enticements as these? If a cup of drink, or a whore, or a little gain, could draw him more than all your love and interest, I do not think you would hold him excused.

And whereas you speak of the nearness and continuance of these allurements, I would fain know was not God as near you, and continually near you to draw you to himself? Faith might have seen him, though flesh and blood cannot. Did he not stand by you when you were in your cups and lustful pleasures? Did he not tell you of the danger, and offer you far better things, if you would obey him and despise those baits? But you would hearken to none of this; you should have remembered that he stood over you, and was looking on you, and you should have said, as Joseph, "How can I do this great wickedness, and sin against God?" Gen. xxxix. 9. You had also Scripture near you, and reason near you, and conscience near you, as well as the bait was near you, and therefore this is a vain excuse.

The twentieth excuse: It was God that let loose the devil to tempt me, and he was too subtle for me to deal with, and therefore what wonder if I sinned, and were overcome?

Answ. 1. He did not let loose the devil to constrain you to sin. He could but entice, and you might choose whether you would yield. The devil could neither make you sin against your will, nor yet necessitate you to be willing.

2. You were a sure friend to Christ that while, that would forsake him as oft as you were tempted by the devil. Is that a friend or a servant worthy to be regarded, that will disobey you, or betray you, as oft as he is tempted to it?

3. Will you excuse your servant if he leave your work undone, and follow cards or dice, or the alehouse, and say, I was tempted to it by one that was cunninger than I? Shall every murderer or thief escape hanging because the devil was too cunning for him in his temptations? Would you have the jury or the judge to take this for a good excuse?

4. And why did you not hearken to God, that enticed you the other way? You forgot what helps he afforded you to discover the wiles of Satan, and to vanquish the temptation. He told you it was an enemy that tempted you, and would you hearken to an enemy? He told you it was a dream, a shadow, a painted pleasure, a gilded carcass, a lying promise, and deceitful vanity, by which you were tempted, and yet would you regard it before your God? He told you that it was your God, your Saviour, your hope, your everlasting happiness that the tempter would beguile you of, and yet would you be beguiled? He told you, and plainly, and often told you, that the tempter would lead you to eternal fire, and undo you everlastingly before you were aware, and that a fatal hook was covered with that bait; and yet would you swallow it?

5. It is plain by all this that it was not your natural weakness of faculties that caused you to be overcome by the subtleties of the devil, as a silly child is deceived by a crafty fellow that overwits him. But it was your careless inconsiderateness, your sensual inclinations, and vicious disposition, that drew you to a wilful obeying of the tempter, and rejecting the wholesome advice of Christ. This, therefore, is a frivolous excuse of your sin.

The one-and-twentieth excuse: But I hope you will not say that all men have free-will, and if my will were not free, how could I choose but sin?

Answ. 1. Your will was not free from God's rule and government; 2. Nor was it free from its natural inclination to good in general; for either of these were more properly slavery. 3. Nor was it free from the influence of a dark understanding. 4. Nor free from its own contracted, vicious inclination. 5. Nor freed from the temptations of the flesh, the world, and the devil.

But it was, 1. Free from any natural determination to evil, or to any thing that was doubtful. 2. And free from the co-action or violence of any. 3. And free from an irresistible determination of any exterior cause, at least ordinarily. So that naturally, as men, you have the power or faculty of determining your own wills, of ruling your inferior faculties in a great measure, yea, of ruling the senses and the fantasy itself, which doth so much to dispose of our understanding. And if your wills, which are naturally free, are yet so habitually vicious that they incline you to do evil, that is not an excuse, but an aggravation of your sin. But of this more under the next.

The two-and-twentieth excuse: But I have not power of myself to any thing that is good. What can the creature do? Without Christ, we can do nothing. It is God that must give me ability, or I can have none, and if he had given it me, I had not been an unbeliever or impenitent. I can no more believe of myself, than I can fulfil the law of myself.

Answ. 1. These are the vain cavils of learned folly, which God will easily answer in a word. The word "power" is taken in several senses. Sometimes, and most commonly and fitly, for a faculty or a strength by which a man can do his duty if he will. This physical power you have, and the worst of sinners have, while they are men on earth. Were they actually willing, they might acceptably perform sincere obedience; and were they dispositively willing, they might actually believe and will. And thus the ungodly have power to believe.

Sometimes the word "power" is taken for authority or leave, for legal or civil power. And thus you have all not only power or liberty to believe, but also a command which makes it your duty, and a threatening adjoined, which will condemn you if you do not.

Sometimes the word "power" is taken ethically, and less properly, for a disposition, inclination, habit, or freedom from the contrary habit or disposition. And in this sense it is true that none but the effectually called have a power to believe. But then observe, 1. That this is but a moral less proper, and not a physical proper impotency; and therefore Austin chooseth rather to say that all men have power to believe, but all have not a will, or faith itself, because we use to difference power from willingness, and willingness actuateth the power which we had before. And therefore our divines choose rather to call grace a habit, when they speak exactly, than a power; and Dr. Twiss derides the Arminians for talking of a power subjected in a power. 2. Note, that this impotency is but the same thing with your unwillingness and wilful blindness in another word. 3. Note, that this impotency is long of yourselves as to the original, and much more as to the not curing, or removing of it. Hath God given you no means towards the cure of this disability, which you have neglected? 4. Note, that this impotency is no just excuse, but an aggravation of your sin. If you were willing to be the servant of Christ, and yet were not able, either because he would not accept you, or because of a want of natural faculties, or because of some other natural difficulty which the willingest mind could not overcome, this were some excuse; but to be habitually wilful in refusing grace, is worse than to be merely, actually unwilling. If a man have so accustomed himself to murder, drunkenness, stealing, or the like wickedness, so far that he cannot leave it, will you therefore forgive him? or will any judge or jury hold him excused? or rather think him the more unfit for mercy? 5. Note, also, that the want of a supernatural habit, no, nor the presence of the contrary habit, do not efficiently determine the will to particular acts, much less take away its natural freedom. 6. And that till habits attain an utter predominancy, (at least,) there is a power remaining in the will to resist them, and use means against them, though eventually the perverse inclination may hinder the use of it.

The three-and-twentieth excuse: I have heard from learned men that God doth determine all actions, natural and free, as the first efficient physical immediate cause, or else nothing could act. And then it was not long of me that I chose forbidden objects, but of him that irresistibly moved me thereto, and whose instrument I was.

Answ. This is a trick of that wisdom which is foolishness with God, and to be deceived by vain philosophy.

1. The very principle itself is most likely to be false, and those that tell you this do err. Much more, I think, may be said against it than for it.

2. I am sure it is either false, or reconcilable with God's holiness, and man's liberty and culpability; so that it is a mad thing to deceive yourselves with such philosophical uncertainties, when the truth which you oppose by it is infallibly certain. That God is not the author of sin, but man himself, who is justly condemned for it, is undoubtedly true, and would you obscure so clear a truth by searching into points beyond human reach, if not unsound, as you conclude them.

The four-and-twentieth excuse: But at least those learned divines among us that doubt of this, do yet say that the will is necessarily and infallibly determined by the practical understanding, and that is as much irresistibly necessitated by objects; and therefore whatever act was done by my understanding or will, was thus necessitated, and I could not help it. They say, liberty is but the acting of the faculty agreeably to its nature; and it was God, as Creator, that gave Adam his faculties, and God, by providential dispose, that presented all objects to him, by which his understanding, and so his will, were unavoidably necessitated.

Answ. This is of the same nature with the former, uncertain, if not certainly false. Were this true, for aught we can see, it would lay all the sin and misery of this world on God, as the irresistible, necessitating cause, which because we know infallibly to be false, we have no reason to take such principles to be true which infer it. The understanding doth not by a necessary efficiency, determine the will, but morally; or rather, is regularly a condition, or necessary antecedent, without which it may not determine itself. Yea, the will, by commanding the sense and fantasy, doth much to determine the understanding. As the eye is not necessary to my going, but to my going right, so is not the understanding's guidance necessary to my willing, (there the simple apprehension may suffice,) but to my right willing. There are other ways of determining the will. Or, if the understanding did determine the will, efficiently and necessarily, it is not every act of the understanding that must do it. If it be so when it saith, This *must* be done, and saith importunately, yet not when it only saith, This may be done, or you may venture on it, which is the common part which it hath in sin.

I am not pleased that these curious objections fall in the way, nor do I delight to put them into vulgar heads; but finding many young scholars, and others that have conversed with them, assaulted with these temptations, I thought meet to give a touch, and but a touch, to take them out of their way, as Mr. Fenner hath done more fully in the preface to his "Hidden Manna," on this last point, to which I refer you. I only add this:

The will of man in its very dominion doth bear God's image. It is a self-determining power, though it be biassed by habits, and needs a guide. As the heart and vital spirits by which it acteth are to the rest of the body, so is it to the soul. The light of nature hath taught all the world to carry the guilt of every crime to the will of man, and there to leave it. Upon this all laws and judgments are grounded. From ignorance and intellectual weakness, men commonly fetch excuses for their faults, but from the will they are aggravated. If we think it strange that man's will should be the first cause, so much as of a sinful mode, and answer all occurring objections, it may suffice that we are certain the Holy Majesty is not the author of sin; and he is able to make all this as plain as the sun, and easily answer all these vain excuses, though we should be unable: and if we be much ignorant of the frame and motions of our own souls, and especially of that high, self-determining principle, free-will, the great spring of our actions, and the curious engine by which God doth sapiently govern the world, it is no wonder, considering that the soul can know itself but by reflection, and God gave us a soul to use, rather than to know itself, and to know its qualities and operations, rather than its essence.

The five-and-twentieth excuse: No man can be saved, nor avoid any sin, nor believe in Christ, but those whom God hath predestinated thereto. I was under an irreversible sentence before I was born, and therefore I do nothing but what I was predestinated to do; and if God decreed not to save me, how could I help it?

Answ. 1. God's judgments are more plain, but his decrees or secret purposes are mysterious; and to darken certainties by having recourse to points obscure, is no part of christian wisdom. God told you your duty in his word, and on what terms you must be judged to life or death; hither should you have recourse for direction, and not to the unsearchable mysteries of his mind.

2. God decreeth not to condemn any but for sin. Sin, I say, is the cause of that condemnation, though not of his decree.

3. God's decrees are acts immanent in himself, and make no change on you, and therefore do not necessitate you to sin, any more than his foreknowledge doth. For both cause only a necessity of consequence which is logical, as the divines on both sides do confess. And therefore this no more caused you to sin, than if there had been no such decree. And it is a doubt whether that decree be not negative, a willing suspending of the divine will, as to evil, or at most a purpose to permit it.

The sixth-and-twentieth excuse: If it be no more, yet doth it make my perdition unavoidable, for even God's foreknowledge doth so; for if he foreknow it, all the world cannot hinder it from coming to pass.

Answ. Must God either be ignorant of what you will do, or else be the cause of it? You foreknow that the sun will rise to-morrow, that doth not cause it to rise. If you foreknow that one man will murder another, you are not the cause of it by foreknowing it. So is it here.

The seven-and-twentieth excuse: God might have hindered my sin and damnation if he would.

Answ. And will you wilfully sin, and think to

escape, because God doth not hinder you? The prince that makes a law against the murder, could lock you up, and keep you from being a murderer. But are you excusable if he do not? We are certain that God could have hindered all the sin, and death, and confusion, and misery that is in the world, and we are as certain that he doth not hinder it but by forbidding it, and giving men means against it; and we are certain that he is just, and good, and wise in all, and not bound to hinder it, and what his reasons are you may better know hereafter. In the mean time, you had better have looked to your own duty.

The eight-and-twentieth excuse: How could I be saved if Christ did not die for me? He died but for his elect, and none could be saved without his death.

Answ. He did die for you, and for more than his elect, though he absolutely purposed only their salvation. Your sins crucified him, and your debt lay upon him, and he so far ransomed you, that nothing but your wilful refusal of the benefits could have condemned you.

The nine-and-twentieth excuse: It was Adam's sin that brought me into this depravedness of will, which I can neither cure, nor could prevent.

Answ. 1. If Adam cast away his holiness, he could no more convey that to us which he cast away, than a nobleman that is a traitor can convey his lost inheritance or honours to his son.

2. You perish, not only for your original sin, but for rejecting the recovering mercy of the Redeemer. You might have had Christ and life in him for the accepting.

The thirtieth excuse: God will require no more than he gives. He gave me not grace to repent and believe, and without his gift I could not have it.

Answ. 1. God will justly require more than he giveth, that is, the improvement of his gifts, as Matt. xxv. shows. He gave Adam but a power to persevere, and not actual perseverance, yet did he justly punish him for want of the act, even for not using by his own will the power which he had given him.

2. It is long of yourself if God did not give you grace to believe; it was because you wilfully refused some preparatory grace. Christ found you at a great distance from him, and he gave you grace sufficient to have brought you nearer to him than you were; you had grace sufficient to have made you better than you were, and restrained many sins, and brought you to the means, when you turned your back on them. Though this were not sufficient to cause you to believe, it was sufficient to have brought you nearer to believing, and through your own wilfulness became not effectual; even as Adam had sufficient grace to have stood, which was not effectual. So that you had not only Christ offered to you, if you would but accept him, but you had daily and precious helps and means to have cured your wills, and caused you to accept him, for neglect of which, and so for not believing, and so for all your other sins, you justly perish.

The one-and-thirtieth excuse: Alas! man is a worm, a dry leaf, (Job xiii. 25,) a silly, foolish creature, and therefore his actions be not regardable, nor deserve so great a punishment.

Answ. Though he be a worm, and as nothing to God, and foolish by sin, yet he is naturally so noble a creature, that the image of God was on him, Gen. xii. 26, and v. i; James iii. 9; and the world made his servants, and angels his attendants, Heb. i. 14. So noble, that Christ died for him, God takes special care of him; he is capable of knowing and enjoying God, and heaven is not thought too good for him if he will obey. And he that is capable of so great good, must be capable of as great evil, and his ways not to be so overlooked by that God that hath undertaken to be his governor. When it tendeth to infidelity, the devil will teach you to debase man, even lower than God would do.

The two-and-thirtieth excuse: Sin is no being; and shall men be damned for that which is nothing?

Answ. 1. It is such a mode as deformeth God's creature. It is a moral being; it is a relation of our actions and hearts to God's will and law.

2. They that say sin is nothing, say pain and loss are nothing too. You shall, therefore, be paid with one nothing for another. Make light of your misery, and say it is nothing, as you did of your sin.

3. Will you take this for a good excuse from your children or servants if they abuse you? or, from a thief or a murderer? Shall he escape by telling the judge that his sin was nothing? or, rather have death, which is nothing, as the just reward of it?

The three-and-thirtieth excuse: But sin is a transient thing; at least it doth God no harm, and therefore why should he do us so much harm for it?

Answ. 1. It hurts not God, because he is above hurt. No thanks to you if he be out of your reach.

2. You may wrong him, when you cannot hurt him; and the wrong deserves as much as you can bear. If a traitor endeavour the death of the prince in vain, his endeavour deserves death, though he never hurt him. You despise God's law and authority; you cause the blaspheming of his name, Rom. ii. 24; he calls it a pressing him as a cart is pressed with sheaves, (Amos ii. 13,) and a grieving of him.

3. And you wrong his image, his church, the public good, and the souls of others.

The four-and-thirtieth excuse: But God's nature is so good and merciful, that sure he will not damn his own creature.

Answ. 1. A merciful judge will hang a man for a fault against man; by proportion, then, what is due for sin against God?

2. All the death and calamity which you see in the world, comes from the anger of this merciful God; why, then, may not future misery come from it?

3. God knoweth his own mercy better than you do; and he hath told you how far it shall extend.

4. He is infinitely merciful; but it is to the heirs of mercy, not to the final rejecters of his mercy.

5. Hath not God been merciful to thee in bearing with thee so long, and offering thee grace in the blood of Christ till thou didst wilfully reject it? Thou wilt confess, to thy everlasting woe, that God was merciful; had he not been so merciful, thou wouldst not have been so miserable for rejecting it.

The five-and-thirtieth excuse: I would not so torment mine enemy myself.

Answ. No reason you should. Is it all one to wrong you, and to wrong the God of heaven? God is the only judge of his own wrongs.

The six-and-thirtieth excuse: All men are sinners, and I was but a sinner.

Answ. All were not impenitent, unbelieving, rebellious sinners, and therefore all are not unpardoned, condemned sinners. All did not live after the flesh, and refuse to the last to be converted, as you did. God will teach you better to difference between sinners and sinners.

The seven-and-thirtieth excuse: But if Christ have satisfied for my sins, and died for me, then how can I justly suffer for the same sins? will God punish one sin twice?

Answ. 1. Christ suffered for man in the nature of man, but not in your person, nor you in him. It was not you that provided the price, but God himself; Christ was not man's delegate in satisfying, and therefore received not his instructions from us, nor did it on our terms, but his own. It was not the same thing which the law threatened that Christ underwent; for that was the damnation of the sinner himself, and not the suffering of another for him; it cannot therefore be yours, but on Christ's own terms. He died for thy sin, but with this intent, that for all that, if thou refuse him, thou shalt die thyself. It is therefore no wrong to thee to die, for it was not thou that diedst before: and Christ will take it for no wrong to him; for he will judge thee to that death. It is for refusing a Christ that died for thee that thou must perish for ever.

The eight-and-thirtieth excuse: But I did not refuse Christ: I believed and trusted in him to the last; and repented for my sins, though I sometimes was overtaken with them.

Answ. Had this been true, thy sin would not have condemned thee: but there is no mocking God; he will show thee then thy naked heart, and convince thousands that thought they believed and repented, that indeed they did not. By thy works, also, will this be discovered, that is, by the main bent and scope of thy life, as Matt. xxv. throughout, and James ii.

The nine-and-thirtieth excuse: I did many good works; and I hope God will set those against my evil works.

Answ. Thy good works were thy sins, because, indeed, they were not good, being not done in sincerity of heart for God. The best man's works have some infirmity, which nothing can cleanse but the blood of Christ, which thou hast made light of, and therefore hast no part in. If all thy life had been spent in perfect works except one day, they would not make satisfaction for the sins of that day, for they are but part of thy duty. Woe to him that hath no better a saviour at judgment than his own good works!

The fortieth excuse: I have lived in poverty and misery on earth, and therefore I hope I have had my suffering here, and shall not suffer in this world and another too.

Answ. 1. By that rule all poor men, and murderers and thieves that are tormented and hanged, should be saved. But as godliness hath the promise of this life, and that to come, so impenitency and wickedness hath the threatening of this life and that to come.

2. The devils and the damned have suffered much more than you already, and yet they are never the nearer a deliverance. When thou hast suffered ten thousand years, thy pain will be never the nearer an end. How, then, can a little misery on earth prevent it? Alas! poor soul, these are but the foretastes and beginnings of thy sorrow. Nothing but pardon through the blood of Christ could have prevented thy condemnation; and that thou rejectest by infidelity and impenitency. His sufferings would have saved thee if thou hadst not refused him, but all thy own sufferings will yield thee no relief.

So much for the answering of the vain excuses which poor sinners are ready to make for themselves, wherein I have been so large, as that this part, I confess, is disproportionable to the rest: but it was for these two reasons.

1. That poor careless souls might see the vanity of such defences: and consider, if such a worm as I can easily confute them, how easily and how terribly will they be all answered by their Judge!

2. I did it the rather, that godly christians might the better understand how to deal with these vain excuses when they meet with them, which will be daily, if they deal with men in this sad condition.

X. We have done with that part of the judgment which consisteth in the exploration or trial of the cause. We now come to that which is the conclusion and consummation of all; and that is, to show you what the sentence will be, and on whom.

And for this we must go straight to the word of God for our light, it being impossible for any man to have any particular knowledge of it, if Christ had not there revealed it unto us. Indeed, almost all the world do acknowledge a life after this, where it shall go well with the good, and ill with the bad. But who shall be then accounted righteous, and who unrighteous, and on what terms and grounds, by whom they shall be judged, and to what condition, they know not.

The sentence in judgment will be, 1. Either on those that never had means to know Christ; 2. Or on those that had.

1. For the former, as it less concerneth us to inquire of their case, so it is more obscurely revealed to us in the Scripture. It is certain that they shall be judged according to their use of the means which they had, (Rom. ii. 11—16,) and the talents which they received, Matt. xxv. But that it falleth out that he that hath but the one talent of natural helps doth improve it to salvation; or that ever they, who knew not Christ, are justified and saved without that knowledge, (being at age and use of reason,) I find not in the Scriptures. I find, indeed, that as many as have sinned without law, shall also perish without law; and as many as have sinned in the law, shall be judged by the law, Rom. ii. 12. But not that any that are justified by the works of nature, such as are here said to be without law. I find also that "they have the work of the law written in their hearts, their conscience also bearing witness, and their thoughts the mean while accusing, or else excusing, one another; in the day when God shall judge the secrets of men by Jesus Christ according to the gospel," Rom. ii. 15, 16. And I believe it is a just excuse, and not an unjust, which is here meant. But it will be but an excuse so far as they were guiltless; and that will be but *in tanto*, and not *in toto*, in part only, and so not a full justification. A heathen's conscience may excuse him from those sins which he was never guilty of, but not from all. But no more of them.

2. The case of those who have had the gospel is more plainly opened to us in God's word. Their sentence is opened in many places of Scripture, but most fully in Matt. xxv. whence we will now collect it.

There we find that Jesus Christ, the Redeemer, as King of the world, shall sit in judgment on all men at the last, and shall separate them one from another as a shepherd divideth his sheep from the goats, and so shall pass the final sentence. This sentence is two-fold, according to the different condition of them that are judged. To them on the right hand there is a sentence of justification, and adjudication to everlasting glory; to them on the left hand there is a sentence of condemnation to everlasting punishment.

The sentence on each of these containeth both the state which they are judged to, and the reason or cause of the judgment to that state: for as God will not judge any to life or death without just cause, so he will publish this cause in his sentence, as it is the manner of judges to do; if you say, Christ will not use a voice, let it satisfy that though we know not the manner, yet if he do it but by mental discovery, as he shows men what shall everlastingly befall them, so he will show them why it shall so befall them.

1. The sentence on them on the right hand will contain, 1. Their justification, and adjudication to

blessedness, and that both as generally denominated, and as particularly determined and described. 2. And the cause of this judgment. 1. In general they shall be pronounced blessed; Satan would have had them cursed and miserable. The law did curse them to misery; many a fearful thought hath possessed their own breasts, lest they should prove at last accursed and miserable: but now they hear the contrary from their Judge. All the promises in the gospel could not perfectly overcome those their fears; all the comfortable words of the ministers of the gospel could not perfectly subdue them; all the tender mercies of God in Christ did not perfectly subdue them; but now they are vanquished all for ever. He that once had heard his Redeemer in judgment call him "blessed," will never fear being cursed more; for he that Christ blesseth, shall be blessed indeed.

The description of their blessedness followeth, "Come, inherit the kingdom prepared for you from the foundation of the world:" and also they are called "blessed of the Father." Here is the fountain of their blessedness—the Father, and the state of their blessedness in being the Father's; for I suppose they are called "the blessed of the Father," both because the Father blessed them, that is, makes them happy, and because these blessed ones are the Father's own: and so Christ will publish it to the world in judgment, that he came to glorify the Father, and will proclaim him the principal efficient, and ultimate end of his work of redemption, and the blessedness of his saints; and that himself is, as Mediator, but the way to the Father. It is the Father that "prepared" the kingdom for them, and "from the foundation of the world" prepared it; both for them, as chosen ones, and for them as future believers and righteous ones. It is called a kingdom, partly in respect to God, the King, in whose glory we shall partake in our places; and partly metaphorically, from the dignity of our condition. For so it is that ourselves are said to be made kings, (Rev. i. 6; v. 1; 1 Pet. ii. 9,) and not that we are properly kings, for then we must have subjects who must be governed by us.

Thus we see their blessedness in the fountain, end, and state of dignity. As to the receptive act on their part, it is expressed by two words; one signifying their first entrance on it—"come," the other their possession—"inherit;" that is, possess it as given by the Father, and redeemed by the Son, and hold it in this tenure for ever.

The true believer was convinced in this life that, indeed, there was no true blessedness but this enjoyment of God in the kingdom of heaven. The Lord revealed this to his heart by his word and Spirit; and therefore he contemned the seeming happiness on earth, and laid up for himself a treasure in heaven, and made him friends with the mammon of unrighteousness, and ventured all his hope in this vessel. And now he findeth the wisdom of that choice in a rich return. God made him so wise a merchant as to sell all for this pearl of greatest price, and therefore now he shall find the gain. As there is no other true happiness but God in glory, so is there nothing more suitable and welcome to the true believer. Oh! how welcome will the face of that God be, whom he loved, whom he sought, whom he longed and waited for! How welcome will that kingdom be which he lived in hope of; which he parted with all for, and suffered for in the flesh! How glad will he be to see the blessed face of his Redeemer, who, by his manifold grace, hath brought him unto this! I leave the believing soul to think of it, and to make it the daily matter of his delightful meditation; what an unconceivable joy, in one moment, this sentence of Christ will fill his soul with undoubtedly, it is now quite past our comprehensions, though our imperfect forethoughts of it may well make our lives a continual feast.

Were it but our justification from the accusations of Satan, who would have us condemned either as sinners in general, or as impenitent, unbelieving rebels against him that redeemed us in special, it would lift up the heads of the saints in that day. After all the fears of our own hearts, and the slanderous accusations of Satan and the world, that we were either impenitent infidels, or hypocrites, Christ will then justify us, and pronounce us righteous. So much for the condition to which they are judged.

2. The reason or cause of this justification of the saints is given us both, 1. In a general denomination, and, 2. In a particular description. 1. In general, it is because they were righteous, as is evident, Matt. xxv. 46, "The righteous shall go into life everlasting." And, indeed, it is the business of every just judge to justify the righteous, and condemn the unrighteous: and shall not the Judge of all the earth judge righteously? Gen. xviii. 25. God makes men righteous before he judges them so, and judgeth them righteous because they are so. He that abominateth that man who saith to the righteous, Thou art wicked, or to the wicked, Thou art righteous, who justifieth the wicked, and condemneth the righteous, will certainly never do so himself.

Indeed, he will justify them who are sinners, but not against the accusation that they are sinners, but against the accusation that they are guilty of punishment for sin: but that is because he first made them just, and so justifiable, by pardoning their sin through the blood of Christ.

And it is true also that he will justify those that were wicked, but not those that are wicked: but judgment findeth them as death leaveth them; and he will not take them for wicked who are sanctified and cleansed of their former wickedness. So that Christ will first pardon them before he justify them against the charge of being sinners in general; and he will first give men faith, repentance, and new obedience, before he will justify them against the charge of being impenitent infidels, or hypocrites, and consequently unpardoned, and doubly guilty of damnation. This two-fold righteousness he will first give men, and so constitute them just, before he will declare it, and sentence them just.

2. The reason of the sentence particularly described, is from their faith and love to Christ, expressed in their obedience, self-denial, and forsaking all for him. "For I was hungry, and ye fed me; I was thirsty, and ye gave me drink; I was a stranger, and ye took me in; naked, and ye clothed me; I was sick, and ye visited me; I was in prison, and ye came to me. Verily, I say unto you, inasmuch as ye have done it to one of the least of these my brethren, ye have done it unto me," Matt. xxv. 35—41. Here is, 1. The causal conjunction "for." 2. And the cause or reason itself.

Concerning both which observe, 1. How it is that man's obedience and self-denial is the reason and cause of his justification. 2. Why it is that God will have the reason of cause thus declared in the sentence.

For the first, observe that it is one thing to give a reason of the sentence, and another thing to express the cause of the benefit given us by the promise, and judged to us by the sentence. Man's obedience was no proper cause why God did, in this life, give pardon of sin to us, or a right to glory; much less of his giving Christ to die for us: and therefore, as to our constitutive justification at our conversion, we must not say or think that God doth justify us, for, or because of, any works of our obedience, legal or evangelical. But when God hath so justified us, when he comes to give a reason of his sentence in judgment, he may and will fetch that reason partly from our obedience, or our performance of the conditions of the new covenant: for, as in this life, we had a righteousness consisting in free pardon of all sin through the blood of Christ, and a righteousness consisting in our personal performance of the conditions of the promise which giveth that pardon, and continueth it to us, so at judgment we shall accordingly be justified. And as our evangelical personal righteousness, commonly called inherent, was at first only in our faith and repentance, and disposition to obey; but afterwards in our actual sincere obedience, in which sense we are constitutively justified, or made righteous here by our works, in James's sense, James ii. 24; so, accordingly, a double reason will be assigned of our sentential justification; one from our pardon by Christ's blood and merits, which will prove our right to impunity and to glory, the other from our own faith and holy obedience, which will prove our right to that pardon through Christ, and to the free gift of a right to glory: and so this last is to be pleaded in subordination to the former, for Christ is become the author of eternal salvation to all them that obey him, Heb. v. 9. He, therefore, that will be saved, must have a Christ to save him as the author, and an obedience to that Christ as the condition of that salvation; and consequently both must be declared in the judgment.

The reason why the Judge doth mention our good works, rather than our believing, may be because those holy, self-denying expressions of faith and love to Christ do contain or certainly imply faith in them, as the life of the tree is in the fruit; but faith doth contain our works of obedience but only as their cause. These works also are a part of the personal righteousness which is to be inquired after; that is, we shall not be judged righteous merely because we have believed, but also because we have added to our faith virtue, and have improved our talents, and have loved Christ to the hazard of all for his sake: for it is not only, or principally, for the goodness of the work considered in itself, or the good that is done by it to the poor; but it is as these works did express our faith and love to Christ by doing him the most costly and hazardous service; that by faith we could see Christ in a poor beggar, or a prisoner; and could love Christ in these better than our worldly goods or liberties, which we must part with, or hazard by the works that are here mentioned.

2. The reasons why Christ will so publicly declare the personal righteousness of men to be the reason or cause of his justifying sentence, are because it is the business of that day, not only to glorify God's mere love and mercy, but eminently to glorify his remunerative justice; and not only to express his love to the elect as such, but to express his love to them as faithful and obedient, and such as have denied all for Christ, and loved God above all; and to show his justice to the men, and faithfulness in fulfilling all his promises, and also his holiness in the high estimation of the holiness of his people. I shall express this in the words of a learned divine: (Dr. Twiss against Mr. Cotton, page 40:) "Was there no more in God's intention when he elected some, than the manifestation of the riches of his glorious grace? Did not God purpose also to manifest the glory of his remunerative justice? Is it not undeniable that God will bestow salvation on all his elect (of ripe years) by way of reward and crown of righteousness, which God the righteous Judge will give? 2 Tim. iv.; 2 Thess. i. It is great pity this is not considered, as usually it is not, especially for the momentous consequence thereof in my judgment." So far he.

So much of the sentence of justification which shall be passed by Christ, at judgment, upon the righteous.

2. We are next to consider of the sentence of condemnation which shall then, by Christ, be passed on the unrighteous; which is delivered to us by Christ, (Matt. xxv.) in the same order as the former.

This sentence containeth, 1. The condemnation itself. 2. The reason or cause of it.

The condemnation expresseth the misery which they are judged to. 1. Generally, in the denomination "cursed." 2. Particularly, by description of their cursed state.

To be cursed, is to be a people destinated and adjudged to utter unhappiness, to all kinds of misery without remedy.

2. Their cursed condition is described in the next words; "Depart from me into everlasting fire, prepared for the devil and his angels."

1. "Depart:" From whom? From the God that made them in his image; from the Redeemer that bought them by the price of his blood, and offered to save them freely for all their unworthiness, and many a time entreated them to accept his offer, that their souls might live; from the Holy Ghost the Sanctifier and Comforter of the faithful, who strove with their hearts, till they quenched and expelled him. Oh! sad departing! Who would not then choose rather to depart from all the friends he had in the world, and from any thing imaginable; from his life, from himself, if it were possible, than from Christ? "Depart:" From what? Why, from the presence of the Judge, from all further hopes of salvation for ever, from all possibility of ever being saved, and living in the joyful inheritance of the righteous. "Depart:" Not from God's essential presence, for that will be with them to their everlasting misery, but from the presence of his grace, in that measure as they enjoyed it. "Depart:" Not from your fleshly pleasures, and honours, and profits of the world; these were all gone and past already, and there was no further need to bid them depart from these. Houses and lands were gone, mirth and recreations were gone, their sweet morsels and cups were gone, all the honour that men could give them was gone, before they were set at Christ's bar to be judged. But from all expectations of ever enjoying these again, or ever tasting their former delights, from these they must depart; not from their sin, for that will go with them. But the liberty of committing that part of it which was sweet to them, as gluttony, drunkenness, whoredom, idleness, and all voluptuousness—from these they must depart. But this is consequential. It is Christ and the possibility of salvation that they are sentenced to depart from.

But whither must they depart? 1. Into fire. 2. Into that fire which was prepared for the devil and his angels. 3. Into everlasting fire.

1. Not into a purifying, but a tormenting fire. Whether elementary or not, whether properly or metaphorically called fire, let us not vainly trouble ourselves to inquire. It is enough to know, that as fire is one of the most grievous tormentors of the flesh, so grievous will be those infernal torments to the whole man, soul and body, such as is most fitly represented to us under the notion of fire, and of burning. It is easy for a secure, unbelieving soul to read and hear of it; but woe, and ten thousand woes, to them that must endure it! In this life they had their good

things, when it went harder as to the flesh with better men; but now they are tormented, when the godly are comforted, Luke xvi. 25.

2. But why is it called "a fire prepared for the devil and his angels?" 1. What is this devil that hath angels? 2. Who are his angels? 3. When was it prepared for them? 4. Was it not also prepared for wicked men? To these in order.

1. It seems by many passages in Scripture that there is an order among spirits, both good and bad; and that there is one devil, who is the prince over the rest.

2. It seems, therefore, that it is the rest of the evil spirits that are called "his angels." And some think that the wicked who served him in this life shall be numbered with his angels in the life to come. Indeed, the apostle calls him "the god of this world," (2 Cor. iv. 4,) as is ordinarily judged by expositors; and "the prince of the power of the air, the spirit that now worketh in the children of disobedience," Eph. ii. 2; and he calleth false, seducing teachers, "the ministers of Satan," 2 Cor. xi. 15: but that wicked men are here meant as part of his angels is not clear.

3. If it be the preparation of God's purpose that is here meant, then it was from eternity; but if it be any commination of God as ruler of the angels, then was this fire prepared for them conditionally, from the beginning of that commination, and was due to them at their fall.

4. It seems that the reason why here is no mention of preparing hell-fire for the wicked, but only the devils, is not because, indeed, it was not prepared also for the wicked; but to note that it is the torment which was first prepared for, or assigned to, the devils; thereby showing the greatness of the misery of the wicked, that the devil and his angels must be their companions. Though some think, as is said before, that the reason why wicked men are not mentioned here, is because they are part of the angels of the devil, and so included. And some think it is purposely to manifest God's general love to mankind, that prepared not hell for them, but they cast themselves into the hell prepared for the devils. But the first seems to be the true sense.

And how apparently righteous are the judgments of the Lord! that those men who would here entertain the devil into their hearts and daily familiarity, should be then entertained by him into his place of torments, and there remain for ever in his society! Though few entertained him into visible familiarity with their bodies, as witches do, who so make him their familiar, yet all wicked men do entertain him in a more full and constant familiarity with their souls than these witches do with their bodies. How familiar is he in their thoughts, to fill them with vanity, lust, or revenge! How familiar is he in their hearts, to fill them with covetousness, malice, pride, or the like evils; and to banish all thoughts of returning to God, and to quench every motion that tendeth to their recovery! How familiar is he with them, even when they seem to be worshipping God in the public assemblies, stealing the word out of their hearts, filling them with vain and wandering thoughts, blinding their minds that they cannot understand the plainest words which we are able to speak to them, and filling them with a proud rebellion against the direction of their teachers, and an obstinate refusal to be ruled by them, be the matter never so necessary to their own salvation! How familiar are these evil spirits in their houses, filling them with ignorance, worldliness, and ungodliness, and turning out God's service, so that they do not pray together once in a day, or perhaps at all! How familiarly doth Satan use their tongues, in cursing, swearing, lying, ribaldry, backbiting, or slandering! And is it not just with God to make these fiends their familiars in torment, with whom they entertained such familiarity in sin? As Christ, with all the blessed angels and saints, will make but one kingdom or family, and shall live all together in perpetual delights; so the devil and all his hellish angels and wicked men shall make but one household, and shall live all together in perpetual misery. O poor sinners! you are not troubled now at his presence and power in your hearts; but will you not then be troubled at his presence and tormenting power? As long as you do not see him, let him do what he will with you, it grieves you little or nothing at all; but what will you say when you must see him, and abide with him for ever? O sirs, his name is easily heard, but his company will be terrible to the stoutest heart alive. He showeth you a smiling face when he tempteth you, but he hath a grimmer face to show you when temptations have conquered you, and torments must succeed. As those who write of witches say, he appeareth at first to them in some comely, tempting shape, till he have them fast tied to him, and then he beats them, and affrights them, and seldom appears to them but in some ugly hue. Believe it, poor sinners, you do not hear or see the worst of him when you are merry about your sinful pleasures, and rejoicing in your hopes of the commodities or preferments of the world. He hath another kind of voice which you must hear, and another face to show you, that will make you know a little better whom you had to do with! You would be afraid now to meet him in the dark. What will it be to live with him in everlasting darkness? Then you will know who it was that you entertained and obeyed, and played with in your sins.

3. And as the text tells us, that it is "a fire prepared for the devil and his angels," so it telleth us that it is "an everlasting fire." It had a beginning, but it shall have no end. If these wretches would have chosen the service of God, they would have met with no difficulty or trouble, but what would have had a speedy end. Poverty and injuries would have had an end; scorns and abuses would have had an end; fasting, humiliation, sorrow for sin, watching, and fighting against our spiritual enemies, would all have had an end. But to avoid these, they chose that ease, that pleasure, which hath brought them to that torment which never will have end. I have said so much of these things already in my book called "The Saints' Rest," that I will now say but this much. It is one of the wonders of the world how men who do believe, or think they do believe, this word of Christ to be true, that "the wicked shall go into everlasting fire," can yet venture on sin so boldly, and live in it so fearlessly, or sleep quietly, till they are out of this unspeakable danger. Only the commonness of it, and the known wickedness of man's heart, doth make this less wonderful: and were there nothing else to convince us that sinners are mad, and dead as to spiritual things, this were enough, that ever the greatest pleasures or profits of the world, or the most enticing baits which the devil can offer them, should once prevail with them to forget these endless things, and draw them to reject an everlasting glory, and cast themselves desperately into everlasting fire; yea, and all this, under daily warnings and instructions, and when it is told them beforehand by the God of truth himself! For the Lord's sake, sirs, and for your souls' sakes, if you care not what ministers say, or what such as I say, yet will you soberly read now and then this twenty-fifth chapter of Matthew, and

regard what is told you by him that must be your Judge? and now and then bethink yourselves, soberly, whether these are matters for wise men to make light of; and what it is to be everlastingly in heaven or in hell-fire?

2. We have seen what is the penalty contained in the sentence against the ungodly; the next thing that the text directs us to is the cause or reason of the sentence, verse 42, "For I was hungry, and ye gave me no meat," &c. The reason is not given expressly either for their sin against the law of works, that is, because they were sinners, and not perfectly innocent, nor yet from their unbelief, which is the great sin against the law of grace; but it is given from their not expressing their faith and love to Christ in works of mercy and self-denial. And why is this so?

1. We must not suppose that these words of Christ do express the whole judicial process in every point, but the chief parts. It is supposed that all men are convicted of being sinners against the perfect law of the Creator, and that they are guilty of death for that sin, and that there is no way but by Christ to obtain deliverance. But because all this must be acknowledged by the righteous themselves, as well as by the wicked, therefore Christ doth not mention this, but that only which is the turning point or cause in the judgment. For it is not all sinners that shall be finally condemned, but all impenitent, unbelieving sinners, who have rebelled finally against their Redeemer.

2. And the reason why faith itself is not expressed, is, 1. Because it is clearly implied, and so is love to Christ as Redeemer, in that they should have relieved Christ himself in his members; that is, as it is expressed in Matt. x. 42, they should have received a prophet in the name of a prophet, and a disciple in the name of a disciple; all should be done for Christ's sake, which could not be unless they believed in him, and loved him. 2. Also because that the bare act of believing is not all that Christ requireth to man's final justification and salvation, but holy, self-denying obedience must be added; and therefore this is given as the reason of their condemnation, that they did not so obey.

We must observe, also, that Christ here putteth the special for the general; that is, one way of self-denying obedience, and expression of love, instead of such obedience in general. For all men have not ability to relieve those in misery, being perhaps some of them poor themselves; but all have that love and self-denial which will some way express itself, and all have hearts and a disposition to do thus, if they had ability; without such a disposition, none can be saved.

It is the fond conceit of some, that if they have any love to the godly, or wish them well, it is enough to prove them happy. But Christ here purposely lets us know that whoever doth not love him at so high a rate as that he can part with his substance, or any thing in the world, to those uses which he shall require them, even to relieve his servants in want and sufferings for the Master's sake, that man is none of Christ's disciples, nor will be owned by him at the last.

XI. The next point that we come to, is to show you the properties of this sentence at judgment.

When man had broken the law of his Creator at the first, he was liable to the sentence of death, and God presently sat in judgment on him, and sentenced him to some part of the punishment which he had deserved; but upon the interposition of the Son, he before the rest resolved on a way that might tend to his recovery, and death is due yet to every sinner for every sin which he commits, till a pardon do acquit him. But this sentence, which will pass on sinners at the last judgment, doth much differ from that which was passed on the first sin, or which is due according to the law of works alone; for,

1. As to the penalty called the pain of loss, the first judgment did deprive man of the favour of his Creator, but the second will deprive him of the favour both of the Creator and Redeemer: the first judgment deprived him of the benefits of innocency; the second deprives him of the benefits of redemption, the loss of his hopes, and possibility of a pardon, of the Spirit of justification and adoption, and of the benefits which conditionally were promised and offered him. These are the punishments of the last judgment, which the law of works did never threaten to the first man, or to any, as it stood alone.

Also the loss of glory as recovered, is the proper penalty of the violated law of grace, which is more than the first loss. As if a man should lose his purse the second time, when another hath once found it for him; or rather, as if a traitor redeemed by another, and having his life and honours offered him if he will thankfully accept it and come in, should by his refusal and obstinacy lose this recovered life which is offered him, which is an addition to his former penalty.

Besides, that the higher degree of glory will be lost, which Christ would bestow on him, more than was lost at first. The very work of the saints in heaven will be to praise and glorify him that redeemed them, and the Father in him, which would not have been the work of man if he had been innocent.

2. As to the pain of sense, the last judgment by the Redeemer will sentence them to a far sorer punishment than would have befallen them if no Saviour had been offered them, Heb. x. 29. The conscience of Adam, if he had not been redeemed, would never have tormented him for rejecting a Redeemer, nor for refusing or abusing his gracious offers and his mercies; nor for the forfeiting of a recovered happiness; nor for refusing the easy terms of the gospel, which would have given him Christ and salvation for the accepting; nor for neglecting any means that tended to recovery; no, nor for refusing repentance unto life, nor for disobeying a Redeemer that bought him by his blood. As all these are the penalties of the Redeemer's law and judgment, so is it a sorer penalty than conscience would have inflicted merely for not being perfectly innocent, and they will be far sorer gripings and gnawings of the never-dying worm for the abuse of these talents, than if we had never been trusted with any after our first forfeiture. Yea, and God himself will accordingly proportion his punishments. So that you see that privatively and positively, or as to their loss and their feeling, the Redeemer will pass on them a heavier doom than the Creator did, or would have done, according to the first law to perfect man.

3. Another property of the judgment of Christ is, that it will be final, peremptory, and excluding all further hopes or possibilities of a remedy. So was not the first judgment of the Creator upon fallen man. Though the law of pure nature knew no remedy, nor gave man any hope of a Redeemer, yet did it not exclude a remedy, nor put any bar against one, but God was free to recover his creature if he pleased. But in the law of grace he hath resolved that there shall be no more sacrifice for sin, but a fearfu' looking-for of judgment and fire which shall devour the adversary, Heb. x. 26, 27; and that the fire shall be everlasting, the worm shall not die, and the fire shall not be quenched, Matt. xxv. 46; xiii. 42, 50; John v. 27; Matt. v. 26; iii. 12;

Luke iii. 17; Mark ix. 43—48. He that now breaketh that pure law that requireth perfect innocency, (as we have all done,) may fly to the promise of grace in Christ, and appeal to the law of liberty, or deliverance, to be judged by that; but he that falls under the penalty of that law which should have saved him, as all final unbelievers and impenitent, ungodly persons do, hath no other to appeal to. Christ would have been a sanctuary and refuge to thee from the law of works, hadst thou but come in to him; but who shall be a refuge to thee from the wrath of Christ? The gospel would have freed thee from the curse of the law of works, if thou hadst but believed and obeyed it; but what shall free thee from the condemnation of the gospel? Had there no accusation lain against thee, but that thou wast in general a sinner, that is, that thou wast not perfectly innocent, Christ would have answered that charge by his blood. But seeing thou art also guilty of those special sins which he never shed his blood for, who shall deliver thee from that accusation? When Christ gave himself a ransom for sinners, it was with this resolution, both in the Father and himself, that none should ever be pardoned, justified, or saved by that ransom that did not, in time of this life, sincerely return to God by faith in the Redeemer, and live in sincere obedience to him, and persevering herein. So that he plainly excepted final infidelity, impenitency, and rebellion from pardon; he never died for the final non-performance of the conditions of the new covenant, so that his judgment for these will be peremptory and remediless. If you say, Why cannot God find out a remedy for this sin as well as he did for the first? I say, God cannot lie, Tit. i. 2. He must be true and faithful, as necessarily as he must be God, because of the absolute perfection of his nature, and he hath said and resolved that there shall be no more remedy.

Many other properties of God's judgment general there are, as righteousness, impartiality, inflexibility, and the like; which, because I would not make my discourse too long, I will pass over, contenting myself with the mention of these which are proper to the judgment of the Redeemer, according to his own laws in special.

XII. The twelfth and last thing which I promised to unfold, is the execution of this judgment. Here I should show you both the certainty of the execution, and by whom it will be, and how; but having done all this already in the third part of the aforesaid Book of Rest, I shall now only give this brief touch of it.

No sooner is the dreadful sentence passed, "Go, ye cursed, into everlasting fire," but away they must be gone; there is no delay, much less any reprieve to be expected, and yet much less is there any hope of an escape. If the Judge once say, Take him, gaoler, and if Christ say, Take him, devils, you that ruled and deceived him, now torment him, all the world cannot rescue one such soul. It will be in vain to look about for help. Alas! there is none but Christ can help you, and he will not, because you refused his help. Nay, we may say he cannot, not for want of power, but because he is true and just, and therefore will make good that word which you believed not. It is in vain then to cry to hills to fall on you, and the mountains to cover you from the presence of him that sitteth on the throne. It will be then in vain now to repent, and wish you had not slighted your salvation, nor sold it for little pleasure to your flesh. It will be then in vain to cry, Lord, Lord, open to us; O spare us; O pity us; O do not cast us into these hideous flames! Do not turn us among devils! Do not torment thy redeemed ones in this fire! All this will then be too late.

Poor sinner, whoever thou art that readest or hearest these lines, I beseech thee, in compassion to thy soul, consider how fearful the case of that man will be that is newly doomed to the everlasting fire, and is haled to the execution without remedy! And what mad-men are those that now do no more to prevent such a misery, when they might do it on such easy terms, and now have so fair an opportunity in their hands!

The time was when repentance might have done thee good, but then all thy repentings be in vain. Now, while the day of thy visitation lasteth, hadst thou but a heart to pray and cry for mercy, in faith and fervency through Christ, thou mightest be heard; but then praying and crying will do no good, shouldst thou roar out in the extremity of thy horror and amazement, and beseech the Lord Jesus but to forgive thee one sin, or to send thee on earth once more, and to try thee once again in the flesh, whether thou wouldst not love him, and lead a holy life, it would be all in vain. Shouldst thou beseech him by all the mercifulness of his nature, by all his sufferings and bloody death, by all the merciful promises of his gospel, it would be all in vain. Nay, shouldst thou beg but one day's reprieval, or to stay one hour before thou were cast into those flames, it would not be heard, it would do thee no good. How earnestly did a deceased gentleman (Luke xvi. 24) beg of Abraham for one drop of water from the tip of Lazarus's finger to cool his tongue, because he was tormented in the flame! And what the better was he? He was sent to remember that he had his good things in this life, and that remembrance would torment him more. And do not wonder or think much at this, that Christ will not then be entreated by the ungodly. You shall then have a Remember, too, from Christ or conscience. He may soon stop thy mouth, and leave thee speechless, and say, Remember, man, that I did one day send thee a message of peace, and thou wouldst not hear it. I once did stoop to beseech thee to return, and thou wouldst not hear. I besought thee by the tender mercies of God, I besought thee by all the love that I had showed thee, by my holy life, by my cursed death, by the riches of my grace, by the offers of my glory, and I could not get thee to forsake the world, to deny the flesh, to leave one beloved sin for all this! I besought thee over and over again, sent many a minister to thee in my name, I waited on thee many a day and year, and all would not do, thou wouldst not consider, return, and live, and now it is too late. My sentence is past, and cannot be recalled. Away from me, thou worker of iniquity, Matt. vii. 22, 23.

Ah sirs, what a case then is the poor desperate sinner left in! How can I write this, or how can you that read or hear it, without trembling once think of the condition that such forlorn wretches will be in! When they look above them, and see the God that hath forsaken them, because they forsook him first; when they look about them, and see the saints on one hand, whom they despised, now sentenced unto glory, and the wicked on the other hand, whom they accompanied and imitated, now judged with them to everlasting misery; when they look below them, and see the flames that they must abide in, even for evermore; and when the devils begin to hale them to the execution; oh! poor souls, now what would they give for a Christ, for a promise, for a time of repentance, for a sermon of mercy, which once they slept under, or made no account of! How is the case altered now with them!

Who would think that these are the same men that made light of all this on earth, that so stoutly scorned the reproofs of the word, that would be worldly, and fleshly, and drunk, and proud, let preachers say what they would, and perhaps hated those that did give them warning. Now they are of another mind, but all too late. Oh, were there any place for resistance, how would they draw back, and lay hold of any thing, before they would be dragged away into those flames! But there is no resisting; Satan's temptations might have been resisted, but his executions cannot; God's judgments might have been prevented by faith and prayer, repentance and a holy life, but they cannot be resisted when they are not prevented. Glad would the miserable sinner be if he might but turn to nothing, and cease to be, or that he might be any thing rather than a reasonable creature; but these wishes are all in vain. There is one time, and one way of a sinner's deliverance; if he fail in that one, he perisheth for ever; all the world cannot help him after that. "I have heard thee in a time accepted, and in a day of salvation have I succoured thee; behold, now is the accepted time; behold, now is the day of salvation," 2 Cor. vi. 2. Now, he saith, "Behold, I stand at the door and knock, if any man hear my voice and open the door, I will come to him, and will sup with him, and he with me," Rev. iii. 20. But for the time to come hereafter, hear what he saith: "Because I have called, and ye refused; I have stretched out my hand, and no man regarded; but ye have set at nought all my counsel, and would none of my reproof: I also will laugh at your calamity; I will mock when your fear cometh; when your fear cometh as desolation, and your destruction cometh as a whirlwind; when distress and anguish cometh upon you. Then shall they call upon me, but I will not answer; they shall seek me early, but they shall not find me: for that they hated knowledge, and did not choose the fear of the Lord: they would none of my counsel: they despised all my reproofs. Therefore shall they eat of the fruit of their own way, and be filled with their own devices. For the turning away of the simple shall slay them, and the prosperity of fools shall destroy them. But whoso hearkeneth unto me shall dwell safely, and shall be quiet from fear of evil," Prov. i. 24—33. I have recited all these words, that you may see and consider whether I have spoke any other thing than God himself hath plainly told you of.

Having said this much of the certainty of the execution, I should next have spoken somewhat of the manner and the instruments, and have showed how God will be for ever the principal cause, and Satan and their own consciences the instruments, in part, and in what manner conscience will do its part, and how impossible it will be to quiet or resist it. But having spoken so much of all this already elsewhere, as is said before, I will forbear here to repeat it, leaving the reader that desireth it there to peruse it.

The uses.—Use 1. Beloved hearers, it was not to fill your fancies with news that God sent me hither this day, nor to tell you of matters that nothing concern you, nor by some terrible words to bring you to an hour's amazement, and no more; but it is to tell you of things that your eyes shall see, and to foretell you of your danger while it may be prevented, that your precious souls may be saved at the last, and you may stand before God with comfort at that day: but because this will not be every man's case, no, nor the case of most, I must, in the name of Christ, desire you to make, this day, an inquiry into your own souls, and, as in the presence of God, let your hearts make answer to these few questions, which I shall propound and debate with you.

Quest. 1. Do you soundly believe this doctrine which I have preached to you? What say you, sirs? Do you believe it as a most certain truth, that you and I, and all the world, must stand at God's bar and be judged to everlasting joy or torment? I hope you do all, in some sort, believe this; but blame me not if I be jealous whether you soundly believe it, while we see in the world so little of the effect of such a belief. I confess I am forced to think that there is more infidelity than faith among us, when I see more ungodliness than godliness among us; and I can hardly believe that man that will say or swear that he believeth these things, and yet liveth as carelessly and carnally as an infidel. I know that no man can love to be damned; yea, I know that every man that hath a reasonable soul hath naturally some love to himself, and a fear of a danger which he verily apprehendeth; he therefore that liveth without all fear, I must think liveth without all apprehension of his danger. Custom hath taught men to hold these things as the opinion of the country; but if men soundly believed them, surely we should see stranger effects of such a faith, than in the most we do see. Doth the sleepy soul that liveth in security, and followeth this world as eagerly as if he had no greater matters to mind; that never once trembled at the thoughts of this great day, nor once asked his own soul in good sadness, My soul, how dost thou think then to escape? I say, doth this man believe that he is going to this judgment? Well, sirs, whether you believe it or not, you will find it true; and believe it you must, before you can be safe. For if you do not believe it, you will never make ready. Let me therefore persuade you in the fear of God to consider that it is a matter of undoubted truth.

1. Consider that it is the express word of the God of truth revealed in Scripture as plainly as you can desire; so that you cannot be unbelieving without denying God's word, or giving him the lie, Matt. xiii. 38—50; xxv. throughout; Rom. ii. 5—10, 16; i. 32. John v. 28, 29, "The hour is coming in which all that are in the graves shall hear his voice, and shall come forth; they that have done good unto the resurrection of life, and they that have done evil unto the resurrection of damnation." "It is appointed to all men once to die, and after this the judgment," Heb. ix. 27. "So then every one of us shall give account of himself to God," Rom. xiv. 9, 12. "And I saw the dead, small and great, stand before God, and the books were opened; and another book was opened, which is the book of life; and the dead were judged out of those things which were written in the books according to their works," Rev. xx. 12. "But I say unto you, that every idle word that men shall speak, they shall give account thereof at the day of judgment; for by thy words thou shalt be justified, and by thy words thou shalt be condemned," Matt. xii. 36, 37. Many more most express texts of Scripture do put the truth of this judgment out of all question to all that believe the Scripture, and will understand it. There is no place left for a controversy in the point. It is made as sure to us as the word of the living God can make it; and he who will question that, what will he believe? What say you, sirs? Dare you doubt of this, which the God of heaven hath so positively affirmed? I hope you dare not.

2. Consider it is a master-part of your faith, if you are christians, and a fundamental article of your creed, that Christ shall come again to judge the quick and the dead: so that you must believe it, or renounce your christianity; and then you renounce Christ, and all the hopes of mercy that you have in him. It is impossible that you should soundly believe in Christ,

and not believe his judgment and life everlasting; because, as he came to bring life and immortality to light in the gospel, (2 Tim. i. 10,) so it was the end of his incarnation, death, and resurrection, to bring you thither; and it is part of his honour and office which he purchased with his blood, to be the Lord and Judge of all the world, Rom. xiv. 9; John v. 22. If, therefore, you believe not heartily this judgment, deal plainly and openly, and say you are infidels, and cast away the hypocritical visor of christianity, and let us know you, and take you as you are.

3. Consider that it is a truth which is known by the very light of nature, that there shall be a happiness for the righteous and a misery for the wicked, after this life; which is evident,

1. In that we have undeniable natural reason for it. 1. God is the righteous Governor of the world, and therefore must make a difference among his subjects, according to the nature of their ways; which we see is not done here, where the wicked prosper and the good are afflicted; therefore it must be hereafter. 2. We see there is a necessity that God should make promises and threatenings of everlasting happiness or misery for the right governing of the world: for we certainly perceive that no lower things will keep men from destroying all human society, and living worse than brute beasts; and if there be a necessity of making such threats and promises, then there is, certainly, a necessity of fulfilling them; for God needeth no lie, or means of deceiving, to rule the world.

2. And as we see it by reason, so by certain experience, that this is discernible by the light of nature; for all the world, or almost all, do believe it. Even those nations where the gospel never came, and have nothing but what they have by nature, even the most barbarous Indians, acknowledge some life after this, and a difference of men according as they are here. Therefore you must believe thus much, or renounce your common reason and humanity, as well as your christianity. Let me, therefore, persuade you all, in the fear of God, to confirm your souls in the belief of this, as if you had heard Christ or an angel from heaven say to you, O man, thou art hasting to judgment.

Quest. 2. My next question is, Whether you do ever soberly consider of this great day? Sirs, do you use, when you are alone, to think with yourselves how certain and how dreadful it will be; how fast it is coming on; and what you shall do, and what answer you mean to make at that day? Are your minds taken up with these considerations? Tell me, is it so, or not.

Alas, sirs! is this a matter to be forgotten? Is not that man even worse than mad who is going to God's judgment and never thinks of it? When, if they were to be tried for their lives at the next assize they would think of it, and think again, and cast a hundred times which way to escape. Methinks you should rather forget to go to bed at night, or to eat your meat, or do your work, than forget so great a matter as this.

Truly, I have often, in my serious thoughts, been ready to wonder that men can think of almost any thing else, when they have so great a thing to think of. What! forget that which thou must remember for ever? forget that which should force remembrance, yea, and doth force it with some, whether they will or not? A poor despairing soul cannot forget it: he thinks, which way ever he goes, he is ready to be judged. Oh! therefore, beloved, fix these thoughts as deep in your hearts as thoughts can go. Oh! be like that holy man, who thought that which way ever he went he heard the trumpet sound, and the voice of the angel calling to the world, "Arise, ye dead, and come to judgment." You have warning of it from God and man to cause you to remember it; do not then forget it. It will be a cold excuse another day, Lord, I forgat this day, or else I might have been ready. You dare not, sure, trust to such excuses.

Quest. 3. My next question to you is, How are you affected with the consideration of this day? Barely to think of it will not serve. To think of such a day as this with a dull and senseless heart is a sign of fearful stupidity. Did the knees of king Belshazzar knock together with trembling when he saw the hand-writing on the wall? Dan. v. 6. How then should thy heart be affected, that seeth the hand-writing of God as a summons to his bar!

When I began to preach of these things long ago, I confess the matters seemed to me so terrible, that I was afraid that people would have run out of their wits with fear; but a little experience showed me, that many are like a dog that is bred up in a forge or furnace, that being used to it, can sleep, though the hammers are beating, and the fire and hot iron flaming about him, when another that had never seen it would be amazed at the sight. When men have heard us seven years together, yea, twenty years, to talk of a day of judgment, and they see it not, nor feel any hurt, they think it is but talk, and begin to make nothing of it. This is their thanks to God for his patience; because his sentence is not executed speedily, therefore their hearts are set in them to do evil, Eccles. viii. 11; as if God were slack of his promise, as some men account slackness, (2 Pet. iii. 9,) when one day with him is as a thousand years, and a thousand years as one day. What if we tell you twenty years together that you must die, will you not believe us, because you have lived so long, and seen no death coming?

Three or four things there be that should bring any matter to the heart. 1. If it be a matter of exceeding weight. 2. If it concern not others only, but ourselves. 3. If it be certain. 4. If near.

All these things are here to be found, and therefore how should your hearts be moved at the consideration of this great day!

1. What matter can be mentioned with the tongue of man of greater moment? For the poor creature to stand before his Maker and Redeemer, to be judged to everlasting joy or torment? Alas! all the matters of this world are plays, and toys, and dreams to this; matters of profit or disprofit are nothing to it; matters of credit or discredit are unworthy to be named with it; matters of temporal life or death are nothing to it. We see the poor brute beasts go every day to the slaughter, and we make no great matter of it, though their life be as dear to them as ours to us. To be judged to an everlasting death or torment, this is the great danger that one would think should shake the stoutest heart to consider it, and awake the dullest sinner to prevent it.

2. It is a matter which concerneth every one of yourselves, and every man or woman that ever lived upon the earth, or ever shall do. I am not speaking to you of the affairs of some far country that are nothing to you but only to marvel at, which you never saw, nor ever shall do. No: it is thy own self, man or woman, that hears me this day, that shall as surely appear before the judgment-seat of Christ, as the Lord liveth, and as he is true and faithful; and that is as sure as thou livest on this earth, or as the heaven is over thee. That man who heareth all this with the most careless and blockish heart, shall be awakened, and stand with the rest at that day. That man who never thought of it, but

spent his time in worldly matters, shall leave all, and there appear. That man that will not believe these things to be true, but maketh a jest of them, shall see and feel what he would not believe, and he also shall be there. The godly that waited in hope for that day, as the day of their full deliverance and coronation, they shall be there; those who have lain in the dust these five thousand years shall rise again, and all stand there. Hearer, whoever thou art, believe it, thou mayst better think to live without meat, to see without light, to escape death, and abide for ever on earth, than to keep away from that appearance. Willing or unwilling, thou shalt be there: and should not a matter, then, which so concerneth thyself, go near to thy heart, and awake thee from thy security?

3. That it is a matter of unquestionable certainty, I have partly showed you already, and more would do if I were preaching to known infidels. If the careless world had any just reason to think it were uncertain, their carelessness were more excusable. Methinks a man should be affected with that which he is certain shall come to pass, in a manner as if it were now in doing. "Ye perfectly know that the day of the Lord so cometh," &c. saith the apostle, 1 Thess. v. 2.

4. This day is not only certain, but it is near, and therefore should affect you the more. I confess, if it were never so far off, yet seeing it will come at last, it should be carefully regarded; but when the Judge is at the door, (Jam. v. 9,) and we are almost at the bar, and it is so short a time to this assize, what soul that is not dead will be secure?

Alas! sirs, what is a little time when it is gone? How quickly shall you and I be all in another world, and our souls receive their particular judgment, and so wait till the body be raised and judged to the same condition! It is not a hundred years, in all likelihood, till every soul of us shall be in heaven or hell; and it is like not half, or a quarter, of that time, but it will be so with the greater part of us: and what is a year or two, or a hundred? How speedily is it come! How many a soul that is now in heaven or hell, within a hundred years dwelt in the places which you now dwell in, and sat in the seats you now sit in! And now their time is past, what is it? Alas! how quickly will it be so with us! You know not, when you go to bed, but you may be judged by the next morning; or, when you rise, but you may be judged before night; but certainly you know that shortly it will be: and should not this, then, be laid to heart? yea, the general judgment will not be long; for certainly we live in the end of the world.

Quest. 4. My next question is, Whether are you ready for this dreadful judgment when it comes, or not? Seeing it is yourselves who must be tried, I think it concerns you to see that you be prepared. How often hath Christ warned us in the gospel, that we be "always ready," because we know not the day or hour of his coming, Matt. xxiv. 42, 44, and xxv. 13; 1 Thess. v. 6; and told us how sad a time it will be to those that are unready, Matt. xxv. 11, 12. Did men but well know what a meeting and greeting there will be between Christ and an unready soul, it would sure startle them, and make them look about them. What say you, beloved hearers, are you ready for judgment, or are you not? Methinks a man that knoweth he shall be judged should ask himself the question every day of his life, Am I ready to give up my account to God? Do not you use to ask this of your own hearts? Unless you be careless whether you be saved or damned, methinks you should, and ask it seriously.

Quest. But who are they that are ready? How shall I know whether I be ready or not?

Answ. There is a two-fold readiness: 1. When you are in a safe case. 2. When you are in a comfortable case, in regard of that day. The latter is very desirable, but the first is of absolute necessity. This, therefore, is it that you must principally inquire after.

In general, all those, and only those, are ready for judgment, who shall be justified and saved, and not condemned, when judgment comes—they who have a good cause in a gospel sense. It may be known beforehand who these are; for Christ judgeth, as I told you, by his law. And therefore find out whom it is that the law of grace doth justify or condemn, and you may certainly know whom the Judge will justify or condemn; for he judgeth righteously.

If you further ask me who these are, remember that I told you before, that every man that is personally righteous, by fulfilling the conditions of salvation in the gospel, shall be saved; and he that is found unrighteous, as having not fulfilled them, shall perish at that day.

Quest. Who are those?

Answ. I will tell you them in a few words, lest you should forget, because it is a matter that your salvation or damnation dependeth upon.

1. The soul that unfeignedly repenteth of his former sinful course, and turneth from it in heart and life, and loveth the way of godliness which he hated, and hateth the way of sin which he loved, and is become thoroughly a new creature, being born again, and sanctified by the Spirit of Christ, shall be justified; but all others shall certainly be condemned.

Good news to repenting converted sinners; but sad to impenitent, and him that knows not what this means.

2. That soul that feeling his misery under sin and the power of Satan, and the wrath of God, doth believe what Christ hath done and suffered for man's restoration and salvation, and thankfully accepteth him as his only Saviour and Lord, on the terms that he is offered in the gospel, and to those ends, even to justify him, sanctify, and guide him, and bring him at last to everlasting glory; that soul shall be justified at judgment; and he that doth not, shall be condemned.

Or, in short, in Scripture phrase, "He that believeth shall be saved; and he that believeth not, shall be condemned," Mark xvi. 16.

3. The soul that hath had so much knowledge of the goodness of God, and his love to man in creation, redemption, and the following mercies; and hath had so much conviction of the vanity of all creatures, as thereupon to love God more than all things below, so that he hath the chiefest room in the heart, and is preferred before all creatures ordinarily in a time of trial: that soul shall be justified at judgment, and all others shall be condemned.

4. That soul that is so apprehensive of the absolute sovereignty of God, as Creator and Redeemer, and of the righteousness of his law, and the goodness of his holy way, as that he is firmly resolved to obey him before all others; and doth accordingly give up himself to study his will, of purpose that he may obey it; and doth walk in these holy ways, and hath so far mortified the flesh, and subdued the world and the devil, that the authority and word of God can do no more with him than any other; and doth ordinarily prevail against all the persuasion and interest of the flesh; so that the main scope and bent of the heart and life is still for God; and when he sinneth, he riseth again by true repentance: I say, that soul,

and that only, shall be justified in judgment, and be saved.

5. That soul that hath such believing thoughts of the life to come, that he taketh the promised blessedness for his portion, and is resolved to venture all else upon it; and in hope of this glory, doth set light comparatively by all things in this world, and waiteth for it as the end of this life; choosing any suffering that God shall call him to, rather than to lose his hopes of that felicity; and thus persevereth to the end: I say that soul, and none but that, shall be justified in judgment, and escape damnation.

In these five marks I have told you, briefly, who shall be justified and saved, and who shall be condemned, at the day of judgment. And if you would have them all in five words, they are but the description of these five graces—repentance, faith, love, obedience, hope.

But though I have laid these close together for your use; yet, lest you should think, that in so weighty a case, I am too short in the proof of what I so determine of, I will tell you, in the express words of many Scripture texts, who shall be justified, and who shall be condemned. "Except a man be born again, he cannot enter into the kingdom of God," John iii. 3. "Without holiness none shall see God," Heb. xii. 14. "Except ye repent, ye shall all likewise perish," Luke xiii. 3, 5. "I send thee to open their eyes, and to turn them from darkness to light, and from the power of Satan unto God, that they may receive forgiveness of sins, and an inheritance among the sanctified by faith that is in me," Acts xxvi. 18. "Whoever believeth in him, shall not perish, but have everlasting life. He that believeth on him is not condemned: he that believeth not is condemned already, because he hath not believed in the name of the only begotten Son of God. And this is the condemnation, that light is come into the world, and men loved darkness rather than light, because their deeds were evil," John iii. 15, 18, 19. "The hour is coming in which all that are in the graves shall hear his voice, and shall come forth; they that have done good, to the resurrection of life; and they that have done evil, to the resurrection of damnation," John v. 28, 29. "Cast the unprofitable servant into outer darkness; there shall be weeping and gnashing of teeth," Matt. xxv. 30. "But those, mine enemies, which would not that I should reign over them, bring hither and slay them before me," Luke xix. 27. "Friend, how camest thou in hither, not having on a wedding garment? And he was speechless. Then said the king to the servants, Bind him hand and foot, and take him away, and cast him into outer darkness," &c. Matt. xxii. 12, 13. "For I say unto you, that except your righteousness exceed the righteousness of the scribes and Pharisees, ye shall in nowise enter into the kingdom of heaven," Matt. v. 20. "Not every one that saith, Lord, Lord, shall enter into the kingdom of heaven; but he that doeth the will of my Father which is in heaven," Matt. vii. 21. "He is become the author of eternal salvation to all them that obey him," Heb. v. 6. "Blessed are they that do his commandments, that they may have right to the tree of life, and may enter in by the gate into the city," Rev. xxii. 14. "There is then no condemnation to them that are in Christ Jesus, that walk not after the flesh, but after the Spirit. For if ye live after the flesh, ye shall die; but if ye through the Spirit do mortify the deeds of the body, ye shall live," Rom. viii. 1, 13. "If any man have not the Spirit of Christ, he is none of his," Rom. viii. 9. "But if ye be led of the Spirit, ye are not under the law," Gal. v. 18. "Be not deceived; God is not mocked: for whatsoever a man soweth, that shall he also reap. For he that soweth to the flesh, shall of the flesh reap corruption; but he that soweth to the Spirit, shall of the Spirit reap life everlasting," Gal. vi. 7, 8. "For where your treasure is, there will your heart be also," Matt. vi. 21. Read Psalm i. and many other texts to this purpose, of which some are cited in my "Directions for Peace of Conscience," Direct. xi.

And thus I have told you from God's word, how you may know whether you are ready for judgment; which is the fourth thing that I would advise you to inquire after.

O sirs! what shift do you make to keep your souls from continual terrors as long as you remain unready for judgment? How do you keep the thoughts of it out of your mind, that they do not break your sleep, and meet you in your business, and haunt you every way you go; while judgment is so near, and you are so unready? But I shall proceed to my next question.

Quest. 5. And in the last place, to those of you that are not yet ready, nor in a condition wherein you may be safe at that day, my question is, How are you resolved to prepare for judgment for the time to come? Will you do no more than you have done hitherto? Or, will you now set yourselves, with all your might, to make preparation for so great a day? Methinks you should be now past all demurs, delays, or further doubtings about such a business; and by the consideration of what I have said already, you should be fully resolved to lose no more time, but presently to awake, and set upon the work. Methinks you should all say, We will do any thing the Lord shall direct us to do, rather than we will be unready for this final doom! Oh that there were but such hearts in you, that you were truly willing to follow the gracious guidance of the Lord, and to use but those sweet and reasonable means which he hath prescribed you in his word, that you may be ready for that day! Alas! it is no hard matter for me to tell you or myself what it is that we must do, if we will be happy; and it is no very hard matter to do it, so far as we are truly willing; but the difficulty is to be truly and thoroughly willing to this work. If I shall tell you what you must do for preparation, shall I not lose my labour? Will you resolve and promise, in the strength of grace, that you will faithfully and speedily endeavour to practise it, whoever shall gainsay it? Upon hope of this I will set you down some brief directions, which you must follow, if ever you will, with comfort, look the Lord Jesus in the face at the hour of death, or in the day of judgment.

The first direction is this: See that your souls be sincerely established in the belief of this judgment and everlasting life; for if you do not soundly believe it, you will not seriously prepare for it. If you have the judgment and belief of an infidel, you cannot have the heart or the life of a christian. Unbelief shuts out the most of the world from heaven: see that it do not so by you. If you say you cannot believe what you would, I answer, feed not your unbelief by wilfulness and unreasonableness: use God's means to overcome it, and shut not your eyes against the light, and then try the issue, Heb. iii. 12—19.

The second direction: Labour diligently to have a sound understanding of the nature of the laws and judgment of God. On what terms it is that he dealeth with mankind, and on what terms he will judge them to life or death, and what the reward and punishment is. For if you know not the law by which you must be judged, you cannot know how to prepare for the judgment. Study the Scripture, therefore, and mark who they be that God promiseth to save, and who they be that he threateneth to condemn; for, according to that word, will the judgment pass.

The third direction: See that you take it as the very business of your lives to make ready for that day. Understand that you have no other business in this world but what doth necessarily depend on this. What else have you to do but to provide for everlasting, and to use means to sustain your own bodies and others of purpose for this work, till it be happily done? Live therefore as men that make this the main scope and care of their lives, and let all things else come in but on the by. Remember every morning, when you awake, that you must spend that day in preparation for your account, and that God doth give it you for that end. When you go to bed, examine your hearts what you have done that day in preparation for your last day, and take that time as lost which doth nothing to this end.

The fourth direction: Use frequently to think of the certainty, nearness, and dreadfulness of that day, to keep life in your affections and endeavours, lest by inconsiderateness your souls grow stupid and negligent; otherwise, because it is out of sight, the heart will be apt to grow hardened and secure. And do not think of it slightly, as a common thing, but purposely set yourselves to think of it, that it may rouse you up to such affections and endeavours as in some measure are answerable to the nature of the thing.

The fifth direction: Labour to have a lively feeling on thy heart of the evil and weight of that sin which thou art guilty of, and of the misery into which it hath brought thee, and would further bring thee if thou be not delivered, and so to feel the need of a deliverer. This must prepare thee to partake of Christ now, and if thou partake not of him now, thou canst not be saved by him then. It is these souls that now make light of their sin and misery, that must then feel them so heavy, as to be pressed by them into the infernal flames. And those that now feel little need of a Saviour, they shall then have none to save them when they feel their need.

The sixth direction: Understand and believe the sufficiency of that ransom and satisfaction to justice which Christ hath made for thy sins, and for the world, and how freely and universally it is offered in the gospel. Thy sin is not uncurable or unpardonable, nor thy misery remediless: God hath provided a remedy in his Son Christ, and brought it so near thy hands, that nothing but thy neglecting or wilful refusing it can deprive thee of the benefit. Settle thy soul in this belief.

The seventh direction: Understand and believe that for all Christ's satisfaction there is an absolute necessity of sound faith and repentance to be in thy own self before thou canst be a member of him, or be pardoned, adopted, or justified by his blood. He died not for final infidelity and impenitency as predominant in any soul. As the law of his Father, which occasioned his suffering, required perfect obedience or suffering; so his own law, which he hath made for the conveyance of his benefits, doth require yet true faith and repentance of men themselves before they shall be pardoned by him, and sincere obedience and perseverance before they shall be glorified.

The eighth direction: Rest not, therefore, in an unrenewed, unsanctified state, that is, till this faith and repentance be wrought on thy own soul, and thou be truly broken off from thy former sinful course, and from all things in this world, and art dedicated, devoted, and resigned unto God. Seeing this change must be made, and these graces must be had, or thou must certainly perish, in the fear of God see that thou give no ease to thy mind till thou art thus changed. Be content with nothing till this be done. Delay not another day. How canst thou live merrily or sleep quietly in such a condition, as if thou shouldst die in it, thou wouldst perish for ever? especially when thou art every hour uncertain whether thou shalt see another hour, and not be presently snatched away by death? Methinks while thou art in so sad a case, which way ever thou art going, or whatever thou art doing, it should still come into thy thoughts, Oh! what if I should die before I be regenerate, and have part in Christ!

The ninth direction: Let it be the daily care of thy soul to mortify thy fleshly desires, and overcome this world, and live as in a continual conflict with Satan, which will not be ended till thy life do end. If any thing destroy thee by drawing away thy heart from God, it will be thy carnal self, thy fleshly desires, and the allurements of this world, which is the matter that they feed upon. This, therefore, must be the earnest work of life, to subdue this flesh, and set light by this world, and resist the devil, that by these would destroy thee. It is the common case of miserable hypocrites, that at first they list themselves under Christ as for a fight; but they presently forget their state and work, and when they are once in their own conceit regenerate, they think themselves so safe, that there is no further danger; and thereupon they do lay down their arms, and take that which they miscall their christian liberty, and indulge and please that flesh which they promised to mortify, and close with the world which they promised to contemn, and so give up themselves to the devil, whom they promised to fight against. If once you apprehend that all your religion lieth in mere believing that all shall go well with you, and that the bitterness of death is past, and in a forbearance of some disgraceful sins, and being much in the exercise of your gifts, and in external ways of duty, and giving God a cheap and plausible obedience in those things only which the flesh can spare, you are then fallen into that deceitful hypocrisy which will as surely condemn you as open profaneness, if you get not out of it. You must live as in a fight, or you cannot overcome. You must live loose from all things in this world, if you will be ready for another. You must not live after the flesh, but mortify it by the Spirit, if you would not die, but live for ever, Rom. viii. 13. These things are not indifferent, but of flat necessity.

The tenth direction: Do all your works as men that must be judged for them. It is not enough (at least in point of duty and comfort) that you judge this preparation in general to be the main business of your lives, but you should also order your particular actions by these thoughts, and measure them by their respects to this approaching day. Before you venture on them, inquire whether they will bear weight in judgment, and be sweet or bitter when they are brought to trial? Both for matter and manner this must be observed. Oh that you would remember this when temptations are upon you! When you are tempted to give up your minds to the world, and drown yourselves in earthly cares, will you bethink you soberly whether you would hear of this at judgment; and whether the world will be then as sweet as now; and whether this be the best preparation for your trial? When you are tempted to be drunk, or to spend your precious time in ale-houses, or vain, unprofitable company, or at cards, or dice, or any sinful or needless sports, bethink you then whether this will be comfortable at the reckoning; and whether time be no more worth to one that is so near eternity, and must make so strict an account of his hours; and whether there be not many better works before you, in which you might spend your time to your greater advantage, and to your greater comfort when it comes to a review? When you are tempted to wantonness, fornication, or any other fleshly intemperance, bethink you soberly with what face these actions will appear at judgment, and whether they will be then pleasant or unpleasant to you. So when you are tempted to neglect the daily worshipping of God in your families, and the catechising and teaching of your children or servants, especially on the Lord's day, bethink yourselves then what account you will give of this to Christ, when he that intrusted you with the care of your children and servants, shall call you to a reckoning for the performance of that trust.

The like must be remembered in the very manner of our duties. How diligently should a minister study; how earnestly should he persuade; how unweariedly should he bear all oppositions and ungrateful returns; and how carefully should he watch over each particular soul of his charge (as far as is possible); when he remembers that he must shortly be accountable for all in judgment! And how importunate should we all be with sinners for their conversion, when we consider that we ourselves also must shortly be judged! Can a man be cold and dead in prayer that hath any true apprehension of that judgment upon his mind, where he must be accountable for all his prayers and performances? O remember, and seriously remember, when you stand before the minister to hear the word, and when you are on your knees to God in prayer, in what a manner that same person, even yourselves, must shortly stand at the bar of the dreadful God! Did these thoughts get thoroughly to men's hearts, they would waken them out of their sleepy devotions, and acquaint them that it is a serious business to be a christian. How careful should we be of our thoughts and words if we believingly remembered that we must be accountable for them all! How carefully should we consider what we do with our riches, and with all that God giveth us, and how much more largely should we expend it for his service in works of piety and charity, if we believingly remembered that we must be judged according to what we have done, and give account of every talent that we receive! Certainly the believing consideration of judgment might make us all better christians than we are, and keep our lives in a more innocent and profitable frame.

The eleventh direction: As you will certainly renew your failings in this life, so be sure that you daily renew your repentance, and fly daily to Christ for a renewed pardon, that no sin may leave its sting in your souls. It is not your first pardon that will serve the turn for your latter sins. Not that you must purpose to sin, and purpose to repent when you have done, as a remedy, for that is a hypocritical and wicked purpose of repenting, which is made a means to maintain us in our sins; but sin must be avoided as far as we can, and repentance and faith in the blood of Christ must remedy that which we could not avoid. The righteousness of pardon in Christ's blood is useful to us only so far as we are sinners, and cometh in where our imperfect inherent righteousness doth come short, but must not be purposely chosen before innocency; I mean, we must rather choose, as far as we can, to obey and be innocent, than to sin and be pardoned, if we were sure of pardon.

The twelfth direction: In this vigilant, obedient, penitent course, with confidence upon God as a Father, rest upon the promise of acceptance and remission, through the merits and intercession of him who redeemed you; look up in hope to the glory that is before you, and believe that God will make good his word, and the patient expectation of the righteous shall not be in vain. Cheerfully hold on in the work that you have begun; and as you serve a better master than you did before your change, so serve him with more willingness, gladness, and delight. Do not entertain hard thoughts of him, or of his service, but rejoice in your unspeakable happiness of being admitted into his family and favour through Christ. Do not serve him in drooping dejection and discouragement, but with love, and joy, and filial fear. Keep in the communion of his saints, where he is cheerfully and faithfully praised and honoured, and where is the greatest visible similitude of heaven upon earth, especially in the celebration of the sacrament of Christ's supper, where he seals up a renewed pardon in his blood, and where, unanimously, we keep the remembrance of his death, until he come. Do not cast yourselves out of the communion of the saints, from whom to be cast out by just censure and exclusion is a dreadful emblem, and forerunner of the judgment to come, where the ungodly shall be cast out of the presence of Christ and his saints for ever.

I have now finished the directions, which I tender to you for your preparation for the day of the Lord; and, withal, my whole discourse on this weighty point. What effect all this shall have upon your hearts the Lord knows: it is not in my power to determine. If you are so far blinded and hardened by sin and Satan, as to make light of all this, or coldly to commend the doctrine, while you go on to the end in your carnal, worldly condition as before, I can say no more, but tell thee again that judgment is near, when thou wilt bitterly bewail all this, too late. And among all the rest of the evidence that comes in against thee, this book shall be one which shall testify to thy face, before angels and men, that thou wast told of that day, and entreated to prepare.

But if the Lord shall show thee so much mercy as to open thy eyes, and break in upon thy heart, and, by sober consideration, turn it to himself, and cause thee faithfully to take the warning that hath here been given thee, and to obey these directions, I dare assure thee from the word of the Lord, that this judgment, which will be so dreadful to the ungodly, and the beginning of their endless terror and misery, will be as joyful to thee, and the beginning of thy glory. The Saviour that thou hast believed in, and sincerely obeyed, will not condemn thee, Psal. i. 5, 6; Rom. viii. 1; John iii. 16. It is part of his business to justify thee before the world, and to glorify his merits, his kingly power, his holiness, and his rewarding justice, in thy absolution and salvation. He will account it a righteous thing to recompense tribulation to thy troublers, and rest to thyself, when the Lord Jesus shall be revealed from heaven with his mighty angels, in flaming fire, taking vengeance on them that know not God, and that obey not the gospel of our Lord Jesus Christ; who shall be punished with everlasting destruction from the presence of the Lord, and from the glory of his power. Even then shall he come to be glorified in his saints, and to be admired in all them that believe, in that day, even because his servants' testimony, and his Spirit's among them, was believed, 2 Thess. i. 6—10. That day will be the great marriage of the Lamb, and the reception of thee and all the saints into the glory of thy Beloved, to which they had a right at their first consent and contract upon earth; and when the bridegroom comes, thou who art ready shalt go in to the marriage, when the door shall be shut against the sleepy, negligent world; and though they cry "Lord, Lord, open to us," they shall be repulsed with a "Verily, I know you not," Matt. xxv. 10—13. For this day, which others fear, mayst thou long, and hope, and pray, and wait, and comfort thyself in all troubles with the remembrance of it, 1 Cor. xv. 55—58; 1 Thess. iv. 17, 18. If thou were ready to be offered to death for Christ, or when the time of thy departing is at hand, thou mayst look back on the good fight which thou hast fought, and on the course which thou hast finished, and on the faith which thou hast kept, and mayst confidently conclude, that henceforth there is laid up for thee "a crown of righteousness, which the Lord the righteous Judge shall give thee at that day: and not to thee only, but unto all them also that love his appearing," 2 Tim. iv. 6—8. "Even so, come, Lord Jesus," Rev. xxii. 20.

A SERMON OF REPENTANCE.

PREACHED BEFORE

THE HONOURABLE HOUSE OF COMMONS,

ASSEMBLED IN PARLIAMENT AT WESTMINSTER,

AT THEIR LATE SOLEMN FAST FOR THE SETTLING OF THESE NATIONS,

April 30, 1660.

Tuesday May 1, 1660.

ORDERED,

That the thanks of this House be given to Mr. BAXTER, for his great pains in carrying on the work of preaching and prayer, before the House, at Saint Margaret's, Westminster, yesterday, being set apart by this House for a day of fasting and humiliation; and that he be desired to print his sermon, and is to have the same privilege in printing the same that others have had in the like kind, and that Mr. Swinfin do give him notice thereof.

W. JESSOP,

Clerk of the Commons' House of Parliament.

TO THE HONOURABLE THE HOUSE OF COMMONS,

ASSEMBLED IN PARLIAMENT.

As your order for my preaching persuaded me you meant attentively to hear, so your order for my publishing this sermon persuadeth me that you will vouchsafe considerately to read it; (for you would not command me to publish only for others that which was prepared for and suited to yourselves;) which second favour if I may obtain, especially of those that need most to hear the doctrine of repentance, I shall hope that the authority of the heavenly Majesty, the great concernment of the subject, and the evidence of reason, and piercing beams of sacred verity, may yet make a deeper impression on your souls, and promote that necessary work of holiness, the fruits whereof would be effectual remedies to these diseased nations, and would conduce to your own everlasting joy. Shall I think it were presumption for me to hope for so high a reward for so short a labour? Or shall I think it were uncharitableness not to hope for it? That here is nothing but plain English, without any of those ornaments that are by many thought necessary to make such discourses grateful to ingenious, curious auditors, proceeded not only from my present want of advantages for study, (having and using no book but a Bible and a Concordance,) but also from the humbling and serious nature of the work of the day, and from my own inclination, less affecting such ornaments in sacred discourses than formerly I have done. It is a very great honour that God and you have put upon me, to conclude so solemn a day of prayer, which was answered the next morning by your speedy, and cheerful, and unanimous acknowledgment of his Majesty's authority. May I but have the second part, to promote your salvation, and the happiness of this land, by your considering and obeying these necessary truths, what greater honour could I expect on earth? Or how could you more oblige me to remain

A daily petitioner to Heaven for these mercies,
on your own and the nation's behalf,
RICHARD BAXTER.

EZEKIEL XXXVI. 31.

THEN SHALL YE REMEMBER YOUR OWN EVIL WAYS, AND YOUR DOINGS THAT WERE NOT GOOD, AND SHALL LOATHE YOURSELVES IN YOUR OWN SIGHT FOR YOUR INIQUITIES AND FOR YOUR ABOMINATIONS.

THE words are a part of God's prognostics of the Jews' restoration, whose dejection he had before described. Their disease began within, and there God promiseth to work the cure. Their captivity was but the fruit of their voluntary captivity to sin, and their grief of heart was but the fruit of their hardness of heart, and their sharpest suffering of their foul pollutions; and therefore God promiseth a methodical cure, even to take away their old and stony heart, and cleanse them from their filthiness, and so to ease them by the removing of the cause. How far, and when, this promise was to be made good to the Jews, as nationally considered, is a matter that requires a longer disposition than my limited hour will allow, and the decision of that case is needless, as to my present end and work. That this is part of the gospel covenant, and applicable to us believers now, the Holy Ghost, in the epistle to the Hebrews, hath assured us.

The text is the description of the repentance of the people, in which the beginning of their recovery doth consist, and by which the rest must be attained. The evil which they repent of is, in general, all their iniquities, but especially their idolatry, called their abominations. Their repentance is foretold, as it is in the understanding and thoughts, and as in the will and affections. In the former, it is called "remembering their own evil ways." In the latter, it is called "loathing themselves in their own sight, for their iniquities and abominations." Montanus translates it *reprebabitis in vos;* but in c. xx. 43, *fastidietis vos.* The same sense is intended by the other versions; when the Septuagint translates it by displeasure, and the Chaldee by groaning, and the Syriac by the wrinkling of the face, and the Sept. in c. xx. 43, by smiting on the face: the Arabic here perverts the sense by turning all to negatives, ye shall not, &c. yet in c. xx. 43, he turns it by the tearing of the face. I have purposely chosen a text that needs no long explication, that in obedience to the foreseen straits of time I may be excused from that part, and be more on the more necessary. This observation contains the meaning of the text, which, by God's assistance, I shall now insist on, viz.:

The remembering of their own iniquities, and loathing themselves for them, is the sign of a repenting people, and the prognostic of their restoration, so far as deliverance may be here expected.

For the opening of which, observe these things following.

1. It is not all kind of remembering that will prove you penitent. The impenitent remember their sin that they may commit it; they remember it with love, desire, and delight. The heart of the worldling goeth after his airy or earthen idol; the heart of the ambitious feedeth on his vain-glory, and the people's breath; and the filthy fornicator is delighted in the thoughts of the object and exercise of his lust. But it is a remembering, 1. From a deep conviction of the evil and odiousness of sin; 2. And with abhorrence and self-loathing; 3. That leadeth to a resolved and vigilant forsaking; that is the proof of true repentance, and the prognostic of a people's restoration.

2. And it is not all self-loathing that will signify true repentance, for there is a self-loathing of the desperate and the damned soul, that abhorreth itself, and teareth and tormenteth itself, and cannot be restrained from self-revenge, when it finds that it hath wilfully, foolishly, and obstinately been its own destroyer. But the self-loathing of the truly penitent hath these following properties:

1. It proceedeth from the predominant love of God, whom we have abused and offended. The more we love him, the more we loathe what is contrary to him.

2. It is much excited by the observation and sense of his exceeding mercies, and is conjunct with gratitude.

3. It continueth and increaseth under the greatest assurance of forgiveness, and sense of love, and dieth not when we think we are out of danger.

4. It containeth a loathing of sin as sin, and a love of holiness as such, and not only a love of ease and peace, and a loathing of sin as the cause of suffering.

5. It resolveth the soul against returning to its former course, and resolveth it for an entire devotedness to God for the time to come.

6. It deeply engageth the penitent in a conflict against the flesh, and maketh him victorious, and setteth him to work in a life of holiness, as his trade and principal business in the world.

7. It bringeth him to a delight in God and holiness, and a delight in himself, so far as he findeth God, and heaven, and holiness within him. He can, with some comfort and content, own himself and his conversation so far as God (victorious against his carnal self) appeareth in him. For as he loveth Christ in the rest of his members, so must he in himself. And this is it that self-loathing doth prepare for.

This must be the self-loathing that must afford you comfort as a penitent people in the way to restoration.

Where you see it is implied, that materially it containeth these common acts. 1. Accusing and condemning thoughts against ourselves. It is a judging of ourselves, and makes us call ourselves, with Paul, foolish, disobedient, deceived; yea, mad;

as Acts xxvi. 11; and with David to say, I have done foolishly, 2 Sam. xxiv. 10. 2. It containeth a deep distaste and displeasure with ourselves, and a heart-rising against ourselves. 3. As also a holy indignation against ourselves, as apprehending that we have played the enemies to ourselves and God. 4. And it possesseth us with grief and trouble at our miscarriages. So that a soul in this condition is sick of itself, and vexed with its self-procured woe.

2. Note also, that when self-loathing proceedeth from mere conviction, and is without the love of God and holiness, it is but the tormentor of the soul, and runs it deeper into sin, provoking men here to destroy their lives; and in hell it is the never-dying worm.

3. Note also, that it is themselves that they are said to loathe, because it is ourselves that conscience hath to do with, as witness, and as judge; it is ourselves that are naturally nearest to ourselves, and our own affairs that we are most concerned in. It is ourselves that must have the joy or torment, and therefore it is our own actions and estate that we have first to mind. Though yet, as magistrates, ministers, and neighbours, we must next mind others, and must loathe iniquity wherever we meet it, and a vile person must be contemned in our eyes, while we honour them that fear the Lord, Psal. xv. 4.

And as by nature, so in the commandment, God hath given to every man the first and principal care and charge of himself, and his own salvation, and consequently of his own ways, so that we may with less suspicion loathe ourselves than others, and are more obliged to do it.

4. Note also, that it is not for our troubles, or our disgrace, or our bodily deformities, or infirmities, or for our poverty and want, that penitents are said to loathe themselves, but for their iniquities and abominations. For, 1. This loathing is a kind of justice done upon ourselves, and therefore is exercised, not for mere infelicities, but for crimes. Conscience keepeth in its own court, and meddleth but with moral evils, which we are conscious of. 2. And also it is sin that is loathed by God, and makes the creature loathsome in his eyes; and repentance conformeth the soul to God, and therefore causeth us to loathe as he doth, and on his grounds. And, 3. There is no evil but sin, and that which sin procureth, and therefore it is for sin that the penitent loathes himself.

5. Note also, that it is here implied, that, till repentance, there was none of this remembering of sin, and loathing of themselves. They begin with our conversion, and, as before described, are proper to the truly penitent. For, to consider them distinctly, 1. The deluded soul that is bewitched by its own concupiscence, is so taken up with remembering of his fleshly pleasures, and his alluring objects, and his honours, and his earthly businesses and store, that he hath no mind or room for the remembering of his foolish, odious sin, and the wrong that he is doing to God, and to himself. Death is oblivious, and sleep hath but a distracted, ineffectual memory, that stirreth not the busy dreamer from his pillow, nor despatcheth any of the work he dreams of. And the unconverted are asleep, and dead in sin. The crowd of cares and worldly businesses, and the tumultuous noise of foolish sports, and other sensual passions and delights, do take up the minds of the unconverted, and turn them from the observation of the things of greatest everlasting consequence. They have a memory for sin and the flesh, to which they are alive, but not for things spiritual and eternal, to which they are dead. They remember not God himself as God, with any effectual remembrance. God is not in all their thoughts, Psal. x. 4. They live as without him in the world, Eph. ii. 12. And if they remember not God, they cannot remember sin as sin, whose malignity lieth in its opposition to the will and holiness of God. They forget themselves, and therefore must needs forget their sinfulness. Alas! they remember not, effectually and savingly, what they are, and why they were made, and what they are daily nourished and preserved for, and what business they have to do here in the world. They forget that they have souls to save or lose, that must live in endless joy or torment. You may see by their careless and ungodly lives that they forget it. You may hear by their carnal, frothy speech that they forget it. And he that remembereth not himself, remembereth not his own concernments. They forget the end to which they tend; the life which they must live for ever; the matters everlasting, whose greatness and duration, one would think, should so command the mind of man, and take up all his thoughts and cares, in despite of all the little trifling matters that would avert them, that we should think almost of nothing else; yet these, even these, that nothing but deadness or madness should make a reasonable creature to forget, are daily forgotten by the unconverted soul, or uneffectually remembered. Many a time have I admired that men of reason that are here to-day, and in endless joy or misery to-morrow, should be able to forget such inexpressible concernments! Methinks they should easier forget to rise, or dress themselves, or to eat, or drink, or any thing, than to forget an endless life, which is so undoubtedly certain, and so near. A man that hath a cause to be heard to-morrow, in which his life or honour is concerned, cannot forget it; a wretch that is condemned to die to-morrow, cannot forget it. And yet poor sinners, that are continually uncertain to live an hour, and certain speedily to see the majesty of the Lord, to their unconceivable joy or terror, as sure as now they live on earth, can forget these things for which they have their memory; and which one would think should drown the matters of this world, as the report of a cannon doth a whisper, or as the sun obscureth the poorest glow-worm. Oh wonderful stupidity of an unrenewed soul! Oh wonderful folly and distractedness of the ungodly! That ever men can forget, I say again, that they can forget eternal joy, eternal woe, and the Eternal God, and the place of their eternal, unchangeable abode, when they stand even at the door, and are passing in, and there is but the thin veil of flesh between them and that amazing sight, that eternal gulf; and they are daily dying, and even stepping in. Oh could you keep your honours here for ever; could you ever wear that gay attire, and gratify your flesh with meats, and drinks, and sports, and lusts; could you ever keep your rule and dignity, or your earthly life in any state; you had some little poor excuse for not remembering the eternal things (as a man hath, that preferreth his candle before the sun): but when death is near and inexorable, and you are sure to die as you are sure to live; when every man of you that sitteth in these seats to-day can say, I must shortly be in another world, where all the pomp and pleasure of this world will be forgotten, or remembered but as my sin and folly, one would think it were impossible for any of you to be ungodly, and to remember the trifles and nothings of the world, while you forget that everlasting all, whose reality, necessity, magnitude, excellency, concernment, and duration are such, as should take up all the powers of your souls, and continually command the service and attendance of your thoughts against all seekers and contemptible competitors whatsoever. But alas,

though you have the greatest helps, (in subservience to these commanding objects,) yet will you not remember the matters which alone deserve remembrance. Sometimes the preachers of the gospel do call on you to remember; to remember your God, your souls, your Saviour, your ends, and everlasting state, and to remember your misdoings, that you may loathe yourselves, and in returning may find life; but some either scorn them, or quarrel with them, or sleep under their most serious and importunate solicitations, or carelessly and stupidly give them the hearing, as if they spoke but words of course, or treated about uncertain things, and spoke not to them from the God of heaven, and about the things that every man of you shall very shortly see or feel. Sometimes you are called on by the voice of conscience within, to remember the unreasonableness and evil of your ways; but conscience is silenced, because it will not be conformable to your lusts. But little do you think what a part your too late awakened conscience hath yet to play, if you give it not a more sober hearing in time. Sometimes the voice of common calamities, and national or local judgments, call on you to remember the evil of your ways; but that which is spoken to all, or many, doth seem to most of them as spoken unto none. Sometimes the voice of particular judgments, seizing upon your families, persons, or estates, doth call on you to remember the evil of your ways; and one would think the rod should make you hear; and yet you most disregardfully go on, or are only frightened into a few good purposes and promises, that die when health and prosperity revive. Sometimes God joineth all these together, and pleadeth both by word and rod, and addeth also the inward pleadings of his Spirit; he sets your sins in order before you, (Psal. l. 21,) and expostulateth with you the cause of his abused love, despised sovereignty, and provoked justice; and asketh the poor sinner, Hast thou done well to waste thy life in vanity, to serve thy flesh, to forget thy God, thy soul, thy happiness; and to thrust his service into corners, and give him but the odious leavings of the flesh? But these pleas of God cannot be heard. Oh horrible impiety! By his own creatures, by reasonable creatures, (that would scorn to be called fools or mad-men,) the God of heaven cannot be heard! The brutish, passionate, furious sinners will not remember. They will not remember what they have done, and with whom it is that they have to do, and what God thinks and saith of men in their condition; and whither it is that the flesh will lead them; and what will be the fruit and end of all their lusts and vanities; and how they will look back on all at last; and whether a holy or a sensual life will be sweetest to a dying man; and what judgment it is that they will all be of, in the controversy between the flesh and Spirit, at the latter end. Though they have life, and time, and reason for their uses, we cannot entreat them to consider of these things in time. If our lives lay on it, as their salvation, which is more, lieth on it, we cannot entreat them. If we should kneel to them, and with tears beseech them, but once a day, or once a week, to bestow one hour in serious consideration of their latter end, and the everlasting state of saints and sinners, and of the equity of the holy ways of God, and the iniquity of their own, we cannot prevail with them. Till the God of heaven doth overrule them we cannot prevail. The witness that we are forced to bear is sad; it is sad to us; but it will be sadder to these rebels that shall one day know that God will not be outfaced; and that they may sooner shake the stable earth and darken the sun by their reproaches, than outbrave the Judge of all the world, or by all their cavils, wranglings, or scorns, escape the hands of his revenging justice.

But if ever the Lord will save these souls, he will bring their misdoings to their remembrance. He will make them think of that which they were so loth to think on. You cannot now abide these troubling and severe meditations; the thoughts of God, and heaven, and hell, the thoughts of your sins, and of your duties, are melancholy, unwelcome thoughts to you: but oh that you could foreknow the thoughts that you shall have of all these things! even the proudest, scornful, hardened sinner, that heareth me this day, shall shortly have such a remembrance, as will make him wonder at his present blockishness. Oh when the irresistible power of Heaven shall open all your sins before you, and command you to remember them, and to remember the time, and place, and persons, and all the circumstances of them, what a change will it make upon the most stout or stubborn of the sons of men! what a difference will there then be between that trembling, self-tormenting soul, and the same that now in his gallantry can make light of all these things, and call the messenger of Christ who warneth him, a puritan, or a doting fool! Your memories now are somewhat subject to your wills; and if you will not think of your own, your chief, your everlasting concernments, you may choose. If you will choose rather to employ your noble souls on beastly lusts, and waste your thoughts on things of nought, you may take your course, and chase a feather with the childish world, till, overtaking it, you see you have lost your labour. But when justice takes the work in hand, your thoughts shall be no more subject to your wills; you shall then remember that which you are full loth to remember, and would give a world that you could forget. Oh then one cup of the waters of oblivion would be of an inestimable value to the damned! Oh what would they not give that they could but forget the time they lost, the mercy they abused, the grace which they refused, the holy servants of Christ whom they despised, the wilful sins which they committed, and the many duties which they wilfully omitted! I have oft thought of their case when I have dealt with melancholy or despairing persons. If I advise them to cast away such thoughts, and turn their minds to other things, they tell me they cannot; it is not in their power; and I have long found that I may almost as well persuade a broken head to give over aching. But when the holy God shall purposely pour out the vials of his wrath on the consciences of the ungodly, and open the books, and show them all that ever they had done, with all the aggravations, how then shall these worms be able to resist?

And now I beseech you all, consider, is it not better to remember your sins on earth, than in hell? before your Physician, than before your Judge? for your cure, than for your torment? Give me leave, then, before I go any further, to address myself to you as the messenger of the Lord, with this importunate request, both as you stand here in your private and in your public capacities. In the name of the God of heaven, I charge you, remember the lives that you have led! remember what you have been doing in the world! remember how you have spent your time! and whether, indeed, it is God that you have been serving, and heaven that you have been seeking, and holiness and righteousness that you have been practising in the world till now! Are your sins so small, so venial, so few, that you can find no employment on them for your memories? or is the offending of the eternal God so slight and safe a thing as not to need your consideration? God forbid you should have such atheistical conceits! Surely God made not his laws for nought; nor doth he make such a stir by his word, and messengers, and providences, against a harmless thing; nor doth he threaten hell to men for small, indifferent matters; nor did Christ need to have died, and done all that he hath done, to cure a small and safe disease. Surely that which the God of heaven is pleased to threaten with everlasting punishment, the greatest of you all should vouchsafe to think on, and with greatest fear and soberness to remember.

It is a pitiful thing, that with men, with gentlemen, with professed christians, God's matters, and their own matters, their greatest matters, should seem unworthy to be thought on; when they have thoughts for their honours, and their lands, and friends; and thoughts for their children, their servants, and provision; and thoughts for their horses, and their dogs, and sports. Is God and heaven less worth than these? are death and judgment matters of less moment? Gentlemen, you would take it ill to have your wisdom undervalued, and your reason questioned; for your honour's sake do not make it contemptible yourselves in the eyes of all that are truly wise. It is the nobleness of objects that most ennobles your faculties, and the baseness of objects doth debase them. If brutish objects be your employment and delight, do I need to tell you what you make yourselves? If you would be noble indeed, let God and everlasting glory be the object of your faculties; if you would be great, then dwell on greatest things; if you would be high, then seek the things that are above, and not the sordid things of earth, Col. iii. 1—3; and if you would be safe, look after the enemies of your peace; and as you had thoughts of sin that led you to commit it, entertain the thoughts that would lead you to abhor it. Oh that I might have but the grant of this reasonable request from you, that among all your thoughts you would bestow now and then an hour in the serious thoughts of your misdoings, and soberly in your retirement between God and your souls remember the paths that you have trod, and whether you have lived for the work for which you were created! One sober hour of such employment might be the happiest hour that ever you spent, and give you more comfort at your final hour, than all the former hours of your life; and might lead you into that new and holy life, which you may review with everlasting comfort.

Truly, gentlemen, I have long observed that Satan's advantage lieth so much on the brutish side, and that the work of man's conversion, and holy conversation, is so much carried on by God's exciting of our reason; and that the misery of the ungodly is, that they have reason in faculty, and not in use, in the greatest things, that I persuade you to this duty with the greater hopes: if the Lord will now persuade you but to retire from vanity, and soberly exercise your reason, and consider your ways, and say, What have we done? and what is it that God would have us do? and what shall we wish we had done at last? I say, could you now be but prevailed with to bestow as many hours on this work, as you have cast away in idleness, or worse, I should not doubt but I should shortly see the faces of many of you in heaven that have been recovered by the use of this advice. It is a thousand pities, that men that are thought wise enough to be intrusted with the public safety, and to be the physicians of a broken state, should have any among them that are untrusty to their God, and have not the reason to remember their misdoings, and prevent the danger of their immortal souls. Will you sit all day here to find out the remedy of a diseased land; and will you not be entreated by God or man to sit down one hour, and find out the disease of, and remedy for, your own souls? Are those men likely to take care of the happiness of so many thousands, that will still be so careless of themselves? Once more therefore, I entreat you, remember your misdoings, lest God remember them; and bless the Lord that called you this day, by the voice of mercy, to remember them upon terms of faith and hope. Remembered they must be, first or last. And believe it, this is far unlike the sad remembrance at judgment, and in the place of woe and desperation.

And I beseech you observe here, that it is your own misdoings that you must remember. Had it been only the sins of other men, especially those that differ from you, or have wronged you, or stand against your interest, how easily would the duty have been performed! How little need should I have had to press it with all this importunity! How confident should I be that I could convert the most, if this were the conversion! It grieves my soul to hear how quick and constant high and low, learned and unlearned, are this uncharitable, contumelious remembering the faults of others; how cunningly they can bring in their insinuated accusations; how odiously they can aggravate the smallest faults, where difference causeth them to distaste the person; how ordinarily they judge of actions by the persons, as if any thing were a crime that is done by such as they dislike, and all were virtue that is done by those that fit their humours; how commonly brethren have made it a part of their service of God to speak or write uncharitably of his servants, labouring to destroy the hearer's charity, which had more need, in this unhappy time, of the bellows than the water! How usual it is with the ignorant that cannot reach the truth, and the impious that cannot bear it, to call such heretics that know more than themselves, and to call such precisians, puritans, (or some such name which hell invents as there is occasion,) who dare not be so bad as they! How odious men pretending to much gravity, learning, and moderation, do labour to make those that are dear to God! and what a heart they have to widen differences, and make a sea of every lake; and that, perhaps, under pretence of blaming the uncharitableness of others! How far the very sermons and discourses of some learned men are from the common rule of doing as we would be done by! and how loudly they proclaim that such men love not their neighbours as themselves; the most uncharitable words seeming moderate, which they give; and all called intemperate that savoureth not of flattery, which they receive! Were I calling the several exasperated factions now in England to remember the misdoings of their supposed adversaries, what full-mouthed and debasing confessions would they make! What monsters of heresy and schism, of impiety, treason, and rebellion, of perjury and perfidiousness, would too many make of the faults of others, while they extenuate their own to almost nothing! It is a wonder to observe how the case doth alter with the most, when that which was their adversary's case becomes their own. The very prayers of the godly, and their care of their salvation, and the fear of sinning, doth seem their crime in the eyes of some that easily bear the guilt of swearing, drunkenness, sensuality, filthiness, and neglect of duty in themselves, as a tolerable burden.

But if ever God indeed convert you, (though you will pity others, yet,) he will teach you to begin at home, and take the beam out of your own eyes, and to cry out, I am the miserable sinner.

And lest these generals seem insufficient for us to confess on such a day as this, and lest yet your memories should need more help, is it not my duty to remind you of some particulars? which yet I shall not do by way of accusation, but of inquiry. Far be it from me to judge so hardly of you, that when you come hither to lament your sins you cannot with patience endure to be told of them.

1. Inquire, then, whether there be none among you that live a sensual, careless life, clothed with the best, and faring deliciously every day; in gluttony and drunkenness, chambering and wantonness, strife and envying; not putting on Christ, nor walking in the Spirit, but making provision for the flesh, to satisfy the lusts thereof? Rom. xiii. 13, 14. Is there none among you that spend your precious time in vanities, that is allowed you to prepare for life eternal? that have time to waste in compliments, and fruitless talk, and visits, in gaming, and unnecessary recreations, in excessive feasting and entertainments, while God is neglected, and your souls forgotten, and you can never find an hour in a day to make ready for the life which you must live for ever? Is there none among you that would take that man for a puritan or fanatic that should employ but half so much time for his soul, and in the service of the Lord, as you do in unnecessary sports and pleasures, and pampering your flesh? Gentlemen, if there be any such among you, as you love your souls, remember your misdoings, and bewail these abominations before the Lord, in this day of your professed humiliation!

2. Inquire whether there be none among you, that, being strangers to the new birth, and to the inward workings of the Spirit of Christ upon the soul, do also distaste a holy life, and make it the matter of your reproach, and pacify your accusing consciences with a religion made up of mere words, and heartless outside, and so much obedience as your fleshly pleasures will admit, accounting those that go beyond you, especially if they differ from you in your modes and circumstances, to be but a company of proud, pharisaical, self-conceited hypocrites, and those whom you desire to suppress. If there should be one such person here, I would entreat him to remember that it is the solemn asseveration of our Judge, that "except a man be converted, and be born again, of water and the Spirit, he cannot enter into the kingdom of heaven," John iii. 3, 5; Matt. xviii. 3; that "if any man have not the Spirit of Christ, he is none of his," Rom. viii. 9; that "if any man be in Christ, he is a new creature; old things are passed away, and all things are become new," 2 Cor. v. 17; that "without holiness none shall see God," Heb. xii. 14; that "the wisdom that is from above is first pure, and then peaceable," Jam. iii. 17; that "God is a Spirit, and they that worship him must worship him in spirit and in truth," John iv. 23, 24; that "they worship in vain that teach for doctrines the commandments of men," Matt. xv. 8, 9; and that "except your righteousness exceed that of the scribes and Pharisees, ye shall in no wise enter into the kingdom of heaven," Matt. v. 20. And I desire you to remember that it is hard to kick against the pricks, and to prosper in rage against the Lord: and that it is better for that man that offendeth one of his little ones to have had a millstone fastened to his neck, and to have been cast into the bottom of the sea, Matt. xviii. 6. It is a sure and grievous condemnation that waiteth for all that are themselves unholy; but to the haters or despisers of the holy laws and servants of the Lord, how much more grievous a punishment is reserved!

3. Inquire also whether there be none among you that let loose your passions on your inferiors, and oppress your poor tenants, and make them groan under the task, or at least do little to relieve the needy, nor study not to serve the Lord with your estates, but sacrifice all to the pleasing of your flesh, unless it be some inconsiderable pittance, or fruitless drops, that are unproportionable to your receivings. If there be any such, let them remember their iniquities, and cry for mercy before the cry of the poor to heaven do bring down vengeance from him that hath promised to hear their cry, and speedily to avenge them, Luke xviii. 7, 8.

4. Inquire whether there be none that live the life of Sodom, in pride, fulness of bread, and idleness, Ezek. xvi. 49; and that are not puffed up with their estates and dignities, and are strangers to the humility, meekness, patience, and self-denial of the saints: that ruffle in bravery, and contend more zealously for their honour and pre-eminence, than for the honour and interest of the Lord. For pride of apparel, it was wont to be taken for a childish or a womanish kind of vice, below a man; but it is now observed among the gallants, that (except in spots) the notes of vanity are more legibly written on the hair and dress of a multitude of effeminate males, than on the females: proclaiming to the world that pride, which one would think even pride itself should have concealed; and calling by these signs to the beholders to observe the emptiness of their minds, and how void they are of that inward worth which is the honour of a christian and of a man: it being a marvel to see a man of learning, gravity, wisdom, and the fear of God, appear in such an antic dress.

I have done with the first part, "the remembering of your own evil ways and doings." I beseech you practically go along with me to the next, "the loathing of yourselves in your own eyes, for all your iniquities and abominations."

Every true convert doth thus loathe himself for his iniquities: and when God will restore a punished people upon their repentance, he bringeth them to this loathing of themselves.

1. A converted soul hath a new and heavenly light to help him to see those matters of humbling use, which others see not.

2. More particularly, he hath the knowledge of sin, and of himself. He seeth the odious face of sin, and seeth how much his heart and life in his sinful days abounded with it, and how great a measure yet remains.

3. He hath seen by faith the Lord himself; the majesty, the holiness, the jealousy, the goodness of the eternal God whom he hath offended, and therefore must needs abhor himself, Job xlii. 6.

4. He hath tasted of God's displeasure against him for his sin already. God himself hath set it home, and awakened his conscience, and held it on, till he hath made him understand that the consuming fire is not to be jested with.

5. He hath seen Christ crucified, and mourned over him. This is the glass that doth most clearly show the ugliness of sin, and here he hath learned to abhor himself.

6. He hath foreseen by faith the end of sin, and the doleful recompence of the ungodly; his faith beholdeth the misery of damned souls, and the glory which sinners cast away. He heareth them beforehand repenting, and lamenting, and crying out of their former folly, and wishing in vain that all this were to do again, and that they might once more be tried with another life, and resolving then how holily, how self-denyingly they would live! He knows that if sin had had its way he had been

plunged into this hellish misery himself; and therefore he must needs loathe himself for his iniquities.

7. Moreover, the true convert hath had the liveliest taste of mercy, of the blood of Christ, of the offers and covenant of grace, of reprieving mercy, of pardoning mercy, of healing and preserving mercy, and of the unspeakable mercy contained in the promise of everlasting life; and to find that he hath sinned against all this mercy doth constrain him to abhor himself.

8. And it is only the true convert that hath a new and holy nature, contrary to sin; and, therefore, as a man that hath the leprosy doth loathe himself because his nature is contrary to his disease, so is it (though operating in a freer way) with a converted soul as to the leprosy of sin. Oh! how he loathes the remnants of his pride and passion; his excessive cares, desires, and fears; the backwardness of his soul to God and heaven! Sin is to the new nature of every true believer, as the food of a swine to the stomach of a man; if he have eaten it, he hath no rest until he hath vomited it up; and then when he looketh on his vomit, he loatheth himself to think how long he kept such filth within him; and that yet in the bottom there is some remains.

9. The true convert is one that is much at home, his heart is the vineyard which he is daily dressing, his work is ordinarily about it; and, therefore, he is acquainted with those secret sins, and daily failings, which ungodly men that are strangers to themselves do not observe, though they have them in dominion.

10. Lastly, a serious christian is a workman of the Lord's, and daily busy at the exercise of his graces; and, therefore, hath occasion to observe his weaknesses and failings, and from sad experience is forced to abhor himself.

But with careless, unrenewed souls it is not so: some of them may have a mild, ingenuous disposition, and the knowledge of their unworthiness; and customarily they will confess such sins as are small disgrace to them, or cannot be hid; or under the terrible gripes of conscience, in the hour of distress, and at the approach of death, they will do more; and abhor themselves, perhaps, as Judas did; or make a constrained confession through the power of fear; but so far are they from this loathing of themselves for all their iniquities, that sin is to them as their element, their food, their nature, and their friend.

And now, honourable, worthy, and beloved auditors, it is my duty to inquire, and to provoke you to inquire, whether the representative body of the Commons of England, and each man of you in particular, be thus affected to yourselves or not. It concerns you to inquire of it, as you love your souls, and love not to see the death-marks of impenitency on them. It concerneth us to inquire of it, as we love you and the nation, and would fain see the marks of God's return in mercy to us, in your self-loathing and return to God. Let conscience speak as before the Lord that sees your hearts, and will shortly judge you, have you had such a sight of your natural and actual sin and misery, of your neglect of God, your contempt of heaven, your loss of precious, hasty time, your worldly, fleshly, sensual lives, and your omission of the great and holy works which you were made for? Have you had such a sight and sense of these as hath filled your souls with shame and sorrow; and caused you in tears, or hearty grief, to lament your sinful, careless lives, before the Lord? Do you loathe yourselves for all this, as being vile in your own eyes, and each man say, What a wretch was I! what an unreasonable, self-hating wretch, to do all this against myself! what an unnatural wretch, what a monster of rebellion and ingratitude, to do all this against the Lord of love and mercy! what a deceived, foolish wretch, to prefer the pleasing of my lusts and senses, a pleasure that perisheth in the fruition, and is past as soon as it is received, before the manly pleasures of the saints, and before the soul's delight in God, and before the unspeakable everlasting pleasures! Was there any comparison between the brutish pleasures of the flesh, and the spiritual delights of a believing soul, in looking to the endless pleasure which we shall have with all the saints and angels in the glorious presence of the Lord? Was God and glory worth no more, than to be cast aside for satiating of an unsatisfiable flesh and fancy, and to be sold for a harlot, for a forbidden cup, for a little air of popular applause, or for a burdensome load of wealth and power, for so short a time? Where is now the gain and pleasure of all my former sins? What have they left but a sting behind them? How near is the time when my departing soul must look back on all the pleasures and profits that ever I enjoyed, as a dream when one awaketh; as delusory vanities, that have done all for me that ever they will do, and all is but to bring my flesh unto corruption, (Gal. vi. 8,) and my soul to this distressing grief and fear! And then I must sing and laugh no more! I must brave it out in pride no more! I must know the pleasures of the flesh no more! but be levelled with the poorest, and my body laid in loathsome darkness, and my soul appear before that God whom I so wilfully refused to obey and honour. Oh wretch that I am! where was my understanding, when I played so boldly with the flames of hell, the wrath of God, the poison of sin! when God stood by and yet I sinned! when conscience did rebuke me, and yet I sinned! when heaven or hell were hard at hand, and yet I sinned! when, to please my God, and save my soul, I would not forbear a filthy lust, or a forbidden vanity of no worth! when I would not be persuaded to a holy, heavenly, watchful life, though all my hopes of heaven lay on it! I am ashamed of myself; I am confounded in the remembrance of my wilful, self-destroying folly! I loathe myself for all these abominations! Oh that I had lived in beggary and rags when I lived in sin! And oh that I had lived with God in a prison, or in a wilderness, when I refused a holy, heavenly life, for the love of a deceitful world! Will the Lord but pardon what is past, I am resolved through his grace to do so no more, but to loathe that filth that I took for pleasure, and to abhor that sin that I made my sport, and to die to the glory and riches of the world, which I made my idol; and to live entirely to that God that I did so long ago and so unworthily neglect; and to seek that treasure, that kingdom, that delight, that will fully satisfy my expectation, and answer all my care and labour, with such infinite advantage. Holiness or nothing shall be my work and life, and heaven or nothing shall be my portion and felicity.

These are the thoughts, the affections, the breathing of every regenerate, gracious soul. For your souls' sake inquire now, is it thus with you? Or have you thus returned with self-loathing to the Lord, and firmly engaged your souls to him at your entrance into a holy life? I must be plain with you, gentlemen, or I shall be unfaithful; and I must deal closely with you, or I cannot deal honestly and truly with you. As sure as you live, yea, as sure as the word of God is true, you must all be such converted men, and loathe yourselves for your iniquities, or be condemned as impenitent to everlasting fire. To hide this from you is but to deceive you, and that in a matter of a thousand times greater moment than your lives. Perhaps I could have made shift, instead of such serious admonitions, to have wasted this hour in flashy oratory, and neat expressions, and ornaments of reading, and other things that are the too common matters of ostentation with men that preach God's word in jest, and believe not what they are persuading others to believe. Or if you think I could not, I am indifferent, as not much affecting the honour of being able to offend the Lord, and wrong your souls, by dallying with holy things. Flattery in these things of soul concernment is a selfish villany, that hath but a very short reward, and those that are pleased with it to-day, may curse the flatterer for ever. Again, therefore, let me tell you, that which I think you will confess, that it is not your greatness, not your high looks, not the gallantry of your spirits that scorns to be thus humbled, that will serve your turn when God shall deal with you, or save your carcasses from rottenness and dust, or your guilty souls from the wrath of the Almighty. Nor is it your contempt of the threatenings of the Lord, and your stupid neglect or scorning at the message, that will endure when the sudden, irresistible light shall come in upon you, and convince you, or you shall see and feel what now you refuse to believe! Nor is it your outside, hypocritical religion, made up of mere words, or ceremonies, and giving your souls but the leavings of the flesh, and making God an underling to the world, that will do any more to save your souls than the picture of a feast to feed your bodies. Nor is it the stiffest conceits that you shall be saved in an unconverted state, or that you are sanctified when you are not, that will do any more to keep you from damnation than a conceit that you shall never die will do to keep you here for ever. Gentlemen, though you are all here in health, and dignity, and honour, to-day, how little a while is it, alas! how little, until you shall be every man in heaven or hell! Unless you are infidels you dare not deny it. And it is only Christ and a holy life that is your way to heaven; and only sin, and the neglect of Christ and holiness, that can undo you. Look, therefore, upon sin as you should look on that which would cast you into hell, and is daily undermining all your hopes. Oh that this honourable assembly could know it in some measure as it shall be shortly known! and judge of it as men do, when time is past, and delusions vanished, and all men are awakened from their fleshly dreams, and their naked souls have seen the Lord! Oh then what laws would you make against sin! How speedily would you join your strength against it as against the only enemy of your peace, and as against a fire in your houses, or a plague that were broken out upon the city where you are! Oh then how zealously would you all concur to promote the interest of holiness in the land, and studiously encourage the servants of the Lord! How severely would you deal with those, that by making a mock of godliness, do hinder the salvation of the people's souls! How carefully would you help the labourers that are sent to guide men in the holy path! and yourselves would go before the nation as an example of penitent self-loathing for your sins, and hearty conversion to the Lord! Is this your duty now? or is it not? If you cannot deny it, I warn you from the Lord do not neglect it; and do not by your disobedience to a convinced conscience prepare for a tormented conscience. If you know your Master's will, and do it not, you shall be beaten with many stripes.

And your public capacity and work doth make your repentance and holiness needful to others as well as to yourselves. Had we none to govern us, but such as entirely subject themselves to the government of Christ; and none to make us laws, but such as have his law transcribed upon their hearts; oh what a happy people should we be! Men are unlikely to make strict laws against the vices which they love and live in; or if they make them, they are more unlikely to execute them. We can expect no great help against drunkenness, swearing, gaming, filthiness, and profaneness, from men that love these abominations so well, as that they will rather part with God and their salvation than they will let them go. All men are born with a serpentine malice and enmity against the seed of Christ, which is rooted in their very natures. Custom in sin increaseth this to more malignity; and it is only renewing grace that doth overcome it. If, therefore, there should be any among our rulers that are not cured of this mortal malady, what friendship can be expected from them to the cause and servants of the Lord? If you are all the children of God yourselves, and heaven be your end, and holiness your delight and business, it will then be your principal care to encourage it, and help the people to the happiness that you have found yourselves. But if in any the original (increased) enmity to God and godliness prevail, we can expect no better (ordinarily) from such, than that they oppose the holiness which they hate, and do their worst to make us miserable. But woe to him that striveth against his Maker! Shall the thorns and briers be set in battle against the consuming fire and prevail? Isaiah xxvii. 4, 5. Oh! therefore, for the nation's sake, begin at home, and cast away the sins which you would have the nation cast away! All men can say, that ministers must teach by their lives, as well as by their doctrines; (and woe to them that do not!) and must not magistrates as well govern by their lives as by their laws? Will you make laws which you would not have men obey? Or would you have the people to be better than yourselves? Or can you expect to be obeyed by others, when you will not obey the God of heaven and earth yourselves? We beseech you, therefore, for the sake of a poor distressed land, let our recovery begin with you. God looks so much at the rulers of a nation in his dealings with them, that ordinarily it goes with the people as their rulers are. Until David had numbered the people, God would not let out his wrath upon them, though it was they that were the great offenders. If we see our representative body begin in loathing themselves for all their iniquities, and turning to the Lord with all their hearts, we should yet believe that he is returning to us, and will do us good after all our provocations. Truly, gentlemen, it is much from you that we must fetch our comfortable or sad prognostics of the life or death of this diseased land. Whatever you do, I know that it shall go well with the righteous; but for the happiness or misery of the nation in general, it is you that are our best prognostication. If you repent yourselves, and become a holy people to the Lord, it promiseth us deliverance; but if you harden your hearts, and prove despisers of God and holiness, it is like to be our temporal, and sure to be your eternal undoing, if saving grace do not prevent it.

And I must needs tell you, that if you be not brought to loathe yourselves, it is not because there is no loathsome matter in you. Did you see your inside you could not forbear it. As I think it would somewhat abate the pride of the most curious gallants, if they did but see what a heap of phlegm, and filth, and dung, (and perhaps crawling worms,) there is within them; much more should it make you loathe yourselves if you saw those sins that are a thousand times more odious. And to instigate you hereunto, let me further reason with you.

1. You can easily loathe an enemy; and who hath been a greater enemy to any of you than yourselves? Another may injure you; but no man can everlastingly undo you, but yourselves.

2. You abhor him that kills your dearest friends; and it is you by your sins that have put to death the Lord of life.

3. Who is it but yourselves that hath robbed you of so much precious time, and so much precious fruit of ordinances, and of all the mercies of the Lord?

4. Who is it but yourselves that hath brought you under God's displeasure? Poverty could not have made him loathe you, nor any thing besides your sins.

5. Who wounded conscience, and hath raised all your doubts and fears? Was it not your sinful selves?

6. Who is it but yourselves that hath brought you so near the gulf of misery, and endangered your eternal peace?

7. Consider the loathsome nature of your sins, and how then can you choose but loathe yourselves?

1. It is the creature's rebellion or disobedience against the absolute universal Sovereign.

2. It is the deformity of God's noblest creature here on earth, and the abusing of the most noble faculties.

3. It is a stain so deep that nothing can wash out but the blood of Christ. The flood that drowned a world of sinners did not wash away their sins. The fire that consumed the Sodomites did not consume their sins. Hell itself can never end it, and, therefore, shall have no end itself. It dieth not with you when you die; though churchyards are the guiltiest spots of ground, they do not bury and hide our sin.

4. The church must loathe it, and must cast out the sinner as loathsome, if he remain impenitent; and none of the servants of the Lord must have any friendship with the unfruitful works of darkness.

5. God himself doth loathe the creature for sin, and for nothing else but sin. "My soul loathed them," Zech. xi. 8. "When the Lord saw it, he abhorred them, because of the provoking of his sons and daughters," Deut. xxxii. 19. "My soul shall abhor you," Lev. xxvi. 30. "When God heard this, he was wroth, and greatly abhorred Israel," Psalm lxxviii. 59. "He abhorred his very sanctuary," Lam. ii. 7. "For he is of purer eyes than to behold iniquity," Hab. i. 13. In a word, it is the sentence of God himself, that a "wicked man is loathsome and cometh to shame," Prov. xiii. 5; so that you see what abundant cause of self-abhorrence is among us.

But we are much afraid of God's departure, when we see how common self-love is in the world, and how rare this penitent self-loathing is.

1. Do they loathe themselves that on every occasion are contending for their honour, and exalting themselves, and venturing their very souls, to be highest in the world for a little while?

2. Do they loathe themselves that are readier to justify all their sins, or at least to extenuate them, than humbly confess them?

3. Do they loathe themselves for all their sins that cannot endure to be reproved, but loathe their friends and the ministers of Christ that tell them of their loathsomeness?

4. Do they loathe themselves that take their pride itself for manhood, and christian humility for baseness, and brokenness of heart for whining hypocrisy or folly, and call them a company of priest-ridden fools that lament their sin, and ease their souls by free confession? Is the ruffling bravery of this city, and the strange attire, the haughty carriage, the feasting, idleness, and pomp, the marks of such as loathe themselves for all their abominations? Why then was fasting, and sackcloth, and ashes, the badge of such in ancient times?

5. Do they loathe themselves for all their sins, who loathe those that will not do as they, and speak reproachfully of such as run not with them to the same excess of riot, (1 Pet. iv. 4,) and count them precisians that dare not spit in the face of Christ, by wilful sinning as venturously and madly as themselves?

6. Or do they loathe themselves for all their sins, that love their sins even better than their God, and will not by all the obtestations, and commands, and entreaties of the Lord, be persuaded to forsake them? How far all these are from this self-loathing, and how far that nation is from happiness, where the rulers or inhabitants are such, is easy to conjecture.

I should have minded you what sins of the land must be remembered, and loathed, if we would have peace and healing. But as the glass forbids me, so alas, as the sins of Sodom, they declare themselves. Though through the great mercy of the Lord, the body of this nation, and the sober part, have not been guilty of that covenant-breaking, perfidiousness, treason, sedition, disobedience, self-exalting, and turbulency, as some have been, and as ignorant foreigners through the calumnies of malicious adversaries may possibly believe; yet must it be for a lamentation through all generations, that any of those who went out from us have contracted the guilt of such abominations, and occasioned the enemies of the Lord to blaspheme; and that any in the pride or simplicity of their hearts have followed the conduct of jesuitical seducers, they know not whither or to what.

That profaneness aboundeth on the other side, and drunkenness, swearing, fornication, lasciviousness, idleness, pride, and covetousness, doth still survive the ministers that have wasted themselves against them, and the labours of faithful magistrates to this day! And that the two extremes of heresy and profaneness do increase each other; and while they talk against each other, they harden one another, and both afflict the church of Christ. But especially woe to England for that crying sin, *the scorning of a holy life*, if a wonder of mercy do not save us! That people, professing the christian religion, should scorn the diligent practice of that religion which themselves profess! That obedience to the God of heaven, that imitation of the example of our Saviour, who came from heaven to teach us holiness, should not only be neglected, unreasonably and impiously neglected, but also by a transcendent impious madness should be made a matter of reproach! That the Holy Ghost, into whose name, as the Sanctifier, these men were themselves baptized, should not only be resisted, but his sanctifying work be made a scorn! That it should be made a matter of derision for a man to prefer his soul before his body, and heaven before earth, and God before a transitory world, and to use his reason in that for which it was principally given him, and not to be wilfully mad in a case where madness will undo him unto all eternity! Judge, as you are men, whether hell itself is like much to exceed such horrid wickedness! And whether it be not an astonishing wonder that ever a reasonable soul should be brought to such a height of abomination! That they that profess to believe the holy catholic church, and the communion of saints, should deride the holiness of the church, and the saints, and their communion! That they that pray for the hallowing of God's name, the coming of his kingdom, and the doing of his will, even as it is done in heaven, should make a mock at all this that they pray for! How much further, think you, is it possible for wicked souls to go in sinning? Is it not the God of heaven himself that they make a scorn of? Is not holiness his image? Did not he make the law that doth command it; professing that none shall see his face without it? Heb. xii. 14. O sinful nation! O people laden with iniquity! Repent, repent speedily, and with self-loathing, repent of this inhuman crime, lest God should take away your glory, and enter himself into judgment with you, and plead against you the scorn that you have cast upon the Creator, the Saviour, the Sanctifier, to whom you were engaged in your baptismal vows! Lest when he plagueth and condemneth you, he say, "Why persecuted you me?" Acts ix. 4. "Inasmuch as ye did it to one of the least of these my brethren, ye did it unto me." Read Prov. i. 20, to the end. When Israel mocked the messengers of the Lord, and despised his words, and misused his prophets, his wrath arose against his people till there was no remedy, 2 Chron. xxvi. 16; and oh that you who are the physicians of this diseased land would specially call them to repentance for this, and help them against it for the time to come!

Having called you first to remember your misdoings, and, secondly, to loathe yourselves in your own eyes for them, I must add a third, that you stop not here, but proceed to reformation, or else all the rest is but hypocrisy. And here it is I that most earnestly entreat this honourable assembly for their best assistance. O make not the forementioned sins your own, lest you hear from God, *quod minus crimine quam absolutione peccatum est.* Though England hath been used to cry out for liberty, let them not have liberty to abuse their Maker, and to damn their souls, if you can hinder it. *Optimus est reipublicæ status, ubi nulla libertas deest, nisi licentia pereundi,* as Nero was once told by his unsuccessful tutor. Use not men to a liberty of scorning the laws of God, lest you teach them to scorn yours; for can you expect to be better used than God. And *cui plus licet quam par est, plus vult quam licet,* Gell. i. 17, c. 14. We have all seen the evils of liberty to be wanton in religion. Is it not worse to have liberty to deride religion? If men shall have leave to go quietly to hell themselves, let them not have leave to mock poor souls from heaven. The suffering to the sound in faith is as nothing; for what is the foaming rage of mad-men to be regarded? But that in England God should be so provoked, and souls so hindered from the paths of life, that whoever will be converted and saved must be made a laughing-stock, which carnal minds cannot endure; this is the mischief which we deprecate.

The eyes of the nation, and of the christian world, are much upon you, some high in hopes, some deep in fears, some waiting in dubious expectations for the issue of your counsels. Great expectations, in deep necessities, should awake you to the greatest care and diligence. Though I would not, by omitting any necessary directions or admonitions to you, invite the world to think that I speak to such as cannot endure to hear, and that so honourable an assembly doth call the ministers of Christ to do those works of their proper office, which yet they will be offended if they do, yet had I rather err in the defective part than by excess, and therefore shall not presume to be too particular. Only in general, in the name of Christ, and on the behalf of a trembling, yet hoping nation, I most earnestly beseech and warn you, that you own and promote the power and practice of godliness in the land; and that as God, whose ministers you are, (Rom. xiii. 4,) is a rewarder of them that diligently seek him, (Heb. xi. 6,) and hath made this a principal article of our faith, so you would imitate your absolute Lord, and honour them that fear the Lord, and encourage them that diligently seek him. And may I not freely tell you that God should have the precedency? and that you must first seek his kingdom, and the righteousness thereof, and he will facilitate all the rest of your work? Surely no powers on earth should be offended, that the God from whom, and for whom, and through whom, they have what they have, is preferred before them, when they should own no interest but his, and what is subservient to it. I have long thought that pretences of a necessity of beginning with our own affairs, hath frustrated our hopes from many parliaments already; and I am sure that by delays, the enemies of our peace have got advantage to cross our ends and attain their own. Our calamities begun in differences about religion, and still that is the wound that most needs closing. And if that were done, how easily, I dare confidently speak it, would the generality of sober, godly people, be agreed in things civil, and become the strength and glory of the sovereign, under God. And though, with grief and shame, we see this work so long undone, (may we hope that God hath reserved it to this season,) yet I have the confidence to profess, that, as the exalting of one party, by the ejection and persecuting of the rest, is the sinful way to your dishonour and our ruin, so the terms on which the differing parties most considerable among us may safely, easily, and suddenly unite, are very obvious, and our concord a very easy thing, if the prudent and moderate might be the guides, and selfish interests and passion did not set us at a further distance than our principles have done. And to show you the facility of such an agreement, were it not that such personal matters are much liable to misinterpretations, I should tell you, that the late reverend primate of Ireland consented, in less than half an hour's debate, to five or six propositions which I offered him, as sufficient for the concord of the moderate episcopal and presbyterians, withou forsaking the principles of their parties. Oh that the Lord would yet show so much mercy to a sinful nation, as to put it into your hearts to promote but the practice of those christian principles which we are all agreed in! I hope there is no controversy among us whether God should be obeyed, and hell avoided, and heaven first sought, and Scripture be the rule and test of our religion, and sin abhorred and cast out. Oh that you would but further the practice of this with all your might! We crave not of you any lordship or dominion, nor riches, nor interest in your temporal affairs; we had rather see a law to exclude all ecclesiastics from all power of force. The God of heaven that will judge you and us, will be a righteous judge betwixt us, whether we crave any thing unreasonable at your hands. These are the sum of our requests: 1. That holiness may be encouraged, and the overspreading profaneness of this nation effectually kept down. 2. That an able, diligent ministry may be encouraged, and not corrupted by temporal power. 3. That discipline may be seriously promoted, and ministers no more hindered by magistrates in the exercise of their office than physicians and schoolmasters are in theirs, seeing it is but a government like theirs, consisting in the liberty of conscionably managing the works of our own office, that we expect. Give us but leave to labour in Christ's vineyard with such encouragement as the necessity of obstinate souls requireth, and we will ask no more. You have less cause to restrain us from discipline than from preaching. For it is a more flesh-displeasing work that we are hardlier brought to. I foretell you that you shut out me, and all that are of my mind, if you would force us to administer sacraments without discipline, and without the conduct of our own discretion, to whom the magistrate appoints it, as if a physician must give no physic but by your prescript. The antidisciplinarian magistrate I could as resolutely suffer under as the superstitious, it being worse to cast out discipline, than to err in the circumstances of it. The question is not, whether bishops or no, but whether discipline or none? And whether enough to use it? 4. We earnestly request that Scripture sufficiency, as the test of our religion, and only universal law of Christ, may be maintained, and that nothing unnecessary may be imposed as necessary, nor the church's unity laid on that which will not bear it, nor ever did. Oh that we might but have leave to serve God only as Christ hath commanded us, and to go to heaven in the same way as the apostles did! These are our desires, and whether they are reasonable, God will judge.

Give first to God the things that are God's, and then give Cæsar the things that are Cæsar's. Let your wisdom be first pure, and then peaceable. Not but that we are resolved to be loyal to sovereignty, though you deny us all these. Whatever malicious men pretend, that is not, nor shall not be, our difference. I have proved more publicly, when it was more dangerous to publish it, that the generality of the orthodox, sober ministers, and godly people of this nation, did never consent to king-killing, and resisting sovereign power, nor to the change of the ancient government of this land, but abhorred the pride and ambition that attempted it. I again repeat it, the blood of some, the imprisonment and displacing of others, the banishment or flight of others, and the detestations and public protestations of more; the oft-declared sense of England, and the wars and sad estate of Scotland; have all declared before the world, to the shame of calumniators, that the generality of the orthodox, sober protestants of these nations, have been true to their allegiance, and detesters of unfaithfulness and ambition in subjects, and resisters of heresy and schism in the church, and of anarchy and democratical confusions in the commonwealth. And though the land hath ringed with complaints and threatenings against myself, for publishing a little of the mixture of jesuitical and familistical contrivances, for taking down together our government and religion, and setting up new ones for the introduction of popery, infidelity, and heresy; yet I am assured that there is much more of this confederacy for the all-seeing God to discover in time, to the shame of papists, that cannot be content to write themselves for the killing of kings when the pope hath once excommunicated them, and by the decrees of a general council at the Lateran, to depose princes that will not extirpate such as the pope calls heretics, and absolve all their subjects from their fidelity and allegiance, but they must also creep into the councils and armies of protestants, and taking the advantage of successes and ambition, withdraw men at once from their religion and allegiance, that they may cheat the world into a belief that treasons are the fruits of the protestant profession, when these masked jugglers have come by night, and sown and cherished these Romish tares. As a papist must cease to be a papist if he will be truly and fully loyal to his sovereign, (as I am ready to prove against any adversary,) so a protestant must so far cease to be a protestant, before he can be disloyal. For Rom. xiii. is part of the rule of his religion. Unhappily there hath been a difference among us which is the higher power, when those that have their shares in the sovereignty are divided; but whether we should be subject to the higher power, is no question with us.

Gentlemen, I have nothing to ask of you for myself, nor any of my brethren, as for themselves, but that you will be friends to serious preaching and holy living, and will not insnare our consciences with any unscriptural inventions of men. This I would beg of you as on my knees: 1. As for the sake of Christ, whose cause and people it is that I am pleading for. 2. For the sake of thousands of poor souls in this land, whose salvation or damnation will be much promoted by you. 3. For the sake of thousands of the dear servants of the Lord, whose eyes are waiting to see what God will do by your hands. 4. For your own sakes, who are undone if you dash yourselves on the rock you should build on, and set against the holy God, and turn the cries of his servants to heaven for deliverance from you, Luke xviii. 8. If you stumble on Christ, he will break you in pieces; but if he fall upon you, he will grind you to powder. 5. For the sake of your posterity, that they may not be bred up in ignorance or ungodliness. 6. For the honour of the nation and yourselves, that you turn by all the suspicions and fears that are raised in the land. 7. For the honour of sound doctrine and church government, that you may not bring schism into greater credit than now you have brought it to deserved shame. For if you frown on godliness under pretence of uniformity in unnecessary things, and make times worse than when libertinism and schism so prevailed, the people will look back with groans, and say, What happy times did we once see! And so will honour schism, and libertinism, and usurpation, through your oppression. 8. Lastly, I beg this of you, for the honour of sovereignty, and the nation's peace. A prince of a holy people is most honourable. The interest of holiness is Christ's own. Happy is that prince that espouseth this, and subjecteth all his own unto it: see Psalm i. 1, 2, and ci. and xv. 4. It is the conscionable, prudent, godly people of the land, that must be the glory and strength of their lawful sovereign. Their prayers will serve him better than the hideous oaths and curses of the profane. Woe to the rulers that set themselves against the interest of Christ and holiness! (read Psalm ii.;) or that make snares for their consciences, that they may persecute them as disobedients, who are desirous to obey their rulers in subordination to the Lord: see Dan. iii. and vi. 5, 10, 13. I have dealt plainly with you, and told you the very truth. If God have now a blessing for you and us, you will obey it, but if you refuse, then look to yourselves, and answer it if you can. I am sure, in spite of earth and hell, it shall go well with them that live by faith.

RIGHT REJOICING:

OR

THE NATURE AND ORDER OF RATIONAL AND WARRANTABLE JOY;

DISCOVERED IN

A SERMON PREACHED AT ST. PAUL'S,

BEFORE THE LORD MAYOR AND ALDERMEN, AND THE SEVERAL COMPANIES OF THE CITY OF LONDON, ON MAY 10, 1660, APPOINTED BY BOTH HOUSES OF PARLIAMENT TO BE A DAY OF SOLEMN THANKSGIVING FOR GOD'S RAISING UP AND SUCCEEDING HIS EXCELLENCY, AND OTHER INSTRUMENTS, IN ORDER TO HIS MAJESTY'S RESTORATION, AND THE SETTLEMENT OF THESE NATIONS.

TO THE RIGHT HONOURABLE THOMAS ALEYNE,

LORD MAYOR OF THE CITY OF LONDON,

WITH THE RIGHT WORSHIPFUL ALDERMEN, HIS BRETHREN.

As, in obedience to your favourable invitation, this Sermon was first preached; and the author, conscious of his great unworthiness, employed in so honourable a work; so is it your pleasure, against which my judgment must not here contest, that hath thus exposed it to the public view; which yet I must confess doth not engage you in the patronage of any of the crudities and imperfections of this hasty work, it being the matter, which is of God, that so far prevailed for your acceptance as to procure your pardon of the manner, which is too much my own. Rejoicing is so highly valued, even by nature, that I thought it a matter of great necessity to help to rectify and elevate your joys. The corruption of a thing so excellent must needs be very bad; and it being the great and durable good that must feed all great and durable joy, and seeing these little transitory things can cause but little and transitory delight, I thought it my duty to insist most on the greatest, on which, in your meditations, you most insist; which I repent not of, especially now you have given my doctrine a more loud and lasting voice, because it is only our heavenly interest that may be the matter of universal continued delight: and so the subject may make the sermon to be of the more universal and continued use, when a subject of less excellency and duration than heaven would have depressed and limited the discourse, as to its usefulness. And also I was forced in this, as in all these sublunary things, to estimate the mercy in which we did all so solemnly rejoice but as a means, which is so far to be valued as it conduceth to its end; and is something or nothing as it relateth to eternity. Since I placed my hopes above, and learned to live a life of faith, I never desire to know any mercy in any other form or name, nor value it on any other account, as not affecting to make such reckonings which I daily see obliterated in grief and shame by those that make them; and remembering who said, that if we had known Christ himself after the flesh, henceforth we know him so no more. As it was my compassion to the frantic, merry world, and also to the self-troubling, melancholy christian, and my desire methodically to help you in your rejoicings about the great occasions of the day, which formed this exhortation to what you heard, and chose the subject which, to some, might seem less suitable to the day; so, if the publication may print so great and necessary a point on the hearts of any that had not the opportunity to hear, as God shall have the praise, and they the joy, so you shall have, under God, the thanks, and I the attainment of my end which is my reward. I rest,

Your servant in the work of Christ

RICHARD BAXTER.

LUKE X. 20.

NOTWITHSTANDING IN THIS REJOICE NOT, THAT THE SPIRITS ARE SUBJECT UNTO YOU; BUT RATHER REJOICE, BECAUSE YOUR NAMES ARE WRITTEN IN HEAVEN.

RIGHT HONOURABLE, WORSHIPFUL, AND BELOVED AUDITORS,

IF any of you shall say, upon the hearing of my text, that I have chosen a subject unsuitable to the occasion, and that a "rejoice not," is out of season on a day of such rejoicing, they may, I hope, be well satisfied by that time they have considered the reason of these words, as used by Christ to his disciples, and the greater joy that is here commanded, and so the reason of my choice.

When Christ had sent forth his seventy disciples to preach the gospel through the cities of Judea, and to confirm it by miraculous cures, for which he endued them with power from above, upon their return they triumph especially in this, that "the devils themselves were subject to them through the name of Christ," ver. 17. A mercy which Christ is so far from extenuating, that, 1. He sets it forth more fully than they, (ver. 18,) "I beheld Satan as lightning fall from heaven." 2. He promiseth them yet more of it, "giving them power to tread on serpents, and on scorpions, and over all the power of the enemy, and that nothing should by any means hurt them." 3. He rejoiceth in spirit, and thankfully acknowledgeth it to the Father himself, ver. 21. And yet he seems here to forbid them to rejoice in it, commanding them another joy. What! was it not a mercy to be rejoiced in? or is there any contradiction in the words of Christ? Neither: he doth not absolutely forbid them to rejoice in it; but he saw that their corruption took an advantage by it, to puff them up with pride and vain-glory, and that they savoured it too carnally, and were much taken with it, as it was a visible triumph and honour to themselves the instruments, and too much overlooked the end and use of it. Christ therefore aggravateth the mercy in its proper notion, as it was to the honouring of the Father and himself, and the advancement of his kingdom, and the saving of men's souls, by the confirmation of the gospel, and the fall of Satan. But the shell or grosser substance of the mercy, applied to a wrong end, and by corruption made another thing, being deprived of its proper soul, this Christ admonisheth them to keep out of their estimation and affection. He meeteth his returning messengers rejoicing too much in themselves: and this proud, inordinate, selfish joy, is it that he would take from them by his caution or prohibition, "In this rejoice not." But that they may see that he doth not envy them their comforts, he showeth them cause of a greater joy, which he alloweth and commandeth them as more suitable to his ends and their felicity: "But rather rejoice that your names are written in heaven."

For the better understanding of this you may observe; 1. What matter of joy the subjection of the devils might afford them. 2. What manner of joy they were affected with, which Christ forbad them. 3. What manner of joy it is that Christ alloweth them, when he seemeth to restrain it wholly to their heavenly interest.

I. No doubt, to have the devils subject to them was a great mercy, in which they might rejoice. For, 1. It was the gift of Christ; and all is perfumed that hath touched his hand. Nothing but good can come from him that is so good, by way of gift.

2. It was a gift foretold by the prophets, as reserved for the gospel time, that is eminently called the kingdom of God; and an extraordinary gift in respect to the precedent and subsequent generations. It was no usual thing for men to exercise such authority over the very devils, as to command them to come forth, and to heal the bodies that they had long afflicted.

3. It was a victory over the strongest enemy, that can make more effectual resistance than the most numerous armies of poor mortals, and would laugh at your horse and arms, your fire and sword, your greatest cannons; and cannot be expugned but by the power of the Almighty. A stronger than he must come upon him, and bind him, and cast him out of his possession, before he will surrender the garrison, goods, and prisoners, which he hath held in peace, Luke xi. 21, 22.

4. It was a victory over the most subtle enemy, that is not conquerable by any stratagems of human wit.

5. It was a victory over the most malicious enemy, that sought more than the subversion of men's temporal peace, and by afflicting the body intended the hurting of the soul.

6. It was a conquest of him that had long possession, and one way or other kept in bondage the prisoners that justice had subjected to his rage.

7. It was a victory exceeding honourable to Christ, whose very messengers, by his name alone, could make the powers of hell submit. He that refused to be made a king, as having not a kingdom of this world, (John xviii. 36,) and that had not a place to lay his head on, Matt. viii. 22; commanded him that had presumed to tempt him with all the kingdoms and the glory of the world! Matt. iv. 8, 9; and that not only by the bare word of his mouth, but by the word of his meanest, most despised messengers; which made the people stand amazed, saying, What manner of man is this?

8. It was a victory tending to the successes of the gospel, to convince the unbelieving world, and so to enlarge the kingdom of Christ, and to save the people's souls.

9. And also from so great a work it was no small honour that accrued to the instruments: an honour which, in its proper place, they might lawfully regard.

10. And all this was aggravated by the congruency of the mercy to the low, despised condition of the instruments, (and of Christ himself,) when they were destitute of all common advantages and means, for the carrying on of so great and necessary a work, surpassing all the strength of flesh: how seasonable was it that the omnipotency of Heaven should then appear for them, and thus engage itself for their success. So that in all this you may easily see that here was abundant matter for a rational, warrantable joy to the disciples.

II. But where then was their fault? And what was that joy which Christ forbad them? *Answer.* Having already told you in general, I shall tell you more particularly. 1. They looked too much at the matter of dominion over the subjected and ejected devils, and relished most delightfully the external part. As the Jews looked for a Messiah that should come in grandeur, and bring the nations under his dominion; so the disciples, that had yet too much of these conceits, began to be lifted up with the expectation of some earthly glory, when they saw the powers of hell submit, and Christ thus begin with the manifestation of his omnipotency. But the great end of these miracles they too much overlooked; they too much left out of their rejoicings the appearances of God, the advantages of faith, the promotion of the spiritual kingdom of Christ, and the greater mercies of the gospel, as to themselves and others.

2. They took too great a share of the honour to themselves, being more affected to see what great things they were made the instruments to accomplish, than what honour did thereby accrue to God and benefit to man; and thus, while they arrogate too much to themselves, and withal too much overlook those higher, greater mercies, to which all their miracles were but means, they deservedly fall under Christ's reproof; and he is employed in the cure of their diseased joys, by amputation of the superfluities, and rectifying the irregularities, and supplying the defects, lest Satan should take possession of their souls, by carnality, selfishness, and pride, when they thought they had conquered him, by dispossessing him of men's bodies.

III. By this you may understand what joy it is that Christ alloweth and commandeth them.

1. As to themselves, to kill their pride, and to increase their kindly joy and thankfulness, and to advance their estimation of the riches of the gospel, and rectify their judgment of the work and kingdom of their Lord, he calls them to mind that higher mercy, which is worthy of their greatest joy. An interest in heaven is another kind of mercy than healing the sick, or casting out devils here on earth.

2. In reference to his honour, he would have them first look at the greatest of his gifts, and not forget the glory which he finally intends them, while they are taken up with these wonders in the way; for his greatest honour ariseth from his greatest mercies.

3. As to the degrees of their rejoicing, he would not have them give the greater share to the lesser mercy, but to rejoice so much more in their heavenly interest, as that all other joy should be as none in comparison of it: so that this "Rejoice not in this," &c. is as much as if he had said, Let your rejoicing in this power over the devils be as nothing in comparison of your rejoicing that your names are written in heaven. Just as he forbiddeth care and labour for these earthly things, when he saith, "Care not what ye shall eat," &c. Matt. vi. 25; "Labour not for the meat that perisheth, but for that which endureth to everlasting life, which the Son of man will give you," John vi. 27. Our care and labour for earthly things must be nothing, in comparison of the care and labour we are at for heaven: and so our joy, in the greatest of these outward mercies, should be as nothing, in comparison of our joy in higher things.

4. As to the nature and order of the thing, he alloweth them no joy in this, or any temporal or created thing whatsoever, but as it proceedeth from God, and tendeth to him as our ultimate end. We must not rejoice in our victories over Satan, or any other enemy, for itself, and as our end, but as it is a means to the glory of God and men's salvation. In all which, it is evident that Christ doth but regulate and advance their joy, and calleth them first to rejoice in that which is their end and all, and animateth all their lower mercies; he then alloweth and requireth them to rejoice, even in this, which he seemed to forbid them to rejoice in, viz. that the devils were subject to them, so they do it in due subordination to its end.

The only difficulty in the preceptive part of the text is, what is meant here by the "writing of their names in heaven." In a word, the meaning is, that they are "fellow-citizens of the saints, and of the household of God;" and having a room among the saints on earth, have a title to the celestial glory. As in some well-ordered cities there were rolls kept of the names of all the citizens, or free-men, as distinct from all the inferior, more servile sort of subjects; and as muster-rolls are kept of the listed soldiers of the army; so all that are saints are enrolled citizens of heaven, that is, are the heirs of the heavenly felicity.

We are decreed to this state before the foundations of the world; we are redeemed to it by the death of Christ; but we are not actually entered into it till we are sanctified by the Holy Ghost, and heartily engaged to God the Father, Son, and Spirit, in the holy covenant.

The doctrine of the text is contained in this proposition—To have our names written in heaven is the greatest mercy, and first, and chiefly, and only for itself to be rejoiced in; which so puts the estimate on all inferior mercies, that further than they refer to this they are not to be the matter of our joy.

Though we had seen the devils subjected to our ministration, departing from the possessed when we command them in the name of Christ, and the bodies of the afflicted miraculously relieved; yet all this were not, comparatively, to be rejoiced in, nor as separated from our title to the heavenly glory.

When I have, first, given you the reasons of the prohibition—"Rejoice not in this," and then of the command—"But rather rejoice," &c. you may, by fuller satisfaction about the sense and truth of the proposition, be better prepared for the further application.

I. "Rejoice not," though the devils themselves were subject to you, further than as this refers to heaven; 1. Because all these common mercies may possibly consist with the present misery of the persons that receive them. A man may be the slave of the devil, as to his soul, when he is casting him out of another man's body. He may be conquered by his own concupiscence, that hath triumphed over many an enemy. These times have showed it, to our grief, that heresy, and pride, and ambition, and self-conceit, may conquer those that have been famous for their conquests. He may be a slave to himself that is the master of another.

And what I say of the instance in my text, you may, upon a parity or superiority of reason, all along give me leave to apply to the great occasion of the day, it being a matter of much greater glory to conquer infernal powers than mortal enemies, and to have the devils subject to us than men. To be such a conqueror of men or devils is no sure proof of the pardon of sin, the favour of God, and saving of your souls. Alas! how many, called valiant, are the basest cowards in the warfare that their everlasting life dependeth on! How many that are renowned for their victories by men, are wretches despised and abhorred by the Lord? What christian so poor and despicable in the world, that would change his state with a Catiline or Sejanus, yea, with a Cæsar or Alexander, if he might? Could you see the inside of a glittering gallant, or an adored prince, that is a stranger to the life of faith, what a sad disparity would you see! the vermin of the most filthy lusts continually crawling in the soul, while the body is set out by the most exquisite ornaments that pride can invent, and their purses can procure, for the increasing of their esteem in the eyes of such as judge of souls by the colour and cover of the bodies. To see the same man sumptuously feasted, attended, honoured, magnified by men, and at the same time dead in sin, unacquainted with the life and comforts of believers, and under the curse and condemnation of the law of God, would tell you that such a wretch is far from the state in which a reasonable man is allowed to rejoice. There are not more naked, leprous souls in the world, than some that are covered with a silken, laced, painted case; nor any more poor and sordid, than such as abound with earthly riches. And for such a one to rejoice is as unseemly as for a man to glory that his gangrened foot hath a handsome shoe; or that his diseased, pained flesh doth suffer in the fashion: or that his wounds and ulcers are searched with a silver instrument. God seeth the rottenness and filth that is within these painted sepulchres, and therefore judgeth not of them as the ignorant spectator, that seeth no further than the smoothed, polished, gilded outside. And therefore we find his language of such to differ so much from the language of the world. He calls those poor, and miserable, and blind, and naked, and foolish, and mad, and dead, and cursed, that perhaps hear nothing lower from the world than honourable, worshipful, rich, and wise; and men are admiring them, while God is loathing them; and men are applauding them, while God condemneth them. And hence it is that the servants of the Lord do lament the case of those that worldlings count most happy. What Paul speaks of those "whose God is their belly, whose glory is their shame, and who mind earthly things," he doth it weeping, Phil. iii. 18, 19; when a frantic sensualist would but have derided his compassionate tears, and bid him keep them for himself.

2. Rejoice not in these outward common things comparatively, or for themselves, because they are not only consistent with most deplorable misery, but also are the strong and ordinary means of making men miserable, and fixing them in it, and increasing it. Many that have seemed humble, fruitful, flourishing, and stedfast, while they dwelt in the valleys of a mean, a low, afflicted state, have proved sun-burnt, weather-beaten sinners, apostates, proud, vain-glorious, and barren, when they have removed their habitations to the mountains of prosperity. Alas! we find it hard enough to be serious, faithful christians, under the less and ordinary temptations of a poor, or mean, or suffering condition. And should I rejoice if I were but to pass to heaven as a camel must pass through a needle's eye? We have difficulties enough already, unless our wisdom, strength, and courage, were greater to encounter them; and shall we rejoice if these difficulties be increased to impossibilities, (as with men,) leaving us no hope but that human impossibilities are conquerable by divine Omnipotency, Luke xviii. 27. Is it not hard enough to have a lowly mind in a low condition? (but much more in a high!) to despise the world when the world despiseth us? to walk in heaven when faith is not interrupted by the noise or shows of the distracted actors of these Bedlam tragedies? and to converse with our everlasting company, when we are freest from these crowds and tumults? And shall we rejoice that we, who already stumble at a straw, have rocks of offence and mountains of difficulty cast before us? How few are advanced to higher measures of faith and holiness by their advancements in the world! For the most part, if they seemed to have something of plain honesty and fidelity before, when they come to be advanced, it is drowned in carnal policies, self-love, and hypocritical dissimulation. And if they seemed before to be humble and heavenly, and to live to God, and to his interest and service, how strangely doth prosperity and dignity transform them, and make them forget their former apprehensions, their convictions, purposes, and vows, yea, their God, their happiness, and themselves! And should we not be very cautelous how we rejoice in an air that few men have their health in? and in a diet, how sweet soever, that corrupts and kills the most that use it? in the tables that prove snares, and the sumptuous houses that are traps to the inhabitants?

3. Rejoice not in these common things, for they are but such as are often made the devil's tools to do his work by, and are used against the Lord that gave them, to the hinderance of the gospel, and injury of the church of Christ. While men are low, and live by faith, they do good with the little which they have; and have the blessing of the will, (when they are unable for the deed,) and of hearts disposed to do good if they had opportunity: when usually those that are lifted up, having more of power, and less of will, do less when they might and should do more; and use their talents to aggravate their sin and condemnation: to further piety, or charity, they have power without will; but to hinder it, they have both power and will. And while the poor of the world, that are rich only in faith, would help on the work of God, and cannot, (by the great assistances which the great might give,) and the rich and honourable can and will not, but can and will promote the interest of the flesh, you may easily see the church's case, how sure it is to know adversity, and how much of our expectation must be from God, and how little from any of the sons of men. Is it as common for one that is very rich to part with all to follow Christ for the hopes of heaven, as it is for one that hath not much in the world to part with? Is it as common for one that hath many thousands a year, to cast all his substance into the treasury, as for a widow to do it that hath but two mites? Luke xxi. 2.

4. Oh how much easier were it like to go with the church of God if greatness and ungodliness were not so commonly conjunct! But usually, as riches, and dignities, and honours, do much increase their carnal interest, so do they increase their carnal-mindedness, and their engagements against that life of faith and holiness which is contrary to their interests; so that none are such malignant adversaries to godliness, and none have such advantage to execute their malice. Seeing, then, that all such honours and advancements are made by corruption too ordinary instruments of the vilest works of serving Satan, and opposing Christ, and oppressing piety, honesty, and innocence, rejoice not in them as for themselves, nor any way but in subservience to your heavenly rejoicings.

5. And it should much abate our carnal joy to consider that all these things are such as may end in misery, and leave the owner in everlasting woe. He that is feasting in purple and fine linen to-day, may be to-morrow in remediless torments, and want a drop of water to cool his tongue, Luke xvi. He that is to-day triumphing over mortal enemies, may to-morrow be led in triumph to hell-fire, and lie in chains of darkness till the judgment of the great day. He that is now prophesying in the name of Christ, and casting out devils, and doing many great and wonderful works, may shortly be condemned at his bar, with a "Depart from me, ye workers of iniquity, I never knew you," Matt. vii. 22, 23. And who would be merry at a feast that he must cast up

again, in griping pain, or mortal sickness? You see now where the great ones of the world do take their places, and how they are admired and honoured by men; but you see not where the tide will leave them, and how they shall be used by infernal spirits, if they have not a better preventive and security than all the renown and dignities of the world. Be cautelous, therefore, in your rejoicing for that which may end in everlasting sorrows.

Yea, more than so, these outward honours and successes may plunge men deeper in perdition than ever they had been without them. And thousands shall wish that they had never known them; and that they had rather been the lowest and obscurest persons, than by the temptations of prosperity to have been led into that misery. And should you not be very cautelous in your rejoicing in that which you may possibly wish you had never known? You see then the reasons for the prohibition, "Rejoice not."

II. But, on the contrary, that the precept, "Rejoice that your names are written in heaven," is backed with such reasons from the nature of the thing, as should much excite us to the practice, is a truth so manifest, that a tedious demonstration of it might seem at best unnecessary, and so an error, in these straits of time. 1. What should be rejoiced in, if not the Lord of life himself, who is the everlasting joy and glory of the saints? If felicity itself cannot make us happy, and life itself is insufficient to quicken us, and the sun itself cannot illuminate us, it is in vain to expect this light, this life, this happiness and joy from any other. From others we may have joy derivatively at the second hand, but only from God as the original and first cause. Other things may be means of the conveyance, but God is the matter of our joy. A creature may be his medicine, but he is our life and health itself. Comfort may be offered by others, but it is he that gives it. Others may direct us to it, but he effecteth it. If God be not to be rejoiced in, the affection of joy is made in vain; for he is goodness itself, and there is nothing lovely or delectable but what is in him. And what is heaven but the fruition of God?

2. It is congruous that we now rejoice in that which we must everlastingly rejoice in. Heaven is the state of everlasting joy, and, therefore, the foresight of it by faith is the only way to rational, solid comfort here. If you knew the place in which you should live but a hundred years in earthly pleasures, or the friend in whom you should as long have sweet delight, the foreknowledge of it would make that place and friend more delightful to you than any other. Mutable joys are the shame of man, and show his levity or his folly in choosing these things to comfort him that are insufficient to perform it. But if your heavenly interest be the matter of your joy, you may rejoice to-morrow as well as to-day, and the next day as well as to-morrow, and the next year as well as this. If prosperity be your joy, your joy must be short, for your worldly prosperity will be so. If victory, and dignity, and overtopping others, be your joy, it will be short; for death is ready to leave the conqueror, the honourable, the prince, with the conquered, and the meanest subject. If the solemnity and feasting of such a day as this should be the greatest matter of your joy, the day will have a night, and the feast an end, and so will your joy. But if heaven be the matter of your joy, you may go on in your rejoicing, and every day may be your festival; for God is the same both yesterday, and to-day, and for ever. You only have the day that hath no night, and the feast that hath no end, or intermission, unless as it is caused by your errors and misapprehensions. There can nothing fall out of so hurtful a nature as to turn your feast into gall and wormwood, for God will be still God, and Christ still your Head, and heaven will be heaven, and nothing is of any considerable moment to put into the scales against your happiness. If once you have a God, a Christ, a heaven to rejoice in, you may rationally indulge a constant joy, and may rationally rejoice in poverty, reproach, contempt, and calumny, in imprisonment, banishment, sickness, or in death, as well as in a prosperous state: and you transgress the laws of reason if you do not.

3. Rejoice if your names are written in heaven; for this is a divine, a pure, a profitable, and a warrantable joy. When God and his ministers rebuke your mirth, it is not this holy mirth that they rebuke, but your dreaming mirth, or waking folly. As we beat down your presumption, but to set up your faith; and beat down men's deceitful hopes, to prepare them for the hopes that will not fail them, and not to bring them to despair; so do we call you from your frothy, foolish, childish mirth, that we may lead you to the highest joys. Here is joy that you need not be ashamed of; of which you can scarcely take too much; of which you need not to repent. Be as joyful and merry as you will, if this may but be the matter of your joy. The more you are thus joyful, the more acceptable to God. It is Satan, and not God, that is the enemy of this joy; that pleads against it, and fills a christian's mind with groundless scruples, and doubts, and objections against it. Oh that our souls and our assemblies did more abound with this holy joy! And oh that christians understood the excellency and usefulness of it, and would set themselves more constantly to the promoting and maintaining of it in themselves! Whoever of you is most joyful in the Lord, I dare persuade you to be more joyful yet; and so far should you be from checking yourselves for this holy joy, that the rest of your duties should intend it, and you should make it your work by the help of all God's ordinances and mercies to increase it. He is the best christian that hath most love, and joy, and gratitude; and he that is best at this, is like to be best in the performance of his other duties, and in the conquest of remaining sins. But more of this in the application.

And now I am approaching to a closer application, I hope I may suppose that I have removed the objection that met me in the beginning, and that by this time you see that I am not unseasonably suppressing your warrantable joy; but, 1. Preventing that which is unwarrantable; and, 2. Showing you the higher joys, which must animate these, or they will be but dead, corrupted things: it is only the regulation and the exaltation of your joys that I am endeavouring; and, for the first, my text affordeth me so full instruction, that you may see this observation meeting you in the first perusal of the words.

That when the Lord hath vouchsafed us matter of rejoicing in his wonders of mercy, and our great successes, the best of us are too prone to take up a selfish, carnal joy, and have need of Christ's prohibition or caution, "Rejoice not in this."

The soul is active, and will be doing; and there is nothing that it is more naturally inclined to than delight. Something or other, which may be suitable to it, and sufficient to answer its desires, it fain would be rejoicing in. And the spiritual part of all our mercies is pure and refined, and too subtle for the discerning of our carnal minds, and, therefore, is invisible to the dark, ungodly world; and, also, it is contrary to the interest of the flesh, and to the present bent of man's concupiscence: and therefore it is that spiritual mercies are not perceived, nor relished by the flesh; yea, that they are refused, as food by a sick stomach, with enmity and loathing, as if they were judgments or plagues, and not mercies; and hence it is that a carnal mind doth as unwillingly accept of any mercies of this sort, as if it were some heavy service that made God almost beholden to him to accept them. But the objects of sense, the matters of commodity, or honour, or sensual pleasure, are such as the worst of men are more eager after than any other; they are things that flesh itself doth savour, and can judge of, and is naturally, now, too much in love with. And, therefore, there being too much of this concupiscence yet within us, the best have need, as to be excited to the spiritual part of their rejoicing, so to be warned and called off from the carnal part. Our successes, and our other common mercies, have all of them both a carnal and a spiritual part; somewhat that is suited to our bodies, and somewhat to our souls. And as we are all too prone to be sensible and regardful of our bodily affairs and interests, and too insensible and neglectful of the matters of our souls; so we can easily pick out so much of providences and mercies as gratify and accommodate our flesh; and there we would stop and know no more; as if we had no spiritual part to mind, nor the mercy of any spiritual part to be improved. To rejoice in mere prosperity and success may be done without grace, by pride and sensuality, as easily as a drunkard can be merry with his cups, or any other sinner in his sin. Think it not needless, then, to hear this admonition, Take heed that you rejoice not carnally in the carcass, or outside only of your mercies; as such an outside religion, consisting in the shell of duty, without God, who is the life and kernel, is not religion indeed, but a hypocritical, self-deceiving show; so you may turn a day of thanksgiving into a day of fleshly mirth, more sinful than a morris-dance or may-game, because of the aggravation of conjunct hypocrisy, if you set not a faithful guard upon your hearts.

For the rectifying, therefore, and elevating of your joys, I am first to tell you, that there is matter of far greater joy before you than all the successes or prosperity of the world: and if it be yours, it may be the matter of your present joy; and if it be not, yet being freely offered you, your acceptance may quickly make it such. Eternal joy and glory is at hand, the door is open, the promise is sure, the way made plain, the helps are many, and safe, and powerful; you may have the conduct of Christ, and the company of thousands, (though the smaller number,) if you will go this way: there are passengers every day going on, and entering in; many that were here the last year, are this year in heaven; yea, many that were yesterday on earth, are in heaven to-day. It is another kind of assembly and solemnity than this that they are now beholding, and you may behold. One strain of their celestial melody doth afford more ravishing sweetness and delight than all that ever earth could yield. If a day in God's courts here be better than a thousand in common employments or delights, then, sure, a day in heaven is better than ten thousand. That is the court; and (except the church, which is a garden that hath some celestial plants, and is a seminary or nursery for heaven) this world is the dunghill. There all is spiritual, pure, and perfect; the soul, the service, and the joy; but here they are all so mixed with flesh, and, therefore, so imperfect and impure, that we are afraid of our very comforts, and are fain, upon the review, to sorrow over many of our joys. We come now from cares and troubles to our feasts; and our wedding garments smell of the smoke; and a secret disquietness in the midst of our delights doth tell us, that the root of our troubles doth remain, and that yet we are not where we should be, and that this is not our resting-place. We lay by our cares and sorrows on these days with our old clothes, to take them up again to-morrow, and alas! they are our ordinary week-day habits: and it were well if it were only so; but even in laughter the heart is sorrowful; and in our sweetest joys we feel such imperfections as threateneth a relapse into our former troubles. But the face of God admitteth no such imperfections in the joy of the beholders; there we shall have joy without either feeling or fear of sorrow, and praises without any mixtures of complaint. Our sweetest love to the Lord of love will feel no bounds and fear no end. Oh what unspeakable delights will fill that soul that now walks mournfully, and feedeth upon complaints and tears! How the glory of God will make that face to shine for ever, that now looks too dejectedly, and is darkened with griefs, and worn with fears, and daily wears a mourning visage! No trouble can enter into the heavenly Jerusalem; nor is there a mournful countenance in the presence of our King! Self-troubling was the fruit of sin and weakness, of ignorance, mistakes, and passion, and, therefore, is unknown in heaven, being pardoned and laid by with our flesh among the rest of our childish weaknesses and diseases. That poor, afflicted, wounded soul, that breathes in trouble as its daily air, and thinks it is made up of grief and fear, shall be turned into love and joy, and be unspeakably higher in those heavenly delights than ever it was low in sorrow. O blessed face of the most glorious God! O happy presence of our glorified Head! O blessed beams of the eternal love, that will continually shine upon us! O blessed work! to behold, to love, to delight and praise! O blessed company of holy angels and perfect saints, so perfectly united, so exactly suited to concord in those felicitating works! Where all these are what sorrow can there be? what relics of distress, or smallest scars of our ancient wounds? Had I but one such friend as the meanest angel in heaven to converse with, how easily could I spare the courts of princes, the popular concourse, the learned academies, and all that the world accounteth pleasure, to live in the sweet and secret converse of such a friend! How delightfully should I hear him discourse of the ravishing love of God, of the glory of his face, the person of our Redeemer, the continued union of the glorified human nature with the divine, and of the Head, with all the glorified members, and his influences on his imperfect ones below; of the dignity, quality, and work of saints and angels, and of the manner of their mutual converse! How gladly would I retire from the noise of laughter, the compliments of comic gallants, the clutter and vain-glory of a distracted world, or any the more manly inferior delights, to walk with one such heavenly companion! Oh how the beams of his illuminated intellect would promote my desired illumination! and the flames of his love to the most glorious God would reach my heart! What life and heavenly sweetness there would be in all his speeches! That little of heaven that I have perceived on some of the servants of the Lord, that are conversant above in the life of faith, doth make them more amiable, and their converse much more delectable to me, than all the feastings, music, or merriments in the world. Oh then what a world of joy and glory will that be, where we shall not only converse with them that have seen the Lord, and are perfected in the beatifical vision and fruition, but also shall ourselves everlastingly behold him, and enjoy him in perfection! That world all true believers see;

they see it by faith in the holy glass which the Spirit in the apostles and prophets hath set up: and they have the earnest and first-fruits of it in themselves, even that Spirit by which they are sealed hereunto; that world we are ready to take possession of; we are almost there; we are but taking our leave of the inhabitants and affairs of earth, and better putting on our heavenly robes, and we are presently there. A few nights more to stay on earth, a few words more to speak to the sons of men, a few more duties to perform, and a few more troublesome steps to pass, will be a small, inconsiderable delay. This room will hold you now but an hour longer, and this world but a few hours more, but heaven will be the dwelling-place of saints to all eternity. These faces of flesh that we see to-day, we shall see but a few times more, if any; but the face of God we shall see for ever. That glory no dismal times shall darken, that joy no sorrow shall interrupt, no sin shall forfeit, no enemy shall endanger or take from us, no changes shall ever dispossess us of. And should not a believer then rejoice that his name is written in heaven? and that every providence wheels him on, and whether the way be fair or foul it is thither that he is travelling? O sirs! if heaven be better than vanity and vexation; if endless joy be better than the laughter of a child that ends in crying; and if God be better than a delusory world; you have then greater matters set before you to be the matter of your joy than prosperity and success, or any thing that flesh and blood delights in.

And this being so, I am next, in faithfulness to your souls, obliged to call you to inquire, whether the rejoicing of this day, and the rejoicing of your lives, do here begin? Is God the beginning and the end of all? Oh that the Lord would awaken you to perceive, in all your mirth, how nearly it concerneth you to know first whether your names are written in heaven, and whether your chiefest joy be fetched from thence!

Alas! sirs, it is a most pitiful sight to see men frisk about in jollity, with the marks of death and wrath upon them; and to see men so franticly merry in their sin, as to forget the misery that will so quickly mar their mirth; and to see men live as quietly and pleasantly as if all were well with them, when they have taken no successful care for their precious souls, nor made any considerable sure provision for their endless life! Poor sinner! the Lord who sent me on this message to thee, knows that I envy thee not thy mirth or pleasure, but only would have it better for thee, or have thee set thy mind on better. But let me so far interrupt thee in thy mirth, as to ask thee whether thou art sure of heaven? or, at least, whether thou hast given diligence to make it sure? 2 Pet. i. 10. If this night thy soul be called away, canst thou truly say that thou art an heir of life, and hast laid up thy treasure there beforehand? If thou say that thou hopest well, and no man can do more, and thus dost desperately cast thy everlasting life upon a careless venture, I must tell thee first that assurance may be had. Would God bid us rejoice that our names are written in heaven, if it were a thing that could not by any means be known? Would he bid us give diligence to make our calling and election sure, if it were a thing that could not by any diligence be attained? And I must add, that presumption is no sign of a safe condition. It shall not go well with you because you imagine it shall go well. A man in a dropsy or consumption will not live by saying that he hopes he shall not die. Yea, more, I must add, that a careless venturousness is a mark of misery. For a man that valueth God and his salvation, cannot put off a matter of such eternal consequence so slightly and disregardfully. And a fear and care about your salvation would be a far better sign. For the most part, they are safest that fear their danger, and they are in the saddest case that are never sad at the consideration of their case. It is not your bold and confident conceits that will open heaven to you, and therefore, I beseech you, presently look out for surer grounds of peace than these.

If you say, How can it be known to me whether my name be written in heaven or not? I shall briefly, but satisfactorily, answer it.

In general, if thou know that thou art one that God hath promised heaven to, thou mayst know thy title, which is meant by the writing of thy name in heaven, and thou mayst know that this promise shall be made good.

More particularly, 1. If thou hast had such an effectual sight of the vanity of earth, and of the heavenly felicity, that heaven hath the pre-eminence in thy practical estimation and choice, and thou hast resolved that heaven or nothing shall be thy happiness, and art so far at a point with all things under the sun, as that thou art resolved to stick closer to Christ than unto them, and whatever it cost thee, to take the fruition of God for ever as thy portion; if, upon consideration of the difference between heaven and earth, God and the creatures, eternity and time, thou hast heartily devoted thyself to God, and art willing to be his servant upon the terms that he inviteth thee on, thou mayst be assured that thy name is written in heaven, Matt. vi. 19—21; xvi. 24—26; xiii. 45, 46; Luke xviii. 33.

But if earth be the place of thy highest estimation and choice, where thou placest thy chief affections, and which thou adherest to more resolutely than to God, and which thou wilt not leave whatever thou lose by it, then, as earth hath thy heart, so earth is thy treasure, and thy name is not written in heaven, but in the dust.

2. If the obtaining of heaven be the principal part of thy care and business, the principal work which thou mindest in the work, it is certain that thy name is written in heaven, Col. iii. 1—4; otherwise not.

3. If, finding thyself lost and filthy in thy sin, thou seest the necessity and sufficiency of Christ, and, being desirous of his grace and righteousness, dost unfeignedly take him for thy Saviour and Lord, and give up thyself to be healed, and justified, and saved by him, as the only Physician of souls, thou art then his member, and thy name is written in heaven, John i. 12; iii. 16, 18.

4. If the heavenly nature be most amiable in thine eyes, and the heavenly life be it that thou most desirest; if thou hadst rather be holy than be unholy, and hadst rather perfectly obey the Lord, than live in sin, and longest to be better, and studiest to live in obedience to the Lord, thy name is in heaven, and thither thou art passing, and it will be thy reward. But if thou love not holiness, but hadst rather be excused from it, and live in thy sins, thou art as yet no heir of heaven, John iii. 19; xii. 26; Psal. i.; cxix. 11.

5. If thy name be written in heaven, thou hast a special love to the heirs of heaven. And the more of heaven thou findest in their hearts and lives, the more amiable they are unto thee, and the sweeter is their converse, 1 John iii. 14; Psal. xv. 4.

I shall name no more. These evidences are sure. By these you may know, while you sit here in these seats, yea, if you lay in the darkest dungeon, that you are the heirs of heaven, and your names are there.

But where there is no such work, no high estimation of heaven, and resolution for it, no mortification or conquest of the world, no prevalent care and diligence for heaven, no resignation of the soul to Christ, that by faith and holiness we might follow him to that glory, no love to holiness, and no delight in the heirs of heaven, such persons are yet aliens to the heavenly nature and inheritance, and cannot rejoice that their names are written in heaven.

And now I have set the glass before you, I earnestly entreat you that you will here seriously view the complexion of your souls. It more nearly concerneth you to know whether your names are written in heaven, and where it is that you must dwell for ever, than to know how to manage your trades and business, or to know whether you shall stir from this place alive, or ever see another day. O sirs, take heed of living in self-deceit till your trying and recovering time is past! This is it that your enemy aims at; he will do all that malice and subtlety can do to keep such matters from your sober thoughts, or to make you groundlessly presume that you are safe, or securely to cast your souls upon a desperate venture, under pretence of trusting in Christ, till he hath you where he would have you; and then he will himself take off the veil, and let you know that you had time and light to have acquainted you with your disease and misery, while you might have had a free, and sure, and full remedy. Then you shall know that it was long of your self-deceit if you would not understand and believe in time, that if you lived after the flesh, you should die, (Rom. viii. 13,) and that it is the pure in heart that shall see God, Matt. v. 8. "Know ye not that the unrighteous shall not inherit the kingdom of God? Be not deceived; neither fornicators, nor idolaters, nor adulterers, nor effeminate, nor thieves, nor covetous, nor drunkards, nor revilers, nor extortioners, shall inherit the kingdom of God," 1 Cor. vi. 9, 10. "For this ye know, that no whoremonger, nor unclean person, nor covetous man, who is an idolater, hath any inheritance in the kingdom of Christ, and of God. Let no man deceive you with vain words, for because of these things cometh the wrath of God on the children of disobedience," Eph. v. 5, 6. And can any thing justify the rejoicing of men in so sad a state?

Give me leave, therefore, to make a little closer application of the several parts of my text to the several sorts of persons whom they do concern. And first to all that yet are not become the heirs of heaven: Rejoice not though devils were subject to you, till your souls are subject to him that bought them. Rejoice not though you had conquered all the world, and had your wills of all your adversaries, as long as you are conquered by your fleshly lusts, and Satan leads you captive at his will, 2 Tim. ii. 25, 26. Rejoice not though you had all the riches of the earth, as long as you are void of the riches of grace, and have nothing to do with the riches of glory. Rejoice not though all men should honour you, and bow to you, and proclaim your fame, as long as you are the drudges of the devil and the flesh, and the God of heaven proclaimeth you his enemies, and resolveth on your destruction, if you do not soundly and seasonably repent, Luke xix. 27; xiii. 3, 5.

Be not offended with me, that, on a day of thanksgiving, I thus far forbid you to rejoice, for it is not you that are qualified for it, or have any part or fellowship in this business, being in the gall of bitterness, and bonds of your iniquity, your hearts being not right in the sight of God. Though the invitation be general, it supposeth that you come prepared; and therefore even he that calls men to his joys, will find out him that hath not on the wedding garment, "and will bind him, and cast him into outer darkness, where shall be weeping and gnashing of teeth," Matt. xxii. 12, 13. 1. Alas! sirs, if God would allow you to rejoice, how willingly could I allow it you. But hear whether he approve it, James v. 1—3, "Go to now ye rich men, weep and howl for the miseries that are coming on you. Your riches are corrupted, and your garments moth-eaten; your gold and silver is cankered, and the rust of them shall be a witness against you, and shall eat your flesh as it were fire. Ye have heaped treasure together for the last days." Luke vi. 24—26, "Woe unto you that are rich, (if you have no better riches,) for ye have received your consolation! Woe unto you that are full, for ye shall hunger! Woe unto you that laugh now, for ye shall mourn and weep! Woe unto you when all men shall speak well of you!" &c. You may find your lesson, Joel ii. 12, 13, "Therefore also now, saith the Lord, turn ye even to me with all your heart, with fasting, and with weeping, and with mourning; and rend your heart." You see what God calls such men to. And if he allow you not to rejoice till you are converted, if I or any man should flatter or cheat you into joy, it would be but a curse to you, and not a benefit.

2. Were your joy but reasonable, I would not discourage it. But a mad-man's laughter is no very lovely spectacle to yourselves. And I appeal to all the reason in the world, whether it be reasonable for a man to live in mirth that is yet unregenerate, and under the curse and wrath of God, and can never say, in the midst of his greatest pomp or pleasure, that he is sure to be an hour out of hell, and may be sure he shall be there for ever, if he die before he have a new, a holy, and a heavenly nature: though he should die with laughter in his face, or with a jest in his mouth, or in the boldest presumption that he shall be saved; yet, as sure as the word of God is true, he will find himself everlastingly undone, as soon as ever his soul is departed from his body, and he sees the things that he would not believe. Sirs, is it rational to dance in Satan's fetters, at the brink of hell, when so many hundred diseases are all ready to mar the mirth, and snatch away the guilty soul, and cast it into endless desperation? I exceedingly pity the godly in their unwarrantable, melancholy griefs; and much more an ungodly man that is bleeding under his wounds of conscience. But a man that is merry in the depth of misery, is more to be pitied than he. Methinks it is one of the most pitiful sights in all the world to see a man ruffle it out in bravery, and spend his precious time in pleasures, and melt into sensual, foolish mirth, that is a stranger to God, and within a step of endless woe! When I see their pomp, and feasting, and attendance, and hear their laughter and insipid jests, and the fiddlers at their doors or tables, and all things carried as if they had made sure of heaven, it saddeneth my heart to think, alas! how little do these sinners know the state that they are in, the God that now beholdeth them, the change that they are near! how little do they think of the flames that they are hastening to, and the outcries and lamentations that will next ensue!

3. Your mirth is disingenuous and dishonest as long as you are without a title to heaven. You slight the Lord that can find such matters of rejoicing, when you have not his favour to rejoice in, and are under his displeasure. While you are refusing Christ, abusing grace, resisting the Spirit, serving the flesh, and undoing your own souls, it cannot be an honest or ingenuous thing for such as you to live in joy.

4. If your mirth were truly honourable to you, it were the more excusable. But to laugh in sin and misery, and make merry so near the endless woe, is a greater shame to your understandings, than to make

sport to set your house on fire. This is the laughter of which Solomon might well say, "Thou art mad," and the mirth of which he saith, "What doth it?" Eccl. ii. 2.

5. Would thy mirth do thee any good, we would not discourage it, yea, if it did not do thee harm. But oh how many are now in sorrow by the means of their unseasonable, sinful mirth! they are too jocund to hear the preacher or their consciences, or to observe the checks and motions of God's Spirit, or to spend now and then an hour in retired, sober thoughts of their everlasting state. Should we but presume to call them to exercise their reason, and mind them of these most needful things, and tell them, O poor distracted mortals, your time is given you for greater things than to fiddle, and dance, and drink, and jest, and prate, and compliment it away! should we not be thought morose, or melancholy, or fanatics? And should we not have some such answer as their ancestors in Sodom gave to Lot? Gen. xix. 9, "Stand back. This one fellow came in to sojourn, and he will needs be a judge: now will we deal worse with thee than with them;" we will take a course with these controllers. Alas! it is this foolish mirth that casteth men's reason and conscience asleep, and drowns the voice of sober words, so that God himself cannot be heard. Could we but get men to retired soberness and seriousness, we should hope that we might find a friend within them, and that we speak to men; and that reason would take part with the most reasonable motions that are made to them from the Lord.

6. Lastly, Would your groundless mirth endure, we would not say so much against it. But, alas! to be merry for a day, and then to lie in misery for ever, is a thing deserving no encouragement. We see it is a merry world with many that have least cause of mirth; but how long will they continue it? To see a man laugh, and play, and feast in a chariot that drives on so fast to death, in a vessel that is on so swift a stream that ends in the gulf of endless horror, is a doleful sight. Oh how quickly will that merry countenance turn sad! those proud looks be turned to an earthy paleness! and those wanton eyes be mouldered to dust, and leave the empty holes to warn the next spectator to use his eyes more wisely while he hath them! How quickly will these same sensual persons exchange their mirth for sighs, and groans, and endless torments, and fruitless lamentations, when they shall have everlasting leisure to peruse their lives, and to consider of their ways, which now there is no persuading them to consider of! Who can encourage such hurtful and unseasonable mirth as this? "Rejoice not, O Israel, for joy, as other people, for thou hast gone a whoring from thy God," Hos. ix. 1. "Rejoice not in a thing of nought," (Amos vi. 13,) much less in the sufferings of your brethren, (Obad. 12,) and, least of all, in any hurt that befalls the church. If enmity to holiness, and exalted impiety, should take occasion to triumph, we answer, as Micah vii. 8, 9, "Rejoice not against me, O mine enemy; when I fall I shall arise: when I sit in darkness the Lord shall be a light unto me. I will bear the indignation of the Lord, because I have sinned against him, until he plead my cause, and execute judgment for me: he will bring me forth to the light, and I shall behold his righteousness."

If you think I have stood too long on the first part of my text, it is not to rebuke your holy joy, but only to promote it, and repress that carnal joy which is more destructive to it than sorrow itself. As you must "seek first the kingdom of God and its righteousness, and then other things shall be added to you," Matt. vi. 33; so must you rejoice first in the kingdom of heaven, and the righteousness that is the way thereto; and then you may add a moderate rejoicing in the things below in a due subordination thereunto. You have the sum in the words of the Holy Ghost, "Thus saith the Lord, Let not the wise man glory in his wisdom, neither let the mighty man glory in his might; let not the rich man glory in his riches; but let him that glorieth glory in this, that he understandeth and knoweth me, that I am the Lord," &c. Jer. ix. 23, 24.

2. My next address must be to them whose names are written in heaven, and that with a twofold exhortation.

I. "Rejoice for your names are written in heaven." It is you, christians, that joy of right belongs to. Little know the lovers of pleasure more than God, that they lose a thousandfold more pleasure than they win; and that by running from a holy life for pleasure, they run from the fire into the water for heat, and from the sun into a dungeon for light. O show the unbelieving world by your rejoicing, how they are mistaken in their choice! Be ashamed that an empty sot, and one that must be for ever a firebrand in hell, should live a more joyful life than you! O do not so wrong your Lord, your faith, your endless joys, as to walk in heaviness, and cast away the joy of the Lord which is your strength, and to be still complaining, when those that are prepared for the slaughter are as frolic as if the bitterness of death were past. It is well that you have so much life as to feel your sicknesses; but it is not well, that because you are yet diseased, the life of grace and of glory should be so uneffectual to your comfort. And yet, alas! how common is it to see the most miserable frisk and fleer, while the heirs of life are sinfully vexing themselves with the inordinate fears of death. Lift up thy head, christian, and remember whence came thy graces, even thy least desires, and whither do they tend. Where is thy Father and thy Head, and the most of thy dear companions? Where is it that thou must live to all eternity? Doth it beseem a companion of angels, a member of Christ, a child of God, an heir of heaven, to be grieved at every petty cross, and to lay by all the sense of his felicity, because some trifle of the world falls cross to his desires and commodity? Is it seemly for one that must be everlastingly as full of joy as the sun is full of light, to live in such a self-troubling, drooping state, as to disgrace religion, and frighten away the ungodly from the doors of grace, that, by your joyful lives, might be provoked to enter? I know as to your happiness, the matter is not comparatively great; because if mistakes and the devil's malice should keep you sad here a hundred years, yet heaven will wipe away all tears, and those joys will be long enough when they come; and as the joy of the ungodly, so the sorrows of the humble, upright soul will be but for a moment; and though you weep and lament when the world rejoiceth, as their joy shall be turned into sorrow, so your sorrow shall be turned into joy, and your joy shall no man take from you. But, in the mean time, is it not shame and pity that you should live so unanswerable to the mercies of the Lord? that you should sinfully grieve the comforting Spirit by the wilful grieving of yourselves, and that you should peevishly cast away your precious mercies, when you so much need them, by reason of the troubles of a vexatious world, which you cannot avoid? that you, even you, that are saved by the Lord, should still be questioning it, or unthankfully denying his great salvation, and so much hinder the salvation of others? For the Lord's sake, christians, and for your souls' sake, and in pity to the ungodly, yield not to the tempter, that would trouble you when he cannot damn you! Is God your Father, and Christ your Saviour, and the Spirit your Sanctifier, and heaven your home? And will you make all, for the present, as nothing to you, by a causeless, obstinate denial? If you are in doubt, let not mere passionate fears be heard; and let not the devil, the enemy of your peace, be heard: but peruse your evidences, and still remember, as the sum of all, that the will is the man, and what you would be that you are before the Lord. If you cannot see the sincerity of your hearts, go to your faithful, able guides, and open the case to them, and let not passion prevail against the Scripture and reason which they bring. Yea, if in your trouble you cannot by all their helps perceive the uprightness of your hearts, I must tell you, you may stay yourselves much upon their judgment of your state. Though it cannot give you full assurance, it may justly help to silence much of your self-accusations, and give you the comfort of probability. If a physician that feels not what you feel, shall yet, upon your speeches, and other evidences, tell you that he is confident your disease is not mortal, nor containeth any cause of fear, you may rationally be much encouraged by his judgment, though it give you no certainty of life. As wicked men through contempt, so many godly people through melancholy, do lose much of the fruit of the office of the ministry, which lieth much in this assisting men to judge of the life or death of their souls. Alas! say they, he feels not what I feel: he is used to judge charitably, and he knoweth not me so well as I know myself. But when you have told him faithfully, as you do your physician, what it is that you know by yourself, he is able to pass a far sounder judgment of your life or death than yourselves can do, for all your feeling: for he knows better what those symptoms signify, and what is used to be the issue of such a case as yours. Be not then so proud or wilful as to refuse the judgment of your faithful pastors, about the state of your souls, in a confidence on your own.

And look not for more, as necessary to your comforts, than God hath made necessary. Is it nothing to have a title to eternal life, unless you be also as holy as you desire? Yea, is it nothing to have a desire to be more holy? Will you have no comfort, as long as you have distractions, or dulness, or such like imperfection in duty; and till you have no disease of soul to trouble you, that is, till you have laid by flesh, and arrived at your perfect joy? Dare not to disobey the voice of God: "Be glad in the Lord, and rejoice, ye righteous; and shout for joy, all ye that are upright in heart," Psal. xxxii. 11. "Rejoice evermore," 1 Thess. v. 16. Let it be something that heaven cannot weigh down that shall suppress thy joy. Art thou in poverty, and is not heaven sufficient riches? Art thou in disgrace, and shalt thou not have honour enough in heaven? Art thou in danger from the injustice or the wrath of man, and is he not almighty that hath undertaken to justify thee? Rom. viii. 33, 34. Dost thou languish under pining sicknesses, and is there not everlasting health in heaven? Art thou weak in knowledge, in memory, in grace, in duty; troubled with uncommanded thoughts and passions; and was it not so on earth with all who are now in heaven? O christians, make conscience of obeying this command; "Rejoice that your names are written in heaven." Did you but know how God approveth such rejoicing, and how much it pleaseth him above your pining sorrows; and how it strengtheneth the soul, and sweeteneth duty, and easeth suffering, and honoureth religion, and encourageth others, and how suitable it is to gospel grace, and to your high relations and ends; and how much better it serves to subdue the very sins that trouble you, than your fruitless, self-weakening complainings do; I say, did you well consider all these things, it would sure revive your drooping spirits.

And do not say now, I would rejoice if I were sure that my name were written in heaven; but I am not sure. For, 1. Who is it long of that you are not sure? You may be sure that he that valueth and seeketh heaven as better than earth, and that loveth the holy way to heaven and the most heavenly people, is indeed an heir of heaven; and you may be sure, if you will, that this is your own case: and yet you say you are not sure that your names are written in heaven. If God give you his grace, and you deny it, will you therefore deny your right to glory, and make one sin the excuse for another.

2. And if you are not sure, is it nothing to have your probabilities, and hopes, and the judgment of your able, faithful pastors, that your souls are in a safe condition? We dare not say so to the careless world, nor to the most of men, as we do to you.

Especially take heed lest melancholy habituate you to fears and griefs; and then religion must bear the blame, and you undergo a calamitous life, though you are the heirs of heaven. To this end, 1. Use not musing, serious thoughts beyond the strength of your brain and intellect. 2. Place not too much of your religion in the perusals and study of your hearts; but (for such as are inclined to melancholy) it is the fruitfullest way to be much in expending duties abroad, and labouring to do good to others. Such duties have less of self, and have much of God, and divert the troubling, melancholy thoughts, and bring in more comfort by way of reward, than is usually got by more direct inquiring after comfort. 3. Use not too much solitariness and retiredness: man is a sociable creature; and as his duty lieth much with others, so his comfort lieth in the same way as his duty. 4. Take heed of worldly sorrows, and therefore of overvaluing worldly things. 5. Take heed of idleness, or of thinking that the duties of holiness are all that you have to mind; but make conscience of being diligent in a particular calling, which diverts the hurtful, troubling thoughts, and is pleasing unto God. 6. Take not every sickness of your souls for death, but rejoice in that life which enableth you to be troubled at your diseases. Keep under melancholy by these means, (and the advice of the physician,) and you will escape a very great hinderance to this high and holy duty of heavenly rejoicing.

II. But you think, perhaps, that I have all this while forgotten the duty proper to the day. No; but I was not fit to speak for it, nor you fit to hear and practise it, till the impediment of carnal rejoicing was removed, and till we had begun with heavenly joy. It is heaven that must animate all our comforts. They are so far sweet as heaven is in them, and no further. Now, therefore, if you first rejoice for your heavenly interest, I dare safely then persuade you to rejoice in the mercies which we are to be thankful for this day. And though some of them are but yet in the birth, if not in the womb, and we are yet uncertain what they will prove, that will not excuse us for any unthankfulness for the first conception or infancy of our mercies. And though Satan seek to get advantage by them, that will not excuse us for our overlooking the mercy in itself. And though there are yet abundance of fears and troubles on the hearts of many of Christ's servants through the land, we cannot by any such accidents be excused from the thankful observation of the workings of the Lord.

All mercies on earth, even spiritual mercies, have their mixtures of trouble, and their imperfections; but must not therefore be denied or extenuated. And though many that are dear to us, smarting by the change, will be offended and grieved at our most moderate thanksgiving, we must not therefore offend the Lord by our disregardfulness of his works.

There are these things to be commemorated by us this day, which I dare not overlook. 1. That God hath so honoured his justice and impartiality, as to show how he hateth sin in whomsoever. And indeed the justice of God itself would seem more amiable to us, were we not so selfish as to think hardly of all that is hurtful unto us. Justice demonstrateth the holiness of God, and all the appearances of his holiness are lovely in themselves.

2. That the holy God hath disowned heresy and divisions on the one side, as well as impiety and profaneness on the other; and that his wisdom thought meet to acquaint us experimentally with the hurtfulness of both, and our danger of both, as he did in former ages of the church. We first found the serpentine malice of the ungodly, and God delivered us when they would have swallowed us up. But while we only heard and read of heresy and schism, and that too often abusively applied to many of the most peaceable servants of the Lord, we understood not the mischief of those evils, but were ready to take the very names to be but the reproaches of piety itself. But God saw meet to let out a flood of this sort of calamities, and to suffer heresy to disgrace itself by its unrighteous fruits, that by those fruits we might the better know it. We never knew before how much we are beholden to him for saving us from this sort of evils; and should never have sufficiently hated them, if we had not smarted by them.

3. It is a mercy to be thankful for, that thus the church is notably fortified against ever relapsing into heresy or schism for the time to come.

4. And that the frailties of men professing godliness having so lamentably appeared, they are taught to take heed of spiritual pride, and to know and distrust themselves, and not to be high-minded, but to fear.

5. It is a very great mercy, for which I must profess I was thankful from the first appearance of it,[a] that so many that I hope are dear to God, have the advantage of his frowns to further their conviction, and repentance, and salvation. As prosperity was the temptation by which ambition got advantage, and Providence misunderstood was pleaded against the holy rule, what a mercy it is that Providence also should undeceive them, and vindicate itself, and teach men hereafter by the example of this age to stay till the end before they take the sense of Providence, or rather to adhere to the holy word because the longest liver shall be too short-lived to see the end, so far as to furnish him for such an interpretation. And therefore that word that is the glass in which we can foresee the end must be our guide. I had rather have my friend poor and penitent, than wealthy and impenitent; and rather in a prison, than in the chains of pride. And am glad that God hath taken away the snare that brought so many souls to so sad a pass; and hath undeceived them in part, that had carnal thoughts of the happiness of saints, and looked for temporal reign and dignity; forgetting that rich men must pass through a needle's eye to heaven; and that lowliness, meekness, humility, patience, forbearing, forgiveness, self-denial, contempt of this world, and living all upon things unseen, is the life that Christ by his doctrine and example taught us, and how ill prosperity befriendeth these. I am in far more hope to see many Peters go out and weep bitterly, than I was when they prospered in a sinful way. And if yet any be so far unhumbled, as to deny it to have been a sinful way, I am in far greater hope of their conviction now than heretofore. In their greatness few durst tell them of their crimes; and those of us that did it were voluminously reproached, threatened, calumniated, and represented as turbulent to the world. (It being usual with base-spirited men to take the judgment of the greatest for their rule, and to think all suffering to be just and honourable that is inflicted by such as few dare contradict.) But now I hope plain-dealing may recover many that before lived under flatteries, and were above reproof. I must profess that my hopes of the saving of many that are dear to me, by the furtherance of this providence, is matter of so much thankfulness to me, that were I sure to suffer with them I would yet give thanks.

6. It is matter of thanksgiving to me that God hath so far owned a unanimous, painful, faithful ministry, (for all their many sad infirmities,) as first to break the profane opposers of them, and then to scatter the adversaries on the other side. Ever since I heard it so familiar among them to call Christ's faithful servants by so many reproachful names, as priests, (in scorn,) presbyters, divines, jack presbyters, black-coats, pulpiteers, &c., and their friends priest-ridden; to suffer quakers openly in the streets to revile them as deceivers, dogs, wolves, hirelings, false prophets, liars, and all the names that hell could teach them; I waited in fear for the judgments of the Lord; which he hath executed in our sight, and caused us to know, that his delays are no desertions of his servants, nor justification of our revilers. And let it stand as a warning to you that have seen it, and you that have executed the punishments of God upon the reproachers, that you take heed of falling into the same crime, and dashing on the rock on which they have been broken; but let all England hear and fear, and do no more so malignantly or presumptuously.

And oh that we the unworthy ministers of Christ, may remember that we are not vindicated and delivered to contend, or to imitate our afflicters, in seeking greatness to ourselves, nor to live in idleness, and neglect the souls committed to our care.

7. It is very great cause of thankfulness in my eyes, that from first to last God hath been so tender of the honour of his unanimous sober people, and his cause, and of the innocency and consciences of his servants, as to execute his afflictions mostly by the hands of erring men; and to keep the rest by imprisonments, seclusions, and other means, so far from all appearance of consent or irregularities: and that at last he hath put an opportunity into their hands to declare to the world their innocency in things with which they were reproached; and that while profane opposers of religion did boast and vapour, and swear and curse, and drink healths for his Majesty's restitution, it is those whom they reproached that have silently and effectually accomplished it, and that with speed, as soon as they had power.

8. It is some matter of thankfulness to me, that whereas, to our perpetual shame, we could not in so many years compose the disagreements in church affairs among us, we are not altogether without hope that agreement may be now more effectually procured; not only because those carnal advantages that hindered it with some are taken from them, and suffering will dispose some more to peace; but be-

[a] We kept this thanksgiving voluntarily in Worcestershire, by agreement among the associated ministers, as we do here this day. See the Agreement published by *The Weekly Mercury*.

cause we are persuaded the disposition, and we are sure the interest, of his Majesty, standeth for our reconciliation and unity. And verily we are the most inexcusable people in the world, if our own long and sad experiences do not resolve us to do the utmost in that work ourselves, which, if we are not horridly proud and wilful, is easy to accomplish.

9. And it is matter of thanksgiving that God hath been all along so wonderfully seen in the work; which makes us hope that the issue will yet be for our good. The first sparks that set fire on the last foundation are yet much unknown, but were so little as makes it the more strange. The wonderful whirlwind that suddenly finished the subversion was marvellous, though sad, because of the wickedness of men. The introducing of the remnant of the members; the stop that was given them, when they had voted in a committee a liberty in religion, that excepted not popery; the casting them out by those that set them up; the discoveries of the fallaciousness of some of their chiefs, who then were tempted into a compliance with the army, and were fabricating a new form of a commonwealth; the breaking of them and of the army, in part by the returning members; the unexpected stop that was given first to their proceedings by his Excellency in the north; the expeditiousness, the constancy, the unanimity, and strange successfulness of that attempt; that an army who thought themselves only fit to be the nation's security for liberty and religion, and were thought necessary to be entailed upon us to that end; that were so heightened in their own and other men's esteem, by their many and wonderful successes, should in a moment (we scarce know how) fly all into pieces as a grenado that is fired; that Ireland at the same time should be so strangely and easily reduced, and that by sober, faithful hands, and by so few, and with such speed; that this famous city should be so unanimously excited to concur so eminently, and contribute very much to the success; that his Excellency should conquer without any blows, and all be despatched that since is done with no considerable resistance: all this, and much more, do make us wonder at the hand of God. And seldom is there so wonderful an appearance of the Lord, but it holds forth matter that is amiable as well as admirable to his church.

Lastly, That all this is done with little or no effusion at all of blood, when so much blood was shed in the foregoing changes, advanceth the wonder to a greater height: and I hope his Majesty and the two houses of parliament will take notice how God hath gone before them in a tender and unbloody change; and will not hearken to them that protest against revenge, while they would use it under the name of justice. When the wheel of Providence turneth so fast, if all that have the advantage of executing their wills under the name of justice should take their advantage, you know what names and sufferings multitudes of the usefullest members in such nations, in the several vicissitudes, must incur to the detriment of the commonwealth and governors.

III. You see what cause we have of thankfulness: but I must tell you that these, as all inferior mercies, are imperfect things; and being but means to greater matters, the heavenly interest first treated on, they are no further significant or valuable than they have some tendency to their end: and I must further tell you, that it is much committed into the hands of man, under God, whether such beginnings shall have a happy or unhappy end. If Christ become to many a stumbling-stone, and be set for the fall of many in Israel,(Luke ii. 34,) and if the gospel itself prove the savour of death to some, no wonder if it be yet possible and too easy for a sinful land to turn these forementioned mercies and successes into most heavy judgments, and to rob themselves of all the honour and the benefit. And therefore, above all, for the Lord's sake, and for a poor, tired, yet hoping nation's sake, and for the sake of the cause of Christ through the world, I beseech you all, from the highest to the lowest, that you will be awakened to a holy vigilancy, and look about you in your several places, lest the enemy of Christ and you should play his after-game more successfully than now you can foresee; and lest the return of a sinful nation to their vomit should make the end yet worse than the beginning. It is not enough to have begun; the fruit of all is yet behind. I must here deal plainly with you, however it be taken, lest I be charged with unfaithfulness at the dreadful tribunal, to which both you and I are hastening. If these beginnings, through your neglects, or any others that have been the instruments, should now be turned to the reviving and strengthening of profaneness, and malignity against the holy ways of God; to the introduction of mere formality in religion; to the casting out, or weakening the hands, of the faithful ministers in the land; to the destruction of order and discipline in the churches; to the suppression of orderly and edifying meetings for mutual assistance in the matters of salvation; or to the cherishing of ignorance or popery in the people; it will blast the glory of all that you have done, and turn the mercy into gall. Believe it, the interest of Christ and holiness will be found at last the surest ground for any prince to build his interest upon; and the owning of corrupt and contrary interests, that engage men in quarrels with the interest of Christ, is it that hath undone so many princes and states already, that it should make the greatest learn at last, to account it their highest honour to be the servants of the King of saints, and to devote their power to the accomplishment of his will. I need not tell you that it is the sober, godly, conscionable sort of men that know what they do, and why, that will be the honour of their governors, and the usefullest of their subjects; and not the barbarous, malignant rabble, that understand not what belongs to the pleasing of God, the happiness of themselves, the good of the commonwealth, or the honour of their king. And do you not think that remissness, to say no worse, of magistrates, who should restrain the insolences of such, is not a great dishonour to our nation, and a great temptation to many in the country, that stand at a distance from the fountain of affairs, to continue their fears lest we have changed for the worse? Put yourselves in their cases, and tell me whether you could, with equal cheerfulness, keep this day, if you were used as many able, faithful ministers and people are in the cities and countries of the land, who have their persons assaulted, their windows battered, their ministrations openly reviled, and that go in danger of their lives from the brutish rabble that were formerly exasperated by the magistrates' punishing them, or the ministers' reproof, or crossing them in their sins. As physicians are judged of, not so much by the excellency of their remedies, as by their success, and the people think of them as they see the patients live or die, so will they do by your great performances which you mention before the Lord this day. Should they prove to the suppression of serious godliness, and the setting up of the wicked of the land, I need not tell you what a name it will leave unto the actors to all generations. But if you vigilantly improve them, as you have given us abundant reason to expect, and the issue shall be the healing concord of the churches, the curbing of profaneness, the promoting of a plain and serious ministry, and of the diligent service of the Lord; this is it that will make your names immortal, that have been the happy instruments of so blessed a work. How joyfully, then, will the subjects commemorate the happy introduction of their sovereign! With what love and honour will they hear his name! How readily will they obey him! How heartily will they pray for him! How precious will your memory be! And this will be numbered among the wonderful deliverances of England. If godliness be persecuted, or made a common scorn in the land, the holy God will vindicate his honour, and make their names a scorn and curse that shall procure it; but if you exalt him, he will exalt you. Protect his lambs, and he will be your Protector. He is with you while you are with him, 2 Chron. xv. 2. "Those that honour him, he will honour; and those that despise him shall be lightly esteemed," 1 Sam. ii. 30.

WHAT LIGHT MUST SHINE IN OUR WORKS.

MATTHEW V. 16.

LET YOUR LIGHT SO SHINE BEFORE MEN, THAT THEY MAY SEE YOUR GOOD WORKS, AND GLORIFY YOUR FATHER WHICH IS IN HEAVEN.

THE work designed for this time is to resolve this practical case, What is that light which must shine before men in the works of Christ's disciples for the glorifying of God?

But the explication of the text is therein included.

The Sun of Righteousness, Jesus Christ, who "giveth light to every one that cometh into the world," or, coming into the world, giveth light to all, from his fulness hath bespangled the inferior heavens, his church, with many refulgent stars, appointed freely to communicate the heavenly light which they had freely received. In his corporeal presence he prepared them; and his Spirit having moved on the darkened world, he irresistibly said, at the descent of the Holy Ghost, "Let there be light, and there was light," beginning at Jerusalem, but not fixed to any determinate place; but what he gave them necessarily and antecedently they were to exercise as free agents, by a command more resistible, which here he gives them. Having told them their office, and given them their names, ver. 14, "Ye are the lights of the world," he next tells them how they must be useful. They must be conspicuous, 1. Because the church where they are placed "is like a city on a hill which cannot be hid." 2. Because it is the end of him that lighteth them, and sets them up, not to put them under a bushel, but on a candlestick, to give light to all his house. And therefore no men's silencing or prohibitions, no difficulties or sufferings, will excuse them from their duty: lights they are, and shine they must: but lest they should think that it is preaching only which he meaneth, he here, commanding them their duty, lets them know that the splendour of christianity is in works as well as words; and thereby giveth us cause to think that it is all his disciples, or christians, that he speaketh to, though first and eminently to the apostles and teachers of the world.

1. By "light" he meaneth both the illuminating knowledge, which must be uttered by words, and the splendour or glory of holiness, which must be refulgent in their lives.

2. He calls it "your" light, as being their own in his graces, as the subjects, and their own in exercise, as the actors, though both under him.

3. It must "shine," that is, appear in its splendour, for the illumination and conviction of the world.

4. It must "so" shine as is fittest to attain these ends: it is not every twinkling that will answer their great obligations.

5. It must be "before men;" that is, both those within, and especially those without, the church, that are but men.

6. It must be a light shining in "good works," and their own works: for that is the grand difference between the disciples of Christ and others. He teacheth them not only to know and talk well, but to do well; and he maketh men such as he teacheth them to be: *Non magna loquimur, sed vivimus*, said Tertullian.

7. "That men may see," doth signify both the necessary refulgent quality of their works, and also the end of God and them.

8. But it is not hypocritical ostentation of what they are not, nor of what they are and have, as for their own glory, to be honoured and praised of men, but for the glorifying of God.

Who is called "their Father," to show their obligation to him, and to encourage them by the honour and comfort of their relation, and to show why their works will tend to the glorifying of God, even because they are so nearly related to him.

And he is said to be "in heaven," because there he appeareth operatively in his glory to the beautifying of holy spirits. As the soul is said to be in the head, and we look a man in the face when we talk to him, as if there principally we saw the man; because it is in the head that it operateth by reason. So much of the meaning of the words.

Many doctrines the text affordeth us: as,

1. Christ's disciples are the lights of the world, both in the splendour of wisdom and holiness.

2. Their most eminent and convincing splendour is in their good works.

3. Their light and good works are their own, though by the grace of Christ; and it is no injury to Christ, or his righteousness, or grace, to say, that they are their own.

4. The splendour of christians in their good works must be such as may be seen of men.

5. The glorifying of God must be the end of our good works, and of their appearance unto men.

6. As bad as corrupted nature is, there is yet something in mankind which tendeth to the approving of the good works of christians, and to their glorifying God thereupon.

7. God is glorified even by common men, when they approve of the glory of holiness in believers; it is not only by saints that God is glorified.

8. As contrary as holiness is to corrupted nature, there is such resplendent goodness in true christians' work, which common men may glorify God for; and so somewhat in them, and in christianity, which hath such agreeableness as may tend to further good.

9. The excellency and splendour of the good works of christians, especially teachers, is a grand means, ordained by God himself, for the conviction of the world, and the glorifying of God.

But the resolving the question, What the splendour of these works must be, is my present undertaken task.

God is not glorified by our adding to him, but by our receiving from him; not by our making him greater, or better, or happier than he is, but by owning him, loving him, and declaring him as he is, that we and others may thereby be wise, and good, and happy.

He is his own glory, and ours; and by his own light only we must know both him and all things. We are not called to bring our candle to show the world that there is a sun, but to persuade them into its light, to open the windows and curtains, to disperse the clouds, and to open the eyes of blinded sinners.

I. The way of doing this, and glorifying God, is in the order following.

1. The first thing that our works must show is their own goodness; they can never prove the cause good until it is clear that they are good themselves; therefore, doubtless, Christ here intendeth that we must abound especially in those good works which the world is capable of knowing to be good, and not only in those which none but christians themselves approve. If believers and unbelievers agreed in no common principles, we were not capable of preaching to unbelievers, nor convincing them, nor of conversing with them. There are many excellent things which nature doth approve, and which both parties are agreed to be good; by the advantage of these, as granted principles, we must convince them of the conclusions which they yet deny; and not as the scandalous christian, so absurdly affect singularity, as to make light of all good which is taken for good by unbelievers, and to seek for eminency in nothing but what the world thinks evil. There is a glory in some good works, which all do honour, and which manifesteth itself.

2. And then the goodness of the work doth manifest the goodness of the doer. Every man's work is so far his own, that he is related to it, and by it, either as laudable, or as culpable; as it is Gal. vi. 4, 5, "Let every man prove his own work, and then shall he have rejoicing in himself alone, and not in another; for every man shall bear his own burthen." God himself will judge men according to their works; and so will men; and so must we (much) do by ourselves; for it is the rightest judging which is likest God's.

This subordinate honour God grants to his servants:

If their works were not an honour to them, as the next agents, they could be none to him in their morality, as man's acts; though they might, as acts in general, be ordered to good by his own goodness. If God's natural works of creation (sun, and moon, and earth, &c.) were not praiseworthy in themselves, God would not be praised for them as their Maker. There are works that God is said to be dishonoured by, Rom. ii. 23, 24; and what are they but such as are really bad, and a dishonour to the authors? It is so far from being true, that no praise, or honour, or comfort from good works, is to be given to man; that God himself is not like else to be honoured by them as morally good, if the actors be not honoured by them: the world must first be convinced that christians are far better than other men, and the righteous more excellent than his neighbour, before they will glorify God as the author of their goodness. In God's own judgment, "Well done," is the first word, and "Good and faithful servant," is the second, and "Enter thou into the joy of thy Lord," is the third.

Two sorts of scandalous persons rob God of his honour in his saints.

1. Those that professing christianity live wickedly, or, at least, no better than other men: whose lives tell the world that christians are but such as they.

2. Those that slander and belie true believers, and would hide their goodness, and make them odious to the world.

As for them that say only that we have no righteousness in ourselves by which we can be justified, I shall not differ with them, if they do but grant that all shall be judged according to their works; and that he that is accused as an infidel, impenitent, a hypocrite, or an unregenerate, ungodly person, must against that accusation be justified by his own faith, repentance, sincerity, and holiness, or be unjustified for ever.

3. The next thing to the work, and the person that is hereby honoured, is the christian religion itself, with the Spirit's operations on the souls of christians; the outward doctrine and example of Christ, who teacheth his servants to be better than the world; and the inward sanctification of the Spirit, which maketh them better. The air and food are commended which make men healthy, and the medicines are praised which cure the disease: that is accounted good, as a means and cause, which doth good, and which maketh men good: if christians were more commonly and notoriously much better than all other men, the world would believe that the gospel and the christian religion were the best.

But when scandalous christians appear as bad, or worse than infidels, the world thinks that their religion is as bad, or worse than theirs.

4. The next ascent of honour is to the Maker or Author of our religion; the world will see that he is good that maketh so good a law and gospel, and that maketh all his true disciples so much to excel all other men. And here the first honour will be to the Holy Spirit, which reneweth souls, and maketh them holy; and the next will be to the Son, our Saviour, who giveth us both the word and Spirit; and the highest or ultimate glory will be to God the Father, who giveth us both his Son and his Spirit.

And thus honour ascendeth to the highest by these steps, and the world beginneth at that which is nearest to them, and reason will proceed by these degrees: 1. The excellent holy lives of christians are better than other men's. 2. Therefore christians are better than other men. 3. Therefore their religion is the best, or the word and work which make them such. 4. Therefore the Spirit is good which makes them good; the Saviour is good who giveth them the word and Spirit; and God, the Fountain of all, even the Father of mercies, is the Fountain of all good, and consequently the end of all. And thus God is known and glorified by our works.

II. The works which thus glorify him are first to be described in general, and then enumerated in special.

I. In general, 1. They must be such as make or show men to be in their places like to God; they must be such as represent the particular perfections of God, which are called his communicable attributes; and such as declare his relations to us; and such as declare his attributes, as so related, and his works.

As, 1. We must so live that men may see that indeed we take not ourselves to be our own, but God to be our absolute Owner; and that it is not ourselves, but he, that must of right dispose both of us and ours, and that we willingly stand to his disposal. 1 Cor. vi. 19, " Ye are not your own."

2. We must so live as may declare that we are not lawless, nor the mere servants of men, but the resolved subjects of God, the sovereign King of all; and that really we are ruled by his laws and will, and not by our own lusts or wills, nor by the wills of any, but as under him; and that we fear not any hurt to the flesh, or them that can but kill the body, in comparison of that one Lawgiver and Judge, who is able to save or to destroy for ever, Luke xii. 4; James iv. 12; 1 Cor. vii. 23; and that we are moved more by his promises, than by all that mortal men can give us; and trust wholly to the heavenly reward of glory, and not to the transitory prosperity of this world, believing that God is true and just, and none of his word shall ever fail. 1 Pet. i. 3, " We are begotten again unto a lively hope, through the resurrection of Christ, to an inheritance incorruptible," &c.

3. We must so live as may declare that God is our grand Benefactor, from whom we have all the good that ever we received, and from whom we hope for all that ever we shall possess; and that he is infinitely good, the original and end of all created good: we must live as those that believe that we are made for God, even to glorify him, and please his blessed will; not by making him beholden to us, but by a willing receiving of his mercies, and a willing improvement of them to our own felicity; and as those that believe that his love is better than life itself, and that to know him, and love him, and glorify him for ever, is the ultimate end and happiness of man: Psal. iv. 7, 8, and lxiii. 3, and lxxiii. 25, 26, 28; Phil. iii. 7, 8; Matt. vi. 33; 1 Pet. i. 5, 6, 8, 9; 2 Cor. v. 1.

2. And we must so live in relation to Christ, and to his Spirit, as may declare to the world that the mercy of the Father is conveyed to us by the Son, and the grace of the Father and the Son by the Spirit; and what wonders of wisdom, goodness and power, truth and justice, holiness and mercy, are manifest in Christ, and his mediation to mankind: Gal. ii. 20; Eph. iii. 16, 17; Phil. i. 20, 21; John xvii. 10.

3. In some the works that glorify God must have these three parts of his likeness upon them.

1. They must be works of light, like the light which from the Father of lights doth illuminate us. Christians must be much wiser than the men of the world, in holy, though not in worldly things, Col. i. 9, 28, and iii. 16. Darkness is the state of Satan's kingdom, and ignorant christians are scandalous, and a dishonour to Christ; not those that are ignorant of unnecessary, unprofitable, or unrevealed things, but those that are ignorant of revealed, necessary, saving truths: 1 Cor. iii. 2; Heb. v. 11, 12.

2. They must be works of holy love to God and man, which show that God and goodness have our hearts, and that we would imitate God in doing good to all, according to our places and power: Gal. vi. 10; Rom. xiii. 10—12.

3. They must be works of life and power, where serious diligence expresseth zeal; and that we set ourselves no lower bounds, than with all our heart, and mind, and might: 2 Tim. i. 7; Rom. xii. 11. Thus much for the general description of them.

II. The description of a christian, whose works glorify God, according to Scripture and experience, may be given you in the following particulars.

I. He is one that placeth his saving religion in the practical knowledge of the only true God, and Jesus Christ the Saviour, whom he hath sent, John xvii. 3. He puts no limits to his endeavours after useful knowledge, but what God hath put by his word or providence; he would abound in holy wisdom, and thinks it worth his greatest diligence, and is still upon the increasing hand: he hath so much knowledge of the lesser matters of religion, as to keep him from scandalous miscarriages about them; but it is the knowledge of God, and of a crucified and glorified Christ, in which he taketh wisdom to consist, John xvii. 3; 1 Cor. ii. 2. This is the light in which he hath his daily conversation, the light which governeth his will and practice, which feedeth his meditations, his prayers, and his discourse; which repelleth his temptations, which maintaineth his hope, and is his daily work of recreation, his food, and feast.

For they will now perceive, 1. That his religion is not a matter of names and words, and trifling controversies, but hath the greatest and most excellent subject in the world; and as nature teacheth all to reverence God, so it will tell them that they must reverence that religion, that conversation, and that person, who is most divine, and where the most of God appeareth.

2. And they will see that his religion consisteth not in uncertainties, which no man can be sure of when he hath done his best; but in things so sure as none should doubt of; which will easily bring men over to consent, and shame or silence contradicters.

3. And then they will see that it is a religion which all sober persons are united in, and doth not lose its authority or reverence, by the divisions, wranglings, and digladiations of sects of different minds; for God is denied by no sober man, nor the essentials of christianity by any true christian.

4. And men will see that our religion is no matter of indifferency, which one may do well enough without, but of absolute necessity to salvation, and that which man was made and redeemed for: and a religion of the greatest subject, the greatest certainty, the greatest consent, and the greatest necessity, will honour itself and its Author in the world, if it be rightly represented in the lives of them that do profess it.

But when men's overdoing shall pretend that all this is too little, and shall seek to raise it, as to more perfection, by their own inventions, or uncertain opinions in doctrine, worship, church-discipline, or practice, they presently cast it as a foot-ball before the boys in the streets, and make it a matter of doubtful, endless disputations, or multiplied sects of pernicious contentions and cruel persecutions; and then the reverence and glory of it is gone, and every philosopher will vie with it in subtilty, and every stranger will presume to censure it, if not to blaspheme it, and deride it. And thus overdoers are the scandals of the world.

II. The christian that will glorify God, and his profession, must be conscionable in the smallest matters; but he must ever describe and open the nature of his religion, as consisting in great and certain things, and not talk too much of smaller matters, as if it were those that men were to be saved by. Tell men of the necessity of believing, fearing, obeying, trusting, and loving God, and of coming to him by Jesus Christ, the great Mediator between God and man; tell them of the intrinsic evil of sin, and of God's justice, and of man's corruption, and of the nature and excellency of holiness, and of the necessity of being new-born of the Holy Spirit, and of mortifying the desires and deeds of the flesh; and tell them of judgment, heaven, and hell, especially the certainty and excellency of the everlasting promised glory; persuade them to believe all this, to think much of all this, and to be true to what they know, and to make it the work of life to be always prepared for death. Let this be your discourse with sinners, (as I told you in the first character it must be your own religion,) and then men will perceive that religion is a matter that doth indeed concern them, and that they are indeed great and necessary things in which you differ from ungodly men: but the scandalous christian talketh most of external church orders, and forms, and opinions, and parties; and thereby maketh the ignorant believe that the difference is but that one will sit when the other kneeleth; and one will pray by the book, and the other without book; and one is for this church government, and another for that; and one for praying in white, and the other in black. And talking too much of such things as these deceiveth the hearers; some it maketh formal hypocrites, who take up this for their religion, and the rest it hardeneth, and maketh them think that such people are only more humorous, and self-conceited, and giddy, and factious than others, but no whit better.

III. The genuine christian hath a humble and cautelous understanding; sensible when he knoweth most how little he knoweth, and how much he is still unacquainted with, in the great mysterious matters of God. His ignorance is his daily grief and burden, and he is still longing and looking for some clearer light. Not a new word of revelation from God, but a clearer understanding of his word. He knoweth how weak and slippery man's understanding is, and he is humbly conscious of the darkness of his own. Therefore he is not conceitedly wise, nor a boaster of his knowledge; but saith, as Paul, 1 Cor. viii. 2, "If any man think that he knoweth any thing, (that is, is proudly conceited of his own knowledge,) he knoweth nothing yet as he ought to know."

And hence it is that though he daily grow in the firmer apprehension of necessary truths, yet he is never confident and peremptory about uncertain, doubtful things; and therefore he is not apt to be quarrelsome and contentious, nor yet censorious against those that differ from him in matters of no greater moment. And hence it is that he runneth not into sects, nor burneth with the feverish dividing zeal, nor yet is scandalously mutable in his opinions; because, as one that is conscious of his ignorance, he doth not rashly receive things which he understands not, but suspendeth his judgment till evidence make him fit to judge; and joineth with neither of the contending parties, till he is sure to know, indeed, which of them is right: and thus he avoideth that dishonouring of religion which the scandalous christian is woefully guilty of; who, with an unhumbled understanding, groweth confident upon quick and insufficient information, and judgeth before he understandeth the case, and before he hath heard or read, and considered, what on both sides may be said, and what is necessary to a true understanding. And thus, either by audacious prating of what he never understood, or reviling and censuring men wiser than himself, or by making himself a judge where he hath need to be many years a learner, or making a religion of his own mistakes, and setting up dividing sects to propagate them, or else by shameful mutability and unsettledness, he becometh a scandal to harden unbelievers, and a disease to the church, and a shame to his profession. Read James iii. 15—17. Conceited wisdom kindleth a contentious zeal, and is not of God, but from beneath.

IV. The christian who glorifieth God by his religion, is one that so liveth that men may perceive that his carnal interest is not the end and ruler of his life; but that God is his end, and to please him is his work and his reward, in which he is comforted, though the flesh and the world be never so much displeased; and that the perfect light and love of God in the unseen glory of another life, is the sanctifying sum of all his hopes, for which all the world must be forsaken. To talk much of heaven, and to be as much and as eager for the world as others, is the way by which the scandalous hypocrite doth bring religion into contempt. It is no high, nor very honourable work, to talk of the vanity of the world; but to live above it, and to be out of the power of it: nor is it any great matter to speak honourably of heaven; but to live as believing seekers of it, and as those that have there their treasure and their hearts, (Matt. vi. 20, 21,) and are comforted more by the hopes of the life to come, than by all their possessions or pleasures in the world. If we will glorify God, our lives must persuade men that he will certainly be our everlasting portion, and the sure and plentiful rewarder of them that diligently seek him, Heb. xi. 6. It is much of the use of a true christian's life to convince unbelievers that there is a heaven for saints; and the scandalous worldling persuadeth them that there is none: Matt. v. 5, 11, 12; Phil. iii. 26, 21; Col. iii. 1—5.

V. Therefore it glorifieth God and our religion when christians live in greater joy, or at least in greater contentedness and peace, than other men. When they can answer all the crosses in the world sufficiently with this, that God is their God, and his love shall be their endless joy, Psal. lxxiii. 1, 25, 26; and when they can live by faith, and not by sight, 2 Cor. v. 7; and can rejoice in hope of the glory of God, Rom. v. 3, 5; and can comfort themselves and one another with this, that they shall for ever be with the Lord, 1 Thess. iv. 17, 18; and can trust him to the death, who hath said, I will never fail thee, nor forsake thee, Heb. xiii. 5. If you would have other men honour your God and your religion, and desire to be such as you, you must really show them that you are on safer grounds and in a happier state than they; and that you will hardly do, if you be not more comfortable than they, or at least settled in more peace and contentedness of mind, as those that have a certain cure for the fears of death, and the danger that ungodly men are in of the revenging justice of the final Judge.

I confess it is possible for trembling, troubled, and distressed christians to be saved. But oh that they knew what a scandal they are to unbelievers, and what a dishonour to God, whom their lives should glorify! What man will fall in love with terrors and unquietness of mind? If you would glorify God by your fears and tears, they must be such as are accompanied with faith and hope; and you must not only show men what would make you happy, if you could obtain it, but also that it is attainable. Happiness is every man's desire, and none will come to Christ unless they believe that it tendeth to their happiness; they take up with the present pleasures of the flesh, because they have no satisfying apprehensions of any better. And if no man show them the first-fruits of any better here, they will hardly believe that they may have better hereafter; it is too hard a talk to put a poor drunkard, fornicator, or a proud and covetous worldling on, to believe that a poor, complaining, comfortless christian is happier than he; and that so sad and unquiet a life must be preferred before all his temporal contentments and delights. You must show him better, or the signs and fruits of better, before he will part with what he hath: you must show him the bunch of grapes, if you will have him go for the land of promise, when he is told of giants that must be overcome: and oh what a blessing is reserved for every Caleb and Joshua, that encourage souls, and glorify the promise! And how much do dejected discouragers of sinners dishonour God, and displease him! I have known some ungodly men, when they have seen believers rejoicing in God, and triumphantly passing through sufferings in the joyful hopes of glory, to sigh and say, Would I were such a one, or in his case; but I have seldom heard any say so of a person that is still sad, or crying, or troubling themselves and others with their scruples, crosses, or discontents; unless it be in respect to their blameless living, perhaps condoling them, they may say, Would I had no more sin to trouble me than you have. I confess that some excellent christians do show no great mirth in the way of their conversation; either because they are of a grave and silent temper, or taken up with severe studies and contemplations, or hindered by bodily pains or weakness. But yet their grave and sober comforts, their peace of conscience, and settled hopes, and trust in God, delivering them from the terrors of death and hell, may convince an unbeliever that this is a far better state than the mirth and laughter of fools in the house of feasting, and in the vanities of a short prosperity. The grave and solid peace and comfort of those that have made their calling and election sure, is more convincing than a lighter kind of mirth, John xvi. 22.

VI. The dominion of love in the hearts of christians, appearing in all the course of their lives, doth much glorify God and their religion; I mean a common hearty love to all men, and a special love to holy men, according to their various degrees of loveliness. Love is a thing so agreeable to right reason, and to social nature, and to the common interest of all mankind, that all men commend it; and they that have it not for others, would have it from others: who is it that loveth not to be loved? and who is it that loveth not the man that he is convinced loveth him, better than him that hateth him, or regardeth him not? And do you think that the same course, which maketh men hate yourselves, is like to make them love your religion? Love is the powerful conqueror of the world; by it God conquereth the enmity of man, and reconcileth to himself even malignant sinners; and by it he hath taught us to conquer all the tribulations and persecutions by which the world would separate us from his love; yea, and to be more than conquerors through him that loved us, and thereby did kindle in us our reflecting love, Rom. viii. 34—36; and by it he hath instructed us to go on to conquer both his enemies and our own; yea, to conquer the enmity rather than the enemy, in imitation of himself, who saveth the sinner, and kills the sin; and this is the most noble kind of victory. Every soldier can end a fever, or other disease, by cutting a man's throat, and ending his life; but it is the work of the physician to kill the disease, and save the man. The scandalous pastor is for curing heresy in the Roman way, by silencing sound preachers, and tormenting and burning the supposed heretics; or, at least, to trust for the acceptance and success of his labours to the sword: and if that which will restrain men from crossing the pastor, would restrain them from resisting the Spirit of God, and constrain them to the love of holiness, it were well; then the glory of conversion should be more ascribed to the magistrate and soldier than to the preacher. But the true pastor is armed with a special measure of life, light, and love, that he may be a meet instrument for the regenerating of souls, who by holy life, and light, and love, must be renewed to their Father's image. Every thing naturally generateth its like, which hath a generative power. And it is the love of God which the preacher is to bring all men to that must be saved: this is his office, this is his work, and this must be his study; he doth little or nothing if he doth not this. Souls are not sanctified till they are wrought up to the love of God and holiness. And, therefore, the furniture and arms which Christ hath left us in his word are all suited to this work of love. We have the love of God himself to preach to them; and the love of a humbled, dying, and glorified Redeemer; and all the amiable blessings of heaven and earth to open to them; and all the loving promises and invitations of the gospel; and must not our hearts, our ministry, and our lives be answerable to all this? Believe it, it must be a preacher, whose matter and manner of preaching and living doth show forth a hearty love to God, and love to godliness, and love to all his people's souls, that is the fit instrument to glorify God by convincing and converting sinners. God can work by what means he will; by a scandalous, domineering, self-seeking preacher, but it is not his ordinary way. Foxes and wolves are not nature's instruments to generate sheep. I never knew much good done to souls by any pastors but such as preached and lived in the power of love, working by clear, convincing light, and both managed by a holy, lively seriousness. You must bring fire if you would kindle fire. Trust not here to the Cartesian philosophy, that mere motion will turn another element into fire. Speak as loud as you will, and make as great a stir as you will, it will be all in vain to win men's love to God and goodness, till their hearts be touched with his love and amiableness; which usually must be done by the instrumentality of the preacher's love. Let them hate me, so they do but fear me and obey me, is the saying of such as set up for themselves, (and but foolishly for themselves,) and, like Satan, would rule men to damnation. If love be the sum and fulfilling of the law, love must be the sum and fulfilling of our ministry. But yet by love I mean not flattery: parents do love as necessarily as any, and yet must correct; and God himself can love and yet correct; yea, he chasteneth every son that he receiveth, Heb. xii. 6, 7; and his love consisteth with paternal justice, and with hatred of sin, and plain and sharp reproof of sinners; and so must ours; but all as the various operations of love, as the objects vary.

And what I say of ministers, I say of every christian in his place. Love is the great and the new commandment, that is, the last which Christ would leave, at his departure, to his disciples. Oh could we learn of the Lord of love, and Him who calleth himself love itself, to love our enemies, to bless them that curse us, and to do good to the evil, and pray for them that hurt and persecute us, we should not only prove that we are genuine christians, the children of our heavenly Father, Matt. v. 44, 45; but should heap coals of fire on our enemies' heads, and melt them into compassion and some remorse, if not into a holy love. I tell you, it is the christian who doth truly love his neighbour as himself; who loveth the godly as his co-heirs of heaven, and loveth the ungodly with a desire to make them truly godly; who loveth a friend as a friend, and an enemy as a man that is capable of holiness and salvation; it is he that liveth, walketh, speaketh, converseth, yea, suffereth, which is the great difficulty in love, and is, as it were, turned, by the love of God shed abroad upon his heart, into love itself; who doth glorify God in the world, and glorify his religion, and really rebuke the blasphemer, that derideth the Spirit in believers, as if it were but a fanatical dream.

And it is he that by tyranny, cruelty, contempt of others, and needless, proud singularities and separations, magisterially condemning and vilifying all that walk not in his fashion, and pray not in his fashion, and are not of his opinion, where it is like enough he is himself mistaken, that is the scandalous christian, who doth as much against God, and religion, and the church, and men's souls, as he doth against love. And though it be Satan's way, as an angel of light, and his ministers' way as ministers of righteousness, to destroy Christ's interest by dividing it, and separating things that God will have conjoined, and so to pretend the love of truth, the love of order, or the love of godliness, or discipline, against the love of souls, and to use even the name of love itself against love, to justify all their cruelties, or censures, and alienations; yet God will keep up that sacred fire in the hearts of the sound christians which shall live and conquer these temptations; and they will understand and regard the warning of the Holy Ghost, Rom. xvi. 17, "I beseech you, mark them which cause divisions and offences, contrary to the doctrine which you have learned, and avoid them" (in their sinful, dividing, offensive ways); "for they that are such serve not the Lord Jesus," (though they may confidently think they do,) "but their own bellies," or carnal interests, though, perhaps they will not see it in themselves; "and by good words and fair (or flattering) speeches, deceive the hearts of the simple." The word is *τῶν ἀκάκων*, *hominum minime malorum*, no bad men, or harmless, well-meaning men; who in case it be not to mortal errors, perhaps, may be in the main sincere, and may be saved when their stubble is burnt; but whether sincere or not, they are scandals in the world, and great dishonourers of God, and serve Satan when they little think so, in all that they do contrary to that universal love, by which God must be glorified, and sinners overcome.

VII. A public mind that is set upon doing good, as the work of his life, and that with sincere and evident self-denial, doth greatly glorify God in the world. As God maketh his goodness known to us by doing good, so also must his children do. Nothing is more communicative than goodness and love; nothing will more certainly make itself known whenever there is opportunity. That a worldly barren love, which doth not help, and succour, and do good, is no true christian love, St. James hath told us fully in his detection of a dead and barren faith. No man in reason can expect that others should take him for a good man, for something that is known to no one but himself, save only that public converse and communion must be kept up by the charitable belief of professions, till they are disproved. The tree is known by its fruits, and the fruits best by the taste, though the sight may give some lower degree of commendation. The character of Christ's purified, peculiar people, is, that they are zealous of good works, Tit. ii. 14. The scandalous christian may be zealous against others, and zealous to hurt them, to persecute them, to censure them, to disparage them, and to avoid them, but the genuine christian is zealous in loving them, and doing them all the good he can. To do a little good upon the by, and from a full table to send an alms to Lazarus at the door, yea, to give to the needy as much as the flesh can spare, without any suffering to itself, or any abatement of its grandeur, pomp, and pleasure in the world, will prove you to be men not utterly void of all compassion, but it will never prove you to be christians, nor better than infidels and heathens. Look not that men should think you better than your fruits do manifest you to be, nor that they take you to be good for saying that you are good, nor judge you to excel others any further than your works are better than others. And marvel not if the world ask, What do you more than others? when Christ himself doth ask the same, Matt. v. 47. If ye salute your brethren, and those of your own opinion and way, and if ye love them that love you, and say as ye say, do not even publicans and infidels do the same? Matt. v. 46. Marvel not if men judge you according to your works, when God himself will do so, who knoweth the heart. He that is all for himself, may love himself, and think well of himself, but must not expect much love from others. Selfishness is the bile or imposthume of societies, where the blood and spirits have an inordinate efflux, till their corruption torment or gangrene the part. While men are all for themselves, and would draw all to themselves, instead of loving their neighbour as themselves, and the public good above themselves, they do but hurt and destroy themselves, for they forfeit their communion with the body, and deserve that none should care for them, who care for none but themselves. To a genuine christian, another's good rejoiceth him as if it were his own, (and how much, then, hath such a one continually to feed his joy!) and he is careful to supply another's wants as if they were his own. But the scandalous, selfish hypocrite doth live quietly, and sleep easily, if he be but well himself, and it go well with his party, however it go with all his neighbours, or with the church, or with the world. To himself he is fallen, to himself he liveth, himself he loveth, himself he seeketh, and himself, that is, his temporal prosperity, he will advance and save, if he can, whatever his religion be; and yet himself he destroyeth, and will lose. It is not well considered in the world, how much of sin consisteth in the narrow contraction of men's love, and regard unto their natural selves, and how much of goodness consisteth in a community of love, and what a glory it is to the government and laws of God that he maketh it so noble and necessary a part of every man's duty, to love all men, and to do good to all, as he is able, though with a difference. God could do us all good enough by himself alone, without one another. But what a mercy is it to the world, that as many persons as there are, so many there are obliged by God to love their neighbours as themselves, and to do good to all about them! And what a mercy is it to the actor, that God will thus make him the instrument and messenger of his beneficence!

Ministers and christians all, would you be thought

better than others? Are you angry with men that think otherwise of you? What good do you more than others in your places? What good do you that other men can see, and feel, and taste, and judge of? Every man loveth himself, and can feel what doth him good in natural things; and God, that by giving you food, and other mercies to your bodies, would have you therein taste his love to your souls, would use you just so for your brethren's good. Do you give them good words and counsel? It is well. But that is not it that they can yet taste and value. You must do that sort of good for them which they can know and relish; not that this will save them, or is any great matter of itself, no more than God's common bodily mercies to you, but this is the best way to get down better. And "he that seeth his brother have need, and shutteth up the bowels of his compassion from him, how dwelleth the love of God in him?" 1 John iii. 17. "Give to him that asketh, and from him that would borrow of thee turn not thou away," Matt. v. 42. That is, let not want of charity hinder thee at any time from giving, though want of ability may hinder thee, and prudence may restrain thee and must guide thee. If you say, Alas! we have it not to give. I answer, 1. Do what you can. 2. Show by your compassion, that you would, if you could, take care of your poor brethren. 3. Beg of others for them, and put on those that can to do it.

Say not, These carnal people value nothing but carnal things, and cannot perceive a man's love by spiritual benefits; for it is not grace, but the means and outside of things spiritual, that you can give them; and for aught I see, the most of us all do very hardly believe God's own love to us, if he deny us bodily mercies. If you languish in poverty, crosses, and painful sickness any thing long, your murmuring showeth that you do not sufficiently taste God's goodness without the help of bodily sense. And can you expect that natural men believe you to be good for your bare words, when you so hardly think well of God himself, though he promise you life eternal, unless he also give you bodily supplies?

VIII. He that will glorify his religion, and God, before men, must be strictly just in all his dealings; just in governing, just in trading and bargaining, just to superiors and to inferiors, to friends and to enemies, just in performing all his promises, and in giving every man his right. He that in love must part with his own right for his neighbour's greater good, must not deprive another of his right; for charity includeth justice, as a lower virtue is included in a higher and more perfect. He must not be unjust for himself, for riches, or any worldly ends; he must not be unjust for friends or kindred; he must not be drawn to it by fear or flattery; no price must hire them to do an unrighteous deed. But above all, he must never be unjust as for religion, as if God either needed or countenanced a lie, or any iniquity. No men are more scandalous dishonourers of religion, and of God, than they that think it lawful to deceive, or lie, or be perjured, or break covenants, or be rebellious, or use any sinful means to secure or promote religion, as if God were not able to accomplish his ends by righteous means. This cometh from atheism and unbelief, when men think that God will lose his cause, unless our wits and sinful shifts preserve it; as if we, and not he, were the rulers of the world. The unrighteous shall not inherit the kingdom of God, (1 Cor. vi. 9,) and seldom escape the hatred or contempt of men.

IX. He that will glorify God, must know and observe the order of commands and duties, and that God will have mercy and not sacrifice, and must prefer the end before the means as such. He must not pretend a lesser duty against a greater, nor take the lesser at that time for a duty, but for a sin, when the greater should take place. God hath made his laws, and our duty, to be the means of our own good. It is no profaneness, but duty, to omit that which else would be a duty, when a greater is to be preferred. God calls it the sacrifice of a fool, who knoweth not that he doth evil under the name of duty, when sacrifice is preferred before an obedient hearing of God's commands, Eccles. v. 1—3. It was no want of holy zeal in Christ, which made him bid the unreconciled, "Leave thy gift at the altar, and first go and be reconciled to thy brother, and then come and offer thy gift," Matt. v. 24. Some zealous persecutors, censurers, and dividers, now, would think I speak like an ungodly person if I should say to them, Let your liturgy, and your prayers, and your worship stay till you have confessed and lamented your injuries to your brethren, and then come and offer your service to God, and lift up pure hands to him, without wrath and doubting. Yet it is no more than God often calls for to the hypocritical Jews. Isa. i. 11, &c. "To what purpose is the multitude of your sacrifices? When ye come to appear before me, who hath required this at your hands, to tread my courts? Bring no more vain oblations; incense is an abomination to me. When ye spread forth your hands, I will hide mine eyes; when ye make many prayers, I will not hear: your hands are full of blood. Wash you, make you clean, relieve the oppressed." Isa. lviii. 2, 3, &c. "They seek me daily, and delight to know my ways, as a nation that did righteousness, and forsook not the ordinance of their God: they ask of me the ordinances of justice; they take delight in approaching to God. Wherefore have we fasted, and thou seest not? have we afflicted our soul, and thou takest no knowledge? Ye fast for strife and debate, and to smite with the fist of wickedness: ye shall not fast as this day, to make your voice to be heard on high. Is it such a fast that I have chosen? a day for a man to afflict his soul? to bow down his head as a bulrush, and to spread sackcloth and ashes under him? wilt thou call this a fast, and an acceptable day to the Lord? Is not this the fast that I have chosen? to loose the bands of wickedness, and to let the oppressed go free, and that ye break every yoke? Is it not to deal thy bread to the hungry, and that thou bring the poor that are cast out to thy house? when thou seest the naked, that thou cover him; and that thou hide not thyself from thy own flesh? Then shall thy light break forth as the morning, and thy health shall spring forth speedily: and thy righteousness shall go before thee; the glory of the Lord shall be thy rereward. Then shalt thou call, and the Lord shall answer; thou shalt cry, and he shall say, Here I am."

It is a point that our Lord Jesus layeth a great stress upon. He purposely healeth on the sabbath day, and tells the censorious Pharisees "the sabbath was made for man, and not man for the sabbath;" that is, the end, which is man's good, is to be preferred before the means; nay, it is no means, and so no duty, which is against it. He defendeth his disciples for getting themselves food as they passed in the corn-fields; and he teacheth them the lawfulness of the priest's labour on the sabbath, and of David's eating the shew-bread; and at two several times doth tell them that God "will have mercy, and not sacrifice;" and biddeth them "go learn what that meaneth," Matt. iv. 13; xii. 7.

And it is not only Pharisees, but many better men, who have need to go learn the meaning of that sentence. The meaning is this, that *(cæteris paribus)* the great duties of the law of nature are to take place before the positive institutions. God's institutions are for man's good: whatever is a duty is also a means to the happiness of man, and pleasing of God, which is the end of all. Love to God and man are greater than all the instituted means of them as such; therefore that is no duty which is no means, or is against the instituter's end. Preaching and prayer must be omitted for some works of love and human good. Discipline is a duty when it is a means to the end for which it is ordained; but when it would hinder or destroy that end (the reputation of religion, and the glory of God's holiness, and the church's good) it is no duty, but a sin. To omit a sacrament, to break the rest of the Lord's day, to forbear the sacred assemblies, may be a duty when the good of men requireth them. Ordination is a duty when it is a means to its proper end; but if it were pleaded against those ends, and order set against the thing ordered, even the work of the ministry, the case would be altered.

When men mistake, and mistime and misplace God's institutions, to the excluding of the great moral duties, which are their end, and persuade men to that as a part of religion, which would certainly do more hurt than good, they scandalously drive men away from religion. Thus imprudent, scandalous professors can backbite and reproach others, and make them odious, and destroy christian love, and peace, and concord, on pretence of zeal for order, government, ceremonies, forms, or for this or that mode of discipline or worship; not having learned what this meaneth, "I will have mercy and not sacrifice;" nor, that forms and external institutions were made for man, and not man for them. And yet I know that this will not justify the familist or hypocrite, who thinks he may do any thing to save his flesh.

Do you think it is not a scandal to Turks, or other infidels, tempting them to deride or hate christianity, to find the papists placing their merits in hurtful pilgrimages, which waste that time which should be spent, and in multitude of unprofitable ceremonies, and in unwholesome food, and injuries to health, under the names of abstinence and mortification? By this rule they may next persuade us, that it will please God if men famish or hang themselves; and consequently if they do so by others, for we must love our neighbour but as ourselves. God himself hath made all our religion so suitable to our good, that he expecteth not that we should take any thing for our duty, but what he giveth us evidence in the thing, or security by his promise, shall be our gain. He that worketh upon self-love, and winneth man by a Saviour, and a glorious reward, and proveth the goodness of all his word and ways, as to our happiness, hath instituted none of his ordinances to our hurt. The apostles had their power only to edification, and not the destruction or hurt of souls, 2 Cor. x. 8; xiii. 10. "Let all things be done to edifying," (1 Cor. xiv. 26,) is a word of greater comprehension and use than many do conceive. When it is against edification, it is not acceptable to God. One would think Christ had broken his own law of discipline when he did familiarly eat with publicans and sinners; and yet that very act of his is one of those which he justifieth by the aforesaid rule, "I will have mercy and not sacrifice," Matt. ix. 11—13. Learn this lesson of preferring mercy before sacrifice, if ever you will glorify God.

The right manner of worshipping God is of great moment to the honour of him and of our religion before the world: that we give no false descriptions of God, or dishonourable attributes: that we teach no dishonourable doctrine as his, especially of his own will and counsels, and of his government, laws, and judgment: that we neither take down the glory of the gospel mysteries, by reducing them to the rank of common providence, nor yet be deceived by Satan or his ministers, as the promoters of light and righteousness, 2 Cor. xi. 15; to abuse and dishonour them by overdoing: that we seek not to glorify God by our lies, or by our own mistaken interpretations or inventions. God must be worshipped as a Spirit, in spirit and truth, and not with popish toys and fopperies, which make others think that our religion is but like a puppet-play and ludicrous device, to keep the people in servitude to the priests by a blind devotion. God must be worshipped rationally, and with all holy wisdom, and not with childish shadows and trifles, nor with slovenly and imprudent words, which tend to breed in the hearers derision or contempt. Neither the cantings or scenical actions, or affected repetitions of the papists, nor the rude, disorderly, incongruous expressions of unskilful men, are fit to be offered to the glorious God. Prudence, and holiness, and seriousness, and reverence, must appear in that worship which must honour God. Oh with what holiness should we hear from and speak to the holy, holy, holy God! who will be sanctified in all that draw near him, (Lev. x. 3,) and will not hold him guiltless that taketh his name in vain! They that will do it acceptably must serve him with reverence and godly fear, (Heb. xii. 28,) as knowing that he is a "consuming fire;" and yet, with alacrity, love, and delight, as knowing that in his favour is life, and that he is the infinitely amiable good, the hope and only portion of believers.

XI. The humility, meekness, and patience of christians are greatly necessary to their glorifying of God. I join all three together for brevity's sake.

1. It is a thing very amiable in the eyes of all, when men have not too high thoughts of themselves, and seek not to be overvalued by others, either as great, or wise, or good: when they seek not precedency, preferment, or honour, but take the lowest place, and envy not the precedence or honour of others, but take another's honour as their own, and take another to be fitter *(cæteris paribus)* for places of power, trust, or eminency, than themselves: when they do, according to the measure of their worth, honour all men, 1 Peter ii. 17; and are "kindly affectioned one to another in brotherly love, in honour preferring one another," Rom. xii. 10; not dissemblingly and complimentally saying, Your servant, sir, while they would fain have others below them, and to be obedient to their wills; but really to think meanly of their own worth and wisdom. Rom. xii. 3, "For I say, through the grace given me, to every man that is among you, not to think of himself more highly than he ought to think, but to think soberly, as God hath dealt to every man the measure of faith." Not thinking himself something when he is nothing, Gal. vi. 3; nor to be more learned, or wise, or pious than he is. We must be, indeed, his disciples, who "humbled himself, and made himself of no reputation," Phil. ii. 7, 8; and washed and wiped the feet of his disciples, to teach them what to be and do to one another: who hath taught us the necessity of cross-bearing and self-denial, and to humble ourselves as little children, if ever we will enter into the kingdom of heaven, Matt. xvi. 24; xviii. 3, 4; and hath decreed and foretold us that whosoever shall exalt himself shall be abased, and he that humbleth himself shall be exalted; and therefore the greatness which his ministers must seek must be to be the servants of the rest, Matt. xxiii.

11—13. "Honour shall uphold the humble in spirit, but a man's pride shall bring him low," Prov. xxix. 23. "Better is it to be of an humble spirit with the lowly, than to divide the spoils with the proud," Prov. xvi. 19. He that will honour his religion must "put on, as the elect of God, bowels of mercy, kindness, humbleness of mind, (not of tongue only,) meekness, long-suffering; forbearing one another, and forgiving one another, if any man have a quarrel against any," Col. iii. 12, 13. He must not set out himself like the richest, and desire to seem high or notable to others, nor set up himself with his superiors, nor swell or grudge, if he be not regarded or taken notice of; nor if he be reproved or dishonoured: but must learn of a humbled Christ to be meek and lowly, Matt. xi. 29; and must not mind or desire high things, but condescend to men of low estate, and not be wise in his own conceit, Rom. xii. 16. "I beseech you, therefore, that you walk worthy the vocation wherewith ye are called, with all lowliness and meekness, with long-suffering, forbearing one another in love," Eph. iv. 1, 2. "Let nothing be done through strife or vain-glory, but in lowliness of mind let each esteem others better than themselves," Phil. ii. 3. What man loveth not such a spirit and conversation? Oh that it were more common and eminent among us, and then we should find that the disaffection of the ignorant would be much abated, and that when a man's ways thus please God, his enemies will be the more at peace with him, Prov. xvi. 7. But when they are proud, and we are proud, and we cannot yield, nor bow, nor give place to the wrathful, but must jostle and contend with them for our place and honour, we lose our christian honour by seeking carnal honour, and appear to be but like other men; and even the proud themselves will disdain the proud.

2. And though we may be angry and not sin, and must be plain and zealous against sin, and for God; though guilty, galled sinners be displeased by it, yet meekness must be our temperature; for a turbulent, rough, unquiet spirit, is displeasing both to God and man; such persons have seldom peace with others or themselves. A meek and quiet spirit is in the sight of God of great price, 1 Pet. iii. 4. "Blessed are the meek, for they shall inherit the earth;" they shall speed better than others, even in this world, Matt. v. 5. "The wisdom from above is first pure, then peaceable, gentle, easy to be entreated, full of mercy and good fruits." Paul tells us what the good works are which we must be always ready to; "To speak evil of no man, to be no brawlers; but gentle, showing all meekness to all men," Tit. iii. 1, 2. The Scripture speaks more of this than I have leisure to recite: see Gal. v. 23; vi. 1; 1 Tim. vi. 11; 2 Tim. ii. 25; 1 Pet. iii. 15; Jam. iii. 13; Zeph. ii. 13; Isa. xxix. 19; Psalm cxli. 4; lxxvi. 9; cxlvii. 6; xxxvii. 11.

3. And patience both towards God and man is a necessary companion of humility and meekness. This greatly differeth from natural dulness, and an insensible temperature. When a man's soul is partly so much awed by God's authority and presence, and partly so much taken up with the great matters of his service, and partly so much contented with his favour and grace, and the hopes of glory, as to make light of all the interests of the flesh as such; and therefore to bear patiently such losses, and crosses, and wants, and sufferings, as touch the flesh, as taking it for no great matter to lose all the world if we save our souls; this is true patience by which God is glorified. For by this men will see that christians have indeed such great things in their hopes, as set them quite above the transitory things of the flesh and the world; but when they are much troubled at every cross and loss, and whine and complain as if they were undone, if they live in poverty or reproach; and are at their wit's end in every danger, and fret and storm at every ill word, or every one that wrongeth them; they are the shame of their profession, and scandals to the world. It is not a sudden anger which is the great sin of impatience; but an impotent disability to suffer in the flesh, in estate or name, and a repining under every want, which showeth a fleshly, worldly mind, and a want of true believing the heavenly felicity; though I confess that pity must make some excuse for many poor women, whose natural temper maketh their passions, troubles, and fears invincible. He that said, "In your patience possess your souls," (Luke xxi. 19,) doth intimate, that we have lost ourselves, and the government, order, and peace of our souls, when we have lost our patience: see Eccl. vii. 8; Jam. v. 7, 8; 1 Pet. ii. 20; 1 Thess. v. 14, "Be patient towards all men;" 1 Tim. vi. 11; Col. i. 11. Whatever zeal you seem to have in prayer, in preaching, and for purity of worship, if you can bear wants and sickness, and the loss of all the world, no better than others, you will appear no better in their eyes; for "if you faint in the day of adversity, your strength is small," Prov. xx. 10.

XII. And as a special fruit of humility, an easy and thankful bearing of reproof, and readiness to confess a fault upon due conviction, is a necessary duty to the honouring of God. It will show men that you are enemies to sin indeed, and that you are not hypocrites, who weed only their neighbours' fields, and see the mote in another's eye, and not the beam which is in your own. "If the righteous smite us by reproofs, it must be taken as a kindness, and as a precious balsam which doth not break our head, but heal us," Psal. cxli. 5. Not that we are bound to belie ourselves in compliance with every man's censorious humour that will accuse us; but we must be readier to censure ourselves than others, and readier to confess a fault, than to expect a confession from others whom we reprove. Sincerity and serious repentance will be honourable in that person who is most careful to avoid sin, and most ready penitently to confess it when he hath been overcome, and truly thankful to those that call him to repentance; as being more desirous that God, and his laws and religion, have the glory of their holiness, than that he himself should have the undue glory of innocency, and escape the deserved shame of his sin.

It is one of the most dangerous diseases of professors, and greatest scandals of this age, that persons taken for eminently religious, are more impatient of plain (though just) reproof, than many a drunkard, swearer, or fornicator: and when they have spent hours or days in the seeming earnest confession of their sin, and lament before God and man that they cannot do it with more grief and tears, yet they take it for a heinous injury in another that will say half so much against them, and take him for a malignant enemy of the godly who will call them as they call themselves. They look that the chief business of a preacher should be to praise them, and set them above the rest, as the only people of God; and they take him for an enemy that will tell them the truth. But the scandal is greatest in those preachers themselves, who cannot endure to hear that they are sinners. So tender and impatient of reproof are some, yea, some that for their learning, and preaching, and piety, are ranked in the highest form, or expect to be so, that almost nothing but flattery or praise can please them: and they can hardly bear the gentlest reproof, no, nor a contradiction of any of their opinions; but they seem to tell men that it is their part and privilege to be the reprovers of others, and to have no reprover, and to tell other men of sin, and be themselves accounted innocent; and to call other men to repentance for particular sins, while they themselves must have no other repentance, than in general to say that they are sinners; and to proclaim to all that their public confessions are formalities, and that it is a Christ to heal the souls of others that they preach, while they acknowledge but little work for his remedies on themselves. But he that "refuseth reproof doth err, and he that hateth it is brutish," how learned, or reverend, or pious soever he would be accounted, Prov. xi. 17, and xii. 1. "He that regardeth reproof is prudent, and he that hateth it shall die," Prov. xv. 5, 10. As ready, humble, penitent confession of sin doth tend to our pardon from God, so doth it tend to our acceptation with man; when God and man will condemn the Pharisee, that justifies himself till confession be extorted from him.

XIII. It is another very honourable fruit of humility, to have a learning disposition, and not to be magisterial; and to be swift to hear, and slow to speak. All Christ's disciples must be as little children, Matt. xviii. 3, 4; especially in a learning, teachable disposition. A child doth not use to set his wit against his master's, or any other that will teach him, nor to rise up against instruction, as a disputer that must have the better, and be accounted the wisest; but his daily business is submissively to learn. A genuine christian is indeed communicative, and willing that others should partake with him in the wisdom and happiness which God hath revealed to him. But he is ready first to learn himself, and knoweth that he must receive before he can communicate: and there is none so far below him but he is willing to hear and learn of; but especially among his equals he is readier to hear and learn than to teach, because he is still conscious of his ignorance, and honoureth the gifts of God in others, which the proud despise, Jam. iii. 1, and i. 19.

But the scandalous christian is so wise in his own eyes, that he is ever of a teaching humour, and those please him best that will sit and hear, and reverence him as an oracle, and magnify every word that drops from his lips. He is so full of himself, that he hath scarce the patience to observe well what another speaks or writeth; and so valueth his own conceptions, that he thinks they should be valued by the hearers: and so scandalous is the teaching humour of some learned men, that they have not the common good manners or civility to suffer another to speak to the end, but they must needs interrupt him, that they may speak, as being more worthy. They take other men's speeches to be so tedious, that their patience cannot hold out the length of them. I mean not that a wise man is bound to lose his time in hearing every self-conceited person talk; but when men are engaged in conference, or disputes, for a man to have such a list to speak, that he cannot stay till another (though long) come to the end, it is scandalous incivility: yea, some can scarce stay till two or three sentences be uttered, but their haste must tell you that they take themselves to be much the wiser, and to be fitter to teach than to hear and learn. And they are so overladen with their own conceited wisdom, that they can carry it no longer without some vent; and so full of their own, that they can have no room to receive any more from others: and being all masters, they receive from God and man the greater condemnation, James iii. 1; Prov. xii. 17; i. 5; xviii. 13.

XIV. The genuine christian hateth backbiting, and disgraceful reports of others, and yet can bear it from others to himself. He hath learned to love all, and to speak evil of no man, nor to receive or vend ill reports of others. He knoweth that this is the work of the devil, the mortal enemy of love. He modestly rebuketh the backbiting tongue, and, with an angry countenance, driveth it away, Psalm xv. 3; Tit. iii. 2; Prov. xxv. 23. Backbiters tell us that they are haters of men; and the apostle joins them with haters of God, Rom. i. 30. Debates, backbitings, whisperings, envyings, are the scandalous christian's work, 2 Cor. xii. 20. He that heareth them will either distaste them, or catch the disease, and be as bad as they. And he that heareth that he is calumniated or reproached by them behind his back, is tempted to abhor both them and their profession. But to deal with men as faithful friends, and in plainness (but with prudence and love) to tell them secretly of their defects and faults, this tendeth to good, and to reconcile the minds of men at last, and to the honour of the christian way: Matt. xviii. 15, 16; Lev. xix. 17; Prov. ix. 8; xxiv. 25; xxvii. 5; Eccl. vii. 5; Prov. xxviii. 23.

But yet, when we are belied and reproached of ourselves, though by christians, or teachers, or superiors, it beseemeth us not to make too great a matter of it, as being tender of our own reputation, but only to be sorry for the slanderer's or backbiter's sin and misery. For men's corruption will have vent; the angry, and malicious, and envious, will speak from the abundance of their hearts; and the guilty will be tender; and children will cry and quarrel; and proud contenders will be impatient. And how small a matter is it, as to us, to be judged of man, who must all be shortly judged of the Lord!

XV. He is one that would keep open to the notice of all the great difference between the godly and the wicked; and aspireth after the highest degrees of holiness, as knowing the corruptions and calamities of the weak, and how much of heaven is in holiness itself; and yet, he loveth, honoureth, and cherisheth the least spark of grace in the weakest christian; and is none of them that censoriously despise such, nor that tyrannically tread them down, or cast them injuriously out of the church.

1. To make men believe that there is little difference between the holy and the profane, is to bring all religion into contempt, and is a wickedness which God's laws throughout condemn, and his judgment shall publicly confute: Matt. iii. 18; 2 Thess. i. 6—11; Jude 15; Matt. xiii. 25, throughout.

2. To take up with a little goodness, which consisteth with scandalous corruptions, is to be a scandal in the church.

3. And yet to be supercilious, and to disdain the weak, or shut out any as ungodly whom Christ hath not warranted us to shut out, and to make stricter rules of trial and Church communion than he hath made, this is justly displeasing both to God and man. It tempteth men to abhor that religion which tendeth more to men's reproach than to their cure, and causeth professors to set themselves higher above the weak, and at a greater distance from their neighbours, than God would have them. Christ is tender of little ones, and would not have them scandalized. His own apostles were very low in knowledge all the time that he was with them on earth. It is not mere want of words that will warrant us to take men for ungodly; even he that is "weak in faith must be received, but not to doubtful disputations," Rom. xiv. 15. To cull out a few that have learned to speak better than the rest, and shut out with the dogs all the infant christians, who must be fed with milk,

because they want expressions, is one of Satan's ways of overdoing, by which he would banish religion out of the world.

XVI. He that will glorify God by his good works must be zealous and diligent in them, and make them the serious business of his life; he must live so that men may see that indeed he doth believe and hope for heaven. That which a man coldly speaks of, and coldly seeketh, men will think he coldly desireth; and therefore that he doth but doubtingly believe it. A cold, slothful christian proclaims his unbelief to others, and so inviteth them to the like. When christians bestir themselves as for their lives, and ply God's work with greatest diligence, and redeem their lives, as knowing that all is short enough to prepare for an endless life, this wakeneth others to life and thoughtfulness, to inquire into the matter of our hopes.

XVII. He that will glorify God must be wise and watchful, to see and take the opportunities of good before they are passed by, and to avoid temptations to error and iniquity, and especially temerity in matters of great and public consequence.

1. Good works have their season. You lose them if you take them not in their time; that may be done now, which if you pass this time you can never do.

2. Temptations also have their season, and must just then be resisted, lest many a year repair not an hour's loss; and they are very many: and narrow-sighted careless persons, who avoid two and fall into the third, or avoid nineteen and are conquered by the twentieth, are always scandalous.

3. And rash adventures on any opinions or actions, but especially of public consequence, are usually most scandalous and pernicious to the church. As in military affairs, and in physic, *ubi non licet bis errare*, men's lives must pay for our temerity and error, and all the world cannot remedy the effects of one mistake; so in matters of religion, if we mistake by our rash conceitedness, and take not time for necessary trial, and proceed not as a man on the ice, or among quicksands, with great care and deliberation, the shaking of kingdoms, the ruin of churches, the silencing of ministers, the corruption of doctrine, worship, and discipline, and the sin and damnation of many souls, may be the effect of our proud presumption and temerity; but the humble, self-suspecting man, that suspendeth his judgment and practice till he hath thoroughly proved all, doth preserve the honour of religion, and avoid such late and dear repentance.

XVIII. The man whose works shall glorify God, must be devoted to the unity and concord of believers, and be greatly averse to dividing and love-killing opinions, words, and practices; and, as much as in him lies, he must live peaceably with all men, 1 Cor. i. 10; Phil. ii. 1—3; Eph. iv. 3, 4, 14—16; Rom. xvi. 17; xii. 18; 1 Thess. v. 17; John xvii. 24. When Paul saith that dividers "serve not the Lord Jesus, but their own bellies," he intimateth to us, that though truth and purity be in their mouths, and really intended by them, as they take it, yet there is usually a secret self-interest that is carried on that biasseth the judgment. And when he telleth them, (Acts xx. 30,) that "of their own selves should men arise, speaking perverse things," which they called (and it is like believed to be) the truth; yet self-interest lay at the bottom, to be somebody in drawing disciples after them; for it is so notorious a truth, that unity and concord are indispensably necessary to the church, as it is to our body, to families, to kingdoms, that men could not do so destructive a thing as dividing is, if some sin had not first caused the error of their minds. It greatly honoureth Christ and religion in the world, when believers live in love and unity: and their discords and divisions have in all ages been the scandal of the world, and the great reproach and dishonour of the church. When Christ's disciples are one in him, it is the way to the infidel world's conversion, that they may believe that the Father sent him, John xvii. 24.

And here the devil has two sorts of servants: 1. The true schismatic, or heretic, who fearlessly and blindly divideth the churches. 2. The overdoing papist, and church tyrant, who will have a greater unity than Christ will here give us, that so we may have none. And when Christ prays that we may be one in him, the pope saith that we shall also be one in him, or we shall be accounted schismatics, and destroyed as such. And when the ancient church, according to Christ's institution, united all in the baptismal covenant, explained in the creed, and Paul numbered the necessary terms of unity, Eph. iv. 4—6. 1. One body (or church of Christ) into which we are baptized. 2. One spirit of holiness in all. 3. One hope of the glorious reward. 4. One Lord by whom we do attain it. 5. One faith, even christian verity. 6. One baptism, or covenant of christianity. 7. And one God and Father of all. And in these God would have all his servants to be one; then come in these overdoers, and they must have us to be all one in all their papal policy, and all the decrees of their pope and councils *de fide*, and in their multitude of corruptions and ceremonious impositions: which is as much as to say, You shall have no unity; for he that saith to all the city or kingdom, you shall be destroyed for discord, or reproached as dividers, if you are not all of one complexion, or have not all the same appetite, age, or bodily stature, doth pronounce reproach or destruction on them absolutely: so is it with all others that put their self-devised terms on their brethren as necessary to unity and peace, on how pious or fair pretences soever; impossible conditions make the thing impossible. These are the church-tearing scandals. These are the snares by which Satan hath made the church a scorn, and our religion a stumblingblock to Turks and heathens; but had the peacemakers been heard, who learned of the Holy Ghost (Acts xv.) to impose nothing on the brethren but necessary things, and who have laboured to revive love, and shame emulations and divisions, God had been more glorified by men, and the reproach of the churches and solemn assemblies taken away. When all sects and parties have bustled and raised a dust in the world to foul the church, and to blind each other; if ever the church's glory be restored, and our shame taken away, it will be by men of love and peace, by healing, uniting, reconciling principles and means.

XIX. He that will glorify God, must live in and to the will of God, and seek to reduce his own will wholly into God's, and to destroy in himself all will that striveth against God's will.

1. The disposing will of God, our Owner, must be absolutely submitted to, and the bounteous will of God, our Benefactor, thankfully and joyfully acknowledged.

2. The ruling will of God our Lawgiver must be with daily study and care obeyed, and his punishing and rewarding justice glorified.

3. The final felicitating will and love of God, our ultimate end and object, that we may please him, and be everlastingly pleased in him, love him, and be loved by him, must be totally desired and sought, as the only and perfect rest of souls.

Oh! that is the holy, the joyful, the honourable

christian, who daily laboureth, and in some good measure doth prevail, to have no will but the will of God, and that which wholly is resolved into it; who looketh no further to know what he should do, but to know by his word what is the law or will of God; who believeth that all that God willeth is good, and had rather have his life, and health, and wealth, and friends, at God's will and disposal, than his own; who knoweth that God's will is love itself, and that to please him is the end of all the world, and the only felicity of men and angels; and resteth wholly in the pleasing of that will. What can be more wise and just, than to have the same will (objectively) with him who is infinitely wise and just? What can be more honourable, than to have the same will as God himself, and (so far) as his children, to be like our Father? What can be more orderly and harmonious, than for the will of the creature to move according to the Creator's will, and to be duly subservient to it, and accurately compliant with it? What can be more holy, nay, what else is holiness, but a will and life devoted and conformed to the will of God? What can be more safe, or what else can be safe at all, but to will the same things which the most perfect wisdom doth direct to, and infinite love itself doth choose? And what can be more easy and quieting to the soul, than to rest in that will which is always good, which never was misguided, and never chose amiss, and never was frustrated, or missed of its decreed ends? If we have no will but what is (objectively) the same with God's, that is, if we wholly comply with, and follow his will as our guide, and rest in his will as our ultimate end, our wills will never be disordered, sinful, misled, or frustrated. God hath all that he willeth (absolutely) and is never disappointed; and so should we if we could will nothing but what he willeth. And would you not take him unquestionably for a happy man, who hath whatsoever he would have? yea, and would have nothing but what is more just and good? There is no way to this happiness but making the will of God our will. God will not mutably change his will to bring it to ours; should holiness itself be conformed to sinners, and perfection to imperfection? But we must, by grace, bring over our wills to God's, and then they are in joint; and then only will they find content and rest. Oh what would I beg more earnestly in the world, than a will conformed wholly to God's will, and cast into that mould, and desiring nothing but what God willeth!

But contrarily, what can be more foolish, than for such infants and ignorant souls as we, to will that which infinite wisdom is against? What more dishonourable, than to be even at the very heart so contrary or unlike to God? What can be more irregular and unjust, than for a created worm to set his will against his Maker's? What else is sin, but a will and life that is cross to the regulating will of God? What can be more perilous and pernicious, than to forsake a perfect, unerring guide, and to follow such ignorant judgments as our own in matters of eternal consequence? What can that soul expect, but a restless state in an uncomfortable wilderness, yea, perpetual self-vexation and despair, who forsakes God's will to follow his own, and hath a will that doth go cross to God's? Poor self-tormenting sinners! consider that your own wills are your idols, which you set up against the will of God, and your own wills are the tyrants to which you are in bondage; your own wills are your prison, and the executioners that torment you with fear, and grief, and disappointments. What is it that you are afraid of, but lest you miss of your own wills? for sure you fear not lest God's will should be overcome and frustrated. What are your cares about but this? What are your sighs, and groans, and tears for? And what is it else that you complain of, but that your own wills are not fulfilled? It is not that God hath not his will. What is it that you are so impatient of, but the crossing of your own wills? This person crosseth them, and that accident crosseth them, and God crosseth them, and you cross them yourselves; and crossed they will be while they are cross to the will of God: for all this while they are as a bone out of joint; there is no ease till it be set right. In a word, a will that is contrary to God's will, and striveth and struggleth against it, is the offspring of the devil, the sum of all sin, and a foretaste of hell, even a restless self-tormentor; and to will nothing but what God willeth, and to love his will, and study to please him, and rest therein, is the rectitude and only rest of souls; and he that cannot rest contentedly in the will of God must be for ever restless.

And when such a holy will and contentment appeareth in you, mankind will reverence it, and see that your natures are divine; and as they dare not reproach the will of God, so they will fear to speak evil of yours: when they see that you choose but what God first chooseth for you, and your wills do but follow the will of God, men will be afraid of provoking God against them as blasphemers, if they should scorn, deride, or vilify you. And could we convince all men that our course is but the same which God commandeth, it would do much to stop their reproach and persecution. And if they see that we can joyfully suffer reproach, or poverty, or pains, or death, and joyfully pass away to God when he shall call us, and live and die in a contented complacency in the will of God, they will see that you have a beginning of heaven on earth, which no tyrant, no loss, or cross, or suffering, can deprive you of, while you can joyfully say, "The will of the Lord be done," Acts xxi. 14.

Object. But if it be God's will for sin to punish me, or forsake me, should I contentedly rest in that revenging will?

Answ. 1. That sin of ours which maketh us uncapable objects of the complacential will of God, is evil, and to be hated. But that will of God which is terminated on such an object, according to the nature of it, by just hatred, is good, and should be loved. And punishment is hurtful to us; but God's will and justice is good and amiable. 2. If you will close with God's will you need not fear his will. If your will be unfeignedly to obey his commanding will, and to be and do what he would have you, his will is not to condemn or punish you. But if God's will prescribe you a holy life, and your will rebel, and be against it, no wonder if God's will be to punish you when your wills would not be punished: John i. 13; Heb. x. 10; John vii. 17; Luke xii. 47.

XX. It glorifieth God and religion in the world when christians are faithful in all their relations, and diligently endeavour the sanctifying and happiness of all societies which they are members of.

I. Holy families, well ordered, do much glorify God, and keep up religion in the world.

1. When husbands live with their wives in wisdom, holiness, and love, and wives are pious, obedient, meek, and peaceable, (Eph. v. 22, 25; Col. iii. 18, 19,) yea, unto such husbands as "obey not the word, that without the word they may be won by the conversation of the wives," 1 Pet. iii. 1, 2.

2. When parents make it their great and constant care and labour, with all holy skill, and love, and diligence, to educate their children in the fear of God, and the love of goodness, and the practice of a

holy life, and to save them from sin, and the temptations of the world, the flesh, and the devil; and have more tender care of their souls than of their bodies, that so the church may have a succession of saints; and when children love, honour, and obey their parents, and comfort them by their forwardness to all that is good, and their avoiding the ways and company of the ungodly: Eph. vi. 1; Col. iii. 20: Psal. i. 1, 2.

3. When masters rule their servants as the servants of God; and servants willingly obey their masters, and serve them with cheerful diligence and trust, and are as careful and faithful about all their goods and business as if it were their own; Eph. vi. 5, 9; Col. iii. 21; iv. 1; 1 Pet. ii. 18.

When the houses of christians are societies of saints, and churches of God, and live in love and concord together, and all are laborious and faithful in their callings, abhorring idleness, gluttony, drunkenness, pride, contention, and evil speaking, and dealing justly with all their neighbours, and denying their own right for love and peace: this is the way to glorify religion in the world.

II. Well-ordered churches are the second sort of societies which must glorify God and propagate religion in the world.

When the pastors are learned in the holy Scriptures, and skilful in all their sacred work, and far excel all the people in the light of faith and knowledge, and in love to goodness, and to men's souls, and in lively, zealous diligence for God, and for men's salvation, thinking no labour, cost, or suffering too dear a price for the people's good; when no sufferings or reproaches move them, nor account they their lives dear to them, that they may but finish their course and ministry with joy. When their public preaching hath convincing light and clearness, and powerful, affectionate application; and their private oversight is performed with impartiality, humility, and unwearied diligence, and they are able to resolve the people's cases of conscience solidly, and to exhort them earnestly, with powerful reason and melting love: this honoureth religion, and winneth souls.

When they envy not one another, nor strive who shall be greatest or uppermost; but contrariwise, who shall be most serviceable to his brethren, and to the people's souls. When they oversee and feed the flock of God which is among them, not by constraint, but willingly; not for filthy lucre, but of a ready mind; neither as being lords over God's heritage, but being ensamples to the flock; and seeking not theirs but them; are willing to spend and be spent for their sakes; yea, though the more they love them the less they are beloved; not minding high things, but condescending to men of low estate: this is the way for ministers to glorify God: 1 Pet. v. 1—4; Acts xx.; 2 Tim. i. 14, 15; 1 Tim. iv. 10; Heb. iv. 11—13; Acts xx. 24; 1 Thess. ii. 8; 2 Tim. iv. 1—3; Luke xxii. 24—26; 2 Cor. xii. 14, 15; Rom. xii. 16.

When ministers are above all worldly interest, and so teach and live that the people may see that they seek not the honour which is of men, but only that which is of God; and lay not up a treasure on earth, but in heaven; and trade all for another world, and are further from pride than the lowest of their flock; when they have not only the clothing of sheep, but their harmless, profitable nature, and not the ravenousness or bloody jaws of destroying wolves. When they use not carnal weapons in their warfare, but by an eminency of light, and love, and life, endeavour to work the same in others; when they are of more public spirit than the people, and more self-denying, and above all private interests, and envyings, and revenge, and are more patient in suffering than the people, through the power of stronger faith, and hope, and love. When they are wholly addicted to holiness and peace, and are zealous for the love and unity of believers, and become all things to all men to win some; in meekness instructing opposers, abhorring contention, doing nothing in strife or vainglory, but preferring others before themselves; not preaching Christ in pride or envy, nor seeking their own praise, but thirsting after men's conversion, edification, and salvation. Thus must Christ be honoured by his ministers in the world.

When they speak the same things, being of one mind and judgment, uniting in the common faith, and contending for that against infidels and heretics, and, so far as they have attained, walk by the same rule, and mind the same things; and where they are differently minded or opinioned, wait in meekness and love till God reveal to them the reconciling truth. When they study more to narrow controversies, than to widen them, and are skilful in detecting those ambiguous words, and verbal and notional differences, which to the unskilful seem material. When they are as chirurgeons, and not as soldiers, as skilful to heal differences, as the proud and ignorant are ready to make them, and can plainly show the dark contenders wherein they agree, and do not know it. When they live in that sweet and amicable concord, which may tell the world that they love one another, and are of one faith and heart, being one in Christ. This is the way for ministers to glorify God in the world. And with thankfulness to God I acknowledge that such, for many years, I had my conversation with, of whom the world that now despiseth them is not worthy: Phil. ii. 21; Matt. vi. 19—21; John v. 44; 2 Cor. x. 4; 2 Tim. ii. 25, 26; 1 Cor. ix. 19, 20, 22; x. 33; Phil. ii. 1—3; 1 Tim. vi. 3, 4; Jam. iii. 14—16; 2 Tim. ii. 14, 24; Phil. iii. 15—17; John xvii. 24; Eph. iv. 3—5; 1 Cor. i. 10; James iii. 17, 18.

And the maintaining of sound doctrine, spiritual, reasonable, and reverent worship, without ludicrous and unreverent trifling, or rudeness, or ignorance, or superstition, or needless singularity, much honoureth God (as is aforesaid). And so doth the exercise of holy discipline in the churches. Such discipline whereby the precious may be separated from the vile, and the holy from the profane, by authority and order; and not by popular usurpation, disorder, or unjust presumptions. Where the cause is fairly tried and judged before men are cast out, or denied the privileges of the church. Where charity appears in embracing the weakest, and turning away none that turn not away from Christ, and condemning none without just proof: and justice and holiness appeareth in purging out the dangerous leaven, and in trying and rejecting the obstinately impenitent heretic and gross sinner after the first and second admonition, and disowning them that will not hear the church: Matt. xviii. 15, 16; Tit. iii. 10; 1 Cor. v. 11. When the neglect of discipline doth leave the church as polluted a society as the infidel world, and christians that are owned in the public communion are as vicious, sensual, and ungodly, as heathens and Mahometans, it is one of the greatest injuries to Christ and our religion in the world. For it is by the purifying of a peculiar people, zealous of good works, that Christ is known to be really the Saviour of the world; and by making his followers better than others, that he, and his doctrine and religion, are known to be the best. Travellers tell me that nothing so much hindereth the conversion of the Mahometans as their daily experience that the lives of the Greek christians, and others that live among them, are too ordinarily worse than theirs. More drunkenness, and more falsehood, lying, deceit, it is said are among those christians than among the Turks. If that be true, those are no true christians; but woe be to them by whom such offence cometh! I have oft heard those soldiers justly censured as profane who turn churches into stables (without great necessity). But how much more hurtfully profane are they who, for carnal ends, confound the world and the church, and keep the multitude of the most sensual, ungodly persons in their communion, without ever calling them personally to repentance! and use the church keys but to revenge themselves on those that differ from them in some opinions, or that cross their interest and wills, or that seem too smart and zealous in the dislike of their carnality, sloth, and church pollutions! When the churches are as full of scandalous sinners as the assemblies of infidels and heathens, the world will hardly ever believe that infidelity and heathenism is not as good as the christian faith. It is more by persons than by precepts that the world will judge of Christ and christianity. And what men on earth do more scandalize the world, more expose christianity to reproach, more harden infidels, more injure Christ, and serve the devil, than they that fill the church with impious, carnal pastors, (as in the church of Rome,) and then with impious, carnal people, maintained constantly in her communion, without any open disowning by a distinguishing, reforming discipline? When such pastors are no better than the soberer sort of heathens, save only in their opinion and formal words, and when their ordinary communicants are no better, it is no thanks to them if all turn not infidels that know them, and if christianity be contemned, and decay out of the world; and it is long of such that disorderly separations attempt that discipline, and distinguishing of the godly and the notoriously wicked, which such ungodly pastors will not attempt. See Lev. xix. 17; Matt. xviii. 15, 16; 1 Cor. v.; Tit. iii. 10: Jer. xv. 19; Psal. xv.; 2 Thess. iii.; Rom. xvi. 17; 2 Tim. iii. 4, 5.

III. But oh how great an honour is it to God and to religion, when kings, princes, and states, do zealously devote their power to God, from whom they do receive it, and labour to make their kingdoms holy! When truth, sobriety, and piety have the countenance of human powers, and rulers wholly set themselves to further the faithful preaching and practising of the holy faith, and to unite and strengthen the ministers and churches, and to suppress iniquity, and to be a terror to evil-doers, it taketh Satan's great advantage out of his hand, and worketh on carnal men by such means as they can feel and understand. Not that God needs the help of man, but that he hath settled officers and a natural order, by which he usually worketh in the world: and as it cannot be expected that an unholy parent and master should have a holy family, or an unholy pastor a holy church, unless by extraordinary mercy; no more can we expect that ungodly magistrates should have a godly kingdom or commonwealth, of which the sacred history of the Jewish and Israelitish kings doth give you a full confirmation. But this I must now say no more of. And thus I have told you, in twenty particulars, what are those good works in which the light of christians must shine before men to the glory of God.

Object. Doth not Matt. v. 10—12, contradict all this? "Blessed are ye when men revile you and persecute you, and say all manner of evil against you falsely for my sake."

Answ. No. You must here distinguish, first, of men; secondly, of righteousness and good works.

I. The men that we have to do with are, first, ordinary, natural men, corrupted by original sin, but yet not hardened to serpentine malignity, as some are: secondly, or they are men that, by sinning against nature and common light, are forsaken and given up to malignant minds.

II. The good works which natural light and human interest can discern and commend, do differ from those which are merely evangelical, of supernatural revelation.

1. Malignant persons hardened in enmity, will scorn and persecute holiness itself, and even that good which reason justifies, and therefore are called unreasonable wicked men, 2 Thess. iii. 2. Good works with these men make us odious, unless they are such as gratify their lusts.

2. But there are natural men not yet so hardened and forsaken, who are usually them that the gospel doth convert: and these have not yet so blinded nature, nor lost all sense of good and evil, but that they honour him that doth good in all the twenty particulars which I have named, and think ill of those that do the contrary, though yet they relish not the christian righteousness, and things of supernatural revelation, for want of faith.

Let us briefly apply it.

Use 1. This informs us what an honourable state christianity and true godliness is. When God hath made us to be the lights of the world, to shine before men to the glory of his holiness, as the sun and stars do to the glory of his power, no wonder if in glory we shall shine as stars in the firmament of our Father, if we do so here, Dan. xii. 3; Matt. xiii. 43; Phil. ii. 15. This must not make us proud, but thankful; for our pride is our shame, and our humility is our glory.

Use 2. And what wonder if all the powers of darkness do bend their endeavours to obscure this sacred light? The prince of darkness is the enemy of the Father of lights; and this is the great war between Christ and Satan in the world. Christ is the light of the world, and setteth up ministerial lights for the world and for his house. His work is to send them forth, to teach them and defend them, to send his Spirit to work in and by them, to bring men to the everlasting light. And Satan's work is to stir up all that he can against them, high and low, learned and unlearned, and to put Christ's lights, both ministers and people, under a bushel; and to make the world believe that they are their enemies, and come to hurt them, that they may be hated as the scorn and offscouring of the world; and to keep up ignorance in ministers themselves, that the church's eyes being dark, the darkness may be great.

But let us pray that God would "forgive our enemies, persecutors, and slanderers, and turn their hearts;" and that he would "open our lips, that our mouths may show forth his praise:" and though his ministers and people have their faulty weaknesses, that he would "be merciful to our infirmities, and grant that those things which the craft and subtlety of the devil or man worketh against us may be brought to nought, and by the providence of his goodness may be dispersed; that we, his servants, being hindered by no persecution, may give thanks to him in his holy church, and serve him in holiness and pureness of life, to his glory," through Jesus Christ.

Use 3. You may see hence how much those men are mistaken, who talk of the good works or lives of christians, as that which must have no honour, lest it dishonour God; as if all the honour were taken from Christ which is given to good works, and the patient's health were the dishonour of the physician; when we are redeemed and purified to be zealous of good works, and created for them in Christ Jesus, as Titus ii. 14; Eph. ii. 10; yea, and shall be judged according to our works.

Use 4. This informeth you that the good works or lives of christians, is a great means ordained by Christ for the convincing of sinners, and the glorifying of God in the world. Preaching doth much, but it is not appointed to do all. The lives of preachers must also be a convincing light; and all true christians, men and women, are called to preach to the world by their good works: and a holy, righteous, and sober life, is the great ordinance of God, appointed for the saving of yourselves and others. Oh that the Lord would bring this close to all our hearts! Christians, if you abhor dumb teachers, because they starve and betray souls, take heed lest you condemn yourselves: you owe men the convincing helps of a holy, fruitful life, as well as the preacher owes them his ministry. Preach by well doing, shine out in good works, or else you are no lights of Christ, but betrayers of men's souls: you rob all about you of a great ordinance of God, a great means appointed by him for men's salvation. The world will judge of the Scriptures by your lives, and of religion by your lives, and of Christ himself by your lives. If your lives are such as tend to persuade men that christians are but like other men, yea, that they are but self-conceited sinners, as carnal, sensual, uncharitable, proud, self-seeking, worldly, envious, as others, and so that christianity is but such, this is a horrid blaspheming of Christ, how highly soever your tongues may speak of him, and how low soever your knees may bow to him. Oh that you knew how much of God's great work of salvation in the world is to be done by christians' lives. Your lives must teach men to believe that there is a heaven to be won, and a hell to be escaped: your lives must help men to believe that Christ and his word are true: your lives must tell men what holiness is, and convince them of the need of regeneration; and that the Spirit of sanctification is no fancy, but the witness of Jesus Christ in the world: your lives must tell men, by repentance and obedience, that sin is the greatest evil; and must show them the difference between the righteous and the wicked: yea, the holiness of God must be glorified by your lives. Father, Son, and Holy Ghost, the Scripture, the church, and heaven itself, must be known much by our lives. And may not I say, then, with the apostle, (2 Pet. iii. 11,) "What manner of persons, then, ought we to be, in all holy conversation and godliness, when the grace of God, which bringeth salvation, hath appeared to all men, teaching us to deny ungodliness and worldly lusts, and to live soberly, righteously, and godly, in this present world?" Tit. ii. 11, 12.

Use 5. But alas! what suitable and plentiful matter doth this offer us for our humiliation and lamentation on such a day as this! A flood of tears is not too much to lament the scandals of the christian world. With what wounded hearts should we think of the state of the churches in Armenia, Syria, Egypt, Abassia, and all the oppressed Greeks, and all the poor deceived and oppressed papists, and all the ignorant, carnal protestants! Oh! how unlike are your lives to your christian faith, and to the pattern left them by their Lord! Doth a worldly, proud, and fleshly, and contentious clergy glorify God? Doth an ignorant ministry glorify him, who understand not the message which they should deliver? Will the world turn christians by seeing christians seek the blood and ruin of each other? and hearing even preachers reproach each other? or seeing them silence or persecute each other? or by seeing the people run into many sects, and separate from one another, as unworthy of christian communion? Will proud, ignorant, censorious, fleshly, worldly professors of religion ever draw the world to love religion? Or will peevish, self-willed, impatient, discontented souls, that are still wrangling, crying, and repining, make men believe that their religion rejoiceth, blesseth, and sanctifieth the soul, and maketh men far happier than all others in the world? Alas! what wonder that so small a part of the world are christians, and so few converted to the love of holiness, when the great means is denied them by you which God hath appointed for their conversion, and the world hath not one helper for a hundred or thousand that it should have? You cry out of those that put out the church lights, under pretence of snuffing them, while yourselves are darkness, or as a stinking snuff.

O brethren, and christians all, I beseech you let us now, and often, closely ask ourselves, what do we more than an Antonine, a Seneca, or a Cicero, or a Socrates did, beyond opinions, words, and formalities? What do you which is like to convert the world, to convince an infidel, or glorify God? Nay, do not some among us think that it is the height, or part, of their religion, to live so contrary to the world, as to be singular from others, even in lawful or indifferent things, and to do little or nothing which the world thinks well of? As if crossing and displeasing men needlessly were their winning conversation. O, when once we go as far beyond them in love, humility, meekness, patience, fruitfulness, mortification, self-denial, and heavenliness, as we do in opinions, profession, and self-esteem, then we shall win souls, and glorify God, and he will also glorify us.

Use 6. And here we see the wonderful mercy of God to the world, who hath appointed them so much means for their conviction and salvation. So many christians as there be in the world, so many practical preachers and helps to men's conversion are there appointed by God; and let the blame and shame lie on us, where it is due, and not on God, if yet the world remain in darkness. It is God's will that every christian in the world should be as a star, to shine to sinners in their darkness; and oh then how gloriously would the world be bespangled and enlightened! If you say, Why, then, doth not God make christians better? That is a question which cannot be well answered, without a larger opening of the methods of grace than we can now have leisure for, and therefore must be done in its proper season.

Use 7. Those that honour God he will honour, and therefore let us also give them that honour which is their due. The barren professors, who honour themselves by overvaluing their poor knowledge, gifts, and grace, and affecting too great a distance from their brethren, and censuring others as unworthy of their communion without reproof, are not the men that honour God, and can lay claim to no great honour from men. But God hath among us a prudent, holy, humble, laborious, patient ministry, that glorify him by their works and patience, and he hath among us a meek and humble, a blameless, and a loving and fruitful sort of christians, who imitate the purity, charity, and simplicity, yea, and concord of the primitive church. These tell the world, to their sight and experience, that religion is better than ignorance and carnality. These tell the world, that Christ and his holy word are true, while he doth that in renewing and sanctifying souls, which none else in the world can do. These show the world, that faith, and holiness, and self-denial, and the hopes of immortality, are no deceits. These glorify God, and are the great benefactors of the world. I must solemnly profess, that did I not know such a people in the world, who, notwithstanding their infirmities, do manifest a holy and heavenly disposition in their lives, I should want myself so great a help to my faith in Christ, and the promise of life eternal, that I fear, without it, my faith would fail. And had I never known a holier ministry and people than those that live but a common life, and excel heathens in nothing but their belief or opinions, and church orders and formalities, I should find my faith assaulted with so great temptations as I doubt I should not well withstand. No talk will persuade men that he is the best physician that healeth no more nor worse diseases than others do. Nor would Christ be taken for the Saviour of the world, if he did not save men. And he saveth them not if he make them not holier and better than other men.

Oh, then, how much do we owe to Christ for sending his Spirit into his saints, and for exemplifying his holy word on holy souls, and for giving us as many visible proofs of his holiness, power, and truth, as there are holy christians in the world! We must not flatter them, nor excuse their faults, nor puff them up. But because the righteous is more excellent than his neighbour, we must accordingly love and honour them, and Christ in them. For Christ telleth us, that he is glorified in them here, John xvii. 10; and that what is done to them, his brethren, even the least, is taken as done to him, Matt. xxv.; and he will be glorified and admired in them when he cometh in his glory at the last, 2 Thess. i. 8—10; and he will glorify their very works before all the world, with a "Well done, good and faithful servant, enter thou into the joy of thy Lord."

THE CURE

OF

MELANCHOLY AND OVERMUCH SORROW,

BY FAITH.

Question.—What are the best preservatives against melancholy and overmuch sorrow?

---

1 CORINTHIANS II. 7.

LEST PERHAPS SUCH A ONE SHOULD BE SWALLOWED UP WITH OVERMUCH SORROW.

THE brevity of a sermon not allowing me time for any unnecessary work, I shall not stay to open the context, nor to inquire whether the person here spoken of be the same that is condemned for incest in 1 Cor. v. or some other; nor whether Chrysostom had good tradition for it, that it was a doctor of the church, or made such after his sin? Nor whether the late expositor[a] be in the right, who thence gathers that he was one of the bishops of Achaia; and that it was a synod of bishops that were to excommunicate him; who yet held that every congregation then had a bishop, and that he was to be excommunicated in the congregation; and that the people should not have followed or favoured such a teacher; it would have been no schism, or sinful separation, to have forsaken him? All that I now intend is, to open this last clause of the verse, which gives the reason why the censured sinner, being penitent, should be forgiven and comforted; viz. Lest he should be swallowed up with overmuch sorrow; as it includeth these three doctrines, which I shall handle all together, viz.

1. That sorrow, even for sin, may be overmuch.
2. That overmuch sorrow swalloweth one up.
3. Therefore it must be resisted and assuaged by necessary comfort, both by others, and by ourselves.

In handling these, I shall observe this order: 1. I shall show you when sorrow is overmuch. 2. How overmuch sorrow doth swallow a man up. 3. What are the causes of it. 4. What is the cure.

I. It is too notorious that overmuch sorrow for sin is not the ordinary case of the world. A stupid, blockish disposition is the common cause of men's perdition. The plague of a hard heart, and seared conscience, keeps most from all due sense of sin, or danger, or misery, and of all the great and everlasting concerns of their guilty souls. A dead sleep in sin doth deprive most of the use of sense and understanding; they do some of the outward acts of religion as in a dream; they are vowed to God in baptism by others, and they profess to stand to it themselves; they go to church, and say over the words of

[a] Dr. Hammond.

the creed, and Lord's prayer, and commandments, they receive the Lord's supper, and all as in a dream! They take on them to believe that sin is the most hateful thing to God, and hurtful to man, and yet they live in it with delight and obstinacy; they dream that they repent of it, when no persuasion will draw them to forsake it, and while they hate them that would cure them, and will not be as bad and mad as they who feel in them any effectual sorrow for what is past, or effectual sense of their present badness, or effectual resolution for a new and holy life. They dream that there is a judgment, a heaven, and a hell, but would they not be more affected with things of such unspeakable consequence if they were awake? Would they be wholly taken up with the matters of the flesh and world, and scarce have a serious thought or word of eternity, if they were awake? Oh how sleepily and senselessly do they think, and talk, and hear of the great work of man's redemption by Christ, and of the need of justifying and sanctifying grace, and of the joys and miseries of the next life; and yet they say that they believe them! When we preach or talk to them of the greatest things, with the greatest evidence, and plainness, and earnestness that we can, we speak as to the dead, or to men asleep; they have ears, and hear not, nothing goeth to their hearts. One would think that a man that reads in Scripture, and believes the everlasting glory offered, and the dreadful punishment threatened, and the necessity of holiness to salvation, and of a Saviour to deliver us from sin and hell, and how sure and near such a passage into the unseen world is to us all, should have much ado to moderate and bear the sense of such overwhelming things. But most men so little regard or feel them, that they have neither time nor heart to think of them as their concern, but hear of them as of some foreign land, where they have no interest, and which they never think to see. Yea, one would think by their senseless neglect of preparation, and their worldly minds and lives, that they were asleep, or in jest, when they confess that they must die; and that when they lay their friends in the grave, and see the sculls and bones cast up, they were but all this while in a dream, or did not believe that their turn is near. Could we tell how to awaken sinners, they would come to themselves, and have other thoughts of these great things, and show it quickly by another kind of life. Awakened reason could never be so befooled and besotted as we see the wicked world to be. But God hath an awakening day for all, and he will make the most senseless soul to feel, by grace or punishment.

And because a hardened heart is so great a part of the malady and misery of the unregenerate, and a soft and tender heart is much of the new nature promised by Christ, many awakened souls under the work of conversion think they can never have sorrow enough, and that their danger lies in hard-heartedness, and they never fear overmuch sorrow till it hath swallowed them up; yea, though there be too much of other causes in it, yet if any of it be for sin, they then cherish it as a necessary duty, or at least perceive not the danger of excess: and some think those to be the best christians who are most in doubts, and fears, and sorrows, and speak almost nothing but uncomfortable complaints; but this is a great mistake.

1. Sorrow is overmuch when it is fed by a mistaken cause. All is too much where none is due, and great sorrow is too much when the cause requireth but less.

If a man thinketh that somewhat is a duty, which is no duty, and then sorrow for omitting it, such sorrow is all too much, because it is undue, and caused by error. Many I have known who have been greatly troubled, because they could not bring themselves to that length or order of meditation, for which they had neither ability nor time; and many, because they could not reprove sin in others, when prudent instruction and intimation was more suitable than reproof. And many are troubled, because in their shops and callings they think of any thing but God, as if our outward business must have no thoughts.

Superstition always breeds such sorrows, when men make themselves religious duties which God never made them, and then come short in the performance of them. Many dark souls are assaulted by the erroneous, and told that they are in a wrong way; and they must take up some error as a necessary truth, and so are cast into perplexing difficulties, and perhaps repent of the truth which they before owned. Many fearful christians are troubled about every meal that they eat, about their clothes, their thoughts, and words, thinking or fearing that all is sinful which is lawful, and that unavoidable infirmities are heinous sins. All such as these are troubles and sorrows without cause, and therefore overmuch.

2. Sorrow is overmuch when it hurteth and overwhelmeth nature itself, and destroyeth bodily health or understanding. Grace is the due qualification of nature, and duty is the right employment of it, but neither of them must destroy it. As civil, and ecclesiastic, and domestic government are for edification and not for destruction, so also is personal self-government. God will have mercy and not sacrifice; and he that would not have us kill or hurt our neighbour on pretence of religion, would not have us destroy or hurt ourselves, being bound to love our neighbour but as ourselves. As fasting is a duty no further than it tendeth to some good, as to express or exercise true humiliation, or to mortify some fleshly lust, &c. so is it with sorrow for sin: it is too much when it doth more hurt than good. But of this next.

II. When sorrow swalloweth up the sinner, it is overmuch, and to be restrained. As,

1. The passions of grief and trouble of mind do oft overthrow the sober and sound use of reason, so that a man's judgment is corrupted and perverted by it, and is not in that case to be trusted. As a man in raging anger, so one in fear or great trouble of mind, thinks not of things as they are, but as his passion represents them; about God and religion, and about his own soul, and his actions, or about his friends or enemies, his judgment is perverted, and usually false, and, like an inflamed eye, thinks all things of the colour which is like itself. When it perverteth reason it is overmuch.

2. Overmuch sorrow disableth a man to govern his thoughts; and ungoverned thoughts must needs be both sinful and very troublesome: grief carrieth them away as in a torrent. You may almost as easily keep the leaves of trees in quietness and order in a blustering wind, as the thoughts of one in troubling passions. If reason would stop them from perplexing subjects, or turn them to better and sweeter things, it cannot do it; it hath no power against the stream of troubling passions.

3. Overmuch sorrow would swallow up faith itself, and greatly hindereth its exercise. They are matters of unspeakable joy which the gospel calleth us to believe: and it is wonderful hard for a grieved, troubled soul to believe any thing that is matter of joy, much less of so great joy as pardon and salvation are. Though it dare not flatly give God the lie, it hardly believes his free and full promises, and the

expressions of his readiness to receive all penitent, returning sinners. Passionate grief serveth to feel somewhat contrary to the grace and promises of the gospel, and that feeling hinders faith.

4. Overmuch sorrow yet more hindereth hope; when men think that they do believe God's word, and that his promises are all true to others, yet cannot they hope for the promised blessings to themselves. Hope is that grace by which a soul that believeth the gospel to be true, doth comfortably expect that the benefits promised shall be its own; it is an applying act. The first act of faith saith the gospel is true, which promiseth grace and glory through Christ. The next act of faith saith, I will trust my soul and all upon it, and take Christ for my Saviour and help: and then hope saith, I hope for this salvation by him: but melancholy, overwhelming sorrow and trouble is as great an adversary to this hope as water is to fire, or snow to heat. Despair is its very pulse and breath. Fain such would have hope, but they cannot. All their thoughts are suspicious and misgiving, and they can see nothing but danger and misery, and a helpless state. And when hope, which is the anchor of the soul, is gone, what wonder if they be continually tossed with storms.

5. Overmuch sorrow swalloweth up all comfortable sense of the infinite goodness and love of God, and thereby hindereth the soul from loving him; and in this it is an adversary to the very life of holiness. It is exceeding hard for such a troubled soul to apprehend the goodness of God at all, but much harder to judge that he is good and amiable to him: but as a man that in the deserts of Libya is scorched with the violent heats of the sun, and is ready to die with drought and faintness, may confess that the sun is the life of the earth and a blessing to mankind, but it is misery and death to him; even so, these souls, overwhelmed with grief, may say that God is good to others, but he seems an enemy to them, and to seek their destruction. They think he hateth them, and hath forsaken them; and how can they love such a God who they think doth hate them, and resolve to damn them, and hath decreed them to it from eternity, and brought them into the world for no other end? They that can hardly love an enemy that doth but defame them, or oppress and wrong them, will more hardly love a God that they believe will damn them, and hath remedilessly appointed them thereto.

6. And then it must needs follow that this distemper is a false and injurious judge of all the word and works of God, and of all his mercies and corrections. Whatever such a one reads or hears, he thinks it all makes against him: every sad word and threatening in Scripture he thinks meaneth him, as if it named him. But the promises and comforts he hath no part in, as if he had been by name excepted. All God's mercies are extenuated, and taken for no mercies, as if God intended them all but to make his sin the greater, and to increase his heavy reckoning and further his damnation. He thinks God doth but sugar over poison to him, and give him all in hatred, and not in any love, with a design to sink him the deeper in hell: and if God correct him, he supposeth that it is but the beginning of his misery, and God doth torment him before the time.

7. And by this you see that it is an enemy to thankfulness. It rather reproacheth God for his mercies, as if they were injuries, than giveth him any hearty thanks.

8. And by this you may see that this distemper is quite contrary to the joy in the Holy Ghost, yea, and the peace in which God's kingdom much consisteth: nothing seemeth joyful unto such distressed souls. Delighting in God, and in his word and ways, is the flower and life of true religion. But these that I speak of can delight in nothing; neither in God, nor in his word, nor any duty. They do it as a sick man eateth his meat, for mere necessity, and with some loathing and averseness.

9. And all this showeth us that this disease is much contrary to the very tenor of the gospel. Christ came as a deliverer of the captives, a Saviour to reconcile us to God, and bring us glad tidings of pardon and everlasting joy: where the gospel was received it was great rejoicing, and so proclaimed by angels and by men. But all that Christ hath done, and purchased, and offered, and promised, seems nothing but matter of doubt and sadness to this disease.

10. Yea, it is a distemper which greatly advantageth Satan to cast in blasphemous thoughts of God, as if he were bad, and a hater and destroyer even of such as fain would please him. The design of the devil is to describe God to us as like himself; who is a malicious enemy, and delighteth to do hurt: and if all men hate the devil for his hurtfulness, would he not draw men to hate and blaspheme God, if he could make men believe that he is more hurtful? The worshipping God, as represented by an image, is odious to him, because it seems to make him like such a creature as that image representeth. How much more blasphemous is it to feign him to be like the malicious devils! Diminutive, low thoughts of his goodness, as well as of his greatness, is a sin which greatly injureth God: as if you should think that he is no better or trustier than a father or a friend, much more to think him such as distempered souls imagine him. You would wrong his ministers if you should describe them as Christ doth the false prophets, as hurtful thorns, and thistles, and wolves. And is it not worse to think far worse than this of God?

11. This overmuch sorrow doth unfit men for all profitable meditation; it confounds their thoughts, and turneth them to hurtful distractions and temptations; and the more they muse, the more they are overwhelmed.

And it turneth prayer into mere complaint, instead of child-like believing supplications.

It quite undisposeth the soul to God's masses, and especially to a comfortable sacramental communion, and fetcheth greater terror from it, lest unworthy receiving will but hasten and increase their damnation.

And it rendereth preaching and counsel too oft unprofitable: say what you will that is never so convincing, either it doth not change them, or is presently lost.

12. And it is a distemper which maketh all sufferings more heavy, as falling upon a poor diseased soul, and having no comfort to set against it: and it maketh death exceeding terrible, because they think it will be the gate of hell; so that life seemeth burdensome to them, and death terrible; they are weary of living, and afraid of dying. Thus overmuch sorrow swalloweth up.

III. *Quest.* What are the causes and cure of it?

Answ. With very many there is a great part of the cause in distemper, weakness, and diseasedness of the body, and by it the soul is greatly disabled to any comfortable sense. But the more it ariseth from such natural necessity, it is the less sinful, and less dangerous to the soul, but never the less troublesome, but the more.

Three diseases cause overmuch sorrow.

1. Those that consist in such violent pain as natural

strength is unable to bear; but this being usually not very long, is not now to be chiefly spoken of.

2. A natural passionateness, and weakness of that reason that should quiet passion. It is too frequent a case with aged persons that are much debilitated, to be very apt to offence and passion; and children cannot choose but cry when they are hurt; but it is most troublesome and hurtful to many women, (and some men,) who are so easily troubled, and hardly quieted, that they have very little power on themselves; even many who fear God, and who have very sound understandings, and quick wits, have almost no more power against troubling passions, anger, and grief, but especially fear, than they have of any other persons.

Their very natural temper is a strong disease of troubling, sorrow, fear, and displeasedness. They that are not melancholy, are yet of so childish, and sick, and impatient a temper, that one thing or other is still either discontenting, grieving, or affrighting them. They are like an aspen leaf, still shaking with the least motion of the air. The wisest and most patient man cannot please and justify such a one; a word, yea, or a look, offendeth them; every sad story, or news, or noise, affrighteth them; and as children must have all that they cry for before they will be quiet, so is it with too many such. The case is very sad to those about them, but much more to themselves. To dwell with the sick in the house of mourning is less uncomfortable. But yet while reason is not overthrown, the case is not remediless, nor wholly excusable.

3. But when the brain and imagination are crazed, and reason partly overthrown by the disease called melancholy, this maketh the cure yet more difficult; for commonly it is the foresaid persons, whose natural temper is timorous and passionate, and apt to discontent and grief, who fall into crazedness and melancholy; and the conjunction of both the natural temper and the disease does increase the misery.

The signs of such diseasing melancholy I have often elsewhere described. As,

1. The trouble and disquiet of the mind doth then become a settled habit; they can see nothing but matter of fear and trouble. All that they hear or do doth feed it; danger is still before their eyes; all that they read and hear makes against them; they can delight in nothing; fearful dreams trouble them when they sleep, and distracted thoughts do keep them long waking; it offends them to see another laugh, or be merry; they think that every beggar's case is happier than theirs; they will hardly believe that any one else is in their case, when some two or three in a week, or a day, come to me in the same case, so like, that you would think it were the same person's case which they all express; they have no pleasure in relations, friends, estate, or any thing; they think that God hath forsaken them, and that the day of grace is past, and there is no more hope; they say they cannot pray, but howl, and groan, and God will not hear them; they will not believe that they have any sincerity and grace; they say they cannot repent, they cannot believe, but that their hearts are utterly hardened; usually they are afraid lest they have committed the unpardonable sin against the Holy Ghost: in a word, fears, and troubles, and almost despair, are the constant temper of their minds.

2. If you convince them that they have some evidences of sincerity, and that their fears are causeless, and injurious to themselves, and unto God, and they have nothing to say against it, yet either it takes off none of their trouble, or else it returneth the next day; for the cause remaineth in their bodily disease; quiet them a hundred times, and their fears a hundred times return.

3. Their misery is, that what they think they cannot choose but think. You may almost as well persuade a man not to shake in an ague, or not to feel when he is pained, as persuade them to cast away their self-troubling thoughts, or not to think all the enormous, confounding thoughts as they do, they cannot get them out of their heads night or day. Tell them that they must forbear long musings, which disturb them, and they cannot. Tell them that they must cast out false imaginations out of their minds, when Satan casts them in, and must turn their thoughts to something else, and they cannot do it. Their thoughts. and troubles, and fears, are gone out of their power, and the more, by how much the more melancholy and crazed they are.

4. And when they are grown to this, usually they seem to feel something besides themselves, as it were, speak in them, and saying this and that to them, and bidding them to do this or that; and they will tell you now it saith this or that, and tell you when and what it hath said to them, and they will hardly believe how much of it is the disease of their own imagination.

5. In this case they are exceeding prone to think they have revelations; and whatever comes into their minds they think some revelation brought it thither. They use to say, this text of Scripture at such a time was set upon my mind, and that text at another time was set on my mind; when oft the sense that they took them in was false, or a false application of it made to themselves, and perhaps several texts applied to contrary conclusions, as if one gave them hope, and another contradicted it.

And some of them hereupon are very prone to prophecies, and verily believe that God hath foretold them this or that, till they see that it cometh not to pass, and then they are ashamed.

And many of them turn heretics, and take up errors in religion, believing verily that God believed them, and set such things upon their minds: and some of them that were long troubled, get quietness and joy by such changes of their opinions, thinking that now they are in God's way, which they were out of all this while, and therefore it was that they had no comfort. Of these I have known divers persons comforted that have fallen into the clean contrary opinions; some have turned papists and superstitious, and some have run too far from papists, and some have had comfort by turning anabaptists, some antinomians, some contrarily called Arminians, some perfectionists, some quakers; and some have turned from christianity itself to infidelity, and denied the life to come, and have lived in licentious uncleanness. But these melancholy heretics and apostates usually by this cast off their sadness, and are not the sort that I have now to deal with.

6. But the sadder, better sort, feeling this talk and stir within them, are oft apt to be confident that they are possessed by the devil, or at least bewitched, of which I will say more anon.

7. And most of them are violently haunted with blasphemous injections, at which they tremble, and yet cannot keep them out of their mind; either they are tempted and haunted to doubt of the Scripture, or christianity, or the life to come, or to think some ill of God; and oftentimes they are strangely urged, as by something in them, to speak some blasphemous word of God, or to renounce him, and they tremble at the suggestion, and yet it still followeth them, and some poor souls yield to it, and say some bad word against God, and then, as soon as it is spoken, somewhat within them saith, Now thy

damnation is sealed, thou hast sinned against the Holy Ghost, there is no hope.

8. When it is far gone, they are tempted to lay some law upon themselves never to speak more, or not to eat, and some of them have famished themselves to death.

9. And when it is far gone, they often think that they have apparitions, and this and that likeness appeareth to them, especially lights in the night about their beds. And sometimes they are confident that they hear voices, and feel something touch or hurt them.

10. They fly from company, and can do nothing but sit alone and muse.

11. They cast off all business, and will not be brought to any diligent labour in their callings.

12. And when it cometh to extremity, they are weary of their lives, and strongly followed with temptations to make away themselves, as if something within them were urging them either to drown themselves, or cut their own throats, or hang themselves, or cast themselves headlong, which, alas! too many have done.

13. And if they escape this, when it is ripe, they become quite distracted.

These are the doleful symptoms and effects of melancholy; and therefore how desirable is it to prevent them, or to be cured while it is but beginning, before they fall into so sad a state!

And here it is necessary that I answer the doubt whether such persons be possessed with the devil, or not? And how much of all this aforesaid is from him?

And I must tell the melancholy person that is sincere, that the knowledge of the devil's agency in his case, may be more to his comfort than to his despair.

And first, we must know what is meant by Satan's possession, either of the body or the soul. It is not merely his local presence and abode in a man that is called his possession, for we know little of that, how far he is more present with a bad man than a good, but it is his exercising power on a man by such a stated, effectual operation. As the Spirit of God is present with the worst, and maketh many holy motions to the souls of the impenitent, but he is a settled powerful agent in the soul of a believer, and so is said to dwell in such, and to possess them, by the habit of holiness and love; even so Satan maketh too frequent motions to the faithful, but he possesseth only the souls of the ungodly by predominant habits of unbelief and sensuality.

And so also he is permitted by God to inflict persecutions, and crosses, and ordinary diseases, on the just; but when he is God's executioner of extraordinary plagues, especially on the head, depriving men of sense and understanding, and working above the bare nature of the disease, this is called his possession.

And as most evil notions on the soul have Satan for their father, and our own hearts as the mothers, so most or many bodily diseases are by Satan, permitted by God, though there be causes of them also in the body itself. And when our own miscarriages, and humours, and the season, weather, and accidents, may be causes, yet Satan may, by these, be a superior cause.

And when his operations are such as we call a possession, yet he may work by means and bodily dispositions, and sometimes he worketh quite above the power of the disease itself, as when the unlearned speak in strange languages, and when bewitched persons vomit iron, glass, &c. And sometimes he doth only work by the disease itself, as in epilepsies, madness, &c.

From all this it is easy to gather, 1. That for Satan to possess the body is no certain sign of a graceless state, nor will this condemn the soul of any, if the soul itself be not possessed. Nay, there are few of God's children but it is like are sometimes afflicted by Satan, as the executioner of God's correcting them, and sometimes of God's trials, as in the case of Job; whatsoever some say to the contrary, it is likely that the prick in the flesh, which was Satan's messenger to buffet Paul, was some such pain as the stone, which yet was not removed, that we find, after thrice praying, but only he had a promise of sufficient grace.

2. Satan's possession of an ungodly soul is the miserable case, which is a thousand times worse than his possessing of the body; but every corruption or sin is not such a possession, for no man is perfect without sin.

3. No sin proveth Satan's damnable possession of a man but that which he loveth more than he hateth it, and which he had rather keep than leave, and wilfully keepeth.

4. And this is matter of great comfort to such melancholy, honest souls, if they have but understanding to receive it, that of all men none love their sin which they groan under so little as they; yea, it is the heavy burden of their souls. Do you love your unbelief, your fears, your distracted thoughts, your temptations to blasphemy? Had you rather keep them than be delivered from them? The proud man, the ambitious, the fornicator, the drunkard, the gamester, the time-wasting gallants that sit out hours at cards, and plays, and idle chats, the gluttonous pleasers of the appetite, all these love their sins, and would not leave them; as Esau sold his birthright for one morsel, they will venture the loss of God, of Christ, and soul, and heaven, rather than leave a swinish sin. But is this your case? Do you so love your sad condition? You are weary of it, and heavy laden, and therefore are called to come to Christ for ease, Matt. xi. 28, 29.

5. And it is the devil's way, if he can, to haunt those with troubling temptations whom he cannot overcome with alluring and damning temptations. As he raiseth storms of persecution against them without, as soon as they are escaping from his deceits, so doth he trouble them within, as far as God permitteth him.

We deny not but Satan hath a great hand in the case of such melancholy persons; for,

1. His temptations caused the sin which God corrects them for.

2. His execution usually is a cause of the distemper of the body.

3. And, as a tempter, he is the cause of the sinful and troublesome thoughts, and doubts, and fears, and passions, which the melancholy causeth. The devil cannot do what he will with us, but what we give him advantage to do. He cannot break open our doors, but he can enter if we leave them open. He can easily tempt a heavy, phlegmatic body to sloth, a weak and choleric person to anger, a strong and sanguine man to lust, and one of a strong appetite to gluttony or to drunkenness, and vain, sportful youth to idle plays, and gaming, and voluptuousness, when to others such temptations would have small strength. And so, if he can cast you into melancholy, he can easily tempt you to overmuch sorrow and fear, and to distracting doubts and thoughts, and to murmur against God, and to despair, and still think that you are undone, undone; and even to blasphemous thoughts of God; or, if it take not this way, then to fanatic conceits of revelation, and a prophesying spirit.

6. But I add, that God will not impute his mere temptations to you, but to himself, be they never so bad, as long as you receive them not by the will, but hate them; nor will he condemn you for those ill effects which are unavoidable from the power of a bodily disease, any more than he will condemn a man for raving thoughts, or words in a fever, frenzy, or utter madness. But so far as reason yet hath power, and the will can govern passions, it is your fault if you use not the power, though the difficulty make the fault the less.

II. But usually other causes go before this disease of melancholy, (except in some bodies naturally prone to it,) and therefore, before I speak of the cure of it, I will briefly touch them.

And one of the most common causes is sinful impatience, discontents, and cares, proceeding from a sinful love of some bodily interest, and from a want of sufficient submission to the will of God, and trust in him, and taking heaven for a satisfying portion.

I must necessarily use all these words to show the true nature of this complicated disease of souls. The names tell you that it is a conjunction of many sins, which in themselves are of no small malignity, and were they the predominant bent and habit of heart and life, they would be the signs of a graceless state; but while they are hated, and overcome not grace, but our heavenly portion is more esteemed, and chosen, and sought than earthly prosperity, the mercy of God, through Christ, doth pardon it, and will at last deliver us from all. But yet it beseemeth even a pardoned sinner to know the greatness of his sin, that he may not favour it, nor be unthankful for forgiveness.

I will therefore distinctly open the parts of this sin which bringeth many into dismal melancholy.

It is presupposed that God trieth his servants in this life with manifold afflictions, and Christ will have us bear the cross, and follow him in submissive patience. Some are tried with painful diseases, and some with wrong by enemies, and some with the unkindness of friends, and some with froward, provoking relatives and company, and some with slanders, and some with persecution, and many with losses, disappointments, and poverty.

1. And here impatience is the beginning of the working of the sinful malady. Our natures are all too regardful of the interest of the flesh, and too weak in bearing heavy burdens; and poverty hath those trials which full and wealthy persons, that feel them not, too little pity, especially in two cases.

1. When men have not themselves only, but wives and children in want, to quiet.

2. And when they are in debt to others, which is a heavy burden to an ingenuous mind, though thievish borrowers make too light of it. In these straits and trials, men are apt to be too sensible and impatient. When they and their families want food, and raiment, and fire, and other necessaries to the body, and know not which way to get supply; when landlords, and butchers, and bakers, and other creditors, are calling for their debts, and they have it not to pay them; it is hard to keep all this from going too near the heart, and hard to bear it with obedient, quiet submission to God, especially for women, whose nature is weak, and liable to too much passion.

2. And this impatience turneth to a settled discontent and unquietness of spirit, which affecteth the body itself, and lieth all day as a load, or continual trouble at the heart.

3. And impatience and discontent do set the thoughts on the rack with grief and continual cares how to be eased of the troubling cause; they can scarce think of any thing else, and these cares do even feed upon the heart, and are, to the mind, as a consuming fever to the body.

4. And the secret root or cause of all this is the worst part of the sin, which is, too much love to the body, and this world. Were nothing overloved, it would have no power to torment us. If ease and health were not overloved, pain and sickness would be the more tolerable; if children and friends were not overloved, the death of them would not overwhelm us with inordinate sorrow; if the body were not overloved, and worldly wealth and prosperity overvalued, it were easy to endure hard fare, and labour, and want, not only of superfluities and conveniences, but even of that which is necessary to health, yea, or life itself, if God will have it so, at least, to avoid vexations, discontents, and cares, and inordinate grief and trouble of mind.

5. There is yet more sin in the root of all, and that is, it showeth that our wills are yet too selfish, and not subdued to a due submission to the will of God, but we would be as gods to ourselves, and be at our own choosing, and must needs have what the flesh desireth. We want a due resignation of ourselves and all our concerns to God, and live not as children, in due dependence on him for our daily bread, but must needs be the keepers of our own provision.

6. And this showeth that we be not sufficiently humbled for our sin, or else we should be thankful for the lowest state, as being much better than that which we deserved.

7. And there is apparently much distrust of God and unbelief in these troubling discontents and cares. Could we trust God as well as ourselves, or as we could trust a faithful friend, or as a child can trust his father, how quiet would our minds be in the sense of his wisdom, all-sufficiency, and love!

8. And this unbelief yet hath a worse effect than worldly trouble: it showeth that men take not the love of God and the heavenly glory for their sufficient portion; unless they may have what they want, or would have, for the body in this world, unless they may be free from poverty, and crosses, and provocations, and injuries, and pains, all that God hath promised them here or hereafter, even everlasting glory, will not satisfy them; and when God, and Christ, and heaven, are not enough to quiet a man's mind, he is in great want of faith, hope, and love, which are far greater matters than food and raiment.

III. Another great cause of such trouble of mind is the guilt of some great and wilful sin; when conscience is convinced, and yet the soul is not converted; sin is beloved, and yet feared; God's wrath doth terrify them, and yet not enough to overcome their sin. Some live in secret fraud and robbery, and many in drunkenness, in secret fleshly lusts, either self-pollution or fornication, and they know that for such things the wrath of God cometh on the children of disobedience; and yet the rage of appetite and lust prevaileth, and they despair and sin; and while the sparks of hell fall on their consciences, it changeth neither heart nor life: there is some more hope of the recovery of these than of dead-hearted or unbelieving sinners, who work uncleanness with greediness, as being past feeling, and blinded to defend their sins, and plead against holy obedience to God. Brutishness is not so bad as diabolism and malignity. But none of these are the persons spoken of in my text; their sorrow is not overmuch, but too little, as long as it will not restrain them from their sin.

But yet, if God convert these persons, the sins which they now live in may possibly hereafter plunge their souls into such depths of sorrow in the review as may swallow them up.

And when men truly converted yet dally with the bait, and renew the wounds of their consciences by their lapses, it is no wonder if their sorrow and terrors are renewed. Grievous sins have fastened so on the conscience of many, as have cast them into incurable melancholy and distraction.

IV. But, among people fearing God, there is yet another cause of melancholy, and of sorrowing overmuch, and that is, ignorance and mistakes in matters which their peace and comfort are concerned in. I will name some particulars.

1. One is, ignorance of the tenor of the gospel or covenant of grace, as some libertines, called antinomians, more dangerously mistake it, who tell men that Christ hath repented and believed them, and that they must no more question their faith and repentance, than they must question the righteousness of Christ: so many better christians understand not that the gospel is tidings of unspeakable joy to all that will believe it; and that Christ and life are offered freely to them that will accept him, and that no sins, however great or many soever, are excepted from pardon, to the soul that unfeignedly turneth to God by faith in Christ; and that whoever will may freely take the water of life, and all that are weary and athirst are invited to come to him for ease and rest.

And they seem not to understand the conditions of forgiveness, which is but true consent to the pardoning, saving (baptismal) covenant.

2. And many of them are mistaken about the use of sorrow for sin, and about the nature of hardness of heart: they think that if their sorrow be not so passionate as to bring forth tears, and greatly to afflict them, they are not capable of pardon, though they should consent to all the pardoning covenant; and they consider not that it is not our sorrow for itself that God delighteth in, but it is the taking down of pride, and that so much humbling sense of sin, danger, and misery, as may make us feel the need of Christ and mercy, and bring us unfeignedly to consent to be his disciples, and to be saved upon his covenant terms. Be sorrow much or little, if it do this much the sinner shall be saved.

And as to the length of God's sorrow, some think that the pangs of the new birth must be a long-continued state; whereas we read in the Scripture, that, by the penitent sinners the gospel was still received speedily with joy, as being the gift of Christ, and pardon, and everlasting life: humility and loathing must continue and increase, but our first great sorrows may be swallowed up with holy thankfulness and joy.

And as for hardness of heart, in Scripture, it is taken for such a stiff, rebellious obstinacy, as will not be moved from their sins to obedience by any of God's commands or threats, and is called oft an iron sinew, a stiff neck, &c.; but it is never taken for the mere want of tears or passionate sorrow in a man that is willing to obey: the hard-hearted are the rebellious. Sorrow, even for sin, may be overmuch, and a passionate woman or man may easily grieve and weep for the sin which they will not leave; but obedience cannot be too much.

3. And abundance are cast down by ignorance of themselves, not knowing the sincerity which God hath given them. Grace is weak in the best of us here, and little and weak grace is not very easily perceived, for it acteth weakly and unconstantly, and it is known but by its acts; and weak grace is always joined with too strong corruption; and all sin in heart and life is contrary to grace, and doth obscure it; and such persons usually have too little knowledge, and are too strange at home, and unskilful in examining and watching their heart, and keeping its accounts: and how can any, under all these hinderances, yet keep any full assurance of their own sincerity. If, with much ado, they get some assurances, neglect of duty, or coldness in it, or yielding to temptation, or unconstancy in close obedience, will make them question all again, and ready to say it was all but hypocrisy. And a sad and melancholy frame of mind is always apt to conclude the worst, and hardly brought to see any thing that is good, and tends to comfort.

4. And in such a case there are too few that know how to fetch comfort from bare probabilities, when they get not certainty, much less from the mere offers of grace and salvation, even when they cannot deny but they are willing to accept them; and if none should have comfort but those that have assurance of their sincerity and salvation, despair would swallow up the souls of most, even of true believers.

5. And ignorance of other men increaseth the fears and sorrows of some. They think, by our preaching and writing, that we are much better than we are; and then they think that they are graceless, because they come short of our supposed measures; whereas if they dwelt with us, and saw our failings, or knew us as well as we know ourselves, or saw all our sinful thoughts and vicious dispositions written in our foreheads, they would be cured of this error.

6. And unskilful teachers do cause the griefs and perplexities of very many. Some cannot open to them clearly the tenor of the covenant of grace: some are themselves unacquainted with any spiritual, heavenly consolations; and many have no experience of any inward holiness, and renewal by the Holy Ghost, and know not what sincerity is, nor wherein a saint doth differ from an ungodly sinner, as wicked deceivers make good and bad to differ but a little, if not the best to be taken for the worst; so some unskilful men do place sincerity in such things as are not so much as duty, as the papists in their manifold inventions and superstitions, and many sects in their unsound opinions.

And some unskilfully and unsoundly describe the state of grace, and tell you how far a hypocrite may go, so as unjustly discourageth and confoundeth the weaker sort of christians, and cannot amend the misexpression of their books or teachers;[b] and too many teachers lay men's comforts, if not salvation, on controversies which are past their reach, and pronounce heresy and damnation against that which they themselves understand not. Even the christian world, these one thousand three hundred, or one thousand two hundred years, is divided into parties by the teachers' unskilful quarrels about words which they took in several senses. Is it any wonder if the hearers of such are distracted?

IV. I have told you the causes of distracted sorrows, I am now to tell you what is the cure; but, alas! it is not so soon done as told; and I shall begin where the disease beginneth, and tell you both what the patient himself must do, and what must be done by his friends and teachers.

I. Look not on the sinful part of your troubles, either as better or worse than indeed it is.

1. Too many persons in their sufferings and sorrows think they are only to be pitied, and take little notice of the sin that caused them, or that they still continue to commit; and too many unskilful friends and ministers do only comfort them, when a round chiding and discovery of their sin should be the better part of the cure; and if they were more sensible how much sin there is, in their overvaluing the

[b] One of my hearers fell distracted with reading some passages in Mr. Shepherd's "Sincere Believer," which were not justifiable or sound.

world, and not trusting God, and in their hard thoughts of him, and their poor, unholy thoughts of his goodness, and in their undervaluing the heavenly glory, which should satisfy them in the most afflicted state, and in their daily impatiences, cares, and discontents, and in denying the mercies or graces received, this would do more to cure some than words of comfort, when they say as Jonah, "I do well to be angry," and think that all their denials of grace, and distracting sorrows and wrangling against God's love and mercy, are their duties, it is time to make them know how great sinners they are.

2. And yet when as foolishly they think that all these sins are marks of a graceless state, and that God will take the devil's temptations for sins, and condemn them for that which they abhor, and take their very disease of melancholy for a crime, this also needs confutation and reprehension, that they may not by error cherish their passions or distress.

II. Particularly, give not way to a habit of peevish impatience: though it is carnal love to somewhat more than to God and glory which is the damning sin, yet impatience must not pass for innocence. Did you not reckon upon sufferings, and of bearing the cross, when you first gave up yourselves to Christ? And do you think it strange? Look for it, and make it your daily study to prepare for any trial that God may bring you to, and then it will not surprise you, and overwhelm you. Prepare for the loss of children and friends, for the loss of goods, and for poverty and want; prepare for slanders, injuries, or poisons, for sickness, pain, and death. It is your unpreparedness that maketh it seem unsufferable.

And remember that it is but a vile body that suffereth, which you always knew must suffer death, and rot to dust: and whoever is the instrument of your sufferings, it is God that trieth you by it; and when you think that you are only displeased with men, you are not guiltless of murmuring against God, or else his overruling hand would persuade you to submissive patience.

Especially make conscience of a settled discontent of mind. Have you not yet much better than you deserve? And do you forget how many years you have enjoyed undeserving mercy? Discontent is a continued resistance of God's disposing will, that I say not some rebellion against it. Your own wills rise up against the will of God. It is atheistical to think that your sufferings are not by his providence; and dare you repine against God, and continue in such repining? To whom else doth it belong to dispose of you and all the world?

And when you feel distracting cares for your deliverances, remember that this is not trusting God. Care for your own duty, and obey his command, but leave it to him what you shall have; tormenting cares do but add to your afflictions; it is a great mercy of God that he forbiddeth you these cares, and promiseth to care for you. Your Saviour himself hath largely, though gently, reprehended them, (Matt. vi.) and told you how sinful and unprofitable they are, and that your Father knoweth what you need; and if he deny it you, it is for just cause, and if it be to correct you, it is yet to profit you; and if you submit to him, and accept his gift, he will give you much better than he taketh from you, even Christ and everlasting life.

III. Set yourselves more diligently than ever to overcome the inordinate love of the world. It will be a happy use of all your troubles if you can follow them up to the fountain, and find out what it is that you cannot bear the want or loss of, and consequently what is it that you overlove. God is very jealous, even when he loveth, against every idol that is loved too much, and with any of that love which is due to him. And if he take them all away, and tear them out of our hands and hearts, it is merciful as well as just. I speak not this to those that are troubled only for want of more faith, and holiness, and communion with God, and assurance of salvation. These troubles might give them much comfort if they understood aright from whence they come, and what they signify. For as impatient trouble under worldly crosses doth prove that a man loveth the world too much, so impatient trouble, for want of more holiness and communion with God, doth show that such are lovers of holiness and of God. Love goeth before desire and grief. That which men love they delight in if they have it, and mourn for want of it, and desire to obtain it. The will is the love; and no man is troubled for want of that which he would not have.

But the commonest cause of passionate melancholy is at first some worldly discontent and care; either wants or crosses, or the fear of suffering, or the unsuitableness and provocation of some related to them, or disgrace, or contempt, do cast them into passionate discontent, and self-will cannot bear the denial of something which they would have, and then when the discontent hath muddied and diseased a man's mind, temptations about his soul do come in afterwards; and that which begun only with worldly crosses, doth after seem to be all about religion, conscience, or merely for sin and want of grace.

Why could you not patiently bear the words, the wrongs, the losses, the crosses, that did befall you? Why made you so great a matter of these bodily, transitory things? Is it not because you overloved them? Were you not in good earnest when you called them vanity, and covenanted to leave them to the will of God? Would you have God let you alone in so great a sin as the love of the world, or giving any of his due to creatures. If God should not teach you what to love, and what to set light by, and cure you of so dangerous a disease as a fleshly, earthly mind, he should not sanctify you, and fit you for heaven. Souls go not to heaven as an arrow is shot upward, against their inclination; but as fire naturally tendeth upward, and earth downward, to their like, so when holy men are dead, their souls have a natural inclination upward; and it is their love that is their inclination; they love God, and heaven, and holy company, and their old godly friends, and holy works, even mutual love, and the joyful praises of Jehovah. And this spirit and love is as a fiery nature, which carrieth them heavenward; and angels convey them not thither by force, but conduct them as a bride to her marriage, who is carried all the way by love.

And on the other side, the souls of wicked men are of a fleshly, worldly inclination, and love not heavenly works and company, and have nothing in them to carry them to God; but they love worldly trash, and sensual, bestial delights, though they cannot enjoy them; and as poor men love riches, and are vexed for want of what they love; and therefore it is no wonder if wicked souls do dwell with devils in the lower regions, and that they make apparitions here when God permits them, and if holy souls be liable to no such descent. Love is the soul's poise and spring, and carrieth souls downward or upward accordingly.

Away, then, with the earthly, fleshly love. How long will you stay here; and what will earth and flesh do for you? So far as it may be helpful to holiness and heaven, God will not deny it to submissive children; but to overlove is to turn from God, and is the dangerous malady of souls, and the poise that sinks them down from heaven. Had you learnt better to forsake all for Christ, and to account all but as loss and dung, as Paul did, (Phil. iii. 8,) you could more easily bear the want of it. When did you see any live in discontent, and distracted with melancholy, grief, and cares, for want of dung, or a bubble, a shadow, or a merry dream? If you will not otherwise know the world, God will otherwise make you know it to your sorrow.

IV. If you are not satisfied that God alone, Christ alone, heaven alone, is enough for you, as matter of felicity and full content, go, study the case better, and you may be convinced. Go, learn better your catechism, and the principles of religion, and then you will learn to lay up a treasure in heaven, and not on earth, and to know that it is best to be with Christ; and that death, which blasteth all the glory of the world, and equalleth rich and poor, is the common door to heaven or hell: and then conscience will not ask you whether you have lived in pleasure or in pain, in riches or in want; but whether you have lived to God or to the flesh; for heaven or for earth? and what hath had the pre-eminence in your hearts and lives? If there be shame in heaven, you will be ashamed when you are there, that you whined and murmured for want of any thing that the flesh desired upon earth, and went thither grieving because your bodies suffered here. Study more to live by faith and hope, on the unseen promised glory with Christ, and you will patiently endure any sufferings in the way.

V. And study better how great a sin it is to set our own wills and desires in a discontented opposition to the wisdom, will, and providence of God; and to make our wills instead of his, as gods to ourselves. Does not a murmuring heart secretly accuse God? All accusation of God hath some degree of blasphemy in it. For the accuser supposeth that somewhat of God is to be blamed, and if you dare not open your mouths to accuse him, let not the repinings of your hearts accuse him; know how much of religion and holiness consisteth in bringing this rebellious self-will to a full resignation, submission, and conformity to the will of God. Till you can rest in God's will you will never have rest.

VI. And study well how great a duty it is wholly to trust God, and our blessed Redeemer, both with soul and body, and all we have. Is not infinite power, wisdom, and goodness, to be trusted? Is not a Saviour, who came from heaven into flesh, to save sinners by such incomprehensible ways of love, to be trusted with that which he hath so dearly bought? To whom else will you trust? Is it yourselves, or your friends? Who is it that hath kept you all your lives, and done all for you that is done? Who is it that hath saved all the souls that are now in heaven? What is our christianity but a life of faith? And is this your faith, to distract yourselves with care and troubles, if God do not fit all his providences to your wills? Seek first his kingdom and righteousness, and he hath promised that all other things shall be added to you, and not a hair of your head shall perish, for they are all, as it were, numbered. A sparrow falls not to the ground without his providence, and doth he set less by those that fain would please him? Believe God, and trust him, and your cares, and fears, and griefs will vanish.

Oh that you knew what a mercy and comfort it is for God to make it your duty to trust him! If he had made you no promise, this is equal to a promise. If he do but bid you trust him, you may be sure he will not deceive your trust. If a faithful friend that is able to relieve you, do but bid you trust him for your relief, you will not think that he will deceive you. Alas! I have friends that durst trust me with their estates, and lives, and souls, if they were in my power, and would not fear that I would destroy or hurt them, that yet cannot trust the God of infinite goodness with them, though he both commands them to trust him, and promise them he will never fail them nor forsake them. It is the refuge of my soul, that quieteth me in my fears, that God, my Father and Redeemer, hath commanded me to trust him with my body, my health, my liberty, my estate, and when eternity seemeth strange and dreadful to me, that he bids me trust him with my departing soul! Heaven and earth are upheld and maintained by him, and shall I distrust him?

Object. But it is none but his children that he will save.

Answ. True; and all are his children that are truly willing to obey and please him. If you are truly willing to be holy, and to obey his commanding will, in a godly, righteous, and sober life, you may boldly rest in his disposing will, and rejoice in his rewarding and accepting will, for he will pardon all our infirmities through the merits and intercession of Christ.

VII. If you would not be swallowed up with sorrow, swallow not the baits of sinful pleasure. Passions, and dulness, and defective duties have their degrees of guilt, but it is pleasing sin that is the dangerous and deep-wounding sin. O fly from the baits of lust, and pride, and ambition, and covetousness, and an unruly appetite to drink or meat, as you would fly from guilt, and grief, and terror. The more pleasure you have in sin, usually the more sorrow it will bring you; and the more you know it to be sin, and conscience tells you that God is against it, and yet you will go on, and bear down conscience, the sharplier will conscience afterwards afflict you, and the hardlier will it be quieted when it is awakened to repentance. Yea, when a humbled soul is pardoned by grace, and believeth that he is pardoned, he will not easily forgive himself. The remembrance of the wilfulness of sinning, and how poor a bait prevailed with us, and what mercies and motives we bore down, will make us so displeased and angry with ourselves, and so to loathe such naughty hearts, as will not admit a speedy or easy reconciliation. Yea, when we remember that we sinned against knowledge, even when we remembered that God did see us, and that we offended him, it will keep up long doubts of our sincerity in the soul, and make us afraid lest still we have the same hearts, and should again do the same if we had the same temptations. Never look for joy or peace as long as you live in wilful and beloved sin. This thorn must be taken out of your hearts before you will be eased of the pain, unless God leave you to a senseless heart, and Satan give you a deceitful peace, which doth but prepare for greater sorrow.

VIII. But if none of the forementioned sins cause your sorrows, but they come from the mere perplexities of your mind about religion, or the state of your souls, as fearing God's wrath for your former sins, or doubting of your sincerity and salvation, then these foregoing reproofs are not meant to such as you; but I shall now lay you down your proper remedy, and that is, the cure of that ignorance and those errors which cause your troubles.

1. Many are perplexed about controversies in religion, while every contending party is confident, and hath a great deal to say, which to the ignorant seemeth like to truth, and which the hearer cannot answer, and when each party tells them that their

way is the only way, and threateneth damnation to them if they turn not to them. The papists say, There is no salvation out of our church; that is, to none but the subjects of the bishop of Rome. The Greeks condemn them, and extol their church, and every party extols their own. Yea, some will convert them with fire and sword, and say, Be of our church, or lie in gaol; or make their church itself a prison, by driving in the uncapable and unwilling.

Among all these, how shall the ignorant know what to choose?

Answ. The case is sad, and yet not so sad as the case of the far greatest part of the world, who are quiet in heathenism, or infidelity, or never trouble themselves about religion, but follow the customs of their countries, and the prince's laws, that they may not suffer. It is some sign of a regard to God and your salvation, that you are troubled about religion, and careful to know which is the right; even controversy is better than atheistical indifference, that will be on the upper side, be it what will. If you cast acorns or pulse among them, swine will strive for it; or if it be carrion, dogs will fight for it; but if it be gold or jewels, dogs and swine will never strive for them, but tread them in the dirt. But cast them before men, and they will be all together by the ears for them. Lawyers contend about law, and princes about dominion, which others mind not; and religious persons strive about religion; and what wonder is this? It doth but show that they value their souls and religion, and that their understandings are yet imperfect. But if you will follow these plain directions, controversies need not break your peace.

I. See that you be true to the light and law of nature, which all mankind is obliged to observe. If you had no Scripture nor christianity, nature (that is, the works of God) do tell you that there is a God, and that he is the rewarder of them that diligently seek him. It tells you that God is absolutely perfect in power, knowledge, and goodness, and that man is a reasonable, free agent made by him, and therefore is his own, and at his will and government. It tells you that a man's actions are not indifferent, but some things we ought to do, and some things we ought not to do; and that virtue and vice, moral good and evil, do greatly differ; and therefore that there is some universal law which obligeth us to the good, and forbids the evil, and that this can be none but the law of the universal Governor, which is God. It tells all men that they owe this God their absolute obedience, because he is their most wise and absolute Ruler; and that they owe him their chiefest love, because he is not only the chief Benefactor, but also most perfectly amiable in himself. It tells us that he hath made us all sociable members of one world, and that we owe love and help to one another. It tells us that all this obedience to God can never be in vain, nor to our loss; and it tells us that we must all die, and that fleshly pleasures and this transitory world will quickly leave us. There is no more cause to doubt of all or any of this, than whether man be man. Be true to this much, and it will be a great help to all the rest.

II. And as to God's supernatural revelation, hold to God's word, the sacred Bible, written by the special inspiration of the Holy Ghost, as the sufficient records of it.

It is not divine faith if it rest not on divine revelation, nor is it divine obedience which is not given to divine government or command. Man's word is to be believed but as it deserveth, with a human faith, and man's law must be obeyed according to the measure of his authority, with a human obedience; but these are far different from a divine. There is no universal ruler of all the world or church but God; no man is capable of it, nor any council of men. God's law is only in nature, and in the holy Scripture; and that being the law by which he will judge us, it is the law which is the only divine rule of our faith or judgment, our hearts and lives. Though all in the Scripture is not of equal clearness or necessity, but a man may be saved that understandeth not a thousand sentences therein, yet all that is necessary to salvation is plainly there contained, and God's law is perfect to its designed use, and needeth no supplement of man's. Hold close to Scripture sufficiency, or you will never know what to hold to. Councils and canons are far more uncertain, and there is no agreement among their subjects which of them are obligatory, and which not, nor any possible way to come to an agreement.

III. Yet use with thankfulness the help of men, for the understanding and obeying the word of God.

Though lawyers, as such, have none of the legislative power, you need their help to understand the use of the law aright. And though no men have power to make laws for the church universal, yet men must be our teachers to understand and use the laws of God. We are not born with faith or knowledge; we know nothing but what is taught us, except what sense or intuition perceiveth, or reason gathereth from thence.

If you ask, Who must we learn of? I answer, of those that know, and have learned themselves. No name, or title, or relation, or habit, will enable any man to teach you that which he knoweth not himself.

1. Children must learn of their parents and tutors.
2. People must learn of their able, faithful pastors and catechisers.
3. All christians must be teachers by charitable helps to one another.

But teaching and law-making are two things. To teach another is but to show him that same scientific evidence of truth, by which the teacher knoweth it himself, that the learner may know it as he doth. To say, You shall believe that is true which I say is true, and that this is the meaning of it, is not teaching, but law-giving; and to believe such a one, is not to learn or know, though some human belief of our teachers is necessary to learners.

IV. Take nothing as necessary to the being of christianity and to salvation, which is not recorded in the Scripture, and hath not been held necessary by all true christians in every age and place.

Not that we must know men first to be true christians, that by them we may know what christian truth is, but the plain Scripture tells all men what christianity is, and by that we know whom to take for christians. But if any thing be new, and risen since the apostles' writing of the Scripture, that can be no point essential to christianity, else christianity must be a mutable thing, and not the same now as it was heretofore, or else there were no christians before this novelty in the world. The church were not the church, nor were any man a christian, if they wanted any essential part of faith or practice.

But here take heed of sophisters' deceit; though nothing is necessary to salvation but all sound christians have still believed, yet all is not necessary, or true, or good, which all good christians have believed or done; much less all which the tempted worse part have held: for though the essence of christianity has been ever and every where the same, yet the opinions of christians, and their mistakes and faults, have been none of their imitable faith or practice. Human nature is essentially the same in Adam, and in all men, but the diseases of nature are another thing. If all men have sin and error, so have all churches; their christianity is of God, but the corruptions and maladies of christians are not. You must hold nothing but what christians of old have held as received from God's word; but because they have all some faults and errors, you must not hold and do all those.

V. Maintain the unity of the Spirit in the bond of peace with all true christians as such, and live in love in the communion of saints.

That is, with them that live in the belief, and in holy obedience to the christian faith and law. By their fruits you shall know them. The societies of malignants, who suppress true practical knowledge and piety, and hate the best men, and cherish wickedness, and bloodily persecute those that in conscience obey not their usurpations and inventions, are not the communion of saints; wolves, thorns, and thistles, are not the sheep or vines of Christ.

VI. Prefer not any odd or singular sect before the universal consent of the faithful in your learning or communion, so far as the judgment of men is to be regarded.

Though we take not our faith from the number of believers, and though the most be usually none of the best, and some few are much wiser than the most, and in a controversy a few men of such knowledge are to be believed before the multitude of less knowledge, yet Christ is the head of all true christians, and not of an odd sect or party only; and he hath commanded them all to live as brethren, in love and holy communion; and in all sciences, the greater number of agreeing men are liker to be in the right, than some straggling persons, who show otherwise no more ability than they: at least, which side soever you like best in less necessary points, you must always be in unity with all true christians, and not unnecessarily differ from them.

VII. Never set a doubtful opinion against a certain truth or duty; reduce not things certain to things uncertain; but contrarily, uncertain things to certain: for instance, it is certain that you ought to live in love and peace with all that are true christians, and to do good to all, and wrong to none; let not any doubtful difference make you violate this rule, and hate, and slander, and backbite, and hurt them for a doubtful, indifferent, or unnecessary thing; set not your mint or cummin, tithes or ceremonies, against love and justice, and the great and certain things of the law; it is an ill sect or opinion that is against the nature and common duty of christianity and humanity.

VIII. Faithfully serve Christ as far as you have attained, and be true to all the truth that you know; sin not by omission or practice against the knowledge which you have, lest God in justice give up your understanding to believe a lie.

IX. Remember that all men on earth are ignorant, and know but as in a glass, and in part, and therefore the best have many errors; no man knoweth the smallest grass or worm with an adequate perfect knowledge. And if God bear with multitudes of errors in us all, we must bear with such as are tolerable in each other; it is well if men be humble, and teachable, and willing to know. As we have seen few more imperfect than the sects that have asserted sinless perfection, so we see few so fallible and erroneous as the Roman sect, which pleadeth their infallibility: when they tell you that you must believe their popes and councils, that you may come to an end of controversy, ask them whether we may here hope for any end of ignorance, error, and sin; if not, what hope of ending all controversies before we come to heaven, where ignorance is ended? The controversies against the essentials of christianity were ended with us all when we became true and adult christians, and the rest will be lessened as we grow in knowledge. Divinity is not less mysterious than law and physic, &c. where controversies abound.

X. Yet stint not yourselves in knowledge, nor say, We have learned enough, but continue as Christ's scholars in learning more and more to the death: the wisest know little, and may still increase. There is a great difference in excellency, usefulness, and comfort, between men of clear, digested knowledge, and confused, undigested apprehensions.

These ten rules practised, will save you from being perplexed with doubts and controversies of all pretenders in religion.

II. But if your trouble be not about doctrinal controversies, but about your sins, or want of grace, and spiritual state, digest well these following truths and counsels, and it will cure you.

I. God's goodness is equal to his greatness; even to that power that ruleth heaven and earth. His attributes are commensurate; and goodness will do good to capable receivers. He loved us when we were enemies; and he is, essentially, love itself.

II. Christ hath freely taken human nature, and made satisfaction for the sins of the world, as full as answereth his ends, and so full that none shall perish for want of sufficiency in his sacrifice and merits.

III. Upon these merits Christ hath made a law, or covenant of grace, forgiving all sin, and giving freely everlasting life to all that will believingly accept it; so that all men's sins are conditionally pardoned by the tenor of this covenant.

IV. The condition of pardon and life is not that we sin no more, or that by any price we purchase it of God, or by our own works do benefit him, or buy his grace; but only that we believe him, and willingly accept of the mercy which he freely giveth us, according to the nature of the gift; that is, that we accept of Christ as Christ, to justify, sanctify, rule, and save us.

V. God hath commissioned his ministers to proclaim and offer this covenant and grace to all, and earnestly entreat them in his name to accept it, and be reconciled to him; he hath excepted none.

VI. No man that hath this offer is damned, but only those that obstinately refuse it to the last breath.

VII. The day of grace is never so passed to any sinner but still he may have Christ and pardon if he will; and if he have it not, it is because he will not. And the day of grace is so far from being passed, that it is savingly come to all that are so willing; and grace is still offered urgently to all.

VIII. The will is the man in God's account, and what a man truly would be and have, he is, and shall have: consent to the baptismal covenant is true grace and conversion, and such have right to Christ and life.

IX. The number and greatness of former sins is no exception against the pardon of any penitent, converted sinner: God pardoneth great and small to such; where sin aboundeth, grace superaboundeth; and much is forgiven, that men may be thankful, and love much.

X. Repentance is true, though tears and passionate sorrow be defective, when a man had rather leave his sin than keep it, and sincerely, though imperfectly, endeavoureth fully to overcome it; no sin shall damn a man which he more hateth than loveth, and had truly rather leave than keep, and showeth this by true endeavour.

XI. The best man hath much evil, and the worst have some good; but it is that which is preferred, and predominant in the will, which differenceth the godly and the wicked. He that in estimation, choice, and life preferreth God, and heaven, and holiness, before the world, and the pleasure of sin, is a true godly man, and shall be saved.

XII. The best have daily need of pardon, even for the faultiness of their holiest duties, and must daily live on Christ for pardon.

XIII. Even sins against knowledge and conscience are too oft committed by regenerate men; for they know more than others do, and their consciences are more active: happy were they indeed if they could be as good as they know they should be, and love God as much as they know they should love him, and were clear from all the relicts of passion and unbelief, which conscience tells them are their sins.

XIV. God will not take Satan's temptations to be our sins, but only our not resisting them. Christ himself was tempted to the most heinous sin, even to fall down to the devil and worship him. God will charge Satan's blasphemous temptations on himself alone.

XV. The thoughts, and fears, and troubles, which melancholy and natural weakness and distemper irresistibly cause, hath much more of bodily disease than of sin, and, therefore, is of the least of sins; and, indeed, no more sin than to burn or be thirsty in a fever, further than as some sin did cause the disease that causeth it, or further than there is left some power in reason to resist them.

XVI. Certainty of our faith and sincerity is not necessary to salvation, but the sincerity of faith itself is necessary. He shall be saved that giveth up himself to Christ, though he know not that he is sincere in doing it. Christ knoweth his own grace, when they that have it know not that it is sound. It is but few true christians that attain to certainty of salvation; for weak grace clogged with much corruption is hardly known, and usually joined with fear and doubting.

XVII. Probability of sincerity and trust in Christ may cause a man, justly, to live and die in peace and comfort, without proper certainty; else few christians should live and die in peace; and yet we see by experience that many do so. The common opinion of most church writers for four hundred years after Christ, was, that the uncontinued sort of christians might fall from a state of grace, in which, had they continued, they had been saved, and, therefore, that none but strong, confirmed christians, at most, could be certain of salvation; and many protestant churches still are of that mind, and yet they live not in despair or terror. No man is certain that he shall not fall as heinously as David and Peter did; and yet while they have no cause to think it likely, they need not live in terror for the uncertainty. No wife or child is certain that the husband or father will not murder them, and yet they may live comfortably, and not fear it.

XVIII. Though faith be so weak, as to be assaulted with doubts whether the gospel be true, and there be any life to come; and though our trust in Christ be not strong enough to banish our fears and troubles; yet if we see so much evidence of credibility in the gospel, and probability of a better life hereafter, as causeth us here to fix our hopes and choice, and to resolve for those hopes to seek first the kingdom of God and his righteousness, and let go all the world rather than sell those hopes, and live a holy life to obtain it, this faith will save us.

XIX. But God's love and promise through Christ is so sure a ground for faith and comfort, that it is the great duty and interest of all men, confidently and quietly, to trust him, and then to live in the joy of holy trust and hope.

XX. If any man doubt of his salvation because of the greatness of his sins, the way to quietness is presently to be willing to forsake them. Either he that complaineth is willing to be holy and forsake his sins, or not. If you be not willing to leave them, but love them, and would keep them, why do you complain of them, and mourn for that which you so much love? If your child should cry and roar because his apple is sour, and yet will not be persuaded to forbear to eat it, you would not pity him, but whip him, as perverse. But if you are truly willing to leave it, you are already saved from its damning guilt.

XXI. If you are in doubt of the sincerity of your faith, and other graces, and all your examination leaveth you uncertain, the way is presently to end your doubt by actual giving up yourself to Christ. Do you not know whether you have been hitherto a true believer? You may know that Christ is now offered to you; consent but to the covenant, and accept the offer, and you may be sure that he is yours.

XXII. Bare examining is not always to be done for assurance, but labour to excite and exercise much the grace that you would be assured of; the way to be sure that you believe and love God, is to study the promises and goodness of God, till active faith assure you that you believe, and you love God and glory, till you are assured that you love them.

XXIII. It is not by some extraordinary act, good or bad, that we may be sure what state the soul is in, but by the predominant bent, and drift, and tenor of heart and life.

XXIV. Though we cry out that we cannot believe, and we cannot love God, and we cannot pray aright, Christ can help us; without his grace we can do nothing; but his grace is sufficient for us, and he denieth not his further help when once he hath but made us willing, but hath bid us ask and have; and if any lack wisdom let him ask it of God, who giveth to all liberally, and upbraideth not with former folly, but gives his Spirit to them that ask him.

XXV. This sin, called the blasphemy of the Holy Ghost, is the sin of no one that believeth Jesus to be the Christ, nor of any that fear it, no, nor of every infidel, but only of some few obstinate, unbelieving enemies, for it is only this: when men see such miracles of Christ and his Spirit as should or could convince them that he is of God, and when they have no other shift, they will rather maintain that he is a conjurer, and wrought them by the devil.

XXVI. Though sinful fear is very troublesome, and not to be cherished, God often permitteth and useth it to good, to keep us from being bold with sin, and from those sinful pleasures and love of the world, and presumption, and security, which are far more dangerous, and to take down pride, and keep us in a sensible, watchful state; for just fear is made to preserve us from the hurt and danger feared.

XXVII. He that goeth fearing and trembling to heaven, will there quickly be past all fear, and doubts, and heaviness, for ever.

XXVIII. When Christ for our sins was in his agony, and when he cried out, "My God, my God, why hast thou forsaken me?" he was then nevertheless beloved of his Father; and he was tempted that he might succour them that are tempted, and suffered such derision that he might be a compassionate High Priest to sufferers.

XXIX. By how much the more the troubles, and blasphemous temptations, and doubts, and fears of a man are grievous, displeasing, and hateful to him, by so much the more he may be assured that they shall not condemn him, because they are not beloved sins.

XXX. All our troubles are overruled by God; and it is far better for us to be at his choice and disposal than our own, or our dearest friend's; and he hath promised that all things shall work together for our good, Rom. viii. 28.

XXXI. A delight in God and goodness, and a joyful, praising frame of soul, from the belief of the love of God through Christ, is far more to be desired than grief and tears, which do but sweep away some dirt, that love, joy, and thankfulness may enter, which are the true evangelical, christian temper, and likest to the heavenly state.

Digest these truths, and they will cure you.

III. But if melancholy have got head already, there must be, besides what is said, some other and proper remedies used; and the difficulty is great, because the disease makes them self-conceited, unreasonable, wilful, and unruly, and they will hardly be persuaded that the disease is in their bodies, but only in the souls, and will not believe but they have reason for all what they think and do; or if they confess the contrary, they plead disability, and say, We can think and do no otherwise than we do.

But supposing that there is some use of reason left, I will give them yet some further counsel; and what they cannot do, their friends must help them to their power, which I shall add.

1. Consider that it should be easy for you in your confounding, troubling thoughts, to perceive that your understandings are not now so sound and strong as other men's; and therefore be not wilful and self-conceited, and think not that your thoughts are righter than theirs, but believe wiser men, and be ruled by them.

Answer me this question, Do you know any minister, or friend, that is wiser than yourself? If you say no, how foolishly proud are you! If you say yea, then ask the minister, or friend, what he thinketh of your condition, and believe him, and be ruled by him rather than by your crazed self.

2. Do you find that your troubles do you more good or hurt? Do they make you fitter or unfitter to believe and love God, and rejoice in him, and praise him? If you feel that they are against all that is good, you may be sure that they are so far from the devil's temptations, and are pleasing to him; and will you cherish or plead for the work of Satan, which you find is against yourselves and God?

3. Avoid your musings, and exercise not your thoughts now too deeply, nor too much. Long meditation is a duty to some, but not to you, no more than it is a man's duty to go to church that hath his leg broken, or his foot out of joint: he must rest and ease it till it be set again, and strengthened. You may live in the faith and fear of God, without setting yourself to deep, disturbing thoughts.

Those that will not obey this counsel, their friends must rouse them from their musings, and call them off to something else.

4. Therefore you must not be much alone, but always in some pleasing, cheerful company: solitariness doth but cherish musings.

Nor must such be long in secret prayer, but more in public prayer with others.

5. Let those thoughts which you have be laid out on the most excellent things: pore not all on yourselves, and on your distempered hearts; the best may find there much matter of trouble. As millstones wear themselves if they go when they have no corn, so do the thoughts of such as think not of better things than their own hearts. If you have any power of your own thoughts, force them to think most of these four things:

1. The infinite goodness of God, who is fuller of love than the sun is of light.

2. Of the unmeasurable love of Christ in man's redemption, and of the sufficiency of his sacrifice and merits.

3. Of the free covenant and offer of grace, which giveth pardon and life to all that do not prefer the pleasure of sin before it, and obstinately refuse it to the last.

4. Of the unconceivable glory and joy which all the blessed have with Christ, and which God hath promised with his oath and seal, to all that consent to the covenant of grace, and are willing to be saved and ruled by Christ. These thoughts will cure melancholy fears.

5. Use not yourselves to a complaining talk, but talk most of the great mercies of God which you have received. Dare you deny them? If not, are they not worthier of your discourse than your present sufferings? Let not all men know that you are in your troubles: complaining doth but feed them, and it discourageth others. Open them to none but your secret counsellors and friends. Use much to speak of the love of God, and the riches of grace, and it will divert and sweeten your sourer thoughts.

6. Especially, when you pray, resolve to spend most of your time in thanksgiving and praising God. If you cannot do it with the joy that you should, yet do it as you can. You have not the power of your comforts; but have you no power of your tongues? Say not that you are unfit for thanks and praises, unless you had a praising heart, and were the children of God; for every man, good and bad, is bound to praise God, and to be thankful for all that he hath received, and to do it as well as he can, rather than leave it undone: and most christians want assurance of their adoption; and must they, therefore, forbear all praise and thanksgiving to God? Doing it as you can is the way to be able to do it better. Thanksgiving stirreth up thankfulness in the heart, but by your objection you may perceive what the devil driveth at, and gets by your melancholy. He would turn you off from all thankfulness to God, and from the very mention of his love and goodness in your praises.

7. When vexatious or blasphemous thoughts are thrust into your mind by Satan, neither give them entertainment, nor yet be overmuch troubled at them: first, use that reason and power that is left you resolutely to cast them out, and turn your thoughts to somewhat else; do not say, I cannot. If you can no otherwise command and turn away your thoughts, rise up and go into some company or to some employment which will divert you, and take them up. Tell me what you would do if you heard a scold in the street reviling you, or heard an atheist there talk against God? would you stand still to hear them, or would you talk it out again with them, or rather go from them, and disdain to hear them, or debate the case with such as they? Do you, in your case, when Satan casts in ugly, or despairing, or murmuring thoughts, go away from them to some other thoughts or business.

If you cannot do this of yourself, tell your friend when the temptation cometh; and it is his duty who hath the care of you to divert you with some other talk or words, or force you into diverting company.

Yet be not too much troubled at the temptation, for trouble of mind doth keep the evil matter in your memory, and so increase it, as pain of a sore draws the blood and spirits to the place. And this is the design of Satan, to give you troubling thoughts, and then to cause more by being troubled at those; and so, for one thought and trouble to cause another, and that another, and so on, as waves in the sea do follow each other. To be tempted is common to the best. I told you to what idolatry Christ was tempted. When you feel such thoughts, thank God that Satan cannot force you to love them, or consent.

8. Again, still remember what a comfortable evidence you carry about with you that your sin is not damning, while you feel that you love it not, but hate it, and are weary of it. Scarce any sort of sinners have so little pleasure in their sins as the melancholy, nor so little desire to keep them; and only beloved sins undo men.

Be sure that you live not idly, but in some constant business of a lawful calling, so far as you have bodily strength. Idleness is a constant sin, and labour is a duty. Idleness is but the devil's home for temptation, and for unprofitable, distracting musings. Labour profiteth others, and ourselves: both soul and body need it. Six days must you labour, and must not eat the bread of idleness, Prov. xxxi. God hath made it our duty, and will bless us in his appointed way. I have known grievous, despairing melancholy cured, and turned into a life of godly cheerfulness, principally by setting upon constancy and diligence in the business of families and callings. It turns the thoughts from temptations, and leaveth the devil no opportunity: it pleaseth God if done in obedience, and it purifieth the distempered blood. Though thousands of poor people that live in want, and have wives and children that must also feel it, one would think should be distracted with griefs and cares, yet few of them fall into the disease of melancholy, because labour keepeth the body sound, and leaveth them no leisure for melancholy musings: whereas, in London, and great towns, abundance of women that never sweat with bodily work, but live in idleness, especially when from fulness they fall into want, are miserable objects, continually vexed, and near distraction with discontent and a restless mind.

If you will not be persuaded to business, your friends, if they can, should force you to it.

And if the devil turn religious as an angel of light, and tell you that this is but turning away your thoughts from God, and that worldly thoughts and business are unholy, and fit for worldly men; tell him that Adam was in innocency to dress and keep his garden, and Noah that had all the world was to be husbandman, and Abraham, Isaac, and Jacob kept sheep and cattle, and Paul was a tent-maker, and Christ himself is justly supposed to have worked at his supposed father's trade, as he went on fishing with his disciples. And Paul saith, idleness is disorderly walking, and he that will not work let him not eat. God made soul and body, and hath commanded work to both.

And if Satan would drive you unseasonably upon longer secret prayer than you can bear, remember that even sickness will excuse the sick from that sort of duty which they are unable for, and so will your disease; and the unutterable groans of the spirit are accepted.

If you have privacy out of hearing, I would give you this advice, that instead of long meditation, or long secret prayer, you will sing a psalm of praise to God, such as the twenty-third, or the one hundred and thirty-third, &c. This will excite your spirit to that sort of holy affection which is much more acceptable to God, and suitable to the hopes of a believer, than your repining troubles are.

IV. But yet I have not done with the duty of those that take care of distressed, melancholy persons, especially husbands to their wives, (for it is much more frequently the disease of women than of men,) when the disease disableth them to help themselves, the most of their helps, under God, must be from others; and this is of two sorts: 1. In prudent carriage to them; 2. In medicine and diet; a little of both.

1. A great part of their cure lieth in pleasing them, and avoiding all displeasing things, as far as lawfully can be done. Displeasedness is much of the disease; and a husband that hath such a wife is obliged to do his best to cure her, both in charity, and by his relative bond, and for his own peace. It is a great weakness in some men, that if they have wives, who by natural passionate weakness, or by melancholy or crazedness, are wilful and will not yield to reason, they show their anger at them to their further provocation. You took her in marriage for better and for worse, for sickness and health. If you have chosen one that, as a child, must have every thing that she crieth for, and must be spoken fair, and as it was rocked in the cradle, or else it will be worse, you must condescend to do it, and so bear the burden which you have chosen, as may not make it heavier to you. Your passion and sourness towards a person that cannot cure her own unpleasing carriage, is a more unexcusable fault and folly than hers, who hath not the power of reason as you have.

If you know any lawful thing that will please them in speech, in company, in apparel, in rooms, in attendance, give it them: if you know at what they are displeased, remove it. I speak not of the distracted, that must be mastered by force, but of the sad and melancholy: could you devise how to put them in a pleased condition you might cure them.

2. As much as you can, divert them from the thoughts which are their trouble; keep them on some other talks and business; break in upon them, and interrupt their musings; rouse them out of it, but with loving importunity; suffer them not to be long alone; get fit company to them, or them to it; especially, suffer them not to be idle, but drive or draw them to some pleasing works which may stir the body, and employ the thoughts. If they are addicted to reading, let it not be too long, nor any books that are unfit for them; and rather let another read to them than themselves. Dr. Sibbes's books, and some useful, pleasing history or chronicles, or news of great matters abroad in the world, may do somewhat to divert them.

3. Often set before them the great truths of the gospel which are fittest to comfort them; and read them informing, comforting books; and live in a loving, cheerful manner with them.

4. Choose for them a skilful, prudent minister of Christ, both for their secret counsel and public audience; one that is skilled in such cases, and one that is peaceable, and not contentious, erroneous, or fond of odd opinions; one that is rather judicious in his preaching and praying than passionate, except when he urgeth the gospel doctrines of consolation, and then the more fervently the better; and one that they much esteem and reverence, and will regardfully hear.

5. Labour to convince them frequently how great a wrong it is to the God of infinite love and mercy, and to a Saviour who hath so wonderfully expressed his love, to think hardlier of him than they would do of a friend, yea, or of a moderate enemy; and so hardly to be persuaded of that love which hath been manifested by the most stupendous miracle. Had they but a father, husband, or friend, that had ventured his life for them, and given them all that ever

they had, were it not a shameful ingratitude and injury to suspect still that they intended all against them, and designed mischief to them, and did not love them? How hath God and our Saviour deserved this? And many that say it is not God that they suspect, but themselves, do but hide their misery by this mistake, while they deny God's greatest mercies; and though they would fain have Christ and grace, will not believe that God who offereth it them will give it them, but think he is one that will remedilessly damn a poor soul that desireth to please him, and had rather have his grace than all the sinful pleasures of the world.

6. Carry them oft abroad into strange company. Usually they reverence strangers, and strange faces do divert them, especially travelling into other parts, if they can bear the motion.

7. It is a useful way, if you can, to engage them in comforting others that are deeper in distresses than they; for this will tell them that their case is not singular, and they will speak to themselves while they speak to others. One of the chief means which cured my fears of my soul's condition, about forty-eight years ago, was oft comforting others that had the same doubts, whose lives persuaded me of their sincerity.

And it would be a pretty diversion to send to them some person that is in some error, which they are most against, to dispute it with them, that, while they whet their wits to convince them, and confute them, it may turn their thoughts from their own distress. Forester tells us that a melancholy patient of his, who was a papist, was cured when the Reformation came into the country, by eager and oft disputing against it. A better cause may better do it.

8. If other means will not do, neglect not physic; and though they will be averse to it, as believing that the disease is only in the mind, they must be persuaded or forced to it. I have known the lady deep in melancholy, who a long time would neither speak, nor take physic, nor endure her husband to go out of the room, and with the restraint and grief he died, and she was cured by physic put down her throat with a pipe by force.

If it were, as some of them fancy, a possession of the devil, it is possible physic might cast him out, for if you cure the melancholy, his bed is taken away, and the advantage gone by which he worketh. Cure the choler, and the choleric operations of the devil cease. It is by means and humours in us that he worketh.

But choose a physician who is specially skilled in this disease, and hath cured many others. Meddle not with women, and ignorant boasters, nor with young, unexperienced men, nor with hasty, busy, over-doing, venturous men, who cannot have time to study the patient's temper and disease, but choose experienced, cautelous men.

Medicinal remedies and theological used not to be given together by the same hand; but in this case of perfect complication of the maladies of mind and body, I think it not unfit, if I do it not unskilfully. My advice is, that they that can have an ancient, skilful, experienced, honest, careful, cautelous physician, neglect not to use him.

The disease called melancholy is formally in the spirits, whose distemper unfits them for their office, in serving the imagination, understanding, memory, and affections; so, by their distemper, the thinking faculty is diseased and become like an inflamed eye, or a foot that is sprained or out of joint, disabled for its proper work.

The matter which is the root and foundation is usually a depravation of the mass of blood, which is the vehicle of the spirits; and that is usually accompanied with some diseases of the stomach, spleen, liver, or other parts, which are for the due concoction, motion, and purification of the blood; which diseases are so various, that they are seldom the same in many persons, and hardly known to the wisest physicians. The spleen is most commonly accused, and often guilty, and the stomach, pancreas, mesentery, omentum, liver, yea, and reins, not rarely are the root, sometimes by obstructing humours, and that of several qualities, and sometimes by stones, and sometimes by various sorts of humours, and sometimes by vesicles; but obstructed, if not tumefied, spleens, are most suspected.

Such a black, distinct humour called melancholy, which hath oft of old been accused, is rarely, if ever, found in any, unless you will call either blood or excrementitious humours by that name, which are grown black by mortification, for want of motion and spirits. But the blood itself may be called melancholy blood, when it hath contracted that distemper and pravity by feculency, sluggishness, or adustion, which disposeth it to the melancholy effects.

But sometimes persons that are sound, are suddenly cast into melancholy by a fright, or by the death of a friend, or by some great loss or cross, or some sad tidings, even in an hour, which shows that it cometh not always from any humour called melancholy, nor for any foregoing disease at all.

But the very act of the mind doth suddenly disorder the passions, and perturb the spirits; and the disturbed spirits, in time, vitiate the blood which containeth them; and the vitiated blood doth, in time, vitiate the viscera and parts which it passeth through; and so the disease beginning in the senses and soul, doth draw first the spirits, and then the humours, and then the parts, into the fellowship, and soul and body are sick together.

And it is of great use to the physician to know where the depravation did begin, whether in the mind or in the body; and if in the body, whether in the blood, or in the viscera, for the cure must be fitted accordingly.

And yet the melancholy brains may be eased, and the mental depravation much kept under, though an obstructed, yea, a scarified spleen, continue uncured many years.

And though the disease begin in the mind and spirits, and the body be yet sound, yet physic, even purging, often cureth it, though the patient say that physic cannot cure souls, for the soul and body are wonderfully co-partners in their diseases and cure; and if we know not how it doth it, yet when experience telleth us that it doth it, we have reason to use such means.

The devil hath another cure for the sad and melancholy than such as I have here prescribed, which is to cast away all belief of the immortality of the soul and the life to come, or at least not to think of it; and for to take religion to be a superstitious, needless fancy; and for to laugh at the threatenings of the Scripture, and to go to play-houses, and cards, and dice, and to drink and play away melancholy: honest recreations are very good for melancholy persons, if we could get them to use them; but, alas! this satanical cure is but like the witches' bargain with the devil, who promiseth them much, but payeth them with shame and utter misery. The end of that mirth is uncurable sorrow, if timely repentance cure not the cause. The garrison of Satan in the hearts of sinners is strongly kept when they are in peace, but when they have fooled away time, and mercy, and hope, die they must, there is no remedy; and to go merrily and unbelievingly to hell, after all

God's calls and warnings, will be no abatement of their torment; to go out of the world in the guilt of sin, and to end life before they would know the use of it, and to undergo God's justice for the mad contempt of Christ and grace, will put a sad end to all their mirth, for "There is no peace to the wicked, saith my God," Isa. xlviii. 22; lvii. 21. But Christ saith to his mourners, (Matt. v. 4,) "Blessed are you that mourn, for you shall be comforted:" and, (John xvi. 20,) "Ye shall weep and lament, but the world shall rejoice; and ye shall be sorrowful, but your sorrow shall be turned into joy." And Solomon knew that the house of mourning was better than the house of feasting; and that the heart of the wise is in the house of mourning, but the heart of fools is in the house of mirth, Eccles. vii. 2—4; but holy joy of faith and hope is best of all.

HOW TO DO GOOD TO MANY:

OR,

THE PUBLIC GOOD IS THE CHRISTIAN'S LIFE.

DIRECTIONS AND MOTIVES TO IT.

INTENDED FOR AN AUDITORY OF LONDON CITIZENS; AND PUBLISHED FOR THEM FOR WANT OF LEAVE TO PREACH THEM.

"Who gave himself for us, that he might redeem us from all iniquity, and purify to himself a people zealous of good works."—TITUS ii. 14.

TO THE TRULY CHRISTIAN MERCHANTS,

AND OTHER

CITIZENS OF LONDON.

As my disease, and the restraint of rulers, seem to tell me that my pulpit work is at an end, so also my abode among you, or in this world, cannot be long. What work I have lived for I have given the world more durable notice than transient words; it hath been such as men in power were against, and it seems, will no longer endure. What doctrine it was that I last prepared for you, I thought meet to desire the press thus to tell you; not to vindicate myself, nor to characterize them who think that it deserves six months' imprisonment, but to be in your hands a provocation and direction for that great work of a christian life, which, sincerely done, will prepare you for the safety, joy, and glory, which London, England, or earth, will not afford, and which men or devils cannot take from you. When through the meritorious righteousness of Christ, your holy love and good works to him in his brethren shall make you the joyful objects of that sentence, "Come, ye blessed, inherit the kingdom," &c.; this is the life that need not be repented of, as spent in vain.

Dear friends, in this farewell I return you my most hearty thanks for your extraordinary love and kindness to myself, much more for your love to Christ, and to his servants, who have more needed your relief. God is not unjust to forget your work and labour of love. You have visited those that others imprisoned, and fed those that others brought into want; and when some ceased not to preach for our affliction, it quenched not your impartial charity. It has been an unspeakable mercy unto me almost all my days, (when I received nothing from them,) to have known so great a number as I have done, of serious, humble, holy, charitable christians, in whom I saw that Christ hath an elect, peculiar people, quite different from the brutish, proud, hypocritical, malignant, unbelieving world! Oh how sweet hath the familiarity of such been to me, whom the ignorant world hath hated! Most of them are gone to Christ, I am following: we leave you here to longer trial: it is like you have a bitter cup to drink, but be faithful to the death, and Christ will give you the crown of life. The word of God is not bound, and the Jerusalem above is free, where is the general assembly of the first-born, an innumerable company of angels, the spirits of the just made perfect, with Christ their glorified Head. The Lord guide, bless, and preserve you.

GALATIANS VI. 10.

AS WE HAVE THEREFORE OPPORTUNITY, LET US DO GOOD UNTO ALL MEN, ESPECIALLY UNTO THEM WHO ARE OF THE HOUSEHOLD OF FAITH.

Good is an epithet of the highest signification of any in human language. Some think the name of God is thence derived. Greatness and wisdom are equally his attributes, but goodness is the completion, and sweetest to the creature. Christ appropriateth it to God to be good, that is, essentially, primarily, and perfectly, and universally communicative: when it is said that God is love, the sense is the same, that he is the infinite, essential, and efficiently and finally amiable, perfect good.

But though no one of his attributes in propriety and perfection are communicable, (else he that hath one part of the Deity must have all,) yet he imprinteth his similitude and image on his works; and the impress of his love and goodness is the chief part of his image on his saints: this is their very holiness; for this is the chief part of their likeness to God, and dedication to him: when the Spirit of sanctification is described in Scripture, as given upon believing, it signifieth that our faithful perception of the redeeming, saving love of God in Christ, is that means which the Spirit of Christ will bless, to the operating of the habit of holy love to God and man, which becomes a new and divine nature to the soul, and is sanctification itself, and the true principle of a holy, evangelical conversation. And as it is said of God, that he is good, and doth good, so every thing is inclined to work as it is; Christ tells us the good tree will bring forth good fruits, &c.; and we are God's workmanship created in Christ Jesus to good works, which God hath ordained, that we should walk in them, Eph. ii. 10.

Yet man doth not good as the sun shineth, by a full bent of natural necessitation, else the world would not be as it is; but as a free, undetermined agent, which hath need to be commanded by a law, and stirred up by manifold motives and exhortations, such as the Holy Ghost here useth in the text.

Where, 1. Doing good is the substance of the duty. 2. Men are the objects. 3. To all men is the extent. 4. Especially to them of the household of faith is the direction for precedency. 5. And while we have opportunity is the season, including a motive to make haste. So large and excellent a theme would require more than my allotted time to handle it fully, therefore I shall now confine myself to the duty extended, "Do good to all men."

Doct. To do good to all men is all men's duty, to which every christian especially must apply himself.

All men should do it: true christians can do it, through grace, and must do it, and will do it. A good man is a common good; Christ's Spirit in them is not a dead or idle principle. It makes them in their several measures the salt of the earth, and the lights of the world; they are fruitful branches of the true vine. Every grace tendeth to well-doing, and to the good of the whole body, for which each single member is made. Even hypocrites, as wooden legs, are serviceable to the body, but every living member much more, except some diseased ones, who may be more troublesome and dangerous than the wooden leg. It is a sign he is a branch cut off and withered who careth little for any but himself. The malignant diabolist hateth the true and spiritual good; the ignorant know not good from evil; the erroneous take evil for good, and falsehood for truth; the slothful hypocrite wisheth much good, but doth little; the formal, ceremonious hypocrite extols the name and image of goodness; the worldly hypocrite will do good if he can do it cheaply, without any loss or suffering to his flesh; the libertine hypocrite pleadeth Christ's merits against the necessity of doing good, and looketh to be saved because Christ is good, though he be barren and ungodly; and some ignorant teachers have taught them to say, when they can find no true faith, repentance, holiness, or obedience in themselves, that it is enough to believe that Christ believed and repented for them, and was holy and obedient for them. He was, indeed, holy and obedient for penitent believers; not to make holiness and obedience unnecessary to them, but to make them sincerely holy and obedient to himself, and to excuse them from the necessity of that perfect holiness and obedience here, which is necessary to those that will be justified by the law of works or innocency. Thus all sorts of bad men have their oppositions to doing good; but to the sincere christian it is made as natural; his heart is set upon it; he is created, and redeemed, and sanctified for it, as the tree is made for fruit. He studieth it as the chief trade and business that he liveth for; he waketh for it; yea, he sleepeth, and eateth, and drinketh for it; even to enable his body to serve his soul, in serving that Lord whose redeemed, peculiar people are all zealous of good works, Tit. ii. 14. The measure of this zeal of doing good is the utmost of their power, with all their talents, in desire and sincere endeavour; the extent of the object is to all, (though not to all alike,) that is, to as many as they can.

But for order's sake we must here consider,

I. Who this all meaneth, and in what order.

II. What is good; and what is that good which we must do.

III. What qualifications he must have that will do good to many.

IV. What rules he must observe in doing it.

V. What works are they that must be done by him that would do good to many.

VI. What motives should quicken us to the practice.

VII. Some useful consectaries of the point.

I. It is God's prerogative to do good to all; man's ability will not reach it. But our all is, as many as we can do good to. 1. To men of all sorts, high and low, rich and poor, old and young, kindred, neighbours, strangers, friends, enemies, good and bad; none excepted that are within our power.

2. Not to a few only, but to as many persons of all sorts as we can; as he that hath true grace would still have more for himself, so he that doth good would fain do more good; and he that doth good to some would fain do good to many more. All good is progressive, and tendeth towards increase and perfection; why are the faithful said to love and long for the day of Christ's appearing, but because it is the great marriage day of the Lamb, when all the elect shall be perfected in our heavenly society? And that makes it a much more desirable day than that of our particular glorification at death.

The perfection of the whole body addeth to the perfection of every part, for it is a state of felicity in perfect love; and love maketh every man's good whom we love to be as sweet to us as our own, yea, maketh it our own; and then the perfection and glory of every saint will be our delight and glory; and to see each single one's love united in one perfect joy and glory, will add to each person's joy and glory. And can you wonder if our little sparks of grace do tend towards the same diffused multiplication; and if every member long for the completing of the body of Christ? Oh how much will this add to every faithful christian's joy! It will not be then a little flock; not despised for singularity, nor hid in the crowd of impious sinners, nor dishonoured by infirmities, or paltry quarrels among ourselves, nor with the mixture of hypocrites; it will not be overvoted, or trod down, and persecuted by the power or number of the ignorant enemies. O christians! go on in doing good to all men with cheerfulness, for it all tendeth to make up the body of Christ, and to prepare for that glorious state and day; every soul you convert, every brick that you lay in the building, tendeth to make up the house and city of God.

But as all motion and action is first upon the nearest object, so must ours; and doing good must be in order: first we must begin at home with our own souls and lives; and then to our nearest relations, and friends, and acquaintance, and neighbours; and then to our societies, church, and kingdom, and all the world. But mark that the order of execution, and the order of estimation and intention, differ. Though God set up lights so small as will serve but for one room, and though we must begin at home, we must far more esteem and desire the good of multitudes, of city, and church, and commonwealth; and must set no bounds to our endeavours, but what God and disability set.

II. But what is that good that we must do? Good is an attribute of being, and is its perfection, or well-being: God's goodness is perfection itself; and as he is the fountain of being, so also of goodness; and, therefore, his goodness is called love, whose highest act is his essential self-love, which is infinitely above his love to the world; but yet it is communicative love, which made all things good, and rested in seeing them all good. And as he is the fountain, so the same will or love is the measuring rule, and the end of all derived good. The prime notion of the creature's goodness is its conformity to the will of God; but the second is its own perfection as its own, which, indeed, is but the same conformity.

Therefore, the true good which you must do men, is to make them conformable to the regulating will of God, that they may be happy in the pleased will of God; and to help them to all means for soul and body necessary hereunto; and this for as many as possibly we can.

III. The rules for judging and doing good are these. 1. That is the greatest good which is God's greatest interest; and his interest is his glory, and the complaisance of his fulfilled will.

2. Therefore, the good of the world, the church, of nations, of multitudes, is greater than the good of few.

3. The good of the soul is greater than of the body.

4. The avoiding the greatest evil is better than avoiding less.

5. Everlasting good is better than short.

6. Universal good which leaveth no evil, is better than a particular good.

7. That is the best good, as to means, which most conduceth to the end.

8. There is no earthly good that is not mixed with some evil, nor any commodity that hath not some inconvenience, or discommodity.

9. No sin must be done for any good.

10. Some things may be done for good which would be sin, were it not for the good which they are done for. It would be sin to give a robber your money, were it not to save your life, or some other commodity: it would be sin to do some things on the Lord's day, which necessity, or a greater good, may make a duty: your own defence may make it a duty to strike another, which else would be a sin.

11. In such cases there is need of great prudence and impartiality to know whether the good or the evil do preponderate; and a great part of the actions of our lives must be managed by that prudence, or else they will be sinful.

12. Therefore it is no small part of a minister's duty to counsel men, as a wise, skilful, and faithful casuist.

IV. To do good to many requireth many excellent qualifications; this is so far from being every one's performance, that we should be glad if a great part of mankind did not do more hurt than good.

1. He that will do his country good, must know what is good, and what is bad: a fool's love is hurtful; he knoweth not how to use it; he will love you to death, as an unskilful physician doth his most beloved patients; or love you into calamity, as amorous fondlings oft do each other. This is the great enemy of human peace, men know not good from evil; like him that killed his son, thinking he had been a thief; or like routed soldiers, that run by mistake into the army of the enemy. Malignity and error make mad and doleful work in the world, and worst in those that should be wisest, and the greatest instruments of public good: the Scripture mistaketh not, which tells us of enemies, and haters of God; and most of the world are professed adversaries to Christ: the Jews crucified him as an enemy to Cæsar, and to the safety of their law and country; and if we may judge by their enmity to holiness, the Spirit of Christ is taken for an intolerable enemy by no small part of nominal christians; the laws of Christ are judged too strict; the hypocrites that bow to him, and hate his laws, do call them hypocrites that are but serious in the practice of christianity, and hate them that have any more religion than compliments, ceremony, and set words; the image of a christian and a minister is set up in militant opposition to them that are christians and ministers indeed; if men that are called to the sacred office would save souls in good earnest, and pull souls out of the fire, and go any further than pomp and stage-work, they pass for the most insufferable men in the world: Elias is taken for the troubler of Israel, and Paul for a pestilent, seditious fellow, and the apostles as the offscouring of all things. Many a martyr hath died by fire, for seeking to save men from the fire of hell; and when the Bedlam world is at this pass, what good is to be expected from such men? When men, called christians, hate and oppose the God, the Christ, the Holy Ghost, to whom they were vowed in baptism; when drunkenness, and whoredom, and perjury, and lying, and all debauchery, is taken for more friendly and tolerable than the most serious worship of God, and obedience to his laws, and avoiding sin; in a word, when the greatest good is taken for insufferable evil, you may know what good to expect from such.

They will all tell you that we must love God above all, and our neighbours as ourselves; but to fight against his word, and worship, and servants, is but an ill expression of their love to God; and seeking their destruction, because they will not sin, is an ill expression of love to their neighbours. When men judge of good and evil, as Satan teacheth them, and as selfish pride and worldly interest incline them, what wonder if such love have murdered thirty thousand, or forty thousand, at once, in France, and two hundred thousand in Ireland, and have filled the christian world with religious blood? Read but the doleful histories of church contentions for one thousand three hundred years, the stories of their wars and mutual persecutions, the streams of blood that have been shed in East and West, the inquisition, and bloody laws still kept up, and all this as good works, and done in love; and you would think that the sacred Roman hierarchy did believe that Christ hath put down the legal sacrificing of beasts, that he might, instead of it, have the blood of men; and that he who requireth his disciples to lay down their lives for him, would have a priesthood kept up to sacrifice their lives to him, that will not wilfully break his laws. And all this is but as Christ foretold us, that his servants should be killed as a piece of service to God. No wonder if such men offer God a ludicrous, mimical sort of service, and worship him in vain, by heartless lip-labour, according to the traditions of men, when they dare sacrifice saints to the Lord of saints, and quiet their consciences by calling them such as they are themselves. But to the honour of goodness, and the shame of sin, to show that they sin against the light of nature itself, they put the name of evil upon good before they dare openly oppose and persecute it; and they put the names of good upon evil before they dare defend and justify it.

But, alas! it is only the ungodly that do mischief, thinking verily that it is good. How many doth the church suffer by, while they prosecute their mistakes, who yet do much good in promoting the common truth which christians are agreed in!

2. He that will do good to all or many, must have an unfeigned love to them. Hatred is mischievous, and neglect is uprofitable. Love is the natural fountain of beneficence. Love earnestly longeth to do good, and delighteth in doing it: it maketh many to be as one, and to be as ready to help others as each member of the body is to help the rest. Love maketh another's wants, sufferings, and sorrows, to be our own: and who is not willing to help himself? Love is a principle ready, active, ingenuous, and constant: it studieth to do good, and would still do more: it is patient with the infirmities of others, which men void of love do aggravate into odiousness, and make them their excuse for all their neglects, and their pretence for all their cruelties. Could you make all the slanderers, backbiters, revilers, despisers, persecutors, to love their neighbours as themselves, you may easily judge what would be the effect; and whether they would revile, or prosecute, or imprison, or ruin themselves, or study how to make themselves odious, or suborn perjured witnesses against themselves.

3. Yea, he that will do good to many, must love many better than himself, and prefer the common good much before his own, and seek his own in the common welfare. He that loveth good, as good, will best love the best: and an honest old Roman would have called him an unworthy beast that preferred his estate, or life, before the common welfare. To be ready to do, suffer, or die, for their country, was a virtue which all extolled. A narrow-spirited, selfish man, will serve others no further than it serveth himself, or, at least, will stand with his own safety or prosperity. He will turn as the weathercock, and be for them that are for his worldly interest. I confess that God oft useth such for common good; but it is by raising such storms as would sink them with the ship, and leaving them no great hope to escape by being false, or by permitting such villanies as threaten their own interest. A covetous father may be against gaming and prodigality in his children; the men of this world are wise in their generation: many that have abbey lands will be against popery; and even atheists, and licentious men, may be loth to be slaves to politic priests, and to come under confession, and perhaps the inquisition; and those that have not sinned themselves into madness or gross delusions, will be loth to set up a foreign jurisdiction, and become the subjects of an unknown priest, if they can help it. God often useth vice against vice; and if no worldly, selfish men were the country's or the church's helpers, it must suffer, or trust to miracles.

But yet there is no trust to be put in these men further than their own interest must stand or fall with the common good. If God, and heaven, and conscience, be not more powerful with a man than worldly interest, trust him not against the stream and tide, or when he thinks he can make a better bargain for himself. He that will sell heaven and Christ for the world, will sell you for it, and sell his country for it, and sell religion, truth, and honesty for it: and if he escape here the end of Ahithophel and Judas, he will venture on all that is out of sight. Christ was the grand Benefactor to the world, and the most excellent Teacher of love, and self-denial, and contempt of the world, to all that will follow him in doing good to many.

4. He that will do much good must be good himself. Make the tree good if you would have good fruit. *Operari sequitur esse.* A bad man is an enemy to the greatest good that he should do. Malignity abhorreth serious piety, and will such promote it? If Elias be a man of miracles, he shall hear, "Hast thou found me, O my enemy!" And Micaiah shall hear, "I hate him, for he prophesieth not good of me, but evil: feed him with the bread and water of affliction."

And a bad man, if by accident he be engaged for a good cause, is still suspected by those that know him. They cannot trust him, as being a slave to lust, and to strong temptations, and a secret enemy to the true interest of his country. Alas! the best are hardly to be trusted far, as being liable to miscarry by infirmity; how little then is to be hoped for from the wicked!

5. He that will do much good in the world, must be furnished with considerable abilities, especially prudence and skill in knowing when, and to whom, and how to do it. Without this, he will do more harm than good. Even good men, when they have done much good, by some one miscarriage, tempted by the remnants of selfishness and pride, and by unskilful rashness, have undone all the good they did, and done as much hurt as wicked enemies. There goeth so much to public good, and so many snares are to be avoided, that rash, self-conceited, half-witted men do seldom do much, unless under the conduct of wiser men.

6. He that will be a public blessing to the world, must have a very large prospect, and see the state of all the world, and foresee what is like to come. He must not live as if his neighbourhood were all the land, or his country or his party were all the church, or all the world: he must know what relation all our actions have to other nations, and to all the church of Christ on earth. The want of this universal prospect involveth many in censorious and dividing sects, who would abhor that way if they knew the case of all the church and world.

And we must not look only to a present exigent or advantage, but foresee how our actions will look hereafter, and what changes may put them under other judgments, and what the fruits may be to posterity. Many things cause death which give the patient present ease.

7. He that will do good to many must have christian fortitude, and not be discouraged with difficulties and opposition. He must serve God for the good of men with absolute resolution, and not with the hypocrite's reserves. He must be armed with patience against not only the malice of enemies, but the ingratitude of friends. The follies, and quarrels, and mutinies, and divisions, and often the abuses of those that he would do good to, must not overcome him. He must imitate God, and do good to the evil, and bless those that curse him, and pray for them that despitefully use him. He must not promise himself more success than God hath promised him, nor yet despair and turn back discouraged; but conscience must carry him on to the end through all, whatever shall befall him.

8. Therefore he must look for his reward from God, and not expect too much from man. Men are insufficient, mutable, and uncertain: their interests and many accidents may change them. The multitude are of many minds and tempers; and if you please some, you shall displease others, and it is hard to please even one person long. Some great ones will not be pleased, unless you will prefer their wills before the will of God, your country's good, and your own salvation. The poor are so many and so indigent, that no man can answer their desires. If you give twenty pounds to twenty of the poor, forty, or a hundred, that expected the like, will murmur at you, and be displeased. What man ever did so much good in the world as not to be accused by some, as if he were a covetous or a hurtful man?

Therefore, he that will do much good, must firmly believe the life to come, and must do that he doth as the work of God, in obedience to him, and look for his reward in heaven, and not as the hypocrite, in the praise of men, much less as the worldling, in the hope of temporal advantage. He must not wonder if he be rewarded as Socrates was at Athens, and as Christ and his apostles were in the world. Themistocles likened himself to a great fruit tree, which men run for shelter under in a storm, and when the storm is over, they throw stones and cudgels at it, to beat down the fruit. Reckon not on a reward from men, but from God. By what is said, you may perceive what are the great impediments of doing good to many, which must be overcome.

I. One, and the worst, is malignity, which is an enmity to spiritual good; for who will promote that which he is against?

II. Another is unbelief of God's commands and promises, when men take not themselves to be his subjects and stewards, nor can take his promise for good security for their reward.

III. Another is the fore-mentioned sin of selfishness, which makes a man's self to be his chiefest love and care, and more to him than Christ's interest, or the church or kingdom.

IV. Another is a false conceit that a man is so obliged to provide for his children and kindred, that all that he can get, how rich soever he be, must be left to make them rich, except some inconsiderable pittance.

V. Another is a great neglect of parents to prepare their children to be profitable to the commonwealth, but only to live in prosperity to themselves. 1. Children should be taught as much as may be to become persons of understanding, and such wisdom as may make them useful. 2. And especially to be truly religious; for then they will be devoted to do good, in love and obedience to God. 3. They should be taught what it is to be members of societies, and what duty they owe to church and state, and how great a part of their duty lieth in caring for the common good, and how sinful and damnable it is to live only to themselves, and how much this selfishness is the sum of all iniquity. 4. Those callings should be chosen for them which they are fittest for, and in which they may do most public good.

VI. And a timorous, cowardly disposition is a great hinderance to public good; for such will be still for the self-saving way, and afraid of the dangers that attend the greatest duties. If they are called to liberality, they will fear lest they should want themselves. In all costly or hazardous duty there will still be a lion in their way. They cannot trust God; and no wonder, then, if they are not to be trusted themselves.

VII. Lastly, sloth and idleness are constant enemies to well-doing. There are two sorts especially guilty of this; one, and the better, is some religious people, who think that their business is only with God and their own hearts, and that if they could spend all their time in meditation, prayer, and such-like exercises, it would be the best kind of life on earth. Among the papists, multitudes, by this conceit, turn friars and nuns. Among us, such spend all their time in hearing sermons, and in reading, and meditating, and prayer, and such-like exercises of religion towards God, if they are but rich enough to live without bodily labour; and the example of Mary and Martha, they think, will make this good.

I know that this is no common error. The wicked are of a far different mind. And I know no man can do too much to save his soul: but we may do one sort of our work too much to the neglect of other parts. We have souls in flesh, and both parts have their proper necessity and work. Mary did somewhat else than hear, though she wisely preferred it in its season. And no one is made for himself alone. You feel that religious exercises do you good, but what good is it that you do to others? I confess a monk's prayers for others is a good work. But God will have praying and endeavouring go together, both for yourselves and others. Bare praying God to relieve the poor, and to teach your children, and instruct the ignorant, will not excuse you from relieving, teaching, or instructing them. Yea, and your own good will best come in by your fullest obedience to God. Do what he bids you, and he will take care of your salvation. Your own way may seem best, but will not prove best: it will but cast you into melancholy and disability at last. "Six days shalt thou labour," is more than a permission. It is St. Paul's canon, "He that will not work, (if able,) let him not eat:" and it was King Solomon's mother who taught him the description of a virtuous woman, Prov. xxxi. 27, "She eateth not the bread of idleness." God will have mercy and obedience as better than sacrifice. The sentence in judgment is upon doing good to Christ in his members, Matt. xxv.; when many that heard much, and prophesied, shall be cast out, Matt. vii. 21. Doing good is the surest way of receiving good. The duties of the first and second table must go together. He that is not zealous to do good, as well as to get good, hath not the peculiar nature of Christ's flock, Tit. ii. 14; and zeal will be diligent, and not for sloth.

2. The other sort of the idle are rich, ungodly, worldly persons, who live as if God did give them plenty for nothing but to pamper their own flesh, and feed their own and others' sensuality. They

think that persons of wealth and honour may lawfully spend their time in idleness, that is, in Sodom's sin, (Ezek. xvi. 49,) as if God expected least where he giveth most. How little conscience do many lords and ladies make of an idle hour, or life! When poor men's labour is such as tendeth to the common good, the rich, by luxury, sacrifice to the flesh the fruits of other men's endeavours; and instead of living in any profitable employment, devour that which thousands labour for.

It is not the toilsome drudgery of the vulgar which we take to be all rich folk's duty; but idleness and unprofitableness is a sin in the richest. Any of them may find good work enough that is fit for them if they be willing. Children, and servants, and friends, and neighbours, and tenants, have souls and bodies which need their help. None can say, God found us no work to do, or that God gave them more time or wealth than they had profitable use for. Little do they think what it will be, ere long, to reckon for all their time and estates, and to be judged according to their works: and their own flesh often payeth dear for its ease and pleasure, by those pains and diseases which God hath suited to their sins; and which usually shorten the lives which they no better use, or snatch them away from that time and wealth which they spent in preparing fuel for hell, and food for the worm that never dieth.

V. But what is it that a man should do that would do good to all or many? There are some good works which are of far greater tendency than others, to the good of many; some of them I will name to you.

I. Do as much good as you are able to men's bodies, in order to the greater good of souls. If nature be not supported, men are not capable of other good. We pray for our daily bread before pardon and spiritual blessings, not as if it were better, but that nature is supposed before grace, and we cannot be christians if we be not men; God hath so placed the soul in the body, that good or evil shall make its entrance by the bodily senses to the soul. This way God himself conveyeth many of his blessings, and this way he inflicteth his corrections; ministers that are able and willing to be liberal, find by great experience that kindness and bounty to men's bodies openeth their ear to counsel, and maketh them willing to hear instruction: those in France, that are now trying men's religion in the market, and are at work with money in one hand, and a sword in the other, do understand this to be true. All men are sensible of pain or pleasure, good or evil, to the flesh, before they are sensible what is necessary for their souls. You must therefore speak on that side which can hear, and work upon the feeling part, if you will do good.

Besides this, your charity may remove many great impediments and temptations. It is no easy thing to keep heavenly thoughts upon your mind, and especially to delight in God, and keep the relish of his law upon your hearts, while pinching wants are calling away your mind, and disturbing it with troublesome passions. To suffer some hunger, and go in vile apparel, is not very difficult; but when there is a family to provide for, a discontented wife and children to satisfy, rents, and debts, and demands unpaid, it must be an excellent christian that can live contentedly, and cast all his useless care on God, and keep up the sense of his love, and a delight in all his service. Do your best to save the poor from such temptations, as you would yourselves be saved from them.

And when you give to the poor that are ignorant and ungodly, give them after it some counsel for their souls, or some good book which is suited to their cases.

II. If you would do good to many, set yourselves to promote the practical knowledge of the great truths necessary to salvation.

1. Goodness will never be enjoyed or practised without knowledge. Ignorance is darkness, the state of his kingdom who is the prince of darkness, who by the works of darkness leadeth the blind world to utter darkness. God is the Father of lights, and giveth wisdom to them that ask and seek it: he sent his Son to be the light of the world; his word and ministers are subordinate light; his servants are all the children of light: ignorance is virtually error, and error the cause of sin and misery. And men are not born wise, but must be made wise by skilful, diligent teaching: parents should begin it, ministers should second them; but alas! how many millions are neglected by both! and how many neglect themselves, when ministers have done their best! Ignorance and error are the common road to wickedness, misery, and hell.

2. But what can any others do for such? Two things I will remember you of: 1. Set up such schools as shall teach children to read the Scriptures, and learn the catechism or principles of religion. Our departed friend, Mr. Thomas Gouge, did set us an excellent pattern for Wales. I think we have grammar schools enough. It is not the knowledge of tongues, and arts, and curious sciences, which the common people want, but the right understanding of their baptismal covenant with God, and of the creed, Lord's prayer, decalogue, and church communion. A poor honest man, or a good woman, will teach children thus much for a small stipend, better than they are taught it in most grammar schools; and I would none went to the universities without the sound understanding of the catechism; yea, I would none came thence, or into the pulpit, without it.

2. When you have got them to read, give them good books, especially Bibles, and good catechisms, and small practical books, which press the fundamentals on their consciences. Such books are good catechisms; many learn the words of the creed, Lord's prayer, commandments, and catechism, by rote, and never understand them, when a lively book that awakeneth their consciences, bringeth them to sensible consideration, and to a true understanding of the same things, which before they could repeat without sense or savour. It is the catechetical truths which most of our English sermons press; and the lively pressing them maketh them pierce deeper than a catechism.

If men that in life, or at death, give a stated revenue for good works, would settle the one half on a catechising English school, and the other half on some suitable good books, it might prove a very great means of public reformation. When a good book is in the house, if some despise it, others may read it; and when one parish is provided, every year's rent may extend the charity to other parishes, and it may spread over a whole country in a little time. Most of the good that God hath done for me, for knowledge or conscience, hath been by sound and pious books.

III. A great means of public good is the right ordering of families all the week, but especially on the Lord's day: though the ministry be the usual means of converting heathens and infidels, christian education by parents is the first means appointed by God for the holy principling of youth: parents must teach them with unwearied diligence, lying down and rising up, Deut. vi. 11. And they that will expect God's blessing must use his appointed means. Nature teacheth men and brutes to provide for their offspring with diligence and patience: and as grace teacheth believers to expect far greater things for themselves and their children than this world affordeth, so it obligeth them to be at so much greater diligence to obtain it. An everlasting kingdom deserveth more labour than a trade or full estate for the flesh. If all parents did their parts to make their children sanctified believers, as well as they expect the schoolmaster should do his part to make them scholars, and the master do his part to teach them their trades, we might hope that ministers would find them fitter for church work, and that godliness would not be so rare, nor so many wicked children break their parents' hearts. But of this I have spoken lately in my "Counsel to Young Men."

Religion is never like to prosper if it be not made a family work. If it be there made the chief business of the house, and done with reverent seriousness and constancy, if magistracy and ministry should fail, yet families would propagate and preserve it. Begin with a reverent begging the help and blessing of God, then read his word, and call upon his name; speak serious words of counsel to inferiors; spend the Lord's day as much as may be in public worship, and the rest in reading godly books, and in singing God's praise, and calling on his name; put suitable books into the hands of servants and children to read when they have leisure; encourage them in it with love and rewards; and keep them out of the way of temptation; and then God's blessing will dwell in your families, and they will be as churches of God. If any complain of negligent ministers, or persecuting magistrates, and will not do their own family duties, which none forbid, they condemn themselves.

IV. If you would be public blessings, and do good to many, do your best to procure a skilful, faithful ministry in the church.

1. Send no son to the university who doth not first show these three qualifications: a capable, natural wit and utterance; a love to serious, practical religion; a great desire to serve God in the ministry, though it should be in suffering from men. If they want any one of these, design them to some other calling; devote not an undisposed lad to the ministry, in hope that God will make him better, but stay till he is better.

2. Seeing pastors are here obtruded upon the flock, it is a work of great importance, for religious gentlemen to buy as many advowsons or presentations as they can, that they may introduce the best that they can get.

God hath hitherto made use of the qualifications of the ministers as the special means for the welfare of his church. The bare title and office is so far from sufficing, without the skill and fidelity of the persons, that such have been the great corrupters and disturbers of the church. When pious men have heaped up riches and honours on the clergy, these have been baits for the worst men to become seekers, and make the sacred ministry but a trade for wealth: and if carnal, worldly men be ministers, alas! what plagues may they be to the people and themselves! They will hate the spiritual practice of doctrine which they preach; when they have told men of a heaven and hell, and the necessity of a holy heart and life, as if they had been in jest, they will take those for hypocrites that believe them, and live accordingly: they will take the best of the flock for their enemies, because they are enemies to their hypocrisy and vice. Instead of imitating St. Paul, (Acts xx.) who taught them publicly, and from house to house, day and night, with tears, they will turn the ministry into compliment and formality, and think that by saying a cold, unskilful sermon, and by roting over a few heartless words, they have laudably performed their part. They will take those for their best hearers who will most honour them, and best pay them, though never so ignorant and ungodly; and their spleen will swell against the best and most religious people, because they dislike their unfaithful lives and ministration. If religion should be in public danger, these will be the Judases that will sell it for gain. They will do any thing rather than suffer much. They are ministers of the world, and not of Christ; readier to make crosses for others than to bear the cross of Christ; for it is gain that is their godliness: and when their treachery is seen and hated, they will hate the haters of it; and the studies of malignant men will be their laboratories, and the pulpits the place where the sublimate and essence of malice must be vended. How effectually will Satan's work be done when it is performed in the formalities of the sacred ministry, and in the name of Christ! Oh what hath the church suffered by a worldly, graceless ministry these thousand years and more! and what doth it yet suffer by them in the East and West!

But, on the other side, a skilful, faithful minister will preach sound doctrine, and worship God with serious devotion, and live to Christ and the church's good. He will speak the word of truth and life with truth and liveliness, as one that believeth what he saith, and feeleth the power of it on his heart. Though he must have food and raiment as other men, it is the saving and edifying of souls which is his work, to which he bendeth all his studies, for which he prayeth and longeth, and in which he rejoiceth, and to which all his worldly interest not only giveth place, but is made to serve. He will think no price, no pains or suffering, too dear, so that the souls of men be saved; this is the riches and preferment which he desireth. He hath nothing too good or too dear for Christ, or for the meanest of his servants, when Christ requireth it. He is willing to spend and be spent for their sakes. It is them, and not theirs, that he desireth. He feareth the unbelief and hard-heartedness of his hearers, and lest they should reject their own salvation, more than all the slanders or persecutions of the enemies. In a word, his heart, his study, his life and business, is to do all the good he can, and they that under such a ministry remain impenitent, and hardened in sin, are the most hopeless, miserable people in the world.

V. And it greatly conduceth to public good to keep up true order and christian discipline in the particular churches. Though popish church tyrants have turned the church keys into a military, reigning, or revenging sword, yet Christ did not in vain commit them into his ministers' hands. Religion seldom prospereth well where the church is no enclosure, but a common, where all sorts, undistinguished, meet; where, as the people know not who shall be made their pastors, but must trust their souls to the care of any that a patron chooseth, so the pastor knoweth not who are his communicating flock until he see them come to the Lord's table, no, nor when he seeth them. When it goeth for a sufficient excuse to the pastors if the rabble of wicked men communicate, or pass for his church members, though they communicate not, if he can but say, I knew them not to be wicked, (and how should he when he knew them not at all?) and that none accused them, when they are mere strangers to each other. In Christ Jesus, neither circumcision nor uncircumcision availeth any thing, but a new creature, and faith that worketh by love. And if Christ made his servants no better than the world, who would believe that he is the Saviour of the world? There will be some tares in Christ's field till his judgment cast them out for ever. But if it be not a society professing holiness, and disowning unholiness, and making a difference between the clean and the unclean, him that sweareth, and him that feareth an oath, him that serveth God, and him that serveth him not; Christ will disown them as workers of iniquity, though they had ate and drank with him, and done miracles in his name, Matt. vii. Much more if it be a society where godliness is despised, and the most godly excommunicated, if they differ but in a formality or ceremony from Diotrephes, and the wicked rabble tolerated and cherished in reviling serious godliness, on pretence of opposing such dissenters. Christ will not own that pastor nor society which owneth not conscience and serious piety.

If the pastors set up their wills and traditions before the laws and will of Christ, and call out, Who is on our side? instead of Who is on Christ's side? and fall out with the sheep, and worry and scatter them, and cherish the goats, and tolerate the wolves, woe to those shepherds, when Christ shall judge them! I wonder not if such incline to infidelity, though they live by the name and image of christianity, and if they be loth to believe that there will be such a day of judgment which they have so much cause to fear.

But the prudent, loving guidance of faithful pastors is so necessary to the church, that without it there will be envy and strife, confusion, and every evil work, and a headless multitude, though otherwise well-meaning, pious people, will be all wise, and all teachers, till they have no wise teachers left, and will crumble all into dissolution, or into shameful sects. St. Paul told us of two games that Satan hath to play, (Acts xx.) one by grievous wolves, that shall devour the flock, (though in sheep's clothing, yet known by their bloody jaws,) the other by men from among yourselves, who shall speak perverse things, to draw disciples after them.

VI. If you would promote the good of all or many, promote the love and concord of all that deserve to be called christians.

To which end you must, 1. Know who those are; and, 2. Skilfully and faithfully endeavour it.

1. Far be it from any christian to think that Christ hath not so much as told us what christianity is, and who they be that we must take for christians, when he hath commanded them all so earnestly to love each other. Is not baptism our christening? Every one that hath entered into that covenant with Christ, and understandingly and seriously professeth to stand to it, and is not proved by inconsistent words or deeds to nullify that profession, is to be taken for a christian, and used in love and communion as such.

Consider of these words, and consider whether all churches have walked by this rule, and whether swerving from it have not been the cause of corruption and confusion.

He is a christian fit for our communion, who is baptized in infancy, and owneth it solemnly at age; and so is he that was not baptized till he himself believed.

He is a christian that believeth Christ to be true God and true man in one person, and trusteth him as our only Redeemer, by his merits and passion, and our Mediator in the heavens; and obeyeth him as our sovereign Lord, for pardon, for his Spirit, and for salvation. And as a christian this man is to be loved and used, though he have not so much skill in metaphysics as to know whether it be a proper speech to call Mary the mother of God, or that one of the Trinity was crucified; or to know in what sense Christ's natures might be called one or two; and in what sense he might be said to have one will or two wills—one operation or two; and know not whether the *tria capitula* were to be condemned; yea, though he could not define, or clearly tell, what *hypostasis, persona*, yea, or *substantia*, signifieth in God; nor tell whether "God of gods" be a proper speech.

This man is a christian, though he know not whether patriarchal, and metropolitical, and diocesan church forms, be according to the will of Christ, or against it; and whether symbolical signs in the worship of God may lawfully be devised and imposed by men; and whether some doubtful words, in oaths and subscriptions of men's imposing, being unnecessary, be lawful; and how far he may, by them, incur the guilt of perjury, or deliberate lying: and though he think that a minister may preach and pray in fit words of his own, though he read not a sermon or prayer written for him by others, who think that no words but theirs should be offered to God or man.

2. If Christ's description of a christian be forsaken, and mere christianity seem not a sufficient qualification for our love and concord, men will never know where to rest, nor ever agree in any one's determination but Christ's. All men that can get power will be making their own wills the rule and law, and others will not think of them as they do; and the variety of fallible, mutable church laws, and terms of concord, will be the engine of perpetual discord, as Ulpian told honest Alexander Severus the laws would be, which he thought to have made for sober concord, in fashions of apparel. Those that are united to Christ by faith, and have his sanctifying Spirit, and are justified by him, and shall dwell with him in heaven, are certainly christians; and such as Christ hath commanded us to love as ourselves. And seeing that it is his livery by which his disciples must be known, by loving one another, and the false prophets must be known by the fruits of their hurtfulness, as wolves, thorns, and thistles, I must profess (though order and government have been so amiable to me as to tempt me to favourable thoughts of some Roman power in the church) I am utterly irreconcilable to it, when I see that the very complexion of that hierarchy is malice and bloodiness against men most seriously and humbly pious, that dare not obey them in their sinful usurpations, and that their cause is maintained by belying, hating, and murdering true christians.

And, on the other side, too many make laws of love and communion to themselves, and confine Christ's church within their little various, and perhaps erroneous, sects; and all others they love with pity; but only those of their cabin and singular opinions they love with complacency and communion: those that condemn such as Christ justifieth, and say that christians are not his, are near of kin to one another, though one sort show it by persecution, and the other but by excommunication, or schismatical separation. "We are all one in Christ Jesus," Gal. iv. 28. And, therefore, I advise all christians to hate the causes and ways of hatred, and love all the causes and means of love. Frown on them that so extol their singular sentiments as to backbite others, and speak evil of what they understand not: especially such as the pamphleteers of this age, whose design is weekly and daily to fight against christian love, and to stir up all men, to the utmost of their power, to think odiously of one another, and plainly to stir up a thirst after blood; never did Satan write by the hand of man if he do it not by such as these: the Lord of love and mercy rebuke them!

And take heed of them that can find enough in the best that are against their way to prove them dishonest, if not intolerable; and can see the mote of a ceremony, or nonconformity to a ceremony, in their brother's eye, and not the beam of malice, or cruelty, in their own. Take heed of those that are either for confounding toleration of all, or for dissipating cruelty on pretence of unity.

That land, or church, shall never truly prosper where these three sorts are not well distinguished: 1. The approved, that are to be encouraged. 2. The tolerable, that are to be patiently and lovingly endured. 3. The intolerable, that are to be restrained. They may as well confound men and beasts, wise men and mad-men, adults and infants, as confound these three sorts, in reference to religion.

I add this note to prevent objections, that though meekness and gentleness promote peace; yet, to speak sharply and hatefully of hatred, unpeaceableness, and cruelty, and all that tends to destroy love, is an act of love, and not of an uncharitable, unpeaceable man.

VII. If you love the common good of England, do your best to keep up sound and serious religion in the public parish churches, and be not guilty of any thing that shall bring the chief interest of religion into private assemblies of men only tolerated, if you can avoid it.

Indeed, in a time of plagues, and epidemical infection, tolerated churches may be the best preservatives of religion, as it was in the first 300 years, and in the Arians' reign, and under popery; but where sound and serious religion is owned by the magistrate, tolerated churches are but as hospitals for the sick, and must not be the receptacle of all the healthful. And, doubtless, if the papists can but get the protestant interest once into prohibited or tolerated conventicles, (as they will call them,) they have more than half overcome it, and will not doubt to use it next as they do in France, and by one turn more to cast it out. The countenance of authority will go far with the vulgar against all the scruples that men of conscience stick at, and they will mostly go to the allowed churches, whoever is there. Let us, therefore, lose no possession that we can justly get, nor be guilty of disgracing the honest conformists, but do all we can to keep up their reputation for the good of souls: they see not matters of difference through the same glass that we do; they think us unwarrantably scrupulous: we think the matter of their sin to be very great; but we know that before God the degree of guilt is much according to the degree of men's negligence or unwillingness to know the truth, or to obey it; and prejudice, education, and converse, maketh great difference on men's apprehensions. Charity must not reconcile us to sin, but there is no end of uncharitable censuring each other.

It hath made me admire to hear some men's words against comprehension, as they call it; that they would not have rulers revoke that which they judge to be heinous sin in their impositions, unless they will revoke all that they think unlawful, lest it should strengthen the parish churches, and weaken the tolerated or suffering part. I will not here open the sin of this policy as it deserves; but I wish them to read a small book called, "The Whole Duty of Nations," said to be Mr. Thomas Beverley's.

VIII. If you love the common good, take heed lest any injuries tempt you into sedition or unlawful wars; no man, that never tried them, can easily believe what enemies wars and tumults are to religion, and to common honesty and sobriety. Men are there so serious about their lives and bodily safety that they have no room or time for serious worshipping of God; the Lord's day is by necessity made a common day; and all men's goods are almost common to the will of soldiers: either power seems to authorize them, or necessity to allow them, to use the goods of others as their own; as if they were uncapable of doing wrong; it is their honour that can kill most; and how little place there is for love it is easy to conceive.

I doubt not but it is lawful to fight for our king or country, in a good cause. As nature giveth all private men a right of private self-defence, and no more, so the same law of nature, which is God's law, giveth all nations a right of public self-defence against its public enemies; that is, against any that by his religion, or his own profession, bindeth himself to destroy that nation if he can, or by open arms seeketh no less than their destruction; but as few calamities are worse to a land than war, so much is to be endured to prevent it. It is like a red-hot iron which fools lay hold on, thinking it is gold, till it fetch off skin and flesh to the bones, and perhaps set the house on fire. If your cause be bad, God will not be for you; and he that so taketh the sword shall perish with the sword; and if you bite and devour one another, you shall be devoured one of another. And, alas! thousands of the innocent usually perish, or are ruined, in the flames which furious men do kindle; no doubt as suffering in prison, so venturing in war, is a duty, when God calls you to it; but in itself a prison is a far more desirable sort of suffering than a war. Therefore, between the danger of the miseries of an unlawful war, and the danger of betraying our king or kingdom, for want of necessary defence, how cautelous should all sober christians be!

IX. If you would promote the common good, do your best to procure wise and faithful rulers.

Quest. What can private men do in this?

Answ. 1. In cases where they have choosing voices they ought to prefer the best with greatest resolution, and not for slothfulness to omit their part, nor for worldly interest, or the fear of men, betray their country, as ever they would escape the punishment of the perfidious. Woe to that Judas that sells his country and conscience for any bribe, or by self-saving fear!

2. In other cases, where you have no choosing vote with men, you have a praying voice with God: pray for kings, and all in authority, that we may live a quiet and peaceable life, in all godliness and honesty. God hath commanded no duty in vain: do it earnestly and constantly, and hope for a good issue from God; do it not selfishly that you may have prosperity or preferment by them, but sincerely for their own and the common good. God is the fountain of power, the absolute Sovereign of all the world: men are but his provincial officers; none claimeth a universal government of the world but one that pretendeth to be Christ's vicar-general, and none believe his claim but blinded men. There is no power but of and under God, who hath made rulers his ministers for our good, to be a praise to them that do well, and a terror to evil-doers; that they that will not be moved with the hopes of God's future rewards, and the fears of his punishments, may be moved by that which is near them, within the reach of sense. And all men regard their bodies, though only believers are ruled by the everlasting interest of their souls.

Therefore, pray hard for kings and magistrates; for if they be good they are exceeding great blessings to the world. They will remember that their power is for God, and the common good, and that to

God they must give a strict account; they will take God's law for the only universal law to the world, and conform their own as by-laws to it. They will take their own interest to consist in pleasing God, and promoting the gospel and kingdom of Christ, and the piety and saving of men's souls. They will be examples of serious godliness, of justice and sobriety, trustiness, and temperance, and chastity, to their subjects; in their eyes a vile person will be contemned, but they will honour those that fear the Lord, Psal. xv. 4. They will love those most that love Christ best, and most diligently obey him, and tenderly fear to sin against him: those please him best that please God best, and are most useful to the common good. They will set their hearts on the people's welfare, and are watching for all, while all securely live under their vigilancy. They will cherish all that Christ cherisheth, and especially the faithful pastors of the churches, that seek not the world, but the welfare of the flocks: when some are saying, In this mountain we must worship God, and some at Jerusalem, they will teach them all to worship God in spirit and truth. When pastors and people grow peevish and quarrelsome for their several interests, opinions, and wills, a Constantine will cast all their libels into the fire, and rebuke the unpeaceable, and restrain the violent, and teach them to forgive and love each other, and will be the great justice of peace to all the churches in the land, and pare their nails that would tear and scratch their brethren; he will countenance the sound and peaceable, and tolerate all the tolerable, but will tie the hands of strikers, and the tongues of revilers; he will contrive the healing of exasperated minds, and take away the occasions of division, and rebuke them that call for fire from heaven, or for the sword, to do that which belongeth to the word, or to execute their pride and wrath: godliness will have all the encouragement they can give it, and innocency a full defence; malignity, and persecution, and perjury, and unpeaceable revenge, will be hateful where they rule; and they had rather men feared sin too much than too little; and would have all men prefer the law and honour of God to theirs: where the righteous bear rule, the people rejoice. The wisdom, piety, and impartiality of their governors suppresseth profaneness, oppression, and contention, and keepeth men in the way of love and peace; and as the welfare of all is the care of such a ruler above his own pleasure, wealth, or will, so he will have the hearts, and hands, and wealth of all with readiness to serve him: no wonder if such are called nursing-fathers, and the light of our eyes, and the breath of our nostrils, and the shadow of a rock in a weary land. As they bear the image of God's supereminency, and doubly honour him, they are doubly honoured by him; so that the names of pious princes show not only the sense of mankind, but the special providence of God in making the memory of the just to be blessed; and as they could not endure to see in their days ungodliness triumph, or serious godliness made a scorn, or conscience and fear of sinning made a disgrace, or the gospel hindered, and faithful ministers forbid to preach it; so God will not suffer their consciences to want the sense of his love, nor their departing souls to fail of their everlasting hopes, nor their memories to be clouded by obscurity or reproach. Even among heathens what a name have those emperors left behind them who lived in justice, charity, and all virtue, and wholly studied the good of all! What a wonder is it that M. Antonine should be so extolled by so many writers, and not one of them all, that I remember, speak one word of evil of him, save that a small, short persecution of the christians was made by some in his time, till he restrained it! And all the people almost deified him, and would have perpetuated his line and name in the throne, but that the horrid wickedness of his posterity forced them to a change. What a name hath excellent Alexander Severus left behind him! And what a blessing have wise, and godly, and peace-making christian princes been in divers ages to the world!

And both the inferior magistrates and the clergy usually much conform themselves, at least in outward behaviour, to their example; for they will choose men of wisdom, conscience, and justice, under them, to judge and govern. The bishops and pastors which they choose will be able, godly, laborious men; not seekers of worldly wealth and honour, nor envious silencers of faithful preachers, nor jealous hinderers of religious duties, nor flattering men-pleasers, nor such as lord it over God's heritage; but such as rule not by constraint, but willingly, as examples of love and piety to the flock. Pray hard, therefore, for kings, and all in authority, and honour all such as unspeakable blessings for the good of all.

But, on the contrary, wicked rulers will be Satan's captains against Jesus Christ, and men's sanctification and salvation. They will be wolves in the place of shepherds, and will study to destroy the best of the people, and to root out all serious godliness and justice. Conscience, and fearing sin, will be to them a suspected, yea, a hated thing. If any abuse it, it serves them for a pretence against it. They take the people's welfare and their own interest to be enemies, and presently look on these, whom they should rule and cherish, as the adversaries whom they must tread down. They will purposely make edicts and laws that are contrary to God's law, that they may have advantage to persecute the faithful, and to destroy them as disobedient. They will study to conquer conscience and obedience to God, lest his authority should be regarded above theirs; and Christ is used by them as if he were a usurper, and not their Sovereign, but were again to be taken for an enemy to Cæsar; and their hatred to true ministers will be such as Paul's accusers intimate, who said, "He preached another king, one Jesus." Wicked rulers will be the capital enemies to all that will be enemies to wickedness, and resolved to please God and save their souls. They will not be obeyed under God, but before him, nor served by the faithful servants of Christ, nor pleased but at the rate of men's damnation, by displeasing God. All men love their like. The worst men, if flatterers, will seem the best to them, and the best the worst and most intolerable, and church and state is like to be written by their copy. Oh what dreadful plagues have wicked rulers been to the world, and what a dismal case do they continue the earth in to this day! Not but that people, and especially priests, do contribute hereto, but the chief authors are men in greatest power. Five parts of six of the world at this day are heathens and infidels. And what is the cause? Rulers will not suffer the gospel to be preached to them. The eastern christians were all torn in pieces by the wickedness and contention of the governors of the state and church, banishing and murdering one another; so that when the Turks invaded them, the promise of liberty to exercise their religion tempted them to make the less resistance, thinking they could not be much worse than before. But the vulgar are so apt to follow the rulers, that ever since, the most of the Easterns are apostatized from Christ, and turned to Mahometanism; though in those countries where the Turk alloweth the christian people to have governors of their own, religion somewhat prospereth, yet where that privilege is denied them, and Turks only are their rulers, it withereth away, and comes to almost nothing.

And what keepeth out reformation, that is, the primitive simple christianity, from the popish countries that have religion corrupted by human superfluities, but the seduction of priests, and the tyranny of rulers, that will not endure the preaching of the gospel, and the opening of the Scriptures to the people in a known tongue? How much holy blood have Roman and Spanish inquisitors, and French and Irish murderers, and most other popish rulers, to answer for! Even Walsh, the papist, in his Irish history, tells us all, out of Ketin and others, how commonly, for ages, they lived there in the sin of bloody wars and murders, yea, even when they professed greatest holiness. Wicked rulers are as the pikes in the pond, which live by devouring all about them. It is Satan's main design in the world to corrupt God's two great ordinances of magistracy and ministry, and turn them both against Christ's kingdom, and to destroy christians in Christ's name. Oh! therefore, pray hard that all christian nations may have good rulers, and be very thankful to God for such.

X. And if you would be instruments of public good, know what are public sins and dangers, that you may do your part against them, and join not with any that will promise never to endeavour any reforming alteration. The chiefest are ignorance, pride, and self-willedness in teachers and people, malignant enmity to goodness, impatience with the infirmities of good men, judging of persons and things by self-interest, covetousness, sensuality, and taking christianity but as the religion of the land, without diligent study to be rooted in the truth. And the scandals of hypocrites and tempted christians hardening the enemies, especially by divisions, and public temerities, and miscarriages, is not the least.

XI. I would also, in order to public good, persuade serious christians to be more zealous in communication with their neighbours, and live not over-strangely to others, and say not as Cain, "Am I my brother's keeper?" Be kind and loving to all about you, and live not as unknown men to them; nor alienate them by sourness, contempt, or needless singularity, but become all things lawful, to all men, to save some; lend them good books, and draw them to hear God's faithful ministers; persuade them to pray in their families, even with a form or book, till they need it not.

XII. Lastly, if you would do good, be such as you would have others be, and teach them by examples of piety, charity, patience, self-denial, forbearing, and forgiving, and not by mere words contradicted by your lives. These are the materials by which you must do good to all.

VI. What now remaineth but that we all set ourselves to such a fruitful course of life? I greatly rejoice in the grace of God, which I daily see in many such of my familiar acquaintance, who study to do good to all, and to live in love, and peace, and holiness, by example, and by self-denial, and constant charity, using Christ's talents to their Master's ends, for the temporal and eternal good of many. But, alas! too many live as if it were enough to do no harm, and say, as the slothful servant, "Here is thy talent which I hid."

And some there be that, in a blind jealousy of the doctrine of justification, (not understanding what the word justification signifieth,) cry down even the words of James, as if they were irreconcilable with Paul's, and can scarce bear him that saith as Christ, (Matt. xii.) "By thy words thou shalt be justified, and by thy words thou shalt be condemned;" as if they had never read, "Well done, good and faithful servant," &c.; "For I was hungry, and ye fed me," &c.; nor Heb. v. 9, "He is the author of eternal salvation to all them that obey him;" or, Heb. xiii. "With such sacrifice God is well pleased;" or, "He that doeth righteousness is righteous;" or that "we shall be judged according to our works;" or, Rev. xxii. 14, "Blessed are they that do his commandments, that they may have right to the tree of life, and may enter in by the gates into the city;" or, Gal. vi. 7, 8, "What a man soweth, that shall he reap. He that soweth to the Spirit, of the Spirit shall reap everlasting life:" with many such.

No man well in his wits can think that any thing we do can merit of God in commutative justice, as if he received any thing from us. This were even to deny God to be God. But are we not under a law of grace? And doth not that law command us obedience, and the improvement of our talents in doing good? And shall we not be judged by that law? And what is judging, but justifying or condemning? No works of ours can stand the trial by the law of innocency or works, but only the perfect righteousness of Christ. But he that is accused of final impenitency, infidelity, hypocrisy, or unholiness, if truly accused, shall never be justified, and if falsely, must be justified against that charge by somewhat besides what is done out of him by Jesus Christ.

It is an easier thing to be zealous for an opinion, which is sound, or supposed such, about works and grace, than to be zealous of good works, or zealously desirous of grace. How sad use did Satan make of men's zeal for orthodox words, when the Nestorian, Eutychian, and Monothelite controversies were in agitation! He went for a hollow-hearted neuter that did not hereticate one side or other. And I would that factious, ignorant zeal were not still alive in the churches. How many have we heard on one side reviling Lutherans, Calvinists, Arminians, episcopalians, presbyterians, independents, &c. to render them odious, that never understand the true state of the difference! And how fiercely do some papists and others cry down solifidians, and persuade men that we are enemies to good works, or think that they are not necessary to salvation, (because some rashly maintained that in a faction against George Major, long ago,) or at least that they are no further necessary, but as signs to prove that which God knoweth without them! And, on the other side, how many make themselves and others believe that the true expositors of Saint James's words are almost papists, and teach men dangerously to trust to works for their justification, while they understand not what either of the apostles mean by justification, faith, or works. Many so carefully avoid trusting to good works, that they have none or few to trust to. No doubt nothing of man must be trusted to for the least part that belongs to Christ, but all duty and means must be both used and trusted for its own part.

Consider well these following motives, and you will see why all christians must be zealous of doing all the good they can.

1. It rendereth a man likest to God to be good, and to do good; on which account Christ requireth it even towards our enemies, (Matt. v.) that we may be perfect, as our heavenly Father is perfect, who doth good even to the unjust; and he that is likest God is the best man, most holy, and most happy, and shall have most communion with God.

2. And when Christ came down in flesh to call man home by making God better known to the

world, he revealeth him in his attractive goodness, and that was by his own beneficence to man. He came to do the greatest good; to be the Saviour of the world, and to reconcile revolted man to God; and all his life, yea, his death and heavenly intercession, is doing good to those that were God's enemies. And to learn of Christ, and imitate his example, is to be his true disciples. And what else do his laws command us? They are all holy, just, and good; and our goodness is to love them, and obey them. By keeping these we must show that we are his disciples. When he tells you who you must do good to, in the instance of the Samaritan, he addeth, "Go thou and do likewise," John xv. He largely tells us of what importance it is for every branch that is planted into him to bring forth fruit.

3. It is much of the end of all the sanctifying operations of the Holy Spirit. Grace is given us to use; even natural powers are given us for action. What the better were man for a tongue, or hands, or feet, if he should never use them? Life is a principle of action. It were as good have no life, as not to use it. And why doth God make men good, but that they may do good, even in their duty to God, themselves, and one another?

4. It is God's great mercy to mankind, that he will use us all in doing good to one another; and it is a great part of his wise government of the world, that in societies men should be tied to it by the sense of every particular man's necessity; and it is a great honour to those that he maketh his almoners, or servants, to convey his gifts to others; God bids you give nothing but what is his, and no otherwise your own than as his stewards. It is his bounty, and your service or stewardship, which is to be exercised. He could have done good to all men by himself alone, without you, or any other, if he would; but he will honour his servants to be the messengers of his bounty. You best please him when you readily receive his gifts yourselves, and most fully communicate them to others. To do good, is to receive good; and yet he will reward such for doing and receiving.

5. Self-love, therefore, should persuade men to do good to all. You are not the least gainers by it yourselves. If you can trust Christ, sure you will think this profitable usury. Is not a cup of cold water well paid for, when Christ performs his promise? And is it not a gainful loss which is rewarded in this life a hundred-fold, and in the world to come with life eternal?

Those that live in the fullest exercise of love, and doing good, are usually most loved, and many are ready to do good to them. And this exercise increaseth all fruitful graces: and there is a present delight in doing good, which is itself a great reward. The love of others makes it delightful to us; and the pleasing of God, and the imitation of Christ, and the testimony of conscience, make it delightful. An honest physician is far gladder to save men's lives or health, than to get their money. And an honest soldier is gladder to save his country, than to get his pay. Every honest minister of Christ is far gladder to win souls, than to get money or preferment. The believing giver hath more pleasure than the receiver; and this without any conceit of commutative meriting of God, or any false trust to works for justification.

6. Stewards must give account of all. What would you wish were the matter of your true account, if death or judgment were to-morrow? Would you not wish you had done all the good you could? Do you believe that all shall be judged according to their works? Did you ever well study that great prediction of Christ? Matt. xxv.

And it is some part of a reward on earth, that men that do much good, especially that to whole nations, are usually honoured by posterity, however they be rewarded by the present age.

7. Every true christian is absolutely devoted to do good. What else is it to be devoted to God, our Creator and Redeemer? What live we for, or what should we desire to live for, but to do good?

II. But this exhortation is especially applicable to them that have special opportunity.

I. Magistrates are the capitals in the societies and public affairs of mankind. They are placed highest that they may have a universal influence. Though it be too high a word to call them gods, or God's vicegerents, (unless *secundum quid*,) yet they are his officers and regent ministers; but it is for the common good. In them God shows what order can do in the government of the world. As the placing of the same figure before many, doth accordingly advance its value in signification, so it is a wonder to note what the place of one man signifieth at the head of an army, of a city, of a kingdom. They are appointed by God to govern men in a just subordination to God's government, and not otherwise. To promote obedience to God's laws by theirs, and by their judgment and execution to give men a foretaste what they may at last expect from God; and by their rewards and punishments to foretell men whom God will reward and punish; and by their own examples to show the subjects how temperately, and soberly, and godly, God would have them live. Atheists can see and fear a magistrate, that fear not God, because they know him not.

They that prefer those as the most worthy of honour whom God abhorreth for their wickedness, and hate and oppress those whom God will honour, do show themselves enemies to him that giveth them all their power. And they that by countenance or practice do teach men to despise the fear of God, and to make light of drunkenness, whoredom, lying, perjury, and such-like odious crimes, do, in a sort, blaspheme God himself, as if he who exalted them were a lover of sin, and a hater of his own laws and service. There are few rulers that are unwilling of power, or to be accounted great; and do they not know, that it is a power to do good that God has given them; and that obligation to do it is as essential to their office as authority? and that they who govern as the officers of God, and pretend to be liker him in greatness than their subjects, must also be liker to him in wisdom and goodness?

Woe to that man who abuseth and oppresseth the just and faithful in the name of God, and by pretence of authority from him to do it! Woe to him that in God's name, and as by his authority, countenanceth the wicked whom God abhorreth, and under Christ's banner fighteth against him! As Christ saith of the offensive, "It were good for that man that he had never been born." Prov. xxiv. 24, "He that saith to the wicked, Thou art righteous, him shall the people curse; nations shall abhor him." Prov. xvii. 15, "He that justifieth the wicked, and he that condemneth the just, even they both are an abomination to the Lord."

God looketh for great service from great men; great trust and talents must have great account; a prince, a lord, a ruler, must do much more good, in promoting piety, conscience, virtue, than the best inferiors; to whom men give much, from them they expect the more. It greatly concerneth such men seriously to ask their conscience, Can I do no more to encourage godliness, conscience, and justice, and to disgrace malignity, brutish sensuality, and fleshly lusts, than I have done? Oh when they must hear,

"Give account of thy stewardship, thou shalt be no longer steward," little think many rulers what an account it is that will be required of them! Oh what a deal of good may the rulers of the earth do, if, instead of over-minding their partial interests, and serving the desires of the flesh, they did but set themselves with study and resolution to promote the common good, by disgracing sin, and encouraging wisdom, piety, and peace! And where this is not sincerely done, as surely as there is a righteous God, and a future judgment, they shall pay for their omissive treachery. And if Satan do prevail to set his own captains over the armies of the Lord, to betray them to perdition, they shall be deepest in misery, as they were in guilt. One would think the great delight that is to be found in doing good to all, should much more draw men to desire authority and greatness, than either riches, or voluptuousness, or a domineering desire that all men should fulfil their wills.

II. The ministers of Christ also have the next opportunity to do good to many; and it is a debt that by many and great obligations they owe to Christ and men. But it will not be done without labour, and condescension, and unwearied patience. It is undertaken by all that are ordained to this office, but oh that it were performed faithfully by all! What a doleful life would the perfidious soul-betrayers live, if they knew what a guilt they have to answer for! even the contempt of the people's souls, and of the blood of Christ that purchased them! O hear that vehement adjuration, (2 Tim. iv. 1, 2,) "I charge thee before God and the Lord Jesus Christ, who shall judge the quick and the dead at his appearing and kingdom, preach the word; be instant, in season and out of season; reprove, rebuke, exhort, with all long-suffering and doctrine." Speak with holy studied skill; speak with love and melting pity; speak with importunity; take no denial; speak as St. Paul, (Acts xx.) publicly, and from house to house; speak before you are silenced in the dust; speak before death have taken away your hearers. It is for souls, it is for Christ, it is for yourselves too: while you have opportunity, do good to all. But of this I have formerly said more in my "Reformed Pastor."

III. And let all men take their common and special opportunities to do good: time will not stay; yourselves, your wives, your children, your servants, your neighbours, are posting to another world; speak now what you would have them hear; do them now all the good you can. It must be now or never; there is no returning from the dead to warn them. O live not as those infidels, who think it enough to do no harm, and to serve their carnal minds with pleasure, as born for nothing but a decent and delightful life on earth! You are all the vineyard or harvest of the Lord; work while it is day, the night is at hand when none can work: woe to the slothful, treacherous hypocrite when the judgment cometh!

Stay not till you are entreated to do good; study it, and seek it. Give while there are men that need, and while you have it, especially to the household of faith. Fire and thieves may deprive you of it; at the furthest, death will quickly do it. Happy are they that know their day, and, trusting in Christ, do study to serve him in doing good to all.

And the doctrine in hand doth further teach us some consectaries which all do not well consider.

I. That living chiefly to the flesh in worldly prosperity, and dropping now and then some small good on the by, to quiet conscience, is the property of a hypocrite. But to sound christians, fruitfulness in doing good is the very trade of their lives, of which they are zealous, and which they daily study.

II. That all christians should be very careful to avoid doing public hurt: it woundeth conscience to be guilty of wronging of any one man: we find it in dying men, that cannot die in peace till they have confessed wrongs, and made satisfaction, and asked forgiveness. And who knoweth but the many apparitions that have certainly been on such occasions, may be done by miserable souls, to seek some ease of the torment of their own consciences? But to hurt many, even whole parishes, cities, churches, kingdoms, how much more grievous will it prove! And yet, alas! how quickly may it be done! and how ordinarily it is done! What grievous mischief may even well-meaning men do by one mistaken practice, or rash act! by the fierce promoting one error; by letting loose one passion, or carnal affection; by venturing once on secret sin; yea, by one rash, sinful word! How much more if they are drawn and set in an unlawful interest and way! And little know we when a spark is kindled how it will end, or how many ways Satan hath to improve it. And one hurtful action, or unwarrantable way, may blast abundance of excellent endowments, and make such a grievous damage to the church, who else might have been an eminent blessing. And if good men may do so much hurt, what have the enemies of godliness to answer for, who, by worldliness and malignity, are corrupters, dividers, and destroyers?

III. The text plainly intimateth that it is a great crime in them, that instead of doing good while they have opportunity, think it enough to leave it by will to their executors to do it. When they have lived to the flesh, and cannot take it with them, they think it enough to leave others to do that good which they had not a heart to do themselves; but a treasure must be laid up in heaven beforehand, and not be left to be sent after, Matt. vi. 20, 21; and he that will make friends of the mammon of unrighteousness must now be rich towards God, Luke xii. 21; it is no victory over the world to leave it when you cannot keep it; nor will any legacy purchase heaven for an unholy, worldly soul.

IV. Yet they that will do good neither living nor dying are worst of all. Surely the last acts of our lives, if possible, should be the best; and as we must live in health, so also in sickness, and to the last in doing all the good we can; and, therefore, it must needs be a great sin to leave our estates to those that are like to do hurt with them, or to do no good, so far as we are the free disposers of them.

The case, I confess, is not without considerable difficulties, how much a man is bound to leave to his children, or his nearest kindred, when some of them are disposed to live unprofitably, and some to live ungodlily and hurtfully. Some think men are bound to leave them nothing; some think they ought to leave them almost all; and some think that they should leave them only so much as may find them tolerable food and raiment. I shall do my best to decide the case in several propositions.

1. The case is not with us as it was with the Israelites, who might not alienate their inheritances from the tribes; yet even they had power to prefer a younger son, that was more deserving, before an elder, that was worse.

2. Where either law or contract have disabled a man to alienate his estate from an ungodly heir, there is no room for a doubt what he must do.

3. Nature teacheth all men to prefer a child that is pious and hopeful in his provisions and legacies, before a stranger that is somewhat better, and not to alienate his estate for want of a higher degree of goodness.

4. When there is just cause to disinherit an elder

son, a younger is to be preferred before a stranger; or a kinsman, if there be no tolerable son.

5. And a son that ought not to be trusted with riches, or a great estate, yet ought to have food and raiment; (unless he come to that state of obstinate rebellion in sin, for which God's law commanded the Israelites to bring forth their sons to be put to death; in such cases the house of correction is fittest for them;) yet should he have such food as may humble him, and not to gratify his lust.

6. If a man that hath the full power to dispose of his estate, real or personal, have sons and kindred, that according to the judgment of sound reason, are like, if they had his estate, to do mischief with it, or maintain them in a wicked life, or in a mere unprofitable life of idleness, living only to themselves, and fleshly ease and pleasure, that man ought to give his estate from such to some that are liker to do good with it, and to use it for God, and the public benefit.

This is much contrary to the common course of most, that think no estate too great for their heirs, nor any portion too great for their daughters, be they what they will, or what use soever they are like to make of it: but these following reasons prove it to be true.

1. Every man hath his estate from God, and for God, and is bound, as his steward, accordingly to use it. This is past doubt; and how doth that man use it for God, who leaveth it to one that is liker to use it for the devil, in a fleshly, unprofitable life? What account can such a steward give? Did God give it you to maintain idleness and sin?

Object. Oh, but it is a son whom I am bound to provide for. *Answ.* Are you more bound to your son than to yourself? God doth not allow you to spend it on yourself, to maintain idleness and vice. Rom. xiii. 13, 14, "Make no provision for the flesh to satisfy the lust (or will) thereof." And may you leave it for such a use as is forbidden both your son and you? It is God that is the owner of it, and it is to him that you must both use and leave it: "Whether you eat or drink, or whatever you do, do all to the glory of God." And will you leave it to be the fuel of lust and sin?

Object. I leave it not for sin; but if he misuse it I cannot help it. *Answ.* Would that excuse you if you put a sword into a mad-man's hand to say, I cannot help it if he use it ill? You might have helped it; it is supposed that you foreknew how he was like to use it.

Object. But he may prove better hereafter, as some do. *Answ.* It is not bare possibilities that must guide a wise man's actions when probability is against them. Would you commit your children to the care of a mad-man, or a knave, because he may possibly come to his wits, or become honest? Have you not long tried him, and have you not endeavoured to cure him of his idleness, wickedness, or lust? If it be not done, what ground have you to presume it will be done when you are dead? You may have so much hope as not utterly to despair of him, but that will not allow you to trust him with that which God made you steward of for his use and service.

But if such hopes may be gratified, give your estate in trust to some conscionable friend, with secret order to give it your son, or kinsman, if he become hereafter fit to use it according to the ends for which God giveth it.

Reas. 2. The obligation in my text of doing good to all, extendeth to the end of our lives, and, therefore, to our last will and testament. Therefore, you must make your wills so as may do good to all, and not to cherish sin and idleness.

Reas. 3. You are bound to do your best to destroy sin and idleness, and, therefore, not to feed and cherish it.

Reas. 4. Doing good is the very thing which you are created, redeemed, and sanctified for; and, therefore, you must extend your endeavours to the utmost, and to the last, that as much as may be may be done when you are dead. If magistrates and ministers took care for no longer than their own lives, what would become of the state or church?

Reas. 5. The common good is better than the plenty of a sinful child; yea, it is to be preferred before the best child, and before ourselves; and, therefore, much more before the worst.

Reas. 6. It is a dreadful thing to be guilty of all the fleshly sins which your ungodly sons will commit with your estate, when they shall by it maintain the sins of Sodom, pride, fulness of bread, and abundance of idleness, if not to strengthen their hands for oppression or persecution, to think that they will spend their days in voluptuousness, because you give them provision for the flesh.

Reas. 7. It is cruelty to them that are already so bad to make their temptations to sin much stronger, and their place in hell the worse, and to make the way to heaven as hard to them as for a camel to go through the eye of a needle; to prepare them to want a drop of water in hell, who were clothed richly, and fared sumptuously on earth; to entice them to say, Soul, take thine ease, thou hast enough laid up for many years, till they hear, Thou fool, this night shall they require thy soul; to cherish that love of the world which is enmity to God, by feeding that lust of the flesh, and lust of the eyes, and pride of life, which are not of the Father, but of the world.

Reas. 8. When this preferring unprofitable and ungodly children before God and the common good is so common and reigning a sin in the world, it is a great fault for religious men to encourage them in it by their example, and to do as they.

Reas. 9. It is a sin to cast away any of God's gifts. When Christ had fed men by a miracle, he saith, "Gather up the fragments that nothing be lost:" if you should cast your money into the sea, it were a crime; but to leave it to such as you foresee are most likely to use it sinfully, is more than casting it away.

If you saw men offer sacrifice to Bacchus, or Venus, you would abhor it; do not that which is so like it, as to leave bad men fuel for fleshly lust.

Reas. 10. It is the more dreadful, because it is dying in studied sin, without repentance. To put so much sin into one's will, shows a full consent, and leaveth no room and time to repent of it.

On all these accounts, I advise all the stewards of God, as they love him, and the public good, and their own souls, while they have opportunity, even to the last breath, to do good to all, and to provide more for the common good than for superfluities to any, and than for the maintaining ungodly children in sin, to the increase of their guilt and misery.

Indeed, in the choice of a calling, employment, and condition of life, and place for their children, doing good should be preferred before their rising in the world: and they that justly endeavour to raise their families in wealth, honour, or power, should do it only that they might do the more good. But it is Satan's design to turn all God's mercies to the cherishing of wickedness, and even the love of parents to their children to the poisoning of their souls, the strengthening of their snares, and the hinderance of their own and other men's salvation. But it is shame and pity that they who in baptism devoted their children to God, the Father, Son, and Holy Ghost, renouncing the world, the flesh, and the devil, as under the banner of the cross, should labour all their life, that impenitently at death they may leave all that they can get to such as, in all probability, will use it in pride, fulness, and idleness, for the flesh, the world, and the devil, against him and his interest, from whom they received it; and to whom both they and all they had were once devoted.

When men are loth that their estates should remove from the name and family, (for which there may be just cause,) I take it for the safest way, as aforesaid, to trust some, as men do their children with guardians, by the advice of lawyers, to secure all from their unworthy heirs, for the next, or some other of the name and lineage, that proveth worthy.

There are many other good works by which some rich men may be very profitable to the commonwealth, such as setting all the poor on work, and building hospitals for the impotent, &c.; but these this city is happily acquainted with already; and though still there be much wanting, yet there is much done.

V. But one more I will presume to name only to you that are merchants, for I am not one who have the ear of princes, who are more able. Might not somewhat more be done than yet is, to further the gospel in your factories, and in our plantations? Old Mr. Eliot, with his helpers in New England, have shown that somewhat may be done, if others were as charitable and zealous as they. The Jesuits and friars showed us, in Congo, Japan, China, and other countries, that much might be done with care and diligence. Though the papal interest was a corrupt end, and all the means which they used were not justifiable, when I read of their hazards, unwearied labours, and success, I am none of those that would deprive them of their deserved honour, but rather wish that we who have better ends and principles, might do better than they, and not come so far behind them as we do, if half be true that Peter Maffæus, and the Jesuits' epistles, and many other writers, tell us of them. I know that they had the advantage of greater helps from kings, and pope, and prelates, and colleges endowed with trained men and copious maintenance. But might not somewhat more be done by us than is yet done?

I. Is it not possible to send some able, zealous chaplains to those factories which are in the countries of infidels and heathens; such as thirst for the conversion of sinners, and the enlargement of the church of Christ, and would labour skilfully and diligently therein? Is it not possible to get some short christian books, which are fitted for that use, to be translated into such languages that infidels can read, and to distribute them among them? If it be not possible also to send thither religious, conscionable factors, who would further the work, the case of London is very sad.

II. Is it not possible, at least, to help the poor ignorant Armenians, Greeks, Muscovites, and other christians, who have no printing among them, nor much preaching or knowledge; and, for want of printing, have very few Bibles, even for their churches or ministers? Could nothing be done to get some Bibles, catechisms, and practical books printed in their own tongues, and given among them? I know there is difficulty in the way; but money, and willingness, and diligence, might do something.

III. Might not something be done in other plantations, as well as in New England, towards the conversion of the natives there? Might not some skilful, zealous preachers be sent thither, who would promote serious piety among those of the English that have too little of it, and might invite the Americans to learn the gospel, and teach our planters how to behave themselves christianly towards them, to win them to Christ?

IV. Is it not possible to do more than hath been done, to convert the blacks that are our own slaves, or servants, to the christian faith? Hath not Mr. Goodwin justly reprehended and lamented the neglect, yea, and resistance of this work in Barbadoes, and the like elsewhere? 1. Might not better teachers be sent thither for that use? 2. Is it not an odious crime of christians to hinder the conversion of these infidels, lest they lose their service by it, and to prefer their gain before men's souls? Is not this to sell souls for a little money, as Judas did his Lord? And whereas the law manumits them from servitude when they turn christians, that it may invite them to conversion, (and this occasioneth wicked christians to hinder them from knowledge,) were it not better move the government, therefore, to change that law, so far as to allow these covetous masters their service for a certain time, using them as free servants? 3. And whereas they are allowed only the Lord's day for their own labour, and some honest christians would willingly allow them some other time instead of it, that they might spend the Lord's day in learning to know Christ, and worship God, but they dare not do it, lest their wicked neighbours rise against them, for giving their slaves such an example; might not the governors be procured to force the whole plantation to it by a law, even to allow their infidel servants so much time on another day, and cause some to congregate them for instruction on the Lord's days? Why should those men be called christians, or have any christian reputation or privileges themselves, who think both christianity and souls to be no more worth than to be thus basely sold for the gain of men's servilest labours? And what though the poor infidels desire not their own conversion, their need is the greater, and not the less.

V. I conclude with this moving inference: The great opposition that is made against doing good by the devil and his whole army through all the world, and their lamentable success, doth call aloud to all true christians to overdo them. Oh what a kingdom of malignants hath Satan, doing mischief to men's souls and bodies through the earth! hating the godly; oppressing the just; corrupting doctrine; introducing lies; turning Christ's labourers out of his vineyard; forbidding them to preach in his name the saving word of life; hiding or despising the laws of Christ, and setting up their own wills and devices in their stead; making dividing, distracting engines, on pretence of order, government, and unity; murdering men's bodies, and ruining their estates, and slandering their names, on pretence of love to the church and souls; encouraging profaneness, blasphemy, perjury, whoredom, and scorning conscience, and fear of sinning. What diligence doth Satan use, through the very christian nations, to turn Christ's ordinances of magistracy and ministry against himself, and to make his own officers the most mischievous enemies to his truth and kingdom, and saving work; to tread down his family and spiritual worship, as if it were by his own authority and commission. To preach down truth, and conscience, and real godliness, as in Christ's own name, and fight against him with his own word, and to teach the people to hate his servants, as if this pleased the God of love.

And, alas! how dismal is their success! In the East, the church is hereby destroyed by barbarous Mahometans: the remnants by their prelates continued in sects, in great ignorance, and dead formality, reproaching and anathematizing one another, and little hope appearing of recovery. In the West, a dead image of religion, and unity, and order, dressed up with a multitude of gauds, and set up against the life and soul of religion, unity, and order, and a war hereupon maintained for their destruction, with sad success: so that, usually, the more zealous men are for the papal and formal human image, the more zealously they study the extirpation of worshipping God in spirit and truth, and thirst after the blood of the most serious worshippers; and cry down them as intolerable enemies who take their baptism for an obliging vow, and seriously endeavour to perform it, and live in good earnest, as christianity bindeth them: and they take it for an unsufferable crime to prefer God's authority before man's, and to plead his law against any thing that men command them. In a word, he is unworthy to be accounted a christian with them, who will be a christian indeed, and not despise the laws of Christ, and unworthy to have the liberty and usage of a man that will not sin and damn his soul: so much more cruel are they than the Turkish tyrants, who, if they send to a man for his head, must be obeyed.

And is the devil a better master than Christ? And shall his work be done with greater zeal and resolution? Will he give his servants a better reward? Should not all this awaken us to do good with greater diligence than they do evil? and to promote love and piety more earnestly than they do malignity and iniquity? Is not saving church and state, souls and bodies, better worth resolution and labour than destroying them?

And the prognostics are encouraging. Certainly, Christ and his kingdom will prevail. At last, all his enemies shall be made his footstool; yea, shall from him receive their doom to the everlasting punishment, which rebels against omnipotency, goodness, and mercy, do deserve. If God be not God, if Christ will not conquer, if there be no life to come, let them boast of their success: but when they are rottenness and dust, and their souls with devils, and their names are a reproach, Christ will be Christ, his promises and threatenings all made good. 2 Thess. i. 6, &c. He will judge it righteous to recompense tribulation to your troublers, when he cometh with his mighty angels in flaming fire, to take vengeance on rebels, and to be glorified in his saints, and admired in all true believers. And when that solemn judgment shall pass on them that did good, and that did evil, described Matt. xxv. with a "Come, ye blessed, inherit the kingdom," and, "Go, ye cursed, into everlasting fire;" doing good and not doing it, much more doing mischief, will be better distinguished than now they are, when they are rendered as the reason of those different dooms.

THE

LAST WORK OF A BELIEVER;

HIS PASSING PRAYER,

RECOMMENDING HIS DEPARTING SPIRIT TO CHRIST,

TO BE RECEIVED BY HIM.

PREPARED FOR THE FUNERAL OF MARY THE WIDOW, FIRST OF FRANCIS CHARLTON, ESQ. AND AFTER OF THOMAS HANMER, ESQ.; AND PARTLY PREACHED AT ST. MARY MAGDALEN'S CHURCH, IN MILK-STREET, LONDON, AND NOW, AT THE DESIRE OF HER DAUGHTER, BEFORE HER DEATH, REPRINTED.

"If any man serve me, let him follow me; and where I am, there shall also my servant be. If any man serve me, him will my Father honour."—John xii. 26.

TO THE READER.

READER,

THE person whose death did occasion this discourse was one that about five years ago removed from her ancient habitation, at Appley, in Shropshire, to Kidderminster, where she lived under my pastoral care till I was come up to London; and before she had lived there a twelvemonth (for thither she removed) she died of the fever, then very common in the city. She lived among us an example of prudence, gravity, sobriety, righteousness, piety, charity, and self-denial, and was truly what I have described her to be, and much more; for I use not to flatter the living, much less the dead. And though I had personal acquaintance with her for no longer a time than I have mentioned, yet I think it worthy the mentioning, which I understand by comparing her last years with what is said of her former time, by those that were then nearest to her, and so were at her death, that whereas (as I have said) sudden passion was the sin that she was wont much to complain of, she had not contented herself with mere complainings, but so effectually resisted them, and applied God's remedies for the healing of her nature, that the success was very much observed by those about her, and the change and cure so great herein, as was a comfort to her nearest relations that had the benefit of her converse; which I mention as a thing that shows us, 1. That even the infirmities that are found in nature and temperature of body are curable, so far as they fall under the dominion of a sanctified will. 2. That even in age, when such passions usually get ground, and infirmities of mind increase with infirmities of body, yet grace can effectually do its work. 3. That to attend God in his means, for the subduing of any corruption, is not in vain. 4. That as God hath promised growth of grace, and flourishing in old age, so in his way we may expect the fulfilling of his promise. 5. That as grace increaseth, infirmities and corruptions of the soul will vanish.

This makes me call to mind that she was once so much taken with a sermon which I preached at the funeral of a holy aged woman,[a] and so sensibly oft recited the text itself as much affecting her—"For which cause we faint not; but though our outward man perish, yet the inward man is renewed day by day," &c. 2 Cor. iv. 16, 17; that I am persuaded both the text itself, and the example opened (and well known) to her, did her much good.

Her work is done, her enemies are conquered, (except the remaining fruits of death upon a corrupting body, which the resurrection must conquer,) her danger, and temptations, and troubles, and fears, are at an end. She shall no more be discomfited with evil tidings; nor no more partake with a militant church in the sorrows of her diseases or distresses. We are left within the reach of Satan's assaults and malice, and of the rage and violence which pride, and faction, and Cainish envy, and enmity to serious holiness, do ordinarily raise against Christ's followers in the world. We are left among the lying tongues of slanderous, malicious men, and dwell in a wilderness among scorpions; where the sons of Belial, like Nabal, are such that a man cannot speak to them, 1 Sam. xxv. 17. The best of them is as a brier, the most upright sharper than a thorn hedge, Mic. vii. 4. "But the sons of Belial shall be all of them as thorns thrust away, because they cannot be taken with hands; but the man that shall touch them must be fenced with iron, and the staff of a spear, and they shall be utterly burned with fire in the same place," 2 Sam. xxiii. 6, 7. We are left among our weak, distempered, sinful, afflicted, lamenting friends; the sight of whose calamities, and participation of their sufferings, maketh us feel the strokes that fall upon so great a number, that we are never like to be free from pain. But she is entered into the land of peace, where pride and faction are shut out; where serpentine enmity, malice, and fury, never come; where there is no Cain to envy and destroy us; no Sodomites to rage against us, and in their blindness to assault our doors; no Ahithophels to plot our ruin; no Judas to betray us; no false witnesses to accuse us; no Tertullus to paint us out as pestilent fellows, and movers of sedition among the people; no Rehum, Shimshai, or their society, to persuade the rulers that the servants of the God of heaven are hurtful unto kings, and against their interest and honour, Ezra iv. 9, 12—14, 22; v. 11; no rabble to cry, "Away with them, it is not fit that they should live;" no Demas that will forsake us for the love of present things; no such contentious, censorious friends as Job's to afflict us, by adding to our affliction; no cursed Ham to dishonour parents; no ambitious, rebellious Absalom to molest us, or to lament; no sinful, scandalous, or impatient friends to be our grief: and, which is more than all, no earthly, sinful inclinations in ourselves; no passions or infirmities; no languishings of soul; no deadness, dulness, hard-heartedness, or weaknesses of grace; no backwardness to God, or estrangedness from him, nor fears or doubtings of his love, nor frowns of his displeasure. None of these do enter into that serene and holy region, nor ever interrupt the joy of saints.

The great work is yet upon our hands, to fight out the good fight, to finish our course, to run with patience the remainder of the race that is before us; and as we must look to Jesus, the Author and Finisher of our faith, as our great Exemplar, so must we look to his saints and martyrs as our encouraging examples under him. Put the case you were now dying, (and oh, how near is it, and how sure!) what would you need most, if the day were come? That is it that you need most now. Look after it speedily while you have time. Look after it seriously, if you have the hearts of men, and sin have not turned you into idiots or blocks. What a disgrace is it to mankind, to hear men commonly at death cry out, Oh! for a little more time. And, Oh! for the opportunities of grace again. And, Oh! how shall I enter upon eternity thus unprepared? as if they had never heard or known that they must die till now. Had you not a life's time to put these questions? And should you not long ago have got them satisfactorily resolved? And justly doth God give over some to that greater shame of human nature, as not to be called to their wits, even by the approach of death itself; but as they contemned everlasting life in their health, God justly leaveth them to be so sottish as to venture presumptuously with unrenewed souls upon death; and the conceit that they are of the right church, or party, or opinion, or that the priest hath absolved them, doth pass with them for the necessary preparation; and well it were for them if these would pass them currently into heaven. But, oh, what heart can now conceive how terrible it is for a new-departed soul to find itself remedilessly disappointed, and to be shut up in flames and desperation, before they would believe that they were in danger of it!

Reader, I beseech thee, as ever thou believest that thou must shortly die, retire from the crowd and noise of worldly vanity and vexation. O, bethink thee, how little a while thou must be here, and have use for honour, and favour, and wealth; and what it is for a soul to pass into heaven or hell, and to dwell among angels or devils for ever; and how men should live, and watch, and pray, that are near to such a change as this. Should I care what men call me, (by tongue or pen,) should I care whether I live at liberty or in prison, when I am ready to die, and have matters of infinite moment before me to take me up? Honour or dishonour, liberty or prison, are words of no sound or signification, scarce to be heard or

[a] Good old Mrs. Doughty, sometime of Shrewsbury, who had long walked with God and longed to be with him, and was among us an excellent example of holiness, blamelessness, contempt of the world, constancy, patience, humility, and (which makes it strange) a great and constant desire to die, though she was still complaining of doubtings, and weakness of assurance.

taken notice of, to one of us that are just passing to God, and to everlasting life. The Lord have mercy upon the distracted world! How strangely doth the devil befool them in the daylight, and make them needlessly trouble themselves about many things, when one thing is needful; and heaven is talked of, (and that but heartlessly and seldom,) while fleshly provision only is the prize, the pleasure, the business of their lives. Some are diverted from their serious preparation for death by the beastly avocations of lust, and gaudiness, and meats, and drinks, and childish sports; and some by the businesses of ambition and covetousness, contriving how to feather their nests, and exercise their wills over others in the world! And some that will seem to be doing the work, are diverted as dangerously as others, by contending about formalities and ceremonies, and destroying charity and peace; rending the church, and strengthening factions, and carrying on interests hypocritically under the name of religion, till the zeal that St. James describeth, (James iii. 13, 14, &c.) having consumed all that was like to the zeal of love and holiness in themselves, proceed to consume the servants and interest of Christ about them, and to bite and devour, till their Lord come and find them in a day that they looked not for him, smiting their fellow-servants, and eating and drinking with the drunken, and cut them asunder, and appoint them their portion with the hypocrites, where shall be weeping and gnashing of teeth, Matt. xxiv. 49—51.

O, study, and preach, and hear, and pray, and live, and use your brethren that differ from you in some opinions, as you would do if you were going to receive your doom, and as will then be most acceptable to your Lord! The guilt of sensuality, worldliness, ambition, of uncharitableness, cruelty, and injustice, of losing time, and betraying your souls by negligence, or perfidiousness, and wilful sin, will lie heavier upon a departing soul, than now, in the drunkenness of prosperity, you can think. Christ will never receive such souls in their extremity, unless upon repentance, by faith in his blood, they are washed from this pollution. It is unspeakably terrible to die, without a confidence that Christ will receive us; and little knows the graceless world what sincerity and simplicity in holiness is necessary to the soundness of such a confidence.

Let those that know not that they must die, or know of no life hereafter, hold on their chase of a feather, till they find what they lost their lives, and souls, and labour for. But if thou be a christian, remember what is thy work: thou wilt not need the favour of man, nor worldly wealth, to prevail with Christ to receive thy spirit. O, learn thy last work before thou art put upon the doing of it! The world of spirits, to which we are passing, doth better know than this world of fleshly darkened sinners, the great difference between the death of a heavenly believer and of an earthly sensualist. Believe it, it is a thing possible to get that apprehension of the love of Christ, that confidence of his receiving us, and such familiar, pleasant thoughts of our entertainment by him, as shall much overcome the fears of death, and make it a welcome day to us when we shall be admitted into the celestial society: and the difference between one man's death and another's, dependeth on the difference between heart and heart, life and life, preparation and unpreparedness.

If you ask me, How may so happy a preparation be made? I have told you in this following discourse, and more fully elsewhere formerly. I shall add now these directions following.

1. Follow the flattering world no further; come off from all expectation of felicity below; enjoy nothing under the sun, but only use it in order to your enjoyment of the real, sure delight; take heed of being too much pleased in the creature. Have you houses, and lands, and offices, and honours, and friends, that are very pleasing to you? Take heed, for that is the killing snare! Shut your eyes, and wink them all into nothing; and cast by your contrivances, and cares, and fears, and remember you have another work to do.

2. Live in communion with a suffering Christ: study well the whole life and nature of his sufferings, and the reason of them, and think how desirable it is to be conformed to him. Thus, look to Jesus, that for the joy that was set before him, despised the shame, endured the cross, and the contradiction of sinners against himself. Dwell upon this example, that the image of a humbled, suffering Christ, being deeply imprinted on thy mind, may draw thy heart into a juster relish of a mortified state. Sure he is no good christian that thinks it not better to live as Christ did, (in holy poverty and sufferings in the world,) than as Crœsus, or Cæsar, or any such worldling and self-pleaser lived. Die daily by following Jesus with your cross, and when you have a while suffered with him, he will make you perfect, and receive your spirits, and you shall reign with him: it wonderfully prepareth for a comfortable death to live in the fellowship of the sufferings of Christ. He is most likely to die quietly, patiently, and joyfully, that can first be poor, be neglected, be scorned, be wronged, be slandered, be imprisoned, quietly, patiently, and joyfully. If you were but at Jerusalem, you would, with some love and pleasure, go up mount Olivet, and think, Christ went this very way. You would love to see the place where he was born, the way which he went when he carried his cross, the holy grave where he was buried (where there is a temple which pilgrims use to visit, from whence they use to bring the mark as a pleasing badge of honour); but how much more of Christ is there in our suffering for his cause and truth, and in following him in a mortified, self-denying life, than in following him in the path that he hath trodden upon earth! His enemies saw his cross, his grave; his mother, his person. This did not heal their sinful souls, and make them happy; but the cross that he calleth us to bear is a life of suffering for righteousness' sake; in which he commandeth us to rejoice, and be exceedingly glad, because our reward is great in heaven, though all manner of evil be spoken of us falsely by men on earth, Matt. v. 11, 12. This is called a being partakers of Christ's sufferings, in which we are commanded to rejoice, "that, when his glory shall be revealed, we may be glad also with exceeding joy," 1 Pet. iv. 13. And as "the sufferings of Christ abound in us, so our consolation aboundeth by Christ," 2 Cor. i. 5. Till we come up to a life of willing mortification, and pleased, contented suffering with Christ, we are in the lower form of his school, and, as children, shall tremble at that which should not cause our terror; and, through misapprehensions of the case of a departing soul, shall be afraid of that which should be our joy. I am not such an enemy to the esteem of relics, but if one could show me the very stocks that Paul and Silas sat in when they sung psalms in their imprisonment, (Acts xvi.) I could be contented to be put (for the like cause) into the same stocks, with a special willingness and pleasure: how much more should we be willing to be conformed to our suffering Lord in a spirit and life of true mortification!

3. Hold communion also with his suffering members: desire not to dwell in the tents of wickedness, nor to be planted among them that flourish for a time, that they may be destroyed for ever, Psal. xcii. 6, 7. I had rather have Bradford's heart and faggot than Bonner's bishopric. It was holy Stephen, and not those

that stoned him, that saw heaven opened, and the Son of man sitting at the right hand of God, (Acts vii. 56,) and that could joyfully say, "Lord Jesus, receive my spirit." He liveth not by faith (though he may be a hanger-on that keepeth up some profession for fear of being damned) who chooseth not rather to suffer affliction with the people of God, than to enjoy the pleasures of sin for a season; and esteemeth not the very reproach of Christ greater riches than the treasures of the world, as having respect to the recompence of reward, Heb. xi. 25, 26.

4. Live as if heaven were open to your sight, and then dote upon the delights of worldlings if you can; then love a life of fleshly ease and honour, better than to be with Christ, if you can. But of this I have spoken at large in other writings.

Christian, make it the study and business of thy life to learn to do thy last work well, that work which must be done but once; that so death, which transmits unholy souls into utter darkness and despair, may deliver thy spirit into thy Redeemer's hands, to be received to his glory, according to that blessed promise, John xii. 26. And while I am in the flesh beg the same mercy for

Thy brother and companion in tribulation,
and in the kingdom and patience of Jesus Christ,

RICHARD BAXTER.

London, Jan. 31, 1661.

ACTS VII. 59.

LORD JESUS, RECEIVE MY SPIRIT.

The birth of nature, and the new birth of grace, in their measure resemble the death of saints, which is the birth of glory. It is a bitter-sweet day, a day that is mixed of sorrow and joy, when nature must quit its familiar guest, and yield to any of these changes. Our natural birth is not without the throes, and pain, and groanings of the mother, though it transmit the child into a more large, and lightsome, and desirable habitation. Our spiritual birth is not without its humbling and heart-piercing sorrows; and when we are brought out of darkness into the marvellous light, we leave our old companions in displeasure, whom we forsake, and our flesh repining at the loss of its sensual delights. And our passage into glory is not without those pangs and fears which must needs be the attendants of a pained body ready to be dissolved, and a soul that is going through so strait a door into a strange, though a most blessed place; and it leaveth our lamenting friends behind, that feel their loss, and would longer have enjoyed our company, and see not (though they believe) the glory of the departed soul. And this is our case that are brought hither this day, by an act of Providence sad to us, though joyous to our departed friend; by a voice that hath called her into glory, and called us into this mourning plight: even us that rejoice in the thoughts of her felicity, and are not so cruel as to wish her again into this corruptible flesh, and calamitous world, from the glorious presence of the Lord; and yet should have kept her longer from it, for our own and others' sakes, if our wisdom had been fit to rule, or our wills to be fulfilled, or if our prayers must have been answered, according to the measure of our failing apprehensions or precipitant desires. But folly must submit to the incomprehensible wisdom, and the desire of the creature must stoop to the will of the Creator. The interest of Christ must be preferred when he calleth for his own, and our temporary interest must give place: flesh must be silent and not contend, and dust must not dare to question God; he knoweth best when his fruit is ripe, and though he will allow our moderate sorrows, he will not so much damnify his saints as to detain them with us from their joyful rest, till we are content to let them go.

Thus also did blessed Stephen depart from glory to glory; from a distant sight of the glory of God, and of Jesus standing at his right hand, into the immediate presence and fruition of that glory. But yet he must pass the narrow port; enraged malice must stone him till he die, and he must undergo the pains of martyrdom before he reach to the glory which he had seen. And when he was arrived in safety, he leaveth his brethren scattered in the storm, and devout men make great lamentation at his burial, Acts viii. 2. Though it is probable by the ordinary acceptation of the word ἄνδρες εὐλαβεῖς, that they were not professed christians, but devout proselytes, (such as Cornelius and the Æthiopian eunuch were,) that buried and thus lamented Stephen, as knowing him to be an excellent person, cruelly murdered by the raging Jews; yet their example, in a case not culpable, but commendable, may be imitated by believers, upon condition that, with our sense of the excellency of the persons, and of our loss by their removal, we exceed them that had but a darker revelation in our joyful sense of the felicity of the translated souls.

The occasion of the death of this holy man was partly that he surpassed others, as being full of faith, and of the Holy Ghost; and partly that he plainly rebuked the blind and furious persecuting zeal of the Jews, and bore a most resolute testimony of Christ. It is an ill time when men must suffer because they are good, and deserve not suffering, but reward; and they are an unhappy people that have no more grace or wit but to fight against heaven, and set themselves under the strokes of God's severest justice, by persecuting them that are dear to Christ, and faithfully perform their duty. It is no strange thing for the zeal and interest of a faction to make men mad; so mad as implacably to rage against the offspring of heaven, and to hate men because they are faithful to their great Master, and because they are against their faction; so mad as to think that the interest of their cause requireth them to destroy the best with the greatest malice, because they stand most in their way, and to forget that Christ, the revenger of his elect, doth take all as done to him that is done to them; so mad as to forget all the terrible threatenings of God, and terrible instances of his avenging justice against the enemies of his servants, whom he taketh as his own; and to ruin their own reputations by seeking to defame the upright, whose names God is engaged to honour, and whose righteousness shall shine forth as the sun, when foolish malignity hath done its worst. When Christ had pleaded his cause effectually with Saul, that was one of the persecutors of Stephen, he maketh him confess that he was περισσῶς ἐμμαινόμενος, exceedingly, excessively, or beyond measure mad against the christians.

But this blessed protomartyr, in despite of malice, doth safely and joyfully pass through all their rage to heaven. By killing him they make him more than conqueror, and send him to receive his crown. And he shuts up all the action of his life in imitation of his suffering Lord with a twofold request to Heaven, the one for himself, that his spirit may be received, the other for his persecutors, that this sin may not be laid to their charge, Acts vii. 59, 60; for so you may find Christ did before him, "Father, forgive them; for they know not what they do;" and, "Father, into thy hands I commend my spirit," Luke xxiii. 34, 46. Only Christ directeth his prayer immediately to the Father, and Stephen to Christ, as being one that had a mediator, when Christ had none, as needing none; and being now bearing witness, by his suffering, to Christ, and therefore it was seasonable to direct his prayer to him; but especially because it was an act of mediation that he petitioneth for, and therefore directeth his petition to the Mediator.

This first request of this dying saint, which I have chosen to handle, as suitable and seasonable for our instruction at this time, in a few words containeth not a few exceeding useful, wholesome truths.

As, I. It is here plainly intimated that Jesus Christ is exalted in glory, in that he hath power to receive departed souls.

II. That Christ is to be prayed to, and that it is not our duty to direct all our prayers only to the Father. Especially those things that belong to the office of the Mediator, as interceding for us in the heavens, must be requested of the Mediator. And those things which belong to the Father to give for the sake of the Mediator, must be asked of the Father for his sake. I cannot now stay to tell you in particular what belongeth to the one, and what unto the other.

III. That man hath a spirit as well as a body; of which more anon.

IV. That this spirit dieth not with the body (unless you will call a mere separation a dying).

V. That Christ doth receive the spirits of his saints when they are separated from the body.

VI. That a dying christian may confidently and comfortably commend his spirit to Christ, to be received of him.

VII. That prayer in general, and this prayer in special, That Christ will receive our departing souls, is a most suitable conclusion of all the actions of a christian's life.

The first and second of these doctrines, offered us by this text, I shall pass by.

The third is not questioned by any that knoweth himself to be a man: but that we may understand it, and the rest, we must consider what the word "spirit" doth here signify. By "spirit," here can be meant nothing but the rational soul, which is the principal constitutive part of the man. For though the word do sometimes signify the wind or breath, and sometimes the moral and intellectual qualifications, and have divers other senses, I need not stay to prove that it is not here so taken. Stephen prayeth not to Christ to receive his breath, his graces, or the Holy Ghost, but to receive his rational, immortal soul.

It is not only the soul, but God himself, that is called "a Spirit:" and though the name be fetched from lower things, that is, because that as we have no adequate positive conception of God or spirits, so we can have no adequate proper names for them, but must take up with borrowed names, as answerable to our notions.

Sometimes the word spirit (as Heb. iv. 12, &c.) is distinguished from the soul; and then it either signifieth the superior faculties in the same soul, or the same soul as elevated by grace.

Do you ask, What the soul is? You may also ask, What a man is? And it is pity that a man should not know what a man is. It is our intellectual nature, containing also the sensitive and vegetative; the principle, or first act, by which we live, and feel, and understand, and freely will. The acts tell you what the faculties or powers are, and so what the soul is. If you know what intellection, or reason and free-will are, you may know what it is to have a spiritual nature, essentially containing the power of reasoning and willing. It is thy soul by which thou art thinking and asking what a soul is; and as he that reasoneth to prove that man hath no reason, doth prove that he hath reason by reasoning against it; so he that reasoneth to prove that he hath no soul, doth thereby prove that he hath a reasonable (though abused) soul.

Yet there are some so blind as to question whether they have souls, because they see them not; whereas if they could see them with eyes of flesh they were no souls, for spirits are invisible. They see not the air or wind, and yet they know that air or wind there is. They see not God or angels, and yet they are fools indeed if they doubt whether there be a God and angels. If they see not their eyes, yet they know that they have eyes, because with those eyes they see other things. And if they know not directly and intuitively that they have rational souls, they might know it by their knowing other things, which without such souls cannot be known. It is just with God that those that live as carnally, and brutishly, and negligently, as if they had no souls to use or care for, should at last be given up to question whether they have souls or no.

O woeful fall! depraved nature! O miserable men, that have so far departed from God, as to deny both themselves and God! or to question whether God be God, and man be man. Return to God, and thou wilt come to thyself. Forget not, man, thy noble nature, thy chiefest part: think not that thou art only shell, because thou seest not through the shell. It is souls that converse by the bodies while they are in flesh. It is thy soul that I am speaking to, and thy soul that understandeth me. When thy soul is gone, I will speak to thee no more. It is thy soul that is the workmanship of God by an immediate or special way of fabrication. "The souls which I have made," Isa. lvii. 16. "He breathed into man the breath of life, and he became a living soul," Gen. ii. 7. It is thy soul that is said to be made after God's image; in that thou art ennobled with a capacious understanding and free-will; and it is thy soul that is the immediate subject of his moral image, even spiritual wisdom, righteousness, and holiness. God hath not hands, and feet, and other members, as thy body hath. How noble a nature is that which is capable of knowing not only things in the world, (in its measure,) but God himself, and the things of the world that is to come; and capable of loving and enjoying God, and of seeking and serving him in order to that enjoyment! Christ thought not basely of a soul that redeemed souls at such a price, when he made his soul an offering for sin, Isa. liii. 10. Were it not for our immortal souls would God ever honour us with such relations to him as to be his children? (For he is first the Father of spirits, (Heb. xii. 9,) and then the Father of saints.) Should we be called the spouse and the members of Christ? would he be at so much cost upon us? should angels attend us as ministering spirits, if we had not spirits fit to minister to God? Would the Spirit of God himself dwell in us, and quicken and beautify us with his grace, should a world of creatures (whose corporeal substance seems as excellent as ours) attend and serve us, if we were but an ingenious sort of brutes, and had not rational, immortal souls? Should such store of mercies be provided for us, should ministers be provided to preach, and pray, and labour for us, if we had not souls to save or lose? "They watch for your souls as they that must give account," Heb. xiii. 17. Why should they preach in season and out of season, and suffer so much to perform their work, but that they know that "he that winneth souls is wise," Prov. xi. 30; and that "he which converteth the sinner from the error of his way, doth save a soul from death, and hide a multitude of sins," James v. 20. The devil himself may tell you the worth of souls when he compasseth the earth, (Job i. 7,) and goeth about night and day to deceive them, and devour them, (1 Pet. v. 8,) and yet can he make you believe that they are so worthless as to be abused to the basest drudgery, to be poisoned with sin and sensuality, to be ventured for a thing of nought?

O sirs! have you such immortal souls, and will you sell them for a lust, for a beastly pleasure, for liberty to glut your flesh, or for the price that Judas sold his Lord for? Is thy soul no more worth than honour, or wealth, or foolish mirth? Is thy soul so base as not to be worth the care and labour of a holy life? Is the world worth all thy care and labour, and shall less be called too much ado, when it is for thy precious soul? Alas! one would think by the careless, fleshly lives of many, that they remember not that they have souls. Have they not need, in the depth of their security, in the height of their ambition, and in the heat of fleshly lusts, to have a monitor to call to them, Remember that thou art a man, and that thou hast a soul to save or lose? What thinkest thou of thy negligence and carnal life, when thou readest that so holy a man as Paul must keep under his body, and bring it into subjection, lest he should be a cast-away after all his labours? 1 Cor. ix. 25—27. O, live not as if the flesh were the man, and its pleasure your felicity; but live as those that have spirits to take care of.

Doct. IV. The spirit of man doth survive the body; it dieth not with it. It is not annihilated; it is not resolved into the essence of some common element of souls, where it loseth its specific form and name. It was still the spirit of Stephen that was received by Christ. It sleepeth not. To confute the dream of those that talk of the sleeping of souls, or any lethargic, unintelligent, or inactive state, of so excellent, capacious, and active a nature, were but to dispute with sleeping men. When we say it is immortal, we mean not that it, or any creature, hath in itself a self-supporting or self-preserving sufficiency; or that they are necessary beings, and not contingent; or primitive beings, and not derived from another by creation. We know that all the world would turn to nothing in a moment if God did but withdraw his preserving and upholding influence, and but suspend that will that doth continue them. He need not exert any positive will or act for their destruction or annihilation. Though *ejusdem est annihilare, cujus est creare,* none can annihilate but God; yet it is by a positive, efficient act of will that he createth; and by a mere cessation of the act of his preserving will he can annihilate. I mean not by any change in him, but by willing the continuance of the creature but till such a period; but yet he that will perpetuate the spirit of man, hath given it a nature (as he hath done the angels) fit to be perpetuated; a nature not guilty of composition and elementary materiality, which might subject it to corruption. So that as there is an aptitude in iron, or silver, or gold to continue longer than grass, or flowers, or flesh; and a reason of its duration many be given *a natura rei,* from that aptitude in subordination to the will of God; so there is such an aptitude in the nature of the soul to be immortal, which God maketh use of to the accomplishment of his will for its actual perpetuity.

The heathenish Socinians, that deny the immortality of the soul, (yea, worse than heathenish, for most heathens do maintain it,) must deny it to Christ himself, as well as to his members; for he used the like recommendation of his soul to his Father when he was on the cross, as Stephen doth here to him. If "Lord Jesus, receive my spirit," be words that prove not the surviving of the spirit of Stephen; then, "Father, into thy hands I commend my spirit," will not prove the surviving of the spirit of Christ. And, then, what do these infidels make of Christ, who also deny his Deity; and, consequently, make him nothing but a corpse, when his body was in the grave? How then did he make good his promise to the penitent malefactor? "This day shalt thou be with me in paradise." But he that said, "Because I live, ye shall live also," (John xiv. 19,) did live in the Spirit, while he was put to death in the flesh, 1 Pet. iii. 18; and receiveth the spirits of his servants unto life eternal, while their flesh is rotting in the grave. This very text is so clear for this, if there were no other, it might end the controversy with all that believe the holy Scriptures.

I confess there is a sleep of souls, a metaphorical sleep in sin and in security, or else the drowsy opinions of these infidels had never found entertainment in the world; a sleep so deep that the voice of God, in the threatenings of his word, and the alarm of his judgments, and the thunder of his warnings by his most serious ministers, prevail not to awaken the most: so dead a sleep possesseth the most of the ungodly world, that they can quietly sin in the sight of God, at the entrance upon eternity, at the doors of hell, and the calls of God do not awaken them: so dead a sleep, that Scripture justly calls them dead, Eph. ii. 1, 5; and ministers may well call them dead, for alas, it is not our voice that can awake them; they are as dead to us: we draw back the curtains to let in the light, and show them that judgment is at hand, and use those true but terrible arguments from wrath and hell, which we are afraid should too much frighten many tender hearers, and yet they sleep on; and our loudest calls, our tears, and our entreaties, cannot awaken them. We cry to them in the name of the Lord, "Awake, thou that sleepest, arise from the dead, and Christ shall give thee light," Eph. v. 14. This moral sleep and death of souls, which is the forerunner of everlasting death in misery, we cannot deny. But after death even this sleep shall cease; and God will awaken them with his vengeance, that would not be awaked by his grace. Then, sinner, sleep under the thoughts of sin and God's displeasure if thou canst. There is no sleeping soul in hell; there are none that are past feeling. The mortal stroke that layeth thy flesh to sleep in the dust, lets out a guilty soul into a world where there is no sleeping; where there is a light irresistible, and a terror and torment, that will keep them waking. If God bid thee awake by the flames of justice, he will have no nay. The first sight and feeling which will surprise thee when thou hast left this flesh, will awake thee to eternity, and do more than we could do in time, and convince thee that there is no sleeping state for separated souls.

Doct. V. Christ doth receive the spirits of the saints when they leave the flesh.

Here we shall first tell you what Christ's receiving of the spirit is. The word signifieth, to take it as acceptable to himself; and it comprehendeth these particulars.

1. That Christ will not leave the new-departed soul to the will of Satan, its malicious enemy. How ready is he to receive us to perdition, if Christ refuse us, and receive us not to salvation! He that now seeketh as a roaring lion night and day, as our adversary, to devour us by deceit, will then seek to devour us by execution. How glad was he when God gave him leave but to touch the goods, and children, and body of Job! And how much more would it please his enmity to have power to torment our souls! But the soul that fled to the arms of Christ by faith in the day of trial, shall then find itself in the arms of Christ in the moment of its entrance upon eternity. O christian, whether thou now feel it to thy comfort or not, thou shalt then feel it to the ravishing of thy soul, that thou didst not fly to Christ in vain, nor trust him in vain to be thy Saviour. Satan shall be for ever disappointed of his desired prey. Long wast thou combating with him; frequently and strongly wast thou tempted by him. Thou oft thoughtest it was a doubtful question, who should win the day, and whether ever thou shouldst hold out and be saved: but when thou passest from the flesh, in thy last extremity, in the end of thy greatest and most shaking fears, when Satan is ready, if he might, to carry thy soul to hell; then, even then, shalt thou find that thou hast won the day. And yet not thou, but Christ is he that hath been victorious for thee; even as when thou livedst the life of faith, it was not thou, but Christ, lived in thee, Gal. ii. 20. Thou mayst fear at thy departure, and leave the flesh with terror, and imagine that Satan will presently devour thee; but the experience of a moment will end thy fears, and thou shalt triumph against thy conquered foe. He that saved thee from the dominion of a tempting devil, will certainly save thee from him when he would torment thee. Here he would have us that he may sift us, and get advantage on our weakness; but Christ prayeth for us, and strengtheneth us, that our faith may not fail, Luke xxii. 31. And he that saveth us from the sin, will save us from the punishment, and from Satan's fury, as he did from his fraud.

2. Christ's receiving us, doth include his favourable entertainment and welcoming the departed soul. Poor soul, thou wast never so welcome to thy dearest friend, nor into the arms of a father, a husband, or a wife, as thou shalt be then into the presence and embracements of thy Lord. Thou hearest, and readest, and partly believest, now how he loveth us, even as his spouse and members, as his flesh and bone, Eph. vi. But then thou shalt feel how he loveth thee in particular. If the angels of God have joy at thy conversion, what joy will there be in heaven at thy entrance into that salvation. And sure those angels will bid thee welcome, and concur with Christ in that triumphant joy. If a returning prodigal find himself in the arms of his father's love, and welcomed home with his kisses, and his robe and feast, what welcome then may a cleansed, conquered soul expect when it cometh into the presence of glorious love, and is purposely to be received with such demonstrations of love, as may be fitted to magnify the love of God, which exceedeth all the love of man, as omnipotency doth exceed our impotency, and therefore will exceed it in the effects! Though thou hast questioned here in the dark, whether thou wert welcome to Christ when thou camest to him in prayer, or when thou camest to his holy table, yet then doubt of thy welcome if thou canst.

Oh had we but one moment's sense of the delights of the embraced soul that is newly received by Christ into his kingdom, it would make us think we were in heaven already, and transport us more than the disciples that saw the transfiguration of Christ; and make us say, in comparing this with all the glory of the world, " Master, it is good for us to be here;" but in consideration of the full, to say, It is better to be there. But it must not be: earth must not be so happy as to have a moment's sense of the unconceivable pleasures of the received soul; that is the reward and crown, and therefore not fit for us here in our conflict.

But low things may, by dark resemblance, a little help us to conceive of something that is like them in a low degree. How would you receive your son, or husband, the next day after some bloody fight, where he had escaped with the victory? or your child, or friend, that arrived safely after a long and a dangerous voyage? Would you not run and meet him, and with joy embrace him, if he had been many years absent, and were now come home? I tell thee, poor soul, thy Saviour hath a larger heart, and another kind of love, than thou; and other reasons of greater force to move him to bid thee welcome into his presence.

3. Christ's receiving the departed soul includeth the state of blessedness into which he doth receive it. If you ask what that is, I answer, it is unto himself, to be with him where he is; and that in general is full of comfort, if there were no more; for we know that Christ is in no ill place; he is glorified at the " right hand of the Majesty on high," Heb. i. 3. And that the souls of the righteous, and at last their bodies, are received to himself, he often telleth us: " If any man serve me, let him follow me; and where I am, there shall also my servant be," John xii. 26. " And if I go and prepare a place for you, I will come again and receive you unto myself; that where I am, there ye may be also," John xiv. 3. And, in the mean time, when we once are absent from the body, we are present with the Lord, (2 Cor. v. 8,) and that is in " the building of God, an house not made with hands, eternal in the heavens," verse 1. Paul, therefore, desired " to depart, and to be with Christ," as being far better, Phil. i. 23; and Christ promised the converted thief, " This day shalt thou be with me in paradise," Luke xxiii. 43. And our state after the resurrection hath the same description, " And so shall we ever be with the Lord," 1 Thess. iv. 17. And what it shall be he declareth himself, " Father, I will that they also, whom thou hast given me, be with me where I am; that they may behold my glory, which thou hast given me," John xvii. 24. The soul of Lazarus (Luke xvi.) was

received into Abraham's bosom, where he is said to be comforted. The heavens receive Christ, (Acts iii. 21,) and therefore the heavens receive the spirits that go to him, even the spirits of the just made perfect, Heb. xii. 23; that is, that are crowned with Christ in glory, and freed from the imperfections and evils of this life. And so that is plain, though some would pervert it, that "whether we wake or sleep, we may live together with him," 1 Thess. v. 10. Not whether we wake to righteousness, or sleep in sin, for such sleepers live not with him; nor whether we wake by solicitude, or sleep in security; nor whether we naturally wake or sleep only, but whether we live, or die, and so our bodies sleep in death, yet we live together with him. In a word, Christ will receive us into a participation of his joy and glory; into a joy as great as our nature shall be capable of, and more than we can now desire, and that the largest heart on earth can justly conceive of or comprehend. And because all this tells you but to the ear, stay yet but a little while, and experimental sight and feeling shall tell you what this receiving is, even when we receive the kingdom that cannot be moved, (Heb. xii. 28,) and when we receive the end of our faith, the salvation of our souls, 1 Pet. i. 9.

Doct. VI. A dying christian may confidently and comfortably commend his spirit to Christ, to be received by him.

Though he have formerly been a grievous sinner, though at the present he be frail and faulty, though he be weak in faith, and love, and duty, though his body by sickness be become unfit to serve his soul, and as to present sensibility, activity, or joy, he seem to be past the best, or to be nothing, though the tempter would aggravate his sins, and weakness, and dulness to his discouragement, yet he may, he must, with confidence recommend his spirit to Christ, to be received by him.

O learn his doctrine, christians, that you may use it in the hour of your last distress. The hour is near; the distress will be the greatest that ever you were in. As well as we seem now while we are hearing this, our turn is nigh. The midwife is not so necessary to the life of the child that receiveth it into the world, as Christ's receiving will be then to our everlasting life. To say over heartlessly these words, "Lord Jesus, receive my spirit," will be no more than a dead-hearted hypocrite may do. Such formal lip-service in life or at death doth profit nothing to salvation; now make such necessary preparation, that at death you may have well-grounded confidence that Jesus Christ will receive your spirits.

1. And first, let me bring this to the carnal, unprepared sinner.

Poor sinner, what thoughts hast thou of thy dying hour, and of thy departing soul? I wonder at thee what thoughts thou hast of them, that thou canst sin so boldly, and live so carelessly, and talk or hear of the life to come so senselessly as thou dost! Thou mightest well think I wronged thee, if I took thee to be such a brute as not to know that thou must die. Thy soul that brought thy body hither, that causeth it now to hear and understand, that carrieth it up and down the world, must very shortly be required of thee, and must seek another habitation. What thoughts hast thou of thy departing soul? Will Christ receive it? Hast thou made sure of that? Or hast thou made it thy principal care and business to make sure? Oh, what doth intoxicate the brains of sensual, worldly men, that they drown themselves in the cares of this life, and ride and run for transitory riches, and live upon the smoke of honour and applause, and never soberly and seriously bethink them whether Christ will receive their departed souls! That they can fill their minds with other thoughts, and fill their mouths with other talk, and consume their time in other inconsiderable employments, and take no more care, and spend no more thoughts, and words, and time about the entertainment of their departing souls! When they are even ready to be gone, and stand, as it were, on tiptoe; when fevers, and consumptions, and many hundred diseases are all abroad so busily distributing their summonses; and when the gates of death have so many passengers crowding in, and souls a remaking such haste away, will you not consider what shall become of yours? Will you say that you hope well, and you must venture? If God had appointed you nothing to do to prepare for your safe passage and entertainment with Christ, you might then take up with such an answer; but it is a mad adventure to leave all undone that is necessary to your salvation, and then to say, you must put it to the venture. If you die in an unrenewed and unjustified state, it is past all venture; for it is certain that Christ will not receive you. You may talk of hoping, but it is not a matter to be hoped for. Hope that God will make good every word of his promise, and spare not; but there is no more hope that Christ will receive the souls of any but of his members, than there is that he will prove a liar. He never promised to save any others; and that is not all, but he hath declared and professed frequently that he will not. And you are no believers if you will not believe him; and if you believe him, you must believe that the unbelievers, the unregenerate, the unholy, and the workers of iniquity, shall not be received into the kingdom of heaven, for he hath professed it, John iii. 3, 36; Heb. xii. 14; Matt. vii. 23.

If Christ would receive the souls of all, your venture then had reason for it; or if he had left it as a thing that depended only on his unrevealed will, and not on any preparations of our own, we might then have quit ourselves of the care, and cast it all on him, as being his part, and none of ours. But it is not so, I hope I need not tell you that it is not so. Believe it, the question must be now resolved, and resolved by yourselves, whether Christ shall receive your departed souls, or cast them off as firebrands for hell. He hath made the law, and set down the terms already to which he will unalterably stand, and which we must trust to. It is now that you must labour to be accepted of him, "for we must all appear before the judgment-seat of Christ; that every one may receive the things done in his body, according to that he hath done, whether it be good or bad," 2 Cor. v. 10. O sirs! this the reason of our importunity with you. "Knowing the terror of the Lord, we persuade men," saith the apostle in the next words, ver. 11. We know that the sentence will be just, and that it is now in your own hands what judgment then shall pass upon you. And if just now your souls were passing hence, before you went from the place you sit in, would you think any care could be too great to make sure that they should go to happiness. Oh that you would consider how much it is your own work, and how much it resteth on yourselves what Christ shall then do with you! Then you will cry to him for mercy, O cast not away a miserable soul! Lord, receive me into thy kingdom! But now he must entreat you to be saved, and to be the people that he may then receive, and you will not hear him. And if you will not hear him when he calleth on you, and beseecheth you to repent and to prepare, as sure as Christ is Christ, he will not hear you when you cry and call for mercy too late in your extremity. Read Prov. i. and you will see this is true. It is you that are to be entreated that Christ may receive you, for the unwillingness and backwardness is on your part. You are now poisoning your souls by sin; and when we cannot entreat you either to forbear, or to take the vomit of repentance, yet when you are gasping and dying of your own wilful self-murder, you will then cry to Christ, and think he must receive you upon terms inconsistent with his justice, holiness, and truth. But flatter not yourselves, it will not be. This is the accepted time; behold, now is the day of salvation. Refuse it now, and it is lost for ever. O sirs, if this were the hour, and you were presently to be received or refused, would you blame me to cry and call to you with all the fervour of my soul, if I knew that it were in your own choice whether you would go to heaven or hell? Why now it is in your choice. Life and death are set before you. Christ will receive you if you will but come within the capacity of his acceptation. If you will not, there will then be no remedy. It is a doleful thing to observe how Satan doth bewitch poor sinners. That when time is gone, and the door of mercy is shut against them, they would think no cries too loud for mercy, and no importunity too great. For Christ telleth us, that then they will cry, "Lord, Lord, open to us," Matt. xxv. 10, 11. And yet now, when the door stands open, no arguments, no earnestness, no tears, can entreat them to enter in. Then there is not the most senseless sinner of you all but would cry more strongly than Esau for the blessing, when his tears could find no place for repentance, Heb. xii. 16, 17; Lord, receive a miserable soul! O whither shall I go if thou receive me not! I must else be tormented in those scorching flames. And yet now you will sell your birthright for one morsel; for a little of Judas's or Gehazi's gain, for the applause of worms, for the pleasing of your flesh that is turning to corruption, for the delights of gluttony, drunkenness, sports, or lust. There is not a man of you but would then pray more earnestly than those that you now deride for earnest praying, as if they whined, and were ridiculous. And yet now you will neither be serious in prayer, nor hear Christ, or his messengers, when he maketh it his earnest request to you to come in to him that you may have life, John v. 40. Then you will knock when the door is shut, and cry, Lord, open to a miserable sinner! and yet now you will not open unto him, when by his word and Spirit, his mercies and afflictions, he standeth at the door of your stubborn hearts, and calleth on you to repent and turn to God; now our entreaties cannot so much as bring you on your knees, or bring you to one hour's serious thoughts about the state of those souls that are so near their doom. O sirs! for your souls' sake, lay by your obstinacy. Pity those souls that then you will beg of Christ to pity. Do not you damn them by your sloth and sin in the day of your visitation, and then cry in vain to Christ to save them when it is too late. Yet the door of grace is open, but how speedily will it be shut! One stroke of an apoplexy, a consumption, a fever, can quickly shut it, and then you may tear your hearts with crying, "Lord, open to us," and all in vain. O did you but see departed souls, as you see the corpse that is left behind; did you see how they are treated at their removal from the flesh; how some are taken and others left; how some are welcomed to Christ, and others are abhorred, and turned over to the tormenter, and thrust out with implacable indignation and disdain, Luke xiii. 28; Prov. i. 24, 26, 27; sure you would enter into serious consideration this day, what it is that makes this difference, and why Christ so useth the one and the other, and what must be done now by the soul that would be received then. Alas! men will do any thing but that which they should do. Among the superstitious papists the conceit of a deliverance from purgatory makes them bequeath their lands and moneys to priests and friars to pray for them when they are dead, and to have other men cry to Christ to receive them, and open to them, when time is past; and yet now in the accepted time, now when it is at your choice, and the door is open, men live as if they were past feeling, and cared not what became of them at the last, and would not be beholden to Christ to receive them, when the deceitful world hath cast them off.

And now, beloved hearers all, I would make it my most earnest request to you, as one that knoweth we are all passing hence, and foreseeth the case of a departed soul, that you would now, without any more delay, prepare and make sure that you may be received into the everlasting habitations: and to this end, I shall more distinctly, though briefly, tell you, 1. What souls they are that Christ will receive, and what he will not; and, consequently, what you must do to be received. 2. What considerations should stir you up to this preparation.

1. Nothing is more sure than that Christ will not receive, 1. Any unregenerate, unconverted soul, John iii. 3, 5; Matt. xviii. 3; that is, not renewed and sanctified by his Spirit, Rom. viii. 9; Heb. xii. 14; Acts xxvi. 18. They must have the new and heavenly nature that will ever come to heaven. Without this you are morally uncapable of it. Heaven is the proper inheritance of saints, Col. i. 12. This heavenly nature and Spirit is your earnest: if you have this you are sealed up unto salvation, 2 Cor. i. 22; Eph. i. 13; iv. 30.

2. Christ will receive none but those that make it now their work to lay up a treasure in heaven, rather than upon the earth, Matt. vi. 20, 21; and that seek it in the first place, Matt. vi. 33; and can be content to part with all to purchase it, Matt. xiii. 44, 46; Luke xiv. 33; xviii. 22. An earthly-minded worldling is uncapable of heaven in that condition, Phil. iii. 17, 18; Luke xvi. 13. You must take it for your portion, and set your hearts on it, if ever you will come thither, Matt. vi. 21; Col. iii. 1—3.

3. Christ will receive no soul at last, but such as sincerely received him as their Lord and Saviour now, and gave up themselves to him, and received his word, and yield obedience to it, and received his Spirit, and were cleansed by him from their iniquities, John i. 11, 12; Luke xix. 27. "That all they might be damned that believed not the truth, but had pleasure in unrighteousness," 2 Thess. ii. 10, 12. They are God's own words; be not offended at them, but believe and fear. "He hateth all the workers of iniquity," and will say to them, "Depart from me, I know you not," Psalm v. 5; Matt. vii. 23.

4. He will receive none but those that loved his servants, that bore his holy image, and received them according to their abilities, Matt. xxv. 40, 41, &c. And if he will say to those that did not entertain them, "Depart from me, ye cursed, into everlasting fire," what will he say to those that hate and persecute them? 1 John iii. 14; v. 2.

5. He will receive none but those that live to him in the body, and use his gifts and talents to his service, and make it their chief business to serve, and honour, and please him in the world, Matt. xxv. 21, 26; 2 Cor. v. 9, 15; Gal. vi. 7, 8; and live not to the pleasing of the flesh, but have crucified it and its lusts, Rom. viii. 1, 13; Gal. v. 24.

Examine all these texts of Scripture, (for the matter is worthy of your study,) and you will see what souls they are that Christ will then receive, and what he will reject. You may see also what you must now be and do, if you will be then received. If you are not regenerate by the Spirit of God; (though you may be sacramentally regenerate in baptism;) if you are not justified by Christ; (though you may be absolved by a minister;) if you seek not heaven with higher estimation and resolutions than any felicity on earth, and take not God for your satisfying portion; (though you be never so religious in subserviency to a fleshly, worldly happiness;) if you receive not Christ as your only Saviour, and set him not in the throne and government of your hearts and lives; (though you may go with men for current christians;) if you hate not sin, if you love not the holy image and children of God, and use them not accordingly; if you crucify not the flesh, and die not to the world, and deny not yourselves, and live not unto God, as making it your chief business and happiness to please him; I say, if this be not your case, as sure as you are men, if you died this hour in this condition, Christ will not own you, but turn you off with a "Depart, ye cursed." You may as well think of reconciling light and darkness, or persuade a man to live on the food of beasts, or the stomach to welcome deadly poison, as to think that Christ will receive an ungodly, earthly, guilty soul.

Deceive not yourselves, sinners. If God could have entertained the ungodly, and heaven could hold unholy souls, answer me, then, these two or three questions.

Quest. 1. What need Christ, then, to have shed his blood, or become a sacrifice for sin? If he could have received the ungodly, he might have done it upon cheaper rates. This feigned him to have died to no purpose, but to bring the unsanctified to heaven, that might have been as well entertained there without his sufferings.

Quest. 2. To what use doth Christ send the Holy Ghost to sanctify his elect, or send his word and ministers to promote it, if they may come to heaven unsanctified?

Quest. 3. If the ungodly go to heaven, what use is hell for? There is no hell, if this be true. But you will quickly find that to be too good news to the ungodly to be true.

2. In Luke xvi. Christ teacheth us our duty by the parable of the steward, that asketh himself beforehand, what he shall do when he must be no longer steward, and contriveth it so that others may receive him when he is cast off; and he applieth it to us that must now so provide, that when we fail we may be received into the everlasting habitations. This is the work that we have all to mind. We always knew that this world would fail us. Oh how uncertain is your tenure of the dwellings that you now possess! Are you provided, certainly provided, whither to go, and who shall receive you when your stewardship is ended, and you must needs go hence? O think of these considerations that should move you presently to provide.

1. Your cottages of earth are ready to drop down, and it is a stormy time, there are many sicknesses abroad. One blast may quickly lay them in the dust; and then the flesh that had so much care, and was thought worthy to be preferred before the soul, must be laid and left to rot in darkness, to avoid the annoyance of the living: and when you may justly look every hour when you are turned out of these dwellings that you are in, is it not time to be provided of some other?

2. Consider, if Christ should not receive thy spirit, how unspeakably deplorable thy case will be. I think there is no man in all this assembly so mad, that would take all the world now to have his soul refused then by Christ, that would professedly make and subscribe such a bargain; and yet, alas, how many are they that will be hired for a smaller price, even for the pleasure of a sin, to do that which Christ himself hath told them will cause him to refuse them! O sirs, for aught you know, before to-morrow, or within this week, you may be put to know these things by trial, and your souls may be refused or received; and woe to you that ever you were men, if Christ receive you not!

Consider, 1. If Christ receive thee not, thou hast no friend left then to receive thee. Thy house, and land, and riches, and reputation, are all left behind; none of them will go with thee; or, if they did, they could afford thee no relief. Thy bosom friends, thy powerful defenders, are all left behind; or if they go before thee, or with thee, they can do nothing there, that could do so much for thee here. No minister so holy, no friend so kind, no patron so powerful, that can give thee any entertainment, if Christ refuse to entertain thee. Look to the right hand or to the left, there will be none to help thee, or care for thy forsaken soul. Then thou wilt find that one Christ had been a better friend than all the great ones upon earth.

2. If Christ, then, receive not thy departed soul, the devils will receive it. I am loth to speak so terrible a word, but that it must be spoken, if you will be awaked to prevent it. He that deceived thee will then plead conquest, and claim thee as his due that he may torment thee. And if the devil say, This soul is mine, and Christ do not rescue and justify thee, but say so too, no heart is able to conceive the horror that will then overwhelm thee. Doth not the reading of the sentence make thee tremble, "Depart from me, ye cursed, into everlasting fire, prepared for the devil and his angels?" Matt. xxv. 41. This is that dreadful delivering up to Satan, when the soul is excommunicated from the city of God. O, therefore, if thou be yet unreconciled to God, agree with him quickly, while thou art here in the way, lest he deliver thee to this terrible jailer and executioner, and thou be cast into the prison of the bottomless pit: "Verily, I say unto thee, thou shalt by no means come out thence till thou hast paid the uttermost farthing," Matt. v. 25, 26.

3. The greatness of the change will increase the amazement and misery of thy spirit, if Christ receive it not. To leave a world that thou wast acquainted with; a world that pleased thee, and entertained thee; a world where thou hadst long thy business and delight, and where, wretched man, thou hadst made the chief provision, and laid up thy treasure: this will be a sad part of the change. To enter into a world where thou art a stranger, and much worse, and see the company and the things that before thou never sawest, and to find things go there so contrary to thy expectation; to be turned, with Dives, from thy sumptuous dwelling, attendance, and fare, into a place of easeless torment: this will be a sadder part of thy change. Here the rich would have received thee, the poor would have served and flattered thee, thy friends would have comforted thee, thy play-fellows would have been merry with thee. But there, alas! how the case is altered! all these have done; the table is withdrawn, the game is ended, the mirth is ceased, and now succeedeth, "Son, remember that thou in thy life-time receivedst thy good things, and Lazarus evil things: but now he is comforted, and thou art tormented," Luke xvi. 25. Oh, dreadful change to those that made the world their home, and little dreamed, or did but dream, of such a day! Never to see this world again, unless by such reviews as will torment them; never to have

sport or pleasure more; and for these to have such company, such thoughts, such work and usage, as God hath told us is in hell.

4. If Christ receive thee not, the burden of thy sins will overwhelm thee, and conscience will have no relief. Sin will not then appear in so harmless a shape as now: it will then seem a more odious or frightful thing. Oh, to remember these days of folly, of careless, sluggish, obstinate folly, of sottish negligence, and contempt of grace, will be a more tormenting thing than you will now believe. If such sermons and discourses as foretell it are troublesome to thee, what then will that sad experience be!

5. The wrath of an offended God will overwhelm thee. This will be thy hell. He that was so merciful in the time of mercy, will be most terrible and implacable when that time is past, and make men know that Christ and mercy are not neglected, refused, and abused at so cheap a rate, as they would needs imagine in the time of their deliration.

6. It will overwhelm the soul if Christ receive it not, to see that thou art entering upon eternity, even into an everlasting state of woe. Then thou wilt think, O whither am I going? What must I endure? and how long, how long? When shall my miseries have an end? and when shall I come back? and how shall I ever be delivered? Oh now what thoughts wilt thou have of the wonderful design of God in man's redemption! Now thou wilt better understand what a Saviour was worth, and how he should have been believed in, and how his gospel and his saving grace should have been entertained.

Oh that the Lord would now open your hearts to entertain it, that you may not then value it to your vexation, that would not value it now to your relief! Poor sinner, for the Lord's sake, and for thy soul's sake, I beg now of thee, as if it were on my knees, that thou wouldst cast away thy sinful cares and pleasures, and open thy heart, and now receive thy Saviour and his saving grace, as ever thou wouldst have him then receive thy trembling, departed soul! Turn to him now, that he may not turn thee from him then. Forsake him not for a flattering world, a little transitory, vain delight, as ever thou wouldst not then have thy departed soul forsaken by him! O delay not, man, but now, even now receive him, that thou mayst avoid so terrible a danger, and put so great a question presently out of doubt, and be able comfortably to say, I have received Christ, and he will receive me; if I die this night he will receive me: then thou mayst sleep quietly, and live merrily, without any disparagement to thy reason. O yield to this request, sinner, of one that desireth thy salvation. If thou wert now departing, and I would not pray earnestly to Christ to receive thy soul, thou wouldst think I were uncharitable. Alas! it will be one of these days; and it is thee that I must entreat, and thyself must be prevailed with, or there is no hope. Christ sendeth me to thyself, and saith, that he is willing to receive thee, if now thou wilt receive him, and be sanctified and ruled by him. The matter stops at thy own regardless, wilful heart. What sayest thou? Wilt thou receive Christ now, or not? Wilt thou be a new creature, and live to God, by the principle of his Spirit, and the rule of his word, to please him here, that thou mayst live with him for ever? Wilt thou take up this resolution, and make this covenant with God this day? O give me a word of comfort, and say, thou art resolved, and wilt deliver up thyself to Christ. That which is my comfort now on thy behalf, will be ten thousand-fold more thy comfort then, when thou partakest of the benefit. And if thou grieve us now, by denying thy soul to Christ, it will be at last ten thousand-fold more thy grief. Refuse not our requests and Christ's request now, as ever thou wouldst not have him refuse thee then, and thy requests. It is men's turning away now from Christ that will cause Christ then to turn from them. "The turning away of the simple slayeth them, and they then eat but the fruit of their own way, and are filled with their own devices," Prov. i. 31, 32. "See then that ye now refuse not him that speaketh; for there is no escaping if you turn away from him that speaketh from heaven," Heb. xii. 25.

What would you say yourselves to the man that would not be dissuaded from setting his house on fire, and then would pray and cry importunately to God that he would keep it from being burnt? Or of the man that will not be dissuaded from taking poison, and then when it gripeth him will cry to God to save his life? Or of the man that will go to sea in a leaking, broken vessel, yea, himself will make those breaches in it that shall let the water in, and when it is sinking will cry to God to save him from being drowned? And will you do this about so great a matter as the everlasting state of your immortal souls? Will you now be worldlings, and sensualists, and ungodly, and undo yourselves, and then cry, "Lord Jesus, receive my spirit," at the last? What! receive an unholy spirit? Will you not knock till the door is shut? when he telleth you, that "it is not every one that will cry Lord, Lord, that shall enter into the kingdom of heaven, but he that doth the will of his Father which is in heaven," Matt. vii. 21.

Lastly, consider with what unspeakable joy it will fill thy soul to be then received by the Lord. Oh what a joyful word will it be, when thou shalt hear, "Come, ye blessed of my Father, inherit the kingdom prepared for you." If thou wilt not have this to be thy case, thou shalt see those received to the increase of thy grief whom thou refusedst here to imitate: "There shall be weeping and gnashing of teeth, when ye shall see Abraham, Isaac, and Jacob, and all the prophets in the kingdom of God, and those that from east, west, north, and south, shall sit there with them, and thou thrust out," Luke xiii. 27—29.

I have been long in this part of my application, having to do with souls that are ready to depart, and are in so sad an unprepared state, as is not to be thought on but with great compassion; I am next to come to that part of the application which I chiefly intended, to those that are the heirs of life.

2. O you that are members of Jesus Christ, receive this cordial which may corroborate your hearts against all inordinate fears of death. Let it come when it will, you may boldly recommend your departing souls into the hands of Christ. Let it be by a lingering disease or by an acute, by a natural or a violent death, at the fulness of your age or in the flower of your youth, death can but separate the soul from flesh, but not from Christ: whether you die poor or rich, at liberty or in prison, in your native country or a foreign land, whether you be buried in the earth or cast into the sea, death shall but send your souls to Christ. Though you die under the reproach and slanders of the world, and your names be cast out among men as evil-doers, yet Christ will take your spirits to himself. Though your souls depart in fear and trembling, though they want the sense of the love of God, and doubt of pardon and peace with him, yet Christ will receive them.

I know thou wilt be ready to say, that thou art unworthy, Will he receive so unworthy a soul as mine? But if thou be a member of Christ thou art worthy in him to be accepted. Thou hast a worthiness of aptitude, and Christ hath a worthiness of merit.

The day that cometh upon such at unawares, that have their hearts overcharged with surfeiting, drunkenness, and the cares of this life, and as a snare surpriseth the inhabitants of the earth, shall be the day of thy great deliverance; "Watch ye, therefore, and pray always, that ye may be accounted worthy to escape all these things that shall come to pass, and to stand before the Son of man," Luke xxi. 34—36. "They that are accounted worthy to obtain that world can die no more; for they are equal unto the angels, and are the children of God," Luke xx. 35, 36.

Object. Oh but my sins are great and many; and will Christ ever receive so ignorant, so earthly and impure a soul as mine?

Answ. If he have freed thee from the reign of sin, by giving thee a will that would fain be fully delivered from it, and given thee a desire to be perfectly holy, he will finish the work that he hath begun; and will not bring thee defiled into heaven, but will wash thee in his blood, and separate all the remnant of corruption from thy soul, when he separateth thy soul from flesh: there needs no purgatory, but his blood and Spirit in the instant of death shall deliver thee, that he may present thee spotless to the Father.

O fear not then to trust thy soul with him that will receive it; and fear not death that can do thee no more harm. And when once thou hast overcome the fears of death, thou wilt be the more resolute in thy duty, and faithful to Christ, and above the power of most temptations, and wilt not fear the face of man, when death is the worst that man can bring thee to. It is true, death is dreadful; but it is as true that the arms of Christ are joyful. It is an unpleasing thing to leave the bodies of our friends in the earth; but it is unspeakable pleasure to their souls to be received into the heavenly society by Christ.

And how confidently, quietly, and comfortably you may commend your departing spirits to be received by Christ, be informed by these considerations following.

1. Your spirits are Christ's own; and may you not trust him with his own? As they are his by the title of creation, "All souls are mine, saith the Lord," Ezek. xviii. 4; so also by the title of redemption, "We are not our own, we are bought with a price," 1 Cor. vi. 19.

Say therefore to him, Lord, I am thine much more than my own; receive thine own, take care of thine own. Thou drewest me to consent to thy gracious covenant, and I resigned myself and all I had to thee. And thou swarest to me, and I became thine, Ezek. xvi. 8. And I stand to the covenant that I made, though I have offended thee. I am sinful, but I am thine, and would not forsake thee, and change my Lord and Master, for a world. O know thine own, and own my soul that hath owned thee, though it hath sinned against thee. Thy sheep know thy voice, and follow not a stranger; now know thy poor sheep, and leave them not to the devourer. Thy lambs have been preserved by thee among wolves in the world, preserve me now from the enemy of souls. I am thine, O save me, (Psal. cxix. 94,) and lose not that which is thine own!

2. Consider that thou art his upon so dear a purchase, as that he is the more engaged to receive thee. Hath he bought thee by the price of his most precious blood, and will he cast thee off? Hath he come down on earth to seek and save thee, and will he now forsake thee? Hath he lived in flesh a life of poverty, and suffered reproach, and scorn, and buffetings, and been nailed to the cross, and put to cry out, "My God, my God, why hast thou forsaken me?" and will he now forget his love, and sufferings, and himself forsake thee after this? Did he himself on the cross commend his spirit into his Father's hands, and will he not receive thy spirit when thou at death commendest it to him? He hath known himself what it is to have a human soul separated from the body, and the body buried in a grave, and there lamented by surviving friends. And why did he this, but that he might be fit to receive and relieve thee in the like condition? O, who would not be encouraged to encounter death, and lie down in a grave, that believeth that Christ did so before him, and considereth why he went that way, and what a conquest he had made!

I know an argument from the death of Christ will not prove his love to the souls of the ungodly so as to infer that he will receive them; but it will prove his reception of believers' souls: "He that spared not his own Son, but gave him up for us all, how shall he not with him also freely give us all things?" (Rom. viii. 32,) is an infallible argument as to believers, but not as to those that do reject him.

Say therefore to him, O my Lord! can it be that thou couldst come down in the flesh, and be abused, and spit upon, and slandered, and crucified; that thou couldst bleed, and die, and be buried for me, and now be unwilling to receive me? that thou shouldst pay so dear for souls, and now refuse to entertain them? that thou shouldst die to save them from the devil, and now wilt leave them to his cruelty? that thou hast conquered him, and yet wilt suffer him at last to have the prey? To whom can a departing soul fly for refuge, and for entertainment, if not to thee that diedst for souls, and sufferedst thine to be separated from the flesh, that we might have all assurance of thy compassion unto ours? Thou didst openly declare upon the cross, that the reason of thy dying was to receive departed souls, when thou didst thus encourage the soul of a penitent malefactor, by telling him, "This day shalt thou be with me in paradise." O give the same encouragement or entertainment to this sinful soul that flieth unto thee, that trusteth in thy death and merits, and is coming to receive thy doom!

3. Consider that Jesus Christ is full of love and tender compassion to souls. What his tears over Lazarus compelled the Jews to say, "Behold how he loved him," John xi. 36; the same his incarnation, life, and death should much more stir us up to say, with greater admiration, Behold how he loved us. The foregoing words, though the shortest verse in all the Bible, "Jesus wept," (verse 35,) are long enough to prove his love to Lazarus: and the Holy Ghost would not have the tears of Christ to be unknown to us, that his love may be the better known. But we have a far larger demonstration of his love; "He loved us and gave himself for us," Gal. ii. 20. And by what gift could he better testify his love? "He loved us, and washed us in his blood," Rev. i. 5. He loved us, as the Father loveth him, John xv. 9. And may we not comfortably go to him that loved us? Will love refuse us when we fly unto him?

Say then to Christ, O thou that hast loved my soul, receive it! I commend it not unto an enemy. Can that love reject me, and cast me into hell, that so oft embraced me on earth, and hath declared itself by such ample testimonies!

Oh had we but more love to Christ, we should be more sensible of his love to us, and then we should trust him, and love would make us hasten to him, and with confidence cast ourselves upon him!

4. Consider that it is the office of Christ to save

souls, and to receive them, and therefore we may boldly recommend them to his hands. The Father sent him to be the Saviour of the world, 1 John iv. 14; and he is effectively the Saviour of his body, Eph. v. 23. And may we not trust him in his undertaken office, that would trust a physician or any other in his office, if we judge him faithful? Yea, he is engaged by covenant to receive us: when we gave up ourselves to him, he also became ours; and we did it on this condition, that he should receive and save us. And it was the condition of his own undertaking; he drew the covenant himself and tendered it first to us, and assumed his own conditions, as he imposed ours.

Say then to him, My Lord, I expected but the performance of thy covenants, and the discharge of thine undertaken office: as thou hast caused me to believe in thee, and love and serve thee, and perform the conditions which thou laidest on me, though with many sinful failings, which thou hast pardoned; so now let my soul, that hath trusted on thee, have the full experience of thy fidelity, and take me to thyself according to thy covenant. "O now remember the word unto thy servant, upon which thou hast caused him to hope!" Psal. cxix. 49. How many precious promises hast thou left us, that we shall not be forsaken by thee, but that we shall be with thee where thou art, that we may behold thy glory! For this cause art thou the Mediator of the new covenant, that by means of death for the redemption of the transgressions that were under the first testament, they which are called might receive the promise of eternal inheritance, Heb. ix. 15. According to thy covenant, "Godliness hath the promise of the life that now is, and of that which is to come," 1 Tim. iv. 8. And when we have done thy will (notwithstanding our lamentable imperfections) we are to receive the promise, Heb. x. 36. O, now receive me into the kingdom which thou hast promised to to them that love thee! James i. 12.

5. Consider how able Christ is to answer thine expectations. All power is given him in heaven and earth, (Matt. xxviii. 19,) and all things are given by the Father into his hands, John xiii. 3. All judgment is committed to him, John v. 22. It is fully in his power to receive and save thee; and Satan cannot touch thee but by his consent. Fear not, then; he is the first and last, that liveth, and was dead; and behold he liveth for evermore, amen; and hath the keys of hell and death, Rev. i. 17, 18.

Say then, If thou wilt, Lord, thou canst save this departing soul! O, say but the word, and I shall live! Lay but thy rebuke upon the destroyer, and he shall be restrained. When my Lord and dearest Saviour hath the keys, how can I be kept out of thy kingdom, or cast into the burning lake? Were it a matter of difficulty unto thee, my soul might fear lest heaven would not be opened to it; but thy love hath overcome the hinderances; and it is as easy to receive me, as to love me.

6. Consider how perfectly thy Saviour is acquainted with the place that thou art going to, and the company and employment which thou must there have; and, therefore, as there is nothing strange to him, so the ignorance and strangeness in thyself should therefore make thee fly to him, and trust him, and recommend thy soul to him, and say, Lord, it would be terrible to my departing soul to go into a world that I never saw, and into a place so strange, and unto company so far above me; but that I know there is nothing strange to thee, and thou knowest it for me, and I may better trust thy knowledge than mine own. When I was a child I knew not mine own inheritance, nor what was necessary to the daily provisions for my life; but my parents knew it that cared for me. The eyes must see for all the body, and not every member see for itself. Oh, cause me as quietly and believingly to commit my soul to thee, to be possessed of the glory which thou seest and possessest, as if I had seen and possessed it myself, and let thy knowledge be my trust!

7. Consider that Christ hath provided a glorious receptacle for faithful souls, and it cannot be imagined that he will lose his preparations, or be frustrate of his end. All that he did and suffered on earth was for this end. He therefore became the Captain of our salvation, and was made perfect through sufferings, that he might bring many sons to glory, Heb. ii. 10. He hath taken possession in our nature, and is himself interceding for us in the heavens, Heb. vii. 25. And for whom doth he provide this heavenly building, not made with hands, but for believers? If, therefore, any inordinate fear surprise thee, remember what he hath said: "Let not your hearts be troubled: ye believe in God, believe also in me. In my Father's house are many mansions: if it were not so, I would have told you. I go to prepare a place for you; and if I go and prepare a place for you, I will come again, and receive you unto myself; that where I am, there ye may be also," John xiv. 1—3.

Say, therefore, Lord, when thou hadst made this lower narrow world, thou wouldst not leave it uninhabited; for man thou madest it, and man thou placedst in it. And when thou hast prepared that more capacious, glorious world for thy redeemed flock, it cannot be that thou wilt shut them out. O, therefore, receive my fearful soul, and help me to obey thy own command, Luke xii. 32, "Fear not, little flock, for it is your Father's good pleasure to give you the kingdom." O, let me hear that joyful sentence, "Come, ye blessed of my Father, inherit the kingdom prepared for you from the foundation of the world," Matt. xxv. 34.

8. Consider that Christ hath received thy soul unto grace, and therefore he will receive it unto glory. He hath quickened us who were dead in trespasses and sins, wherein in times past we walked, &c. But God, who is rich in mercy, for his great love wherewith he loved us, even when we were dead in sins and trespasses, quickened us together with Christ, and raised us up together, and made us sit together in heavenly places in Christ Jesus, Eph. ii. 1—6. The state of grace is the kingdom of heaven, as well as the state of glory, Matt. iii. 2; x. 7; xiii. 11, 24, 31, 33, 44, 45, 47. By grace thou hast the heavenly birth and nature: we are first-born to trouble and sorrow in the world; but we are new-born to everlasting joy and pleasure. Grace maketh us heirs, and giveth us title, and therefore at death we shall have possession. The Father of our Lord Jesus Christ, according to his abundant mercy, hath begotten us again unto a lively hope, by the resurrection of Jesus Christ from the dead, to an inheritance incorruptible and undefiled, and that fadeth not away, reserved in heaven for us, 1 Pet. i. 3, 4. The great work was done in the day of thy renovation; then thou wast entered into the household of God, and made a fellow-citizen with the saints, and receivedst the Spirit of adoption, Eph. ii. 19; Gal. iv. 6. He gave thee life eternal, when he gave thee knowledge of himself, and of his Son, John xvii. 3. And will he now take from thee the kingdom which he hath given thee? Thou wast once his enemy, and he hath received thee already into his favour, and reconciled thee to himself; and will he not then receive thee to his glory? Rom. v. 8—11, "God commendeth his love toward us, in that, while we were yet sinners, Christ died for us. Much more then, being now justified

by his blood, we shall be saved from wrath through him. For if, when we were enemies, we were reconciled to God by the death of his Son, much more, being reconciled, we shall be saved by his life. And not only so, but we also joy in God through our Lord Jesus Christ, by whom we have now received the atonement." And when we have peace with God, being justified by faith, (Rom. v. 1,) why should we doubt whether he will receive us? The great impediments and cause of fear are now removed: unpardoned sin is taken away, our debt is discharged. We have a sufficient answer against all that can be alleged to the prejudice of our souls: yea, it is Christ himself that answereth for us; it is he that justifieth, who then shall condemn us? Will he not justify those at last whom he hath here justified? Or will he justify us, and yet not receive us? That were both to justify and condemn us.

Depart, then, in peace, O fearful soul; thou fallest into his hands that hath justified thee by his blood; will he deny thee the inheritance of which he himself hath made thee heir, yea, a joint-heir with himself? Rom. viii. 17. Will he deprive thee of thy birthright, who himself begot thee of the incorruptible seed? If he would not have received thee to glory, he would not have drawn thee to himself, and have blotted out thine iniquities, and received thee by reconciling grace. Many a time he hath received the secret petitions, complaints, and groans which thou hast poured out before him; and hath given thee access with boldness to his throne of grace, when thou couldst not have access to man; and he hath taken thee up, when man hath cast thee off. Surely he that received thee so readily in thy distress, will not now at last repent him of his love. As Manoah's wife said, "If the Lord were pleased to kill us, he would not have received a burnt-offering and a meat-offering at our hands, neither would he have showed us all these things," Judg. xiii. 23. He hath received thee into his church, and entertained thee with the delights and fatness of his house, (Psal. xxxvi. 8,) and bid thee welcome to his table, and feasted thee with his body and his blood, and communicated in these his quickening Spirit; and will he then disown thee, and refuse thee, when thou drawest nearer him, and art cast upon him for thy final doom? After so many receptions in the way of grace, dost thou yet doubt of his receiving thee?

9. Consider how nearly thou art related to him in this state of grace; thou art his child, and hath he not the bowels of a father? When thou didst ask bread, he was not used to give thee a stone; and will he give thee hell, when thou askest but the entertainment in heaven, which he hath promised thee? Thou art his friend, (John xv. 14, 15,) and will he not receive his friends? Thou art his spouse, betrothed to him the very day when thou consentedst to his covenant; and where then shouldst thou live but with him? Thou art a member of his body, of his flesh and bone, Eph. v. 30; and no man ever yet hated his own flesh, but nourisheth and cherisheth it, even as the Lord the church, verse 29: as he came down in flesh to be a suitor to thee, so he caused thee to let go all for him; and will he now forsake thee? Suspect it not, but quietly resign thy soul into his hands, and say, Lord, take this soul that pleads relation to thee; it is the voice of thy child that crieth to thee; the name of a father, which thou hast assumed towards me, is my encouragement. When thou didst call us out of the world unto thee, thou saidst, I will receive you, and I will be a father to you, and ye shall be my sons and daughters, 2 Cor. vi. 17, 18. O our Father, which art in heaven, shut not out thy children, the children of thy love and promise. The compassion that thou hast put into man engageth him to relieve a neighbour, yea, an enemy, much more to entertain a child; our children and our friends dare trust themselves upon our kindness and fidelity, and fear not that we will reject them in their distress, or destroy them, though they do sometimes offend us: our kindness is cruelty in comparison of thine; our love deserveth not the name of love in comparison of thy most precious love. Thine is the love of God, who is love itself, 1 John iv. 8, 16; and who is the God of love, 2 Cor. i. 13, 11; and is answerable to thine omnipotency, omniscience, and other attributes: but ours is the love of frail and finite sinful men. As we may pray to thee to forgive us our trespasses, for we also forgive those that have trespassed against us; so we may pray to thee to receive us, though we have offended thee, for even we receive those that have offended us. Hath thy love unto thine own its breadth, and length, and height, and depth; and is it such as passeth knowledge? Eph. iii. 17—19. And yet canst thou exclude thine own, and shut them out that cry unto thee? Can that love, which washed me and took me home when I lay wallowing in my blood, reject me, when it hath so far recovered me? Can that love now thrust me out of heaven, that lately fetched me from the gates of hell, and placed me among thy saints? "Whom thou lovest, thou lovest to the end," John xiii. 1. "Thou art not as man, that thou shouldst repent," Numb. xxiii. 19. "With thee is no variableness, or shadow of turning," Jam. i. 17. If yesterday thou so freely lovedst me as to adopt me for thy child, thou wilt not to-day refuse me, and cast me into hell. Receive, Lord Jesus, a member of thy body; a weak one, indeed, but yet a member, and needeth the more thy tenderness and compassion, who hast taught us not to cast out our infants, because they are small and weak. "We have forsaken all to cleave unto thee, that we might with thee be one flesh and spirit," Eph. v. 31; 1 Cor. vi. 17. O cut not off, and cast not out, thy members that are ingrafted into thee. "Thou hast dwelt in me here by faith, and shall I not now dwell with thee?" Eph. iii. 17. Thou hast prayed to the Father, that we may be one in thee, and may be with thee to behold thy glory, John xvii. 20—24; and wilt thou deny to receive me to that glory, who pray but for what thou hast prayed to thy Father? Death maketh no separation between thee and thy members; it dissolveth not the union of souls with thee, though it separate them from the flesh; and shall a part of thyself be rejected and condemned?

10. Consider that Christ hath sealed thee up unto salvation, and given thee the earnest of his Spirit; and therefore will certainly receive thee, 2 Cor. i. 22; v. 5; Eph. i. 13, 14; iv. 30. Say, therefore, to him, Behold, Lord, thy mark, thy seal, thine earnest: flesh and blood did not illuminate and renew me; thy Spirit which thou hast given me is my witness that I am thine, Rom. viii. 16. And wilt thou disown and refuse the soul that thou hast sealed?

11. Consider that he that hath given thee a heavenly mind, will certainly receive thee into heaven. If thy treasure were not there, thy heart would never have been there, Matt. vi. 21. Thy weak desires do show what he intends thee for; he kindled not those desires in vain. Thy love to him (though too small) is a certain proof that he intends not to reject thee; it cannot be that God can damn, or Christ refuse, a soul that doth sincerely love him: he that loveth, "dwelleth in God, and God in him," 1 John iv. 15, 16. And shall he not then dwell with God for ever? God fitteth the nature of every creature to its use,

and agreeably to the element in which they dwell; and, therefore, when he gave thee the heavenly nature, (though but in weak beginnings,) it showed his will to make thee an inhabitant of heaven.

Say, therefore, to him, O Lord, I had never loved thee if thou hadst not begun and loved me first; I had not minded thee, or desired after thee, if thou hadst not kindled these desires: it cannot be that thy grace itself should be a deceit and misery, and intended but to tantalize us; and that thou hast set thy servants' souls on longing for that which thou wilt never give them. Thou wouldst not have given me the wedding garment, when thou didst invite me, if thou hadst meant to keep me out: even the grain of mustard seed which thou sowedst in my heart, was a kind of promise of the happiness to which it tendeth. Indeed I have loved thee so little, that I am ashamed of myself, and confess my cold indifferency deserves thy wrath; but that I love thee, and desire thee, is thy gift, which signifieth the higher satisfying gift: though I am cold and dull, my eyes are towards thee; it is thee that I mean when I can but groan: it is long since I have bid this world away; it shall not be my home or portion: O perfect what thou hast begun; this is not the time or place of my perfection; and though my life be now hid with thee in God, when thou appearest, let me appear with thee in glory, Col. iii. 4. And, in the mean time, let this soul enjoy its part that appeareth before thee; give me what thou hast caused me to love, and then I shall more perfectly love thee, when my thirst is satisfied, and the water which thou hast given me shall spring up to everlasting life, John iv. 14.

12. Consider, also, that he that hath engaged thee to seek first his kingdom, is engaged to give it them that do sincerely seek it. He called thee off the pursuit of vanity when thou wast following the pleasures and profits of the world; and he called thee to labour for the food that perisheth not, but endureth to everlasting life, John vi. 27. Since then it hath been thy care and business, (notwithstanding all thine imperfections,) to seek and serve him, to please and honour him, and so to run that thou mightest obtain.

Say, then, Though my sins deserve thy wrath, and nothing that I have done deserve thy favour, yet godliness hath thy promise of the life to come; and thou hast said, that "he that seeks shall find," Matt. vii. 7, 8. O now let me find the kingdom that I have sought, and sought by thy encouragement and help: it cannot be that any should have cause to repent of serving thee, or suffer disappointment that trusts upon thee. My labour for the world was lost and vain, but thou didst engage me to be stedfast and abound in thy work, on this account, that my labour should not be in vain, 1 Cor. xv. 58. Now give the full and final answer unto all my prayers: now that I have done the fight, and finished my course, let me find the crown of righteousness which thy mercy hath laid up, 2 Tim. iv. 8. O crown thy graces, and with thy greatest mercies recompense and perfect thy preparatory mercies, and let me be received to thy glory, who have been guided by thy counsel, Psal. lxxiii. 24.

13. Consider that Christ hath already received millions of souls, and never was unfaithful unto any. There are now with him the spirits of the just made perfect, that in this life were imperfect as well as you. Why, then, should you not comfortably trust him with your souls? and say, Lord, thou art the common salvation and refuge of thy saints; both strong and weak, even all that are given thee by the Father, shall come to thee, and those that come thou wilt in nowise cast out. Thousands have been entertained by thee that were unworthy in themselves, as well as I. It is few of thy members that are now on earth, in comparison of those that are with thee in heaven. Admit me, Lord, into the new Jerusalem: thou wilt have thy house to be filled; O, take my spirit into the number of those blessed ones that shall come from east, west, north, and south, and sit down with Abraham, Isaac, and Jacob in the kingdom; that we may, together with eternal joys, give thanks and praise to thee that hast redeemed us to God by thy blood.

14. Consider that it is the will of the Father himself that we should be glorified. He therefore gave us to his Son, and gave his Son for us, to be our Saviour, "That whosoever believeth in him should not perish, but have everlasting life," John iii. 16, 17. All our salvation is the product of his love, Eph. ii. 4; John vi. 37. John xvi. 26, 27, "I say not that I will pray the Father for you, for the Father himself loveth you, because ye have loved me," &c. John xiv. 21, "He that loveth me shall be loved of my Father, and I will love him, and will manifest myself to him."

Say, therefore, with our dying Lord, "Father, into thy hands I commend my spirit." By thy Son, who is the way, the truth, and the life, I come to thee, John xiv. 6. "Fulness of joy is in thy presence, and everlasting pleasures at thy right hand," Psal. xvi. 11. Thy love redeemed me, renewed and preserved me; O now receive me to the fulness of thy love. This was thy will in sending thy Son, that of all that thou gavest him he should lose nothing, but should raise it up at the last day. O let not now this soul be lost that is passing to thee through the straits of death. I had never come unto thy Son if thou hadst not drawn me, and if I had not heard and learned of thee, John vi. 44, 45. I thank thee, O Father, Lord of heaven and earth, that thou hast revealed to me, a babe, an idiot, the blessed mysteries of thy kingdom, Luke x. 21; Acts iv. 13. O now as the veil of flesh must be withdrawn, and my soul be parted from this body, withdraw the veil of thy displeasure, and show thy servant the glory of thy presence: that he that hath seen thee but as in a glass, may see thee now with open face; and when my earthly house of this tabernacle is dissolved, let me inhabit thy building not made with hands, eternal in the heavens, 2 Cor. v. 1.

15. Lastly, Consider that God hath designed the everlasting glory of his name, and the pleasing of his blessed will, in our salvation; and the Son must triumph in the perfection of his conquest of sin and Satan, and in the perfecting of our redemption; and, doubtless, he will not lose his Father's glory and his own. Say, then, with confidence, I resign my soul to thee, O Lord, who hast called and chosen me, that thou mightest make known the riches of thy glory on me, as a vessel of mercy prepared unto glory, Rom. ix. 23. Thou hast predestinated me to the adoption of thy child by Christ unto thyself, to the praise of the glory of thy grace, wherein thou hast made me accepted in thy Beloved, Eph. i. 5, 6, 11, 12. Receive me now to the glory which thou hast prepared for us, Matt. xxv. 34. The hour is at hand; Lord, glorify thy poor adopted child, that he may for ever glorify thee, John xvii. 1. It is thy promise to glorify those whom thou dost justify, Rom. viii. 30. As "there is no condemnation to them that are in Christ," (Rom. viii. 1,) so now let him present me faultless before the presence of his glory with exceeding joy; and to thee "the only wise God our Saviour, be the glory, majesty, dominion, and power for evermore. Amen." Jude 24, 25.

What now remaineth, but that we all set ourselves to learn this sweet and necessary task, that we may joyfully perform it in the hour of our extremity; even to recommend our departing souls to Christ, with confidence that he will receive them. It is a lesson not easy to be learned; for faith is weak, and doubts and fears will easily arise, and nature will be loth to think of dying; and we that have so much offended Christ, and lived so strangely to him, and been entangled in too much familiarity with the world, shall be apt to shrink when we should joyfully trust him with our departing souls. O, therefore, now set yourselves to overcome these difficulties in time. You know we are all ready to depart; it is time this last important work were thoroughly learned, that our death may be both safe and comfortable.

There are divers other uses of this doctrine, that I should have urged upon you, had there been time. As, 1. If Christ will receive your departing souls, then fear not death, but long for this heavenly entertainment.

2. Then do not sin for fear of them that can but kill the body, and send the soul to Christ.

3. Then think not the righteous unhappy because they are cast off by the world; neither be too much troubled at it yourselves when it comes to be your case; but remember that Christ will not forsake you, and that none can hinder him from the receiving of your souls. No malice nor slanders can follow you so far as by defamation to make your justifier condemn you.

4. If you may trust him with your souls, then trust him with your friends, your children that you must leave behind, with all your concernments and affairs: and trust him with his gospel and his church; for they are all his own, and he will prevail to the accomplishment of his blessed pleasure.

But, 5. I shall only add that use which the sad occasion of our meeting doth bespeak. What cause have we now to mix our sorrows for our deceased friend, with the joys of faith for her felicity! We have left the body to the earth, and that is our lawful sorrow, for it is the fruit of sin; but her spirit is received by Jesus Christ, and that must be our joy, if we will behave ourselves as true believers. If we can suffer with her, should we not rejoice also with her? And if the joy be far greater to the soul with Christ, than the ruined state of the body can be lamentable, it is but reason that our joy should be greater for her joy, than our sorrow for the dissolution of the flesh. We that should not much lament the passage of a friend beyond the seas, if it were to be advanced to a kingdom, should less lament the passage of a soul to Christ, if it were not for the remnant of our woeful unbelief.

She is arrived at the everlasting rest, where the burden of corruption, the contradictions of the flesh, the molestations of the tempter, the troubles of the world, and the injuries of malicious men, are all kept out, and shall never more disturb her peace. She hath left us in these storms, who have more cause to weep for ourselves, and for our children, that have yet so much to do and suffer, and so many dangers to pass through, than for the souls that are at rest with Christ. We are capable of no higher hopes than to attain that state of blessedness which her soul possesseth; and shall we make that the matter of our lamentation as to her, which we make the matter of our hopes as to ourselves? Do we labour earnestly to come thither, and yet lament that she is there? You will say, it is not because she is clothed upon with the house from heaven, but that she is unclothed of the flesh: but is there any other passage than death unto immortality? Must we not be unclothed before the garments of glory can be put on? She bemoaneth not her own dissolved body; the glorified soul can easily bear the corruption of the flesh; and if you saw but what the soul enjoyeth, you would be like-minded, and be moderate in your griefs. Love not yourselves so as to be unjust and unmerciful in your desires to your friends. Let Satan desire to keep them out of heaven, but do not you desire it. You may desire your own good, but not so as to deprive your friends of theirs; yea, of a greater good, that you may have a lesser by it. And if it be their company that you desire, in reason you should be glad that they are gone to dwell where you must dwell for ever, and therefore may for ever have their company; had they staid on earth you would have had their company but a little while, because you must make so short a stay yourselves. Let them therefore begin their journey before you; and grudge not that they are first at home, as long as you expect to find them there. In the mean time he that called them from you hath not left you comfortless; he is with you himself, who is better than a mother, or than ten thousand friends: when grief or negligence hindereth you from observing him, yet he is with you, and holdeth you up, and tenderly provideth for you: though turbulent passions injuriously question all his love, and cause you to give him unmannerly and unthankful words, yet still he beareth with you, and forgiveth all, and doth not forsake you for your peevishness and weakness, because you are his children; and he knoweth that you mean not to forsake him. Rebuke your passions, and calm your minds; reclaim your thoughts, and cast away the bitterness of suspicious, quarrelsome unbelief; and then you may perceive the presence of your dearest Friend and Lord, who is enough for you, though you had no other friend. Without him all the friends on earth would be but silly comforters, and leave you as at the gates of hell; without him all the angels and saints in heaven would never make it a heaven to you. Grieve not too much that one of your candles is put out while you have the sun; or if indeed it be not day with any of you, or the sun be clouded or eclipsed, let that rather be the matter of your grief; find out the cause, and presently submit and seek reconciliation: or if you are deprived of this light, because you are yet asleep in sin, hearken to his call, and rub your eyes: "Awake, thou that sleepest, and arise from the dead, and Christ shall give thee light," Eph. v. 14. "Knowing that it is now high time to awake out of sleep, our salvation being nearer than when we first believed: the night is far spent, the day of eternal light is even at hand; cast off therefore the works of darkness, and put on all the armour of light; walk honestly and decently as in the day," Rom. xiii. 11—14. And whatever you do, make sure of the Friend that never dieth, and never shall be separated from you; and when you die will certainly receive the souls which you commend unto him.

And here, though contrary to my custom, I shall make some more particular mention of our deceased friend on several accounts. 1. In prosecution of this use that now we are upon, that you may see in the evidences of her happiness how little cause you have to indulge extraordinary grief on her account; and how much cause to moderate your sense of our loss, with the sense of her felicity. 2. That you may have the benefit of her example for your imitation, especially her children that are bound to observe the holy actions as well as the instructions of a mother. 3. For the honour of Christ, and his grace, and his servant: for as God hath promised to honour those that honour him, (1 Sam. ii. 30,) and Christ hath said, "If any man serve me, him will my Father honour," John xii. 26; so I know Christ will not take it ill to be honoured in his members, and to have his ministers subserve him in so excellent a work: it is a very considerable part of the love or hatred, honour or dishonour, that Christ hath in the world, which he receiveth as he appeareth in his followers. He that will not see a cup of cold water given to one of them go unrewarded, and will tell those at the last day that did or did not visit and relieve them, that they did or did it not to him, will now expect it from me as my duty to give him the honour of his graces in his deceased servant; and I doubt not will accordingly accept it, when it is no other indeed than his own honour that is my end, and nothing but the words of truth and soberness shall be the means.

And here I shall make so great a transition as shall retain my discourse in the narrow compass of the time in which she lived near me, and under my care, and in my familiar acquaintance, omitting all the rest of her life, that none may say I speak but by hearsay of things which I am uncertain of; and I will confine it also to those special gifts and graces in which she was eminent, that I may not take you up with a description of a christian as such, and tell you only of that good which she held but in common with all other christians. And if any thing that I shall say were unknown to any reader that knew her, let them know that it is because they knew her but distantly, imperfectly, or by reports; and that my advantage of near acquaintance did give me a just assurance of what I say.

The graces which I discerned to be eminent in her were these. 1. She was eminent in her contempt of the pride, and pomp, and pleasure, and vanity of the world; and in her great averseness to all these, she had an honest impatience of the life which is common among the rich and vain-glorious in the world: voluptuousness and sensuality, excess of drinking, cards and dice, she could not endure, whatever names of good house-keeping or seemly deportment they borrowed for a mask. In her apparel she went below the garb of others of her rank; indeed in such plainness as did not notify her degree; but yet in such a grave and decent habit as notified her sobriety and humility. She was a stranger to pastimes, and no companion for time-wasters; as knowing that persons so near eternity, that have so short a life, and so great a work, have no time to spare. Accordingly, in her latter days she did, as those that grow wise by experience of the vanity of the world, retire from it, and cast it off before it cast off her: she betook herself to the society of a people that were low in the world, of humble, serious, upright lives, though such as had been wholly strangers to her; and among these poor inferior strangers she lived in contentment and quietness; desiring rather to converse with those that would help her to redeem the time, in prayer and edifying conference, than with those that would grieve her by consuming it on their lusts.

2. She was very prudent in her converse and affairs, (allowing for the passion of her sex and age,) and so escaped much of the inconveniences that else in so great and manifold businesses would have overwhelmed her: as "a good man will guide his affairs with discretion," Psal. cxii. 5; so "discretion will preserve him, and understanding will keep him, to deliver him from the way of the evil man, who leaveth the paths of uprightness to walk in the way of darkness," Prov. ii. 11—13.

3. She was seriously religious, without partiality, or any taint of siding or faction, or holding the faith of our Lord Jesus Christ in respect of persons. I never heard her speak against men, or for men, as they differed in some small and tolerable things: she impartially heard any minister that was able, and godly, and sound in the main, and could bear with the weaknesses of ministers when they were faithful. Instead of owning the names or opinions of prelatical, presbyterian, independent, or such like, she took up with the name and profession of a christian, and loved a christian as a christian, without much respect to such different, tolerable opinions. Instead of troubling herself with needless scruples, and making up a religion of opinions and singularities, she studied faith and godliness; and lived upon the common certain truths, and well-known duties, which have been the old and beaten way, by which the universal church of Christ hath gone to heaven in former ages.

4. She was very impartial in her judgment about particular cases, being the same in judging of the case of a child and a stranger; and no interest of children, or other relations, could make her swerve from an equal judgment.

5. She very much preferred the spiritual welfare of her children before their temporal; looking on the former as the true felicity, and on the latter without it but as a pleasant, voluntary misery.

6. Since I was acquainted with her, I always found her very ready to good works, according to her power. And when she hath seen a poor man come to me, that she conjectured solicited me for relief, she hath reprehended me for keeping the case to myself, and not inviting her to contribute; and I could never discern that she thought any thing so well bestowed as that which relieved the necessities of the poor that were honest and industrious.

7. She had the wonderful mercy of a man-like, christian, patient spirit, under all afflictions that did befall her; and under the multitude of troublesome businesses, that would have even distracted an impatient mind. Though sudden anger was the sin that she much confessed herself, and therefore thought she wanted patience, yet I have oft wondered to see her bear up with the same alacrity and quietness, when Job's messengers have brought her the tidings that would have overwhelmed an impatient soul. When law-suits and the great afflictions of her children have assaulted her like successive waves, which I feared would have borne her into the deep, if not devoured all her peace, she sustained all as if no great considerable change had been made against her, having the same God and the same Christ, and promises, and hope, from which she fetched such real comfort and support as showed a real, serious faith.

8. She was always apt to put a good interpretation upon God's providences; like a right believer, that having the spirit of adoption, perceiveth fatherly love in all, she would not easily be persuaded that God meant her any harm: she was not apt to hearken to the enemy that accuseth God and his ways to man, as he accuseth man and his actions to God: she was none of those that are suspicious of God, and are still concluding death and ruin from all that he doth to them, and are gathering wrath from misinterpreted expressions of his love; who weep because of the smoke before they can be warmed by the fire. Yet God is good to Israel; and it shall go well with them that fear before him, (Psalm lxxiii. 1; Eccles. viii. 12, 13,) were her conclusions from the sharpest providences: she expected the morning in the darkest night, and judged not of the end by the beginning; but was always confident if she could

but entitle God in the case that the issue would be good. She was not a murmurer against God, nor one that contended with her Maker; nor one that created calamity to herself by a self-troubling, unquiet mind: she patiently bore what God laid upon her, and made it not heavier by the additions of uncomfortable prognostics, and misgiving or repining thoughts. She had a great confidence in God, that he was doing good to her and hers in all; and where at present she saw any matter of grief, she much supported her soul with a belief that God would remove and overcome it in due time.

9. She was not troubled, that ever I discerned, with doubtings about her interest in Christ, and about her own justification and salvation; but whether she reached to assurance or not, she had confident apprehensions of the love of God, and quietly reposed her soul upon his grace. Yet not secure through presumption or self-esteem, but comforting herself in the Lord her God; by this means she spent those hours in a cheerful performance of her duty, which many spend in fruitless self-vexation for the failings of their duty, or in mere inquiries whether they have grace or not; and others spend in wrangling, perplexed controversies about the manner or circumstances of duty: and I believe that she had more comfort from God by way of reward upon her sincere obedience, while she referred her soul to him, and rested on him, than many have that more anxiously perplexed themselves about the discerning of their holiness, when they should be studying to be more holy, that it might discover itself. And by this means she was fit for praises and thanksgiving, and spent not her life in lamentations and complaints; and made not religion seem terrible to the ignorant, that judge of it by the faces and carriage of professors. She did not represent it to the world as a morose and melancholy temper, but as the rational creature's cheerful obedience to his Maker, actuated by the sense of the wonderful love that is manifested in the Redeemer, and by the hopes of the purchased and promised felicity in the blessed sight and fruition of God. And I conjecture that her forementioned disposition to think well of God, and of his providences, together with her long and manifold experience, (the great advantage of ancient, tried christians,) did much conduce to free her from doubtings and disquieting fears about her own sincerity and salvation; and I confess, if her life had not been answerable to her peace and confidence, I should not have thought the better, but the worse, of her condition; nothing being more lamentable than to make haste to hell, through a wilful confidence that the danger is past, and that they are in the way to heaven as well as the most sanctified.

10. Lastly, I esteemed it the height of her attainment that she never discovered any inordinate fears of death, but a cheerful readiness, willingness, and desire, to be dissolved, and be with Christ. This was her constant temper both in health and sickness, as far as I was able to observe. She would be frequently expressing how little reason she had to be desirous of longer life, and how much reason to be willing to depart. Divers times in dangerous sickness I have been with her, and never discerned any considerable averseness, dejectedness, or fear. Many a time I have thought how great a mercy I should esteem it if I had attained that measure of fearless willingness to lay down this flesh, as she had attained. Many a one that can make light of wants, or threats, or scorns, or any ordinary troubles, cannot submit so quietly and willingly to death. Many a one that can go through the labours of religion, and contemn opposition, and easily give all they have to the poor, and bear imprisonments, banishment, or contempt, can never overcome the fears of death. So far, even the father of lies spake truth; "Skin for skin, yea, all that a man hath will he give for his life," Job ii. 4. I took it, therefore, for a high attainment and extraordinary mercy to our deceased friend, that the king of terrors was not terrible to her. Though I doubt not but somewhat of averseness and fear is so radicated in nature's self-preserving principle, as that it is almost inseparable, yet in her I never discerned any troublesome appearances of it. When I first came to her in the beginning of her last sickness, she suddenly passed the sentence of death upon herself, without any show of fear or trouble, when to us the disease appeared not to be great. But when the disease increased, her pains were so little, and the effect of the fever was so much in her head, that, after this, she seemed not to esteem it mortal, being not sensible of her case and danger: and so, as she lived without the fears of death, she seemed to us to die without them. God, by the nature of her disease, removing death as out of her sight, when she came to that weakness, in which else the encounter was like to have been sharper than ever it was before. And thus, in one of the weaker sex, God hath showed us that it is possible to live in holy confidence, and peace, and quietness of mind, without distressing griefs or fears, even in the midst of a troublesome world, and of vexatious businesses, and with the afflictions of her dearest relations almost continually before her: and that our quiet or disquiet, our peace or trouble, dependeth more upon our inward strength and temper than upon our outward state, occasions, or provocations; and that it is more in our hands than of any or all our friends and enemies, whether we shall have a comfortable or uncomfortable life.

What remaineth now, but that all we that survive, especially you that are her children, do follow her as she followed Christ? Though the word of God be your sufficient rule, and the example of Christ be your perfect pattern, yet as the instructions, so the example of a parent must be a weighty motive to quicken and engage you to your duty; and will else be a great aggravation of your sin. A holy child of unholy parents doth no more than his necessary duty; because whatever parents are, he hath a holy God: but an unholy child of holy parents is inexcusable in sin, and deplorably miserable, as forsaking the doctrine and pattern both of their Creator and their progenitors, whom nature engageth them to observe; and it will be an aggravation of their deserved misery to have their parents witness against them, that they taught them, and they would not learn; and went before them in a holy life, but they would not follow them. "My son, hear the instruction of thy father, and forsake not the law of thy mother; for they shall be an ornament of grace unto thy head, and chains about thy neck," Prov. i. 8, 9. Read and consider Prov. xxx. 17; xv. 20; xxiii. 22, 25. Sins against parents have a special curse affixed to them in this life, as the case of Ham showeth; and the due observance and honouring of parents hath a special promise of temporal blessings, as the fifth commandment showeth. "Children, obey your parents in the Lord, for it is right: honour thy father and thy mother, (which is the first commandment with promise,) that it may be well with thee, and thou mayst live long on the earth," Eph. vi. 1—3. The histories of all ages are so full of the instances of God's judgments, in this life, upon five sorts of sinners, as may do much to convince an atheist of the government and special providence of God; that is, upon persecutors, murderers, sacrilegious, false witnesses, (especially by perjury,) and abusers and dishonourers of parents. And the great honour that is due to parents when they are dead, is to give just honour to their names, and to obey their precepts, and imitate their good examples. It is the high commendation of the Rechabites, that they strictly kept the precepts of their father, even in a thing indifferent, a mode of living; not to drink wine, or build houses, but dwell in tents: and God annexeth this notable blessing, "Thus saith the Lord of hosts, the God of Israel; Because ye have obeyed the commandment of Jonadab your father, and kept all his precepts, and done according unto all that he hath commanded you: therefore thus saith the Lord of hosts, the God of Israel; Jonadab the son of Rechab shall not want a man to stand before me for ever," Jer. xxxv. 6, 7, 18, 19. But, especially in the great duties of religion, where parents do but deliver the mind of God, and use their authority to procure obedience to divine authority, and where the matter itself is necessary to our salvation, the obligation to obedience and imitation is most indispensable; and disobedience is an aggravated iniquity, and the notorious brand of infelicity, and prognostic of ensuing woe; the ungodly children of godly parents being the most deplorable, unhappy, unexcusable persons in the world (if they hold on).

There is yet another doctrine that I should speak to.

Doct. 7. Prayer in general, and this prayer in particular, that Christ will receive our departing souls, is a most suitable conclusion of all the actions of a christian's life.

Prayer is the breath of a christian's life: it is his work and highest converse, and therefore fittest to be the concluding action of his life, that it may reach the end at which he aimed. We have need of prayer all our lives, because we have need of God, and need of his manifold and continued grace. But in our last extremity we have a special need. Though sloth is apt to seize upon us, while prosperity hindereth the sense of our necessities, and health persuadeth us that time is not near its journey's end, yet it is high time to pray with redoubled fervour and importunity when we see that we are near our last. When we find that we have no more time to pray, but must now speak our last for our immortal souls, and must at once say all that we have to say, and shall never have a hearing more. Oh, then, to be unable to pray, or to be faithless, and heartless, and hopeless in our prayers, would be a calamity beyond expression.

Yet I know, for ordinary observation tells it us, that many truly gracious persons may accidentally be undisposed and disabled to pray when they are near to death. If the disease be such as doth disturb the brain, or take them up with violence of pain, or overwhelm the mind by perturbation of the passions, or abuse the imagination, or notably waste and debilitate the spirits, it cannot be expected that a body thus disabled should serve the soul in this or any other duty. But still the praying habit doth remain, though a distempered body do forbid the exercise. The habitual desires of the soul are there; and it is those that are the soul of prayer.

But this should move us to pray while we have time, and while our bodies have strength, and our spirits have vigour and alacrity to serve us, seeing we are so uncertain of bodily disposition and capacity so near our end. O pray, and pray with all your hearts, before any fever or deliration overthrow your understandings or your memories; before your thoughts are all commanded to attend your pains, and before your decayed spirits fail you, and deny their necessary service to your suits; and before the apprehensions of your speedy approach to the presence of the most holy God, and your entrance upon an endless state, do amaze, confound, and overwhelm your souls with fear and perturbation. O christians! what folly, what sin and shame is it to us, that now while we have time to pray, and leave to pray, and helps to pray, and have no such disturbing hinderances, we should yet want hearts, and have no mind, no life and fervour for so great a work! O pray now, lest you are unable to pray then; and if you are then hindered but by such bodily indisposedness, God will understand your habitual desires, and your groans, and take it as if you had actually prayed. Pray now, that so you may be acquainted with the God that then you must fly unto for mercy, and may not be strangers to him, or unto prayer; and that he may not find then that your prayers are but the expression of your fears, and not of your love, and are constrained, and not voluntary motions unto God: pray now in preparation to your dying prayers. Oh what a terrible thing it is to be to learn to pray in that hour of extremity, and to have then no principle to pray by, but natural self-love, which every thief hath at the gallows! To be then without the spirit of prayer, when without it there cannot an acceptable word or groan be uttered; and when the rejection of our suits and person will be the prologue to the final judicial rejection, and will be a distress so grievous as presumptuous souls will not believe, till sad experience become their tutor. Can you imagine that you shall then at last be taught the art of acceptable prayer merely by horror, and the natural sense of pain and danger, as seamen in a storm, or a malefactor by the rack, when in your health and leisure you will not be persuaded to the daily use of serious prayer, but number yourselves with the families that are under the wrath of the Almighty, being such as call not on his name, Jer. x. 25; Psalm lxxix. 6.

Indeed, there are many prayers must go before, or else this prayer, "Lord Jesus, receive my spirit," will be in vain, when you would be loth to find it so. You must first pray for renewing, sanctifying grace, for the death of sin, and the pardon of sin, for a holy life, and a heavenly mind, for obedience, patience, and perseverance; and if you obtain not these, there is no hope that Jesus Christ should receive your spirits, that never received his sanctifying Spirit.

How sad is it to observe that those that have most need of prayer, have least mind to pray, as being least sensible of their needs! Yea, that those that are the next step to the state of devils, and have as much need of prayer as any miserable souls on earth, do yet deride it, and hate those that seriously and fervently perform it; a man of prayer being the most common object of their malicious reproach and scorn. O miserable Cainites, that hate their brethren for offering more acceptable sacrifice than their own! Little do they know how much of the very satanical nature is in that malice, and in those reproachful scorns. And little do they know how near they are to the curse and desperation of Cain, and with what horror they shall cry out, "My punishment is greater than I can bear," Gen. iv. 11, 13. If God and good men condemn you for your lip-service, and heartless devotions, and ungodly lives, will you therefore hate the holy nature and better lives of those that judge you, when you should hate your own ungodliness and hypocrisy? Hear what God said to the leader of your sect, "Why art thou wroth? and why is thy countenance fallen? If thou doest well, shalt thou not be accepted? and if thou doest not well, sin lieth at the door," Gen. iv. 6. Have you not as much need to pray as those that you hate and reproach for praying? Have you not as much need to be oft and earnest in prayer as they? Must Christ himself spend whole nights in prayer, (Luke vi. 12,) and shall an ignorant, sensual, hardened sinner think he hath no need of it, though he be unconverted, unjustified, unready to die, and almost past the opportunity of praying? O miserable men, that shortly would cry and roar in the anguish of their souls, and yet will not pray while there is time and room for prayer! Their Judge is willing now to hear them, and now they have nothing but hypocritical, lifeless words to speak! Praying is now a wearisome, tedious, and unpleasant thing to them, that shortly would be glad if the most heart-tearing lamentations could prevail for the crumbs and drops of that mercy which they thus despise, Luke xvi. 24. Of all men in the world it ill becomes one in so deep necessities and dangers to be prayerless.

But for you, christians, that are daily exercised in this holy converse with your Maker, hold on, and grow not strange to heaven, and let not your holy desires be extinguished for want of excitation. Prayer is your ascent to heaven; your departure from a vexatious world to treat with God for your salvation; your retirement from a world of dangers into the impregnable fortress where you are safe, and from vanity unto felicity, and from troubles unto rest, which, though you cannot come so near, nor enjoy so fully and delightfully, as hereafter you shall do, yet thus do you make your approaches to it, and thus do you secure your future full fruition of it. And let them all scoff at hearty, fervent prayer as long as they will, yet prayer shall do that with God for you which health, and wealth, and dignity, and honour, and carnal pleasures, and all the world shall never do for one of them. And though they neglect and vilify it now, yet the hour is near when they will be fain to scamble and bungle at it themselves; and the face of death will better teach them the use of prayer, than our doctrine and example now can do. A departing soul will not easily be prayerless, nor easily be content with sleepy prayers; but, alas! it is not every prayer that hath some fervency from the power of fear that shall succeed. Many a thousand may perish for ever that have prayed, "Lord Jesus, receive my spirit." But the soul that breatheth after Christ, and is weary of sinning, and hath long been pressing toward the mark, may receive encouragement for his last petitions, from the bent and success of all the foregoing prayers of his life. Believe it, christians, you cannot be so ready to beg of Christ to receive your souls, as he is ready and willing to receive them. As you come praying, therefore, into the world of grace, go praying out of it into the world of glory. It is not a work that you were never used to, though you have had lamented backwardness, and coldness, and omissions. It is not to a God that you were never with before; as you know whom you have believed, so you may know to whom you pray. It is indeed a most important suit to beg for the receiving of a departed soul; but it is put up to him to whom it properly doth belong, and to him that hath encouraged you by answering many a former prayer with that mercy which was the earnest of this, and it is to him that loveth souls much better than any soul can love itself. O live in prayer, and die in prayer, and do not, as the graceless, witless world, despise prayer while they live, and then think a, Lord, have mercy on me, shall prove enough to pass them into heaven. Mark their statues and monuments in the churches, whether they be not made kneeling and lifting up the hands, to tell you that all will be forced to pray, or to approve of prayer, at their death, whatever they say against it in their life. O pray, and wait but a little longer, and all your danger will be past, and you are safe for ever! Keep up your hands a little longer, till you shall end your conflict with the last enemy, and shall pass from prayer to everlasting praise.

A SERMON

PREACHED AT

THE FUNERAL OF THAT HOLY, PAINFUL, AND FRUITFUL MINISTER OF CHRIST,

MR. HENRY STUBBS;

ABOUT FIFTY YEARS A SUCCESSFUL PREACHER AT BRISTOL, WELLS, CHEW, DURSLEY, LONDON, AND DIVERS OTHER PLACES.

ACTS XX. 24.

BUT NONE OF THESE THINGS MOVE ME, NEITHER COUNT I MY LIFE DEAR UNTO MYSELF, SO THAT I MIGHT FINISH MY COURSE WITH JOY, AND THE MINISTRY, WHICH I HAVE RECEIVED OF THE LORD JESUS, TO TESTIFY THE GOSPEL OF THE GRACE OF GOD.

THIS hour being designed to such a commemoration of our deceased friend, Mr. Stubbs, as is laudably used at such men's funerals, I have chosen words of this text, which the heart and life of this holy man did so constantly express, that, doubtless, the same Spirit suggested them to blessed Paul and him. They are the profession of a full devotedness to God, in his christian and ministerial work, notwithstanding all expected difficulties and oppositions, which he resolved with unmoved patience to undergo to the joyful finishing of his course.

The witness of the Holy Ghost, with his own experience, did teach him to expect bonds and afflictions at Jerusalem, it being the ordinary entertainment which every where did abide him; but how much worse might come he knew not, but was resolvedly prepared for all. The joyful finishing of his course was so desirable to him, that no suffering, though it were the loss of life itself, did seem too dear or hard a means for its accomplishment.

Here is then, first, The great and desirable prize for which nothing could be too dear. Secondly, The cheerful resolution of the apostle to go on, and part with life itself to attain it.

The first, though the words have no great difficulty, yet, as to the matter, may need some brief explication, viz.

1. What is meant by his "course."
2. What by his "ministry, and testifying the gospel of the grace of God."
3. How this was "received of the Lord Jesus."
4. What is meant by the "finishing of his course."
5. How it was to be done "with joy."
6. Why he was not moved by foreseen sufferings, nor accounted his "life dear" to attain this end.

And for brevity, I shall now observe this method, to add the instructions and other applications to each part of the text as I explain it.

First, The word translated "course," signifieth a race to be swiftly run: and a threefold race is here included. 1. The race of human life, which is short and uncertain; we are not born for nothing; nor doth God give us life, and time, and maintenance, to live in idleness, or to serve the flesh. The sun stands not still whether we sleep or wake; our breath, our pulse are still in motion, our glass is running. And oh! how quickly shall we see and hear, that time on earth shall be to us no more! This course will be certainly and quickly finished; but whether "with joy," it concerneth us timely to foresee. For the review of time, of precious time, and the work of time, will be no contemptible part of our everlasting work.

2. The "course" (or race) of christianity, is the necessary improvement of our time. This is not a play, nor an idle, brutish, or a jesting life. It is a great work for a self-destroying, undone sinner, to believe in a Saviour, and in such a Saviour, and wholly to trust his merits, sacrifice, counsel, and conduct, his powerful operations, and effectual intercessions, for all our present and our future hopes. It was not a dream of war that we were listed for in our baptism under the Captain of our salvation. The resisting of temptations, the quenching of the devil's fiery darts, the denial of ourselves, and forsaking friends, reputation, estate, and liberty, and life, for the sake of Christ, and renouncing the flesh, the world, and the devil, for the hopes of a promised, unseen glory, is a real work. To believe in Christ and his promise of heaven, to the forsaking of all worldly hopes, is a serious business. To love God above all, and our neighbour as ourselves, and to do as we would be done by, how easily soever mentioned and professed, are works not unworthy to be ascribed to the Spirit of the living God, and to the grace of the Almighty. He that well finisheth the christian course, shall certainly receive the crown of righteousness; and though none of these works do in the least participate in the office of the justifying sacrifice, merits, or grace of Jesus Christ, yet shall we be judged according to them; and we must live to Christ, if we will live with Christ.

3. The apostolical, ministerial course was also to be finished with joy. His call was wonderful, his office honourable, his gifts powerful, his sufferings great, his labours greater; his successes by miracles in themselves miraculous: yet all this would not have saved himself, if he had not faithfully finished his course. To begin hopefully is more common than to end happily. The sun of persecution withereth much fruit that seemed flourishing: Judas's end did more difference him from the rest of the apostles, than his beginning.

Secondly, His ministry was considerable as common to all the clergy, or as apostolical. To preach the word as he commanded Timothy, to be instant in season and out of season, to reprove, rebuke, exhort, with all long-suffering and doctrine, to rule well, and labour in the word and doctrine, to take heed to ourselves and unto doctrine, and continue therein that we may save ourselves and them that hear us; to take heed to ourselves and all the flock, to hold back nothing profitable to them, but to teach them publicly, and from house to house, day and night with tears, (Acts xx.) in meekness instructing those that oppose themselves, if God, at any time, will give them repentance: all this is not a dream or play.

And to go over much of the world, from nation to nation, by sea and land, to preach this gospel to strangers of various languages, through all difficulties and sufferings, to confirm all by miracles, to leave his sacred doctrine infallibly in records to the church, as a rule to the end of the world, to teach men to observe all things Christ had commanded them, as well as to disciple nations, and baptize them, and to settle the orders and government of the churches according to the will of Christ, this was the extraordinary part of his ministry.

Thirdly, This ministry was received of the Lord Jesus, by an extraordinary call, a voice from heaven, and an inspiration of others that were ministerially to send him; and the special inspiration of his own soul, for apostolical qualifications. But do not ordinary ministers also receive their office from the Lord Jesus? Yes; and though the way of their reception differ, their obligation to finish their course is divine, as well as Paul's. Christ called Paul by himself, and by inspired prophets; and he calleth us by his qualifying grace, and by his stated law, (as the king maketh mayors and bailiffs of corporations by his charters,) wherein the ordainers and electors orderly determine of the recipient persons, and the ordainers ministerially invest them; but the office, power, and obligation is directly from the law of Christ. And if any breach or interruption should be made in human ordination and tradition, the law still standeth to direct men in the choice and investiture, and to confer authority, and to oblige, as well as the Holy Ghost, to give men the necessaries thereto.

Therefore, as we receive our office from Christ, we must use it for Christ, and not for carnal self, nor as the servants of men; and we must use it according to the laws of Christ, whose laws soever shall gainsay them.

Fourthly, The finishing of Paul's course, is the bringing his work of christianity and ministry to the desired joyful end. 1. To the end of duration; not to be weary of well-doing, nor, having put his hand to Christ's plough, to look back and repent, nor forsake the warfare in which he was engaged. "He that endureth to the end shall be saved; and in due time we shall reap if we faint not." 2. To the end of intention: 1. To do his own appointed work, that his grace being exercised and increased, he may be acceptable to God, and fit with joy to meet the Lord. 2. To call and save sinners, and to build up saints, and to gather churches unto Christ, and edify them, and leave to all ages his doctrine and example, a certain word and powerful motive. 3. To glorify Christ and God the Father in all this; not to sit warm in a reverend habit, for men to honour for the sake of the office and bare name of an apostle.

But to "testify the gospel of the grace of God," to declare the truth of it, the necessity of it, the privileges, and the honour, the great love of God, revealed by the Son of his love to sinners, and the great and manifold benefits given them in Christ; the hope of glory set before them, and the just and reasonable means and conditions of obtaining it. Thus did he, as immediately sent, and thus must we, as sent by Christ's appointed order in his law, testify the gospel of the grace of God.

Fifthly, Concerning Paul's "finishing his course with joy," we must consider, 1. What joy it is that is here meant. 2. How much of this joy each faithful minister may expect. 3. And whence and on what account he may expect it.

I. The joy here meant, which Paul expected, is, first, The joy which the nature of the work affordeth; divine, certain, great, and holy truth is pleasant to him that understandeth it, believeth it, and is exercised in the serious meditation of it. It is sweet to read, and think, and speak of the essential love of God; and of his unspeakable grace in Christ, of his free reconciliation, justification, adoption, and salvation of those that were his enemies; of the wonderful mysteries and methods of God's love in our redemption and salvation; of the heavenly glory which we and all the elect of God shall enjoy for ever. What sweeter food or business for our minds, than such things as these?

Secondly, The success of our work is an addition to our joy. The success of it on our own souls, while they increase in holiness, and are raised to the greater knowledge of God, and greater love to him, and communion with him; and our success on others while they are brought home to God and saved. If it be pleasant to a successful physician to save men's lives, it must be more so to a successful minister of Christ, to further men's regeneration, and to save men's souls. To add more to the number of them that love the Lord Jesus, that are his members, that are enemies to sin, examples of holiness, that pray for the world, and that shall live in glory; is not this a joyful work? There is joy among the angels in heaven for every sinner that repenteth, Luke xv. 10. Christ rejoiceth in it, and all good men that know it rejoice in it, and shall not the minister of it then rejoice? "I rejoiced greatly," saith St. John, and "I have no greater joy," 3 John 3, 4. "Ye are our joy and crown of rejoicing," 1 Thess. ii. 19.

Thirdly, The honour of Christ, and the pleasing of God in our labours, and the success, is the top of all our joy, 2 Cor. v. 9; Heb. xii. 28; Eph. v. 10; Heb. xiii. 21; xi. 5. For to please God, and to be perfectly pleased in him, is our heavenly felicity itself.

Fourthly, It is our joy to foresee the blessed end, the everlasting, glorious reward; to live in the belief and hope of this, and to taste the love of God in Christ, which is the first-fruits. All this is the joy in which we may hope to finish our course.

II. How much of this joy may we here expect?

Answ. 1. So much as shall satisfy us that in our dedication of ourselves to God, we make a wise and happy choice, which we need not to repent of; though we might easily have chosen a way more likely for wealth and pleasure to the flesh, and in which we should not have kindled the indignation of so many against us; nor have brought on ourselves so much envy and malice, so much slanders and reproaches, to name no worse, yet experience tells us, that God taught us to choose the most pleasant life, as our deceased brother and I have truly oft told one another that we have found it. Even when we are sorrowful, we are always rejoicing, 2 Cor. vi. 10. When we are falsely reported of, our rejoicing is this, the testimony of our consciences, that in simplicity and godly sincerity, and not in fleshly wisdom, we have had our conversation in the world, 2 Cor. i. 12. Paul and Silas could sing with their backs sore with scourging, and their feet fast in the stocks, Acts xvi.; and the apostles rejoiced that they were accounted worthy to suffer reproach and abuse for Christ, Acts v. 41. Never yet did difficulty, or suffering, much tempt me to repent that I had not chosen another calling; much less to repent of the christian choice; for, saith Peter, "Whither shall we go? Lord, thou hast the words of eternal life," John vi. 68.

Secondly, We may expect so much joy as shall make the duties of christianity and ministry easy and delightful to us, (Psal. i. 2,) and make us say, that "a day in his courts is better than a thousand, and to be a door-keeper in his house than to dwell in the tents or palaces of wickedness." And that it is good for us to draw near to God. And if at any time our diseased appetites shall lose their pleasure, we are yet sure that we have chosen the only wholesome and delicious food; and God hath physic that can recover our appetites.

Thirdly, We may expect so much joy as shall keep us from thirsting again for the world, or longing for the forbidden pleasures of sin; and shall make even the house of mourning and godly sorrow pleasanter to us than mirth and feasting is to the ungodly, and never desire to partake of their delights.

Fourthly, We may expect so much joy as shall make all our sufferings very tolerable, especially those that are for truth and righteousness, Matt. v. 10—12. Believers took joyfully the spoiling of their goods, and accepted not offered deliverance, Heb. xi.; as seeing him that is invisible, and expecting a better and more enduring substance. And that which is not joyous, but grievous at the present, will bring forth the quiet fruit of righteousness, Heb. xii.

Fifthly, We may expect so much joy as shall encourage us to hold out to the end, and never to forsake Christ and a holy life, as weary or as hoping for a better.

Sixthly, We may expect so much joy, as shall be some foretaste of the heavenly joy, and some reward here of all our labours. Yea, some may be filled with joy and peace in believing, and have unspeakable glorious joy, Rom. xv. 13; 1 Pet. i. 7, 8.

Seventhly, We may expect so much as shall convince the ungodly, that we live a more comfortable life than they. Paul and Silas singing in the stocks, it is like, had some part in the conviction of the gaoler.

III. Whence, and on what accounts, may we expect this joy?

Answ. This may be gathered from what is said before. 1. From the love and acceptance of the Father. 2. From the grace of the Son. 3. From the communion of the Holy Spirit. And, therefore, 1. From the goodness of our work before mentioned. 2. From the truth of the promises of God. 3. From the communion of saints. 4. From the continued protection, and other mercies, of God. 5. And from the certain hopes of glory: all which I must now but thus only name.

There is another kind of joy, which too many seek in this sacred office, thereby corrupting and profaning it; and the best things corrupted become the worst, and such men most pernicious to mankind, and these rotten pillars the greatest betrayers and enemies to the church; I mean such as Gregory Nazianzen sadly describeth in his time, even at the first general council at Constantinople; and such as Isidore Pelusiota in his Epistles to Zosimus, and some such others, freely reprehendeth; and such as Gildas describeth in this land; and such as Salvian rebuketh; and such as, the canons of abundance of councils tell us, swarmed heretofore.

First, Had there not been prelates and priests, that had placed their joy in dominion over their brethren, and getting into exalted thrones, in being rich and idle, and bowed to even by princes, and mastering kings and kingdoms by cursing them from Christ; making themselves as the soul, and princes as the body; themselves as the sun, and princes as the moon and stars, abusing *Tibi dabo claves*, and "the disciple is not above his master," to the mastering of kings and states, as their sheep and disciples; a great part of the church history had been unwritten, or otherwise written than it is.

Secondly, Yea, far be it from any minister of Christ to expect their joy from human applause, and the multitude of followers or disciples; to be accounted a learned or a holy man, an excellent preacher, and so to have the respect and love of many.

A good name and love are not to be despised when they follow fidelity as its shadow; and as they signify the good of those that profit by the word. The Galatians would once have even pulled out their eyes for Paul; but, alas! what is the thought and breath of man, that is hastening to the dust, and to the impartial Judge? How small a matter should it be to us to be judged of many, that are so near the final judgment; and what a terrible sentence is it to the hypocrites! "Verily they have their reward," Matt. vi. 2. O poor and miserable reward! And yet what age hath not seen that verified, "Of your own selves shall men arise, that shall speak perverse things to draw away disciples after them," Acts xx. 30. And (Rom. xvi. 17) such still have been as have caused divisions and offences, contrary to apostolical doctrine, not serving the Lord Jesus, but their own bellies, being ever fleshly, worldly men; and, by good words and fair speeches, deceive the hearts of the simple. And men that have had the form of godliness, (or the lifeless image,) but deny the power of it by wicked lives, are those from whom we must turn away.

Thirdly, Yea, and far be it from any faithful minister, or christian, to take up his joy from a conceit that he hath commutatively merited of God, by the excellency of his faith or labours. Alas! who is sufficient for these things? And what have we that we have not received? Or who hath given to God that it may be repaid him? Or what faithful minister of Christ did ever come out of the pulpit, or from his private duty, without grief and shame that his faith and love, his skill and zeal, have been so vastly unsuitable to such great and excellent things that he was about? And yet the conscience of simplicity and godly sincerity, and God's forgiveness, assistance, and acceptance, may set our joy above that shame and grief.

Sixthly, And now it is easy to see the reason why Paul accounted not his life dear, nor was moved by the foresight of any sufferings, so he might but finish his course with joy.

For, first, He well knew that the end would pay for all, and no man shall ever lose by God, nor shall the most abundant labour be in vain, 1 Cor. xv. 48. Is there any repentance in heaven for their labours or sufferings for Christ on earth? Do they think that God is in their debt? "Faith ever reckoneth that the sufferings of this present time are not worthy to be compared with the glory which shall be revealed in us," Rom. viii. 18. "For which cause we faint not; but though our outward man perish, yet the inward man is renewed day by day. For our light affliction, which is but for a moment, worketh for us a far more exceeding and eternal weight of glory; while we look not at the things which are seen, which are temporal; but at the unseen things, which are eternal," 2 Cor. iv. 16—18.

Secondly, And Paul well knew that he and all the world were in the hands of God, and that he served such a Master as could easily preserve him as far as he saw meet, from all his enemies and sufferings. And that sufferings chosen for us by God, are better than if we had the kingdoms of the world by the gift of Satan, Matt. iv. Balak's words to Balaam, methinks, were words of honour and joy, "The Lord hath kept thee from honour." Oh! who would not be ambitious of being so kept from honour? The poverty and shame that is by and for God, is better than the preferment and honour of men; and the reproach of Christ is greater riches than the treasures of Egypt. And if God see it best, he knoweth how to save the righteous from trouble, and if not, to give them suffering, strength, and joy.

And it is a wonder of providence how God preserveth their names and honour, that despise honour and life for him, so that even they that killed the present prophets and just men, yet build the sepulchres of those that were killed by their fathers, and say, If we had lived in the days of our fathers we would not have been partakers with them in the blood of the prophets, Matt. xxiii. 27, 28. The wonder of that foreigner in Henry VIII.'s days, *Deus bone quomodo hic vivunt gentes*, that saw men killed for being protestants, and for being papists, was not so contradictory a subject as the papists' usage of the saints, a stupendous instance of man's madness and Satan's methods, that at the same time can rack, and burn, and murder saints, and yet honour the relics, names, and memories of the dead that were before them. That while they zealously cast away men's lives and treasure, to recover the holy land where saints had lived, at the same time murdered those by thousands that did most nearly imitate them; and to this day kill the living saints, under the name of schismatics or heretics, (for not obeying the king of Rome before God,) and keep holy days for the dead, and reverence their shrines and relics. What contempt did poor St. Martin undergo from his neighbour bishops, as suspected of Priscilleanism, and as an unlearned hypocrite, that was for liberty for heretics, so that he separated from their synods and communion; and yet what a name hath he left behind him even in that church whose prelates thus despised him!

Thirdly, Moreover, Paul had now tried both the ways, of being against Christ, and being for him; and was so fully convinced by experience and revelation of the evil of the one and the goodness of the other, that he had great reason to be resolved and unmoved, as knowing that no suffering can make the servants of Christ as miserable as his enemies, nor any preferment or prosperity make any one of the worldlings as happy as the poorest saint. Because he had rather be Lazarus than Dives hereafter, and had rather stand on the right hand of Christ than on the left, therefore he accordingly made his choice. For he well knew how bad a bargain it would prove to win all the world and lose his soul, and to lay up a treasure on earth, so as also to treasure up wrath against the day of wrath, and to prepare for such an even-song as Luke xii. 20, "Thou fool! this night shall they require thy soul; and then whose are the things that thou hast provided?"

Alas! what gain is it to save an estate a little while, that at death must certainly be forsaken? to save a life this year, this month, this day, that may be gone on sadder terms the next, and certainly will ere long be gone? Are not the bishops of Winchester and London, Gardiner and Bonner, now dead, as well as the martyrs whom they burnt? Are not Alexander the Third, and Innocent the Third and Fourth, and such other persecuting popes, now dead, as well as all the godly christians whom they murdered? Alas! what a nothing is time, and how little difference between to-day and to-morrow, this year and next! that which hath been, that which is, and that which will be! Shall a man part with his God, and his everlasting hopes, that he may be able to say in hell, I was once a lord, a man of honour, I had once full provision for the flesh; I had pleasure in the way to the torment which I undergo?

In the expounding of these words of St. Paul, I have but given you the image, or rather the spirit, of Mr. Stubbs. Funeral praises, by flatterers brought into disgrace, will be here blamed by no wise man that knew the person, no more than in Nazianzen for his orations for Cyprian, Basil, and others, unless it be for the defect, which is unavoidable.

I. This faithful servant of Christ hath run his race; what that was, and how he performed it, the county of Gloucester knoweth, and the city of Wells in Somersetshire knoweth, and this city and this congregation partly know. And I will speak but little of him but what I know myself, and have by unquestionable testimony. His birth, parentage, and youthful life, I am not acquainted with. He was a minister of Christ about fifty years, dying at the age of seventy-three. His studies, and parts, and labours, lay not in the critical or controversial way; and as he was so happy as not to waste his time in contentious studies, so he was so humble and honest as not to trouble his auditory with such matters, nor to pretend to have studied what he had not, nor, like many proud ignorants, to boast or contend most where they know least. His soul was taken up with the great things of religion. His preaching was most on the baptismal covenant, on the articles of the creed, the Lord's prayer, and decalogue, and such necessary things which essentially constitute a christian. I never heard him meddle with controversies in public, or in his private talks; but all, how to know God in Christ, and how to seek and serve him, and how to resist temptations and sin, and what a life we shall live with Christ for ever; and how to live in love, righteousness, peace, and profitableness to one another, especially how to serve God entirely, and in what state we shall live with him for ever. He was the freest of most that ever I knew from that deceit of the serpent mentioned 2 Cor. xi. 3, who corrupteth men by drawing them from the simplicity which is in Christ. His breath, his life, his preaching, his prayers, his conference, his conversation, was christian simplicity and sincerity. Not as the world calleth simplicity, folly, but as it is contrary to hypocrisy, to a counterfeit zeal, to mere affectation, to a divided heart. He knew not how to dissemble nor wear a mask; his face, his mouth, his whole conversation, laid bare his heart. While he passed by all quarrels and controversies, few quarrelled with him; and he had the happiness to take up head, heart, and time, with only great, sure, and necessary things.

II. Of all men that ever I knew, he seemed to me one of the most humble. His preaching, his discourse, his garb, and all his behaviour, spake pure humility, and were far from pride; never did I hear from him a word of ostentation, much less of envy at the precedence of others; he came to Christ as a teachable child, and preached as a learner, and I never heard that he strove with any. He had learned of Christ to be meek and lowly, and to make himself of no reputation, nor seek the honour that is of man. Oh, how far was he from striving to be above his brethren, or troubling the church by a proud, imperious, or turbulent spirit!

III. He was exceedingly peaceable in his principles and in his practice; never contending with opinionators, or those that cry down this and that error of their brethren, to get the reputation of being free from errors. He put not his finger into the fire of contention; nor ever, that I heard of, made himself of a sect or faction, nor preached for this party against that, except for Christ's party against the devil's. Nor did I ever hear him, in his private talk, backbite any; nor exercise the too common liberty against others, in carping at their infirmities, or making himself their judge. Had the church had no more unpeaceable pastors, we had not been in the sad condition that we are in, denying peace and concord, obstinately, to the servants of Christ, and militating, by forbidden arms, against one another. Long would it have been before he would have reviled, vexed, or hindered any true minister of Christ from preaching his gospel, or living in peace.

IV. He was an honourer of his superiors, and obedient to authority, as far as would stand with his obedience to God. I never heard that, publicly or privately, he spake a disloyal or irreverent word of the king, or others in authority. After he had here preached awhile in London, he had a preferment to a parish church in Gloucestershire, of eight pounds per annum maintenance, and it had many and many years had no minister; and by the honest connivance or forbearance of the reverend bishop of Gloucester, he there preached, for some years past, in peace; of which I am past doubt that bishop hath no cause to repent. He used part of the liturgy, not sticking at the censure of them that called this as their judgments led them. His judgment, his work, his age, and experience, set him above all factious inducements, and taught him to please God, whoever were displeased. And when, at last, he was driven away, I never heard him speak of it with any bitterness. He is now where God's praises are celebrated, and whence no holy soul shall ever be cast out.

V. His labour was such as beseemed one absolutely devoted to God: his preaching was very plain and familiar, fitted rather to country auditors than to curious ears; and he chose accordingly; but it was wholly for faith, love, and holiness. He was much in catechising, and very moving in his familiar exhortations, setting his whole heart upon the winning and edifying of souls, and longing for the success, as much as covetous merchants do for rich returns. He kept a private weekly meeting for the young people, to deal with them as a catechiser, by way of familiar questions; which was much of his labour wherever he came. And he much rejoiced in the young people's willingness, and his success. The greatest benefice cannot please one that worketh for the fleece, so much as he was pleased that his unwearied labour profited his flock. How thankful was he to God, and the bishop's connivance, for that short liberty to work! And to their honour I must say, that he praised not only the friendly peaceableness of the magistrates and gentry of the county, but also of his neighbour conformable ministers, that lived by him in love, and envied not his liberty.

This holy man so little cared for the hypocrite's reward, that no reproach of men did move him; nor did he count his great labour or life dear to him, that he might subserve him that came to seek and save the lost. He took that for the joyful finishing of his course, from which Satan and many mistaken men would have discouraged him. As it was one of the greatest aggravations of Christ's sufferings, that he was crucified as a reputed sinner, even as a blasphemer, and an enemy to Cæsar, and a contemner of the law; so he knew that all things must be accounted dung that we may be found in Christ, and conformed to him even in his sufferings. And if a Seneca could say, that no man more showeth himself to be a good man than he that will lose the reputation of being a good man, lest he should lose his goodness itself, and defile his conscience; no wonder if this holy man accounted not his fame too dear to preserve his conscience. And, indeed, his friends and physicians suppose that his labours hastened his death.

He came from the country to London, again to work, and, after his journey, preaching almost every day, and some days twice, even after he began to be ill, no wonder if the fever and dysentery, that followed, despatched him. At first he fell down in the pulpit, but recovering, went on; and so again, after, till he was disabled. Some will censure him for imprudence in such labours; but they must consider what it is to be above the inordinate love of life, and to long for the good of souls. And withal, that which much imboldened him, was, that he was wont to go somewhat ill into the pulpit, and to come better out: but the heat of the season, seventy-and-three years of age, gave advantage to the messenger which God did send to end his labours and all his sufferings.

Two things especially I commend to imitation. 1. That he was more in instructing and catechising children by familiar questions than almost any man that I have known; which showed that he laboured not for applause. 2. He prayed as constantly as he preached, and no wonder, then, that his labours had much success. He omitted not his duty to God in his family, by the greatness of his public labours. And a man of prayer is a man of power with God.

For my part, I never saw him till his coming to live in London, I think not seven years ago, though I long heard of his successful preaching. But to show you how great his charity was, and what a loss I have myself, and how faulty I and others are in too much forgetting of our friends, I will tell you that he hath oft told me that (as I remember, above twenty years) he never went to God in prayer, but he particularly remembered me. But his love hath not tempted me to say a word of him which I verily believe not to be true. And I conclude it with this profession, that I scarce remember the man, that ever I knew, that served God with more absolute resignation and devotedness, in simplicity and godly sincerity, and not with fleshly wisdom, and lived like the primitive christians, without any pride or worldly motives, or in whose case I had rather die. And, therefore, no wonder that he lived in peace of conscience, and died with Paul's words, "I have fought a good fight, I have finished my course. Henceforth is laid up for me a crown of righteousness, which God, the righteous Judge, shall give." Which both Paul and he might say without any injury to Christ, or grace, or free justification. Thus did he finish his course in eminent fidelity, and constant peace of conscience; and what was wanting in fuller joy, is now made up.

Use 1. And what use should we make of all, but to imitate such examples, and not to be moved by any trials, nor count our lives dear, that we may finish our course with joy, and the ministry which we have received of the Lord Jesus Christ, to testify the gospel of the grace of God? Run the same race, and you may have the same joy and blessed end. Would you have more particular counsel how to finish your course with joy? I shall briefly give you some; the Lord cause you and me to follow it.

I. He that never began well, cannot finish well. Search the Scriptures, and advise with the wise; prove all things, and hold fast that which is good. Take heed that you take not evil for good, and good for evil. Set out in the way of truth. If you are out of the way, the faster and the farther you go, the more you have to repent of, and lament. Be honest and faithful in seeking truth, and God will forsake not you. But go not with Balaam's covetous heart, and pre-engaged purpose. O, fear a false heart, and false teachers, especially men that plainly prosecute a worldly interest and design.

II. If God, Christ, grace, and glory, be not enough for you, and seem not a sufficient portion, unless you have also prosperity to the flesh, undertake not the ministry, nor profess christianity; for, without self-denial, contempt of the world, taking up the cross, forsaking all, you have but the delusory name and image of christianity. Absolutely devote yourselves to God, and hope not for great matters in the world. Except nothing from him; suspect and fear the hypocrite's reserves; serve Christ and trust him; trust him with estate, and liberty, and life, and soul, and all; study your duty for your part, and cast your care on him for his part. Take no thought what ye shall eat or drink, but seek first God's kingdom and the righteousness thereof. You will never finish your course with joy, if you be not absolutely devoted to God.

III. Preach to yourselves first, before you preach to the people, and with greater zeal. O Lord, save thy church from worldly pastors, that study and learn the art of christianity, and ministry; but never had the christian, divine nature, nor the vital principle which must difference them and their services from the dead. Do you love other men's souls more than your own? will a dead nurse give a warm and vital milk? Nothing doth more to make you good preachers, than that which doth most to make you good christians: I thank the Lord for the method of his grace and providence, that cast me divers years into the care of my own soul, before I purposed to preach to others, and made me read over the most of all our English practical divines, to make me a christian indeed, before I set myself to the artificial part. I repent not of this unusual method.

IV. Let your joyful part of religion be most of your meditations: the infinite goodness of God, who is love; the wonder of man's redemption; the freeness and fulness of the promise; and the certainty and glory of our future state: these are the chief part of our religion, and of chiefest use; which must resolve us, fix us, quicken us, and help us to live in thankfulness and joy.

V. Above all, labour to strengthen faith in Christ, his word, and the life to come, and to live in the constant exercise thereof. Faith is it that showeth us the matter and reason of our duty and our joy. And if believing meditation have too long intermissions, our joy will also intermit. And if affliction or weakness make our present state to be grievous to us, and keep us from much present joy, yet faith and hope can see that which is to come. Many of God's faithful servants labour in peace of conscience and in hope; who, through infirmities of the flesh, have no great joys: and yet may be well said to finish their course with joy, because everlasting joy is the end, which at the finishing of it they obtain.

VI. Stick not at labour or suffering; hearken not to the repining and seducing flesh. Think nothing too much or too dear; your work is good, and much better wages in itself than fleshly pleasure. Labour for God and souls, and keep out selfishness and carnal ends, and God will secure your reward. Labour faithfully, and trust God confidently; fulfil his commanding will, whoever countermand you; and then rest in his accepting, disposing, and rewarding will, whatever befall you in the world. His will is the only infallible rule; and his will is the only secure and felicitating rest. They that conscionably do his will, may comfortably say, "The will of the Lord be done;" as our brother in his sickness often did.

His will made us, his will hath maintained and preserved us, and multiplied mercies to us. By his will we live, and by his will we die, and in his will we hope to rest for ever. Mr. Stubbs is gone before; this will hath guided him, and this will hath received him. In the same good hand I am closely following him. Our separation is like to be very short; and none of you will stay long behind. Farewell, vain, vexatious world! farewell, malignant, lying, cruel world! Welcome life, light, and love, delightful, perfect, and eternal! Let it be our care so to finish our course with joy, that we may hear, "Well done, good and faithful servant, enter thou into the joy of thy Lord." Blessed is that servant whom his Lord, when he cometh, shall find so doing. Come, Lord Jesus, come quickly. Amen.

Use 2. But methinks, I should not let you, that have been the hearers of Mr. Stubbs, and such as he, go without some notice what it is that this text and this providence of God do call you specially to consider. Which is, 1. Whether you have furthered the joy of your teacher's course. 2. Whether you take care that your own course may be finished with joy, and why it must be done, and how.

I. Do not think that you are not much concerned in the matter, whether your teachers live and die in joy; neither say, when they are dead, it is too late to mind that which is past and gone. As much as it is past, your account is not past. You may hear of it again in another manner than now you do.

You are concerned in it, 1. For your own interest. 2. For their relation to you, and labours for you, in gratitude and humanity. 3. As you are obliged to the church of Christ, and regard its interest. And, 4. As you are men, and lovers of mankind.

First, What is their ministry but the seeking of your salvation? And what is their joy but their success (next God's acceptance of their labours)? And if they miss of this, is it not you that will be the greatest sufferers? If you fall out with your physician, or cast away, or cast up, the only physic that can cure you, is not death more to you, than the loss of his labour and physic to him? Shall the physician mourn over his dying patient, and shall the patient think it nothing to him? If the child prosper not, or die, the nurse's sorrow is a smaller matter than the child's death. Is your unconverted, unpardoned, miserable state, and your danger of damnation, more to us than to you? Will your hell be no more painful than our compassion? And when your worm never dieth, and your fire will be unquenchable, our compassion will cease, and we shall grieve for you no more.

The God that forbade Samuel to mourn any more for Saul, will call us to approve of his righteous judgment, and to rejoice in the glorifying of his justice on you. Abraham did but upbraid Dives with his former sinful pleasures. Your teachers, yea, your own parents, will not mourn in heaven for all the torments that you undergo in hell, nor consent to ease you by a drop of water, Luke xvi.

Oh what a pitiful sight it is now to see a teacher or parent mourning over the misery of ignorant, careless, wilful sinners; and they themselves rejoicing, and despising compassion, and laughing at the brink of hell. I heard of a passionate wife that cut her own throat to anger her husband. And they tell us, that the Circumcellian Donatists, that separated from other christians, in a practical zeal for their own bishop, did murder themselves to bring the odium upon their adversaries as persecutors.

But that poor sinners should merrily run towards hell, to anger their teachers, yea, that multitudes should do thus, what an instance is it of the madness of corrupted minds! One saith, I will never hear him more: and another saith, Shall I be catechised like a boy? and another saith, These preachers would make us mad, if we should believe and lay to heart what they say: and another saith, Cannot one drink and be merry, and please his flesh, but he must be damned for it? Are none saved but puritans and precisians? And who is it that will have the worst of this at last? God will not condemn us for your sins. If you will needs be miserable for ever, our desires and endeavours to have saved you shall not be lost at all to us. Oh! how dear will impenitent sinners pay for all the tears and groans which now they do constrain from their compassionate teachers!

That God who is love itself, and putteth love into parents for the education of their children, hath also put a tender love to souls, and especially to their own flocks, into every faithful minister of Christ; which maketh all their study, and labour, and sufferings, easy to them, or tolerable, at least, for the comfortable hope which they have of men's salvation. Oh! may we but serve the Saviour of the world, in the gathering of his chosen flock; and in bringing sinners from darkness to light, and from the power of Satan unto God, in making reconciled and adopted sons of those that were the enemies of God and holiness, what a joy would it be to every true minister of Christ! Did a damned wretch cry, Send Lazarus to warn my brethren, that they come not to this place of torments? And shall not we rejoice if we cannot only keep sinners from those flames, but also help them to live in joy with Christ and holy spirits for ever? May we see souls in heaven for ever praising God, and know that this is the fruit of our labours and God's grace? Yea, may we here see holy persons living to God, and calling upon his name, and rejoicing in hope, and serving and honouring him in a wicked world, and say, These are they that God hath given to Christ by our embassage; how much sweeter will this be to us than fleshly pleasures! and will you not allow us the joy of your salvation? If so, judge yourselves whether the loss of Christ, and grace, and heaven, and happiness, and all hope, will be a smaller loss to you, than the loss of such comfort, in your hoped welfare, will be to us.

Oh! all you that are yet unconverted, fleshly, worldly persons, strangers to a holy, heavenly life, under the ministry of such holy men as I am speaking of, think in time, I beseech you, of these two particulars!

First, What a loss is it to lose the blessing and fruit of a holy ministry. God giveth not such to all the world. Many kingdoms of heathens and infidels have no such helps. Nay, most of the christian world have too little such; all ears are not so happy as to hear the joyful tidings, the sound instructions, the close convictions, the earnest exhortations which you have heard, and these not mixed with the poison of heresies. And will you lose, will you wilfully lose all this? What! have the best of physicians, and be yet unhealed? have the best of teachers, that long, and labour, and pray for your salvation, and yet be ignorant unbelievers, or base neglecters of this great salvation? Will you, as Capernaum, be lift up to heaven in mercies, and cast down to hell by your contempt? Oh that you knew in time how great a loss it is to lose one counsel, one sermon, much more all the life and labours of one such a minister of Christ, that prayed, and studied, and laboured for your souls! Do you ever hope to be saved, or not? If not, despair is a beginning of hell. If yea, do you hope to be saved without preaching, or by it? If without it, what reason have you for such hopes, when God hath made this his ordinary means? Whatever hope they may have that can have no preaching, you can have none that might have had it, and would not; or that had it, and despised and disobeyed it. But if it be by preaching that you hope to be instructed, converted, and saved, what preaching is it? Do you look for better than such as you have lost; or are smaller and weaker remedies like to cure you, that, to the last, despised greater?

Secondly, And remember that all this will aggravate your sin, and rise up in judgment against you to your condemnation. Do you think all these sermons, and prayers, and tears, shall never more be thought on? Yes. God, that sent his ministers, sets not so light by their labours as you do. He knoweth, and thy conscience shall one day consider, what importunate exhortations thou didst neglect. How, on such a day, on such a text, his minister earnestly pleaded with thy soul, and thou hadst nothing to say against the word, and yet thou wentest on and did not repent. Oh! for your soul's sake, put us not to come in against you as witnesses to your condemnation, instead of rejoicing in your sanctification and salvation!

Oh! put us not to shake off the dust of our feet against you! Turn not all our love and labours to kindle a greater fire for your misery. Remember, that even the merciful Saviour of souls hath said, that it shall be easier yet for Sodom and Gomorrah in the day of judgment than for such. Fire from heaven declared the wrath of God against Sodom and Gomorrah; and will you yet have a more dreadful fire? And what moveth you to all this? Do they persuade you to any thing dishonest, or to your hurt? Will you despise all our counsel, and go to hell rather than love God, and learn and do his holy will, and live in the delightful hopes of heaven, and in love, peace, and good works towards one another? This is all that we persuade you to: and will it not torment your consciences for ever to remember that this was all that you fled from God for, and that you avoided more than sin and hell?

Secondly, I have told you that your own interest is more concerned in the success of our ministry than our joy. I next tell you that it is inhuman ingratitude to deny us such a joy as this. Our relation and labours for you make it our due: shall children deny their parents the comfort of their love, when it is only their well-doing and happiness that they desire? As Christ and angels rejoice at a sinner's conversion, so do true ministers in their degree. And is it not base ingratitude to deny Christ, angels, and ministers, this joy, by refusing obstinately to be saved?

Thirdly, And why do you take on you to be christians, and no more regard the interest of the church of Christ? Those are the church's enemies that will not give up themselves to Christ, that would not have him to reign over them, and subdue their fleshly minds and lusts, Luke xix. 27; Rom. viii. 6, 7, 13; that hinder the success of the ministers of Christ that would build up his church. And what is our building, but to bring home souls? Our office is not of man, but of Christ. He giveth us our commission, though man deliver it us. He commandeth you to receive and obey his word which we deliver you, and terribly threateneth those that will not, Heb. xiii. 17; John xiii. 20; Matt. ix. 36, 37; Luke ix. 18, &c. Is it not rebellion against him, then, to be refusers? Nay, what do you but as much as in you lieth to destroy the ministerial office, and so destroy the church of God. For if we are but to stand here and talk to you awhile, and not to win your souls to God, this is but an image or carcass of the ministry, as to the success and end. As you mortify all God's ordinances, and turn them into a lifeless image, so you do the ministry to you; and make it to you but "as sounding brass or tinkling cymbal." Is it worth your tithes, or are we worthy of your reverence, merely to talk to you, and never to convert and save you?

Oh the blindness of the minds of the ungodly! If the seekers, or other heretics, do but cry down ministers and universities, you jusfly rise up against them as enemies to christianity and the church; and yet you yourselves destroy their ministry as to yourselves, and would have but the name, and garb, and image. He that would have the tenth part of all men's revenues to be settled to maintain physicians in the land, and yet would not have men be healed by them, is foolisher and a worse enemy to the country, than he that would have none at all.

Fourthly, And as you are lovers of mankind, you should not deny us so reasonable a joy as your own salvation; especially to such as, for the hope of this, renounce the pleasures and honours of the world. If you could do well enough without instructers, Christ would not have appointed them, nor if there had been any better way for your salvation. And for our parts, we could have found out work and callings that would better have served us for worldly ends; and we could live idle, and seek preferment, and flatter and please you, and neglect your souls in this calling that we are in.

But then, woe to us, as well as you! O, remember who hath said, "Obey them that have the rule over you, for they watch for your souls, as they that must give account, that they may do it with joy, and not with grief, for that is unprofitable for you," Heb. xiii. 17. He is not worthy to be called a man, that will deny any joy or good to his neighbour, which doth no hurt to himself or others. But, consider whether he be not herein worse than a devil, that will deny another the comfort of seeing him happy, and freely do him the greatest good?

Do you not see, now, how much you are concerned, that you further our joyful finishing of our course? I beseech you, let conscience judge you, before God judge you. Speak as before God. Have you been turned by them from darkness to light; and from unbelief to a lively faith; and from a fleshly to a spiritual life; and from worldly love and hopes to the love of God, and the hope of endless joys in heaven? Are you at a point with the flattering world and fleshly lusts; and have you heartily taken God and heaven for your portion, and Christ for your Saviour, and the Holy Spirit for your Sanctifier and Comforter, and the word of God for your law and charter, and the servants of God for your pleasantest company, and the service and praises of God for your best and pleasantest work, and sin for your worst and greatest enemy? If this be so, bless God that made the word so effectual to you. But if it be not, you have wronged your teachers in robbing them of the joy which was their due. This is it that we studied, prayed, and preached for; this is it that we live and labour for. This was to have been the chief part of our reward from you. It is not your tithes and money, without this, that will satisfy any but an hireling.

Many old canons of the church forbade ministers to receive any offerings or gifts from unbelievers and wicked men; as if they had said, Keep your money to yourselves, and think not to stop our mouths with gifts. Give up yourselves to Christ, or you give us nothing. I tell you it is you that are our great afflicters, and you shall answer for it. It is much more to us to lose the joy of your salvations, than to lose our estates or liberties, or worldly honour and reputation; and you can never be saved if you will not be sanctified, nor happy if you will not be holy. O, yet look back and remember what counsel God sent you by his ministers, and what importunities they used with you; and if you have denied them yet their joy, O pity yourselves if you regard not them; and deny not yourselves still the present joy of a holy life, and the everlasting joy of heavenly glory, which yet you may attain.

II. And have not you also a course that should be finished with joy, as well as we? O sirs! time is precious, short, and hasty. This race is for all eternity, and is to be run but once. Heaven will be quickly won or lost for ever. Can any one hear and believe this that hath the heart of a man, and not be awakened presently to make haste? Dare you die in an unholy, unpardoned state? Dare you go out of the world more foolishly than the unjust steward out of his stewardship, before you have provided another habitation? Dare you appear before God without his Spirit and image, and without the wedding garment of sincere holiness, and so without a part in Christ? O sirs! no heart can now conceive what a dreadful appearing that will be. Alas, sirs! we are dying, we are all dying, one to-day and another to-morrow, and we are all quickly gone; and do you take no care whether you shall go next, when God bids you care, in a manner, for nothing else? Your course will soon be finished. Shall it be with joy, or the beginning of everlasting misery? Oh! resolve now, resolve this day, as you would speed for ever! God's grace must save you; but it lieth more on your present choice and resolution than careless sinners will well consider of.

Quest. But how should I finish my course with joy?

Answ. You may gather it from what is said already. Are you willing, if I tell you to do your part? Asking questions will not serve instead of work.

I. Will you see that you perish not through your own mere carelessness, and wilful neglect of what you can do for your souls? If you will not do what you can, what good will directions do you? If men will live as if they had not reason and self-love, and knew not that they must die, or care not what becomes of them for ever, what can one do for the safety of such men? As men cannot dispute, that agree not in some granted principles; so we cannot lead you to Christ by the gospel, if you agree not in some principles of humanity and self-preservation. A sottish carelessness is the undoing of the most.

II. Set yourselves to study the gospel of Christ, till you understand what salvation is, and what is the way to it, and know the nature of true religion: and then you will see in it so much truth, so much necessity, so much amiable beauty and fitness to make you wise, good, and happy, that it will win your hearts to love and pleasure in it.

III. Study thoroughly the true meaning of your baptismal covenant; and solemnly, before God, consent to it with tongue and heart, and live as under the obligation of it all your days; and also live in the belief of all the promises of it, and expectations of all the benefits promised. The sum of all your religion for duty and comfort is comprised in your baptismal covenant. Though it be an error to be oft baptized, it is a hundred times worse error, never truly to understand, consent, and practise, after so solemn a vow and covenant.

IV. When you have given up yourselves to God, as your God and Father, your Saviour and your Sanctifier, remember that your great relations have engaged you in the greatest business and the highest hopes in all the world. And, therefore, now live as fellow-citizens of the saints and the household of God, that have nobler converse, work, and hope, than worldly unbelievers. Remember, now, with whom and what you have to do; and that it is not a by and trifling business, but the best and greatest, that you have undertaken.

V. Join with those that are for heaven, whose counsel and company may be your help; separate from no christians by way of division, further than God commandeth you; and do not easily forsake the judgment of the generality of godly men: but make few your familiar friends, and those such as are most wise, and humble, and sincere, and cheerful in the belief and hopes of glory, and suitable to your use and converse.

VI. In all doubts and difficulties of religion, judge not hastily before you have thoroughly heard and tried. Prefer a suspended judgment, that stayeth till it have tried, before a rash and hasty judgment of what you know not, and may repent of.

VII. Carefully govern your fleshly appetites and sense, and avoid needless temptations, especially to sinful pleasure: for lust will conceive else, and bring forth sin; and sin being finished will bring forth death. You will find sin and comfort contrary.

VIII. Especially, fear the flatteries of the world, and hopes of a pleasant life to the flesh on earth, and an itch after riches, plenty, or preferment, and designs for the attaining them; love not the world, nor the things that are in the world, the lust of the flesh, the lust of the eyes, and pride of life, the portion of the wicked; for if any man love the world (for the flesh and itself) so far the love of the Father is not in him, 1 John ii. 15, 16.

IX. Value precious time, and live not in idleness; spend time as you would hear of it at last, and as those that know what it is to have but one short life to determine where they shall live for ever. Hear and abhor all pastimes and triflings that would rob you of your time.

X. Converse daily in heaven while you are on earth; let faith still see it; let hope still make after it, and let love desire it, and delightfully remember it. There is our Father, our Saviour, our Comforter, our friends, with whom we must live for ever. There let our hearts be as the place of all our hopes. And let the strain of your religion be as heavenly as you can; let it consist in love, in unity and concord, in the joyful praises of Jehovah, and in a pure, holy life. This will raise you above the sinful love of this transitory life, and the fear of death, and give you the foretastes of heaven on earth, while you do God's will on earth as it is done in heaven. But it is the Spirit and grace of Christ which you must beg and seek, and on which you must obediently depend, for the performance of all this, and not upon your unconstant wills. Without Christ we can do nothing; but by his strengthening us we can do all things necessary to our salvation; and we are more than conquerors, even in our patient sufferings, through the Captain of our salvation, who hath conquered for us.

Thus we may finish our course with joy.

A

TRUE BELIEVER'S CHOICE AND PLEASURE,

INSTANCED IN

THE EXEMPLARY LIFE OF MRS. MARY COXE,

THE LATE WIFE OF DR. THOMAS COXE.

TO MY WORTHY AND MUCH HONOURED FRIEND,

DR. THOMAS COXE.

Sir,

Though your great kindness and care of the health of me and mine much oblige me to you, and your personal worth much more, and your worthy children command my great respect and love; yet none of these should have moved me to say a word of all that I have said of your deceased wife, which I had not verily believed to be true; and it was God's grace in her which much more commanded it than all my debt to you and yours.

She was so exemplary, as that I think it my duty, for the good of others, to make this publication of her character, and of this sermon.

But one great defect is here to be notified to the reader, that almost all her secret way of duty and particular converse is omitted, which you that were still with her could have described; for I thought meet to say no more than I either knew myself, or was obvious and known to many.

The words which I heard but yesterday from the mouth of your brother in discourse, were such as I doubt can be said of few, that in so many years, from the hour of her marriage to her death, she was never known to do one disobliging action, or speak one disobliging word, of or to any one of her husband's kindred or relations.

Had it seemed meet to you, or to your worthy and ingenuous son, and your pious daughter, (the true image of her mother,) to have been the describer of the soul and life of this exemplary saint, how much more fully could you have done it than I, that was so much less acquainted with her!

She is gone home, and you and I are at the door. The Lord give us so to live by faith on the promise and love of God, and the things unseen, that thence we may daily fetch our ruling motives, and establishing consolations, and not from a transitory, deceitful world; and, following Christ and his saints under the cross, may with them possess the incorruptible crown, and be found at his call among those that love his appearing, and be for ever with the Lord. Amen, Amen.

November 19th, 1679.

PSALM CXIX. 111.

THY TESTIMONIES HAVE I TAKEN AS AN HERITAGE FOR EVER; FOR THEY ARE THE REJOICING OF MY HEART.

A text that speaketh of rejoicing, and that in an heritage, and an heritage for ever, may seem unsuitable to a mournful funeral; but it was chosen by our deceased friend, and not without justifiable reason. That which was a day of sorrow to us, was a day of rest and joy to her; and it was meet that she should foresee that joy, and, tasting it in the first-fruits, should commend that to us which she had found so sweet, and would bring us to the felicity which she hath now obtained. If the damned sensualist (Luke xvi.) would have had one sent from another world, in hope to save his unbelieving brethren, no wonder if a holy person were desirous that others should partake of her pleasure and inheritance, and, like the lepers that found the siege of Samaria raised, would not feast and rejoice alone. She chose this, no doubt, as that which was most lively imprinted on her own heart, with a just desire that it might be printed also on the hearts of others; that so we may not only rejoice with her that now rejoiceth in the heavenly possession, but, as Paul saith, "every man may prove his own works, and so may have rejoicing in himself alone, and not (only) in another," Gal. vi. 4. Let us, therefore, by God's assistance, so improve these words, as may conduce to this desired end.

By God's "testimonies" here is meant that supernaturally revealed law and promise, which was possessed by the church of the Jews, as God's peculiar people, supposing the law of nature, and the common mercies which God had given to all the rest of fallen mankind. Both the precepts and promises are here included, the types, and their signification of the thing typified.

"I have taken them," signifieth, I have believed them, implying that God revealed them; and I have accepted them, implying that God had offered them; and I have chosen them, implying the preferring them before all competitors; and I have trusted them, as signifying their special use for the guiding, stablishing, quieting, and saving of the soul.

"For an heritage," signifieth,

1. As that which I trust to as my security for a heavenly inheritance.

2. And as that which now is my best portion while I am in the way, including the things connoted.

3. And as that which I prefer before all wealth, and worldly heritage. Alexander and Cæsar had larger dominions than David, but neither of them was king of God's peculiar people, that had possession of his oracles, nor had the promises which he had, that Christ should be his son and successor on his throne.

The words "for ever," relateth both to the inheritance as everlasting, and also to David's choice, as immutably hereupon determined.

They are said to be the rejoicing of the heart aptitudinally in themselves, which caused him to choose them, and actually, because he had chosen, believed, loved, and obeyed them.

So that this is the sum of the sense: Worldly men make choice of a worldly inheritance and hopes, and on this they trust; and in this they seek their chiefest pleasure: but I, though blessed largely with thy bounty, have suffered many afflictions in the world; but thy word hath been my guide, and thy promises still fulfilled to me; and experience hath confirmed my faith and resolution to lay all my hope upon thy word or covenant, both for this life and that to come, and from it I seek and fetch my comfort: it hath been my joy in all my sorrows, and in it to the last will I rejoice. This is the sense of the text, from which we are all taught,—

Doct. That God's covenant or testimonies are the true believer's heritage for ever, and as such are trusted and chosen by him; and therefore, among all the allurements and the crosses of this world, are the support and rejoicing of his heart.

In the handling this I shall show you,

I. What it is in God's testimonies which make them fit to be our heritage and our joy.

II. How they are called an heritage for ever.

III. How they are so taken by believers.

IV. How far they are their joy.

I. In God's covenant or testimonies there is, 1. The Author. 2. The Mediator. 3. The applying Agent. 4. The ascertaining revelation. 5. The donative or benefit given. 6. The guiding doctrine and law. 7. And the persons or subjects connoted, to whom all this is suited, to be an heritage for ever, and the rejoicing of their hearts.

1. The Author is God, the Lord of us and all; in whose hand and will is our soul and body, our life and death, our health and sickness, our joy and sorrow; whose loving-kindness is life, and better than life, Psal. lxiii. 3; who, if he will, can make us whole and happy, and who hath told us what he will do by his covenant. He wanteth not love, for he is love itself; essential, infinite self-love, communicating to his creatures such love as his wisdom seeth meet for them to receive. The love that gave us the Mediator and the covenant, will certainly perform it; it was of mercy that he promised, it is now of mercy and justice that he performs it. He wanteth not wisdom to rule the world by truth and goodness, and needeth not deceit and falsehood hereunto, nor to flatter such worms as we into obedience. Nor doth he, that maintaineth heaven and earth, want power to make good all his word; nor is there any adverse power to make it difficult, and hazard the success. Indeed, he that seriously considereth the divine perfection, will think it were more strange and incredible that God should not bless and glorify the faithful, according to his word. If it be credible that the sun sends forth its illuminating and enlivening beams so far and wide, to so many millions of various creatures, (though it scorch the unsuitable objects that are too near,) it is credible that God, who is infinite goodness, should bless the capable with heavenly glory. And did we not see that sin maketh many uncapable, it would be harder to reason to believe that all shall not be blessed by such a God, than that all the faithful shall be blessed. And we find, that though both be hard to unbelievers, they are of the two more hardly brought to believe the threatenings, than the promises, of God. What wonder is it that infinite power, wisdom, and love, should make some of his creatures blessed by communication, and man in special, when he hath made him capable of it?

And what greater satisfaction and security can a fearful, troubled, dying man have, than the infallible word of the most glorious God? Surely he that firmly believeth it to be his word, can hardly choose but believe that it is true, and meet for our most quieting trust.

2. The angels and Moses were the mediators of the Jewish law; but the eternal Word incarnate is the Mediator of the new covenant; promised only before, to Abraham, David, &c. yea, to Adam, but sent, when made man, in the fulness of time, Gal. iv. 4. And it must needs be a sure and excellent covenant which is made and confirmed by such a Mediator, named in the prophecy, "Wonderful, Counsellor, The Mighty God, The everlasting Father, The Prince of Peace," Isa. ix. 6; of the increase of whose government and peace there is no end. He is the heir of all things, by whom the worlds were made; the brightness of God's glory; the express image of his person; and upholding all things by the word of his power; made better than angels, having by inheritance obtained a more excellent name; whom all the angels of God do worship; and for whom they disdain not to minister to the faithful. It is a sure and comfortable doctrine which must have such a Preacher sent from heaven, and a certain covenant which hath a such wonderful Mediator.

3. But it is not like the powerless word of man, but the holy Spirit of the Father and the Son undertaketh to accompany it; and, as the arm of God, to set it home, and make it effectual to its proper ends: we have not only heard this word, but felt it; as we hear and feel the powerful winds, though we see them not, and perceive not whence they come, or

whither they go. All have felt this who are born of the Spirit, John iii. 8. God spake not like man when he said, "Let there be light," Gen. i.; and he teacheth not like man, when his Spirit, by his word, doth quicken, illuminate, and regenerate souls. It is a sure covenant that hath such an inward Mediator, such an agent, and advocate, and witness of Christ, speaking operatively from God to man, and speaking prevailingly in man to God.

4. And the sure manner of revelation doth make it fit to be our trust and joy. As it beareth on itself the image or impress of God's power, wisdom, and goodness; so by powerful miracles, and manifold wisdom, and unmeasurable goodness, it hath been delivered, sealed, defended, and propagated; and by a communicated spirit of life, light, and love, in all sound believers, confirmed to this day.

5. And what is it that with such glory and certainty is delivered to us from heaven? It is a deed of gift, (thus sealed by Christ's blood and Spirit,) of grace, and glory; of Christ to be our Head, and Lord, and Husband, and Life, in and with him, John v. 10, 12; of the free pardon of all our sins, how many and great soever, and of reconciliation with God, and of justification by the blood and righteousness of our Redeemer, and of the continued teaching, preserving, sanctifying, strengthening, comforting aid of the Holy Spirit; of adoption and title to the heavenly inheritance, that being sons, and having the Spirit of the Son, by it we shall be sealed up to glory, and be made the habitation and temples of God. In a word, it is a promise of this life, so far as that all things shall work together for our good, Rom. viii. 28; and of the life which is to come, where we shall live in glory with Christ for ever. This is the sure and blessed covenant of God.

6. And what are the doctrine and laws of God? are they not also suited to our trust and joy? Is it not a delightful thing to read that which no mere man could tell us? How God made man and all the world, and what laws he gave him. How sin came into the world, and death by sin. How God hath governed the world from the beginning, and how he hath redeemed us. What Christ is, and what he hath done, and what he will do. And what man is, and what he should be, and what he shall be, and do, and have for ever.

And what is there in God's laws but that which is our safety, and should be our joy? If good laws be the safety and honour of kingdoms, are not God's laws so to all the world? What an ugly dungeon were the world without them; and what a worse than brutish thing were man! Oh! how happy were man, were families, were cities, were kingdoms, if all had made God's laws their rule, and all men's laws and lives had been ruled by them! Then there would have been none but wise, just, and holy rulers, that would have governed for God, and for the common good; and princes would have been indeed the fathers of their countries, and masters of their families, abhorring all contradicting selfish interests, and all injustice, tyranny, and oppression. Then subjects would have, with reverence, readiness, and fidelity, obeyed God, in obeying and honouring their parents, princes, and masters. Then all men would love their neighbours as themselves, and do as they would be done by; love and justice would reign among all, and injury, partiality, and selfishness would be abhorred. And which of us cannot say, Had I been ruled by God's laws, I had escaped all the guilt, the shame, the corrections, the terrors that have befallen me. It is our sin against that sacred rule, which is the cause of all our sorrows; else what peace might we have had in our consciences, in our bodies, in our houses, in our cities, and country, as having peace with God. God's strictest laws are but his strict forbidding us to destroy or hurt ourselves and others, as you forbid fire, and water, and knives, and gunpowder, surfeiting, and poison, to your children, for their preservation.

Oh! how glad would every true christian be, if God's laws were fullier written on his heart, and he could but be and do all that God therein commandeth. For want of this perfect conformity it is that he crieth out with Paul, "To will is present with me, but to do I find not. O wretched man that I am! who shall deliver me from the body of this death?" Rom. vii. 24.

How joyful should we be if we could but trust God, and love him, and obey him, and be free from sins, as much as the law of God commandeth us! We testify, therefore, that the law is holy, and just, and good, while we repent that we break it, and wish that we could better keep it. For this would keep our souls from guilt, and shame, and terrors, and our bodies from much calamity and pain; all God's ways are pleasantness, and all his paths are peace. Great peace have they that love his law, and nothing shall offend them: let papists hide it and accuse it, and let the ignorant and malignant scorn it, yet will believers judge it fit for their confidence and delight.

7. And the rather, because that all this is admirably suited to our necessity. We are undone sinners, and had perished for ever, without a Saviour and a pardoning covenant. We are dark and foolish, and should have erred to damnation, without this sure and heavenly guide. We are beset with temptations, and how should we overcome them without God's promise of better things than this world can give us? We are under manifold pains and sorrows, and must shortly die; and how should we undergo all this in peace, if we had not hopes of future happiness, and of that which will compensate all our losses? We have a life of service to God which must be faithfully and cheerfully done; and how should we so do it without good persuasion of this reward? He that cometh to God, must believe that God is, and that he is the rewarder of them that diligently seek him.

Oh! then, what a joyful word should that be to us, which is sent from God himself thus to guide, to secure, to strengthen, and comfort us, by the promise of all that we need, and can well desire, sealed by the blood, miracles, and Spirit of Christ; and bearing the impress of God the author, and that to such miserable sinners as we are.

II. But how are God's testimonies our heritage for ever, when in heaven we shall have no need of Scriptures?

Answ. 1. "For ever" sometimes signifieth, to the end of my life, as David saith, "I shall dwell in the house of the Lord for ever," Psal. xxiii. and so oft. And so God's testimonies were taken for his heritage, or chiefest portion, and rejoicing constantly, and to his life's end, as securing him of an everlasting heritage.

2. And the heritage promised by them, and connoted, is everlasting; and the holiness imprinted by them on his soul will be perpetuated and perfected in heaven.

III. What is it for believers to take God's testimonies for their heritage?

Answ. It is supposed that the flattering world, and the pleasures of the flesh, do stand here in competition, and are by many taken for their best, and this because they either think not of, or believe not, the better things of a life to come, and the comforts of a holy prospect and preparation. In this case, every true believer, seriously weighing all, and what can be said on both sides, what the world and flesh will be and do for him, and what God, and grace, and glory will be and do, doth wisely discern and resolve,

1. That the world is vanity, and sin abominable.

2. That God is all-sufficient, infinitely good, and to be trusted, and his word most wise, and just, and true; and therefore, though his belief have its imperfections and assaults, yet he so far believeth God's promises to be sure, and his precepts to be good and necessary, as that he resolveth here to place his hope and trust for his whole felicity in this life and hereafter, and to give up himself to the study, love, and obedience of God's laws, as the guide, and security, and comfort of his soul, renouncing all the flatteries of the flesh and world which stand against it, and are preferred by sensual unbelievers.

In few words, this was David's faith and choice, and this is the faith and choice of all true believers, by which we may discern whether we are such; though all have not the same degree of trust and fixed resolution, yet all have this much in sincerity.

IV. *Quest.* But can all say, They are the rejoicing of my heart?

Answ. All of them can say,

1. We see that there is in the word and covenant of God in Christ, unspeakably more matter fit to be our joy, than in all the pleasures, and wealth, and honours of this world.

2. And therefore we prefer it before them all, in our desire and our fixed choice.

3. And we find so much goodness and suitableness to us in this sacred word, as that we love it as our food and our security, though not with the appetite and love which we desire.

4. And though we have not that joy in this our love to it, and in the hopes of promised glory, which a stronger faith and love would cause, yet we find that it is our best, and we perceive more good in it than in sinful pleasures; and the true and chief support of our souls in all our fears and troubles, and in our prospect of another life, is from the love and word of God through Christ.

And though our pleasure in it be not sensual and luscious, it is much more solid and satisfying to our souls, than we find in any other thing.

And the sweetness which we taste in it, is greater at some times than at others.

And the comfort which we have in our bodily health and welfare is much, as it signifieth to us the love of God performing to us his promises, and helping us to serve him with joy and gladness, in order to everlasting joy.

This is the ordinary case of true believers, though extraordinarily, 1. Some tempted, troubled, melancholy christians, overwhelmed with grief and fears, do not perceive this much in themselves. 2. And the healthfuller, stronger sort of christians have yet a more sweet and constant pleasure, in the testimonies and ways of God.

Having said thus much for explication, a little more may suffice to show you why and whence it is that believers receive the testimonies of God with this fixed choice, and trust, and pleasure.

1. It is from honest self-love and interest. They certainly find that it is their best, that it is true and good, and that there is nothing else to be found in this world that will serve instead of it, to be a quieting security, guide, and comfort to the soul. They perceive what they need, and that nothing else can supply those needs. This must be their hope, or they must despair.

2. It is from holy suitableness and love to God, and the goodness which they relish in his word. As God giveth every living creature an appetite suitable to his food and benefits, so doth he to the new creature. Holiness is mostly the soul's appetite to God, and spiritual good. The word which promiseth and guideth us to the incorruptible crown of glory, is an incorruptible seed, 1 Pet. i. 3—6; and it is our milk or food, 1 Pet. ii. 2; and by it we are made partakers of the divine nature, 2 Pet. i. 4; and it is the ingrafted or innaturalized word which is able to save our souls, Jam. i. 21. And as the whole stock is marvellously turned to serve a little graft which is planted into it, and as if it had lost its former kind, doth bring forth only the fruit of the graft, so is God's word implanted in us to the change of our nature and our fruits. And it is no sound appetite which hath no pleasure. No wonder if a strong belief do cause us to "rejoice with joy unspeakable and full of glory, that we may receive the end of our faith, our salvation," 1 Pet. i. 6—8.

All God's commands and promises have, by the divine impression of them on our souls, left somewhat there which is like them, and connatural; even a holy light to understand their truth and goodness, and a holy love to them and the things revealed, to desire them, and take pleasure in them, and a holy liveliness to pursue the good desire. And this is the writing of the law and gospel on our hearts; and in this sense it may be said that God, that Christ, that the Holy Ghost is in our souls, and dwelleth in us, even as an efficient principle, and a beloved object, and desired end. And if this be all that they intend, those called quakers have no reason to accuse us for not preaching a God and a Christ within us. And if this be it that is meant by those who tell the world, that by saying that the Holy Ghost is in us, we are more arrogant than the pope, that claimeth a visible monarchy; we glory in this joyful privilege, this earnest, seal, and first-fruits of heavenly glory, and humbly thank him, who hath vouchsafed it, and assured us of it in his word, Rom. viii. 9, 11; 2 Cor. vi. 16; Eph. iii. 17; 1 John iv. 13; 1 Cor. iii. 16; 2 Tim. i. 14; 1 John iii. 24; iv. 12, 15, 16. And if the scorners have any belief of the Scriptures, let them read and tremble, "If any man have not the Spirit of Christ, the same is none of his," Rom. viii. 9.

I have given you the sense and the reason of this doctrine; we come hither to learn what use to make of it. And I think if I preach also on the copy or impress of this text, whose relics we have laid in the dust, and tell us what use she made of such doctrine, it will be a considerable help to our own application.

I have never loved or used to adorn sepulchres, or hang out specious signs at the doors of pride, ambition, tyranny, or worldliness, to entice others to imitate prosperous sinners in their sin; were I to preach at the funerals of an Alexander or a Cæsar, I had rather say that which may save the living from following them in pride and bloodshed, than to tempt men to the like sin and misery.

To praise damned men, because they had the pleasures of sin for a season, is to be more foolish and uncharitable than the tormented gentleman, (Luke xvi.) who would have had one sent from the dead to warn his brethren, lest they should follow him to that place of torment, by preferring fleshly pleasure and prosperity before the life and hope of saints. Our praises ease not tormented souls. It is a mark of the citizens of the holy city, that "A vile person is contemned in their eyes;" but withal, that they "Honour those that fear the Lord; for God doth honour them."

My duty, therefore, to God, and my love to holiness and holy persons, and to you in special that are her children and other relations, commandeth me to tell you (though some of you know it better than I) that our deceased friend, in the course of her pilgrimage, did speak of herself by her constant practice, what David professed in this text. Though I speak but from eighteen or nineteen years' acquaintance with her myself, I have full evidence of it for the former part of her life; and my acquaintance with her by neighbourhood, and mutual esteem, hath been such as hath given me more advantage to know her, than most have had; though I remember not ever to have spoken with one person that hath known her, that did not take her for an extraordinary and eminent example of the piety and virtues which I shall mention.

If the hypocrites seek the praise of men, verily they have their reward; (a poor reward!) but she, seeking first the kingdom of God, and the honour that is of him, had this cast in as overplus. I never heard that any person of any persuasion did speak evil of her, or question her eminent sincerity and worth.

Had she come to this by sinful compliance, she might have feared Christ's words, "Woe unto you, when all men speak well of you!" Luke vi. 26; but as God hath not left himself without witness to the very heathens, so he hath not left innocency, wisdom, love, peace, and piety, without some witnesses in the consciences of the ungodly; few of them have the face to speak against these in their proper names: and if he could not dishonour them by our mixed faults, and by the slanderous affixed names of heresy, schism, disobedience, hypocrisy, fanaticism, folly, and what else ignorance and malignity can devise, the devil knew not how to dishonour holiness and virtue, nor to encourage the blind world to so common a hatred and opposition of them, as they show in all nations of the earth.

When she chose this text, it was from such a suitable spirit, as all men choose the food, the friends and company, the business and discourse, which by agreeableness they most delight in. That she made God's word and covenants (connoting God's love, Christ, grace, and glory, the spring, matter, and end) her best, her heritage, her all, contemning all that stood in competition, and that these were the rejoicing of her heart, she showed to us that knew her, by these notable effects.

I. By her constant, serious, diligent use of the word of God, by hearing, reading, conference, and meditation. Her food was not more constantly used, nor, I believe, so sweet to her. Her hearing in the public assemblies, nothing but necessity could interrupt; and her private constancy her relations know. She practically told us that the blessed man's "delight is in the law of the Lord, and therein doth he meditate day and night," Psal. i. 2.

II. She made so much (in esteem, use, and thankfulness) of every little of the help she could get in these spiritual things, as showed that they were her heritage and joy. When some come home with accusations of the sermon, as dry, dull, or weak, she found in it something for profit and solace. I am sure my own conversation and duties have been truly guilty of the foresaid faults; and yet how gladly would she come over the way to us at prayer-time! How much did she value now and then a little (too dull, unprofitable) conference, and took it for a loss that she could have no more! How glad was she of now and then a too dry and short letter, and how carefully would she keep them! as if, with the woman of Canaan, she had been begging for the crumbs. Alas! our duller appetites seldom so desire after, or delight in, much larger portions of well-dressed food, but fulness hath loathing, and we call it dry manna, which we are weary of; or every little fault in the dressing turneth our stomach against it: full souls loathe the honeycomb, but to the hungry every bitter thing is sweet.

III. She loved and received the word of God from any faithful minister that brought it. It is true that she more frequented and desired some than others; but her religion was not faction, or siding with this party, or with that; she was far from a schismatical mind or practice. When one party separate from all that preach in the parish churches, and another from all that preach elsewhere; she separated from neither.

IV. Accordingly, she loved all persons that feared God as such; not confining her affections or kindness to those of this or that controvertible opinion; but that candour, and holy simplicity, and serious practical religion which she had herself, was it that she loved in all others whomsoever.

V. And accordingly, her conference was not about controversies or matters of contention, in which too many spend their hours in these times, but that which tendeth to edification, and to administer grace to the hearers. She was not such as Paul oft reproveth for striving about words, and little things, that tend not to edify, but subvert.

VI. Much less was she tainted with any heresy or dangerous error in religion, nor ever drawn from the truth, and her spiritual stedfastness; but cleaved to the form of wholesome words, and the simplicity that is in Christ, and to them that held the unity of the Spirit in the bond of peace; avoiding the vain janglings of men of contention, pride, and corrupt minds.

VII. She was not of a censorious, backbiting temper, nor used, as too many faulty christians, to make it her discourse to find fault with others, and make herself the judge of controversies, cases, actions, and persons, which she understood not; but had learned that lesson, "Speak evil of no man;" and to know and be called to it, before she judged.

VIII. She was very desirous of the good of all, and glad of any thing which tended to promote the conversion and saving of men's souls.

IX. She was charitable and liberal also to their bodies, in an unusual degree; as I am able to say by particular experience, in which I have known it exercised to the poor.

X. Her humility and detestation of pride was manifest, not only in her garb and behaviour, but in her low thoughts of herself, and the lowliness of all her conversation, and great dislike of all that savoured of pride.

XI. She was not morose, nor a refuser of converse or useful visits, when reason required them; but she took it for a great affliction to have much diversion by company, or by-matters, from her constant course of better work; and (besides her health) was, therefore, the more inclined to be much in the country, that her mind and time might not be at the mercy of too much intruding diversions and unprofitable discourse.

XII. Much more was she averse to all sorts of sensuality; such pleasing of the flesh as corrupteth the mind, and turneth it from holy work and pleasure; and such vain recreations as waste precious time, and profit not ourselves or others. Holy things were her food and feast, her work and recreation.

XIII. Her prudence in all matters was very exemplary; being much more against unadvised rashness, and actions which tend to ill effects, than most of us of the stronger sex; and I confess I should think much better of myself if I could equal her herein. In which her acquaintance commonly admired her, though this is a point which all must acknowledge much imperfection in.

XIV. And her gentleness, meekness, and calmness of mind and carriage was very amiable to her friends, and most that did converse with her. She was a great adversary to passionate behaviour, which surely came from that power of grace, which had made love and meekness become a nature in her, seeing no such thing could be else expected in one of her sex, and complexion, and bodily weaknesses.

XV. She did not, as the hypocrite, give God the second place in her heart and life, and the world the first, nor put off Christ with the leavings of the flesh, nor take this world for her best or heritage, and the next only for a reserve when she must needs leave this; she seemed to prize no heritage but God, nor to set much by any transitory vanity whatsoever.

XVI. She excelled in the earnest desire of her children's good, and in the care of their well-doing and salvation. How oft hath she desired me to pray for them! How glad was she if I would at any time but converse with them, and advise them! They know better themselves (though I know much) how much she prayed for them; how oft and tenderly she counselled them; what letters of serious, holy counsel she would write to them; and how like she was to Job, who prayed and sacrificed for his children when they were merry and feasting together, fearing lest they should forget God, and sin against him!

XVII. This kind of life which I have described, was her calling and trade, and in a manner her only business in the world. It was not now and then in a good mood, like a feast or recreation; but as she knew that one thing is needful, so she chose that better part, which never was, nor will be taken from her. She so lived as if she had but this one thing to mind and do in the world, to please God by obeying him, and to cleave to Christ; and to do good, and to be saved. Nothing else seemed to be much in her mind, thoughts, care, and business; her life seemed to be but this one thing. But I must confess that poor and tempted persons, that are under many worldly wants, crosses, and employments, cannot be expected to reach her measure in this; though one thing be their best and portion, they may be tossed with many troublesome cares and businesses. But God gave her both mind, opportunity, and help to live in as even a course of constant holiness in a family, as monks can pretend to or hope for in their community or solitude. Religion was her very life.

XVIII. In this life she had also a constant peace of conscience, bewailing her imperfections, but not living in melancholy, despair, hard thoughts of God, or an uncomfortable sort of religion. I have oft heard her speak of her lamented weakness of faith, love, and heavenly desires and joy; but never, that I remember, one doubting word of her own sincerity and salvation: but her ordinary speech was lamenting that we were all so weak in our belief of the word of God, and the unseen world, and what excellent persons we should be, if herein we had a stronger faith, that were liker unto sight; and how much it should be the business of all believers, to pray and labour for an increased powerful belief hereof, as that which would set all right in us.

XIX. Her patience under her bodily infirmities also was exemplary. Her weakness made her so liable to dangerous coughs while she was in London air, that by this she was constrained to live much from home; and most of all her life she was tormented with a frequent headache; but in her patience in all this she did possess her soul, and patience furthered experience, and experience hope; and she learned more the quiet fruits of righteousness by being much exercised herein.

XX. And as by this she daily learned to die, so the expectation and preparation for death was her continual work and state. She lived, and heard, and prayed, and wrote her letters to her children, as at the brink of the grave, and the door of eternity. Not that her diseases did seem to us to be very mortal, or threaten this sudden change; but she knew the brevity of man's life, and that death is ready to remove us all, and what a moment it is till that certain hour.

And as she lived holily and in peace with God and man, so she died with ease and little likelihood of the ordinary miseries of fear or pain. A little soreness and swelling of her leg, and pain towards the hip, turned to two swooning fits, and in the third or fourth, having been in quiet discourse with her husband, she as quietly sunk and died away, desiring that I should be sent for to pray with her: she was dead before I came, without any signs of nature's striving. And she had said to her daughter after her former fits, she did not think that one could have died so easily as she had almost done. A death thus expected, and thus prepared for, is not to be called sudden. Thus God can make death easy to some of us, that are apt to over-fear the antecedent pain. And, now, what can be more (almost) desired in this world, than such a life, and such a death? Our dear friend is at home with Christ, and God's will, which is goodness and love itself, is so fulfilled; even that will which must dispose of all things, and in which only we must seek our rest.

And having described this true copy of the text, I may boldly speak of it to the several sorts.

I. I may ask again both quakers and scorners, whether the Holy Spirit do not dwell and work in such among us, as our dear friend now deceased was?

II. I may ask unbelievers and Sadducees, whether these operations of the Spirit of God on believers be not a sign that God owneth the gospel by which he thus worketh? and that Christ liveth and reigneth, who can thus still send a sanctifying Spirit into believers' souls? And whether it be not blasphemy to think and say, either that these excellent endowments of souls are not of God, or that he giveth them all in vain; and that believers are all deceived by God, and labour and hope all their days for that which hath no being; and that the better God maketh them, the more deluded, vain, and frustrate he maketh them, and ruleth and amendeth the world by falsehood?

III. I may ask the papists, with what face they can say, as they use to do, that they never heard of a protestant saint? And whether we may not be as religious in the places that God hath set us in, as if we turned recluses, monks, or nuns, and shut up ourselves from doing any good in the world?

IV. I may ask the malignant, that call all serious godliness hypocrisy, whether such a life as this doth savour of dissimulation? and whether such seriousness and hypocrisy are not contraries, and hypocrisy be not a profession without that seriousness, which is sincerity? And whether they that in baptism solemnly vow to take God for their God, and Christ for their Lord and Saviour, and the Holy Ghost for Christ's Advocate and Witness, and their Sanctifier and Comforter, and to renounce the flesh, the world, and the devil; and, when they have done, perform none of this which they vowed; but to live to the flesh and world which they renounced, and take a holy life as needless, yea, and hate it; I say, whether these be not the impudent hypocrites that vow and profess that holiness which they abhor, rather than they that with all their diligence perform the holy vow which they have made? And if wives promise fidelity to their husbands, servants to their masters, and subjects to their princes, are they the hypocrites that are serious and keep their promise? or they that were never serious in it, but scorn the keeping of it?

V. And as to those malignant persons that take this strict and serious diligence for men's souls to be but scrupulosity, or the character of some over-zealous bigots or puritans who are most inclined to schism, and to be troublesome or dangerous to states, I ask them,

1. What is there in all the description which I have here truly given you, which is injurious or dangerous to church or state, or any person? Will it hurt any one that God and men are seriously loved? and that God's testimonies are trusted and delighted in and obeyed? and that God's kingdom and righteousness is first sought?

2. Is it not Christ, and christianity, and Scripture that you accuse? If it be schismatical and dangerous to be serious in performing what we profess and vow, surely it is bad in baptism to vow it, and still by calling ourselves christians to profess it. To accuse, hate, and scorn the serious practice of your own professed religion, is to be the most foolish self-condemners, and, in some respects, worse than Mahometans, infidels, and heathens.

VI. But my most earnest desire is to you the loving husband and beloved children of our departed friend, that you will not overlook,

1. The correction,
2. The sin,
3. The mercy,
4. Or the duty which God now calleth you seriously to consider.

(1.) I need not persuade such as are rather apt to over-much sorrow, not to despise this chastening of the Lord, but rather not to faint under his rebuke. But I cannot dissuade you from a sense of your loss; we that are your neighbours feel it; but you much more, to whom it is much greater. What saints in heaven do know of us, or think of us, or do for us, we shall better know when we are there: but here you are deprived of the daily prayers which she sent up for you; of the continuance of her loving care of your souls, and watchfulness over you; of her wise and faithful counsels to you, and of her imitable example, as it was still before you; a husband of a pious, prudent helper, and children of a tender, affectionate mother: your great sorrows tell me you feel your loss.

(2.) And all correction is for sin, which is worse than suffering. Oh! fall down before God, and with penitent tears bewail your sin, which hath caused your loss. Humbly confess how unworthy you were of such a mother, and beg of God to forgive that sin.

(3.) But mercy also, as well as sin and loss, must be acknowledged. Your sorrow must give due place to thankfulness and comfort. Your mother is taken from you, but remember,

1. What a mercy it was and is to you, that you are so related to such parents, seeing God hath promised special mercy to the faithful and their seed; and if any of you miss it, it will be through your own ingratitude and contempt.

2. What a mercy is it that all her prayers for you are yet in force, and more of the answer of them may yet be sent you, if you reject it not.

3. You have yet all her holy counsels to remember, and they may profit you while you live.

4. And though she be gone, I hope her example will never be forgotten by you.

5. And what a mercy is it that, under all her infirmities, you enjoyed her so long.

6. And yet how much greater cause of thankfulness have you that she so lived and so died; and that you may think of her with comfort as being with Christ, and hope to be with her for ever. Every one hath had a mother, but every one had not such a mother as you have had.

(4.) And I have intimated your duty, while I have mentioned your loss and mercy.

1. Think over often what sin she reproved in you, and what counsel she gave you; and now revive your resolution to obey it.

2. Remember what she was wont to pray for on your behalf; and let it not now be long of your neglect or wilfulness that you are without it.

3. Remember her humble, moderate, holy example; and think whether your souls have not as much need of the greatest care and diligence as hers had? And why should not you be as studious to please God, and make sure of heaven, as she was? Bless God that you have such a pattern, that hath so long dwelt with you, for your imitation, next your imitation of Christ. Holy simplicity is despised by the world, but it will prove the only wisdom at the last.

I have told you what use to make of the example of our deceased friend; let me now tell you what use of the text, which she so much loved, transcribed, and chose.

I. And, first, here you may learn the nature of true faith and sound religion. It taketh God's testimonies and promises for our heritage, and for the comfort of our hearts. It is not true faith, unless we so trust God's promises for this life and that to come, as to take what he promiseth for our best, and our inheritance, and his promise for our best security and title, and his law for our governing rule that we may obtain it.

So that, 1. Here you see how we differ from infidels, that do not trust their everlasting hopes and happiness on the promise of God.

2. And how we differ from hypocrites, who speak best of heaven, but really look for their best on earth, which Christ calleth " trusting in their riches," because that is, indeed, their trust, from which they have their greatest expectations, and for which they most labour and will leave all: this a believer doth for promised happiness; and this the worldly hypocrite doth for the prosperity of the flesh on earth.

3. And here you see that faith and godliness are not melancholy, uncomfortable things, as the devil and the flesh would persuade unexperienced fools and unbelievers, unless it be sad to have security from God of a heavenly heritage, and rejoice therein.

And here you see the differences between the mirth of a fleshly infidel and of a believing saint. One is like a drunkard that is merry for an hour in a brutish kind of befooling pleasure; or like one that hath a pleasant dream, or one that heareth a jest or merry tale, or seeth a pretty comedy or show. The other is more rational and heart-contenting than it should be to any one of you, to have good security for many hundred years' life, and health, and prosperity here on earth. Such a birthright do profane fools sell for such a morsel, not knowing that the fear of God caused by true faith is the beginning of wisdom.

II. Hence, therefore, we may learn how to try our sincerity of faith. Doth it make us take God's promise, and the thing promised, as our heritage? Though we are not without temptations to doubting, nay, nor without the remnants of unbelief, but our hearts are troubled, when we look beyond death, with many fears; yet if we so far trust God's word, as resolvedly to take it for that which we will adhere to, and lay our chiefest hopes upon, we have a faith that will entitle us to the promised benefits.

Object. But some may say, I cannot say that it is the rejoicing of my heart.

Answ. 1. Can you say that you take it for that in which you place and seek your joy, though you cannot yet attain it? and that you prefer not any other pleasure in your esteem, and choice, and seeking? If so, you show that you truly believe and trust to the faithfulness of God's word, though yet you reach not what you seek. Desire is the first-fruit of faith and love, and holy joy is the flower and perfection.

2. Cannot you say that it is this word that maketh you hope that there is for man a better life, and that you shall not perish like the beasts? and that your fears and sorrows are somewhat abated by the promises of God?

3. Cannot you say that you perceive a pleasing goodness in the word of God, which maketh it welcome and acceptable to you?

By what I have mentioned, you may find,

1. That the word hath not been in vain unto you, when it hath caused such effects.

2. And that the same Spirit is in you which wrote the word, or else you would not love and desire it, and take it for suitable food and pleasure, yea, your heritage and joy.

3. And you may hence perceive that you are not without the love of God himself, though you see him not, and have not such sensible conceptions of him as you have of men and things which you have seen; for if you love truth, and goodness, and holiness in God's word, because it is such, you sure love best the greatest truth, goodness, and holiness, and that is God.

4. And hence you may perceive that though our nature love not death, and a weak faith will not overcome all fears, when we think of coming into an unseen world, yet really you are lovers of heaven, in that you are lovers of that which constituteth heaven, and is its desirableness to man; even holiness, and God's love, and glorious presence, and our perpetual joy herein. If you desire this, you desire heaven, though the fear of death do make you doubt of it.

5. And hence you may find that you are not worldly hypocrites, else it is not God's promises and law that you would take for your heritage and joy; but worldly prosperity and fleshly pleasure; and God and heaven should have but the leavings of the flesh, for fear of an after-reckoning at death.

6. And though your joy be small, you may know that it is of the right kind, when it is chiefly sought in God's love and promises; and you would not let go the word of God, and lose your part in it, for all the vanities of this world.

III. Hence also you may learn why all true christians so much value the testimonies or word of God; why they so much read it, think of it, talk of it, and hear of it, and are loth that papists should corrupt it, or conceal it in an unknown tongue, or that any should deny them the necessary use of it, or silence the ministers that preach it to them: who would willingly be deprived of his heritage or heart rejoicing?

IV. Yea, indeed, hence we see how much we should set by it and use it, how dear it should be to us, how strictly we should obey it, with what delight we should read and meditate in it, how diligent we should be to confirm our belief of it, and how we should fetch our hope and comfort from it in life and at our death?

V. And you may see hence, that it is no wonder that the devil and all his servants in the world are enemies to the word of God, because they are enemies to our heritage and joy: and there are few better signs while many pretend to be for Christ, to know who are really for him, and who are against him and his greatest enemies, than to judge of men as they further or hinder, love or hate, the word of God as to its proper use, as the heritage and joy of holy souls.

VI. But the chief part of my application is to commend this wise and holy choice, and solid comfort, to you all; and to beseech you presently to imitate David, and turn away from all inconsistent pleasures. If you live in sorrow or deceit, and die in desperation, it is not for want of an offer from God of better things. Have you lived hitherto as thus resolved? If you have, the Lord confirm you; and, be sure, such hopes shall not deceive you. If you have not, what will you now choose and do? If you live not to some end, you live not like men, according to reason. If you have chosen what end to live for and seek, what is it? Consider, I beseech you, of these things following, before it be too late.

1. What will you take for your heritage, or your best, if not the future promised joys? and what will you take for your security but God's word? What is it that you place your chiefest hopes in? Shall health, and wealth, and pleasure to the flesh, and honour among men, be taken for your heritage? Dare you, under your hands, make a covenant for these to quit all your hopes of the life to come? If not, which is it you prefer, and which would you quit, if one must be hazarded or lost? Which hath the nearest and highest place in your hearts? Which seek you first, and make all other things give place to? O sirs! it is a shame to our stupid hearts, that we have need to be so often told by preachers that we must die, and that our flesh must shortly lie neglected in dust and darkness till the resurrection, and that we, and all the deceitful trifles of this world, are ready to part for ever! It is a shame that we must be oft told that which every fool and child, at the use of reason, may know, how poor and how short a heritage, or pleasure, all those have, who have no better than this world can give them!

What say you; will you die in hope, or in despair? If unbelief make you hope that there is no hell, yet hope of heaven you can have none, unless you trust the word of God. The light of nature, indeed, is such a natural word, or revelation, as may tell us much of a future life of retribution; but God's supernatural revelation is so much clearer, that we cannot expect that he will see by a lesser, who wilfully rejects a greater light. Sure all men would live for ever if they could, and all would be for ever happy. You would not sure die like dogs, without any hope of a better life hereafter, if you could have good security for such hopes? And what better security is there to be found by mortal men, than the promises of God, confirmed by Christ's blood and miracles, and by the seal of his Holy Spirit?

In a word, without all doubt, either heaven must be your heritage, or you must have none that is worthy of a serious thought, and enough to keep a man from wishing that he had never been born, or been a brute that had not reason to know the matter of his griefs and fears; and either God's word, seconding the light of nature, must give you hopes of a better life, or you must live and die in mere despair. And shall that be your wilful choice?

2. Consider how invaluable a mercy it is to man, yea, to sinful, miserable man, that God should vouchsafe to give him such an everlasting heritage, and such security for it; and that on the mere thankful acceptance of the sinner. And how worthily will they be undone, that by wilful refusal are deprived of freely offered felicity.

3. And consider how suitable a heritage and security it is that is offered us, and how fit for our joyful acceptance and esteem.

The thing promised is no less than endless glory with God our Redeemer, and all the blessed. It is in the world where we must be for ever: it is the perfection of that which every holy soul desireth: it is our best, our all: it must be that or nothing; that or hell.

The word or covenant which is our trust,

1. Is God's own word.

2. It perfecteth and secondeth natural revelation and hope.

3. It beareth on itself the impress of God, even his power, wisdom, and love, in wonders, prophecies, and grace. It is sealed by the blood of Christ, by his own and his disciples' multitude of miracles, and by the gift of his sanctifying Spirit to all true believers, to the end. It is confirmed to our souls by the experience of the power of it, and the blessed effects, and this indwelling Spirit, the witness of Christ; and by the answer of prayers, by many providences, and by the experience of all believers to this day.

It is excellently suited to all our needs, to our wants, our dangers, our fears, our doubts, yea, and our sinful unworthiness in the freeness of God's mercy, and all his gifts.

Indeed, man had rather live by sight, and would fain know, by seeing, whither souls go, and what they are, and have, and do, hereafter. But it is not we, but God that is the ruler, and fittest to choose both the gift and means, the end and way. If we thankfully trust and improve a promise, we shall quickly see and have possession. Blessed be God for the light of his gospel, to guide us up to the light of glory! Oh that we had hearts to trust it, love it, and rejoice in it, as we have just cause!

4. And is it not a great mercy of God, that he hath herein called us to a life of happiness and present joy? If he had bid us only weep for sin to the last breath, the condition had been easy, as for pardon, and hope of endless mercy; but he hath given us a word which he would have to be the rejoicing of our hearts, and do we not love joy, or have we any better?

I have not now time, and I much more want myself such a mind and heart as I should have, to tell what cause of daily joy God hath given us in his word and covenants. But this I will tell you, that our want of joy is our daily sin and shame, as well as our loss and suffering, and among all the discoveries of the sinful weakness of our faith, hope, and love, our want of rejoicing in the word of promise, and hope of glory, is not the less. Oh what an enemy is death in this respect, that standing between it darkeneth and affrighteth us from our joys! but Christ hath conquered death to deliver those that through fear of it are subject to bondage, Heb. ii. 14, 15. And though we cry, O miserable men! who shall deliver us? we yet thank God through Jesus Christ our Lord.

And I must second the testimony of our deceased friend, in professing for your encouragement my own experience: I have taken God's testimonies for my heritage, and they have been these fifty years, or near, the pleasure of my life, and sweeter than honey, and preciouser than thousands of gold or silver. As we tell men, in charity, of the things which we have found good, the medicines that have healed us, and commend the persons that have been friendly to us; and as man's nature is inclined to propagate the knowledge and communicate the good which we partake of, and grace increaseth this inclination, so I take it to be my duty to add herein my own experience, if it may contribute to the determining of your choice; and reason teacheth all men to regard that means, and remedy, and good the more, which many have had experience of; and it is not to be taken for vain ostentation, to profess that which all must have in some degree that will be saved.

Though the natural and sinful fears of pain and death too long deprived me of much of the joy which I should have had in the thoughts of the unseen world, and too much doth so to this day, yet I must say that the word of God, and the persons that love and practise it, and the holy way of life and peace, and all things that here savour of heaven, have been so good and pleasant to me, as enableth me to assure you, that on earth there is nothing so worthy of your desire and joy.

And to encourage you, I will tell you, by my own experience, what benefit may be expected from this kind of delight, agreeable to David's and our friend's experience.

1. By this means my life hath been almost a constant pleasure.

2. This pleasure hath much upheld me under almost constant bodily infirmity and pain.

3. It hath made all my sufferings from men, and crosses in the world, to be tolerable, and very easy to me: had not God's word been my delight, I had lived uncomfortably, in constant pains and sorrows, and had perished in my trouble.

4. It hath saved me from the snares of sinful pleasures. Man's nature will seek for some delight, and they that have it not in good, will seek it in things hurtful and forbidden: it is only greater things that can overcome our mistaken choice of lesser. In my childhood, I was sinfully inclined to the pleasure of romances, and of childish sports; but when I tasted the sweetness of God's testimonies and ways, I needed no other, but spit out those luscious, unwholesome vanities. And though common knowledge, called learning, be pleasant to man's nature, and I cannot say that I have not overvalued it, yet I must say, that the relish of these greater matters hath made me see how much of it is vanity, and hath saved me from the pursuit of that part of it which doth but please curiosity and fancy, and tendeth not to use, and to greater things; and sensual pleasures I had no need of.

5. It hath by this means made that pleasure which I had, to be such as my reason did approve and justify, whereas if I had sought it in preferment, wealth, or sensuality, a foreseeing conscience would have affrighted me out of all my pleasure, and I should have had more of the pricks than of the rose, of the sting than of the honey. Of this pleasure you need not fear too much, but of the sensual pleasure we more easily catch a mortal surfeit.

6. This sweetness of God's word hath made also my calling and daily labour sweet; so that it had my heart, and not my forced hand and tongue.

7. And this hath helped my constancy herein, for when we have no delight in our work, we grow weary, and weariness tendeth to give it over, or to do it heartlessly, and slubber it over in unacceptable hypocrisy.

8. And this hath much saved me from the sinful loss of time. Pleasure causeth trifling and delays. Who needeth vain pastimes that delighteth in God's word and work?

9. And this hath been to me an excellent help for the increase of knowledge; for the mysteries of godliness have still more to be learned by the wisest man; and as boys at school, so the scholars of Christ, learn best who have most pleasure in their books.

10. And this pleasure hath much confirmed my belief of the truth of Scripture, when it hath borne its own witness to my mind, and I have tasted that goodness which is agreeable to its truth. I easily believe him that commendeth a thing to me, when I taste or feel that it is good.

11. And this pleasure hath helped me against vain thoughts and talk, while the truths of God were sweet, and so continually welcome; it is easy to think of that which we delight in, and sinful delights corrupt the thoughts and speech with constant sin.

12. And this pleasure hath somewhat fed my daily thankfulness to God, in the constant experience of the goodness of his truth and ways.

13. And it cured the error of my beginnings, when I strove for nothing so much as to weep for sin, and perceived not that the joy of the Lord is our strength, and the flower of holiness, and likest to the heavenly state; and that the Spirit sanctifieth, by making God and goodness pleasant to us.

14. And hereby it made me find, that the praises of God are the sweetest and noblest exercises of religion; when before I placed more in lamenting sin and misery.

15. And this maketh many things needless to me that else would seem needful. I want not more company; I want no recreation but for my body. If I have not what I would have, I see where only it is to be found.

16. And I am assured that the constant pleasure of my mind hath not only kept me from melancholy, but from greater sicknesses, and tended to the lengthening of my life (as Scaliger saith pleasant studies do); for constant pleasure must needs tend to health.

17. And this taste hath made me long for more, and had I not felt that it is good to draw near to God, and very desirable to know him and his will, I should never have so earnestly begged for clearer light, and more near and sweet communion with him. Pleasure is the cause of strong desire.

18. It hath been one of my greatest helps against many temptations of subtle enemies, that tempt men to sadducism, and doubt of the life to come.

19. It hath made me more communicative to others, for we would all have partakers in our delights.

20. And it hath greatly furthered my repentance and hatred of sin, when I have tasted what pleasure it depriveth us of, and the abhorrence and loathing of myself that can delight in such a God, and Saviour, and word no more. When I taste how good it is, and see so much reason to rejoice in it, and the hopes of glory, a thousand-fold more than I do, none of all the actual sins of my life do make me half so much loathe my naughty heart, as to think that my want of greater joy in so great and near a good, doth show so much weakness in my faith, and hope, and love. Oh that I had more faith and love, that I might have more of this delight!

Hearers, I have sincerely told you what comfort you may have, if you will not refuse it, from the word of God, and from the experience of David, and (because things near are aptest to affect) from the experience of our deceased friend, and of myself, and, indeed, of all God's servants in their degree. You would live in joy, you would die in joy; we need it in a life of so much trouble, and for a change that else is terrible, and it is sure and near. O sirs! we need another kind of comfort than sport, or appetite, or wealth, or any such fading vanity will give us; you may have some of it, if you will. And though joy be the top of grace, which we arrive not at with a wish, nor in an hour, yet the nature of the new creature relisheth, or savoureth, the things of the Spirit, Rom. viii. 5—7. And the spirit of adoption is a spirit of filial love, and crieth, Abba, Father; and the love of God the Father, the grace of the Son, and the communion of the Holy Spirit, which are the believer's part, are all of them the greatest comforters; and Christ giveth believers that seek and trust him, that spring of living waters which tendeth to everlasting satisfaction, and cureth indigent and sinful thirst.

Will you then have any portion, heritage, and joy, which will be worthy of a man, and shall go further with you than the grave? If you will you may: God and this congregation are witnesses that it was offered you. But think not to refuse it, and prefer the transitory pleasures of sin before it, and at last have it, and find that which you refused, or which you sought not first, Matt. vi. 33; nor to find a treasure in heaven, where you never laid it up or sought it. The hopes of the wicked perish, and the hypocrite's hopes are as the giving up of the ghost; but the righteous hath hope in his death, and therefore may die in peace and joy, Job viii. 13, 14; xi. 20; Prov. xi. 7; xiv. 32.

Perhaps some will say, that such a discourse of rejoicing is unsuitable to the mourning of a funeral. I think not, of such a funeral, in which we commemorate the holy life and death, and believe the present and everlasting joy, of such a friend, and one with whom we have long joined in seeking and waiting for that felicity, and hope ere long, and for ever, to rejoice with Christ, and her, and all the blessed. And funeral sermons are not for the benefit (though for the due honour) of the dead, but of the living, to teach us all to prepare for death, which, indeed, is so much of the business of our whole life, that all the rest is but a vain show, and foolish trifling, or much worse. And wherein doth our preparation for death so much consist, as foreseeing what so great a change will need, and what a trial it will put our faith and hope to, to seek and get such security for our everlasting state, and such sound belief of it, and settled content and comfort in it, which the fears of death, judgment, and hell, may not shake or overcome; that so we may finish our course with joy, and pass through the valley of the shadow of death and fear no evil, but may comfort one another and ourselves with this, that we shall for ever be with the Lord; and may say with Paul, "I have fought a good fight; I have finished my course; henceforth is laid up for me a crown of righteousness," which God, the righteous Judge, will give to me and to all that love Christ's appearance, when he shall come to be glorified in his saints, and admired in all them that do believe, and shall say, "Well done, good and faithful servant! enter thou into the joy of thy Lord."

Woe, and for ever woe, to every soul of you that shall finally reject or neglect the offer of such a heritage and joy! And blessed be that grace which hath caused all true believers to prefer it in their highest esteem, and choice, and seeking. I have looked about to see if there were any better and surer to be had, and I am fully satisfied it must be this or none. I offer you but what God hath caused me and all that he will save to choose; and, Lord, grant that I may never look back to any other. Let the love of God my heavenly Father, the grace of Jesus Christ my Lord, and the joy of the sanctifying Spirit, sealing up the promise of God as my security, and writing his law and gospel in my heart, be my heritage and joy; and I shall never envy the most prosperous sinner their portion in this life, but shall live and die in the thankful praise of the God of my salvation, who is essential, infinite, joyful love. Amen, Amen.

FAITHFUL SOULS SHALL BE WITH CHRIST:

THE

CERTAINTY PROVED,

AND

THEIR CHRISTIANITY DESCRIBED AND EXEMPLIFIED,

IN

THE TRULY CHRISTIAN LIFE AND DEATH

OF THAT EXCELLENT, AMIABLE SAINT,

HENRY ASHHURST, ESQUIRE, CITIZEN OF LONDON.

BRIEFLY AND TRULY PUBLISHED FOR THE CONVICTION OF HYPOCRITES AND THE MALIGNANT, THE STRENGTHENING OF BELIEVERS, AND THE IMITATION OF ALL, ESPECIALLY THE MASTERS OF FAMILIES IN LONDON.

TO MY WORTHY FRIENDS,

MRS. JUDITH ASHHURST, WIDOW OF HENRY ASHHURST, ESQ., AND MR. HENRY ASHHURST, THEIR SON, WITH ALL HIS BRETHREN AND SISTERS,

GRACE AND PEACE.

Dear Friends,

I am persuaded that the image of so good a husband and father cannot but be deeply printed on your minds; but yet may it not be wholly needless to be told of the comfort and the duty thence to be inferred. It was you, sir, his eldest son and executor, who called me to the public performance of that which I have thought meet to make more public. I have long known you so well, that I am comfortably persuaded, that your father had great cause to place that great affection on you and confidence in you which he did. Your dear love to him, and great reverence of him, and hearty love to the good which he loved, and your singleness and uprightness of mind and life, are your amiableness, and better than the greatest earthly birthright. But I did purposely say little in the following discourse of your father's example, as consolatory and obligatory to all his nearest relations, because I thought that their special interest in him did give them right to a special address, which is the intent of this epistle. God's Scripture blessings of the faithful and their seed, doth make this relation honourable and comfortable to you all. How cheerfully may you all follow the footsteps of one so near you, who sped so well in following Christ! The greatest comforts and blessings are the greatest obligations to further duty; and that duty is the way to get greater blessings. It will be some help to you to love God and goodness, good men, and all men, to remember how much all these were loved by one who so tenderly loved yourselves. You have not only heard, but seen and felt, that holiness is not a bare name or dream, and religion a mere art or image, but a divine nature, a real renovation of heart and life, and that the effects of God's Spirit, in sanctifying souls, do greatly difference them from carnal minds. You have seen that godliness, genuine and real, is not a wearisome, uncomfortable life. Live as he did, and it will be a cure of melancholy, passions, and discontents, and a constant tranquillity and delight.

What a help is his example to you, to live in true love to one another; to be of a humble, meek, and quiet spirit, neither vexatious to yourselves or others: as also to be absolutely devoted to God, of public minds, and comforts to the poor and needy, and to use all that you have as his stewards, daily preparing for your great account. You have seen how you may live above the world, even while you prosper in it; and how to expound, "Love not the world, nor the things that are in the world: if any man love the world, the love of the Father is not in him," 1 John ii. 15. "For where your treasure is, there will your hearts be also," Matt. vi. 21. The Spaniards have a proverb, The world is a carrion, and they are the dogs that love it, much more that snarl and fight about it. One would think, that to read and believe, Matt. v. and

vi. Luke xii. and xvi. and James iv. should affright men from being deceived by such a shadow, whose speedy vanishing all foresee.

You have seen what it is to be a christian indeed, and how your affairs, your conversations, and your families, should be ordered. And you have seen how the best may suffer and must die; and, therefore, what need we all have to be prepared with strong and well-exercised faith, hope, and patience, and, by daily conversing in the heavenly regions, to get sweeter thoughts of heaven than of the most prosperous state on earth, that we may die like serious believers, and joyfully commit our departing souls to Christ, when we leave these corruptible bodies to the grave. O dear friends, the day is at hand; the change is of unspeakable importance; the work of faith and hope is high and difficult: set to it speedily with heart and might, and let not flesh and the world entangle and deceive you.

The great love which your father had to me, and much more which he had to Christ, his church, and all the faithful, obliged me to be the larger in describing his example for your use and comfort; for as Christ, gone to heaven, hath left here his servants, called his brethren, that men in them may show their love and thankfulness to him, which he will reward as done unto himself, so the way which I must take to express my love and gratitude to your deceased father, is by desiring and endeavouring the true felicity of his wife and children, whom he so dearly loved; and that must be, by taking God for your God and Father; Christ for your Saviour; the Holy Spirit for your Sanctifier; the holy Scriptures for your rule; the church for the body of which you are members; true pastors for your teachers; the faithful for your most beloved companions; (especially each other who are by so many bonds obliged to more than ordinary endearedness and love;) and Christ for your chief pattern, and such as your father in following him; heaven for your felicity, home, and hope; and this short life for the day of your preparation and salvation; and the world, flesh, and devil, so far as they are against any of this, for the enemies which, with all vigilancy and resolution, must be overcome.

Oh how great, how good, and absolutely necessary a work is this, which if any one of you should miscarry about, you would be more inexcusable than most persons in the world! But that you will all faithfully imitate such an example of holiness, humility, meekness, mortification, peace, and dearest love to one another, and to all good men, is the comfortable hope and hearty prayer, as it is the present faithful counsel. of

Your servant for such ends,

RICHARD BAXTER.

December 7, 1680.

JOHN XII. 20.

IF ANY MAN SERVE ME, LET HIM FOLLOW ME; AND WHERE I AM, THERE SHALL ALSO MY SERVANT BE: IF ANY MAN SERVE ME, HIM WILL MY FATHER HONOUR.

If our judgments and wills had been the choosers and disposers of human events, as the affairs of the world would be otherwise managed than they are, so the meeting of this day would rather have been for a joyful thanksgiving for our deceased friend's recovery to health, than a mourning solemnizing of his funeral; but it is not we that made the world, or our own or others' souls, and it is not our right to determine of their time and events. It is one prime Agent, supreme Ruler, and ultimate end, one that is infinite in power, wisdom, and goodness, who is omnipresent, immutable, and every way perfect, that must actuate, order, and bless a world of such imperfect and differing individuals; and not such ignorant understandings, such partial and ill-guided wills, and such impotent powers, as ours are: he that maketh the watch, determineth how many hours it shall go. The Giver of life and time, must give us the measures of it; it is our part to spend it well: it is because the Creator having left us to some liberty and trust about ourselves, we are the misusers of it, that there are so many disorders, and, consequently, calamities, in the world, and on ourselves and ours, as there are. And if the God of love did not keep the overruling determination in his hand, and bring good out of all our evil, and harmony out of our discords and confusions, what a chaos, or hell, would the world become! Let us, therefore, humbly and willingly leave God's own work to himself, (he will do all well, and at last we shall understand it,) and let us mind our own. He hath taken up our brother's soul from earth; it is our part to think how to improve this: our own are following: our hour is at hand: our oil is wasting apace: our glass is almost run: every pulse, every breath, every word leaveth us one less of the number appointed us. It is our great concern to look inwards, and look upwards, and with our utmost diligence to study how to spend the short time that remaineth, that we may die in safety, peace, and hope, and follow the departed saints to glory.

To instruct myself and you herein, I have chosen this text, as giving us both sure directions, and such great and comfortable promises, as in life, and at death, we may boldly trust.

They are spoken by no doubtful messenger, but by the mouth of Christ himself; and that to men who were under our temptations, and earnestly desired to see Christ glorified on earth, and to partake of outward greatness here; to see that famous man who had wrought so many miracles, and lately raised the dead. But he tells them that both he and they must die before they can be glorified, and that they must overcome the inordinate love of this life, if ever they would attain a life of blessedness, John xii. 23—25; and that they might not, by uncertainty of the end or way, say, as Philip, "We know not whither thou goest, and how shall we know the way," he summarily tells them both: the way is, to serve him, and follow him; the end that is promised is, to be where he is, and to be honoured of his Father.

As if he should say, I know that your weakness and remaining carnality is such, that you would fain see me reign as a universal King on earth, that you might be advanced by me in the flesh; and it is a hard lesson to you to learn to lay down this life, which is so dear to you, and to pass into a world which you never saw, and know so little of. But have I not, by my doctrine, life, and frequent miracles, and newly by raising Lazarus from the dead, convinced you that I am the true Messiah, sent of God, to whom you may boldly trust the conduct and disposal of your lives and souls? If so, then see that you absolutely trust me, learn of me, serve me, and follow me. And let this satisfy you living and dying, that you shall speed as I myself do, and be with me where I am, though the place and state be yet unseen to you; and there you shall, by my Father, be advanced to far greater dignity and honour, than in this sinful life and world you are capable of. And of all this I give here my promise, which you must believe and trust, if you will be saved by me.

This is the plain exposition of the text. But let us more distinctly inquire, I. What is here meant by serving Christ. II. What it is to follow him. And, afterwards, III. What it is to be where he is. IV. And what to be honoured by his Father.

I. Some, that by false and narrow notions have received a wrong opinion of saving faith, may be puzzled at this, that serving Christ and following him are made the necessary terms or conditions of being where he is. And some say, that justifying faith, and saving faith, are two different things; and some say, that Christ himself did not clearly preach the doctrine of justification by faith, but left it for St. Paul. But the plain truth is, that in the gospel it is all one, to be a believer, a christian, and a disciple of Christ, in covenant with him as the true Messiah. And in those times the disciples of any great and famous teachers were taken into their families, and were their servants; not in a worldly, common work, but in order to the ends of their office and instructions; it is the same word which we often translate "deacons:" and as it was then usual with Jews and heathens, at their great feasts, for the servitors to give every guest his part, by the appointment of the ruler of the feast; so the Spirit, by the apostles, did institute church deacons to be servants to distribute the provisions made at their love-feasts, and the proportions allowed for each one's relief, to look to the poor, and to execute such church orders as the present bishops or elders did appoint (by which you may see how big the bishop's church then was). And so Christ calleth all christians his deacons, ministers, or servants, and some above others, peculiarly in office, as those that were to serve him as the Saviour of the world, for their own and other men's salvation; as his relation to us partaketh by analogy of many, so is our service to him. It is as the service of a scholar in obedient and diligent, humble learning; as the obedience of a patient to his physician; as the obedience of a beggar in asking, and thankfully accepting; as the obedience of a malefactor, who thankfully taketh a pardon; and if a rebel, promiseth to lay down arms, and live in true subjection to his prince; as the service of a child that liveth dependently in dutiful gratitude or love. It is not to give Christ any thing that he needeth; but to be readier to hear him, than to offer him the sacrifice of fools, who, by thinking to oblige him by their gifts, do but offend him.

The matter of our required service is, 1. To confess, with grief, our sin, our misery, and our need of him, his grace and mercy.

2. To learn, understand, and believe his word.

3. Thereby to know God, from whom we were revolted; and to return to him in the hand of our Mediator, by absolute resignation, devotion, and subjection; to obey, and trust, and love him, and joyfully to hope for everlasting happiness in this love.

4. To give up ourselves to Christ as our Saviour, by his sacrifice, merits, teaching, government, and intercession; to bring us home to God, by justifying, sanctifying, and finally glorifying us.

5. To obey the motions of his Spirit to that end, which are but to bring us to a conformity of his word.

6. To love God in his saints and creatures, and do all the good to one another that we can, and cherish a holy unity and peace, and to do wrong to none.

7. To watch against and resist all the temptations of the flesh, the world, and the devil, which would draw us from any of this duty.

8. To bear our medicinal corrections patiently and profitably, and pray, seek, and wait for blessed immortality.

9. To pray long and labour for the public good, the church's welfare, and the conversion of the dark, unbelieving world.

10. To do all this for the glorifying of God and our Redeemer, and the pleasing of his holy will, as the end and only rest of souls.

This is the service which Christ requireth; and is there any thing in all this which is not safe, delightful, honourable, profitable, and exceedingly desirable, to every one that knoweth what it is to hope for happiness, and to live like a christian or a man?

II. And what is it that is meant by following Christ? Disciples then were wont to dwell with their Master, that they might be always at hand to do what he bid them.

To follow Christ, includeth, 1. The absolute taking him for the Guide and Saviour, to whom we trust our bodies and souls. 2. The obedient following of his instruction and commands. 3. The following of his example, in all the imitable parts of his life. 4. The submissive following him through all the sufferings wherewith God trieth us, and by what death he chooseth for us, into the heavenly mansions, whither he is ascended. This is the following of Christ, which the straits of this hour allow me but to name.

Use. Before we proceed, let us consider how to improve what is said, and open the two promises after in our application.

1. And, first, it is hence evident what it is to be indeed a christian: it is to serve and follow Christ in trust, as the Procurer, the Captain, the Giver of salvation. Our relation to him, by a sacred covenant and vow, is the thing from which we are named christians. Deceitful covenanting may give us the name among men, that cannot see the heart, and may deceive ourselves and others; but if the soul consent not, God doth not consent to justify or save us. O sirs! try quickly, try faithfully, before death say, It is now too late, whether you are such as God, as well as men, will judge to be christians indeed. Oh! be not self-deceivers, for God will not be mocked with names and shadows, and heartless words, and the false pretences of a worldly, fleshly, unsanctified mind! You will find one day that Christ came not to be a shadow, nor a stepping-stone to worldly ends, nor a patron of pride and fleshly lusts. You will find, ere long, that to be a christian is a great and

serious business, on which lieth the everlasting saving of our souls; greater than life or death, crowns and kingdoms, or any concerns of this corruptible flesh; a business which will not be done asleep, nor with a careless mind, nor with a slothful, unresolved soul, nor with the thoughts and hours which pride and vanity can spare, and which are the leavings of fleshly lusts and pleasures. To be a christian is to turn our backs on all these deceitful vanities and sinful pleasures, and to place our absolute trust in Christ, and to serve and follow him to the death, in hope of everlasting glory obtained by his manifold grace. Have you no careful thoughts of another life? and no fear what will become of your departing souls at death? If not, your reason is asleep. If you have, what is it that quieteth and comforteth you? Is it only a careless venture, because God is merciful, as if his mercy saved all? God forbid that your souls should go out of your bodies without a better preparation than this! But if, finding yourselves undone by sin, and liable to God's destroying justice, and believing that Christ is the only sufficient and faithful Saviour, you give up soul and body in trust to him, resolvedly consenting to serve and follow him who hath purchased and promised you blessedness with himself; this is true christianity, and this is a trust which will not deceive. Sirs, you send for us in sickness, and perhaps we cannot come, or we find men overwhelmed with pain and fear, and with a feeble body and fainting spirits, unfit to try and judge themselves, and to do so great a work as is here described, if not unable to hear much discourse of it. Oh! what a sad time is that for a minister to give you that instruction, which a long time of strength was too little to improve! What a dreadful thing is it for a soul then to have all the work that you lived for to begin and do, and for to have but a sick and fainting hour or day to do that which you could not do in all your lives, and which turneth the key for heaven or hell! The Lord give you awakened reason and wisdom before it be too late. The name of christians is not to be used to deceive fleshly men into damning presumption, but to signify a soul that trusteth in Christ, and followeth him in obedience and patience to salvation.

Oh that you all feelingly knew how much it concerneth you, presently to set home and resolve this question, Do I trust, serve, and follow Christ? Let us now a little look to his footsteps, that we may know.

1. Christ lived in the world to do his Father's work and will, to glorify and please him: see John iv. 34; ix. 4; viii. 29; xii. 27, 28; xvii. 4. Is it God's work that you live for, and his will that you chiefly study to please in your inferior degree and place?

2. Christ was the greatest lover of souls. His business on earth was to seek and save them, and he is still about that work in heaven. He thought not his strange condescending incarnation, his sufferings and heart-blood, his labour and life, too dear to save them. Are your own and others' souls thus precious in your eyes? Do you think no labour loss, no cost or suffering too dear, to save yourselves and others? Do your prayers and your practices prove this to be true?

3. Christ's great work was to gather a church on earth, which should be his peculiar kingdom, spouse, and body, to glorify God, and be glorified with him, Eph. iv. 1—17; v. 25—32; iii. 21; Acts xx. 28. If you are christians indeed, Christ's church is to you as your body to the members, that are all ready to serve it, abhorring abscission and separation from it, and every painful, perilous disease.

You love, you long, you pray for the true enlargement, concord, and holy prosperity of the church: that God's name may be hallowed, his kingdom come, and his will done on earth as it is in heaven, is the first and chief of your desire: see 1 Cor. xii.; Col. i. 18, 24. Are you thus followers of Christ?

4. Love to God and man was the very nature, and life, and work of Christ; manifested in constant doing good, and praying for his persecutors, and reconciling enemies to God, Rom. v. 8—10; 2 Cor. v. 19, 20; John xv. 13; Mark x. 21; John xv. 9; Gal. ii. 20; Eph. ii. 4. And if you follow Christ, love will be your nature, life, and work, and you will walk in love as Christ loved us, Eph. v. 2; 1 John iv. 11. Even as he hath loved us, he requireth that we love one another, John xiii. 34; xv. 9, 12; which is not with a barren, unprofitable love, James ii. 14, &c.; John xiii. 35.

5. In order to these ends, Christ lived quite above all the pomps and vanities of the world, and above the love of worldly dominion, and fleshly pleasure, and life itself; and refused not to die a shameful death, as a reputed malefactor, to redeem us, "making himself of no reputation, enduring the cross and despising the shame," Phil. ii. 7, 10; 1 Pet. iii. 18; iv. 1. And if you follow Christ, though you must not be cross makers, you must be cross bearers, and above the love of worldly vanity, and life itself in comparison of eternal life. For Christ suffered for us, leaving us an example, (1 Pet. ii. 21,) and will have us take up our cross and follow him, forsaking all that stands against him, (Luke xiv. 29, 32, 33,) and submit to be in our flesh partakers of his sufferings, 1 Pet. iv. 13. We cannot equal him in patience, but we must so far imitate him, as not to sin and forsake the truth for fear of suffering, nor to account our lives dear, that we may finish our course with joy, Matt. v. 11, 12; Acts xx. 24.

6. Christ, though he were the Lord of all the world, did condescend to a humble, low condition, and chose not a prince's court for converse, but the poor, and men of low degree. And he hath commanded us to learn of him to be meek and lowly, (Matt. xi. 29,) and to be the servants of all, as that which is above worldly greatness, Mark ix. 35; x. 44. And he blesseth the meek, and the poor in spirit, Matt. v. Do we follow him in this; and condescend to men of low estate, (Rom. xii. 16,) remembering that not many great and noble are called, (1 Cor. i. 26,) and that God hath chosen the poor of the world, that are rich in faith, to be heirs of his kingdom, Jam. ii. 5; 1 Cor. i. 27, 28; or do you not (as those reproved, Jam. iv.) show a worldly, carnal mind, by too much valuing the high and rich, and too much vilifying the poor? Our flesh and health is nearer us far than our clothes and riches. And yet how far is flesh and strength from making a bad man more valuable and amiable than a weak and sickly saint!

7. Though Christ was the greatest lover of souls, yet was he the greatest hater of sin; so great that he came into the world to destroy it, as the devil's work; and would rather die than sin should not be condemned and die, 1 John iii. 7, 8; Matt. i. 21; and to save men from it was his office. And for all his meekness, he forbeareth not to call Herod, fox, and sharply reprove the scribes and Pharisees, (Matt. xxiii.) yea, and to give Peter the rebuke which he gave the devil, when he did his work, by dissuading him from his sufferings: "Get thee behind me, Satan," Matt. xvi.

And if we look on sin as a harmless thing, and the profit, honour, or pleasures reconcile us to it, and we are indifferent towards it on pretence of moderation and avoiding rash zeal and indiscretion; this is not to be followers, but enemies of Christ, reproaching his office and cross, as if he had needlessly been born and died.

8. A heavenly mind and life is the chief imitation of Christ: his kingdom was not of this world; his glory is at the right hand of the Father; and our glory must be in seeing his glory, John xvii. 22, 24. It is in heaven that he promiseth his followers a reward, Matt. v. 12; Heb. xi. 16; xii. 22; Luke xvi. 9; xxiii. 43. And it is in heaven that our treasure must be laid up, and our hearts, affections, and hopes must be set, and our conversation must be, Matt. vi. 19—21; Col. iii. 1, 3, 4; Phil. iii. 19, 20.

You see now what it is to be followers of Christ; is this your case? I mean not in degree, but in sincere imitation. Oh try and judge!

Use 2. Whatever it hath been, shall it be so for the time to come? Oh that this might be a day of effectual resolution and engagement to us all! Do I need to tell you that it is not Christ that leadeth men to gluttony or drunkenness, or chambering and wantonness, to idleness, and pride, and worldly vanity, and fleshly lust? Rom. xiii. 13; Gal. v. 21, 22; Rom. viii. 1, &c. It is not Christ that teacheth men to doubt of the immortality of the soul, and of the life to come, and of the truth of the gospel: nor is it Christ that teacheth them to play the hypocrites, and scorn, and hate, and persecute the serious practice of that religion which their tongues profess: these are the works of the devil, which Christ came to destroy. O bethink you whom you follow, and whither you go, before you come to your journey's end. The world, flesh, and devil have undone all that ever followed them to the end. But if you will serve Christ and follow him, I will tell you what encouragements you have.

1. You have the greatest and most honourable Master in all the world, that is able to make good all his undertakings.

2. You have the surest, infallible Leader, that never was deceived, nor did deceive, nor hath he need of deceit to govern us.

3. You have love itself to lead you; one that hath done more than all the world besides can do, to show you that he loveth you, and therefore doth all for your good.

4. You have a humbled, condescending Leader; God in flesh, that hath spoken face to face with man, and came near us to bring us up to God.

5. You have a plain, familiar Teacher, who hath not set your wits on artificial, logical tricks, like the undoing of a pair of tarrying irons, but hath brought light and immortality to light, and taught us to know God and our everlasting hopes, and a safe and joyful way thereto.

6. And yet you have a complete, perfect Teacher, who teacheth you by words and works and inspiration, and can make you what he bids you be, and leaveth out nothing that is necessary to your salvation.

7. And you have the only sufficient Guide to happiness. He is the way, the truth, and the life; and no man cometh to the Father but by him. No man but he hath revealed the God and glory which he hath fully seen and known. All men are liars and deceivers, not to be trusted, further than some way they have learned of him, by the teaching of his works, or word, or Spirit.

And now shall we need to say more to men, that are already vowed to Christ in their baptism, who profess themselves christians, who know that they must die, and who know that there is no other hope or way, to persuade them to be what they profess, that they may not miss of what they hope for? But the following promises, if believed, will persuade you.

III. "Where I am there shall my servant be." They that serve and follow Christ, shall, in their measure, speed as he doth, and be with him where he is. *Quest.* And where is that? *Answ.* It is certainly in no ill place: though it be a controversy, whether Christ descended to hell, it is certain that now he is not there; and therefore his members shall not be there. He is certainly in paradise, for there he promised the converted thief to be that day with him. He is in heaven: Acts i. 11, "This same Jesus, which is taken up from you into heaven, shall so come in like manner as ye have seen him go into heaven." Acts iii. 21, "Whom the heaven must receive till the time of restitution of all things." John xvii. "And now, O Father, glorify me with thine own self." Verse 13, "And now I come to thee." It is in the glorious presence of God that Christ now abideth in our nature; even at the right hand of God, Matt. xxvi. 64; Mark xiv. 62; xvi. 19; Luke xxii. 6, 9; Acts vii. 55, 56; Rom. viii. 34; Eph. i. 20; Col. iii. 1; Heb. i. 3, 13; viii. 1; xii. 2; x. 12; 1 Pet. iii. 22.

Therefore, though many texts do seem to intimate that he will return to earth again, and that the new Jerusalem shall come down from heaven, and that we look for a new heaven and earth in which righteousness shall dwell, yet these texts do fully prove that faithful souls go presently to Christ who is in heaven, and that there will be no such descent to earth as shall be any diminution of the glory of the saints: for it shall be no diminution of the glory of Christ; and we shall be where Christ will be. If heaven come down to earth, and the veil be drawn, it will be no loss.

2. That departed, faithful souls go to him, the Scripture elsewhere also tells us. "Father, I will that they also whom thou hast given me, be with me where I am, that they may behold my glory which thou hast given me," John xvii. 24. "To-day shalt thou be with me in paradise," Luke xxiii. 43. When we "fail" here, we shall "be received into" the everlasting habitations, Luke xvi. 9. "The beggar died, and was carried by angels into Abraham's bosom," ver. 22; "now he is comforted," ver. 25. "We know that if our earthly house of this tabernacle were dissolved, we have a building of God, a house not made with hands, eternal in the heavens. For in this we groan, earnestly desiring to be clothed upon with our house which is from heaven, that mortality might be swallowed up of life," 2 Cor. v. 1, 2. "We are confident, and willing rather to be absent from the body and present with the Lord," ver. 8. "To me to live is Christ, and to die is gain—having a desire to depart to be with Christ, which is far better," Phil. i. 21, 23. "We are come to mount Sion, and to the city of the living God, the heavenly Jerusalem, and to an innumerable company of angels, to the general assembly and church of the first-born, which are written in heaven, and to God the Judge of all, and to the spirits of just men made perfect, and to Jesus the Mediator of the new covenant," Heb. xii. 22—24. "Blessed are the dead that die in the Lord from henceforth: Yea, saith the Spirit, that they may rest from their labours; and their works do follow them," Rev. xiv. 13.

I heap all these texts together for myself as well as you, that we may see that as the faithful shall certainly have a blessed resurrection, so their departing souls at death shall certainly be with Christ in glory. For I take the assurance of the soul's immortality, and felicity at death, to be a point that deserveth as much of our thoughtful diligence, as any one that we have to think of. He is mad that doubteth whether there be a God, if he live with his eyes open in the world; and as for christianity, it is life and immortality which Christ came to secure us of and bring to light. And he that by the light of nature doth but believe the soul's immortality and a life of retribution, is much prepared to be a christian; so suitable will he find christianity to our everlasting interest.

But yet all will be dark to men, and seem uncertain, till Christ be their teacher, and they truly believe in him, and take it on his certain word.

Truly believe that Jesus is the Christ, and his gospel true, and there is no room for a doubt of the immortality of souls, and future blessedness, so plainly is it expressed in all the gospel. The Socinians, that look for nothing till the resurrection, dream of a dreaming sleep of souls, but dare not talk of any cessation or annihilation of them. For then a resurrection is a contradiction; another soul may be created, but it cannot be the same that was annihilated.

And as no man can believe that Christ speaketh truth and is Christ indeed, but he must needs believe his promise, that the faithful soul shall be where he is, so no man can truly believe that all faithful souls, and only such, shall be with Christ and partake of blessedness; but it will constrain him to a life of serious holiness at least, if it feast him not with the foretaste of heavenly joys. Can you imagine that any man can firmly believe that all and only holy souls go to Christ in glory when they leave the body, and yet not seek first the kingdom of God, and make the securing of this his chiefest care and business in the world? It cannot be: every man loveth himself; and no man can be indifferent whether his soul be in heaven or hell for ever. Dulness and present diverting things, may make a man negligent and inconsiderate about lesser matters, where the loss seemeth tolerable; but I cannot believe that if a man be awake and in his wits, any thing but secret unbelief and doubting can make one so dull or inconsiderate about his everlasting joy or misery, as not to make it his chiefest care. For I see that if a man have but a law-suit, on which all his estate depends, or a trial on which his life depends, he cannot forget it or make light of it: he will not drink, or jest, or play away the little time in which his business must be done. And can any one soundly believe that his soul at death shall go to Christ in glory, and not set more by such a hope than by all the riches, and sport, and pleasure, and vain-glory of so short a life as this? Or can any man soundly believe that the wicked and unholy shall go to everlasting punishment, and yet not make it his chief care to escape it? Sure, as mad and bad as man's corrupted mind is, this will scarce stand with human nature. I judge of others by myself; if I had never had at the worst a secret uncertainty whether the gospel be true, and souls immortal, I might have been surprised indeed to a sudden temptation to some sin, but I could never have thought that a man in his wits should choose any life but resolved holiness, nor could I have chosen any other.

If I see a man a careless neglecter of his soul, that maketh no great matter of sin or duty, or maketh not God, and Christ, and heaven the subject of his most serious ruling thoughts, and his greatest business in the world; but showeth us that his health, and wealth, and honour, and pleasure, are better loved, and more earnestly sought, and faster held; I will not believe that this man taketh the gospel, and the soul's future state therein described, to be a certain truth; let him say what he will, he doubteth of it at his heart: and such men use to say when they speak out, I know what I have here, but I know not what I shall have hereafter: could I keep what I have, I would let others take what is promised in heaven.

But, O man, thou knowest thou canst not keep what thou hast. Shortly thy soul must be required and called away, and then whose are the things which thou hast loved? Luke xii. 19, 20.

I will therefore say more. Though men had no certainty of dwelling with Christ, and doubted whether his word be true, yet it were worse than madness not to prefer the bare probability (that I say not possibility) of a future, endless glory, (when endless misery is probable to the refusers,) before all here that can be set against it. Oh! what is this transitory dream of worldly, fleshly pleasure to everlasting joy or misery! Verily every man at his best estate (in worldly respects) is altogether vanity, Psalm xxxix. 5. Oh! mark how emphatical every word is! Verily (it is no doubt) every man (high and low, good and bad, in bodily and worldly respects only) at his best or settled estate (not only in pain, and poverty, and age, but in his strength, and wit, and wealth, and honour, on the throne as well as on the dunghill) is vanity. That is an untrusty lie and shadow that seemeth something and is next to nothing, and this altogether (in mere worldly, corporal respects, in all that he hath to glory or take pleasure in). What need we more to prove all this, than to foresee how the dream and tragedy endeth? A little while we run up and down, and eat and drink, and talk and sport, and sometimes laugh, and sometimes weep, and then change our pomp and pride for a shroud and coffin, and are laid to rot in a grave of earth, where these idol, pampered bodies, be turned themselves into the quality of their darksome habitation. And if these were our best, were not every man at his best estate altogether vanity?

And if a mere probability of the life to come, in reason should resolve all men for serious holiness, how can we think that a certain or firm belief would not do it?

By this, then, it is past doubt, that hypocrisy reigneth in all mere, nominal christians, and in all that live not a holy life, and, indeed, in most men in the world. They are false in professing to believe that Christ is true, and his gospel certain truth, and that at death they must go to heaven or hell, if their lives show not that heaven and hell are greater, and more prevailing matters with them, than all the fleshly provisions, pleasures, and glory of this world.

Hypocrites are distinguished from professed infidels; but if they were not unbelievers at the heart, they were not hypocrites in professing faith. The Scripture giveth these titles or attributes therefore to saving faith; it is called, "faith unfeigned," or not hypocritical or dissembled, 1 Tim. i. 5; Philem. 6, it is called "effectual;" and Gal. v. 6, "faith that works by love;" and James ii. "faith that is not dead, but working to perfection;" it is not "unfeigned," if it be not "effectual." You cannot make a man believe that a bear pursueth him, or his house is on fire, or his life in danger, but he will accordingly bestir him. You cannot draw a man to other business from the care of his life, if he believe that it lieth on his present care.

O sirs! the hypocrite's belief of another world, and his lifeless opinion, conquered by secret unbelief, will shortly fall as a house built on the sand, Matt. vii. 23; and no heart can now fully conceive how terrible to him the fall will be. When you see that there is no more tarrying here, and that death and an endless life are come, a dead profession, and secret unbelief, will leave you then to despair and horror. It is not the name of a christian that will then serve to comfort, or to save your souls. I do not say, that no man shall be saved that hath any doubting, even of the gospel and the life to come; but I say, you cannot be saved, if your belief of it prevail not to engage you in a holy life, and conquer not the flesh, the world, and the devil. It must be a prevailing faith.

But, I suppose, you are convinced, that a sound and firm belief of the passage of departing souls to Christ, or unto misery, would certainly resolve men for a holy life; but some say, If we be uncertain, how can we help it? We are out of sight, and we have not the command of our own understandings. We would be sure what becomes of souls with all our hearts, but we cannot attain it.

Answ. Christ came into the world to teach it us; such knowledge is too high and precious to be attained with a slothful wish, or to be had without the use of the means which Christ hath appointed us. Have you learned of Christ, with a humble and teachable, willing mind? Have you not been diverted and blinded by the things which you knew were but deceitful vanity? Have you set your understandings at work with such serious consideration, and so long, as the trial of so great a matter doth require? Have you sought to able and faithful ministers of Christ to help you where you found yourself insufficient? Have you daily begged the help of the Spirit of God, as knowing that heavenly things must be discerned by a heavenly light? Have you honestly obeyed so much as you did know? If you have done this, which reason requireth, I do not think that thus waiting on God, he will leave you to any damnable unbelief, or to an unholy, sensual life.

But because the strengthening of our belief herein is the most needful thing, even to the best, both for their hope, and joy, and duty, and all that understand themselves must earnestly desire, that their belief of the gospel, and the life to come, did reach to a satisfying certainty; I will shortly repeat the proofs that must ascertain us, though I have largely done it in my books called "The Life of Faith," and "The Reasons of the Christian Religion," and "The Unreasonableness of Infidelity." I care not how oft (when necessary) I repeat them, and wish that they were more of the daily study of those that now study controversies, or only superstructures.

I. And first, nature giveth us the arguments to prove man's future state.

1. God hath made man with an essential capacity, to think and care, as his greatest concern, what shall become of his soul when he dieth; and God maketh none of his works in vain, much less so noble a one as man.

2. A bare probability of the life to come, as now revealed, with our certainty of the brevity and vanity of this life, maketh it the interest and certain duty of all men in the world, to be far more careful for their future state, than for the body, and this present life. He liveth against reason that doth not this.

3. And can a wise man believe that God bindeth all men, by their essential reason, to make the care of a thing that is not, or ever shall be, to be the chief business of their lives, and that deceit and falsehood should be the guide of all our greatest actions, and man should be made to follow a lie, to his everlasting disappointment? Judge reasonably, whether this be like to be the work of the most great, and wise, and holy God.

4. History and experience assureth us, that it is the expectation of a life to come, the hope of reward there, and the fear of punishment, which are God's means, for the actual government of mankind. And though many atheists are in the world, and more Sadducees and unbelievers, yet few, if any, are wholly such, but have consciences that keep them in some awe; and laws and professed religion tell you, that it is hopes and fears of another life, which are the ruling principles; which, as they reign in the best, so few of the worst will directly contradict; and were it not for such fears of punishment hereafter, the lives of no princes or enemies would be safe from destroying malice, policy, or power. And is it likely that this world is governed by a lie, by that God who wants no power, wisdom, or love, to govern it by truth; and who maketh the best men the greatest haters of lying, that they may be like him?

5. And how comes the belief of the soul's immortality to be so common a principle in the nature of man, if it be not true?

II. But seeing it is the gospel that must give us the full and satisfying certainty, keep these few evidences of its truth continually printed on your minds.

1. Remember that promises, types, and prophecies foretold Christ's coming long before; even prophecies sealed with miracles and fulfilled.

2. Remember that Christ's own person and doctrine did bear that image of God, which is unimitable; and had that power, wisdom, and love, which prove them to be of God. God's image and superscription, discernible by holy minds, doth difference the gospel from all the words of fallible men.

3. Remember that it was proved to be of God, by multitudes of open and uncontrolled miracles; and God will not work miracles remedilessly to deceive mankind, especially the great miracle of Christ's resurrection, (long by him foretold,) and his visible ascending up to heaven.

4. The sending down the promised Spirit on the apostles, and on other believers then, for languages, miracles, prophesyings, &c.; and the long exercise of these tongues and miracles by many, and in many parts of the world, and the gathering of the churches by them.

5. The full and certain historical conveyance of these matters of fact to us, in and by the sacred Scriptures, church ordinances, and tradition, (as the statutes of the land are delivered us,) without any weakening contradiction of the said history or fact.

6. Above all, the continued testimony of God's Spirit in all true believers, that is, the same Spirit which indited the Scripture, writeth it out on all holy souls, or formeth, reneweth, and disposeth them to answerable holiness; even to the image of God, in holy light, and love, and life, and to a heavenly mind and conversation, and to be sober, just, and loving to all. And God would never bless a lie, to do the greatest work in this world, to make men good and like himself; and, remember, that the whole frame and tendency of the Spirit's sanctifying work on souls, is to prepare them for a life to come, by causing them to believe it, desire it, hope for it, and seek it, and hate sin, and part with any thing to obtain it. All sound believers have this work upon them, and are of such a mind and spirit; and this Spirit or holy nature in them, is Christ's witness and theirs. They have the witness in themselves, 1 John v. 10.

7. And remember that even the malice of Satan affordeth us much help to confirm our faith. It is notorious that he keepeth up through all the world a war against Christ, and against our hopes of future

glory. How he followeth men with inward, importunate temptations against their own interest and reason, and what proof of his malice we have in human wickedness, and in witches, witchcrafts, or operations on bodies, apparitions, &c. I have so often proved to you, that I will now forbear the repetition. And doth not all this contain assuring evidence of the truth of Christ, his gospel, and our future hopes?

Use. Come, then, fellow-christians; let us pray, "Lord, increase our faith;" let us detest all suggestions which tend to unbelief, and so would bring us to the rank of brutes, and to despair; let us live according to our most holy faith, and show ourselves and others that we heartily believe that the servants of Christ that follow him, shall be with him where he is. O, pray for faith. Meditate for faith. Lament your unbelief. O fools that we are, and slow of heart to believe a gospel so revealed and confirmed! Why are we so fearful of dying, O we of little faith? Were but this one text written on our hearts, and turned into faith and hope; yea, did we believe Christ speaking it but as confidently as we believe and trust a parent, or a tried friend, for any thing promised which is in their power; yea, or but as confidently as we can trust their love without a promise, oh, how joyfully should we live and die! O, bend your prayers and best endeavours against the unbelief and doubtings of the gospel, and the unseen world. Were your faith here strong, it would bring you to that holiness which would much end your doubts of your own sincerity and part in Christ.

Had we nothing else to prove the sinful weakness of our faith, but our uncomfortable thoughts of the life to come, and the state of our departing souls, alas! how sad an evidence is it! Come on, then, christians. Think further what this text containeth, and beg of God that you and I may believe it as we need, and as Christ deserveth to be believed. Think what it is to be with Christ. We shall be with our compassionate, great High Priest; with him that came down in flesh to us; with him that loved us to the death, and redeemed us by his blood to God, and will make us kings and priests for ever. We shall be with him that is gone to prepare a place for us; in his Father's house he hath many mansions, John iv. 3. It was not a mere man, it was not an angel, that made us this promise, but the Son of God, who hath confirmed it by four seals, his blood, his miracles and resurrection, his sacraments, and his Spirit.

Are you afraid that your souls shall die with your bodies? Christ is not dead, and we shall be with him. It is his promise, "Because I live, ye shall live also," John xiv. 19. The article of his descending to hades, called hell, is to tell us that Christ's soul died not with his body, yea, it went that day to paradise. Our Head and we shall not be separated. Are you afraid of going to hell? Christ is not there. Are you afraid lest God forsake you? He forsaketh not Christ, though, for our sakes, he once in part forsook him that we might not be forsaken.

Can you fear devils, or any enemies? Where Christ is glorified, there come no devils, enemies, or fears. We are here with him as chickens under the wings of the hen, Matt. xxiii. 37. How safely and how joyfully then shall we be lodged in the bosom of eternal love!

But we see not the place, nor what our departed friends enjoy. But Christ seeth it, who is there.

But we see not Christ. But firm belief will make us love him, and rejoice with unspeakable, glorying joy, 1 Pet. vi. 8, 9.

But we cannot conceive of the state and operations of a separated soul, nor where it is, nor how God is there enjoyed.

But is it not enough to believe that we shall be with Christ, and fare (in our measure) no worse than he? If you are afraid lest Christ be deceived, or deceive you, that is a sinful fear indeed. But if you only fear lest you have no part in him, consent to his covenant, do but give up yourselves in obedience and trust, though not in perfection, yet in sincere desire and resolution, and then you have no just cause to fear it.

O sirs! why do not our hearts rejoice, when we think that we shall shortly be with Christ? Here we have ill company too oft; implacable enemies, unsuitable and sinful friends, and worst of all, a foolish and perverted heart, that is, in effect, our greatest enemy. But where Christ is, none of this is so. With him we shall have the company of our holy, departed friends; even all of them that we conversed with in the flesh, whom we lamented and wept over as if they had been lost. We shall with Christ have the company of innumerable angels, and all the faithful from the days of Adam.

And oh! how much better will Christ's own glorious presence be, than his presence in humbled flesh was to his followers on earth. Here Christ was a despised, crucified man. There even his body is more glorious than the sun, and the heaven or holy city needs no sun, because God and the Lamb is the light thereof. Spirits are there in confirmed holiness, and not left to that imperfect liberty of will, which lets in by abuse all sin and misery on the world. They strive not in the dark in ignorant zeal, or mixtures of error and selfish partiality, as we do here. There are no silencers of the holy ministers that continually sing Jehovah's praises. There is no malignant calumny or persecution, no envious reproach of one another, or striving who shall have his will, or be master of the rest. But holy love uniteth, animateth, and delighteth all, for it is God that they love in one another. There is no selfish, foolish fear lest individuation cease, and saints shall be too much one, and all be one common soul. In a word, to be with Christ is to be perfect in holiness and glory, in God, in the heavenly society, in the joys of sight, and love, and praise, delivered from the bondage of corruption, from sin and fear, and from temptation and troubles of all our enemies.

IV. But yet the promise here saith more, "If any man serve me, him will my Father honour." The Father's love did give us the Redeemer, and the Father's love shall glorify us with him. What is the honour that is here meant? Honour sometimes signifieth advancement in general, making one great and happy, Numb. xxii. 17, 37; xxiv. 11; xxvii. 20; 1 Kings iii. 13; 1 Chron. xvi. 27; Psal. viii. 5; 1 Sam. ii. 30. And sometimes it signifieth the provision and maintenance which is due to deserving superiors, which is half the double honour due to the elders that rule well, especially that labour in the word and doctrine, 1 Tim. v. 17. And sometimes it is taken for a magnified, praised state. God will honour faithful christians all these ways; he will advance them to the highest dignity they are meet for; he will give them the most bounteous provisions of his household, even more than they can now desire or believe. He will make them kings and priests to God, and coheirs with Christ in the glorious inheritance, Rom. viii. 17; Rev. i. 6; v. 10; xx. 6. They shall judge the world, and angels, 1 Cor. vi. 2, 3. They shall see God, (Matt. v.) and be called his children, and all together the spouse and body of Christ, Eph. v.; Rev. xxi. and xxii. &c. They shall at Christ's appearing (who is their life) appear with him in glory, Col. iii. 4. When he cometh to be admired in his saints, and glorified in all them that believe, 2 Thess. i. 10, &c. We shall see face to face, and shall see him as he is, 1 John iii. 2. We shall behold the glory that God hath given him, John xvii. 24. The righteous shall have dominion in that morning, and shall shine as stars, (Dan. xii. 3,) yea, as the sun in the firmament of the Father, Matt. xiii. 34. God will put his name upon them, and they shall be pillars in his temple, and go out no more, Rev. ii. and iii. Yea, they shall be equal with the angels, Luke xx. 36. Thus shall it be done to them whom God delighteth to honour, even to all in their several degrees who faithfully serve and follow Christ.

And yet, christians, are we afraid of dying? I even hate my own heart for the remnant of its unbelief, which no more rejoiceth, and no more longeth to be with Christ, while I read and speak of all this to you. I know that clear and full apprehensions are proper to possessors, and therefore not to be here expected; but, Lord, give us such a light of faith as may let in some such tastes of glory, as are needful to us in our hoping state. How can we cheerfully labour, and suffer, and overcome without them? How shall we go through a tempting and troubling world, and entertain with joy the sentence of death, and lay down the body in the dust, without the joy of the Lord, which is our strength? Had our hearts this one promise deeply written in them, we should live in holiness and die in joy.

I have spoken of my text to myself and you. I have now a copy of it to describe. Let none think that the praise of the dead is a needless or inconvenient work, Christ himself praiseth them, and will praise them when he justifieth them before all the world. "Well done, good and faithful servant," &c. Matt. xxv. "He will be admired and glorified in them," 2 Thess. i. 2. The 11th chapter of the Hebrews is the praise of many of them, of whom the world was not worthy (this wicked world, which know neither how to value them or to use them). Christ will have the tears and costly love of a poor penitent woman who anointed him, to be spoken of wherever the gospel is read. The Orations of excellent Gregory Nazianzen, (greater than Gregory the Great,) with many such, show us that the ancients thought this a needful work. Many live in times and places where few such men are known, and they have need to know from others that there are and have been such. Had not I known such, I had wanted one of the greatest arguments for my faith. I should the hardlier have believed that Christ is a Saviour, if I had not known such as he hath begun to save; nor that there is a heaven for souls, if I had not known some disposed and prepared for it, by a holy mind and life. I thank God, I have known many, many, many such, of several ranks, some high, more low. Oh! how many such (though not all of the same degree of holiness) have I lived with, who are gone before me; holy gentlemen, holy ministers of Christ, and holy poor men! I love heaven much the better when I think that they are there. And while I am so near them, and daily wait for my remove, though I here breathe and speak in flesh, why may I not think that I am nearlier related to that congregation than to this? The saying is, A friend is half our soul. If so, sure the greater half of mine is gone thither long ago. It is but a little of me that is yet in painful, weary flesh. And now one part of me more is gone, the holy and excellent Henry Ashhurst; and God will have me live so long after him, as to tell you what he was, to his Father's and Redeemer's praise, and to provoke you to imitation.

God saith, "The memory of the just shall be blessed, while the wicked's name shall rot." Methinks even the natural pride of princes, who would not be the scorn of future ages, but the praise, should accidently incline them to do good, and seem good at the least; while the common experience of all the world tells us, that God doth wonderfully show himself the Governor of the world, by ruling fame, to the perpetual honour of good, and the shame and scorn of evil.

Even among heathens, what a name is left of Titus, Trajan, Adrian, and above all the Roman emperors, of Antonine the philosopher, and Alexander Severus! And who nameth a Nero, Domitian, Commodus, Heliogabalus, &c. without reproach? Yea, I have observed that though malefactors hate that prince that punisheth them, and ungodly men hate piety and the persons that condemn and trouble them in their sins, yet such a testimony for goodness is left in common nature, that even the generality of the profane and vicious world speak well of a wise, just, godly prince, even living, and much more when he is dead. And so they do of other public persons, magistrates and ministers of the gospel; and they will praise goodness in others that will not practise it, especially that which brings sensible good to men's bodies or to the commonwealth.

And therefore great men should hate that counsel which crieth down popularity, as a trick to make them contemn the sense of those below them. For usually it is the best rulers that are most praised by the vulgar, by reason of the self-glorifying light by which true goodness shineth in the world, and by reason of the experience of mankind, that good men will do good to others. How commonly will even drunkards, whoremongers, and unjust men, reproach a magistrate or teacher that is a drunkard, whoremonger, or unjust, and praise the contrary! Much more will the wise and good do it, who indeed are as the soul of kingdoms and other societies, and the chief in propagating fame. It is true that the *bellua multorum capitum* is liable to disorders, and unfit for secrets or uniting government, and it is hypocrisy to affect popular applause as our felicity or reward, or to be moved by it against God and duty. But many men see more and hear more than one, and single men are apter to be perverted and judge falsely by personal interest and prejudice, than the multitude are. *Vox populi* is ofttimes *vox Dei*. I have read Dr. Heylin, vilifying a bishop, Abbot, and saying, The church had no greater a plague than a popular prelate (or to that sense). And I have heard some reproach the late Judge Hale as a popular man; but as my intimacy with the last assured me that he set very little by the opinion of high or low, in comparison of justice and conscience, so, while God keeps up a testimony for goodness in human nature, men will not think ill of a man because his goodness hath constrained even the most to praise him. Nor will it prove the way to please God or profit themselves or others, to make themselves odious by cruelty or wickedness, and then to despise their judgments that dispraise them, and to cry down popularity. "Woe to you when men speak well of you," meaneth, when either you do the evil that the wicked praise, or forsake truth and duty lest they dispraise you; or, as hypocrites, make men's praise your end.

It is not so low a matter as great birth or riches, or any other worldly honour, which I am to remember of our deceased friend. Multitudes that are now in misery, did once excel him in all these. But yet, as a touch of the history of his life is fit to go before his exemplary character, (which is my work,) and because it is a great honour and blessing to the seed of the faithful, I shall premise a little first of his parentage, and then of that part of his life which I knew not, but give you on the unquestionable credit of others.

He was the third son of Henry Ashhurst, of Ashhurst, in Lancashire, Esq. by Cassandra, his wife, daughter of John Bradshaw, of Bradshaw, of the same county, Esq. His father was a gentleman of great wisdom and piety, and zealous for the true reformed religion in a country where papists much abounded. And when King James (the more to win them) was prevailed with to sign the book for dancing and other such sports on the Lord's day, he being then a justice of peace, (as his ancestors had been,) and the papists, thus imboldened, sent a piper not far from the chapel to draw the people from the public worship, he sent him to the house of correction; and being for this misrepresented to the king and council, he was put to justify the legality of what he did, at the assizes; which he so well performed, that the judge was forced to acquit him (though he was much contrary to him); and an occasion being offered to put the oath of allegiance on his prosecutors, their refusal showed them papists, as was before suspected.

God blessed this gentleman in his three sons. The eldest was a man eminent for his wisdom, integrity, and courage, a member of the long parliament called 1640; though all such by interested, partial men are accounted and called what their prejudice and enmity doth suggest, and though, with many more such, he was by the conquering army abused and cast out. The second son was a colonel; and Henry, the youngest, about fifteen years old, was sent to London, and bound apprentice to a master somewhat severe. And whereas such severity tempteth many proud and graceless young men to be impatient and weary of their masters, and to break out to seek forbidden pleasure, at play-houses, taverns, and perhaps with harlots, and to rob their masters to maintain these lusts, till they are hardened in sin, and break their own hopes, and their parents' hearts, (alas! how many such wretches hath this city!) God's grace in our friend did teach him to make a clean contrary use of it. This affection did help to drive him to hear good preachers for his comfort, and to betake himself to God in prayer, and to search the Scripture for direction, in which way he found the teaching and blessing of his heavenly Master, which helped him to bear all harshness and hardness in his place.

And having no place of retirement but a cold hole in the cellar, in the coldest nights he spent much time in prayer and meditation; and his good father allowing him a yearly pension for his expenses, he spent it mostly in furnishing his poor closet with good books—not play-books, or romances and idle tales, but such as taught him how to please God and to live for ever.

From his childhood he had a humble meekness, and sweetness of temper, which made his life easy to himself and others, and made him so acceptable to godly ministers and people, that their acquaintance and converse and love became to him a great confirmation and help to his growth in grace, especially good Mr. Simeon Ash, a man of his plainness, and of the primitive strain of christianity.

His master, I need not tell how, so wasted his estate, that he shut up shop when Mr. Ashhurst was gone from him, whose great fidelity had helped to keep him up, and he took care of his indigent children afterwards.

His portion was but five hundred pounds and a small annuity, and one Mr. Hyet, a minister, lent him three hundred pounds more; with which stock he set up in partnership with one Mr. Row, a draper, and so continued three years. Mr. Row took up his stock, and was a major in the Earl of Essex's army, and left Mr. Ashhurst to the whole trade. Narrowly escaping the misery of an unsuitable match, he married, on Mr. Ash's motion, the daughter of one Mr. Risby, who is now his sorrowful widow, having with her about fifteen hundred pounds. He began his trade at the beginning of the wars, when others left off theirs. He dedicated yearly a good part of his gain to God, in works of charity; and it increased greatly: and as his known trustiness made men desirous to deal with him, so God strangely kept those men that he trusted from breaking, when the most noted tradesmen in the same towns broke, to the undoing of those that trusted them. And though his trading was great about thirty years, he managed it with ease and calmness of mind, and was not by it diverted from duties of religion. He usually was at one word in his trading.

His body being healthful, he rose about four o'clock, or five, and in secret usually spent about two hours in reading, meditation, and prayer, and then went to his family duties, as is afterward described. He was a great improver of his time, or else he could never have done what he did for so many persons, usually saying, he desired to live no longer than he might be serviceable to God and men. But he was most regardful to lose no part of the Lord's day, in which he did all towards God and his family with great reverence and humble seriousness; and as he much desired godly, trusty servants, he had much of his desire, and his house was as a school of piety, meekness, and as a church.

When his faithful pastor, Mr. Simeon Ash, was buried, (the very day before the new Act of Uniformity would have silenced him, being an old nonconformist,) he used to go, at the end of the week, to Hackney, to his country house, and there spend the Lord's day.

In the common fire his house was burnt, as well as others, but is rebuilt with advantage: and all God's corrections, and the hurt which, by his permission, we undergo from bad men, will turn to our gain, if we believe and patiently expect the end.

Thus far I have given you, for the most part, but what his best knowing friends have most credibly given me of the history of his pilgrimage; but I will next tell you what I knew myself, in above twenty years' familiarity with him; and that shall be more descriptive than historical, though, in what is already said from others, you may much know what he was.

Mr. Ash's praise, and his own free love, first brought on our acquaintance; and, indeed, my many restraining hinderances have kept me from so much familiarity with many.

Those that knew him need little of my description. Those that have been much in his house, and seen his children and servants carry themselves as reverently and respectfully to him as if he had been a lord, when yet he was so lovingly familiar with them, will think there was some cause for this. Those that hear it the common speech of magistrates, godly ministers, and people, We have lost the most excellent pattern of piety, charity, and all virtue that this city hath bred in our times, will think that there is some reason for this praise. Some of us seem to shine to strangers, who are cloudy and contemptible to those that are near us; and many excellent, obscure, poor christians are taken little notice of, in a low, retired, or unobserved station: but his esteem, and honour, and love, was at home and abroad, by his children, servants, neighbours, fellow-citizens, that I say not even by some that loved not his religiousness, or that took him to be too much a friend to those whom their opinions and interest engaged them against.

And if you would truly know what was the meritorious cause of all this love and honour, I will tell you: it was the image of Christ, and the fruits of his holy doctrine and his Spirit. No man believeth that there is a God, who doth not believe that the liker is any man to God, the better and the more honourable he is. All is glorious that is holy, that is, of God, and for God, separated to him from all that is common and unclean. Base fools may more admire and reverence a proud man, or gilded idol; but all that know God, and the almost nothingness of vain man, do value all things and persons in the measure, as they are dispositively, actively, and relatively divine. The Spirit of God, by David, begins the Psalms with describing such blessed men as these; and Christ, next after his preaching repentance, begins with such men's characters and blessedness, Matt. v. I shall, therefore, now truly tell you what our deceased brother was, and what of God so shined in him as commanded all this love and praise; while far greater men, by their filth and folly, their sin and hurtful cruelty, have made themselves the plague and burden of their times, as the children of him whose name is but the contract of do-evil.

I. His religion was only the Bible, as the rule. He was a mere Scripture christian, of the primitive spirit and strain. No learning signified much with him, but what helped him to understand the Scripture. The Bible was his constant book, and in it he had great delight; and he loved no preaching so well as that which made much and pertinent use of Scripture, by clear exposition and suitable application. He liked not that which worthy Dr. Manton was wont to call gentleman preaching, set out with fine things, and laced and gilded, plainly speaking self-preaching, man-pleasing, and pride; for when pride chooseth the text, the method, and the style, the devil chooseth it, though the matter be of God: therefore he also highly valued those books which are much in such wise and seasonable use of Scripture; of which he commended, above all, the Lectures of Mr. Arthur Hildersham.

II. He neither much studied books of controversy, nor delighted in discourse of any of our late differences. I scarce ever heard him engage in any of them; but his constant talk was of practical matter, of God, of Christ, of heaven, of the heart and life, of grace and duty, or of the sense of some practical text of Scripture. He so little savoured and minded the quarrels that many lay out their greatest zeal on, and find matter in them to condemn and backbite one another, that he either carried it as a stranger or an adversary to such discourse.

III. Accordingly, while men were guilty of no damning heresy or sin, but held all great and necessary truths in love, and holiness, and righteousness of life, he made little difference in his respects and love. A serious, godly independent, presbyterian, or episcopal christian, was truly loved and honoured by him. Indeed, he loved not church tyranny, nor hypocritical images of religion, on one hand, nor confusion on the other; but the primitive spirit of seriousness, purity, and charity, he valued in all. A differing tolerable opinion never clouded the glory of sincere christianity in his eyes. He was of no sect, and he was against sects as such, being of a truly catholic spirit; but he could see true godliness and honesty in many whose weakness made them culpable, in too much adhering to a side or sect.

IV. He greatly hated backbiting and obloquy. "Speak evil of no man," was a text which he often had in his mouth. I never knew any noted men so free from that vice as Judge Hale and Mr. Ashhurst. If a man had begun to speak ill of any man behind his back, either they would say nothing, or divert him to something else, or show their distaste of it. Sin he would speak against, but very little of the person. Only one sort of men he would take the liberty to express his great dislike of, and that was the hinderers of the gospel, and silencers of faithful preachers of it, and persecutors of godly christians, and oppressors of the poor; and their pretences of government, and order, and talk against schism, could never reconcile him to that sort of men; but his distaste was never signified by scurrility, nor any thing that savoured of an unruly or seditious spirit.

V. His heart was set on the hallowing of God's name, the coming of his kingdom, and the doing of his will on earth as it is done in heaven; on the propagating of religion, and encouraging of all able, faithful preachers and practisers of it to his power. Ever since I knew him, it seemed much more of his serious business in the world than his trade or worldly gain was. He was a right hand to his faithful pastor, good old Mr. Simeon Ash. How seldom did I visit Mr. Ash, at any time, but I found or left them together! and now they are together with Christ. He did not love with barren words, nor serve God of that which cost him nothing. Few but I knew from his own mouth, that he gave these eighteen years (since August 24, 1662) a hundred pounds a year to the ejected ministers of Lancashire, and some schools there and in the neighbouring parts, and many Bibles, catechisms, and other good books, to divers places, besides the said one hundred pounds a year: and a friend of his and mine tells me that it was to him that he yearly delivered it to be distributed, save that lately twenty pounds a year of it went to Northumberland.

VI. Indeed, charity was his life and business. Another mean man that was oft with him, saith that he hath had of him many score pounds to give away, which few ever knew of. I do not think that there are many that can say that ever they were denied when they asked him for money to a charitable use. I am sure I never was.

About 1662 and 1663, he endeavoured hard to have got the pious citizens of London to contribute yearly to the relief of the poor ejected ministers of the several counties where they were born; and I was employed to the Lord Chancellor Hide to acquaint him with it and get his consent, that it might not be taken for a fomenting of faction; but though he said, God forbid that he should be against men's charity, yet most durst not trust him, and so it fell.

Since then he and others set up a conventicle, which, methinks, might be tolerated by bishops themselves. They met often to consult and contribute for the relief of poor housekeepers; and they chose an ancient, active, godly man, fit for that work, to be as a deacon; I mean, to go about the city, and find out such housekeepers as were very poor, sick, or impotent, or any way in want, and to bring in a catalogue of their names, places, and degrees of need; always preferring the pious, honest poor. And they made Mr. Thomas Gouge their treasurer, (one of the same trade, whose hands could not be tied from doing good when his tongue was tied by the silencers,) and the foresaid messenger brought them their contributions, with good instructions, and prayer when there was need; for which use, sometimes, they procured a minister for the ignorant.

Indeed, he was the common comforter and reliever of distressed ministers and others. I know of none in London that they so commonly resorted to as him.

VII. And so large was his desire of doing good, that not only England, Scotland, and Ireland knew it, but it specially extended to the natives in America; of whose conversion to christianity he had a fervent desire. In Oliver Cromwell's time, a public collection was made all over England for the educating of scholars, and defraying other charges in New England, for that work, of which good old Mr. Eliot, the Indians' evangelist, was the chief operator: with that money lands were purchased to the value of about eight hundred pounds a year, and settled on a corporation of citizens in trust, and Mr. Ashhurst must be the treasurer, on whom lay the main care and work. When the king was restored, the corporation was dead in law; and one that sold most of the lands which were settled for that use (Colonel Bedingfield, a papist) seized on his sold land, and yet refused to repay the money. The care of the recovery, and of restoring the corporation, and all the work, was the business of Mr. Ashhurst; for which he desired my solicitation of the Lord Chancellor Hide, who did readily own the justness of the cause and goodness of the work, and first gave us leave to nominate the new corporation, and Mr. Boyle for president, and Mr. Ashhurst for treasurer; and afterwards, when it came to suit before him, did justly determine it for the corporation.

And so these nineteen years last past, it was he, by the help of Mr. Boyle, and the rest, who hath had the main care of the New England assistance, by which a printing-press hath been there set up, and the Bible translated into the Indians' tongue, and other books also for their instruction, and the agents encouraged to help them, till the late unhappy war there interrupted much of their endeavours; and of their victory in that war the converted Indians were not the least cause.

Oh! how sad will the news of his death be to old Mr. Eliot, if he live to hear it, and to his American converts! And he hath left by his will a hundred pounds to the college there, and fifty pounds to their corporation.

VIII. Some may think that he wanted a public spirit, because he avoided being a magistrate, and paid his fine rather than take an alderman's place; but it was only to keep the peace of his conscience, which could not digest, 1. The corporation declaration and oath; nor, 2. The execution of the laws against nonconforming ministers and people. I never heard him plead that the solemn oath, called the National Covenant, was not unlawfully imposed or taken. His thoughts of that I knew not; but he was not ignorant that the words showed that it was a promise or vow to God, and that a vow made sinfully bindeth, notwithstanding, to the lawful and necessary part of the matter: and he thought that to oppose, in our places, profaneness, popery, and schism, and to repent of sin and amend, were lawful and necessary things; and therefore to say that there is no obligation, by that oath, on me or any other person, without excepting any of these aforesaid, was a thing that he would rather, I believe, have suffered death than do. He would not do that which he thought perjury himself, much less justify it in thousands whom he never knew; and he feared lest he should become guilty of constituting all the cities and corporations of England by perjury, and stigmatizing the front of the nation with such a fearful brand. Some men think that the mark of the beast in Revelation, without which none might buy or sell, was perjury and persecution; finding that the Lateran council, sub Innoc. III. and others which are of their religion, do absolve subjects of their temporal lords, whom the pope excommunicateth from their oaths of allegiance, which was ordinarily practised against emperors and kings; and finding that these lords or princes themselves were to swear to exterminate all called heretics, on pain of excommunication, deposition, and damnation; and that every such ruler that professeth himself a papist knowingly, bindeth himself to destroy all protestants, or exterminate them, if he can do it without danger to the papal church; and also finding that all their clergy must swear the Trent oath, by which they cannot but be perjured: and they say that they never heard or read that ever such a thing was done by heathens, infidels, or Mahometans: and Mr. Ashhurst was afraid of any thing that seemed to him such a brand. Yet I never heard him speak uncharitably of those worthy men who do what he refused, supposing that they in words or writing declared as openly as they sware and took the declaration, that they took it but in such or such a lawful sense; though he could not do so himself.

IX. He had an earnest desire of the welfare of the city, that it might flourish in piety, sobriety, justice, and charity, and that good men might be in power; believing that the welfare of the world lieth not so much in the forms of government, as in the goodness of the men; and that that is the best form which best secureth us from bad men. And all such service as he could do, no man was readier to do, as when he was master of the Merchant Tailors' Company, and on many other occasions, he showed. His relations tell me, that he then gave them about 300*l.* of his own money, and greatly promoted the improvement of their stock, to the rebuilding of their hall, and abatement of their debts.

X. He never was a soldier, even when London was a garrison, but always for the ways and works of peace. He was ever against tumults, sedition, and rebellion; and I never heard a word from him injurious to the king and higher powers. He was greatly troubled at the late resistance made by the assemblies in Scotland, and glad when his letters thence told him, that they were but a few hot-headed men, whom the generality of the godly presbyterians disclaimed, and would oppose. Peace was his temper, and peace with all men, to his power, he kept and promoted; and I never knew man that lived in more peace with his conscience, and with all men, good and bad. I never heard that he was an enemy, or had an enemy, save sin, the devil, the world, and the flesh, as all good men renounce them. Nay, I never heard of any one man that ever spake evil of him, so strange a reconciling power hath such a mind, and such a life.

XI. He excelled all that ever I knew in the grace of meekness; and Christ saith, "That such shall inherit even the earth." For men know not how to fall out with such, while no public employment doth, by cross interest, cause it. They that were nearer him than I, say, that they never saw him in any undecent passion: he knew not how to show himself angry, no, nor displeased, otherwise than by mild and gentle words. His countenance was still serene, and his voice still calm and quiet; never fierce or loud, no, not to a servant. He oft used to women the words of St. Peter, "A meek and a quiet spirit is in the sight of God of great price," 1 Peter iii. 4; which is the ornament there commended, instead of gold and gaudiness, which now are grown into so common and excessive use, as if it were the design to avoid the imputation of hypocrisy, by wearing the open badges of folly and pride, lest they should seem wise and humble; as some will rant and scorn, lest they should be thought religious hypocrites.

God fitted him for his place; had he been a magistrate or a preacher, a little more sharpness had been needful. And though I once knew one, that, for want of just anger, was too like Eli, and could not sufficiently reprove or correct a child, yet it pleased God, that his mildness had no such ill effect; but his family loved and reverenced him the more.

XII. I never observed a father carry himself to his children (as well as to his wife) with more constant expressions of love, and with a greater desire of their holiness and salvation. He spake to his children with that endeared kindness, as men used to do to a bosom friend, in whom is their delight. And, indeed, love is the vital spirit, which must make all education and counsel effectual, which, without it, usually is dead, both to children, and all others; though there are seasons when we must be angry and not sin.

XIII. Indeed, he was so made of love and gentleness, that I may say, that love was his new nature, and his temper, his religion, and his life, and that he dwelt in love; and, therefore, in God, and God in him. His looks, his smiles, his speech, his deeds, were all the constant significations of love.

XIV. And no less eminent was his humility; his speech, company, garb, behaviour, and all his carriage, did declare it. He was a great disliker of proud, vain attire, boasting speech, and pomp, and inordinate, worldly spendour, especially that which was chargeable, while so many thousands were in want. He was poor in spirit, suited to a low condition, though he was rich, and condescended to men of low estate. The poor were his pleasing friends. He loved the rich, that were rich to God, but he hated ambition, and flattering great men.

XV. Indeed, he was a plain christian, of the primitive stamp, strange to hypocrisy and affectation, and all that is called the lust of the flesh, the lust of the eye, and pride of life; and the sins of Sodom, pride, idleness, and fulness: his habit, his furniture, his provisions were all plain; nothing for excess, as provision for the flesh, to satisfy the lust thereof; yet all that was needful for right ends. No niggardly parsimony, but sparing to do good; sparing from all the ways of pride and pomp, but never sparing from decency, or good works.

XVI. The government of his family, and the worship of God there performed, was wise, cheerful, grave, and constant. He worshipped God as other good christians use to do: besides his secret devotions, reading the Scriptures, (after the craving of God's help,) and giving some plain, short notes, which were suited to his family's use, catechising, and taking an account of their profiting, singing psalms, and prayer; and, on the Lord's day, hearing and repeating the sermons; a nonconformist preaching an early sermon to many in his house, which so ended, that none might be hindered from the further work of the day. The whole day seemed not too long to him for the delightful employment of his soul toward God. Oh! how far was he from being weary, or needing any vain recreation! In his family worship he played not the orator, nor was very tedious; but in conference of good things, and in his counsels, plain and short; much like the style of Mr. Greenham's writings.

XVII. He had a special care to place his children in a way of employment, and with good relations; out of the way both of idleness and ill company, and worldly vanity and temptations. And God hath so blessed him in his wise and holy endeavours for them, that of four sons and two daughters, there is not one whom we have not good cause to hope well of, that they will, in piety and welfare, answer his endeavours.

XVIII. Others can tell you more than I of his management of his trade; only this I will say, that God greatly blessed his honesty and liberality; and men knew that they might trade with him, without any danger of deceit, so that he grew up to a very considerable estate; and yet was never so intent on his trade, but he was ready for any service of God, and help to others, or public work.

And those that say, they shall lose their custom, except they tipple and make their bargains in alehouses, coffee-houses, or taverns, or use much prating and enticing words, may see here that one hath thriven more than most have done, that yet took a quite contrary course.

XIX. He was a stranger to vain talk and frothy jests, and also to a sour, morose converse; but good, short, cheerful discourse, was his ordinary entertainment.

XX. It is no wonder if, in such a life, so absolutely devoted to God, he lived in a constant serenity of mind; he that had peace with God and men, had peace of conscience. I never heard him speak one word which savoured of any doubt of his salvation, or discouraging thoughts of the life to come; he lived not in bondage to tormenting fears, or sad apprehensions; but studied fully to please God, and joyfully trusted him, rejoiced in his love, and hoped for his kingdom; but without any overvaluing of his own worth, or works; having much in his mouth those words of St. Paul, "I have nothing to glory of," and, "I am nothing."

XXI. The last part of his example, which I have to commend to you, and specially to myself, is his marvellous patience, as through all his life, so specially in his last and sharp affliction. It was a providence which posed many of us, that God should so smartly handle such a man as this; till God's oracles told our faith enough to silence all murmuring thoughts of God. For God had given him before the blessings of Job, a healthful body, and constant prosperity; and shall sinners taste no correction, and receive nothing of God, but pleasant things? All God's graces must have their exercise and trial; and faith and patienee are most tried and exercised in a suffering state: God loveth not martyrs less than others. 2. And he had served God before by action, and usually our last service is by patience; and Lazarus, in sores and wants, was in a safer way to Abraham's bosom, than Dives in his silks and sumptuous fare. 3. And we are naturally so loth to leave this world and flesh, that God seeth it meet to help our willingness, by making us weary of it; and affliction, though grievous to the present, tendeth to the quiet fruit of righteousness; and making us partakers of God's holiness, certainly tendeth to make us partakers of his glory: cross-bearing, and partaking of the sufferings of Christ, is an indispensable christian duty; we must be conformed to him in his sufferings, if we will reign with him, and be partakers of our Master's joy. And in heaven all tears are wiped away, and there are no groans nor moans, no sorrows nor repining, or accusing God, for any of our former sufferings. What need have I, yea, what need have you all, to remember this!

Flesh will feel, and faith will not avoid pain and present torment, no more than death; but it fortified our dear brother's soul, that it should not too much suffer with his body.

Several years he was molested most with some cloudy troubles of his head, which Tunbridge waters eased for a time; and next with acrimony of urine; and next it too painfully appeared to be the stone in the bladder. He long resolved to endure it to the death; but at last extremity of torment and despair of any other ease, did suddenly cause him to choose to be cut. Two stones were found, and one of them in the operation was broken into pieces; many of which were taken out, by very terrible search, and about thirty pieces after came away through the wound. Physicians and all present admired at his patience. No word, no action, signified any distressing sense; and, though he was about sixty-five years old, God did recover him, and heal the wound: but we were too unthankful, and his pains returned; gently at first, but afterwards as terribly as before. And, after that, a strong fever, of which, unexpectedly, he recovered. And then, oft inflammations, and at last, a dangerous one; and finally, so great torment, that a French lithotomist being here, he was over-persuaded to be searched, and cut again, and a third stone was taken away, with competent speed and ease, and divers big fragments of it, which had been broken off in the first operation. Thus was he cut twice in about a year's space; and the wound seemed marvellously to heal for divers months: and when we had prayed hard for him, we turned it to thanksgiving, and thought the danger of death was past; but after, his strength failed, and he died in peace. God gave him those months of ease and calmness, the better to bear his approaching change.

In all this, none heard him express any querulous impatience. Most of his words were telling men how tolerable his pain was, and how good God was, and thankfully acknowledging his mercy. The last words which I had from him, were of the goodness of God, Oh that we could love God more. And when he thought he should recover, he was very solicitous in his inquiry, what God would have him do in gratitude. And one of the chief things which he resolved on to one of his old friends, was, that he would set upon as many parliament men as he could speak with, to repeal all the laws which hinder good men from preaching Christ's gospel. Adding moreover, And, countrymen, saith he, you and I will take care for Lancashire, that the gospel may be more preached among them. (It being their native country, and abounding with papists, and many parts have scarcity of preachers.)

But suddenly he passed from the exercise of faith and patience unto sight and rest.

His last words (save his farewell, and "Come, Lord Jesus") were to an old friend, Mr. Nathaniel Hulton, "to walk in the way of God, will be comfort at death;" being not of their mind, who for fear of fetching too much comfort from our own duty (which they call works) do think Christ's merits injured by such thoughts and words as these; as if the cure were a disgrace to our physician; or Christ (Matt. xxv.) had mis-described the last judgment; or God were no "rewarder of them that diligently seek him;" and "laying up our treasure and hearts in heaven," were no means to be "received into the everlasting habitation."

And thus passed this faithful soul to Christ.

And now, reader, have I not shown thee a true copy of the first part of my text; one that indeed served Christ and followed him? Is not this his image and imitation? And is it not sure then that he is where Christ is? and that God that maketh it our duty to honour his memory on earth, hath given him another kind of honour in the heavens?

And to what other end have I said all this of him? In general, "Go and do thou likewise."

I. I do it much for the use of the magistrates and people of this city. I commend this example to them all. Oh, what an honourable and happy city would this be, if you were all such as our deceased brother was! We joyfully thank God for so much goodness as flourished among you. The Lord make London still the glory of the cities on earth. But were all families used as his family was, and all men here lived as this man lived, we should suspect we had the "new earth, wherein dwelt righteousness." And were princes and nobles such, the world such, or but the christian church such, what a taste of heaven should we have on earth! But should we not then be too loth to die? and too little difference earth from heaven? But, oh that London, who know that I do not over-praise this holy man, would but imitate his example!

II. I do it much for his children's use; their honour, their comfort, but especially their everlasting good. Will they ever forget the instructions, the love, and the life of such a father?

III. I do it partly for the use of the clergy and their agents, that have judged such men as this to be worthy of all the reproach and sufferings which some canons and late laws have laid on such. I write not to cast reproach back upon them. But, reverend fathers and brethren, as you believe a God, a Christ, a judgment, and a life to come, bethink you whether such men as this should be fined, or excommunicated, *ipse facto*, as your canon doth it? And when Christ hath promised, that if they serve him, they shall be where he is, and his Father will honour them, dare you make your church-doors too narrow to receive them, when Dr. Heylin tells us how far Bishop Laud would have had it widened to receive the papists, if they would come in? Do not such men as this serve and follow Christ? And are they yet excommunicate schismatics if they will not serve and follow you, in the things that neither Christ nor his apostles commanded or practised? yea, which they forbid (as I have proved in my "First Plea" and my "Treatise of Episcopacy")? I am in great hope that if you knew but the tenth part of the now silenced ministers, and prosecuted people, that I do, your consciences would constrain you to publish your repentance, and petition king and parliament for better terms of unity and peace. For I will hope that most silencers and afflicters do it more through ignorance and unacquaintedness with the men than in diabolical malignity.

IV. And I have done this for my own use; to discharge my duty; to set before me this pattern of sincerity, love, and patience, for my reproof and imitation. We were of the same year for age; and of the same judgment, and desire, and aim; but I have not attained to his degree of goodness and patience. Being not unlikely to be exercised with some like afflictions, after a life of wonderful mercy, and quickly to follow my departed friend; I beg of God that he will not try me beyond the strength which he will give me, but so increase my faith and patience, that I may finish my course with joy.

V. Lastly, I have written this for the comfort of all serious, suffering believers. Christians, let us not think that we serve Christ for nought, or that our labour for holiness and heaven is in vain. Nor let us faint when we are tried and chastised. Labour and sorrow will quickly have an end: angels are ready to convoy us home: how low soever you are here in your bodies, estates, employment, or reputation, you have Christ's promise that his Father will honour you. Look then to Jesus, the Author and Perfecter of your faith, who, for the joy that was set before him, endured the cross, and despised the shame, lest you be weary and faint in your minds; and comfort one another with these words, that "we shall be ever with the Lord." Amen.

A SERMON

PREACHED AT

THE FUNERAL OF THAT FAITHFUL MINISTER OF CHRIST,

MR. JOHN CORBET.

WITH HIS TRUE AND EXEMPLARY CHARACTER

---

2 COR. XII. 1—9.

IT IS NOT EXPEDIENT FOR ME DOUBTLESS TO GLORY. I WILL COME TO VISIONS AND REVELATIONS OF THE LORD. I KNEW A MAN IN CHRIST ABOUT FOURTEEN YEARS AGO, (WHETHER IN THE BODY, I CANNOT TELL; OR WHETHER OUT OF THE BODY, I CANNOT TELL: GOD KNOWETH;) SUCH AN ONE CAUGHT UP TO THE THIRD HEAVEN. AND I KNEW SUCH A MAN, (WHETHER IN THE BODY, OR OUT OF THE BODY, I CANNOT TELL: GOD KNOWETH;) HOW THAT HE WAS CAUGHT UP INTO PARADISE, AND HEARD UNSPEAKABLE WORDS, WHICH IT IS NOT LAWFUL FOR A MAN TO UTTER. OF SUCH AN ONE WILL I GLORY: YET OF MYSELF I WILL NOT GLORY, BUT IN MINE INFIRMITIES. FOR THOUGH I WOULD DESIRE TO GLORY, I SHALL NOT BE A FOOL; FOR I WILL SAY THE TRUTH: BUT NOW I FORBEAR, LEST ANY MAN SHOULD THINK OF ME ABOVE THAT WHICH HE SEETH ME TO BE, OR THAT HE HEARETH OF ME. AND LEST I SHOULD BE EXALTED ABOVE MEASURE THROUGH THE ABUNDANCE OF THE REVELATIONS, THERE WAS GIVEN TO ME A THORN IN THE FLESH, THE MESSENGER OF SATAN TO BUFFET ME, LEST I SHOULD BE EXALTED ABOVE MEASURE. FOR THIS THING I BESOUGHT THE LORD THRICE, THAT IT MIGHT DEPART FROM ME. AND HE SAID UNTO ME, MY GRACE IS SUFFICIENT FOR THEE: FOR MY STRENGTH IS MADE PERFECT IN WEAKNESS. MOST GLADLY THEREFORE WILL I RATHER GLORY IN MY INFIRMITIES, THAT THE POWER OF CHRIST MAY REST UPON ME.

IT is but lately that we were here lamenting the loss of this city and the church of God, in the removal of an excellent saint: we are now come on the like occasion. It is a year of jubilee for holy souls, and a harvest for heaven. The ripest are gathered, and the green and sour fruit is yet left on earth. But, oh! what a heavy judgment is it to the needy world, which wants such lights as God is taking in! But we are not the choosers. It is well if we be obedient learners, and can follow such to life in the holy path.

The text read to you hath so much matter of instruction, that will excuse me if I scarce name the most. It is part of Paul's vindication against the accusers of his person and ministry, which were some erroneous judaizing teachers. He confesseth that glorying is an inexpedient thing, and sounds like folly; but yet, in case of necessary defence, it may be modestly and sincerely done. Especially the opening of those divine revelations and gifts which make for the strength of the faith of others. The explication shall be taken in as we go.

Observ. 1. It is no new thing for the wisest and holiest of Christ's ministers to be accused even by the teachers of christianity.

For, 1. There are many erroneous teachers, that are confident they are in the right, and oppose the teachers of truth as if they were the erring men.

2. And there are worldly, proud, malignant hypocrites, who bring their unsanctified hearts into the sacred office, and manage it as men do common trades, but with greater enmity and strife.

3. And there are abundance of ignorant or half-wise injudicious men, who have self-conceitedness enough to be peremptory and confident, but neither knowledge nor humility enough to perceive their own weakness and mistakes.

Use 1. Therefore let it not become a scandal to you, if you hear some teachers accusing and vilifying others.

Use 2. And think not that a minister is erroneous or faulty, merely because others, though of great name, do accuse him, or so represent him. It hath still been so, and while Satan is Satan, and man is corrupt man, and there is so much darkness, and so much worldly temptations, and cross interests, it will be so; and preachers will be made the common and dangerous hinderers of preachers; and where they have power, will silence them, and disgrace their work.

Observ. 2. Glorying or boasting, is in itself an inexpedient thing. It savours of pride, and selfishness, and folly, when it is not necessary and just. And therefore all christians should be backward to it.

Observ. 3. Yet that which is so inexpedient, may, on just occasions, become good, and a duty.

That is, 1. When it is made needful to God's honour, and the vindication and success of our ministry and the truth. And,

2. When these are our true needs. And,

3. When we speak nothing but the truth.

Use 3. Oh that men knew how great a sin it is, by their confident errors and rash accusations, to put Christ's ministers upon such a defence; much more to seek their silence and destruction.

And here you see that inconveniences will not excuse us from necessary duties; nor prove that all is unlawful which hath such. What is it in this confused and imperfect world that hath not its inconveniences? In government, both monarchy, aristocracy, and democracy, absolute and limited, have their many inconveniences. In churches, the power of people and pastors, equality and subordination, riches and poverty, severity and lenity, to use discipline or neglect it, have their inconveniences. In worship, imposed words or free, and all human forms and modes, have their inconveniences. In houses, a married life and a single, to have children and to have none, to have servants or none, to have much business or little, to be high or low, rich or poor, to rule gently or severely, have all their inconveniences. In our conversations, to be yielding or not, to converse with few or many, with high or low, to speak or to be silent, have all their inconveniences.

And yet there are men that on one side can silence Christ's faithful ministers by hundreds or thousands, and persecute the true members of Christ, and cast out true discipline, and corrupt the churches, and justify all this by urging some inconveniences. And there are others that can unchurch most churches in the world, and separate from their worship, and think the charge of inconveniences will justify all. And so we should have no government, no ministry, no worship, no families, wives, or children, or servants, no books, no trades, no food, no physic, if all mere inconveniences forbid them.

By this our instance, Solomon may be understood, what it is to be wise and righteous over-much: some are so wise and righteous (materially, not formally) that they can find faults in all persons, all duties, all speeches, all actions, and on pretence of doing all better, would hinder us from doing what we can, and undo all as if it were for amending. Not but that inconveniences may make actions sinful; but the great part of christian prudence lieth in holding the balance, and trying wisely whether the good or hurt, the benefit or inconvenience, do weigh down; we shall never preach or pray, nor converse with mankind, without some inconvenience.

Observ. 4. Divine revelations acquainting the soul with heaven, are matters most worthy of lawful, humble, modest glorying.

It was Paul's heavenly visions which he gloried in as his advancement, when he had mentioned his many persecutions and sufferings in the way.

These tend to that perfection and felicity of souls: in these men have to do with the glorious Jehovah, the angelic choir, the heavenly society, our glorified Head, our highest hopes, and matter of the greatest everlasting joys. Oh, if God would but give you and me this heavenly sight, and let us but once see what Paul saw, what little things would crowns and lordships seem to us when we look down from such a height! What trifling should we think most of the bustles of this world! What toys and dreams, their wealthy honour and sinful delights! I should then say, Now I see what it is that we seek, and hope, and suffer for, what it is to enjoy God and our Redeemer; and therefore now I know what it is to be a believer, a saint, a man indeed. Oh! what a help to mortification would such a sight of paradise be! How easily should we after resist temptations, deny the flesh, contemn the world, and hate our sins! Oh! how it would overcome all these distrustful, trembling fears of death, and make us long, and groan, and cry to be with Christ! What life would it put into all holy duty! How easily should we bear our short afflictions! How would it mellow our sour, contentious minds toward one another, and teach us better whom to love and live in peace with, than pride and worldliness or faction will teach us!

Fellow-christians, though you and I may not expect such raptures and ecstasies as Paul's; yet we have the gospel of Jesus, a divine revelation of this same heavenly glory; not to be set light by, because we see it not ourselves. It is by the Son of God that saw it, and now is there preparing it for us; it is sealed by a certain word, and the heavenly beams are sent down from him upon our hearts, to show it us, and lead us up. We are capable of a lively belief, of the full assurance of hope, of the pledges, earnest, and first-fruits; and of rejoicing with unspeakable, glorying joy. We are capable in our manner, and are sure of traffic for heaven, and with heaven, of sending up our treasures, and there conversing in spirit, as in the city which is our home, and hearing by faith the joyful harmony of the heavenly songs and praises of Jehovah. Here we are capable of such a powerful touch with the loadstone of divine love, or to have our spirits so refined and sublimated, as shall make it as natural to them to make upward towards Christ, and long for full and perfect union. Oh! had we lived as believers should have lived, how much more of heavenly-mindedness and delight might we have attained than we have done! Oh! thank God for the gospel revelation, and beg grace to bring it in power on your hearts. And then, let worldlings take their earthly portion; we can spare them all that hindereth not the gathering and edification of the church, and the heavenly interest of souls.

Observ. 5. There is a third heaven and heavenly paradise, where are the concerns and hopes of holy souls.

Paul was taken thither up: had he no interest there, no hopes, no friends, no business there; why then should he have been rapt up thither? How many heavens there be, and why it is here called the third, I will not interrupt your more necessary thoughts by conjecturing inquiries. Most say, the air is called the first; the starry heaven, the second; and the place of the glorified spirits, the third; but these are vain conjectures. No man knoweth how many there be: the globes or stars are at vast distance from each other: some great philosophers have been tempted to think, that world is infinite, as an adequate effect of infinite power, because God hath no unactive power: all this is profane rashness. The heavens, which are our inheritance, are the place where perfect glorious spirits shall live in blessed society with Christ and one another; joyfully beholding the glory of God, and feeling the delights of mutual love; and yet there are different degrees of glory from the different degrees of the capacity of spirits; whether also from any difference in the place, and communicating causes, we shall shortly better know: there are more sorts of spirits than we can now know. Though I know not how to receive Aquinas's doctrine, that no two angels are of the same species; the diversity, as well as the incomprehensible glory and numbers, are unknown to us. Those that God employeth under Christ as his pursuivants, messengers, and servants for his church, are called angels. Whether there be orders over orders, quite above angels, and how angels differ from the perfected spirits of the just, we know not.

As it is designed for saints, its glory consisteth,

1. In the glory of the place.

2. In the perfecting and glorifying the natures and persons that enjoy it.

3. In the glory of the heavenly society, Christ, angels, and saints.

4. In the glory of their high and excellent work, to love and magnify God for ever.

5. In the communication of the joyful love, and light, and life of God, upon these glorified spirits. Oh! what doth every one of these words signify! Is not this a paradise indeed, that is, a place of purest, greatest pleasure?

Use. And are we not taught by such a glass as this, how great and how good a God we serve? Oh, look up to the heavens, and see what he is by that which he hath made. Yea, it is said, (Psal. cxiii. 6,) that he humbles himself to behold the things in heaven, as well as upon earth. O sinners! what a God do you despise, neglect, and forget! and what a heaven do you sell for fleshly lust, and to feed a corruptible body for the grave! O christians! what a God have we to serve and fear, and how zealously and purely should we serve him! What a God have we to trust and hope in, and how great a sin is it to distrust him! What a heaven have we to seek and hope for, and how cheerfully and constantly should we do it! Alas! our cold hearts, and slothful lives, and worldly cares, and sinking spirits, beseem not such a God and heaven. Were we designed but to inhabit the sun, or some resplendent star, how high is it above this earth! Shall we creep only on earth and feed on dust, and defile our souls as if we were preparing them by sin for hell, when we have a third heaven and paradise to look up to, and seek and hope for?

Doth Satan say, What is that to thee, that is so far above thee? It is to us; it is the place where the glory of God is which we seek; where our glorified Head is. The place of holy spirits, whither also Enoch and Elias were translated; where Abraham, Isaac, and Jacob live; whither Christ's spirit went at death, and where he received the believing thief; where Lazarus is in Abraham's bosom; which Stephen foresaw, and to which he was received. It is the place which we are set on earth to seek, dearly purchased, surely promised, to which God's Spirit is now preparing us, and of which it is our pledge and seal. Were it not for such an end and hope, how vain were man, and what a dream this world! Take heaven from us, and take our lives, our joys, yea, more than many such lives as these. Oh that we could be more deeply sensible for what we are christians, and for what we hope! what holy, patient, joyful christians should we then be! But it is not a wavering belief, a divided heart, and a few cold, strange, and staggering thoughts of heaven, that will do this as we desire it.

Observ. 6. Souls are not so closely tied to the body, but now they may be rapt up into paradise, or the third heavens.

When Paul could not tell whether it was in the body or out of it, it showeth somehow the soul was there, and that it is possible it might be out of the body.

Obj. If it were in the body, the body must go with it. If out of the body, it must leave the body dead.

Answ. It might be in the body, and not take up the body. If man were born blind, the lucid spirits and visive faculty would act only within, but as soon as a miracle opened his eyes, he would see as far as the sun and stars. And the sun sends down even its beams to this earth. Should God open this dark lantern of the body, we little know how far a soul may see without any separation from the body. Did not Stephen's soul in the body see Christ in glory?

And if it went out of the body, it followeth not that it must be separated from the body and leave it dead. When London was on fire, how high did the flame go above the fuel, and yet it was not separated from the fuel. A soul can stay in the body, and yet not be confined to it as a chicken in the shell, but may see and mount above it to the heavens.

Use. Therefore think not of souls as you do of bodies, which are circumscribed in their proper places. We know not what formal thoughts to have of the dimensions or locality of spirits. Somewhat such *eminenter* they have, (for they have individuation and numeral quantity, and some passivity,) but not *formaliter* as gross bodies have. While the soul is in the body it worketh on it, and is a substance distinct from it, and such a form as hath also its own form, even its formal power or virtue, of vital activity, sensitive and intellective perception, and sensitive and rational appetite. It is active life itself, as the principle; it perceiveth itself, and loveth itself, it understandeth what other spirits are by itself, it remembereth innumerable things past, it riseth up to some knowledge of God, it can seek, love, and obey him, and all this though not out of the body, yet above any efficiency of bodily organs. Oh! what a sad part of man's fall is it, to lose so much as the world hath done, of the knowledge of ourselves! And to begin to know ourselves, our souls, and how man differs from a beast, is the first part of recovering knowledge, leading up towards the knowledge of God, which is the highest.

O then, sirs, do not only own the heavenly dignity of souls, but use your souls accordingly. Are they good for no better than to serve the body in lust and appetite, and keep it in motion and some pleasure, or at least from stinking, awhile in the world? Sinners, hear and consider, if you wilfully condemn your own souls to bestiality, God will condemn them to perpetual misery. Yea, you do it yourselves, and pass from brutishness to the devilish nature and woeful state.

Observ. 7. The things of the heavenly paradise are to mortal men unutterable.

That is,

I. Such as cannot be uttered. And,

II. Such as must not be uttered. It is not lawful to Paul that saw them.

Not that nothing of it may or must be uttered. Christ hath brought life and immortality to light. They are great things and glorious which are by him revealed. Enough well believed and used to overcome the temptation of this flesh and world, and to raise us to a holy life, and joyful hope, and comfortable sufferings and death. Christ best knoweth the just measure of revelation meet for earth. Candles must serve for narrow and dark rooms, and are more worth than all the gold on earth. The sun by day must not come too near us lest it burn us up, but send us its beams at the distance that we can bear them. And all souls are not here meet for the same measures, much less for that sight which the glorified enjoy. The pure in heart do see God, (Matt. v.) and even here more than impure souls.

1. There is no human language that hath words fit to reveal that part of the heavenly things which God hath shut up from us as his secrets. Man's words are only fitted to man's use and to man's concerns, and not to angels and the secrets of heaven. We speak not a word of God himself, which signifieth formally what God is, but only analogically or by similitude, and yet not in vain. Paul saw, and holy

souls see, that which no human language can properly express.

2. And if it could, yet mortals could not understand it, no more than a language which they never heard.

3. And Paul had it revealed in a manner suited to his own use, and not in a manner meet for communication.

II. And it was unlawful also to utter it. 1. For God saw not all that meet for the dark world of undisposed sinners, which was allowed to one eminent saint.

2. Nor would he have so much more revealed by a minister than the Son of God from heaven had himself before revealed.

3. And the revelation is to be suited to the fruition. Full knowledge is fit only for those that must fully enjoy it.

Use. Therefore remember with what measures of heavenly knowledge we must be here content, so much as Christ hath revealed and is suitable to a distant life of faith. I have known some run into greater calamities than I will mention, by an expectation of visible communion with angels, and others by rash conceits of visions, dreams, and prophetical revelations; but the common error of christians is, to content themselves with a feeble faith, (or at least get no better,) and then think it should be made up by somewhat like to sight or corporal sense, and to be unsatisfied because they know no more than by believing they can reach to. As if believing were but an uncertain apprehension, (with which we are unsatisfied,) and we are not content to live on that which God hath revealed, but we would fain know more, before we are ready for it; whereas we must explicitly believe all that is explicitly revealed, and implicitly believe and trust God for the rest.

We are here used to live by sight and sense, and the soul is strange to such apprehensions as are quite above sense and without it. And fain we would have God bring down the unseen things to these sensations and perceptions; and we would fain have distinct and formal knowledge of that which God hath but generally revealed. It is somewhat excusable for a soul to desire this, as it is the state of perfection to which we do aspire. But it is not well that we remember not more that sight and full fruition are reserved together for the life to come, and that we live no more thankfully and joyfully on so much as we may in the body by believing know.

Quest. What may we conjecture those things are which Paul had seen, and must not utter?

Why should we inquire when they must not be uttered? We may mention a possibility to rebuke our bold, unquiet thoughts.

Our souls would fain have not only analogical, but formal conceptions of the essence, substance, glory, immensity, eternity of God. Hope for much in heaven, but never for an adequate comprehension. But this is the very highest of all those things which are not to be uttered, and therefore not to be here attained.

Our souls would fain be perfect extensively and intensively in philosophy, and know heaven and earth, the spheres, or orbs, or vortices; the magnitudes, number, distances, motions, and the nature of all the stars, and the compagination of the whole frame of being. But this is unutterable, and not here to be known.

Our souls would fain know more of the angelical nature; what such spirits are, whether absolutely immaterial as mere acts and virtues, or substances which are purer matter; and what their number and differences are; and how vast, and many, and distant their habitations; and what are their offices on earth or elsewhere; and how much they know of us and our affairs, and in what subordination men, churches, and kingdoms stand to them, and they to one another, and how they are individuated, and how far one. But all these are unutterable, and locked up from us.

Our souls would fain know whether there was any world before this earth, and the creation of the six days; and whether there was any spiritual Being, which was an eternal effect by emanation from an eternal cause, as light from the sun; and whether the sun and stars are intellectual or sensitive, and exceed man in form, as well as in matter, and what the noble nature of fire is. But these things are unutterable, and so not knowable to us.

Our souls would fain have more sensible perceptions of themselves, as to their substance, and their separate state. Whether they are substances utterly immaterial; how they are generated, how they subsist and act out of the body, and how they do enjoy. How they are individuate, and yet how far one. How far one or not one with Christ, and one another. Whether they are divisible in substance as continued quantities, as well in number as *quantitates discretæ*. What place and limits do confine them (being not infinite). How far they have still sensation; and how they see, praise, and enjoy God; and how they converse with one another; and how far they know the things on earth; and how their state before the resurrection differs from what it will be after; and how far the soul will be instrumental in the raising of the body. But all these are unutterable things.

We would fain know more of the decrees of God, and how all his acts are eternal, and yet produce their effects in time. How they are many, and yet but one, producing divers contrary effects. Many such things inquisitive nature would fain know which are unutterable.

But this must satisfy us:

1. That sinful souls, and dark, in a dark body, and a dark world, are not fit for so great a light, nor capable of it. It will put out our eyes to gaze so nearly on the sun.

2. That Christ hath revealed so much of the greatness and certainty of the heavenly glory, as he seeth meet and suitable to God's holy ends and us.

3. That the church hath so much clearer a revelation than the heathen and infidel world, as should make us thankful for our light.

4. That, if we believe the revelation of the gospel soundly, we may live a holy, joyful life, and die in the peace and triumph of our hopes.

5. That it is not by sight, but by faith, that we must here live, in our wilderness, expectant state.

6. That the more we cleave to God, and live by faith above the flesh and world whilst we are in it, the clearer and sweeter our apprehensions of heaven will be.

7. That God must be trusted implicitly about that which is yet unknown to us, as well as explicitly for what we know. And,

8. That what we know not now, we shall know hereafter, and the day is near. Let these things quiet our souls in health and sickness, though we are yet in darkness as to the unutterable things.

9. And always add, that what we know not, Christ knoweth for us, to whom it belongeth to prepare the place for us, and us for it, and to receive us. Had we but a friend in heaven whom we could trust, we could partly take up with their knowledge. Our Head is there, and the eyes that we must trust to are in our Head.

But how was Paul in danger of being exalted above measure by the abundance of revelations?

Answ. 1. It might have been above the measure meet for man in flesh, and so unsuitable to his present state.

2. It might have been unto sinful pride, as the angels fell from God, and as Adam fell, desiring to be as a god in knowledge.

Observ. 8. Even heavenly revelations may be made the matter and occasion of unmeet and sinful exaltation.

For, 1. It is the nature of sin to turn all our objects into itself to feed it. Not as they are without us *in esse reali*, but within us *in esse cognito*, the ideas in our minds. Austin saith, indeed, that grace is that *quo nemo male utitur*, but he must mean it, 1. As in itself. 2. And efficiently, grace never doth evil. But objectively, in the idea or remembrance of it, it may be abused to pride.

2. And the greatest and most excellent objects as ours, give pride the greatest advantage. Heavenly revelations are far more excellent than gold, and dominion, and worldly pomp. Children are proud of fine clothes, and worldly fools of vain-glory, but saints may be more tempted to be proud of wisdom, holiness, and things above the reach of others.

3. And Satan knoweth how to fetch temptations from the highest, best, and holiest things; and his malice being as much against them as against us, he will be here most malignantly industrious.

Use. We see, then, that pride is such a sin as the holiest saint is not fully secured from; no, not when he hath been hearing unutterable words, and seeing the heavenly paradise itself; no, not if he came down from the third heavens, and bring his imperfect nature with him. Though he came newly from converse with angels, much more when he cometh from the most fervent prayers, or holiest meditations, or most heavenly and successful studies, and from hearing the most seraphic preacher, or preaching as such a one himself. He is not out of danger when he newly cometh from the most self-denying acts of mortification, or the greatest victory against temptation, or the greatest suffering for Christ. What a sad description do Cyprian and Epiphanius make of the miscarriages of some confessors that had offered to die for Christ.

Let none, therefore, abuse the grace of Christ, and the doctrine of perseverance, by thinking that it sets him above all danger or fears of falling, unless he can say, that he is better than Paul was, and hath seen and heard more than he did in paradise; or than Peter did with Christ; and Moses and Elias on the holy mount. Oh that this age did not loudly tell us, how much the real or supposed knowledge of divine things may be abused to sinful exaltations. By one side, even by most famed teachers, to contempt of others, and lording it over the heritage of God, and racking and rending his church by their needless, yea, wicked, convulsive, imposing devices. And, by the other side, by hurtful, unwarrantable censures and separations, and speaking evil of the things which they know not. Have you heard and seen more of heaven than others? Be, then, more holy, loving, merciful, and peaceable, and liker those in heaven than others. Read over and over James iii. Show out of a good conversation your works with meekness of wisdom; for the wisdom from above, neither befriendeth enmity to piety or peace, but is first pure, then peaceable, &c.

But how is Paul kept from being exalted above measure? God gave him a thorn in the flesh. Note,

Observ. 9. God seeth our danger, when we see not our own, and saveth us from that which we saw not, or had not else prevented. Thanks to him, and not to us.

But how doth God do it? By a thorn in the flesh.

Observ. 10. It is better that the flesh smart, than the soul be over-much exalted.

No pain or suffering of the flesh is so bad as pride, nor hath so bad effects.

Use. Why, then, do we so little fear exaltation? How greedily do some religious people desire it! How impatient of any thing that crosses it, and humbleth them! How little do they lament it, and confess it! Is pride so rare, or so small a sin, even among preachers and zealous men?

And why do we so much fear every thorn in the flesh, every sickness, pain, or cross, as if pride could be prevented or killed at too dear a rate? And why do we quarrel with God for our sufferings, as if our disease were not so bad as his remedy? Who ever heard you in health cry out of your pride, as in sickness you do of your pain? It is a happy thorn, which lets out this corrupt and pestilent blood.

But what was this thorn in the flesh of Paul?

Answ. The Greek word signifieth, a sharp stake, pale, nail, stub, or thorn, or any such sharp thing, that runs into the flesh, as it falls out with barefoot travellers, among such thorns and stubs.

It is strange how many expositors came to take up that injurious conceit, that it was fleshly lust; which hath not the least colour in the text.

1. Lust would be rather likened to a fire or itch, than to a thorn.

2. It would be called an alluring, rather than a buffeting.

3. Paul had a life of labour and suffering, which would keep down fleshly lust.

4. This thorn is given him, as sent from God, to save him from sin; but where is God said to give men lust, to save them from pride.

5. This thorn was the buffeting of a messenger of Satan; but it is not like, that Satan could so excite lust in Paul.

6. Paul prayeth thrice, that it might be taken from him; it is not like, that Satan could so follow him with lustful motions, and that Paul would not have mentioned fasting, and other means of cure.

7. God doth not yet say, that he will yet take it from him; but under his weakness, manifest his sustaining grace, which sounds not like an answer of a prayer against lust.

8. Paul is vindicating his ministry against accusers, by mentioning his infirmities, that is, his bodily sufferings, and his revelations; and is the telling them of his lust a meet means for this?

9. It is called his weakness, which is his usual title for his sufferings; but you may see, (Rom. vii.) that he calleth lust by more odious names.

I doubt not, but it was some bodily suffering which was this thorn; but whether by persecutors, or by a disease, is the chief doubt: many think that it was by persecution,

1. Because it was by a messenger of Satan.

2. Because wicked men are, in Scripture, likened to thorns.

I more incline to think it was a fit of some violent pain in the flesh, and most likely the stone, (or some such thing,) which, indeed, is a tormenting thorn in the flesh. For,

We read of his frequent persecutions; but never that he so named them, or that he so much prayed against them; but rejoiced, as Christ bids such, with exceeding joy, Matt. v. 11, 12. And when he and all the apostles so much exhort believers to rejoice in such sufferings for Christ, is it like he would here tell men how he prayed against it?

And as to the reasons for the contrary sense:—

1. Wicked men are called thorns, as hurtful; and

so are other hurting things. Christ had a crown of thorns on his head, John xix. 5; and Paul must feel one in his flesh. Any thing hurtful is likened to thorns, Job xli. 2; Prov. xxvi. 9; xxii. 5; Hos. ii. 6; ix. 6.

2. And Satan is, in Scripture, usually mentioned as God's executioner, even in trying his children. It was into his hands that Job was put; hurting work is fittest for an evil and destroying angel. He would sift the apostles as wheat, by outward affrighting, as well as inward tempting. However, suffering it was.

Observ. 11. A thorn in the flesh is one of God's means to keep the best from being over-much exalted.

You have heard, that the best may need it.

1. And the flesh hath so much hand in our sin, that it is fit to bear its part of suffering.

2. And it is the most ignoble part, and therefore its suffering hath less of hurt, and less to signify God's displeasure. Soul sufferings are the sore sufferings; and it is the soul that is the chief agent in our duties; and, therefore, where it is spared, we are least disabled for God's work, and our communion with him.

3. And the nearness of body and soul is such, that God can use the body to keep the soul in a humble and a safe condition.

Use 1. Mistake not the nature and meaning of the flesh's sufferings. Grudge not at God, if he exercise thus his greatest saints. Wonder not if the best men have sharp persecutions, pinching wants, and painful sickness, a long and sharp tormenting stone, or other such-like thorn in the flesh.

1. It is but the flesh, in our brutish part, common to beasts. If flesh must die and rot, why may it not first feel the thorn?

2. We grudged not at that health, and youth, and ease, and pleasure of it, which was the danger and temptation to the soul; why, then, should we grudge at the pain, which tendeth to our cure.

3. If you feel not the need of suffering, you know not yourselves. Did you know your pride, and overmuch love of flesh and ease, you would say, that pain is a physic which you need, were it but to help on your willingness to die.

4. Pain here depriveth us of none of our true felicity; it hindereth not God's love to us; it keeps us not from heaven: Lazarus was in a fairer way than Dives. It takes nothing from us, but what we covenanted to forsake for Christ.

5. Do we not find that we are better when we suffer, than when we are high? Were religious people better when victories and successes did lift them up, than they have been in their sufferings? Did they live then more humbly, peaceably, and heavenly?

6. The thorn will soon be taken out; flesh will not endure long, and therefore this pain will not be long. A few more painful nights and days, and the porter which we fear, will break open our prison doors, and end these weary, grievous sufferings.

Use 2. And think not the thorn is a mark that such are worse than others. Paul was not worse; and shall we censure such as he?

Use 3. But let us all know the use of suffering: what cure hath this medicine wrought? Blessed be our wise and gracious Physician, we find it a powerful, though unpleasant remedy. It keepeth Lazarus from the sins of Dives; from living a worldly, sensual life, and loving the prosperity of the flesh, instead of heavenly, true felicity. It keepeth us from a beastly living to our appetites and lust; which would divert and deprave the spiritual appetite. It keepeth us from being deluded by worldly flatteries, and looking for a portion in this life, and laying up a treasure on earth; and from growing senseless and impenitent in sin. It awakeneth the soul to serious expectations of eternity, and keepeth us as within the sight or hearing of another world; and tells us to the quick, that we must make ready to die, and to be judged; and that we have much more to do with God, than with man; and for heaven, than earth. It taketh down pride, and all excessive respects to human approbation; and keeping us still in the sight of the grave, doth tell us what man's body is, *mors sola fatetur, quantula sunt hominum corpuscula.* Juv. What faithful soul, that hath been bred up in the school of afflictions, doth not by experience say, that it was good for him? How dull, how proud, how worldly might we else have been, and trifled away our lives in sloth and vanity!

And it is not for nothing that our thorns (or nails) in the flesh, are kin to the nails that pierced our Saviour on the cross, and that we tread in his steps, and as cross-bearers, are thus far conformable to his sufferings.

Be patient, then, under the pain, and careful to improve it, and thankful for the profit. And let not the soul too much condole the flesh, as if it had not at hand a better habitation and interest. It is but this "vile body," (Phil. iii. 9,) lent us for a little time, as our clothes till night, or as our horse in a journey; when we have done with them, be content of God's separation; and till then, let us not take our correcter for our enemy. I groan too much, Lord; I complain too much; I fear too much; but my soul doth acknowledge the justice, and love, and wisdom of thy dealings, and looketh that this thorn should bring forth sweet and happy fruit; and that all the nails of my cross, being sanctified by the blood of my crucified Redeemer, should tend to make me partaker of thy holiness.

But who put this thorn into Paul's flesh? It was one of Satan's messengers.

Observ. 12. The sufferings of the holiest persons in the flesh, may be the buffetings of a messenger of Satan.

No wonder; he that hath got somewhat of his own in us all, defiling us with sin, if he also may answerably be permitted to afflict us. He possessed many in Christ's time, and it was devils that made them dumb, and deaf, and mad; whom Christ at once delivered from devils and diseases. He is called the accuser and destroyer, and he that had the power of death, (Heb. ii. 14,) whom Christ by death and resurrection conquered. Christ calleth his healing the palsy-man the forgiving of his sin. And James saith, upon prayer and anointing, the sick should be healed, and his sins forgiven. And for the cause of sin, many christians were sick and weak, and many fallen asleep. I cannot say, that good angels may not hurt men, and execute God's judgments; but Scriptures maketh evil ones his ordinary executioners.

Use. Therefore it is no proof, that a man is not a child of God, though the devil have permission to torment his flesh. "The devil shall cast some of you into prison," Rev. ii. 10.

Please God, and Satan hath no power; and Christ will take out the thorn ere long, which Satan is permitted to put in.

But how doth Paul endure the thorn? He prayeth that it might depart from him.

Observ. 13. The best men are sensible of the suffering of the flesh, and may pray God to take it from them.

Grace doth not make the flesh insensible, nor

separate the soul from it, though it set us above it; nor make us despise it, though it show us a higher interest and better habitation, and teach us to bear the cross, and resign the body to the will of God. A godly man may groan under his pain, and take it as a fruit of sin, and an act of the chastising justice of an offended Father, and pray against it as hurtful, though not as a remedy. They that ignorantly dispute that because Christ hath suffered all our punishment, therefore there is no penal hurt in pain or death, confute themselves if they complain under it, or pray against it, or desire such prayers from the church or any. Yea, one use of the thorn is to awaken and quicken us to prayer, like Jonas's storm.

Use. Go, then, to God in all affliction, but not with carnal, discouraged hearts. He maketh you thus feel the need of his mercy, that you may, with the prodigal, think of home, and cry for mercy, and abuse it no more. Christ did not blame the blind and lame for crying out, "Jesus, thou Son of David, have mercy on us;" nor the Canaanite woman for begging for the crumbs. Is any afflicted, let him pray, and send for the elders' prayers. The thorn in the flesh will make us feel, and feeling will teach us to repent and pray, and prayer is the means of hope for the deliverance of body and soul. Grace maketh us not stupid, yet there are some that think a man behaveth not himself like a believer, if he cry and pray that the thorn may depart. What think they of David, in Psalm vi. and xvii. and lxxxviii. and many more? What think they of Christ, that prayed that, if possible, the cup might pass by him? He did it to show that even innocent nature is averse to suffering and death, though grace make us submit to the will of God. (We continue men when we are believers.) We must mourn with them that mourn, and yet not love others better than ourselves, nor feel their thorns more sensibly than our own. We must neither despise chastenings, nor faint.

But how doth Paul pray? Doth he make any great matter of his thorn? He besought the Lord thrice that it might depart.

Observ. 14. Even earnest and oft prayer is suitable to sharp afflictions.

There is a kind of devils, and so of Satan's thorns, which go not out by fasting and prayer; no, not by Christ's own apostles. The sense and means must be suited to the malady. God can do it upon one prayer, or upon none; but we are not so easily fitted to receive it.

And Paul, in this also, is conformed to Christ, who, in his agony, prayed thrice against his cup, though with submission.

Use 1. You see here that the apostles' gift of healing was not to be used at their own wills, nor for their own flesh that it might not suffer; but for the confirmation of the faith, when it pleased the Holy Spirit. Trophimus and Epaphroditus might be sick, and Timothy need a little wine with his water, though Paul had the gift of healing.

Use 2. Oh let our pains drive us all to God: who hath not some? Sicknesses are all abroad: what house, how few persons have not some; and yet is there a prayerless house or person? If faith have not taught you to pray as christians, methinks feeling should teach you to pray as men. I say not that prayer must shut out food and physic; but food and physic will not do, if prayer prevail not with the Lord of all.

Use 3. And think not thrice or continued praying to be too much, or that importunity is in vain. "Christ spake a parable to this end, that men ought always to pray, and not wax faint," Luke xviii. 1. Whether God deliver us or not, prayer is not lost: it is a good posture for God to find us in; we may get better if we get not what we ask. Obey and pray, and trust God.

But what answer doth the Lord give to Paul's thrice praying? He saith, "My grace is sufficient for thee, and my strength is manifested in weakness."

1. It was not a promise that the thorn should depart.

2. It seems to be rather a denial at the present, and that Paul must not be yet cured of his thorn; for it is called a weakness that must continue for the manifesting of God's strength: and what was the sufficiency of grace and strength for, but to endure and improve the thorn?

3. But this promised grace and strength is better than that which was desired.

Observ. 15. Even oft and earnest prayer of the greatest saint for deliverance from bodily pains, may not be granted in the kind, or thing desired.

For, 1. We are not lords, but beggars, and must leave the issue to the donor: and God hath higher ends to accomplish than our ease or deliverance. It is meet that he should first fit all his actions to his own will and glory, and next to the good of many, and to his public works in the world, and then to look at our interest next.

2. And we are utterly unmeet judges of matter, manner, time, or measure, what God should give us for the body, and how much, and how, and when. When should we be sick, or pained, or persecuted, or die, if all our prayers must be absolutely granted? We know not how much better God is preparing us for by pain, and bringing us to by dismal death. He will not keep us from grace and glory because our flesh is loth to suffer and to die.

3. And in this Paul also was conformed to Christ. He was heard in the thing that he feared, when, in his agony, he prayed with strong cries; but it was not by the removing of the bitter cup, but by divine strength and acceptance. And so it is with Paul; sufficient grace and strength to bear is the thing promised.

Use 1. We see, then, that they are mistaken that think Christ's promise of giving believers whatever they ask, will prove him a breaker of his promise, if the strongest believer receive not all that he asketh for the body. Was not Paul a strong believer? All that God hath promised, and we are fit to receive, God will be sure to give.

Use 2. Let not unbelief get advantage by God's not granting such prayers for the body. Say not, Why, then, is it my duty to pray? 1. You know not beforehand but God may give it: possibility bids you beg. 2. Why did Christ pray against his cup? 3. You lose not prayer; you draw nearer God; you exercise repentance and desire; you signify your dependence; you are prepared for much greater gifts.

Observ. 16. When God will not take the thorn out of our flesh, and deliver us when we pray, from bodily sufferings, he will be sure to do better for prepared persons, even to give them his sufficient grace, and manifest his strength in their pain and weakness.

It is not for want of love or power that he lets us tumble on our beds in pain, or lie under slanderers' or persecutors' rage. He that with a word could make the world, with a word can save us from all this. But if we suffer not, how shall suffering graces be exercised; faith, patience, self-denial, and hope? Is not grace better than ease or life? How shall we get the benefit of suffering if we feel it not? How shall grace and divine strength be manifested to ourselves and others?

Quest. What is it that grace is sufficient for?

Answ. 1. Not to set us up above the frailties of humanity and mortality, nor to raise us to the joy that souls in heaven have. 2. Not to every one alike, but in our several measures. Some fear pain and death more than others; some have greater patience and joy, and long to depart and be with Christ.

But to all the faithful it shall suffice, 1. To keep them from revolting from Christ, and repenting of their choice and hope. 2. To save them from charging God foolishly, as if he did them wrong. 3. It shall keep them from damning despair. When Satan sifteth them, Christ's intercession shall keep their faith from failing. Grace shall humble them, and save them from sin, and the flesh, and world: they shall cast soul and body upon Christ, and trust him in hope in their several degrees: and those that have been more believing, heavenly, and fruitful than the rest, are likest to have the greatest peace and comfort, especially in their greatest need.

Quest. And how is God's strength manifested in our weakness?

Answ. 1. It is manifested to ourselves, by keeping us from sin, and sinking into despair, and enabling us to bear, and trust, and wait, and usually in the peace or joy of hope. We know we are insufficient for this ourselves. When flesh and heart, as natural, fail us, God is the strength of our hearts, and our portion for ever, Psal. lxxiii. 26. We do not think oft before that ever we can bear and overcome, as grace enableth us.

2. And it is manifest oft to others, who shall see that power of grace in the sufferings of believers, which they did not see in their prosperity.

Use. Let not, then, our own weakness and insufficiency too much distress us with fears of suffering and death; yea, when we feel the thorn, let us not forget our help and strength. By grace here is meant, the loving and merciful help of God, especially giving us the inward strength by which we may not only bear, but improve the sufferings of the flesh. This body was not made to be here incorruptible or immortal; we were born in sin, and therefore born to pain and death. We have lived in sin, and no wonder if we live in sorrow; but the sufferings of our Redeemer have sanctified our sufferings. The cross is not now such a cursed thing as guilt had made it. "He took our suffering flesh and blood, that he might destroy by death the devil that had the power of death, and deliver us who, by the fear of death, were all our life-time subject to bondage," Heb. ii. 14, 15. Our pain prepareth us for endless pleasures, and our sorrows for our Master's joy. When we have suffered with him, we shall reign with him: he liveth, and we shall live by him: he is risen, and we shall rise by him: he is in glory, and we must be with him.

In the mean time, his grace is sufficient for us, not only in health and ease, but in all our pain and sickness. He is not so unskilful or unkind, as to give such physic to his own, which shall do them more harm than good. Though it be grievous at the present, it brings forth the quieting fruit of righteousness; but we must first be exercised therein. Let us not, then, be his impatient patients; grace can support us and overcome. Men are not sufficient: our wit, our power, our worthiness are not sufficient; but God's grace is sufficient. If ease and life had been better than grace and glory, we might have had them; but God giveth us better than flesh would choose. Though the body be weak, the head weak, the memory weak, the stomach weak, and all weak, yet God is strong, and his strength will support us, and bring us safe to our journey's end. Lazarus lay among dogs in weakness, at the rich man's doors, but the angels conveyed him in strength to Abraham's bosom. We must lie, and languish, and groan, in weakness, but Omnipotence is engaged for us. We must die in weakness, but we shall be raised in power, by him who will change these vile bodies, and make them like to his glorious body, by the power by which he can subdue all things to himself, Phil. iii. 20, 21. Let us, therefore, "lift up the hands that hang down, and the feeble knees," Heb. xii. 12; looking to Jesus the Author and Finisher of our faith, who, for the joy that was set before him, endured the cross.

And let us beg more for divine grace and strength, than for the departing of the thorn. Grace is better than ease and health. If the soul be a nobler part than the body, the health of it is more desirable. Bodily ease is common to brutes and wicked men: strength of grace is proper to saints: ease and health in this life are short, but holiness will be everlasting. Health fits us for fleshly pleasure, but holiness for communion with God. Oh, pray not carnally, for the flesh more than for the Spirit, for earth more than for heaven! Pray, that while the outward man is perishing, the inward man may be renewed day by day; and that our light afflictions, which are but for a moment, may work for us an exceeding and eternal weight of glory, while we look not at the temporal things which are seen, but at the eternal things which are unseen to us, 2 Cor. iv. 16—18. Why should we grudge at any sufferings, which are for the glory of God's grace and strength: as Christ said of Lazarus, "This sickness is not unto death, (that is, the end of it is not to end his life, though he die,) but that the glory of God may be revealed;" so pain and death are not God's ends, but the manifesting of his grace and strength.

But, alas! it is not only the flesh that is weak, but grace itself; (as it is in us, though not as it is in God and of God;) nor is it flesh only that hath the thorn, but the heart or conscience also hath its part. The spirit of a man (if sound and well) will sustain his (bodily) infirmities: but a wounded spirit who can bear? If faith were not weak, if hope, and love, and desire were not weak, the weakness of the body might well be borne. If sin and guilt were no wound or thorn in the soul and conscience, we could be more indifferent as to the flesh, and almost as quietly bear our own pain and death as our neighbour's. Though it is hard to say as Tertullian, *Nihil crus sentit in nervo, cum animus est in cœlo;* yet our content and joy would overcome the evil of our suffering. But, alas! when soul and body must be both at once lamented, this, this is hardly borne. Lord! seeing it is thy sufficient grace, and not my bodily ease, which I must trust to, and my weakness must manifest thy strength, O let not grace also be in me insufficient and weak! O let not faith be weak, nor hope, nor love, nor heavenly desires and foretastes be weak; nor patience and obedience weak! Head is weak, and heart is weak; but if faith also be weak, what shall support us? at least let it be unfeigned and effectual, and attain its end, and never fail. Flesh is failing, and health (as to its proper strength) is failing. But be thou my God, the strength of my heart, and my portion for ever. And whatever thorn the flesh must feel, yet let me finish my course with joy. Amen.

I have run over many things in a text so suitable, that I could not well spare any of them. Those that well knew our deceased friend, will say, that except Paul's extraordinary rapture, and apostolical privileges, in Paul's case I have been describing his.

I come not to gratify the interest of any of his

relations, to speak to you according to custom of a stranger whom I knew not; but for the honour of God's grace, and our own edification, to tell you what I knew by my most faithful and familiar friend. It is almost forty years since I heard him preach in the city of Gloucester; there was his entrance, and there he lived (under a papist bishop of the protestant church, Godfry Goodman, as his last testament in print professed); there he abode during the civil wars, and wrote the history of what happened there. He was after removed to the city of Chichester, and from thence to Bramshot in Hampshire, where he continued till 1662, when, silenced with the rest, he was cast out. He lived peaceably in London, without gathering any assembly for public preaching. Dwelling in Totteridge with Alderman Web, his great love drew him there, to remove to me, with whom awhile he took up his habitation. In all the time that he was with me, I remember not that ever we differed once in any point of doctrine, worship, or government, ecclesiastical or civil, or that ever we had one displeasing word.

The king's licences encouraged his old flock at Chichester to invite him thither, though they had the help of another nonconformist before, with whom he joined with love and concord. God many years afflicted him with the disease that was his death: while the pain was tolerable to nature, he endured it, and ceased not preaching till a fortnight before he was carried up to London to have been cut. But before that could be done, in about a fortnight more he died. This is the short history of his course.

But I will next give you his true character, and then tell you how like his case was to Paul's here in my text, and then tell you to what use I do all this.

I. He was a man so blameless in all his conversation, that I may say, as I did here lately of another, (Alderman Ashhurst,) that I never heard one person accuse or blame him, except for nonconformity, and that difference from others in these divided times, which his book expresses. Of which more anon.

II. Were it not that I have said we never differed, and so made myself an incompetent judge, I should have said that I thought him a man of great clearness and soundness in religion, much by the advantage of the calmness and considerateness of his mind.

III. He was of so great moderation and love of peace, that he hated all that was against it, and would have done any thing for concord in the church, except sinning against God, and hazarding salvation. In the matter of the five articles, or Arminianism, he went the reconciling way, and I have seen a compendium of his thoughts in a manuscript, which is but the same with what I have delivered in my "Cath. Theol." but better fitted to readers that must have much in a few words.

He constantly at Totteridge joined in all the worship with the public assembly, and had no sinful, separating principles. He was for catholic union, and communion of saints, and for going no further from any churches or christians than they force us, or than they go from Christ. He then preached only to such neighbours as came into the house between the times of the public worship. He was for loving and doing good to all, and living peaceably with all as far as was in his power. Some things in episcopacy, presbytery, and independenby, he liked, and some things he disliked in all; but with all sorts lived in love and peace, that did seek the furtherance of men's salvation. Many parts of conformity he could have yielded to, but not to all; nothing less than all would satisfy.

IV. In all he was true to his conscience, and warped not for a party's interest or faction. If all the nonconformists in England had refused, he would have conformed alone, if the terms had been reduced to what he thought lawful. And he studied that with great impartiality.

V. He managed his ministry with faithfulness and prudence: he took it for heinous sacrilege to alienate himself from the sacred office to which he was devoted, though men forbad it him. But he thought not the same circumstances of ministration necessary to all times and places: he was not for open preaching to great numbers, when it was like by accident to do more hurt than good; nor yet for forbearing it, when it was like to do more good than hurt. He spared not his flesh, but held on from year to year under his great pain of the stone in the bladder, till within a month before he died. Much less would the prohibition of any restrain him, to whom God gave no such forbidding power.

VI. He served God with self-denial, not with any selfish or worldly designs: he never looked after preferment or riches, or any great matters in the world: he had daily bread, and was therewith content.

VII. He suffered his part in our common lot, 1662, Aug. 22, (ejected and silenced with about 2000 more,) with as little murmuring as any man that I knew. I never heard him dishonour the king, nor speak much against those by whom he suffered, or rip up their faults, unless a rare and necessary self-defence be called an accusing them. I never heard him so much as complain how much church maintenance he was deprived of, nor of the difficulties of his low, dejected case.

VIII. He was a great hater of that base pride and envy, which possesseth too many of the sacred office, who grudge if others be preferred before them; and if the people go from them to others for their greater edification; and think themselves wronged if they be not followed and applauded, either above or equal with more worthy men. He was very careful to preserve the reputation of his brethren, and rejoiced in the success of their labours, as well as of his own, and a most careful avoider of all divisions, contentions, or offences. And he was very free in acknowledging by whom he profited, and preferring others before himself.

IX. He was very much in the study of his own heart by strict examination, as his cabinet-papers, which may come to light, make known, as I had also occasion otherwise to know.

X. By this examination he was confidently assured of his own sincerity in the true love of God, and of holiness, for itself, and such-like evidences, which he wrote down, renewing his examination as occasion required: and though he had known what it was to be tempted to doubt of the life to come, he was fully settled against all such doubts and temptations.

XI. But though he had a settled assurance both of the truth of the gospel and the life to come, and of his own satisfaction and sincerity; yet, so lively were his apprehensions of the greatness of his approaching change, and the weight of an everlasting state, and what it is to enter upon another world, that he was not without such fears, as, in our frail condition here, poor mortals that are near death are liable to. And indeed fear signifieth a belief of the word of God, and the life to come, much more than dull insensibility: but he signified his belief both by fear and hope, and strong assurance.

XII. He had the comfort of sensible growth in grace. He easily perceived a notable increase of his faith, and holiness, and heavenliness, and humility, and contempt of worldly vanity, especially of late years, and under his affliction, as the fruit of God's correcting rod.

I have truly given you the description of the man, according to my familiar knowledge. I shall yet review the similitude of his case with this of Paul described in my text.

I. Paul was accused by envious, contentious teachers: and so was he; though I never heard any one person else speak evil of him: as is said, they that upbraided not Paul with his former persecution, nor had any crime to charge him with, yet accused his ministry: as they said of Daniel, " We shall find no fault against him, except it be concerning the law of his God." His preaching and writings, though all for peace, were the matter of his accusations: the bishop blamed him for preaching, even when the king had licensed him: and a nameless writer published a bloody invective against his pacificatory book, called, " The Interest of England," as if it had been written to raise a war. The enemies of peace were his enemies.

II. He took boasting to be inexpedient, as Paul did: and when he was silenced as unworthy to be suffered in the ministry, he once offered a modest defence to the bishop, and wrote a short and peaceable account of his judgment about the sin of schism, in his own vindication.

III. He had (though not the ecstasy of Paul, yet) great knowledge of things divine and heavenly to have been the matter of his glory.

IV. The heavenly paradise was the place of his hopes, where he daily studied to lay up his treasure, which had his chiefest thoughts and care.

V. He found by experience that an immortal soul is not so tied to this body of flesh, but that it can get above it, and all its interest and pleasure, and live on the hopes of unseen glory.

VI. As he knew the incapacity of mortals to have formal and adequate conceptions of the state of the heavenly paradise and separated souls; so he submitted to God's concealing will, and lived on the measure of gospel revelation.

VII. He knew the danger of being exalted above measure, by occasion of holy knowledge; and how apt man is to be so puffed up.

VIII. God himself saved him from that danger, by his humbling, wholesome, sharper remedy.

IX. A thorn in the flesh was God's remedy to keep him in a serious, humble frame: three great stones were found in his bladder, and one small one in a corrupted kidney; and how painful a thorn these were for many years, it is easy to conjecture.

X. Satan was permitted to try him as Job, not only by the pain of his flesh, but also by reproaches, as aforesaid, and by casting him out of his ministry, as unworthy to preach the gospel of Christ, unless he would say, swear, and do all that was by men imposed; and the rest of those afflictions, which are contained in such an ejected, impoverished, calumniated state, are described in the late and former experience of many such.

XI. Though I never heard him pray against poverty or reproach, yet for the liberty of his ministry he did, that he might preach that gospel of salvation. And pain forced him to have recourse to God, for deliverance from the thorn in his flesh. And if Christ and Paul prayed thrice with earnestness, no wonder if continued pain made him continue his suit to God.

XII. As Christ was heard in the thing which he feared, and yet must drink that cup, and Paul, instead of the departing of the one, was promised sufficient grace, and the manifesting of God's strength in his pain and weakness; so it pleased not God to take away the thorn from our dear brother's flesh; but he did better for him, and gave him his supporting help, and an increase of grace, and showed his own strength in all his weakness; and also hastened his final deliverance, beyond expectation.

And now he is past all, at rest with Christ and all the blessed. We see not them, but they see God, and God seeth us, and is preparing us for the same felicity; and if it be by the same means, and we must bear the cross, and feel the thorn, it will be wholesome and short, and good is the will and work of God. Lord, let me not account ease, honour, or life dear to me, that I may finish my course with joy, and the ministry received of the Lord, and come in season and peace to thee.

And is not this providence of God, and this example of our deceased friend, of use to us? Yes, no doubt, of manifold use.

I. It is of great use to all the land, to good and bad, to observe God's threatening in the removal of his servants. Oh! how many excellent christians, and faithful ministers of Christ, have been taken hence within a few months! the same week we hear of four or five more besides our brother, and some of them the most excellent, useful men. And is it not time, 1. To repent of our neglect of such helps as God is now removing? 2. And to be presently awakened to use them better before the rest be taken away? Alas! poor souls, what a case are you in, if you die, or the word be taken from you, before you are regenerated, and prepared for a better life! It is not so much their loss and hurt, as yours, which Satan endeavoureth in silencing so many hundred such; and it is your heavy punishment, more than theirs, which God inflicteth by their death. O speedily repent, before that death have stopped the mouths which called you to repentance. And it should awaken the best to prepare for death, and for public suffering: it seems there is some great evil to come, when God thus takes away the best. Yea, if it should be a forerunner of a better state, yet all, save two of the old stock, that dishonoured God in the wilderness, must fall, and it was by bloody wars, (a dreadful means,) that Joshua, and the new generation, were to possess the land of promise.

II. It is of use to us, unworthy ministers of Christ, who yet survive. 1. It calleth loudly to us, to work while it is day, for our night is near, when we cannot work; death will shortly silence us all more effectually than men have done. Do God's work prudently, do it patiently, peaceably, and in as much concord, and true obedience, as you can; but be sure you do it, whoever forbid it, or be against it, as long as God or yourselves have not rendered you uncapable. Whatever silencers say against it, necessity is upon you; God calls for it, souls call for it. The charge is dreadful, 2 Tim. iv. 1, 2. Your vows call for it: Satan's malice, and the number of soul-betrayers and murderers, must provoke you: our time is short: souls are precious: Christ the chief Shepherd dearly purchased them, and will judge you according to your works. It will not justify your neglect to say, Men forbade me; sufferings were prepared for me; bishops and famous divines wrote learned books to prove that preaching was to me a sin, and that I was bound to forbear it when forbidden. 2. And it telleth us, that we, as well as others, must prepare for the sharpest trials from God; no thorn in the flesh so sharp and painful, which we may not feel; no death so violent or sudden, but we may undergo: love and hatred are not known by outward events, prosperity or adversity. A great difference Solomon acknowledgeth between the good and the bad, the righteous and wicked; him that sacrificeth, (or worshippeth God,) and him that doth not; him that sweareth, (perjuriously, or profanely,) and him that feareth (such) an oath: some are loved of God, and some are hated. And this difference is manifest in such disposals, even of prosperity and adversity, as tend to their greater holiness and happiness, which shall manifest the difference fully, and for ever: but outward events manifest it not in themselves; all such things come alike to all; yea, the cross is more laid on the godly than the wicked. Eccles. ix. 1—3. O, therefore, away with the two disciples' desires of church preferment, and worldly dignity, and prepare to drink of Christ's cup, and be baptized with his baptism, Matt. xx. 22, 23. Learn daily how to bear slanders and persecutions from men, even from christian teachers; and how to lie in fleshly pains, night and day; and how to die: and all this in faith, and peace, and joy, at least in the quiet hope of everlasting joy.

III. And without any disgracing or provoking design, but merely in conscience and compassion to the souls of the people, and of our reverend brethren themselves. I do humbly entreat the right reverend and reverend imposing clergy, to lay by awhile, if possible, all unrighteous prejudice, and partiality, and worldly interests and respects, and consider that they also must die; and as they will stand to it at last, to resolve these questions:

I. Whether those terms of church concord and peace be wisely and justly made, which are too narrow to receive such men as this (for faith, knowledge, peaceableness, blamelessness, holiness, &c.) into the ministry, communion of their church, or to endure them out of a gaol? Whether wise and good men could find no better? And whether Christ ever directed the church to exclude such, or did not plainly require the contrary? And whether the apostles ever excluded such, or made such rules?

II. Whether they think in their hearts, that it were better all the good were undone, which hath been done by nonconformists these eighteen years, to the ministerial furthering of knowledge, repentance, holiness, and salvation, than that such should have preached the gospel when forbidden?

III. Whether it will be peace to your consciences at the judgment of Christ, that any of you have furthered the silencing of such, and their other sufferings?

IV. Whether they that have written and preached against their preaching, or for their silencing, and the execution of the laws against them, or persuaded them to give over their work themselves, and reproached and accused them for doing it, be not engaged in this frightful cause?

V. Is it not gross partiality, if you will cherish men of ignorance, viciousness, or far less worth, while such as these are thought intolerable, merely because the former are more obedient to you, than fear of sinning will suffer these to be?

VI. Was that church therein guided by the Spirit of Christ, which made the canon which *ipso facto* excommunicateth such?

VII. If you had known as many of the (about) two thousand silenced, and as well as I have done, how much of the grace of God shined in them; is it possible, that any man, that hath the true fear and love of God, and sense of everlasting things, could ever, by any pretences of church government or order, or upon any bias of interest, have consented to their silencing and sufferings?

Some will think, that in partiality I over-magnify men, because they were of my own mind and party. I have (besides some pious women) written the characters and published the praises of divers; of Mr. Richard Vines, Mr. John Janeway, Mr. Joseph Alleine, Mr. Henry Stubbs, Mr. Wadsworth, and now Mr. John Corbet, and lately one layman, Alderman Ashhurst; and he that hath now received them, whom such as you cast out, or vilified, knoweth that I have in knowledge of them, and love to Christ, whose grace shined in them, spoken simply the truth from my heart; and it is in a time and place where it is fully known, and feareth no confutation. And the history shall live, to the shame of church-dividing, tearing principles, and all thorny, hurtful dispositions, and to the encouragement of the faithful, and the imitation of those that in time to come shall by faith, patience, and well-doing, seek for immortality and eternal life, by serving our Redeemer, and pleasing God.

THE

FAREWELL SERMON

OF

RICHARD BAXTER;

PREPARED TO HAVE BEEN PREACHED TO HIS HEARERS AT KIDDERMINSTER AT HIS DEPARTURE, BUT FORBIDDEN.

TO THE INHABITANTS OF THE BOROUGH AND FOREIGN OF KIDDERMINSTER, IN THE COUNTY OF WORCESTER.

Dear Friends,

While I was lately turning up the rubbish of my old papers, I found this sermon in the bottom, which I had quite forgotten that I kept, but thought it had been cast away with many hundred others. Much of the last sheet was added to the sermon after I came from you; and I remember that when I intended to send you this sermon as my farewell, I durst not then have so much converse with you, for your own sakes, lest it should raise more enmity against you, and your displeasing circumstances of religious practice should be said to come from my continued counsels to you.

I have lately taken my farewell of the world, in a book which I called "My Dying Thoughts:" my pain of body and debility increasing, and my flesh being grown to me more grievous than all my enemies or outward troubles. I remembered the benefit I often received upon your prayers; and craving the continuance of them, till you hear of my dissolution, therewith I send this, as my special farewell to yourselves, whom I am bound to remember with more than ordinary love and thankfulness, while I am

RICHARD BAXTER.

JOHN XVI. 22.

AND YE NOW THEREFORE HAVE SORROW: BUT I WILL SEE YOU AGAIN, AND YOUR HEART SHALL REJOICE, AND YOUR JOY NO MAN TAKETH FROM YOU.

My dearly beloved in our dearest Lord,

I will so far consent to your troubled thoughts of this unwelcome day, as to confess that to me, as well as you, it somewhat resembleth the day of death. 1. Death is the separation of the dearest consorts, soul and body; and how near the union is betwixt us, both that of relation, and that of affection, which must admit this day of some kind of dissolution, I will rather tell to strangers than to you. 2. Death is unwelcome both to soul and body of itself (though it destroy not the soul, it doth the body). So dear companions part not willingly. Your hearts and minds are here so over-forward in the application, that words may be well spared, where sense hath taken so deep possession. 3. Death is the end of human converse here on earth. We must see and talk with our friends here no more. And this our separation is like to end that converse between you and me, which formerly we have had in the duties of our relations. We must no more go up together, as formerly, to the house of God; I must no more speak to you publicly in his name, nor solace my own soul, in opening to you the gospel of salvation, nor in the mention of his covenant, his grace, or kingdom. Those souls that have not been convinced and converted, are never like to hear more from me for their conviction or conversion. I have finished all the instruction, reproof, exhortation, and persuasion, which ever I must use, in order to their salvation. I must speak here no more to inform the ignorant, to reform the wicked, to reduce the erroneous, to search the hypocrite, to humble the proud, to bow the obstinate, or to bring the worldly, the impenitent, and ungodly to the knowledge of the world, themselves, and God. I must speak no more to strengthen the weak, to comfort the afflicted, nor to build you up in faith and holiness. Our day is past; our night is come, when we cannot work as formerly we have done. My opportunities here are at an end. 4. Death is the end of earthly comforts, and our separation is like to be the end of that comfortable communion, which God for many years hath granted us. Our public and private communion hath been sweet to us. The Lord hath been our Pastor, and hath not suffered us to want. He made us lie down in his pleasant pastures, and hath led us by the silent streams, Psal. xxiii. 1, 2. He restored our souls, and his very rod and staff did comfort us. But his smiting and scattering time is come. These pleasures now are at an end. 5. Death is the end of human labours; there is no ploughing or sowing, no building or planting, in the grave. And so doth our separation end the works of our mutual relation in this place. 6. Death is the effect of painful sickness, and usually of the folly, intemperance, or oversight of ourselves. And, though our conscience reproach us not with gross unfaithfulness, yet are our failings so many, and so great, as force us to justify the severity of our Father, and to confess that we deserve this rod. Though we have been censured by the world as being over-strict, and doing too much for the saving of our own and others' souls, yet it is another kind of charge that conscience hath against us. How earnestly do we now wish that we had done much more; that I had preached more fervently, and you had heard more diligently, and we had all obeyed God more strictly, and done more for the souls of the ignorant, careless, hardened sinners that were among us! It is just with God that so dull a preacher should be put to silence, that could ever speak without tears and fervent importunity to impenitent sinners, when he knew that it was for no less than the saving of their souls, and foresaw the joys which they would lose, and the torment which they must endure, if they repented not. With what shame and sorrow do I now look back upon the cold and lifeless sermons which I preached! and upon those years' neglect of the duty of private instructing of your families, before we set upon it orderly and constantly! Our destruction is of ourselves: our undervaluings and neglects have forfeited our opportunities. As good Melancthon was wont to say, *In vulneribus nostris proprias agnoscimus pennas,* The arrow that woundeth us was feathered from our own wings. 7. Death useth to put surviving friends into a dark and mourning habit. Their lamentations are the chief part of funeral solemnities. And in this also we have our part. The compassion of condolers is greater than we desire, for sorrow is apt to grow unruly, and exceed its bounds, and bring on more sufferings by lamenting one; and also to look too much at the instruments, and to be more offended at them than at our sins. 8. But death is the end of all the living. The mourners also must come after us; and, alas! how soon! It maketh our fall more grievous to us, to foresee how many must ere long come down! How many hundred pastors must shortly be separated from their flocks! If there were no epidemical malady to destroy us, our ministry hath its mortality. Your fathers, where are they? and the prophets, do they live for ever? Zech. i. 5. This made us the more importunate with you in our ministry, because we knew that we must preach to you, and pray with you, and instruct you, and watch over you, but a little while. Though we knew not what instrument death would use, we knew our final day was coming, when we must preach, and exhort, and pray our last with you. We knew that it behoved us to work while it was day, (and oh that we had done it better!) because the night was coming when none could work, John ix. 4. 9. And as it is appointed to all men once to die, so after death there followeth judgment. And we also have our further judgment to undergo. We must expect our hour of temptation. We must be judged by men, as well as chastened by God. We must prepare to bear the reproach and slanders of malicious tongues, and the unrighteous censures of those that know us not, and of those who think it their interest to condemn us. And we must also call ourselves to judgment. We are like to have unwelcome leisure, to review the days and duties which are past. It will then be time for us to call ourselves to account of our preaching and studies, and other ministerial works, and to sentence our labours and our lives; and it will be time for you to call yourselves to account of your hearing and profiting, and to ask, How have we used the mercies which are taken from us? Yea, God himself will judge us according to our works. He will not justify us, if we have been unfaithful in our little, and have been such as Satan and his instruments, the accusers of the brethren, do report us. But if we have been faithful, we may expect his double justification. 1. By pardon, he will justify us from our sins. 2. By plea and righteous sentence, he will justify us against the false accusations of our enemies: and that is enough. How small a thing should it seem to us, to be judged of man, who must stand or fall to the final sentence of the Almighty God! 10. The separated soul and body do retain their relations, and the soul its inclination to a re-union with its body. And though our nearest obligations may be now dissolved, and the exercise of our communion hindered, yet I know we shall never forget each other, nor shall the bond of love which doth unite us be ever loosed and made void. And so much of our relation shall still continue, as is intimated in those texts, 1 Cor. iv. 15, 16; xii. 14; Phil. iv. 1, &c. 11. And the power of death will not be everlasting, a resurrection and re-union there will be at last; but whether in this world, I cannot prophesy. I am apter to think that most of us must die in the wilderness, and that our night must bear some proportion with our day. But things unrevealed belong only unto God. It sufficeth me to be sure of this, that as our kingdom, so our comforts are not of this world; and that as Christ, so his servants under him, may say, "Behold I and the children which God hath given me," Heb. ii. 13; and that we shall "present you as chaste virgins unto Christ," 2 Cor. xi. 2. And "therefore we have preached, taught, and warned, that we might present you perfect in Christ Jesus," Col. i. 28. "For what is our hope, or joy, or crown of rejoicing? Are not even ye in the presence of our Lord Jesus Christ at his coming? For ye are our glory and our joy," 1 Thess. ii. 19, 20.

But yet the resemblance between death and this our separation holdeth not in all things. 1. It is not I, nor any pastor, that is the church's soul or life. This is the honour of Christ, the Head. Being planted into him, you may live, though all his ministers were dead, or all your teachers driven into corners, Isa. xxx. 20. 2. The continuance of your church state dependeth not on the continuance of any one single pastor whatsoever. God can provide you others to succeed us, that may do his work for you more successfully than we. And could I but hope that they should be as able, and holy, and diligent as I desire, how little should I partake with you in this day's sorrows! Had I not given you these exceptions, malicious tongues would have reported that I made myself your life or soul, and take the churches to be all dead when such as I are silenced and cast out. But I remember Psalm xii.

Though what I have said, and what you feel, may make you think that a funeral sermon is most seasonable on such a day, yet I have rather chosen to preach to you the doctrine of rejoicing, because you sorrow not as men that have no hope, and because I must consider what tendeth most to your strength and stedfastness; and that you may see herein I imitate our Lord, I have chosen his words to his troubled disciples, before his departure from them, John xvi. 22. And though I make no question but it will be said with scorn, that thus I make myself as Christ, and that I seditiously encourage you by the expectations of my restitution, yet will I not therefore forbear to use my Saviour's consolatory words, but will remember to whom, and on what occasion, he said, "Every plant, which my heavenly Father hath not planted, shall be rooted up. Let them alone: they be blind leaders of the blind. And if the blind lead the blind, both shall fall into the ditch," Matt. xv. 13, 14.

The words are Christ's comforts to his orphan, sorrowful disciples, expressing, first, their present condition, and that which they were now to taste of; and, secondly, their future state. Their present case is a state of sorrow, because that Christ must be taken from them. Their future case will be a state of joy, which is expressed, 1. In the futurity of the cause, "but I will see you again." 2. In the promise of the effect, "and your heart shall rejoice." 3. In the duration and invincibility of it, "and your joy no man taketh from you," or "shall take from you." He had before likened their sorrows on this occasion, to the pains of a woman in her child-bearing, which are but short, and end in joy. And in relation to that similitude, the Syriac translateth λύπην, sickness, and the Persian translateth it, calamity. Some expositors limit the cause of their sorrows to the absence of Christ, or that death of his which will for a time both shake their faith, and astonish their hopes, and deprive them of their former comforts. And others limit the word therefore to the following crosses or sufferings which they must undergo for the sake of Christ, and accordingly they interpret the cause of their succeeding joy. But I see no reason but both are included in the text; but principally the first, and the other consequently. As if he had said, When you see me crucified, your hearts and hopes will begin to fail, and sorrow to overwhelm your minds, and you will be exposed to the fury of the unbelieving world; but it will be but for a moment, for when you see that I am risen again, your joy will be revived; and my Spirit afterwards, and continual encouragements, shall greatly increase and perpetuate your joys, which no persecutions or sufferings shall deprive you of, but they shall at last be perfected in the heavenly, everlasting joys. The cause of their sorrow is, first his absence, and next their sufferings with him in the world, when the bridegroom is taken from them they must fast, that is, live an afflicted kind of life in various sorrows; and the causes of their succeeding joy are, first his resurrection, and next his Spirit, which is their Comforter, and lastly, the presence of his glory at their reception into his glorious kingdom. Their sorrow was to be short, as that of a woman in travail, and it was to have a tendency to their joy. And their joy was to be sure and near, "I will see you again," and great, "your heart shall rejoice," and everlasting, "your joy no man taketh from you."

The sense of the text is contained in these six doctrinal propositions.

Doct. 1. Sorrow goeth before joy with Christ's disciples.

Doct. 2. Christ's death and departure was the cause of his disciples' sorrows.

Doct. 3. The sorrows of Christ's disciples are but short. It is but now.

Doct. 4. Christ will again visit his sorrowful disciples, though at the present he seem to be taken from them.

Doct. 5. When Christ returneth or appeareth to his disciples, their sorrows will be turned into joy.

Doct. 6. The joy of christians in the return or reappearing of their Lord is such as no man shall take from them.

Of these, by God's assistance, I shall speak in order, and therefore be but short on each.

Doct. 1. Sorrow goeth before joy with Christ's disciples.

The evening and the morning make their day. They must sow in tears before they reap in joy. They must have trouble in the world, and peace in Christ. God will first dwell in the contrite heart, to prepare it to dwell with him in glory. The pains of travail must go before the joy of the beloved birth.

Quest. What kind of sorrow is it that goeth before our joy?

Answ. 1. There is a sorrow positively sinful, which doth, but should not, go before our joy. Though this be not meant directly in the text, yet it is too constant a foregoer of our comforts. It is not the joys of innocency that are our portion, but the joys of restoration; and the pains of our disease go before the ease and comfort of our recovery. We have our worldly sorrows, and our passionate and peevish sorrows, like Jonah's for the withering of his gourd. According to the degree of our remaining corruption, we have our sorrows, which must be sorrowed for again. Sometimes we are troubled at the providences of God, and sometimes at the dealings of men; at the words or doings of enemies, of friends, of all about us. We are grieved if we have not what we would have, and when we have it, it becomes our greater grief: nothing well pleaseth us, till we so devote ourselves to please our God, as to be pleased in the pleasing of him.

2. And we have our sorrows which are sinful through our weakness and imperfection, when, through the languishing feebleness of our souls, we are over-much troubled at that which we may lawfully sorrow for with moderation; when impatience causeth us to make a greater matter of our afflictions than we ought. If God do but try us with wants or crosses; if we lose our friends, or if they prove unkind; we double the weight of the cross by our impatience. This cometh from the remnants of unmortified selfishness, carnality, and overloving earthly things. Were they less loved, they would be less sorrowed for. If we had seen their vanity, and mortification had made them nothing to us, we should then part with them as with vanity and nothing. It is seldom that God or men afflict us, but we therefore afflict ourselves much more. As the destruction of the wicked, so the troubles of the godly, is chiefly of themselves.

3. There is a mere natural suffering or sorrow, which is neither morally good or bad; as to be weary with our labour; to be pained with our diseases; to be sensible of hunger and thirst, of cold and heat; to be averse to death, as death, as Christ himself was; and at last to undergo it, and lie down in the dust. There are many sorrows which are the fruits of sin, which yet, in themselves, are neither sin nor duty.

4. There are castigatory sorrows from the hand of God, which have a tendency to our cure, if we use them according to his appointment. Such are all the foresaid natural sufferings, considered as God's means and instruments of our benefit. He woundeth the body to heal the soul: he lanceth the sore to let

out the corruption: he letteth us blood to cure our inflammations and apostemated parts: he chasteneth all that he loveth and receiveth; and we must be subject to a chastening Father if we will live; for he doth it for our profit, "that we may be partakers of his holiness," Heb. xii. 1—14.

5. There are honourable and gainful sufferings from blind, malicious, wicked men, for the cause of Christ and righteousness, such as the gospel frequently warneth believers to expect. These are the sorrows that have the promises of fullest joy: not that the mere suffering in itself is acceptable to God; but the love which is manifested by suffering for him, is that which he cannot but accept: so that the same measure of sufferings are more or less acceptable, as there is more or less love to God expressed by them, and as the honour of Christ is more or less intended in them. For to give the body to be burned without love will profit us nothing, 1 Cor. xiii. 3. But when the cause is Christ's, and the heart intendeth him as the end of the suffering, then "blessed are they which are persecuted for righteousness' sake, for theirs is the kingdom of heaven," &c. Matt. v. 10—12.

6. There are penitential and medicinal sufferings, for the killing of sin, and helping on the work of grace, which are made our duty. In the former we are to be but submissive patients, but in these we must be obedient agents, and must inflict them on ourselves. Such are the sorrows of contrition and true repentance; the exercises of fasting, abstinence, and humiliation; the grief of the soul for God's displeasure, for the hiding of his face, and the abatement of his graces in us; and all the works of mortifying self-denial, and forbearing all forbidden pleasures, which God doth call his servants to. Though in the primitive and principal part of holiness there is nothing but what is sweet and pleasant to a soul, so far as it is holy; (as the love of God and the love of others, and worshipping God, and doing good, and joy, and thanks, and praise, and obedience, &c.;) yet the medicinal parts of grace, or holiness, have something necessarily in them that is bitter, even to nature as nature, and not only as corrupt, such as are contrition, self-denial, mortification, abstinence, as aforesaid.

7. There are charitable sorrows for the dishonour of God, and for the sin, hurt, and miseries of others. These, also, are our duties, and we must be agents in them as well as patients. As we must first pray for the hallowing of the name of God, and the coming of his kingdom, and the doing of his will on earth as it is done in heaven; so we must most grieve for the abuse and dishonour of God's name, the hindering of his kingdom, and the breaking of his laws; that so many nations see not the peril, and know not God, and have not the gospel, or will not receive it, but live in rebellion against their Maker, and in blindness, obstinacy, and hardness of heart, and are given up to commit uncleanness with greediness, Eph. iv. 18, 19; that so many nations which are called christians, are captivated in ignorance and superstition, by the blindness, pride, carnality, and covetousness of their usurping, self-obtruding guides; that so many men professing christianity have so little of the knowledge or power of what they generally and ignorantly profess, and live to the shame of their profession, the great dishonour and displeasure of their Lord, and the grief or hardening of others; that the church of Christ is broken into so many sects and factions, possessed with such an uncharitable, destroying zeal against each other, and persecuting their brethren as cruelly as Turks and heathens do; that the best of christians are so few, and yet so weak and liable to miscarriages: all these are the matter of that sorrow which God hath made our duty; and all these sorts of sorrow do go before a christian's fullest joy.

Reason 1. God will have some conformity between the order of nature and of grace. Non-entity was before created entity; the evening before the morning; infancy before maturity of age; weakness before strength; the buried seed before the plant, the flower, and fruit; and infants cry before they laugh; weakness is soon hurt, and very querulous. No wonder, then, if our sorrows go before our joys.

2. Sin goeth before grace, and therefore our sorrows are before our joys. The seed is first fruitful which was first sown. Joy, indeed, hath the elder parent, *in esse reali et absoluto,* but not *in esse causali et relativo.* We are the children of the first Adam, before we are children of the second; we are born flesh of flesh, before we are born spiritual of the Spirit, 1 Cor. xv.; John iii. 6. And where Satan goeth before Christ, it is equal that sorrow be before joy.

3. Our gracious Father and wise Physician doth see that this is the fittest method for our cure. That we may deny ourselves, we must know how little we are beholden to ourselves, and must smart by the fruit of our sin and folly before we are eased by the fruit of love and grace. It is the property of the flesh to judge by sense, and therefore sense shall help to mortify it. The frowns of the world shall be an antidote against its flatteries. It killeth by pleasing, and therefore it may help our cure by displeasing us. Loving it is men's undoing; and hurting us is the way to keep us from overloving it. These wholesome sorrows do greatly disable our most dangerous temptations, and preserve us from the pernicious poison of prosperity. They rouse us up when we are lazy and ready to sit down; they awake us when we are ready to fall asleep; they drive us to God when we are ready to forget him, and dote upon a deceiver; they teach us part of the meaning of the gospel; without them we know not well what "a Saviour," a "promise," a pardon," "grace," and many other gospel terms, do signify. They teach us to pray, and teach us to hear and read with understanding; they tell us the value of all our mercies, and teach us the use of all the means of grace; they are needful to fix our flashy, light, inconstant minds, which are apt to be gazing upon every bait, and to be touching or tasting the forbidden fruit, and to be taken with those things which we had lately cast behind our backs, till medicinal sorrow doth awake our reason, and make us see the folly of our dreams. Yea, if sorrow check us not, and make us wise, we are ready to lay by our grace and wit, and to follow any goblin in the dark, and, like men bewitched, to be deceived by we know not what, and to go on as a bird to the fowler's snare, as an ox to the slaughter, and as a fool to the correction of the stocks, Prov. vii. 22, 23.

4. Moreover, precedent sorrows will raise the price of following joys. They will make us more desirous of the day of our deliverance, and make it the welcomer to us when it comes. Heaven will be seasonable after a life of so much trouble; and they that come out of great tribulation, will joyfully sing the praises of their Redeemer, Rev. vii. 14.

5. And God will have the members conformed to their Head, Luke xiv. 27, 33: this was Christ's method, and it must be ours: we must take up the cross, and follow him, if ever we will have the crown, Rom. viii. 17, 18; and we must suffer with him if we will be glorified with him, 2 Tim. ii. 12. Though the will of God be the reason which alone

should satisfy his creatures, yet these reasons show you the equity and goodness of his ways.

Use 1. If sorrow before joy be God's ordinary method of dealing with his most beloved servants, learn hence to understand the importance of your sorrows. You say as Baruch, "Woe is me now! for the Lord hath added grief to my sorrow; I fainted in my sighing, and I find no rest," Jer. xlv. 3. You are ingenious in recounting and aggravating your afflictions. But are you as ingenious in expounding them aright? do you not judge of them rather by your present sense, than by their use and tendency? You will not do so by the bitterness of a medicine, or the working of a purge or vomit. You will like it best when it worketh in that way as usually it doth with them that it cureth. And should you not be glad to find that God taketh that way with you, which he most usually takes with those that he saveth? Sure you do not set light by the love of God. Why, then, do you complain so much against the signs and products of it? Is it not because you have yet much unbelief, and judge of God's love as the flesh directeth you, instead of judging by the effects and prognostics which he himself hath bid you judge by? We will grant to the flesh, that no "chastisement for the present seemeth joyous, but grievous;" if you will believe the Spirit, that, "nevertheless, afterward it yieldeth the peaceable fruit of righteousness to them that are exercised thereby;" and that "whom the Lord loveth he chasteneth, and scourgeth every son whom he receiveth," Heb. xii. 6, 11. Misunderstand not, then, the prognostics of your present sorrows. Think how they will work as well as how they taste. They bode good, though they are unpleasant. If you were bastards and reprobates you might feel less of the rod. When the ploughers make furrows on you, it prepareth you for the seed; and the showers that water it prognosticate a plenteous harvest. Think it not strange if he thresh and grind you, if you would be bread for your Master's use. He is not drowning his sheep when he washeth them, nor killing them when he is shearing them. But by this he showeth that they are his own: and the new-shorn sheep do most visibly bear his name or mark, when it is almost worn out, and scarce discernible, on them that have the longest fleece. If you love the world and prosperity best, rejoice most in it, and grieve most for the want of it. But if you love God best, and take him for your part and treasure, rejoice in him, and in that condition which hath the fullest significations of his love; and grieve most for his displeasure, and for that condition which either signifieth it, or most enticeth you to displease him. If things present be your portion, then seek them first, and rejoice in them, and mourn when they are taken from you, 2 Cor. iv. 18; Matt. vi. 20, 21. But if really your portion be above with Christ, let your hearts be there; and let your joys and sorrows and endeavours signify it, Col. iii. 1—4. The sense of brutes doth judge of pain and pleasure only by their present feeling; but the reason of a man, and the faith of a christian, do estimate them according to their signification and importance. I know that it is in vain to think by reason to reconcile the flesh and sense unto its sufferings; but if I may speak to you as to men, much more if as to christians, and reason with your reasonable part, I shall not at all despair of the success.

Quest. 1. Tell me, then, who it is that you suffer by; that hath the principal disposing hand in all? Is it one that you can reasonably suspect of any want of power, wisdom, or goodness? Is he not much fitter to dispose of you, than you or any mortals are? If the physician be fitter than the patient to determine how he shall be ordered, and if you are fitter than your infant child, and if you are fitter than your beast to determine of his pasture, work, and usage, sure then you will grant, that God is much more fit than we. And if he would give you your choice, and say, It shall go with thee all thy days, for prosperity or adversity, life or death, as thou wilt thyself, or as thy dearest friend will; you should say, Nay, Lord, but let it be as thou wilt; for I and my friend are foolish and partial, and know not what is best for ourselves. Not our wills, but thy will be done.

Quest. 2. Do you not see that carnal pleasure is far more dangerous than all your sorrows? Look on the ungodly that prosper in the world, and tell me whether you would be in their condition? If not, why do you long for their temptations; and to live in that air whose corruption causeth such epidemical mortalities? If you would not, with the rich man, (Luke xvi.) be damned for sensuality, nor with the fool, (Luke xii. 19, 20,) say, Soul, take thy ease, &c. when your souls are presently to be taken from you, or with him, (Luke xviii. 22, 23,) go away sorrowful from Christ, desire not the temptations which brought them to it. If you would not oppress the people of God with Pharaoh, nor persecute the prophets with Ahab and Jezebel, nor resist the gospel, and persecute the preachers of it, with the scribes and Pharisees, (1 Thess. ii. 14—16,) desire not the temptations which led them to all this.

Quest. 3. Would not you follow your Saviour, and rather be conformed to him and to his saints, than to the wicked that have their portion in this life? I doubt you do not well study the life and sufferings of Christ, and the reason of them, when you find yourselves so little concerned in them, and so desirous of another way. And would you not go to heaven in the common way that the saints of old have gone before you in? Read the Scripture and all church history, and observe which is the beaten path of life; and whether even among believers and the pastors of the church, it was the persecuted or the prosperous that most honoured their profession; and which of them it was that corrupted the church with pride and domination, and kindled in it those flames of contention which are consuming it to this day, and sowed those seeds of divisions whose sour fruit have set their children's teeth on edge. Mark whether it was the suffering or the prospering part that hath had the greatest hand in her after-sufferings.

Quest. 4. What saith your own experience, and how hath God dealt with you in the time that is past? Hath not your suffering done you good? If it have not, you may thank yourselves; for I am sure God's rod hath a healing virtue, and others have received a cure by it. How much is mankind beholden to the cross! When David went weeping up mount Olivet, he was in a safer case than when he was gazing on Bathsheba from his battlements. And when Christ was sweating blood upon mount Olivet, (Luke xxii. 44,) it was a sign that man's redemption was in hand; and when he was bleeding on the cross, and drinking vinegar and gall, it was almost finished. And if the cross hath borne such happy fruit, what reason have we to be so much against it? If it have proved good for you that you were afflicted, and no part of your lives have been more fruitful, why should your desires so much contradict your own experience? If bitter things have proved the most wholesome, and a full and luscious diet hath caused your disease, what need you more to direct your judgment, if you will judge as men, and not as brutes?

Obj. But (you will say) it is not all sorrow that foretelleth joy: some pass from sorrow unto greater sorrow. How then shall we know whether our sorrows tend to worse or unto better?

Answ. It is true that there are sorrows which have no such promise as these have in the text. As, 1. The mere vindictive punishment of the wicked. 2. The sinful sorrows which men keep up in themselves, proceeding from their sinful love of creatures. 3. And the corrections which are not improved by us to our amendment and reformation.

But the promise belongeth, 1. To those sorrows which in sincerity we undergo for the sake of Christ and righteousness. 2. To those sorrows which we ourselves perform as duties, either for the dishonour of God, or the sins or miseries of others; or our penitential sorrows for our own offences. 3. And to those sorrows of chastisement which we patiently submit to, and improve to a true amendment of our hearts and lives. For though sin be the material cause, or the meritorious cause, yet love which maketh reformation the effect, will also make the end to be our comfort.

Use 2. If this be God's method, condemn not then the generation of the just, because you see them undermost in the world, and suffer more than other men. Think it not a dishonour to them to be in poverty, prisons, banishment, or reproach, unless it be for a truly dishonourable cause. Call not men miserable, for that which God maketh the token of his love, and the prognostic of their joy. Methinks he that hath once read the Psalms xxxvii.; lxxiii.; Matt. v. 10—12; Job xiii. and xv.; 2 Thess. i., and well believeth them, should never err this old condemned error any more. And yet it is common among carnal men to do as some beasts do, when one of their fellows is wounded they all forsake him: so these stand looking with pity, or fear, or strangeness upon a man that is under sufferings and slanders, as if it must needs be a deserved thing; and think it a great dishonour to a man, how innocent soever, when they hear that he is used as offenders and malefactors are; forgetting how by this they condemn their Saviour, and all his apostles and martyrs, and the wisest, best, and happiest men that the earth hath borne. And all this is but the blind and hasty judgment of sense and unbelief, which hath neither the wit to judge by the word of God, nor yet the patience to stay the end, and see how the sorrows of the godly will conclude, and where the triumph of the hypocrite will leave them.

And yet some there be that are apt to err on the other extreme, and to think that every man is happy that is afflicted, and that such have all their sorrow in this life, and that the suffering party is always in the right; and therefore they are ready to fall in with any deluded sect, which they see to be under reproach and suffering. But the cause must be first known, before the suffering can be well judged of.

Doct. 2. Christ's death and departure was the cause of his disciples' sorrows.

This is plain in the words, "Ye now therefore have sorrow; but I will see you again." And the causes of this sorrow were these three conjunct: 1. That their dear Lord, whom they loved, and whom they had heard, and followed, and put their trust in, must now be taken from them. If the parting of friends at death do turn our garments into the signs of our sad and mournful hearts, and cause us to dwell in the houses of mourning, we must allow Christ's disciples some such affections, upon their parting with their Lord.

2. And the manner of his death, no doubt, did much increase their sorrows. That the most innocent should suffer as a reputed malefactor; that he that more contemned the wealth, and pleasures, and glory of the world, than ever man did, and chose a poor, inferior life, and would not have a kingdom of this world, and never failed in any duty to high or low, should yet be hanged ignominiously on a cross, as one that was about to usurp the crown; that deluded sinners should put to death the Lord of life, and spit in the face of such a Majesty, and hasten destruction to their nation and themselves; and that all Christ's disciples must thus be esteemed the followers of a crucified usurper; judge if we had been in their case ourselves, whether this would have been matter of sorrow to us or not. Had it not been enough for Christ to have suffered the pain, but he must also suffer the dishonour, even the imputation of sin, which no man was so far from being guilty of? and of that particular sin, usurpation of dominion, and treason against Cæsar, which his heart and life were as contrary to as light to darkness? And was it not enough for christians to suffer so great calamities of body for righteousness' sake, but they must also suffer the reproach of being the seditious followers of a crucified malefactor whom they would have made a king? No; our Lord would stoop to the lowest condition for our sakes, which was consistent with his innocency and perfection. Sin is so much worse than suffering, that we may take this for the greatest part of his condescension, and strangest expression of his love, that he should take not only the nature and the sufferings of a man, but also the nature and the imputation of sinners. Though sin itself was inconsistent with his perfection, yet so was not the false accusation and imputation of it: he could not become a sinner for us; but he could be reputed a sinner for us, and die as such. And when our Lord hath submitted to this most ignominious kind of suffering, it is not fit that we should be the choosers of our sufferings, and say, Lord, we will suffer any thing except the reputation of being offenders, and the false accusations of malicious men. If in this we must be made conformable to our Head, we must not refuse it, nor repine at his disposal of us.

3. And their sorrow for Christ's departure was the greater, because they had so little foresight of his resurrection and return. It is strange to see how dark they were in these articles of the faith, for all their long converse with Christ, and his plain foretelling them his death and resurrection; and how much of their teaching Christ reserved to the Spirit after his departure from them. "Then took he unto him the twelve, and said unto them, Behold, we go up to Jerusalem, and all things that are written by the prophets concerning the Son of man shall be accomplished. For he shall be delivered unto the gentiles, and shall be mocked, and spitefully entreated, and spit upon: and they shall scourge him and put him to death: and the third day he shall rise again. And they understood none of these things: and this saying was hid from them, neither knew they the things which were spoken," John xii. 16; Luke xviii. 31—34. Had they known all that would follow, and clearly foreseen his resurrection and his glory, they would then have been troubled the less for his death; but when they saw him die, and foresaw him not revive, and rise, and reign, then did their hearts begin to fail them, and they said, "We trusted that it had been he which should have redeemed Israel," Luke xxiv. 21. Even as we use to lament immoderately, when we lay the bodies of our friends in the grave, because we see not whither the soul is gone, nor in what triumph and joy it is received unto Christ; which if we saw it would moderate our griefs. And

even so we over-pity ourselves and our friends in our temporal sufferings, because we see not whither they tend and what will follow them. We see Job on the dunghill, but look not so far as his restoration. "Behold, we count them happy which endure. Ye have heard of the patience of Job, and have seen the end of the Lord; that the Lord is very pitiful, and of tender mercy," Jam. v. 11. There is no judging by the present, but either by staying the end, or believing God's predictions of it.

Use. It is allowable in Christ's disciples to grieve (in faith and moderately) for any departure of his from them: they that have had the comfort of communion with him in a life of faith and grace, must needs lament any loss of that communion. It is sad with such a soul, when Christ seemeth strange, or when they pray and seek, and seem not to be heard. It is sad with a believer when he must say, I had once access to the Father by the Son; I had helps in prayer, and I had the lively operations of the Spirit of grace, and some of the joy of the Holy Ghost; but now, alas, it is not so. And they that have had experience of the fruit and comfort of his word, and ordinances, and discipline, and the communion of saints, may be allowed to lament the loss of this, if he take it from them. It was no unseemly thing in David, when he was driven from the tabernacle of God, to make that lamentation, "As the hart panteth after the water-brooks, so panteth my soul after thee, O God. My soul thirsteth for God, for the living God: when shall I come and appear before God? My tears have been my meat day and night, while they continually say unto me, Where is thy God? O my God, my soul is cast down within me," Psalm xlii.; xliii. And, "My soul longeth, yea, even fainteth for the courts of the Lord: my heart and my flesh crieth out for the living God. Yea, the sparrow hath found an house, and the swallow a nest," &c. "Blessed are they that dwell in thy house: they will be still praising thee. For a day in thy courts is better than a thousand. I had rather be a door-keeper in the house of my God, than to dwell in the tents of wickedness," Psal. lxxxiv. 2—4, 10. It signifieth ill when men can easily let Christ go, or lose his word, or helps and ordinances. When sin provoketh him to hide his face, and withdraw his mercies, if we can senselessly let them go, it is a contempt which provoketh him much more. If we are indifferent what he giveth us, it is just with him to be indifferent too, and to set as little by our helps and happiness as we set by them ourselves. But we little know the misery which such contempt prepareth for: "Be thou instructed, O Jerusalem, lest my soul depart from thee; lest I make thee desolate, a land not inhabited," Jer. vi. 8. "Yea, woe also unto them when I depart from them," Hos. ix. 12. When God goeth, all goeth; grace and peace, help and hope, and all that is good and comfortable, is gone, when God is gone. Wonder not, therefore, if holy souls cry after God, and fear the loss of his grace and ordinances; and if they lament the loss of that, which dead-hearted sensualists are weary of, (Luke viii. 37,) and would drive away; it will be the damning sentence, (Matt. xxv. 41,) "Depart from me, all ye workers of iniquity," Luke xiii. 27; Matt. vii. 23. And, therefore, all that is but like it, is terrible to them that have any regard of God or their salvation.

Doct. 3. The sorrows of Christ's disciples are but short. It is but now that they have sorrow: and how quickly will this now be gone!

Reas. 1. Life itself is but short, and, therefore, the sorrows of this life are but short. "Man that is born of a woman is of few days, and full of trouble. He cometh forth like a flower, and is cut down: he fleeth also as a shadow, and continueth not," Job xiv. 1, 2. Though our days are evil, they are but few, Gen. xlvii. 9. As our time maketh haste, and posteth away, so also do our sorrows, which will attain their period together with our lives. As the pleasure of sin, so the sufferings of the godly, are but for a season, Heb. xi. 25. "Now, for a season, if need be, ye are in heaviness through manifold temptations," 1 Pet. i. 6. The pleasures and the pains of so short a life, are but like a pleasant or a frightful dream; how quickly shall we awake, and all is vanished! If we lived as long as they did before the flood, then worldly interest, prosperity, and adversity, would be of greater signification to us, and yet they should seem nothing in comparison of eternity: for where now are all the fleshly pains or pleasures of Adam or Methuselah? Much more are they inconsiderable in so short a life as one of ours. Happy is the man whose sorrows are of no longer continuance than this short and transitory life!

Reas. 2. God's displeasure with his servants is but short, and, therefore, his corrections are but short. Psal. xxx. 5, "His anger endureth but for a moment, but in his favour is life." Isa. liv. 7, 8, "For a small moment have I forsaken thee; but with great mercy will I gather thee. In a little wrath I hid my face from thee for a moment; but with everlasting kindness will I have mercy on thee, saith the Lord thy Redeemer." Isa. xxvi. 20, "Come, my people, enter into thy chambers, and shut thy doors about thee: hide thyself as it were for a little moment, until the indignation be overpast." Thus even in judgment doth he remember mercy, and consumeth us not, because his compassions fail not, Lam. iii. "He will not always chide, nor will he keep his anger for ever. For he knoweth our frame; he remembereth that we are dust," Psal. ciii. 9, 14. His short corrections are purposely fitted to prepare us for endless consolations.

Reas. 3. Our trial also must be but short, and, therefore, so must be our sorrows. Though God will not have us receive the crown without the preparation of a conflict and a conquest, yet will he not have our fight and race too long, lest it overmatch our strength, and his grace, and we should be overcome. Though our faith and we must be tried in the fire, yet God will see that the furnace be not over-hot, and that we stay no longer but till our dross be separated from us, 1 Pet. i. 6, 7, 9. God putteth us not into the fire to consume us, but to refine us, (Psal. cxix. 67, 75,) that when we come out we may say, (Psal. cxxix. 1—3,) "It is good for us that we were afflicted," Psal. cxix. 71; Isa. xlix. 13; and then he will save the afflicted people, Psal. xviii. 27.

Reas. 4. The power of those that afflict God's servants wrongfully, is but short; and, therefore, the sorrows of such affliction can be but short. Though it be foreign churches of whom I speak, I hope it is to such as take their case to be to them as their own. While they are breathing out threatenings, they are ready to breathe out their guilty souls. If a man in a dropsy or consumption persecute us, we would not be over-fearful of him, because we see he is a dying man. And so little is the distance between the death of one man and another, that we may well say, All men's lives are in a consumption, and may bear their indignation, as we would do the injuries of a dying man. How short is the day of the power of darkness! Christ calleth it but an hour; "This is your hour, and the power of darkness," Luke xxii. 53. How quickly was Herod eaten of worms, and many another cut off in the height of their prosperity when they have been raging in the heat of persecution! Little thought Ahab that he had been so near his woeful day, when he had given order that Micaiah should be fed with the bread and water of affliction, till he returned in peace. What persecutions have the death of a Licinius, a Julian, a Queen Mary, &c. shortened! While they are raging they are dying; while they are condemning the just, they are going to be condemned by their most just avenger. How quickly will their corpses be laid in dust, and their condemned souls be put under the chains of darkness, till the judgment of the great and dreadful day! 2 Pet. ii. 4. He is not only an unbeliever, but irrational or inconsiderate, that cannot see their end, (Jude 6,) in the greatest of their glory. How easy is it to see these bubbles vanishing, and to foresee the sad and speedy period of all their cruelties and triumphs! "Knowest thou not this of old, since man was placed upon earth, that the triumphing of the wicked is short, and the joy of the hypocrite but for a moment? Though his excellency mount up to the heavens, and his head reach unto the clouds; yet he shall perish for ever like his own dung: they which have seen him shall say, Where is he? He shall fly away as a dream, and shall not be found: yea, he shall be chased away as a vision of the night. The eye also which saw him shall see him no more; neither shall his place behold him," Job xx. 4—9. Though pride do compass them about as a chain, and violence cover them as a garment, and they are corrupt, and speak oppression, or calumny, wickedly, they speak loftily, or from on high. Though they set their mouth against the heavens, and their tongue walketh through the earth, yet surely they are set in slippery places. God doth cast them down into destruction. How are they brought into desolation as in a moment! They are utterly consumed with terrors: as a dream [a] from one that awaketh; so, O Lord, in awaking, (or rising up, that is, saith the Chaldee paraphrase, in thy day of judging, or as all the other translations, *in civitate tua*, in thy kingdom or government,) thou shalt despise their image, that is, show them and all the world how despicable that image of greatness, and power, and felicity was which they were so proud of. If such a bubble [b] of vain-glory, such an image of felicity, such a dream of power and greatness, be all that the church of God hath to be afraid of, it may be well said, "Cease ye from man, whose breath is in his nostrils: [c] for wherein is he to be accounted of?" Isa. ii. 22. "His breath goeth forth, he returneth to his earth; in that very day his thoughts perish," Psa. cxlvi. 4. And, "Behold, the Lord God will help me, who is he that shall condemn me? lo, they all shall wax old as a garment; the moth shall eat them up," Isa. l. 9. And, "Hearken unto me, ye that know righteousness, the people in whose heart is my law; fear ye not the reproach of men, neither be ye afraid of their revilings. For the moth shall eat them up like a garment, and the worm shall eat them like wool: but my righteousness shall be for ever, and my salvation from generation to generation," Isa. li. 7, 8. The sorrows which so short-lived power can inflict, can be but short. You read of their victories and persecutions in the news-books one year, and quickly after of their death.

Use 1. Hence, therefore, you may learn how injudicious they are, that think religion is disparaged by such short and small afflictions of believers; and how inexcusable they are who yield unto temptation, and venture upon sin, and comply with the ungodly, and forsake the truth, through the fear of so short and momentary sorrows, when there is none of them but would endure the prick of a pin, or the scratch of a brier, or the biting of a flea, to gain a kingdom, or the opening of a vein, or the griping of a purge, to save their lives. Oh! how deservedly are ungodly men forsaken of God! for how short a pleasure do they forsake him, and the everlasting pleasures! And how short a trouble do they avoid by running into everlasting trouble! If sin had not first subdued reason, men would never make it a matter of question, whether to escape so small a suffering they should break the laws of the most righteous God; nor would they once put so short a pain or pleasure into the balance against the endless pain and pleasure; nor would a temptation bring them to deliberate on a matter, which should be past deliberation with a man that is in his wits. And yet, alas! how much do these short concernments prevail through all the world! Unbelievers are short-sighted, they look only or chiefly to things near and present. A lease of this empty world for a few years, yea, an uncertain tenure of it, is preferred before the best security for eternal life. Its present pleasures which they must have, and its present sorrows which they take care to escape. As Christ hath taught us to say about these worldly things, so the devil hath taught them to say about everlasting things, "Care not for to-morrow, for the morrow shall take thought for the things of itself: sufficient to the day is the evil thereof," Matt. vi. 34. Therefore when the day of their calamity shall come, a despairing conscience will perpetually torment them, and say, This is but the sorrow which thou chosest to endure, or the misery which thou wouldst venture on, to escape a present inconsiderable pain.

If there be any of you that shall think that present sufferings are considerable things, to be put into the scales against eternity, or that are tempted to murmuring and impatience under such short afflictions, I desire them but to consider, 1. That your suffering will be no longer than your sin. And if it endure but as long, is it any matter of wonder or repining? Can you expect to keep your sickness, and yet to be wholly freed from the pain? Can sin and suffering be perfectly separated? Do you think to continue ignorant, and proud, and selfish, and in so much remaining unbelief, carnality, worldliness, and sloth, and yet never to feel the rod or spur, nor suffer any more than if you had been innocent? Deceive not yourselves, it will not be. Sin lieth at the door, and be sure at last it will find you out, Gen. iv. 7; Numb. xxxii. 23. "Behold, the righteous shall be recompensed in the earth: much more the ungodly and the sinner," Prov. xi. 31. "Judgment must begin at the house of God, and the righteous are saved with much ado," 1 Pet. iv. 17, 18. God is not reconciled to the sins of any man, and as he will show by his dealings that he is reconciled to their persons, so will he show that he is not reconciled to their sins. If God continue your sufferings any longer than you continue your sin, and if you can truly say, I am afflicted though I am innocent, then your impatience may have some excuse.

2. Your sorrows shall be no longer than you make

[a] Or as Amyraldus Paraphras. Cum olim evigilabunt, præsens eorum felicitas erit instar somnii, quod somno discusso dissipatum est: quin etiam antequam evigilent, in ipsa illa urbe in qua antea florebant vanam istam felicitatis pompam, in qua antea volitabant, reddes contemnendam, tanquam umbram aut imaginem evanescentem; in qua nihil solidi est.

[b] Nubecula est cito evanescit, said Athanasius of Julian.

[c] When Julian's death was told at Antioch, they all cried out, Maxime fatue! ubi sunt vaticinia tua? Vicit Deus et Christus ejus. Abbas Urspargens, page 91.

them necessary, and will you grudge at your own benefit? or at the trouble of your physic while you continue your disease? It is but "if need be, that now for a season, ye are in heaviness through manifold temptations," 1 Pet. i. 6. And who maketh the need? Is it God or you? Who maketh you dull, and slothful, and sensual? Who turneth your hearts to earthly things, and deprives you of the sweetness of things spiritual and heavenly? Who maketh you proud, and unbelieving, and uncharitable? Is it he that doth this, that causeth the need of your afflictions, and is to be blamed for the bitterness of them? But it is your Physician that is to be thanked and praised, for fitting them so wisely to your cure.

3. Your sorrows shall not be so long as you deserve. It is strange ingratitude, for that man to grudge at a short affliction that is saved from everlasting misery, and confesseth he hath deserved the pains of hell. Confess with thankfulness, that "it is his mercy that you are not consumed and condemned, because his compassions fail not. If God be your portion, hope in him; for the Lord is good to them that wait for him, to the soul that seeketh him. It is good that you both hope and quietly wait for the salvation of the Lord. It is good for a man that he bear the yoke in his youth. He sitteth alone and keepeth silence, because he hath borne it upon him. He putteth his mouth in the dust; if so be there may be hope. He giveth his cheek to him that smiteth him: he is filled full with reproach. For the Lord will not cast off for ever: but though he cause grief, yet he will have compassion according to the multitude of his mercies," Lam. iii. 22—32. All that is come upon us is for our evil deeds, and for our great trespasses, and God hath punished us less than our iniquities, Ezra ix. 13.

4. Your sorrows shall not be so long as the sorrows of the ungodly, nor as those that you must endure, if you will choose sin to escape these present sorrows. Abel's sorrow is not so long as Cain's; nor Peter's or Paul's so long as Judas's. If the offering of a more acceptable sacrifice do cost a righteous man his life, alas, wha is that to the punishment that malignant, envious Cainites, or treacherous Judases must endure! What is the worst that man can do, or the most that God will here inflict, to the reprobates' endless, hellish torments! Oh! had you seen what they endure, or had you felt those pains but a day or hour, I can hardly think that you would ever after make so great a matter of the sufferings of a christian here for Christ, or that you would fear such sufferings more than hell. It is disingenuous to repine at so gentle a rod, at the same time whilst millions are in the flames of hell, and when these sufferings tend to keep you thence.

5. Your sorrows shall not be so long as your following joys, if you be persevering, conquering believers. What is a sickness, or a scorn, or a prison, or banishment, or shame, or death, when it must end in the endless joys of heaven? Oh! do but believe these with a lively, sound, effectual faith, and you will make light of all the sufferings in the way. *Nihil crus sentit in nervo*, saith Tertullian, *cum animus est in cœlo*, Heb. xi. 25, 26, &c. The mind that is in heaven, and seeth him that is invisible, will easily bear the body's pains. Mistake not in your accounts, and you will reckon that the sufferings of this present time are not worthy to be compared with the glory which shall be revealed in us, Rom. viii. 18. "For our light affliction, which is but for a moment, doth work for us a far more exceeding and eternal weight of glory; while we look not at the things which are seen, but at the things which are not seen: for the things which are seen are temporal; but the things which are not seen are eternal," 2 Cor. iv. 17, 18.

Use 2. And if it be but for a "now" that you must have sorrows, how reasonable is it that those sorrows be moderated and mixed with joy! And how just are those commands: "Rejoice evermore," 1 Thess. v. 16. "Rejoice and be exceeding glad, for great is your reward in heaven," Matt. v. 10—12. "Rejoicing in hope; patient in tribulation," Rom. xii. 12. How rational was their joy, who being beaten and forbidden to preach, "departed from the presence of the council, rejoicing that they were counted worthy to suffer shame for the name of Christ!" Acts v. 41. "Rejoice, inasmuch as ye are partakers of Christ's sufferings. If ye be reproached for the name of Christ, happy are ye; for the spirit of glory and of God resteth upon you: on their part he is evil spoken of, but on your part he is glorified," 1 Pet. iv. 13, 14. It is a shame to be dejected under a short and tolerable pain, which is so near to the eternal pleasure; and to suffer as if we believed not the end, and so to sorrow as men that are without hope.

Doct. 4. Christ will again visit his sorrowful disciples. He removeth not from them with an intent to cast them off. When he hideth his face, he meaneth not to forsake them. When he taketh away any ordinances or mercies, he doth not give them a bill of divorce. When he seemeth to yield to the powers of darkness, he is not overcome, nor will he give up his kingdom or interest in the world. When he letteth the boar into his vineyard, it is not to make it utterly desolate, or turn it common to the barren wilderness: for,

1. He hath conquered the greatest enemies already, and therefore there remaineth none to conquer him. He hath triumphed over Satan, death, and hell: he hath conquered sin, and what is there left to depose him from his dominion?

2. He retaineth still his relation to his servants; whether he be corporally present or absent, he knoweth his own; and it is their care also that, whether present or absent, they may be accepted of him, 2 Cor. v. 7—9. He is their Head while they are suffering on earth; and therefore he feeleth their sufferings and infirmities, Heb. iv. 15. And hence it is that he thus rebuketh a persecuting zealot, "Saul, Saul, why persecutest thou me?" Acts ix. 4.

3. He hath not laid by the least measure of his love; he loveth us in heaven as much as he did on earth: "Having loved his own which were in the world, to the end he loved them," John xiii. 1. And as Joseph's love could not long permit him to conceal himself from his brethren, but broke out the more violently after a short restraint, so that he fell on their necks and wept; so will not the more tender love of Christ permit him long to hide his face, or estrange himself from the people of his love; and when he returneth, it will be with redoubled expressions of endearment.

4. His covenant with his servants is still in force; his promises are sure, and shall never be broken, though the performance be not so speedy as we desire. "Know therefore that the Lord thy God, he is God, the faithful God, which keepeth covenant and mercy with them that love him and keep his commandments to a thousand generations; and repayeth them that hate him to their face to destroy them: he will not be slack to him that hateth him, he will repay him to his face," Deut. vii. 9, 10. "He keepeth covenant and mercy with his servants that walk before him with all their heart," 1 Kings viii. 23; Dan. ix. 4; Neh. i. 5; ix. 32. And it is the promise of Christ when he departed from his servants, that "He will come again, and take them to himself; that

where he is, there they may be also, John xiv. 3; xii. 26.

5. His own interest, and honour, and office, and preparations, do engage him to return to his disconsolate flock: his jewels and peculiar treasure are his interest, Mal. iii. 17; 1 Pet. ii. 9; Exod. xix. 5. He that hath chosen but a little flock, (Luke xii. 32,) and confined his interest and treasure into such a narrow compass, will not forsake that little flock, but secure them to his kingdom. He that hath made it his office to redeem and save them, and hath so dearly bought them, and gone so far in the work of their salvation, will lose none of all his cost and preparations; but for his people, and his blood, and his honour, and his Father's will, and love, will certainly finish what he hath undertaken. And, therefore, his withdrawings shall not be everlasting.

6. It is for their sakes that he withdraweth for a time; though the bitter part be for their sin, it is intended as medicinal for their benefit: sometimes he doth it to awake and humble them, and stir them up to seek him, and call after him; to show them what they have done in provoking him to withdraw and hide his face, that renewed repentance may prepare them for the comforts of his return. Sometimes he hath such work for them to do, which is not so agreeable to his presence; as fasting, and mourning, and confessing him in sufferings, Matt. ix. 15. And sometimes he hath comforts of another kind to give them in his seeming absence. "I tell you the truth; it is expedient for you that I go away: for if I go not away, the Comforter will not come unto you; but if I depart, I will send him to you," John xvi. 7. As there were comforts which the disciples were fittest for in Christ's bodily absence, so when he will take away his ordinances, or our prosperity, or friends, there are comforts of another sort, in secret communion with him, and in suffering for him, which his people may expect; not that any can expect it, who, on that pretence, do reject these ordinances and mercies, no more than the disciples could have expected the Comforter, if they had rejected the corporal presence of Christ; but God hath such supplies for those that mourn for his departure.

Use 1. Misunderstand not then the departings of your Lord. It is too bad to say with the evil servant, "My Lord delayeth his coming;" and worse to say he will never return. 1. He will return at his appointed day to judge the world; to justify his saints, whom the world condemned; to answer the desires, and satisfy all the expectations, of believers; and to comfort, and everlastingly reward, the faithful that have patiently waited his return. And when he returneth with salvation, then shall we also return from our calamities, and shall "discern between the righteous and the wicked, between him that served God and him that served him not," Mal. iii. 18. Undoubtedly our "Redeemer liveth, and shall stand at the latter day upon the earth: and though after our skin worms devour these bodies, yet in our flesh we shall see God," Job xix. 25, 26. "Behold, he cometh with clouds; and every eye shall see him, and they also which pierced him: and all kindreds of the earth shall wail because of him. Even so. Amen," Rev. i. 7. Though unbelieving scoffers shall say, "Where is the promise of his coming?" 2 Pet. iii. 4; yet believers consider, "That a day is with the Lord as a thousand years, and a thousand years but as a day; and that the Lord is not slack of his promise, but long-suffering," ver. 8, 9. "He will not leave us comfortless, but will come unto us," John xiv. 18. The patient expectation of the just shall not be forgotten, nor in vain, Psal. ix. 18. "Seeing it is a righteous thing with God to recompense tribulation to them that trouble you; and to you who are troubled rest with us, when the Lord Jesus shall be revealed from heaven with his mighty angels, in flaming fire taking vengeance on them that know not God, and that obey not the gospel of our Lord Jesus Christ: who shall be punished with everlasting destruction from the presence of the Lord, and from the glory of his power; when he shall come to be glorified in his saints, and admired in all them that believe in that day," 2 Thess. i. 6—10.

2. And he will return also to the seemingly forsaken flocks of his disciples. He hath his times of trial, when the shepherds being smitten, the sheep are scattered; and he hath his times of gathering the scattered ones again together, and "giving them pastors after his own heart, that shall feed them with knowledge and understanding," Jer. iii. 15. And shall say, "What is the chaff unto the wheat?" Jer. xxiii. 28. When we cry, "Woe is me for my hurt! my wound is grievous;" we must also say, "Truly this is a grief, and I must bear it. My tabernacle is spoiled, and all my cords are broken: my children are gone forth of me, and they are not: there is none to stretch forth my tent any more, and to set up my curtains. For the pastors are become brutish, and have not sought the Lord. O Lord, correct me, but with judgment; not in thine anger, lest thou bring me to nothing," Jer. x. 19—21, 24. "Many pastors have destroyed my vineyard, they have trodden my portion under-foot, they have made my pleasant portion a desolate wilderness: and being desolate it mourneth to me; the whole land is made desolate, because no man layeth it to heart," Jer. xii. 10, 11. But "woe be unto the pastors that destroy and scatter the sheep of my pasture! saith the Lord. Therefore thus saith the Lord against the pastors that feed my people; Ye have scattered my flock, and driven them away, and have not visited them: behold, I will visit upon you the evil of your doings, and I will gather the remnant of my flock. And I will set up shepherds over them which shall feed them: and they shall fear no more, nor be dismayed, neither shall they be lacking, saith the Lord," Jer. xxiii. 1—4. "Woe to the shepherds of Israel that feed themselves! should not the shepherds feed the flocks? Ye eat the fat, and clothe you with the wool, ye kill them that are fed: but ye feed not the flock. The diseased have ye not strengthened, neither have ye healed that which was sick, neither have ye bound up that which was broken, neither have ye brought again that which was driven away, neither have ye sought that which was lost; but with force and with cruelty have ye ruled them. Thus saith the Lord; Behold, I am against the shepherds; and I will require my flock at their hand, and cause them to cease from feeding the flock; neither shall the shepherds feed themselves any more; for I will deliver my flock from their mouth. Behold, I, even I, will both search my sheep, and seek them out; and will deliver them out of all places where they have been scattered in the cloudy and dark day. And as for you, O my flock, Behold, I judge between cattle and cattle, between the rams and the he-goats. Is it a small thing to you to have eaten up the good pasture, but ye must tread down with your feet the residue of your pastures? and to have drunk of the deep waters, but you must foul the residue with your feet? And as for my flock, they eat that which you have trodden with your feet; and they drink that which ye have fouled with your feet. Therefore thus saith the Lord God unto them; Behold, I, even I, will judge between the fat cattle and the lean. Because ye have thrust with side and with shoulder, and pushed all the diseased

with your horns, till ye have scattered them abroad," &c. Ezek. xxxiv. Read the rest. Particular churches may be scattered to dissolution, but none of the faithful members.

3. And Christ hath his returning time, to the souls of his servants which seem to be forsaken by him: "Weeping may endure for a night, but joy cometh in the morning," Psal. xxx. 5. When he seemeth their enemy, and writeth bitter things against them, he is their surest Friend, and will justify them himself from their accusers. Though they may be troubled when they remember God, and their spirit be overwhelmed in them, and their souls refuse to be comforted, and say, Will the Lord cast off for ever? and will he be favourable no more? Is his mercy clean gone for ever? Doth his promise fail for evermore? Hath God forgotten to be gracious? Hath he in anger shut up his tender mercies? Yet must we rebuke this unbelief, and say, This is my infirmity; I will remember the works of the Lord: surely I will remember thy wonders of old. I will meditate of thy works, and talk of thy doings, Psal. lxxvii. The long night that hath no day, the long winter that hath no summer, is the reward of the ungodly; but light ariseth to the righteous in his darkness, and joy to them that are upright in heart, Psal. cxii. 4. Light is sown for them, and in season will spring up, Psal. xcvii. 11. The righteousness which was hid from the world by false accusations, and from ourselves by the terrors and mistakes of darkness, will God "bring forth as light, and our judgment as the noon-day," Psal. xxxvii. 6. Our eclipse will vanish when the sun returneth, and our sins no longer interpose: and though all our inquiries and complainings have not brought us out of the dark, yet "God is the Lord who showeth us light," Psal. cxviii. 27; and "in his light we shall see light," Psal. xxxvi. 9. Say then, O distrustful, trembling christian, "Why art thou cast down, O my soul? and why art thou thus disquieted within me? hope thou in God: for I shall yet praise him, who is the health of my countenance, and my God," Psal. xlii. 5, 11; xliii. 5. Though now you go mourning because of the oppression of the enemy, God will send out his light and truth, and they shall lead you, and bring you to his holy hill and tabernacle: and then you shall go with praise to the altar of God, even of God your exceeding joy, Psal. xliii. 2—4.

Use 2. Learn, then, how to behave yourselves in the absence of your Lord, till his return. If you ask me how;—Answer, 1. Be not contented and pleased with his absence. You must bear it, but not desire it. Else you are either enemies, or children that have run themselves into such guilt and fears, that they take their father for their enemy. 2. Nay, be not too indifferent and insensible of your Lord's departure. Love is not regardless of the company of our Beloved. He may well take it ill, when you can let him go, and be as merry without him as if his absence were no loss to you. If you care no more for him, he will make you care, before you shall feel the comforts of his presence. Such contempt is the way to a worse forsaking: call after him till he return, if he hide his face. 3. Turn not aside to the creature for content; and seek not to make up the loss of his presence with any of the deceitful comforts of the world. Let him not see you take another in his stead, as if riches, or power, or worldly friends, or fleshly pleasure, would serve your turn instead of Christ. If once you come to this, he may justly leave you to your vain contents, and let them serve your turn as long as they can, and see how well they will supply his room. Oh! see that no idol be admitted into his place till Christ return. 4. Be not imboldened, by his absence, to sin. Say not as the evil servant, in your hearts, My Lord delayeth his coming, and so begin to smite your fellow-servants, and to eat and drink with the drunken, lest your Lord come in a day when you look not for him, and cut you asunder, and appoint your portion with the hypocrites: there shall be weeping and gnashing of teeth, Matt. xxiv. 48—51. Because Christ cometh not to judge the wicked as soon as they have sinned, they are imboldened to sin more fearlessly: and "because sentence against an evil work is not speedily executed, therefore the hearts of the sons of men are fully set in them to do evil," Eccles. viii. 11. But, "behold, the Judge is at the door," Jam. v. 9. He that cometh will not tarry; and for all these things you must come to judgment, Eccles. xi. 9; xii. 14. 5. Be not discouraged by your Lord's delay, but wait his coming in faith and patience. Can you not wait for him so short a time? Oh! how quickly will it be accomplished! Sink not into despondency of mind. Be not dismayed in the duties or sufferings to which you are called. "Lift up the hands that hang down, and the feeble knees; and make straight paths for your feet, lest that which is lame be turned out of the way; but let it rather be healed," Heb. xii. 12, 13. "Be stedfast, unmoveable, always abounding in the work of the Lord, forasmuch as ye know that your labour is not in vain in the Lord," 1 Cor. xv. 58. "Be sober, and hope unto the end," 1 Pet. i. 13. "Ye are the house of Christ, if ye hold fast the confidence and the rejoicing of the hope firm unto the end," Heb. iii. 6, 14; vi. 11. "Ye have need of patience, that having done the will of God, ye may inherit the promises," Heb. x. 36.

Doct. 5. When Christ shall again appear to his disciples, their sorrows shall be turned into joy: when Christ returneth, joy returneth. Saith David, (Psal. xxx. 7,) "Thou didst hide thy face, and I was troubled." But, (ver. 11, 12,) "Thou hast turned for me my mourning into dancing: thou hast put off my sackcloth, and girded me with gladness; to the end that my glory may sing praise to thee, and not be silent. O Lord my God, I will give thanks unto thee for ever." When the sun ariseth it is day, and its approach dispelleth the winter frosts, and reviveth the almost dying creatures, and calleth up the life which was hidden in the seed, or retired unto the root. After a sharp and spending winter, how quickly doth the sun's return recover the verdure and beauty of the earth, and clothe it in green, and spangle it with the ornaments of odoriferous flowers, and enrich it with sweet and plenteous fruits! the birds, that were either hid or silent, appear and sing, and the face of all things is changed into joy. So is it with the poor deserted soul, upon the return of Christ: unbelieving doubts and fears then vanish; the garments of sadness are laid aside, and those of gladness are put on; the language of distrust and despairing lamentations are first turned into words of peace, and then into joyful thankfulness and praise. The soul that was skilled in no spiritual discourse, but complaining of a dead and frozen heart, of dull, and cold, and lifeless duties, is now taken up in the rehearsals of the works of infinite love, and searching into the mysteries of redemption, and reciting the great and precious promises, and magnifying the name and grace of its Redeemer, and expatiating in the praises of the everlasting kingdom, the heavenly glory, the blessed society, and especially of the Lamb, and of the eternal God. You would not think that this is the same person, that lately could scarce think well of God;

or that dwelt in tears, and dust, and darkness, and could think of nothing but sin and hell, and from every text and every providence, concluded nothing, but undone, or damned. Would you think this joyful, thankful soul, were the same that lately was crying on the cross, "My God, my God, why hast thou forsaken me?" that could find nothing written on the tables of his heart, but forsaken, miserable, and undone; that daily cried out, It is too late, there is no hope, I had a day of grace, but it is past and gone. When Christ returneth, and causeth his face to shine upon them, all this is turned into praise, and honour, and glory, unto the Lamb, and to the almighty and most holy God, that liveth for ever, and is the everlasting joy and portion of his saints. And, sooner or later, thus will it be with all the upright, that wait on God in the day of trial, and deal not falsely in his covenant. The Son who was brought up with the Father, and was daily his delight, rejoicing always before him, rejoicing also in the habitable parts of the earth, whose delights were with the sons of men, doth bless the children of Wisdom with a participation of his delights; for "blessed are they that keep his ways."—"Blessed is the man that heareth him, watching daily at his gates, waiting at the posts of his doors: for he that findeth him findeth life, and shall obtain favour of the Lord," Prov. viii. 30—36. Though Christ had left his disciples so lately under fears and trouble, guilty of deserting him, and seemingly now deserted by him, yet early on the third day he ariseth for their consolation, and presently sendeth them these joyful words, in the first speech he uttereth, and that by a woman that had been sorrowful and a sinner: "Go to my brethren, and say unto them, I ascend to my Father, and your Father; and to my God, and your God," John xx. 17. Those that his ministers have long been comforting in vain, when Christ returneth he will revive and comfort them in a moment, and with a word. The soul that now crieth, Oh it is impossible, it will never be, doth little know how easy it is with Christ. It is but saying, "Lazarus, arise;" or, "Let there be light," and there will be life and light immediately at his command.

2. And so when he restoreth his ordinances and order to a forsaken church, and restoreth their holy opportunities and advantages of grace, what gladness and praising their Redeemer will there be! As it was with the churches upon the death of Julian, and after the heathen and the Arian persecutions, in the happy reign of Constantine, Theodosius, Marcian, &c. How joyfully did the English exiles return to worship God in their native land, upon the death of queen Mary; and see the fall of Bonner and Gardiner, that had sacrificed so many holy christians in the flames! How gladly did they grow in the soil that was manured with the blood and ashes of their faithful brethren, and reap the fruit of their fortitude and sufferings! When Christ whipped the buyers and sellers out of the temple, and would not let them make the house of prayer a place of merchandise, what hosannahs were sounded in Jerusalem! Matt. xxi. 15, 16. "When the salvation of Israel cometh out of Zion, and the Lord bringeth back the captivity of his people, Jacob shall rejoice, and Israel shall be glad," Psal. xiv. 7. "Blessed are they that dwell in his house; for they will be still praising him. For a day in his courts is better than a thousand," Psal. lxxxiv. 4, 10. "Blessed is the people that know the joyful sound: they shall walk, O Lord, in the light of thy countenance. In thy name shall they rejoice all the day: and in thy righteousness shall they be exalted. For the Lord is our defence; and the Holy One of Israel is our King," Psal. lxxxix. 15—18. What gladness was there at a private meeting of a few christians that met to pray for Peter, when they saw him delivered and come among them! Acts xii. 12; v. 14. When the churches had rest, they were edified, and walked in the fear of the Lord, and in the comfort of the Holy Ghost, Acts ix. 31.

3. But the great joy will be when Christ returneth in his glory at the last day. What a multitude of sorrows will then be ended! And what a multitude of souls will then be comforted! What a multitude of desires, and prayers, and expectations will then be answered! How many thousand that have sowed in tears, shall then reap in everlasting joy! When the creature shall be delivered from the bondage of corruption, into the glorious liberty of the sons of God, Rom. viii. 26, 27. When all the faith, and labour, and patience of all the saints from the beginning of the world, shall be rewarded with the rivers of celestial pleasure, and the just shall enter into their Master's joy, Matt. xxv. 21.

That you may the better understand the sweetness of all these sorts of joy, which Christ's return will bring to saints, observe these following ingredients in them.

1. It is Christ himself that is the object of their joy: he that is the dearly beloved of their souls; that for their sakes was made a man of sorrows: it is he who is their hope and help; with whom they are in covenant as their only Saviour; in whom they have trusted, with whom they have deponed their souls. If he should fail them, all would fail them; and they were of all men most miserable: they would be comfortless if he should not come unto them, and were not their comfort. The world cannot help and comfort them, for it is empty, vain, a transient shadow: it will not, for it is malignant, and our professed enemy. For we know that we are of God, and the whole world is *in maligno positus*, set on wickedness, (or as some think, because ὁ πονηρός is put for the devil in the foregoing verse, and the article here also used,) is as it were planted into the devil, or put under the devil, to war against Christ and the holy seed; and indeed Satan seemeth in this war against the church, to have somewhat like success as he had against Christ himself: as Christ must be a man of sorrows and scorn, and be crucified as a blasphemer and a traitor, before he rejoice the hearts of his disciples by his resurrection; so the church was a persecuted, scorned handful of men, for the first three hundred years, and then it rose by christian emperors to some reputation, till Satan, by another game, overcame them by Judas's successors: that, for "What will you give me," by pride and worldliness betrayed them into that deplorable state, in which they have continued these 900 years at least: so that the christian name is confined to a sixth part of the world; and serious, sanctified believers are persecuted more by the hypocrites that wear the livery of Christ, than by heathens and infidels themselves. And when the church is so low, almost like Christ on the cross and the grave, will not a resurrection be a joyful change? When it crieth out on the cross, "My God, my God, why hast thou forsaken me?" will not Christ appearing for its deliverance be a welcome sight?

It was when Adam had brought a curse on himself and his posterity, and all the earth, that redemption by the holy seed was promised; and when Satan had conquered man, that Christ was promised to conquer him. It was when the world was destroyed by the deluge, that its reparation was promised to Noah. It was when Abraham was a sojourner in a strange land, that the peculiar promises were made to him and his seed. It was when the Israelites were enslaved to extremity, that they were delivered.

And it was when the sceptre was departing from Judah, and they and the world were gone from God, that Christ the Light of the world was sent. And when the Son of man cometh, shall he find faith on the earth? When we see how vast the heathen and infidel kingdoms are, and what a poor despised people those are that set their chief hopes on heaven; and how Satan seemeth every where to prevail against them, and most by false and worldly christians, what a trial is this to our faith and hope! As the disciples said of a crucified Christ, We trusted it had been he that should have redeemed Israel; we are almost ready in the hour of temptation to say, We trusted that God's name should have been hallowed, and his kingdom come, and his will be done on earth as it is in heaven. And oh, how seasonable and how joyful will the church's resurrection be after such low and sad distress! Many a sad christian under the sentence of death, is going hence with fear and trouble; when a moment shall transmit them into the joyful presence of their Lord, and the possession of that which with weakness and fear they did but believe.

2. And Christ will not come or be alone: with him will come the new Jerusalem: he will put glory on each member, but much more on the whole. Oh how many of our old companions are now there! not under temptation, or any of the tempter's power; not under the darkness of ignorance, error, or unbelief; not under the pains of a languid, diseased, corruptible body; not under the fear of sin, or Satan, or wicked men; not under the terror of death or hell, of an accusing conscience, or the wrath of God. Oh, with what joy shall we see and enjoy that glorious society! To be translated thither from such a world as this, from such temptations, sins, such fears and sorrows, such perfidious, malignant wickedness, what will it be but to be taken as from a gaol unto a kingdom, and from the suburbs of hell unto the communion of blessed saints and angels, and into the joy of our Lord!

Doct. 6. Your joy shall no man take from you: the joy that cometh at Christ's return will be a secure, everlasting joy; impregnable as heaven itself. Christ and his church will be crucified no more. Look not then for Christ or his church in the grave. He is not here; he is risen. Who can we fear will deprive us of that joy?

1. Not ourselves; and then we need to fear no other: our folly and sin is our enemies' strength; they can do nothing against us without ourselves. The arrows that wound us are all feathered from our own wings. But our trying time will then be past, and confirmation will be the reward of conquest. He that hath kept us in the day of our trial, will keep us in our state of rest and triumph. How the (now) fallen angels came to lose their first innocency and welfare, is unknown to us: but we have a promise of being for ever with Christ.

2. Nor shall devils deprive us of that joy: neither by those malicious temptations wherewith they now molest and haunt us; nor by the unhappy advantages which we have given them by our sin, to corrupt our imaginations, and thoughts, and affections, or to disturb our passions, or pervert our understandings. Nor by any terror or violence to molest us.

3. Nor shall any men take from us that joy. The blessed will increase it; their joy will be ours: and the wicked will be utterly disabled; they will be miserable themselves in hell. They will no more endanger us by flattering temptations; nor terrify us by threats; nor tread us down by their power; no hurt us in their malice; nor render us odious by false accusations; nor triumph over us with pride and false reproach. They that said of the church, as of Christ, "He trusted in God; let him deliver him now, if he will have him: for he hath said, I am the Son of God," Matt. xxvii. 43; they shall see that God hath delivered his church, and he will have it.

Use 1. And will not a firm belief of all this rejoice the soul under all disappointments and sufferings on earth? And doth not our dejectedness and want of joy declare the sinful weakness of our faith? O sirs, our sadness, our impatience, our small desire to be with Christ, the little comfort that we fetch from heaven, do tell us, that christianity, and a life of faith, is a harder work than most imagine; and the art, and form, and words of holiness, are much more common than a holy, heavenly mind and life. Christ speaketh many words of pity to his servants under sorrows and sinking grief, which some mistake for words of approbation or command. "Why are ye afraid, O ye of little of faith?" were words both of compassion and reproof. I am sure the great unbelief that appeareth in much of our dejectedness and sorrow, deserveth more reproof than our sufferings deserve to be entertained with those sorrows.

Use 2. I will therefore take my farewell of you, in advising and charging you as from God, that you be not deceived by a flattering world, nor dejected by a frowning world; but place your hopes on those joys which no man can take from you. If you cannot trust the love of God, and the grace and promises of our Saviour, and the witness of the Holy Spirit, you must despair; for there is no other trust.

So many of you seem to have chosen this good part, the one thing necessary, which shall never be taken from you; that in the midst of our sorrows, I must profess that I part with you with thankfulness and joy. And I will tell you for what I am so thankful, that you may know what I would have you be for the time to come.

I. I thank the Lord, that chose for me so comfortable a station, even a people whom he purposed to bless.

II. I thank the Lord that I have not laboured among you in vain; and that he opened the hearts of so great a number of yours, to receive his word with a teachable and willing mind.

III. I thank the Lord that he hath made so many of you as helpful to your neighbours in your place, as I have been in mine; and that you have not been uncharitable to the souls of others, but have with great success endeavoured the good of all.

IV. I rejoice that God hath kept you humble, that you have not been addicted to proud ostentation of your gifts or wisdom, nor inclined to invade any part of the sacred office, but to serve God in the capacity where he hath placed you.

V. I rejoice that God hath made you unanimous, and kept out sects, and heresies, and schisms, so that you have served him as with one mind and mouth; and that you have not been addicted to proud wranglings, disputings, and contentions, but have lived in unity, love, and peace, and the practice of known and necessary truths.

VI. I rejoice that your frequent meetings in your houses, spent only in reading, repeating your teacher's sermons, prayer, and praise to God, have had none of those effects which the conventicles of proud opiniators and self-conceited persons use to have; and which have brought even needful converse and godly communication into suspicion, at least with some, that argue against duty from the abuse.

Yea, I rejoice that hereby so much good hath been done by you. You have had above forty years' experience of the great benefit of such well-ordered christian converse, increasing knowledge, quickening holy desires, prevailing with God for marvellous, if not miraculous, answers of your earnest prayers, keeping out errors and sects.

VII. I am glad that you have had the great encouragement of so many sober, godly, able, peaceable ministers, in all that part of the country round about you, and mostly through that and the neighbour countries: men that avoided vain and bitter contentions, that engaged themselves in no sects or factions; that of a multitude, not above two, that I know of, in all our association had ever any hand in wars; but their principles and practices were reconciling and pacificatory: they consented to catechise all their parishioners, house by house, and to live in the peaceable practice of so much church discipline, as good christians of several parties were all agreed in. And you have lived to see what that discipline was, and what were the effects of such agreement.

VIII. I am glad that you were kept from taking the solemn league and covenant, and the engagement, and all consent to the change of the constituted government of this kingdom. I took the covenant myself, of which I repent, and I will tell you why: I never gave it but to one man, (that I remember,) and he professed himself to be a papist physician newly turned protestant, and he came to me to give it him: I was persuaded that he took it in false dissimulation, and it troubled me to think what it was to draw multitudes of men by carnal interest so falsely to take it; and I kept it, and the engagement, from being taken in your town and country. At first it was not imposed, but taken by volunteers; but after that it was made a test of such as were to be trusted or accepted. Besides the illegality, there are two things that cause me to be against it.

1. That men should make a mere dividing engine, and pretend it a means of unity. We all knew at that time when it was imposed, that a great part, if not the greatest, of church and kingdom were of another mind; and that as learned and worthy men were for prelacy, as most the world had, (such as Usher, Morton, Hall, Davenant, Brownrig, &c.) And to make our terms of union to be such, as should exclude so many and such men, was but to imitate those church-dividers and persecutors, who in many countries and ages, have still made their own impositions the engines of division, by pretence of union. And it seemeth to accuse Christ, as if he had not sufficiently made us terms of concord, but we must devise our own forms as necessary thereto.

2. And it was an imposing on the providence of God, to tie ourselves by vows to that as unchangeable, which we knew not but God might after change, as if we had been the masters of his providence. No man then knew but that God might so alter many circumstances, as might make some things sins, that were then taken for duty; and some things to be duty, which then passed for sin. And when such changes come, we that should have been content with God's obligations, do find ourselves insnared in our own rash vows.

And I wish that it teach no other men the way of dividing impositions, either to cut the knot, or to be even with the covenanters.

IX. I greatly rejoice that family religion is so conscionably kept up among you, that your children and apprentices seem to promise us a hopeful continuation of piety among you.

X. And I thank God that so great a number of persons, eminent for holiness, temperance, humility, and charity, are safely got to heaven already, since I first came among you; and being escaped from the temptations and troubles of this present evil world, have left you the remembrance of their most imitable examples.

And having all this comfort in you, as to what is past, I shall once more leave you some of my counsels and requests, for the time to come, which I earnestly entreat you not to neglect.

I. Spend most of your studies in confirming your belief of the truth of the gospel, the immortality of the soul, and the life to come, and in exercising that belief, and laying up your treasure in heaven: and see that you content not yourselves in talking of heaven, and speaking for it; but that your hopes, your hearts, and your conversation be there; and that you live for it, as worldlings do for the flesh.

II. Flatter not yourselves with the hopes of long life on earth, but make it the sum of all your religion, care, and business, to be ready for a safe and comfortable death; for till you can fetch comfort from the life to come, you can have no comfort that true reason can justify.

III. Live as in a constant war against all fleshly lusts, and love not the world, as it cherisheth those lusts. Take heed of the love of money, as the root of manifold evils: think of riches with more fear than desire; seeing Christ hath told us how hard and dangerous it maketh our way to heaven. When once a man falls deeply in love with riches, he is never to be trusted, but becomes false to God, to all others, and to himself.

IV. Be furnished beforehand with expectation and patience, for all evils that may befall you; and make not too great a matter of sufferings, especially poverty, or wrong from men. It is sin and folly in poor men, that they overvalue riches, and be not thankful for their peculiar blessings. I am in hopes that God will give you more quietness than many others, because there are none of you rich: it is a great means of safety to have nothing that tempteth another man's desire, nor that he envieth you for: despised men live quietly, and he that hath an empty purse, can sing among the robbers; he that lieth on the ground, feareth not falling. When Judea (and so when England by Saxons, Danes, &c.) was conquered, the poor were let alone to possess and till the land, and had more than before. It was the great and rich that were destroyed, or carried or driven away. Is it not a great benefit to have your souls saved from rich men's temptations, and your bodies from the envy, assaults, and fears, and miseries that they are under?

V. Take heed of a self-conceited, unhumbled understanding, and of hasty and rash conclusions: it is the fool that rageth, and is confident; sober men are conscious of so much darkness and weakness, that they are suspicious of their apprehensions: proud self-conceitedness, and rash, hasty concluding, causeth most of the mischiefs in the world; which might be prevented, if men had the humility and patience to stay till things be thoroughly weighed and tried. Be not ashamed to profess uncertainty, where you are indeed uncertain. Humble doubting is much safer than confident erring.

VI. Maintain union and communion with all true christians on earth; and therefore, hold to catholic principles of mere christianity, without which you must needs crumble into sects. Love christians as christians, but the best most; locally separate from none, as accusing of them further than they separate from Christ, or deny you their communion, unless you will sin. The zeal of a sect, as such, is partial, turbulent, hurtful to dissenters, and maketh men as thorns and thistles; but the zeal of christianity, as such, is pure and peaceable, full of mercy and good fruits, mellow, and sweet, and inclineth to the good of all. If God give you a faithful, or a tolerable public minister, be thankful to God, and love, honour, and encourage him; and let not the imperfections of the Common Prayer make you separate from his communion: prejudice will make all modes of worship different from that which we prefer, to seem some heinous, sinful crime; but humble christians are most careful about the frame of their own hearts, and conscious of so much faultiness in themselves, and all their service of God, that they are not apt to accuse and aggravate the failings of others, especially in matters which God has left to our own determination. Whether we shall pray with a book, or without, in divers short prayers, or one long one; whether the people shall sing God's praise in tunes, or speak it in prose, &c. is left to be determined by the general rules of concord, order, and edification. Yet do not withdraw from the comcommunion of sober, godly nonconformists, though falsely called schismatics by others.

VII. Be sure that you maintain due honour and subjection to your governors: "Fear the Lord and the king: and meddle not with them that are given to change," Prov. xxiv. 21. "And that in regard of the oath of God," Eccles. viii. 2. "Curse not the king, no not in thy thought; and curse not the rich in thy bed-chamber: for a bird of the air shall carry the voice, and that which hath wings shall tell the matter," Eccles. x. 20. Obey God with your first and absolute obedience, and no man against him: but obey the just commands of magistrates, and that out of obedience to God; and suffer patiently when you cannot obey. And if God should ever cast you under oppressing and persecuting governors, in your patience possess your souls; trust God and keep your innocency, and abhor all thoughts of rebellion or revenge: he that believeth will not make haste. Do nothing but what God will own, and then commit yourselves and your way to him. Repress wrath, and hate unpeaceable counsels; our way and our time must be only God's way and time. Self-saving men are usually the destroyers of themselves and others. Peter, that drew his sword for Christ, denied him the same night with oaths and curses. Fools trust themselves, and wise men trust God: fools tear the tree, by beating down the fruit that is unripe and harsh; and wise man stay till it is ripe and sweet, and will drop into their hands: fools rip up the mother for an untimely birth; but wise men stay till maturity give it them: fools take red-hot iron to be gold, till it burn their fingers to the bone; they rush into seditions and blood, as if it were a matter of jest; but wise men sow the fruit of righteousness and peace, and as much as in them lieth, live peaceably with all men. All men are mortal, both oppressors and oppressed: stay a little, and mortality will change the scene: God's time is best. Martyrdom seldom killeth the hundredth part so many as wars do: and he is no true believer that taketh martyrdom to be his loss: and Christ is more interested in his gospel, church, and honour, than we. Queen Mary's cruelties, and the bishops' bonfires, made religion universally received the more easily when her short reign was ended. We may learn wit of the fool, that seeing great guns and muskets, asked, what they were to do; and the answerer said, to kill men: saith he, Do not men die here without killing? In our country they will die of themselves.

VIII. Be sure that you keep up family religion; especially in the careful education of youth. Keep them from evil company, and from temptations; and especially of idleness, fulness, and baits of lust. Read the Scripture and good books, and call upon God, and sing his praise; and recreate youth with reading the history of the church, and the lives of holy men and martyrs: instruct them in catechisms and fundamentals.

IX. Above all, live in love to God and man; and let not selfishness and worldliness prevail against it. Think of God's goodness, as equal to his greatness and wisdom; and take yourselves as members of the same body with all true christians. Blessed are they that faithfully practise those three grand principles which all profess, viz. 1. To love God as God above all (and so to obey him). 2. To love our neighbours as ourselves. 3. And to do as we would be done by. Love is not envious, malignant, censorious; it slandereth not; it persecuteth not; it oppresseth not; it defraudeth not; it striveth not to gain by another's loss: get men once to love their neighbours as themselves, and you may easily prognosticate peace, quietness, and concord; happiness to the land, and salvation to the people's souls.

Finally, brethren, live in love, and the God of love and peace shall be among you. The Lord save you from the evils of which I have here and often warned you. Remember with thankfulness the many years of abundant mercy which we have enjoyed (though too much mixed with our sins, and vilified by some). "Comfort yourselves together, and edify one another, even as also ye do. And I beseech you, brethren, to know them which labour among you, and are over you in the Lord, and admonish you; and to esteem them very highly in love, for their work's sake: and be at peace among yourselves," 1 Thess. v. 11—13. And the Lord deeply write on our hearts these blessed words, "We have known and believed the love that God hath to us. God is love; and he that dwelleth in love dwelleth in God, and God in him," 1 John iv. 16. And remember, "Seeing all these things shall be dissolved, what manner of persons ought ye to be in all holy conversation and godliness, looking for and hasting unto the coming of the day of God, wherein the heavens being on fire shall be dissolved, and the elements shall melt with fervent heat? nevertheless we, according to his promise, look for new heavens and a new earth, wherein dwelleth righteousness," 2 Pet. iii. 11—13.

I need not lengthen my counsels further to you now, having been called by the will and providence of God to leave behind me a multitude of books, which may remember you of what you heard, and acquaint the world what doctrine I have taught you; and if longer studies shall teach me to retract and amend any failings, in the writings or practice of my unripe and less experienced age, as it will be to myself as pleasing as the cure of bodily disease, I hope it will not seem strange or ungrateful to you: though we must hold fast the truth which we have received, both you and I are much to be blamed, if we grow not in knowledge, both in matter, words, and method: the Lord grant that also we may grow in faith, obedience, patience, in hope, love, and desire to be with Christ.

"Now the God of peace, that brought again from the dead our Lord Jesus, that great Shepherd of the sheep, through the blood of the everlasting covenant, make you perfect in every good work to do his will, working in you that which is well-pleasing in his sight, through Jesus Christ; to whom be glory for ever and ever. Amen," Heb. xiii. 20, 21.

DIRECTIONS TO JUSTICES OF PEACE,

ESPECIALLY IN

CORPORATIONS,

FOR THE DISCHARGE OF THEIR DUTY TO GOD.

WRITTEN AT THE REQUEST OF A MAGISTRATE, AND PUBLISHED FOR THE USE OF OTHERS THAT NEED IT, BY RICHARD BAXTER; IMPELLED BY THE LOVE OF GOD AND MEN, TO BECOME THEIR SUBMISSIVE MONITOR.

I SHALL suppose that you begin with God, in public hearing his word for your direction, and by fasting and prayer, to beg his blessing on your endeavours; and I must suppose, that you are resolved to do God's will when you know it. Yet be very jealous of your own heart, lest there be any latent reserves; for in this is your greatest danger. Read Jer. xlii. 1—5, with Jer. xliii. 1—4.

Direct. 1. Remember the original and nature of authority. It is a beam from the sovereign authority of God: it can have no lower spring; as there can be no being but from God's being, Rom. xiii. 1, 2, 4, 6. You are all God's officers. The sense of this will teach you, 1. Whose work you have to do, and to abhor the doctrine that would make you so human, as to have nothing to do in matters of religion, or of soul-concernment. 2. And whose will you must consult. 3. And to take heed of abusing so divine a thing, by negligence or misemployment. 4. And to use your authority reverently and religiously, and not carelessly as a common thing. As ministers must speak with reverence, because they are God's messengers; so must you rule with pious reverence, as being God's officers. 5. Nor must others be suffered to despise your authority, because it is of God, and necessary to the common good. 6. And this will teach you to look to God, for protection, approbation, encouragement, and reward.

Direct. 2. Be sure that it be not self, but God, that is your ultimate end, and next to that, the public good. Let the pleasing and honouring God, and the benefit of men, be the very thing that you intend and seek; and not any carnal content in your own exaltation, or power, or honour. If you do the best works for self, and not for God, you debase them and lose them; and make them sins, and serve yourselves, and not God, in them; and your reward will be accordingly. Be exceeding jealous of your hearts in this; for selfishness is deep-rooted, and it is the common cause of men's perdition, and the sin that overturneth the governments of the earth, and destroyeth the governors. Look not at sin only as a troubler of the nation, and wrong to men, but as an offence to God, and a cause of damnation. Do all your work with respect to God and everlasting life. It is the pope's device, to make men believe that magistrates have nothing to do but for men's bodies, and temporal affairs, except as executioners of his decrees. If that were generally believed, how base would the magistracy seem in comparison of the ministry, to all men that believe a life to come! They that count all dung for Christ, would be tempted to count the magistrate no better, if his office no more respected Christ and salvation than some imagine; 2 Chron. xix. 6; Prov. viii. 15, 16; Matt. xxviii. 18; John ix. 11; Rom. xiii. 6, 4; xi. 36; 1 Cor. x. 31.

Direct. 3. That your ends and actions may be right, remember the labour, the difficulties, and danger of your place, and that the honour is but the clothing of your office, and as sugar to tice down that labour and suffering which is bitter to your flesh. Look upon greatness and government as that which in patience you must submit to undergo, when it is for God and the common good, but not as a thing that a wise man should be ambitious of. He is unlikely to rule for God, that proudly seeks the power for himself, 2 Sam. xv. 4.

Direct. 4. Forget not the two great summaries of your work; to encourage the good, and be a terror and avenger to the evil, Rom. xiii. And therefore be not the same to persons that are not the same; but be a lamb to the lambs, and a lion to the wolves, Psal. xviii. 25, 26. God, that is no respecter of persons, is yet the greatest distinguisher of persons. Many actions and accusations may come before you, which are indited by mere malignant enmity against the fear of God; and if the enemies of a holy life can find but magistrates that will fit their turns, they will make your power but an engine to do the devil's work; and will never want pretences and covers for their malice: see Dan. vi. 5. The godly and sober you must put in your bosom, and honour them that fear the Lord, or else you are no christians, Psal. xv. 4; 1 John iii. 14. But a vile person you must contemn, and the wicked you must cast out as dross, Psal. xv. 4; Prov. xxv. 4; Psal. cxix. 119. A ruler that is himself ungodly, and distasteth holiness, will make but a churlish nursing father to the church, Isa. xlix. 23.

Direct. 5. Never make the law an instrument of evil: set not the letter against the sense; interpret not the sense to be against the end. As the sense is the law, so the end informs the means, and is above it. The law of the land may restrain you from doing some good, that the law of God commandeth to the sovereign rulers, but it cannot warrant you to do any evil. There is no power but from God, and God gives none against himself, Rom. xiii. 4.

Direct. 6. See that you be such yourselves, as you would have others be. Be examples of holiness, temperance, and righteousness to all the people.

1. Let your practice commend a holy life, and all God's ordinances, public and private, to them. Order your families as they should do theirs. As ministers must preach by their lives, so you must govern by your lives. If you neglect holy worship, despise discipline, or have profane and prayerless families, the people take it for a licence to be profane. 2. Avoid the sins which you would have them avoid; especially be as little as may be in ale-houses, or unlawful sports. Honour godliness, and disgrace all sin, by your daily speeches and examples. If you will disobey God and the laws, how can you expect obedience yourselves?

Direct. 7. Set yourselves to do good with all your skill, and care, and industry. Have no restriction, but disability. Study it and make it your daily work to do all the good you can: you have an office to discharge, and not a work on the by to do. Abhor the principles and spirit, that entice magistrates to shift off all the displeasing and troublesome work, and to do no more than is thrust upon them, and they know not how with honour to avoid. If you know of unlicensed or abusive ale-houses, or other wickedness that calls for redress, stay not till you are urged, and conviction is offered you; but make inquiry, and procure them convicted, and think it not below you or too much to seek after vice, and do all that you are able to suppress it. If the law of the land oblige you not to this, God's law doth, by which you shall be judged. 1. Is not sin God's enemy? 2. Have you not taken up arms against it by a double engagement, as christians, and as magistrates? 3. Doth it not bring down judgments, and is it not the fire in our thatch, and the plague of the commonwealth? 4. Did it not kill the Lord Jesus? 5. Doth it not damn men to the everlasting misery? 6. Is it not fearful to draw on your own heads, the guilt of a thousand oaths, and of the drunkenness and other abominations which you connive at? 7. Your power is one of God's talents, of which he will require the improvement. 8. If your offices be good and necessary to the commonwealth, then make the best of them. If you do little in them, you teach men to esteem them little worth. 9. Every man is bound to do all the good he can in his place, and therefore so are you. 10. If negligent and scandalous ministers must be cast out, what must be done with negligent and scandalous magistrates? If you make your office more consistent with sin than ours, you so far vilify it. If magistrates were but dealt with, as ministers be, by the sequestering act, what work would be made! 11. Can a man do too much for such a God, such a reward, such an end, and in such a cause? You have more from God than others, in honour and greatness, and therefore you should be more diligent than others, Luke xii. 48. 12. When you have done your best, you shall find that sin will be too hard for you, and the devil too cunning for you. Sin is so strong, its friends so many and violent, its enemies so few, despised, discouraged, and weak, and their impediments so very many and great, that when you have all done your best, it will be too little. Never were there stricter laws and endeavours, and yet drunkenness and wickedness rage in our streets, as if it were to scorn or dare the magistrate; and many honest people are so tired in the costly and fruitless prosecution, that they are tempted to sit down, and meddle no more, and to entertain unworthy thoughts of magistracy. Deut. xiii. 14, if there were but a fame of a seducing idolater, they were to inquire and make search, and ask diligently whether it were true or not. See what work Nehemiah made with the sabbath-breakers, Neh. xiii. Job saith, (xxix. 16,) "I was a father to the poor, and the cause which I knew not, I searched out." And if in wrongs against men you must search, much more when against God. And if magistrates be not bound to search after sin, nobody is; for why should poor private men do it more than you? Read Psal. ci.

Direct. 8. Think not of a conscionable discharge of your duty, without many temptations to take you off. See therefore that you be fortified with self-denial and resolution: those that smart by you will complain, scarce a sinner but will have a friend to solicit you for his impunity: your own selfishness will be tempting you to be partial to your friends, to gentlemen, and such as may do you a pleasure or a displeasure. If you cannot deny both self and all for Christ, you cannot be true to him, Luke xiv. 26, 33. Be at a point with all the world, as one that is resolved that God must be pleased, if all be displeased. You are captains in Christ's army against sin and Satan, and therefore must excel in courage, Josh. i. 7; 1 Chron. xxii. 12; xxviii. 10, 20; 2 Chron. xv. 7; xix. 6, 7. He that cannot deny his friend, or self, will deny God: see 1 Sam. ii. 29, 30. Pity more the nation and men's souls, than the body of a sinner: see Prov. xix. 18; xxiii. 13, 14. If punishment will do the sinner no good, it will restrain many others, and so is a due to the commonwealth.

Direct. 9. Remember still, that your opportunity will be short, both of office and life; and therefore be up and doing, lest you give a dreadful account of your stewardship; as an unprofitable servant that hath borne the sword in vain, and only rubbed out the time in sitting in the seat and wearing the clothes of a magistrate. Keep you a daily reckoning with yourself; and call yourself to an account: what good have you done this day, this week, with your power? And lament it if any opportunity hath been lost, Rom. xiii. 4, 6.

Direct. 10. Be especially careful to suppress unnecessary abusive ale-houses, for there is the devil's shop; where drunkenness, dissension, ribaldry, whoredom, swearing, cursing, mocking at godliness, and a world of wickedness is committed. Oh how much is God abused in ale-houses in one day! And hitherto they have stood as in despite of all that we can do. If constables be not driven on, and clerks be not watched, and profane gentlemen that uphold sin well checked; and if honest men be not much encouraged against the malice of the ungodly, that count them but busy, troublesome fellows, for seeking to suppress this and other sins, (Gen. xix. 9,) wickedness will still reign, and the laws be as ciphers, to the ruin of souls and families, the guilt and shame of negligent magistrates, the grief of the upright, and the reproach and danger of the commonwealth.

Direct. 11. Defraud not the poor of any thing that the law hath made their due. If the mulcts of unlicensed and abusive ale-sellers, and of swearers, drunkards, &c. be their due, how dare you deprive them of it? I doubt at judgment, abundance of magistrates will have so many pounds to answer for, of which the poor have been defrauded, that the sums charged on highway robbers will come far short of theirs. Usurp not a power that is not given you, to dispense with the laws, which you are bound to obey and execute.

Direct. 12. Let zeal and prudence go together. Hearken not to the impious that would destroy your zeal, and plunge you into mortal guilt, on pretence of prudence and moderation; nor yet to any that would draw you to rash, imprudent actions, on pretences of piety or zeal. In cases where your duty lies plain before you, go through with it, whatever it cost you. But in cases that are too hard for you, if it be a law difficulty, consult with the skilful in the law (lest the malicious take advantage of your mistakes); and if it be a doubt about the laws of God, advise with some judicious ministers of Christ, whose office it is to teach you, and rule by God's word, as it is yours to command and rule them by the sword. It is never well, but where magistrates and ministers go together, each knowing his proper place and work, Mal. ii. 6, 7; Deut. xvii. 8, 9, 12; 1 Cor. iv. 1; 1 Thess. v. 12; Heb. xiii. 7, 17, 24.

"When the righteous are in authority, the people rejoice: but when the wicked beareth rule, the people mourn," Prov. xxix. 2.

Oct. 20, 1657.

MR. BAXTER'S LETTER

IN ANSWER

TO THE CASE OF MARRYING WITH A PAPIST.

SIR,

THOUGH I cannot be insensible how inconvenient to myself the answer of this case may possibly prove, by displeasing those who are concerned in it, and meddling about a case of persons utterly unknown to me; yet because I take it to be a thing which fidelity to the truth and charity to a christian soul requireth, I shall speak my judgment whatever be the consequence. But I must crave the pardon of that noble lord, who desired my answer might be subscribed to the case, because necessity requireth more words than that paper will well contain.

The question about the marriage, is not *An factum valeat?* but *An fieri debeat?* There is no affirming, or denying, without these necessary distinctions: 1. Between a case of necessity, and of no necessity. 2. Between a case where the motives are from the public commodity of church or state, and where they are only personal or private. 3. Between one who is otherwise sober, ingenuous, and pious, and a faithful lover of the lady, and one that either besides his opinion is of an ungodly life, or seeketh her only to serve himself upon her estate. 4. Between a lady well grounded and fixed in truth and godliness, and one that is weak and but of ordinary settledness. Hereupon I answer,

Prop. 1. In general, It cannot be said to be simply and in all cases unlawful to marry an infidel or heathen, much less a papist.[a]

2. In particular, It is lawful in these following cases:

1. In case of true necessity: when all just means have been used, and yet the party hath a necessity of marriage, and can have no better.[b] If you ask, Who is better? I answer, a suitableness in things of greatest moment to the party's good determineth that: an impious, hypocritical protestant is worse than a sober, godly papist (for such I doubt not but some be). But he that is sound both in judgment and in life is better than either.

2. In case it be very likely to prove some great commodity to church or state.[c] For so I doubt not but a protestant lady might marry a papist prince, or other person, on whom the public good doth eminently depend; so be it, 1. That she be stable and of good understanding herself. 2. And like to keep such interest in him as may conduce to his own and the public good. 3. And in case she may not be as well disposed of to the good of the public other ways. When all these concur, the probability of public utility is so great, that the person (I think) may trust God to make up personal incommodities, and preserve the soul who aimeth at his glory, and keepeth in his way. But small, inconsiderable probabilities are not enough to move one to hazard their soul in so perilous a way.

3. Besides these two cases (of real necessity and public utility) I remember no case at the present, in which it is lawful for such a protestant lady to marry a papist: at least in the ordinary case of persons in this land, I take it to be undoubtedly sinful, what hopes soever may be imagined of his conversion. My reasons are these:

1. A husband is especially to be a meet helper in matters of the greatest moment;[d] and this help is to be daily given, in counselling in the things that concern salvation, instructing in the Scriptures, exciting grace, subduing sin, and helping the wife in the constant course of a holy life, and in her preparation for death and the life to come. And a humble soul that is conscious of its own weakness, will find the need of all this help; which how it can be expected from one who only promiseth not to disturb her in her religion, I cannot understand. I should as soon advise her to take a physician in her sickness who only promiseth not to meddle with her health, as a husband who only promiseth not to meddle with her in matters of religion.

2. A husband who is no helper in religion, must needs be a hinderer; for the very diversions of the mind from holy things, by constant talk of other matters, will be a very great impediment: and as not to go forward is to go backward, so not to help is to hinder, in one of so near relation. How hard it is to keep up the love of God, and a delight in holiness, and heavenly desires, and a fruitful life, even under the greatest helps in the world, much more among hinderances, and especially such as are in our bosom, and continually with us, I need not tell a humble and self-knowing christian. And of what importance these things are, I shall not declare till I am speaking to an infidel or impious person.

3. And as for the conversion of another, marriage is none of the means that God hath commanded for

[a] Esther's case. [b] 1 Cor. vii. 29. [c] Esth. ii. 17.
[d] Gen. ii. 18, 20; 1 Cor. xiv. 35; Eph. iv. 29; v. 11, 15, 19, 20, 25—27, to the end; Col. iii. 16; Heb. iii. 13; 1 Cor. i. 10; Rom. xv. 6.

that end (that ever I could find):[e] preaching, or conference with judicious persons, are the means of such conversion: and if it be a hopeful thing, it may be tried and accomplished first; there are enow of us who are ready to meet any man of the papal way, and to evince the errors of their sect (by the allowance of authority). If reason, or Scripture, or the church, or sense itself may be believed, we shall quickly lay that before them that hath evidence enough to convince them; but if none of this can do it before-hand, how can a wife hope to do it? she ought not to think a husband so fond and weak, as in the matters of his salvation to be led by his affections to a woman, against his reason, his party, and his education: or if she can do more than a learned man can do, let her do it first, and marry him after. I had rather give my money or my house and land in charity, than to give myself in charity, merely in hope to do good to another. It is a love of friendship and complacence, and not a love of mere benevolence, which belongeth to this relation. Moreover, error and sin are deep-rooted things, and it is God only that can change such hearts; and women are weak, and men are the rulers; and therefore to marry, if it were a vicious, ungodly protestant, merely in hope to change him, is a course which I think not meet here to name or aggravate as it deserveth.

4. Yea, she may justly fear rather to be changed by him; for he hath the advantage in authority, parts, and interest. And we are naturally more prone to evil than to good. It is easier to infect twenty men than to cure one. And if he speak not to her against her religion, enow more will.

5. Or if she be so happy as to escape perversion, there is little hope of her escaping a sad calamitous life; partly by guilt, and partly by her grief for her husband's soul, and partly by family disorders and sins, and also by daily temptations, disappointment, and want of those helps and comforts in the way to heaven, which her weakness needeth, and her relation should afford. So that if her soul escape, she must look that her great affliction should be the means: and yet we cannot so confidently expect from God, that he sanctify to us a self-chosen affliction as another.

6. Supposing him to be one that loveth her person truly, and not only her estate, (for else she must expect to stand by a contemned thing,) yet his religion will not allow him otherwise to love her, than as a child of the devil in a state of damnation may be loved. For their religion teacheth them, that none can be saved but the subjects of the pope.

If it be objected, It seemeth it is no sin, in that you can allow it in a case of necessity, or for the notable benefit of the church or state. I answer, It is no sin in those cases, but out of them it is. It is no sin, but my duty, to lay down my life for my king or country; but it followeth not that I may therefore do it without sufficient cause: so it is in this case.

Having plainly given you my judgment in the proposed case, I leave it to that noble lord who sent for it, to use it, or conceal it, or burn it, as he please. For it being not the lady that sent to desire my resolution, but he; my answer is not hers, but his that sent for it. But I humbly crave, that if she be at all acquainted with my answer, (or any one else,) it may not be by report, but by showing it her entire, as I have written it. And as I doubt not but his honour will find itself engaged to preserve me from the displeasure of such as he acquainteth with it, (it being but the answer of his desire, and not an employment which I sought for,) so it must be remembered, 1. That I have purposely avoided the meddling with the particular errors of the Romanists' religion. 2. That I speak not a word against any christian love to papists, or amicable correspondence with them as our neighbours: much less am I passing any sentence on their souls, or countenancing those who run from them into any contrary extreme. But a husband and a bosom friend are relations which require such a special suitableness, as is not to be found in all whom we must love. 3. And what I say of the papist, I say also of any debauched, ungodly protestant: for it is not names and parties that make men good, or save their souls. A papist who is holy, heavenly, of an upright, mortified life, and not of a bloody or uncharitable mind to those that differ from him, is in a far happier state as to himself; though I think that the heart and life of the one, and the judgment of the other, do make them both unsuitable to such a lady as the case describeth. And though God may possibly convert and make suitable, and do wonders hereafter; yet it being things likely, and not things only possible, which reason must expect, I must say that the consequents of such an unsuitable match are like to be more bitter to her, than one that is indifferent and regardless of the concernments of a soul can understand. 4. Change but the tables, and put the case to a judicious papist, and he will resolve it as I have done, and tell you that a dispensation may be given but in such cases. 5. If the case had been, whether such a lady might give all her estate to a papist without her person, I should not think she had half so much reason to be unwilling.

R. BAXTER.

Acton, July 21, 1665.

[e] Unequal yoking with others, as well as unbelievers, by parity of reason, is proportionably evil: righteousness with unrighteousness, light with darkness, hath no communion, 2 Cor. vi. 14, 15.

MR. BAXTER'S PREFACE

TO

MR. ALLEINE'S ALARM.

TO ALL THE IGNORANT, CARNAL, AND UNGODLY, WHO ARE LOVERS OF PLEASURE MORE THAN GOD, AND SEEK THIS WORLD MORE THAN THE LIFE EVERLASTING, AND LIVE AFTER THE FLESH, AND NOT AFTER THE SPIRIT.

He that hath an ear to hear, let him hear.

MISERABLE SOUL!

THERE is that life, and light, and love, in every true believer, but especially in every faithful minister of Christ, which engageth them to long and labour for your salvation. Life is communicative and active; it maketh us sensible that faith is not a fantasy, nor true religion a stage-play, nor our hopes of our eternal happiness a dream. And as we desire nothing more for ourselves, than to have more of the holy life, which we have, alas! in so small a measure; so what is it that we should more desire for others? With the eye of an infallible (though too weak) faith we see the heaven which you neglect; and the blessed souls in glory with Christ, whose companions you might be for ever: we see the multitude of souls in hell, who came thither by the same way that you are going in; who are shut out of the glorious presence of God, and are now among these devils that deceived them, remembering that they had their good things here, Luke xvi. 25; and how they spent the day of their visitation; and how light they once set by God, by Christ, by heaven, by mercy, whilst mercy was an earnest solicitor for their hearts. And with our bodily eyes we see at the same time abundance of poor sinners living about us as if there were no God, no Christ, no heaven, no hell, no judgment, no, nor death, to be expected; as if a man were but a master-beast, to rule the rest, and feed upon them, and perish with them. And if it were your own case, to see what souls do in heaven and hell, and at once see how unbelievingly, carelessly, and senselessly most men live on earth, as if there were no such difference in another world, would it not seem a pitiful sight to you? If you had once seen the five brethren of Dives on earth, eating, drinking, laughing, and merry, clothed and faring daily with the best; and at the same time seen their brother's soul in hell, begging in vain for a little ease, and wishing in vain that one from the dead might go warn his brethren, that they come not to the place of torment; would it not seem to you a pitiful sight? Would not pity have made you think, Is there no way to open these gentlemen's eyes? no way to acquaint them what is become of their brother, and where Lazarus is, and whither they themselves are going? No one driveth or forceth them to hell, and will they go thither of themselves? And is there no way to stop them, or keep them back? Did you but see yourselves what we see by faith, (believing God,) and at once behold the saints in heaven, the lost, despairing souls in hell, and the senseless, sensual sinners on earth, that yet will lay none of this to heart, sure it would make you wonder at the stupidity of mankind. Would you not say, Oh what a deceiver is the devil, that can thus lead on souls to their own damnation! Oh what a cheater is this transitory world, that can make men so forget the world where they must live for ever! Oh what an enemy is this flesh, that thus draweth down men's souls from God! Oh what a besotting thing is sin, that turneth a reasonable soul into worse than a beast! What a Bedlam is this wicked world, when thousands are so busily labouring to undo themselves and others, and gratifying the devil, against the God and Saviour who would give them everlasting, blessed life!

And as we have such a sight as this by faith to make us pity you; so have we so much taste of the goodness of God, the sweetness of his ways, and the happiness of believers, as must needs make us wish that you had but once tried the same delights, which would turn the pleasures of sin into detestation. God knoweth that we desire nothing more for ourselves than the perfection and eternity of this holiness and happniess which we believe and taste. And should we not desire the same for you?

And being thus moved with necessary pity, we ask of God what he would have us to do for your salvation. And he hath told us in Scripture, that the preaching of his gospel, to acquaint you plainly with the truth, and earnestly and frequently entreat you to turn from the flesh and world, to God by Jesus Christ, is the means with which his grace is ready to concur for your salvation, when obstinate resistance causeth the Holy Spirit to forsake the sinner, and leave him to himself, to follow his own counsels, lusts, and wills.

In this hope we undertook the sacred ministry, and gave up ourselves to this great and most important work. In the great sense of our unworthiness, but yet in the sense of your souls' necessity, we were not such fools at our first setting out, as not to know it must be a life of labour, self-denial, and patience, and the devil would do his worst to hinder us; and that all sorts of his instruments would be ready to serve him against our labours, and against your souls. Christ our Captain saved by patient conquest, and so must we save ourselves and you: and so must you save yourselves under Christ, if ever you be saved. It was no strange thing to Paul that bonds and afflictions did every where abide him; nor did he account his life dear that he might finish his course with joy, and the ministry committed to him by the Lord, Acts xx. 23, 24. It was no strange thing to him to be forbidden to preach to the gentiles, that they might be saved, by such as were filling up the measure of their sins, and were under God's utmost wrath on earth, 1 Thess. ii. 15, 16. Devils and Pharisees, and most where they came, both high and low, were against the apostles' preaching of the gospel, and yet they would not sacrilegiously and cruelly break their covenant with Christ, and perfidiously desert the souls of men; even as their Lord for the love of souls did call Peter Satan, that would have tempted him to save his life and flesh, instead of making it a sacrifice for our sins, Matt. xvi. 23.

What think you should move us to undertake a calling so contrary to our fleshly ease and interest? Do we not know the way of ease and honour, of wealth and pleasure, as well as others? And have not we flesh as well as others? Could we not be content that the cup of reproach, and scorn, and slander, and poverty, and labours, might pass from us, if it were not for the will of God and your salvation? Why should we love to be the lowest, and trodden down by malignant pride, and counted as the filth of the world, and the offscouring of all things; and represented to rulers whom we honour, as schismatics, disobedient, turbulent, unruly, by every church usurper whom we refuse to make a god of? Why give we not over this preaching of the gospel at the will of Satan, that is, for the everlasting suffering of your souls, under the pretence of making us suffer? Is not all this that you may be converted and saved? If we be herein beside ourselves, it is for you. Could the words of the ignorant or proud have persuaded us, that either your wants and dangers are so inconsiderable, or your other supplies and helps sufficient, that our labours had been unnecessary to you, God knoweth we should have readily obeyed the silencing sort of pastors, and have betaken us to some other land, where our service had been more necessary. Let shame be the hypocrite's reward, who taketh not the saving of souls, and the pleasing of God, for a sufficient reward, without ecclesiastical dignities, preferments, or worldly wealth.

I have told you our motives; I have told you our business, and the terms of our undertaking. It is God and you, sinners, that next must tell us what our entertainment and success shall be. Shall it still be neglect, and unthankful contempt, and turning away your ears and heart, and saying, We have somewhat else to mind? Will you still be cheated by this deceiving world? and spend all your days in pampering your guts, and providing for your flesh, that must lie rotting very shortly in a grave? Were you made for no better work than this? May not we bring you to some sober thoughts of your condition, not one hour seriously to think whither you are going? What! not one awakened look into the world where you must be for ever? nor one heart-raising thought of everlasting glory? Not one heart-piercing thought of all your Saviour's love? nor one tear for all your sinful lives? O God, forbid! Let not our labours be so despised. Let not your God, your Saviour, and your souls, be set so light by. O let there be no profane person among you like Esau, who for one morsel sold his birthright.

Poor sinners! we talk not to you as on a stage in customary words, and because that talking thus was our trade. We are in as good earnest with you as if we saw you all murdering yourselves, and we are persuading you to save yourselves. Can any man be in jest with you who believeth God? who by faith foreseeth whither you are going, and what you lose, and where the game of sin will end? It is little better to jest with you now in a pulpit or in private, than to stand jesting over your departing souls when at death you are breathing out your last.

Alas! with shame and grief we do confess, that we never speak to you of these things as their truth and weight deserve; not with the skill and wisdom, the affection and fervency, which beseemeth men engaging in the saving of poor souls. But yet you may perceive that we are in good sadness with you. (For God is so.) What else do we study for, labour for, suffer for, live for? Why else do we so much trouble ourselves, and trouble you with all this ado, and anger them that would have made us silent?—For my own part, I will make my free confession to you to my shame, That I never grew cold, and dull, and pitiless to the souls of others, till I first grew too cold and careless of my own (unless when weakness or speculative studies cool me, which I must confess they often do). We never cease pitying you till we are growing too like you, and so have need of pity ourselves.

When, through the mercy of my Lord, the prospect of the world of souls, which I am going to, hath any powerful operation on myself, O then I could spend and be spent for others. No words are too earnest, no labour too great, no cost too dear; the frowns and wrath of malignant opposers of the preaching of Christ's gospel are nothing to me. But when the world of spirits disappear, or my soul is clouded, and receiveth not the vital, illuminating influences of heaven, I grow cold, first to myself, and then to others.

Come then, poor sinners, and help us, who are willing at any rate to be your helpers. As we first crave God's help, so we next crave yours. Help us, for we cannot save you against your wills, nor save you without your consent and help. God himself will not save you without you, and how shall we? Know that the devil is against us, and will do his worst to hinder us; and so will all his ministers, by what names or titles soever dignified or distinguished. But all this is nothing, if you will but take our parts yourselves; I mean, if you will take Christ's part, and your own, and will not be against yourselves. Men and devils cannot either help or hinder us in saving you as you may do yourselves. If God and you be for us, who shall be against us?

And will you help us? Give over striving against God and conscience; give over fighting against Christ and his Spirit. Take part no more with the world and the flesh, which in your baptism you renounced. Set your hearts to the message which we bring you. Allow it your man-like, sober thoughts; search the Scriptures, and see whether the things which we speak be so or no. We offer you nothing but what we have resolvedly chosen ourselves, and that after the most serious deliberation that we can make. We have many a time looked round about us, to know what is the happiness of man; and had we found better for ourselves, we had offered better to you. If the world would have served our turns, it should have served yours also, and we would not have troubled you with the talk of another world; but it will not, I am sure it will not serve your turns to make you happy; nor shall you long make that sorry, self-deceiving shift with it as now you do.

But if you will not think of these things, if you will not use the reason of men, alas, what can we do to save your souls? O pity them, Lord, that they may pity themselves. Have mercy on them, that they may have some more mercy on themselves. Help them, that they may help themselves and us. If you still refuse, will not your loss be more than ours? If we lose our labour, (which to ourselves we shall not,) if we lose our hopes of your salvation, what is this to your everlasting loss of salvation itself? And what are our sufferings for your sakes, in comparison of your endless sufferings?

But O, this is it that breaketh our hearts, that we leave you under more guilt than we found you; and when we have laid out life and labour to save you, the impenitent souls must have their pains increased for their refusing of these calls. And that it will be part of your hell to think for ever how madly you refused our counsel, and what pains, and cost, and patience, were used to have saved you, and all in vain. It will be so. It must needs be so. Christ saith, It shall be easier for Sodom and Gomorrah in the day of judgment, than for the rejecters of his gospel calls. The nature of the thing, and the nature of justice, certainly tell you that it must be so.

O turn not our complaints to God against you! Turn us not from beseeching you to be reconciled to God, to tell him you will not be reconciled. Force us not to say, that we earnestly invited you to the heavenly feast, and you would not come. Force us not to bear this witness against you. Lord, we could have borne all our labour and sufferings for them much easilier, if they would but have yielded to thy grace. But it was they themselves that broke our hearts, that lost our labour, that made us preach and entreat in vain: it was easier to preach without maintenance than without success. It was they that were worse to us than all the persecutors in the world. How oft would we have gathered them, but they would not, but are ungathered still! How many holy, faithful ministers have I known these eleven years last past who have lived in pining poverty and want, and hardly by charity got bread and clothing, and yet if they could but have truly said, Lord, the sermons which I preach privately, and in danger, have won many souls to thee, it would have made all their burden easy! But I tell thee, senseless and impenitent sinner, thou that deniest God in thy heart, and thou that deniest them thy conversion, which was the end of all their labours, thou hast dealt much more cruelly with them than they that denied the Levites bread.

Poor sinners! I know that I am speaking all this to those that are dead in sin; but it is a death consisting with a natural life, which hath a capacity of spiritual life; or else I would no more speak to you than to a stone. And I know that you are blind in sin; but it is a blindness consisting with a reasonable faculty, which is capable of spiritual illumination; or else I would no more persuade you than I do a beast. And I know that you are in the fetters of your own lusts; your wills, your love, your hearts, are turned away from God, and strongly bewitched with the dreams and dalliances with the flesh and world. But your wills are not forced to this captivity. Surely those wills may be changed by God's grace, when you clearly see sufficient reason for to change them; else I would as soon preach (were I capable) to devils and damned souls. Your case is not yet desperate, O make it not desperate! There is just the same hope of your salvation as there is of your conversion and perseverance, and no more. Without it there is no hope. And with it you are safe, and have no cause to doubt and fear. Heaven may be yet yours, if you will. Nothing but your own wills, refusing Christ and a holy life, can keep you out. And shalt thou do it? Shall hell be your own choice? And will you, I say, will you not be saved?

O think better what you do! God's terms are reasonable; his word and ways are good and equal; Christ's yoke is easy, and his burden light, and his commandments are not grievous to any, but so far as blindness and a bad and backward heart doth make them so. You have no true reason to be unwilling; God and conscience shall one day tell you and all the world, that you have no reason for it. You may as wisely pretend reason to cut your throats, to torment yourselves, as plead reason against a true conversion unto God. Were I persuading you not to kill yourselves, I would make no question but you would be persuaded. And yet must I be hopeless when I persuade you from everlasting misery, and not to prefer the world and flesh before your Saviour and your God, and before a sure, everlasting joy? God forbid.

Reader, I take it for a great mercy of God, that before my head lieth down in the dust, and I go to give up my account unto my Judge, I have this opportunity once more earnestly to bespeak thee for thy own salvation. I beg it of thee as one that must shortly be called away, and speak to thee no more till we come unto our endless state, that thou wouldst but sometimes retire into thyself, and use the reason of a man, and look before thee whither thou art going; and look behind thee how thou hast lived, and what thou hast been doing in the world till now; and look within thee, what a case thy soul is in, and whether it be ready to enter upon eternity; and look above thee, what a heaven of glory thou dost neglect, and what God thou hast to be thine everlasting friend or enemy, as thou choosest, and as thou livest, and that thou art always in his sight; yea, and look below thee, and think where they are that died unconverted. And when thou hast soberly thought of all these things, then do as God and true reason shall direct thee. And is this an unreasonable request? I appeal to God, and to all wise men, and to thine own conscience, when it shall be awakened. If I speak against thee, or if all this be not for thy good, or if it be not true and sure, then regard not what I say. If I speak not that message which God hath commanded his ministers to speak, then let it be refused as contemptuously as thou wilt. But if I do but in Christ's name and stead beseech thee to be reconciled to God, (2 Cor. v. 19, 20,) refuse it at thy peril. And if God's beseeching thee shall not prevail against thy sloth, lust, thy appetite, against the desires of the flesh, against the dust and shadows of the world, remember it when with fruitless cries and horror thou art beseeching him too late.

I know, poor sinner, that flesh is brutish, and lust and appetite have no reason. But I know that thou hast reason thyself, which was given thee to overrule them; and that he that will not be a man, cannot be a saint, nor a happy man. I know that thou livest in a tempting and a wicked world, where things or persons will be daily hindering thee. But I know that this is no more to a man that by faith seeth heaven and hell before him, than a grain of sand is to a kingdom, or a blast of wind to one that is fighting or flying for his life, Luke xii. 4. O man! that thou didst but know the difference between that which the devil and sin will give thee, if thou wilt sell thy soul and heaven, and that which God hath promised and sworn to give thee, if thou wilt heartily give up thyself to him. I know thou mayst possibly fall into company (at least among some sots and drunkards) that will tell thee, all this is but troublesome preciseness, and making more ado than needs. But I know withal what that man deserveth who will believe a fool before his Maker. (For he can be no better than a miserable fool, that will contradict and revile the word of God, even the word of grace, that would save men's souls.)

And, alas, it is possible thou mayst hear some of the tribe of Levi (or rather of Cain) deriding this serious godliness as mere hypocrisy, and fanaticism, and self-conceitedness: as if you must be no better than the devil's slaves, lest you be proud in thinking that you are better than they; that is, you must go with them to hell, lest in heaven ye be proud hypocrites for thinking yourselves happier than they.

It may be they will tell you, that this talk of conversion is fitter for pagans and infidels to hear, than christians and protestants; because such men's big looks or coat may make the poison the easilier taken down. I will entreat thee but as before God to answer these following questions, or to get them answered, and then judge whether it be they or we that would deceive thee; and whether as men use to talk against learning that have none themselves, so such men prate not against conversion, and the Spirit of God, because they have no such thing themselves.

Quest. 1. I pray ask them whether it be a puritan or fanatic opinion that men must die? And what all the pomp, and wealth, and pleasure of the world will signify to a departing soul? Ask them whether they will live on earth for ever, and their merry hours and lordly looks will have no end? And whether it be but the conceit of hypocrites and schismatics that their carcass must be rotting in a darksome grave?

Quest. 2. Ask them whether a man have not an immortal soul, and a longer life to live when this is ended? Luke xii. 41.

Quest. 3. Ask them whether reason require not every man to think more seriously of the place or state where he must be for ever, than of that where he must be for a little while, and from whence he is posting day and night? And whether it be not wiser to lay up our treasure where we must stay, than where we must not stay, but daily look to be called away, and never more to be seen on earth? Matt. vi. 19, 20; 2 Cor. iv. 16—18; v. 1—3, 6—8.

Quest. 4. Ask them whether God should not be loved with all our heart, and soul, and might? Matt. xxii. 27. And whether it be not the mark of an ungodly miscreant to be a lover of pleasure more than God, (2 Tim. iii. 4,) and a lover of this world above him? 1 John ii. 15, 16. And whether we must not seek first God's kingdom and his righteousness, (Matt. vi. 33,) and labour most for the meat that never perisheth, (John vi. 27,) and strive to enter in at the strait gate, (Luke xiii. 24,) and give all diligence to make our calling and election sure? 2 Pet. i. 10.

Quest. 5. Ask them whether without holiness any shall see God? Heb. xii. 14; Matt. v. 8; Tit. ii. 14. And whether the carnal mind is not enmity to God, and to be carnally-minded is not death, and to be spiritually-minded is life and peace? And whether if you life after the flesh you shall not die, and be condemned; and they shall live and be saved that walk after the Spirit? And whether any man be Christ's that hath not his Spirit? Rom. viii. 1, 5—10.

Quest. 6. Ask them whether any man have a treasure in heaven whose heart is not there? Matt. vi. 21. And whether this be not the difference between the wicked and the godly, that the first do make their bellies their gods, and mind earthly things, and are enemies to the cross of Christ (though perhaps not his name); and the latter have their conversation in heaven, and being risen with Christ, do seek and set their affections on things above, and not on things that are on earth, to which they are as dead, and their life is hid (or out of sight) with Christ in God, till Christ appear, and then they shall appear (even openly to all the world) with him in glory? Phil. iii. 18—20; Col. iv. 1—5.

Quest. 7. Ask them whether it be credible, or suitable to God's word or working, that he that will not give them the fruits of the earth without their labour, nor feed and clothe them without themselves, will yet bring them to heaven without any care, desire, or labour of their own, when he hath bid him care not for the one, and called for their greatest diligence for the other? Matt. vi. 23, 25, 33; John vi. 27. Yea, ask them whether these be not the two first articles of all faith and religion: 1. That God is. 2. That he is the rewarder of them that diligently seek him? Heb. xi. 6.

Quest. 8. Ask them, yea, ask your eyes, your ears, your daily experience in the world, whether all or most that call themselves christians, do in good sadness thus live to God in the Spirit, and mortify the flesh with its affections and lusts, and seek first God's kingdom and righteousness, love him above all, and lay up treasure and heart in heaven? or rather, whether most be not lovers of the world, and lovers of pleasures more than God, and live not after the flesh, and mind not most the things of the flesh? I mention not now the drunkards, the flesh-pleasing gentlemen, that live in pride, fulness, and idleness, and sport, and play away their precious time; nor the filthy fornicators, nor the merciless oppressors, nor the malignant haters of a godly life, nor the perjured and perfidious betrayers of men's souls and of the gospel, or of their country's good, nor such other men of seared conscience, whose misery none questioneth but such as are blind and miserable. It is not those only I am speaking of, but the common, worldly, fleshly, and ungodly ones.

Quest. 9. Ask them whether the name of a christian will save any of these ungodly persons? And whether God will like men the better for lying, and calling themselves christians, when they are none indeed? And whether they dare preach to the people that a christian drunkard, or a christian fornicator or oppressor, or a christian worldling, needeth no conversion?

Quest. 10. Ask them whether they say not themselves that hypocrisy is a great aggravation of all other sins? And whether God hath not made the hypocrites and unbelievers to be the standards in hell? Luke xxv. 51. And whether seeking to abuse God by a mock religion, do make such false christians better than the poor heathens and infidels, or much worse? And whether he be not a hypocrite that professeth to be a christian, and a servant of God, when he is none, nor will be? And whether he that knoweth his master's will, and doth it not, shall not have the sorest stripes or punishment? Luke x. 47.

Quest. 11. Ask them whether in their baptism (which is their christening as a covenant) they did not renounce the flesh, the world, and the devil, and vow and deliver up themselves to God their Father, their Saviour, and their Sanctifier? And whether all or most men perform this vow? And whether a perjured covenant-breaker against God, is fitter for salvation than one that never was baptized?

Quest. 12. Ask them whether the holy nature of God be not so contrary to sin, as that it is blasphemy to say that he will bring to heaven, and into the bosom of his eternal delights, any unholy, unrenewed soul? 1 Pet. i. 15, 16.

Quest. 13. Ask them why it was that Christ came into the world? Whether it was not to save his people from their sins, Matt. i. 21; and to destroy the works of the devil, 1 John iii. 8; and to purify to himself a peculiar people, zealous of good works, Tit. ii. 11; and to bring home straying souls to God, Luke xv.; and to be the way to the Father? John xiii. 6. And whether Christ will save that soul that is not converted by him, and saved from his sins? Or whether it be the dead image only of a crucified Jesus that is all their Saviour while they will have no more of him?

Quest. 14. Ask them why they believe, and were baptized into the Holy Ghost? And whether a man can enter into the kingdom of heaven that is not born of the Spirit as well as of water? John iii. 3, 5, 6; and that is not converted, and begins not the world as it were anew, in a teachable, tractable newness of life, like a little child? Matt. xviii. 3. And whether it be not a certain truth, that if any man have not the Spirit of Christ, the same is none of his? Rom. viii. 9.

Quest. 15. Ask them why Christ gave the world so many warnings of the damnableness of the Pharisees' hypocrisy, if hypocritical christians may be saved? And what were these Pharisees? They were the masters of the Jewish church; the rabbies that must have high places, high titles, and ceremonies, formal garments, and must be reverenced of all; that gave God lip-service without the heart, and made void his commands, and worshipped him in vain, teaching for doctrines the commandments of men, and strictly tithed the mint and cummin, while lovely mercy and justice were passed by; who worshipped God with an abundance of ceremonies, and built the tombs and garnished the sepulchres of the saints, while they killed and persecuted those that did imitate them, and hated the living saints, and honoured the dead. They were the bitterest enemies and murderers of Christ, on pretence that he was a blasphemer, and a seditious enemy to Cæsar and the common peace, and one that spake against the temple. They were the greatest enemies of the apostles, and silencers of those that preached Christ's gospel, and persecuted them that called upon his name. And had these no need of conversion because they could say, God is our Father, (when the devil was their father, John viii. 44,) and they were Abraham's seed? And are not hypocritical christians, drunken christians, fornicating christians, carnal, worldly, infidel christians, (the contradiction is your own,) persecuting christians, false-named, hypocritical christians, as bad, yea, worse, as they abuse a more excellent profession? Matt. xv. 7, 8; xxiii.; xxii. 18; vi. 2, &c.; Luke xii. 1.

Quest. 16. Doth not the holy state of heaven require holiness in all that shall possess it? Can an unholy soul there see, and love, and praise, and delight in God for ever, and in the holy society and employment of the saints? Rev. xxi. 27. Is he not liker a Mahometan than a christian, that looketh for a sensual and unholy heaven?

Quest. 17. What is the difference between the church and the world? Is not the church a holy society of regenerate souls? Yea, the church visible is only those that in baptism vow holiness and profess it. Look those hypocrites in the face, and see whether they do not blush when they repeat in the creed, I believe in the Holy Ghost; I believe in the holy catholic church, and the communion of saints, who shall have the forgiveness of sins, and life everlasting. Ask them whether they mean holy adulterers, holy worldlings, holy perjured persons? Ask them whether they mean a communion of saints in a tavern, in a play-house, in a gaming-house, in a whore-house, or a jesting, canting, stage-play communion? If the church be holy, be holy if you will be of the church: if it be a communion of saints, make it not a communion of swine; and make not saints and their communion seem odious either for their infirmities, or their crossness to your carnal interests or conceits.

Quest. 18. Ask them whether there be a heaven and a hell or not? If not, why are they pretended christians? If there be, will God send one man to heaven, and another to hell, to so vast, so amazing a difference of states, if there be no great difference between them here? If holiness no more differenced christians from others, than saying a sermon or saying over a prayer doth difference one from an infidel, where were the justice of God in saving some and damning others? And what were christianity better than the religion of Antonine, Plato, Socrates, Seneca, Cicero, Plutarch, if not much worse? Go into London streets, and when you have talked with living, prudent men, then go to the painter's shop, and see a comely picture; and to the looking-glass, and see the appearance of each passenger in a glass; and to the periwig shops, and set a wooden-head with a periwig upon the bulk; and you have seen something like the difference of a holy soul and of a dead and dressed formal hypocrite.

Quest. 19. Ask them whether kings, and all men, make not a great difference between man and man; the loyal and perfidious, the obedient and disobedient? And whether they difference not themselves between a friend and foe; one that loveth them, and one that robbeth, beateth, or would kill them? And shall not the most holy God make more difference between the righteous and the wicked? Mal. iii. 17, 18.

Quest. 20. But if they are dead in every point, save carnal interests, ask them why they are preachers or priests? And if conversion and holiness be a needless thing, what life they themselves are of? And why the country must be troubled with them, and pay them tithes, and give them reverence? When these twenty questions are well answered, conclude that you may be saved without conversion.

But if, poor soul, thou art fully convinced, and askest, What should I do to be converted? the Lord make thee willing, and save thee from hypocrisy, and I will quickly tell thee in a few words.

1. Give not over sober thinking of these things till thy heart be changed, Psal. cxix. 59.

2. Come to Christ, and take him for thy Saviour, thy Teacher, thy King, and he will pardon all that is past, and save thee, John i. 12; iii. 16; v. 40; 1 John v. 11, 12.

3. Believe God's love, and the pardon of sin, and the everlasting joys of heaven, that thou mayst feel that all the pleasure of the world and flesh are dung in comparison of the heavenly delight of faith, and hope, and holy love, and peace of conscience, and sincere obedience.

4. Sin no more wilfully, but forbear that which thou mayst forbear, Isa. lv. 7.

5. Away from temptations, occasion of sin and evil company, and be a companion of the humble, holy, heavenly, and sincere, Psal. cxix. 115, 63.

6. Wait on God's Spirit in the diligent, constant use of his own means. Read, hear, meditate, pray; pray hard for that grace that must convert thee. Wait thus, and thou shalt not wait in vain, Psal. xxv.; xxxvii. 34; lxix. 6.

Pity, O Lord, and persuade the souls; let not

Christ's blood, his doctrine, his example, his Spirit, be lost unto them, and they lost for ever. Let not heaven be as no heaven to them, while they dream and dote on the shadows in this world. And oh save this land from the greater destruction than all our late plagues, and flames, and divisions, which our sins and thy threatenings make us fear. O Lord, in thee have we trusted, let us never be confounded.

R. BAXTER.

OF

REDEMPTION OF TIME.

THE usual vice of human nature, to be weary of good things when they grow old and common, and to call for novelties, is especially discernible in men's esteem and use of books. Abundance of old ones are left neglected to the worms and dust, whilst new ones of a far less worth are most of the booksellers' trade and gain. It is not easy to give a reason of it, but it is not to be denied, that this age hath few such writers as the last, either controversial or practical. Even among the papists, there are now few such as Suarez, Vasquez, Valentia, Victoria, Penottus, Ruiz, Alvarez, Bellarmine, &c. And among us, too few such as Jewel, Whittaker, Reignolds, Field, Usher, White, Challoner, Chillingworth, &c. which the papists understanding, would fain have the monuments of these worthies forgotten; and are calling for new answers to the schisms that have been so long ago confuted, to keep those old, unanswerable writings from the people's hands. And thus doth the envious enemy of holiness, by the practical writings of those holy men who are now with God. The solid, grave, and pious labours of Richard Rogers, Perkins, Greenham, Deering, Dent, Smith, Dod, Hildersham, Downame, Samuel Ward, Hall, Bolton, Dike, Stocke, Elton, Taylor, Harris, Preston, Sibbs, Ball, and many more such, are by the most neglected, as if we were quite above their parts; but it were well if more injudicious or undigested writings possessed not their room. Though I may hereby censure myself as much as others, I must needs say, that the reprinting of many of our fathers' writings, might have saved the labour of writing many later books, to the greater commodity of the church.

Among the rest, I well remember that even in my youth (and since much more) the writings of Mr. Whately were very savoury to me; especially his Sermon of Redeeming Time.

I must so far venture on the displeasure of the guilty, as to say, that the doleful condition of two sorts of persons, the SENSUAL GENTRY and the idle beggars, is it that hath compelled me to this service; but especially of the former sort, who though slothful, may possibly be drawn to read so small a book. What man that believeth a life hereafter, and considereth the importance of our business upon earth, and observeth how most persons, but especially our sensual gentry, live, can choose but wonder that ever reason can be so far lost, and even self-love and the care of their own everlasting state so laid asleep, as men's great contempt of time declareth? Ladies and gentlewomen, it is you whom I most deeply pity and lament: think not that I am too bold with you; God, who employeth us on such service, will be bolder with you than this comes to. And Christ was bold with such as you, when he spake the histories or parables of the two rich men in Luke xii.; xvi.; and when he told men how hardly the rich should enter into the kingdom of heaven. And James was bold with such when he wrote, chap. v. "Go to now, ye rich men, weep and howl for your miseries that shall come upon you. Your riches are corrupted, and your garments moth-eaten. Your gold and silver is cankered; and the rust of them shall be a witness against you, and shall eat your flesh as it were fire, &c.——Ye have lived in pleasure on earth, and been wanton; ye have nourished your hearts as in a day of slaughter."——And he was neither ignoble nor unlearned, but of honourable birth, and the orator of an university, who was so bold with the English gentry (when, they say, they were much wiser and better than they are now) as to bespeak them thus:——(Herbert's Church-porch.)

"Fly idleness; which yet thou canst not fly
By dressing, mistressing, and compliment;
If those take up the day, the sun will cry
Against thee; for his light was only lent:
God gave thy soul brave wings; put not those feathers
Into a bed to sleep out all ill weathers.
O England! full of sin, but most of sloth,
Spit out thy phlegm, and fill thy breast with glory;
Thy gentry bleats, as if thy native cloth
Transfused a sleepiness into thy story.
Not that they all are so, but that the most
Are gone to grass, and in the pasture lost.
This loss springs chiefly from our education:
Some till their ground, but let weeds choke their son:
Some mark a partridge; never their child's fashion:
Some ship them over, and the thing is done.
Study this art; make it thy great design;
And if God's image move thee not, let thine.
Some great estates provide; but do not breed
A mast'ring mind; so both are lost thereby:
Or else they breed them tender; make them need
All that they leave: this is flat poverty.
For he that needs five hundred pounds to live,
Is full as poor as he that needs but five."

When I peruse the map of Sodom, in Ezek. xvi. 49, 50, methinks I am in an infected city, where instead of LORD HAVE MERCY ON US, it is written on the GENTRY'S doors, PRIDE, FULNESS OF BREAD, ABUNDANCE OF IDLENESS, UNMERCIFULNESS, AND ABOMINATION. "Behold, this was the iniquity of thy sister Sodom, pride, fulness of bread, and abundance of idleness was in her and in her daughters, neither did she strengthen the hand of the poor and needy: and they were haughty, and committed abomination before me." The title over the leaves of these verses might be, THE CHARACTER OF THE SENSUAL GENTRY.

Mistake me not, I am so far from accusing all the rich and honourable, that I must say it is as a testimony against the rest, that I know many such who spend their time as fruitfully and diligently as the poor (though in another sort of service): and such might the rest have been if their bodies had not got the mastery of their souls. It is not your PRIDE or FULNESS of BREAD that I am now to speak of, but your IDLENESS. Many of the old philosophers thought that when sickness or age had made one unserviceable to the commonwealth, it was a shame to live, and a duty to make away themselves, as being but unprofitable burdens to the world. Christians are not of their mind, because it is a mercy even under pain to have time of preparation for another world, and because we may serve God in patience, and heavenly desires, and hope, when we cannot serve him by an active life. But christians and heathens will proclaim those persons to be the shame of nature, who wilfully make themselves unprofitable, and live in their health as if they were disabled by sickness; and are condemned by their sensuality to a prison or a grave: so that their epitaph may be written on their doors, HERE LIETH SUCH A ONE, rather than it can be said, Here he liveth. Oh what a rock is a hardened heart! How can you choose but tremble when you think how you spend your days? and how all this time must be accounted for? that those that have a death and judgment to prepare for, a heaven to get, a hell to escape, and souls to save, can waste the day in careless idleness, as if they had no business in the world, and yet their consciences never tell them what they do, and how all this must be reviewed?

Compare together the life of a christian and of a fleshly brute, and you will see the difference. Suppose them both ladies or gentlewomen of the same rank: the one riseth as early as is consistent with her health; with thoughts of thankfulness and love her heart also awaketh, and riseth up to Him that night and day preserveth her. She quickly despatcheth the dressing of her body, as intending no more but serviceable warmth and modest decency: and then she betaketh herself to her closet, where she poureth out her soul in confession, supplication, thanksgiving, and praise to God, her Creator, Redeemer, and Sanctifier. And as one that delighteth in the law of the Lord, she reverently openeth the sacred Scripture, and readeth over some part of it with some approved commentary at hand, in which she may see the sense of that which of herself she could not understand: what is plain she taketh in, digesteth, and layeth up for practice; and that which is too hard for her, as a humble learner she waiteth in patience, till by her teacher's help in time she can come to understand it. As she hath leisure, she readeth such holy books as interpret and apply the Scriptures, to enlighten her mind, and resolve her will, and quicken her affections, and direct her practice. And as she liveth in an outward calling or course of labour, in which her body as well as her mind may have employment, she next addresseth herself to that. She looketh with prudence and carefulness to her family. She taketh care of her servants' labours, and their manners; neither suffering any to live in idleness, nor yet so overlabouring them, as to deny them some time to read the Scriptures, and call upon God, and mind their souls. She endureth no profane despisers of piety or vicious persons in her house. She taketh fit seasons to speak to her servants such sober words of holy counsel, as tend to instruct and save their souls. She causeth them to learn the principles of religion in some catechism, and to read such good books as are most suitable to their capacity. In her affairs, she avoideth both sordid parsimony and wasteful prodigality; and is thrifty and sparing, not in covetousness, but that she may do the more good to them that want. She indulgeth no excess or riotousness in her house, though the vices of the times should make it seem needful to her honour. If she want recreation, or have leisure for more work, she steps out to her poor tenants' and neighbours' houses, and seeth how they live, and what they want, and speaketh to them some sober words of counsel about the state of their immortal souls, and stirreth them up to a holy life. She causeth the souls of the poor to bless her, and is an example of piety to all about her. But her special care and labour is in the education of her children (if she have any). She watcheth over them, lest the company, and example, and language of ungodly persons should infect them. She causeth them to read the Scriptures, and other holy books, and to learn the principles of religion, and teacheth them how to call upon God, and give him thanks for all his mercies. She acquainteth them with the sins of their depraved natures, and laboureth to humble them in the sense thereof. She openeth to them the doctrine of man's salvation by Christ, and the necessity of a new birth and of a heavenly nature: she disgraceth all sin to them, especially the radical and master-sins; even ignorance, unbelief, selfishness, pride, sensuality, and voluptuousness, the love of this world, and unholiness of heart and life. She sweetly and seriously insinuateth into them the love and liking of faith and holiness; and frequently enlargeth her speech to them of the greatness, wisdom, and goodness of God, and what he is to man, and how absolutely we owe him all the service, obedience, and love that our faculties can possibly perform. She sweeteneth their thoughts of God and godliness, by telling them what God hath done for man, and what he will be to his own for ever; and by acquainting them with the reasons of a holy life, and the folly of ungodly men; and what a beastly thing it is to be sensual, and to pamper and please this flesh, which must shortly turn to dust, and to neglect a soul which must live for ever. She remembereth them oft that they must die, and telleth them how great a change death makes, and how the change of regeneration must prepare us for it. She openeth to them the blessedness of holy souls, that shall be for ever with the Lord, and the misery of the damned, who cast away themselves by the wilful neglect of the time of their visitation. In a word, it is her daily care and calling, to prepare her children for the service of God, and to be blessings to the world in their generation, and to be happy themselves for evermore; and to destroy and prevent that sin and wickedness, which would make them a plague and curse in their generation. Her meals are not luxurious nor long, nor her feastings unnecessary, to the wasting of estate or precious time; but seasonable, frugal, charitable, and pious, intended to promote some greater good. She keepeth up the constant performance of religious duties in her family; not mocking God with formal compliment, but worshipping him in reverence and serious devotion, reading the holy Scriptures, and seriously calling upon God, and singing to him psalms of praise. If her mind need recreation, she hath some profitable history, or other fruitful books to read, and variety of good works, and a seasonable diversion to the affairs of her family, instead of cards and dice, and the abused fooleries of the sensual world. When she is alone, her thoughts are fruitful to herself; either examining her heart and life, or looking seriously into eternity, or rejoicing her soul in the remembrance of God's mercies, or in the foresight of endless blessedness with him, or in stirring up some of his graces in her soul. When she is with others, her words are savoury, sober, seasonable; as the oracles of God for piety and truth, tending to edification, and to administer instruction and grace to the hearers, and rebuking the idle talk, or filthy scurrility, or backbiting of any that would corrupt the company and discourse. At evening she again returneth to the more solemn worshipping of God, and goeth to rest, as one that still waiteth when she is called to rest with Christ, and is never totally unready for that call. Thus doth she spend her days, and accordingly doth she end them; being conveyed by angels into the presence of her Lord, and leaving a precious memorial to the living: the poor lamenting the loss of her charity, and all about lamenting the removal of a pattern of piety and righteousness, and loving holiness the better for the perfume of such a heavenly and amiable example.

On the other side, how different is the life of the sensual ladies and gentlewomen to whom I am now writing! When they have indulged their sloth in unnecessary sleep, till the precious morning hours are past, they arise with thoughts as fruitless as their dreams. Their talk and time, till almost half the day is gone, is taken up only about their childish trifling ornaments: so long are they dressing themselves, that by that time they can but say over or join in a few formal words, which go for prayer, it is dinner-time (for an image of religion some of them must have, lest conscience should torment them before the time). And when they have sat out an hour or two at dinner, in gratifying their appetites, and in idle talk, they must spend the next hour in talk which is as idle. A savoury word of the life to come must not trouble them, nor interrupt their fleshly converse. Perhaps they must next go to cards or dice, and it may be to a play-house, or at least on some unprofitable visitation, or some worthless visitors that come to them, must take up the rest of the afternoon in frothy talk, which all set together comes to nothing, but vanisheth as smoke. And they choose such company, and such a course of life, as shall make all this seem unavoidable and necessary; and that it would run them into contempt and great inconveniences if they did otherwise. If they look after their affairs, it is merely through covetousness: but more usually they leave that care to others, that they may do nothing that is good for soul or body. They use their servants as they do their beasts, for their service only; and converse with them as if they had no souls to save or lose: they teach them by their example to speak vainly, and live sensually, and to forget the life to come. Their children they love but as the brutes do their young; they teach them how to bow and dance, and carry themselves decently in the sight of men; but never labour to heal their souls of ignorance, unbelief, and pride; nor open to them the matters of everlasting consequence; but rather persuade them that serious holiness is but hypocrisy, and the obedience of God's laws is a needless thing. They teach them by their example, to curse, and swear, and lie, and rail, and to deride religion, or at least to neglect God, and life eternal, and mind only the transitory vanities of this life. They leave them to Satan, to wicked company and counsel, and to their fleshly lusts and pride; and when they have done, take care only to get them sufficient maintenance, to feed this sensual fire while they live. They train them up for the service of sin and Satan, that at age they may have ignorance and vice sufficient to make them the plagues and misery of their country, and to engage them in enmity against that gospel and ministry which is against their lusts; that rebelling against Christ, they may have at last the reward of rebels, instead of salvation. In a word, they do more against their poor children's souls, than all their enemies in the world; if not more than the devil himself could do, at least, they most effectually serve him, for their children's damnation. Thus do they spend their days, and at night conclude them as carelessly as they begun them; and at death (without a true conversion) shall end them as miserably as they spent them sinfully. And while they are pampering their flesh and saying, I have enough, I will eat, drink, and be merry, they suddenly hear, "Thou fool, this night shall thy soul be required, and then whose shall all this be which thou possessest?" Luke xii. 19, 20. And when they have a while been clothed in purple and silks, and "fared sumptuously every day," they must hear at last, "Remember that thou in thy life-time receivedst thy good things, and Lazarus evil things: but now he is comforted, and thou art tormented." And when the time which they now despise is gone, oh what would they give for one other year or hour of such time, to do the work which they now neglected! Luke xvi. 24—26; Matt. xxv. 8—12.

Is there not a great difference now between these two sorts of persons, in the expense of time? And is it any wonder if there be a difference in their rewards? In Matt. xxv. 30, it is not only, Cast the whoremonger, the drunkard, the perjurer, the persecutor; but, "Cast the unprofitable servant into outer darkness: there shall be weeping and gnashing of teeth."

Compare, I beseech you, the time which you spend, 1. In idleness. 2. In excessive sleep. 3. In adorning you. 4. In feasting and long meals. 5. In curiosity and pomp, employing most of your servants' time in impertinencies, as well as your own. 6. In excessive worldly cares. 7. In vain company and idle talk. 8. In vain thoughts. 9. In sensual recreations, in cards, dice, huntings, hawkings, plays, romances, fruitless books, &c. I say, compare this time with the time which you spend in examining your hearts and lives, and trying your title to eternal life; in bewailing sin, and begging mercy of God, and returning thanks and praise to your great Benefactor; in instructing your children and servants; in visiting the sick, relieving the poor, exhorting one another; in meditating on eternity, and the way thereto; in learning the word and will of God; and in the sanctified labours of your outward calling. And let your consciences tell you, which of these hath the larger share? And whether those things which should have none, and those which should have little, have not almost all? And whether God have not only the leavings of your flesh?

Gentlemen and ladies, I envy not your pleasures. I have myself a body with its proper appetites, which would be gratified, as well as you. And I have not wanted opportunity to gratify it. If I thought that this were the most manly life, and agreeable to reason, and that we had no greater things to mind, I could thus play away my time as you do. But it amazeth me to see the world's stupidity, that people who are posting away into eternity, and have so much to do in a little time, and of such inconceivable importance, can yet waste their days in sleeping, and dressing, and feasting, and complimenting; in pastime, and plays, and idle talk, as if they were all but a dream, and their wits were not so far awakened as to know what it is to be a man. And to increase our pity, when they have done, they ask, What harm is there in cards and dice, in stage-plays and romances? Is it not lawful to use such and such recreations? Suppose they were all unquestionably lawful, have you no greater matter that while to do? Have you no more useful recreations, that will exercise your bodies and minds more profitably, or at least with less expense of time? To a sedentary person, recreation must be such as stirs the body: to a labouring person, variety of good books and pious exercises are fitter recreations than cards or dice. Is your recreation but as the mower's whetting of his scythe? no oftener nor no longer than is necessary to fit you for those labours and duties, which must be the great and daily business of your lives? If this be so, I am not reprehending you: but I beseech you consider, have you not souls to regard, as well as others? Have you not a God to serve? and his word and will to learn and do? Have you not servants and children to instruct and educate? (And oh what a deal of labour doth their ignorance and obstinacy require!) Have you not death and judgment to prepare for? Have you not an outward calling to follow? (Though I say not that you must do the same labours as the poor, I say that you must labour and be profitable to the commonwealth.) Have you not many good works of charity to do? And will you leave the most of this undone, and waste your time in plays, and cards, and feasts, and idleness, and then say, What harm is in all this, and are they not lawful? Oh that the Lord would open your eyes, and show you where you must be ere long; and tell you what work you have here to do, that must be done, or you are lost for ever! And then you would easily tell yourselves whether playing and fooling away precious time be lawful for one in your condition. If your servants leave most of their work undone, and spend the day in cards, and stage-plays, and feasting, and in merry chat, and then say, Madam, are not cards, and plays, and jesting lawful? will you take it for a satisfactory answer? And is it not worse that you deal with God?

It is a most irrational and ungrateful error, to think that you may spend one hour's time the more in idleness, because that you are rich. The reason were good, if labour were for nothing but to supply your own bodily necessities. But do you not believe that God is your Lord and Master? and that he giveth you not an hour's time in vain, but appointeth you work for every hour (except your necessary rest)? And that your time and wealth are but his talents? And bethink yourselves whether a servant may say, I will do less work than my fellow-servants, because I have more wages? And whether you may do less for God, because he giveth you more than others? But of this I have said so much in my preface to my book called "The Crucifying of the World," that I shall now dismiss it.

And what I have said especially to the rich, (who think their loss of time no sin,) I must say also to all others: O value time before it is gone. Use it before it is taken from you. Despatch the work that you were made for. Repent and turn to God unfeignedly. Prepare for death without delay. Time will not stay; nor will it ever be recovered. Were it not lest I should write a treatise instead of a preface, I would especially press this on all these following sorts of people. 1. Those that are young, who have yet the flower of their time to use, that they cast it not away on childish vanity or lusts. 2. Those that have lost much time already, that they show the sincerity of their repentance, by redeeming the rest, and lose no more. 3. Those that are yet ignorant, ungodly, and unprepared for death and the world to come; oh what need have these to make haste, and quickly get into a safer state, before their time be at an end! 4. Those that in sickness resolved and promised, if God would recover them, to redeem their time. 5. The weak and aged, whom nature and sickness do call upon to make haste. 6. The poor and servants, whose opportunities for spiritual means are scant, and therefore have need to take them when they may; especially on the Lord's day. 7. Those that live under excellent helps and advantages for their souls; which if they neglect, they may never have again. 8. And those that by office or power have especial opportunity to do good. All these have a double obligation to value and redeem their time.

But because in my book called "Now or Never," I have already urged these to diligence, I shall only add this one request, to sportful youth, to sensual brutes, to the idle sort of the gentry, to impenitent loiterers, to gamesters, and to all that have time to spare, that they will soberly use their reason in the answer of these following questions, before they proceed to waste the little time that is remaining, as vainly as they have done the rest. And I earnestly beseech them, and require them, as in the sight and hearing of their Judge, that they deny me not so friendly and reasonable a suit.

Quest. 1. Do you consider well the shortness and uncertainty of your time? You came but lately into the world, and it is but a very little while till you must leave it. The glass is turned upon you; and it is incessantly running. A certain number of motions your pulse must beat, and beyond that number it shall not be permitted to strike another stroke. Whatever you are thinking, or saying, or doing, you are posting on to your final state. And oh how quickly will you be there! Suppose you had seventy years to live, how soon will they be gone! But you are not sure of another hour. Look back on all your time that is past, and tell me whether it made not haste? And that which is to come will be as hasty. Will not the tolling of the bell instruct you? Will not graves, and bones, and dust instruct you? While many are hourly crowding into another world, will conscience permit you to be idle? Doth it not tell you what you have to do, and call upon you to despatch it? Can you play away your time, and idle it away, whilst the bell is tolling, whilst the sick are groaning, whilst every pulse and breath is telling you that you are hasting to your end? Do you consider what a wonder of providence it is, that all your humours, parts, and organs, that so many arteries, nerves, and veins, should be kept in order one year to an end? If you have no pains of sickness to admonish you, do you not know what a fragile thing is flesh; which, as the flower fadeth, doth hasten to corruption and to dust? How short is your abode in your present dwelling like to be, in comparison of your abode in dust and darkness! And can you have while now to waste so many hours in the adorning, the easing, and the pampering of such a lump of rottenness, and forget the part that lives for ever? Must you stay on earth so short a time, and have you any of this little time to spare? yea, so much of it as you daily waste in idleness, play, and vain curiosity?

Quest. 2. Do you soberly consider what work you have for all your time? and on how important a business you come into the world? Believe it, O man and woman, it is to do all that ever must be done, to prepare for an everlasting life. Endless joy or misery is the certain reward and consequent of the spending of your present time. And oh that God would open your eyes, to see how much you have to do in order to this eternal end! You have ignorant minds which must be instructed, and knowledge is not easily and quickly got. Poor ministers of Christ can tell you that, who with many years' labour can scarce bring one half a parish to understand the very principles of the christian religion. You have souls depraved by original sin, and turned from God. and enslaved to the world and flesh; and these must be renewed and regenerated. You must have a new and holy nature, that you may have a new and holy life. How many false opinions have you to be untaught! How many weighty lessons to learn! How many pernicious customs to be changed! How many powerful corruptions to be mortified! How many temptations to be overcome! How many graces to be obtained; and then to be exercised, and strengthened, and preserved! Is it easy to get a solid faith; a tender heart; a faithful conscience; a fervent desire and love to God; a quieting confidence and trust; a well-guided zeal, and preserving fear; an absolute resignation, self-denial, and obedience; a hatred of all sin; a love to holiness; a fitness and ability for every duty; a love to our neighbour as ourselves; a true love to our enemies; a contentedness with our condition; a readiness and joyful willingness to die; a certainty of the pardon of all our sins, and of our title to eternal happiness; a longing after the coming of Christ; a public spirit, wholly devoted to the common good? Is it nothing to do all that which you have to do in meditation, in self-examination, in prayer, in educating children, in teaching and governing your families; in all duties of your other relations; to superiors, to inferiors, to equals, to neighbours, to enemies, to all? Is it nothing to order and govern your hearts, your thoughts, your passions, your tongues? Alas! sirs, have you all this to do; and yet can you have while to slug, and game, and play, and fool away your time? If a poor man had but sixpence in his purse to buy bread for himself and for his family, and would give a groat of it to see a puppet-play, and then dispute that puppet-plays are lawful, how would you judge of his understanding and his practice? Oh how much worse is it in you, (as the case is more weighty,) when you have but a little uncertain time, to do so much, so great, so necessary work in, to leave it almost all undone, and throw away that time on cards, and plays, and sensuality, and idleness! I tell you time is a most precious thing; more precious than gold, or jewels, or fine clothes: and he is incomparably more foolish that throws away his time, than he that throws away his gold, or trampleth his clothes or ornaments in the dirt. This, this is the foolish, pernicious prodigality.

Quest. 3. Have you deeply considered that everlasting condition which all your time is given you to prepare for? Doth it not awaken and amaze thy soul, to think what it is to be for ever, I say, *for ever*, in joy or misery, in heaven or hell? One of these will certainly and shortly be thy portion, whatever unbelief may say against it. Oh what a heart hath that stupified sinner, that can idle away that little time which is allotted him to prepare for his everlasting state! that knoweth he shall have but this hasty life to win or lose eternal glory in, and can play it away as if he had nothing to do with it; and heaven or hell were indifferent to him, or were but insignificant words!

Quest. 4. What maketh you so loth to die, if time be no more worth than to cast away unprofitably? The worth of time is for the work that is to be done in time. To a man in a palsy, an apoplexy, a madness, that cannot make use of it, it is little worth. If you were sick and like to die this night, would you not pray that you might live a little longer? I beseech you cheat not your souls by wilful self-deceit. Tell me, or tell your consciences, How would you form such a prayer to God for your recovery if you were now sick? Would you say, Lord, give me a little more time to play at cards and dice in? Let me see a few more masks and plays? Let me have a little time more to please my flesh, in idleness, feastings, and the pleasures of worldliness and pride? Did you ever find such a prayer in any prayer book? Would you not rather say, Lord, vouchsafe me a little more time to repent of all my loss of time, and to redeem it in preparation for eternal life, and to make my calling and election sure? And will you yet live so contrary to your prayers, to your conscience, and to reason itself?

Quest. 5. Is the work that you were made for, hitherto well done? Are you regenerated and renewed to the heavenly nature? Are you strong and established in grace? Have you made sure of pardon and salvation? Are your hearts in heaven? and is your daily conversation there? And are you ready with well-grounded hope and peace, to welcome death, and appear in judgment? If all this were done, you had yet no excuse for idling away one day or hour; because there is still more work to do, as long as you have time to do it. (And if this were done, you would have that within you, which would not suffer you to cast away your time.) But for these men or women to be passing away time in sloth or vanity, who are utterly behindhand, and have lost most of their lives already, and are yet unregenerated, and strangers to a new and heavenly life, and are unpardoned, and in the power and guilt of sin, and unready to die, and shall certainly be for ever lost, if they die before that grace renew them; I say again, for such as these to be sporting away their time, is a practice which fully justifieth the holy Scriptures, when they call such persons fools, and such as have no understanding, unless it be to do evil, and successfully destroy themselves.

Quest. 6. Do you think if you neglect and lose your time, that ever you shall come again into this world, to spend it better? If you idle away this life, will God ever give you another here? If you do not your work well, shall you ever come again to mend it? O no, sirs, there is no hope of this. Act this part well, for as you do it, you must speed for ever; there is no coming back to correct your errors. I have elsewhere told you, that it must be *now* or *never*. And yet have you time to spare on vanity?

Quest. 7. Do you mark what dying men say of time, and how they value it (unless they be blocks that are past feeling)? How ordinarily do good and bad then wish that they had spent time better, and cry out, Oh that it were to spend again! Then they are promising, Oh if it were to do again, we would spend that time in heavenly lives and fruitful obedience, which we spent in curiosity, idleness, and superfluous, sensual delights. Then they cry, Oh that God would renew our time, and once more try us how we will spend it! Alas! sirs, why should wise men so much differ in health and sickness? Why should that time be vilified now, which will seem so precious then?

Quest. 8. How think you the miserable souls in hell would value time, if they were again sent hither, and tried with it again on the terms as we are? Would they feast it away, and play it away, as you do now; and then say, Are not plays, and cards, and feastings lawful? Every fool will be wise too late, Matt. xxv. 3, 8, 11. Bethink you what their experience teacheth them, and let warning make you wise more seasonably, and at a cheaper rate.

Quest. 2. Do you believe that you must give an account of your time? and that you must look back from eternity on the time which you now spend? If you do, what account will then be most comfortable to you? Had you not rather then find ur your accounts that all your hours have been spent to the best advantage of your souls, than that abundance of them have been cast away on fruitless toys? Will you have more comfort than in the hours which you spent in heart-searching, and heart-reforming, and learning and practising the word of God, or in those which you spent upon needless sports, curiosity, or idleness? Do now as you would desire you had done.

Quest. 10. How do you now wish that you had spent the time which is already past? Had you not rather that it had been spent in fruitful holiness and good works, than in idleness and fleshly pleasures? If not, you have not so much as a shadow of repentance; and therefore can have no just conceit that you are forgiven. If yea, then why will you do that for the time to come, which you wish for the time past that you had never done? And hereby show that your repentance is hypocritical, and will not prove the pardon of your sin? For so far as any man truly repenteth, he is resolved not to do the like, if it were to do again, under the like temptations.

Quest. 11. Do you know who attendeth you while you are loitering away your time? I have elsewhere told you, that the patience and mercy of God is waiting on you; that Christ is offering you his grace, and the Holy Spirit moving you to a wiser and a better course; that sun and moon, and all the creatures here on earth, are offering you this service; besides ministers and all other helpers of your salvation: and must all these wait upon you while you serve the flesh, and vilify your time, and live as for nothing?

Quest. 12. Do you consider what you lose in the loss of time? That time which you are gaming or idling away, you might have spent in entertaining grace, in heavenly converse, in holy pleasures, in making your salvation sure. And all this you lose in your loss of time; which all your sports will never compensate.

Quest. 13. Is the devil idle while you are idle? Night and day he is seeking to devour you; and will you, like the silly bird, sit chirping and singing in your wanton pleasures, when the devil's gun is ready to give fire at you? If you saw but how busy he is about you, and for what, you would be busier yourselves for your own preservation, and less busy in doing nothing than you are.

Quest. 14. Do you really take Christ, and his apostles and saints, to be the fittest pattern for the spending of your time? If you do not, why do you usurp the name of christians? Is he a christian who would not live like a christian? or that taketh not Christ for his Master and example? But if you say, Yea; I pray you then tell us how much time Christ or any of his apostles did spend at cards, or dice, or stage-plays? how much in curiosity about dressing and superfluous ornaments; about unnecessary pomp, and courtship? how much in sluggishness, idleness, and vain discourse? or how much in furnishing their bodies, their attendants, their habitations, with matter of splendour and vain-glory? Did they waste so much of the day in nothings and need-nots, as our slothful, sensual gentry do? or did they not rather spend their time in holy living, and fervent praying, and in doing all the good they could to the souls and bodies of all about them, and in the labours of a lawful bodily employment? Write after this copy, rather than after that which is set by the sensual fools of the world, if you make any account of God's acceptance. Do as the saints did, if you will speed as they; or else for shame never honour their names and memorials to your own condemnation. If you will spend your time as the flesh and the world teach you, rather than as Christ hath taught you, you must look for your payment from the flesh and the world. And why then in baptism did you renounce them and vow to follow Christ? "Be not deceived; God is not mocked: for whatsoever a man soweth, that shall he also reap. For he that soweth to his flesh shall of the flesh reap corruption; but he that soweth to the Spirit shall of the Spirit reap life everlasting," Gal. vi. 7, 8. Bethink you what the reason was that the ancient fathers and churches so much condemned the going to the spectacles of theatres; and why the canons made it such a crime for a minister to play at dice. (Read Dr. Jo. Reignolds's Cloud of Witnesses of all sorts against Stage-plays.)

Reader, if thou think this counsel or reprehension too precise or strict, grant me but this reasonable request, and I have my end. Live in the world but with a soul that is awake, that soberly considereth what haste time maketh, and how quickly thy glass will be run out; how fast death is coming, and how soon it will be with thee. What a work is it to get a carnal, unprepared soul to be renewed and made holy, and fitted for another world! What a terrible thing it will be to lie on a death-bed with a guilty conscience, unready to die, and utterly uncertain whither thou must next go, and where thou must abide for ever! Foresee but what use of thy present times will be most pleasing or displeasing to thy thoughts at last; and spend it now but as thou wilt wish thou hadst spent it; and value it but as it is valued by all when it is gone: use it but as true reason telleth thee will make most to thy endless happiness, and as is most agreeable to the ends of thy creation and redemption; and as beseemeth that man who soberly and often thinketh what it is to be either in heaven or hell for ever, and to have no more but this present short, uncertain life, to decide that question, which must be thy lot; and to make all the preparation that ever must be made for an endless life. I say, do but thus lay out thy time as reason should command a reasonable creature, and I desire no more. I have warned thee in the words of truth and faithfulness; the Lord give thee a heart to take this warning.

Thy compassionate Monitor,

RICHARD BAXTER.

September 23, 1667.

MR. BAXTER'S

SENSE OF THE ARTICLES

OF THE

CHURCH OF ENGLAND:

IN ANSWER TO THE SCRUPLES PROPOSED TO HIM BY SOME THAT WERE CALLED UPON TO SUBSCRIBE THEM.

I TAKE not this form of words, called, *The Articles of the Church of England*, to be essential to the said church; nor any thing in them to be essential to the christian religion, which was not so from its beginning, and in the first ages of christianity, yea, and in every following age. Nor do I take such form or matter to be instead of the Scripture and the ancient creeds, a necessary rule of divine faith, or necessary to the being of ministry, membership, and communion in the church of England: but that they were subordinate to the Scriptures and the said creeds, a laudable profession of this church at the Reformation; that they misexpounded not the divine rule by any heresy, thereby to promote our communion with other reformed churches, and to guide novices at home in the exposition of the said rule: far be it from us to be of a religion and church which is of no older date than the said Articles or Common Prayer. But holding, with excellent Augustine, that *contra rationem nemo sobrius, et contra Scripturam nemo christianus*, so also that *contra ecclesiam nemo pacificus;* (the church still being supposed to be for reason and Scripture, sober and christian;) and wishing that God's own word were taken for the sufficient terms of our consent and concord in order to union and communion; and knowing that the ambiguity of words, and our common imperfection in the art of speaking, do leave an uncertainty in the sense of most human writings till explained; and yet supposing that the authors of these Articles meant them orthodoxly, that I may not seem needlessly scrupulous, I subscribe them; and that I may not be unconscionably rash in subscribing, I here tell all whom it may concern, how I understand the words which I subscribe.

ART. II. *A sacrifice for all the sin of man, original and actual.* Though *omnibus* be also in the Latin, *all* is left out in King James's edition. I suppose they meant not, for any man's final, predominant impenitence, infidelity, atheism, or unholiness; but for all sorts of sin, on condition of faith and repentance, actually pardoning them to penitent believers.

ART. III. *He went down into hell.* That is, into *hades*, the state of separated souls: of which see Archbishop Usher's Answer to the Jesuits.

ART. IV. *Took again his body with flesh and bones, and all things appertaining to the perfection of man's nature, wherewith he ascended into heaven, and there sitteth, &c.*

That is, he sitteth in heaven with the same body glorified, which was flesh and bones on earth, and catachrestically is by some so called. Now it is a celestial, incorruptible, spiritual, glorious body; but indeed is not now the same thing which we call formally flesh, bones, or blood, nor will admit of the same definition. For, 1. The Scripture saith plainly, that "flesh and blood cannot inherit the kingdom of God," 1 Cor. xv. 50. "There is a natural body, and there is a spiritual body," ver. 43, 44. The context showeth that it is not moral, sinful corruption that is called flesh and blood here, but that natural corruptibility which flesh and blood hath. See Hammond on the text.

Christ's body will not be worse than ours, (but ours made like to his, Phil. iii. 20.) But ours shall not be flesh, blood, and bones.

2. When there is not the same form or definition, there is not to be the same proper formal denomination: but no sober philosopher or physician ever gave such a definition of flesh, blood, or bones, as will truly agree with Christ's glorified body: the name therefore can be but equivocal.

3. There is a symmetry in God's works, Christ being in his glorified humanity advanced above angels in power, is not below them in natural perfection: his spiritual, celestial body is congruous to his soul; and all the angels obey and worship him. When we are the children of the resurrection, we shall be equal to the angels, and neither marry nor die; and so not have bodies of mortal constitution. I dare not say that the sun or light is a more glorious body than Christ's; nor encourage those disputers that ask how many feet long and broad his body is, or the place that containeth it.

4. I dare not incur the guilt of contradicting two general councils in a matter of faith, when they anathematize the dissenters, and agree therein, though disagreeing in other things, and pleading the tradition of the fathers, and the Scripture.

The seventh general council at C. P. under Const. Copion. condemning image-worship, saith, (as Binnius translateth it,) p. 378. Defin. 7. *Siquis non confessus fuerit Dominum nostrum Jesum Christum post assumptionem animatæ rationalis et intellectualis carnis, simul sedere cum Deo et Patre, atque ita quoque rursus venturum cum Paterna Majestate, judicaturum vivos et mortuos, non amplius quidem carnem, neque incorporeum tamen, ut videatur ab iis a quibus compunctus est, et maneat Deus extra crassitudinem carnis, anathema.*

To which saith the second Nicene (their adversaries) by Epiphanius, *Huc usque recte sentiunt et Patrum traditionibus consentientiæ dicunt.*

5. The long church divisions, which have for 1300 years followed the rash determinations about some dark invisible things, maketh me more inclined to suspend, than rashly to affirm, in doubtful cases, especially about God, and Jesus Christ.

6. It is not the perfection of glorified humanity to be flesh and bones.

7. I cannot say, that earth (as flesh and bones are) dwells in ethereal regions.

ART. VI. *Holy Scripture containeth all things necessary to salvation.* I consent: therefore if the ministry, sacraments, and church communion be necessary to salvation, the Scripture containeth all necessary to them.

IBID. *In the name of the holy Scriptures we understand those canonical books of the Old and New Testament, of whose authority was never any doubt in the church.*

Expos. Not excluding the epistle to the Hebrews; James; 2 Peter; Jude; 2 and 3 John; Revelation, which divers churches long doubted of.

ART. VII. *The civil precepts thereof* (the law given from God by Moses) *ought not of necessity to be received in any commonwealth.*

Expos. Civilia sunt præcepta quæ dantur ad regendas civitates (seu societates civiles); God's laws are the supreme civil laws; man's laws are but by-laws (such as corporations make under the laws of the land) about things mutable, left undetermined by God, and subordinate to his laws. God hath two sorts of civil laws: 1. Such as are universal or common to all christian nations at least: as, that there shall be rulers and subjects; that rulers obey and promote the laws of God and the kingdom of Christ, and do nothing against them; that they seek the common good, and rule in righteousness, and be a terror to evil works, and encourage piety, and virtue, and peace; that they restrain blasphemy, perjury, profaneness, murder, adultery, theft, false witness, and false judging, &c. These civil laws bind all nations, as the law of nature; and all christian nations, as the law of Christ; but not as the law of Moses promulgate to the Jews. 2. But there are also particular civil laws that were proper to the Jews' commonwealth in specie: I suppose the Article meaneth these, and includeth the former in the word *moral laws*, though indeed they be the most eminent civil laws.

ART. VIII. *The three Creeds,* viz. *Nice Creed, Athanasius' Creed, and that commonly called the Apostles' Creed, ought thoroughly to be received and believed* (omnino).

Expos. Rightly understood: viz. 1. That by *God of God, very God of very God,* be not meant two Gods: 2. Nor the damnatory clauses taken for part of Athanasius' Creed, though they be part of the liturgy assented and consented to.

ART. IX. *This infection of nature doth remain even in them that are regenerate.*

Expos. That is, in a mortified, subdued degree, but not predominant, or unpardoned.

ART. X. *We have no power* (nihil valemus): viz. Our natural powers or faculties are not sufficient without grace.

ART. XI. *We are accounted righteous before God only for the merit of our Lord and Saviour Jesus Christ, and not for our own works or deservings: wherefore that we are justified by faith only, is a most wholesome doctrine, &c.*

Expos. Though he that doth righteousness is righteous, and the Scripture throughout and frequently mentioneth an inherent personal righteousness necessary to salvation, yet this is no universal righteousness, nor such as will justify us according to the law of innocency or works; but is merely subordinate to the merit and efficacy of the sacrifice and righteousness of Christ, which only meriteth for us as a price; our faith being only the requisite (yet given) moral qualification for the reception of the free gift of pardon, justification, and adoption, and hath not the least part of the office or honour of Christ: yet are Christ's words true, "that by men's words they shall be justified or condemned: and all men shall be judged according to their works:" and James truly saith, "that by works a man is justified, and not by faith only." Not by works of perfection or of Moses' law, nor any that as a price or commutation do make the reward to be of debt, and not of grace; but by a practical faith or christianity. Such acts as faith itself is, and prove our belief to be such as Christ hath promised justification and salvation to; such as by justifying belief to be sincere, do justify the person against the charge of infidelity, hypocrisy, impenitence, and ungodliness. Christianity is that faith which Paul opposeth to works.

ART. XII. *Good works spring out necessarily of a true and lively faith; insomuch that by them a lively faith may as evidently be known as a tree discerned by the fruit.*

Expos. 1. It is a hypothetical necessity that is here meant, consistent with freedom. 2. And a truth of evidence, and not an equal degree.

ART. XIII. *Works done before the grace of Christ and the inspiration of the Spirit, are not pleasant to God; forasmuch as they spring not of faith in Jesus Christ: neither do they make men meet to receive grace, or as the schools say, deserve grace of congruity, yea, rather they have the nature of sin.*

Expos. 1. No good is done before all common grace. 2. Preparatory grace usually goeth before special grace; and those that resist it, are further from the kingdom of God, than they that have it. And to him that hath (by improvement) shall be given; and in every nation, he that feareth God, and worketh righteousness, is accepted of him. Believing that God is, and that he is the rewarder of them that diligently seek him, is better than nothing, and than mere sin.

ART. XIV. *Voluntary works, besides, over and above God's commandments, which they call works of supererogation, cannot be taught without arrogancy and iniquity.*

Expos. I suppose they meant not that voluntary canons, impositions, oaths, and church offices are so bad.

ART. XVI. *Expos.* I suppose this Article meaneth only the unpardoned sin against the Holy Ghost, and of a total departure from common grace, and some degree of habit and act from special grace; but determineth not the controversy, whether any totally and finally fall from such an unconfirmed grace as else would save.

ART. XVIII. *They are to be had accursed that presume to say, that every man shall be saved by the law or sect which he professeth, so that he be diligent to frame his life according to that law and the light of nature. For holy Scripture doth set out to us only the name of Jesus Christ whereby men must be saved.*

Expos. Some sects contradict the light of nature; they worship devils, and offer their children in sacrifice to them, and murder the just: this will save none.

But if the meaning be to curse all that hope that some are saved, who never heard of the name of Christ, and that his Spirit and grace go farther than the knowledge of his name, I will not curse such. All were not accursed that hoped well of Socrates, Antonine, Alexander Severus, Cicero, Epictetus, Plutarch, &c. There is no name, that is, no other Messiah, to be saved by but Christ. But, 1. God judgeth men by no other law but that which they were under; and the law of grace made to fallen mankind in Adam and Noah, was not repealed by the Jews' peculiarity. 2. God had more people than the Jews and proselytes of old. 3. The old Jews knew less of Christ than his apostles before his resurrection. 4. The apostles then believed not his dying for our sins, his resurrection, ascension, heavenly intercession, &c. 5. It is no christianity now that believeth not these. If I durst curse all the world who now believe no more than the old Jews and the apostles then did, yet durst I not curse all christians that hope better of them.

Art. XXIII. *Those we ought to judge lawfully called and sent, which be chosen and called to this work by men, who have public authority given them in the congregation, to call and send ministers into the Lord's vineyard.*

Expos. Given them, that is, by Christ in his Scripture institution, and by those that Christ authorizeth under him.

Art. XXV. *Sacraments be certain sure witnesses and effectual signs of grace, and God's good will, &c.*

Expos. They signify what God offereth. They invest the true believing receiver in the right of pardon, adoption, and salvation. They are morally operative signs of exciting and increasing inherent grace in believers.

Art. XXVI. *Nor is the effect of Christ's ordinances taken away by their (ministers') wickedness.*

Expos. Sacraments are not void, because a bad man administered them; but prayer, and preaching, and example, are usually more effectual from able, godly men, than from the ignorant and wicked. The blind man could say, "God heareth not sinners; but if any be a worshipper of God, and do his will, him he heareth." To the wicked saith God, "What hast thou to do to take my covenant into thy mouth?" &c. Psal. l. It is a sin to prefer a bad man before a better. And it is dangerous to encourage men in daily sin, who usurp the sacred office of bishops or pastors, having neither the qualifications essentially necessary thereto, nor that which is essentially necessary to a call.

The excepted Articles, and those that need no exposition, I pass by. If I have hit on the true meaning, I subscribe my assent: and I thank God that this national church hath doctrine so sound, and pity them that write, preach, or practise contrary to the Articles which they subscribe, and accuse them that refuse subscribing them; and take them for sinners, who take them not for their pastors, because that their wickedness nulleth not their sacramental administrations.

MR. BAXTER'S LETTER TO MR. BROMLEY,

1680,

CONTAINING HIS JUDGMENT ABOUT FREE-WILL,

IN AS FEW WORDS AS POSSIBLE, FOR THE SATISFACTION OF SOME PERSONS, WHO MISUNDERSTOOD SOME OF HIS BOOKS.

The dispute about free-will is one of the hardest in the world, and hath tired doctors these 1200 years; and therefore cannot be made easy to you, much less in a few words: but thus much is easy and sure:

1st. That all good is of God, and all our willingness to good is of his grace.

2dly. The deliverance of the will from its ill disposition, and disposing it to good, is of absolute necessity to salvation; and this holy freedom no man hath further than he hath grace.

3dly. The will hath a self-determining power, which is its natural freedom in all its actions.

4thly. Common grace enableth men to do more good and less hurt than they do; and it is for not using this power that they suffer.

5thly. If these short words satisfy you not, be satisfied with shorter; that all sin, and consequently punishment, is of ourselves; and all grace and deliverance is from God. Obey his Spirit, and you shall shortly understand his counsel.

Yours,

RICHARD BAXTER.

REASONS FOR MINISTERS

USING

THE GREATEST PLAINNESS AND SERIOUSNESS POSSIBLE,

IN ALL THEIR

APPLICATIONS TO THEIR PEOPLE.

To show the reasonableness that all ministers should deal thus faithfully and plainly with such as are under their ministry, I will lay open somewhat of the case before you, and then judge reasonably of it as you are men. The eternal God, delighting in the wonderful diversity of his creatures, hath made man of a middle nature, between brutes and angels, giving him vital power, reason, and free-will. He hath placed him in this world, as for a race or warfare; resolving that as he behaveth himself it shall go with him in another world for ever: for though his body be dust, and must to dust return, his soul is from above, and liveth in blessedness or misery for ever. By sin we have all forfeited our right to heaven: but eternal love hath given us a Redeemer, who is God and man, who as our Surety became a sacrifice for our sins, and by his merits hath purchased a conditional grant of free forgiveness, and of renewing grace, and endless glory. And being ascended into heaven, possesseth it in our nature, and intercedeth for us, being now as Redeemer, Lord of all. And as the sun above us sendeth down its beams on earth, so doth our glorified Lord his Spirit, to quicken, enlighten, and sanctify souls, who were dead, and dark, and disaffected to God, to holiness, and heavenly perfection. And he hath appointed the ministerial office, that men might be his messengers to men, to acquaint them with his grace, and with the glory which he prepareth for them, that they may truly believe it, soberly think of it, duly value it, heartily choose it, and diligently seek it, and live and die in the joyful expectation of it. And as our souls converse not with our neighbours immediately, but in and by our bodies in which they work; so the Spirit of Christ doth not ordinarily work on men's souls without any means, but by his word and works which his ministers must declare. Man is not now put upon satisfying God's justice, or purchasing his salvation by a price. Christ hath done these, and made a free gift of grace and glory to all that will but penitently and believingly accept it. Under God's grace men's everlasting salvation now lieth on their own wills; no men or devils can damn or undo any one soul, but by his own consent to the cause of his damnation. No men or devils can keep one soul from the heavenly glory, but by tempting him to refuse it, undervalue and neglect it, and prefer the pleasures of sin before it, and by keeping him from loving, desiring, and seeking it: for every one shall certainly have it who had rather be a holy christian on earth, and live in perfect love and joy with God in heaven for ever, than for his filthy pleasure to enjoy the prosperity of this world. To acquaint men with this, is our ministerial office; we are charged to set before them the great salvation which Christ hath procured, and importunately to beseech them to mind it, believe it, and accept it, that it may be theirs for ever. We believe God, and therefore we speak to men as he hath commanded us. We entreat them in his name, to turn from sinful enmity and folly, and to be reconciled to God, and be wise for their salvation. We tell them but what God's word, sent from heaven, telleth us and them, that holiness is the love of God and goodness, and the hatred of sin; that the pure in heart are blessed, for they shall see God: but without holiness none can see him. We tell them from God, that heaven is won or lost on earth; and that none shall have it but such as hence learn to love a holy and heavenly life; and that the dislike of holiness is the forfeiture of happiness, and the beginning or forerunner of hell. We assure them, that God will never say, Depart from me, ye workers of iniquity, if they do not first by iniquity depart from God; and that God will not damn them, except they damn themselves, by the obstinate final refusing and resisting of his mercy. We entreat men therefore but to live as men should do that love themselves, and that are not indifferent whether they live in heaven or hell for ever. We entreat them not to be worse to themselves, than the devil and all their enemies are, who cannot make them commit one sin against their wills. And yet after all this warning, entreaty, and importunity, there are thousands and ten thousands that will not be persuaded, nor regard the warning given them from God. Some will not believe but that a man dies like a dog; and what wonder if such live like dogs? And some will not believe but that they may be saved without regenerating grace and holiness, though Christ's own mouth hath protested the contrary, and told us verily that it cannot be, John iii. 3, 5, 18, 19; Matt. xviii. 3; Heb. xii. 14; Rom. viii. 6—9, 13, &c. Multitudes will not be brought to understand what we say; but when we talk of redemption, sanctification, and salvation, they hear us as if we spake Greek or Hebrew to them, and under teaching, grow old in sottish, grossest ignorance. Multitudes are taken up with the love of prosperity, and the love of this deceiving world. Multitudes are carried away with aspiring ambition and foolish pride; and more with the love of fleshly pleasures, and satisfying their appetites and lusts. Many poor people (who every where are the most) are so oppressed with want, and wearied with their daily labour, and taken up with cares to pay their rents and debts, and maintain their families, that they think it excusable in them if they little mind the pleasing of God and saving of their souls; supposing that they have no leisure for it, and God requireth it not at their hands. And the same most servants think, who have time little enough for their masters' work. Multitudes have such dead and hardened hearts, that, when we tell them that they must shortly be in heaven or hell, as they are here prepared, we speak almost as to blocks, or men asleep: they feel not what we say, as if they did not hear us.

We are bid cry aloud, and tell them of their sin and danger, (Isa. lviii. 1. 2,) and yet we cannot get them to regard and feel. God saith, "Awake, thou that sleepest, and Christ shall give thee light;" and yet we cannot get them to awake, nor hear us like men that have the use of reason, and love themselves. Alas, how many thousands are there whom we could never persuade to consider with deep and serious thoughts, what will become of their souls when they are dead, nor seek to be resolved of it from the infallible word of God! that never set apart one hour in their lives to consider seriously, whether they have any title to salvation, which they can make good by the word of God by which they must be judged!

Sirs, this, this is the case of multitudes of our neighbours; and what would you have a minister to do in such a case? Should we flatter and smooth them up in an unholy life, what thanks would they give us for this ere long, when they find themselves in hell?

Would you have us stand by in silence, and look on, while Satan thus leadeth thousands to perdition? Would you have us let them quietly go to hell, for fear of displeasing them or others, or seeming to be unmannerly or uncivil with them? Would you have us whisper to men that must be awakened or undone for ever, whom thunder and lightning will not awake?

Alas, we see men dying daily, and we are dying ourselves, and daily look when we speak our last, and when they hear their last, even all that ever they shall hear more for their salvation. We see how time doth pass away; much is lost already, the rest is short, and utterly uncertain: and the ignorance, unbelief, hard-heartedness, fleshliness, worldliness, pride, malignity, and unholiness of sinners, are deep-rooted, strong, and damnable evils. We see men, when they are convinced that they must repent or perish, (Luke xiii. 3, 5,) putting it off from day to day; when they are certain to be gone ere long, and never certain of one more hour. And, alas, a long life is little enough for a willing, awakened, serious christian to work out his salvation, and make his calling and election sure.

Sirs, tell us as christians, or at least as men, what faith, and reason, and human love command us to do in such a case? Shall we forbear, or speak to them in formality as on a stage, as if we were players, and not preachers, and would persuade them not to believe what we say? should we let them alone, be damned, and take it for our excuse, that they or others were unwilling of our labours? Shall we pretend charity, and hope that they have already enough to save them, while we see not so much as knowledge, or any love to holiness, nor forsaking of mortal sin, nor any serious care of their salvation? Is it the office of charity to further men's delusions and damnation? If we believed not another life ourselves, and that there is a God who will reward them, and only them, that diligently seek him, (Heb. xi. 6,) we would quickly renounce this ungrateful ministry and work; we would wish that all the preachers in the world were silenced, and that the people would better use their tithes than to maintain such troublers of the world. But God hath shined into our minds with the heavenly, convincing light. He hath given us the first-fruits and pledge of glory. We believe a heaven and a hell, and the absolute necessity of a holy and heavenly mind and life; and we know why we do believe it. Here we have, upon our sober consideration, laid up all our hopes and comforts; and what should we persuade our neighbours to choose, but that which God hath taught us to choose ourselves? And woe to him that ever he was born, that maketh not this choice, and taketh not the heavenly for his portion!

RICHARD BAXTER.

December 18, 1676.

THE END

JOHN CHILDS AND SON, BUNGAY.